THE LAW OF TRUSTS

ONE WEEK LOAN

A fine will be charged if not returned by the date stamped above

THE LAW OF TRUSTS

by

Geraint Thomas

BA (Wales), D. Phil. (Oxon), Barrister (Inner Temple),
Professor of Equity and Property Law at Queen Mary, University of London

AND

Alastair Hudson

LLB LLM PhD (Lond), Barrister (Lincoln's Inn),
Professor of Equity and Law at Queen Mary, University of London

OXFORD
UNIVERSITY PRESS

OXFORD
UNIVERSITY PRESS

Great Clarendon Street, Oxford OX2 6DP

Oxford University Press is a department of the University of Oxford.
It furthers the University's objective of excellence in research, scholarship,
and education by publishing worldwide in

Oxford New York

Auckland Bangkok Buenos Aires Cape Town Chennai
Dar es Salaam Delhi Hong Kong Istanbul Karachi Kolkata
Kuala Lumpur Madrid Melbourne Mexico City Mumbai Nairobi
São Paulo Shanghai Taipei Tokyo Toronto

Oxford is a registered trade mark of Oxford University Press
in the UK and in certain other countries

Published in the United States
by Oxford University Press Inc., New York

British Library Cataloguing in Publication Data

Data available

Library of Congress Cataloging-in-Publication Data

Thomas, Geraint W.
  The law of trusts / by Geraint Thomas and Alastair Hudson.
    p. cm.
  Includes bibliographical references and index.
  ISBN 0-19-829894-3 (alk. paper)
  1. Trusts and trustees—England. I. Hudson, Alastair. II. Title.
  KD1480.T478 2004
  346.4205'9—dc22

                                        2004021774

ISBN 0-19-829894-3

1 3 5 7 9 10 8 6 4 2

Typeset by Newgen Imaging Systems (P) Ltd., Chennai, India
Printed in Italy
on acid-free paper by
Legoprint S.p.A. Italy

ABOUT THE CONTRIBUTORS

Francis Barlow, BA, MA (Oxon), Barrister (Inner Temple); Bencher (Lincoln's Inn). Publications: joint editor of *Williams on Wills*, 4th, 5th, 6th, 7th and 8th editions (1974, 1980, 1987, 1996, and 2002); joint editor of the 'Wills' and 'Executors' titles in *Halsbury's Laws of England*, 4th edition, vols 50 (reissue) and 17 (2) (reissue); consultant editor of and contributor to *Tolley's Trust Drafting and Precedents*.

John Glasson is an English solicitor specializing in the international aspects of trusts. He is a consultant to the London firms of Eversheds and Dawsons, and to Stuart Smalley & Co in the Isle of Man. He is founding editor of the loose-leaf encyclopaedia *International Trust Laws* and editor of the hardback publication *The International Trust*. John Glasson is a registered legal practitioner in the Isle of Man and is admitted as a solicitor in the British Virgin Islands.

Dr Alastair Hudson, LlB, LlM, PhD (London), Barrister (Lincoln's Inn) and Professor of Equity & Law at Queen Mary, University of London. He is the author of a number of books, including: *Equity & Trusts* (2003), *The Law on Financial Derivatives* (2002), *Understanding Equity and Trusts* (2004), *The Law on Investment Entities* (2000), *Swaps, Restitution and Trusts* (1999), *Towards a Just Society: law, labour and legal aid* (1999), and *The Law on Homelessness* (1997); he edited *New Perspectives on Property Law, Obligations and Restitution* (2004), *New Perspectives on Property Law, Human Rights and the Home* (2004), *Modern Financial Techniques, Derivatives and Law* (2000) and *Credit Derivatives: law, regulatory and accounting issues* (1999). He also writes 'Part 5: Capital Issues' and 'Part 5A: Open-ended Investment Companies' of *Palmer's Company Law*.

Christopher J McKenzie, MA (Oxon), TEP, practised as an English solicitor between 1987 and 1996. He was admitted to practise in the BVI in 1996, and in Anguilla in 1998, and now heads up the trusts and estates team in the private client department of Walkers in the BVI. He has contributed to numerous books on trusts and estates, is a frequent lecturer at international conferences and chaired the sub-committee of the BVI branch of STEP, the proposals of which led to the enactment of VISTA.

Karen Mumgaard, MA (Oxon), has specialized in pensions law since qualification as a solicitor in 1994. She is currently part of the pensions team at CMS Cameron

McKenna and is a part-time lecturer at the University of the West of England. She is also editor of International Pension Lawyer.

Christopher Sly, MA (Cantab.), TEP, is a partner in the Private Client Department of Payne Hicks Beach, solicitors. He has specialized in international tax, trusts and estate planning for most of his career and acts for a number of international trust companies as well as advising individuals and families. Christopher is a member of the International Academy of Estate and Trust Law.

Professor Geraint Thomas, BA (Wales), D.Phil (Oxon), Barrister (Inner Temple), Professor of Equity and Property Law and Head of the Department of Law at Queen Mary, University of London. Publications include: *Thomas on Powers* (1998); chapters on 'Asset Protection Trusts' and 'Purpose Trusts', in *International Trust Laws* (loose-leaf encyclopaedia: Jordans, updated to 2001) and *The International Trust* (2002) both edited by John Glasson; and numerous articles on various aspects of the Law of Trusts and Pension Schemes.

Michael Waterworth, MA (Cantab.), Barrister (Lincoln's Inn), practises at the Chancery Bar, at 10 Old Square, Lincoln's Inn. He is a joint editor of *Williams on Wills*, 8th Edition, the 'Executors' title in the current edition of *Halsbury's Laws of England, Mellows: Taxation for Executors and Trustees, Parker's Modern Wills Precedents*, 4th Edition and is author of *A Practitioner's Guide to Drafting Trusts*.

PREFACE

This book is concerned both to present a scholarly account of the principles on which the general law of trusts is based and also, significantly, to consider the ways in which those general concepts have been applied in particular contexts in practice. The structure of the book is, we think, unique among trusts law texts in its division between **Section One: General Principles** and **Section Two: Specific Trusts**. The purpose of that division is to perform the usual task required of a book of this sort in examining the core principles relating to the formation of express trusts, the duties of trustees, the function of trusts implied by law, and liability of trustees for breach of trust, before applying those general principles to speci fic forms of trusts which the practitioner will recognize. It has been our aim, then, to consider the law of trusts in a manner which will be of particular use to those practitioners for whom the trust is in the core of their practice and of use also to those who encounter trusts only from time to time.

In writing this book one cannot help but be aware of the long shadows cast by Lewin on *Trusts*, Snell on *Equity*, and Underhill and Hayton on the *Law on Trusts and Trustees*, books which were first published in 1837, 1868, and 1878 respectively. Everyone working and writing in this field owes the successive authors of those books a great intellectual debt. From their very beginnings their self-appointed task was to map out the paths through the thickets of ancient precedent and to give the trusts practitioner and scholar an idea of the general lie of the land. Without them, as with so many of the great nineteenth-century writers of legal textbooks like Chitty, Palmer, and Benjamin in their various fields, the coherence in the law of trusts today might not have been possible. Whereas those books have always constituted elegant syntheses of centuries of often conflicting authority on the nature of the trust, this book attempts both to give an account of those foundational principles and also to apply those principles to the many different forms which modern trusts have taken. It is hoped that this extra dimension to the discussion of trusts in this book will help the reader to understand the progress which has taken place in this field since those books were first written.

In the modern practice of trusts law there are, of course, different principles at play in different contexts: for example, there are great differences between the statutes and the case law dealing with pension fund trusts and trusts of the family home. This differentiation between types of trust is an established feature, it is suggested, of modern trusts law practice. There is ever more legislation dealing with the various forms of trust, whether asserting default provisions for ordinary trusts which lack certain types of power (as provided by the Trustee Act 2000), or those legislative and regulatory codes dealing specifically with unit trusts, pension funds, trusts of land, will trusts, and so forth. In writing this book we considered it important to give an account of those varying forms of trust, not simply with the intention of splitting the concepts of the law of trusts up into their various contexts, but rather to analyse the common bedrock of principle which has given birth to each type of trust. In so doing it is hoped that practitioners will find the information they need to answer specific questions relating to the use of trusts in their practices, and that all readers of this book will find this analysis of the law of trusts gives a full account of the general principles underlying the trust. There follows in the Introduction a synopsis of the contents of this book and in Chapter 1 'The Nature of the Trust' an introduction to the concept of the trust.

We should like to thank, first and foremost, our fellow contributors to this book who have brought to it their expertise in particular areas of trusts practice: Francis Barlow, John Glasson, and Karen Mumgaard. For those readers who take an interest in such things, the division of labour was as follows. Geraint Thomas was responsible for Chapters 2 to 23, the first part of Chapter 24, Chapters 38 and 39, and the first part of Chapter 40. Alastair Hudson was responsible for Chapter 1, Chapters 25 to 33, Chapters 47 to 57, contributions to Chapters 5 and 10, and the Introduction. Chapters 34 to 37 were written by Francis Barlow; Chapters 41 and 42 by John Glasson, the final section of Chapter 42 being co-authored with Chris Sly. Chapters 43 to 46 by Karen Mumgaard; the second part of Chapter 24 by Michael Waterworth; and the second part of Chapter 40 by Christopher McKenzie. We acknowledge and thank various publishers for kind permission to make use of certain material already published elsewhere in some form: to Sweet & Maxwell Ltd, in respect of material in Chapters 4, 11, 13, 16 to 20, and 24 in particular; to Jordan Publishing Ltd in respect of Chapters 6, 9, 38, and 39; and to Cavendish Publishing Ltd. We are extremely grateful to Chris Rycroft, Annabel Macris, and, in particular during the latter stages, Meg Zawadzki and Amanda Greenley of Oxford University Press and Rob Dickinson, also Bob Burns, the Law Librarian at Queen Mary, University of London, for their enthusiastic support for this project, the professional way in which the manuscript was transformed into the book which you now hold in your hands, and for their patience throughout the long and careful process of writing this book.

Our greatest debts of thanks, though, go to those loved ones who have suffered both our long absences as we crafted this book and the, possibly, even longer expositions of the ideas herein contained. Any errors or infelicities which have crept into this work are, we recognize in time-honoured fashion, entirely our fault alone. We have endeavoured to state the law as we found it from the materials available to us in late January 2004.

GWT

ASH

CONTENTS—SUMMARY

D. TRUSTS IMPLIED BY LAW

E. BREACH OF TRUST

SECTION TWO: SPECIFIC TRUSTS

F. PRIVATE CLIENT TRUSTS

K. TRUSTS OF LAND AND OF THE HOME

TABLE OF CONTENTS

SECTION ONE: GENERAL PRINCIPLES OF THE LAW OF TRUSTS

A. INTRODUCTION TO THE LAW OF TRUSTS

Introduction: The Scope of the Book

1. The Nature of the Trust

B. EXPRESS PRIVATE TRUSTS

C. THE DUTIES AND POWERS OF TRUSTEES

10. The Duties of Trustees: Part One

D. TRUSTS IMPLIED BY LAW

Contents

SECTION TWO: SPECIFIC TRUSTS

F. PRIVATE CLIENT TRUSTS

34. Private Client Trusts: Inheritance Tax and Interest in Possession Trusts

Contents

Contents

Contents

J. TRUSTS USED IN COMMERCIAL CONTEXTS

53. Trusts Which Conduct a Business

Contents

Contents

TABLE OF CASES

lvii

TABLES OF NATIONAL LEGISLATION

UK STATUTORY INSTRUMENTS

Australia

Bahamas

Belize

Bermuda

TABLE OF INTERNATIONAL LEGISLATION

TABLE OF NON-STATUTORY MATERIALS

LIST OF ABBREVIATIONS AND ACRONYMS

AEA 1925	Administration of Estates Act 1925
COB	*Conduct of Business Sourcebook of the Financial Services Authority*
CPR	Civil Procedure Rules
CREST	Central Securities Depository for the UK market and Irish equities
ECJ	European Court of Justice
FA	Finance Act
FDA 1991	Fraudulent Dispositions Act 1991
FIFO	First in, first out
FSA	Financial Services Authority
FSMA 2000	Financial Services and Markets Act 2000
GMP	Guaranteed Minimum Pension
GT	Grupo Torras SA
ICTA	Income and Corporation Taxes Act
IHTA 1984	Inheritance Tax Act 1984
IR SPSS	Inland Revenue Savings, Pensions, Share Schemes section
ITA 1984	International Trusts Act 1984
ITL 1992	International Trusts Law 1992
LIFFE	International Financial Futures and Options Exchange
LOTA 1996	Labuan Offshore Trusts Act 1996
LPA 1925	Law of Property Act 1925
LPI	Limited price indexation
MAR 1	Published under the FSA, Market Conduct Sourcebook Instrument 2001
MFR	Minimum Funding Requirement
MFR Regulations	(The) Occupational Pension Schemes (Minimum Funding Requirement) Regulations
MNT Regulations	(The) Occupational Pension Schemes (Member-nominated Trustees and Directors) Regulations

MNTs	Member nominated trustees
Opra	Occupational Pensions Regulatory Authority
PPF	Pensions Protection Fund
PTA 1996	Purpose Trusts Act 1996 (Isle of Man)
RPI	Retail Prices Index
RSC	Rules of the Supreme Court
SLA 1925	Settled Land Act 1925
SLA settlements	Settled Land Act settlements
STAR Trust	Special Trusts (Alternative Regime) Law of the Cayman Islands
TA 1925	Trustee Act 1925
TA 1992	Trusts Act 1992 (Belize)
TAA 1993	Trustee (Amendment) Act 1993 (British Virgin Islands)
TAA 2003	Trustee (Amendment) Act 2003 (British Virgin Islands)
TCGA 1992	Taxation of Chargeable Gains Act 1992
TGLA 1989	Trusts (Choice of Governing Law) Act 1989 (The Bahamas)
(the) 1989 Law	Fraudulent Dispositions Law 1989 (Cayman Islands)
(the) 1992 Law	International Trusts Law 1992
TJL 1984	Trusts (Jersey) Law 1984
TLATA 1996	Trusts of Land and Appointment of Trustees Act 1996
TSPA 1989	Trusts (Special Provisions) Act 1989 (Bermuda)
TSPAA 1998	Trusts (Special Provisions) Amendment Act 1998 (Bermuda)
TUPE	Transfer of Undertakings (Protection of Employment) Regulations 1981
UCITS Directive	Undertaking for Collective Investment of Transferable Securities Directive
UCTA 1977	Unfair Contract Terms Act 1977
UKLA	UK Listing Authority
VISTA 2003	Virgin Islands Special Trusts Act 2003

LIST OF BIBLIOGRAPHIC ABBREVIATIONS

Baker	P Baker, 'Transnational Enforcement of Tax Liability' in *Tolleys International Tax Planning* (4th edn, Butterworths, 1999)
Briggs and Rees	Briggs and Rees, *Civil Jurisdiction and Judgments* (3rd edn, LLP, 2002)
Campbell	E Campbell, *Changing the Terms of Trusts* (Butterworths, 2002)
Cheshire and Burn	E Burn, *Cheshire and Burn's The Modern Law of Real Property* (16th edn, Butterworths, 2000)
Cheshire and North	North and Fawcett, *Cheshire and North's Private International Law* (13 edn, Butterworths, 1999)
Collier	J Collier, *Conflict of Laws* (3rd edn, Cambridge University Press, 2001)
Dicey and Morris	L Collins (ed), *Dicey and Morris, The Conflict of Laws* (13th edn, Sweet & Maxwell, 2000) with Third Supplement (2003).
Duckworth in Glasson	A Duckworth, 'Forced Heirship and the Trust' in Glasson (ed), *The International Trust* (Jordans, 2002)
Farwell	Sir George Farwell and FK Archer, *A Concise Treatise on Powers* (3rd edn, 1916)
Ford and Lee	Ford and Lee, *The Law of Trusts* (3rd edn, Law Book Co, 1996)
Goff and Jones	R Goff and G Jones, *The Law of Restitution* (6th edn, Sweet & Maxwell, 2002)
Harris *Hague Trusts Convention*	J Harris, *The Hague Trusts Convention—Scope, Application, and Preliminary Issues* (Hart Publishing, 2002)
Harris *Transnational Trusts Litigation*	J Harris, 'Transnational Trusts Litigation—Jurisdiction and Enforcement of Foreign

	Judgments' in J Glasson (ed), *The International Trust* (Jordans, 2002)
Hayton in Glasson	D Hayton, 'The International Recognition of Trusts' in Glasson (ed), *The International Trust* (Jordans, 2002)
Hudson	AS Hudson, *Equity & Trusts* (3rd edn, Cavendish Publishing, 2003)
Jaffey	Clarkson and Hill, *Jaffey on the Conflict of Laws* (2nd edn, Butterworths, 2002)
Jarman	RW Jennings and JC Harper, *Jarman on Wills* (8th edn, 1951)
Lewin	J Mowbray, L Tucker, N Le Poidevin and E Simpson, *Lewin on Trusts* (17th edn, Sweet Maxwell, 2000) with First Supplement (2003)
Lupoi	M Lupoi, *Trusts—a Comparative Study* (Cambridge University Press, 2000)
Martin	J Martin, *Hanbury and Martin's Modern Equity* (16th edn, Sweet & Maxwell, 2001)
Matthews *Capacity*	P Matthews, 'Capacity to create a trust: the onshore problem, and the offshore solutions' (2002) 6 Edinburgh Law Review 176–198.
Matthews *Jurisdiction Clauses*	P Matthews, 'What is a Jurisdiction Clause?' (2003) Jersey Law Review 232
Matthews *Migration*	P Matthews, *Trusts: Migration and Change of Proper Law* (Key Haven, 1997)
Meagher, Gummow and Lehane	R Meagher, J Heydon and M Leeming, *Meagher, Gummow and Lehane's Equity: Doctrines and Remedies* (4th edn, Butterworths, 2002)
Megarry and Wade	C Harpum, *Megarry and Wade's The Law of Real Property* (6th edn, Sweet & Maxwell, 2000)
Nygh	PE Nygh, *Conflicts of Law in Australia* (6th edn, 1995)
Oakley	A Oakley, *Constructive Trusts* (3rd edn, Sweet & Maxwell, 1997)
Overbeck	Alfred E von Overbeck, *Explanatory Report on the Hague Trusts Convention*, English

	Translation by the Permanent Bureau, Hague Conference on Private International Law
Parker and Mellows	A Oakley, *Parker and Mellows' The Modern Law of Trusts* (8th edn, Sweet & Maxwell, 2003)
Pettit	P Pettit, *Equity and Trusts* (9th edn, Butterworths, 2001)
Scott	W Fratcher, *Scott on Trusts* (4th edn, Little, Brown, 1987)
Sly and Glasson in Glasson	C Sly and J Glasson, 'Payment by Trustees of Foreign Taxes' in J Glasson (ed), *The International Trust* (Jordans, 2002)
Snell	J McGhee, *Snell's Equity* (30th edn, Sweet & Maxwell, 2000)
Spry	I Spry, *Equitable Remedies* (Sweet & Maxwell, 2001)
Sugden	Edward Sugden (Lord St Leonards), *A Practical Treatise on Powers* (8th edn, 1861)
Sykes and Pryles	Sykes and Pryles, *Australian Private International Law* (3rd edn, The Law Book Co, 1991)
Thomas	GW Thomas, *Powers* (Sweet & Maxwell, 1998)
Underhill and Hayton	A Underhill and DJ Hayton, *Law of Trusts and Trustees* (16th edn, Butterworths, 2002)

SECTION ONE

GENERAL PRINCIPLES OF THE LAW OF TRUSTS

Part A

INTRODUCTION TO THE LAW OF TRUSTS

PART A

INTRODUCTION TO THE LAW OF TRUSTS

INTRODUCTION: THE SCOPE OF
THE BOOK

A. The Approach of this Book Within the Development of
the Law of Trusts

The law of trusts is a discipline of great antiquity but the trust has nevertheless always demonstrated itself to be capable of adapting its core principles to fit new social and economic circumstances. It was ever thus with the history of the trust, as the use gave way to the great aristocratic family settlements which in turn are giving way to an extraordinary diversity of trusts used in relation to occupational pension funds, unit trusts, the family home, wills, domestic and international tax planning, domestic and international asset protection, and taking security in commercial transactions. These institutional uses of the trust are above and beyond the ordinary use of express, implied, constructive, and resulting trusts concepts to ensure that the common law owners of property behave conscionably in relation to others who also have rights in that property. Out of this general principle of good conscience and out of the general principles of equity have grown sophisticated techniques, doctrines, and presumptions which recognize claims to property based on ideas as different as the duties of trusteeship, the beneficiary principle, and tracing in equity. All of these principles have been developed through hundreds of years of cases, scholarly debate, and the ceaseless ingenuity of the members of the legal profession, and they answer some of the most fundamental questions to face human societies as to the resolution of disputes concerning the extent of various people's rights and duties in private property.

The elegant simplicity of the device which the law of trusts uses to resolve these disputes is its greatest strength. That is, the recognition that more than one person can have rights in property at the same time such that a bundle of rights and obligations are created between those people. In consequence, equity will recognize that some owners of property, the trustees, will bear obligations towards other owners of the same property. The trust, therefore, embodies a sophisticated and yet very simple synthesis of rights based on property and on obligations. The justification for the imposition of such a network of rights and obligations in the form of a trust is the unconscionability of the defendant denying the claimant either rights in equity in the trust property or some equitable remedy against the defendant personally if the trust property or its traceable substitute is not recoverable. The adaptability of the law of trusts to changing circumstances is due to

5

the inherent durability of this core concept: by recognizing that more than one person has rights to property at the same time, unconscionable treatment of that property can be prevented, complex dealings with property over long periods of time can be managed effectively, and the competing rights and obligations of the various owners can be marshalled efficiently.

Consequently, this idea can be used to ensure that trustees observe the wishes of those who create trusts in situations as diverse as that in which such a person (a set-tlor) has died and left that property by will or where a group of settlors have bonded together to create a fund of money with which to pay themselves pensions when they retire. It can be used to prevent the person whose name appears on the Land Register as being the proprietor of the family home from unconscionably denying the rights of those other people who may have contributed in common with him to the purchase price of that property or to its maintenance or improvement thereafter. It can be used to trace and to recover for a company the value of property looted from it by its directors in breach of their fiduciary duties of loyalty and good faith, even if the original property taken from the company has passed through a number of hands and been converted into other property on a number of occasions, by means of the imposition of a constructive trust on the person who ultimately holds the traceable proceeds of that property. In these ways as in many others, the law of trusts reinforces the lawful wishes of the owner of property and protects others from the unconscionable abstraction of their property.

This book focuses, however, on the English law on private trusts. It contains no discussion of the law of charities nor of any other public trusts: the reader is referred to the appropriate textbooks on that subject, *Tudor on Charities* or *Picarda on Charities*.

B. The Lay-Out of This Book

Section One: General Principles

Section One: General Principles considers the fundamental principles on which the law of trusts rests and the modern shape of the law. Section One is divided into five parts. The first part deals with the definition and classification of the various forms of trust under the general law, while observing trends in the international, commercial as well as the municipal and domestic use of the trust.

Part A Introduction to the Law of Trusts attempts a definition of the term 'trust' by evaluating the various literatures around the Commonwealth which have undertaken the same task. Then the difference between express, resulting, implied, and constructive trusts are considered, together with the differences between the various forms of express private trusts. That chapter considers, in introductory terms, the role of settlor, trustee, and beneficiary in the trust structure before considering the various purposes for which trusts are used in practice.

Part B Express Private Trusts deals with the manner in which express trusts are declared, constituted, and recognized. Chapter 2 'The Three Certainties' considers both the requirements of certainty necessary for the creation of an express trust, whether by will or *inter vivos*. 'Chapter 3' Certainty of Subject Matter' then considers specifically the requirement of certainty of subject matter, before Chapter 4 'Certainty of Objects' considers the various practical issues surrounding the identification of the beneficiaries of various forms of express trust.

Chapter 5 'The Constitution of an Express Private Trust' considers the manner in which express trusts are constituted by means of the transfer of property to trustees or the situation in which the settlor declares himself to be trustee, the issues surrounding contracts and covenants to create trusts, and trusts of future property. Chapter 6 considers the centrality of 'The Beneficiary Principle' including analyses of trusts created specifically for the benefit of people and trusts for non-charitable purposes. Chapter 7 'The Nature of a Beneficiary's Interest' considers the various forms of express private trusts, dividing between fixed interest trusts (including vested interests, contingent interests, conditional interests, interests in possession, and interests in remainder), discretionary trusts, protective trusts, accumulation and maintenance trusts, and issues relating to the assignability of interests and rights, as well as the surrender and forfeiture of interests and rights. Chapter 8 analyses 'Trusts with Unlawful Purposes', including infringements of public policy, the rule against perpetuities, the rule against excessive accumulations, restrictions on alienation, and trusts to defeat dependants and to defraud creditors. Chapter 9 'Trusts and Insolvency' considers the various ways in which the trust device represents a security device in the event of bankrupty.

Part C The Duties and Powers of Trustees deals with the core concepts of trusteeship. The discussion spread across Chapter 10 'The Duties of Trustees, Part One' and Chapter 11 'The Duties of Trustees, Part Two' divides between general duties in relation to the trust and general duties in relation to the exercise of the trustees' powers. The general duties relating to the trust relate to the duties of trustees on acceptance of trust, to obey directions of trust, to exercise reasonable care, to act properly in relation to the payment of outgoings, to invest the trust fund, to distribute income and capital to the right people, not to delegate their trusteeship, to act jointly, to act gratuitously, not to profit from the trust, to account to the beneficiaries, and to provide particular forms of information as to the management of the trust to the beneficiaries. The general duties in relation to the exercise of trustees' powers include: the duty to consider the exercise of a power or discretion, the duty to exercise an active discretion, the duty not to act under the dictation of another, the duty not to fetter the discretion, the duty to exercise the power in such a way that the intended result is achieved (or an unintended one is not achieved), and the duty to take account of relevant considerations and to ignore irrelevant ones; the duty to treat beneficiaries and objects even-handedly, the duty not to act capriciously or unreasonably, and an implied duty of good faith. Of central significance to the beneficiaries' ability to control trustees' discharge of their duties is the access to information as to the trustees' decisions and also, in certain circumstances, the reasons for their decisions: as considered in Chapter 12 'Disclosure of Information by Trustees'.

By contrast with the duties of trustees are the complex questions associated with the manner in which trustees exercise their powers. Chapters 13 and 14 divide 'Powers of Trustees' into two parts. The first deals with general principles relating to trustees' powers (the definition and classification of powers, the excessive exercise of a power, frauds on a power, the effect of powers of revocation, powers to release, contingent and conditional powers, and the duration of powers) and the second to specific powers of trustees (relating to sale; giving receipts; compounding liabilities and settling claims; and effecting insurance, delegation, maintenance, advancement, and amendment). Associated with the exercise of these powers are the powers of delegation, considered in Chapter 15 'Delegation by Trustees'.

The discussion of powers then ranges across a series of detailed questions in Chapter 16 relating to 'Powers of Revocation', in Chapter 17 'Disclaimer, Release, and Extinguishment of Powers', in Chapter 18 to 'The Excessive Execution of a Power', and in Chapter 19 to 'Fraud on a Power'. Chapter 20 'The Judicial Review of the Exercise of Trustees' Discretions' considers the manner in which the courts maintain control over the powers of trustees. By contrast again, Chapter 21 'Rights of Trustees' considers the rights which trustees have, to indemnity, to recover their disbursements, and so forth, in contrast to the range of positive and negative obligations which they bear in relation to the observance of their duties and the performance of their powers.

Chapter 22 'Death, Retirement, Removal, and Appointment of Trustees' deals with the appointment, retirement, and removal of the trustees, as well as the rights of beneficiaries to remove trustees and to terminate the trust. Chapter 23 'Particular Trustees and Protectors' then analyses specific forms of trustee such as judicial trustees, the role of the Public Trustee, custodian trustees, trust corporations, and the use of protectors in jurisdictions other than England and Wales. Chapter 24 'Variation and Amendment of Trusts' considers the manner in which trusts can be varied under the Trustee Act 1925, the Variation of Trusts Act 1958, and other miscellaneous provisions. This chapter also considers the line between mere variations and comprehensive resettlements of trusts.

The focus then shifts away from express trusts to trusts implied by law. **Part D, Trusts Implied by Law** considers implied, resulting, and constructive trusts, as well as equitable doctrines such as proprietary estoppel. Chapter 25 'An

Introduction to Trusts Implied by Law' analyses the bases on which such trusts come into existence: whether in the form of resulting trusts, implied trusts, the various forms of constructive trust arising *sui generis* or under particular headings, and the associated equitable doctrines of proprietary estoppel and estoppel by representation. Chapter 26 'Resulting Trusts' analyses the two principal forms of resulting trust. Automatic resulting trusts arise in circumstances in which there is no declaration of trust by mistake, a failure of trust, or surplus property after the performance of a trust and loans for a specified purpose. Resulting trusts arising on the purchase of property are then surveyed, together with the equitable presumptions in favour and against resulting trusts, as well as limits on resulting trusts on grounds of illegality, of mistake, and in relation to void contracts.

The group of chapters on constructive trusts is based on the fundamental principle that a constructive trust is predicated on the legal owner of property acting unconscionably and knowingly. That general principle is then applied in a variety of contexts. So, Chapter 27 'Constructive Trusts in Response to Unconscionable Behaviour' considers the ambit of that general principle, and then the imposition of constructive trusts in relation to unlawful killing; theft; bribery; unconscionable dealing with property; undue influence and constructive fraud; circumstances in which statute is used as an engine of fraud; the enforcement of voluntary agreements; fraud, void and voidable contracts. Then in Chapter 28 'Constructive Trusts to Enforce Agreements' considers constructive trusts in relation to contracts and in relation to voluntarily assumed liability. Those in relation to contracts are demonstrated to arise over specifically enforceable contracts, commercial joint ventures, agreements to stay out of the market, part performance of agreements, and purchaser's undertakings; those in relation to voluntarily assumed liability arise in relation to common intention constructive trusts, secret trusts, mutual wills, and in limited circumstances around incompletely constituted trusts.

Chapter 29 'Constructive Trusts in Response to Abuse of Fiduciary Position' considers the ways in which constructive trusts arise in relation to unauthorized profits from a fiduciary office, the acceptance of bribes, situations in which there is a conflict of interest, and the relationship of these principles with express trust. Chapter 30 on *The Liability of Strangers* to the trust considers those situations in which people who are not trustees of an express trust are construed to be liable as though trustees, or as trustees de son tort, or on the basis of knowing receipt of property in breach of trust or who assist such a breach of trust dishonestly.

Finally for Section One, **Part E, Breach of Trust** considers the potential avenues of redress which are open to beneficiaries in the event of a breach of trust. Chapter 31 'Avoidance of Breach of Trust' considers the means by which settlors might structure their settlements to reduce the liability of a breach of trust and the means by which the beneficiaries can prevent a breach of trust, particularly through freezing injunctions, the removal of trustees, and the appointment of judicial trustees. Chapter 32 'Trustees' Liability for Breach of Trust' then considers the potential liability of express trustees for breach of trust, the nature of the remedies of account and equitable compensation, the available defences to breach of trust, and the beneficiaries' right of election between remedies. As considered in Chapter 30, this liability of trustees frequently operates in tandem with the liability of third parties who have received property in breach of trust or who have dishonestly assisted that breach. A further aspect of such litigation in practice is considered in Chapter 33 'Tracing and Proprietary Claims' in relation to the recovery of trust property passed away in breach of trust, by contradistinction to the imposition of personal liability on the trustees or some third party. The discussion of tracing divides between common law tracing and equitable tracing, where the latter considers tracing the trust property into mixed funds, considering the available claims and remedies, the loss of the right to trace in certain circumstances, and the possible defences to a tracing claim.

Section Two: Specific Trusts

Section Two: Specific Trusts then progresses from the discussion of general principle to consider the manner in which such principles function in identified contexts which are common features of trusts law practice.

Part F, Private Client Trusts considers the manner in which the trust device is used to organize the estates of private clients. Chapter 34, 'Private Client Trusts' considers the functioning of trusts in which the rights of the beneficiary have vested in that beneficiary. Chapter 35 focuses on 'Accumulation and Maintenance Trusts' created for the purpose of caring for family members by providing for the investment of capital to provide for their maintenance and for the accumulation of earned income. By contrast Chapter 36 'Discretionary Trusts and Disabled Trusts' considers the flexibility which the discretionary trust gives to those planning their personal affairs and ordering their estates both during their lifetimes and in preparation for their deaths. Chapter 37 'Testamentary Trusts' considers testamentary trusts and the functions of executors in relation to trusts created by will.

Part G, International Trusts reflects the increasing significance of the use of trusts in cross-border contexts. In particular there are discussions in Chapter 38 of 'Offshore Asset Protection Trusts', in Chapter 39 of 'Offshore Purpose Trusts', in Chapter 40 Cayman Islands STAR Trusts and the Virgin Islands' Special Trusts Act 2003. Questions of private international law and trusts are considered in Chapter 41 'Choice of Law' and Chapter 42 'Jurisdiction, Remedies, and the Recognition and Enforcement of Foreign Judgments'.

One of the most significant contexts in which the trust concept is used in modern practice is the pension fund used in the employment context as considered in

Part H, Occupational Pension Scheme Trusts. The fundamental basis of such trusts is analysed in Chapter 43 'Nature and Structure of Occupational Pension Scheme Trusts'. The statutory and regulatory context within which pension funds operate is balanced by the power of the settlors of the trust fund in establishing occupational pension funds, as delineated in Chapter 45 'Legislation Affecting Benefits' and, by contrast in relation to trustees, in Chapter 44 'Trusteeship and Duties of Trustees of Occupational Pension Scheme Trusts' both in relation to the nature and context of pension fund trusts and the specific statutory provisions. Chapter 46 then considers the 'Amendment, Termination, and Regulation of Occupational Pension Schemes'.

Trusts are used increasingly frequently in financial markets, as set out in **Part I, Trusts in Financial Transactions.** In Chapter 47 'Trustees in the Law of Finance' there is a discussion of the liability of trustees to comply with the provisions of the Financial Services and Markets Act 2000, regulation by the Financial Services Authority, and the need to comply with principles as to the conduct of business between professional trustees and inexpert beneficiaries. Chapter 48 'Trusts of Financial Instruments and of Money' considers the manner in which financial instruments can be made the subject matter of a trust and the particular complexities associated with the constitution of trusts over money held in electronic bank accounts. By extension, then, in Chapter 49 'Trusts Used to Take Security in Commercial Transactions' is an analysis of the means by which *Quistclose* trust techniques and retention of title techniques, as considered in Chapter 9, are applied specifically to financial contracts: ranging from ordinary loan contracts through to complex financial derivatives. The trust device is particularly significant when taking security in financial transactions by means of margin or collateralization. The dematerialization of financial products creates particular problems concerning the subject matter of such trusts and of tracing the proceeds of such trust funds. Chapter 50 'Trusts in Relation to Debt Securities' analyses the particular role of the trustee in the regulation of the issue of eurobonds and the issue of debentures. Chapter 51 'Unit Trusts' considers the interaction of both forms of fiduciary, scheme manager and trustee, in unit trusts and, by way of brief comparison, in open-ended investment companies. Chapter 52 'Investment of Private Express Trusts' considers the use of private trusts as investment vehicles, the provisions of the Trustee Act 2000 relating to the need for standard investment criteria, to the general duty of care owed by trustees towards the beneficiaries, the requirements of portfolio investment theory, and the beneficiaries' remedies for breach of these duties of investment.

Part J, Trusts Used In Commercial Contexts considers how the principles of the general law of trusts have been adapted specifically for use in commercial situations. Chapter 53 'Trusts Which Conduct a Business' considers the practical problems relating to the establishment and management of trading trusts, the limitation of the trustees' liabilities, the distinction between trusts and partnerships, and the means of ensuring the pursuit of such a trust's commercial purpose. Chapter 54 'Fiduciary Liability in the Creation of Financial and Commercial Transactions' considers how the seller of goods or an expert commercial party dealing with a customer in a regulated market may be held liable as a constructive trustee of any benefit taken from a commercial relationship or any unauthorized profit taken from a fiduciary office. Chapter 55 'Trusts and the Termination of Contracts' then analyses the means by which property advanced under a void or otherwise ineffective contract can be recovered by the contracting parties.

Part K, Trusts of Land and of the Home considers the complex network of trusts concepts which arise in relation to the family home and the statutory rules relating to trusts of land. Chapter 56 'Trusts of the Family Home' analyses the means by which rights are acquired in the family home by means of express trusts, purchase price resulting trusts, common intention constructive trusts, and proprietary estoppel. Chapter 57 'Trusts of Land' considers the operation of the Trusts of Land and Appointment of Trustees Act 1996 and the residual operation of the Settled Land Act 1925.

1

THE NATURE OF THE TRUST

A. The Definition of the Term 'Trust'

The essence of the trust

The essence of a trust is the imposition of an equitable obligation on a person who **1.01**
is the legal owner of property (a trustee) which requires that person to act in good
conscience when dealing with that property in favour of any person (the
beneficiary) who has a beneficial interest recognized by equity in the property.[1]

---

[1] The nature of this form of 'conscience' has been the subject of scholarly debate for centuries.
For jurists such as St German and for Sir Thomas More conscience bound the Lord Chancellor to
follow the rules set out in the common law and conscience bound a trustee not simply to follow his

The trustee is said to 'hold the property on trust' for the beneficiary. There are four significant elements to the trust: that it is equitable, that it provides the beneficiary with rights in property, that it also imposes obligations on the trustee, and that those obligations are fiduciary in nature. This chapter introduces these facets of the trust, and describes the general categories into which trusts fall.

1.02 A trust comes into existence either by virtue of having been established expressly by a person (the settlor) who was the absolute owner of property[2] before the creation of the trust (an express trust); or by virtue of some action of the settlor which the court interprets to have been sufficient to create a trust but which the settlor himself did not know was a trust (an implied trust);[3] or by operation of law either to resolve some dispute as to ownership of property where the creation of an express trust has failed (an automatic resulting trust)[4] or to recognize the proprietary rights of one who has contributed to the purchase price of property (a purchase price resulting trust);[5] or by operation of law to prevent the legal owner of property from seeking unconscionably to deny the rights of those who have equitable interests in that property (a constructive trust).[6]

1.03 The rights and obligations of the various parties to the trust are considered by way of introduction in this chapter before being analysed more fully in the appropriate chapters later in the book. The following paragraphs consider the principal features of the trust and the various ways in which trusts have been defined and understood by courts, legislatures, and other commentators in various jurisdictions.

The equitable nature of the trust

1.04 The common thread between all of the various categories of trusts is the obligation of the trustee to act in good conscience in relation to any dealings with the property at issue and in recognition of the rights of beneficiaries.[7] The central role of conscience in the operation of a trust was identified by Lord Browne-Wilkinson in

---

own conscience but rather conscience bound a trustee to observe the wishes of his beneficiary (see, for example, *Gresley v Saunders* (1522) Spelman Rep 22–23). However, as the notion of conscience is rendered by Lord Browne-Wilkinson in *Westdeutsche Landesbank v Islington* [1996] AC 669 there is a suggestion of a greater subjectivity in that a person will only be subject to the duties of a trustee if he knows of the matter which is said to affect his conscience: see para 27.01 in this regard in relation to constructive trusts arising on the basis of conscience.

[2] Such that the 'property' in question is best understood to be 'rights in property' and need not be absolute title in the property. Thus, a lease over land may itself be the subject matter of a trust even though it is not the largest property right in that land (*Keech v Sandford* (1726) Sel Cas Ch 61). An equitable interest in a trust may itself be the subject matter of a trust (*re Lashmar* (1891) 1 Ch 258, *Grainge v Wilberforce* (1889) 5 TLR 436). See paras 5.09 *et seq* below.

[3] *Re Kayford* [1975] 1 WLR 279; *Paul v Constance* [1977] 1 WLR 527.

[4] *Vandervell v IRC* [1967] 2 AC 291.   [5] *Dyer v Dyer* (1788) 2 Cox Eq Cas 92.

[6] *Westdeutsche Landesbank Girozentrale v Islington LBC* [1996] AC 669.

[7] See A S Hudson, *Equity and Trusts* (3rd edn, Cavendish Publishing, 2003) ('*Hudson*'), 952.

Westdeutsche Landesbank v Islington[8] in the first of his four 'relevant principles of trust law':

> (i) Equity operates on the conscience of the owner of the legal interest. In the case of a trust, the conscience of the legal owner requires him to carry out the purposes for which the property was vested in him (express or implied trust) or which the law imposes on him by reason of his unconscionable conduct (constructive trust).[9]

This opening paragraph of his lordship's definition of a trust makes no explicit mention of the resulting trust, although it could be treated as having been subsumed within the reference to 'implied trust' in his first principle. There is a distinction drawn here between the motivation behind express and implied trusts on the one hand, and constructive trusts on the other. The express trust is conceived of here as an institutional[10] device which obliges the trustee to perform the duties identified by the settlor when the trust was created. By contrast the function of the constructive trust is as a response to the unconscionable behaviour of the trustee. Whereas the express trust is deliberately created and performed by reference to the settlor's wishes, the constructive trust is responsive to the conduct of the trustee and seeks to control his conduct by making him subject to the fiduciary duties associated with the status of a constructive trustee.[11] The constructive trust comes into existence only when the defendant acts unconscionably in the knowledge that his behaviour is unconscionable.[12]

The classic definition of a trust is generally taken to be that of Sir Arthur Underhill **1.05** which he set out in the following terms:

> A trust is an equitable obligation, binding a person (called a trustee) to deal with property owned[13] by him (called trust property, being distinguished from his private property) for the benefit of persons (called beneficiaries or, in old cases,

---

[8] *Westdeutsche Landesbank Girozentrale v Islington LBC* [1996] AC 669, [1996] 2 All ER 961,988, *per* Lord Browne-Wilkinson. [9] ibid.

[10] The term 'institutional' in relation to trusts was imported to English trusts law by Prof Maudsley ('Proprietary Remedies for the Recovery of Money' (1959) 75 LQR 234, 237) from an article by the American jurist Prof Pound ('The Progress of Law' (1920) 33 Harv L Rev 420, 421). That a trust is 'institutional' (or perhaps 'substantive', see para 25.33) means that it arises automatically at the time when the trustee is aware of some factor which affects his conscience, and is not a remedy which only comes into existence at the time when a court gives an order to that effect. This sense of the trust is considered below at para 25.39.

[11] The constructive trust is considered in detail in Chapters 27 through 30.

[12] *Westdeutsche Landesbank v Islington* [1996] AC 669. On the notion of conscience in equity generally and in the trust in particular see *Hudson* 6 *et seq* and 977 *et seq*.

[13] Interestingly, Prof David Hayton in the most recent edition of A Underhill and DJ Hayton, *Law of Trusts and Trustees* (16th edn, Butterworths, 2002)('*Underhill and Hayton*') 5, explains that he has altered Sir Arthur Underhill's definition of the trust slightly to recognize that the trustee is an *owner* of the legal title in trust property (on which see *Smith v Anderson* (1880) 15 Ch D 247, 275 *per* James LJ) and not simply a person who has the trust property under his control: a person may

cestuis que trust), of whom he may himself be one, and any one of whom may enforce the obligation[14].[15]

This definition recognizes that the trust is enforced by equity, rather than by the common law. The common law does not recognize the rights of any person to property other than the legal owner of that property and consequently the common law will not recognize the equitable interests of beneficiaries. By means of the trust, equity ensures that the legal owner of property observes the rights of other people who have beneficial rights in the property. The trust property is deemed to be separate from the trustee's own, personal property, even though the trustee is the common law owner of that property.

1.06   Sir Arthur Underhill's definition is one which can be applied so as to cover all forms of trust, although its focus is primarily on the express trust. The most effective definition of the trust is that of Lord Browne-Wilkinson in *Westdeutsche Landesbank v Islington*,[16] based as it is on a broadly based notion of conscience which covers all forms of trust whether expressly declared or implied by the court. That the trust functions on the basis of the trustee's conscience is evident from the second of Lord Browne-Wilkinson's principles of the law of trusts:

> (ii) Since the equitable jurisdiction to enforce trusts depends upon the conscience of the holder of the legal interest being affected, he cannot be a trustee of the property if and so long as he is ignorant of the facts alleged to affect his conscience . . . [17]

To put that proposition another way: to be a trustee, one must have knowledge of some factor which affects one's conscience. The trust is imposed only from the time at which the trustee had the requisite knowledge of the factor which is said to affect his conscience. By way of example: simply because a person took possession of a bicycle that would not necessarily render him a trustee of that bicycle, unless and until he became aware that the bicycle belonged to another person and therefore that it was unconscionable for him to purport to retain beneficial

---

have control of the trust property as a bailee or depositary for that property without having any legal title in it. The definition in previous editions had read: 'A trust is an equitable obligation, binding on a person (who is called a trustee) to deal with property over which he has control (called trust property, being distinguished from his private property) for the benefit of persons (called beneficiaries or, in old cases, *cestuis que trust*), of whom he may himself be one, and any one of whom may enforce the obligation.'

[14]   Pettit adds to the end of this definition the following: ' . . . or for a charitable purpose, which may be enforced at the instance of the Attorney-General, or for some other purpose permitted by law though unenforceable': P Pettit, *Equity and Trusts* (9th edn, Butterworths, 2001) ('*Pettit*') 25.

[15]   *Underhill and Hayton* 3. Cited with approval in *Re Marshall's WT* [1945] Ch 217, at 219; *Green v Russell* [1959] 2 QB 226, at 241. J McGhee, Snell's Equity (30th edn, Sweet & Maxwell, 2000) ('*Snell's, Equity*') suggesting that there is no satisfactory definition of a trust was cited with approval in *Allen v Distillers Company (Biochemicals) Ltd* [1974] QB 384, at *Snell* 394.

[16]   [1996] AC 669.

[17]   *Westdeutsche Landesbank Girozentrale v Islington LBC* [1996] AC 669, [1996] 2 All ER 961, 988, *per* Lord Browne-Wilkinson.

title in it. This notion is considered further below in relation to constructive trusts.[18] Another judicial conceptualization of this point ran as follows:

> The typical case of a trust is one in which the legal owner of the property is constrained by a court of equity so to deal with it as to give effect to the equitable rights of another.[19]

The core of the trustee's obligation is therefore to recognize the equitable rights of the beneficiaries: an obligation which gives rise to a broad range of fiduciary duties considered in Part D of this book. The principal focus of the law of trusts is the protection of the beneficiaries' equitable interests. Consequently, the main questions in relation to the analysis of any trust are the identification of the applicable equitable interests to be protected, their nature and their extent.

That the trust relates to property

The focus of the trust is on property

The roots of the trust, and those of its precursor the medieval use, were in land law. **1.07** Many of the developments and perturbations which have been caused in trusts law in recent years have been the result of the attempt to apply trusts law concepts which were developed originally to deal with land to contexts involving personal property and, in particular, intangible property such as money held in electronic bank accounts.[20] In relation to intangible property in particular, the need in the general law of trusts to be able to identify the subject matter of the trust is much more complex than in relation to real property.

That uses and trusts arose originally from dealings in land is evident from Coke's **1.08** definition of the trust as being:

> ... a confidence reposed in some other, not issuing out of the land but as a thing collateral thereto, annexed in privity to the estate of the land, and to the person touching the land, for which *cestui que trust* has no remedy but by subpoena in the Chancery.[21]

The trust emerges as an action exercisable by the beneficiary in connection with land in the form of a 'confidence': one sense of which term equates to the notion of conscience which is used by equity to describe the trust in many other contexts[22] and which gives a flavour of the trustee's fiduciary duties of loyalty and confidentiality towards the beneficiary. That trusts are property holding devices emerges from Lord Browne-Wilkinson's third principle of trusts law:

> (iii) In order to establish a trust there must be identifiable trust property...[23]

---

[18] See para 27.01. [19] *Re Astor's Settlement Trusts* [1952] Ch 534, 541, *per* Roxburgh J.
[20] See para 33.97. [21] Co Litt 272b.
[22] *Westdeutsche Landesbank Girozentrale v Islington LBC* [1996] AC 669.
[23] *Westdeutsche Landesbank Girozentrale v Islington LBC* [1996] AC 669, [1996] 2 All ER 961, 988, *per* Lord Browne-Wilkinson.

The ramifications of this principle are that there cannot be a valid trust unless there is some property which is distinct from all other property such that it can be identified as being the subject matter of the trust,[24] and also that the trust is an institution which is concerned with the allocation of rights in property and is not simply an institution connected with obligations.[25] This principle gives rise to the requirement of certainty of the subject matter of the trust, considered in Chapter 3,[26] and the beneficiary principle, considered in Chapter 6,[27] the combination of which require that there be identified property held on trust for the benefit of identified people for a limited perpetuity period, as opposed to being held on trust for abstract purposes which confer no beneficial rights on any identified person.[28] In short, there cannot be a valid trust unless there is some identified property held on trust for some identified person.[29]

1.09 To be a beneficiary under a trust is to be a person with proprietary rights in the property which comprises the trust fund.[30] The trust may be either a trust which identifies property which belongs to one individual beneficiary, or which identifies that single beneficiary as being one of a class of beneficiaries who own rights in property collectively, or which identifies the beneficiary as having rights in property subject to the satisfaction of some contingency (whether the satisfaction of that contingency is within the control of the trustees or not).[31] As Lord Browne-Wilkinson held in his fourth principle of trusts law:

> (iv) Once a trust is established, as from the date of its establishment the beneficiary has, in equity, a proprietary interest in the trust property, which proprietary interest will be enforceable in equity against any subsequent holder of the property (whether the original property or substituted property into which it can be traced) other than a purchaser for value of the legal interest without notice.[32]

That the beneficiary has proprietary rights in the subject matter of the trust leads to a number of other, legal effects. If the trust property is transferred out of the trust in breach of the trustees' obligations, the beneficiaries have a right to recover the property taken from the trust fund,[33] or to trace their rights in that property into any other property for which it is substituted,[34] or to recover its value from

---

[24] *Re Goldcorp Exchange Ltd* [1995] AC 74.

[25] On the difficulties caused by this principle in modern trusts practice see AS Hudson, 'The unbearable lightness of property' in AS Hudson (ed), *New Perspectives on Property Law, Obligations and Restitution* (Cavendish Publishing, 2004) 1, 11 and 23.

[26] See para 3.01.   [27] See para 6.01.   [28] See para 6.13.

[29] There are complications in relation to discretionary trusts, as considered in Chapter 34, when it may be difficult to identify which property is held on trust for which beneficiaries. However, the statement given above will constitute a sufficient conceptual platform at this stage.

[30] See the discussion of *Saunders v Vautier* (1841) 4 Beav 115 at paras 1.45, 7.05.

[31] See paras 4.01 *et seq* below.

[32] *Westdeutsche Landesbank Girozentrale v Islington LBC* [1996] AC 669, [1996] 2 All ER 961, 988, *per* Lord Browne-Wilkinson.   [33] As discussed in Chapter 32.

[34] As discussed in Chapter 33.

the trustees personally[35] or from any third party who has interfered with the trust personally.[36] Further, because the trust fund constitutes the property of the beneficiaries in equity it will not form a part of the trustee's own estate either in the event of his insolvency or on his death.[37]

That the trustees own the property

The trustees are the owners at common law of the trust fund. The point has been **1.10** made by Prof Hayton,[38] as considered above,[39] that Sir Arthur Underhill's original definition of the trust required a slight, but significant, amendment to the effect that we should recognize that a trustee *owns* the trust property and does not simply have it under his control. That the trustees are the owners of the trust fund at common law means two things. First, a trust does not have legal personality and therefore cannot contract on its own behalf nor can it own property as a legal person: rather, it acts through the trustees. It is the trustees who are recorded at the Land Registry as being the proprietors of land held on trust, it is the trustees who are empowered to sign cheques to make payments out of the trust's bank account, and so on. The trustees operate and manage the trust's affairs. Secondly, the trustees' powers of operation and their legal ownership of the property is tempered by equity's recognition of the rights of the beneficiaries. The nature of that equitable ownership is considered below.[40] In relation to the control of the trustees, the beneficiaries are able to hold the trustees to account for the performance of their fiduciary duties in the manner considered in Part D and for breach of trust in Chapter 32.

The nature of the property which can comprise a trust fund

The 'property' which constitutes a trust fund can be any form of right in property **1.11** and need not be equivalent to outright dominium in the underlying property. Thus, a lease over land may itself be the subject matter of a trust[41] even though it is not the largest possible property right in that land, and an equitable interest in a trust may itself be the subject matter of a trust[42] even though it does not constitute the entirety of the rights in that property. Provided that any asset or thing can be described as being property or a right in property, then it is capable of forming the subject matter of a trust. It has been accepted latterly that even the benefits to be derived from property which cannot itself be transferred, such as the future

---

[35] As discussed in Chapter 32.
[36] As discussed in Chapter 30.   [37] As discussed in Chapter 7.
[38] *Underhill and Hayton* 5, explains that he has altered Sir Arthur Underhill's definition of the trust slightly to recognize that the trustee is an *owner* of the legal title in trust property in recognition of the arguments made to that effect in *Smith v Anderson* (1880) 15 Ch D 247, 275 *per* James LJ.
[39] See para 1.05.   [40] See para 1.35 and paras 7.01 *et seq.*
[41] *Keech v Sandford* (1726) Sel Cas Ch 61.
[42] *Grainge v Wilberforce* (1889) 5 TLR 436; *Re Lashmar* (1891) 1 Ch 258.

income which may be derived from a non-transferable promotions contract,[43] can nevertheless form the subject matter of a trust.[44] The reference above[45] to a settlor needing 'absolute title' in the property which is to be subjected to the trust indicates that the settlor must own all of the rights which are purportedly settled on trust.[46] Therefore, as mentioned, a lease can be the subject matter of a trust. The settlor need not be the owner of the fee simple in the land over which the lease takes effect. The settlor cannot create a valid settlement over property which he does not own at the time when the settlement is created[47] but he must be the owner of those rights which are to be the subject matter of the trust.

That the trust imposes obligations

1.12   While the trust is a property holding device, the means by which trusts law effects the holding of property and the protection of the rights of the beneficiaries is by means of imposing obligations on the trustees. The trustees' obligations fall into two kinds: first, fiduciary obligations of good conscience which include requirements that those trustees avoid conflicts of interest, that they deal fairly between the beneficiaries, and that they refrain from making unauthorized profits from the trust;[48] secondly, obligations of good management which include requirements that the trustees do the best for the beneficiaries, that they act prudently when making investments, and that they provide given kinds of information to the beneficiaries.[49] These obligations are considered in detail in Part C of this book. Some of these principles of trusteeship arise under the general law of trusts, or are read into a trust by the Trustee Act 2000, or are adapted for their particular purpose by the terms of a trust instrument. If the trustees breach these general obligations, or any specific obligations identified in the trust instrument, or any duty of care imposed on them by the Trustee Act 2000, then the trustees face liability for breach of trust, in the manner discussed in Chapter 32.[50]

1.13   To this extent, the law of trusts appears to be made up of obligations imposed on the trustee; albeit, importantly, obligations which relate to the beneficiaries' rights

---

[43] *Don King Productions Inc v Warren* [1998] 2 All ER 608, Lightman J; affirmed [2000] Ch 291, CA.

[44] *Re Celtic Extraction Ltd (in liquidation), Re Bluestone Chemicals Ltd (in liquidation)* [1999] 4 All ER 684; *Don King Productions Inc v Warren* [2000] Ch 291; *Swift v Dairywise Farms* [2000] 1 All ER 320.   [45] See para 1.11.

[46] While the settlor must own absolute title in the property settled on trust—for example, a lease— he need not hold absolute title in the property to which those rights relate—to continue the example, he need not own the freehold in the land over which the lease takes effect.

[47] *Re Brook's Settlement Trusts* [1939] 1 Ch 993. Cf *Re Ralli's Will Trusts* [1964] 2 WLR 144.

[48] See the discussion of these concepts in Chapter 29, paras 29.19 *et seq.*

[49] See the discussion of these concepts in Chapter 11.   [50] See para 32.01.

in the trust property. The definition of the trust used by Hanbury and Martin contains a sense of these obligations:

> A trust is a relationship recognised by equity which arises where property is vested in (a person or) persons called the trustees, which those trustees are obliged to hold for the benefit of other persons called *cestuis que trust* or beneficiaries. The interests of the beneficiaries will usually be laid down in the instrument creating the trust, but may be implied or imposed by law. The beneficiary's interest is proprietary in the sense that it can be sold, given away or disposed of by will; but it will cease to exist if the legal estate in the property comes into the hands of a bona fide purchaser for value without notice of the beneficial interest. The subject matter of the trust must be some form of property... There may also be trusts for charitable purposes; such trusts are enforced at the suit of the Attorney-General.[51]

The first half of that definition highlights the obligations borne by the trustee; the second half deals with other parts of the definition which rehearse that given by Lord Browne-Wilkinson in *Westdeutsche Landesbank v Islington*.[52]

Again, the nature of the obligation, or compulsion, imposed on the trustee is **1.14** evident in the definition of the trust provided by Keeton and Sheridan:

> A trust is the relationship which arises wherever a person (called the trustee) is compelled in equity to hold property, whether real or personal, and whether by legal or equitable title, for the benefit of some persons (of whom he may be one and who are termed beneficiaries) or for some object permitted by law, in such a way that the real benefit of the property accrues, not to the trustees, but to the beneficiaries or other objects of the trust.[53]

The obligations which are borne by the trustees are nevertheless obligations imposed by equity and are not in the manner of contractual or tortious obligations. They are obligations of good conscience, and as such operate on the basis of much wider, foundational principles as well as on the basis of narrow rules of trusts law developed by the case law in the Chancery courts as considered in this book. In that vein Maitland attempted a broad definition of the obligations characteristic of the trust:

> When a person has rights which he is bound to exercise upon behalf of another or for the accomplishment of some particular purpose he is said to have those rights in trust for that other or for that purpose and he is called a trustee. It is a wide, vague definition, but the best that I can make. I shall comment on it by distinguishing cases of trust from some other cases.[54]

In this sense the trustee is someone who bears 'rights'. This is an important dimension of trusteeship not dealt with explicitly by the other definitions considered thus far. A trustee does have rights: the rights of the legal owner of property to sell that

---

[51] *Hanbury and Martin's Modern Equity* (16th edn, Sweet & Maxwell, 2001) ('*Martin*') 47–48.
[52] [1996] AC 669.   [53] Sheridan and Keeton, *The Law of Trusts* (12th edn, 1993) 3.
[54] Maitland, *Lectures on Equity* (2nd edn, 1936) 44.

property, to mortgage it, and so forth. The trustee's name is the name which appears on the Land Register, on the bank account's cheque book, and so forth. Those rights are rights which he is 'bound to exercise upon behalf' of the beneficiaries, which is the same as saying that the trustee owes obligations to the beneficiaries but coming at it from the other direction. The trustee's position is therefore a combination of the rights of the common law owner of property and equitable obligations to observe the rights of the beneficial owners of that property and to obey the principles of fiduciary law. Importantly, the nature of the trust is identified by Maitland as being observable only from an analysis of the decided cases rather than being readily capable of definition in the abstract.

1.15   A judicial definition of the trust similarly recognized the obligational aspect of the trust.

> No definition of a 'trust' seems to have been accepted as comprehensive and exact . . . Strictly it refers, I think, to the duty or aggregate accumulation of obligations that rest upon a person described as a trustee. The responsibilities are in relation to property held by him, or under his control. That property he will be compelled by a court in its equitable jurisdiction to administer in the manner lawfully prescribed by the trust instrument, or where there be no specific provision written or oral, or to the extent that such provision is invalid or lacking, in accordance with equitable principles. As a consequence the administration will be in such a manner that the consequential benefits and advantages accrue, not to the trustee, but to the persons called cestuis que trust, or beneficiaries, if there be any, if not, for some purpose which the law will recognise and enforce. A trustee may be a beneficiary, in which case advantages will accrue in his favour to the extent of his beneficial interest.[55]

In the vernacular sense of the word 'trust', the beneficiaries are therefore obliged to repose confidence in the good conscience of the trustee.[56] Unlike the vernacular meaning of the word trust, however, the beneficiaries' faith in the trustees is bolstered by the obligations which the law of trusts imposes on them. The special quality of these obligations in the law of trusts is encapsulated in the trustees' obligations being fiduciary obligations, as considered in the next section.

That the trustee's obligations are fiduciary in nature

1.16   That the obligations of the trustee are fiduciary obligations emerges most clearly from Scott's definition of the term 'trust':[57]

---

[55]   *Re Scott* [1948] SASR 193, 196 *per* Mayo J. Cited with approval in J Mowbray et al, *Lewin on Trusts* (17th edn, Sweet & Maxwell, 2000) ('*Lewin*') 4.

[56]   Cotterrell, 'Trusting in law: legal and moral concepts of trust' (1993) 46(2) Current Legal Problems 75.

[57]   Albeit that his definition is prefaced by the following, perfectly sensible caveat: 'Even if it were possible to frame an exact definition of a legal concept, the definition would not be of great practical value. A definition cannot properly be used as though it were a major premise so that rules governing conduct can be deduced from it. Our law, at least, has not grown in that way. When the rules have been arrived at from other sources, it may be possible to attempt to frame a definition. But the

It is possible to state the principal distinguishing characteristics of the concept [trust] so that others responsible for the Restatement of Trusts proposed the following definition or description of an express trust. It is 'a fiduciary relationship with respect to property, subjecting the person by whom the title to property is held to equitable duties to deal with the property for the benefit of another person, which arises as a result of a manifestation of an intention to create it'. In this definition or description the following characteristics are to be noticed: (1) a trust is a relationship; (2) it is a relationship of a fiduciary character; (3) it is a relationship with respect to property, not one involving merely personal duties; (4) it involves the existence of equitable duties imposed upon the holder of the title to the property to deal with it for the benefit of another; and (5) it arises as a result of a manifestation of an intention to create the relationship. The combination of these things characterizes the notion of the trust as that notion has been developed in the Anglo-American law.[58]

The fiduciary nature of a trustee's duties are not capable of simple definition. It could be said that the remainder of this book is concerned with their description: therefore an off-the-cuff summary here would not be helpful. That they are fiduciary in nature suggests, in the broadest terms, that they oblige the trustees to act with the utmost loyalty, fidelity, and care towards the beneficiaries.

B. The Different Forms of Trust

It is difficult to create a definition of the trust which will fit all contexts without dealing at a level of high abstraction because trusts fall into different categories which function in different ways. There are four types of trust identified in the Law of Property Act 1925: express trusts, implied trusts, resulting trusts, and constructive trusts.[59] However, this fourfold division conceals the fact that different forms of resulting and constructive trusts operate in different ways from one another and that the category of implied trusts has all but fallen into disuse.   **1.17**

Express trust

Express trusts are created consciously by the absolute owner of the property (the settlor) either declaring himself to be trustee of the property for identified beneficiaries, or declaring that some other person is to be trustee of the property for identified beneficiaries and then transferring legal title in the trust property to those trustees. The formalities required for the constitution of an express trust are considered in Chapter 5, and the effects of a failure to constitute the trust properly by vesting legal title in the subject matter of the trust in the trustees are considered in Chapter 6.   **1.18**

---

definition results from the rules, and not the rules from the definition. All that one can properly attempt to do is give such a description of a legal concept that others will know in a general way what one is talking about.'

[58] Scott, *Trusts* (4th edn) para 2.3.   [59] Law of Property Act 1925, s 53(2).

1.19　The settlor may be a trustee and also a beneficiary of the trust property. Thus, a settlor may declare himself to be trustee of property for appointed beneficiaries such that, assuming the declaration of trust has satisfied any applicable formalities,[60] an equitable interest in that property is created in favour of those beneficiaries with the settlor holding that property as trustee from that time. The settlor can reserve himself the rights of a sole beneficiary or one of a class of beneficiaries provided that the property is held on trust by at least one other person as trustee. The only impossible permutation would be for the settlor to be the sole trustee and the sole beneficiary of the trust because in that case that person would remain, in effect, the absolute owner of the property and no trust would have been created.

The various categories of express trust are considered below.[61]

Implied trust

1.20　The category of implied trust does seem to have all but withered on the vine. In the seventeenth century Lord Nottingham suggested that the term 'implied trusts' referred to all trusts which were not express trusts, although that usage is not continued today: in this book the term 'trusts implied by law' is instead used to cover resulting and constructive trusts.[62] That the term implied trusts continues to have some continued existence is suggested by a reference to implied trusts in section 53(2) of the Law of Property Act 1925. The implied trust, it is suggested, might cover the situation in which a settlor unknowingly performs actions which the court subsequently interprets as being the creation of a trust. For example, in circumstances in which the legal owner of a bank account declared that the contents of that account were to be considered to be the property of both himself and his sexual partner, the court interpreted this arrangement to have constituted a trust even though the settlor had no knowledge that that would have been the effect of his actions.[63] The modern cases[64] have, however, defined trusts created in such circumstances as being express trusts, as opposed to implied trusts.

Resulting trust

1.21　Resulting trusts arise in one of two contexts: either to restore the equitable interest in property to its original beneficial owner where a declaration of trust or other disposition of property has not exhausted the equitable interest in that property,[65] or to recognize that someone who has contributed to the purchase price of

---

[60] See para 5.01.　　[61] See para 1.27.

[62] *Cook v Fountain* (1676) 3 Swanst 585.　　[63] *Paul v Constance* [1977] 1 WLR 527.

[64] *Paul v Constance* [1977] 1 WLR 527.

[65] *Vandervell v IRC* [1967] 2 AC 291, HL; *Westdeutsche Landesbank v Islington LBC* [1996] AC 669; *Air Jamaica Ltd v Charlton* [1999] 1 WLR 1399, PC. See also trusts effected further to the principle in *Barclay's Bank v Quistclose Investments Ltd* [1970] AC 567, considered at para 49.14.

property has acquired an interest in that property in proportion to his contribution to its purchase price.[66] The doctrine of resulting trusts is therefore a limited one, divided as it is between these two limited categories. The purpose of the former type of resulting trust is, in truth, a means of ensuring that there is no 'gap' in the ownership of property;[67] that is, the resulting trust supplies a means of resolving disputes as to the ownership of property by means alternatively of a declaration that the equitable interest in that property results back to the person who last owned that property or that a proprietary interest in it results to the person who contributed the means of acquiring it. The purpose of the latter type of resulting trust is to prevent the legal owner of property from unconscionably denying the rights of some other person who has contributed to the acquisition of property when it was the common intention of the parties that each should take some proprietary right in that property.[68]

Constructive trust

The constructive trust exemplifies equity's role as a means of ensuring good conscience. When a person deals with property in a way which is deemed to be unconscionable, a court of equity will *construe* that person to be a trustee of that property. The effect of the imposition of this constructive trusteeship is that the defendant will be required to hold that property on trust for the claimant,[69] or to account in cash for the loss caused to the claimant if there is no property left in his hands.[70] The former example is a proprietary constructive trust, whereas the latter is a personal liability to account as a constructive trustee: the former example is analysed in detail in Chapter 27 and the latter in Chapter 30. **1.22**

Constructive trusts arise in general terms in any circumstance in which the defendant deals unconscionably with property with knowledge of the nature of his actions.[71] Therefore, constructive trusts can be said to arise on a very broad principle, while also being capable of being separated out into a number of distinct categories which have been applied in the decided cases. The circumstances in which a constructive trust will arise are in relation to: general circumstances in which the defendant has knowledge of some factor affecting his conscience;[72] **1.23**

---

[66] *Dyer v Dyer* (1788) 2 Cox Eq Cas 92; *Tinsley v Milligan* [1994] 1 AC 340; *Westdeutsche Landesbank v Islington LBC* [1996] AC 669.

[67] C Rickett and R Grantham, 'Resulting trusts—a rather limited doctrine' in P Birks and F Rose (eds), *Restitution and Equity, Vol 1* (Oxford: Mansfield Press, 2000) 39.

[68] *Westdeutsche Landesbank v Islington LBC* [1996] AC 669.

[69] *Westdeutsche Landesbank v Islington LBC* [1996] AC 669.

[70] *Royal Brunei Airlines v Tan* [1995] 2 AC 378.

[71] *Westdeutsche Landesbank v Islington LBC* [1996] AC 669.

[72] *Westdeutsche Landesbank v Islington LBC* [1996] AC 669.

unconscionable dealings with land;[73] contracts to convey land[74] or other property;[75] profits from unlawful acts such as receiving bribes,[76] theft,[77] or killing;[78] fiduciaries making unauthorized profits from their offices;[79] common intention in relation to the acquisition of land;[80] secret trusts[81] and mutual wills;[82] interference with the trust so as to assume the role of trustee;[83] dishonest assistance in a breach of trust;[84] and knowing receipt of property in breach of trust.[85]

1.24 One significant distinction between an express trust and a constructive trust is that an express trust necessarily comes into existence from the moment at which the settlor declared it, whereas a constructive trust cannot exist but for the unconscionable behaviour of the defendant which brings it into existence: therefore the express trust is brought into existence by the deliberate act of the settlor whereas a constructive trust is brought into existence by means of the wrongful act of the trustee. By way of example, taking the constructive trust imposed on a thief on stealing property,[86] suppose the following. If a man refrained from stealing an item of property, there would not be any need to impose a constructive trust on him as a means of restoring to the victim his property rights; whereas if that same man had stolen that property, then he will be deemed to become a constructive trustee of that property from the moment at which he performed the unconscionable act of theft.[87] Thus, the constructive trust is dependent on the unconscionability of the defendant's actions.

1.25 Whereas the constructive trust can be observed as coming into existence only on the wrongful and knowing act of the trustee, it nevertheless operates on an institutional basis.[88] That is, the constructive trust is taken by the court to have come into existence retrospectively and automatically at the date of the defendant's wrongful and knowing act.[89] In English equity, the constructive trust does not come into existence on a remedial basis, that is prospectively from the date of the

---

[73] *Paragon Finance plc v Thakerar & Co* [1999] 1 All ER 400; *Banner Homes v Luff Development* [2000] Ch 372; [2000] 2 WLR 772.

[74] *Lysaght v Edwards* (1876) 2 Ch D 499; *Chinn v Collins* [1981] AC 533; *Neville v Wilson* [1997] Ch 144.

[75] *Chinn v Collins* [1981] AC 533; *Neville v Wilson* [1997] Ch 144.

[76] *Attorney-General for Hong Kong v Reid* [1994] 1 AC 324.

[77] *Westdeutsche Landesbank v Islington LBC,* [1996] AC 669.

[78] *Re K (Deceased)* [1986] Ch 180; *Re H (Deceased)* [1990] 1 FLR 441.

[79] *Boardman v Phipps* [1967] 2 AC 46.

[80] *Lloyds Bank v Rosset* [1991] 1 AC, 107; [1990] 1 All ER 1111.

[81] *Ottaway v Norman* [1972] Ch 698.

[82] *Dufour v Pereira* (1769) 1 Dick 419; *Stone v Hoskins* [1905] P 194.

[83] *Mara v Browne* [1896] 1 Ch 199, 209.   [84] *Royal Brunei Airlines v Tan* [1995] 2 AC 378.

[85] *Re Montagu* [1987] Ch 264.   [86] *Westdeutsche Landesbank v Islington* [1996] AC 669.

[87] *Westdeutsche Landesbank v Islington* [1996] AC 669.

[88] *Westdeutsche Landesbank v Islington* [1996] AC 669.

[89] *Westdeutsche Landesbank v Islington* [1996] AC 669.

court judgment on terms dictated at the discretion of the court, unlike its American comparator.[90]

The only general definition of conscience in this context is one based entirely on observation of the decided cases. No more certain definition of that principle exists in the case law than that which can be culled from observation of the decided cases.[91] The various categories of constructive trust are considered in Part D, Chapters 27 through 30.   **1.26**

C. Forms of Express Trust

Bare trusts

A bare trust arises where the trustees hold property on trust for a single, absolutely **1.27** entitled beneficiary. The beneficiary therefore holds the entire equitable interest in the trust fund. Consequently, the trustee has no discretion nor any obligation other than the stewardship of the trust property on behalf of that beneficiary. The beneficiary herself must not be subject to any contingency or encumbrance which will interfere with her equitable interest in the property. She will hold the entirety of the possible equitable interest in that property. The trustee in such a situation is generally referred to as being a 'nominee'. That is, one who holds property in the name of another. Further to the principle in *Saunders v Vautier* [92] the beneficiary is able to direct the trustee how to deal with the property even if the trust instrument purports to direct the trustee to hold the property in a manner which is contrary to the beneficiary's wishes.[93]

Fixed trusts

The term 'fixed trust' refers to the situation in which the trustees hold property **1.28** on trust for a certain, defined list of beneficiaries.[94] An example of such a class of beneficiaries would be: 'on trust for my two children Anna and Bertha'. The 'fixed' nature of the trust refers then to the fixed list of people who can benefit from the trust. There is no discretion for the trustees as to the beneficiaries nor as to the interests which they can take from the trust. Rather, the trustees are bound by the limited, fixed nature of their trusteeship. The role of trustee is comparatively straightforward in this situation because the trustee is required simply to perform the terms of the trust slavishly.[95]

---

[90] *Westdeutsche Landesbank v Islington* [1996] AC 669.
[91] See perhaps the discussion of the notion of conscience taken from ethical philosophy in *Hudson* 977, para 37.2.
[92] (1841) 4 Beav 115.   [93] For a full consideration of this principle see para 7.05.
[94] *IRC v Broadway Cottages Trust* [1955] 2 WLR 552.   [95] See para 10.07.

Discretionary trusts and powers of appointment

1.29 As its name suggests, a discretionary trust grants the trustees some discretion in the manner in which the trust operates. A discretionary trust may give some discretion to the trustee as to the manner in which property is to be distributed or the people to whom that property is to be distributed.[96] Suppose, by way of example, a situation in which a settlor has three adult children and wishes to empower trustees to use as much of a fund of money as they may think appropriate to help whichever one of them earns the least money in any given calendar year. The trustee has discretion to distribute the amount of money necessary to make good that person's lack of funds. The role of trustee is therefore more complicated than in respect of the fixed trust because the trustee is required to exercise discretion, always ensuring that such exercise of her discretion remains within the terms of the settlement.[97] Suppose the settlor set aside a fund of money 'such that my trustee shall pay £5,000 per year out of that fund to whichever of my children shall have the greatest need of it'. In such a situation the trustee is compelled to make the payment but she has discretion as to which child will receive it.[98] In a discretionary trust, the discretionary class of beneficiaries may have equitable interests in the property to the extent that each of them can compel the trustees to perform their obligations and to exercise their discretion properly. However, no individual beneficiaries acquire any specific beneficial right in any identifiable property until the trustees' discretion has been exercised formally.[99]

1.30 Alternatively, a settlor may decide that a trustee is to have a power of appointment between a number of potential beneficiaries. That the trustee has a power of appointment means that the trustee is empowered to decide which people from among an identified class of beneficiaries are entitled to take absolute title in property which is advanced to them by the trustees.[100] A power in this sense is a term of art[101] connoting a capacity in its holder to do something with the property which has been placed under his control.[102] A power of appointment has been defined as meaning 'a power of disposition given to a person over property not his own by someone who directs the mode in which that power shall be exercised by

---

[96] *McPhail v Doulton* [1970] 2 WLR 1110.   [97] See para 4.08.
[98] The issue in such situations will often be whether or not the ambit of the trustee's discretion has been identified with sufficient certainty.
[99] The question of the settlor's power to effect change, if acting as one of the trustees, is considered in para 13.34.
[100] *Breadner v Granville-Grossman* [2001] Ch 523, [2000] 4 All ER 705. Suppose, by way of example, that the settlor sets aside a fund 'to be held on trust by Trustee with a power to appoint the sum of £10,000 to whichever of the named beneficiaries has the greatest need of it [where the concept "need" is defined elsewhere in the instrument]'. The trustee therefore has discretion to choose which of the identified class is to receive absolute title in that £10,000 per season.
[101] GW Thomas, *Powers* (Sweet & Maxwell, 1998) ('*Thomas*') 1.
[102] *Re Armstrong* (1886) 17 QBD 521, 531, *per* Fry LJ.

a particular instrument'.[103] The donee (or, holder) of a power is not in the same position as a trustee,[104] although a power of appointment may be contained in a trust instrument and the donee of a power is always obliged to carry out his duties in accordance with the terms of his power.[105] An example of a trust provision containing a power of appointment might be as follows: 'the trustee shall have the discretion to select which of my children shall receive £5,000 (a discretionary trust obligation) subject to a power that the trustees may pay an amount of up to £1,000 to my wife (a power of appointment)'. The distinction between a trust and a power can be defined in the following manner. A trust, including a discretionary trust, will compel the performance of an obligation, even if the trustee has some room for manoeuvre as to the precise manner in which that obligation is exercised;[106] whereas the exercise of a power is at the option of the donee of that power[107] and a court cannot do more than compel any holder of such a power, even if it is contained in a trust, to consider whether or not the power should be exercised.[108]

Accumulation and maintenance trusts

A settlor may seek to create an endowment trust from which the needs and living   **1.31** expenses of the settlor's children, for example, are to be provided. Consequently, the principal responsibility of the trustee is to invest the trust property and then to apply it according to the needs identified in the terms of the trust. The beneficiaries have rights against the trustees to have the trust performed in accordance with the terms of the trust and to have property advanced for their benefit at the time identified in the trust (subject to any discretion in the trustees). This form of trust is considered in detail in Chapter 35.

Sham trusts

Equity will look to the substance and not simply at the form of any purported   **1.32** trust. Therefore, it is not sufficient to create a trust that the settlor creates what is in truth some other legal device but labels it as a trust in the hope that this will lead the court to consider his device to be a trust. In such a situation the court will find that the device and its trust label is a sham and will refuse to enforce it as though a trust. It is in relation to cases of insolvency that sham trusts arise most frequently. A clear example is that of *Midland Bank v Wyatt*[109] in which Mr Wyatt sought, on the advice of his solicitor, to put property beyond the reach of his trade creditors

---

[103] *Freme v Clement* (1881) 18 Ch D 499, 504 *per* Lord Jessel MR.   [104] *Thomas* 20.
[105] See generally *Re Armstrong* (1886) 17 QBD 521, 531, *per* Fry LJ. For an extended discussion of the nature of a power see *Thomas* 4 *et seq*, and para 13.01.
[106] *McPhail v Doulton* [1970] 2 WLR 1110.
[107] *Re Gulbenkian* [1968] Ch 126; *McPhail v Doulton* [1970] 2 WLR 1110.
[108] *Re Hay's Settlement Trusts* [1981] 3 All ER 786.   [109] [1995] 1 FLR 697.

when he thought that his textiles business and consequently Mr Wyatt himself might go into bankruptcy. Mr Wyatt's matrimonial home was held on trust for himself and his wife equally. Mr Wyatt purported to declare a trust over his rights in the property in favour of his wife and daughters so that, in the event of his bankruptcy, his home would be safe from his creditors not being a part of Mr Wyatt's personal estate but rather being held on trust by him on the terms of the trust. Mr Wyatt made no mention of this arrangement to any member of his family; when he was divorced from his wife, Mrs Wyatt did not know of the trust which had purportedly granted her the majority share in the home; and Mr Wyatt continued to use his share in the house as security for business loans as though the trust had never been created. Consequently, it was held that the purported trust had been a sham created solely for the purpose of putting property beyond the reach of his creditors and that no valid trust had therefore been created.[110]

By contrast it may also be the case that a person seeks to deny the existence of a trust and to claim that property which he holds is in fact his property absolutely. The courts will construe the defendant to be a trustee of that property[111] or recognize the existence of a valid express trust over that property, as appropriate.[112] The imposition of trust obligations on the basis of ensuring that the defendant acts in good conscience in recognition of the claimant's rights in equity in property necessarily means that the defendant's unconscionable designs are considered to be shams in circumstances in which the defendant seeks to deny the rights of the claimant in the property at issue.

Public and private trusts

1.33 This book is concerned with private trusts. There are public trusts in the form of charitable trusts which are beyond the scope of this work: the reader is referred to the standard works on charities: *Tudor on Charities* and *Picarda on Charities*. There are also other forms of public body which have attracted the moniker 'trust' but which are, in truth, bodies corporate and not trusts at all. Examples of these bodies corporate are NHS trusts[113] and Housing Action Trusts. Private trusts are trusts which conform to the pattern considered so far in this book.

---

[110] The court also considered points under s 423 of the Insolvency Act 1986 which are of no particular moment at this juncture.
[111] Such that the defendant will be a constructive trustee of that property, as considered at para 1.22 above.
[112] *Paul v Constance* [1977] 1 WLR 527, where the defendant sought to allege that no express trust had been created by her husband such that money held in a bank account in his name passed to her as his next of kin, whereas the court held that her husband had in fact intended to create an express trust over that bank account in favour of himself and his lover absolutely.
[113] On which see AS Hudson, *The Law on Investment Entities* (London: Sweet & Maxwell, 2000) 309.

The various forms of trust considered in Section Two: Specific Trusts

It is the contention of the authors of this book that the practice of the law of trusts **1.34** can be best understood as a combination of the general principles considered in this Section One and also by consideration of the means by which those general principles are applied to the particular forms of trust considered in Section Two: Specific Trusts. What has been considered so far in this chapter are the well-established divisions between various forms of trust as understood by the general principles of trusts law. By recognizing that trusts occupy different contexts in their practical application as well, it is possible to understand the effects of the various case law, statutory and regulatory codes which deal with particular species of the genus trust on those general principles. An outline of the structure of this book, and of the key features of these specific trusts is to be found in the Introduction.

D. The Nature of the Rights and Obligations of Settlor, Trustee, and Beneficiary

The nature of the trust

This chapter is concerned with describing the nature of the trust. That description **1.35** can only be conducted in outline terms precisely because the true nature of the trust will only become apparent after a close scrutiny of the case law, statutory provisions, and equitable principles which form the subject matter of the thousand and more pages of this book. It is important, however, to construct a basic ideology of the manner in which the trust functions to enable us to clear a path through the thicket of ostensibly conflicting authority in many areas. That ideology can be based on an understanding of the nature of the rights of, variously, the settlor, the trustees, and the beneficiaries in relation to one another and in relation to the trust property. The purpose, then, of the following three sections is to consider the shape of these three central concepts, but it is in the remainder of the book that they shall be analysed in detail.

The settlor's rights and duties

The termination of the settlor's role in the trust

The role of settlor is simply that of creator. Once creation has taken place, then **1.36** there is no evident role for the settlor in the operation of the trust *in his capacity as settlor*. So, as considered above, the settlor may declare himself to be one of the trustees or the sole trustee, and the settlor may declare himself to be one of the beneficiaries.[114] The settlor is significant only in relation to express trusts and those

---

[114] But not the sole beneficiary if he is also the sole trustee because that would not create any trust as there would be no separation of the legal and the equitable title: *Re Cook* [1948] Ch 121, [1948]

31

implied trusts which have been described by the courts as being a form of express trust.[115] In relation to constructive trusts, there will be no settlor: rather the trust will come into existence to prevent unconscionable behaviour by the constructive trustee in relation to property of which he is not the rightful beneficial owner. In relation to resulting trusts, the role of the absolute owner of the property will be of significance only to the extent that he failed to make his intentions to create an express trust or otherwise to transfer property sufficiently clear.

1.37   When an express trust is declared the settlor is required to demonstrate an intention to create such a trust, and to identify with sufficient certainty the property which is to be held on trust and those who are to take beneficial interests in that property. Beyond that, however, the settlor has no further role to play in the trust *qua* settlor. The settlor, instead, drops from the picture absolutely[116] and has no rights, *qua* settlor, either to direct the trustees how to deal with the trust property or to reclaim the property which has been settled on trust.[117] In consequence, on the creation of an express trust, the beneficiaries acquire ultimate beneficial title in the trust fund and the settlor *qua* settlor relinquishes all property claims against that property. The authorities are clear: if the settlor intended to create a trust, then it is by reference to the law of trusts that any question must be answered; whereas if that person's intention were to do anything other than create a trust, then the law of trusts has no part to play.[118] However, the purposes which motivated the settlor's intention to create the trust and the terms of any instrument by which the trust was declared will be of importance in the interpretation both of the trustees' obligations and the beneficiaries' rights under that trust.

No recovery of settled property unless some reservation of power

1.38   A settlor has no power to countermand or terminate a trust once it has been validly constituted. Therefore, trusts law operates on the conscience of the settlor as well as on the trustee, requiring the settlor to vest legal title in the trust property in the trustee in line with the terms of the trust.[119] By way of example, if a settlor declared a trust over property just before her marriage in favour of herself, her husband, and any prospective children, then if the marriage failed the settlor would not be entitled in her capacity as settlor to unwind the trust and recover the trust property.[120] Once a trust has been created, it remains inviolate. For a settlor to interfere with a trust once constituted, it would be necessary for the settlor to reserve to himself a specific authority under the terms of the trust to unwind the trust, whether acting as trustee or enjoying the property as a beneficiary. The precise terms of the trust

---

1 All ER 2311; *Re Lord Grimthorpe* [1908] 2 Ch 675. Also see *Rye v Rye* [1962] AC 496, [1962] 1 All ER 146.

[115] eg *Paul v Constance* [1977] 1 WLR 527.   [116] *Paul v Paul* (1882) 20 Ch D 742.
[117] *Re Ralli's Will Trusts* [1964] 2 WLR 144.   [118] *Milroy v Lord* (1862) 4 De GF & J 264.
[119] *Re Ralli's WT* [1964] 2 WLR 144.   [120] *Paul v Paul* (1882) 20 Ch D 742.

will be decisive of the settlor's ability to act in this way, unless those terms transgress any rule of statute or of public policy.[121] In any event, it is likely that, in such a situation, the person who acted as settlor would then reserve rights as a form of trustee rather than as settlor.

The nature of the beneficiary's equitable interest

The distinction between rights in personam *and* in rem

A key component of this book will be the nature of the equitable interest which the **1.39** beneficiary acquires under a trust: it is twinned with the nature and extent of the trustees' obligations. It is important to distinguish between the beneficiary having rights *in rem* and rights *in personam*. Rights *in rem* (from the Latin, meaning 'in a thing') refer to the beneficiaries' rights in the trust property itself, as considered immediately below. Each beneficiary is said to have an equitable proprietary interest within the context of the terms of the trust. The trust instrument may specify that particular classes of beneficiary have particular forms of right in identified portions of the trust fund. Nevertheless, as a general proposition, the beneficiaries are recognized as having proprietary rights in the trust property, or in its traceable proceeds in the event that the trust property is passed away in breach of trust.[122] Alternatively, the beneficiaries may also have purely personal rights—that is, rights *in personam*—against the trustees in the event that the trustees commit some breach of trust. As considered in Chapter 32, the trustees bear obligations in such circumstances to effect specific restitution of the property passed away from the trust or personal obligations to pay equitable compensation to the beneficiaries.[123] Similarly, any third person who has knowingly received that property in breach of trust[124] or who has acted as a dishonest assistant to the breach of trust,[125] will bear personal obligations to account to the beneficiaries for any loss suffered by the trust: as considered in Chapter 30.

Consequently, it can be seen that the beneficiary's rights are predicated both on his proprietary rights and on his personal rights against the trustees.[126] Typically, a proprietary right is considered to be a right in a specific item of property. Thus, in *Re Goldcorp Exchange Ltd*[127] customers of a bullion exchange, who held contracts entitling them to have bullion of a given type and quantity delivered to them, had only personal rights against the exchange when it was declared to be bankrupt because there was no specific bullion segregated from the general store of bullion held by the exchange which was capable of being held on trust for them. It was held that, because there was no specific property in which the customers could

---

[121] *Midland Bank v Wyatt* [1995] 1 FLR 697. [122] See para 32.01.
[123] *Target Holdings v Redferns* [1996] 1 AC 421. [124] *Re Montagu* [1987] Ch 264.
[125] *Royal Brunei Airlines v Tan* [1995] 2 AC 378; *Twinsectra Ltd v Yardley* [2002] UKHL 12, [2002] 2 AC 164; *Dubai Aluminium v Salaam* [2002] 3 WLR 1913.
[126] See Chapter 7. [127] [1995] 1 AC 74.

assert any rights, they had no proprietary rights at all. Therefore, the customers were required to rely on their contractual claims for damages which were effectively worthless given that the exchange had gone into insolvency.

1.40 On the other hand, in *Attorney-General for Hong Kong v Reid*,[128] the former Attorney-General had taken bribes not to prosecute particular criminals. It was held that these bribes were held on constructive trust for the defendant's employers. The question was whether those employers could be entitled to proprietary rights over the bribes and also any profits made from the investment of those bribes. It was held that the defendant held the bribes on proprietary constructive trust, and consequently any investments bought with those bribes, from the moment that the bribes were received. It was on the basis that equity would look upon as done that which ought to have been done that equitable proprietary rights in the bribes were deemed to pass to the employers on constructive trust automatically on their receipt by the defendant. Therefore, in *Reid*, the proprietary rights arose in relation to property in which the plaintiff had never previously had any rights as a result of an equitable claim against the defendant's conscience. Importantly, these proprietary rights did not need to be linked to any particular item of property: rather, they attached to any property representing the value of those original bribes at any time. This approach should be contrasted with *Re Goldcorp*, in which the identity of the property was considered to be the more vital element, to indicate the flexible manner in which proprietary rights may be created in some situations.[129]

Different qualities of beneficial interest

1.41 The foregoing discussion of the varying types of trusts indicates not only that the precise obligations of the trustees will differ from case to case but also that the rights of the beneficiaries will vary in quality. The most important distinction will be between vested rights and rights which remain contingent on some eventuality provided for under the terms of the trust. Under a mere power of appointment, the beneficiary will have no vested rights in any property until the trustee exercises her power of appointment in favour of that beneficiary.[130] The right of the beneficiary

---

[128] [1994] 1 AC 324.

[129] These two cases are capable of being reconciled in that in *Re Goldcorp* the focus of the case was on the identity of those persons out of a number of plaintiffs to whom property rights could be allocated, as compared with *Attorney-General for Hong Kong v Reid* in which the question concerned the identity of property in which pre-existing rights could be allocated to a single plaintiff. The former concerned too many plaintiffs fighting over too little property; whereas the latter concerned only a single plaintiff selecting from an array of available property. However, the underlying issue is whether a plaintiff ought to lose a claim once the specific property which attached to those rights disappears, or whether those rights should be said to have some intrinsic value in themselves such that it is not important that there be specific, segregated property to which those rights ought to attach.

[130] *Re Brook's ST* [1939] 1 Ch 993.

is merely an unenforceable hope (or *spes*) that the trustee will decide to exercise her power in favour of that beneficiary.[131] A power of appointment does not give the beneficiary any right in the money: all that the beneficiary has is an unenforceable hope that the holder of the power will choose to benefit her. Under a discretionary trust the beneficiary will not acquire a vested right in any particular property under the trust until the trustees' discretion is exercised in her favour—but under a discretionary trust the beneficiary will acquire a personal right in common with the other beneficiaries to ensure that the trustees observe the terms of the trust. A beneficiary under a discretionary trust has a right to require the trustees to consider her case fairly: that in itself has been held to constitute some right in the trust property.[132]

It is important to note that beyond that personal claim against the trustee, the beneficiary will not have rights to any specific property under a discretionary trust before the trustee has exercised her discretion. This should be compared with a bare trust under which the beneficiary will have equitable proprietary rights in the trust property from the moment at which the trust is created. Under a bare trust there is no interest to compete with that of the bare beneficiary—therefore, the right of the beneficiary is vested in the trust fund itself. Similarly, where trust property is held 'on trust for A for life, remainder to B' it is A who will have a vested proprietary interest in the trust fund and a right to receive the income from the trust fund, whereas B will acquire a right to ensure that the trustees respect her rights to the property after A's death but no vested interest until A's death. **1.42**

The rights of the beneficiary, as has emerged from the preceding discussion, will depend on the specific terms and nature of the trust. The beneficiary will always have a right to compel the trustees to carry out the terms of the trust. It is a necessary part of the law of trusts that there be some person for whose benefit the court can decree performance of the trust.[133] Beneficiaries will occupy subtly different positions depending upon the terms of the trust under which they take their particular interests. **1.43**

The nature of the beneficiaries' proprietary rights in the trust

The nature of the beneficiary's interest is considered in detail in Chapter 7. What follows here is a short, introductory consideration of the nature of those rights. There is a dichotomy between the nature of the trust as a creature of equity which acts *in personam* on the conscience of the trustee but which nevertheless grants the beneficiaries proprietary rights in the trust property subject always to the precise nature of those beneficiaries' interests as expressed in the trust instrument. **1.44**

---

[131] ibid.   [132] *Re Ralli's WT* [1964] 2 WLR 144.
[133] *Morice v Bishop of Durham* (1805) 10 Ves 522, considered in Chapter 4 below. Cf *Medforth v Blake* [2000] Ch 86.

The roots of the beneficiaries' rights as proprietary rights in the trust fund can be observed by reference to the rule in *Saunders v Vautier*[134] whereby all of the beneficiaries, constituting the entirety of the equitable interest in a trust fund, provided that they are all *sui juris* and acting together, can direct the trustees how to deal with that trust fund. As Megarry J has described this proposition[135] in relation to the ability of beneficiaries using the rule in *Saunders v Vautier* to rearrange the terms of a trust:

> If under a trust every possible beneficiary was under no disability and concurred in the re-arrangement or termination of the trusts, then under the doctrine in *Saunders v Vautier* those beneficiaries could dispose of the trust property as they thought fit; for in equity the property was theirs. Yet if any beneficiary was an infant, or an unborn or unascertained person, it was held that the court had no general inherent or other jurisdiction to concur in any such arrangement on behalf of that beneficiary.

The significance of the rule is that it establishes that the beneficiary has a right in the trust fund itself and not merely personal claims against the trustees or against the settlor.

1.45 The case of *Saunders v Vautier*[136] itself concerned a testator who bequeathed £2,000 worth of East India stock on trust for V. The trust provided that the capital of the fund should be held intact until V reached the age of 25 and that the dividends from the stock should be accumulated with the capital. V reached the age of maturity (at that time, 21 years of age) and sought delivery of the capital and dividends to him immediately rather than having to wait until he reached the age of 25. Lord Langdale MR held as follows:

> I think that principle has been repeatedly acted upon; and where a legacy is directed to accumulate for a certain period, or where the payment is postponed, the legatee, if he has an absolute indefeasible interest in the legacy, is not bound to wait until the expiration of that period, but may require payment the moment he is competent to give a valid discharge.

In short, even though the trust specifically provided that the beneficiary was not to be entitled to take the property until he reached the age of 25, it was held that the rights of the beneficiary take priority over the directions of the settlor. This right of the beneficiary was held to be capable of enforcement even though, in the submission of the residuary legatees, V's interest was contingent on reaching the age of 25 and therefore ought not to have been satisfied if the settlor's instructions were to be strictly observed.

The rule in *Saunders v Vautier* has its roots in the principles relating to wills applied in the ecclesiastical courts, traceable to *Green v Spicer*[137] and *Younghusband v*

---

[134] (1841) 4 Beav 115. [135] *In Re Holt's Settlement* [1969] 1 Ch 100, 111.
[136] (1841) 4 Beav 115. [137] (1830) 1 Russ & M 395.

Grisborne.[138] Page Wood V-C in *Gosling v Gosling*[139] and subsequently the Court of Appeal in *Re Nelson*[140] have identified the beneficiaries as having proprietary rights in the trust property on this basis.[141] While the case of *Saunders v Vautier* was itself concerned with the rights of one beneficiary under a will, subsequent cases have interpreted that decision as founding the broader proposition that groups of beneficiaries, even in relation to discretionary trusts, are entitled to call for the property or to require that the trustees deal with the property in a manner which may appear tantamount to a variation of the existing trust or alternatively a resettling of that property. So, in *Re Bowes,*[142] in which a trust fund was created over £5,000 for the express purpose of planting trees on a large estate, the human beneficiaries who were entitled under other provisions of that same trust were permitted to call for the fund reserved for the maintenance of trees so that they could alleviate the financial problems which they were experiencing at that time immediately. This approach was also applied by the Court of Appeal in *Re Nelson*[143] where it was held that 'the principle [in *Saunders v Vautier*] is that where there is what amounts to an absolute gift cannot be fettered by prescribing a mode enjoyment'. In other words, where all of the equitable interest is settled for the benefit of a group of beneficiaries absolutely, that is tantamount to transferring title outright to them by means of an assignment.

Similarly, in *Re Smith*[144] it was held that even in relation to a discretionary trust held for two classes of potential beneficiaries the trustees would be required to treat those beneficiaries 'as though they formed one person' absolutely entitled to the trust. Romer J held that in circumstances in which the trustees have a discretion as to the amount of the fund to be passed to one beneficiary and are also obliged to pass any remainder outstanding after exercising that discretion to other beneficiaries, where all of those beneficiaries present themselves to the trustees demanding a transfer of the trust fund, the trustees are required to make that transfer. The court in *Stephenson v Barclays Bank*[145] permitted a beneficiary to take delivery of her divisible share in the whole of the trust fund without needing to act together with the other beneficiaries: this approach would require that the property be capable of such division and that the beneficiary's precise entitlement is calculable. By contrast in *Lloyds Bank v Duker*[146] a beneficiary was prevented from removing his part of the trust property because the removal of his portion from the total fund would have robbed the other beneficiaries of a majority shareholding in a private company. Therefore, it was held that the countervailing obligation

---

[138] (1844) 1 Col 400.   [139] (1859) John 265.
[140] [1928] Ch 920.   [141] *See Curtis v Lukin* (1842) 5 Beav 147.
[142] [1896] 1 Ch 507.   [143] [1928] Ch 920.   [144] [1928] Ch 915.
[145] [1975] 1 All ER 625.   [146] [1987] 3 All ER 193.

to act fairly between the beneficiaries overrode the individual claimant's desire to realize his proprietary rights.[147]

The beneficiary principle

1.46 As considered in Chapter 6, the beneficiary principle requires that there be some person with an interest in the trust property in whose favour the court can decree performance:[148] a principle which emphasizes the centrality of the beneficiary to the functioning of a trust. If there is no such beneficiary for whom the court can decree performance then the trust will not be valid.[149]

The obligations of the trustee

The extent of the trustee's fiduciary obligations

1.47 On creation of a trust the legal title in the trust property must be vested in the trustee and held by the trustee on trust for the beneficiaries. Suppose a trust created over a fund of £1,000 held in a current bank account. The legal title in that bank account will be vested in the trustee. In practice, this means that the trustee's name appears on the cheque book, the trustee is empowered to authorize transfers of any money held in that account, the trustee has a contract with the bank as to the administration of the bank account, it is the trustee who would sue the bank for any negligence in the handling of the account, and so forth. The trustee has all of the common law rights in the bank account. Any litigation between the trust and third persons is conducted by the trustee as legal title holder in the trust property. Therefore, for the remainder of this book we shall refer to the trustee as the 'legal owner' of property. This is a technical use of the term 'legal owner' which means that the trustee is vested with all of the common law rights in the property. It is not meant to be used in opposition to the colloquial use of the word 'illegal'.

However, the most important feature of the trust is that the trustee is not entitled to assert personal, beneficial ownership in the trust property. Rather, it is the beneficiary who has all of the beneficial title in property, as considered immediately below. Therefore, suppose that S dies leaving a will which appoints T to hold a house on trust for his children. T will be the person whose name appears on the legal title to the property at the Land Registry. However, T would not be entitled to sell the property and keep the money for herself beneficially. Rather, she would be required to hold the sale proceeds on trust for the beneficiaries.

1.48 Two important points arise. First, a practical point. It will always be important to consider the precise terms of the trust. As will become apparent throughout this

---

[147] *Tito v Waddell (No 2)* [1977] Ch 106.
[148] *Morice v Bishop of Durham* (1805) 10 Ves 522; *Leahy v Att-Gen for New South Wales* [1959] AC 457; *Re Denley* [1969] 1 Ch 373; *Re Lipinski* [1976] Ch 235.
[149] See para 6.01.

book, the courts will tend to look very closely at the precise written terms of a trust or at the verbal expression of the settlor's intentions. Therefore, if, in the example above, T was required to hold the house on trust so that S's children could live there until the youngest of them reached the age of 18, T would be committing a breach of trust by selling the property before the child reached the age of 18. Consequently, not only would T hold the sale proceeds of the house on trust for the children but T would also be required to pay compensation to the trust to make good any loss suffered by the trust fund from the breach of trust.[150] However, if the terms of the trust gave T a discretionary power to sell whenever T chose, then T would not have committed a breach of trust, prima facie, in selling the house.

Secondly, the trustee is required to hold the original trust property, or any substitute property, on trust for the beneficiaries. Therefore, unless there is something expressly to the contrary on the terms of the trust, a trust attaches not simply to specific property and that property only. Rather, the trust attaches to bundles of property rights which may be transferred from one piece of property to another. Suppose a trust with a defined purpose of maintaining a house for the beneficiaries with a power for the trustees to sell that house if the beneficiaries wish to move elsewhere. At the outset the original house is held on trust. When the house is sold, the trust attaches instead to the sale proceeds and then to the second house which is bought with that money. If the trust attached rigidly to one piece of property it would be impossible for the beneficiaries to acquire rights in the second house. In truth, a trust attaches to property rights and to value, not to specific items of property. What is important to bear in mind is that the particular property which makes up the trust fund from time to time may change, it is the trust fund in whatever form at any particular time which the trustees are required to hold on trust. **1.49**

The precise obligations on the trustee are therefore to be found in the trust document itself. However, there are more general obligations on the trustee imposed by the general law of trusts. These issues are considered in more detail in Part C. Among the issues to be considered are the amount of information which trustees are required to give to beneficiaries, the manner in which the trust fund should be invested while it is being held on trust, the appointment or retirement of trustees, and the termination of the trust. As may have become apparent by now, much will depend upon the nature and terms of the trust. **1.50**

Trusts law acts in personam *against the conscience of the trustee*

In trusts law theory, the trustee is always posited as being the defendant. That emerges from the assertion that a trust operates by means of the court controlling **1.51**

---

[150] *Target Holdings v Redferns* [1996] 1 AC 421, considered in Chapter 32.

his conscience. In the context of an express trust the trustee's obligations arise from the dictates of conscience in his observation of his express fiduciary duties; in the context of trusts implied by law it is the necessity of preventing the trustee from dealing unconscionably with property which founds the trust in the first place. In relation to the law on express trusts more generally, the doctrines of certainty of subject matter and of objects are targeted at the need for the court to ensure sufficient certainty for the court to be able to police the trustee's obligations under the trust instrument. Similarly, the beneficiary principle, which might otherwise be thought to focus attention on the beneficiary, is expressed by Lord Greene MR in *Morice v Bishop of Durham*[151] in terms of the need for there to be a beneficiary in existence who can bring the trustee to court in the event of any breach of trust:[152] thus centring the obligations on the conscionability of the trustee yet again. Consequently, the law of trusts is directed almost entirely at the obligations incumbent on the trustee. In that sense the law of trusts operates on the basis of the maxim that 'Equity acts *in personam*' because in enforcing a trust the court is acting against the conscience of the trustee. Significantly, that does not mean that the beneficiary acquires only rights of a personal nature against the trustee. Rather, the beneficiary acquires both proprietary rights in relation to the trust property and also personal rights against the trustee either to prevent the trustee from committing a breach of trust or against the trustee once a breach of trust has been committed, as considered above.

All trustees are fiduciaries

1.52 It is suggested that trustees always occupy a fiduciary office in relation to the beneficiaries, even if a trustee is merely a bare trustee. A bare trustee who is required simply to maintain property for safekeeping—for example as a nominee over land or even as the depositary in relation to collective investment schemes—does not have to balance the competing claims of beneficiaries with claims against the same property, albeit that their rights have different incidents and extents. Indeed some commentators would go so far as to say that the bare trustee is not a fiduciary at all because her obligations are similar, in effect, to a bailee of property required to mind that property for its true owner.[153] It is said by the proponents of this opinion that it is only when a trustee is charged with some discretion or some power in relation to the trust property that he is properly considered to be a fiduciary in relation to it.[154]

---

[151] (1805) 10 Ves 522.
[152] cf financial regulation which displaces the primacy of the trustee's role and represents a reversal in part of the trust theory relationship, as considered above.
[153] J Penner, 'Exemptions' in P Birks (ed), *Breach of Trust* (Hart Publishing, 2002) 241.
[154] ibid.

This view is, however, incorrect. The bare trustee is a fiduciary. There are two forms of fiduciary duty. First, there are *active* fiduciary duties which police the manner in which trustees and others carry out their express powers. Secondly, however, there are *latent* fiduciary duties which apply equally to a bare trustee as to a trustee charged with some active power. Such latent fiduciary duties are only evident when the bare trustee performs some act which, even if not mentioned in the express terms of her trusteeship, nevertheless offend against fiduciary law. Examples of such latent fiduciary duties are the rule against self-dealing, and the rule against making secret profits from the fiduciary office.[155] These rules apply to a bare trustee as to any other type of trustee. If the bare trustee behaves properly then no mention of them need be made. However, that does not mean that they do not apply to such a bare trustee. A little like the station platforms which slip from view as our train pulls away: just because we cannot see them, it does not mean that they are not always there.

The core of trusteeship

The duties of trustees divide broadly between duties of good management and **1.53** duties of good faith. The mandatory content of the principles governing trustee-ship are considered in Part C in relation to the trustees' obligations not to permit conflicts of interest, not to generate secret profits, not to advantage one beneficiary over another, to provide limited categories of information to the beneficiaries, not to breach the terms of the trust, and to manage the investment of the trust fund in accordance with the Trustee Act 2000 or with the terms of the trust where the latter contradict the former.

The identification of any rigid, quasi-statutory notion of 'trusteeship' is not pos- **1.54** sible in English law, even though it may seem desirable to commercial users of trusts. There are cases such as *Armitage v Nurse*[156] which suggest that there is no objective, mandatory core of rules binding on all trustees because trustees are enti-tled to limit their obligations by means of contract; whereas there are other authorities such as *Walker v Stones*[157] which deny trustees the right to limit their liabilities by contract so as to exclude liability for their own dishonesty. It is sug-gested that no court of equity would permit dishonesty on the part of trustees in the same way that no common law court would condone an ordinary fraud which would fall under the tort of deceit.

The search for a core to the notion of trusteeship must then focus on the question **1.55** 'how much further can mandatory principles of trusteeship extend?' The answer to this question is satisfactorily answered by recognizing that any trusteeship is predi-cated on a decision as to whether or not the trustee has acted in good conscience. The core of the trustees' obligation under an express trust is expressed in the

---

[155] See Chapter 29.   [156] [1998] Ch 241.   [157] [2001] QB 902.

mandatory terms of any trust instrument which is supplemented by the ordinary rules of trusts law in the absence of such an instrument. What is more significant is not any 'core' of trusteeship but rather any 'sense' of trusteeship: that is, the true nature of the trust is contained in the obligations of the trustees to act in good conscience. This notion of good conscience is, by definition, a deliberately open-textured, moral notion. A moral notion which has specific legal and equitable consequences. It is not possible in this short section to account for the varied nature of trusteeship: the nature of that office can only be revealed by a close study of the principles in Parts C and D of this book.

E. The Trust Compared to Other Legal Relationships

The trust compared to other legal concepts

1.56   There are conceptions of the trust which focus on its institutional, almost quasi-contractual nature: in so doing, it is suggested, these definitions have in mind express trusts more than those forms of trusts which are implied by law. One example of this approach is the definition of the trust provided in The Hague Convention on the Law Applicable to Trusts and on their Recognition for the purposes of that Convention in the following terms:

> ...the term 'trust' refers to the legal relationships created—*inter vivos* and on death—by a person, the settlor, when assets have been placed under the control of a trustee for the benefit of a beneficiary or for a specified purpose. A trust has the following characteristics—(a) the assets constitute a separate fund and are not part of the trustee's own estate; (b) title to the trust assets stands in the name of the trustee or in the name of another person on behalf of the trustee; (c) the trustee has the power and the duty, in respect of which he is accountable, to manage, employ or dispose of the assets in accordance with the terms of the trust and the special duties imposed upon him by law. The reservation by the settlor of certain rights and powers, and the fact that the trustee may himself have rights as a beneficiary, are not necessarily inconsistent with the existence of a trust.[158]

That understanding of the trust may appear, at first blush, to be explicable in terms of ordinary contracts, contracts of agency, bailment, and gift. The following sections, however, set out the differences between each category.

---

[158] The Hague Convention on the Law Applicable to Trusts and on their Recognition, art 2. Cited with approval in *Lewin* 3, and A Oakley, *Parker and Mellow's The Modern Law of Trusts* (8th edn, Sweet & Maxwell, 2003)(*'Parker and Mellows'*)12–13.

Contract

Fundamental distinctions between the contract and the trust

A contract is a bilateral agreement (resulting from an offer, an acceptance of that **1.57** offer, and consideration passing between the parties) created at common law between two parties who do not necessarily have any other relationship in existence between them. By contrast to the bilateral nature of the contract, an express trust arises from the unilateral act of the settlor in declaring a trust. There is no contract between settlor and trustee necessarily. For example, a settlor may declare himself to be trustee of property which he already owns for the benefit of some other person. Even if the settlor were to appoint some other person to act as trustee, the trustee's obligations, absent any other circumstances, would be imposed upon him by equity and would be obligations which are owed to the beneficiaries once the trust has been properly constituted, and not to the settlor.[159]

Far from being merely a party to a contract, a trustee holds a fiduciary office requir- **1.58** ing the utmost good faith from him in relation to the management of the trust property and his behaviour in relation to the beneficiaries.[160] The trustee will become liable to account personally to the beneficiaries for any breach of trust.[161] It might be, if a professional trustee is appointed (perhaps a bank or a solicitor), that the trustee may require payment from the settlor to act as trustee and may require that an agreement be put in place between settlor and trustee so as to limit the liability of the trustees for breach of trust in particular contexts.[162] In such circumstances there will be a trust and also a contract created between settlor and trustee. However, the contract does not form a part of the trust—rather, it is collateral to it.

A contract creates merely personal obligations between the two contracting parties, **1.59** which may be supported by specific performance or by common law damages in the event of any breach of contract. The rights to damages arise in common law from the very existence of the contract. By contrast, in relation to a trust, there are personal obligations between trustee and beneficiary in relation to the treatment of the trust fund and the performance of the trustee's obligations under the trust.[163] The trustee will be liable to the beneficiary both to reinstate the trust fund and for compensation if there is any breach of trust. The beneficiary is also entitled to require the trustee to carry out her obligations.[164] The remedies available for a breach of trust differ markedly from those available for a breach of contract,

---

[159] *Paul v Paul* (1882) 20 Ch D 742.

[160] See para 10.01.

[161] See para 32.01.

[162] See, for example, *Armitage v Nurse* [1998] Ch 241.

[163] See Chapter 31.

[164] Beneficiaries who are absolutely entitled to the trust property, and acting *sui juris*, are empowered to direct the trustees to deliver the trust property to them: *Saunders v Vautier* (1841) 4 Beav 115.

involving obligations to effect specific restitution of the trust property and to provide equitable compensation, without the need for the beneficiaries to satisfy common law tests as to causation or remoteness of damage.[165] Significantly, a trust takes effect over property creating equitable proprietary rights in favour of the beneficiaries whereas no such arrangement is created by an ordinary contract. Furthermore, trustees owe fiduciary duties to the beneficiaries not to make unauthorized profits nor to allow any conflict of interest nor to self-deal[166] with the trust property. Ordinary contracts do not create such fiduciary obligations, although contracts of agency and contracts of partnership will create fiduciary duties but of a different quality to those of a trustee.

Express trusts cannot be interpreted as being merely contracts

1.60 Some commentators have suggested that the essence of the express trust[167] is the relationship between settlor and trustee and that the trust is concerned with a form of contract between trustee and settlor whereby the trustee agrees to act for the settlor on the terms of an arrangement between themselves as to the extent of the trustee's obligations, the trustee's right to remuneration, and the purposes of the trust. This approach treats the trust as being simply made up of obligations borne by the trustee to the settlor in contract.[168] This fundamental assertion is, however, wrong. Many trusts are not predicated on a contract. In relation to commercial practice it will commonly be the case that there will be a commercial contract which uses a trust as a device to hold security for payment or a contract for services whereby some person will be limiting their liability and identifying their fee in return for acting as trustee, and in that sense there will tend to be a contract. This position, however, fails to provide a complete analysis of even express trusts given that there are express trusts which are recognized as having come into existence without the conscious action of the parties,[169] in situations like that in *Paul v Constance*[170] or *Re Kayford*,[171] let alone the formation of a contract between settlor and trustee.[172] Furthermore this argument does not describe constructive,

---

[165] *Target Holdings v Redferns* [1996] 1 AC 421, [1995] 3 WLR 352, [1995] 3 All ER 785. See para 32.70.

[166] See para 29.01.

[167] It can only be the express trust which is intended here. A resulting or constructive trust does not require any contract between 'settlor' and trustee of necessity because either form of trust arises by operation of law and not by means of the consensual act of the parties. There may be agreement between the parties which is the context within which, for example, common intention constructive trusts come into existence, but such agreement is not a necessary precondition for the creation of such trusts implied in law in general terms.

[168] Langbein, 'The contractarian basis of the law of trusts' (1995) 105 *Yale Law Journal*, 625.

[169] eg *Paul v Constance* [1977] 1 WLR 527; *Re Kayford* [1975] 1 WLR 279.

[170] [1977] 1 WLR 527.   [171] [1975] 1 WLR 279.

[172] Particularly in circumstances in which the settlor is also the sole trustee.

resulting, or implied trusts, which arise by operation of law in the manners discussed in Part D of this book. Trusts and contracts are therefore two very different institutions.[173]

While it has become fashionable, by the time of writing, to suppose that the oblig-   **1.61** ational element within the law relating to express trusts leads to the conclusion that the trust is really a subset of the law of obligations,[174] it is suggested that this approach is misconceived for four reasons. First, trusts impose fiduciary relationships on trustees whereas contracts do not impose fiduciary obligations of necessity.[175] Secondly, it is possible for trusts to come into existence without there being any contract in place between the settlor and any of the trustees.[176] Thirdly, trusts come into existence in relation to property and therefore occupy a place as part of property law, albeit that they also impose fiduciary obligations on trustees. Trusts are, in truth, hybrids of property law and fiduciary obligations. Fourthly, trusts arise both by operation of law, in the form of implied, resulting, and constructive trusts, as well as by means of a declaration of trust by a settlor: the contractarian notion of trusts has no explanation for such trusts implied by law.

Bailment

The important element of the trust is that property is held by the trustee for the   **1.62** benefit of the beneficiary. Therefore, a division between legal and equitable title occurs in the ownership of that property in circumstances in which a settlor declares the trust.[177] That forms a useful comparison with the law of bailment—again a combination of property law and of contract law obligations. In bailment, a person delivers property into the control of another person on the understanding that the property is to be returned to its owner. Thus, in a theatre, a member of the audience may leave a coat with the cloakroom attendant during the performance. There is no transfer of property law rights. Rather, the theatre becomes bailee of the coat during the performance, on the understanding that the coat is to be returned at the end of the performance. This may form part of the contract for the acquisition of the theatre ticket, or be the subject of a separate contract requiring payment for each garment left at the cloakroom, or it may be a purely gratuitous service offered by the theatre.[178] In either case, the bailee is not subjected to

---

[173] See also *Underhill and Hayton* 9.

[174] See for example Langbein, 'The contractarian basis of the law of trusts' (1995) 105 *Yale Law Journal* 625; J Penner, 'Exemptions' in P Birks (ed), *Breach of Trust* (Hart Publishing, 2002) 241.

[175] While it is accepted that contracts of agency or contracts of partnership will create fiduciary obligations, ordinary contracts do not; whereas all trusts do impose fiduciary obligations on trustees for the reasons given in the text.

[176] eg *Paul v Constance* [1977] 1 WLR 527.

[177] *Westdeutsche Landesbank v Islington* [1996] AC 669.

[178] For a radical restructuring of this topic see G McMeel, 'On the redundancy of the concept of bailment' in AS Hudson (ed), *New Perspectives on Property Law, Obligations and Restitution*, (Cavendish Publishing, 2003) 247.

that range of equitable obligations relating to the management and investment of property which are imposed on a trustee: their obligations are of a very different order. The bailor of the coat deposited in the theatre cloakroom does not surrender any of his ownership rights in the coat, unlike the situation in which property is settled on trust whereby the trustee becomes the legal owner of that property. That the trustee acquires these property rights is essential to the functioning of the trust,[179] whereas a bailee of property does not acquire any property rights in the objects put into her control.

Agency

1.63 The law of agency arises in general principles of the law of contract being a contract between a principal and its agent. The extent of the agent's liability will depend upon the terms of its agency.[180] There is no particular formality necessary to constitute someone an agent,[181] except in relation to land.[182] It is possible to imply a contract of agency from the behaviour of the principal and the agent.[183] The most significant difference between the relationship of principal and agent and that of settlor and trustee is that there is no contract necessarily in place between settlor and trustee, the agent does not necessarily hold property on terms set out by another person, and in any agency relationship there is no third party who occupies the rights of a beneficiary in such property. In general terms, the liabilities of the principal and the agent will be dependent upon the terms of the agency agreement between them on the ordinary principles of the law of contract, not on a code of principles akin to trusts law and in particular the incidents of trusteeship considered in Part C of this book. The agent is a fiduciary in a similar manner to the trustee being a fiduciary. The most significant similarity between trustee and agent is in relation to the fiduciary obligations created by each office. Trustees and agents owe fiduciary duties to the beneficiaries and principals respectively, precluding them from making unauthorized profits from their arrangements or becoming otherwise unjustly enriched. If an agent seeks to retain profits for himself, over and above any commission to which he is contractually entitled, the agent will hold those profits on constructive trust for its principal[184] in a similar way to a trustee but that similarity is based on the common feature of trusteeship and agency that both are fiduciary offices.

Gift

1.64 A gift involves the outright transfer of property rights in an item of property from an absolute owner of those rights to a volunteer (that is, someone who has given

[179] *Milroy v Lord* (1862) 4 De GF & J 264. [180] *Kelly v Cooper* [1993] AC 205.
[181] *Heard v Pilley* (1869) 4 Ch App 548. [182] Law of Property Act 1925, s 53.
[183] *Garnac Grain Co Inc v HMF Faure and Fairclough Ltd* [1968] AC 1130.
[184] *Boardman v Phipps* [1967] 2 AC 46.

no consideration for the transfer). The recipient (or donee) becomes absolute owner of that property as a result of the transfer. In some senses the recipient of a gift appears to occupy a similar position to the beneficiary under a trust. The settlor transfers absolute title in property by dividing between the legal title vested in the trustee and the equitable title vested in the beneficiary. The beneficiary is not required (by the general law of trusts) to have given consideration for that transfer. In that sense the beneficiary is a volunteer. One of the core equitable principles already considered is that equity will not assist a volunteer.[185] However, the significant difference between a gift and a trust is that legal title has been assigned to the trustee on the basis that the trustee is required to deal with the property for the benefit of the beneficiary. In short, equity is acting on the conscience of the trustee in her treatment of the trust fund, rather than seeking to benefit a beneficiary. It is a by-product of the control of the trustee's conscience that the beneficiary takes equitable title in the property.

F. The Uses of the Trust

A property holding device

The trust is best recognized as being a property holding or management device. In its broadest terms, whether commercial or domestic, the trust device is a valuable technique for the organization of any property rights so that their common ownership between a group of people can be made plain, or so that their ownership can be obscured behind the office of the trustee and among a group of beneficiaries, or so that those rights can be protected against third persons, or so that they can be made available to a group of people in identified circumstances over a given period of time. That one person, the trustee, acts on behalf of another person, the beneficiary, but in a way that both are recognized as having different rights to the property which the trustee holds means that it is possible for the trustee to deal as freely with the property as the settlor would wish but also so that the beneficiary can enforce her own, collateral rights. Some trusts can facilitate the management of property by the design of the settlor, while others can intrude by order of the court to frustrate the unconscionable designs of a scoundrel, while others yet can resolve disputes as to ownership. Their seemingly limitless appeal is due to their flexibility and the simplicity of their conceptual roots.

1.65

Domestic, familial uses of the trust

The trust has been used since time immemorial to provide for the means by which property can be made available for successive generations within a family but always

1.66

---

[185] See para 5.36.

in the confidence that no one family member would be able to use that property for any personal advantage not permitted by the settlor. The patriarchs in old landed families were thus able to settle their land and their chattels for the benefit of future generations with detailed provision as to which members of the family and which sorts of relative (whether male or female, whether blood descendants or those marrying into the family) were entitled to take interests in which types of property. The selection of trustees caused a difficulty for settlors because they were required to choose people in whom they could repose sufficient confidence not only during their own lifetimes but also in the future, but those trustees also offered the power to have the settlors' wishes carried loyally into effect down the generations because the office of trustee continues in effect even if the human holders of that office from time to time should succumb to the inherent weakness of the flesh and die. The only limitation on the power of the settlor were the rules against excessive perpetuities or accumulations.[186] The rules concerning settlements of land and of chattels in the grand style are considered in Chapter 5,[187] although they are of waning significance. Nevertheless, the trust has provided almost limitless possibilities, within the bounds of public policy and the criminal law, for the owner of property to deal with it *inter vivos* or by means of trusts contained in his will. The more modern use of trusts has been in the resolution of disputes as to ownership of the family home either where no document has made the division of ownership plain or where events subsequent to the creation of any arrangement suggest an alternative allocation of property rights, as considered in Chapter 56.[188]

Commercial uses of the trust

1.67 The principal rules of trusts law in relation to commercial transactions are considered in detail in Part J of this book.[189] Commercial people use trusts to take security in their transactions, in common with a range of other devices such as pledges, floating and fixed charges, liens, escrow accounts, and so forth.[190] The trust continues to establish itself as a very flexible method of structuring the means by which money might be paid under a contract in advance of the delivery of goods or the performance of services such that the recipient is not paid until the goods or services are supplied, thus giving security to the payer, but such that the seller of the goods or services can have confidence that he will be paid once he performs his part of the transaction. As Lord Browne-Wilkinson held in *Target Holdings v Redferns*:[191]

---

[186] See para 8.01.   [187] See para 5.01.   [188] See para 56.01.
[189] For a more wide-ranging account of the commercial uses of trusts, the reader is referred to *Hudson* 671 *et seq.*
[190] See para 49.01.   [191] [1996] 1 AC 421.

In the modern world the trust has become a valuable device in commercial and financial dealings. The fundamental principles of equity apply as much to such trusts as they do to the traditional trusts in relation to which those principles were originally formulated. But in my judgment it is important, if the trust is not to be rendered commercially useless, to distinguish between the basic principles of trust law and those specialist rules developed in relation to traditional trusts which are applicable only to such trusts and the rationale of which has no application to trusts of quite a different kind.

As his lordship said, there is a need for equity to winnow out those principles which are of use only in family and similar situations. Similarly, his lordship suggested that equity must ensure that it does develop specialist rules which are appropriate to the decision of commercial cases. It is perhaps somewhat ironic that Lord Browne-Wilkinson both set out this call for the possible need for equity to adopt a new approach in the commercial context and then delivered the leading speech in the House of Lords in *Westdeutsche Landesbank v Islington*[192] in which the traditional rules were consolidated in contradistinction to laying the groundwork for the development of such new commercial principles.

1.68 An illustration of the commercial utility of the trust is given by the case of *Re Kayford*[193] in which a company which operated a mail order business, on the advice of its accountants who considered the company to be in financial difficulties, paid the moneys which it received from those of its customers who paid in advance for their goods into a bank account which was held separately from the other bank accounts and all other money owned by the company. When any customer received their goods, the money constituting their prepayment was taken from the segregated bank account and paid into the company's ordinary bank accounts. After this arrangement had been established, the company went into insolvency. The question arose as to the ownership of the advance payments held in the segregated bank account. The court held that an express trust had been created over those advance payments in favour of the customers who had made prepayments without receiving their goods. The act of segregating those moneys coupled with the intention that they be capable of being repaid to customers in the event that the company could not fulfil their orders was sufficient to satisfy the court that the effect of the accountant's actions had been the constitution of a trust.

1.69 The important commercial by-product of the creation of a trust in such circumstances is that the beneficiary under the trust retains a property right in the trust fund and is protected against the trustee's insolvency because the trust property is not subsumed into that part of the insolvent person's estate which is distributed to the insolvency creditors. In commercial terms, the trust is a core technique in taking security in a transaction. Where one party is concerned about the ability of the

---

[192] [1996] 1 AC 669.   [193] [1975] 1 WLR 279.

other party to perform its obligations, any property (including money) which is to be passed as part of the transaction can be held on trust until such time as both parties' contractual obligations have been performed.

Fiscal uses of the trust

Basic techniques in the use of trusts for tax planning purposes

1.70 The settlor may have a number of motivations in creating the trust, one of which may be the reduction of his liability to tax. The core, technical advantage of the trust in this sense is the possibility that more than one person owns the trust property at one and the same time such that the question as to which of them is to bear the liability to pay tax on any income or capital gain of the trust is a complex one. While UK revenue law has developed sophisticated rules governing the allocation of liability to tax and the rate at which tax will be paid by means of statute, and frequently ever more sophisticated rules preventing the avoidance of tax through the use of trusts by means of statute and of case law, trusts nevertheless offer great possibilities for the minimization of the settlor's personal liability to tax due to the division in the ownership of property between trustee and beneficiary on the creation of a trust, coupled with the opportunities for structuring the ownership of property and selecting the people who should own it, which the trust device presents.

1.71 As considered above, the trust enables one person (the settlor) to have property held by another (the trustee) for the benefit of some other person (the beneficiary). Suppose that the property involved is a bundle of valuable shares which are expected to generate a large dividend annually. The shareholder will be liable to a form of income or corporation tax on those dividends and a form of capital gains tax on the disposal of the shares for profit. However, if those shares were transferred onto a trust to be held on trust for the benefit of third parties, the settlor would be able to deny any prima facie liability for tax due in relation to that shareholding. UK revenue law has developed a complex web of statutory provisions and case law principles which will deem the settlor to be liable for the tax in any event in many situations in which the avoidance of tax was the purpose behind the creation of this trust, and many other situations in which the unwary and innocent settlor may not have intended to avoid liability to tax at all. This book cannot hope to cover all of these situations and therefore will restrict itself to this very brief account of the ways in which trusts might be used for fiscal purposes.[194]

The settlor may have been seeking to minimize his own liability to tax, in which case the tax treatment of the trust will be of significance. There are a number of principles of revenue law dealing specifically with the situation in which the settlor

---

[194] The reader is referred to the standard works on revenue law such as *Simon's Taxes* and in relation to the core principles underpinning the taxation of trusts to GW Thomas, *Taxation and Trusts* (Sweet & Maxwell, 1981) generally.

is deemed to have reserved some benefit or interest for himself. So, for fiscal purposes the settlor will seek the appearance that he, the settlor, retains no beneficial interest in the settled property from the moment of the declaration of that trust. Otherwise, the trust property may be deemed by operation of statute to remain his property beneficially so that the trust's liability to tax is treated as being the liability which the settlor would have faced had he retained the property absolutely.

As considered below, the law of taxation will frequently levy liability to tax at the rate   **1.72**
of tax which would have been payable by the beneficiary as if no trust had existed and particularly in relation to bare trusts where the sole beneficiary is treated for tax purposes as being in effect the absolute owner of the trust property.[195] However, the settlor may have been a good deal more cunning, or well advised, than that. The settlor may name persons other than himself to be the beneficiaries of the trust and therefore claim to have no rights to the shares. Those beneficiaries might be the settlor's own infant children (who would probably have no other taxable income) or a company controlled by the settlor. Other common tax avoidance schemes using trusts involve using trustees resident in other tax jurisdictions where little or no tax is payable (such as the Cayman Islands or the British Virgin Islands) to raise an argument that the trust ought not to be liable to UK taxation in any event but rather to tax at the lower rate applicable in that other jurisdiction.

Tax statutes have become increasingly complex in recent years to combat these transparent attempts to avoid liability to UK tax. The flexibility afforded by the trust means that the ingenuity of lawyers practising in the field of taxation can be applied to construct ever more sophisticated structures to avoid the letter of the law. In response to this tax avoidance industry, the Inland Revenue has adopted the approach of promoting legislation that is targeted at very specific forms of avoidance. The more effective approach appears to be that developed by the courts to ignore any 'artificial steps' in such tax avoidance structures, so that the true substance of the transaction can be taxed without the sham devices of a tax avoidance scheme.[196] However, there is nothing per se to prevent a person from ordering her own affairs in a way which reduces her liability to tax.[197]

Principles of the taxation of trusts

The difficulty with reference to the taxation of trusts is that there is more than one   **1.73**
person with proprietary rights in the trust fund. This short section does not attempt to do more than outline some of the main principles involved in the taxation of trusts. Nevertheless Part F, in relation to Private Client Trusts, considers many of the fiscal encumbrances on the use of trusts for clients organizing their

---

[195] *Baker v Archer-Shee* [1927] AC 844.
[196] *Ramsay v IRC* [1982] AC 300; *Furniss v Dawson* [1984] 2 WLR 226.
[197] See perhaps *Ingram v IRC* [1985] STC 835.

affairs. Readers with a more detailed interest than that discussion penetrates are directed to books dealing with the taxation of trusts.[198]

1.74 The general principle is that it is the trustee who must account for any taxable income deriving from the trust property.[199] There are those who doubt that this principle does create quite such an all-embracing rule as that for which this case is typically taken to be authority.[200] However, where the trust is a bare trust (that is, a trustee holds as bare nominee for a single beneficiary absolutely), it is the beneficiary who is liable for taxable income generated by that trust.[201] It is suggested that this latter decision must be correct, otherwise a taxpayer liable to higher rate income tax would simply be able to create a number of trusts, each receiving a portion of the income belonging beneficially to the taxpayer but so that those portions fell below the threshold for payment of higher rate tax.

1.75 Different rules apply to accumulation and discretionary trusts. A special rate of tax is applicable to trusts under sections 686(1), (1A) and 832(1) of the Income and Corporation Taxes Act (TA) 1988. The creation of settlements in which the settlor retains some equitable interest (however small) will typically be caught by anti-avoidance legislation. Therefore, where the settlor retains a benefit under such a discretionary or accumulation trust, the taxpayer will be liable for any difference between the rate of tax applicable to trusts and the taxpayer's own effective rate of tax.[202] Similarly, under inheritance tax rules, where a taxpayer makes a gift with a reservation of some benefit in that gift to herself, tax will be chargeable on the taxpayer's estate.[203]

1.76 In the Finance Act 1995, a broad range of tax avoidance rules were introduced in relation to settlements by addition to Part XV of the TA 1988. These provisions consolidated the piecemeal anti-avoidance legislation passed in connection with settlements hitherto. Within the technical tax term 'settlement' for this purpose fell 'any disposition, trust, covenant, agreement, arrangement or transfer of assets'.[204] The underlying intention of these provisions was to prevent tax avoidance in situations in which a settlor seeks to retain some benefit to herself under a settlement.[205] The tax position in relation to non-resident trusts is particularly complex and not within the compass of this book.[206]

---

[198] GW Thomas (n 194 above); A Shipwright and E Keeling, *Revenue Law* (Blackstone Press, 1998); J Tiley, *Revenue Law* (Hart, 2001).
[199] *Williams v Singer* [1921] 1 AC 65, *per* Viscount Cave.
[200] *Reid's Trustees v IRC* (1926) 14 TC 512; Shipwright and Keeling (n 198 above) 401 *et seq.*
[201] *Baker v Archer-Shee* [1927] AC 844.
[202] TA 1988, s 687.
[203] Finance Act 1986, s 102.
[204] TA 1988, s 660G.
[205] ibid, s 660(2).
[206] Readers are referred to R Venables, *Taxation of Offshore Trusts* (6th edn, London: Key Haven, 2002) generally.

Part B

EXPRESS PRIVATE TRUSTS

2

THE THREE CERTAINTIES

A. The Three Certainties: Introduction

A trust necessarily imposes onerous obligations of a particular kind on a trustee with **2.01** respect to the trust property and towards its beneficiaries—obligations which a court may be called upon to enforce. Failure to fulfil such obligations may be a breach of trust for which the trustee may be held personally liable at the instance of the beneficiaries. It is therefore self-evident that, in order for an express trust to be capable of being carried into effect and enforced, it must be clear that it was intended to impose 'trust obligations', as opposed to some other kind of legal or equitable obligation; that the property in respect of which such obligations exist is known and certain; and that the identity of the beneficiaries or objects of the trust is ascertained or ascertainable. These are the 'three certainties' essential for the creation of an express private trust: certainty of intention to create a trust; certainty of subject matter; and certainty of beneficiaries (or objects). They are simple to state—indeed, they are simple in concept. However, they also give rise to some difficult questions.

The 'three certainties' are dealt with separately, because it is convenient to do so. **2.02** However, it must always be remembered that they can seldom be segregated in practice. In particular, the absence of certainty of subject matter or of objects is usually a sound indicator of a lack of intention to create a trust. As Lord Eldon warned in *Morice v Bishop of Durham*:[1]

> wherever the subject to be administered as trust property, and the objects, for whose benefit it is to be administered, are to be found in a will, not expressly creating a trust,

---

[1] (1805) 10 Ves 522, 536. Similarly, in *Wright v Atkyns* (1823) Turn & Russ 143, 157, 159, *per* Lord Eldon: 'Where a trust is to be raised characterised by certainty, the very difficulty of doing it is

the indefinite nature and quantum of the subject, and the indefinite nature of the objects, are always used by the Court as evidence that the mind of the testator was not to create a trust; and the difficulty that would be imposed upon the Court to say what should be so applied, or to what objects, has been the foundation of the argument that no trust was intended.

Similarly, in *Mussoorie Bank Ltd v Raynor*,[2] in relation to precatory trusts, Sir Arthur Hobhouse stated:

> If there is uncertainty as to the amount or nature of the property that is given over, two difficulties at once arise. There is not only difficulty in the execution of the trust because the Court does not know upon what property to lay its hands, but the uncertainty in the subject of the gift has a reflex action upon the previous words, and throws doubt upon the intention of the testator, and seems to shew that he could not possibly have intended his words of confidence, hope or whatever they may be,—his appeal to the conscience of the first taker,—to be imperative words.

B. Certainty of Intention

2.03 A trust clearly ought to be declared by means of express words, such as 'on trust' or plain equivalent.[2A] However, technical or formal words are not required for the creation of an express private trust. Equity has regard to the substance and not the form. There must simply be a sufficiently clear manifestation of an intention to create such a trust.[3] 'As for the requisite certainty of words, it is well settled that a trust can be created without using the words "trust" or "confidence" or the like: the question is whether in substance a sufficient intention to create a trust has been manifested.'[4] There is no magic in the word 'trust'.[5] Although it is the most common pointer to an intention to create a trust, it is clearly a word capable of different meanings.

> The word is in common use in English language, and whatever may be the position in this court, it must be recognised that the word is often used in a sense different from that of an equitable obligation enforceable as such by the courts. Many a man may be in a position of trust without being a trustee in the equitable sense . . . At the

---

an argument which goes, to a certain extent, towards inducing the Court to say it is not sufficiently clear what the testator intended.' Also *Mussoorie Bank Ltd v Raynor* (1882) 7 App Cas 321, 331, *per* Sir Arthur Hobhouse.

[2] (1882) 7 App Cas 321, 331. See also *BMF Trading v Abacus Holdings Ltd* (2002) 5 ITELR 473.

[2A] The normal meaning of the words 'on trust' is a technical one and cannot be ignored: *Bath and North East Somerset Council v A-G* (2002) 5 ITELR 274.

[3] *Re Atkinson* (1911) 80 LJ Ch 370, 371; *Moore v Darton* (1851) 4 De G & Sm 517; *Page v Cox* (1852) 10 Hare 163; *Dipple v Corles* (1853) 11 Hare 183; *Brisbane City Council v A-G (Qld)* (1978) 19 ALR 681, 684–685. See also *Malim v. Keighley* (1794) 2 Ves. 333, at 335; *OT Computers Ltd v First National Tricity Finance Ltd*, Pumfrey J, 9 May 2003: Lawtel ACO105027.

[4] *Re Kayford Ltd (in Liquidation)* [1975] 1 WLR 279, 282; *Hunter v Moss* [1994] 1 WLR 452, 455–456.

[5] *Kinloch v Secretary of State for India in Council* (1882) 7 App Cas 619, 631.

same time, it can hardly be disputed that a trust may be created without using the word trust. In every case one has to look to see whether in the circumstances of the case, and on the true construction of what was said and written, a sufficient intention to create a true trust has been manifested.[6]

Thus, in appropriate circumstances, an express trust may be created by means of an informal declaration,[7] or may be inferred from the acts of the settlor or the circumstances of the case.[8] So, in *Paul v Constance*,[9] the words 'the money is as much yours as mine', referring to moneys in a bank account, were held, in the circumstances of the case, to have created a trust. A similar result was reached in *Rowe v Prance*,[10] where the legal owner of a yacht referred to it, in many conversations with his mistress, as 'ours' or as 'our boat'.

It is not even necessary that the creator of the trust should be aware that it is a trust that he was creating: all that is required is that he has a sufficiently clear intention to create a state of affairs (such as the creation of successive equitable interests in property)[11] which requires a trust for its implementation or to impose an obligation of the kind which in law is regarded as a trust obligation.[12] He is presumed to intend the legal consequences of his acts.[13]   **2.04**

Mere conduct without the requisite intention will not be effectual to impose a trust.[14] On the other hand, a clear intention to create a trust will not necessarily   **2.05**

---

[6] *Tito v Waddell (No 2)* [1977] Ch 106, 211. Megarry V-C added (at 216): 'Certainly in common speech in legal circles "trust" is normally used to mean an equitable relationship enforceable in the courts and not a governmental relationship which is not thus enforceable.' He also pointed out that '. . . the term "trust" is one which may properly be used to describe not only relationships which are enforceable by the courts in their equitable jurisdiction, but also other relationships such as the discharge, under the direction of the Crown, of the duties or functions belonging to the prerogative and the authority of the Crown. Trusts of the former kind [are] . . . "trusts in the lower sense"; trusts of the latter kind [are] "trusts in the higher sense".'

[7] *Paul v Constance* [1977] 1 WLR 527.

[8] *Re Kayford Ltd* [1975] 1 WLR 279 (mail order company paid customers' payments into a separate bank account until orders were fulfilled); *Re Chelsea Cloisters Ltd* (1981) 41 P & CR 98 (tenants' damage deposits held on trust by landlord); *Re Lewis's of Leicester Ltd* [1995] 1 BCLC 428 (customers' moneys paid into separate trust account). In such cases, if the trust is declared in respect of moneys which have become part of the assets of the settlor, there might be an improper preference of creditors under the provisions of the Insolvency Act 1986. See (1980) MLR 489, esp 496–498 (W Goodhart and G Jones); and (1992) 12 OJLS 333 (M Bridge). See also *White v Briggs* (1848) 2 Ph 583; *R v Clowes (No 2)* [1994] 2 All ER 316 (terms of brochures for a collective investment scheme indicating that funds were received on trust for investors).

[9] [1977] 1 WLR 527.   [10] [1999] 2 FLR 787.

[11] *Re Armstrong* [1960] VR 202 (oral self-declaration of trust by depositor of sums in bank accounts, reserving right to income, his sons taking capital if he died during period of deposit).

[12] As, for example, in *Paul v Constance* [1977] 1 WLR 527; *Re Vandervell's Trusts (No 2)* [1974] Ch 269; and *Re Chelsea Cloisters Ltd* (1981) 41 P & CR 98.

[13] cf *Swiss Bank Corporation v Lloyds Bank Ltd* [1981] AC 584, 595–596 (in relation to an equitable charge).

[14] *Commissioner of Stamp Duties (Qld) v Jolliffe* (1920) 28 CLR 178, 189. See also *Trident General Insurance Co Ltd v McNiece Bros Pty Ltd* (1988) 80 ALR 574, 602.

constitute a trust obligation.[15] If, for example, one of the other essential requirements of a trust, such as certainty of subject matter or of objects, is absent, the purported trust will still fail. In other cases, what was contemplated as a trust may in fact be an obligation of an entirely different character, such as a charge[16] or a debt.[17]

2.06   A trust may be created by will or *inter vivos.* In the latter case, the trust may be created (i) by an effectual declaration by the holder of property that he thereafter holds that property on specified trusts or (ii) by means of a transfer of that property by the settlor to some other person to hold on specified trusts.[18] The intention to create an *inter vivos* trust of land or any interest in land must be manifested in writing.[19] The creation of an express private trust on death must be effected by means of a valid testamentary instrument executed in conformity with the requirements of section 9 of the Wills Act 1837 and duly admitted to probate.[20] In each case, however, there must be certainty of intention to create a trust. In the much quoted words of Lord Alvanley MR, in *Malim v. Keighley*:[21] 'wherever any person gives property, and points out the object, the property, and the way in which it shall go, that does create a trust, unless he shews clearly that his desire expressed is to be controlled by the party, and that he shall have an option to defeat it'. The required manifestation is usually satisfied by an express declaration of trust and, subject to any question of inaccurate use of terminology, generally presents no difficulty.

2.07   However, where it is a matter of inference, considerable uncertainty can arise: the question whether a trust has been created is then primarily one of construction, of ascertaining the true meaning of the words used, viewed in the particular context in which they appear or were uttered.[22]

C. Absolute Gift or Trust

2.08   In some cases, it is difficult to establish whether a disposition of property was intended to be an absolute one or to impose a trust. As James V-C pointed out,

---

[15] *Commissioner of Stamp Duties (Qld) v Jolliffe* (1920) 28 CLR 178, 189. See also *Ernst & Young Inc v Central Guaranty Trust Co* (2001) 3 ITELR 605.

[16] *Clough Mill Ltd v Martin* [1985] 1 WLR 111; *Re Bond Worth Ltd* [1980] Ch 228.

[17] *Commissioners of Customs and Excise v Richmond Theatre Management Ltd* [1995] STC 257. The relationship between a prisoner and a prison governor who holds the prisoner's cash is that of debtor and creditor, and not that of beneficiary and trustee: *Duggan v Governor of Full Sutton Prison* [2004] 1 WLR 1010. It is suggested that a better solution would have been to hold that the governor is a bare trustee not subject to any duty to invest.

[18] See generally Chapter 5, Sections B and C, below.

[19] See paras 5.09–5.14 below.   [20] See paras 5.06–5.08 below.

[21] *Keighley* (1794) 2 Ves 333, 335.

[22] *Richards v Delbridge* (1974) LR 18 Eq 11, 14; *Trident General Insurance Co Ltd v McNiece Bros. Pty Ltd* (1988) 80 ALR 574, 603; *OT Computers Ltd v First National Tricity Finance Ltd*, decision of Pumfrey J, 9 May 2003. Lawtel AC0105027.

in *Irvine v Sullivan*,[23] the word 'absolutely' may be used in different senses: it 'may refer to extent of interest; that is to say, the entire unlimited interest. It may mean that, but it may mean something a great deal more; and I think the natural grammatical meaning of the word "absolutely" is unfettered and unlimited. It implies . . . that it is unlimited in point of estate, and unfettered in respect of any condition or trust.' It is trite law that, when used in the latter sense, ie, where there is an absolute, indefeasible gift, whether of real or personal property, to a person, any restriction imposed by the donor upon the future disposal of that property is inconsistent with the absolute gift and is, therefore, repugnant and void. As James LJ put it in *Re Stringer's Estate*:[24]

> It is settled by authority that if you give a man some property, real or personal, to be his absolutely, then you cannot by your will dispose of that property which becomes his. You cannot say that, if he does not spend it, if he does not give it away, if he does not will it, that which he happened to have in his possession, or in his drawer, or in his pocket at the time of his death, shall not go to his heir at law if it is realty, or to his next of kin if it is personalty, or to his creditors who may have a paramount claim to it. You cannot do that if you once vest property absolutely in the first donee. That is because that which is once vested in a man, and vested de facto in him, cannot be taken from him out of the due course of devolution at his death by any expression of wish on the part of the original testator.

There are several instances in the law reports of absolute gifts being made which are then followed by purported gifts over if certain circumstances arise or certain events occur: for example, if the donee should die intestate,[25] or 'without a will and childless';[26] or if he shall not have disposed of the property;[27] or if he should die mentally unfit to manage his own affairs;[28] or if he should die without leaving lawful issue;[29] or if the property should otherwise pass to the Crown as *bona vacantia*.[30] Similarly, absolute gifts may be accompanied by precatory words.[31] In all these cases, the donee takes absolutely and the gift over is repugnant and void. The same principle applies where the absolute gift is followed by words purporting to confer a power, whether general or limited, coupled with a gift over if the power is not exercised: both the gift over and the power are repugnant and void.[32]

2.09

---

[23] (1869) LR 8 Eq 673, 680.   [24] (1877) 6 Ch D 1, 14–15.

[25] *Holmes v Godson* (1856) 8 De GM & G 152; *Hughes v Ellis* (1855) 20 Beav 193; *Barton v Barton* (1857) 3 K & J 512; *Ross v Ross* (1819) 1 Jac & W 154; *Bull v Kingston* (1816) 1 Mer 314.

[26] *Re Dixon* [1903] 2 Ch 458; see also *Gulliver v Vaux* (1746) 8 De GM & G 167n.

[27] *Re Jones* [1898] 1 Ch 438; *Re Mortlock's Trust* (1857) 3 K & J 456; *Hales v Margerum* (1796) 3 Ves 299.

[28] *Re Ashton* [1920] 2 Ch 481.   [29] *Re Parry and Daggs* (1885) 31 Ch D 130.

[30] *Re Wilcock's Settlement* (1875) 1 Ch D 299.

[31] *Re Byrne's estate* (1892) 29 LR Ir 250; *Creagh v Murphy* (1873) 7 Ir R Eq 182; *Re Atkinson* (1911) 80 LJ Ch 370; *Re Johnson* [1939] 2 All ER 458. For 'precatory trusts', see paras 2.17–2.23 below.

[32] *Bradly v Westcott* (1807) 13 Ves 445, esp 453.

A gift of income only, unlimited as to time, is equivalent to an absolute gift. Consequently, a superadded power will not cut down that gift.[33]

2.10 The underlying doctrine in these cases is that of repugnancy; and it may sometimes have unexpected results. It might have been thought that, once it is established that the intention was to give A an absolute interest, the intended gift would simply fail if A predeceased the testator. However, this is not so. Under the so-called principle in *Re Lowman*,[34] the gift which would otherwise have been repugnant and void is accelerated and takes effect, the doctrine of repugnancy being no longer applicable. Lindley LJ reviewed earlier cases in *Re Lowman* and concluded:[35]

> ... where there are successive limitations of personal estate in favour of several persons absolutely, the first of them who survives the testator takes absolutely, although he would take nothing if any other legatee had survived and taken; or, in other words, in the case supposed the effect of the failure of an earlier gift is to accelerate, and not destroy, the later gift ...
> ... The doctrine of repugnancy has no application to gifts which fail; the doctrine does not come into operation until somebody takes, and it is only those limitations which defeat the interest some one takes that are void, on the ground that they are inconsistent with what is given to him.

Lindley LJ expressly did not decide the issue in relation to land. However, in *Re Dunstan*,[36] Neville J concluded that 'no sound distinction' can be drawn between real and personal estate. In that case, a testatrix gave freeholds absolutely to A, subject to a gift that whatever of the freeholds should remain after death should be given to a named charity. The gift to the charity would have been repugnant and void and A would have taken absolutely if he had survived the testator, but he failed to do so and the gift to the charity took effect.

2.11 In any event, what may at first sight appear to be an absolute, unfettered gift may be construed, in context, to be a gift on trust. In *Parnall v Parnall*,[37] for example, property was left to a widow 'for her sole use and benefit. It is my wish that

---

[33] *Southouse v Bate* (1851) 16 Beav 132; *Weale v Ollive (No 2)* (1863) 32 Beav 421. See GW Thomas, *Powers* (Sweet & Maxwell, 1998) ('*Thomas*'), 55.

[34] [1895] 2 Ch 348.   [35] ibid 354, 358.

[36] [1918] 2 Ch 304. See also *Re Stringer's Estate* (1877) 6 Ch D 1, 15, *per* James LJ.

[37] (1878) 9 Ch D 96. See also *Mackett v Mackett* (1872) LR 14 Eq 49; *Perry v Merritt* (1874) LR 18 Eq 152; *Re Jones* [1898] 1 Ch 438. In *Breton v Mockett* (1878) 9 Ch D 95, where there was a gift of personal estate, including farming stock, live and dead, for a widow's life, without being liable to account for any diminution or depreciation in the implements and stock; and, after her death, the residue of his personal estate was given to his children, it was held that the widow took an absolute interest. There was no obligation to carry on the farm here. Cf *Cockayne v Harrison* (1872) LR 13 Eq 432, where there was a gift for life of farming stock, made in connection with a gift for life of the farming business, the stock being necessary to carry on the business, so the legatee was bound to keep up the stock. It was said that, where there is no trade, the legatee takes an absolute interest. See, too, *Randall v Russell* (1817) 3 Mer 190; *Phillips v Beal* (1858) 32 Beav 25; *Groves v Wright* (1856) 2 K & J 347.

whatever property my wife might possess at her death be equally divided between my children.' It was held that she took an absolute interest. On the other hand, in *Curnick v Tucker*,[38] where property was left to a widow 'for her sole use and benefit, in the full confidence that she will so dispose of it amongst all our children, both during her lifetime and at her decease, doing equal justice to each and all of them', it was held that the widow had a life interest only, coupled with a power of disposition among her children, by deed or by will. The wording was similar in each case, but the intention and the effect were found to be different. According to Byrne J, in *Re Jones*,[39] the principles by which the courts are guided in such cases can be broadly summarized as follows:

> There are one or two rules which the Court is obliged to observe in construing wills containing gifts of this class. It is clear that if a gift is made in terms to a person absolutely, that can only be reduced to a more limited interest by clear words cutting down the first estate. There is a principle also which one must observe—represented in a class of cases like *Constable v Bull*[40]—that, although the words are absolute in the first instance, you may find subsequently occurring words sufficiently strong to cut down the first apparent absolute interest to a life interest. Then there have been a great many decisions ... in cases in which the testator has given an absolute interest in the first instance and has superadded words indicating that the person taking that interest is to have a power of disposition, and then has followed that up by purporting to give what shall remain, or what may not have been disposed of by the first taker. After all, in all these cases it is a question of construction; but the law requires that if there is an absolute gift in the first instance, you must have clear words to cut down that estate.

Thus, although there may be a presumption that a gift which is expressed to be absolute is intended to be unfettered by any trust, the terms of the disposition, taken as a whole and viewed in the context in which they appear, may manifest an intention to create a trust and to confer a more limited interest (with or without a power of disposition).

Absolute gift with engrafted trusts

One class of such cases comprises those instances in which the word 'absolute' is used, but there is found nonetheless to be a valid executory limitation over upon a certain event. In such a case, the fact that there is a power to appoint among the persons intended to take by virtue of the gift over does not, of itself, make the limitation void, provided that the contingency upon which the gift over is expressed to take effect is not solely the non-exercise of that power.[41] Similarly, where the rule in *Lassence v Tierney*[42] applies, what appears in the first instance as an absolute

2.12

---

[38] (1874) LR 17 Eq 320. See also *Le Marchant v Le Marchant* (1874) LR 18 Eq 414; *Re Sanford* [1901] 1 Ch 939 (a will and codicil); *Re Beesty's Will Trusts* [1966] Ch 223.
[39] [1898] 1 Ch 438, 441.   [40] (1849) 3 De G & Sm 411.
[41] *Comiskey v Bowring-Hanbury* [1905] AC 84.   [42] (1849) 1 Mac & G 551.

gift to the donee is then cut down by trusts which are engrafted or imposed on that absolute interest. Only if those trusts fail, through lapse or invalidity or any other reason, does the absolute gift take effect.[43]

Life interest coupled with power of disposition[44]

2.13 In principle, there is a clear distinction between an absolute gift, on the one hand, and a disposition which confers a life (or other limited) interest on the donee of the property, coupled with a power of disposition by deed or will. Nevertheless, it may be difficult to distinguish one from the other in practice. Certainly, it is obvious that no absolute gift is made where A has a life interest coupled with a special power of appointment in favour of others (say, A's children). However, the result is less clear where A has a general power of appointment, exercisable by deed or will, and can therefore appoint the property to himself or into his estate.[45] Thus, in *Re Ryder*,[46] a testatrix directed that income of her estate be paid to her husband for his life (or until he should marry again) and also authorized him 'so long as he is entitled to the income of part or of the whole of my estate to apply such portion of the corpus of my estate as he shall think fit for his own use and benefit'. It was held that the husband had power in his lifetime to appoint the corpus to himself, and had actually done so. Similarly, in *Re Richards*[47] and *Re Shuker's Estate*,[48] a widow was held to have a life interest coupled with a general power of appointment during her lifetime. A general power exercisable by will,[49] or by deed or will,[50] is similar. If the donee of the power of appointment, be it general or special, does not exercise it, the property passes under the gift over in default of appointment, and not as part of the donee's estate.[51] If there is no gift over, the property results back to the donor's estate.

2.14 In such cases, however, the gift over itself was not in favour of the donee or his estate.[52] Where, in contrast, there is a gift of personal or real property to A for life,

---

[43] *Hancock v Watson* [1902] AC 14; *Watson v Holland* [1985] 1 All ER 290; *Re Burton's Settlement Trusts* [1955] Ch 348; *Smither v Willock* (1803) 9 Ves 233; *Hodgson v Smithson* (1856) 8 De GM & G 604; *Gatenby v Morgan* (1876) 1 QBD 685; *Re Cohen* [1915] WN 361; *Re Bernard's Settlement* [1916] 1 Ch 552; *O'Connor v Tanner* [1917] AC 25; *Re Marshall* [1928] Ch 661; *Fyfe v Irwin* [1939] 2 All ER 271; *Re Hatch* [1948] Ch 592.
[44] See *Thomas* 53–54. See also *Re Sanford* [1901] 1 Ch 939; *Re Beesty's Will Trusts* [1966] Ch 223.
[45] A may be treated as absolute owner of the property in certain circumstances, however: see *Thomas* 12–15.
[46] [1914] 1 Ch 865.   [47] [1902] 1 Ch 76; cf *Re Pedrotti* (1859) 27 Beav 583.
[48] [1937] 3 All ER 25.
[49] *Nannock v Horton* (1802) 7 Ves 391; *Archibald v Wright* (1838) 9 Sim 161.
[50] *Reith v Seymour* (1828) 4 Russ 263.
[51] *Pennock v Pennock* (1871) LR 13 Eq 144; *Re Thomson's Estate* (1880) 14 Ch D 263. See also *Scott v Josselyn* (1859) 26 Beav 174, and *Re Pounder* (1886) 56 LJ Ch 113.
[52] See, for example, *Re Ryder* [1914] 1 Ch 865 (charitable purposes); *Re Richards* [1902] 1 Ch 76 (other residuary legatees); *Re Shuker's Estate* [1937] 3 All ER 25 (to trustees of other trusts).

with remainder as A should by deed or will (or by will only)[53] appoint, with remainder in default of appointment to A himself, or to A's executors, administrators, or assigns, this is usually (but not necessarily always)[54] construed as an absolute gift to A.[55] This is a development of the rule that, where personal property is bequeathed by will to a person for life and, after his death, to his personal representative, the bequest is ordinarily construed as an absolute gift to him.[56] Consequently, A could call for a transfer to him of any property held subject to the power of appointment, which (subject to any question of duty)[57] could be safely handed over to A, and A could give a valid receipt for it, without any necessity for A to exercise or release the power.[58] A's personal representatives could take the property only as part of A's estate, and if A disposed of it during his lifetime they could not dispute or claim in opposition to the act of A.[59] A limitation to A's next of kin, or to *persona designata*, would not, of course, give A complete dominion over the property.[60] Moreover, a general power of appointment exercisable only with the consent of another does not confer an absolute interest.[61]

In some cases, where the life interest has been severed from the power of appointment for the purpose of introducing other distinct and contingent separate interests which never, in fact, arise, it has been held that the donee nonetheless took absolutely. Thus, in *Goodtitle d Pearson v Otway*,[62] where there was a devise to A for life, with remainder to her issue, and if A had no issue with power to A to dispose of the property at her will and pleasure, it was held that A, who had no issue, took absolutely.[63]

2.15

---

[53] *Sed quaere* where the power is exercisable by will only.

[54] For example, in the context of covenants to settle after-acquired property: *Re Gerard (Lord) Oliphant v Gerard* (1888) 58 LT 800; *Tremayne v Rashleigh* [1908] 1 Ch 681; cf *Re O'Connell* [1903] 2 Ch 574.

[55] *The London Chartered Bank of Australia v Lempriere* (1873) LR 4 PC 572, 595–596. See also *Devall v Dickens* (1845) 9 Jur 550; *Saberton v Skeels* (1830) 1 Russ & M 587; *A-G v Malkin* (1846) 2 Ph 64; *Page v Soper* (1853) 11 Hare 321. Such a gift was common in marriage settlements. See *Re Best's Settlement Trusts* (1874) LR 18 Eq 686, 691; *Smith v Iliffe* (1875) LR 20 Eq 666.

[56] *Holloway v Clarkson* (1843) 2 Hare 521; *Alger v Parrott* (1866) LR 3 Eq 328; *Avern v Lloyd* (1868) LR 5 Eq 383; *Wing v Wing* (1876) 24 WR 878; *Re Brooks* [1928] Ch 214.

[57] *Jackson v Commr of Stamps* [1903] AC 350.

[58] *Re Davenport* [1895] 1 Ch 361; *Re Onslow* (1888) 39 Ch D 622. Although these cases deal with the effect of the Married Women's Property Act 1882 on a married woman (A), it is clear that the same result had long been established in the case of a man and a feme sole. See also *Holloway v Clarkson* (1843) 2 Hare 521; *Devall v Dickens* (1845) 9 Jur 550; *Page v Soper* (1853) 11 Hare 321; *Gardiner v Young* (1876) 34 LT 348; *Kirkpatrick v Capel* (1819) refd to in Edward Sugden (Lord St Leonards), *A Practical Treatise on Powers* (8th edn, 1861) ('*Sugden*') 75, n (e).

[59] *Anderson v Dawson* (1808) 15 Ves 532; *Daniel v Dudley* (1841) 1 Ph 1; *Page v Soper* (1853) 11 Hare 321.

[60] *Anderson v Dawson*, above, at 536, which now applies to real as well as personal property. See, too, *Brookman v Smith* (1871) LR 6 Exch 291; *Evans v Evans* (1892) 2 Ch 173; *Re Davison's Settlement* [1913] 2 Ch 498.

[61] *Sympson v Hornby* (1716) Prec Ch 452.   [62] (1753) 2 Wils 6.

[63] See also *Re Maxwell's Will* (1857) 24 Beav 246; and *Nowlan v Walsh* (1851) 4 De G & Sm 584 (where the contingency was remarrying).

2.16 It is, of course, a matter of construction whether an absolute indefeasible gift is intended or not. In *Reid v Atkinson*,[64] for instance, a gift of real and personal property to A 'to have, hold, and enjoy in the fullest and amplest manner for the term of her life, with full power to dispose of all the aforesaid property, both real and personal, as she may judge wisest and best', was said to indicate an absolute gift. As Christian LJ said:[65] 'Full enjoyment during life, full power to dispose of, these things exhaust the advantages of property, and are comprised in the very idea of property...'; there was here 'a lavish accumulation of language directed to show that her enjoyment and dominion were to be as boundless as the limit of human life and the nature of human proprietorship admitted the possibility of'. Similarly, a gift 'to A, her heirs and assigns for ever, with the intention that she enjoy the property during her life, and by her will dispose of it as she thinks proper', created an absolute gift.[66] On the other hand, in *Le Marchant v Le Marchant*,[67] a gift to a widow of all property 'for her sole use and benefit, in the full confidence that she will so bestow it on her decease to my children in a just and equitable spirit, and in such manner and way as she feels would meet with my full approval' was held to confer on the widow a life interest only, coupled with a power of disposition. Moreover, a gift in default of the exercise of a power of appointment, not being a mere residuary gift, is evidence (though, no doubt, not conclusive) of an intention to create a series of limitations coupled with a power, rather than absolute interest.[68]

Precatory trusts

2.17 Closely related to the present issue, namely whether there is an absolute gift or a limited interest under a trust, is the question whether or not a testator intended to create a 'precatory trust'. Historically, the use of precatory words in wills[69]—that is, words expressing a hope, wish, desire, expectation or confidence that a named legatee should use his legacy in a particular way—have often posed difficult questions of construction. The typical case is that where property is given (often expressed to be given 'absolutely') to an individual (often the surviving spouse), but where the

---

[64] (1871) 5 IR Eq 373.
[65] ibid 382–383.
[66] *Doe d Herbert v Thomas and Lewis* (1835) 3 Ad & Ell 123. See, too, *Hoy v Master* (1834) 6 Sim 568; *Anon* (1732) 2 Kel CC 6; *Bradley v Peixoto* (1797) 3 Ves 324; *Espinasse v Luffingham* (1846) 3 Jo & Lat 186; *Reith v Seymour* (1828) 4 Russ 263; *Archibald v Wright* (1838) 9 Sim 161.
[67] (1874) LR 18 Eq 414. See also *Curnick v Tucker* (1874) LR 17 Eq 320.
[68] *Re Maxwell's Will* (1857) 24 Beav 246, 250; *Healy v Donnery* (1853) 3 ICLR 213.
[69] Since the issue is one of the meaning of words, a precatory trust might, in principle, be created by a non-testamentary instrument or even orally. In *Hill v Hill* [1897] 1 QB 483, a letter or memorandum recording a conversation was under consideration, but was held not to have created a precatory trust. Lord Esher MR stated (at 488): 'Whether a precatory trust can be created by word of mouth or by anything less than a will, it is unnecessary to consider, because I do not think that the words used here, even if occurring in a will, would create such a trust.' However, it seems clear that the court was willing to contemplate the possibility.

words of gift are accompanied by an expression of confidence or hope or expectation that the donee will apply that property in a particular way or will dispose of it, on his or her own death, in favour of others (usually the donor's children or other members of the family). Depending on the context in which they are used, such words may impose moral, but legally unenforceable, obligations, or they may impose a binding 'precatory trust' on the legatee. As Lindley LJ pointed out in *Re Williams*:[70] 'The term "precatory" only has reference to forms of expression. Not only in wills but in daily life an expression may be imperative in its real meaning although couched in language which is not imperative in form. A request is often a polite form of command. A trust is really nothing except a confidence reposed by one person in another, and enforceable in a court of equity.' He added that there is 'abundant authority for saying that, if property is left to a person in confidence that he will dispose of it in a particular way as to which there is no ambiguity, such words are amply sufficient to impose an obligation'. However, a 'precatory trust' is simply a trust inferred from 'precatory' words: it is not a special kind of trust. As Rigby LJ observed, also in *Re Williams*,[71] referring to 'what are awkwardly and, in my opinion, incorrectly called "precatory trusts" . . . this phrase is nothing more than a misleading nickname. When a trust is once established, it is equally a trust, and has all the effects and incidents of a trust, whether declared in clearly imperative terms by a testator, or deduced upon a consideration of the whole will from language not amounting necessarily and in its prima facie meaning to an imperative trust.'[72]

It is, therefore, a matter of inference whether a trust was intended or not; but the **2.18** readiness of the courts to infer a trust has varied over time: 'in some of the older cases obligations were inferred from language which in modern times would be thought insufficient to justify such an inference'.[73] By the end of the seventeenth century and at least until the mid-nineteenth century or thereabouts, very slight indications of a trust were sufficient in a will.[74] Certainly, there was a marked tendency throughout this period to regard a request in a will as imperative. As Kindersley V-C stated in *Palmer v Simmonds*:[75]

> In most of the cases of this class the Court is called upon to do what it is persuaded was never the intention of the testator; for when a testator expresses his *confidence* that the devisee will do so and so, what he really means is to say that he expresses the *confidence*, because he does not mean to create a *trust*. He gives absolutely, because he

---

[70] [1897] 2 Ch 12, 18 – 19.   [71] ibid 27.

[72] In *Re Atkinson* (1911) 80 LJ Ch 370, 371, Cozens-Hardy MR stated: 'I am not very fond of the word "precatory". But I think we all understand what it means.'

[73] *Re Williams* [1897] 2 Ch 12, 18, *per* Lindley LJ.

[74] *Eales v England* (1704) 1 Eq Cas Abr 297; *Jones v Nabbs* (1718) 1 Eq Cas Abr 404; *Vernon v Vernon* (1737) Amb 3; *Harding v Glyn* (1739) 1 Atk 469; *Massey v Sherman* (1739) Amb 520; *Adlington v Cann* (1744) 3 Atk 152; *Parsons v Baker* (1812) 18 Ves 476; *Eade v Eade* (1820) 5 Madd 118; *Cary v Cary* (1804) 2 Sch & Lef 173; *Palmer v Simmonds* (1854) 2 Drew 221; *Gully v Cregoe* (1857) 24 Beav 185.

[75] (1854) 2 Drew 221, 225. Here, there was no certainty of subject matter.

has confidence. But then this Court has said that is a reason why the Court should create a trust.

Thus, all of the following precatory expressions, construed in their particular contexts, were held to have created trusts: 'in the fullest confidence';[76] 'the most entire and explicit confidence';[77] 'trusting';[78] 'not doubting';[79] 'in the full belief';[80] 'well knowing';[81] 'under the firm conviction';[82] 'requesting';[83] 'recommending';[84] 'beg';[85] and 'desire'.[86] In cases of doubt, the settlor's contemporaneous and subsequent acts may be taken into consideration.[87]

2.19 However, this apparent readiness of the courts to construe precatory words as imperative[88] is said to have been brought to a halt by the decision of the Court of Appeal in Chancery in *Lambe v Eames*,[89] where a gift by a testator to his widow of his entire estate, 'to be at her disposal in any way she may think best for the benefit of herself and family', was held to be an absolute gift and not to create a trust. James LJ, referring to earlier cases cited to the court, stated[90] that 'the officious kindness of the Court of Chancery in interposing trusts where in many cases the father of the family never meant to create trusts, must have been a very cruel kindness indeed'.[91] In *Re Atkinson*,[92] Cozens-Hardy MR, referring to *Lambe v Eames*, observed:

---

[76] *Wright v Atkyns* (1809–10) 17 Ves 255. [77] *Smith v Smith* (1856) 2 Jur (NS) 967.

[78] *Baker v Mosley* (1848) 12 Jur 740; but not a trust in *Hoy v Master* (1834) 6 Sim 568 or *Ellis v Ellis* (1875) 44 LJ Ch 225.

[79] *Massey v Sherman* (1739) Amb 520. See also *Parsons v Baker* (1812) 18 Ves 476.

[80] *Fordham v Speight* (1875) 23 WR 782.

[81] *Briggs v Penny* (1851) 3 Mac & G 546. Cf *Bardswell v Bardswell* (1838) 9 Sim 319.

[82] *Barnes v Grant* (1857) 26 LJ Ch 92.

[83] *Re O'Bierne* (1844) 7 Ir Eq R 171. Cf *House v House* (1974) LT 427.

[84] *Malim v Keighley* (1795) 2 Ves 529; *Malim v Barker* (1796) 3 Ves 150; *Tibbits v Tibbits* (1816) 19 Ves 656; *Ford v Fowler* (1840) 3 Beav 146. But Cf *Cunliffe v Cunliffe* (1770) Amb 686; *Young v Martin* (1843) 2 Y & CCC 582; *Johnson v Rowlands* (1848) 2 De G & Sm 356.

[85] *Corbet v Corbet* (1873) Ir R 7 Eq 456. Cf *Green v Marsden* (1853) 1 Drew 646.

[86] *Re Jevons* (1911) 56 SJ 72.

[87] *Bentley v Mackay* (1851) 15 Beav 12, 19. See also *Shephard v Cartwright* [1955] AC 431.

[88] It has been suggested that it was founded on the desire of the Court of Chancery to undermine the rule that, prior to the Executors Act 1830, an executor was permitted by the ecclesiastical courts to retain any part of the residuary estate undisposed of by the will. The cases suggest, however, that the courts were more concerned with certainty (of subject matter and objects, as well as of intention) and enforceability.

[89] (1871) 6 Ch App 597. Although this decision was distinguished in both *Curnick v Tucker* (1874) LR 17 Eq 320 and *Le Marchant v Le Marchant* (1874) LR 18 Eq 414, the change of approach which it is supposed to have introduced was reaffirmed in *Re Hutchinson and Tenant* (1878) 8 Ch D 540.

[90] ibid 599.

[91] The undesirable results that might ensue were highlighted by Fry LJ in *Re Diggles* (1888) 39 Ch D 253, 258. A testatrix had given her property to her daughter, expressing a 'desire' that she allow A an annuity of £25 during her life. Fry LJ stated: 'Now consider the inconvenience of what we are asked to decide, that there is a precatory trust affecting the whole property—that the whole property is held in trust to pay £25 a year to Anne Gregory for her life. No fund is directed to be set apart, so if there be a trust, it is a trust affecting the whole property. If so, the residuary legatee could not sell a bedstead or give away a ring without committing a breach of trust. This is a monstrous result . . .'.

[92] (1911) LJ Ch 370, 372.

And it is beyond all doubt that, in years gone by, words which were in form merely expressing hope, desire, wish, intention, and so on, were construed by very learned Judges in a manner which would not now be followed. It has been pointed out by the Courts for the last quarter of a century and longer that the current has turned. The leaning of the Courts is now undoubtedly not to extend the doctrine of precatory trusts. And I think I may go further and say that the leaning of the Courts is now not to construe words used in a will, not being words of a strict definite legal character or words that are beyond doubt - equivalent words, in short—as creating a trust.

In fact, the courts had been leaning strongly in this direction well before the decision in *Lambe v Eames*.[93] There are numerous reported examples to this effect and, in all the following cases, most of which were decided before *Lambe v Eames*, the relevant precatory words were held *not* to have created a trust: 'it is my earnest wish';[94] 'in confidence';[95] 'upon the fullest trust and confidence';[96] 'having full confidence';[97] 'in full assurance and confidence';[98] 'feeling confident';[99] 'it is my dying request';[100] 'beg';[101] 'in order that she might provide for';[102] and 'desire'.[103] These non-imperative precatory words and expressions are indistinguishable from the trust-creating ones. Nor can they be classified by reference to some specified date.

2.20 Quite apart from general statements, made well before 1871, to the effect that, where property was given absolutely by will and without restriction, the courts would not lightly impose upon it a trust upon mere words of recommendation or confidence,[104] it is clear from the earlier cases themselves that precatory words were not regarded in isolation, but were always construed in the context in which they appeared.[105] In particular, unless they were accompanied by words indicating sufficient certainty of subject matter and certainty of objects—being essential prerequisites for enforceability of any trust—precatory words were not generally considered to be imperative. Wherever the subject matter to be administered as

[93] *Re Williams* [1897] 2 Ch 12, 35, *per* Rigby LJ.
[94] *Bland v Bland* (1745) 2 Cox 349; *Hood v Oglander* (1865) 34 Beav 301.
[95] *Anon* (1603) Cary 22. [96] *Webb v Wools* (1852) 2 Sim (NS) 267.
[97] *Fox v Fox* (1859) 27 Beav 301; *Palmer v Simmonds* (1854) 2 Drew 221; *Creagh v Murphy* (1873) Ir R 7 Eq 182.
[98] *Macnab v Whitbread* (1853) 17 Beav 299.
[99] *Mussoorie Bank Ltd. v Raynor* (1882) 7 App Cas 221.
[100] *Pierson v Garnet* (1786) 2 Bro CC 38. [101] *Green v Marsden* (1853) 1 Drew 646.
[102] *Morrin v Morrin* (1886) 19 LR Ir 37.
[103] *M'Culloch v M'Culloch* (1863) 11 WR 504; *Stead v Mellor* (1877) 5 Ch D 225; *Re Diggles* (1888) 39 Ch D 253.
[104] See, for example, *Lawless v Shaw* (1835) Ll & G temp Sug 154,164 and *Re Byrne's Estate* (1892) 29 LR Ir 250. As early as 1849, Lord St Leonards observed, in his *Law of Real Property*, 375–376: '. . . the law as to the operation of words of recommendation, confidence, request, or the like, attached to an absolute gift, has in late times varied from the earlier authorities. In nearly every recent case, the gift has been held to be uncontrolled by the request or recommendation made, or confidence expressed.'
[105] *Godfrey v Godfrey* (1863) 8 LT 200.

trust property, and the objects, for whose benefit it is to be administered, are to be found in a will, not expressly creating a trust, the indefinite nature and quantum of the subject, and the indefinite nature of the objects, were used by the court as evidence that the intention of the testator was not to create a trust; 'and the difficulty that would be imposed upon the Court to say what should be so applied, or to what objects, has been the foundation of the argument that no trust was intended'.[106] Only 'where the property to be given is certain, and the objects to whom it is given are certain, there a trust is to be created'.[107] Such statements long pre-dated the more commonly cited observations made at the end of the nineteenth century.[108] Precatory words therefore tended not to give rise to a trust in those cases where the legatee or devisee could actually dispose of the whole of the property to himself in his own lifetime and where there was no certainty as to what should remain at his death, or where the 'trust' failed for some other reason.[109] As Rigby LJ pointed out in *Re Williams*,[110] when he reviewed several of the older authorities:

> I have dealt with these authorities at length in order to shew that a substantial agreement as to principle had been arrived at long before the decisions beginning with *Lambe v Eames*, which have been cited as though they in some way altered the law on this subject. Without going through these seriatim, I may say that in every case the conclusion that the words relied upon did not create an imperative trust was based, as I think, upon some uncertainty either as to the subject or as to the objects of the supposed trust.

Similarly, in *Re Oldfield*,[111] although Kekewich J was prepared to say that 'what Lord Langdale laid down[112] is no longer law', it is clear that, in the Court of Appeal, both the old and new cases were regarded as broadly consistent and differing only on points of construction. Vaughan-Williams LJ even pointed out[113] that 'it all depends on how you read the words of Lord Alvanley.[114] If you

---

[106] *Morice v Bishop of Durham* (1805) 10 Ves. 522, 536. See also *Wright v Atkyns* (1810) Turner & Russell 157, 159, and *Knight v Knight* (1840) 3 Beav 148, 172–173; and (post-*Lambe v Eames*) *Mussoorie Bank Ltd v Raynor* (1882) 7 App Cas 321, 331. For an example of the absurdity of finding a trust in some situations, see *Re Diggles* (1888) 39 Ch D 253, 256–257.

[107] See, for example, *Pierson v Garnet* (1786) 2 Bro CC 38, 45, referring to the principles extracted from earlier cases by Lord Thurlow in *Harland v Trigg* (1782) 1 Bro CC 142 and *Wynne v Hawkins* (1782) 1 Bro CC 179.

[108] *Mussoorie Bank Ltd v Raynor* (1882) 7 App Cas 321, 331; *Re Williams* [1897] 2 Ch 12, 18–19.

[109] *A-G v Hall* (1735) mentioned in 2 Cox 314; *Bland v Bland* (1745) 2 Cox 349; *Pierson v Garnet* (1786) 2 Bro CC 38; *Sprange v Barnard* (1789) 2 Bro CC 585; *Moggridge v Thackwell* (1803) 7 Ves 36; *Paul v Compton* (1803) 8 Ves 375; *Morice v Bishop of Durham* (1805) 10 Ves 522; *Dashwood v Peyton* (1811) 18 Ves 41; *Tibbits v Tibbits* (1816) 19 Ves 656; *Forbes v Ball* (1817) 3 Mer 437; *Briggs v Penny* (1849) 3 De G & Sm 525; *Palmer v Simmonds* (1854) 2 Drew 221.

[110] [1897] 2 Ch 12, 35.   [111] [1904] 1 Ch 549.

[112] In *Knight v Knight* (1840) 3 Beav 148, 172.   [113] [1904] 1 Ch 549, 554.

[114] ie, the words which Lord Langdale followed in *Knight v Knight*.

read those words as meaning "the way in which the property shall go" (in the imperative), there is nothing, to my mind, in any of those cases[115] to shew that that would be contrary to what was affirmed in the House of Lords in *Knight v Boughton*.'

Thus, in so far as there was a change during the course of the nineteenth century **2.21** in the courts' approach to precatory trusts, it was, at most, a change in approach to construction, or even just in emphasis, rather than a change in principle. As Rigby LJ put it, 'the Court of Appeal cannot in recent cases be assumed to have intended in any way to alter the settled law on the subject, or to have assumed a jurisdiction to deal with the question as if it were independent of authority'.[116] In any event, the modern view is that 'there is established in the older authorities no binding or overriding rule of construction which would disentitle one to look at each will and to extract from that will what was the true intention of the particular testator or testatrix'.[117] As Collins LJ explained in *Re Adams and the Kensington Vestry*,[118] both *Lambe v Eames* and *Re Hutchinson and Tenant*[119] established that the aim was really to find out what, upon the true construction, was the meaning of the testator, rather than to lay hold of certain words which in other wills had been held to create a trust, although on the will before them they were satisfied that that was not the intention: 'I have no hesitation in saying myself, that I think some of the older authorities went a great deal too far in holding that some particular words appearing in a will were sufficient to create a trust.'

The true intention of the testator must be ascertained from the wording and form **2.22** of his will as a whole, taking into account any admissible extrinsic evidence, and not be presumed on the basis of earlier decisions on other wills which happened to have used similar words. Precatory words will not be presumed to indicate an intention to create a trust. 'You must take the will which you have to construe and see what it means, and if you come to the conclusion that no trust was intended you say so, although previous judges have said the contrary on some wills more or less similar to the one you have to construe.'[120] The appropriate approach and,

---

[115] ie, *Re Diggles* (1888) 39 Ch D 253; *Re Hamilton* [1895] 2 Ch 370; *Re Williams* [1897] 2 Ch 12. It was argued in *Re Oldfield* that, when Lindley LJ delivered judgment in *Re Hamilton*, he was unaware that *Malim v Keighley* had been approved by the House of Lords in *Knight v Boughton* (1844) 11 Cl & Fin 513, 548, 551; and the same was also true of the Court of Appeal's decisions in *Re Williams* and *Re Diggles*.

[116] [1897] 2 Ch 12, 35. He also pointed out that 'a substantial agreement as to principle had been arrived at long before the decisions beginning with *Lambe v Eames*, which have been cited as though they in some way altered the law on this subject'.

[117] *Re Steele's Will Trusts* [1948] Ch 603, 606.

[118] (1884) 27 Ch 394, 410. This is a curious case in that it was brought under a vendor and purchaser summons to determine good title, and neither the widow nor the children (the persons directly interested in the relevant disposition) were before the court.

[119] (1878) 8 Ch D 540.   [120] *Re Hamilton* [1895] 2 Ch 370, 373.

indeed, the proper scope and purpose of the so-called doctrine of precatory trusts, was stated even more clearly by Fletcher Moulton LJ in *Re Atkinson*:[121]

> The principle is that you have to find from the words of the will the intention of the testator. The doctrine of precatory trusts does not mean that the Courts may create an intention which they do not think from the will was in the mind of the testator. It means that they may come to the assistance of weak or even inapt words and recognise his intention to create a trust in spite of the language being such that lawyers would not have used it for that purpose. It only meets the case of recognition of the intention of the testator, and is not a doctrine by which an intention that did not exist is read into the will.

2.23 There is no doubt, therefore, that, depending on the context, precatory words and expressions may create a trust. 'It would . . . be an entire mistake', as Lindley LJ put it in *Re Williams*,[122] 'to suppose that the old doctrine of precatory trusts is abolished.' Similarly, Cozens-Hardy MR stated in *Re Atkinson*:[123]

> I am in no way lending colour to the idea . . . that the doctrine of precatory trust is at an end; certainly, in my opinion, there is no foundation for that. I believe that the doctrine of precatory trusts remains. But I also believe that at the present time, having regard to the decisions of the last quarter of a century, it is a doctrine which must be viewed with some strictness. Its application must be carefully limited in considering any particular document.

Thus, in *Comiskey v Bowring-Hanbury*,[124] where the testator had given his entire estate to his widow, 'in full confidence that she will make such use of it as I should have made myself and that at her death she will devise it to such one or more of my nieces as she may think fit', the House of Lords held that a trust had been created. However, it is clear that little, if any, significance was attributed to the words 'in full confidence' and that the determining factor was the presence of an express provision in default of such testamentary disposition by the wife. A trust was held to have been created also in *Re Steele's Will Trusts*,[125] where the relevant provision[126] was in terms *mutatis mutandis* exactly corresponding with that considered and held to have created a trust in *Shelley v Shelley*.[127] The decision in *Steele* has been criticized[128] on the basis that *Shelley* itself would be decided differently today, but Wynn-Parry J regarded it as a binding authority instead of construing the will before him on its own merits. However, such criticism is misplaced. The

---

[121] (1911) 80 LJ Ch 370, 374.

[122] [1897] 2 Ch 12, 18. See also *Godfrey v Godfrey* (1863) 8 LT 200.

[123] (1911) LJ Ch 370, 373.

[124] [1905] AC 84, reversing the Court of Appeal and Kekewich J; Lord Lindley dissented. Interestingly, Cozens-Hardy LJ had dissented in the Court of Appeal, holding that a precatory trust had been created: [1904] 1 Ch 415.

[125] [1948] Ch 603.

[126] Including the words 'I request my said son to do all in his power by his will or otherwise to give effect to this my wish'.

[127] (1868) LR 6 Eq 540.   [128] See (1968) 32 Conv (NS) 361 (P Langan).

adoption of a reasonably lengthy and complex form of words (and not just a few precatory words) known to have been held judicially to have a particular effect affords 'the strongest indication', as Wynn-Parry J put it, that the testatrix intended, with professional assistance, to produce that same effect. The fact that a modern court might have placed a different construction on that formula if it had recently arisen for consideration for the first time is immaterial.

Section 22 of the Administration of Justice Act 1982[129]

The scope for precatory trusts has been limited further by the provisions of section 22 of the Administration of Justice Act 1982, which provides: **2.24**

> Except where a contrary intention is shown it shall be presumed that if a testator devises or bequeaths property to his spouse in terms which in themselves would give an absolute interest to the spouse, but by the same instrument purports to give his issue an interest in the same property, the gift to the spouse is absolute notwithstanding the purported gift to the issue.

This provision is limited in scope. It applies only to testamentary gifts between spouses and only where it is 'issue' who might, apart from the spouse, have an interest in the property. Thus, it has no application where (say) mistresses, brothers, sisters, nieces, or nephews are involved;[130] or where the situation described in the section is brought about by a marriage settlement or by an appointment under a special power[131] (even a testamentary power) for there is no devise or bequest in such a case. On the other hand, where a general power of appointment is deemed to have been exercised by virtue of section 27 of the Wills Act 1837, section 22 of the 1982 Act would presumably apply to the property which is subject to that power.

The gift to the spouse and the purported gift to issue must also be in the same **2.25** instrument. A will and a codicil are considered separate instruments, even though the codicil may republish the will. The supposition seems to be that, if the testator has dealt with the same subject matter in different instruments, he will necessarily have manifested a different intention in respect of each instrument or manifested the same intention on two separate occasions. However, inconsistency between a will and a codicil is perhaps just as possible as inconsistency within the same instrument.

Section 22 can only apply where the devise or bequest is 'in terms which in them- **2.26** selves give an absolute interest to the spouse'; and where no 'contrary intention is

---

[129] See *Thomas*, 56–58.

[130] The (no less common) gifts in cases such as *In the Estate of Lupton* [1905] P 321, *Re Jones* [1898] 1 Ch 438, *Re Connolly* [1910] 1 Ch 219, and *Bibbens v Potter* (1879) 10 Ch D 733 would thus remain unaffected. And the result in *In the Estate of Last* [1958] P 137 might well be different if the gift were to a surviving spouse rather than a brother (who was held to have a life interest).

[131] cf *Pennock v Pennock* (1871) LR 13 Eq 144.

shown'. The purpose of the section is to catch the kind of gift commonly found in home-made wills, such as 'I leave all my property to my wife and after her death to my children'.[132] In order to make sense of the section, one must first consider whether the gift to the spouse is 'in terms which in themselves' would give him/her an absolute interest (ie, the words 'all my property to my wife' in the above example). If the gift as a whole is considered, then it is no longer clear that an absolute gift was indeed intended and the purpose of the section would be defeated. The fact that the will purports to give issue, as well as the spouse, an interest in the relevant property clearly does not, in itself, render the gift to the spouse absolute: indeed, the opposite is the case. If a testator leaves property to his wife 'so that she may have full possession of it and entire power and control over it, to deal with it or act with regard to it as she may think proper',[133] are these terms sufficient to give an absolute interest to the spouse? Section 22 does not require the word 'absolutely' to be used. In any event, there are many instances in which the words 'absolutely' or 'absolute' did not prevent a more limited interest being held to exist.[134] The question is whether the will discloses a 'contrary intention' and it is the terms of the purported gift to the issue that is the likely source of such contrary intention, so such terms clearly cannot be ignored entirely. The overall effect of section 22, therefore, seems to be that, where a gift is made which is clearly absolute, very clear words will be required to cut down that gift and impose a trust. Consequently, it is probably only in the simplest of cases that section 22 is likely to have any application.

2.27 Indeed, there is nothing in section 22 itself to indicate how it is to be applied. It does provide relief from liability to an executor who has formed a view that section 22 applies to a particular disposition and distributed on that basis. This is particularly important where the estate is large or where infant beneficiaries are involved (as is likely to be the case). Section 48 of the Administration of Justice Act 1985 and Order 93, rule 21, of the Rules of the Supreme Court provide a quick and inexpensive solution in such a case, in that an application may be made for the directions of the court as to the proper construction of the will in question. The application is made by way of *ex parte* originating summons, with a supporting affidavit exhibiting the opinion of counsel of at least ten years' standing; and the court may then make an order authorizing the distribution of the estate in

---

[132] This example is given in the Law Commission's 19th Report, *The Interpretation of Wills*, Cmnd 5301 (1973) paras 60–62. Another example might be: 'I give and bequeath unto my wife A my entire estate. In the event of my wife remarrying I wish the residue of my estate at that time to be shared equally between my two children B and C.'

[133] *Re Sanford* [1901] 1 Ch 939 (wife took a life interest with a general power of appointment). Cf *Reid v Atkinson* (1871) 5 IR Eq 373, esp. 382–383.

[134] See, for example, *Pennock v Pennock* (1871) LR 13 Eq 144; *Bibbens v Potter* (1879) 10 Ch D 733; *Comiskey v Bowring-Hanbury* [1905] AC 84.

accordance with such opinion without hearing argument.[135] Nevertheless, in all but the simplest cases, the only safe course remains to seek the court's guidance in construction proceedings. Section 22 will probably be of little, if any, assistance where the terms of the will are ambiguous, or the intention behind the gift uncertain, or in determining whether a will intends to create an absolute gift or to confer a lesser interest coupled with a power.

---

[135] See the Practice Direction of 28 January 1987, *Supreme Court Practice* (1997), Vol 2, para 867, for the procedural requirements.

3

CERTAINTY OF SUBJECT MATTER

A. General Principle

All property, of whatever nature and wherever situated,[1] may be the subject **3.01** matter of a trust. However, the property which constitutes the trust fund—the subject matter of the trust—must be certain or be capable of being ascertained.[2] In principle, this is self-evident and straightforward. It would be impossible to execute or enforce a trust whose subject matter was not known. No sensible obligation can be imposed in respect of 'some of my property', or 'some of my best linen',[3] or even 'a handsome gratuity',[4] unless the meaning which such expressions were intended to bear has been or can be made sufficiently clear. This requirement of certainty applies not only to the description of the trust fund itself, ie the conceptual certainty of the item(s) of property of which it is to be composed, but also to the extent or quantum of the interest of a particular beneficiary in that trust

---

[1] Land is generally subject to the *lex loci situs* and many foreign jurisdictions prohibit or restrict the holding of land in foreign trusts, either under specific statutory provisions or as a matter of public policy.

[2] Thus, a gift of 'my old farm' or 'my favourite picture' would seem, at first sight, to be uncertain. However, the context of the will as a whole and such extrinsic evidence as may be admissible may render the gift certain, eg, if it can be shown that the testator had only one farm or one picture. Cf *Pettingall v Pettingall* (1842) 11 LJ Ch 176 ('favourite black mare').

[3] *Peck v Halsey* (1726) 2 P W 387.   [4] *Jubber v Jubber* (1839) 9 Sim 503.

fund. It is self-evident that, even where the trust fund as a whole is indisputably 'certain', a declaration that a particular beneficiary is entitled to 'a share', or 'some', or 'a suitable proportion' of that fund clearly cannot be executed or enforced unless such expressions have also been ascribed an ascertainable meaning or may be rendered certain by some known person in the exercise of a power or discretion. In order 'to create a trust it must be possible to ascertain with certainty not only what the interest of the beneficiary is to be but to what property it is to attach'.[5]

3.02 There are fewer cases than one might think, however, in which an intended trust has actually failed on the ground of uncertainty of subject matter (in either of these senses). Many of the decisions often cited in support of the general principle were actually decided on some completely different basis (such as the absence of any intention to create a trust).[6] Many of them are also frequently referred to without regard to the particular instrument in which they appeared or the context with which they were concerned. Moreover, the courts have generally striven to make sense of what might, at first sight, seem meaningless. Thus, a simple, straightforward requirement actually embraces a number of difficult strands.

3.03 An express private trust may be created *inter vivos* or on death. The creation of such a trust on death must, like any other testamentary disposition, comply with the requirements of the Wills Act 1837.[7] An *inter vivos* trust may be created by means of either a transfer of property to a trustee or a declaration by the owner of property that he himself shall thenceforth hold that property as a trustee. In order to be effectual, a transfer of property may be subject to its own peculiar formal requirements: different forms of property are subject to different requirements, or subject to none at all.[8] Where the owner of property merely declares himself a trustee of that property, there is clearly no transfer of property at all. Whichever method is used, it must be effective.[9]

B. Relationship Between Certainty of Intention and Certainty of Subject Matter

3.04 The requirement of certainty of intention to create a trust has already been dealt with.[10] However, one specific point ought to be emphasized. Many of the cases frequently cited as instances of uncertainty of subject matter—and especially what might be termed the 'anything that is left' cases[11]—were, in fact, concerned less

---

[5] *Re London Wine Co (Shippers) Ltd* [1986] PCC 121, 137, *per* Oliver J; *Russell-Cooke Trust Co v Prentis* (2002) 5 ITELR 532; *Re The Double Happiness Trust* (2002) 5 ITELR 646.
[6] See paras, 2.03–2.12 above.   [7] See paras, 5.06–5.08 below.
[8] See paras, 5.09–5.30 below.
[9] *Milroy v Lord* (1862) 4 De GF & J 264, 274–275 (quoted in para 5.01 below).
[10] See Chapter 2 above.   [11] See paras 3.07–3.09 below.

with certainty of subject matter than with certainty of intention, ie they were cases in which the central question was whether it was intended to make an absolute gift or to create a trust. If the intention is to make an absolute gift, then any apparent gift over of what may be left or undisposed of is repugnant and void. Thus, a gift to T on trust for A absolutely, with a direction that anything remaining in T's hands at the death of A should go to B, operates as an absolute gift to A.[12] Even in *Palmer v Simmonds*,[13] although it is clear that the expression of confidence that the legatee should, at his death, 'leave the bulk of my said residuary estate' to others would have been too uncertain as a description of the subject matter of any trust, the actual decision was that the precatory words in the testatrix's will did not manifest an intention to impose a trust and the legatee took the estate absolutely.[14] Such cases therefore do not necessarily have any direct bearing on the issue of certainty of subject matter and must be approached with considerable caution. They certainly do not support the conclusion that expressions such as 'what is left' or 'anything that is left' are necessarily too vague and uncertain to constitute an identifiable trust fund.[15]

C. Identifying the Trust Fund

In the unlikely event that a person declared himself a trustee of his entire estate, or the more likely event that he transferred all his assets to trustees (as, indeed, may sometimes happen on death), there would generally be no uncertainty of subject matter,[16] and only perhaps some administrative difficulties in securing or collecting **3.05**

---

[12] See, for example, *Malim v Keighley* (1795) 2 Ves 529; *Grey v Montagu* (1764) 2 Eden 205; *Ross v Ross* (1819) 1 Jac & W 154; *A-G v Hall* (1731) 1 Jac & W 158n; *Lightburne v Gill* (1764) 3 Bro PC 250; *Bourn v Gibbs* (1831) 1 Russ & Myl 614; *Cuthbert v Purrier* (1822) Jac 415; *Green v Harvey* (1842) 1 Hare 428; *Watkins v Williams* (1851) 3 Mac & G 622; *Re Yalden* (1851) 1 De GM & G 53; *Holmes v Godson* (1856) 8 De GM & G 152; *Re Mortlock's Trust* (1857) 3 K & J 456; *Bowes v Goslett* (1857) 27 LJ Ch 249; *Henderson v Cross* (1861) 29 Beav 216; *Weale v Ollive* (1863) 32 Beav 421; *Perry v Merritt* (1874) LR 18 Eq 152; *Re Wilcocks' Settlement* (1875) 1 Ch D 229; *Re Percy* (1883) 24 Ch D 616, esp. 617–618; *Re Jones* [1898] 1 Ch 438; *Re Walker* [1898] 1 Ir R 5; *Re Dunstan* [1918] 2 Ch 304; *Re Gouk* [1957] 1 WLR 493; *Re Minchell's Will Trusts* [1964] 2 All ER 47.

[13] (1854) 2 Drew 221.

[14] The absolute gift apparently took effect under what became known as the rule in *Lassence v Tierney* (1849) 1 Mac & G 551, ie, where trusts which have been engrafted on an absolute interest fail for some reason, the absolute gift remains. In *Sprange v Barnard* (1789) 2 Bro CC 585, a wife gave property (which was itself identified with certainty) to her husband for his use 'and, at his death, the remaining part of what is left, that he does not want for his own wants and use, to be divided' between others. It was held that the property vested absolutely in the husband, on the basis that it was a trust which would be impossible to be executed, but it is not clear whether this meant lack of certainty of intention (which would indeed result in an absolute gift) or of certainty of subject matter (which should have produced a resulting trust).

[15] Such cases are dealt with below: see paras 3.07–3.09 below.

[16] Even the word 'all' was held uncertain in *Bowman v Milbanke* (1878) 1 Lev 130 ('all to my mother': did it carry land?) disapproved in *Smyth v Smyth* (1878) 8 Ch D 561; but today it is likely to be given its prima facie meaning (as in *Re Shepherd* (1914) 58 SJ 304: 'all' passed realty). See, generally, *Halsbury's Laws of England*, vol 50 (4th edn, 1998 Reissue) paras 525–537.

in the assets. More typically (and whichever method may be employed), trusts are intended to be declared of some particular assets in the estate or some part or proportion or share thereof, or of the balance or remainder of the estate once some other gift or disposition has taken effect. In such cases, the asset in question or that part of the estate that is to constitute the initial trust fund must be described or identified with sufficient certainty to enable the court, if asked, to make an order for the execution of the purported trust.[17] This is a simple and elementary principle. Yet, it can be difficult to apply and some sweeping conclusions have all too often been drawn (erroneously) from a few peculiar cases.

Conceptual uncertainty

3.06 Often, the difficulty is one of conceptual certainty: the words or expressions used to describe the initial trust fund are such that they fail to identify the property or assets intended to constitute that fund. Whether this is the case or not depends on the normal processes of construction; and, depending on the context, expressions which might appear 'uncertain' (and which may even have been held uncertain in other contexts) may be held to be workable and valid (and vice versa). For example, even a testamentary gift or trust of 'all'[18] or a bequest of 'everything else at my house'[19] may or may not mean what they appear to suggest. Frequently cited examples of uncertainty of subject matter include 'the bulk of my property',[20] 'the remaining part of what is left',[21] 'anything that is left',[22] 'such parts of my estate as she shall not have sold',[23] a direction to make 'ample provision',[24] and so forth.[25] These may be good examples of uncertainty in their own particular context, but there is no reason why such phrases should necessarily be uncertain wherever they appear. The problem usually appears in relation to testamentary trusts rather than *inter vivos* settlements. Nevertheless, wherever it occurs, it is always a question of construction of the relevant instrument; and the meaning will depend on the context.[26] Indeed, it is clear from the mass of authorities on this subject that the courts

---

[17] *Hunter v Moss* [1993] 1 WLR 934, 945, *per* Colin Rimer QC; *Ernst & Young Inc v Central Guaranty Trust Co* (2001) 3 ITELR 605.

[18] See *Bowman v Milbanke, supra* and *Re Shepherd, supra* as to whether or not it includes realty. See also *Choithram International SA v Pagarani* [2001] 1 WLR 1 (certainty of gift of 'all my wealth' left open).

[19] *Boon v Cornforth* (1751) 2 Ves Sen 277: held to include such things as would properly go with a house, such as heirlooms, furniture, curtains, and ornaments, but not watches. Cf *Beaufort (Duke) v Dundonald (Lord)* (1716) 2 Vern 739; *Shaftesbury (Earl) v Shaftesbury (Countess)* (1716) 2 Vern 748.

[20] *Palmer v Simmonds* (1854) 2 Drew 221.   [21] *Sprange v Barnard* (1789) 2 Bro CC 585.

[22] *Re Last* [1958] P 137.   [23] *Re Jones* [1898] 1 Ch 438.

[24] *Winch v Brutton* (1844) 14 Sim 379; *Fox v Fox* (1859) 27 Beav 301.

[25] See further J Mowbray et al, *Lewin on Trusts* (17th edn, Sweet & Maxwell, 2000) ('*Lewin*'), 31–32; A Underhill and DJ Hayton, *Law of Trusts and Trustees* (16th edn, Butterworths, 2002) ('*Underhill and Hayton*'), 78–81.

[26] In *Mohun v Mohun* (1818) 1 Sw 201, for example, the court held uncertain a provision which read 'I leave and bequeath to all my grandchildren, and share and share alike' and refused to transpose the word 'all' for the purpose of giving meaning to an instrument that had none.

have always leaned in favour of certainty and validity (especially in relation to testamentary trusts) rather than uncertainty and invalidity. Some of the more common problematic cases will be dealt with specifically below.

Trusts of 'anything that is left' etc

It is *not* the case, as often seems to be suggested,[27] that a trust of 'anything that is left' (or of a similar description of property, such as 'anything remaining' or 'anything that he does not want') is necessarily uncertain and void. It is self-evident that, if the initial trust fund is certain (X) and if the amount taken out of that fund (Y) is certain or ascertainable, the remainder (or 'anything that is left') (Z) must also be certain or ascertainable, ie $X-Y=Z$.[28] An obvious example of such a process is the case where a fund is held on trust for (say) A for life, where A has a general power of appointment over the fund, and on A's death, and subject to and in default of any appointment by A, the remainder of the fund is to be held on trust for another or others. **3.07**

Thus, where a gift of 'what shall be left' is preceded by a power of appointment (or of appropriation, selection, or other similar dispositive power), the gift clearly points to that part or portion of the property which is unappointed (or unappropriated or not otherwise disposed of) under the relevant power.[29] The law reports are full of such examples. In *Constable v Bull*,[30] for example, it was held that the expression 'whatever remains of my said estate and effects' did not create an absolute gift but gave others an interest in the estate; in *Re Sheldon and Kemble*,[31] a gift of what might remain of a testator's estate to be divided equally between surviving children was held valid; and in *Re Thomson's Estate*,[32] all property was left to a wife 'to be disposed of as she may think proper for her own use and benefit', but 'should there be anything remaining of the said property or any part thereof' at her death, it should go to certain named persons, there was no uncertainty.[33] Even in *Re Last*,[34] where a testatrix left her estate to her brother, saying 'At his death **3.08**

---

[27] *Lewin*, 31; *Underhill and Hayton*, 79–80.
[28] Another obvious example is a trust of the residue of a deceased's estate after payment of debts, taxes, and legacies. Numerous other examples could be suggested.
[29] See, for example, *Surman v Surman* (1820) 5 Madd 123.　　[30] (1849) 3 De G & Sm 411.
[31] (1885) 53 LT 527.
[32] (1879) 13 Ch D 144 (widow took life interest with power of disposition during her lifetime only).
[33] See, for example, *Surman v Surman, supra*; *Scott v Josselyn* (1859) 26 Beav 174; *Pennock v Pennock* (1871) LR 13 Eq 144; *Re Adam's Trust* (1865) 14 WR 18; *Re Stringer's Estate* (1877) 6 Ch D 1; *Bibbens v Potter* (1879) 10 Ch D 733; *In the Estate of Lupton* [1905] P 321; *Re Holden* (1888) 57 LJ Ch 648; *Re Sanford* [1901] 1 Ch 939; *Re Ryder* [1914] 1 Ch 865; *Re Cammell* (1925) 69 SJ 345; *Re Shuker's Estate* [1937] 3 All ER 25. Cf *Re Maxwell's Will* (1857) 24 Beav 246.
[34] [1958] P 137. The Crown claimed that it was an absolute gift to the brother and, therefore, claimed the property as *bona vacantia. Re Last* is often cited as an example of uncertainty of subject matter, but it is plainly not one.

anything that is left, that came from me to go to my late husband's grandchildren', and where the brother died intestate, Karminski J held that, upon the true construction of the will, the brother's interest was a life interest only and the grandchildren were entitled to the estate in equal shares. Similarly, in *Re Richards*,[35] where there was a bequest of income of an estate to a wife for life, with a direction that 'in case such income shall not be sufficient she is to use such portion of' the capital 'as she may deem expedient', and, on her death, 'what is left' of the capital was to be divided among certain legatees, Farwell J held that the wife had a life interest, a general power of appointment over the capital during her life, and the named persons took what was left at her death.

3.09   On the other hand, in other contexts, where it is not possible to ascertain the intended subject matter (even on a benign construction), the gift or trust will indeed fail. In *Wynne v Hawkins*,[36] for example, a devise to the testator's wife, 'not doubting she will give what shall be left to my grandchildren', was not sufficiently certain to create a trust.[37] Similarly, a gift to A for life 'and whatever she can transfer to go to her daughters' is void for uncertainty as to the daughters;[38] and so, too, is a gift of whatever a life tenant 'can save out of the income'.[39] In each case, the words of the gift must be construed in their own context and according to the form of the intended gift.

That which is 'reasonable' or 'satisfactory'

3.10   Gifts of a 'reasonable' or 'satisfactory' amount may also be sufficiently certain and valid in appropriate circumstances. It has long been accepted that, where a will furnished some ground on which to estimate the amount intended to be bequeathed, there is sufficient certainty. Thus, in *Jackson v Hamilton*,[40] where a testator directed his trustees 'to retain in their hands any reasonable sum or sums of money which should be sufficient to remunerate them for the trouble they

---

[35]   [1902] 1 Ch 76, followed in *Re Shuker's Estate, supra*. Farwell J distinguished *Re Pedrotti's Will* (1859) 27 Beav 583, where there was also a life interest for the wife, coupled with the words 'in case anything should occur that her income is not sufficient, she shall be at liberty to go to the principal', and where it was held that the word 'sufficient' meant 'sufficient for the widow's wants', so as to afford her a maintenance suitable to her condition in life (so she did not have a general power of appointment). Here, it was 'sufficient for her desires'. See also *Re Willatts* [1905] 2 Ch 135.

[36]   (1782) 1 Bro CC 179. Where the property consists of perishable goods or household furniture, the words make sense in that there is an expected wear and tear during lifetime.

[37]   See also *Bland v Bland* (1745) 2 Cox 349; *Sprange v Barnard* (1789) 2 Bro CC 585; *Pushman v Filliter* (1795) 3 Ves 7; *Wilson v Major* (1805) 11 Ves 205; *Bull v Kingston* (1816) 1 Mer 314; *Forbes v Ball* (1817) 3 Mer 437; *Eade v Eade* (1820) 5 Madd 118; *Lechmere v Lavie* (1832) 2 My & Cr 197; *Horwood v West* (1823) 1 Sim & St 387; *Ex p Payne* (1837) 2 Y & C 636. Cf *Duhamel v Ardovin* (1750–51) 2 Ves Sen 162.

[38]   *Flint v Hughes* (1843) 6 Beav 342.

[39]   *Cowman v Harrison* (1852) 10 Hare 234, 22 LJ Ch 993; see also *Hudson v Bryant* (1845) 1 Coll 681 (more than tenant for life wants to live on).

[40]   (1846) 3 J & Lat 702.

should have' in executing the trusts of his will, it was referred to a Master to determine what would be a reasonable sum. Similarly, where there is a bequest for the maintenance, support, and education of an infant or an adult, or to set him up in business, but no amount is specified, the court will determine the amount to be applied for that purpose,[41] unless the amount is left to the discretion of a named person instead,[42] or the words are too vague to furnish a basis of calculation.[43] In *Re Golay's Will Trusts*,[44] a testator directed his executors to let T enjoy one of his flats during her lifetime 'and to receive a reasonable income from my other properties'. Ungoed-Thomas J held that the words 'reasonable income' directed an objective determinant of the amount which the court could, if necessary, apply. Accordingly, the direction was sufficient and the bequest was not defeated by uncertainty.

> ... the yardstick indicated by the testator is not what he or any other specified person subjectively considers to be reasonable but what he identifies objectively as 'reasonable income'. The court is constantly involved in making such objective assessments of what is reasonable and it is not to be deterred from doing so because subjective influences can never be wholly excluded. In my view the testator intended by 'reasonable income' the yardstick which the court could and would apply in quantifying the amount so that the direction in the will is not in my view defeated by uncertainty.[45]

In other circumstances (albeit not in this case), that which is 'reasonable' might be interpreted to mean what the testator *subjectively* meant, and that meaning might be determined by looking at surrounding circumstances under 'the armchair rule'.[46]

Trusts of 'the bulk of' property

Even a seemingly clear-cut example of conceptual uncertainty such as the expression 'the bulk of' an estate[47] may be held to be certain in an appropriate context. **3.11** Thus, in *Bromley v Tryon*,[48] where a shifting clause in a will was expressed to operate should any of the issue of B become entitled to a specified settled estate 'or the bulk thereof', the House of Lords upheld the clause, despite the fact that the estate might be altered substantially in size, character, and value before the opening of

---

[41] *Broad v Bevan* (1823) 1 Russ 511n; *Pride v Fooks* (1840) 2 Beav 430; *Kilvington v Gray* (1839) 10 Sim 293; *Batt v Anns* (1841) 11 LJ Ch 52; *Thorp v Owen* (1843) 2 Hare 610; *Re Pedrotti's Will* (1859) 27 Beav 583.
[42] *Lewis v Lewis* (1785) 1 Cox 162; *Re Sanderson's Trust* (1857) 3 K & J 497; and see RW Jennings and JC Harper, *Jarman on Wills* (8th edn, 1951) ('*Jarman*') 883.
[43] *Abraham v Alman* (1826) 1 Russ 509; *Anthony v Donges* [1998] 2 FLR 775 ('such minimal part of my estate as [my wife] might be entitled to under English law for maintenance purposes' held void).
[44] [1965] 1 WLR 969.　　　[45] ibid 972.
[46] See (1965) 81 LQR 481 (REM).　　[47] See *Palmer v Simmonds, supra.*
[48] [1952] AC 265.

any particular succession and might be composed of land and money. As Lord Simonds LC observed:[49]

> Then it was said that even so the words are uncertain in content, for it is purely a question of degree what constitutes the 'bulk'. I cannot accept this contention. I think that according to the ordinary use of language the bulk means the greater part, which may according to the subject matter refer to an area, number or value. And that I may not be thought guilty of a solution which is equally obscure, I will add that 'greater part' means anything over one-half.

The House of Lords held that, in this particular context, the reference to 'the bulk' was to value and not to area or size, and the expression meant anything over half. Therefore, as a 'triggering event', the clause was not void for uncertainty. However, a trust of 'the bulk of my estate' would probably still fail, for a more precise amount would need to be established.

Separation or segregation of assets from the estate as a whole

3.12 Where an *inter vivos* declaration of trust is made in respect of certain assets (especially chattels) which form part of a larger collection or holding of similar, but not identical, assets, then such assets must generally be identified by a sufficiently specific description or separated, segregated, or appropriated from the mass. This is a problem peculiar to *inter vivos* trusts. It cannot arise in the case of testamentary trusts, for the entire estate vests in the executors and, in the nature of things, all trust property, like all legacies and other gifts, must be raised out of the estate by the executors and clearly need not be segregated by the deceased before death.[50] In the case of testamentary trusts, the problem is likely to be one of identification of the subject matter from the description given or adequacy of the estate. In any event, even in the case of *inter vivos* trusts, the requirement of 'certainty of subject matter' is not precisely the same for all forms of property.

Chattels

3.13 Where it is intended to declare a trust of chattels forming part of a larger mass, the settlor must, as a preliminary matter, separate, segregate, or appropriate those chattels from the mass, or declare a trust of a proportion or fraction of the mass as a whole (ie create a form of co-ownership of the whole), or otherwise identify the relevant chattels in a sufficiently clear and unambiguous manner. Whichever

---

[49] ibid 275–276. Lord Morton agreed at 279. The clause was 'of respectable antiquity', being derived from Davidson's *Precedents and Forms in Conveyancing* vol IV (2nd edn, 1864) 516, and adopted by Key and Elphinstone's *Precedents in Conveyancing* vol II (2nd edn, 1883) 556; and its validity had never been questioned, not even in *Re Hinckes* [1920] 2 Ch 511. This conclusion was based on the fact that the testatrix had referred to land, money, chattels, and investments and not just to land (which might have raised an uncertainty as to value or area).
[50] See, for example, *Re Clifford* [1912] 1 Ch 29 and *Re Cheadle* [1900] 2 Ch 620.

82

method is used, there must also be an intention to pass title to those chattels. As Oliver J put it in *Re London Wine Co (Shippers) Ltd*:[51]

> I cannot see how, for instance, a farmer who declares himself to be a trustee of two sheep (without identifying them) can be said to have created a perfect and complete trust whatever rights he may confer by such declaration as a matter of contract. And it would seem to me to be immaterial that at the time he has a flock of sheep out of which he could satisfy the interest. Of course, he could by appropriate words, declare himself to be a trustee of a specified proportion of his whole flock and thus create an equitable tenancy in common between himself and the named beneficiary, so that a proprietary interest would arise in the beneficiary in an undivided share of all the flock and its produce. But the *mere* declaration that a given number of animals would be held upon trust could not ... without very clear words pointing to such an intention, result in the creation of an interest in common in the proportion which that number bears to the number of the whole at the time of the declaration. And where the mass from which the numerical interest is to take effect is not itself ascertainable at the date of the declaration such a conclusion becomes impossible.

In *London Wine* itself, dealers of wine had deposited stocks of wine in various warehouses. Quantities of wine were then sold to customers, but, in many instances, the wine remained at the warehouse; there was no appropriation from bulk of any wine to answer any particular contracts. The customer received a certificate of title for wine for which he had paid which declared him the sole and beneficial owner of certain wine of a certain vintage. The customer was charged for storage and insurance but there was no segregation of specific cases. A receiver was appointed under a floating charge. The judge held that it could not be said that the legal title to the wine had passed to the customers; the description of wine did not adequately link it with any given consignment at any given warehouse: indeed, in some cases, the certificates had been issued even before the wine had been received by the company. Moreover, the company had not declared itself a trustee of any wine for, as Oliver J stated, 'to create a trust it must be possible to ascertain with certainty not only what the interest of the beneficiary is to be but to what property it is to attach', and this could not be done here.[52]

The same requirement of unconditional segregation was applied, with a different result, in *Re Stapylton Fletcher Ltd*.[53] This case concerned two wine merchants who held stocks of wine for customers. When a customer purchased wine, it was physically removed from the company's trading stock and placed in the company's reserve. In the case of one of them ('ESV') the wine was stored by type and vintage and a master card index was maintained which showed the names of customers and the number of cases of wine allocated to each customer. The individual cases

3.14

---

[51] [1986] PCC 121, 137. See also *Re Wait* [1927] 1 Ch 606; and (1987) 103 LQR 438 (R Goode).

[52] There was not even an ascertainable bulk in *London Wine*: see *Re Stapylton Fletcher* [1995] 1 All ER 192 below.

[53] [1995] 1 All ER 192. See also (1995) 48 CLP 117, 131 (A Clarke).

of wine were not, however, marked with a particular customer's name. As wine was delivered to each customer and new wines acquired, the master index was updated. Some wines were ordered '*en primeur*' directly from the producers and stored for them in bonded warehouses. In the case of ESV, those wines were individually allocated to customers and details were recorded accurately on the master index. The other merchant ('SFL') made no attempt to allocate the wines, either to specific customers or as between the company and its customers generally. Joint administrative receivers were appointed over the assets of the two companies. They subsequently sought directions from the court on whether and to what extent the wines held by ESV's customers' reserve or in bond had been sufficiently ascertained for property in the goods to have been transferred.[54]

3.15 Section 16 of the Sale of Goods Act 1979 provided that 'where there is a contract for the sale of unascertained goods no property in the goods is transferred to the buyer unless and until the goods are ascertained'. In the case of goods forming part of a bulk, ascertainment for the purposes of section 16 was held not to occur until those goods were separated from the bulk, usually immediately prior to delivery. Title was acknowledged to have passed to customers where an individual case of wine had a specific customer's reference on it and the allocation tallied with the company's records of wine ordered and paid for; where a stack of cases had a label showing the cases as belonging to one individual; or where records showed that other cases in a stack have already been removed, leaving a number of cases which exactly tallies with a remaining individual's order. In such cases, there is an actual allocation or appropriation of individual cases to individual customers, as opposed to a mere 'entitlement' to a certain number of cases, ie where there are no discernible features identifying a particular case or cases as belonging to an individual customer.[55] The present case was different from *London Wine* in that wine purchased by customers had been segregated in a separate part of the warehouse and careful records maintained by the company.[56]

---

[54] In the sale of goods context, these problems are now subject to the Sale of Goods Amendment Act 1995; but the Act applies only where there has been a prepayment for goods and also the bulk itself is identified (which was not the case in *London Wine*).

[55] Applying *Carlos Federspiel & Co SA v Charles Twigg & Co Ltd* [1957] 1 Lloyd's Rep 240.

[56] Legal title had passed, so the question of certainty for trusts did not arise. In the sale of goods context, the intention of the parties is central. Section 17(2) of the 1979 Act provides that, for the purpose of ascertaining the intention of the parties, regard shall be had to the terms of the contract, the conduct of the parties, and the circumstances of the case. Thus, if a number of cases or bottles of identical wine are held, not mingled with the trading stock, in store for a group of customers, those cases or bottles will be ascertained for the purposes of s16 of the 1979 Act, even though they are not immediately appropriated to each individual customer. In other words, if there is to be no delivery, but merely a segregation in the hands of the seller for retention by him, it is the segregation of the stock from the company's trading assets (whether done physically or by giving instructions to a bonded warehouse keeper) which causes the goods to be ascertained for the purposes of s16. In such a case, property will pass by common intention and the customers will take as tenants in common in the proportion that their goods bear to the entire stock.

In any event, segregation of individual chattels alone is not sufficient: it must be **3.16** an unconditional segregation amounting to an appropriation. As Pearson J put it, in *Carlos Federspiel & Co SA v Charles Twigg & Co Ltd*:[57]

> A mere setting apart or selection of the seller of the goods which he expects to use in the performance of the contract is not enough. If that is all, he can change his mind and use some other goods in performance of this contract. To constitute an appropriation of the goods to the contract, the parties must have had, or be reasonably supposed to have had, an intention to attach the contract irrevocably to those goods, so that those goods and no others are the subject of the sale and become the property of the buyer. Secondly, it is by agreement of the parties that the appropriation, involving a change of ownership, is made, although in some cases the buyer's assent to an appropriation by the seller is conferred in advance by the contract itself or otherwise. Thirdly, an appropriation by the seller, with the assent of the buyer, may be said always to involve an actual or constructive delivery. If the seller retains possession, he does so as bailee for the buyer.

In *London Wine*, there was no such unconditional segregation and customers' orders could have been fulfilled from any source, not necessarily even from existing stocks. Moreover, 'the passing of property is concerned with the creation of rights *in rem*, which the purchaser can assert not only against the vendor but against the world at large, and which he can alienate in such a way as to create similar rights in a transferee'.[58] Without unconditional segregation, it would not be possible to say whether subsequent dealings with some of the goods were dealings with the purchaser's property or with the seller's own property.

The issue of certainty in relation to chattels arose again in the Privy Council in *Re* **3.17** *Goldcorp*,[59] where, however, the central question was not appropriation (or segregation) but ascertainment. As Lord Mustill pointed out:[60] 'It makes no difference what the parties intended, if what they intend is impossible: as is the case with an immediate transfer of title to goods whose identity is not yet known.' In *Goldcorp*, a company which dealt in gold and other precious metals sold unascertained bullion to non-allocated claimants for future delivery. The company's brochure provided that it would be responsible for storing and insuring customers' bullion and that physical delivery of gold and silver could be taken on seven days' notice. Each customer received an invoice or certificate verifying his ownership. Customers were also told that the company would maintain a separate and sufficient stock of each type of bullion to meet their demands, but it failed to do so. The company got into difficulties and receivers were appointed. The receivers applied to court for directions as to the disposal of the company's remaining stock of bullion.

---

[57] ibid 255.
[58] *Karlshamns Oljefabriker v Eastport Navigation Corp, The Elafi* [1982] 1 All ER 208, 214.
[59] [1995] 1 AC 74. See also *Associated Alloys Pty v CAN* (2000) 71 Aus LR 568.
[60] [1995] 1 AC 74, 90.

3.18   There were three categories of claimant. The first category comprised a group of non-allocated claimants who had contracted to purchase unascertained generic goods. The second category comprised a customer who had agreed to purchase specific gold maple coins from the company on a non-allocated basis. The company acquired a substantial quantity of maple coins but not expressly for him, ie he, too, had purchased generic goods. The Privy Council held that no property in any bullion passed in law or in equity to this individual or to the other non-allocated claimants. They could not acquire title until it was known to what goods that title related. There was no fixed and identified bulk in existence from which a title could be created by a deemed appropriation. There had been no appropriation of bullion or coins to their contracts. Indeed, no separate and sufficient stock of bullion to meet the customers' requirements actually existed. On the other hand, in respect of the third class of customers, there had been sufficient ascertainment and appropriation of bullion to transfer title to each of them and thereafter they had a shared interest in the pooled bullion stored on their behalf. The company had misappropriated that bullion by mixing it with its own bullion. The bullion belonging to them which was held by the receivers comprised bullion equal to the lowest balance thereof held by the company at any time; and it would have been inequitable to impose a lien in their favour on all the company's assets at the date of receivership.

3.19   The company had not, by its collateral promises, declared itself a trustee of bullion in favour of customers. What could the subject matter of the trust have been? It could not have been the company's current stock of bullion answering the contractual description (and there was no other bullion to which the trust could relate) for this would have inhibited any dealings with it otherwise than for the purpose of delivery under the non-allocated sale contracts. [61] It was acknowledged that a vendor of goods ex-bulk [62] can declare himself a trustee of the bulk in favour of a buyer, but this was inconsistent with the nature of the contracts here. The customers had contracted to buy generic goods without any stipulation as to their source. They had purchased for the physical delivery on demand of the precise quantity of bullion fixed by their contracts, not a shifting proportion of a shifting bulk, prior to delivery.

3.20   Thus, where the subject matter of a trust is intended to be chattels forming part of a larger mass, and the declaration of trust does not take the form of co-ownership,

---

[61]   [1995] 1 AC 74, 91.

[62]   Two species of unascertained goods may be distinguished: 'generic goods', which are sold on terms which preserve the vendor's freedom to decide for himself how and from what source he will obtain goods answering the contractual description; and 'goods sold ex-bulk', which are to be supplied from a fixed and pre-determined source, from within which the seller may make his own choice but outside which he may not go: ibid 89.

the question is simply whether those chattels have been identified with sufficient certainty to render the intended trust enforceable by the court. This may, and perhaps generally would, be achieved by an irrevocable physical segregation or appropriation of the relevant chattels. However, this is surely not essential: the required 'certainty' may be provided by other means, for example where gold bars or cases of wine, though forming part of a larger bulk, are identified specifically by reference to distinct numbers, codes, or other identification marks. In all cases, the 'identification' must be irrevocable in that the settlor cannot thereafter use the goods for other purposes or substitute other goods to be the subject matter of the trust. There is no certainty where the declaration relates to generic goods.

This result may be a necessary consequence of the nature of the property, ie the fact **3.21** that tangible assets are generally distinguishable from each other. As Rimer QC stated, when referring to *London Wine* in *Hunter v Moss*:[63]

> The decision was concerned solely with an alleged declaration of trust in respect of tangible assets in the nature of cases of wine. Even tangible assets which are regarded as forming part of a homogeneous mass are physically separate, and so distinguishable, from other assets comprised within the same mass. Further, certain of the assets in a group of ostensibly similar or identical assets may in fact have characteristics which distinguish them from other assets in the class. Consignments of wine provide a good example. Some of the cases within it may contain wine that is corked, or may have been stored badly and have deteriorated or may have other inherent defects.

This is generally the case, no doubt; and failure to identify which (distinguishable) chattels were intended to be the subject matter of a trust will be fatal. However, it may be wondered whether all tangible assets are indeed distinguishable from each other, for example a trust of '100 of my (completely indistinguishable) 1,000 gold bars'. In view of the decision in *Hunter v Moss* itself,[64] one may wonder why there would not be certainty of subject matter in such a case, without specific identification or segregation or appropriation of any particular 100 gold bars. *Re Goldcorp* does not rule out this possibility, for it was concerned with generic goods, with bullion which the company had not even acquired.

The answer, of course, is that it is not simply a question of identifying the relevant **3.22** chattels out of a distinguishable mass but also of establishing that the trust is attached irrevocably to those chattels and no others, so that property in those chattels has passed and the original owner can no longer use them for his own or any other purpose and cannot substitute other goods to be held on trust. Segregation or appropriation identifies relevant assets and may be strong evidence of an intention to subject them to a trust, but in itself it is not enough. On the other hand, a failure to segregate or otherwise identify specific indistinguishable tangible assets makes it difficult, if not impossible, to ascertain which assets were

---

[63] [1993] 1 WLR 934, 940.   [64] See paras 3.25–3.29 below.

intended to be irrevocably dedicated to the trust. This is not necessarily due to the nature of the asset, but it may lead to the same result.

3.23　In any event, it seems that the principles applicable in relation to tangible assets need not also govern other forms of property. As Rimer QC noted in *Hunter v Moss*:[65]

> I do not, however, consider that the principle . . . applied with regard to the certainties requisite for the purposes of a trust relating to tangible assets is one which is necessarily also applicable by analogy to trusts of intangible assets, for example, to a purported trust of a specific sum of money forming part of a larger credit balance in a particular bank account. The latter trust will of course only be valid if its subject matter is certain. But the determination of whether the requisite degree of certainty has been achieved is, in my judgment, not necessarily governed by principles analogous to those which apply in the case of tangible assets.

Choses in action

3.24　The general principle that the subject matter of a trust must be identified with sufficient certainty to enable the court to make an order for the execution of that trust applies equally to choses in action. However, the strict requirements applied in relation to tangible assets need not apply, and have not been applied, in relation to intangible assets.[66]

3.25　In *Hunter v Moss*,[67] the defendant was the registered holder of 950 shares in a company with an issued share capital of 1,000 shares. At first instance, the judge (Colin Rimer QC) held that he had made a valid oral declaration of trust constituting himself trustee for the plaintiff of 5 per cent of the company's issued share capital, and that the trust applied to 50 of the defendant's 950 shares. The defendant appealed on the ground that the purported trust failed for want of certainty of subject matter. The Court of Appeal dismissed his appeal, holding that, in the case of a declaration of trust of personalty, the requirement of certainty of subject matter did not necessarily entail segregation of the property which was to form the subject matter of the trust; that the declaration of trust here was sufficiently certain as to subject matter, since the shares held by the defendant were of such a nature as to be indistinguishable from each other and were all therefore capable of satisfying the trust without identifying any particular 50 shares.[68]

---

[65] [1993] 1 WLR 934, 940.

[66] *Hunter v Moss* [1993] 1 WLR 934, 940, 945, [1994] 1 WLR 452.

[67] ibid. See also (1994) 110 LQR 335 (DJ Hayton); (1994) CLJ 443 (LS Sealy); (1995) 48 CLP 113 (A Clarke); (1994) CLJ 448 (M Ockleton); (1995) 9 Tr Law Int 43 (P Birks); [1996] Conv 223 (J Martin).

[68] All the shares had in fact been sold for cash and shares in another company (B & F), so the trust attached to the equivalent proportion of the consideration received. Following the sale, the defendant paid to the plaintiff the net dividends paid on B & F's shares on what was thought to be the appropriate proportion attributable to the plaintiff's 5%.

According to Dillon LJ,[69] there was no question of an imperfect transfer: it was **3.26** an oral declaration of trust. It would not be good enough to declare a trust of 50 shares, without indicating the company the settlor had in mind; but here there was just one class of shares in the one company. If A holds 200 shares and executes a transfer of 50 such shares to an individual donee or trustee, and hands over his certificate for 200 shares and the transfer to give effect to the transfer, there is a valid gift of the 50 shares without any further identification of their numbers: it would be a completed gift without waiting for the registration of the transfer.[70] A new share certificate would then be issued in the ordinary way.

At first instance in *Hunter*,[71] Rimer QC stated:

> ... the question of whether in any particular case there is such uncertainty depends, or ought to depend, not on the application of any immutable principle based on the requirements of a need for segregation or appropriation, but rather on whether, immediately after the purported declaration of trust, the court could, if asked, make an order for the execution of the purported trust. In any particular case it could and will only do so if, *inter alia*, the subject matter of the trust is identified with sufficient certainty.

Referring to the point that, without segregation, it would not be possible to say whether subsequent dealings were with trust property or the settlor's own property, he added: 'if any such uncertainty were to arise, that would not be because the trust fund was uncertain as to subject matter, but rather because the trustee failed to keep proper accounts showing how he had subsequently dealt with it'.

Hunter v Moss has been criticized.[72] Nevertheless, it was followed in *Re Harvard* **3.27** *Securities*,[73] where a dealer in financial securities purchased shares on behalf of clients and retained legal title in the shares as nominee for each client. However, shares were not actually allocated or segregated for them. The company went into liquidation and the question arose as to whether the clients had beneficial interests in the shares. Neuberger J held in their favour: *Hunter v Moss* was distinguishable from other cases on the ground that it, unlike them, was not concerned with chattels; and it showed that it was possible to create a trust of some shares from a class of shares without actual segregation or appropriation.

Thus, in relation to certainty of subject matter, there has emerged a distinction **3.28** between tangible and intangible assets. Whether there is any need to draw such a distinction is doubtful, however. If the decision in *Hunter v Moss* is correct, there is surely no obvious reason why it could not also apply equally in the (perhaps unlikely) event that the owner of indistinguishable chattels purported to create a trust of a certain number of them, without segregation. However, the key issue

---

[69] [1994] 1 WLR 452, 457. [70] *Re Rose* [1952] Ch 499.
[71] [1993] 1 WLR 934, 945. [72] See, in particular, (1994) 110 LQR 335 (DJ Hayton).
[73] [1997] 2 BCLC 369. Academic criticism of *Hunter v Moss* was noted. So, too, was the fact that the House of Lords had refused leave to appeal in *Hunter v Moss after* the decision in *Re Goldcorp*.

seems to have been ignored in *Hunter v Moss*. In the case of shares, as with chattels, there can surely not be a trust (even where the number of identical shares is certain) if the owner of those shares has retained a right to use those shares for his own purposes or to substitute others as the subject matter of that trust. Whatever the form of the property, it is a question not just of adequate identification but also of intention in relation to that identified property.

3.29 Part of the difficulty here arises from a misunderstanding of what the law requires in order to have 'certainty'. This question is discussed in greater detail below, in relation to 'certainty of objects',[74] where it is suggested that the law does not seek or require absolute, mathematical certainty: it looks for 'workability'. All that is required is that, in the given case or the particular circumstances, there is sufficient 'certainty' to enable the court to enforce the trust. In *Hunter v Moss*, such a workable solution was considered possible: it was unnecessary and, indeed, unreasonable not to give effect to what the settlor had intended. The objection that, without segregation or some other form of identification of the precise number of shares in question, it would not be possible to determine whether subsequent dealings with shares were with trust property or the settlor's own property, was addressed and dealt with in *Hunter v Moss* itself. The settlor-trustee would be guilty of a breach of trust if he were to fail to keep accounts, which presumably also implies a duty on his part to segregate or appropriate the shares (or treat them as if they had been segregated or appropriated). Moreover, as against the trustee, other rules of trusts law, such as the presumption against a breach of trust or that a trustee is presumed to spend his own money first,[75] could be invoked to resolve such issues. If it transpires that the beneficiary has no remedy against a third party, such as a bona fide purchaser from the trustee, this would be because of the application of principles which would affect a beneficiary of any trust where the trustee had failed to deal with trust property properly. However, such reasoning tends to assume that which it seeks to prove. If the 'settlor' has retained a right to use the assets for his own purposes, there can be no trust. But if he has not retained such a right, there is still a need to ascertain precisely in respect of which assets he has not done so.

Money

3.30 The same general principles apply to money. A requirement that moneys be kept separate is normally an indicator that they are impressed with a trust; and the absence of such a requirement, if there are no other indicators of a trust, normally (but not necessarily) negatives it.[76] However, where an identified or identifiable

---

[74] See Chapter 4 below.   [75] *Re Hallett's Estate* (1880) 13 Ch D 696.
[76] *R v Clowes (No 2)* [1994] 2 All ER 316, where, however, Watkins LJ said (at 325): 'The fact that a transaction contemplates the mingling of funds is, therefore, not necessarily fatal to a trust.' See also *Henry v Hammond* [1913] 2 KB 515, 521; *Burdick v Garrick* (1870) LR 5 Ch App 233; and *Re Nanwa Gold Mines Ltd* [1955] 1 WLR 1080.

sum of money is paid over, the crucial question is whether or not the recipient is entitled to treat that money as his own: if he is not, then he is a trustee of it; but if he is, then he is not a trustee. As Channell J put it, in *Henry v Hammond*:[77]

> It is clear that if the terms upon which the person receives the money are that he is bound to keep it separate, either in a bank or elsewhere, and to hand that money to be so kept as a separate fund to the person entitled to it, then he is a trustee of that money and must hand it over to the person who is his *cestui que trust*. If, on the other hand, he is not bound to keep the money separate, but is entitled to mix it with his own money and deal with it as he pleases, and when called upon to hand over an equivalent sum of money, then, in my opinion, he is not a trustee of the money, but merely a debtor.

Similarly, in *Re Andrabell Ltd* [78] (a retention of title case, in which the question of uncertainty of subject matter was not raised), Peter Gibson J said that the relationship between A and B, under which A is lawfully at liberty to mix moneys or other assets which he receives with moneys and assets of his own, and is not obliged to keep the moneys or assets so received in a separate account or fund, is a relationship which is inconsistent with A being a trustee for B in respect of the moneys or assets received by him.

3.31 A separate question is whether there is sufficient certainty of subject matter to constitute a trust where the owner of money declares a trust of a portion (as opposed to a proportion)[79] of it, whether that money is in a bank account or actual coinage or notes. At first instance in *Hunter v Moss*,[80] the judge (Colin Rimer QC) referred to the example of a declaration of trust of £1,000 out of moneys in a bank account and concluded that there is nothing uncertain about it.[81]

3.32 In *Mac-Jordan Construction Ltd v Brookmount Erostin Ltd*,[82] M were subcontractors for B as main contractors. B was contractually obliged to retain money (representing a percentage of a building contract price) on trust for M. However, the money had been paid into a general bank account and had not been set aside as a separate fund when a receiver was appointed. It was consequently held that there was no trust applicable to the retention fund: at best, there was merely a general bank account. M was, therefore, not entitled to the money in priority to the receiver and a secured creditor. M merely had a contractual right to have B maintain a separate account;

---

[77] [1913] 2 KB 515, 521 (cited with approval by Slade J in *Re Bond Worth Ltd* [1980] Ch 228, 260–261. See also *Re Nevill* (1871) LR 6 Ch App 397 (affirmed in the HL sub nom *John Towle & Co v White* (1873) 29 LT 78); *Foley v Hill* (1848) 2 HL Cas 28; *South Australian Insurance Co v Randell* (1869) LR 3 PC 101; and *Hinckley Singapore Trading Pte Ltd v Sogo Department stores (S) Pte Ltd* (2001) 4 ITELR 301.

[78] [1984] 3 All ER 407.

[79] As in the case of any other form of property, there ought to be no difficulty where the declaration relates to a proportion or fraction (one-half, one-quarter, or whatever) of the fund.

[80] [1993] 1 WLR 934, 946.

[81] *Hunter v Moss* [1993] 1 WLR 934, 946. See paras 3.25–3.29 above. *Underhill and Hayton* (at 78) adopt the view that this is uncertain, however.

[82] [1992] BCLC 350.

and, if it had in fact been maintained, it would have been impressed with a trust in favour of B.[83] However, it was not a declaration of trust of a certain sum of money in the general bank account: there was no identifiable source of the money. *Mac-Jordan* is therefore not inconsistent with what was said in *Hunter v Moss*. It is suggested that, if *Hunter v Moss* is correct, there is nothing uncertain about a declaration of trust of £1,000 out of moneys in a bank account. Nor, it is suggested, is there anything necessarily uncertain about a similar declaration in respect of money in its physical form (coinage, bank notes, and so forth), provided it is all indistinguishable.[84] The consequences and implications are the same as those established in *Hunter v Moss* in relation to indistinguishable shares. However, the same criticisms as have been directed at *Hunter v Moss* apply equally in this context.

Trusts of parts or portions of the property

3.33 Where property is intended to be divided into parts or portions, so that there is effectively a separate gift of each individual part, then, if one such part cannot be ascertained, the gift(s) of the other part(s) to the other legatee(s) will fail. Sometimes, the failure to ascertain is that of the testator, as in *Jerningham v Herbert*,[85] where the testatrix gave to A such of her jewels as should at her death be deposited at a specified place, and gave the rest of her jewels to B. At her death, there were no jewels deposited at that place and Leach MR held that the whole gift failed: the will referred to a future act to be done by the testatrix in order to complete her gift and that act had not been completed. A division or selection by the testator himself is incompatible with a selection by the legatee. As Romer J stated in *Asten v Asten*:[86]

> If a will shews that a testator intends to give a particular property to a legatee, and, owing to the testator having several properties answering the description in the will of the particular property given you are unable to say, either from the will itself or from extrinsic evidence, which of the several properties the testator referred to, then on principle the gift must fail for uncertainty, and the Court cannot, in order to avoid an intestacy, change the will, or construe it as giving to the legatee the option of choosing any one of the properties.

Although the court will strive, by means of extrinsic evidence, to discover which property or asset was intended for which legatee, it cannot rewrite the will in order to save the gift.[87]

---

[83] *Re Goldcorp* [1995] 1 AC 74, 100.

[84] If it comprises different currencies, presumably the same problem as with shares in companies arises and there is a need to identify which amounts of which currencies were intended.

[85] (1828) 4 Russ 388. See also the peculiar case of *Edwards v Jones (No 2)* (1866) 35 Beav 474 where a testator devised to his daughter a house to be built by his executors; the executor, who was also residuary legatee, built a house at the daughter's request; otherwise, the gift would apparently have been void for uncertainty.

[86] [1894] 3 Ch 260, 263. See also *Richardson v Watson* (1833) 4 B & Ad 787.

[87] ibid; *Richardson v Watson, supra*; *Blundell v Gladstone* (1851–52) 3 Mac & G 692.

The requisite certainty may be provided by conferring an express power of selec-   **3.34**
tion on someone. Thus, a gift of portions to daughters, to be determined by the
testator's wife or executors, according to the value of their services to the family (or
even, in the case of a daughter's marriage, according to the match she might
make), was upheld because the discretion conferred on the wife or executors
removed any potential uncertainty.[88] If property is given to trustees with a discretionary power to apply or distribute it, or any part of it, for specific objects or purposes or in a certain way, and any part of it which is not so applied or distributed
is given to A, then this operates as an absolute gift to A subject to any exercise of
that discretion or power (as in a typical discretionary trust or a trust with an overriding power of appointment).[89] An equal division is made where the donee of a
power of distribution fails to exercise the power.[90]

Where the specified mechanism or formula for selection breaks down, however, the   **3.35**
entire gift may fail. In *Boyce v Boyce*,[91] for example, several houses were left on trust
for a widow for life and, after her death, to convey to his daughter (A) one house as
she should choose, all the others to be conveyed to another daughter (B). A died in
the testator's lifetime, so could not choose. The trust in favour of B therefore failed.[92]
Such harsh consequences may not always follow, however. For example, a gift to two
(and presumably more) persons 'in such shares as shall be determined by [blank]' has
been held to make them tenants in common in equal shares.[93]

In other cases, the court has been ready to imply a power of selection, or has gone   **3.36**
even further, in order to save the gift. The fact that the legatee is to be able to select
may appear either by express words used in the will, or by reasonable inference
from it.[94] In *Re Knapton*,[95] for example, a testatrix who owned several small
houses bequeathed 'one house to each of my nephews and nieces and one to N.H.
One to F.K. One to my sister. One to my brother.' Simonds J held that the right
of choice should go in the first place to the persons benefiting as 'nephews and
nieces' and afterwards to the other persons in the order in which they were named.

---

[88] *Re Conn* [1898] 1 Ir R 337.
[89] *Lancashire v Lancashire* (1848) 2 Ph 657, 1 De G & S 288; *McPhail v Doulton* [1971]
AC 424.
[90] *Salusbury v Denton* (1857) 3 K & J 529. See also *Liddard v Liddard* (1860) 28 Beav 266;
Greville v Greville (No 1) (1859) 27 Beav 594.
[91] (1849) 16 Sim 476. *Jarman*, at 485, states that this decision 'seems somewhat technical',
because it was clear that the testator intended B to take whatever A did not choose and it might well
have been held that B should take the whole lot.
[92] It may be otherwise, however, where the gift comprises a definite portion of a larger quantity,
the devisee or legatee being entitled to select, eg, a devise of two out of four acres lying together. See
Grace Marshal's case Dyer 281b, n; 8 Vin Abr 48, pl 11; *Hobson v Blackburn* (1833) 1 My & K 571;
Jacques v Chambers (1846) 2 Coll 441.
[93] *Robinson v Wheelwright* (1855) 21 Beav 214.   [94] *Asten v Asten, supra* 262.
[95] [1941] Ch 428. Following *Duckmanton v Duckmanton* (1860) 5 H & N 219; and *Asten v
Asten* [1894] 3 Ch 260.

Moreover, in the event of disagreement among the nephews and nieces, the choice among them was to be determined by lot, in accordance with the analogy of Roman Law.[96] Prima facie, if the testator gives one of such properties to a legatee without saying more, then the reasonable inference is that the testator intended the legatee to select.[97] He was also prepared to hold that, where a testator gives one of such properties to each of several legatees, then he intends (prima facie) to give the right of selection to the legatees according to the priority of the bequests.[98]

3.37   Similarly, where a testator bequeaths a certain number of shares in a company, and it appears that at the date of the will he held shares in that company of two different classes, one of which is more valuable than the other, and either of which is sufficient to satisfy the bequest, then the legatee apparently has a right of selection.[99] If the more valuable shares are not sufficient to satisfy the bequest, it is a question of construction out of which class the bequest ought to be satisfied.[100]

Trust of surplus funds after providing for illegal object

3.38   Another class of case is that where the gift is of the surplus of a specified fund remaining after providing for an object which is illegal or unattainable and the exact amount to be laid out on that object is not specified. Generally, the gift of the surplus is void for uncertainty, unless the court is able to determine from the terms of the gift what would have been the proper amount to be expended had that object been legal or attainable, or the gift of surplus actually carries with it all that is not otherwise effectually disposed of. In *Re Coxen*[101] (a case concerning the intermingling of charitable purposes with potentially non-charitable ones) Jenkins J stated that the result of the authorities appeared to be as follows:

(a)   Where the amount applicable to the non-charitable purpose can be quantified, the trusts fail *quoad* that amount but take effect in favour of the charitable purpose as regards the remainder. Here, the question is essentially one of evidence: has the testator furnished fair and reasonable data to enable the relevant sum (otherwise applicable towards the non-charitable purpose) to be ascertained (and then deducted).[102]

---

[96]   Justinian's Institutes, Book II, title 20, s 23.

[97]   Whether it appears on the face of the will that the testator had several such properties, as in *Duckmanton v Duckmanton, supra,* or whether the fact otherwise appears, as in *Tapley v Eagleton* (1879) 12 Ch D 683.

[98]   *Boyce v Boyce, supra,* was not referred to in *Re Knapton,* but it was in *Asten v Asten, supra.*

[99]   *Jaques v Chambers* (1846) 15 LJ Ch 225, 16 LJ Ch 243; *Millard v Bailey* (1866) LR 1 Eq 378; *O'Donnell v Welsh* [1903] 1 Ir R 115.

[100]   *Re Cheadle* [1900] 2 Ch 620.

[101]   [1948] Ch 747, 752. See also *Chapman v Brown* (1801) 6 Ves 404; *Re Birkett* (1878) 9 Ch D 576; *Re Taylor* (1888) 58 LT 538; *Re Porter* [1925] Ch 746; *Re Dalziel* [1943] Ch 277; *Re Parnell* [1944] Ch 107.

[102]   See, for example, *Mitford v Reynolds* (1842) 1 Phil 185.

(b) Where the amount applicable to the non-charitable purpose cannot be quantified, both the charitable and non-charitable trusts wholly fail because it cannot then be held that any ascertainable part of the fund or the income thereof is devoted to charity.[103]

(c) There is an exception to the general rule in what are commonly known as the 'tomb cases', ie, cases in which there is a primary trust to apply the income of a fund in perpetuity in the repair of a tomb not in a church, followed by a charitable trust in terms extending only to the balance or residue of such income. The established rule in such cases is that the invalid trust for the repair of the tomb is ignored and the entire income is regarded as devoted to the charitable purpose.[104]

(d) There is an exception of a more general character where, as a matter of construction, the gift to charity is a gift of the entire fund or income subject to the payments thereout required to give effect to the non-charitable purpose, in which case the amount set free by the failure of the non-charitable gift is caught by, and passes under, the charitable gift.[105]

If a part of a particular fund be given to one person and the residue to another, **3.39** it is a question of intention, not subject to any particular rule, whether the gift of the residue is to be read as a gift of the mere balance of the fund after deducting the amount of the sum first given out of it,[106] or a gift of the entire fund subject to the gift previously made out of it.[107] In the latter case, if the gift of the part fails, the gift of the residue may carry the whole fund: in the former case, this is not so.[108]

Where a fund has been bequeathed for two definite purposes, one of which is ille- **3.40** gal and the other charitable, the question that arises is how far the charitable purpose can be carried into effect. If the fund has been given for two such purposes *pari passu*, the court will endeavour to ascertain what portion of the fund would be sufficient to satisfy the illegal purpose if it were legal; this part of the gift fails and the charity takes the balance of the fund. If it is impossible to make such a calculation, the court may apparently divide the fund between the two purposes.[109]

---

[103] *Chapman v Brown*, supra; *Re Porter* [1925] Ch 746; *A-G v Hinxman* (1820) 2 J & W 270; *A-G v Davies* (1803–04) 9 Ves 535; *A-G v Goulding* (1788) 2 Bro CC 428; *Re Taylor* (1888) 58 LT 538; *Re Dalziel* [1943] Ch 277.

[104] *Fisk v A-G* (1867) LR 4 Eq 521; *Hunter v Bullock* (1872) LR 14 Eq 45; *Dawson v Small* (1874) LR 18 Eq 114; *Re Williams* (1877) 5 Ch D 735; *Re Birkett* (1878) 9 Ch D 576; *Re Vaughan* (1886) 33 Ch D 187; *Re Rogerson* [1901] 1 Ch 715.

[105] *Re Parnell* [1944] Ch 107.

[106] *Page v Leapingwell* (1812) 18 Ves 463; *Easum v Appleford* (1840) 5 My & Cr 56.

[107] *Falkner v Butler* (1765) Amb 514; *Carter v Taggart* (1848) 16 Sim 423; *Re Harries' Trust* (1859) Johns 199.

[108] Hawkins and Ryder, *The Construction of Wills* (London: Sweet & Maxwell, 1965) by EC Ryder, based on the 3rd edition of *Hawkins on the Construction of Wills* (1925) 53.

[109] *Hoare v Osborne* (1866) LR 1 Eq 585; *Re Rigley's Trust* (1866) 36 LJ Ch 147; *Champney v Davy* (1879) 11 Ch 949; *Re Vaughan* (1886) 33 Ch D 187.

The maxim *id certum est quod certum reddi potest* may be applied in order to save gifts which would otherwise be void for uncertainty.

D. Joint Bank Accounts

3.41 Joint bank accounts are subject, in general, to the same principles as other personal property. However, joint bank accounts (whether current or deposit accounts) pose peculiar problems of their own. A joint bank account (often in the names of husband and wife) may have been opened simply for the convenience of one party, so that the other party has only rights of withdrawal for specified purposes and the moneys in the account form part of the estate of the party who opened the account. Alternatively, the presumption of advancement may be said to apply to the account, in which case difficult questions arise as to when the presumption is intended to operate (ie immediately or on death?) and also in respect of what (such an account having a fluctuating balance). It is trite law that, where a husband and wife (or, indeed, any other parties) have a joint bank account, the beneficial ownership of money in it, and of assets acquired by means of such money, will depend upon their intentions.[110] There are various possibilities.

Pooled assets

3.42 The first possibility is that the joint account is intended to be a pool of their joint resources, in which case the money in the account will belong to them jointly: there is no need to apportion the money according to their respective contributions.[111] In *Re Bishop*,[112] for example, a husband and wife opened a bank account, to which they both contributed, in unequal amounts, out of their own resources, and for no specific purpose. Each spouse withdrew money at will, for both housekeeping and investment purposes. Some investments were acquired in the name of one of the spouses only. Stamp J held that, where a joint account was opened by spouses, on the terms that either could draw from it, then, in the absence of evidence that it was opened for a specific purpose, each spouse could draw on it for his or her own benefit (and not necessarily for the benefit of both); and that if one of them purchased a chattel for his or her own benefit or made an investment in his or her own name, that chattel or investment belonged to the person in whose name it was purchased or invested. He further held that, on the death of the husband, the moneys standing to the credit of the joint account accrued beneficially to his wife. It is also clear from the decision that, where shares have been purchased

---

[110] Very often the issue is one of certainty of intention rather than certainty of subject matter and this must be borne in mind when considering the case law.
[111] See, for example, *Jones v Maynard* [1951] Ch 572.   [112] [1965] Ch 450.

in the name of one spouse only, any 'rights issue' made in respect of those shares also belongs to that spouse and does not become joint property.[113]

Such arrangements between husband and wife do not necessarily have to be **3.43** attended with legal consequences as between the two spouses while the marriage is still subsisting.[114] They do not necessarily 'result in contracts even though there may be what as between other parties would constitute consideration for the agreement'.[115]

Presumption of advancement

Where a joint account is opened by a husband in the joint names of husband and **3.44** wife, and the only money paid into the account is that of the husband, a different question arises, namely whether the presumption of advancement operates in favour of the wife. This again is a matter of intention. If the purpose of opening the account was mere convenience[116] (or, indeed, any purpose which rebuts the presumption of advancement) the surviving wife will not take the balance. However, if the intention was to make provision for the surviving wife, then she will be so entitled.[117]

It is not entirely clear how such an arrangement should be analysed. In the case of **3.45** a certain and unchanging asset, there ought not to be any difficulty; but an active bank account is very different. One possibility is that, as soon as a cheque is paid into the joint account, it thereupon constitutes a gift to the wife, although it is a gift liable to be diminished by the husband exercising his power to draw upon the account, so that in the end the wife would only get the balance remaining. However, as Megarry J pointed out, in *Re Figgis*,[118] such an analysis is 'quite unreal'.

> A husband who over 50 years has paid into a joint account some £10,000 a year, and at his death has drawn out all but £1,000, would on this analysis have made gifts of £500,000 to his wife, only to take back £499,000 of what he has given. This may be the law; it might even be equity; but it is indisputably remarkable.

On the other hand, a gift of whatever stands to the credit of the bank account at the husband's death runs the peril of being accounted testamentary in nature, so as to require due execution as a will.[119]

---

[113] See also *Re Young* (1885) 28 Ch D 705; *Gage v King* [1961] 1 QB 188.

[114] *Gage v King* [1961] 1 QB 188.

[115] *Balfour v Balfour* [1919] 2 KB 571, 578–579, *per* Atkin LJ.   [116] See para 3.49 below.

[117] *Re Figgis* [1969] 1 Ch 123. See also *Re Pattinson* (1885) 1 TLR 216; *Re Harrison* (1920) 90 LJ Ch 186.

[118] [1969] 1 Ch 123, 149.

[119] ibid. In an Irish case, *Owens v Greene* [1932] IR 225, and three Canadian cases, *Hill v Hill* (1904) 8 Ont LR 710, *Shortill v Grannan* (1920) 55 DLR 416 and *McKnight v Titus* (1933) 6 Mar Prov R 282, it was held that an attempt to pass interests on death by putting money into joint accounts was an attempted testamentary disposition and as such it was invalid. *Young v Sealey, supra,* held otherwise; and *Re Reid, supra,* held that there was an immediate gift.

3.46 However, the appropriate analysis, according to the High Court of Australia, in *Russell v Scott*[120] is as follows:

> A person who deposits money in a bank on a joint account vests the right to the debt or the chose in action in the persons in whose names it is deposited, and it carries with it the legal right to title by survivorship... The vesting of the right and title to the debt or chose in action takes effect immediately, and is not dependent upon the death of either of the persons in whose names the money has been deposited. In short it is not a testamentary disposition.

In other words, 'by placing the money in the joint names, the deceased did then and there and by that act give a present right of survivorship'.

3.47 Thus, it seems that the correct analysis is that there is an immediate gift of a fluctuating and defeasible asset, consisting of the chose in action for the time being constituting the balance in the bank account.[121] The fact that the account is in joint names and that the presumption of advancement might apply does not prevent the husband from withdrawing moneys from the account for his own purposes: indeed, withdrawals would be regarded as withdrawals of his own money. In effect, he is considered to have reserved for himself a power of revocation. What the wife takes by way of advancement is the balance remaining at the husband's death. If this is correct (and it probably is), then it follows that the moneys in the account during the husband's lifetime belong to him: at least, he could withdraw sums of money from the account and spend or apply them for his own purposes, so that, if he were to buy some asset with the money, that asset would belong to him alone and he would not have held it on trust for his wife (or for himself and his wife). In any event, the result in such a case is still that the balance in the account at the date of death accrues to the wife by survivorship.[122]

3.48 The presumption of advancement can also operate in a similar manner and with similar results in relation to bank accounts in the joint names of father and child,[123] although the presumption may be rebutted by evidence to the contrary. Thus, in *O'Neill v IRC*,[124] where the deceased, a resident of Northern Ireland, had opened bank accounts in the Isle of Man in his and his daughter's joint names, it was held that the presumption did not operate because he retained de facto control of the accounts and his motive in creating them was to conceal his interest from the Inland Revenue and from his estranged wife.

---

[120] (1936) 55 CLR 440, esp 448, 455.   [121] *Re Figgis, supra*, at 149.
[122] ibid 146. Megarry J explicitly did not decide this point, however, and commented that 'the subject is worthy of academic disputation'. See also *Young v Sealey* [1949] Ch 278 and *Russell v Scott* (1936) 55 CLR 440.
[123] See, for example, *Re Warwick* (1912) 56 SJ 253; *Re Reid* (1921) 50 OLR 595.
[124] [1998] STC (SCD) 110. See also *Lavelle v Lavelle* The Times, 9 March 2004.

Joint accounts for specific purposes

A joint account may be opened for a specific purpose only, as in *Marshal v*   **3.49**
Crutwell,[125] where an ailing husband put his account in joint names only for
greater convenience in the management of his affairs and where the wife drew all
cheques at the direction of her husband. In such a case, the surviving wife will not
take the balance of the account upon the first death.[126]

No beneficial joint tenancy

Although property, including a bank account, is put in joint names, it clearly   **3.50**
does not follow that the beneficial interest is also held jointly, as in *Standing v
Bowring*,[127] where a widow transferred Consols into the joint names of herself and
her godson, with the express intention that he, in the event of his surviving her,
should have the Consols for his own benefit, but that she should have the dividends during her life. The Court of Appeal held that the legal title of the godson
as joint tenant of the stock was complete, although he had not assented to the
transfer until he was called upon to re-transfer it; and the evidence showed clearly
that she did not, when she made the transfer, intend to make her godson a mere
trustee for her except as to the dividends. The relationship did not give rise to the
presumption of advancement, but the presumption of a resulting trust was nega-
tived by the evidence. In other words, this was an irrevocable settlement for herself
for life, remainder to the godson absolutely.

---

[125] (1875) LR 20 Eq 328. See also *Young v Sealey* [1949] Ch 278 and *Russell v Scott* (1936) 55
CLR 440 (in which the presumption could not have applied, but where there was direct evidence of
a lack of intention to make a gift). Cf *Beecher v. Major* (1865) 2 Dr & Sm 431.

[126] However, as Megarry J noted in *Re Figgis* [1969] 1 Ch 123, 145:'. . . in the nature of things a
deposit account is far less appropriate than a current account as a provision for convenience'.

[127] (1885) 31 Ch D 282. See also *Re Harrison* (1920) 90 LJ Ch 186, 191. Cf *Beecher v Major*
(1865) 2 Dr & Sm 431.

4

CERTAINTY OF OBJECTS[1]

A. Introduction

Trusts must have 'certainty of objects'. It is well established[2]—and probably **4.01** self-evident—that, in the case of a private trust,[3] the beneficiaries must be defined with sufficient certainty to enable the trustees to execute the trust properly, according to the settlor's intentions. The settlor must 'mark out the metes and bounds which are to fetter the trustees'.[4] The trustees must be in a position to know, with certainty, in favour of whom trust income or capital must be distributed; and, in the event of some error or default on the part of the trustees, the court must know, with certainty, how it should execute the trusts, or what remedy, if any, it ought to provide or make available to whom. 'The principle can be concisely stated by saying that, in order to be valid, a trust must be one which the

---

[1] See generally G W Thomas, *Powers* (Sweet & Maxwell, 1998) ('*Thomas*') Ch 3, on which much of this present chapter is based; (1982) 98 LQR 551 (CT Emery); (1971) 29 CLJ 68 (JA Hopkins); (1971) 87 LQR 31 (JW Harris); (1971) 24 CLP133 (H Cohen); (1974) 37 MLR 643 (Y Grbich); (1974) 38 Conv (NS) 269 (L McKay); (1973) 7 VUWLR 258 (L McKay); (1975) 4 Anglo-Am LR 442 (S Fradley); [1980] Conv 263 (L McKay); [1982] Conv 432 (A Grubb); [1984] Conv 22 (P Matthews); [1984]Conv 304 (J Martin) and 307(DJ Hayton).

[2] See, for example, *Morice v Bishop of Durham* (1805) 10 Ves Jr 522, 540, *per* Lord Eldon LC.

[3] Charitable trusts are not subject to the same requirement of certainty of objects. Provided there is a clear intention to devote property exclusively to charity, the generality of the description of the charitable purpose or object will not be fatal and a specific charitable purpose or object will be found.

[4] *Re Park* [1932] 1 Ch 580, 583, *per* Clauson J.

Court can control and execute.'[5] Similarly, in the case of a power, the objects in whose favour the power has been conferred must be defined with sufficient certainty to enable the donee of the power to exercise it properly, in accordance with the donor's intentions. The donee must be able to know, for example, whether a particular individual qualifies as an object—and in whose favour he may properly exercise his discretion—and thus be sure that the proposed exercise will not be excessive. The court must likewise be in a position to determine whether the power has been exercised excessively, or whether a particular individual has standing to complain of some other error or default on the part of the donee.[6] Thus, a requirement of 'certainty of objects' is common to all private trusts and powers alike.

4.02 However, the test of what constitutes 'certainty of objects' need not be—and indeed is not—the same for all trusts and powers. The intentions of a settlor or donor will differ according to the kind of trust imposed or the kind of power conferred; and, in consequence, the duties owed by trustees towards their beneficiaries or by donees of powers towards their objects will also vary.

B. Fixed Trusts

4.03 In its simplest form, a 'fixed trust' could simply be a direction to trustees to hold the trust fund (or its income) on trust for named individuals, or for a class of existing beneficiaries (for example the settlor's living grandchildren), in equal or (specified) unequal shares. In these cases, the settlor's overriding intention (ie a distribution of the trust fund in equal or unequal shares) cannot be carried into effect unless it is possible to identify all the named individuals or all the members of the class (as the case may be), ie to compile a complete list of all the qualifying beneficiaries.[7] There 'can be no division in equal shares amongst a class of persons unless all the members of the class are known'.[8] In both these examples (the named individuals and the existing class), such a complete list can be compiled immediately on the creation of the trust. In many cases—most notably those which involve the fulfilment of some condition or contingency—the actual number and specific identity of beneficiaries (and thus the quantum or extent of each beneficiary's interest) cannot be determined at the inception of the trust. Indeed, it is possible that no such beneficiary ever satisfies the relevant condition or contingency, in which case there

---

[5] *IRC v Broadway Cottages Trust* [1955] Ch 20, 30, *per* Jenkins LJ.

[6] *Re Gulbenkian's Settlement Trusts* [1970] AC 508, 524, *per* Lord Upjohn. See also *Wild v Smith* [1996] OPLR 129.

[7] *IRC v Broadway Cottages Trust* [1954] 1 All ER 878, 881, *per* Wynn-Parry J, and [1955] Ch 20, 29, *per* Jenkins LJ; *Re Gulbenkian's Settlement Trusts* [1970] AC 508, 524, *per* Lord Upjohn. See also [1984] Conv 304 (J Martin) and 307 (D Hayton).

[8] *IRC v Broadway Cottages Trust* [1955] Ch 20, 29.

will be a resulting trust for the settlor (or his estate). Nevertheless, in all these cases, both the maximum number and the extent of beneficial interests as at the relevant time (and at any given time) have been fixed by the settlor: the trusts themselves identify precisely who is or will become entitled to what at the relevant time and entitlement is not dependent on the discretion of any person. The same is true of a trust to divide the income of a trust fund, during an appointed period, among a class of persons for the time being living or in existence, and if more than one in equal shares: all the members of the class at any given time must be known.[9] The fundamental principle is simple: if it is clear, from the terms of the intended trusts, that the trustees will not be able to compile a complete list of all qualifying beneficiaries at the relevant time, those trusts will fail.

C. Powers of Appointment

The object of a power, unlike the beneficiary of a trust, is not entitled to a partic-   **4.04**
ular share of or interest in the property which is the subject matter of the power, unless and until that power is actually exercised in his favour. The object of a power merely has a hope that the donee of the power, in his discretion, will exercise it in his favour. Equitable ownership of the relevant property, pending the exercise of the power, rests with others. A particular disposition may (*inter alia*) take the form of a direct gift to, or an express or implied trust in favour of, a class of beneficiaries, coupled with a power to select (or exclude or appoint) one or more of those beneficiaries, or, alternatively, a power to appoint (or select or exclude) in favour of one or more of a class of objects, coupled with an express or implied gift in default of appointment.[10] In each of these cases, the objects of the relevant power, will not have any interest in the relevant property, by virtue of their status as objects, unless and until the power is exercised in their favour. Instead, the beneficiaries of the direct gift or fixed trust (in the first case) and those entitled in default of appointment (in the second case) will have vested, but defeasible, interests in the property; and those interests will be defeated, wholly or partially, upon any exercise of the power. Thus, in such a case, there can be no question of any particular object *qua* object being entitled to a particular fixed interest: who (if anybody at all) gets what (if anything), and when, are matters within the discretion of the donee of the power (who may or may not be a trustee).

The duties owed by a donee of a power vary considerably according to whether the   **4.05**
donee is an ordinary individual or a trustee (or other fiduciary). These duties are

---

[9] *IRC v Broadway Cottages Trust* [1955] Ch 20, 29. The 'relevant time' will, of course, vary according to the precise form of the trusts, but the underlying principle remains the same: see *Thomas* 81–82.
[10] For a detailed discussion of the differences between these types of disposition, see *Thomas* paras 2-61–2-75.

examined in greater detail below.[11] However, one feature which all powers have in common (irrespective of their nature or the status or character of the donee) is that they can be exercised only in favour of those who are proper objects of the power.[12] Any exercise of a power in favour of a non-object will be an excessive, if not a fraudulent, execution, in respect of which the appointor will be liable. Thus, putting it at its lowest, it is essential, for the protection of the donee, that he knows with certainty whether a particular individual is a qualifying object or not. Similarly, if a particular individual complains to the court (as he could do if the donee of the power is a trustee) that, as a qualifying object, he has not been considered as a potential recipient of bounty by the trustee-donee, the court must be able, as a preliminary step, to determine whether or not that individual really is a member of the class of objects. Thus, even in the case of a simple power, there must be some degree of certainty of objects.

In some cases, the class of objects may be so small and well defined that there would be no difficulty in identifying and compiling a complete list of each and every one of its members, if this were required, for example under a trust for a widow for life, with remainder to such of her children as she may appoint. At the other extreme, the class of objects may be comprised of thousands—or even millions—of persons.[13] In such a case, it would be impossible to compile, at any given time, a complete list of all the members of the relevant class of objects. Nevertheless, the relevant power is capable of being valid. It is also clear that the donor of such a power does not intend that each and every member of the class should receive some benefit: whether any member does so or not is left to the discretion of the donee.

4.06 Moreover, it is not reasonable to attribute to the donor an intention that, when the donee is exercising or considering exercising the power, he should nonetheless survey and consider a complete list of all the objects. What is needed is 'an appreciation of the width of the field'.[14] As Harman J stated in *Re Gestetner Settlement*,[15] in relation to trustees upon whom a mere power had been conferred:

> ... they are bound, as I see it, to consider at all times during which the trust is to continue whether or no they are to distribute any and if so what part of the fund and, if so, to whom they should distribute it. To that extent, I have no doubt that there is a duty on these trustees: a member of the specified class might, if he could show that the trustees had deliberately refused to consider any question at all as to the want or suitability of any member of the class, procure their removal; but there is not ... any duty, as I see it, on the trustees to distribute the whole of either income or capital

---

[11] See Chapter 11 below.
[12] See, for example, *Re Gulbenkian's Settlement Trusts* [1970] AC 508, 518, *per* Lord Reid.
[13] *Re Park* [1932] 1 Ch 580; *Re Gulbenkian's Settlement Trusts* [1970] AC 508; *Blausten v IRC* [1972] Ch 256; *Re Manisty's Settlement* [1974] Ch 17; *Re Hay's Settlement Trusts* [1982] 1 WLR 202.
[14] *Re Hay's Settlement Trusts* [1982] 1 WLR 202, 210, *per* Megarry V-C.
[15] [1953] Ch 672, 688–689. See also *Re Coates* [1955] Ch 495; *Re Sayer* [1957] Ch 423; *Re Hain's Settlement* [1961] 1 WLR 440, 445; *Re Gulbenkian's Settlement Trusts* [1970] AC 508.

among the members of the specified class; ... there is no obligation on the trustees to do more than consider—from time to time, I suppose—the merits of such persons of the specified class as are known to them and, if they think fit, to give them something. The settlor had good reason ... to trust the persons whom he appointed trustees; but I cannot see here that there is such a duty as makes it essential for these trustees, before parting with any income or capital, to survey the whole field, and to consider whether A is more deserving of bounty than B. That is a task which was and which must have been known to the settlor to be impossible, having regard to the ramifications of the persons who might become members of this class.

If, therefore, there be no duty to distribute, but only a duty to consider, it does not seem to me that there is any authority binding me to say that this whole trust is bad. In fact, there is no difficulty, as has been admitted, in ascertaining whether any given postulant is a member of the specified class ... There being no uncertainty in that sense, I am reluctant to introduce a notion of uncertainty in the other sense, by saying that the trustees must worry their heads to survey the world from China to Peru, when there are perfectly good objects of the class in England ... There is no uncertainty in so far as it is quite certain whether particular individuals are objects of the power. What is not certain is how many objects there are; and it does not seem to me that such an uncertainty will invalidate a trust worded in this way.

Thus, the donee must be able to say, with certainty, whether a particular individual is or is not an object of the power; and those entitled in default of appointment must clearly be entitled to restrain the donee from exercising the power save among those who are clearly qualifying objects.[16]

Although this test—the so-called 'any given postulant test'—referred to 'any' individual, some subsequent decisions took the view that it was not necessary that the donee should be able to say of literally any individual, no matter who, whether he was or was not a member of the class of objects, but that it was sufficient that this could be said of one single individual, even if there might be considerable uncertainty as to other possible claimants.[17] However, this alternative interpretation of the test of certainty for a mere power was decisively rejected by the House of Lords in *Re Gulbenkian's Settlements*.[18] Thus, a trustee, as the donee of a mere power, and the court must be in a position in which it can be said with certainty 'who is within and who is without the power',[19] or (in another formulation) whether it can be said with certainty 'that any given individual is or is not a member of the class',[20] and 'the accent must be upon that word "any", for it is not simply the individual whose claim you are considering who is spoken of'.[21] The stricter version of

4.07

---

[16] *Re Gulbenkian's Settlement Trusts* [1970] AC 508, 525, *per* Lord Upjohn.
[17] *Re Gibbard's Will Trusts* [1967] 1 WLR 42; *Re Leek* [1967] Ch 1061, 1076; *Re Gulbenkian's Settlements* [1967] Ch 126, 134.
[18] [1970] AC 508, esp. 524, *per* Lord Upjohn. Lord Hodson and Lord Guest agreed (at 520). Lord Donovan, though inclined to share this view, reserved his opinion on it (at 526). See also *Thomas* 85–86.
[19] [1970] AC 508, 525.
[20] *McPhail v Doulton* [1971] AC 424, 456, *per* Lord Wilberforce.
[21] *Re Baden's Trusts (No 2)* [1973] Ch 9, 28, *per* Stamp LJ.

the 'any given postulant test' must therefore be satisfied if the power is to be valid.[22]

D. Discretionary Trusts

4.08 In addition to a fixed trust, a mere power and a trust power, there is also something called a 'power in the nature of a trust' or, as it is now more commonly called, a 'discretionary trust'. In simple terms, a discretionary trust partakes of the character of both a fixed trust and a power of appointment. The trustees of an exhaustive discretionary trust, like the trustees of a fixed trust, are under a duty to distribute the trust income or capital (or both) but, like the donees of a power of appointment, they have a discretion as to which members of the class of objects will actually receive some benefit, as well as to the amounts and times of, and perhaps conditions attached to, distributions.[23] They are obliged to exercise the discretion conferred upon them: they must not only consider from time to time whether or not to make a distribution, but they must also actually exercise their discretion.

4.09 As in the case of a power of appointment, the class of discretionary objects under a discretionary trust may be so small and well defined that a complete list of its members could be compiled without difficulty. On the other hand, the class of objects may be enormously wide.[24] In such a case, the trustee 'would surely never require the preparation of a complete list of names, which anyhow would tell him little that he needs to know'. The trustees only have to 'make such a survey of the range of objects or possible beneficiaries as will enable them to carry out their fiduciary duty'.[25] They are under a duty to consider exercising their discretion, just as in the case of a mere power conferred upon them, but they must carry out a fuller and more comprehensive inquiry: the difference is one of degree and not one of principle.[26]

4.10 Until *McPhail v Doulton*,[27] the test of certainty of objects of a discretionary trust was the same as that for fixed trusts, ie the 'complete list test'.[28] Behind this strict

---

[22] The nature of the test may be illustrated by reference to a simple mathematical example. A 'prime number' is a number which is divisible, without remainder, only by itself and by the number 1. On the basis of this certain definition, there should be no difficulty in ascertaining whether any given number (any given postulant) is a prime number or not.

[23] See, generally, *Thomas* 86–91; [1970] ASCL 197 (JD Davies); (1974) 37 MLR 643 (Y Grbich); (1976) 54 Can BR 229 (MC Cullity).

[24] *McPhail v Doulton* [1971] AC 424.

[25] Sachs LJ pointed out, in *Re Baden's Deed Trusts (No 2)* [1973] Ch 9, 20, that the word 'range' has 'an inbuilt and obvious element of elasticity, and thus provides for an almost infinitely variable range of vision suitable to the particular trust to be considered'. He concluded: 'Assessing in a businesslike way "the size of the problem" is what the trustees are called on to do.'

[26] *McPhail v Doulton* [1971] AC 424, 457, *per* Lord Wilberforce.

[27] [1971] AC 424. See also *Re Beckbessinger* [1993] 2 NZLR 362.

[28] *IRC v Broadway Cottages Trust* [1955] Ch 20; *Re Ogden* [1933] Ch 678.

approach lay the fundamental principle that the court would have to intervene in order to execute the trust in the event of default by the trustees. It was assumed, largely on the basis of nineteenth-century authorities,[29] that the only means of executing the trust available to the court was to order an equal distribution. This meant that the discretionary trust was regarded, in effect, as a 'fixed' trust; and, in order to make an equal distribution, the court would need to know, with sufficient certainty, the identity of all the beneficiaries. However, in *McPhail v Doulton*,[30] the House of Lords overruled *Broadway Cottages* and held that the test for certainty of objects of a discretionary trust was similar to that for mere powers, namely the 'any given postulant test'. Equal division might be sensible in many instances, but there was nothing inherent in the nature of a discretionary trust, nor in the court's powers over trusts, which called for any such rigid rule. Indeed, there were numerous examples in the law reports where a different type of execution had been ordered, as appropriate to the circumstances.[31] If called upon to execute a discretionary trust, the court could do so in the manner best calculated to the settlor's or testator's intentions: this might be by the appointment of new trustees, by authorizing or directing representatives of the class of beneficiaries to prepare a scheme of distribution, or even, in a proper case, by directing the trustees to make a distribution.[32] Thus freed from the requirement to make an equal distribution, there was no compelling need to insist on a complete list of all qualifying objects; and, consequently, the House of Lords established that the test for certainty of objects of discretionary trusts ought to be similar to that accepted by the House of Lords in *Re Gulbenkian's Settlements*[33] for mere powers, namely that 'the trust is valid if it can be said with certainty that any given individual is or is not a member of the class'.[34]

This test did not remain long in this simplified state. The House of Lords simply determined the question of law (ie what correct test of certainty of objects should be applied in the case of a discretionary trust) in *McPhail v Doulton*. The actual application of that test to the *Baden* trusts was remitted to the Chancery Division. Brightman J held the trusts valid. On appeal from his decision[35] (which was upheld), the judges in the Court of Appeal clearly had difficulty in applying the

4.11

---

[29] Such as *Kemp v Kemp* (1801) 5 Ves Jr 849 and *Morice v Bishop of Durham* (1805) 10 Ves Jr 522. Trusts of the kind found in *Burrough v Philcox* (1840) 5 My & Cr 72 are not considered to be discretionary trusts here, but rather to be a combination of a fixed trust and a mere (fiduciary) power. *Burrough v Philcox* was not even cited to the House of Lords in *McPhail v Doulton*.

[30] [1971] AC 424 (Lord Reid, Viscount Dilhorne, and Lord Wilberforce; Lords Hodson and Guest dissenting).

[31] For example, *Mosely v Moseley* (1673) Fin 53; *Clarke v Turner* (1694) Free Ch 198; *Warburton v Warburton* (1702) 4 Bro PC 1; *Harding v Glyn* (1739) 1 Atk 469; and *Richardson v Chapman* (1760) 7 Bro PC 318.

[32] [1971] AC 424, 457, *per* Lord Wilberforce.   [33] [1970] AC 508.

[34] [1971] AC 424, 456, *per* Lord Wilberforce. Lord Keith and Viscount Dilhorne agreed (at 437 and 446–447).

[35] [1973] Ch 9.

new test in the strict form in which it was enunciated in the House of Lords in both *Re Gulbenkian's Settlements* and *McPhail v Doulton*.[36] One of the main difficulties centred on the significance of the words 'or is not' in the strict version of the test: how does one prove a negative? This difficulty, if not impossibility, was avoided by the majority in the Court of Appeal by adopting the view that, if it cannot be proved affirmatively that a particular postulant is a qualifying member of the class of objects, then he must be regarded as someone who is not within it.[37] As long as there is a 'substantial number' of objects clearly within the class, the discretionary trust will be valid.[38] Thus, although it can be said that the appropriate test of certainty of objects for discretionary trusts is the 'any given postulant test', there remains some uncertainty as to its precise meaning and operation.

E. Conceptual and Evidential Certainty

4.12 It is also necessary to distinguish between two forms of certainty, namely 'conceptual certainty' and 'evidential certainty'.[39] Whether a complete list has to be compiled (for a 'fixed' trust) or the 'any given postulant test' satisfied (for mere powers and discretionary trusts), the basic issue remains the same: is it possible to ascertain *with certainty* those persons whom the settlor or donor intended should qualify as beneficiaries or objects? Whichever test of 'certainty of objects' applies, the trustees need to know whether any particular individual is or is not a member of the relevant class and, therefore, to be included in a complete list, in one case, or as an object of a discretion in the other. In order to answer this question, it is necessary to have a sufficiently clear and unambiguous definition or description of the beneficiaries or objects; and it must also be possible to determine, on the evidence available, whether any particular individual actually meets, or answers to, that description or definition. As Upjohn LJ stated in *Re Hain's Settlement*:[40]

---

[36] For a detailed discussion of the difficulties encountered by the Court of Appeal, see *Thomas* 89–96.

[37] This view leans towards the more relaxed test of certainty advocated in relation to mere powers in *Re Gibbard's Will Trusts* [1967] 1 WLR 42, and which had been decisively rejected in *Re Gulbenkian's Settlements* [1970] AC 508.

[38] See, in particular, [1973] Ch 9, 19–20, *per* Sachs LJ; 22–23, *per* Megaw LJ. What, however, is meant by a 'substantial number'?

[39] In *Re Tuck's Settlement Trusts* [1978] Ch 49, 59, Lord Denning MR referred to this distinction as 'most unfortunate'. Nevertheless, it has become a central feature in the context of 'certainty of objects': see, for example, *Re Baden's Deed Trusts (No 2)* [1973] Ch 9, 19 and 20, *per* Sachs LJ. What the reported cases do not tell us is what is (or might be) meant by 'conceptual certainty' itself (or linguistic or semantic certainty, which are assumed to be synonymous and interchangeable expressions) or how it may be determined. Judges have used these expressions in different senses, without ever addressing the basic question of what they mean by them or what they hope to achieve by using them: see generally *Thomas* 91–96.

[40] [1961] 1 All ER 848, 853. See also *Re Sayer* [1957] Ch 423, 432; *Re Gulbenkian's Settlements* [1970] AC 508, 524; and *McPhail v Doulton* [1971] AC 424, 457.

... first the language used to describe the class may be ambiguous or uncertain as a matter of construction or secondly, on the evidence the class may in fact be incapable of ascertainment.

Conceptual certainty

It is clear that the words or concepts used by a settlor or the donee of a power to define or describe the beneficiaries of the trust, or the objects in whose favour the power may (or, in the case of a discretionary trust, must) be exercised, must be sufficiently precise and unambiguous for it to be possible to determine in principle whether a particular individual is or is not a member of the relevant class. Clearly, where the objects of the power are named individuals, or where the words or concepts used are unambiguous—for example, 'sons', 'daughters', 'children', 'first cousins'—there should be no difficulty in principle in determining what it is that a particular individual must establish or satisfy if he is to qualify as a member of the class.[41] On the other hand, the words or concepts used by the donor may be ambiguous or imprecise—so much so that their meaning cannot be rendered precise and unambiguous even by process of construction—so that it is impossible to say with certainty whether they apply to or describe a particular individual. Examples which have been suggested (rightly or wrongly) include 'old friends',[42] 'a good citizen', a 'pure blooded Englishman',[43] and 'persons having a moral claim on X'.[44] In such cases, the concept is said to be so imprecise that it is impossible to say with certainty that *even one* qualifying individual can be found who falls within it. On the other hand, the concept may simply be imprecise in the sense that it cannot be said with certainty whether or not any individual, 'no matter who', falls within its boundaries, but it may nonetheless be said with some certainty that a particular individual does so (or even that a few individuals do so). Thus, it may be said that A, B, and C were all clearly 'old friends' of X on the basis of any reasonable meaning that might be attributed to that phrase, but that it is impossible to say with certainty whether D, E, or F were also 'old friends' of X, unless and until that phrase is seen to have a definite and precise meaning.   4.13

However, the search for 'conceptual certainty' has not generally been regarded as an abstract, philosophical exercise. The court usually seeks to find an acceptable   4.14

---

[41] There may also be a question, of course, as to whether the class is intended to exclude illegitimate, legitimated, or adopted persons. In broad terms, such persons will be deemed to be included under statutory provisions (if not included expressly) and their exclusion will depend on the presence of a contrary intention (which may have to be determined by process of construction), unless the relevant instrument preceded the relevant statute (none of which had retrospective effect). However, this does not render the underlying defining concepts uncertain.

[42] See *Re Coates* [1955] Ch 495; *Re Gibbard* [1966] 1 All ER 273; *Re Gulbenkian's Settlements* [1970] AC 508, 524; *Re Barlow's Will Trust* [1979] 1 WLR 278.

[43] An example given by Lord Evershed MR in *Re Allen* [1953] Ch 810, 819, of a phrase which would be too conceptually uncertain even in the context of a condition precedent.

[44] See *Re Leek* [1969] 1 Ch 563, 579.

workable meaning or sense for a particular word or description, one based on a sufficient degree of probability as to what or whom the settlor had in mind, and bearing in mind that what is sufficient may well vary according to the nature of the disposition, the context in which it appears, and the circumstances of the case. Wherever possible, resolving a question of certainty will be guided by pragmatism. As Lord Wilberforce stated in *Blathwayt v Baron Cawley*[45] (in relation to a condition subsequent) a judge should 'judge the degree of certainty with some measure of common sense and knowledge and without excessive astuteness to discover ambiguities'. The meaning of particular words and expressions will depend upon the context in which they are used; and the same words or expressions may be held insufficiently precise in one disposition while being found certain in another.[46] Pragmatism will generally not be sacrificed to theory. As Roxburgh J observed in *Re Coates*:[47]

> ... I find no necessity to introduce into this subject the difficult doctrine of conceptions having an *a priori* certainty.
> This question of uncertainty is a vexed question. Of course, language draws a series of mental pictures in the mind of the person hearing the words spoken. Those pictures are sometimes fairly well defined, and sometimes blurred in outline, but they are never very precise. Language is a medium which disdains mathematical rules ...

Thus, all that is really meant by conceptual certainty in this context is simply whether or not it is possible to read or peruse the language used by the settlor or donor and thereby ascertain, sufficiently unambiguously, what he meant by them; or, in other words, whether it is possible to determine (if necessary, by process of construction and resorting to any admissible evidence), by reference to the description or criteria laid down by the settlor or donor, which persons or classes of persons he intended should be the beneficiaries of the trust or the objects of the power.[48]

4.15 The court will generally adopt a benevolent construction of any provision, if it can, in order to save it from invalidity. The approach outlined by Megarry J in *Re Lloyd's Trust Instruments*[49] applies to trusts and powers as much as anything else. What is required is that some 'fair meaning'[50] be put on the phrase used. The difficulty must simply not be so great as to make it impossible to give meaning

---

[45] [1976] AC 397, 425. See also *Re Allen* [1953] Ch 810, 816; *Re May* [1917] 2 Ch 126; *Re May (No 2)* [1932] 1 Ch 99; *Re Wright* (1937) 158 LT 368; *Re Morrison's Will Trusts* [1940] Ch 102; *Re Evans* [1940] Ch 629; *Re Samuel* [1942] Ch 1; *Re Tepper's Will Trusts* [1987] Ch 358; *Re McKenna* [1947] IR 277; *McCausland v Young* [1948] NI 72, [1949] NI 49. Cf *Re Borwick* [1933] Ch 657.

[46] *Sifton v Sifton* [1938] AC 656, 675–676; *Fillingham v Bromley* (1823) Turn & R 530; *Re Wright* [1907] 1 Ch 231; *Re Coxen* [1948] Ch 747.

[47] [1955] Ch 495, 497, 499 (gift to friends nominated by the testator's wife).

[48] See the broad principles set out by Lord Upjohn in *Re Gulbenkian's Settlements* [1970] AC 508, 522–524.

[49] Unreported decision of 24 June, 1970, cited in *Brown v Gould* [1972] Ch 53, 56–57.

[50] The phrase is that of Lord Jessel MR in *Re Roberts* (1881) 19 Ch D 520, 529: see *Brown v Gould* [1972] Ch 53, 56.

to the expression.[51] Thus, it would be more accurate, perhaps, to talk in terms of a high degree of probability, rather than invoke 'conceptual certainty'. A particular word, expression, or concept may be clear and unambiguous in one context, but completely uncertain and ambiguous in another (as in the case of conditions).[52] Thus, it is possible (albeit perhaps unlikely) that a seemingly irredeemably ambiguous expression may, in the right context, bear a clear and certain meaning, for example a gift to 'pure blooded Englishmen' might be valid if (say) the testator was the President of The Pure Blooded Englishmen Society.

This should be distinguished, however, from those cases in which a particular word **4.16** or expression may not be uncertain or ambiguous in itself, but, rather, may be capable of bearing more than one meaning, all equally certain. In these latter cases, it is simply a question of deciding (if possible) which meaning was actually intended. Thus, in both wills and deeds, the primary meaning of the word 'children' is 'the first generation only of legitimate descendants by any marriage'.[53] However, the particular context may indicate that the word 'children' was intended to refer to more remote generations of descendants or even the whole line capable of inheriting from the named person, that it refers to illegitimate children, stepchildren, or adopted children,[54] or that it is confined to children of a first or particular marriage, and so forth. Similarly, the word 'issue' prima facie means 'descendants of every degree',[55] but the context may show that it actually refers only to children. In other words, the precise intended meaning of the word or expression may differ in accordance with, and will depend on, the context in which it is used.[56] Nevertheless, each of these possible meanings is clear. There is no conceptual uncertainty here: it is simply a question of ascertaining which of several certain concepts was actually intended. If this task proves impossible, then the disposition will indeed fail for uncertainty, but this will not necessarily be failure due to conceptual uncertainty.

Evidential certainty

On the assumption that a sufficient degree of precision is present in the definition **4.17** or description of the class of beneficiaries or objects, the question of evidential

---

[51] *Doe d Winter v Perratt* (1843) 9 Cl & Fin 606, 689; *Brown v Gould* [1972] Ch 53, 56.
[52] On conditions, see *Thomas* 96–102.
[53] *Williams on Wills* (7th edn, 1995) vol 1, 698; *Norton on Deeds* (2nd edn, 1928), 462.
[54] Questions as to the inclusion or exclusion of legitimated, illegitimate, and adopted children are now determined in accordance with (i) the provisions of the relevant statute, (ii) the presence of a contrary intention in the relevant instrument, and (iii) the date of the relevant disposition. The legislation (the Legitimacy Acts 1926 and 1976, the Adoption Acts 1950, 1958, and 1976, the Family Law Reform Act 1969, the Children Act 1975) did not have retrospective effect. See *Williams on Wills*, vol 1, 688–694, 701–703.
[55] *Williams on Wills*, vol 1, 704; *Norton on Deeds*, 467.
[56] Consider the word 'dependants', for example. See *Re Ball* [1947] Ch 228; *Re Sayer* [1957] Ch 423; *Re Saxone Shoe Co Ltd's Trust Deed* [1962] 2 All ER 904; *Re Baden's Deed Trusts (No 2)* [1973] Ch 9, 21; *Simmons v White Brothers* [1899] 1 QB 1005, 1007; *Wild v Smith* [1996] OPLR 129.

certainty remains to be resolved, ie does a particular individual actually meet the stipulated criteria, or answer to the description or definition laid down, so as to qualify as a member of the relevant class? As Sachs LJ put it in *Re Baden's Deed Trusts (No 2)*,[57] 'once the class of persons to be benefited is conceptually certain it then becomes a question of fact to be determined on evidence whether any postulant has on inquiry been proved to be within it . . .'. Suppose, for example, that the class of beneficiaries or objects includes employees and ex-employees of a particular company and their respective relatives, and that there is no uncertainty in the meaning of the words 'relative' and 'ex-employee'. Suppose, too, that A claims that he is a distant relative of an employee of the company, or that B claims that he was employed by the company many years ago. Suppose, however, that there is no satisfactory evidence that A is related to the relevant employee, nor that B is an ex-employee, for example because all relevant records have disappeared or been destroyed. In these circumstances, there is no uncertainty in the meaning of the concepts employed, but there is evidential uncertainty as to whether A or B qualifies as a member of the class.

4.18 The effect of evidential uncertainty varies according to the kind of trust or power in question. In broad terms, evidential uncertainty is fatal to the validity of a 'fixed' trust, but it is not so in the case of a discretionary trust or a mere power.

Evidential certainty for 'fixed' trusts

4.19 Since, in the case of a 'fixed' trust, a complete list of all beneficiaries is required for certainty and validity, any evidential uncertainty will be fatal. If the primary duty imposed on the trustees is to distribute the trust property or its income in equal (or specified unequal) shares, such a trust cannot be carried into effect unless the maximum number of qualifying beneficiaries is known.[58]

4.20 However, once again, the issue must be viewed pragmatically: 'absolute' certainty is not required; and a remote theoretical possibility that there is some qualifying beneficiary whose existence is not known to the trustees can be ignored. What is required in the case of a 'fixed' trust, where a complete list of beneficiaries is essential, is a high degree of probability (perhaps as high a degree of probability as one can reasonably achieve) that all those who should be in the relevant class can be and have been found. In *Re Saxone Shoe Co Ltd's Trust Deed*,[59] Cross J expressed the view that:

> . . . the answer depended on what was probable and not on what was theoretically possible. When the court directs an inquiry to ascertain next of kin, or distributes a

---

[57] [1973] Ch 9, 19.

[58] *Re Sayer* [1957] Ch 423; *Re Saxone Shoe Co Ltd's Trust Deed* [1962] 2 All ER 904.

[59] [1962] 2 All ER 904, 912. Earlier authorities did not really contradict this view: in *IRC v Broadway Cottages Trust* [1955] Ch 20, it had been admitted that the class of beneficiaries in question was not ascertainable; in *Re Hooper's 1949 Settlement* (1955) 34 ATC 3, Danckwerts J held that lack of completeness was merely a possibility, and not definite; and in *Re Eden* [1957] 2 All ER 430 it was clear that considerable difficulty would be encountered in ascertaining all the objects.

fund on the master's certificate given in answer to the inquiry, it is always possible that the class will never be or has not been completely ascertained. Someone, for example, may have gone abroad, married and had children, and then returned home without telling his relatives of his marriage and died supposedly a bachelor. All that is necessary is that the court should be satisfied that it is probable that the class can be or has been ascertained.

Similarly, in *Re Eden*,[60] Wynn-Parry J pointed out that:

> . . . mere difficulty of ascertainment is not of itself fatal to the validity of the gift. As has been pointed out, it is a matter of degree, and it is only when one reaches, on the evidence, a conclusion that is so vague, or that the difficulty is so great that it must be treated as virtually incapable of resolution, that one is entitled, to my mind, to say that a gift of that nature is void for uncertainty.

These cases were, of course, concerned with discretionary trusts, and not fixed trusts; and, following *McPhail v Doulton*,[61] the test of certainty of objects which would now be applicable to them would be the 'any given postulant test' and not the 'complete list test'. Nevertheless, having been decided at a time when a complete list of beneficiaries was considered necessary, they are probably still relevant to the question of the degree of evidential 'certainty' required for a fixed trust. There is no compelling reason to think that absolute certainty should now be essential. In many instances, trustees could never say, with absolute certainty, that they have found all those who qualify as beneficiaries: it is always theoretically possible that someone has been overlooked. The trustees must simply be in a position in which there is a probability that a complete list of all beneficiaries can be compiled.[62] The governing consideration must be that the primary duty of the trustees of a fixed trust is to distribute the fund to all those who are entitled and, in order to fulfil that duty, they must be in a position in which they are able, by means of all reasonable inquiries (and, if necessary, with the assistance of the court), to compile a complete list of all those persons intended to take an interest in the fund, and not just those who are clearly shown to be qualifying beneficiaries on the current state of available evidence. It would clearly be impossible to determine the maximum number and identity of all beneficiaries intended to qualify if there is either an ambiguous set of criteria which have to be satisfied (ie conceptual uncertainty) or if the state of available evidence is such that there is reasonable doubt concerning the status of any individual, ie doubt as to whether that individual should be placed on the list at all (for example because of the destruction or loss of relevant evidence), as opposed to doubt as to his continued existence or whereabouts. Thus, a reasonably or substantially complete list of all those 'persons with whom the donor had ever travelled in a railway coach'[63] could not be **4.21**

---

[60] [1957] 2 All ER 430, 433.   [61] [1971] AC 424.
[62] As to the degree of probability required, see *Thomas* 115–116.
[63] An example given in argument in *Re Baden's Deed Trusts (No 2)* [1973] Ch 9, 13.

compiled, not because the basic concept is unclear but because insufficient evidence is available to enable the task to be carried out.

4.22   Evidential uncertainty is usually distinguished from an inability to ascertain the continued existence or whereabouts of a beneficiary, although, arguably, they are but different aspects of the same thing.[64] The basis of this distinction is that there may be no conceptual uncertainty and the state of available evidence is such that there is no difficulty in compiling a complete list of all those persons who satisfy the criteria laid down by the settlor; and yet there may be uncertainty as to the continued existence or whereabouts of some of those persons.[65] In such circumstances, the trustees can apply to the court for directions.[66] The court may then declare that the relevant share of the fund be placed and held in a separate account, or paid into court, in the hope that the missing beneficiary is found in the future, or it may make a *Benjamin* order[67] and distribute the fund on the assumption that the individual is dead. The latter course does not prevent a 'missing' beneficiary who later appears from recovering his share from those to whom it was distributed. A *Benjamin* order 'does not vary or destroy beneficial interests. It merely enables trust property to be distributed in accordance with the practical probabilities.'[68] However, the trustees themselves will then be protected.

4.23   Trustees (or personal representatives) who distribute property among only those beneficiaries of whose claims they then had notice may also be protected by the provisions of section 27 of the Trustee Act 1925,[69] provided the relevant procedures as to giving appropriate notices and making advertisements are complied with. Again, this provision does not extinguish the beneficial interest of a beneficiary of whose claim the trustees had no notice: such a beneficiary may still follow the property representing his entitlement into the hands of any recipient (other than a purchaser). Such a provision therefore does not indicate that a complete list of beneficiaries need not be compiled. On the contrary, the trustees may distribute the property among only 'the persons entitled thereto' and it assists early distribution by indicating a method by which the trustees could carry out an inquiry without resorting to court and thereby achieve what is in substantial probability a complete list.

---

[64]   See (1982) 98 LQR 551, esp 556–551, 568, and 578 (CT Emery). The distinction is said to be based on the observations of Lord Upjohn in *Re Gulbenkian's Settlements* [1970] AC 508, 524. See also *Thomas* 116–117; [1984] Conv 22, 29, n 61 (P Matthews) and [1984] Conv 304, 306 (J Martin).

[65]   See *Re Gulbenkian's Settlements* [1970] AC 508, 524, *per* Lord Upjohn; *McPhail v Doulton* [1971] AC 424, 457, *per* Lord Wilberforce. Cf *Re Baden's Deed Trusts (No 2)* [1973] Ch 9, 19, *per* Sachs LJ.

[66]   *Re Gulbenkian's Settlements* [1970] AC 508, 524, *per* Lord Upjohn.

[67]   *Re Benjamin* [1902] 1 Ch 723. See also *Re Green's Trusts* [1985] 3 All ER 455.

[68]   *Re Green's Trusts* [1985] 3 All ER 455, 462, *per* Nourse J.

[69]   Similar provisions in s 17 of the Family Law Reform Act 1969 have been repealed: Family Law Reform Act 1987, s 20.

Evidential certainty for discretionary trusts and mere powers

In order to satisfy the 'any given postulant test', there must be conceptual certainty, **4.24** so as to have a clear set of criteria which any claimant must satisfy. In addition, there must also be evidential certainty in order to establish whether any given postulant actually does satisfy those criteria. Thus, it is not enough, in practical terms, that the words 'relative' or 'ex-employees', for instance, bear a sufficiently clear and precise meaning: it must also be possible to determine, as a factual matter, whether A actually is or is not a 'relative' or whether B actually is or is not an 'ex-employee' in the context of the disposition in question.[70] The question in such a case is whether the 'any given postulant test' can be satisfied or not, and therefore whether the discretionary trust or mere power is valid or void for uncertainty.

As in the case of 'fixed' trusts, it is essential to bear in mind the difference between **4.25** conceptual uncertainty and 'evidential difficulties'.[71] The court, it is said, is never defeated by evidential uncertainty. As Lord Upjohn made clear, in *Re Gulbenkian's Settlements*,[72] 'if the trustees feel difficulty or even doubt upon the point the Court of Chancery is available to solve it for them'. Thus, if there is any uncertainty as to whether a particular individual is or is not *as a matter of fact* a member of the class of objects, the trustee of a discretionary trust (or the donee of a mere power) can obtain a ruling on the matter from the court, as well as directions as to how to deal with such a situation.[73]

However, this still leaves open the question of what exactly it is that has to be **4.26** proved. If the 'any given postulant test' favoured by the House of Lords in both *Re Gulbenkian's Settlements* and *McPhail v Doulton* requires that it be possible to say *affirmatively* of *any* individual (no matter who) that he is a member of the class of objects or, alternatively, to say *affirmatively* that he is not, then there is no room for a category of ambiguous or borderline cases. However, the apparent strictness of this test—especially the need to prove a negative which seems to be encapsulated in the words 'or is not'—can lead to major difficulties.[74] Thus, in

---

[70] In the *Baden* litigation, for example, the trustees could not trace a number of short-term ex-employees of the company, or their relatives and dependants: *Re Baden's Deed Trusts (No 2)* [1972] Ch 607.

[71] ibid [1973] Ch 9, 19, *per* Sachs LJ. See also [1970] AC 508, 523, 524.

[72] [1970] AC 508, 523, 524 (but see (1982) 98 LQR 551, 557 (CT Emery)).

[73] It is clear, from both *IRC v Broadway Cottages Trust* [1955] Ch 20 and *Re Gulbenkian's Settlements* [1970] AC 508 (see, especially, the arguments in favour of invalidity at 512–513), that uncertainty of fact was considered fatal only to a 'fixed' trust or a discretionary trust, and not to a mere power. The assimilation of discretionary trusts and mere powers (for certainty purposes) in *McPhail v Doulton* [1971] AC 424 removed the objection to factual uncertainty in the case of discretionary trusts: indeed, it seems to have been conceded that, provided there is conceptual certainty, the next question ('where are these objects to be found?') was 'an administrative matter'.

[74] For a more detailed discussion of the difficulties thrown up by the 'any given postulant test', including uncertainties as to its actual meaning and effects, see *Thomas* 119–126.

Re Baden's Deed Trusts (No 2),[75] it was argued that the trusts were void for uncertainty on the basis that it was not possible to say affirmatively of *any* individual that he or she was *not* one of the 'relatives' or 'dependants' of one of the specified groups of objects. In *Re Baden*, although Stamp LJ took the strict and literal version of the 'any given postulant test', the majority in the Court of Appeal (Sachs LJ and Megaw LJ) concluded that such an argument was 'totally irrelevant' and 'wholly fallacious'. Any claimant who could not prove he was a qualifying object could be assumed not to be one.[76] Indeed, Megaw LJ added[77] that 'the test is satisfied if, as regards at least a substantial number of objects, it can be said with certainty that they fall within the trusts; even though, as regards a substantial number of other persons, if they ever for some fanciful reason fell to be considered, the answer would have to be, not "they are outside the trust", but "it is not proven whether they are in or out"'. What a 'substantial number' might be was 'a question of common sense and of degree in relation to the particular trust'. All three judges concluded (as Brightman J had done at first instance)[78] that the relevant provision was not void for uncertainty, although there are clearly inconsistent interpretations of the 'any given postulant test' and of the precise requirements of evidential certainty in the various judgments.

Summary

4.27 By way of summary, it can be said that the test of certainty of objects for 'fixed' trusts remains 'the complete list test' and that the test of certainty of objects for discretionary trusts (as well as mere powers conferred on trustees) is the 'any given postulant test'. Conceptual certainty is an essential prerequisite of both tests. However, if the expression 'conceptual certainty' is to be used at all (in lieu of a more flexible phrase such as 'sufficient degree of precision'), it is suggested that it must be viewed and applied in a pragmatic and flexible manner, so that fanciful possibilities and purely theoretical possibilities can be ignored. What is required is a high degree of probability as to the intended sense of the word or expression under scrutiny (the degree of probability varying with the particular context). It can also be said that evidential certainty is essential for the validity of a 'fixed' trust (otherwise a complete list of beneficiaries cannot be compiled) but that it is not essential for discretionary trusts (or mere powers). However, even in the case of a 'fixed' trust, this requirement ought not to be exaggerated. That which is purely fanciful or a mere theoretical possibility ought not to prevent such a trust from being carried out and enforced.

[75] [1973] Ch 9.   [76] ibid 20, *per* Sachs LJ and at 22–23, *per* Megaw LJ.
[77] ibid 22–23.   [78] [1972] Ch 607.

F. Mere Powers Conferred on Non-Fiduciaries[79]

It is not uncommon to find that, under the terms of a trust, a power of appointment **4.28**
(or some analogous power) has been conferred not on the trustees but on someone
who holds no fiduciary office and owes no fiduciary duties whatsoever. A common
example is the case of a power of appointment in favour of children or issue, conferred by a testator's will on his widow. *Re Gulbenkian's Settlements*[80] clearly
involved a mere power conferred on a trustee. As a fiduciary power, such a power
carries with it a duty to consider its exercise from time to time and this, in turn,
requires the trustee to survey the class of objects (although the extent of that duty
is not as great as in the case of a discretionary trust). A mere power conferred on a
non-fiduciary, on the other hand, carries no such duty at all. The donee can put
aside the power and need not address the question of its exercise at all, and the
court will not interfere. The application of the same 'any given postulant test' in
determining the certainty of objects of such a power (a bare power) may, therefore,
be 'unnecessarily draconian'.[81] Thus, a power of appointment in favour of the
donor's 'friends' ought to be valid, it is argued, if the donee could appoint in
favour of a person who is on any view a 'friend', even if there are other persons of
whom it cannot be said with certainty whether they are 'friends' or not. In other
words, the power is valid if it can be said, in principle, that just one person meets
the stipulated criteria (in effect, applying the *Re Allen*[82] test). In such a case, it is
said that any conceptual uncertainty would not prevent the court from restraining either an improper appointment or one which could not be shown to be
proper.

Whether this looser test is the correct test remains to be determined. There is some **4.29**
slight support for it in *Re Leek*,[83] but this may not have survived *Re Gulbenkian*.[84]
In any event, whether this view is accepted or not, the fact remains that conceptual certainty is not based solely on the need for the donee of a power to be able to
distinguish between a proper and an improper object, but also on the right of
those entitled in default of appointment not to have their interests divested or
determined otherwise than by means of a valid appointment in favour of a qualifying object. And, of course, no distribution can be determined to be proper
unless there is conceptual certainty. The suggestion that some looser test than the
'any given postulant test' should apply to a non-fiduciary mere power seems to
assume that it might be possible to ascertain with certainty that one person
is clearly within the class of objects. However, this would not be conceptual

---

[79] See *Thomas* 126–130.   [80] [1970] AC 508.
[81] See (1982) 98 LQR 551, 582 (CT Emery).
[82] [1953] Ch 810 (a case of a condition precedent).   [83] [1967] Ch 1061, 1076.
[84] [1970] AC 508, esp 525.

certainty. Nor would it be the same 'any given postulant test' as was laid down in *Gulbenkian* and *McPhail v Doulton*.

4.30 On the other hand, such a strict approach may be too harsh in relation to a non-fiduciary mere power. Suppose, for example, that a testator left his estate to his widow for life and, subject thereto, on trust for such of *his* 'old friends' as his widow (who is not a trustee) may by will appoint. Many would regard the conferring of such a power as a reasonable act and, indeed, one which does not misuse or abuse ordinary language in any way. Therefore, it might seem unreasonable for the law to strike it down on the ground of uncertainty. There must, of course, be some test of validity here, for otherwise the widow could appoint in favour of someone who was a complete stranger in relation to the testator. One possible analysis is that what the testator meant by the expression 'old friends' was simply what his widow says it means, ie his 'old friends' (in his usage) were those persons identified as such by his widow. However, even this construction does not necessarily resolve the uncertainty unless some test of conceptual 'certainty' is adopted which is looser or more relaxed than the seemingly over-strict 'any given postulant test' (which might just as well be called the 'necessary and sufficient conditions' test). Whether the courts consider a looser test to be appropriate at all and, if so, what form it might take, are questions that remain to be resolved.[85]

G. Time to Establish Certainty[86]

4.31 *Conceptual* certainty must exist at the date of creation of the relevant trust or power. This is the case irrespective of whether trust income or capital is to be distributed immediately or at some point in the future (for example at the end of the perpetuity period). It is the intention of the settlor or donor and the meanings which he attached to particular expressions that dictate what is and what is not permissible in any given case, and not the meanings that others may ascribe to them in the future.

4.32 It does not necessarily follow, however, that *evidential* certainty must also be shown to exist at the date of creation of the trust or power. In the case of 'fixed' trusts, a complete list of beneficiaries is required, and the relevant trusts may be such that a complete list can be compiled *ab initio* and at all times during the subsistence of the trusts. On the other hand, it is sometimes the case that it is impossible for the trustees to know, at the creation of the trust, who will qualify as beneficiaries at the relevant time, let alone the extent of their respective interests, and therefore impossible for them to compile a complete list of such

---

[85] See *Thomas* 129–130 for further discussion of these questions.   [86] ibid 131–133.

beneficiaries from the outset. This is so, for example, in the common case of ultimate trusts in remainder (following discretionary trusts) for such of the settlor's issue living at the expiry of the relevant perpetuity period (of, say, eighty years) and, if more than one, in equal shares absolutely. Thus, it would seem reasonable that the relevant date at which sufficient evidential certainty must exist is the date on which the required complete list needs to be available and must therefore be compiled. It may be that the issue has little practical impact in any event, in that it should be possible, other than in the most fanciful cases, to determine, at the date of creation of the trust, whether the trustees ought to be able, in principle, to compile a complete list of beneficiaries entitled under the 'fixed' trusts when the relevant time arrives. On the assumption that the terms of the trust—and specifically the definition or description of those who are intended to qualify as beneficiaries, and also the extent or quantum of their respective interests—are sufficiently certain, then, if it can be seen that there is insufficient evidential certainty to enable the trustees to compile such a complete list at the date of the settlement, if that were the relevant date, it is difficult to see how there could be sufficient evidential certainty in the future.

In the case of a discretionary trust and also a mere power conferred on a trustee, **4.33** there must be *evidential* certainty, it seems, at all times during the duration of the trust or power. *Conceptual* certainty must be seen to exist *ab initio*. Once this is established, it is then a question of fact, to be determined on evidence, whether any particular individual is or is not a member of the relevant class of objects. Therefore, as soon as the discretionary trust or power becomes exercisable, there must be sufficient *evidential* certainty to enable the trustees to exercise it effectively.

It seems clear, however, that, if there is sufficient *evidential* certainty to enable a **4.34** complete list to be compiled at the creation of the settlement, then the trusts cannot fail thereafter on the ground of evidential uncertainty.[87] This approach seems unobjectionable. Once the trust is established, the trustees are under a duty to ensure that sufficient information is acquired and retained, and proper records are maintained, by them, in order for them to fulfil their duties at the appropriate times: hence, there should not be any difficulty about being able to ascertain the identity of those who were, are, and in due course become beneficiaries. If they fail to do so, this should give rise to a claim for breach of trust, and not to an argument for invalidity. If, for some reason beyond their control, there is some evidential uncertainty which they cannot resolve themselves, the court is always available to assist them in doing so.

---

[87] *Re Hain's Settlement* [1961] 1 All ER 848.

H. Resolution of Uncertainty by a Third Party

4.35 It is well established that questions of *evidential* uncertainty may be resolved by referring the determination of a factual question to a third party.[88] The extent to which *conceptual* uncertainty may be resolved (if at all) by the same means is less clear, however. In *Re Coxen*,[89] for example, the testator had devised a dwelling house to his trustees with a direction that it should fall into residue 'if in the opinion of my trustees she shall have ceased permanently to reside therein'. Jenkins J held that two conditions were laid down: (i) the ceasing of personal residence; and (ii) such cesser being permanent (which required intention); and that the opinion of the trustees that the event had happened, and not just the happening of the event, was what brought about the cesser of the interest.[90] This, in his view, made 'a very material difference':

> If the testator had insufficiently defined the state of affairs on which the trustees were to form their opinion, he would not I think have saved the condition from invalidity on the ground of uncertainty merely by making their opinion the criterion, although the declaration by the trustees of this or that opinion would be an event about which there could be no uncertainty. But ... the relevant double event is sufficiently defined to make it perfectly possible for the trustees (as the judges of fact for this purpose) to decide whether it has happened or not, and in my view the testator by making the trustees' opinion the criterion has removed the difficulties which might otherwise have ensued from a gift over in a double event the happening of which, though in itself sufficiently defined may necessarily be a matter of inference involving nice questions of fact and degree.

Thus, there is a clear distinction between the resolution of a factual question by the trustees (which is acceptable) and the resolution of conceptual uncertainty. If there is such conceptual uncertainty that the court cannot resolve it, no other person can do so either.

4.36 This was followed in *Re Jones*,[91] where a testator directed his trustees to purchase an annuity for his daughter and directed that 'if at any time ... [she] shall in the uncontrolled opinion of [the trustees] have social or other relationship with' a named person, then she would forfeit one-half of the annuity payments. Danckwerts J held that the provision for forfeiture was insufficiently certain to enable the trustees to come to a proper decision and the condition subsequent was therefore void for uncertainty. The 'mere fact that the decision of the question is referred to the trustees' opinion does not overcome the difficulty of uncertainty'.[92]

---

[88] *Dundee General Hospitals Board of Management v Walker* [1952] 1 All ER 896.
[89] [1948] Ch 747, esp 758–762.   [90] ibid 761.
[91] [1953] Ch 125.   [92] ibid 130. Cf *Donner v Knight* (1809) 1 Taunt 417 ('associate, continue to keep company with, or cohabit, or criminally correspond with' held valid); and *Jeffreys v Jeffreys* (1901) LT 417 ('associate' held uncertain).

Similarly, in *Re Burton's Settlements*,[93] Upjohn J accepted that 'the fact that the decision is given to the trustees cannot give certainty to a clause which is otherwise uncertain'.

The courts have not always been consistent, however. In *Re Tuck's Settlement* **4.37** *Trusts*,[94] for example, it was provided that, in the event of any dispute or doubt as to whether a wife was 'an approved wife', the decision of the Chief Rabbi in London of the Portuguese or Anglo-German community should be conclusive. Of this particular provision, Lord Denning MR stated: 'if there is any conceptual uncertainty in the provisions of this settlement, it is cured by the Chief Rabbi clause'.[95] It is not entirely clear whether this was intended to be a general statement of principle or not. It would appear, from the context in which this statement was made, that Lord Denning regarded the Chief Rabbi as having been asked to give a decision on the interpretation of words used 'in the business in which he is expert'.[96] If so, there is much to be said for such an approach. In any event, if it is accorded wider significance, it would have been a minority view. Indeed, it would then be difficult to see how it could have been relevant, for the clause itself restricted the Chief Rabbi to decisions 'as to . . . facts' only, and all three judges agreed that there was sufficient conceptual certainty without regard to 'the Chief Rabbi clause'. However, such an approach is not unique.[97] Nevertheless, there is no strong authority for the proposition that *conceptual* uncertainty, as well as evidential uncertainty, can be cured or resolved by reference to the opinion of a third party.

This is not to say, however, that the required conceptual certainty can never be **4.38** provided by a third party. This is illustrated by Eveleigh LJ's view of 'the Chief Rabbi clause' in *Re Tuck's Settlement Trusts*,[98] which he construed as saying, in effect, that the settlor's definition of 'Jewish faith' was the same as the Chief Rabbi's.

> I therefore do not regard the settlor as leaving it to the Chief Rabbi to discover what
> the settlor meant or to provide a meaning for the expression used by the settlor

---

[93] [1955] Ch 82, 95. See also *Re Wright's Will Trusts* [1981] LS Gaz R 841; *Nichols v Allen* (1881) 130 Mass 211, 39 Am Rep 445; *Brody Estate* (1962) 26 D & C 2d 409; *Tatham v Huxtable* (1950) 81 CLR 639. Cf *Re Mills* [1930] 1 Ch 654.

[94] [1978] Ch 49.

[95] ibid 62. Russell LJ expressly refrained from ruling on the provision. Eveleigh LJ construed it differently (at 66). See also *Re Saxone Shoe Co Ltd's Trust Deed* [1962] 2 All ER 904, 912, where Cross J clearly thought that the words 'in the opinion of the directors' removed any doubt there may otherwise have been as to whether certain persons were 'dependants'. According to *Re Badens Deed Trusts (No 2)* [1973] Ch 9, it is difficult to argue now that the word 'dependants' is conceptually uncertain; but, at the time of *Re Saxone*, this was not entirely clear: see, for example, *Re Ball* [1947] Ch 228; *Re Sayer* [1957] Ch 423.

[96] [1978] Ch 49, 61.

[97] See, for example, *Re Leek* [1969] Ch 563, esp at 579, *per* Harman LJ; *Re Coates* [1955] Ch 495, esp 499, *per* Roxburgh J.

[98] [1978] Ch 49, 66.

when the meaning is in doubt. The court itself will not do so and I doubt if *Dundee General Hospitals*... allows me to say that the court will permit the Chief Rabbi to do so. The fact is that the Chief Rabbi knows what he means by 'Jewish faith' and the testator has said that he means the same thing. There is no element of speculation here. *Id certum est.*

Indeed, it is possible to read Lord Denning's observations on 'the Chief Rabbi clause' as expressing the same view.

4.39 In any event, there is clearly a difference between asking a third party to determine, with any reasonable degree of certainty, what a settlor or donor meant by some expression such as 'old friends' and asking that third party to decide which persons he or she would consider to be, or have been, 'old friends' of the settlor or donor. If and in so far as the relevant expression is conceptually uncertain in the first case, it is because the precise meaning ascribed to it by the settlor or donor is unknown; and any meaning which the third party might ascribe to it might or might not coincide with what the settlor or donor intended. In the second case, however, the precise meaning of the expression is known: it is that which the third party himself chooses to ascribe to it. On this analysis, the main question would seem to be whether it is clear that the settlor or testator left the definition of the word or expression—the giving of content to the concept—to the third party (as opposed to leaving it to the third party to determine the meaning which the settlor or testator himself intended it to have). However, even here, there must presumably be some means of controlling the decision of the third party: it can hardly be the case, for instance, that a third party could claim that, in his opinion, someone who was a complete stranger to the testator was actually an old friend of his. Thus, if such provisions are effective at all (and, it is suggested, in the appropriate context, such as conditions precedent, there is no reason why they should not be so), it is not because they provide a means by which certainty is provided for a particular concept (in the essentialist sense) but because the settlor or testator has indicated that something less strict than 'conceptual certainty' is required, and because the law allows the disposition to be effective on this basis. In effect, the third party is acting as an expert: the sense which he ascribes to a word or expression can be said to be acceptable if it is a sense which other similar experts might ascribe to it, but it is not necessarily a sense which would be universally recognized or applicable.

4.40 However, it is difficult to see how such an analysis could assist in relation to the objects of discretionary trusts or mere powers. The 'any given postulant test', by its very nature, cannot be applied unless there is conceptual certainty. If the court cannot discern the meaning of a word or expression, it is difficult to see how a third party can do so, for both are operating under the same handicap. A third party can provide evidential certainty, but he or she is not better placed than anyone else to determine the essential quality of an 'old friend' of the settlor or donor (or whatever the expression may be). In so far as decisions such as *Re Tuck's Settlement Trusts*[99] and similar cases suggest otherwise, they can be distinguished on the basis that they are concerned with conditions precedent, in relation to which there is a much looser approach.

I. Administrative Unworkability[100]

The requirement of 'certainty of objects' for both trusts and powers alike is closely **4.41** linked with the nature and extent of the duties imposed on trustees and donees and, in turn, on the issue of enforcement by the court in the case of any default by such trustee or donee. In broad terms, it may be said that, whereas a non-fiduciary donee of a mere power owes neither a duty to exercise the power nor even a duty to *consider* its exercise, a trustee upon whom a mere power has been conferred *qua* trustee owes a duty to consider periodically whether to exercise the power or not (even if there is no duty actually to exercise it); and a trustee of a discretionary trust is under a duty both to consider the exercise of, and actually to exercise, his discretion. One outstanding question is the extent to which such duties can be carried out (if at all) if and when the class of objects is very large—comprising, say, hundreds of thousands or even millions of people.[101] Strictly speaking, this is not a question of (un)certainty of objects. Rather, it seems that this issue is concerned more with the duties of trustees and donees of powers, and specifically with the question whether those duties can be carried out or, in default, enforced by the court.[102] Nevertheless, even if conceptual and evidential certainty are established, there may still exist a third kind of 'uncertainty' (often referred to as 'administrative unworkability') which is related to the excessive size of the class of objects and which, in the case of a 'fixed' trust and a discretionary trust (but not a mere power), may result in invalidity. This issue is discussed in greater detail below.[103]

---

[99] [1978] Ch 49.   [100] See *Thomas* 138–139, 274–291.

[101] *Re Baden's Deed Trusts (No 2)* [1973] Ch 9, 20; *Re Hay's Settlement Trusts* [1982] 1 WLR 202, 210.

[102] cf *Re Beatty's Will Trusts* [1990] 1 WLR 1503 (noted in (1991) 107 LQR 211 (JD Davies)).

[103] See para 11.15 below.

5

THE CONSTITUTION OF
AN EXPRESS PRIVATE TRUST

A. General Principle

The general principles governing the constitution of trusts were set out by Turner LJ in *Milroy v Lord*:[1]   **5.01**

> ...in order to render a voluntary settlement valid and effectual, the settlor must have done everything which, according to the nature of the property comprised in the settlement, was necessary to be done in order to transfer the property and render the settlement binding upon him. He may of course do this by actually transferring the property to the persons for whom he intends to provide, and the provision will then be effectual, and it will be equally effectual if he transfers the property to a trustee for the purposes of the settlement, or declares that he himself holds it in trust for those purposes; and if the property be personal, the trust may, as I apprehend, be declared either in writing or by parol; but, in order to render the settlement binding, one or other of these modes must, as I understand the law of this court, be resorted to, for there is no equity in this court to perfect an imperfect gift. The cases go further to this extent, that if the settlement is intended to be effectuated by one of the modes to which I have referred, the court will not give effect to it by applying another

---

[1] (1862) 4 De GF & J 264, 275.

of those modes. If it is intended to take effect by transfer, the court will not hold the intended transfer to operate as a declaration of trust, for then every imperfect instrument would be made effectual by being converted into a perfect trust.

5.02 Two of the most common methods of creating and constituting an express private trust are (a) a transfer of property, whether during the owner's lifetime or on his death,[2] to a trustee, coupled with an effective declaration that the property is to be held on specified trusts; (b) an express (and necessarily lifetime) declaration of trust by the owner of property of himself as trustee of that property ('self-declaration').[3] To these may be added a third, namely (c) the exercise of an appropriate dispositive power (such as a power of appointment or power of advancement) so as to create trusts of the property which is the subject matter of the power.

B. Transfer to Trustees

5.03 The most common method of creating an express private trust is by means of a transfer of property to a trustee, coupled with an effective declaration of the applicable trusts. Such a transfer may take place during the settlor's lifetime (thereby creating an *inter vivos* settlement) or on his death (thereby creating testamentary trusts). In order to be an effective disposition and constitute such a trust, the relevant formalities must be complied with.

5.04 A trust intended to be created by a transfer of property to a trustee is not completely constituted unless and until the transfer of that property is complete and enforceable. If it is not, the intended trustee is a mere volunteer; and equity will not come to the aid of a volunteer. 'There is no equity . . . to perfect an imperfect gift.'[4] Thus, in *Jones v Lock*,[5] where a father placed a cheque payable to himself in the hands of his baby, saying 'I give this to baby', the gift failed, because the cheque was not endorsed and could not pass by delivery. Similarly, in *Richards v Delbridge*,[6] where the lessee of a mill wrote and signed a memorandum on his lease 'This deed and all thereto belonging I give to [ERR] from this time forth, with all the stock in trade', and delivered the lease to ERR's mother, the gift failed, because the lease could be transferred effectively only by assignment by deed.[7] Moreover, a failed transfer will not be construed instead as a self-declaration of trust: a clear intention to give the property, even if ineffective, is inconsistent with an intention to retain it as trustee.[8]

---

[2] Trusts may also arise on death under statute, eg on an intestacy, under ss 46 and 47 of the Administration of Estates Act 1925.

[3] Trusts may also be constituted under contract: see paras 5.57 *et seq* below.

[4] *Milroy v Lord* (1862) 4 De GF & J 264.   [5] (1865) 1 Ch App 25.

[6] (1874) LR 18 Eq 11.   [7] See also *Antrobus v Smith* (1806) 12 Ves Jr 39.

[8] *Richards v Delbridge, supra; Milroy v Lord, supra; Pappadakis v Pappadakis* [2000] WTLR 719. See, however, *Re Rose* [1952] Ch 499, 510–511.

There are certain limited exceptions (or apparent exceptions) to the principle **5.05**
that equity will not assist a volunteer, and these are considered below.[9] First, however, the basic provisions governing the effective constitution of a trust will be
considered.

Testamentary trusts

An effective testamentary disposition must be made by a will or codicil executed **5.06**
in compliance with the formal requirements of section 9 of the Wills Act 1837.
A will is 'an instrument by which a person makes a disposition of his property to
take effect after his decease and which is in its own nature ambulatory and revocable during his life'.[10] Section 9 of the Wills Act 1837 provides:

No will shall be valid unless—

(a) It is in writing, and signed[11] by the testator, or by some other person in his
presence and by his direction;[12] and
(b) It appears that the testator intended by his signature to give effect to the
will;[13] and
(c) the signature is made or acknowledged[14] by the testator in the presence of[15]
two or more witnesses present at the same time;[16] and
(d) each witness either—
(i) attests[17] and signs the will; or
(ii) acknowledges[18] his signature, in the presence of the testator (but not necessarily in the presence of any other witness),

but no form of attestation shall be necessary.

Thus, a testamentary disposition, properly so-called, whether of a legal estate
or equitable interest, cannot be made unless it complies with section 9 of the
1837 Act.

Where property is given by will or codicil to a person as trustee, the trusts cannot **5.07**
be validly declared by a subsequent instrument other than a new will or codicil

---

[9] See paras 5.36–5.45 below.
[10] *Baird v Baird* [1990] 2 AC 548, 556, *per* Lord Oliver. He added: 'It is, of course, axiomatic
that an essential characteristic of a will is that, during the lifetime of the testator, it is a mere declaration of his present intention and may be freely revoked or altered.'
[11] *Hindmarsh v Charlton* (1861) 8 HL Cas 160; *Re Chalcraft* [1948] P 222; *Re Colling* [1972] 3
All ER 729; *In the Estate of Cook* [1960] 1 All ER 689; *Rhodes v Peterson* 1972 SLT 98.
[12] *In the Goods of Clark* (1839) 2 Curt 329.
[13] *Weatherhill v Pearce* [1995] 2 All ER 492; *Wood v Smith* [1992] 3 All ER 556; *Re Mann's Goods*
[1942] P 146; *Re Beadle* [1974] 1 All ER 493.
[14] *Smith v Smith* (1866) 1 P & D 143.
[15] *Casson v Dade* (1781) 1 Bro CC 99; *Weatherhill v Pearce* [1995] 2 All ER 492; *Re Groffman*
[1969] 2 All ER 108; *Brown v Skirrow* [1902] P 3; *Tribe v Tribe* (1849) 1 Rob Ecc 775; *In the Goods
of Piercy* (1845) 1 Rob Ecc 278.
[16] *Wyatt v Berry* [1893] P 5; *Re Davies* [1951] 1 All ER 920.
[17] *In the Goods of Sharman* (1869) 1 P & D 662.   [18] *Couser v Couser* [1996] 3 All ER 256.

which itself satisfies section 9.[19] Failure to do so means that the property will be held on resulting trust for the person(s) entitled to the testator's residuary estate or on his intestacy (as the case may be).

5.08 On death, there is necessarily a complete and effective transfer of property (the deceased's estate) to a personal representative (the executor or administrator, as the case may be). A testamentary trust is therefore completely constituted and (subject to payment of debts, taxes, and other prior charges on the estate) will be enforced, even where the intended trustee has predeceased the testator, or disclaims, or lacks capacity.[20] Equity will not allow a trust to fail for want of a trustee (unless, exceptionally, the identity of the named trustee is an essential prerequisite or condition of the trust).[21]

Inter vivos settlements

Creation of trusts of land

5.09 Section 53(1) of the Law of Property Act 1925 provides:

(1) Subject to the provisions hereinafter contained with respect to the creation of interests in land by parol:

(a) No interest in land can be created or disposed of except by writing signed by the person creating or conveying the same, or by his agent thereunto lawfully authorised in writing, or by will, or by operation of law;[22]

(b) A declaration of trust respecting any land or any interest therein must be manifested and proved by some writing signed by some person who is able to declare such trust or by his will;

…

(2) This section does not affect the creation or operation of resulting, implied or constructive trusts.

The word 'land' is defined widely to include land of any tenure, mines and minerals, corporeal and incorporeal hereditaments, easements, rights and privileges or benefits in land, and also undivided shares in land.[23] Thus, chattels real[24] are included, as are undivided shares in land,[25] but not chattels personal,[26] or

---

[19] *Adlington v Cann* (1744) 3 Atk 141; *Habergham v Vincent* (1793) 2 Ves 204; *Briggs v Penny* (1851) 3 Mac & G 546; *Re Boyes* (1884) 26 Ch D 531. For the operation of secret trusts, however, see paras 28.31–28.53 below.

[20] *Sonley v Clock Makers' Company* (1780) 1 Bro LL 81; *Re Smithwaite's Trusts* (1871) LR 11 Eq 251.

[21] *Re Armitage* [1972] Ch 438, 445.

[22] Oddly, the scope of s 53(1)(a) is not entirely clear. It seems to cover the creation of equitable interests in land other than interests under a trust, eg restrictive covenants. It cannot be limited to legal interests because of s 52(1).

[23] Law of Property Act 1925, s 205(1)(ix), as amended by the Trusts of Land and Appointment of Trustees Act 1996, s 25(2) and Sch 4.

[24] *Forster v Hale* (1798) 3 Ves Jr 696; *Re De Nicols (No 2)* [1900] 2 Ch 410.   [25] See n 23 above.

[26] *Fordyce v Willis* (1791) 3 Bro CC 577, 587; *Bayley v Boulcott* (1828) 4 Russ 345; *Grant v Grant* (1842) 34 Beav 642; *Peckham v Taylor* (1862) 31 Beav 250.7

a partnership in land,[27] or money secured by a mortgage of land,[28] and probably not an interest in the proceeds of sale of land.[29]

Section 53(1)(b) does not require a declaration of trust of land actually to be in writing: it must only be 'manifested and proved' by some writing, ie written evidence will suffice.[30] Such evidence may take the form of a subsequent acknowledgement by the 'person having the right to declare himself a trustee',[31] or a declaration or memorandum to the same effect;[32] a recital in a deed or other instrument, such as a will, a bond, or a marriage settlement;[33] a statement in an affidavit or in a pleading;[34] or in a letter.[35] The 'writing' must be signed by 'some person who is able to declare such trust', who is usually, but not necessarily, the legal owner of the land, for example where property is held by T on bare trust for B, it is B who is able to declare a trust and whose signature is required.[36] It was held in some early authorities that, where S had transferred land to T on trust for B, without signing a declaration of trust in favour of C, it was T (and not S) who had to produce the required signed evidence subsequently.[37] However, the beneficial interest is presumably still vested in S and it is difficult to see why it should not be S who has to provide the requisite evidence of the trust; or, put another way, how T could be the 'person who is able to declare such trust'.

Signature by an agent is not authorized under section 53(1)(b).[38]   **5.11**

A trust found to exist by appropriate evidence satisfying the statute takes effect as   **5.12** from the date of its creation, and not the date on which the evidence comes into existence or the date on which the question is determined[39] or there is part

---

[27] *Forster v Hale* (1798) 3 Ves Jr 696; *Dale v Hamilton* (1847) 16 LJ Ch 126 and 397; *Re De Nicols (No 2)* [1900] 2 Ch 410.

[28] *Benbow v Townsend* (1883) 1 Myl & K 506.

[29] *Stevens v Hutchinson* [1953] Ch 299; *Irani Finance Ltd v Singh* [1971] Ch 59. Cf *Cooper v Critchley* [1955] Ch 431; *Barclay v Barclay* [1970] 2 QB 677. Such an interest is clearly within s 53(1)(c), however.

[30] *Forster v Hale* (1798) 3 Ves Jr 696, 707; *Smith v Matthews* (1860) 3 De GF & J 139; *Re Tyler* [1967] 1 WLR 1269.   [31] *Forster v Hale* (1798) 3 Ves Jr 696, 707.

[32] *Ambrose v Ambrose* (1716) 1 P Wms 321; *Bellamy v Burrow* (1735) Cas t Talb 97.

[33] *Deg v Deg* (1727) 2 P Wms 412; *Moorecroft v Dowding* (1725) 2 P Wms 314; *Re Hoyle* [1893] 1 Ch 84; *Re Holland* [1902] 2 Ch 360.

[34] *Barkworth v Young* (1856) 4 Drew 1; *Hampton v Spencer* (1693) 2 Vern 288; *Cottington v Fletcher* (1740) 2 Atk 155.

[35] *Forster v Hale* (1798) 3 Ves Jr 696; *Morton v Tewart* (1842) 2 Y & C Ch 67.

[36] *Tierney v Wood* (1854) 19 Beav 330; *Kronheim v Johnson* (1877) 7 Ch D 60; *Dye v Dye* (1884) 13 QBD 147. See also *Bridge v Bridge* (1852) 16 Beav 315 (personal property). See also [1984] CLJ 306, esp 316–320 (TG Youdan).

[37] *Gardner v Rowe* (1828) 5 Russ 258; *Smith v Matthews* (1861) 3 De GF & J 139. See also *Mountain v Styak* [1922] NZLR 131; and [1984] Camb LJ 306, 316–320 (TG Youdan).

[38] Or so it has always been assumed. But why should a duly authorized agent not be a person 'able to declare such trust'?

[39] *Gardner v Rowe* (1825) 2 S & S 346; (1828) 5 Russ 258; *Rochefoucauld v Boustead* [1897] 1 Ch 196, 206.

performance of the trusts.[40] In other words, the trust is unenforceable but not void, which may have significant implications, for example, in the event of the settlor's insolvency.

5.13 It must be clear from the 'writing' not only that a trust has been created but also what the terms of the trust were supposed to be.[41] If the precise terms cannot be ascertained, the trust cannot be enforced.[42] However, such terms may be supplied by some unsigned writing, provided it is incorporated by reference into the signed writing or can clearly be connected with it.[43]

5.14 Charitable trusts are also subject to these provisions.[44] The statute, being concerned with questions of proof, may also probably be pleaded as a defence to proceedings in England and Wales for the enforcement of a trust of land outside the jurisdiction.[45]

Dispositions of equitable interests

5.15 Section 53(1)(c) of the Law of Property Act 1925 provides:

> (1) Subject to the provisions hereinafter contained with respect to the creation of interests in land by parol:
>
> ...
>
> (c) A disposition of an equitable interest or trust subsisting at the time of the disposition, must be in writing signed by the person disposing of the same, or by his agent thereunto lawfully authorised in writing or by will.
>
> (2) This section does not affect the creation or operation of resulting, implied or constructive trusts.

Section 53(1)(c), unlike section 53(1)(b), is not restricted to land, but applies to equitable interests in and trusts of both real and personal property. It applies only to a *subsisting* equitable interest: it does not apply to the creation of an equitable interest. Prior to the creation of a trust, the equitable interest is merged in the legal estate and can pass automatically with it and is not treated as separate and distinct.[46] Thus, there is no disposition within section 53(1)(c) when the legal and beneficial owner of property creates a trust: there is no subsisting equitable interest, but the creation of a new one.

---

[40] Law of Property Act 1925, s 55(d).
[41] *Forster v Hale* (1798) 3 Ves Jr 696, 707; *Smith v Matthews* (1860) 3 De GF & J 139, 152; *Mountain v Styak* [1922] NZLR 131.
[42] *Forster v Hale, supra; Morton v Tewart, supra; Smith v Matthews, supra.*
[43] *Forster v Hale* (1798) 3 Ves Jr 696. See also *Morton v Tewart* (1842) 2 Y & C Ch 67, 77.
[44] *Addlington v Cann* (1744) 3 Atk 141.
[45] *Rochefoucauld v Boustead* [1897] 1 Ch 196, 207; *Leroux v Brown* (1852) 12 CB 801. The Act must be pleaded specifically.
[46] *Vandervell v IRC* [1967] AC 291; *Westdeutsche Landesbank v Islington Borough Council* [1996] AC 669, 706; *Re Cook* [1948] Ch 212; *DKLR Holding Co v CSD (NSW)* (1982) 40 Aus LR 1. See also (1967) 31 Conv 174 (SM Spencer); [1979] Conv 17 (G Battersby); (1967) 30 MLR 461 (N Strauss); [1966] CLJ 19 (G Jones).

The disposition must actually be in writing, and not simply evidenced in writ- **5.16**
ing.[47] However, where the equitable interest is assigned upon trust, the writing
need not contain the particulars of the trust, which may themselves be made
known orally[48] (but if not made known at all the assignee will hold the interest on
resulting trust).

The word 'disposition' bears a wide meaning.[49] In addition to a straightforward **5.17**
assurance or assignment, it includes a release or surrender of a subsisting equitable
interest,[50] but not a disclaimer[51] or a power of nomination under a pension
scheme.[52] Variations of trusts under the Variation of Trusts Act 1958 are also not
within section 53(1)(c), either because they are impliedly excluded by the 1958
Act or because there is a constructive trust (which is excluded under section
53(2)).[53] It may also be the case that, where there is a change in the membership
of an unincorporated association, where trustees hold property on trust for members, or in the membership of a deed of settlement company, some writing signed
by the transferor within section 53(1)(c) may not be necessary.[54] The members are
considered to be contractually bound to each other, but it is not entirely clear why
this should exclude the need for writing when their interests are enlarged or
reduced or acquired from other members. Paperless dealings in the CREST system in shares in UK public companies are excluded by subsidiary legislation from
the scope of section 53(1)(c).[55]

Where trustees hold property on trust for B and, in the exercise of a power of **5.18**
appointment, they appoint the property away from B in favour of C (or a class
of persons), this is not a 'disposition' of a subsisting equitable interest: it is a case
of extinguishing B's interest and creating a new one in C. Similarly, if B himself
exercised the power of appointment, it may still not be a 'disposition' by him of his
interest to C: it is certainly not an assignment or other transfer of that interest; nor

---

[47] *Grey v IRC* [1958] Ch 690, 706–707. See also (1984) 47 MLR 385, 392 (B Green). The 'writing' may consist of several documents, only one of which is signed, provided they are clearly referable to one another: *Re Danish Bacon Co Ltd Staff Pension Fund Trusts* [1971] 1 WLR 248.
[48] *Re Tyler* [1967] 1 WLR 1269. If it is an equitable interest in land, the particulars of the trust
must be evidenced in writing under s 53(1)(b).
[49] Section 205(1)(ii) of the Law of Property Act 1925 states that 'disposition' includes a conveyance and also a devise or bequest. A 'conveyance' is defined to include a disclaimer, which has,
however, been held not to be a disposition for the purposes of s 53(1)(c); and devises and bequests
are governed by s 9 of the Wills Act 1837 and are not within s 53 at all.
[50] Law of Property Act 1925, s 205(1)(ii). See also [1979] Conv 17, 20–21 (G Battersby).
[51] *Re Paradise Motor Co Ltd* [1968] 1 WLR 1125. See also Law of Property Act 1925, s 52(2)(b).
[52] *Re Danish Bacon Co Ltd Staff Pension Fund Trusts* [1971] 1 WLR 248; *Baird v Baird*
[1990] 2 AC 548. See also *Gold v Hill* (1998–99) 1 ITELR 27 (oral nomination of rights under life
insurance policy).
[53] *Re Holt's Settlement* [1969] 1 Ch 100.
[54] *Ashby v Blackwel & Milton Bank* (1765) Amb 503.
[55] Uncertified Securities Regulations 1995 (SI 1995/3272), Reg 32(5). See also Stock Transfer
Act 1982, s 1(2).

would it seem to be a surrender of that same interest to another: the interest seems to determine automatically on the creation of a new interest in the exercise of the power.[56]

5.19 Section 53(1)(c) does not require that a declaration of trust of personalty (other than such an equitable interest) must be in writing: such a declaration needs no writing at all.[57]

Exclusion of section 53

5.20 Section 53(2) provides that section 53 'does not affect the creation or operation of resulting, implied or constructive trusts'. A statute may not be used as an instrument of fraud.[58] Thus, where land is transferred by S to T on trust but does not comply with section 53(1)(b), it would be fraudulent on T's part to point to the failure to satisfy the statutory formalities and claim the land for himself. S can prove the trust by means of oral evidence; and T would hold the land on trust for S.[59] This applies not just to the transferee/trustee, but also to creditors or volunteers claiming under or through him.[60] The principle is straightforward in the case where S transferred land to T to hold on trust for S, but its application is less clear where T was intended to hold it on trust for B. Can B, a volunteer, enforce the trust; or will T still hold the land on constructive trust for S? This question appears to be unresolved.[61] Upon whom does the fraud have to be perpetrated? On the one hand, it may be said to be S alone, which is supported by the fact that S can apparently assert his beneficial ownership and defeat any intended trust by 'revoking' his declaration or dying, leaving B with no recourse.[62] On the other hand, it ought to be remembered that, long before the Statute of Uses, uses were

---

[56] This is uncertain, however. See *Re Vandervell's Trusts (No 2)* [1974] Ch 269, 320, *per* Lord Denning. The observations of Viscount Simonds in *Grey v IRC* [1960] AC 1, 12 do not seem in point, because he was referring to the continued existence of the same interest. Cf *Re Tyler's Fund Trusts* [1967] 3 All ER 389, at 391–392; and *Oughtred v IRC* [1960] AC 206, 253.

[57] *Paul v Constance* [1977] 1 WLR 527; *Rowe v Prance* [2000] WTLR 249; *M'Fadden v Jenkyns* (1842) 1 Ph 153; *Milroy v Lord* (1862) 4 De GF & J 264.

[58] *Rochefoucauld v Boustead* [1897] 1 Ch 196; *McCormick v Grogan* (1869) LR 4 HL 82; *Pallant v Morgan* [1953] Ch 43; *Paragon Finance plc v Thakerar & Co* [1999] 1 All ER 400, 409.

[59] *Lincoln v Wright* (1859) 4 De G & J 16, 22; *Davies v Otty (No2)* (1865) 45 Beav 208; *Childers v Childers* (1857) 1 De G & J 482; *Haigh v Kaye* (1872) 7 Ch App 469; *Booth v Turle* (1873) LR 16 Eq 182; *Rochefoucauld v Boustead* [1897] 1 Ch 196; *Bannister v Bannister* [1948] 2 All ER 133; *Hodgson v Marks* [1971] Ch 892. See also *Dalton v. Christofis* [1978] WAR 42; *South Yarra Project Pty Ltd v Gentsis* [1985] VR 29; *Bahr v Nicolay (No 2)* (1988) 164 CLR 604. Whether T holds on an express trust, or a resulting trust, or a constructive trust is unclear: *Rochefoucauld v Boustead, supra*, clearly refers to an express trust; *Hodgson v Marks, supra*, suggests a resulting trust; but see *Paragon Finance plc v Thakerar & Co* [1999] 1 All ER 400, 409.

[60] *Lincoln v Wright* (1859) 4 De G & J 16; *Re Duke of Marlborough* [1894] 2 Ch 133.

[61] See [1984] CLJ 306, esp 335–336 (TG Youdan); [1987] Conv 246 (JD Feltham); Underhill and Hayton, *The Law Relating to Trusts and Trustees* (16th edn, 2003) 255–256; Ford and Lee, *Principles of the Law of Trusts* (2nd edn) 209–211; Scott, *The Law of Trusts* (4th edn) vol 1, s44, 436–437; A Oakley, *Constructive Trusts* (3rd edn, Sweet & Maxwell, 1997) ('*Oakley*') 55–56.

[62] *Rudkin v Dolman* (1876) 35 LT 791; *Scheuerman v Scheuerman* (1916) 52 SCR 625, 636.

enforced, in order to prevent fraud, not by declaring that the trustee held the land on a resulting use for the settlor (which would have defeated the object of creating the use in the first place) but by ordering the trustee to carry out the trust: the trustee was held to the agreement into which he had entered in favour of B.

A trust created for value gives rise to a contract capable of being specifically **5.21** enforced, which in turn gives rise to a constructive trust. The intended trust can therefore be enforced, despite the absence of writing.[63]

Secret trusts and 'common intention' constructive trusts also fall within section **5.22** 53(2), either because the avoidance of fraud is involved or there is an enforceable agreement for value.[64]

Methods of transfer for common forms of trust property

The appropriate form of transfer from settlor to trustee depends on the particular **5.23** property being transferred. Different kinds of property are governed by different rules, often different statutes, and, in case of any doubt, guidance must be sought in the relevant area of property law. What follows is but a brief outline of the basic rules governing the most common forms of property.

Land.   Section 52(1) of the Law of Property Act 1925 provides: **5.24**

> All conveyances of land or of any interest therein are void for the purpose of conveying or creating a legal estate unless made by deed.

A deed is not required in the case of grants of leases taking effect in possession for **5.25** a term not exceeding three years at the best rent which can reasonably be obtained without taking a fine: indeed they can be created by parol.[65] In the case of registered land, the transferee must be registered as proprietor on the Land Register.[66] The creation or disposal of other interests in land requires writing.[67] Otherwise, they have the force and effect of interests at will only, notwithstanding that consideration may have been given for them.[68]

Chattels.   Chattels are transferred by actual or constructive delivery, coupled **5.26** with an intention to give, or the delivery of an executed deed of gift.[69]

---

[63] *Oughtred v IRC* [1960] AC 206, esp 227, 230, 233, and 239; *Neville v Wilson* [1997] Ch 144, esp 155–158. See also [1996] CLJ 436 (CA Nolan); [1996] Conv 368 (Thompson).

[64] For secret trusts and common intention constructive trusts, see paras 28.23–28.53 below.

[65] Law of Property Act 1925, s 54(2).

[66] Land Registration Act 1925, ss 5, 9, 20, 23, and 69; Land Registration Rules 1925, SI 1925/1093, r 83(3). The transferee becomes registered proprietor as from the date on which the relevant documents are delivered to the Land Registry. See also *Mascall v Mascall* (1984) 50 P & CR 119 (an application of the principle in *Re Rose* [1949] Ch 78).

[67] Law of Property Act 1925, s 53(1)(a).   [68] ibid, s 54(1).

[69] *Cochrane v Moore* (1890) 25 QBD 57; *Re Cole* [1964] Ch 175; *Thomas v Times Book Co Ltd.* [1966] 1 WLR 911. See also *Jaffa v Taylor Gallery Ltd* The Times, 21 March 1990 (trust instrument referring to chattel held effective to vest title).

5.27 **Shares and securities.**   Shares in companies are transferred by means of a duly executed form of transfer together with the share certificates, followed by registration of the new owner by the company.[70] Bearer securities are transferable by delivery.

5.28 **Negotiable instruments.**   A negotiable instrument is transferred by delivery. A cheque is merely a revocable mandate to the bank to pay the presenter. Payment takes effect only when the cheque is cleared. The mandate may be revoked by the donor and will be revoked automatically on his death.[71] In contrast, an irrevocable banker's draft would take effect at once.[72]

5.29 **Other choses in action.**   The appropriate method to transfer a (legal or equitable) debt or other chose in action[73] is by means of an absolute assignment by writing, under the hand of the assignor, in accordance with section 136(1) of the Law of Property Act 1925. If a purported assignment does not comply with section 136(1), it may still be effective as a valid equitable assignment.[74] An equitable assignment of an equitable interest, for no consideration, is clearly permissible, provided it is in writing and satisfies section 53(1)(c) of the Law of Property Act 1925. Moreover, there can be a valid equitable assignment where there is consideration.[75] However, there is considerable uncertainty over the validity of a voluntary oral or written equitable assignment of a legal debt;[76] and, as a result, the principles of equitable assignment should be invoked only in a salvage operation and not relied on as the basis for making an effective transfer.

5.30 **Future property.**   Assignments of future property and expectancies are valid in equity, provided they are made *for value*.[77] There are numerous examples in the cases of such assignments being enforced, in relation, for example, to an interest

---

[70]   Companies Act 1985, s 182(1)(b); Companies (Tables A to F) Regulations 1985, Table A, Art 23; Stock Transfer Act 1963. See also Companies Act 1989, s 207 and Uncertified Securities Regulations 1995 (SI 1995/3272) (uncertified stock).

[71]   *Re Swinburne* [1926] Ch 38; *Re Owen* [1949] 1 All ER 901.

[72]   *Carter v Sharon* [1936] 1 All ER 720.

[73]   Many choses in action are subject to their own statutory provisions, eg shares in companies (see above); life insurance (Policies of Assurance Act 1867); patents (Patents Act 1977); copyrights (Copyright, Designs and Patents Act 1988, ss 90, 94); and so on.

[74]   Which survived the introduction of statutory assignment: *William Brandt's Sons & Co v Dunlop Rubber Co Ltd* [1905] AC 454, 461.

[75]   ibid.; *Olsson v Dyson* (1969) 120 CLR 365, 375–376, 386.

[76]   It is not valid in Australia: *Olsson v Dyson* (1969) 120 CLR 365. The authorities in England are contradictory: *Re Westerton* [1919] 2 Ch 104, 111 (consideration necessary); *Ex p Pye* (1811) 18 Ves Jr 140; *Fortescue v Barnett* (1834) 2 Myl & K 36; *Kekewich v Manning* (1851) 1 De GM & G 176; *Richardson v Richardson* (1867) LR 3 Eq 686; *Re King* (1879) 14 Ch D 179; *Harding v Harding* (1886) 27 QBD 442, 445; *Re Patrick* [1891] 1 Ch 82; *Re McArdle* [1951] Ch 669 (consideration unnecessary). For a full discussion of the case for and against validity, see Mowbray et al, *Lewin on Trusts* (17th edn, Sweet & Maxwell, 2000) ('*Lewin*') 43–44.

[77]   *Tailby v Official Receiver* (1888) 13 App Cas 523; *Siebe Gorman & Co Ltd v Barclays Bank Ltd* [1979] 2 Lloyd's Rep 142.

under the will of a living testator,[78] the mere expectancy of next of kin,[79] future income,[80] book debts,[81] damages recoverable in a pending action,[82] the copyright in unwritten songs,[83] and future royalties.[84] A covenant for value to transfer future property has the effect of vesting the beneficial interest in that property in the covenantee when it is acquired by the covenantor.[85] An assignment for value which purports to have immediate effect takes effect as a contract to assign the relevant property when it comes into existence and is acquired by the assignor (when the beneficial interest will vest in the assignee).[86]

An assignment *not made for value*, however, is invalid.[87] Equity will not assist a **5.31** volunteer. Thus, a voluntary assignment to trustees by a settlor, of her expectation of inheriting the property of then living persons (ie her mere *spes successionis*),[88] could not be enforced by the trustees when the settlor actually became entitled to property on the deaths of those persons.[89]

Similarly, an attempt, made for no value, by an object of a power of appointment **5.32** to settle any property or interest to which he may become entitled in the event that the power is exercised in his favour will not be valid, and a transfer of any property or interest eventually appointed will not be enforced in favour of the purported assignee.[90]

A distinction must be drawn, of course, between a mere expectancy and a contin- **5.33** gent interest: whereas the former, as we have seen, can be assigned only for value, a contingent interest under a trust may be assigned without consideration.[91] The distinction is not always obvious. A 'future interest' is an interest which confers a right to enjoyment of property at a future time; and it may be vested or contingent. Even a 'vested future interest' (ie one vested in interest but not yet vested in possession) confers an immediate or present right to future enjoyment, and can

---

[78] *Bennett v Cooper* (1846) 9 Beav 252; *Re Clarke* (1887) 36 Ch D 348.
[79] *Re Lind* [1915] 2 Ch 345.
[80] *Re Gillott's Settlement* [1934] Ch 97; *Syrett v Egerton* [1957] 1 WLR 1130.
[81] *Tailby v Official Receiver* (1888) 13 App Cas 523. [82] *Glegg v Bromley* [1912] 3 KB 474.
[83] *Performing Rights Society v London Theatre of Varieties* [1942] AC 1; *Campbell Connelly & Co Ltd v Noble* [1963] 1 WLR 252; see also Copyright, Designs and Patents Act 1988, s 91.
[84] *Re Trytel* (1952) 2 TLR 32.
[85] *Re Lind* [1915] 2 Ch 345; *Re Gillott's Settlement* [1934] Ch 97; *Re Haynes' Will Trusts* [1949] Ch 5.
[86] *Holroyd v Marshall* (1860) 10 HLC 191; *Horwood v Millar's Timber & Trading Co Ltd* [1917] 1 KB 305, 315.
[87] The presence of a seal made no difference: *Meek v Kettlewell* (1842) 1 Hare 464; (1843) 1 Ph 342; *Re Ellenborough* [1903] 1 Ch 697; *Re Brooks' Settlement Trusts* [1939] Ch 993.
[88] *Clowes v Hilliard* (1876) 4 Ch D 413; *Re Parsons* (1890) 45 Ch D 51, 55.
[89] *Re Ellenborough* [1903] 1 Ch 697.
[90] *Re Brooks' Settlement Trusts* [1939] Ch 993. The result ought to be different, however, where the settlor settles an interest, though defeasible, in default of appointment.
[91] *Lord Dursley v Fitzhardinge* (1801) 6 Ves Jr 251, 260.

thus easily be assignable. A 'contingent future interest', strictly speaking, confers no right at all until the contingency or future event occurs; and, in this sense, it is only a possibility that an interest may arise in the future.[92] Nevertheless, equity came to enforce assignments of contingent remainders by compelling the assignor to transfer the property to the assignee when it fell into possession;[93] and, by now, it is well established that contingent interests are assignable without consideration. However, although the distinction between a mere expectancy and a contingent interest is one of substance and effect, there may sometimes be some difficulty in identifying which has been created.[94]

5.34 An interest in an estate still in course of administration may be settled,[95] apparently on the basis that the beneficiary-settlor has a present right to have the estate duly and properly administered, despite the fact that it is also well established that he has no equitable, proprietary interest in any assets in the estate.[96]

5.35 A right to rectify a deed or rescind it for fraud or mistake, and thereby recover property, is not a future interest (or a chose in action): it is a present equitable interest in that property and, as such, may be assigned without consideration or transferred by will.[97]

Unusual cases of trusts becoming completely constituted

5.36 Provided the relevant property becomes vested in the trustees, equity will generally enforce the trust. Assuming there is no impropriety involved, equity is not concerned with the manner in which the trust became constituted, nor with the fact that it would not have lent its assistance to constitute the trust.

The rule in Strong v Bird

5.37 The rule in *Strong v Bird* [98] operates where the owner of property intends to make an immediate specific gift of that property (but clearly does not complete it), where that intention continues until the owner's death (ie he does not change his

---

[92] Thus, at common law, such interests were regarded as inalienable: *Lampet's Case* (1612) 10 Co Rep 46b.

[93] *Wright v Wright* (1750) 1 Ves Sen 409; *Crofts v Middleton* (1856) 8 De GM & G 192. The process was assisted by the Statute of Wills 1540 and the Wills Act 1837, s 3. They became fully alienable at law following the Real Property Act 1845, s 6.

[94] See, for example, *Re Midleton's Will Trusts* [1969] 1 Ch 600 and *Re St Albans Will Trusts* [1963] Ch 365. See also *Meek v Kettlewell* (1842) 1 Hare 464; (1843) 1 Ph 342; *Clowes v Hilliard* (1876) 4 Ch D 413; *Re Parsons* (1890) 45 Ch D 51; *Molyneux v Fletcher* [1898] 1 QB 648; *Re Mudge* [1914] 1 Ch 600.

[95] *Commr of Stamp Duties (Queensland) v Livingston* [1965] AC 694; *Re Leigh's Will Trusts* [1970] Ch 277; *Marshall v Kerr* [1995] 1 AC 148.

[96] *Commr of Stamp Duties (Queensland) v Livingston, supra; Sudeley v A-G* [1897] AC 11.

[97] *Phillips v Phillips* (1862) 4 De GM & G 208, 218; *Dickinson v Burrell* (1866) LR 1 Eq 337; *Latec Investments Ltd v Hotel Terrigal Pty Ltd* (1965) 113 CLR 265.

[98] (1874) LR 18 Eq 315.

mind), and where the intended donee then becomes the owner's personal representative. The gift is then perfected. There must be an intention to make an immediate gift, and not a testamentary one.[99] The property in question may be real or personal, but must be specific and existing.[100] The donee may be appointed an executor or an administrator[101] of the donor's estate, or one of the executors or administrators (the whole of the estate vesting in each one).[102] Despite the fact that the personal representative receives the property in a fiduciary as well as a personal capacity, his personal interest prevails. The reasoning behind this conclusion, as explained in *Re Stewart*,[103] is as follows:

> ... first, that the vesting of the property in the executor on the testator's death completes the imperfect gift made in the lifetime, and, secondly, that the intention of the testator to give the beneficial interest to the executor is sufficient to countervail the equity of beneficiaries under the will, the testator having vested the legal estate in the executor.

In *Re Ralli's Will Trusts*,[104] the settlor intended to transfer into settlement an equit-   **5.38** able interest which she enjoyed under her father's will and, indeed, she had entered into a covenant to settle the property in question. In the event, and entirely by chance, the trustee of the settlement became sole trustee of both the settlement and the settlor's will. Buckley J held that the property was subject to the trusts of the settlement:

> ... the circumstance that the plaintiff holds the fund because he was appointed a trustee of the will is irrelevant. He is at law the owner of the fund and the means by which he became so have no effect on the quality of his legal ownership. The question is: For whom if anyone does he hold the fund in equity?

In *Re Ralli* itself, the covenant to settle the property in question was evidence of a continuing intention to complete the gift.

Constitution of a trust without completing the transfer of property

As we have seen, in order to constitute a trust, the settlor must make a complete   **5.39** and effective transfer of the subject matter of the trust to the trustee. If he fails to do so, the intended trust will fail. Equity will not assist a volunteer and will not

---

99   *Re Innes* [1910] 1 Ch 188; *Re Freeland* [1952] Ch 110; *Re Hyslop* [1894] 3 Ch 522.
100   *Re James* [1935] Ch 449; *Wankford v Wankford* (1704) 1 Salk 299; *Strong v Bird, supra*; *Re Applebee* [1891] 3 Ch 422; *Re Innes, supra*; *Morton v Brighouse* [1927] 1 DLR 1009; *Re Harvey* (1932) 41 OWN 299.
101   The application of the rule to an administrator, and not just an executor, is not beyond question, but it seems to have been adopted: *Re Gonin* [1979] Ch 16, 35. Cf *Re Pagarani* (1998/99) 2 OFLR 1.
102   *Strong v Bird, supra*; *Re Stewart* [1908] 2 Ch 251; *Re James* [1935] Ch 449
103   [1908] 2 Ch 251, 254.
104   [1964] Ch 288. See also *Re Bowden* [1936] Ch 71; *Re Adlard* [1954] Ch 29. *Re Brooks' Settlement Trusts* [1939] Ch 993 is not a decision to the contrary because the relevant property never became vested in the trustee: see *Lewin* 53–54; but cf *Underhill and Hayton* 142–143.

perfect an imperfect gift.[105] However, there are cases in which the transfer may not be complete and final, but in which neither a further act by the settlor-donor nor the assistance of equity is required to perfect the title; and, in such cases, a trust will be properly constituted. In other words, if the settlor has done everything that he himself can or needs to do in the making of an effective transfer, and the trustee has within his control the power to perfect his title, without recourse to equity, then, until the transfer is actually completed, the settlor will hold the property on trust.[106] Such cases are not really exceptions to the principle that equity will not assist a volunteer, for the assistance of equity is not invoked or required, and they are not inconsistent, therefore, with the basic propositions laid down in *Milroy v Lord.*

Land

5.40 Although the principle applies to land generally, it is particularly apposite in relation to registered land. In *Mascall v Mascall*,[107] for example, the registered proprietor of land handed over a completed transfer and the land certificate to his son. Before the transfer was registered, the transferor argued that he was not bound by it. The Court of Appeal held, however, that the transferor had done everything in his power and that needed to be done in order to enable the son to register himself as the new proprietor, so the gift was complete.[108] The assistance of equity to perfect the gift was not required.

Company shares

5.41 Shares in companies are transferred by means of a two-stage process, namely (a) the delivery by the transferor to the transferee of a duly executed form of transfer together with the share certificates and (b) the registration by the company of the transferee as the new shareholder.[109] However, as soon as stage (a) is complete, the transferor has done everything that he can or needs to do; and the transferee is then in a position to procure his registration as the new shareholder and thereby perfect the gift, without any further act on the part of the transferee and without the assistance of equity.[110] If the consent of the company's directors is required

---

[105] *Milroy v Lord* (1862) 4 De GF & J 264.

[106] *Re Rose* [1952] Ch 78. It is unclear, but also immaterial, whether the settlor is then a trustee for the intended beneficiaries or for the trustees of the intended trust.

[107] (1989) 50 P & CR 119.

[108] See also *Brown & Root Technology Ltd v Sun Alliance and London Assurance Co Ltd* [1996] Ch 51 (reversed [2002] 2 WLR 566); *Corin v Paton* (1990) 169 CLR 540.

[109] See para 5.27 above.

[110] *Re Rose* [1949] Ch 78; *Re Rose* [1952] Ch 499; *Hurst v Crampton Bros (Coopers) Ltd* (2003) 1 BCLC 304, where Jacobs J held that, although it was a perfectly constituted gift, it also infringed the right of pre-emption conferred on existing members of the company by its articles of association; and, on appeal, *Pennington v Waine* [2002] 1 WLR 2075, where the CA upheld the gift, apparently on the basis that it would have been unconscionable for the donor to recall it.

before such registration can take place (as is often the case with shares in private companies) and the directors refuse to give their consent, the intending transferor holds the shares on trust for the intended transferee.[111] Clearly, the principle cannot apply in the case of an improperly executed transfer or where some further document needs to be executed by the settlor: unless and until the settlor completes everything that he needs to do, there is simply an imperfect gift.[112]

Debts and other choses in action

The legal assignment of a debt or other *chose in action* requires writing, signed by the assignor, coupled with notice to the debtor. However, the assignee himself can give notice of the assignment to the debtor, without the assistance of equity. The assignor has done everything that he needs to do in order to perfect the gift, and he is a trustee for the assignee of the debt or other chose in action from the time the signed writing is produced and before notice is given.[113]   **5.42**

Although the position is not entirely clear,[114] the position would seem to be the same in relation to an assignment which is not an effective statutory absolute assignment, for example because it is not in writing or only a partial assignment.   **5.43**

Cheques

A cheque is merely a revocable mandate to the bank to pay the presenter. Payment takes effect only when the cheque is cleared. It does not operate as an appropriation of, or confer a right to, any asset. The principle of *Re Rose* therefore does not apply to cheques.   **5.44**

Estoppel and incompletely constituted trusts

Both promissory and proprietary estoppel may operate in such a way that an imperfect transfer into settlement is perfected. In *Re Vandervell's Trusts (No 2)*,[115] an option to purchase shares was vested in a trust company, but owned beneficially by the settlor. The trustee used trust money to exercise the option, the intention of the settlor and trustee being that the shares became part of the trust fund. Subsequent dividends on the shares were paid to the trustee. However, the settlor had failed to comply with section 53(1)(c) of the Law of Property Act 1925 and it was argued by the settlor's personal representatives that he had not, therefore, disposed of his beneficial interest. The Court of Appeal held (*inter alia*) that the personal representatives were estopped[116] from denying the trustee's title.   **5.45**

---

[111] *Re Rose* [1949] Ch 78, 88–89; *Re Rose* [1952] Ch 499, 513 and 518.

[112] *Milroy v Lord* (1862) 4 De GF & J 264; *Re Rose* [1952] Ch 499; *Mascall v Mascall* (1989) 50 P & CR 119; *Re Trustee of Pehrsson (a bankrupt)* (1999) 2 ITELR 230, 238–239.

[113] *Olsson v Dyson* (1969) 120 CLR 365, 386–387.

[114] See above. See also *Lewin* 51.   [115] [1974] Ch 269, 320–321 and 325.

[116] The Court of Appeal seems to have thought in terms of promissory estoppel, but it seems more appropriate to regard the circumstances as giving rise to proprietary estoppel.

Similarly, an incomplete and imperfect transfer of land to trustees could well be perfected under the doctrine of proprietary estoppel if the trustees were subsequently to act to their detriment in reliance on some assurance or encouragement on the part of the settlor (say, by expending money on the improvement of the land). Such circumstances are likely to be exceedingly rare, however.

C. Express Lifetime Declaration of Trust

Declaration of trust

5.46   The owner of property ('the settlor') can declare himself a trustee of property which he owns. No particular or technical form of words is required, provided the intention to constitute himself a trustee is clear. If the property is not vested in the settlor's own name, but held by a nominee or other trustee for him, the declaration will take the form of a direction to the nominee or trustee to hold the property on specified trusts.[117] Where one of a larger body of trustees has property vested in him and declares himself a trustee of that property for the existing trusts, his declaration is effective and he is bound to transfer it into the names of all the trustees.[117A]

Certainty of subject matter

5.47   The settlor must identify, with sufficient precision to make the trust workable, the property which is to be the subject matter of the trust. This is particularly problematic where the settlor declares himself a trustee of property, rather than transferring property to another. If the settlor is declaring himself a trustee of only a part of a larger holding of undifferentiated assets, rather than the whole, he should always identify clearly the precise assets over which the trust is being declared, preferably by segregating or appropriating those assets from the larger holding, or declare himself a tenant in common (with other beneficiaries) of the entire holding, in specified shares.[118] Otherwise, it may be difficult to identify the precise assets subject to the trust. The recent decision of the Court of Appeal in *Hunter v Moss*[119] may have relaxed these requirements, but it ought, perhaps, to be relied on as part of a salvage operation rather than an approach which may safely be relied upon.[120]

---

[117]   *Paul v Constance* [1977] 1 WLR 527. See also paras 2.03–2.07 above.
[117A]   *Choithram International SA v Pagarani* [2001] 1 WLR 1.
[118]   *Re Wait* [1927] 1 Ch 606; *Re London Wine Co (Shippers) Ltd* [1986] PCC 121; *MacJordan Construction Ltd v Brookmount Erostin Ltd* [1992] BCLC 350; *Re Stapylton Fletcher Ltd* [1994] 1 WLR 1181; *Re Goldcorp Exchange Ltd* [1995] 1 AC 74. See also *OT Computers Ltd v First National Tricity Finance Ltd*, Pumfrey J, 9 May 2004: Lawtel AC0105027.
[119]   [1994] 1 WLR 452, CA; followed in *Re Harvard Securities Ltd* [1997] 2 BCLC 369. See also *Re CA Pacific Finance Ltd* [2000] 1 BCLC 494 (Hong Kong); and *Herdegen v Federal Commr of Taxation* (1988) 84 ALR 271.
[120]   See paras 3.12–3.32 above.

Referential trusts[121]

Trusts and powers may be, and often are, created by reference to other trusts and   **5.48**
powers declared and contained in a completely separate instrument or elsewhere
in the same instrument.[122] In broad terms, referential trusts and powers operate
and apply as if the original provisions to which reference is made had been written
out fully in the instrument making the reference.[123] In *Re Shirley's Trusts*,[124] for
example, the words 'in like manner to all intents and purposes as if such trusts and
provisions were here fully repeated' were held to require the repetition or importation of all provisions; and, in *Re Sutton*,[125] PO Lawrence J stated that a reference
to 'the trusts hereinbefore declared' in a will would include all those trusts, including a direction that the property should fall into residue, in the absence of words
confining the phrase to particular trusts. Similarly, powers created by reference
to other powers will be taken to be of the same extent and nature as such other
powers.

A direction that certain property be held so as to constitute a separate and inde-   **5.49**
pendent fund, the trusts and powers applicable to which are simply created by reference, must, of course, be distinguished from a direction that property should
simply accrue to the funds of a prior settlement and be held on the trusts (or the
trusts for the time being) thereof. This distinction may be crucial for a number of
different purposes. Suppose, for example, that a settlement confers on a life tenant a power to appoint one-half of the income of the trust fund in favour of a surviving spouse. Suppose, too, that other property is given 'upon the same trusts and
with and subject to the powers and provisions' as those in the settlement. If the
other property is intended as an accrual to the fund of the existing settlement, an
exercise of the power of appointment will extend to one-half of the income of the
entire fund, including all accruals thereto.[126] On the other hand, if the other property is intended to constitute an independent fund subject to trusts and powers
created by reference to the original settlement, there is a question as to whether the
relevant power is to be imported by reference[127] and, if it is, whether it will then
constitute a separate power which must be exercised independently if it is to operate as an effective appointment of one-half of the income of the other property.
Similarly, where there is an accretion to an existing fund, a hotchpot clause will
apply to the entire fund, including all accretions, so that appointees in favour of

---

[121] See, generally, *Thomas* 42–50.
[122] For example, by declaring that a particular share of the trust fund is to be held 'upon such
trusts and under and subject to such powers and provisions as are hereinbefore contained concerning' another share: see, for example, *Pugh v Drew* (1869) 17 WR 988; *Boyd v Boyd* (1863) 9 LT 166;
Hindle v Taylor (1855) 5 De GM & G 577; *Surtees v Hopkinson* (1867) LR 4 Eq 98.
[123] *Re Playfair* [1951] Ch 4, 9.   [124] (1863) 32 Beav 392.
[125] [1921] 1 Ch 257, 267.   [126] *Re Pauls' Settlement Trusts* [1920] 1 Ch 99.
[127] See, for example, *Hindle v Taylor* (1855) 5 De GM & G 577; *Cooper v Macdonald* (1873) LR
16 Eq 258; *Trew v The Perpetual Trustee Company* [1895] AC 264.

whom the original funds have been appointed (before the accruals) will not take a share in the accruals without bringing their appointed shares into hotchpot.[128] On the other hand, if there are two independent funds, the first question will be whether a hotchpot clause is to be imported and made applicable to the later fund; and, if it is, it will apply only in respect of that fund.[129] As Sargant J said in *Re Fraser*:[130]

> ... it seems to me that the question really turns upon this: Is the second set of words which settles the additional fund really a separate settlement of the additional fund upon the like trusts as the first or original fund, the words being merely words of reference so as to operate by way of compendious introduction of the earlier trusts, or does the second set of trusts operate as an amalgamation of the second fund with the first fund so as to make it an augmentation of or an accretion to the first fund?

A similar question may arise in relation to covenants to settle after-acquired property.[131]

5.50 It is a question of construction whether a new and separate settlement has been created by reference or whether there is simply an accrual to an existing settlement. There is no law and no presumption: it depends simply on the meaning and effect of the instrument in question.[132] In broad terms, where there are separate settlors dealing with separate shares of a fund, by means of separate instruments, there will almost certainly be separate settlements of such shares created by reference. As Russell J stated in *Re Campbell's Trusts*,[133] 'in no instance in the case of separate instruments, at separate dates, and with separate settlors, has the fund ever been treated as one aggregate fund, either for the purposes of hotchpot, or as regards multiplication of charges, or for any other purpose'. However, it does not follow that, where there is only one instrument and one settlor, there must be a single settlement. Thus, where a testator gives separate funds or shares of his estate to trustees upon trusts for his children respectively for life, with remainder to such of their issue as they should appoint, with a gift over in default of appointment to their children in equal shares, and a further gift over in favour of other children, the trusts of each fund or share may constitute a separate settlement, so that a beneficiary may take a share of an unappointed fund without bringing into hotchpot another fund which she took under an appointment.[134]

---

[128] *Re Perkins* [1893] 1 CR 283, 67 LT 743; *Re Fraser* [1913] 2 Ch 224; *Re Playfair* [1951] Ch 4.
[129] *Re North* (1897) 76 LT 186; *Re Marquis of Bristol* [1897] 1 Ch 946; *Re Cavendish* [1912] 1 Ch 704; *Re Marke Wood* [1913] 1 Ch 303, and [1913] 2 Ch 574; *Re Beaumont* [1913] 1 Ch 325; *Re Fraser* [1913] 2 Ch 224.
[130] [1913] 2 Ch 224, 232.
[131] *Re Beaumont, supra*; *Re Cavendish, supra*. Cf *Re Fraser, supra*. It is doubtful whether such a covenant is either a 'trust or a power' for the purposes of being incorporated by reference, although it may be a 'provision'.
[132] *Re Marke Wood* [1913] 2 Ch 574, 583. Whether the principles of construction are the same or different in the cases of a will and a settlement is uncertain. Cf *Re Cavendish* [1912] 1 Ch 794, 803 and *Re Marke Wood* [1913] 1 Ch 303, 311. See also *Re Marquis of Bristol* [1897] 1 Ch 946, 949.
[133] [1922] 1 Ch 551, 562.
[134] *Re Marke Wood* [1913] 2 Ch 574. Cf *Re Marquis of Bristol* [1897] 1 Ch 946.

Creating trusts by reference requires careful thought and precise language. There **5.51**
are many observations in the authorities on the dangers of referential trusts[135] and
warnings that they give rise 'to a great deal of uncertainty and confusion'[136] and
that the only safe course is to set out comprehensively words creating the trusts
and powers intended to apply to each of the different funds or properties.[137]
Clearly, much may depend on subtle differences in the actual terms of reference.
A reference to 'such or the like' trusts and powers, for example, does not necessarily indicate identical trusts and powers.[138] Reference may also be made to 'the
same trusts with the same powers' as those declared or created elsewhere, or to
trusts and powers 'as nearly corresponding thereto as the circumstances of the case
will admit'[139] (or some such similar expressions). According to Malins V-C, in
Surtees v Hopkinson,[140] 'corresponding with' means 'effectuating the like object
corresponding with what [the testator] had said': the 'like' limitations are the same
as 'corresponding' limitations and, once again, neither requires complete identity.
In such cases, it is the degree of 'correspondence' that needs to be determined and
which may prove problematic.[141] In some cases, the guiding principle may simply
be the spirit rather than the strict form,[142] although the court does not, of course,
have a free-ranging discretion in such matters: it is engaged in a process of construing the terms of reference and determining the true intention of the settlor.[143]

One particular danger is that circumstances may have changed considerably **5.52**
between the date of creation of the original trusts and powers to which reference
is made and the date on which such referential trusts and powers themselves come
into operation.[144] This fact will have to be taken into account in determining
the extent to which the original trusts and powers are to be 'rewritten' into the
new instrument and the degree of 'correspondence' which must be achieved.
Moreover, a general reference to the trusts and powers created by a former

---

[135] See, for example, *Trew v The Perpetual Trustee Company* [1895] AC 264, 267–268; *Re Finch and Chew's Contract* [1903] 2 Ch 486, 493; *Re Arnell* [1924] 1 Ch 473, 478.

[136] *Re Shelton's Settled Estates* [1945] Ch 158, 164.

[137] *Trew v The Perpetual Trustee Company* [1895] AC 264, 267; *Re Finch and Chew's Contract* [1903] 2 Ch 486, 493. As Pearson J put it in *Brigg v Brigg* (1885) 54 LJ Ch 464, 465: 'the draftsman has unfortunately forgotten the line, *brevis esse laboro, obscurus fio*. A few more words would have prevented all confusion.'

[138] *Re Smith* (1881) 45 LT 246; *Brigg v Brigg, supra*. See also *Countess Berchtoldt v Marquis of Hertford* (1844) 7 Beav 172; *Surtees v Hopkinson* (1867) LR 4 Eq 98; *Minton v Kirwood* (1868) 3 Ch App 614.

[139] See, for example, *Re Shelton's Settled Estates* [1945] Ch 158; *Surtees v Hopkinson, supra*.

[140] (1867) LR 4 Eq 98, 105.

[141] *Re Shelton's Settled Estates* [1945] Ch 158, 165, *per* Vaisey J: 'The "correspondence" must be as near as the circumstances will admit, which of course implies that it may be more or less near and also more or less distant.'

[142] *Key v Key* (1853) 4 De GM & G 73, 84. See also *Sweeting v Prideaux* (1876) 2 Ch D 413; and *Towns v Wentworth* (1858) 11 Moo PC 526.

[143] The meaning may, of course, be totally unclear or simply absurd: *Re Powell* [1918] 1 Ch 407.

[144] See, for example, *Re Shelton's Settled Estates* [1945] Ch 158; *Re Gooch* [1929] 1 Ch 740.

disposition may lead to uncertainty as to the time when the referential trusts and powers themselves take effect.[145]

5.53 Where, under a special power of appointment, a testator appoints property on the trusts of an antecedent instrument or such of them as are 'capable of taking effect', such an expression may be construed as meaning what the law allows to take effect and it need not be confined to a reference to the trusts and powers which, by reason of the death of parties or other intervening circumstances, are still in fact existing or capable of coming into existence. Thus, if some of the appointed trusts fail because some of the intended beneficiaries are not objects of the power, or because the rule against perpetuities is infringed, those trusts may be excluded from the appointment and the remainder allowed to take effect.[146] In an extreme case, a combination of changed circumstances and what the law allows to take effect may result in the complete failure of the intended referential trusts.[147]

5.54 Express differences and variations must obviously be observed. For example, if trusts and powers in favour of A are declared by reference to trusts and powers previously created in favour of B, but the later referential trusts and powers (unlike the original ones) include a direction that no part of the capital is to be paid or advanced to or for the benefit of A, such a restriction will clearly operate as a modification of the original provisions.[148] Similarly, if the original trusts or powers are inconsistent with the limitations and conditions attached to the new trusts or powers, the former will be made to conform to the intention displayed by such limitations.[149] Moreover, if there is any contingency or restriction which is *personal* to the donee of the original power, that contingency or restriction will not be attached to the power created by reference,[150] although other contingencies or restrictions (for example that the power be exercisable by will only, or that a power be exercisable only if and when the donee has attained a specified age) will no doubt apply equally, in the absence of some express provision to the contrary or a clear inconsistency.[151]

5.55 There seems to be a general reluctance to construe referential trusts and powers in such a way that charges, or trusts in the nature of charges, are duplicated[152] (in the

---

[145] See, for example, *Hare v Hare* (1876) 24 WR 575; *Re Walpole* [1903] 1 Ch 928.
[146] *Re Finch and Chew's Contract* [1903] 2 Ch 486, esp 493.
[147] *Re Powell* [1918] 1 Ch 407 (where the effect was that the testator purported to bequeath his own property to himself). See also *Re Currie's Settlement* [1910] 1 Ch 329, 333; *Culsha v Cheese* (1840) 7 Hare 236.
[148] *Re Sutton* [1921] 1 Ch 257 (power to revoke and resettle).
[149] *Crossman v Bevan* (1859) 27 Beav 502.
[150] *Harrington (Earl) v Harrington (Countess Dowager)* (1868) LR 3 HL 295.
[151] Sir George Farwell and FK Archer, *A Concise Treatise on Powers* (3rd edn, 1916) ('*Farwell*') 116; *Shrewsbury (Earl) v Keightley* (1866) LR 2 CP 130.
[152] *Boyd v Boyd* (1863) 9 LT 166; *Trew v The Perpetual Trustee Company* [1895] AC 264; *Re Berners* (1892) 67 LT 849. This probably does not amount to a rule of construction, however: *Re Marke Wood* [1913] 1 Ch 303, 310.

absence of express provision to that effect).[153] In fact, there is a broad distinction in the cases between (a) cases where the relevant property is subject to a power to raise a definite sum (or the income of a definite sum) and (b) cases where the power is to raise a charge not exceeding a certain proportion of the value (or income) of the property. In the latter cases, the rule against duplication of charges does not apply (in the absence of a contrary indication) and the power to charge is increased in proportion to the value of the additional property.[154]

On all these questions, however, the central issue is one of establishing intention **5.56** by construing the relevant instrument.[155] 'The rule of construction which ought to be applied', as Pearson J stated in *Brigg v Brigg*,[156] 'is that the instrument must be looked at, as the saying is, at all its four corners, for the purpose of discovering what the governing intention of the parties was...'. Simple prudence thus dictates that, when referential trusts are created, the words and expressions used should not only identify the precise trusts and powers which are to be imported by reference but also precisely how and when they are intended to operate (particularly where, as is almost invariably the case, they are intended to apply in relation to additional or different beneficiaries).

D. Contracts to Create Trusts, Covenants to Settle After-Acquired Property

A trust once constituted cannot be revoked by the settlor acting *qua* settlor,[157] **5.57** unless he reserves to himself an express power to do so in the trust instrument. A mere promise made by a person that at some point in the future he will settle property on trust, or that he will settle on trust property in which he has no proprietary rights at the time of making that promise, will not be binding on that person.[158] The issue relating to the purported declaration of a trust over property in which the settlor has no proprietary rights is referred to as a purported trust over 'after-acquired' property, in that the rights in the property are acquired only after the purported declaration of trust. The settlor has no proprietary rights which can be settled on trust and no trust is impressed on the property if and when the settlor subsequently receives it. However, if that promise to settle the property had been made in a deed of covenant then the parties to that covenant would be entitled to enforce the terms of that covenant at common law.[159] Trustees who are parties to

---

[153] *Cooper v Macdonald* (1873) LR 16 Eq 258, esp 266–267. See also *Hindle v Taylor* (1855) 5 De GM & G 577.
[154] *Re Arnell* [1924] 1 Ch 473, esp 480–481. Cf *Re Beaumont* [1913] 1 Ch 325.
[155] *Re Oxenden's Settled Estates* (1904) 74 LJ Ch 234.   [156] (1885) 54 LJ Ch 464, 465.
[157] *Paul v Paul* (1882) 20 Ch D 742.   [158] *Re Brook's ST* [1939] 1 Ch 993.
[159] *Cannon v Hartley* [1949] Ch 213.

a covenant will not be capable of being forced by the beneficiaries under the trust to enforce that covenant,[160] unless the covenant itself constitutes the trust fund.[161] The Contracts (Rights of Third Parties) Act 1999 provides a right under contract law for a third party identified in the contract to enforce that contract. This section considers the scope of these principles.

Enforceability of a promise

5.58   This section considers the circumstances in which promises made by means of a deed of covenant or a contract will be enforceable. A promise made in a deed of covenant will have the full force and effect of a binding contract, given that a deed replaces the need for consideration in the formation of a contract.[162]

A validly constituted settlement cannot be unmade

5.59   Clearly, there may be situations in which the parties create marriage settlements, or other trusts, under which they promise to deal with property in a particular manner. However, it is possible that subsequent events may make the terms of the settlement appear to be unattractive. For example, in *Paul v Paul*,[163] where a couple who were parties to a complex marriage settlement subsequently sought to separate, they also sought to undo the marriage settlement and reallocate the property between themselves. It was held by the court that a settlement, once created, could not be undone.[164] The only circumstances in which the beneficiaries would be entitled to undo a trust would be in accordance with the rule in *Saunders v Vautier*[165] whereby absolutely entitled beneficiaries, acting *sui juris*, are empowered to direct the trustees to deliver legal title in the property to them.

Parties to the covenant can enforce the covenant

5.60   In relation to covenants to deal with property in a particular manner, the parties to the covenant are entitled to enforce the covenant under the ordinary principles of the law of contract. In the trusts context, the importance of a covenant would be as an obligation entered into by a person to settle specified property on trust for the benefit of other people. On the basis that there is no trust created, the covenant itself will give the parties to the covenant the right to sue to enforce the promise at common law, without the need for resort to the law of trusts. For example, where a person had undertaken by deed of covenant to settle property on his daughter, she would be entitled to enforce that obligation if she were a party to the covenant and consequently to receive an award of damages at common law.[166]

---

[160]   *Re Pryce* [1917] 1 Ch 234; *Re Kay* [1939] Ch 329; *Re Cook* [1965] Ch 902.
[161]   *Fletcher v Fletcher* (1844) 4 Hare 67.
[162]   *Hall v Palmer* (1844) 3 Hare 532; *Macedo v Stroud* [1922] 2 AC 330.
[163]   (1882) 20 Ch D 742.   [164]   *Paul v Paul* (1882) 20 Ch D 742.
[165]   (1841) 4 Beav 115.   [166]   *Cannon v Hartley* [1949] Ch 213.

It would be in the capacity of a party to the covenant that the daughter would be entitled to seek performance of the obligation in the covenant. However, she would not be able to sue on the promise in her capacity as a beneficiary under that trust.

Rights to specific performance are only available to those who have given consid- **5.61** eration.[167] So, in *Pullan v Koe*[168] the claimant was entitled to claim a right in contract where she had given consideration as part of a marriage settlement and in consequence was entitled to specific performance of the defendant's promise to settle after-acquired property on trust for her. If the claimant had not given consideration for the promise then her only claim would be based on an entitlement to damages at common law if she were a party to the covenant. However, equity does not recognize this principle, and, in equity, parties to a deed of covenant are volunteers because they will usually not have given any other form of consideration. Equity will not assist a volunteer. Specific performance is, therefore, not available to a volunteer.[169] In the case of *Cannon v Hartley*[170] a father entered into a covenant to settle after-acquired property on his daughter, among others. His daughter was a party to the covenant but had given no other consideration. She was entitled to damages at common law for breach of covenant when her father refused to perform his covenant. Such an action, quite apart from its rarity in any event, does not, therefore, result in the settlement becoming completely constituted (for the benefit of other beneficiaries who were not parties to such a covenant): this situation contrasts, therefore, with that in *Pullan v Koe*[171] where the claimant had given consideration within the terms of a marriage settlement.

The Contracts (Rights of Third Parties) Act 1999

The Contracts (Rights of Third Parties) Act 1999 has introduced into English **5.62** contract law a right for a third party, for whose benefit a contract has been entered into, to enforce that contract, thereby abrogating in part the old common law rules of privity of contract. In relation to the issue of after-acquired property, the purported beneficiary will be able to enforce the contract[172] if she is identified in the contract either personally or as part of a class of persons for whose benefit the contract has been created.[173] The claimant is entitled to rely on all of the rights accorded by contract law, including damages and specific performance— therefore the contract takes effect at common law and in equity.[174]

The limits on the operation of the Act appear to be as follows. First, there must be **5.63** a contract and not a mere promise. The promise made by the promisor must be in

---

[167] *Pullan v Koe* [1913] 1 Ch 9; *Cannon v Hartley* [1949] Ch 213.   [168] [1913] 1 Ch 9.
[169] *Jefferys v Jefferys* (1841) Cr & Ph 138.   [170] [1949] Ch 213.
[171] [1913] 1 Ch 9.   [172] But only those entered into after 11 May 2000.
[173] Contracts (Rights of Third Parties) Act 1999, s 1.
[174] Contracts (Rights of Third Parties) Act 1999, s 1.

the form of a contract with consideration or made in a deed. The principal argument against the operation of the 1999 Act in many situations would be that the promise made by the promisor to settle after-acquired property would not constitute a contract because typically there would be no consideration passing between the promisor and either the trustee or the purported beneficiary. In many commercial situations there will be a commercial contract (into which the trust is incorporated) or there may be a contract between settlor and trustee in situations like an occupational pension fund (as considered in Chapter 43).

5.64 Secondly, it is not clear the extent to which the identified class of persons able to enforce the contract will correlate with the rules for certainty of objects in trusts law. To make the point another way: what is the class which must be identified? Will that level of certainty correspond with the trusts law rules for the identity of beneficiaries under, for example, a discretionary trust? It would seem sensible to suppose that if the class of beneficiaries is sufficiently certain, it ought to be sufficiently certain for the purposes of the 1999 Act. What remains unclear, however, is whether or not the beneficiary would be required to have vested rights within the terms of the contract or whether the Act would also apply to people who potentially fall within a class of objects of a mere power of appointment:[175] in the latter case it could not be contended that the contract was for the benefit of the beneficiary because there was no vested interest on the part of the third party.

5.65 Thirdly, a contract creates personal rights but an ordinary contract will create neither proprietary rights nor fiduciary obligations.[176] Suppose therefore that the promise made is a promise to transfer money—the claimant's entitlement is unlikely to be enforceable by specific performance because it is merely a money claim.[177] In consequence the claimant receives only personal rights and not rights in property against that fund. If the contract provided the third party with rights in identified property (other than money) then there would be no principled reason to suppose that specific performance would not grant that third party rights in the property when received by the promisor. However, even in such a case, it is not clear whether the claimant can recover only what he or she has lost (or the equivalent) or whether the trust can be completely constituted for the benefit of all other beneficiaries.

5.66 It is important to remember that, while a contract may also create a trust as a by-product,[178] the contract will not *be* a trust in itself. A contract will not grant equitable title in property—only a trust or a charge or a similar right will do that.

---

[175] *Re Brook's ST* [1939] 1 Ch 993.
[176] That is, unless the contract were a contract of agency or of partnership, or a contract for the sale of property.
[177] *South African Territories Ltd v Wallington* [1898] AC 309; *Beswick v Beswick* [1968] AC 58.
[178] *Re Kayford* [1975] 1 WLR 279.

A trust will give certain remedies which a mere contract cannot. The principal advantage of the trust over the remedies available under contract law (principally common law damages and equitable specific performance) is that the trust will entitle the claimant to proprietary rights in that property which is held on trust. A beneficiary under a trust will be able to acquire preferential rights in an insolvency[179] and will be entitled to receive compound interest on amounts owing to it[180] rather than merely simple interest. Significantly, also, a trustee is bound by obligations of utmost good faith and prevented from allowing any conflicts of interest or the making of secret profits.[181]

The 1999 Act may affect the rights of an intended beneficiary in relation to **5.67** covenants to settle after-acquired property. However, this is not clear, and there may be difficulties in the application of the Act.

Trustee not permitted to enforce the covenant

The question here is whether the trustees, as parties to the settlor's covenant, can **5.68** enforce that covenant, recover damages for breach, and then hold those damages on trust for the intended beneficiaries. The established position in English law is that trustees must not only take no action to enforce the covenant but will be barred from doing so.[182] Several reasons have been put forward to explain and justify this rule, for example that the court will not allow a beneficiary to do indirectly, through the trustees, that which he could not achieve directly;[183] that, even if the trustee were to succeed in an action on the covenant, he would recover nominal damages only, for he has suffered no loss;[184] and that, even if he recover substantial damages, he could not take a beneficial interest so that there would then be a gap in the beneficial ownership, requiring that the equitable interest be held on resulting trust for the settlor, thereby rendering the process futile.[185]

In *Re Kay's Settlement*,[186] for example, a woman conveyed property to herself for **5.69** life and in remainder to other people while she was a spinster. The conveyance contained a covenant to settle after-acquired property. Subsequently the woman married and had children. In later years she received property which fell within the terms of the covenant but to which she had had no entitlement at the time of creating the covenant. The woman refused to settle the property on trust in accordance with the covenant. None of the beneficiaries could establish any rights

---

[179] *Re Goldcorp* [1995] 1 AC 74. [180] *Westdeutsche Landesbank v Islington* [1996] AC 669.
[181] *Boardman v Phipps* [1967] 2 AC 46.
[182] *Re Pryce* [1917] 1 Ch 234; *Re Kay* [1939] Ch 329; *Re Cook* [1965] Ch 902.
[183] *Re Pryce* [1917] 1 Ch 234. [184] See (1950) 3 CLP 30, 43 (O Marshall).
[185] cf *Re Cavendish-Browne's Settlement Trusts* [1916] WN 341, an obscure, briefly reported case, decided before *Re Pryce* and *Re Kay*. In any event, it concerned specific land and not after-acquired property.
[186] [1939] Ch 329.

in the after-acquired property. The question arose whether or not the trustees, as parties to the covenant, could enforce it so as to compel the woman to settle the after-acquired property. In line with the earlier decision in *Re Pryce*,[187] where it was held that the trustees would not be permitted to sue on such a covenant, the Court held that the trustees would actually be directed not to do so. This principle was followed in *Re Cook*:[188] the trustees ought not to be permitted to commence such litigation because it would be vexatious and wasteful.[189] If the trustee were allowed to commence the litigation and enforce the covenant there would be no trust on which the property could be held.

5.70   The correctness of these decisions and of such reasons has been the subject of a vast body of literature.[190] Nevertheless, unless and until these questions are challenged on appeal, the current position in English law is that a trustee will be prevented by the court from enforcing covenants to settle after-acquired property.

Trust of the promise itself

5.71   An exception to the approach set out above appears in the decision in *Fletcher v Fletcher*.[191] A father covenanted with a trustee to settle an after-acquired sum of £66,000 on his sons, Jacob and John. The property was passed to the trustee on the father's death. In reliance on the principles set out in the line of cases culminating in *Re Cook*[192] (above), the trustee contended that there had been no valid trust and that the trustee ought therefore to be absolutely entitled to the money. The court held, however, that the surviving beneficiary, Jacob, was entitled to sue under the terms of the trust on the basis that there had been property which could have been settled on the purported trust. The relevant trust property identified by the court in *Fletcher* was *the benefit of the covenant itself*.

5.72   In itself, the concept of creating a trust of the benefit of a contract or covenant is not particularly problematic or novel. The benefit of a contract or covenant is itself a form of property, ie a chose in action. A party to such a contract or covenant can assign that benefit to another and deal with it as with any other form of property, for example mortgaging or charging it as security. He can also declare trusts of that chose in action in favour of another. The basis of the decision in *Fletcher*, therefore, is that, in addition to a straightforward covenant to settle after-acquired property

---

187   [1917] 1 Ch 234.   188   [1965] Ch 902.
189   cf *Hirachand Punanchand v Temple* [1911] 2 KB 330.
190   See, for example, (1950) 3 CLP 30 (O Marshall); (1960) 76 LQR 100 (DW Elliott); (1962) 78 LQR 228 (JA Hornby); (1965) 23 CLJ 46 (GH Jones); (1966) 29 MLR 397 (D Matheson); (1966) 8 Malaya LR 153 (M Scott); [1967] ASCL 387 (JD Davies); (1969) 85 LQR 213 (WA Lee); (1975) 91 LQR 236 (JL Barton); (1976) 92 LQR 427 (RP Meagher and JRF Lehane); (1979) 32 CLP 1; (1981) 34 CLP 189 (CEF Rickett); [1982] Conv 280 (M Friend) and 352 (S Smith); (1982) 98 LQR 17 (JD Feltham); (1986) 60 ALJ 387 (S Lindsay and P Ziegler); [1988] Conv 19 (D Goddard); *Underhill and Hayton*, 166–182; *Lewin* paras 10-06–10-26A.
191   (1844) 4 Hare 67.   192   [1965] Ch 902.

on trust, there is also an immediate declaration of trust of the benefit of the covenant, thereby resulting immediately in a fully constituted trust. When the covenant is subsequently performed (either voluntarily or as a result of enforcement of the trust by one of its beneficiaries), one form of trust property (the chose in action) is replaced by another. The weakness of the actual decision in *Fletcher* is that a trust of the benefit of a covenant, just like a trust of any other form of property, requires a clear manifestation of an intention to create that trust; and there is no indication in *Fletcher* that the settlor had ever possessed any such intention in respect of a chose in action.

In the case of *Don King v Warren*[193] two boxing promoters entered into a series of **5.73** partnership agreements whereby they undertook to treat any promotion agreements entered into with boxers as being part of the partnership property. It was held by Lightman J and subsequently the Court of Appeal that this disclosed an intention to settle the benefit of those promotion agreements on trust for the members of the partnership. This demonstrates a principle akin to *Fletcher v Fletcher* whereby a contract was held to have been capable of forming the subject matter of a trust despite the fact that the agreements themselves were not capable of assignment.[194] However, the principle underlying *Fletcher* is not in question: it is the absence of intention to create an immediately binding trust that makes its application questionable. In any event, it is difficult to see how *Fletcher* could affect the situation in the 'after-acquired property' cases, for even in *Fletcher* the covenant related to specific, existing property.

Contracts to create trusts of land

Section 2 of the Law of Property (Miscellaneous Provisions) Act 1989 provides: **5.74**

(1) A contract for the sale or other disposition of an interest in land can only be made in writing and only by incorporating all the terms which the parties have expressly agreed in one document or, where contracts are exchanged, in each.
(2) The terms may be incorporated in a document either by being set out in it or by reference to some other document.
(3) The document incorporating the terms or, where contracts are exchanged, one of the documents incorporating them (but not necessarily the same one) must be signed by or on behalf of each party to the contract.

Thus, section 2 applies to a contract (executed after 26 September 1989) to create   **5.75** a trust of any interest in land or to dispose of an equitable interest in land, including an interest in co-owned land.[195] All the terms of the contract must be in one

---

[193] [1998] 2 All ER 608, Lightman J; affirmed [2000] Ch 291.

[194] For other examples of trusts of property which was in itself non-assignable, see *Re Celtic Extraction Ltd (In Liquidation), Re Bluestone Chemicals Ltd (In Liquidation)* [1999] 4 All ER 684; *Swift v Dairywise Farms* [2000] 1 All ER 320.

[195] Section 2 has been interpreted somewhat liberally and has been held not to apply to a collateral agreement (*Record v Bell* [1991] 1 WLR 853), an option (*Spiro v Glencrown Properties Ltd*

document or, where contracts are exchanged, in each.[196] The relevant document must be signed by, or on behalf of, both parties. If section 2 is not complied with, there is no contract, ie it is void and not simply unenforceable.

5.76 Subject perhaps to the possible application of section 53(1)(c) of the Law of Property Act 1925,[197] a contract to create a trust of property other than land or an interest in land does not need to satisfy any formalities.

Contracts to dispose of subsisting equitable interests in pure personalty

5.77 If T holds pure personalty on trust for B1, and B1 enters into a specifically enforceable contract to sell his equitable interest to B2, and if B1 is then a bare trustee for B2, with no active duties to perform, so that B1 can effectively be ignored in the ensuing relationship and T holds the property on trust for B2, the question is whether there has been a disposition by B1 to B2 which, in order to be valid, must be in writing and comply with section 53(1)(c).[198] If it is a specifically enforceable contract, it gives rise to a constructive trust in favour of B2, and the creation of such a trust is excluded from the scope of section 53(1)(c) by section 53(2).[199] In reality, in very few cases is it conceivable that B1 would simply be a bare trustee for B2, and a sub-trust will have been created and section 53(1)(c) would not be applicable.[200] Indeed, in *Chinn v Collins*,[201] the House of Lords held that no formalities needed to be satisfied for a contract relating to an equitable interest in publicly quoted shares, despite the fact that such a contract is not specifically enforceable and therefore does not give rise to a constructive trust. 'Dealings related to the equitable interest in these [shares] required no formality. As soon as there was an agreement for their sale accompanied or followed by payment of the price, the equitable title passed at once to the purchaser and all that was needed to perfect his title was notice to the trustee or the nominee.'[202]

[1991] Ch 537), a supplemental agreement following an executed contract (*Tootall Clothing Ltd v Guinea Properties Management Ltd* (1992) 64 P & CR 452), or a 'lock-out' agreement (*Pitt v PHH Asset Management Ltd* [1994] 1 WLR 327); but it has been applied to a variation of the original contract (*McCausland v Duncan Lawrie* [1996] 4 All ER 995).

[196] A document omitting an agreed term can be rectified so as to comply with s 2: *Wright v Robert Leonard (Developments) Ltd* [1994] EGCS 69.

[197] See next paragraph.

[198] *Oughtred v IRC* [1960] AC 206, 233, per Lord Denning; *Grey v IRC* [1958] Ch 375, 382, per Lord Evershed MR; [1958] Ch 690, 715; *Grainge v Wilberforce* (1889) 5 TLR 436; *Re Lashmar* [1891] 1 Ch 258.

[199] *Neville v Wilson* [1997] Ch 144. The same view had been expressed earlier in *Oughtred v IRC* [1958] Ch 383; [1960] AC 206, 227–228; *Re Holt's Settlement* [1969] 1 Ch 100; *DHN Food Distributors Ltd v London Borough of Tower Hamlets* [1976] 3 All ER 462.

[200] Or so it is generally assumed. It may well be asked, however, why there has not simply been a part disposal of B1's equitable interest, to which s 53(1)(c) ought to apply. See (1984) 47 MLR 385, 396–399 (B Green).

[201] [1981] AC 533.   [202] ibid 548.

6

TRUSTS FOR NON-CHARITABLE PURPOSES: THE BENEFICIARY PRINCIPLE[1]

---

[1] A Underhill and DJ Hayton, *Law of Trusts and Trustees* (16th edn, Butterworths, 2002) ('*Underhill and Hayton*') 110–129; P Baxendale-Walker, *Purpose Trusts for Commercial and Private Use* (Butterworths Tolley, 1999); Morris and Leach, *The Rule Against Perpetuities* (2nd edn, Sweet & Maxwell, 1962) Ch 12; Maudsley, *The Modern Law of Perpetuities* (Butterworths, 1979) 166–178; Gray, *The Rule Against Perpetuities* (4th edn, Sweet & Maxwell, 1942) App H, 894–909; Scott, *The Law of Trusts* (4th edn, Little Brown & Co, 1987), 119, 123, 124; RW Jennings and JC Harper, *Jarman on Wills* (8th edn, 1951), ('*Jarman*') 284–290, 898–899; (1892) 5 Harv LR 389 (JB Ames); (1902) 15 Harv LR 509 (JC Gray); (1917) 33 LQR 342 (C Sweet); (1937) 53 LQR 24, 33 (WO Hart); (1949) 13 Conv (NS) 418 (DC Potter); (1950) 14 Conv (NS) 374 (AKR Kiralfy); (1952) 68 LQR 449 (RE Megarry); (1953) 17 Conv (NS) 46 (LA Sheridan); (1953) 6 CLP 151 (OR Marshall); (1955) 18 MLR 120 (L Leigh); (1958) 4 Univ of West Aus LR 235 (LA Sheridan); (1970) 34 Conv (NS) 77 (PA Lovell); (1971) 87 LQR 31 (JW Harris); (1973) 37 Conv (NS) 420 (L McKay); (1977) 40 MLR 397 (N Gravells); (1977) 41 Conv (NS) 179 (K Widdows); A Duckworth, *STAR Trusts: the Special Trusts (Alternative Regime) Law 1997* (Gostick Hall Publications, 1997); HAJ Ford, 'Dispositions for Purposes' in PD Finn (ed), *Essays on Equity* (1985), 159–178; RBM Cotterrell, 'Some Sociological Aspects of the Controversy Around the Legal Validity of Private Purpose Trusts' in Stephen Goldstein (ed), *Equity and Contemporary Legal Developments* (The Hebrew University of Jerusalem, 1990) 302–334; P Matthews, 'The New Trust: Obligations Without Rights?' in AJ Oakley (ed), *Trends in Contemporary Trust Law* (Clarendon Press, 1997), 1–31; [2000] JTCP 237; (2001) 117 LQR 96 (DJ Hayton); see GW Thomas, 'Purpose Trusts' in J Glasson (ed), *The International Trust* (Jordans, 2002) 237; T Honore, 'Trusts: The Inessentials' in J Getzler (ed), *Rationalizing Property, Equity and Trusts* (LexisNexis, 2003) 7. No recommendation is made in the Law Commission's Report on *The Rules Against Perpetuities and Excessive Accumulations* (Law Com No 251) as to purpose trusts; see paras 1.14, 8.36.

A. General Principle

6.01   The generally accepted rule in English law is that, in order to be valid, a trust must have an ascertainable beneficiary (individual or corporate) in whose favour performance of the trust may be decreed.[2] A trust is obligatory: it imposes a duty; and there cannot be an obligation unless there is a corresponding right. On this basis, trusts for purposes or objects are invalid, for a purpose or object cannot sue. Trusts for charitable purposes, however, are valid because they are enforceable by the Attorney-General.[3] As Lord Parker stated in *Bowman v Secular Society Ltd*:[4]

> A trust to be valid must be for the benefit of individuals . . . or must be in that class of gifts for the benefit of the public which the courts in this country recognise as charitable in the legal as opposed to the popular sense of that term.

On this basis, the courts have, for example, declared invalid trusts for 'objects of benevolence and liberality',[5] for 'the purpose of providing some useful memorial to myself',[6] for 'the maintenance . . . of good understanding between nations . . . and . . . the preservation of the independence and integrity of newspapers',[7] or for the purpose of bricking up a house for 20 years after a testatrix's death.[8]

6.02   However, there are several examples of non-charitable purpose trusts being held valid by the courts. These have been judicially described as 'concessions to human weakness or sentiment',[9] as 'troublesome, anomalous and aberrant',[10] and as 'occasions when Homer has nodded'.[11] Nevertheless, their existence clearly indicates that some non-charitable purpose trusts may be valid, and in turn raises the question whether such instances 'are to be regarded as anomalous or whether they are destructive of the supposed principle'.[12] Roxburgh J's conclusion, in *Re Astor's Settlement Trusts*,[13] was that the principle was well founded, both in theory and practical considerations:

> The typical case of a trust is one in which the legal owner of the property is constrained by a court of equity so to deal with it as to give effect to the equitable

---

[2] *Morice v Bishop of Durham* (1804) 9 Ves 399, 404; *Bowman v Secular Society Ltd* [1917] AC 406, 441; *Re Chardon* [1928] Ch 464; *Re Diplock* [1941] Ch 253, 259; *Re Wood* [1949] Ch 498; *Re Astor's Settlement Trusts* [1952] Ch 534; *Leahy v Attorney-General (NSW)* [1959] AC 457, 478; *Re Denley's Trust Deed* [1969] 1 Ch 373; *Re Vandervell's Trusts (No 2)* [1974] Ch 269, 319.
[3] *Leahy v Attorney-General (NSW)* [1959] AC 457 at 478, 479.
[4] [1917] AC 406, 441. There is no shortage of statements to the same effect; see, eg, *Re Endacott* [1960] Ch 232, 246; *Re Recher's Will Trusts* [1972] Ch 526, 538.
[5] *Morice v Bishop of Durham* (1804) 9 Ves 399.   [6] *Re Endacott* [1960] Ch 232.
[7] *Re Astor's Settlement Trusts* [1952] Ch 534.
[8] *Brown v Burdett* (1882) 21 Ch D 667. See also *M'Caig's Trustees v Kirk Session of United Free Church of Lismore* 1915 SC 426 and *Aitken's Trustees v Aitken* 1927 SC 374.
[9] *Re Astor's Settlement Trusts* [1952] Ch 534, 541.   [10] *Re Endacott* [1960] Ch 232, 251.
[11] ibid 250.   [12] *Re Astor's Settlement Trusts* [1952] Ch 534, 541, *per* Roxburgh J.
[13] ibid 541–542.

rights of another. These equitable rights have been hammered out in the process of litigation in which a claimant on equitable grounds has successfully asserted rights against a legal owner or other person in control of property. Prima facie, therefore, a trustee would not be expected to be subject to an equitable obligation unless there was somebody who could enforce a correlative right, and the nature and right of that obligation would be worked out in proceedings for enforcement . . . At an early stage, however, the courts were confronted with attempts to create trusts for charitable purposes which there was no equitable owner to enforce . . . But if the purposes are not charitable, great difficulties arise both in theory and in practice. In theory, because having regard to the historical origins of equity it is difficult to visualize the growth of equitable obligations which nobody can enforce, and in practice, because it is not possible to contemplate with equanimity the creation of large funds devoted to non-charitable purposes which no court and no department of state can control, or in the case of maladministration reform. Therefore, Lord Parker's . . . proposition would prima facie appear to be well founded. Moreover, it gains no little support from the practical considerations that no officer has ever been constituted to take, in the case of non-charitable purposes, the position held by the Attorney-General in connexion with charitable purposes, and no case has been found in the reports in which the court has ever directly enforced a non-charitable purpose against a trustee.

Thus, the emphasis here is on the unenforceability of non-charitable purpose trusts, which is itself seen as an inevitable consequence of the absence of any beneficiary—or, to be precise, of anyone who can claim 'equitable rights' in or to the trust property—to whom the trustees could owe any equitable duties.

However, well established though this view has become, it does not provide a **6.03** comprehensive analysis of the position in English law. It seems clear that the lack of a beneficiary with enforceable equitable rights in the trust property may not have been the sole reason why English courts have generally refused to uphold purpose trusts: indeed, the few reported cases suggest that such trusts might also be held invalid on one or more of many other grounds. Indeed, it is arguable that the lack of such a beneficiary may not always have been regarded as a fundamental obstacle to the validity of purpose trusts: some of the older decisions suggest that English law may originally have accorded greater significance to the intentions of the settlor or testator (provided they were lawful and clear) and to the need to enforce a moral obligation of conscience, which the trustees had recognized and accepted, rather than to questions of equitable proprietary rights or issues of practical difficulty in enforcement.[14]

---

[14] A more sweeping analysis has been put forward by P Baxendale-Walker in *Purpose Trusts for Commercial and Private Use* (Butterworths Tolley, 1999). He argues that there is actually no rule against non-charitable purpose trusts in English law; or, alternatively, that, if there is such a rule, it is erroneous, being based on what he alleges is a misunderstanding of early equity jurisprudence and a misreading of early authorities by judges and lawyers over several centuries. It is suggested that such a view is simply untenable, however: see GW Thomas, 'Purpose Trusts' in J Glasson (ed), *The International Trust* (Jordans, 2002) 237, 268–281.

B. Valid Non-Charitable Purpose Trusts

6.04 Those trusts for non-charitable purposes which have been held valid were classified by Morris and Leach[15] into the following categories:

(a) trusts for the erection or maintenance of monuments or graves;
(b) trusts for the saying of masses (where such trusts are not regarded as charitable);
(c) trusts for the maintenance of particular animals;
(d) trusts for the benefit of unincorporated associations (although this group is more doubtful);
(e) miscellaneous cases.

Monuments and graves

6.05 Reasonable provision for the erection of a gravestone or the building of a tomb for a deceased person is apparently regarded as a funeral expense, and as valid independently of any principle or concession relating to private purpose trusts.[16] However, a trust to erect a monument to some member of the testator's family, or to erect headstones on specified graves, or to maintain a grave or keep it in repair, is valid, provided it does not infringe the rule against perpetuities.[17] As Lindley LJ stated in *Re Tyler*,[18] 'There is nothing illegal in keeping up a tomb; on the contrary, it is a very laudable thing to do.' (If such a trust involves the maintenance or repair of the fabric of the church, or the upkeep of the churchyard as a whole, it may be charitable.[19])

Masses

6.06 Trusts for the saying of masses may be charitable if the masses are said in public and the gifted property is used for the provision of stipends for the priests who are to say the masses (thereby relieving church funds).[20] If these requirements are not satisfied, the trust may possibly be valid as a non-charitable purpose trust, provided the rule against perpetuities is not infringed.[21]

---

[15] Morris and Leach, *The Rule Against Perpetuities* (Sweet & Maxwell, 2nd edn, 1962) 310. This classification was adopted by Lord Evershed MR in *Re Endacott* [1960] Ch 232, 246.

[16] *Mellick v President and Guardians of the Asylum* (1821) Jac 180; *Trimmer v Danby* (1856) 25 LJ Ch 424. Cf Gray in Morris and Leach (n 15 above) 311.

[17] *Masters v Masters* (1718) 1 P Wms 421; *Trimmer v Danby* (1856) 25 LJ Ch 424; *Mussett v Bingle* [1876] WN 170; *Pirbright v Salwey* [1896] WN 86; *Re Hooper* [1932] 1 Ch 38. See also the Parish Councils and Burial Authorities (Miscellaneous Provisions) Act 1970.

[18] [1891] 3 Ch 252, 258–259.

[19] *Re Vaughan* (1886) Ch D 187; *Re Eighmie* [1935] Ch 524.

[20] *Re Hetherington* [1990] Ch 1; *Re Caus* [1934] Ch 162.

[21] *Bourne v Keane* [1919] AC 815, 874–875; *Re Gibbons* [1917] 1 Ir R 448; *Re Will of Ryan* (1925) 60 Ir LTR 57; *Re Khoo Cheng Teow* [1932] Straits Setts LR 226.

Specific animals

Trusts for the care or maintenance of specific animals have also been upheld, for **6.07** example an annuity to be applied in maintaining the testator's favourite black mare,[22] or a gift for the maintenance of the testator's horses and hounds.[23] The trust must again not be perpetuitous.

Unincorporated associations

An unincorporated association, unlike the individuals of which it is composed or **6.08** a corporation, is not a legal person (unless made so by statute) and therefore cannot be an entity capable of holding property. It has been defined as 'two or more persons bound together for one or more common purposes, not being business purposes, by mutual undertakings each having mutual duties and obligations, in an organisation which has rules which identify in whom control of it and its funds rests and on what terms and which can be joined or left at will'.[24]

The property of an unincorporated association may be held on its behalf in **6.09** different ways.[25] In *Neville Estates Ltd v Madden*,[26] Cross J laid down the often-cited principles which govern the validity of a gift to an unincorporated association:

> Such a gift may take effect in one or other of three quite different ways. In the first place, it may, on its true construction, be a gift to the members of the association at the relevant date as joint tenants, so that any member can sever his share and claim it whether or not he continues to be a member of the association. Secondly, it may be a gift to the existing members not as joint tenants, but subject to their respective contractual rights and liabilities towards one another as members of the association. In such a case a member cannot sever his share. It would accrue to the other members on his death or resignation, even though such members include persons who become members after the gift took effect. If this is the effect of the gift, it will not be open to objection on the score of perpetuity or uncertainty unless there is something in its terms or circumstances or in the rules of the association which precludes the members at any given time from dividing the subject of the gift between them on the footing that they are solely entitled to it in equity. Thirdly, the terms or circumstances of the gift or the rules of the association may show that the property in question is not to be at the disposal of the members for the time being, but is to be held in trust for or applied for the purposes of the association as a quasi-corporate entity. In this case

---

[22] *Pettingall v Pettingall* (1842) 11 LJ Ch 176.   [23] *Re Dean* (1889) 41 Ch D 552.

[24] *Conservative and Unionist Central Office v Burrell* [1982] 1 WLR 522, 525, *per* Lawton LJ. Although the case concerned the meaning of 'unincorporated association' for the purposes of the Income and Corporation Taxes Act 1970, s 238 (1), this definition is considered to be of general application. See also *Re Koeppler's Will Trusts* [1986] Ch 423, 431, *per* Slade LJ.

[25] See *Neville Estates Ltd v Madden* [1962] Ch 832, 849; *Re Recher's Will Trusts* [1972] Ch 526, 538; *Re Bucks Constabulary Fund (No 2)* [1979] 1 WLR 937; *Re Grant's Will Trusts* [1980] 1 WLR 360; *News Group Newspapers Ltd v SOGAT 82* [1986] ICR 716; J Warburton [1985] Conv 318; J Warburton, *Unincorporated Associations, Law and Practice* (1986).

[26] [1962] Ch 832, 849. See also *Leahy v Attorney-General (NSW)* [1959] AC 457, 478; *Radmanovich v Nedeljkovic* (2001) 3 ITELR 802.

the gift will fail unless the association is a charitable body. If the gift is of the second class, ie one which the members of the association for the time being are entitled to divide among themselves, then, even if the objects of the association are in themselves charitable, the gift would not, I think, be a charitable gift.

Similarly, in *Re Recher's Will Trusts*,[27] Brightman J stated:

> A trust for non-charitable purposes, as distinct from a trust for individuals, is clearly void because there is no beneficiary. It does not, however, follow that persons cannot band themselves together as an association or society, pay subscriptions and validly devote their funds in pursuit of some lawful non-charitable purpose. An obvious example is a member's social club. But it is not essential that the members should only intend to secure direct personal advantages to themselves. The association may be one in which personal advantages to members are combined with the pursuit of some outside purpose. Or the association may be one which offers no personal benefit at all to the members, the funds of the association being applied exclusively to the pursuit of some outside purpose. Such an association of persons is bound, I would think, to have some sort of constitution; that is to say, the rights and liabilities of the members of the association would inevitably depend on some form of contract *inter se*, usually evidenced by a set of rules.
>
> ...
>
> In the case of a donation which is not accompanied by any words which purport to impose a trust, it seems to me that the gift takes effect in favour of the existing members of the association as an accretion to the funds which are the subject matter of the contract which such members have made *inter se*, and falls to be dealt with in precisely the same way as the funds which the members themselves have subscribed. So in the case of a legacy. In the absence of words which purport to impose a trust, the legacy is a gift to the members beneficially, not as joint tenants or as tenants in common so as to entitle each member to an immediate distributive share, but as an accretion to the funds which are the subject-matter of the contract which the members have made *inter se*.

The traditional view, therefore, is that a trust for the purposes of an association (as opposed to its members) will fail unless those purposes are charitable or fall within one of the exceptional categories of valid non-charitable purposes.

Miscellaneous cases

6.10 Among the miscellaneous cases are to be found a valid trust for 'the promotion of fox-hunting',[28] (in Ireland) a valid trust to dispose of property to the testator's 'best spiritual advantage',[29] and a trust to provide a maintenance fund for a historic building[30] or a sinking fund for the repair of a block of flats.

---

[27] [1972] Ch 526, 538. [28] *Re Thompson* [1934] Ch 342.

[29] *Re Gibbons* [1917] 1 IR 448. Such a trust would be void for uncertainty in England and Wales, quite apart from the beneficiary principle.

[30] Inheritance Tax Act 1984, s 77; *Glasgow Trades House v IRC* 1970 SC 101, 108, 113. *Quaere* whether this is charitable. It can also be explained as a statutory exception to the general rule.

Trusts to provide an annual cup for yacht racing,[31] to keep a portrait in repair,[32] **6.11**
and (in Australia) to found a Catholic newspaper,[33] have all been held void, but
on the ground of perpetuity and not for lack of a beneficiary.[34]

C. Reasons for Invalidity of Non-Charitable Purpose Trusts

The authorities suggest that the courts have given alternative reasons for holding **6.12**
non-charitable purpose trusts void. More than one reason may apply in any particular case; and it is clearly not the case that, by placing emphasis on one reason,
the court is indicating that another reason would not also be equally fatal to
validity in a particular case. Very often, however, the court's reasons are not kept
distinct.

The beneficiary principle

Lord Parker pointed out in *Bowman v Secular Society Ltd*[35] that there must be **6.13**
someone who can enforce a trust, other than a charitable trust, somebody in
whose favour the court can decree performance. A trust creates an obligation, so
there must be a correlative right in somebody to enforce it. In the case of a private
trust, there is clearly no such difficulty; and, in the case of charitable trusts, the
Attorney-General is charged with the duty of enforcement. A trust for a non-charitable purpose, however, lacks both a beneficiary and an enforcer. On this basis,
trusts for purposes have been declared void in *Re Wood*,[36] *Re Astor's Settlement*,[37]
Re Shaw,[38] and *Re Endacott*.[39]

The beneficiary principle is closely related to the so-called rule in *Saunders v* **6.14**
Vautier,[40] but they are, nonetheless, separate principles. The beneficiary principle
is concerned with enforceability and, as such, it requires that, at all times during
the existence of a trust, there is some person who has a sufficient interest under the
terms of that trust to be able to enforce it. Such a person may be a beneficiary with
a fixed interest, someone (perhaps the settlor himself) entitled under a resulting
trust, or an object of a discretionary trust: in other words, someone who has an
equitable proprietary interest or right in the trust fund. The rule in *Saunders*, on
the other hand, enables a trust to be terminated when, and only when, all the

---

[31] *Re Nottage* [1895] 2 Ch 649.   [32] *Re Gassiot* (1901) 70 LJ Ch 242.
[33] *Re Lawlor* [1934] VR 22.
[34] Where the ground of invalidity is something other than the lack of a beneficiary, it clearly does
not follow that the lack of a beneficiary would not also, or otherwise, be considered equally fatal.
[35] [1971] AC 406, 441. Sir William Grant MR is said to have expressed the same view in *Morice
v Bishop of Durham* (1804) 9 Ves 399, 405. However, his observations seem to have been directed at
the need for certainty of objects rather than the beneficiary principle.
[36] [1949] Ch 498, esp 501.   [37] [1952] Ch 534, esp 547.   [38] [1957] 1 WLR 729.
[39] [1960] Ch 232.   [40] (1841) 4 Beav 115.

beneficiaries (and objects) of the trust are adults, *sui juris,* and between themselves absolutely entitled to the trust fund: when all of these conditions are met, the beneficiaries can direct the distribution of the trust fund to themselves. Indeed, these conditions must always be satisfied at some point (but obviously not at every point) during the existence, or more likely at the natural termination, of any express private trust (and no later than the end of the perpetuity period applicable to that trust). It is immediately obvious that these are distinct principles and, in particular, that the beneficiary principle must be satisfied even when the rule in *Saunders* cannot apply. Given the strict requirements of the rule against perpetuities, it is difficult, if not impossible, to envisage any terms of any valid private trust which do not ensure that someone will have a sufficient direct proprietary interest or right in the trust fund to be able to ask the court for protection and enforcement of the trust. This is the case irrespective of the fact that the interest may be vested, contingent, or defeasible in some way, that it may arise under some provision in default or under a resulting trust, that the beneficiaries may be infants or even unborn, that there may be a trust or power to accumulate income, or, indeed, that it is the proprietary right of a discretionary object (who, of course, has no interest properly so-called).[41] At the risk of labouring the point, this is precisely what the beneficiary principle requires and why it is the absence of such a 'proprietary' basis that is so fatal to the purpose trust.[42]

6.15 In two decisions—*Re Denley*[43] and *Re Lipinski*[44]—the court has once again, arguably, exhibited a more liberal approach to the beneficiary principle. In *Re Denley,* trustees for sale were directed to maintain land as a sports ground 'primarily for the benefit of the employees of the company and secondarily for the benefit of such other person or persons (if any) as the trustees may allow to use the

---

[41] Although an object of a discretionary trust has no 'interest' in the technical sense, he does possess a 'proprietary' right (with several of the characteristics of 'property') and, as such, he has a sufficient interest to require protection and to enable him to enforce the trust: see generally GW Thomas, *Powers* (Sweet & Maxwell, 1998) ('*Thomas*') 377–387, and paras 7.20–7.27 and 7.37–7.38 below.

[42] It has been argued that, in the nineteenth century, English courts upheld purpose trusts without any indication that they were inherently problematic: they were neither condemned nor approved. It was only when wider and more ambitious projects were sought to be achieved in the twentieth century that an explicitly hostile judicial view was instituted, and that the beneficiary principle came to be regarded as one of the fundamental characteristics of a private trust. In essence, the basic conception of a trust changed fundamentally from the position where it was regarded as a moral obligation of conscience capable of fulfilment if the trustee recognized and accepted it to the situation where enforceability depends on the existence of someone who can claim some equitable interest or right in the trust property. See RBM Cotterrell, 'Some Sociological Aspects of the Controversy Around the Legal Validity of Private Purpose Trusts' in Stephen Goldstein (ed), *Equity and Contemporary Legal Developments* (The Hebrew University of Jerusalem, 1990) 302. However, it is difficult to avoid the conclusion that, whatever may be said about the historic position, English law is today wedded to the beneficiary principle in the 'proprietary' sense.

[43] [1969] 1 Ch 373.   [44] [1976] Ch 235.

same'. Goff J held the gift valid. He distinguished between different kinds of purpose trusts:[45]

> I think there may be a purpose or object trust, the carrying out of which would benefit an individual or individuals, where that benefit is so indirect or intangible or which is otherwise so framed as not to give those persons any *locus standi* to apply to the court to enforce the trust, in which case the beneficiary principle would, as it seems to me, apply to invalidate the trust, quite apart from any question of uncertainty or perpetuity. Such cases can be considered if and when they arise. The present is not . . . of that character. . . . Apart from this possible exception, in my judgment the beneficiary principle of *In Re Astor's Settlement Trusts*, which was approved of in *In Re Endacott decd*, . . . is confined to purpose or object trusts which are abstract or impersonal. The objection is not that the trust is for a purpose or object *per se*, but that there is no beneficiary or *cestui que trust* . . .
> Where, then, the trust, though expressed as a purpose, is directly or indirectly for the benefit of an individual or individuals, it seems to me that it is in general outside the mischief of the beneficiary principle.

The trust in question did not infringe the rule against perpetuities; and its beneficiaries were ascertained or ascertainable at any given time.

It is not entirely clear how the trust in *Re Denley* was classified. Goff J clearly **6.16** accepted that a trust expressed as a purpose, but indirectly for the benefit of an individual, was outside the mischief of the beneficiary principle.[46] Moreover, the purpose of extracting the relevant distinction from the authorities seems clearly to have been to justify the conclusion that the trust in question was valid, notwithstanding the fact that it was expressed to be for a non-charitable purpose. On the other hand, his concern that the employees to be benefited should be ascertained or ascertainable at any given time suggests that it was a trust for individuals, and not a purpose trust at all. It is clear, however, that he equated the beneficiary principle simply with the question of enforceability and not with the issue of equitable ownership: the question of whether the employees of the company, together with those others who might be permitted to use the sports ground, could terminate the trust was clearly not regarded as material.

Re Denley leaves many questions unanswered. It does not, for example, identify **6.17** the nature of the 'benefit' and, in particular, whether there has to be some legal or equitable interest or right (other than a right simply to enforce the trust) or whether a de facto advantage is sufficient. Nor does it suggest how 'indirect' a benefit may be before it falls within the beneficiary principle. The employing company presumably derived an indirect benefit from the provision of a fringe benefit to its employees,[47] but it is doubtful whether it would have standing to

---

[45] [1969] 1 Ch 373, 380–382.   [46] ibid 383–384.
[47] cf *Oppenheim v Tobacco Securities Co Ltd* [1951] AC 297.

enforce the trust, any more than a schoolteacher has standing to enforce a trust for the education of a schoolchild.[48]

6.18 *Re Denley* was subsequently approved by Oliver J in *Re Lipinski*. In that case, the testator bequeathed his residuary estate to trustees on trust as to one-half for the Hull Judeans (Maccabi) Association in memory of his late wife, to be used solely in constructing and improving new buildings for the Association. The Hull Judeans were not a charitable body. Oliver J held that, whether the gift was treated as a purpose trust or an absolute gift to an unincorporated non-charitable body with a superadded direction, the gift was valid if the beneficiaries were ascertainable; that the specified purpose of the gift to the Hull Judeans was within the power of that association and its members were the ascertained or ascertainable beneficiaries; and, accordingly, the association's members were the persons who were entitled to enforce that purpose. A gift to an unincorporated non-charitable association for objects upon which the association is at liberty to spend both capital and income will not fail for perpetuity.[49] Oliver J adopted the reasoning of Goff J which, he concluded, accorded both with authority and with common sense. He also pointed out that, although the distinction made by Goff J had not appeared in earlier cases, nevertheless they are consistent with it. For example, in *Re Clarke*[50] (a gift to the Corps of Commissionaires), *Re Drummond*[51] (a gift to the Old Bradfordians Club), *Re Taylor*[52] (a gift to the Midland Bank Staff Association) and *Re Turkington*[53] (a gift to a masonic lodge to build a suitable temple), in each of which the testator had prescribed the purpose for which the gift was to be used, and in each of which the gift was upheld, there were ascertainable beneficiaries. The same can be said of *Re Price*[54] (a gift to the Anthroposophical Society). In contrast, in *Re Wood*[55] (a gift for 'The Week's Good Cause' on the BBC) and *Leahy v Attorney-General (NSW)*[56] (a gift for an order of nuns or the Christian Brothers) the gifts failed because there were none.

6.19 More recently, however, Vinelott J in *Re Grant's Will Trusts*[57] refused to follow the more flexible approach established by *Re Denley* and *Re Lipinski*. In *Re Grant*, a testator had left his estate 'to the Labour Party property committee for the benefit of the Chertsey headquarters of the Chertsey and Walton Constituency Labour Party'. Vinelott J held that the gift failed and devolved as on intestacy. He considered that in *Re Lipinski* Oliver J had construed the gift, not as one on trust for a purpose, but as one under which the members of the association could have resolved to use the property for some other purpose, or indeed to divide it among

---

[48] *Shaw v Lawless* (1838) 5 Cl & Fin 129, 156. See also *Annual Survey of Commonwealth Law* (1968) 439 (D Davies) on a trust for the education of one's relations.
[49] [1976] Ch 235, 245G; *Re Price* [1943] Ch 422.   [50] [1901] 2 Ch 110.
[51] [1914] 2 Ch 90.   [52] [1940] Ch 481.   [53] [1937] 4 All ER 501.
[54] [1943] Ch 422.   [55] [1949] Ch 498.   [56] [1959] AC 457.
[57] [1980] 1 WLR 360.

themselves.[58] Moreover, he considered that *Re Denley*, on a proper analysis, fell outside the categories of gifts to unincorporated associations and purpose trusts. In his judgment, there was no distinction in principle between a trust to permit a class defined by reference to employment to use and enjoy land in accordance with rules to be made at the discretion of trustees, on the one hand, and, on the other hand, a trust to distribute income at the discretion of trustees among a class defined by reference to, for example, relationship to the settlor. In both cases, the benefit to be taken by any member of the class is at the discretion of the trustees.[59] Thus in effect the trust in *Re Denley* was reinterpreted as a trust for the benefit of individuals, thereby satisfying the requirements of the beneficiary principle. In reaching this result Vinelott J concluded that the reasons given for the decisions (if not the decisions themselves) in two cases, namely *Re Drummond*[60] and *Re Price*,[61] were not well founded.

Although the simple logic of *Re Grant* is appealing, it does not deal effectively with **6.20** the discussion of purpose trusts in *Re Denley*. It does not take into account the fact that both Oliver J (in *Re Lipinski*) and Megarry V-C (in *Re Northern Developments (Holdings) Ltd*)[62] accepted the distinction drawn by Goff J. It also ignores several other cases in which there appear to have been purpose trusts, whose validity seems to have been accepted without question. In *Re Abbott's Fund Trusts*,[63] for example, a fund constituted for the maintenance and support of two ladies was held, after their deaths, on resulting trust for the subscribers, apparently on the basis that it was a purpose trust.[64] In *Re Harpur's Will Trusts*,[65] Lord Evershed MR thought that a gift upon trust to apply income during a limited period (of, say, ten years) for certain named persons, some of which are charitable and some not, as the trustees think fit, is by the ordinary law valid. Maintenance funds for historic buildings are often non-charitable purpose trusts.[66] It may also be the case that a trust created with the primary purpose of paying creditors is a type of purpose trust.[67] In any event, the status of Goff J's classification is now, following *Re Grant*, doubtful.

A purpose trust which incidentally benefits persons (as in *Re Denley*) apparently **6.21** cannot be terminated by those persons who indirectly benefit from the purpose,

---

[58] ibid 368.   [59] ibid 368.   [60] [1914] 2 Ch 90.   [61] [1943] Ch 422.

[62] (Unreported) 6 October 1978; referred to in *Carreras Rothmans Ltd v Freeman Mathews Treasure Ltd* [1985] 1 All ER 155; see also (1985) 101 LQR 280 (P Millett).

[63] [1900] 2 Ch 326.

[64] This is doubtful, however: it is relatively easy to analyse the *Abbott* trust as a 'persons trust'.

[65] [1962] Ch 78, 91; and also *per* Harman LJ at 96. See also *Re Aberconway's Settlement Trusts* [1953] Ch 647, 665, *per* Evershed MR and *per* Denning LJ at 669 (and *per* Danckwerts J at first instance: [1952] 2 All ER 981, 986).

[66] Inheritance Tax Act 1984, s 77.

[67] *Carreras Rothmans Ltd v Freeman Mathews Treasure Ltd* [1985] 1 All ER 155, applying *Re Northern Developments (Holdings) Ltd* (unreported).

and they have no right to call for distribution of the property. If this is indeed the case, then *Re Denley* does not satisfy the strict version of the beneficiary principle, namely that it is not just concerned with enforceability, with finding an ascertainable person who is sufficiently benefited by the trust to have *locus standi* to enforce it, but that it is in fact a manifestation of and based on equitable ownership, so that it is only those persons who have actual equitable proprietary interests or rights in the trust property who can enforce that trust: on this view, if there is no such person, there can be no valid trust. Instead, *Re Denley* arguably recognized a hybrid trust, one which is for the benefit of ascertained persons, but under which such persons have no equitable interests or rights in the trust property itself. In contrast, a trust for persons who are to be benefited by the carrying out of a stipulated purpose, for example the education and maintenance of the settlor's children, can be terminated by those persons (assuming they are adults, of full legal capacity, and between them absolutely entitled to the settled property). In the latter case, the purpose is merely the motive for the gift, and the beneficiaries may make the trust property their own.[68]

Uncertainty and impossibility

6.22 If and in the unlikely event that non-charitable purpose trusts are valid in English law, there would presumably be a need for certainty of objects of such a trust and the test for such certainty must then be determined. If a non-charitable purpose trust can exist at all, the definition or description of the purpose must be sufficiently certain. Conceptual certainty would seem to be essential.[69] In *Morice v Bishop of Durham*,[70] for example, the gift was of personal estate upon trust 'to dispose of the ultimate residue to such objects of benevolence and liberality as the Bishop of Durham in his own discretion shall most approve of . . .'. It was held that such language did not confine the objects which the Bishop might choose to charitable objects. The gift can be said to have failed, in this instance, on the ground that the objects had not been described with sufficient certainty to enable the court to determine whether the trustee was properly carrying out his trust. Other similar examples include gifts for 'undertakings of general utility',[71] for 'deserving objects',[72] and 'for such purposes as they should think fit'.[73] The same could be said of *Re Endacott*[74] and *Re Astor's Settlement Trusts*.[75] This reasoning would explain why trusts for the maintenance of specific animals, or for the erection and maintenance of a specific tombstone, have been upheld. The requirement of certainty can be satisfied by the provision of a sufficiently precise description of

---

[68] *Re Andrew's Trusts* [1905] 2 Ch 48; *Re Osoba* [1979] 1 WLR 247; *Re Compton* [1945] Ch 123; *Oppenheim v Tobacco Securities Trust Co* [1951] AC 297.
[69] *McPhail v Doulton* [1971] AC 424. See generally *Thomas* Ch 3.
[70] (1804) 9 Ves 339.   [71] *Kendall v Granger* (1842) 5 Beav 300.
[72] *Harris v Du Pasquier* (1872) 26 LT 689.   [73] *Fowler v Garlike* (1830) 1 Russ & M 232.
[74] [1960] Ch 232.   [75] [1952] Ch 534.

the purpose intended to be provided for. However, certainty of object does not avoid the application of the beneficiary principle: even a specific purpose cannot ask the court to enforce a trust.

Similarly, administrative workability is essential. *Re Denley* could not save the **6.23** trust in *R v District Auditor, ex parte West Yorkshire Metropolitan County Council*,[76] where a local authority, purporting to exercise statutory powers, attempted to create a trust 'for the benefit of any or all or some of the inhabitants of the County of West Yorkshire'. The capital and income of the trust were to be applied in any of four expressed methods. The class of potential beneficiaries numbered around 2,500,000. It was held that the class was so large that the trust was administratively unworkable.

Delegation of power of testamentary disposition

It has been said that testamentary[77] non-charitable purpose trusts are void on the **6.24** grounds that, as there is no one who can enforce the trust, the trustees are left to determine the destination of the subject matter of the trust: 'The testator has imperfectly exercised his testamentary power; he has delegated it, for the disposal of his property lies with them, not with him.'[78] However, it appears that no such trust has ever been struck down for this reason. Indeed, it seems more apt as a description of one of the consequences of a failure caused by other factors, rather than a cause in itself. Indeed, in *Re Beatty's Will Trusts*,[79] in the context of powers of appointment, Hoffmann J stated that 'a common law rule against testamentary delegation, in the sense of a restriction on the scope of testamentary powers, is a chimera, a shadow cast by the rule of certainty, having no independent existence'. Whether it differs from the ancient principle that a testator must make an effective disposition of his property if he were to disinherit his heir is unclear.[80] In any event, neither principle seems to have much significance in the context of non-charitable purpose trusts.

Public policy

If the purpose of a trust is capricious, useless, wasteful, harmful, illegal, or other- **6.25** wise contrary to public policy, it will fail. Thus a direction to trustees to brick up

---

[76] [1986] RVR 24; and see *Thomas* 286–287.

[77] The objection does not apply to *inter vivos* trusts.

[78] *Leahy v Attorney-General (NSW)* [1959] AC 457, 484, *per* Viscount Simonds. See also *Re Wood* [1949] Ch 498, 501, *per* Harman J, and *Re Denley's Trust Deed* [1969] 1 Ch 373, 387, *per* Goff J; *Buckle v Bristow* (1864) 11 LT 265; *Fowler v Garlike* (1830) 1 Russ & M 232.

[79] [1990] 1 WLR 1503; and see (1991) 107 LQR 211 (J Davies); [1991] Conv 138 (J Martin).

[80] *Houston v Burns* [1918] AC 337, esp 342–343; *Attorney-General v National Provincial and Union Bank of England* [1924] AC 262, 268; *Fell v Fell* (1922) 31 CLR 268, 284; *Batson v Morgan* (1894) 13 NZLR 525, 528.

a house for 20 years has been held void.[81] A similar fate befell a trust for the purpose of building statues of the testator and of his whole family and the building of 'artistic towers' at prominent points on his estates;[82] a trust to erect a massive bronze equestrian statue of the testator;[83] and a trust to provide a weekly supply of fresh flowers on the graves of the testatrix and her mother.[84] Such trusts are considered to have 'objects of no utility, private or public, objects which benefit nobody, and which have no other purpose or use than that of perpetuating at great cost, and in an absurd manner, the idiosyncrasies of an eccentric testator'.[85]

Perpetuity

6.26 The rule against perpetuities is generally concerned with the commencement of interests—with the limit of time to which the vesting of future interests may be postponed—and not with the duration of interests. It is a rule directed against remoteness of vesting. In the context of non-charitable purpose trusts, however, it is the duration of the trust that matters: the period for which the trustees may apply the property vested in them for or towards the purpose or object of the trust must be confined to the perpetuity period.

6.27 If and in so far as non-charitable purpose trusts are valid at all, the relevant perpetuity period is apparently the same as for any other trust, namely a period of lives in being plus 21 years. In *Re Howard*,[86] for example, a gift for the feeding of a parrot during the life of the survivor of two servants was upheld. In *Re Moore*[87] a trust for maintaining a tomb and keeping it in repair until the expiry of 21 years from the death of the last survivor of all persons living at the testator's death failed because of uncertainty (ie the impossibility of ascertaining when the last life would be extinguished) and not because of the use of lives in being. A royal lives clause was not challenged in *Re Astor*;[88] and in *Re Khoo Cheng Teow*[89] the Supreme Court of the Straits Settlements upheld a non-charitable purpose trust for a period of royal lives plus 21 years.

6.28 There is no doubt that the 'lives' in question must be human lives, and cannot be the lives of animals, fish, or trees in California.[90] Whether the option of using a perpetuity period of a fixed term of years, not exceeding 80, provided by section 1(1) of the Perpetuities and Accumulations Act 1964 is available in the case of

---

81 *Brown v Burdett* (1882) 21 Ch D 667.

82 *M'Caig v University of Glasgow* 1907 SC 231; and *M'Caig's Trustees v Kirk Session of United Free Church of Lismore* 1915 SC 426. In the latter case, Lord Salvesen said (at 434): 'The prospect of Scotland being dotted with monuments to obscure persons who happened to have amassed a sufficiency of means, and cumbered with trusts for the purposes of maintaining these monuments in all time coming, appears to me to be little less than appalling.'

83 *Aitken's Trustee v Aitken* 1927 SC 374.   84 *Lindsay's Executor v Forsyth* 1940 SC 458.

85 *M'Caig v University of Glasgow* 1907 SC 231, 242.

86 The Times, 30 October 1908.   87 [1901] 1 Ch 936.   88 [1952] Ch 534.

89 [1932] Straits Setts LR 226.   90 *Re Kelly* [1932] IR 255, esp 260–261.

purpose trusts is undecided.[91] If non-charitable purpose trusts are invalid in any event, such a question is clearly otiose.

If the stipulated perpetuity period is excessive, or if the trust is capable of being **6.29** indefinite in its duration (for example because no perpetuity period is stipulated), it will be void. The court will not read into the trust an implied limitation to 21 years or 'for so long as the law allows'.[92] Moreover, the 'wait and see' rules introduced by the Perpetuities and Accumulations Act 1964 do not apply to purpose trusts.[93] Nevertheless, the courts have sometimes shown reluctance to strike down purpose trusts on the ground of perpetuity. A direction to maintain a grave 'for so long as law allows', or for as long as the trustees 'can legally do so', has been held valid for a period of 21 years.[94] On at least one occasion, judicial notice was taken of the fact that the lifespan of an animal is not likely to exceed 21 years, so that a trust for the support of that animal could not exceed the perpetuity period.[95] Indeed, in *Re Dean*[96] North J upheld a gift of an annuity, for a period of up to 50 years, for the upkeep of the testator's horses and hounds, if they should live so long.

D. Alternative Means of Effectuating Non-Charitable Purposes

There are various methods by which a non-charitable purpose may be carried into **6.30** effect without resorting to a trust as the medium. It seems clear[97] that a gift to the members of an association which exists for the advancement of a non-charitable purpose, for example anti-vivisection, as joint tenants or subject to their contract *inter se*, and not for the association's purposes as such, is valid (subject to the rule against perpetuities). A gift to a corporation created to advance non-charitable

---

[91] Morris and Leach, *The Rule Against Perpetuities* (Sweet & Maxwell, 2nd edn, 1962) Supp 21, suggest that s 1(1) of the 1964 Act does not apply to purpose trusts. The contrary has been argued by Maudsley, *The Modern Law of Perpetuities* (Butterworths, 1979) 177–178. See also P Matthews, 'The New Trust: Obligations Without Rights?' in AJ Oakley (ed), *Trends in Contemporary Trust Law* (Clarendon Press, 1997) 12. No recommendation is made by the Law Commission's Report on *The Rules Against Perpetuities and Excessive Accumulations* (Law Com No 251) as to the removal of the uncertainty caused by s 15 in relation to the availability of the 80-year period to non-charitable purpose trusts: see para 8.36 of the Report.

[92] Morris and Leach (n 91 above) 322; *Re Kelly* [1932] IR 255; *Re Compton* [1946] 1 All ER 117. Cf *Re Budge* [1942] NZLR 350.   [93] Perpetuities and Accumulations Act 1964, s 15(4).

[94] *Pirbright v Salwey* [1896] WN 86; *Re Hooper* [1932] 1 Ch 38.

[95] *Re Haines* The Times, 7 November 1952. This contrasts with Meredith J's statement in *Re Kelly* [1932] IR 255 that the court does not enter into a dog's expectation of life.

[96] (1889) 41 Ch D 552. It is clear from North J's judgment that the need to satisfy the rule against perpetuities was present in his mind, but there is no indication why he thought it was satisfied in this particular instance.

[97] From, eg, *Re Lipinski* [1976] Ch 235; *Re Recher* [1972] Ch 526.

purposes would not be received by it on trust[98] and would therefore be free from many of the difficulties facing a trust. Also, a gift of income to a company for as long (within the perpetuity period) as it carries out the expressed purpose would be valid.[99] A gift to a charitable body, subject to a request (but not an obligation) to carry out a particular purpose, such as the maintenance of a tomb or monument, with a gift over to another charitable body if the request is not complied with, has also been held valid.[100]

6.31 There is no reason, in principle, why a non-charitable purpose should not be achieved by means of a mere power (as opposed to a trust power), rather than a trust (subject, of course, to satisfying the law's requirements as to certainty and perpetuity).[101] However, a purpose trust will not be construed as a power simply in order to save it from invalidity.[102]

6.32 Most, if not all, of these alternative methods suffer from some disadvantage or another. For example, an unincorporated association can alter its objects or be dissolved by its members, who could then distribute the gifted property among themselves. A gift to a non-charitable corporation will be applicable for its purposes while it is a going concern, but its objects may be altered or it may be wound up and its property distributed among its members, in accordance with its memorandum and articles, which are capable of alteration in accordance with statutory provisions. There may also be considerable practical difficulty in enforcing a promise or undertaking given by a corporation or charity. And a mere power need not be exercised by the doneer. Nevertheless, in most circumstances, the prudent practitioner will probably opt for one of these alternatives rather than risk the uncertainties of a trust.

E. *Quistclose* Trusts

6.33 Although it has been argued that *Quistclose* trusts[103] are a species of non-charitable purpose trusts, this is not an accurate, or even a plausible, categorization—a

---

[98] *Bowman v Secular Society Ltd* [1917] AC 406, 440–441.

[99] *Re Chardon* [1928] Ch 464. The possibility of reverter in such a case was not subject to the rule against perpetuities until the enactment of the Perpetuities and Accumulations Act 1964, s 12.

[100] *Re Tyler* [1891] 3 Ch 252; *Re Dalziel* [1943] Ch 277. However, if the second charity assigns its contingent interest to the first charity, the latter may presumably ignore its promise to carry out the purpose: *Re Emery* (1928) 34 ALR 167.

[101] *Re Douglas* (1887) 35 Ch D 472, esp 486; *Re Wootton* [1968] 1 WLR 681, 688. See also *Re Harpur's Will Trusts* [1962] Ch 78, 91, 96, and *Re Aberconway's Settlement Trusts* [1953] Ch 647, 665, 669 (and at first instance [1952] 2 All ER 981, 986).

[102] *Re Shaw* [1957] 1 WLR 729, 746; *IRC v Broadway Cottages Trust* [1955] Ch 20, 36; *Re Endacott* [1960] Ch 232, 246.

[103] So-called after *Barclays Bank Ltd v Quistclose Investments Ltd* [1970] AC 567. See also GW Thomas, 'Purpose Trusts' in J Glasson (ed), *The International Trust* (Jordans, 2002), 254–268, and esp the literature and cases listed at 256, n 2.

view that has recently been endorsed by the House of Lords in *Twinsectra Ltd v Yardley*.[104] A detailed treatment of such trusts is provided elsewhere in this work.[105]

F. Summary of Position in English Law

The status of non-charitable purpose trusts in English law is somewhat ambivalent. Despite the obvious judicial hostility towards such trusts, various exceptional instances have been held valid. Moreover, the precise basis upon which purpose trusts are generally considered invalid is, arguably, far from clear. In broad terms, the cases seem to fall into three distinct, although overlapping, categories (leaving aside the unincorporated association cases). First, there are those in which the purposes were minor, indeed trivial, but also specific, such as the tombs, monuments, and animal cases. The second group includes cases in which the purposes were expressed generally, indeed vaguely, as ones which might have been philanthropic or 'public' in nature, but which did not qualify as charitable purposes and therefore failed for conceptual uncertainty. The third category includes those instances which have failed on grounds of 'perpetuity'. All this might suggest that, provided the purposes are specific and are confined to the perpetuity period, a non-charitable purpose trust could be held valid.

6.34

However, these analyses have at least two serious weaknesses. First, the fact that a particular non-charitable purpose trust was held invalid because of one obvious flaw (be it uncertainty, perpetuity, or whatever) actually lends no support to the argument that, but for that flaw, the trust would otherwise be valid: the court may merely have opted for the solution that was most easily established. Secondly, they ignore the existence and primacy of the beneficiary principle and the need for enforceability. The crucial question seems to be whether non-charitable purpose trusts are simply not capable of being trusts at all in English law, ie *because* they have no identifiable beneficiaries, they are not enforceable and controllable and must therefore fail (and cannot even take effect as a power), or whether they are a legitimate form of trust but, because they are unenforceable and uncontrollable by the court, they can have no effect. The traditional view—and it is suggested the correct view—is that the beneficiary principle is one of the fundamental characteristics of a private trust, without which there can be no trust at all.[106] A private trust requires that identifiable beneficiaries have entitlements to trust property in the form of equitable estates and interests, or other enforceable equitable proprietary rights. In English law, there must exist 'an irreducible core of obligations

6.35

---

[104] [2002] 2 WLR 802.   [105] See paras 9.74–9.98 below.
[106] (1917) 33 LQR 342, 357–358 (C Sweet).

owed by the trustees to the beneficiaries and enforceable by them which is fundamental to the concept of a trust. If the beneficiaries have no rights enforceable
against the trustees there are no trusts.'[107]

6.36　It has been argued that the beneficiary principle does not have—or, at least, does
not require—this central defining role.[108] Instead, this view emphasizes a need to
respect and give some effect to the settlor's or testator's intentions (provided they
are lawful and clear). The trust is essentially a moral obligation of conscience,
which is capable of fulfilment if the trustee himself recognizes and accepts it: 'the
defect in the obligatory nature of the trust is not a contradiction in terms, for it is
not the obligation but its enforcement which . . . is at fault'.[109] The lack of means
of enforcement presents merely practical difficulties.[110] After all, it is said to be
doubtful whether anyone can claim an equitable interest or proprietary right in
the trust fund of a charitable trust, but this never seems to have been considered
an obstacle to the validity of such a trust. One of the things that distinguishes a
charitable trust from a non-charitable purpose trust is precisely the availability of
an ever-present enforcer (the Attorney-General). Thus, it can be argued that the
fundamental problem of non-charitable purpose trusts is not one of essential
validity but of enforceability, and, if the problem of enforceability could be
resolved (as in the case of charitable trusts), such trusts would only have to satisfy
the law's requirements as to certainty and perpetuity. In practical terms, this distinction might seem to have no significance, for the fact remains that, under
English law, there is no recognized enforcer of any such trust. Nevertheless, it may
be a material consideration which might affect the response of an English court if,
and when, it is called upon to recognize or deal with a non-charitable purpose
trust created in a different jurisdiction and in respect of which an enforcer has
been appointed.[111]

6.37　Whether this is indeed an accurate assessment of a charitable trust may itself be
debatable. It is arguable that the beneficiaries of a charitable trust (who constitute
an appreciable section of the public) are indeed the equitable 'owners' of the trust
property and that a charitable trust is saved from invalidity, not by the disapplication

---

[107] *Armitage v Nurse* [1997] 2 All ER 705, 713, *per* Millett LJ.

[108] See, for example, (2001) 117 LQR 96 (DJ Hayton); T Honore, 'Trusts: The Inessentials' in
J Getzler (ed), *Rationalizing Property, Equity and Trusts* (LexisNexis, 2003) 7.

[109] L Leigh (1955) 18 MLR 120, 137.

[110] RBM Cotterrell, 'Some Sociological Aspects of the Controversy Around the Legal Validity of
Private Purpose Trusts' in Stephen Goldstein (ed), *Equity and Contemporary Legal Developments*
(The Hebrew University of Jerusalem, 1990) 302 at 312. See also (1949) 13 Conv (NS) 418, 424
(DC Potter); (1937) 53 LQR 24, 33 (WO Hart); (1971) 87 LQR 31, 56–57 (JW Harris); (1950)
14 Conv (NS) 374, 374–375 (AKR Kiralfy); (1952) 68 LQR 449, 451 (RE Megarry).

[111] (2001) 117 LQR 97 (DJ Hayton); P Matthews, 'From Obligation to Property and Back
Again?' in DJ Hayton, *Extending the Boundaries of Trusts and Similar Ring-Fenced Funds* (Kluwer
Law International, 2002) 230; and T Honore (n 108 above).

of the beneficiary principle, but by the disapplication of the rules relating to certainty of objects and/or the rule against perpetuity. In other words, it could be said that the beneficiaries of a charitable trust, which is usually a continuing trust with an open class of beneficiaries,[112] are effectively in the same position as the objects of a private discretionary trust. However, the law's requirements as to certainty of objects and perpetuity have been eliminated; and difficulties of enforcement (which, without certainty of objects, would otherwise be considerable) are resolved by the appointment of the Attorney-General, who performs a duty similar to that allotted to him in public law for the protection of amorphous public rights.[113]

In any event, the uncertainties of English law in relation to non-charitable purpose trusts—even after the decision in *Re Denley*—are such that only the more adventurous or ignorant practitioner would take the risk of deliberately setting up such trusts, even where a specific enforcer is expressly appointed in the trust instrument. Various 'offshore' jurisdictions have attempted, through legislation, to remove the uncertainties and restrictions which are found in English law, thereby encouraging and enabling the creation of non-charitable purpose trusts within their own jurisdictions. In doing so, they have been forced, as we shall see, to deal directly with those vitiating factors—primarily questions relating to enforcement, uncertainty of objects, and perpetuity—which have proved to be such formidable obstacles in English law. Various aspects of 'offshore' trusts are discussed more fully in Chapters 39 and 40 below. **6.38**

---

[112] The rule in *Saunders v Vautier* (1841) 4 Beav 115 could not apply to such a class.

[113] See also *Gaudiya Mission v Brahmacham* [1998] Ch 341, 350; *Weth v A-G* [1999] 1 WLR 686, 691; [1999] 63 Conv 20 (J Warburton).

7

THE NATURE OF A BENEFICIARY'S INTEREST

A. Introduction

The debate on the nature of a beneficiary's interest under a trust, and specifically **7.01** whether a beneficiary's rights are rights *in personam* against the trustee or rights *in rem* against the trust property, has a long history and remains controversial.[1] It is certainly the case that a beneficiary has a right *in personam* to insist upon and compel the due and proper administration of the trust by the trustee and to require the trustee to account for his stewardship of trust assets. However, it also seems clear that, at least in relation to certain kinds of trust, such as a bare trust, a beneficiary has rights *in rem*, in that he can compel the trustee to transfer the legal title to him. Moreover, as a general rule, a beneficial interest under a 'fixed' trust, ie a defined, limited interest (be it vested or contingent, in possession or in remainder), clearly possesses many of the characteristics of 'property'.[2] The beneficiary can alienate such an interest by assignment or otherwise; and he can declare (sub-)trusts of that

---

[1] (1899) 15 LQR 294 (Hart); (1917) 17 Col LR 269; (1917) 17 Col LR 467; (1929) 45 LQR 198 (Hanbury); (1954) 32 Can BR 520 (Latham); (1967) 45 Can BR 219 (Waters); *Baker v Archer-Shee* [1927] AC 844; *Archer-Shee v Garland* [1931] AC 212; *Webb v Webb* [1994] QB 696. [2] *Tinsley v Milligan* [1994] 1 AC 340, 371.

interest. In addition, a beneficiary—including an object of a discretionary trust who has no right to compel the trustee to pay him any trust income or capital, who is dependent on the exercise of the trustees' discretion in his favour, and who cannot, therefore, be said to have an equitable proprietary interest as such—may still trace the trust assets into the hands of third parties (unless that third party is 'equity's darling' or otherwise protected).[3]

7.02 Equity, by its nature and origins, acted *in personam*: it acted on the conscience of the trustee. Where land was conveyed to A in fee simple on trust for B in fee simple, the common law regarded A as the absolute owner who, therefore, held rights *in rem*, enforceable against anyone, whereas B had no recognizable rights at all. Equity compelled A to hold the land for B and allow B to enjoy it, so, at first, B merely had rights *in personam* against A to compel him to perform his trust. However, in a gradual and well-established process of development, equity had to respond effectively when, for example, A died or transferred the land to another. The range of persons against whom the trust could and would be enforced had to be extended: in 1465, it was enforced against anyone who took the land with notice of the trust;[4] in 1483, the trust was enforced against a trustee's heir;[5] in 1522, against anyone to whom the land had been conveyed as a gift (ie volunteers);[6] and later the executors and the execution creditors of the trustee were bound by the trust.[7] Thus, the position in equity was that a person who took the trust property without giving value in exchange (a donee, heir, or executor) took it with all its attaching burdens, equitable and legal; and that even someone who had given value would be bound if, before the conveyance, he knew of (ie had notice of) the existence of the trust. The 'polar star of equity'[8] thus became: legal rights are good against all the world; equitable rights are good against all persons except a bona fide purchaser of the legal estate for value without notice (ie 'equity's darling') and those claiming under such a purchaser.[9] The title of the equitable owner became almost, but not quite, as absolute and indefeasible as the title of a legal owner.[10] The beneficiary's rights clearly became much more than rights *in personam* enforceable only against the trustee: they are rights enforceable against virtually all third parties, so at worst they are hybrid rights.

---

[3] See, eg, *Re Diplock* [1948] Ch 465; Law of Property Act 1925, s 27. See also paras 29. 73–29.79 below, and Chapter 33 generally.   [4] YB 5 Edw IV, Mich pl 16.

[5] YB 22 Edw IV, Pasch pl 18.   [6] YB 14 Hen VIII, Mich pl 5, f 7.

[7] See FW Maitland, *Equity* (ed by JW Brunyate: 1936) 112; C Harpum, *Megarry and Wade's The Law of Real Property* (6th edn, Sweet & Maxwell, 2000) ('*Megarry and Wade*') 113–115.

[8] *Stanhope v Earl Verney* (1761) 2 Eden 81, 85.

[9] *Re Nisbet and Potts' Contract* [1906] 1 Ch 386 (squatter who acquired title by adverse possession bound by restrictive covenant).

[10] It is actually not the case, of course, that legal rights are invariably absolute and indefeasible.

There is no inconsistency between having both rights *in personam* and rights **7.03** *in rem*: they can easily coexist, although it may be necessary in a particular case to focus on one rather than the other.[11] If the trustee is before the court, it is not necessarily relevant that the trust assets are not within the jurisdiction, nor that English law is not the governing law of the trust.[12] On the other hand, the court can also act if the trust assets are within the jurisdiction but the trustees are not.[13]

However, the entitlement and the rights of a beneficiary may vary considerably **7.04** depending on the kind of trust involved. For example, whether or not an object of a discretionary trust has any rights capable of assignment to another, and whether or not those rights may properly be characterized as 'proprietary' in nature (questions which are dealt with in detail below),[14] it is clear that they differ, if only in their extent, from the rights attached to the interest of a beneficiary under a 'fixed' trust or a bare trust. It is therefore more practical to consider both the nature of the 'interest' possessed by a beneficiary and the rights to which he is entitled in the context of the particular kind of trust.

B. The Rule in *Saunders v Vautier*

The proprietary nature of a beneficiary's interest is illustrated most clearly in the **7.05** case of a bare trust or, indeed, any trust, to which the rule in *Saunders v Vautier*[15] applies. Under this rule, an adult beneficiary (or a number of adult beneficiaries acting together) who is (or are) of full legal capacity and has (or between them have) an absolute, vested, and indefeasible interest in the capital and income of trust property may terminate the trust and require the trustee to transfer the property to him (or them).[16] The underlying principle is that a man may deal with his own property as he wishes and the court will not enforce any restraint on his absolute ownership and enjoyment. Thus, if property is given absolutely to an infant beneficiary, with a direction that the income of that property is to be accumulated until some age beyond his age of majority, he may put a stop to the accumulation and demand payment to him of both capital and income as soon as he attains the

---

[11] See *Webb v Webb* [1994] QB 696. This will be material where, for example, the trust assets or trustees are not within the jurisdiction, or for tax purposes.

[12] *Ewing v Orr-Ewing* (1883) 9 App Cas 34; *Re Ker's Settlement Trusts* [1963] Ch 553; *Chellaram v Chellaram* [1985] Ch 409; *Webb v Webb* [1991] 1 WLR 1410, [1994] QB 696.

[13] *Comphania de Mocambique v British South Africa Co* [1892] 2 QB 358; *Hesperides Hotels Ltd v Aegean Turkish Holidays Ltd.* [1979] AC 508. See also the Civil Jurisdiction and Judgments Act 1982 and CPR, Pt 6, rr 6, 17 *et seq.*   [14] See paras 7.2–7.27 and 7.37–7.38 below.

[15] (1841) 4 Beav 115; affirmed, Cr & Ph 240.

[16] *Stokes v Cheek* (1860) 28 Beav 620; *Magrath v Morehead* (1871) LR 12 Eq 491; *Weatherall v Thornburgh* (1878) 8 Ch D 261 at 270; *Re Smith* [1928] Ch 915; *Re Sandeman* [1937] 1 All ER 368. See also *Buschau v Rogers Communications Inc* (2002) 5 ITELR 27.

age of 18 years.[17] Provided the conditions are met, not only may several beneficial co-owners invoke the rule but so, too, may beneficiaries entitled in succession.[18]

7.06 Clearly, the rule cannot apply where the beneficiary does not have an absolute interest, for example because he has a contingent, limited, or future interest;[19] or where his interest is vested but defeasible, for instance by the exercise of an overriding power of appointment; or where unborn or infant beneficiaries have an actual or potential interest; or where the class of beneficiaries is not closed;[20] or where there is no unanimity. Nor does the rule entitle the beneficiaries to direct the trustees to appoint their own nominee as a new trustee of a continuing trust, or to give directions as to the investments that trustees should make, or to demand that the trustees do anything which they are not willing to do beyond handing over the trust property to the beneficiaries or their nominees (against a proper discharge).[20A] Also, the rights of the beneficiaries are subject to the rights of the trustees to be fully protected against such matters as taxes, costs, or other outgoings (for example rent under a lease comprised in the trust fund).[21]

7.07 A single beneficiary who satisfies the conditions of the rule but is absolutely entitled only to an undivided *share* of the trust fund has rights which are similar to, but not quite as extensive as, those of the beneficiaries collectively. In general, he is entitled to have transferred to him (subject to the above-mentioned rights of the trustees) an aliquot share of each and every asset of the trust fund which presents no difficulty as far as division is concerned. This will apply to cash, an unsecured loan, stock exchange securities, and the like, where the property is easily divisible; but not to land or, in some cases, to shares in private companies or mortgage debts, where it is not. In the latter cases, the beneficiary will have to wait until the property is sold before being able to call on the trustees as of right to account to him for

---

[17] *Wharton v Masterman* [1895] AC 186; *Gosling v Gosling* (1859) Johns 265, 272; *Josselyn v Josselyn* (1837) 9 Sim 63; *IRC v Hamilton-Russell's Executors* [1943] 1 All ER 474; *Re Jump* [1903] 1 Ch 129. Before the Perpetuities and Accumulations Act 1964, a beneficiary's incapacity to bear children could not be taken into account in determining whether she had such a right to call for the property: *Jee v Audley* (1787) 1 Cox 324; *Re Dawson* (1888) 39 Ch D 155; *Re Deloitte* [1926] Ch 56 (doubted in *Berry v Geen* [1938] AC 575, 584); *IRC v Bernstein* [1960] Ch 444. However, s 14 of the 1964 Act now provides that the presumption of future parenthood contained in s 2 shall apply to any question as to the right of beneficiaries to put an end to accumulations of income. See also *Figg v Clarke* [1997] 1 WLR 603.
[18] *Haynes v Haynes* (1866) 35 LJ Ch 303; *Re Millner* (1872) LR 14 Eq 245; *Anson v Potter* (1879) 13 Ch D 141; *Re White* [1901] 1 Ch 570; *Re Bowes* [1896] 1 Ch 507; *Re Bellville's ST* [1964] Ch 163.
[19] *M'Donald v Bryce* (1838) 2 Keen 276; *Eyre v Marsden* (1839) 4 My & Cr 231; *Berry v Geen* [1938] AC 575.
[20] *Re Levy* [1960] Ch 346, 363; *Re Westphal* [1972] NZLR 792, 794–795; *Re Trafford's Settlement* [1985] Ch 32; *Re Weir's Settlement* [1971] Ch 145.
[20A] *Re Brockbank* [1948] Ch 206; *Kirby v Wilkins* [1929] 2 Ch 444; *Hotung v Ho Yuen Ki* (2002) 5 ITELR 556. The rule that such beneficiaries can instruct trustees how to vote shares in a company is an exception: *Butt v Kelson* [1952] Ch 197.
[21] *Re Brockbank* [1948] Ch 206; *Stephenson v Barclays Bank Trust Co Ltd.* [1975] 1 WLR 882. On the appointment of trustees, see paras 22.35–22.68 below.

his share of the assets.[22] Where a beneficiary is absolutely entitled to an aliquot share of a trust shareholding, he is generally entitled to call for a transfer to him of a proportionate number of the shares,[23] but the court may refuse to order such a transfer if there is good reason to do so. It has been held that it is not enough that the trust shareholding is a majority holding and that it will be broken up on such a transfer, with a consequent diminution in the value of the undistributed shares.[24] However, this seems inconsistent with the reasoning in *Re Marshall*,[25] and a sale was ordered, rather than a distribution, where the entire shareholding was distributable but one beneficiary would have received a majority holding, the value of which was greater than his proper share of the trust fund.[26] It would also appear that the rights of a beneficiary entitled to an undivided share are subject to, and can be defeated by, an exercise by the trustees of a power of appropriation.

C. Fixed Trusts

Equitable interests were modelled 'into the shape and quality of real estates'.[27] **7.08** A beneficiary under a fixed trust has an equitable, proprietary interest and, as such, it possesses the usual characteristics of property. Thus, the beneficiary may use or enjoy it or its fruits, charge it or assign it to another.[28] The nature and extent of the beneficiary's rights will depend on the nature and extent of the interest itself, for example whether it is limited or absolute, determinable or conditional, and so forth. Subject to this, however, a restraint on the alienation of an equitable interest is generally as ineffective as one imposed on a legal interest.[29]

D. Assignment of Equitable Interests

General principles

The involvement of the trustee is not essential to a valid assignment of an **7.09** equitable interest. Nor is it necessary that notice of the assignment be given to

---

[22] *Stephenson v Barclays Bank Trust Co Ltd*, supra; *Crowe v Appleby* [1975] 1 WLR 1539, 1543; *Re Weiner's Will Trusts* [1956] 1 WLR 579; *Re Horsnaill* [1909] 1 Ch 631; *Re Marshall* [1914] 1 Ch 192, 199; *Lloyds Bank v Duker* [1987] 1 WLR 1324.

[23] *Re Marshall*, supra; *Re Weiner's Will Trusts*, supra; *Re Sandeman's Will Trusts* [1937] 1 All ER 368.

[24] *Re Weiner's Will Trusts*, supra.   [25] [1914] 1 Ch 192

[26] *Lloyds Bank v Duker*, supra.   [27] *Burgess v Wheate* (1759) 1 Eden 177, 249.

[28] *Brydges v Brydges* (1796) 3 Ves 120. An assignment of an equitable interest must comply with s 53(1)(c) of the Law of Property Act 1925: see paras 5.15–5.19 above.

[29] *Brandon v Robinson* (1811) 8 Ves 429; *Green v Spicer* (1830) 1 Russ & M 395; *Re Brown* [1954] Ch 39.

the trustee, although failure to do so may result in subsequent purchasers or incumbrancers acquiring priority over the assignee.[30] As a general rule, an assignee of a beneficial interest will be subject to all the equities that affect that interest.[31] Also as a general rule, equitable interests take priority according to the order of their creation—'first in time, first in right'.[32] Thus, an equitable charge over trust property created by the trustees in breach of trust will not rank ahead of the beneficiary's interest.[33] On the other hand, the beneficiary's interest will be bound by an equitable mortgage or charge to which the trust property was subject at the creation of the trust or validly created by trustees before the assignment. A beneficiary can assign no more than he is entitled to and cannot assign his interest free of such a charge. Moreover, the assignee takes subject to any debt owed by the assignor to the trustees as such, for example to make good a breach of trust or when the beneficiary has received an unauthorized advance.[34] These basic rules apply to an assignee of an equitable interest who is a purchaser for value without notice, and not just to one who is a volunteer.[35]

Exceptions[36]

7.10   (a) A purchaser of an equitable interest in good faith takes free of a 'mere equity' unless he has notice of it.

The general rules described above do not apply at all to 'personal equities', such as, for example, the 'deserted wife's equity' to remain in the matrimonial home,[37] or a right to rescind a contract where rescission will not result in the recovery of any

---

[30] *Burn v Carvalho* (1839) 4 Myl & Cr 690; *Bell v London and North Western Rly* (1852) 15 Beav 548; *Donaldson v Donaldson* (1854) Kay 711; *Justice v Wynne* (1860) 12 Ir Ch R 289; *Gorringe v Irwell India Rubber and Gutta Percha Works* (1886) 34 Ch D 128; *Weddell v JA Pearce & Major* [1988] Ch 26. See also paras 7.11–7.13 below.

[31] *Priddy v Rose* (1817) 3 Mer 86, 107; *Phillips v Phillips* (1862) 4 De GF & J 208; *Shropshire Union Railways and Canal Company v The Queen* (1875) LR 7 HL 496; *Cave v Cave* (1880) 15 Ch D 639; *Cloutte v Storey* [1911] 1 Ch 18; *BS Lyle Ltd v Rosher* [1959] 1 WLR 8, 19.

[32] *Phillips v Phillips, supra*; *Shropshire Union Railways and Canal Company v The Queen, supra*; *Perham v Kempster* [1907] 1 Ch 373; *National Provincial Bank Ltd v Ainsworth* [1965] AC 1175, 1238.

[33] *Shropshire Union Railways and Canal Company v The Queen, supra*; *Cave v Cave, supra*; *Perham v Kempster, supra*.

[34] *Sawyer v Sawyer* (1885) 28 Ch D 595; *Re Patrick* [1891] 1 Ch 82; *Bolton v Curre* [1893] 1 Ch 544. See also *Woodyatt v Gresley* (1836) 8 Sim 180 and *Re Jewell's Settlement* [1919] 2 Ch 161. This rule also applies where the assigning beneficiary is also a trustee. See also *Muscat v Smith* [2003] 1 WLR 2853 (tenant's right to set off rent against assignee-landlord).

[35] *Mangles v Dixon* (1852) 2 HLC 702, 731–732.

[36] See, generally, J Mowbray et al, *Lewin on Trusts* (17th edn, Sweet & Maxwell, 2000) ('*Lewin*') 818–819.

[37] *National Provincial Bank Ltd v Ainsworth* [1965] AC 1175, esp 1328. The right is now registrable (Class F) land charge which, if registered, will bind a purchaser and a trustee in bankruptcy: see the Family Law Act 1996, ss 32–33; Insolvency Act 1986, s 336(2).

property.[38] On the other hand, the rules apply in modified form where the earlier equity is a 'mere equity', ie it is not a 'personal equity' and it is not an actual equitable interest, for example an equity to have a deed rectified where rectification will result in the recovery of property.[39] Such 'mere equities' do not bind an assignee who is a purchaser in good faith without notice of its existence, provided the assignee acquires an equitable interest properly so-called (such as a beneficial interest under a trust) and the 'mere equity' in question is dependent upon that interest.[40]

(b) A purchaser of an equitable interest takes priority if that interest carries with it a better right to acquire the legal title.[41] **7.11**

A simple example of this exception is the case where a purchaser procures a transfer of property not to himself but to another as trustee for him, provided the purchaser and trustee did not have notice of the equity.[42] This rule is consistent with the superiority accorded to the legal estate.

The exception does not, however, extend so as to bind a purchaser of the legal estate itself without notice of a prior equitable interest, for example if a trustee holds property on trust to transfer the legal title to X, but in breach of trust transfers it to Y, then, provided Y is a purchaser in good faith, for value and without notice, he will not be bound by X's prior interest.[43]

(c) The beneficiary's right to priority may be lost as a result of some conduct on the part of that beneficiary or his trustee. **7.12**

Priority may be defeated 'by conduct, by representations, by misstatements of a character which would operate and ensure to forfeit and take away the pre-existing

---

[38] *Gross v Lewis Hillman Ltd* [1969] 3 All ER 1476, 1482.

[39] *Phillips v Phillips* (1862) 4 De GM & G 208, 218. The right of a person in actual occupation of registered land to rectify the register and recover that land enjoys priority over a subsequent purchaser of a legal or equitable estate in the land, unless the purchaser made inquiries of that person and the right was not disclosed: Land Registration Act 1925, s 70(1)(g); *Blacklocks v JB Developments (Godalming) Ltd* [1982] Ch 183; *Nurdin & Peacock plc v DB Ramsden & Co Ltd* [1999] 1 EGLR 119.

[40] ibid; *Cave v Cave* (1880) 15 Ch D 639; *Cloutte v Storey* [1911] 1 Ch 18; *Westminster Bank v Lee* [1956] Ch 7; *National Provincial Bank Ltd v Ainsworth* [1965] AC 1175, esp 1328; *Latec Investments Ltd v Hotel Terrigal Pty Ltd* (1965) 113 CLR 265.

[41] *Wilkes v Bodington* (1707) 2 Vern 599; *Wilmot v Pyke* (1845) 5 Hare 14, 21, 22; *Rooper v Harrison* (1855) 2 K & J 86; *Thorndyke v Hunt* (1859) 3 De G & J 563; *Taylor v London and County Banking Company* [1901] 2 Ch 231, 262, 263; *Assaf v Fuwa* [1955] AC 215, 229–230; *McCarthy & Stone Ltd v Julian Hodge & Co Ltd* [1971] 1 WLR 1547, 1557. A purchaser without notice of another existing equitable interest may sometimes acquire priority by acquiring the legal title subsequently, even if at that later date he then has notice of the prior interest (the *tabula in naufragio* exception), but following its abolition in relation to the tacking of equitable mortgages (LPA 1925, s 94) it is likely to be of limited application: see *Lewin*, 824.

[42] *Stanhope v Earl Verney* (1761) 2 Eden 81, 85: the beneficiary and trustee 'are one'.

[43] *Garnham v Skipper* (1885) 55 LJ Ch 263.

title'. However, 'that which is relied on for such a purpose must be shown and proved by those on whom the burden to show and prove it lies, and … it must amount to something tangible and distinct, something which can have [this] grave and strong effect …'.[44] Thus, where a beneficiary sold his interest and included a receipt in the assignment despite the fact that the purchase money had not been paid, he could not thereafter assert an unpaid vendor's lien against a mortgagee of the interest from the purchaser without notice.[45] It is probable that the basis of this exception is estoppel,[46] although this is not entirely clear.

Also, priority may be waived, expressly or by implication.[47]

7.13   (d) The rule in *Dearle v Hall*.[48]

Under the rule in *Dearle v Hall*, priority between successive assignments of equitable interests is determined not by the order in which they are made but by the order in which notice of an assignment is given to the trustees.[49] In order to apply, there must be a fund holder, a person with a beneficial interest, more than one assignee, consideration moving from the second or subsequent assignee, and the absence of actual or constructive notice on his part of a prior assignment.[50] Priority depended on notice being received and it was not sufficient that the assignee had taken reasonable steps to give notice.[51]

The basis of the rule is unclear, but it seems to be that, as between two innocent assignees, priority should be given to the one who, by giving notice, has prevented the assignor from defrauding others by representing himself as the owner (or unencumbered owner) of the interest,[52] or has taken steps to safeguard his own interests and protect trustees on a distribution of trust property.[53]

---

[44]   *Shropshire Union Railways and Canal Co v The Queen* (1875) LR 7 HL 496, 507.
[45]   *Abigail v Lapin* [1934] AC 491, 503–504. See also *Rice v Rice* (1854) 2 Drew 73; *Lloyds Bank Ltd v Bullock* [1896] 2 Ch 193; *Re King's Settlement* [1931] 2 Ch 294.
[46]   ibid; *Shropshire Union Railways and Canal Co v The Queen, supra*, 512. Cf *Capell v Winter* [1907] 2 Ch 376, 382 (which is the better equity?).
[47]   *Fung Ping Shan v Tong Shun* [1918] AC 403; *ANZ Banking Group Ltd v National Mutual Life Nominees Ltd* (1977) 15 ALR 287.
[48]   (1832) 3 Russ 1. See also *Lewin*, 824–837.
[49]   Notice of an assignment is not essential to the validity of the assignment: *Bell v London and North Western Railway* (1852) 15 Beav 548; *Donaldson v Donaldson* (1854) Kay 711; *Re Lowes' Settlement* (1861) 30 Beav 95; *Gorringe v Irwell India Rubber and Gutta Percha Works* (1886) 34 Ch D 128; *Weddell v JA Pearce & Major* [1988] Ch 26. The rule applied originally only to equitable interests in pure personalty, although it did apply to an interest under a trust for sale of land.
[50]   *Re Holmes* (1885) 29 Ch D 786; *Mutual Life Assurance Society v Langley* (1886) 32 Ch D 460; *Ward v Duncombe* [1893] AC 369, 391; *BS Lyle Ltd v Rosher* [1959] 1 WLR 8 (but see (1961) 77 LQR 69 (L Elphinstone).
[51]   *Calisher v Forbes* (1871) 7 Ch App 109; *Johnstone v Cox* (1880) 16 Ch D 571, affirmed 19 Ch D 17.
[52]   *Ward v Duncombe* [1893] AC 369, 391–392.
[53]   *Hodgson v Hodgson* (1837) 2 Keen 704; *Phipps v Lovegrove* (1873) LR 16 Eq 80; *Low v Bouverie* [1891] 3 Ch 82.

Section 137 of the Law of Property Act 1925

The rule in *Dearle v Hall* has been given statutory form and extended by section **7.14**
137 of the Law of Property Act 1925. In particular, the rule now extends to equitable interests in land,[54] but it does not apply until a trust has been created.[55]
Section 137 provides:

(1) The law applicable to dealings with equitable things in action which regulates
the priority of competing interests therein, shall, as respects dealings with equitable interests in land, capital money, and securities representing capital money
effected after the commencement of this Act, apply to and regulate the priority
of competing interests therein.
This subsection applies whether or not the money or securities are in court.

(2) (i) In the case of a dealing with an equitable interest in settled land, capital
money or securities representing capital money, the persons to be served
with notice of the dealing shall be the trustees of the settlement; and where
the equitable interest is created by a derivative or subsidiary settlement, the
persons to be served with notice shall be the trustees of that settlement.[56]

(ii) In the case of a dealing with an equitable interest in land subject to a trust of
land, or the proceeds of the sale of such land, the persons to be served with
notice shall be the trustees.

(iii) In any other case the person to be served with notice of a dealing
with an equitable interest in land shall be the estate owner of the land
affected.
The persons on whom notice is served pursuant to this subsection shall be
affected thereby in the same manner as if they had been trustees of personal
property out of which the equitable interest was created or arose.[57]
This subsection does not apply where the money or securities are in court.

(3) A notice, otherwise than in writing, given to, or received by, a trustee after the
commencement of this Act as respects any dealing with an equitable interest in
real or personal property, shall not affect the priority of competing claims of
purchasers in that equitable interest.[58]

---

[54] See the Land Registration Act 1986, s 5(1)(b), (2) for the extent of the application of the rule
to registered land.

[55] Law of Property Act 1925, s 137(10).

[56] See also *Ward v Duncombe* [1893] AC 369, 394; *Stephens v Green* [1895] 2 Ch 148, 161. Notice
must be given to the trustees personally, unless their solicitors, for example, are authorized to receive
such notices: *Saffron Walden Second Benefit Building Society v Rayner* (1880) 14 Ch D 406; *Arden v
Arden* (1885) 29 Ch D 702. See also LPA 1925, s 138. There are no requirements as to the content
of any notice, but that which it contains clearly ought to be correct: see *Re Bright's Trusts* (1856) 21
Beav 430; *Woodburn v Grant* (1856) 22 Beav 483; *Whittingstall v King* (1882) 46 LT 520.

[57] See also the Trustee Act 1925, s 28: a trustee or personal representative acting for the purposes
of more than one trust or estate shall not, in the absence of fraud, be affected by notice of any instrument, matter, fact, or thing in relation to any particular trust or estate if he has obtained notice
thereof merely by reason of his acting or having acted for the purposes of another trust or estate.

[58] Before the enactment of section 137, the requisite notice need not have been formal or in
writing.

(4) Where, as respects any dealing with an equitable interest in real or personal property—

   (a) the trustees are not persons to whom a valid notice of the dealing can be given;[59]
   (b) there are not trustees to whom a notice can be given; or
   (c) for any other reason a valid notice cannot be served, or cannot be served without unreasonable cost or delay;

a purchaser[60] may at his owns cost require that—

   (i) a memorandum of the dealing be endorsed, written on or permanently annexed to the instrument creating the trust;
   (ii) the instrument be produced to him by the person having the possession or custody thereof to prove that a sufficient memorandum has been placed thereon or annexed thereto.

Such memorandum shall, as respects priorities, operate in like manner as if notice in writing of the dealing had been given to trustees duly qualified to receive the notice at the time when the memorandum is placed on or annexed to the instrument creating the trust.

(5) Where the property affected is settled land, the memorandum shall be placed on or annexed to the trust instrument and not the vesting instrument.

Where the property affected is land subject to a trust of land, the memorandum shall be placed on or annexed to the instrument whereby the equitable interest is created.

(6) Where the trust is created by statute or by operation of law, or in any other case where there is no instrument whereby the trusts are declared, the instrument under which the equitable interest is acquired or which is evidence of the devolution thereof shall, for the purposes of this section, be deemed the instrument creating the trust.

In particular, where the trust arises by reason of an intestacy, the letters of administration or probate in force when the dealing was effected shall be deemed such instrument.

(7) Nothing in this section affects any priority acquired before the commencement of this Act.

(8) Where a notice in writing of a dealing with an equitable interest in real or personal property has been served on a trustee under this section, the trustees from time to time of the property affected shall be entitled to the custody of the notice, and the notice shall be delivered to them by any person who for the time being may have the custody thereof; and subject to the payment of costs, any person interested in the equitable interest may require production of the notice.[61]

---

[59] An assignor who is also a sole trustee is not a person to whom a valid notice can be given: *Browne v Savage* (1859) 4 Drew 635; *Re Dallas* [1904] 2 Ch 385.

[60] See the Law of Property Act 1925, s 205(1)(xxi).

[61] A trustee is not obliged, apart from this provision, to provide information on incumbrances of equitable interests. If he chooses to do so, he is obliged to do no more than answer to the best of his actual knowledge and belief: *Low v Bouverie* [1891] 3 Ch 82.

(9) The liability of the estate owner of the legal estate affected to produce documents and furnish information to persons entitled to equitable interests therein shall correspond to the liability of a trustee for sale to produce documents and furnish information to persons entitled to equitable interests in the proceeds of sale of the land.

(10) This section does not apply until a trust has been created, and in this section 'dealing' includes a disposition by operation of law.

Section 137 does not appear to have altered the law relating to notices of assignment **7.15** given to just one of several trustees (other than to extend such law to land as well as to personal property). In such a case, the notice provides protection for as long as the notified trustee remains in office: a subsequent assignee or incumbrancer is required to make inquiry of all the trustees.[62] Such notice also remained effective after that trustee's death or retirement,[63] but the notice was not effective against assignees or incumbrancers who paid money after the death or retirement of that trustee, unless he had made the notice known to one or more of the continuing trustees.[64] If the assignee or mortgagee was himself a trustee, his knowledge affected priority, because it could be assumed that, in his own interests, he would disclose his interest;[65] but no such protection could be claimed on the basis that the assignor or mortgagor was a trustee.[66] Giving notice to all trustees is clearly the prudent course, for it remains effective even after they have all died or retired, and notwithstanding the fact that they may not have communicated the notice to their successors.[67]

The rule also applies as between a purchaser for value and a trustee in bankruptcy **7.16** who fails to give notice of the bankruptcy.[68]

In relation to a fund in court, priority as between assignees depends on which one **7.17** first obtains a stop order to prevent the transfer of the fund,[69] unless an assignee has served a proper notice before (as opposed to after) the fund was paid into court,[70] or the assignee had notice of the prior assignment.[71]

---

[62] *Smith v Smith* (1833) 2 Cr & M 231; *Meux v Bell* (1841) 1 Hare 73; *Willes v Greenhill* (1861) 4 De GF & J 147. In certain circumstances, a notice may, of course, be required to be given to all trustees in order to be effective: see, for example, *Sutcliffe v Wardle* (1890) 63 LT 329.

[63] *Ward v Duncombe* [1893] AC 369.

[64] *Timson v Ramsbottom* (1836) 2 Keen 35; *Re Phillips' Trusts* [1903] 1 Ch 183.

[65] *Browne v Savage* (1859) 4 Drew 635, 641; *Newman v Newman* (1885) 28 Ch D 674. See also *Re Lewer* (1876) 4 Ch D 101, affirmed (1877) 5 Ch D 61.

[66] *Lloyds Bank v Pearson* [1901] 1 Ch 865, 873.

[67] *Re Wasdale* [1899] 1 Ch 163; *Freeman v Laing* [1899] 2 Ch 355; *Re Phillips' Trusts* [1903] 1 Ch 183.

[68] *Re Atkinson* (1852) 2 De GM & G 140; *Re Barr's Trusts* (1858) 4 K & J 219; *Re Russell's Policy Trusts* (1873) LR 15 Eq 26; *Palmer v Locke* (1881) 18 Ch D 381; *Re Bright's Settlement* (1880) 13 Ch D 413. Section 137(10) refers expressly to a 'disposition by operation of law'.

[69] *Greening v Beckford* (1832) 5 Sim 195; *Swayne v Swayne* (1848) 11 Beav 463; *Haly v Barry* (1868) 3 Ch App 452, 456; *Mack v Postle* [1894] 2 Ch 449; *Stephens v Green* [1895] 2 Ch 148.

[70] *Brearcliff v Dorrington* (1850) 4 De G & Sm 122; *Livesey v Harding* (1856) 23 Beav 141; *Pinnock v Bailey* (1883) 23 Ch D 497. See also *Lister v Tidd* (1867) LR 4 Eq 462; *Re Eyton* (1890) 45 Ch D 458; *Edgar v Plomley* [1900] AC 431.

[71] *Re Holmes* (1885) 29 Ch D 786. Priority will not be affected, however, if the assignee receives notice after the assignment but before obtaining a stop order: *Mutual Life Assurance Society v Langley* (1886) 32 Ch D 460.

f two or more notices are served simultaneously, they take priority according to
heir dates.[72]

7.19 Section 137 and the rule in *Dearle v Hall* apply only to determine priority as
between purchasers. As between volunteers, priority is determined according to
the time of creation ('first in time, first in right'), irrespective of whether notice
is actually given.[73]

E. Nature of the Interest of an Object of a Discretionary
Trust or of a Mere Power

Objects of a discretionary trust

7.20 The objects or beneficiaries of a discretionary trust have a right to be considered
as potential recipients of benefit from the property which is subject to such trust,
a right to compel the trustees to consider the exercise of their discretion from time
to time, and also, crucially, a right to compel the trustees to distribute the trust
property over which such discretion has been conferred (be it income or capital or
both). In the case of a discretionary trust, there is no one entitled in default of
appointment, or of an exercise of the trustees' discretion, in whom beneficial ownership of the property can be said to be vested.[74] The question, therefore, is
whether the object of a discretionary trust, like the beneficiary under a fixed interest trust, can be said to have a proprietary 'interest' of any kind in the property
which is the subject of the trustees' discretion.[75] If not, what precisely is the nature
of such an object's rights under such a trust?

7.21 In answering these questions, three broad distinctions must be borne in mind:
first, the distinction between the interest of an individual object and that of all the
objects, taken together; secondly, the distinction between an exhaustive discretionary trust (under which the trustees are obliged to distribute the entire income)
and a non-exhaustive discretionary trust (under which they are authorized not to

[72] *Calisher v Forbes* (1871) 7 Ch App 109; *Johnstone v Cox* (1881) 16 Ch D 571, (1882) 19
Ch D 17.
[73] *Justice v Wynne* (1860) 12 Ir Ch Rep 289, 299, 304–305; *United Bank of Kuwait plc v Sahib*
[1997] Ch 107, 119–120.
[74] *Murphy v Murphy* [1999] 1 WLR 282, 290.
[75] In *Re Beckett* [1940] Ch 279, where Simonds J held that the objects of a power of maintenance
did not have a 'prior life or other interest, whether vested or contingent' which took precedence over
the power of advancement in s 32 of the Trustee Act 1925, he also said that 'it is quite true that in
one sense the objects of a discretionary trust have an interest in the fund which is being administered
for their benefit'.

distribute income and may divert it for other purposes, such as accumulation);[76] and thirdly, the distinction between a closed class of objects and one which remains open.

The position of the beneficiaries of an *exhaustive* discretionary trust with a *closed* **7.22** class was established in *Re Smith*[77] and *Re Nelson (Note)*.[78] In *Re Smith*, trustees had a discretion to pay or apply income for the benefit of the testator's daughter and her children and, as to capital, they had a discretion to pay or apply it for her benefit and, subject thereto, to hold it on trust for the children. There were three children, one of whom had died. The daughter was past the age of childbearing (so that the class was closed). The two surviving children and the representatives of the deceased child joined together to assign their interests by way of mortgage. Romer J held that, as they were together the sole objects of the discretionary trust, they were entitled between them to have the whole fund applied to or for their benefit.[79] He stated:

> Where there is a trust under which trustees have a discretion as to applying the whole or part of a fund to or for the benefit of a particular person, that particular person cannot come to the trustees, and demand the fund; for the whole fund has not been given to him but only so much as the trustees think fit to let him have. But when the trustees have no discretion as to the amount of the fund to be applied, the fact that the trustees have a discretion as to the method in which the whole of the fund shall be applied for the benefit of the particular person does not prevent that particular person from coming and saying: "Hand over the fund to me".[80]

Similarly, in *Re Nelson (Note)*,[81] the class of discretionary objects consisted of a man, his wife, and children. There was only one child and she had attained 21.[82] All three of them assigned their interests by way of mortgage. The court held that the income ought to be paid to the mortgagee and not continue to be applied for the benefit of the three of them, on the basis that all the persons interested in the income of the trust had disposed of their interests.

Thus, although an *individual* object of an *exhaustive* discretionary trust (and a for- **7.23** tiori in the case of a *non-exhaustive* one) cannot claim any part of the trust fund or its income (as the case may be) because he is not entitled to any interest in it unless

---

[76] The discretion may relate to capital as well as income.

[77] [1928] Ch 915.   [78] [1928] Ch 920 (reported as a note to *Re Smith, supra*).

[79] ie, the rule in *Saunders v Vautier* (1841) Cr & Ph 240 applied. See also paras. 7.05–7.07 above.

[80] See also *Green v Spicer* (1830) 1 Russ & My 395 and *Younghusband v Gisborne* (1844) 1 Coll 400.

[81] [1928] Ch 920.

[82] As Peter Gibson J pointed out in *Re Trafford's Settlement* [1985] Ch 32, 40, it may be that the wife was beyond the age of childbearing, but, in any event, no question as to the entitlement of a future beneficiary was considered.

and until the trustees exercise their discretion in his favour,[83] and notwithstanding that the class of beneficiaries is a *closed* class, all the objects of such a discretionary trust,[84] where the class is closed, may join together and collectively call upon the trustees to transfer the fund to them or deal with the property subject to the discretion as if they were the absolute owners thereof (for example by assigning their interests by way of mortgage, so that thereafter the trustees must pay the trust income to the mortgagee).[85] Although, as Lord Reid pointed out in *Gartside v IRC*,[86] two or more persons cannot have a single right unless they hold it jointly or in common, and the beneficiaries of a discretionary trust do not have such a right—indeed, they are in competition with each other and what the trustees give to one is his alone—it remains the case that, under the principle laid down in *Saunders v Vautier*,[87] such beneficiaries, as the persons for whom or in whose favour alone the trust property may be applied, have a right to terminate the trust and deal with the property as if it were their own.

In the case of a *non-exhaustive* discretionary trust, or in the case of any discretionary trust where the class of beneficiaries is not closed, the position is different: all the beneficiaries for the time being, even acting collectively, cannot demand payment of the trust fund to them or direct its application on their behalf. In *Gartside v IRC*,[88] trustees had power to apply the income of a fund at their discretion for the maintenance or benefit of all or any of the testator's son, the son's wife, or children (if any), and to accumulate surplus income; and, after the son's death, the trustees were to hold the capital and income (and accumulations) on trust for such of the son's children as being male attained 21 or being female attained that age or married, and if more than one equally. The trustees also had power to advance at any time to a grandchild up to one-half of the presumptive or vested share of that grandchild. The trustees exercised their power of advancement in favour of the only two grandchildren. The testator's son died and the Crown claimed estate duty on the advanced funds. The central point at issue was whether the objects of the discretionary trust had 'interests in possession' in the fund for

---

[83] The position of such a beneficiary and the likelihood of his receiving some benefit from the trust may, nonetheless, be taken into account in assessing his financial resources for the purposes of making an order for financial provision under s 25 of the Matrimonial Causes Act 1973: *Browne v Browne* [1989] 1 FLR 291; *J v J (C intervening)* [1989] Fam 270. It may also be a relevant consideration in applications for financial provision under the Inheritance (Provision for Family and Dependants) Act 1975. In neither case, however, can the beneficiary be assumed to have an actual entitlement under the discretionary trust.

[84] In principle, it may be possible to bring about a similar result even in the case of a non-exhaustive discretionary trust, eg where any authorized accumulations of income accrue solely for the benefit of the same beneficiaries. See *IRC v Hamilton-Russell's Executors* [1943] 1 All ER 474; *Re Jump* [1903] 1 Ch 129.

[85] *Re Nelson* (1918) [1928] Ch 920; *Re Smith* [1928] Ch 915.   [86] [1968] AC 553, 605–606.

[87] (1841) Cr & Ph 240.   [88] [1968] AC 553.

estate duty purposes prior to the date of the advances. The House of Lords held that they did not. Lord Reid stated:[89]

> I think that this idea of a group or class right must have arisen in this way. Where the trustees are bound to distribute the whole income among the discretionary beneficiaries and have no power to retain any part of it or use any part of it for any other purposes, you cannot tell what any one of the beneficiaries will receive until the trustees have exercised their discretion. But you can say with absolute certainty that the individual rights of the beneficiaries when added up or taken together will extend to the whole income. You can have an equation $x+y+z = 100$ although you do not yet know the value of x or y or z. And that may lead to important results where the trust is of that character. But that is not this case.

Similarly, Lord Wilberforce stated:[90]   **7.24**

> No doubt in a certain sense a beneficiary under a discretionary trust has an 'interest': the nature of it may sufficiently for the purpose, be spelt out by saying that he has a right to be considered as a potential recipient of benefit by the trustees and a right to have his interest protected by a court of equity. Certainly that is so, and when it is said that he has a right to have the trustees exercise their discretion 'fairly' or 'reasonably' or 'properly' that indicates clearly enough that some objective consideration (not stated explicitly in declaring the discretionary trust, but latent in it) must be applied by the trustees and that the right is more than a mere spes. But that does not mean that he has an interest which is capable of being taxed by reference to its extent in the trust fund's income: it may be a right, with some degree of concreteness or solidity, one which attracts the protection of a court of equity, yet it may still lack the necessary quality of definable extent which must exist before it can be taxed.

Lord Wilberforce then pointed out[91] that, in this case, not only did no one of the discretionary beneficiaries have at the relevant time any right to receive any income, but also the discretionary beneficiaries, taken together, had no right to receive any or all of the income, because the trustees had power to accumulate so much of the income as they did not distribute (which might have been the whole) for the benefit of persons unborn.

Thus, the discretionary trust in *Gartside* was a non-exhaustive one. Lord   **7.25**
Wilberforce expressly left open[92] the question of the nature of the 'interest' of the members of a class of beneficiaries of an exhaustive discretionary trust.

---

[89] ibid 606. He also stated (at 607): '"In possession" must mean that your interest enables you to claim now whatever may be the subject of the interest. For instance, if it is the current income from a certain fund your claim may yield nothing if there is no income, but your claim is a valid claim, and if there is any income you are entitled to get it. But a right to require trustees to consider whether they will pay you something does not enable you to claim anything. If the trustees do decide to pay you something, you do not get it by reason of having the right to have your case considered: you get it only because the trustees have decided to give it to you.'

[90] ibid 617–618. Lord Hodson agreed (at 613) with Lord Wilberforce.

[91] ibid 615.   [92] ibid 621.

Nevertheless, in *Sainsbury v IRC*[93] and *Re Weir's Settlement Trusts*[94] it was held that the position was the same under the two kinds of discretionary trust. In ✱ *Sainsbury*,[95] Ungoed-Thomas J pointed out that the only right which any object has in an exhaustive, as in a non-exhaustive, discretionary trust is to have the trustees exercise their discretion and to be protected by the court in that right. Before distribution, no object is entitled to any defined part of the income. Moreover, all the individual objects could not dispose of all the income to be distributed without agreeing to do so (and there was no such agreement). To treat separate unquantifiable interests as quantifiable interests or as one quantifiable interest was to 'confuse the conception of group persona with the separate rights of individuals'. Although the class of beneficiaries here was not a closed one,[96] there were several members of it in existence.

7.26 *Re Weir's Settlement Trusts*[97] is equally clear. Here, trustees were directed to pay out the whole income of the trust fund for the benefit of all or such one or more to the exclusion of the others or other of the settlor's daughter, her husband, or their children or remoter issue, as in their absolute discretion they thought fit. There were no children of the marriage and, from the date of their marriage until the son-in-law's death, the trustees paid all the income to the daughter. The Crown claimed estate duty on his death. The trustees asked the Court to determine whether estate duty was payable. The Court of Appeal, following *Gartside*, held in favour of the trustees. The discretionary trust here was again an exhaustive one. Although the daughter was the sole existing object (she was past the age of childbearing), the trustees had power to pay capital to her on a remarriage. The Crown claimed estate duty on the husband's death on the basis that the effect of the trusts was that, on his death leaving the daughter but no issue of the marriage surviving, the trustees were to hold the trust fund on trust to pay the income thereof to the wife for life, ie the discretionary trusts were effectively replaced by a life tenancy in favour of the wife. Of this, Russell LJ said:[98]

> On examination of this analysis … it emerged that it involved the proposition that in a discretionary trust in which there might from time to time be only one object alive, by deaths, and from time to time more than one object alive, by new entrants being born, there could be spelled out a series of discretionary trusts and a series of determinable life interests. Suppose the class to be the children from time to time living of A, B and C: A1 and B1 are the living objects: A1 dies and the property passes, B1 acquiring a defeasible life interest: C1 is born and the discretionary trust revives; but C1 is a sickly child and only survives one week and on his death there is once more a passing … and so on, potentially … The wife became entitled to receive the income by virtue of her being not a tenant for life but the sole object of the discretionary trust and under that same trust. In respect of income in hand and not applied

---

[93] [1970] Ch 712.   [94] [1971] Ch 145.   [95] [1970] Ch 712, 725.
[96] ibid 725E.   [97] [1971] Ch 145.   [98] ibid 166.

at the husband's death, her claim as sole living discretionary object would extend to that as well as to subsequent dividends declared in respect of a period before the husband's death. Conversely, at her death during the trust period ... her estate would have no claim to later-received dividends declared in respect of a period before her death, because her rights under the discretionary trust would not be those of a life tenant but only those of a discretionary object, who must necessarily survive at the time when income comes to the hands of the trustees. Similarly, in the hypothetical case of the class of children of A, B and C already mentioned, a sole object for the time being would not necessarily be entitled as such to insist upon payment over of every penny come to the hands of the trustees: the trustees on learning of an imminent addition to the class of objects, for example a child of an impoverished C would be entitled to keep income in hand with a view to applying it for the benefit of C's child.

Thus, as long as the class of beneficiaries remains open and the trustees' discretion remains potentially exercisable, even a sole existing member of the class of beneficiaries of an exhaustive discretionary trust will not be entitled to demand payment to him of trust income as and when it is received by the trustees, and he will not, therefore, have an interest in the trust fund.

The same analysis has been carried forward and applied for the purposes of capi-   **7.27** tal transfer tax (now inheritance tax). In *Re Trafford's Settlement*,[99] the settlor had directed that, during his lifetime, trustees should pay or apply the income of the trust fund to or for the benefit of himself, any wife whom he might marry, and his child or children or issue 'or any of them', as the trustees in their absolute discretion thought fit. He remained unmarried and had no children. The Inland Revenue asserted that, at his death, the value of the trust fund fell to be included in his estate for capital transfer tax purposes,[100] on the basis that, immediately before his death, he had been beneficially entitled to an interest in possession in the trust fund and was therefore to be treated as having been beneficially entitled to the property in which his interest subsisted. Peter Gibson J held that, on its true construction, the settlement created an immediate discretionary trust; that the single object of a discretionary trust did not immediately before his death have an interest in possession in the settled property if there remained a possibility of further objects of the trust coming into existence at some time in the future; and that the settlor's entitlement to income in the present case was always subject to such a possibility (if he were to marry) and, accordingly, he did not have an interest in possession in the settled property immediately before his death. The trustees would have been justified in withholding income, at least for a while, with a view to considering whether a further beneficiary might come into existence and fall to

---

[99] [1985] Ch 34. See also *Figg v Clark*, The Times, 11 March 1996.
[100] By virtue of ss 22(1) and 23(1) of the Finance Act 1975. See now ss 5 and 6 of the Inheritance Tax Act 1984.

be considered, notwithstanding that such a beneficiary was not living or ascertained at the time when the income accrued or was received. According to Peter Gibson J:[101]

> When income is received by the trustees of a discretionary trust of income, the sole object of a class which is not yet closed cannot in my judgment claim an immediate entitlement to that income. It is always possible that before a reasonable time for the distribution of that income has elapsed another object will come into existence or be ascertained and have a claim to be considered as a potential recipient of the benefit of that income. So long as that possibility exists, the sole object's entitlement is subject to the possibility that the income will be properly diverted by the trustees to the future object once he comes into existence or is ascertained. Indeed, in strictness the entitlement of the sole object is only an entitlement that the trustees should consider whether to pay income to him.

Once it is accepted that income, as it is received, will not necessarily belong to the sole discretionary object for the time being, it cannot be postulated that that object has an immediate absolute right to the income as it accrues.[102] Consequently, where a class of discretionary beneficiaries (whether it is an open or closed class) comprises more than one member, no individual beneficiary has or can claim an interest in the trust fund or its income. The position is the same for the sole existing member of a class of discretionary beneficiaries where that class is not yet closed. In both cases, it is immaterial whether the discretionary trust is exhaustive or non-exhaustive. It would seem to be the case, however, that, where there is only one member of a closed class, and where the discretionary trust is exhaustive, the trustees' discretion is effectively at an end: the sole beneficiary is then entitled to the trust income or capital (as the case may be) and he will then have an interest in the trust fund. Indeed, in *Re Trafford's Settlement*,[103] it was conceded that this was the case and that such a sole beneficiary would have an 'interest in possession' for capital transfer tax purposes. As for all the members of a closed class of beneficiaries, acting collectively, they may, in the case of an exhaustive discretionary trust, terminate the discretionary trust or demand that the property (be it income or capital) which is the subject matter of the discretion be applied at their direction, but this right will not result in each individual member having an aliquot share of or interest in the whole attributed to him. In the case of a non-exhaustive discretionary trust, or indeed any discretionary trust with an open class of beneficiaries, the existing members of the class have no such collective rights.

---

[101] [1985] Ch 32, 40.
[102] See *Pearson v IRC* [1981] AC 753, esp 775, *per* Viscount Dilhorne, and at 786, *per* Lord Keith.
[103] [1985] Ch 32, 39.

Objects of a mere power

The objects of a *non-fiduciary mere power* do not have any interest as such, in their **7.28**
capacity as objects, in the property which is the subject matter of that power. This
is so whether such objects are regarded in their individual capacity or collectively.
Until and subject to any exercise of the power, beneficial ownership of such property lies with those entitled in default of appointment or with the beneficiaries of
an express or implied trust.[104] The objects of such a power do not even have an
enforceable right to be considered as potential recipients of benefit. All they ✳
have are negative rights to ensure that, if and when the power is exercised, such
exercise is not excessive or fraudulent. They will acquire an interest in the property
which is subject to the power (if at all) only if and when it is exercised in their
favour.

The objects of a *fiduciary mere power* are in a similar position in that, both indi- **7.29**
vidually and collectively, they have no interest as such in the subject matter of the ✳
power. Beneficial ownership of the property subject to the power rests, as before,
with those entitled in default of and subject to any exercise of the power, or in the
beneficiaries under an express or implied trust.[105] However, the objects of such a
power, have a range of additional rights which the objects of a non-fiduciary
power do not have, such as a right to be considered as potential recipients of ✳
benefit. They also have rights by which they may ensure that the trustees carry out
their various fiduciary duties honestly and properly, in accordance with the terms
of the particular power or discretion, and only in furtherance of the purpose(s) for
which the power or discretion was conferred. However, the fact remains that,
although the donee of such a power is subject to numerous fiduciary duties,
which the objects of that power are able to enforce, such objects, whether
individually or collectively, do not have any direct 'interest' in the property which
is subject to the power. Just like the objects of a discretionary trust, they will
acquire such an interest (if at all) only if and when the power is exercised in their
favour.

Assignment by a discretionary object

If it is the case that an object of a discretionary trust or of a mere power has no **7.30**
'interest' as such in the property which is the subject matter of that power or discretion, it may be asked whether such object or beneficiary has anything which he

---

✳ [104] *Re Brooks' Settlement Trusts* [1939] Ch 993. See generally *Thomas* 58–66.
[105] *Re Gulbenkian's Settlements* [1970] AC 408; *Re Hay's Settlement Trusts* [1982] 1 WLR 202. See
also *Gartside v IRC* [1968] AC 553, 606; *McPhail v Doulton* [1971] AC 424, 449; *Re Gestetner*
[1953] Ch 672, 687–688; and *Schmidt v Rosewood Trust Ltd* [2003] 2 WLR 1442, 1455. See generally *Thomas* 264–273.

may assign to another or which may vest in his trustee in bankruptcy.[106] It would seem that he does not. According to Lord Walker, in *Schmidt v Rosewood Trust Ltd*,[107] the possibility of 'a collective disposition will be rare, and on his own the object of a discretionary trust has no more of an assignable or transmissible interest than the object of a mere power': 'an individual's interest or right is non-assignable'. However, it is arguable that this conclusion may depend on whether the assignment is voluntary or made for value.

7.31 In *Re Brooks' Settlement Trusts*,[108] a child who was a member of both the class of objects of a power of appointment and also the class entitled in default executed a *voluntary* settlement whereby he assigned to trustees 'all the part or share, parts or shares and other interest whether vested or contingent to which the setttlor is now or may hereafter become entitled whether in default of appointment, or under any appointment hereafter to be made or on failure of any such appointment of and in the trust property'. In due course, his mother appointed a sum of cash to him and surrendered her life interest. Farwell J held that, as at the date of the voluntary settlement, the mother had not exercised the power of appointment in the child's favour; and he was therefore purporting to assign a mere expectancy of something to which he was not then entitled, but to which he might thereafter become entitled. Consequently, the appointed sum had to be paid over to him and he could not be compelled to hand it over to the trustees of the voluntary settlement.

> ... in the case of a special power the property is vested in the persons who take in default of appointment, subject, of course, to any prior life interest, but liable to be divested at any time by a valid exercise of the power, and the effect of such an exercise is to defeat wholly or *pro tanto* the interests which up to then were vested in the persons entitled in default of appointment and to create new estates in those persons in whose favour the appointment had been made. That being so, it is, in my judgment, impossible to say that until an appointment has been made in favour of this son that son had any interest under his mother's settlement other than an interest as one of the people entitled in default of appointment; he had an interest in that; but that interest was liable to be divested, and, if an appointment was made (as in fact it was made)

---

[106] Where the trustees are directed to pay income to a beneficiary and have a discretion only as to the manner in which it may be applied, the income is that of the beneficiary: *Green v Spicer* (1830) 1 Russ & M 395; *Younghusband v Gisborne* (1844) 1 Coll 400. Similarly, where sums are actually appointed or paid over to an object or the trustees exercise their discretion in his favour, such sums become the property of that object: his trustee in bankruptcy will then be able to claim them: *Re Ashby* [1892] 1 QB 872, 877 (at least to the extent that such sums exceed the amount necessary for his mere support). Cf *Edmonds v Edmonds* [1965] 1 WLR 58; and *Webb v Stenton* (1883) 11 QBD 518.
[107] [2003] 2 WLR 1442, 1455; see also 1458 and 1463.
[108] [1939] Ch 993. See also Sir George Farwell and FK Archer, *A Concise Treatise on Powers* (3rd edn, 1916) ('*Farwell*') 310; *Lovett v Lovett* [1898] 1 Ch 82 (where Romer J held that equitable estoppel cannot be applied in favour of a volunteer); *Duke of Northumberland v IRC* [1911] 2 KB 343, 354.

in favour of the son, then to that extent the persons entitled in default were defeated and he was given an interest in the funds which he had never had before and which came into being for the first time when the power was exercised.[109]

The son here had attempted to make a voluntary assignment of a mere expectancy which could not be valid and enforceable in law. Thus, in such a case, a trustee, in exercising his discretion, can properly pay money or transfer property to, and would receive a good discharge from, the 'assignor', notwithstanding that the trustee has notice of the voluntary assignment.[110]

On the other hand, where the assignment is not voluntary, but made for value, it may be valid and enforceable by the assignee: **7.32**

> If value be given, it is immaterial what is the form of assurance by which the disposition is made, or whether the subject of the disposition is capable of being thereby disposed of or not. An assignment for value binds the conscience of the assignor. A Court of Equity as against him will compel him to do that which *ex hypothesi* he has not yet effectually done. Future property, possibilities, and expectancies are all assignable in equity for value.[111]

In *Re Coleman*,[112] for example, the provision in question was construed to mean **7.33**
that no child was entitled to any income from the estate until the youngest child had attained the age of 21, ie until then the income was payable at the discretion of the trustees. The eldest child assigned his 'interest' for value while the younger children were still under age. North J concluded[113] that, if the trustees, in the exercise of their discretion, decided to appropriate income for the benefit of the assignor 'and propose to apply it for his benefit by handing it over to him', then the interest would pass by the assignment; but if, instead of doing that, they were to apply it for his benefit in some other way, the assignee did not take the benefit of that provision at all. In the Court of Appeal, Cotton LJ upheld the point of construction and added[114] that the assignment did not catch everything that the trustees might give to the assignor out of trust income.

> If the trustees were to pay an hotel-keeper to give him a dinner he would get nothing but the right to eat a dinner, and that is not property which could pass by assignment or bankruptcy. But if they pay or deliver money or goods to him, or appropriate money or goods to be paid or delivered to him, the money or goods would pass by the assignment.

---

[109] [1939] Ch 993, 997.   [110] cf *Public Trustees v Ferguson* [1947] NZLR 9.

[111] *Re Ellenborough* [1903] 1 Ch 697, 700, *per* Buckley J; *Tailby v Official Receiver* (1888) 13 App Cas 523. See also *Norman v FCT* (1963) 109 CLR 9.

[112] (1888) 39 Ch D 443. See also *Re Buttock* (1891) 64 LT 736; *Re Neil* (1890) 62 LT 649; *Re Fitzgerald* [1904] 1 Ch 573, 593; *Train v Clapperton* [1908] AC 342; *Re Laye* [1913] 1 Ch 298; *Re Hamilton* (1921) 124 LT 737; *Re Ashby* [1892] 1 QB 872; *Re Allen-Meyrick's Will Trusts* [1966] 1 All ER 740, 743. Cf *Lord v Bunn* (1843) 2 Y & C Ch Cas 98 and *Public Trustees v Ferguson* [1947] NZLR 746.

[113] ibid 447.   [114] ibid 451.

Thus, an assignment for value will carry over to the assignee any money or property appropriated or allocated to an object, or in respect of which an irrevocable decision to pay or transfer the same to the object directly has been made by the trustees, but not necessarily money which is applied indirectly for his benefit, such as by way of payment to another for services to be performed for the object. Moreover, even where the assignment has been made for value, the rights of the assignee cannot be greater than those of the object,[115] ie to have the trust administered properly, and the assignee clearly cannot demand that the trustees should exercise their discretion in his favour. Nevertheless, where there has been an assignment for value, and the trustees have notice of it, the trustees ought to pay the assignee, from whom alone can they receive a good discharge.

7.34   However, this presupposes that the trustee could exercise his discretion in this way. There may be a difficulty in that the circumstances in question may involve either an excessive exercise of the power or a fraud on that power. Neither the trustees of a discretionary trust nor the donee of a power could deliberately pay any income or other property to someone who is a stranger, nor, indeed, to an object, with the intention and knowledge that such an object will simply pass it on to a stranger. On the other hand, the terms of a power may be sufficiently wide to authorize payment to a third party if and in so far as such payment can be said to be of benefit to the object himself.[116] Indeed, in *Re Coleman* itself it would appear that North J, at least, directed his mind to the question of what was of benefit to the object.[117] Even in such a case, however, it is the independent decision and act of the trustee that carries any benefit over to the third party and not the assignment by the object. Similarly, if the trust instrument expressly authorizes the trustee to pay or apply income or capital in favour of an assignee of an object, the correct analysis would seem to be that any such assignee is added to the class of objects (and thereby enjoys the same rights as any other object) and not that the rights of an object can be assigned effectively to another. In principle, it is very difficult, if not impossible, to see how the object of a discretionary trust or of a mere power could assign his rights to another.

7.35   There is a superficial similarity between the right of an object of a discretionary trust or of a mere power, on the one hand, and that of a beneficiary under an unadministered estate, on the other. The latter, like the former, does not have a proprietary interest in the estate until the administration is complete.[118] Nevertheless, it

---

[115]   *Train v Clapperton* [1908] AC 342. Cf *Edmonds v Edmonds* [1965] 1 WLR 58 and *Webb v Stenton* (1883) 11 QBD 518.

[116]   *Re Clore's Settlement Trusts* [1966] 2 All ER 272.

[117]   (1888) 39 Ch D 443, 447. *Daubeny v Cockburn* (1816) 1 Mer 626.

[118]   *Commissioner of Stamp Duties (Queensland) v Livingston* [1965] AC 694; *Eastbourne Mutual Building Society v Hastings Corpn* [1965] 1 All ER 779.

has been held that he has an assignable chose in action.[119] However, a residuary beneficiary, unlike an object of a discretionary trust or mere power, will eventually become entitled to some property (assuming there is anything left when the estate is fully administered); and, in the event that he should die before administration is complete, his chose in action will pass with the remainder of his estate. Such entitlement as he has is not dependent upon the discretion of another. This is clearly not the case in respect of an object's or discretionary beneficiary's rights.

It has been held that an object of a discretionary trust or power can release the **7.36** trustees from their duty to consider whether or not to exercise their discretion in his favour and that, if he did so, he would thereupon cease to be an object.[120]

Are the rights of objects 'proprietary' rights?

Whether such rights as are possessed by an object of a discretionary trust or of a **7.37** mere power can properly be categorized as 'proprietary' in nature, or merely personal, is an important question in several contexts. For example, if a beneficiary's claim or right to disclosure of trust documents depends on the existence of, and is an adjunct to, a proprietary interest in the trust property,[121] a discretionary object is clearly at a disadvantage unless his rights can be said to be proprietary rights. (This may not be of much significance if the Privy Council's analysis in *Schmidt v Rosewood Trust Ltd*,[122] is adopted in English law.) It is also of considerable importance in the context of the 'beneficiary principle' which, it has been argued, is undermined, if not shown to be based on a false premise, by the acceptance of the modern discretionary trust, under which no one need have a proprietary interest at all. This raises a question as to the basis of the beneficiary principle itself—specifically, whether the enforceability of a trust requires a beneficiary with a proprietary interest in the trust fund or whether a proprietary right will suffice. This issue is dealt with elsewhere.[123]

It does not follow, however, that, because the object of a discretionary trust or **7.38** mere power has no fixed or ascertainable entitlement in or to the trust fund, his rights (even if unassignable) are not proprietary rights. Something will not be denied the status of 'property' merely because one of its characteristics is that it may not be assignable: alienability is not an indispensable attribute of a right of property, whether it is because assignment is considered incompatible with its nature, as was the case originally with debts, or because a statute so provides or considerations of public policy so require.[124] In fact, a right is not even prevented

---

[119] *Re Leigh's Will Trusts* [1970] Ch 277; *Marshall v Kerr* [1995] 1 AC 148.
[120] *Re Gulbenkian's Settlements (No 2)* [1970] Ch 408.
[121] *Re Londonderry's Settlement* [1965] Ch 918, esp 937.   [122] [2003] 2 WLR 1442.
[123] See paras 6.13–6.21 above for a fuller discussion of the beneficiary principle.
[124] *Cain's Case* (1954) 91 CLR 540, 583, *per* Kitto J.

from being a proprietary right simply because it is not enforceable:[125] in the case of a discretionary object, of course, his rights clearly are enforceable, both against the trustee and, in appropriate circumstances, against a third party who is not 'equity's darling'. In any event, ownership of a proprietary interest is not a pre-requisite of enforceability. It is sufficient, in the case of an object of a discretionary trust, at least, that he has a right to call on the trustee to administer the trust prop-erly, to account for his dealings with the trust property, and to enforce the exercise of the trustee's discretion. He has an expectancy, an equitable chose in action which cannot be assigned, and which ceases to exist upon the object's death, but which is nonetheless proprietary in nature.

F. The Rights and Interests of Members of Pension Funds

7.39 In broad terms, members (and other beneficiaries) of a typical occupational pen-sion scheme have specified entitlements under the scheme (a pension on retire-ment, a widow(er)'s pension, a 'death in service' benefit, and so forth). They are also usually objects of powers conferred by that scheme and thereby enjoy a status and rights similar to those outlined above in respect of objects of mere powers and discretionary trusts. In *LRT Pension Fund Trustee Co Ltd v Hatt*,[126] Knox J, classified the rights and interests of members of pension funds as follows:

1. At the top of the scale comes the right to receive a pension or other benefit in accordance with the rules as they stand from time to time. I include under this head the right to restrain improper exercises of fiduciary powers vested in the trustees or other bodies involved in the operation of the scheme...

2. Next comes the right which is correlative to the duty of an employer to observe the implied term in contracts of employment that the employer will not act in breach of the implied obligation of good faith... The right of employees is there-fore capable of securing to them as members of a pension scheme benefits over and above what the current rules of the scheme taken by themselves provide as their lawful entitlement.

3. Thirdly, there are the expectations which members might quite legitimately har-bour that discretions will be exercised in their favour where no such breach of a duty of good faith by the employer or abuse of a fiduciary power is involved in the non-exercise of the discretion. Typically this situation arises where there is a sur-plus discerned by the actuary to the fund and one possiblity is for pensions to be increased. No doubt the larger the surplus the livelier the expectation but in the great majority of pension funds it remains an expectation rather than a right. That is not to say that it is either without value or that the law will not protect it in appropriate circumstances...

---

[125] eg, statute-barred debts are still regarded as property; and, formerly, until a right of action against the Crown was permitted by statute, government debts (such as unpaid Crown annuities, for example) could not be sued for in court, but they were always regarded as personal property: *Ex parte Huggins* (1882) 21 Ch D 85, 90–91. [126] [1993] OPLR 225, 265–266.

It is also to be borne in mind that the fact that a beneficiary's interest is only an expectation of an exercise of a discretion in his or her favour does not detract from that beneficiary's right to have the fund in respect of which that discretion may be expected to be exercised dealt with according to law and not improperly. An object of a discretionary trust is entitled to have the fund dealt with properly even in a traditional voluntary settlement. All the more so is a member of a pension fund entitled not to have the pension fund dealt with otherwise than according to law.

A similar analysis of the rights of a member of an occupational pension scheme, **7.40** albeit from a slightly different perspective, was put forward by Lord Oliver in *Baird v Baird*.[127] The scheme under consideration was a typical contributory balance-of-cost scheme, under which the funds were vested in trustees and the scheme itself administered by a committee of management. Scheme benefits were not assignable. On the death of a member of the scheme while still in service, a payment would be made to such person or persons as the member had nominated, or, in default of nomination, to the member's widow(er) or estate. The case concerned the validity of a particular nomination. However, Lord Oliver provided a lucid analysis of such schemes in general:[128]

> Essentially, a pension scheme of the type with which this appeal is concerned is no different from any other *inter vivos* declaration of trust or settlement containing provisions for the destination of the trust fund after the death of the principal beneficiary. By becoming party to the scheme, each employee constitutes himself both a beneficiary and *(quoad* his contributions to the trust fund from which the benefits are payable) a settlor. He retains no proprietary interest in his contributions but receives instead such rights, including the right to appoint interests in the fund to take effect on the occurrence of specified contingencies, as the trusts of the fund confer upon him.
> In essence, the power to appoint the 'death-in-employment benefit' is no different from any other power of appointment. It disposes of no property of the appointor, for the proprietary interest of the estate of the appointor is one which arises only in default of appointment and in the event of there being no surviving widow.
> ... the provisions of [the scheme] exclude any power of *inter vivos* disposition and [which] confer on the appointor an interest of a capital nature only in default or on failure of the prior limitations.

At the stage when the member has made his nomination, there comes immediately into being a trust in favour of the nominated beneficiary, but one defeasible by the revocation of the nomination or appointment (and upon satisfying any other conditions, such as receiving any requisite consents) or by leaving employment (whereupon the 'death-in-employment' benefit ceases to be payable).

This is to be contrasted with the case where the member has an absolute beneficial **7.41** interest in his share of the fund during his lifetime, without any restriction on assignment. In such a case the nomination is ineffective and the share of the fund

---

[127] [1990] 2 AC 548 (appeal to the PC from Trinidad and Tobago).
[128] ibid 556–557.

will pass under the trusts of the member's will.[129] It is also to be contrasted with certain statutory nominations. In the case of nominations under the Provident Societies Acts, the nomination is in its nature testamentary, and the nominator is free to deal with the nominated property during his lifetime, but he is given a statutory power to deal with the property which is separate from the requirements of the Wills Act 1837.[130] Under the Friendly Societies Act 1974 the subject matter of a nomination does not apparently form part of the nominator's estate but passes directly to the nominee by force of the nomination.[131] In contrast, the power conferred by statute on a member of a friendly society to nominate a beneficiary of the proceeds of a life insurance policy, or on a member of an industrial and provident society to nominate a proportion of his property in the society in favour of someone else, is in the nature of a testamentary power.[132]

> No doubt, where the effect of the particular scheme is . . . to confer upon a member a full power of disposition during his lifetime over the amount standing to his credit under the scheme, a disposition of that interest upon his death would normally constitute a testamentary disposition requiring attestation in accordance with the statutory requirements for the execution of a will. But in what is now the normal case of non-assignable interests such as that in the present case and, *a fortiori*, where the power of nomination and revocation requires the prior approval of the trustees or of a management committee, their Lordships see no reason to doubt the correctness of Megarry J's decision in the *Danish Bacon Co* case . . . [133]

7.42   In any event, the exercise of a power to appoint a death benefit under a typical pension scheme is an *inter vivos* disposition: the power is effectively a special power of appointment which operates by force of the rules of the scheme,[134] and which (depending on the precise terms of the scheme) may be exercised revocably or irrevocably,[135] and may defeat interests in default of appointment.[136] As Lord Oliver stated in *Baird*,[137] in this type of scheme, at the stage when a member has made his nomination, there comes immediately into being a trust in favour of the nominated beneficiary, but one defeasible by the revocation of the nomination

---

[129]   *Re MacInnes* [1935] 1 DLR 401; *Re Shirley* (1965) 49 DLR (2d) 474; *Baird v Baird* at 558.

[130]   *Re Barnes* [1940] Ch 267; and *Eccles Provident Industrial Co-operative Society Ltd v Griffiths* [1912] AC 483, 490 and [1911] 2 KB 275, 284.

[131]   *Bennett v Slater* [1899] 1 QB 45.

[132]   *Bennett v Slater* [1899] 1 QB 45; *Griffiths v Eccles Provident, Industrial Co-operative Society Ltd* [1911] 2 KB 275; *Eccles Provident Industrial Co-operative Society Ltd v Griffiths* [1912] AC 483; *Demee v National Independent Mechanics' Friendly Society* [1919] RCR 8; *Re Barnes* [1940] Ch 267. See also *Baird v Baird, supra*, 558.

[133]   ibid 561, *per* Lord Oliver. See *Re Danish Bacon Co Staff Pension Fund Trusts* [1971] 1 WLR 248. The analysis put forward by Lord Oliver is essentially the same as that adopted in the nineteenth century in relation to similar provisions in the statutory Customs Annuity and Benevolent Fund: see *Re William Phillips' Insurance* (1883) 23 Ch D 235; *Re Pocock's Policy* (1871) 6 Ch App 445; *Re Maclean's Trusts* (1874) LR 19 Eq 274; *Urquhart v Butterfield* (1887) 37 Ch D 357.

[134]   *Re Danish Bacon Co Staff Pension Fund Trusts* [1971] 1 WLR 248, 256.

[135]   See *Re Maclean's Trusts* (1874) LR 19 Eq 274; *Demee, supra*.

[136]   *Baird v Baird, supra*, at 557; *Demee, supra*.   [137]   At 558.

(and upon satisfying any other conditions, such as receiving any requisite consents) or by leaving employment (whereupon the death benefit may cease to be payable).[138]

It also seems clear that, in respect of a contributory pension scheme, each member **7.43** is a settlor to the extent of his or her own contributions. Any power reserved by or conferred on such member, and indeed any power conferred on the trustees of the scheme in respect of such member, can therefore be exercised only within, and never outside, the applicable perpetuity period.[139] However, it is also probable that, even in respect of a non-contributory scheme or a scheme under which both employer and employees contribute, contributions paid by the employer are not gratuitous, but represent 'deferred remuneration' of the employee.[140]

---

[138] The statement by Megarry J in *Re Danish Bacon* at 257E, to the effect that a nomination of the type before him was sufficiently testamentary in nature to be wholly ineffective as a disposition or assignment so long as the nominator lived, does not seem to accord with the remarks of Lord Oliver in *Baird*, and seems, in any event, not to have been relevant to the decision which Megarry J actually reached.

[139] See paras 8.69–8.80 below.

[140] See also *Parry v Cleaver* [1970] AC 1, 16; *The Halcyon Skies* [1977] QB 14; *Smoker v London Fire & Civil Defence Authority* [1991] 2 AC 502; *Defrenne v Belgium* [1976] ECR 445; *Bilka-Kaufhaus Gmbh v Weber von Hartz* [1986] ECR 559; *Barber v Guardian Royal Exchange Assurance Group* [1991] 1 QB 344.

8

TRUSTS WITH UNLAWFUL PURPOSES: THE RULES AGAINST PERPETUITIES, AGAINST INALIENABILITY, AND AGAINST EXCESSIVE ACCUMULATIONS[1]

---

[1] Much of this present chapter is based GW Thomas, *Powers* (Sweet & Maxwell, 1998) ('*Thomas*') Chapter 4.

A. Trusts With Unlawful Purposes: Introduction

8.01 Trusts may be wholly or partly ineffective because they are unlawful. The most common and problematic examples of such unlawful trusts are those which contravene the rule against perpetuities, or the rule against inalienability, or the rule against excessive accumulation of income. These three rules are dealt with in detail in Sections B, C and D of this chapter. Trusts may also be unlawful because they seek to defeat or prejudice the rights of creditors: trusts and insolvency are dealt with in detail in Chapter 9 below. Trusts may also fail because they infringe a rule of public policy:[2] these rules are now outlined below.

(1) Trusts Against Public Policy

Trusts purporting to oust the jurisdiction of the court

8.02 A trust or provision in a trust purporting to oust the jurisdiction of the court is void. For example, a provision which purports to authorize trustees 'to determine . . . whether any moneys are to be considered as capital or income . . . and to determine . . . all questions and matters of doubt arising in the execution of the trusts' is void.[3] Such a provision 'is both repugnant to the benefits which are conferred by the will upon the beneficiaries and also . . . contrary to public policy as being an attempt to oust the jurisdiction of the court to construe and control the construction and administration of a testator's will and estate'. The courts alone, and not the trustees, can determine legal questions, for example as to the meaning of 'charity'; and, in most cases where a question of construction arises, it is the intention of the settlor or testator that needs to be ascertained, which is itself a task for the courts and not for the trustees to determine. This is not to say, however, that trustees or third parties can never be made judges of fact, even where the existence of such fact is a precondition of the vesting of a gift or interest.[4] They may even be given power to ascribe meaning to particular terms in a trust; they may be given dispositive discretions which are expressed to be 'absolute and uncontrolled'; and they may be authorized to pay income to capital beneficiaries and capital to income beneficiaries. What is not possible, however, is to declare that their decisions and actions can never be challenged in court and that the courts shall never have jurisdiction to control the trust.

8.03 Similarly, provisions *in terrorem* will have no force or effect. For example, a provision that a bequest of personalty shall be revoked if the legatee contests the

---

[2] *A-G v Pearson* (1817) 3 Mer 353, 399; *Hamilton v Waring* (1802) 2 Bligh 196.
[3] *Re Wynn* [1952] Ch 271; *Re Raven* [1915] 1 Ch 673.
[4] See, for example, *Dundee General Hospitals Board v Walker* [1952] 1 All ER 896. See also paras 4.35–4.40 above.

will or marries without consent, will be disregarded and the bequest will take effect.[5] A provision which is not intended as a threat to the legatee but is a proper determinable interest, with a gift over on new trusts upon the happening of the specified event, is valid, however.[6] Such a provision ought not to be adopted lightly, for the analogy between a gift to A until he becomes bankrupt or attempts to alienate his interest and a gift to A until he makes an application to the court is not a strong one. There is no rule of public policy against preventing a beneficiary from going to court to contest a will,[7] and the same may apply to an *inter vivos* trust. However, there is a difference between contesting the trust itself and challenging some action or decision of the trustees: there may be other good reasons why the latter cannot be challenged in particular circumstances, but it is doubtful whether an absolute bar on taking legal proceedings can ever be lawful.

Trusts for fraudulent purposes

A trust cannot be used for a fraudulent purpose, such as to evade taxation or to hide the real ownership of the property from creditors.[8] Also, the presumption of advancement may not be allowed to be rebutted by evidence of an unlawful purpose which has been carried out.[9]   **8.04**

Conditions in restraint of marriage

A provision that a gift or interest will be divested if the beneficiary gets married is void as being in restraint of marriage.[10] A provision designed to encourage parties to divorce is also void.[11] A partial restraint, such as a condition against marriage with a particular person, is valid.[12] So, too, is a gift over in the event of a second marriage[13] or a requirement for prior consent to marriage.[14] A limitation 'until marriage' will also be valid, provided it is not intended to be a total restraint on marriage.[15]   **8.05**

---

[5] *Re Hanlon* [1933] Ch 254.

[6] *Re Whiting's Settlement* [1905] 1 Ch 96; *Leong v Lim Beng Chye* [1955] AC 648.

[7] *Cooke v Turner* (1846) 15 M & W 727; *Evanturel v Evanturel* (1874) LR 6 PC 1; *Nathan v Leonard* [2002] WTLR 1061. The court has jurisdiction to grant relief from forfeiture to beneficiaries whose interests are forfeit through no fault of their own: *Simpson v Vickers* (1807) 14 Ves 34; *Nathan v Leonard, supra.*

[8] *Sekhon v Alissa* [1989] 2 FLR 94; *Midland Bank plc v Wyatt* [1995] 1 FLR 697. See also Chapter 9 below.

[9] *Tribe v Tribe* [1996] Ch 107. See also *Tinsley v Milligan* [1994] 1 AC 340.

[10] *Lloyd v Lloyd* (1852) 2 Sim (NS) 255; *Re Hewett* [1918] 1 Ch 458.

[11] *Re Caborne* [1943] Ch 224. Cf *Re Thompson* [1939] 1 All ER 681.

[12] *Jenner v Turner* (1880) 16 Ch D 188; *Re Bathe* [1925] Ch 377; *Re Hanlon* [1933] Ch 254.

[13] *Allen v Jackson* (1875) 1 Ch D 399.   [14] *Re Whiting's Settlement* [1905] 1 Ch 96.

[15] *Re Hewett* [1918] 1 Ch 458; *Re Lovell* [1920] 1 Ch 122; *Re Fentem* [1950] WN 543.

Conditions separating parent and child

8.06 A trust which is intended to interfere with the performance of parental duties or to separate parent and child is void.[16]

Trusts adverse to religion and morality

8.07 Trusts which are adverse to the foundation of all religion and subversive of all morality are void.[17]

Consequences of unlawful trust

8.08 A trust for a wholly unlawful purpose will not be enforced by the court; nor will it assist the settlor to recover his property,[18] unless the illegal purpose fails to take effect.[19] An innocent creditor of a deceased settlor may, however, recover the property.[20] Where only part of the trust is unlawful and the amount applicable towards the unlawful purpose can be ascertained, the lawful trusts of the remainder will be saved.[21] However, if this cannot be done, the whole gift will fail.[22]

B. The Rule Against Perpetuities

(1) Statement of The Rule Against Perpetuities

8.09 The rule against perpetuities, which applies to trusts,[23] is a rule invalidating interests which vest too remotely: indeed, it is often called the rule against remoteness of vesting.[24] The classic statement of the common law rule against perpetuities is that of Joyce J in *Re Thompson*:[25]

> The rule against perpetuities requires that every estate or interest must vest, if at all, not later than twenty-one years after the determination of some life in being at the

---

[16] *Re Sandbrook* [1912] 2 Ch 471; *Re Boulter* [1922] 1 Ch 75; *Re Borwick* [1933] Ch 657; *Re Piper* [1946] 2 All ER 503.

[17] *Thornton v Howe* (1862) 31 Beav 14.

[18] *Cottington v Fletcher* (1740) 2 Atk 155; *Muckleston v Brown* (1801) 6 Ves 52; *Davies v Otty (No 2)* (1865) 35 Beav 208; *Haigh v Kaye* (1872) 7 Ch App 469; *Re Great Berlin Steamboat Co* (1884) 26 Ch D 616.

[19] *Symes v Hughes* (1870) LR 9 Eq 475.

[20] *Muckleston v Brown, supra; Joy v Campbell* (1804) 1 Sch & Lef 328, 335, 339; *Miles v Durnford* (1852) 2 De GM & G 641.

[21] *Mitford v Reynolds* (1842) 1 Ph 185; *Re Rigley's Trusts* (1867) 15 WR 190; *Fisk v A-G* (1867) LR 4 Eq 521; *Re Vaughan* (1886) 33 Ch D 187.

[22] *Chapman v Brown* (1801) 6 Ves 404; *Re Birkett* (1878) 9 Ch D 576; *Re Taylor* (1888) 58 LT 538; *Re Porter* [1925] Ch 746.

[23] *Duke of Norfolk's Case* (1683) 3 Ch Cas 1.

[24] Morris and Leach, *The Rule Against Perpetuities* (2nd edn, 1962, and 1st Supp, 1964) 1.

[25] [1906] 2 Ch 199, 202. See also JC Gray, *The Rule Against Perpetuities* (4th edn, 1942) §201; Morris and Leach, *The Rule Against Perpetuities* (2nd edn, 1962, and 1st Supp, 1964); RH

time of the creation of such estate or interest, and not only must the person to take be ascertained, but the amount of his interest must be ascertainable within the pre-scribed period. Or the rule may be stated thus: A grant or other limitation of any estate or interest to take effect in possession or enjoyment at a future time, and which is not, from the time of its creation, a vested estate or interest, will be void *ab initio* if, at the time when the limitation takes effect, there is a possibility that the estate or interest limited will not vest within the period of a life or lives then in being, or within a further period of twenty-one years thereafter.

Any future interest, in real or personal property, must vest in interest (as opposed to vest in possession),[26] within the perpetuity period. An interest will be vested only if: (a) the person(s) entitled is/are ascertained; (b) the interest is ready to take effect in possession forthwith, subject only to any prior interest; and (c) the size of the benefit is known.[27]

Construction

A reference to the rule against perpetuities is taken to indicate the common law **8.10** rule, unless the context makes it clear that something different is intended.[28] Where the language of an instrument is ambiguous, the court will prefer the inter-pretation that will prevent the gift from being void for perpetuity.[29] However, the relevant trusts must first be read and construed as if the rule against perpetuities did not exist; and only then is the rule applied to them.[30] The court will also endeavour to give effect to executory trusts so as to comply with the rule.[31]

On the other hand, the use of expressions such as 'so far as the law permits' will not **8.11** generally be construed so as to prevent a trust from being void for remoteness,[32] unless it is reasonably clear what the intended period was intended to be.[33] A gift

Maudsley, *The Modern Rule Against Perpetuities* (1979); C Harpum *Megarry and Wade's The Law of Real Property* (6th edn, Sweet & Maxwell, 2000) ('*Megarry and Wade*') 238–300; the Law Commission's Consultation Paper No 133 and Report, *The Rules Against Perpetuities and Excessive Accumulations* (Law Com No 251). For the history of the rule, see Gray, §§ 123–200; WS Holdsworth, *A History of English Law* vol 7, 81–144, 193–238; AWB Simpson, *An Introduction to the History of the Land Law* (OUP, 1961) Ch 9; (1965) 81 LQR 106 (DE Allen); (1981) 97 LQR 593 (R Deech); (1986) 102 LQR 250 (Dukeminier); (1986) 36 UTLJ 187 (AI Ogus).

[26] *Evans v Walker* (1876) 3 Ch D 211.
[27] *Megarry and Wade*, 242–243. *Re Hargreaves* (1890) 43 Ch D 401.
[28] *IRC v Williams* [1969] 1 WLR 1197, 1203.
[29] *Pearks v Moseley* (1880) 5 App Cas 714, 719; *Re Mortimer* [1905] 2 Ch 502, 506; *Re Hume* [1912] 1 Ch 693; *Re Leek* [1969] 1 Ch 563, 583–584; *IRC v Williams* [1969] 1 WLR 1197; *Re Deeley's Settlement* [1974] Ch 454.
[30] *Heasman v Pearse* (1871) 7 Ch App 275, 285; *Pearks v Moseley, supra*; *Re Bowen* [1893] 2 Ch 491; *Re Hume* [1912] 1 Ch 693, 698; *Re Legh's Settlement Trusts* [1938] Ch 39, 44; *Re Johnson's Settlement Trusts* [1943] Ch 341.
[31] *Shelley v Shelley* (1868) LR 6 Eq 540; *Re Steele's Will Trusts* [1948] Ch 603.
[32] *Christie v Gosling* (1866) LR 1 HL 279; *Portman v Viscount Portman* [1922] 2 AC 473; *Re Compton* [1946] 1 All ER 117; *Re Abraham's Will Trusts* [1969] 1 Ch 463; *Re Kelly* [1932] IR 255.
[33] *Re Hooper* [1932] Ch 28; *Re Vaux* [1939] Ch 465. See also *Shelley v Shelley, supra*; *Re Beresford Hope* [1917] 1 Ch 287; *Re Steele's Will Trusts, supra*.

over on the 'failure' of a prior interest will not generally be construed to include failure under the rule against perpetuities.[34]

Effect of failure to comply with the rule

8.12 A disposition of a future interest in property which fails to comply with the rule against perpetuities is void. If the disposition was made before 16 July 1964, and is therefore governed by the common law rule alone, the interest is void *ab initio*. In the case of a disposition made after 15 July 1964, and which is subject to the 'wait and see' provisions of the Perpetuities and Accumulations Act 1964, the interest is prospectively void, ie it is presumed to be valid and becomes invalid only if and when it becomes clear that it will vest at too remote a time.

The perpetuity period at common law

8.13 At common law, the perpetuity period consists of any life or lives in being and a further period of 21 years (plus any gestation period).[35] The life or lives in question must be human lives (and not the lives of animals),[36] must be 'in being' at the date when the instrument creating the interest takes effect,[37] and must also be mentioned expressly in the disposition or be identifiable by implication.[38] It is not necessary that a life in being should himself be a beneficiary or even have any relationship with those who are, ie he need not be 'logically relevant' (hence the widespread use of 'royal lives').[39] There is no specific restriction on the number of lives in being selected,[40] provided that the class is not so large as to be void for uncertainty.[41]

8.14 At common law, the validity of every interest must be determined at the date when the instrument creating it takes effect. Moreover, validity depends upon possibilities and not upon probabilities or actual events.[42] If, at the date when the relevant instrument takes effect, there is a remote possibility that the interest will vest outside the perpetuity period, that interest will be void: it is immaterial that it is highly

---

[34] *Re Hubbard's Will Trusts* [1963] Ch 275; *Re Buckton's Settlement Trusts* [1964] Ch 497; *IRC v Williams, supra.* Cf *Re Robinson's Will Trusts* [1963] 1 WLR 628.

[35] *Lord Dungannon v Smith* (1846) 12 Cl & F 546, 563.

[36] *Re Kelly* [1932] IR 255, 260, 261. Cf *Re Dean* (1889) 41 Ch D 552.

[37] ie, if it is a deed, at the time of its execution; and if it is a will, at the time of the testator's death.

[38] In this case, the relevant lives are those who are clearly connected with the trusts in question.

[39] *Re Villar* [1929] 1 Ch 243; *Re Leverhulme (No 2)* [1943] 2 All ER 274.

[40] See, for example, *Pownall v Graham* (1863) 33 Beav 243; *Thellusson v Woodford* (1805) 11 Ves Jun 112, 145; *Caddell v Palmer* (1833) 1 Cl & Fin 372; *Re Villar* [1929] 1 Ch 245; *Re Leverhulme (No 2), supra*; *Re Warren's Will Trusts* (1961) 105 SJ 511.

[41] *Re Moore* [1901] 1 Ch 936; *Re Villar* [1929] 1 Ch 243; *Re Leverhulme (No 2), supra*.

[42] ibid 244; Morris and Leach (n 24 above) 70. Ambiguity may be resolved in favour of validity, however: *Re Deeley's Settlement* [1974] Ch 454.

improbable that this will occur and, indeed, that in the event the possibility does not actually happen.[43] At common law, there is generally no 'wait and see' rule.[44]

The Perpetuities and Accumulations Act 1964

The Perpetuities and Accumulations Act 1964 (which applies only to instruments **8.15** taking effect after 15 July 1964) modified the strict common law position in three major respects.[45] First, an alternative perpetuity period may now be chosen. Secondly, a 'wait and see' principle has been introduced. Thirdly, restrictions have been introduced on the persons who could be used as lives in being for the specific purposes of the 'wait and see' rules.

An alternative perpetuity period

Section 1(1) of the Act provides that, where the instrument by which any disposition **8.16** is made *so provides*, the perpetuity period applicable to the disposition under the rule against perpetuities, instead of being of any other duration, shall be of a duration equal to such number of years not exceeding 80 as is specified in that behalf in the instrument. A 'disposition' includes the *conferring* of a power of appointment; and 'power of appointment' includes any discretionary power to transfer a beneficial interest in property without the furnishing of valuable consideration.[46] However, section 1(1) does not have effect where the disposition is made *in exercise* of a special power of appointment; but it is provided that, where a period of years not exceeding 80 is specified in the instrument creating the power, that period shall apply in relation to any disposition under the power as it applies in relation to the power itself.[47]

The 'wait and see' principle

The 1964 Act introduces a principle of 'wait and see'. Section 3(1) provides that, **8.17** where a disposition would be void[48] on the ground that the interest disposed of

---

[43] *Re Watson's Settlement Trusts* [1959] 1 WLR 732, 739, approving *Megarry and Wade* 244. See also *Re Wood* [1894] 3 Ch 381; *Lord Dungannon v Smith* (1845–46) 12 Cl & Fin 546; *Re Roberts* (1881) 50 LJ Ch 265; *Thomas v Thomas* (1903) 87 LT 58; *Re Bewick* [1911] 1 Ch 116; *Re Engels* (1943) 168 LT 311.

[44] There are two exceptions, namely in cases of alternative contingencies (see *Megarry and Wade* 274–275) and powers of appointment (see paras 8.38–8.58 below).

[45] See, generally, *Megarry and Wade,* 242–295 and Maudsley (n 25 above) *passim.*

[46] Section 15(2) of the 1964 Act.

[47] Section 12(2) of the 1964 Act. Section 1(1) does not apply either to the conferring of an option to acquire for valuable consideration any interest in land, where the perpetuity period is 21 years: s 9(2) of the 1964 Act.

[48] These provisions apply only if the relevant disposition would otherwise be void at common law. It must first be established, therefore, whether it does or does not fail at common law. On the other hand, where other provisions of the 1964 Act, such as age reduction or exclusion of members of a class, may save a particular disposition, the 'wait and see' rule must be applied first; only if and when the disposition is seen not to be capable of being saved by the 'wait and see' rule will these other provisions come into operation. See also the 'class-closing' provisions in s 4 of the Act: paras 8.23–8.26 below.

might not become vested until too remote a time, the disposition shall be treated, until such time (if any) as it becomes established that the vesting *must* occur, if at all, after the end of the perpetuity period, as if the disposition were not subject to the rule against perpetuities. Indeed, its becoming so established shall not even affect the validity of anything previously done in relation to the interest disposed of by way of advancement, application of intermediate income, 'or otherwise'. Thus, instead of the common law rule that validity must be determined as at the date of the instrument creating the interest and in the light of possibilities, the Act provides that a disposition will fail only if and when it is established that vesting *must* occur, if at all, outside the perpetuity period.

Restrictions on lives in being

8.18 The 1964 Act does not affect the validity of 'royal lives' clauses or any other similar perpetuity clause which is valid at common law. However, the Act[49] introduces a detailed definition of the lives in being which are to be used for the purposes of the 'wait and see' provisions. Here, the perpetuity period is to be determined by reference to the lives (in being at the relevant time) of the categories of persons specified in section 3(5). These are:

(a) The person by whom the disposition was made;

(b) a person to whom or in whose favour a disposition was made, that is to say

   (i) in the case of a disposition to a class of persons, any member or potential member of the class;

   (ii) in the case of an individual disposition to a person taking only on certain conditions being satisfied, any person as to whom some of the conditions are satisfied and the remainder may in time be satisfied;

   (iii) in the case of a special power of appointment exercisable in favour of members of a class, any member or potential member of the class;

   (iv) in the case of a special power of appointment exercisable in favour of one person only, that person or, where the object of the power is ascertainable only on certain conditions being satisfied, any person as to whom some of the conditions are satisfied and the remainder may in time be satisfied;

   (v) in the case of any power, option or other right, the person on whom the right is conferred;

(c) a person having a child or grandchild within (b)(i) to (iv) above, or any of whose children or grandchildren, if subsequently born, would by virtue of his or her descent fall within those categories; and

---

[49] Section 3(4) and (5). For a detailed treatment, see *Megarry and Wade* 253–258. These provisions apply only to dispositions made after 15 July 1964; and, of course, they cannot apply where a fixed statutory period is chosen under s 1(1) of the Act (there being no lives in being in any event).

(d) any person on the failure or determination of whose prior interest the disposition
is limited to take effect.[50]

Any person falling within these categories must be in being and ascertainable at
the commencement of the perpetuity period; but so that the lives of 'any description of persons' falling within categories (b) or (c) above shall be disregarded
if the number of persons of that description is such as to render it impracticable to
ascertain the date of death of the survivor.[51] If no life in being is available, the
perpetuity period is 21 years only.[52]

Age of childbearing

The 1964 Act also made some much-needed changes to the common law's absurd   **8.19**
assumptions in connection with the age of childbearing. At common law, a person
was regarded as being capable of having children, irrespective of how young or old
he or she might be.[53] Moreover, evidence was not admissible to prove that a particular
person was not actually capable of having a child.[54] Section 2(1)(a) of the 1964 Act
now provides that, in relation to dispositions taking effect after 15 July 1964, it
shall be presumed for the purposes of the rule against perpetuities that a male cannot have a child under the age of 14 and that a female can have a child at the age of
12 or over, but not under 12 or over 55.[55] In addition, section 2(1)(b) provides that
evidence may now be adduced to prove that a particular person, whatever his or her
age, is or is not capable of having a child at the relevant time.[56]

The rule against perpetuities and class gifts

'A class gift is a gift of property to all who come within some description, the prop-   **8.20**
erty being divisible in shares according to the number of persons in the class.'[57]
Thus, a gift 'to my children who shall live to be 25', or 'to such of my children as
are born hereafter and shall marry', are class gifts.[58] A variation in the number of

---

[50] *Re Thomas Meadows & Co Ltd* [1971] Ch 278.   [51] Section 3(4)(a).
[52] Section 3(4)(b).
[53] Hence the assumed existence of the 'fertile octogenarian'. See *Jee v Audley* (1787) 1 Cox 324;
Lord Dungannon v Smith (1845–46) 12 Cl & Fin 546; *Re Dawson* (1888) 39 Ch D 155; *Re Deloitte*
[1926] Ch 56; *Ward v Van der Loeff* [1924] AC 653; *Figg v Clarke* [1997] STC 247.
[54] *Re Dawson* (1888) 39 Ch D 155; *Re Sayer's Trusts* (1868) LR 6 Eq 319; *Re Deloitte, supra.*
[55] 'Having' a child in this context includes having a child by adoption, legitimation, or other
means: see s 2(4).
[56] 'Having' a child in this context means begetting and bearing children: s 2(4). See also the consequential provisions in s 2(2) and (3).
[57] *Megarry and Wade* 270–271; RW Jennings andSC Harper, *Jarman on Wills* (8th edn, 1951)
('*Jarman*')341, 348; *Pearks v Moseley* (1880) 5 App Cas 714, 723; *Kingsbury v Walter* [1901] AC
187, 192.
[58] See, for example, *Lee v Pain* (1845) 4 Hare 249; *Boreham v Bignall* (1850) 8 Hare 131; *Leigh
v Leigh* (1854) 17 Beav 605; *Re Stanhope's Trusts* (1859) 27 Beav 201; *Re Hornby* (1859) 7 WR 729;
Aspinall v Duckworth (1866) 35 Beav 307; *Dimond v Bostock* (1875) 10 Ch App 358; *Re Jackson*
(1883) 25 Ch D 162; *Re Mervin* [1891] 3 Ch 197; *Kingsbury v Walter* [1901] AC 187.

members of the class will result in a corresponding increase or decrease in the share of each member.[59] If the number of people in the 'class' does not affect the size of each one's share, it is not a class gift.[60] For the purposes of the common law rule against perpetuities, if the size of the class, and therefore the size of each member's share or interest, might increase or decrease outside the perpetuity period, the gift is totally void.[61]

8.21 The harshness of the common law rule was mitigated by means of the so-called rule in *Andrews v Partington*.[62] This is a rule of construction and applies to both settlements *inter vivos* and will trusts[63] and to both realty and personalty.[64] It provides that a class of beneficiaries will close when the first member of that class becomes entitled in possession to his share of capital[65] (usually on attaining a specified age), so that no one born after that date can be a member of the class and take any share or interest. The rule is essentially one of convenience and purports to reconcile two conflicting intentions of the settlor: the first is an intention that all persons qualifying as members of the class should take (which may not be possible if the class is closed prematurely); the second intention is that each one should take at the specified age (which may not be possible if the class is kept open pending the birth of further members).[66] The settlor is presumed, therefore, to have intended that the class should close as soon as the first share or interest vests in possession, at which point the maximum number of shares or interests is fixed.[67] Thus, in the case of a class gift to A's children at 21, where A has no child or no child who has attained the age of 21 at the creation of the settlement, the class closes as soon as the first child of A to attain 21 does so.[68] No child of A born

---

[59] *Re Hornby* (1859) 7 WR 729; *Boreham v Bignall* (1850) 8 Hare 131; *Dimond v Bostock* (1875) 10 Ch App 358; *Re Jackson* (1883) 25 Ch D 162.

[60] *Bain v Lescher* (1840) 11 Sim 397; *Havergal v Harrison* (1843) 7 Beav 49; *Storrs v Benbow* (1853) 3 De GM & G 390; *Wilkinson v Duncan* (1861) 30 Beav 111; *Rogers v Mutch* (1878) 9 Ch D 117; *Re Stansfield* (1880) 15 Ch D 84.

[61] *Leake v Robinson* (1817) 2 Mer 363; *Smith v Smith* (1870) 5 Ch App 342; *Hale v Hale* (1876) 3 Ch D 643; *Pearks v Moseley* (1880) 5 App Cas 714.

[62] (1791) 3 Bro CC 401. See also Morris and Leach (n 24 above) 103–118; *Megarry and Wade* 228–250, 500–504; (1964) 70 LQR 61 (JHC Morris); [1958] CLJ 39 (SJ Bailey); *Jarman* 1660 *et seq*.

[63] *Re Knapp's Settlement* [1895] 1 Ch 91; *Re Wernher's Settlement Trusts* [1961] 1 WLR 136; *Re Chapman's Settlement Trusts* [1977] 1 WLR 1163. *Quaere* whether it applied to marriage settlements: *Andrews v Partington* (1791) 3 Bro CC 401, 404. Being a rule of construction, it can be displaced by a contrary intention.

[64] *Re Canney's Trust* (1910) 101 LT 905.

[65] The rule does not apply to gifts of income only: *Re Stephens* [1904] 1 Ch 322 (joint lives; also accumulation of income); *Re Ward* [1965] Ch 856 (discretionary trusts).

[66] *Re Emmett's Estate* (1880) 13 Ch D 484, 490; *Re Stephens* [1904] 1 Ch 322, 328; *Re Chartres* [1927] 1 Ch 466, 474.

[67] *Barrington v Tristram* (1801) 6 Ves 345, 348.

[68] *Ellison v Airey* (1748) 1 Ves Sen 111; *Congreve v Congreve* (1781) 1 Bro CC 530; *Balm v Balm* (1830) 3 Sim 492; *Armitage v Williams* (1859) 27 Beav 846; *Re Mervin* [1891] 3 Ch 197; *Re Knapp's Settlement* [1895] 1 Ch 91; *Re Deloitte* [1919] 1 Ch 209; *Re Chartres* [1927] 1 Ch 466; *Re Bleckly* [1951] Ch 740, 749; *Re Wernher's Settlement Trusts* [1961] 1 WLR 136. The share of a member of

after that date can take an interest; and if any child born before that date (and is, therefore, a member of the class) fails to attain the age of 21, the share or interest which he or she would otherwise have taken accrues to those members of the class born before that date who do attain the age of 21.[69] Similarly, if the gift is to B for life, with remainder to A's children at 21, the class closes at the natural termination of B's interest, if before that date a child of A has attained the age of 21.[70] If no child of A has then been born, or none has attained 21, the class closes as soon as a child of A does so.[71]

The rule never operated in a straightforward manner, however, and there were several exceptions. For example, where the shares of members of a class were intended to vest at birth, and no member is born when their interests would otherwise fall into possession, then the class stays open and is not closed prematurely. Thus, where there is a gift to the children of A and, at the creation of the settlement, A has no children, then all the children of A, whenever born, will be members of the class.[72] And, of course, the rule in *Andrews v Partington* cannot apply at all where it is excluded expressly, for example where there is an express direction as to the time at which the class is intended to close, such as a gift to members of a class 'whenever born'[73] or living at a specified 'closing date';[74] and it may even be excluded by implication, for instance by conferring a power of advancement which authorizes payment of presumptive shares.[75] On the other hand, the rule is not necessarily excluded by references to 'all' or to 'all or any' members of a class or to those 'now born or who shall be born hereafter'.[76] Where the language is

8.22

---

the class who attained the age of 21, but died before the material date will vest in his or her personal representatives: *Devisme v Mello* (1781) 1 Bro CC 537; *Berry v Briant* (1862) 2 Dr & Sm 1; *Watson v Young* (1885) 28 Ch D 436. The rule applies to a class of any kind: *Kevern v Williams* (1832) 5 Sim 171; *Peyton v Hughes* (1842) 7 Jur 311; *Bainbridge v Cream* (1852) 16 Beav 25; *Baldwin v Rogers* (1853) 3 De GM & G 649; *Maddock v Legg* (1858) 25 Beav 531; *Re Gardiner's Estate* (1875) LR 20 Eq 647; *Dimond v Bostock* (1875) 10 Ch App 358; *Re Chapman's Settlement* [1971] 1 WLR 1163.

[69] *Gillman v Daunt* (1856) 3 K & J 48; *Robley v Ridings* (1847) 11 Jur 813.

[70] *Devisme v Mello* (1781) 1 Bro CC 537; *Ayton v Ayton* (1787) 1 Cox 327; *Berkeley v Swinburn* (1848) 16 Sim 275; *Baldwin v Rogers* (1853) 3 De GM & G 649; *Maddock v Legg* (1858) 25 Beav 531; *Berry v Briant* (1862) 2 Dr & Sm 1; *Re Smith* (1862) 2 J & H 594; *Re Aylwin's Trusts* (1873) LR 16 Eq 585, 590–591; *Watson v Young* (1885) 28 Ch D 436; *Ward v Van der Loeff* [1924] AC 653; *Greenwood v Greenwood* [1939] 2 All ER 150; *Re Brooke* [1953] 1 WLR 439.

[71] *Kevern v Williams* (1832) 5 Sim 171; *Clarke v Clarke* (1836) 8 Sim 59; *Locke v Lamb* (1867) LR 4 Eq 372; *Re Emmet's Estate* (1880) 13 Ch D 484; *Re Bleckly* [1951] Ch 740.

[72] *Weld v Bradbury* (1715) 2 Vern 705; *Shepherd v Ingram* (1764) 1 Amb 448; *Re Chartres* [1927] 1 Ch 466, 471–472; *Re Bleckly* [1951] 1 WLR 740, 749. See also (1954) 70 LQR 66 (JHC Morris). If a child of A is then living, after-born children of A cannot take: *Horsley v Chaloner* (1750) 2 Ves Sen 83; *Kevern v Williams* (1832) 5 Sim 171; *Peyton v Hughes* (1842) 7 Jur 311; *Oppenheim v Henry* (1853) 10 Hare 441; *Re Manners* [1955] 1 WLR 1096.

[73] *Re Edmondson's Will Trusts* [1972] 1 WLR 183; *Re Henderson's Trusts* [1969] 1 WLR 651.

[74] *Re Tom's Settlement* [1987] 1 WLR 1021.   [75] *Re Henderson Trusts* [1969] 1 WLR 651.

[76] *Heathe v Heathe* (1740) 2 Atk 121; *Prescott v Long* (1795) 2 Ves 690; *Re Emmett's Estate* (1880) 13 Ch D 484; *Re Bleckly* [1951] Ch 740; *Re Wernher's Settlement Trusts* [1961] 1 WLR 136; *Re Clifford's Settlement Trusts* [1981] Ch 63.

ambiguous, the court will prefer the interpretation that will prevent the gift from being void for perpetuity.[77]

The effect of the Perpetuities and Accumulations Act 1964

8.23 The first question in relation to a class gift is whether it is valid or void for perpetuity under the common law rules, taking into account the class-closing rules. If it is wholly valid, the 1964 Act does not apply. If it is void under the common law rules, the Act may save it (wholly or in part). The principle that a class gift cannot be partially good and partially bad no longer holds.

8.24 Section 4(4) of the Act provides that, where it is apparent at the time the disposition is made or becomes apparent at a subsequent time that the inclusion of any potential members of a class[78] would cause the disposition to be treated as void for remoteness, those persons shall, unless their exclusion would exhaust the class, be deemed for all the purposes of the disposition to be excluded from the class. However, these provisions apply only if the 'wait and see' provisions in section 3 of the Act have already been applied and have failed to save the gift,[79] or if the class gift has not been saved by the rule in *Andrews v Partington*.

8.25 In addition, the 1964 Act introduced new age-reduction provisions. One cause for failure of trusts under the common law rule against perpetuities was the postponement of the vesting of a beneficiary's interest until he or she attained an excessive age, for example a gift to the first child of A to attain the age of 25 would be void if A was still living, because a child of A might attain that age more than 21 years after the death of A.[80] In order to save such gifts, section 163 of the Law of Property Act 1925 provided that, where a specified age was excessive[81] and would render the gift void (for example 'to the first of A's children to attain 25', where A was still alive and had no child who had yet attained 25), it should be reduced

---

[77] *Pearks v Moseley* (1880) 5 App Cas 714, 719; *Re Mortimer* [1905] 2 Ch 502, 506; *Re Hume* [1912] 1 Ch 693; *Re Deeley's Settlement* [1974] Ch 454.

[78] ie, 'persons, being potential members of a class or unborn persons who at birth would become members or potential members of the class'. A person is treated as a member of a class if in his case all the conditions identifying a member of a class are satisfied, and is treated as a potential member if in his case some only of those conditions are satisfied but there is a possibility that the remainder will in time be satisfied: s 15(3). An unborn person is not a potential member of a class, it seems: see s 4(3),(4).

[79] See the opening words of s 3.

[80] *Merlin v Blagrave* (1858) 25 Beav 125; *Abbiss v Burney* (1881) 17 Ch D 211. If A had already died, his surviving children would themselves be lives in being, or if one of his children was already aged 25, the gift would be valid: *Lachlan v Reynolds* (1852) 9 Hare 796; *Southern v Wollaston* (1852) 16 Beav 276; *Picken v Matthews* (1878) 10 Ch D 264.

[81] Section 163 applied strictly to age-reduction. A gift (say) to such issue as were living at too remote a date could not be saved.

to the age of 21.[82] By means of this substitution, the gift was saved and indeed accelerated.[83]

Section 4(1) of the 1964 Act took the process further.[84] Section 4(1) provides that, where a disposition is limited by reference to the attainment by any person or persons of a specified age exceeding 21 years, and it is apparent at the time the disposition is made, or becomes apparent at a subsequent time, that the disposition would otherwise be void for remoteness, but it would not have been void if the specified age had been 21 years, then the disposition shall be treated for all purposes as if, instead of the age actually specified, the disposition had specified the nearest age that would prevent the disposition from being void. Thus, the age-reduction is not necessarily or automatically to 21 years. Moreover, section 4(1) extends to gifts made by reference to the age of someone other than a beneficiary.[85] Where a class gift provides for the attainment of different ages (exceeding 21) in relation to different persons (for example for sons and daughters), section 4(1) applies so as to reduce each such age to the extent required to save the gift.[86] If necessary, age-reduction and class-reduction may be combined. Again, the age-reduction provisions apply only if the 'wait and see' provisions in section 3 of the Act have already been applied and have failed to save the gift[87] or if the class gift has not been saved by the rule in *Andrews v Partington*. **8.26**

Trusts subsequent to void trusts

Where there are successive trusts, the rule against perpetuities applies to each limitation separately. If each of the limitations is valid, there is clearly no difficulty. Also, a limitation is not rendered void simply because it is followed by a void one,[88] provided the limitations are not so inseparably mixed as to defeat the entire settlement.[89] However, at common law, if one of the limitations is void for remoteness, this may—but does not necessarily—infect and invalidate a subsequent one.[90] This will occur only if the subsequent limitation is *dependent* upon the prior void limitation, ie if it is intended to take effect only if the prior limitation itself takes effect (or not as the case may be): the vesting of a dependent limitation remains uncertain until the fate of the prior gift is known.[91] In contrast, an **8.27**

---

[82] *Re Hooper's Settlement Trusts* [1948] Ch 586; *Re Gilpin* [1954] Ch 1. Section 163 applied only to an instrument executed after 1925 or the will of a testator dying after 1925: s 163(2).

[83] See *Megarry and Wade* 235–236 for a useful illustration of the operation of these provisions.

[84] Section 163 of the LPA was repealed by ss 4(6) and 15(5) of the 1964 Act, but only in relation to instruments taking effect after 15 July 1964, so s 163 still applies to post-1925 and pre-15 July 1964 instruments.

[85] See *Megarry and Wade* 236–237 for a useful illustration of the operation of these provisions.

[86] Section 4(2).   [87] See the opening words of s 3.

[88] *Garland v Brown* (1864) 10 LT 292.   [89] *Re Abraham's Will Trusts* [1969] 1 Ch 463.

[90] 'Invalidity by contagion': *Re Hubbard's Will Trusts* [1963] Ch 275, 285.

[91] See, for example, *Re Mill's Declaration of Trust* [1950] 1 All ER 789; *Re Buckton's Settlement Trusts* [1964] Ch 497.

independent limitation is intended to vest in interest at its own time, whether or not the prior limitation does so.[92] Thus, the safe course and common practice is to ensure that subsequent gifts are vested, not contingent, and not 'subject to' the prior limitations.[93]

8.28   Limitations which follow void limitations have been divided into three classes for the purposes of the rule at common law.[94]

(a) Vested limitations. Interests which are vested *ab initio* cannot be defeated by the rule against perpetuities.[95]

(b) Contingent but independent limitations. An interest which is not dependent on a prior (void) limitation will be valid, provided that the contingency attached to the subsequent limitation itself does not infringe the rule against perpetuities.[96]

(c) Contingent but dependent limitations. The subsequent interest, being dependent upon a prior void limitation, will fail, even though it may itself be bound to vest (if at all) within the perpetuity period.[97]

Effect of the 1964 Act

8.29   Section 6 of the Perpetuities and Accumulations Act 1964 has abolished these common law rules relating to dependent limitations in relation to a disposition made after 15 July 1964. Section 6 provides that such a disposition shall not be treated as void for remoteness by reason only that the interest disposed of is ulterior to and dependent upon an interest under a disposition which is void; and the vesting of an interest shall not be prevented from being accelerated on the failure of a prior interest by reason only that the failure arises because of remoteness. Thus, the rule against perpetuities must be applied to each limitation separately and independently.

Alternative contingencies

8.30   If there are two alternative contingencies, one void for remoteness and one not, and the latter is genuinely an alternative to and not dependent upon the void

---

[92] *Proctor v Bishop of Bath and Wells* (1794) 2 H Bl 358; *Palmer v Holford* (1828) 4 Russ 403; *Re Thatcher's Trusts* (1859) 26 Beav 365; *Re Abbott* [1893] 1 Ch 54, 57; *Re Hooper's Settlement Trusts* [1948] Ch 586; *Re Hubbard's Will Trusts* [1963] Ch 275; *Re Leek* [1967] Ch 1061. The dependent limitation is void even though it must itself vest (if at all) within the perpetuity period.

[93] *Re Canning's Will Trusts* [1936] Ch 309.   [94] *Megarry and Wade* 240–241.

[95] *Lewis v Waters* (1805) 6 East 336; *Re Allan* [1958] 1 WLR 220; *Re Hubbard's Will Trusts* [1963] Ch 275. Cf *Re Backhouse* [1921] 2 Ch 51.

[96] *Re Abbott* [1893] 1 Ch 54; *Re Canning's Will Trusts* [1936] Ch 309; *Re Coleman* [1936] Ch 528; *Re Hubbard's Will Trusts, supra.*

[97] *Re Thatcher* (1859) 26 Beav 365, 369; *Re Hewett's Settlement* [1915] 1 Ch 810; *Re Hubbard's Will Trusts, supra; Re Ramadge* [1919] 1 IR 205.

contingency, the gift is valid at common law if the valid contingency occurs. Even the common law adopted a 'wait and see' rule.[98] However, this approach was permitted only if the alternative contingencies were expressed in the instrument creating the interest.[99] The 1964 Act does not change this rule.

Conditional and determinable interests and resulting trusts[100]

A *condition precedent* is one that must be fulfilled before a beneficiary becomes **8.31** entitled to a vested interest, for example 'to A if he attains 21', or 'to A if he survives B'.[101] The condition must be satisfied within the perpetuity period; and any possibility that it might not be meant that the interest was void at common law. Conditions precedent are now subject to the 'wait and see' provisions in section 3 of the Perpetuities and Accumulations Act 1964.

A *condition subsequent* is one which authorizes the grantor or his representatives **8.32** to determine an existing interest.[102] Thus, where there is a gift of land to trustees on condition that it shall always be used as an orphanage (or a hospital or whatever), the grantor and his successors in title have a right of re-entry if the condition is broken. If the condition infringes the rule against perpetuities and is void for remoteness, the interest which was made subject to it is not also rendered void: indeed, it can take effect unconditionally and becomes an absolute interest.[103]

A *determinable interest* differs from a condition subsequent in that it determines **8.33** automatically at common law. The rule against perpetuities, as Romer J put it in *Re Chardon*,[104] 'is not dealing with the duration of interests but with their commencement, and so long as the interest vests within lives in being and twenty-one years it does not matter how long that interest lasts'. Thus, an interest was not rendered void simply because it may have terminated outside the perpetuity period, for example a gift of premises for so long as they are used for the purposes of a public library,[105] or of income to pay outgoings of a house for as long as it is occupied by

---

[98] *Longhead d Hopkins v Phelps* (1770) 2 Wm Bl 704; *Leake v Robinson* (1817) 2 Mer 363; *Miles v Harford* (1879) 12 Ch D 691; *Re Davey* [1915] 1 Ch 837; *Re Curryer's Will Trust* [1938] Ch 952.

[99] *Proctor v Bishop of Bath and Wells* (1794) 2 H Bl 358; *Lord Dungannon v Smith* (1845–46) 12 Cl & Fin 546; *Re Bence* [1891] 3 Ch 242.

[100] See *Megarry and Wade* 244–250.

[101] ibid 246–247, where it is also pointed out that a discretionary trust is essentially a type of condition precedent, although now, under s 15(2) of the 1964 Act, discretionary trusts rank as powers of appointment.

[102] ibid 248.

[103] *Re Da Costa* [1912] 1 Ch 337; *Re Macleay* (1875) LR 20 Eq 186; *Dunn v Flood* (1883) 25 Ch D 629; *Re Elliott* [1952] Ch 217; *Imperial Tobacco Co Ltd v Wilmott* [1964] 1 WLR 902.

[104] [1928] Ch 464, 468.   [105] *Hopper v Corporation of Liverpool* (1944) 88 SJ 213.

a beneficiary.[106] The grantor's possibility of reverter was also not subject to the rule, it seems, despite the fact that it was necessarily contingent.[107]

8.34 Resulting trusts are not subject to the common law rule against perpetuities. The beneficial interest exists or arises because the settlor has failed to dispose of it and it is therefore vested in the settlor *ab initio*.[108]

8.35 Section 12 of the Perpetuities and Accumulations Act 1964 now provides that, in relation to dispositions made after 15 July 1964, the rule against perpetuities shall apply to the possibility of reverter on the determination of a determinable interest, and also the possibility of a resulting trust on the determination of any other determinable interest in property, in the same way that it would apply if the relevant provision were expressed in the form of a condition subsequent. If the possibility of reverter or the resulting trust (as the case may be) fails for remoteness, the determinable interest becomes an absolute interest. Thus, where there is a disposition of premises to trustees, in an instrument taking effect after 15 July 1964, for the purposes of an orphans' home or public library (or whatever) for as long as that purpose exists, with a gift over to A, the 'wait and see' provisions of the 1964 Act are applied: if the premises cease to be used for the specified purposes within 21 years, A takes absolutely; but, after 21 years have elapsed, A and the settlor (and his successors in title) are excluded and the gift becomes unconditional and absolute.

Powers and the rule against perpetuities.[109]

8.36 Generally, the rule against perpetuities applies to powers as it does to proprietary interests.[110] Thus a power given to trustees to lease,[111] or to sell,[112] which may be exercisable during the lifetime of an unborn person, is void *ab initio* at common law. In many cases, of course, powers are annexed or incidental to an interest and will, therefore, stand or fall according to the (in)validity of that interest.[113] In

---

[106] *Re Cassel* [1926] Ch 358. See also *Re Randell* (1888) 38 Ch D 213; *Wainwright v Miller* [1897] 2 Ch 255; *Re Gage* [1898] 1 Ch 498; *Re Blunt's Trusts* [1904] 2 Ch 767; *Re Chardon, supra*; *Re Chamber's Will Trusts* [1950] Ch 267; *Re Cooper's Conveyance Trusts* [1956] 1 WLR 1096.

[107] Although this was not settled beyond doubt: see *Megarry and Wade* 244–245; and see also *Re Tilbury West Public School Board and Hastie* (1966) 55 DLR (2d) 407.

[108] *Re Cooper's Conveyance Trust* [1956] 1 WLR 1096; *Re Randell* (1888) 38 Ch D 213; *Re Blunt's Trusts* [1904] 2 Ch 767; *Re Chardon* [1928] Ch 464. See also (1938) 54 LQR 264 (MJ Albery).

[109] See *Thomas*, Ch 4; Morris and Leach, (n 24 above) Ch 5; Maudsley (n 25 above) 58–64; *Megarry and Wade* 279–287.

[110] Indeed, since the enactment of the Perpetuities and Accumulations Act 1964, most perpetuity problems tend to arise, in practice, in connection with the exercise of dispositive powers, rather than the head settlement itself.

[111] *Re Allott* [1942] 2 Ch 498.

[112] *Goodier v Johnson* (1881) 18 Ch D 441, 446; see also *Re Daveron* [1893] 3 Ch 421 and *Re Wood* [1894] 3 Ch 381.

[113] *Peters v Lewes & East Grinstead Rly* (1881) 18 Ch D 429, 433, 434; *Re Wills' Will Trusts* [1959] Ch 1.

other cases, statutory provisions may now apply to prevent the invalidation of powers,[114] and, indeed, in some cases, such as the powers conferred on trustees of charitable trusts or on the trustees of qualifying occupational pension schemes,[115] there need be no restriction to any perpetuity period.

The application of the rule against perpetuities differs according to the nature of the power. It is convenient, if not essential, to distinguish between general and special powers, and between dispositive powers (such as powers of appointment, powers of advancement, discretionary trusts, and other analogous powers) and administrative powers (such as powers of investment, of sale, or of leasing). **8.37**

(2) Powers of Appointment

General powers and special powers

The first task is one of definition. For the specific purposes of the rule against perpetuities, a power is regarded as a *general* power only if it is equivalent to absolute ownership by the donee of the power of the property which is subject to the power.[116] Thus, an intermediate (or hybrid) power to appoint to anyone in the world except the donee himself,[117] or to anyone in the world with the consent of X (who could be, for example, the trustees of a settlement or the parent of the donee),[118] as well as a joint power,[119] are all regarded as *special* powers in this context. Similarly, a power to appoint by will to any person or persons living at the death of the donee is also probably a *special* power for perpetuity purposes.[120] On the other hand, if the donee is a member of a limited class of objects but can appoint in his own favour,[121] or where he may appoint to anyone except X and he himself is not X,[122] the power is regarded as a *general* power. Moreover, a general power to appoint by will only is also treated as a *special* power for the specific purpose of determining the validity of the power,[123] but as a *general* power for the purpose of determining the validity of an appointment made thereunder.[124] **8.38**

---

[114] See para 8.58 below.   [115] Section 163 of the Pension Schemes Act 1993.
[116] *Re Earl of Coventry's Indentures* [1974] Ch 77, 93, *per* Walton J.
[117] *Re Park* [1932] 1 Ch 580. See also *Blausten v IRC* [1972] Ch 256; *Re Manisty's Settlement* [1974] Ch 17; *Re Hay's Settlement Trusts* [1982] 1 WLR 202.
[118] *Webb v Sadler* (1873) 8 Ch App 419; *Re Watts* [1931] 2 Ch 302; *Re Triffitt's Settlement* [1958] Ch 852, 860, 861.
[119] *Re Churston Settled Estates* [1954] Ch 334; *Re Earl of Coventry's Indentures, supra.*
[120] *Re Jones* [1945] Ch 105.
[121] *Re Penrose* [1933] Ch 793; see also *Taylor v Allhusen* [1905] 1 Ch 529.
[122] *Re Penrose, supra*, 805–807. *Quaere* if he holds the power in a fiduciary capacity: see, for example, *Re Beatty* [1990] 1 WLR 1503.
[123] *Wollaston v King* (1868) LR 8 Eq165; *Morgan v Gronow* (1873) LR 16 Eq 1.
[124] *Rous v Jackson* (1885) 29 Ch D 521; *Re Flower* (1885) 55 LJ Ch 200.

8.39 Section 7 of the Perpetuities and Accumulations Act 1964[125] confirms the common law position. It provides that, for the purposes of the rule against perpetuities, a power of appointment shall be treated as a *special* power unless

(a) in the instrument creating the power it is expressed to be exercisable by one person only, and

(b) it could, at all times during its currency when that person is of full age and capacity, be exercised by him so as immediately to transfer to himself the whole of the interest governed by the power without the consent of any other person or compliance with any other condition, not being a formal condition relating only to the mode of exercise of the power.

It also provides that the old rule relating to powers exercisable by will only is to be retained.[126] However, whereas under the old law a power to appoint to anyone in the world with the consent of X, though classified as a special power at its creation, could probably have become a general power in the event of X's death,[127] it seems that, under the terms of section 7, this is no longer possible and the character of a power is determined once and for all at the outset.[128] The first task, then, is to determine the nature of the power in question; and the effects of the rule against perpetuities on powers can be understood only if the specific distinction between general and special powers is borne in mind.

8.40 In general, the rule can operate so as to invalidate the power itself, so that no appointment is possible; or, alternatively, it can invalidate a particular appointment made under a valid power. It can also invalidate a gift in default of appointment.

Validity of the power

General powers

8.41 The donee of a general power is not, technically, the owner of the property which is the subject matter of the power (power and property being fundamentally different concepts). However, for the purposes of the rule against perpetuities (as for many other purposes) the law looks to the substance rather than the form: property subject to a general power is regarded as beneficially owned by the donee of the power.[129] 'There exists, by the existence of the power, a present, immediate,

---

[125] The provisions of the Act apply to general powers created or exercised after 15 July 1964; but to special powers only if they were both created and exercised after that date. The provisions of s 7 apply in all cases for construing whether the power is general or special for perpetuity purposes: see s 15(5).

[126] Section 7, proviso.   [127] See, eg, *Re Dilke* [1921] 1 Ch 34; *Re Phillips* [1931] 1 Ch 347.

[128] See *Megarry and Wade* 283.

[129] *Thomas* 150; Sir George Farwell and FK Archer, *A Concise Treatise on Powers* (3rd edn, 1916) ('*Farwell*') Edward Sugden (Lord St Leonard), *A Practical Treatise on Powers* (8th edn, 1861) 396.

and unrestrained alienability, and there is no necessity to consider in that case how far a perpetuity may be created any more than it is necessary to consider it in the case of an absolute owner.'[130] Consequently, in order to be valid, a general power, like an absolute interest in property, must be acquired, if at all, by the donee within the perpetuity period. Thus, the donee must be ascertainable within that period: a general power given, for instance, to the survivor of a class of unborn persons[131] would be void. Similarly, a general power may be void because it is not exercisable until the occurrence of an event which itself may not happen within the perpetuity period, such as, for example, on the marriage of an unborn person,[132] or on the failure of issue of a particular marriage.[133] On the other hand, although a general power which is exercisable by deed alone, or by deed or by will, must become exercisable within the perpetuity period, it will not be invalidated simply because it is, in fact, exercised outside that period.[134] As in the case of absolute ownership, the time and manner of its exercise are irrelevant.[135] By contrast, a general power which is exercisable by will alone must be exercisable within the perpetuity period and there must be no possibility of its being exercised outside that period.[136]

The 'wait and see' provisions of the Perpetuities and Accumulations Act 1964 **8.42** apply to general powers. Section 3(2) provides that, where a disposition (made by an instrument taking effect after 15 July 1964) consisting of the conferring of a general power of appointment would otherwise be void on the ground that the power might not become exercisable until too remote a time, the disposition shall be treated, until such time (if any) as it becomes established that the power will not be exercisable within the perpetuity period, as if the disposition were not subject to the rule against perpetuities. The relevant 'lives in being' for the purposes of the 'wait and see' provisions are set out in section 3(5) and, although it is not entirely clear how some of the categories might be relevant to general powers, the person upon whom the power has been conferred is one of them.[137]

Special powers

A special power of appointment is valid only if it can be said, at the time of its cre- **8.43** ation, that it must be exercised, if at all, within the perpetuity period. Thus, if the donee will not necessarily be ascertained within the period,[138] or if the power may

---

[130] *Re Fane* [1913] 1 Ch 404, 413–414, *per* Buckley LJ.
[131] *Re Hargreaves* (1889) 43 Ch D 401.   [132] *Morgan v Gronow* (1873) LR 16 Eq 1.
[133] *Bristow v Boothby* (1826) 2 S & St 465.
[134] *Bray v Hammersley* (1830) 2 Sim 513; affirmed on appeal (1834) 2 Cl & F 453; *Re Meredith's Trusts* (1876) 3 Ch D 757; *Morgan v Gronow, supra*. See also *Re Fasken* [1961] OR 891; *O'Donohue v Comptroller of Stamps* [1969] VR 431, 433.
[135] *Re Fane* [1913] 1 Ch 404, 413.
[136] *Wollaston v King* (1868) 8 Eq 165; *Morgan v Gronow, supra*.
[137] Section 3(5)(b)(v). See para 8.17 above.   [138] *Re Hargreaves* (1889) 43 Ch D 401.

be exercised beyond that period, it is void.[139] As Parker J stated in *Re De Sommery*:[140]

> A special power which, according to the true construction of the instrument creating it, is capable of being exercised beyond lives in being and twenty-one years afterwards is, by reason of the rule against perpetuities, absolutely void; but if it can only be exercised within the period allowed by the rule, it is a good power, even although some particular exercise of it might be void because of the rule. If a power be given to a person alive at the date of the instrument creating it, it must, of course, if exercised at all, be exercised during his life, and is therefore valid. Again, if a power can be exercised only in favour of a person living at the date of the instrument creating it, it must, if exercised at all, be exercised during the life of such person, and is therefore unobjectionable. Further, the instrument itself may expressly limit a period, not exceeding the legal limits, for the exercise of the power. Lastly, where the settlor has used language from which the court may fairly infer that he contemplated the creation, not of a single power, but of two distinct powers, one of which only is open to objection because of the rule against perpetuities, the court will avoid the latter only and will give effect to the power which is not open to this objection.

The same principles apply to a *general* power exercisable *by will only*.[141] Thus, if, under a settlement, A has a power of appointment in favour of his children and appoints in favour of his son S for life, and then to such person or persons as S shall by will appoint, the power given to S is valid only if he was alive at the date of the settlement.[142]

8.44 The separation of those powers which are not open to objection from those which are depends on the settlor having intended to create separate powers rather than a single one. If the settlor has not himself separated the different powers, the court will not do it for him.[143] Thus, a power vested in the trustees for the time being of a settlement is invariably regarded as a single and indivisible power which may therefore be void, for the successors need not necessarily be lives in being.[144] However, a power given to A and B or other the trustees of the settlement for the time being to appoint to unborn persons was divided into two powers: one was held to be a valid power vested in A and B, the other to be an invalid power vested

---

[139] *Re Abrahams* [1969] 1 Ch 463; *Re Norton* [1911] 2 Ch 27; *Re De Sommery* [1912] 2 Ch 622; *Re Fane* [1913] 1 Ch 404; *Kennedy v Kennedy* [1914] AC 215; *Re Symm* [1936] 3 All ER 236; *Re Vaux* [1939] Ch 465; *Re Watson* [1959] 2 All ER 676; see also *O'Donohue v Comptroller of Stamps, supra,* 439; Morris and Leach (n 24 above) 141; Gray, §§ 475, 477.

[140] [1912] 2 Ch 622, 630–631, approved in *Kennedy v Kennedy* and *Re Watson, supra.*

[141] See para 8.38 above.

[142] *Phipson v Turner* (1838) 9 Sim 227; *Morse v Martin* (1865) 34 Beav 500; *Wollaston v King* (1868) LR 8 Eq 165; *Morgan v Gronow* (1873) LR 16 Eq 1; *Slark v Dakyns* (1874) LR 10 Ch 35; *Hutchinson v Tottenham* [1898] 1 IR 403, [1899] 1 IR 344; *Tredennick v Tredennick* [1900] 1 IR 354.

[143] *Innes v Harrison* [1954] 1 WLR 668; *Re Watson, supra.*

[144] *Re De Sommery, supra,* 631; *Re Symm's Will Trusts* [1936] 3 All ER 236; *Re Vaux* [1939] Ch 465. The same is true if the trustee is a trust corporation: Morris and Leach (n 24 above) 142.

in their successors.[145] Similarly, a power given to the trustees for the time being of a will to appoint capital or income either for the benefit of X (which was capable of being exercised only during his lifetime) or for the benefit of his wife and children (which was capable of being exercised outside the perpetuity period) was construed as two separate powers, a valid one in favour of X and an invalid one in favour of his wife and children.

Discretionary trusts

8.45 A power given to trustees to allocate income under a discretionary trust is void if it is exercisable during the life, or in favour of, an unborn person, unless the discretionary trust as a whole is expressed to be subject to a lawful perpetuity period (usually a specific period of up to 80 years,[146] or a 'royal lives' clause within which the power may be exercised). Gray[147] argued that discretionary trusts of income were a series of separate and independent powers exercisable at successive periods in respect of each instalment of income, so that only those powers exercisable outside the perpetuity period were void, while those exercisable within it were valid.[148] Whatever may be said in favour of this view, the courts have actually treated discretionary trusts of income as creating one indivisible power to apply income as it arises, and therefore void or valid in its entirety.[149]

8.46 Section 1(1) of the Perpetuities and Accumulations Act 1964 permits the express selection of a period of years not exceeding eighty as the relevant perpetuity period for a particular disposition.[150] A 'disposition' includes the *conferring* of a power of appointment; and 'power of appointment' includes any discretionary power to transfer a beneficial interest in property without the furnishing of valuable consideration.[151] The period must be specified in the instrument by which the disposition is made.[152]

8.47 The Act applies (except as provided in section 8(2), dealing with administrative powers of trustees) only in relation to instruments taking effect after 15 July 1964;

[145] *Attenborough v Attenborough* (1855) 1 K & J 296; *Re De Sommery, supra,* 631; *Re Watson, supra.* Cf *Re Abbott* [1893] 1 Ch 54; *Bandon v Moreland* [1910] 1 IR 220; *Re Wills' Will Trusts* [1959] Ch 1, 10.
[146] Under s 1(1) of the 1964 Act.　　[147] See Gray, §§ 410.1–410.5.
[148] A view supported by *Lyons v Bradley* (1910) 169 Ala 505, 33 So 244, and perhaps by *Re Kelly* [1932] IR 255, but opposed by *Bundy United States Trust Co* (1926) 257 Mass 72, 153 NE 337. See also *Re Bullen* (1915) 17 WALR 73 and *Shenandoah Valley etc v Taylor* (1951) 192 Va 135, 63 SE (2d) 786.
[149] *Re Blew* [1906] 1 Ch 624; *Re Coleman* [1936] Ch 528; *Innes v Harrison* [1954] 1 All ER 884; *Re Allan* [1958] 1 All ER 401; and see also *Re Bullen* (1915) 17 WAR 73; *Re Antrobus* [1928] NZLR 364; *Re Hyne* [1958] Qd R 431; Morris and Leach (n 24 above) 143–144; IJ Hardingham and R Baxt, *Discretionary Trusts* (2nd edn, 1984) 73–74.
[150] See para 8.16 above.　　[151] Section 15(2) of the 1964 Act.
[152] Although it is considered that the chosen period may be evident by necessary implication from the terms of the settlement.

and, in the case of an instrument made in the *exercise* of a special power of appointment (as defined), the Act applies only where the instrument *creating* the power takes effect after that date.[153] Where a disposition is made otherwise than by an instrument, the Act applies as if the disposition had been contained in an instrument taking effect when the disposition was made.[154] The crucial date, therefore, is the date of creation of the special power. Section 1(2) provides that subsection (1) shall not have effect where the disposition is made in *exercise* of a *special* power of appointment, but, where a period is specified under that subsection in the instrument creating such a power, the period shall apply in relation to any disposition under the power as it applies to the power itself. Consequently, if a fixed period of years is adopted as the relevant perpetuity period at the creation of the settlement, that same period shall also govern the exercise of any special power of appointment conferred by that settlement and, upon any such exercise, the original perpetuity period cannot be extended by the appointor (by reference to lives in being plus 21 years, or to section 1(1) of the 1964 Act, or otherwise).[155] Similarly, where the original perpetuity period adopted by the settlement is based expressly on lives in being plus 21 years, that period cannot be extended (by reference to a fixed period under section 1(1) of the 1964 Act or otherwise) by any exercise of a special power under that settlement.

8.48 Where a special power is not governed by section 1(1) of the Act and is not subject to a valid perpetuity period at common law, it may still be saved from invalidity by the 'wait and see' provisions. Section 3(3) of the Act[156] provides that, where a disposition consisting of the conferring of any power, option, or other right would otherwise be void on the ground that the right might be exercised at too remote a time, the disposition shall be treated as regards any exercise of the right within the perpetuity period as if it were not subject to the rule against perpetuities and shall be treated as void for remoteness only if, and so far as, the right is not fully exercised during that period. Consequently, a power or discretion created by an instrument taking effect after 15 July 1964, will not necessarily be void *ab initio*, for the 'wait and see' provisions of the Act will now apply.

8.49 For the purposes of these 'wait and see' provisions (but not otherwise), the statutory list of 'lives in being' in section 3(5) must be used in order to determine the relevant perpetuity period. This list includes any of the following who are individuals in being and ascertainable at the commencement of the perpetuity period,

---

[153] Section 15(5).   [154] Section 15(6).

[155] An appointment may, of course, provide for the vesting of interests on the happening of the *earlier* of (i) the termination of the original perpetuity period or (ii) the expiry of a period of lives in being plus 21 years.

[156] Section 163 of the Law of Property Act 1925 applies to appointments made under special powers exercised after 31 December 1925, and before 16 July 1964.

namely the donee of the power, any member or potential member of the class in favour of whom the power is exercisable, the sole object of the power, and, where an object of the power is ascertainable only on certain conditions being satisfied, any person as to whom some of the conditions are satisfied and the remainder may in time be satisfied, and the parents and grandparents of the objects of the power.[157]

Effect of a power being invalid

If a power is invalid, it simply cannot be exercised.[158]　　　　　　　　　　　**8.50**

Validity of the appointment

General powers

Given that a general power is regarded, for the purposes of the rule against per-　**8.51** petuities, as tantamount to absolute ownership of the property which is subject to the power, an appointment under a general power is regarded as equivalent to a disposition of the donee's own property. Thus, the appointees need only be capable of taking under the instrument which exercises the power; and the perpetuity period runs from the date of the appointment, not from the date of the creation of the power.[159]

However, general powers exercisable *by will only* are regarded as special powers for　**8.52** the purpose of determining their validity, but as general powers for the purpose of determining the validity of any appointment made thereunder. Thus, in their case, too, the perpetuity period runs from the date of the appointment.[160] This rule is expressly preserved by the proviso to section 7 of the Perpetuities and Accumulations Act 1964.

Special powers

In the case of a special power of appointment, the donee 'has merely been given　**8.53** the power of saying on behalf of the settlor which objects shall take the property under the settlement and in what proportions. It is as though the settlor had left a blank in the settlement which [the appointor] fills up for him if and when the power of appointment is exercised. The appointees' interests come to them under

---

[157] See para 8.18 above.
[158] *Bristow v Boothby* (1826) 2 S & St 465; *Morgan v Gronow* (1873) LR 16 Eq 1; *Blight v Hartnoll* (1881) 19 Ch D 294; *Re Hargreaves* (1889) 43 Ch D 401.
[159] *Re Thompson* [1906] 2 Ch 199, 202; *Muir v Muir* [1943] AC 468, 483; *Pilkington v IRC* [1964] AC 612, 641.
[160] *Rous v Jackson* (1885) 29 Ch D 521; *Re Flower* (1885) 55 LJ Ch 200; *Stuart v Babington* (1891) 27 LR Ir 551. *Rous v Jackson* has been much criticized: see, eg, Morris and Leach (n 24 above) 148–149. In the United States, general testamentary powers are generally assimilated to special powers, so that the perpetuity period runs from the date of the instrument of creation.

the settlement alone and by virtue of that document.'[161] Thus, the appointees must be capable of taking under the instrument creating the power, and the perpetuity period is measured from the date of the creation of the power, not from the date of its exercise.[162] Thus, if A creates a settlement and reserves to himself a power of appointment in favour of his issue, an appointment to his son S for life with remainder to such of S's children born in A's lifetime as shall attain the age of 21 years will be valid.[163] On the other hand, if S has power to appoint among his issue and he appoints to his son B (unborn at the date of the creation of the power) for life, with remainder to B's children equally, the appointment to B's children is too remote. Similarly, where an appointed interest is liable to forfeiture, with a gift over to other objects of the power, the act or event causing forfeiture must occur within the appropriate period if it is to be effectual.[164]

8.54 Deeds and wills must be distinguished. A deed speaks from its own date,[165] whereas a will speaks from the date of death of the testator,[166] by which time limitations which would have been bad when the will was made might well prove good.[167] Moreover, a power of appointment is well executed by an appointment to an object (A) for life, with power to A to dispose of the capital by deed or will, whether A was living at the date of the creation of the original power or not, for the effect of the appointment is, in substance, to give the whole beneficial interest to A, thereby not transgressing the rule against perpetuities.[168] On the other hand, an appointment to A for life, with a power of disposition by will only, is valid only if A was alive at the date of the creation of the power; if he was not, the exercise is void for perpetuity, at least in respect of all that is subsequent to the

---

[161] *Muir v Muir* [1943] AC 468, 483, *per* Lord Romer.

[162] *Robinson v Hardcastle* (1788) 2 TR 241; *Routledge v Dorril* (1794) 2 Ves 357; *Thomas v Thomas* (1844) 14 Sim 234; *Wilkinson v Duncan* (1861) 30 Beav 111; *Re Brown and Sibly's Contract* (1876) 3 Ch D 156; *Re Gage* [1898] 1 Ch 498; *Whitby v Van Luedecke* [1906] 1 Ch 783; *Re Crichton's Settlement* (1912) 106 LT 588; *Re Staveley* (1920) 90 LJ Ch 111; *Re Samuda's Settlement* [1924] 1 Ch 61; *Re Legh's Settlement* [1938] Ch 39; *Re Johnson's Settlement* [1943] Ch 341; *Re Pratt's Settlement* [1943] Ch 356; *Massey v Barton* (1844) 7 Ir Eq Rep 95; *D'Abbadie v Bizoin* (1871) IR 5 Eq 205; *Re Hallinan's Trusts* [1904] 1 IR 452; *Re Ramadge* [1919] 1 IR 205.

[163] *Re Bowles* [1902] 2 Ch 650.

[164] *Hodgson v Halford* (1879) 11 Ch D 959; *Webb v Sadler* (1873) 8 Ch App 419; *Stockbridge v Story* (1871) 19 WR 1049; *Wainright v Miller* [1897] 2 Ch 255; *Re Gage* [1898] 1 Ch 498.

[165] A voidable deed, if subsequently confirmed, still speaks from its own date (of execution) for these purposes: *Cooke v Cooke* (1887) 38 Ch D 202, where an infant confirmed the original settlement when she came of age.

[166] *Vanderplank v King* (1843) 3 Hare 1; *Faulkner v Daniel* (1843) 3 Hare 199; *Lord Dungannon v Smith* (1845–46) 12 Cl & Fin 546; *Williams v Teale* (1847) 6 Hare 239; *Peard v Kekewich* (1852) 15 Beav 166; *Southern v Wollaston* (1852) 16 Beav 166 and 276; *Catlin v Brown* (1853) 11 Hare 382; *Wilkinson v Duncan* (1861) 30 Beav 111; *Re Mervin* [1891] 3 Ch 197.

[167] *Peard v Kekewich* (1852) 15 Beav 166; *Wilkinson v Duncan* (1861) 30 Beav 111; *Re Russell* [1895] 2 Ch 698; *Re Game* [1907] 1 Ch 276.

[168] *Bray v Bree* (1834) 2 Cl & Fin 453; *Jebb v Tugwell* (1855) 7 De GM & G 663.

life interest.[169] There is no objection, of course, to giving an unborn individual or a class of unborn persons an interest for life simply, without any remainder over;[170] nor to a life interest to an unborn person with an absolute gift in remainder to an ascertained living person, or to one necessarily ascertainable within the prescribed period.[171]

Powers of advancement

The same principle applies to a power of advancement, whether express or statu-   **8.55**
tory. A power of advancement authorizes the resettlement of funds in favour of a beneficiary and, indeed, others, provided it is for that beneficiary's benefit.[172] If it were the rule that advancements were not to be 'read back' into the original or head settlement, property could be resettled in perpetuity and need never become absolutely vested in anyone. In fact, it is clear that there is 'an effective analogy between powers of advancement and special powers of appointment'; the advanced beneficiary is 'the passive recipient of the benefit extracted for her from the original trusts; . . . it is the property subjected to the trusts by the settlers and passed over into the new settlement through the instrumentality of a power which by statute is made appendant to those trusts'. For the purposes of the rule against perpetuities, the new settlement 'is only effected by the operation of a fiduciary power which itself "belongs" to the old settlement'.[173]

An advancement (just like an appointment) may be partially void for perpetuity   **8.56**
and partially valid.[174] Provided the valid trusts and powers are severable from the invalid ones—which may not be difficult where successive interests have been created, but very difficult in the case of class gifts—the advancement should generally be partially valid. However, the extent of the invalidity may be so substantial as 'to alter the intended consequences of an advancement so drastically that the trustees cannot reasonably be supposed to have addressed their minds to the questions relevant to the true effect of the transaction'.[175]

---

[169] *Phipson v Turner* (1838) 9 Sim 227; *Slark v Dakyns* (1874) 10 Ch App 35; *Morse v Martin* (1865) 34 Beav 500; *Morgan v Gronow* (1873) LR 16 Eq 1; *Hutchinson v Tottenham* [1899] 1 IR 344; *Tredennick v Tredennick* [1900] 1 IR 354.

[170] *Williams v Teale* (1847) 6 Ha 239, 250; *Hampton v Holman* (1877) 5 Ch D 183, 188; *Re Roberts* (1881) 19 Ch D 520.

[171] *Evans v Walker* (1876) 3 Ch D 211; *Re Hargreaves* (1889) 43 Ch D 401; *Garland v Brown* (1864) 10 LT 292.

[172] *Roper-Curzon v Roper-Curzon* (1871) LR 11 Eq 452; *Re Halsted's Will Trusts* [1937] 2 All ER 570; *Re Ropner's Settlements* [1956] 1 WLR 902; *Re Wills' Will Trusts* [1959] Ch 1; *Pilkington v IRC* [1964] AC 612; *Re Clore's Settlement Trust* [1966] 1 WLR 955; *Re Abraham's Will Trusts* [1969] 1 Ch 463; *Re Hastings-Bass* [1975] Ch 25.

[173] *Pilkington v IRC, supra*, 642, *per* Viscount Radcliffe. The same also applies to an express power of advancement.

[174] *Re Hastings-Bass* [1975] Ch 25.

[175] ibid 41. This was the case in *Re Abrahams' Will Trusts* [1969] 1 Ch 463.

The 'second look' doctrine

8.57 Notwithstanding the fact that, in the case of a special power of appointment (and a power of advancement), the perpetuity period is measured from the date of the creation of the power, not from the date of its exercise, it is permissible to take into account not only facts and circumstances existing at the date of the instrument creating that power (into which the appointment or advancement must be read back) but also facts and circumstances existing at the date of the exercise of that power. In other words, a 'second look' is taken at that time.[176] Thus, a gift to A for life, remainder to such of his children as shall attain the age of 25, would be too remote at common law. However, if the gift were to A for life, remainder to such of A's children as he appoints, and A appointed to such of his children as shall attain the age of 25, then, provided all A's children are aged over four years when he dies, his appointment will be valid.[177]

Validity of appointments under special powers under the 1964 Act

8.58 Under the 1964 Act, an instrument creating a special power and which takes effect after 15 July 1964, may adopt an express fixed period of years (not exceeding 80) as the relevant perpetuity period for its purposes, and that period will also govern any appointment (or advancement) made thereafter in exercise of the power. Moreover, the 'wait and see' provisions of the Act apply to special powers of appointment, so that any such powers as would otherwise be void for perpetuity at common law (and, of course, are not subject to an express perpetuity period of a fixed number of years) shall actually be treated as void for remoteness only if, and so far as, they are not fully exercised within the relevant perpetuity period (which period must be determined by reference to the statutory list of lives in being in section 3(5) of the Act). Nevertheless, whether the power of appointment is subject to the 'wait and see' provisions, the validity for perpetuity purposes of any appointment made in exercise of that power must be tested by reading it back into

---

[176] *Wilkinson v Duncan* (1861) 30 Beav 111; *Von Brockdorff v Malcolm* (1885) 30 Ch D 172; *Re Coulman* (1885) 30 Ch D 186; *Re Thompson* [1906] 2 Ch 199; *Re Paul* [1921] 2 Ch 1; *Re Hallinan* [1904] 1 IR 452; *White v Commr for Stamps* (1908) 8 SR (NSW) 287; *Re Eliot* (1913) 11 DLR 34; *Davy v Clarke* [1920] 1 IR 137; *Re McLean* [1926] VLR 21; *Re Liverton* [1951] NZLR 351; *Re Fasken* [1961] OR 891; *Re Murdoch* [1970] 1 NSWR 265; Morris and Leach (n 24 above) 152–154; Maudsley (n 25 above) 62–63.

[177] *Wilkinson v Duncan* (1861) 30 Beav 111; *Re Paul* [1921] 2 Ch 1. Under s 15(5) of the 1964 Act, the provisions of that Act apply where the instrument creating the power took effect after 15 July 1964. See also the 'class closing' provisions in s 4 of the Act. In exceptional circumstances, the doctrine in *Langston v Blackmore* (1755) Amb 289 may operate, ie where a power of appointment is executed with the concurrence of an object to whom the appointor might validly have appointed the entire property, and the appointment provides for the settlement of that property, the appointment may be regarded as one to that object absolutely, followed by a resettlement by him, and therefore not open to objection on the ground of perpetuity or for introducing a 'non-object': see *Thomas* 158.

the creating instrument and the dispositions effected by the appointment must be regarded as having been made by that instrument.

Severance of good trusts from the bad

An appointment which is partly good and partly bad may be wholly void unless it **8.59** is possible to sever the good from the bad.[178] The invalidity of one limitation may lead to the invalidity of another. The property which is the subject of the appointment cannot be given to those to whom it might have been lawfully appointed.[179] However, where there are successive limitations in one instrument, the rule against perpetuities must be applied to each limitation separately. Also, if a gift or appointment expresses alternative contingencies upon which an interest may vest, and one event is not too remote whereas the other is, the gift is still good if, in fact, the valid contingency occurs.[180]

Bad appointment after good

The typical case here is the appointment of a valid life interest, followed by ulterior **8.60** limitations which are too remote. The effect is that the life interest remains good, but the ulterior limitations are void.[181]

Good appointment after bad

A limitation is not void simply because it is preceded by a void limitation,[182] **8.61** unless perhaps both valid and void limitations are so intermixed or so drastic in their consequences as to vitiate the entire settlement.[183] On the other hand, the general rule at common law is that a limitation which is subsequent to and dependent (or expectant) upon a void limitation is itself void, notwithstanding that otherwise it must itself vest (if at all) within the perpetuity period.[184] A limitation is

---

[178] *Gooding v Read* (1853) 4 De GM & G 510; *Read v Gooding* (1856) 21 Beav 478; see also *Re Wise* [1896] 1 Ch 281; *Hancock v Watson* [1902] AC 14; *Re Bowles* [1905] 1 Ch 371; *Re Davies and Kent's Contract* [1910] 2 Ch 35; *Re Norton* [1911] 2 Ch 27; *Re Davey* [1915] 1 Ch 837. See also *Re Abrahams' Will Trusts* [1969] 1 Ch 463; *Re Hastings-Bass* [1975] Ch 25.

[179] *Jee v Audley* (1787) 1 Cox 324; *Routledge v Dorril* (1794) 2 Ves 357; *Sugden* 505; *Farwell* 340.

[180] *Longhead d Hopkins v Phelps* (1770) 2 Wm Bl 704; *Monypenny v Dering* (1852) 2 De GM & G 145; *Hodgson v Halford* (1879) 11 Ch D 959; *Watson v Young* (1885) 28 Ch D 436 (doubted by *Farwell* 342).

[181] *Bristow v Warde* (1794) 2 Ves 336, 350; *Routledge v Dorril, supra*; *Garland v Brown* (1864) 10 LT 292; *Wollaston v King* (1868) LR 8 Eq 165; *Stuart v Cockerell* (1870) 5 Ch App 713; *D'Abbadie v Bizoin* (1871) IR 5 Eq 205; *Morgan v Gronow* (1873) LR 16 Eq 1; *Hutchinson v Tottenham* [1898] 1 IR 403; [1899] 1 IR 344; *Tredennick v Tredennick* [1900] 1 IR 354; *Re Abrahams' Will Trusts* [1969] 1 Ch 463; and *Re Hastings-Bass* [1975] Ch 25.

[182] *Garland v Brown* (1864) 10 LT 292.

[183] *Re Abrahams' Will Trusts* [1969] 1 Ch 463; see also *Pilkington v IRC* [1961] Ch 466, 488, 489, *per* Upjohn LJ and [1964] AC 612, 641, 642, *per* Viscount Radcliffe.

[184] *Proctor v Bishop of Bath and Wells* (1794) 2 Hy Bl 358; *Beard v Westcott* (1822) 5 B & Ald 801; *Re Thatcher* (1859) 26 Beav 365; *Re Abbott* [1893] 1 Ch 54, 57; *Re Hewett's Settlement* [1915] 1 Ch 810; *Re Davey* [1915] 1 Ch 837; *Re Robinson* [1963] 1 WLR 628; *Re Hubbard's Will Trusts* [1963] Ch 275; *Re Buckton's Settlement Trusts* [1964] Ch 497; *Re Leek* [1967] Ch 1061.

'dependent' if it is intended to take effect only if the prior limitation itself takes effect; its vesting remains uncertain until the fate of the prior limitation is established. An 'independent' limitation is intended to take effect in any event; it vests in interest at its own separate time. Therefore, subsequent vested limitations are safe.[185] Subsequent contingent limitations are also safe provided they are independent (and provided, of course, their own particular contingencies do not infringe the rule against perpetuities).[186] On the other hand, subsequent contingent and dependent limitations will fail unless the prior limitation is valid.[187]

8.62 Most cases are now governed by the Perpetuities and Accumulations Act 1964, section 6[188] of which provides that a disposition shall not be treated as void for remoteness by reason only that the interest disposed of is ulterior to and dependent upon an interest under a disposition which is so void. Moreover, the vesting of an interest shall not be prevented from being accelerated on the failure of a prior interest by reason only that the failure arises because of remoteness.

Severance and appointment to a class

8.63 As we have seen,[189] 'a class gift is a gift of property to all who come within some description, the property being divisible in shares according to the number of persons in the class'.[190] Thus, a gift 'to my children who shall live to be 25', or 'to such of my children as are born hereafter and shall marry', are class gifts.[191] A variation in the number of members of the class will result in a corresponding increase or decrease in the share of each member.[192] If the number of people in the 'class' does not affect the size of each one's share, it is not a class gift.[193] Where there is an appointment to a class, some members of which must take (if at all) within the perpetuity period, but others may not, and the share of each member cannot be

---

[185] *Lewis v Walters* (1805) 6 East 336; *Re Allan* [1958] 1 WLR 220; *Re Hubbard, supra.* Cf *Re Backhouse* [1921] 2 Ch 51.

[186] *Re Abbott, supra*; *Re Canning's Will Trusts* [1936] Ch 309; *Re Coleman* [1936] Ch 528; *Re Hubbard, supra.*

[187] *Proctor v Bishop of Bath and Wells, supra*; *Palmer v Holford* (1828) 4 Russ 403; *Re Thatcher, supra*; *Re Hewitt, supra*; *Re Ramadge* [1919] 1 IR 205; *Re Mill's Declaration of Trust* [1950] 2 All ER 292; *Re Hubbard, supra.*

[188] Applicable after 15 July 1964, and independently of the 'wait and see' provisions.

[189] See paras 8.20–8.22 above.

[190] *Megarry and Wade* 270–271; *Jarman*, 341, 348; *Pearks v Moseley* (1880) 5 App Cas 714, 723; *Kingsbury v Walter* [1901] AC 187, 192.

[191] See, for example, *Lee v Pain* (1845) 4 Hare 249; *Boreham v Bignall* (1850) 8 Hare 131; *Leigh v Leigh* (1854) 17 Beav 605; *Re Stanhope's Trusts* (1859) 27 Beav 201; *Re Hornby* (1859) 7 WR 729; *Aspinall v Duckworth* (1866) 35 Beav 307; *Dimond v Bostock* (1875) 10 Ch App 358; *Re Jackson* (1883) 25 Ch D 162; *Re Mervin* [1891] 3 Ch 197; *Kingsbury v Walter* [1901] AC 187.

[192] *Re Hornby* (1859) 7 WR 729; *Boreham v Bignall* (1850) 8 Hare 131; *Dimond v Bostock* (1875) 10 Ch App 358; *Re Jackson* (1883) 25 Ch D 162.

[193] *Bain v Lescher* (1840) 11 Sim 397; *Havergal v Harrison* (1843) 7 Beav 49; *Storrs v Benbow* (1853) 3 De GM & G 390; *Wilkinson v Duncan* (1861) 30 Beav 111; *Rogers v Mutch* (1878) 9 Ch D 117; *Re Stansfield* (1880) 15 Ch D 84.

ascertained within that period, the whole appointment is void, even in respect of the shares of those who have already satisfied any required contingency and whose shares are therefore vested.[194] On the other hand, an appointment of some specified sum or share—for example, of £2,000 'to each of my daughters'—is not a class gift, but a group of separate gifts.[195] If the individual shares of the members of the group can be ascertained within the period, the appointment is valid as to those who take within it and void as to the rest.

8.64 Class gifts are not severable at common law. However, in some cases, what appeared to be a class gift was held to be separate gifts to separate classes, so that one gift was valid even though another one was void. The test is whether the size of the shares of members of a class is liable to be affected by a subsequent or further contingent gift which is too remote: if it is not, the first gift is valid.[196] The harshness of the common law was and is mitigated by the so-called rule in *Andrews v Partington*,[197] under which a numerically uncertain class of beneficiaries normally closes when the first member becomes entitled to claim his share, ie as soon as the first share vests in possession.[198]

8.65 The introduction by section 3(1) of the Perpetuities and Accumulations Act 1964 of the principle of 'wait and see', ie that a disposition 'shall be treated, until such time (if any) as it becomes established that the vesting must occur, if at all, after the end of the perpetuity period, as if the disposition were not subject to the rule against perpetuities', has undermined the destructiveness of the common law rules. Statutory age-reduction provisions in section 163 of the Law of Property Act 1925[199] and section 4 of the 1964 Act[200] may also operate to save class gifts which would otherwise be void.[201] Moreover, the principle that a class gift cannot be partially good and partially bad has itself been abandoned in respect of class gifts made after 15 July 1964. Section 4(4) of the Act provides that, where it is apparent at the time the disposition is made or becomes apparent at a subsequent time that the inclusion of any persons, being potential members of a class, or unborn persons who at birth would become members or potential members of the class, would cause the disposition to be treated as void for remoteness, those persons shall,

---

[194] *Leake v Robinson* (1817) 2 Mer 363; *Pearks v Moseley, supra*; *Smith v Smith* (1870) 5 Ch App 342; *Re Gage* [1898] 1 Ch 498; *Re Lord's Settlement* [1947] 2 All ER 685; *Re Hooper* [1948] Ch 586. Cf *Wainwright v Miller* [1897] 2 Ch 255.

[195] *Wilkinson v Duncan* (1861) 30 Beav 111; *Re Smith's Trusts* (1878) 9 Ch D 117; *Rogers v Mutch* (1878) 10 Ch D 25; *Re Stansfield* (1880) 15 Ch D 84.

[196] See *Megarry and Wade* 262–263.   [197] (1791) 3 Br CC 401.

[198] *Barrington v Tristram* (1801) 6 Ves 345, 348; *Picken v Matthews* (1878) 10 Ch D 264; *Re Bleckly* [1951] Ch 740; *Jarman* 1660, 1671.

[199] Applicable to instruments executed, and wills of testators dying, after 31 December 1925, but before 16 July 1964: s 163 was repealed by s 4(6) of the 1964 Act in respect of instruments taking effect after 15 July 1964.

[200] Applicable to instruments taking effect after 15 July 1964.

[201] See *Megarry and Wade* 266–270.

unless their exclusion would exhaust the class, be deemed for all the purposes of the disposition to be excluded from the class. This is subject to the prior application of the Act's 'wait and see' rule.[202] Only if that fails to save the gift will the question of class-reduction arise. Nevertheless, the effect of these provisions is that the Act will, if necessary, treat a class gift as a gift to those members of the class who take within the perpetuity period.[203] The same rules apply to appointments in favour of classes.

Gifts in default of appointment

8.66 The invalidity of a power of appointment, or an invalid exercise of a valid power, will not invalidate a gift in default of appointment; and an invalid discretionary trust will not invalidate subsequent limitations.[204]

8.67 The validity of a gift in default of appointment, where a valid power is not exercised, is governed by the following principle:

> If, at the moment when the power expires (by death of the donee, release or other-wise) the donee had made an appointment in the exact terms of the gift in default of appointment, and if such appointment would have been valid under the Rule against Perpetuities, then the gift in default of appointment is also valid; otherwise it is invalid.[205]

The failure of the donee of the power to make an appointment, or the release of the power by the donee, has the same effect (for perpetuity purposes) as if he had made an appointment in favour of the takers in default. Just as a 'second look' may be taken at the circumstances existing at the date of exercise of a special power, a similar 'second look' may be taken at circumstances existing at the date when the power ceases to be exercisable, or is released, and the gift in default takes effect. In *Re Edwards*,[206] for example, a share of residue had been left to A for life, with remainder to such of A's children as A should appoint and, in default of appointment, to such of A's children as should be living when the youngest child attained the age of 35. A died without exercising the power, leaving four daughters, the youngest of whom was 25 years of age. In the circumstances as they existed at A's death, the youngest daughter was bound to attain the age of 35 (if at all) within 21 years of A's death, and the gift in default of appointment was therefore held valid.

8.68 In the case of a *general* power exercisable by *deed*, the validity of the gift in default of appointment is determined as if the donee of the power had appointed to

---

[202] Section 3(1) of the Act. There is also special provision for cases where class-reduction has to be combined with age-reduction: see s 4(3).

[203] See *Megarry and Wade* 266, for an example of the operation of these rules.

[204] *Wollaston v King* (1868) LR 8 Eq 165; *Webb v Sadler* (1873) LR 8 Ch 419; *Freme v Clement* (1881) 18 Ch D 499; *Re Abbott* [1893] 1 Ch 54; *Re Hay* [1932] NI 215; *Re Coleman* [1936] Ch 528; *Re Allan* [1958] 1 WLR 220.

[205] Morris and Leach (n 24 above) 159, quoted with approval in *Re Edwards* (1960) DLR (2d) 755 (Ont).

[206] ibid, following *Sears v Coolidge* (1852) 329 Mass 340, 108 NE 2d 563.

himself and thereby become the absolute owner of the appointed property, and then made a gift to the takers in default.[207] The same principle also seems to apply to unexercised general powers exercisable by deed or by will, or by will only (although, in view of section 27 of the Wills Act 1837, only rarely will there be an unexercised general power of this kind).[208]

(3) Occupational Pension Schemes and Appointments of 'Death Benefits'[209]

Both occupational and personal pension schemes are generally[210] exempt from the operation of any rules of law relating to perpetuities. Section 163(1) of the Pension Schemes Act 1993[211] provides: **8.69**

> The rules of law relating to perpetuities shall not apply to the trusts of, or any disposition made under or for the purposes of, a personal or occupational pension scheme at any time when this section applies to it.

This exemption applies whether the trusts or dispositions in question are created or made before or after section 163 first applies to the scheme in question, but it does not validate with retrospective effect any trusts or dispositions which the rules of law relating to perpetuities (including, where applicable, the 'wait and see' provisions of section 3(1) of the 1964 Act) already require to be treated as void before section 163 applies to the scheme.[212] Moreover, if section 163 ceases to apply to a scheme, trusts created and dispositions made under it or for its purposes shall then again be subject to the rules of law relating to perpetuities as if the section had never applied to it.[213]

---

[207] Morris and Leach (n 24 above) 159–160; *Re Fasken* (1961) DLR (2d) 193.

[208] Morris and Leach (n 24 above) 159–160; Gray §524.1.

[209] For a more detailed treatment of this topic, see *Thomas* 162–172; and (1995) *Private Client Business*, Issue 2, 133–148 (GW Thomas).

[210] Only those schemes which qualify under s 163 of the Pension Schemes Act 1993 are exempt. A public service so qualifies at all times. Otherwise, a scheme qualifies at any time when it is contracted out or an appropriate personal pension scheme in relation to any employment or if it satisfies the requirements of the Personal and Occupational Pension Schemes (Perpetuities) Regulations 1990 (SI 1990/1143), as amended by SI 1994/1962, Reg 24. A personal pension scheme qualifies under s 163 at any time when it is approved by the Inland Revenue for the purposes of Chap IV of Part XIV of the Income and Corporation Taxes Act 1988. See also the Law Commission's Report, *The Rules Against Perpetuities and Excessive Accumulations*, (Law Com No 251) 38–42 (paras 3-58–3-62) and 88 (paras 8-33–8-34).

[211] In force as from 7 February 1994; replacing s 69(1) of the Social Security Act 1973 (in force as from 5 September 1973).

[212] Section 163(3). But for statutory exemption, pension fund trusts are subject to the rule against perpetuities: *Re Flavel's Will Trusts* [1969] 1 WLR 444; *Re Meadows (Thomas) & Co Ltd and Subsidiary Companies (1960) Staff Pension Scheme Rules* [1971] Ch 278; and *Air Jamaica Ltd v Charlton* [1999] 1 WLR 1399.

[213] Section 163(7). When an occupational or personal pension scheme ceases to be a qualifying scheme, it will nevertheless be treated as continuing to qualify for a further period of two years from the cesser, or for such longer period as the Occupational Pensions Board consider reasonable in the case of the particular scheme. If the scheme does not specify a perpetuity period (and few now do),

8.70 Where a pension scheme is not exempt, however, the rule against perpetuities must clearly be complied with, although the precise manner in which the rule applies is not at all clear. Even where a scheme is exempt, there may be difficult perpetuity issues. For example, such schemes invariably contain provisions to ensure that, if a member of the scheme dies while still in service and before retirement benefits under the scheme have been paid, a lump sum ('death benefit') will become payable.[214] The rules of the scheme may provide that the death benefit may be paid to the member's personal representatives, or to a nominated beneficiary, or distributed at the discretion of the trustees (or administrator) of the scheme. Although it is common practice to limit any nomination or distribution to the member's dependants, this is not required by the Inland Revenue as a condition of approval of the scheme. Indeed, it has become common practice to provide that the trustees shall have an absolute discretion as to the manner in which, and in favour of whom, any death benefit is to be applied. The class of objects is usually widely defined; and the trustees' discretion is often sufficiently broad to enable them to settle the death benefit on wide-ranging discretionary trusts, or to transfer it to the trustees (even foreign trustees) of another discretionary trust.[215] The question, even in relation to an exempt scheme, therefore, is how far (if at all) do the provisions of section 163 of the 1993 Act apply to any settlement or sub-settlement of such death benefit. It seems clear that the statutory exemption in section 163 extends no further than the pension scheme itself: if it were otherwise, and the exemption also applied to appointed trusts of any 'death benefit', it might be possible to create perpetual private trusts. However, if, as seems certain, section 163 is not applicable, what is the perpetuity period applicable to the new trusts and powers thus appointed? Most exempt schemes, acting in reliance on statute, no longer include an express perpetuity period; and, even if they did, to which aspects of the scheme does it apply?

8.71 In order to answer these questions, the nature of a pension scheme needs to be examined. There are two main ways of viewing a typical occupational or personal pension scheme. The first would be to regard the scheme as the equivalent of a 'head settlement', so that, for example, any exercise by the trustees (or the member) of the scheme of a power of appointment or of nomination in respect of any death benefit must, for perpetuity purposes, be read back into that 'head

---

and if withdrawal of approval occurs more than 21 years after the creation of the scheme, the consequences for the scheme could be dire: see, for example, *Re Meadows (Thomas) & Co Ltd, supra*; and *Re Flavel's Will Trusts, supra*.

[214] The amount may be considerable and usually represents a multiple of (not exceeding four times) the member's final remuneration, less any retained benefits. The mechanism for disposing of the death benefit may be a power of appointment or of nomination or even of advancement.

[215] Some difficult questions arise in relation to the inheritance tax treatment of such discretionary trusts, eg when will the tenth anniversary fall for the purposes of the ten-yearly charge under s 64 of the Inheritance Tax Act 1984?

settlement'.[216] However, there are many difficulties with such an analysis. The second way of viewing such arrangements is that there is no disposition by, or in respect of, an individual member until he or she becomes a member of the scheme and probably not until the first contribution is paid (by the member or his employer or both). These alternative views and the difficulties to which they give rise are examined below, where it is also suggested that the second analysis referred to above is the correct one.

The position and rights of a member of an occupational pension scheme were **8.72** described, in general terms, by Lord Oliver in *Baird v Baird*.[217] The scheme under consideration was a typical contributory balance-of-cost scheme, under which the funds were vested in trustees and the scheme itself administered by a committee of management. Scheme benefits were not assignable. On the death of a member of the scheme while still in service, a payment would be made to such person or persons as the member had nominated, or, in default of nomination, to the member's widow(er) or estate. These are typical standard terms of occupational pension schemes. The specific point at issue concerned the validity of a deceased member's nomination. However, as we have seen, Lord Oliver provided a lucid analysis of such schemes in general.[218]

At the stage when the member has made his nomination, there comes immedi- **8.73** ately into being a trust in favour of the nominated beneficiary, but one defeasible by the revocation of the nomination or appointment (and upon satisfying any other conditions, such as receiving any requisite consents) or by leaving employment (whereupon the 'death-in-employment' benefit ceases to be payable).[219]

---

[216] *Muir (or Williams) v Muir* [1943] AC 468, 483, *per* Lord Romer; *Re Paul* [1921] 2 Ch 1; and see paras 8.51–8.53 above.

[217] [1990] AC 548. This was a decision of the Privy Council on appeal from the Court of Appeal of Trinidad and Tobago. The analysis put forward by Lord Oliver is essentially the same as that adopted in the nineteenth century in relation to similar provisions in the statutory Customs Annuity and Benevolent Fund: see *Re William Phillips' Insurance* (1883) 23 Ch D 235; *Re Pocock's Policy* (1871) 6 Ch App 445; *Re Maclean's Trusts* (1874) LR 19 Eq 274; *Urquhart v Butterfield* (1887) 37 Ch D 357. In contrast, the power conferred by statute on a member of a friendly society to nominate a beneficiary of the proceeds of a life insurance policy, or on a member of an industrial and provident society to nominate a proportion of his property in the society in favour of someone else, is in the nature of a testamentary power: *Bennett v Slater* [1899] 1 QB 45; *Griffiths v Eccles Provident Industrial Co-operative Society Ltd* [1911] 2 KB 275; *Eccles Provident Industrial Co-operative Society Ltd v Griffiths* [1912] AC 483; *Demee v National Independent Mechanics' Friendly Society* [1919] RCR 8; *Re Barnes* [1940] Ch 267. See also *Re MacInnes* [1935] 1 DLR 401; *Re Shirley* (1965) 49 DLR (2d) 474.

[218] ibid 556–557. See para 7.40 above.

[219] This is to be contrasted with the case where the member has an absolute beneficial interest in his share of the fund during his lifetime, without any restriction on assignment. In such a case, the nomination is ineffective and the share of the fund will pass under the member's will: *Re MacInnes* [1935] DLR 401; *Re Shirley* (1965) 49 DLR (2d) 474; and *Baird v Baird* at 558. It is also to be contrasted with certain statutory nominations. In the case of nominations under the Provident Societies

No doubt, where the effect of the particular scheme is . . . to confer upon a member a full power of disposition during his lifetime over the amount standing to his credit under the scheme, a disposition of that interest upon his death would normally constitute a testamentary disposition requiring attestation in accordance with the statutory requirements for the execution of a will. But in what is now the normal case of non-assignable interests such as that in the present case and, a fortiori, where the power of nomination and revocation requires the prior approval of the trustees or of a management committee, their Lordships see no reason to doubt the correctness of Megarry J's decision in the *Danish Bacon Co,* case . . . [220]

Thus, on this analysis, it seems clear that, in respect of a contributory pension scheme, each member is a settlor to the extent of his or her own contributions. Interests arising in consequence of his or her membership must vest, and any power reserved by or conferred on such member, and indeed any power conferred on the trustees of the scheme in respect of such member, can therefore be exercised only within, and never outside, the applicable perpetuity period. It is also probable that, even in respect of a non-contributory scheme or a scheme under which both employer and employees contribute, contributions paid by the employer are not gratuitous, but represent 'deferred remuneration' of the employee. Admittedly, there are some cases which might indicate the contrary, namely that rights under a pension scheme constitute a gratuitous provision by the employing company without any bargain or agreement between it and its employees.[221] However, these cases are concerned with old-style schemes, under which it was not unusual for a member's benefits to be entirely dependent upon the discretion of his employer.[222] They are also contradicted by more recent authorities which have taken the view that pension benefits and rights are the products of sums paid into the pension fund by the employer as deferred or delayed remuneration for the

---

Acts, the nomination is in its nature testamentary, and the nominator is free to deal with the nominated property during his lifetime, but he is given a statutory power to deal with the property which is separate from the requirements of the Wills Act: see *Re Barnes* [1940] Ch 267; and *Eccles Provident Industrial Co-operative Society Ltd v Griffiths* [1912] AC 483, 490 and [1911] 2 KB 275, 284. Under the Friendly Societies Act 1974 the subject matter of a nomination does not apparently form part of the nominator's estate but passes directly to the nominee by force of the nomination: *Bennett v Slater* [1899] 1 QB 45.

[220] *Baird v Baird* at 561, *per* Lord Oliver. See *Re Danish Bacon Co Staff Pension Fund Trusts* [1971] 1 WLR 248.

[221] *Re J Bibby & Sons Pension Trust Deed* [1952] 2 All ER 483; *Beach v Reed Corrugated Cases Ltd* [1965] 1 WLR 807; *Armour v Liverpool Corporation* [1939] 1 All ER 363. Many schemes still include an express provision to the effect that neither the rules of the scheme nor the granting of any benefits thereunder shall have any contractual effect. However, the purpose of such a provision is generally regarded to be to avoid claims (such as that made in *Ward v Barclay Perkins & Co Ltd* [1939] 1 All ER 287) that it was an implied term of joining the scheme that the employee was entitled to permanent employment. Such a provision does not, of course, negative the contractual effect of the employee's (separate) contract of employment.

[222] See *Re J Bibby, supra*, in particular. In *Armour, supra*, the result seems to have turned on the fact that no contract was proved.

employee's current work: they are akin to insurance.[223] In addition, the older cases pre-date both the 'preservation requirements' introduced by the Social Security Act 1973 and the cases decided on Article 119 of the Treaty of Rome.[224] The modern view is that the provision of pension benefits is regarded as an implied (if not an express) term of the contract of employment, such benefits being provided in return for the work of the employee and/or his continuous loyal service.[225]

> ... the beneficiaries under a pension scheme such as this are not volunteers. Their rights have contractual and commercial origins. They are derived from the contracts of employment of the members. The benefits provided under the scheme have been earned by the service of the members under those contracts and, where the scheme is contributory, *pro tanto* by their contributions.[226]

This is also the view of the Inland Revenue (contributions to non-exempt schemes being taxed as remuneration received by the employee), of the Occupational Pensions Board, and of the trade unions.

In any event, the relevant disposition for perpetuity purposes seems to occur when **8.74** an individual becomes a member of the scheme and contributions are paid by or in respect of that member. However, this does not in itself identify the applicable perpetuity period. The sensible course of action is to ensure that, when each member joins the scheme, an appropriate perpetuity period is expressly made applicable to any interests that may be created under an appointment, nomination, or advancement of that member's 'death benefit' under the scheme and also that, in respect of such interests, such perpetuity period commences on the date on which that person became a member. [227] However, most schemes do not contain any such express perpetuity period, for any purpose. Consequently, one must be implied. But who are the logically relevant 'lives in being' for perpetuity purposes in these circumstances? Are they all the members of the scheme living at the date of its creation, or all the members of the scheme living at the date of the creation of the sub-trusts? Are they the members of some more limited group, such as the lives which are logically relevant to the appointed sub-trusts? And do the

---

[223] *Parry v Cleaver* [1970] AC 1, 16; *The Halcyon Skies* [1977] QB 14; *Smoker v London Fire & Civil Defence Authority* [1991] 2 AC 502.

[224] *Defrenne v Belgium* [1976] ECR 445; *Bilka-Kaufhaus Gmbh v Weber von Hartz* [1986] ECR 559; *Barber v Guardian Royal Exchange Assurance Group* [1991] 1 QB 344.

[225] *Mettoy Pension Trustees Ltd v Evans* [1990] 1 WLR 1587; *Imperial Group Pension Trust Ltd v Imperial Tobacco Ltd* [1991] 1 WLR 589, 597; *Mihlenstedt v Barclays International Ltd* [1989] IRLR 522; *Kerr v British Leyland (Staff) Trustees Ltd* (CA, 26 March 1986); *Cullen v Pension Holdings Ltd* [1992] PLR 135, 146; *Uncle v Parker* (1995) IR 120, 123; *Vas v Stadt Bielefeld* [1996] 389, 392.

[226] *Mettoy, supra*, at 1610, *per* Warner J.

[227] The Law Commission has recommended in its Report (Law Com No 251) that, in respect of interests created under a nomination or advancement under a pension scheme, the perpetuity period should be taken to start on the date on which the person making the nomination became a member of the scheme: see 133, para 11-11.

'wait and see' provisions of the Perpetuities and Accumulations Act 1964 apply here?[228]

8.75 In *Re Meadows (Thomas) & Co Ltd and Subsidiary Companies (1960) Staff Pension Scheme Rules*,[229] Goff J had to consider a peculiar arrangement set up in 1960, whereby the employing company took out a group deferred annuity policy with an insurance company to provide pensions for its staff. Pensions would be paid to the company. The company kept a register (made up on 1 September each year) showing the name of each person entitled to benefit, the particulars from which the amount of pension entitlement could be calculated (updated to show any entitlement to a higher pension), and the premium payable. In the event that an employee retired on pension before pension age or withdrew from service before pension age, the scheme's rules provided that a proportion of the provision made under the policy was surrendered for a sum of money. Such sums would be returned to the employing company which then paid them over to a benevolent fund (to which additional sums could be contributed by the employing company) and the committee of that fund could apply it in various ways for the benefit of employees, their widows, and dependants. The committee also had power to wind up the fund and distribute it among employees. The question at issue was whether the committee's powers infringed the rule against perpetuities, or whether they were saved by section 3 of the Perpetuities and Accumulations Act 1964.

8.76 In *Meadows*, there were only two possible instruments, namely the rules of the scheme and the group insurance policy. Neither of these disposed of an interest in property: the rules merely set out terms to affect the policy when it arose; the group policy created nothing until persons were brought within its ambit. There were two other possibilities as to what was the relevant disposition: (a) each annual premium; and (b) the entry of each name on the register. Possibility (a) was clearly incorrect, because it drew a distinction between the policy and its fruits. Possibility (b), however, was 'plainly right' (subject to the qualification that, where a person had been promoted to a higher grade and consequently enjoyed higher benefits, there was a fresh disposition as from the date when the preferment was entered on the register). Section 15(5) of the 1964 Act provides that the Act applies only in relation to instruments taking effect after the commencement of the Act, but by section 15(6) the Act is made to apply to a disposition made otherwise than by an instrument as if the disposition had been contained in an instrument taking effect when the disposition was made. If, therefore, interests in the benevolent fund created by the 1960 scheme were interests arising out of a disposition made by an instrument (ie the rules of the policy), the Act would not apply

---

[228] It is arguable that the 'wait and see' provisions cannot apply (see *Thomas* 165) but this is not the conclusion reached by the courts.
[229] [1971] Ch 278.

by virtue of section 15(5). But if they were interests under a disposition not so made, the Act applied by virtue of section 15(6). Goff J concluded that the latter was the case.

Consequently, the 'wait and see' provisions of the 1964 Act applied and the **8.77** scheme's powers concerning the benevolent fund were valid under section 3(3) in so far as they were exercised within the perpetuity period. It was held that section 3(5)(d) was the applicable provision (ie 'any person on the failure or determination of whose prior interest the disposition is limited to take effect).[230] 'In the case of each person, there is a disposition of his part of the global sum in favour of the benevolent fund taking effect on the failure of his prior pension rights.'[231] In relation to each individual, one had to look to see when he was entered on the register: if it was before the 1964 Act came into force, the Act did not apply except as to any increments to which he became entitled after that date; but if he was entered after the Act came into force, it wholly applied. Where it applied, then as long as any powers with regard to the monies returned were exercised within 21 years of his death, they were valid.

In general terms, the identity of relevant 'lives in being' remains unclear, however. **8.78** It seems to have been conceded in *Meadows* that section 3(5)(iii) of the 1964 Act (under which the relevant lives, in the case of a special power of appointment exercisable in favour of members of a class, would be any member or potential member of the class) could not apply, on the ground that the number of persons falling within the class was such as to render it impracticable to ascertain the date of death of the survivor. In a typical modern pension scheme, however, the class of objects in whose favour any death benefit may be appointed, though often wide, is likely to be confined to a member's spouse, children, and certain defined dependants— a class of persons seldom so numerous as to make it impracticable to ascertain the date of death of the survivor. Therefore, on the (safe) assumption that the analysis put forward in *Meadows* is correct and the relevant 'disposition' occurs when an individual becomes a member of the scheme and contributions are paid by or in respect of that member, it is not necessarily the case that the applicable perpetuity period is confined to the 21 years following the death of that individual.

Nevertheless, the effect of this uncertainty, it is suggested, is that the prudent **8.79** approach, where a perpetuity period has to be *implied*, is to assume that the member himself is the only 'life in being' for perpetuity purposes and that, in relation to an appointment of a member's death benefit, the only perpetuity period that can safely be adopted is the period of 21 years from the death of that member.

---

[230] The peculiar circumstances of the case meant that s 3(5)(a) and (b)(iii) were considered inapplicable; but, in other, more straightforward cases, they could well apply.
[231] [1971] Ch 285.

8.80 However, there is no reason why these uncertainties could not be circumvented by the adoption of an *express* perpetuity period in respect of the relevant disposition. In other words, a better solution would be to ensure that, when each member joins the scheme, an appropriate perpetuity period is expressly made applicable to any interests that may be created under an appointment, nomination, or advancement of that member's 'death benefit' under the scheme; and also that, in respect of such interests, such perpetuity period commences on the date on which that person became a member. Indeed, such an express period may, presumably, even be a period of years not exceeding eighty, as allowed by section 1(1) of the 1964 Act (and which period would then also apply to any appointment of the death benefit by virtue of section 1(2)).

(4) Proposals for Reform

8.81 The Law Commission has recently proposed a number of changes to the law relating to perpetuities.[232] It recommends that the rule against perpetuities should only apply to successive interests in property held in trust (including those subject to conditions precedent or subsequent and those arising under a right of reverter under the determination of a determinable interest); to powers of appointment; and to successive legal interests in chattels under the doctrine of executory bequests.[233] It further recommends that there should be one, fixed, overriding perpetuity period of 125 years, to which no express reference need be made and which should apply irrespective of any stipulation to the contrary.[234] As a general rule, this period should commence when the instrument creating the estate, interest, right, or power to which the rule applies takes effect.[235] Subject to two exceptions, the proposed period should only apply prospectively to instruments taking effect on or after the date on which any legislation is brought into force (including wills executed before such date, but where the testator dies thereafter).[236] One exception to this principle is the recommendation that trustees of a trust that was in existence at that date should have power to elect (by irrevocable deed) that their trust should be subject to the new 125-year period if the trust contained an express perpetuity period of lives in being plus 21 years and the trustees believe that it is impracticable to ascertain the existence or whereabouts of the measuring lives in being and cannot, therefore, determine the date at which the perpetuity period would come to an end.[237] The other exception to the principle of prospectivity is the case of dispositions made after any legislation is brought into force under special powers of appointment that were created by instruments

---

[232] *The Rules Against Perpetuities and Excessive Accumulations*: Law Com No 251.
[233] ibid 88 (para 7.31) and 138 (Clause 1 of the Draft Bill).
[234] ibid 101 (paras 8.13–8.14); 133 (para 11.8); 140 (Clause 5(1) and (2) of the Draft Bill).
[235] ibid 101 (para 8.15); and 142 (Clause 6(1) of the Draft Bill).
[236] ibid 102–105 (paras 8.18–8.24).   [237] ibid 103–104 (para 8.20).

that took effect before that date. In such cases, the recommendation is that the perpetuity period applicable to any such disposition should be 125 years commencing on the effective date of the instrument which created the special power of appointment.[238]

Subsidiary proposals are then made to cater for two specific cases. First, in relation **8.82** to any estate, interest, or right created by the exercise of a *special power of appointment*, the perpetuity period should commence when the instrument creating the power takes effect, ie the old common law rule is retained.[239] For these purposes, a power of appointment exercisable otherwise than by will (whether or not it is also exercisable by will) is a *special* power unless (a) the instrument creating it expresses it to be exercisable by one person only and (b) at all times during its currency, when that person is of full age and capacity, it could be exercised by him so as immediately to transfer to himself the whole of the interest governed by the power, without the consent of any other person or compliance with any other condition (ignoring a formal condition relating only to the mode of exercise of the power). Also, a power of appointment exercisable by will (whether or not it is also exercisable otherwise than by will) is a *special* power unless (a) the instrument creating it expresses it to be exercisable by one person only and (b) that person could exercise it so as to transfer to his personal representatives the whole of the estate or interest to which it relates. If a power of appointment which is exercisable by will or otherwise would be a special power under one but not both of the foregoing provisions then it is also provided that it is a special power.[240] Thus, joint powers and consent powers still cannot be general powers under these proposals, which, in fact, seem to have the same broad effect as section 7 of the Perpetuities and Accumulations Act 1964.[241] It is also provided that, as in section 15(1) of the 1964 Act, a 'power of appointment' includes 'a discretionary power to transfer a beneficial interest in property without the provision of valuable consideration' (so that the rule will continue to apply to powers of maintenance and advancement and to discretionary trusts of capital or income).[242]

The Law Commission also recommends that the rule against perpetuities should **8.83** not apply to an interest or right arising under an occupational pension scheme, a personal pension scheme, a public service pension scheme, or self-employed pension arrangements. The effect of this change in the law would be that all (or virtually all) *'genuine pension schemes'* were outside the ambit of the rule.[243] However,

---

[238] ibid 104–105 (paras 8.21–8.23).

[239] ibid 101–102 (para 8.16); and p. 142 (Clause 6(2) of the Draft Bill).

[240] ibid 144, 146 (Clause 11 of the Draft Bill).

[241] As in the case of s 7, the character of the power would seem to be fixed, once and for all, at the time of creation.

[242] Law Com No 251, 150 (Clause 20(3) of the Draft Bill). In both statutes, the word 'transfer' is presumably intended to include 'creation'.

[243] ibid 90 (para 7.36).

it also recommends that the rule should apply to interests created by a nomination of benefits made by a member of a pension scheme or by the exercise of a power of advancement by the trustees, and that the period shall be taken to start at the date on which the person making the nomination became a member of the scheme.[244] This will apply even if the person making the nomination became a member of the scheme before the legislation was brought into force.

C. The Rule Against Inalienability[245]

8.84   Property must not be rendered inalienable. English law prohibits not only future interests which are too remote but also immediate gifts, whether of real or personal property, which are subject to a permanent restraint on alienation. Such restraints (whether absolute or conditional) attached to an absolute gift are repugnant to the gift and therefore void. This topic is dealt with elsewhere.[246] However, the intention of a settlor may be to create a 'perpetual trust'[247] or a 'purpose trust': perhaps the trustees are to hold the capital indefinitely; or a beneficial interest may be given to an institution, such as a club or an unincorporated association, of indefinite duration; or the trust fund is to be applied in furtherance of some non-charitable purpose.[248] In such cases, the property is effectively rendered inalienable. The rule against perpetuities as such cannot prevent perpetual duration, because there are no 'lives in being' in whom any interest can vest.

8.85   As a general rule, a trust is void if the disposition of the settled property, or the beneficial interest in it, is prohibited or rendered impossible. This may be the case because of the terms of the gift,[249] or because the rules of the club, association, or society which it was intended to benefit prohibit alienation.[250] If the gift requires property to be held essentially as an endowment, and the capital and income applied indefinitely for a specified purpose, it is void.[251] Examples include a bequest to trustees to maintain a tomb;[252] a devise of land to be held in perpetuity for use as a private burial ground;[253] a bequest to provide an annual yachting

---

[244]   ibid 102 (para 8.17) and 142 (Clause 6(3) of the Draft Bill).
[245]   *Megarry and Wade* 268–271.   [246]   See paras 2.08–2.11 above.   [247]   Gray, §909.1.
[248]   The rule does not apply to charitable trusts: *Chamberlayne v Brockett* (1872) 8 Ch App 206, 211; *A-G v Webster* (1875) LR 20 Eq 483.
[249]   *Re Patten* [1929] 2 Ch 276.
[250]   ibid; *Re Gwyon* [1930] 1 Ch 255. However, if the members of the club can change the rules and remove the prohibition, there seems to be no reason why the gift should not be valid: *Re Clarke* [1901] 2 Ch 110.
[251]   *Cocks v Manners* (1871) LR 12 Eq 574, 585, 586.
[252]   *Rickard v Robson* (1862) 31 Beav 244. See also *Re Dean* (1889) 41 Ch D 552, 557; *Re Elliott* [1952] 1 All ER 145; *Re Dalziel* [1943] Ch 277.
[253]   *Yeap Cheah Neo v Ong Cheng Neo* (1875) LR 6 PC 381.

cup;[254] and a bequest to trustees to pay income to a company for the holiday expenses of workpeople.[255] On the other hand, if the gift is an absolute one, there can be no valid restraint on alienation and the gift is therefore valid.[256] For example, a gift to a club, association, or society will be valid if the members can dispose of it as they wish.[257]

If the right to income is itself free from any restraint on alienation, and may therefore **8.86** be assigned or otherwise disposed of, it does not matter that the capital vested in trustees is inalienable. For example, in *Re Chardon*,[258] a trust to pay the income of a legacy to a cemetery company, for as long as it maintained a particular grave, was held valid. Romer J pointed out that the rule against perpetuities was directed against interests which might vest outside the perpetuity period, and not against interests which vested within the period but then continued beyond it. Here, the company and the residuary legatees had vested interests and could join together to dispose of the entire fund. Similarly, a life interest may be given to an unborn beneficiary and, provided such interest itself vests within the perpetuity period, it is permissible for the trustees to hold the capital of the trust fund until that beneficiary's death, which may occur outside the perpetuity period.[259]

Inalienability is permitted if it is restricted to the perpetuity period: it is perma- **8.87** nent inalienability or inalienability for an excessive or uncertain period that is impossible.[260] The permissible period for this purpose seems to be the period of human lives in being plus 21 years;[261] and, in this sense, in relation to purpose trusts, the rule against inalienability may be said to be a rule against purpose trusts of *excessive* duration. The Perpetuities and Accumulations Act 1964 did not affect the law relating to purpose trusts. Section 15(4) expressly provides that nothing in the Act is to affect the operation of the rule rendering void for remoteness certain dispositions under which property is limited to be applied for purposes other than the benefit of any person or class of persons, where the property may be so applied after the end of the perpetuity period applicable to the relevant disposition under

---

[254] *Re Nottage* [1895] 2 Ch 649.   [255] *Re Drummond* [1914] 2 Ch 90.

[256] See, for example, *Cocks v Manners* (1871) LR 12 Eq 574; *Re Smith* [1914] 1 Ch 937; *Re Drummond, supra*; *Re Prevost* [1930] 2 Ch 383; *Re Ogden* [1933] Ch 678.

[257] *Re Ray's Will Trusts* [1936] 2 All ER 93, 97, 98; *Re Turkington* [1937] 4 All ER 501; *Leahy v A-G for NSW* [1959] AC 457, 478; *Neville Estates Ltd v Madden* [1962] Ch 832; *Re Recher's Will Trusts* [1972] Ch 526; *Re Lipinski's Will Trusts* [1976] Ch 235; *Re Grant's Will Trusts* [1980] 1 WLR 360.

[258] [1928] Ch 464. See also *Re Chambers' Will Trusts* [1950] Ch 267; (1937) 53 LQR 24 (WO Hart); (1938) 54 LQR 258 (MJ Albery). Cf *Re Wightwick's Will Trusts* [1950] Ch 260.

[259] *Wainwright v Miller* [1897] 2 Ch 255; *Re Gage* [1898] 1 Ch 498.

[260] *Kennedy v Kennedy* [1914] AC 215; *Re Wightwick's Will Trusts* [1950] Ch 260.

[261] *Thellusson v Woodford* (1805) 11 Ves 112, 135, 146; *Carne v Long* (1860) 2 De GF & J 75, 80; *Re Dean* (1889) 41 Ch D 552, 557 (which, in adopting the lives of animals, was wrong); *Re Moore* [1901] 1 Ch 936; *Re Astor's Settlement Trusts* [1952] Ch 534; *Re Khoo Cheng Teow* [1932] Straits Sett Reps 226.

such rule. The choice, as a perpetuity period, of a period of years not exceeding 80, under section 1(1) of the Act, would seem not to be available in such cases.[262]

8.88   The status of non-charitable purpose trusts in English law is uncertain, to say the least: with the exception of a few anomalous instances, they are almost certainly invalid. Similarly, gifts to unincorporated associations can be construed in several different ways and give rise to difficulties of their own. These issues are discussed separately, elsewhere in this book, in the context of the 'beneficiary principle'.[263]

D. The Rule Against Excessive Accumulations

General principles

8.89   At common law, the rule against excessive accumulation of income[264] went hand in hand with the rule against perpetuities: the basic principle was that the accumulation of income could validly be directed for so long as the vesting of interests in the property itself might validly be postponed.[265] However, the Accumulations Act 1800 (the 'Thellusson Act') imposed restrictions on the period allowed for accumulations. In their present form, these restrictions are found in sections 164–166 of the Law of Property Act 1925 and section 13 of the Perpetuities and Accumulations Act 1964.[266] Their effect is to direct that:

> no person may by any instrument or otherwise settle or dispose of any property in such manner that the income thereof shall . . . be wholly or partially accumulated for any longer period than one[267] of the following six periods:

---

[262] At least, this seems to be the safer conclusion. The wording of s 15(4) is notoriously ambiguous and unclear. See P Matthews, 'The New Trust: Obligations without Rights?' in *Trends in Contemporary Trust Law* (Oxford, 1996) 1, 12 and 17.

[263] See Chapter 6 generally.

[264] 'Accumulation' seems to have been construed both in a narrow and a wide meaning. According to Harman LJ, in *Re Earl of Berkeley* [1968] Ch 744, 772, it 'involves the addition of income to capital, thus increasing the estate in favour of those entitled to capital and against the interests of those entitled to income'. This narrow view would seem to exclude accumulation of the kind involved in *Re Rochford's Settlement Trusts* [1965] Ch 111. Widgery LJ doubted whether it 'signifies any more than a simple aggregation of instalments of income to create a single fund': [1968] Ch 744, 780. Russell LJ did not give a definition. See also *Theobald on Wills* (15th edn, 1993) 633–634.

[265] *Thellusson v Woodford* (1805) 11 Ves 112.

[266] These provisions apply to a power of accumulation as well as a direction to accumulate: *Re Robb* [1953] Ch 459; and s 13(2) of the 1964 Act. They apply whether accumulation is at simple or compound interest: *Re Phillips* (1880) 49 LJ Ch 198; *Re Clutterbuck* [1901] 2 Ch 285, 287; *Re Hawkins* [1916] 2 Ch 570, 577; *Re Garside* [1919] 1 Ch 132, 137; and s 13(2) of the 1964 Act. Cf *Crawley v Crawley* (1835) 7 Sim 427; *Re Pope* [1901] 1 Ch 64, 69, 70. They also apply whether the whole or just part of the income is accumulated: *Re Travis* [1900] 2 Ch 541.

[267] And not more than one: *Re Errington* (1897) 76 LT 616; *Wilson v Wilson* (1851) 1 Sim (NS) 288; *Jagger v Jagger* (1883) 25 Ch D 729; *Re Watt's Will Trusts* [1936] 2 All ER 1555.

(a) the life of the grantor or settlor;

(b) a term of 21 years from the death of the grantor, settlor or testator;

(c) the minority or respective minorities of any person or persons living or *en ventre sa mere* at the death of the grantor, settlor or testator;

(d) the minority or respective minorities of any person or persons who under the limitations of the instrument directing accumulations would for the time being, if of full age, be entitled to the income directed to be accumulated;

(e) a term of 21 years from the date of the making of the disposition;

(f) the duration of the minority or respective minorities of any person or persons in being at that date.

Alternatives (e) and (f) were added by section 13 of the 1964 Act and are available **8.90** only in the case of dispositions taking effect after 15 July 1964. Alternative (a) is the only period of a life available for accumulation: and the life in question must be that of the grantor or settlor himself, and not of some other person.[268] Alternative (b) starts to run at the beginning of the day after the testator's death.[269] Alternatives (c), (d), and (f) refer to minority, which, as from 1 January 1970, ends at the age of 18.[270] However, this change does not affect the validity of any direction for accumulation in a settlement or other disposition made by a deed, will,[271] or other instrument made before that date with reference to a minority ending at 21.[272] Alternatives (c) and (f) refer to minorities of persons living or *en ventre sa mere* at the relevant time, whereas alternative (d) is not so confined.[273] Alternatives (c) and (f) do not require those persons to be prospectively entitled to any benefit from the gift, but alternative (d) does.[274] Accumulation under alternatives (c) and (f) cannot exceed a single minority: where there are several minorities, the maximum period will be the longest minority. Alternative (d), however, authorizes accumulation during the 'minorities' of beneficiaries who are not in existence or *en ventre sa mere* at the date on which the trust is created and, indeed, accumulation may continue during the successive minorities of such beneficiaries[275]—but there can be accumulation under alternative (d) (just like alternatives (c) and (f)) when no such beneficiary is living at all.[276]

---

[268] *Re Lady Rosslyn's Trusts* (1848) 16 Sim 391.

[269] *Webb v Webb* (1840) 2 Beav 493; *Gorst v Lowndes* (1841) 11 Sim 434; *A-G v Poulden* (1844) 3 Hare 555.

[270] Family Law Reform Act 1969, s 1.

[271] A will or codicil made before 1 January 1970 is not to be treated as having been made on or after that date merely because it has been confirmed by a codicil executed on or after that date: s 1(7).

[272] Section 1(4); and Sch 3, para 7.   [273] *Sidney v Wilmer* (1863) 4 De GJ & S 84.

[274] *Jagger v Jagger* (1883) 25 Ch D 729, 733, where Kay J. thought that alternative (d) indicated a person who could at any time say: 'But for this accumulation I should be absolutely entitled to the dividends'. But, in *Re Cattell* [1914] 1 Ch 177, 189, Lord Parker declared that this was clearly not its true meaning.

[275] *Re Cattell* [1914] 1 Ch 177. See also *Ellis v Maxwell* (1841) 3 Beav 587.

[276] *Haley v Bannister* (1819) 4 Madd 275, 277; *Ellis v Maxwell* (1841) 3 Beav 587, 596–597; see also *Longdon v Simson* (1806) 12 Ves 295.

Effect of excessive direction to accumulate

8.91 Where a direction to accumulate is excessive, the consequences differ according to whether the direction simply exceeds one of the six statutory periods or infringes the common law perpetuity period of lives in being plus 21 years. A direction or power to accumulate which exceeds the perpetuity period is wholly void, so that no income can be accumulated at all.[277] The 'wait and see' provisions of the 1964 Act do not seem to apply: section 3(1) applies only where an interest may be void for remoteness of vesting, and remote vesting is not the basis of the rule against excessive accumulations, although it is possible that the words 'any power, option or other right' in section 3(3) could be construed so as to apply to accumulations.[278]

8.92 Where the selected period of accumulation exceeds a permitted statutory period but cannot exceed the perpetuity period, it is good *pro tanto*: only the excess over the appropriate accumulation period is void.[279] What is the 'appropriate' period depends on what (if anything) the settlor or testator had, or may have had, in mind, which is sometimes a question of construction, taking into account the circumstances of the case (for example whether the disposition is made by will or *inter vivos*).[280]

8.93 Where excessive accumulation is directed, the income so released belongs to the person(s) who would have been entitled if accumulation had not been directed[281] (which may be under a resulting trust or a residuary gift or on an intestacy).[282] Subsequent interests are not accelerated.[283]

---

[277] *Marshall v Holloway* (1820) 2 Swans 432; *Boughton v James* (1844) 1 Coll CC 26, 45; *Curtis v Lukin* (1842) 5 Beav 147. This is also the case where the accumulation was intended for charity: *Martin v Maugham* (1844) 14 Sim 230.

[278] *Megarry and Wade* 304–305; E Burn, *Cheshire and Burn's The Modern Law of Real Property* (16th edn, Butterworths, 2000) ('*Cheshire and Burn*') 330.

[279] *Griffiths v Vere* (1803) 9 Ves 127; *Eyre v Marsden* (1838) 2 Keen 564 (affirmed 4 My & Cr 231); *Leake v Robinson* (1817) 2 Mer 363, 389. The reason is said to be that the statutory provisions merely cut down the wider powers permitted at common law: *Megarry and Wade* 305.

[280] *Re Watt's Will Trusts* [1936] 2 All ER 1555, 1562; *Re Ransome* [1957] Ch 348, 361; *Talbot v Jevers* (1875) LR 20 Eq 255; *Re Lady Rosslyn's Trust* (1848) 16 Sim 391; *Webb v Webb* (1840) 2 Beav 493; *Longdon v Simson* (1806) 12 Ves 295, 298; *Griffiths v Vere* (1803) 9 Ves 127. See, generally, *Megarry and Wade* 305–306.

[281] Section 164(1) of the Law of Property Act 1925; *Green v Gascoyne* (1865) 4 De GJ & S 565; *Combe v Hughes* (1865) 2 De GJ & S 657; *Trickey v Trickey* (1832) 3 My & K 560.

[282] *Re O'Hagen* [1932] WN 188; *O'Neill v Lucas* (1838) 2 Keen 313; *Ellis v Maxwell* (1841) 3 Beav 587; *Morgan v Morgan* (1851) 4 De G & Sm 164; *Mathews v Keble* (1868) 3 Ch App 691; *Re Garside* [1919] 1 Ch 132; *Re Walpole* [1933] Ch 431; *Re Ransome* [1957] Ch 348.

[283] *Eyre v Marsden* (1838) 2 Keen 564, 574; *Green v Gascoyne* (1865) 4 De GJ & S 565, 569; *Weatherall v Thornburgh* (1878) 8 Ch D 261, 269, 271, 272; *Re Parry* (1889) 60 LT 489; *Berry v Geen* [1938] AC 575; *Re Robb* [1953] Ch 459.

Accumulation and the rule in *Saunders v Vautier*[284]

The so-called rule in *Saunders v Vautier* enables a beneficiary of full age (or, where **8.94**
there are more than one, all adult beneficiaries acting together), who has (or
between them have) an absolute, vested, and indefeasible interest in the capital
and income of property, to call for the transfer of that property to him (or them)
and thereby terminate any trusts otherwise applicable to it. This right is exercisable notwithstanding any direction to accumulate income. Thus, if property is
given absolutely to an infant beneficiary, with a direction that the income of that
property is to be accumulated until some age beyond his age of majority, he may
put a stop to the accumulation and demand payment to him of both capital and
accumulated income as soon as he attains the age of 18 years.[285] In such a case,
section 164 does not apply. (This is not the case, of course, if the beneficiary has
a vested interest only in the accumulated income, to which section 164 applies,
and is not also entitled to the capital.)[286]

Before the Perpetuities and Accumulations Act 1964, a beneficiary's incapacity to **8.95**
bear children could not be taken into account in determining whether she had
such a right to call for the property.[287] However, section 14 of the Act now provides that, in relation to dispositions made after 15 July 1964, the presumption as
to future parenthood contained in section 2 shall apply to any question as to the
right of beneficiaries to put an end to accumulation of income.[288]

Exceptions to the rule

There are various exceptions to the rule against excessive accumulations.[289] These **8.96**
include:

(a) Provisions for the payment of the debts of any other person.[290] If they are the
    debts of the settlor or testator, such a provision is valid even if it outlasts the
    perpetuity period.[291] If they are the debts of any other person, the direction

---

[284] (1841) 4 Beav 115 (affirmed, Cr & Ph 240). See also *Wharton v Masterman* [1895] AC 186.
[285] *Wharton v Masterman* [1895] AC 186; *Gosling v Gosling* (1859) Johns 265, 272; *Josselyn v Josselyn* (1837) 9 Sim 63; *IRC v Hamilton-Russell's Executors* [1943] 1 All ER 474; *Re Jump* [1903] 1 Ch 129.
[286] *Shaw v Rhodes* (1835) 1 My & Cr 135; *Evans v Hellier* (1837) 5 Cl & Fin 114.
[287] *Jee v Audley* (1787) 1 Cox 324; *Re Dawson* (1888) 39 Ch D 155; *Re Deloitte* [1926] Ch 56 (doubted by the House of Lords in *Berry v Geen* [1938] AC 575, 584); *IRC v Bernstein* [1960] Ch 444.
[288] See para 8.19 above. See also *Figg v Clarke* [1997] 1 WLR 603.
[289] See ss 164–166 of the Law of Property Act 1925; and *Megarry and Wade* 308–310.
[290] Section 164(2)(i); *Viscount Barrington v Liddell* (1852) 2 De GM & G 480, 497, 498. The accumulation must, of course, be bona fide: *Mathews v Keble* (1868) 3 Ch App 691, 697. A provision for recoupment of debts already paid is not within the section: *Bateman v Hotchkin* (1847) 10 Beav 426; *Tewart v Lawson* (1974) LR 18 Eq 490; *Re Heathcote* [1904] 1 Ch 826.
[291] *Lord Southampton v Marquis of Hertford* (1813) 2 V & B 54, 65; *Bateman v Hotchkin* (1847) 10 Beav 426. A similar exception is made for accumulations to pay the National Debt.

must be confined to the perpetuity period.[292] The debts may be existing or contingent debts, but they must derive from an existing obligation,[293] so that, for example, accumulation to discharge an existing mortgage,[294] or to cover a potential liability under an (as yet) unbroken leasehold covenant, would be included, but not accumulation to pay inheritance tax on the death of a living person.[295]

(b) Provisions for raising portions for any legitimate issue[296] (including unborn issue)[297] of the grantor, settlor, or testator, or of any person taking any interest under the settlement or disposition or to whom any interest is thereby limited.[298] Such a provision must be limited to the perpetuity period. Although the phrase 'raising portions' is 'a technical phrase of conveyancing',[299] its meaning in this context is not entirely clear,[300] for example it is not confined to younger children of a marriage;[301] and the 'portions' may be created by the instrument directing the accumulation or by a separate instrument.[302] A direction to accumulate the entire income of the trust property, or even the bulk of it, does not fall within this exception, however, for this is not a case of 'raising portions' but of giving everything.[303] Similarly, accumulations must also not be merely by way of addition to capital, with a power or discretion for someone to use them for raising portions: the accumulations must be 'themselves, as separate items, used for the purpose of portions'.[304] The person 'taking an interest' need not take an interest in the property the income of which is being accumulated: it may be any interest whatsoever under the instrument in question, no matter how small or remote it may be.[305]

---

[292] *Viscount Barrington v Liddell* (1852) 2 De GM & G 480, 498.

[293] *Varlo v Faden* (1859) 1 De GF & J 211, 224, 225.

[294] *Bateman v Hotchkin, supra*; *Re Hurlbatt* [1910] 2 Ch 553.

[295] *Re Rochford's Settlement Trusts* [1965] Ch 111. The actual decision in this case might have been different if the settlement had been made after the 1964 Act came into force, when another (new) accumulation period would have been available; but this would not affect the proposition in the text above.

[296] *Shaw v Rhodes* (1836) 1 My & Cr 135, 159; Family Law Reform Act 1969, s 15.

[297] *Beech v Lord St Vincent* (1850) 3 De G & Sm 678; *Re Stephens* [1904] 1 Ch 322.

[298] Section 164(2)(ii) of the Law of Property Act 1925.

[299] *Re Bourne's Settlement Trusts* [1946] 1 All ER 411.

[300] *Watt v Wood* (1862) 2 Dr & Sm 56, 60; *Re Elliott* [1918] 2 Ch 150.

[301] *Re Stephens* [1904] 1 Ch 322. See also *Re Elliott, supra*.

[302] *Beech v Lord St Vincent* (1850) 3 De G & Sm 678; *Halford v Stains* (1849) 16 Sim 488, 496; *Barrington v Liddell* (1852) 2 De GM & G 480; *Middleton v Losh* (1852) 1 Sm & G 61.

[303] *Bourne v Buckton* (1851) 2 Sim (NS) 91; *Wildes v Davies* (1853) 1 Sm & G 475; *Edwards v Tuck* (1853) 3 De GM & G 40, 58.

[304] *Re Bourne's Settlement Trusts* [1946] 1 All ER 411, 415.

[305] *Bourne v Buckton, supra*; *Barrington v Liddell, supra*; *Morgan v Morgan* (1850) 4 De G & Sm 164; *Edwards v Tuck* (1853) 3 De GM & G 40.

(c) Provisions for accumulations of the produce of timber or wood.[306] They must be confined to the perpetuity period.[307]

(d) Where accumulations of surplus income are made during a minority under any statutory power or under the general law, the period for which such accumulations are made is not to be taken into account in determining the periods for which accumulations are permitted to be made under section 164 of the 1925 Act.[308] Under section 31 of the Trustee Act 1925, where any property is held in trust for a minor, the trustees have power to apply the income of that property for the maintenance, education, or benefit of the minor and, subject thereto, they are directed to accumulate the residue of that income.[309] The period during which such accumulation is made is disregarded for the purposes of determining any permissible period of accumulation. Thus, accumulation may be directed for a period of 21 years after a testator's death and, if the beneficiary is still a minor at the expiry of that period, accumulation may validly continue under section 31.[310] This has given rise to the practice of making a series of revocable appointments in favour of a succession of infant beneficiaries, thereby maximizing the available periods for accumulation.[311] On the other hand, although an express period may be combined with section 31 in this way, section 31 may also be excluded by a contrary intention manifested in the trust instrument.[312] Consequently, an express direction to accumulate income will amount to an exclusion of section 31 (at least for the duration of the expressly chosen period); and this will be the case even where such a direction is invalid as being in excess of one of the permitted accumulation periods: in such a case, the income will be treated as undisposed of.[313]

(e) None of these restrictions apply to bodies corporate, so that a company can direct or authorize trustees to accumulate income for any period not exceeding the perpetuity period applicable to the settlement, ie the original common law principle continues to operate.[314]

(f) Various commercial arrangements are also not subject to the rule, because they are not true settlements or dispositions within the meaning of the statute and are essentially contractual in nature. For example, unit trusts which capitalize

---

[306] Section 164(2)(iii).   [307] *Ferrand v Wilson* (1845) 4 Hare 344.

[308] Section 165 of the Law of Property Act 1925.

[309] For s 31 of the Trustee Act 1925, see paras 14.08–14.25 below.

[310] *Re Maber* [1928] Ch 88.

[311] Care must be taken, of course, not to commit a fraud on the power when making such revocable appointments: see generally Chapter 19 below.

[312] Section 69(2) of the Trustee Act 1925. See also *Re Turner's Will Trusts* [1937] Ch 15; *Re McGeorge* [1963] Ch 544; *Re Geering* [1964] Ch 136.

[313] *Re Ransome* [1957] Ch 348; *IRC v Bernstein* [1961] Ch 399; *Re Erskine's Settlement Trusts* [1971] 1 WLR 162.

[314] *Re Dodwell & Co's Trust* [1979] Ch 301; *Dinari Ltd v Hancock Prospecting Pty Ltd* [1972] 2 NSWLR 385.

part of their income;[315] the payment of premiums on a life insurance policy;[316] and partnership agreements which provide for accumulation of profits.[317]

8.97 Directions for keeping property in repair are also often included as exceptions to the rule, but it is doubtful whether there is a proper 'accumulation' in such cases, because the capital value is being maintained and not enhanced.[318] Similarly, the retention of income to meet a potential future income need is not necessarily an 'accumulation' in the technical sense, for example where surplus income of a trust fund is retained in order to meet a possible future shortfall in an annuity which was a continuing charge on the income of a trust fund.[319] Section 164 applies only to England and Wales.[320]

Application to powers

8.98 These principles apply equally to an appointment or advancement made in the exercise of a power conferred by the settlement. Moreover, the 'relation back' doctrine operates in relation to such an exercise for the purposes of the rule against excessive accumulations as it applies for the purposes of the rule against perpetuities. Consequently, if and in so far as a power of appointment or power of advancement seeks to make provision for the accumulation of the income of the appointed or advanced property, it can do so only for the unexpired portion (if any) of the accumulation period selected in, and for the purposes of, the original settlement by which the power is conferred and/or during the minority of any infant beneficiary (under section 31 of the Trustee Act 1925).

Application of the rule to occupational pension schemes

8.99 It is not entirely clear how the rule against excessive accumulations applies (if at all) to occupational pension schemes and any trust declared of death benefits arising under them.[321] A preliminary distinction must be drawn between (i) the accumulation of income of the trust fund of the scheme itself and (ii) the accumulation of the income of the death benefit under the express trusts declared by an appointment.

---

[315] *Re AEG Unit Trust (Manager's) Ltd's Deed* [1957] Ch 415. Another explanation is that all the unit holders could join together to end the accumulations.

[316] *Bassil v Lister* (1851) 9 Hare 177, 184 (doubted recently: *Carver v Duncan* [1985] AC 1082, 1100, *per* Oliver LJ). See also *Re Vaughan* [1883] WN 89; *Cathcart's Trustees v Heneage's Trustees* (1883) 10 R 1205.

[317] *Bassil v Lister, supra.*

[318] *Re Gardiner* [1901] 1 Ch 697, 699, 700; *Vine v Raleigh* [1891] 2 Ch 13; *Re Mason* [1891] 3 Ch 467. See also *Bassil v Lister* (1851) 9 Hare 177, 184.

[319] *Re Berkeley* [1968] Ch 744; *Vine v Raleigh* [1891] 2 Ch 13; *Re Earle* (1924) 131 LT 383; *Re Coller* [1939] Ch 277. It is sometimes referred to as '*de facto* accumulation'.

[320] Section 209(3) of the Law of Property Act 1925.

[321] See *Thomas* 178–183; (1995) *Private Client Business*, Issue 3, 223–232.

The income of the scheme itself

It is arguable, in the case of a non-contributory scheme, that it is the employing **8.100**
company that is the settlor and, accordingly, the statutory limits on accumulation
do not apply (under *Re Dodwell*).[322] However, if, as seems likely, the employer's
contributions represent the deferred or delayed remuneration of the employee, it
is the employee who is the settlor[323] and *Re Dodwell* will not apply. The mere
interposition of a company in the chain by which a settlement is effected will not
enable the statutory restrictions on accumulation to be avoided. 'In most cases it
will be an individual human being who, when you trace the provision of the funds
back, turns out to be the real settlor and then, of course, section 164 will apply in
all its ferocity.'[324]

An alternative analysis is that there is no 'accumulation' of income in the techni- **8.101**
cal sense. The mere retention of income does not alter its nature as income.[325]
Such retention is not an accumulation: it is analogous to the retention of money
against liabilities for repairs or breaches of covenants in leases; it is 'only *de facto*
accumulation caused by uncertainty as to the availability of assets'.[326] Support for
such an analysis in the context of an employee-benefit scheme may be derived
from *Re Saxone Shoe Co Ltd's Trust Deed*,[327] where Cross J held that the primary
object of the trust deed was to benefit the employees of the company and, in that
context, the relevant provision was a power to hold up income so that it could be
applied later for their benefit rather than a trust to accumulate surplus income for
the benefit of those interested in capital.

Also, as we have seen,[328] the statutory restrictions do not apply to commercial **8.102**
transactions, such as payments of premiums under insurance policies. As Turner
V-C pointed out, in *Bassil v Lister*,[329] the premiums became part of the general
funds of the insurance company and subject to its expenses; and the estate did not
receive back any accumulations of income, but a sum payable by the insurance
company under a contract with the testator, and such a sum was not an accumulation within the meaning of the statute. (It does not follow, of course, that the
rule is inapplicable when the policy itself or its proceeds are settled: in that case,
the rule applies as to any other property.)

It is sometimes argued that the members of a pension scheme are essentially **8.103**
investors in a unit trust, to which section 164 of the 1925 Act has been held to

---

[322] *Re Dodwell & Co's Trusts* [1979] Ch 301.   [323] See para 8.73 above.
[324] *Re Dodwell & Co's Trusts* [1979] Ch 301, 311.   [325] See para 8.97 above.
[326] *Re Berkeley* [1968] Ch 744, 776 (*per* Russell LJ); see also at 772 (*per* Harman LJ), and 780 (*per*
Widgery LJ); *Vine v Raleigh* [1891] 2 Ch 13; *Re Earle* (1924) 131 LT 383; *Re Coller* [1939] Ch 277.
[327] [1962] 1 WLR 943.   [328] See para 8.96 above.
[329] (1851) 9 Hare 177. See also *Re Vaughan* [1883] WN 89; *Cathcart's Trustees v Heneage's Trustees*
(1883) 10 R 1205; *Bassil v Lister* has been doubted recently: *Carver v Duncan* [1985] AC 1082,
1100, *per* Oliver LJ.

have no application.[330] However, members of a unit trust usually have power to control its management and, if acting unanimously, even to terminate the unit trust. Members of an occupational pension scheme have no such power. The analogy is therefore a weak one.

8.104   The better view, it is suggested, is that the retention of monies by the trustees of an occupational pension scheme is precisely that, a mere retention pending its application, and not an accumulation in the strict sense, with the result that section 164 of the 1925 Act does not apply.[331]

The income of the death benefit

8.105   On the other hand, where express trusts are declared in respect of the death benefit, and the accumulation of income is then directed or authorized, it is difficult to see how section 164 could fail to apply. The material questions at this stage are similar to those which arise in the context of the rule against perpetuities: what is the maximum period available for the accumulation of income of the death benefit (whether the period is expressly chosen or has to be implied)? And when does that period commence?

8.106   None of the six periods listed in section 164 seems appropriate: some of them clearly cannot apply at all; and the application of others is either uncertain and ambiguous or seems to be of little value.[332] Period (a) (life of the settlor) clearly cannot apply. Period (b) (21 years from the death of the settlor) is often chosen, but it is not clear that it is available. It undoubtedly applies to a testamentary disposition (which an appointment of a death benefit is not), but it also seems capable of applying to some lifetime dispositions as well.[333] However, period (b) seems to require a single settlor or testator. The deceased member would almost certainly be the 'settlor' or 'disponor' to the extent of his own contributions to the scheme; and, if the employer's contributions are properly regarded as deferred remuneration, probably also of those contributions too. Nevertheless, although the member is *a* settlor in relation to the death benefit, he may not be *the sole* settlor. The fund of the pension scheme, out of which the death benefit is carved, will have been constituted, in theory, by means of the contributions of all past and present members of the scheme, all of whom could equally be described as 'settlors'.[334]

---

[330] *Re AEG Unit Trust (Managers) Deed* [1957] Ch 415. See also HC Deb vol 697, col 1499 (1 July 1964).

[331] See Law Com No 133, para 3.32; and Law Com No 251, para 10.5.

[332] See *Thomas* 179–183 for a more detailed analysis.

[333] *Re Cattell* [1914] Ch 177, 186.

[334] *Bassil v Lister* (1851) 9 Hare 177; *Re Pocock's Policy* (1871) 6 Ch App 445; *Re Maclean's Trusts* (1874) LR 19 Eq 274; *Re William Phillips Insurance* (1883) 23 Ch D 235; *Urquhart v Butterfield* (1887) 37 Ch D 357; *Re Meadows (Thomas) & Co Ltd and Subsidiary Companies (1960) Staff Pension Scheme Rules* [1971] 1 Ch 278, 284C–E and 285D–E.

Moreover, there is no obvious mathematical correlation between the death benefit and the contribution of the deceased member. The scheme's funds are usually not unitized; and contributions are therefore not converted into a specific number of 'units' as and when they are made. If this is the correct analysis, it may well be the case that period (b) is not available in these circumstances.

On the other hand, it may be said that, as soon as an individual becomes a mem- **8.107** ber of the scheme and begins to pay contributions, he acquires various rights, including a right, if the relevant events occur and a death benefit becomes payable, to have that death benefit appointed or dealt with by the trustees of the scheme. It is difficult to see how the death benefit differs from the proceeds of an insurance policy, the benefit of which may never become payable but which, nonetheless, is capable of being settled (including on discretionary trusts).[335] In neither case is there an obvious mathematical correlation between the amount of the premiums or contributions paid and the proceeds or benefits produced on the happening (if at all) of the relevant contingency. On this analysis, the relevant disposition for the purposes of section 164 takes place when a member first joins the scheme. Thus, period (e) (21 years from the date of the disposition), if available, is not likely to be of much use. Similarly, periods (c), (d), and (f) (the duration of the minority of certain classes of persons),[336] would also be of little use in practice.

Consequently, when an appointment of a death benefit declares trusts which **8.108** include a direction or power to accumulate income, it would seem that period (b) may be available, subject to certain uncertainties, but that the only safe period available in practice—and possibly the only period available at all—is that permitted by section 31 of the Trustee Act 1925 or under the general law, namely during the infancy of the appointed beneficiaries.

Accumulation to purchase land

Section 166 of the Law of Property Act 1925 provides: **8.109**

> (1) No person may settle or dispose of any property in such manner that the income thereof shall be wholly or partially accumulated for the purchase of land[337] only, for any longer period than the duration of the minority or respective minorities of any person or persons who, under the limitations of the instrument directing the accumulation, would for the time being, if of full age, be entitled to the income so directed to be accumulated.[338]
> (2) This section does not, nor do the enactments which it replaces, apply to accumulations to be held as capital money for the purposes of the Settled Land Act 1925, or the enactments replaced by that Act, whether or not the accumulations are primarily liable to be laid out in the purchase of land.

---

[335] *Re Kilpatrick's Policies Trusts* [1966] Ch 730.   [336] See para 8.89 above.
[337] See s 205(1)(ix) of the Law of Property Act 1925; and *Re Clutterbuck* [1901] 2 Ch 285.
[338] See para 8.89 above for s 164(1)(d).

(3) This section applies to settlements and dispositions made after the 27 June, 1892.

Proposals for reform

8.110   The Law Commission has recently recommended that the statutory restrictions on accumulations should be repealed (subject to an exception in relation to charitable trusts), but only in relation to instruments taking effect after any legislation was brought into force.[339] The maximum period for accumulation will then be commensurate with the proposed new perpetuity period, ie 125 years.

8.111   As an exceptional case, in which abolition would have retrospective effect, it is proposed that special powers of appointment which were created before such legislation was brought into force, but which were exercised thereafter, should be subject to the new and not the old law. For these purposes, therefore, the exercise of a special power of appointment would be regarded as an instrument taking effect *after* any legislation was brought into force, even though the power was created before that date.[340] This is a radical proposal, for it authorizes appointments which will enable accumulation of income to continue well beyond the period applicable to the original settlement or to permit accumulation to recommence after the original period has expired. This might well run counter to the settlor's wishes; it could result in an alteration of entitlements under the settlement; and it might also lead to undesirable and unforeseen fiscal disadvantages. Although elsewhere in the Draft Bill special powers of appointment are referred to separately from a power of advancement or a nomination under a pension scheme,[341] it is intended, presumably, that, in this context, a 'power of appointment' includes a power of advancement and a nomination under such a scheme.[342] However, the difficulties outlined earlier in this section in relation to appointments of 'death benefits' under pension schemes will cease to arise if these proposal are enacted.

---

[339] Law Com No 251, 128–131 (paras 10.15–10.21) and 146 (Clause 13 of the Draft Bill).
[340] ibid, 129 (para 10.16) and 150 (Clause 15(1) of the Draft Bill).
[341] See, for example, Clause 6 at 142.
[342] See Clause 20(3) at 150. Also, the word 'transfer' is presumably intended to include 'create'.

9

TRUSTS AND INSOLVENCY

A. Protective Trusts

Introduction

An interest to which a beneficiary is *absolutely* entitled under a trust cannot be **9.01**
made inalienable and any attempt to make it so is repugnant and void.[1] Nor is it
possible to impose a condition or proviso that the beneficiary's interest shall not
be subject to the claims of creditors in the event of his insolvency:[2] the interest
(whether absolute or limited) will vest in his trustee in bankruptcy. It is, of course,
a question of construction of the trust instrument in each case whether the

---

[1] *Hunt-Foulston v Furber* (1876) 3 Ch D 285; *Re Dugdale* (1888) 38 Ch D 176; *Re Mabbett*
[1891] 1 Ch 707. See also *Re Rosher* (1884) 26 Ch D 801; *Re Ashton* [1920] 2 Ch 481; *Re Cockerill*
[1929] 2 Ch 131; *Re Brown* [1954] Ch 39; *Re Wenger's Settlement* (1963) 107 SJ 981. A contractual
term attempting to impose a total restraint on alienation is also void: *Hall v Busst* (1960) 104 CLR
106. A few (much-criticized) partial restraints were held valid: *Re Macleay* (1875) LR 20 Eq 186. Cf
Re Rosher (1884) 26 Ch D 801; *Re Brown* [1954] Ch 39.
[2] *Brandon v Robinson* (1811) 18 Ves 429; *Graves v Dolphin* (1826) 1 Sim 66; *Green v Spicer*
(1830) 1 Russ & M 395; *Snowdon v Dales* (1834) 6 Sim 524; *Younghusband v Gisborne* (1844) 1 Coll
400, (1846) 15 LJ Ch 355.

beneficiary has a vested interest or is simply the object of the trustees' discretion.[3] The test, it seems, is whether the executors of the beneficiary, if he were dead, would have a right to demand the payment of any arrears of income from the trustees. If so, the beneficiary has a vested interest in such income and his creditors are prospectively entitled to future payments.[4]

9.02 Nevertheless, a beneficiary's interest may be made *determinable* upon his bankruptcy or on the occurrence of some other event. Also, he may simply be made an object of a discretionary trust, thereby ensuring that he has no interest as such which could vest in a trustee in bankruptcy.

Determinable interests

9.03 A determinable interest is one which will automatically determine on the occurrence of some specified event which may never occur.[5] Such an interest is typically created by the use of words such as 'until', 'during', and 'as long as'. The determining event itself limits the interest created.[6] It must be distinguished from an interest subject to a condition subsequent, where the condition is an independent forfeiture provision which is added to an absolute interest and merely confers a right to enter and determine the interest when the specified event occurs: the interest continues unless and until entry is made.[7] Such an interest is typically created by the use of words such as 'but if', 'on condition that', or 'provided that'. At common law, the implications and consequences of creating an interest subject to a condition subsequent could differ appreciably from those arising from the creation of a determinable interest.[8] One of the more important was that, because the operation of a condition subsequent effected a forfeiture of an estate or interest, the law treated them more strictly (for example by requiring precise wording)[9] than determinable interests. These differences were adopted by equity; and, when

---

[3] In several decisions, mostly from the early 19th century, the beneficiary was held to have a vested interest despite the presence of words which conferred a discretion on the trustees: see, for example, *Graves v Dolphin* (1826) 1 Sim 66; *Green v Spicer, supra*; *Piercy v Roberts* (1832) 1 Myl & K 4; *Snowdon v Dales, supra*; *Younghusband v Gisborne, supra*; *Re Johnston* [1894] 3 Ch 204; *Re Nelson* (1916), reported in [1928] Ch 920n; *Re Smith* [1928] Ch 915.

[4] *Re Sanderson's Trusts* (1857) 3 K & J 497.

[5] *Mary Portington's Case* (1613) 10 Co Rep 35b and 41b. This is based on the ancient principle that every fee may possibly last forever, so that, if the event is bound to happen, the estate could not be a determinable fee.

[6] *Morley v Rennoldson* (1843) 2 Hare 570, 580; *Re Leach* [1912] 2 Ch 422.

[7] *Matthew Manning's Case* (1609) 8 Co Rep 94b and 95b; *Re Evans's Contract* [1920] 2 Ch 469, 472.

[8] For example, in relation to the rule against perpetuities, a right of entry was void if it might possibly arise at too remote a date, in which case the right was void and the interest became absolute, whereas the possibility of reverter following a determinable interest was not subject to the rule at all. The position has now been altered by statute: see para 8.35 above.

[9] See, for example, *Clavering v Ellison* (1859) 7 HLC 707; *Sifton v Sifton* [1938] AC 656; *Clayton v Ramsden* [1943] AC 320; *Re Gape* [1952] Ch 743; *Re Tarnpolsk* [1958] 1 WLR 1157; *Re Krawitz* [1959] 1 WLR 1192.

it became possible to create equitable estates and interests of both kinds, the advantages of determinable interests were reaffirmed.[10] Although, in *Re Leach*,[11] the interest in question was a determinable fee simple, the decision was criticised[12] and it is now general practice to create determinable *life* interests only.

Express protective trusts

A person cannot settle his own property[13] on *himself* until bankruptcy.[14] **9.04** However, this rule—which is probably based on public policy—applies only to *bankruptcy* and only for the benefit of the trustee in bankruptcy acting on behalf of the general creditors. A determining event other than bankruptcy, even though created by the settlor to protect his own interest, is effective and will serve to defeat the claim of an individual creditor. Thus, in *Re Detmold*,[15] for example, the settlor had a life interest which was determinable if he 'shall become bankrupt, or shall do or suffer something whereby [the income], or some part thereof, would . . . by operation or process of law, if belonging absolutely to him, become vested in or payable to some other person'; and, if such determination occurred, the income was payable to his wife. In the event, an order was made appointing a judgment creditor of the settlor as receiver of the income; and, subsequently, the settlor was adjudicated bankrupt. North J held that the income was payable to the settlor's wife: the settlor's entitlement to income had ceased before his bankruptcy, when the receiver was appointed.[16] There was a limited exception to this strict principle in the case of a marriage settlement under which the husband settled property on himself for life or until his bankruptcy, with remainder to his wife, in which case the husband's interest would vest in his trustee in bankruptcy only to the extent that his contribution to the settlement exceeded that of his wife.[17] However, this exception applies only where the wife's contribution on the marriage was not also settled so as to give her a protected life interest and only where her contribution is of definite property free of conditions or contingencies. In effect, this is a case where the settlement, though ostensibly created by the husband, was regarded as one created (at least in part) with property provided by the wife. How far the

---

[10] *Re Leach* [1912] 2 Ch 422. See also (1917) 33 LQR 14 (Jenks) and 236 (C Sweet).
[11] [1912] 2 Ch 422.
[12] (1917) 33 LQR 236, 241 (C Sweet).
[13] *Re Holland* [1902] 2 Ch 360.
[14] *Knight v Browne* (1861) 7 Jur NS 894; *Brooke v Pearson* (1859) 27 Beav 181; *Re Burroughs-Fowler* [1916] 2 Ch 251; *Re Wombwell* (1921) 125 LT 437. This principle even applies to marriage settlements: *Higinbotham v Holme* (1812) 19 Ves 88; *Ex p Hodgson* (1812) 19 Ves 206; *Re Pearson* (1876) 3 Ch D 807.
[15] (1889) 40 Ch D 585. See also *Re Johnson* [1904] 1 KB 134; *Re Perkin's Settlement Trusts* [1912] WN 99; *Re Balfour's Settlement* [1938] Ch 928.
[16] [1938] Ch 928.
[17] *Ex p Hodgson* (1812) 19 Ves 206; *Lester v Garland* (1832) 5 Sim 205; *Mackintosh v Pogose* [1895] Ch 505.

exception could apply beyond marriage settlements generally to cases where valuable consideration of the right kind has been given is hard to say: for example, it has been held not to apply to a partnership agreement which provided for the forfeiture of a partner's interest upon his bankruptcy.[18]

9.05 There is no objection, however, to one person settling property until the bankruptcy of another. Indeed, a beneficiary's life interest may be limited so as to be determinable not just on his bankruptcy but also on any attempt by the beneficiary to alienate his interest. Such provisions are strictly construed and their scope will depend on the words used. Thus, an interest made determinable on 'alienation' will generally be determined only by a disposition by the act of the party and will not be affected by bankruptcy or by a transfer by operation of law;[19] and the words 'until he attempts . . . to become bankrupt' have been held not to apply to bankruptcy generally, and not to have occurred on the appointment of a receiver on a creditor's petition.[20] Nor, in the absence of a clear indication to the contrary, will past, as opposed to future, acts and omissions cause a determination of the interest;[21] and 'attempting' to assign, as opposed to an actual assignment, will not necessarily cause a forfeiture.[22] On the other hand, an alienation of part of the income has been held to cause a forfeiture, even though an express reference to 'any part thereof' was not included.[23] Consequently, it has become standard practice to adopt wide words: for example, by settling property on A 'until he shall assign charge or otherwise dispose of the same or some part thereof or become bankrupt . . . or do something whereby the said annual income or some part thereof would become payable to or vested in some other person';[24] or 'until he . . . does or attempts to do or suffers any act or thing, or until any event happens . . . whereby, if the said income were payable during the trust period to the principal beneficiary absolutely during that period, he would be deprived of the right to receive the same or any part thereof'.[25] Thus, where determinable interests are framed in such wide terms, the relevant protected life interest will be forfeited

---

[18] *Whitmore v Mason* (1861) 2 J & H 204.

[19] *Wilkinson v Wilkinson* (1819) 3 Swans 515; *Lear v Leggatt* (1829) 2 Sim 479; (1829) 1 Russ & My 690; *Whitfield v Prickett* (1838) 2 Keen 608. Cf *Cooper v Wyatt* (1821) 5 Madd 482; *Ex p Eyston* (1877) 7 Ch D 145.

[20] *Re Evans* [1920] 2 Ch 304. For other examples, see *Re Griffiths* [1926] Ch 1007; *Ex p Lovell* [1901] 2 KB 16; *Re Amherst's Trusts* (1872) LR 13 Eq 464; *Ex p Dawes* (1866) 17 QBD 275.

[21] *West v Williams* [1899] 1 Ch 132, 148.

[22] cf *Re Wormald* (1890) 43 Ch D 630; *Re Adamson* (1913) 29 TLR 594. Cf *Re Porter* [1892] 3 Ch 481.

[23] *Re Dennis's Settlement Trusts* [1942] Ch 283; *Re Haynes' Will Trusts* [1949] Ch 5.

[24] *Re Leach, supra.* See also *Billson v Crofts* (1873) LR 15 Eq 314; *Re Aylwin's Trusts* (1873) LR 16 Eq 585; *Re Jenkins* [1915] 1 Ch 46; *Re Longman* [1955] 1 WLR 197.

[25] Trustee Act 1925, s 33(1)(i).

- in the event of bankruptcy;[26]
- when a receiver of the income is appointed;[27]
- when the trustees assert their right to impound the income following a breach of trust by the beneficiary;[28]
- where the interest is subjected to a sequestration order;[29]
- where the income is redirected under a family arrangement;[30]
- where an attempt is made to surrender the life interest in a tax-saving scheme;[31]
- when an equitable charge is created by a maintenance order;[32]
- when an attachment of earnings order is made to secure a former wife's maintenance;[33]
- where the principal beneficiary became an 'enemy' for the purposes of the Trading with the Enemy Act 1939.[34]

On the occurrence of any of the specified events, A's interest would determine; but if none of them occurred before he died, the estate would then become absolute.[35]

On the other hand, it has been held that there was no forfeiture

- when the life tenant appointed trustees as his attorneys to receive trust income and pay management expenses;[36]
- where a beneficiary went abroad and appointed an attorney to receive income and apply it for his benefit;[37]

---

[26] *Re Scientific Investment Pension Plan Trusts* [1999] Ch 58; *Trappes v Meredith* (1871) 7 Ch App 248; *Metcalfe v Metcalfe* (1889) 43 Ch D 633; *Re Evans* [1920] 2 Ch 304. There is a forfeiture even if the clause looks to the future. Also, a discharge from bankruptcy, unlike an annulment, does not re-vest the interest in the beneficiary: *Re Walker* [1939] Ch 974.

[27] *Re Detmold* (1889) 40 Ch D 585.   [28] *Re Balfour's Settlement* [1938] Ch 928.

[29] *Re Baring's Settlement Trusts* [1940] Ch 737. The other person need not take a proprietary interest in the income. However, if the forfeiture clause is narrower and applies only when the income becomes 'vested in or charged in favour of' another, it seems there is no forfeiture unless the person to whom the income is payable acquires a proprietary interest in it: see *Lewin* 150–151; *Re Gourju's Will Trusts* [1943] Ch 24; *Re Wightman* [1947] 2 All ER 647n; *Re Pozot's Settlement Trusts* [1952] Ch 427.

[30] *Re Dennis's Settlement Trusts* [1942] Ch 283. See also *Re Smith's Will Trusts* (1981) 131 NLJ 292.

[31] *Gibbon v Mitchell* [1990] 1 WLR 1304.

[32] *Hurst v Hurst* (1882) 21 Ch D 278; *Re Richardson's Will Trusts* [1958] Ch 504. However, see *General Accident Fire and Life Assurance Corporation Ltd v IRC* [1963] 1 WLR 1207 and para 9.09 below.

[33] *Edmonds v Edmonds* [1965] 1 All ER 379n.

[34] *Re Gourju's Will Trusts* [1943] Ch 24; *Re Wittke* [1944] Ch 166. Cf *Re Hall* [1944] Ch 46; *Re Harris* [1945] Ch 316 (the last two cases involving express, and not the statutory, trusts).

[35] ibid 429. See also *Rochford v Hackman* (1852) 9 Hare 475.

[36] *Re Tancred's Settlement* [1903] 1 Ch 715 (which must be doubtful: merely appointing an attorney should not be problematic, but there was also an assignment of the interest here). See also *Croft v Lumley* (1858) 6 HL Cas 781; *Alvison v Holmes* (1861) 1 J & H 530; *Re Kelly's Settlement* (1889) 59 LT 494.

[37] *Re Swannell* (1909) 101 LT 76.

- where trustees are directed to pay a debt out of income already accrued and due to the beneficiary;[38]
- where the life tenant was certified as a person of unsound mind and a statutory receiver was appointed;[39]
- where an order was made under section 57 of the Trustee Act 1925 authorizing trustees to raise money to enable the tenant for life to pay 'certain pressing liabilities';[40]
- where the life interest is assigned to trustees for the benefit of the assignor;[41]
- where the beneficiary received a capital sum to pay his debts and agreed to repay it by means of a policy, the premiums for which he paid out of his own resources and not out of trust income.[42]

9.06   An assignment by the beneficiary of arrears of income already accrued and payable to him, but not of future income, is effective and will generally not determine his interest.[43] Indeed, it would be somewhat pointless if it were otherwise, for the beneficiary, once he had received the income, would be free to dispose of it as he saw fit in any event. An assignment made expressly subject to a restriction or condition against alienation, or declared to have effect only so far as the beneficiary could assign, will not necessarily cause a forfeiture: such an assignment has no effect at all or only to the extent authorized.[44]

9.07   Where there is provision for the determination of the interest if the income 'would' become vested in another, there is a forfeiture as soon as an immediate right to any income is given, even if the right is revoked before any income actually arises.[45] On the other hand, it has also been held that, where a beneficiary authorized his trustees to pay money out of future dividends and the company in question did not declare a dividend, there was no forfeiture: the authority was 'completely nugatory' and there was nothing on which it could operate.[46]

---

[38]   *Dunan v Dunan* (1904) 91 LT 819; *Re Mair* [1909] 2 Ch 280.

[39]   *Re Oppenheim's Will Trusts* [1950] Ch 633. See also *Re Westby's Settlement* [1950] Ch 296; Mental Health Act 1983, s 106(6).

[40]   *Re Mair* [1935] Ch 562. That which is authorized by an order under s 57 is deemed to have been inserted in the trust instrument as an overriding power. However, the authorized scheme may still include some provision which could lead, in future, to the tenant for life committing some act which results in a forfeiture: ibid 565; and *Re Salting* [1932] 2 Ch 57.

[41]   *Lockwood v Sikes* (1884) 51 LT 562.   [42]   *Re Salting* [1932] Ch 57.

[43]   *Re Stulz's Trusts* (1853) 4 De GM & G 404; *Cox v Bockett* (1865) 35 Beav 48; *Hurst v Hurst* (1882) 21 Ch D 278; *Re Richardson's Will Trusts* [1958] Ch 504.

[44]   *Samuel v Samuel* (1879) 12 Ch D 152 (where Jessel MR summed up such a provision thus: 'I charge if I can charge, and I do not if I cannot charge'); and *Re Stulz's Trusts, supra*.

[45]   *Re Baker* [1904] 1 Ch 157.

[46]   *Re Longman* [1955] 1 WLR 197. This is confined to an assignment of specific income which never arises.

If the determining event requires the beneficiary to do, permit, or suffer something, there will not be a forfeiture if the income becomes payable to another as a result of an act or event beyond his control.[47]   **9.08**

The effect of a court order, made in matrimonial proceedings,[48] on a protected life   **9.09**
interest under a marriage settlement is uncertain. In *Re Richardson's Will Trusts*,[49]
where the court ordered the principal beneficiary to charge his interest with an
annual payment to his divorced wife, the charge was held to have effected a forfeiture. However, in *General Accident Fire and Life Assurance Corporation Ltd v
IRC*,[50] a forfeiture was held not to have occurred as a result of an order directing
payment of part of the beneficiary's income to a former wife. Although
Re Richardson was not referred to in *General Accident*, another case which had
reached the same conclusion in favour of forfeiture, *Re Carew*,[51] was overruled.
Despite attempts to differentiate between these two decisions on grounds of construction of section 33 of the Trustee Act 1925,[52] they are difficult to distinguish.
It is not plausible to suggest, as Donovan LJ did in *General Accident*,[53] that forfeiture should not occur because section 33 was intended simply 'as a protection to
spendthrift or improvident or weak life tenants', unless it is intended to include
protection against the consequences of divorce as well as against financial imprudence. A charge on a protected life interest, whether pursuant to a court order in
matrimonial proceedings or not, clearly ought to effect a forfeiture under the general law, so a specific reason is required to justify why this does not happen. One
explanation is that a protective trust is, throughout, 'potentially subject in all its
trusts to such an order' as might be made in matrimonial proceedings.[54] Another
is that, in *General Accident*, unlike *Re Richardson*, the court was varying the trusts
of the settlement and not simply charging the beneficiary's interest. Either of these
explanations would place *General Accident* in the same category as the cases dealing with the effects of section 57.[55]

Statutory protective trusts

The need for some form of protection for the beneficiaries of settled property, and   **9.10**
particularly against the profligacy and even bankruptcy of the principal
beneficiary, was met by a statutory form of protective trusts in section 33 of the
Trustee Act 1925.[56] This relates to the income of trust property and is based on a

---

[47] *Re Hall* [1944] Ch 46; *Re Harris* [1945] Ch 316. Cf the wider wording of s 33(1) of the Trustee
Act 1925: para 9.12 below.
[48] Matrimonial Causes Act 1973, s 24(1).   [49] [1958] Ch 504.
[50] [1963] 1 WLR 1207.   [51] (1910) 103 LT 658.
[52] ibid, 1217 and 1221. See also (1963) 27 Conv (NS) 517 (FR Crane).
[53] [1963] 1 WLR 1207, 1218.
[54] As suggested by Russell LJ at 1222, although he refrained from basing his decision on this
ground.
[55] See para 9.05 above.   [56] (1957) 21 Conv (NS) 110 (L Sheridan).

combination of (a) a determinable life interest and (b) a discretionary trust in favour of the specified classes of objects. The broad effect is that, if one of the specified determining events happens, the life interest is determined and the statutory discretionary trusts spring into operation instead.[57] Section 33 provides the settlor with a simple shorthand mechanism by which to create a wide form of protective trusts by implication: he need only declare that the property is to be held 'on protective trusts' or, indeed, use any words which make the same intention clear,[58] although he can, by express provision in the trust instrument, vary the trusts otherwise implied by the section.[59] Section 33 provides:

(1) Where any income,[60] including an annuity or other periodical income payment, is directed to be held on protective trusts for the benefit of any person[61] (in this section called 'the principal beneficiary') for the period of his life or for any less period, then, during that period (in this section called 'the trust period') the said income shall, without prejudice to any prior interest, be held on the following trusts, namely:—

(i) Upon trust for the principal beneficiary during the trust period or until he, whether before or after the termination of any prior interest, does or attempts to do or suffers any act or thing, or until any event happens,[62] other than an advance under any statutory or express power,[63] whereby, if the said income were payable during the trust period to the principal beneficiary absolutely during that period, he would be deprived of the right to receive the same[64] or any part thereof, in any of which cases, as well as on the termination of the trust period, whichever first happens, this trust of the said income shall fail or determine;

(ii) If the trust aforesaid fails or determines during the subsistence of the trust period, then, during the residue of that period, the said income shall be held upon trust for the application thereof for the maintenance or support, or otherwise for the benefit, of all or any one or more exclusively of the other or others of the following persons (that is to say)—

(a) the principal beneficiary and his wife or husband, if any, and his or her children or more remote issue, if any, or

(b) if there is no wife or husband or issue of the principal beneficiary in existence, the principal beneficiary and the persons who would, if he were

---

[57] *Re Allsopp's Marriage Settlement Trusts* [1959] Ch 81.

[58] *Re Wittke* [1944] Ch 166 ('upon protective trusts for the benefit of my sister'); *Re Platt* [1950] CLY 4386 ('for protective life interests').

[59] Section 33(2).

[60] Including income distributed under a discretionary trust: *Re Isaacs* (1948) 92 SJ 336.

[61] Meaning 'natural persons' only and not companies: *IRC v Brandenburg* [1982] STC 555.

[62] The principal beneficiary need not be responsible for the occurrence of the event: *Re Hall* [1944] Ch 46; *Re Pozot's Settlement Trust* [1952] Ch 427.

[63] The giving of consent by the principal beneficiary to the making of an advance does not cause a forfeiture: *Re Rees* [1954] Ch 202; *Re Haris's Settlement* (1940) 162 LT 358. See also *Re Hodgson* [1913] 1 Ch 34; *Re Stimpson's Settlement* [1931] 2 Ch 77; *Re Shaw's Settlement* [1951] Ch 833.

[64] Meaning 'deprived of the right to receive the same on the day it becomes due': *Re Greenwood* [1901] Ch 887, 891; *Re Westby's Settlement* [1950] Ch 296.

actually dead, be entitled to the trust property or the income thereof or the annuity fund, if any, or arrears of the annuity, as the case may be;

as the trustees in their absolute discretion, without being liable to account for the exercise of such discretion, think fit.

(2) This section does not apply to trusts coming into operation before the commencement of this Act, and has effect subject to any variation of the implied trusts aforesaid contained in the instrument creating the trust.

(3) Nothing in this section operates to validate any trust which would, if contained in the instrument creating the trust, be liable to be set aside.

(4) In relation to the dispositions mentioned in section 19(1) of the Family Law Reform Act 1987, this section shall have effect as if any reference (however expressed) to any relationship between two persons were construed in accordance with section 1 of that Act.

Application of income

The trustees are bound to apply income for the stated purposes and have no power **9.11** under section 33 to accumulate or otherwise deal with it.[65] There is no apportionment of income by reference to the date of forfeiture: income received after that date is applicable under the discretionary trusts.[66] However, there is apportionment at the death, so that the trustees must apply, under the discretionary trusts of section 33(1)(ii), not only such income as they have already received but not yet applied but also income apportioned to the period before death.[67] The trustees must cease to pay income to the principal beneficiary as soon as they have notice of forfeiture, but they are not liable for continuing to do so before they have such notice.[68] The extent to which the trustees can properly apply income for the benefit of a bankrupt principal beneficiary after his interest has determined and he has become an object of the discretionary trusts is discussed below.

Determining events

In broad terms, the nature of the events and circumstances that will cause a pro- **9.12** tected life interest to determine under section 33 are the same as those already discussed in relation to expressly created determinable life interests.[69] One important consideration is that the extent and effect of expressly created trusts may be more limited than is the case with section 33, the wording of which is very wide.[70] For example, under section 33, a protected life interest may determine before the termination of a prior interest, which is unusual in an express protective trust. Also, as we have seen,[71] an express trust may require the beneficiary to 'do, permit, or suffer' something before his interest will determine, in which case

---

[65] *Re Gourju's Will Trusts* [1943] Ch 24.   [66] ibid.
[67] *Re Forster's Settlement* [1942] Ch 199; *Re Locker's Settlement* [1977] Ch 1323.
[68] *Re Long* [1901] WN 166.   [69] See para 9.03 above.
[70] *Re Pozot's Settlement* [1952] Ch 427, 446.   [71] See para 9.04 above.

there will not be a forfeiture if the income becomes payable to another as a result of an act or event beyond his control.[72] In contrast, section 33(1)(i) applies when 'any event happens', which may be beyond the principal beneficiary's control. On the other hand, section 33 itself may be varied in the trust instrument, and it is therefore a question, in each case, of construing the terms of the settlement.

Discretionary trusts following forfeiture

9.13 Upon the determination of the protected life interest, the statutory discretionary trusts specified in section 33(1)(ii) come into operation; and the trustees must apply the income 'for the maintenance or support, or otherwise for the benefit' of all or any one or more exclusively of the other or others of the persons comprised in the relevant class of objects. The class includes the principal beneficiary himself. The nature of the rights of a mere object of a discretionary trust are discussed more fully elsewhere.[73] For present purposes, it is sufficient to recall that such an object has no title in or right to any trust income: he simply has a right to require, and if necessary compel, the trustees to consider exercising their discretion from time to time, and a mere hope or expectancy (a *spes*) that the trustees will actually exercise it in his favour. A voluntary assignment of a mere expectancy is not valid and enforceable; and, in such a case, the trustees, in exercising their discretion, can properly pay money or transfer property to, and would receive a good discharge from, the 'assignor', notwithstanding that they have notice of the voluntary 'assignment'.[74] On the other hand, the object can assign his *spes* for value. Unless and until the trustees exercise their discretion in favour of that object, his assignee or creditor will be entitled to none of the income.[75] However, if there is an assignment for value, the object's assignee becomes entitled to any income which the trustees decide to pay to the object and any goods which they have appropriated to him,[76] and the trustees will be liable to the assignee if they pay the income or deliver the goods to the assignor after receiving notice of the assignment.[77]

9.14 This raises a difficult question of whether, or to what extent, the trustees can properly exercise their discretion in favour of an object who has assigned his *spes* or become bankrupt (as would have happened to the principal beneficiary under a protective trust). His bankruptcy or act of assignment clearly does not disqualify him from being a member of the class of objects: indeed, section 33(1)(ii) explicitly includes him in the class. The trustees' discretion is not terminated or suspended

---

[72] *Re Hall* [1944] Ch 46; *Re Harris* [1945] Ch 316. Cf the wider wording of s 33(1) of the Trustee Act 1925.

[73] See paras 7.20–7.27 and 7.37–7.38 above.

[74] cf *Public Trustee v Ferguson* [1947] NZLR 9.

[75] *Twopenny v Peyton* (1840) 10 Sim 487; *Holmes v Penney* (1856) 3 K & J 90.

[76] *Re Coleman* (1888) 39 Ch D 443; *Tailby v Official Receiver* (1888) 13 App Cas 523; *Re Ellenborough* [1903] 1 Ch 697, 700.

[77] *Re Neil* (1890) 62 LT 649.

and they are clearly authorized to apply income for his benefit.[78] Although, in the context of bankruptcy, there seems to be no compelling reason why discretionary payments of income to a bankrupt object should not be 'property' vesting in his trustee in bankruptcy,[79] statute provides that the bankrupt's income may not be reduced below what is required for his and his family's reasonable domestic needs.[80] This seems to be a statutory recognition of what was formerly (and, outside the context of bankruptcy, presumably still is) acknowledged under the general law, ie that, despite assignment or bankruptcy, payments could still properly be made to a beneficiary for what he needed for his maintenance and support[81] (and he would have to account to his assignee or creditors only for any surplus above such amounts). As Cotton LJ stated, in *Re Coleman*,[82] any such assignment by the object does not catch everything that the trustees might give to him:

> If the trustees were to pay an hotel-keeper to give him a dinner he would get nothing but the right to eat a dinner, and that is not property which could pass by assignment or bankruptcy. But if they pay or deliver money or goods to him, or appropriate money or goods to be paid or delivered to him, the money or goods would pass by the assignment.

There remains some uncertainty as to the extent to which the trustees can properly pay or apply income to or for the benefit of an object who has assigned his rights or become bankrupt. Nevertheless, it is generally considered to be entirely proper for discretionary trustees to pay income directly to the object for his and his family's maintenance or basic needs. It would also be proper to apply income for his benefit indirectly, for example by paying it to his or her spouse, provided the recipient is a proper object of the trustees' discretion (which is usually the case)[83] and that any such payments are not subject to conditions.

The assignee, creditor, or trustee in bankruptcy does not become a member of the class of objects and remains a stranger in relation to the trustees' discretion. Therefore, any payment by the trustees directly to such assignee, creditor, or trustee in bankruptcy may be excessive and void,[84] although the terms of the discretion may be sufficiently wide to authorize payment to a third party if and in so far as such payment can be said to be of benefit to the object himself.[85] The rights of an assignee or creditor cannot be greater than those of the object himself:[86] **9.15**

---

[78] *Chambers v Smith* (1878) 3 App Cas 795; *Re Bullock* (1891) 64 LT 736; *Re Coleman, supra.*
[79] Insolvency Act 1986, ss 306, 436; *Re Landau (A Bankrupt)* [1998] Ch 223, 232.
[80] Insolvency Act 1986, s 310. See also *Re Roberts* [1900] 1 QB 122, 129 (after-acquired property).
[81] *Re Ashby* [1892] 1 QB 872.   [82] (1888) 39 Ch D 443, 451.
[83] See Trustee Act 1925, s 33(1)(ii)(a).
[84] *Re Bullock* (1891) 64 LT 736; *Train v Clapperton* [1908] AC 342; *Re Laye* [1913] 1 Ch 298; *Re Hamilton* (1921) 124 LT 737.
[85] *Re Clore's Settlement Trusts* [1962] 2 All ER 272.
[86] *Train v Clapperton* [1908] AC 342. cf *Edmonds v Edmonds* [1965] 1 WLR 58; and *Webb v Stenton* (1883) 11 QBD 518.

he would have the right to have the trust administered properly but no right to demand that the trustees exercise their discretion in his favour.

Variation of the statutory protective trusts

9.16   It is common practice, where protective trusts are considered desirable at all, either to create complete express trusts or to modify section 33 extensively. For example, powers may be conferred on the trustees to enlarge the principal beneficiary's interest (wholly or in part) into an unrestricted life interest;[87] or to reinstate the protected life interest once it has been determined (especially if such determination was accidental rather than a deliberate act, or if it occurred during the subsistence of a prior interest); or to allow the trustees to appoint (even on wide-ranging trusts) the underlying capital (and not just advance it) without causing a forfeiture; or to introduce a power to accumulate income. Entirely different objects of the discretionary trusts may also be specified.

9.17   In practice, however, the same effects, and even greater flexibility, can be achieved more easily by two other methods: first, by creating a revocable (unprotected) life interest, ie one which can be revoked by the trustees in the event of the life tenant's bankruptcy (or, indeed, his attempting to alienate his interest or committing some other unacceptable act); and, secondly, by means of a discretionary trust. There is also the additional advantage that, in both cases, the settlor himself can be the life tenant or a discretionary object (as the case may be).

Miscellaneous

9.18   The effect of section 33(3) is that it remains impossible for a settlor to settle property on himself for life or until he should become bankrupt.[88]

9.19   Where the principal beneficiary also becomes entitled to the trust capital, the two interests will not merge.[89]

Discretionary trusts generally

9.20   Far greater flexibility can be achieved by the creation of discretionary trusts *ab initio*, rather than by relying on the statutory discretionary trusts (even if modified extensively by the trust instrument) arising *in futuro* on the determination of a protected life interest. Protection against insolvency or assignment is just as effective, but it is then just one of several advantages provided by wide and flexible discretionary trusts (not least the fact that the discretionary trusts are not limited to the lifetime of a principal beneficiary). All the difficulties and uncertainties surrounding determinable life interests are avoided. Consequently, the creation of protective trusts is now relatively uncommon.

---

[87] *Re Gordon's Will Trusts* [1977] Ch 27.
[88] See Para. 9.04 above.   [89] *Re Chance's Settlement Trusts* [1918] WN 34.

B. Trusts and the Insolvency Act 1986

Introduction

Prior to the enactment of the Insolvency Act 1985 (which was itself replaced by **9.21**
the Insolvency Act 1986), the two main statutory provisions in English law preventing the use of trusts as a means of avoiding liability to creditors were
section 172 of the Law of Property Act 1925 and section 42 of the Bankruptcy Act
1914. Both of these provisions could be traced back to earlier statutes.[90] Both
section 172 and section 42 have been repealed.[91] Nevertheless, they remain
important because they are the basis of similar, if not identical, legislation in
several overseas jurisdictions. For example, there are provisions which are identical
with (or broadly similar to) those in section 42 and/or section 172 (or even the
provisions of the 1571 Act) still in force in each of the Australian States, in the
British Virgin Islands, Gibraltar,[92] Hong Kong, and New Zealand. Similar
provisions were recently in force in the Bahamas, Bermuda, the Cayman Islands,
and the Turks and Caicos Islands.[93]

The Insolvency Act 1986

The Insolvency Act 1986 (the 1986 Act) provides a comprehensive legislative **9.22**
framework for both individual and corporate insolvency. On bankruptcy, a bankrupt's[94] estate vests in the trustee in bankruptcy immediately on his appointment
taking effect, and it so vests without any conveyance, assignment, or transfer.[95]
A bankrupt's 'estate' comprises all property belonging to or vested in the bankrupt
at the commencement of the bankruptcy, subject to certain exceptions—in particular, property held by the bankrupt in trust for any other person.[96] As well as
money, goods, things in action, and land, 'property' includes every description of
property, wherever situated, and also obligations and every description of interest,
whether present or future or vested or contingent, arising out of or incidental to

---

[90] Section 172 of the Law of Property Act 1925 re-enacted the provisions of para 31 of Part II of
Sch 3 to the Law of Property (Amendment) Act 1924 (which never came independently into operation). The provisions of para 31 replaced in very substantially different terms the provisions of the
statute 13 Eliz I, c 5 (the 1571 Act). Section 42(1) of the Bankruptcy Act 1914 reproduced s 47(1)
of the Bankruptcy Act 1883, which in turn re-enacted the first part of s 91 of the Bankruptcy Act
1869 (save that the latter provision applied only to traders, and subject to other minor amendments). See also *Lloyds Bank Ltd v Marcan* [1973] 1 WLR 339, 344, *per* Pennycuick V-C.
[91] Insolvency Act 1985, Sch 10.
[92] See *Hess v Line Trust Corporation Ltd* (1998/99) 1 ITELR 249.
[93] For a detailed analysis of the 1571 Act, s 172 of the LPA 1925, and s 52 of the Bankruptcy Act
1914, see GW Thomas, 'Asset Protection Trusts' in J Glasson (ed), *The International Trust* (Jordans,
2002) 337, 339–370.
[94] Insolvency Act 1986, s 381(1).   [95] ibid, s 306.
[96] ibid, s 283; *Schuppan v Schuppan* [1997] 1 BCLC 258.

property.[97] Thus, an interest under a trust, such as a life interest or interest in remainder, is included, but not a mere *spes* enjoyed by the bankrupt as an object of a discretionary trust, nor a special power of appointment exercisable by the bankrupt but of which he himself is not an object.[98]

9.23 A bankruptcy petition may not be presented to the court unless the debtor:

(a) is domiciled in England and Wales,

(b) is personally present in England and Wales on the day on which the petition is presented, or

(c) at any time in the period of three years ending with that day has been ordinarily resident, or has had a place of residence, in England and Wales, or has carried on business in England and Wales.[99]

9.24 The Insolvency Act 1986 also includes several provisions dealing with transactions defrauding creditors; and they are not all dependent on bankruptcy. Settlements and prior transactions made by a person who is adjudicated bankrupt[100] are dealt with in sections 339–342 of the 1986 Act;[101] and transactions defrauding creditors[102] are dealt with in sections 423–425 of the 1986 Act.[103] In broad terms, the policy underlying these provisions—unlike that which underpins recent asset protection legislation in certain offshore jurisdictions—is an attempt to make life easier for the creditor by clarifying and simplifying, and indeed widening, the basis on which he may seek to set aside dispositions made by his debtor.

---

[97] Insolvency Act 1986, s 436. See also *Morgan v Morris* (1998) Lawtel Document No C0004394 (1 April 1998); and *Re Landau* [1998] Ch 223. cf *Re Scientific Investment Plan* [1998] PLR 141.

[98] See, for example, *Clarkson v Clarkson* [1994] BCC 921.

[99] Insolvency Act 1986, s 265. In *Theophile v Solicitor-General* [1950] AC 186, the House of Lords held that a debtor continues to carry on business, as far as bankruptcy jurisdiction is concerned, until all trade debts and liabilities, including tax liabilities, arising out of the carrying on of the business have been paid.

[100] Which were formerly within the scope of s 42 of the Bankruptcy Act 1914.

[101] Under the 1986 Act, s 284(1), where any person is adjudged bankrupt, any disposition of property made by that person in the period to which the section applies is void except to the extent that it is or was made with the consent of the court, or is or was subsequently ratified by the court. In *Re Flint* [1993] Ch 319, three weeks after a bankruptcy petition had been presented against the husband, an order was made in divorce proceedings, pursuant to the Matrimonial Causes Act 1973, s 24, ordering him to transfer his interest in the matrimonial home to the wife. A week later the husband was adjudicated bankrupt. The husband's trustee in bankruptcy obtained a declaration that the order was void as a disposition of property within the 1986 Act, s 284(1) and was void unless subsequently ratified by the court dealing with the bankruptcy.

[102] Which were formerly within s 172 of the Law of Property Act 1925.

[103] See [1998] 62 Conv 362 (JG Miller).

Transactions at an undervalue and preferences in the event of bankruptcy

Under section 339 of the Insolvency Act 1986, where an individual is adjudged **9.25** bankrupt and he has, at a relevant time, entered into 'a transaction with any person at an undervalue', the trustee of the bankrupt's estate may apply to the court; and, on such an application, the court may make such order as it thinks fit for restoring the position to what it would have been if that individual had not entered into that transaction. Section 339(3) then provides that, for these purposes, an individual enters into a 'transaction at an undervalue' if:

(a) he makes a gift to that person or he otherwise enters into a transaction with that person on terms that provide for him to receive no consideration,

(b) he enters into a transaction with that person in consideration of marriage, or

(c) he enters into a transaction with that person for a consideration the value of which, in money or money's worth, is significantly less than the value, in money or money's worth, of the consideration provided by the individual.

Section 436 provides that a 'transaction' includes 'a gift, agreement or arrange- **9.26** ment, and references to entering into a transaction shall be construed accordingly'. The meaning of the expression 'transaction at an undervalue' has been considered in several cases[104] in the context of sections 423–425 of the 1986 Act, where the same expression is used. The observations made in those cases apply equally in relation to section 339 and ought to be referred to accordingly. Moreover, in *Re Paramount Airways Ltd*,[105] the Court of Appeal held (in relation to the virtually identical provisions in section 238 of the 1986 Act, relating to transactions at an undervalue made by a company) that the words 'any person' had to be given their literal meaning, unrestricted as to persons or territory, and an order could therefore be made against a foreigner resident abroad.

Similar provision is made in section 340 of the Insolvency Act 1986 for the case **9.27** where an individual is adjudged bankrupt and he has, at a relevant time, 'given a preference' to 'any person'. For these purposes, an individual has given a preference to a person if:

(a) that person is one of the individual's creditors or a surety or guarantor for any of his debts or other liabilities, and

---

[104] See, eg, *Arbuthnot Leasing International Ltd v Havelet Leasing Ltd* [1990] BCC 636; *Chohan v Sagar* [1992] BCC 306; *Pinewood Joinery (a firm) v Starelm Properties Ltd* [1994] 2 BCLC 412; *National Bank of Kuwait v Menzies* [1994] 2 BCLC 306; *Agricultural Mortgage Corp plc v Woodward* [1995] 1 BCLC 1, [1994] BCC 688; *Royscot Spa Leasing v Lovett* [1995] BCC 502; *Schuppan v Schuppan* [1997] 1 BCLC 258; *Jyske Bank (Gibraltar) Ltd v Spjeldnaes (No 2)* [1999] BPIR 525. See also *Re MC Bacon Ltd* [1990] BCLC 324 (on the Insolvency Act 1986, s 238(4)(b), which corresponds to s 423(1)(c)).
[105] [1993] Ch 223. See also *Jyske Bank (Gibraltar) Ltd v Spjeldnaes (No 2)* [1999] BPIR 525.

(b) the individual does anything or suffers anything to be done which (in either case) has the effect of putting that person into a position which, in the event of the individual's bankruptcy, will be better than the position he would have been in if that thing had not been done.[106]

9.28 In relation to section 340 (but not section 339), the court is directed not to make an order in respect of a preference given to any person unless the individual who gave it was influenced, in deciding to give it, by a desire to produce in relation to that person the effect mentioned in paragraph (b) above.[107] On the other hand, an individual who has given a preference to an 'associate of his (otherwise than by reason only of being his employer)' is presumed, unless the contrary is shown, to have been influenced by such a desire.[108]

9.29 A 'relevant time' for the purposes of both section 339 and section 340 is defined in section 341 as follows:

(a) in the case of a transaction at an undervalue, at a time in the period of 5 years ending with the day of the presentation of the bankruptcy petition on which the individual is adjudged bankrupt,

(b) in the case of a preference which is not a transaction at an undervalue and is given to a person who is an associate of the individual . . . at a time in the period of 2 years ending with that day, and

(c) in any other case of a preference which is not a transaction at an undervalue, at a time in the period of 6 months ending with that day.

9.30 It is further provided[109] that (subject to a 'two-year exception' mentioned below), none of the times specified above is 'a relevant time' unless the individual:

(a) is insolvent at that time; or
(b) becomes insolvent in consequence of the transaction or preference.

For these purposes, an individual is 'insolvent' if:

(a) he is unable to pay his debts as they fall due; or
(b) the value of his assets is less than the amount of his liabilities, taking into account his contingent and prospective liabilities.[110]

9.31 These requirements are presumed to be satisfied, unless the contrary is shown, where the individual has entered into a transaction at an undervalue with an 'associate' of his. Moreover, if the individual has made a transaction at an under-value (as opposed to given a preference) at a time less than two years before the

---

[106] Insolvency I Act 1986, s 340(3).   [107] ibid s 340(4).
[108] ibid, s 340(5). An 'associate' is defined in s 435.   [109] ibid, s 341(2).
[110] ibid, s 341(3); *Schuppan v Schuppan* [1997] 1 BCLC 258.

presentation of the bankruptcy petition, that time will be 'a relevant time' irrespective of his insolvency.[111]

An 'associate', for the purposes of the Act, is defined widely in section 435, which **9.32** provides *inter alia* that a person is an associate of an individual if that person is the individual's husband or wife, or is a relative, or the husband or wife of a relative, of the individual or of the individual's husband or wife. A person is also an associate of any person with whom he is in partnership, and of the husband or wife or a relative of any individual with whom he is in partnership. He is also an associate of any person whom he employs or by whom he is employed. A person in his capacity as trustee of a trust (other than some specified exceptions) is an associate of another person if the beneficiaries of the trust include, or the terms of the trust confer a power that may be exercised for the benefit of, that other person or an associate of that other person.[112]

The broad effect of these provisions is that, where an individual is adjudged bank- **9.33** rupt and he has entered into a transaction at an undervalue within two years of the presentation of the bankruptcy petition, then the court must make an order in respect thereof on the application of the individual's trustee in bankruptcy; and that, where he has entered into such a transaction within five years, but not within two years, of the presentation of the bankruptcy petition, similar consequences follow, but only if it is shown that the individual was insolvent at the time of the transaction or became so in consequence thereof (bearing in mind the presumption made against him if the transaction was made with an 'associate'). On the other hand, where the individual has given a preference to any person and such preference is not a transaction at an undervalue, a distinction is drawn between (a) a preference given to an 'associate' (where the relevant time limit is within two years of the date of the presentation of the bankruptcy petition) and (b) one given to any other person (where the relevant time limit is the period of six months ending with that date).

The court may make such order 'as it thinks fit' under section 339 or section 340, **9.34** but section 342 lists various forms of order which the court may wish to make. For example, an order may:

(a) require any property transferred as part of the transaction, or in connection with the giving of the preference, to be vested in the trustee of the bankrupt's estate as part of that estate;

---

[111] ibid, s 341(2).
[112] ibid, s 435(1), (2), (3), (4), and (5). Any provision that a person is an associate of another person is taken to mean that they are associates of each other: s 435(1).

(b) require any property to be so vested if it represents in any person's hands the application either of the proceeds of sale of property so transferred or of money so transferred;

(c) release or discharge (in whole or in part) any security given by the individual;

(d) require any person to pay, in respect of benefits received by him from the individual, such sums to the trustee of his estate as the court may direct.[113]

9.35 An order under section 339 or section 340 may affect the property of, or impose any obligation on, any person whether or not he is the person with whom the individual in question entered into the transaction or, as the case may be, the person to whom the preference was given. However, such an order will not prejudice any interest in property which was acquired from a person other than that individual and was acquired in good faith and for value, or prejudice any interest deriving from such an interest; and it will not require a person who received a benefit from the transaction or preference in good faith, for value, and without notice of the relevant circumstances, to pay a sum to the trustee of the bankrupt's estate, except where he was a party to the transaction or the payment is to be in respect of a preference given to that person at a time when he was a creditor of that individual.[114]

9.36 In addition, sections 335A,[115] 336, and 337 of the 1986 Act deal with the powers of the court in certain specific cases, namely cases where a trustee in bankruptcy applies (under section 14 of the Trusts of Land and Appointment of Trustees Act 1996) for an order for the sale of a dwelling house of which the bankrupt and his spouse (or former spouse) are trustees for sale; cases where a spouse claims rights of occupation under Part IV of the Family Law Act 1996; and also cases where the bankrupt has rights of occupation by virtue of a beneficial interest and has infant children living with him.

9.37 A number of decisions—many of which show that some of the principles enunciated in the pre-1986 cases continue to be relevant—illustrate the operation of sections 339 and 340 of the 1986 Act. In *Clarkson v Clarkson*,[116] A, B, and C were directors and shareholders of a prosperous company. In 1989, they each took out a life insurance policy for £500,000 in order to provide cash for the other two to buy out the insured director's interest in the company when he died. C's policy was held on trust by A, B, and C, who had a power to appoint the

---

[113] ibid, s 342(a)–(d). See s 342 generally for the remaining forms of order and also for supplementary provisions

[114] Section 342(2), as amended by the Insolvency (No 2) Act 1994, s 2. The purpose of the 1994 Act is to provide protection for an innocent purchaser from a donee who received property from a person subsequently declared bankrupt. See paras 9.46–9.47 below for a discussion of identical provisions in the Insolvency Act 1986, s 425 and of cases decided thereon.

[115] Inserted by the Trusts of Land and Appointment of Trustees Act 1996, Sch 3, para 23. See also *Re Raval* [1998] 2 FLR 718; *Judd v Brown* [1991] 1 FLR 1191.

[116] [1994] BCC 921.

policy and its proceeds for the benefit of the insured director's spouse, children, and grandchildren, and the other two directors; and, in default of appointment, on trust for A and B equally. In June 1991, the company went into administrative receivership. In June 1992, the trustees appointed the proceeds of the policy to C's wife. In January and February 1993, all three directors were adjudicated bankrupt. The trustees in bankruptcy of A and B claimed that the appointment (having been made within two years of the bankruptcies) was a transaction at an undervalue within section 339. The Court of Appeal rejected the claim, holding that the creation of the trust by C in 1989 had been a gift, but not the appointment made in 1992.

Hoffmann LJ stated:

> The appointment was merely the exercise of a fiduciary power to select the person to whom the gift should go. It has been for centuries a principle of the law of powers that an appointment under a special power takes effect as if it had been written into the instrument creating the power. The appointee takes the property of the settlor and not that of the donee of the power.

The court was willing to give section 339 a purposive construction, holding that it was clearly intended to enable a trustee in bankruptcy to recover for the benefit of creditors any property which the bankrupt had given away or transferred at an undervalue during the relevant period (as defined in section 341). What 'property' did A and B have at the relevant time? Under the settlement, each had a vested interest in the trust fund in default of appointment: however, such an interest was, in its nature, liable to defeasance. Each was a potential object of the power of appointment; but this was nothing more than a right to be considered as a potential appointee. Each was a trustee and donee of the power (along with C), but this clearly conferred no beneficial interest in the property[117] at all and the power had to be exercised jointly by all three trustees.

In *Re Kumar*,[118] a husband and wife were joint tenants of the matrimonial home, which was worth about £140,000 and was mortgaged to a bank. On 11 June 1990, the husband executed a transfer of his interest to the wife (to which the bank consented on condition that the mortgage was reduced). The wife thereupon became sole proprietor of the house and assumed sole liability for the mortgage. On 9 July, an action brought against the husband by former clients for negligence was compromised and a consent order made against him for payment of damages of £30,000 and costs by instalments or the immediate payment of £56,000 in default. On 24 July, the wife petitioned for divorce. On 20 December,

9.38

---

[117] The wide definition of a bankrupt's estate in the 1986 Act, s 283, clearly included a general power of appointment but not a power exercisable over property not for the time being comprised in the bankrupt's estate, and it did not extend to property held by the bankrupt on trust: s 283(3)(a) and (4).

[118] [1993] 2 All ER 700.

the husband's former solicitors entered a default judgment against him for non-payment of their costs of some £22,500 and on 31 December the plaintiffs in the negligence action signed judgment for £56,000 and costs against him under the consent order, the terms of which he had been unable to satisfy. On 21 January 1991, a decree nisi was granted on the wife's petition. On 25 March, a bankruptcy petition was presented by the husband's former solicitors. On 19 April, under a consent order made in the divorce proceedings, the wife agreed to her claim for financial provision being dismissed in consideration of the husband's transfer of his interest in the matrimonial home to her and his agreement to make periodical payments. On 24 July, a bankruptcy order was made against the husband. The trustee in bankruptcy applied to the court for an order under section 339 of the Insolvency Act 1986 reversing the husband's transfer of the matrimonial home to the wife on 11 June 1990, on the ground that it was a transaction at an undervalue and was void as against his creditors.

9.39 Ferris J held that the compromise of a claim to financial provision in matrimonial proceedings was capable of being consideration in money or money's worth for the purposes of determining whether a transaction had been entered into at an undervalue for the purposes of section 339. However, whether it was a relevant consideration depended on the value of the claim for relief which was compromised. Since the husband's interest in the matrimonial home had already been transferred to the wife by way of gift and there was no evidence that the transfer had been executed in return for an agreement by the wife not to seek any further capital provision, and as she must have been aware that he had no other assets out of which to make any further capital provision, the purported compromise of the wife's claim did not amount to relevant consideration for the purposes of section 339. Furthermore, having regard to the difference in value between the equity of redemption and the amount of the mortgage, the wife's assumption of sole liability for the mortgage was significantly less than the consideration provided by the husband and was not sufficient to prevent the transaction being at an undervalue. The transfer of the husband's interest was therefore a transaction at an undervalue within section 339. Even if there had been a compromise of the wife's prospective claim for capital provision—which the judge held was not the case—his conclusion would have been the same. The husband had made a disposal of his only remaining capital asset of any substance and it involved a substantial element of bounty on his part.[119]

9.40 In contrast, in *Re Ledingham-Smith*,[120] A and B carried on a business in partnership. They employed the services of accountants whose fees were paid by monthly

---

[119] Ferris J referred to the decision of Goff J in *Re Windle* [1975] 1 WLR 1628 and to *Re Abbott* [1983] Ch 45.
[120] [1993] BCLC 635.

standing order for £1,000. By the end of September 1989, A and B owed the accountants almost £8,000 for services rendered. By the end of 1989, they owed around £24,000. In January 1990, the accountants declared that they would not continue to act for the partnership unless their outstanding fees were paid. The parties agreed that the partnership would pay £5,000 a week, first to satisfy any fees incurred during that week and then to be used towards reducing the balance of outstanding fees. The partnership was declared bankrupt in April 1990, and the trustee in bankruptcy sought to recover, under section 40 of the Insolvency Act 1986, sums which had been paid to the accountants pursuant to the agreement.

Morritt J held that there were three issues before the court.   **9.41**

(1) The first issue was whether A and B had put the accountants in a position which, in the event of their bankruptcy, would be better than if the thing had not been done (called a 'preference in fact').
(2) Secondly, if there was a preference in fact, whether A and B were influenced by a desire to confer a benefit (called 'the relevant influence').
(3) Thirdly, upon whom did the burden of proving the relevant influence rest?

As to the first issue, the judge held that there was no preference in fact. Section 340(3)(b) required that the recipient's position 'will be better' (not 'may be') in a bankruptcy after the doing of the thing in question. On the facts, the accountants could not be said to have been benefited: services were still being provided and expenses incurred. As to the second issue, it was not helpful to consider whether the words 'influenced . . . by a desire' in section 340(4) posed a greater or lesser test than the test under the former legislation of a dominant intention to prefer.[121] 'Intention', 'motive', and 'desire' were different concepts. The words 'desire' and 'influence' were not susceptible to any further definition and the question was simply one of applying them to the facts of a given case. Here, it was not possible to infer from the facts a desire to prefer on the part of A and B. As to the third issue, it was clear from section 340(5) that the burden was on the trustee to show that a preference had been conferred.[122]

Transaction defrauding creditors

Section 423 of the Insolvency Act 1986 (unlike section 339 above) applies **9.42** whether or not insolvency proceedings of any kind have been taken, and however long before the application to the court the transaction being impugned was

---

[121] Millett J pointed out in *Re MC Bacon Ltd* [1990] BCLC 324, 335 that the tests predicated by s 340 are completely different and consideration of the position under the old legislation cannot assist.
[122] See also *Bishopsgate Investment Management Ltd v Maxwell* The Times, 11 February 1993 (hearing, 28 January 1993), where the defendant had charged his flat in favour of his solicitors to secure payment of unpaid costs and disbursements.

entered into. However, like section 339, it applies to a 'transaction at an undervalue', an expression which is defined in terms identical to those used in relation to section 339.[123] Section 423(1) provides that, apart from gifts and transactions made in consideration of a marriage, a person enters into a 'transaction at an undervalue' with another person if he enters into a transaction with the other for a consideration the value of which, in money or money's worth, is significantly less than the value, in money or money's worth, of the consideration provided by himself. An almost identical provision (in section 238(4)(b) of the 1986 Act) was considered in *Re MC Bacon Ltd*,[124] where the issue was whether the granting of a debenture by a company was a transaction at an undervalue, and in respect of which provision Millett J made the following observations:[125]

> To come within that paragraph the transaction must be (i) entered into by the company; (ii) for a consideration; (iii) the value of which measured in money or money's worth; (iv) is significantly less than the value; (v) also measured in money or money's worth; (vi) of the consideration provided by the company. It requires a comparison to be made between the value obtained by the company for the transaction and the value of the consideration provided by the company. Both values must be measurable in money or money's worth and both must be considered from the company's point of view... The mere creation of a security over a company's assets does not deplete them and does not come within the paragraph. By charging its assets the company appropriates them to meet the liabilities due to the secured creditor and adversely affects the rights of other creditors in the event of insolvency. But it does not deplete its assets or diminish their value. It retains the right to redeem and the right to sell or remortgage the charged assets. All it loses is the ability to apply the proceeds otherwise than in satisfaction of the secured debt. That is not something capable of valuation in monetary terms and is not customarily disposed of for value.

This passage in Millett J's judgment was approved by the Court of Appeal in *National Bank of Kuwait v Menzies*,[126] which held that the analysis applied equally to section 423(1)(c) of the 1986 Act. It was also applied in *Agricultural Mortgage Corporation plc v Woodward*,[127] where the Court of Appeal held that, in assessing the consideration moving between the parties to an impeached transaction, the court will look at the totality of the transaction, examine it realistically, and take into account the real value of the benefits and advantages accruing to either side, in the context of the purpose with which the transaction is found to have been carried out. In that case, the debtor had mortgaged his farm to the plaintiff (AMC) as security for a loan. He fell into arrears with the mortgage payments and AMC gave him a deadline to clear the arrears. Two days before the deadline, the debtor granted his wife a tenancy of the mortgaged property. The value of the mortgaged farm with vacant possession was over £1 million, whereas its value, subject to the

---

[123] Section 423(1)(a)–(c); and see also s 339(2).   [124] [1990] BCLC 324.
[125] ibid, 340–341.   [126] [1994] 2 BCLC 306.
[127] [1995] 1 BCLC 1, [1994] BCC 688; *Barclays Bank v Eustice* [1995] 1 WLR 1238.

tenancy, was less than £500,000. AMC sought to have the tenancy set aside. AMC conceded that the rent reserved under the tenancy agreement represented a full market value, but nonetheless argued that the consideration received by the debtor was less than the value of the consideration provided by him, on the basis that the value of his freehold interest was diminished by the grant of the tenancy and that this detriment was part of the consideration provided by him. This argument was rejected at first instance and, even on appeal, the Court of Appeal preferred to leave this specific question open.[128] Nevertheless, the Court of Appeal allowed the appeal on the ground that the transaction had to be viewed as a whole and the tenancy gave the debtor's wife additional benefits, beyond the rights granted by the tenancy, for which she did not pay, namely the safeguarding of the family home, the acquisition of the farming business, and, in particular, the surrender value of the tenancy (ie the wife was placed in a 'ransom position' in that AMC would have to negotiate with her and pay her a high price in order to get vacant possession of the farm and sell it for the purpose of enforcing its security). On the other hand, where a company transferred property worth £750,000, but encumbered with a mortgage for £2.65 million, to an associated company for £1, the transaction could not be said to be one at an undervalue.[129] Similarly, a letter of instructions from the debtor which did not create any security and simply gave effect to an agreement providing for the future allocation, as between two creditors, of sums to which they were already entitled as secured creditors, was not a transaction at an undervalue.[130]

Those who may apply for an order under section 423

An application for an order under section 423 may not be made in relation to **9.43** a transaction except:

(a) in a case where the debtor has been adjudged bankrupt (or is a body corporate which is being wound up or in relation to which an administration order is in

---

[128] [1995] 1 BCLC 1, 10 and 12, *per* Sir Christopher Slade and Neill LJ.

[129] *Pinewood Joinery (A Firm) v Starelm Properties Ltd* [1994] 2 BCLC 412. The 'hope' value of property (ie any additional value arising from the hope or possibility that planning permission may be obtained) must obviously be taken into account in determining the value of the consideration given by the transferor. However, in this case, there was no evidence as to what the 'hope' value of the property might be.

[130] *National Bank of Kuwait v Menzies* [1994] 2 BCLC 306. However, such an arrangement could well be open to attack as a preference. See also *National Westminster Bank plc v Jones* [2001] 1 BCLC 98. In *Knights v Seymour Pierce Ellis Ltd* (unreported decision of Robert Englehart QC, 13 June 2001: Lawtel Doc No C0101502) it was held that the mere transmission by a company of money from A to a third party B did not involve any kind of 'transaction' for the purposes of ss 238 and 423 of the 1986 Act. And in *Treharne v Brabon* [2001] 1 BCLC 11, it was held that a sale effected by a bankrupt's wife as mortgagee was not 'entered into' by the bankrupt.

force) by the Official Receiver, by the trustee of the bankrupt's estate (or by the liquidator or administrator of the body corporate), or, with the leave of the court, by a victim of the transaction;

(b) in a case where a victim of the transaction is bound by an approved.[131] voluntary arrangement, by the supervisor of the voluntary arrangement or by any person who (whether or not so bound) is such a victim; or

(c) in any other case, by a victim of the transaction.[132.]

An application made under any of paragraphs (a)–(c) is to be treated as made on behalf of every victim of the transaction.[133] A 'victim' for these purposes means a person who is, or is capable of being, prejudiced by the transaction at an undervalue.[134]

Provision which may be made by order under section 423

9.44 Where a person (individual or corporate) has entered into a transaction at an undervalue with another person (individual or corporate), the court[135] may, if satisfied under section 423(3), make such order as it thinks fit for:

(a) restoring the position to what it would have been if the transaction had not been entered into, and

(b) protecting the interests of persons who are victims of the transaction.[136]

There is an element of discretion involved here (implicit in the word 'may'). Indeed, the Court of Appeal held, in *Re Paramount Airways Ltd*,[137] that this provision confers on the court an overall discretion, which is wide enough, if justice so requires, to enable the court to make no order against the other party to the transaction or the person to whom the preference was given. In particular, if a foreign element is involved, the court will need to be satisfied that, in respect of the relief sought against him, the defendant is sufficiently connected with England for

---

[131] ie approved under the 1986 Act, Part I or Part VIII.

[132] ibid, s 424(1).

[133] ibid, s 424(2).

[134] ibid, s 423(5). See also *Pinewood Joinery (A Firm) v Starelm Properties Ltd* [1994] 2 BCLC 412, 417–418.

[135] 'The court' means the High Court or any other court which has jurisdiction in relation to a bankruptcy petition relating to the individual or to wind up the company: s 423(4). But cf *Moon v Franklin* [1996] BPIR 196; and *TSB Bank plc v Katz* [1997] BPIR 147.

[136] Insolvency Act 1986, s 423(2).

[137] [1993] Ch 223, especially, 239–240. See also *Jyske Bank (Gibraltar) Ltd v Spjeldnaes (No 2)* [1999] BPIR 525; *Polly Peck International Ltd v Citibank NA* The Times, 20 October 1993; *Polly Peck International plc v Nadir* [1993] BCC 886; *Mackinnon v Donaldson* [1986] Ch 482; *Barclays Bank plc v Homan* [1993] BCLC 680; and *Hughes v Hannover Ruckversicherungs-Aktiengesellschaft* [1997] 1 BCLC 497.

it to be just and proper to make the order against him despite the foreign element (which might be shown, for example, by his residence).

However, the discretion conferred by section 423(2) is not apparently an absolute **9.45** and uncontrolled discretion: 'the courts must set their faces against transactions which are designed to prevent plaintiffs in proceedings, creditors with unimpeachable debts, from obtaining the remedies by way of execution that the law would normally allow them'.[138] It is true that an order shall be made only if the court is satisfied that the transaction was entered into:

> for the purpose—
> (a) of putting assets beyond the reach of a person who is making, or may at some time make, a claim against him, or
> (b) of otherwise prejudicing the interests of such a person in relation to the claim which he is making or may make.[139]

However, the fact that the transaction was carried out (say) pursuant to legal advice from solicitors or counsel and without dishonest intent does not by itself mean that the purpose of the transaction is not caught by section 423(3).[140]

Section 425 provides that, without prejudice to the generality of section 423 (and **9.46** the discretion conferred on the court), an order made with respect to the transaction may:

(a) require any property transferred as part of the transaction to be vested in any person, either absolutely or for the benefit of all the persons on whose behalf the application for the order is treated as made;

(b) require any property to be so vested if it represents, in any person's hands, the application either of the proceeds of sale of property so transferred or of money so transferred;

(c) release or discharge (in whole or in part) any security given by the debtor;

(d) require any person to pay to any other person in respect of benefits received from the debtor such sums as the court may direct;

(e) provide for any surety or guarantor whose obligations to any person were released or discharged (in whole or in part) under the transaction to be under such new and revived obligations as the court thinks appropriate;

(f) provide for security to be provided for the discharge of any obligation imposed by or arising under the order, for such an obligation to be charged on any property and for such security or charge to have the same priority as a

---

[138] *Arbuthnot Leasing International Ltd v Havelet Leasing Ltd (No 2)* [1990] BCC 636, 645, *per* Scott J.
[139] Insolvency Act 1986, s 423(3).
[140] *Arbuthnot Leasing International Ltd v Havelet Leasing Ltd (No 2)* [1990] BCC 636, 644.

security or charge released or discharged (in whole or in part) under the transaction.

9.47 Section 425(2) then provides further that, although an order under section 423 may affect the property of, or impose any obligation on, any person whether or not he is the person with whom the debtor entered into the transaction, those exclusions which apply in relation to section 339 also apply in relation to section 423.[141] Thus, no order may be made which would prejudice the interests of a bona fide mortgagee.[142]

9.48 In any event, the court must attempt to provide for the restoration of the antecedent position 'as far as possible' and to protect the interests of the victims of the transaction so far as practicable. Thus, where the transaction is made up of more than one component, the court has power to set aside one component but not the other(s).[143] The court may also order the transferee under the impeached transaction to hold the property on trust for the transferor, but without prejudice to the claims of the creditors of the transferee himself, who may have become creditors after the date of the transfer.[144]

'For the purpose of'

9.49 One of the key requirements of section 423 is that the court must be satisfied that the transaction at an undervalue must have been entered into for one of the purposes specified in section 423(3).[145] This requirement replaces the all-important 'intent to defraud' in section 172 of the Law of Property Act 1925. It was a recommendation of the Cork Committee (whose work prepared the way for the 1986 Act) that the law should be changed so as to make clear that:

> the necessary intent on the part of the debtor is an intent to defeat, hinder, delay or defraud creditors, or to put assets belonging to the debtor beyond their reach, and that such intent may be inferred whenever this is the natural and probable consequence of the debtor's actions, in the light of the financial circumstances of the debtor at the time, as known, or taken to have been known, to him.[146]

It is not at all clear that section 423 has given full effect to this particular recommendation. In particular, the expression 'for the purpose of' is itself not free from ambiguity; and, in this respect at least, it is not at all obvious that the position of a person seeking to set aside a relevant transaction has been improved.

[141] See Insolvency Act 1986 s 342(2).
[142] *Chohan v Saggar* [1994] 1 BCLC 706; *Judd v Brown* [1999] 1 FLR 1191.
[143] Insolvency Act 1986, s 423(2)(a); *Chohan v Saggar* [1992] BCC 306, on appeal [1994] 1 BCLC 706; *Arbuthnot Leasing International Ltd v Havelet Leasing Ltd (No 2)* [1990] BCC 636.
[144] ibid, 645.   [145] See para 9.42 above.
[146] *Report of the Review Committee on Insolvency Law and Practice* Cmnd 8558 (1982), 277, para 1215(b) and 291, para 1283(b).

The meaning of the word 'purpose' in section 423 was considered in *Chohan v* **9.50**
Saggar,[147] where Edward Evans-Lombe QC (sitting as a deputy High Court
judge) held that section 423(3) required a dominant purpose to remove assets
from the reach of actual or potential claimants or creditors. The facts of the case
were as follows. A transferred a house to B, subject to a legal charge in favour of a
building society and apparently pursuant to a sale to B as a sitting tenant. B then
executed a trust deed under which the property was held on trust for C, to whom
A owed money. It was found that, at the date of the transfer, A was under great
pressure from his creditors and was probably insolvent on an asset basis: certainly,
he could not pay his debts as they fell due. (He was subject, for example, to two
awards of damages for libel made against him.) It was also found that, in the
circumstances of the case, the property had been disposed of at a significant
undervalue. However, it was argued that, even if A might have intended to put
assets out of the reach of his creditors, this was not his sole purpose: he also
intended to benefit B.

The judge considered that the word 'purpose' had to be construed 'bearing in
mind the mischief against which the section in which that word appears is
aimed'[148]—which, in the case of section 423, was the removal of assets by their
owner, in anticipation of claims being made or contemplated, out of the reach of
such claimants. He stated[149] that the words 'for the purposes of' in section 423
were equivalent to the words 'with intent to' in section 172 of the Law of Property
Act 1925, and he saw no reason to give section 423 a different meaning, or to
approach it differently, from the way in which the Court of Appeal approached
section 172 in *Lloyds Bank v Marcan*[150]

> I propose to construe section 423(3) as requiring a plaintiff to demonstrate a domi-
> nant purpose to remove assets from the reach of actual or potential claimants or cred-
> itors, but as not excluding the possibility that there might also be other purposes
> behind the relevant transfer. To do otherwise would seem to me to remove section
> 423 from any practical use in restraining the mischief to which it was directed.[151]

In this case, A's dominant purpose had been to remove property from the reach
of creditors, and the application of section 423 was not affected by the presence
of another intention, namely one to benefit B and others. The transaction was
therefore set aside. The Court of Appeal upheld this decision (subject to a slight
variation in the form of order). Nothing was said in the judgments in the Court of
Appeal regarding Evans-Lombe QC's views on the meaning of the expression 'for

---

[147] [1992] BCC 306, on appeal [1994] 1 BCLC 706.
[148] Applying the remarks of Lord Oliver in *Brady v Brady* [1989] AC 755, 779. The remarks of
Evans-Lombe QC were approved by the Court of Appeal in both *Royscot Spa Leasing Ltd v Lovett*
[1995] BCC 502 and *Barclays Bank plc v Eustice* [1995] 1 WLR 1238, 1247.
[149] [1992] BCC 306, 321, 323.   [150] [1973] 1 WLR 1387.
[151] [1992] BCC 306, 323.

the purpose of' and it may therefore be assumed that his observations were thus approved by implication. The same approach seems clearly to have been adopted in *Arbuthnot Leasing International Ltd v Havelet Leasing Ltd (No 2)*,[152] *Agricultural Mortgage Corporation plc v Woodward*,[153] *Royscot Spa Leasing Ltd v Lovett*,[154] *Barclays Bank plc v Eustice*,[155] *Schuppan v Schuppan*,[156] and *Jyske Bank (Gibraltar) Ltd v Spjeldnaes (No 2)*.[157] Thus, a transaction may be set aside if just *one* of its purposes is to put assets beyond the reach of creditors or otherwise prejudice them. Indeed, such a purpose need not even be the dominant purpose.

9.51 This approach was recently confirmed by the Court of Appeal in *IRC v Hashmi*.[158] The statutory purpose under section 423(3) does not have to be the sole, or even the predominant, purpose behind the impugned transaction; it is sufficient if it is a purpose and not merely a consequence of the transaction. The Court of Appeal pointed out that it will frequently be the case that a person's intention to move assets beyond the reach of creditors and, for example, his intention to provide for his family will be so similar that he himself will not know which purpose was dominant. The crucial requirement is that a section 423(3) purpose is a purpose, rather than a by-product, of the transaction: if it is not of significance to the person or makes no contribution to his decision to effect the transaction, or if it is trivial, it can be excluded. The question whether a particular purpose is a 'dominant' purpose is presumably a question of fact and will need to be decided on the particular circumstances of each case. It may involve difficult inquiries and give rise to distinctions of some nicety. Communications between the transferor and his legal advisers on how to structure the transaction in question at an undervalue are likely to be considered sufficiently iniquitous not to be subject to the protection of legal professional privilege and, therefore, for public policy to require that they be disclosed on discovery.[159]

9.52 Another difficulty is that the words 'intent', 'motive', 'desire', and 'purpose' may have different meanings, but they overlap and, in a particular context, can mean the same thing. As we have seen, in *Re Ledingham-Smith*,[160] Morritt J took the view that, in relation to the words 'influenced . . . by a desire' in section 340(4) of the 1986 Act, 'intention', 'motive', and 'desire' were different concepts. On the other hand, in *Arbuthnot Leasing International Ltd v Havelet Leasing Ltd (No 2)*[161]

---

[152] [1990] BCC 636. [153] [1995] 1 BCLC 1. [154] [1995] BCC 502.
[155] [1995] 1 WLR 1238, 1247. [156] [1997] 1 BCLC 258.
[157] [1999] BPIR 525. See also *DEFRA v Feakins* (unreported decision of Penry-Davey J, 10 December 2001: Lawtel Doc No C01022527); *National Westminster Bank plc v Jones* [2001] 1 BCLC 98.
[158] [2002] All ER (D) 71, affirming the decision of Hart J at [2002] BPIR 271.
[159] *Barclays Bank plc v Eustice* [1995] 1 WLR 1238; *Royscot Spa Leasing Ltd v Lovett* [1995] BCC 502. See also *Derby & Co v Weldon (No 10)* [1990] 1 WLR 660.
[160] [1993] BCLC 635: see paras 9.40–9.41 above. [161] [1990] BCC 636, 643.

in relation to section 423 itself, Scott J referred to 'the intentions, the purpose, the motive—one may choose what word one will'; and Edward Evans-Lombe QC clearly adopted the same approach in *Chohan v Saggar*.[162]

In the recent case of *Pagemanor Ltd v Ryan*,[163] it seems to have been held that the wording of section 423 requires a *subjective* test of the transferor's state of mind and intentions in making the relevant transfer. Whether this is indeed the case, without any qualification, is surely doubtful. Is the transferor free to set his own standards of honesty, for example? Must he not be presumed to intend the natural consequences of his actions? In the classic type of case to which section 423 is intended to apply, the motive to defeat creditors and the motive to secure the transferor's family often coexist, so that even the transferor would be unable to say which was uppermost in his mind;[164] and it seems unduly onerous for any defeated creditor to have to prove a subjective intention on the part of the transferor in such cases. The word 'purpose' must be construed in its particular context, which, in this case, is the mischief at which section 423 is aimed, namely: **9.53**

> the removal of assets by their owner, in anticipation of claims being made or contemplated, out of the reach of such claimants if those claims ultimately prove to be successful. It would defeat that purpose if it were possible successfully to contend that if the owner was able to point to another purpose, such as the benefit of his family, friends or the advantage of business associates, the section could not be applied.[165]

However, if it is indeed the case that the words 'for the purpose of' in section 423 are 'equivalent to' the words 'with intent to' in section 172 of the Law of Property Act 1925 (as was stated in *Chohan v Saggar*), then it seems to follow that the cases decided on section 172 (and on the provisions of the 1571 Act which preceded it) remain relevant.[166]

Public policy

In addition to the specific statutory provisions, English law prohibits a settlor, on the grounds of public policy, from creating a settlement upon himself until bankruptcy. In such a case, a determinable interest has been created, the determining event is regarded as void as against the trustee in bankruptcy, and the settlor's interest vests   **9.54**

---

[162] On the difficulties of ascribing meaning to the word 'purpose' in other contexts, see, for example, *Chandler v DPP* [1962] 3 All ER 142; *Sweet v Parsley* [1970] AC 132; *Newton v Commissioner of Taxation of the Commonwealth of Australia* [1958] AC 450.

[163] Unreported decision of Sonia Proudman QC, 5 February 2002: Lawtel Doc No C0102643.

[164] *Commissioners of Inland Revenue v Hashmi* [2002] BPIR 271.

[165] *Chohan v Saggar* [1992] BCC 306, 321, *per* Edward Evans-Lombe QC.

[166] In *Chohan v Saggar* itself, the judge was clearly guided by the decision in *Lloyds Bank v Marcan* [1973] 1 WLR 1387.

in that trustee.[167] This is so even in the case of an antenuptial settlement.[168] On the other hand, if a determining event other than bankruptcy is stipulated (and occurs), allowing the gift over to take effect prior to the bankruptcy of the settlor, the trustee in bankruptcy will be excluded.[169]

Domicile of a trust

9.55 The rules of private international law governing the domicile of a trust will clearly have a significant effect on the validity of a trust created to avoid the consequences of insolvency and on the jurisdiction of a particular court to set it aside. These rules are dealt with in detail elsewhere in this work.[170] In England the position is governed, in broad terms, by section 45(3) of the Civil Jurisdiction and Judgments Act 1982[171] which must be read and applied in conjunction with Articles 7 to 10 and 22 of the Hague Convention on the Law Applicable to Trusts and on their Recognition 1985[172] and Articles 5(6) and 60(3) of the Brussels Regulation 2002.[173] Even so, it is often not immediately obvious how the domicile of a trust is to be determined and the process of doing so involves numerous considerations, most of which are usually finely balanced.[174]

Reciprocal enforcement of insolvency laws and orders[175]

9.56 The effect of an English bankruptcy order is that all the bankrupt's property[176] (apart from specific exempted items) vests automatically in his trustee in

---

[167] *Re Burroughs-Fowler* [1916] 2 Ch 251; *Re Wombwell* (1921) 125 LT 437; *Knight v Browne* (1861) 7 Jur NS 894; *Brooke v Pearson* (1859) 27 Beav 181.
[168] *Higinbotham v Holme* (1812) 19 Ves 88; *Ex p Hodgson* (1812) 19 Ves 206; *Re Pearson* (1876) 3 Ch D 807.
[169] *Re Detmold* (1889) 40 Ch D 585.   [170] See Chapters 41 and 42 below.
[171] Now re-enacted in para 12 of Sch 1 to the Civil Jurisdiction and Judgments Order 2001, SI 2001/3929.
[172] Enacted by the Recognition of Trusts Act 1987. See also J Harris, *The Hague Trusts Convention* (Hart Publishing: Oxford, 2002).
[173] Replacing the Brussels Convention on Jurisdiction and the Enforcement of Judgments in Civil and Commercial Matters 1968 (as from 1 March 2002). Article 5(6) applies only to express trusts and not to constructive trusts (on which see generally T Yeo, 'Constructive Trustees and the Brussels Convention' (2001) 117 LQR 560). See also the Lugano Convention on Jurisdiction and the Enforcement of Judgments in Civil and Commercial Matters 1988 (between EC Member States and EFTA States), which is itself currently being revised in order to bring it into line with the Brussels Regulation 2002.
[174] For a thorough survey and analysis of many of these considerations, and the applicable rules of law, as well as the relevant English procedural rules as to service, see the recent judgment of Lawrence Collins J in *Chellaram v Chellaram (No 2)* [2002] EWHC 632 (Ch).
[175] See generally J Harris, 'Trusts and the Conflict of Laws' in J Glasson (ed), *The International Trust* (Jordans, 2002) Part 1, Chapters 1 and 2.
[176] The Insolvency Act 1986, s 436 defines 'property' so as to include 'every description of property wherever situated'.

bankruptcy, ie it purports to have worldwide effect. In practice, however, the trustee's title to property situated outside the jurisdiction must be established in accordance with the local law. Similarly, it is a matter for the private international law of the *situs* to determine whether recognition will be accorded to the English adjudication, to the trustee's status, and to his title. The trustee's title to foreign assets is likely to be subject to any real rights in the property arising under the *lex situs*; and it is also likely that the courts of the *situs* will accord priority to certain personal rights arising in favour of local creditors.[177] The detailed principles and rules of private international law, as applied in England and Wales, are beyond the scope of this chapter.[178]

The United Kingdom subscribes to the Brussels Convention 1968[179] (which was implemented by the Civil Jurisdiction and Judgments Act 1982 (CJJA 1982) and which, as from 1 March 2002, has been replaced for those EC States bound thereby by the Brussels Regulation).[180] Article 1 of the Brussels Convention specifically excluded from its scope 'bankruptcy, proceedings relating to the winding up of insolvent companies or other legal persons, judicial arrangements, compositions and analogous proceedings'. Article 1 of the new Brussels Regulation includes an exclusion in identical terms. This exclusion is wide enough to include proceedings under sections 339 and 238 of the Insolvency Act 1986. Section 1(3) of the Civil Jurisdiction and Judgments Act 1991 (inserting Schedule 3C into the CJJA 1982) also excludes the same matters.[181] Indeed, the European Court of Justice has held that Article 1 extends also to proceedings derived from and closely connected to such insolvency proceedings.[182] However, there are exceptions to this seemingly absolute exclusion. For example, section 25(1) of the Civil

9.57

---

[177] I Fletcher, *Cross-Border Insolvency* (JCB Mohr, 1992), 227–229. See also P St J Smart, *Cross-border Insolvency* (Butterworths, 1998); *Re Roy Clifford Turner* Guernsey Court of Appeal, 27 September 1988.

[178] See L Collins (ed), *Dicey and Morris, The Conflict of Laws* (13th edn, Sweet & Maxwell, 2000), (*'Dicey and Morris'*) esp vol I, Chs 14–16; North and Fawcett, *Cheshire and North's Private International Law* (13th edn, Butterworths, 1999), (*'Cheshire and North'*) esp Ch 15; J Harris, *supra*; and esp Chapters 41 and 42 below.

[179] The Brussels Convention on Jurisdiction and the Enforcement of Judgments in Civil and Commercial Matters (27 September 1968). Article 1 is set out in Sch 1 to the Civil Jurisdiction and Judgments Act 1982.

[180] Introduced pursuant to Art 65 of the EC Treaty (inserted by the Treaty of Amsterdam). The UK reserved the right to opt out of Art 65, but opted back into this particular initiative. Denmark, which also has an opt-out, has decided not to adopt the Regulation and will continue to apply the Brussels Convention 1968. The basic principle of the Regulation (like the Convention) is that a defendant should be sued in the courts of his domicile. There is no definition of 'domicile' in relation to an individual, so each Member State must apply its own rules in that regard (in the UK, s 41 of the CJJA 1982). However, Art 60(1) defines the 'domicile' of a company (thereby replacing s 42 of the CJJA 1982 in the UK).

[181] See the Civil Jurisdiction and Judgments Act 1991, Sch 1 (Title 1, Art 1(2) of the Lugano Convention, which forms the new Sch 3C to the CJJA 1982).

[182] *Gourdain v Nadler* Case 133/78 [1979] ECR 733.

Judgments and Jurisdiction Act 1982 (as amended) permits an English court to grant interim relief in aid of any foreign 'proceedings', even if the subject matter of those proceedings falls outside the scope of Article 1 (and thus extends to foreign insolvency proceedings).[183]

9.58 In any event, English law has traditionally afforded assistance and co-operation to office holders in overseas insolvency proceedings, to enable them to act in relation to property located in England and Wales. Thus, foreign bankruptcy proceedings are recognized if they take place in the jurisdiction in which the debtor is domiciled in the eyes of English law, or if the debtor has submitted to the proceedings. Where a foreign adjudication is recognized, English law will also recognize the person appointed under those proceedings as the equivalent of an English trustee in bankruptcy. In respect of the proprietary effects of a foreign adjudication, English law distinguishes between movable and immovable property. The bankrupt's movable property within the jurisdiction of the courts of England and Wales vests automatically in his trustee in bankruptcy (or equivalent) from the time of adjudication, subject, however, to any rights over, or claims to, the property which existed at the time when the trustee's title was acquired. In the case of English immovable property, the foreign adjudication is not capable of effecting a transfer of title, although, in practice, English courts have often been willing to assist the foreign trustee in procuring the vesting of title in himself, for example by compelling the bankrupt to execute a conveyance, or by appointing the foreign trustee as receiver of (and with power to sell) the bankrupt's property.

9.59 As from 31 May 2002, a new EU Council Regulation[184] on Insolvency Proceedings has come into force, which introduces provisions governing jurisdiction for opening insolvency proceedings[185] (whether the debtor is a natural or a legal person, a trader or an individual); judgments delivered directly on the basis of insolvency proceedings and closely connected with such proceedings; and also the recognition of those judgments and the applicable law. The Regulation sets out, among other things, but only for the matters covered by it, uniform rules on conflict of laws which replace, within their scope of application, national rules of private international law. Broadly, the law of the Member State of the opening of the proceedings should be applicable, a rule that should be valid both for the main proceedings and for local proceedings, and should determine all the effects of the

---

[183] Civil Jurisdiction and Judgments Act 1982 (Interim Relief) Order 1997, SI 1997/302. See also Rules of the Supreme Court (Amendment) 1997 (SI 1997/415); *Re International Power Industries NV* [1985] BCLC 128, esp 137; (1997) 16 CJQ 185 (IR Scott) and (1998) 17 CJQ 149 and (1998) 114 LQR 46 (P St J Smart).

[184] Council Regulation (EC) 1346/2000 of 29 May 2000: (2000) OJ L160/1. The UK and Ireland have adopted the Regulation, but not Denmark.

[185] The term 'insolvency proceedings' means the proceedings listed in Sch A of the Regulation, which, in relation to the UK, means winding up by or subject to the supervision of the court, creditors' voluntary winding up (with confirmation by the court), and administration.

insolvency proceedings, both procedural and substantive, on the persons and legal relations concerned.

Proceedings to set aside an alleged transaction at an undervalue under section 423 **9.60** of the Insolvency Act 1986 (at least, in circumstances where there is no bankruptcy or winding up) were not excluded by Article 1 of the 1968 Convention,[186] and Article 1 of the new Brussels Regulation will be construed in the same way. Indeed, it is likely that a claim under section 423 brought by a liquidator or trustee in bankruptcy is also not excluded, for the cause of action is still independent of bankruptcy. Thus, reliance on section 423 will have obvious advantages (in comparison, say, with section 339) where the defendant has assets overseas, because questions of service and enforcement ought to be resolved in accordance with standard procedures. Moreover, section 423 almost certainly applies extraterritorially.[187] It will be recalled that section 425(1) of the 1986 Act authorizes the court, when making an order under section 423, to require 'any property' transferred as part of the transaction to be vested in 'any person', or to require 'any person' to pay 'any other person' such sums as the court may direct. Section 436 declares that 'property' includes all types of property 'wherever situated'; and there seems to be no reason, in principle, why the words 'any person' should be confined to persons within the United Kingdom.[188]

However, section 426 of the 1986 Act[189] now provides a legislative framework for **9.61** inter-jurisdictional co-operation and reciprocal enforcement of insolvency orders of all kinds (relating to both corporate and individual insolvencies). This framework is intended to apply not only in relation to England, Wales, Scotland, and Northern Ireland, but also to 'any relevant country or territory'.[190] For these purposes, a 'relevant country or territory' means:

(a) any of the Channel Islands or the Isle of Man, or

---

[186] *Reichert v Dresdner Bank* (Case 115/88) [1990] ECR 1–27; *Reichert v Dresdner Bank (No 2)* (Case 261/90) [1992] ILPr 404; *Aiglon Ltd v Gau Shan Co Ltd* [1993] 1 Lloyd's Rep 164.
[187] *Aiglon Ltd v Gan Shan Co Ltd* [1993] 1 Lloyd's Rep 164 (accepted that s 423 could apply to a transfer of money from an English company to a Swiss one). See also *Re Paramount Airways Ltd* [1993] Ch 223 (on s 238); *Re Mid-East Trading Ltd (No 2)* [1997] 3 All ER 481, affirmed [1998] 1 All ER 577 (on s 236); and *Rousou's Trustee v Rousou and Another* [1955] 2 All ER 169, [1955] 3 All ER 486 (transfer of money from one bank account in Cyprus to another attacked under the Law of Property Act 1925, s 172).
[188] See *Re Paramount Airways Ltd* [1993] Ch 223, esp 235–239.
[189] Earlier provisions were founded in the Bankruptcy Act 1869, s 74, the Bankruptcy Act 1883, s 118, and the Bankruptcy Act 1914, s 122. Cases on these earlier provisions include *Re Levy's Trusts* (1885) 30 Ch D 119; *Galbraith v Grimshaw* [1910] AC 508; *Re Osborn* (1931–32) B & CR 189; *Re Jackson* [1973] NI 67; and *Re a Debtor, ex parte the Viscount of the Royal Court of Jersey* [1981] Ch 384. On s 426 generally, see R Woloniecki (1986) 35 ICLQ 644.
[190] Insolvency Act 1986, s 426(4).

(b) any country or territory designated for the purposes of section 426 by the Secretary of State by order made by statutory instrument.

The list of countries currently so designated includes: Anguilla, Australia, the Bahamas, Bermuda, Botswana, Brunei Darussalam, Canada, the Cayman Islands, the Falkland Islands, Gibraltar, Hong Kong, Republic of Ireland, Malaysia, Montserrat, New Zealand, St Helena, Republic of South Africa, the Turks and Caicos Islands, Tuvalu, and the British Virgin Islands.[191] However, the operation of section 426 is confined to cases where a request for co-operation is made by a court in the overseas country or territory, and it is not competent for an office holder to make a direct approach for assistance. Moreover, major trading partners such as the United States, France, Germany, and Japan are not included in the list of designated countries. Section 426 does not abolish or curtail the pre-existing common law rules dealing with international co-operation in insolvency matters: on the contrary, it now provides an additional basis for affording assistance to certain jurisdictions. One of the limiting factors under the common law rules was (and is) the requirement that the foreign adjudication was final and for a definite sum, and assistance is not directly available for restitution of assets. Section 426, however, is not so confined and thereby seems to extend the scope of remedies which may be granted. Section 426(4) declares that the courts having jurisdiction in relation to 'insolvency law' in any part of the United Kingdom 'shall assist' the courts having the corresponding jurisdiction[192] in any other part of the United Kingdom or any relevant country or territory. For the purposes of section 426 'insolvency law' means, in relation to any relevant country or territory, so much of the law of that country or territory as corresponds to provisions falling within paragraphs (a)–(c) of section 426(10).[193] A request made to a court in any part of the United Kingdom by a court in a relevant country or territory is authority for the court to which the request is made to apply, in relation to any matters specified in the request, the insolvency law which is applicable by either court in relation to comparable matters falling within its jurisdiction.

9.62 Thus, a foreign office holder (acting through a request made by the relevant foreign court) could apparently enlist the assistance of an English court in impeaching a transaction made at an undervalue, or even in applying some remedy of foreign law. In exercising its discretion under subsection (5), a court is directed to

---

[191] SI 1986/2123 (The Co-operation of Insolvency Courts (Designation of Relevant Countries and Territories) Order 1986); SI 1996/253; SI 1998/2766.

[192] As Lawrence Collins J pointed out in *Re Television Trade Rentals Ltd* [2002] EWHC 211 (Ch) (unreported), 19 February 2002, at [12], 'having a corresponding jurisdiction' means that the foreign court must be the court with jurisdiction in insolvency matters, and not the court which would have jurisdiction in the foreign country to do what is asked in England. See also *Re Dallhold Estates (UK) Pty Ltd* [1992] BCLC 621 and *Re Bank of Credit and Commerce International SA (No 9)* [1994] 3 All ER 764.

[193] Insolvency Act 1986, s 426(10), (11).

have regard in particular to the rules of private international law. It is not entirely clear how this restriction will be interpreted and applied. It has been suggested that the discretion being referred to is that of the *requesting* court,[194] but this has been rejected and, instead, it has been suggested that it means the discretion of the *requested* court to refuse assistance on the ground, for example, that the request infringes the rule that foreign tax claims will not be enforced.[195] In *Re Television Trade Rentals Ltd*,[196] Lawrence Collins J suggested (obiter) that this 'obscure and ill-thought out provision' meant that the court should take into account the foreign elements in deciding which law to apply, such as the connections of the parties with England and with the foreign country.[197] In any event, there seems to be no obvious reason why it should prevent an English court, in appropriate circumstances, from assisting a foreign court in the avoiding of voidable transactions. The underlying principle of section 426 is that a trustee in bankruptcy may obtain the assistance of the local court in gaining control of assets; and the international effect of a foreign (or an English) adjudication remains subject to the local rules of the private international law of each jurisdiction in which assets of the debtor are located.

The interpretation and scope, as well as the legislative history, of section 426 were **9.63** considered by the Court of Appeal in *Hughes v Hannover Ruckversicherungs-Aktiengesellschaft*.[198] According to Morritt LJ, the reference to 'insolvency law' in section 426(4) serves to identify the courts in any part of the United Kingdom on which the obligation to assist is cast. There is nothing in section 426 to exclude the general jurisdiction and powers vested in those courts as such under the laws of England and Wales. The purpose of subsection (5) is not to reduce that jurisdiction or those powers, but to extend them for the purposes of subsection (4). Thus, a court in England, faced with a request from a relevant country, may, in respect of the matters specified in such request, apply either the insolvency law of the relevant country concerned or its own insolvency law. The concluding words of subsection (5) introduce the hypothesis that the matters specified in the request fall within the jurisdiction of the court applying the insolvency law under consideration in so far as 'comparable matters' do so. There is available to an English court, when asked for assistance by the court of a relevant country under section 426:

---

[194] *Re Dallhold Estates (UK) Pty Ltd* [1992] BCLC 621, 626.

[195] *Re BCCI SA (No 9)* [1994] 3 All ER 764, 785; *Re Television Trade Rentals Ltd* [2002] EWHC 211 (Ch) (unreported), 19 February 2002, at [17].

[196] ibid.

[197] In the case before him, this issue did not arise because there was no case for the application of Isle of Man law.

[198] [1997] 1 BCLC 497.

(a) its own general jurisdiction and powers;[199] and either

(b) the insolvency law of England and Wales as provided for in the Insolvency Act 1986, the specified sections of the Company Directors Disqualification Act 1986, and the subordinate legislation made under any of those provisions;[200] or

(c) so much of the law of the relevant country as corresponds to that comprised in (b).[201]

The request has a dual effect: it informs the English court what assistance is sought for the purposes of subsection (4); and it is the trigger to the enlarged jurisdiction for which subsection (5) provides.

9.64 Nevertheless, the obligation to assist is imposed on a court and not some executive agency. The function of the court under section 426 must be to consider whether, in accordance with the three sources of law identified earlier, the assistance may properly be granted. If it may, then it should be; if not, then it should be withheld. If the English court cannot do exactly what is sought, then it should consider whether it can properly assist in some other way in accordance with any of the available sources of law. Public policy may be one reason for refusing assistance, but it is not the only reason. The assistance is discretionary. The fact of the request is itself a weighty factor to be taken into account; and the English court may be expected to accept without further investigation the views of the requesting court. Moreover, the response of the English court will depend on the interaction of section 426 of the Insolvency Act 1986 and the provisions of the Civil Jurisdiction and Judgments Act 1982. Thus, if an English court has made an order at the suit of a creditor under section 423 of the 1986 Act, such an order must be enforced (if enforced at all) in Scotland or Northern Ireland under section 426(1), but it would be enforceable in (say) France or Germany under the Brussels Regulation 2002 (not being excluded by Article 1 of that Regulation and not being included within section 426 of the 1986 Act). If a Scottish resident creditor enters a claim in an English insolvency, but has also attached the debtor's property in France, an injunction granted by the English court restraining the creditor from continuing with French proceedings cannot be enforced in France (being excluded by Article 1 of the Brussels Regulation 2002 and being outside the scope of section 426). However, it could be enforced in Scotland under section 18 of the 1982 Act (requiring reciprocal enforcement of judgments as between different

---

[199] The judges in *Re Osborn* (1931–32) B & CR 189, *Re Jackson* [1973] NI 67, and *Re a Debtor, ex parte the Viscount of the Royal Court of Jersey* [1981] Ch 384, were said to have applied (a).

[200] Chadwick J was said to have applied (b) in *Re Dallhold Estates (UK) Pty Ltd* [1992] BCLC 621.

[201] Rattee J was said to have applied (b) and (c) in *Re Bank of Credit and Commerce International SA (No 9)* [1994] 2 BCLC 636. See also *Re JN Taylor Finance Property Ltd, England v Purves* [1999] BCC 197; *Re Television Trade Rentals Ltd* [2002] EWHC 211 (Ch), (unreported) 19 February 2002.

parts of the United Kingdom) because, according to *Hughes v Hannover*, the jurisdiction to grant an extraterritorial injunction is derived from the court's general equitable jurisdiction and is not part of its 'insolvency law' jurisdiction under section 426.[202]

Nevertheless, the request itself can never be conclusive as to the manner in which **9.65** the discretion of the court should be exercised. Thus, the approach of Richard Scott V-C in *Re Focus Insurance Company*[203]—summarizing the views of Chadwick J in *Re Dallhold Estates (UK) Pty Ltd*[204] ('do what you are asked unless there is a compelling reason not to do so') and Rattee J in *Re Bank of Credit and Commerce International SA (No 9)*[205] ('do what you are asked unless there is some good reason for not doing so')—was approved.

In *Hughes* itself, assistance in response to a letter of request from the Supreme Court of Bermuda was refused, on the basis that the property and the dispute in question were substantially in Massachusetts and there was no sufficient connection with England.[206] Section 426 was considered further in *Re Southern Equities Corp Ltd*,[207] where the Supreme Court of South Australia requested the English court to exercise its jurisdiction to assist it by making an order requiring the oral examination of the respondent (a partner in a firm of UK accountants) in accordance with Australian law and procedure. The respondent, who was a potential witness at a trial in South Australia, was not obliged, under Australian procedural rules, to provide a witness statement of his evidence to a liquidator in advance of the trial. The Court of Appeal allowed the appeal of the liquidator. According to the Court of Appeal, when faced with such a request the court had a choice, afforded by section 426(5) of the 1986 Act, of applying either section 236 of the 1986 Act or section 596B of the Australian Corporations Law. Once the court had chosen to apply section 596B, it had to direct itself by reference to the law of Australia, and section 236 of the 1986 Act ceased to have any relevance. Were it otherwise, section 426 of the 1986 Act would be deprived of much of its effect, since the choice of law of the requesting court would be circumscribed by limitations to be found in the corresponding provisions of the insolvency law of England. Furthermore, since one of the objects of section 426 was to provide for some form of reciprocal assistance for insolvencies with an international dimension,[208] it would be inconsistent with the

---

[202] See (1998) 17 CJQ 149, 162 (P St J Smart).   [203] [1996] BCC 659.
[204] [1992] BCLC 621. It is not entirely clear, in fact, whether Chadwick J was prepared to concede any discretion to the court: see 626.
[205] [1994] 2 BCLC 636.
[206] See also *Re JN Taylor Finance Property Ltd, England v Purves* [1999] BCC 197.
[207] [2000] 2 WLR 1141, [2000] 2 BCLC 21.
[208] As Morritt LJ pointed out ([2000] 2 BCLC 21, 64), this is confined, of course, to countries or territories with insolvency laws corresponding to the Insolvency Act 1986, as designated by the Secretary of State.

need for comity evident in the framework provided for by the section to stigmatize either the substantive law or the exercise by the requesting court of the jurisdiction thereby conferred as oppressive. Moreover, in both jurisdictions the principles observed by the courts were directed to avoiding oppression of the witness, although the method by which that aim was to be achieved was different.[209]

Other considerations

9.66 There are other considerations which anyone involved in setting up, administering, or even advising upon, asset protection trusts must bear in mind. In particular, there are several grounds on which the adviser himself, and not just the debtor-client, may be pursued by, and perhaps held liable to, a creditor. In addition, there are specific sanctions in English criminal law of which an adviser must be aware.

Constructive trusteeship

9.67 There is a risk that an adviser may become liable to a creditor as constructive trustee. The danger is illustrated by *Finers (A Firm) v Miro*,[210] for example, where a partner in a firm of solicitors had set up an intricate network of overseas companies and trusts to hold the client's assets. Subsequently, an investigation into the affairs of one of these companies gave rise to allegations of fraud against the client. The solicitors became concerned that some of the client's assets held by them may have been acquired from misappropriated funds. They froze the client's account and assets and applied to the court for directions as to how they should deal with these assets. The client applied to have the proceedings struck out. The Court of Appeal held that, where a solicitor had strong evidence of suspected fraud on the part of a client, he was entitled, under the rule that fraud unravelled all obligations of confidence, to apply to the court (either under its inherent jurisdiction or under the Rules of the Supreme Court) for directions as to how to deal with the client's assets, notwithstanding the inevitable breach of the solicitor's duty of confidence to his client. Because the solicitor was potentially liable as constructive trustee at the suit of those entitled to assets misappropriated by the fraud, the court could direct the solicitor to notify interested persons of the existence of the proceedings.

9.68 There are, of course, several ways in which an adviser may become liable as constructive trustee—in particular, as a knowing recipient of trust property or as a dishonest assistant in a breach of trust. These heads, as well as constructive trusts generally, are dealt with in detail in Chapters 30 to 33 below.

---

[209] See also *Re Television Trade Rentals Ltd* [2002] EWHC 211 (Ch), (unreported) 19 February 2002, at [13]. Also *Governor and Company of the Bank of Scotland v A Limited* (2001) 3 ITELR 503.
[210] [1991] 1 All ER 182.

Criminal offences and criminal conspiracy[211]

Chapter VI of Part IX of the Insolvency Act 1986 contains a number of provisions **9.69** prescribing offences which may be committed under the Act and the penalties for those offences. In particular, section 357(1) of the 1986 Act declares that a bankrupt is guilty of an offence if he makes, or causes to be made, or has in the period of five years ending with the commencement of the bankruptcy made or caused to be made, any gift or transfer of, or any charge on, his property. (This includes causing or conniving at the levying of any execution against the property.)[212] The bankrupt is also guilty of an offence if he conceals or removes, or has at any time before the commencement of the bankruptcy concealed or removed, any part of his property after, or within two months before, the date on which a judgment or order for the payment of money has been obtained against him, being a judgment or order which was not satisfied before the commencement of the bankruptcy.[213] (The 'commencement of bankruptcy' means the day on which a bankruptcy order is made.)[214] He is not guilty of an offence if he proves that, at the time of the conduct constituting the alleged offence, he had no intent to defraud or to conceal the state of his affairs.[215] If he is found guilty of an offence, the bankrupt is liable to imprisonment or a fine or both.[216]

Of more direct concern to those who advise a transferor on a course of action **9.70** intended to defraud his creditors, or who assist him in such a course, is the possibility that they could themselves be guilty of the common law offence of conspiracy to defraud (preserved by section 5(2) of the Criminal Law Act 1977) or of the offence of aiding and abetting the debtor to commit the statutory offence of conspiracy.

Section 1(1) of the 1977 Act provides as follows:

> Subject to the following provisions of this Part of this Act, if a person agrees with any other person or persons that a course of conduct shall be pursued which will necessarily amount to or involve the commission of any offence or offences by one or more of the parties to the agreement if the agreement is carried out in accordance with their intentions, he is guilty of conspiracy to commit the offence or offences in question.

Although the offence of conspiracy at common law was abolished by section 5(1) of the 1977 Act, this did not extend to the offence of conspiracy so far as it relates to conspiracy to defraud.[217]

---

[211] See, generally, Smith and Hogan, *Criminal Law* (Butterworths, 8th edn, 1996) 277–313.
[212] Insolvency Act 1986, s 357(2). [213] ibid, s 357(3).
[214] ibid, ss 278(a), 381(2). [215] ibid, s 352. [216] ibid, s 350(6).
[217] The Criminal Justice Act 1987, s 12 effectively provides that statutory conspiracy and conspiracy to defraud are not mutually exclusive.

9.71 Most agreements to defraud will be agreements to commit offences under the Theft Acts but it is clear that they need not be and, indeed, that there can be cases of fraud which are not substantive offences.[218] A person is defrauded when he is 'prejudiced', and conspirators have a sufficient *mens rea* if it is their purpose to cause that prejudice. However, in *Wai Yu-tsang v R*,[219] the Privy Council thought this was not necessarily required and that it is enough that the parties have agreed to cause the prejudice: if they have agreed to defraud, they intend to defraud, and it is immaterial that defrauding is not their purpose (their purpose usually being to benefit themselves, and not necessarily to cause loss to another).[220] 'Prejudice' includes putting at risk: if the conspirators know that the effect of carrying out the agreement will be to put the victim's property at risk, then they intend prejudice to him and, if they are dishonest, they are guilty of conspiracy to defraud him (and this is so if it turns out that the property is not impaired or even if the victim makes a profit).[221]

9.72 An agreement in England to carry out a fraud abroad is not indictable as a conspiracy to defraud in England. However, it is often difficult to determine where the fraud has been committed.

9.73 In addition to the above, it is possible, in principle, for an adviser to be charged with other offences, for example money laundering, breaches of relevant exchange control regulations, breach of professional codes and regulations or of his duty to the court, and so forth. Similarly, he may find himself being sued for tortious conspiracy.[222]

These and other matters are beyond the scope of this book.

C. *Quistclose* Trusts[223]

The *Quistclose* trust

9.74 *Quistclose* trusts deserve special mention because of their increasing use and importance in modern commercial transactions. In essence, it is a simple commercial

[218] Smith and Hogan, *Criminal Law* (Butterworths, 8th edn, 1996), 294.
[219] [1992] 1 AC 269.
[220] cf *Attorney-General's Reference (No 1 of 1982)* [1983] QB 751.
[221] See also *Scott v Metropolitan Police Commissioner* [1975] AC 819, esp 840; *Bolton* (1991) 94 Cr App Rep 74, 80; *R v Seillon* (CA (Criminal Division), 14 May 1982), *DPP v Alsford* [1978] CAR 116.
[222] See, eg, *Crofter Hand Woven Harris Tweed Co Ltd v Veitch* [1942] AC 435, esp 439, *per* Viscount Simon; *Lonrho plc v Fayed* [1991] BCC 641; *Yukong Lines Ltd of Korea v Rendsburg Investments Corp* [1998] BCC 870; *Brown v Bennett* [1999] BCC 91.
[223] This section is based on GW Thomas, 'Purpose Trusts' in J Glasson (ed), *The International Trust* (Jordans, 2002) 254–268.

arrangement akin to a retention of title clause (though with a different object) which enables the borrower to have recourse to the lender's money for a particular purpose without entrenching on the lender's property rights more than necessary to enable the purpose to be achieved. The money remains the property of the lender unless and until it is applied in accordance with his directions, and in so far as it is not so applied it must be returned to him, notwithstanding the borrower's insolvency.[224] It is, therefore, a form of asset protection.

The *Quistclose* trust takes its name from the case of *Barclays Bank Ltd v Quistclose* **9.75** *Investments Ltd*,[225] the facts of which were as follows. R Ltd was a company in serious financial difficulties: it had an overdraft with Barclays Bank (in excess of the permitted limit). In order to pay a dividend (of roughly £210,000) which it had already declared, R Ltd borrowed money from Quistclose Investments. The loan was made on the agreed condition that it would be used to pay the dividend. It was paid into a separate account, opened especially for the purpose, with Barclays, who knew that the money was borrowed and who agreed with R Ltd that it would be used only for the purpose of paying the dividend. Before the dividend was paid, however, R Ltd went into voluntary liquidation. Quistclose brought an action against R Ltd and Barclays claiming that the money had been held by R Ltd on trust to pay the dividend; that, as the trust had failed, it was held on resulting trust for Quistclose; and that Barclays had had notice of the trusts and were, accordingly, constructive trustees of the money for Quistclose.

The House of Lords, affirming the decision of the Court of Appeal, held that first, **9.76** arrangements of this character for the payment of a person's creditors by a third person gave rise to a relationship of a fiduciary character or trust in favour, as a primary trust, of the creditors, and, secondly, if the primary trust failed, of the third person. This had been recognized in a series of cases over some 150 years.[226] The fact that the transaction was one of a loan, giving rise to a legal action of debt, did not exclude the implication of a trust enforceable in equity. There was no difficulty in recognizing the coexistence in one transaction of legal and equitable rights and remedies: when the money was advanced, the lender acquired an equitable right to see that it was applied for the primary designated purpose; when the purpose had been carried out (ie the debt paid) the lender had his remedy against the borrower in debt; if the primary purpose could not be carried out, the question arose as to whether a secondary purpose (ie repayment to the lender) had been agreed, expressly or by implication; if it had, the remedies of equity might be invoked to give effect to it, and, if not (and the money was intended to fall into the general

---

[224] *Twinsectra Ltd v Yardley* [2002] 2 AC 164, 187–193.
[225] [1970] AC 567.
[226] ibid 580. These cases included *Toovey v Milne* (1819) 2 B & A 683; *Edwards v Glynn* (1859) 2 El & El 29; *Re Rogers* (1891) 8 Morr 243; *Re Drucker (No. 1)* [1902] 2 KB 237; *Re Hooley* [1915] HBR 181.

assets of the debtor), there was the appropriate remedy of a loan. Here, there was a clear intention to create a secondary trust for the benefit of the lender, Quistclose, to arise if the primary trust could not be carried out. Barclays had, on the facts, accepted the money with knowledge of the circumstances which made it trust money and could not retain it against Quistclose. Lord Wilberforce, delivering the decision of the House of Lords, clearly thought[227] that it was the 'mutual intention' of the lender and borrower—indeed 'the essence of the bargain'—that the sum advanced should not become part of the assets of R Ltd, but should be used *exclusively* for the payment of a particular class of creditors, the shareholders entitled to the dividend.

9.77   The decision in *Quistclose* left unanswered a range of difficult questions, such as the location of the beneficial interest pending the application of the monies for the stipulated purpose, the respective rights (if any) of the lender, the borrower, and the third party ultimately intended to benefit—all of which have subsequently given rise to an extensive literature.[228] However, it is relevant to highlight two preliminary points in particular. First, it is clear that the case was not argued before the House of Lords in terms of a non-charitable purpose trust. The appellants clearly contended that there was no trust at all. The respondents clearly thought in terms of a 'persons trust', for their counsel, in summarizing their argument,[229] and having referred to a payment by A to B 'to be applied for a specific purpose' as creating a trust, stated:

---

227   [1970] AC 567, 580.
228   See, eg, R Chambers, *Resulting Trusts* (Clarendon Press, 1997) Ch 3; S Worthington, *Proprietary Interests in Commercial Transactions* (Clarendon Press, 1996) Ch 3; RM Goode, *Principles of Corporate Insolvency Law* (Sweet & Maxwell, 1990); LJ Priestley, 'The Romalpa Clause and the *Quistclose* Trust' in PD Finn (ed), *Equity and Commercial Relationships* (Law Book Co Ltd, 1987), 217; (1985) 101 LQR 269 (PJ Millett); (1988) 11 UNSWLJ 66 (RP Austin); (1991) 107 LQR 608 (CEF Ricketts); (1992) 18 Mon LR 147 (FR Burns); (1992) 12 OJLS 333 (M Bridge); J Payne '*Quistclose* and Resulting Trusts' in P Birks and F Rose (eds), *Restitution and Equity— Volume One: Resulting Trusts and Equitable Compensation* (Mansfield Press, 2000) 77–95; (2001) 21 OJLS 267 (L Ho and P St J Smart). See also *Re EVTR Ltd* [1987] BCLC 646; *Twinsectra Ltd v Yardley* [1999] Lloyd's Rep Bank 438; *Re Branston & Gothard Ltd* [1999] 1 All ER (Comm) 289; *Burton v FX Music Ltd* The Times, 8 July 1999; *Re Australian Elizabethan Theatre Trust* (1991) 102 ALR 681; *Re McKeown* [1974] NILR 226; *General Communications Ltd v Development Finance Corporation of New Zealand Ltd* [1990] 3 NZLR 406; *Re Associated Securities Ltd* [1981] 1 NSWLR 742; *Guardian Ocean Cargoes Ltd v Banco da Brasil SA* [1991] 2 Lloyd's Rep 68. There are also some recent unreported decisions: *Hurst-Bannister v New Capital Reinsurance Corp Ltd* [2000] Lloyd's Rep IR 166; *Re Griffin Trading Co* [2000] BPIR 256; *R v Common Professional Examination Board, ex parte Sally Mewling-McLeod* The Times, 2 May 2000; and *Shanshal v Al-Kishtaini* [1999] TLR 448. See now *Twinsectra Ltd v Yardley* [2002] 2 AC 164, discussed, at para. 9.86–9.94 below. See also *The Quistclose Trust: Critical Essays*, ed W Swadling (Hart, 2004) which appeared after this section was submitted for publication: some of the essays (eg Chapter 4, by Lionel Smith) raise interesting questions, but others persist in unnecessarily complicating the analysis of the *Quistclose* trust.
229   [1970] AC 567, 576.

If the specified purpose is for the benefit of identified persons or for charity (subject to exceptions not here material) the court in the exercise of its equitable jurisdiction in the execution of trusts will enforce the equitable obligation of B.

The House of Lords was not asked to consider and determine the possible exist-   **9.78**
ence or validity of a non-charitable purpose trust and it did not do so. Secondly, it is clear that Lord Wilberforce attached considerable importance to the intentions of the parties—not just whether there was an intention to create a trust of any kind, as opposed to a mere loan or a charge or an assignment, but also in whose favour, or for whose benefit, such a trust was intended. There does not seem to be any compelling reason why the parties to a *Quistclose*-type transaction should always have the same intentions: the fact that the third party creditors were intended to have a beneficial interest in one case surely does not make it a requirement of a *Quistclose* trust that they must always have such an interest.

Nature of the *Quistclose* trust

Nevertheless, subsequent English cases confused, rather than clarified, these issues,   **9.79**
and the nature and operation of a *Quistclose* trust became matters of considerable debate and uncertainty. In *Carreras Rothmans Ltd v Freeman Mathews Treasure Ltd*[230] and *Re Northern Developments Holdings Ltd*,[231] for example, it was held that a *Quistclose* trust was a type of non-charitable purpose trust under which the beneficial interest remained in suspense pending the application of the moneys for the stipulated purpose. In *Carreras*, the plaintiff (a manufacturer of tobacco products) advertised its products extensively in newspapers and periodicals, using the services of the defendant, an advertising agency. Such services included buying advertising space in publications and on billboards; and, in doing its work, the defendant negotiated favourable discounts and incurred debts *as a principal* to third parties for the space bought and for certain technical services. The plaintiff paid the defendant an annual fee in monthly instalments for the placement work, and each month the plaintiff would pay the defendant a sum equivalent to the amount of the invoices received by the defendant from third parties for liabilities incurred the previous month. The plaintiff paid the money in time for the defendant to pay the third parties when the debts became due for payment. When the defendant fell into financial difficulties, it was agreed that a special account should be opened into which the plaintiff would pay a sum equivalent to the monies due to third parties. The defendant then went into voluntary liquidation and its liquidator arranged for the special account to be frozen before cheques were cleared. The third party publishers reacted to non-payment by threatening that, unless the plaintiff met the defendant's liabilities to them, they would not publish any advertisement of the

---

[230] [1985] Ch 207.
[231] Unreported decision of Megarry V-C, 6 October 1978.

plaintiffs products. The plaintiff paid the debts incurred by the defendant to the third parties and took an assignment of those debts. The plaintiff then brought an action against the defendant and its liquidator for a declaration that the monies in the special account were held on trust for the sole purpose of paying the third party creditors and for an order for those monies to be repaid to the plaintiff. Peter Gibson J (unfortunately in an unreserved judgment) held that the monies paid into the special account were never held by the defendant beneficially; that, since the monies had been paid in for a specific purpose, equity required that the monies be used only for that purpose; that accordingly, the agreement created a trust and the plaintiff had a right to enforce the payment over of the monies to the third parties and the third parties had an interest in the orderly administration of those trust funds.

9.80 His conclusion on the first question, namely whether or not the loaned monies were subjected to a trust, was relatively unproblematic. This was a question of ascertaining the mutual intentions of the parties, and the circumstances of this case pointed clearly to a trust. However, none of this indicated the capacity in which, or the mechanism by which, the plaintiff recovered the money: was it as the original lender and under a resulting trust? Or was it as assignee of the third party creditors and under an express trust? A strict application of the decision of the House of Lords in *Quistclose* would seem to point clearly to the first of these two alternatives. However, Peter Gibson J (despite the fact that his judgment was unreserved) refused to accept *the joint submission* of counsel that the third party creditors for the payment of whose debts the plaintiff had paid the monies into the special account had no enforceable rights.[232] Instead, he preferred to base his conclusions on an earlier, unreported decision of Megarry V-C in *Re Northern Developments (Holdings) Ltd*.[233]

9.81 In none of the earlier cases, other than *Re Northern Developments*, had any consideration been given to the question of whether the person intended to benefit from the carrying out of the specific purpose (ie, the third party creditor) had any enforceable rights. In *Quistclose* itself and earlier cases, either the primary purpose had been carried out, and the contest was between the borrower's trustee in bankruptcy or liquidator and the person to whom the money had been paid, or the purpose was treated as having failed, and the contest was between the trustee in bankruptcy or liquidator and the lender. Prior to *Re Northern Developments*, the position where the primary purpose was still capable of being carried out had not

---

[232] It is clear that counsel for both plaintiff and defendant had submitted that the third party creditors had no enforceable rights; and it seems equally clear that the plaintiff claimed that, in default of the stipulated purpose being fulfilled, there was a resulting trust in favour of the plaintiff: [1985] Ch 207, 222, 223.

[233] Unreported decision of Megarry V-C, 6 October 1978.

been considered.[234] In *Re Northern Developments*, a group of banks paid money into an account in Northern's name for the express purpose of paying the unsecured creditors of a subsidiary company (Kelly) in financial difficulties and for no other purpose. Over half the fund remained unexpended when Kelly was put into receivership. Megarry V-C held that there was a *Quistclose*-type trust here and that the trust was a non-charitable purpose trust enforceable by identifiable individuals, namely the banks as lenders, Kelly itself, and Kelly's creditors. On his analysis, the third party creditors did not have a beneficial interest as such under a *Quistclose* trust: instead, they had a 'right' to compel performance of the trust in their favour, such 'right' being similar to the right of a beneficiary entitled to a share of residue under a will to compel due administration of the estate. In the light of this authority, Peter Gibson J concluded, in *Carreras*, that the beneficial interest is in suspense until the payment is made.

This novel approach to the problem—one for which there is no trace of support in *Quistclose* itself—gives rise to several difficult questions.[235] First, the nature of this 'right' is ambiguous. The analogy with the position of a beneficiary interested in unadministered residue seems completely inappropriate. Such a beneficiary has no proprietary interest at all—only a mere *spes* or hope of benefit—unless and until the estate is fully administered (or there is an earlier appropriation) and he may never actually receive such an interest at all. On the other hand, once a *Quistclose* trust is completely constituted (when monies are transferred to the borrower), there is no obvious reason why the purpose cannot be fulfilled, ie why the third party creditors should not be able to demand its immediate performance. Why should the beneficial interest need to be in suspense at any stage and why should the purpose of the trust fail simply because the borrower had become insolvent? Indeed, in *Carreras* itself, the order made was that the liquidator should forthwith apply the money in the special account in carrying out the purpose of the trust.[236] If this was the case in *Carreras*, then why could it not equally be the case with other *Quistclose* trusts (including *Quistclose* itself), in which case how could a resulting trust arise in favour of the lender? Under a *Quistclose* trust, the borrower trustee has the option of carrying out the purpose of the loan (according to the terms of the loan agreement) or returning the money to the lender: he has no other duties to perform; and, by definition, the trust fund cannot be diminished by any prior claims. This is the language of powers and not simply of trust. A personal representative, on the other hand, takes absolute ownership of the assets in an unadministered estate, has a range of duties to perform which take priority over distribution to beneficiaries, and may, in fact, have no property left to

9.82

---

[234] *Twinsectra Ltd v Yardley* [2002] 2 AC 164.
[235] See GW Thomas (n 223 above) 260–262.   [236] [1985] Ch 207, 232.

give to any of them. But, in this latter case, non-payment is the result of the inadequacy of the assets and not a change in the status of the 'trustee'.

9.83 A second difficulty is that the *Carreras* analysis said nothing about the rights of the lender. It is well recognized that the lender in a *Quistclose* transaction acquires an equitable right to ensure that the monies that he has lent are applied for the primary designated purpose[237] (or, at least, a right to prevent their misapplication).[238] However, it is trite law that a settlor who retains no beneficial interest, and no express power of control over trustees, cannot enforce a trust which he has created.[239] Consequently, the settlor/lender must have some right which an ordinary settlor would not have, and the most likely explanation is that he has such a right because he has a beneficial interest under the trust.[240] Moreover, in several cases—including *Twinsectra Ltd v Yardley*[241]—the primary trust, if it can be said to have been a non-charitable purpose trust at all, must have been for an abstract purpose, with no one but the lender to enforce performance or restrain misapplication. However, as we have seen,[242] abstract purpose trusts are not recognized in English law: even *Re Denley* was not prepared to contemplate the possibility that they might be valid.

9.84 An alternative and much more straightforward analysis of the *Quistclose* trust as an express trust was put forward in Australia, in *Re Elizabethan Theatre Trust*,[243] where Gummow J argued persuasively that the *Quistclose* trust could be analysed easily in terms of existing principles and norms and that there was 'scarcely a need' for another kind of trust. It was an express trust with two limbs, rather than an express trust in favour of the shareholders and a resulting trust in favour of Quistclose.[244]

9.85 There is much to be said for this analysis. Under a *Quistclose* trust, the borrower holds the money on trust for the lender, but with a power to apply the money for (and only for) the stipulated purpose. If and when the borrower exercises that power, the purpose of the loan is fulfilled and the lender's beneficial interest is extinguished. It is a power exercisable for the 'benefit' of the borrower, but it is not a general power, for it can be exercised only in particular circumstances and in

---

[237] [1970] AC 567, 581.
[238] *Edwards v Glyn* (1859) 2 El & El 29, 50–51; *Re Rogers* (1891) 8 Morr 243, 248.
[239] See (1985) 101 LQR 269, 287 (PJ Millett); *Twinsectra Ltd v Yardley* [2002] 2 AC 164.
[240] As argued, eg, by Millett, ibid—save that he went on to argue that the trust is actually an 'illusory trust', which seems unlikely and unnecessary. The 'settlor' presumably has a contractual right, arising from his contract with the borrower, to prevent (by injunction) the misapplication of the monies (*Palmer v Carey* [1926] AC 703, 706; *Swiss Bank Corporation v Lloyds Bank Ltd* [1982] AC 584, 613), but generally has no right to compel its application in a particular way (by specific performance).
[241] [2002] 2 AC 164.   [242] See paras 6.01–6.03, 6.13–6.21, 6.34–6.38 above.
[243] (1991) 102 ALR 681.   [244] ibid 691.

favour of a particular object or class of objects. It is also then largely immaterial whether one views the objects of the power as a 'purpose' or a class of persons. Moreover, it is clearly not the case that, if the settlor/lender is regarded as the beneficiary under such a trust, he could then revoke the trust prior to the carrying out of the stipulated purpose. The settlor would have no such right either under the contract or in equity. If S directs T to hold property on trust for S, but T has a power to distribute the property to X (or a class comprised of A to F), then, for as long as that power subsists, S alone is not absolutely and indefeasibly entitled to that property.[245] The question that would then arise is: what happens to the power when the borrower becomes insolvent, assuming it has not by then been exercised? The obvious answer is that it then ceases to exist, or at least to be exercisable. If the intention is to save the borrower from insolvency, the power—whether it be classified as a mere power or a fiduciary power—can be exercised only when, and for as long as, the borrower is solvent. There would then be no question of the power vesting in the borrower's trustee in bankruptcy, receiver, or liquidator and being exercisable by any one of them (as the case may be).[246] It is conceivable, but highly unlikely, that the power conferred on the borrower is a trust power (in the sense that it must be exercised by the borrower). In that case, the creditors would have a right to compel its execution and the lender would then not have a beneficial interest. However, such an analysis would not be consistent with *Quistclose* itself or any of the subsequent *Quistclose*-type cases.

A settled analysis?

Many of these issues were recently addressed and partially resolved by the House **9.86** of Lords in *Twinsectra Ltd v Yardley*.[247] Twinsectra loaned £1 million on the terms of a solicitors' undertaking to the effect that the money would 'be utilised solely for the acquisition of property' on behalf of the latter's client 'and for no other purpose', and would be retained by the solicitors until such time as it was so applied. In the event, and contrary to the terms of this undertaking, not all the money was used for this purpose but was simply paid over upon the client's instructions. The loan was not repaid. The first question at issue was whether the loan monies were subject to any form of trust in the solicitors' hands. All five Law Lords concluded that the money was held on trust.

In his speech, Lord Millett provided a lengthy and detailed analysis of the **9.87** *Quistclose* trust and addressed, in particular, the location of the beneficial interest under such a trust. He favoured the view that, pending the carrying out of the

---

[245] See also R Chambers, *Resulting Trusts*, 74. It is, therefore, nonsense to suggest that the rule in *Saunders v Vautier* (1841) 4 Beav 115 would apply so as to enable S to call for the trust fund, as is suggested in the first essay in *The Quistclose Trust: Critical Essays*, ed W Swadling (Hart, 2004) at 27, 28. (Cf ibid at 73.)

[246] See G W Thomas, *Powers* (Sweet & Maxwell, 1998) ('*Thomas*') 194–210.

[247] [2002] 2 AC 164.

stated purpose, the beneficial interest under a *Quistclose* trust rests with the lender. As for the alternative analyses, he made the following observations.

9.88   First, it was plain that the beneficial interest is not vested unconditionally in the borrower so as to leave the money at his free disposal. The borrower's interest pending the application of the money for the stated purpose or its return to the lender is minimal. He must keep the money separate; he cannot apply it except for the stated purpose; unless the terms of the loan otherwise provide he must return it to the lender if demanded; he cannot refuse to return it if the stated purpose cannot be achieved; and if he becomes bankrupt it does not vest in his trustee in bankruptcy.[248]

9.89   Secondly, the beneficial interest was clearly not vested in the contemplated beneficiary. Lord Millett pointed out that the purpose of the loan in *Re Northern Developments* was not solely to enable the debtor to avoid bankruptcy by paying off existing creditors, but to provide it with working capital. Moreover, the lenders' object was not to benefit the creditors, but to protect their own interests.

9.90   Thirdly, the 'purpose trust' analysis was neither workable nor necessary. In several cases, including *Twinsectra* itself, the primary trust was for an abstract purpose with no one but the lender to enforce performance or restrain misapplication. There was no reason to make an arbitrary distinction between money paid for an abstract purpose and money paid for a purpose which can be said to benefit an ascertained class of beneficiaries, and the cases rightly draw no such distinction: 'Any analysis of the *Quistclose* trust must be able to accommodate gifts and loans for an abstract purpose.'

9.91   Fourthly, the argument that the beneficial interest remained in suspense until the stated purpose was carried out was also defective: 'The difficulty with this (apart from its unorthodoxy) is that it fails to have regard to the role which the resulting trust plays in equity's scheme of things, or to explain why the money is not simply held on a resulting trust for the lender.'

9.92   Lord Millett concluded his analysis by saying that all the alternative analyses have their difficulties, but that there are two problems, in particular, which they fail to solve—problems which are easily solved if the beneficial interest remains throughout in the lender. The first is the fact, well established by the authorities, that the primary trust is enforceable by the lender. On what basis can he do so? Clearly not as beneficiary of the secondary trust and not as settlor. The second problem relates to the basis on which the primary trust is said to have failed. Given that the money does not belong to the borrower, his/its insolvency should not prevent the original purpose being fulfilled, unless the purpose is said to have been to

---

[248] [2002] 2 AC 188.

avoid insolvency or collapse. However, one must not confuse the purpose of the trust with the settlor's motive: the frustration of the latter does not necessarily mean that the purpose of the trust has failed, '[b]ut if the borrower is treated as holding the money on a resulting trust for the lender but with power (or in some cases a duty) to carry out the lender's revocable mandate, and the lender's object in giving the mandate is frustrated, he is entitled to revoke the mandate and demand the return of money which never ceased to be his beneficially'. His conclusion, therefore, is as follows:

> I . . . hold the *Quistclose* trust to be an entirely orthodox example of the kind of default trust known as a resulting trust. The lender pays the money to the borrower by way of loan but he does not part with the entire beneficial interest in the money, and insofar as he does not it is held on a resulting trust for the lender from the outset. Contrary to the opinion of the Court of Appeal, it is the borrower who has a very limited use of the money, being obliged to apply it for the stated purpose or return it. He has no beneficial interest in the money, which remains throughout in the lender subject only to the borrower's power or duty to apply the money in accordance with the lender's instructions. When the purpose fails, the money is returnable to the lender, not under some new trust in his favour which only comes into being on the failure of the purpose, but because the resulting trust in his favour is no longer subject to any power on the part of the borrower to make use of the money. Whether the borrower is obliged to apply the money for the stated purpose or merely at liberty to do so, and whether the lender can countermand the borrower's mandate while it is still capable of being carried out, must depend on the circumstances of the particular case.[249]

Thus, according to Lord Millett, the *Quistclose* trust, far from being *sui generis*, is in essence an entirely orthodox trust based on existing and well-understood principles and norms.[250]

9.93 Whether the other four Law Lords agreed with the details of Lord Millett's analysis is unclear, however. Lord Hoffmann alone dealt directly with the nature of the trust created by the solicitors' undertaking. However, he did not expressly endorse Lord Millett's analysis; nor did he attempt to analyse a *Quistclose* trust himself—indeed, nowhere in his speech is *Quistclose* mentioned. According to Lord Hoffmann, the undertaking made it clear that the money 'was not to be at the free disposal' of the client and that the solicitors 'were not to part with the money to [the client] or anyone else except for the purpose of enabling him to acquire property': ' . . . the effect of the undertaking was to provide that the money . . . should remain Twinsectra's money until such a time as it was applied for the acquisition

---

[249] ibid 192–193.

[250] An attempt is made in the first essay in *The Quistclose Trust: Critical Essays*, ed W Swadling (Hart, 2004) to challenge the correctness of Lord Millett's analysis (and indeed, the proposition that the *Quistclose* trust is a trust at all). However, the challenge is mostly sound and fury: several of the key arguments (eg the application of the rule in *Saunders v Vautier*, the risk of 'double recovery') are clearly flawed; and some important material (eg *Re Australian Elizabethan Theatre Trust* (1991) 102 ALR 681) is not addressed at all.

of property in accordance with the undertaking'. His analysis of the trust in question was that the solicitors 'held the money in trust for Twinsectra, but subject to a power to apply it by way of loan' to the borrower in accordance with the undertaking. Lord Slynn agreed with Lord Hoffmann and made no reference to Lord Millett's speech. Lord Steyn agreed with the judgments of Lord Hoffmann and Lord Hutton, and did not refer to Lord Millett. Lord Hutton, for his part, indicated that he had read the draft speeches of both Lord Hoffmann and Lord Millett and, for the reasons they had given, agreed that the solicitors' undertaking 'created a trust', despite the fact that their reasons may not have been entirely in accord. Thus, even if it can be said that Lord Steyn and Lord Hutton agreed, directly or indirectly, with Lord Millett, it is not clear whether their agreement extended to the detailed analysis of a *Quistclose* trust put forward by Lord Millett or was simply confined to the conclusion that the solicitors' undertaking had created a trust—even a *Quistclose* trust—which is all that needed to be established in order for the second point in the case (the 'dishonest assistance' point) to be raised. In other words, once a trust (even a *Quistclose* trust) had been found to exist, there was no need to analyse the nature of that trust and the majority of the House of Lords did not attempt to do so.

9.94   Indeed, the analysis put forward by Lord Millett may raise uncertainties of its own. It is clear that, for Lord Hoffmann, the solicitors held Twinsectra's money on trust, 'but subject to a power to apply it by way of loan'. Although he acknowledged that the solicitors owed 'fiduciary obligations . . . in respect of the exercise of the power', there is no hint that he considered that they were actually under a duty to exercise it. Lord Millett seems to have reached the same conclusion in that he too held that the money belonged to Twinsectra subject only to a 'right to apply it' for the stated purpose. Moreover, he clearly acknowledged that the lender's right may simply be a right to prevent misapplication for an unauthorized purpose and not to compel application for an authorized one.[251] All of this clearly supports the analysis of a *Quistclose* trust in favour of the lender but with a mere *power* for the borrower to use the money for the stated purpose. However, at various points in his judgment, he also referred to the borrower being under a *duty* to apply the money.[252]

9.95   Similarly, when dealing with the question of certainty of objects, he says: 'the borrower is authorized (or directed) to apply the money for a stated purpose, but this is a mere power and does not constitute a purpose trust'.[253] In other words, Lord Millett contemplated the possibility that the idea of a *Quistclose* trust encompassed a range of different arrangements, including not just cases where

---

[251] [2002] 2 AC 188–189, 193. See also *Re Rogers* (1891) 8 Morr 243.
[252] ibid 186, 191; see also *Gilbert v Gonard* (1884) 54 LJ Ch 439.
[253] ibid 193.

the borrower-trustee had a power to apply the loan for the specific purpose, but also where the borrower-trustee was under a duty to do so. 'Whether the borrower is obliged to apply the money for the stated purpose or merely at liberty to do so, and whether the lender can countermand the borrower's mandate while it is still capable of being carried out, must depend on the circumstances of the particular case.' Of course, there is no reason, in principle, why a lender could not impose such an obligation on the borrower. However, once this point is reached and he is held to have done so, then the implications and consequences must surely be different from those outlined by Lord Millett.

First, if the borrower is *obliged* to apply the money for the stated purpose, and does **9.96** not merely have a right or power to do so, then it is difficult to see how the beneficial interest can then be said to be vested in the lender. The borrower will hold the money on trust for the intended ultimate beneficiary (the unpaid creditors in the typical case). Even if the borrower is said to have a 'trust power'—in the sense of a power which he must exercise, as opposed to a mere power—it is surely the intended ultimate beneficiary who is the beneficiary and not the lender. The problematic question as to whether the 'beneficiary' of the trust or trust power was a human being (such as the creditors) or a purpose, and whether in the latter case there could be a valid trust at all, would need to be addressed all over again.

Secondly, where such an arrangement has been created, can the primary trust ever **9.97** fail? If not, how could a resulting trust ever arise in favour of the lender? Thirdly, how and why would the lender have any interest in enforcing the trust under such an arrangement? If the primary trust can be and is enforced and carried into effect, as it surely ought to be, there can be no secondary trust in favour of the lender. These are the very difficulties that were discussed at length by Lord Millett and which would not arise if the *Quistclose* trust were analysed simply as a trust for the lender, coupled with a power for the borrower to apply the money for the stated purpose, but which, it is suggested, would be as alive as ever once the borrower is held to be under an obligation to do so.

Some uncertainties as to the nature of a *Quistclose* trust therefore remain. It is sug- **9.98** gested that a *Quistclose* trust is an express trust, under which the settlor-lender retains the beneficial interest and the borrower possesses a power to pay the funds to a creditor. *Twinsectra*, and especially the judgment of Lord Millett, concludes that (in general) it is indeed a trust in favour of the lender, coupled with a power in the borrower, but that it is a resulting and not an express trust. It is not entirely clear why this should be the case. If A lends money to B for the specific purpose of paying debts, Lord Millett would say that the beneficial interest is not wholly disposed of (pending exercise of the power) and it therefore results back to A. This makes his analysis consistent with the decision in *Quistclose* itself. However, it could also be argued that this is an express trust. Indeed, it is difficult to imagine that any adviser acting for a lender, when asked by his client to ensure that money loaned to a borrower for a specific purpose was used solely for that purpose and would be returned to the lender in the event of the borrower becoming insolvent before that purpose could be implemented, would not seek to avoid the uncertainties of the law in this area. Surely such an adviser would seek to ensure that the difficult issues outlined above would never arise and the simple and obvious way to do so would be to create an express trust (coupled with a power) in terms which made it abundantly clear that, pending application of the money, the beneficial interest was vested in the lender and no one else, and also that the borrower had a mere power (exercisable subject to certain conditions) and no more. The form of such an express trust would be identical to Lord Millett's resulting trust. In any event, there is surely very little scope after *Twinsectra* to argue in favour of an analysis of a *Quistclose* trust as a non-charitable purpose trust—even one falling under *Re Denley*—or as a trust under which the beneficial interest remains in suspense until the creditor is paid. There is simply no need to do so.

PART C

THE DUTIES AND
POWERS OF TRUSTEES

10

THE DUTIES OF TRUSTEES: PART ONE[1]

[1] A Underhill and DJ Hayton, *Law of Trusts and Trustees* (16th edn, Butterworths, 2002) ('*Underhill and Hayton*') 484–687.

A. General Duties in Relation to the Trust

10.01   Trusteeship is primarily about duty and obligation. It is an onerous and complicated matter which ought not to be undertaken lightly. Trustees are invariably required to discharge numerous duties and obligations, and failure to do so may result in serious liability. Different kinds of trust involve different kinds of duties and, even in relation to trusts of the same kind, the precise content of any particular duty may be curtailed or modified by express provision in the trust instrument or by the particular circumstances of the case. Many trustees' duties are often rendered less onerous, not just by provisions exempting trustees from liability for breach of those duties, but also by means of powers which confer on them a wide discretion as to the manner in which those duties may be carried out. The duties of trustees therefore go hand in hand with their powers.

10.02   Some of the duties and powers of trustees are sufficiently important to merit separate detailed treatment in various parts of this work. The duty of trustees to provide information to their beneficiaries and objects, for example, is dealt with in Chapter 12. Several of these duties are surrounded and qualified almost out of existence by exceptions, usually in the form of powers conferred on trustees. Delegation by trustees is an obvious example: this is dealt with separately in Chapter 15 below. Similarly, the duty to invest, which is dealt with briefly in this chapter, is explored fully in Chapter 52. This chapter deals with some of the general duties of trustees in relation to the trust.

B. Duties on Acceptance of a Trust

10.03   The duties of a trustee on acceptance of a trust are essentially matters of common sense. The trustee is required to take an active role and will, therefore, need and want to familiarize himself with all the information relevant to the task. As Kekewich J put it, in *Hallows v Lloyd*:[2]

> ... when persons are asked to become new trustees, they are bound to inquire of what the property consists that is proposed to be handed over to them, and what are the trusts. They ought also to look into the trust documents and papers to ascertain what notices appear among them of incumbrances and other matters affecting the trust.

The precise details will obviously vary according to whether the trustee is an original trustee or appointed subsequently in place of or in addition to an existing trustee, but his duties are broadly the same whenever he is appointed. He will require the production of the trust instrument, all deeds of appointment (of beneficial interests or of trustees), trust accounts, investment schedules, and all

---

[2] (1888) 39 Ch D 686, 691.

documents and papers relating to the administration of the trust, including, in general, all correspondence and memoranda relevant to trusteeship,[3] and even information of relevance which is not evident from such documents.[4] In short, a trustee must familiarize himself with the state of the trusts, the circumstances in which he is to operate, and the potential liability to which he may expose himself.

The trustee must acquaint himself with the identity of the current trustees and **10.04** beneficiaries, the nature of the trusts and trust assets, the range of powers available to the trustees (and, in case of doubt, obtain legal advice on the matter).[5] He must review trust investments,[6] and ensure that they are authorized and appropriate to the trust and are vested in his name jointly with his co-trustees (or under their joint control).[7] If he discovers that loss has been caused, he is obliged to investigate the circumstances and decide whether action for recovery is possible and appropriate.[8] A trustee is liable only for such acts and matters as he knows or ought to have known.[9]

For his own protection, a trustee will also wish to know whether, on acceptance of **10.05** trusteeship, there might be an unauthorized conflict between self-interest and his fiduciary duty, whether there are provisions for remuneration of trustees and for exempting them from liability and their extent, whether he can retire when he wishes, without prior consent, whether he can be removed and, if so, by whom and in what circumstances, and so forth. Professional trustees ought also to be aware of their statutory duties to report certain matters, for example under the Terrorism Act 2000, the Proceeds of Crime Act 2002, not to mention various requirements in Revenue legislation.

A new trustee is entitled to assume that his predecessors acted properly and he **10.06** need not, therefore, conduct extensive investigations into past actions.[10] However, if there are suspicious circumstances, he should take legal advice and take appropriate steps. Otherwise, he himself may be liable for breach of trust.

C. Duty to Obey the Directions of the Trust

A trustee must obey and carry out the directions laid down in the trust, **10.07** unless he is authorized not to do so by the trust instrument, by statute, or by

---

[3] *Tiger v Barclays Bank Ltd* [1952] 1 All ER 85.   [4] *Mond v Hyde* [1999] QB 1097, 1104.
[5] *Nestle v National Westminster Bank* [1993] 1 WLR 1260, 1265.   [6] ibid.
[7] *Underwood v Stevens* (1816) 1 Mer 712; *Lewis v Nobbs* (1878) 8 Ch D 591. If he retains money in his hands for an unreasonable time, without investing it, he may be liable: *Moyle v Moyle* (1831) 2 Russ & M 710.
[8] *Bennett v Burgis* (1846) 5 Hare 295.
[9] *Re Hurst* (1892) 67 LT 96; *Youde v Cloud* (1874) LR 18 Eq 634.
[10] *Ex p Geaves* (1856) 8 De GM & G 291, 309; *Re Forest of Dean Coal Mining Co* (1878) 10 Ch D 450, 453–454; *Harvey v Olliver* (1887) 57 LT 239. *Rawsthorne v Rowley* [1909] 1 Ch 409n.

the court.[11] As a general rule, trustees cannot depart from the duties imposed on them, and cannot assume powers not conferred on them, not even if they consider that, by doing so, they would be acting to the benefit of their beneficiaries.[12] A trustee must obviously pay trust income and capital to those entitled (without demand);[13] and, if he has discretion as to distribution, he must exercise it within a reasonable time.[14] If he is directed to sell certain property[15] or to invest only in specified assets, he must obviously comply with such directions.[16]

10.08 In some cases, the trustee is required to act only in accordance with the advice of a third party expert, such as a competent valuer or actuary, or a financial intermediary authorized under the Financial Services and Markets Act 2000, in which case the trustee must accept and act promptly in reliance on that advice, unless there is a strong reason why he considers the expert to have acted improperly or on the basis of some substantial mistake.[17] In other cases, a trustee may be directed to satisfy some condition before taking action, for example obtaining the consent of a beneficiary, the settlor, or a third party, in which case he must satisfy that condition.[18]

D. Duty to Safeguard Trust Assets

10.09 A trustee must take all reasonable and practicable steps to safeguard trust assets. Thus, he must ensure that debts owed to the trust are repaid timeously and, if

---

[11] The trustees may have a power of amendment (as to which see Chapter 24 below). The beneficiaries may authorize the trustee to act otherwise if the principle in *Saunders v Vautier* applies. As for occupational pension schemes, see s 68 of the Pensions Act 1995; and, for the powers of the court, see Chapter 24 below.

[12] *Clough v Bond* (1838) 3 My & Cr 490, 496–497; *Target Holdings Ltd v Redferns* [1966] AC 421, 434. Of course, it is not a rule of strict liability. There are exceptions, eg where the directions are unlawful or impracticable, or rendered impossible. Trustees may also be able to rely on an exemption clause or invoke s 61 of the Trustee Act 1925, but only a foolish trustee would embark on a course of action intending to rely on these.

[13] *Hawkesley v May* [1956] 1 QB 304.

[14] *Re Alleyn-Meyrick's Will Trusts* [1966] 1 WLR 499; *Re Gulbenkian's Settlement Trusts (No 2)* [1970] Ch 408; *Re Locker's Settlement Trusts* [1977] 1 WLR 1323. The consequences of such failure vary according to whether the trustees have a mere power or a trust power: for the duties of trustees in relation to their discretions, see Chapter 11 below.

[15] *Fry v Fry* (1859) 27 Beav 144; *Craven v Craddock* [1868] WN 229 (see also (1869) 20 LT 638); *Wentworth v Wentworth* [1900] AC 163. For trustees' powers of sale, see paras 14.46–14.57 below.

[16] For trustees' duties and powers of investment, see Chapter 52 below.

[17] *Re George Newnes Group Pension Fund* [1968] 2 All ER 802; *Re Imperial Food Ltd's Pension Scheme* [1986] 1 WLR 717; *Stannard v Fisons Pension Trust Ltd* [1992] IRLR 27. See also *Dean v Prince* [1954] Ch 409 and *Wrightson Ltd v Fletcher Challenge Nominees Ltd* [2001] OPLR 249.

[18] See, generally, GW Thomas, *Powers* (Sweet & Maxwell, 1998) ('*Thomas*'), Ch 12. See also *Bateman v Davis* (1818) 3 Madd 98. Cf *Stevens v Robertson* (1868) 37 LJ Ch 499. An action taken without meeting such precondition is not necessarily void.

necessary (and acting jointly with his co-trustees), take legal proceedings to enforce payment.[19] (This is without prejudice to the trustee's powers to compound liabilities.[20]) He must ensure that title to trust property is vested or registered in the trustees' names;[21] must not allow rent to fall into arrears;[22] he must keep up the premiums on an insurance policy (unless it is surrendered or paid up for good cause)[23] and must ensure that notice is given to the assurer of an assignment of a policy to the trust.[24] He must compile a complete and accurate inventory of trust chattels, including a valuation of their worth;[25] and he must invest trust monies within a reasonable time.[26]

When selling trust property, a trustee must use his best endeavours to obtain the **10.10** best terms, notwithstanding that he may already be under a moral (but not a legal) obligation to sell to another.[27] He must invite competition, inform himself of the value of the property, fix a reserve price, take advice from a person reasonably qualified to give it, and generally ensure that a sale is not improvident or made on unreasonable terms.[28] He ought not do anything that depreciates the value of the property (although a sale shall not be impeachable by any beneficiary on the ground that any of the conditions subject to which the sale was made may have been 'unnecessarily depreciatory', unless it appears that the consideration for the sale was thereby rendered inadequate).[29] A trustee should ensure that trust property does not fall into decay.[30]

---

[19] *Buxton v Buxton* (1835) 1 My & Cr 80; *Fenwick v Greenwell* (1847) 10 Beav 412; *Grove v Price* (1858) 26 Beav 103; *Re Brogden* (1888) 38 Ch D 546; *Millar's Trustees v Polson* (1897) SLR 798; *Re England's Settlement Trusts* [1918] 1 Ch 24.

[20] As to which, see paras 14.72–14.75 below. A trustee in any doubt ought to seek the directions of the court: *Public Trustee v Cooper* [2001] WTLR 901; *Representation of I* (2001) 4 ITELR 446; *Bradstock Group Pension Scheme Trustees Ltd v Bradstock Group plc* [2002] PLR 327.

[21] *Lewis v Nobbs* (1878) 8 Ch D 591; *Wyman v Paterson* [1900] AC 271; *Macnamara v Carey* (1867) IR 1 Eq 9 (where the settlor was able to mortgage the property).

[22] *Tebbs v Carpenter* (1816) 1 Madd 290.

[23] *Re Godwin's Settlement* (1918) 87 LJ Ch 645.

[24] *Kingdon v Castleman* (1877) 25 WR 345; *Re Godwin's Settlement* (1918) 87 LJ Ch 645. See also *Re McGaw* [1919] WN 288.

[25] *Temple v Thring* (1887) 56 LJ Ch 767.

[26] *Gilroy v Stephens* (1882) 30 WR 745; *Re Jones* (1883) 49 LT 91; *Cann v Cann* (1884) 51 LT 770.

[27] *Buttle v Saunders* [1950] 2 All ER 193; *Cowan v Scargill* [1985] Ch 270. See also *Selby v Bowie* (1863) 8 LT 372; *R v Commission for New Towns, ex p Tomkins* [1988] RVR 106 (affirmed (1989) 58 P & CR 57). As to joint sales by trustees with owners of contiguous property, see *Re Cooper and Allen's Contract* (1876) 4 Ch D 802; *Rede v Oakes* (1864) 4 De GJ & SM 505; *Re Parker and Beech's Contract* [1887] WN 27.

[28] *Oliver v Court* (1820) 8 Price 127; *Ferraby v Hobson* (1847) 2 Ph 255 (leasehold); *Re Cooper and Allen's Contract* (1876) 4 Ch D 802, 816; *Campbell v Walker* (1800) 5 Ves 678; *Ord v Noel* (1820) 5 Madd 438; *Pechel v Fowler* (1795) 2 Anst 549. See also *Norris v Wright* (1851) 14 Beav 291.

[29] Trustee Act 1925, s 13.

[30] *Re Hotchkys* (1886) 32 Ch D 408. Whether the costs of repair fall on capital or income is another matter: see *Re Fowler* (1881) 16 Ch D 723; *Re Courtier* (1886) 34 Ch D 136.

10.11   Specific duties apply to a trustee where the trust fund includes a controlling share-holding in a private company. In *Re Lucking's Will Trusts*,[31] Cross J stated:

> What steps, if any, does a reasonably prudent man who finds himself a majority shareholder in a private company take with regard to the management of the company's affairs? He does not content himself with such information as to the management of the company's affairs as he is entitled to as shareholder, but ensures that he is represented on the board. He may be prepared to run the business himself as managing director or, at least, to become a non-executive director while having the business managed by someone else. Alternatively, he may find someone who will act as his nominee on the board and report to him from time to time as to the company's affairs. In the same way trustees holding a controlling interest ought to ensure so far as they can that they have such information as to the progress of the company's affairs as directors would have. If they sit back and allow the company to be run by the minority shareholders and receive no more information than shareholders are entitled to, they do so at their risk if things go wrong.

These observations have subsequently been interpreted so that they do not impose an absolute duty on trustees to ensure that one of their number, or a nominee, is on the company's board, but simply as outlining convenient methods by which a trustee (and any prudent man of business) with such a controlling holding would place himself in a position to make an informed decision whether any action is appropriate to be taken for the protection of his asset.[32] Alternative methods of achieving the same end might include the receipt of copies of the agenda and minutes of board meetings, the receipt of monthly management accounts in the case of a trading concern, or quarterly reports. As Brightman J noted, in *Bartlett v Barclays Bank Trust Co Ltd*:[33]

> The purpose to be achieved is not that of monitoring every move of the directors, but of making it reasonably probable . . . that the trustees or one of them will receive an adequate flow of information in time to enable the trustees to make use of their controlling shareholding should this be necessary for the protection of their trust asset, namely the shareholding.

10.12   If a trustee has acted 'with reasonable care, prudence and circumspection', but has nonetheless committed an error of judgment, he may not be liable for any resulting loss.[34] Nor will he be liable if the trust property is stolen, provided he took reasonable care of it.[35]

---

[31] [1968] 1 WLR 866.

[32] *Re Miller's Deed Trusts* [1978] LS Gaz 454; *Bartlett v Barclays Bank Trust Co Ltd* [1980] Ch 515.

[33] ibid 533–534.

[34] *Re Chapman* [1896] 2 Ch 763, esp 778; *Re Lucking's Will Trusts* [1968] 1 WLR 866; *Bartlett v Barclays Bank Trust Co Ltd* [1980] Ch 515. See also *Buxton v Buxton* (1835) 1 My & Cr 80; *Sculthorpe v Tipper* (1871) LR 13 Eq 232; *Robinson v Robinson* (1851) 1 De GM & G 247.

[35] *Jones v Lewis* (1751) 2 Ves Sen 240; *Job v Job* (1877) 6 Ch D 562; *Jobson v Palmer* [1893] 1 Ch 71. If the trustee himself is guilty of some other unauthorized act, eg in paying trust money to a stranger, the result may well be otherwise.

E. Duty to Act Even-Handedly as Between Beneficiaries[36]

It is a well-established general principle that, in the absence of some provision to the contrary, a trustee must be impartial in the execution of his trust. As Turner LJ stated in *Re Tempest*,[37] 'it is of the essence of the duty of every trustee to hold an even hand between the parties interested under the trust. Every trustee is in duty bound to look to the interests of all, and not of any particular member or class of members of his *cestuis que trusts*.' Similarly, in *Re Lepine*,[38] Fry LJ stated: 'I agree, as fully as it can be expressed, that it is the duty of trustees to hold a perfectly even hand between all their *cestuis que trust*.' Most of the traditional duties of trustees seem to be examples of the duty to act fairly or with an even hand as between beneficiaries with different interests. In broad terms, members of the same class of beneficiaries or objects ought to be treated equally, on the basis that they enjoy equal rights, interests, or expectations. Where beneficiaries have different interests, or where there are different classes which, in relation to each other, enjoy different degrees of importance or dissimilar rights, trustees ought to treat them fairly (or impartially, or with an even hand). However, the extent to which this duty applies (if at all) depends on the nature, terms, and purpose of the particular trust.

Discretionary dispositive powers

One of the more common situations in which the duty needs to be considered is that where trustees are exercising discretionary dispositive powers. This aspect of the matter is dealt with in detail elsewhere, in the context of the specific duties owed by trustees in relation to the exercise of their powers.[39] This section deals with other less common instances of the application of the duty.

Impartiality in relation to investments[40]

'The obligation of a trustee is to administer the trust fund impartially or fairly, having regard to the different interests of the beneficiaries.'[41] As a rule, he must hold a reasonable balance between capital and income and must not choose investments which yield a high income for the life tenant but the capital value of which is insecure or bound to depreciate.[42] There may be circumstances, arising

10.13

10.14

10.15

---

[36] *Thomas*, paras 6-165–6-179.
[37] (1866) 1 Ch App 485, 487–488. See also *Re Pauling's Settlement Trusts (No 2)* [1963] Ch 576, 586; *Nestle v National Westminster Bank plc* [1993] 1 WLR 1260.   [38] [1892] 1 Ch 210, 219.
[39] *Edge v Pensions Ombudsman* [2000] Ch 602, 618, 627; *Nestle v National Westminster Bank plc* [2000] WTLR 795, 803. See Chapter 11 generally and paras 11.03–11.29 in particular.
[40] The trustees' duty to invest is dealt with in detail below: see paras 10.58–10.84 and Chapter 52.
[41] *Nestle v National Westminster Bank* [1994] 1 All ER 118, 136, *per* Staughton LJ.
[42] *Re Pauling's Settlement (No 2)* [1963] Ch 576; *Raby v Ridehalgh* (1855) 7 De GM & G 104; *Stuart v Stuart* (1841) 3 Beav 430; *Re Mulligan* [1998] 1 NZLR 481. See also *JW v Morgan Trust Company of the Bahamas Ltd* (2000) 4 ITELR 541. Where a trustee has a lien over the trust fund, he must also act even-handedly as between himself and the beneficiaries: *X v A* [2000] 1 All ER 490, 495.

from the relative poverty of the beneficiaries or their relationship to the settlor, for example, to justify a departure from this rule. As was said in *Nestlé v National Westminster Bank*:[43] 'it would be an inhuman rule which required trustees to adhere to some mechanical rule for preserving the real value of the capital when the tenant for life was the testator's widow who had fallen upon hard times and the remainderman was young and well-off'.[44] However, such circumstances are exceptions to the general rule.

Annuities

10.16 The law relating to annuities is complex.[45] Where an annuity is payable out of trust income, the trustees may have no power to accumulate surplus income in order to secure the annuity, although express provision may be made to the contrary and the position be different if the annuity is a continuing charge on income.[46] If the income is insufficient to pay the annuity, surplus income of future years must be applied to discharge the arrears.[47] If trustees have resorted to capital in such a case of insufficiency of income, the capital beneficiaries are apparently not entitled to be reimbursed out of the surplus income of future years.[48]

10.17 If a will directs that an annuity be purchased, the annuitant can call for payment to him of the purchase money instead of the annuity.[49] Similarly, if the trustee has power to purchase an annuity, he can pay over the purchase money instead of buying the annuity.[50] However, an annuitant is not entitled to ask for the capitalized value of his annuity without the consent of the beneficiaries entitled to capital.[51]

Receipts and outgoings

10.18 The same principle broadly underpins the rules relating to the classification of receipts and the incidence of outgoings, such as the rule that an augmentation of the capital of the trust fund must generally accrue for the benefit of all beneficiaries and be treated as capital and not income,[52] and the rule requiring income to bear current expenses and the corpus to be subject to capital charges.

---

[43] *Nestle v National Westminster Bank* [1994] 1 All ER 118, 136, *per* Staughton LJ.
[44] *Re Pauling's ST* [1964] Ch 303.   [45] *Underhill and Hayton*, 532–535.
[46] *Re Platt* [1916] 2 Ch 563; *Re Coller's Deed Trusts* [1939] Ch 277; *Re Chance* [1962] Ch 593; *Re Berkeley* [1968] Ch 744.
[47] ibid; *Torre v Browne* (1855) 5 HL Cas 555. The annuitant is not entitled to interest, however.
[48] *Re Berkeley* [1968] Ch 744; *Re Croxon* [1915] 2 Ch 290.
[49] *Stokes v Cheek* (1860) 28 Beav 620; *Re Robbins* [1907] 2 Ch 8.
[50] *Messeena v Carn* (1870) LR 9 Eq 260; *Re Mabbett* [1891] 1 Ch 707.
[51] *Wright v Callender* (1852) 2 De GM & G 652. For the income tax treatment of 'tax-free' annuities, see the so-called 'rule in *Re Pettit*': [1922] 2 Ch 765. See also *Festing v Taylor* (1862) 3 B & S 217; *Burroughes v Abbott* [1922] 1 Ch 86; *Re Jones* [1933] Ch 842; *Re Kingcome* [1936] Ch 566; *Re Goodson's Settlement* [1943] Ch 101; *IRC v Cooke* [1946] AC 1; *Ferguson v IRC* [1970] AC 442;
[52] *Re Barton's Trusts* (1868) LR 5 Eq 238; *Bouch v Sproule* (1887) 12 App Cas 385.

These rules are outlined below.[53] In such cases, although the purpose of the rule is said to be to attain 'equal' treatment for all beneficiaries, it is more accurate to regard it as achieving a broad fairness.

Distribution of assets

It is often the case, especially with class gifts, that one beneficiary attains a vested **10.19** interest in possession in the trust fund before another or others do so. An immediate distribution of assets to that beneficiary may, depending on the value of those assets and of the trust fund in future, result overall in unequal distributions as between all the beneficiaries. Nevertheless, it is well established that, as a general rule and in the absence of a direction to the contrary in the trust instrument, the trustees must make an immediate distribution and cannot wait until all beneficiaries have attained vested interests in possession. Indeed, a beneficiary of full age and legal capacity, with such an interest, is entitled to call on the trustees to make the distribution to him. They are not liable merely because, subsequently, the retained assets prove insufficient to provide other beneficiaries with an equal share.[54]

There are exceptions, however, which Walton J summarized in *Stephenson v* **10.20** *Barclays Bank Trust Co Ltd*:[55]

> When the situation is that a single person who is *sui juris* has an absolutely vested beneficial interest in a share of the trust fund, . . . he is entitled to have transferred to him . . . an aliquot share of each and every asset of the trust fund which presents no difficulty so far as division is concerned. This will apply to such items as cash, money at the bank or an unsecured loan, stock exchange securities and the like. However, as regards land, certainly in all cases, as regards shares in a private company in very special circumstances (see *In re Weiner* [1956] 1 WLR 579) and possibly (although the logic of the addition in fact escapes me)[56] mortgage debts (see *In re Marshall* [1914] 1 Ch 192 *per* Cozens-Hardy MR) the situation is not so simple, and even a person with a vested interest in possession in an aliquot share of the trust fund may have to wait until the land is sold, and so forth, before being able to call upon the trustees as of right to account to him for his share of the assets.

The basis of the exceptional treatment of land is that 'an undivided share of real estate never fetches quite its proper proportion of the proceeds of sale of the entire estate; therefore, to allow an undivided share to be elected to be taken as real estate by one of the beneficiaries[57] would be detrimental to the other beneficiaries'.[58]

---

[53] See paras 11.79–11.88 and 14.63–14.65 below.
[54] *Re Hurst* (1892) 67 LT 96, 99; *Re Swan* (1864) 2 Hem & M 34, 37; *Re Winslow* (1890) 45 Ch D 249; *Re Lepine* [1892] 1 Ch 210; *Re Gardiner* [1942] NZLR 199; *Re Chirnside* [1974] VR 160.
[55] [1975] 1 WLR 882, 889–890.
[56] The explanation is that mortgages include not just the debt but also the estate and powers of the mortgagee: *Crowe v Appleby* [1975] 1 WLR 1539, 1543.
[57] Or a direction to trustees to make such a 'distribution'.
[58] *Re Marshall* [1914] 1 Ch 192, 199, *per* Cozens-Hardy MR.

10.21   Where land is held on trust for sale, the trustees have a discretionary power to postpone sale, and the vesting in possession of a beneficiary's share neither determines that power nor entitles the beneficiary to call for an immediate sale.[59]

10.22   The same considerations do not generally apply to personalty. However, in exceptional circumstances, such as the case of a private company in which the trust holds a majority of the shares,[60] the transfer to one beneficiary of his share might prejudice the interests of the other beneficiaries, and the same principle might then apply.[61]

10.23   Similar considerations arise in relation to the appropriation of assets by trustees. Appropriation is dealt with in greater detail elsewhere.[62]

Conversion[63]

Express direction

10.24   An express duty to convert property must be implemented by the trustees, in accordance with the directions given.[64] If the trustees have a discretion as to whether to convert or not, then, as long as they exercise their discretion properly, the court will not interfere with their decision.[65]

The rule in Howe v Lord Dartmouth

10.25   In addition, a duty to convert may arise by necessary implication, on the basis that there is a duty to maintain an even hand as between the beneficiaries and from the nature of the property. Modern trust instruments invariably exclude such a duty and it will, therefore, be dealt with briefly here. The rule in *Howe v Lord Dartmouth*[66] applies only where (i) there is a gift of residuary personalty, (ii) to or in trust for persons in succession, (iii) such residue comprises wasting, hazardous, or unauthorized assets, and (iv) there is no express duty to convert or other exclusion of the rule.[67] Thus, the rule has no application to realty,[68] to *inter vivos* trusts,[69] to authorized investments (even if wasting and hazardous),[70] to specific bequests,[71]

---

[59]   *Re Horsnaill* [1909] 1 Ch 631; *Re Kipping* [1914] 1 Ch 62; *Crowe v Appleby, supra.*
[60]   *Re Marshall, supra.*   [61]   *Re Sandeman* [1937] 1 All ER 368; *Re Weiner* [1956] 2 All ER 482.
[62]   See paras 14.77–14.83 below.
[63]   J Mowbray et al, *Lewin on Trusts* (17th edn, Sweet & Maxwell, 2000) ('*Lewin*') paras 25-27–25-88; *Underhill and Hayton*, 548–563.
[64]   *Bate v Hooper* (1855) 5 De GM & G 338, 344.   [65]   See Chapter 20 generally.
[66]   (1802) 7 Ves 137.
[67]   *Lichfield v Baker* (1840) 2 Beav 481; *Sutherland v Cooke* (1843) 1 Coll 498; *House v Way* (1848) 12 Jur 959; *Bate v Hooper* (1855) 5 De GM & G 338; *Re Smith's Estate* (1879) 48 LJ Ch 205; *Re Brooker* [1926] WN 93; *Re Trollope's Will Trusts* [1927] 1 Ch 596; *Re Berton* [1939] Ch 200.
[68]   *Re Woodhouse* [1941] Ch 332.   [69]   *Re Van Straubenzee* [1901] 2 Ch 779, esp 782.
[70]   *Re Gough* [1957] Ch 323.
[71]   *Lord v Godfrey* (1819) 4 Madd 455; *Pickering v Pickering* (1839) 4 Myl & Cr 289, 299; *Hubbard v Young* (1847) 10 Beav 203; *Harris v Poyner* (1852) 1 Drew 174 and 181.

or intestacies.[72] Nor does it apply where there is a contrary intention that the property is to be enjoyed in specie,[73] or where the trustees have express authority to retain assets in the state in which they are found at the testator's decease,[74] or to postpone the sale of his business.[75] On the other hand, the rule is not necessarily excluded by the conferral on trustees of a power to postpone conversion for the more convenient realization of the estate.[76]

Apportionment[77]

Where there is a duty to convert

Where there is a duty to convert, whether under an express trust for sale[78] or one **10.26** implied under the rule in *Howe v Lord Dartmouth*[79] or imposed by statute,[80] the tenant for life is entitled, pending conversion, to the fair equivalent of the income he would have received if conversion had taken place, ie the property is treated as if it had been sold and the proceeds invested in authorized investments. This is often referred to as the second limb of the rule in *Howe v Lord Dartmouth*. Unlike the first limb, the second limb applies to all settled property subject to an immediate trust for sale and is not confined to residuary estates; it also applies even where there is an express trust for sale and to intestacies.[81]

This rule does not apply to land (freehold or leasehold) held on trust for sale, for **10.27** the life tenant is entitled to the entire income.[82] A power to postpone conversion or retain investments will not, by itself, exclude a duty to apportion.[83] A power to retain the property will only exclude the duty if the power is actually and consciously exercised.[84] The rule does not apply where the direction is to sell *in the future*,[85] or to unauthorized investments by the trustees, in which case the tenant for life is entitled to the entire income from that investment.[86] Nor does the rule

---

[72] Administration of Estates Act 1925, s 33(1) imposes an express trust for sale.
[73] See also *Vincent v Newcombe* (1832) You 599; *Macdonald v Irvine* (1878) 8 Ch D 101; *Re Game* [1897] 1 Ch 881; *Re Wareham* [1912] 2 Ch 312; *Re Guinness's Settlement* [1966] 1 WLR 1355. The burden of proving such intention falls on the life tenant.
[74] *Gray v Siggers* (1880) 15 Ch D 74.
[75] *Re Crowther* [1895] 2 Ch 56; *Re Elford* [1910] 1 Ch 814. Cf *Re Smith* [1896] 1 Ch 171.
[76] *Re Berry* [1962] Ch 97, disapproving *Re Fisher* [1943] Ch 377 on this point.
[77] *Lewin*, paras 25-27–25-88; *Underhill and Hayton*, 548–563.
[78] *Gibson v Bott* (1802) 7 Ves 89; *Dimes v Scott* (1827) 4 Russ 195.
[79] *Re Appleby* [1903] 1 Ch 565, 566; *Stroud v Gwyer* (1860) 28 Beav 130.
[80] For example, the Administration of Estates Act 1925, s 33(5).
[81] *Re Sullivan* [1930] 1 Ch 84. Cf *Re Fisher* [1943] Ch 377.
[82] *Casamajor v Strode* (1809) 19 Ves 390n; *Hope v D'Hedouville* [1893] 2 Ch 361; *Re Searle* [1900] 2 Ch 829; *Re Earl of Darnley* [1907] 1 Ch 159; *Re Oliver* [1908] 2 Ch 74; *Re Berton* [1939] Ch 200.
[83] *Re Woods* [1904] 2 Ch 4; *Re Inman* [1915] 1 Ch 187; *Re Sheldon* (1888) 39 Ch D 50; *Re Rogers* [1915] 2 Ch 437.
[84] *Re Guinness's Settlement* [1966] 1 WLR 1355; *Rowlls v Bebb* [1900] 2 Ch 107.
[85] *Re North* [1909] 1 Ch 625; *Re Barratt* [1925] Ch 550.
[86] *Stroud v Gwyer* (1860) 28 Beav 130; *Slade v Chaine* [1908] 1 Ch 522.

apply where (as is usual) there is an express or implied provision to the contrary[87] in the trust instrument (which must be construed according to its terms).[88]

10.28 Where the duty applies, the tenant for life is entitled to be credited with the fair equivalent of the income that he would have received if conversion had taken place. This is calculated on the basis of the value of the asset on the first anniversary of the testator's death or, if sold within that year, the actual sale proceeds.[89] If there is a power to postpone sale, the value at death is taken.[90] Interest (traditionally at the rate of 4 per cent) runs from the date of death to the date of conversion.[91]

Future and reversionary interests

10.29 The same broad principle of maintaining equality between life tenant and remainderman applies in relation to the testator's future or reversionary property which will yield no income for the life tenant. This, the so-called rule in *Re Earl of Chesterfield's Trusts*,[92] is complementary to the first limb of the rule in *Howe v Lord Dartmouth*. It does not apply, therefore, to *inter vivos* trusts. It applies to future or reversionary property and pure personalty (other than leaseholds), not currently yielding income, which is directed to be sold, but the sale of which is deferred by the trustees in their discretion. The life tenant is entitled (i) in the case of personalty (other than leaseholds), to a fair equivalent of the income he would have received if the property had been sold and invested in authorized securities;[93] and (ii) in the case of property of a reversionary nature, when it falls in, to a proportionate part of the capital, representing compound interest (with yearly rests) on the true actuarial value of the property at the testator's death.[94]

The Apportionment Act 1870

10.30 Unless it is expressly excluded (and it is common practice to do so), section 2 of the Apportionment Act 1870 provides:

> All rents, annuities, dividends, and other periodical payments in the nature of income . . . shall, like interest on money lent, be considered as accruing from day to day, and shall be apportioned in respect of time accordingly.

---

[87] See, for example, *Miller v Miller* (1872) LR 13 Eq 263; *Thursby v Thursby* (1875) LR 19 Eq 395; *Re Chancellor* (1884) 26 Ch D 42; *Re Elford* [1910] 1 Ch 814. See also *Parry v Warrington* (1820) 6 Madd 155; *Wing v Wing* (1876) 34 LT 941.

[88] Thus, an exclusion of apportionment of 'dividends rents interests of moneys of the nature of income' was held not to extend to the profits of a business: *Re Berry* [1962] Ch 97. See also *Re Lewis* [1907] 2 Ch 296. [89] *Re Fawcett* [1940] Ch 402, 407, 409.

[90] *Re Parry* [1947] Ch 23. [91] ibid; *Re Fawcett, supra.*

[92] (1883) 24 Ch D 643. See also *Re Goodenough* [1895] 2 Ch 537; *Re Duke of Cleveland's Estate* [1895] 2 Ch 542; *Re Morley* [1895] 2 Ch 738; *Re Hobson* (1885) 53 LT 627.

[93] *Brown v Gellatly* (1867) 2 Ch App 751; *Meyer v Simonsen* (1852) 5 De G & Sm 723; *Wentworth v Wentworth* [1900] AC 163.

[94] *Underhill and Hayton*, 552; *Lewin*, paras 25-67–25-71.

'Dividends' include all payments (whether or not declared at fixed times) made by the name of dividend, bonus, or otherwise out of the revenue of trading or other registered companies (public and private).[95] Dividends within the Act must be declared in respect of a definite, though not necessarily regularly recurring, period.[96] 'Rent' includes rent service, rentcharge, and all periodical payments in lieu of or in the nature of rent[97] (but not rent payable in advance).[98] 'Annuities' include salaries and pension.[99] The Act also applies to mortgage interest,[100] but not to insurance monies or the profits of a private business or partnership.[101]

Unless excluded, the Act will require apportionment of income whenever a new **10.31** or different beneficiary becomes entitled to income, such as, for example, on the death of a life tenant, or on the forfeiture of a determinable life interest, or on the birth of a new member of a class of beneficiaries contingently entitled on attaining a specified age.[102]

F. Duty to Exercise Reasonable Care

A trustee's duty of care, as established in the late nineteenth century, was **10.32** to take such care as an ordinary prudent man of business would take in managing his own affairs.[103] In relation to trust investments, he had to act as an ordinary prudent man of business would act when investing for the benefit of others for whom he felt morally obliged to provide (thus excluding the possibility of making a speculative investment).[104] A higher standard probably applied to a professional trustee, who was required to take such care and exercise such skill as he (or it) professed himself (or itself) to possess;[105] and a higher standard was also probably required of a paid trustee in comparison with an unpaid one.[106]

---

[95] Apportionment Act 1870, s 5; *Re Griffith* (1879) 12 Ch D 655; *Re Lysaght* [1898] 1 Ch 115; *Re White* [1913] 1 Ch 231.   [96] *Re Jowitt* [1922] 2 Ch 442.

[97] Section 5.   [98] *Ellis v Rowbotham* [1900] 1 QB 740.

[99] Section 5.   [100] *Re Lewis* [1907] 2 Ch 296.

[101] Section 6; *Jones v Ogle* (1872) 8 Ch App 192.

[102] *Lawrence v Lawrence* (1884) 26 Ch D 795; *Re Piercy (No 2)* [1907] 1 Ch 289; *Re Muirhead* [1916] 2 Ch 181; *Re Joel's Will Trusts* [1967] Ch 14.

[103] *Speight v Gaunt* (1883) 9 App Cas 1, 19 (affirming (1883) 22 Ch D 727, esp 736, 754). See also *Brice v Stokes* (1805) 11 Ves 319; *Massey v Banner* (1820) 1 Jac & W 241; *Bullock v Bullock* (1886) 56 LJ Ch 221.

[104] *Re Whiteley* (1886) 33 Ch D 347, esp 355, 358; *Cowan v Scargill* [1985] Ch 270, 288; *Nestle v National Westminster Bank* [1994] 1 All ER 118, esp 126, 140.

[105] *Bartlett v Barclays Bank Trust Co Ltd* [1980] Ch 515, 534.

[106] *Re Waterman's Will Trusts* [1952] 2 All ER 1054, 1055; *National Trustees Co of Australia v General Finance Co* [1905] AC 373, 381.

10.33   A statutory duty of care has now been introduced by the Trustee Act 2000,[107] section 1 of which provides:

> (1) Whenever the duty under this subsection applies to a trustee, he must exercise such care and skill as is reasonable in the circumstances, having regard, in particular—
>
> > (a) to any special knowledge or experience that he has or holds himself out as having, and
> >
> > (b) if he acts as trustee in the course of a business or profession, to any special knowledge or experience that it is reasonable to expect of a person acting in the course of that kind of business or profession.

The duty imposed by subsection (1) is called 'the duty of care' and Schedule 1 to the Act makes provision about when the duty of care applies to a trustee.[108]

10.34   Section 1 does not impose any positive duty actually to *do* anything, for example it does not impose a duty to invest: it merely deals with the standard of care required if and when a trustee decides to act, in the carrying out of a duty imposed, or in the exercise of a power conferred, on him by the trust instrument or the general law.

10.35   Secondly, the duty of care may be excluded or curtailed: paragraph 7 of Schedule 1 declares that 'the duty of care does not apply if or in so far as it appears from the trust instrument that the duty was not meant to apply'. The duty will therefore not apply automatically to all trustees: indeed, the likelihood is that professional trustees will ensure that the statutory duty of care is excluded or curtailed.[109] Thus a professional trustee, of whom special knowledge or experience may reasonably be required, may exclude liability for failing to display or exercise such special knowledge or experience.

10.36   Thirdly, limb (a) of section 1(1) directs one to have regard to any special knowledge that a trustee 'holds himself out as having'. Thus, an ignorant non-professional trustee, or one who has a misplaced notion of his own abilities, but who has held himself out as an expert, may be liable, unless it can be said that it is 'not reasonable in the circumstances' to have believed him. Given the ease with which a professional trustee may avail himself or itself of an express exemption clause, section 1 is essentially a trap for the ignorant and the idiotic and not an effective means of controlling trustees at all.

10.37   Fourthly, limbs (a) and (b) of section 1(1) may both apply to a professional trustee. For example, where the trustee is a professional trustee, regard must be

---

[107] The Trustee Act 2000 came into force on 1 February 2001: The Trustee Act 2000 (Commencement) Order 2001, SI 2001/49. Part I of, and Sch 1 to, the Act deal with the 'duty of care' of trustees. The Act is based on the Law Commission's Consultation Paper No 146 (*Trustees' Powers and Duties*) and their Report No 260, of the same title.

[108] Trustee Act 2000, ss 1(2), 2.

[109] The availability of exemption clauses to professional trustees was raised as a matter of concern in debates on the Bill and it was formally referred to the Law Commission: *Hansard*, HL, vol 612, col 384; Standing Comm A, 24 October 2000, cols 23–24.

had not only to any special knowledge or experience that 'it is reasonable to expect' of that trustee, but also any further or additional knowledge or experience that he has or 'holds himself out as having'.

Fifthly, it seems clear that the statutory duty of care is not a general duty at all: it **10.38** does not apply to *all* aspects of a trustee's activities, because section 2 of the Act declares that Schedule 1 'makes provision about when the duty of care applies'. Schedule 1 merely lists, under six headings, those *powers* to the exercise of which the duty applies (unless excluded or curtailed). These are as follows:

Investment

The duty of care applies to a trustee (a) when exercising the general power of **10.39** investment (ie, the power conferred by section 3(1) of the Act) or any other power of investment, however conferred, and also (b) when carrying out a duty to which he is subject under section 4 or 5 of the Act (being duties relating to the exercise of a power of investment or the review of investments).[110] Part II of the Act deals with the investment powers of trustees.[111] Section 3(1) provides that, subject to the provisions of Part II, 'a trustee may make any kind of investment that he could make if he were absolutely entitled to the assets of the trust'.[112]

Acquisition of land

The duty of care applies to a trustee (a) when exercising the power to acquire free- **10.40** hold or leasehold land conferred by section 8 of the Act, or (b) any other power to acquire land, however conferred, and also any power in relation to land acquired under a power mentioned in (a) or (b).[113]

Agents, nominees, and custodians

The duty of care applies to a trustee when entering into arrangements under **10.41** which (a) a person is authorized under section 11 of the Act to exercise the func- tions as an agent, or (b) a person is appointed under section 16 of the Act to act as a nominee, or (c) a person is appointed under section 17 or 18 of the Act to act as a custodian; (d) when entering into arrangements under which, under any other power, however conferred, a person is authorized to exercise functions as an agent

---

[110] Schedule 1, para 1(a), (b).

[111] Part II of the Act applies in relation to trusts whether created before or after its commence- ment: s 7(1). Restrictive provisions in pre-3 August 1961 trust instruments which might otherwise have been revived will not be treated as restricting the general power of investment: s 7(2). Also, pro- visions in trust instruments made before the commencement of the new Part II provisions, and which confer powers on trustees to invest in investments authorized by law, are to be treated as conferring the new general power of investment: s 7(3).

[112] For trustees' powers of investment, see paras 10.58–10.84 and Chapter 52 below.

[113] Schedule 1, para 2(a), (b), (c). For trustees' powers in relation to land, see paras 14.48–14.70 and Chapters 56 and 57 below.

or is appointed to act as a nominee or custodian; and (e) when carrying out his duties under section 22 of the Act (review of agents, nominees, and custodians). For these purposes, 'entering into arrangements' includes, in particular, selecting the person who is to act, determining any terms on which he is to act, and, if the person is being authorized to exercise 'asset management functions', the preparation of a policy statement under section 15 of the Act.[114]

Compounding of liabilities

10.42 The duty of care applies to a trustee when exercising (a) the power under section 15 of the Trustee Act 1925 to do any of the things referred to in that section, or (b) any corresponding power, however conferred.[115] Section 15, in its original form, declared that a trustee or trustees would not be responsible for any loss occasioned by any act or thing done by him or them under that section, provided it was done 'in good faith'. These words have now been replaced with the words 'if he has or they have discharged the duty of care set out in section 1(1) of the Trustee Act 2000'.[116] Even so, the test remains whether the acts or things 'seem expedient' to him or them, and not whether they are necessary.

Insurance

10.42A The duty of care applies to a trustee when exercising the power under section 19 of the Trustee Act 1925 to insure property,[116A] and also when exercising any corresponding power, however conferred.

Reversionary interests

10.43 The duty of care also applies to a trustee (a) when exercising the power under section 22(1) or (3) of the Trustee Act 1925 to do any of the things referred to there (reversionary interests and valuations); and (b) when exercising any corresponding power, however conferred.

10.44 The new statutory duty of care does not apply to many of the functions of 'pension scheme'[117] trustees, ie their functions in relation to investment and the acquisition of land; in relation to arrangements with agents, nominees, and custodians to the extent that they relate to trustees authorizing a person to exercise

---

[114] Schedule 1, para 3(1) (a), (b), (c), (d), (e) and (2)(a), (b), (c). For trustees' powers to delegate, see Chapter 15 below.
[115] Schedule 1, para 4(a), (b). For trustees' powers to compound liabilities, see paras 14.72–14.75 below. [116] Schedule 2, para 20.
[116A] For Section 19, see paras 14.66–14.70 below.
[117] Defined as 'an occupational pension scheme (within the meaning of the Pension Schemes Act 1993) established under a trust and subject to the law of England and Wales': ibid, s 36(1).

their functions with respect to investment or appointing a person to act as their nominee or custodian.[118] Nor does it apply to trustees of authorized unit trusts.[119]

G. Duties in Relation to Payment of Outgoings

Duties in relation to receipts and outgoings[120]

The first question is to decide whether a particular receipt is income or capital. It is unclear whether the trustees can properly be given discretion to decide the question: certainly, if any such provision purports to oust the jurisdiction of the court, it will not be valid.[121]
10.45

In broad terms, the following propositions are generally correct. Dividends are income,[122] to which a life tenant (or other income beneficiary) is entitled, even if they are paid after his death.[123] Payment of cumulative dividends (or 'arrears') also constitutes income at the date of payment.[124] If a company makes a distribution in specie to its shareholders of shares which it owns in a *subsidiary* company, such shares, too, are income in the hands of the trustees.[125] If a distribution in specie is directed, but the shares are actually sold and the proceeds of sale distributed instead, there must be an apportionment of income up to the death of the life tenant.[126]
10.46

However, this is not the case in relation to a distribution made from a company's share premium account.[127] Also, where a company purchases its own shares out of a reserve fund, which are then distributed to existing shareholders as fully paid (or redeems redeemable preference shares), the proceeds are capital in the hands of
10.47

---

[118] ibid, s 36(2). Parts II and III and ss 16 to 20 of the Act do not apply to the trustees of any pension scheme. Part IV applies only to a limited extent: see s 36(3) to (8).

[119] ibid, s 37. The duty is not excluded for trustees managing funds under a common investment scheme: ibid, s 38.   [120] *Lewin*, 645–652.

[121] *Re Wynn* [1952] Ch 271. Whether a particular receipt is capital or income is a question of fact and law, which trustees cannot alter. However, it is difficult to see why trustees could not *treat* or *deem* one to be the other.   [122] *De Gendre v Kent* (1867) LR 4 Eq 283.

[123] ibid. Also, even if they are payable out of the profits of an earlier year (*Re Joel* [1936] 2 All ER 962) or out of capital assets or profits (*Re Doughty* [1947] Ch 263; *Re Harrison's Will Trusts* [1949] Ch 678). Cf *Re Sale* [1913] 2 Ch 697; *Re Grundy* (1917) 117 LT 470. The Apportionment Act 1870 may apply, however.

[124] *Re Wakley* [1920] 2 Ch 205; *Re Taylor's Trusts* [1905] 1 Ch 734; *Re Sale* [1913] 2 Ch 697; *Re Marjoribanks* [1923] 2 Ch 307. See also *Re Pennington* [1915] WN 333; *Re Sandbach* [1933] Ch 505; *Re MacIver's Settlement* [1936] Ch 198; *Re Smith's Will Trusts* [1936] 2 All ER 1210.

[125] *Hill v Permanent Trustee Co of New South Wales Ltd* [1930] AC 720 (PC); *Re Doughty* [1947] Ch 263; *Re Harrison's Will Trusts* [1949] Ch 678; *Re Sechiari* [1950] 1 All ER 417; *Re Kleinwort's Settlement Trusts* [1951] Ch 860; *Rae v Lazard Investment Co Ltd* [1963] 1 WLR 555. Cf *Re Rudd's Will Trusts* [1952] 1 TLR 44 and *Re Winder's Will Trusts* [1951] Ch 916.

[126] *Bulkeley v Stephens* [1896] 2 Ch 241; *Re Oppenheimer* [1907] 1 Ch 399; *Re Muirhead* [1916] 2 Ch 181; *Re Henderson* [1940] Ch 368.   [127] *Re Duff's Settlements* [1951] Ch 923.

the trustees.[128] The status of bonuses depends on what they represent: if paid *as capital* they will also be capital in the hands of the trustees, but if they are actually additional dividends they will be income.[129]

10.48 Shares bought 'cum dividend', ie where dividends have been declared but not yet paid, are capital and not income in the hands of the trustees: there is no need to apportion.[130] Similarly, in the absence of special circumstances, there is no need to apportion income when such shares are sold.[131] This is purely a rule of convenience; and the interested beneficiaries 'ought to take the rough with the smooth'.

10.49 Where trustees hold units in a unit trust, any distribution by the managers should be treated as capital or income on the basis of the above principles and as if they directly held the shares in the unit trust.[132]

10.50 Directors' fees received by trustees and for which they are required to account to the trust are capital.[133]

10.51 The proceeds of sale of land are capital, as are the proceeds of the sale of timber not in the ordinary course,[134] periodical payments (even if received from the income of another fund),[135] and undisposed of income of another settlement received under a resulting trust.[136] On the other hand, rent from land is income,[137] as are the proceeds of the sale of wood in the ordinary course,[138] rent and royalties (for example from a lease of an open mine, or a brickfield, or a gravel pit, peat bog, and so forth),[139] and interest on a mortgage debt.[140]

---

[128] *Bouch v Sproule* (1887) 12 AC 385; *Re Northage* (1891) 60 LJ Ch 488; *Re Whitfield* [1920] WN 256; *IRC v Fisher's Executors* [1926] AC 395; *Re Joel* [1936] 2 All ER 962; *Re Wright's Settlement Trusts* [1945] Ch 211; *Re Outen's Will Trusts* [1963] Ch 291.

[129] *Bouch v Sproule* (1887) 12 AC 385, 397; *Re Bouch* (1885) 29 Ch D 635, 653; *Hill v Permanent Trustee Co of NSW* [1930] AC 720, esp 730–732. As capital: *Re Evans* [1913] 1 Ch 23; *Re Ogilvie* (1919) 35 TLR 218; *IRC v Blott* [1921] 2 AC 171; *Re Taylor* [1926] Ch 923; *IRC v Wright* [1927] 1 KB 333. As income: *Re Northage* (1891) 60 LJ Ch 488; *Re Tindal* (1892) 9 TLR 24; *Re Malam* [1894] 3 Ch 578; *Re Despard* (1901) 17 TLR 478; *Re Hume Nisbet's Settlement* (1911) 27 TLR 461. The company's classification determines the nature of the receipt in the hands of the trustees: *Re Outen's Will Trusts* [1963] Ch 291. See also *Lubbock v British Bank of South America* [1892] 2 Ch 198 and *Re Taylor* [1926] Ch 923.

[130] *Re Sir Robert Peel's Settled Estates* [1910] 1 Ch 389.

[131] *Scholefield v Redfern* (1863) 2 Dr & Sm 173, 182; *Re Henderson* [1940] Ch 368; *Re MacLaren's Settlement Trusts* [1951] 2 All ER 414; *Hitch v Ruegg* [1986] TL & P 62 (or as *Re Ellerman* in [1984] LS Gaz 430), disapproving of *Re Winterstoke's Will Trusts* [1938] Ch 158.

[132] *Re Whitehead's Will Trusts* [1959] Ch 579.

[133] *Re Francis* (1905) 74 LJ Ch 198; *Re Macadam* [1946] Ch 73, 76–77.

[134] *Earl of Cowley v Wellesley* (1866) 35 Beav 635.

[135] *Re Fisher* [1943] Ch 377; *Re Hey's Settlement* [1945] Ch 294, 308; *Re Payne* (1943) 169 LT 365.

[136] *Re Guinness's Settlement* [1966] 1 WLR 1355; *Re Whitehead* [1894] 1 Ch 678.

[137] *Brigstocke v Brigstocke* (1878) 8 Ch D 363; *Re Wix* [1916] 1 Ch 279; *Sinclair v Lee* [1993] Ch 496, 506.   [138] *Earl of Cowley v Wellesley, supra*; *Dashwood v Magniac* [1891] 3 Ch 306.

[139] *Earl of Cowley v Wellesley, supra Re Kemeys-Tynte* [1892] 2 Ch 211.

[140] *Re Lewis* [1907] 2 Ch 296; *Caulfield v Maguire* (1842) 2 Jo & Lat 141.

Incidence of expenses[141]

The general principle is as follows: **10.52**

> Trustees are entitled to be indemnified out of the capital and income of their trust
> fund against all obligations incurred by the trustees in the due performance of their
> duties and the exercise of their powers. The trustees must then debit each item of
> expenditure either against income or against capital. The general rule is that income
> must bear all ordinary outgoings of a recurrent nature, such as rates and taxes, and
> interest on charges and incumbrances. Capital must bear all costs, charges and
> expenses incurred for the benefit of the whole estate.[142]

Trustees may resort to capital to meet an income charge if no income is immediately available, but must reimburse capital out of future income, and vice versa.[143]

Thus, rent and other recurring outgoings in respect of leases comprised in the trust   **10.53**
fund are payable out of income, including the costs of repairing breaches of
covenant[144] and even the costs of complying with dangerous structure notices,
provided the works do not constitute improvements.[145] Rates and taxes have been
held payable out of income,[146] as were the charges of professional trustees fixed by
reference to trust income,[147] and the charges of estate agents for finding tenants.[148]

Expenditure which is incurred for the trust or estate as a whole falls on capital.[149]   **10.54**
This includes the costs of changing investments,[150] the costs of obtaining advice as
to trust investments or legal advice,[151] or of seeking the directions of the court,[152] of
administration proceedings,[153] of appointing new trustees,[154] of paying money into
court under the Trustee Act,[155] and of litigation for protecting the trust assets,[156] in
addition to more obvious charges, such as the costs of improvements to property.

---

[141] *Lewin* 652–658.

[142] *Carver v Duncan* [1985] AC 1082 1120, *per* Lord Templeman.

[143] *Stott v Milne* (1885) 25 Ch D 710; *Honywood v Honywood* [1902] 1 Ch 347.

[144] *Re Gjers* [1899] 2 Ch 54; *Re Shee* [1934] Ch 345, 399. But not the costs of repairing breaches committed before the trust was created: *Re Betty* [1899] 1 Ch 821.

[145] *Re Copland's Settlement* [1900] 1 Ch 326. If they are improvements, they ought to be met out of capital or apportioned between capital and income.

[146] *Re Redding* [1897] 1 Ch 876; *Re Cain's Settlement* [1919] 2 Ch 364; *Carver v Duncan, supra.*

[147] *Re Hutton* [1936] Ch 536; *Re Roberts' Will Trusts* [1937] Ch 274; *Re Godwin* [1938] Ch 341.

[148] *Re Watson* [1928] WN 309. Cf *Re Leveson-Gower's Settled Estate* [1905] 2 Ch 95.

[149] *Carver v. Duncan, supra.* These include costs of fencing (*Earl of Cowley v Wellesely, supra*) and road charges (*Re Leigh's Settled Estates* [1902] 2 Ch 274).   [150] *Carver v Duncan, supra.*

[151] *Poole v Pass* (1839) 1 Beav 600; *Carver v Duncan, supra; Alsop Wilkinson v Neary* [1996] 1 WLR 1220.

[152] *Re Elmore's Will Trusts* (1860) 9 WR 66; *Re Leslie's Settlement Trusts* (1876) 2 Ch D 185.

[153] *Re Turnley* (1866) 1 Ch App 152.

[154] *Re Fellows' Settlement* (1856) 2 Jur NS 62; *Re Fulham* (1850) 15 Jur 69; *Ex p Davis* (1852) 16 Jur 882. See also the Trustee Act 1925, s 60, which confers a discretion on the court.

[155] *Re Whitton's Trusts* (1869) LR 8 Eq 352.

[156] *Stott v Milne* (1884) 25 Ch D 710; *Hamilton v Tighe* [1898] 1 IR 123; *More v More* (1889) 37 WR 414; *Re McClure's Trusts* (1906) 76 LJ Ch 52.

Premiums on insurance policies, such as endowment policies to protect the trust against inheritance tax charges, are generally payable out of trust capital.[157]

10.55 The costs of preparing annual trust accounts are generally paid out of income.[158] However, if such accounts include capital accounts and are for the benefit of the trust as a whole (as is likely to be the case), such costs may properly be paid out of capital or, preferably, apportioned between capital and income. If trustees audit trust accounts not more than once in every three years, or more frequently if the nature of the trust or any 'special dealings' with trust property so require, they have an absolute discretion under section 22(4) of the Trustee Act 1925 to pay the costs out of capital or income (or partly in one way and partly in the other); but, in default of any direction by the trustees to the contrary in any special case, costs attributable to capital shall be borne by capital and costs attributable to income shall be borne by income.

10.56 Most modern trust instruments make express provision for the payment of out-goings and generally confer on the trustees an absolute discretion to pay out of income expenses which would otherwise fall on trust capital or to pay out of capital expenses which would otherwise fall on income. The above-mentioned general principles are, therefore, usually expressly modified or excluded. This flexibility is reflected in section 31 of the Trustee Act 2000, which provides:

> (1) A trustee—
>
> > (a) is entitled to be reimbursed from the trust funds, or
> > (b) may pay out of the trust funds,
>
> expenses properly incurred by him when acting on behalf of the trust.
> (2) This section applies to a trustee who has been authorised under a power con-ferred by Part IV or any other enactment or any provision of subordinate legisla-tion, or by the trust instrument—
>
> > (a) to exercise functions as an agent of the trustees, or
> > (b) to act as a nominee or custodian,
>
> as it applies to any other trustee.

The expression 'trust funds' is defined simply as 'income or capital funds of the trust'.[159]

10.57 The general wording of section 31 would now seem to confer on trustees a very broad discretion as to the incidence of outgoings. However, how broad it is and for what purpose is not at all clear. One view is that section 31 merely authorizes

---

[157] *Macdonald v Irvine* (1878) 8 Ch D 101; *Re Sherry* [1913] 2 Ch 508; *Carver v Duncan* [1985] AC 1082, 1120. See also *Re Morley* [1895] 2 Ch 738; *Re Betty* [1899] 1 Ch 821, 829; *Re McEacharn* (1911) 103 LT 900, 902. For trustees' powers to insure, see paras 14.66–14.70 below.

[158] There seems to be no authority for this practice. *Shore v Shore* (1859) 4 Drew 501 and *Earl of Cowley v Wellesley* (1866) LR 1 Eq 656 are not directly in point.

[159] Trustee Act 2000, s 39(1).

trustees to resort to capital or income to meet proper expenses in the first instance, but that the ultimate incidence of such expenses would still need to be allocated or adjusted subsequently, in accordance with the general rules outlined above.[160] Another view is that section 31 ought to be read literally.[161] It is improbable that the legislation was intended to confer an uncontrolled discretion on the trustees, so that, if they wished, they could, for example, throw on income all expenses normally falling on capital. Thus, even if section 31 has widened trustees' discretion in this area, it would seem that some constraints on that discretion are required, such as a requirement that they act fairly as between the income and capital beneficiaries. If this is the case, it would seem likely that the general principles outlined earlier in this section could furnish the appropriate constraints, and it is unlikely, therefore, that section 31 has simply made them redundant.

H. Duty to Invest

Introduction

The discussion of the trustee's obligations to invest the trust fund are considered in outline terms in this section but receive a more detailed, contextual treatment in Chapter 52. In line with the underlying philosophy of this book, this section is concerned to analyse the general principles associated with the trustee's obligations in relation to the investment of private, express trusts, whereas the context of the investment of trust funds in practice is considered in Section Two of this work, specifically in chapter 52 within Part I, **Trusts in Financial Transactions**, in relation to pension fund trusts in Part H and in relation to authorized unit trusts in Chapter 51 of Part I. This discussion relates exclusively to express, private trusts because occupational pension funds and authorized unit trusts have their own statutory schemes as considered in their respective chapters. **10.58**

With the enactment of the Trustee Act 2000, the trustee's obligations to invest the trust fund fall into three general parts: first, those incumbent on him under statute; secondly, those incumbent on him by virtue of express trusts powers; and, thirdly, the development of the principles governing investment of the trust by decided cases. These various aspects of the trustee's obligations are considered here; Chapter 52 then places these principles in context. **10.59**

The Trustee Act 2000 sets out the statutory code relating to the investment of trust funds and the delegation of the trustees' duties to agents, custodians, and nominees. It introduces a general power of investment for trustees permitting them to act as though they were the absolute owners of the trust property. That general power of investment comes with a duty of care on trustees and further **10.60**

---

[160] *Lewin*, para 25-26B. *Underhill and Hayton*, 564–565, seems to adopt the broader view.
[161] J Kessler, *Drafting Trusts and Will Trusts* (6th edn), para 20.28.

obligations to consider the standard investment criteria provided for by statute and to take proper advice on their investment policies and decisions. That Act also makes specific provision for investment in land. The Trustee Delegation Act 1999 makes provision for enduring powers of attorney relating to trustees' obligations.

10.61 It is usual for the express provisions of a trust to provide for a code of powers and obligations incumbent on trustees when investing the trust fund. The trustee will typically seek to limit his own liability for any loss suffered by the beneficiaries through those investments in that code. Those provisions may also seek to exclude the operation of the general law of trusts.

10.62 The trustee's general duties of investment, developed through the case law, require that the trustee is to act prudently and safely, to act fairly between beneficiaries, and to act in the best interests of the beneficiaries. The best interests of the beneficiaries are generally taken to be their financial interests. Therefore, non-financial considerations will typically not be taken into account when reviewing the trustees' investment activities, except in the exceptional circumstances where all the actual or potential beneficiaries are adults with strict moral views on particular matters or where the terms of the trust provide that other considerations are to be taken into account.

The scope of the Trustee Act 2000

10.63 The Trustee Act 2000 replaced the restrictive Trustee Investments Act 1961 with a far more permissive approach to the investment of trust funds. The 1961 Act, in broad terms, required the trustees to separate the trust fund into wide range and narrow range investments with the intention that no more than half of the trust fund should be invested in any investment carrying even that risk associated with publicly quoted companies on the London Stock Exchange. This cautious attitude to trust investment sought to preserve the capital of trust funds from losses which might result from more progressive financial speculation. This structure prevented trustees from generating a return on investment for the beneficiaries equivalent to an ordinary market return on investment funds. In consequence, the Trustee Act 2000 sought to expand the powers of trustees to make investments both by treating them as though absolutely entitled to the trust fund, and therefore empowered to make a much broader range of investments, and also subject to a duty of care to the beneficiaries which is considered below.

10.64 The Trustee Act 2000 does not set out mandatory rules for the administration and investment of trusts in that the provisions of a trust instrument may exclude the operation of the Act either by express provision or by inference from the construction of any such provisions.[162] For example, the Act provides that 'the duty

---

[162] See eg Trustee Act 2000, Sch 1, para 7 and other provisions referred to in the text to follow.

of care [imposed on trustees][163] does not apply if or in so far as it appears from the trust instrument that the duty is not meant to apply'.[164] At one level the exclusion of the Act by inference may relate simply to the fact that the Act applies to trusts created before the passage of the Act and therefore a provision which excludes the Trustee Act 1925[165] may therefore be reasonably construed so as to exclude any successor in the Trustee Act 2000 also. As drafted, the Trustee Act 2000 does appear to permit the general provisions of a trust created before or after the passage of the Trustee Act 2000 to be read so as to exclude its operation.

Significantly, then, settlors and their trustees are to have freedom to create trusts   **10.65** arrangements without the interference of mandatory rules which would prohibit certain trusts structures. Indeed the strict nature of equitable principles like the prohibition on trustees making unauthorized profits from their fiduciary office would almost make any such statutory provisions pointless.[166] The role of the Trustee Act 2000 is therefore to supply trusts provisions where otherwise there would be a gap in the trusts provisions.

The general power of investment under statute

The Trustee Act 2000 provides that 'a trustee may make any kind of investment   **10.66** that he could make if he were absolutely entitled to the assets of the trust': this is referred to in the legislation as a 'general power of investment'.[167] Therefore, the trustee is not constrained as to the form of investments which he may make by reason only of his status as a trustee. It should, however, be remembered that the trust instrument may impose restrictions on the trustees' powers to make investments and also that financial regulation may in effect preclude certain types of investment by persons who are considered to be insufficiently expert to make them.[168] There remain restrictions on the power of trustees to make investments in land unless by way of loans secured on land, as is considered below.[169] This general power of investment operates in addition to anything set out in the trust instrument unless it is excluded by that trust instrument.[170] Therefore, the settlor could preclude the trustees from making particular forms of investment.[171]

---

[163] Considered below at paras 10.67–10.69.
[164] Trustee Act 2000, Sch 1, para 7.
[165] eg ibid, ss 7, 10, 27.
[166] See eg *Boardman v Phipps* [1967] 2 AC 46.   [167] Trustee Act 2000, s 3(1).
[168] See the discussion of the obligations placed on trustees by the Financial Services and Markets Act 2000 in Chapter 47.
[169] Trustee Act 2000, s 3(3).   [170] ibid, s 6(1).
[171] In contradistinction to the 1961 code, this means that the trustee is presumed to be free to make any suitable investments in the absence of any express provision to the contrary whereas the trustee was previously presumed to be capable only of making a limited range of investments in the absence of any provision to the contrary. The 1961 code is now replaced by the Trustee Act 2000 in this regard: Trustee Act 2000, s 7(3).

The duty of care under statute

10.67 The Trustee Act 2000 provides for a statutory duty of care which imposes a duty of 'such skill and care as is reasonable in the circumstances' on trustees.[172] That 'duty of care'[173] is relative to the context in which the trustee is acting. Where the trustee has, or holds himself out as having, any 'special knowledge or experience' then the precise scope of that trustee's duty of care will be shaped by that knowledge or experience.[174] In consequence, a trustee who is a professional stockbroker would be expected to have the knowledge and experience of such a stockbroker when making investments on behalf of the trust in shares. The standard expected of such a trustee would therefore be higher than that of an inexpert trustee when considering the liability of such a trustee for loss resulting to the trust fund arising, for example, from the negligence of a trustee in selecting a particular investment strategy. If the duties of a trustee are performed 'in the course of a business or profession' then the duty of care is applied in the context of any special knowledge or experience which such a professional could be expected to have.[175]

10.68 As considered above, the provisions of the Act can be expressly or impliedly displaced by the trust instrument.[176] In consequence this duty of care may be limited by the express provisions of the trust, or even by a construction of those provisions which suggests that the settlor's intention was to exclude such a liability.[177]

10.69 The duty of care is not expressed by the 2000 Act to be a general duty in the form of an all-encompassing statutory tort. Rather, the Act provides that the duty will only apply in limited circumstances.[178] The principal instance in which the statutory duty of care applies[179] is in relation to a trustee exercising a 'general power of investment'[180] under the Act or any other power of investment 'however conferred'.[181] Alternatively the duty of care applies when trustees are carrying out obligations under the Act in relation to exercising or reviewing powers of investment.[182] The duty of care also applies in relation to the acquisition of land,[183] which would seem to cover the use of appropriate advice and appropriate levels of care in selecting the land, contracting for its purchase, and insuring it.[184] It applies in general terms in relation to the appointment of agents, custodians, and nominees,[185] which would include the selection of reasonable agents with appropriate qualifications for the task for which they were engaged.

---

[172] Trustee Act 2000, s 1(1).

[173] ibid, s 1(2).   [174] ibid, s 1(1)(a).   [175] ibid, s 1(1)(b).

[176] ibid, Sch 1, para 7.   [177] cf paras 52.91–52.92 below.   [178] Trustee Act 2000, s 2.

[179] ibid, Sch 1, para 1.   [180] As defined by ibid, s 3(2) and considered below.

[181] With the effect that this provision may be the only mandatory provision in the legislation because it appears to apply to powers of investment in general and not simply to that set out in s 3(2). However, the Act does permit an express exclusion in the trust to obviate the operation of any of the provisions in the Act and therefore it would appear possible to circumscribe the operation of this provision: Sch 1, para 7.   [182] Trustee Act 2000, ss 4, 5.

[183] ibid, Sch 1, para 2.   [184] ibid, Sch 1, para 5; Trustee Act 1925, s 19.

[185] ibid, Sch 1, para 3.

Standard investment criteria under statute

The Trustee Act 2000 requires that the trustees have regard to something **10.70** described in the statute as the 'standard investment criteria'[186] when exercising their investment powers: that is whether making new investments or considering their existing investments.[187] The 'standard investment criteria' to which the trustees are to have regard comprise two core principles of prevailing investment theory: first, the obligation to make 'suitable' investments and, secondly, the need to maintain a diverse portfolio of investments to spread the fund's investment risk.

First, then, the trustees are required to consider:

> the suitability to the trust of investments of the same kind as any particular invest-
> ment proposed to be made or retained and of that particular investment as an invest-
> ment of that kind.[188]

The expression 'suitability'[189] requires that investment managers are required to consider whether or not the risk associated with a given investment is appropriate for the client proposing to make that investment. Those providing financial services, including trustees making investment decisions on behalf of beneficiaries, are required to allocate their clients to one of a list of categories of customer ranging from the expert to the ordinary retail customer.[190] The trustee is required to consider whether the trust fund for which he is making an investment would be dealing in a suitable manner in making the proposed investment. It is presumed that the trustee would be liable for breach of trust in the event that an unsuitable investment were made which caused loss to the trust.[191]

Secondly, the trustees must observe 'the need for diversification of investments of **10.71** the trust, in so far as is appropriate to the circumstances of the trust'.[192] Two points arise from this provision. The first question which arises is as to the amount of diversification which is necessary. The answer is that the level of diversification of investments is dependent on the nature of the trust. A trust which requires the trustees to hold a single house on trust for the occupation of a named beneficiary does not require that the trustees make a range of investments: rather, the trustees are impliedly precluded from making a range of investments. Similarly, a trust with only a small amount of capital could not afford to buy a large number of investments. The second issue relates to the need for diversification which is itself

---

[186] ibid, s 4(1).   [187] ibid, s 4(2).   [188] ibid, s 4(2)(a).
[189] See eg Securities and Investment Board Rulebook, as supplemented from time to time, Ch III, Part 2; Securities and Futures Authority Rulebook, as supplemented from time to time, Rule 5.31; New York Stock Exchange 'Know Your Customer Rule', CCH NYSE Guide, s 2152 (Art III, s 2).
[190] See the general discussion of the conduct of business regulations effected by the Financial Services Authority under the Financial Services and Markets Act 2000 in Chapter 47.
[191] *Target Holdings v Redferns* [1996] 1 AC 421; [1995] 3 WLR 352; [1995] 3 All ER 785.
[192] Trustee Act 2000, s 4(2)(b).

bound up with need to dilute the risk of investing in only a small number of investments. This is frequently referred to as 'portfolio theory'.[193] The term 'portfolio theory' expresses the notion that if an investor invests in a number of different investments across a number of different markets then the impact of loss in value suffered by any individual market or individual investment will be balanced out by the investments made in other markets which will not have suffered from that particular fall in value.

10.72 The Trustee Act 2000 imposes a positive obligation on the trustees to seek out professional advice on the investments to be made.[194] Similarly, when considering whether or not to vary the investments which the trust has made, the trustees are required to take qualified investment advice.[195] This is unless it appears reasonable to the trustee in the circumstances to dispense with such advice.[196] The type of advice which the trustee must acquire is 'proper advice': being advice from someone whom the trustee reasonably believes is qualified to give such advice.[197]

The acquisition of land as an investment or otherwise

10.73 Under the Trustee Act 2000, trustees are empowered to acquire freehold and leasehold land for any purpose.[198] That acquisition can be made for the purposes of investment or for the occupation of a beneficiary but also it may be made for 'any other reason':[199] the purpose of listing the two specific contexts is to avoid any doubt that those two reasons are permissible. The trustee has the powers of 'the absolute owner in relation to the land'.[200] This presumably means that the trustee is free to deal with the land on behalf of the trust in terms of conveying it, securing it, and so forth. However, it is not supposed that this could be taken to mean that the trustee is entitled to ignore the equitable interests of any beneficiaries in that land when held on trust. In line with the general scheme of the 2000 Act the legislation provides for additions to any terms of any trust instrument so that there are default provisions if a trust should lack them.[201] It is nevertheless open to the settlor to exclude the operation of the statute in any particular circumstances.

Express investment powers

10.74 An express power on a trustee to make an investment may be general, giving the trustees power to invest in whatever they wish, or limited to specific types of investment. The trustee will nevertheless be subject to certain limitations. Although in *Re Harari's Settlement Trusts*[202] it was held that such a power would not be interpreted restrictively, the case of *Re Power's Will Trusts*[203] established that

---

[193] Considered below at paras 10.77–10.78.   [194] Trustee Act 2000, s 5(1).
[195] ibid, s 5(2).   [196] ibid, s 5(3).   [197] ibid, s 5(4).
[198] These particular powers do not apply to land that was settled land before 1996: ibid, s 10.
[199] ibid, s 8(1).   [200] ibid, s 8(3).   [201] ibid, s 9.   [202] [1949] 1 All ER 430.
[203] [1951] Ch 1074; distinguishing *Re Wragg* [1919] 2 Ch 58.

the word 'invest' implied a yield of income and, thus, non-income producing property would not constitute an investment. In *Re Power's Will Trusts* the trustee was relying on the investment provision to justify the acquisition of a house for the beneficiaries to live in. It was held that this acquisition did not include the necessary element of income generation for the trust. Thus in *Re Wragg*[204] it was permitted to acquire real property on the basis that that property was expected to generate income. It should be remembered that the trustee will have powers of investment both under any express power and under the Trustee Act 2000.

Power to vary investment powers

Section 57 of the Trustee Act 1925 gives the court power to vary the powers of investment under a trust. That section provides that: **10.75**

> Where in the administration of any property vested in trustees [any investment] is in the opinion of the court expedient, but the same cannot be afforded by reason of the absence of any power for that purpose vested in the trustees by the trust instrument, if any, or by law, the court may by order confer upon the trustees, either generally or in any particular instance, the necessary power for the purpose . . .

Therefore, the court is entitled to permit investments of a broad range, from mortgages and loans through to purchase or sales of assets generally, where the court considers it to be expedient. That power can be exercisable on a one-off basis or can be by way of an effective variation of the terms of the trust. Such transactions must be for the benefit of all of the beneficiaries and not for any particular beneficiary.[205] In cases involving large funds, the court may permit a large expansion of the trust investment powers to enable the retention of a professional fund investment manager. Thus, in *Anker-Peterson v Anker-Peterson*,[206] a fund containing £4 million was expanded in this way such that the investment manager would be able to invest the fund in a commercially reasonable manner. Each case is treated on its own merits and recourse to court may be necessary even after the Trustee Act 2000 if the trust instrument had some express restriction on investment.[207]

The trustee's duty to act prudently and safely under the general law of trusts

The trustee's general duties of investment can be summarized in the following three core principles: to act prudently and safely;[208] to act fairly between beneficiaries;[209] and to acquire the best return for the beneficiaries.[210] Evidently there is a contradiction in these principles between acting prudently and making the highest available return on the property. In most cases, there will be an   **10.76**

---

[204] [1919] 2 Ch 58.   [205] *Re Craven's Estate* [1937] Ch 431.   [206] [1991] LS Gaz 32.
[207] *Trustees of the British Museum v Attorney-General* [1984] 1 WLR 418.
[208] *Learoyd v Whiteley* (1887) 12 App Cas 727.   [209] *Bartlett v Barclays Bank* [1980] Ch 515.
[210] *Cowan v Scargill* [1984] 3 WLR 501.

increased element of risk required in seeking to generate a higher investment return. So, in *Learoyd v Whiteley*[211] it was held that, when the trustee is investing trust property, she must not only act as a business person of ordinary prudence, but must also avoid all investments of a hazardous nature.

10.77   A rule which prevents the trustee from undertaking any financial risk of a hazardous nature was emblematic of an older approach to trustees' investment obligations and is one which conflicts with the modern portfolio theory that an investment manager is necessarily always taking risk and that what is required is to balance the amount of risk taken with the risk appetite of the client. Evidently, the *Learoyd v Whiteley* principle can be made to correlate with the conduct of business rules developed by the Financial Services Authority (FSA) under the Financial Services and Markets Act 2000 in relation to which the service provider is required to deal with the customer in a manner appropriate to the customer's level of expertise in financial investments. Thus, one could identify something which constituted a hazardous risk in a particular context as being different from something which bore some milder level of risk. The case of *Bartlett v Barclays Bank*[212] drew such a distinction between a prudent degree of risk and something which amounted to 'hazard', whereby it would be acceptable for a trustee to take a prudent risk but a risk which put the trust fund in hazard would be considered to be an invalid exercise of the trustee's powers.

10.78   The *Learoyd v Whiteley* principle was altered slightly by Hoffmann J in *Nestle v National Westminster Bank plc*[213] in which it was said that:

> Modern trustees acting within their investment powers are entitled to be judged by the standards of current portfolio theory, which emphasises the risk level of the entire portfolio rather than the risk attaching to each investment taken in isolation.[214]

Thus a more modern approach was taken to the business of investing trust property. Rather than seeking simply to protect the beneficiaries' capital and their income stream in a world of comparatively stable markets, it is suggested that modern financial theory should have a place. The epitome of modern investment theory is the notion that given the differentiation between various financial markets—whereby, for example, bond markets and real property markets may surge when equity markets fall—the most profitable and the most prudent policy is to spread one's investments across a range of different products, companies, and markets so that one is insulated from a failure of any one market or company and also exposed to the possibility of profit across a range of markets. In that light, portfolio theory includes a relic of prudence by avoiding investing completely in one form of investment which may fall in

---

[211] (1887) 12 App Cas 727.
[212] [1980] Ch 515.   [213] [1993] 1 WLR 1260; see also *Underhill and Hayton* 598 *et seq.*
[214] A discretionary portfolio manager is someone who is given freedom to decide what investments are made and what risks are taken—see generally A Hudson, *Swaps, Restitution and Trusts* (London: Sweet & Maxwell, 1999) 1.

value. Nevertheless, it also encourages trustees to invest outwith a narrow range of investments, as required by the Trustee Investment Act 1961.

It is in this regard that the requirements in the Trustee Act 2000, that the trustees **10.79** consider standard investment criteria and that the trustees take advice from qualified persons, become significant. In many cases it will only be possible to decide with hindsight whether an investment constituted a prudently taken risk, which generated a profit or only a small loss in calm market conditions, or a hazardous investment, which caused a great loss to the trust due to some aberration which the trustee (presumably) did not foresee at the time of making that investment. Of course, it may be the case that a successful investment was nevertheless outwith the classes of investment envisaged by the terms of the trust or that it was an investment of a sort which reasonable investment managers would not have made on behalf of the particular client in question. That, it is suggested, is a different question from the success or failure of the investment to generate a profit: hazardous investments may still be profitable investments in benign market conditions. What the Trustee Act 2000 seeks to do is to cause trustees to reflect, with the advice of appropriately qualified professionals, on the investments which they propose to make so that trustees will demur from investments which present an unacceptable level of risk. It will always be impossible for trustees to know in advance whether or not the investments they make will be profitable.

It is important to recall that the trustee is acting as a fiduciary in relation to any **10.80** investment decision which he makes. Consequently, a trustee will not be allowed to invest in anything in which he has a personal interest[215] nor in any other investment which would otherwise cause a conflict of interest.[216]

Trustee's obligation to secure the best available return for the beneficiaries

In contrast to the obligation not to take imprudent risk, there is a suggestion on **10.81** the authorities that the trustee generate the optimum return for the trust. This obligation to make the highest available return is in opposition to prioritizing any other objective, such as promoting some ethical or other non-financial objective. This issue arose in the case of *Cowan v Scargill*[217] in which the board of trustees of a mineworkers' pension fund was divided between executives of a trade union, to which most of the members of a pension fund belonged, and executives from the Coal Board which had employed most of those members. The most profitable investment identified by the trustees was in oil companies and in companies working in apartheid South Africa. The defendant, on behalf of the trade union membership of the board of trustees, refused to make such investments on the grounds that it was ethically wrong for the fund to invest in apartheid South

---

[215] *Re David Feldman Charitable Foundation* (1987) 58 OR (2d) 626.
[216] *Boardman v Phipps* [1967] 2 AC 46.   [217] [1984] 3 WLR 501.

Africa and also contrary to the interests of the members of the fund to invest in an industry which competed with the coal industry, in which all the members worked or had worked previously.

10.82　Megarry V-C held that '[w]hen the purpose of the trust is to provide financial benefits for the beneficiaries, the best interests of the beneficiaries are their best financial interests'. Therefore, the duty of the trustees to act in the best interests of the beneficiaries is to generate the best available return on the trust fund regardless of other considerations. The scope of the duty of investment was summarized by his lordship as the need to bear in mind the following: 'The prospects for the yield of income and capital appreciation both have to be considered in judging the return from the investment.'

10.83　His lordship therefore focused on the objections which the defendant trustee had raised in respect of the particular form of investment which had been suggested. He held that while 'the trustees must put on one side their own personal interests and views …', and later that '… if investments of this type would be more beneficial to the beneficiaries than other investments, the trustees must not refrain from making the investments by reasons of the views that they hold'. The irony is that, in relation to the moral nature of the obligations on the trustee to deal equitably with the trust fund, the trustee is not permitted to bring decisions of an ethical nature to bear on the scope of the investment powers. As his lordship put it: 'Trustees may even have to act dishonourably (though not illegally) if the interests of their beneficiaries require it.' What is not clear from the judgment is what the court's approach would have been if the trust had expressly excluded investment in South Africa. It must be the case that such an express provision would have had to be enforced.

Application of Trustee Act 2000 to trusts implied by law

10.84　What remains unclear within the terms of the Trustee Act 2000 is what exactly is meant by the term 'trustee' itself. The legislation itself makes general reference only to a 'trustee' but does not make clear whether or not that is to apply only to express trustees (that is, trustees who have accepted the office subject to a detailed trust instrument) or whether it refers also to constructive trustees, trustees of resulting trusts, or trustees of implied trusts like that in *Paul v Constance*:[218] the common feature between all those latter forms of trust being that the trustees would not know of their trusteeship until the court order which confirms it. Therefore, it is possible that there are trustees who do not know of their obligations and who are in breach of the positive obligations in the Trustee Act 2000 which apply in the absence of an exclusion clause—such as to produce a policy statement for the investment of trust funds and so forth.[219] The structure of the Act, and its references to exclusion of

---

[218] [1977] 1 WLR 527; considered above at para 2.03.　　　[219] Trustee Act 2000, s 4.

liability in the trust instrument, indicate that the legislative drafts person was focused on such express trusts formed by way of an instrument.[220]

I. Duty to Distribute Property to Right Persons

General principle

A trustee must obviously distribute trust capital and income only to those entitled to it, as specified in the trust instrument or as selected by the trustees (or other authorized person) in pursuance of a proper exercise of a dispositive power conferred by the settlement. In addition, for administrative purposes, trustees may also transfer trust property to a third party, such as an agent or custodian, or as security for a loan to the trust, but only if they are authorized to do so by the trust instrument or by statute.   **10.85**

In most instances, this particular duty overlaps with the trustee's duty to obey and act only in accordance with the trust instrument and his duty not to delegate his trust to another. If a trustee pays trust funds to the wrong person, he will be liable for a breach of trust, even if he did so on the basis of a forged authority from a beneficiary,[221] or a forged marriage certificate.[222] If he hands over trust money before he is supposed to receive security for it, he will be liable for any loss.[223] Similarly, if he hands over the trust fund for management by another, *without authority* to do so, the trustee will have to make good any resulting loss, 'however unexpected the result, however little likely to arise from the course adopted and however free such conduct may have been from any improper motive'.[224]   **10.86**

Circumstances affecting distribution[225]

Unmarried minor beneficiaries cannot give a valid receipt and trustees should not distribute funds to them unless they are expressly authorized to do so by the trust instrument.[226] Trustees should also not distribute to a beneficiary lacking mental capacity, other than in accordance with an order of the Court of Protection or a person authorized and registered under an enduring power of attorney. Divorce does not in itself affect the trusts of a settlement, although they may have been varied by an order of the court.[227]   **10.87**

---

[220] eg ibid, ss 9, 22, Sch 1 para 7: all of which make reference to existing trust instruments or provisions.

[221] *Ashby v Blackwell* (1765) Eden 299. Cf *Re Smith* (1902) 71 LJ Ch 411.

[222] *Eaves v Hickson* (1861) 30 Beav 136. See also *Bostock v Floyer* (1865) LR 1 Eq 26; *Sutton v Wilders* (1871) LR 12 Eq 373.

[223] *Target Holdings Ltd v Redferns* [1996] AC 421; (1998) 114 LQR 214, esp 225–227 (Lord Millett).   [224] *Clough v Bond* (1838) 3 My & Cr 490, 496–497.

[225] *Lewin*, paras 26-26–26-45.

[226] A married infant can give a valid receipt: Law of Property Act 1925, s 21.

[227] Matrimonial Causes Act 1973, s 24; Family Law Act 1996, s 15, Sch 2, paras 1, 2, and 5.

10.88 If the estate of a deceased beneficiary is entitled to a distribution, the trustees must require his personal representative to prove his title by producing an English grant of representation but, subject to this, must hand over the property. If a trustee pays a foreign personal representative without production of an English grant, he will become an executor *de son tort*.[228] Although there is a presumption of death if there is no trace of a beneficiary for a period of at least seven years,[229] a trustee should not rely on such a presumption: they should require actual proof of death or seek the directions of the court before distributing the trust property.[230]

10.89 Similarly, trustees who distribute funds on the assumption that a woman is past the age of childbearing do so at their own risk.[231] They must obtain medical evidence to that effect[232] or obtain the authority of the court to do so.[233]

10.90 A beneficiary who assigns his interest to a third party ought, as a matter of prudence, to notify the trustee of his assignment and the trustee ought to make a note of the same on the trust instrument. If a trustee subsequently pays trust funds to that beneficiary and not to his assignee, he will be liable.[234] Similarly, the trustee is liable if he pays money to an assignee whose title is bad, if the trustee has failed to investigate that title properly.[235] However, a trustee is not bound to know of derivative titles and, provided he makes reasonable inquiries, he will not necessarily be liable because it subsequently transpires that he acted on erroneous information.[236]

Protection for trustees

Section 27 of the Trustee Act 1925

10.91 Trustees may protect themselves by advertising for beneficiaries of whose claims they are not aware by utilizing the procedure set out in section 27 of the Trustee Act 1925, which provides as follows:

> (1) With a view to the conveyance to or distribution among the persons entitled to any real or personal property, the trustees of a settlement, trustees of land, trustees for sale of personal property or personal representatives, may give notice by advertisement in the Gazette, and in a newspaper circulating in the district in which the land is situated,

---

[228] *Smith v Bolden* (1863) 33 Beav 262; *New York Breweries Co Ltd v A-G* [1899] AC 62.
[229] *Re Watkins* [1953] 1 WLR 1323. There is no presumption of death without issue: *Re Jackson* [1907] 2 Ch 354. [230] ie, obtain a *Benjamin* order: *Re Benjamin* [1902] 1 Ch 723.
[231] It is sometimes said that trustees ought to act without a court order in a clear case: *Re Pettifor's Will Trusts* [1966] Ch 257. Cf *National Trustees, Executors and Agency Co Ltd of Australia Ltd v Tuck* [1967] VR 847. [232] *Bullas v Public Trustee* [1981] 1 NSWLR 641.
[233] *Re National Westminster Bank Ltd's Declaration of Trust* [1963] 1 WLR 820. The position will presumably be reviewed periodically in line with advances in medical science.
[234] *Hallows v Lloyd* (1888) 39 Ch D 686; *Re Neil* (1890) 62 LT 649; *Lord v Bunn* (1843) 2 Y & C Ch Cas 98. A trustee is not entitled, on payment to an assignee, to the custody of the deed of assignment, although he can ask for a statutory acknowledgement for production and an undertaking for safe custody (*Re Palmer* [1907] 1 Ch 486). [235] *Davis v Hutchings* [1907] 1 Ch 356.
[236] *Re Cull's Trusts* (1875) LR 20 Eq 561; *Cothay v Sydenham* (1788) 2 Bro CC 391; *Leslie v Baillie* (1843) 2 Y & C Ch Cas 91.

and such other like notices, including notices elsewhere than in England and Wales, as would, in any special case, have been directed by a court of competent jurisdiction in an action for administration, of their intention to make such conveyance or distribution as aforesaid, and requiring any person interested to send to the trustees or personal representatives within the time, not being less than two months, fixed in the notice or, where more than one notice is given, in the last of the notices, particulars of his claim in respect of the property or any part thereof to which the notice relates.

(2) At the expiration of the time fixed by the notice the trustees or personal representatives may convey or distribute the property or any part thereof to which the notice relates, to or among the persons entitled thereto, have regard only to the claims, whether formal or not, of which the trustees or personal representatives then had notice and shall not, as respects the property so conveyed or distributed, be liable to any person of whose claim the trustees or personal representatives have not had notice at the time of conveyance or distribution; but nothing in this section

(a) prejudices the right of any person to follow the property, or any property representing the same, into the hands of any person, other than a purchaser, who may have received it; or

(b) frees the trustees or personal representatives from any obligation to make searches or obtain official certificates of search similar to those which an intending purchaser would be advised to make or obtain.

(3) This section applies notwithstanding anything to the contrary in the will or other instrument, if any, creating the trust.

Section 27 applies to claims by beneficiaries and not just by creditors.[237] The protection afforded is available only if the trustees comply with its requirements, so, in difficult cases, the trustees ought to seek the directions of the court as to appropriate notices.[238] If it is impracticable to advertise in a foreign country, the court may even dispense with this requirement.[239] Section 27 protects trustees only in respect of claims of which they have no notice: they clearly cannot ignore claims of which they do have notice, even if the beneficiary does not respond to the advertisement.[240]

Reliance on counsel's opinion

Where a question of construction arises on the provisions of a trust or will, the **10.92** trustee may obtain the opinion in writing of a barrister of at least ten years' standing and may then safely proceed to take such steps in reliance on that opinion as the High Court may specify, without hearing argument.[241] This summary procedure is inappropriate, however, and the High Court will not make an order where there is a serious dispute in the matter.[242]

---

[237] *Re Aldhous* [1955] 1 WLR 459.
[238] *Re Letherbrow* [1935] WN 34 and 48; *Re Holden* [1935] WN 52.
[239] *Re Gess* [1942] Ch 37.
[240] *Markwell's Case* (1872) 21 WR 135; *Guardian Trust and Executor Co of New Zealand Ltd v Public Trustee of New Zealand* [1942] AC 115 (PC).
[241] Administration of Justice Act 1985, s 48(1); Practice Direction, Pt 8, Section A, paras A.1(1) and A.2(1) and CPD 12, section A.   [242] Section 48(2).

Section 61 of the Trustee Act 1925

10.93   If it appears to the court that a trustee is or may be personally liable for any breach of trust, but he has acted honestly and reasonably, and ought fairly to be excused for the breach of trust and for omitting to obtain the directions of the court in the matter in which he committed such breach, then the court may relieve him either wholly or partly from personal liability for the same.[243]

Distribution to an agent of a beneficiary

10.94   A trustee dealing with someone purporting to act under a power of attorney granted by a beneficiary has limited protection under section 5 of the Powers of Attorney Act 1971, which provides as follows:

> (1) A donee of a power of attorney who acts in pursuance of the power at a time when it has been revoked shall not, by reason of the revocation, incur any liability (either to the donor or to any other person) if at that time he did not know that the power had been revoked.
>
> (2) Where a power of attorney has been revoked and a person, without knowledge of the revocation, deals with the donee of the power, the transaction between them shall, in favour of that person, be as valid as if the power had then been in existence.
>
> (3) Where the power is expressed in the instrument creating it to be irrevocable and to be given by way of security then, unless the person dealing with the donee knows that it was not in fact given by way of security, he shall be entitled to assume that the power is incapable of revocation except by the donor acting with the consent of the donee and shall accordingly be treated for the purposes of subsection (2) of this section as having knowledge of the revocation only if he knows that it has been revoked in that manner.
>
> (4) Where the interest of a purchaser depends on whether a transaction between the donee of a power of attorney and another person was valid by virtue of subsection (2) of this section, it shall be conclusively presumed in favour of the purchaser that that person did not at the material time know of the revocation of the power if
>
> > (a) the transaction between that person and the donee was completed within twelve months of the date on which the power came into operation; or
> >
> > (b) that person makes a statutory declaration, before or within three months after the completion of the purchase, that he did not at the material time know of the revocation of the power.
>
> (5) Without prejudice to subsection (3) of this section, for the purposes of this section knowledge of the revocation of a power of attorney includes knowledge of the occurrence of any event (such as the death of the donor) which has the effect of revoking the power.
>
> (6) In this section 'purchaser' and 'purchase' have the meanings specified in section 205(1) of the Law of Property Act 1925.
>
> (7) This section applies whenever the power of attorney was created but only to acts and transactions after the commencement of this Act.

---

[243] Trustee Act 1925, s 61. See para 32.87 below.

Adopted, illegitimate, and legitimated persons

A trustee is not under a duty to inquire before distributing property whether any **10.95** adoption has been effected or revoked or whether any person is illegitimate or has been adopted by one of his natural parents or could be legitimated. A trustee will not be liable for any distribution made without regard to any such fact if he did not have notice thereof before such distribution was made.[244]

J. Duty Not to Delegate

It is a fundamental principle of trusts law that a trustee may not delegate his duties **10.96** and functions to another, unless he is expressly authorized to do so by the trust instrument: *delegatus non potest delegare*. The office of trustee is one of personal trust and confidence. The person who holds it is required to exercise his own judgment and discretion. In the absence of express provision to the contrary, an individual trustee or the trustees collectively cannot refer or commit the trust or the exercise of trustee powers to a co-trustee or to another.[245] 'Such trusts and powers are supposed to have been committed by the testator to the trustees he appoints by reason of his personal confidence in their discretion, and it would be wrong to permit them to be exercised by [another].'[246] 'Trustees who take on themselves the management of property for the benefit of others have no right to shift their duty on other persons; and if they employ an agent, they remain subject to responsibility towards their *cestuis que trust*, for whom they have undertaken the duty.'[247]

Originally, trustees were not able to appoint agents to carry out even managerial **10.97** functions, save where the act was purely ministerial or where the necessity of the case required it. The basic rule against delegation, though still one of the pillars of the trust, has by now been modified and relaxed considerably. In addition to the widespread use in modern trust instruments of wide express provisions authorizing delegation (of trusts as well as administrative powers), trustees now have available to them a wide range of statutory powers to delegate—so much so that the basic rule often seems to be more honoured in the breach. Delegation by trustees is dealt with in detail in Chapter 15 below.

---

[244] Adoption Act 1976, s 45; Legitimacy Act 1976, s 7. This does not prejudice the right of such a person to follow the property into the hands of another who has received it, other than a purchaser: Adoption Act 1976, s 45(3); Legitimacy Act 1976, s 7(3).

[245] *A-G v Glegg* (1738) 1 Atk 356; *Crewe v Dicken* (1798) 4 Ves 97; *Chambers v Minchin* (1802) 7 Ves 186; *Langford v Gascoyne* (1805) 11 Ves 333; *Adams v Clifton* (1826) 1 Russ 297; *Clough v Bond* (1838) 3 My & Cr 490; *Cowell v Gatcombe* (1859) 27 Beab 568; *Wood v Weightman* (1872) LR 13 Eq 434; *Re Bellamy and Metropolitan Board of Works* (1883) 24 Ch D 387; *Re Flower and Metropolitan Board of Works* (1884) 27 Ch D 592.

[246] *Robson v Flight* (1865) 4 De GJ & S 608, 613, *per* Lord Westbury LC.

[247] *Turner v Corney* (1841) 5 Beav 515, 517, *per* Lord Langdale MR. See also *Rowland v Witherden* (1851) 3 Mac & G 568; *Speight v Gaunt* (1883) 22 Ch D 727, 756, *per* Lindley LJ; *Re Airey* [1897] 1 Ch 164, 170 *per* Kekewich J; *Re Parry* [1969] 1 WLR 614, 618, *per* Pennycuick J.

K. Duty to Act Jointly

10.98   As a general rule, where there are two or more trustees, they must act jointly.[248] This rule follows from the fact that trustees cannot delegate their duties: a trustee cannot appoint a co-trustee to perform his duties for him. The acts and decisions of a majority of trustees cannot, therefore, bind a dissenting minority or the trust. Thus, for example, a trust for sale must be carried into effect unless the trustees unanimously agree to exercise their power to postpone sale.[249] Trustees must ensure that trust assets do not get into the hands of just one or some of them,[250] and so must join in the receipt of money, unless they have authority to the contrary;[251] and, if a co-trustee is authorized to receive money, he must not be allowed to retain it for longer than the circumstances require.[252] Trust investments ought to be made and retained in joint names,[253] unless necessity demands otherwise,[254] or the trustees lawfully appoint nominees or custodians.[255] Trustees must not authorize a bank to honour cheques signed by one or some only of their number.[256] Also, all trustees must act jointly in exercising an option to renew a lease, surrendering a lease, applying for relief against forfeiture, or operating a break clause.[257]

There are exceptions to the general rule, however.

  (a) Trustees of charitable trusts may act by majority.[258]
  (b) Trustees of pension trusts may act by majority.[259]

---

[248] *Luke v South Kensington Hotel Co* (1879) 11 Ch D 121; *Re Dixon* (1826) 2 GL & J 114; *Swale v Swale* (1856) 22 Beav 584; *Re Flower and Metropolitan Board of Works* (1884) 27 Ch D 592; *Re Roth* (1896) 74 LT 50; *Re Hilton* [1909] 2 Ch 548; *Re Whiteley* [1910] 1 Ch 600; *Re Butlin's Settlement Trust* [1976] Ch 251.

[249] *Re Roth* (1896) 74 LT 50; *Re Mayo* [1943] Ch 302; *Jones v Challenger* [1961] 1 QB 176. Trustees must also meet to discuss and reach decisions: *A-G v Scott* (1750) 1 Ves Sen 413.

[250] *Re Flower and Metropolitan Board of Works* (1884) 27 Ch D 592.

[251] Whether under the trust instrument or statute: see, for example, the Law of Property Act 1925, s 27, and the Trustee Act 2000, s 11. Some older cases held that, where a trustee could prove that he joined in a receipt for the sake of conformity, but that he did not in fact receive the money, he would not be liable: *Brice v Stokes* (1805) 11 Ves 319; *Re Fryer* (1857) 3 K & J 317. This seems a doubtful conclusion. See now Trustee Act 2000, ss 11, 12(1).

[252] *Brice v Stokes, supra*; *Styles v Guy* (1849) 1 Mac & G 422; *Wiglesworth v Wiglesworth* (1852) 16 Beav 269; *Egbert v Butter* (1856) 21 Beav 560; *Thompson v Finch* (1856) 8 De GM & G 560; *Lewis v Nobbs* (1878) 8 Ch D 591; *Carruthers v Carruthers* [1896] AC 659; *Re Munton* [1927] 1 Ch 262.

[253] *Lewis v. Nobbs, supra Swale v Swale* (1856) 22 Beav 584.

[254] See, for example, *Consterdine v Consterdine* (1862) 31 Beav 330.

[255] Trustee Act 2000, ss 16, 17.

[256] *Clough v Bond* (1838) 3 My & Cr 490; *Trutch v Lamprell* (1855) 20 Beav 116. A trustee who gave his co-trustee a crossed cheque for delivery to a beneficiary was not liable (*Lake Bathurst Australasian Gold Mining Co v Bagshaw* (1862) 3 De GJ & Sm 355). If one trustee forges the signature of another trustee on a cheque in order to withdraw money from a bank, to whom instructions have been given to honour joint cheques only, the bank does not obtain a good discharge: *Welch v Bank of England* [1955] Ch 508. Cf *Brewer v Westminster Bank Ltd* [1952] 2 All ER 650.

[257] *Hammersmith and Fulham LBC v Monk* [1992] 1 AC 478.

[258] *Re Whiteley* [1910] 1 Ch 600, 608.   [259] Pensions Act 1995, s 32.

(c) Where the trust instrument (or the court) expressly directs otherwise.[260]

(d) Where a trustee may lawfully delegate.[261]

(e) Where a trustee receives income.[262]

As to (e), it has long been established that one trustee may be authorized by his co-trustees to receive income, such as the collection of rents, or the receipt of dividends.[263]

L. Duty Not to Profit from the Trust; Duty to the Trust Must Not Conflict With Self-Interest[264]

Basic principle

A trustee must not place himself in a position where his duty to the trust and his own self-interest may come into conflict.[265] Consequently, a trustee must not profit from his trusteeship, and he must not use or deal with trust property for his own personal benefit or advantage.[266]

10.99

It is a well-established rule of equity that a person in a fiduciary position may not, in the absence of authority to the contrary, enter into engagements in which he has or may have a personal interest, or which possibly may conflict with the interests of those whom he is bound to protect.[267] As Lord Herschell put it, in *Bray v Ford*:[268]

10.100

> It is an inflexible rule of a Court of Equity that a person in a fiduciary position . . . is not, unless otherwise expressly provided, entitled to make a profit; he is not allowed

---

[260] *Re Butlin's Settlement Trust* [1976] Ch 251.   [261] See Chapter 15 below.

[262] *Townley v Sherborne* (1634) J Bridg 35; *Gouldsworth v Knights* (1843) 11 M & W 337; *Gough v Smith* [1872] WN 18. See also Companies Act 1985, s 360.

[263] *Townley Sherborne, supra; Gough v Smith, supra.* See also Companies Act 1985, s 360.

[264] Finn, *Fiduciary Obligations* (1977) Ch 21, 199–251; AJ Oakley, *Constructive Trust* (3rd edn, 1997), Section 3, 85–179; *Underhill and Hayton*, 651–671; *Lewin*, paras 20-01–20-158.

[265] *Boardman v Phipps* [1967] 2 AC 46.

[266] *A-G for Hong Kong v Reid* [1994] 1 AC 324; *Ex p Lacey* (1802) 6 Ves 625; *Aberdeen Town Council v Aberdeen University* (1877) 2 App Cas 544; *Rochefoucauld v Boustead* [1898] 1 Ch 550.

[267] *Aberdeen Railway Company v Blaikie Brothers* (1854) 1 Macq 461, 471, *per* Lord Cranworth LC. The following formulation of the obligations of a fiduciary, put forward by PD Finn in his essay on 'Fiduciary Law and the Modern Commercial World' (in *Commercial Aspects of Trusts and Fiduciary Obligations*, ed E McKendrick (Oxford, 1992) 9, has attracted considerable support. He stated: 'A fiduciary (a) cannot misuse his position, or knowledge or opportunity resulting from it, to his own or to a third party's possible advantage; or (b) cannot, in any matter falling within the scope of his service, have a personal interest or an inconsistent engagement with a third party— unless this is freely and informedly consented to by the beneficiary or is authorised by law.' This is acknowledged to be an adaptation of the formulation of Deane J in *Chan v Zacharia* (1983) 53 ALR 417, 435. Although this formulation suffices as a starting point, it does not cover all the ground or resolve all issues. It does not identify when a fiduciary 'misuses' his position. It does not deal with the question whether these are duties imposed on a fiduciary (and, if so, how they interact with other positive duties) or whether they are simply disabilities. Nor does it address the issue of conflict between duty and duty, or indeed between power and power. See also *Equity, Fiduciaries and Trusts*, ed Youdan (1989), 1–56; and RP Austin in *Trends in Contemporary Trust Law*, ed AJ Oakley (Oxford: 1996), 159.

[268] [1896] AC 44. See also *NZ Netherlands 'Oranje' Society Inc v Kuys* [1973] 1 WLR 1126, 1129.

to put himself in a position where his interest and duty conflict. It does not appear to me that this rule is . . . founded upon principles of morality. I regard it rather as based on the consideration that, human nature being what it is, there is danger, in such circumstances, of the person holding a fiduciary position being swayed by interest rather than by duty, and thus prejudicing those whom he was bound to protect. It has, therefore, been deemed expedient to lay down this positive rule.

This 'inflexible rule' applies, with differing degrees of severity and in a bewildering variety of circumstances, to trustees,[269] agents,[270] directors,[271] partners,[272] and others, whether they were expressly appointed to such offices or simply took it upon themselves to act as if they had been. It also applies to different kinds of trustees and all types of trusts, including occupational pension schemes.[273]

Nature of the rule

10.101 Whether there is in fact only one rule with several limbs, or several different but connected rules, is not entirely clear. Thus, a distinction has emerged between what is called the 'profit rule' and the 'conflict rule' (although the two clearly overlap),[274] and also between a 'self-dealing' rule, where the fiduciary is, in effect, transacting with himself (for example as both vendor and purchaser) and a 'fair-dealing' rule, where he is not.[275] Although the 'self-dealing' and 'fair-dealing' rules are usually discussed exclusively in the context of a purchase by the fiduciary of his principal's property, or of a beneficial interest (as the case may be), there seems to be no reason why the two rules should not apply equally in relation to other transactions. Indeed, it has been held that the self-dealing and fair-dealing rules should not be regarded as imposing duties on trustees not to purchase trust property, or

---

[269] See, eg, *Re Edwards' Will Trusts* [1982] Ch 30, 40, *per* Buckley LJ: 'It is well established law that a trustee cannot use his position or his powers as a trustee to acquire Property for his own benefit.'

[270] *Lowther v Lowther* (1806) 13 Ves 95, 103; *Powell & Thomas v Evan Jones & Co* [1905] 1 KB 11; *English v Dedham Vale Properties Ltd* [1978] 1 WLR 93. Cf *Lord Napier and Ettrick v RF Kershaw Ltd* [1993] 1 All ER 385.

[271] *Selangor United Rubber Estates Ltd v Cradock (No 3)* [1968] 1 WLR 1555. See also [1967] CLJ 83 (LS Sealy).   [272] *Bentley v Craven* (1853) 18 Beav 75.

[273] *Brooke Bond & Co Ltd's Trust Deed* [1963] Ch 357.

[274] In *Swain v The Law Society* [1982] 1 WLR 17, 29, Stephenson LJ regarded the 'profit rule' as but one aspect of the wider 'conflict rule', but this has not found universal acceptance: see, for example, *Chan v Zacharia* (1984) 53 ALR 417, 433; *Warman International v Dwyer* (1995) 69 ALR 362, 368.

[275] *Tito v Waddell (No 2)* [1977] Ch 106, 224–225, 240–244. Megarry V-C concluded that, although both rules, or both limbs of the one rule, had common origins in that equity is astute to prevent a trustee from abusing his position or profiting from his trust, there were two rules for all practical purposes: at 241. In practice, the two rules overlap, because trustees usually derive a profit at the expense of their beneficiaries. However, a trustee may make a profit where there is no obvious conflict of duty and interest, eg in a joint investment with the beneficiaries, so that it is the 'profits rule' that dominates; or the trustee may be pursuing his own interest, without making a profit, in conflict with his duty as trustee, so that the 'conflict rule' dominates.

not to purchase a beneficiary's interest without proper disclosure, but essentially as general rules of equity which subject trustees to particular disabilities in cases falling within those rules.[276]

Purchase of trust property: the self-dealing rule

In any event, whether it is viewed as imposing duties or establishing disabilities, **10.102** the general principle is a strict one. According to Lord Eldon LC, in *Ex p James*,[277] in a case where a trustee has purchased trust property, 'the purchase is not permitted in any case, however honest the circumstances; the general interests of justice requiring it to be destroyed in every instance; as no Court is equal to the examination and ascertainment of the truth in much the greater number of cases'. Similarly, in *Ex p Lacey*,[278] he declared that, in such a case, it is impossible for the court to determine whether the trustee has obtained an advantage or not. And, in *Parker v McKenna*,[279] James LJ stated that the rule was 'an inexorable rule, and must be applied inexorably by this Court, which is not entitled . . . to receive evidence, or suggestion or argument as to whether the principal did or did not suffer any injury in fact by reason of the dealing of the agent; for the safety of mankind requires that no agent shall be able to put his principal to the danger of such an inquiry as that'. Thus, it is a rule of policy, rather than a technical rule of law;[280] and, therefore, a transaction may be set aside even where it was perfectly fair and honest,[281] and even if it resulted in a profit to the trust fund.[282] It is the possibility of conflict that matters and must be guarded against. [283]

Indirect transactions intended to avoid the rule

The rule cannot easily be avoided by indirect methods. For example, a trustee **10.103** cannot sell trust property to a nominee,[284] or to a person with the intention of

---

[276] *Tito v Waddell, supra,* 247–250. As a result, breaches of those rules are not (or not necessarily) breaches of trust and therefore not subject to the six-year limitation period laid down in s 21 of the Limitation Act 1980.
[277] (1803) 8 Ves 337, 345. See also *Ex p Lacey* (1802) 6 Ves 625; *Ex p Bennett* (1805) 10 Ves 381; *Randall v Errington* (1805) 10 Ves 423; and *Parker v McKenna* (1874) 10 Ch App 96.
[278] (1802) 6 Ves 625.   [279] (1874) 10 Ch App 96, 124–125.
[280] In *British Coal Corporation v British Coal Staff Superannuation Scheme Trustees Ltd* [1993] PLR 303, 312–313, Vinelott J stated that the rule was based on common sense and it was not a technical rule of trust law. See also the remarks of Lord Herschell in *Bray v Ford* [1896] AC 44, cited at para 10.100 above. In *Holder v Holder* [1968] Ch 353, Danckwerts and Sachs LJJ (at 398, 402–403) considered it to be a rule of practice only, and not one of jurisdiction; but this view is difficult to sustain in the light of earlier cases.
[281] *Campbell v Walker* (1800) 5 Ves 678, 680; *Dyson v Lum* (1866) 14 LT 588; *Wright v Morgan* [1926] AC 788 (a sale of trust property to one trustee-beneficiary was expressly authorized; but he assigned his beneficial interest to another trustee, who then bought the property at a price fixed by an independent valuer: sale still set aside by the Privy Council).
[282] *Ex p Lacey* (1802) 6 Ves 625; *Ex p Bennett* (1805) 10 Ves 381; *Re Thompson's Settlement* [1986] Ch 99.   [283] *Brooke Bond & Co Ltd's Trust Deed* [1963] Ch 357.
[284] *Silkstone & Haigh Moor Coal Co v Edey* [1900] 1 Ch 167; *Re Postlethwaite* (1888) 60 LT 514.

repurchasing that property from him.[285] It does not matter that the sale may have been at auction and that the trustee paid well above the reserve price, for the rule is based on his status as trustee and not on his conduct.[286] Nor can he retire from the trust in order to purchase trust property, or simply opt out of the decision to sell or the conduct of sale.[287] A sale by a trustee to his wife is also likely to be impeachable, although the circumstances may be such that it will be upheld.[288] Similarly, a sale to a limited company which is essentially the *alter ego* of the trustee, or substantially owned by him (and a close member of his family), or to a partnership of which the trustee is a member, will also be viewed with suspicion.[289] Certainly, if the beneficiaries question the sale, the onus is on the purchaser to prove that the sale was proper, in good faith, and at the best price then available.[290]

10.104   Trustees cannot lease trust property to one or more of themselves;[291] nor, probably, can a trustee lease his own property to the trust.[292] It would also seem to be the case that a trustee could not become a mortgagee of trust property, with all the powers and rights over that property which his status as mortgagee would entail.[293] If a trustee can sell his property to the trust, he must sell at cost price and not make a profit.[294] If a trustee lends money to the trust, he may not charge interest.[295] Although a personal representative can appropriate to himself cash, or assets which are the equivalent of cash (but not shares in an unquoted company), in order to satisfy a legacy to him, he must do so fairly and cannot appropriate to himself assets which are more likely to appreciate more than others.[296]

10.105   A purchase by a trustee is voidable rather than void.[297] A beneficiary may seek to avoid the sale even as against a person to whom the property has subsequently

---

[285] *Sanderson v Walker* (1807) 13 Ves 601; *Parker v McKenna* (1874) 10 Ch App 96; *Williams v Scott* [1900] AC 499; *Delves v Gray* [1902] 2 Ch 606; *Re Sherman* [1954] Ch 653. If the purchase by the trustee occurs many years later, it may not be impeachable: *Baker v Peck* (1861) 4 LT 3; *Re Postlethwaite, supra* (20 years later).

[286] *Campbell v Walker* (1800) 5 Ves 678; *Ex p Lacey* (1802) 6 Ves 625; *Movitex Ltd v Bulfield* [1988] BCLC 104.

[287] *Wright v Morgan* [1926] AC 788; *Re Boles and British Land Co's Contract* [1902] 1 Ch 244.

[288] *Tito v Waddell (No 2)* [1977] Ch 106; *Burrell v Burrell's trustees* 1915 SC 333; *Re King's Will Trust* (1959) 173 Estates Gazette 627.

[289] *Silkstobe & Haigh Moor Coal Co v Edey, supra; Re Thompson's Settlement* [1986] Ch 99; *Movitex Ltd v Bulfield, supra.*

[290] *Farrar v Farrars Ltd* (1880) 40 Ch D 395. See also *Tse Kwong Lam v Wong Chit Sen* [1983] 1 WLR 1349.

[291] *Re Dumbell* (1802) 6 Ves 617; *Re John's Assignment Trusts* [1970] 1 WLR 955, 960. Of course, a sole trustee could not lease property to himself in any event: *Rye v Rye* [1962] AC 496.

[292] *Bentley v Craven* (1853) 18 Beav 75; *Re Cape Breton Co* (1885) 29 Ch D 795.

[293] Notwithstanding *A-G v Hardy* (1851) 1 Sim NS 338; *Re Mason's Orphanage* [1896] 1 Ch 54, 59.

[294] *Re Williams* (1892) 40 WR 636; *Re Sykes* [1909] 2 Ch 241.

[295] *Gordon v Trail* (1820) 8 Price 416; *Re Jones* [1917] St R Qd 74.

[296] *Kane v Radley-Kane* [1999] Ch 274; *Lloyds Bank v Duker* [1987] 3 All ER 193; *Barclay v Owen* (1889) 60 LT 220; *Re Richardson* [1896] 1 Ch 512.

[297] *Re Sherman* [1954] Ch 653; *Holder v Holder* [1968] Ch 353.

been transferred, other than 'equity's darling';[298] and, if the transfer is set aside, the transferee (just like a trustee) is entitled to be refunded the purchase money with interest.[299]

The conflict rule

Most examples of the application of the self-dealing rule (or the profit rule) are **10.106** also instances of the application of the conflict rule. Trustees are under a duty not to put themselves in a position where their duty to the trust conflicts with their self-interest, and a breach of this duty usually manifests itself in one of the forms of self-dealing. However, it is possible for a trustee to engage in an activity on his own account, which does not necessarily result in profit or which does not necessarily involve self-dealing. For example, a trustee who derives incidental profits from his position as trustee is not usually dealing with himself in the strict sense. In such cases, he is in breach of the conflict rule.

Renewal of trust lease

The classic illustration of the conflict rule is *Keech v Sandford*,[300] where the trustee **10.107** had attempted, unsuccessfully, to persuade the lessor of a lease (of the profits of a market), which the trustee held on trust for an infant beneficiary, to renew the lease in favour of the trust; and only after such refusal did the trustee renew the lease in his own favour. Lord Chancellor King held that the trustee must hold the renewed lease on trust for the beneficiary. The same trusts that applied to the original lease also apply to the renewed one.[301] If any profits are made from the renewed lease, for example of business premises, the trustee is accountable for them. The same principle applies if the spouse of the trustee renews the lease.[302] It also applies to the renewal of contracts.[303]

Purchase of reversion on trust lease

The position where the trustee purchases the reversion expectant on a lease to the **10.108** trust is not entirely clear, but the rule in *Keech v Sandford* almost certainly applies. Early authorities took a different view, and the rule was applied to a reversion only

---

[298] *Aberdeen Town Council v Aberdeen University* (1877) 2 App Cas 544.

[299] *Rowley v Ginnever* [1897] 2 Ch 503. A trustee is entitled to a charge on the property to secure his entitlement: ibid.

[300] (1726) Sel Cas t King 61. See also *Re Edwards' Will Trusts* [1982] Ch 30; *Elder's Trustee and Executor Co Ltd v Higgins* (1963) 113 CLR 426; *Chan v Zacharia* (1984) 154 CLR 178; and (1969) 33 Conv (NS) 161 (S Cretney). There is no such principle where there is no fiduciary relationship: *Re Biss* [1903] 2 Ch 40.

[301] *Re Jarvis* [1958] 1 WLR 815 (no liability because of laches and acquiescence).

[302] *Ex p Grace* (1799) 1 Bos & P 376; *Re Biss, supra*. The principle also applies to executors: *Re Morgan* (1881) 18 Ch D 93; *James v Dean* (1808) 15 Ves 236.

[303] *Don King Productions Inc v Warren* [2000] Ch 291.

where the lease was renewable by contract or by custom.[304] However, in *Prothero v Prothero*,[305] the Court of Appeal, without considering earlier relevant authorities, held that the rule was indeed applicable: 'if a trustee who owns the leasehold gets in the freehold, that freehold belongs to the trust and he cannot take the property for himself'. Subsequently, in *Thompson's Trustee in Bankruptcy v Heaton*,[306] Pennycuick V-C concluded that he was bound by *Prothero* and that the decision 'is really in modern times an application of the broad principle that the trustee must not make a profit out of the trust estate'. Many leases today are renewable under statute; and lessees often have rights of enfranchisement, so the rule in *Keech v Sandford* ought to apply without qualification. In other cases, it may be said that the trustee ought to be liable only if the trustee has derived some personal benefit from his position as trustee, for example by virtue of possessing significant information about the premises or the lease which he would not otherwise have had. However, even in such a case, it ought to be remembered that the conflict rule may apply even where the trustee has not derived a personal benefit from the transaction.[307] Nor does it seem to be relevant that the reversion is a different item of property from the lease itself. The rule is designed to prevent a potential conflict of interest from arising. In any event, a trustee has available to him the right to seek the sanction of the court and a prudent trustee would invoke that right.

Other incidental profits

10.109   'If the person in a fiduciary position does gain or receive any financial benefit arising out of the use of the property of the beneficiary he cannot keep it unless he can show authority.'[308] Thus, where a trustee uses votes attached to shares held on trust to appoint himself a director of the company, any remuneration derived from his directorship must be accounted for to the trust,[309] unless, perhaps, where he was already a director before being appointed trustee.[310] If a trustee uses trust moneys in his own business,[311] or gives trust business to a firm of which he is a

---

[304] *Phipps v Boardman* [1964] 2 All ER 187, 201–202, *per* Wilberforce J. See also *Randall v Russell* (1817) 3 Mer 190; *Hardman v Johnson* (1815) 3 Mer 347; *Longton v Wilsby* (1897) 76 LT 770; *Bevan v Webb* [1905] 1 Ch 620. Cf *Re Lord Ranelagh's Will* (1884) 26 Ch D 590.

[305] [1968] 1 WLR 519. See also (1968) 31 MLR 707 (P Jackson); (1968) 84 LQR 309 (L Megarry); (1968) 32 Conv (NS) 220 (F Crane).

[306] [1974] 1 WLR 605. See also (1974) 38 Conv (NS) 288; (1975) 38 MLR 226 (P Jackson).

[307] *Elder's Trustee and Executor Co Ltd v Higgins* (1963) 113 CLR 426.

[308] *Brown v IRC* [1965] AC 244, *per* Lord Reid. See also *Huntingdon Copper Co v Henderson* (1872) 4 R 294, 308. Cf the unusual facts of *Patel v Patel* [1981] 1 WLR 1343.

[309] *Re Macadam* [1946] Ch 73, esp 82; *Re Francis* (1905) 92 LT 77; *Williams v Barton* [1927] 2 Ch 9. It is otherwise if the trustee's appointment as director is not dependent upon the trust shareholding or if he is remunerated under an entirely independent bargain: *Re Gee* [1948] Ch 284; *Re Lewis* (1910) 103 LT 495.

[310] *Re Dover Coalfield Extension Ltd* [1908] 1 Ch 65. There is then a question as to whether, if he reappoints himself as a director after becoming trustee, he ought then to account for his remuneration.   [311] *Brown v IRC, supra.*

member, he must account for the profit.[312] A trustee must not compete with the trust, for example by setting up his own business in competition with a trust business,[313] at least if it is a specialized business or if the trustee attempts to solicit customers from the trust business A trustee was even compelled to account for a sum paid to him to induce him to retire.[314]

The basic rule is always the same: 'that which is the fruit of trust property or of the **10.110** trusteeship is itself trust property'.[315] If this is the case, it is immaterial that the beneficiary himself might not otherwise have derived the profit; that the trustee acted honestly and, indeed, consciously in what was considered to be the beneficiary's best interests; or even that the trustee used his own assets and skills.[316] The profit may arise, not from the unauthorized use of trust property or even be the fruit of trust property, but from misuse by the trustee of his position, for example a bribe or secret commission,[317] but it must still be accounted for.

Exceptions to the self-dealing rule and conflict rule

Notwithstanding such statements as to the absolute and inflexible nature of these **10.111** rules, it is now well recognized that there are exceptions to them. Even in *Bray v Ford*,[318] Lord Herschell remarked that he was 'satisfied that [they] might be departed from in many cases, without any breach of morality, without any wrong being inflicted, and without any consciousness of wrong-doing. Indeed, it is obvious that it might sometimes be to the advantage of the beneficiaries that the trustee should act for them professionally rather than a stranger, even though the trustee were paid for his services.' Thus, an express provision in the trust instrument (or other relevant terms of appointment of the fiduciary) may effectively exclude the application of the rule.[319] For example, the rule obliges a trustee to act without remuneration, but an express provision is usually incorporated in the trust instrument authorizing him to charge for doing so[320] (although such a provision will

---

[312] *Williams v Barton, supra.* Cf *Jones v AMP Perpetual Trustee Company NZ Ltd* [1994] 1 NZLR 690; *HSBC (HK) Ltd v Secretary for Justice* (2001) 3 ITELR 763.

[313] *Re Thomson* [1930] 1 Ch 203 (yacht broking business); *Warman International Ltd v Dwyer* (1995) 69 ALJR 362. It may depend, however, on the nature of the business: cf *Moore v M'Glynn* [1894] 1 IR 74 (general store).

[314] *Sugden v Crossland* (1856) 3 Sm & G 192; *Re Smith* [1896] 1 Ch 71.

[315] *Swain v Law Society* [1981] 3 All ER 797, 813, *per* Oliver LJ.

[316] *Boardman v Phipps* [1967] 2 AC 46; *A-G for Hong Kong v Reid* [1994] 1 AC 324;

[317] *A-G for Hong Kong v Reid, supra; Swain v Law Society* [1981] 3 All ER 797. See also *Logicrose Ltd v Southend United Football Club Ltd* [1988] 1 WLR 1256.

[318] [1896] AC 44, 51, notwithstanding the quotation in para 10.100 above.

[319] *Swain v The Law Society* [1982] 1 WLR 17, 37, *per* Oliver LJ (approved by Lord Brightman in [1983] AC 598 at 619). See also *Space Investments Ltd v Canadian Imperial Bank of Commerce Trust Co (Bahamas) Ltd* [1986] 1 WLR 1072; *Hahn v Bank International Ltd* [1987] CILR 407; and *The Cotomo Trust Case* (decision of Smellie J: GC of Cayman Islands, 2 June 1997).

[320] *Webb v Earl of Shaftesbury* (1802) 7 Ves 480; *Willis v Kibble* (1839) 1 Beav 559. See also *Space Investments Ltd v Canadian Imperial Bank of Commerce Trust Co (Bahamas) Ltd* [1986] 1 WLR

always receive a strict interpretation from the courts).[321] Similarly, In *Sargeant v National Westminster Bank plc*,[322] a sale by the trustees of a testator's will to themselves of certain farms comprised in the testator's estate, made in reliance upon an express power in the will authorizing the trustees to purchase trust property, was upheld by the Court of Appeal. Nourse LJ stated:[323]

> The rule that a trustee must not profit from his trust holds that prevention is better than cure. While it invariably requires that a profit shall be yielded up, it prefers to intervene beforehand by dissolving the connection out of which the profit may be made. At that stage the rule is expressed by saying that a trustee must not put himself in a position where his interest and duty conflict. But to express it in that way is to acknowledge that if he is put there, not by himself, but by the testator or settlor under whose dispositions his trust arises, the rule does not apply.

10.112 On this basis, the rule against conflict may be excluded, in appropriate cases, by implication, and not by express provision, for example in cases where a testator directs the sale of property to a named individual who is then appointed an executor of the will, or where an original trustee is included as a beneficiary or an object in whose favour certain powers may be exercised. The application of the rule may also be excluded by the person entitled to the benefit of the rule. As Upjohn LJ stated in *Boulting v Association of Cinematograph, Television and Allied Technicians*:[324]

> Like all rules of equity, it is flexible, in the sense that it develops to meet the changing situations and conditions of the time . . . The rule, however, is essentially for the protection of the persons to whom the duty is owed.
> To sum up the position, it is clear that the person entitled to the benefit of this positive rule is the person who is protected by it, but he, and he alone, can in proper circumstances relax it to such extent as he thinks proper. It cannot be used as a shield by the person owing the duty; that is clear; it is a sword and as such only can it be used by the person entitled to the benefit of it, and he may sheath the weapon.

1072. In *Re William Makin & Son Ltd* [1993] OPLR 171, 176, Vinelott J alluded to 'the doubtful and difficult question whether the application of this principle [ie the rule against conflict of interests] can in fact be excluded by an express provision in a trust instrument' (a question which he did not have to consider in the case before him). It may be that he was referring to some particular point which had arisen in that case or more generally to potential difficulties which might arise from the application of an express exclusion clause. However, if he intended to question the *principle* of an effective exclusion provision, his view cannot be supported by authority.

[321] *Re Gee* [1948] Ch 284; *Re Chalinder & Herington* [1907] 1 Ch 58, 61; *Re Chapple* (1884) 27 Ch D 584; *Clarkson v Robinson* [1900] 2 Ch 722; *Re Ames* (1883) 25 Ch D 72; *Re Fish* [1893] 2 Ch 413; *Re Orwell's Will Trusts* [1982] 3 All ER 177. See also *Bogg v Raper*, 12 April 1998.

[322] (1990) 61 P & CR 518. The trustees already had tenancies granted to them by the testator during his lifetime. The central question was whether the trustees could sell the property while their pre-existing tenancies continued to subsist. They were under a duty to obtain the best possible price for the property, which, it was alleged, could only be achieved if it could be sold with vacant possession. Not surprisingly, it was held that, as tenants, they were not obliged to move out. As trustees, they could sell only what they had, namely freehold interests subject to tenancies. Ordinarily, they could still not sell the farms to themselves, but the will expressly authorized them to do so here.

[323] ibid 519. See also *Edge v The Pensions Ombudsman* [1998] PLR 15.

[324] [1963] 2 QB 606, 636, 637, and 638.

It must be applied realistically to a state of affairs which discloses a real conflict of duty and interest and not to some theoretical or rhetorical conflict. It is quite unnecessary to invoke the rule in the case of a director who takes too long a holiday or stays at too expensive an hotel; that is just a plain breach of his duty to serve the company faithfully . . . But it would be quite wrong to attempt any definition of the ambit of the rule. It is there, firm and untrammelled, waiting to be applied to the changing times and conditions of the times as circumstances may require, only to be relaxed where those entitled to the benefit of it are of full age, *sui juris* and have all the requisite knowledge, not only of all the relevant facts but of their rights.

Departures from the strict rule may also be authorized by the court. It may, for instance, authorize the remuneration of a trustee (prospectively or retrospectively) under its inherent jurisdiction, or under certain statutory provisions.[325] Indeed, the court can give a trustee leave to purchase trust property, provided the trustee (and preferably his co-trustees) can satisfy the court that the proposed transaction is of benefit to the beneficiaries generally, but it will generally not do so if the beneficiaries object on reasonable grounds, until all other ways of selling the property at an adequate price have failed.[326] If the purchaser has contracted to purchase the property before he became a trustee, he will not lose his rights under the contract and will not be required to account as a trustee.[327]   **10.113**

It has been suggested that *Holder v Holder*[328] indicates that the court might now be more prepared to exercise its discretion in this regard and, indeed, that the so-called strict rule is a rule of practice only,[329] and that perhaps the courts should apply the 'fair-dealing' rule, rather than the 'self-dealing' rule, to purchases by trustees of trust property. However, the facts of *Holder* were exceptional and the decision has not been interpreted in this way subsequently. In *Re Thompson's Settlement*,[330] Vinelott J held that the decision was based on the ground that the vendor and purchaser had not been the same person, and therefore the 'self-dealing' rule did not apply. Indeed, he reiterated the traditional view that the rule 'is   **10.114**

---

[325] See paras 21.04–21.08 below.

[326] *Farmer v Dean* (1863) 32 Beav 327; *Tennant v Trenchard* (1869) 4 Ch App 537; *Campbell v Walker* (1800) 5 Ves 678. See also *Public Trustee v Cooper* [2001] WTLR 901. The Public Trustee, just like any other trustee, cannot enter into a bargain with himself: *Re New Haw Estate Trusts* (1912) 107 LT 191. The court may approve a sale to a trustee, even when a beneficiary objects, if the interests of the trust as a whole demand it: *Tennant v Trenchard* (1869) 4 Ch App 537, 547; *Union Trustee Co of Australia Ltd v Gorrie* [1962] Qd R 605. The court cannot, of course, authorize a transaction under this jurisdiction if it would otherwise be unauthorized, eg because it is expressly prohibited by the trust instrument or because a requisite consent cannot be obtained: see, for example, *Re Robinson* (1885) 31 Ch D 247; *Re Walley* [1884] WN 144. The instructions to the valuer must be exhibited and the valuer should exhibit his valuation with his own affidavit. The court can approve a sale, purchase, compromise, or other transaction by a person in his capacity as trustee. This has been construed to cover an advance to a tenant for life of a portion of capital for the purpose of stocking and cultivating a farm: *Re Household* (1884) 27 Ch D 553.

[327] *Re Taylor* [1950] VLR 476. Cf *Re Mulholland's Will Trusts* [1949] 1 All ER 460.

[328] [1968] Ch 353.   [329] ibid 398, *per* Danckwerts LJ; and 402–403 *per* Sachs LJ.

[330] [1986] Ch 99.

applied stringently in cases where a trustee concurs in a transaction which cannot be carried into effect without his concurrence and who also has an interest in or holds a fiduciary duty to another in relation to the same transaction'.[331]

Purchase of a beneficiary's interest: the fair-dealing rule

10.115   The purchase by a trustee of the equitable interest of a beneficiary under the trust is not subject to the same objections, ie the 'fair-dealing' rule applies, and not the 'self-dealing' rule.[332] As Megarry V-C put it in *Tito v Waddell (No 2)*:[333]

> The fair-dealing rule is . . . that if a trustee purchases the beneficial interest of any of his beneficiaries, the transaction is not voidable *ex debito justitiae*, but can be set aside unless the trustee can show that he has taken no advantage of his position and has made full disclosure to the beneficiary, and that the transaction is fair and honest.

The court regards such a purchase with suspicion and, if the beneficiary seeks to have it set aside, the court will do so, unless the trustee can show that he dealt with the beneficiary at arm's length, that the purchase was beneficial to the beneficiary, and that the trustee fully disclosed all facts known to him which might have influenced the trustee's decision to purchase,[334] for example a valuation which was not made known to the beneficiary.[335] The trustee is not required, however, to advise the beneficiary. It will also assist the trustee if the transaction was initiated by the beneficiary.[336]

Application to trustees' powers

10.116   It is generally the case, of course, that the operation of the rule presupposes the existence, and applies specifically to the exercise, of some power,[337] ie it can be relevant only in situations where the fiduciary has authority to act in a particular way in the first place. For instance, a particular disposition of, or dealing with, trust property by a trustee (whether in favour of himself or another) must be shown to be an authorized act, carried out in exercise of a subsisting and sufficiently wide power or in pursuance of an enforceable duty. If the terms of the trust or power expressly or implicitly prohibit a sale of trust property to A, it is irrelevant whether or not A is himself a trustee of that property: that specific act would be *ultra vires* and void and the question of a possible conflict of interests arising out of that act

---

[331] [1986] Ch 115. See also *Public Trustee v Cooper* [2001] WTLR 901.

[332] *Coles v Trecothick* (1804) 9 Ves 234; *Clarke v Swaile* (1762) 2 Eden 134.

[333] [1977] Ch 106, 241.

[334] *Coles v Trecothick, supra*; *Thomson v Eastwood* (1877) 2 App Cas 215, 236; *Williams v Scott* [1900] AC 499.

[335] *Dougan v Macpherson* [1902] AC 197. See also *Hill v Langley* The Times, 28 January 1988.

[336] *Coles v Trecothick, supra.*

[337] It may be a duty to act, of course. The trustee must, however, be able to identify the lawful basis which enables him to act.

could not then be an issue. As a bare minimum, the particular act or transaction must not be one which would be impeachable if carried out in favour of, or with, an independent third party. In this sense, the effect of the rule against conflict of interests is to exclude (whether by implication of law or by the implied intention of the donor is not clear) a fiduciary himself from the category of persons in favour of, or with whom, he could otherwise deal or transact business; and, as such, the rule could be regarded simply as another aspect of the excessive exercise of a power.

This is indeed an appropriate way to view matters where the power in question is   **10.117**
an administrative or managerial power. Although such powers must be exercised solely for the purposes for which they were conferred (for example powers of investment or of sale are conferred on trustees in order to enable them the better to carry out their trusts), in the absence of some direction that a specified person is not to be benefited by their exercise, they will usually authorize the trustee to deal or transact business with the world generally. The rule against conflict of interests operates so as to exclude the trustee himself from the range of persons with whom he may deal, so that a trustee, for example, may invest trust funds with, or sell trust property to, anyone at all, other than himself.

However, in relation to dispositive powers, such as powers of appointment, pow-   **10.118**
ers of advancement, and other similar powers, it is less clear whether the rule against conflict of interests operates in the same way or, indeed, whether it applies at all. A dispositive power is exercisable only in favour or for the benefit of its named or identified objects. If the donee, whether he is a trustee or not, is not included as an object of such a power, any exercise of that power which benefits the donee, directly or indirectly, will be either excessive or fraudulent, in which case there seems to be no need or place for the rule against conflict of interests. On the other hand, if the donee, whether he is a trustee or not, is expressly included as an object of the power, this fact in itself would seem to exclude the application of the rule: otherwise, what appears to be the manifest intention of the donor, namely to confer a dual status on the donee, would be defeated. Thus, although the application of the rule against conflict of interests may perform some function in relation to the exercise of an administrative power, it is not immediately obvious why or how the rule can or should apply in relation to an exercise of a dispositive power. Indeed, it has been argued elsewhere[338] that the rule against conflict of interests may have a role to play, in some instances, in relation to exercise of dispositive powers, but that, generally, it does not, because other doctrines (such as those relating to the excessive or fraudulent exercise of a power) will apply instead.

---

[338] See *Thomas*, paras 11-10–11-33. See also *Taylor v Allhusen* [1905] 1 Ch 529; *Re Penrose* [1933] Ch 793; *Re Edward's Will Trusts* [1947] 2 All ER 521; *Re Wills' Trust Deeds* [1964] Ch 219; *Re Beatty* [1990] 1 WLR 1503; *Sargeant v National Westminster Bank plc* (1990) 61 P & CR 518; *Re William Makin &Son Ltd* [1993] OPLR 171.

M. Duty to Act Gratuitously

10.119 As a general rule, a trustee holds office voluntarily and is required to perform his duties gratuitously.[339] In broad terms, this is merely one aspect of the trustee's duty of loyalty and his duties not to place himself in a position where his fiduciary duty and his self-interest come into conflict and not to profit from his trust. Put in narrower terms, the basis of the principle is that, if it were otherwise, 'the trust estate might be loaded and made of little value'.[340]

10.120 The rule applies equally to a professional trustee, such as a solicitor, and a layman. Indeed, the rule was so strictly applied that a solicitor-trustee could not employ one of his partners if he himself might derive a direct or indirect benefit from such employment.[341] There was a limited exception, under the so-called rule in *Cradock v Piper*,[342] whereby a solicitor-trustee could charge costs if he had acted for his co-trustee(s) as well as himself in connection with trust litigation, provided his actions had not increased the expense to the trust.[343] The application and scope of the strict principle have long since been qualified, however. Indeed, a professional trustee, far from being obliged to act for no payment, now has a statutory right to remuneration.[344] Consequently, it is more appropriate to regard remuneration as a right of a trustee: this is dealt with in Chapter 21 below.

N. Duty to Keep and Render Accounts

10.121 A trustee is under a duty to provide his beneficiaries with a full and accurate record of his stewardship and management of the trust property, from which the beneficiaries can see whether the trustee has obeyed the provisions of the trust instrument and the manner in which he has done so. He is, therefore, required to keep and render proper, clear, and accurate financial accounts, with supporting vouchers, receipts, and other documents.[345] The trustee must be able, at the request of a beneficiary, to give the latter full and accurate information on the state and value of the trust fund;[346] and the trustee must allow the beneficiary, or his

---

[339] *Re Barber* (1886) 34 Ch D 77; *Dale v IRC* [1954] AC 11, 27.

[340] *Robinson v Pett* (1734) 3 P Wms 249, 251.

[341] *Christophers v White* (1847) 10 Beav 523; *Clark v Carlon* (1861) 30 LJ Ch 639; *Re Gates* [1933] Ch 913; *Re Hill* [1934] Ch 623. Trust work and the firm's general work had to be separate.

[342] (1850) 1 Mac & G 664.

[343] *Lyon v Baker* (1852) 5 De G & Sm 622; *Re Corsellis* (1887) 34 Ch D 675. Involvement in litigation was essential, although it need not have been hostile.

[344] Trustee Act 2000, Part V: see paras 21.04–21.5 below.

[345] *Springett v Dashwood* (1860) 2 Giff 521; *Burrows v Walls* (1855) 5 De GM & G 233; *Newton v Askew* (1848) 11 Beav 145, 152; *Clarke v Earl of Ormonde* (1821) Jac 108, 120; *Pearse v Green* (1819) 1 Jac & W 135.

[346] *Armitage v Nurse* [1998] Ch 241, 261; *Re Tillott* [1892] 1 Ch 86; *Re Page* [1893] 1 Ch 304, 309; *Talbot v Marshfield* (1868) 3 Ch App 622; *Ryder v Bickerton* (1743) 3 Swan 30n.

solicitor or accountant, to inspect the trust accounts and documents,[347] including legal advice which pertains to the trust as opposed to the trustees personally,[348] unless these fall into that category of information which the trustee is not obliged to disclose.[349] However, the trustee is not required to provide copies of the trust accounts or other trust documents free of charge.[350] The nature and extent of a trustee's duty to provide information, and to whom it is owed, are dealt with in detail in Chapter 12 below.

The process whereby accounts may be challenged is referred to by the archaic **10.122** terminology of falsifying or surcharging accounts. The falsification of accounts involves showing that an entry is false or wrongly inserted, for example that the trustee has applied trust money in an unauthorized investment, or distributed it to the wrong beneficiary. In a somewhat artificial process of reasoning, the trustee is presumed to have acted honestly and reasonably and thus to have applied or spent his own money in such cases, and not trust money: the amount expended ought to have remained in the trust fund and, therefore, the trustee is personally liable to account for it.[351] Issues relating to foreseeability of loss and causation are not relevant. If an authorized investment has been wrongfully transferred or sold and replaced with an unauthorized investment, the trustee must lay out whatever it costs to restore the trust fund to the state it would have been in but for the breach of trust. [352]

Surcharging involves showing that an item that should have been credited to the **10.123** trust fund has been omitted. This may have been caused because the trustee has negligently failed to supervise an unauthorized agent, or to bring proceedings against another trustee for breach of trust, or indeed against a third party for committing a tort or a breach of contract in respect of trust property. It appears that the core element is a failure to take care; and it has been said that the relationship of trustee and beneficiary is merely an incidental factor.[353] The crucial feature,

---

[347] *Kemp v Burn* (1863) 4 Giff 348; *Re Cowin* (1886) 33 Ch D 179; *Re Londonderry's Settlement* [1965] Ch 918; *Schmidt v Rosewood Trust Ltd* [2003] 2 WLR 1442; *Ottley v Gilbey* (1845) 8 Beav 602; *Clarke v Earl of Ormonde* (1821) Jac 108, 120. See also *Butt v Kelson* [1952] Ch 197 in relation to the (lack of) rights of beneficiaries to inspect accounts of a company, shares in which are held by trustees who are also directors.   [348] *Hawkesley v May* [1956] 1 QB 304.

[349] For example, information relating to another beneficiary's interest, or relating to the reasons of trustees for exercising their discretions, or which would prejudice the trustees in their management of the trust: *Hawkeley v May, supra*; *Re Rabbaiotti's Settlement* [2000] WTLR 953; *Rouse v 100F Australian Trustees Ltd* [2000] WTLR 111. See also *Lawrence v Berbrier* (2002) 5 ITELR 9 (Ontario).

[350] *Ottley v Gilbey* (1845) 8 Beav 602; *Kemp v Burn* (1863) 4 Giff 348; *Re Bosworth* (1889) 58 LJ Ch 432; *Re Watson* (1904) 49 SJ 54.

[351] *Clough v Bond* (1838) 3 My & Cr 490, 496–497; *Knott v Cottee* (1852) 19 Beav 77; *Wallersteiner v Moir* (N0 2) [1975] QB 373 397; *Target Holdings v Redferns* [1996] I AC 421, 434. See also [1993] Restitution LR 7, 20 (Lord Millett); (1998) 114 LQR 214 (Lord Millett).

[352] *Target Holdings v Redferns, supra*; *Re Massingberd* (1890) 63 LT 296.

[353] *Bank of New Zealand v New Zealand Guardian Trust Co* [1999] 1 NZLR 664, 687; *Bristol & West Building Society v Mothew* [1998] Ch 1, 17.

however, is that the trust fund and the beneficiaries should be compensated[354] for the loss actually suffered as a result of the breach of trust.[355] It is often a matter of some difficulty to establish that a particular loss has been caused by trustee's failures, for example where it is alleged that loss resulted from a failure to sell specific investments,[356] or to diversify investments,[357] or to exercise adequate supervision over a private company a majority of whose shares are held by the trustees.[358] It must be proved that the trustee failed to do what a reasonable, careful, and properly informed trustee would have done and that such failure caused the loss. Nevertheless, if such causation is proved, the accounts should be surcharged with the amount of the loss.[359] No deduction is made for any tax that would have been payable but for the breach of trust.[360] Nor can the trustee rely on any contributory negligence on the part of a beneficiary: the latter is entitled to expect the trustee to perform his duties properly. [361]

10.124   In appropriate circumstances, the court may order the falsification and surcharge of accounts on the basis of wilful default, in which case the trustee is required to account for both what he has actually received and what might have been received but for his wilful default or misconduct. 'Wilful default' includes deliberate, reckless, and negligent breaches of trust.[362] In such cases, the court needs to be satisfied that at least one instance of wilful default has been proved and that the conduct of the trustees is such as to raise a reasonable suspicion that other undisclosed breaches of trust may also have occurred.[363]

10.125   A trustee cannot plead lack of understanding, inability, or inexperience as a defence to his failure to keep proper accounts,[364] especially as he has statutory powers enabling him to employ an agent to do so. If he has failed to keep accounts, the trustee will be subject to costs in subsequent proceedings.[365] However, if he has kept accounts but, through an honest mistake, they contain errors, he will

---

[354] The trust is entitled to 'compensation' and not 'damages': *Target Holdings v Redferns, supra.*

[355] *Target Holdings v Redferns, supra,* 439.

[356] *Wight v Olswang (No 2)* [2000] WTLR 783 (reversed [2001] WTLR 291).

[357] *Nestle v National Westminster Bank* [1993] 1 WLR 1265, 1281.

[358] *Bartlett v Barclays Bank Trust Co Ltd* [1980] Ch 515.

[359] *Wight v Olswang (No. 2), supra.*

[360] *Barlett v Barclays Bank Trust Co Ltd, supra,* 543; *Re Bell's Indenture* [1980] 1 WLR 1217; *John v James* [1986] STC 352, 361.

[361] *Magnus v Queensland National Park* (1888) 37 Ch D 466. Punitive damages and damages for distress and inconvenience are not relevant in equitable claims: *West v Lazard Brothers & Co Jersey Ltd* [1993] JLR 165; *Miller v Stapleton* [1996] 2 All ER 449.

[362] *Partington v Reynolds* (1858) 4 Drew 253; *Re Stevens* [1898] 1 Ch 162; *Re Tebbs* [1976] 1 WLR 924; *Bartlett v Barclays Bank Trust Co Ltd, supra; Coulthard v Disco Mix Club* [1999] 2 All ER 457.

[363] For an excellent description of the principles of trustee accounting. See *Glazier v Australian Men's Health (No 2)* [2001] NSW SC 6.   [364] *Wroe v Seed* (1863) 4 Giff 425, 429.

[365] On costs, see *Eglin v Sanderson* (1862) 3 Giff 434; *Ottley v Gilbey, supra; Newton v Askew* (1848) 11 Beav 145; *Thompson v Clive* (1848) 11 Beav 475; *Re Skinner* [1904] 1 Ch 289; *Re Linsley* [1904] 2 Ch 785; *Re Holton's Settlement Trusts* [1918] WN 78; *Re Den Haag Trust* (1998) 1 OFLR 495.

generally be awarded costs.[366] If the trustee is a trustee of more than one trust, he must keep the funds of each trust separately and must keep proper and separate accounts for each trust.[367] Trust accounts ought not to be destroyed when the trust terminates: even if the trustee is released by the beneficiaries, they may be required at a subsequent date. [368]

The trustee is under a duty to correct any errors in the accounts. Thus, if the trustee **10.126** has overpaid a beneficiary, he must recover the overpayment, either from that beneficiary's remaining share of the trust fund or from future income to which that beneficiary would otherwise be entitled.[369] This is subject to the control of the court, however, and may be modified if hardship would be caused.[370] A trustee may also be able to recoup in the same way his own commission that he should have retained from prior distributions, but this is not entirely clear.[371] An overpayment which cannot be recovered from the beneficiary's share of the trust fund or from future income, for example because the fund has been fully distributed, can be recovered from the beneficiary himself only if the trustee himself cannot make good the loss.[372]

If a trustee is alleged to have profited from his office, or from some misuse of trust **10.127** property, the court may order a specific account of profits, rather than an account of the general administration of the trust. The trustee is liable to restore to the trust fund and the beneficiaries the highest value attained by the relevant assets between the date of breach and the date of judgment.[373]

Subject to the payment of costs, any person interested in the equitable interest **10.128** may require production of any notice in writing of a dealing with an equitable interest which has been served upon the trustee under section 137 of the Law of Property Act 1925.[374]

The trustee's duty extends beyond the keeping of accounts to the disclosure of **10.129** information and, indeed, beyond that to a positive duty to inform a beneficiary of full age and capacity of his interest and rights under the trust.[375] If this is not done,

---

[366] *Smith v Cremer* (1875) 24 WR 51.
[367] *Freeman v Fairlie* (1817) 3 Mer 29, 41. The position is different in the case of unit trusts and common investment funds.
[368] *Payne v Evens* (1874) LR 18 Eq 356; *Re Page* [1893] 1 Ch 304; *Gray v Haig* (1854) 20 Beav 219. If accounts have not been kept, the trustee's own papers and accounts can be inspected: *Stainton v Carron Co* (1857) 21 Beav 346.
[369] *Dibbs v Goren* (1849) 11 Beav 483; *Re Horne* [1905] 1 Ch 76 , 79. The trustees may recoup such overpayment even against an assignee for value of that beneficiary's share: *Dibbs v Goren, supra*.
[370] See *Perpetual Executors and Trustees Association v Simpson* [1906] 12 ALR 95; *Re Ettelson* [1946] VLR 217.
[371] *Re Horne* [1905] 1 Ch 76 (trustee cannot do so); dist in *Re Ainsworth* [1915] 2 Ch 96 and *Re Musgrave* [1916] 2 Ch 417. [372] *Re Diplock* [1948] Ch 465.
[373] *Nant-y-glo and Blaina Ironworks Co v Grave* (1878) 12 Ch D 738; *Target Holdings v Redferns* [1996] 1 AC 421, 440. [374] Section 137(8).
[375] *Hawkesley v May* [1956] 1 QB 304. See also (1970) 34 Conv 29 (A Samuels).

the beneficiaries will not be able to enforce their rights and the trustee's duty would be diminished, if not rendered meaningless.[376]

10.130   The duty of a trustee to account cannot be excluded by express provision in the trust instrument. As Millett LJ said in *Armitage v Nurse*,[377] in English law, there must exist 'an irreducible core of obligations owed by the trustees to the beneficiaries and enforceable by them which is fundamental to the concept of a trust. If the beneficiaries have no rights enforceable against the trustees there are no trusts . . . '. According to Millett LJ, 'the duty of the trustees to perform the trusts honestly and in good faith for the benefit of the beneficiaries is the minimum necessary to give substance to the trusts'. In other words, these particular fiduciary duties—to act honestly and in good faith—cannot be excluded (by, for example, an exemption clause). The absolute minimum that a trustee must do if there is to be a trust is that he must (i) at least hold and safeguard the trust property (ii) provide information to the beneficiaries concerning the terms of the trust, so that they are in a position to check that the trusts are being carried out, and (iii) keep accurate and reliable accounts and records of his custodianship to prove that the trusts were observed. Accountability of the trustees to the beneficiaries is one of the fundamental defining features of the trust: the trustee cannot be allowed to treat the trust property as his own; he cannot be relieved of the duty to explain his custodianship; and the beneficiary cannot be deprived of the information he needs to check on, and possibly challenge, the trustee's performance.

O. Duty to Provide Information

10.131   This duty, its nature and extent, and the person to whom it is owed, is dealt with in detail in Chapter 12 below.

P. Breach of Duty

10.132   A trustee who fails, without authority, to carry out his duties commits a breach of trust for which he may be held liable. Breach of Trust is dealt with in detail in Chapters 31 to 33 below.

10.133   A trustee who has retired remains liable for breaches of trust committed during his trusteeship, but not for those committed after he retires, provided he did not retire in order to facilitate the subsequent breach of trust.[378]

---

[376] See *Scally v Southern Health and Social Services Board* [1992] 1 AC 294 , 306–307.

[377] [1998] Ch 241, 253. See also DJ Hayton, 'The Irreducible Core of Trusteeship' in AJ Oakley (ed), *Trends in Contemporary Trust Law* (Oxford, 1996) 47–62.

[378] *Head v Gould* [1898] 2 Ch 250; *Norton v Pritchard* (1845) 5 LT(OS) 2; *Webster v Le Hunt* (1861) 9 WR 918; *Palairet v Carew* (1863) 32 Beav 564; *Clark v Hoskins* (1868) 37 LJ Ch 561.

The conduct of a trustee must be judged with reference to the facts and circum- **10.134**
stances existing at the time when he had to act and which were known, or ought
to have been known, by him at that time.[379]

---

[379] *Re Hurst* (1892) 67 LT 96, 99; *Re Chapman* [1896] 2 Ch 763, 777–778; *Nestle v National Westminster Bank (No 2)* [1993] 1 WLR 1260.

11

THE DUTIES OF TRUSTEES: PART TWO

A. Introduction to the Duties of Trustees in Relation to the Exercise of Their Powers[1]

All donees of special and intermediate (or hybrid) powers and discretions owe **11.01** some obligation to the objects of their powers. This is often described as a duty to act 'honestly' or 'properly'. However, such a general formulation, true though it is, is not particularly helpful, for it fails to distinguish the several elements and disparate strands of which such a duty is comprised, not all of which apply to all powers or to all donees. Some obligations are indeed common to all—trustees,

---

[1] The substance of this chapter is based on Chapter 6, GW Thomas, *Powers* (Sweet & Maxwell, 1998) ('*Thomas*') which, unlike the present chapter, also deals with the general duties owed (or not owed, as the case may be) by other fiduciaries and by non-fiduciaries.

other fiduciaries and non-fiduciaries alike—for example the duty not to commit a fraud on the power, or the duty not to exercise it 'excessively', or the duty not to delegate its exercise to another.[2] However, other duties are attached only to fiduciary powers, and they do not arise at all in relation to a non-fiduciary power, for example a duty to consider the exercise of the power. In addition, powers, all of which necessarily confer discretion of some sort, may be expressly enlarged so as to be exercisable 'in the absolute and uncontrolled discretion' of the donees. In such cases, a tension may sometimes arise between the duties to which the donees are undoubtedly subject and the considerable (indeed, the seemingly unlimited) width of the discretion conferred upon them. Difficult questions may then arise as to the extent (if any) to which a particular exercise of the power may be open to review by, and interference from, the court. In this chapter, we shall consider some of the general duties imposed on trustees in the exercise of their powers and discretions. The associated question of the 'reviewability' of any such exercise will then be dealt with in Chapter 20.

11.02   The specific duties dealt with in this chapter (many of which overlap) are the following:

(1) The duty to consider the exercise of a power or discretion. (This duty extends to giving equal consideration to objects and beneficiaries with similar rights; and to giving fair consideration to objects and beneficiaries with dissimilar rights.)

(2) The duty to exercise an active discretion.

(3) The duty not to act under the dictation of another.

(4) The duty not to fetter the discretion.

(5) The duty to exercise the power in such a way that the intended result is achieved (or an unintended one is not achieved); and the duty to take account of relevant considerations and to ignore irrelevant ones.

(6) The duty to treat beneficiaries and objects even-handedly.

(7) The duty not to act capriciously or unreasonably.

(8) An implied duty of good faith.

B. The Duty to Consider the Exercise of a Power or Discretion[3]

11.03   In broad terms, both the existence and extent of the duty to consider the exercise of a power or discretion depend on the nature of the power and the status of the

---

[2] These three duties are dealt with in separate chapters of their own: see Chapters 19, 18, and 15 below.

[3] For a fuller discussion of the points and issues raised under this head, see *Thomas* 263–297. See also IJ Hardingham and R Baxt, *Discretionary Trusts* (2nd edn, 1984) Chs 2 and 5; DM Maclean, *Trusts*

donee. The donee of a power of appointment (or indeed any other power) who is
not in a fiduciary position—such power being referred to in this work as a non-
fiduciary mere power—is not subject to any such duty: he can simply ignore or
even forget the existence of the power. By contrast, powers of appointment (and
other powers) conferred on trustees *qua* trustees (or on other fiduciaries *qua*
fiduciaries) carry with them a duty to consider periodically whether or not the
power should be exercised. Of course, all powers conferred on trustees *qua*
trustees are fiduciary powers. However, dispositive powers conferred on trustees
generally take one of two forms: (i) those powers in respect of which the trustee
has a discretion as to whether he will actually exercise them or not ('fiduciary mere
powers', or 'trust powers'); and (ii) those powers which are coupled with a duty to
exercise them, where the trustee has no discretion as to whether or not to carry out
the duty—indeed, he will be liable for a breach of trust if he fails to do so—but he
has a discretion as to which of the objects are to benefit, or the manner in which
or the time at which the duty will be performed ('discretionary trusts', or 'powers
in the nature of a trust', or even 'trust powers'). In both cases, however, the trustee
is under a duty to consider the exercise of the relevant power. Indeed, the nature
and content of that duty is similar in both cases. However, it is not identical and
it is convenient, therefore, to deal with them separately, even if this involves an element of repetition.

Fiduciary mere powers

11.04 In this case, the trustee holds the trust fund on trust for those entitled in default of
appointment, subject to any distribution by the trustee in exercise of the power of
appointment conferred upon him *qua* trustee (and which power he therefore
holds in a fiduciary capacity). Such a power may be a special power, an intermediate power, or even a qualified general power.[4] Although the trustee is not obliged
to *exercise* such a power, he is, nonetheless, under a duty to *consider* from time to
time whether or not such a power ought to be exercised.[5]

11.05 Precisely what the 'duty to consider' consists of is not entirely clear. In one sense,
it seems to be merely a more positive formulation of other, well-established negative

---

and Powers (1989) 17–25; (1971) 87 LQR 31 (JW Harris); (1974) 38 Conv (NS) 269 (L McKay);
[1982] Conv 432 (A Grubb).

[4] See *Re Park* [1932] 1 Ch 580; *Blausten v IRC* [1972] Ch 256; *Re Manisty's Settlement* [1974]
Ch 17; *Re Hay's Settlement Trusts* [1982] 1 WLR 202. See also *Re Beatty* [1990] 1 WLR 1503, where
the power in question authorized the trustees to distribute 'among such persons...as they think fit',
and the trustees exercised the power in favour of themselves. Hoffmann J held that the power was a
fiduciary power and not a general power 'in the sense of the traditional classification which equates
such a power with an outright beneficial disposition'.

[5] *Re Gulbenkian's Settlements* [1970] AC 508, esp 518, *per* Lord Reid; *Re Hay's Settlement
Trusts* [1982] 1 WLR 202, 209, 210, *per* Megarry V-C; *McPhail v Doulton* [1971] AC 424,449;
Gartside v IRC [1968] AC 553,606; *Re Gestetner* [1953] Ch 672 at 687–688.

obligations imposed on a trustee. Imposing a positive duty to consider reinforces the general principle that a fiduciary power may not be released, a principle which might otherwise be breached de facto by persistent inaction on the part of the donee. Similarly, a duty to consider underlines the importance of the duty not to delegate the exercise of a power to another. In this sense, it could be said that the donee is simply under a duty to remind himself periodically that he is the holder of a fiduciary power, which he (and no one else) ought to consider exercising. An alternative view is that the duty merely refers to the well-recognized cases of failure to consider the exercise of a discretion in specific instances,[6] rather than a more general and continuing positive duty to consider.

11.06 It is reasonably clear, however, that there is more to it than this. The duty to consider implies a positive requirement to take some active steps, to take an affirmative decision from time to time whether or not the power is to be exercised. Moreover, given that any consideration of the exercise of the power cannot realistically take place in the abstract, the duty to consider also seems to require the trustee not just to inquire into and examine, in broad terms at least, the size and composition of the class of objects, but also to address those considerations which might make a possible exercise of the fiduciary power appropriate or inappropriate in the then existing circumstances. The duty to consider, then, can properly be referred to as a duty to inquire and ascertain.

11.07 However, a mere statement that there is a duty to consider does not, in itself, indicate how the trustee is supposed to discharge that duty. Where and how does he begin? His first duty, no doubt, is to consider the width of the class of objects, to inquire into and ascertain its composition, by category, group, and size. But he ought then to move on to consider the claim to priority of any particular category or the claim to benefit of any particular individual.

> He must first consider what persons or classes of persons are objects of the power within the definition in the settlement or will. In doing this, there is no need to compile a complete list of the objects, or even to make an accurate assessment of the number of them: what is needed is an appreciation of the width of the field . . . Only when the trustee has applied his mind to 'the size of the problem' should he then consider in individual cases whether, in relation to other possible claimants, a particular grant is appropriate. In doing this, no doubt he should not prefer the undeserving to the deserving; but he is not required to make an exact calculation whether, as between deserving claimants, A is more deserving than B . . .
> . . . the duties of a trustee which are specific to a mere power seem to be threefold. Apart from the obvious duty of obeying the trust instrument, and in particular of making no appointment that is not authorised by it, the trustee must, first, consider periodically whether or not he should exercise the power; second, consider the range of objects of the power; and third, consider the appropriateness of individual appointments.[7]

---

[6] See, for example, *Klug v Klug* [1918] 2 Ch 67, 71.   [7] *Re Hay, supra*, 210 *per* Megarry V-C.

Although this threefold classification segregates the duty to consider exercising a power from the duty to consider the range of objects and the duty to consider the appropriateness of individual appointments, it is often neither necessary nor fruitful to do so. In reality, these three duties are often but different aspects of the same exercise: they overlap and merge into one another.

The nature and extent of the trustee's 'duty to consider' in relation to a power of appointment conferred on him *qua* trustee clearly varies with the circumstances of each case and with the nature of the power (be it special, hybrid, or general).[8] Every power must be exercised only for the purpose for which it was conferred, or, at least, in accordance with what the trustees honestly consider to have been the purpose. The particularity with which that purpose may be described will vary from case to case. The trust instrument itself may indicate a specific or general purpose, for example to maintain or educate, or to provide retirement benefits, or some order of priority among objects.[9] In some cases, the donor expressly accords priority to some objects, for example by specifying a 'primary' and a 'secondary' class, or by directing that primary regard is to be had to one beneficiary, such as an eldest son. **11.08**

In the absence of an express provision to this effect, the terms of the particular power and the context in which it is conferred may, by clear implication, provide some guidance to the trustees with regard to the proper mode of considering how to exercise it.[10] For example, where a special power of appointment is conferred in favour of a limited number of objects (for instance the children and grandchildren of the settlor), the trustees are able, and may be expected, to inquire into and ascertain and compare the personal needs, merits, and circumstances (including age, state of health, educational requirements, financial circumstances, employment, and so forth) of all, or virtually all, of the objects, both as individuals and as members of the family as a whole.[11] Indeed, in the case of a power of maintenance or of advancement—which are said to be powers with only one object, namely the person maintained or advanced[12]—the trustees would be expected to consider all such matters in relation to that one object. Similarly, trustees must make appropriate inquiries before exercising their discretion in respect of any 'death benefit' payable under the provisions of a pension scheme, especially if such exercise will override the terms of any nomination which they have received affecting that benefit.[13] **11.09**

---

[8] See, for example, *Re Beatty* [1990] 1 WLR 1503.

[9] eg, *Richardson v Chapman* (1760) 7 Bro PC 318.

[10] *Re Manisty's Settlement* [1974] Ch 17, 25, *per* Templeman J.

[11] See, for example, *Maberley v Turton* (1808) 14 Ves 499.

[12] See *Re Abraham's Will Trusts* [1969] 1 Ch 463, 484–485.

[13] See *Wild v Smith* [1996] PLR 275; *Harris v Lord Shuttleworth* [1994] ICR 989, 999; *Packwood v Trustees of Airways Pension Scheme* [1995] OPLR 369. See also *Re Boston's Will Trusts* [1956] Ch 395, 406, in the different context of the Settled Land Act 1925, s 73(1)(iv) and s 28 of the Law of Property Act 1925 (which has been repealed by the Trusts of Land and Appointment of Trustees Act 1996, s 25(2) and Sch 4).

Even where the class of objects is large and comprised of different categories, the terms of the power may sometimes imply an order of priority or preference, as was the case in *Re Gulbenkian's Settlement*,[14] for example, where it was clear that the trustees were expected to have regard to the best interests of one named beneficiary (Nubar Gulbenkian). In yet other cases, the relevant purpose may be ascertainable only by process of construction. As Templeman J pointed out, in *Re Manisty's Settlement*,[15] the trustees will endeavour to give effect to the wishes and intentions of the donor, and they 'will derive that intention not from the terms of the power necessarily or exclusively, but from all the terms of the settlement, the surrounding circumstances and their individual knowledge acquired or inherited'. Thus, in many instances, the trustees may have to rely on knowledge acquired by them outside the trust instrument (for example changes in the circumstances of the family) or even on the consent of a third party, such as the settlor himself.[16] In addition, the trustees would probably also be expected to take account of wider considerations, such as anticipated changes in government policy or tax legislation. Moreover, none of these considerations remain fixed and immutable. The duty to consider may therefore vary with the passage of time, as the range of objects and their circumstances alter.

11.11   In some cases, the class of objects may not only be relatively large but also be comprised of several different (and seemingly unconnected) groups or categories. In *Re Manisty's Settlement*,[17] Templeman J not only provided an illustration of such a class but also made some observations on the nature of the trustees' duty in such a case:

> If a settlor creates a power exercisable in favour of his issue, his relations and the employees of his company, the trustees may in practice for many years hold regular meetings, study the terms of the power and the other provisions of the settlement, examine the accounts and either decide not to exercise the power or to exercise it only in favour, for example, of the children of the settlor. During that period the existence of the power may not be disclosed to any relation or employee and the trustees may not seek or receive any information concerning the circumstances of any relation or employee. In my judgment it cannot be said that the trustees in those circumstances have committed a breach of trust and that they ought to have advertised the power or looked beyond the persons who are most likely to be the objects of the bounty of the settlor. The trustees are, of course, at liberty to make further inquiries, but cannot be compelled to do so at the behest of any beneficiary. The court cannot judge the adequacy of the consideration given by the trustees to the exercise of the power, and it cannot insist on the trustees applying a particular principle or any principle in reaching a decision.

---

[14] [1970] AC 508.   [15] [1974] Ch 17, 26.
[16] See generally *Re Manisty's Settlement* [1974] Ch 17, 26; *Re Coates* [1955] Ch 495; *Blausten v IRC* [1972] Ch 256, 273.   [17] [1974] Ch 17, 25.

This echoes the view of Harman J in *Re Gestetner*,[18] to the effect that:

> there is no obligation on the trustees to do more than consider—from time to time, I suppose—the merits of such persons of the specified class as are known to them and, if they think fit, to give them something . . . I cannot see here that there is such a duty as makes it essential for these trustees, before parting with any income or capital, to survey the whole field, and to consider whether A is more deserving of bounty than B.

The trustees did not have to 'worry their heads to survey the world from China to Peru, when there are perfectly good objects of the class in England'. Certainly, the trustees are expected, irrespective of the width of the class of objects, to consider such requests as are actually made by objects (irrespective of which sub-group or category they may fall into) for the power to be exercised in their favour, and to consider the claims and needs of those who are actually known to them.[19] In addition, the trustees are required to consider the circumstances of those who are entitled in default of appointment, whose interests will be defeated or divested by any appointment. These would seem to be minimum requirements, however. The interests and claims of all objects, other than those at hand or those in a favoured category, cannot be ignored entirely. Such a sweeping conclusion would seem to be at odds with the views expressed by Lord Wilberforce in *McPhail v Doulton*,[20] and with statements in *Re Baden's Deed Trusts (No 2)*[21] (which, admittedly, concerned discretionary trusts, rather than mere powers), and they directly contradict the conclusion of Megarry V-C in *Re Hay's Settlement Trusts*,[22] that 'the trustee must not simply proceed to exercise the power in favour of such of the objects as happen to be at hand or claim his attention'.

11.12 The question remains as to whether it is meaningful in any sense to say that trustees are under a duty to consider the exercise of a power where the class of objects extends to millions of people. To whom would such a duty be owed; and would it be enforceable by the court? These questions are of even greater significance in another, related context, namely that of 'administrative workability' in relation to discretionary trusts, and are therefore discussed in greater detail in that context.[23]

Discretionary trusts

11.13 In the case of a discretionary trust, the trustee is obliged to exercise the power and his discretion is therefore limited to the selection of those objects who are to benefit and the manner in which, or the time at which, they will do so. As in the case of a mere power, the trustee is under a duty to make such a survey of the range

---

[18] [1953] Ch 672, 688, 689.
[19] *Re Manisty's Settlement* [1974] Ch 17, 25, *per* Templeman J. [20] [1971] AC 424, 449, 457.
[21] [1973] Ch 9, esp 20, 27. [22] [1982] 1 WLR 202, 209–210. See also *Thomas* 269–272.
[23] See para 11.15 below.

of objects or possible beneficiaries as will enable him to carry out his fiduciary duty.[24] The underlying principle is the same in each case, but there is a difference of degree. In the case of a discretionary trust, a wider and more comprehensive range of inquiry is called for.[25] In simple terms the trustee has to do more and try harder. This duty of inquiry and ascertainment was described by Lord Wilberforce in the following terms:[26]

> ...a trustee with a duty to distribute, particularly among a potentially very large class, would surely never require the preparation of a complete list of names, which anyhow would tell him little that he needs to know. He would examine the field, by class and category; might indeed make diligent and careful inquiries, depending on how much money he had to give away and the means at his disposal, as to the composition and means of particular categories and of individuals within them; decide upon certain priorities or proportions, and then select individuals according to their needs or qualifications...

> ...Such distinction as there is [between discretionary trusts and fiduciary mere powers] would seem to lie in the extent of the survey which the trustee is required to carry out: if he has to distribute the whole of a fund's income, he must necessarily make a wider and more systematic survey than if his duty is expressed in terms of a power to make grants. But just as, in the case of a power, it is possible to underestimate the fiduciary obligation of the trustee to whom it is given, so, in the case of a trust (trust power), the danger lies in overstating what the trustee requires to know or to inquire into before he can properly execute his trust. The difference may be one of degree rather than of principle...

11.14　The precise manner in which a trustee would be expected to carry out this process of inquiry and ascertainment will therefore vary from case to case. As Sachs LJ pointed out, in *Re Baden's Deed Trust (No 2)*,[27] when it is said that trustees must make such a survey of the range of objects or possible beneficiaries as will enable them to carry out their fiduciary duty, the word 'range' has 'an inbuilt and obvious element of considerable elasticity, and thus provides for an almost infinitely variable range of vision suitable to the particular trust to be considered'. 'Assessing in a businesslike way "the size of the problem" is what trustees are called upon to do.'[28]

Size of the class and administrative workability

11.15　Given that the nature and extent of the trustees' duty to consider varies according to the size of the class, it may reasonably be asked whether a class may be so large as to dilute the duty to the point where it becomes meaningless to refer to it as a 'duty' at all. If so, does the power or discretion remain valid, but subject to no duty to consider, or is it simply invalid? The answer to this question is that neither the

---

[24] cf *Re Hain's Settlement* [1961] 1 WLR 440.　[25] *McPhail v Doulton* [1971] AC 424, 457.
[26] ibid 449.　[27] [1973] Ch 9, 20.
[28] *Re Baden's Deed Trust (No 2)* [1973] Ch 9, 20, *per* Sachs LJ.

size of the class of objects nor 'administrative difficulties' (which are probably different factors) will in itself prevent a trustee upon whom a *mere power* has been conferred from carrying out his duty to *consider* the exercise of that power. Certainly, neither factor will render such a power invalid. On the other hand, the position is different in relation to a *discretionary trust*: 'administrative unworkability' will render a discretionary trust void.

Size of class of mere powers conferred on trustees

It has long been established that an intermediate (or hybrid) power or a wide special power can validly be conferred on a person *not occupying any fiduciary position*.[29] The reasoning behind this conclusion is that such a donee owes no duty to anyone when deciding whether or not to exercise his power. For some time, however, there was some doubt as to whether such a power could validly be conferred on trustees as such. The leading authorities, especially *Blausten v IRC*[30] and *Re Manisty's Settlement*,[31] were not entirely consistent or convincing.[32]

11.16

The difficulty facing trustees was that they would be faced with the need to discharge their fiduciary duty to consider whether and in what circumstances to exercise a power so widely framed that it did not in itself afford any indication which could guide them.[33] As Megarry V-C put it, when he reviewed earlier authorities[34] in *Re Hay's Settlement Trusts*:[35] 'The difficulty comes when the power is given to trustees as such, in that the number of objects may interact with the fiduciary duties of the trustees and their control by the court.' In *Re Hay*, trustees held a trust fund 'for such persons or purposes . . . as the trustees shall by any deed . . . appoint', other than the settlor, any husband of hers, and any past or present trustee. The question was whether this power was valid. Megarry V-C, having concluded that the duties of the trustees included a duty to consider periodically whether or not they should exercise their power, to consider the range of objects of the power, and also to consider the appropriateness of individual appointments, went on to ask whether there is something in the nature of an intermediate power which conflicts with these duties.[36] He considered Buckley LJ's observations in *Blausten* and rejected them. There was no ground on which the power in question could be said to be void. It was administratively workable (the words of Lord Wilberforce in *McPhail v Doulton*[37] being held to be directed

11.17

---

[29] *Re Park* [1932] 1 Ch 580; *Re Jones* [1945] Ch 105; *Re Byron's Settlement* [1891] 3 Ch 474.
[30] [1972] Ch 256, esp 272, 274, 275; see also *Re Abrahams' Will Trusts* [1969] 1 Ch 463; *Re Eyre* (1883) 49 LT 259; *Re Edward's Will Trusts* [1947] 2 All ER 521.   [31] [1974] Ch 17.
[32] See the discussion in *Thomas* 276–280.
[33] *Blausten v IRC* [1972] Ch 256, 273, *per* Buckley LJ; *IRC v Schroder* [1983] STC 480, 498.
[34] Principally *Re Gestetner Settlement* [1953] Ch 672; *Re Gulbenkian's Settlements* [1970] AC 508; *McPhail v Doulton* [1971] AC 424; *Re Baden's Deed Trusts (No 2)* [1973] Ch 9.
[35] [1982] 1 WLR 202 at 208–209.   [36] ibid at 210.   [37] [1971] AC 424, 457.

at discretionary trusts only, and not mere powers). Nor was the power capricious.[38] He added that, 'if there is some real vice in a power, and there are real problems of administration or execution, the court may have to hold the power invalid' (although no examples of such problems were given), but the court 'should be slow to do this'.[39]

11.18 The powers in question in *Blausten, Manisty,* and *Hay* were all contained in *inter vivos* settlements. However, in *Re Beatty*,[40] similar powers conferred by will were also upheld. According to Hoffmann J, these were fiduciary powers which required the trustees to give consideration to whether they should be exercised and to act in accordance with what they honestly consider to have been the purpose for which the testatrix had created the powers. These powers, 'being fiduciary, are not general powers in the sense of the traditional classification which equates such a power with an outright beneficial disposition to the donee himself. Nor are they special powers in the traditional sense. The objects of the power can hardly be described as a class. They are intermediate or hybrid powers of the kind considered in *Re Park*[41] . . .'[42] Such powers would have been valid if created by deed, delegating to the trustees the disposal of the testatrix's property in accordance with her known wishes; and there was no rule of law invalidating the powers merely because they were contained in a will.

11.19 Although all these authorities are decisions at first instance, it seems now to be established that a *mere* power conferred on a trustee (as in the case of an ordinary individual) will not be invalid simply on the basis that the class of objects is exceptionally large. The size of the class is not regarded as an obstacle to the carrying out by the trustees of their duty to *consider* the exercise of their power. It will not prevent them from administering such obligations as have been imposed upon them. Indeed, it seems clear (*Blausten* apart) that the objects of such a power need not constitute even a loose 'class'. This, however, raises other difficult questions. For example, does it make any sense, in these circumstances, to say that the trustees are under a *duty* to consider the exercise of their power? If there is such a duty, is there a point at which it becomes so diluted that it is theoretical only and can effectively be ignored? Would it not make more sense to distinguish more clearly between special and intermediate powers, at least in relation to trustees' duties to *consider exercise* (despite Templeman J's observation that the duties of trustees of an intermediate power were 'precisely similar' to the duties of trustees of special powers)?[43]

---

[38] [1971] AC 424 at 212. He questioned Templeman J's example (in *Re Manisty's Settlement* [1974] Ch 17, 27) of a power to benefit the 'residents of Greater London' as one of capriciousness, but pointed out that Templeman J had indicated that this consideration did not apply to an intermediate power in any event.   [39] ibid, 212.
[40] [1990] 1 WLR 1503.   [41] [1932] 1 Ch 580.   [42] [1990] 1 WLR 1503, 1506.
[43] *Re Manisty's Settlement* [1974] Ch 17. See *Thomas* 280–281 for a fuller discussion of these questions.

Size of class of discretionary trusts

The position is different in relation to discretionary trusts. It is well established **11.20**
that a discretionary trust cannot be created in favour of a class of objects which is
virtually without limit. In *Yeap Cheah Neo v Ong Cheng Neo*,[44] for example, the
Privy Council held that a trust of residue 'to apply and distribute the same, all circumstances duly considered, in such manner and to such parties as to them [the
executors] may appear just' failed 'for want of adequate expression of it'. Similarly,
in *Re Carville*,[45] a gift of residue 'to be disposed of as my executors shall think fit'
was held invalid on the ground that the testatrix had failed to define 'the manner
in which the distribution is to take place, or the object of the share'. And in *Re
Chapman*,[46] a gift of residue to 'be applied for charitable purposes, as I may in
writing direct, or to be retained by my executor for such objects and such purposes
as he may in his discretion select, and to be at his own disposal', was held by Eve J
to be neither an exclusively charitable gift nor a trust sufficiently definite for the
court to execute.[47] In all these cases, the executor or trustee (as the case may be)
could not take beneficially. The fatal flaw in each case was the absence of any
specificity in the form or nature of the trusts: there were no identifiable criteria
which the trustee had to observe or which the court could use to enforce the trust.

This, it seems, is the kind of situation that Lord Wilberforce had in mind in **11.21**
McPhail v Doulton,[48] where, having emphasized the distinction between conceptual certainty and evidential certainty,[49] he added:

> There may be a third case where the meaning of the words used is clear but the
> definition of beneficiaries is so hopelessly wide as not to form 'anything like a class'
> so that the trust is administratively unworkable or in Lord Eldon's words one that
> cannot be executed (*Morice v Bishop of Durham*, 10 Ves Jr 522, 527). I hesitate to give
> examples for they may prejudice future cases, but perhaps 'all the residents of Greater
> London' will serve. I do not think that a discretionary trust for 'relatives' even of a liv-
> ing person falls within this category.

Although the references to 'the definition' of the beneficiaries being hopelessly
wide, and to Lord Eldon's observations in *Morice v Bishop of Durham*, suggest
strongly that this is simply another example of conceptual uncertainty, it is clear
that Lord Wilberforce was deliberately not referring to conceptual uncertainty.
Rather, what he envisaged was something that would make a trust administratively unworkable.[50]

---

[44] (1875) LR 6 PC 381, 390–392.
[45] [1937] 4 All ER 464, esp 467: the residue passed to the statutory next of kin under a partial
intestacy.   [46] [1922] 1 Ch 287.
[47] See also *Re Park* [1932] 1 Ch 580, 583; *Re Pugh* [1967] 1 WLR 1262; *Re White* [1963] NZLR
788; *Re Hollole* [1945] VLR 295.   [48] [1971] AC 424, 457.
[49] See paras 4.12–4.27 above.
[50] See *Thomas* 283–284; (1974) 37 MLR 643 (Y Grbich); (1975) 49 ALJ 10 (IJ Hardingham).

11.22 The two pivotal ideas in his statement are (i) *administrative* difficulties and (ii) *execution* of a discretionary trust by the court. In *McPhail v Doulton*,[51] the House of Lords held that, in the event of default by the trustees of a discretionary trust, the court need not distribute the trust fund among the beneficiaries in equal shares, but could, instead, ensure that the trustees' duty was carried into effect by a variety of other means, such as by directing an unequal distribution, by removing the defaulting trustees and appointing new trustees, or by sanctioning a scheme of distribution prepared by the beneficiaries. The fact remains, however, that discretionary trustees (whether original or substituted) are obliged to give effect to their trust, and, in the event of any default, a discretionary trust may have to be executed by the court. A discretionary trust differs from a mere power in this respect.[52] It is therefore essential that, if an enforceable duty is to be imposed on the trustees, that duty must be one which they can actually comprehend and carry out, and one which, if the trustees default, the court can enforce. There must be some reference point, some guiding principle, or objective criteria, to enable the trustees and the court to identify what it is that they *have* to do. Without this, there is no enforceable trust. On this basis, Megarry V-C indicated, in *Re Hay's Settlement Trusts*,[53] that he would, if necessary, have held an intermediate *trust* in favour of such a wide class as that before him void as being administratively unworkable.

11.23 In *Re Manisty's Settlement*,[54] Templeman J attempted to explain Lord Wilberforce's observations by reference to capricious purposes. His attempt was subsequently questioned by Megarry V-C in *Re Hay's Settlement Trusts*.[55] However, even if it may not actually be what Lord Wilberforce had in mind, it may nonetheless be an appropriate way to describe the same phenomenon. Templeman J regarded a power to benefit 'the residents of Greater London' as a capricious power only because, in his view (rightly or wrongly), the class constituted 'an accidental conglomeration of persons who have no discernible link with the settlor or with any institution'. If this is applied to a discretionary trust, it seems to be another way of expressing the view that the description of the class of objects is such that it is impossible to discern the guiding principle by which the trustees are intended to carry out their duties; or, as Stamp LJ put it in *Re Baden's Deed Trusts (No 2)*,[56] no principle can be discerned by which any survey of the range of objects or possible beneficiaries could be conducted or to indicate where it should start or finish. Therefore, it may reasonably be said, in defence of Templeman J, that it may well be capricious to purport to impose a duty on trustees which they cannot possibly implement, or which the court could not enforce. There may be other, different

---

[51] [1971] AC 424.   [52] *Re Hay's Settlement Trusts* [1982] 1 WLR 202, 213–214.
[53] ibid 213.   [54] [1974] Ch 17, 27.
[55] [1982] 1 WLR 202, 212. See also (1975) 49 ALJ 10 (IJ Hardingham).
[56] [1973] Ch 9, 28.

examples of capriciousness, but it is not at all obvious why this should not be one too. The observations of Megarry V-C, in *Re Hay's Settlement Trusts*,[57] do not affect Templeman J's view, for the latter was clearly referring to 'an accidental conglomeration' of persons who have 'no discernible link' with the settlor, whereas Megarry V-C's example (where the settlor was a former chairman of the Greater London Council) and also the intended trust in *West Yorkshire* (see below) are both clearly cases where there is such a 'discernible link'.

In only one case thus far, it seems, has 'administrative unworkability' been an issue, namely *R v District Auditor, ex p West Yorkshire Metropolitan County Council*.[58] Here, a local authority which anticipated its abolition, and in exercise of powers conferred on them by section 137(1) of the Local Government Act 1972 to incur expenditure 'which in their opinion is in the interests of their area or any part of it or all or some of its inhabitants', resolved to create a trust under which the trustees were directed to apply the capital and income of a trust fund in such manner as they thought fit 'for the benefit of any or all or some of the inhabitants of the County of West Yorkshire'. The disposition was held to create a discretionary trust and not a power, but it was not a charitable trust. The class of objects numbered some two-and-a-half million people. Lloyd J assumed, without deciding the point, that the class was defined with sufficient clarity. Nevertheless, he concluded that it was invalid as an express private trust because, being in favour of such a huge class, it was 'quite simply unworkable'. The definition of beneficiaries was so hopelessly wide as to be incapable of forming anything like a class.

11.24

Although *West Yorkshire* is not a satisfactory decision, for a number of reasons,[59] it now seems clear that, in principle, *a discretionary trust*, unlike a mere power, may be declared invalid on the ground that it is 'administratively unworkable'. It is not entirely clear, however, whether the sheer size of the class alone, the simple question of numbers or potential numbers, is the fatal ingredient or simply a relevant factor in determining invalidity on this ground. In *Re Baden's Deed Trusts (No 2)*,[60] Sachs LJ clearly did not think that numbers alone would be fatal, for he seems to have referred to two potentially large classes, namely 'those who have served in the Royal Navy' and 'the wide-ranging discretionary trusts . . . of the Army Benevolent Fund', as examples of classes which were clearly valid. However, even these examples do not come close to the size of the classes of objects of the intermediate powers at issue in *Re Manisty's Settlement Trusts*[61] and *Re Hay's Settlement Trusts*.[62] In principle, it is not difficult to envisage a case where the settlor has purported to create discretionary trusts in respect of a very small trust fund in favour of a very large class of

11.25

---

[57] [1982] 1 WLR 202, 212.
[58] [1986] RVR 24. See also *Thomas* 285–287; [1986] CLJ 391 (C Harpum).
[59] See *Thomas* 286–287. [60] [1973] Ch 9, 20. [61] [1974] Ch 17.
[62] [1982] 1 WLR 202.

jects, in which case the administration of the trusts may prove well-nigh impossible and the size of the class would be a significant factor. Indeed, this may well be a question of degree, depending on the purpose of the trust. Nevertheless, the real vice is not so much the size of the class as the absence of identifiable and objective criteria or clear principles to guide the trustees in the performance of their duties. As Lord Wilberforce pointed out in *McPhail v Doulton*,[63] in relation to the trustees' duty to inquire and ascertain, 'in each case the trustees ought to make such a survey of the range of objects or possible beneficiaries as will enable them to carry out their fiduciary duty'. Earlier,[64] he had described what this entailed:

> The trustee [should] examine the field, by class and category; might indeed make diligent and careful inquiries, depending on how much money he had to give away and the means at his disposal, as to the composition and needs of particular categories and of individuals within them; decide upon certain priorities or proportions, and then select individuals according to their needs or qualifications.

11.26 This suggests that, if a 'class' does not comprise one group of objects, all of whom possess a common nexus or defining characteristic, it is at least already categorized and sub-classified by the terms of the trust. The trustees' duty, therefore, seems to be one to examine and survey such categories and subclasses, to determine priorities, to apportion, and select. Where such broad criteria are identified, this duty can be carried out even in relation to a large class of objects, such as that in *Re Gestetner*[65] (which included named individuals, descendants of two named persons, named charities, and employees of various companies). In contrast, it cannot be executed in relation to a class of 'all the residents of Greater London', which is comprised of persons who are not categorized by the relevant disposition, and who have no obvious connection with each other or with the settlor, or with some institution (such as a company or charity) with its own identity and favoured by the settlor, other than the accidental and arguably irrelevant fact of their residence in a geographical area: they are, as Templeman J put it in *Re Manisty's Settlement*,[66] 'an accidental conglomeration of persons who have no discernible link with the settlor or with any institution'. In such a case, no principle has been provided by which the trustees could conduct a survey of the objects or know where or with whom to begin or finish.[67]

Objects' remedy where there is a failure to consider exercise

11.27 If a trustee is under an obligation to consider periodically whether or not to exercise a *mere power* of appointment conferred on him, it would seem to follow that,

---

63 [1971] AC 424, 457.   64 ibid 449.   65 [1953] Ch 672.
66 [1974] Ch 17, 27.
67 *Re Baden's Deed Trusts (No 2)* [1973] Ch 9, 28, *per* Stamp LJ. What, then, of a trust in favour of 'relatives'? If 'relatives' are defined as the descendants of an unidentified common ancestor, there must remain a question as to whether the trust is administratively workable: see *Thomas* 290–291.

in the event that the trustee refused to carry out his obligation, any member of the class of objects of that power could complain. The trustee cannot 'simply fold his hands and ignore' the power: 'he must from time to time consider whether or not to exercise the power, and the court may direct him to do this'.[68] However, it is difficult to see how the trustee could be forced to consider exercising the power. Certainly, such a remedy would probably be of little value to the complaining object. His remedy, therefore, would seem to be the removal of the refusing trustee and his replacement by another. 'A member of the specified class [of objects] might, if he could show that the trustees had deliberately refused to consider any question at all as to the want or suitability of any member of the class, procure their removal...'[69] Of course, the same difficulty could apply, in principle, to a replacement trustee who 'might equally be inert or recalcitrant'.[70]

In principle, an object could complain of two things. First, he could complain that the trustee was refusing to give any consideration at all to the exercise of the power, for example by refusing to conduct any survey at all of the range of objects of the power. In practice, such a complaint would be difficult to establish. A persistent failure by the trustee to make any distribution at all might be a relevant factor, but it could not in itself found a complaint, for the trustee could well have decided, in a proper exercise of his discretion, not to make any distribution. Secondly, the object could complain that the trustee was refusing to consider that object's own particular position and circumstances. In this case, it would seem to be a necessary prerequisite that the existence and circumstances of the object be known to, or have been brought to the attention of, the trustee. A mere power does not require a trustee to discover the identity of all its objects. Therefore, the fact that a particular object may not have been considered by the trustee is not necessarily sufficient in itself to found any complaint. However, the trustee may manifestly have failed to consider any exercise of the power, such as, for example, where he has purported to delegate or release the power without authority. In any event, the difficulties facing a complaining object are essentially evidential difficulties; and there seems to be no obstacle, in principle, to the making of a complaint.

Remedies of objects of discretionary trust on failure to distribute

A *discretionary trust*, unlike a mere power, imposes on the trustee not just a duty to consider exercising his discretion (or to inquire and ascertain) but also a duty to   **11.28**

---

[68] *Re Hay's Settlement Trusts* [1982] 1 WLR 202, 209, *per* Megarry V-C. See also *Re Bryant* [1894] 1 Ch 324, 331–332, *per* Chitty J: 'If, however, ... there is an obligation to entertain the question of duty to consider the matter, and then a discretion arising in the execution of the duty, then I may inquire whether the four trustees are acting honestly or not, in the discharge of their duty....'
[69] *Re Gestetner Settlement* [1953] Ch 672, 688, *per* Harman J. See also *Gartside v IRC* [1968] AC 553, 606, *per* Lord Reid; *Re Manisty's Settlement* [1974] Ch 17, 25, *per* Templeman J. See also *Tempest v Lord Camoys* (1882) 21 Ch D 571, 578, 579 and 580. For further discussion, see *Thomas* 291–292.
[70] *IRC v Broadway Cottages Trust* [1955] Ch 20, 31. See also (1971) 87 LQR 31 (JW Harris).

distribute the subject matter of that discretion. These duties are owed to the objects of the power. There are no beneficiaries entitled in default of appointment in this case; and no duty is owed to the donor of the power.[71] If the trustee fails to carry out his duties, he is in breach of trust. Only the objects of the power (and any non-defaulting trustee) can complain to the court. The trustee cannot be compelled to make any distribution in favour of any particular object (whether he is the complaining object or not). It may be the case that he cannot even be compelled to consider the position, circumstances, and needs of every object, although this would seem to depend on the width or range of the class: there is no obvious reason why he should not be expected to do so where the class is small. In any event, each object can complain that the trustee is refusing to consider the exercise of his discretion under the discretionary trust, whether by failing to inquire into and ascertain the range of potential beneficiaries or to consider any particular claimant, and thereby failing to administer his trust properly.

11.29   The court can then take steps to ensure that the duty is executed. The court may appoint a new trustee in place of the defaulting trustee;[72] it may direct the trustees to distribute (at least, where the proper basis for distribution is readily apparent);[73] it may direct that the subject matter be distributed equally or unequally among the objects; or it may direct representatives of the different classes of beneficiaries to prepare a scheme of distribution or authorize them to distribute in accordance with a scheme already prepared.[74] The precise remedy will vary according to the circumstances of each case, but the court will endeavour, in all cases, to execute the trust power 'in the manner best calculated to give effect to the settlor's or testator's intention'.[75]

C. The Duty to Exercise an Active Discretion

11.30   A trustee must apply his mind to the actual exercise of any power or discretion. It is 'an inherent requirement of the exercise of any discretion that it be given real and genuine consideration'.[76] There must be the 'exercise of an active

---

[71] *Re Astor's Settlement Trusts* [1952] Ch 534, 542, *per* Roxburgh J.
[72] *McPhail v Doulton* [1971] AC 424, 457; *Re Gestetner Settlement* [1953] Ch 672, 688; *Gartside v IRC* [1968] AC 553 ,606; *Re Manisty's Settlement* [1974] Ch 17, 25. See also *Tempest v Lord Camoys* (1882) 21 Ch D 571, 578, 579, and 580. Cf *IRC v Broadway Cottages Trust* [1955] Ch 20, 35.
[73] See, for example, *Bennett v Honywood* (1772) Amb 708; *Re J Bibby & Sons Ltd's Pension Trust Deed* [1952] 2 All ER 483, 486. Cf *Re Astor's Settlement* [1952] Ch 534, 548.
[74] See, for example, *Re Drexel Burnham Lambert UK Pension Plan* [1995] 1 WLR 32; *Mettoy Pension Trustees Ltd v Evans* [1990] 1 WLR 1587. Cf *Re William Makin & Sons Ltd* [1993] OPLR 171; and *British Coal Corporation v British Coal Staff Superannuation Scheme Trustees Ltd* [1993] PLR 303; *Liley v Hey* (1841) Hare 580; and (1971) 29 CLJ 68, 95–100 (J Hopkins).
[75] *McPhail v Doulton* [1971] AC 424, 457, *per* Lord Wilberforce.
[76] *Karger v Paul* [1984] VR 161, 164, *per* McGarvie J. See also *Re Beloved Wilkes' Charity* (1851) 3 Mac & G 440, 448 ('with a fair consideration').

discretion'.[77] Clearly, if a trustee simply acts under dictation or pursuant to instructions, he cannot be said to have applied his own mind to the exercise and, in this sense, there is clearly an overlap between this head and the next one. However, it is possible for a trustee to exercise a power himself and still not apply his mind properly to the implications and consequences of his act. In *Turner v Turner*,[78] for example, trustees, who had a discretionary power to distribute capital or income of a trust fund, executed a series of deeds placed before them by the settlor, and by which they purported to exercise their powers. At no time did the trustees appreciate their powers and duties; they were unaware that they had any discretion; and they did not read or understand the effects of the documents they were signing. Mervyn Davies J held that they had never applied their minds to the exercise of their discretion and that the power to appoint had not been validly exercised. The trustees had a duty to consider the need for, and the wisdom and implications of, the appointment before exercising their power; and this they did not carry out.[79] He concluded that the authorities[80]

> permit the inference that, in a clear case on the facts, the Court can put aside the purported exercise of a fiduciary power, if satisfied that the trustees never applied their minds at all to the exercise of the discretion entrusted to them. If appointers fail altogether to exercise the duties of consideration . . . then there is no exercise of the power and the purported appointment is a nullity.

He then held that the purported appointment at issue was a nullity.

Other reported instances are common. In *Klug v Klug*,[81] for example, where one trustee was prepared to exercise a power of advancement in order to relieve a beneficiary from a liability to pay legacy duty, but the other trustee refused to concur because the beneficiary had married without her consent, Neville J held that the court, in exercise of its control over the discretion of the trustees, could direct the trustees to raise the required sum.[82] He stated,[83] as his reason for interfering, that the refusing trustee had declined to exercise the power 'not because she has considered whether or not it would be for her daughter's welfare that the advance should be made, but because her daughter has married without her consent, and her letters show, in my opinion, that she has not exercised her discretion at all'.[84] In *Wilson v Turner*,[85] where trustees, who had a discretion as to payment of

11.31

---

[77] *Partridge v The Equity Trustees Executors and Agency Co Ltd* (1947) 75 CLR 149, 164.
[78] [1984] Ch 100.   [79] ibid 109–110.
[80] *Re Pilkington's Will Trusts* [1961] Ch 466; *Re Abrahams' Will Trusts* [1969] 1 Ch 463; *Re Hastings-Bass* [1975] Ch 25.   [81] [1918] 2 Ch 67.
[82] Although interfering with the exercise of a trustee's discretion is accepted practice in such circumstances, directing that it be exercised in a particular manner is unusual: a more normal response would be the removal of the refusing trustee.   [83] ibid 71.
[84] It is also possible to justify the court's interference in this case on the ground that the mothertrustee had exercised her discretion by deciding not to exercise her power, but that she had done so for an improper motive or purpose (as, for example, in *Cochrane v Cochrane* [1922] 2 Ch 230).
[85] (1883) 22 Ch D 521.

income for the maintenance of a child, had simply paid income to the father during the infancy of that child, the Court of Appeal held that the trustees had not exercised their discretion as to its application (and the father's estate was liable to repay the whole amount received). And in *Partridge v Equity Trustees Executors and Agency Co Ltd*,[86] trustees were held liable for improper exercise of their powers where they allowed debts to remain unpaid until the debtor went bankrupt: the relevant power involved 'the use of an active discretion, not the mere passive attitude of leaving matters alone, and no relief afforded where (as here) loss has arisen from carelessness or supineness'.[87]

11.32 If the trustees decide not to exercise their discretion or, alternatively, decide to do so in a particular way, the court will not generally interfere with their decision, even if a different result might seem more reasonable or advantageous, provided always that the trustees have acted in good faith. Such reluctance to intervene is particularly evident where the trustees' discretion has been enlarged so as to be 'absolute and uncontrolled'. However, this does not alter the fact that, if and when trustees do exercise a power or discretion, they must do so actively and consciously. The requirements of a valid exercise raise questions which are distinct from those which may apply to the validity of the decision reached pursuant to a valid exercise, and the two issues must be kept separate.

D. The Duty Not to Act Under the Dictation of Another

Personal nature of the discretion

11.33 The discretion conferred on a trustee (or any donee of a power) is of a personal nature; and any exercise of the power must be a personal and conscious act of the trustee himself, a result of his own consideration and deliberation. This broad principle underlies, among other things, the rule against delegation *delegatus non potest delegare*.[88] If the power or discretion is conferred on trustees as such, it is personal to the holders of that office for the time being.

11.34 As a general rule, a trustee cannot exercise a power or discretion under the dictation or instructions of another person. Thus, a beneficiary cannot insist that trustees accept a particular offer to purchase trust property,[89] or appoint a particular person to act as trustee.[90] Similarly, a trustee in bankruptcy has been held

---

[86] (1947) 75 CLR 149.

[87] ibid 164. Cf *National Trustees Executors and Agency Co of Australasia Ltd v Dwyer* (1940) 63 CLR 1; *Cotton v Dempster* (1918) 20 WAR 14; *Re Greenwood* (1911) 105 LT 509; *Hitch v Leworthy* (1842) 2 Hare 200.   [88] Delegation by trustees is dealt with in Chapter 15.

[89] *Selby v Bowie* (1863) 8 LT 372. Of course, the trustee must bear in mind his duty to accept the highest offer: see *Buttle v Saunders* [1950] 2 All ER 193.

[90] *Re Brockbank* [1948] Ch 206; *Re Gadd* (1883) 23 Ch D 134; *Re Higginbottom* [1892] Ch 132. See also s 19 of the Trusts of Land and Appointment of Trustees Act 1996.

personally liable for implementing instructions given to him by his 'stupid committee of inspection'.[91] Other examples can easily be envisaged, for instance
trustees of a pension scheme who exercise their powers on the directions of the
employer, or trustees of a family trust who obey the instructions of the settlor.

Where trustees make a considered and bona fide exercise of a particular power, no **11.35**
object or beneficiary can direct otherwise and, as a general rule, the court will not
intervene. In *Re Steed's Will Trusts*,[92] for example, the Court of Appeal refused to
interfere, at the instance of a primary beneficiary, with the exercise by trustees of
their discretionary powers of sale. Lord Evershed MR stated:[93]

> ... ought the trustees to exercise their discretion as they propose by a sale, or should
> they rather succumb to the plaintiff's wishes, she being the person who has such an
> overwhelmingly preponderant interest in the trust property? ... It may well be that
> other trustees might have been ... submissive ... but they have not taken that line.
> The line they have taken has been a deliberate exercise of the discretion and a delib-
> erate discharge of the duty. There is no ground whatever for suggesting that they have
> done any wrong thing, as that word is ordinarily understood. How then can the
> Court now be asked to override the discretion which the testator conferred upon
> them, particularly in the circumstances which ... were in his mind, and for the pur-
> poses of preventing which the trusts were imposed?
> ... I am quite satisfied, upon the general principles which are applicable to these mat-
> ters, that this Court ought not to interfere, and will not interfere here, with the exer-
> cise of the trustees' discretion. Why, after all, one may ask, when the testator who has
> given this bounty has made plain what his purpose is, if the trustees have established
> they have done their utmost to give effect to the duty which is imposed upon them,
> should the Court disregard the testator and overrule the trustees out of a natural sym-
> pathy for the plaintiff? I think the answer to that is, there is no reason whatever.

The prohibition against acting under dictation does not prevent a trustee from **11.36**
seeking advice from others, including the settlor or the objects of the power.
Dialogue and discussion with objects and beneficiaries is entirely proper: indeed,
in many cases, it ought to be encouraged. A trustee is expected to familiarize himself with the circumstances and needs of his beneficiaries and to keep himself
informed of how they think their interests would be best served. Moreover, a
trustee can properly exercise his powers in order to give effect to the wishes of an
object (or of the settlor), provided the trustee himself has considered the matter
and himself takes the final decision. Similarly, there is no reason why a trustee
should not follow the instructions given to him, even if they lead to a course
of action which he would not otherwise have adopted, provided he does not
simply obey such instructions blindly, without exercising his own judgement and

---

[91] *Ex p Brown. Re Smith* (1886) 17 QBD 488, esp 492–493. See also *Selangor United Rubber
Estates v Craddock (No 3)* [1968] 1 WLR 1555; *Automatic Self Cleansing Filter Syndicate v
Cuninghame* [1906] 2 Ch 34.   [92] [1960] Ch 407.
[93] At 417–419.

discretion first.[94] Trustees, it has been said, can 'freely discuss with beneficiaries the reasons for and against a particular decision, without running the risk of being held to act against their own judgment, if they should disregard, in the end, objections to which they had thought it right in the first instance to direct their attention'.[95] Indeed, in some instances, trustees are required by the terms of their trust, or even by statute to consult with, or obtain the prior consent of, their beneficiaries.[96]

11.37 It seems to be a matter of some doubt whether trustees can be compelled by their beneficiaries as to how to exercise, or refrain from exercising, votes attached to trust shares. In *Butt v Kelson*,[97] the Court of Appeal held that beneficiaries were entitled to be treated as though they were the registered shareholders in respect of trust shares and that they could compel the trustee-directors, if necessary, to use their votes as the beneficiaries or the court (if the beneficiaries were not in agreement) thought proper. Subsequently, in *Re Whichelow*,[98] Upjohn J pointed out that this decision was difficult to reconcile with *Re Brockbank*[99] (which was not cited in *Butt v Kelson*). It is possible to confine *Butt v Kelson* to cases where all the beneficiaries are *sui juris* and between them entitled to the entire beneficial interest. However, even then, it is difficult to see how they have any rights other than the right to terminate the trust.[100] *Butt v Kelson* is an exceptional case and it may have to be confined to its own particular facts or to cases where trustees are both shareholders and directors.

E. The Duty Not to Fetter the Discretion

11.38 A trustee (like any other donee of a special power, whether or not it is a fiduciary power) cannot, as a general rule, fetter the exercise of any of his powers and discretions. He cannot covenant to exercise it in a particular way. Nor can he enter into any undertaking, or adopt an inflexible policy or a premature and irrevocable view, as to the future exercise of a power or discretion. In the absence of authority to the contrary, a trustee can exercise a power or discretion properly only by giving honest and appropriate consideration to those relevant facts and circumstances which exist at the time or times at which the power becomes or is exercisable. 'The conduct of trustees ought to be regarded with reference to the facts and circumstances existing at the time when they had to act and which were

---

[94] *Re Poole* (1882) 21 Ch D 397, 404; *Ex p Brown, Re Smith* (1886) 17 QBD 488; *Wilson v Turner* (1883) 22 Ch D 521; *Re Pauling's Settlement Trusts* [1964] Ch 303; *Turner v Turner* [1984] Ch 100. See also *Matter of Osborn* (1937) 252 App Div 438, 299 NY Supp 593.

[95] *Fraser v Murdoch* (1881) 6 App Cas 855, 864–865, *per* Lord Selborne LC. See also *Hitch v Leworthy* (1842) 2 Hare 200.

[96] See, for example, s 32 of the Trustee Act 1925; ss 6(5) and 7(3) of the Trusts of Land etc Act 1996. For the position of trustees of settled land and other fiduciaries, see *Thomas* 301–303.

[97] [1952] Ch 197, esp 207, *per* Romer LJ.   [98] [1954] 1 WLR 5.   [99] [1948] Ch 206.

[100] Under *Saunders v Vautier* (1841) 4 Beav 115.

known or ought to have been known by them at that time.'[101] If the trustee could commit himself irrevocably, in advance, to a particular mode or form of exercise in the future, by which time circumstances may have changed, the actual execution of the power could have an entirely different and unintended effect.[102] Thus anything which might prevent the trustee from exercising an active discretion at the relevant time is capable of amounting to a fetter on his power and will be regarded with suspicion.

The 'relevant' time will vary from case to case, depending on the nature and purpose of the power and the nature of the transaction which it is intended to effect. For example, a power to pay or apply annual income must be exercised as and when such income arises (or within a reasonable time thereafter)[103] and a once and for all decision cannot be made simply to apply the income automatically to a certain person or for a particular purpose.[104] A trustee may not undertake to exercise a power or discretion in a particular way at some point in the future,[105] whether by covenant or otherwise, for this is regarded as imposing a fetter upon the trustee's discretion: it is not a proper discharge of the trustee's duty and the undertaking is not enforceable by the covenantee.[106] Moreover, if the trustee himself cannot fetter the exercise of his power, the court cannot do so in his place.[107]   **11.39**

This general principle (or prohibition) is not confined to dispositive powers, but extends also to administrative and managerial powers.[108] It also applies irrespective of whether the agreement, undertaking, or fetter is a beneficial one.[109]   **11.40**

An attempt to impose an unauthorized fetter on a power or discretion is totally ineffective, it seems; and the power or discretion can subsequently be exercised, at the proper time or times, entirely free from the fetter.   **11.41**

The application of the principle (or prohibition) may be excluded or restricted by an express provision (although, unlike express provisions authorizing the release of powers, this is perhaps neither common nor always easy to draft). Moreover, it must be doubtful whether fetters and restrictions of all kinds are prohibited,   **11.42**

---

[101] *Re Hurst* (1892) 67 LT 96, 99, *per* Lindley LJ. See also *Nestle v National Westminster Bank plc* [1993] 1 WLR 1260 and *Cowan v Scargill* [1985] Ch 270.
[102] See, for example, *Stannard v Fisons Pension Trust Ltd* [1992] IRLR 27.
[103] *Re Allen-Meyrick's Will Trusts* [1966] 1 WLR 499, 505.
[104] *Re Vestey's Settlement* [1950] 2 All ER 891, 895. See also *Weller v Ker* (1866) LR 1 HL Sc 11, esp 16; *Gilbey v Rush* [1906] 1 Ch 11, 22–24; *Thomas* 304–306 and Ch 12.
[105] *Re Gibson's Settlement Trusts* [1981] Ch 179.
[106] *Thacker v Key* (1869) LR 8 Eq 408, 411; *Palmer v Locke* (1880) 15 Ch D 294; *Re Bradshaw* [1902] 1 Ch 436; *Re Cooke* [1922] 1 Ch 292. A covenant *not* to exercise a power may be valid and enforceable, because this is regarded as a release of the power; the question then is whether the trustee was authorized to effect any such release.
[107] *Re Allen-Meyrick's Will Trusts* [1966] 1 WLR 499.
[108] *Moore v Clench* (1875) 1 Ch D 447, esp 453; *Clay v Rufford* (1852) 5 De G & Sm 768.
[109] *Oceanic Steam Navigation Company v Sutherbery* (1880) 16 Ch D 236.

irrespective of the circumstances. Thus, on a sale or purchase of land by trustees, are they prohibited (in the absence of express provision to the contrary) from entering into a covenant which restricts their future use of either retained land or the land thus purchased ? Would they be acting properly if they were to grant a short-term option as part of the transaction, for example so as to enable the purchaser to arrange finance?[110] In these specific examples, the wide statutory powers conferred on trustees of land by section 6(1) of the Trusts of Land and Appointment of Trustees Act 1996 would probably suffice to enable the trustees to enter into the relevant covenant or grant the particular option. However, section 6(1) may have been disapplied by the disposition creating the trust of land; and, in any event, the general question may still arise in other contexts, for example a covenant by trustees not to compete with a business which they have sold off. Clearly, if any such fetter was expressly prohibited, or if it amounted in substance to an unauthorized release of a power, it could not then be adopted or upheld. Nevertheless, in those cases in which the purpose for which the primary power (particularly a dispositive power) was created may be better achieved by adopting some fetter or restriction on another, ancillary power, it may be that the prohibition may have been impliedly excluded.

F. The Duty to Take Account of Relevant Considerations and to Ignore Irrelevant Ones; and the Duty to Exercise the Power in Such a Way that the Intended Result Is Achieved (or an Unintended One Avoided)[111]

11.43 If a trustee (or other donee of a fiduciary power) exercises, or purports to exercise, a power, but fails entirely to appreciate that he has a discretion in the matter or to address his mind to any of the implications and consequences of the exercise (as in *Turner v Turner*)[112] it is clear that he has failed to carry out his duties at all and that, in principle, the exercise or purported exercise is null and void.[113] This is a case of no exercise at all. However, this is clearly not the only ground upon which it may be open to challenge: there are others (although they often overlap and tend to merge with one another). A trustee may have been fully aware that the discretion and decision is his but, in exercising that discretion, he has made an appointment which is not actually authorized by the terms of the power. These are cases of unauthorized exercise—being excessive or fraudulent executions of their power.[114]

---

110 See *Meek v Bennie* [1940] NZLR 1.   111 See further *Thomas* 309–324.
112 [1984] Ch 100.
113 This is sometimes referred to as the equitable equivalent of *non est factum*.
114 See Chapters 18 and 19 below.

A trustee may also have failed to take account of, or give proper weight to, all rele- **11.44**
vant considerations (or, alternatively, he took account of, or gave undue weight to,
irrelevant considerations)[115] or the exercise may have had an effect, or brought
about a state of affairs, which differs from that actually intended.[116] He may have
acted in ignorance of some crucially material factor. He may have addressed his
mind to the apparent wisdom and implications of the particular exercise, but has,
nonetheless, misconstrued or been misguided as to its actual effects and consequences.[117] In some of these cases, the result may be so absurd or extreme that it
might be possible to conclude that it could not possibly have been authorized by
the terms of the power. However, in other cases, that which has been done may be
authorized by the terms of the power (in the sense of not being excessive, fraudulent, deliberately capricious, and so on), but the effects or consequences may be
such that the actual *exercise* may be open to challenge. In such cases, the question
is not one of the existence or non-existence of legitimate authority (which is essentially a question of construction and one which is not dependent on the trustee's
knowledge or ignorance of any particular consideration) but one of improper
exercise of legitimate authority (which may be materially affected by such ignorance). This section is concerned with those cases in which the exercise of a power
or discretion is based on ignorance of some kind. In all such cases, the crucial
questions are the same: what are relevant and irrelevant considerations? How
significant must they be to infect the trustees' decision? What are the consequences of such an exercise based on, or induced by, error? Is the purported exercise of the power null and void or voidable or does it stand?

Relevant and irrelevant considerations

It is, of course, impossible to lay down any hard and fast rules as to what might or **11.45**
might not be a relevant or irrelevant consideration in relation to the exercise of a
power or discretion. It is simple enough to state that a discretion must be exercised
in good faith and upon real and genuine consideration, but it must also be exercised in accordance with the purposes for which the discretion was conferred; and,
as such purposes vary from one instance to the next, so too will the nature of what
is a relevant or irrelevant consideration.[118] The exercise of a dispositive power or
discretion which is exercisable in favour of one object only (whether it is a power

---

[115] *Stannard v Fisons Pension Trust Ltd* [1991] PLR 225. See also *Wild v Smith* [1996] PLR 275;
Harris v Lord Shuttleworth [1994] ICR 989, 999; *Law Debenture Trust Corp Ltd v PO* [1998] 1 WLR
1329; *Re the Green GLG Trust* (2002) 5 ITELR 590.
[116] *Re Abrahams' Will Trusts* [1969] 1 Ch 463.
[117] See, for example, *Hampden v Earl of Buckinghamshire* [1893] 2 Ch 531, 544, where Lindley LJ
stated: '. . . an honest trustee may fail to see that he is acting unjustly towards those whose interests
he is bound to consider and to protect: and, if he is so acting, and the Court can see it although he
cannot, it is in my opinion the duty of the Court to interfere.'
[118] See *Thomas*, paras 6-15–6-33; and also *Harris v Lord Shuttleworth* [1994] ICR 989.

of advancement or otherwise) may well require consideration of factors which are different from those which might arise in the exercise of a power which is exercisable in favour of a large class of objects. Among the relevant factors which a trustee must take into account are the tax consequences of his decision.[119]

11.46 Other considerations may also need to be taken into account. For example, will the duty of 'real and genuine consideration' differ in cases where the objects or beneficiaries have given some form of consideration for their status (as in pension fund cases)?[120] Is it necessary to take into account the claims or interests of, or indeed information concerning, others (such as those entitled in default of appointment); and, if so, to what extent? In the case of occupational pension schemes, to what extent (if at all) should trustees take into account the rights and interests of the employer?[121] Moreover, administrative powers, such as powers to invest[122] or to buy and sell property, clearly raise different considerations (and it may be the case that the court will intervene if there is an improper or imprudent exercise of such a power).[123]

11.47 In any event, as we have already seen,[124] trustees are under a duty to *consider* exercising the powers conferred on them (whether or not they are also obliged actually to exercise those powers). In reality, in order to discharge that duty to consider effectively, trustees must in practice take into account many of the considerations which would be relevant to an actual exercise. The question of what might or might not be a relevant consideration in relation to a particular power has, therefore, already been touched upon, and it will not be repeated here.[125] The basic principle is that, even if the court interferes at all, it will merely examine *whether* the discretion was exercised properly and will not examine *how* it was exercised, ie if the court is satisfied that there is no material flaw in the decision-making process, it will not interfere with the actual decision reached (although the latter may, of course, indicate the existence of such a flaw).

---

[119] *Green v Cobham* [2002] STC 820, [2000] WTLR 1101; *Abacus Trust Company (Isle of Man) Ltd v NSPCC* [2001] STC 1344, 1353. See also *Re the Green GLG Trust* (2002) 5 ITELR 590 (RC of Jersey); *AMP (UK) plc v Barker* [2001] WTLR 1237; *Hearn v Younger* [2001] EWHC 963.

[120] See, for example, the observations of Fox LJ in *Kerr v British Leyland (Staff) Trustees Ltd* (1986) [2001] WTLR 1071, cited by Knox J in *LRT Pension Fund Trustee Co Ltd v Hatt* [1993] OPLR 225, 255; and by Dillon LJ in *Stannard v Fisons Pension Trust Ltd* [1991] PLR 225, 233; *Wilson v Law Debenture Trust Corp* [1995] 2 All ER 337, 347–348.

[121] See, for example, *Re Imperial Foods Pension Scheme* [1986] 1 WLR 717; *Lock v Westpac Banking Corporation* [1991] PLR 167, esp 179; *Stannard v Fisons Pension Trust Ltd, supra.*

[122] *Cowan v Scargill* [1985] Ch 270.

[123] At least, if it is a statutory power, eg of the kind conferred on a tenant for life under the Settled Land Act 1925: *Hampden v Earl of Buckinghamshire* [1893] 2 Ch 531; *Re Hunt's Settled Estates* [1905] 2 Ch 418. Cf *Cowan v Scargill* [1985] Ch 270, 286–287 and *Edge v Pensions Ombudsman* [1998] PLR 15, 29–30.   [124] See paras 11.03–11.29 above.

[125] For the operation of this point in two contrasting contexts, see the discussion of *Karger v Paul* [1984] VR 161 and *Stannard v Fisons Pension Trust Ltd* [1991] PLR 225 in *Thomas*, paras 6-149–6-163.

If the particular exercise of a power or discretion by, or act of, a trustee is to be open **11.48** to challenge under this head, common sense and practical necessity would seem to dictate that the relevant consideration that was ignored (or given undue weight) or the irrelevant consideration that was taken into account (and given too much weight) must have had an appreciable and significant impact on the trustee's final decision.[126] Otherwise, a trustee's decisions and actions could be open to challenge, at any point in the future, on the slightest grounds: it would be all too easy for any interested party, including the trustees themselves, to claim that a particular decision had been reached in ignorance of some marginally relevant factor. However, some considerations may require greater attention and carry greater weight than others; some may be relevant but relatively trivial, and a failure to consider them may have little (if any) bearing on the trustee's decision, while others may be central and crucial. It is certainly true that any failure to consider that which is relevant is a breach of the trustee's fiduciary duty to exercise his discretion properly.[127] Nevertheless, surely what matters for a proper exercise of the trustee's discretion, and a proper discharge of his duty, is a proper consideration of that which is significantly relevant?

What is 'significantly relevant'? One obvious answer is to say that, had the trustee **11.49** not failed to consider that which was relevant (or had not considered that which was irrelevant), he *would not* have made the decision that he did actually make and *would* have acted differently. In other words, a significantly relevant consideration is one which, but for its absence, *would* have led to a different outcome; and, likewise, a significantly irrelevant consideration is one which, but for its presence, would also have produced a different result. Such a 'but for' test would seem to be essential if trustees' decisions are not to be merely provisional and vulnerable. However, in recent decisions involving the so-called 'rule in *Hastings-Bass*' (which is discussed below),[128] the emphasis has not been placed on what the trustee *would* otherwise have done but on what he *might* have done.[129] In *Abacus Trust Co (Isle of Man) v Barr*,[130] for example, Lightman J stated that the said rule

> does not require that the relevant consideration unconsidered by the trustee should make a fundamental difference between the facts as perceived by the trustee and the facts as they should have been perceived and actually were. All that is required in this regard is that the unconsidered relevant consideration would or might have affected the trustee's decision, and in a case such as the present that the trustee would or might have made a different appointment or no appointment at all.

If this is correct, the threshold is rather low and, as a result, all sorts of potential difficulties may arise. It is all too easy to claim that some unknown factor *might*

---

[126] See, eg, *Wild v Smith* [1996] PLR 275.

[127] *Scott v National Trust* [1998] 2 All ER 705, 717; *Edge v Pensions Ombudsman* [2000] Ch 602, 627–628.   [128] See paras 11.51–11.78 below.

[129] *AMP (UK) plc v Barker* [2001] OPLR 191, [2001] PLR 77; *Hearn v Younger* [2002] All ER (D) 223; *Abacus Trust Co (Isle of Man) v Barr* [2003] 2 WLR 1362. See also *Stannard v Fisons Pension Trust Ltd* [1991] PLR 227, paras 46, 64, and 66.   [130] [2003] 2 WLR 1362 1369.

have affected a particular decision. The finality of trustees' decisions may be undermined, not just by the beneficiaries but also by the trustees themselves. As Park J stated, in *Breadner v Granville-Grossman*:[131] 'It cannot be right that whenever trustees do something which they later regret and think they ought not to have done, they can say they never did it in the first place.' There must be some finality. At the very least, the courts should not give any encouragement to trustees not to stand by what should have been a proper exercise of their discretion.

11.50 Indeed, if it is the case that the basis for the court's interference is not the absence of authority,[132] but an improper exercise of legitimate authority, it must surely be clear, on objective grounds, that, but for their ignorance or misunderstanding of a significantly relevant consideration, the trustees *would* or certainly *ought to have* acted differently or not at all. It is suggested below[133] that the true test—or, at least, a more workable test—ought to be to ask what the consequences would have been if the *same* effects had been brought about by trustees *with* actual knowledge of the relevant consideration. The court should intervene so as to reverse only that which, had it been done with full knowledge and understanding of the significantly relevant consideration, would have been capricious, absurd, or such that no reasonable trustee with such knowledge and understanding would ever have done.

The principle in *Hastings-Bass*

11.51 A failure to take account of relevant considerations may be a breach of fiduciary duty on the part of the trustee, for which he will be liable to a beneficiary who is adversely affected. The trustee may have failed, for example, to make reasonable (or any) inquiries that might have disclosed the relevant consideration, or to give any serious thought to the matter; he may not have sought advice or considered such advice as he received. Such a trustee will usually be able to invoke a provision in the trust instrument exempting him from liability; and, if the transaction cannot be annulled in some way, the beneficiaries would be left without remedy. In other cases, the trustees' ignorance does not arise out of a breach of fiduciary duty, for example because they could not, with reasonable inquiry, have discovered the relevant consideration.[134] According to Lightman J, in *Abacus Trust Company (Isle of Man) v Barr*,[135] in the absence of any such breach of duty, neither the trustee nor a beneficiary has a right to have a decision declared invalid because the trustee's decision was in some way mistaken or has unforeseen or unpalatable

---

[131] [2001] Ch 523, 543.

[132] As clearly seems to be the case, although this view has been challenged: see paras 11.55–11.56, 11.70 below.   [133] See paras 11.73–11.74 below.

[134] *Abacus Trust Company (Isle of Man) v Barr* [2003] 2 WLR 1362, 1370, para 24.

[135] [2003] 2 WLR 1362: judgment delivered on 6 February 2003. See paras 11.64–11.70 below.

consequences. However, if this were correct (and it is suggested that it cannot be), the negligent trustee could claim a right which would not be available to the innocent trustee.

Indeed, at first sight, it seems rather odd that trustees can themselves invoke the **11.52** principle in *Hastings-Bass* in order to reverse the consequences of their own breach of fiduciary duty. However, it is clear from the cases that they can indeed do so.[136] It is the failure to exercise a power properly that underlies the principle; it is not intended to be an escape route for negligent trustees. A beneficiary or object whose interest or rights are defeated or adversely affected by an exercise by the trustees of a discretion conferred on them is entitled to insist that, if it be done at all, it should be done properly. If the trustees do not make an application to court, the beneficiaries or objects presumably can do so instead. In appropriate circumstances, there is no reason why the negligent trustee should not have to pay the costs of any such application; and, in a case where the trustee has deliberately committed a breach, or where the principle in *Hastings-Bass* cannot be applied (for example because third parties would be adversely affected), the appropriate remedy may be compensation for the trustee's breach of fiduciary duty.

The more important, and much more controversial, question is whether the exer- **11.53** cise of the discretion is itself null and void or whether it stands. The answer depends, it seems, on the extent to which the actual result or effect differs from that intended.[137] In *Re Vestey's Settlement*,[138] for example, Lord Evershed MR held that a power to distribute income among a large class had been effectively exercised because the result which was actually achieved was not 'substantially or essentially different from that which was intended'. On the other hand, in *Re Pilkington's Will Trusts*,[139] Upjohn LJ intimated that an advancement by way of sub-settlement which had an entirely different result from that intended (by reason of the application of the rule against perpetuities) would not be valid under section 32 of the Trustee Act 1925: this would be a matter to which the trustees would not have addressed their minds. Subsequently, in *Re Abrahams' Will Trusts*,[140] a settlement created by exercise of a power of advancement was declared wholly void because the trustees had not appreciated the impact of the rule against perpetuities—which altered the settlement completely—and had not therefore had a right appreciation of their discretion.

Both *Re Pilkington* and *Re Abrahams* concerned powers of advancement, and not **11.54** powers of appointment (let alone any other kind of power or discretion). When a

---

[136] ibid; and *Abacus Trust Company (Isle of Man) Ltd v NSPCC* [2001] STC 1344.

[137] See, for example, *Gilbey v Rush* [1906] 1 Ch 11 (consent to sale based on trustees' ignorance still upheld).

[138] [1951] Ch 209, 221 (an appointment intended to create accumulation and maintenance trusts actually conferred an absolute interest in income). [139] [1961] Ch 466, 489.

[140] [1969] 1 Ch 463.

similar question (again involving a power of advancement) arose in *Re Hastings-Bass*,[141] the Court of Appeal concluded that the decision of Cross J in *Re Abrahams* should not 'be treated as laying down any principle applicable in any case other than one in which the effect of the perpetuity rule has been to alter the intended consequences of an advancement so drastically that the trustees cannot reasonably be supposed to have addressed their minds to the question relevant to the true effect of the transaction'.[142] In *Hastings-Bass,* an advancement had created a valid life interest but also purported to create other powers and trusts which were void for perpetuity. The Court of Appeal held that the prime consideration of the trustees was to confer an immediate and indefeasible life interest in possession, with its attendant saving of estate duty. The trustees undoubtedly considered it beneficial to make some provision for the life tenant's issue, and to confer on him a power to make provision for his widow. However, these 'indirect and contingent benefits (had they been capable of taking effect) should be regarded as mere make-weights which might be treated as enhancing the benefit . . . of the scheme as a whole, but which were of far less significance than the major benefits of the saving of death duties coupled with an acceleration of [his] interest . . . The law cannot . . . require the trustees' exercise of their discretion to be treated as a nullity on the basis of an absurd assumption that, had they realised its true legal effect, they would have reached an unreasonable conclusion as the result of the weighing operation.'[143]

11.55 These early cases could, therefore, be analysed as having a narrow and limited application. They were restricted to powers of advancement, and it is clear, for example, that Cross J, in *Re Abrahams,* considered this to be a crucial factor.[144] A power of advancement is exercisable in favour of only one object and, indeed, only for that object's 'benefit'.[145] If it is exercised in a manner which is manifestly not for that object's benefit, it is not so much a question of taking into account irrelevant considerations or failing to consider relevant ones, but rather an attempt to do something which is not authorized by the power. The effect of the advancement (or, indeed, appointment)[146] is so non-beneficial to the object(s) that the purported exercise itself is excessive[147] and, therefore, *ultra vires* and void. As Buckley LJ put it, in *Re Hastings-Bass*:[148] 'If the resultant effect of the intended advancement were such that it could not reasonably be regarded as being beneficial to the person intended to be advanced, the advancement could not stand, for it would not be within the powers of the trustees under section 32.'

---

[141] [1975] Ch 25.   [142] ibid 41.   [143] ibid 39, 40.
[144] [1969] 1 Ch 466, 484–485.
[145] See paras 15.59–15.67 below. In fact, it is not necessarily true that a power of appointment may not also be exercisable in favour of just one object: see *Thomas* 315.
[146] As in *Re Vestey's Settlement, supra.*
[147] For the excessive exercise of a power, see Chapter 18 below.   [148] [1975] Ch 25, 40–41.

On this basis, the principle in *Hastings-Bass* could be said to be a narrow one: it is merely one example of an excessive exercise of a power.[149] As such, the same consequences should follow as for any other excessive execution of a power, ie the exercise may be wholly void or it may be good in part and void in part. The general principle is that, where something is added which is improper, the execution may be good and the excess alone void if it is possible to distinguish the two, but, where the boundaries between the excess and the execution are not distinguishable, the whole appointment fails.[150] On this narrow view, if *Hastings-Bass* has added anything new to the jurisprudence in this area, it is that it has made it possible (or perhaps just easier) to identify and categorize the object or purpose of an entire advancement or appointment as 'unauthorized' by looking at the totality of its effects rather than individual parts or separate interests. Only in a rare case is it likely, or even arguable, that the result of the trustees' exercise of their discretion is 'substantially or essentially different'[151] from that intended; and only rarely would such an exercise then be set aside. Nevertheless, the narrow interpretation of the principle in *Hastings-Bass* is somewhat academic at present: it was argued and rejected in *Mettoy Pension Trustees Ltd v Evans*.[152]

Another way of looking at the principle is to say that the exercise of a power by **11.56** trustees might be regarded as a nullity by analogy with the rescission of a disposition on the grounds of fundamental mistake of fact or law. Rescission enables a voluntary disposition to be set aside for mistake in circumstances where the disposition fails to carry out the intention of the parties in some fundamental way, and where the mistake is as to the effect (and not just the consequences) of the disposition.[153] However, not only is this distinction between 'effects' and 'consequences' difficult to draw (and even somewhat spurious),[154] but also the requirement that the relevant mistake be 'fundamental' clearly does not accord with the decisions on the rule in *Hastings-Bass*.[155] Alternatively, the appropriate analogy may be the common law doctrine of *non est factum*, where, again, the transaction must be essentially different in substance or in kind from that intended.[156] However, this analogy seems more appropriate in relation to the case where there has been no exercise of the discretion at all, as in *Turner v Turner*.[157] If the narrow

---

[149] The 'excess' in a particular case may, of course, involve the transgression of a rule of law or of the scope of the power. The categories of what may be 'excessive' are not closed (and cannot be, given that the scope of each power may be different).

[150] See para 11.77 below; and *Thomas* 434–435.

[151] *Re Vestey's Settlement* [1951] Ch 209, 221. See also *Hastings-Bass, supra,* 40–41.

[152] [1990] 1 WLR 1587, 1622–1623.

[153] *Lady Hood of Avalon v Mackinnon* [1909] 1 Ch 476; *Re Walton's Settlement* [1922] 2 Ch 509; *Gibbon v Mitchell* [1990] 1 WLR 1304, 1309; *Anker-Petersen v Christensen* [2002] WTLR 313.

[154] *Underhill and Hayton* 697–698, adheres to the distinction. But see *Anker-Petersen v Christensen* [2002] WTLR 313 para 38; *Abacus Trust Company (Isle of Man) Ltd v NSPCC* [2001] STC 1344, para 16.

[155] See *Abacus Trust Co (Isle of Man) v Barr* [2003] 2 WLR 1362, for example.

[156] *Gallie v Lee* [1971] AC 1004.   [157] [1984] Ch 100.

view (the 'excessive exercise' view) were adopted, there would be no need to draw such analogies.[158] In any event, there is no support for such alternatives in any of the reported cases.

11.57   In fact, the way in which the law has developed in subsequent cases has been by way of adopting a much broader interpretation of the principle in *Hastings-Bass*. In *Hastings-Bass* itself, Buckley LJ seems to have enunciated a much wider principle, namely that, in certain cases, a trustee's exercise of a discretion could be challenged or interfered with on the grounds that he had failed to take into account relevant considerations or had taken into account irrelevant considerations:

> . . . where by the terms of a trust (as under section 32) a trustee is given a discretion as to some matter under which he acts in good faith, the Court should not interfere with his action notwithstanding that it does not have the full effect which he intended, unless (1) what he has achieved is unauthorised by the power conferred upon him, or (2) it is clear that he would not have acted as he did (a) had he not taken into account considerations which he should not have taken into account, or (b) had he not failed to take into account considerations which he ought to have taken into account.

Head (1) covers cases of excessive execution of a power. Head (2) is clearly a separate and wider ground for interference. It differs from the case where there has been no exercise of the discretion at all (as in *Turner v Turner*). It is also clearly directed not at what is authorized by a power or discretion, but at the considerations which a trustee ought, or ought not, to take into account in exercising that power or discretion. If the intended or actual effect of an exercise of a power is unauthorized by the power, such exercise is ineffective precisely because, and to the extent that, it is an excessive exercise; and the considerations taken or not taken into account by the donee of the power are irrelevant in determining its invalidity. Thus, a donee cannot justify an action beyond the scope of his powers, even if he considers such action to be beneficial—indeed, even if it is manifestly beneficial—to an object of the power, for example because he considers that a testator has made a will in ignorance of the amount of his assets and that different dispositions would be more morally acceptable,[159] or because he is acting in the best interests of the objects of the power.[160]

11.58   Head (2), however, contemplates the possibility that the intended or actual effect of an exercise of a power may well be authorized by the terms of the power (ie not an excessive exercise) and, yet, that such exercise may be impeachable because the trustee failed to consider relevant considerations or took irrelevant considerations

---

[158] Rectification and rescission do not just apply to trustees, of course, and do not depend on a breach of fiduciary duty.

[159] *Ellis v Barker* (1871) 7 Ch App 104.

[160] See, for example, *Re Wreck Recovery and Salvage Company* (1880) 15 Ch D 353; *Niemann v Niemann* (1889) 43 Ch D 198.

into account. Support for such a broad principle may perhaps be found in earlier cases.[161] However, they are all capable of being explained on narrower grounds than the broad principle enunciated in *Hastings-Bass*.

Nevertheless, the existence of this wider ground of challenge, which is really what **11.59** has come to be called 'the rule in *Hastings-Bass*'—or, more appropriately, 'the principle in *Hastings-Bass*'[162]—was recognized by Warner J in *Mettoy Pension Trustees Ltd v Evans*.[163] In *Mettoy*, one of the issues concerned the validity of a particular deed which had been executed by the trustees of a pension scheme, in exercise of a power of amendment held jointly with the employing company, and intended to consolidate the rules of that scheme and to correct certain past errors. It was argued that the trustees had failed to take into account or consider a number of changes to the provisions of the scheme effected by the deed, the most important of which was the introduction of a rule which provided that any surplus funds on the winding up of the scheme were to be applied at the discretion of the employing company and not, as had previously been the case, at the discretion of the trustees.[164] It was therefore argued that the deed ought to be declared wholly or partially invalid under 'the rule in *Hastings-Bass*'.[165] In the event, Warner J held that the discretion conferred on the employer was a fiduciary power. This fact was not known by the trustees when they executed the relevant deed, but there was no evidence that, if they had known it, they would have declined to execute it in the form in which it was presented to them. Consequently, Warner J held that the rule in *Hastings-Bass* did not apply.[166]

Nevertheless, the judgment in *Mettoy* contains many important observations **11.60** (although perhaps obiter) on the nature and scope of the 'principle which may be labelled "the rule in *Hastings-Bass*"'. According to Warner J, it was a rule which was not confined to cases where an exercise by trustees of a discretion vested in them was partially ineffective because of some rule of law or because some limit on their discretion had been overlooked: 'the reason for the application of the principle is the failure by the trustees to take into account considerations that they ought to have taken into account'.[167] For the principle to apply, however, it is not sufficient to show that the trustees did not have a proper understanding of the effect of their act. It must also be clear that, had they had a proper understanding of it, they *would* not have acted as they did.[168]

---

[161] *Ellis v Barker* (1871) 7 Ch App 104; *Re Hodges* (1878) 7 Ch D 754; *Re Roper's Trusts* (1879) 11 Ch D 272; *Wilson v Turner* (1883) 22 Ch D 521; *Re Lofthouse* (1885) 29 Ch D 921; *Re Bryant* [1894] 1 Ch 324; *Klug v Klug* [1918] 2 Ch 67; *Re Moxon's Will Trusts* [1958] 1 WLR 165; *Re Pauling's Settlement Trusts* [1964] Ch 303.   [162] See, for example, *Green v Cobham* [2002] STC 820, 827.
[163] [1990] 1 WLR 1587 1622–1626.   [164] ibid 1605, 1621–1622.
[165] The formulation of the rule adopted by Warner J was as follows: 'where a trustee acts under a discretion given to him by the terms of the trust, the Court will interfere with his action if it is clear that he would not have acted as he did had he not failed to take into account considerations which he ought to have taken into account': ibid, 1621H.   [166] ibid 1629–1630.
[167] ibid 1624B.   [168] ibid 1624C–D.

11.61 In a case where it is claimed that the rule might apply, three questions were said to arise.[169] First, what were the trustees under a duty to consider? Secondly, did they fail to consider it? Thirdly, if so, what would they have done if they had considered it? In *Mettoy* itself, Warner J indicated that, if the discretion conferred on the employer (in relation to the application of surplus funds on a winding up) had not been a fiduciary power, and if, in that event, the trustees had failed to appreciate that the effect of the relevant amendment was to transfer such discretion from themselves to the employer, he would have concluded that they would not then have executed the deed in the form in which it was presented to them. In the event, the discretion was a fiduciary power and he could not say (because of the absence of evidence) that the trustees would have acted differently if they had appreciated this fact.[170] Warner J also observed that, where the material error concerned just a part of the instrument in question, there was no reason why the entirety should be annulled. If the court was satisfied that the trustees would have acted in the same way, but with the omission, for instance, of a particular clause, it could declare only that provision void: 'the remedy to be adopted by the court must depend on the circumstances of each case'.[171]

11.62 The principle has been reviewed, and seemingly extended yet further, in more recent decisions.[172]

11.63 In *Green v Cobham*,[173] the will of a testator, who was domiciled in the British Virgin Islands, directed his executors to pay part of his residuary estate to the trustees of a UK discretionary trust, the objects of which included his grandchildren. The trustees of the discretionary trust disclaimed any interest under the will.[174] The executors then executed a deed, the effect of which was that new trustees held the share of residue on trusts identical with those in the UK settlement but under the trusts of the will. The trust assets included shares in a company in which a substantial reserve of retained profits had built up. It was decided that the retained profits be distributed to the trustees of the will trust. The latter then distributed them to the grandchildren, three of whom were under the age of 18; and, in their case, the trustees executed appointments on accumulation and maintenance trusts. The trustees were not aware that the will trust and the accumulation and maintenance settlements constituted a single composite settlement

---

[169] [1990] 1 WLR 1625B.   [170] ibid 1629.

[171] ibid 1624–1625. This is similar to the court's jurisdiction in cases of an excessive exercise of a power.

[172] Despite some criticism of earlier cases: see, for example, Sir Robert Walker, 'Some Trust Principles in the Pensions Context' in AJ Oakley (ed), *Trends in Contemporary Trust Law* (OUP, 1996) 123, who pointed out (at 129) that a balance had to be struck 'between the pursuit of perfectly informed decision-making and the need for practical certainty'.

[173] [2002] STC 820: judgment delivered on 19 January 2000.

[174] It was common ground that the disclaimer was effective. It must be doubtful, however, whether trustees, whose primary duty is to get in all assets, can disclaim property which is not 'onerous'.

with a single body of trustees for capital gains tax purposes. Initially, the trustees were non-resident,[175] but one of the trustees then retired from practice as a solicitor, while remaining as a trustee, and as a result the majority of trustees of the composite settlement became resident in the UK, with ensuing adverse capital gains tax consequences for the settlement on its ceasing to be non-resident. The trustees sought a declaration that the appointment in favour of the infant grandchildren was made by an invalid exercise of the will trustees' power of appointment and was void. They contended that the trustees had failed to take into account the capital gains tax consequences of the appointment and that the principle in *Hastings-Bass* therefore applied. Parker J held in favour of the trustees: had they directed their minds, as they should have done, to the tax considerations, they would not under any circumstances have made an appointment which gave rise to any significant risk that the will trust might thereafter become a UK resident trust for capital gains tax purposes.[176] The principle in *Hastings-Bass* therefore applied to the appointment, which was void in its entirety.

Abacus Trust Company (Isle of Man) Ltd v NSPCC[177] involved a complicated tax **11.64** avoidance scheme in relation to a non-resident trust, whose beneficiaries included the settlor and his wife, both of whom were resident in the UK. The essence of the scheme was that a potential charge to capital gains tax would be avoided by the creation of new trusts and the exclusion of the settlor and his wife as beneficiaries (which had to take place before 6 April 1998) and an appointment in favour of charity (which had to take place after that date). In the event, the deed of appointment in favour of charity was executed early (on 3 April 1998) and, as a result, occasioned a charge to capital gains tax. Having referred to *Green v Cobham*, Patten J stated:[178]

> That decision is clear authority that trustees, when exercising powers of appointment, are bound to have regard to the fiscal consequences of their actions and that where it can be demonstrated that a proper consideration of these matters would have led to the appointment not going ahead the court is entitled to and should treat that as an invalid exercise of the power in the sense of it being void ab initio ... The financial consequences for the beneficiaries of any intended exercise of a fiduciary power cannot be assessed without reference to their fiscal implications. The two seem to me inseparable.

He concluded that the appointment was void.

Abacus Trust Company (Isle of Man) v Barr[179] was concerned with an Isle of Man **11.65** settlement under which the settlor was entitled to a life interest subject to an

---

[175] Under s 52(1) and (2) of the Capital Gains Tax Act 1979. See now s 69 of the Taxation of Chargeable Gains Tax Act 1992.
[176] The trustees were apparently concerned about the income tax implications (under s 740 of ICTA 1988). [177] [2001] STC 1344: judgment delivered on 17 July 2001.
[178] ibid 1353. [179] [2003] 2 WLR 1362: judgment delivered on 6 February 2003.

overriding power of appointment. The power was exercisable by the trustee, with the consent of a protector, in favour of members of a class of discretionary objects, which included the settlor, his wife, and two sons. The settlor wished the trustee to exercise the power so as to appoint 40 per cent of the trust fund on discretionary trusts for the benefit of his sons, to the exclusion of the settlor himself and his wife. The request, as relayed to the trustee by an intermediary, referred to an appointment of 60 per cent of the trust fund; and the trustee appointed 60 per cent of the fund accordingly. Some ten years after the error was discovered, proceedings were commenced to challenge the appointment under the *Hastings-Bass* principle. The court's jurisdiction to order rectification or rescission was not invoked, because the trustee intended to appoint 60 per cent of the fund.

11.66 Four questions were identified by Lightman J. First, was the trustee's mistake sufficiently fundamental to bring *Hastings-Bass* into play? The answer was 'yes':[180]

> It is clear that the Rule does not require that the relevant consideration unconsidered by the trustee should make a fundamental difference between the facts as perceived by the trustee and the facts as they should have been perceived and actually were. All that is required in this regard is that the unconsidered relevant consideration would or *might* have affected the trustee's decision, and in a case such as the present that the trustee would or might have made a different appointment or no appointment at all.

11.67 Secondly, was it sufficient to bring *Hastings-Bass* into play that there was a mistake on the part of the trustee, however it arose? Lightman J concluded that it was not enough:

> What has to be established is that the trustee in making his decision has . . . failed to consider what he was under a duty to consider. If the trustee has in accordance with his duty identified the relevant considerations and used all proper care and diligence in obtaining the relevant information and advice relating to those considerations, the trustee can be in no breach of duty and its decision cannot be impugned merely because in fact that information turns out to be partial or incorrect . . . In the absence of any such breach of duty the rule does not afford the right to the trustee or any beneficiary to have a decision declared invalid because the trustee's decision was in some way mistaken or has unforeseen or unpalatable consequences.[181]

11.68 Thirdly, was the trustee at fault in giving effect to the misunderstanding of the settlor's wishes? Lightman J concluded that it was, because here the error was made by an intermediary who was held to have been acting as agent for the trustee and not for the settlor.[182]

11.69 Fourthly, was the appointment void or voidable? Having emphasized the differences between public and private law, Lightman J held that the appointment was merely voidable[183] and that equitable defences were therefore available

---

[180] [2003] 2 WLR 1369, para 21.   [181] ibid 1369–70, paras 23–24.
[182] ibid 1371, para 27.
[183] He dismissed *Cloutte v Storey* [1911] 1 Ch 18 (a case of fraud on a power, which held the appointment is void in equity) as 'problematic'.

(for example, bona fide purchaser, laches, acquiescence, change of position). Indeed, the court can now, it seems, set aside the deed on terms, rather than hold the offending parts void.

Abacus has been heavily criticized on a number of grounds.[184] As Green points out,[185] a straightforward application of the *Hastings-Bass* principle would have required the judge to decide whether the trustee had taken account of the actual wish of the settlor and, if not, whether doing so would/might have made any difference. It is the failure to take account of the relevant information that constitutes the breach of fiduciary duty. However, the judge held that this was not in itself sufficient; he went further and held that it was also necessary to find that the trustee had committed a separate breach of fiduciary duty, which he did, because the trustee's agent (the intermediary) had failed to 'use all proper care and diligence' to ascertain the settlor's actual wish. This is an entirely novel feature and seems inconsistent with earlier decisions on *Hastings-Bass*. It means that 'the relief is available in respect of the acts of the negligent trustee but not in respect of the acts of the careful trustee, even though the substantive basis for impugning the trustee's decision is the same in each case'.[186] It also means that, if trustee negligence becomes the requirement for relief, trustees themselves are not likely to bring proceedings.[187] Moreover, holding the trustee vicariously liable for the acts of its agent, appointed in good faith, raises more general issues of a trustee's liability for the acts of his agent.

11.70

Summary

A narrow interpretation of the original principle in *Hastings-Bass* would suggest that it is another example of an excessive exercise of a power or discretion. However, as it has been developed in subsequent cases, it can be seen to have a broader application and to be capable of being invoked to annul an exercise of a power on erroneous grounds. The principle is not concerned primarily (or at all) with the existence or non-existence of legitimate authority (which is not dependent on the trustee's knowledge or ignorance of any particular consideration): indeed, it is doubtful whether it would have any role to play in relation to such a question, where other doctrines could apply with better effect. Rather, it deals with the improper exercise of legitimate authority (which may be materially affected by such ignorance). That which has been done may be authorized by the

11.71

---

[184] See, for example, [2003] PCB 173 (E Nugee); (2003) Trust Law Int 114 (B Green).
[185] ibid 119–122. See also Nugee (n 184 above) 177.
[186] Green (n 184 above) 121. See also *Breadner v Granville-Grossman* [2000] WTLR 829.
[187] Green points out, however, that this additional element of negligence will probably be present in most cases. Also, in *Abacus* itself, the judge found that the trustee's agent had been negligent, so the requirement was met in any event. However, it is not at all clear why an innocent failure to take account of a relevant consideration should not be sufficient.

terms of the power (in the sense of not being excessive, fraudulent, deliberately capricious, and so on), but the effects or consequences may be such that the actual *exercise* may be open to challenge.

11.72 In order to justify interference by the court, two requirements must be satisfied. First, relevant considerations (and, it is suggested, they must be *significantly* relevant considerations) must have been unknown or ignored or, alternatively, irrelevant considerations (and again, it is suggested, they must have been *significantly* irrelevant considerations) must have been given undue weight. Secondly, it must be established that the trustees *would* not have taken the decision they took, or acted as they did, if they had known or had not ignored such relevant consideration (or had not taken account of such irrelevant consideration). The word 'would' does not indicate a requirement of absolute certainty, but simply a likelihood on a balance of probabilities. Recent decisions suggest that it is sufficient to show that the trustees 'might' have acted differently. In so far as this suggests that even the slightest possibility would suffice, it is suggested that they are in error: at the very least, the court must be satisfied, on a balance of probabilities, that a different decision or action was a realistic possibility. The court should be reluctant to interfere with the exercise of discretion by trustees and should not annul their decisions lightly. With the benefit of hindsight, trustees could often say that they would not have acted as they did had they known, or appreciated the significance of, a relevant consideration. However, if the general principle against interference with the exercise of discretion is to be preserved, and if the finality of trustees' decisions is regarded as having important practical significance, the principle in *Hastings-Bass* ought to apply only where there is a material irregularity in the decision-making process and the actual outcome is fundamentally flawed: it ought not to be a mechanism simply to give trustees a second chance.

11.73 It is suggested that the appropriate test for the application of the principle ought to be to ask what, on a balance of probabilities, the consequences would have been if the *same* effects had been brought about by trustees *with* actual knowledge of the relevant consideration (or without taking account of the irrelevant consideration). The court should intervene so as to reverse only that which, had it been done with full knowledge and understanding of the significantly relevant consideration, would have been capricious, absurd, or such that no reasonable trustee with such knowledge and understanding would ever have done. This is not the same as saying that the trustee has actually acted capriciously, absurdly, or unreasonably, for, if he acted out of ignorance or negligently, he could not be said to have the requisite state of mind to have done so.[188] It is simply saying that, if he had had *mens rea* and deliberately acted in the same way, his decision or action would have been capricious, absurd or unreasonable. Such an approach would

---

[188] For the trustee's duty not to act capriciously, see paras 11.89–11.90 below.

impose necessary limitations on the principle in *Hastings-Bass* and would also make it consistent with other grounds for judicial interference with, and control of, the exercise of trustees' discretions.

Recent authorities are not necessarily inconsistent with such a view. It would have **11.74** been utterly unreasonable and absurd, even capricious, for the trustee in *Abacus Trust Company (Isle of Man) Ltd v NSPCC*[189] intentionally to have executed the relevant deed of appointment prematurely; or for the trustee in *Abacus Trust Company (Isle of Man) v Barr*[190] deliberately to have ignored the settlor's 'instructions' to appoint 40 per cent of the trust fund rather than 60 per cent. The same could be said of *Green v Cobham*,[191] which is viewed as the most liberal application of the *Hastings-Bass* principle. It is said that there were no adverse capital gains tax consequences for the trustees to consider: the adverse effects came about when the solicitor retired from practice and not as a result of the appointment. However, Parker J concluded that this argument was 'not sustainable' because 'the damage was done' as soon as the deed of appointment was executed in the sense that the status of the will trust as a non-resident settlement became determinable by reference to the status of the trustees of the deed as well as that of the will trustees. This conclusion has been criticized.[192] However, it is suggested that it is correct. Immediately the deed of appointment was executed, the non-resident status of the will trust might have been jeopardized, not just by the retirement from practice of one of the trustees, but also by some entirely freakish accident, such as a non-resident trustee falling under a bus or being eaten by a cayman. This is not a result that any reasonable trustee, with full knowledge and proper understanding of the tax implications, would have brought about. Whether such a test is adopted remains to be seen.

Void or voidable exercise?

On the question whether an instrument which is successfully challenged under **11.75** the *Hastings-Bass* principle is void or voidable, Lightman J's conclusion that it is merely voidable, and that equitable defences are available, has generally been welcomed. This may have its advantages. However, its correctness has also been questioned. It is said that there is no basis for it in any of the earlier decisions on the *Hastings-Bass* principle.[193] However, the issue does not seem to have been addressed directly in those cases. It is also said to be inconsistent with *Cloutte v Storey*,[194] in which the Court of Appeal is said to have held that a document

---

[189] [2001] STC 1344.   [190] [2003] 2 WLR 1362.   [191] [2002] STC 820.
[192] See, for example, (2003) Trust Law Int 114, 127 (B Green).
[193] See *AMP (UK) plc v Barker* [2001] WTLR 1237; *Stannard v Fisons Pension Trust Ltd* [1991] PLR 225; *Kerr v British Leyland (Staff) Trustees Ltd* (1986) [2001] WTLR 1071; *Mettoy Pension Trustees Ltd v Evans* [1990] 1 WLR 1587.
[194] [1911] 1 Ch 18: Lightman J. found this decision 'problematic'. See also *Aleyn v Belchier* (1758) 1 Eden 132; *Daubeny v Cockburn* (1816) 1 Mer 626, 628; *Birley v Birley* (1858) 25 Beav 299; *Topham v Duke of Portland* (1863) 1 De GJ & Sm 517, 574.

executed in fraud of a power is void, and therefore defeats even a bona fide purchaser.[195] However, the Court of Appeal did not express itself in such absolute terms. The Court of Appeal held that an appointment under a common law power, by which the legal estate has passed, is at most voidable, and a purchaser for value of the legal estate without notice is not affected by the fraudulent execution of the power. In contrast, an appointment in fraud of an equitable power, not operating so as to pass the legal estate, is void, and a purchaser for value without notice can only rely on such equitable defences as are open to purchasers without the legal title who are subsequent in time against prior equitable titles. The settled interests under consideration were equitable and the purchasers did not have the legal title.[196] At first instance, Neville J observed that a purchaser for valuable consideration from an appointee who has acquired the legal title without notice is not affected by the fraudulent execution of the power.[197] In the Court of Appeal, Farwell LJ added:[198]

> If an appointment is void at law, no title at law can be founded on it; but this is not so in equity: the mere fact that the appointment is void does not prevent a Court of Equity from having regard to it: eg, an appointment under a limited power to a stranger is void, but equity may cause effect to be given to it by means of the doctrine of election . . .
>
> It is said that if the appointed fund has been paid over to the [appointees], either by transfer of the stocks and securities to them by the trustees, or by payment to them of the proceeds of the realization thereof by the trustees, they would have obtained the full legal title and possession, and restitution could not have been obtained from them; and in my opinion this, as a general proposition, is correct.[199]

Thus, it is not the case that a fraudulent appointment is void in all circumstances.

11.76 In any event, it is difficult to see how the doctrine of fraud on a power, and therefore the decision in *Cloutte v Storey*, could be relevant to the *Hastings-Bass* principle. A fraudulent appointment is *ultra vires*: it will be set aside because there is no authority to make it, and the question whether the trustee took account of relevant or irrelevant considerations is immaterial.

11.77 If the *Hastings-Bass* principle is seen as an application of the doctrine of *excessive* exercise of a power (which it probably is not), then the result ought to be the same, ie the entirety is not necessarily void. Where something is added which is improper, the execution may be good and the excess alone void if it is possible to distinguish the two; but, where the boundaries between the excess and the execution are not distinguishable, the whole appointment fails.

---

[195] (2003) Trust Law Int 114, 122 (B Green).   [196] ibid 30.   [197] ibid 24.
[198] ibid 31, 34.
[199] It must surely be incorrect to say that assets improperly transferred to appointees cannot be recovered.

If the principle operates so as to reverse what is essentially a capricious, absurd, or **11.78** unreasonable exercise of the power (as suggested above), the exercise ought to be voidable only. Those affected adversely have a right to have the transaction set aside, but such a right is a 'mere equity';[200] and a mere equity cannot take priority over or defeat the rights of a bona fide purchaser, whether of the legal estate or equitable interest.

G. The Duty to Treat Beneficiaries and Objects Even-Handedly[201]

In the absence of some provision to the contrary, a trustee must be impartial in the **11.79** execution of his trust.[202] As Turner LJ stated, in *Re Tempest*,[203] 'it is of the essence of the duty of every trustee to hold an even hand between the parties interested under the trust. Every trustee is in duty bound to look to the interests of all, and not of any particular member or class of members of his *cestuis que trusts.'* Such statements actually encapsulate two different duties. In broad terms, it may be said that members of the same class of beneficiaries or objects ought to be treated equally, on the basis that they enjoy equal rights and interests. However, where beneficiaries have different interests, or where there are different classes which, in relation to each other, enjoy different degrees of importance or dissimilar rights, trustees ought to treat them fairly (or impartially, or with an even hand). In many cases, however, it is difficult to distinguish these two separate duties.

Most of the traditional duties of trustees would seem to be examples of the duty to **11.80** act fairly or with an even hand as between beneficiaries with different interests. Thus, an augmentation of the capital of the trust fund must generally accrue for the benefit of all beneficiaries and be treated as capital and not as income.[204] The same general duty also requires a trustee to act impartially between a life tenant and the remainderman and to maintain a reasonable balance between the provision of income for the former and the preservation of capital for the benefit of the latter.[205] It underpins certain specific rules requiring the conversion of trust property[206] and the apportionment of the proceeds of sale or value of such property as between

---

[200] See, for example, *Bowen v Evans* (1844) 1 Jo & Lat 178; *Wade v Dixon* (1858) 28 LJ Ch 315; *Phillips v Phillips* (1862) 4 De F & J 208; *Cave v Cave* (1880) 15 Ch D 639, 646.
[201] See, generally, *Thomas,* paras 6-165–6-179; *Underhill and Hayton,* 529–548; and PD Finn, *Fiduciary Obligations* (1977), 56–74.   [202] *Lloyds Bank v Duker* [1987] 1 WLR 1324.
[203] (1866) 1 Ch App 485, 487–488. See also *Re Lepine* [1892] 1 Ch 210, 219; *Re Pauling's Settlement Trusts (No 2)* [1963] Ch 576, 586; *Nestle v National Westminster Bank plc* [1993] 1 WLR 1260.
[204] *Re Barton's Trusts* (1868) LR 5 Eq 238; *Bouch v Sproule* (1887) 12 App Cas 385.
[205] cf. *Cowan v Scargill* [1985] Ch 270; *Nestle v National Westminster Bank plc* [1993] 1 WLR 1260.
[206] Under the so-called 'rule' in *Howe v Earl of Dartmouth* (1802) 7 Ves 137. See also s 33 of the Administration of Estates Act 1925.

income and capital.[207] It also manifests itself in relation to the incidence of out-goings, such as, for example, in the rules requiring income to bear current expenses and the corpus to be subject to capital charges.[208] In such cases, although the purpose of the particular rule is often said to be to attain 'equal' treatment for all beneficiaries, it would seem to be more accurate to regard it as achieving (a broad) fairness.

11.81 The administrative or managerial powers of trustees are, of course, ancillary to their duties and are conferred in order to enable them the better to carry out those duties. Trustees must not, therefore, exercise such powers in a way which is inconsistent with their primary duties.[209] In this sense, it may be said that, in the exercise of their administrative or managerial powers, trustees are under a similar duty to treat the beneficiaries and objects of their trust impartially. Thus, trustees for sale of land ought generally to exercise their power to postpone sale where the share of one beneficiary has vested in possession, but the shares of others have not.[210]

11.82 Similarly, in the simple case where trustees have wide powers of investment in order to enable them to carry out their duty to invest more effectively, it would not be a proper exercise of their discretion to change an investment merely for the sake of increasing the income of the tenant for life, if, in doing so, the security of the capital is diminished.[211] They may not exercise those powers which are conferred on them for the benefit of a class of beneficiaries or objects generally so as to give undue advantage to one beneficiary or object at the expense of the others. It is a trustee's 'bounden duty to have regard to the rights and interests of all parties concerned', and if he invests trust moneys 'at the instance and for the benefit of one or more of *cestuis que trustent* [sic], without having regard to the interests of the others, and loss has resulted from the investment, that is a breach of trust for which he and his estate must be made responsible'.[212] In *Knox v Mackinnon*,[213]

---

[207] For example, under the so-called 'rule' in *Re Earl of Chesterfield's Trusts* (1883) 24 Ch D 643. Similar requirements of equality of treatment also operate in other areas, eg the payment of debts in bankruptcy; the distribution of assets on liquidation; abatement in the case of an insufficient estate; and so forth.

[208] Costs of administration of trust property, including legal proceedings, are payable out of corpus, unless they relate exclusively to the tenant for life (or presumably to any beneficiary whose interest is solely in income).

[209] *Balls v Strutt* (1841) 1 Hare 146, 149; *Raby v Ridehalgh* (1855) 7 De GM & G 104, 108; *Re Sandys* [1916] 1 Ch 511.

[210] *Re Horsnaill* [1909] 1 Ch 631. See also *Re Kipping* [1914] 1 Ch 62; *Re Marshall* [1914] 1 Ch 192; *Re Weiner* [1956] 1 WLR 579; *Stephenson v Barclays Bank Trust Co Ltd* [1975] 1 WLR 882. The same does not apply to shares or property other than land and mortgages: *Re Sandeman's Will Trusts* [1937] 1 All ER 368.

[211] *Re Dick* [1891] 1 Ch 423, 431. See also *Cowan v Scargill* [1985] Ch 270, 286–287; *Raby v Ridehalgh* (1855) 7 De GM & G 104, 108.

[212] *Raby v Ridehalgh* (1855) 7 De Gm & G 104, 109.

[213] (1888) 13 App Cas 753. See also *Re National Provincial Marine Insurance Co* (1870) 5 Ch App 559; and *Re Denver Hotel Company* [1893] 1 Ch 495 (but cf *British and Amercian Trustee and Finance Corporation v Couper* [1894] AC 399).

for example, trustees sold a tenement comprised in the trust fund to one of seven beneficiaries under the trust. The purchaser was unable to pay the whole of the purchase price and the trustees allowed him to retain the balance on loan. He conveyed three houses (including the purchased trust property) to the trustees as security for the loans, but all the properties were subject to prior incumbrances exceeding two-thirds of their estimated value. The trustees also held the personal obligation of the borrower and his father-in-law. Some of the other beneficiaries protested on two occasions, but the moneys were allowed to remain on loan, on these securities, until the borrower and his father-in-law both became bankrupt some ten years later. Some £10,000 was lost to the trust. Although the trust deed contained a power authorizing the trustees to lend the trust fund on such securities as they might think proper, and also an exemption clause declaring that they should not be liable for 'omissions, errors, or neglect of management', the trustees were held[214] not to have acted with perfect impartiality between the beneficiaries. There was evidence that the trustees, 'from very worthy motives', had placed themselves in the position of champions of one side of the family; and the whole transaction was essentially 'an accommodation' to enable one beneficiary to buy the property and not a bona fide investment of trust funds.[215]

The same broad principles apply in the context of occupational pension schemes. **11.83** Trustees dealing with surplus funds under such schemes are bound to exercise their powers fairly as between the beneficiaries.[216] When considering a proposed amendment to the trust deed of a pension scheme, trustees are entitled and probably obliged to take into account the interests of the employer in any surplus funds. They have to be satisfied that 'the overall package' is 'fair' to both the employer and the members of the scheme.[217] Similarly, when dealing with transfer payments from one scheme to another, they have to act fairly as between the transferring members and the remaining members.[218]

The extent to which such impartiality or even-handedness is required in respect of **11.84** *dispositive* powers is less clear. In some cases, any such duty is necessarily excluded. Certain powers, such as statutory and express powers of advancement, for example, are not usually exercisable in favour of a class of beneficiaries as such: rather, they apply in respect of a particular beneficiary's own vested, presumptive, or contingent share of the capital of the trust fund. The size or extent of each such share

---

[214] By the Court of Session; affirmed by the House of Lords.

[215] *Knox v Mackinnon* (1888) 13 App Cas 753, 763, 766, 769. See also *Re Brogden* (1888) 38 Ch D 546; *Ward v Ward* (1843) 2 HLC 777n. Cf *Harris v Black* (1983) 46 P & CR 366. For similar reasons, a person with declared views favourable to one class of beneficiaries is an unsuitable appointee as trustee: *Re Tempest* (1866) 1 Ch App 485, 489–490.

[216] *UEB Industries Ltd v WS Brabant* [1991] PLR 109, 116.

[217] *Lock v Westpac Banking Corporation* [1991] PLR 167, 179.

[218] *Stannard v Fisons Pension Trust Ltd* [1991] PLR 225, 230.

(which need not be an equal share) is usually established by the trusts of the settlement; and, in exercising such a power in respect of any such share, the trustees are not generally concerned with maintaining an even hand in relation to other beneficiaries: there is no requirement, for instance, that, if one beneficiary is advanced, all others must also be benefited in a similar way or to the same extent. Indeed, it would be absurd to suggest any such requirement.[219]

11.85 Other powers, such as powers of appointment and discretions over income, almost by their very nature and purpose, exclude any requirement of equality in the *effects* of their execution.[220] As Fox J stated, in *Pearson v IRC*:[221] 'A power over income which can be exercised only by distributing income equally among the objects would, if such a power has ever been created at all, be most unusual; it is difficult to see any point in such a provision.' Similarly, in *Edge v Pensions Ombudsman*,[222] Scott V-C observed: 'In relation to a discretionary power of that character it is, in my opinion, meaningless to speak of a duty on the trustees to act impartially. Trustees, when exercising a discretionary power to choose must, of course, not take into account irrelevant, irrational or improper factors. But, provided they avoid doing so, they are entitled to choose and to prefer some beneficiaries over others.'

11.86 *Edge* itself concerned an appeal from a decision of the Pension Ombudsman in which he had annulled an amendment by trustees of the rules of a pension scheme so as to use surplus funds to benefit members of the scheme, without providing any benefit at all to pensioners. The Pension Ombudsman held that the trustees were in breach of their duty to act impartially. Scott V-C reversed this decision and commented:[223]

> What is 'undue partiality'? The trustees are entitled to be partial. They are entitled to exclude some beneficiaries from particular benefits and to prefer others. If what is meant by 'undue partiality' is that the trustees have taken into account irrelevant or improper or irrational factors, their exercise of their discretion may well be flawed. But it is not flawed simply because someone else, whether or not a judge, regards the partiality as 'undue'. It is the trustees' discretion that is to be exercised.

In such cases, there clearly cannot be any duty to exercise the power or discretion so as to produce equality of outcome in respect of all objects.

11.87 It is less clear, however, whether, in the absence of some provision to the contrary, trustees must give *equal consideration* to all objects of the same class, ie although

---

[219] An element of even-handedness is preserved by the Trustee Act 1925, s 32(1), Provisos (b) and (c).

[220] Such a power may, of course, be conferred, subject, eg, to a discretion as to the time or manner of execution, but this would be unlikely.   [221] [1980] Ch 1, 14.

[222] [1998] Ch 602, 618, [1998] PLR 15, 29–30. As Scott V-C pointed out, the observations of Megarry V-C, in *Cowan v Scargill* [1985] Ch 270, 286–87, relating to 'the duty of trustees to ... [hold] the scales impartially between different classes of beneficiaries', were clearly intended to be confined to an investment power.   [223] ibid 30.

only one or some of the objects in a class may actually be benefited, whether the circumstances of all must be considered first. This is not to suggest that an identical inquiry must be conducted in respect of each and every object, using some kind of checklist. The circumstances of individual objects (for example children) may—indeed, probably will—differ considerably. Nevertheless, where the class of objects is small, for instance the children of the settlor or of some other individual, it is probable that all members of that class of objects have an equal right to be considered for receipt of bounty; and trustees cannot properly select some objects without an even-handed regard to the competing rights and potential claims of others. On the other hand, such equality of consideration becomes an impossibility where the class of objects is extremely large (as in the case of hybrid or intermediate powers) or comprised of numerous different categories of objects. In such cases, equal consideration may be required in respect of all those objects in the same class or category who are known to the trustees (whether as a result of their own inquiries or of claims put forward by objects themselves or otherwise), but even this seems doubtful. The degree of 'fairness' required will vary considerably from case to case, depending on the nature of the power or discretion (a mere power or a discretionary trust), on the size and constitution of the class of objects, and on whether different objects (or categories of objects) have similar or dissimilar rights or claims. In some cases, this may demand equality of treatment, but not in others.

A duty to treat all objects and beneficiaries of the same class even-handedly can, of **11.88** course, be excluded expressly in the trust instrument (and it is common practice to do so). It may also be the case that the rigour with which the duty will affect the trustees may be modified or diminished by prevailing circumstances. In *Nestle v National Westminster Bank plc*,[224] Staughton LJ stated: 'If the life tenant is living in penury and the remainderman already has ample wealth, common sense suggests that a trustee should be able to take that into account, not necessarily by seeking the highest possible income at the expense of capital but by inclining in that direction.' This, however, seems to be a recognition that the duty to act impartially between life tenant and remainderman has never been applied with mathematical precision (it does not, for example, impose a general duty to convert and to reinvest). In this sense, the duty to act impartially could often be regarded simply as one to act fairly (and not 'equally').

H. Duty Not to Act Capriciously

Although, as a general rule, the court will not review the decisions of trustees, it **11.89** may intervene where the exercise of a power or discretion is capricious. These are

---

[224] [1993] 1 WLR 1260, 1279.

exceptional instances where the exercise cannot be said, on any reasonable view, to be for the benefit of the objects or beneficiaries or in furtherance of the purpose for which the power was actually created. They are cases which go well beyond mere error of judgement and in which the conduct of the trustees has been capricious, arbitrary, absurd, wanton, oppressive, vexatious, mischievous, or ruinous.[225] As Lord Jessel MR stated in *Ex parte Lloyd*,[226] where a trustee in bankruptcy had decided not to sell a contingent reversionary interest: 'Here the appellant says that the refusal to sell is an absurd exercise of the discretion of the trustee. But the Court will not interfere unless the trustee is doing that which is so utterly unreasonable and absurd that no reasonable man would so act.'

11.90 A clear example of such conduct is provided by *Re Chapman*,[227] where a trustee who had paid income to a tenant for life for some fifteen years ceased to do so when he suspected that she was an impostor. Lord Herschell, having accepted the trustee's submission that 'what is reasonable must be measured by the responsibility which the law imposes on a trustee', stated:[228]

> I do not think that a trustee is bound to run any risks. I think that he is entitled to satisfy himself by all reasonable inquiry and investigation, because, if he pays money to any person who is not properly entitled to receive it, he may be held liable. But if he sees risk where none in fact exists, and if he refuses to be satisfied by evidence which would satisfy all reasonable men, then I think that he must bear all the expenses which his conduct causes ...
>
> The appellant contends that the trustee is the only judge of what is reasonable, and that he is entitled to be satisfied in such a way as he considers proper. I most entirely dissent from that proposition. The appellant asked how the Court could decide whether a trustee had been acting reasonably, and suggested that this point must be left to the trustee himself. But the Courts have every day in a variety of cases to determine whether men are acting reasonably; and I can see no ground why they should not determine what is reasonable in the case of a trustee, just as in any other case ...
>
> I do not believe that he acted dishonestly, or that he had any personal ends to serve. I think that it was sheer unreasonableness on his part. Sometimes a man gets an idea into his head, and nothing will shake him.

---

[225] See, for example, *Re Brittlebank* (1881) 30 WR 99; *Ex p Lloyd* (1882) 47 LT 64; *Ex p Brown* (1886) 17 QBD 488; *Re Bell Bros Ltd* (1891) 65 LT 245; *Re Chapman* (1895) 72 LT 66. These descriptions are used interchangeably in the cases. There may be differences of degree between capriciousness and perverseness (ie behaviour which no reasonable body of trustees would engage in: see, for example, *Harris v Lord Shuttleworth* [1994] ICR 989, 999) and the other descriptions of conduct referred to above, but this seems immaterial, provided the conduct, act, or decision is sufficiently unreasonable to warrant interference by the court.

[226] (1882) 47 LT 64, 65. See also *Dundee General Hospitals Committee of Management v Walker* [1952] 1 All ER 896, 901 ('whether these errors were so extravagant that no reasonable man could have fallen into them') and 903 ('no reasonable man, fairly considering the facts, could have taken the view which the trustees took'); *Harris v Lord Shuttleworth, supra*, 1111 ('a decision at which no reasonable body of trustees could arrive'); *Wild v Smith* [1996] PLR 275; and *Edge v Pensions Ombudsman* [1998] PLR 15, 30 ('decision ... that no reasonable body of trustees properly directing themselves could have reached'). [227] (1895) 72 LT 66.

[228] ibid 67–68.

Similarly, Lindley LJ concluded:[229]

> A trustee may be honest, and yet, from over-caution or some other cause, he may act unreasonably; and if, as in this case, his conduct is so unreasonable as to be vexatious, oppressive, or otherwise wholly unjustifiable, and he thereby causes his *cestuis que trust* expense which would not otherwise have been incurred, the trustee must bear such expense, and it ought not to be thrown on the trust estate or on his *cestuis que trust*.

In some instances, capricious conduct may be indistinguishable from a failure to take into account relevant considerations or an insistence on taking into account irrelevant ones. In other words, the duty 'to give properly informed consideration to the problem' may sometimes be said to be but one aspect of the duty not to act capriciously.[230] Thus, where a trustee refuses to acknowledge plain facts or to accept an unequivocal statement of the law, his conduct may properly be described as capricious because he is failing to consider all that is relevant to the decision he has to make. It is also possible to categorize those cases in which the principle in *Hastings-Bass* has been applied[231] as examples of capricious behaviour (defined broadly) on the part of the trustees. Certainly, the conduct of the trustees in such cases was 'so unreasonable as to be vexatious, oppressive, or otherwise wholly unjustifiable'. Similarly, where a trustee acts on the basis of an absurd premise, as would be the case, for example, if he were to exercise a power of appointment in favour of certain objects solely on the ground that they had red hair or blue eyes, he could be said to be ascribing undue weight to a totally irrelevant consideration. In other cases, capricious conduct is similar to lack of good faith. In all cases, however, the conduct or behaviour of the trustees, or the consequences of their actions, must be so unreasonable as to be absurd in some way. However, although all these heads may overlap, they are not necessarily identical in all cases. A trustee may reach a perverse decision in perfect good faith[232] and on the basis of a consideration of all relevant considerations, and without regard to any irrelevant ones. Moreover, capriciousness seems to involve a positive state of mind rather than omissions. Therefore, it seems that the duty not to act capriciously merits separate treatment. **11.91**

---

229 ibid 68.

230 *Harris v Lord Shuttleworth* [1993] PLR 39, 47 (where the trustees had to consider whether they were satisfied that there had been a retirement occurring by reason of incapacity). See also *Kerr v British Leyland (Staff) Trustees Ltd* (1986) [2001] WTLR 1071; *Mihlenstedt v Barclays Bank* [1989] IRLR 522, 525; and *Dean v Prince* [1954] Ch 409, 418, 427.

231 See paras 11.43–11.74 above.

232 In *Hutton v West Cork Railway Co* (1883) 23 Ch D 654, 671, Bowen LJ stated, in relation to payments made by a company by way of gratuities to its directors and servants: '*Bona fides* cannot be the sole test, otherwise you might have a lunatic conducting the affairs of the company, and paying away its money with both hands in a manner perfectly *bona fide* yet perfectly irrational.' This is sometimes referred to as the case of 'the amiable lunatic'.

I. An Implied Duty of Good Faith[233]

11.92 Where a power is held by a person who is not a trustee (or other fiduciary), he owes no duty to anyone to consider the exercise of that power. Indeed, he may ignore the power entirely; and he is at liberty to declare that he will never exercise it. In the event that he does exercise the power, he must do so honestly and properly: he cannot, for example, exercise it excessively or fraudulently. Nevertheless, in broad terms, he remains free from most of the obligations and restrictions (such as the rule against conflict of interests) which fall on a trustee or other donee of a fiduciary power. To this general proposition, however, there is one possible exception. It is of recent origin and, as yet, seems to apply only in the context of occupational pension schemes. It is generally referred to as 'the *Imperial* implied obligation of good faith', after the decision in which it originated. However, both its scope and the manner in which it differs from other truly 'fiduciary' obligations remain unclear.[234] Although it is merely of indirect concern to trustees, it merits a brief discussion in this chapter.

11.93 In *Imperial Group Pension Trust Ltd v Imperial Tobacco Ltd*[235] the relevant provision in a company's contributory pension scheme[236] provided that, on its determination, any surplus in the fund was to be applied solely for the employees, the pensioners, and their dependants, and in no circumstances was any part of the surplus to revert to the company. The fund was managed by a committee exercising the powers conferred on it by the trust deed and the rules. All members of the committee had to be employees of the company, and were appointed, and were capable of being removed, by the company.[237] There was no express provision for increasing pensions, but the committee did so by exercising its power to amend the rules with the consent of the company. Shortly before a takeover of the company, the committee of management and the company altered the rules to provide for the automatic closure of the fund to new members in the event of takeover, and to create a new rule which guaranteed pension increases of 'at least' the lesser of 5 per cent and the increase in the rate of inflation. When the rate of inflation

---

[233] See, generally, *Thomas,* paras 6-187–6-200.

[234] In *Re National Grid Company* [1997] PLR 157, Walker J said: 'The scope and limits of the *Imperial Tobacco* duty will no doubt be worked out, on a case by case basis, in coming years. It will probably be found to have more than one attribute in common with fiduciary duties. But it will not, I think, assist the development of the law to try to blend the two together, or to dilute the Vice-Chancellor's clear statement . . . that an employer can consistently with its duty of good faith have regard to its own financial interests.' See also (1996) 25 ILJ 121 (D Brodie); (1996) 24 Austr Business LR 341 (A Nolan); (1997) 11 Tr Law Int 93 (D Pollard).   [235] [1991] 1 WLR 589.

[236] This was a contributory, balance-of-cost scheme, ie one under which the members paid contributions, and the company was bound to pay such sums as the scheme actuary might certify were necessary to make the fund actuarially solvent.

[237] These powers of appointment and removal were presumably fiduciary powers, properly so-called: *Re Skeats' Settlement* (1889) 42 Ch D 522; *Re Shortridge* [1895] 1 Ch 278; *Pepper v Tuckey* (1844) 2 Jo & Lat 95.

increased to above 5 per cent, the committee sought, but failed to obtain, an assurance from the new management of the company that it would consent to inflation-linked increases in benefits greater than 5 per cent. The company then created a new non-contributory pension scheme, for new employees, under which any ultimate surplus would revert to the company. The company offered an inflation-linked increase of up to 15 per cent to any member of the original scheme who transferred to the new scheme, taking his aliquot share of the fund with him. The committee issued a summons to determine whether it could increase the scale of benefits under the original scheme without the consent of the company. Browne-Wilkinson V-C held that *the power of the company* to give or withhold its consent was *not* a fiduciary power (which, in the circumstances, was clearly correct). However, he also held that it was a power that was subject to an implied obligation that it would not be exercised so as seriously to damage the relationship of confidence between the employer and the employees and ex-employees. In exercising that *obligation of good faith*, the company could have regard to its own financial and other interests in the future operation of the scheme (which it clearly could not do if the power had been fiduciary). However, it was required to exercise its rights with a view to the efficient running of the scheme and not for the collateral purpose of forcing the members to give up their accrued rights in the fund in order that the company should obtain a benefit for itself. Consequently, if the company exercised its right in pursuance of such a collateral purpose in breach of its obligation of good faith, the exercise of the power to withhold consent would be invalid.

If there had been an express restriction or constraint on the company's power to give or withhold consent to an amendment, this would have been valid and enforceable according to its terms, irrespective of whether the power was a fiduciary one or not. If the power had been a fiduciary power, the company would have been limited by its obligations to consider the interests of members only. However, it had been conceded that the power of consent was not a fiduciary power.[238] The question, therefore, was whether the company's power was subject to any implied constraint or not. A restriction on the company's right to give or withhold consent to the effect that it could not be unreasonably withheld[239]

11.94

---

[238] 'If this were a fiduciary power the company would have to decide whether or not to consent by reference only to the interests of the members, disregarding its own interests. This plainly was not the intention': [1991] 1 WLR 589, 596E. In *Re The National Grid Company plc* [1997] PLR 157, the Pensions Ombudsman regarded the duty of good faith as one 'approaching a fiduciary duty'. However, Walker J emphasized the fact that the employer could have regard to its own interests; and, in the circumstances of the case, where the trustees had recommended a 50:50 split of surplus funds but National Grid had opted for a 70:30 split instead, he found that the company had not acted in breach of its duty of good faith.

[239] As, for example, in cases where a restrictive covenant required the consent of the dominant owner to any building works: *Wrotham Park Estates Co Ltd v Parkside Homes Ltd* [1974] 1 WLR 798; *Cryer v Scott* (1986) 55 P & CR 183, 194 and 202.

would be unworkable and could not, therefore, be implied.[240] However, a pension scheme trust differed in nature from a traditional family trust in that, in relation to the former, the employer was not conferring a bounty and the beneficiaries were not volunteers. Consequently, a restriction on the employer's power would be implied; and that restriction was 'the implied obligation of good faith' which was implied into every contract of employment, namely that the employer will not, without reasonable and proper cause, conduct himself in a manner calculated or likely to destroy or seriously damage the relationship of confidence and trust between employer and employee.[241] This obligation applied as much to the exercise of the employer's rights and powers under a pension scheme as it did to the other rights and powers of an employer. It was open to the company to look after its own interests, financially and otherwise, in the future operations of the scheme in deciding whether or not to give its consent.

> However, in my judgment the obligation of good faith does require that the company should exercise its rights (a) with a view to the efficient running of the scheme established by the fund and (b) not for the collateral purpose of forcing the members to give up their accrued rights in the existing fund subject to this scheme.[242]

As to (a), it would be a breach of the obligation of good faith if the company were to resolve that it would never consider whether or not to consent to an amendment increasing benefits. It should consider each proposal put forward by the committee. If the company had given a blanket refusal to consider, such refusal was improper. Thus, in this respect alone, the employing company, though possessed of a non-fiduciary power, was subject to duties of a kind which normally attach only to fiduciary powers. As to (b), the starting point must be that there is in existence a trust to provide pension benefits for a closed class of employees. The obligation of good faith requires that the company should not exercise its rights for the collateral purpose of coercing that class to give up its rights under the existing trust. The duty of good faith requires the company to preserve its employees' rights and pension fund, not destroy them.[243]

11.95 All this is expressed very much in the language of fraudulent exercise of a power. Indeed, although no cases on the doctrine of fraud on a power are mentioned in the judgment, or apparently cited in argument, it is difficult to avoid the conclusion that at the root of the problem in *Imperial* lay a straightforward attempt by the company to exercise its power to give or withhold consent for an ulterior purpose, rather than the purpose for which that power had been conferred.[244] There

---

[240] [1991] 1 WLR 589, 596F–H.

[241] ibid 597F–598C. *Woods v WM Car Services (Peterborough) Ltd* [1981] ICR 666, 670; *Lewis v Motorworld Garages Ltd* [1986] ICR 157.

[242] [1991] 1 WLR 589, 599. See also *Bates v BP Oil New Zealand Ltd* [1996] 1 ERNZ 657, esp 670–671.   [243] [1991] 1 WLR 589, 599D–E.

[244] For the fraudulent exercise of a power, see Chapter 19 below. See also *Re Courage Group Pension Schemes* [1987] 1 WLR 495, 505; *Re National Bus Company* [1997] PLR 1, 19.

was no evidence to explain why the company could not, by agreement with the committee, offer the same benefits under the original scheme that it was offering under the new scheme: so why was the company seeking to induce the members to give up their rights in the fund of the original scheme?[245] The only reasonable inference would seem to be that it was in order to obtain the surplus, which was a collateral and unlawful purpose.

If so, whether the power in question was a fiduciary or a non-fiduciary one would   **11.96**
be immaterial. However, the difficulty facing the judge in *Imperial* was that the case was not argued on the basis of fraud on a power and no conclusive evidence was put before him to that effect. Indeed, much of the judgment is based on hypo-thetical assumptions rather than on proved or agreed facts. Nevertheless, the deci-sion clearly laid down that, in the exercise of a non-fiduciary power or discretion conferred on it under the provisions of an occupational pension scheme, an employing company owes a duty not to damage the relationship of confidence between the employer and its employees and ex-employees; that the company (unlike any other non-fiduciary) cannot refuse to consider the exercise of its power and, indeed, must consider proposals each time they are put to it; and that, although the company could have regard to its own interests in the future opera-tion of the pension scheme, it is required to exercise its rights with a view to the efficient running of the scheme.

The existence of the '*Imperial* obligation of good faith' has been recognized and   **11.97**
approved by courts at different levels, from the House of Lords down, and in many different jurisdictions.[246] In most cases, it has arisen and been applied in some context other than that of occupational pension schemes:[247] indeed, it was plainly imported from the wider field of industrial relations, where its contrac-tual origins are relatively clear. However, it has clearly taken root in the pensions

---

[245] At 599H–600B.

[246] See, for example, *Malik v Bank of Credit and Commerce International SA (in liquidation)* [1998] AC 20; [1995] 3 All ER 545 (CA); *Mahmud v Bank of Credit and Commerce International SA (in liquidation)* [1998] AC 20; [1996] ICR 406 (CA); *South West Trains Ltd v Wightman* [1998] PLR 113; *Laceys Footwear (Wholesale) Ltd v Bowler International Freight Ltd* [1997] 2 Lloyd's Rep 369; *Kevin Adin v Sedco Forex International Resources Ltd* [1997] IRLR 280; *Independent Pension Trustee Ltd v Law Construction C Ltd* (1997) SLT 1105; *Hillsdown Holdings plc v Pensions Ombudsman* [1997] 1 All ER 862; *Wilson v Law Debenture Trust Corp plc* [1995] 2 All ER 337; *McDonald v Horn* [1995] 1 All ER 961; *British Coal Corporation v British Coal Staff Superannuation Scheme Trustees Ltd* [1995] 1 All ER 912; *Auckland Electric Power Board v Auckland Provincial District Local Authorities Officers Industrial Union of Workers (Inc)* [1994] 2 NZLR 415; *Harris v Lord Shuttleworth* [1994] IRLR 547; *LRT Pension Fund Trustee Company Limited v Halt* [1993] PLR 227; *Walden Engineering Co Ltd v Warrener* [1993] IRLR 420; *Woodward's Ltd v Montreal Trust Co of Canada* (1992) 97 DLR (4th) 516; *Stannard v Fisons Pensions Trust Ltd* [1992] IRLR 27; *Re UEB Industries Ltd Pension Plan* [1992] 1 NZLR 294; *Telecom South Ltd v Post Office Union (Inc)* [1992] 1 NZLR 275; *White v Reflecting Roadstuds Ltd* [1991] IRLR 331. See also (1996) 25 ILJ 121 (D Brodie).

[247] In *Malik v BCCI, supra,* for example, the employer was held to be subject to an implied obli-gation not to carry on a dishonest and corrupt business (see at 34–35, *per* Lord Nicholls).

context. In *Hillsdown Holdings plc v Pensions Ombudsman*,[248] for example, Knox J held, where an employer had a power to suspend or determine its contributions to the scheme, such power had been given to it for its own benefit and was therefore not a fiduciary power, but its exercise, in combination with the exercise of a power to adhere further employees to the scheme, was a breach of the employer's obligation of good faith. It was one thing for an employer to take a 'contributions holiday' in respect of a category of existing members and quite another to introduce a large class of new members and take a 'contributions holiday' in relation to them so as to accelerate the effect of the 'contributions holiday' in relation to existing members.

11.98 However, the scope and effects of the duty of good faith remain uncertain.[249] As between the employee-member and the employer, the employer's obligation of good faith is founded on the contract of employment and any breach of that duty would therefore seem to be a breach of contract, in respect of which the employee could recover damages[250] (or even, in appropriate cases, an injunction or specific performance). In this sense, the fact that the obligation is implied, rather than express, seems to be immaterial. Thus, in the same way that an employer who contracted expressly to pay pension contributions of a certain amount could be sued for breach of contract if he failed to fulfil that obligation, an employer who (as in *Imperial*) attempted indirectly to undermine the employee's legitimate expectations under the 'pensions promise'[251] would equally be in breach of contract.[252] In the circumstances under consideration in *Imperial*, the obligation operated, in effect, as a fetter on the exercise by the employer of those powers and discretions conferred on it by the provisions and rules of the pension scheme.[253] There was no obstacle to the assumption by the company of a contractual limitation or fetter on its power which effectively subordinated its own self-interest to the paramount

---

[248] [1997] 1 All ER 862, esp 889–891. See also *Hillsdown Holdings plc v Pension Ombudsman* [1997] 1 All ER 862; *Re The National Grid Company* [1997] PLR 157. Cf *Mair v Stelco Inc* [1995] 9 CCPB 140.

[249] It does not, for example, impose an obligation on the employer to act reasonably: *Imperial Group Pension Trust Ltd v Imperial Tobacco Ltd* [1991] 1 WLR 589; *White v Reflecting Road Studs* [1991] IRLR 331; *Post Office v Roberts* [1980] IRLR 347. But it is an objective matter: *Malik v BCCI* [1998] AC 20. For examples of the application of the doctrine in employment cases, see (1997) 11 Tr Law Int 93, 97 and 102–105 (D Pollard).

[250] ibid. Cf *Burazin v Blacktown City Guardian Pty Ltd* (1996) 142 ALR 144.

[251] See *LRT Pension Fund Trustee Co Ltd v Hatt* [1993] OPLR 225, 265–267.

[252] *Mihlenstedt v Barclays Bank* [1989] IRLR 522, 525 and 531. In *Stannard v Fisons Pension Trust Ltd* [1991] PLR 225, 235, where the question of the employees having a legitimate expectation of benefit from surplus funds was raised and where Dillon LJ indicated that, if the employer were to decrease its rate of contributions, this would 'in some circumstances be a breach of contract with its employees'. See also *UEB Industries v Brabant* [1992] 1 NZLR 294, 297; *Hillsdown Holdings plc v Pensions Ombudsman* [1997] 1 All ER 862, 890; *Re The National Grid Company* [1997] PLR 157; and *Re National Bus Company* [1997] PLR 1.

[253] [1998] 1 WLR 589, 598 (although the analogy with the position of a co-owner of land is difficult to sustain).

interests of its employees who were members of the scheme, and which imposed on the company duties in respect of that power to which it would not otherwise have been subject. As an implied term of the contract, however, such an obligation of good faith may, presumably, be excluded by some express provision to the contrary,[254] whether it be one of general application or directed specifically at the employer's powers and discretions under a pension scheme.

It is clear, however, that, in *Imperial,* Browne-Wilkinson V-C did not regard the implied obligation of good faith as being governed exclusively by the contract of employment. Indeed, he indicated that a claim based on such an obligation need not be founded in contract alone, for the pension trust deed and rules themselves are to be taken as impliedly subject to the limitation that the rights and powers of the company can only be exercised in accordance with the implied obligation of good faith.[255] This extension of the principle was approved in *LRT Pension Fund Trustee Company Limited v Hatt,*[256] where Knox J said that 'the right thus recognised in employees to restrain the employer from withholding its consent in breach of the implied obligation of good faith goes beyond the right to receive the benefits currently prescribed by the Rules and I follow Sir Nicholas Browne-Wilkinson V-C in adopting the view that such a right can arise as a matter of trust law'.[257] **11.99**

Such an extension of the duty seems to be necessary in order to enable those beneficiaries under the pension scheme who were not parties to any contract of employment (such as the dependants of a deceased member and possibly also pensioners) to enforce the duty of good faith against the employer. However, the precise manner in which the duty has become enforceable in trust law remains unclear. It is axiomatic that the employer is not a trustee (indeed, not in a fiduciary position of any kind) and it is clear, therefore, that the court could not provide many of the remedies which would normally be available against a defaulting trustee, such as the removal of the donee and its replacement with another or, indeed, undertaking to exercise the power itself in the face of opposition from the employer. The most plausible analysis is in terms of an excessive execution of a power, ie there is a failure to comply with the implied duty of good faith (or, indeed, with any other implied limitation). On this basis, what the employer can or cannot do in exercise of the powers conferred on it by the provisions of the pension scheme is a matter of trusts law (or the law of powers) as much as contract. Another possible analysis of the situation might be that any requirement that an employer upon whom a power or discretion has been conferred by the provisions **11.100**

---

[254] cf *Adin v Sedco Forex International Resources Ltd* [1997] IRLR 280, 284 (and see the cases referred to at 283–284 generally).

[255] [1991] 1 WLR 589, 597–598. He did not regard himself as bound by anything said in *Mihlenstedt v Barclays Bank* [1989] IRLR 522, 525.   [256] [1993] PLR 227, 255; see also, 265.

[257] See also *Re National Bus Company* [1997] PLR 1, 17.

of the pension scheme must exercise that power or discretion in 'good faith' does no more than confirm that any such exercise must be 'honest' and 'proper' in the sense that it cannot be fraudulent. In other words, the power or discretion was conferred on the employer for a particular primary purpose (broadly, to assist in the provision and protection of rights and benefits under the pension scheme) and it cannot, therefore, be exercised in a manner which seeks to subvert that purpose. However, this analysis is not consistent with the reasoning in *Imperial* itself (where fraud on the power was neither argued nor proved). Moreover, the *Imperial* obligation of good faith is clearly wider than a duty not to commit a fraud on the power, for it effectively imposes a duty on the donee of a non-fiduciary power to *consider* the exercise of that power as and when called upon to do so, which is a duty to which only the donee of a fiduciary power is normally subject.

11.101   Another possible analysis is that, in the exercise of any power conferred upon it under the pension scheme, the employer must take into account all crucially relevant factors and exclude from consideration all irrelevant ones. One of the most important factors is the impact of the exercise or non-exercise of a power on the employer-employee relationship, construed in a wide sense, and, in particular, the preservation of the employer's duty of good faith which underpins that relationship. It is not uncommon, even in the context of family settlements, to confer powers (whether fiduciary or non-fiduciary in nature) which are expressly limited in scope or restricted as to the time or manner of their exercise. In some instances, where such a limitation or restriction is not expressed, it may have to be implied in order to give effect to the underlying purpose of the settlement. Similarly, there seems to be no objection, in principle, to the imposition of a limitation or restriction on a power which effectively compels the donee thereof to *consider* some particular factor or circumstance before he decides whether or not to exercise that power. Indeed this would seem possible whether it is a non-fiduciary power (as in *Imperial*) or a fiduciary power (provided, in the case of the latter, that the limitation or restriction is an essential element of the original power and not imposed later by the fiduciary donee). Moreover, there can be no objection to the donee of a non-fiduciary power entering into an undertaking to *consider* its exercise when called upon to do so (the donee of a fiduciary power already being subject to such a duty in any event), provided he does not bind himself to a particular form of exercise. The reality of the situation is that the *Imperial* duty of good faith involves a willing assumption by the employer of a restriction or fetter on its powers and, indeed, of duties in relation to such powers to which it would not otherwise be subject in the law of powers or the law of trusts. It may be an unusual instance, but it can nonetheless be subsumed under well-recognized general principles, without confining its operation to contract. The alternative view would be that the decision in *Imperial* created a quasi-fiduciary power, one which is clearly not a fiduciary power properly so-called[258] but one which, nonetheless, partakes of some of the characteristics of a fiduciary power, most notably the duty to consider its exercise when called upon to do so. However, it is suggested that there is no need to adopt such a view.

It is also unclear how the duty may affect the trustees of the pension scheme. Such trustees are not parties to any contract; the power in question is that of the employer, and not theirs; and, in any event, in the absence of express provision to the contrary they could not restrict or fetter their own powers or discretions. Therefore, no member or beneficiary of the scheme could have any cause of action against the trustees in the event of a breach by the employer of its duty of good faith. It does not follow, however, that the trustees may not be liable for some associated breach of their own. The employer's obligation of good faith (and, indeed, any obligation founded in the contract of employment, whether on the part of employer or employee) is a material consideration which the trustees ought to take into account in carrying out their own duties and in exercising their own powers and discretions; and, in principle, any failure to do so would constitute a breach of their own duties for which they would be liable to the beneficiaries of the scheme. Thus, if the contract of employment of a particular member of the scheme stipulates that his pay for the purposes of calculating his pension is a lower sum than would otherwise be the case, this particular term of the contract will probably bind the trustees, as would be the case where, under a private family settlement, a particular beneficiary had effectively released or surrendered part of his interest.[259] It was also suggested in *South West Trains Ltd v Wightman*[260] (but without deciding the point) that the trustees of the scheme might be able to resist any claim by a beneficiary to a pension in excess of that provided for in the relevant contract by asking for the claim to be dismissed as an abuse of the process of the court.[261]

11.102

The operation and effects of the *Imperial* duty are not without limit, however. If and to the extent that the employer's duty of good faith operates and is enforceable as part of the trusts themselves, it seems safe to assume that it can be excluded by an express provision to the contrary in the trust deed or rules of the scheme, in the same way that a power which is explicitly fiduciary in nature (and cannot, without more, be exercised for the benefit of the donee at all) can, by express declaration, be exercised in favour of the donee.[262] Moreover, it is difficult to see how

11.103

---

[258] In *The National Grid Company plc* [1997] PLR 157, the Pensions Ombudsman took the view that the duty of good faith was a duty 'approaching a fiduciary duty'. Although Walker J thought that the criticisms of this view were put too high, he nonetheless concluded that the Ombudsman had lost sight of the essential point that a fiduciary power would not permit the employer to look after its own financial interests. See also *Hillsdown Holdings plc v The Pensions Ombudsman* [1997] 1 All ER 862.   [259] *South West Trains Ltd v Wightman* [1998] PLR 113, 132–135.
[260] ibid.   [261] Relying on *Hirachand Punamchand v Temple* [1911] 2 KB 330.
[262] cf *Poole v Trustees of the Cytec Industries (UK) Ltd Pension Scheme*: decision of the Pensions Ombudsman, 16 May 1997, referred to in (1997) Trust Law Int 93, 102 (D Pollard).

any term (express or implied) in the contract of employment could impose direct restrictions on the trustees of a pension scheme or amend the duties imposed on them by the general law, unless the trust instrument itself and the rules of the scheme expressly incorporate such restriction or amendment. Thus, it is immaterial whether the employer and employee consider (and indeed expressly agree) that it is desirable, whether in the interests of enhancing the employer-employee relationship or otherwise, that the trustees of a pension scheme ought to disclose the reasons upon which they based an exercise of one of their powers or discretions. The trustees are entitled to rely on the general and well-established principle of law against such disclosure, unless it is expressly excluded or amended by the trust instrument or rules under which they accepted office and now operate.

12

DISCLOSURE OF INFORMATION
BY TRUSTEES

A. Introduction

This chapter deals with the question whether and, if so, the extent to which **12.01** trustees are obliged to disclose information (in the form of trust documents or otherwise) to their beneficiaries. This issue is connected to a second question, namely whether trustees are obliged to disclose to their beneficiaries the reasons for exercising a discretion or power in a particular way, which, in turn, is connected to the broader question whether any such exercise may be interfered with or reviewed by the court. All these questions clearly overlap; and there is no doubt that the connection between the presence or absence of any obligation to disclose information, on the one hand, and the courts' unwillingness to interfere with or review trustees' exercise of their discretions, on the other, is a close one. Indeed, where the focus of the inquiry is the extent to which a right to disclosure of information is to be restricted by the need to protect confidentiality in relation to the exercise of a dispositive discretion, the issue can often be analysed as an inquiry to determine whether confidential communications are trust documents.[1] It remains the case, however, that they are separate questions and the rule against having to give reasons can be justified on a number of different grounds. It is also the case that, even if a duty to provide information (including the giving of reasons) were imposed, it does not necessarily follow that the exercise of a discretion would then become reviewable, nor that the information, once acquired, could be

---

[1] *Schmidt v Rosewood Trust Ltd* [2003] 2 WLR 1442, 1457. See also *Re Londonderry's Settlement* [1965] Ch 918, 928, 936–937.

used to support a claim for such review. In any event, it is more convenient to deal with these two questions separately; and the judicial review of the exercise of trustees' discretions is considered separately elsewhere.[2]

B. The Orthodox View

12.02 Trustees are obliged to inform adult beneficiaries, properly so-called, of the existence and terms of a trust (which will indicate the interests and rights of the beneficiaries created by the trust instrument), whether or not those beneficiaries have requested the information.[3] They are also probably obliged to tell the beneficiaries the names and addresses of the trustees.[4] In relation to the objects of a discretionary trust or of a fiduciary power, however, trustees are required only to take reasonable steps to inform,[5] so that they are not expected to search out and inform all the objects of their status under the trust. In this, as in other matters, fulfilling the duty is a matter of degree. In any event, trustees are under no duty to give advice or explanations to beneficiaries concerning their rights,[6] nor to advise them that such rights may have been improperly exercised.[7] Indeed, it may be inappropriate for them to do so, for this may well place the trustees in a position in which they are advancing the interests of one class of beneficiaries at the expense of another. As Collins J explained, in *Hamar v Pensions Ombudsman*,[8] trustees are not obliged 'to give information as to how a particular beneficiary may obtain his portion in a particular trust fund or may exercise his statutory rights particularly where, as here, they form the view that it was not in the interests of the remaining beneficiaries that he should be able to obtain the money in question'.

---

[2] See, generally, Chapter 20 below.
[3] See, for example, *Hawkesley v May* [1956] 1 QB 304; *Re Emmet's Estate* (1881) 17 Ch D 142; *Burrows v Walls* (1855) 5 De GM & G 233, 253; *Brittlebank v Goodwin* (1868) LR 5 Eq 545, 550; *Re Lewis* [1904] 2 Ch 656; *Re Mackay* [1906] 1 Ch 25. But see also *Tito v Waddell No 2* [1977] Ch 106, 242–243. Cf *Hartigan Nominees v Rydge* (1992) 29 NSWLR 405, 431–432; *Corin v Patton* (1990) 169 CLR 540, 584; and *Hawkins v Clayton* (1988) 164 CLR 539 at 553–554. Oddly enough, a settlor is not obliged to disclose his trust to the trustees or beneficiaries: *Fletcher v Fletcher* (1844) 4 Hare 67. There is no duty on *executors* to disclose to beneficiaries their entitlements under a will (unless the will expressly requires them to do so): *Re Lewis* [1904] 2 Ch 656; *Chauncy v Graydon* (1743) 2 Atk 616. However, this rule is itself inappropriate in modern circumstances.
[4] *Murphy v Murphy* [1999] 1 WLR 282.
[5] The trustees need take only such steps as are reasonably practicable: *Re Hay's Settlement* [1982] 1 WLR 202.
[6] *Hamar v Pensions Ombudsman* [1996] PLR 1 10–11; *NGN Staff Pension Plan Trustees Ltd v Simmons* [1994] OPLR 1; *Tito v Waddell (No 2)* [1977] Ch 106, 242.
[7] *Hamar v Pensions Ombudsman, supra*; *NHS Pensions v Beechinor* [1997] OPLR 99; *Outram v Academy Plastics* [2000] PLR 283. See also *Miller v Stapleton* [1996] 2 All ER 449, 463; and *Stevens v Montpelier Group plc*, Pensions Ombudsman's determination No M00251, 5 June 2003. If a trustee takes it upon himself to give advice to a beneficiary, which turns out to be negligent, he may well be liable in tort. It may also constitute 'maladministration' within s 146(1) of the Pensions Act 1995. Cf *Westminster City Council v Haywood* [1996] 2 All ER 467, 480, 482 and *Miller v Stapleton, supra*, 463.
[8] [1996] PLR 1, 10–11.

Nevertheless, the orthodox view, at least under English law, has been that a   **12.03**
beneficiary was entitled to see trust documents and to be given information concerning trust affairs; and, moreover, that such rights had a proprietary basis, ie
they were founded on the basis that trust documents were trust property in which
the beneficiary had a proprietary interest. The basic position was summed up by
Lord Wrenbury, in *O'Rourke v Darbishire*,[9] namely that a beneficiary

> is entitled to see all the trust documents because they are trust documents and
> because he is a beneficiary. They are in a sense his own. Action or no action, he is en-
> titled to access to them. This has nothing to do with discovery. The right to discov-
> ery is a right to see someone else's documents. A proprietary right is a right to access
> to documents which are your own.

It has been pointed out recently[10] that this general statement was certainly apposite in *O'Rourke* itself, on the basis that, if the claimant had succeeded in his claim
(alleging fraud against an executor), the grant of probate would have been revoked
and the claimant (and others interested on an intestacy) would have been entitled
to the whole of the estate, including any documents forming part of it. It is not the
case, however, that a beneficiary has an absolute right to all and any trust documents. A beneficiary's individual right 'might in some circumstances run counter
to the collective interest of the beneficiaries as a body'.[11] Moreover, a trustee is not
bound to give a beneficiary information about a share in which he has no interest.[12] Saying that the trustees are under 'a duty to inform' is but the beginning and
not the end of the matter: the kind of information that may have to be disclosed,
and to whom, probably varies with the nature of the trust.

Another limitation on the beneficiary's right to disclosure is the need to protect   **12.04**
the confidentiality of communications between trustees, especially in relation to
the exercise of their discretions. As Salmon LJ pointed out in *Re Londonderry's
Settlement*,[13] because the exercise by trustees of a discretion is not open to challenge in the courts, their reasons for acting as they did are therefore immaterial
and need not be disclosed:

> Another ground for this rule is that it would not be for the good of the beneficiaries
> as a whole, and yet another that it might make the lives of trustees intolerable should
> such an obligation rest upon them...Nothing would be more likely to embitter
> family feelings and the relationship between the trustees and members of the family,
> were trustees obliged to state their reasons for the exercise of the powers entrusted to

---

[9] [1920] AC 581, 626; *AT & T Istel Ltd v Tully* [1993] AC 45; *The Den Haag Trust* (1997/98)
1 OFLR 495.   [10] *Schmidt v Rosewood Trust Ltd* [2003] 2 WLR 1442, 1457C, *per* Lord Walker.
[11] *Re Cowin* (1886) 33 Ch D 179, 197, *per* North J.
[12] *Re Tillott* [1892] 1 Ch 86, 89, *per* Chitty J; *Re Cowin* (1886) 33 Ch D 179. A beneficiary
entitled to capital does not necessarily have a right to see the income accounts: *Nestle v National
Westminster Bank* [2000] WTLR 795, 822. However, this must depend on the circumstances of the
case, eg if there is an allegation that the trustees have failed to maintain an even hand.
[13] [1956] Ch 918, 936–937. *O'Rourke v Darbishire* was referred to by all three judges, but only
Salmon LJ seems to have adopted the proprietary basis expressly (at 937).

them. It might indeed well be difficult to persuade any persons to act as trustees were a duty to disclose their reasons, with all the embarrassments, arguments and quarrels that might ensue, added to their present not inconsiderable burdens.

Similarly, Harman LJ stated:[14]

> This is a long-standing principle and rests largely, I think on the view that nobody could be called upon to accept a trusteeship involving the exercise of a discretion unless, in the absence of bad faith, he was not liable to have his motives or his reasons called in question either by the beneficiaries or by the Court.

Thus, *Re Londonderry* is not so much concerned with establishing the basis of a beneficiary's right to disclosure of information or to fix the limits of any such right, but rather to confirm the principle that there is no right to have confidential information disclosed. In any event, the orthodox position in English law is that a beneficiary has a right to disclosure of trust documents, in so far as they concern him and his interest, because he has a proprietary interest in those documents, but he has no right to disclosure of confidential information (whether recorded in a document or not).

12.05 This position has been criticized on a number of grounds, most of which, it is suggested, have exaggerated the difficulties involved. One criticism is that there is no clarity as to what is or is not a 'trust document'.[15] However, it is doubtful whether this is a serious problem. Prima facie a beneficiary is entitled to inspect, either personally or through his solicitor,[16] all documents held by a trustee in that character;[17] he is also entitled, at his own expense, to obtain copies of all such documents.[18] These include documents creating the trusts[19] (even if the beneficiary's interest has been defeated by the exercise of an overriding power of appointment);[20] all instruments effecting changes in trusteeship; all documents exercising or releasing powers of appointment, at least in so far as the interest of that beneficiary is affected; all vouchers for payments made by the trustees or their agents;[21] and all written notices received by the trustees in relation to that beneficiary's interest.[22] Instructions submitted by trustees to counsel, and

---

[14] [1956] Ch 928–929.

[15] In *Re Londonderry's Settlement* [1965] Ch 918, 935, Danckwerts J referred to one of the definitions of 'trust documents' suggested to the court ('everything in the trustees' hands as such') as 'quite hopeless': 'That will cover practically everything that reaches the trustees in their official capacity, from advertisements for pink pills to blackmailing letters from people who think they have a grudge against the trustees.'   [16] *Re Cowin* (1886) 33 Ch D 179, 186–187.

[17] *Simpson v Bathurst* (1869) LR 5 Ch App 193 at 202; *Bursill v Tanner* (1885) 16 QBD 1; *Re Cowin, supra*, 186–187; *Re Ojjeh Trust* [1993] CILR 348.

[18] *Ex p Holdsworth* (1838) 4 Bing NC 386; *Ottley v Gilbey* (1845) 8 Beav 602.

[19] *Ex p Holdsworth, supra*; *Bhander v Barclays* (1997/98) 1 OFLR 497.

[20] *Bugden v Tylee* (1856) 21 Beav 545; *Newton v Askew* (1848) 11 Beav 145.

[21] *Clarke v Lord Ormonde* (1821) Jac 108, 120; *Re Ellis* [1908] WN 215.

[22] Sections 137(8), (9) and 138 of the Law of Property Act 1925; *Re Postlethwaite* (1887) 35 Ch D 722, 727; *Re Booth's Settlement Trusts* (1853) 1 WR 444; *Hallows v Lloyd* (1888) 39 Ch D 686, 691.

opinions obtained from counsel, to guide them in the administration of the trust (including, presumably, to resolve points of construction) are also regarded as trust documents,[23] but not such as relate to the trustees' own defence in any litigation against them, nor any documents produced in connection with the case.[24] Correspondence (and copies thereof) passing between the trustees and their solicitors relating to the affairs of the trust also rank as trust documents,[25] but not if it relates to legal proceedings against the trustees.[26] Correspondence between the trustees and other beneficiaries may not be so, however,[27] although this would seem to depend on the purpose and content of such correspondence. Actuarial reports obtained by the trustees are also normally disclosable trust documents.[28] Thus, in broad terms, trust documents are documents which are in the possession of trustees as trustees, which record the history and current state of the trusts and their administration, and which would have to be handed on to new trustees[29] (and, indeed, for which such new trustees would have to search, if necessary, amongst their trust papers)[30] if the latter are to be able to understand what the trusts are and have been and what their obligations in respect thereof now are.

On the other hand, trust documents do not generally include the agenda or **12.06** minutes of trustees' meetings, nor any documents which relate to or record their deliberations or disclose the reasons for their decisions or the material upon which they were based. As Sheller JA stated, in *Hartigan Nominees v Rydge*[31] (referring to *Re Londonderry's Settlement*), the 'material upon which reasons were or might have been based cannot generally be withheld, unless it reveals the reasons themselves or the reasoning process'. He added: 'What is restricted is, I think, access to documents which are of a class which would or might reveal the reasoning process of the trustees.' Mahoney JA agreed. Similarly, correspondence and other communications (which, presumably, now extend to electronic communications) between the trustees and individual beneficiaries, of concern only to such beneficiaries and dealing with matters which are either personal to them or affect only their own interests under the trusts, have also been said not to be

---

[23] *Devaynes v Robinson* (1855) 20 Beav 42; *Wynne v Humberston* (1858) 27 Beav 421, 423–424; *Talbot v Marshfield* (1865) 2 Dr & Sm 549.
[24] *Brown v Oakshott* (1849) 12 Beav 42; *Wynne v Humberston, supra; Talbot v Marshfield, supra; Thomas v Secretary of State for India* (1870) 18 WR 312.
[25] *Re Londonderry's Settlement* [1965] Ch 918, 934; *Re Mason* (1883) 22 Ch D 609; *Re Postlethwaite* (1887) 35 Ch D 722.
[26] *Holmes v Baddeley* (1844) 1 Ph 476, 483; *Bacon v Bacon* (1876) 34 LT 349. See also *CAS Nominees v Nottingham Forest* [2001] 1 All ER 954; *Woodhouse & Co (Ltd) v Woodhouse* (1914) 30 TLR 559.
[27] *Re Londonderry's Settlement, supra*, 934. Cf *Tugwell v Hooper* (1847) 27 Beav 348.
[28] *Tierney v King* [1983] 2 Qd R 580; *Hartigan Nominees v Rydge* (1992) 29 NSWLR 405, 445.
[29] *Re Booth's Settlement Trusts* (1853) 1 WR 444.
[30] *Hallows v Lloyd* (1888) 39 Ch D 686, 691.
[31] (1992) 29 NSWLR 405, 445. See also *Wilkinson v Clerical Administrative and Related Employees Superannuation Pty Ltd* [1998] 79 FCR 469, 480; *Attorney-General v Breckler* [1999] 197 CLR 83, 99. Cf *Telstra Super Pty Ltd v Flegeltaub* [2000] 2 VR 276, 286.

trust documents[32] and which therefore need not be disclosed to other beneficiaries. These are flexible propositions, however, and the purpose of the document or the surrounding circumstances may be such that the beneficiaries can claim that a document is a trust document which they are entitled to inspect. Only in unusual circumstances is it likely that there will be an issue as to whether a particular document is or is not a 'trust document' and, even then, it is certainly not beyond the wit of a judge to resolve it easily.

12.07 The equation of rights of inspection of trust documents with the beneficiaries' equitable rights of property has also been criticized on a number of grounds.[33] One objection is that beneficiaries who have an equitable proprietary interest in the assets of their trust are not entitled, while the trust continues to exist, to possession of those assets, and the same principle should apply to trust documents. However, this, too, exaggerates the problem unduly. Surely, it has never been seriously argued that actual possession of original trust documents (as opposed to copies thereof or details of the information contained therein) should vest in the beneficiaries (at least, not until the trust terminates).[34] Another objection is that, if the question is made to hinge on the existence of a trust document, it seems to follow that an absurd distinction would have to be drawn between reasons which have been reduced into writing (and which would then be disclosable) and those which have not (which would not have to be disclosed).[35] However, this again adopts too literal an approach. The relevant 'property' may, in some circumstances, be the actual trust documents but, in most instances, it is the *information* which those documents contain that matters; and information can be as much trust 'property' as the documents themselves or any other asset.[36] The crucial question in relation to information is usually whether it is confidential (and therefore non-disclosable) or not (and therefore disclosable); and this question has to be resolved irrespective of whether the information is recorded in a document or not.

12.08 A more fundamental objection is that the property-based approach necessarily prevents the objects of discretionary trusts (and also objects of powers of appointment) from being able to claim any right to disclosure of information. In *Re Londonderry* itself, the claim for disclosure was made by a beneficiary with an entitlement in default, and not by an object of a discretionary trust or power. If the right of inspection is founded on a proprietary interest in such documents, it is

---

[32] *Re Londonderry's Settlement, supra*, 934, 935.
[33] See, for example, Ford and Lee, *Principles of the Law of Trusts* (2nd edn: looseleaf) 423.
[34] In *O'Rourke v Darbishire* [1920] AC 581, for example, Lord Parmoor referred (at 619–620) to a beneficiary's entitlement 'to the production *for inspection* of all documents relating to the affairs of the trust'; and even Lord Wrenbury (at 626–627) referred to the beneficiary's right as one 'to *access* to them'. See also *Breen v Williams* (1996) 186 CLR 71, 89; *Rouse v IOOF Australia Trustees* (1999) 73 SASR 484. [35] *Re Londonderry's Settlement* [1965] Ch 918, 937.
[36] *Boardman v Phipps* [1967] 2 AC 46. See also *Hartigan Nominees Pty Ltd v Rydge* (1992) 29 NSWLR 405, 435 and 444.

said that it must be denied to such objects because they cannot be said to have a proprietary interest in the assets held by trustees;[37] and such a conclusion would be harsh and unfair. However, the property-based analysis does not demand such an extreme conclusion, for it all depends on the meaning attached to the word 'property' in this context. The nature of the 'interest' and rights of an object of a discretionary trust is dealt with in greater detail elsewhere.[38] For present purposes, it will suffice to say that it does not follow that, because the object of a discretionary trust or mere power has no fixed or ascertainable entitlement in or to the trust fund, his rights (even if unassignable) are not proprietary rights. An object of a discretionary trust has, at least, a right to call on the trustee to administer the trust properly, to account for his dealings with the trust property, and to enforce the exercise of the trustee's discretion. He has an expectancy, an equitable chose in action which cannot be assigned and which ceases to exist upon the object's death, but which is nonetheless proprietary in nature. This chose in action is surely sufficiently 'proprietary' to enable such an object to call for the disclosure of relevant documents and information relating to the trust in so far as it concerns him.[39]

Indeed, in the recent case of *Murphy v Murphy*,[40] Neuberger J concluded that a **12.09** discretionary object was entitled to require trustees to provide information as to the nature and value of trust property, the trust income, and how it had been invested and distributed. The claimant wished to find out what had happened to the trust assets and also to make out a case as to why he should receive some of those funds. It was held that the court had a broad equitable jurisdiction to order a third party to disclose to the object the names and addresses of the trustees of the settlement. However, Neuberger J emphasized that the court had a discretion, essentially as part of its jurisdiction to control trusts, whether to order such disclosure or not; and, in the circumstances of the case, he ordered disclosure of the identity of the trustees of one settlement but not of another. Nevertheless, *Murphy* is simply a case on the proper administration of the trust: it contains nothing on the question of disclosure of reasons for the exercise of a discretion, nor indeed on the disclosure of confidential information generally. Nor does it suggest that a trustee is under any obligation greater than the duty to give information to the object who has asked for (and, of course, is entitled to) it: the trustee is not necessarily under a duty to search out all objects in order to apprise them of their rights.

Pension schemes might have been regarded differently from traditional family **12.10** settlements, on the basis that the members of such schemes may have provided some

---

[37] See, however, *Spellson v George* (1987) 11 NSWLR 300, 315–316.
[38] See paras 7.20–7.38 above.
[39] *Murphy v Murphy* [1999] 1 WLR 282; *Stuart-Hutcheson v Spread Trustee Co Ltd* [2002] WTLR 1213. See also *Millar v Hornsby* (2000) 3 ITELR 81.   [40] [1999] 1 WLR 282.

form of consideration for their rights and benefits under that scheme.[41] However, it is the orthodox approach of English law that has been held to apply to the trustees of pension funds. In *Wilson v Law Debenture Trust Corpn plc*,[42] the plaintiffs were former employees of Company A who had contributed to the company's pension scheme. The defendant was the trustee of that scheme. Company A sold the relevant business to Company B, and employees were transferred to Company B and became members of that company's own scheme. Company A's scheme was in substantial actuarial surplus. The trustee determined to transfer to the new scheme an amount calculated on the 'past service reserve' method in respect of the transferred employees.[43] The effect was to leave substantially the whole of the surplus funds in Company A's scheme. Two members then asked the transferring trustee to disclose to them all the documents in the trustee's possession, including minutes of trustee meetings, which might indicate the reason for the determination. The trustee, relying on *Re Londonderry*, refused, on the basis that it was not required to disclose documents which would disclose the trustee's reasons for exercising its discretion in the way that it did. The plaintiffs therefore brought proceedings for an order to compel such disclosure. Rattee J held that, where a discretion was entrusted to a trustee by the relevant trust instrument, the trustee was not required to give reasons for the exercise of that discretion 'and, in the absence of evidence (apart from such disclosure) that the trustee had acted improperly, whether from an improper motive or by taking account of factors which the trustee should not have taken into account or not taking into account factors which the trustee should have taken into account,[44] the court would not interfere with the exercise of the trustee's discretion since, in general, the principles applicable to private trusts as a matter of trust law applied equally to pension schemes. In the absence of any impropriety, the trustee was under no obligation to disclose documents containing evidence of its reasons for the manner in which it exercised its discretion. Rattee J accepted that a pension scheme differs from a private trust in that, in particular, the members of a pension scheme have purchased their interests. However, even in this context, the crucial question is what is the nature of the interest which they have purchased; and this depends 'upon the

---

[41] Trustees and managers of occupational pension schemes are subject to statutory requirements with regard to the disclosure of information about such schemes to members: see s 41 of the Pensions Act 1995; ss 113–117 of the Pension Schemes Act 1993; the Occupational Pension Schemes (Disclosure of Information) Regulations 1996, SI 1996 1655.

[42] [1995] 2 All ER 337. See also *Tierney v King* [1983] Qd R 580; *Stuart v Armourguard Security* [1996] 1 NZLR 484; *Crowe v Stevedoring Employees Retirement Fund* [2003] PLR 343.

[43] The trustees' discretion, as set out in Clause 22(b) of the scheme's trust deed ([1995] 2 All ER 337, 340), did not confer an absolute discretion: the relevant words were 'as the Trustee determines to be appropriate' (having taken actuarial advice).

[44] As was the case in *Kerr v British Leyland (Staff) Trustees Ltd* (CA, 26 March 1986) and *Stannard v Fisons Pension Trust Ltd* [1991] PLR 225, [1992] IRLR 27.

application to the relevant trust instrument . . . of well-established principles of trust law'. He added:[45]

> It would . . . be wrong in principle to hold that the long-established principles of trust law as to the exercise by trustees of discretions conferred on them by their trust instruments, in the context of which parties to a pension scheme such as the present entered into those schemes, no longer apply to them and that the trustees are under more onerous obligations to account to their beneficiaries than they could have appreciated when appointed, on the basis of the relevant trust law as it has stood for so long.

This decision has been criticized,[46] partly on the specific ground that it treats *Re Londonderry* as a more precise and definitive statement of principle than it may be and partly on the more general and somewhat nebulous ground that it did not distinguish sufficiently (or at all) between the basic principles of trust law and those specialist rules developed in relation to traditional trusts.[47] In any event, whether such criticisms are justified or not,[48] *Wilson* is a straightforward illustration of one aspect of the orthodox approach to the question of disclosure of information, ie that no beneficiary[49] is entitled to compel a trustee to disclose his reasons for exercising a discretion.

C. Other Analyses

Other jurisdictions have adopted a different analysis which, in essence, is that **12.11** the trustee's duty to disclose trust information is one aspect of his wider fiduciary duty to administer and carry out his trust—a duty which he owes both to a beneficiary with a proprietary interest and to a discretionary object. Sometimes, this is described as a corollary of the trustee's duty to account.[50] However, it must clearly be broader than this, for a duty to account does not necessarily extend to or include a duty to disclose all trust information (and certainly not what may be regarded as confidential information). In Ireland, for example, in *Chaine-Nickson v Bank of Ireland*,[51] the disclosure of information by trustees, even to the object of a discretionary trust, has been held to be part of their duty to account for their management of the trust fund, and not to be dependent upon

---

[45] [1995] 2 All ER 337, 348. See also *Caboche v Ramsay* (1993) 119 ALR 215, 228.

[46] See, for example, Robert Walker, 'Some Trust Principles in the Pensions Context' in *Trends in Contemporary Trust Law* (Oxford, 1996) 131; also [1997] JBL 514 (M Thomas).

[47] See *Target Holdings v Redferns* [1996] AC 421, 435. Cf *R v Commonalty and Citizens of the City of London, ex p Matson* [1996] 3 Admin LR 49 (a public law case with different considerations).

[48] See further GW Thomas, *Powers* (Sweet & Maxwell, 1998) ('*Thomas*') 372–374.

[49] Not even one with a vested and absolute interest in the trust fund.

[50] *Low v Bouverie* [1891] 3 Ch 82, 99. Taken out of context, a requirement that a trustee is 'accountable' for his actions is potentially misleading: it may indicate the narrow duty 'to keep and produce accounts' or a broad requirement to justify and explain all the trustee's decisions and actions; and, without more, a 'duty to account' may be meaningless. [51] [1976] IR 393.

the existence of a proprietary interest. In New South Wales, in *Spellson v George*,[52] Powell J stated:

> The question then is, whether a person whose status is only that of a potential object of the exercise of a discretionary power can properly be regarded as one of the *cestuis que trust* of the relevant trustee. I do not doubt that he can, and should, properly be so regarded, for although it is true to say that, unless, and until, the trustee exercises his discretion in his favour, he has no right to receive, and enjoy, any part of the capital or income of the trust fund, it does not follow that, until that time arises, he has no rights against the trustee. On the contrary, it is clear that the object of a discretionary trust, even before the exercise of the trustee's discretion in his favour, does have rights against the trustee . . . —those rights, so it seems to me, are not restricted to the right to have the trustee *bona fide* consider whether or not to exercise his (the trustee's) discretion in his (the object's) favour, but extend to the right to have the trust property properly managed and to have the trustee account for his management . . .

Similarly, in *Hartigan Nominees Pty Ltd v Rydge*,[53] where the issue concerned the disclosure of a memorandum of wishes addressed to the trustees by the real settlor, Kirby P (dissenting) stated:[54]

> I do not consider that it is imperative to determine whether that document is a 'trust document' (as I think it is) or whether the respondent, as a beneficiary, has a proprietary interest in it (as I am also inclined to think he does). Much of the law on the subject of access to documents has conventionally been expressed in terms of the 'proprietary interest' in the document of the party seeking access to it. Thus, it has been held that a *cestui que trust* has a 'proprietary right' to seek all documents relating to the trust: see *O'Rourke v Darbishire* [1920] AC 581, 601, 603. This approach is unsatisfactory. Access should not be limited to documents in which a proprietary right may be established. Such rights may be *sufficient*; but they are not *necessary* to a right of access which the courts will enforce to uphold the *cestui que trust's* entitlement to a reasonable assurance of the manifest integrity of the administration of the trust by the trustees.

Kirby P agreed with the comments on this issue made in Ford and Lee's *Principles of the Law of Trusts*,[55] namely:

> The beneficiary's rights to inspect trust documents are founded therefore not upon any equitable proprietary right which he or she may have in respect of those documents but upon the trustee's fiduciary duty to keep the beneficiary informed and to render accounts. It is the extent of that duty that is in issue.

12.12 And in Canada, in *Attorney-General of Ontario v Stavro*,[56] a case involving an application for disclosure by a beneficiary with a contingent interest in an unadministered estate, Lederman J considered that a proprietary basis for a right to disclosure 'leads one astray'.

---

[52] (1987) 11 NSWLR 300, 316.   [53] (1992) 29 NSWLR 405.   [54] ibid 421.
[55] 2nd edn (Sydney 1990) 425.
[56] (1995) 119 DLR (4th) 750, 756. Cf *Lawrence v Berbrier* (2002) 5 ITELR 9.

It must be asked, however, whether this alternative basis actually amounts to any- **12.13**
thing different in substance from an extension, and therefore an endorsement, of
the proprietary analysis.[57] The objects of discretionary trusts (and of fiduciary
mere powers of appointment) have various rights against the trustees (and others),
including the right to insist upon the proper administration of the trust and, as a
corollary, a right to require the trustees to account for their stewardship and management of the trust property.[58] If such rights can properly be categorized as 'proprietary' in nature—and it is suggested that they can be[59]—then the 'alternative'
analysis seems consistent with the 'proprietary' one. Moreover, the alternative
analysis does not seem to make it any easier to distinguish between what is disclosable and what is not. 'Information'—indeed, 'trust information'—takes many
different forms. The difficulty of deciding whether certain information is
confidential or not and, if it is, whether it is disclosable remains as great.

D. The Current Position in English Law: A Different Approach?

In the recent case of *Schmidt v Rosewood Trust Ltd*,[60] the Privy Council reviewed **12.14**
the law on this subject and suggested a radically different basis for a trustee's duty
to disclose information. *Rosewood* involved an appeal to the Privy Council from
the Isle of Man, in which the petitioner sought disclosure of documents relating
to two settlements of which his late father had been a co-settlor and under which
he claimed discretionary interests, both in his own capacity and as the administrator of his father's estate. The respondent trustees opposed disclosure on the
ground that the petitioner was not a beneficiary under the settlements and his
father was never more than an object of a power and, as such, had no entitlement
to trust documents or information. An order for disclosure was made by the High
Court of the Isle of Man but set aside on appeal to the Staff of Government
Division. The Privy Council allowed the appeal and remitted the matter for
further consideration by the High Court.

According to the Privy Council, although a beneficiary's right to seek disclosure of **12.15**
trust documents could be described as a proprietary right, it was best approached
as one aspect of the court's inherent jurisdiction to supervise and, if appropriate,
intervene in the administration of a trust, including a discretionary trust.
The jurisdiction did not depend on any distinction between transmissible and

---

[57] cf *Breen v Williams* (1996) 186 CLR 71, 89; *Rouse v IOOF Australia Trustees* (1999) 73 SASR 484.
[58] In *Hartigan Nominees, supra*, 421, Kirby P stated that a proprietary right was not necessary
to 'a right of access which the courts will enforce to uphold the *cestui que trust's* entitlement to a
reasonable assurance of the manifest integrity of the administration of the trust by the trustees'.
See also *Murphy v Murphy* [1999] 1 WLR 282.
[59] See paras 7.20–7.38 above. It is submitted that such rights are 'proprietary' even if they are
non-assignable (which is itself not an absolute proposition).   [60] [2003] 2 WLR 1442.

non-transmissible or discretionary interests, or between the rights of an object of a discretionary trust and those of an object of a mere power of a fiduciary character. 'The object of a discretion (including a mere power) may also be entitled to protection from a court of equity, although the circumstances in which he may seek protection, and the nature of the protection he may expect to obtain, will depend on the court's discretion . . .'.[61] No beneficiary had an absolute right to disclosure of information. Lord Walker pointed out[62] that recent Commonwealth authorities (which were extensively quoted and which were clearly influential) confirmed that

> no beneficiary (and least of all a discretionary object) has any entitlement as of right to disclosure of anything which can plausibly be described as a trust document. Especially when there are issues as to personal or commercial confidentiality, the court may have to balance the competing interests of different beneficiaries, the trustees themselves, and third parties. Disclosure may have to be limited and safeguards may have to be put in place. Evaluation of the claims of a beneficiary (and especially of a discretionary object) may be an important part of the balancing exercise which the court has to perform on the materials placed before it. In many cases the court may have no difficulty in concluding that an applicant with no more than a theoretical possibility of benefit ought not to be granted any relief.

Disclosure of information is, therefore, within the discretion of the court. How should the court exercise its discretion in such cases? According to Lord Walker:[63]

> There are three such areas in which the court may have to form a discretionary judgment: whether a discretionary object (or some other beneficiary with only a remote or wholly defeasible interest) should be granted relief at all; what classes of documents should be disclosed, either completely or in a redacted form; and what safeguards should be imposed (whether by undertakings to the court, arrangements for professional inspection, or otherwise) to limit the use which may be made of documents or information disclosed under the order of the court.

12.16   Thus, not only has the property-based analysis been abandoned in *Rosewood*, but also an alternative basis for a duty to disclose has been put forward which seems to go much further than the Commonwealth decisions relied upon. The Commonwealth authorities may have ruled out the need to establish a proprietary basis for a right to disclosure, but they are consistent with such a basis. Whether one views those decisions as broadening the meaning of a proprietary right so as to include the rights of the objects of discretionary trusts and fiduciary powers, or simply as declaring that such objects may *also* be entitled to disclosure, the status of those beneficiaries who clearly have a proprietary interest (in the orthodox sense of an actual, assignable entitlement) was not undermined. Indeed, in *Hartigan Nominees Pty Ltd v Rydge*,[64] even Kirby P (dissenting) said that, although

---

[61] [2003] 2 WLR 1458.   [62] ibid 1463–1464.   [63] ibid, 1459.
[64] (1992) 29 NSWLR 405, 421.

access should not be limited to documents in which a proprietary right may be established, such rights 'may be *sufficient*; but they are not *necessary*'. *Rosewood* states categorically that such rights are 'neither sufficient nor necessary': 'there may be circumstances (especially of confidentiality) in which even a vested and transmissible beneficial interest is not a sufficient basis for requiring disclosure of trust documents'.[65]

There may well be good reason to deny a beneficiary what would otherwise be a clear right of access to trust information, but it must be doubtful whether it requires, or even justifies, the broader conclusion that a right to seek disclosure of information is, in all circumstances, an aspect of the court's jurisdiction to supervise, and where appropriate intervene in, the administration of trusts. Indeed, as Lord Hoffmann has pointed out, the Privy Council had merely been asked in *Rosewood* to answer a narrow and negative question, namely 'whether persons in the position of the Schmidts [as objects of a power of appointment] could in no circumstances demand information about the trust'.[66] There was no need to go further. Moreover, by insisting that, ultimately, the disclosure of trust information rests on a broad judicial discretion, the Privy Council's approach seems to place the emphasis in the wrong place: it is one thing for the court to have discretion to refuse to order disclosure in appropriate circumstances (where, presumably, there is a presumption in favour of the beneficiary and the burden of justifying non-disclosure rests on the trustee)[67] and quite another for the right to seek disclosure itself to be dependent on the court's discretion (where, presumably, it is for the beneficiary to justify his claim). It may well be the case that, once the issue is before the court, there is not 'a lot of difference between a discretion to order the production of information and a discretion to refuse it'.[68] However, it is surely a significant difference when deciding whether or not to go to court in the first place. What is needed is a set of general, predictive rules or principles and not discretionary responses to individual applications to court.

It remains to be seen whether the position of a beneficiary with a proprietary interest has been undermined by *Rosewood*. It would also be an odd state of affairs if (say) a beneficiary under a bare trust, or even a beneficiary under a simple

12.17

12.18

---

[65] [2003] 2 WLR 1442, 1459.

[66] 6th Annual Nottingham Lecture, delivered in Miami on 30 September, 2003. Indeed, the Privy Council refrained from deciding whether they were actually entitled to information or what that information might be. It remitted that matter for decision in the Isle of Man after a fuller examination of the facts.

[67] Or, indeed, to order the disclosure of what might otherwise not be disclosable: *Re the Rabaiotti 1989 Settlement* (2000) 2 ITELR 763 (Royal Court of Jersey—jurisdiction claimed to order disclosure of otherwise non-disclosable documents, such as a letter of wishes). Cf *Stuart-Hutcheson v Spread Trustee Co Ltd* [2002] WTLR 1213 (Guernsey, where the position is different); and *Re the M and L Trusts* (2003) 5 ITELR 656.

[68] Lord Hoffmann in 6th Annual Nottingham Lecture, *supra*.

fixed-interest trust, could not simply point to his proprietary interest as the basis of his claim to compel his trustee to disclose trust information. It may be that, in such a case, *Rosewood* will be interpreted as doing no more than confirm what has essentially long been the case, namely that there is a presumption that a beneficiary with a proprietary interest is entitled to disclosure of trust information, but not in all cases and subject to the court's discretion to sanction non-disclosure, ie it is a qualified right. The statement that a proprietary right is not sufficient (to confer an absolute right) is entirely consistent with this view. Moreover, if one were to ask why there should be such a presumption in favour of such a beneficiary, the obvious answer, it seems, is precisely because he has such a proprietary interest. Arguably, *Rosewood* is concerned only with, and should be confined to, claims to disclosure of information made by objects of discretionary trusts and fiduciary powers. Invoking the court's general supervisory jurisdiction so as to assist such objects (in appropriate circumstances) may have been justifiable if the orthodox property-based analysis was not considered sufficient or appropriate to encompass them (as was the case). However, there was no need to stray beyond the specific and narrow issue under consideration and to re-evaluate the rights of all beneficiaries under all kinds of trusts.[69] Nevertheless, the wide terms in which Lord Walker's advice is couched, and the breadth of the discretion apparently claimed for the courts, indicate that this is precisely what *Rosewood* purported to do.

12.19　In any event, *Rosewood* was not concerned with the question of disclosure by trustees of the reasons for the exercise of their discretions. The claimant made no claim for such disclosure: indeed, there is no indication that the trustees had actually exercised any of the several powers and discretions conferred on them by the various settlements. The application was an attempt 'to obtain trust accounts and other information from the trustees of the two settlements' and for 'fuller disclosure of trust accounts and information about the trust assets'. Trust assets had not been fully disclosed, and there was incomplete information about a web of associated companies incorporated in different parts of the world; and the allegation was that the claimant was 'entitled to know what the trustees have done with the money'.[70] The detailed terms of the original order made by the High Court are not set out in the report,[71] but it seems clear that it was not at all concerned with the disclosure by the trustees of reasons for exercising a discretion. The advice of Lord Walker refers to 'issues as to personal or commercial confidentiality',[72] but

---

[69] On a broader level, the decision may even be said to undermine the orthodox view that a trust is, and must necessarily be, an equitable property holding vehicle and to support the alternative view that proprietary interests are not essential, provided there is an effective enforcement mechanism.
[70] [2003] 2 WLR 1442 at 1444G–H, 1445G, 1448G–H, 1449H.　　[71] ibid 1450A–B.
[72] ibid 1463G. The astonishingly brief references (at 1457–1458 and 1459) to *Re Londonderry's Settlement* [1965] Ch 918 seem to be part of the analysis of the basis (proprietary or otherwise) on

in an entirely different context, and there is no reason to assume that he intended to include such reasons within the category of 'confidential' (and, therefore, potentially disclosable) information.[73] Moreover, when he referred to the three areas in which the Court has to form a discretionary judgment in relation to the disclosure of information,[74] there is no explicit reference to the disclosure of such information. Thus, even if some of the reasoning in *Re Londonderry* was regarded as inconclusive, there is no reason to assume that the Privy Council disapproved of the decision or sought to restrict the protection afforded to trustees in the exercise of their dispositive discretions. Nevertheless, *Rosewood* raises the possibility that the courts may now invoke the same broad, discretionary jurisdiction so as to intervene in areas of trust administration which have, hitherto, been beyond reach.

12.19A The post-*Rosewood* status of *Re Londonderry* has been considered in Australia in *Crowe v Stevedoring Employees Retirement Fund*,[75] where Balmford J in the Supreme Court of Victoria followed the majority decision in *Hartigan Nominees* (which had held that a letter of wishes need not be disclosed) and concluded that *Re Londonderry* continued to apply in Australia. In the event, the material under scrutiny (including an actuarial report) was ordered to be disclosed, but only because there was no evidence that it revealed the reasons for any decision of the trustee. It is suggested that the position ought to be the same in England. Thus, letters of wishes, for example, should continue not to be disclosable, as in *Hartigan*, if they constitute (as they usually do) 'documents which evidence the reasons why trustee have made their decisions', as opposed to 'material obtained by trustees to assist them in administering the trust'.

12.19B A similar conclusion was reached in the High court of New Zealand, in *Foreman v Kingstone*,[75A] in which Potter J adopted *Rosewood* and held that discretionary objects were entitled to receive information which would enable them to ensure the accountability of the trustees in terms of the trust deed. They were entitled to have the trust property properly managed and to have the trustees account for their management. These rights were subject to the discretion of the court when trustees sought directions or beneficiaries sought relief against refusal by trustees to disclose, and the court could take into account: whether there were issues of personal or commercial confidentiality; the nature of the interests of the beneficiaries seeking access; the impact on the trustees, other beneficiaries, and

which a claim for disclosure of trust information might be made. Lord Walker did not (and did not need to) conclude that, once a non-proprietary basis for the claim was accepted, 'confidentiality in communications between trustees as to their exercise of their dispositive discretions' might then be potentially disclosable too.

[73] These words seem to refer, for example, to information about one beneficiary and his circumstances which is of no concern to another, private communications to the trustees from other beneficiaries, letters of wishes, and so forth. [74] ibid 1459; and see para 12.15 above.
[75] [2003] PLR 343. [75A] [2004] 1 NZLR 841.

third parties; whether some or all of the documents could be disclosed in full or redacted from; whether safeguards could be imposed on the use of the trust documents; and whether, in the case of a family trust, disclosure would be likely to embitter feelings and relationships between the trustees and beneficiaries to the detriment of the beneficiaries as a whole. It was a fundamental duty of trustees to inform beneficiaries of their rights, which must carry with it the right for the beneficiaries to inspect documents of the trust from which their rights may be deduced and the rendering of trust accounts. Moreover, he accepted that the right of a beneficiary to trust information was not founded on any proprietary interest but was, rather, an aspect of the court's inherent jurisdiction to supervise the administration of trusts.[75B] However, Potter J also clearly accepted that *Rosewood* had no effect on the right of trustees not to disclose their *reasons* for exercising their powers and discretions. Beneficiaries had to respect the autonomy of the trustees pursuant to broad discretions conferred on them by the trust instrument. Consequently, in *Foreman v Kingstone* itself, the judge ordered disclosure of financial information, accounts covering winding up of the trusts and distributions, details of beneficiaries to whom distributions had been made, legal opinions obtained by the trustees for the purposes of their trusts and funded from trust funds, deeds of appointment of trustees, details of the trustees' reasons for the exercise of their discretions (as distinct from information which informed their decisions), including their reasons for making distributions and decisions relating to the management of the trust property.

E. Exclusion of The Right of Access to Trust Information

12.20 It has been argued that the claimant's right to information ought to depend on what information the settlor intended him to have, instead of the broad discretionary approach based on the distinction between trusts and powers; and that, even under the *Rosewood* approach, the settlor's intention should be the clearest guide to the exercise of the court's general discretion, because such intention lies at the foundation of the trust obligation and the extent thereof.[76] Indeed, there is probably little doubt that a settlor can go a long way towards excluding or restricting a beneficiary's, or object's, right to trust information.[77] On the other hand, it has been pointed out[78] that such a view may be excellent advice in theory but it soon runs into practical difficulties. The settlement may not say anything about the matter, in which case it may be difficult to discern the settlor's intention.

[75B] Potter J seems to have rejected the argument that there was a distinction (alleged to have been confirmed in *Rosewood*) between 'core trust documents', which trustees were obliged to disclose, and those 'which may only peripherally be included within the category of trust documents', which were not subject to automatic disclosure.

[76] See [2003] 10 JITCP 139 (DJ Dayton).

[77] See for example, *Tierney v King* [1983] 2 Qd R 580; *Hartigan Nominees v Rydge* (1992) 29 NSWLR 405, 446.   [78] Lord Hoffmann in 6th Annual Nottingham Lecture, *supra*.

It would not be safe to assume that, because the settlor conferred a fiduciary power rather than imposed a discretionary trust, he was actually signalling his intentions about disclosure of information (especially if, as in *Rosewood*, the settlor is a Russian oligarch and the drafting of the settlement was plainly 'miserable'). There may even be a problem of finding out who the settlor actually was.

There seems little doubt that, even if *Rosewood* takes root in English law, the **12.20A** settlor's intentions are and will be a material factor in the court's exercise of its discretion. However, it also seems clear that they cannot be decisive—especially if the restriction on the right to information may be so great as to render the trust unenforceable and therefore void. In *Armitage v Nurse*,[79] Millett LJ, having stated that, 'if the beneficiaries have no rights enforceable against the trustees, there are no trusts', added that 'every beneficiary is entitled to see the trust accounts'. A right of enforcement is effective only if the beneficiaries not only know that they are beneficiaries but also have a right to call on the trustees to account for their stewardship of and dealings with the trust property. This, in turn, seems of necessity to import a right to call on the trustees to provide relevant trust information. The question therefore arises whether such duties as to disclosure of information as are imposed on trustees by the general law can be restricted, or indeed annulled entirely, by express provision in the trust instrument.[80]

First, it seems clear, following *Armitage v Nurse*, that the duty of the trustees to **12.21** provide the beneficiaries with trust accounts cannot be excluded totally: otherwise, there would not be a trust. Indeed, it also seems to follow that, when *Rosewood* refers to the disclosure of trust documents being a matter within the discretion of the court and not an absolute entitlement, trust accounts must be excluded from the ambit of that discretion or, alternatively, that the discretion applies only where the claim for disclosure is made by the object of a discretionary trust or fiduciary power (and where there is, nonetheless, a beneficiary who is entitled to such disclosure) or only so as to restrict partially the extent of what the trustees are required to disclose to a particular claimant.

Secondly, there may be a distinction, notwithstanding *Rosewood*, between the **12.22** rights to disclosure of a beneficiary (properly so-called) and those of an object of a discretionary trust or fiduciary power, and while the latter may be restricted or abrogated by the trust instrument the former may not.[81] Thus, as long as there is

---

[79] [1998] Ch 241, 255. See also *Low v Bouverie* [1891] 3 Ch 82, 99.

[80] See (1994) 3 Jo Int Trust & Corp Plg 134 (JRF Lehane). It should be borne in mind (as the Law Commission's recent Consultation Paper No 171, *Trustee Exemption Clauses*, makes clear) that such express provisions may take the form of exemption clauses, duty exclusion clauses, extended powers clauses, and indemnity clauses. In this section, references to express provisions include all these possibilities.

[81] See A Underhill and DJ Hayton, *Law of Trusts and Trustees* (16th edn, Buttetworths, 2002) ('*Underhill and Hayton*') 672–673.

an ascertained beneficiary who possesses the requisite rights of enforcement (including the right to call for trust accounts), any such rights as others may or would otherwise also possess can be excluded by the trust instrument. However, this must be doubtful: it surely cannot be an absolute rule. The interests of a beneficiary (or a class of beneficiaries) may differ fundamentally from those of another (or others) and especially from those of objects of a discretionary trust or fiduciary power; and the fact that the former have rights (which they may or may not exercise) to call on the trustees to account may be of no assistance whatsoever to the latter. Indeed, it is not actually a requirement of trusts law that there must always be some ascertained person, at all times and any given time during the duration of the trust, who possesses such rights of enforcement. Thus, a settlor may create a perfectly valid and binding trust when he declares himself a trustee of property which he already owns in favour of his as yet unborn grandchildren, despite the fact that, until a grandchild is born, there is no practical means of enforcing the trust. All that is required is that, at some relevant time during the duration of the trust, there be an ascertainable person capable of enforcing the trust in so far as it concerns or affects him. Thus, in the last example, if the settlor had also created a power of appointment exercisable in favour of his children, pending the birth of a grandchild, it is difficult to identify the principle which would permit him to exclude the rights of any child to enforce the trust against him or to call on him to account for his trusteeship in so far as it affected the rights of that child.

12.23 It is, of course, undeniable that express provision in the trust instrument may restrict or abrogate many of the duties imposed on trustees by the general law. However, it is suggested that the rights of a beneficiary, or indeed of an object of a discretionary trust or fiduciary power, to call on the trustees to disclose information cannot be excluded or restricted in so far as such information is necessary in order to enable that beneficiary or object to enforce the trust and to compel the trustees to account for their stewardship of the trust property (but only in so far as such enforcement or accounting affects his own interests). It is also suggested that, notwithstanding *Rosewood*, the court's discretion in relation to issues of enforcement and accounting extends only to imposing restrictions or conditions on the extent and use of disclosable information, and cannot validate a total abrogation of the trustees' duty to account. If the effect of *Rosewood* is that no beneficiary has an absolute right to disclosure of any trust information, including trust accounts, it must follow that trustees are not under an absolute duty to disclose. Trustees would then have a discretion as to whether to make disclosure or not; and their exercise of such discretion would itself have to be honest and in good faith and so forth. If and in so far as they acted improperly and thereby committed a breach of trust, they could presumably invoke and rely on any available exemption clause exonerating them from liability. However, if this avenue were open to trustees in respect of their duty to account, it would render the core, defining feature of the trust meaningless. Consequently, it is suggested that *Rosewood* cannot, or ought not to, be interpreted as extending this far.

Another issue arises from the common practice of settlors of providing trustees with a letter or memorandum of wishes.[82] Such a document has no binding force. It may also be the case that the settlor has expressly directed the trustees not to disclose its contents to any beneficiary or object. In *Hartigan Nominees Pty Ltd v Rydge*,[83] a majority in the Court of Appeal of New South Wales held that trustees were not obliged to disclose such a confidential memorandum of wishes on the basis that it was not a 'trust document'. Kirby P (dissenting) thought otherwise and regarded the memorandum as 'an essential component of or companion to the trust deed itself'; and the latter, 'being understood in the light of the memorandum of wishes is effectively to be taken to be supplemented by it'.[84] It is, presumably, a question of construction in each case whether such a memorandum is or is not a 'trust document'. However, what lies at the heart of this issue is the broader question whether or not confidential information ought to be disclosed.[85] The majority in *Hartigan* (and subsequently the Supreme Court of Victoria in *Crowe*)[86] followed the *Re Londonderry* approach and held that trustees should not be required to disclose confidential information relating to the exercise of their discretion or the confidential expression of wishes by the settlor. If this remains the position in English law after *Rosewood* (and it is suggested that it ought to be), then a settlor may properly direct trustees not to disclose such information, either within or outside the trust instrument. On the other hand, if *Rosewood* has the effect of rendering such confidential information potentially disclosable, at the discretion of the court, the extent to which a settlor will be able to direct non-disclosure will presumably depend on the same considerations as would govern similar directions in respect of any other form of trust information. In other words, such a direction would not be effective if it prevented the enforcement of the trust or relieved the trustees from their duty to account, or to the extent that it purported to curtail the jurisdiction of the court to supervise and control such matters.

12.24

F. Discovery of Documents in Legal Proceedings

As Harman LJ made clear in *Re Londonderry's Settlement*,[87] 'very different considerations apply when it comes to a question of discovery in an action where

12.25

---

[82] See, for example, *Schmidt v Rosewood Trust Ltd* [2003] 2 WLR 1442, 1444E–F. See also *Hartigan Nominees v Rydge, supra*; and [2003] 10 JITCP 139 (DJ Hayton).

[83] (1992) 29 NSWLR 405 (followed in *Crowe v Stevedoring Employees Retirement Fund* [2003] PLR 343). [84] ibid 419. See also *Talbot v Marshfield* (1865) 2 Dr & Sm 549.

[85] This issue is dealt with in greater detail in Chapter 20 below. [86] See para 12.19A above.

[87] [1965] Ch 918, 934.

a beneficiary is impeaching the validity of the trustees' actions'. This does not suggest, however, that the general rule against reviewing the exercise of a power or discretion, as outlined above, can somehow be circumvented when an aggrieved object or beneficiary commences legal proceedings against a trustee and then seeks to rely on the process of discovery in order to have that trustee's decisions re-opened.[88] Order 24 of the Rules of the Supreme Court (which, it seems clear, is what Harman LJ had in mind) provided that 'after the close of pleadings in an action begun by writ there shall ... be discovery by the parties to the action of the documents which are or have been in their possession, custody or power relating to matters in question in the action'. Order 24 and 'discovery' has now been replaced by 'disclosure' under the Civil Procedure Rules.[89] However, a claimant cannot, by this means, be provided with a cause of action which he did not and could not have had previously. He must still be able to demonstrate a plausible prima facie case against the trustee, as opposed to a speculative 'fishing expedition' which can be struck out. Disclosure applies only to 'documents'. Although it is not confined to paper writings, but extends to anything upon which evidence or information is recorded in a manner intelligible to the sense or capable of being made intelligible by the use of equipment (for example a tape recording or a computer database),[90] it does not extend to information which has not been recorded in any document of any kind. Thus, a beneficiary may obtain discovery from a trustee of what is acknowledged to be a 'trust document' (in the above extended sense) or, indeed, to aid him when he is suing a trustee for any breach of trust. However, as we have seen, a right to production of trust documents is not necessarily the same as a right to information from the trustees. Similarly, an order for the administration of interrogatories to trustees in appropriate circumstances, in order to elicit the discovery of facts, would assist a beneficiary pursuing such a claim. However, as we have seen, even where the reasons upon which a trustee has exercised his discretion are known, the merits of his decision cannot be questioned or reviewed. Interrogatories cannot be administered where there is no obligation to give answers. Rules of procedure are relevant and will assist only where the claimant already has an independent claim or cause of action, such as an allegation that the decision-making process itself was flawed; neither can they provide a cause of action where none could otherwise exist.

---

[88] Nothing in *McDonald v Horn* [1994] OPLR 281 (prospective costs order) affects the above statement.

[89] CPR r 31 and Practice Direction.

[90] *Grant v Southwestern and County Properties Ltd* [1975] Ch 185; *Barker v Wilson* [1980] 1 WLR 884; *Derby & Co Ltd v Weldon (No 9)* [1991] 1 WLR 652; *Dubai Bank v Galadari (No 7)* [1992] 1 WLR 106.

13

THE POWERS OF TRUSTEES: PART ONE

A. Powers Generally:[1] Basic Terminology and Distinctions

Definition of 'power'

The word 'power' is said to be a term of art and means 'an individual personal **13.01** capacity of the donee of the power to do something'.[2] In this sense, it signifies an ability, as a matter of public or private law, to affect property and interests in property or to determine the relations between persons without reference to property of any kind and, as such, is clearly too broad for present purposes. In a narrower sense, the word 'power' has been regarded as synonymous with 'power of appointment', which is 'a power of disposition given to a person over property not his own by some one who directs the mode in which that power shall be exercised'.[3] Not all powers are powers of appointment, or even dispositive in nature, however. A more appropriate definition for present purposes, therefore, is that a power signifies an authority or mandate conferred on a trustee to deal with, as well as dispose of, property which he holds.

---

[1] The law of powers clearly encompasses far more than merely the powers of trustees. For an extensive and detailed survey of the law of powers, including the powers of trustees, see GW Thomas, *Powers* (Sweet & Maxwell, 1998) ('*Thomas*') on which much of this section is based. See also DM Maclean, *Trusts and Powers* (1989); *Halsbury's Laws of England*, 4th edn, vol 36(2) (reissue); Sir George Farwell and FK Archer, *A Concise Treatise on Powers* (3rd edn, 1916) ('*Farwell*'); Edward Sugden (Lord St Leonards), *A Practical Treatise or Powers* (8th edn, 1861) ('*Sugden*'); *Chance on Powers*, 3 vols (1841).

[2] *Re Armstrong* (1886) 17 QBD 521, 531, *per* Fry LJ.

[3] *Freme v Clement* (1881) 18 Ch D 499, 504, *per* Lord Jessel MR; *Sykes v Carroll* [1903] 1 IR 17.

Power and property

13.02 The distinction between 'power' and 'property' is fundamental. A power relates to property which the donee of the power does not himself own beneficially and is distinct from the dominion a man has over his own property.[4] Such a distinction may seem to have little relevance to a trustee, who clearly does not own the trust fund beneficially. However, even a trustee may be an object of a power of appointment over that trust fund. Nevertheless, the distinction still holds and such a power does not make the fund the property of the trustee (or of any other object) unless and until the power is properly exercised.[5] 'The power of a person to appoint an estate to himself is . . . no more his "property" than the power to write a book or to sing a song. The exercise of any one of these three powers may result in property, but in no sense which the law recognises are they "property".'[6]

Classification of powers[7]

13.03 Powers have been classified in a number of ways. Traditionally, powers were classified according to the donee's interest in the property over which the power was given, and were called powers collateral, powers in gross, and powers appendant (or appurtenant).[8] This classification has a residual, albeit minor, significance for certain rare purposes,[9] but in general it has been abandoned. Another, and a more useful and commonly used, classification is based on the purpose for which powers are created or conferred, and distinguishes between administrative or managerial powers, on the one hand, and dispositive powers (often erroneously limited to powers of appointment)[10] on the other. This broad distinction is clearly central to the position and authority of trustees.

13.04 *Administrative* or managerial powers, as their name suggests, are conferred on a trustee for the purpose of managing trust property. Such powers may be created expressly by the trust instrument or by necessary implication or conferred by statute—the most obvious example of the latter being the powers conferred by

---

[4] *Re Armstrong* (1886) 17 QBD 521, 531, *per* Fry LJ. *Commissioner of Stamp Duties v Stephen* [1904] AC 137, 140, *per* Lord Lindley; *Duke v A-G* (1843) 10 Cl & F 257; *Platt v Routh* (1840) 6 M & W 756; *Goatley v Jones* [1909] 1 Ch 557; *Van Grutten v Foxwell (Third Appeal)* (1901) 84 LT 545; *Re Reeve* [1935] Ch 110.   [5] *Pennock v Pennock* (1871) LR 13 Eq 144.

[6] *Re Armstrong, supra*, 531. As a general rule, the distinction applies equally to both general and special powers. However, there are exceptions: see *Thomas* 3–4.

[7] See generally *Thomas* 4–30. Nevertheless, the position may be otherwise in specific contexts (eg for taxation purposes): see *Melville v IRC* [2002] 1 WLR 407.   [8] *Thomas* 4.

[9] For example, infants could (and presumably still can) exercise a power simply collateral, whether over realty or personalty, but could (and can) exercise a power in gross, and probably a power appendant, over personal property only.

[10] Powers of appointment are clearly dispositive powers, but not all dispositive powers are powers of appointment: powers of advancement, for example, are also dispositive powers (though not, perhaps, for all purposes: see *Lord Inglewood v IRC* [1983] 1 WLR 866, 873), and so, too, are powers of selection and nomination.

the Trustee Act 1925. A range of specific administrative powers will be considered at various points in this work.

Dispositive powers are powers which authorize one person to create or dispose of **13.05** beneficial interests or proprietary rights in property which that person does not himself own. In this sense, a common law power of attorney is capable of being a dispositive power. In relation to trustees, powers of appointment, which can subsist only in equity,[11] are clearly the most important kind of dispositive power, although other powers which may have a similar dispositive effect, such as powers of advancement, powers of maintenance, powers to select, and discretions relating to capital or income, are all common and are all considered here.

Powers of appointment have traditionally been sub-classified by reference to their **13.06** objects as general powers, special powers, or hybrid (or intermediate) powers.

A simple[12] *general* power is a power which the donee can exercise in favour of such **13.07** person or persons as he pleases, including himself and his executors and administrators.[13] A truly general power would also permit the donee to appoint in favour of any purpose or purposes, as he pleases.[14] It might be thought that a power which is subject to some restriction or limitation as to the mode or manner of its exercise could not be a general power and, indeed, this is generally the case. However, the law does not always take this view and a general power which is exercisable by will only, for example, is still regarded as a general power[15] (presumably because, when the time for its exercise actually arises, there is then no restriction).

A *special* power (sometimes referred to as a limited power), on the other hand, is a **13.08** power which can be exercised only in favour of certain specified persons (or even just one person) or classes, such as children, issue, or relations.[16] The donee 'is restricted to some objects designated in the deed [or will] creating the power'.[17] The donee of the power may himself be an object of the power, for example a power given by a wife to her husband to appoint to 'any issue of my husband's late father'.[18] Nor is there any objection to a special power being conferred on two or more persons jointly (a joint power).[19] Moreover, even a trustee upon whom a

---

[11] Law of Property Act 1925, s 1(7).

[12] ie, one that has not been given a special meaning for some statutory purpose.

[13] *Irwin v Farrer* (1812) 19 Ves 86; *Mackenzie v Mackenzie* (1851) 3 Mac & G 559; *Re Park* [1932] 1 Ch 580, 583–584; *Re Penrose* [1933] 793.

[14] See *Re Dilke* [1921] 1 Ch 34, 40, 43, where the omission of the words 'and purposes' after 'such person or persons' was considered unimportant. Cf *Re Jones* [1945] Ch 105.

[15] *Hawthorn v Shedden* (1856) 3 Sm & G 293; *Re Powell's Trusts* (1869) 39 LJ Ch 188.

[16] See, for example, *Re Dilke* [1921] 1 Ch 34, 41, 42; *Re Johnston's Estate* (1922) 56 ILT 153; *Eland v Baker* (1861) 29 Beav 137; *Re Gestetner Settlement* [1953] Ch 672; *Re Sayer* [1957] Ch 423.

[17] *Sugden* 394.

[18] *Re Penrose* [1933] Ch 793, 804–805; *Taylor v Allhusen* [1905] 1 Ch 529. Cf *Tharp v Tharp* [1916] 1 Ch 142, 152.

[19] *Re Churston Settled Estates* [1954] Ch 334; *Re Earl of Coventry's Indentures* [1974] Ch 77.

power of appointing the trust property has been conferred may himself be an object of that power (in fact, this is fairly common in the case of both private family settlements and occupational pension schemes).

13.09 Not all powers fit into one or other of these two categories. A power to appoint to all persons except a named or specified person, persons, or class of persons (for example, a power to appoint 'to any person except AB or CD, or any relatives of the said AB or CD')[20] is clearly not exercisable in favour of any person in the world and is not, therefore, a general power.[21] Similarly, neither a power to appoint by deed to anyone other than the donee of the power,[22] nor a power to appoint to all persons living at the death of the donee,[23] is unlimited as to its objects and neither, therefore, can be a general power. On the other hand, none of these powers is a special power in the ordinary sense. Consequently, a third category of powers, that of *hybrid* (or *intermediate*) powers has been recognized, and these are essentially powers to appoint to anyone in the world with the exception of certain specified persons or groups of persons.[24] It is in this sense that the expression is used in this work.

13.10 *Construction and context.* It is a question of construction whether a general, special, or hybrid power has been created.[25] For example, a power to appoint among an unlimited class of objects, and which is subject to no restriction on the manner or mode of its exercise, may look like a general power, but it may still not be one if it is exercisable only with the consent of another person (ie, if it is a 'consent power').[26] There may be a restriction on the power in the form of a postponement of the period of distribution of the property in question, but this will not necessarily prevent it from being a general power.[27] A power may partake of several of the characteristics mentioned above.[28] For example, a power may be given to A and B to appoint, with the consent of C, to anyone except a defined class of persons, which includes A and B. This would be described as a joint, hybrid consent

---

[20] AB and CD often being the settlor and his/her spouse and the trustees of the settlement.

[21] *Re Byron's Settlement* [1891] 3 Ch 474; *Re Park* [1932] 1 Ch 580, 584–585; *Re Jones* [1945] Ch 105; *Blausten v IRC* [1972] Ch 256; *Re Manisty's Settlement* [1974] Ch 17; *Re Hay's Settlement Trusts* [1982] 1 WLR 202.   [22] *Re Park* [1932] 1 Ch 580.

[23] *Re Jones* [1945] Ch 105.

[24] *Re Byron's Settlement* [1891] 3 Ch 474; *Re Park* [1932] 1 Ch 580; *Re Jones* [1945] Ch 105; *Re Abrahams' Will Trusts* [1969] 1 Ch 463, 474; *Re Lawrence's Will Trusts* [1972] Ch 418; *Re Manisty's Settlement* [1974] Ch 17; *Re Hay's Settlement Trusts* [1982] 1 WLR 202; *Re Beatty's Will Trusts* [1990] 1 WLR 1503.

[25] See, for example, *Re Johnston's Estate* (1922) 56 ILT 153; *Eland v Baker* (1861) 29 Beav 137; *Bannerman's Trustees v Bannerman* 1915 SC 398.

[26] *Re Churston Settled Estates* [1954] Ch 334; *Re Earl of Coventry's Indentures* [1974] Ch 77. The position may be different where the relevant consent is required only as to the actual exercise of the power and not as to the selection or approval of the appointee: *Re Dilke* [1921] 1 Ch 34; *Re Phillips* [1931] 1 Ch 347; *Re Watts* [1931] 2 Ch 302; *Re Joicey* (1932) 76 Sol Jo 459; *Re Triffitt's Settlement* [1958] Ch 852.   [27] *Re Keown's Estate* (1867) 1 IR Eq 372.

[28] (1962) 26 Conv (NS) 25, 27 (AD Hughes).

power. Some powers do not fit comfortably in the class in which they have been placed. For example, a power to appoint to a specified (and perhaps narrow) class, but where the donee himself is a member of that class, is still a special power, despite the fact that the donee could appoint the property to himself, as in the case of a general power.[29] A power may also change its status and category as circumstances change: for example, a power to appoint to anyone except a specified person (ie, a hybrid power) may become a general power if and when that excluded person dies or can no longer come into existence;[30] and a power conferred on a spinster to appoint to anyone except any husband she may marry is regarded as a general power while she remains unmarried, but will become a hybrid power if she marries.[31] The classification of powers of appointment into general, special, and hybrid powers is both simple and convenient, but it is not precise or exhaustive. Just as the distinction between power and property, though fundamental, is sometimes ignored for particular purposes, powers of appointment, too, may often be classified in different ways for different purposes,[32] and questions of construction must always be addressed, therefore, in the context of the specific purpose under consideration.

Status of donee. Another basis for sub-classifying powers is by reference to the differences and extent of the duties and obligations (if any) attaching to different kinds of powers, or arising from the differences in status of particular donees.[33] The **13.11** distinction between 'power' and 'trust' is obviously fundamental. A trust imposes an obligation, or creates a duty; a power confers an option. A trust is imperative, whereas a power is discretionary. The court will compel the execution of a trust, but it cannot compel the actual execution of a power[34]—not even where the power is conferred on trustees. However, although the two concepts are fundamentally  different, the dividing line can often be blurred, particularly where powers are conferred on trustees *qua* trustees. Although the trustee then has a discretion which, as a general rule, he is not obliged to exercise, the fact that the power has been conferred on him in his capacity as trustee clearly distinguishes it from a power conferred on an ordinary individual: it has been conferred specifically in order to enable the trustee the better to carry out the trusts imposed upon him. A trustee, unlike an ordinary individual, is therefore subject to certain duties in relation to

---

[29] Indeed, for some purposes (eg, the rule against perpetuities) it would be treated as a general power.   [30] *Re Byron's Settlement* [1891] 3 Ch 474, 480; *Re Harvey* [1950] 1 All ER 491.

[31] *Re Harvey* [1950] 1 All ER 491. Such a change of status is not possible for all purposes, however: see *Thomas* 17–18.   [32] See *Thomas* 13–20.

[33] In broad terms, this is the basis of the classification of powers put forward by Warner J in *Mettoy Pension Trustees Ltd v Evans* [1990] 1 WLR 1587, 1613–1614.

[34] *Re Gulbenkian's Settlements* [1970] AC 508, 518, 525; *McPhail v Doulton* [1971] AC 424, 440–441, 444, 449; *Gisborne v Gisborne* (1877) 2 App Cas 300; *Tempest v Lord Camoys* (1882) 21 Ch D 571; *Wilson v Turner* (1883) 22 Ch D 521; *Re Gadd* (1883) 23 Ch D 134; *Re Courtier* (1886) 34 Ch D 136; *Re Bryant* [1894] 1 Ch 324; *Re Charteris* [1917] 2 Ch 379.

such a power. This basic principle applies to all powers conferred on a trustee, whether they be administrative or dispositive in nature, although, obviously, some powers may be subject to more or wider duties than others.

13.12 *Non-fiduciary and fiduciary mere powers.* Where the power in question is a power of appointment—whether it is conferred on trustees or ordinary individuals—the objects of the power, *qua* objects, are not entitled to any share of or interest in the trust fund, the subject matter of the power. Such share or interest as they become entitled to must be given to them by an actual exercise of the power. Subject to any such exercise, others will have vested, but defeasible, interests in the trust fund.[35] There is a variety of different ways in which powers of this kind can be combined with trusts. For example, there might be an express or implied trust in favour of a class of beneficiaries, subject to a power to exclude some members of that class. Alternatively, a power of appointment might be combined with an express or implied gift in default of appointment. In either of these cases, pending and subject to the exercise of the particular power, someone will have a vested interest in the trust fund, such interest being defeasible (wholly or partly) by its exercise. In the nineteenth century, such a power, being found in the context of a trust, was often called a 'trust power'. However, this is misleading and of little value, for it does no more than indicate that there is a dual arrangement, comprising of a power of appointment and an element of duty, and it does not aid an understanding of the essential nature of the arrangement.[36] Powers of this kind are better regarded as '*mere powers*' and are so called in this work. Such powers may be conferred on trustees *qua* trustees or on ordinary individuals: in neither case is there any obligation actually to exercise the power, but a trustee, unlike an ordinary individual, is subject to certain duties (such as the duty to *consider* exercising the power) imposed by virtue of his status or office. It is appropriate, therefore, to distinguish between simple '*mere powers*' conferred on ordinary individuals, albeit in relation to a trust fund (for example, a power of appointing a trust fund conferred by a settlor on his or her non-trustee spouse), and '*mere fiduciary powers*', which are mere powers conferred on trustees.[37] It is in these senses that these expressions are used generally in this work. However, it is important to appreciate that such expressions are not confined or used solely in relation to powers of appointment. The need to distinguish between mere powers and mere fiduciary powers arises

---

[35] *Thomas* 21; *Re Brooks Settlement Trusts* [1939] Ch 993, 996–997; *Duke of Northumberland v IRC* [1911] 2 KB 343, 354.   [36] See [1984] Conv 227 (R Bartlett and C Stebbings).
[37] It has been suggested (Bartlett and Stebbings (n 36 above) 228–229) that a power of appointment given to a fiduciary as such should be called a 'trust power'. However, it is preferable to avoid using the term altogether if possible. Recent cases (eg, *Re Hay's Settlement Trusts* [1982] 1 WLR 202) use the term 'mere power' in relation to trustees. The expression 'mere fiduciary power' is used here in order to distinguish trustees' powers from those powers (identical in form) conferred on ordinary individuals. Under Warner J's classification in *Mettoy Pension Trustees Ltd v Evans* [1990] 1 WLR 1587, 1613–1614, 'mere powers' are 'category 1' powers and 'mere fiduciary powers' are 'category 2' powers.

from the fundamental difference between the status of their respective donees and this difference affects all powers, both dispositive and administrative.

Discretionary trusts. Trustees may also be given powers which they *must* exercise: **13.13** they may be under a duty to *exercise* such a power but still have a discretion as to the manner in which to do so or as to the choice of objects and so forth. The element of duty (to exercise the power) will be enforced by the court, by one means or another, but there is generally no compulsion as to the manner in which it is executed. Because of this combination of obligation and discretion, such powers were often referred to in the past as 'powers in the nature of trusts', 'powers coupled with a duty', or 'trust powers'. However, in view of the element of duty involved, they are more commonly referred to nowadays as '*discretionary trusts*'.[38]

Discretionary trusts, in turn, are usually sub-classified into two kinds: the '*exhaus-* **13.14** *tive* discretionary trust', under which the trust fund or trust income (as the case may be) must be distributed *simpliciter*; and the '*non-exhaustive* discretionary trust', under which trust property or trust income (as the case may be) must be distributed unless the trustees have power not to distribute it, which usually means that they have power to dispose of or utilize it in some other way, such as, for example, a power to accumulate income. The basic idea in each case, however, is that of a power or discretion that must be exercised.[39]

Powers, express and implied trusts, gifts in default, and discretionary trusts[40]

What this makes clear is that different kinds of obligations attach to different **13.15** kinds of powers and different kinds of trust. It is essential, therefore, that, in order to establish the nature and extent of such obligations and rights, the kind of trust that has been imposed or the kind of power that has been conferred must be determined. In many instances, this task is relatively straightforward. However, the ease and frequency with which powers and duties may be combined within one arrangement often leads to uncertainty and may involve a difficult exercise of construction. This is particularly so in the following cases which, broadly described, involve combinations of powers of appointment and express or implied trusts, powers of appointment and gifts in default of appointment, and discretionary trusts.[41]

---

[38] These would be 'category 4' powers under Warner J's classification in *Mettoy Pension Trustees Ltd v Evans* [1990] 1 WLR 1587, 1613–1614.

[39] Once again, although this applies primarily to dispositive powers, it can, in principle, apply to administrative powers as well.

[40] See generally *Thomas* 58–70; (1962) 26 Conv 92 (MG Unwin); (1967) 31 Conv 364 (FR Crane); (1971) 29 CLJ 68 (J Hopkins); [1984] Conv 227 (R Bartlett and C Stebbings).

[41] See generally *Thomas* 58–70; and also the five types of gift identified by Buckley J in *Re Leek* [1967] Ch 1061, 1073–1074.

Power of appointment coupled with an express or implied trust

13.16 Under this arrangement, there is a direct trust for all members of a specified class of beneficiaries, subject to a power of selection or a power of exclusion of one or more members of the class.[42] In *Re Hughes*,[43] for example, a testator appointed A as his executor and trustee and gave him all his estate 'upon trust for all my children and their issue in such shares and in such manner as I shall by codicil direct or appoint or, failing any such direction or appointment by me, then in such shares as . . . . A shall in his discretion think fit and proper'. In the event, the testator left no codicil; but he had children, grandchildren, and a great-grandchild. Sargant J held that the children and their issue living at the death of the testator were entitled to the estate, subject to the power of selection given to A.

13.17 Where there is no such express gift, the question is whether one will be implied. There are many examples of cases where there was a power to appoint among a class of objects, but no express gift to those objects and also no gift over in default of appointment, and where the court nonetheless implied a gift to the objects of the power equally in the event of that power not being exercised.[44] In other words, these are cases where a trust is implied from the words of the power itself. According to Lord Cottenham, in *Burrough v Philcox*,[45] the underlying principle of such cases is as follows:

> Where there appears a general intention in favour of a class, and a particular intention in favour of individuals of a class to be selected by another person, and the particular intention fails, from that selection not being made, the Court will carry into effect the general intention in favour of the class.

Thus, in *Re Caplin*,[46] for example, property was held for a wife for life and, after her death, for such of the relations or friends of the wife as she should by will appoint. There was no gift in default of appointment. It was held that there was an implied trust in favour of the objects.

---

[42] It might seem as if, in the light of s 158 of the Law of Property Act 1925, there is no appreciable difference between (a) a gift for such of a class as the donee of a power might *select* (an exclusive power) and (b) a gift to the entire class with a superadded power merely to ascertain shares (a non-exclusive power). See also *Farwell* 414; *Gainsford v Dunn* (1874) LR 17 Eq 405. However, as Sargant J pointed out, in *Re Hughes* [1921] 2 Ch 208, 214, although there may not be any difference in the extent of the power, there may still be a material difference for the purpose of construing the gift itself. [43] [1921] 2 Ch 208.

[44] *Farwell* 528.   [45] (1840) 5 My & Cr 72, 92.

[46] (1865) 2 Dr & Sm 527 (next of kin being held to be entitled, the word 'friends' being held to be synonymous with relations). See also *Wilson v Duguid* (1883) 24 Ch D 244; *Re White's Trusts* (1860) John 656; *Stolworthy v Sancroft* (1864) 33 LJ Ch 708; *Lambert v Thwaites* (1866) LR 2 Eq 151; *Carthew v Enraght* (1872) 20 WR 743; *Re Llewellyn's Settlement* [1921] 2 Ch 281; *Re Arnold* [1947] Ch 131; *Re Scarisbrick* [1951] Ch 622; *Re Hargrove* (1873) 8 IR Eq 256; *Sinnott v Walsh* (1880) 5 LR Ir 27; *Perpetual Trustee Co Ltd v Tindal* (1940) 63 CLR 232; and (1911) 25 Harv LR 1 (Gray). A similar approach is used in relation to both settlements and wills: *Lambert v Thwaites, Wilson v Duguid, Re Llewellyn's Settlement, supra.*

This construction is clearly not possible if there is a gift over in default of an exer- **13.18** cise of the power: such a gift over is inconsistent with a trust in favour of the members of the class.[47] This is so even where the gift over is void for some reason: you cannot imply a trust for the objects of the power where there is gift over to somebody else: in such a case, nothing can be implied.[48] On the other hand, even if the donee of the power could have excluded one class entirely from benefit, a gift may still be implied;[49] and so, too, where events have rendered it impossible to exercise the power;[50] or where there is a gift over in default of there being any objects of the power[51] or because of a residuary gift.[52]

In this type of gift, the existence of a power of appointment does not prevent the **13.19** vesting of the trust property in the members of the class until and in default of the execution of the power:[53] they have vested, but defeasible, interests in the trust property, independently of the power.[54] Even if the power is exercisable by will only, this will not postpone the time of vesting, and it is not the case that only those to whom an appointment might have been made will be held to have an interest.[55] If the power to select or exclude is exercised, the interests of the beneficiaries are defeated (or simply varied), either completely or *pro tanto*.[56] On the other hand, if the power to select or exclude is not exercised, the gift in favour of the class simply becomes indefeasible. Thus, if the donee dies without exercising the power, the share or interest of each member of the class becomes indefeasible at the time of the donee's death; and the personal representatives of a member who has predeceased the donee will become entitled to his share.[57] Moreover, the donee of the power under this kind of arrangement is not obliged and cannot be compelled to exercise it: the power is a fiduciary mere power if it is conferred on a trustee *qua* trustee, and a non-fiduciary mere power if it is conferred on an ordinary individual.

---

[47] *Roddy v Fitzgerald* (1857) 6 HLC 823; *Goldring v Inwood* (1861) 3 Giff 139; *Richardson v Harrison* (1885) 16 QBD 85, 102, 104; *Re Mills* [1930] 1 Ch 654; *Re Gestetner* [1953] Ch 672; *Re Lyons and Carroll's Contract* [1896] 1 IR 383.　　　　[48] *Re Sprague* (1880) 43 LT 236.

[49] *Longmore v Broome* (1802) 7 Ves 124; *Penny v Turner* (1848) 2 Ph 493; but cf *Jones v Torin* (1833) 6 Sim 255.　　　　[50] *Carthew v Enraght* (1872) 20 WR 743.

[51] *Re Leek* [1969] 1 Ch 563 (failure of trusts because of uncertainty of objects).

[52] *Re Brierley* (1894) 43 WR 36; *Re Weekes* [1897] 1 Ch 289, 293; *Re Hall* [1899] 1 IR 308. See also *Thomas* 61.　　　　[53] *Doe d Willis v Martin* (1790) 4 TR 743.

[54] *Lambert v Thwaites* (1866) LR 2 Eq 151; *Bradley v Cartwright* (1867) LR 2 CP 511; *Wilson v Duguid* (1883) 24 Ch D 244; *Casterton v Sutherland* (1804) 9 Ves 445 (where all five beneficiaries had died, but all were held to have been tenants in common).

[55] *Heron v Stokes* (1842) 2 Dr & War 89. If, on the other hand, the power is contingent on the donee leaving children, and there is a gift over in the event of there being no such child, no one can take by implication under the power if no child survives the donee: *Winn v Fenwick* (1849) 11 Beav 438; *Stolworthy v Sancroft* (1864) 33 LJ Ch 708; cf *Faulkner v Lord Wynford* (1845) 15 LJ Ch 8.

[56] *Re Hughes* [1921] 2 Ch 208, 214.

[57] *Lambert v Thwaites* (1866) LR 2 Eq 151, esp 155; *Doe v Martin* (1790) 4 TR 39; *Casteron v Sutherland* (1804) 9 Ves 445; but cf *Brown v Pocock* (1833) 6 Sim 257 (which seems to be an isolated decision in favour of a joint tenancy).

Power of appointment coupled with a gift over in default of appointment

13.20 A different form of disposition is made where a power of appointment is conferred on a donee in favour of a class, coupled with an express gift in default of appointment,[58] for example a power conferred on trustees to appoint in favour of the settlor's children and remoter issue, coupled with a gift over in default in favour of the settlor's children in equal shares. Where there is a gift over in default of appointment—whether to the objects of the power themselves or to other persons—the terms of the power cannot operate to vest the estate in the objects of it by implication.[59] (However, a gift over intended to take effect on an event which does not happen will not necessarily prevent an implied gift arising from the terms of the power itself.[60])

13.21 The members of the class entitled in default of appointment, just like the beneficiaries of a direct gift or trust (see above), have vested, but defeasible, interests in the appointable property. The general principle, as stated in *Re Brooks' Settlement Trusts*[61] by Farwell J, is as follows:

> . . . in the case of a special power the property is vested in the persons who take in default of appointment, subject, of course, to any prior life interest, but liable to be divested at any time by a valid exercise of the power, and the effect of such an exercise of the power is to defeat wholly or pro tanto the interests which up to then were vested in the persons entitled in default of appointment and to create new estates in those persons in whose favour the appointment had been made.

13.22 If (or to the extent that) the power has not been exercised, the interests of those entitled in default of appointment become indefeasible. The power conferred in such a case must, by the very nature of the disposition, be a mere power—a fiduciary mere power if conferred on a trustee and a non-fiduciary mere power if conferred on an ordinary individual.

13.23 Where there is no express gift in default, the question is whether one can be implied. According to Lord Evershed MR in *Re Scarisbrick's Will Trusts*,[62] it was 'clear that, where there is a power to appoint among a class, there will prima facie be implied a gift over in default of appointment to all the members of the class in equal shares'. However, such an implication will not always be made. In order to imply a gift in default of the power being exercised, there must be a clear indication to this effect in, and upon the construction of, the relevant trust instrument (be it a will or a settlement).[63] As Romer J stated in *Re Weekes' Settlement*,[64] there

---

[58] See, for example, *Re Gestetner Settlement* [1953] Ch 672; *Re Leek* [1967] Ch 1061, 1074.

[59] *Jenkins v Quinchant* (1745) 5 Ves 596n; *Pattison v Pattison* (1854) 19 Beav 638; *Richardson v Harrison* (1885) 16 QBD 85; *Re Sprague* (1880) 43 LT 236.

[60] *Kennedy v Kingston* (1821) 2 J & W 431.

[61] [1939] Ch 993, 997; see also *Duke of Northumberland v IRC* [1911] 2 KB 343, 354.

[62] [1951] Ch 622, 635.

[63] *Lambert v Thwaites* (1866) LR 2 Eq 151; *Wilson v Duguid* (1883) 24 Ch D 244.

[64] [1897] 1 Ch 289, 292. See also *Re Combe* [1925] Ch 210, 216, *per* Tomlin J; *Re Leek* [1967] Ch 1061, 1074–1075; *Healy v Donnery* (1853) 3 ICLR 213; *Re Hall* [1899] 1 IR 308; *Perpetual*

is 'no hard and fast rule that a gift to A for life with a power to A to appoint among a class and nothing more must, if there is no gift over in the will, be held a gift by implication to the class in default of the power being exercised'. One factor militating against any such implication is the size of the class in question,[65] but even this is not conclusive. The question is whether, on the facts of each particular case, it is proper to infer a gift in default in favour of the objects of the power.[66]

If a gift over in default of appointment is implied, the consequences are the same **13.24** as in the case of an express gift over: the members of the class entitled in default have vested, but defeasible, interests in the trust fund; and, if the power to appoint is not exercised, the gift in default simply becomes indefeasible. The power of appointment must be a mere power (a fiduciary or non-fiduciary mere power depending on the status of the donee).

It might seem as if there is no practical difference between these two types of dis- **13.25** position: in the case of both a power of appointment coupled with an express or implied trust and a power of appointment coupled with a gift over in default of appointment, there is, in effect, a combination of a mere power of appointment and a 'fixed' trust. In each case, the power of appointment is a mere power and the beneficiaries of the trust have vested but defeasible interests in the trust property. However, there may be important differences in some cases, especially where the primary trust or gift in default is implied. For example, in the case of an implied primary trust, coupled with a power to exclude (or select or appoint) which is exercisable by will only, the beneficiaries of such trust are not restricted to those living at the death of the donee of the power, ie those in whose favour the power might have been exercised.[67] On the other hand, in the case of an implied gift over in default, and where the power of appointment is again exercisable by will only, the class entitled in default is limited to those living at the donee's death.[68]

The *time* at which the identity of those entitled is determined—under either type **13.26** of gift—varies according to whether or not there is a prior life interest and, indeed, according to whether it is the life interest of the donee of the power or of some other person. If it is the life of the donee of the power, those entitled are generally ascertainable at the death of the life tenant, and not at the death of the donor of the power.[69] If the life interest is that of some person other than the donee, the

---

Trustee Co Ltd v Tindal (1940) 63 CLR 232, 257; *Lutheran Church of Australia v Farmers' Co-operative Executors* (1970) 121 CLR 628, 638.

[65] *Re Perowne* [1951] Ch 785; see also *Re Combe* [1925] Ch 210, esp 219.
[66] *Re Wills' Trust Deeds* [1964] Ch 219, 230, *per* Buckley J.
[67] *Heron v Stokes* (1842) 2 Dr & War 89.
[68] *Lambert v Thwaites* (1866) LR 2 Eq 151, 155; *Walsh v Wallinger* (1830) 2 Russ & My 78; *Kennedy v Kingston* (1821) 2 Jac & W 431; *Woodcock v Renneck* (1841) 4 Beav 190. Where the power is exercisable by deed as well as by will, there is no requirement that the objects should survive the donee if they are to take: *Re Arnold* [1947] Ch 131, 136. See generally *Thomas*, 64–65.
[69] *Finch v Hollingsworth* (1855) 21 Beav 112.

relevant time is usually the death of the survivor of the life tenant or the donee.[70] Thus, the composition of the class is left in suspense long enough to let in all those who might be born while the power is in existence. This is not an inflexible rule, however, and each case must be decided on its facts.[71] Where there is no prior life interest, membership of the class entitled in default of appointment is prima facie determined at the time when the instrument creating the power came into effect.[72]

Nature of the interest of takers

13.27 Those who take in default (in the case of both a power of appointment coupled with an express or implied trust and a power of appointment coupled with a gift over in default of appointment) will almost certainly do so as tenants in common and not as joint tenants. The fact that the power permits the donee to select objects or to fix proportions is taken to be a sufficient reference to plurality of interest among objects to create a tenancy in common.[73] In general, in the absence of an express indication to the contrary,[74] the court adopts the rule that equality is equity and the property vests in those entitled equally.[75] This is the case, of course, only where the court is simply executing a trust and the power in question is a mere power. In the case of a discretionary trust (see below), the court will ensure, by one means or another, that the power itself is exercised, in default of the donee/trustee doing so.[76]

Discretionary trusts[77]

13.28 Discretionary trusts are dealt with in detail later in this work.[78] At this stage, we shall address only the fundamental definitional characteristics of such trusts. As we have already seen,[79] trustees may sometimes be given powers which they *must* exercise: they may be under a duty to *exercise* such a power but still have a

---

[70] *Re White's Trusts* (1860) John 656.   [71] See also *Carthew v Enraght* (1872) 20 WR 743.
[72] *Walter v Maunde* (1815) 19 Ves 424, 426; *Cole v Wade* (1806–7) 16 Ves 27 (cf Sugden 662); *Longmore v Broom* (1802) 7 Ves 124.
[73] *Re Arnold* [1947] Ch 131, 137, *per* Wynn-Parry J, approving *Hawkins on Wills* (3rd edn) 75, and noting that *Brown v Pocock* (1833) 6 Sim 257 (joint tenancy) was an isolated case.
[74] This might be an indication of unequal shares or of a joint tenancy (see *Brown v Pocock, supra*), or that the division is to be based on a judgment as to certain facts, such as necessity or the circumstances of the family (see *Gower v Mainwaring* (1750) 2 Ves Sen 87; *A-G v Price* (1810) 17 Ves 371; *Mahon v Savage* (1803) 1 Sch & Lef 111; *Hewett v Hewett* (1765) 2 Ed 332.
[75] *Salusbury v Denton* (1857) 3 K & J 529; *Doyley v A-G* (1735) 2 Eq Cas Abr 194.
[76] As in *Brown v Higgs* (1803) 8 Ves Jr 561.
[77] See generally (1957) 21 Conv 55 (LA Sheridan); (1967) 31 Conv 117 (AJ Hawkins); (1976) 54 Can Bar Rev 229 (MC Cullity); [1977] Mon LR 210 (Y Grbich); [1982] Conv 118 and 177 (AR Everton); [1984] Conv 227 (R Bartlett and C Stebbings).   [78] See Chapter 36 below.
[79] See paras 11.03–11.29 above, where it was also pointed out that, in the past, such arrangements were often (misleadingly) called 'powers in the nature of trusts', 'powers coupled with a duty', or 'trust powers'.

discretion as to the manner in which to do so or as to the choice of objects and so forth. The element of duty (to exercise the power) will be enforced by the court, by one means or another, but there is generally no compulsion as to the manner in which it is executed. As Lord Eldon stated in *Brown v Higgs*:[80]

> Where there is a mere power of disposing and it is not exercised, the court cannot execute it; but wherever a trust is created and the execution of that trust fails by the death of the trustee or by accident, the court will execute the trust. But there are not only a mere trust and a mere power, but there is also known to the court a power which the party to whom it is given is intrusted and required to execute; and with regard to that species of power, the court considers it as partaking so much of the nature and qualities of a trust, that if a person who has that duty imposed on him does not discharge it, the court will to a certain extent discharge the duty in his room and place. The principle is that if the power is one which it is the duty of the donee to execute, made his duty by the requisition of the will, put upon him as such by the testator, who has given him an interest extensive enough to enable him to discharge it, he is a trustee for the exercise of the power, and has not a discretion whether he will exercise it or not. The court adopts the principle as to trusts, and will not permit his negligence, accident or other circumstances to disappoint the interests of those for whose benefit he is called upon to execute it.

Under such an arrangement, the donor of the power intends that its objects will take, if at all, under and by virtue of an exercise of that power and not under any (express or implied) trust or gift in default of appointment. There can be no gift in default in this instance, because such a gift would be inconsistent with the essential nature of the power itself:[81] one cannot say that the power *must* be exercised and, at the same time, provide for the eventuality that it is not. The trustee/donee of a pure power in the nature of a trust (or *exhaustive* discretionary trust) is under a duty to exercise the primary discretion conferred on him; and, in broad terms, he must (and not merely may) carry out the obligation imposed on him to exercise the power and distribute the subject matter of that discretion (whether it be trust income or capital or both), although, like the donee of a mere power, he may have discretion as to which members of the class of objects will actually receive some benefit, as well as in relation to the amounts and times of, and perhaps conditions attached to, any distribution. Under a *non-exhaustive* discretionary trust, the trustee has an additional discretion, namely whether or not to make a distribution at all. In such a case, the trustee may, for example, be empowered to accumulate trust income instead of distributing it.[82] However, this

13.29

---

[80] (1803) 8 Ves Jr 561, 570–571.

[81] *Roddy v Fitzgerald* (1857) 6 HLC 823; *Goldring v Inwood* (1861) 3 Giff 139; *Richardson v Harrison* (1885) 16 QBD 85, 102, 104; *Re Mills* [1930] 1 Ch 654; *Re Gestetner* [1953] Ch 672. This is the case even where there is a gift in default which is invalid for some reason (*Re Sprague* (1880) 43 LT 236), although the presence of such a gift will inevitably have some effect on the construction of the arrangement as a whole.

[82] See [1970] ASCL 187 (JD Davies); (1974) 37 MLR 643 (Y Grbich); (1976) 54 Can Bar Rev (MC Cullity); (1990) 4 Tr L & P 177 (F Spearing).

is still a discretionary trust and not a mere power. Thus, if, for example, the trustee omits or fails to take a conscious decision not to distribute, or if there is disagreement among the trustees on the question, a distribution must take place and the overriding duty to do so will be enforced by the court. As we have seen, this would not be the case if the power were a mere power.

13.30 A member of the class of objects of a discretionary trust, like the object of a mere power, is dependent for any benefit upon the exercise of the trustee's discretion in his favour and has no proprietary interest[83] in, or entitlement to, any trust income or capital. Like the object of a fiduciary mere power (but not the object of a non-fiduciary mere power), he merely has the right to be *considered* as a potential recipient of benefit and a hope of benefiting.[84] In certain rare circumstances, the discretionary objects as a class may, however, be said to be entitled to the beneficial interest under a discretionary trust.[85]

13.31 Whether or not a discretionary trust has been created is a question of 'intention or presumed intention to be derived from the language of the instrument'.[86] In broad terms, the issue is whether the relevant provision is mandatory in form. In *Re Saxone Shoe Co Ltd's Trust Deed*,[87] for example, the words 'shall ... be applicable' were construed, in their context, as 'shall be applied' and thereby to constitute an imperative trust to apply. In *McPhail v Doulton*,[88] where the question of construction was said to be 'one of some nicety, and, indeed, artificiality',[89] the words 'the trustees *shall apply* the net income of the fund' were held to constitute an imperative direction to the trustees. There was a primary trust to distribute, albeit coupled with a power to accumulate.[90] In each case, the instrument as a whole must, of course, be considered, and not just isolated expressions.[91]

13.32 Where there is a discretionary trust, the court will ensure by one means or another that it is carried into effect. The power or discretion conferred on the trustees will itself be exercised, in default of the trustees doing so.[92] Until *McPhail v Doulton*,[93] it was thought that the court would and could do so only by making an equal division of the trust fund among the objects; and, indeed, in simple cases, such as small family trusts, this is probably the appropriate course. However, *McPhail v*

---

[83] The word 'interest' is used here in its technical sense. It is not intended to imply that such an object has no proprietary *rights*.

[84] *Gartside v IRC* [1968] AC 553; *Re Weir's Settlement* [1969] 1 Ch 657; *Sainsbury v IRC* [1970] 1 Ch 712; *Re Trafford's Settlement* [1985] Ch 32.   [85] *Re Smith* [1928] Ch 915.

[86] *Re Scarisbrick's Will Trusts* [1951] Ch 622, 635, *per* Evershed MR.

[87] [1962] 2 All ER 904.   [88] [1971] AC 424.

[89] See *Re Baden's Deed Trusts* [1969] 2 Ch 388, 400, *per* Russell LJ.

[90] See [1971] AC 424, 438, 444, 450. Cf *Re Leek* [1967] Ch 1061, 1075 and [1969] Ch 563, 580, 582.

[91] *Re Hain's Settlement* [1961] 1 WLR 440, 443; *McPhail v Doulton* [1971] AC 424, 438; *Pearson v IRC* [1981] AC 753.   [92] As in *Brown v Higgs* (1803) 8 Ves Jr 561.

[93] [1971] AC 424.

Doulton established that the Court could exercise the trustee's discretion, in appropriate circumstances, by making an unequal distribution.[94]

A person who is not a trustee as such of any trust property may nonetheless have been made a trustee of a particular power or discretion, although this would be very unusual.[95] **13.33**

B. Powers Conferred on Trustees as Office Holders[96]

Strictly speaking, there are two related, but distinct, issues here. The first concerns powers conferred on several persons, where the question is whether that power is simply a joint power or a joint and several one. A power may be granted, for example, to A, B, and C, but A may die before the power is exercised, or B may disclaim, or C may refuse to act. The second issue concerns the survivorship of powers. If a power is conferred on A, B, and C, there is a question as to whether the survivor of A, B, and C can exercise that power, but also whether D, E, and F, as their successors, can do so. There is nothing in the nature of a power that precludes it from surviving;[97] on the other hand, nothing in its nature guarantees survival. In broad terms, and subject to statutory provisions, the answers to both questions depend on the intention of the donor of the power, as evidenced by his express words or by necessary implication.[98] **13.34**

Such questions are not likely to be common in relation to trustees. The general principle is that, where a power is annexed to an office—something that may be determined by asking whether the power would have been conferred on the donees 'but for their office'[99]—then all persons who hold or fill that office can exercise the power.[100] There is a presumption that a power given to trustees to enable them to deal with or dispose of the trust property is conferred on them *virtute officii*.[101] Such a power is annexed to the office. Thus, where one of several trustees disclaims or dies, the other or surviving trustee(s) can exercise any power annexed to the trusteeship.[102] The power vests in those who act and the consent **13.35**

---

[94] Even in *Burrough v Philcox* (1840) 5 My & Cr 72, it is not entirely clear whether the court was actually exercising the power itself, but doing so by means of an equal distribution.

[95] See, for example, *Re Mills* [1930] 1 Ch 654, 669, *per* Romer LJ; and *Re Wills' Trust Deeds* [1964] Ch 219, 228, 236–237, *per* Buckley J.   [96] See, generally, *Thomas* 213–217.

[97] *Mansell v Mansell* (1757) Wilm 36, 50.

[98] *Re Bacon* [1907] 1 Ch 475, 478–479. See also *Bersel Manufacturing Co Ltd v Berry* [1968] 2 All ER 552.   [99] *Crawford v Forshaw* [1891] 2 Ch 261, 266, *per* Lindley LJ.

[100] *Att-Gen v Fletcher* (1835) 5 LJ Ch 75; *Crawford v Forshaw, supra.*

[101] *Jones v Price* (1841) 11 Sim 557; *Lane v Debenham* (1853) 11 Hare 188; *Byam v Byam* (1854) 19 Beav 58; *Re Smith* [1904] 1 Ch 139; *Re Bacon* [1907] 1 Ch 475; *Re De Sommery* [1912] 2 Ch 622; *Re Hampton* (1918) 88 LJ Ch 103; *Innes v Harrison* [1954] 1 All ER 884.

[102] *White v M'Dermott* (1872) IR 7 CL 1; *Clarke v Parker* (1812) 19 Ves 1; *Worthington v Evans* (1823) 1 Sim & St 165; *Sharp v Sharp* (1819) 2 Barn & Ald 405. The same applies to powers conferred on executors *virtute officii*: *Re Robinson* [1912] 1 IR 410.

of one who disclaims or renounces is not necessary.[103] This applies not just to trusts, including 'trust powers' or discretionary trusts, but also to mere powers and discretions annexed to the trustee's office.[104] It does not necessarily matter that the office itself will not endure beyond the lives of the persons who hold it.[105] Nor is it conclusive that the power is conferred (say) on the trustees 'and their successors', or on the trustees, A, B, and C, by name (or 'the said trustees' or other equivalent). In each case, the question is the same: was the power conferred on them as individuals or as holders of the office of trustee?[106] A power annexed to an office, and not conferred on an individual as such, may, however, be void as infringing the rule against perpetuities,[107] although administrative, as opposed to dispositive, powers are no longer subject to the rule.

13.36 In the case of trustees, section 18(1) of the Trustee Act 1925 provides that, where a trust is imposed on, or a power is given to, two or more trustees jointly, the same may be exercised by the survivor or survivors of them for the time being. 'Trust' and 'trustee' here include implied and constructive trusts and cases where a trustee has a beneficial interest in the trust property, as well as personal representatives.[108] Section 18(2) provides further that, until the appointment of new trustees, the personal representatives or representative for the time being of a sole trustee or, where there are two or more trustees, of the last surviving or continuing trustee, shall be capable of exercising any power which was given to, or capable of being exercised by, the sole or last surviving or continuing trustee or other the trustees or trustee for the time being of the trust. 'Personal representative' here does not include an executor who has renounced or has not yet proved.[109]

---

[103] *Bersel Manufacturing Co Ltd v Berry* [1968] 2 All ER 552. Section 36(8) of the Trustee Act 1925 provides expressly that, in relation to the statutory power to appoint trustees, 'continuing trustee' includes a refusing or retiring trustee if willing to act: see *Re Norris* (1884) 27 Ch D 333; *Re Coates to Parsons* (1886) 34 Ch D 370.

[104] *Re Smith* [1904] 1 Ch 139, 144; *Crawford v Forshaw* [1891] 2 Ch 261; *Warburton v Sandys* (1845) 14 Sim 622.

[105] *Re De Sommery* [1912] 2 Ch 622; *Kennedy v Kennedy* [1914] AC 215.

[106] *Re Smith* [1904] 1 Ch 139, 144; *Crawford v Forshaw* [1891] 2 Ch 261; *Re Cooke's Contract* (1877) 4 Ch D 454; *Hall v May* (1857) 3 K & J 585; *Lane v Debenham* (1853) 11 Hare 188. Cf *Re Beesty's Will Trusts* [1966] Ch 223.   [107] Perpetuities and Accumulations Act 1964, s 8.

[108] Trustee Act 1925, s 67(17).   [109] Section 18(4). See also s 68(9).

14

THE POWERS OF TRUSTEES: PART TWO

A. Specific Powers of Trustees : Introduction

Trustees have available to them, and may exercise, only those powers as are conferred **14.01** on them by the trust instrument, by statute, and by the court. This basic principle applies to managerial and administrative powers as it applies to dispositive ones.[1] Equity might have taken the view that, because trustees were the absolute owners of the legal estate, they could and should have all the powers of management that any

---

[1] One common classification of powers distinguishes between administrative or managerial powers, on the one hand, and dispositive powers, on the other. However, it must be borne in mind that it is not a technical distinction and that what appears clearly to be an administrative power may have a dispositive effect (eg a power to partition) while powers which are generally clearly dispositive in nature (eg powers of maintenance and advancement) may actually be regarded, for a particular purpose, as administrative ones: see, for example, *Lord Inglewood v IRC* [1983] 1 WLR 366, 373, *per* Fox LJ.

absolute owner would normally have. However, it did not: instead, during the late eighteenth and early nineteenth centuries, there gradually emerged a strict principle that trustees could exercise only the powers actually conferred upon them.[2] The response to such a restrictive doctrine is well known. Trust instruments became longer and more complicated, as settlors sought to make adequate provision for all sorts of future eventualities by conferring an ever-increasing range of powers on trustees; and, gradually, the process was supplemented by a series of statutes (of which the Trustee Act 1925 remains the most important) which expanded the range of powers available to trustees and established a code of 'default rules' on which they could fall back if their trust instrument was inadequate. This is a process that continues to the present day; and many of the powers in a modern trust instrument directly reflect constant changes in investment practices and, especially, in tax legislation.

14.02 As the number and range of trustees' powers has expanded, greater emphasis has come to be placed on the fiduciary obligations of trustees in relation to their exercise. All powers conferred on trustees as such are fiduciary powers[3] and are conferred to enable them the better to perform their duties as trustees and to give effect to the trust. In broad terms, the exercise by trustees of their managerial or administrative powers is subject to the same considerations as the exercise of fiduciary powers generally. For example, they must consciously address their minds, from time to time, to the question whether they ought or ought not to exercise their powers in furtherance of their trust. These general considerations, which are fundamental to the proper exercise by trustees of any powers conferred on them, including administrative powers, are dealt with in greater detail elsewhere.[4] Nevertheless, the basic historical principle remains the same: trustees are limited in what they can or cannot do by the powers made available to them: they cannot act in the absence of authority to do so, not even if they honestly and reasonably believe it to be in the best interests of their trust.[5]

---

[2] See, for example, *Holmes v Dring* (1788) 2 Cox Eq Cas 1.

[3] It is possible, though unusual, to confer a power on a person who is a trustee in a personal capacity; but a power conferred on a person *as trustee* (ie by virtue of his office) is necessarily a fiduciary power.

[4] See Chapter 11 above. The law would be much simpler if trustees had all the powers that would be available to them if they were absolute beneficial owners of the trust property (thereby removing the question of *vires* entirely) and controlled simply by reference to their overriding fiduciary obligations. Bare trustees have all the powers of an absolute owner: Trusts of Land and Appointment of Trustees Act 1996, ss 1(1), (2)(a), and 6(1).

[5] In such a case, the appropriate course of action is to apply to the court under s 57 of the Trustee Act 1925: see paras 24.16–24.18 below. If trustees exceed their powers in the case of necessity, they may subsequently be excused, but their action is still unauthorized and they clearly act at their own risk: *Harrison v Randall* (1852) 9 Hare 397; *Forshaw v Higginson* (1857) 8 De GM & G 827. See also s 61 of the Trustee Act 1925.

Trustees must familiarize themselves, therefore, with the nature and scope of the **14.03** powers conferred on them by the trust instrument and by law. The administrative powers contained in modern trust instruments often vary slightly in order to reflect and fit in with the particular beneficial provisions of the individual settlement,[6] but they generally tend to be in standard form.[7] Such express powers are generally required because there is no, or no adequate, statutory provision; and they often take the form of appropriate extensions or modifications of particular statutory powers. It is also common practice to confer on trustees a power to extend or modify their own *administrative* powers if this is regarded as being expedient and in the best interests of the trust.[8] The actual scope of express powers will be determined by their own terms and in the particular context in which they appear.[9]

Some of the more important powers, such as the power to delegate and powers of **14.04** investment, are dealt with separately elsewhere.[10] In this chapter, the two most important statutory dispositive powers[11]—namely the power of maintenance and the power of advancement—are dealt with first in sections C and D and then some of the more important statutory administrative powers will be examined briefly in sections E and following.

B. Contrary Intention

Section 69(2) of the Trustee Act 1925 provides that the powers conferred by that Act **14.05** on trustees are in addition to the powers conferred by the instrument, if any, creating the trust, but those powers, unless otherwise stated, apply if and so far only as a contrary intention is not expressed in the instrument, if any, creating the trust, and have effect subject to the terms of that instrument.[12] This provision does not require an express exclusion or some equivalent positive expression: there is an effective exclusion 'if, on a fair reading of the instrument in question, one can say that such application would be inconsistent with the purport of the instrument'.[13]

---

[6] For example, the powers in an 'interest in possession' settlement for inheritance tax purposes will usually be subject to restrictions not found or required in a discretionary trust.

[7] See, for example, J Kessler, *Drafting Trusts and Will Trusts* (6th edn, 2000).

[8] *Re Rank's Settlement Trusts* [1979] 1 WLR 1242.

[9] See, for example, *Re Maryon-Wilson's Estate* [1912] 1 Ch 55; *Re Harari's Settlement Trusts* [1949] WN 79; *Re Peczenik's Settlement Trusts* [1964] 1 WLR 720.

[10] See Chapters 15 (delegation), 52 (investment).

[11] See footnote 1 to para 14.01 above and paras 14.06–14.45 below. Despite the fact that, in *Lord Inglewood v IRC* [1983] 1 WLR 366, 373, Fox LJ regarded a power of advancement as analogous, in some respects, to an administrative power, it is (like the power of maintenance) considered that, in most contexts and for most purposes, it is actually a dispositive power.

[12] Despite its broad words, there are exceptions: see, for example, ss 14(3), 16(2), 26(2), and 27(3).

[13] *IRC v Bernstein* [1961] Ch 399, 412, *per* Lord Evershed MR. See also *Re Evans's Settlement* [1967] 1 WLR 1294; *Re Gertsman* [1966] VR 45, 55; *Re Havill* [1968] NZLR 1116, 1126.

Consequently, if the intention is that a statutory power should be available to the trustees in addition to any express power, this should be made clear in the trust instrument.

C. Powers of Maintenance[14]

14.06 In the absence of express provision in the trust instrument or statute, trustees would not be able to pay trust income or capital to an infant,[15] whether by way of maintenance or otherwise, because the infant would not be able to give a valid receipt for it.[16] From early on, the courts claimed and exercised an inherent jurisdiction to authorize, or to enlarge inadequate express powers for, the application of trust income for the maintenance and education of infant beneficiaries. As Pearson J stated, in *Re Collins*:[17]

> ... where a testator has made a provision for ... the children of a particular *stirps* in succession or otherwise, but has postponed the enjoyment either for a particular purpose or generally for the increase of the estate, it is assumed that he did not intend that these children should be left unprovided for in a state of such moderate means that they should not be educated properly for the position and fortune which he designs them to have, and the court has accordingly found from the earliest time that where an heir-at-law is unprovided for, maintenance ought to be provided for him.

This inherent jurisdiction was exercised even where the infant's interest was merely contingent or defeasible (for example by the exercise of an overriding power of appointment).[18] In any event, it became standard practice to confer on trustees an express (and usually wide) power to maintain infant beneficiaries out of trust income, and indeed to do so by paying such income to the infant's parent or guardian. Eventually, a statutory power was made available in section 43 of the Conveyancing Act 1881; and this, in turn, was replaced by section 31 of the Trustee Act 1925. Although most modern trust instruments contain express powers of maintenance, such powers tend to take the form of specific modifications to the provisions of section 31.

---

[14] (1953) 17 Conv (NS) 273 (BS Ker); [1973] CLJ 246 (AM Prichard); (1963) 79 LQR 184 (PV Baker).

[15] As from 1 January 1970, the age of majority was reduced from 21 to 18 years: Family Law Reform Act 1969, s 1.

[16] A *married* infant may now give a valid receipt: s 21 of the Law of Property Act 1925. This does not seem to include a widowed infant. See also *Rotheram v Fanshaw* (1748) 3 Atk 628, 629.

[17] (1886) 32 Ch D 229, 232. For a more direct expression of the same sentiment, see *Re Christian* (1882) 3 LR (NSW) Eq 13, 18, *per* Manning PJ. In *Chapman v Chapman* [1954] AC 429, 456, Lord Morton said that the provision of maintenance was the only exception to the rule that a court would not alter a man's will because it thinks it beneficial to do so.

[18] See, for example, *De Witte v Palin* (1877) LR 14 Eq 251; *Re Boulter* [1918] 2 Ch 40.

In broad terms, section 31 confers on trustees powers to apply trust income for the maintenance and education of minor beneficiaries and also directs the accumulation of income not so applied. **14.07**

Section 31 of the Trustee Act 1925

Section 31(1) and (2) provides as follows: **14.08**

(1) Where any property is held by trustees in trust for any person for any interest whatsoever,[19] whether vested or contingent, then, subject to any prior interests or charges affecting that property—

   (i) during the infancy of any such person, if his interest so long continues, the trustees may, at their sole discretion, pay to his parent or guardian, if any, or otherwise apply for or towards his maintenance, education or benefit, the whole or such part, if any, of the income of that property as may, in all the circumstances, be reasonable, whether or not there is—

      (a) any other fund applicable to the same purpose; or
      (b) any person bound by law to provide for his maintenance or education; and

   (ii) if such person on attaining the age of eighteen years has not a vested interest in such income, the trustees shall thenceforth pay the income of that property and of any accretion thereto under subsection (2) of this section to him, until he either attains a vested interest therein or dies, or until failure of his interest:

Provided that, in deciding whether the whole or any part of the income of the property is during a minority to be paid or applied for the purposes aforesaid, the trustees shall have regard to the age of the infant and his requirements and generally to the circumstances of the case, and in particular to what other income, if any, is applicable for the same purposes; and where trustees have notice that the income of more than one fund is applicable for those purposes, then, so far as practicable, unless the entire income of the funds is paid or applied as aforesaid or the court otherwise directs, a proportionate part only of the income of each fund shall be so paid or applied.

(2) During the infancy of any such person, if his interest so long continues, the trustees shall accumulate all the residue of that income by investing it, and any profits from so investing it,[20] from time to time in authorised investments, and shall hold those accumulations as follows—

   (i) If any such person—

      (a) attains the age of eighteen years, or marries under that age, and his interest in such income during his infancy or until his marriage is a vested interest; or

---

[19] Including an interest subject to defeasance: *Re Sharp's Settlement* [1973] Ch 331; *Re Delamere's Settlement* [1984] 1 WLR 813, 818; *Re Buckley's Trusts* (1883) 22 Ch D 583. However, a vested interest does not include a deferred interest: *Re McGeorge* [1963] Ch 544 (where there was a devise of land declared not to take effect until after the death of the testator's wife).

[20] As from 1 February 2001: The Trustee Act 2000 (Commencement) Order 2001, SI 2001/49.

(b) on attaining the age of eighteen years or on marriage under that age becomes entitled to the property from which such income arose in fee simple, absolute or determinable, or absolutely, or for an entailed interest;[21]

the trustees shall hold the accumulations in trust for such person absolutely, but without prejudice to any provision with respect thereto contained in any settlement by him made under any statutory powers during his infancy, and so that the receipt of such person after marriage, and though still an infant, shall be a good discharge; and

(ii) In any other case the trustees shall, notwithstanding that such person had a vested interest in such income, hold the accumulations as an accretion to the capital of the property from which such accumulations arose, and as one fund with such capital for all purposes, and so that, if such property is settled land, such accumulations shall be held upon the same trusts as if the same were capital money arising therefrom;

but the trustees may, at any time during the infancy of such person if his interest so long continues, apply those accumulations, or any part thereof, as if they were income arising in the then current year.

Section 31 may be excluded wholly or modified by express provision in the trust instrument.[22] Common amendments include: the alteration of the age(s) of the beneficiaries, so that accumulation and maintenance can continue beyond the age of 18 years;[23] the total exclusion of sub-paragraphs (i)(a) and (b) of subsection (1) and also the proviso to subsection (1); and the substitution of a wider discretion, such as 'as the trustees in their absolute discretion think fit', in place of the words 'as may, in all the circumstances, be reasonable'.

Applicability of section 31

14.09 Section 31 does not apply to an instrument (under which the relevant interest arises) which came into operation before 1 January 1926.[24] Instead, its predecessor, section 43 of the Conveyancing Act 1881, applies to the rare case of a pre-1926 instrument. Where a special power of appointment conferred by a pre-1926 instrument is

[21] Entailed interests can no longer be created: Trusts of Land and Appointment of Trustees Act 1996, s 2(6) and Sch 1, para 5.
[22] Section 69(2) of the Trustee Act 1925; *Re Turner's Will Trusts* [1937] Ch 15; *Re Watt's Will Trusts* [1936] 2 All ER 1555; *Re Rees* [1954] Ch 202.
[23] But, obviously, not beyond any period permitted by statute or by common law, for which see paras 8.13–8.26 above. Very often, the amendment of s 31 is part of a scheme of 'accumulation and maintenance trusts' created for inheritance tax purposes (as defined in the Inheritance Tax Act 1984, s 71) and is intended to enable accumulation of income for the maximum period of time while ensuring that the beneficiaries still attain interests in possession in the trust fund on or before attaining the age of 25. In simple cases, this entails no more than the substitution of the age of 25 for the age of 18; but, in more complex trusts, eg where some beneficiaries are unborn or under the age of 4 at the creation of the trusts, the extent to which, and manner in which, s 31 may be amended requires careful thought and is far from straightforward: see, generally, Chapter 35 below.
[24] Section 31(5).

exercised after 1925, the appointment itself (and not the head settlement) is the relevant instrument for this purpose and section 31 applies to the appointed interests.[25] Section 31 also applies to post-1925 intestacies.[26]

As from 1 January 1970, the age of majority was reduced from 21 to 18 years and **14.10** section 31 now applies accordingly.[27] Where a special power of appointment conferred by a pre-1970 instrument is exercised after 1969, the appointment itself is the relevant instrument for this purpose and section 31 applies to the appointed interests subject to the reduction in the age of majority,[28] although, in such a case, it is possible, by express provision, to preserve the original form and age of majority.[29] However, the 1969 Act did not affect pre-1970 instruments[30] or pre-1970 intestacies.[31] Nor does the 1969 Act affect the application of section 31 to an interest under a pre-1970 will, whether or not the testator died before or after 1 January 1970, and irrespective of the fact that the will is confirmed by a post-1969 codicil.[32] However, where the unamended section 31 still applies, trustees who apply income for the maintenance of a beneficiary who has attained the age of 18 may do so by paying such income directly to that beneficiary.[33]

Specific points on the construction of section 31

'Maintenance, education or benefit'

These words are generally regarded as authorizing the application of trust income **14.11** for routine, recurring expenses of a beneficiary; they are words 'of the widest import'[34] and, in appropriate cases, include capital investment, for example to buy a house in which the beneficiary can live or a share in a partnership, or even placing money on deposit.[35] Although trustees usually pay over the money so applied, it may also be given to trustees to hold on trust for the beneficiary absolutely,[36] or contingently upon attaining the age of majority.[37] In appropriate circumstances, trustees may pay income in respect of past maintenance;[38] and, in exceptional cases, they may even make reasonable donations to charity,[39] and the

---

[25] *Re Dickinson's Settlements* [1939] Ch 27; *Re De La Bere's Settlement Trusts* [1941] Ch 443; *Begg-McBrearty v Stilwell* [1996] 4 All ER 205.
[26] Section 47(1)(ii) of the Administration of Estates Act 1925.
[27] Family Law Reform Act 1969, s 1(2), (3) and Sch 1.
[28] *Begg-McBrearty v Stilwell* [1996] 4 All ER 205.
[29] ibid 222–223: subject, of course, to the restrictions in s 164 of the LPA 1925.
[30] Family Law Reform Act 1969, s 1(4) and Sch 3, para 5(1)(a).
[31] ibid, s 1(4) and Sch 3, para 5(1)(b).   [32] ibid, s 1(7).
[33] ibid, s 1(4) and Sch 3, para 5(2).
[34] *Re Heyworth's Contingent Reversionary Interest* [1956] Ch 364, 370.
[35] ibid; and *Allen v Coster* (1839) 1 Beav 202.   [36] *Re Vestey's Settlement* [1951] Ch 209.
[37] *Pilkington v IRC* [1964] AC 612. Provided the 'benefit' is established, the contingency need not be limited to attaining the age of majority.
[38] *Stopford v Lord Canterbury* (1840) 11 Sim 82; *Re Kirwan* (1869) 8 SCR (NSW) Eq 21; *Re Lawrence* (1908) 25 WN (NSW) 79; *Perpetual Trustee Co Ltd v Shelley* (1921) 21 SR (NSW) 426.
[39] *Re Walker* [1901] 1 Ch 879.

court may ratify payments made in excess of those which are actually authorized by the relevant power.[40]

Considerations relevant to the exercise of the trustees' discretion

14.12 The proviso to subsection (1) (which is usually excluded expressly in most trust instruments) directs that, in deciding whether to exercise their powers of maintenance, the trustees shall have regard to the age of the infant and his requirements and generally to the circumstances of the case, and in particular to what other income, if any, is applicable for the same purposes; and where trustees have notice that the income of more than one fund is applicable, then, so far as practicable, a proportionate part only of the income of each fund shall be so paid or applied, unless the entire income of all the funds is thus paid or applied.

14.13 The trustees must consider what is of benefit to, and in the best interests of, the beneficiary (a duty which applies whether or not the proviso to section 31(1) has been excluded). The beneficiary's needs and circumstances will clearly vary according to age[41] and status and will almost invariably require consideration of his parents' circumstances also, as Cotton LJ pointed out in *Re Lofthouse*:[42]

> . . . the trustees in exercising their discretion must consider what is most for the benefit of the infant. In considering that, they should take into account that the father is not of sufficient ability properly to maintain his child, and that it is for her benefit not merely to allow him enough to pay her actual expenses, but to enable him to give her a better education and a better home. They must not be deterred from doing what is for her benefit because it is also a benefit to the father, though, on the other hand, they must not act with a view to his benefit apart from hers.

Thus, although trustees can clearly pay trust income to the beneficiary's parent(s) and, indeed, may do so even if the payment incidentally benefits the parent(s),[43] they must not do so simply because it is of benefit to the parent(s): they must form the view that it is beneficial to the beneficiary to do so.[44] And, of course, it is a clear breach of trust if the trustees fail to give any consideration at all to any application of income and do so automatically.[45]

---

[40] *Brown v Smith* (1878) 10 Ch D 377; *Kerferd v Perpetual Executors and Trustees Association of Australasia Ltd* (1893) 19 VLR 700; *Irwin v Jones* [1924] NZLR 58.

[41] This will include considering whether to apply undistributed income as the beneficiary approaches the age of majority.

[42] (1885) 29 Ch D 921, 932.   [43] *Fuller v Evans* [2000] 1 All ER 636.

[44] *Wilson v Turner* (1883) 22 Ch D 521; *Re Senior* [1936] 3 All ER 196; *Re Moxon's Will Trusts* [1958] 1 WLR 165; *Re Pauling's Settlement Trusts* [1964] Ch 303; *Re Hodges* (1878) 7 Ch D 754; *Re Roper's Trusts* (1879) 11 Ch D 272; *Re Bryant* [1894] 1 Ch 324. See also *Craig v National Trustees Executors and Agency Co of Australasia Ltd* [1920] VLR 569.

[45] *Wilson v Turner* (1883) 22 Ch D 521; *Turner v Turner* [1984] Ch 100.

Accumulation of unapplied income

While the beneficiary is under the age of 18 (and his interest still continues), the **14.14** trustees *must* accumulate such income as is not applied for that beneficiary's maintenance, education, or benefit, although they may, during that same time, resort to and apply such accumulations as if they were income arising in the then current year.[46]

The next question is: what then happens to such accumulated income? This **14.15** depends on the nature of the beneficiary's interest under the trust. If he has an absolute and indefeasible vested interest in capital during infancy, he is entitled to the income (including accumulated income) produced by that capital as and when it arises. He has an immediate right to the money and simply cannot, by virtue of being an infant, give a good receipt for it.[47] If he dies in infancy, the capital and accumulated income pass with his estate. If he becomes entitled to an absolute and indefeasible vested interest in capital when he attains the age of 18 (or marries under that age), he again becomes entitled to all accumulations of income of that capital.[48] His interest is not 'absolute' if it is capable of being defeated by, for example, a power of appointment.[49] If, during his infancy (or until his marriage), the beneficiary has a vested interest in income only (for example he has a vested life interest), one of the peculiar effects of section 31(2)(i)(a) is that his vested interest is, in fact, for all practical purposes in precisely the same position *as if* his interest in surplus income *were contingent*. Despite having a vested interest in the income, he becomes entitled to accumulations of that income only if he attains the age of 18 years; and, if he dies before attaining that age (and unmarried), such accumulations will not fall into and form part of his estate. As Lord Greene MR put it, in *Stanley v IRC*:[50]

> The infant does not during infancy enjoy the surplus income. It is not his in any real sense. The title to it is held in suspense to await the event, and if he dies under [18] his interest in it (whether or not it be truly described as a vested interest) is destroyed ... If he attains [18] he takes the accumulations, if he dies under [18] he does not ... We are disposed to think that the effect of the section is better described, not as leaving the interest of the infant as a vested interest subject to defeasance, but as engrafting on the vested interest originally conferred on the infant ... a qualifying trust of a special nature which confers on the infant a title to the accumulations if and only if he attains [18] or marries.

---

[46] Section 31(2): see above.
[47] *IRC v Blackwell* [1924] 2 KB 351, 363, *per* Rowlatt J; *Stanley v IRC* [1944] 1 KB 255, 259 *per* Lord Greene MR.
[48] Section 31(2)(i)(b), which actually refers (see above) to entitlement in fee simple, absolute or determinable (in respect of realty), or absolutely (in respect of personalty), or for an entailed interest (in respect of realty or personalty): *Re Sharp's Settlement Trusts* [1973] Ch 331, 333.
[49] ibid.   [50] [1944] 1 KB 255, 261.

This peculiar effect may be countered by express provision in the trust instrument.[51]

14.16 In any other case, section 31(2)(ii) provides that the accumulations shall be held as an accretion to the capital of the property from which they arose and as one fund with such capital for all purposes. If a beneficiary has a contingent interest in capital, his interest in its income during infancy will also be contingent; and, if he becomes entitled to the capital, he becomes entitled to the accumulations (which are then in the form of capital and not income).

14.17 If he remains contingently entitled to the capital when he attains the age of 18 (when the power to maintain ceases), for example because it is held on trust for him if he attains the age of 25, then the trustees must pay the income of that property, and of any accretion thereto under section 31(2), to him, until he either attains a vested interest therein or dies, or until failure of his interest.[52] In other words, he acquires a vested interest in income at the age of 18, notwithstanding that his interest in capital remains contingent; and the effect may even be to accelerate the vesting of his interest in income, for example if he had been given a life interest if he attained the age of 25. Section 31(1)(ii) may be excluded expressly in the trust instrument, or by necessary implication where there is some alternative provision for the relevant income, such as, for example, a direction to accumulate[53] (although it is not obvious why accumulation of income is necessarily inconsistent with a power to maintain),[54] or where the trustees have power to pay the income to others.[55]

Intermediate income

14.18 The maintenance of a beneficiary under section 31 is clearly possible only where the income of the relevant property or interest is available, and it may not always be so for a number of reasons.

---

[51] *Re Delamere's Settlement Trusts* [1984] 1 WLR 813 (trust for grandchildren 'in equal shares absolutely' held to exclude s 31(2)(i)(b). It is often the case that, in complex accumulation and maintenance trusts which seek to maximize the available period of accumulation and yet satisfy the requirements of s 71 of the Inheritance Tax Act 1984, it is essential that this provision be excluded so as to ensure that the beneficiaries take vested interests in possession in time.

[52] Section 31(1)(ii), which, in terms, does not apply to vested interests: *Re McGeorge* [1963] Ch 544.

[53] *Re Reade-Revell* [1930] 1 Ch 52; *Re Turner's Will Trusts* [1937] Ch 15; *Re Watt's Will Trusts* [1936] 2 All ER 1555; *Re Stapleton* [1946] 1 All ER 323; *IRC v Bernstein* [1961] Ch 399. Cf the position in Australia: *Re Nathan* [1938] VLR 72; *Re Linton* [1944] VLR 118; *Re Watts* [1949] VLR 64; *Re Lesser* [1954] VLR 435, 439. Since it is the intention to exclude that matters, it will be effective even where the direction to accumulate is void: *Re Ransome* [1957] Ch 348; *Re Erskine's Settlement Trusts* [1971] 1 WLR 162; *Brotherton v IRC* [1978] 1 WLT 610, 616.

[54] *Re Thatcher's Trusts* (1884) 26 Ch D 426; *Re Collins* (1886) 32 Ch D 229.

[55] *Re Geering* [1964] Ch 136. See also *Re McGeorge* [1963] Ch 544, 552–553 (interest both contingent and deferred).

First, the trust instrument may make an express alternative provision directing **14.19** that income is to be paid to someone other than the infant beneficiary during the latter's infancy, or be accumulated[56] (even if the direction to accumulate is void),[57] or be held on discretionary trusts.[58] Indeed, section 31 itself is expressed to apply 'subject to any prior interests or charges affecting that property'.[59] Clearly, it cannot apply to income, whether by way of application for maintenance or accumulation or payment to a beneficiary who has attained his majority, if that income is not available because it has been disposed of in some other manner. Income which must be paid to A for life is not available for the maintenance of B.[60] Other cases are not as straightforward, however. For example, those entitled in remainder who will or may become entitled to trust capital, including accretions thereto by way of accumulations, may be said to have a 'prior interest' in trust income. It would seem likely that they do not, and that a person with a 'prior interest' during a period of accumulation must have a right to call for the income, but this point was expressly left undecided by Clauson J in *Re Spencer*[61] and by the Court of Appeal in *Re Turner's Will Trusts*.[62]

Secondly, not all gifts carry intermediate income. *Vested* interests generally carry **14.20** the right to income unless there is a contrary intention (and subject, of course, to any prior interest). There will be such a contrary intention if the vested interest is deferred[63]—provided there is no provision indicating that the income is indeed to be carried.[64] Section 31 applies to a *contingent* interest only if the limitation or trust carries the intermediate income of that property.[65] It has no application, therefore, to a beneficiary who has a mere *spes successionis* (such as an object of a discretionary trust or someone interested in an unadministered estate)[66] or, indeed, to an infant object of a discretionary trust to whom trust income has been allocated absolutely.[67] The question, therefore, is: which interests do carry

---

[56] *Re Turner's Will Trusts* [1937] Ch 15; *Re Watt's Will Trusts* [1936] 2 All ER 1555; *Re Stapleton* [1946] 1 All ER 323; *IRC v Bernstein* [1961] Ch 399.

[57] *Re Ransome* [1957] Ch 348; *Re Erskine's Settlement Trusts* [1971] 1 WLR 162; *Brotherton v IRC* [1978] 1 WLR 610, 616.

[58] *Re Vestey's Settlement* [1951] Ch 209. Once the trustees exercise their discretion in favour of an object and allocate trust income to him absolutely, s 31 still does not apply, although it may do so in relation to income subsequently arising from that income.

[59] See, for example, *Re Spencer* [1935] Ch 533; *Re Gertsman* [1966] VR 45, 54–56.

[60] *Re Williams* [1950] St R Qd 148, 200.   [61] [1935] Ch 533.

[62] [1937] Ch 15. See also *IRC v Bernstein* [1960] Ch 444 and [1961] Ch 399 (esp 418, *per* Harman LJ), where a similar point arose, and was left undecided, in relation to s 32 of the Trustee Act 1925.

[63] *Berry v Geen* [1938] AC 575; *Re Oliver* [1947] 2 All ER 162; *Re Gillett's Will Trusts* [1950] Ch 102; *Re McGeorge* [1963] Ch 544; *Re Geering* [1964] Ch 136; *Re Nash's Will Trusts* [1965] 1 WLR 221.

[64] *Re Geering, supra.*   [65] Section 31(3).

[66] *Re Beckett's Settlement* [1940] Ch 279; *Re Midleton's Will Trusts* [1969] 1 Ch 600 (trust for a future successor to a peerage).

[67] *Re Vestey's Settlement* [1951] Ch 209.

intermediate income? Section 175(1) of the Law of Property Act 1925[68] provides expressly that, in the absence of express provision to the contrary, certain testamentary interests shall carry the intermediate income:

> A contingent or future specific devise or bequest of property, whether real or personal, and a contingent residuary devise of freehold land, and a specific or residuary devise of freehold land to trustees upon trust for persons whose interests are contingent or executory shall, subject to the statutory provisions relating to accumulations, carry the intermediate income of that property from the death of the testator, except so far as such income, or any part thereof, may be otherwise expressly disposed of.

All the rules relating to gifts carrying intermediate income are subject to a contrary intention, ie a gift which would normally carry the intermediate income may be declared not to do so and vice versa.

In the case of wills, a contingent residuary gift of personalty,[69] or of a mixed fund of realty and personalty,[70] carries with it the intermediate income which it produces after the testator's death, unless there is a contrary intention in the will: 'the undisposed of income becomes part of residue'.[71] A contingent residuary gift, which is not just contingent but also deferred to a future date which must come sooner or later does not carry the intermediate income, unless, again, it is provided that the intermediate income is to be carried.[72] In the case of contingent interests created by *inter vivos* settlements, similar principles will apply but, essentially, the question will be one of intention, and express provision should always be made for the destination of intermediate income.

14.21 A future or contingent general legacy or a pecuniary legacy does not generally carry the intermediate income.[73] The normal rule in relation to such a legacy is that it is paid at the appropriate time out of residue and the legatee is not entitled to any income or interest in respect of the period before the legacy becomes payable.[74] However, there are exceptions to this general rule. First, it does not apply where the pecuniary legacy is directed to be severed from the rest of the

---

[68] It applies only to wills coming into operation on or after 1 January 1926: s 175(2). For which gifts carry intermediate income (or not), see, generally, *Theobald on Wills* (15th edn) 266–267; and see also (1953) 17 Conv (NS) 273 (B Ker); (1963) 79 LQR 184 (PV Baker).

[69] *Re Adams* [1893] 1 Ch 329; *Re Holford* [1894] 3 Ch 30.

[70] *Genery v Fitzgerald* (1822) Jac 468; *Countess of Bective v Hodgson* (1864) 10 HLC 656.

[71] *Re Adams, supra*, 334.

[72] *Re Oliver* [1947] 2 All ER 162, 166; *Re Gillett's Will Trusts* [1950] Ch 102; *Re McGeorge* [1963] Ch 544, 551; *Re Geering* [1964] Ch 136.

[73] *Re Woodin* [1895] 2 Ch 349; *Re George* (1877) 5 Ch D 837; *Re Raine* [1929] 1 Ch 716; *Re Gertsman* [1966] VR 45.

[74] *Re Raine, supra*; *Re Dickson* (1885) 29 Ch D 331; *Re Boulter* [1918] 2 Ch 40. The time at which an immediate legacy becomes payable is either (a) the time specified in the will or (b) one year after the testator's death and, if not actually paid then, interest will then also be payable: *Re Hall* [1951] 1 All ER 1073. A future or contingent legacy becomes payable when the deferred event occurs or the contingency is satisfied: *Re Raine, supra*.

estate and retained as a separate fund: here, the actual intermediate income (and not just a fixed rate of interest) is payable from the date on which the separate fund is created or (if later) the end of the executor's year.[75] Secondly, if (i) the testator was the parent of, or stood *in loco parentis* to, the infant legatee, (ii) the legacy is given directly to him and not to trustees to hold for him, (iii) no other fund was set aside for the maintenance of the infant, and (iv) if the legacy is contingent, the contingency is the attaining by the infant of an age not exceeding the age of majority, the legacy will carry interest (at 5 per cent per annum)[76] and be payable out of the income of the residuary estate.[77] Thirdly, the testator may indicate in his will that the future or contingent legacy should carry interest from his death until payment for the maintenance of the infant legatee: in such a case, the testator need not be the parent of, or stand *in loco parentis* to, the legatee; and the contingency may be the attaining by the infant of an age greater than the age of majority.[78] Fourthly, a *vested* legacy given in satisfaction of a debt carries interest.[79] Fifthly, a *vested* legacy charged on real property alone also carries interest.[80] If, in the last four cases, the actual income attributable to the legacy exceeds the rate of interest, the excess falls into residue.

It does not follow, however, that section 31 applies to all of the above legacies, ie it **14.22** is not sufficient that they carry intermediate income or interest. If the will expressly directs that section 31 applies, there is clearly no difficulty; and it may be possible, in the case of the first-mentioned exception (a direction to create a separate fund) to infer that such application was intended by the testator. However, subject to these considerations, section 31(3) provides expressly that section 31 applies to a future or contingent legacy by the parent of, or a person standing *in loco parentis* to, the legatee, if and for such period as, under the general law, the legacy carries interest for the maintenance of the legatee. In other words, the second exception mentioned above is explicitly included, which strongly suggests that section 31 does not apply in the case of the other exceptions: such application would be possible only if the reference in section 31(3) to 'intermediate income' were to be construed to include interest on those other excepted legacies, and this seems improbable. Thus, section 31 would seem not to apply even to the third of the above-mentioned exceptions, despite the fact that the interest is explicitly made available for the maintenance of the infant.

---

[75] *Re Medlock* (1886) 55 LJ Ch 738; *Re Woodin* [1895] 2 Ch 309; *Re Couturier* [1907] 1 Ch 470; *Re Gertsman, supra.*

[76] Section 31(3) of the Trustee Act 1925, which applies 'subject to any rules of court to the contrary': thus, RSC Ord 44, r 10 (CPR Pt 50, r 50.1) may arguably have increased it to 6%, but this must be doubtful.

[77] *Re George* (1877) 5 Ch D 837; *Re Bowlby* [1904] 2 Ch 685; *Re West* [1913] 2 Ch 345; *Re Abrahams* [1911] 1 Ch 108; *Re Pollock* [1943] Ch 338.

[78] *Re Churchill* [1909] 2 Ch 431; *Re West* [1913] 2 Ch 345; *Re Stokes* [1928] Ch 716; *Re Selby Walker* [1949] 2 All ER 178; *Re Jones* [1932] 1 Ch 108 (where the headnote is wrong). See also (1953) 17 Conv (NS) 273, 279, 283–284 (BS Ker).

[79] *Re Rattenberry* [1906] 1 Ch 667.   [80] *Shirt v Westby* (1808) 16 Ves 393.

14.23 Where a pecuniary legacy is given to trustees upon trust for an infant beneficiary with a contingent interest, the legacy carries interest from the end of the executor's year. The interest will be invested by the trustees and section 31 will apply to the intermediate income of the invested fund.[81]

Apportionment of trust income

14.24 The Apportionment Act 1870 requires the income of trust assets to be apportioned on a day-to-day basis. It applies, therefore, when an infant beneficiary attains the age of 18.[82] Where income accrued before, but is not received until after, that date, it cannot be applied for maintenance: at the date of receipt, the beneficiary is no longer an infant; and it cannot be applied before that date because trustees cannot exercise their discretion in advance, in anticipation of the receipt.[83]

14.25 Apportionment of income is also required when a class of beneficiaries increases or decreases as a result of death or birth. Suppose, for example, that there are six members of the class (A to F). The trustees should divide trust income into six shares. The share of an adult beneficiary must be paid to him, whether or not he has attained a vested interest;[84] and the share of an infant beneficiary must be accumulated, as a separate fund and not as part of the general trust fund,[85] or applied for his maintenance.[86] If one of the beneficiaries dies before attaining a vested interest, income accruing up to the date of his death must be apportioned[87] and, thereafter, it must be divided into five shares. Income which had been accumulated as part of the dead beneficiary's share accrues to the trust fund as a whole.[88] If the class is increased by the birth of another beneficiary, income must be apportioned as at the date of his birth (and he will not have an interest in income arising before then and his birth will not affect accumulations already made),[89] and thereafter it must be divided into the greater number of shares.

D. Powers of Advancement

14.26 Just as in the case of powers of maintenance in relation to trust income, it has long been common practice to confer on trustees wide powers to pay or apply a portion

---

[81] *Kidman v Kidman* (1871) 40 LJ Ch 359; *Re Medlock* (1886) 55 LJ Ch 738; *Re Clements* [1894] 1 Ch 665; *Re Woodin* [1895] Ch 309; *Re Pollock* [1943] Ch 338.
[82] *Re Joel's Will Trust* [1967] Ch 14.   [83] ibid 29.
[84] Section 31(1)(ii) of the Trustee Act 1925.
[85] *Re Joel's Will Trust, supra*; *Re Sharp's Settlement Trusts* [1973] Ch 331.
[86] Section 31(1), (2).   [87] *Re Joel's Will Trust, supra*; *Re Sharp's Settlement Trusts, supra*.
[88] *Re Joel's Will Trust, supra* (not following *Re King* [1928] Ch 330). In this instance, a member of the class may become entitled to accumulations made before he was born.
[89] *Re King, supra*, 336; *Re Joel's Will Trust, supra*. Income accumulated for an infant beneficiary who attains a vested interest belongs to him, even if, at the time of the accumulation, the class was smaller than it eventually turns out to be.

of trust capital for the advancement or benefit (and even the maintenance and education) of beneficiaries, notwithstanding that their interests were contingent or in remainder.[90] The general purpose of such powers was described by Viscount Radcliffe in *Pilkington v IRC*:[91]

> No one doubts that such a power was frequently conferred upon trustees under settlements of personalty and that its general purpose was to enable them in a proper case to anticipate the vesting in possession of an intended beneficiary's contingent or reversionary interest by raising money on account of his interest and paying or applying it immediately for his benefit. By so doing they released it from the trusts of the settlement and accelerated the enjoyment of his interest (though normally only with the consent of a prior tenant for life); and, where the contingency on which the vesting of the beneficiary's title depended, failed to mature or there was a later defeasance or, in some cases, a great shrinkage in the value of the remaining trust funds, the trusts as declared by the settlement were materially varied through the operation of the power of advancement. This possibility was recognised and accepted as an incidental risk attendant upon the exercise of such a power, whose presence was felt on the whole to be advantageous in a system in which the possession of property interests was often deferred long beyond adult years.

Express powers of advancement

It is still common practice to include express powers of advancement in settle-**14.27** ments (and essential in the case of a discretionary trust or capital money arising under the Settled Land Act 1925, to which section 32 does not apply), although the usual method of doing so is by means of the incorporation of a modified form of section 32 of the Trustee Act 1925. An express power may be as wide or as narrow as the settlor intends and as its terms permit. The more common modifications to section 32 are intended to widen its scope by removing some of the restrictions to which it is subject, for example by express reference to purposes (such as maintenance and education) in respect of which there may be some uncertainty whether they fall within the words 'advancement or benefit',[92] or to authorize advancements on discretionary or protective trusts, and by the exclusion of parts (or even all) of the proviso to subsection (1) so as to permit the application of the whole of a beneficiary's presumptive or vested share and to remove the need for the consent of any person with a prior life or other interest. It is also possible to apply the power of advancement to the whole of the trust fund and not just a beneficiary's share in it. Indeed, an express power should always specify the capital out of which an advancement may be made.[93] If the express power is intended to be narrower than section 32, for example by restricting advancement to specific property or a limited sum, or to specific purposes, its terms must be well

[90] See, for example, *Re Hodgson* [1913] 1 Ch 34; *Re Winch's Settlement* [1917] 1 Ch 633.
[91] [1964] AC 612, 633–634.   [92] *Re Patterson* [1941] VLR 45, 57.
[93] *Re Aldridge* (1886) 55 LT 554.

considered, specific, and clear. For example, advancement for 'the purchase of a business' was held not to be wide enough to permit placing a deposit at Lloyd's,[94] whereas, in a case where the power permitted 'the advancement of any business' in which the beneficiary was concerned and the beneficiary was a doctor, it was held that the purchase of a house with surgery was authorized.[95] There is no reason why an express power of advancement can not coexist with the statutory power, although the latter may be excluded (wholly or in part), either expressly in the trust instrument[96] or by implication, for example because there would otherwise be some inconsistency with a specific provision of the trust (for instance relating to the amount that may be advanced)[97] or the general purpose of the trust as a whole.[98]

The statutory power

14.28 Section 32 (which, unlike section 31, was a new provision and did not replace an earlier version)[99] was expressed in terms that corresponded closely with the previous common form recommended in books of conveyancing precedents and adopted in practice before 1926.[100] It provides:

> (1) Trustees may at any time or times pay or apply any capital money subject to a trust, for the advancement or benefit, in such manner as they may, in their absolute discretion, think fit, of any person entitled to the capital of the trust property or of any share thereof, whether absolutely or contingently on his attaining any specified age or on the occurrence of any other event,[101] or subject to a gift over on his death under any specified age or on the occurrence of any other event, and whether in possession or in remainder or reversion, and such payment or application may be made notwithstanding that the interest of such person is liable to be defeated by the exercise of a power of appointment or revocation,[102] or to be diminished by the increase of the class to which he belongs:
>
> Provided that—
> (a) the money so paid or applied for the advancement or benefit of any person shall not exceed altogether in amount one-half of the presumptive or vested share or interest of that person in the trust property; and

---

94 *Re Craven's Estate (No 2)* [1937] Ch 431.
95 *Re Williams' Will Trusts* [1953] Ch 138.   96 Section 69(2) of the Trustee Act 1925.
97 *Re Evans' Settlement* [1967] 1 WLR 1294. See also *Re Collard's Will Trusts* [1961] Ch 293.
98 *IRC v Bernstein* [1961] Ch 399 (where the purpose was to build up capital over a period of time). Cf *Re Henderson's Trusts* [1969] 1 WLR 651. Accumulation of income is not generally inconsistent with a power of advancement, however.
99 Section 32 does not apply to trusts created or constituted before 1 January 1926. A trust in a will is not created or constituted until the death of the testator: *Re Darby* (1943) 59 TLR 418. Trusts created by the exercise of a special power of appointment conferred by a will are constituted by the will (as from the testator's death): *Re Batty* [1952] Ch 280; *Re Bransbury's Will Trusts* [1954] 1 WLR 496. Trusts created by deed by the exercise of a general power of appointment conferred by will are constituted by the deed: ibid.
100 *Pilkington v IRC* [1964] AC 612, 634; *Re Stimpson's Trusts* [1931] 2 Ch 77.
101 *Re Garrett* [1934] Ch 477.   102 *Re Hodgson* [1913] 1 Ch 34.

(b) if that person is or becomes absolutely and indefeasibly entitled to a share in the trust property the money so paid or applied shall be brought into account as part of such share; and

(c) no such payment or application shall be made so as to prejudice any person entitled to any prior life or other interest, whether vested or contingent, in the money paid or applied unless such person is in existence and of full age and consents in writing to such payment or application.

(2) This section does not apply to capital money arising under the Settled Land Act 1925.[103]

Meaning of 'advancement' and 'benefit'

'Advancement' in this context[104] means the establishment in life of the beneficiary, **14.29** or some step that will contribute to his establishment: it must provide some permanent benefit or advantage in life for that beneficiary.[105] In the nature of things, it is more relevant to an early period of the beneficiary's life,[106] but this is not necessarily so, and it is certainly not restricted to minority.[107] The word 'benefit' has a much wider meaning: indeed, it has been said to be 'the widest possible word one could have',[108] although it is not completely without limit. The difference between an 'advancement' and an application of money for the beneficiary's 'benefit' is often slight and, nowadays, of little relevance except in those rare instances where an express power narrows, rather than widens, the scope of section 32. For example, paying a beneficiary's debts has been held not to be a proper 'advancement',[109] but it may be a proper application for his 'benefit'.[110] In any event, given that both express powers and the statutory power invariably include both words, there is little, if any, point in attempting to differentiate between what constitutes an 'advancement' as opposed to a 'benefit'. Examples of purposes for which trust capital has been advanced include the following: establishing the beneficiary (and even the husband of a beneficiary) in business;[111] payment on

---

[103] Substituted by the Trusts of Land and Appointment of Trustees Act 1996, s 25(1), Sch 3, para 3(1), (8).

[104] The word 'advancement' bears different connotations in the context of the presumption of advancement and resulting trusts and also, to a lesser degree, in that of s 47(1)(iii) of the Administration of Estates Act 1925.   [105] *Pilkington v IRC* [1964] AC 612, 634.

[106] *Re Kershaw's Trust* (1868) LR 6 Eq 322; *Molyneux v Fletcher* [1898] 1 QB 648, 653. This must depend to a great extent on the nature of the beneficiary's interest.

[107] *Clarke v Hogg* (1871) 19 WR 617.

[108] *Re Moxon's Will Trusts* [1958] 1 WLR 165. See also *Re Breed's Will* (1875) 1 Ch D 226; *Re Brittlebank* (1881) 30 WR 99; *Re Buckinghamshire's Settlement Trusts* The Times, 29 March 1977.

[109] *Talbot v Marshfield* (1868) 3 Ch App 622; *Re Hall* (1887) 14 OR 557; *Re Gerbich* (2001) 4 ITELR 589.   [110] *Lowther v Bentinck* (1874) LR 19 Eq 166. Cf *Re Price* (1887) 34 Ch D 603.

[111] *Phillips v Phillips* (1853) Kay 40; *Re Kershaw's Trust* (1868) LR 6 Eq 322; *Re Mead* (1919) 119 LT 724. Similar (now outdated) purposes include the purchase of a commission in the army (*Cope v Wilmot* (1772) Amb 704; *Lawrie v Banks* (1858) 4 K & J 142) and an apprenticeship (*Simpson v Brown* (1865) 11 LT 593). Modern equivalents might include payment of fees and costs of qualifying for a profession, retraining, payment of school fees by way of lump sum, and so forth, especially if trust income was insufficient or not available.

marriage;[112] assisting emigration;[113] furnishing a house;[114] and payment of legacy duty.[115] Examples of applications of capital for a beneficiary's 'benefit' (though not necessarily 'advancements') include: paying a beneficiary's debts;[116] providing a house for infant beneficiaries to live in with their parents;[117] making provision to ameliorate the beneficiary's tax liability;[118] maintaining and supporting the beneficiary;[119] settling capital on the trusts of a marriage settlement for the benefit of the beneficiary, his wife, and children;[120] safeguarding against the possibility of the premature death of a beneficiary on military service;[121] paying for a cruise as part of the beneficiary's recuperation following a mental breakdown;[122] and making donations to charity in order to satisfy a moral obligation which the beneficiary felt he owed.[123] Paying money direct to a beneficiary may be an advancement or for his benefit,[124] provided there is a specific and considered purpose in doing so, but simply putting money in his pocket will not be.[125]

Trustees' discretion

14.30 The trustees must exercise their discretion honestly and only if they have formed a considered view that it is truly for the benefit of the advanced beneficiary[126] (which may be by way of payment or transfer to another person).[127] This requires balancing the interests of the advanced beneficiary against those of others who will be disappointed or whose entitlements will be defeated by the advancement.[128] If they fail to give proper consideration to the decision to advance, the exercise of the power may be void;[129] and, if they cannot agree whether to exercise the power or not, the court may take appropriate steps.[130] However, provided the trustees have acted properly, the court will not interfere with their exercise of their

---

[112] *Lloyd v Cocker* (1860) 27 Beav 645.   [113] *Re England's Estate* (1830) 1 R & M 499.
[114] *Perry v Perry* (1870) 18 WR 482.   [115] *Klug v Klug* [1918] 2 Ch 67.
[116] *Lowther v Bentinck* (1874) LR 19 Eq 166. See also *Perpetual Trustee Co Ltd v Smith* (1906) 6 SR (NSW) 542.
[117] *Re Lesser* [1947] VLR 366. One of the more common forms of advancement, in practice, is the purchase of a house, furniture, and domestic chattels for a beneficiary, either on marriage or simply on leaving home.
[118] *Re Ropner's Settlement Trusts* [1956] 1 WLR 902; *Re Meux's Trusts* [1958] Ch 154.
[119] *Re Breed's Will* (1875) 1 Ch D 226.
[120] *Re Halsted's Will Trusts* [1937] 2 All ER 570; *Roper-Curzon v Roper-Curzon* (1871) LR 11 Eq 452.
[121] *Re Wills' Will Trusts* [1959] Ch 1.
[122] *Re Dick* [1940] VLR 166.
[123] *Re Clore's Settlement Trusts* [1966] 1 WLR 955. Cf *Re Reddington* (1828) 1 Moll 256; *Re Bayly* [1944] NZLR 868. See also *Re the S Settlement* (2001) 4 ITELR 206 and *Re the X Trust* (2002) 5 ITELR 119 (RC, Jersey).   [124] *Re Moxon's Will Trusts* [1958] 1 WLR 165.
[125] *Roper-Curzon v Roper-Curzon* (1871) LR 11 Eq 452.
[126] *Phillips v Phillips* (1853) Kay 40; *Re Kershaw's Trusts* (1840) LR 6 Eq 322; *Re Moxon's Will Trusts* [1958] 1 WLR 165.
[127] See, for example, *Re Kershaw's Trusts, supra.*
[128] *Re Pauling's Settlement Trusts* [1964] Ch 303.
[129] *Turner v Turner* [1984] Ch 100.
[130] *Klug v Klug* [1918] 2 Ch 67. See also *McPhail v Doulton* [1971] AC 424.

discretion.[131] The duties of trustees in relation to the exercise of powers generally, including a power of advancement, are dealt with in greater detail elsewhere.[132]

Advancement by way of resettlement

Powers of advancement (or, more likely, powers to benefit) are commonly exercised so as to create a new (or enlarge an existing) separate settlement under which not only the advanced beneficiary but also others, such as his wife and children, have interests or may derive some benefit.[133] Sometimes, the purpose of such settlements is to postpone the age at which a beneficiary's interest will vest (for example because he is immature or a spendthrift) but, more commonly, it is to obtain a tax advantage of some kind. There are two key issues in such cases: first, is it a proper exercise of the power to confer (often substantial) benefits on non-objects and, if so, to what extent? Secondly, is it a valid objection that, in creating such a separate settlement, the trustees are delegating their duties and powers to others? **14.31**

Benefiting non-objects

On the first question, it has long been established that trustees may exercise their powers of advancement by way of resettlement of the relevant trust property, whether by creating an entirely new settlement on the advancement or by transferring it to an existing receptacle settlement, and notwithstanding that persons who are not objects of the power benefit under the trusts of the new or receiving settlement.[134] This was confirmed by the House of Lords in *Pilkington v IRC*,[135] where the trustees exercised the statutory power of advancement by applying one-half of an infant beneficiary's expectant share in the trust fund by adding it to the trust fund of another settlement, the purpose being to avoid death duties. Although the primary trusts of the receiving settlement were in favour of the advanced beneficiary (being, essentially, accumulation and maintenance trusts in her favour during her infancy, and an absolute interest in capital contingently on attaining the age of 30), others, who were not objects of the power of advancement, were potentially interested under the default trusts. The House of Lords saw no objection to this resettlement. In fact, in appropriate circumstances, the interests of the non-objects (for example the advanced beneficiary's spouse and children) need not be minor or merely incidental: provided that the advancement is made for the demonstrable benefit of the advanced beneficiary, their interests **14.32**

---

[131] *Re Brittlebank* (1881) 30 WR 99; *Re Ropner's Settlement Trusts* [1956] 1 WLR 902.

[132] See Chapter 11 above.

[133] See, generally, GW Thomas *Powers* (Sweet & Maxwell, 1998) ('*Thomas*') 418–429; (1981) 9 NZULR 247 (J Prebble); [1994] PCB 402 (R Oerton).

[134] *Roper-Curzon v Roper-Curzon* (1871) LR 11 Eq 452; *Re Halsted's Will Trusts* [1937] 2 All ER 570; *Re Ropner's Settlement Trusts* [1956] 1 WLR 902; *Re Wills' Will Trusts* [1959] Ch 1; *Pilkington v IRC* [1964] AC 612. See also *Re Hampden's Settlement Trusts* [1977] TR 177, [2001] WTLR 195 (a case of a power of appointment); *Re Esteem Settlement* [2001] WTLR 641.

[135] [1964] AC 612.

may be substantial and extensive.[136] Indeed, the advanced beneficiary need not be a beneficiary at all under the trusts of the advancement. In *Re Clore's Will Trust*,[137] it was held that the trustees could properly pay capital to the trustees of a charity which the beneficiary wished to benefit. The power had to be exercised for the improvement of the material situation of the beneficiary, but this was not confined to his direct financial advantage: it could include, for instance, certain moral or social obligations on his part, such as those he might have towards dependants.[138] In the case of a wealthy man, it might also include enabling him to discharge the moral obligations that he recognized to make charitable donations.[139] The nature and amount of those donations depended on all the circumstances of the case, including the position in life of the beneficiary, the amount of the fund, and the amount of his other resources. If the obligation were not to be met out of the trust fund, the beneficiary would have to meet it out of his own pocket, if at all. Thus, the use of trust money improved his material situation.

Delegation

14.33 As to the second question, is it a proper objection to an advancement that it involves a delegation by the trustees of their duties and powers? In *Pilkington v IRC*,[140] Viscount Radcliffe dealt with this objection as follows:

> I am unconvinced by the argument that the trustees would be improperly delegating their trust by allowing the money raised to pass over to new trustees under a settlement conferring new powers on the latter. In fact I think that the whole issue of delegation is here beside the mark. The law is not that trustees cannot delegate: it is that trustees cannot delegate unless they have authority to do so. If the power of advancement which they possess is so read as to allow them to raise money for the purpose of having it settled, then they do have the necessary authority to let the money pass out of the settlement into the new trusts. No question of delegation of their powers or trusts arises. If, on the other hand, their power of advancement is so read as to exclude settled advances, *cadit quaestio*.

There is no doubt that the word 'benefit' in a power of advancement is wide enough to permit an application of funds by way of resettlement and, therefore, by necessary implication, to authorize the delegation of the trustees' powers.[141] In *Pilkington*, an actual transfer of assets to different trustees was not contemplated, for the trustees of the will which conferred the power and the trustees of the

---

[136] *Re Halsted's Will Trusts, supra; Pilkington v IRC, supra; Re Abraham's Will Trust* [1969] 1 Ch 463 at 484.
[137] [1966] 1 WLR 955.
[138] ibid 957–958 See also *Pilkington v IRC, supra.*
[139] cf *Re Walker* [1901] 1 Ch 879. See also *Re the S Settlement* (2001) 4 ITELR 206 and *Re the X Trust* (2002) 5 ITELR 119 (RC, Jersey).
[140] [1964] AC 612, 638–639.
[141] *Re Abraham's Will Trust* [1969] 1 Ch 463 (challenged on grounds of perpetuity not delegation).

proposed new settlement were the same persons. However, no importance was attached to this factor. 'So long as there are separate trusts, the property effectually passes out of the old settlement into the new one, and it is of no relevance that, at any rate for the time being, the persons administering the new trust are the same individuals.'[142]

Discretionary and protective trusts

It seems to follow that a similar power of advancement is also sufficiently wide to permit the creation of discretionary trusts or protective trusts, or indeed any kind of trust, notwithstanding that the advanced beneficiary himself may not be a beneficiary or object of such newly created trusts or, alternatively, may see his interest or expectations defeated by the trustees of such new trusts. If it is the case (as *Re Clore* clearly indicates it may be) that the power is even wide enough, in special circumstances, to authorize the complete diversion or divestment of a beneficiary's share in favour of a stranger and to the entire exclusion of the beneficiary himself, it is difficult to identify any convincing principle by which the creation of discretionary trusts could logically be classified as being, of its very nature, a non-beneficial purpose and be distinguished from *Re Clore*.[143] The crucial factor in each case is whether the particular purpose which it is proposed to effect or achieve by means of an exercise of the power of advancement is actually of benefit to the specific object of the power. It is only in exceptional circumstances that an application of the trust fund as in *Re Clore* could be said to be beneficial to any particular beneficiary or object. Similarly, even if the creation of discretionary or protective trusts by means of an advancement is not an unauthorized purpose per se, it is only in unusual cases that it could be justified as a proper exercise of the relevant power. **14.34**

It must be emphasized, however, that this analysis applies strictly to common-form powers of *advancement* (for the 'benefit' of a beneficiary) and not to express powers of advancement formulated in narrower terms. Nor does it necessarily follow that the same conclusion can be reached in relation to powers of *appointment* which are also exercisable for the 'benefit' of beneficiaries. There is an obvious difference between powers of *appointment* and powers of *advancement* in that no object of a power of *appointment* has any interest in the appointable property unless and until the power is exercised in his favour, whereas a common-form power of *advancement* applies to and operates in respect of a particular beneficiary's interest in the capital of the trust fund.[144] On the other hand, the two kinds of **14.35**

---

[142] *Pilkington v IRC* [1964] AC 612, 639; *Re Pilkington's Will Trusts* [1959] Ch 699, 705.

[143] This is the view expressed originally in *Thomas* 422–423, at a time when other works suggested the contrary. The current edition of J Mowbray et al, *Lewin on Trusts* (17th edn, Sweet & Maxwell, 2000) ('*Lewin*') 806, reversing its earlier view, now also accepts that discretionary and protective trusts may be created by way of advancement.

[144] Even if his interest exists under a revocable appointment: *Re Hodgson* [1913] 1 Ch 34.

power also have much in common. In any event, the delegation of powers of appointment is dealt with separately later in this work.[145]

Consent from persons with prior interests

14.36   Proviso (c) to section 32(1)[146] stipulates that no payment or application shall be made so as to prejudice any person entitled to any prior life or other interest, whether vested or contingent, in the money paid or applied, unless such person is in existence and of full age and consents in writing to such payment or application. This includes a person with a protected life interest, who, in giving such consent to an advance, will not forfeit his life interest. If he has a protected life interest under section 33 of the Trustee Act 1925, such consent to an advancement (whether made under section 32 or an express power), is expressly declared not to be a forfeiting event by section 33(1)(i). If the protected life interest is created under express protective trusts (and section 33 is not applicable), such consent is not a forfeiting event if the trust instrument includes an express power of advancement or the statutory power applies by implication.[147]

14.37   The objects of a prior discretionary trust are not persons entitled to any 'interest', so their consent is not required.[148] It is also probable that unborn children who may become entitled to capital, and have an interest in accumulated income prior to the relevant interest in capital, also have no 'prior interest' for these purposes, but this remains undecided. In *IRC v Bernstein*,[149] the settlor had directed that income should be accumulated during his lifetime 'in augmentation of the capital of the trust fund and for the benefit of the person or persons who shall eventually become entitled thereto'. On the settlor's death, part of the trust fund was to be held on trust for his wife absolutely or, if she had died, for the children of the marriage. No children had been born. Although it was held that the statutory power of advancement was not available in any event, the question was raised whether, if it had been, the unborn children would have had a 'prior interest' in the accumulated income (as opposed to the original capital). At first instance, Danckwerts J held that they would not. The Court of Appeal, however, left the question undecided,[150]

---

[145]   See, generally, Chapter 15 below.

[146]   Which is usually expressly excluded in modern trust instruments. The mere extension of s 32 to the entire fund, instead of one-half, will not affect the requirement for consent: *Henley v Wardell* The Times, 21 September 1988.

[147]   *Re Shaw's Settlement* [1951] Ch 833 (following *Re Hodgson* [1913] 1 Ch 34 and distinguishing *Re Stimpson's Trusts* [1931] 2 Ch 77); *Re Rees' Will Trusts* [1954] Ch 202. The consent of the objects of the discretionary trusts that would arise on the forfeiture of the protected life interest is not required: *Re Harris' Settlement* (1940) 162 LT 358.

[148]   *Re Beckett's Settlement* [1940] Ch 279.

[149]   [1961] Ch 399 (CA); and [1960] Ch 444 (Danckwerts J).

[150]   The Court of Appeal regarded this question as the same one that had arisen and also been left undecided in relation to s 31 of the Trustee Act 1925 in *Re Spencer* [1935] Ch 533 and *Re Turner's Will Trusts* [1937] Ch 15.

although they seem to have preferred the view that only persons who have a present right to call for income can be said to have a 'prior interest' and there was no such right during the accumulation period.[151]

The court has no power to dispense with the consent of the person with a prior **14.38** interest who is not under a disability.[152] If such person has become bankrupt, his consent is still required, although the sanction of his trustee in bankruptcy must then be obtained.[153] If the power to consent is exercisable by someone in a fiduciary position (and a person with a 'prior interest' in the context of a power of advancement would seldom be so), and he fails to give due and proper consideration to its exercise, the court may interfere.[154]

Hotchpot

Proviso (b) to section 32 (1)[155] provides that, if a person is or becomes absolutely **14.39** and indefeasibly entitled to a share in the trust property, the money paid or applied for his advancement or benefit shall be brought into account as part of such share. The value to be brought into account is the actual sum advanced, or the value of the advanced assets as at the date of the advancement; and it is set against the value of the trust property (or the relevant share therein) as at the date of its ultimate distribution.[156]

Exhaustive exercise of the power

Proviso (a) to section 32(1)[157] provides that the money paid or applied for the **14.40** advancement or benefit of any person shall not exceed altogether in amount more than one-half of that person's presumptive or vested share in the trust property. If the trustees exercise the power to its full extent and advance one-half of a beneficiary's share, the power is exhausted in so far as it concerns that beneficiary. It cannot be exercised subsequently, even though the value of retained assets increases and the amount advanced is then less than one-half the value of those assets.[158] In order to avoid this result, the trust instrument should declare that the

---

[151] [1961] Ch 399, 418.
[152] *Re Forster's Settlement* [1942] Ch 199. The judge added, however (at 207): 'I desire to add that nothing in this judgment is directed to the powers of the court under s 57 of the Trustee Act 1925. No application under that section is before me.' See also *Re Beale's Settlement Trusts* [1932] 2 Ch 15.
[153] *Re Cooper* (1884) 27 Ch D 565. See also *Re 90 Thornhill Road, Tolworth, Surrey* [1970] Ch 261; *Alexander v Alexander* (1870) LR 6 Ch 124.
[154] *Gilbey v Rush* [1906] 1 Ch 11; *Klug v Klug* [1918] 2 Ch 67.
[155] Which is usually expressly excluded in modern trust instruments.
[156] *Re Crocker* [1916] 1 Ch 25; *Re Poyser* [1908] 1 Ch 828; *Re Forster-Brown* [1914] 2 Ch 584; *Re Cooke* [1916] 1 Ch 480; *Re Tod* [1916] 1 Ch 576; *Re Willis* [1939] Ch 705; *Re Hillas-Drake* [1944] Ch 235; *Re Slee* [1962] 1 WLR 496, 507–508; *Re Gollin's Declaration of Trust* [1969] 1 WLR 1858.
[157] Which is usually replaced by a provision that the power of advancement extends to the whole of a beneficiary's vested or presumptive share.
[158] *Re Marquess of Abergavenny's Estate Act Trusts* [1981] 1 WLR 843.

power continues to be exercisable in respect of one-half of any increase in value of retained assets or the trustees should ensure that slightly less than one-half is advanced in the first place.

Advancements and the rule against perpetuities

14.41 The rule against perpetuities applies to a power of advancement in the same way that it applies to a power of appointment, and the trusts of the advanced fund must be read back into the head settlement which conferred the power in the first place. Thus, where a new settlement is created (or a transfer made to an existing separate one), the perpetuity period governing that new settlement (or the existing separate settlement) must be commensurate with, or at least cannot exceed, that which governs the head settlement out of which the advanced funds are derived.[159]

14.42 If some of the trusts created by an advancement are void for perpetuity and some are not, for example there is a valid life interest but the remainder interests are too remote, the general rule is that the advancement will stand in so far as the valid interests are concerned. However, if the overall effects of the advancement are so drastically different from those intended that it cannot reasonably be said to be for the benefit of the advanced beneficiary, the entire advancement may be void and the advanced funds will be treated as never having left the original settlement.[160] This is the effect of the so-called 'rule in *Hastings-Bass*', the scope and application of which are uncertain and which is discussed in greater detail elsewhere.[161]

Mode of exercising the power of advancement

14.43 Advancements are often effected by deed, although express powers frequently authorize advancements merely in writing, while section 32 of the Trustee Act 1925 specifies no requirement at all. Thus, a mere resolution of the trustees may suffice,[162] as will a transfer of assets to the trustees of another settlement (although prudent trustees will always want to retain a record of their actions). Where the consent of a person with a prior interest is required, it is customary, but not essential, to make such person a party to the deed or other instrument effecting or recording the advancement and to record the fact that such consent has been given.

14.44 The power, which is one to 'pay or apply any capital money', may be exercised by a resolution to allocate the relevant property to the beneficiary or by appropriating it on the trusts of a new settlement;[163] and also by advancing land, quoted investments,

---

159 *Pilkington v IRC, supra.*
160 *Re Hastings-Bass* [1975] Ch 25; *Re Abraham's Will Trusts* [1969] 1 Ch 463; *Mettoy Pension Trustees Ltd v Evans* [1990] 1 WLR 1587.
161 See paras 11.51–11.78 above.   162 *Re Wills' Will Trusts* [1959] Ch 1.
163 *Re Baron Vestey's Settlement* [1951] Ch 209; *Pilkington v IRC* [1964] AC 612.

or any other asset to the beneficiary: the court will not insist on a payment of cash with which the beneficiary could then buy the asset from the trustees.[164] Although the statutory power does not expressly authorize trustees to 'raise' money for advancement, this seems implicit in the section and, in any event, section 16(1) of the Trustee Act 1925 is available to them.[165]

Ensuring purpose is effected

Advancements may be made to the beneficiary directly, especially if made for general purposes, provided that the trustees can reasonably take the view that the beneficiary can be trusted to use the advanced money or assets for such purposes. If the advance is for a particular purpose, the trustees must not only make it clear to the beneficiary what that purpose is, but they must also inquire as to its application and do whatever they can in order to ensure that it is used only for that purpose.[166] **14.45**

E. Powers Relating to Sales and Other Dealing with Land and Other Property

Powers of sale are usually conferred on trustees expressly, either as general administrative powers or in relation to specific property or particular transactions. Occasionally, such powers must be implied, for example where there is direction to distribute the trust property among several beneficiaries and the nature of the property requires a prior sale; or where there is a direction to the trustees to carry on a business.[167] **14.46**

Such express or implied powers are supplemented by a large number of statutory powers. Several of these powers are dealt with in detail in other parts of this book,[168] although some of them will also be touched on briefly below. Most of them are part of a wide range of statutory powers conferred on trustees in relation to the purchase of or investment in, or other dealings with, land; and, therefore, the focus here is necessarily on powers relating to land. However, it must be borne in mind that some of these powers (such as the powers to sell by auction or to sell trust property in order to raise money for distribution of capital) actually apply to property of any kind. In any event, just a few of them can be noted here. **14.47**

---

[164] *Re Collard's Will Trusts* [1961] Ch 293; *Pilkington v IRC* [1964] AC 612, 639.

[165] See also *Re Wills' Will Trusts* [1959] Ch 1.

[166] *Re Pauling's Settlement Trust* [1964] Ch 303. In practice, there is little that the trustees can do if the advance is misapplied. See also *Will of Raphael* [1914] VLR 557; *Re Williams* [1950] St R Qd 148.

[167] See, for example, *Grant v Grant* (1914) 14 SR (NSW) 271; *Pagels v MacDonald* (1936) 54 CLR 519; *Re Bennett* (1912) 12 SR (NSW) 695, 698–699; *Re Wheaton* [1937] SASR 19.

[168] See Chapters 52 (investment) and 57 (Trusts of Land).

Powers conferred by the Trusts of Land and Appointment of Trustees Act 1996

14.48 As from 1 January 1997, when the Trusts of Land and Appointment of Trustees Act 1996 came into force,[169] a new regime for creating settlements of land (the 'trust of land') has replaced the former strict settlement and trust for sale. A 'trust of land' means 'any trust of property which consists of or includes land', other than 'settled land'.[170] Thus, the inclusion of *any* land in the trust fund will make the trust (including a bare trust)[171] a trust of land subject to the 1996 Act. Trusts for sale of land can still be created, but the doctrine of conversion (whereby the land was regarded as personal property, notwithstanding that it had not been sold) no longer applies.[172]

Power to postpone sale

14.49 Where trustees hold land on an immediate *trust* for sale created by a 'disposition', section 4(1) of the 1996 Act implies a power to postpone sale, despite any contrary provision in the disposition. Moreover, the trustees are not liable in any way for postponing sale of the land, in the exercise of their discretion, for an indefinite period.[173] A 'trust for sale' means 'an immediate trust for sale, whether or not exercisable at the request or with the consent of any person'.[174] A trust for sale is not 'immediate' and, therefore, a power to postpone sale is not required, if it is directed to be carried out on the occurrence of some future date or event (for example when a beneficiary attains a specified age), at which time section 4 of the 1996 Act becomes applicable. A 'disposition' includes a 'conveyance' (which itself includes a mortgage, charge, lease, assent, vesting declaration, vesting instrument, disclaimer, release, and every other assurance of property or of an interest therein by any instrument, except a will) and also a devise, bequest, or an appointment of property contained in a will.[175]

---

[169] Trusts of Land and Appointment of Trustees Act 1996 (Commencement) Order 1996, SI 1996/2974.

[170] The 1996 Act, s 1(1)(a) and (3). Land to which the Universities and Colleges Estates Act 1925 applies is also excluded from the new regime. A 'trust' includes any description of trust, whether express, implied, resulting, or constructive, including a trust for sale and a bare trust. Although settled land (strict settlements) can no longer be created, those created before 1997 could continue to exist and to be governed by the Settled Land Act 1925: see s 2. For the meaning of 'land', see the 1996 Act, s 23(2) and the Law of Property Act 1925, s 205(1)(ix).

[171] It would appear, somewhat oddly, that a constructive trustee also has the wide powers (eg to sell and reinvest) conferred by the 1996 Act.

[172] The 1996 Act, s 3(1). The abolition of the doctrine of conversion applies to trusts created or arising before or after 1 January 1997, but not to one created by the will of a testator who died before that date: s 3(2),(3).

[173] This applies to trusts created or arising before as well as after the commencement of the Act: s 4(2). Trustees are not liable in any way for postponing sale of the land, in the exercise of their discretion, for an indefinite period.

[174] The 1996 Act, ss 23(2), 25(1) and Sch 4, and the Law of Property Act 1925, s 205(1)(xxix).

[175] The 1996 Act, s 23(2), and the Law of Property Act 1925, s 205(1)(ii). A merely *oral* declaration of trust of land clearly does not constitute an 'assurance', but it is possible that it is still included in 'disposition'.

Powers of an absolute owner

Section 6(1) of the 1996 Act provides that, for the purpose of exercising their **14.50** functions as trustees,[176] the trustees of land have in relation to the land subject to the trust all the powers of an absolute owner. They have powers to acquire freehold or leasehold land in the United Kingdom as an investment, for occupation by a beneficiary, or for any other reason, and they have all the powers of an absolute owner in relation to such land.[177] In exercising such powers (which clearly include a power of sale), the trustees must have regard to the rights of their beneficiaries; and they must not contravene any other enactment or rule of law or equity.[178] Moreover, such wide powers (unlike the power to postpone sale) can be excluded or modified in the disposition creating the trust of land, and their exercise may be made subject to consent.[179]

Section 6(1) on its own would not allow trustees to decide unilaterally to termi- **14.51** nate their trust, and transfer the trust property to beneficiaries absolutely entitled, if the trust was intended to be a continuing one, or, indeed, if all the beneficiaries did not wish this to happen. Section 6(2) provides specifically:

> Where in the case of any land subject to a trust of land each of the beneficiaries inter-ested in the land is a person of full age and capacity who is absolutely entitled to the land, the powers conferred on the trustees by subsection (1) include the power to convey the land to the beneficiaries even though they have not required the trustees to do so; and where land is conveyed by virtue of this subsection—
>
> (a) the beneficiaries shall do whatever is necessary to secure that it vests in them, and
>
> (b) if they fail to do so, the court may make an order requiring them to do so.

This provision clearly applies only to land, and not any other property, comprised in a trust of land. The power is exercisable when all the beneficiaries (ie all the beneficial joint tenants or tenants in common) are, or, it seems, the sole beneficiary is, absolutely entitled to the land and of full age and capacity. The reference to 'each of the beneficiaries' seems to be an attempt to exclude cases where absolute entitlement could be claimed by the joint action of beneficiaries who are successive owners, one or more of whom may be a limited owner, rather than con-current owners. The power may also be exercised without the consent of the beneficiaries—indeed, against their wishes—but it can be excluded by the trust instrument or relevant disposition.[180] However, in the situation contemplated by section 6(2), the beneficiaries could, presumably, forestall the trustees' action by

---

[176] And for no other or wider purpose, eg they cannot make gifts of trust property.

[177] Trusts of Land and Appointment of Trustees Act 1996, s 6(3); Trustee Act 2000, s 8.

[178] Section 6(5),(6) of the 1996 Act. What exactly these provisions add to the general law is unclear. [179] ibid, s 8(1),(2).

[180] ibid, ss 8(1), 11(2)(c).

compelling the latter to appoint new trustees of the land under section 19 of the 1996 Act.[181]

14.52 When exercising the powers conferred by section 6 of the 1996 Act, the duty of care imposed by section 1 of the Trustee Act 2000 will apply.[182]

Power to partition

14.53 A power of sale on its own, or a power to exchange on its own, does not authorize trustees to effect a partition of land comprised in the trust fund, although a power of sale coupled with a power to exchange may suffice, at least where the property is held on trust for several beneficiaries.[183] In many cases, the same result can be achieved by means of a power of appropriation.[184]

14.54 Where beneficiaries of full age are absolutely entitled in undivided shares to land held in a trust of land, section 7(1) of the 1996 Act authorizes trustees to partition the land, or any part of it, and provide, by way of mortgage or otherwise, for the payment of equality money.[185] The trustees must give effect to any such partition by conveying the partitioned land in severalty (whether or not subject to any legal mortgage created for raising equality money), either absolutely or in trust, in accordance with the rights of those beneficiaries.[186] Before exercising the powers conferred by section 7(2), the trustees must obtain the consent of each of those beneficiaries.[187] If there is disagreement, the trustees may apply to the court, which can make such order as it thinks fit, including an order for the partition of the property.[188]

14.55 Where a share in the land is affected by an incumbrance, the trustees may either give effect to it or provide for its discharge from the property allotted to that share as they think fit.[189] If a share in the land is absolutely vested in a minor, these powers are still exercisable as if he were of full age, except that the trustees may act on his behalf and retain land or other property representing his share in trust for him.[190] If improvements have been made to the property by a beneficiary, account may be taken of the fact on an apportionment (as on a sale).[191]

---

[181] See paras 57.30–57.39 generally below.
[182] Section 6(9), inserted by the Trustee Act 2000, s 40 and Sch 2, Pt II, para 45(3). The Trustee Act 2000 came into force on 1 February, 2001: The Trustee Act 2000 (Commencement) Order 2001, SI 2001/49.
[183] *Bradshaw v Fane* (1856) 3 Drew 534; *Re Frith and Osborne* (1876) 3 Ch D 618.
[184] See paras 14.77–14.83 below.
[185] Section 7(1) is subject to ss 21 and 22 of the Commonhold and Leasehold Reform Act 2002.
[186] The 1996 Act, s 7(2). There is nothing in s 7 to suggest that a partition must involve *all* the beneficiaries.
[187] ibid, s 7(3).   [188] ibid, s 14; *Rodway v Landy* [2001] Ch 703.   [189] ibid, s 7(4).
[190] ibid, s 7(5).   [191] *Re Pavlou* [1993] 1 WLR 1046.

Exclusion and restriction of powers

The powers conferred by sections 6 and 7 of the 1996 Act (ie their powers as **14.56** absolute owners, to transfer land to those absolutely entitled, to acquire land, and to partition) 'do not apply in the case of a trust of land created by a disposition in so far as provision to the effect that they do not apply is made by the disposition',[192] ie they can be expressly excluded. Thus, in theory, even a power of sale may be excluded, although not to the extent of depriving the trustees of their power of sale under section 16(1) of the Trustee Act 1925.[193] Moreover, the exercise of any power conferred by sections 6 and 7 of the 1996 Act can be made subject, by the relevant disposition, to a requirement of consent.[194]

Delegation of powers by trustees of land

Section 9(1) of the 1996 Act authorizes trustees of land, by power of attorney, to **14.57** delegate to any beneficiary or beneficiaries of full age and beneficially entitled to an interest in possession in land subject to the trust any of their functions as trustees which relate to the land. Such delegation may be for any period or indefinite.[195] Beneficiaries to whom functions have been delegated under section 9(1) are, in relation to the exercise of the functions, in the same position as trustees (with the same duties and liabilities); but such beneficiaries shall not be regarded as trustees for any other purposes.[196] The provisions of section 9, together with the supplementary provisions of section 9A (inserted by the Trustee Act 2000),[197] are dealt with in greater detail in the chapter on Delegation of Powers.[198]

Other specific powers to deal with trust property

Power to sell by auction

In relation specifically to sales of property (real or personal) by auction, section 12 **14.58** of the Trustee Act 1925 provides:

(1) Where a trustee has a duty or power to sell property, he may sell or concur with any other person in selling all or any part of the property, either subject to prior charges or not, and either together or in lots, by public auction or by private contract, subject to any such conditions respecting title or evidence of title or other matter as the trustee thinks fit, with power to vary any contract for sale, and to buy in at any auction, or to rescind any contract for sale and to re-sell, without being answerable for any loss.
(2) A duty or power to sell or dispose of land includes a duty or power to sell or dispose of part thereof, whether the division is horizontal, vertical, or made in any other way.

---

[192] ibid, s 8(1). The exclusion must be in 'the disposition' creating the trust.
[193] ibid, s 8(4) and Trustee Act 1925, s 16(2); and see paras 14.46–14.52 above.
[194] ibid, s 8(2). The requirement must be in 'the disposition' creating the trust.
[195] ibid, s 9(5).   [196] ibid, s 9(7).
[197] Trustee Act 2000, s 40 and Sch 2, Pt II, para. 47.   [198] See Chapter 15 below.

(3) This section does not enable an express power to sell settled land to be exercised where the power is not vested in the tenant for life or statutory owner.

Subsection (2) ('in any other way') seems wide enough to authorize trustees to sell or reserve minerals separately from the land itself, and also to grant an easement to the purchaser.

Power to sell subject to depreciatory conditions

14.59 A sale by trustees may be subject to reasonable conditions of sale, but not anything that cannot be justified by the state of their title.[199] In *Dance v Goldingham*,[200] for example, trustees who sold land on condition that the purchaser should accept a short and inadequate title, which depreciated the value of the property, were held to have committed a breach of trust. It was held, in *Dunn v Flood*,[201] that the court would not order specific performance of a contract for a sale made on depreciatory conditions, as a result of which section 13 of the Trustee Act 1925 was enacted.[202] Section 13 provides:

(1) No sale made by a trustee shall be impeached by any beneficiary upon the ground that any of the conditions subject to which the sale was made may have been unnecessarily depreciatory, unless it also appears that the consideration for the sale was thereby rendered inadequate.
(2) No sale made by a trustee shall, after the execution of the conveyance, be impeached as against the purchaser upon the ground that any of the conditions subject to which the sale was made may have been unnecessarily depreciatory, unless it appears that the purchaser was acting in collusion with the trustee at the time when the contract for sale was made.
(3) No purchaser, upon any sale made by a trustee, shall be at liberty to make any objection against the title upon any of the grounds aforesaid.
(4) This section applies to sales made before or after the commencement of this Act.

Section 13 merely protects the purchaser by safeguarding the transaction (and even then not in all cases): it does not protect the trustee who makes a sale subject to unnecessary and unjustifiable conditions from liability for breach of trust. Indeed, given that trustees can, and usually do, include in a contract of sale a right to rescind the contract if they are unable or unwilling on reasonable grounds to remove a purchaser's objections,[203] they may also be liable if they fail to include such a term.

Power to raise money by sale, mortgage, etc

14.60 Section 16(1) of the Trustee Act 1925 provides:

Where trustees are authorised by the instrument, if any, creating the trust or by law to pay or apply capital money subject to the trust for any purpose or in any manner,

---

[199] *Hobson v Bell* (1839) 2 Beav 17; *Rede v Oakes* (1864) 4 De GJ & SM 505; *Dunn v Flood* (1883) 25 Ch D 629; (1885) 28 Ch D 586.   [200] (1873) LR 8 Ch App 902.   [201] ibid.
[202] Originally in s 3 of the Trustee Act 1888 and then s 14 of the Trustee Act 1893.
[203] See, for example, *Re Jackson and Haden's Contract* [1906] 1 Ch 412; *Selkirk v Romar Investments Ltd* [1963] 1 WLR 1415.

they shall have and be deemed always to have had power to raise the money required *by sale*, conversion, calling in, or mortgage of all or any part of the trust property for the time being in possession.

Section 16 applies notwithstanding anything to the contrary contained in the trust instrument and thus cannot be excluded.[204] However, its purpose is somewhat limited: for example, it does not authorize trustees to mortgage existing assets in order to raise money to purchase further investments.[205] Indeed, in so far as land is concerned, it is difficult to see the purpose of section 16 now that trustees have the powers of an absolute owner under section 6(1) of the 1996 Act, although it may still be relevant occasionally in relation to personal property.

Duties of trustees in relation to sale of trust property

The powers of trustees, including their powers of sale, are conferred the better to enable them to perform their trusts.[206] In any sale, trustees must act in the interests, and for the financial benefit, of their beneficiaries; and, where the beneficiaries have different interests, with a due consideration of those interests.[207] Thus, where trustees had struck a bargain for the sale of trust property but had not bound themselves by a legally enforceable contract, they were under a duty to consider and explore a higher offer that they had received, and not to carry through the bargain to which they felt in honour bound.[208] They have 'an overriding duty to obtain the best price which they can for their beneficiaries'.[209] If they fail to observe this principle, they are liable for a breach of trust. Similarly, trustees will be liable if they turn down a better offer because a beneficiary [210] expresses a preference for another purchaser offering a lower price.[211] Indeed, if there are several offers, all of them equally advantageous, the trustees must form their own opinion as to which one to accept and must not simply follow a beneficiary's preference.[212] The general principle does not apply, of course, once a binding contract for sale has been concluded, and

14.61

---

[204] Section 16(2). Although it does not apply to trustees for charitable purposes or to trustees for the purposes of the Settled Land Act 1925, not being also statutory owners.

[205] *Re Suenson-Taylor's Settlement* [1974] 1 WLR 1280.

[206] *Balls v Strutt* (1841) 1 Hare 146, 149; see also *Re Wyvern Developments Ltd* [1974] 1 WLR 1097, 1106.

[207] *Downes v Grazebrook* (1817) 3 Mer 200; *Ord v Noel* (1820) 5 Mad 438, 440; *Re Cooper and Allen's Contract* (1876) 4 Ch D 802; *Cowan v Scargill* [1985] Ch 270.

[208] *Buttle v Saunders* [1950] 2 All ER 193; *Cowan v Scargill, supra*, 280; *R v Commission for New Towns, ex p Tomkins* (1988) 58 P & CR 57.

[209] *Buttle v Saunders, supra*, 195.

[210] Unless the beneficiary is solely and absolutely entitled to the property in question.

[211] *Taylor v Tabrum* (1833) 6 Sim 281.

[212] *Selby v Bowie* (1863) 4 Giff 300. If all offers are equally advantageous, the trustees may, of course, properly decide to accept the beneficiary's preferred offer, as long as it is their decision to do so and not simply in compliance with his wishes.

the court will not allow the trustees to withdraw from it[213] (unless the contract itself amounts to a breach of trust).[214]

14.62   For similar reasons, trustees must ensure that the management of the sale is conducted properly, that it takes place in a reasonably competitive market, and is not carried out within an unreasonable time frame.[215]

Powers to repair or improve trust property

14.63   Historically, trustees not only had power, but were actually under a duty, to *repair* trust property and ensure that it did not fall into decay from want of repair. However, in the absence of express provision to the contrary, they were neither under a duty nor empowered to *improve* trust property.[216] Before 1997, trustees for sale of *land* had the extensive range of powers to improve land made available by the Settled Land Act 1925,[217] which were made applicable by section 28 of the Law of Property Act 1925. Section 28 was repealed by the Trusts of Land and Appointment of Trustees Act 1996.[218] Trustees of land now have all the powers of an absolute owner in relation to trust land, which include extensive powers to repair and improve that land.[219] However, not only are these enlarged powers restricted to land (and trustees may hold property requiring repair and improvement other than land), but they also do not indicate whether a particular authorized work constitutes an 'improvement' and not a mere 'repair'. Thus, trustees of land, like trustees generally, must fall back on general equitable principles,[220] which, in broad terms, require the trustees to maintain an even hand as between beneficiaries[221] and to ensure that the burden is not borne unfairly by those entitled to income as opposed to those entitled to capital (and vice versa). In the absence of express provision to the contrary in the trust instrument, the cost of 'improvements' ought, therefore, to fall on trust capital; and the cost of mere 'repair' ought to fall on trust income.

---

[213] *Harper v Hayes* (1860) 2 De GF & J 542.

[214] The court will not order specific performance of a contract which is a breach of trust, and the purchaser must seek damages from the trustees: *Wood v Richardson* (1840) 4 Beav 174, 176; *Fuller v Knight* (1843) 6 Beav 205; *Thompson v Blackstone* (1843) 6 Beav 470; *Sneesby v Thorne* (1855) 7 De GM & G 399; *Oceanic Steam Navigation Co v Sutherberry* (1880) 16 Ch D 236; *Dunn v Flood* (1883) 25 Ch D 629; (1885) 28 Ch D 586; *Gas Light and Coke Co v Towse* (1887) 35 Ch D 519.

[215] *Ord v Noel* (1820) 5 Mad 438, 440; *Harper v Hayes, supra*; *Tomlin v Luce* (1889) 41 Ch D 573 and (1889) 43 Ch D 191; *Grove v Search* (1906) 22 TLR 290.

[216] See, for example, *Harkness v Harkness* (1903) 20 WN (NSW) 269; *Amos v Fraser* (1906) 4 CLR 78, 84.

[217] For details of the Settled Land Act 1925 and the specific powers of trustees of settled land, see *Lewin*, 1064–1139. SLA settlements still exist, but are of declining importance.

[218] Section. 25(2) and Sch 4.   [219] The 1996 Act, s 6(1); and Trustee Act 2000, s 8(3).

[220] *Re Hotchkys* (1886) 32 Ch D 408; *Re Conquest* [1929] 2 Ch 353; *Re Smith* [1930] 1 Ch 88; *Re Wynn (No 2)* [1955] 1 WLR 940.   [221] See paras 11.79–11.88 above.

As to whether particular works are properly categorized as 'improvements' or **14.64** 'repairs', in broad terms 'the test is whether the act to be done is one which in substance is the renewal or replacement of substantially the whole'.[222] A more helpful formulation is provided in the Australian case of *Wilkie v Equity Trustees Executors and Agency Co Ltd*,[223] despite the fact that Madden CJ clearly used the word 'repairs' to encompass improvements as well as minor works of maintenance:

> So we have three kinds of repairs to consider. First, those ordinary recurring repairs which more fully appertain to the enjoyment of the tenant for life and which last only for a short time—such as papering and painting. Income must bear all such repairs. Secondly, where structural repairs are very great or considerable, they are to be charged wholly to corpus because the advantage obtained from them tells very much more in favour of the remainderman. Thirdly, there is a middle position where you have repairs which are structural in some degree, being more than the ordinary recurring repairs which a tenant, as between a landlord and tenant—ordinarily carries out—a class of repairs which is midway between the two first classes indicated. The cost of these should be borne in due proportion by income and corpus. We think that the rule is that trustees should be trusted in their just discretion to appropriate the proportion which either should bear.

Generally, trust income would bear the burden, for example, of the equivalent of **14.65** 'tenant's repairs',[224] rent payable for the property,[225] rates and taxes relating to the property,[226] and fire insurance.[227] On the other hand, trust capital would be expected to bear the burden of large-scale works required by the local authority to remedy structural defects;[228] or of putting in repair property purchased when out of repair;[229] or of connecting the property to the public sewers.[230] In other cases, especially where the trustees have to borrow money, and where the benefit of the works (be they categorized as 'repairs' or 'improvements') is enjoyed by all beneficiaries, the cost may be apportioned, for example the loan is repaid out of capital but payments of interest come out of trust income.[231] It is a question of fact in each case whether a particular act constitutes a repair or an improvement. However, a power to pay for repairs out of trust capital or income is still conferred for the benefit of the estate as a whole and the trustees would not necessarily be

---

[222] *Lurcott v Wakely and Wheeler* [1911] 1 KB 905, 924, per Buckley LJ.
[223] [1909] VLR 277, 281.
[224] *Re Redding* [1897] 1 Ch 876; *Re Betty* [1899] 1 Ch 821. See also *Re Kingham* [1897] 1 IR 170.
[225] *Re Gjers* [1899] 2 Ch 54.
[226] *Will of Jackson* [1905] VLR 16; *Foley v Cannon* (1936) 53 WN (NSW) 223; *Re Dawes* [1854] VLR 76.
[227] *Perpetual Trustee Co Ltd v Adams* (1923) 24 SR (NSW) 87, 92; *Re Cross* [1943] VLR 38.
[228] *Re Robins* [1928] Ch 721. See also *Eyre v O'Rorke* (1905) 25 NZLR 182; *Re Smart's Settlement* (1933) 33 SR (NSW) 412.
[229] *Re Freman* [1898] 1 Ch 28. Cf *Lord De Tabley* (1896) 75 LT 328; *Re Jervis* (1919) 146 LT Jo 215.
[230] *Read v Deane* [1906] VLR 138. Cf *Re Partington* [1902] 1 Ch 711.
[231] *Re Courtier* (1886) 34 Ch D 136; *Re Redding* [1897] 1 Ch 876; *Re Betty* [1899] 1 Ch 821; *Re Kingham* [1897] 1 IR 170. See also *Re Gjers* [1899] 2 Ch 54.

exercising that power properly if they were to throw on capital the costs of repairs that ought to be borne by income: the power must be exercised fairly and equitably and not, in effect, to readjust beneficial entitlements.[232] On general principles, however, unless the trustees manifestly exercise their powers unreasonably or unfairly in the circumstances of the particular case, their decision ought to stand.

Powers to insure trust property

14.66 Trustees are generally[233] not under a duty to insure trust property, but it has long been accepted that they have power to do so.[234] In any event, trustees now have extensive statutory powers to insure.

14.67 Section 19 of the Trustee Act 1925 (as amended)[235] provides:

(1) A trustee may—

(a) insure any property which is subject to the trust against risks of loss or damage due to any event, and

(b) pay the premiums out of the trust funds.

(2) In the case of property held on a bare trust, the power to insure is subject to any direction given by the beneficiary or each of the beneficiaries—

(a) that any property specified in the direction is not to be insured;

(b) that any property specified in the direction is not to be insured except on such conditions as may be so specified.

(3) Property is held on a bare trust if it is held on trust for—

(a) a beneficiary who is of full age and capacity and absolutely entitled to the property subject to the trust, or

(b) beneficiaries each of whom is of full age and capacity and who (taken together) are absolutely entitled to the property subject to the trust.

---

[232] *Re Lord De Tabley* (1896) 75 LT 328; *Re Earl of Stamford and Warrington* [1916] 1 Ch 404; *Re Lord Boston's Will Trusts* [1956] Ch 395.

[233] Although it must surely be the case that a trustee ought to act, in relation to insurance, in the same way as an ordinary prudent man would act; and there must also be cases where such a duty surely ought to be implied from the nature of the property, or the circumstances of the case: see, for example, *London and North Western Railway Co v Glyn* (1859) 1 El & El 652; *North British and Mercantile Insurance Co v Moffatt* (1871) LR 7 CP 31; *Ebsworth v Alliance Marine Insurance Co Ltd* (1873) LR 8 CP 596; and *Re Betty* [1899] 1 Ch 821, 829. See also *Pateman v Heyen* (1993) 33 NSWLR 188; *Re South Australian Perpetual Forests Ltd 1964 Trust Deed* (1995) 64 SASR 434; *Kingham v Kingham* [1897] 1 IR 170; *Re Wythes* [1893] 2 Ch 369, 375 (court order).

[234] *Re McEarcharn* (1911) 103 LT 900, 902; *Ex p Yallop* (1808) 15 Ves 60, 67–68; *Bailey v Gould* (1840) 4 Y & C Ex 221; *Garner v Moore* (1855) 3 Drew 277; *Kingham v Kingham* [1897] 1 IR 170, 174. Cf *Re Bennett* [1896] 1 Ch 778, 786. See also Law Commission's Report (*Trustees' Powers and Duties*), Law Com No 260 (1999) 162–163. There can be no general duty to insure because some trustees would not have the money to pay premiums.

[235] By the Trusts of Land and Amendment of Trustees Act 1996, s 25(1) and Sch 3, para 3(1),(5), and the Trustee Act 2000, ss 34, 40(3) and Sch 4, Pt II. Under the original version of s 19 of the 1925 Act, there was a limit on the amount of insurance (a maximum of three-quarters of the full value of the property) and premiums were payable out of trust income. The 1996 Act, s 6(1) of which conferred on trustees of land all the powers of an absolute owner, restricted s 19 to personalty. The new version of s 19 does not amend s 6(1).

(4) If a direction under subsection (2) of this section is given, the power to insure, so far as it is subject to the direction, ceases to be a delegable function for the purposes of section 11 of the Trustee Act 2000 (power to employ agents).

(5) In this section 'trust funds' means any income or capital funds of a trust.

Thus, section 19, which may be excluded or modified by the trust instrument,[236] **14.68** applies to all kinds of property. Trustees will be subject to the statutory duty of care imposed by section 1(1) of the Trustee Act 2000 (which may itself be excluded or modified)[237] when exercising these powers.

Insurance premiums are payable out of trust capital or income, but there is no guid- **14.69** ance as to which ought to be applied in what circumstances. Although the trustees appear to have a wide discretion in this regard, they are subject to general equitable principles, such as the duty to act fairly and maintain an even hand as between the beneficiaries. In most cases, they will still be guided by the established general principle that, in the absence of express directions to the contrary, if the insurance is intended to preserve trust capital or is for the benefit of the entire fund (for example, policies to meet inheritance tax liabilities), the premiums are payable out of trust capital.[238] If premiums that ought to have fallen on capital were actually paid out of income, they must be reimbursed (with interest).[239] In other cases, for example where beneficiaries are personally allowed to enjoy trust property (usually chattels) on such terms and conditions as the trustees think fit, the costs of insuring that property might fairly be shared between the trust and the beneficiary or between capital and income, depending on the beneficiary's interest in the trust fund.

The *application* of insurance money where the policy is kept up under any trust or **14.70** power is governed by section 20 of the Trustee Act 1925 (as amended):[240]

(1) Money receivable by trustees or any beneficiary under a policy of insurance against the loss or damage of any property subject to a trust or to a settlement within the meaning of the Settled Land Act 1925 . . . shall, where the policy has been kept up under any trust in that behalf or under any power statutory or otherwise, or in performance of any covenant or of any obligation statutory or otherwise, or by a tenant for life impeachable for waste, be capital money for the purposes of the trust or settlement, as the case may be.

(2) If any such money is receivable by any person, other than the trustees of the trust or settlement, that person shall use his best endeavours to recover and receive the money, and shall pay the net residue thereof, after discharging any costs of recovering and receiving it, to the trustees of the trust or settlement, or, if there are no trustees capable of giving a discharge therefor, into court.

---

[236] Trustee Act 1925, s 69(2).   [237] Trustee Act 2000, Sch 2, para 7.

[238] *Macdonald v Irvine* (1878) 8 Ch D 101; *Re Sherry* [1913] 2 Ch 508; *Carver v Duncan* [1985] AC 1082, 1120. See also s 20(1) of the Trustee Act 1925 as to the application of insurance money.

[239] *Re Morley* [1895] 2 Ch 738.

[240] By the Trusts of Land and Appointment of Trustees Act 1996, s 25(1) and Sch 3, para 3(5) and the Trustee Act 2000, ss 34(2), 40(3), Sch 4, Pt II.

(3) Any such money—

(a) if it was receivable in respect of settled land within the meaning of the Settled Land Act 1925, or any building or works thereon, shall be deemed to be capital money arising under that Act from the settled land, and shall be invested or applied by the trustees, or, if in court, under the direction of the court, accordingly;

(b) if it was receivable in respect of personal chattels settled as heirlooms within the meaning of the Settled Land Act 1925, shall be deemed to be capital money arising under that Act, and shall be applicable by the trustees, or, if in court, under the direction of the court, in like manner as provided by that Act with respect to money arising by a sale of chattels as settled heirlooms as aforesaid;

(c) if it was receivable in respect of land subject to a trust of land or personal property held on trust for sale, shall be held upon the trusts and subject to the powers and provisions applicable to money arising by a sale under such trust;

(d) in any other case, shall be held upon trusts corresponding as nearly as may be with the trusts affecting the property in respect of which it was payable.

(4) Such money, or any part thereof, may also be applied by the trustees, or, if in court, under the direction of the court, in rebuilding, reinstating, replacing, or repairing the property lost or damaged, but any such application by the trustees shall be subject to the consent of any person whose consent is required by the instrument, if any, creating the trust to the investment of money subject to the trust, and, in the case of money which is deemed to be capital money arising under the Settled Land Act 1925, be subject to the provisions of that Act with respect to the application of capital money by the trustees of the settlement.

(5) Nothing contained in this section prejudices or affects the right of any person to require any such money or any part thereof to be applied in rebuilding, reinstating, or repairing the property lost or damaged, or the rights of any mortgagee, lessor, or lessee, whether under any statute or otherwise.

(6) This section applies to policies effected either before or after the commencement of this Act, but only to money received after such commencement.

F. Power to Give Receipts

14.71   A power to give a receipt is implicit in and incidental to any power of sale conferred on trustees. However, without more, this would not necessarily provide the purchaser or other recipient of the receipt with protection against a subsequent claim that the trustees had acted improperly and that he had actual or constructive notice of the trust. Thus, trust instruments invariably conferred (and often still do confer) express powers to give receipts on trustees, usually for general purposes but sometimes in relation to specific transactions or assets. In any event, section 14 of the Trustee Act 1925 provides:

(1) The receipt in writing of a trustee for any money, securities, investments[241] or other personal property or effects payable, transferable, or deliverable to him

---

[241]   Inserted by the Trustee Act 2000, s 40(1), Sch 2, Pt II, para 19.

under any trust or power shall be a sufficient discharge to the person paying, transferring, or delivering the same and shall effectively exonerate him from seeing to the application or being answerable for any loss or misapplication thereof.

(2) This section does not, except where the trustee is a trust corporation, enable a sole trustee to give a valid receipt for—

(a) proceeds of sale or other capital money arising under a trust of land;[242]

(b) capital money arising under the Settled Land Act 1925.

(3) This section applies notwithstanding anything to the contrary in the instrument, if any, creating the trust.

G. Power to Compromise

Trustees have powers, under section 15 of the Trustee Act 1925, to compromise claims and settle disputes out of court. Section 15 provides: **14.72**

(1) A personal representative,[243] or two or more trustees acting together,[244] or, subject to the restrictions imposed in regard to receipts by a sole trustee not being a trust corporation,[245] a sole acting trustee[246] where by the instrument, if any, creating the trust, or by statute, a sole trustee is authorised to execute the trusts and powers reposed in him, may, if and as he or they think fit—

(a) accept any property, real or personal, before the time at which it is made transferable or payable; or

(b) sever and apportion any blended trust funds or property; or

(c) pay or allow any debt or claim on any evidence that he or they think sufficient; or

(d) accept any composition or any security, real or personal, for any debt or for any property, real or personal, claimed; or

(e) allow any time of payment of any debt; or

(f) compromise, compound, abandon, submit to arbitration, or otherwise settle any debt, account, claim, or thing whatever relating to the testator's or intestate's estate or to the trust;

and for any of those purposes may enter into, give, execute, and do such agreements, instruments of composition or arrangement, releases, and other things as to him or them seem expedient, without being responsible for any loss occasioned by any act or thing so done by him or them if he has or they have discharged the duty of care set out in section 1(1) of the Trustee Act 2000.[247]

---

[242] Inserted by the Trusts of Land and Appointment of Trustees Act 1996, s 25(1), Sch 3, para 3(1),(3). See also (1969) 33 Conv (NS) 240 (J Garner).

[243] *Re Houghton* [1904] 1 Ch 622 (one executor compromising claim of a co-executor).

[244] This does not remove the general requirement that, where there are more than two trustees of a private trust, they must all act unanimously.

[245] See Law of Property Act 1925, s 27(2); Trustee Act 1925, s 14(2); Settled Land Act 1925, s 94(1).   [246] *Re Ridsdel* [1947] Ch 597 (custodian trustee).

[247] Before the 2000 Act came into effect, the relevant words were 'in good faith', which suggested that the trustees need not have acted prudently: *Re Owens* (1882) 47 LT 61.

The section has a wide operation and the powers conferred by it will be construed broadly.[248] Thus, although the compromise of a claim will normally arise in the context of a commercial dispute with a stranger to the trust, it need not do so. The section may also be relied on in order to compromise a claim by a beneficiary under the trust, as in *Re Earl of Strafford*,[249] where the compromise involved the surrender by beneficiaries of life interests in certain chattels in return for the abandonment of a claim against them in respect of other chattels, and where Megarry V-C stated:[250]

> Nor is strict mathematical and actuarial calculation of benefits the only criterion: a compromise which, on the best estimate available, confers unequal financial benefits may nevertheless be a good compromise which ought to be accepted if it is likely to resolve long-standing family disputes and promote family peace. A beneficiary who benefits least in money may benefit most in the value that he or she places on peace of mind.

However, there must be a compromise of a genuine dispute: the section cannot be used in the context of an artificial 'dispute' simply in order to effect a variation of the trusts.[251]

14.73 Although trustees may exercise these powers if they 'think fit' and essentially have a discretion whether to do so or not, they must, nonetheless, exercise them actively and consciously. As was stated in an Australian case, *Partridge v Equity Trustees Executors and Agency Co Ltd*,[252] dealing with a similar provision, the section 'involves the use of an active discretion, not the mere passive attitude of leaving matters alone, and no relief is afforded where (as here) loss has arisen from carelessness or supineness'. (In this case, the trustees had failed to enforce certain debts before the debtor became bankrupt.) In the case of a debt owed to the trust, the trustees must, of course, ensure that it does not become time barred. However, provided the trustees take a conscious, considered, and honest decision not to press for the immediate payment of a debt, they will not be liable if, in the event, it proves irrecoverable.[253]

14.74 It is not necessary, in order to justify a compromise, to show that the claim in question would otherwise have succeeded.[254] Indeed, if it were otherwise, the powers would be deprived of their force and purpose. However, there must be a genuine claim that can be compromised. Rights which are not disputed and which are easily enforced need not be compromised, for example where a purchaser from

---

[248] *Re Ezekiel's Settlement Trusts* [1942] Ch 230; *Re Earl of Strafford* [1980] Ch 28.
[249] ibid.
[250] ibid 33.
[251] ibid; *Re Powell-Cotton Resettlement* [1956] 1 WLR 23.
[252] (1947) 75 CLR 149, 164.
[253] See, for example, *Re Greenwood* (1911) 105 LT 509; *Cotton v Dempster* (1918) 20 WAR 14; *National Trustees Executors and Agency Co of Australasia Ltd v Dwyer* (1940) 63 CLR 1. The trustees are also entitled to have regard to the expressed wishes of the settlor: *Hitch v Leworthy* (1842) 2 Hare 200.
[254] *Re Ridsdel* [1947] Ch 597.

the trustees has simply forfeited his deposit on failure to complete.[255] Trustees should pay attention to the views and wishes of their beneficiaries before entering into a compromise, but they are not bound by them or obliged to obtain consent: indeed, trustees can act against their beneficiaries' wishes if they so choose.[256]

In a great many instances, trustees still prefer to obtain the directions and sanction of the court before entering into a compromise. This is especially the case, and probably prudent, where large sums are involved, where the claim or dispute involves difficult legal or factual questions, where the interests of infant or unborn beneficiaries are involved, or where there may be a conflict of interest and duty. The costs of any such application would normally be paid out of the trust fund. Thus, despite the width of section 15, it is surprisingly little used by trustees in practice. **14.75**

H. Power to Pay Statute-Barred Debts

It might seem obvious that debts owed by the trust, and which have become statute-barred, ought not to be paid by the trustees and that they would be liable for a clear breach of trust if they did so. However, the law is somewhat anomalous on this point. Certainly, a *personal representative* should not pay a statute-barred debt when it has been judicially held to be statute-barred,[257] although it seems, in other cases, he can do so and not be guilty of a *devastavit*.[258] If a residuary legatee directs the personal representative to plead the statute, he must comply.[259] Trustees, on the other hand, may not be similarly compelled by their beneficiaries; and, apparently, they may also pay statute-barred debts. In *Budgett v Budgett*,[260] for example, a trustee had failed to pay the costs of the solicitor to the trust before the debt became statute-barred and asked the court for directions as to whether he could then pay it. Kekewich J held that the trustee should do so, because a trustee's position differed from that of an executor. An executor was paying the testator's debts, not his own, and thereby 'admitting a creditor to prove against another's estate'. A trustee, on the other hand, was paying his own debt 'and he, although the legal liability may be gone, still owes the money. It may not be recoverable, but still the debt is not gone. It is a debt due from him.'[261] Indeed, the trustee had a right to pay such a debt even if the beneficiaries objected. How far one can extrapolate a general principle from this instance is debatable, however. **14.76**

---

[255] ibid; *Re Hoobin* [1957] VR 341.
[256] *Re Ezekiel's Settlement Trusts* [1942] Ch 230; *Re Earl of Strafford* [1980] Ch 28.
[257] *Midgely v Midgely* [1893] 3 Ch 282.
[258] ibid 297–299. See, generally, Williams, Mortimer and Sunnucks, *Executors, Administrators and Probate* (17th edn) 735–737. [259] *Re Wenham* [1892] 3 Ch 299.
[260] [1895] 1 Ch 202. [261] ibid 217.

I. Powers of Appropriation[262]

Inherent powers

14.77　Trustees have inherent powers of appropriation, although their extent is somewhat uncertain: they would seem to be exercisable in certain specific situations, rather than generally. The original basis of the trustees' power was the avoidance of circuitous acts. A beneficiary who is entitled to a share of the trust fund may prefer to receive a specific asset from the fund instead of a sum of money. If the trustees have power to sell the asset to the beneficiary, and the beneficiary is immediately entitled to a sum of money equal to the purchase price, the trustees may short circuit the proposed transaction by appropriating the asset directly to the beneficiary.[263] In such a case, the consent of the beneficiary is required (if he does not initiate the transaction) and the appropriation is regarded as the equivalent of a sale,[264] which may have adverse capital gains tax implications.[265] If the beneficiary is absolutely entitled, he can call for the immediate transfer of the appropriated assets as soon as the appropriation is made.[266] However, trustees may also appropriate assets, it seems, in favour of infant beneficiaries, who would be bound by it if it is done fairly and at a proper valuation, even though the beneficiaries are incapable of giving consent.[267]

14.78　An appropriation under the inherent power (unlike the statutory power) is valid only if the appropriated assets are authorized investments at the date of appropriation.[268] Appropriation may be made in favour of one beneficiary only, and there

---

[262] Distinguished, of course, from a *duty* to appropriate, which must be carried out: *Fraser v Murdoch* (1881) 6 App Cas 855; *Re Walker* (1890) 62 LT 449; *Re Ruddock* (1910) 102 LT 89.

[263] *Re Beverly* [1901] 1 Ch 681; *Re Ruddock* (1910) 102 LT 89; *Re Craven* [1914] 1 Ch 358; *Re Nicholson's Will Trusts* [1936] 3 All ER 832; *Wigley v Crozier* (1909) 9 CLR 425, 438. See also the power to partition of trustees of land under s 8(3) of the Trustee Act 2000.

[264] Despite the general rule that a trustee may not sell trust property to himself, a trustee (or personal representative) who is also a beneficiary may appropriate trust assets to satisfy his share, provided that he acts fairly: *Elliott v Kemp* (1840) 7 M & W 306, 313; *Barclay v Owen* (1889) 60 LT 220; *Re Richardson* [1896] 1 Ch 512; *Kane v Radley-Kane* [1999] Ch 274; *Re Pearce* [1936] SASR 137. It is prudent, however, to ensure that express provision is made to authorize such an eventuality and to pre-empt any argument of breach of fiduciary duty.

[265] ie if there is a sufficient contractual element. However, see also Taxation of Chargeable Gains Act 1992, ss 62(4), 64(3).

[266] *Re Marshall* [1914] 1 Ch 192. A beneficiary who is absolutely entitled to a fraction of personal property is generally able to call for the transfer of an *aliquot* part of that personalty even if there has been no appropriation. This rule does not apply to realty or to special kinds of personalty, such as shares in private companies and mortgages: see *Re Kipping* [1914] 1 Ch 62; *Re Sanderman's Will Trusts* [1937] 1 All ER 368; *Re Weiner's Will Trusts* [1956] 1 WLR 579; *Stephenson v Barclays Bank Trust Co Ltd* [1975] 1 WLR 882, 889–890; *Crowe v Appleby* [1975] 1 WLR 1539, 1543.

[267] *Re Ruddock* (1910) 102 LT 89.

[268] *Stewart v Sanderson* (1870) LR 10 Eq 26, 28; *Re Waters* [1889] WN 39.

need not be a contemporaneous appropriation in favour of all,[269] provided the trustees act fairly.[270]

The trustees' inherent power also extends to the appropriation of assets to a settled share,[271] but not, it seems, where the beneficiaries are entitled only to shares of income, because an undivided share of income of the entire trust fund is not the same thing as the entire income of an appropriated share of the trust fund.[272] (The position is different under the statutory power and a suitably drafted express power.) **14.79**

Appropriated assets are valued as at the date of appropriation.[273] Once appropriated, any increase or decrease (as the case may be) in their value will accrue to, or fall upon, the beneficiary to whom they were appropriated.[274] If the appropriation is intended to satisfy the beneficiary's entire interest in, or share of, the trust fund at the time the appropriation is made, he will not be able to claim any share of any increase in value of assets retained by the trustees on the account of other beneficiaries.[275] However, where the appropriation is partial, in the sense that it is intended to satisfy only a fraction of the beneficiary's share of the fund, the beneficiary must bring into account, on the final distribution of the trust fund, that which has been previously appropriated to him. As a general rule, it is the *cash value* (as at the date of appropriation) that is brought into account.[276] There is no requirement to bring into account notional interest on the cash value.[277] Whether this accords with the settlor's true intention, and whether it is beneficial to the beneficiary of the appropriation or to the other beneficiaries, depends on the circumstances of the case, but it may be prudent to ensure that the trust instrument expressly authorizes the appropriation of assets by reference to their value as a specified fraction or proportion of the value of the trust fund as a whole.[278] **14.80**

If the value of the appropriated assets exceeds the value of the beneficiary's share or interest in the trust fund, the appropriation may still be made, by way of sale and set-off, with the beneficiary paying equality money in order to make up the difference.[279] **14.81**

---

[269] *Re Richardson* [1896] 1 Ch 512; *Re Nickels* [1898] 1 Ch 630. No doubt, the trustee must consider the effect of an appropriation on other beneficiaries.
[270] *Re Lepine* [1892] 1 Ch 210, 218; *Re Brookes* [1914] 1 Ch 558.
[271] *Re Nickels, supra.*
[272] *Re Freeston's Charity* [1978] 1 WLR 741; and see also *Macculloch v Anderson* [1904] AC 55.
[273] *Re Charteris* [1917] 2 Ch 379; *Re Collins* [1975] 1 WLR 309.
[274] *Fraser v Murdoch* (1881) 6 App Cas 855; *Re Waters* [1889] WN 39 ('for better or worse', as Kay J put it); *Re Richardson* [1896] 1 Ch 512. Moreover, the trustees cannot claim any indemnity against the general trust fund for any subsequent loss to the appropriated assets: *Fraser v Murdoch, supra*, 865.
[275] *Re Marquess of Abergavenny's Estate Act Trusts* [1981] 1 WLR 843.
[276] *Re Richardson, supra*; *Re Gollin's Declaration of Trust* [1969] 1 WLR 1858.
[277] *Re Marquess of Abergavenny's Estate Act Trusts, supra*, 847.
[278] *Re Leigh's Settlement Trusts* [1981] CLY 2453.
[279] *Re Phelps* [1980] Ch 275, 277–278; and see s 33 of the Administration of Estates Act 1925.

Statutory powers

14.82 There are also extensive statutory powers of appropriation in section 41 of the Administration of Estates Act 1925. Although these powers are conferred on *personal representatives* (which, in this context, does not include trustees),[280] it is common practice for trust instruments to confer these statutory powers expressly on trustees, usually subject to modifications (such as the exclusion of the requirement for consent). The provisions of section 41 are largely self-explanatory and are as follows:

> (1) The personal representative may appropriate any part of the real or personal estate, including things in action, of the deceased in the actual condition or state of investment thereof at the time of appropriation in or towards satisfaction of any legacy bequeathed by the deceased, or of any other interest or share in his property, whether settled or not, as to the personal representative may seem just and reasonable, according to the respective rights of the persons interested in the property of the deceased:
>
> Provided that—
>
> (i) an appropriation shall not be made under this section so as to affect prejudicially any specific devise or bequest;
>
> (ii) an appropriation of property, whether or not being an investment authorised by law or by the will, if any, of the deceased for the investment of money subject to the trust, shall not (save as hereinafter mentioned) be made under this section except with the following consents:—
>
> > (a) when made for the benefit of a person absolutely and beneficially entitled in possession, the consent of that person;
> >
> > (b) when made in respect of any settled legacy share or interest, the consent of either the trustee thereof, if any (not being also the personal representative), or the person who may for the time being be entitled to the income:
>
> If the person whose consent is so required as aforesaid is an infant or is incapable, by reason of mental disorder within the meaning of the Mental Health Act 1983 of managing and administering his property and affairs, the consent shall be given on his behalf by his parents or parent, testamentary or other guardian or receiver, or if, in the case of an infant, there is no such parent or guardian, by the court on the application of his next friend;[281]
>
> (iii) no consent (save of such trustee as aforesaid) shall be required on behalf of a person who may come into existence after the time of appropriation, or who cannot be found or ascertained at that time;
>
> (iv) if no receiver is acting for a person suffering from mental disorder, then, if the appropriation is of an investment authorised by law or by the will, if

---

280 Administration of Estates Act 1925, s 55(1)(xi).

281 The county court has jurisdiction under this proviso where the amount or value of the estate does not exceed the county court limit: s 41(1A).

any, of the deceased for the investment of money subject to the trust, no consent shall be required on behalf of the said person;

(v) if, independently of the personal representative, there is no trustee of a settled legacy share or interest, and no person of full age and capacity entitled to the income thereof, no consent shall be required to an appropriation in respect of such legacy share or interest, provided that the appropriation is of an investment authorised as aforesaid.

(2) Any property duly appropriated under the powers conferred by this section shall thereafter be treated as an authorised investment, and may be retained or dealt with accordingly.

(3) For the purposes of such appropriation, the personal representative may ascertain and fix the value of the respective parts of the real and personal estate and the liabilities of the deceased as he may think fit, and shall for that purpose employ a duly qualified valuer in any case where such employment may be necessary; and may make any conveyance (including an assent) which may be requisite for giving effect to the appropriation.

(4) An appropriation made pursuant to this section shall bind all persons interested in the property of the deceased whose consent is not hereby made requisite.

(5) The personal representative shall, in making the appropriation, have regard to the rights of any person who may thereafter come into existence, or who cannot be found or ascertained at the time of appropriation, and of any other person whose consent is not required by this section.

(6) This section does not prejudice any other power of appropriation conferred by law or by the will (if any) of the deceased, and takes effect with any extended powers conferred by the will (if any) of the deceased, and where an appropriation is made under this section, in respect of a settled legacy, share or interest, the property appropriated shall remain subject to all trusts and powers of leasing, disposition, and management or varying investments which would have been applicable thereto or to the legacy, share or interest in respect of which the appropriation is made, if no such appropriation had been made.

(7) If after any real estate has been appropriated in purported exercise of the powers conferred by this section, the person to whom it was conveyed disposes of it or any interest therein, then, in favour of a purchaser, the appropriation shall be deemed to have been made in accordance with the requirements of this section and after all the requisite consents, if any, had been given.

(8) In this section, a settled legacy, share or interest includes any legacy, share or interest to which a person is not absolutely entitled in possession at the date of the appropriation, also an annuity, and 'purchaser' means a purchaser for money or money's worth.

(9) This section applies whether the deceased died intestate or not, and whether before or after the commencement of this Act, and extends to property over which a testator exercises a general power of appointment, including the statutory power to dispose of entailed interests, and authorises the setting apart of a fund to answer an annuity by means of the income of that fund or otherwise.

14.83 When incorporated into a trust instrument, section 41 thus provides a reasonably comprehensive code enabling trustees to appropriate assets. It is usually modified so as to exclude the need for any consents, thereby making the administration of the trust easier and simpler and also ensuring that an appropriation is not categorized as an agreement for sale with and to the beneficiary. Section 41, unlike the inherent power of trustees, applies to an appropriation of property whether or not being an investment authorized by law or by the will. In other respects, the operation of the statutory power is subject to the same principles as are applicable to the trustees' inherent power (and which have been described above), save to the extent that the trust instrument specifies otherwise.

J. Power to Conduct Business

14.84 Trustees generally have no power to conduct a business unless they are expressly authorized to do so by the trust instrument.[282] This seems self-evident where the question is whether the trustees can invest the trust fund in the acquisition of a business which they then intend to carry on, given the commercial skills required and the risks involved. However, the position is broadly the same where the original settled property is itself a business or includes a business. Even in such a case, if the trustees are intended to continue the business, clear and express powers to do so ought to be conferred on them. It cannot be assumed that, in settling the business on trustees, the settlor or testator impliedly expected or authorized them to retain it and carry it on: if this had been his true intention, he would be expected to have conferred the necessary powers to enable them to do so. In such cases, the general presumption is that trustees are authorized to carry on the business only until such time as they are able to sell it as a going concern: they may not do so indefinitely and must sell it within a reasonable time.[283] If they satisfy this requirement, they are entitled to an indemnity out of the trust fund in respect of any liabilities properly incurred.[284] However, if they fail to sell the business when they could have obtained a fair price for it, they will be personally liable for losses incurred thereafter.[285]

14.85 In some instances, an implied power to carry on a business may be apparent from the context or the circumstances of the case, but this is unusual and ought not to

---

[282] *Kirkman v Booth* (1848) 11 Beav 273; *Collinson v Lister* (1855) 20 Beav 356. This is clearly different from investing in trading companies (including cases where trustees hold a controlling shareholding in a trading company), in relation to which the crucial issues are the scope of the trustees' powers of investment, their authority to delegate, and their duties of supervision.

[283] *Garrett v Noble* (1834) 6 Sim 504; *Collinson v Lister* (1855) 20 Beav 356, 365–366; *Re Chancellor* (1884) 26 Ch D 42; *Dowse v Gorton* [1891] AC 190; *Re Crowther* [1895] 2 Ch 56; *Re East* (1914) 111 LT 101. Although these cases deal with personal representatives, it is generally regarded that the same principles apply to trustees. See also *Re Morish* [1902] St R Qd 245; *Re Hansford* [1949] St R Qd 143.

[284] *Dowse v Gorton, supra.*

[285] *West Australian Trustee, Executor and Agency Co Ltd v Perpetual Executors, Trustees and Agency Co Ltd (WA)* (1942) 44 WALR 64.

be relied upon.[286] However, where a business is settled on trust for sale and a power to postpone sale is also conferred on the trustees, this will not suffice, without more, to justify the carrying on of the business, other than for the purpose of selling it as a going concern.[287]

Even where trustees are authorized to carry on a business, they may not, in the absence of express provision to the contrary, make use of any assets other than those employed by the settlor or testator. Otherwise, a personal representative could hold up the administration of an estate, and a trustee could postpone the distribution of a trust fund, by retaining all its assets in order to make use of them in running the business.[288]   **14.86**

In the absence of express provision to the contrary, trustees of a private trust must act unanimously when exercising their powers: if one fails or refuses to join with the others, the power cannot be exercised.   **14.87**

K. Power to Lend Trust Moneys

Trustees were authorized under the Trustee Investment Act 1961[289] to invest trust money in loans secured on land (as narrower range investments requiring advice). These provisions are repealed by the Trustee Act 2000, section 3 of which confers wider power of investing in mortgages on trustees. These powers are available to existing, as well as new, trusts, although they can be excluded by the trust instrument. Powers of investment conferred by the Trustee Act 2000 are considered in greater detail elsewhere.[290]   **14.88**

Where trustees are authorized by the trust instrument or by law to pay or apply capital money 'for any purpose or in any manner', section 16 of the Trustee Act 1925[291] also authorizes them to raise the money required by mortgaging the trust property (realty or personalty), and to hold an equity of redemption as a trust   **14.89**

---

[286] See, for example, *Re Chancellor, supra* (authority to carry on business for 22 years); *Re Smith* [1896] 1 Ch 71 (authority for 2 years only). See also a number of Australian authorities where the issue has been canvassed extensively, with differing results: *Cain v Watson* (1890) 16 VLR 88; *Re Bridget Quigley's Will* (1895) 16 LR (NSW) Eq 45; *Hill v Hill* (1901) 1 SR (NSW) Eq 228; *Re Astill and Freeman* [1906] QWN 5; *Re Crago* (1908) 8 SR (NSW) 269; *Fomsgard v Fomsgard* [1912] VLR 209; *McCarthy v McCarthy* (1919) 19 SR (NSW) 122; *Re Reynolds* [1921] VLR 575; *Re Benjamin* [1938] VLR 76; *Re Francis* [1948] SASR 287; *Re May* [1948] QWN 5; and also *Re George Benson* (1915) 34 NZLR 639; *Re Lees* (1915) 34 NZLR 1054.

[287] *Re Smith* [1896] 1 Ch 171.

[288] *Ex parte Garland* (1803) 10 Ves 110, 119–121. Cf *Re Dimmock* (1885) 52 LT 494.

[289] First Schedule, Part II, para 13.

[290] See paras 10.58–10.84 above and Chapter 52 below.

[291] See para 14.60 above.

asset. In relation to land, section 6 of the Trusts of Land and Appointment of Trustees Act 1996 confers even wider powers on trustees.[292]

14.90 In the absence of statutory powers such as these (and others) or of an express power in the trust instrument, trustees may not lend trust moneys.[293] It is common practice, therefore, to confer on trustees express powers to lend, with or without interest, with or without security or on personal security only. Even the widest power must be exercised reasonably and prudently, however. Trustees ought not to lend on speculative ventures;[294] and, even if authorized to lend on personal security only, they ought to secure a personal covenant to repay that is likely to be honoured (and perhaps even obtain guarantees).[295] Trustees should not leave trust moneys in an ordinary bank account for an unreasonable length of time:[296] they should pay them into a responsible bank and only for a temporary purpose.[297] Section 11(1) of the Trustee Act 1925[298] authorizes trustees to pay any trust money into a bank to a deposit or other account, but only pending the negotiation and preparation of any mortgage or charge, or during any other time while an investment is being sought for.

14.91 A trustee should not generally lend trust moneys jointly with the moneys of another, or the moneys of the trustee himself.[299] Trustees should not lend trust moneys to one or more of themselves (in breach of the rule against self-dealing).[300] It is also ill-advised for them to lend their own money to the trust (in breach of the rule against conflict of interests).[301]

---

[292] See paras 14.49–14.52 above.

[293] In some cases, the requisite power may be implied, eg if trustees are authorized to carry on a business, it may be inferred that they are also authorized to extend credit in transactions in which such credit is normally allowed in that kind of business.

[294] *Fouche v Superannuation Fund Board* (1952) 88 CLR 609.

[295] *Re Smith's Trusts* (1905) 5 SR (NSW) 500.

[296] *Lord Londesborough v Somerville* (1854) 19 Beav 295; *Astbury v Beasley* (1868) 17 WR 638; *Cann v Cann* (1884) 33 WR 40. Trustees were authorized to invest in bank deposits under the Trustee Investments Act 1961, as will be the case under the Trustee Act 2000, s 3, but an ordinary account is not an investment.

[297] *Massey v Banner* (1820) 1 J & W 241, 248; *Johnson v Newton* (1853) 11 Hare 160; *Wilks v Groome* (1856) 3 Drew 584; *Ex p Kingston* (1871) 6 Ch App 632; *Re Marcon's Estate* (1871) 40 LJ Ch 537.

[298] Which is repealed by the Trustee Act 2000, s 40, Sch 2, para 18 and Sch 4, Pt II. The effect of its repeal will probably be to revive pre-1926 law and the propositions set out in the text above will become more significant.

[299] *Will of Margaret MacPherson* [1963] NSWR 268.

[300] *Anon v Walker* (1828) 5 Russ 7; *Re Waterman's Will Trusts* [1952] 2 All ER 1054; *Space Investments Ltd v Canadian Imperial Bank of Commerce Trust Co (Bahamas) Ltd* [1986] 1 WLR 1072.

[301] Notwithstanding the charity case of *A-G v Hardy* (1851) 1 Sim (NS) 338, and its approval in *Re Mason's Orphanage and London and North Western Rly* [1896] 1 Ch 54, 59.

L. Power to Borrow

Historically, trustees have had power to borrow money for the purposes of their trust, for example for the payment of debts arising from the management of the trust property, the repair and improvement of trust property, running an authorized business, and so on. Trustees also have available specific statutory powers authorizing borrowing for specific purposes, for example the powers conferred by section 16 of the Trustee Act 1925,[302] or on trustees of land by section 6(1) of the Trusts of Land and Appointment of Trustees Act 1996.[303] **14.92**

In the absence of express provision to the contrary, trustees of a private trust must act unanimously when exercising their powers: if one fails or refuses to join with the others, the power cannot be exercised.[304] **14.93**

---

[302] See para 14.60 above; and *Re Suenson-Taylor's Settlement* [1974] 1 WLR 1280. The kind of transaction held not to be authorized by section 16 could be sanctioned, of course, by the beneficiaries, if they are all of full age and capacity: *Re White* [1901] 1 Ch 570. See also *Scott v Murray* (1888) 14 VLR 187. [303] See paras 14.48–14.52 above.

[304] *Luke v South Kensington Hotel Co* (1879) 11 Ch D 121.

15

DELEGATION BY TRUSTEES[1]

A. General Principle

The office of trustee is one of personal trust and confidence. The person who **15.01** holds it is required to exercise his own judgement and discretion. In the absence of express provision to the contrary, an individual trustee or the trustees collectively cannot refer or commit the trust or the exercise of trustee powers to a co-trustee or to another, for *delegatus non potest delegare*.[2] 'Such trusts and powers are supposed to have been committed by the testator to the trustees he appoints by reason of his personal confidence in their discretion, and it would be wrong to permit them to be exercised by [another].'[3] 'Trustees who take on themselves the management of property for the benefit of others have no right to shift their duty

---

[1] See, generally, GW Thomas, *Powers* (Sweet & Maxwell, 1998) ('*Thomas*') Ch 7 (which pre-dates both the Trustee Delegation Act 1999 and the Trustee Act 2000, however).

[2] *A-G v Glegg* (1738) 1 Atk 356; *Crewe v Dicken* (1798) 4 Ves 97; *Chambers v Minchin* (1802) 7 Ves 186; *Langford v Gascoyne* (1805) 11 Ves 333; *Adams v Clifton* (1826) 1 Russ 297; *Clough v Bond* (1838) 3 My & Cr 490; *Cowell v Gatcombe* (1859) 27 Beav 568; *Wood v Weightman* (1872) LR 13 Eq 434; *Re Bellamy and Metropolitan Board of Works* (1883) 24 Ch D 387; *Re Flower and Metropolitan Board of Works* (1884) 27 Ch D 592.

[3] *Robson v Flight* (1865) 4 De GJ & S 608, 613, *per* Lord Westbury LC.

on other persons; and if they employ an agent, they remain subject to responsibility towards their *cestuis que trust*, for whom they have undertaken the duty.'[4]

15.02 The most common application of the rule against delegation is in the context of the exercise of dispositive powers and discretions conferred on trustees and others who hold fiduciary office. However, the principle is much wider than this: even a non-fiduciary power cannot be delegated if (as is likely to be the case) the donor intended the donee to exercise his own discretion and not commit its exercise to another.[5] Nor is it the case that only dispositive powers are subject to the rule: it also applies to administrative powers. The crucial question is whether the exercise of the particular power requires the exercise of a personal discretion; and such a requirement can be (and generally is) inherent in any special power, whether it is conferred on a trustee or other fiduciary or on a non-fiduciary.[6]

15.03 The strict rule could always be excluded or modified by express provision in the trust instrument. Moreover, there were limited exceptions to the rule. In particular, trustees could delegate tasks which were merely ministerial and involved no personal discretion or confidence. Trustees were themselves required to exercise discretions—to distribute trust property, to select investments, to sell or lease trust property,[7] and so on—but, once they had done so, the mere 'mechanical' task of implementing their decision could then be delegated to another. Thus, trustees could execute a deed by an attorney if it involved no discretion, such as simply passing a legal estate.[8] Similarly, provided it is clear that the trustee had exercised his own judgement and discretion (which fact should, for safety, be recorded in the deed itself), there is no reason why he should not delegate to an attorney the formal execution of a deed of appointment, or of any ministerial act, in order to complete the appointment.[9] A trustee could also delegate in cases of necessity, for instance where the trust property and beneficiaries were overseas.

15.04 Eventually, it was established that, if, according to ordinary business practice, it was prudent to employ an agent to carry out a particular task, such as a broker to deal in stocks on behalf of the trustees, or solicitors to transact legal business, then

---

[4] *Turner v Corney* (1841) 5 Beav 515, 517, *per* Lord Langdale MR. See also *Rowland v Witherden* (1851) 3 Mac & G 568; *Speight v Gaunt* (1883) 22 Ch D 727, 756, *per* Lindley LJ; *Re Airey* [1897] 1 Ch 164, 170, *per* Kekewich J; *Re Parry* [1969] 1 WLR 614, 618, *per* Pennycuick J.

[5] *Re Joicey* [1915] 2 Ch 115.

[6] See, for example, *Re Brown's Trusts* (1865) LR 1 Eq 74; *Carr v Atkinson* (1872) LR 14 Eq 397; *Webb v Sadler* (1873) 8 Ch App 419, esp 424; *Williamson v Farwell* (1887) 35 Ch D 128. See also *Hawkins v Kemp* (1803) 3 East 410.

[7] *Rowland v Witherden* (1851) 3 Mac & G 568; *Clarke v The Royal Panopticon* (1857) 4 Drew 26; *Robertson v Flight* (1865) 4 De GJ & Sm 608, 614; *Green v Whitehead* [1930] 1 Ch 38. Cf *Re Muffett* (1887) 56 LJ Ch 600.

[8] *Re Hetling and Merton's Contract* [1893] 3 Ch 269, 280. See also *A-G v Scott* (1750) 1 Ves Sen 413 and *Offen v Harman* (1859) 29 LJ Ch 307.   [9] *Re Airey* [1897] 1 Ch 164, 170.

trustees, too, could employ and pay such an agent.[10] The trustees would be liable for any loss which occurred except in cases of 'legal' or 'moral' necessity. If the trustees' agent, having been properly appointed, committed some act in the course of his employment for which the trustees were held liable, they were entitled to an indemnity from the trust fund.[11] The appointment of an agent to advise them did not, however, enable trustees to escape the consequences of some inherently unauthorized or improvident act.[12] Nor did it authorize the appointment of an agent to carry out some task outside the agent's competence.[13] Trustees could not delegate the selection of an agent to one or just some of their number;[14] and, where money was payable to trustees, all the trustees would have to sign a discharge if the payer was to receive a valid receipt:[15] in the exercise of all their functions, trustees were and are obliged to act jointly and unanimously.[16] Nevertheless, the position was reached where, under the general law, trustees could employ an agent where (i) such employment was expressly authorized by the trust instrument, or (ii) *ex necessitate rei* it was impossible for the trustee to do the particular act himself, or (iii) the act was merely ministerial and the employment of an agent was reasonably necessary in the circumstances or was in accordance with ordinary business practice.[17] However, trustees still could not delegate the execution of their trusts at 'their own mere will and pleasure'.[18]

B. Statutory Authority to Delegate

The powers of trustees to delegate have been widened considerably by statute— **15.05** most notably by section 25 of the Trustee Act 1925 and Part IV of the Trustee Act 2000.[19] These statutory provisions authorize individual trustees and trustees collectively to delegate, but only to a limited extent and subject to specific restrictions. In particular, there is still no general statutory power for trustees to delegate

---

[10] *Speight v Gaunt* (1883) 9 App Cas 1; *Bonithon v Hockmore* (1685) 1 Vern 316; *Joy v Campbell* (1804) 1 Sch & Lef 328; *Clough v Bond* (1838) 3 My & Cr 490; *Speight v Gaunt* (1883) 22 Ch D 727, 756, 763; 9 App Cas 1, 4, 19; *Re Gasquoine* [1894] 1 Ch 470, 475, 476, 478.

[11] *Benett v Wyndham* (1862) 4 De GF & J 259.

[12] *Learoyd v Whiteley* (1887) 12 App Cas 727.

[13] *Fry v Tapson* (1884) 28 Ch D 268; *Budge v Gummow* (1872) 7 Ch App 719; *Re Dewar* (1885) 54 LJ Ch 830; *Ex p Townsend* (1828) 1 Moll 139.

[14] *Robinson v Harkin* [1896] 2 Ch 415. See also *Re Bellamy and Metropolitan Board of Works* (1883) 24 Ch D 387; *Re Flower and Metropolitan Board of Works* (1884) 27 Ch D 592.

[15] *Ex p Belchier* (1754) Amb 218, 219.

[16] *Luke v South Kensington Hotel Co* (1879) 11 Ch D 121, 125.

[17] *Re Parsons* (1754) Amb 218; *Speight v Gaunt* (1883) 9 App Cas 1.

[18] ibid 5, *per* Earl of Selborne LC. The Law Commission's Consultation Paper No 146 (*Trustees' Powers and Duties*), which preceded the Trustee Delegation Act 1999, contains a useful summary of the history and restrictive scope of the rule against delegation: see paras 3.7–3.15 in particular.

[19] The Trustee Act 2000 came into force on 1 February 2001: The Trustee Act 2000 (Commencement) Order 2001, SI 2001/49.

their dispositive discretions. Subject to a limited exception in section 25 of the Trustee Act 1925, trustees may delegate dispositive discretions only if they are expressly authorized to do so by their trust instrument and only to the extent authorized by the terms of the particular power. Such express powers (which are now common) and some of the difficult questions to which they have given rise will be dealt with later in this chapter.[20] First, however, we shall look in detail at the main statutory powers of delegation available to trustees.

Delegation by individual trustees: section 25 of the Trustee Act 1925

15.06 A limited and temporary form of delegation of discretions (including dispositive discretions) by an individual trustee was authorized by section 25 of the Trustee Act 1925 (as subsequently amended).[21] The Trustee Delegation Act 1999[22] has now substituted a new version of section 25, which provides as follows:

> (1) Notwithstanding any rule of law or equity to the contrary, a trustee may, by power of attorney, delegate the execution or exercise of all or any of the trusts, powers and discretions vested in him as trustee either alone or jointly with any other person or persons.
>
> (2) A delegation under this section—
>
> (a) commences as provided by the instrument creating the power or, if the instrument makes no provision as to the commencement of the delegation, with the date of the execution of the instrument by the donor; and
>
> (b) continues for a period of twelve months or any shorter period provided by the instrument creating the power.
>
> (3) The persons who may be donees of a power of attorney under this section include a trust corporation.
>
> (4) Before or within seven days after giving a power of attorney under this section the donor shall give written notice of it (specifying the date on which the power comes into operation and its duration, the donee of the power, the reason why the power is given and, where some only are delegated, the trusts, powers and discretions delegated) to—
>
> (a) each person (other than himself), if any, who under any instrument creating the trust has power (whether alone or jointly) to appoint a new trustee; and
>
> (b) each of the other trustees, if any;
>
> but failure to comply with this subsection shall not, in favour of a person dealing with the donee of the power, invalidate any act done or instrument executed by the donee.

---

[20] See paras 15.38–15.67 below.

[21] In broad terms, the original section 25 authorized delegation, for an unlimited period, in the case of a trustee who was absent from the UK for more than a month (cf s 36(1) of the Trustee Act 1925). The Powers of Attorney Act 1971, s 9, introduced a general power of delegation for individual trustees, but the period of delegation was restricted to 12 months. A further amendment by s 3(3) of the Enduring Powers of Attorney Act 1985 dealt with delegation by a trustee for sale who was also a beneficial co-owner.

[22] Which came into force on 1 March 2000: The Trustee Delegation Act 1999 (Commencement) Order 2000, SI 2000/216.

(5) A power of attorney given under this section by a single donor—

(a) in the form set out in subsection (6) of this section; or
(b) in a form to the like effect but expressed to be made under this subsection,

shall operate to delegate to the person identified in the form as the single donee of the power the execution and exercise of all the trusts, powers and discretions vested in the donor as trustee (either alone or jointly with any other person or persons) under the single trust so identified.

(6) The form referred to in subsection (5) of this section is as follows—

'THIS GENERAL TRUSTEE POWER OF ATTORNEY is made on [*date*] by [*name of one donor*] of [*address of donor*] as trustee of [*name or details of one trust*]. I appoint [*name of one donee*] of [*address of donee*] to be my attorney [*if desired, the date on which the delegation commences or the period for which it continues (or both)*] in accordance with section 25(5) of the Trustee Act 1925.

[*To be executed as a deed*]'.

(7) The donor of a power of attorney given under this section shall be liable for the acts or defaults of the donee in the same manner as if they were the acts or defaults of the donor.

(8) For the purpose of executing or exercising the trusts or powers delegated to him, the donee may exercise any of the powers conferred on the donor as trustee by statute or by the instrument creating the power, including power, for the purpose of the transfer of any inscribed stock, himself to delegate to an attorney power to transfer, but not including the power of delegation conferred by this section.

(9) The fact that it appears from any power of attorney given under this section, or from any evidence required for the purposes of any such power of attorney or otherwise, that in dealing with any stock the donee of the power is acting in the execution of a trust shall not be deemed for any purpose to affect any person in whose books the stock is inscribed or registered with any notice of the trust.

(10) This section applies to a personal representative, tenant for life and statutory owner as it applies to a trustee except that subsection (4) shall apply as if it required the notice there mentioned to be given—

(a) in the case of a personal representative, to each of the other personal representatives, if any, except any executor who has renounced probate;
(b) in the case of a tenant for life, to the trustee of the settlement and to each person, if any, who together with the person giving the notice constitutes the tenant for life; and
(c) in the case of a statutory owner, to each of the persons, if any, who together with the person giving the notice constitute the statutory owner and, in the case of a statutory owner by virtue of section 23(1)(a) of the Settled Land Act 1925, to the trustees of the settlement.

15.07 Thus, by way of summary, an individual trustee may now delegate all or any of his trusts, powers, and discretions, but still only for a maximum period of twelve months (from the relevant date). Delegation is effected by a statutory short-form power of attorney (or one to the like effect). A power of attorney given under section 25 may take effect as an enduring power of attorney. A trustee may now delegate to a co-trustee, but sub-delegation remains unauthorized. The trustee must give the appropriate notice of the delegation; and he remains liable for the acts and defaults of his delegate.

A trustee who is also a beneficial co-owner

15.08   Specific provision is made for the case where a trustee is also a beneficial co-owner of land.[23] Subject to any contrary intention in, and the terms of, the instrument creating the power of attorney and the trust instrument, the donee of a power of attorney is not prevented from doing an act in relation to land, the capital proceeds of a conveyance of land, or income from land, by reason only that the act involves the exercise of a trustee function of the donor if, at the time when the act is done, the donor has a beneficial interest in the land, proceeds, or income.[24] Such a person may therefore confer, by ordinary power of attorney, a power of the appropriate kind which is not limited in its duration, and without having to give notice to anyone. He remains liable, however, for the donee's acts and defaults.[25]

Collective delegation by trustees: section 11 of the Trustee Act 2000

15.09   Since 1925, trustees collectively had available a wide power to employ agents under section 23 of the Trustee Act 1925.[26] However, section 23 has been repealed and replaced by section 11 of the Trustee Act 2000[27] which provides that, subject to the provisions of Part IV of the Act, the trustees of a trust collectively 'may authorise any person to exercise any or all of their delegable functions as their agent'. In the case of a trust other than a charitable trust,[28] the trustees' 'delegable functions' consist of 'any function' other than those listed in section 11(2), which are:

(a)   any function relating to whether or in what way any assets of the trust should be distributed,

(b)   any power to decide whether any fees or other payment due to be made out of the trust funds should be made out of income or capital,

(c)   any power to appoint a person to be a trustee of the trust, or

(d)   any power conferred by any other enactment or the trust instrument which permits the trustees to delegate any of their functions or to appoint a person to act as a nominee or custodian.

Thus, dispositive discretions of trustees may not be delegated under section 11. In addition, in the case of property held on a bare trust, if the beneficiaries have

---

[23]   Replacing s 3(3) of the Enduring Powers of Attorney Act 1985 which itself was enacted to deal (somewhat inadequately) with the decision in *Walia v Michael Naughton Ltd* [1985] 1 WLR 1115.

[24]   Trustee Delegation Act 1999, s 1(1)–(5).   [25]   ibid, s 1(4).

[26]   An agent appointed under 23 of the Trustee Act 1925 will be treated as if he had been authorized to act as an agent under s 11 of the 2000 Act: ibid, Sch 3, para 5.

[27]   Trustee Act 2000, s 40, Sch 2, Pt II, para 23, Sch 4, Pt II. The Trustee Act 2000 came into force on 1 February 2001: The Trustee Act 2000 (Commencement) Order 2001, SI 2001/49.

[28]   The delegable functions of charity trustees are narrower and dealt with separately: see s 11(3)–(5) of the Trustee Act 2000.

given a direction that any trust property is not to be insured (or only on specified conditions), the trustees' power to insure ceases to be a delegable function.[29]

15.10 The power conferred by section 11 is available to a sole trustee.[30] However, the trustees of a pension scheme may not authorize any person to exercise any functions relating to *investment* as their agent. They must also not authorize a person (to exercise any other function) who is (a) an employer in relation to the scheme, or (b) connected with or an associate of such an employer.[31]

15.11 The power conferred by section 11 is in addition to powers conferred on trustees otherwise than by the Act itself[32] and is subject to any restriction or exclusion imposed by the trust instrument or by any enactment or any provision of subordinate legislation.[33]

Duty of care

15.12 The trustees are subject to the statutory duty of care created by the Act when entering into arrangements under which a person is authorized under section 11 to exercise functions as an agent and when entering into arrangements under which, under any other power, however conferred, a person is authorized to exercise functions as an agent. For these purposes, entering into arrangements under which a person is authorized to exercise functions includes, in particular, selecting the person who is to act, and determining any terms on which he is to act.[34] However, the duty of care does not apply if or in so far as it appears from the trust instrument that the duty is not meant to apply.[35]

Persons who may act as agents

15.13 The trustees may appoint any person (including one of themselves) other than a beneficiary, to act as their agent. Section 12 of the Trustee Act 2000 provides:

(1) Subject to subsection (2), the persons whom the trustees may under section 11 authorise to exercise functions as their agent include one or more of their number.
(2) The trustees may not authorise two (or more) persons to exercise the same function unless they are to exercise the function jointly.

---

[29] Section 19(2),(4) of the Trustee Act 1925, substituted by 34 of the Trustee Act 2000.
[30] ibid, s 25(1).
[31] ibid, s 36(5), (6). The word 'employer' has the same meaning as in the Pensions Act 1995; and ss 249 and 435 of the Insolvency Act 1986 apply for the purpose of determining whether a person is connected with or an associate of an employer: s 36(7).
[32] For example, trustees' power under the general law to delegate trust discretions in relation to foreign property (previously in s 23(2) of the Trustee Act 1925, which has been repealed by the Trustee Act 2000) will continue to be available, independently of the Trustee Act 2000. The trust instrument is also likely to include wider or additional express powers.
[33] ibid, s 26(a), (b). A sole trustee may prefer to exercise the new power conferred by s 25 of the Trustee Act 1925, which is wider in scope but restricts delegation to a maximum of 12 months.
[34] Trustee Act 2000, ss 1 and 2, and Sch 1, para 3(1)(a),(d), and (2). [35] ibid, Sch 1, para 7.

(3) The trustees may not under section 11 authorise a beneficiary to exercise any function as their agent (even if the beneficiary is also a trustee).

(4) The trustees may under section 11 authorise a person to exercise functions as their agent even though he is also appointed to act as their nominee or custo-dian[36] (whether under section 16, 17 or 18 or any other power).

Subsection (3) will not prevent the trustees from delegating some function to a beneficiary under an express power in the trust instrument or some other enact-ment, for example under section 9 of the Trusts of Land Act 1996, a function relating to land can be delegated to a beneficiary of full age who is entitled to an interest in possession in the land.[37]

Linked functions

15.14　A person who is authorized under section 11 to exercise a function is (whatever the terms of the agency) subject to any specific duties or restrictions attached to the function. For example, a person who is authorized under section 11 to exercise the statutory general power of investment is subject to the duties (the standard invest-ment criteria) under section 4 of the Act in relation to that power.[38] An agent will owe a duty of care to his trustee principal under the general law and will not be sub-ject to the statutory duty of care imposed by section 1 of the Act, which applies only to the trustee. A person who is authorized under section 11 to exercise a power which is subject to a requirement to obtain advice is not subject to the requirement if he is the kind of person from whom it would have been proper for the trustees, in compliance with the requirement, to obtain advice,[39] for example someone com-petent to act as an investment adviser who is employed to make trust investments.

15.15　Special provisions were required to deal with trusts to which section 11 of the Trusts of Land and Appointment of Trustees Act 1996 applies, ie trusts where there are duties to consult beneficiaries and give effect to their wishes. First, the trustees may not, under section 11 of the 2000 Act, authorize a person to exercise any of their func-tions on terms that prevent them from complying with section 11(1) of the 1996 Act.[40] Secondly, the agent authorized under section 11 of the 2000 Act to exercise any function relating to land subject to the trust is not himself subject to section 11(1) of the 1996 Act.[41] These provisions are not likely to have much impact, for it is standard practice to exclude the application of section 11 of the 1996 Act in any event.

Terms of agency

15.16　The trustees may authorize a person to exercise functions as their agent on such terms as to remuneration and other matters as they may determine.[42] However,

---

[36] And vice versa: ibid, s 19(6)(b), (7)(b).
[37] The trustees must act jointly and by means of a power of attorney.
[38] Trustee Act 2000, s 13(1).　　[39] ibid, s 13(2).　　[40] ibid, s 13(3), (4).
[41] ibid, s 13(5).　　[42] ibid, s 14(1).

they may not authorize any such person to exercise functions as their agent on any of the specified terms unless it is 'reasonably necessary' for them to do so.[43] These specified terms are:

(a) a term permitting the agent to appoint a substitute;
(b) a term restricting the liability of the agent or his substitute to the trustees or any beneficiary;
(c) a term permitting the agent to act in circumstances capable of giving rise to a conflict of interest.

What is 'reasonably necessary' will clearly vary from case to case. What may be reasonable for the performance of a one-off function may not be so in the case of an ongoing one, and vice versa. The appointment may need to be justified by reference to the standard terms of such an engagement or, at least, any alternative terms that were available. A term permitting an agent to appoint a substitute, ie to sub-delegate, may be reasonable if the prior consent (or even subsequent approval) of the trustees is required for any appointment made, but not if it is an uncontrolled authority. There are many occasions on which it is expedient, if not necessary, for trustees to appoint agents whose self-interest will conflict with their duties, for example discretionary fund managers. Any term restricting the liability of the agent must be difficult to justify. In any event, in many, perhaps most, cases, trustees and their agents will stand in some contractual relationship and the Unfair Contract Terms Act 1977 will therefore apply. The statutory duty of care will also apply to the trustees when determining the terms on which the agent is to act, but the duty may itself be excluded or modified by the trust instrument.[44]

Asset management

Specific restrictions are imposed by section 15 of the Act in relation to agents exercising any of the trustees' 'asset management functions'. The 'asset management functions' of trustees are their functions relating to (a) the investment of assets subject to the trust; (b) the acquisition of property which is to be subject to the trust; and (c) managing property which is subject to the trust and disposing of, or creating or disposing of an interest in, such property.[45] First, the trustees may not even authorize a person to exercise any such functions as their agent except by an agreement which is in writing, or evidenced in writing.[46] (There is no such requirement for agency agreements generally.) Secondly, the trustees may not authorize a person to exercise such functions unless:

(a) they have prepared a statement that gives guidance as to how the functions should be exercised ('a policy statement'), and

15.17

---

[43] ibid, s 14 (2).   [44] ibid, s 2, Sch 1, para 7.   [45] ibid, s 15(5).   [46] ibid, s 15(1).

(b) the agreement under which the agent is to act includes a term to the effect that he will secure compliance with

    (i) the policy statement, or

    (ii) if the policy statement is revised or replaced (under section 22)[47] the revised or replacement policy statement.[48]

Thirdly, the trustees must formulate any guidance given in the policy statement with a view to ensuring that the functions will be exercised in the best interests of the trust.[49] Fourthly, the policy statement itself must be in, or evidenced in, writing.[50]

Power to appoint nominees

15.18 Under the general law, a trustee is under a duty to take reasonable steps to get in, secure, and retain control of trust assets; and, where there are two or more trustees, their duty is to ensure that the assets are vested in joint names. Trustees cannot, in the absence of express provision in the trust instrument or statute,[51] vest assets in the names of nominees or custodians. This is clearly inconvenient, especially in relation to the investment of trust funds, where it is standard practice and beneficial to the trust to be able to use nominees for the administration of trust assets, to join CREST, or to make use of discretionary fund management and other mechanisms of modern investment management. This defect in the law is redressed in section 16(1) of the Trustee Act 2000, which authorizes trustees (subject to the provisions of Part IV of the Act):

(a) to appoint a person to act as their nominee in relation to such of the assets of the trust as they determine (other than settled land), and

(b) to take such steps as are necessary to secure that those assets are vested in a person so appointed.

Any appointment made under section 16 must be in, or evidenced in, writing.[52] This section does not apply, however, to any trust having a custodian trustee or in relation to any assets vested in the official custodian for charities.[53] Nor does it apply to pension schemes,[54] authorized unit trusts,[55] common investment schemes for charities,[56] or where legislation otherwise provides.[57]

Power to appoint custodians

15.19 Section 17(1) of the Trustee Act 2000 authorizes trustees (subject to the provisions of Part IV of the Act) to appoint a person to act as a custodian in relation to

---

[47] See paras 15.24–15.26 below.   [48] Trustee Act 2000, s 15(2)(a), (b).   [49] ibid, s 15(4).
[50] ibid, s 15(5).   [51] See, for example, s 4(2) of the Public Trustee Act 1906.
[52] Trustee Act 2000, s 16(2).   [53] ibid, s 16(3).   [54] ibid, s 36(8).
[55] ibid, s 37(1).   [56] ibid, s 38.   [57] ibid, s 26(b).

such of the assets of the trust as they may determine. For the purposes of the Act, a person is a custodian in relation to assets if he undertakes the safe custody of the assets or of any documents or records concerning the assets.[58] Any appointment made under section 17 must be in, or evidenced in, writing.[59] This section does not apply, however, to any trust having a custodian trustee or in relation to any assets vested in the official custodian for charities.[60] Nor does it apply to pension schemes,[61] authorized unit trusts,[62] common investment schemes for charities,[63] or where legislation otherwise provides.[64]

Investment in bearer securities

If the trustees retain or invest in securities payable to bearer, they must appoint **15.20** a person to act as a custodian of the securities.[65] This direction does not apply, however, if the trust instrument or any enactment or provision of subordinate legislation contains provision which (however expressed) permits the trustees to retain or invest in securities payable to bearer without appointing a person to act as custodian.[66] It also does not apply, however, to any trust having a custodian trustee or in relation to any assets vested in the official custodian for charities.[67] Nor does it apply to pension schemes,[68] authorized unit trusts,[69] common investment schemes for charities,[70] or where legislation otherwise provides.[71]

Person who may be appointed as a nominee or custodian

A person may not be appointed under section 16, 17, or 18 as a nominee or **15.21** custodian unless one of the 'relevant conditions' is satisfied.[72] The 'relevant conditions'[73] are that

(a) the person carries on a business which consists of or includes acting as a nominee or custodian;
(b) the person is a body corporate which is controlled by the trustees;[74]
(c) the person is a body corporate recognized under section 19 of the Administration of Justice Act 1985.

Subject to these conditions (and to subsection (4)), the persons whom the trustees may appoint include

(a) one of their number, if that one is a trust corporation, or

---

[58] ibid, s 17(2).   [59] ibid, s 17(3).   [60] ibid, s 17(4).   [61] ibid, s 36(8).
[62] ibid, s 37(1).   [63] ibid, s 38.   [64] ibid, s 26(b).   [65] ibid, s 18(1).
[66] ibid, s 18(2).   [67] ibid, s 18(4).   [68] ibid, s 36(8).   [69] ibid, s 37(1).
[70] ibid, s 38.   [71] ibid, s 26(b).
[72] ibid, s 19(1). Trustees of a charitable trust which is not an exempt charity must act in accordance with any guidance given by the Charity Commissioners: ibid, s 19(4).   [73] ibid, s 19(2).
[74] Control by the trustees is determined in accordance with s 840 of the Income and Corporation Taxes Act 1988: Trustee Act 2000, s 19(3).

(b) two (or more) of their number, if they are to act as joint nominees or joint custodians.[75]

15.22 The trustees may appoint a person as their nominee (under section 16) even though he is also appointed to act as their custodian (under section 17 or 18 or any other power) or authorized to exercise functions as their agent (under section 11 or any other power).[76] Similarly, they may appoint a person to act as their custodian (under section 17 or 18) even though he is also appointed to act as their nominee (under section 16 or any other power) or authorized to exercise functions as their agent (under section 11 or any other power).[77]

Terms of appointment of nominees and custodians

15.23 Subject to sections 29 to 32 of the Act, trustees may appoint a person to act as a nominee or custodian (under section 16, 17, or 18) on such terms as to remuneration and other matters as they may determine.[78] However, they may not make such an appointment on any of the following terms, unless it is reasonably necessary for them to do so, that is to say:

(a) a term permitting the nominee or custodian to appoint a substitute;

(b) a term restricting the liability of the nominee or custodian or his substitute to the trustees or to any beneficiary;

(c) a term permitting the nominee or custodian to act in circumstances capable of giving rise to a conflict of interest.[79]

Review of agents, nominees, and custodians

15.24 Section 22 of the Trustee Act 2000 ensures that, once an agent, nominee, or custodian has been appointed, the trustees are subject to a continuing obligation to supervise him. However, the Act distinguishes between (a) agents, nominees, or custodians appointed under section 11, 16, 17, or 18 of the Act itself and (b) similar agents, nominees, or custodians appointed under an express power conferred by the trust instrument or by any enactment or any provision of subordinate legislation.[80] The duty of continuing supervision imposed by section 22 applies to all of them, but not in relation to those in category (b) if its application is inconsistent with the terms of the trust instrument or the enactment or provision of subordinate legislation.[81] Thus, where an express power to appoint agents, nominees, or custodians is conferred on trustees, the trust instrument may exclude or modify the duty of continuous supervision.

---

[75] Trustee Act 2000, s 19(5).   [76] ibid, s 19(6).   [77] ibid, s 19(7).   [78] ibid, s 20(1).
[79] ibid, s 20(3). See also para 15.16 above for similar restrictions in s 14(3) in relation to the terms of appointment of an agent.   [80] See ibid, s 21(1),(2).   [81] ibid, s 21(3).

In any event, section 22(1) of the Act provides: **15.25**

 While the agent, nominee or custodian continues to act for the trust, the trustees—

(a) must keep under review the arrangements under which the agent, nominee or custodian acts and how these arrangements are being put into effect,
(b) if circumstances make it appropriate to do so, must consider whether there is a need to exercise any power of intervention that they have, and
(c) if they consider that there is a need to exercise such a power, must do so.

For these purposes, 'power of intervention' includes (a) a power to give directions to the agent, nominee, or custodian and (b) a power to revoke the authorization or appointment.[82]

In relation specifically to an agent who has been authorized to exercise asset man- **15.26** agement functions, the duty of continuous supervision is elaborated further in section 22(2), so as to include, in particular :

(a) a duty to consider whether there is any need to revise or replace the policy statement made for the purposes of section 15,
(b) if they consider that there is a need to revise or replace the policy statement, a duty to do so, and
(c) a duty to assess whether the policy statement (as it has effect for the time being) is being complied with.

Section 15(3) and (4) applies to the revision of or replacement of a policy statement under section 22 as it applies to the making of a policy statement under section 15.[83]

Liability for agents, nominees, and custodians

A trustee is not liable for any act or default of the agent, nominee, or custodian unless he has failed to comply with the duty of care applicable to him, under paragraph 3 of Schedule 1, (a) when entering into the arrangements under which the **15.27** person acts as agent, nominee, or custodian, or (b) when carrying out his duties of supervision under section 22.[84] If a trustee has agreed a term under which the agent, nominee, or custodian is permitted to appoint a substitute, the trustee is not liable for any act or default of the substitute unless he has failed to comply with the duty of care applicable to him, under paragraph 3 of Schedule 1, when (a) agreeing that term or (b) when carrying out his duties of supervision under section 22 in so far as they relate to the use of the substitute.[85]

As to the effect of trustees exceeding their powers, section 24 provides: **15.28**

---

[82] ibid, s 22(4).   [83] ibid, s 22(3).   [84] ibid, s 23(1).   [85] ibid, s 23(2).

A failure by the trustees to act within the limits of the powers conferred by this Part—

(a) in authorising a person to exercise a function of theirs as an agent, or

(b) in appointing a person to act as nominee or custodian,

does not invalidate the authorisation or appointment.

Third parties can, therefore, deal with the trustees' agent, nominee, or custodian, without being concerned whether his appointment conformed with the requirements of the Act.

Sole trustee

15.29 Part IV of the Act applies to a trust having a sole trustee as it applies to other trusts, save that section 18 (investment in bearer securities) does not impose a duty on a sole trustee if that trustee is a trust corporation.[86]

Remuneration of agents, nominees, and custodians

15.30 If a person other than a trustee[87] has been authorized[88] to exercise functions as an agent of the trustees, or appointed to act as nominee or custodian, the trustees may remunerate the agent, nominee, or custodian out of the trust funds for services if (a) he is engaged on terms entitling him to be remunerated for those services and (b) the amount does not exceed such remuneration as is reasonable in the circumstances for the provision of those services by him to or on behalf of the trust.[89] The trustees may also reimburse the agent, nominee, or custodian out of the trust funds for any expenses properly incurred by him in exercising functions as an agent, nominee, or custodian.[90] The expression 'trust funds' means income or capital funds of the trust.[91]

Delegation by trustees of land to a beneficiary

15.31 Section 9(1) of the Trusts of Land and Appointment of Trustees Act 1996 authorizes trustees of land, by power of attorney, to delegate to any beneficiary or beneficiaries of full age and beneficially entitled to an interest in possession in land subject to the trust any of their functions as trustees which relate to the land. Such delegation may be for any period or indefinite,[92] but it cannot be an enduring power of attorney.[93] The power of attorney must be given by all the trustees jointly and (unless expressed to be irrevocable and to be given by way of security) may be revoked by one or more of them. Moreover, the power of attorney is automatically

---

[86] Trustee Act 2000, s 25(1), (2).

[87] The trustee may still be remunerated *as trustee*, provided this is itself authorized.

[88] However appointed, whether under a power conferred by Part IV of the Trustee Act 2000, or any other enactment, or any provision of subordinate legislation, or by the trust instrument.

[89] ibid, s 32(1),(2).

[90] ibid, s 32(3). See also s 31 (*reimbursement* of a trustee, whether acting as trustee or as an agent).

[91] ibid, s 39(1).   [92] 1996 Act s 9(5).   [93] ibid, s 9(6).

revoked by the appointment of a new trustee, though not by the death of a trustee or his otherwise ceasing to be a trustee.[94] Beneficiaries to whom functions have been delegated under section 9(1) are, in relation to the exercise of the functions, in the same position as trustees (with the same duties and liabilities); but such beneficiaries shall not be regarded as trustees for any other purposes (including, in particular, the purposes of any enactment permitting the delegation of functions by trustees or imposing requirements relating to the payment of capital money).[95] Thus, there can be no sub-delegation.

Only functions relating to land may be delegated, and not those relating to any **15.32** other assets comprised in a trust of land, or even the proceeds of sale of land. Although not made explicit, it seems clear that only managerial, and not dispositive, functions are delegable. Moreover, delegation is possible only to (and, therefore, obviously when there is) a beneficiary of full age beneficially entitled[96] to an interest in possession in land subject to the trust. Thus, trustees may delegate the relevant functions to a beneficiary who has a present entitlement to occupy the land[97] or to receive its rents and profits.[98] On the other hand, such functions cannot be delegated to a beneficiary with a contingent interest, an interest in remainder or reversion, or an object of a discretionary trust—any of whom may, in a particular case, be permitted by the trustees to occupy trust property.

Where a beneficiary to whom functions are delegated under section 9 (1) ceases to **15.33** be a person beneficially entitled to an interest in possession in land subject to the trust, the consequences differ according to whether those functions were delegated to that beneficiary alone or to him and others, and, if the latter is the case, whether they were delegated on a joint or several basis. If the functions were delegated to that beneficiary alone, the power of attorney is automatically revoked. If they were delegated to him and to other beneficiaries[99] to be exercised by them jointly (but not separately), the power is revoked if each of the other beneficiaries ceases to be so entitled (but otherwise functions exercisable in accordance with the power are so exercisable by the remaining beneficiary or beneficiaries). If the functions are delegated to him and other beneficiaries to be exercised by them separately (or either separately or jointly), the power is revoked in so far as it relates to him.[100]

---

[94] ibid, s 9(3).   [95] ibid, s 9(7).

[96] Not including a trustee or personal representative: ibid, s 22(1), (2).

[97] Whether under the declared trusts or s 12 of the 1996 Act.

[98] ibid, s 23(2) and the Law of Property Act 1925, s 205(1)(xix). An entitlement to income (eg as life tenant) but subject to a power to accumulate income is not an 'interest in possession' for inheritance tax purposes (*Pearson v IRC* [1981] AC 753). However, as a proposition of general property law, this view is hard to justify and there is no obvious reason why it should apply in relation to s 9(1) of the 1996 Act.

[99] All of whom must, of course, also be beneficially entitled to an interest in possession.

[100] ibid, s 9(4).

Statutory duty of care applies

15.34   The new statutory duty of care under section 1 of the Trustee Act 2000 applies to trustees of land in deciding whether to delegate any of their functions under section 9 of the 1996 Act[101] (unless it is excluded, or to the extent that it is modified, by the trust instrument).[102] Once they have delegated, and the delegation is not irrevocable, then while the delegation continues the trustees must keep the delegation under review; if circumstances make it appropriate to do so, they must consider whether there is a need to exercise any power of intervention that they have; and, if they consider that there is a need to exercise such a power, must do so.[103] The statutory duty of care applies (again subject to being excluded or modified) to trustees in carrying out any of these duties to review and intervene.[104] For the purposes of section 9A, a 'power of intervention' includes a power to give directions to a beneficiary and a power to revoke the delegation.[105] Unless he fails to comply with the statutory duty of care in deciding to delegate any of the trustees' functions under section 9, or in carrying out any duty to review and intervene, a trustee of land is not liable for any act or default of the beneficiary or beneficiaries to whom the functions have been delegated.[106]

Protection of purchasers

15.35   Where trustees purport to delegate to a person, by a power of attorney under section 9(1), functions relating to any land, and another person in good faith deals with the delegate in relation to the land, the delegate shall be presumed in favour of that other person to have been a person to whom the functions could be delegated, unless that other person has knowledge[107] at the time of the transaction that the delegate was not such a person. It shall be conclusively presumed in favour of any purchaser whose interest depends on the validity of that transaction that that other person dealt in good faith and did not have such knowledge if that other person makes a statutory declaration to that effect before or within three months after the completion of the purchase.[108]

Miscellaneous cases

15.36   Charity trustees and the trustees of certain pension funds are subject to additional statutory provisions. The Charity Commissioners have statutory power to authorize dealings with charity property which would otherwise be beyond the powers of the trustees.[109] This power can be and has been used to extend trustees' powers of delegation.[110]

---

[101]   1996 Act, s 9A(1), inserted by the Trustee Act 2000, s 40(1), Sch 2, Pt II, para 47.
[102]   Trustee Act 2000, Sch 1, para 7.   [103]   1996 Act, s 9A(2),(3).   [104]   ibid, s 9A(5).
[105]   ibid, s 9A(4).   [106]   ibid, s 9A(6).   [107]   Actual or just constructive knowledge?
[108]   ibid, s 9(2).   [109]   Charities Act 1993, s 26.
[110]   The Charity Commissioners have even produced a Model Order for the purpose: (1994) 2 Decisions of the Ch Commrs 29.

In relation to the trustees of an occupational pension scheme established under a   **15.37**
trust (called 'a trust scheme'),[111] section 34(1) of the Pensions Act 1995 provides
that such trustees have (subject to any restriction imposed by the scheme) the
same power to make an investment of any kind as if they were absolutely entitled
to the assets of the scheme. Section 34(2) then declares that any discretion of such
trustees to make a decision about investments may be delegated to a fund manager
who satisfies certain requirements. The trustees must ensure that a written statement of the principles governing investment decisions for the purpose of the pension scheme is prepared, maintained, and periodically revised.[112] Moreover,
section 34(5) of the Act authorizes the trustees (subject to any restriction imposed
by the trust scheme) to delegate the exercise of their discretion relating to investment decisions, to two or more of their number or, as regards investment business
overseas, to a fund manager operating outside the United Kingdom.[113]

C. Delegation of Trusts, Dispositive Powers, and Discretions[114]

Despite substantial statutory intervention, there is still no general authority   **15.38**
enabling trustees to delegate their dispositive functions. Subject to certain limited
or short-term exceptions (such as section 25 of the Trustee Act 1925), the rule
against delegation continues to apply to a trustee's trusts and dispositive powers
and discretions. Trustees generally may delegate such dispositive functions only if,
and to the extent that, they are expressly authorized to do so by the trust instrument. The scope and extent of any such authority in any particular case clearly
depends on the terms of the specific power in question. However, this simple
statement conceals a number of complex issues and difficult problems. These
issues and problems are considered in this section.

General principles again

As we have seen, a trust or power involving the exercise of a personal discretion   **15.39**
or confidence by the trustee or donee cannot be delegated, unless there is
express authority to do so: *delegatus non potest delegare*.[115] The trustee or donee's
decision cannot be made for him, not even by the donor of the power
himself. Where trustees delegate their dispositive discretions and duties, without authority to do so, it is a breach of trust and they will be liable for any
consequent loss.[116]

---

[111] Pensions Act 1995, s 124(1).   [112] ibid, s 35(1)–(6)   [113] See also ibid, ss 34, 37.
[114] See, generally, *Thomas*, Ch 7, esp 402–430; [1994] Private Client Business 317 and 402
(R Oerton); [1980] BTR 174 (B McCutcheon).
[115] See paras 15.01–15.04 above.
[116] *Rowland v Witherden* (1851) 3 Mac & G 568.

Consultation with beneficiaries

15.40 Trustees do not delegate when they consult with experts or with their beneficiaries. They are not prohibited from inquiring into and taking account of the wishes of others—indeed, they are encouraged to do so—nor from allowing the arguments of others to influence their conduct.

> It would be extremely dangerous to hold that the trustees, having such a discretion to exercise, might not freely discuss with the beneficiaries the reasons for and against a particular decision, without running the risk of being held to act against their own judgment, if they should disregard, in the end, objections to which they had thought it right in the first instance to direct attention.[117]

Although trustees generally are not obliged to consult their beneficiaries before exercising their powers,[118] trustees of *land* are subject to a specific statutory requirement to do so.[119] Moreover, if trustees apply to the court for directions, they ought first to consult their beneficiaries (or their representatives) before doing so.[120]

General and hybrid powers

15.41 A *general* power is regarded for many purposes as equivalent to absolute ownership. Such a power may therefore be delegated.[121] The donee of a general power may direct different trustees to hold the appointed property on new (including discretionary) trusts. If a trustee confers a general power upon a beneficiary, the appointment is, in effect, regarded as a gift of an interest and not as a delegation of the power.[122] If new trusts are created by the exercise of a general power and the appointment nominates new trustees to carry them out, the existing trustees must transfer the appointed property to the new trustees. If such an appointment is made by a testamentary instrument, the position is different, for the appointor, in exercising the general power, has made the appointed property 'assets' which are available for the payment of his debts in due course of administration (even where the trustees had to consent to the exercise of the power).[123] Consequently, the existing trustees must transfer the appointed property to the appointor's personal representatives, or

---

[117] *Fraser v Murdoch* (1881) 6 App Cas 855, 864–865; *Hitch v Leworthy* (1842) 2 Hare 200; *Re Pauling's Settlement Trusts* [1963] Ch 576, 586.   [118] *X v A* [2000] 1 All ER 490.

[119] Trusts of Land and Appointment of Trustees Act 1996, s 11: see paras 15.09–15.16 above. A similar, but more limited, requirement appeared in (the now repealed) s 26(3) of the Law of Property Act 1925, on which see: *Re Jones* [1931] 1 Ch 375; *Bull v Bull* [1955] 1 QB 234; *Waller v Waller* [1967] 1 WLR 451; *Crawley Borough Council v Ure* [1996] 1 QB 13.

[120] RSC Ord 85, para 7.7.

[121] *Combe's Case* (1613) 9 Co Rep 75a; *White v Wilson* (1852) 1 Drew 298, 304; *Re Triffitt's Settlement* [1958] Ch 852.

[122] *Bray v Bree* (1834) 2 Cl & Fin 453; *Phipson v Turner* (1838) 9 Sim 227; *Slark v Dakyns* (1874) LR 10 Ch App 35; *Morse v Martin* (1865) 34 Beav 500; *Re Hughes* [1921] 2 Ch 208, 212. *Re Mclean* (1929) 35 ALR 216.   [123] See *Thomas* 14–15.

at their direction. If the appointed property is not required for the payment of debts, the personal representatives must, in due course, transfer the appointed property (or such of it as remains after any such payment) to the new trustees.[124]

Although a *hybrid* (or intermediate) power is not necessarily excluded from the rule against delegation,[125] it may nonetheless be delegated where it virtually amounts to a general power. In *Re Triffitt's Settlement*,[126] where a marriage settlement conferred a power of appointment on the settlor herself, in favour of 'such person or persons other than and except [the settlor's father] and any wife of his and in such manner generally as the [settlor] shall from time to time or at any time by deed revocable or irrevocable with the consent in writing of the trustees for the time being...appoint', Upjohn J held (*inter alia*) that, although the words 'in such manner' would not confer any power to delegate a discretion if they occurred in an ordinary limited power of appointment, this was a wide, non-fiduciary power created by the settlor for her own benefit (and which she could exercise in her own favour). In such circumstances, it was to be implied that the settlor/appointor could delegate the exercise of discretionary powers completely. **15.42**

On the other hand, where such a hybrid power is conferred on trustees, the rule against delegation applies, unless there is something in the trust instrument to exclude it. In *Re Hay's Settlement Trusts*,[127] for example, a hybrid power had been conferred on trustees to appoint in favour of 'such persons or purposes' other than the settlor, any husband of hers, and any trustee or past trustee of the settlement. The trustees purported to exercise this power by declaring that the trust fund was to be held on trust to pay the income 'to or for the benefit of any person or persons whatsoever...or to any charity' as the trustees thought fit. Megarry V-C held that this exercise had not designated the 'persons' to whom the appointment was made, but merely provided the mechanism whereby a person or persons might be ascertained from time to time by the exercise of the discretion given to the trustees. This was 'a plain case of delegation': the power in the settlement was not being exercised by appointing the persons who were to benefit, but by creating a discretionary trust under which the discretionary trustees would from time to time select those who would benefit. There was nothing in the settlement to exclude the normal rule against delegation and the trustees' purported exercise of their power was therefore an excessive execution of the power.[128] **15.43**

---

[124] *Lassells v Cornwallis* (1704) 2 Vern 465; *Holmes v Coghill* (1802) 7 Ves 499 and (1806) 12 Ves 206; *Pardo v Bingham* (1868) LR 6 Eq 485; *Re Hoskin's Trusts* (1877) 5 Ch D 229 and (1877) 6 Ch D 281; *Hayes v Oatley* (1872) LR 14 Eq 1; *Re Philbrick* (1865) 13 WR 570; *Re Peacock's Settlement* [1902] 1 Ch 552; *Re Phillips* [1931] 1 Ch 347.
[125] *Re Hay's Settlement Trusts* [1982] 1 WLR 202, 213; *Re Beatty* [1990] 1 WLR 1503.
[126] [1958] Ch 852.   [127] [1982] 1 WLR 202.
[128] ibid 212–213. The fact that the trustees who purported to exercise the power and the trustees of the intended discretionary trust were the same persons was immaterial. For the doctrine of excessive execution of a power, see Chapter 18 below.

Special powers

15.44 'By the terms of its creation the obligation of the donee to exercise personal discretion is inherent in a special power, which can, therefore, never be delegated.'[129] Thus, a joint power of appointment may not be exercised in such a way as to confer a power of revocation on one only of the appointors.[130] Similarly, 'a person whose consent is required to the execution of a power cannot, by a general power of attorney given to another to consent for him to any deed which the attorney shall think fit, effectually delegate his power of consent, but the execution of the power will be altogether void'.[131]

Authorized delegation

15.45 A trustee or donee of a discretionary power may delegate its exercise to another if, and in so far as, he is authorized to do so.[132] It is common to include, in modern settlements and wills, a clear and express authority for the trustees (or other donee) to delegate their powers, dispositive as well as administrative, to another. Such authority may be incorporated in the terms of the particular power itself or it may be conferred by a separate clause (which may authorize the delegation of any powers conferred by the settlement or will in question).[133] Sometimes, however, the extent (if any) to which delegation is authorized may be a matter of implication. Thus, for example, in *Re Ainsworth*,[134] where there was a power to appoint land 'in such shares and proportions manner and form and for such interests and subject to such restrictions conditions and limitations over' as the donee should appoint, Eve J held that it was not an excessive exercise of the power to appoint the land to trustees on trust for sale, or to confer on them a discretionary power to postpone sale with the fullest powers of management and leasing pending sale. Similarly, in *Re Rank's Settlement Trusts*,[135] Slade J held that a special power of appointment on trusts 'with such provisions for maintenance education and advancement and otherwise at the discretion of any person and with such gifts over and generally in such manner' was wide enough to authorize the donee of the power to confer on new trustees all such administrative powers as were reasonably ancillary to any appointed beneficial interests.

15.46 The extent to which *a special power of appointment* can be delegated (if at all) depends largely on the construction of the instrument creating the power. A bare power to appoint to or among a class of objects will not, without more,

---

[129] Sir George Farwell and FK Archer, *A Concise Treatise on Powers* (3rd edn, 1916) ('*Farwell*') 499; *Re Boulton* [1928] Ch 703; *Re Morris* [1951] 2 All ER 528; *Re Hunter* [1963] Ch 372; *Re Triffitt's Settlement* [1958] Ch 852, 861.

[130] *Burnaby v Baillie* (1889) 42 Ch D 282.

[131] *Hawkins v Kemp* (1803) 3 East 410. Cf *Stuart v Norton* (1860) 9 WR 360 (a trustee could, out of necessity, delegate his trust in respect of foreign property); and see also Trustee Act 1925, s 25 and paras 15.06–15.08 above.   [132] *Pilkington v IRC* [1964] AC 612, 638–639.

[133] See, eg, James Kessler, *Drafting Trusts and Will Trusts* (London: Sweet & Maxwell, 2nd edn, 1995), 253–255.   [134] [1921] 2 Ch 179.   [135] [1979] 1 WLR 1242.

authorize an appointment on discretionary or protective trusts.[136] Nor, it seems, will a power simply to determine or vary the shares of beneficiaries. The scope of other powers may be more difficult to establish, however.[137]

D. Powers to Appoint 'in Such Manner and Form' and Other Analogous Powers

A power to appoint 'in such manner', or 'in such manner and form', as the donee **15.47** shall or may appoint, will not generally permit delegation (at least, not of any dispositive power),[138] but, exceptionally, it may properly be exercised so as to confer *a common-form power of advancement* on the trustees of a settlement, whether the appointed interests are vested[139] or contingent.[140] In *Re May's Settlement*,[141] for example, a widow had a special power to appoint to her issue 'in such manner and form in every respect' as she should by deed or will appoint. She appointed property to her two infant children as tenants in common in equal shares, and gave the trustees an ordinary power of advancement. Astbury J held that, as she had appointed vested, absolute interests, the power of advancement was in no sense a delegation of her special power, but was merely ancillary to the absolute appointment. The same conclusion was reached in *Re Mewburn's Settlement*[142] in relation to contingent interests. A power of advancement is 'a purely ancillary power, enabling the trustees to anticipate by means of an advance under it the date of actual enjoyment by a beneficiary selected by the appointor of the interest appointed to him or her, and it can only affect the destination of the fund indirectly in the event of the beneficiary failing to attain a vested interest'.[143] Although the 'common form' or 'ordinary' power of advancement under consideration in these cases extended to only half of the fund in question (as does the statutory power in section 32 of the Trustee Act 1925), it has long been the practice to extend such a power to the entire fund; and there seems to be no obvious reason why the principle established in the decisions should not apply equally to such an extended power of advancement.[144]

---

[136] *Re Boulton's Settlement Trusts* [1928] Ch 703 (the precise wording of the power is not reported); *Re Hunter's Will Trusts* [1963] Ch 372; *Re Morris's Settlement Trusts* [1951] 2 All ER 528; *Ingram v Ingram* (1740) 2 Atk 88; *Alexander v Alexander* (1755) 2 Ves Sen 640; *Carr v Atkinson* (1872) LR 14 Eq 397; *Burnaby v Baillie* (1889) 42 Ch D 282; *Williamson v Farwell* (1887) 35 Ch D 128.

[137] cf *Re Hay's Settlement Trusts* [1982] 1 WLR 202 (hybrid power).

[138] *Re Joicey* [1915] 2 Ch 115, 120; *Re Mewburn's Settlement* [1934] Ch 112, 116; *Re May's Settlement* [1926] Ch 135; *Re Triffitt's Settlement* [1958] Ch 852.

[139] *Re May's Settlement* [1926] Ch 135.

[140] *Re Mewburn's Settlement* [1934] Ch 112; *Re Morris's Settlement Trusts* [1951] 2 All ER 528; *Re Wills' Will Trusts* [1959] Ch 1, 11–13. [141] [1926] Ch 135.

[142] [1934] Ch 112.   [143] *Re Morris's Settlement Trusts* [1951] 2 All ER 528, 532.

[144] If the trust instrument contains an express power of advancement, does it continue to apply to an appointed share? Different views were held on this issue before 1926 (see, for example, *Re Greenslade* [1915] 1 Ch 155, 160–161. This is of less importance today, but it may still be an issue in certain circumstances: see *Thomas* 407–408.

15.48   On the other hand, the appointment can easily go too far and make an unauthorized delegation. In *Re Joicey*,[145] for example, a testator had settled a fund on trust for his daughter for life and, after her death, for her issue 'for such interests in such proportions *and in such manner in all respects*' as she should by deed or will appoint, and in default of appointment to her children equally. The daughter by will appointed the fund in favour of all her children and declared certain trusts of the share of each child. During the period of 21 years after her death, the income of the share was to be paid to him or her; the child was given a general testamentary power of appointment; trusts in default of appointment were declared in favour of the child's issue; and provision was made for cross-accruer to other shares in the event of the failure of the primary trusts. A proviso was added to the effect that trustees of the testator's will 'shall (if and so far as I can authorise the same) have power from time to time or at any time... in their absolute discretion to transfer and make over the share or shares for the time being of the appointed funds' to a son absolutely. The Court of Appeal held that the power conferred on the trustees by the proviso was an attempt to delegate the power given by the testator to his daughter and was therefore invalid. According to Warrington LJ:[146]

> It is not even a power of advancement which might possibly be said to be so common an incident to such interests as the donee has here created as to be fairly within the words 'in such manner in all respects'—as to this I express no opinion. It is I think impossible to deny that under the provision in question the trustees might of their own volition and without reference to the circumstances of the son or any other consideration convert a contingent interest into an absolute one and thus completely alter the dispositions made by the testatrix. To give such a power as this to the trustees is in my opinion to delegate to them an authority reposed in the appointor alone, and the provision in question is accordingly void as being in excess of the power.

The power in *Re Joicey* was not regarded as a simple power of advancement, but was one which was 'not confined in any way to circumstances requiring maintenance or advancement and [could] be exercised by the trustees irrespective of such considerations'.[147] A power of such width was more akin to a power of appointment and therefore more easily caught by the rule against unauthorized delegation.

15.49   There seems to be no reason why the same principles should not apply to *powers of maintenance*. In *Re Greenslade*,[148] however, it was held that a power of maintenance could not be delegated. A testator had given a share of his estate to trustees upon trust to pay the income thereof to his daughter for life, and, after her death, to hold the share and its income in trust for her children or any of their issue in such manner as she should by deed or will appoint. The testator's will contained an express provision enabling the trustees to apply any part of the annual income

---

[145] [1915] 2 Ch 115. See also *Re Fox* [1904] 1 Ch 480.
[146] [1915] 2 Ch 115, 123; see also at 120, 122.
[147] ibid 122, *per* Pickford LJ; see also at 123, *per* Warrington LJ.   [148] [1915] 1 Ch 155.

of the share to which an infant might be entitled towards the maintenance, education or benefit of such infant, but, by a codicil, the testator declared that the powers of maintenance should only apply to income to which the infant was, or if of full age would be, entitled. The daughter, by her will, appointed the share and the income thereof to all her children who should attain 25 before the expiration of 21 years from her death, or should be living at the expiration of such period without having attained 25, with a substitutional proviso in favour of the children of a deceased child. The appointment also empowered the trustees of the settled share to apply the income of the expectant share of any child (or grandchild) for or towards his maintenance, education, or benefit. Eve J held that conferring such a power was an attempt to delegate to the trustees a personal discretion exercisable by the daughter, and therefore wholly inoperative.

> ...it cannot, I think, be denied that the trustees, acting under that power, could divert income from objects of the power of appointment, who become ultimately entitled in possession under the appointment to other objects who, in the event, may never become entitled in possession...It must, therefore, be admitted that the power enables the trustees to modify in some respects the appointment made by the donee, a result which is for practical purposes tantamount to what would have arisen had the appointment of the income accruing to the period of distribution been made in express terms to such of the objects as the trustees might select. In other words, I think the power is, in effect, an attempt to delegate to the trustees a personal discretion exercisable by the donee.

Also, the power contained in the original will was inapplicable to the appointed share.[149]

The reasoning in *Re Greenslade* is clearly similar to that in *Re Joicey*. In both cases, **15.50** it was a material factor that the power in question did not necessarily accelerate the enjoyment of the person who would ultimately be entitled to the capital or income, but had the effect of converting a contingent entitlement into a vested one, thereby defeating other contingent interests, at the discretion of someone other than the appointor. In both cases, the power in question was not considered to be a 'common form' or 'ordinary' power. Whereas there was no statutory power of advancement to which reference could be made in *Re Joicey*, there was a statutory power of maintenance in section 43 of the Conveyancing Act 1881, but this was held not to apply to the trusts in *Re Greenslade*. Section 31 of the Trustee Act 1925[150] will now apply, by implication and in the absence of an indication to the contrary, to the original trusts declared by the trust instrument and to any trusts created by an appointment, or to the shares produced by an allocation or division. Nevertheless, difficult questions may still arise in connection with the extent to which an appointment may create a power of maintenance where none existed before, or may affect the nature or extent of a power of maintenance conferred by

---

[149] ibid 160–161.   [150] See paras 14.08–14.25 above.

the original settlement. The impact of *Re Greenslade* and *Re Joicey* may now be limited, but they are still more than mere examples of the rule against delegation: they could still apply where an appointment purports to create unorthodox powers of maintenance and advancement, or where it purports to confer such powers on persons who are not trustees (to whom sections 31 and 32 of the Trustee Act 1925 do not apply). It therefore remains important to ensure that the terms of any power of appointment are sufficiently wide and flexible to permit the creation and delegation of wide and flexible powers of maintenance and advancement.

E. Delegation by Transfer to Separate Trustees

15.51 Even where the terms of a special power would authorize a wide and far-reaching appointment of beneficial interests, it is not necessarily the case that the donee can properly make an appointment to or in favour of new trustees of his own choosing, whether those trustees are intended to hold the appointed property on sub-trusts within the head settlement or as trustees of a separate settlement.[151] This is an issue of considerable importance for certain tax purposes (especially capital gains tax), but it may also arise in other contexts, for example in relation to questions of title. Clearly, it is possible for the person who has power to appoint new or additional trustees (whether it be an express power or the statutory power conferred by sections 36 and 37 of the Trustee Act 1925)[152] to appoint as trustees of an existing settlement, or of trusts appointed under a power conferred by an existing settlement, those persons who are also trustees of a separate settlement (or those who would have been such trustees if the relevant power of appointment had been wide enough to permit the donee thereof to create a separate settlement). However, such trustees would then become trustees of the existing settlement, or of sub-trusts within the existing settlement. They would not be trustees of a new and separate settlement (at least as far as the appointed property is concerned) and would have been appointed not by the donee of the power to appoint beneficial interests but by the donee of the power to appoint trustees, who would have to apply his own mind to the exercise of this fiduciary power.

15.52 As to the question whether a new and separate settlement has come into existence, Lord Wilberforce observed in *Roome v Edwards*:[153]

> One might expect to find separate and defined property; separate trusts; and separate trustees. One might also expect to find a separate disposition bringing the separate settlement into existence. These indicia may be helpful, but they are not decisive. For example, a single disposition, eg a will with a single set of trustees, may create what are clearly separate settlements, relating to different properties, in favour of different

---

[151] *Thomas* 410–411; *Farwell* 374. [152] See paras 22.42–22.57 below.
[153] [1982] AC 279, 292–293.

beneficiaries, and conversely separate trusts may arise in what is clearly a single settlement, eg when the settled property is divided into shares. There are so many possible combinations of fact that even where these indicia or some of them are present, the answer may be doubtful, and may depend upon an appreciation of them as a whole.

... To take two fairly typical cases. Many settlements contain powers to appoint a part or a proportion of the trust property to beneficiaries: some may also confer power to appoint separate trustees of the property so appointed, or such power may be conferred by law: see Trustee Act 1925, section 37. It is established doctrine that the trusts declared by a document exercising a special power of appointment are to be read into the original settlement ... [154] If such a power is exercised, whether or not separate trustees are appointed, I do not think that it would be natural for such a person as I have presupposed[155] to say that a separate settlement had been created: still less so if it were found that provisions of the original settlement continued to apply to the appointed fund, or that the appointed fund were liable, in certain events, to fall back into the rest of the settled property. On the other hand, there may be a power to appoint and appropriate a part or portion of the trust property to beneficiaries and to settle it for their benefit. If such a power is exercised, the natural conclusion might be that a separate settlement was created, all the more so if a complete new set of trusts were declared as to the appropriated property, and if it could be said that the trusts of the original settlement ceased to apply to it. There can be many variations on these cases each of which will have to be judged on its facts.

Thus, if a power of appointment is exercised in such a manner as to vary the age of vesting or to vary the shares in which contingent beneficiaries are to take, all the other trusts, powers, and provisions of the settlement remaining intact, the appointment merely varies the original settlement; and the settlement and the appointment together constitute a single settlement.[156] However, appropriately drafted powers may also be capable of authorizing trustees to execute an instrument or do some act which has the effect not merely of altering the presently subsisting trusts of the settlement in relation to specified assets, but of subjecting those assets to the trusts of an entirely different settlement, in such manner that the trustees exercising the power are to be discharged from any further responsibilities in relation to those assets in their capacity as trustees of the original settlement.[157] If such a power is exercised so that, for example, the appointed or advanced assets become vested in distinct trustees and all the trusts, powers, and provisions of the original settlement are irrevocably gone, and completely new trusts, powers, and provisions are created to take their place, so that no one will ever again need to refer to the original settlement except to confirm that it has ceased to exist, the original settlement will not so much have been varied as have ceased to exist.[158]

---

[154] *Muir v Muir* [1943] AC 468.

[155] ie 'a person with knowledge of the legal context of the word ["settlement"] under established doctrine and applying this knowledge in a practical and common-sense manner to the facts under consideration'.   [156] *Hart v Briscoe* [1979] Ch 1, 8.

[157] *Bond v Pickford* [1983] STC 517, 522h.   [158] ibid; *Roome v Edwards* [1982] AC 279, 292.

15.53 For capital gains tax purposes, the creation of a separate settlement will involve a deemed disposal by the trustees of the original settlement, under which the trustees of the separate settlement will have become absolutely entitled to the subject matter of the appointment or advancement. This deemed disposal is an occasion of charge to tax under section 71 of the Taxation of Chargeable Gains Act 1992.[159] If a separate settlement is not created, the trustees of the original settlement and the trustees of the new sub-trusts will be regarded as a single and continuing body of trustees.[160] Consequently, any liability for tax on capital gains realized by the trustees of the sub-trusts (who may be non-resident) may fall on the trustees of the head settlement.[161] There may also be other tax implications, such as the availability and extent of any reliefs, or the rate of charge (in the context of capital gains tax), or the ascertainment of the applicable charging regime and valuation of chargeable property (in the context of inheritance tax).

15.54 There are two separate issues here. The first is whether the terms of the power in question are wide enough to authorize the creation of a new settlement and the delegation of trusts and powers. Clearly, there can be no such separate settlement if the power is too restricted to permit its creation. The second issue is whether a separate settlement has actually been created by the exercise of a suitable power. It clearly does not follow that, because the terms of a power authorize the creation of a separate settlement, any exercise of that power must produce that result. Whether this is the effect or not depends largely on the intention of the donee when he exercised the power. Where the intention is not expressed and clear, the guidelines put forward by Lord Wilberforce in *Roome v Edwards*[162] as to whether a particular set of facts amounts to a new settlement are clearly relevant. However, it is the first issue (that of the extent to which the particular power permits delegation) that is of greater relevance here.

15.55 The statutory power of *advancement* (unless expressly curtailed), as well as an express power of advancement in a similar form, will be wide enough to permit such a resettlement and delegation.[163] The extent to which a special power of *appointment* will do so is less straightforward. Generally, and in the absence of express provision to the contrary, a power simply to appoint which of the beneficiaries shall take the trust property, and to determine their interests, does not authorize trustees to delegate their discretion or to transfer the trust property into a new settlement. In older cases, the question centred around powers to

---

[159] 'Hold-over' relief may be available in certain limited circumstances, under ss 165 and 260 of the 1992 Act. [160] Taxation of Chargeable Gains Act 1992, s 69(1).

[161] *Roome v Edwards* [1982] AC 279. See also *Hart v Briscoe* [1979] Ch 1; *Bond v Pickford* [1983] STC 517; *Ewart v Taylor* [1983] STC 721; *Swires v Renton* [1991] STC 490.

[162] [1982] AC 279, 292–293.

[163] *Pilkington v IRC* [1964] AC 612. See paras 14.26–14.45 above for a full discussion of section 32 of the Trustee Act 1925.

appoint 'in such manner' or 'in such manner and form', and it was far from certain whether such powers were sufficiently wide to authorize the appointment of new and separate trustees to hold the appointed fund—some were held to be so, but others were not.[164] However, there is nothing inherent in the nature of a power of advancement which permits delegation, or in the nature of a power of appointment which does not. Indeed, the same question may arise in connection with powers which are not strictly powers of advancement or of appointment, such as powers to pay or apply capital, or to allocate or appropriate assets. In each case, it depends on the width of the power whether or not delegation and the creation of a new settlement are authorized.[165]

More recent cases have focused, therefore, on the question whether the power in question is one 'in the wider form', as opposed to one 'in the narrower form',[166] as described by Slade LJ in *Bond v Pickford*.[167] Slade LJ referred to the rule against delegation and concluded:[168] **15.56**

> . . . as a matter of trust law trustees, who are given a discretionary power to direct which of the beneficiaries shall take the trust property and for what interests, do *not* have the power thereby to remove assets from the original settlement, by subjecting them to the trusts of a separate settlement, unless the instrument which gave them the power expressly or by necessary implication authorizes them to do so. In the absence of such authority, any exercise of the power, other than one which renders persons beneficially absolutely entitled to the relevant assets, will leave those assets subject to the trusts of the original settlement . . . and the trustees of the original settlement will remain responsible for them, in that capacity.
>
> Thus, there is in my opinion a crucial distinction to be drawn between (a) powers to alter the presently operative trusts of a settlement which expressly or by necessary implication authorizes the trustees to remove assets altogether from the original settlement (without rendering any person absolutely beneficially entitled to them); and (b) powers of this nature which do not confer on the trustees such authority.

In *Bond v Pickford* itself, the trust instrument clearly included a power which was wide enough to permit the trustees to delegate by creating a new settlement (ie a power in the wider form). However, the trustees exercised, instead, a separate, narrower power to allocate or appropriate sums or investments in favour of

---

[164] *Re Tyssen* [1894] 1 Ch 56; *Busk v Aldam* (1874) LR 19 Eq 16; *Scotney v Lomer* (1886) 31 Ch D 380; *Re Redgate* [1903] 1 Ch 356; *Re Adams' Trustees and Frost's Contract* [1907] 1 Ch 695; *Re Mackenzie* [1916] 1 Ch 125. See, generally, *Thomas* 411–414.

[165] It is appropriate to refer to delegation and resettlement together, for resettlement inevitably involves some degree of delegation. It is not suggested that delegation always involves resettlement: this is clearly not the case.

[166] This terminology is not intended to be synonymous with 'general powers' or 'hybrid powers', on the one hand, and 'special powers' on the other. A special power may or may not authorize delegation and resettlement; and a hybrid power, despite its width, may do neither: see *Re Hay's Settlement Trusts* [1982] 1 WLR 202. A general power will clearly do so.

[167] [1983] STC 517, 522–523. See also *Roome v Edwards* [1982] AC 279, esp 292–293; and *Swires v Renton* [1991] STC 490. [168] At 522–523, (emphasis in original).

a beneficiary—a power which the Court of Appeal held to be too narrow to authorize the transfer of assets to a new settlement.

15.57 In *Swires v Renton*,[169] the power under consideration was clearly wide enough to authorize the creation of a new setlement, and the question was whether the exercise of that power by the trustees had had this effect. The terms of the power were as follows:

> It shall be lawful for the trustees at any time or times during the appointed period . . . at their absolute discretion to pay or apply any part or parts of the capital of the trust fund to or for the benefit of all or any one or more to the exclusion of the others or other of the specified class freed and released from the trusts concerning the same . . .

It was argued that, because of its concluding words, this power permitted *only* an outright payment to a beneficiary or the creation of a new settlement. Hoffmann J held that the power authorized the trustees (a) to dispose of the trust fund to themselves as trustees of a new settlement, or (b) to declare that it was to be subject to new trusts within the existing settlement.[170] Although he did not state explicitly that the trustees could also transfer the fund to different trustees of another settlement, this is implicit in (a). Although the entire beneficial interest in the trust property was dealt with, in the circumstances (not least that some of the administrative powers in the original settlement were expressed to *continue* to apply) it was held that a new settlement had not been intended or created.

15.58 In contrast, where trustees of a discretionary trust exercised a power to apply capital for the benefit of objects by resolving that they themselves would thereafter hold the trust fund, as trustees of a new and separate settlement, on certain fixed trusts, it was held that the original settlement had been terminated and an entirely new settlement had been created.[171] Similarly, where trustees, in the exercise of a special power of appointment, appointed the entire beneficial interest, created a new power to appoint new trustees, and *expressly* incorporated the administrative powers of the original settlement (ie they were not expressed to *continue* to apply), and where trust accounts had been drawn up on the basis that the appointed property was no longer subject to the original settlement, it was held that a new and separate settlement had been created.[172]

F. Delegation Under Powers to 'Benefit'[173]

15.59 It is often the case that a power of appointment (or other power) is expressed in terms which do not state explicitly that delegation or resettlement is authorized.

---

[169] [1991] STC 490. [170] ibid 501a. [171] *Hart v Briscoe* [1979] Ch 1.
[172] *Ewart v Taylor* [1983] STC 721.
[173] For a fuller discussion of this question, see *Thomas* 423–429.

The most common example, perhaps, is a power which is simply expressed to be exercisable 'for the benefit' of one or more or all of a class of objects. Several of the powers under consideration in the older cases[174] were powers of this kind. However, no argument seems to have been put forward in these cases to the effect that an appointment in favour of new and separate trustees would have been beneficial and therefore authorized and valid. On the other hand, in *Re Pocock's Policy*,[175] for example, a statutory benevolent fund established for the benefit of widows, children, and other relatives of officers of the Customs came under consideration. Under the rules of the fund, a proportion of the fund was directed to 'be applied or paid in any manner or proportion which [the subscriber] might propose for the benefit of his widow, children or relatives, or his nominees who should have been duly admitted by the directors'. A subscriber appointed his share of the fund to the trustees of his daughter's marriage settlement upon trust for his daughter for life, with remainder for her husband (who was not a relative) for life, with remainder for their issue. Neither the trustees nor the husband were formally admitted to the scheme. Nevertheless, it was held that the settlement by the subscriber on his daughter, her husband, and issue, was a valid application of the fund 'for the benefit' of his daughter within the meaning of the rules, and that no admission of the trustees or of the husband was necessary.[176] It is not entirely clear why, in principle, this approach should not apply generally so as to authorize delegation and resettlement wherever the power is exercisable 'for the benefit' of the objects. It seems that, in *Bond v Pickford*, both Slade LJ[177] and Nourse J at first instance[178] thought that the power conferred by Clause 3(i) of the trust instrument alone (without the benefit of the additional specific authorization to resettle in Clause 3(i)(b)) was manifestly a power in the wider form. Hoffmann J seems to have taken a similar view in *Swires v Renton*.[179] It might still be difficult, in the circumstances of a particular case, to justify the act of delegation or a re-settlement as 'beneficial'. Nevertheless, it is suggested that a power which may be exercised 'for the benefit' of an object might, in principle, authorize delegation and resettlement.

15.60 As we have seen,[180] it is now well established that the statutory power of *advancement* (and an express power of advancement in similar terms) authorizes trustees to delegate and resettle trust assets[181]—even, in appropriate cases, to create discretionary trusts. In this specific context, the word 'benefit' has been construed very widely indeed.[182] However, it is less clear whether a special power of *appointment* which is exercisable 'for the benefit' of objects should be construed in the same way or more narrowly.

---

[174] See, for example, *Scotney v Lomer* (1886) 31 Ch D 380 and *Re Tyssen* [1894] 1 Ch 56.
[175] (1871) 6 Ch App 445.   [176] See esp 452, *per* James LJ.   [177] [1983] STC 517, 525d.
[178] [1982] STC 403, 411.   [179] [1991] STC 490.   [180] See paras 14.28–14.38 above.
[181] *Pilkington v IRC* [1964] AC 612.   [182] *Re Clore's Settlement Trusts* [1966] 1 WLR 955.

15.61   A power of appointment differs from a power of advancement in a number of ways. First, an advancement, unlike an appointment, is said to remove the advanced funds entirely out of the original settlement for all purposes, and any trusts created of such funds are not read back into the settlement (except for perpetuity purposes).[183] An appointment, by contrast, is said not to have such an effect.[184] However, this argument simply presupposes that which had to be established. Such consequences may indeed be the effect where the powers in question are simple in form, but this is a function of the width of the power and not something intrinsic to its nature. A power of advancement may be exercised so as to make only minor amendments to the trusts of a settlement, for instance by postponing the age at which a beneficiary takes a vested interest, and a power of appointment may be exercised so as to remove funds entirely into a separate settlement.

15.62   Secondly, a power of advancement is said to be exercisable only for the benefit of the individual beneficiary who is being advanced.[185] An appointment, on the other hand, may benefit an entire class of objects, some of whom may not even have been born. However, this argument would seem to favour a more liberal interpretation of the word 'benefit' in the context of an appointment, rather than an advancement, and not the reverse.

15.63   Thirdly, it is well established that an exercise of a power of appointment in favour of a stranger (ie someone who is not a member of the class of objects of the power) is excessive and void (either wholly or *pro tanto*).[186] On the other hand, upon the exercise of a power of advancement, persons who are not objects of the power may be benefited and, indeed, the 'advanced' beneficiary may be excluded altogether.[187] Although this may seem to indicate a material difference between the nature of the two kinds of power, it is not clear that this is indeed so. The doctrine of excessive execution applies to a power of advancement as it applies to a power of appointment: in neither case can the power be exercised purely and simply in favour of a stranger, without regard to the object(s) of the power. In each case, the exercise must be for the benefit of a proper object. The manner in which a power is exercised, or the way in which the object is benefited (and, therefore, whether a stranger can derive some benefit from its exercise) depends on the terms, and therefore the scope, of the power and not, it seems, on some inherent characteristic of that particular power. If a power of appointment is exercisable for the

[183] *Re Gossett's Settlement* (1854) 19 Beav 529; *Lawrie v Bankes* (1858) 4 K & J 142; *Re Fox* [1904] 1 Ch 480; *Re Pilkington's Will Trusts* [1959] Ch 699, 705; *Pilkington v IRC* [1964] AC 612, 639; *Re Marquess of Abergavenny's Estate Act Trustees* [1981] 1 WLR 843.
[184] *Muir v Muir* [1943] AC 468.
[185] See, for example, *Re Abrahams' Will Trusts* [1969] 1 Ch 463, 484–485.
[186] See, for example, *Re Boulton's Settlement Trusts* [1928] Ch 703; *Re Hoff* [1942] Ch 298; *Re Brinkley* [1968] Ch 407; and see Chapter 18 generally.
[187] *Re Kershaw's Trusts* (1868) LR 6 Eq 322; *Pilkington v IRC* [1964] AC 612; *Re Clore's Settlement Trusts* [1966] 1 WLR 955.

'benefit' of its objects, and if the question is simply one of construction, there seems to be no obvious reason why it should be construed more narrowly than a power of advancement. The word 'benefit' also appears in section 1 of the Variation of Trusts Act 1958, where it has also been interpreted widely.[188] Indeed, if a narrower view is adopted, trustees would be presented with difficult problems in familiar situations, for example in cases where they have power to permit an object to occupy a house comprised in the trust fund, and the question arises whether the object's spouse can also live in it, or continue to live in it after the object's death.

There is, of course, an obvious difference between powers of appointment and powers of advancement in that no object of a power of appointment has any interest in the appointable property unless and until the power is exercised in his favour, whereas a common-form power of advancement applies to and operates in respect of a particular beneficiary's interest in the capital of the trust fund. It may be that, in the absence of clear authority, the courts are more reluctant to countenance the possibility that a power to defeat existing interests can be delegated to another.[189] In the case of a power of appointment, the interests of those entitled in default are divested and defeated (wholly or *pro tanto*). Thus, there may be good reason to distinguish between a power which is exercisable for the 'benefit' of a beneficiary who already has some interest (even if it is only a presumptive or contingent interest) in the property which is subject to the power, on the one hand, and a power which is exercisable for the 'benefit' of its objects, who do not as yet have any such interest in such property, on the other. However, this particular distinction does not seem to have been raised in the cases and may well be found to be a distinction without a difference. **15.64**

There is much to be said for adopting the same approach to special powers of appointment, powers of advancement, powers of maintenance, and, indeed, any powers which are expressed to be for the benefit of a beneficiary or an object, ie the word 'benefit' should be construed in the same way in each case. If this were the case, there should be no obvious reason why one should presume that an appointment by way of resettlement cannot be beneficial; and, if this is conceded, it is implicit in the power that it permits delegation, that it authorizes the introduction of non-objects, and that, in appropriate circumstances, it even allows the total exclusion of the particular object, as in the case of a power of advancement. Nevertheless, the decisions in *Re Hunter*[190] and *Re Morris*[191] have generally been taken to suggest otherwise. However, it is difficult to see how *Re Hunter* could **15.65**

---

[188] See, for example, *Re Holt's Settlement* [1969] 1 Ch 100, 121, where Megarry J expressed the view that 'the word "benefit" is . . . plainly not confined to financial benefit, but may extend to moral or social benefit'. See also *Re T's Settlement Trusts* [1964] Ch 158; *Re Weston's Settlement* [1969] 1 Ch 223; *Re CL* [1969] 1 Ch 587; *Re Remnant's Settlement Trusts* [1970] Ch 560.
[189] *Re Joicey* [1915] 2 Ch 115, 123.   [190] [1963] Ch 372.   [191] [1951] 2 All ER 528.

have survived *Pilkington* (in which it was apparently not cited). In fact, in *Re Hunter*, Cross J considered himself bound by the Court of Appeal's decision in *Re Morris*, but the power under consideration in *Re Morris* was not one to 'benefit' anyone, so the decision in that case was not directly in point in either *Re Hunter* or *Pilkington* (in which it was cited). In any event, a continuing adherence to the restrictive construction of special powers manifested in cases such as *Re Hunter* may well be pointless in practice. As we have seen,[192] even a narrow power of appointment (for example one exercisable 'in such manner and form') may be exercised in such a way that a standard-form power of advancement may be created over or in respect of the appointed fund. *Pilkington* has established that a power of advancement may be exercised in such a way that powers and discretions may be delegated. As a result, the personal discretion which is said to be inherent in a special power of appointment may effectively be delegated to another by means of two operations, namely a limited exercise of the power of appointment followed by an exercise of the newly created power of advancement.[193] If the two transactions are separated by a reasonable period of time and one is not made dependent upon the other, it would be very difficult to challenge them on the grounds that there is an excessive or fraudulent appointment.[194]

15.66 The question whether there is any remaining difference of substance between a power of advancement and a power of appointment exercisable for the 'benefit' of a certain object—at least in relation to delegation—does not seem to have been addressed directly in any reported case.[195] As we have seen, in 1871, in the context of a statutory benevolent fund, a power to pay or apply a fund 'for the benefit of' certain objects was held to have been exercised effectually notwithstanding that a non-object had been introduced and the appointment made to trustees of a separate settlement.[196] More recently, in *Re Hampden's Settlement Trusts*,[197] a similar power was considered in the context of a discretionary family settlement. The relevant power provided as follows:

> Notwithstanding the trusts and powers hereinbefore contained the trustees ... shall have power ... to pay transfer or apply the whole or any part or parts of the capital of the trust property to or for the benefit of all or such one or more exclusive of the other or others of the capital beneficiaries for the time being living as the trustees shall in their absolute discretion think fit.

Thus, under the power in question, the trustees were limited to making payments or applications of trust property for 'the benefit of capital beneficiaries for the time

---

[192] See paras 14.29–14.35 above.   [193] See, however, *Re Joicey* [1915] 2 Ch 115.

[194] cf ss 36 and 37 of the Trustee Act 1925, which authorize trustees to appoint new trustees of the whole or a segregated part of the trust fund.

[195] See, however, the exchanges of Upjohn J and Danckwerts J in *Re Wills' Will Trusts* [1959] Ch 1, 12–13; *Re Pilkington's Will Trusts* [1959] Ch 699, 705, 706–707; and [1961] Ch 466, 490.

[196] *Re Pocock's Policy* (1871) 6 Ch App 445. See para 15.59 above.   [197] [1977] TR 177.

being living', which, in the circumstances of the case, meant a named 'designated heir' (A) and his daughter (B). He and the trustees were of the view that it would be beneficial to him if an application were made in favour of all his children, including those who were not yet born (and who were, therefore, not existing objects of the power). The trustees executed a deed of appointment to this effect, and the question was whether they had acted properly in doing so.

The appointment in *Re Hampden* was challenged on two grounds: first, that it was **15.67** not possible to benefit unborn persons in any way whatsoever; secondly, that the words 'pay transfer or apply' did not justify a simple resettlement in this manner. In the event, Walton J held that the trustees had acted properly. He was more than willing to believe that the draftsman of the head settlement may never have contemplated 'the kind of resettlement which is here in question', but it was nonetheless warranted by the wording of the power.[198] However, much as it is to be welcomed, *Re Hampden* cannot be taken as strong support for the view that a special power of appointment for the 'benefit' of objects can be exercised in a similar manner. The power in question was not strictly a power of advancement, but a power to 'pay transfer or apply... for the benefit of' certain objects. However, despite the trustees' apparent conception of it, it was more analogous to a power of advancement and not strictly a power of appointment. Moreover, certain fundamental issues were not apparently argued and certainly not decided—for example, questions relating to the difference (if any) in the nature of powers of appointment and of advancement, the interrelationship of the doctrines against excessive or fraudulent executions of powers and the construction, of the power by the court, or the precise status of pre-*Pilkington* cases such as *Re Hunter* and *Re Morris*. Thus, the extent to which the word 'benefit' can be said to authorize the delegation of a power of *appointment* (if at all) remains uncertain and the only prudent course is to ensure that appropriate express provision is made in order to put matters beyond doubt.[199]

G. Effect of Invalid Delegation

The attempted delegation of a trust or power, without authority to do so, is a mere **15.68** nullity, but this does not generally affect any appointed trusts, estates, or interests, which are authorized by the original power. Thus, in *Williamson v Farwell*,[200] for example, where the donee of a special power to appoint among his own children appointed the fund to his son for life, with remainder to the son's children as the

---

[198] ibid, 181.
[199] Indeed, it is the common practice to do so. See, for example, J Kessler, *Drafting Trusts and Will Trusts* (London: Sweet & Maxwell, 2nd edn, 1995) 293, 299, 311, 324.
[200] (1887) 35 Ch D 128.

son should appoint, and, in default of appointment, to his son absolutely, it was held that, although the power conferred on the son amounted to an unauthorized attempt to delegate, the life interest and the ultimate gift in default were valid. Where an unauthorized attempt is made to delegate a power, it makes no difference whether the objects of the delegated power were also the objects of the original power[201] or were strangers.[202] On the other hand, there may be rare cases in which not only is the purported delegation of a discretionary power held invalid, but also the entire appointment fails, on the ground that there is no indication of what the appointor would have done if he had realized the extent to which his appointment was invalid.[203]

H. Involuntary Delegation

15.69 The delegation of a power may be involuntary by operation of law, as on the bankruptcy[204] or mental disorder[205] of the donee of the power. In broad terms, any general power vested in a bankrupt, and any special or hybrid power of which he himself is an object, will vest in his trustee in bankruptcy, but not 'any power exercisable . . . over or in respect of property not for the time being comprised in the bankrupt's estate' or one that 'cannot be exercised for the benefit of the bankrupt'.[206] Powers exercisable by will only cannot pass to a trustee in bankruptcy, for such a power is purely personal; and no man can make a will for another.[207] Also, a trustee in bankruptcy cannot release a special power even where to do so would be for the benefit of the bankrupt.[208]

---

[201] [1887] 35 Ch D 128.
[202] *Carr v Atkinson* (1872) LR 14 Eq 397. See also *Webb v Sadler* (1873) 8 Ch App 419 and *Re Boulton's Settlement Trusts* [1928] Ch 703, 709.
[203] *Coats' Trustees v Tillinghast* [1944] SC 466. See also the 'rule in *Hastings-Bass*' at paras 11.51–11.78 above.
[204] Insolvency Act 1986, ss 306, 283(4). See also *Re Baker* [1936] Ch 61, 66.
[205] Mental Health Act 1983, s 96.   [206] Insolvency Act 1986, s 283(1).
[207] *Nicholls to Nixey* (1885) 29 Ch D 1005.
[208] *Re Rose* [1904] 2 Ch 348. See also *Coffin v Cooper* (1865) 2 Dr & Sm 365, 375; and (in relation to a similar point under s 120 of the Lunacy Act 1890) *Re Hirst* [1892] WN 177.

16

POWERS OF REVOCATION[1]

A. Nature of a Power of Revocation

A power of revocation is not a power of appointment. A power of revocation and **16.01**
new appointment confers two separate and distinct powers which may be exercisable at different times. As Turner LJ stated in *Evans v Saunders*:[2]

> I think, also, that powers of revocation and new appointment are separate and dis-
> tinct powers; that the power of new appointment may continue after the power of
> revocation has been exercised, and that the exercise of the power of revocation will
> not of itself extinguish or destroy the power of new appointment. Further, I think,
> that where under the exercise of a general power of appointment, a power of revoca-
> tion, and of new appointment is reserved, the power of appointment so reserved is a
> new power, and cannot be held to be the old power which has been already exercised.

Often, the exercise of a power of revocation is a condition precedent to the exercise of a power of appointment.[3] A simple power to appoint new trusts includes in
itself a power to revoke the subsisting trusts, for, without a revocation of the old
trusts, there could obviously be no appointment of new ones.[4] A power in the
original settlement to revoke trusts may also, of itself, authorize new trusts.[5]

---

[1] See generally, GW Thomas, *Powers* (Sweet & Maxwell, 1998) ('*Thomas*') Ch 13, on which this
chapter is based.

[2] (1855) 6 De GM & G 654, 671, agreeing with Kindersley V-C at first instance.

[3] *Re Thursby's Settlement* [1910] 2 Ch 181, 186.

[4] Edward Sugden (Lord St Leonards), *A Practical Treatise on Powers* (8th edn, 1861) ('*Sugden*') 364.

[5] ibid 371.

Moreover, a power of revocation and a power of new appointment are usually exercised in the same document. Nevertheless, the two powers remain distinct; and a power of revocation, as the name suggests, is simply a power to revoke subsisting trusts (whether they be the original trusts or appointed trusts) and its exercise does not necessarily affect or revoke the power to appoint new trusts itself.

> It is said, very truly, . . . you cannot revoke the power to appoint new uses. No doubt the power, is to revoke the old uses and to appoint new ones. In one sense it is one power. We all know that, by the same instrument, you constantly execute the two powers. You revoke the old uses, and you proceed instantly upon the same sheet of paper, before the revocation can have operated, to appoint new uses. The revocation and the new appointment go together, not by separate deeds, but by one deed. No doubt the power of revocation is to revoke the old uses, and not to revoke the power of new appointment.[6]

B. Creation of a Power of Revocation

16.02 A power of revocation is usually expressly created or reserved by the person who declares the trusts (whether created by the original settlement or by an appointment) or who confers the power of appointment in respect of some property. Any form of words will suffice, of course, provided their intention and effect are clear. On the exercise of a power of appointment, a power of revocation and a power of new appointment may be expressly reserved, although the instrument creating the original power of appointment did not itself expressly reserve a power of revocation.[7] It may also be possible (subject to what is said below) to imply a power to revoke. For example, a simple power to appoint new trusts includes in itself a power to revoke the subsisting trusts, for, without a revocation of the old trusts, there could be no appointment of new ones.[8] This principle would seem to apply equally whether the power to appoint new trusts is found in the original settlement or in an instrument exercising a power of appointment.[9] On the other hand, a settlement may obviously declare itself to be wholly irrevocable, and a power of appointment may be so worded as to show that an irrevocable appointment alone is permitted and that no power of revocation may be reserved.[10]

C. Revocation of Appointment by Deed

16.03 Where an appointment under a power is made *by deed,* it cannot be revoked unless an express power of revocation be reserved in the deed by which the power is

---

[6] *Saunders v Evans* (1861) 8 HL Cas 721, 739.
[7] *Adams v Adams* (1777) 2 Cowp 651; *Hele v Bond* (1717) Prec Ch 474.   [8] *Sugden* 364.
[9] cf *Beecher v Major* (1865) 2 Dr & Sm 431, esp 436. See also *Marshall v Crutwell* (1875) LR 20 Eq 328; *Young v Sealey* [1949] Ch 278; *Re Warwick* (1912) 56 SJ 253; *Re Reid* (1921) 50 OLR 595; *Russell v Scott* (1936) 55 CLR 440; *Re Figgis* [1969] 1 Ch 123; *Re Bishop* [1965] Ch 450.
[10] *Piper v Piper* (1834) 3 My & K 159; *Alexander v Young* (1848) 6 Hare 393.

executed. Nor will a revocation then be authorized by a general prospective power in the deed *creating* the power of appointment which is being exercised.[11]

> . . . where the power is executed *by deed,* unless a power of revocation is reserved in that deed, the appointment cannot be revoked; no, not even if the original power expressly authorize the donee in the most unlimited terms to appoint and to revoke his appointments from time to time; for the law will not endure a prospective power like this, but on every execution a new power of revocation must be reserved.[12]

This principle does not necessarily apply to an appointment not made by deed. In **16.04** *Re Beesty's Will Trusts,*[13] for example, Wilberforce J held that an appointment made in writing, and not by deed, was revocable notwithstanding that no express power of revocation was reserved. It does not follow, however, that an appointment not made by deed is necessarily revocable. An intention that it be revocable must still be reasonably clear from the surrounding circumstances, or be manifested by some means. Otherwise, if *Re Beesty* were regarded as laying down a general principle, it could lead to considerable inconvenience.

Every power reserved in a deed executing a power will be construed strictly. Thus, **16.05** for example, the reservation of a mere power of revocation in such a deed will not in itself authorize a new appointment,[14] although the effect of a simple revocation is to restore the original trusts and powers, under which a further appointment is likely to be authorized.[15]

Where a power of appointment is expressed to be exercisable only in accordance **16.06** with certain peculiar formalities or requirements, these must of course be observed. Provided this has been done, and a power of revocation and new appointment has been reserved, a subsequent new appointment (whether reserving a power of revocation and new appointment or not) apparently need not observe the same formalities. The objects of the power cannot be changed, but the formal mode of execution may be altered.[16] There is no reason to suppose that the exercise of a power of revocation cannot also be subject to compliance with certain specified formalities (for example exercise by deed alone).

---

[11] *Hele v Bond* (1717) Free Ch 474; 1 Eq Cas Abr 342; *Worrall v Jacob* (1817) 3 Mer 256; *Marlborough (Duke) v Godolphin (Lord)* (1750) 2 Ves Sen 61; Sugden 367–373.

[12] Sugden 369, 370: 'The decision has avoided great inconvenience, and led to none.' *See also Hele v Bond, supra.*   [13] [1966] Ch 223, 233.

[14] *Ward v Lenthall* (1667) 2 Keb 269. Cf the apparently unique case of *Young v Cattle* (1707) 1 P Wms 101, where an office holder appointed his successor by deed, without reserving a power of revocation, and later countermanded this with another appointment. Cowper LC held that it was a mere authority and was clearly countermandable.

[15] *Montagu v Kater* (1853) 8 Exch 507; *Evans v Saunders* (1855) 6 De GM & G 654; *Sheffield v Von Donop* (1848) 7 Hare 42.

[16] *Sugden,* 366; *Brudenell v Elwes* (1802) 7 Ves 382; *Adams v Adams* (1777) 2 Cowp 651.

D. Revocation of Testamentary Appointments

16.07 These rules do not apply to powers which are executed or reserved by will or codicil, for a will or codicil by its very nature is a revocable instrument.[17] Thus, a power of revocation need not be expressly reserved in a will or a codicil; and an appointment by will or codicil is revocable by a subsequent appointment by deed, as well as by another will or codicil.[18]

E. Time of Exercise

16.08 It would seem to be the case that, if a power of appointment is expressed to be exercisable on a fixed date, its exercise on that date could not, in the absence of an indication to the contrary, be revocable. A power exercisable on or before a given date may be revocably exercised, but only so that a new appointment under it is made on or before that given date, ie the whole execution must be within the limits prescribed.[19] Thus, an appointment may be revocable only before the end of the relevant perpetuity period, or before the death of a named individual, or before a beneficiary attains a specified age.[20]

F. Power Given to Two or More Persons

16.09 A power of appointment given to two or more persons or the survivor of them, with or without a power of revocation, may be executed by a joint appointment reserving to the survivor a power to revoke and appoint again.[21]

> Once one has accepted . . . that the power can, in the first instance, be exercised either by the donees jointly or by the survivor of them during the life of the survivor, it must surely follow logically that an appointment made by the donees jointly can be revoked by the survivor. Otherwise, if it were not so, one could be in this position: that, once the power has been exercised in fact, the power then becomes converted into a joint power, and it would only be in the case of non-exercise that the power would be one exercisable by either survivor. That seems to me to be an illogical result . . . Once one reaches the conclusion . . . that, by implication or by interpretation of the will,[22] the survivor has a power of appointment, then one reaches . . . the conclusion that the joint appointment must be capable of being revoked by a similar appointment made by the survivor.[23]

---

[17] *Lisle v Lisle* (1781) 1 Bro CC 533; *Lawrence v Wallis* (1788) 2 Bro CC 319.

[18] *Lisle v Lisle, supra.*   [19] *Piper v Piper* (1834) 3 My & K 159, 166, 167.

[20] As would be common in trusts intended to satisfy s 71 of the Inheritance Tax Act 1984. These are really examples of conditional powers, for which see *Thomas*, Ch 12.

[21] *Sugden* 364; *Brudenell v Elwes* (1802) 7 Ves 382.

[22] There is no reason to suppose that the principle is any different in the case of a settlement.

[23] *Re Beesty's Will Trusts* [1966] Ch 223, 233–234.

It must, of course, be a question of construction in each case (a) whether the original power of appointment authorizes a revocation by the survivor(s) of two or more persons, as opposed to a joint revocation only, and also (b) whether the execution of the joint power itself effectually reserves such a power of revocation to the survivor(s).[24]

It is a different case altogether, however, where a joint power is conferred and is exercised so as to reserve a power of revocation to one of the appointors, exercisable during the lifetimes of both of the appointors, ie not simply by the survivor. Such an exercise is likely to involve an improper delegation of the power and, as such, would be invalid.[25]

16.10

G. Intention to Revoke[26]

As in the case of the execution of any power, there must be a sufficiently clear manifestation of an intention to exercise a power of revocation. Where a new appointment is made, there must be an intention not only to appoint but also to revoke the existing appointment.[27] Thus, an appointment expressed to be made in exercise of every power enabling the appointor does not extend to property which he cannot appoint without the exercise of a power of revocation, if there is other property to which the words might apply. Similarly, where a donee of a power to appoint by deed or will partially executed the power by deed, reserving a power of revocation, and afterwards, by will, by virtue of every power conferred on her by the settlement and 'otherwise howsoever', purported to appoint all the property which, under the settlement, she had power to appoint, it was held that her will operated on the unappointed part only and was not an exercise of the power of revocation and new appointment.[28] An appointment by a husband and wife in exercise of a special power of appointment 'and of every or any other power enabling them in that behalf' did not operate to exercise a power of revocation and new appointment contained in an earlier deed of appointment.[29] Nor does a reappointment by will exercise a power of revocation exercisable by deed only.[30]

16.11

However, if the intention to revoke is clear, it is not essential to refer expressly to the power of revocation.[31]

16.12

---

[24] *Brudenell v Elwes*, supra; *Montagu v Kater* (1853) 8 Exch 507; *Re Harding* [1894] 3 Ch 315; *Re Weightman's Settlements* [1915] 2 Ch 205.   [25] *Burnaby v Baillie* (1889) 42 Ch D 282, 301.
[26] See generally *Thomas*, paras 5-177–5-213.
[27] *Re Wells' Trusts* (1889) 42 Ch D 646; *Pomfret v Perring* (1854) 5 De GM & G 775, esp 780; *Eilbeck v Wood* (1826) 1 Russ 564; *Tebbott v Voules* (1833) 6 Sim 40.
[28] *Pomfret v Perring*, supra; *Re Hall* (1903) 19 TLR 420.
[29] *Re Thursby's Settlement* [1910] 2 Ch 181.
[30] *Re Hambro's Marriage Settlements* [1949] Ch 111.
[31] *Re Chatterton's Settlement* [1946] Ch 284.

Wherever there has been a complete appointment under a power, an appointment which entirely disposes of the property, you must get rid of that appointment in some way or another before any further appointment can be made. In other words, you must displace that which has operated as a complete appointment before there can be room for any further exercise of the original power, or, to put it in legal language, you must revoke the existing uses or trusts, and create new ones to take their places. It is not of course necessary that this should be done by technical words. Though there are two things to be done—a revocation of the existing uses and a subsequent substitution of other uses—the two may be done *uno flatu* just as well as by two separate processes. The revocation of the old uses and the declaration of new ones may be contained in different instruments, or they may be in one and the same instrument, and, moreover, it is clear law as well as common sense that the thing may be done, without any express revocation of the old uses, by the use of words which can take effect only if a revocation of the old uses is implied ... But, although the two processes may be combined in that way, you must be able to find that the first appointment, so far as it is effectual, is displaced by something which is afterwards done.[32]

Thus, if the purported appointment would be entirely ineffectual if it were not to be treated as exercising the power of revocation, a revocation will be regarded as having been made.[33]

16.13 If the intention to revoke is clear, it generally makes no difference that the appointees substituted in place of the original appointees cannot take for some reason: the revocation is still effective.[34] However, if the appointment is revoked only in order to make an appointment or gift in favour of another person, and there is no intention to revoke except for that purpose, the removal of the ground of revocation nullifies the revocation.[35] The reported cases[36] concern the defective execution of a subsequent will or a codicil which, of their very nature, are revocable. In each case, 'the whole question depends on the intention of the testator. If a will is simply revoked in order to make a gift in favour of another person, and you can see that there is no intention to revoke unless for that purpose, then the doctrine of *Onions v Tyrer* applies.'[37] Much depends on the circumstances of each case. If a subsequent will or codicil contains no express revocation of the earlier will or codicil, and the interests appointed or created by the subsequent

---

[32] *Re Brace* [1891] 2 Ch 671, 675, *per* North J. See also *Re Reilly and Brady's Contract* [1910] 1 IR 258; and *Re Thursby's Settlement* [1910] 2 Ch 181, 186, *per* Farwell LJ: 'It is, however, of course open to the claimants to show that there are other *indicia* besides the reference to the power, shewing an intention to execute; for example a reference to property which can only pass by means of an execution of both power of revocation and of appointment.'

[33] *Re Moses* [1902] 1 Ch 100; *Re Barker's Settlement* [1920] 1 Ch 527; *Re Lees' Trusts* [1926] WN 220; *Re Butler's Settlement* [1942] Ch 403; *Cooper v Martin* (1867) 3 Ch App 47, 56.

[34] *Quinn v Butler* (1868) LR 6 Eq 225; *Re Bernard's Settlement* [1916] 1 Ch 552, esp 560.

[35] *Duguid v Fraser* (1886) 31 Ch D 449, esp 452.

[36] See, for example, *Re Bernard's Settlement* [1916] 1 Ch 552; *Quinn v Butler, supra; Re Fleetwood* (1880) 15 Ch D 594; *Onions v Tyrer* (1716) 1 P Wms 343; *Tupper v Tupper* (1855) 1 K & J 665.

[37] *Quinn v Butler, supra*, at 227; *Onions v Tyrer, supra; Tupper v Tupper, supra*.

instrument fail, the earlier will or codicil is likely to remain unaffected,[38] but this is not necessarily the case. Although the nature of a deed differs in this respect, there seems to be no compelling reason why the same principles should not also apply where the subsequent instrument is a deed. It will still be a question of the intention of the person executing the power.

A general devise or bequest taking effect under section 27 of the Wills Act 1837 **16.14** does not in itself show a sufficient intention to revoke as well as appoint.[39] In *Charles v Burke*,[40] Kay J cited and commented on Sir John Romilly's words in *Palmer v Newell*:[41]

> '. . . although a will does, by virtue of the statute, operate as a general exercise of all[42] powers of appointment, yet that it does not operate as an exercise of a power of revoking a previous instrument.' I can only say that that seems to me to be a most reasonable restriction to put upon this general provision in the Wills Act, because although no doubt you may exercise the power of revocation by simply appointing, if you refer to the power, yet you have a double operation to go through, you revoke and reappoint, and the fact of such an appointment does revoke a previous instrument and make a new appointment.

This principle applies where the power of revocation and new appointment is that **16.15** contained in the instrument originally creating it, as well as to the case where it is reserved by an appointment made in exercise of the original power.[43]

H. Effect of Revocation

Where an original power of appointment is exercised, with a reservation of a **16.16** power of revocation, and it is followed by a revocation, the original power of appointment is revived (and may be exercised again and again after each revocation).[44] Similarly, if, on the first exercise of the power of appointment, there is

---

[38] *Re Fleetwood* (1880) 15 Ch D 594, 609; *Duguid v Fraser, supra; Re Walker* [1908] 1 Ch 560; *Re Bernard's Settlement, supra; Ward v Van der Loeff* [1924] AC 653.

[39] *Re Jones* (1886) 34 Ch D 65, where Kay J stated (at 68) that in *Pomfret v Perring* (1854) 5 De GM & G 775 there was another power to which the appointment by will could apply. *Re Gibbes' Settlement* (1887) 37 Ch D 143; *Charles v Burke* (1888) 43 Ch D 223n; *Re Brace* [1891] 2 Ch 671; *Re Salvin* [1906] 2 Ch 459; *Re Goulding's Settlement* (1899) 48 WR 183; *Re Hall* (1903) 19 TLR 420; *Re Thursby's Settlement* [1910] 2 Ch 181; *Palmer v Newell* (1855) 20 Beav 32, 38; *Nanney v Williams* (1856) 22 Beav 452; *In the Goods of Merritt* (1858) 1 Sw & Tr 112; *Re Wallinger's Estate* [1898] 1 IR 139. [40] (1888) 43 Ch D 223 n, 224 n.

[41] (1855) 20 Beav 32, 38.

[42] Section 27 operates, in fact, only so as to exercise all general powers of appointment.

[43] *Re Goulding's Settlement* (1899) WR 183.

[44] If the (revoked) appointment was made in exercise of a power conferred by the settlement itself, the effect is generally to restore the original settlement: it is highly unlikely that, on such a revocation, the settlement itself had inadvertently been destroyed. See *Sugden* 376; *Re Watts* [1931] 2 Ch 302. Cf *Ward v Lenthall* (1667) 1 Sid 343; *Hele v Bond* (1717) Prec Ch 474.

reserved a power of revocation and new appointment, the original power is not thereby exhausted and at an end. Upon the revocation of the instrument of execution, such original power remains unaffected and exists in full force. Nor will such an instrument constitute a new settlement destructive of the first.[45]

16.17   In the same way, where an irrevocable appointment is made, under which a new power of appointment is created, it is generally the case that, where a revocable appointment is made in exercise of that new power and such revocable appointment is subsequently revoked, the trusts, powers, and provisions existing before that revocable appointment was made (ie those in the irrevocable appointment) will be revived, including the power to make a further new appointment.

16.18   The law is illustrated in the leading case of *Evans v Saunders*.[46] Here, the donee of a power of appointment exercisable by deed or will appointed the whole fee by deed, reserving a power of revocation and new appointment by deed. By a subsequent deed, she revoked all the trusts appointed by the first appointment, and made a further appointment of the whole fee, again reserving a power of revocation and new appointment. By a third deed, she revoked the trusts of the second appointment, but did not, on this occasion, declare new trusts. She subsequently exercised her power of appointment by will. It was held that she had not precluded herself from exercising the original power by way of testamentary appointment. Knight Bruce LJ summed up the position thus:[47]

> . . . a power, which in any mode or to any extent whatsoever has been exercised, but exercised revocably, and the revocable appointment made under which has been well revoked, without having been acted on, is generally, if not universally, in the same force and exercisable in the same manner as if the revoked appointment had not existed, and that a power cannot necessarily be exhausted by a revocable act, though executing otherwise the power to the utmost, more than by a conditional act or by an act of merely partial execution . . .

The original power in the settlement was well created and those who disputed its exercise had to show why it had become incapable of exercise. There had been no release of it, and no act done to affect it, unless it had been exhausted by the several appointments, or destroyed by new powers created by those deeds. This was not the case. The uses were not exhaustive because they were at all times revocable.

16.19   Whether the original power is destroyed by the creation of new powers is a question of intention. It is one thing to argue, where a power of appointment is exercisable only by a deed attested by two witnesses, and it is properly exercised so as to create a power of appointment exercisable by deed witnessed by three people, that this has created a new power, and that the former could not be exercised

---

[45]   *Saunders v Evans* (1861) 8 HL Cas 721.
[46]   (1855) 6 De GM & G 654, affirmed by the House of Lords in (1861) 8 HL Cas 721.
[47]   (1855) 6 De GM & G 654, 665.

while the latter was still subsisting. However, in this case, 'what we are called upon here to say is, that a power to appoint by deed only, has operated to destroy the original power to appoint by deed or will. I think that very clear evidence of intention would be necessary to justify such a conclusion, for the substitution of the less extensive power would be in derogation of an existing right.'[48]

If, in the original settlement, a power of revocation only is reserved, a power to appoint new trusts may be implied and may be executed accordingly,[49] unless a contrary intention can be collected from the whole settlement, or the estate is expressly limited on other trusts.[50]   **16.20**

I. Partial Revocation

It is possible, of course, both to reserve a power of revocation only in respect of some, rather than all, appointments (or parts of an appointment) and also to exercise a power of revocation only in respect, or to the extent, of some revocable appointments (or parts of a revocable appointment). If a clause reserving a power of revocation extends, by necessary grammatical construction, to one or some only of several appointments made by the same instrument, a subsequent execution of the power does not, and cannot, revoke all the appointments made by the instrument.[51] Similarly, the exercise of a power of revocation will extend only to such appointments (or parts of an appointment) as are expressed to be revoked, or which are revoked by necessary implication.   **16.21**

A deed of appointment containing a power of revocation and new appointment must be acted upon even if there is evidence that a subsequent appointment in unascertainable terms has been made.[52] In other words, the revocable appointment stands until it is proved to have been revoked and the extent to which it has been revoked is established, for example where there is evidence of a subsequent deed of revocation and new appointment, but it is impossible to find it or prove its contents.   **16.22**

J. Defective Execution of a Power of Revocation

There appears to be no case in which an exercise of a power of appointment is defective in form[53] but which has been construed as an implied revocation of   **16.23**

---

[48] ibid 675–676. See also *Sheffield v Von Donop* (1848) 7 Hare 42; *Montagu v Kater* (1853) 8 Exch 507; *Ward v Lenthall* (1667) 2 Keb 269; *Witham v Bland* (1674) 3 Swan 311; *Sugden* 381–383.
[49] *Fowler v North* (1673) 3 Keb 7.   [50] *Atwaters v Birt* (1601) Cro Eliz 856.
[51] *Morgan v Gronow* (1873) LR 16 Eq 1, 13.
[52] *Rawlins v Rickards* (1860) 28 Beav 370, 374. See also *Hougham v Sandys* (1827) 2 Sim 95, 136–137.   [53] For the defective exercise of a power, see *Thomas*, Ch 10.

some earlier appointment. In *Re Hambro's Marriage Settlements*,[54] Roxburgh J held that the appointment by will in that case could not operate. It had been contended that the doctrines relating to the defective execution of a power applied to defective execution of powers of revocation; but he did not consider it necessary to decide the point in order to decide the case. The Court of Appeal[55] also considered it unnecessary to decide the point.

K. Fraud on a Power

16.24 It is unclear whether the doctrine of fraud on a power applies to the revocation of an appointment. In principle, it seems that it might be capable of doing so. Suppose, for instance, that a trustee has made a valid appointment of a trust fund in favour of A, but subject to an overriding power of appointment in favour of B, C, and D. The trustee then exercises this power and revocably appoints the trust fund in favour of B, C, and D. Subsequently, A marries the trustee's daughter. A and the trustee agree that, if the appointment is revoked, A will use the trust fund for the benefit of the daughter, or, indeed, that A and the trustee will simply divide the trust fund between them.[56] There seems to be no reason why this revocation should not be regarded as fraudulent, in the same way that the original appointment in favour of A would itself have been fraudulent if it had then been accompanied by such an agreement.

16.25 Astbury J had no difficulty in finding, in *Re Jones' Settlement*,[57] that the doctrine applied to a revocation. However, the Court of Appeal held, in *Re Greaves*,[58] that it does not, and *Re Jones' Settlement* was overruled. The reasoning of Lord Evershed MR[59] rests heavily on the premise that, as the appointor owed no duty to the objects to exercise the power at all, they could therefore have no valid ground for complaint if the appointor chose to recall a revocable exercise of it.

> The 'duty' in relation to any exercise of the power of appointment is no more than a 'duty' not to exercise the power otherwise than for the single benefit of the members of the designated class of objects. If, therefore, the 'duty' applies to the revocation of an appointment already made, to whom is it owed? Clearly not to the original appointees or to the class of possible appointees; for the donee of the power never owed any duty to them to exercise it at all, and they can, therefore, have no valid ground for complaint if he chooses to recall a revocable exercise of it. Moreover, if the 'duty' were held to be owed to these persons, it could only be a duty not to exercise the power of revocation otherwise than for their single benefit; and as revocation *per*

---

[54] [1949] Ch 111.   [55] ibid 484.
[56] cf *Shirley v Fisher* (1882) 47 LT 109 (where, it seems, no fraud was found on the facts).
[57] [1915] 1 Ch 373.
[58] [1954] Ch 434. Vaisey J, at first instance, held that the revocation was fraudulent and ineffective.
[59] ibid 447–448.

se can never benefit the objects of the power as such, this would mean that the power of revocation could never be exercised save with a view to re-appointment... Equally, ... the 'duty' cannot be owed to the class of possible appointees plus the persons to take in default of appointment, since the interests of the latter might be directly in conflict with the interests of the former. Finally, the 'duty' cannot be owed to the persons to take in default of appointment, so as (for the first time) to disable the donee of the power from taking or even (we suppose) permitting anyone else to take directly or indirectly any benefit from or through any of such persons: for those persons have taken, once and for all, vested interests granted to them by the original donor, subject only to the power of the appointor wholly or partly to divest them. And revocation without re-appointment must necessarily benefit the persons taking in default as such, so that the conception of a duty to them not to revoke an existing revocable appointment is a contradiction in terms. Further, as the donee of the power is plainly under no obligation to them to revoke the existing appointment but is free to revoke it or not as he pleases, it follows that there is no objection in law to his stipulating for some benefit to himself or some third party as a condition of revocation.

However, this seems to confuse the rights of an object of a power in relation to **16.26** whether it ought to be, or can be, exercised at all, with the rights of an object to prevent or control an unauthorized or improper exercise. It is certainly true that an object of a mere power has no right to call on the appointor to exercise that power (in his favour or at all). However, if the power is actually exercised, the object clearly has the right to have it exercised properly, in accordance with its terms and for the purpose for which it was created or conferred. Similarly, the object or beneficiary of an executed revocable appointment cannot prevent or object to a lawful and proper revocation of that appointment. However, if the *purpose or object* of a revocation is to benefit the donor himself, it is difficult to see why that revocation should be unimpeachable. Moreover, once an appointment has been made, the objects who have benefited thereunder may have vested, albeit defeasible interests; and in this respect it is difficult to see how their rights differ from the rights of those who are entitled in default of appointment, whose interests may also be defeated and who are entitled to ensure that any such defeasance occurs only upon a proper exercise of the power of appointment.

The Court of Appeal was careful, in *Re Greaves*, to emphasize[60] that the judgment **16.27** was confined to the facts of that case and to facts strictly analogous thereto:

> that is, when the following conditions are found: (1) a special power of appointment expressed to be exercisable by deed, revocable or irrevocable, or by will, with a gift over in default of and subject to any such appointment; (2) an exercise of that power by deed expressed to be liable to be revoked at any time; and (3) a subsequent total revocation followed by, or (if you will) coupled with, a general release of the power.

---

[60] ibid 449–450.

It was stated[61] that it was possible to conceive of a case in which the power to revoke is so closely related to a power of reappointment that, as a matter of construction, the former power should be held to be only exercisable for the purposes of, and as an essential step towards, a reappointment. In such a case, if the reappointment were ineffective, the revocation might also fall with it. In practice, however, it is very unlikely that there would be such close interdependence between the powers of revocation and reappointment.

16.28   It is also doubtful whether the same liberal attitude would be adopted in relation to a revocation by a trustee (or any other person in a fiduciary position). In *Re Greaves*, the relevant powers of appointment and revocation were not vested in a trustee, but in the life tenant. Trustees owe duties to the objects of their powers which non-trustees generally do not.[62] It may also be that *Re Greaves* could be confined to cases where the revocation does no more than produce a state of affairs that could properly have been brought about in the first instance by a simple release (and no appointment) by the appointor. It would be much simpler if it could be said that a revocation will be fraudulent if it is made for any purpose which would render an appointment made under a special power, if made for the same purpose, invalid. However, the wide statements in *Re Greaves* seem to make this conclusion impossible.

---

⁶¹ [1954] Ch 450.   ⁶² See Chapter 11 above.

17

DISCLAIMER, RELEASE, AND EXTINGUISHMENT OF POWERS[1]

A. Disclaimer of Powers

17.01 Section 156(1) of the Law of Property Act 1925 provides that a person to whom any power, whether coupled with an interest or not, is given may by deed disclaim the power, and, after disclaimer, shall not be capable of exercising or joining in the exercise of the power.[2] On such a disclaimer, the power may be exercised by the other person or persons, or the survivor or survivors of the other persons, to whom the power is given, unless the contrary is expressed in the instrument creating the power.[3] Section 156 seems to place the disclaimer of a power on the same footing as the disclaimer of an estate.[4] A trustee must disclaim his entire trust and a partial disclaimer has no effect at all: 'He must disclaim *in toto*, or he remains a trustee as to all.'[5] Thus, a person may disclaim the office of trustee, and thereby disclaim all powers conferred on or by the office, but he may not accept the office and then disclaim a power conferred on him *virtute officii* so as to vest it in his co-trustees. Nor does section 156 enable a tenant for life under the Settled Land Act to

---

[1] See, generally, G W Thomas, *Powers* (Sweet & Maxwell, 1998) ('*Thomas*') Ch 15, on which this chapter is based.

[2] Section 156 applies to powers created or arising either before or after the commencement of the Act: s 160.   [3] Section 156(2).

[4] *Re Fisher and Haslett* (1884) 13 LR Ir 546.

[5] *Re Lord and Fullerton's Contract* [1986] 1 Ch 228, 233; *Re Eyre* (1883) 49 LT 259; *Saul v Pattinson* (1886) 34 WR 561.

disclaim powers conferred on him by that Act (although a statutory owner may release his powers).[6] Subject to these exceptions, however, the section seems to authorize the disclaimer by a donee of a joint power, leaving the other joint donee(s) to exercise the power alone: whether this is actually the case in any specific instance probably depends, however, on the intention of the donor of the power.[7]

B. Release of Powers

17.02 Prior to the enactment of section 52 of the Conveyancing Act 1881 (with effect from 1 January 1882), all powers, except powers collateral and powers coupled with a duty or trust,[8] could be suspended or destroyed, either wholly or in part, by the donees thereof. The old classification of powers was therefore of considerable importance in this context.

Traditional classification

17.03 (1) A power simply collateral is a power given to a person who has no interest whatsoever in the property over which the power is given. A typical example would be a mere power conferred upon an individual to appoint property vested in trustees among several objects, and in which property the donee has no interest of his own. Such a power is given, or supposed to have been given, for the benefit of some third person and could not be released.[9]

17.04 (2) A power in gross is a power given to a person who has an interest in the property over which the power extends, but such an interest as cannot be affected by the exercise of the power. The most common instance is that of the tenant for life who has a power to appoint the destination of capital after his death.[10]

17.05 (3) A power appendant (or appurtenant) is a power exercisable by a person who has an interest in the property and which interest is capable of being affected, diminished, or disposed of to some extent by the exercise of the power.[11]

---

[6] Settled Land Act 1925, s 104(1); *Re Craven Settled Estates* [1926] Ch 985.

[7] cf *Burnaby v Baillie* (1889) 42 Ch D 282, esp 301.

[8] *Weller v Ker* (1866) LR 1 Sc & D 11; *Re Eyre, supra; Saul v Pattinson, supra; Re Dunne's Trusts* (1878) 1 LR Ir 516.

[9] *West v Birney* (1819) 1 Russ & M 431; *Smith v Death* (1820) 5 Madd 371; *Willis v Shorral* (1739) 1 Atk 474; *Thacker v Key* (1869) LR 8 Eq 408; *Chambers v Smith* (1878) 3 App Cas 795; *Shirley v Fisher* (1882) 47 LT 109. Where the grantor reserved a power *for his own benefit* he could release it, whether he had retained an interest in the estate or not: *West v Birney, supra; Bird v Christopher* (1653) Sty 389.

[10] *Smith v Death* (1820) 5 Madd 371; *Barton v Briscoe* (1822) Jac 603; *Horner v Swann* (1823) Turn & R 430; *Malcolm v O'Callaghan* (1835) 5 LJ Ch 137; *Smith v Houblon* (1859) 26 Beav 482; *Re Radcliffe* [1892] 1 Ch 227. A tenant for life's power of jointuring is also a power in gross.

[11] *Re D'Angibau* (1880) 15 Ch D 228, 232–233; *Re Mills* [1930] 1 Ch 654.

An example of such a power would be a tenant for life's power to grant leases in possession.

(4) A power coupled with a duty or trust is a power conferred on trustees (or other fiduciaries) by virtue of their office. Thus, whether a trustee has a mere power of appointment or a trust power, he is under a duty in respect of the power: to consider its exercise, in the first case, and to consider its exercise and to distribute in the second case. 'A trustee who has a power which is coupled with a duty is . . . bound, so long as he remains trustee, to preserve that power, and to exercise his discretion as circumstances arise from time to time, whether the power should be used or not, and he could no more, by his voluntary act, destroy a power of that kind than he can voluntarily put an end to or destroy any other trust that may be committed to him.'[12]   **17.06**

The right to release a power, if it existed at all, applied whether the power was present or future,[13] and whether the property was real or personal.[14]   **17.07**

Section 155 of the Law of Property Act 1925

Since 1 January 1882, powers collateral (as well as powers in gross and powers appendant) can be suspended or destroyed. Section 52 of the Conveyancing Act 1881 provided that any person to whom any power, whether coupled with an interest or not, was given, and irrespective of whether the power came into operation before or after the commencement of the Act, could by deed release or contract not to exercise the power. The Act did not apply, however, where the release of the power would be a breach of trust. Therefore, powers coupled with a duty or trust[15] still cannot be suspended or destroyed in the absence of an express authority to that effect in the instrument creating the power. Nor, if the power was to arise at a future time, could the donee fetter his right to exercise it by any act or undertaking prior to that time.[16]   **17.08**

Section 155(1) of the Law of Property Act 1925 replaced section 52 of the 1881 Act, but it did not alter the law in relation to the release of powers. Section 155 simply provides: **17.09**

> A person to whom any power, whether coupled with an interest or not, is given may by deed release, or contract not to exercise, the power.

A power coupled with a trust or duty still cannot be released in the absence of express authority to do so. Nor can the donee of such a power contract not to   **17.10**

---

[12] *Re Eyre* (1883) 49 LT 259, 260, *per* Kay J; *Weller v Ker* (1866) LR 1 Sc & D 11; *Saul v Pattinson* (1886) 34 WR 561.   [13] *Albany's Case* (1586) 1 Co Rep 110b.
[14] *Noel v Lord Henley* (1825) M'Cl & Yo 302.
[15] ie a 'fiduciary power in the full sense of the term': *per* Chitty J in *Re Somes* [1896] 1 Ch 250, 255.
[16] *Re Eyre, supra; Saul v Pattinson, supra.*

exercise it. All powers conferred on trustees, *virtute officii,* will be of this kind. However, a power conferred on a donee who also happens to be a trustee need not be conferred on him in his capacity as trustee, in which case it may not be coupled with any duty or trust and may be released. Contrariwise, a power may be conferred on an individual who is not a trustee as such, but who is nonetheless placed under a fiduciary duty in relation to that specific power.[17] Thus, the real distinction in this context is that between fiduciary powers (or powers coupled with a trust or a duty), which, in the absence of authority, may not be released, and non-fiduciary powers which may be released under section 155. Identifying or classifying a particular power may not be easy, however.[18]

Beneficial powers and vicarious powers

17.11 In *Re Wills' Trust Deeds,*[19] Buckley J suggested that powers broadly fall into two classes, namely 'beneficial powers' (so-called because they are such as to confer a benefit of a kind on the donee) and 'vicarious powers' (so-called because their distinguishing characteristic is the donor's intention that the donee shall in the exercise of the power act on the donor's behalf to achieve an end desired by the donor, in respect of which he placed his confidence in the donee of the power). As an alternative, the latter 'would not inappropriately be called a power coupled with a duty or coupled with a trust, or a power in the nature of a trust'. Given that the donee of a 'beneficial power' is 'unlikely' to be under any obligation to the settlor, either legal or moral, to exercise such a power, he could properly release it: the donee could not be regarded as acting unconscientiously in debarring himself from its use. On the other hand, the donee of a 'vicarious power', 'even if under no legal or moral obligation to exercise the power, ought not in good conscience to deprive himself of the capacity to exercise it until the period within which it must be exercised, if at all, has run out, for by doing so he would disenable himself during the remainder of that period from discharging the confidence reposed in him by the settlor, should an occasion arise after the release on which the donee, if still free to exercise the power, would have done so'.[20]

17.12 However, in view of the clear, unqualified language of section 155 of the Law of Property Act 1925, Buckley J recognized that the class of powers which cannot be released 'should not be extended beyond the field indicated by authority'.[21] He therefore considered the circumstances in which judges in the past had treated powers as being incapable of being released because of their fiduciary character.

---

[17] See *Re Wills' Trust Deeds* [1964] Ch 219, 228; *Re Mills* [1930] 1 Ch 654, 669.

[18] See, for example, *Re Mills, supra* (power conferred on one of two trustees held to be a power appendant and not a trust power).   [19] [1964] Ch 219, esp 227–229.

[20] ibid, 229.   [21] ibid.

Following a review of some of the main authorities,[22] Buckley J concluded that the following propositions were established:[23]

1. If a power is granted to appoint among a class of objects and, in default of appointment, there is a trust, express or implied, in favour of the members of that class, the donee of the power cannot, by failure to appoint or by purporting to bind himself not to appoint or, which comes to the same thing, by purporting to release his power, defeat the interest of the members of the class of objects.
2. A 'power of the kind just mentioned cannot be released, for the donee is under a duty to exercise it, notwithstanding that the Court may not be able to compel him personally to perform that duty, and can remedy his default only by executing the trust in default of appointment'.
3. Where a power is conferred on trustees *virtute officii* in relation to their trust property, they cannot release it or bind themselves not to exercise it.
4. The same is true if the power is conferred on persons who are in fact trustees of the settlement but is conferred on them by name and not by reference to their office, if on the true view of the facts they were selected as donees of the power because they were the trustees.
5. Where a power is conferred on someone who is not a trustee of the property to which the power relates or, if he be such a trustee, is not conferred on him in that capacity, then, in the absence of a trust in favour of the objects of the power in default of appointment, the donee is, at any rate prima facie, not under any duty recognizable by the court to exercise a power such as to disenable him from releasing the power.

The third and fourth propositions seem to be unobjectionable, subject to the **17.13** addition of the caveat that trustees may nonetheless have express authority to release some or all of their powers.[24] There are other difficulties with these propositions,[25] especially after the decision of the House of Lords in *Re Gulbenkian's Settlements*[26] and *McPhail v Doulton*.[27] It has subsequently been doubted,[28] with justification, whether *Re Wills* could stand in the light of the subsequent decision of the Court of Appeal in *Muir v IRC*.[29] In *Muir* itself, the Court of Appeal preferred to distinguish *Re Wills* on the ground that it was primarily concerned with a point of construction:[30] it was not necessary to say whether *Re Wills* was wrongly decided and the Court of Appeal expressly refrained from doing so. However,

---

[22] *Brown v Higgs* (1803) 8 Ves 561; *Weller v Ker* (1866) LR 1 Sc & D 11; *Re Eyre* (1883) 49 LT 259; *Saul v Pattinson* (1886) 34 WR 561; *Re Mills* [1930] 1 Ch 654.
[23] [1964] Ch 219, 236–237.   [24] *Muir v IRC* [1966] 1 WLR 1269.
[25] See *Thomas*, para 15-11.   [26] [1970] AC 508.   [27] [1971] AC 424.
[28] *Mettoy Pension Trustees Ltd v Evans* [1990] 1 WLR 1587, 1614.
[29] [1966] 1 WLR 1269.   [30] ibid 1283.

both cases confirmed the fundamental principle that powers conferred on trustees *qua* trustees cannot be released, in the absence of express authority to do so.

The *Mettoy* classification of powers

17.14 In *Mettoy Pension Trustees Ltd v Evans*,[31] Warner J was attracted by the submission that the classification of powers into powers simply collateral, powers in gross, and powers appendant or appurtenant (as set out in *Re D'Angibau*)[32] is now of antiquarian interest only. A 'more pertinent' classification was accepted instead, namely one which classified fiduciary powers into four categories:

> Category 1 comprises any power given to a person to determine the destination of trust property without that person being under any obligation to exercise the power or to preserve it. Typical of powers in this category is a special power of appointment given to an individual where there is a trust in default of appointment. In such a case the donee of the power owes a duty to the beneficiaries under that trust not to misuse the power, but he owes no duty to the objects of the power. He may therefore release the power but he may not enter into any transaction that would amount to a fraud on the power, a fraud on the power being a wrong committed against the beneficiaries under the trust in default of appointment: see *In Re Mills* [1930] 1 Ch 654 and *In Re Greaves* [1954] Ch 434. It seems to me to follow that, where the donee of the power is the only person entitled under the trust in default of appointment, the power is not a fiduciary power at all, because then the donee owes no duty to anyone. That was the position in *In Re Mills* [1930] 1 Ch 654 ...
>
> Category 2 comprises any power conferred on the trustees of the property or on any other person as a trustee of the power itself: *per* Romer LJ at 669 ... 'a fiduciary power in the full sense'.[33] ... A power in this category cannot be released; the donee of it owes a duty to the objects of the power to consider, as and when may be appropriate, whether and if so how he ought to exercise it; and he is to some extent subject to the control of the Courts in relation to its exercise: see, for instance, *In Re Abrahams' Will Trusts* [1969] 1 Ch 463, 474, *per* Cross J, *In Re Manisty's Settlement* [1974] Ch 17, 24, *per* Templeman J; and *In Re Hay's Settlement Trusts* [1982] 1 WLR 202, 210, *per* Sir Robert Megarry V-C.
>
> Category 3 comprises any discretion which is really a duty to form a judgment as to the existence or otherwise of particular circumstances giving rise to particular consequences. Into this category fall the discretions that were in question in such cases as *Weller v Ker* (1866) LR 1 Sc & Div 11; *Dundee General Hospitals Board of Management v Walker* [1952] 1 All ER 896, and ... *Ker v British Leyland (Staff) Trustees Ltd* ... and *Mihlenstedt v Barclays Bank International Ltd* [1989] PLR 124 ...
>
> Category 4 comprises discretionary trusts, that is to say cases where someone, usually but not necessarily the trustees, is under a duty to select from among a class of beneficiaries those who are to receive, and the proportions in which they are to receive, income or capital of the trust property ...

Although it is not stated explicitly, it seems clear that Warner J accepted that powers and discretions within Categories 3 and 4 cannot be released.

---

[31] [1990] 1 WLR 1587, 1613–1614.   [32] (1879) 15 Ch D 228, 232.

[33] Such as the powers of the managers of a unit trust.

The power under consideration in *Mettoy* was a power conferred on an employing **17.15**
company to apply surplus funds on the winding up of a pension scheme 'at the
absolute discretion' of the company. Warner J concluded that it was a fiduciary
power in the full sense, ie it fell within Category 2 of his classification. In this particular context, Buckley J's twofold classification of 'beneficial' and 'vicarious'
powers was not considered relevant.

Although Buckley J's decision in *Re Wills* has never been overruled, his classifi- **17.16**
cation of powers has not subsequently been followed or adopted. Despite the
obvious differences between the particular contexts in which Buckley J and
Warner J put forward their respective classifications, it must be doubtful whether
the two can stand together. Certainly, there is a great deal of common ground
between them: both recognize, for example, that powers conferred on trustees as
such, or on an individual as a trustee of a particular power, are non-releasable
fiduciary powers in the full sense. However, there are also marked differences. In
particular, a power falling within Warner J's Category 1 is said to be releasable in
Mettoy, whereas the same power, falling within Buckley J's first category, is said to
be incapable of being released in *Re Wills*. On this specific point, the views
expressed in *Mettoy* seem to be more in accord with the authorities: there seems to
be no convincing reason why a non-fiduciary donee of a mere power should not
be able to release his power. Moreover, the classification of powers and discretions put forward in *Mettoy* provides a more accurate reflection of modern law and
practice, particularly after *Re Gulbenkian* and *McPhail v Doulton*.

Binding effect of a release

If trustees (or other holders of an office) properly release a power which has been **17.17**
conferred on them *virtute officii,* will that release bind their successors in office, or
will it completely extinguish the power? *In Re Wills' Trust Deeds,*[34] Buckley J
thought that such a release would bind only those executing the release (ie the
current office holders) and would not bind their successors in office.

> A power granted to successive holders of an office is unlike trust property the entire
> ownership of which is vested in the trustees for the time being of the settlement and
> devolves on each change of trustee by succession. Where a power is granted to suc-
> cessive holders of an office all that is vested in the incumbent for the time being of the
> office is the capacity to exercise the power while he holds that office. In other words,
> the power is granted by the original donor directly to each successive holder of the
> office and none of them acquires the power by succession from his predecessor. It
> appears to me to follow that none of the successive holders of the office is capable of
> binding any subsequent holder of the office not to exercise the power...They might
> by a complete exercise of it exhaust the power and so exclude their successors in office
> from being capable of any further exercise of it.

---

[34] [1964] Ch 219, 238.

17.18   If this is correct, it could lead to undesirable and peculiar consequences. For example, if the trustees for the time being were to release a power of appointment, those entitled in default of appointment would not have an indefeasible interest in the relevant property unless and until the office itself ceased to exist, for a change in the identity of the office holders might lead to the defeasance of their interests. Moreover, where a power is conferred on trustees as such (which is certainly the most common example of this point), it is not generally considered to be the case that the trustees for the time being have but a fraction of that power or, alternatively, that each succeeding set of trustees have their own separate power out of a series of powers. The general view is that a power conferred on trustees as such is a single, undivided power.[35] The reasoning on which Buckley J based his different conclusion is not made apparent in *Re Wills.*[36] It is not surprising, therefore, that *Re Wills,* though never overruled, has not found favour with practitioners, and its correctness on this point has been doubted. Indeed, it may well be that this aspect of *Re Wills* is inconsistent with the Court of Appeal's judgment in *Muir v IRC,* where it seems to have been implicit in the circumstances of that case that the release effected by the trustees was not only authorized but also complete and binding.[37] The prudent course of action in order to avoid any uncertainty on this issue is clearly to make express provision in the trust instrument to the effect that, in the absence of a declaration to the contrary, a release shall extinguish the power for all time.

Methods of releasing powers

17.19   A release may be effected expressly or by implication.[38] An express release of a power under section 156(1) of the Law of Property Act 1925 must be made by deed. It is also usually the case that the settlement or other instrument conferring express authority to release a power requires any such release to be by deed, although this is not necessary. As Plowman J pointed out in *Re Courtauld's Settlement*:[39]

> A power of appointment can be extinguished in a number of ways. It can be extinguished expressly, for example by a deed of release, or by a contract not to exercise the power, or it can be extinguished impliedly by any dealing with the property by the donee of the power which is inconsistent with its further exercise.

---

[35] See, for example, *Re De Sommery* [1912] 2 Ch 622, esp 631; *Innes v Harrison* [1954] 1 WLR 668. This is also unavoidably implied by other authorities, such as *Re Blew* [1906] 1 Ch 624; *Re Whiteford* [1915] 1 Ch 347; *Re Cassel* [1926] Ch 358; *Re Vaux* [1939] Ch 465; *Re Symm's Will Trusts* [1936] 3 All ER 236; *Re Watson's Settlement Trusts* [1959] 2 All ER 676; and *Re Bullen* (1915) 17 WAR 73. Cf *Re Kelly* [1932] IR 255, esp 263; *Lyons v Bradley* (1910) 168 Ala 505, 33 So 244; *Bundy v US Trust Co* (1926) 257 Mass 72, 153 NE 337. See also *Gooding v Read* (1853) 4 De GM & G 510; *Re Watson* [1892] WN 192, and *Re Wise* [1896] 1 Ch 281 (which were all reviewed and not followed in *Re Blew, supra*).   [36] See *Thomas,* paras 15-24–15-28.

[37] [1966] 1 WLR 1269 esp 1283–1284; *Mettoy Pension Trustees Ltd. v Evans* [1990] 1 WLR 1587 1614.

[38] *Cunynghame v Thurlow* (1832) 1 Russ & M 436; *Smith v Houblon* (1859) 26 Beav 482; *Re Courtauld's Settlement* [1965] 2 All ER 544.

[39] ibid 545. See also *Foakes v Jackson* [1900] 1 Ch 807; *Re Hancock* [1896] 2 Ch 173.

Such a dealing may occur, for example, when the donee of the power propounds an arrangement under the Variation of Trusts Act 1958 which is inconsistent with the continued existence of the power.[40] A power may also be released by a recital in an order, whether made under the Variation of Trusts Act or otherwise.[41] Such an implied release may be effective notwithstanding that an *exercise* of the particular power would require a deed.[42] However, in cases which are not subject to the court's jurisdiction under the 1958 Act, if the instrument conferring authority to release a power expressly requires a release to be made by deed, such a requirement must be complied with and there ought to be no room for an implied release. If a revocable appointment is revoked in part only, the remainder of the appointment being 'confirmed', such confirmation will not in itself amount to a release of the power to revoke the remainder of the appointment.[43]

Extent and effect of release

A power exercisable in favour of a number of objects need not be released in respect of the entire class, but may be released in respect of only one (or some) of those objects.[44] Similarly, there seems to be no objection to a 'temporary' release, such as a release which has the effect of excluding an object from the class for a period of time or until he attains a specified age. A power need not be released in respect of the entirety of the property which is the subject matter of the power, but may be released in respect of only part of that property.[45]   **17.20**

If a power can be released at all, it is generally irrelevant that the donee of the power himself derives some benefit from the release, even where the release is made with the intention of benefiting the donee.[46] The doctrine applicable to the fraudulent exercise of a power will not make the release fraudulent and void. Thus, where a tenant for life has power to appoint a trust fund in favour of his children and issue, with remainder in default of appointment to a particular child absolutely, a release of the power by the tenant for life and the subsequent disposal of the trust fund by him and that child jointly will be valid, notwithstanding that the same result brought about by an actual appointment in favour of the child would probably have been fraudulent and void.[47]   **17.21**

It does not follow, however, that the same can be said of a release of a fiduciary power. Even where a trustee has authority to release a power, it is not necessarily   **17.22**

---

[40] *Re Courtauld, supra*, at 546; *Re Ball's Settlement* [1968] 2 All ER 438, 440.
[41] *Re Christie-Miller's Settlement Trusts* [1961] 1 All ER 855, 856; *Boyd v Petrie* (1872) 7 Ch App 385; *Re Sugden's Trusts* [1917] 2 Ch 92.   [42] *Foakes v Jackson, supra*.
[43] *Re Lees' Trusts* [1926] WN 220.   [44] *Re Brown's Settlement* [1939] Ch 944.
[45] *Green v Green* (1845) 2 Jo & Lat 529, 541; *Re Evered* [1910] 2 Ch 147, esp 156–157, 161.
[46] *Cunynghame v Thurlow* (1832) 1 Russ & M 436; *Smith v Houblon* (1859) 26 Beav 482; *Re Little* (1889) 40 Ch D 418; *Re Radcliffe* [1892] 1 Ch 227; *Re Somes* [1896] 1 Ch 250.
[47] *Re Somes, supra*, 254.

the case that he may do so in a manner which may benefit himself. Thus, where the authority to release is conferred on trustees, that authority, like the fiduciary power itself, may be said to be conferred on them for the benefit of the beneficiaries and for the general purposes of the trust, and, if the trustees derive some benefit from a release, the rule against conflict of interests may well apply.

17.23 Once a power has been validly released, it ceases to be exercisable thereafter, either entirely or to the extent of the release.[48]

Covenants and the release of powers

17.24 A covenant or contract to exercise a *general* power of appointment which is exercisable *by deed* (or otherwise than by will) may be the subject of a decree of specific performance.[49]

17.25 However, specific performance of a covenant or contract to exercise a *general testamentary* power of appointment will not be granted, because the objects are clearly intended to take under a testamentary instrument and such a decree would effectively allow an appointment to be made by deed, although damages may be awarded for breach of such a covenant.[50]

17.26 A covenant to exercise a *special testamentary* power in a particular way is regarded as imposing a fetter on the donee's discretion. It is not regarded as a proper discharge of the donee's duty and is, therefore, altogether void and is neither enforceable by the covenantee nor remediable by an award of damages.[51] It is not necessarily the case, however, that a testamentary appointment will be invalid simply because it conforms with a covenant to appoint which the appointor entered into, especially if his will pre-dates the covenant,[52] or presumably if it can be shown that he reconsidered the terms of the appointment when the will was executed and up to the date of his death. Section 155 of the Law of Property Act 1925 clearly does not affect these propositions, for it deals only with contracts not to exercise powers and not contracts to exercise them in a particular way.

17.27 In relation to special testamentary powers, there seem to have been two main objections to such a covenant or contract. First, the express terms of the power could and would be departed from, for, in effect, a power to appoint by will would then be executed by deed. Secondly, such special powers were generally regarded as 'fiduciary' in nature; and, as such, the donee was required to be able to have regard, up to the last moment of his life, to the circumstances then affecting the

---

[48] *Smith v Plummer* (1848) 17 LJ Ch 145; *Hurst v Hurst* (1852) 16 Beav 372; *Re Brown's Settlement* [1939] Ch 944; *Re Evered* [1910] 2 Ch 147.
[49] *Re Dykes' Estate* (1869) LR 7 Eq 337.   [50] *Re Parkin* [1892] 3 Ch 510.
[51] *Thacker v Key* (1869) LR 8 Eq 408, 415; *Palmer v Locke* (1880) 15 Ch D 294; *Re Bradshaw* [1902] 1 Ch 436; *Re Cooke* [1922] 1 Ch 292, esp 300; *Coffin v Cooper* (1865) 2 Dr & Sm 375.
[52] *Palmer v Locke, supra*, 303.

various objects of the power, and he could not fetter his discretion by a pre-existing contract.[53] In this context (as in others) a 'fiduciary power' bore a wide meaning and was clearly not confined to a power conferred on a trustee (or someone holding a fiduciary office as such).[54]

Although there seems to be no decision involving a similar covenant or contract **17.28** in relation to the exercise of a *special power* which is exercisable *by deed* (probably because the same effect could easily be achieved simply by an actual immediate exercise of the power), the same principles are still capable of applying. Certainly, the execution of a fiduciary power must be made in the light of circumstances existing at the time of its exercise, and an exercise by anticipation is generally not possible. Indeed, since the cases referred to above did not involve trustees or any person holding a fiduciary office as such, it would seem that the same principles apply also to non-fiduciaries.

In contrast, a voluntary covenant *not* to exercise a *special power* may be valid. **17.29** Indeed, section 155 of the Law of Property Act 1925 expressly authorizes the donee of any power to contract not to exercise it. Such a covenant or contract effects a release of the power.[55] However, the manner in which this actually operates is not always straightforward (and is not referred to in section 155). The decision of the Court of Appeal in *Re Evered*[56] provides a good illustration of this, as well as a summary of relevant principles by Cozens-Hardy MR:[57]

(1) A power to appoint by will cannot be executed by deed.
(2) A covenant to appoint by will in a particular way cannot be the subject of specific performance or have any legal operation.[58]
(3) An exercise of the power by will is not rendered invalid by reason of the fact that the appointor has covenanted to make such an appointment, there being no other circumstance which might render the appointment invalid apart from the covenant.[59]
(4) The appointor may covenant *not* to exercise his power in favour of a particular object of the power, and in such case the power could thereafter only be exercised subject to the fetter or limitation thus imposed by the negative covenant.
(5) In so far as the whole or any part of the settled property is released from the power, it goes as unappointed to the persons entitled in default of appointment, subject to the provisions of any hotchpot clause which may be found in the settlement.

---

[53] See, for example, *Re Cooke* [1922] 1 Ch 292, 300.
[54] *Thacker v Key, supra,* 414–415; *Re Bradshaw, supra,* 447; *Palmer v Locke, supra,* 299.
[55] *Isaac v Hughes* (1870) LR 9 Eq 191.　　[56] [1910] 2 Ch 147.
[57] ibid 158–160. See also 161, *per* Buckley LJ.　　[58] *Palmer v Locke* (1880) 15 Ch D 294, 303.
[59] ibid; see also *Coffin v Cooper* (1865) 2 Dr & Sm 375.

(6) If the power is to appoint by deed or will, a deed by which the appointor purports to release a portion of the fund in favour of an object of the power may
be construed—*ut res magis valeat*—as an appointment in favour of the object.
But this cannot be so if the power is testamentary only. The deed must operate as a release or not at all.[60]

17.30 In *Re Evered*, the documents operated upon the footing of an obligation on the
appointor to refrain from exercising her power, or not to exercise her power in a
particular way, and the benefits derived by the sons flowed from the trusts in
default of appointment. A covenant, though negative in form, may, however, be
held to be positive in substance.[61]

17.31 Section 155 of the Law of Property Act 1925 now provides that a person to whom
'any' power is given may 'contract not to exercise it', but this does not extend to
powers coupled with a trust or duty. Therefore, a trustee cannot contract not to
exercise a power conferred on him *qua* trustee unless he is expressly authorized
to do so (or expressly authorized to release his powers).

Releases and fraud on a power

17.32 The doctrine of fraud on a power does not apply to a release of a power.[62]

C. Extinguishment of Powers

17.33 Powers may be extinguished for a number of different reasons and in a variety of
different circumstances. A power may be exhausted by an effectual, irrevocable
exercise. The purposes for which a power was created may cease to exist or may
never come into existence. The time during which a power is exercisable may
expire. Some essential precondition which would render the power exercisable
may not be satisfied. Powers may even be extinguished by order of the court.

Exercise and satisfaction

17.34 Some powers are extinguished by a single effectual exercise. Thus, a power to
sell specific property is necessarily exhausted once the property is sold. Most
powers are capable of being exercised more than once: indeed, they are commonly expressed to be exercisable 'from time to time' or 'at any time' (which
amounts to the same thing).[63] Powers to appoint among children,[64] powers to

---

[60] cf *Davies v Huguenin* (1863) 1 Hem & M 730, doubted in *Palmer v Locke, supra*, 302.
[61] *Re Cooke* [1922] 1 Ch 292.   [62] *Re Greaves* [1954] Ch 434.
[63] *Digges's Case* (1600) 1 Co Rep 173a.
[64] *Cuninghame v Anstruther* (1872) LR 2 Sc & D 223; *Doe d Milborne v Milborne* (1788) 2 Term
Rep 721.

lend money,[65] and a whole host of other powers—such as powers of investment, maintenance, advancement, and so forth—may generally be exercised repeatedly. In each case, however, it is a question of intent and construction whether a particular power has been exhausted by a particular exercise. Thus, where the trustee intends to make, and does make, an absolute and irrevocable appointment of the property which is subject to the power, the power is exhausted.[66] It cannot be exercised further unless a power of revocation and further appointment is reserved (either expressly or by necessary implication), irrespective of a change of mind or circumstances.[67]

Any dealing with property by the donee of a power inconsistent with the exercise of the power releases it, on the general principle that a person is not permitted to defeat his own grant.[68] Thus, if the donee joins with those who are entitled in default of appointment in an assignment to some person of the property which is subject to the power, he may be taken to have released his power and any subsequent purported exercise of the power will be inoperative.[69] It may be difficult in some cases to ascertain what the precise intention may have been, however.[70] A different result may follow where a release is expressly required to be made by deed or in accordance with other specified requirements and also, of course, if the dealing with the property is by a trustee. **17.35**

Where there is a primary power, and in default of appointment a secondary power, a partial exercise of the primary power does not exclude the exercise of the secondary power. Thus, where there is a joint power of appointment and, in default of appointment, a power for the survivor to appoint, a joint appointment of part of the property will not necessarily prevent the survivor from appointing the remainder.[71] Similarly, to the extent that a primary power to appoint given to one donee is not exercised (or only partially exercised) a secondary power given in default of exercise of the primary power may become exercisable by a second donee.[72] **17.36**

Other extinguishing events

A power may be extinguished when the purposes for which it was created have ceased to exist. For example, powers of maintenance or of advancement during **17.37**

---

[65] *Webster v Boddington* (1848) 16 Sim 177; *Versturme v Gardiner* (1853) 17 Beav 338. Cf *Harrold v Harrold* (1861) 3 Giff 192.

[66] *Re Hancock* [1896] 2 Ch 173. Cf *Nottidge v Dering* [1909] 2 Ch 647.

[67] *Re Marquess of Abergavenny's Estate Act Trusts* [1981] 1 WLR 843.

[68] *Smith v Death* (1820) 5 Madd 371; *Barton v Briscoe* (1822) Jac 603; *Walford v Gray* (1865) 5 New Rep 235.   [69] *Foakes v Jackson* [1900] 1 Ch 807; *Re Hancock, supra*, 183.

[70] See, for example, *Re Lees' Trusts* [1926] WN 220; *Re Thursby's Settlement* [1910] 2 Ch 181, 186; *Morgan v Gronow* (1873) LR 16 Eq 1; *IRC v Cookson* [1977] 1 WLR 962.

[71] *Re Simpson's Settlement* (1851) 4 De G & Sm 521. Cf *Simpson v Paul* (1761) 2 Eden 34.

[72] *Mapleton v Mapleton* (1859) 4 Drew 515.

minority cease when the object attains the age of majority.[73] A power may become incapable of being exercised when some precondition fails to materialize, for example where there is a power to appoint in favour of the children of a named individual, and that individual dies without issue,[74] or when the time for its exercise expires, for example a power which is exercisable until the donee marries,[75] or when some other essential contingency is not fulfilled.[76]

17.38 A power may be extinguished by merger when the donee becomes absolutely entitled to the property which was the subject matter of the power.[77] Also, a power may, by express direction or by necessary implication, be exercisable only during the duration of some particular interest.[78] However, a power may, in exceptional circumstances, coexist with the fee.[79] Indeed, a power often remains exercisable despite the alienation of the property which is its subject matter. Thus, a power appendant may be exercised notwithstanding the alienation of the estate to which it was appendant, provided the exercise does not derogate from the grant.[80] Alienation will not, therefore, necessarily destroy a power to appoint new trustees,[81] or a power of sale,[82] or a power of appointment over property not alienated.[83] A power in gross, being independent of the donee's interest, may be exercised during the continuance, or after the determination, of that interest.[84] In all cases, however, it is a matter of intention and construction whether the power in question has been extinguished or ceased to be exercisable.[85]

Order of the court

17.39 Powers may occasionally be extinguished by order of the court, although it is more often the case that they are simply suspended in the course of legal proceedings.[86]

---

[73] *Clarke v Hogg* (1871) 19 WR 617.
[74] *Lancashire v Lancashire* (1848) 2 Ph 657. See also *Bond v Taylor* (1861) 2 John & H 473 and *Re Ward's Trusts* (1872) 7 Ch App 727.   [75] *Kenny v Kenny* [1940] 1 DLR 243.
[76] For Contingent Powers generally, see *Thomas*, Ch 12.
[77] *Cross v Hudson* (1789) 3 Bro CC 30. See also *Sing v Leslie* (1864) 2 Hem & M 68.
[78] *Haswell v Haswell* (1860) 2 De GF & J 456.
[79] *Maundrell v Maundrell* (1805) 10 Ves 246, 255; *Cross v Hudson, supra*, 35; *Mortlock v Buller* (1804) 10 Ves 292; *Grice v Shaw* (1852) 10 Hare 76; *Sing v Leslie, supra*.
[80] *Long v Rankin* (1822), Edward Sugden (Lord St Leonards), *A Practical Treatise on Powers* (8th edn, 1861) ('*Sugden*') 895; *Warburton v Farn* (1849) 16 Sim 625; *Alexander v Mills* (1870) 6 Ch App 124; *Earl of Lonsdale v Lowther* [1900] 2 Ch 687.
[81] *Hardaker v Moorhouse* (1884) 26 Ch D 417.
[82] *Tyrrell v Marsh* (1825) 3 Bing 31; *Walmesley v Butterworth* (1835) 5 Sweet's Bythewood 168.
[83] *Re Sprague* (1880) 43 LT 236; *Jones v Winwood* (1841) 10 Sim 150.
[84] *Reresby v Newland* (1723) 2 P Wms 93; *Parsons v Parsons* (1744) 9 Mod Rep 464; *Re Master's Settlement* [1911] 1 Ch 321.
[85] *Daniel v McCabe* [1951] IR 133; *Re Jump* [1903] 1 Ch 129; *Bickley v Guest* (1831) 1 Russ & M 440.
[86] A Underhill and DJ Hayton, *Law of Trusts and Trustees* (16th edn, Butterworths, 2002) (*Underhill and Hayton*) 832–847; J Mowbray et al, *Lewin on Trusts* (17th edn, Sweet & Maxwell, 2000) ('*Lewin*') paras 29-69–29-70, 36-80–36-83.

Variation of Trusts Act 1958

Section 1(1) of the Variation of Trusts Act 1958 authorizes the court to approve **17.40**
(on behalf of the categories of persons specified) any arrangement varying or
revoking all or any of the trusts on which any property is held, or enlarging the
powers of trustees of managing or administering such property. There seems to be
no doubt that the court may sanction arrangements under the Act which are
inconsistent with the continued existence of dispositive or administrative powers,
thereby effectively extinguishing those powers. The absence of express authority
in the trust instrument to release a power, or the absence of an actual express
release, seems to be immaterial.[87] The court's order may even control the future
exercise of a power.[88] The Variation of Trusts Act is dealt with in detail below.[89]

Marriage settlements

Powers in a marriage settlement are not extinguished by a decree absolute of **17.41**
divorce.[90] The judicial separation of husband and wife does not affect their capacity
to exercise a joint power.[91] However, the court may, in the exercise of its jurisdiction to vary marriage settlements conferred by sections 23 and 24 of the
Matrimonial Causes Act 1973, affect or extinguish powers conferred by a settlement. Thus, a wife may be treated as if she were dead, so that her husband alone
can exercise a joint power as the deemed survivor;[92] or a power of appointment
may be extinguished or postponed.[93]

Administration orders [94]

A decree for administration does not absolve a trustee or a personal representative **17.42**
from the performance of his duties,[95] but he should obtain the sanction of the court
to each transaction thereafter.[96] This extends to the institution or defence of legal
proceedings,[97] the execution of a power of sale,[98] the appointment of trustees,[99]

---

[87] *Re Courtauld's Settlement* [1965] 1 WLR 1385; *Re Turner's Will Trusts* [1960] Ch 122; *Re Ball's Settlement* [1968] 1 WLR 899.
[88] *Re Drewe's Settlement* [1966] 1 WLR 1518.   [89] See Chapter 24 below.
[90] *Fitzgerald v Chapman* (1875) 1 Ch D 563; *Burton v Sturgeon* (1876) 2 Ch D 318; *Re Pilkington's Settlement* (1923) 129 LT 629; *Re Monro's Settlement* [1933] Ch 82.
[91] *Halsbury's Laws*, 4th edn, vol 13, paras 1136–1141.
[92] *Re Poole* [1959] 1 WLR 651; *Smith v Smith* [1970] 1 WLR 155.
[93] *Evered v Evered* (1874) 31 LT 101; *Noel v Noel* (1885) 10 PD 179; *Pryor v Pryor* (1887) 12 PD 165; *Bosvile v Bosvile* (1888) 13 PD 76.
[94] See (1968) 84 LQR 64 (AJ Hawkins) esp 64–77; CPR Pt 64; *Re Wilson* (1885) 28 Ch D 457; *Re Blake* (1885) 29 Ch D 913; *McLean v Burns Philp Trustee Co Pty Ltd* (1985) 2 NSWLR 623.
[95] *Bernhardt v Galsworthy* [1929] 1 Ch 549; *Cardigan v Curzon-Howe* (1885) 30 Ch D 531.
[96] *Re Viscount Furness* [1943] Ch 415, 419. See also *Bethell v Abraham* (1873) LR 17 Eq 24; *Minors v Battison* (1876) 1 App Cas 428.
[97] *Jones v Powell* (1841) 4 Beav 96.   [98] *Walker v Smalwood* (1768) Amb 676.
[99] *Webb v Earl of Shaftesbury* (1802) 7 Ves 480; *Middleton v Reay* (1849) 7 Hare 106; *Re Gadd* (1883) 23 Ch D 134; *Thomas v Williams* (1883) 24 Ch D 558; *Re Norris* (1884) 27 Ch D 333; *Tempest v Lord Camoys* (1888) 58 LT (NS) 221.

doing repairs,[100] or investment.[101] It is the duty of the trustee or personal representative to bring before the court the question upon which the direction of the court is required. If he acts without such direction he does so at his peril,[102] although good title can probably be conferred on innocent purchasers.[103] An administration decree probably does not suspend dispositive powers, or, perhaps, powers which are expressed to be exercisable at the absolute or uncontrolled discretion of the trustees, but this seems uncertain.[104] However, a prudent trustee would seek the court's directions even in such a case; and, in any event, the effect of the order is not to extinguish the power.[105] Where trustees have an absolute discretion in the exercise of a power, the court will not force them to exercise it, but, if it is exercised, the court will ensure that it is exercised properly. If the power is coupled with a trust, the court will ensure that it is exercised, but it will not generally interfere with the trustees' discretion as to the precise manner of its exercise.[106]

17.43 If a partial (as opposed to a general) administration order is made, the powers of trustees or personal representatives are not affected, except to the extent that the exercise of such powers may conflict with the order made.[107]

Institution of proceedings

17.44 The mere issue of a writ for administration does not deprive a trustee of his powers or discretions in dealing with trust property, although he may be required to satisfy the court that a particular exercise was right and proper.[108] Nor does the issue of an originating summons relating to the execution of a trust or the administration of a deceased's estate,[109] except in so far as the particular relief sought necessarily involves some interference with an exercise of a power or discretion.[110]

Payment into court

17.45 Where trustees pay the trust fund into court under section 63 of the Trustee Act 1925, they retire from the trusts and are no longer permitted to exercise any

---

[100] *Mitchelson v Piper* (1836) 8 Sim 64.

[101] *Bethell v Abraham* (1873) LR 17 Eq 24; *Re Lofthouse* (1885) 29 Ch D 921; *Widowson v Duck* (1817) 2 Mer 494.

[102] *Garner v Moore* (1855) 3 Drew 277.   [103] *Berry v Gibbons* (1873) 8 Ch App 747.

[104] *Sillibourne v Newport* (1855) 1 K & J 602; *Talbot v Marshfield* (1867) LR 4 Eq 661; *Brophy v Bellamy* (1872) 8 Ch App 798. Cf *Bethell v Abraham, supra*, 26.

[105] *Thomas v Williams* (1883) 24 Ch D 558.

[106] *Brophy v Bellamy, supra*; *Re Blake* (1885) 29 Ch D 913.

[107] *Stevens v Theatres Ltd* [1903] 1 Ch 857. Cf *Duff v Devlin* [1924] 1 IR 56; *Dolan v Murphy* [1930] IR 60.

[108] *Berry v Gibbons* (1873) 8 Ch App 747; *Neeves v Barrage* (1849) 14 QB 504; *Adams v Scott* (1859) 7 WR 213; *Att-Gen v Clack* (1839) 1 Beav 467; *Jones v Powell* (1841) 4 Beav 96; *Peatfield v Benn* (1853) 17 Beav 522; *Sillibourne v Newport* (1855) 1 K & J 602.

[109] Under CPR Pt 64, r 64 and Practice Direction to CPR Pt 64 (preserving the old RSC Ord 85, with amendments).

[110] *Café v Bent* (1843) 3 Hare 245. See also *Re Radcliffe* (1878) 7 Ch D 733 and *Re Barrett* (1889) 43 Ch D 70.

of the powers conferred on them as trustees.[111] Whether this results in the powers being extinguished or remaining exercisable by the court itself, or in the appointment of new trustees to exercise the powers, seems to depend on the circumstances of each case.[112]

Directions of the court

Applications for directions may be made[113] on 'any question arising in the administration of the estate of a deceased person or in the execution of a trust'. This extends to directions as to the mode of exercise of a power or discretion, and the trustee will generally be allowed his costs of making the application.[114] However, although trustees may surrender to the court their powers or discretions in respect of existing funds and in relation to existing circumstances (as opposed to any future exercise of a discretion),[115] this is seldom done; and applications for directions do not usually involve the surrender or extinguishment of a power or discretion.[116]

17.46

In appropriate circumstances, the court may make prospective orders as to costs, for example where members of pension schemes represent significant classes of members and do not have the resources for, or should not reasonably be expected to meet the costs involved in, participating in the application.[117] Normally, however, a prospective costs order in favour of one party, especially in hostile litigation, would be unjust to the other party and might be seen to fetter the trial judge's discretion.[118]

17.47

---

[111] *Re Nettlefold's Trust* (1888) 59 LT (NS) 315; *Re Coe's Trusts* (1858) 4 K & J 199; *Re Tegg* (1866) 15 WR 52; *Re Mulqueen* (1871) 7 LR Ir 127. Cf, however, *Re London's Trusts* (1871) 40 LJ Ch 370 and *Joel v Mills* (1861) 30 LJ Ch 354.

[112] *Re Coe's Trusts, supra; Re Tegg, supra; Re Nettlefold's Trusts, supra; Re Ashburnham's Trust* (1885) 54 LT (NS) 84; *Klug v Klug* [1918] 2 Ch 67; and *McPhail v Doulton* [1971] AC 424.

[113] Under CPR Pt 64; *Re Beddoe* [1893] 1 Ch 547. See also *Alsop Wilkinson v Neary* [1996] 1 WLR 1220; *Breadner v Granville-Grossman (Costs)* [2001] WTLR 377, 390.

[114] *Turner v Turner* (1862) 30 Beav 414. Such costs will usually be on an indemnity basis: *Re Buckton* [1907] 2 Ch 406 (which has not been superseded by CPR: *D'Arbo v Page (No 2)* The Times, 10 August 2000); *McDonald v Horn* [1995] 1 All ER 961, esp 969–970; *Chessels v British Telecommunications plc* [2002] WTLR 719; CPR r 48.4. A trustee ought not to appeal against the directions given, however: if he does so, he is liable to pay the costs: *Re Londonderry's Settlement* [1965] Ch 918. On actions that are unreasonable, see *Re Spurling's Will Trusts* [1966] 1 WLR 920.

[115] *Re Alleyn-Meyrick's Will Trusts* [1966] 1 All ER 740, 744; *Re Berens* [1888] WN 95.

[116] See, eg, *Re Alleyn-Meyrick's Will Trusts, supra; Marley v Mutual Security Merchant Bank and Trust Co Ltd* [1991] 3 All ER 198; *Public Trustee v Cooper* [2001] WTLR 901; *Joel v Mills* (1861) 30 LJ Ch 354; *Prendergast v Prendergast* (1850) 3 HLC 195. The court may approve a particular transaction, but it cannot order that it be carried out: *Re Robinson* (1885) 31 Ch D 247.

[117] *McDonald v Horn* [1995] 1 All ER 961; *Re British Airways Pension Schemes* [2000] PLR 311. See also *Re Omar Family Trust* [2000] WTLR 713.

[118] *National Anti-Vivisection Society Ltd v Duddington* The Times, 23 November 1989. See also *STG Valmet Trustees Ltd v Brennan* [2002] WTLR 273 (CA of Gibraltar).

18

THE EXCESSIVE EXECUTION
OF A POWER[1]

A. General Principle

'Excess in the exercise of a power consists in the transgression either of the rules of **18.01** law or of the scope of the power.'[2] In other words, excessive execution involves an attempt to go beyond that which is authorized by the express or implied terms of the particular power or by law. All powers, whether they are dispositive or administrative, and whether they are conferred on trustees or others in a fiduciary position or on ordinary (ie non-fiduciary) persons, are subject to the principle. Common examples of excessive execution of powers conferred on trustees (or on others in relation to a trust) are the improper delegation of the power;[3] attempts to impose or annex unauthorized conditions;[4] the creation of excessive interests; and the inclusion of persons who, or purposes which, are not proper objects of the power.[5] Moreover, an exercise of a power which transgresses the rule against

---

[1] See generally GW Thomas, *Powers* (Sweet & Maxwell, 1998) ('*Thomas*') Ch 8, which forms the basis of this present chapter.

[2] Sir George Farwell and FK Archer. *A Concise Treatise on Powers* (3rd edn, 1916) ('*Farwell*') 324; *Thomas* 433.   [3] *Re Boulton's Settlement Trust* [1928] Ch 703.

[4] *Pawlet v Pawlet* (1748) 1 Wils KB 224. Cf *Re Witty* [1913] 2 Ch 666.

[5] *Re Boulton's Settlement Trust* [1928] Ch 703; *Leadenhall Independent Trustees Ltd v Welham*,Park J, 19 March 2004: Lawtel AC 9200701. It is also arguably the case that the application of the rule against

perpetuities or the rule against excessive accumulations is also an excessive execution of that power: indeed, these particular rules of law, unlike certain others, cannot be excluded by the express terms of the power.[6]

18.02   Whether or not a particular exercise is excessive depends, in each case, on the scope of the specific power. Although the extent and limits of any power ought to be delineated expressly, in many cases they may have to be implied and may give rise to difficult questions of construction.

B. Excessive Execution Distinguished from Valid Execution With Unintended Effects

18.03   There is clearly an overlap between an excessive execution of a power and a valid exercise which simply fails to achieve the intended result of that exercise. In *Re Hastings-Bass*[7] and *Re Abrahams' Will Trusts*,[8] for example, a question arose as to whether a particular exercise of a power of advancement was wholly void, or just partially void, on the basis that the application of the rule against perpetuities had drastically altered the trusts intended to be created by the relevant advancement. At first sight, such a question would seem to be simply one of an excessive execution of a power[9] (as most perpetuitous executions would be). However, in *Re Hastings-Bass*,[10] Buckley LJ indicated that the principle enunciated by Cross J in *Re Abrahams* was directed at the case where:

> the effect of the perpetuity rule has been to alter the intended consequences of an advancement so drastically that the trustees cannot reasonably be supposed to have addressed their minds to the question relevant to the true effect of the transaction.

Buckley LJ clearly distinguished between an excessive exercise of a power, on the one hand, and a failure to take into account relevant considerations or to exclude from consideration irrelevant factors, on the other. It is the latter that has come to be regarded as the substance of the so-called 'rule in *Hastings-Bass*'.[11] The donor of a fiduciary power does not authorize any exercise of that power without prior careful consideration by the donee and, in this sense, any careless exercise which fails to ensure that the intended result is achieved could itself be said to be excessive.

---

conflict of interests in relation to the exercise of a power is but another instance: see paras 10.116–10.118 above.

[6] The rules against perpetuities and excessive accumulations, the delegation of powers and discretions, and the rule against conflict of interests, are all dealt with separately in other chapters: see Chapters 8, 10, 15, and 29.

[7] [1975] Ch 25. See also *Thomas*, paras 6-132–6-145.   [8] [1969] 1 Ch 463.

[9] This point was argued, unsuccessfully, in *Mettoy Pension Trustees Ltd v Evans* [1990] 1 WLR 1587, 1622–1623.   [10] [1975] Ch 25, 41.

[11] *Mettoy Pension Trustees Ltd v Evans* [1990] 1 WLR 1587, 1624, *per* Warner J.

Nevertheless, despite the fact that many factors are common to both topics, the principles applicable to an excessive exercise of a power and those involved in the duty of a trustee or other fiduciary to have a proper understanding of the effect of an exercise of a power operate in different ways and serve different functions. Thus, an exercise of a power of appointment, irrespective of whether it is a fiduciary or a non-fiduciary power, will fail entirely if it is exclusively in favour of non-objects, without any need to investigate or question the considerations which the appointor may or may not have taken into account; and it will fail *pro tanto* if it is in favour of both objects and non-objects, provided that the valid interests are severable from the invalid. On the other hand, an exercise of a power (which must probably be a fiduciary power) which infringes the rule in *Hastings-Bass* may be exclusively in favour of objects of the power and yet still be invalid on the basis that the actual effect of the exercise is materially different from that intended, or because insufficient account was taken of crucially relevant factors, or too much account was taken of irrelevant ones.[12]

C. Excessive and Fraudulent Execution Distinguished

The dividing line between excessive execution of a power and fraud on the **18.04** power[13] can be very fine, especially in relation to powers of appointment, partly because the cases in both areas tend to involve the introduction of non-objects (indeed, fraudulent appointments are generally attempts to achieve the effects of an excessive appointment without actually making one) and partly because the central issue in each case is the intention of the appointor when he exercised the power. The distinction is also crucial, in that a fraudulent execution is generally entirely (and not just partially) invalid. As Sargant J said in *Re Holland*:[14]

> If, on the one hand, there is a genuine appointment to an object of the power, coupled with an attempt to impose on that appointment conditions or trusts in favour of persons who are not objects, then the appointment stands good free from the conditions. If, on the other hand, there is no genuine appointment to an object of the power, but the appointment actually made to that object is for purposes foreign to the power, then the whole appointment fails as being an appointment unwarranted by the power, and that whether the real purposes of the appointment have or have not been communicated to the nominal appointee and assented to by him.

The mere fact that the appointor purports to attach a condition intended to compel the appointee to settle the appointed funds, or to make provision for

---

[12] See, eg *Stannard v Fisons Pension Trust Ltd* [1991] PLR 225; and see also *Thomas*, paras 6-158–6-162. The rule in *Hastings-Bass* and the duties which it purports to enforce are therefore dealt with separately elsewhere: see paras 11.51–11.78 above.

[13] The doctrine of fraud on a power is discussed in detail in Chapter 19 below.

[14] [1914] 2 Ch 595, 601. In *Re Burton* [1955] Ch 82, 99, Upjohn J said it was 'plain' that this passage was referring to the doctrine of fraud on a power.

non-objects, is not of itself sufficient to constitute a fraud on the power (although it is often a good indication of it). If fraud is not established, the question is whether the appointment can still stand and the condition alone rejected as being excessive. Moreover, where a condition is annexed, not to the appointed fund but to the appointor's own property, the exercise of the power is not necessarily excessive. In such a case, the doctrine of election applies: the appointee can choose to take the appointed fund, free from any unauthorized condition, and forfeit any interest in the appointor's own property, or he can accept the latter subject to the condition.[15]

18.05 Since an excessive exercise of a power or discretion is essentially an unauthorized exercise, one which is *ultra vires*, the doctrine is clearly capable of applying in innumerable instances. Some of these, for example appointments which infringe the rule against perpetuities or the rule against excessive accumulations, are dealt with in different chapters. In other cases, what might be termed an excessive execution may be better regarded as a fraud on the power or a failure by the trustee to address his mind properly to the exercise in which he was engaged: such other heads of potential invalidity ought, therefore, to be borne in mind as well. This chapter considers some of the more common examples of an excessive execution of a power or discretion by trustees, namely those which seek to (a) annex unauthorized conditions to an appointment, or (b) grant excessive interests, or (c) include persons who, or purposes which, are not proper objects of the power.

Excess by way of annexing conditions

18.06 Clearly, conditions cannot be imposed by the exercise of a power unless the trustee or other donee is authorized to do so by the terms of that power.[16] It is immaterial whether the power is a fiduciary or non-fiduciary power. Unauthorized conditions cannot be introduced even if they are intended to, and would, benefit an object of the power. A simple power of selection or distribution, for instance, will not be wide enough.[17] On the other hand, the words 'in such manner and form' are probably sufficient.[18] In other cases, it may be that it is only the particular condition which it is sought to impose that is unauthorized.[19] In each case, it is a matter of the construction of the terms of the power.

18.07 The cases also distinguish between a limitation over on a given event and a simple condition which it is attempted to attach to the execution of a power.[20] It is clear that a person with an exclusive power of appointment can appoint an interest

---

[15] *Re Burton* [1955] Ch 82; *Re Neave* [1938] Ch 793; *King v King* (1864) 15 Ir Ch R 479; *Churchill v Churchill* (1867) LR 5 Eq 44, 49; *Roach v Trood* (1876) 3 Ch D 429, 444.
[16] *Burleigh v Pearson* (1749) 1 Ves Sen 281, 282, *per* Lord Hardwicke. See generally *Thomas* 436–438.   [17] *Butler v Butler* (1880) 7 LR Ir 407.
[18] *Pawlet v Pawlet* (1748) 1 Wils KB 224; *Dillon v Dillon* (1809) 1 Ball & B 77.
[19] See, eg, *Vatcher v Paull* [1915] AC 372.   [20] *Stroud v Norman* (1853) Kay 313.

subject to a contingency.[21] Therefore, an appointment to one object, on condition that he carries out a specified act and, if he fails to do it, then over to another object, may be valid, for an act to be performed by the appointee is no different in substance from any other contingency, such as attaining a particular age or the birth of other children. Nevertheless, this must be treated with caution. The fact that a power of appointment is exclusive (as most now are) is but one relevant factor: the donee may exclude an object altogether, but it remains the case that, if he purports to exercise the power in an object's favour, he must do so in accordance with the terms of that power.[22] For example, a power to appoint property unconditionally will be exercised excessively if the appointor directs that the property is to go over in the event of the donee dying under the age of 21.[23]

If an appointment is indeed made subject to an unauthorized condition, and there **18.08** is no fraud, the appointment itself is valid, and the condition alone held void, provided the invalid condition is separable; if it is not, the appointment as a whole is infected and fails.[24] The fact that a condition is separable clearly does not indicate, of itself, that the donee possessed an overriding and genuine intention to benefit an object, but this is often overlooked (at least, where there is present some intention to benefit the object). Thus, an appointment to an object subject to a charge for an unauthorized object is valid, but the charge is void.[25] Similarly, if A has power to appoint £1,000 among his children, and he appoints the entire sum to them subject to a condition that they shall release a debt owing to them, the appointment of the £1,000 stands, the condition annexed thereto alone being void, for 'the boundaries between the excess and proper execution are precise and apparent'.[26] Where a power to divide a fund ('in such shares and proportions') was exercised in favour of six children equally, but the share of one of them was to be held on trust until he attained the age of 30 years, at which time it would pass to the other five if his conduct proved 'unworthy' in the meantime, it was held that the power did not authorize the annexing of conditions and the son took absolutely.[27] An appointment to two objects, with conditions annexed that one should not sell

---

[21] See, eg *Caulfield v Maguire* (1842) 2 Jo & Lat 141; *Graham v Angell* (1869) 17 WR 702.

[22] *Butler v Butler* (1880) 7 LR Ir 401.

[23] See Edward Sugden (Lord St Leonards), *A Practical Treatise on Powers* (8th edn, 1861) ('*Sugden*') 527; *Dillon v Dillon* (1809) 1 Ball & B 77.

[24] This proposition is not affected by either *Stroud v Norman* (1853) Kay 313 or *Vatcher v Paull* [1915] AC 372, in both of which the relevant power authorized the annexing of conditions.

[25] *Re Jeaffreson's Trusts* (1866) LR 2 Eq 276; *Dowglass v Waddell* (1886) 17 LR Ir 384.

[26] *Alexander v Alexander* (1755) 2 Ves Sen 640, 644; *Re Holland* [1914] 2 Ch 595. See also *Richardson v Simpson* (1846) 3 Jo & Lat 540; *Watt v Creyke* (1856) 3 Sm & G 362; *Rooke v Rooke* (1862) 2 Drew & Sm 38; *Roach v Trood* (1876) 3 Ch D 429; *Re Staveley* (1920) 90 LJ Ch 111; *Re Neave* [1938] Ch 793 (on which see *Re Simpson* [1952] Ch 412 and *Re Burton's Settlements* [1955] Ch 82). Cf *Stuart v Lord Castlestuart* (1858) 8 Ir Ch Rep 408, where an appointment to a son on condition that he released his father's estate from a loan raised in the son's favour, was upheld on the basis that the father's motive was to prevent injustice to his other children and he derived no benefit himself.   [27] *Butler v Butler* (1880) 7 LR Ir 401.

or dispose of the property and the other should create a strict settlement of her appointed share, was held valid but the conditions void.[28]

18.09 On the other hand, an appointment fails in its entirety if it is subject to an inseparable condition. In *Webb v Sadler*,[29] for instance, the donee of a power of appointment among children appointed to trustees upon such trusts as one of the children with the consent of the donee of the power during his life and, after his death, with the consent of the trustees, should appoint. The requirement as to consent was held to be inseparable from the power and thus rendered it wholly void.[30] Similarly, an appointment by will of £200 to an object, subject to payment of burial expenses and the appointor's small debts, was held not severable and therefore wholly void.[31]

18.10 If the excessive condition were a condition precedent, the whole appointment may well fail, for the event on which the appointment arose or became effective would not have occurred.[32]

Creating excessive interests

18.11 Under the same principles, where excessive interests are created on the execution of a power, then, provided the boundary between that which is permitted and the excess is distinguishable, the execution will be good and only the excess void. Thus, if a power to lease for 21 years is exercised so as to grant a lease for 40 years, the power is well executed to the extent of 21 years: in such a case, it is clear by how much the donee has exceeded his power.[33] A power, and indeed a trust, to accumulate income for a period in excess of any available accumulation period is good *pro tanto* and only the excess is void (provided the relevant perpetuity period is not also exceeded).[34] Where a power becomes ineffective as to part of the property, an appointment of the whole is also good *pro tanto*.[35] A power to charge a particular sum will be duly executed by a charge of a larger sum, only the excess being void.[36] An appointment of a greater interest than that authorized by the power may also be cut down and saved.[37] And where a power to appoint £25,000 was exercised so

---

[28] *Palsgrave v Atkinson* (1884) 1 Coll 190. See also *Sadler v Pratt* (1833) 5 Sim 632 and *Thomas* 437. But see also category (c) below para 18.12.   [29] (1873) 8 Ch App 419.
[30] See also *Re Perkins* [1893] 1 Ch 283; *Re Cohen* [1911] 1 Ch 37. *D'Abbadie v Bizoin* (1817) 5 Ir Eq 205 is probably better regarded as a case of fraud on the power.
[31] *Hay v Watkins* (1843) 3 Dr & War 339.   [32] *Farwell* 345.
[33] *Campbell v Leach* (1775) Amb 740; *Parry v Brown* (1663) 2 Freem 171; *Alexander v Alexander* (1755) 2 Ves Sen 640, 644. See also *Thomas* 439–440. At common law, however, the excess would have been fatal: *Roe d Prideaux Brune v Prideaux* (1808) 10 East 158; *Sugden* 520–521. So, too, where the power is controlled by statutory provisions (unless the terms of those provisions suggest otherwise): *Bishop of Bangor v Parry* [1891] 2 QB 277; and see *Smortle v Penhallow* (1701) 2 Lord Raym 995, 1000.
[34] *Griffiths v Vere* (1803) 9 Ves 127; *Leake v Robinson* (1817) 2 Mer 363, 389; *Eyre v Marsden* (1838) 2 Keen 564 (affirmed 4 My & Cr 231).
[35] *Re Turner* [1932] 1 Ch 31.   [36] *Parker v Parker* (1714) Gilb Rep 168.
[37] *Peters v Morehead* (1730) Fort 339; but see *Wykham v Wykham* (1811) 18 Ves 395.

as to appoint £15,000 clear of death duties, it was held effective as an appointment of £15,000 together with any death duties up to a ceiling of £10,000.[38]

Including persons or purposes which are not proper objects of the power

There is clearly an excessive execution of a power of appointment if such execution **18.12** is in favour of strangers (ie non-objects), for example where a power to appoint to children is exercised in favour of grandchildren,[39] or where the trustees of a pension scheme with a power to distribute surplus funds by way of augmentation of benefits for prospective pensioners seek to exercise it so as to make discretionary payments to existing persons.[39a] Here, again, the question is whether or not the interests given to the strangers are separable from those given to authorized objects: if they are, the appointment is effective *pro tanto*; if not, the appointment is wholly void.

D. Appointment of an Interest to an Object, Followed by an Interest to a Stranger

A simple example in this category is the appointment of a life interest to an object **18.13** (O) with remainder to a stranger (S). Here, O obtains a valid life interest (and no more), but the appointment to S fails, so that the property purported to be appointed to S goes as in default of appointment (or is held on resulting trust, as the case may be).[40]

Another instance (though less common) is an appointment of a vested but defeas- **18.14** ible interest to object O, with a gift over to a stranger by way of executory limitation, to take effect on the happening of some event or contingency, for example 'to O in fee simple, but if O should die in his father's lifetime, remainder to S in fee simple'.[41] Similarly, an appointment 'to O in fee simple until he ceases to reside in the family home, remainder to S in fee simple'.[42] Notwithstanding that the gift over to S can never take effect, or that it is distinct and severable from the gift to O, the happening of the stipulated event or the satisfying of the stated contingency will still divest O of his interest.[43] This was the intention of the appointor,

---

[38] *Re Keele Estates (No 2)* [1952] Ch 603.

[39] *Re Hepworth* [1936] Ch 750; *Re Hoff* [1942] Ch 298; *Re Brinkley's Will Trusts* [1968] Ch 407.

[39a] *Leadenhall Independent Trustees Ltd v Welham*, Park J, 19 March 2004: Lawtel AC 9200701.

[40] *Adams v Adams* (1777) 2 Cowp 651; *Brudenell v Elwes* (1801) 1 East 442; *Bristow v Warde* (1794) 2 Ves 336; *Reid v Reid* (1858) 25 Beav 469; *Rucker v Schofield* (1862) 1 Hem M 36. See also *Routledge v Dorril* (1794) 2 Ves 357; *Crompe v Barrow* (1799) 4 Ves 681; *Smith v Lord Camelford* (1793–1795) 2 Ves 698. Cf *Re Hastings-Bass* [1975] Ch 25.

[41] *Brown v Nisbett* (1750) 1 Cox Eq Cas 13.

[42] John Chapman Gray, *The Rule Against Perpetuities* (4th edn, 1942) by Roland Gray, §114, n 3.

[43] *Brown v Nisbett, supra*; *Doe d Blomfield v Eyre* (1848) 5 CB 713; *Re Staples* [1933] IR 126; and see *Bate v Willats* (1877) 37 LT 221. Cf *Gatenby v Morgan* (1876) 1 QBD 685 and *Re Jones* [1915] 1 Ch 246, both involving 'pre-Wills Act 1837' devises.

as inferred from the form of the appointment. It follows, however, that, if divesting should not occur unless the gift over is effective, the original gift to O becomes absolute.[44] Moreover, the gift to O may become absolute where the gift over to S is void for remoteness, for that is not dependent on any intention of the appointor.[45]

18.15   Where there is no absolute appointment to an object of the power but, instead, a series of invalid limitations which form one system of trusts, the whole appointment will fail.[46] It may be otherwise if the appointment indicates sufficiently clearly that, in the event of the failure of the trusts declared in respect of some shares, those shares are to accrue to the other shares, the trusts whereof have not failed.[47]

18.16   Where there is an appointment to an object of a special power of appointment in trust for strangers, it is unclear whether the object will take the fund absolutely, on the basis that the appointment is one and indivisible,[48] or because the so-called rule in *Lassence v Tierney*[49] applies, or whether it fails entirely on the basis that the appointor did not intend to benefit that object and had not addressed his mind properly (or at all) to the effect of the appointment,[50] or, indeed, because it is a fraudulent exercise of the power. In *Woolridge v Woolridge*,[51] Page Wood V-C stated:

> where there is an absolute appointment by will in favour of a proper object of the power, and that appointment is followed by attempts to modify the interest so appointed in a manner which the law will not allow, the Court reads the will as if all the passages in which such attempts are made were swept out of it, for all intents and purposes, ie not only so far as they attempt to regulate the quantum of interest to be enjoyed by the appointee in the settled property, but also so far as they might otherwise have been relied upon as raising a case of election.[52]

---

[44]   *Webb v Sadler* (1873) 8 Ch App 419, 426; *Re Rooke* [1953] Ch 716.

[45]   *Brown v Nisbett, supra*; *Re Brown and Sibly's Contract* (1876) 3 Ch D 156; *Re Staveley* (1920) 90 LJ Ch 111; *Re Pratt's Settlement Trusts* [1943] Ch 356. General rules of law as to the distinction between, and the characteristics of, determinable interests and interests defeasible by condition subsequent apply to appointments.

[46]   *Rucker v Scholefield* (1862) 1 Hem & M 36. See also *Re Finch and Chew's Contract* [1903] 2 Ch 486; *Hall v Hall* (1873) 43 LJ Ch 107, 108.

[47]   *Re Swinburne* (1884) 27 Ch D 696. Cf *Tomkyns v Blane* (1860) 28 Beav 422 (where the object was put to his election).

[48]   *Farwell* 347; *Sugden* 518; *Rucker v Scholefield* (1862) 1 Hem & M 36; *Gerrard v Butler* (1855) 29 Beav 541. See also *Tomkyns v Blane* (1860) 28 Beav 422 (where the object was put to his election).

[49]   (1849) 1 Mac & G 551. The essence of the rule is that 'if you find an absolute gift to a legatee in the first instance, and trusts are engrafted or imposed on that absolute interest which fail, either from lapse or invalidity or any other reason, then the absolute gift takes effect so far as the trusts have failed, to the exclusion of the residuary legatee or next of kin, as the case may be': *Hancock v Watson* [1902] AC 14, 22, *per* Lord Davey. See also *Rucker v Scholefield* (1862) 1 Hem & M 36.

[50]   *Hamilton v Royse* (1804) 2 Sch & Lef 315, 332; *Re Cohen* [1911] 1 Ch 37. Such a case also seems capable of falling under the head of failure to exercise an active discretion at all (*Turner v Turner* [1984] Ch 100) or within the scope of the rule in *Re Hastings-Bass* [1975] Ch 25. See *Thomas* 441.   [51]   (1859) Johns 63, 69.

[52]   See also *Churchill v Churchill* (1869) LR 5 Eq 44; *Re Neave* [1938] 3 All ER 220.

It is difficult to see, however, how such an appointment could stand if the appointor cannot be shown to have intended to confer some benefit on the object himself.

E. Appointment to a Stranger, Followed by an Interest to an Object

Two separate questions need to be addressed here. First, is the appointment in remainder in favour of an object valid, or does it perish along with the prior invalid appointment in favour of a stranger? Secondly, if it is valid, is it accelerated so as immediately to vest in possession?[53]   **18.17**

On the first question, the basic approach is that set out by Lord St Leonards in *Crozier v Crozier*,[54] namely that 'although the life interest is void, yet it would still further defeat the testator's intention if the remainder...were not supported'. Thus, an appointment to stranger S for life, remainder to object O, will be valid as to O but clearly not as to S.[55] Where there is an appointment to stranger S, but with a gift over to object O on a contingency, the appointment to S is clearly void, but the gift over to O will take effect if (and only if) the contingency is satisfied.[56] Thus, if, under a power to appoint to children, there is an appointment to grand-child S, but if he dies before attaining the age of majority then gift over to child O, the gift over will take effect only if S dies during his minority; if he does not, the property subject to the power passes in default of appointment.[57] The same consequence ensues presumably when the gift over to object O depends on the happening of some particular event or the satisfying of some stipulated condition (be it precedent or subsequent).   **18.18**

As to the second question, namely whether the interest of the object is accelerated because the prior gift to a stranger is void, there is no reason why limitations under an appointment should not be subject to the same rules as limitations which do not so arise. As a general rule 'the effect of a disclaimer or other destruction of the particular estate is to accelerate the estates in remainder'.[58] More precisely, acceleration depends both on the nature of the remainder and on a discernible   **18.19**

---

[53] See generally *Thomas* 442–449. Both questions were once tied up with the common law's complex rules governing the validity of remainders, rules which are no longer in force: see AWB Simpson, *An Introduction to the History of the Land Law* (OUP, 1961) 199–200.

[54] (1843) 3 Dr & War 353, 370.

[55] *Crozier v Crozier* (1843) 3 Dr & War 353; *Alexander v Alexander* (1755) 2 Ves Sen 640; *Doe d Duke of Devonshire v Lord Cavendish* (1782) 4 Term Rep 741n; *Robinson v Hardcastle* (1788) 2 Bro CC 344; *Reid v Reid* (1858) 25 Beav 469.

[56] *Alexander v Alexander, supra*; *Robinson v Hardcastle, supra*; *Routledge v Dorril* (1794) 2 Ves 357; *Re Enever's Trusts* [1912] 1 IR 511. Cf *Crompe v Barrow* (1799) 4 Ves 681; *Hewitt v Lord Dacre* (1838) 2 Keen 622.

[57] *Long v Ovenden* (1881) 16 Ch D 691.   [58] *Re Scott* [1911] 2 Ch 374.

intention that it be accelerated. As Jenkins LJ put it, in *Re Flower's Settlement Trusts*:[59]

> The principle, I think, is well settled, at all events in relation to wills, that where there is a gift to some person for life, and a vested gift in remainder expressed to take effect on the death of the first taker, the gift in remainder is construed as a gift taking effect on the death of the first taker or on any earlier failure or determination of his interest, with the result that if the gift to the first taker fails . . . or . . . does not take effect because it is disclaimed, then the person entitled in remainder will take immediately upon the failure or determination of the prior interest, and will not be kept waiting until the death of the first taker.

This general principle applies to both real and personal property; it applies to both wills and settlements *inter vivos* although 'it may well be more difficult, in the case of a settlement, to collect the intention necessary to bring the doctrine of acceleration into play';[60] it applies where the remainder is a class gift;[61] and it applies to any interest, including partial (such as an annuity) and residuary interests.[62] Thus, in order 'to bring acceleration into operation something must be found . . . equivalent to the gift of a vested remainder'.[63] However, it need not be both vested and indefeasible, for a vested defeasible remainder will suffice.[64] On the other hand, if, at the time of the determination of the prior interest, the remainder following that interest is still contingent, there can be no acceleration, for it will then not be possible to tell whether it will take effect.[65] Strictly speaking, even an express provision that, on the failure or determination of a prior interest, a subsequent contingent interest should vest in possession immediately would not bring about an acceleration of that interest; rather, it would simply be the satisfaction of an alternative contingency.[66]

18.20 The second requirement for acceleration—an intention that it should occur—is of equal importance. Equity 'carried out the intention of the testator by giving effect

---

[59] [1957] 1 WLR 401, 405; the requisite intention was in fact absent here. [60] *Loc cit.*

[61] *Eavestaff v Austin* (1854) 19 Beav 591; *Jull v Jacobs* (1893) 68 LT 20; *Re Crothers' Trusts* [1915] 1 Ir R 53.

[62] *Re Hodge* [1943] Ch 300, where Simonds J said, at 301–302: 'An interest is postponed that a prior interest may be enjoyed. If that prior interest is determined, whether by the death of a prior beneficiary or for any other cause, the reason for postponement disappears and there is no reason why there should not be acceleration.'

[63] *Re Flower's Settlement Trusts, supra*, 408; *Re Dawson's Settlement* [1966] 1 WLR 1456; *Re Harker's Will Trusts* [1969] 1 WLR 1124.

[64] *Re Willis* [1917] 1 Ch 365; *Re Conyngham* [1921] 1 Ch 491; *Re Taylor* [1957] 1 WLR 1043; *Re Hatfeild's Will Trusts* [1958] Ch 469.

[65] *Re Townsend's Estate* (1886) 34 Ch D 357; *Re Taylor, supra*; *Re Scott* [1975] 1 WLR 1260.

[66] The position of legal estates was formerly complicated by various feudal rules, under which only vested and indefeasible remainders could be accelerated. However, the position was otherwise in equity and, of course, it is the equitable rules that now prevail. See further *Re Scott, supra*, 378–380 (criticized in (1916) LQR 83 and 392 (FE Farrer) but referred to with approval by an unrepentant Warrington LJ in *Re Conyngham* [1921] 1 Ch 491, 498); *Abbiss v Bumey* (1881) 17 Ch D 211, 229, 233; *Re Hatfeild's Will Trusts* [1958] Ch 469, 475.

to the equitable limitations according to the terms of his will';[67] and the same applies to deeds.[68] Although this is a question of the construction of each instrument, the cases suggest that, wherever possible, the court will try to find such an intention that acceleration should occur. The words 'with remainder' alone have been held sufficient, for example.[69] Similarly, the words 'from and after his decease' have been taken to indicate only the order of succession of the limitations and not the precise time at which they are to vest in possession;[70] and the expression 'after the death' has been readily treated as equivalent to 'subject to the foregoing trust'.[71] In another instance, where there was a gift to A for life 'and then to be divided equally between her issue', the court construed the word 'then' as equivalent to 'at her death', or 'after her death', or perhaps 'subject to her life interest'.[72]

In very few cases has the requisite intention to accelerate not been found. In *Re Flower's Settlement Trusts*,[73] for instance, the settlor had given discretionary powers to trustees to apply trust income during his lifetime in favour of a wide variety of objects (excluding himself, his wife, and his children); there followed other trusts, including a life interest for his widow, which were to take effect 'after the death of the settlor'. The trusts which were to have operated during his lifetime were void for uncertainty. The Court of Appeal held that such indications of intention as there were in the trust deed pointed strongly against acceleration; 'after the death' was intended literally in this case. Similarly, in *Re Young's Settlement Trusts*,[74] Harman J concluded that the doctrine of acceleration was inapplicable to the 'very peculiar limitations' which he had to consider. Although Harman J acknowledged that the doctrine of acceleration could involve some alteration of beneficial interests,[75] he was not prepared, in the circumstances of *Re Young*, to infer such an intention on the part of the settlor. Given the peculiar form of the trusts, acceleration would have produced anomalous and unfair results.[76] He also noted that he had been referred to 'no case in which the effect of a disclaimer or surrender was to alter vested interests in possession, as is suggested to be the result here'.[77] However, although this may well be a significant factor in determining whether an intention to accelerate is present, there is no reason why it should, in itself, prevent such an intention being found.

18.21

---

[67] *Abbis v Bumey, supra*, 233; *D'Eyncourt v Gregory* (1864) 34 Beav 36; *Re Willis* [1917] 1 Ch 365, 372–373; *Re Conyngham* [1921] 1 Ch 491; *Re Hatfeild's Will Trusts* [1958] Ch 469; *Re Dawson's Settlement* [1966] 1 WLR 1456; *Re Harker's Will Trusts* [1969] 1 WLR 1124.

[68] *Re Flower's Settlement Trusts, supra.*   [69] *Re Hatfeild's Will Trusts, supra*, 475.

[70] *Lainson v Lainson* (1854) 5 De GM & G 754, 756; *Re Conyngham, supra*, 498.

[71] *Re Taylor supra*, 1047; *Re Young's Settlement Trusts* [1959] 2 All ER 74, 78.

[72] *Re Davies* [1957] 1 WLR 922.   [73] [1957] 1 WLR 401.   [74] [1959] 2 All ER 74.

[75] Referring to *Re Davies* [1957] 1 WLR 922, *Re Johnson* (1893) 68 LT 20, and *Re Flower's Settlement Trusts* [1957] 1 WLR 401.

[76] [1959] 2 All ER 74, 78B–D, 79E–F. Harman J referred to 'a startling result'. See also *Re Faux* (1915) 113 LT 81, esp 89.   [77] [1959] 2 All ER 74, 79D.

18.22   Where there is a contingent remainder and the contingency has not been satisfied at the time of the determination of the prior interest, what happens to the income which accrues in the interim? In the absence of some indication to the contrary (which is unlikely), accumulation of such income is not possible, for by giving away the prior interest (usually a life interest) the testator or settlor has evinced an intention not to have that income accumulated. The income, therefore, is undisposed (and passes under a residuary gift or on a partial intestacy or under a resulting trust as the case may be).[78]

18.23   Another question is whether acceleration closes the class of beneficiaries who are entitled in remainder. The cases suggest that this may indeed be what happens, but they are not entirely consistent. In *Re Johnson*,[79] for example, there was a devise to the testator's son (A) for life, with remainder to A's wife for life, with remainder 'after the death of the survivor of them' to trustees upon trust for 'all my children who shall then be living'. The life interests of A and his wife were later revoked by codicil. Stirling J held not only that the class gift took effect immediately but also that the class closed at once, its members being all the living children of the testator (which, presumably, would include A himself). More recently, in *Re Davies*,[80] Vaisey J held that, where a share of residue had been left to A for life 'and then to be divided equally between her issue', and A disclaimed her life interest, the principle of acceleration applied so as to give the share to A's three children to the total exclusion of other unknown members of the class.

18.24   The remainder must, of course, be vested, for otherwise it could not be accelerated at all.[81] As a general rule, where there is a gift to a class subject to a contingency (for example 'to the children of A who shall attain the age of 21') the class closes when the first member of that class to fulfil that contingency does so, and the class is limited to those in existence when the first capital share[82] becomes payable, to the exclusion of anyone born thereafter: until that happens, the class remains open.[83]

---

[78] *Re Taylor* [1957] 1 WLR 1043, 1045, where 'acceleration' is printed for 'accumulation': see [1957] 3 All ER at 58c; *Re Scott* [1975] 1 WLR 1260. In *Re Hatfeild's Will Trusts* [1958] Ch 469 it was argued that the income should be accumulated under the provisions of 175 of the Law of Property Act 1925, but this was rejected on the grounds that the section does not apply where 'such income, or any part thereof, may be otherwise expressly disposed of'.

[79] (1893) 68 LT 20, applied in *Re Crothers' Trusts* [1915] 1 Ir R 53.

[80] [1957] 1 WLR 922. This, it is submitted, is an unsatisfactory decision in some respects, though approved of obiter in *Re Taylor* [1957] 1 WLR 1043: see *Thomas* 446, n 7.

[81] *Jull v Jacobs* (1876) 3 Ch D 703; *Re Townsend's Estate* (1886) 34 Ch D 357 (and see the observations thereon in *Re Davies, supra*, 926, and in *Re Taylor, supra*, 1048); *Re Scott* [1975] 1 WLR 1260.

[82] The rule does not apply to gifts of income only (*Re Stephens* [1904] 1 Ch 322) or to discretionary trusts of income (*Re Ward* [1965] Ch 856); but it is not excluded simply because land is held on trust for sale and sale is postponed (*Re Edmondson's Will Trusts* [1972] 1 WLR 183).

[83] *Andrews v Partington* (1791) 3 Bro CC 401; the rule applies also to deeds: *Re Knapp's Settlement* [1895] 1 Ch 91. See also *Re Chartres* [1927] 1 Ch 466; (1954) 70 LQR 61 (JHC Morris); and [1958] CLJ 39 (SJ Bailey). It is often said that class-closing rules are 'not founded on any view of the testator's intention' (*Re Emmet's Estate* (1880) 3 Ch D 484, 490) for there are, in fact, two conflicting

On the other hand, although the decision of Vaisey J in *Re Davies* was approved by **18.25** Upjohn J in *Re Taylor*,[84] such approval was obiter and the doctrine of acceleration was not applied in the latter case. In *Re Kebty-Fletcher's Will Trusts*,[85] Stamp J easily distinguished the case before him, where there had been an assignment of the life interest to trustees on the trusts which would have been applicable if the tenant for life were dead, from *Re Davies*, where there had been a disclaimer of the life interest. Nevertheless, Stamp J clearly doubted whether *Re Davies* was correctly decided; and, in *Re Harker's Will Trusts*,[86] Goff J refused to follow it. In *Re Harker*, the life tenant had executed a deed of release and surrender of his life interest and the two questions before the court were (i) whether the interests in remainder of his children had been accelerated into possession and (ii) if so, whether the rule in *Andrews v Partington* applied so as to close the class of children. As to question (i), Goff J held that the children's interests had indeed been accelerated, but, as to question (ii), he held that the rule in *Andrews v Partington* did not apply. According to Goff J, the rule is adopted only when the court is endeavouring to reconcile two inconsistent directions, one that the whole class of beneficiaries shall take, and the other that the fund shall be divided at a moment when the whole class cannot be ascertained,[87] ie, where the testator intended, or may be taken to have intended, a distribution at a moment which may be anterior to the birth of all the members of the class.[88] In the case before him, there was no such inconsistency:

> Where the class are independent of the tenant for life, then, of course, the testamentary dispositions are such that the testator may be taken to have intended a distribution before they are ascertained but when they are the children of the tenant for life that is not so.[89]

He therefore refused to follow *Re Davies*. He explained *Re Johnson*[90] on the basis that a conflict arose in that case on the documents; and he distinguished *Jull v Jacobs*[91] and *Re Townsend's Estate*[92] on the ground that the problem did not present itself in either case. *Re Chartres*,[93] where Astbury J applied the rule so as to close a class entitled in default of appointment upon the release of a power of appointment, was explained on the ground that the testator himself had specified the expiration of the period of distribution.[94] Thus, whether the rule applies so as

---

intentions: one that all class members take, the other that they take at a certain time or event. In any event, they are rules of convenience, or perhaps better called 'artificial rules of construction'. See *Mainwaring v Beevor* (1849) 8 Hare 44, 49; *Re Stephens* [1904] 1 Ch 322, 328; *Re Chartres* [1927] 1 Ch 466, 474–475; *Re Ransome* [1957] Ch 348, 358.

84 [1957] 1 WLR 922.   85 [1969] Ch 339.   86 [1969] 1 WLR 1124.
87 Citing Buckley J in *Re Stephens* [1904] 1 Ch 322, 328.
88 *Re Kebty-Fletcher* [1969] Ch 339, 344, *per* Stamp J.   89 [1969] 1 WLR 1124, 1128.
90 (1893) 68 LT 20.   91 (1876) 3 Ch D 703.   92 (1886) 34 Ch D 357.
93 [1927] 1 Ch 466.
94 This was also the view taken by Stamp J in *Re Kebty-Fletcher* [1969] Ch 339. However, it is difficult to justify in view of Astbury J's general approach and particularly his observations at [1927] 1 Ch 466, 478.

to close a class comprised of the tenant for life's own children, on the acceleration of their interests into possession on the disclaimer or surrender of the life interest, is seriously in doubt. *Megarry and Wade*[95] states that, where the remainders are accelerated by the premature determination of a prior life interest and a remainderman is already qualified to take, the rule will not apply unless the limitation is one to which the rule would in any case apply. Thus, where there is a gift to A for life, with remainder to his children who attain 21, no remainderman could be born after A's death and so the premature determination of A's life interest will not bring within the rule a limitation which would otherwise stand outside it. However, where the remainder is to A's grandchildren who attain 21, the rule would apply to the limitation, so as to exclude some of the grandchildren, if A's life interest is prematurely determined. This is the distinction which Goff J had in mind in *Re Harker*. Nevertheless, it is still inconsistent with *Re Davies*.

18.26 There seems to be no compelling reason why the same rules should not apply to limitations created by the exercise of a power.[96] It is the intention of the appointor which is the crucial factor: 'The question turns upon the intention, and not upon anything peculiar to powers, beyond the circumstance that the invalidity of the intermediate estates was occasioned by an excess in the execution of the power.'[97] However, according to Farwell,[98] appointments by will differ in this respect from devises and bequests, not in ignoring the importance of intention but in the presumption made in establishing that intention. 'An appointment by will to an object in remainder, after a particular estate to a stranger, is not accelerated, unless a contrary intention can be gathered from the instrument executing the power: but the estate goes during the period over which the particular estate, if valid, would have extended, to the persons entitled in default.' Thus, where a fund is appointed to stranger S for life, remainder to object O, the income of the fund would go as in default of appointment during S's lifetime, unless a contrary intention is evident. However, the only authority referred to by Farwell and Sugden in support of their general proposition is *Crozier v Crozier*,[99] itself a case in which the testator clearly did not intend acceleration[100] and which relied on earlier authorities concerning contingent interests.[101] Therefore, even if there is such a presumption as that suggested, it seems to be a weak one and certainly easily displaced by any evidence of a contrary intention.[102] On this basis, where there was an appointment on trusts for stranger S, but if they should become 'incapable

---

[95] At 534.   [96] See *Thomas* 449.
[97] *Crozier v Crozier* (1843) 3 Dr & War 353, 368, *per* Lord St Leonards.
[98] At 355–356, following *Sugden* 515, who was following his own judgment in *Crozier v Crozier*, *supra*.   [99] (1843) 3 Dr & War 353.
[100] *Craven v Brady* (1867) LR 4 Eq 209, 214.
[101] See, eg *Alexander v Alexander* (1755) 2 Ves Sen 640, 642; *Robinson v Hardcastle* (1786) 2 Bro CC 22, 29–30; *Crompe v Barrow* (1791) 4 Ves 681; *Routledge v Dorril* (1794) 2 Ves 357, 363; and see also *Brudenell v Elwes* (1801) 1 East 442.   [102] See *Re Chartres* [1927] 1 Ch 466, for example.

of taking effect' then in favour of object O, a clear contrary intention was manifested and there was an immediate appointment to O.[103] Similarly, O's interest in remainder was accelerated on the determination of a determinable life interest appointed to S and where there was express provision (and hence the requisite contrary intention) that on such event the life interest 'should cease and determine as fully and effectually as it would by [S's] actual decease'.[104]

F. Appointment to a Class Embracing Both Objects and Strangers

The basic position was summed up by Kindersley V-C as follows:[105]   **18.27**

> When an appointment is to a class, some of whom are within and others are not within the proper limits of the power, if the class of persons is ascertained, so that you can point to A, who is within the limits, and say so much is to go to him, though the others are not within the limits, yet the appointment to A shall take effect; but if the appointment is to a class, some of whom may, and others may not, be objects of the power, and there is nothing to point out what portion is to go to those who are within the power, and what to those who are not, the whole fails.

The relevant class must be ascertained or ascertainable at the relevant time and also the share that each member is intended to take must then be known. Thus, in *Re Farncombe's Trusts*,[106] a power to appoint to issue, 'such issue to be born before any such appointment', was exercised in favour of A (an object) for life, remainder to A's children in equal shares at 21. Three children (including one *en ventre sa mere*) were living at the date of the appointment; three others were born afterwards. Hall V-C held[107] that, if all the children attained 21, the three children who were proper objects of the power would take a one-sixth share each, and the remaining three-sixth shares would go as in default of appointment. If any child who was not an object died before he attained 21, his 'share' would 'go to increase in part or wholly, according to circumstances, the shares well appointed'.[108]

The same approach may also apply, it seems, where a fund is appointed to objects   **18.28**
and strangers as joint tenants. In *Re Kerr's Trusts*,[109] Jessel MR refused to apply to a fund the rules of tenure applicable to realty, so that an appointment to O and S as joint tenants was effective to the extent of O's interest, but that of S failed and

---

[103] *Line v Hall* (1873) 43 LJ Ch 107; *Rochford v Hackman* (1852) 9 Hare 475. This, it seems, could equally well be regarded as an instance of alternative sets of trusts, one of which simply could not take effect. See too, *Re Finch and Chew's Contract* [1903] 2 Ch 486.

[104] *Craven v Brady* (1867) LR 4 Eq 209.

[105] *Harvey v Stracey* (1852) 1 Drew 73, 117. See also *Sadler v Pratt* (1833) 5 Sim 632.

[106] (1878) 9 Ch D 652.   [107] At 657–658.

[108] It is not entirely clear how this solution was intended to work out in practice: see *Thomas* 450.

[109] (1887) 4 Ch D 600.

went as in default of appointment. Whether the same conclusion could be reached where land is involved remains undecided. The implication of *Re Kerr* is that it could not. However, on any view, and whether the property is realty or personalty, the *Re Kerr* solution is difficult to analyse[110]—it seems to involve an enforced severance of a joint tenancy, notwithstanding the clear intention of the appointor.

18.29 If it is not possible to ascertain precisely what share or interest an object is intended to take, the whole appointment fails, for example, where the class of appointees remains open or unascertained at the relevant time, so that it is not possible to stipulate even the minimum interest of an object. Similarly, where discretionary trusts are created in favour of a class of objects and non-objects, the appointment will be void *in toto*.[111]

18.30 In the application of this principle, it is permissible to 'wait and see' what the actual state of affairs may be at the time of distribution or vesting. An appointment made to take effect in the future is not void simply because the appointees may, when that time arrives, include strangers as well as objects.[112] Thus, if the power authorizes an appointment in favour of children and issue living at the appointor's death, one must wait and see whether there are then objects to take and whether their respective shares are ascertainable.[113]

---

[110] See *Thomas* 450–451.

[111] *Re Brown's Trusts* (1865) LR1 Eq 74: here, the discretionary trusts, which were to arise on the forfeiture of a protected life interest appointed to an object, were not authorized by the terms of the power in any event.   [112] *Harvey v Stracey, supra,* 133.

[113] *Re Witty* [1913] 2 Ch 666. If there are no objects to take, the rule in *Lassence v Tierney, supra,* may apply.

19

FRAUD ON A POWER[1]

A. General Principles

The donee of a limited power must exercise it bona fide for the end designed by the **19.01**
donor, which requires that the power can be exercised only in favour of the objects of
that power and in furtherance of the purpose for which it was conferred. If the donee,
in good faith, exercises a power in favour of a stranger or in some other way which is
not consistent with the terms and scope of his power, such exercise is excessive.[2]

---

[1] GW Thomas, *Powers* (Sweet and Maxwell, 1998) '*Thomas*' Ch 9, which forms the basis of this chapter; Sir George Farwell and FK Archer, *A Concise Treatise on Powers* (3rd edn, 1916) ('*Farwell*') Ch X; Edward Sugden (Lord St Leonards), *A Practical Treatise on Powers* (8th edn, 1861) ('*Sugden*') Ch 12; Henry Chance, *A Treatise on Powers* (1831) 2 vols, and supplement (1841); *Halsbury's Laws*, vol 36, 275–281; I J Hardingham and R Baxt, *Discretionary Trusts* (2nd edn, 1984) ('*Hardingham and Baxt*') 101–110; LA Sheridan, *Fraud in Equity* (1957), 116–124; (1936) 25 Kentucky LJ 3 (AH Eblen); (1947) 12 Conv (NS) 106 (Benas); (1948) 64 LQR 221 (HL Hanbury); (1977) 3 Monash LR 210 (Y Grbich).

[2] See Chapter 18 above.

If, however, the donee deliberately attempts to secure the effect of an excessive execution without actually making one, the exercise of the power is not simply excessive: it is fraudulent and void.[3] The donee

> ... must act with good faith and sincerity, and with an entire and single view to the real purpose and object of the power, and not for the purpose of accomplishing or carrying into effect any bye or sinister object (sinister in the sense of being beyond the purpose and intent of the power).[4]

19.02 The phrase 'fraud on a power' does not 'carry the sense of deceit which the word "fraud" bears in other contexts' (although, of course, such deceit may be involved): 'it indicates the doing of something which is not right, using those words in their broad sense—at least, *a deliberate defeating* of what the donor of the power authorised and intended'.[5] Or, in Lord Parker's much-cited words:[6]

> The term fraud in connection with frauds on a power does not necessarily denote any conduct on the part of the appointor amounting to fraud in the common law meaning of the term, or any conduct which could properly be termed dishonest or immoral. It merely means that the power has been exercised *for a purpose, or with an intention*, beyond the scope of, or not justified by, the instrument creating the power.

19.03 Thus, there are two basic elements in a fraudulent exercise of a power: first, a disposition by the donee which, in substance if not in form, is beyond the scope of the power; and secondly, a deliberate breach of the implied obligation not to exercise the power for an ulterior purpose. It is the second element which distinguishes a fraud on a power. An appointment to an object subject to an unauthorized condition that he passes on a benefit to a stranger could result in the severance of the condition, leaving a valid appointment to the object (ie as an excessive appointment it would be invalid *pro tanto*) or in a fraudulent and void appointment.[7] The dividing line can sometimes be difficult to discern,[8] but what is of decisive importance is the intention or purpose of the donee in exercising the power:[9] if there is present some 'ulterior purpose' or 'collateral purpose', a 'deliberate defeating'[10] of the donor's intention, there is a fraud on the power.

---

[3] *Aleyn v Belchier* (1758) 1 Eden 132; *Cloutte v Storey* [1911] 1 Ch 18; *Re Courage Group's Pension Schemes* [1987] 1 WLR 495, 505, 509–511. GW Keeton and LA Sheridan, *Equity* (2nd edn, 1976) 258.

[4] *Duke of Portland v Topham* (1864) 11 HLC 32, 54, *per* Lord Hatherley.

[5] *Re Dick* [1953] Ch 343, 360, *per* Lord Evershed MR (emphasis added).

[6] *Vatcher v Paull* [1915] AC 372, 378 (emphasis added).

[7] It could also be a void appointment, of course, as a breach of some other duty, for example, failing to exclude irrelevant considerations or to consider relevant ones.

[8] See, for example, *Re Holland* [1914] 2 Ch 595 and *Re Cohen* [1911] 1 Ch 37.

[9] *Re Crawshay* [1948] Ch 123, 135. See, too, *Palmer v Wheeler* (1811) 2 Ball & B 18; *Wade v Cox* (1835) 4 LJ Ch 105; *Harrison v Randall* (1852) 9 Hare 397; *Humphrey v Olver* (1859) 33 LTOS 83; *Pares v Pares* (1863) 33 LJ Ch 215; *Re Huish's Charity* (1870) LR 10 Eq 5; *Mackechnie v Marjoribanks* (1870) 22 LT 841; *Re Chadwick's Trusts* [1939] 1 All ER 850; *Re Simpson* [1952] Ch 412.

[10] *Re Dick* [1953] Ch 343, 360.

However, the doctrine is not founded upon any state of conscience imputed to the **19.04** donee in equity.[11] Dishonesty of some kind is often present, but it is not essential. The doctrine may apply where the donee honestly believes that, by his exercise of the power, he is disposing of the property in a more beneficial manner, or in a way which he believes would have been the real wish of the donor of the power, in the circumstances prevailing at the date of such exercise.[12] The true intention of the donor of the power as to its scope and purpose is as expressed in, and must be ascertained from, the instrument creating the power, even where the donor and the donee are the same person.[13] This may give rise to difficult questions of construction, particularly where the donor's purpose was to ensure maximum flexibility, as in the case of a typical power of variation in a trust deed.[14]

Although the doctrine is usually considered in the context of special powers of **19.05** appointment and, indeed, in relation to such powers conferred on trustees as such, the doctrine applies to the 'exercise of any limited power where the purpose of such exercise is to defeat the purpose for which the power was conferred',[15] including powers of advancement,[16] powers to jointure or raise portions,[17] and to any power conferred on trustees as such (even powers of investment).[18] Thus, an appointment in favour of a particular object which has been induced by a bribe will be a fraud on the power.[19] Also, the doctrine can apply to a power conferred on the committee of management of a pension scheme (or other analogous body) to amend the scheme's trust deed, 'which can only be exercised for the purpose of promoting the purpose of the scheme, namely to provide pensions for those employed in the undertaking, and not to bring about the unnecessary dissolution of the scheme'.[20]

Where a trustee exercises a power fraudulently, there is, of course, a breach of **19.06** fiduciary duty as well. However, such a fraudulent exercise of a power differs from any other improper exercise of a power by a trustee (for example taking into account an irrelevant consideration, or failing to take into account a crucially relevant one,

---

[11] *Farwell*, 458–459.

[12] *Aleyn v Belchier* (1758) 1 Eden 132; *Duke of Portland v Topham* (1864) 11 HLC 32; *Topham v Duke of Portland* (1869) 5 Ch App 40, 59; *Vatcher v Paull* [1915] AC 372.

[13] *Lee v Fernie* (1839) 1 Beav 483; *Topham v Duke of Portland* (1863) 1 De GJ & Sm 517; *Hutchins v Hutchins* (1876) 10 IR Eq 453.

[14] *Kearns v Hill* [1991] PLR 161; *Re Dyer* [1935] VLR 273; *Re Ball's Settlement Trusts* [1968] 1 WLR 899, 904.

[15] *Re Courage Group's Pension Schemes* [1987] 1 WLR 495.

[16] *Lawrie v Bankes* (1858) 4 K & J 142; *Molyneux v Fletcher* [1898] 1 QB 648.

[17] *Saunders v Shafto* [1905] 1 Ch 126.

[18] *Cowan v Scargill* [1985] Ch 270, 288; *Re Smith* [1896] 1 Ch 71

[19] *Re Wright* [1920] 1 Ch 108, 118; *Rowley v Rowley* (1854) Kay 242, 262.

[20] *Re Courage Group's Pension Schemes* [1987] 1 WLR 495. Millett J's judgment is clearly couched in terms of a fraud on a power (of amendment). *Duke of Portland v Topham* (1864) 11 HLC 32 was cited in argument, but neither it nor any other case on fraud on a power was referred to in the judgment.

or otherwise failing to exercise his discretion properly) in that there will be present an intention, a deliberate attempt (which may be honest or dishonest), to circumvent or even defeat the real purpose and object of the power. However, the donee need not be a trustee or even occupy a fiduciary position.[21] The doctrine of fraud on a power applies to fiduciary and non-fiduciary powers alike. Indeed, it is often the only ground upon which the exercise of a non-fiduciary power may be challenged. The doctrine does not apply, however, to beneficial powers, such as general powers, or hybrid powers conferred on the donee for his own benefit.[22] In addition, where there is a joint power, a fraudulent intent on the part of only one donee is sufficient to render its exercise void.[23]

B. Fraud on Whom?

19.07 It is generally assumed that the persons who would have been 'defrauded' are those entitled in default of appointment. The exercise of a special power of appointment divests (either wholly or partially according to the terms of the appointment) the interests limited in default of appointment and creates new interests in those persons in whose favour the appointment is made.[24] The takers in default of appointment should be divested of their interests (if at all) only by an honest and proper exercise of the power.[25] As Lord Parker stated in *Vatcher v Paull*:[26]

> The limitations in default of appointment may be looked upon as embodying the primary intention of the donor of the power. To defeat this intention the power must be *bona fide* exercised for the purpose for which it was given.

19.08 Clearly, this theory cannot apply to all powers. If the power in question is a power in the nature of a trust (ie a discretionary trust, where trustees are under a duty both to consider and to distribute)[27] there can be no gift over, and thus no takers, in default.[28] A fraud on such a power must therefore be a fraud on its objects. A question then arises as to whether it can be said that the objects of any other kind of

---

[21] See, for example, *Re Crawshay* [1948] Ch 123; *Re Dick* [1953] Ch 343; *Re Brook's Settlement* [1968] 1 WLR 1661.

[22] *Re Triffitt's Settlement* [1958] Ch 852, 863. There seems to be no reason, however, why the doctrine should not apply to a hybrid power of which the donee is an excluded object, but which he attempts to exercise for his own benefit.

[23] *Lawrie v Bankes* (1858) 4 K & J 142.

[24] *Re Brooks' Settlement Trusts* [1939] Ch 933; *Farwell* 310–311; Charles Fearne, *An Essay on the Learning of Contingent Remainders and Executory Devises* (7th edn, 1820) 226–233; *Duke of Northumberland v IRC* [1911] 2 KB 343, 354. See also *Att-Gen v Earl of Selborne* [1902] 1 QB 388, 398.   [25] *Re Greaves* [1954] Ch 434, 447.   [26] [1915] AC 372, 379.

[27] *McPhail v Doulton* [1971] AC 424.

[28] *Re Mills* [1930] 1 Ch 654; *Re Gestetner* [1953] Ch 672; *Roddy v Fitzgerald* (1857) 6 HL Cas 823; *Goldring v Inwood* (1861) 3 Giff 139; *Re Sprague* (1880) 43 LT 236; *Richardson v Harrison* (1885) 16 QBD 85, 102, 104; *Re Brierly* (1894) 43 WR 36; *Re Perowne* [1951] Ch 785; also *Re Lyons and Carroll's Contract* [1896] 1 IR 383; *Re Hall* [1899] 1 IR 308.

power could similarly be 'defrauded'. Lord Parker's dicta in *Vatcher v Paull* are not necessarily inconsistent with such a view, for it may well be that the limitations in default of appointment are the 'primary intention' of the donor of the power, but it does not follow that they are his only intention. Indeed, in *Topham v Duke of Portland*[29] Turner LJ clearly recognized both a primary and a secondary intention:

> The purpose of the author of a settlement, by which a power is created, is to benefit the objects within the range of the power. If the power be exercised beyond that range, his intention is that the property, the subject of the power, shall go to those who are entitled in default of appointment . . . When therefore it is asked that effect may be given to an appointment, which has for its object to go beyond the power, it is in truth asked that the unauthorized purpose of the donee may be preferred to the authorized purpose of the donor, and that to the prejudice of those who would be entitled but for the donee's unauthorized purpose.

Indeed, it seems to be a principle of long standing that, where there are two or more objects, the fraudulent execution of the power may be challenged by any one of them.[30] In *Rowley v Rowley*,[31] Wood V-C distinguished three classes involving the doctrine of fraud on a power. The second class consisted of cases where the fraud 'may be wholly on the parties interested in the distribution of the fund'; and he went on to refer (in the context of severance) to 'the case of distribution among several objects of a power, where there is a clear right in all the parties interested in the distribution . . . the object of the donor of the power being to have a fair and equal distribution of it'.[32] This proposition accords with common sense. There may well not be any benefit to the takers in default even if they were to establish a fraudulent execution, for the appointor is then free to make another, valid appointment in favour of an object not entitled in default. **19.09**

It is well established that a mere power need not be exercised, whether it be conferred on trustees by virtue of their office or on a non-fiduciary.[33] It also seems settled that trustees may be liable to an object for simply refusing to consider whether or not the power ought to be exercised.[34] However, the existence or non-existence of duties to consider or exercise is distinguishable from the duties which arise upon an actual exercise. Both a trustee and a non-fiduciary, if and when they do exercise a power, are under a duty to do so strictly in accordance with its terms, in furtherance of the purpose for which it was created or conferred, and to ensure that any exercise is neither **19.10**

---

[29] (1863) 1 De GJ & Sm 517, 568–569.
[30] See, for instance, *Aleyn v Belchier* (1758) 1 Eden 132; *Daubeny v Cockburn* (1816) 1 Mer 626.
[31] (1854) Kay 242, 258–259.   [32] At 259, 260.
[33] *Re Gulbenkian's Settlements* [1970] AC 408.
[34] *Re Hay's Settlement Trusts* [1982] 1 WLR 202; *Turner v Turner* [1974] Ch 100; *Re Hodges* (1878) 7 Ch D 754; *Re Roper* (1879) 11 Ch D 272; *Re Lofthouse* (1885) 29 Ch D 921; *Re Gestetner* [1953] Ch 672, 688; *Gartside v IRC* [1968] AC 553, 606, 617–618; *Re Manisty* [1974] Ch 17, 25; *Lutheran Church of Australia v Farmers' Co-operative Executors* (1970) 121 CLR 628, 639. These authorities and dicta are clearly inconsistent with the remarks of Lord Hodson in *McPhail v Doulton* [1971] AC 424, 441.

excessive nor fraudulent. In this sense, a donee who is not a trustee must, in making an appointment, nonetheless act as a trustee would act.[35] The object of a discretionary trust, for example, not only has a right to have the trust fund duly and properly administered, but he also has a hope or expectancy of benefit.[36] The object of a mere power vested in a non-fiduciary has a similar hope or expectancy.[37] Both, therefore, have an 'interest' in a loose sense which needs to be protected; both have 'rights' which would be prejudiced, if not defeated, by a fraudulent exercise of the power.

19.11 Indeed, in *Re Nicholson's Settlement*,[38] the Court of Appeal, in discussing the distinction between a power of appointment in favour of one object fulfilling a particular qualification and a power in favour of members of a class, seems to have directed its attention precisely towards the rights of the objects and not anyone entitled in default. Jenkins LJ stated:[39]

> The [sole] appointee and no one else is benefited, as the donor of the power intended should be the case if the appointor decided to exercise the power; and there is no detriment to anyone else. Where, however, there is a power to select among a class, and a particular beneficiary is selected in order to achieve a collateral purpose, the result is *pro tanto* to diminish the interest of the other beneficiaries, a diminution which the appointor is no doubt authorized to effect in a *bona fide* attempt to achieve what he considers justice and fairness as between the beneficiaries, but which he is not authorized to effect in order to achieve a collateral purpose.

In principle, there does not seem to be any good reason why the objects of any power should not have standing to come to court to challenge a particular execution of that power as being fraudulent.[40] This accords with long-standing authority. Indeed, it is suggested that, whatever the nature of the power, any claim alleging its fraudulent exercise can be made, by someone (perhaps also including the donor of the power)[41] who has or had an interest which has been prejudiced or defeated (in whole or in part) by such fraudulent exercise, whether that interest be in default of appointment, in possession or remainder, or by way of resulting trust, and whether vested or contingent; or by someone who is a proper object of the power, or, perhaps, in an appropriate case, by the donor of the power.

---

[35] *Scroggs v Scroggs* (1755) Amb 272, 273.

[36] *Gartside v IRC* [1968] AC 553; *Re Munro's Settlement Trusts* [1963] 1 WLR 145, 148.

[37] *Re Brooks' Settlement Trusts* [1939] Ch 993.

[38] [1939] Ch 11. For a full discussion of this ambiguous decision, see *Thomas* 458–460, 467–472.

[39] At 20. This reflects the arguments put to the court, at 15, 16.

[40] Indeed, in *McPhail v Doulton* [1971] AC 424, 441, Lord Hodson seems to have acknowledged that there is such a right. An analogous right would be that of a beneficiary in an unadministered estate: *Commissioner of Stamp Duties (Queensland) v Livingston* [1965] AC 694; *Re Leigh* [1970] Ch 277. Someone who has a hope of benefiting (as next of kin) if a person should die childless and intestate does not have a sufficient interest, however, to bring an action for fraudulent execution of a power: *Molyneux v Fletcher* [1898] 1 QB 648, 655–656, following *Clowes v Hilliard* (1876) 4 Ch D 413 and *Re Parsons* (1890) 45 Ch D 51.

[41] For a discussion of the question whether or not the donor of the power has standing to complain, see *Thomas* 459–460.

C. Grounds on Which an Exercise of a Power
May Be Fraudulent

19.12

An exercise of a power may be fraudulent if it was made (1) pursuant to an antecedent agreement or bargain between the trustee (or other donee of the power) whereby a non-object is to benefit; or (2) for a corrupt purpose; or (3) for purposes foreign to the power. Heads (1) and (2) are, for most purposes, really subdivisions of head (3). However, this threefold classification is convenient and sanctioned by long usage; and occasionally there are instances which fall within head (1) but not within head (2) or (3).

Antecedent agreement between trustee (or other donee) and object

19.13

The execution of a limited power (of whatever nature) may be fraudulent and void on the ground that it was made pursuant to an antecedent agreement by the appointee to benefit persons who are not objects of the power or entitled in default (or presumably if it was made to effect some purpose not authorized by the power), even if that agreement is in itself unobjectionable.[42] The nature of the advantage, and whether it is intended to accrue to the appointor or someone else (other than the person(s) entitled in default), is generally immaterial, although, of course, where the donee is a trustee (or other fiduciary) the rule against conflict of interest may also apply. The appointor may have bargained for some advantage to himself, such as the return to him of part of the appointed property,[43] or the payment of his debts,[44] or the lending to him (even on good security) of the appointed fund;[45] or on condition that the appointee should buy his (the appointor's) life interest in the appointed property;[46] or that the appointee would not claim restitution of part of a trust fund paid to the appointor in breach of trust.[47] On the other hand, the advantage or benefit may have been intended for some other stranger to the power: the appointee may have agreed or undertaken, for instance, to pay over the appointed funds,[48] or to resettle the appointed property in favour of non-objects.[49] In all such cases, if there is an antecedent agreement, there is fraud. Similarly, where the exercise of a power is induced by a bribe (promised or given) from the object benefited by that exercise, there is a corrupt bargain and the exercise is fraudulent.[50]

---

[42] *Farwell* 471; *Thomas* 460.

[43] *Daubeny v Cockburn* (1816) 1 Mer 626, 644; *Jackson v Jackson* (1840) 7 Cl & Fin 977.

[44] *Farmer v Martin* (1828) 2 Sim 502; *Reid v Reid* (1858) 25 Beav 469.

[45] *Arnold v Hardwick* (1835) 7 Sim 343.

[46] *Duggan v Duggan* (1880) 5 LR Ir 525 (affirmed, 7 LR Ir 152); and see *Stuart v Lord Castlestuart* (1858) 8 Ir Ch R 408.

[47] *Askham v Barker* (1850) 12 Beav 499.   [48] *Lee v Fernie* (1839) 1 Beav 483.

[49] *Salmon v Gibbs* (1849) 3 De G & Sm 343; *Carver v Richards* (1860) 1 De GF & J 548. See, also *Birley v Birley* (1858) 25 Beav 299; *Pryor v Pryor* (1864) 2 De GJ & Sm 205; *Knowles v Morgan* (1909) 54 Sol Jo 117; *Evans v Nevill* The Times, 11 February 1908.

[50] *Re Wright* [1920] 1 Ch 108, 118; *Rowley v Rowley* (1854) Kay 242, 262.

19.14 It does not follow, however, that an appointment to an object of the power, coupled with a contemporaneous settlement by that object of the appointed fund, is automatically void. The court might consider this to be an absolute appointment of the property to the object, followed by a disposition by him of the property in favour of strangers to the power, *unless* it can be shown that the appointment was made in pursuance of an agreement inducing that appointment (or for a corrupt or foreign purpose).[51] The mere existence of a contract or bargain between appointor and appointee for a settlement is not enough to avoid the appointment: it must be shown that, but for the contract or bargain, the appointment would not have been made.[52] Thus, an appointment made in favour of a non-object may, in exceptional circumstances, be upheld if it is made with the consent of an object,[53] whether the subject matter of the power be property in possession or reversion.[54] The question in each case is: in what character does the appointee take the property? If the appointment is in substance for his absolute use and benefit, the appointment is good; but if the appointor's purpose is to effect distribution among persons not objects of the power, the appointee merely being a conduit, the appointment cannot be supported.[55] It is not enough that the appointor *hopes* that the appointee will so dispose of the appointed property as to benefit a non-object, if the appointor intends to benefit the object whatever disposition the latter may subsequently make of the appointed property.[56]

19.15 Given that the limitations in default of appointment (assuming there to be any) are 'looked upon as embodying the primary intention of the donor of the power', a bargain or condition which leads to the fund or property going in default 'can never therefore defeat the donor's primary intention', and will thus not be fraudulent.[57] Thus, an appointor can release his power, even in pursuance of a bargain, even if he himself benefits therefrom: the doctrine of fraud on a power does not apply to a release precisely because the effect of a release is to benefit those entitled in default.[58] (A trustee or other fiduciary must, of course, be authorized to release a power in the first place.) On the same basis, it could be said that it is not

---

[51] *Thompson v Simpson* (1841) 1 Dr & War 459, 487; *Goldsmid v Goldsmid* (1842) 2 Hare 187; *Birley v Birley* (1858) 25 Beav 299; *Daniel v Arkwright* (1864) 2 Hem & M 95; *Whitting v Whitting* (1908) 53 So Jo 100; *Re Foote and Purdon's Estate* [1910] 1 IR 365; *Re Boileau's Will Trusts* [1941] WN 222. The court's willingness to take this view may also be crucial for the purposes of the rule against perpetuities. However, there could be two separate transfers or disposals for tax purposes.

[52] *Re Turner's Settled Estates* (1884) 28 Ch D 205.

[53] *White v St Barbe* (1813) 1 Ves & B 399; *Wright v Goff* (1856) 22 Beav 207; *Cunninghame v Anstruther* (1872) LR 2 Sc & Div 233, 234.

[54] *Re Gosset's Settlement* (1854) 19 Beav 529.

[55] *Farwell* 475; *Re Crawshay* [1948] Ch 123; *Langston v Blackmore* (1755) Amb 289; *Fitzroy v Duke of Richmond (No 2)* (1859) 27 Beav 190; *Birley v Birley, supra*; *Pryor v Pryor* (1864) 2 De GJ & Sm 205; *Cooper v Cooper* (1869) LR 8 Eq 312; *Roach v Trood* (1876) 3 Ch D 429.

[56] *Re Crawshay, supra*, 135. See further *Thomas* 461–462.

[57] *Vatcher v Paull* [1915] AC 372, 379, *per* Lord Parker; *Re Greaves* [1954] Ch 434, 446.

[58] *Re Somes* [1896] 1 Ch 250; *Re Greaves* [1954] Ch 434, 445, 446.

necessarily fraudulent to appoint to an object with the purpose that a benefit is passed on to the person(s) entitled in default.[59] Of course, where the appointee is the sole object of the power and also entitled in default, he is in effect the sole owner of the property, and an agreement with the appointor as to the destination of that property, wherever that might be, will not be fraudulent.[60]

Whether there can be a fraud on the power where the appointor is also the person **19.16** entitled in default is debatable.[61]

In the context of head (1), it does not matter whether the power in question is one **19.17** to appoint to one or other of a class of objects or one to appoint in favour of one object only.[62]

Execution for a corrupt purpose

A power is fraudulently executed and void if the execution was made for a corrupt **19.18** purpose. A simple example is where the appointor intends a benefit to result to himself, such as where he appoints to a child of his (who is a proper object of the power) who is in delicate health and likely to die, intending or hoping that he will take the property as next of kin;[63] or where bonuses accruing on insurance policies held in trust were appointed with the intention that they be used to discharge the premiums payable by the appointor, who was thereby released from having to pay them himself;[64] or where an appointment is made so that the appointees can mortgage the appointed property, the mortgage money being paid to the appointor;[65] or where moneys are advanced to a beneficiary to be applied towards repayment of a debt owed to the trustee by the beneficiary's husband.[66] There is no reason either why a trustee who is bribed to make a particular investment should not fall within this category of fraudulent execution.[67]

---

[59] This may be considered necessary, for instance, where the power is a fiduciary one and cannot be released, and it is intended to benefit those entitled in default sooner rather than later. 'Not necessarily fraudulent' because a fiduciary owes other duties to the objects.

[60] *Wright v Goff* (1856) 22 Beav 207.   [61] See *Thomas* 462–463.

[62] *Re Nicholson's Settlement* [1939] Ch 11.

[63] *Lord Hinchinbroke v Seymour* (1789) 1 Bro CC 395; *Palmer v Wheeler* (1811) 2 Ball & B 18; *Jackson v Jackson* (1840) 7 Cl & Fin 977; *Keily v Keily* (1843) 4 Dr & War 38, 55 (where *Lord Sandwich's Case* (1789) is cited); *Gee v Gurney* (1846) 2 Coll 486; *Rowley v Rowley* (1854) Kay 242; *Lady Wellesley v Earl Mornington* (1855) 2 K & J 143; and see *Warde v Dixon* (1858) 28 LJ Ch 315; *Eland v Baker* (1861) 29 Beav 137; *Davies v Huguenin* (1863) 1 Hem & M 730; *Carroll v Graham* (1865) 11 Jur NS 1012; *Henty v Wrey* (1882) 21 Ch D 332; *Dowager Duchess of Sutherland v Duke of Sutherland* [1893] 3 Ch 169; *Re De Hoghton* [1896] 2 Ch 385; *Chandler v Bradley* [1897] 1 Ch 315; *Middlemas v Stevens* [1901] 1 Ch 574; *Re Cornwallis West* (1919) 88 LJKB 1237.

[64] *Harrison v Randall* (1851) 9 Hare 397.

[65] *Pares v Pares* (1863) 33 LJ Ch 215, where the facts, though suspicious, were held (surprisingly) not to constitute fraud.

[66] *Molyneux v Fletcher* [1898] 1 QB 648.

[67] *Re Smith* [1896] 1 Ch 71; and see *Cowan v Scargill* [1975] Ch 270, 288.

19.19 The nature of the benefit is immaterial; it need not be derived from the appointed property, nor even be financial: for example, an appointment giving preference to a child of a first marriage in order to induce the wife to have the decree nisi of divorce made absolute and so leave the appointor free to marry again was fraudulent and void.[68] Indeed, where the appointor has deliberately set out to benefit a non-object by means of the appointment, there is a fraudulent execution of the power. It is not necessary that the appointee be under 'strong moral suasion' to carry out the wishes of the appointor.[69] Clearly, in any of these cases, if the donee of the power is a trustee, he will also be guilty of a breach of trust.

19.20 However, the mere fact that the donee may possibly derive some benefit from the exercise of his power will not necessarily render that exercise fraudulent. (If the donee is a trustee, there may be a question of conflict of interest in some cases.) Thus, an appointment will not be avoided simply because the appointee is an infant. In *Beere v Hoffmister*,[70] for example, A and his wife had a joint power of appointment in favour of her children; in default of appointment, the fund was settled on the children who attained the age of 21 and, subject thereto, to the wife's next of kin. The power was exercised, reserving a joint power of revocation, in favour of the sole child, then aged three and in good health (although the wife was seriously ill). The child died two years later and A became entitled to her property. The appointment was held valid, there being no evidence of a corrupt purpose. There are many other similar examples.[71] An appointment may also not be impeachable if one of its purposes is ultimately to widen the administrative powers of a settlement under which the appointor is life tenant.[72] Of course, these could equally well be examples of fraudulent execution of a power: it depends on the purpose of the donee and on the circumstances of each case.

> The meaning and the good sense of the rule appears to be that if the appointor, either directly or indirectly, obtain any exclusive advantage to himself, and that to obtain this advantage is the object and the reason of its being made, then that the appointment is bad; but that if the whole transaction taken together shows no such object, but only shows an intention to improve the whole subject-matter of the appointment for the benefit of all the objects of the power, then the exercise of the power is not fraudulent and void, although by the force of circumstances such improvement cannot be bestowed on the property, which is the subject of the appointment, without the appointor to some extent participating therein.[73]

---

[68] *Cochrane v Cochrane* [1922] 2 Ch 230.

[69] *Re Dick* [1953] Ch 343, 359–360, reasserting *Vatcher v Paull* [1915] AC 372, 378, and explaining *Re Crawshay* [1948] Ch 123, 135.

[70] (1856) 23 Beav 101. See also *Butcher v Jackson* (1845) 14 Sim 444; *Hamilton v Kirwan* (1845) 2 Jo & Lat 393; *Domville v Lamb* (1853) 1 WR 246; and *Fearon v Desbrisay* (1851) 14 Beav 635.

[71] See, for instance, *Cockcroft v Sutcliffe* (1856) 2 Jur NS 323; *Pares v Pares* (1863) 10 Jur NS 90; and *Baldwin v Roche* (1842) 5 Ir Eq R 110.

[72] *Re Huish's Charity* (1870) LR 10 Eq 5; *Pickles v Pickles* (1861) 7 Jur NS 1065.

[73] *Re Huish's Charity* (1870) LR 10 Eq 5, 9–10, *per* Lord Romilly MR.

Although an appointor may appoint to himself if he is one of the objects of the power,[74] it does not necessarily follow that, if he does so, 'there is nothing to invalidate'[75] that appointment. This may be the case where the power is a 'beneficial power'; but where the appointor is also a trustee and the power was conferred upon him *qua* trustee, he must exercise that power (and indeed any other power, such as a power to consent to an appointment by another) bona fide for the benefit of the objects.[76] He must at least consider the claims or circumstances of the objects before he can appoint to himself. (Whether this is regarded as a question of executing a power for a 'corrupt purpose' or simply as a breach of trust does not seem to matter.) Difficult questions may arise where the donee of a fiduciary power is also an object of that power; and, although an exercise of such a power in favour of the donee himself may not be fraudulent, it may nonetheless be open to challenge on other grounds, such as the application of the rule against conflict of interests.   **19.21**

Finally, the decision of the Court of Appeal in *Re Nicholson's Settlement*[77] may have established that, *in the absence of an agreement, arrangement, or understanding with the appointee* which fetters the interest given to him, it is not possible to sustain an allegation of fraud *under this head* where the power in question empowers an appointment in favour of one object only, as in the case of someone who answers a particular description or fulfils a particular qualification. Category (2), in other words, may apply only to a power to appoint to several persons or to one or other of the members of a class of objects. This view, it is suggested, does not have much to recommend it and has been severely criticized.[78]   **19.22**

Execution for a foreign purpose

An execution of a power is said to be fraudulent and void if it is for some purpose foreign to the power[79]—in this respect the comments of Turner W in *Topham v Duke of Portland* are of relevance.[80] All cases of fraudulent execution clearly involve an 'unauthorized purpose'. For most purposes, therefore, categories (1) and (2) are effectively subdivisions of the third.[81] In all three cases, however, there must be some ulterior purpose, a 'deliberate defeating' of the donor's intention,[82] for it is this element that distinguishes a fraud on a power from a merely excessive exercise.   **19.23**

---

[74] *Taylor v Allhusen* [1905] 1 Ch 529; *Re Penrose* [1933] Ch 793.
[75] *Halbury's Laws*, vol 36, 277.
[76] See, for instance, *Eland v Baker* (1861) 29 Beav 137, where a good title could not be made; also *Re Beatty* [1990] 1 WLR 1503.
[77] [1939] Ch 11.   [78] See *Thomas* 467–472.
[79] ibid 466; *Farwell* 477; *Halbury's Laws*, vol 36, 277.
[80] See para 19.08 above.   [81] *Farwell* 460.
[82] *Re Dick* [1953] Ch 343, 360.

19.24 Examples of 'foreign purposes' are usually those which benefit someone who is not an object of the power. For instance, in *Re Marsden's Trust*,[83] a donee of a power to appoint in favour of children of her marriage wished to benefit her husband. She proposed an appointment in favour of her daughter on condition that the latter made over half the appointed property to her father. Having been advised that such an appointment was not authorized, the donee then appointed the property to her daughter unconditionally. By arrangement, on the mother's death, her husband would inform the daughter of her mother's real desire and the daughter would thereby be induced to carry out that desire. The appointment was held fraudulent and void.[84] Similarly, an appointment will be void where its purpose is that the appointed property should pass to a non-object under an assignment already executed by the appointee.[85]

19.25 Although many cases of fraudulent execution will involve a bargain between appointor and appointee (and therefore fall under category (1) above) a bargain is not essential. Whether the power is exercised for a corrupt or foreign purpose, if it is the appointor's intention to benefit a non-object or to further an unauthorized purpose the appointment is fraudulent. The appointee need not be under 'strong moral suasion' to carry out the wishes of the appointor.[86] The appointee need not even know of the fraudulent intention or purpose; and it is irrelevant that the purpose never takes effect.[87]

19.26 However, the notion of a 'foreign purpose' embraces far more than an intention to benefit a non-object. In *D'Abbadie v Bizoin*,[88] for example, the foreign purpose was (appropriately) an intention on the part of the donee to induce her son (an object of the power) to reside in France; this was held not to be warranted by the power. Similarly, although the terms of a power may authorize the imposition of a condition, the actual condition stipulated in an appointment to an object may nonetheless be 'foreign' and fraudulent.[89] Another example may be the case where a revocable appointment is made in favour of an infant object (A), with the sole purpose of enabling the period during which the income of the appointed property may be accumulated to be prolonged (by virtue of the application of section 31 of the Trustee Act 1925), but where there is no intention to benefit A himself,

---

[83] (1859) 4 Drew 594.

[84] cf *Re Crawshay* (1890) 43 Ch D 615, doubted in *Re Crawshay* [1948] Ch 123.

[85] *Hay v Watkins* (1843) 3 Dr & War 339, 343; *Weir v Chalmley* (1850) 1 Ir Ch R 295; *Lady Wellesley v Earl Mornington* (1855) 2 K&J 143; *Topham v Duke of Portland* (1863) 1 De GJ & Sm 517, 568; *Re Perkins* [1893] 1 Ch 283; *Re Cohen* [1911] 1 Ch 37; *Re Walker and Elgee's Contract* (1918) 53 Ir LT 22; *Re Dick* [1953] Ch 343.

[86] *Re Dick* [1953] Ch 343, 359–360, explaining *Re Crawshay* [1948] 123.

[87] *Re Crawshay* [1948] Ch 123, 135.   [88] (1871) 5 IR Eq 205.

[89] *Vatcher v Paull* [1915] AC 372, 379; *Re Perkins* [1893] 1 Ch 283; *Re Cohen* [1911] 1 Ch 37. Cf *Hodgson v Halford* (1879) 11 Ch D 959, where a forfeiture clause on marrying anyone not a Jew was held to be authorized by the power.

the concluded purpose being an ultimate appointment of the property (plus accumulations) to another adult object (B). Although such revocable appointments are commonly made in practice, their status remains doubtful (unless, of course, it can be said that some benefit or hope of benefit to A, as well as B, was contemplated and that the appointment would have been made in any event).

It is not necessary that the appointee should be privy to the transaction or that the **19.27** purpose is not communicated to him before the appointment, 'because the design to defeat the purpose for which the power was created will stand just the same, whether the appointee was aware of it or not'.[90] Nor is it relevant that the appointor himself gets no personal benefit from the appointment.[91] According to the decision of the Court of Appeal in *Re Nicholson's Settlement*,[92] this head of fraudulent execution, like category (2) above, does not apply to a power to appoint in favour of *one object only*. An execution of such a power can be said to be fraudulent only if it can be proved that there was some bargain, arrangement, or understanding between the appointor and the appointee which fetters the appointed interest in the appointee's hands in favour of some person or persons other than the appointee himself, ie category (1) alone can be relevant in such a case. This view, it is suggested, does not have much to recommend it and has been severely criticized.[93]

D. Fraud on a Power and Occupational Pension Schemes

The doctrine of fraud on a power applies equally to powers and discretions **19.28** conferred under occupational pension schemes (and other 'commercial' trusts). The exercise of scheme powers by the trustees or by employers for an 'ulterior' or 'foreign' or 'collateral' purpose will be fraudulent and void.[94] As we have seen, the doctrine is capable of applying to powers which are not fiduciary in nature as well as to those which are fiduciary in the strict sense.[95] However, it is clearly not the case that the exercise of every and any power conferred on the employer in relation to a pension scheme will be held fraudulent if or in the event that the purpose or effect of such exercise is to enable the employer to derive some personal benefit or advantage or, indeed, if such exercise is made pursuant to some bargain between the employer and the members or trustees of the scheme. It is in this area, in particular that it becomes difficult to distinguish the boundaries between fraudulent and excessive exercise of powers, to identify what duties (if any) are owed by an employer in the exercise of its scheme powers, and also how all these issues relate to each other. This is particularly difficult because they all tend to revolve around and depend upon strikingly similar facts.

---

[90] *Re Marsden's Trusts* (1859) 4 Drew 594.   [91] See cases in n 85 above.
[92] [1939] Ch 11.   [93] See *Thomas* 467–472.
[94] *Re Courage Group's Pension Scheme* [1987] 1 WL 495.   [95] See para 19.06 above.

19.29 However, this should not disguise the fact that occupational pension schemes are fundamentally different. Suppose, for example, that the employer has a power to amend a pension scheme, or, alternatively, that the trustees have such a power which is exercisable with the consent of the employer. Suppose, too, that the employer wishes to have the scheme amended so as to introduce a new provision conferring some benefit or advantage on the employer (for example, a right to surplus funds, where none existed before; or a right to introduce new participating employers to the scheme). In return for such an amendment, the employer may be willing to accede to a bargain for an increase in benefits. In such a case, the first question is simply whether the intended benefit to the employer (the payment of any part of surplus funds or whatever) is prohibited by the provisions of the scheme. If it is, then any such amendment is excessive and void; and no question of fraudulent exercise of the power need arise. However, the question whether the amendment is indeed excessive is not always straightforward. For example, it is highly material whether the power is exercisable by the employer for its own benefit or in its own interests.[96] If it is a fiduciary power, in the strict sense, then it may not be so exercised in the absence of express authorization; but if it is an 'enlarged' fiduciary power, or not a fiduciary power at all, and if, on the proper construction of the power, one of its purposes or objects is to benefit the employer, then its exercise by the employer in its own favour will not be excessive. The exercise may be open to challenge on the ground that the employer is in breach of its implied duty of good faith, or (if it is a fiduciary power) of one of the duties owed by the donee of such a power. However, it will not be excessive and it will not then be fraudulent. Therefore, in such a case, provided such other obligations (if any) are complied with, it would seem to be entirely proper for the employer to bargain with the objects of the power or with the trustees of the scheme in order to obtain some advantage for itself (whether in the form of a share of surplus, a contributions holiday,[97] or otherwise). If, on the other hand, it is attempted to accomplish a prohibited purpose by some means which is not in terms excessive (for example, by amending the scheme so as to introduce a power to transfer funds to another scheme under which the employer would be entitled to the prohibited benefit;[98] or by entering into a bargain under which a power created for the exclusive benefit of members is exercised in such a way as to deprive them of or derogate from their rights[99]) then such an act would be carried out for a collateral or ulterior purpose and would therefore be fraudulent.

---

[96] As in *Imperial Group Pension Trust Ltd v Imperial Tobacco Ltd* [1991] 1 WLR 589.

[97] *Stannard v Fisons Trust* [1992] IRLR 27; *LRT Pension Trustee Co Ltd v Hatt* [1993] OPLR 225, 266; *Hillsdown Holdings plc v Pensions Ombudsman* [1997] 1 All ER 862; *Re The National Grid* [1997] PLR 157, 180.

[98] *Hillsdown Holdings plc v Pensions Ombudsman* [1997] 1 All ER 862; *FMC Superannuation and Pension Scheme Trustees Ltd* [1995] OPLR 385.

[99] *Imperial Tobacco, supra*; *Hillsdown Holdings, supra*; *Cullen v Pension Holdings Ltd* [1992] PLR 135.

E. Powers to 'Advance' or 'Benefit' the Object

Most settlements incorporate either an express or statutory[100] power to pay or apply capital money 'for the benefit' of a beneficiary. Such a power is dealt with in greater detail elsewhere in this work.[101] Only two specific points need be mentioned here. First, the doctrine of fraud on a power applies to this kind of power as much as to any other.[102] Secondly, the interpretation by the court of the word 'benefit' could have the effect that capital may properly be paid to, or applied for, someone who is not an object.

19.30

'Advancement' suggests the establishing of a beneficiary in life.[103] 'Benefit', on the other hand, is a word of wider import.[104] Thus, a power to pay or apply capital for a beneficiary's 'benefit' has been held to authorize payment from a wife's fund to enable her husband to set up in business in England, thus preventing the separation of the family;[105] and to authorize the creation of sub-settlements under which persons other than the beneficiary (such as members of his family), being strangers to the power, benefited;[106] indeed, to enable a wealthy beneficiary to make charitable donations (to a non-object) in discharge of moral obligations which he felt.[107] In such cases, it is immaterial that non-objects benefit from the exercise of the power: '... if the disposition itself, by which I mean the whole provision made, is for her benefit, it is no objection to the exercise of the power that other persons benefit incidentally as a result of the exercise'.[108] Indeed, there is no need to show that the 'benefit' is 'related to his or her own real or personal needs'.[109] It is generally assumed, in practice, that the law is the same for powers to *appoint* capital for an object's 'benefit'.

19.31

All this is consistent with the doctrine of fraud on a power. Where the power expressly or by necessary implication authorizes the benefiting of an object by means of an indirect benefit to a stranger, then an execution of such a power cannot of itself be fraudulent. Nevertheless, irrespective of the width of a particular power, the donee must still exercise it properly, for good reason, and certainly not

19.32

---

[100] Section 32 of the Trustee Act 1925.   [101] See paras 15.59–15.67 above.

[102] *Lawrie v Bankes* (1858) 4 K & J 142; *Molyneux v Fletcher* [1898] 1 QB 648; and see *Cowan v Scargill* [1975] Ch 270, 288.

[103] *Re Kershaw's Trusts* (1868) LR 6 Eq 322, 323.

[104] *Lowther v Bentinck* (1874) LR 19 Eq 166, 169.

[105] *Re Kershaw's Trusts, supra.* See also *Re the S settlement* (2001) 4 ITELR 206 and *Re the X Trust* (2002) 5 ITELR 119 (RC, Jersey).

[106] *Re Halsted's Will Trusts* [1973] 2 All ER 570; *Pilkington v IRC* [1964] AC 612.

[107] *Re Clore's Settlement Trusts* [1966] 1 WLR 955.

[108] *Pilkington v IRC, supra,* 636, *per* Lord Radcliffe. It is clear from the cases that the benefit conferred on the stranger to the power need not be 'incidental'.

[109] *Re Pilkington's Will Trusts* [1961] Ch 466, 481, *per* Lord Evershed. The benefit can simply be the avoidance of taxation: *Pilkington v IRC, supra,* 640; *Re Wills' Will Trusts* [1959] Ch 1, 11–12, *per* Upjohn J.

with any sinister or by-purpose or intent.[110] Thus, an exercise of a power of advancement, ostensibly for the benefit of its primary object, but in substance and reality for the benefit of a stranger (such as someone towards whom the object felt no legal or moral obligations), is likely to be a fraudulent exercise, irrespective of the use of the word 'benefit' and of the width of the power in other circumstances.

F. Fraud on a Power and the Variation of Trusts[111]

19.33 The doctrine of fraud on a power also gives rise to problems (often unforeseen) in the context of the variation of trusts. For example, it is common to find trusts in favour of A for life (sometimes protective trusts for life) with power for A to appoint in favour of his children and remoter issue. If A were to appoint in favour of (say) his adult children, he and they, together, could then terminate the trust, thus cutting out all other objects and those entitled in default of appointment. If such an exercise is carried out in pursuance of an agreement or arrangement between the parties concerned, the effect of the appointment is that the power has been exercised deliberately for an unauthorized purpose and, as such, the exercise is likely to be fraudulent and void.[112] If there is no such agreement, but the same result is achieved by means of two separate and independent transactions, there is no element of fraud and the transaction should stand. However, if A has a protected life interest, or if he appoints in favour of infant children, the approval of the court must be obtained for the arrangement, either on behalf of 'any person in respect of any discretionary interest of his under protective trusts where the interest of the principal beneficiary has not failed or determined', or on behalf of the infant beneficiaries or both.[113] The court will obviously not exercise its discretion in a way which facilitates or enables a fraudulent exercise of a power, but the manner in which the doctrine interacts with the court's role in the variation of trusts is not entirely clear from the authorities.

19.34 *Re Robertson's Will Trusts*[114] is a typical example. Here, A had a protected life interest and had exercised his special power of appointment in favour of his three children equally. The intention was that the fund be divided between them all on an actuarial basis. One result of the arrangement would be that A would be able to purchase an annuity which would yield a better income than his life interest. Russell J stated that the court would not approve an arrangement if it clearly involves an appointment which is a fraud on the power. Nevertheless, he concluded

[110] *Re Pauling's Settlement Trusts (No1)* [1964] Ch 303.
[111] For the variation of trusts generally, see Chapter 24 below.
[112] *Re Brook's Settlement* [1968] 3 All ER 416, 423.
[113] Variation of Trusts Act 1958, s 1(1)(d), (2); and s 33 of the Trustee Act 1925.
[114] [1960] 1 WLR 1050; see, too, *Re Merton's Settlement* [1953] 2 All ER 707.

that, on the evidence, the appointor intended to benefit his children rather than himself and therefore approved the arrangement. (It became apparent that the arrangement would benefit the appointor only at an intermediate stage.) In similar circumstances, in *Pelham Burn*[115] the Court of Session approved an arrangement on the basis that the liferentrix obtained no more than the actuarial value of her interest, and any benefit to her was incidental and not the purpose of the appointment. And in *Re Wyndham*,[116] although the Court of Session refused to approve the arrangement under which the liferentrix/appointor obtained capital in excess of the actuarial value of her interest, it indicated that it would approve an amended arrangement under which she received only the actuarial value of that interest.

At first sight, these cases seem to suggest that, if the life tenant receives no more than the actuarial value of his interest, he will have committed no fraud on his power. However, this would clearly not accord with earlier authorities on fraudulent execution, for the guiding factor is not what the appointor may have gained from the appointment—indeed he may have derived no benefit at all—but the purpose or intent which he entertained when he exercised the power. It is a question of fact whether his intention was fraudulent or not, and there is nothing in the Variation of Trusts Act which modifies that rule. Certainly, none of the parties before the court in an application under the Act is likely to allege fraud, so of necessity it falls to the court (perhaps through the trustees), in the exercise of its discretion, to ensure that fraud is not present. Nevertheless, although the fact that the appointor receives no benefit at all or receives no more than the actuarial value of his interest is evidence—and may well be cogent evidence—of the absence of any fraud, this is not conclusive. **19.35**

This question was developed further by Megarry J in *Re Wallace's Settlements*:[117] **19.36**

> But between plain fraud, on the one hand, and no fraud, on the other hand, there is a wide spectrum, ranging from strong though not conclusive evidence to far-fetched suspicion. At what point should the Court draw the line?... It cannot be right to say that the Court will grant its approval in every case unless the parties have been incautious enough to provide of a *prima facie* case of fraud on the power. On the other hand, I do not think that it would be right to withhold approval merely by reason of far-fetched suspicions of a possible fraud on the power. If as a result of either the presence of evidence or its absence the Court comes to the conclusion that there is a fair case for investigation whether a fraud on the power is involved, approval should be withheld until such investigation has been made and satisfactorily resolved. In reaching the decision whether there is a fair case for investigation, I would disregard remote possibilities or fantastic suggestions; equally, I would not require cogent evidence. In my judgment, if to a fair, cautious and enquiring mind the circumstances of the appointment, so far as known, raise a real and not merely a tenuous suspicion of a fraud on the power, the approval of the Court ought to be withheld until that suspicion is dispelled.[118]

---

[115] 1964 SLT 9.   [116] 1964 SLT 290, esp 293.   [117] [1968] 2 All ER 209.
[118] ibid 213–214.

19.37   In *Wallace* itself, an inalienable, defeasible life interest was replaced by an absolute interest in capital; also the actuarial valuation was that of an alienable and indefeasible life interest. Such facts gave rise to a case calling for investigation, but, in the event, the evidence showed no real substance in the suspicions.[119] In other words, there was a clear finding here that the appointment in question was not fraudulent.

19.38   On the other side of the line is *Re Brook's Settlement*.[120] Here again, A had a protected life interest, and had exercised his power of appointment in favour of his two children, one of whom was a minor. The court was asked to approve the arrangement (for the division of the trust fund between A and the two children) on behalf of both the minor child and those interested as potential discretionary objects in the event of the forfeiture of A's life interest. Stamp J refused to do so, holding that the execution of the power of appointment was fraudulent. The known effect of the appointment was to produce, by defeating the interests of future children, a state of affairs under which the court might be expected to approve a division more favourable to the tenant for life than would have been the case if the division had had to be shown to be for the benefit of the after-born children; and the tenant for life here was anxious to obtain all he could on the division. Thus, the facts of the case led to the conclusion that there was fraud. However, Stamp J made it plain that, in his view, none of the earlier authorities had established that there could not be fraud where the life tenant received the actuarial value of his life interest.

> . . . if you find an appointment such as is here in question and, on the contemplated division of the fund, the appointor takes no more of the appointed fund than the value of his life interest, the appointment is not invalidated by the mere fact that it is made in contemplation of the division. It does not in my judgement, however, follow that an appointment made by one entitled to a life interest not with an entire and single object of benefiting the appointee, but with a view also to having part of the capital of the appointed fund to spend, would be unobjectionable if the capital to be received was less than the market value of the life interest. The question must be one of fact. If my view of the earlier high authorities[121] is correct and it is the purpose and object of the appointment which is the test of its validity or invalidity, it must, I think, follow that, an appointment made partly for the purpose of enabling part of the capital of the appointed fund, however small, to be put in the pocket of the appointor is a fraud on the power: for if that be part of the motive for the appointment there is not the absence of an ulterior object necessary to support it.[122]

19.39   This, it is submitted, is the correct formulation of the principle that should apply in such cases. It is entirely consistent with *Wallace*.[123] Thus, if it can be shown that

---

[119]   ibid 214. See, too, the explanation of *Wallace* in *Re Brook's Settlement* [1968] 3 All ER 416, 422, *per* Stamp J.

[120]   [1968] 3 All ER 416; [1968] 1 WLR 1661.

[121]   *Duke of Portland v Lady Topham* (1864) 11 HL Cas 32; and *Vatcher v Paull* [1915] AC 372.

[122]   [1968] 3 All ER 416, 423.   [123]   See paras 19.36–19.37 above.

the appointment was a separate and independent transaction made irrespective of the scheme of division sought to be achieved, there would probably be no vice and it would stand.[124] An appointment which facilitates the division of the trust fund is likely to raise a suspicion of fraud which merits investigation. And if the appointor has negotiated for as much as he could fairly get out of a division of the fund and has clearly exercised his power simply to bring that about, there is at least a strong case for inquiry, and the execution is likely to be fraudulent and void.[125]

G. Burden of Proof

What the court looks to is the intention or purpose of the appointor at the date of the exercise of the power.[126] It is this that distinguishes a fraudulent from a merely excessive exercise. The burden of proving a corrupt intention or purpose lies on the person seeking to avoid the transaction.[127] Proof of intention may be difficult to establish, particularly in the absence of a bargain,[128] and especially where (as in many cases) the appointor may have died, and where no presumptions or inferences are made in favour of the impeacher (at the initial stages at least). 'Fraud, improper motives, intentions, objects, or purposes, ought not to be presumed, they must be proved...'.[129] Or, in the words of Jessel MR: 'Fraud is not lightly to be presumed or inferred. In all cases in which fraud is inferred there must be such cogent facts that the Court cannot reasonably come to any other conclusion.'[130] Mere suspicion will not suffice.[131] The position was summarized by Kindersley V-C in *Re Marsden's Trusts*:[132]

19.40

> Unless it can be shown that the trustee having the discretion exercises the trust corruptly or improperly, or in a manner which is for the purpose not of carrying into effect the trust, but defeating the purpose of the trust, the Court will not control or interfere with the exercise of the discretion. There may be a suspicion that the trust has been exercised in a particular manner and from a certain motive, which, if it could be proved, would be held not to be a proper motive; but if it be mere suspicion—though the suspicion is ground for jealous investigation—if it be mere suspicion, and not matter amounting to a judicial inference or conviction from the facts, the Court will not act upon it. But if, on the other hand, it can be proved to the satisfaction of the judicial mind that the power has been exercised corruptly

---

[124] [1968] 3 All ER 416, 422.   [125] ibid.

[126] *Re Crawshay* [1948] Ch 123, 135, propositions (3) and (5), based on *Re Wright* [1920] 1 Ch 108, 117. It must be noted, however, that these propositions were not subject to argument in the Court of Appeal.

[127] *Askham v Barker* (1853) 17 Beav 37.   [128] *Re Crawshay, supra,* 135.

[129] *Henty v Wrey* (1882) 21 Ch D 332, 354, *per* Lindley MR.   [130] ibid 350.

[131] *Campbell v Home* (1842) 1 Y & C Ch Cas 664; *M'Queen v Farquhar* (1805) 11 Ves 467; *Pares v Pares* (1863) 10 Jur NS 90; *Henty v Wrey* (1882) 21 Ch D 332; *Re De Hoghton* [1896] 2 Ch 385; *Re Boileau* [1921] WN 222; *Re Merton* [1953] 1 WLR 1096.

[132] (1859) 4 Drew 594, 599–600.

or for a purpose which defeats instead of carrying into effect the purpose of the trust, then the Court will not permit such an exercise of the power to prevail.

19.41 The purpose or intention must be ascertained as a matter of substance, and not solely by analysing the effect of the exercise of the power.[133] Fraud will not necessarily be inferred by the court from, for instance, the mere fact that the donee (or any other non-object) is found in possession of the appointed property at some later date,[134] although it may raise a case for inquiry.[135]

19.42 Evidence is admissible as to the state of mind of the appointor, including statements by the appointor which go to show his or her state of mind at the material date. Such statements may be material though they are not contemporaneous with the date of the exercise of the power.[136] However, notwithstanding references to the appointor's 'state of mind'[137] or 'motive',[138] evidence of *motive*—such as anger and resentment—under which it is alleged the exercise took place is apparently not sufficient by itself to establish fraud, for 'there would be no end to such objections, if they were to be admitted as grounds for questioning appointments: in almost all cases, where there has been an inequality in the appointment, something of that kind has existed'.[139] 'It is one thing', said Turner LJ,[140] 'to examine into the purpose with which an act is done, and another thing to examine into the motives which led to that purpose': examining the motives involved both 'danger and inconvenience'.

19.43 It may well be, however, that *motive* may be relevant and thus be investigated in one category of fraud on a power. In *Re Wright*,[141] PO Lawrence J stated:

> In cases where it is not suggested that the donee of a special power has exercised the power with the intention of benefiting himself or some other person not an object of the power the Court will not as a rule examine into the motive which may have induced the donee to exercise the power in favour of a particular object of the power. The donee is entitled to prefer one object to another from any motive he pleases, and however capriciously he exercises the power the Court will uphold it.[142] But in my opinion this rule does not apply where the motive is corrupt or improper even although the appointment is made in favour of an object of the power and the intention and purpose of the appointor is that the appointee should take the whole of the

---

[133] *Re Burton* [1955] Ch 82, 100, *per* Upjohn J.

[134] *Re Merton* [1953] 1 WLR 1096, 1110, *per* Wynn Parry J.

[135] *Jackson v Jackson* (1840) 7 Cl & Fin 977 (involving the creation of a charge in favour of the appointor immediately after the appointment).

[136] *Re Crawshay, supra*, 135, approving proposition (6).   [137] ibid.

[138] *Re Marsden's Trusts, supra*, 599–600.

[139] *Vane v Lord Dungannon* (1840) 2 Sch & Lef 118, 130, *per* Lord Redesdale. *Farwell*, 469, states that 'motives . . . are not to be adverted to', but this is an overstatement.

[140] *Topham v Duke of Portland* (1863) 1 De GJ & S 517, 571; approved in (1869) 5 Ch App 40, 57.

[141] [1920] 1 Ch 108, 117–118.

[142] This is not the case, of course, where the donee is a trustee. A trustee cannot act capriciously: see Chapter 11 generally.

appointed fund unconditionally for his own benefit. An example of such a corrupt or improper motive, where the intention and purpose of the appointment itself cannot be said to be otherwise than in accordance with the end designed by the donor of the power, is to be found in the case of a bribe being given or promised to the donee of the power in order to induce him to make an appointment in favour of the objects of the power to the exclusion or detriment of the others.

Although this is unquestionably an example of a fraudulent exercise of a power, it is difficult to see how these dicta could carry much weight on the question of the relevance of 'motive'.[143] They are certainly inconsistent with earlier authorities. Moreover, they also tend to confuse the form or effect of the transaction with its substance. The donor of the power conferred it on the donee in the expectation that it would be exercised, if at all, in good faith. The passage also makes no distinction between trustees (and other fiduciaries) and non-fiduciaries: trustees cannot exercise their powers capriciously and the objects of such powers who are not benefited or those entitled in default of appointment have rights to see those powers properly and honestly exercised. In any event, it is not necessary that the donee of a power (or any other non-object) should derive some benefit from the appointed property itself.[144] Acceptance of a bribe, from the appointee or from a third party, would be sufficient to constitute a corrupt purpose or intention, so that investigation of motive would thus be unnecessary, though it would clearly have high probative value.[145]

In any event, the general rule is well established: it is for the person alleging fraud- **19.44** ulent exercise of a power to prove the allegation as a matter of substance. Nevertheless, the circumstances may be such that the burden of proof may shift easily. Certainly, there are instances where the court held that it was for those seeking to uphold an appointment to prove that the power had been properly executed. For example, where there is proof that the appointor at one time intended a benefit to accrue to himself, or indeed if a corrupt intention is once shown to have been entertained, it is for those who seek to uphold the appointment to prove that such an intention no longer existed at the time of the appointment.[146] Similarly, it has been held that, where one appointment has already been set aside, a second appointment by the same donee in favour of the same object cannot be upheld in the absence of 'clear proof' that the later appointment is completely free from the original taint which avoided the first.[147]

---

[143] See *Thomas* 479–480.   [144] *Cochrane v Cochrane* [1922] 2 Ch 230.

[145] *Re Crawshay* [1948] Ch 123 approved the observations made in *Re Wright*. The evidence in *Re Wright* seems to have pointed clearly to the existence of a bargain, in fact. *Topham* was not referred to in the case, but it seems clear that PO Lawrence J was fully aware of the principles it had established.

[146] *Humphrey v Olver* (1859) 5 Ch App 40, 62; also see 58–59; *Re Wright, supra,* 120; cf *Re Crawshay, supra,* 137-138. See also *Thomas* 480–481.

[147] *Topham v Duke of Portland* (1869) 5 Ch App 40, 62. See also *Redman v Permanent Trustee Co of NSW* (1916) 22 CLR 84.

19.45　It is unclear from subsequent decisions whether these propositions as to the shifting onus of proof have survived. For example, in *Re Crawshay*[148] the Court of Appeal adopted a more flexible approach. It was argued that, if a corrupt intention is shown ever to have been entertained, the burden of proof lies upon those who support the appointment. However, the Court of Appeal preferred an approach that reached a conclusion on the basis of the evidence as a whole, recognizing that 'the cogency of the inference drawn from the proof of intention must largely depend on the length of the period that elapses between the date as at which the intention is proved and the date on which the power is exercised and on what has happened in the meanwhile'.[149] It may well be that the better approach is to consider all relevant, admissible evidence and see whether the inferences that may be drawn from it, without reference to any presumption or shift in onus, support the fraud which has been alleged. However, this approach seems to be inconsistent with *Topham*, which was cited neither in *Re Crawshay* nor in *Re Wright*. It has been suggested[150] that the matter may perhaps be resolved by distinguishing between the burden of proof imposed by law and the provisional burden which is raised by the state of the evidence. Although the legal burden remains throughout on the person alleging fraud, he goes some way towards discharging it by producing evidence of prior fraudulent conduct; there is then a provisional presumption of fraud, which is by no means conclusive.

19.46　It must also be borne in mind that the donee of a power is generally not obliged to give reasons or explanations for the decisions he has reached or the manner in which he has exercised his discretions. This principle applies not just to the donees of non-fiduciary powers but also to trustees, of both family settlements[151] and occupational pension schemes.[152] Thus, documents such as the minutes and agenda of trustee meetings or correspondence which might evidence a fraudulent exercise of a power cannot be demanded by any beneficiary or object. Of course, this does not prevent beneficiaries and objects from commencing hostile litigation against trustees, alleging fraudulent exercise of a power (or some other impropriety), and appropriate evidence of such fraud (or other impropriety) may emerge during the pre-trial process of discovery.[153] However, they must have some evidence of fraud or impropriety before any such action is commenced: they cannot make speculative allegations based on mere suspicion and then invoke the process of discovery in order to ascertain whether or not a cause of action actually exists.[154]

---

[148] [1948] Ch 123.　　[149] *Re Crawshay, supra*, 137–138.　　[150] *Thomas* 481.

[151] *Re Londonderry's Settlement Trusts* [1965] Ch 918.

[152] *Wilson v Law Debenture Trust Corporation plc* [1995] 2 All ER 337; *Libby v Kennedy* [1999] PLR 143.

[153] See, for example, *Compagnie Financiere et Commerciale de Pacifique v Peruvian Guano Co* (1882) 11 QBD 55, esp 63; *Re Londonderry's Settlement Trusts, supra*, 939; and also (1965) 81 LQR 196 (RE Megarry); H Malek and P Matthews, *Discovery* (London 1993).

[154] *Karger v Paul* [1984] VR 161; *Hartigan Nominees Pty Ltd v Rydge* (1992) 29 NSWLR 405.

H. The Degree of Fraudulent Intent or Purpose

It is not entirely clear from the cases whether the presence of *any* fraudulent intent or purpose is sufficient to avoid the execution of a power, notwithstanding that there may also be present a perfectly honest and sincere intent to benefit one of the objects, or to further one of the purposes, of that power. In other words, would an exercise for 'mixed' purposes fail or not? A power has to be exercised 'with an entire and single view to the real purpose and object of the power',[155] which suggests that the presence of any other purpose, no matter how insignificant, would be fatal and would invalidate the exercise of the power. In some cases, the exercise of a power has been said to be fraudulent if it was not made 'with the *sole object* of benefiting the appointee... [or] *not confined* to benefiting the appointees themselves'.[156] Indeed, the fact that a fraudulent intent on the part of only one donee of a joint power will render void an exercise of that power[157] tends to support this stricter view. On the other hand, the view has also been expressed that a power of appointment, for instance, has been fraudulently exercised if a non-object received a 'material' benefit,[158] which implies that where such benefit is *de minimis* the exercise will be upheld. In yet other cases, an alternative test has been adopted, namely whether or not the particular exercise would have been made 'but for' the fraudulent purpose.[159] Both of these latter views suggest that, provided it is of secondary importance and probably also a merely trivial consideration, the presence of a fraudulent purpose will not necessarily invalidate a particular exercise of a power. It is doubtful, however, whether these formulations are essentially inconsistent with each other.

19.47

The central question is simply whether the donee of the particular power intended to achieve some ulterior purpose by its exercise. It is the donee's intention to benefit a non-object or to further an unauthorized purpose that is crucial, and not the result actually achieved, although, of course, the effects of any execution may provide clear evidence of a fraudulent intent. If the power is executed with a corrupt or foreign purpose, the exercise is fraudulent; and it is irrelevant that the purpose never takes effect,[160] or even that the appointee was not even aware of it.[161] The real question is whether the power was exercised, in substance and not just in form, with the intention and purpose of benefiting the appointee (in which case it will be good) or simply in order to enable the distribution of the property to a stranger, the appointee being regarded merely as a conduit for that

19.48

---

[155] See, for example, *Duke of Portland v Topham* (1864) 11 HLC 32, 54; *Re Greaves* [1954] Ch 434, 447.

[156] *Re Simpson* [1952] Ch 412, 416, 417.   [157] *Lawrie v Bankes* (1858) 4 K & J 142.

[158] *Re Greaves* [1954] Ch 434, 447.

[159] See, for instance, *Pryor v Pryor* (1864) 2 De GJ & Sm 205, 210; *Re Turner's Settled Estates* (1884) 28 Ch D 205, 217, 219; *Birley v Birley* (1858) 25 Beav 299, 307.

[160] *Re Crawshay* [1948] Ch 123, 135.   [161] *Re Marsden's Trusts* (1859) 4 Drew 594.

purpose. Similarly, if the appointor hoped that the appointee would dispose of the appointed property in favour of a stranger, but where there was no bargain or understanding that the appointee would do so, and the appointor would still have exercised the power in the same manner irrespective of any dispositions which the appointee was free to make and may have made, the exercise will not be fraudulent.[162] Indeed, even the existence of a bargain between appointor and appointee as to the destination of the appointed property will not necessarily avoid the appointment: it must be shown that, but for the bargain, the appointment would not have been made.[163] In all these cases, the relevant question is whether the power in question would have been exercised *but for* the *intent* to achieve an ulterior purpose or whether the actual exercise would have been made in any event. Thus, the 'but for' test seems more appropriate, workable, and more consistent with the reported cases.

I. Effect of Fraudulent Execution of a Power

Execution is void not voidable

19.49 A fraudulent execution of a power is wholly void.[164] It is irrelevant that the appointee was entirely ignorant of the appointor's intentions or otherwise innocent;[165] and an appointment in exercise of a joint power will be fraudulent where only one of the appointors is infected with a fraudulent intent.[166] The court acts upon the intention of the donee of the power to exercise it for some foreign purpose. The question to be asked in each case is: would the appointment have been made if it had not been for the improper intention of the appointor? If not, the appointment is invalid; and it remains so even if the appointee, upon being appealed to by the appointor to effectuate the improper purpose, refuses to do so.

> If the appointee refuses to give effect to the wishes of the appointor, he gets what it was never intended he should have, and enjoys property which, if his conduct could have been forseen, might and probably would have been given to another. But the case is exactly the same whether the consent or the agreement to act as desired be given or entered into before or after the appointment. The Court also would be placed in this dilemma:—If it did not enforce compliance with the wishes of the appointor, it would be sanctioning the appointee in taking property never intended for him; and if the Court were to enforce it as binding in conscience on the appointee, the Court

---

162 *Re Crawshay* [1948] Ch 123, 125.
163 *Re Turner's Settled Estates* (1884) 28 Ch D 205.
164 *Re Marsden's Trust* (1859) 4 Drew 594; *Cloutte v Storey* [1911] Ch 18; *Vatcher v Paull* [1915] AC 372, 378.
165 *Re Marsden's Trust, supra*; *Scroggs v Scroggs* (1755) Amb 272.
166 *Farwell* 459; *Lawrie v Bankes* (1858) 4 K & J 142.

would enforce the execution of a power in favour of persons who were not objects of it.[167]

Consequently, it would not matter if (say) the ailing child to whom an appointment had been made were to recover;[168] or if the appointee were to refuse to perform his side of a bargain with the appointor.

Confirmation and ratification

An appointment under a common law power, or a power operating under the **19.50** Statute of Uses, by which the legal estate passed, was voidable only. But an appointment in fraud of an equitable power (ie not operating so as to pass the legal estate) was void. In the case of the former, the persons entitled in default of appointment could ratify or confirm the legal estate created by the appointment, because the legal estate had already passed at law.[169] However, ratification or confirmation of a fraudulent equitable appointment was not possible: 'when no estate has passed, "ratification" in the legal sense has no application: the legal estate has to be conveyed by the persons in whom it is vested, and the persons entitled in default of appointment establish the appointee's interest, not by ratifying or confirming his legal title, for he has none, but by conveying or directing the conveyance of the legal title vested in them or in trustees for them to him'.[170] The original appointment remains totally void. Thus, ratification or confirmation is not possible. Instead, in the case of a fraudulent execution of an equitable power, any purported 'confirmation' is construed as an assignment of their interest by the persons entitled in default of appointment, coupled with a release of his power by the appointor.[171] This would clearly present problems where the appointor had no authority to effect a release.

Since 1925, most powers—and certainly all powers of appointment over, and **19.51** powers to convey or charge, land or any interest therein—operate in equity only.[172] Thus, ratification or confirmation of a power is generally not possible. Nevertheless, in the case of those powers which remain legal, such as a power of attorney or the powers vested in a chargee by way of legal mortgage,[173] a fraudulent execution remains voidable. And a purchaser for value of a legal estate in the subject matter of the power, without notice of the fraud, would not be affected by the fraudulent execution of a legal power.[174]

---

[167] *Topham v Duke of Portland* (1862) 31 Beav 525, 541, *per* Sir John Romilly MR.

[168] *Lady Wellesley v Earl Mornington* (1855) 2 K & J 143. See also *Topham v Duke of Portland* (1863) 1 De GJ & Sm 517, 555.

[169] *M'Queen v Farquhar* (1805) 11 Ves 467; *Preston v Preston* (1869) 21 LT 346.

[170] *Cloutte v Storey* [1911] 1 Ch 18 at 32, *per* Farwell LJ.

[171] ibid 25, *per* Neville J. See also paras 11.75–11.78 above.

[172] See the Law of Property Act 1925, ss 1(7), 3, 205(1)(xi).   [173] ibid.

[174] There is limited statutory protection for a purchaser from an object of fraudulent appointment in s 158 of the LPA 1925.

J. Severance

19.52   It is usually impossible for the court to be able to sever composite appointments into their constituent parts, for it cannot know whether or how the power would ever have been exercised if it had not been for the corrupt purpose or improper intention. Thus, if a trustee were to appoint £3,000 to a child pursuant to an agreement that he be given back £1,000, the appointment is not good as to £2,000, but will fail *in toto*. It is impossible to say whether the appointment was actuated by love for the child or by a wish to provide for him: at least, it cannot be said that so much was to be attributed to a genuine purpose and so much to the intention to benefit himself.[175]

19.53   Nevertheless, there are exceptions to the general rule. Appointments may be severed to the extent that they are bona fide executions of the power, but bad as to the remainder, where (a) some consideration has been given which cannot be restored, or (b) the court can sever the intentions of the appointor, and distinguish the good from the bad.[176]

Consideration which cannot be restored

19.54   The first exception is said to arise where some consideration has been given which cannot be restored. However, the operation and scope—indeed the very existence—of this exception are obscure. The basic principle is simple: a fraudulent appointment is simply void.

> However, upon principle, I do not see how any part of a fraudulent agreement can be supported, except where some consideration has been given, that cannot be restored; and it has, consequently, become impossible to rescind the transaction *in toto*, and to replace the parties in the same situation ... In ordinary cases of fraud, the whole transaction is undone, and the parties are restored to their original situation. If a partially valuable consideration has been given, its return is secured as the condition on which equity relieves against the fraud.[177]

Thus, in the straightforward case where one of a limited class of objects has provided consideration for an appointment in his or her favour, the appointment is totally void and the consideration will be restored. 'To say, it is to be supported to that extent, would be to say that the [object] shall have the full benefit of the fraudulent agreement ... Either, then, you must hold that a child, giving a consideration for an appointment in its favour, is guilty of no fraud on the power; or you must wholly set aside the appointment procured by the fraud.'[178]

---

[175] *Farwell* 487–488; *Daubeny v Cockburn* (1816) 1 Mer 626; *Fanner v Martin* (1828) 2 Sim 502; *Askham v Barker* (1850) 12 Beav 499; *Agassiz v Squire* (1854) 18 Beav 431; *Rowley v Rowley* (1854) Kay 242; *Topham v Duke of Portland* (1863) 1 De GJ & Sm 517; *Re Chadwick's Trusts* [1939] 1 All ER 850.

[176] *Farwell* 488; *Thomas* 485–487.

[177] *Daubeny v Cockburn* (1816) 1 Mer 626, 643–644.   [178] *Loc cit.*

Where, however, the consideration could not be restored, the transaction could not be rescinded *in toto*, for the parties could not be replaced in their former situation. This, at least, is said to be the principle. But it is difficult to find any authority which illustrates its operation.[179]

19.55

From the viewpoint of a stranger, the basic principle was equally simple. 'The payment of a money consideration cannot make a stranger become the object of a power created in favour of children. He can only claim under a valid appointment executed in favour of some, or one, of the children.'[180] A payment of money might have the effect that an appointment ceased to be voluntary, which was of significance if it was not to be avoidable under various statutes as being in fraud of creditors or purchasers, but it could not in itself make the appointment cease to be fraudulent.[181]

19.56

Severance of appointor's intentions

As a second exception to the rule that a fraudulent exercise of a power is totally void, the court may be able to sever the intentions of the appointor and distinguish the good intention from the bad, as in the case where the fraud affects only one of two or more objects. In *Ranking v Barnes*,[182] the donee of a power to appoint in favour of children appointed two-sixths of the fund to a married daughter, one purpose being to enable her husband to use one-half of the appointed funds to pay a debt. The appointment was held invalid, but only as to one-half.[183] Similarly, in *Rowley v Rowley*,[184] a husband had a power of appointment over a sum of £30,000 in favour of his younger children. Pursuant to an agreement with his wife, he fraudulently appointed a sum of £5,000 to one child. By a similar deed, dated the next day and reciting the earlier appointment, he appointed the rest of the fund to his other child. Wood V-C held that the latter appointment was not so connected with the earlier, fraudulent appointment as to be invalid; nor, indeed, was the motive for the latter appointment the same as in the former case. Thus, although the general rule against severance is likely to apply in most instances, the evidence may be such as to enable the court to distinguish what is attributable to an unauthorized intention or purpose from that which is attributable to an authorized one.[185]

19.57

Annexed conditions?

Where there is an appointment to an object of the power, with a condition annexed, severance may well be easier and the appointee left to enjoy the property

19.58

---

[179] See *Thomas* 485–486.   [180] *Daubeny v Cockburn* (1816) 1 Mer 626, 638.
[181] *Daubeny v Cockburn, supra,* 638; *George v Milbanke* (1803) 9 Ves 190 (where the power was general) and comments thereon in *Halifax Joint Stock Banking Co v Gledhill* [1891] 1 Ch 31, 37–38.
[182] (1864) 10 Jur NS 463.   [183] See also *Harrison v Randall* (1851) 9 Hare 397.
[184] (1854) Kay 242.
[185] *Topham v Duke of Portland* (1863) 1 De GJ & Sm 517, 572, *per* Turner LJ.

free from that condition. However, apart from this, there does not seem to be any reason to justify a distinction, in the context of fraudulent execution of a power, between cases involving annexed conditions (be they authorized or unauthorized by the terms of the power) and those which do not.[186] Most instances of severed conditions involve excessive, not fraudulent, execution of a power, and the general principle there is simply

> that an ulterior purpose of this kind, which is *ultra vires* only and not also a fraud on the power, though it may have operated as a motive for the appointment in the mind of the appointor, will, nevertheless not prevent an object of the power from taking for his own benefit the estate appointed to him, if the words used, according to their proper construction... are sufficient to execute the power and vest the property in the appointee.[187]

In relation to fraudulent execution of a power, there is no reason why an annexed condition could not have a sinister purpose or by-purpose. Nor is there any reason why such a condition should be regarded differently from any other kind of fraud. The true principle, it is suggested, is that 'a condition, whether authorized or unauthorized in nature, and whether severable or inseverable, may be an integral part of a fraud on the power rendering the whole appointment bad; in other words, invalidity for fraud and invalidity for excess are not mutually exclusive terms'.[188] If the appointor's intention or purpose cannot be severed into the good and the bad, the execution fails entirely, notwithstanding that a condition annexed to the appointment could otherwise be easily severed.

K. Cases Where the Doctrine of Fraud Does Not Apply

Release of a power

19.59   The doctrine of fraud on a power does not apply to the release of a power.[189] The donee of an ordinary (non-fiduciary) power can release that power by deed, or contract not to exercise it,[190] even if he himself thereby acquires some benefit which he could not have obtained by an exercise of the power.[191] Thus, in *Re Somes*,[192] where a life tenant under a settlement had an exclusive power of appointment for the benefit of his daughter or her issue, the fund passing in default of appointment to the daughter absolutely, and the life tenant, being in want of money, released his power so that he and his daughter could subsequently

---

186   *Thomas* 487; *Farwell* 489.
187   *Macdonald v Macdonald* (1875) LR 2 Sc & Div App Cas 482, 492, *per* Lord Selborne.
188   *Farwell* 489. See also *Vatcher v Paull* [1915] AC 372, 378.
189   For a full discussion of the release of powers, see *Thomas*, Ch 15 and Chapter 17 above.
190   Section 155 of the Law of Property Act 1925. Note that the section has a purely negative effect on contracts: it does not authorize a donee to contract to exercise a power in a particular way.
191   *Re Radcliffe* [1892] 1 Ch 227 (not following *Cunynghame v Thurlow* (1832) 1 Russ & My 436n).
192   [1896] 1 Ch 250. See also *Smith v Houblon* (1859) Ch 227.

mortgage their interests in the fund, the sum borrowed being applied for his own purposes, the release could not be impeached. As Chitty J stated:[193]

> ...there is a fallacy in applying to a release of a power of this kind the doctrines applicable to the fraudulent exercise of such a power. There is no duty imposed on the donee of a limited power to make an appointment; there is no fiduciary relationship between him and the objects of the power beyond this, that if he does exercise the power of appointment, he must exercise it honestly for the benefit of an object or the objects of the power, and not corruptly for his own personal benefit; but I cannot see any ground for applying that doctrine to the case of a release of a power; the donee of the power may, or he may not, be acting in his own interest, but he is at liberty, in my opinion, to say that he will never make any appointment under the power, and to execute a release of it.

19.60 The donee of such a power is under a duty to ensure that the (paramount) interests of those entitled in default of appointment are not divested otherwise than for the purposes and in the way limited by the donor of the power,[194] but he is not obliged to exercise that power at all, or even to consider its exercise. Therefore, not only does the release of such a power not involve a breach of any duty but it also confirms or renders indefeasible those interests in default.[195]

19.61 Whether the same conclusion applies in respect of a power coupled with a duty (a fiduciary power) is unclear. A trustee (or other donee) of such a power cannot release it in the absence of express authorization to do so.[196] If the power cannot be released in any event, then clearly no question of fraudulent release can arise. If release of the power is authorized, the effect of any such release is the same as in the case of a release of a non-fiduciary power: the interests of those entitled in default of appointment are simply confirmed and rendered indefeasible: the releasor 'leaves things as the donor of the power left them'.[197] However, other considerations arise on the release of a fiduciary power (and, in *Re Somes*, Chitty J carefully confined himself to non-fiduciary powers[198]). The fiduciary donee may be in breach of some acknowledged duty, for example in deciding to release his power, he may not have taken into account all crucially relevant considerations or may have been swayed unduly by irrelevant ones.[199] The release of a power by a fiduciary donee may also be in breach of the rule against conflict of interests: for example, the transaction under scrutiny in *Re Somes* might well have been impeachable if the releasor (and ultimate beneficiary) had been a trustee (or someone in a similar fiduciary position). In such cases, and certainly in the more extreme instances, such as where the release of a fiduciary power is induced by a bribe, there may be no need

---

[193] [1896] 1 Ch 250, 255.   [194] *Re Greaves* [1954] Ch 434, 446, *per* Evershed MR.
[195] It must be questionable, however, whether this principle is absolute and cannot affect even an extreme case, such as a release induced by means of a bribe: see *Thomas* 488.
[196] *Re Eyre* (1883) 49 LT 259; *Re Mills* [1930] 1 Ch 65.
[197] *Re Greaves* [1954] Ch 434, 446, *per* Evershed MR.   [198] [1896] 1 Ch 250, 255.
[199] cf *Karger v Paul* [1984] VR 161.

to invoke the doctrine of fraud on a power, for the act is clearly impeachable as a breach of trust (or other fiduciary duty). Indeed, in the absence of a breach of some fiduciary obligation or rule of this kind, or unless the release is an intrinsic and inseparable part of a larger transaction which is itself impeachable under the doctrine of fraud,[200] it is difficult to see how the mere release of a fiduciary power, as a separate and individual act, could be fraudulent.[201]

Revocation of appointment

19.62 The doctrine of fraud on a power is also said not to apply to the revocation of an appointment.[202] Thus, in *Re Greaves*,[203] the revocation of an appointment by a life tenant in order to facilitate the implementation of a scheme of distribution of the capital of the trust fund subject to the power, and under which scheme she herself benefited, was not within the doctrine of a fraud on the power. The underlying reason is the same as that applicable to the release of powers. As Evershed MR stated:[204]

> *prima facie* at least, the appointor, having made a revocable power of appointment,[205] owes no duty to anyone if he revokes the appointment; if he revokes and does not re-appoint, no one can complain of what he has done, for no one can assert the misuse of a power, namely, the power of appointment. *Prima facie*, according to the ordinary use of language, if an appointment has been made subject to a power of revocation, then the appointor has reserved to himself a *locus poenitentiae*, a right to recall the selection or discrimination he has made, to wipe the slate, as it were, clean again, to go back whence he started and to decide afresh, not only what selection or discrimination he will make, but whether he will select or discriminate at all. If he repents of his original selection or discrimination, revokes the appointment he has made and then, without more, releases his power of appointment, he will have, on second thoughts, renounced the power vested in him. The persons entitled to take will be the persons designated by the creator of the trust in the precise event which has happened, that is, the event that the donee of the power to direct a different destination of the trust property will not have effectively availed himself of the opportunity granted to him. As already stated, he is under no positive duty to exercise the power at all. The only relevant duty which he owes is to the persons designated by the donor of the power to take in default of appointment, the duty not to exercise the power of divesting them save strictly to the extent and in the manner prescribed by the donor. No one can, therefore, complain of a fraud on the power if the power has been, in the end, repudiated.

19.63 The exclusion of the doctrine may not be absolute, however. The Court of Appeal could 'conceive' of a case in which there is conferred a power to revoke previously declared trusts which is so closely related to a power of re-appointment that, as a matter of construction, the former power should be held to be only exercisable for

---

[200] See the observations made in relation to a power of revocation in *Re Greaves* [1954] Ch 434, 450.

[201] See, however, *Thomas* 489.

[202] For powers of revocation, see *Thomas*, Ch 13 and Chapter 16 above.

[203] [1954] Ch 434 (overruling *Re Jones' Settlement* [1915] 1 Ch 373).

[204] [1954] Ch 434, 447.

[205] It seems clear that this should read either 'having made a revocable exercise of a power of appointment' or 'having made a revocable appointment'.

the purposes of, and as an essential step towards, a re-appointment'. In such a case, 'if for any reason the re-appointment were ineffective, the revocation might fall with it so as to leave the original trusts persisting'.[206] How far this is a genuine exception to the general rule seems debatable, however.

Different considerations arise, however, where the power of revocation is conferred on a trustee. The power of revocation in *Re Greaves* was not a fiduciary power; and it is clear that, in reaching its conclusion, the Court of Appeal attached considerable significance to the fact that the donee of such a power owed no duty at all to its class of objects (as opposed to those entitled in default).[207] However, where such a power is conferred on a trustee (or similar fiduciary), the position is different: the donee is obliged to consider the exercise of the power from time to time; and the objects have a right to be considered for receipt of bounty. Moreover, in exercising a power to revoke, a trustee must exercise a conscious discretion, must take into account crucially relevant considerations and exclude all irrelevant ones. The exercise of a fiduciary power of revocation may therefore be impeachable on the grounds that some such fiduciary obligation has been breached. It is possible, therefore, that the doctrine of fraud on a power may apply to the exercise of a fiduciary power of revocation, for example where the revocation is induced by a bribe,[208] as in the case of a release; but it is also possible that there is no need for it to do so, because the exercise of that power can be more easily challenged as a breach of some fiduciary obligation. **19.64**

General and hybrid powers

The doctrine of fraud on a power applies to special or limited powers: it does not apply to a general power: it is of the nature of such a power that the donee could exercise the power in his own favour and then pass on the subject matter of the power to anyone he pleases. Similarly, where the donee of a hybrid power is himself an object of that power (or, indeed, of any power which he may exercise in his own favour) the doctrine cannot apply.[209] However, subject to this, there is no reason why the exercise of a hybrid power for a corrupt purpose or pursuant to a bargain should not be subject to the doctrine. Thus, any exercise of such a power which is intended to benefit indirectly someone who is excluded from the class of objects (whether it is the donee himself or anyone else) is fraudulent and void. **19.65**

Power to jointure

A power to jointure—that is, a power for a husband to make provision for his widow—has always been regarded as 'a somewhat peculiar power'.[210] The **19.66**

---

[206] [1954] Ch 434, 450.   [207] ibid 446.
[208] cf *Att-Gen of Hong Kong v Reid* [1994] 1 AC 324; *Re Att-Gen's Reference (No 1 of 1985)* [1986] QB 491; *Lister v Stubbs* (1890) 45 Ch D 1.
[209] *Re Triffitt's Settlement* [1958] Ch 852, 863–864, *per* Upjohn J.
[210] *Saunders v Shafto* [1905] 1 Ch 126, 137, 138.

doctrine of fraud on a power applies to a power of jointuring, but in a modified form.[211]

L. Liability of Trustees

19.67 Trustees ought to be astute in suspecting fraud. If they part with the trust fund improperly, they will have to replace it. 'A trustee who, having good reason to doubt the validity of an appointment, thinks proper to act upon it, must be affected by the consequences which follow upon the act.'[212] Thus, in *Mackechnie v Marjoribanks*,[213] for example, the donee of a special power appointed the entire trust fund to her daughter, who was an object of the power. The daughter requested the trustee, by letter of even date with the appointment, to pay the fund into her mother's bank account, The trustee did so. The mother died insolvent, having used part of the moneys for her own purposes. The trustee was held liable to replace the fund at the suit of those entitled in default of appointment, James V-C finding that the letter and the appointment were part of the same transaction. The measure of damage is not necessarily the amount of benefit received, but the entire loss to the trust fund.[214]

19.68 If the trustees have been misled and innocently transferred the property in accordance with what appeared to be a proper and valid appointment, they cannot be made liable.[215] Indeed, trustees may be made to pay the costs if they raise untenable objections to acting upon appointments.[216]

M. Position of Third Parties

19.69 As a general rule, the payment of money cannot make an appointment cease to be fraudulent.[217] In ordinary cases, the whole transaction is undone and the parties are restored to their original situation. If valuable consideration has been given, its return is secured as the condition on which equity relieves against the fraud.[218]

---

[211] See *Thomas* 491–492. It is an interesting question whether the anomalous treatment of powers of jointuring might be extended to other powers.

[212] *Harrison v Randall* (1851) 9 Hare 397.   [213] (1870) 18 WR 993; 39 LJ Ch 604.

[214] *Re Deane* (1888) 42 Ch D 9.   [215] ibid 18.

[216] *Farwell* 470; *Campbell v Home* (1842) 1 Y & C Ch Cas 664; *Patterson v Wooler* (1876) 2 Ch D 576.

[217] Although it may make an appointment cease to be voluntary. This was important in the context of avoidance of conveyances (or other assurances) under the provisions of the Statutes of 13 Eliz c 5 (Frauds on creditors) (replaced by s 172 of the LPA 1925, itself replaced by s 423 of the Insolvency Act 1986) and 27 Eliz c 4 (Frauds on purchasers) (replaced by s 173(1) of the LPA 1925). See *May on The Law of Fraudulent and Voluntary Conveyances* (3rd edn, 1908) 252–253.

[218] *Daubeny v Cockburn* (1816) 1 Mer 626, 638, 643, 644.

This principle applies, it seems, to anyone (object or non-object) who has given consideration for a fraudulent appointment. The recipient of property under a fraudulent execution of a power gets no title if the power is equitable only (as is likely to be the case) even if he has no notice of the fraud; he will not have the security of the legal estate and will be a subsequent equitable claimant only.[219] The recipient thus holds that property on constructive trust for those lawfully entitled to it.

However, section 157 of the Law of Property Act 1925 provides limited protection for purchasers of interests from objects of fraudulent appointments and for their successors in title.[220] However, there is no protection at all under this provision where there is only one person entitled in default of appointment. A purchaser may be fixed with constructive notice, even if he has no express notice of the fraud. Marriage will not be sufficient consideration. And even if he succeeds in satisfying all conditions, he is protected only to the extent of the amount to which, at the date of the appointment, the appointee was presumptively entitled in default of appointment. Thus, if A has power to appoint £100,000 among his four children and any grandchildren and, in default of appointment, his children take equally, and he fraudulently appoints the entire sum to one child, a purchaser from that child is protected only to the extent of £25,000. If A fraudulently appointed to a grandchild, a purchaser from him would get no protection at all.

19.70

---

[219] *Cloutte v Storey* [1911] 1 Ch 18. See also paras 11.75–11.78 above.
[220] Section 157(3). The section applies to dealings effected after 1925, but whenever the appointment itself was made: s 157(4).

20

THE JUDICIAL REVIEW OF THE EXERCISE OF TRUSTEES' DISCRETIONS[1]

A. Introduction

The exercise by trustees of their powers and discretions is invariably required to be **20.01** 'honest' or 'bona fide', but judges have often deployed a number of other expressions which may or may not be intended to convey the idea that such exercise is not entirely without some limitation: these include words such as 'proper', 'sound', 'reasonable', 'fair', and 'prudent'.[2] As we have already seen, trustees must not act capriciously.[3] Nor must they act 'arbitrarily and unreasonably',[4] 'mischievously or ruinously',[5] 'improperly or unreasonably',[6] 'wantonly or capriciously'.[7] It may be that all these expressions are used simply as synonyms for the overriding requirement of 'good faith', for, as Lord Jessel MR pointed out in *Errington v*

---

[1] See GW Thomas, *Powers* (Sweet & Maxwell, 1998) ('*Thomas*') 343–377; [1998] Conv 244 (NDM Parry); (1975) 25 UTLJ 99 (M Cullity); (1975) 12 UWALR 91 (IJ Hardingham); (1967) 31 Conv 117 (AJ Hawkins); (1961) 61 Colum LR 1425 (EC Halbach); (1957) 21 Conv 55 (LA Sheridan); (1997) 11 Tr Law Int 42 (D Pollard).

[2] See, for example, *Costabadie v Costabadie* (1847) 6 Hare 410; *Re Hodges* (1878) 7 Ch D 754; *Tabor v Brooks* (1878) 10 Ch D 273; *Re Roper's Trusts* (1879) 11 Ch D 272; *Re Bryant* [1894] 1 Ch 324; *Armitage v Nurse* [1998] Ch 241.

[3] See paras 11.89–11.91 above.   [4] *Tabor v Brooks* (1878) 10 Ch D 273.

[5] *Re Brittlebank* (1881) 30 WR 99.

[6] *Re Courtier* (1886) 34 Ch D 136; *Re Radnor's Will Trusts* (1890) 45 Ch D 402.

[7] *Pilkington v IRC* [1964] AC 612, 641. See also *Lutheran Church of Australia (South Australia District) Incorporated v Farmers' Co-operative Executors and Trustees Ltd* (1970) 121 CLR 628, 639.

Metropolitan District Railway Co[8] (a public law case), 'you can shew want of *bona fides* in two ways', either 'by proving . . . some collateral purpose as a fact' or 'by proving that the alleged purpose is so absurd, under the circumstances that it cannot possibly be *bona fide*'. This suggests, rightly, that the concept of 'good faith' is not necessarily synonymous with 'honesty' (although sometimes it clearly is): an honest man may act unreasonably.[9] However, it is difficult to identify in the authorities a consistent usage of terminology.[10] Expressions such as 'good faith', 'honesty', 'reasonableness', and 'prudence' have been used indiscriminately by the courts, and it is not at all clear whether they are intended to convey a common meaning or to indicate that different standards are required in different contexts.

20.02 As a preliminary step, it can be said that the law is generally clear on two associated principles, at least. First, where a mere power is exercisable by trustees in their absolute discretion, the court will not compel the trustees to exercise it.[11] The court will not intervene where there has been a conscious decision, taken in good faith, not to exercise the discretion.[12] Secondly, where there is a discretionary trust, or where the relevant power is coupled with a trust or duty (or cases of 'mixed trust and power'),[13] the court will enforce the proper and timely exercise of that trust or power, and might do so by removing the trustees who refused to join in. However, subject to this overriding consideration, the court will not readily interfere with the discretion of the trustees as to the particular time or manner of their bona fide exercise of it.[14]

20.03 There are, of course, several grounds on which the court may interfere and review the exercise by trustees of their powers and discretions. The trustee may have

---

[8] (1882) 19 Ch D 559, 571. See also *Hartigan Nominees v Rydge* (1992) 29 NSWLR 405, 428; *Lee v Showmen's Guild of Great Britain* [1952] 2 QB 329, 344.

[9] *Re Chapman* (1895) 72 LT 66, 68; *Cowan v Scargill* [1985] Ch 270, 289. Cf *Karger v Paul* [1984] VR 161, 164.

[10] It has been pointed out (rightly) that 'the whole history of this particular area of the law has been what may be called a history of well-meaning sloppiness of thought': see (1975) 12 UWALR 91 (IJ Hardingham). See also *Karger v Paul, supra*, 164.

[11] *Tempest v Lord Camoys* (1882) 21 Ch D 571, 578, 579, and 580. See also *National Trustees Executors and Agency Co of Australasia Ltd v Dwyer* (1940) 63 CLR 1. However, the court will ensure that a discretionary trust is carried into effect.

[12] *Re Gulbenkian's Settlements* [1970] AC 508, 518; *Tempest v Lord Camoys* (1882) 21 Ch D 571, 578, 579 and 580; *Re 90 Thornhill Road, Tolsworth Surrey* [1970] Ch 261, 265; *Re Mays* [1943] Ch 302. This is in contrast to a failure to exercise the discretion at all: see, for example, *Turner v Turner* [1984] Ch 100; *Klug v Klug* [1918] 2 Ch 67; *Re Wells* (1889) 43 Ch D 281; *Wilson v Turner* (1883) 22 Ch D 521.

[13] As they were called by Chitty J in *Re Bryant* [1894] 1 Ch 324, 330. See also *Tempest v Lord Camoys* (1868), noted at (1882) 21 Ch D 576n.

[14] This is what is stated in the headnote of *Tempest v Lord Camoys* (1868) 21 Ch D 571. None of the judgments uses the words 'bona fide' or any equivalent (although they can presumably be implied): they merely held that the dissenting trustee's exercise of his discretion could not be interfered with. See also *Re Blake* (1885) 29 Ch D 913; *Re Kipping* [1914] Ch 62; and *Re Charteris* [1917] 2 Ch 379.

misconstrued the nature or scope of the power and exercised it in favour of some object, or for some purpose, not contemplated or authorized by the donor, in which case the exercise will be excessive and impeachable.[15] The trustee may have exercised the power for some ulterior purpose, in which case he will have acted dishonestly and committed a fraud on the power.[16] Also, as we have seen in Chapter 11, he may have failed entirely to take into account some crucially relevant consideration or wrongly taken into account and attributed too much significance to an irrelevant one, and thereby failed to exercise his discretion properly or at all. Similarly, he may have acted under dictation from another or committed some other act which resulted in a failure to exercise the discretion at all;[17] or he may have acted in a manner which is so completely unreasonable that it is plain that he must have been acting capriciously. In all these cases, the exercise or purported exercise of the power or discretion is capable of being reviewed by the court; and it is often the case that, when a particular exercise is held not to have been carried out 'in good faith', 'honestly', 'reasonably', or 'prudently', the substance of the matter is that there has been a breach of one of these well-recognized heads of challenge. This is not to question the merits of a decision; rather, there has been a flaw in the decision-making process itself. As Lord Truro LC stated, in *Re Beloved Wilkes's Charity*[18] (where the discretion was apparently not an absolute one), 'the duty of supervision on the part of [the] Court will thus be confined to the question of the honesty, integrity, and fairness with which the deliberation has been conducted, and will not be extended to the accuracy of the conclusion arrived at, except in particular cases'. Thus, there is a long-standing distinction between the decision-making process and the actual decision itself. However, it is often a matter of some difficulty to differentiate between them: for example, it is often the inaccuracy or lack of merit of the conclusion arrived at (which is not reviewable per se) that points to a lack of 'fairness' in the trustees' deliberations or consideration (which is reviewable) and vice versa.

B. The Prudent Trustee Standard

At first sight, it would seem self-evident that the act of conferring a power or discretion on a trustee in itself implies that the donor expected the trustee to exercise it reasonably, prudently, and with sound judgement. After all, prudence and reasonableness are expected and required of a trustee in all things connected with **20.04**

---

[15] See Chapter 18 above.   [16] See Chapter 19 above.

[17] *Turner v Turner* (1883) 22 Ch D 521; *Re Bryant* [1894] 1 Ch 324, 330.

[18] (1851) 3 Mac & G 440, 448. He also referred to the trustees' duty to act not only 'with an entire absence of indirect motive [and] with honesty of intention' but also 'with a fair consideration of the subject'.

his office and the discharge of his functions. All trustees, of course, do not have the same duties and liabilities.[19] Nevertheless, as a general rule a trustee is required, in the management of trust affairs, to take all those precautions which an ordinary prudent man of business would take in managing the affairs of other people for whom he felt morally bound to provide.[20] This duty, which is not confined to matters relating to investment of trust funds, necessarily implies a degree of reasonableness. As Lord Wilberforce pointed out, in *McPhail v Doulton*,[21] 'a trustee to whom, as such, a power is given is bound by the duties of his office in exercising that power to do so in a responsible manner according to its purpose'. This would not necessarily mean that the reasonableness of every decision of a trustee might be open to review, for it is well established that reasonable people often differ about what is reasonable,[22] without one of them necessarily being misguided or wrong. Nevertheless, if reasonableness is the standard required of trustees, it is logical that unreasonable behaviour should be capable of being challenged and reviewed by the courts, and there is, indeed, some authority to this effect.[23] It has been suggested[24] that the 'prudent man of business' test is appropriate only in relation to the exercise of administrative, and not dispositive, powers. However, this seems hard to justify. The exercise of a dispositive power which directly affects beneficial entitlement would seem to demand greater scrutiny and control than the exercise of an administrative one. In any event, in a typical trust instrument, there will usually be a general provision to the effect that the exercise of dispositive and administrative powers alike is to be at the discretion of the trustees, so it is the effect of such a provision, rather than the nature of the power, that is usually in issue.

20.05 On the other hand, it is a fundamental principle that the court will not interfere with the exercise of a power or discretion simply on the ground that it might have reached a different or better conclusion. Different people will be influenced by a variety of circumstances and they will have different ideas of what is reasonable in

---

[19] *Earl of Egmont v Smith* (1877) 6 Ch D 469, 475; *Knox v Gye* (1872) LR 5 HL 656. See also *Lonrho plc v Fayed (No 2)* [1992] 1 WLR 1, 12.

[20] *Speight v Gaunt* (1883) 9 App Cas 1, 19; *Re Whiteley* (1886) 33 Ch D 347, 355; *Learoyd v Whiteley* (1887) 12 App Cas 727; *Eaton v Buchanan* [1911] AC 253; *Nestle v National Westminster Bank plc* [1993] 1 WLR 1260, 1267–1268.

[21] [1971] AC 424, 449 (also 457). See also *Re Chapman* (1895) 72 LT 66, 67; *Re Hay's Settlement Trusts* [1982] 1 WLR 202, 209. Mere negligence or carelessness may not in themselves amount to want of good faith or dishonesty (*Royal Brunei Airlines v Tan* [1995] 2 AC 378, 389; *Walker v Stones* [2001] QB 902; *Jones v Gordon* (1877) 2 AC 616, 628–629) but they are still relevant in determining whether a trustee has acted unreasonably or irresponsibly.

[22] See, for example, *Dundee General Hospitals Board of Management v Walker* [1952] 1 All ER 896, 901. See also *Re Chapman, supra*, 68; *Cowan v Scargill* [1985] Ch 270, 289.

[23] See *Re Hodges* (1878) 7 Ch D 754; *Harris v Lord Shuttleworth* [1994] ICR 989, 999; *Wild v Smith* [1996] PLR 275, 280; *Elder's Trustee and Executor Co Ltd v Higgins* (1965) 113 CLR 426; *Edge v Pensions Ombudsman* [1998] PLR 15, 30.

[24] [1989] Conv 244, 250 (NDM Parry). See also *Edge v Pensions Ombudsman, supra*.

the exercise of their discretions.[25] However, the donor has conferred a discretion on the trustee and not on any other person; and it would therefore not be appropriate if the discretion of another (or of the court) were to be substituted for that of the trustee.[26] Indeed, for the same reason, there is a reluctance on the part of the courts to review or permit any challenge to the exercise of a power or discretion on the ground of 'unreasonableness'[27] (which is a different exercise from seeking to 'improve' on what might otherwise be a reasonable, if not the best, decision).

A power, by its very nature, is discretionary. Therefore, it may well be wondered **20.06** whether a declaration that a power is exercisable 'at the trustee's discretion', or 'at the trustee's absolute and uncontrollable discretion', serves any purpose and, if so, what (in either case) that purpose might be. In other words, are these additional words merely surplus, so that an identical discretion is conferred in each case; or do they indicate that different degrees of discretion are being created? If the latter is the case, then it is arguable that the possibility of judicial interference is excluded (and, even then, not totally) only where the power or discretion in question is expressly enlarged by declaring it to be 'absolute', or 'uncontrollable'.[28] In addition, there may be a difference between the kind of discretion which is inherent in a mere power conferred on trustees and the discretion (usually as to quantum, time, or mode of exercise) which is conferred on discretionary trustees. In one case, the trustees are not obliged to exercise their discretion, so that a decision not to do so, taken in good faith and in the appropriate manner, would be within the scope of what the donor contemplated. In contrast, a failure to exercise the relevant discretion in the context of a discretionary trust within a reasonable time (even if it is done in good faith) may well defeat or retard the proper implementation of the overriding obligation imposed by the donor. The authorities do not always provide clear answers to these questions; and, as a survey of the development of the relevant principles shows, there has always been a degree of ambiguity as to the possibility and scope of judicial intervention in relation to different kinds of discretions (or discretions conferred in different contexts).

---

[25] *Dundee General Hospitals Board of Management v Walker* [1952] 1 All ER 896, 901.

[26] The principle of non-interference also applies to fiduciaries other than trustees: see, for example, *Ex parte Lloyd* (1882) 47 LT 64, 65; *Re Bell Bros Ltd* (1891) 65 LT 245; *Re Gresham Life Assurance Company* (1872) 8 Ch App 446; *Moffat v Farquhar* (1877) 7 Ch D 591; *Re Stranton Iron Company* (1873) LR 16 Eq 559; *Pinkett v Wright* (1842) 2 Hare 120; *Robinson v The Chartered Bank* (1865) LR 1 Eq 32.

[27] This general statement is confined, of course, to private law (and the decisions of trustees in particular).

[28] Or 'absolute and uncontrollable', or 'sole, absolute, and uncontrolled', or any other form of expression which has similar effect (eg 'irresponsible').

C. Unenlarged and Enlarged Discretions

20.07 Some of the earlier cases indicate that, where a power or discretion was not enlarged so as to be 'absolute and uncontrollable', the courts might indeed sometimes intervene where the trustees' exercise had been unreasonable. In many instances, however, the possibility of judicial control along these lines was not addressed directly but arose as an adjunct to a point of construction, the question usually being whether an obligation had been imposed on the trustees (coupled with a discretion as to the time and manner of execution) and which created an entitlement on the part of the objects of that discretion, or whether a mere power had been conferred on the trustees, which they were not obliged to exercise and which created no such entitlement.[29] There are indications that the courts were more willing to interfere in the case of a discretionary trust, and where the discretion (as to quantum usually) was not enlarged, and to imply a requirement that that discretion be exercised reasonably.[30] Even in the case of a mere power conferred on trustees, ie where there was no obligation to exercise it, an unenlarged discretion might be required to be exercised reasonably. This seems to have been the implication of the observations of Lord Truro in *Re Beloved Wilkes's Charity*.[31] Similarly, in *Costabadie v Costabadie*,[32] Wigram V-C clearly recognized that a trustee was expected to exercise 'a sound and honest' or a 'proper and honest' discretion, and he referred to 'the honest and reasonable exercise of that discretion', although, in the circumstances of that case, the complainant's allegations of improper exercise were not established.

20.08 In none of these cases, however, were the observations of the court directed at the exercise of a power or discretion which was expressed to be 'absolute' or 'uncontrollable'—as most trust instruments will now provide. The general principle in relation to such enlarged discretions is usually expressed in relatively simple terms: provided the trustees have exercised the discretion conferred on them, and done so in good faith, the courts will not interfere with or review the accuracy of their decision. The leading case (but certainly not the first[33]) on enlarged discretions is *Gisborne v Gisborne*,[34] where a testator gave his trustees a discretion 'of their uncontrollable authority' to pay and apply the annual income of the estate 'as they

---

[29] See, for example, *Costabadie v Costabadie* (1847) 6 Hare 410; *Tempest v Lord Camoys* (1868) 21 Ch D 571; and also *Tempest v Lord Camoys* 1868, noted at (1882) 21 Ch D 576n.

[30] *Ransome v Burgess* (1866) LR 3 Eq 773 (later disapproved in *Wilson v Turner* (1883) 22 Ch D 521, but on the point of construction). See also *Re Bryant* [1894] 1 Ch 324, 331–332; *Mundy v Earl Howe* (1793) 4 Bro CC 223; *Meacher v Young* (1834) 2 My & K 490.

[31] (1851) 3 Mac & G 440, 448.   [32] (1847) 6 Hare 410, 414.

[33] See *Costabadie v Costabadie* (1847) 6 Hare 410; *Re Beloved Wilkes's Charity* (1851) 3 Mac & G 440 and the authorities cited therein; *Holmes v Penny* (1856) 3 K & J 90; *Re Sanderson's Trusts* (1857) 3 K & J 497.   [34] (1877) 2 App Cas 300.

shall think expedient' for specified purposes. As to the nature and scope of the trustees' discretion, Lord Cairns stated:[35]

> My lords, larger words than those, it appears to me, it would be impossible to introduce into a will. The trustees are not merely to have discretion, but they are to have 'uncontrollable', that is, uncontrolled, 'authority'. Their discretion and authority, always supposing that there is no *mala fides* with regard to its exercise, is to be without any check or control from any superior tribunal. What is the subject-matter with regard to which they are to exercise this discretion and this authority? The subject-matter is the payment, or the application, not merely of the whole of the income of his real and personal estate, but of such portion only as they deem it proper to expend. It is for them to say whether they will apply the whole, or only a part, and if so what part. And how are they to decide, if they do not apply the whole, what is the part which they are to apply? They are to decide upon this principle, that it is to be such part as they shall think expedient, not such part as shall be sufficient, not such part as shall be demanded by or for the person to be benefited, but such part as they shall think expedient; and upon the question of what is expedient it is their discretion which is to decide, and that discretion according to which they are to decide is to be uncontrolled.

Similar views were expressed by Lord Penzance and Lord O'Hagan[36] and *Gisborne* effectively became the foundation of the law relating to judicial review of discretionary decisions by trustees. However, the decision should be placed in its proper context. There were other sources of income available to maintain the person on whose behalf the claim was made, namely the testator's widow (a person of unsound mind). It is clear that the trustees' discretion was explicitly made 'uncontrollable': it is not, therefore, an authority on the possibility of judicial interference and review where the relevant power or discretion is not so enlarged.[37] The relevant standard was the trustees' view (and not that of prudent trustees generally) of what was 'expedient' (and not some more objective standard, such as what was necessary or reasonable). Moreover, there is no question in *Gisborne* of the trustees acting otherwise than in good faith and within the limits, and in furtherance of the object, of the discretion conferred on them by the will. Nor was there any failure to exercise that discretion.

Shortly thereafter, in *Re Hodges*,[38] where trustees had an unenlarged discretion to **20.09** apply the income of a legacy for the maintenance and education of legatees as they should think fit, Malins V-C held, notwithstanding the recent decision in *Gisborne* (which was not even referred to),[39] that, in the circumstances, the

---

[35] ibid 305.   [36] ibid 309 and 311.

[37] Neither *Wilkes* nor *Costabadie* was referred to in *Gisborne*, although *Ransome v Burgess* was.

[38] (1878) 7 Ch D 754.

[39] *Gisborne* had been decided some ten months earlier. *Costabadie v Costabadie* (1847) 6 Hare 410 was referred to in *Hodges* in support of the proposition that the court had no jurisdiction to intervene where the discretion is fairly and properly exercised, but not *Gisborne*. In contrast, *Costabadie* was not referred to in *Gisborne*.

trustees had acted improperly in allowing only £60 a year for that purpose and directed that the whole income (£100) be applied instead. He stated:[40] 'I do not think it to the interests of the wards that they should be left uneducated, or that the father should incur debts for the purpose of their education when they have the means of maintaining themselves . . .'. Indeed, there is a strong indication in his judgment that judicial interference in such cases was common practice.[41] Malins V-C emphasized, however, that the court would not have interfered if the trustees' discretion had been absolute and uncontrollable, thus recognizing that the *Gisborne* principle did not extend to unenlarged powers and discretions conferred on trustees. In contrast, Malins V-C readily applied the *Gisborne* principle in *Tabor v Brooks*,[42] where trustees had been given an 'uncontrolled and irresponsible discretion' to sell or convert assets and to apply income for the maintenance of a beneficiary (who was 'addicted to very intemperate habits, and was frequently intoxicated, and violent in his conduct to his wife') and of his wife and children. The trustees refused to pay any income to the wife when asked to do so, other than small sums of money and paying school expenses of the child (amounting to £60 a year), and paid the remainder (of £300 a year) to the beneficiary himself. Malins V-C held, on the authority of *Gisborne*, that the court could not interfere, despite the fact that the trustees would have been acting 'more wisely' if they had divided the income between husband and wife, there being no mala fides.[43]

20.10   It seems clear that, in Malins V-C's view, the crucial distinction of principle that had to be made was that between (i) a discretion which was not enlarged and with which the court would not interfere if it was 'fairly and honestly exercised' and not exercised 'in an arbitrary and unreasonable manner' and (ii) an absolute and uncontrolled discretion, with which the court would not interfere 'so long as there is no *mala fides*' in its exercise.[44] It is not clear where the dividing line between these two categories was considered to fall. In category (i), it is the absence of good faith and reasonableness that apparently need to be established, but in category (ii) bad faith on the part of the trustees must be proved. This, it would seem, suggests a difference of degree; and the dividing line between absence of good faith and presence of bad faith may be difficult to locate.[45] Nevertheless, the distinction

---

[40] (1878) 7 Ch D 761.   [41] ibid 761. One example is *White v Grane* (1854) 18 Beav 571.
[42] (1878) 10 Ch D 273. See also *Marquis Camden v Murray* (1880) 16 Ch D 161, 170.
[43] It is doubtful whether the decision in *Tabor v Brooks* would be the same today: the trustees clearly seem to have exercised their discretion for an ulterior purpose, ie to ensure that Mrs Tabor continued to live with her husband.
[44] *Tabor v Brooks* (1878) 10 Ch D 273, 277, 278.
[45] In *Karger v Paul* [1984] VR 161, 164, McGarvie J said that he did not agree 'that there is any conceptual territory which lies between good faith and bad faith. An act which falls short of good faith is done in bad faith.' It is suggested that this is an oversimplification.

seems to have been well recognized.[46] Thus, in *Re Schneider*,[47] where the trustees had exercised their discretion bona fide, Warrington J stated:

> ... the trustees were given by the testator an uncontrolled discretion. They have exercised such discretion. It is not alleged that they have done so *mala fide*, and they are, therefore, under no liability for the consequences ... the discretion of the trustees is not capable of review by any tribunal, always supposing that there is no *mala fides* with regard to its exercise.

In fact, no charge of mala fides or want of honesty on the part of the trustees was made. It seems clear, however, that despite being an enlarged discretion, its exercise would have been open to review if such an allegation had been made and proved.

However, apart from this consistent refusal to interfere with or review the exercise **20.11** of an enlarged discretion in the absence of bad faith, no other single consistent principle seems to emerge from these cases. Many of these decisions seem to support a general principle of intervention and review in the case of unenlarged discretions, but this is far from clear, because most (if not all) of them are capable of being explained in other ways. Many of them involved powers of support and maintenance of infant beneficiaries, with which the courts were always particularly concerned.[48] Others involved points of construction. In some instances, the trustees had acted capriciously,[49] or on the basis of manifestly improper reasons.[50] In *Re Chapman*,[51] the trustee's conduct amounted to 'sheer unreasonableness': he had exercised his discretion in the face of known facts and his decision was 'so unreasonable as to be vexatious'.[52] Consequently, such authority as there is to support intervention where trustees have exercised their unenlarged powers and discretions unreasonably may be said not to be particularly strong or extensive.

On the other hand, it is possible to conclude that, where the discretion is not **20.12** enlarged in any way, the authorities are entirely consistent with the general principle that trustees are expected to manifest the reasonable behaviour expected of an ordinary prudent man of business managing the affairs of other people for whom he felt morally bound to provide. Although there is a presumption against a breach of trust, so that there is, in effect, a presumption that a trustee has exercised his powers and discretions in good faith, honestly, and reasonably,[53] many of the cases discussed above suggest, nonetheless, that it is possible to persuade the

---

[46] See, for example, *Re Roper's Trusts* (1879) 11 Ch D 272; *Re Wise* [1896] 1 Ch 281, 286; *Re Chapman* (1895) 72 LT 66, 68 .   [47] (1906) 22 TLR 223, 226.

[48] The court even has an inherent jurisdiction to allow maintenance out of an infant's own property.   [49] *Re Hodges* (1878) 7 Ch D 754; *Tabor v Brooks* (1878) 10 Ch D 273, 277.

[50] *Klug v Klug* [1918] 2 Ch 67; *Re Bell Brothers* (1891) 65 LT 245; *Re Roper's Trusts* (1879) 11 Ch D 272.   [51] (1895) 72 LT 66.

[52] ibid 68.   [53] *Re Gresham Life Assurance Society* (1872) 8 Ch App 446, 449, 450, 452.

court to interfere with any such exercise where it can be shown that the decision taken is not a reasonable one in the circumstances.[54] Many of these cases did, indeed, involve trusts or powers to maintain (which are essentially dispositive powers), but others were concerned with administrative powers.[55] However, there is no indication that the courts explicitly distinguished between different kinds of powers and discretions. In all cases, the focus of the inquiry and the basis of the decision seems to have been the presence or absence of some enlarging words, and not the nature of the power itself. They were concerned in all cases with the same issues, ie the presence or absence of enlarging words, of bad faith, and of good faith and honesty.[56] Indeed, it is suggested that there is no logic in the distinction. If, in the exercise of his powers and discretions, a trustee acts in good faith, the presence of enlarging words will ensure that his decision cannot be questioned or reviewed, not even if the court considers that most reasonable men (or the court itself) would have reached a different conclusion in the same circumstances. Only if the decision is so perverse that it indicates a serious flaw in the decision-making process itself will it be open to interference and review, ie if the effect is that the power or discretion cannot be said to have been exercised at all.

20.13 On the other hand, it is suggested that, if there are no such enlarging words, a more objective standard of reasonableness ought to apply, namely that of the 'prudent man', so that any exercise by a trustee of an unenlarged power or discretion is open to review if it can be shown that the decision taken is one which a reasonable trustee would not have reached in the particular circumstances. This would not render the exercise of any and every unenlarged power or discretion by trustees open to review. In the absence of evidence to the contrary, trustees will be presumed to have acted reasonably and in good faith, and not to have committed a breach of trust. Moreover, there is not necessarily just one view of what is reasonable, not even in the case of the 'prudent man'.

D. Distinction Between the Decision-Making Process and the Merits of the Decision

20.14 In addition to the need to distinguish between enlarged and unenlarged discretions, there is also a crucial distinction that must be drawn between the merits of a decision and the propriety of the process by which it was reached. In this context, the decision of the House of Lords in *Dundee General Hospitals Board of*

---

[54] *Costabadie v Costabadie* (1847) 6 Hare 410; *Re Beloved Wilkes's Charity* (1851) 3 Mac & G 440, 448; *Re Hodges* (1878) 7 Ch D 754; *Re Roper's Trusts* (1879) 11 Ch D 272; *Re Chapman* (1895) 72 LT 66.
[55] See, for example, *Bethell v Abraham* (1873) LR 17 Eq 24. See also *Thomas* 360–361.
[56] *Re Knollys' Trusts* [1912] 2 Ch 357. See also *Martin v Martin* [1919] P 283.

Management v Walker[57] figures prominently. Although its relevance may be open to doubt, in that it actually deals with slightly different issues, it merits separate treatment here. A testator had bequeathed a legacy to the Dundee Royal Infirmary, subject to the proviso that it should be payable 'only if my trustees shall in their sole and absolute discretion be satisfied' that, at the testator's death, the Infirmary had not been taken over, wholly or partly, by or placed under the control of the State or of a local authority. In the circumstances, the trustees decided not to pay the legacy. Their decision was challenged on the ground that, in the circumstances, it was an unreasonable one. There was no allegation of bad faith or dishonesty.[58] It was held that the only reasonable interpretation of the words used by the testator was that he intended the trustees to be the sole judges of all the matters which they had to consider in carrying out the duty which he had put on them. Assuming reasonableness on the part of the trustees to be the test of the validity of their decision,[59] they were entitled to take into consideration the matters they had taken into account; and the conclusion they had reached was such as a reasonable man could have reached.

Whether (and, if so, how far) the decision in *Dundee* is relevant to a discussion of **20.15** the reviewability of the exercise of powers and discretions by trustees is unclear. As Lord Morton emphasized:[60]

> The contingency on which the payment depended was the state of mind of the trustees, not the existence in fact or in law of some objective state of control. Although the word discretion is used, this is not a case of the exercise of a discretion in the true sense of the word, as, for instance, when trustees are given a discretion to pay or not to pay money to a beneficiary or a discretion as to the amount of any such payment. I do not, therefore, derive much assistance from authorities dealing with the exercise by trustees of discretionary powers such as these.

Lords Normand, Morton, and Tucker took a similar view,[61] thus distinguishing *Dundee* from the kind of case considered earlier in this section; and this, combined with the (reluctant) assumption made by the House of Lords that 'reasonableness' was the proper test to be applied to the trustees' decision, clearly casts doubt on the wider relevance and usefulness of *Dundee*. Once it is accepted that 'reasonableness' is the appropriate test, other questions undoubtedly arise, for example as to whether a subjective or an objective standard must be satisfied.[62] However, as we have seen, *Gisborne* and the decisions which followed it make it clear that, in the case of absolute powers and discretions conferred on trustees, the

---

[57] [1952] 1 All ER 896.   [58] ibid 899, 901, 903, 904, 906.
[59] It is clear that several of their lordships doubted whether the reasonableness of the course which the trustees had adopted was the proper test of the validity of their decision, rather than their honesty: see, for example, at 901 *per* Lord Normand, 903 *per* Lord Morton, 906 *per* Lord Tucker.
[60] ibid 906.   [61] At 899, 903, 906.
[62] In *Dundee*, the argument that the relevant test was whether any reasonable man, fairly considering the matter, would have arrived at the result at which the trustees arrived was rejected.

'reasonableness' of their exercise cannot (without more) be questioned, and *Dundee* does not in any way contradict this principle. Nor does it express any conclusion as to the reviewability of decisions taken in exercise of an unenlarged power or discretion.

20.16 In at least two respects, however, the approach adopted by the House of Lords in *Dundee* is entirely consistent with the other authorities considered above. First, the overriding importance of ascertaining the intention of the testator (or settlor) was recognized and affirmed. This point, though obvious, is, nonetheless, fundamental to any explanation of the different results reached in different cases. Here, not only was the discretion absolute, but it was also a discretion as to the trustees' own state of mind.[63] Their duty was one to pay the legacy if they were themselves satisfied that a particular state of affairs had not come about.[64] Secondly, it is clear that the House of Lords would have been prepared to intervene and review the trustees' exercise of their discretion (notwithstanding that it was absolute) if bad faith or dishonesty had been alleged and proved or if it 'involved a trespass beyond the limits of what was committed to them by the testator'.[65] In Lord Reid's words:[66]

> But by making his trustees the sole judges of a question a testator does not entirely exclude recourse to the Court by persons aggrieved by the trustees' decision. If it can be shown that the trustees considered the wrong question, or that, although they purported to consider the right question they did not really apply their minds to it or perversely shut their eyes to the facts or that they did not act honestly or in good faith, then there was no true decision and the Court will intervene, but nothing of that kind is alleged in this case.

These observations[67] were clearly not intended to be confined to the peculiar discretion in question in *Dundee*, and were directed more generally at any discretion conferred on a trustee; and, although they are strictly obiter, it is suggested that they provide a useful and accurate summary of the principles applicable to all such powers and discretions, including those which are enlarged and declared to be absolute.

---

[63] As Lord Normand put it (at 899): 'The right to receive the legacy was contingent on the trustees' state of mind, the absence of a state of doubt.' He also suggested that 'if a state of doubt was brought about by one circumstance which cannot successfully be assailed, it does not matter that the doubt was increased or confirmed by other circumstances which the trustees might not be entitled . . . to take into account'. Cf *Harris v Lord Shuttleworth* [1994] ICR 991, [1995] OPLR 79.

[64] [1952] 1 All ER 896, 904, *per* Lord Reid. See also at 901, *per* Lord Normand: 'One may usefully reflect that reasonable people often differ about what is reasonable, and it may be that the testator inserted the words "in their sole and absolute discretion" in order to exclude from the purview of the courts the kind of questions which have occupied so large a part of the time given to this appeal.'

[65] ibid 901, *per* Lord Normand.   [66] ibid 904.

[67] Similar statements were made by Lord Normand (901), Lord Morton (903) and Lord Tucker (906).

The crucial distinction here is that between the decision-making process by which **20.17** a particular decision or conclusion is reached and the merits or correctness of that decision or conclusion itself. Even if the actual decision or conclusion reached in exercise of an enlarged discretion cannot be challenged on its merits, it may still be possible to challenge the decision-making process itself. Such a challenge may be based on an allegation of bad faith, or on a failure by the donee of the discretion to exercise an active discretion or to give real and genuine consideration to the exercise,[68] or, indeed, on a breach of any of the duties owed by the donee and discussed earlier.[69] This is illustrated by *Karger v Paul*,[70] where the power conferred on the trustees was exercisable 'in their absolute and unfettered discretion', and where the exercise of that power was challenged on two grounds: first, that the trustees had not acted honestly and in good faith; and, secondly, that they had acted without any fair and proper consideration as to whether they should do so. McGarvie J (in the Supreme Court of Victoria) pointed out[71] that there were two legal issues: first, as to the grounds on which the exercise by the trustees of the power conferred on them might be examined and reviewed; secondly, whether it was relevant to consider the state of mind of the trustees at the time they decided to exercise the power. He held[72] that, where the power was absolute and unfettered, the exercise by the trustees of their discretion will not be examined or reviewed by the courts 'so long as the essential component parts of the exercise of the particular discretion are present. Those essential component parts are present if the discretion is exercised by the trustees in good faith,[73] upon real and genuine consideration and in accordance with the purposes for which the discretion was conferred.' He went on:[74]

> . . . it is open to the Court to examine the evidence to decide *whether there has been a failure by the trustees to exercise the discretion in good faith, upon real and genuine consideration and in accordance with the purposes for which the discretion was conferred.* As part of the process of, and solely for the purpose of, ascertaining whether there has been any such failure, it is relevant to look at evidence of the inquiries which were made by the trustees, the information they had and the reasons for, and manner of, their exercising their discretion. However, it is not open to the Court to look at those things for the independent purpose of impugning the exercise of discretion on the grounds that their inquiries, information or reasons or the manner of exercise of the discretion, fell short of what was appropriate and sufficient. Nor is it open to the

---

[68] *Re Beloved Wilkes's Charity* (1851) 3 Mac & G 440; *Partridge v The Equity Trustees Executors and Agency Co Ltd* (1947) 75 CLR 149, 164.

[69] See Chapter 11.   [70] [1984] VR 161.   [71] ibid 163.

[72] ibid 163–164.

[73] He indicated that the test of acting honestly is the same as the test of acting in good faith (referring to *R v Holl* (1881) 7 QBD 575, 580–581, *per* Bramwell LJ). It was argued for the plaintiff that gross negligence may of itself amount to an absence of good faith, but McGarvie J did not agree. Honest blundering or carelessness did not of themselves amount to bad faith: *Jones v Gordon* (1877) 2 AC 616, 628–629. See also *Walker v Stones* [2001] QB 902.

[74] [1984] VR 161, 164 (emphasis added).

Court to look at the factual situation established by the evidence, for the independent purpose of impugning the exercise of the discretion on the grounds the trustees were wrong in their appreciation of the facts or made an unwise or unjustified exercise of discretion in the circumstances. *The issues which are examinable by the Court are limited to whether there has been a failure to exercise the discretion in good faith, upon real and genuine consideration and in accordance with the purposes for which the discretion was conferred. In short, the Court examines whether the discretion was exercised but does not examine how it was exercised.*

Thus, the decision-making process may be examined and reviewed in order to ascertain whether the relevant discretion can be said to have been exercised properly or at all; and, if there is a fundamental flaw in the process by which the trustees arrived at a particular decision, they have not, in substance, exercised that power or discretion at all. Similar well-recognized principles operate in public law.[75]

20.18 It may be possible, of course, that the decision actually taken, or the purpose which it is sought to advance, is patently so absurd that, under the circumstances, it indicates some material flaw in the decision-making process itself;[76] or that the circumstances are such that some explanation is clearly called for and the refusal of the trustees to provide one lends support to an inference of a breach of trust.[77] However, provided there is no such flaw nor such circumstances the merits of the decision actually taken by trustees cannot be interfered with or reviewed.

E. Pension Scheme Trusts

20.19 The courts have applied a similar approach in relation to pension scheme trusts. Thus, in *Harris v Lord Shuttleworth*,[78] Glidewell LJ summarized the principles applicable in that case by saying that trustees must ask themselves the correct questions; they must direct themselves correctly in law; in particular, they must adopt a correct construction of the pension scheme rules; they must not arrive at a perverse decision, ie a decision at which no reasonable body of trustees could arrive; and they must take into account all relevant, but no irrelevant, facts. There is no reason why the same principles should not govern the exercise of fiduciary powers and discretions generally. Clearly, their application must take account of, and will vary in effect according to, the particular context. The judicial review of the actions and decision of public bodies involves considerations,

---

[75] See De Smith, *Judicial Review of Administrative Action* (5th edn 1995) 285–286.

[76] *Errington v Metropolitan District Railway Co* (1882) 19 Ch D 559, 571, *per* Jessel MR.

[77] *Taylor v Midland Bank Trust Co Ltd* [2002] WTLR 95. An example might be the case where a legitimate expectation of a beneficiary is unexpectedly defeated: *Scott v National Trust* [1998] 1 WLR 226.

[78] [1994] ICR 989, 999. See also *Wild v Smith* [1996] PLR 275, 280; *Lee v Showmen's Guild of Great Britain* [1952] 2 QB 329, 344.

and is subject to safeguards, which do not apply to pension schemes and certainly not to private family trusts, such as the obvious public interest in the outcome and also the need for leave of the court to make an application for review. There are also obvious differences between pension schemes and family trusts, not least in the 'commercial' origins of the former and the dominating element of 'bounty' in the latter. Nevertheless, the underlying principle of review remains common to all cases, as was confirmed in *Wilson v The Law Debenture Trust Corporation plc*.[79] Unless there is evidence of some flaw in the decision-making process itself that may render it open to challenge, trustees are not bound to disclose the reasons for their decision and the merits of the decision itself cannot be investigated or challenged.

However, the Pensions Ombudsman, who is empowered by section 146 of the **20.20** Pension Schemes Act 1993 to provide a remedy for 'maladministration', seems to have gone much further than the courts have been prepared to go. In various determinations,[80] the Pensions Ombudsman has held that trustees who refused to disclose the reasons for their decisions were guilty of maladministration and liable accordingly. These determinations are unsatisfactory for a number of reasons. They do not always have sufficient (if any) regard to the requirement in section 164 of the 1993 Act that 'injustice' must have been sustained in consequence of the maladministration; they often equate 'injustice' with distress or mere disappointment,[81] which clearly seems to be incorrect,[82] or with a failure to advise a scheme member on his entitlements, which is not a duty of scheme trustees and therefore also an incorrect basis for a determination;[83] and they frequently (and often explicitly) do not distinguish between maladministration and disputes of fact or of law. Above all, in so far as these determinations deal with the question of disclosure of reasons for the exercise of a discretion (and it is not clear that many of them purport to do so directly),[84] they would seem to be inconsistent with *Wilson* and may therefore be overturned in due course by the High Court. Nevertheless, for the present, they represent a gradual whittling away, in the context of pensions trusts at least, of the protection hitherto accorded to trustees in the exercise of their discretions.

---

[79] [1995] 2 All ER 337. See also para 12.10 above.
[80] See, for example, *Allen v TKM Group* [2002] PLR 333; and determinations Nos M00006 (*Mrs K Holding*), 26 August 2003; M00450, 27 August 2003. See also paras 44.41–44.44 below.
[81] See, for example, determination No M00450, 27 August, 2003.
[82] *NHS Pensions Agency v Pensions Ombudsman* (1996) OPLR 119.
[83] See, for example, determination No M00251, 5 June 2003; *NHS Pensions v Beechinor* [1997] OPLR 99; *Outram v Academy Plastics* [2000] PLR 283; *University of Nottingham v Eyett* [1999] I WLR 594.
[84] See, for example, the quotation in para 44.44 below, which is one illustration of the sheer confusion of several distinct principles of review.

F. Judicial Review Where Reasons Are Actually Given

20.21 It is often said that, where reasons are actually provided by the trustees for the exercise of their discretion (irrespective of the kind of trust), their decisions may then be open to review, and the correctness of those reasons may be considered by the court. In *Re Londonderry's Settlement*,[85] for example, Harman LJ, having reaffirmed the general principle that 'trustees exercising a discretionary power are not bound to disclose to their beneficiaries the reasons actuating them in coming to a decision', added a rider, 'namely, that if trustees do give reasons, their soundness can be considered by the Court'. However, no authority was cited in support of this proposition. Reference was made to the observations of James LJ in *Re Gresham Life Assurance Society*[86] on the analogous position of directors, but there is nothing in those observations to suggest that the merits of a decision reached by trustees (or directors) can be questioned or reviewed, even where reasons have been made known. Indeed, it seems clear that James LJ was referring to a case where there was an allegation of improper motive, arbitrariness, or capriciousness (ie some material flaw in the decision-making process itself); and, it is suggested, that this is what Harman LJ had in mind when he referred to the 'soundness' of trustees' decisions. Similarly, in *Re Bell Bros Ltd*,[87] Chitty J clearly took the view that, if directors disclosed their reasons for acting, the court could then consider those reasons, but only in order to ascertain whether the decision-making process itself was flawed: '... the Court must consider the reasons assigned *with a view to ascertain whether they are legitimate or not; or, in other words, to ascertain whether the directors have proceeded on a right or a wrong principle*'.

20.22 There seems to be no English decision holding directly that the exercise of a discretion may be reviewed by the court where trustees have made known their reasons; and various general dicta[88] sometimes referred to as lending support to a right to interfere in such circumstances are actually directed at the validity of the decision-making process itself.[89] Indeed, a conclusion that trustees are at greater risk of having their decisions reviewed if they voluntarily disclose their reasons, than if they remain secretive, is as absurd as the view that a beneficiary is entitled to see that which is reduced into writing but not that which is not. The true position, it is

---

[85] [1965] Ch 918, 928–929.   [86] (1872) 8 Ch App 446, 449, 450.

[87] (1891) 65 LT 245, 246 (emphasis added).

[88] See, for example, *Re Beloved Wilkes's Charity* (1851) 3 Mac & G 440, 447; *Tempest v Lord Camoys* (1882) 21 Ch D 571, 580.

[89] The remarks of the Pensions Ombudsman, in *Re National Bus Company* [1997] PLR 1, 22, must also be read in this light. In the Australian case of *Karger v Paul* [1984] VR 161, 164, McGarvie J seems to have adopted a wider view: 'The exception is that the validity of the trustees' reasons will be examined and reviewed if the trustees choose to state their reasons for their exercise of discretion.'

suggested, is summarized by Lord Normand in *Dundee General Hospitals Board v Walker*:[90]

> It was said for the appellants that the Courts have greater liberty to examine and correct a decision committed by a testator to his trustees, if they choose to give reasons, than if they do not. In my opinion, that is erroneous. The principles on which the Courts must proceed are the same whether the reasons for the trustees' decision are disclosed or not, but, of course, it becomes easier to examine a decision if the reasons for it have been disclosed. Lord Truro's judgment in *Re Wilkes's (Beloved) Charity* ought not to be construed as going beyond that.

The basic principle is that the giving of reasons is not required because (*inter alia*) the merits of a decision taken in the exercise of a discretion cannot be reviewed. It is not that such merits cannot be reviewed because the giving of reasons for the decision is not required. Actual knowledge of reasons should not, therefore, affect the issue.

G. Future Developments

As we have seen,[91] in the recent case of *Schmidt v Rosewood Trust Ltd*,[92] the Privy Council reviewed the law on the subject of a trustee's duty to disclose information and held that a beneficiary's right to seek disclosure of trust documents was best approached as one aspect of the court's inherent jurisdiction to supervise and, if appropriate, intervene in the administration of a trust, including a discretionary trust. Lord Walker pointed out[93] that **20.23**

> no beneficiary (and least of all a discretionary object) has any entitlement as of right to disclosure of anything which can plausibly be described as a trust document. Especially when there are issues as to personal or commercial confidentiality, the court may have to balance the competing interests of different beneficiaries, the trustees themselves, and third parties. Disclosure may have to be limited and safeguards may have to be put in place.

Disclosure of information is, therefore, within the discretion of the court.

One important, and hitherto unanswered, question in the present context is whether *Rosewood* will (or was intended to) have any effect at all on the law relating to the disclosure by trustees of the reasons for the exercise of their discretions. It has already been pointed out[94] that no such claim for disclosure was made in *Rosewood*. Both the original application and appeal were concerned with obtaining trust accounts and other information about the trust assets. It is clear that, after *Rosewood* (and on the assumption that it is adopted in English law), objects of discretionary trusts and of fiduciary powers will have rights to seek and, at the **20.24**

---

[90] [1952] 1 All ER 896, 900.   [91] See paras 12.14–12.19 above.
[92] [2003] 2 WLR 1442.   [93] ibid 1463–1464.   [94] See para 12.19 above.

discretion of the court, to obtain disclosure of such 'trust information' as was formerly disclosable to a beneficiary with a recognizable proprietary interest in the trust fund. It also seems to have been decided (by implication rather than explicitly)[95] that potentially disclosable 'trust information' is not confined to that which is in documentary form. However, it is not at all clear that *Rosewood* has (or was intended to have) any effect at all on the question of *what* is disclosable: it does not purport to define 'trust information' or even extend the range of what has hitherto been regarded as constituting disclosable 'trust information'. Lord Walker referred to 'issues as to personal or commercial confidentiality',[96] but there is no reason to assume that he intended to include the reasons of trustees for the exercise of their discretions. There is no compelling reason to conclude that *Rosewood* has any effect at all on what was said in *Re Londonderry* on this crucial issue or that it sought to restrict the protection afforded to trustees in the exercise of their dispositive discretions.

20.25 Clearly, no one could seriously suggest that the legitimate interests and expectations of beneficiaries should not be safeguarded. However, it is already the case that no discretion conferred on trustees is truly 'absolute': the law already requires trustees to exercise their discretions honestly and in good faith, and not improperly, excessively, fraudulently, arbitrarily, or capriciously; and the decision-making process itself is subject to numerous requirements. It must also be acknowledged that the discretion has been conferred on the trustees and not on the court, and also, presumably, that it is open to a settlor to declare that such discretion is 'uncontrollable' (as is usually the case in modern trust instruments). In exercising their own individual judgement, the trustees are entitled to expect protection against the claims of disappointed beneficiaries. A balance must be struck between the interests of the beneficiaries and those of the trustees; and *Rosewood* and some of the more recent pension trusts cases may represent the beginnings of a movement towards redressing that balance in favour of beneficiaries and objects.

20.26 As Kirby P pointed out in his dissenting judgment in *Hartigan Nominees Pty Ltd v Rydge*,[97] the requirement that a beneficiary should have to show misconduct or wrongdoing on the part of a trustee in order to obtain access to what would otherwise be confidential information imposed 'an unreasonably high barrier to the effective supervision by the court of the actions of trustees'. It was true that

---

[95] Although there are random references to 'documents or information' (eg, ibid 1458C and 1459H) and the like, the focus of the analysis is overwhelmingly on 'trust documents' (see, eg, 1458–1459).

[96] ibid 1463G. The astonishingly brief references (at 1457–1458 and 1459) to *Re Londonderry's Settlement* [1965] Ch 918 seem to be part of the analysis of the basis (proprietary or otherwise) on which a claim for disclosure of trust information might be made. Lord Walker did not (and did not need to) conclude that, once a non-proprietary basis for the claim was accepted, 'confidentiality in communications between trustees as to their exercise of their dispositive discretions' might then be potentially disclosable too. [97] (1992) 29 NSWLR 405, 419–422.

'in some cases hurt, embarrassment and general consternation will accompany the disclosure of documents', but against this must be balanced 'the suspicion which will attend a refusal to give access to a document of great importance to the determination of the financial and other benefits received by the beneficiaries' (a memorandum of wishes in that case). As for the consequences of non-disclosure:

> In the place of knowledge there will be rumour. In the place of a critical examination of the words of the benefactor, there will be opinions resting upon reported benefits received by members of the family who disclose such benefits. In the place of an opportunity to offer comments about disputed assertions of fact, there may be blind acceptance by the trustees of what may be completely unjustified assertions and opinions expressed by the settlor (or instigator). Better decisions are generally made by those who have the relevant information before them . . . The rule of secrecy which the trustees urge is one which may effectively deny the trustees access to relevant information.

Moreover the trustees did not have to fear 'undue harassment' by beneficiaries. As long as they exercised their discretion honestly and without malice, the court would protect them and would refuse to supervise the merits of their decisions. Indeed, the court could punish such 'harassment' by appropriate orders for costs.

On the other hand, in *Crowe v Stevedoring Employees Retirement Fund*[98] (a **20.27** post-*Rosewood* decision[99]) the Supreme Court of Victoria confirmed that *Re Londonderry's Settlement* should be followed in Australia and that it also applied to a superannuation scheme. The question of disclosure of confidential information by trustees was held to be governed by the majority decision in *Hartigan Nominees v Rydge*. In particular, in *Hartigan*, Sheller JA indicated that actuarial reports obtained by the trustees were probably not documents which evidenced the reasons why the trustees had made their decisions, any more than trust accounts or opinions from counsel or, indeed, any other material obtained by the trustees to assist them in administering the trust. However, there was restricted access to documents which are of a class which would or might reveal the reasoning process of the trustees.[100] Material 'upon which reasons were or might have been based cannot generally be withheld, unless it reveals the reasoning process'.[101] The trustees' right not to disclose their reasons for exercising discretionary powers or their 'reasoning process' should be preserved, but the class of documents to which beneficiaries are denied access should not be extended beyond this exceptional category. It is clear from *Crowe* that, in Victoria at least, this position remains the same and has not been affected by *Rosewood*.

---

[98] [2003] PLR 343.   [99] See paras 12.14–12.19 above.
[100] (1992) 29 NSWLR 405, 446. See also paras 12.06 and 12.11 above.
[101] ibid 445, referring to *Jacobs' Law of Trusts in Australia* (5th edn, 1986) para 1716, at p 393.

20.28 Thus, it remains to be seen whether in English law, and if so how, *Rosewood* has affected the principle that trustees are not obliged to disclose confidential information, and especially their reasons for exercising a discretion in a particular way. In any event, in view of the abundant forms of protection afforded to trustees in modern trust instruments and by the general law, there is a strong argument, *Rosewood* apart, for requiring trustees to disclose the reasons for the exercise of a discretion (including, where appropriate, a memorandum of wishes), but to maintain the established principle that their actual decision cannot be challenged unless those reasons disclose some manifest error or impropriety in the decision-making process itself or a failure to satisfy one of the orthodox and long-established standards required by law. This would subject trustees to greater scrutiny but would not necessarily subject them to greater duties than the law already requires of them (apart from the need to make such disclosure).

21

RIGHTS OF TRUSTEES

A. Right to Remuneration

As we have seen,[1] a trustee holds office voluntarily and is required to perform his **21.01** duties gratuitously.[2] This is merely one aspect of the trustee's duty of loyalty and his duties not to place himself in a position where his fiduciary duty and his self-interest come into conflict and not to profit from his trust. However, it is invariably the case that trustees can claim remuneration for their services, either under an express provision in the trust instrument or under statute. It therefore seems more appropriate to deal with this aspect of trusteeship as a right of the trustee rather than a negative duty.

---

[1] See paras 10.119–10.120 above.
[2] *Re Barber* (1886) 34 Ch D 77; *Dale v IRC* [1954] AC 11, 27.

Express remuneration clauses

21.02 The most common exception to the rule is the long-standing practice of including express remuneration provisions in trust instruments. Such provisions are not contracts between settlor and trustee: prior to the Trustee Act 2000, they were regarded as just one of the beneficial dispositions effected by the trust.[3] Consequently, where such a provision is in a will which was witnessed by the trustee, section 15 of the Wills Act 1837 applied and the trustee lost the benefit;[4] it abated along with other legacies if the estate was insufficient,[5] and creditors of the estate had priority.[6] Remuneration may also be conditional on the trustee discharging the duties required.[7]

21.03 Such express provisions will be strictly construed.[8]

Trustee Act 2000

21.04 Part V of the Trustee Act 2000 has now introduced new provisions providing for the 'reasonable remuneration' of professional trustees and trust corporations.[9] Sections 28 and 29 of the 2000 Act are as follows:

> 28 (1) Except to the extent (if any) to which the trust instrument makes inconsistent provision, subsections (2) to (4) apply to a trustee if—
>
> > (a) there is a provision in the trust instrument entitling him to receive payment out of trust funds in respect of services provided by him to or on behalf of the trust, and
> > (b) the trustee is a trust corporation or is acting in a professional capacity.
>
> (2) The trustee is to be treated as entitled under the trust instrument to receive payment in respect of services even if they are services which are capable of being provided by a lay trustee.
>
> (3) Subsection (2) applies to a trustee of a charitable trust who is not a trust corporation only—

---

[3] *Re Duke of Norfolk's Settlement Trusts* [1982] Ch 61. They are not regarded as ousting the jurisdiction of the court: *Will of Shannon* (1977) 1 NSWLR 210.

[4] *Re Pooley* (1888) 40 Ch D 1.

[5] *Re Thorley* [1891] 2 Ch 613; *Re Brown* [1918] WN 118; *Re Dunne* [1934] VLR 307; *SCD (NSW) v Pearse* (1953) 89 CLR 51. A charging clause could still operate in favour of a solicitor who had attested the will but was not appointed a trustee until after death: *Re Royce's Will Trusts* [1959] Ch 626.

[6] *Re White* [1898] 2 Ch 217; *Re Salmen* (1912) 107 LT 108; *Re Duke of Norfolk, supra.* The court may apparently provide otherwise under its inherent jurisdiction: *Re Worthington* [1954] 1 WLR 526, 530.

[7] *Re McCutcheon* [1941] VLR 174. Cf *Winter-Irving v Winter* [1907] VLR 546; *Will of Steele* (1915) 15 SR (NSW) 247.

[8] *Re Chalinder & Herington* [1907] 1 Ch 58; *Re Gee* [1948] Ch 284.

[9] Sections 28 and 29 also apply to personal representatives acting professionally: s 35. Section 29 does not apply to charitable trustees (for which see s 30); s 28 applies to the professional trustee of a charitable trust if he is not the sole trustee (it also does not apply to a trust corporation): s 28(3).

(a) if he is not a sole trustee, and

(b) to the extent that a majority of the other trustees have agreed that it should apply to him.

(4) Any payments to which the trustee is entitled in respect of services are to be treated as remuneration for services (and not as a gift) for the purposes of—

(a) section 15 of the Wills Act 1837 (gifts to an attesting witness to be void), and

(b) section 34(3) of the Administration of Estates Act 1925 (order in which estate to be paid out).

(5) For the purposes of this Part, a trustee acts in a professional capacity if he acts in the course of a profession or business which consists of or includes the provision of services in connection with—

(a) the management or administration of trusts generally or a particular kind of trust, or

(b) any particular aspect of the management or administration of trusts generally or a particular kind of trust,

and the services he provides to or on behalf of the trust fall within that description.

(6) For the purposes of this Part, a person acts as a lay trustee if he—

(a) is not a trust corporation, and

(b) does not act in a professional capacity.

29 (1) Subject to subsection (5), a trustee who—

(a) is a trust corporation, but

(b) is not a trustee of a charitable trust,

is entitled to receive reasonable remuneration out of the trust funds for any services that the trust corporation provides to or on behalf of the trust.

(2) Subject to subsection (5), a trustee who—

(a) acts in a professional capacity, but

(b) is not a trust corporation, a trustee of a charitable trust or a sole trustee,

is entitled to receive reasonable remuneration out of the trust funds for any services that he provides to or on behalf of the trust if each other trustee has agreed in writing that he may be remunerated for the services.

(3) 'Reasonable remuneration' means, in relation to the provision of services by a trustee, such remuneration as is reasonable in the circumstances for the provision of those services to or on behalf of that trust by that trustee and for the purposes of subsection (1) includes, in relation to the provision of services by a trustee who is an authorised institution under the Banking Act 1987 and provides the services in that capacity, the institution's reasonable charges for the provision of such services.

(4) A trustee is entitled to remuneration under this section even if the services in question are capable of being provided by a lay trustee.

(5) A trustee is not entitled to remuneration under this section if any provision about his entitlement to remuneration has been made—

    (a) by the trust instrument, or

    (b) by any enactment or any provision of subordinate legislation.

(6) This section applies to a trustee who has been authorised under a power conferred by Part IV or the trust instrument—

    (a) to exercise functions as an agent of the trustees, or

    (b) to act as a nominee or custodian,

as it applies to any other trustee.

21.05 Such remuneration is payable out of the 'trust funds', which are defined as both the income or capital funds of the trust,[10] but there is no regulation or guidance as to how it is to be paid. Pre-2000 Act authorities therefore still apply and remuneration may be paid out of the income of part only of the trust fund,[11] out of capital under the exercise of a power of appointment,[12] or by some other, more unusual means.[13] Sections 28 and 29 are also subject to any express provision in the trust instrument, so that, for example, a professional trustee may be able to charge only for services of a professional nature.[14]

Remuneration under other statutes

21.06 The Public Trustee is authorized by statute to charge fees as may be fixed by the Treasury for its services,[15] as are persons appointed to be Judicial Trustees.[16] Corporations which act as custodian trustees (they cannot also be a managing trustee) are also authorized to charge such fees as the Public Trustee could charge for acting as custodian trustee.[17] If the court appoints a corporation to be a trustee, either solely or jointly with another person, the court may authorize the corporation to charge such remuneration for its services as trustee as the court may think fit.[18]

The court's inherent jurisdiction

21.07 The court has an inherent jurisdiction to authorize the remuneration (or additional remuneration) of a trustee. This applies to express, resulting, and constructive

---

[10] Trustee Act 2000, s 39(1).
[11] *Public Trustee v IRC* [1960] AC 398. See also (1988) 2 Trust Law & Practice 93 (J Thurston).
[12] *Re Beatty's Will Trusts* [1990] 1 WLR 1503.
[13] *Space Investments Ltd v Canadian Imperial Bank of Commerce Trust Co (Bahamas) Ltd* [1986] 1 WLR 1072 (trustee bank could deposit money with itself and use for its own purposes).
[14] cf *Re Hobson* (1899) 25 VLR 370; *R v Smillie* [1956] NZLR 269.
[15] Public Trustee Act, s 9; Public Trustee (Fees) Act 1957.
[16] Judicial Trustees Act 1896, s 1.   [17] Public Trustee Act 1906, s 4.
[18] Trustee Act 1925, s 42.

trustees; and it extends to prospective as well as retrospective remuneration.[19] It is a jurisdiction which 'should be exercised only sparingly and in exceptional cases',[20] so as not to disturb the arrangement voluntarily entered into by the trustee and not to burden the trust fund unduly. Consequently, the jurisdiction will be exercised, for example, only where the trustee has undertaken exceptionally burdensome work which was not foreseen when the trust was created or which has brought unexpected benefits to the beneficiaries,[21] or where the original provision for remuneration has been seriously undermined by inflation.[22] The jurisdiction was described in the Court of Appeal in *Re Duke of Norfolk's Settlement Trusts*:[23]

> In exercising that jurisdiction the court has to balance two influences which are to some extent in conflict. The first is that the office of trustee is, as such, gratuitous; the court will accordingly be careful to protect the interests of the beneficiaries against claims by the trustees. The second is that it is of great importance to the beneficiaries that the trust should be well administered. If, therefore, the court concludes, having regard to the nature of the trust, to the experience and skill of a trustee and to the amounts which he seeks to charge when compared with what other trustees might require to be paid for their services and to all the other circumstances of the case, that it would be in the best interests of the beneficiaries to increase the remuneration, then the court may properly do so.

Remuneration may even be authorized where the trustee (or other fiduciary) has **21.08** committed an innocent breach of trust (and provided there are exceptional circumstances of the kind described above).[24] The justice of each individual case must be considered on its facts: 'a hard and fast rule that the beneficiary can demand the whole profit without an allowance for the work without which it could not have been created is unduly severe'; and the principle is not confined to cases 'where the personal conduct of the fiduciary cannot be criticised'.[25] It has been said that the jurisdiction will not be exercised where it has 'the effect of encouraging trustees in any way to put themselves in a position where their interests conflict with their duties as trustees'.[26] This has subsequently been said to be too strict and that,

---

[19] *Foster v Spencer* [1996] 2 All ER 672; *Sargeant v National Westminster Bank* (1990) 61 P & CR 518; *Re Drexel Burnham Lambert's Pension Plan* [1995] 1 WLR 32. See also *Re Keeler's Settlement Trusts* [1981] Ch 156; *Re Llewellin's Will Trust* [1949] Ch 225.

[20] *Re Worthington* [1954] 1 WLR 526; *Re Duke of Norfolk's Settlement Trusts* [1982] Ch 61; *Re Masters* [1953] 1 WLR 81; *Re Freeman* (1887) 37 Ch D 148; *Marshall v Holloway* (1820) 2 Swan 431.

[21] *Boardman v Phipps* [1967] 2 AC 46; *Re Duke of Norfolk's Settlement Trusts, supra*; *John v James* [1986] STC 352, 358.

[22] *Re Barbour's Settlement* [1974] 1 All ER 1188, 1192.

[23] [1982] Ch 61, 79.

[24] *Boardman v Phipps* [1967] 2 AC 46.

[25] *O'Sullivan v Management Agency and Music Ltd* [1985] QB 428, 468; *Re Berkeley Applegate Ltd* [1988] 3 All ER 71, 83; *Cheese v Thomas* [1994] 1 All ER 35, 43.

[26] *Guinness plc v Saunders* [1990] 2 AC 663, 701, *per* Lord Goff.

although the question of conflict of interest is an important consideration, it is but one factor in the equation.[27]

Contract with the beneficiaries

21.09 A trustee may contract for remuneration with the agreement of the beneficiaries if they are of full age and capacity and between them absolutely entitled to the trust property, and provided the agreement was not procured through undue influence.[28] It is also possible for a trustee to contract with one beneficiary (or some of them) only for reimbursement out of his or her (or their) particular interest, for example for payment out of a life tenant's income. It is unclear whether the agreement has to be in place before the trustee accepts office: once he has become trustee, he has assumed his duties for no payment and there is no consideration for the agreement.[29] However, this must be doubtful: his assumption of trusteeship under the trust and any contract with a beneficiary are entirely separate transactions; a trustee can always retire and the consideration is his agreement to continue acting as trustee.

B. Right to Reimbursement and Indemnity[30]

Introduction

21.10 A trustee's liabilities can take many different forms: he may be liable simply as property owner; he may incur liability when entering into contracts with third parties, or as a result of his tortious acts or omissions, and so on. The trustee, unlike an agent, incurs personal liability to third parties: in effect, he acts as principal in matters connected with the trust. Neither the settlor nor the beneficiaries will be liable, save in exceptional circumstances, such as where the trustee has also been appointed an agent for them.[31] Historically, the trustee would have been sued in tort or contract at common law, which, of course, did not recognize his peculiar status. His personal liability could, therefore, be unlimited, just like any other individual, for example, if he carries on a trade or business, he is regarded as doing so on his own account and will be liable to trade creditors accordingly.[32] He

---

[27] *Badfinger Music v Evans* [2001] 1 WTLR 1; *University of Nottingham v Fisher* [2000] ICR 1462. Lord Goff's statement seems to have been taken out of context and is still likely to be of considerable importance in relation to trustees.

[28] *Ayliffe v Murray* (1740) 2 Atk 58.

[29] *Re Sherwood* (1840) 3 Beav 338; *Douglas v Archbutt* (1858) 2 De G & J 148.

[30] J Mowbray et al, *Lewin on Trusts* (17th edn, Sweet & Maxwell, 2000) ('*Lewin*') para 21-01; A Underhill and DJ Hayton, *Law of Trusts and Trustees* (16th edn, Butterworths, 2002) ('*Underhill and Hayton*') 810–826.

[31] *Fraser v Murdoch* (1881) 6 App Cas 855, 872–873.

[32] *Wightman v Townroe* (1813) 1 M & S 412. See also *Re Phoenix Life Assurance Co* (1862) 2 J & H 229.

may have a right to recoup, out of the trust fund, expenses which he has properly incurred and to be indemnified in respect of any liability. However, his liability is not limited to the amount or value of the trust assets: he remains personally liable for the difference.

Statutory indemnity

It has long been the case that a trustee is entitled to be indemnified out of the trust **21.11** property in respect of liabilities, costs, and expenses properly incurred by him in connection with the performance of his duties and in the exercise of his powers as trustee.[33] 'Persons who take the onerous and sometimes dangerous duty of being trustees are not expected to do any of the work on their expense.'[34] This general rule has now been given statutory force by section 31(1) of the Trustee Act 2000, which provides that a trustee is entitled to be reimbursed from the trust funds or may pay out of the trust funds expenses properly incurred by him when acting on behalf of the trust.[35]

Routine reimbursement outside litigation

The costs of appointing a new trustee, including the costs of the new trustee in **21.12** investigating the state of the trust property and matters connected with the trust, are payable out of and may be recovered from the trust fund.[36] The costs of former trustees which were paid to their personal representatives in order to get them to transfer the trust property have been recovered by a new trustee.[37] A trustee is entitled to be reimbursed his travelling expenses, if properly incurred;[38] the expenses incurred in connection with the employment of agents;[39] and costs paid to a solicitor for services rendered to the trust.[40] The right exists not only in respect of debts already paid, but also a liability to make payment.[41] If a trustee of a life

---

[33] Law of Property Amendment Act 1859, s 31; Trustee Act 1893, s 24; Trustee Act 1925, s 30(2). See also *Re Earl of Winchilsea's Policy Trusts* (1888) 39 Ch D 168; *Holding and Management Ltd v Property Holding and Investment Trust plc* [1989] 1 WLR 1313. Even before statute intervened, this was the case: see *Worrall v Harford* (1802) 8 Ves 4, 8; *A-G v Mayor of Norwich* (1837) 2 Myl & Cr 406; *Re German Mining Co* (1854) 4 De GM & G 19.

[34] *Re Grimthorpe* [1958] Ch 615, 623, *per* Danckwerts J.

[35] This entitlement is extended to a trustee who acts as agent for the trustees or as nominee or custodian: s 31(2).

[36] *Re Pumfrey* (1882) 22 Ch D 255; *De Vigier v IRC* [1964] 2 All ER 907.

[37] *Harvey v Olliver* (1887) 57 LT 239.

[38] *Malcolm v O'Callaghan* (1837) 3 Myl & Cr 52.

[39] Trustee Act 2000, s 11. See also paras 15.06 and 15.30 above.

[40] *Macnamara v Jones* (1784) 2 Dick 587; *Smith v Dale* (1881) 18 Ch D 516; *McEwan v Crombie* (1883) 25 Ch D 175. A beneficiary may ask the court for an order to tax the costs of the solicitor: Solicitors Act 1974, s 71(3). Even if not taxed, the bill may be moderated: see *Re Park* (1888–89) 41 Ch D 326; *Goodchild v Roberts* [1925] Ch 592; *Warter v Anderson* (1853) 11 Hare 301; *Johnson v Telford* (1827) 3 Russ 477.

[41] *Re Exhall Coal Co Ltd* (1866) 35 Beav 449, 453; *St Thomas's Hospital v Richardson* [1910] 1 KB 271, 276; *Re Suco Gold Pty Ltd* (1983) 33 SASR 99.

insurance policy pays the premium on the policy for its preservation, he is entitled to be indemnified out of the policy proceeds,[42] unless his failure to pay from other available sources was improper.[43] Where a trustee has properly paid calls on shares, he is entitled to be reimbursed.[44] The right arises when the liability is incurred and it is not merely hypothetical.[45] A trustee may also recover the costs incurred in cleaning up contaminated trust land, and for this purpose may even retain trust assets after the beneficiaries have become absolutely entitled to the trust property.[46]

Liability to third parties in contract

21.13 A trustee who enters into a contract with a third party will be subject to a personal liability, just like an ordinary individual, and that liability is potentially unlimited.[47] The trust, unlike a corporation, is not a legal entity. It is possible for the trustee and the other contracting party to agree expressly that the trustee shall not be personally liable, or that his liability shall be limited to a specified amount, or that the other shall look only to the trust assets for payment.[48] However, this is unlikely to be the case in practice. It is not enough for the trustee simply to describe himself as a trustee: there must be evidence that the parties jointly agreed that his liability would be limited.[49] If such an agreement was reached, this does not make the creditor a secured creditor and the trustee would not be taken to have charged the debt on the trust fund.[50]

21.14 As between the trustee and the trust, he is entitled to an indemnity out of the trust fund in respect of his personal liability under a contract if the contract was

---

[42] *Re Leslie* (1881) 23 Ch D 552, 560; *Re Smith's Estate* [1937] Ch 636; *Re Layton's Policy* [1873] WN 49.   [43] *Clack v Holland* (1854) 19 Beav 262.

[44] See also *Re Phoenix Life Assurance Co* (1862) 2 J & H 229; *James v May* (1873) LR 6 HL 328; *Re National Financial Co* (1868) 3 Ch App 791; *Fraser v Murdoch* (1881) 6 App Cas 855; *Hobbs v Wayet* (1887) 36 Ch D 256.

[45] *X v A* [2000] 1 All ER 490; *Custom Credit Corpn Ltd v Ravi Nominees Pty Ltd* (1982) 8 WAR 42, 53–55; *Commissioner of Stamp Duties v ISPT* (1999) 2 ITELR 1, 18; *Hughes-Hallett v Indian Mammoth Gold Mines Co* (1882) 22 Ch D 561. See also *Re Nixon* [1904] 1 Ch 638; *Re Lewis* [1939] Ch 232; *Re Owers* [1941] Ch 389.

[46] *X v A, supra*. See also Environmental Protection Act 1990, Pt 2; *Environment Agency v Hillridge Ltd* [2003] EWHC 3023 (Ch).

[47] *Muir v City of Glasgow Bank* (1879) 4 App Cas 337; *Perring v Draper* [1997] EGCS 109.

[48] *Parsons v Spooner* (1846) 5 Hare 102; *Lumsden v Buchanan* (1865) 4 Macq 950; *Muir v City of Glasgow Bank, supra,* esp 355–356; *Re Robinson's Settlement* [1912] 1 Ch 717, 729.

[49] *Lumsden v Buchanan, supra*; *Burt Boulton & Hayward v Bull* [1895] 1 QB 276, 285; *Watling v Lewis* [1911] 1 Ch 414, 424; *Helvetic Investment Corp Pty Ltd v Knight* (1984) 9 ACLR 773; *General Credits Ltd v Tawilla Pty Ltd.* [1984] 1 Qd R 388.

[50] *Re State Fire Insurance Co* (1863) 1 De GJ & Sm 634; *Swiss Bank Corp v Lloyds Bank Ltd* [1980] 3 WLR 457, 467 (affirmed [1982] AC 584). An intention to charge the trust fund may, of course, be present, but it will not readily be found.

properly entered into in the administration of the trust. Thus, a trustee who carries on a trade or business, and is authorized to do so by the trust instrument or will, is entitled to be indemnified out of the trust estate against any liabilities which he has properly incurred.[51] If he is authorized to employ only a specific portion of the trust assets in the business, his right of indemnity is restricted to those assets.[52] The other contracting party will be entitled not only to his personal claim against the trustee, but will also have a right by subrogation to the trustee's indemnity.[53]

A trustee's liability in tort

A trustee, like any other individual, may be personally liable in tort for his, or his agents' or employees', acts or omissions in connection with the administration of the trust.[54] As in the case of his liability in contract, neither his status as trustee nor the amount or value of the trust assets will be relevant to the third party claimant. The trustee will be entitled to an indemnity out of the trust fund if he acted within his powers and did so reasonably and with due diligence,[55] for example, in the case of vicarious liability, if he employed a properly qualified agent to carry out the act which led to the tortious cause of action.[56] If the trustee did not act reasonably, he is presumably not entitled to such an indemnity. The successful claimant will have a personal claim against the trustee and a right by subrogation to such indemnity (if any) as the trustee can claim.[57]

21.15

Liability as property owner

As registered holder of shares in a company, a trustee will be personally liable for any liability attaching to those shares, for example to pay calls; and his liability cannot be limited to the assets available to him.[58] Each trustee is liable for the whole claim, and not just a proportionate part;[59] and his liability will not cease until he ceases to be a registered holder.[60] If the shares are an authorized investment, the trustee is entitled to an indemnity from the trust fund; and the company has a right by subrogation to that indemnity in addition to its personal claim against the trustee. Similar principles apply where trustees hold land.

21.16

---

[51] *Dowse v Gorton* [1891] AC 190; *Re Oxley* [1914] 1 Ch 604; *Vacuum Oil Co Pty Ltd v Wiltshire* (1945) 72 CLR 319.

[52] *Ex p Garland* (1803) 10 Ves 110; *Re Johnson* (1880) 15 Ch D 548; *Re Webb* (1890) 63 LT 545. Cf *Strickland v Symons* (1884) 26 Ch D 245.

[53] *Ex p Edmonds* (1862) 4 De GF & J 488; *Fraser v Murdoch* (1881) 6 App Cas 855; *Re Johnson* (1888) 15 Ch D 548.

[54] *Flower v Prechtel* (1934) 159 LT 491.   [55] ibid; *Re Raybould* [1900] 1 Ch 199.

[56] *Benett v Wyndham* (1857) 4 De GF & J 259.   [57] *Re Raybould, supra.*

[58] *Re Royal Bank of Australia* (1860) 2 Giff 189; *Barrett's Case* (1864) 4 De GJ & Sm 416; *Re East of England Banking Co* (1865) 2 Dr & Sm 452; *Leifchild's Case* (1865) LR 1 Eq 231, 236.

[59] *Cunninghame v City of Glasgow Bank* (1879) 4 App Cas 607.

[60] *Alexander Mitchell's Case* (1879) App Cas 567; *Rutherford's Case* (1879) App Cas 581. The automatic vesting provisions of the Trustee Act 1925, s 40, do not apply: s 40(4)(c).

Trustee's indemnity and unauthorized transactions

21.17   As a general principle, a trustee who incurs costs, expense, or liability in respect of an unauthorized transaction is not entitled to an indemnity.[61] If the trustee has acted in good faith and the unauthorized transaction has benefited the trust, he may be indemnified to the extent of the benefit, but this seems to be a matter for the discretion of the court rather than an entitlement.[62] If a trustee has committed a breach of trust for which he is liable to compensate the trust, he cannot claim an indemnity from the trust fund, for example for paying trust debts with his own money, until he makes good his default.[63]

Constructive trustees

21.18   If a person has become a constructive trustee of property by reason of his use of trust property or of his fiduciary position, and the beneficiaries seek to recover that property, he will be allowed his costs and expense in obtaining that property: he who seeks equity must do equity.[64] A person who has acted as trustee in good faith, wrongly believing himself to have been duly appointed, is also entitled to an indemnity, just like a properly appointed trustee.[65]

Void and voidable trusts

21.19   A voidable settlement is valid until it is avoided. Consequently, a trustee is entitled to such proper costs and expenses as he incurred in the administration of the trust before it is avoided.[66] A settlement which is void *ab initio* is different, however, and a trustee is not entitled to an indemnity for costs incurred in administering trusts which he ought to have known were void.[67]

Trustee's lien

21.20   The trustee who has a right of indemnity has an equitable lien upon the trust fund (capital and income) in respect of the costs, expenses, and liabilities covered by the

---

[61] *Leedham v Chawner* (1858) 4 K & J 458; *Hosegood v Pedler* (1879) 66 LJ QB 18, 21; *Ecclesiastical Commissioners v Pinney* [1900] 2 Ch 736.
[62] *Vyse v Foster* (1872) 8 Ch App 309, 336–337; *Re German Mining Co* (1854) 4 De GM & G 19; *Re Leslie* (1883) 23 Ch D 552; *Jesse v Lloyd* (1883) 48 LT 656; *Conway v Fenton* (1888) 11 Ch D 512, 518; *Re Smith's Estate* [1937] Ch 636.
[63] *Jacubs v Rylance* (1874) LR 17 Eq 341; *Doering v Doering* (1889) 42 Ch D 203; *Re Geary* [1939] NI 152, 157.
[64] *Rowley v Ginnever* [1897] 2 Ch 503. This is not an entitlement, however; and much must depend on the constructive trustee's conduct.   [65] *Travis v Illingworth* [1968] WN 206.
[66] *Ex p Tomlinson* (1861) 3 De GF & J 745; *Re Holden* (1887) 20 QBD 43; *Re Carter and Kenkerdene's Contract* [1897] 1 Ch 776, 784–785.
[67] *Smith v Dresser* (1866) LR 1 Eq 651; *Re Holden, supra*. This seems unduly harsh, however. The legal estate may have been effectively transferred to the trustee who may have incurred liability in respect of his ownership in ignorance of the fact that the trusts were void.

indemnity.[68] This charge takes priority over the claims of the beneficiaries and even over purchasers and mortgagees from them.[69] The trustee can also probably refuse to transfer the trust assets to new trustees until his lien is satisfied.[70] The right of indemnity includes several different rights:

(1) A right of reimbursement, for instance, where the trustee discharges the relevant liability out of his own resources, he is entitled to be reimbursed out of the trust fund.[71] The trustee is not generally entitled to charge interest in such circumstances.[72]

(2) A right of exoneration, ie where he discharges the liability directly out of the trust fund.[73]

(3) A right of retention, ie a trustee may retain trust assets until he has been indemnified, not just in relation to present liabilities but also future or contingent liabilities.[74] The trustee cannot be compelled to transfer the trust fund, by a beneficiary or his assign, until his entitlement has been satisfied.[75]

(4) A trustee may also realize trust assets in order to recover his costs and expenses.[76] In some cases, the trustee may need an order from the court; and, in exceptional circumstances, for example where the trust would be seriously damaged, the court may not make such an order for sale but will do what it can to protect the trustee.[77]

The rights of retention and reimbursement are proprietary interests in the trust fund and, as such, may be assigned or charged to the creditor to whom the liability

---

[68] *Stott v Milne* (1884) 25 Ch D 710, 715; *Jennings v Mather* [1902] 1 KB 1, 6; *Governors of St Thomas's Hospital v Richardson* [1910] 1 KB 271, 276. *Hardoon v Belilios* [1901] AC 118. See also *Balkin v Peck* (1998) 1 ITELR 717.

[69] *Dodds v Tuke* (1884) 25 Ch D 617, 619; *Re Knapman* (1881) 18 Ch D 300; *Re Griffith* [1904] 1 Ch 807.

[70] *Re Pauling's Settlement Trusts (No 2)* [1963] Ch 576; *Stephenson v Barclays Bank Trust Co* [1975] 1 WLR 882; *X v A* [2000] 1 All ER 490; *Re Suco Gold Pty Ltd* (1983) 33 SASR 99, 109. See also Trusts of Land and Appointment of Trustees Act 1996, s 19(3)(b). Cf *Wilson v Parker* (1846) 10 Jur 979.

[71] *Worrall v Harford* (1802) 8 Ves 4, 8; *Re Exhall Coal Co* (1866) 35 Beav 449, 453; Trustee Act 2000, s 31(1)(a).

[72] *Gordon v Trail* (1820) 8 Price 416; *Foster v Spencer* [1996] 2 All ER 672. If the trustee discharges a debt carrying interest, he is in turn entitled to such interest by way of subrogation: *Re Beulah Park Estate* (1872) LR 15 Eq 43. See also *Finch v Prescott* (1874) LR 17 Eq 554.

[73] *Re Blundell* (1888) 40 Ch D 370, 376–377; *Jennings v Mather* [1902] 1 KB 1, 6; Trustee Act 2000, s 31(1)(b).

[74] *Re Chennell* (1878) 8 Ch D 492, 503; *Jennings v Mather, supra; Governors of St Thomas's Hospital v Richardson* [1910] 1 KB 271.

[75] *Ex p James* (1832) 1 Deac & Ch 272; *Re Norwich Yarn Co* (1843) 22 Beav 143; *Ex p Chippendale* (1853) 4 De GM & G 19; *Re Exhall Coal Co, supra; Re Layton's Policy* [1873] WN 49; *Re Chennell, supra; Jennings v Mather, supra.* Presumably, a trustee cannot justify retention of all assets if part will satisfy his indemnity.   [76] *Re Pumfrey* (1882) 22 Ch D 255, 262.

[77] *Darke v Williamson* (1858) 25 Beav 622.

is owed and in respect of which the indemnity arose.[78] They will also vest in the trustee's own trustee in bankruptcy or liquidator,[79] but only for the benefit of creditors of the trust and not those of the trustee generally.[80] Creditors may also have a claim against the trust fund by way of subrogation, but only if the trustee has a right of indemnity[81] and they cannot claim more than the trustee was entitled to.[82]

21.21   The lien lies over the whole trust fund, both capital and income.[83] If separate funds are held on distinct trusts, however, liabilities incurred in respect of one fund cannot generally be indemnified out of the other.[84]

21.22   A trustee is required, of course, to keep accurate accounts of costs and expenses. If he does not do so, he may not be able to recover them, although the court may order a reasonable allowance in such a case.[85]

21.23   The trustee's right continues to exist, and he continues to have an interest in the trust fund in the form of a non-possessory lien, even after he has been replaced by a new trustee: it is an independent right which does not depend in any way on any right of indemnity that the new trustee may possess.[86] However, it may be that, when a trustee appoints the trust fund (or a part thereof) in favour of a beneficiary or object, he is impliedly overreaching his own equitable interest (commensurate with his right of indemnity) along with any other beneficial interests in the trust fund (or that part):[87] this will be explicit if the appointed property or trusts are expressed to be 'freed and discharged' from the trusts formerly affecting the same.

---

[78] *Octavo Investments Pty Ltd v Knight* (1979) 144 CLR 360, 369–370; *Custom Credit Corporation Ltd v Ravi Nominees Pty Ltd* (1992) 8 WAR 42, 52–59.

[79] *Jennings v Mather, supra*; *Official Assignee v O'Neill* (1898) 16 NZLR 628; *Octavo Investment, supra*; *Re Suco Gold Pty Ltd, supra*.

[80] *Re Richardson* [1911] 2 KB 705; *Re Byrne Australia Pty Ltd* (1981) 1 NSWLR 394; *Re Byrne Australia Pty Ltd (No 2)* (1981) 2 NSWLR 364; *Rye v Ashfield Nominees Ltd* (2001) New Law Digest, 2 August.

[81] *Strickland v Symons* (1884) 26 Ch D 245.

[82] *Ex p Garland* (1803) 10 Ves 110; *Ex p Edmonds* (1862) 4 De GF & J 488, 498; *Re Johnson* (1880) 15 Ch D 548. See also *Re Frith* [1902] 1 Ch 342.

[83] *Stott v Milne* (1884) 25 Ch D 710, 715; *Hardoon v Belilios* [1901] AC 118, 123–124.

[84] *Ex p Garland* (1803) 10 Ves 110; *Price v Loaden* (1856) 21 Beav 508; *Fraser v Murdoch* (1881) 6 App Cas 855; *Dowse v Gorton* [1891] AC 190, 208. See also *Roome v Edwards* [1982] AC 279 in relation to capital gains tax liability.

[85] *Hethersell v Hales* (1679) 2 Rep Ch 158.

[86] *Octavo Investments Pty Ltd v Knight* (1979) 144 CLR 360; *Kemtron Industries Pty Ltd v Commissioner of Stamp Duties* [1984] 1 Qd R 576; *Dimos v Dikeakos Nominees Ltd* (1997) 149 ALR 113; *Rothmore Farms Pty Ltd v Belgravia Pty Ltd* (1999) 2 ITELR 159.

[87] *Octans Investments Pty Ltd v Knight* (1979) 144 CLR 360; *Kemtron Industries Pty Ltd v Commissioner of Stamp Duties* [1984] 1 Qd R 576. See also *Rothmore Farms Pty Ltd v Belgravia Pty Ltd, supra*.

Clubs and societies

Members of a club or other unincorporated association are not liable to anyone **21.24** beyond the amount of their membership subscriptions. Therefore, in the absence of provision to the contrary, the trustees of such a club or other association do not have a right to be indemnified by or against the members; and they are deemed to have accepted office with knowledge of this fact.[88]

Costs of litigation[89]

The trustee is also entitled to an indemnity in respect of costs properly incurred in **21.25** connection with trust proceedings,[90] provided such costs are not improperly incurred.[91] On a taxation, a trustee's costs ought to be taxed on an indemnity basis, unless they were unreasonably incurred or unreasonable in amount.[92] A trustee may be deprived of his costs, however, if he has committed a breach of trust, or if he has acted dishonestly or he is guilty of gross misconduct, negligence, obstinacy, or capriciousness.[93]

A trustee who, without the prior sanction of the court, defends an action relating **21.26** to the trust places himself at considerable risk. If the action succeeds, he must still prove that he had reasonable grounds for defending it and that the costs were properly incurred. If he cannot do so, he cannot recoup from the trust fund the costs of the action beyond such costs as would have been incurred if he had applied for leave to defend.[94] The same applies if a trustee commences such an action without leave of the court. If trustees appeal unsuccessfully against an order of the court, they will have to pay the costs.[95] On an appeal between beneficiaries, trustees may not be entitled to their costs in briefing counsel (although much depends on the circumstances of the case).[96]

---

[88] *Wise v Perpetual Trustee Co* [1903] AC 139.

[89] For an extensive discussion of the costs of trustees in trust proceedings, see *Lewin*, paras 21-41–21-119.

[90] *Turner v Hancock* (1882) 20 Ch D 303; *Re Love* (1885) 29 Ch D 348; *Re Jones* [1897] 1 Ch 190, 197; *Re Grimthorpe* [1958] Ch 615; *Re Harrison's Settlement Trusts* [1965] 1 WLR 1492, 1497; *Re Spurling's Will Trusts* [1966] 1 WLR 920, 930–936; *McDonald v Horn* [1995] 1 All ER 961, 970–971; *Armitage v Nurse* [1998] Ch 241, 262–263.

[91] *Easton v Landor* (1892) 62 LJ Ch 164, 165; *Re Beddoe* [1893] 1 Ch 547, esp 562; *McDonald v Horn* [1995] 1 All ER 961.

[92] CPR, r 44(2), (3), r 48. See also *Bowen-Jones v Bowen-Jones* [1986] 3 All ER 163, 164.

[93] *Taylor v Glanville* (1818) 3 Madd 176, 178; *Springett v Dashwood* (1860) 2 Giff 521, 528; *Re Chennell* (1878) 8 Ch D 492, 502; *Turner v Hancock* (1882) 20 Ch D 303; *Re Silver Valley Mines* (1882) 21 Ch D 381, 386; *Re Evans* (1884) 26 Ch D 58; *Re Love* (1885) 29 Ch D 348; *Re Jones* [1897] 2 Ch 190.

[94] *Leedham v Chawner* (1858) 4 K & J 458; *Re Beddoe* [1893] 1 Ch 547; *Re Yorke* [1911] 1 Ch 370; *Re England's Settlement Trusts* [1918] 1 Ch 24; *Singh v Bhasin* [2000] WTLR 275.

[95] *Re Earl of Radnor's Will Trusts* (1890) 45 Ch D 402.

[96] *Carroll v Graham* [1905] 1 Ch 478; *Catterson v Clark* (1906) 95 LT 42. This seems to be a rule more honoured in the breach than in the observance.

21.27 A trustee should, therefore, always apply to the court, by means of a *Beddoe* summons,[97] for sanction to bring or defend trust proceedings. As Lightman J stated in *Alsop Wilkinson v Neary*:[98] 'Trustees have a duty to protect and preserve the trust estate for the benefit of the beneficiaries and accordingly to represent the trust in a third party dispute . . . trustees are well advised to seek court authorisation before they sue or defend.' They will be entitled to be indemnified against the costs of any such application.

21.28 Where trustees have sought guidance and protection from the court, they ought not to appeal against the subsequent order of the court in those proceedings, but should leave the beneficiaries to do so if they wish.[99]

Basis for trustee's right of indemnity

21.29 The trustee's indemnity has been said to be founded on a contract between him and the settlor.[100] However, this is difficult to justify. It is not consistent with the courts' view of trustee remuneration clauses, in relation to which, as we have seen,[101] the courts have rejected a contractual analysis in favour of the view that they are one of the beneficial provisions of the trust.[102] A trustee generally has no right to sue the settlor in contract to recover costs or satisfy an indemnity: indeed, the trustee has no right of indemnity against the settlor, unless the latter is also a beneficiary.[103] In addition, a settlor who is also the trustee cannot reasonably be said to have entered into a contract with himself. The trustee's right of indemnity is an incident of his trust; in effect, he has a beneficial interest in the trust fund commensurate with his right of indemnity,[104] or, alternatively, he has a non-possessory equitable lien: it is an independent right which exists entirely independently of contract. If necessary, the trustee could be said to have a power to indemnify himself (the exercise of which is conditional on the proper performance of the trust) or his right might even be viewed as an example of the 'benefit and burden principle'.

---

[97] *Re Beddoe, supra.* See also *Re Moritz* [1960] Ch 251; *Re Eaton* [1964] 3 All ER 229n; *Smith v Croft* [1986] 2 All ER 551.   [98] [1995] 1 All ER 431.

[99] *Re Londonderry's Settlement* [1965] Ch 918, 930.

[100] *Darke v Williamson* (1858) 25 Beav 622, 626; *Cotterell v Stratton* (1872) 8 Ch App 295, 302; *Turner v Hancock* (1882) 20 Ch D 303; *Dutton v Thompson* (1883) 23 Ch D 278, 282; *Re Grimthorpe, supra,* 623; *Re Spurling's Will Trusts, supra,* 934; *Armitage v Nurse, supra,* 263.

[101] See para 21.02–21.03 above.

[102] *Re Duke of Norfolk Settlement Trusts* [1982] Ch 61, 77. See now Trustee Act 2000, s 28(4) (which does not effect a rejection of the analysis, however).

[103] *Jervis v Wolferstan* (1874) LR 18 Eq 18; *Fraser v Murdoch* (1881) 6 App Cas 855, 872.

[104] *Octavo Investments Pty Ltd v Knight* (1979) 144 CLR 360; *Kemtron Industries Pty Ltd v Commissioner of Stamp Duties* [1984] 1 Qd R 576, 590.

Indemnity against beneficiaries

Trustees also have a right of indemnity as against their beneficiaries in certain   **21.30**
circumstances. This aspect is dealt with in detail in Chapter 32 below.[104A]

C. Right to Seek Directions from the Court

Trustees are entitled to ask the court for assistance and directions both in relation   **21.31**
to questions of the construction[105] and effect of the trust documents and also the
administration of the trust, so that they can ensure that they act properly and do
not commit a breach of trust.[106] The main matters on which such directions may
be sought are set out in the Practice Direction to Part 64 of the Civil Procedure
Rules. These include claims for the determination of any questions as to the composition of any class of persons having a beneficial interest in trust property or as
to the rights or interests of a person claiming to be beneficially entitled under the
trust; claims for an order approving a sale, purchase, compromise, or other transaction by a trustee,[107] or for an order directing any act to be done in the execution
of a trust which the court could order to be done if the trust were being executed
under the direction of the court. A beneficiary may seek an order requiring the
trustee to provide and verify accounts, to pay trust money into court,[108] or to do
or not to do a particular act.[109]

The circumstances in which trustees might require the directions of the court   **21.32**
clearly vary considerably in nature. Trustees are expected and required to discharge their trusts without being overcautious in seeking the protection of the
court; for example, when the time for distribution of trust property arrives, the
trustees should distribute it and, indeed, may be liable for breach of trust, and for
the consequences of such breach, if they fail to do so or delay doing so unreasonably.[110] However, there may be circumstances, for instance where third parties
are seeking to have the settlement set aside as being in fraud of creditors, in which

---

[104A] See also *Hardoon v Belilios* [1901] AC 118; *Balkin v Peck* (1998) 43 NSWLR 706;
Countryside (No 3) Pty Ltd v Best (2001) 4 ITELR 600.

[105] See *Re Buckton* [1907] 2 Ch 406, esp 414; *McDonald v Horn* [1995] 1 All ER 961, esp 970.

[106] CPR Pt 64, r 64.2 (1) and Practice Direction to CPR Pt 64, para 1. See also *Re Berens* [1888]
WN 95; *Re Freme's Contract* [1895] 2 Ch 256. A beneficiary may also seek such directions, as
may a protector of the trust (*Re Omar Family Trust* [2000] WTLR 713; *Re Hare Trust* (2001) 4
ITELR 288).

[107] *Re Household* (1884) 27 Ch D 553; *Re Robinson* (1885) 31 Ch D 247.

[108] ie, only if he actually has such money: *Nutter v Holland* [1894] 3 Ch 408.

[109] *Suffolk v Lawrence* (1884) 32 WR 899. The court will not interfere with the exercise of a
discretion by the trustee.

[110] See *Midland Bank Trust Co (Jersey) Ltd v Federated Pension Services* [1995] JLR 352; *Moss v
Integro Trust (BVI) Ltd* (1997/98) 1 OFLR 427.

the prudent trustee will seek directions from the court as to whether to distribute at all or whether to litigate the claim.[111] Hypothetical questions or ones that may only arise in the future cannot be raised.[112] Nor should disputes with third parties be dealt with under this procedure.[113]

21.33 The trustees may also surrender their discretion, either generally or in a particular instance, to the court; or they may simply seek the sanction of the court to a proposed exercise of discretion by the trustees themselves.[114] Seeking the court's sanction or guidance does not, of itself, involve a surrender to the court of the trustees' discretion:[115] they may simply be asking whether a proposed transaction is within their powers, or seeking the approval of the court that it would be a proper exercise by them, or they may be asking for a declaration that a decision or action which has already taken place was proper.

D. Right to Have Trust Administered by the Court

21.34 A trustee has a right in exceptional circumstances to have the trust administered by the court. However, this course of action is appropriate, and the court will make an administration order, only where there are difficulties which cannot be resolved or dealt with in some other way,[116] for example by removing the trustees and appointing new ones. A person who applies for an administration order without good reason, for instance a trustee who merely wishes to be released, or a beneficiary who has no basis for impugning the competence of the trustees, or where there is no difficulty in administering the trust, will probably have to pay all the costs.[117] An applicant who acted in good faith, but without good cause, will not get his own costs.[118]

---

[111] *Re Armstrong Whitworth Securities Co Ltd* [1947] Ch 673; *Finers v Miro* [1991] 1 WLR 35; CPR Pt 50, r 50; *Lewin*, paras 27-15–27-19; *Underhill and Hayton*. 832–844.

[112] *Re Berens* [1888] WN 95; *Re Barnato* [1949] Ch 258. The question is whether the trustee is in any immediate difficulty: *Re Freme's Contract, supra,* 278; *Re Staples* [1916] 1 Ch 322.

[113] *Marley v Mutual Security Merchant Bank and Trust Co Ltd* [1991] 3 All ER 198, 201; *Alsop Wilkinson v Neary* [1995] 1 All ER 431, 434.

[114] See, for example, *Re Drexel Burnham Lambert UK Pension Plan* [1995] 1 WLR 32.

[115] *Public Trustee v Cooper* [2001] WTLR 901, 922–924; *Marley v Mutual Security Merchant Bank, supra.* See also *Re the Thyssen-Bornemisza Continuity Trust* (2002) 5 ITELR 340 (Bermuda); *Re the Fletcher Challenge Energy Employee Educational Fund* (2003) 5 ITELR 682 (NZ).

[116] *Talbot v Earl of Radnor* (1834) 3 My & K 252; *Goodson v Ellisson* (1827) 3 Russ 583; *Re Wilson* (1885) 29 Ch D 913; *Re Gyhon* (1885) 29 Ch D 834; *Re Blake* (1885) 29 Ch D 913; *Re De Quetteville* (1903) 19 TLR 383; *McLean v Burns Philp Trustee Co Pty Ltd* (1985) 2 NSWLR 623.

[117] *Forshaw v Higginson* (1855) 20 Beav 485; *Re Stokes' Trusts* (1872) LR 13 Eq 333; *Re Cabburn* (1882) 46 LT 848.

[118] *Re Leake's Trusts* (1863) 32 Beav 135; *Re Heming's Trust* (1856) 3 K & J 40; *Re Hodgkinson* [1895] 2 Ch 190.

E. Right to Pay Money into Court

Trustees (or a majority of them) have a statutory power to pay into court trust **21.35** moneys or securities under their control; and, if they do so, they will obtain a good discharge for the same. Section 63 of the Trustee Act 1925 provides as follows:

(1) Trustees, or the majority of trustees, having in their hands or under their control money or securities belonging to a trust, may pay the same into court.

(2) The receipt or certificate of the proper officer shall be a sufficient discharge to trustees for the money or securities so paid into court.

(3) Where money or securities are vested in any persons as trustees, and the majority are desirous of paying the same into court, but the concurrence of the other or others cannot be obtained, the court may order the payment into court to be made by the majority without the concurrence of the other or others.

(4) Where any such money or securities are deposited with any banker, broker, or other depositary, the court may order payment or delivery of the money or securities to the majority of the trustees for the purposes of payment into court.

(5) Every transfer payment and delivery made in pursuance of any such order shall be valid and take effect as if the same had been made on the authority or by the act of all the persons entitled to the money and securities so transferred, paid, or delivered.

Payment into court is, in effect, retirement from the trust to the extent of the money and securities paid in, and the trustees' dispositive powers thereby cease to be exercisable.[119] The trustee remains liable for past breaches, however.[120]

Trustees must have good reason for paying into court; and, if they do not have any, **21.36** they may be liable for the extra costs occasioned by their action.[121] Trustees already have the protection of a wide array of statutory powers, for example section 27 of the Trustee Act 1925 (advertisements for beneficiaries)[122] and section 42 of the Administration of Estates Act 1925 (appointing trustees of a minor's property), not to mention the right to seek the directions of the court in difficult cases. Only in rare cases, therefore, will trustees be justified in paying into court.[123]

F. Discharge on Termination of Trust

On the completion of his trusteeship and the distribution of the trust fund, a **21.37** trustee loses the security previously afforded to him by possession of that fund. In

---

[119] *Re Williams's Settlement* (1858) 4 K & J 87; *Re Coe* (1858) 4 K & J 199; *Goode v West* (1851) 15 LT 236; *Re Tegg* (1866) 15 LT 236; *Beaty v Curson* (1869) LR 7 Eq 194; *Re Nettlefold* (1888) 59 LT 315.

[120] *Re Waring* (1852) 16 Jur 652; *A-G v Alford* (1855) 2 Sm & G 488; *Barker v Peile* (1865) 2 Dr & Sm 340.   [121] *Re Giles* (1886) 55 LJ Ch 695.   [122] See para 10.91 above.

[123] *Re Jones* (1857) 3 Drew 679; *Re Wylly* (1860) 28 Beav 458; *Re Maclean's Trusts* (1874) LR 19 Eq 274. Cf *Re Waring, supra*; *Re Metcalfe Trusts* (1864) 2 De GJ & Sm122; *Re Elliot's Trusts* (1873) LR 15 Eq 194; *Re Cull's Trusts* (1875) LR 20 Eq 561.

general, a trustee is entitled merely to have his accounts examined and settled by the beneficiaries before handing over the trust fund, and to be given a formal discharge or, alternatively and if necessary, to have the accounts taken in court. His right appertains strictly to the accounts of each separate trust fund and the trustee cannot refuse to hand over one trust fund until his accounts have been settled and he has been discharged in respect of a different one.[124]

21.38 The trustee is not entitled, however, to demand a release by deed from the beneficiaries.[125] As Kindersley V-C put it, in *King v Mullins*:[126]

> In the case of a declared trust, where the trust is apparent on the face of a deed, the fund clear, the trust clearly defined, and the trustee is paying either the income or the capital of the fund, if he is paying it in strict accordance with the trusts, he has no right to require a release under seal . . . such a claim on the part of a trustee would in strictness be improper, if he is paying in accordance with the letter of the trust. In such a case he would have no right to a release.

In other words, in a plain and simple case, the trustee is entitled only to a receipt.[127] The position may be different, however, and the trustee may demand a release, where he has been required to depart from the strict terms of his trust,[128] or where the trust fund has been resettled, although the original trustees are still entitled only to a receipt from the trustees of the new settlement to whom the fund is transferred.[129] A trustee who distributes funds under the direction of the court is not entitled to a release, because he is protected by the order itself.[130] A trustee may not use trust money to pay for insurance against his own liability for a breach of trust.[131]

21.39 As for trust and other relevant documents, a trustee is entitled to retain custody of the trust instrument and deeds of appointment of new trustees, but he cannot retain or demand delivery to him of trust documents generally. Thus, where an interest in the trust fund has been assigned, the trustee cannot require the delivery to him of the assignment; nor can he demand that a power of attorney be handed over.[132] The trustee can demand examined copies of trust documents, but not attested or duplicate copies, except at his own expense.[133] On the other hand, he is probably entitled to demand an acknowledgement for production and an undertaking for safe

---

[124] *Price v Loaden* (1856) 21 Beav 508.

[125] *Chadwick v Heatley* (1845) 2 Coll 137; *King v Mullins* (1852) 1 Drew 308; *Warter v Anderson* (1853) 11 Hare 301; *Re Wright's Trusts* (1857) 3 K & J 419; *Re Roberts' Trusts* (1869) 38 LJ Ch 708; *Re Hoskin's Trusts* (1877) 5 Ch D 229; 6 Ch D 281. [126] (1852) 1 Drew 308, 311.

[127] *King v Mullins, supra; Re Hoskin's Trusts, supra; Re Ruddock* (1910) 102 LT 89.

[128] *King v Mullins, supra.* [129] *Re Cater's Trusts (No 2)* (1858) 25 Beav 366.

[130] *Gillespie v Alexander* (1826–27) 3 Russ 130; *Knatchbull v Fearnhead* (1837) 3 Myl & Cr 122; *Waller v Barrett* (1857) 24 Beav 413; *Smith v Smith* (1861) 1 Dr & Sm 384; *Williams v Headland* (1864) 4 Giff 505. [131] *Kemble v Hicks* [1999] PLR 287.

[132] *Re Palmer* [1907] 1 Ch 486.

[133] *Warter v Anderson* (1853) 11 Hare 301; *Clayton v Clayton* [1930] 2 Ch 12.

custody.[134] The trust instrument ought to make express provision for such matters; and it is not unreasonable for such provision to authorize the trustees to use trust moneys to pay for attested copies. Trustees ought, in any event and as a matter of prudence, to take and retain copies of all crucial trust documents.[135]

G. Exemption for Breach of Trust[136]

General principle

Trustees must carry out the duties and obligations contained in the trust instru-   **21.40**
ment or imposed by law; and a failure to do so constitutes a breach of trust, for which they will be liable to their beneficiaries. Trustees are entitled, as we have seen, to be indemnified out of the trust property in respect of certain liabilities, costs, and expenses properly incurred by them in connection with the performance of their duties and in the exercise of their powers as trustees. However, as a general prin-ciple, trustees are not entitled to be exempted or excused from the consequences of a breach of trust. Nevertheless, modern trust instruments invariably include wide 'exemption clauses' which exclude or restrict any such liability except in cases where the trustee is guilty of fraud. Thus, a typical common-form exemption clause might read: 'No trustee shall be liable for any loss or damage which may happen to the trust fund at any time or from any cause whatsoever unless such loss or damage shall be caused by his own actual fraud.' It seems appropriate, therefore, to consider trustee exemption clauses as one of the rights of trustees.

Trustees may be protected against exposure to legal accountability in a variety   **21.41**
of different ways. The trust instrument may include 'duty exclusion clauses', ie provisions which remove or curtail the duties to which trustees would otherwise be subject. There may be 'extended powers clauses' which expressly authorize that which would otherwise be unauthorized and the doing of which would have been a breach of trust (for example powers to invest in wasting assets). The trustees may also have extended rights of indemnity to cover liabilities to third parties incurred in the administration of the trust. In such cases, provided the trustee acts honestly, prudently, and with due care, and, of course, within the terms and scope of the authority conferred on him, he is not committing a breach of trust. An 'exemption clause' (or 'immunity clause', 'exculpation clause', or sometimes even an 'indemn-ity clause'), on the other hand, is a provision which excludes liability for what is, within the terms of the trust, a breach of trust.

---

[134] *Re Palmer* [1907] 1 Ch 486.   [135] See *Payne v Evens* (1874) LR 18 Eq 356, 367.
[136] See the Law Commission's Consultation Paper No 171, *Trustee Exemption Clauses*; and also [1989] Conv 42 (P Matthews). See also DJ Hayton, 'The Irreducible Core Content of Trusteeship' in *Trends in Contemporary Trust Law* (Oxford, 1996) 47.

651

21.42 Exemption clauses will be construed strictly and restrictively.[137] However, a solicitor-trustee who drafted the trust instrument may rely on an exemption clause contained therein, provided he informed the settlor of its inclusion and advised him as to its effects.[138]

Extent to which trustees may be exempt from liability

21.43 The crucial issue in relation to exemption clauses is the extent to which trustees may properly be exempted from liability for breach of trust. If the protection extends too far, there may be no enforceable duty and, therefore, no trust at all. Current law recognizes that there is an irreducible core of obligations from which trustees cannot escape. That core is said to comprise little more than a duty to act honestly and in good faith. In *Armitage v Nurse*,[139] the Court of Appeal held that exemption clauses were valid and effective to exclude liability for ordinary and gross negligence; and that a clause similar to the example given above excluded the trustee from liability for loss or damage to the trust fund 'no matter how indolent, imprudent, lacking in diligence, negligent or wilful he may have been, so long as he has not acted dishonestly'. Thus, all liability can be excluded except fraud. Millett LJ accepted that there is an 'irreducible core of obligations owed by the trustees to the beneficiaries and enforceable by them which is fundamental to the concept of a trust' and that, in its absence, no trust will have been created. He added that 'the duty of the trustees to perform the trusts honestly and in good faith for the benefit of the beneficiaries is the minimum necessary give substance to the trusts, but in my opinion it is sufficient'. However, the core obligations of a trustee do not include the duties of skill and care or of prudence and diligence.

21.44 This is a somewhat abstract approach to the issue. In practical terms, a duty 'to perform the trusts honestly and in good faith' must have some substance and must be tied to something concrete. In the typical trust, the trustee will be required to carry out a range of complex duties, from investing the trust fund properly to exercising a discretion in making distributions of the trust property to beneficiaries. The trustee is accountable to his beneficiaries for the manner in which he has discharged the duties imposed on him. His accountability lies at the very core of the trust, but it must still be accountability for something specific. His duties may vary enormously, depending on the nature and purpose of the trust. He may be said to be acting 'honestly' and 'in good faith' if he carries them out negligently, but not if he fails to consider acting at all. Nor can he rely on an exemption clause as a justification for committing what is a breach of trust.

---

[137] *Armitage v Nurse* [1998] Ch 241, 255–256.
[138] *Bogg v Raper* The Times, 22 April 1998; (1998/99) 1 ITELR 267, 284–287.
[139] [1998] Ch 241, esp 245, 250, 254. See also *Bogg v Raper, supra*; *Wight v Olswang* The Times, 18 May 1999, (1998/99) 1 ITELR 189; *Taylor v Midland Bank Trust Co* (2000) 2 ITELR 439.

In any event, if one asks (somewhat unrealistically) what is the absolute minimum **21.45** that a trustee must do if there is to be a trust, the answer, it seems, is that he must: (i) at least hold and safeguard the trust property; (ii) provide information to the beneficiaries concerning the terms of the trust, so that they are in a position to check that the trusts are being carried out; and (iii) keep accurate and reliable accounts and records of his custodianship to prove that the trusts were observed. These three duties cannot be excluded and a trustee cannot be exempted from liability for their breach: a trustee cannot be allowed to treat the trust property as his own; he cannot be relieved of the duty to explain his custodianship; and the beneficiary cannot be deprived of the information he needs to check on, and possibly challenge, the trustee's performance. If it were otherwise, there would be no trust at all.

The decision in *Armitage* is certainly not free from doubt.[140] Not only does it **21.46** establish that liability can be excluded for everything other than the trustee's own fraud but it also excludes the possibility of construing 'fraud' so as to include constructive fraud. If the trustee is to be deprived of the protection of the typical, wide exemption clause, ie one where he is protected against everything other than his own 'actual fraud', he must have had actual knowledge that his action was contrary to the interests of the beneficiaries or, at least, have been recklessly indifferent to that fact.[141] There is no need for the trustee to derive a personal benefit.[142] However, fraud in this context is not to be equated with fraud required for a fraudulent misrepresentation, nor with 'equitable fraud'. Indeed, a deliberate breach of trust may also not be fraudulent, for such a breach may have been committed in good faith and in the belief that it was in the best interests of the beneficiaries.[143]

This restricted and undesirable approach seems to have been ameliorated some- **21.47** what in a more recent case, *Walker v Stones*,[144] where the court took the view that, where a solicitor-trustee honestly believed that he was acting in the best interests of the trust, he could still be said to be acting fraudulently if no reasonable solicitor-trustee would have thought that the act was done for the benefit of the

---

[140] The position is different in other jurisdictions: see, for example, Belize Trustee Act 1992, s 50(6); Trusts (Guernsey) Law 1989 s 34(7); Trusts (Jersey) Law 1984, Art 26(9) and *Midland Bank Trustee Jersey Ltd v Federated Pension Services* [1996] PLR 179; (Turks and Caicos) Trusts Ordinance 1990, Art 29(10); and for Scotland, see *Knox v Mackinnon* (1888) 13 App Cas 753; *Rae v Meek* (1889) 14 App Cas 558; *Carruthers v Carruthers* [1896] AC 659, 667; *Wyman v Paterson* [1900] AC 271. See also *Lutea Trustees Ltd v Orbis Trustees Guernsey Ltd*, (1997) SCLR 735; *Re Poche* (1984) 6 DLR (4th) 40; and *Robertson v Howden* (1892) 10 NZLR 609; and also the survey of relevant cases in [1989] Conv 42 (P Matthews).
[141] *Armitage v Nurse, supra*, 251–256. Cf *Re Bell's Indenture* [1980] 1 WLR 1217.
[142] *Armitage v Nurse, supra*, 251; *Taylor v Midland Bank Trust Co Ltd, supra.*
[143] ibid.   [144] [2001] QB 902.

beneficiaries; and, in such a case, the trustee could not invoke the protection of a wide exemption clause.[145]

21.48 In all cases, the extent of the protection conferred on a trustee will depend on the precise terms of the relevant exemption clause. Thus, a clause which excludes a breach of trust caused by 'wilful default' will deny protection to a trustee who deliberately commits a breach, even if he honestly believes that he is acting in the best interests of the beneficiaries.[146] A clause which refers to a 'wilful breach' of trust has been held to require a deliberate act which the trustee knows is a breach of trust;[147] and one which refers to 'gross negligence' requires a serious degree of negligence, probably approaching recklessness.[148]

Special statutory provisions

21.49 Specific statutory provisions impose stricter standards on trustees of certain kinds of trusts or in respect of certain trustee functions.[149]

Proposals for reform

21.50 The Law Commission recently published a Consultation Paper[150] on this topic, in which the view is expressed that there is a strong case for some regulation, because of the reduced level of protection for beneficiaries and the fact that existing law is too deferential to trustees. The Paper asks whether reliance on exemption clauses 'is seriously endangering the interests of those whom the trust relationship is directed to promote'. However, it recognizes that there is a need to maintain a balance between the 'respective interests of settlor, trustee and beneficiary' and that an absolute prohibition on all trustee exemption clauses is not justifiable. Denying settlors all power to modify or restrict the extent of the obligations and liabilities of the trustee would have a very significant impact on the trust relationship. It would restrict the settlor's autonomy to dictate the obligations to be

---

[145] Leave to appeal to the House of Lords was granted but the appeal was abandoned. The Court of Appeal seems to have taken the same view of 'dishonesty' as was adopted by the Privy Council in *Royal Brunei Airlines v Tan* [1995] 2 AC 378, which has itself been affected by *Twinsectra v Yardley* [2002] 2 AC 164.

[146] *Lewis v Great Western Railway Company* (1877) 3 QBD 195; *Forder v Great Western Railway Company* [1905] 2 KB 532. See also *Re City Equitable Fire Insurance Co Ltd* [1925] Ch 407.

[147] *Re Trusts of Leeds City Brewery Ltd's Debenture Stock Trust Deed (1921)* [1925] Ch 532n at 544.

[148] *Midland Bank Trustees (Jersey) Ltd v Federated Pension Services Ltd* [1996] PLR 179. Cf *Hinton v Dibbin* (1842) 2 QB 646; *The Hellespont Argent* [1997] 2 Lloyd's Rep 547, 586–588.

[149] See, for example, Financial Services Act 1986, s 84 (trustee or manager of unit trust scheme); Companies Act 1985, s 192(1) (trust deed for securing issue of debentures); Pensions Act 1995, ss 33, 34 (investment functions of pension scheme trustees).

[150] No 171: *Trustee Exemption Clauses*.

attached to trustees; and excessive regulation may deter lay trustees from accepting the office. Several provisional proposals are put forward:

- All trustees should be given power to pay for indemnity insurance out of the trust fund.
- Professional trustees should not be able to rely on clauses excluding liability for negligence.
- In so far as professional trustees may not exclude liability, they should not be permitted to claim indemnity from the trust fund.
- In determining whether professional trustees have been negligent, the court should have power to disapply duty exclusion clauses or extended power clauses where such reliance would be inconsistent with the overall purposes of the trust and it would be unreasonable in the circumstances for the trustee to be exempted from liability.
- Any regulation of trustee exemption clauses should be made applicable not only to trusts governed by English law but also to persons carrying on trust business in England and Wales.
- Any legislation should not be retroactive.

The Commission also invited views on two further points:

- Whether reliance on an exemption clause should be permitted only where the clause satisfies the test of reasonableness;
- Whether professional trustees should not be able to rely on such clauses where it is not unreasonable to do so by reference to all the circumstances (including the nature and extent of the breach).

22

DEATH, RETIREMENT, REMOVAL, AND APPOINTMENT OF TRUSTEES

A. Death of Trustee

Devolution of the trust property

22.01   Trustees are joint tenants of the trust property. Consequently, no trustee as such can sever the joint tenancy or devise or bequeath an interest in the trust property. On the death of a trustee, the office passes, and the trust property accrues by survivorship, to the other surviving trustee or trustees.[1] On the death of a sole or last surviving trustee, the trust property devolves upon his personal representative(s).[2]

Devolution of trusts and powers

22.02   Apart from statute, a *power* annexed to an office[3] (such as that of trustee) is exercisable by any person who holds that office.[4] Even a power which arises by implication may, if it attaches to the office of trustee, be exercised by the holder(s) for the time being of that office.[5] 'Every power given to trustees which enables them to deal with or affect the trust property is *prima facie* given to them *ex officio* as an incident of their office, and passes with the office to the holders or holder thereof for the time being.'[6] Thus, when a trustee disclaims or dies, the surviving acting trustee(s) can exercise any power annexed to the trusteeship;[7] or where a power is conferred on (say) three executors *virtute officii*, and one of them renounces or dies, the power remains exercisable by the other two.[8] The power vests in those

---

[1] *Warburton v Sandys* (1845) 14 Sim 622; *Eyre v Countess of Shaftesbury* (1725) 2 P Wms 103; *Re Harding* [1923] 1 Ch 182.   [2] See the Administration of Estates Act 1925, ss 1 and 3.
[3] Which may be determined by asking whether the power would have been conferred on the donees 'but for their office': *Crawford v Forshaw* [1891] 2 Ch 261, 266, *per* Lindley LJ.
[4] ibid; *A-G v Fletcher* (1835) 5 LJ Ch 75. See generally GW Thomas, *Powers* (Sweet & Maxwell, 1998) (*Thomas*) 212–217.
[5] *Anon* (1574) 2 Leon 220, case 276; *Anon* (1580) 3 Dyer 371b; *Milward v Moore* (1580) Sav 72; *Forbes v Peacock* (1843) 11 M & W 630; *Sabin v Heape* (1859) 27 Beav 553; *Dean v Dean* [1891] 3 Ch 150, 157.
[6] *Re Smith* [1904] 1 Ch 139, 144, *per* Farwell J. See also *Re De Sommery* [1912] 2 Ch 622; *Re Symm's Will Trusts* [1936] 3 All ER 236; and *Re Will's Trust Deeds* [1964] Ch 219.
[7] *White v M'Dermott* (1872) IR 7 CL 1; *Clarke v Parker* (1812) 19 Ves 1; *Worthington v Evans* (1823) 1 Sim & St 165; *Sharp v Sharp* (1819) 2 Barn & Ald 405.
[8] *Re Robinson* [1912] 1 IR 410.

who act and the consent of the one who disclaims or renounces is not necessary.[9] It does not necessarily matter that the office itself will not endure beyond the lives of the persons who hold it.[10] A dispositive power[11] attached to an office, rather than conferred on an individual, may, however, be more vulnerable to the application of the rule against perpetuities.[12]

Section 18 of the Trustee Act 1925 now governs most cases of the devolution of **22.03** both trusts and powers on the death of a trustee. Section 18(1) deals with the case where there is a surviving trustee:[13]

> Where a power or trust is given to or imposed on two or more trustees jointly, the same may be exercised or performed by the survivors or survivor of them for the time being.

'Trust' and 'trustee' here extend to implied and constructive trusts and to cases where a trustee has a beneficial interest in the trust property, as well as to personal representatives.[14] It is clearly contemplated in section 18 that a sole surviving trustee can carry out a trust, or exercise a power, originally conferred on two or more trustees, *unless* the contrary is expressly provided in the trust instrument (ie that there must always be at least two or more trustees).[15]

Section 18(2) then deals with the case where there is no surviving trustee:

> Until the appointment of new trustees, the personal representatives or representative for the time being of a sole trustee, or, where there were two or more trustees of the last surviving or continuing trustee, shall be capable of exercising or performing any power or trust which was given to, or capable of being exercised by, the sole or last surviving or continuing trustee, or other the trustees or trustee for the time being of the trust.

'Personal representative' here does *not* include an executor who has renounced or has not proved.[16] An executor who has accepted office but who has not yet proved the will can exercise the power of appointment of new trustees under section 36(1) of the Trustee Act 1925.[17] The personal representative automatically ceases to be capable of carrying out the trusts or exercising a power as soon as a new trustee is appointed: he need not be removed.[18] Section 18 does not impose an

---

[9] *Bersel Manufacturing Co Ltd v Berry* [1968] 2 All ER 552.
[10] *Re De Sommery* [1912] 2 Ch 622; *Kennedy v Kennedy* [1914] AC 215.
[11] Administrative powers are no longer subject to the rule.
[12] Perpetuities and Accumulations Act 1964, s 8.
[13] Section 18 takes effect subject to the restrictions imposed with regard to receipts by a sole trustee, not being a trust corporation: s 18(3).   [14] Trustee Act 1925, s 67(17).
[15] ie, s 18(1) can be modified or excluded expressly by the trust instrument: Trustee Act 1925, s 69(2). As for the Public Trustee as sole trustee, see Public Trustee Act 1906, s 5(1); *Re Leslie's Hassop Estates* [1911] 1 Ch 611; *Re Moxon* [1916] 2 Ch 595; and paras 23.06–23.20 below.
[16] Section 18(4); and see s 68(9).   [17] *Re Crowhurst Park* [1974] 1 WLR 583.
[18] *Re Routledge's Trust* [1909] 1 Ch 280.

obligation on a personal representative to act: he may decline to accept the position and duties of trustee if he so chooses.[19] On the other hand, he cannot insist on doing so against the wishes of a person with a power to appoint a new trustee in place of a deceased trustee.[20]

22.04 Section 18 applies only to powers conferred on trustees by virtue of their office as trustees, those which are annexed to the office and form an integral part of it.[21] It does *not* apply to powers—not even *fiduciary* powers[22]—conferred on persons by name and personal to them, even where such persons also happen to be trustees: such a personal power will perish on the death of one of the donees, *unless* it is clear that it continues to be exercisable by the survivor(s). The presumption in such a case continues to be that 'if a man says he will trust two, the law will not say he shall trust one: it is a joint confidence'.[23]

B. Retirement of Trustee

22.05 A trustee may retire from office under an express power conferred by the trust instrument or a similar power which is necessarily implied;[24] under an order of the court; with the informed consent of all the beneficiaries, all of whom must have attained the age of majority and have full legal capacity;[25] and under statutory powers contained in the Trustee Act 1925.

Retirement under an express power

22.06 It is standard practice to include in trust instruments a power enabling a trustee to retire. Such a power must be construed and applied according to its terms, which may

---

[19] *Re Bennet* [1906] 1 Ch 216, 225; *Re Ridley* [1904] 2 Ch 774; *Legg v Mackrell* (1860) 2 De GF & J 551. [20] *Re Routledge's Trust* [1909] 1 Ch 280.
[21] *Warburton v Sandys* (1845) 14 Sim 622; *Crawford v Forshaw* [1891] 2 Ch 261; *Re Bacon* [1907] 1 Ch 475.
[22] Fiduciary powers are usually conferred on holders of a fiduciary office, such as trusteeship. However, this is not necessarily the case: a power may be a fiduciary power (eg a power to appoint new trustees) without being annexed to any office; and it is quite possible (though unusual) for a person who is a trustee to hold a fiduciary power as a personal power and not by virtue of his office.
[23] *Re Harding* [1923] 1 Ch 182; *Re Beesty's Will Trusts* [1966] Ch 223; *Re Edward's Will Trusts* [1947] 2 All ER 521; *Mansell v Mansell* (1757) Wilm 36, 50; *Peyton v Bury* (1731) 2 P Wms 626; *A-G v Gleg* (1738) 1 Atk 356; *Lane v Debenham* (1853) 11 Hare 188. There may be additional complications where the power is conferred on members of a class. Difficulties may also arise where a power is conferred on persons named with their office (eg 'to my trustees, A and B') and it is then a question of construction to determine the donor's actual intention in each case: *Delaney v Delaney* (1885) 15 LR Ir 55; *Paterson's Trustees v Finlay* 1918 SC 713; and *Thomas* 215–217.
[24] *Davis v. Richards and Wallington Industries Ltd* [1990] 1 WLR 1511 (which involved, *inter alia*, an implied *exercise* of a power to remove a trustee).
[25] *Wilkinson v Parry* (1828) 4 Russ 272.

vary from case to case. Such powers rarely require a trustee to retire, or consider retiring, upon attaining a specified age,[26] but this would be prudent practice—and might avoid, for example, difficult questions about the continuing capacity of a trustee.

Retirement under court order

A trustee may retire under an order of the court. This is a rare occurrence. It may **22.07** be necessary to rely on this method where, for example, the person who can appoint a replacement trustee cannot be found, or where the trustee wishing to retire cannot find someone to take his place,[27] or the consent of the continuing trustees cannot be secured.

The court may also discharge a trustee, without necessarily appointing a replace- **22.08** ment, in the course of a claim for the administration or execution of the trusts, but it will generally not do so unless a trust corporation or at least two other trustees remain.[28]

Retirement with consent of all beneficiaries

Where all the beneficiaries of a trust are of full age and legal capacity, and between **22.09** them absolutely entitled to the trust property, they may act together to terminate the trust, by transferring the property to themselves or to others absolutely or on other trusts; and, in doing so, may override the wishes of the settlor or of the trustees.[29] In principle, therefore, all such beneficiaries may secure the retirement of a trustee by terminating the trust. This would be an extreme and unusual course, however. They cannot compel a trustee to carry out new or modified trusts or impose on him any new or increased liabilities.[30] Consequently, the circumstances are likely to be such that the beneficiaries cannot effectively authorize the retirement of a trustee without the consent of his co-trustee(s).

Retirement by compulsion on the direction of beneficiaries

Section 19 of the Trusts of Land and Appointment of Trustees Act 1996 now pro- **22.10** vides that a trustee may be *compulsorily* retired at the direction of beneficiaries, but only in certain specified circumstances. Section 19(1) applies:

> . . . in the case of a trust where—
> (a) there is no person nominated for the purpose of appointing new trustees by the instrument, if any, creating the trust, and

---

[26] cf Companies Act 1985, s 293 (directors of public company).
[27] *Re Humphry's Estate* (1855) 1 Jur NS 921; *Re Somerset* [1887] WN 122. The costs of the application (including those of the retiring trustee himself) would normally be payable out of the trust fund: *Re Chetwynd's Settlement* [1902] 1 Ch 692; *Re Stoke's Trusts* (1872) LR 13 Eq 333.
[28] ibid; *Re Stretton* [1942] WN 95.
[29] This is the principle in *Saunders v Vautier* (1841) 4 Beav 115; affirmed (1841) Cr & Ph 240.
[30] *Re Brockbank* [1948] Ch 206.

(b) the beneficiaries under the trust are of full age and capacity and (taken together) are absolutely entitled to the property subject to the trust.

Where section 19 applies, the beneficiaries may (in broad terms) direct the trustee(s) to retire and also require them to appoint replacement trustees.[31]

22.11   Clearly, the precondition for the application of limb (a) of section 19(1) ('there is no person nominated . . . by the instrument') is not met if the trust instrument includes a subsisting and exercisable express power to appoint new trustees and the donee of the power is (say) simply unwilling or unable to exercise that power, although it will be met if the nominated person is dead. On the other hand, the precondition will be satisfied, it seems, if the statutory power of appointing new trustees conferred by section 36 of the Trustee Act 1925 applies to the trust (and there is still no nominated person). Similarly, an express provision in the trust instrument which incorporates section 36 by reference, but subject to some modifications, will also satisfy the precondition if the words 'nominated person' strictly mean a named person, as opposed to (say) any person who happens to fill a particular office (for example a last surviving trustee) or to enjoy a particular status.

22.12   As for limb (b) of section 19(1), the word 'beneficiaries' means 'any person who under the trust has an interest in property subject to the trust (including a person who has such an interest as a trustee or personal representative)'.[32] It is not clear whether this literally means a person who has a proprietary interest in the technical sense (for example a life or remainder interest) or whether it also includes an object of a discretionary trust and even an object of a (fiduciary or non-fiduciary) power, neither of whom has such an 'interest' at all. Although the definition of 'beneficiary' is intended to apply to the provisions of the Act as a whole, and some of those provisions seem to be limited to beneficiaries with 'interests' properly so-called,[33] this is not clearly the case for all provisions.[34] The narrow interpretation must be that section 19(1)(b) does *not* include objects of discretionary trusts and powers. On the other hand, the purpose of section 19 is to enable those who could, in any event, terminate a trust under the principle in *Saunders v Vautier* to appoint new trustees without actually terminating that trust (which might have adverse tax consequences). If a trust is to be terminated under *Saunders v Vautier*, all interested parties, including all objects of any discretionary trusts or of any (fiduciary and non-fiduciary) dispositive powers would have to act together. Section 19(1)(b), taken on its own terms, is clearly looking to the collective 'interest' of all those who, between them, can be said to be absolutely entitled to the trust property, and not to the separate 'interests' of each individual beneficiary

---

[31] Section 19(2). This right can be excluded by an express provision in the trust; or, in respect of a pre-1997 trust, by a post-1996 deed executed by the settlor: see s 21(5), (6), (7).

[32] Trusts of Land and Appointment of Trustees Act 1996, s 22(1).

[33] ibid, ss 6(2), 7, 9, 10, 11, and 12.   [34] ibid, s 6(4), (5), and (6).

or object. This suggests that the objects of any discretionary trusts or of any (fiduciary and non-fiduciary) dispositive powers are also 'beneficiaries' for the purposes of section 19. However, this is far from clear.

A beneficiary may have assigned his interest to another or it may have passed by **22.13** operation of law to his trustee in bankruptcy or his personal representative, in which case it will be the person(s) now standing in the original beneficiary's shoes who must join with the other beneficiaries for the purposes of section 19. (In such a case, the assignee may or may not, depending on the circumstances, himself hold the interest subject to fiduciary obligations in favour of others.) Where a beneficiary has assigned his interest to a trustee to hold on sub-trusts, a question may arise as to whether section 19 may or can be invoked only by that assignee-trustee and other beneficiaries of the original head settlement or whether the beneficiaries of the sub-settlement must also be included. The answer may vary, it seems, according to the circumstances of the case and depends largely on the nature of the sub-settlement, for example whether it is revocable or irrevocable, whether its trusts are exhaustive and it is truly separate from the head settlement. In some cases, all beneficiaries, of both head and sub-settlement, will need to be involved; in others, only the respective beneficiaries of the head settlement or of the sub-settlement as separate entities will be relevant (so that, for example, the beneficiaries of the sub-settlement could even remove and replace the assignee-trustee of that sub-settlement, without the involvement of the other beneficiaries of the head settlement). It would be prudent, however, to ensure that, on the creation of such a sub-settlement, no such uncertainty could arise, for example by including a person nominated for the purpose of appointing new trustees for the purposes of limb (a), thereby disapplying section 19(1), or by an express disapplication of section 19 altogether.[35]

Kinds of directions that may be given

Where section 19 of the 1996 Act applies, the beneficiaries may then give a direction **22.14** or directions under section 19(2) of either or both of the following descriptions, that is to say:

(a) a written direction to a trustee or trustees to retire from the trust, and
(b) a written direction to a trustee or trustees for the time being (or if there are none, to the personal representative of the last person who was a trustee) to appoint by writing to be a trustee or trustees the person or persons specified in the direction.

Thus, the beneficiaries may direct a trustee to retire (with or without the appointment of a new trustee) or appoint a new trustee without requiring any trustee to retire.

---

[35] ibid, s 21(5).

Form of direction

22.15 The beneficiaries' direction must be in writing, but not necessarily by deed (thereby reflecting similar provisions in section 36 of the Trustee Act 1925). It may take the form of a single direction given by all of the beneficiaries acting jointly or given by each of them (acting alone or jointly with one or more but not all of the others); and, in the latter case, each direction must specify the same person or persons for retirement or appointment.[36] A direction may be withdrawn in writing by any beneficiary before it has been acted upon, in which event the direction(s) given by the other beneficiaries is or are ineffective.[37] A direction for retirement must be served on the retiring trustee(s); and a direction for appointment (whether on the retirement of a trustee or otherwise) must be served on all the trustees for the time being.[38]

Implementation and effect of directions relating to retirement

22.16 Where a trustee has been given a direction to retire from the trust, and provided the requirements of section 19(3) of the 1996 Act have been complied with, he shall make a deed (not just writing) declaring his retirement and he shall be deemed to have retired and be discharged from the trust. The requirements of section 19(3) are that:

(i) Reasonable arrangements have been made for the protection of any rights of the trustee in connection with the trust. A retiring trustee has a right to payment of unpaid fees and an indemnity against existing expenses and liabilities which have been properly incurred, and the continued protection of such rights are clearly within the scope of this provision. However, it also seems to go further and to contemplate that, as in the case of voluntary retirement, a trustee may reasonably seek protection by way of express indemnity from the beneficiaries and continuing trustees in respect of contingent and future liabilities, rather than have to rely on his equitable non-possessory charge (which would be difficult to enforce if the trust assets have been distributed). A retiring trustee can also require his accounts to be settled before he retires and gives up control of trust assets.

(ii) After he has retired there will be either a trust corporation or at least two persons to act as trustees to perform the trust. In other words, if a new trustee is not being appointed, then (as in the case of section 39 of the Trustee Act 1925)[39] at least two existing trustees, or a trust corporation, must remain in office. If all the trustees (or all but one, and that one is not a trust corporation) are being retired, new trustees must be appointed at the same time.

---

[36] 1996 Act, s 21(1) and (2).   [37] ibid, s 21(1).   [38] ibid, s 19(2)(b).
[39] Although, of course, s 39 provides for retirement without the appointment of a new trustee, which may or may not be the case under s 19 of the 1996 Act.

(iii) Either another person is to be appointed to be a new trustee on his retirement (whether in compliance with a direction under section 19(2)(b) or otherwise) or the continuing trustees by deed consent to his retirement. The consent, by deed, of the continuing trustee(s) is required for a compulsory retirement without the appointment of a new trustee, but such consent is not required where a new trustee is appointed.

The retiring trustee and continuing trustees, together with any new trustee, must do whatever is necessary in order to vest the trust property in the continuing trustees (together with any new trustees, where appropriate). If the trustee fails or refuses to implement the directions given without reason, or if there is a dispute which cannot be resolved by agreement (for example because he regards the provision made for his protection as unreasonable), the matter would have to be resolved by the court.[40]

Implementation and effect of directions relating to appointment

A direction given by the beneficiaries to the trustees does not itself appoint new **22.17** trustees. The actual appointment is made by the trustees themselves in accordance with that direction. Although not made explicit in section 19(2)(b), it is clear that, in the nature of things, the appointment must be made by all the trustees for the time being, acting together, and presumably must also be made in writing (as in the case of an appointment under section 36 of the Trustee Act 1925) although, for ease of vesting of trust property, it ought to be made by deed. If the appointment is accompanied by the retirement of a trustee, the retirement must be effected by deed.[41]

Once appointed, a new trustee will occupy the same office, be subject to the same **22.18** fiduciary duties and provisions, and have the same powers and discretions as a trustee originally appointed.

Vesting of trust assets

There is limited provision for the vesting of trust assets following the retirement **22.19** or appointment of a trustee under the provisions of the 1996 Act. Section 19(4) of the 1996 Act provides:

> Where a trustee retires under subsection (3) he and the continuing trustees (together with any new trustee) shall (subject to any arrangements for the protection of his rights) do anything necessary to vest the trust property in the continuing trustees (or the continuing and new trustees).

---

[40] The court could, for example, nominate someone to execute the required deed on the trustee's behalf: Supreme Court Act 1981, s 39. Costs would presumably follow the event.

[41] Trusts of Land and Appointment of Trustees Act 1996, s 19(3). The retirement and new appointment would, in practice, be effected by the one deed.

This provision applies only where a trustee is being retired (with or without the appointment of a new trustee). It does not include the case of an appointment of a new trustee under a direction given by the beneficiaries (under section 19(2)(b)). Such an appointment is presumably intended to be covered by section 37(1)(d) of the Trustee Act 1925. Where a trustee is being retired, without a new appointment being made, the trust property will vest automatically in the continuing trustees under the provisions of section 40(2) of the Trustee Act 1925[42] (other than assets of the kind specified in section 40(4), which must be transferred by the appropriate method).

Exclusion of section 19

22.20   The application of section 19 of the 1996 Act may be excluded by the trust instrument.[43] Where the trust was created before the date of commencement of the Act (1 January 1997), the application of section 19 may be excluded by an irrevocable deed executed by the settlor or settlors (but without prejudice to anything done before its execution in compliance with a valid direction already given under section 19).[44] Section 19 cannot be excluded in relation to a testamentary trust created before 1 January 1997, nor a pre-commencement *inter vivos* trust whose settlor is dead. Indeed, subject to the above-mentioned exclusions, section 19 applies to a trust whenever created.

Voluntary retirement under the Trustee Act 1925 where a replacement trustee is appointed

22.21   Under section 36(1) of the Trustee Act 1925, where a trustee, either original or substituted, desires to be discharged from all or any of the trusts or powers reposed in or conferred on him, the person or persons nominated for the purpose of appointing new trustees by the trust instrument or, if there is no such person or no such person able and willing to act, the surviving or continuing trustees or trustee for the time being or the personal representatives of the last surviving or continuing trustee, may, by writing, appoint one or more trustees to be a trustee or trustees in his place (subject to the restrictions imposed by the Act on the number of trustees).[45]

---

[42]   As amended by the 1996 Act, s 25(1) and Sch 3, para 3(14).
[43]   Trusts of Land and Appointment of Trustees Act 1996, s 21(5).
[44]   ibid, s 21(6), (7), (8); Trusts of Land and Appointment of Trustees Act 1996 (Commencement) Order 1996, SI 1996/2974.
[45]   Section 36 of the Trustee Act 1925 is dealt with in detail below: see paras 22.42–22.47.

Voluntary retirement under the Trustee Act 1925 where a replacement trustee is not appointed

Section 39(1) of the Trustee Act 1925[46] provides: **22.22**

> Where a trustee is desirous of being discharged from the trust, and after his discharge there will be either a trust corporation or at least two persons to act as trustees to perform the trust, then, if such trustee as aforesaid by deed declares that he is desirous of being discharged from the trust, and if his co-trustees and such other person, if any, as is empowered to appoint trustees, by deed consent to the discharge of the trustee, and to the vesting in the co-trustees alone of the trust property, the trustee desirous of being discharged shall be deemed to have retired from the trust, and shall, by the deed, be discharged therefrom under this Act, without any new trustee being appointed in his place.

Thus, this statutory discharge operates only if a trust corporation or at least two persons remain as acting trustees after the retirement, which can pose a problem where, for example, United Kingdom trustees wish to retire and appoint a foreign trust company in their place.[47] This requirement applies even where only one trustee was appointed originally. Although section 39, and therefore this restriction, can probably be excluded or modified by the trust instrument,[48] a retirement under an express, as opposed to the statutory, power would not attract the application of the automatic vesting provisions of section 40(2) of the Trustee Act 1925, in which case the trust property would have to be vested in the continuing trustees (or a trust corporation) by the appropriate method.

Section 39 does not seem to authorize a trustee to retire from part of the trusts: it   **22.23**
refers to 'the trust' as opposed to 'all or any of the trusts' (as in section 36(1)). It is generally thought that, where a separate set of trustees has been appointed under section 37(1)(b) in respect of distinct trusts, retirement of a trustee of one such set of distinct trusts may be permissible under section 39(1).

Retirement and breach of trust

A trustee who retires in order to facilitate a breach of trust by his co-trustees (or the   **22.24**
successor trustees) may himself be held liable for their breach.[49] Indeed, in such circumstances, any indemnity given to the retiring trustee against the consequences of the breach might have no effect, for it would itself be tainted with fraud

---

[46] As amended by the Trusts of Land and Appointment of Trustees Act 1996, s 25(1) and Sch 3, para 3(13).

[47] A foreign trust company will probably not be a 'trust corporation' within the meaning of the Trustee Act 1925, s 68(18).

[48] Trustee Act 1925, s 69(2) (which actually refers to 'powers conferred . . . on trustees'); *LRT Pension Fund Trustee Co Ltd v Hatt* [1993] PLR 227.

[49] *Webster v Le Hunt* (1861) 9 WR 918; *Palairet v Carew* (1863) 32 Beav 564; *Clark v Hoskins* (1868) 37 LJ Ch 561; *Head v Gould* [1898] 2 Ch 250.

and could not be relied on.[50] However, there must be a causal connection between the retirement (and any new appointment) and the breach. The retiring trustee will not be held liable for a breach intended at the date of retirement but not subsequently committed, nor for a breach committed by the successor trustees which was not in contemplation at the date of retirement.[51]

C. Removal of a Trustee

Removal under an express power[52]

22.25 Express powers of removal are not commonly found in domestic trusts, but are increasingly popular, and often essential, in offshore trusts, where they may be reserved by the settlor or, more usually, conferred on a protector. Such powers are strictly construed, whether in relation to the description of the appointor or in respect of the circumstances in which they may be exercised. This is particularly important in cases where trustees have incurred substantial expenses and liabilities for which they remain liable after ceasing to be trustees, but, after removal, will no longer have control of or recourse to the trust assets to meet such liabilities. Nevertheless, section 36(2) of the Trustee Act 1925 expressly recognizes the validity of express powers of removal and provides that, where a trustee has been removed under such a power, a new trustee or new trustees may be appointed in his place, as if he were dead or, in the case of a corporation, as if the corporation desired to be discharged from the trust, and the provisions of section 36 shall apply accordingly (subject to the restrictions imposed by the Act on the number of trustees).

22.26 Powers of removal do not have retrospective effect. Like powers to appoint trustees, powers of removal are fiduciary powers and must be exercised in the best interests of the trust and its beneficiaries and not for the benefit of the person exercising the power or for some ulterior motive.[53]

22.27 The removal of a trustee does not automatically ensure that the trust property will be vested in the remaining (or the remaining and any new) trustees. In England and Wales (and jurisdictions with similar statutory provisions), where a trustee is removed and a new trustee is appointed by deed, the trust property is vested

[50] *Sheppard's Touchstone of Common Assurances*, 7th edn by R Preston (1820) 132, 371. Cf *Warwick v Richardson* (1824) 10 M & W 284 (indemnity recognized at common law) and Supreme Court Act 1981, s 49. Mowbray et al, *Lewin on Trusts* (17th edn, Sweet & Maxwell, 2000) ('*Lewin*'), 370.
[51] *Head v Gould* [1898] 2 Ch 250, 274, *per* Kekewich J; *Clark v Hoskins* (1868) 37 LJ Ch 561, 567.
[52] See *London & County Banking Co v Goddard* [1897] 1 Ch 642.
[53] *IRC v Schroder* [1983] STC 480, 500; *von Knierem v Bermuda Trust Co Ltd* (1994) 1 Offshore Cases and Materials 116 (Bermuda).

automatically in the new set of trustees by virtue of section 40(1) of the Trustee Act 1925 (other than assets of the kind specified in section 40(4)). Where a trustee is removed, without a new trustee being appointed, it would appear that similar provisions in section 40(2) do not apply: the relevant trustee has been removed and is not 'retiring' and the removal is effected under an express and not a statutory power. Other methods of removal are therefore advisable, for example vesting of assets in a nominee.

Statutory provisions for removal of trustees

Section 36(1) of the Trustee Act 1925 provides that a trustee, whether original or substituted, who remains out of the United Kingdom for more than twelve months or refuses or is unfit to act or is incapable of acting, may be removed by the appropriate person and replaced with a new trustee.[54] **22.28**

Section 41 of the Trustee Act 1925 provides that the court may appoint a new trustee or new trustees, whenever it is expedient to do so and it is found inexpedient, difficult, or impracticable to do so without the assistance of the court, and such an appointment may be made in substitution for any existing trustee or trustees.[55] **22.29**

Removal under the court's inherent jurisdiction

The court has an inherent jurisdiction, in the execution of trusts, to remove a trustee, even without his consent and against his wishes.[56] If the court considers it expedient, it may even order removal of a trustee in an administration action without a specific claim for removal having been made.[57] **22.30**

The principles upon which the court will exercise its inherent jurisdiction are broadly the same as those which guide the exercise of its statutory jurisdiction under section 41 of the Trustee Act 1925. **22.31**

> In exercising so delicate a jurisdiction as that of removing trustees, their lordships do not venture to lay down any general rule beyond the very broad principle . . . that their main guide must be the welfare of the beneficiaries . . . It is quite true that friction or hostility between trustees and the immediate possessor of the trust estate is not of itself a reason for the removal of trustees. But where the hostility is grounded on the mode in which the trust has been administered, . . . it is certainly not to be disregarded. . . . if it appears clear that the continuance of the trustee would be detrimental to the execution of the trusts, even if for no other reason than that human infirmity would prevent those beneficially interested, or those who act for them,

---

[54] Section 36(1) is dealt with in detail below: see paras 22.42–22.57.
[55] Section 41 is dealt with in detail below: see paras 22.58–22.77.
[56] *Re Harrison's Settlement Trusts* [1965] 1 WLR 1492. The appropriate procedure is by claim under Part 7 of the Civil Procedure Rules, save where there is no dispute of fact, when Part 8 is appropriate. [57] *Re Wrightson* [1908] 1 Ch 789.

from working in harmony with the trustee, and if there is no reason to the contrary from the intentions of the framer of the trust to give this trustee a benefit or otherwise, the trustee is always advised by his own counsel to resign, and does so. If, without any reasonable ground he refuses to do so, it seems to their lordships that the court might think it proper to remove him…[58]

The court will not automatically remove a trustee for any mistake or neglect of duty or inaccuracy of conduct whatsoever. A mere misunderstanding, without wilful default, may not suffice.[59] In practice, and subject to Lord Blackburn's general guidance, a trustee will be removed only if his acts or omissions or conduct are 'such as to endanger the trust property or to show a want of honesty or a want of proper capacity to execute the duties or a want of reasonable fidelity'.[60] Indeed, the court may not in all cases remove trustees who have been held liable for a breach of trust, for example where the breach was innocent, the trustees are otherwise honest and persons of integrity, and an appeal is pending.[61]

22.32 Examples of the court's exercise of its inherent jurisdiction include cases where trustees took up permanent residence abroad;[62] where a trustee was insolvent;[63] where a trustee could not be traced[64] or had absconded;[65] where a trustee competed with the trust or had a conflict of interest;[66] where a trustee refused to act,[67] or to act promptly,[68] or to implement the orders of the court;[69] and where a trustee allowed a co-trustee to commit a breach of trust.[70] Many of these cases would now fall within the scope of section 36 of the Trustee Act 1925. In any event, such examples must be treated with caution: the specific problem may be capable of being resolved without removal of the trustee, for example the particular conflict of interest may cease.

22.33 Disagreement or friction between trustees and beneficiaries, or between one trustee and another, do not in themselves justify removal of a trustee: indeed,

[58] *Letterstedt v Broers* (1884) 9 App Cas 371, at 386–387, *per* Lord Blackburn.
[59] *A-G v Coopers' Co* (1812) 19 Ves Jr 197; *A-G v Caius College* (1837) 2 Keen 150.
[60] ibid 385–386. See also *Re Wrightson* [1908] 1 Ch 789; *Miller v Cameron* (1936) 54 CLR 572, 580; *Re Roberts* (1983) 70 FLR 158; *Titterton v Oates* [2001] WTLR 319.
[61] *Re Pauling's Settlement Trusts (No 2)* [1963] Ch 576.
[62] *Buchanan v Hamilton* (1801) 5 Ves Jr 702; *O'Reilly v Anderson* (1849) 8 Hare 101.
[63] *Bainbrigge v Blair (No 1)* (1839) 1 Beav 495; *Re Roche* (1842) 2 Dr & War 287, 289; *Charitable Donations v Archbold* (1847) 11 Ir Eq R 187; *Harris v Harris (No 1)* (1861) 29 Beav 107; *Re Hopkins* (1881) 19 Ch D 61, 63.
[64] *Re Ledwick* (1844) 6 Ir Eq R 561; *Re Harrison's Trusts* (1852) 22 LJ Ch 69.
[65] *Re Renshaw's Trusts* (1869) 4 Ch App 783.
[66] *Moore v M'Glynn* [1894] 1 IR 74; *Ex p Phelps* (1742) 9 Mod 357; *Monty Financial Services Ltd v Delmo* [1996] 1 VR 65.
[67] *Howard v Rhodes* (1837) 1 Keen 581; *A-G v Murdoch* (1856) 2 K & J 571; *Palairet v Carew* (1863) 32 Beav 564; *Luke v South Kensington Hotel Co* (1879) 11 Ch D 121, 127; *Reid v Hadley* (1885) 2 TLR 12. A trustee who refuses to exercise his discretion under a discretionary trust may also be removed: *McPhail v Doulton* [1971] AC 424.   [68] *Higginbotham v McGilchrist* 1930 SC 635.
[69] *Clarke v Heathfield (No 2)* [1985] ICR 606.   [70] *Ex p Reynolds* (1800) 5 Ves Jr 707.

disagreements as to the manner in which a trust is administered or its property distributed are not uncommon.[71] Some additional, reasonable and substantial cause must be shown. The court will need to be satisfied that the proper administration of the trust is jeopardized as a result, for example because the trustees entertain views which are inconsistent with their status,[72] or cannot agree to act unanimously.[73] It is the protection of the beneficiaries' interests and of the trust property, and the proper execution of the trusts, that is of paramount importance.

The court can remove a trustee without appointing a replacement, and it will **22.34** sometimes do so, especially in urgent cases.[74] The court will ensure that, after the removal, there remains an appropriate number of trustees for the purposes of the trust.

D. Appointment of New Trustees Under an Express Power

Most trust instruments creating express trusts contain an express power to **22.35** appoint new trustees. Such powers are strictly construed, whether in relation to the description of the appointor or in respect of the circumstances in which they may be exercised. Thus, where the power is conferred on a 'continuing' trustee, it cannot be exercised by a retiring trustee.[75] Similarly, a power which is exercisable when a trustee has become 'incapable' of acting cannot be exercised where the trustee is merely 'unfit' (for example because he is bankrupt)[76] for 'incapacity' has been construed to mean physical or mental incapacity or infancy.[77] A power exercisable only in specified circumstances can be exercised only when those circumstances have actually occurred.[78] A power expressed to be exercisable by deed only cannot be exercised by will (and vice versa).

---

[71] See, for example, *Lee v Young* (1843) 2 Y & C Ch 532; *Forster v Davies* (1861) 4 De GF & J 133; *A-G v Hardy* (1851) 1 Sim (NS) 338, 357; *A-G v Clapham* (1855) 4 De GM & G 591, 632.

[72] *A-G v Pearson* (1835) 7 Sim 290; *A-G v Shore* (1833) 7 Sim 309.

[73] *Re Consiglio's Trusts* (1973) 36 DLR (3d) 658.

[74] *Clarke v Heathfield (No 2)* [1985] ICR 606. In such a case, the court will probably appoint a receiver to act until new trustees are appointed subsequently.

[75] *Lord Camoys v Best* (1854) 19 Beav 414; *Re Norris* (1884) 27 Ch D 333; *Re Coates to Parsons* (1886) 34 Ch D 370. It is otherwise under the statutory power in s 36 of the Trustee Act 1925, for it is expressly provided (s 36(8)) that a continuing trustee includes a refusing or retiring trustee, if willing to act.

[76] *Turner v Maule* (1850) 15 Jur 761; *Re Watts' Settlement* (1851) 9 Hare 106. See also *Withington v Withington* (1848) 16 Sim 104; *Re Harrison's Trusts* (1852) 22 LJ Ch 69; *Re May's Will Trusts* [1941] Ch 109. Cf *Re Bignold's Settlement Trusts* (1872) 7 Ch App 223.

[77] *Re Watts' Settlement* (1851) 9 Hare 106; *Turner v Maule* (1850) 15 Jur 761; *Re East* (1873) 8 Ch App 735; *Re Blake* [1887] WN 173. Section 20 of the Law of Property Act 1925 provides that the appointment of an infant as trustee of a trust shall be void, but without prejudice to the power to appoint a new trustee to fill the vacancy. See also *Re Vinogradoff* [1935] WN 68; and the court's powers to appoint trustees under s 41 of the Trustee Act 1925 (paras 22.58–22.71 below).

[78] *Re Wheeler and de Rochow* [1896] 1 Ch 315.

Fiduciary nature of power

22.36 In the absence of express provision to the contrary, or of some necessary implication, a power to appoint new trustees is a fiduciary power, even where it is conferred on someone who is not a trustee,[79] such as an employer-company in relation to its pension scheme,[80] and even where the appointor may appoint himself.[81] This is also the case where the donee of the power is a protector of the trust.[82] It may be otherwise where the power to appoint is conferred on a beneficiary who is actually or effectively solely and absolutely entitled to the trust property, or on someone upon whom a general power of appointment has also been conferred.[83]

22.37 There is no reason, in principle, why the donee of a power to appoint new trustees, who is not a trustee himself (but who is still a fiduciary in relation to that power), should not be under a duty to consider the exercise of that power from time to time. This seems implicit in the general principle that a fiduciary cannot fetter the exercise of a power or release it.[84] This does not mean that such a person is subject to fiduciary duties as onerous as those applicable to a trustee, but it would require him to act or consider acting, for example, when it came to his attention that the number of trustees had fallen below a required minimum. Nor does it mean that such a person can be forced to accept this fiduciary position, only that, if he does so, he must act accordingly: he can certainly refuse to act, but only after proper consideration.[85]

Capacity to exercise an express power

22.38 A power to appoint new trustees conferred on a person (whether he is a trustee or not) who is incapable, by reason of mental disorder, of executing the power may

---

[79] *Re Skeats' Settlement* (1889) 42 Ch D 522; *IRC v Schroder* [1983] STC 480; *Re Osiris Trustees* (2000) 2 ITELR 404.

[80] *Icarus (Hertford) Ltd v Driscoll* [1990] PLR 1; *Mettoy Pension Trustees Ltd v Evans* [1990] 1 WLR 1587; *Re William Makin & Son Ltd* [1998] OPLR 171; *Simpson Curtis Pension Trustees Ltd v Readson Ltd (in receivership)* [1994] OPLR 231; *Independent Pension Trustee v LAW Construction* [1996] OPLR 259. Cf *Denny v Yeldon* [1995] OPLR 115 (suspect decision on several grounds, but in which the fiduciary nature of the power was not addressed). In these case, which raised the question whether a power could or could not be exercised by a receiver, administrator, or liquidator (as the case may be), the central issue was one of capacity (ie, did the relevant instrument or statute creating the power confer it on the officer in question) and not one of different attributes of different fiduciary powers. See generally *Thomas* 197–209.

[81] As is the case, for example, under s 36(1) of the Trustee Act 1925.

[82] *Steele v Paz* [1993–95] Manx LR 426; *Re Z Trust* [1997] Cayman ILR 248; R Ham, E Campbell and M Tennet, 'Protectors' in J Glasson (ed) *The International Trust* (Jordans, 2002) Ch 5.

[83] cf *Re Triffitt's Settlement* [1958] Ch 852.

[84] *Ayr Harbour Trustees v Oswald* (1883) 8 App Cas 623, 639–640; *Re Gestetner* [1953] Ch 672, 688.

[85] Clearly, a refusal to act or to consider acting can itself be synonymous with a refusal to accept the fiduciary role in the first place, in which case there is no cause for complaint. Cf *Re Knight's Will* (1884) 26 Ch D 82.

be exercised, in appropriate circumstances, by the court (which may also make consequential vesting orders).[86]

An infant can exercise a power to appoint expressly conferred on him, provided that any such exercise does not affect his own interest under the trust.[87] An infant cannot be a trustee, however.[88]   **22.39**

Persons who may be appointed new trustees

A power to appoint new trustees is subject to the same restrictions, and must be exercised by reference to the same principles and considerations, as any other power. Thus, the exercise of the power must not be a fraud on the power or excessive (for example by appointing someone expressly ruled out by the settlor); the appointor must take into account only relevant considerations and must exclude all irrelevant ones; the choice must not be capricious or manifestly unreasonable and inappropriate;[89] and so on.[90] As a general rule, and in the absence of express provision to the contrary,[91] the appointor may not appoint himself.[92] This is also the case under section 36(6) of the Trustee Act 1925 (appointment of additional trustees)[93], although section 36(1) does permit the appointor to appoint himself as a new replacement trustee. Provided the appointor does not infringe or ignore such principles, and provided he acts lawfully (and does not, for example, appoint an infant as trustee), he has considerable discretion as to the choice of a new trustee. Thus, for example, foreign trustees may be appointed in the exercise of an express power: the discretion belongs to the trustees, and the appropriateness of the proposed appointment is for them to decide; and as long as their decision is arrived at properly and honestly and in the best interests of the beneficiaries, the court will not intervene, even if the court itself, in exercise of its statutory jurisdiction to appoint new trustees, may not have acted in the same way. Indeed, in such a case, and in the absence of peculiar factors, the trustees need not even seek the sanction of the court for their decision.[94]   **22.40**

In broad terms, however, the appointor of a new trustee under an express power will probably—and, in prudence, perhaps ought to—follow the same principles as the court will apply when exercising its statutory power.[95]   **22.41**

---

[86] Mental Health Act 1983, ss 94 and 96; *Re Shortridge* [1895] 1 Ch 278; *Re Fuller* [1900] 2 Ch 551; *Re Blake* [1887] WN 173.   [87] *Re Parsons* [1940] Ch 973. See also *Thomas* 188–192.
[88] Law of Property Act 1925, s 20.   [89] *Re Whitehead's Will Trusts* [1971] 1 WLR 833, 837.
[90] See Chapter 11 above and *Thomas*, Chs 6, 8, and 9.
[91] *Montefiore v Guedalla* [1903] 2 Ch 723. Cf *Re Sampson* [1906] 1 Ch 435.
[92] *Re Skeats' Settlement* (1889) 42 Ch D 522; *Re Newen* [1894] 2 Ch 297.
[93] *Re Power's Settlement Trusts* [1951] Ch 1074.
[94] *Richard v Mackay*, unreported judgment of 4 March 1987, noted in (1987) 11 Tr Law Int 23; and *Re Beatty's Will Trust (No 2)*, unreported decision of 28 February 1991, noted in (1991) 11 Tr Law Int 177. The English trustees must ensure that they obtain a proper discharge under s 37(1)(c) of the Trustee Act 1925.   [95] See paras 22.58–22.71 below.

E. Appointment of New Trustees Under the Statutory Power

22.42 New trustees may also be appointed under the statutory power conferred by section 36 of the Trustee Act 1925. The statutory power is supplemental to any express power and is exercisable where there is no express power, or where an express power cannot be exercised in the prevailing circumstances (for example because some precondition for its exercise has not been met), and where the statutory power has not been expressly excluded or modified in such a way as to make it unexercisable.

Circumstances in which an appointment of a new trustee may be made

22.43 Section 36 applies in relation to an original or substituted trustee, and whether appointed by the court or otherwise; and it specifies seven instances in which the statutory power may be exercised.

Where a trustee is dead

22.44 This head is relatively straightforward, but it includes the case of a person who is appointed trustee in a will but who then predeceases the testator. However, it does not include the case where all the intended trustees have so died, for there is then no surviving or continuing trustee.[96] The trust will still not fail: the trust property is vested in the testator's personal representative(s) and a new trustee must be appointed by the court.[97]

Where a trustee remains out of the United Kingdom for more than twelve months

22.45 This head applies where a trustee has resided abroad for an unbroken period of twelve months,[98] even when the trustee has been forced to be absent against his will.[99]

22.46 Under section 25 of the Trustee Act 1925 (as substituted by section 5 of the Trustee Delegation Act 1999) a trustee may, by power of attorney, 'delegate the execution or exercise of all or any of the trusts, powers and discretions vested in him as trustee either alone or jointly with any other person or persons'. However, such delegation is possible only for a maximum period of twelve months (commencing on the date of execution of the power of attorney or on the date expressly specified).[100]

Where a trustee desires to be discharged

22.47 This head applies where a trustee 'desires to be discharged from all or any of the trusts or powers reposed in or conferred on him'. It includes an executor who has

---

[96] *Nicholson v Field* [1893] 2 Ch 511.   [97] *Re Williams* (1887) 36 Ch D 231.
[98] *Re Walker* [1901] 1 Ch 259.   [99] *Re Stoneham's Settlement Trusts* [1953] Ch 59.
[100] See further paras 15.05 – 15.08 above. Presumably, by a judicious use of ss 25 and 36, a trustee could contrive to be outside the United Kingdom for a period just short of two years.

paid funeral and testamentary expenses and debts[101] and then assents to a legacy (whether the legacy is settled or not), whereupon he ceases to be executor as such and holds the legacy as trustee. He may then retire and appoint a new trustee in his stead.[102] In the case of land, however, the personal representatives ought to execute a written assent in their own favour as trustees before appointing new trustees: although the appointment itself will be valid, the legal estate in the land will not vest in the new trustees under section 40 of the Trustee Act 1925.[103]

Where a trustee refuses to act

This head includes the case of a trustee who has disclaimed, and therefore never **22.48** took on, the office of trustee.[104]

Where a trustee is unfit to act

This head applies where a trustee, though capable, is unfit to act on the grounds **22.49** of a conviction for a crime of dishonesty,[105] or where the trustee is in liquidation or is bankrupt[106] (although the nature of the trust property may be such that the bankruptcy of the trustee may give rise to no danger or concern).

Where a trustee is incapable of acting

A power to appoint new trustees conferred on a person (whether he is a trustee or **22.50** not) who is incapable, by reason of mental disorder, of executing the power may be exercised, in appropriate circumstances, by the court (which may also make consequential vesting orders).[107]

Where a trustee who is incapable by reason of mental disorder is also entitled to a **22.51** beneficial interest under the trust, a new trustee may not be appointed in his place under section 36(1)(b) without leave of the court under the Mental Health Act 1983, although a person with an <u>express</u> power to remove and appoint may do so, without leave, under section 36(1)(a).

Appointment of an additional trustee

Section 36(6) provides that, where there are not more than three trustees, the per- **22.52** son with the power to appoint new trustees (being the person nominated for this

---

[101] Administration of Estates Act 1925, s 39.

[102] *Re Cockburn's Will Trusts* [1957] Ch 438; *Re Ponder* [1921] 2 Ch 59; *Re Pitt* (1928) 44 TLR 371; *Re Yerburgh* [1928] WN 208; *Re De Sommery* [1912] 2 Ch 622; *Re Timmis* [1902] 1 Ch 176; *Re Earl of Stamford* [1896] 1 Ch 288; *Re Smith* (1889) 42 Ch D 302; *Re Moore* (1882) 21 Ch D 778.

[103] *Re King's Will Trusts* [1964] Ch 542.

[104] *Re Hadley* (1851) 5 De G & Sm 67; *Re Birchall* (1889) 40 Ch D 436.

[105] *Turner v Maule* (1850) 15 Jur 761.

[106] *Re Barker's Trusts* (1875) 1 Ch D 43; *Re Adams' Trust* (1879) 12 Ch D 634.

[107] Mental Health Act 1983, ss 94 and 96; *Re Shortridge* [1895] 1 Ch 278; *Re Fuller* [1900] 2 Ch 551; *Re Blake* [1887] WN 173. See also paras 22.78–22.85 below.

purpose by the trust instrument or, if there is no such person or none able and willing to act, then the trustee or trustees for the time being) may appoint 'another person or persons' to be an additional trustee or trustees. The appointor cannot appoint himself as an additional trustee under this provision (although he can do so when filling a vacancy under section 36(1)).[108] There is no obligation to appoint such an additional trustee (unless the trust instrument or statute direct the contrary);[109] and the number of trustees shall not be increased beyond four.

Persons by whom an appointment may be made

22.53   An appointment of a new trustee under the statutory power may be made by (a) the person or persons nominated for the purpose by the instrument, if any, creating the trust, or (b) if there is no such person, or no such person able and willing to act, then the surviving or continuing trustees or trustee for the time being, or the personal representatives of the last surviving trustee.[110] A 'continuing' trustee includes a 'refusing' or 'retiring' trustee if able and willing to act;[111] but a 'refusing' or 'retiring' trustee does not include a trustee who is compulsorily removed.[112] A sole surviving trustee can obviously appoint a new trustee during his lifetime, but not by his will.[113]

22.54   A power of appointment conferred on persons jointly must (in the absence of an indication to the contrary) be exercised by them jointly. Where they cannot agree on the choice of appointee, they will be regarded as being 'unable' or 'unwilling' to act, and the statutory power will then be exercisable in the surviving or continuing trustee(s).[114]

Mode of exercising the statutory power

22.55   The statutory power to appoint new trustees (under section 36(1) and (6)) must be exercised 'by writing'. This does not include a will.[115] It is standard practice, however, to exercise the power by deed, so that the automatic vesting provisions of section 40 of the Trustee Act 1925 apply.

Separate sets of trustees for separate parts of the trust property

22.56   A separate set of trustees, not exceeding four, may be appointed for any part of the trust property held on trusts distinct from those relating to any other part or parts of the trust property (even if those parts eventually coalesce for the benefit of the

---

[108]   *Re Power's Settlement Trusts* [1951] Ch 1074; *Re Sampson* [1906] 1 Ch 435.
[109]   See also *Peacock v Colling* (1885) 33 WR 528; *Re Knight's Will* (1884) 26 Ch D 82.
[110]   *Re Shafto's Trusts* (1885) 29 Ch D 247; *Nicholson v Field* [1893] 2 Ch 511; *Re Coates to Parsons* (1886) 34 Ch D 370.
[111]   Section 36(8).   [112]   *Re Stoneham's Settlement Trusts* [1953] Ch 59.
[113]   *Re Parker's Trusts* [1894] 1 Ch 707.
[114]   *Re Sheppard's Settlement Trusts* [1888] WN 234.   [115]   ibid.

same beneficiary), notwithstanding that no new trustees or trustee are or is to be appointed for other parts of the trust property, and any existing trustee may be appointed or remain one of such separate sets of trustees.[116] If only one trustee was originally appointed, then one separate trustee may be so appointed.[117] It is not obligatory to appoint more than one new trustee where only one trustee was originally appointed,[118] or to fill up the original number of trustees where more than two trustees were originally appointed. However, except where only one trustee was originally appointed, and a sole trustee when appointed will be able to give receipts for all capital money, a trustee shall not be discharged from his trust unless there will either be a trust corporation or at least two persons to act as trustees to perform the trust.[119] Moreover, nothing in the Trustee Act shall authorize the appointment of a sole trustee, not being a trust corporation,[120] where the trustee, when appointed, would not be able to give valid receipts for all capital money arising under the trust.[121]

Restrictions on the number of trustees

22.57 There are no restrictions on the number of trustees of a trust of personalty, but, as a matter of administrative convenience, it is unusual and imprudent to have more than four.[122] On the appointment of a trustee for the whole or any part of the trust property under the statutory power, the number of trustees may be increased, but not beyond a maximum of four trustees.[123] Section 34 of the Trustee Act 1925 restricts the number of trustees of land to a maximum of four.[124] Also, although a trust of land may have a sole trustee,[125] at least two trustees are needed (unless the sole trustee is a trust corporation) in order to give a valid receipt for the proceeds of sale or other capital money arising under a trust of land or capital money arising under the Settled Land Act 1925.[126]

F. Appointment of New Trustees by the Court

22.58 In addition to its inherent jurisdiction to appoint new trustees, the High Court (or, where the value of the trust fund does not exceed £30,000, the county court)

---

[116] *Re Hetherington's Trusts* (1886) 34 Ch D 211; *Re Moss's Trusts* (1888) 37 Ch D 513.
[117] Section 37(1)(b) of the Trustee Act 1925. See also *Re Parker's Trusts* [1894] 1 Ch 707.
[118] See *Earl of Lonsdale v Beckett* (1850) 4 De G & Sm 73; *Re Birchall* (1889) 40 Ch D 436.
[119] Section 37(1)(c).   [120] Incorporated in a State of the European Union.
[121] Section 37(2).
[122] Charitable trusts and pension fund trustees can act by majority, so the same practical restriction on numbers does not apply.   [123] Trustee Act 1936, s 36(6).
[124] See, however, s 34(3)(a) (land vested in trustees for charitable, ecclesiastical, or public purposes).
[125] *Re Myhill* [1928] Ch 100; *Williams & Glyn's Bank Ltd v Boland* [1981] AC 487.
[126] Trustee Act 1925, s 14(2); Law of Property Act 1925, s 27(2).

also has statutory jurisdiction conferred by section 41 of the Trustee Act 1925. This jurisdiction is exercisable 'whenever it is expedient to appoint a new trustee or new trustees, and it is found inexpedient difficult or impracticable so to do without the assistance of the court'. The court may make an order appointing a new trustee either in substitution for, or in addition to, any existing trustee, or when there is no existing trustee.[127] The court will not act, however, if an express or statutory power could be exercised and there is someone able and willing to exercise it.[128]

22.59 Thus, the court will act in a variety of circumstances, such as, for example, where there is no original trustee of a settlement (for instance because the person named as trustee disclaims or dies, or the settlor inadvertently omitted to appoint a trustee);[129] where a trustee, or the donee of the power of appointment, has become incapable of acting;[130] where an infant has been appointed trustee;[131] where the donees of an express power to appoint cannot agree on the choice of appointee;[132] where there is doubt as to whether the statutory (section 36) power or an express power is exercisable (for example whether a trustee is 'unfit' or 'incapable' of acting);[133] sometimes,[134] where there is dispute or disagreement between the trustees (for example where they cannot act jointly and it becomes impossible to execute the trusts);[135] where a trustee has been convicted of a crime involving dishonesty or is bankrupt and refuses to concur in the appointment of a replacement trustee;[136] or, indeed, where any of the reasons for removing a trustee specified in section 36(1) of the Trustee Act 1925 applies but the statutory power is not available or cannot be exercised.[137]

22.60 In exercising its jurisdiction, the court considers whether the trustee's acts or omissions are 'such as to endanger the trust property or to show a want of honesty or a want of proper capacity to execute the duties or a want of reasonable

[127] Section 41(1).
[128] *Re Gibbon's Trusts* (1882) 30 WR 287; *Re Higginbottom* [1892] 3 Ch 132.
[129] *Dodkin v Brunt* (1868) LR 6 Eq 580; *Viscountess D'Adhermar v Bertrand* (1865) 35 Beav 19; *Re Smirthwaite's Trusts* (1871) LR 11 Eq 251; *Re Davis' Trusts* (1871) LR 12 Eq 214; *Re Moore* (1882) 21 Ch D 778; *Re Williams' Trusts* (1887) 36 Ch D 231.
[130] *Re Lemann's Trusts* (1883) 22 Ch D 633; *Re Phelps' Settlement Trusts* (1885) 31 Ch D 351.
[131] cf *Re Parsons* [1940] Ch 973.
[132] *Re Sheppard's Settlement Trusts* [1888] WN 234; *Re Somerset* [1887] WN 122.
[133] *Re Woodgate's Settlement* (1856) 5 WR 448.
[134] A dispute may well be better dealt with and resolved not by removing one of the trustees but by invoking the court's jurisdiction to control trustees and the administration and execution of trusts.
[135] *Letterstedt v Broers* (1884) 9 App Cas 371; *Re Henderson* [1940] Ch 764; *Earl of Portsmouth v Fellows* (1820) 5 Madd 450; *Re Consiglio's Trusts* (1973) 36 DLR (3d) 658.
[136] *Coombes v Brookes* (1871) LR 12 Eq 61; *Re Adams' Trusts* (1879) 12 Ch D 634; *Re Foster's Trusts* (1886) 55 LT 479; *Re Danson* (1899) 48 WR 73; *Re Henderson* [1940] Ch 764.
[137] See, for example, *Re Bignold's Settlement Trusts* (1872) 7 Ch App 223; *Hutchinson v Stephens* (1834) 5 Sim 498; *Re May's Will Trusts* [1941] Ch 109.

fidelity';[138] or, in the words of Dixon CJ in *Miller v Cameron*,[139] it is exercised 'with a view to the interest of the beneficiaries, to the security of the trust property and to an efficient and satisfactory execution of the trusts and a faithful and sound exercise of the powers conferred upon the trustee'.

Removal and appointment in cases of breach of trust

These broad considerations apply with even greater force where a breach of trust is **22.61** established or alleged. Thus, where one trustee appointed a new trustee because his co-trustee would not participate in a breach of trust, both the appointor and appointee were removed;[140] and where a trustee, who was charged with breach of trust, appointed a new trustee in the face of objections from the complaining beneficiary, the court again removed both the appointor and appointee.[141] It is not necessarily the case, however, that a trustee will be removed and replaced in cases of breach of trust: such an outcome will depend on the circumstances of the case. Thus, where the trust fund is immediately distributable and there are sufficient safeguards to protect the trust assets and the beneficiaries (say, because the beneficiaries are of full age and capacity and do not support the removal), the trustees may not be removed;[142] or where the trustee, if removed, would be deprived of the funds required to pay taxes for which he or it might remain liable after removal, or of its security for costs (but, again, only if there are sufficient safeguards in place).[143]

The court's inherent jurisdiction

The court also has an inherent jurisdiction, which in some ways is wider than that **22.62** conferred by section 41. For example, section 41 does not seem to confer jurisdiction simply to remove a trustee without appointing a replacement, but the court can do so under its inherent jurisdiction—which it may exercise, for example, in an emergency, or where a receiver is appointed to hold the trust assets, or where there are other remaining trustees.[144]

Persons who may be appointed new trustees

The minimum considerations governing the appointment of a new trustee are the **22.63** need to safeguard the trust assets, the protection of the interests of the beneficiaries,

---

[138] *Letterstedt v Broers* (1884) 9 App Cas 371, 386. See also *Re Wrightson* [1908] 1 Ch 789, 803; *Nissen v Grunden* (1912) 14 CLR 297; *Princess Anne of Hesse v Field* [1963] NSWR 998.

[139] (1936) 54 CLR 572, 580. See also *Re Roberts* (1983) 70 FLR 158; *Titterton v Oates* [2001] WTLR 319; *Monty Financial Services Ltd v Delmo* [1996] 1 VR 65.

[140] *Pepper v Tuckey* (1844) 2 Jo & Lat 95.   [141] *Peatfield v Benn* (1853) 17 Beav 522.

[142] *Re Wrightson* [1908] 1 Ch 789, 803; *Nissen v Grunden* (1912) 14 CLR 297; *Princess Anne of Hesse v Field* [1963] NSWR 998.

[143] *Re Pauling's Settlement Trusts* [1963] Ch 576 (where the trustee in question was a bank).

[144] *Re Harrison's Settlement Trusts* [1965] 3 All ER 795, 799; *Re Chetwynd's Settlement* [1902] 1 Ch 692; *Re Henderson* [1940] Ch 764; *Clarke v Heathfield (No 2)* [1985] ICR 606.

and the need to ensure that the trusts are properly implemented. Someone whose own self-interest may conflict with his duty to the trust will, therefore, not generally be appointed (unless the trust instrument requires or contemplates such an appointment, as in the case of some pension scheme trusts)[145] but there is no absolute bar to such an appointment (for example as in the case of a bank with which the beneficiaries, or the trust itself, may have accounts).[146] Although it is proper, and indeed common practice, to consult with, and seek the views of, the beneficiaries as to who is an appropriate choice as new trustee,[147] the decision must be that of the court; and certainly someone who is likely to promote the interests of some beneficiaries at the expense of others will not be appointed. The choice of appointee must ensure the proper administration of the trust. Moreover, the court will not appoint someone ruled out by the settlor, but will seek to give effect to any preference he may have expressed in the trust instrument. The views of a continuing trustee will be taken into account, but he cannot veto a proposed appointment; and, if necessary, the continuing trustee himself may have to be removed and replaced.[148]

Beneficiary as trustee

22.64   A beneficiary may, in appropriate circumstances, be appointed a trustee. Historically, there seems to have been some reluctance on the part of the court to appoint a beneficiary:[149] although the appointment of a life tenant as trustee has been held not to be improper,[150] the view seems to have been that it was inappropriate because of the lack of protection afforded to the remainderman. Similarly, a remainderman would not be appointed trustee by the court, because of the risk posed to the interest of the life tenant.[151] However, even if there ever was such a rule (which is doubtful), it is certainly not an absolute one. It was inconsistent with one of the main features of strict settlements under the Settled Land Acts; and, in relation to many modern trusts, the inclusion of a beneficiary as one of the trustees is often regarded as a clear benefit to all concerned (not least because of the intimate knowledge of the family that such a trustee can provide). Of greater importance than the fact that the proposed appointee is also a beneficiary are considerations such as the purpose of the trust, the powers and discretions at the disposal of the trustees (especially in relation to the destination of income or capital), and, of course, whether there is (or is likely to be) more than one trustee.

---

145 *Re Drexel Burnham Lambert UK Pension Plan* [1995] 1 WLR 32; *Re Parsons* [1940] Ch 973.
146 cf *Re Northcliffe's Settlements* [1937] 3 All ER 804.
147 *Marshall v Sladden* (1849) 7 Hare 428; *O'Reilly v Alderson* (1849) 8 Hare 101.
148 *Re Tempest* (1866) 1 Ch App 485.   149 *Wilding v Bolder* (1855) 21 Beav 222.
150 *Forster v Abraham* (1874) LR 17 Eq 351; *Briggs v Parsloe* [1937] 3 All ER 831. See also *Ex p Clutton* (1853) 17 Jur 988; *Ex p Conybeare's Settlement* (1853) 1 WR 458.
151 *Re Paine's Trusts* (1885) 28 Ch D 725. The court would appoint a remainderman trustee in special circumstances, however, eg where the life tenant was of full age and consented: *Ex p Conybeare's Settlement* (1853) 1 WR 458. A similar objection used to be raised in relation to a near relative of a beneficiary: *Wilding v Bolder* (1855) 21 Beav 222.

Trust solicitor as trustee

Similarly, the court has been reluctant in the past to appoint as new trustee the **22.65** solicitor to the trust, unless there were special circumstances to justify it.[152] This did not mean, however, that such an appointment made without the court's assistance was not valid.[153] In any event, it is doubtful whether any such reluctance will be manifested today: it is not the status of the proposed appointee that matters, but considerations such as the nature of the trusts, the possibility of a conflict of interest, the protection afforded to the trustee, and whether or not the solicitor will be the sole trustee.

Persons resident overseas as trustee

There is no absolute bar to the appointment of persons resident abroad as trustees **22.66** of an English trust: indeed, such an appointment can and is often made in exercise of an express power to appoint.[154] According to Pennycuick V-C in *Re Whitehead's Will Trusts*,[155] 'apart from exceptional circumstances, it is not proper to make such an appointment, that is to say, the court would not, apart from exceptional circumstances, make such an appointment'. The most obvious exceptional circumstances are those in which the beneficiaries have settled permanently in some country outside the United Kingdom and what is proposed is an appointment of new trustees in that country.[156] However, where an express power is concerned, it is for the appointor to decide whether the circumstances or connection with the foreign jurisdiction are such as to justify the appointment of foreign trustees—which may include beneficial tax treatment overseas or the fact that the beneficiaries have substantial overseas business interests—even if the court itself might not have made such an appointment in exercise of its jurisdiction. More recent cases[157] have adopted a wider and more relaxed attitude towards appointments of foreign trustees under express powers than appears to have been the case in *Re Whitehead*.

Where the court is asked to make the appointment, the approach in *Re* **22.67** *Whitehead* is likely to be followed and the court will need to be satisfied that there are exceptional circumstances (in the sense that the beneficiaries are resident

---

[152] *Re Norris* (1884) 27 Ch D 333; *Re Earl of Stamford* [1896] 1 Ch 288; *Re Kemp's Settled Estates* (1883) 24 Ch D 485; *Re Spencer's Settled Estates* [1903] 1 Ch 75. Cf *Re Cotter* [1915] 1 Ch 307 (appointor's own solicitor). [153] ibid.
[154] Unreported decisions in *Richard v Mackay* (1997) 11 Tr Law Int 23 (Millett J: 4 March 1987); *Re Beatty's Will Trusts (No 2)* (1997) 11 Tr Law Int 77 (Vinelott J: 28 February 1991). See also paras 22.35–22.41 above. [155] [1971] 1 WLR 833, 837.
[156] ibid. See also *Re Weston's Settlements* [1969] 1 Ch 223; *Re Windeatt's Will Trusts* [1969] 1 WLR 692; *Re Chamberlain* (1976) 126 NLJ 1034.
[157] Unreported decisions in *Richard v Mackay* (1997) 11 Tr Law Int 23 (Millett J: 4 March 1987); *Re Beatty's Will Trusts (No 2)* (1997) 11 Tr Law Int 77 (Vinelott J: 28 February 1991).

overseas) and that the new jurisdiction has an adequate trust law or at least recognizes and enforces foreign trusts. If the court is asked to exercise its jurisdiction—whether under section 41 or under the Variation of Trusts Act 1958—the applicant must positively satisfy the court that the proposed appointment of foreign trustees is the right thing to do; and the court is not likely to be so satisfied if the purpose is simply to avoid tax.[158] An English court also has an inherent jurisdiction to remove and replace foreign trustees of a foreign settlement, provided the trustees are within the jurisdiction of the English court and subject to *in personam* orders.[159]

Corporations

22.68 Although a corporation could not originally be a trustee at all (having no conscience capable of being bound), and for a long time could only be a trustee of land if it had a licence in mortmain,[160] it has long been the case that a corporation, including a corporation sole,[161] can be appointed as trustee. A body corporate can even be a joint tenant with a natural person.[162] Thus, a power to appoint 'a new trustee or new trustees' (whether an express power or under section 41) and a power to appoint one or more 'persons' (under section 36) authorize the appointment of a corporate trustee.[163]

Appointment of trustees of land and of proceeds of sale of land

22.69 The persons having power to appoint new trustees (including additional trustees) of land shall be bound to appoint the same persons (if any) who are for the time being trustees of any trust of the proceeds of sale of the land.[164] (There is no requirement, however, for two instruments to be used: a single instrument will suffice, in which case these provisions do not apply.)

22.70 Where new trustees of land are appointed, a memorandum of the persons who are for the time being the trustees of the land shall be endorsed on or annexed to the conveyance by which the land was vested in trustees of land; and such conveyance shall be produced to the persons who are for the time being the trustees of the land by the person in possession of it in order for that to be done when the trustees so require.[165]

---

158 *Re Weston's Settlements* [1969] 1 Ch 223.　　159 *Chellaram v Chellaram* [1985] Ch 409.
160 The Mortmain Acts have been repealed.
161 *Bankes v Salisbury Diocesan Council of Education Inc* [1960] Ch 631.
162 The Bodies Corporate (Joint Tenancy) Act 1899.
163 *Re Thompson's Settlement Trusts* [1905] 1 Ch 229.
164 Law of Property Act 1925, s 24, as substituted by the Trusts of Land and Appointment of Trustees Act 1996, s 25(1) and Sch 3, para 4(7).
165 Trustee Act 1925, s 35(1), (3), and (4), as amended by the Trusts of Land and Appointment of Trustees Act 1996, Sch 3, para 3(10).

Protection of purchaser of land

Section 38 of the Trustee Act 1925 provides: **22.71**

(1) A statement, contained in any instrument...by which a new trustee is appointed for any purpose connected with land, to the effect that the trustee has remained out of the United Kingdom for more than twelve months or refuses or is unfit to act, or is incapable of acting, or that he is not entitled to a beneficial interest in the trust property in possession, shall, in favour of a purchaser of a legal estate, be conclusive evidence of the matter stated.

(2) In favour of such purchaser any appointment of a new trustee depending on that statement, and any vesting declaration, express or implied, consequent on the appointment, shall be valid.

Moreover, a purchaser is not concerned to see that the provisions of section 24(1) of the Law of Property Act 1925 have been complied with.[166]

Miscellaneous matters

Ineffective appointments and retirements

An ineffective appointment of new trustees leaves the existing or 'old' trustees in **22.72** place, and it is the latter alone and not the supposed 'new' trustees who remain obliged to carry out the trusts and who may exercise the powers and discretions conferred on trustees.[167] If the trust property is transferred to the 'new' trustees in pursuance of the invalid appointment and then suffers an unauthorized or improper loss, the 'old' trustees remain trustees, and are therefore liable, and the 'new' trustees will also be liable as constructive trustees on the basis that they have intermeddled with the trust property.[168] In principle, similar consequences should follow where a trustee has not effectually retired or been removed and there is no appointment of a new trustee, ie the purportedly retired or removed trustee remains in office.

Administration proceedings

If the court has made a *general* administration order, the donee of a power to appoint **22.73** new trustees ought to obtain the approval of the court before he exercises that power.[169] If he acts without such approval, the appointment is potentially voidable and not void: the appointor must prove, at his own expense, that the appointment was proper and supportable: if he cannot do so, the appointment will be avoided.[170]

---

[166] Law of Property Act 1925, s 24(2).

[167] *Pearce v Pearce* (1856) 22 Beav 248; *Warburton v Sandys* (1845) 14 Sim 622; *Miller v Priddon* (1855) 1 De GM & G 335. See also *Adam & Co International Trustees Ltd v Theodore Goddard* [2000] WTLR 349.

[168] *Pearce v Pearce* (1856) 22 Beav 248. Cf *Lancashire v Lancashire* (1848) 2 Ph 657, where there was an invalid appointment of a new trustee, but the 'old' trustee was held not to be able to resume his position after a long period of inactivity.

[169] *Webb v Earl of Shaftesbury* (1802) 7 Ves Jr 480; *A-G v Clack* (1839) 1 Beav 467; *Middleton v Reay* (1849) 7 Hare 106; *Re Gadd* (1883) 23 Ch D 134.

[170] *A-G v Clack* (1839) 1 Beav 467, 473; *Café v Bent* (1843) 3 Hare 245.

22.74 On the other hand, where the court has made an order for *partial* administration only,[171] the appointor may exercise his power and appoint a new trustee without the court's approval, unless proceedings are on foot to have new trustees appointed or the court has ordered an inquiry in relation to the appointment of new trustees.[172]

Costs

22.75 The costs of appointing a new trustee, including those of the appointor, are borne by the capital of the trust fund.[173]

Indemnity for former trustee

22.76 Under the general law, a trustee has a right of indemnity, which consists of rights of reimbursement, exoneration, retention, and realization.[174] Once a trustee ceases to hold office and to have trust property vested in him or under his control, he loses his right of retention.[175] However, his rights of reimbursement, exoneration, and realization are not dependent on the retention of trust assets. Moreover, he continues to have an equitable charge over,[176] or an equitable interest in,[177] the trust property even after his retirement or replacement.[178]

22.77 Retiring trustees often seek express indemnities from the new trustees. Sometimes, the granting of such indemnities is authorized by the trust instrument. Where this is not the case, the new trustees may still enter into a covenant for indemnity, but their liability will then be entirely personal: the indemnified former trustee will not have recourse to the trust fund by way of subrogation and the new trustees will not be able to resort to the trust fund to satisfy any claim under the indemnity.[179] It is generally thought that, where the new trustees' express covenant is coextensive with the rights of the outgoing trustee to reimbursement and exoneration under the general law, the trust property may be resorted to in order to satisfy any claim made under the covenant. Whether this is supported by reference to an implied power in the new trustees to enter into such an express covenant, or under section 15(f) of the Trustee Act 1925, it still does

---

[171] Rules of the Supreme Court, Ord 85, r 2(1); CPR Part 50, r 50.1 and Sch 1.

[172] *Re Cotter* [1915] 1 Ch 307.

[173] *Harvey v Oliver* (1887) 57 LT 239; *Carter v Sebright* (1859) 26 Beav 374.

[174] *Lewin*, 371–373, 540–542.

[175] *Re Pauling's Settlement (No 2)* [1963] 1 All ER 857. An outgoing trustee may defer the vesting of trust property in the new trustees pending settlement of claims, but this is seldom satisfactory or desirable.   [176] *Stott v Milne* (1884) 25 Ch D 710, 715.

[177] *Jennings v Mather* [1901] 1 KB 108, 113–114; [1902] 1 KB 1, 6, 9.

[178] *Dimos v Dikeakos Nominees Pty Ltd* (1996) 68 FCR 39; *Rothmore Farms Pty Ltd v Belgravia Farms Pty Ltd* (1999) 2 ITELR 159, 170–172.

[179] *Strickland v Symons* (1884) 26 Ch D 245; *Re Evans* (1887) 34 Ch D 597; *Re Gorton* (1889) 40 Ch D 536, 543; *Jennings v Mather* [1901] 1 KB 108; [1902] 1 KB 1.

not permit the creation of rights of indemnity greater than those authorized by the trust instrument or by the general law.

G. Replacement of Trustee Suffering from Mental Disorder

Section 36 of the Trustee Act 1925 and section 96(1)(k) of the Mental Health Act 1983

One of the grounds for removing and replacing a trustee under section 36(1) of the Trustee Act 1925 is that he is 'incapable' of acting, which clearly includes someone suffering from mental disorder within the meaning of the Mental Health Act 1983.[180] Once this ground is established, the statutory power to appoint a new trustee may be exercised by the person(s) nominated for that purpose by the trust instrument or, if there is no such person nor such person able and willing to act, then the surviving or continuing trustees or trustee for the time being, or the personal representatives of the last surviving or continuing trustee.[181] **22.78**

If the person nominated in the trust instrument himself lacks capacity, then he is not 'able' to act and any appointment ought to be made by the continuing trustees, who need not involve the court.[182] If that person is himself a trustee but has no beneficial interest in possession under the trust, the continuing trustees can, under section 36(1), remove him. If he is a trustee and also has a beneficial interest in possession, then the leave of the Court of Protection is required in order to remove him and make the new appointment.[183] If a trustee is incapable and there is no other trustee available to act, and there is no person nominated by the trust instrument for the purpose, a receiver (if any) of the incapable trustee can appoint new trustees under section 96(1)(k) of the Mental Health Act 1983; but, if there is no receiver, the easier course is for the beneficiaries to ask the court to **22.79**

---

[180] 'Incapacity' for the purposes of s 36 is not restricted to such a person, but also includes someone of unsound mind (*Re East* (1873) 8 Ch App 735; *Re Blake* [1887] WN 173) or too old and infirm to act (*Re Lemann's Trusts* (1883) 22 Ch D 633; *Re Weston's Trusts* [1898] WN 151).

[181] For s 36, see paras 22.42–22.57 above. The power of appointment cannot be exercised by an attorney under an enduring power of attorney: the power cannot be delegated to another and is, in any event, not conferred on the person nominated 'as trustee', so that s 3(3) of the Enduring Powers of Attorney Act 1985 does not apply. It is conceivable that, where the person nominated is a 'patient' under the Mental Health Act 1983 and a receiver has been appointed, such receiver may exercise the power, but this requires an application to the court for leave and would seem, in any event, to be unnecessary.

[182] *Re Coates to Parsons* (1886) 34 Ch D 370. However, unless the trust property vests automatically in the new trustees under s 40(1) of the Trustee Act 1925 (which does not apply to assets of the kind specified in s 40(4)), a vesting order may be needed.

[183] Trustee Act 1925, s 36(9).

make an appointment under its statutory jurisdiction in section 41 of the Trustee Act 1925.[184]

22.80 Under section 96(1)(k) of the Mental Health Act 1983, the judge[185] of the Court of Protection has power to make such orders and give such direction and authorities as he thinks fit for the exercise of any power (including a power to consent) vested in a patient, whether beneficially or as guardian or trustee or otherwise.[186] Among the beneficial powers exercisable under the Act are a power to consent to the exercise of a power of advancement under a settlement;[187] a general power of appointment and a power to revoke a voluntary settlement;[188] and the power to appoint an attorney.[189] The all-embracing words of section 96(1)(k)—'whether beneficially, or as guardian or trustee, or otherwise'—clearly authorize the Court of Protection to exercise powers vested in a patient as trustee. Indeed, there is no obvious reason why the words 'as trustee' should be limited to cases in which the patient is an express trustee,[190] while the words 'or otherwise' are wide enough to cover cases where the patient holds a power in a fiduciary capacity (but not as trustee). However, the Court of Protection is not prepared, as a matter of general practice, to authorize the functions of a patient in the administration of a trust. The proper course is to discharge the patient from the trust, with or without the appointment of a replacement trustee. On the other hand, specific powers (fiduciary or non-fiduciary) may be exercised by the court, such as a joint special power of appointment in favour of children of a marriage,[191] and, of course, powers to appoint new trustees[192] (although, where the patient has no beneficial interest in the trust property, the preferred practice is that the application ought to be made in the Chancery Division).

Section 36(6A) to (6D) of the Trustee Act 1925

22.81 Subsections (6A) to (6D) were inserted into section 36 of the Trustee Act 1925 by section 8 of the Trustee Delegation Act 1999. In broad terms, the purpose of the new provisions is to facilitate the appointment of new trustees under section 36(6) in the situation where one co-owner of land has, before losing capacity, delegated his functions as trustee to the other co-owner by enduring power of attorney (two trustees being required to give a valid receipt for the proceeds of sale of the land). The new subsections, which apply only in relation to enduring powers of attorney

---

[184] See paras 22.58–22.77 above.
[185] As to the meaning of which, see ss 112 and 94 of the 1983 Act.
[186] See *Re RHC* [1963] 1 WLR 1095.   [187] *Re Nevill* (1885) 31 Ch D 161.
[188] *Re Price* (CA, 1909).
[189] See Heywood and Massey, *Court of Protection Practice* (12th edn, 1991) 179–180.
[190] *Re A* [1904] 2 Ch 328, 333.   [191] ibid.
[192] *Re Shortridge* [1895] 1 Ch 278; *Re Fuller* [1900] 2 Ch 551. A vesting order may also be made under s 96(2) of the 1983 Act, but only in conjunction with an order under s 96(1)(k); but a vesting order on its own may be made under s 54 of the Trustee Act 1925.

created on or after the date of commencement of the 1999 Act (1 March 2000), provide:

(6A) A person who is either—

(a) both a trustee and attorney for the other trustee (if one other), or for both of the other trustees (if two others), under a registered power; or

(b) attorney under a registered power for the trustee (if one) or for both or each of the trustees (if two or three),[193]

may, if subsection (6B) of this section is satisfied in relation to him, make an appointment under subsection (6)(b) of this section on behalf of the trustee or trustees.

(6B) This subsection is satisfied in relation to an attorney under a registered power for one or more trustees if (as attorney under the power)—

(a) he intends to exercise any function of the trustee or trustees[194] by virtue of section 1(1) of the Trustee Delegation Act 1999; or

(b) he intends to exercise any function of the trustee or trustees in relation to any land, capital proceeds of a conveyance of land or income from land by virtue of its delegation to him under section 25 of this Act or the instrument (if any) creating the trust.

(6C) In subsections (6A) and (6B) of this section 'registered power' means a power of attorney created by an instrument which is for the time being registered under section 6 of the Enduring Powers of Attorney Act 1985.

(6D) Subsection (6A) of this section—

(a) applies only if and so far as a contrary intention is not expressed in the instrument creating the power of attorney (or, where more than one, any of them) or the instrument (if any) creating the trust; and

(b) has effect subject to the terms of those instruments.

Given that an appointment authorized by these provisions would actually be made under section 36(6)(b) of the Act, they would be displaced (as is section 36(6) itself) where the trust instrument confers the power to appoint trustees on a nominated person.

Section 20 of the Trusts of Land Act 1996

Section 20 of the Trusts of Land and Appointment of Trustees Act 1996[195] provides: **22.82**

This section applies where—

(a) a trustee is incapable by reason of mental disorder of exercising his functions as trustee,

---

[193] Subsection (6A) mirrors the requirement of subsection (6) to the effect that additional trustees may not be appointed if there are already more than three trustees.
[194] It seems that, as long as the attorney has a genuine intention to exercise such functions, paragraphs (a) and (b) of subsection (6B) will be satisfied, and there is no need for the attorney actually to have so acted; nor is there a need, it seems, to prove that the appointment of additional trustees is necessary.
[195] Section 20 is similar to s 19, which is dealt with at paras 22.10–22.20 above.

(b) there is no person who is both entitled and willing and able to appoint a trustee in place of him under section 36(1) of the Trustee Act 1925, and

(c) the beneficiaries under the trust are of full age and capacity and (taken together) are absolutely entitled to the property subject to the trust.

Although section 20 cannot apply where there is someone entitled, willing, and able to make an appointment under section 36 of the Trustee Act 1925, it can apply and, oddly, seems to override an express power to the same effect (although section 20, like section 19, of the 1996 Act itself can be expressly excluded).[196]

Section 20(2) provides:

The beneficiaries may give to—

(a) a receiver of the trustee,

(b) an attorney acting for him under the authority of a power of attorney created by an instrument which is registered under section 6 of the Enduring Powers of Attorney Act 1985, or

(c) a person authorised for the purpose by the authority having jurisdiction under Part VII of the Mental Health Act 1983,

a written direction to appoint by writing the person or persons specified in the direction to be a trustee or trustees in place of the incapable trustee.

A direction given under section 20 is subject to the same rules and requirements as one given under section 19[197] and these are set out in section 21 of the 1996 Act. Section 20, unlike section 19, does not, however, include express provisions for the vesting of trust property, but it seems probable that the usual rules apply. In other words, if the appointment is made by deed, the automatic vesting provisions of section 40(1) of the Trustee Act 1925 apply, save in relation to assets of the kind specified in section 40(4) (in which case a vesting order may be required); and section 37(1)(d) of the 1925 Act also probably applies.

Appointment by the court

22.83 Section 41 of the Trustee Act 1925 authorizes the court to appoint a new trustee in substitution for a trustee who is incapable by reason of mental disorder within the meaning of the Mental Health Act 1983 of exercising his functions as trustee. The court also has power to make ancillary vesting orders.[198] Section 41 is dealt with in detail above.[199]

---

[196] Section 21(5). See paras 22.10–22.20 above.
[197] ibid. However, s 20, unlike s 19, does not contain express directions as to the minimum number of trustees. [198] Trustee Act 1925, ss 41, 51.
[199] See paras 22.58–22.77 above.

Section 54 of the Trustee Act 1925 and the Court of Protection's concurrent jurisdiction

An application for the appointment of a new trustee or a vesting order may be **22.84** made to the Court of Protection in cases which fall within section 54(2)(b) or (d) of the Trustee Act 1925, but in other cases the application must be made to the High Court. Section 54 provides:

(1) Subject to the provisions of this section, the authority having jurisdiction under Part VII of the Mental Health Act 1983 shall not have power to make any order, or give any direction or authority, in relation to a patient who is a trustee if the High Court has power under the Trustee Act 1925 to make an order to the like effect.

(2) Where a patient is a trustee and a receiver appointed by the said authority is acting for him or an application for the appointment of a receiver has been made but not determined, then, except as respects a trust which is subject to an order for administration made by the High Court, the said authority shall have concurrent jurisdiction with the High Court in relation to—

  (a) mortgaged property of which the patient has become a trustee merely by reason of the mortgage having been paid off;
  (b) matters consequent on the making of provision by the said authority for the exercise of a power of appointing trustees or retiring from a trust;
  (c) matters consequent on the making of provision by the said authority for the carrying out of any contract entered into by the patient;
  (d) property to some interest in which the patient is beneficially entitled but which, or some interest in which, is held by the patient under an express, implied or constructive trust.

  The Lord Chancellor may make rules with respect to the exercise of the jurisdiction referred to in this subsection.[200]

(3) In this section 'patient' means a patient as defined by section 94 of the Mental Health Act 1983, or a person as to whom powers are exercisable under section 98 of that Act and have been exercised under that section or section 104 of the Mental Health Act 1959.

Vesting of trust assets without removing trustee

Sections 44(ii)(a) (land) and 51(1)(ii)(a) (stock and things in action) of the Trustee **22.85** Act 1925 authorize the court to make an order vesting trust property in the remaining trustees, without removing the trustee under a disability or appointing a new trustee in his place. This may be an appropriate course of action where the trust is not a continuing one and the trust property simply needs to be distributed to the beneficiaries,[201] but generally, and especially in the case of a continuing trust, the

---

[200] Court of Protection Rules 1994, SI 1994/3046, r 17.
[201] *Re Watson* (1881) 19 Ch D 384; *Re Martyn* (1884) 26 Ch D 745.

appropriate course is to remove the trustee under disability, with or without appointing another in his place, and then make the necessary vesting order.[202]

H. Vesting of Trust Property in New Trustees

22.86 Section 37(1)(d) of the Trustee Act 1925 declares that, on the appointment of a trustee for the whole or any part of trust property, any assurance or thing requisite for vesting the trust property, or any part thereof, in a sole trustee or jointly in the persons who are the trustees shall be executed or done. This may be done by means of an express assurance, executed in accordance with the rules applicable to an effective transfer of the particular kind of property, or by means of a 'vesting declaration' operating under statute, or by means of a vesting order made by a competent court.

Vesting of trust property out of court

22.87 Where a new trustee is appointed by deed, there is an automatic implied vesting of trust property by virtue of section 40(1) of the Trustee Act 1925 (unless the deed provides otherwise or the assets in question fall within section 40(4)). Section 40(1) applies on the appointment of a new trustee and provides:

> Where by a deed a new trustee is appointed to perform any trust,[203] then—
>
> (a) if the deed contains a declaration by the appointor to the effect that any estate or interest in any land subject to the trust, or in any chattel so subject, or the right to recover or receive any debt or other thing in action so subject, shall vest in the persons who by virtue of the deed become or are the trustees for performing the trust, the deed shall operate, without any conveyance or assignment, to vest in those persons as joint tenants and for the purposes of the trust the estate interest or right to which the declaration relates, and
>
> (b) if the deed is made after the commencement of this Act and does not contain such a declaration, the deed shall, subject to any express provision to the contrary therein contained, operate as if it had contained such a declaration by the appointor extending to all the estates interests and rights with respect to which a declaration could have been made.

This provision applies to an appointment of a new trustee under an express power and is not confined to one made under a statutory power.

---

[202] *Re Harrison's Settlement Trusts* [1965] 1 WLR 1492; *Re Nash* (1881) 16 Ch D 503. Cf *Re Leon* [1892] 1 Ch 348 and *Re Lees' Settlement Trusts* [1896] 2 Ch 508 (in both of which there were continuing trusts, but the application was unopposed).
[203] This includes a bare trust and a mortgage effected by a declaration of trust: *London and County Banking Co v Goddard* [1897] 1 Ch 642.

Section 40(2) applies where a trustee retires and is discharged by deed, without a **22.88** new trustee being appointed, and provides:

> Where by a deed a retiring trustee is discharged under section 39 of this Act or section 19 of the Trusts of Land and Appointment of Trustees Act 1996 without a new trustee being appointed, then—
>
> (a) if the deed contains such a declaration as aforesaid by the retiring and continuing trustees, and by the other person, if any, empowered to appoint trustees, the deed shall, without any conveyance or assignment, operate to vest in the continuing trustees alone, as joint tenants, and for the purposes of the trust, the estate, interest or right to which the declaration relates; and
>
> (b) if the deed is made after the commencement of this Act and does not contain such a declaration, the deed shall, subject to any express provision to the contrary therein contained, operate as if it had contained such a declaration by such persons as aforesaid extending to all the estates, interests and rights with respect to which a declaration could have been made.

As the opening words of subsection (2) make clear, it applies only where the trustee retires and is discharged under the specified statutory provisions. It does not apply where a trustee retires or is removed under an express power,[204] in which case the trust property ought to be vested in the continuing trustees by an express assurance.

Excluded Property

Not all kinds of trust property fall within the scope of section 40(1) or (2). **22.89** Section 40(4) provides:

> This section does not extend—
>
> (a) to land conveyed by way of mortgage for securing money subject to the trust, except land conveyed on trust for securing debentures or debenture stock;
>
> (b) to land held under a lease which contains any covenant, condition or agreement against assignment or disposing of the land without licence or consent, unless, prior to the execution of the deed containing expressly or impliedly the vesting declaration, the requisite licence or consent has been obtained, or unless, by virtue of any statute or rule of law, the vesting declaration, express or implied, would not operate as a breach of covenant or give rise to a forfeiture;
>
> (c) to any share, stock, annuity or property which is only transferable in books kept by a company or other body, or in manner directed by or under an Act of Parliament.
>
> In this subsection 'lease' includes an underlease and an agreement for a lease or underlease.

Mortgages are excluded because it is standard practice to transfer them without **22.90** disclosing the trusts, so as to keep them off the face of the mortgagor's title.[205]

---

[204] Presumably, s 40(2) applies where section 39 or section 19 (as the case may be) have been incorporated and simply modified in the trust instrument.

[205] See also the Law of Property Act 1925, ss 111–113.

Stocks and shares are transferred by a transfer registered with the company or bank or through the CREST system. Where trust property is held by nominees, the appointment of new trustees will not affect the legal title, but the equitable interest will be held on trust for different beneficiaries, in which case the trustees for the time being must ensure that the nominee's records are amended accordingly. The equitable interest, which would otherwise need to be assigned by signed writing under section 53(1)(c) of the Law of Property Act 1925, will probably pass by a vesting declaration as an equitable 'thing in action'.

Property 'subject to the trust'

22.91 The implied vesting declaration also applies only to property 'subject to the trust', ie to estates and interests which form part of the trust property. Thus, land held by executors as such who have completed administration of the estate but who have not vested the land in themselves as trustees by written assent (in accordance with section 36 of the Administration of Estates Act 1925) will not pass under a vesting declaration on the appointment of new trustees.[206]

Registered land

22.92 Section 40(5) of the Trustee Act 1925 provides that, for purposes of registration of the deed in any registry, the person or persons making the declaration expressly or impliedly, shall be deemed the conveying party or parties, and the conveyance shall be deemed to be made by him or them under a power conferred by the Act. In relation to registered land, under section 47(1) of the Land Registration Act 1925 a vesting declaration under section 40 takes effect subject to the proper entry being made on the register. The original appointment and a certified copy (for filing) must be sent to the Registrar, who will also need to be satisfied that the appointors were entitled to make the appointment. It is common practice and simpler, however, for the registered proprietor to transfer the land to the newly appointed and continuing trustees.

Vesting orders

22.93 The court's jurisdiction to make vesting orders is set out in sections 44 to 56 of the Trustee Act 1925. The jurisdiction extends to all property in any part of Her Majesty's dominions except Scotland.[207]

---

[206] *Re King's Will Trusts* [1964] Ch 542. Cf *Mohan v Roche* [1991] 1 IR 560.

[207] Trustee Act 1925, s 56. See also *Halsbury's Laws of England* (4th edn) vol 6, para 803. The jurisdiction has been exercised in relation to land in Canada (*Re Groom's Trust* (1869) 11 LT 336) and in Ireland (*Re Taitt's Trusts* [1870] WN 257) but it is doubtful whether an English court would now exercise this wide jurisdiction unless there was good reason why an application was not made in the relevant overseas jurisdiction.

Vesting orders of land

Section 44 of the Trustee Act 1925 provides: **22.94**

> In any of the following cases, namely—
>
>   (i) Where the court appoints or has appointed a trustee or where a trustee has been appointed out of court under any statutory or express power;
> (ii) Where a trustee entitled to or possessed of any land[208] or interest therein, whether by way of mortgage or otherwise, or entitled to a contingent right therein, either solely or jointly with any other person—
>
>   (a) is under disability; or
>   (b) is out of the jurisdiction of the High Court;[209] or
>   (c) cannot be found, or, being a corporation, has been dissolved;[210]
>
> (iii) Where it is uncertain who was the survivor of two or more trustees jointly entitled to or possessed of any interest in land;
> (iv) Where it is uncertain whether the last trustee known to have been entitled to or possessed of any interest in land is living or dead;
>   (v) Where there is no personal representative of a deceased trustee who was entitled to or possessed of any interest in land, or where it is uncertain who is the personal representative of a deceased trustee who was entitled to or possessed of any interest in land;[211]
> (vi) Where a trustee[212] jointly or solely entitled to or possessed of any interest in land, or entitled to a contingent right therein, has been required, by or on behalf of a person entitled to require a conveyance of the land or interest or a release of the right, to convey the land or interest or to release the right, and has wilfully refused or neglected to convey the land or interest or release the right for twenty-eight days after the date of the requirement;[213]
> (vii) Where land or any interest therein is vested in a trustee whether by way of mortgage or otherwise, and it appears to the court to be expedient;
>
> the court may make an order (in this Act called a vesting order) vesting the land or interest therein in any such person in any such manner and for any such estate or

---

208 See Trustee Act 1925, s 68(6).

209 Temporary absence will not suffice: *Hutchinson v Stephens* (1834) 5 Sim 498.

210 See *Re Watson* (1881) 19 Ch D 384; *Re Martyn* (1884) 26 Ch D 745; *Re Currie* (1878) Ch D 93; *Re Holland* (1881) 16 Ch D 672; *Re Harrison's Settlement Trusts* [1965] 1 WLR 1492 (a vesting order under this head is inappropriate if there is a continuing trust and the trustee concerned has not been discharged from office).

211 See *Re William's Trusts* (1887) 36 Ch D 231; *Re Rackstraw's Trusts* (1885) 52 LT 612; *Re Pilling's Trusts* (1884) 26 Ch D 432.

212 See *Jones v Davies* [1940] 1 WN 174 (foreclosed mortgagor held to be a trustee).

213 *Re Mills' Trusts* (1888) 40 Ch D 14; *Re Knox's Trusts* [1895] 1 Ch 538, [1895] 2 Ch 483; *Re Crowe's Mortgage* (1871) LR 13 Eq 26; *Re D Jones & Co's Mortgage* (1888) 59 LT 859; *Re Struve's Trusts* (1912) 56 Sol Jo 551; the Law Reform Committee 23rd Report (Cmnd 8733), para 5.8.

interest as the court may direct, or releasing or disposing of the contingent right to such person as the court may direct:

Provided that—

(a) Where the order is consequential on the appointment of a trustee the land or interest therein shall be vested for such estate as the court may direct in the persons who on the appointment are trustees; and

(b) Where the order relates to a trustee entitled or formerly entitled jointly with another person, and such trustee is under disability or out of the jurisdiction of the High Court or cannot be found, or being a corporation has been dissolved, the land interest or right shall be vested in such other person who remains entitled, either alone or with any other person the court may appoint.

22.95 Thus, of the seven cases in which the court may make a vesting order, the first is concerned with an appointment of new trustees; and the remaining six cases apply only where a new appointment is not being made, and are relevant, for example, where a trustee has retired or been removed under an express power (when section 40 of the Trustee Act 1925 does not apply).

Release of land from contingent rights of unborn persons

22.96 Section 45 of the Trustee Act 1925[214] provides:

Where any interest in land is subject to a contingent right in an unborn person or class of unborn persons who, on coming into existence would, in respect thereof, become entitled to or possessed of that interest on any trust, the court may make an order releasing the land or interest therein from the contingent right, or may make an order vesting in any person the estate or interest to or of which the unborn person or class of unborn persons would, on coming into existence, be entitled or possessed in the land.

Effect of vesting order

22.97 Section 49 of the Trustee Act 1925 provides:

A vesting order under any one of the foregoing provisions shall in the case of a vesting order consequential on the appointment of a trustee, have the same effect

(a) as if the persons who before the appointment were the trustees, if any, had duly executed all proper conveyances[215] of the land for such estate or interest as the court directs; or

(b) if there is no such person, or no such person of full capacity, as if such person had existed and been of full capacity and had duly executed all proper conveyances of the land for such estate or interest as the court directs;

and shall in every other case have the same effect as if the trustee or other person or description or class of persons to whose rights or supposed rights the said provisions respectively relate had been an ascertained and existing person of full capacity, and had executed a conveyance or release to the effect intended by the order.

---

214 See *Hargreaves v Wright* (1853) 1 WR 408.   215 See Trustee Act 1925 s 68(1)(3).

In addition, section 9 of the Law of Property Act 1925 provides that a vesting order concerning a legal estate operates to convey or create the legal estate concerned in like manner as if the same had been a conveyance executed by the owner of it.

Power to appoint person to convey

Section 50 of the Trustee Act 1925 provides: **22.98**

> In all cases where a vesting order can be made under any of the foregoing provisions, the court may, if it is more convenient, appoint a person to convey the land or any interest therein or release the contingent right, and a conveyance or release by that person in conformity with the order shall have the same effect as an order under the appropriate provision.

Whether it is 'convenient' to appoint a person to convey, rather than make a vesting order, depends on the circumstances of the particular case. Thus, if the property is to be sold in lots and there are several parties under some disability, it may be less expensive to appoint such a person;[216] or where a sale is to be made out of court and the purchaser is unknown. [217]

Vesting order relating to stock and things in action

Section 51(1) of the Trustee Act 1925 provides: **22.99**

> In any of the following cases, namely—
>
> (i) Where the court appoints or has appointed a trustee, or where a trustee has been appointed out of court under any statutory or express power;
> (ii) Where a trustee entitled, whether by way of mortgage or otherwise, alone or jointly with another person to stock[218] or to a thing in action[219]—
>
>> (a) is under disability;[220] or
>> (b) is out of the jurisdiction of the High Court;[221] or
>> (c) cannot be found, or, being a corporation, has been dissolved;[222] or
>> (d) neglects or refuses to transfer stock or receive the dividends or income thereof, or to sue for or recover a thing in action, according to the direction of the person absolutely entitled[223] thereto for twenty-eight days next after a request in writing has been made to him by the person so entitled;[224] or

---

[216] *Hancox v Spittle* (1857) 3 Sm & G 478. Cf *Shepherd v Churchill* (1857) 25 Beav 21.
[217] *Hipkin v Hipkin* [1962] 1 WLR 49 (sequestered property sold by sequestrator).
[218] See Trustee Act 1925 s 68(14).
[219] See *Re Defense Supplies Corporation's Application* (1948) 65 RPC 172 (application for letters patent).   [220] *Re Dehaynin (Infants)* [1910] 1 Ch 223.
[221] *Re Trubee's Trusts* [1892] 3 Ch 55.
[222] *Re General Accident Assurance Corporation* [1904] 1 Ch 147; *Re Price* [1894] WN 169; *Re Straithblaine Estates Ltd* [1948] Ch 228.
[223] New trustees are 'absolutely entitled' for this purpose: *Re Cane's Trusts* [1895] 1 IR 172; *Re Ellis's Settlement* (1857) 24 Beav 426.   [224] *Re Knox's Trusts* [1895] 2 Ch 483.

(e) neglects or refuses to transfer stock or receive the dividends or income thereof, or to sue for or recover a thing in action for twenty-eight days next after an order of the court for that purpose has been served on him;

(iii) Where it is uncertain whether a trustee entitled alone or jointly with another person to stock or a thing in action is alive or dead;

(iv) Where stock is standing in the name of a deceased person whose personal representative is under disability;

(v) Where, stock or a thing in action is vested in a trustee[225] whether by way of mortgage or otherwise and it appears to the court to be expedient;

the court may make an order vesting the right to transfer or call for a transfer of stock or to receive the dividends or income thereof, or to sue for or recover the thing in action, in any such person[226] as the court may appoint:[227]

Provided that—

(a) Where the order is consequential on the appointment of a trustee, the right shall be vested in the persons who, on the appointment, are the trustees; and

(b) Where the person whose right is dealt with by the order was entitled jointly with another person, the right shall be vested in that last-mentioned person either alone or jointly with any other person whom the court may appoint.

Appointment of person to make or join in a transfer

22.100 Section 51(2) provides:

In all cases where a vesting order can be made under this section, the court may, if it is more convenient, appoint some proper person to make or join in making the transfer: Provided that the person appointed to make or join in making a transfer of stock shall be some proper officer of the bank, or the company or society whose stock is to be transferred.[228]

Effect of order

22.101 Section 51(3) of the Trustee Act 1925 provides:

The person in whom the right to transfer or call for the transfer of any stock is vested by an order of the court under this Act, may transfer the stock to himself or any other person, according to the order, and the Bank of England and all other companies shall obey every order under this section according to its tenor.

Section 51(4) declares:

After notice in writing of an order under this section it shall not be lawful for the Bank of England or any other company to transfer any stock to which the order relates or to pay any dividends thereon except in accordance with the order.

---

225 *Re Deans* [1954] 1 All ER 496: the President of the Family Division was not a trustee of an intestate's property for this purpose; and the same applies, presumably, to the Public Trustee.

226 If there is a beneficiary who is absolutely entitled to the property, the court may vest it in him directly: *Orwin v A-G* [1998] 2 BCLC 693.

227 *Re Harrison's Settlement Trusts* [1965] 1 WLR 1492.

228 *Re Price's Settlement* [1883] WN 202; *Re Holland* (1881) 16 Ch D 672.

Declarations and directions

Under section 51(5):   **22.102**

> The court may make declarations and give directions concerning the manner in which the right to transfer any stock or thing in action vested under the provisions of this Act is to be exercised.[229]

Shares in ships

Section 51(6) provides: **22.103**

> The provisions of this Act as to vesting orders shall apply to shares in ships registered under the Merchant Shipping Act 1995 as if they were stock.

Vesting orders of charity property

Section 52 of the Trustee Act 1925 provides: **22.104**

> The powers conferred by this Act as to vesting orders may be exercised for vesting any interest in land, stock, or thing in action in any trustee of a charity or society over which the court would have jurisdiction upon action duly instituted, whether the appointment of the trustee was made by instrument under a power or by the court under its general or statutory jurisdiction.

Vesting orders for the maintenance etc of an infant beneficiary

Section 53 of the Trustee Act 1925 provides: **22.105**

> Where an infant is beneficially entitled to any property the court may, with a view to the application of the capital or income thereof for the maintenance, education, or benefit[230] of the infant, make an order—
>
> (a) appointing a person to convey such property;[231] or
> (b) in the case of stock, or a thing in action, vesting in any person the right to transfer or call for a transfer of such stock or to receive the dividends or income thereof, or to sue for and recover such thing in action, upon such terms as the court may think fit.

Trustees who are mental patients

Section 54 of the Trustee Act 1925 is dealt with above.[232]   **22.106**

---

[229] *Re Gregson* [1893] 3 Ch 233; *Re CMG* [1898] 2 Ch 324; *Re New Zealand Trust and Loan Company* [1893] 1 Ch 403; *Re Peacock* (1880) 14 Ch D 212.

[230] *Re Heyworth's Contingent Reversionary Interest* [1956] Ch 364; *Re Ropner's Settlement Trusts* [1956] 1 WLR 902; *Re Baron Vestey's Settlement* [1951] Ch 209; *Re Meux* [1958] Ch 154; *Re Bristol's Settled Estates* [1965] 1 WLR 569; *Re Lansdowne's Will Trusts* [1967] Ch 603.

[231] *Re Gower's Settlement* [1934] Ch 365 (mortgage of infant's interest).

[232] See para 22.84 above.

Conclusive nature of certain vesting orders

22.107 Section 55 of the Trustee Act 1925 provides:

> Where a vesting order is made as to any land under this Act or under Part VII of the Mental Health Act 1983, as amended by any subsequent enactment, or under any Act relating to lunacy in Northern Ireland, founded on an allegation of any of the following matters namely—
>
> (a) the personal incapacity of a trustee or mortgagee; or
> (b) that a trustee or mortgagee or the personal representative of or other person deriving title under a trustee or mortgagee is out of the jurisdiction of the High Court or cannot be found, or being a corporation has been dissolved; or
> (c) that it is uncertain which of two or more trustees, or which of two or more persons interested in a mortgage, was the survivor; or
> (d) that it is uncertain whether the last trustee or the personal representative of or other person deriving title under a trustee or mortgagee, or the last surviving person interested in a mortgage is alive or dead; or
> (e) that any trustee or mortgagee has died intestate without leaving a person beneficially interested under the intestacy or has died and it is not known who is his personal representative or the person interested;
>
> the fact that the order has been so made shall be conclusive evidence of the matter so alleged in any court upon any question as to the validity of the order; but this section does not prevent the court from directing a reconveyance or surrender or the payment of costs occasioned by any such order if improperly obtained.

Jurisdictional limits

22.108 Section 56 of the Trustee Act 1925 provides:

> The powers of the court to make vesting orders under this Act shall extend to all property in any part of Her Majesty's dominions except Scotland.[233]

Persons entitled to apply for orders

22.109 Section 58 of the Trustee Act 1925 provides:

> (1) An order under this Act for the appointment of a new trustee or concerning any interest in land, stock, or thing in action subject to trust, may be made on the application of any person beneficially interested[234] in the land, stock, or thing in action, whether under disability or not, or on the application of any person duly appointed trustee thereof.
> (2) An order under this Act concerning any interest in land, stock, or thing in action subject to a mortgage may be made on the application of any person beneficially

---

[233] As for property in Scotland, the court will give leave to the trustees to apply for a vesting order from an appropriate Scottish court: see *Practice Direction* [1945] WN 80 and [1985] 1 All ER 884.

[234] *Re Sheppard's Trusts* (1862) 4 De GF & J 423 (beneficiary with contingent interest); *Ayles v Cox, ex p Attwood* (1853) 17 Beav 584 (purchaser of trust property).

interested in the equity of redemption, whether under disability or not, or of any person interested in the money secured by the mortgage.[235]

Judgment in absence of trustee

Section 59 of the Trustee Act 1925 provides: 22.110

> Where in any action the court is satisfied that diligent search has been made for any person who, in the character of trustee, is made a defendant in any action, to serve him with a process of the court, and that he cannot be found, the court may hear and determine the action and give judgment therein against that person in his character of a trustee as if he had been duly served, or had entered an appearance in the action, and had also appeared by his counsel and solicitor at the hearing, but without prejudice to any interest he may have in the matters in question in the action in any other character.

---

[235] *Re Peacock* (1880) 14 Ch D 212 (new trustees, or purchasers from them, given right to call for a transfer).

23

PARTICULAR TRUSTEES[1] AND PROTECTORS

A. Judicial Trustees

Judicial trustees are appointed by, and act under the supervision and control of, the **23.01** Court.[2] Their functions are regulated by the Judicial Trustees Act 1896[3] and Rules made under that Act.[4] The appointment of a judicial trustee, which is within the discretion of the court,[5] is usually made when there is a breakdown in the administration of the trust, such as, for example, where trustees fail to account or where

---

[1] Regarding particular trustees see J Mowbray et al, *Lewin on Trusts* (17th edn, Sweet & Maxwell, 2000) ('*Lewin*'), paras 19-411–19-436; A Underhill and DJ Hayton, *Law of Trusts and Trustees* (16th edn, Butterworths, 2002) ('*Underhill and Hayton*') 785–802.

[2] *Re Ridsdel* [1947] Ch 597, 605. The court can appoint a judicial trustee in place of an executor or administrator: Judicial Trustees Act 1896, s 1(2) and *Re Wells* [1968] 1 WLR 44; and also to be a Settled Land Act trustee: *Re Marshall's Will Trusts* [1945] Ch 217.

[3] The Act does not apply to charities. It does not extend to Scotland or Northern Ireland.

[4] Judicial Trustee Rules 1983, SI 1983/370.

[5] *Re Chisholm* (1898) 43 SJ 43; *Re Ratcliffe* [1898] 2 Ch 352; *Re Martin* [1900] WN 129.

the complicated affairs of a pension scheme with many members need to be sorted out, but it is not considered necessary or desirable to order full administration.[6]

Who may be appointed

23.02　Any fit and proper person nominated for the role may be appointed as judicial trustee, including an existing trustee, a beneficiary, a solicitor or accountant, or a bank.[7] If the court is not satisfied of the fitness of the nominated person, or if none is nominated at all, the court may appoint one of its own officials (ie the holder of that office for the time being) to act, or a person recommended by a retiring judicial trustee.[8] The court is reluctant to appoint a judicial trustee to act jointly with a private trustee, although it has jurisdiction to do so.[9]

Terms of appointment

23.03　If the court appoints as judicial trustee a person who is not an official of the court, it may require the appointee to give security, usually by guarantee, for what he will receive as judicial trustee and will give directions as to how he is to deal with and account for the same.[10] The court may also give directions as to the vesting of trust property in the judicial trustee and the custody of trust documents.[11] As to the remuneration of the judicial trustee, the court may, on examination of his accounts, allow his disbursements and authorize his remuneration by reference to such rates of professional charges as it thinks fit, or it may specify, on his appointment, the appropriate scale of professional charges, but such remuneration may not in any year exceed 15 percent of the capital value of the trust fund.[12]

Accounts and administration

23.04　Although subject to certain specific rules, especially with regard to accounts, and also to the control of the court, a judicial trustee may, in general, administer the trust in the same way as an ordinary trustee: he may, for example, exercise powers conferred on trustees, including a power to compromise claims, without seeking the court's directions.[13] The accounts of a judicial trustee must be audited once a year by an officer of the court or a professional accountant appointed by the

---

[6] See *Re Ratcliffe, supra*, 355–356; *McDonald v Horn* The Times, 12 October 1993 (and see [1995] 1 All ER 961); *Chichester Diocesan Fund and Board of Finance Inc v Simpson* [1944] AC 341; *Re Diplock* [1948] Ch 465; *Ministry of Health v Simpson* [1951] AC 251.

[7] Judicial Trustees Act 1896, s 1(3); *Re Cohen* [1918] WN 252; *Re Ridsdel, supra; Bowen-Jones v Bowen-Jones* [1986] 3 All ER 163, 167.

[8] Section 1(3): the Official Solicitor is usually appointed. See also *Douglas v Bolam* [1900] 2 Ch 749; and the Judicial Trustee Rules 1983, r 15 and r 16. An official of the court cannot be appointed as judicial trustee in some cases: ibid, r 15.　　　　[9] Section 1(1); *Re Martin* [1900] WN 129.

[10] Judicial Trustee Rules 1983, r 6.　　　[11] ibid, r 7.　　　[12] ibid, r 11.

[13] *Re Ridsdel* [1947] Ch 597. See also Trustee Act 1925, s 15 and paras 14.72–14.75 above.

court.[14] A judicial trustee or, indeed, any person interested in the trust, may ask the court for directions as to the trust or its administration, including the termination of the judicial trusteeship, without the need for any formal originating process.[15] If a judicial trustee fails to comply with the Act, the Rules or the court's directions, or fails to do anything he is required to do, he may be asked to attend in chambers to account for his actions and the court may give such directions as it sees fit, including discharging the judicial trustee and not allowing his remuneration.[16]

Application to the court

A settlor, including an intending settlor, trustee, or beneficiary may apply to the **23.05** High Court for the appointment of a judicial trustee.[17] The claim form must be served on every existing trustee and on such of the beneficiaries as the applicant thinks fit.[18] The application must be supported by a witness statement or affidavit by the applicant containing a short description of the trust instrument, short particulars of the trust property, with an approximate estimate of its capital value and income, details of any incumbrances affecting the property, the persons in possession of trust documents, the names and addresses of the beneficiaries and a short description of their interests, the name, address, and description of the proposed judicial trustee, and proposals for his remuneration.[19]

B. The Public Trustee

The Public Trustee is a corporation sole, with perpetual succession and an official **23.06** seal, established by the Public Trustee Act 1906.[20] She is a salaried official, barred from acting for personal reward, and who may sue and be sued like any other corporation sole.[21] Any losses to a trust caused by the Public Trustee or her officers, and of the kind that an ordinary trustee would be liable to make good, will be made good to the beneficiaries from the Consolidated Fund.[22]

---

[14] Judicial Trustee Act 1896, s 1(6); Judicial Trustee Rules 1983, rr 9, 12, 13. In the case of a corporate judicial trustee, the accounts must be submitted to the person specified by the court. The judicial trustee's accounts need to be lodged with the court for examination by the court only if such person or a beneficiary objects.

[15] Judicial Trustee Rules 1983, rr 9–14.   [16] ibid, r 14.

[17] Sections 1(1), 2. See also Civil Procedure Rules, Pt 8, rr 8.1(2)(b) and 6, and Practice Direction, Pt 8(b), Section A.3.

[18] Judicial Trustee Rules 1983, r 4. If the application is made by an intending settlor, it need not be served on anyone.   [19] ibid, r 3.

[20] The Act applies to English trusts only: Public Trustee Act 1906, s 17(2). See also *Re Hewett's Settlement* [1915] 1 Ch 228. Cf *Re Ardagh's Estate* [1914] 1 IR 5.

[21] Public Trustee Act 1906, ss 1, 11. The Public Trustee's central office must be in London: Public Trustee Rules 1912, r 3.   [22] Public Trustee Act 1906, s 7.

23.07   The Public Trustee may act alone or jointly with any person or body of persons and has the same duties, powers, and liabilities, rights and immunities as an ordinary trustee acting in the same capacity, and is subject to the control of the court in the same way.[23] Nor is the Public Trustee in a position different from that of a private trustee in respect of conflicts of interest and is, therefore, equally subject, for example, to the self-dealing rule.[24]

Excluded trusts

23.08   The Public Trustee must not accept trusts which are exclusively for religious or charitable purposes;[25] any trust created solely by way of security for money;[26] any trust for the benefit of creditors;[27] and any trust involving the management or carrying on of a business, unless (a) she is merely a custodian trustee without power of management and either holds no property which exposes her to risk or the circumstances are exceptional and she is fully indemnified or secured against loss, or (b) where she accepts as an ordinary trustee, under exceptional circumstances, and either the consent of the Treasury has been obtained or the trusteeship has been accepted for no more than eighteen months and with a view only to winding up the business and she is satisfied that it can be carried on without risk.[28] This prohibition does not prevent the Public Trustee from accepting a trust merely because it holds shares in public or private trading companies. However, if the trust holds a controlling shareholding and the trustee is not authorized to leave the management of the company to another,[29] the position may well be different.

23.09   The Public Trustee may decline to act or may prescribe conditions on which she will accept any trust, but cannot decline to act merely on the ground that the trust property is of small value.[30]

The Public Trustee as an ordinary trustee

23.10   The Public Trustee may, by that name or by any other sufficient description, be appointed trustee of any trust,[31] unless the trust instrument directs the contrary.[32] The appointment may be made by the settlor, by the person having power to appoint a new trustee, or by the court.[33] She may be appointed as an original

---

[23] ibid, s 2(2); *Re Leslie Hassop's Estates* [1911] 1 Ch 611.

[24] *Re New Haw Estates Trusts* (1912) 107 LT 191. See also *Re Phillips* (1931) 101 LJ Ch 338. cf *Re Abercrombie's Will Trusts* [1931] WN 109.

[25] Public Trustee Act 1906, s 2(5). See also *Re Hampton* (1918) 88 LJ Ch 103; *Re Shaw* [1957] 1 WLR 729.   [26] Public Trustee Rules 1912, r 6.

[27] Public Trustee Act 1906, s 2(4).   [28] ibid; Public Trustee Rules 1912, r 7.

[29] *Re Lucking's Will Trusts* [1968] 1 WLR 866; *Bartlett v Barclays Bank Trust Co Ltd* [1980] Ch 515.

[30] Public Trustee Act 1906 s 2(3).

[31] Other than those trusts she is forbidden from accepting: see para 23.08 above.

[32] Public Trustee Act 1906, s 5(1), (3). The court may still override an express provision in the trust instrument.   [33] ibid, s 5(1).

trustee or as a new, substituted, or additional trustee. The consent of the Public Trustee, under her official seal, must be obtained before she is appointed, except where the appointment is by will, when the appointment does not take effect until such consent has been secured.[34] The Public Trustee does not become a trustee until she has accepted her appointment.[35] Notice of any proposed appointment of the Public Trustee must, where practicable, be given in the prescribed manner to all persons beneficially interested who are resident in the United Kingdom and whose addresses are known to the person proposing to make the appointment or, if such persons are infants, to their guardians. Any such person may, within 21 days of the receipt of any such notice, apply to the court for an order preventing such appointment and the court may make such order if, having regard to the interests of all the beneficiaries, it considers it expedient to do so.[36] Failure to give such notice does not invalidate the appointment, however.[37] The court is not likely to appoint the Public Trustee against the wishes of a substantial number of the beneficiaries,[38] nor against the wishes of a continuing trustee if nothing has been alleged against him, unless it is expedient to do so.[39]

The Public Trustee may be appointed sole trustee even in cases where there were **23.11** originally two or more trustees and where the trust instrument stipulates that there shall be more than one trustee; and, when appointed, she may exercise powers expressly declared to be exercisable only by at least two trustees.[40] The Public Trustee, being a trust corporation, can give a good receipt for the proceeds of sale of land.[41]

The Public Trustee as custodian trustee

The Public Trustee is also authorized by the Public Trustee Act 1906 to act as cus- **23.12** todian trustee of any trust.[42] Any banking or insurance company, or other body corporate entitled to act as such, may also be appointed custodian trustee. Custodian trustees generally are dealt with in Section C of this chapter.[43]

---

[34] Public Trustee Rules 1912, r 8(2).   [35] ibid. See also *Re Shaw* (1914) 110 LT 924.
[36] Public Trustee Act 1906, s 5(4). The notice must be addressed to the relevant person's last known place of abode or place of business and be served by post or delivered: Public Trustee Rules 1912, r 40(2), (3). See also Civil Procedure Rules, Pt 8, r 8.1(2)(b) and (6), and Practice Direction, Pt 8(b), Section A.3.
[37] *Re Firth* [1912] 1 Ch 806; *Re Drake's Settlement* [1926] WN 132.
[38] ibid.   [39] *Re Kensit* [1908] WN 235.
[40] Public Trustee Act 1906, s 5(1); *Re Leslie's Hassop Estates* [1911] 1 Ch 611; *Re Ardagh's Estate* [1914] 1 IR 5; *Re Moxon* [1916] 2 Ch 595; *Re Duxbury's Settlement Trusts* [1995] 1 WLR 425.
[41] Trustee Act 1925, s 14(2); Law of Property Act 1925, s 27(2).
[42] Public Trustee Act 1906, s 4(1), (3); Public Trustee Rules 1912, r 6(d). This does not extend to those trusts which the Public Trustee is forbidden from accepting: see para 23.08 above.
[43] See paras 23.21–23.25 below.

Fees of the Public Trustee[44]

23.13 The Public Trustee's fees are regulated by section 9 of the Public Trustee Act 1906, the Public Trustee (Fees) Act 1957, and orders made thereunder.[45] Each such order must specify whether the fee is payable out of capital or income; and, where it is payable out of capital, the Public Trustee has power to direct, with the consent of the beneficiary of full age entitled to income, that it shall be paid out of income if she thinks there are special reasons which make it expedient to do so.[46] Current fees are set out in the Public Trustee (Fees) Order 1999,[47] and include an acceptance fee, an administration fee, a withdrawal fee, and fees for particular services. All these fees are to be paid out of capital except for the following, which are payable out of income:

(a) fees which, under section 1(3) of the 1957 Act, the Public Trustee directs to be paid out of income;

(b) the administration fee payable in respect of annuities and similar terminable payments;

(c) the insurance fee;

(d) the income-collection fee;

(e) the management fee where the Public Trustee acts as a trustee of a superannuation scheme or on behalf of the trustees of a friendly society or runs a common investment scheme;

(f) VAT on a fee which is itself payable out of income.

Where fees are payable out of income, they have to be borne rateably by the persons entitled to the trust income.[48]

Complaints against the Public Trustee

23.14 Any person aggrieved by any act or omission or decision of the Public Trustee in relation to any trust may apply to the court, and the court may make such order as it thinks just.[49]

---

[44] *Underhill and Hayton* 792–793; *Lewin*, para 19-45.

[45] Public Trustee (Fees) Order 1999, SI 1999/ 855. See also Trustee Act 2000, s 29(5)(b) which prevents the application of s 29 to the Public Trustee.   [46] Public Trustee (Fees) Act 1957, s 1.

[47] SI 1999/855.

[48] *Re Roberts' Will Trusts* [1937] Ch 274. See also *Re Bentley* [1914] 2 Ch 456; *Re Hicklin* [1917] 2 Ch 278; *Re Hulton* [1936] Ch 536; *Re Riddell* [1936] Ch 747; *Re Godwin* [1938] Ch 341; *Re Evans' Will Trusts* [1948] Ch 185; *Re Koenigsberg* [1949] Ch 348.

[49] Public Trustee Act 1906, s 10. The application is made to a judge of the Chancery Division in Chambers, by claim form under CPR, Pt 50 r 50(1). See also *Re Wilson* [1964] 1 WLR 214.

Miscellaneous provisions

The Public Trustee may employ such solicitors, bankers, accountants, and brokers **23.15** or other persons as she may consider necessary, having regard to the interests of the trust. She must, where practicable, take into consideration the wishes of the creator of the trust, the other trustees (if any), and the beneficiaries.[50] The Public Trustee may also take and rely on professional advice and assistance in regard to legal and other matters and act on credible information of facts.[51]

The Public Trustee may make advances out of public money for the purposes of **23.16** any trusts estate of which she is a trustee.[52] The Public Trustee, if appointed in any capacity, is not required to give a bond or security, but is subject to the same liabilities as if she had done so.[53]

The Public Trustee is bound to keep a register setting out the date of acceptance of **23.17** a trust, particulars of the trust property, of the person entitled to income, of any notices received as to dealings with any beneficial interest, of the exercise or release of any power, of any decision or opinion of the court in respect of the trust, and also decisions of her own relating to the trust. Such registers are to be kept at the central office in London.[54] A separate account is to be kept for each trust, with separate accounts of capital and income.[55]

The entry of the name of the Public Trustee in the books of a company does not **23.18** constitute notice of a trust, and no one is affected with such notice merely because he deals with the Public Trustee.[56] A company may not object to the entry of the name of the Public Trustee on its books by reason only that she is a corporation.

Trust securities and documents must be kept at the bank to the trust or some other **23.19** safe place allowed by the Treasury.[57]

The Public Trustee may invest money belonging to any trust and coming into her **23.20** hands in any mode of investment (a) expressly or impliedly authorized by the trust instrument or (b) if there is no trust instrument, authorized by law for the investment of trust funds. She may also pay and deposit such money in court for investment in any manner authorized by rules made under section 38(7) of the Administration of Justice Act 1982; or, if authorized by the trust instrument or otherwise by law, retain any investment existing at the date of commencement of the trust. However, the Public Trustee should not invest in or hold any investment

---

[50] Public Trustee Act 1906, s 11(2). This power, being exercisable when considered 'necessary', would appear to be narrower than the general power in s 11 of the Trustee Act 2000.
[51] Public Trustee Rules 1912, r 26.   [52] ibid, r 25.
[53] Public Trustee Act 1906, s 11(4).   [54] Public Trustee Rules 1912, r 16.
[55] ibid, r 19.   [56] Public Trustee Act 1906, s 11(5).
[57] Public Trustee Rules 1912, r 18.

in such manner as to expose her to liability as the holder thereof, unless she is satisfied that she is fully indemnified or secured against loss.[58]

C. Custodian Trustees[59]

23.21 A custodian trustee is usually appointed to hold trust investments or trust documents, while the administration or management of the trust remains in the hands of ordinary trustees (who are usually then called managing trustees). Thus, a custodian trustee undertakes certain duties in relation to the trust and is therefore distinguished from a bare trustee.[60] The use of a custodian trustee saves the expense of transferring trust assets every time a new trustee is appointed; and it is often regarded as a safeguard against potential breaches of trust. In the case of trusts with large trust funds or complicated trust arrangements, such as unit trusts and pension schemes, a custodian trustee is usually appointed expressly under the terms of the trust.

Bodies who may be appointed custodian trustees

23.22 The custodian trustee is a creature of statute. The Public Trustee and any banking or insurance company or other body corporate authorized by the Public Trustee Act 1906 and rules made thereunder may be appointed as custodian trustee.[61] Under rule 30 of the Public Trustee Rules 1912,[62] the following corporations are entitled to act as custodian trustees:

(1) the Treasury Solicitor;
(2) any corporation[63] which:

    (a) is constituted under the law of the United Kingdom or of any part thereof, or under the law of any other Member State of the European Economic Community or of any part thereof;

    (b) is empowered by its constitution to undertake trust business (which for the purpose of this rule means the business of acting as trustee under wills and settlements and as executor and administrator) in England and Wales;

    (c) has one or more places of business in the United Kingdom; and

    (d) is—

        (i) a company incorporated by special Act of Parliament or Royal Charter, or a company registered (with or without limited liability) in the United

---

[58] Public Trustee Rules 1912, r 17. See also SI 1987/821; SI 1988/817; SI 1990/518; SI 1991/1227; SI 1997/177; SI 1999/1021.

[59] *Underhill and Hayton*, 796–800; *Lewin*, paras 19-46–19-51.

[60] *IRC v Silverts Ltd* [1951] Ch 521; *Re Brooke Bond & Co Ltd's Trust Deed* [1963] Ch 357.

[61] Public Trustee Act 1906, s 4(1), (3).

[62] As substituted by SI 1975/1189 (Public Trustee (Custodian Trustee) Rules 1975) and amended by SI 1976/836 (Public Trustee (Custodian Trustee) Rules 1976); SI 1981/358 (Public Trustee (Custodian Trustee) Rules 1981); SI 1984/109 (Public Trustee (Custodian Trustee) Rules 1984); SI 1985/132 (Public Trustee (Custodian Trustee) Rules 1985); SI 1987/1891; SI 1994/2519.

[63] The Bank of Ireland satisfies para (b): see *Re Bigger* [1977] Fam 203.

Kingdom under the Companies Act 1948[64] or under the Companies Act (Northern Ireland) 1960 or in another Member State of the European Economic Community and having a capital (in stock or shares) for the time being issued of not less than £250,000 (or its equivalent in the currency of the State where it is registered) of which not less than £100,000 (or its equivalent) has been paid up in cash,[65] or

(ii) a company which is registered without limited liability in the United Kingdom under the Companies Act 1948 or the Companies Act (Northern Ireland) 1960 or in another Member State of the European Economic Community and of which one of the members is a company within any of the classes defined in this sub-paragraph;

(3) any corporation which is incorporated by special Act or Royal Charter or under the Charitable Trustees Incorporation Act 1872[66] which is empowered by its constitution to act as a trustee for any charitable purposes, but only in relation to trusts in which its constitution empowers it to act;

(4) any corporation which is constituted under the law of the United Kingdom or of any part thereof and having its place of business there, and which is either:

(a) established for the purpose of undertaking trust business for the benefit of Her Majesty's Navy, Army, Air Force or Civil Service or of any unit, department, member or association of members thereof, and having among its directors or members any persons appointed or nominated by the Defence Council or any Department of State or any one or more of those Departments, or

(b) authorised by the Lord Chancellor to act in relation to any charitable, ecclesiastical or public trusts as a trust corporation, but only in connection with any such trust as is so authorised;

(5) any Regional Health Authority, District Health Authority or special health authority, but only in relation to any trust which the authority is authorised to accept or hold by virtue of section 90 of the National Health Service Act 1977;

(6) the British Gas Corporation,[67] or any subsidiary of the British Gas Corporation, but only in relation to a pension scheme or pension fund established or maintained by the Corporation by virtue of section 36 of the Gas Act 1972;

(7) the London Transport Executive,[68] but only in relation to a pension scheme or pension fund—

(a) which is established or administered by the Executive by virtue of section 6 of the Transport (London) Act 1969, or

(b) in relation to which rights, liabilities and functions have been transferred to the Executive by an order under section 74 of the Transport Act 1962 as applied by section 18 of the Transport (London) Act 1969;

---

[64] See now Companies Act 1985.

[65] Meaning capital and not current assets: *Re Skinner* [1958] 1 WLR 1043, 1049–1050.

[66] Repealed by the Charities Act 1993.

[67] Dissolved by the British Gas Corporation Dissolution Order 1990, SI 1990/147, and its undertaking transferred to British Gas plc pursuant to Part II of the Gas Act 1986.

[68] Now London Regional Transport: London Regional Transport Act 1984.

(8) any of the following, namely—

    (a) the Greater London Council;[69]

    (b) the corporation of any London borough (acting by the council);

    (c) a county council, district council, parish council or community council;

    (d) the Council of the Isles of Scilly;

    (e) the Common Council of the City of London;

but only in relation to charitable or public trusts (and not trusts for an ecclesiastical charity or for a charity for the relief of poverty) for the benefit of the inhabitants of the area of the local authority concerned and its neighbourhood, or any part of that area;

(9) any of the following, namely—

    (a) a metropolitan district council[70] or a non-metropolitan county council,

    (b) the corporation of any London borough (acting by the council),

    (c) the Common Council of the City of London,

    (d) the Council of the Isles of Scilly,

but only in relation to any trust under which property devolves for the sole benefit of a person who occupies residential accommodation provided under section 21(l)(a) of the National Assistance Act 1948 by the local authority concerned or is in the care of that authority; and a corporation acting as a custodian trustee by virtue of this paragraph in relation to any trust is entitled to continue so to act in relation to that trust until a new custodian trustee is appointed, notwithstanding that the person concerned ceases to occupy such accommodation or to be in the care of that authority, as the case may be;

(10) the National Coal Board,[71] or any subsidiary of the National Coal Board, but only in relation to a scheme or arrangements established under regulations made under section 37 of the Coal Industry Nationalisation Act 1946;

(11) any corporation acting as trustee of the trusts of any pension scheme or pension fund established or maintained by the British Broadcasting Corporation but only in relation to those trusts;

(12) any corporation appointed by the Secretary of State as a trustee of any scheme having effect by virtue of regulations made under section 37 of the Coal Industry Nationalisation Act 1946 for purposes relating to pensions, gratuities or other like benefits and in relation to which provision is, or has been, made by regulations made under paragraph 2(1) of Schedule 5 to the Coal Industry Act 1994 for the scheme to continue in force notwithstanding the repeal by the Coal Industry Act 1994 of section 37 of the Coal Industry Nationalisation Act 1946 and of the enactments modifying that section, but only in relation to such a scheme.

---

[69] Abolished by the Local Government Act 1985.   [70] Also abolished: ibid.

[71] Replaced by the British Coal Corporation. See regulations under the Coal Industry Act 1994, Sch 5, para 2; and SI 1994/2519.

Duties, rights, and liabilities of custodian trustee

Section 4(2) of the Public Trustee Act 1906 sets out the functions and rights of **23.23** a custodian trustee as follows:

(1) the trust property must be transferred to the custodian trustee as if he were sole trustee (and any vesting orders made under the Trustee Act 1925)[72] and (without prejudice to the rights of any other person) the custodian trustee is to have the custody of all securities and documents of title relating to the trust property, but the managing trustees may have access to them and may make copies of them or extracts thereof;

(2) the management of the trust property and the exercise of any power or discretion exercisable by the trustees of the settlement remains vested in the managing trustees;

(3) the custodian trustee must concur in and perform all acts necessary to enable the managing trustees to exercise their powers of management or any other power or discretion vested in them (including the power to pay money or securities into Court) unless the matter in which such concurrence is required is a breach of trust or involves personal liability;

(4) all sums payable to or out of the income or capital of the trust property must be paid to the custodian trustee, but the custodian trustee may allow the income to be paid to or at the direction of the managing trustees, and in such case is exonerated from seeing to the application thereof and is not answerable for any loss or misapplication thereof;

(5) the power of appointing new trustees, when exercisable by the trustees, is exercisable by the managing trustees alone (and the custodian trustee is not to be counted in the number of trustees), but the custodian trustee has the same power of applying to the court for the appointment of a new trustee as any other trustee;

(6) the custodian trustee, if he acts in good faith, is not liable for accepting as correct and acting upon the faith of any written statement by the managing trustees as to any birth, death, marriage, or other matter of pedigree or relationship, or other matter of fact upon which the title of the trust property or any part thereof may depend nor for acting upon any legal advice obtained by the managing trustees independently of the custodian trustee.

Charges

A custodian trustee may charge fees, and retain or pay the same out of the trust, **23.24** even if there is no charging clause in the trust instrument, provided such fees do not exceed those chargeable by the Public Trustee when acting as custodian trustee.[73] A custodian trustee, like any other trustee, cannot profit from his trust.[74]

---

[72] See paras 22.86–22.100 above.
[73] See Public Trustee Act 1906, s 4(3). A trust corporation cannot be appointed as both custodian trustee and managing trustee so as to charge fees.
[74] *Re Brooke Bond & Co Ltd's Trust Deed* [1963] Ch 357.

Termination of custodian trusteeship

23.25 The court may, on the application of the custodian trustee, or any managing trustee or any beneficiary, make an order terminating the custodian trusteeship if it is satisfied that this is the general wish of the beneficiaries or that it is otherwise expedient to do so.[75] If the custodian trustee is to be appointed sole ordinary trustee, application should be made to the court to have the custodian trusteeship terminated and an order for appointment as ordinary trustee made.[76]

D. Trust Corporations

23.26 The appointment of a trust corporation has numerous advantages, such as avoidance of changes in trusteeship and continuity of administration, and is perceived to provide greater security as well as access to a range of expertise. A trust corporation, unlike an ordinary sole trustee, can also give a good receipt for capital moneys.[77] A trust corporation may act as sole trustee or as a co-trustee with an individual.[78]

23.27 A 'trust corporation' means the Public Trustee or a corporation either (a) appointed by the court in any particular case to be a trustee or (b) entitled to act as custodian trustee under rules made under section 4 of the Public Trustee Act 1906.[79] The qualifications are set out in the Public Trustee (Custodian Trustee) Rules 1975[80] and include any corporation which:

    (a) is constituted under the law of the United Kingdom or any other Member State of the European Union; and

    (b) is authorized by its constitution to undertake trust business in England and Wales;

    (c) has one or more places of business in the United Kingdom; and

    (d) being a registered company has issued capital (in stock or shares) for the time being of not less than £250,000 (or its equivalent in the currency of the State where the company is registered), of which not less than £100,000 (or its equivalent) has been paid up in cash.

---

[75] Public Trustee Act 1906, s 4(2)(i).   [76] *Re Squire's Settlement* (1946) 62 TLR 133.

[77] Trustee Act 1925, s 14(2); Law of Property Act 1925, s 27(2); Settled Land Act 1925, ss 18(1)(c), 94, 95. See also (1997/98) 4 Trusts & Trustees 6 (N Johnson).

[78] Bodies Corporate (Joint Tenancy) Act 1899; *Re Thompson's Settlement Trusts* [1905] 1 Ch 229. This is not recommended in practice, however.

[79] Trustee Act 1925, s 68(18); Law of Property Act 1925, s 205(1)(xxviii). See para 23.22 above.

[80] SI 1975/1189. See para 23.22 above.

The expression generally designates a trust corporation which undertakes, for **23.28** profit, the administration of trusts. For certain purposes,[81] the expression also includes the Treasury Solicitor, the Official Solicitor, and any person holding any other official position prescribed by the Lord Chancellor; and, in relation to the property of a bankrupt and property subject to a deed of arrangement, the trustee in bankruptcy and the trustee under the deed respectively; and, in relation to charitable, ecclesiastical, and public trusts, any local or public authority so prescribed; and any other corporation constituted under the laws of the United Kingdom which satisfies the Lord Chancellor that it undertakes the administration of such trusts without remuneration, or that by its constitution it is required to apply the whole of its net income after payment of outgoings for charitable, ecclesiastical, or public purposes, and is prohibited from distributing, directly or indirectly, any part thereof by way of profits amongst any of its members, and is authorized by him to act in relation to such trusts as a trust corporation.[82]

Position of trust corporations

In general, a trust corporation is subject to the same duties and has the same **23.29** powers as an ordinary trustee.[83] However, it also enjoys a special status for some purposes and is subject to special provisions in some respects.

(a) A trust corporation as sole trustee can give a valid receipt for capital moneys.[84]

(b) A new trustee may be appointed out of court in place of a trust corporation (or any other corporate trustee) which is dissolved.[85]

(c) A higher standard of care is required from a remunerated trust corporation, such as a bank, than an unpaid trustee.[86]

(d) Relief under section 61 of the Trustee Act 1925 will be granted to a trust corporation only in exceptional circumstances.[87]

(e) A new trustee may be appointed in place of a trust corporation (or any other corporate trustee) which has been removed under a power in the trust instrument as if the corporation desired to be discharged.[88]

---

[81] For the purposes of the Law of Property Act 1925, The Settled Land Act 1925, the Administration of Estates Act 1925, and the Supreme Court Act 1981.

[82] Law of Property (Amendment) Act 1925, s 3.

[83] Where a corporate trustee acted as both trustee and banker, a successor trustee will not be in a worse position in respect of information on the bank account and production of documents than if an individual had been a trustee: *Tiger v Barclays Bank Ltd* [1952] 1 All ER 85.

[84] Trustee Act 1925, s 14(2); Law of Property Act 1925, s 27(2); Settled Land Act 1925, ss 18(1)(c), 94, 95.

[85] Trustee Act 1925, s 36(3): the corporation is deemed to be 'incapable' of acting.

[86] *Bartlett v Barclays Bank Trust Co Ltd (No 1)* [1980] Ch 515, 534. See also Trustee Act 2000, s 1.

[87] *Re Pauling's Settlement Trusts* [1964] Ch 303, 338–339.

[88] Trustee Act 1925, s 36(2).

(f) A sole trustee can retire from the trust (notwithstanding section 37 of the Trustee Act 1925) when a trust corporation is appointed as a new trustee.

(g) The court may make an order, under section 41 of the Trustee Act 1925, appointing a new trustee in place of a trust corporation (or any other corporate trustee) which is in liquidation or has been dissolved. The necessary vesting orders may be made under sections 44 and 51 where a trustee, being a corporation, has been dissolved.

Remuneration of trust corporation

Express provision in trust instrument

23.30 The trust instrument will usually make express provision for the remuneration of a trust corporation. It ought to include provision authorizing the charging of scale fees and specifying the different functions for which a charge may be made (and be submitted to the trust corporation for its approval), for the standard professional charging clause will not do so.[89] Section 29 of the Trustee Act 2000 authorizes the remuneration of a trust corporation which is not otherwise entitled to charge for its services, but this seems to be restricted to reasonable remuneration for services actually rendered (and not scale fees). Similarly, section 28 of the 2000 Act authorizes a trust corporation which can invoke an express charging clause in the trust instrument to charge for services capable of being performed by a lay trustee, provided this is not inconsistent with the terms of the trust (and, again, charging scale fees may be inconsistent).

Authorization by the court

23.31 Where the court appoints a trust corporation to act as trustee (solely or jointly), it may authorize the corporation to charge such remuneration for its services as the court may think fit.[90]

Authorization by the beneficiaries

23.32 A trust corporation may be authorized to charge for its services out of the capital or income of the trust fund by those beneficiaries of full age and capacity who are entitled to such capital or income; or, alternatively, it may act in return for covenanted payments directly from such beneficiaries.

Trust corporation as custodian trustee

23.33 A trust corporation which acts as a custodian trustee may charge remuneration in accordance with section 4(3) of the Public Trustee Act 1906. However, it cannot

---

[89] *Re Cooper* (1939) 160 LT 453.
[90] Trustee Act 1925, s 42. See also *Re Young* [1934] WN 106; *Re Masters* [1953] 1 WLR 81.

be appointed to act as both custodian trustee and managing trustee, and any such appointment is wholly void.[91]

E. Protectors[92]

It is increasingly common, especially in relation to 'offshore' trusts, to appoint a **23.34** person, or use a mechanism, independent of the trustees, who or which is intended to monitor, oversee, and even control the trustees in the administration of a trust. Usually, such a person is called a 'protector',[93] but he may also be called an 'appointor' or 'specified person' (although the latter expressions are usually confined to persons involved in the actual exercise of specific powers) or even a 'committee of management' or a 'board'. Whichever expression is used, it is not a term of art. Moreover, protectors may have widely differing functions. In some cases, the protector's role is simply to be consulted by the trustees or to give or withhold consent to a particular exercise of a specific power, such as a power to invest in certain kinds of assets. In other cases, the protector has dispositive powers, or power to remove and appoint new trustees, or power to change the jurisdiction of the trust, or a right to demand the production of trust accounts. Although the protector is independent of the trustees, and does not have any trust property vested in him (and is, therefore, not a trustee himself), very often his primary function is to ensure that the settlor's wishes are implemented in the administration of the trust.[94]

The role of office of protector is usually regarded as a fiduciary one,[95] but it need **23.35** not necessarily be so. Thus, a protector with a power to remove or appoint trustees will be a fiduciary, just like any other person with such a power;[96] but there is no reason why a protector with a dispositive power must necessarily be in a fiduciary

---

[91] *Forster v Williams Deacons Bank Ltd* [1935] 1 Ch 359; *Arning v James* [1936] Ch 158.

[92] See, generally, DWM Waters, 'The Protector: New Wine in Old Bottles?' in AJ Oakley (ed), *Trends in Contemporary Trust Law* (Oxford, 1996) 63; R Ham, E Campbell and M Tennet, 'Protectors' in J Glasson (ed), *The International Trust* (Jordans, 2002) 225; P Matthews, 'Protectors: Two Cases, Twenty Questions' (1995) 9 Trust Law Int 108; A Duckworth, 'Protectors—Fish or Fowl' (1995) 4 JITCP 131 and (1996) 5 JITCP 18; (1995) 1 JITCP 31 (A Penney); (1995) 4 Trusts & Trustees 12 (AJ Conder); (1993) 1 JITCP 88 (RC Lawrence).

[93] Reflecting the historic role of the 'protector' of settled land in the context of the Fines and Recoveries Act 1833. The consent of such a protector was required for certain transactions, but he was not a fiduciary: 1833 Act, s 36.

[94] See, for example, *Re the Hare Trust* (2001) 4 ITELR 288. It is possible, but seldom advisable, for the settlor himself to be the protector.

[95] *IRC v Schroder* [1983] STC 480; *Steel v Paz Ltd* [1993–95] Manx LR 426; *Re the settlements made between X and Charles Richard Blamfield and Abacus (C) Ltd* (RC of Jersey, 28 January 1994); *Von Knierem v Bermuda Trust Co Ltd* (1994) Butterworths Offshore Cases, vol 1, 116–125; *Rawson Trust v Perlman* (SC of Bahamas, 25 April 1995); *Re Osiris Trustees* (2000) 2 ITELR 404.

[96] *Re Skeats' Settlement* (1889) 42 Ch D 522; *Mettoy Pension Trustees v Evans* [1990] 1 WLR 1587, 1620.

position any more than any other non-trustee appointor or a person who holds or reserves a power to revoke or amend the trust. A protector is not a trustee and it cannot be presumed that all and any powers conferred on him are necessarily fiduciary powers.[97] On the other hand, a protector does not have to be a trustee to be in a fiduciary position. Moreover, powers generally are not inherently fiduciary or non-fiduciary and there is little to be gained, in this context at least, from classifying them as such:[98] they become fiduciary powers when they are conferred on a person who occupies a fiduciary office. A protector, unlike an ordinary individual, holds office. This does not necessarily make all his powers fiduciary in nature, but it tends to equate the protector more with the trustee. It may also be added that it would be odd if a protector, unlike a trustee, were not bound, for example, by the rules against self-dealing or profiting from the trust, or could exercise his powers for his own benefit. Clearly, the trust instrument should specify whether or not the office of protector in relation to that trust is intended to be a fiduciary office and whether all the powers (and, if not, which powers) conferred on the protector are intended to be fiduciary powers. However, if this is not done, then, in the final analysis, the court must consider the nature and function of the protector, and of the particular power(s) under scrutiny, within the context of that particular trust and in the light of the purposes for which it or they were conferred. It will be material whether the protector is an office holder without a direct personal interest under the trust or in the beneficiaries, or simply a named individual with such an interest. If the function of the power is crucial to the proper running of the trust as a whole and for the welfare of the beneficiaries as a whole, or if a failure or refusal to act could jeopardize the proper administration of the trust, it is suggested that it is likely that the protector is a fiduciary and, as such, subject to duties similar to those of the trustees. The court's primary function, after all, is to protect the trust and its beneficiaries and not the settlor or the protector. There is also the added advantage to the protector that, as a fiduciary, it becomes easier to claim remuneration and an indemnity from the trust fund.

---

[97] *Re Z Trust* [1997] CILR 248.

[98] See, for example, the classification in *Mettoy Pension Trustees v Evans, supra*, 1613 (and para 17.14 above).

24

VARIATION AND AMENDMENT OF TRUSTS

A. Deviation from the Terms of the Trust: Introduction

24.01 Trustees must make themselves aware of the terms of the trust and must comply with those terms. Trustees who do not carry out the terms of their trust by distributing the trust property to the wrong persons or by exceeding or acting outside the powers given to them by the trust instrument will be liable for breach of trust. A trustee who fails to adhere to the terms of the trust but who has 'acted honestly and reasonably, and ought fairly to be excused for the breach of trust and for omitting to obtain the directions of the court in the matter in which he committed such breach' can apply to the court and may be relieved either wholly or partly from personal liability for the breach.[1]

---

[1] Trustee Act 1925, s 61.

24.02   There are, however, circumstances in which trustees are able to deviate from the terms of the trust without fear of incurring personal liability and without entertaining the uncertainty of an application for relief from liability after the event. This chapter is concerned with lawful deviation from the terms of the trust whether achieved with the consent of the beneficiaries[2] or under the approval of the court. The court may approve a transaction under its inherent jurisdiction to supervise the administration of trusts[3] or by statute under section 57 of the Trustee Act 1925,[4] section 64 of the Settled Land Act 1925,[5] or the Variation of Trusts Act 1958.[6]

B. Variation With the Consent of the Beneficiaries

24.03   A trustee can deviate from the terms of the trust without fear of personal liability if the beneficiaries who are between themselves entitled to the entire beneficial interest are *sui juris*[7] and in agreement that the trustee should be authorized to take the deviant step. Trustees are protected in this way because beneficiaries who concur in a breach of trust are unable to bring proceedings against trustees for the consequences of a breach which they have authorized.[8]

24.04   If all of the beneficiaries entitled to the whole beneficial interest are *sui juris* they can compel the trustees to hand over the property to them or to others to whom they direct and thus bring the trusts to an end.[9] What beneficiaries cannot do is to compel trustees to act in a particular way or to exercise their discretion according to the will of the beneficiaries while maintaining the trusts.[10] In *Stephenson v Barclays Bank Trust Co Ltd*[11] Walton J analysed the position in the following way:

> Now it is trite law that the persons who between them hold the entirety of the beneficial interests in any particular trust fund are as a body entitled to direct the trustees how that trust fund is to be dealt with, and this is obviously the legal territory from which that definition derives. However, in view of the arguments advanced to me by counsel for the respondents, and more particularly that advanced by him on the basis of the decision of Vaisey J in *Re Brockbank*, I think it may be desirable to state what I conceive to be certain elementary principles. (1) In a case where the persons who between them hold the entirety of the beneficial interests in any particular trust fund are all sui juris and acting together ('the beneficial interest holders'), they are entitled to direct the trustees how the trust fund may be dealt with. (2) This does not mean, however, that they can at one and the same time override the

---

[2] See paras 24.03–24.04 below.   [3] See paras 24.05–24.11 below.
[4] See paras 24.16–24.18 below.   [5] See paras 24.12–24.15 below.
[6] See paras 24.19–24.45 below.   [7] That is, of full age and mental capacity.
[8] *Re Pauling's Settlement Trusts* [1963] 3 All ER 1, 11. Where a trustee has reason to suspect that a beneficiary has given consent under the undue influence of another he may yet be liable.
[9] *Saunders v Vautier* (1841) 4 Beav 115.   [10] *Re Brockbank* [1948] Ch 206.
[11] [1975] 1 All ER 625.

pre-existing trusts and keep them in existence. Thus, in *Re Brockbank* itself the beneficial interest holders were entitled to override the pre-existing trusts by, for example, directing the trustees to transfer the trust fund to X and Y, whether X and Y were the trustees of some other trust or not, but they were not entitled to direct the existing trustees to appoint their own nominee as a new trustee of the existing trust. By so doing they would be pursuing inconsistent rights. (3) Nor, I think, are the beneficial interest holders entitled to direct the trustees as to the particular invest-ment they should make of the trust fund. I think this follows for the same reasons as the above. Moreover, it appears to me that once the beneficial interest holders have determined to end the trust they are not entitled, unless by agreement, to the further services of the trustees. Those trustees can of course be compelled to hand over the entire trust assets to any person or persons selected by the beneficiaries against a proper discharge, but they cannot be compelled, unless they are in fact willing to comply with the directions, to do anything else with the trust fund which they are not in fact willing to do. (4) Of course, the rights of the beneficial interest holders are always subject to the right of the trustees to be fully protected against such matters as duty, taxes, costs or other outgoings; for example, the rent under a lease which the trustees have properly accepted as part of the trust property.[12]

C. Inherent Jurisdiction of the Court

The High Court has inherent jurisdiction to supervise the administration of **24.05** trusts.[13] The county court has a statutory jurisdiction where the total value of the fund in question does not exceed £30,000.[14] The court does not have unlimited jurisdiction to authorize a variation of trust in favour of persons who are not *sui juris* such as children and persons who, though interested in the trusts, have not been born.[15] Apart from statute, there are, at most, four cases in which the court has inherent jurisdiction to modify or vary trusts affecting persons who are not *sui juris* subject to the preconditions that all persons who are *sui juris* consent and the modification or variation is clearly for the benefit of all persons interested who are not *sui juris*. The four circumstances in which the court has intervened in the past are: (a) cases in which the court has effected changes in the nature of an infant's property, for example by directing investment of his personalty in the purchase of freeholds; (b) cases in which the court has allowed the trustees of settled property to enter into some business transaction which was not authorized by the settlement; (c) cases in which the court has allowed maintenance out of income which the settlor or testator directed to be accumulated; (d) cases in which the court has approved a compromise on behalf of infants and possible after-born beneficiaries.[16]

---

[12] [1975] 1 All ER 625, 637. See also paras 7.05–7.07 above.
[13] The jurisdiction is exercisable by the Chancery Division.
[14] County Courts Act 1984, s 23.   [15] *Chapman v Chapman* [1954] AC 429.
[16] *Chapman v Chapman* [1954] AC 429, 451.

For these purposes a compromise means an agreement relating to disputed rights and so the court has no inherent jurisdiction to approve a scheme of variation which affects the interests of persons who are not *sui juris*. That jurisdiction derives from the Variation of Trusts Act 1958.[17]

24.06 The first of these cases does not involve a variation of the beneficial interests of the person under a disability but merely the authorization of investment in property which the trustees could not invest in without the approval of the court. The other three cases are generally described as 'salvage' or 'emergency' cases, 'maintenance' cases, and 'compromise' cases.[18]

24.07 The leading decision in relation to the salvage and emergency[19] cases is *Re New*[20] in which case the Court of Appeal authorized trustees to concur in a shareholders' scheme for the reconstruction of a prosperous limited company, shares in which had become vested in the trustees. The evidence showed that the scheme would be greatly to the advantage of all parties interested including infants and unborn persons.

24.08 The jurisdiction in such cases is only available where the case is one which may reasonably be supposed to be one not foreseen or anticipated by the author of the trust, where the trustees are embarrassed by the emergency that has arisen, and the consent of all the beneficiaries cannot be obtained by reason of some of them not being *sui juris* or in existence.[21] This is also an administrative jurisdiction. It does not enable the court to intervene in order to approve the variation of beneficial interests.[22]

24.09 'Maintenance' cases[23] arise where the trust dispositions have provided for accumulations of income in favour of an infant during his minority without providing for his maintenance during that period: but this provision would be stultified if the infant were not maintained while the income was accumulating. The court has in such cases refrained from enforcing the letter of the trusts, and by authorizing maintenance has saved the infant from starving while the harvest designed for him was in the course of ripening.[24]

24.10 Examples include *Re Walker*,[25] *Re Allen*[26] and *Re Collins*.[27] Although providing that income might be paid towards the maintenance of a minor could be said to

---

[17] See paras 24.19–24.45 below.

[18] *Chapman v Chapman* [1954] AC 429, 469–470, *per* Lord Asquith of Bishopstone.

[19] Cases of 'emergency' involve the authorization of an activity which must, of necessity, be undertaken if the trustees are to act in the best interests of the beneficiaries. Cases of 'salvage' involve the authorization of an activity necessary for the preservation of the trust property.

[20] [1901] 2 Ch 534.   [21] *Re New* [1901] 2 Ch 534, 544 per Romer LJ.

[22] *Re Tollemarche* [1903] 1 Ch 457; *Chapman v Chapman* [1954] AC 429.

[23] It would now be unusual to encounter a case in which there is no provision for maintenance, for example, because of the exclusion of Trustee Act 1925, s 31.

[24] *Chapman v Chapman* [1954] AC 429, 469.   [25] *Walker v Duncombe* [1901] 1 Ch 879.

[26] *Re Allen, Havelock v Havelock* (1881) 17 Ch D 807.

[27] *Re Collins, Collins v Collins* (1886) 32 Ch D 229.

result in the variation of beneficial interests it is clear that even this jurisdiction is extremely limited. In *Re Walker* Farwell J said:

> I decline to accept any suggestion that the court has an inherent jurisdiction to alter a man's will because it thinks it beneficial. It seems to me that is quite impossible.

'Compromise' cases involve a compromise of rights (under the settlement or will) **24.11** which are the subject of doubt or dispute. It is then often in the interest of all interested parties, adult or infant or unborn, to have certainty substituted for doubt.[28] This jurisdiction is available in the case of genuine disputes and not where what is proposed is a scheme of variation which does not compromise a genuine dispute. Examples include *Re Trenchard,*[29] *Re Wells,*[30] *Re Hylton's Settlement,*[31] and *Re Chapman.*[32] As in the case of applications under the Variation of Trusts Act 1958, the court can only approve a compromise on behalf of persons who are not *sui juris* or not yet in existence if the compromise is for the benefit of those persons.

D. Settled Land Act 1925, Section 64

The court has a general jurisdiction under section 64 of the Settled Land Act 1925 **24.12** to authorize transactions in respect of settled land. The section provides that:

(1) Any transaction affecting or concerning the settled land, or any part thereof, or any other land (not being a transaction otherwise authorised by this Act, or by the settlement) which in the opinion of the court would be for the benefit of the settled land, or any part thereof, or the persons interested under the settlement, may, under an order of the court, be effected by a tenant for life, if it is one which could have been validly effected by an absolute owner.

(2) In this section 'transaction' includes any sale, exchange, assurance, grant, lease, surrender, reconveyance, release, reservation, or other disposition, and any purchase or other acquisition, and any covenant, contract, or option, and any application of capital money and any compromise or other dealing, or arrangement; and 'effected' has the meaning appropriate to the particular transaction; and the references to land include references to restrictions and burdens affecting land.

The jurisdiction under this section is broader than that under the Trustee Act **24.13** 1925, section 57[33] although the section only applies where a settlement under the Settled Land Act 1925 contains or includes land. Where the land has been sold the section ceases to have any application.[34]

---

[28] *Chapman v Chapman* [1954] AC 429, 469.   [29] [1902] 2 Ch 378.
[30] [1903] 1 Ch 848.
[31] *Re Lord Hylton's Settlement, Barclays Bank Ltd v Joliffe* [1954] 2 All ER 647n; [1954] 1 WLR 1055.
[32] [1954] AC 429.
[33] See paras 24.16–24.18 below. *Re Downshire Settled Estates, Marquess of Downshire v Royal Bank of Scotland* [1953] 218, 253.
[34] *Re Simmons, Simmons v Public Trustee* [1956] Ch 125.

24.14 The breadth of the jurisdiction derives from the definition of 'transaction' in subsection (2) which is not confined to matters of an administrative nature in the management of the trusts[35] although it can be used for those limited purposes.[36] Schemes of variation have been approved under the section which have the effect of reducing liability for tax.[37]

24.15 Schemes approved under section 64 include (1) transferring settled land into another settlement under which the life tenant would continue to have a life interest but his heir, the Marquess of Blandford, would take a life interest in protective trusts;[38] (2) distributing capital to the life tenant in exchange for the release of a power of appointment;[39] (3) the transfer of assets into a maintenance fund the beneficiaries of which included persons who did not benefit under the Settled Land Act 1925 settlement;[40] (4) raising a capital sum to pay the tenant for life's debts backed by a life assurance policy ensuring repayment on his death;[41] and (5) raising £10,000 to enable the tenant for life to live in the mansion house until it could be sold.[42]

The section is no longer available (as was formerly the case in relation to land held on trust for sale) where land is held on a trust of land[43]. Where land is held on a trust of land dealings may be authorized under section 57 of the Trustee Act 1925 or under the Variation of Trusts Act 1958 but not under the Settled Land Act 1925, section 64.

E. Trustee Act 1925, Section 57

24.16 Section 57 of the Trustee Act 1925 extended the inherent jurisdiction of the High Court extant in relation to cases of emergency and salvage to cases of expediency. The section provides that :

(1) Where in the management or administration of any property vested in trustees, any sale, lease, mortgage, surrender, release, or other disposition, or any purchase, investment, acquisition, expenditure, or other transaction, is in the opinion of the court expedient, but the same cannot be effected by reason of the absence of any power for that purpose vested in the trustees by the trust instrument, if any, or by law, the court may by order confer upon the trustees, either

---

[35] *Re Downshire Settled Estates, supra*, 252, *per* Evershed MR; *Re Simmons, supra*.
[36] *Re Scarisbrick's Re-Settlement Estates* [1944] Ch 229.
[37] *Re Downshire Settled Estates, supra*.
[38] *Hambro v Duke of Marlborough* [1994] Ch 154.   [39] *Re Simmons, supra*.
[40] *Raikes v Lygon* [1988] 1 WLR 281.   [41] *Re White-Popham Settled Estates* [1936] Ch 725.
[42] *Re Scarisbrick's Re-Settlement Estates, supra*.
[43] Trusts of Land and Appointment of Trustees Act 1996 repealed Law of Property Act 1925, s 28: the section which provided an essential bridge between the powers of trustees for sale and Settled Land Act trustees.

generally or in any particular instance, the necessary power for the purpose, on such terms, and subject to such provisions and conditions, if any, as the court may think fit and may direct in what manner any money authorized to be expended, and the costs of any transaction, are to be paid or borne as between capital and income.

(2) The court may, from time to time rescind or vary any order made under this section, or may make any new or further order.

(3) An application to the court under this section may be made by the trustees, or by any of them, or by any person beneficially interested under the trust.

(4) This section does not apply to trustees of a settlement for the purposes of the Settled Land Act, 1925.

Unlike section 64 of the Settled Land Act 1925, the jurisdiction under this section **24.17** is expressly limited to the management or administration of trust property. It is not a section intended to enable the court to rewrite trusts in the manner contemplated by the Variation of Trusts Act 1958 and, apart from enabling the court to intervene in non-emergency cases, it has a limited effect on the jurisdiction of the court to authorize deviations from the terms of the trust.[44] Nonetheless, following the introduction of section 57 of the Trustee Act 1925 it is no longer necessary to show that the case is one of salvage or emergency but that the transaction in relation to the management or administration of the trust property is expedient.

The words 'management or administration' contemplate the managerial supervision **24.18** and control of trust property on behalf of beneficiaries[45] and 'expedient' means expedient for the trust as a whole, not for a single beneficiary.[46] The power has been exercised to authorize the purchase of a life tenant's interest[47] and to enable the life tenant's debts to be paid with the backing of an insurance policy.[48] It has also been exercised to approve the partition of land[49] and to authorize sale in circumstances in which the necessary consent was not forthcoming.[50]

F. The Variation of Trusts Act 1958

The difficulties encountered as a result of the limited interpretation of the **24.19** breadth of the court's inherent jurisdiction in *Chapman v Chapman*[51] led to the

---

[44] *Re Downshire Settled Estates, Marquess of Downshire v Royal Bank of Scotland* [1953] Ch 218, 248.

[45] *Re Downshire, supra*, 247; *Re Forster's Settlement, Michelmore v Byatt* [1954] 1 WLR 1450.

[46] *Re Craven's Estate, Lloyds Bank Ltd v Cockburn (No 2)* [1937] Ch 431.

[47] *Re Foster's Settlement, Michelmore v Byatt* [1954] 3 All ER 714.

[48] *Re Salting, Ballie-Hamilton v Morgan* [1932] 2 Ch 57.

[49] *Re Thomas, Thomas v Thompson* [1930] 1 Ch 194.

[50] *Re Beal's Settlement Trusts, Huggins v Beal* [1932] 2 Ch 15.

[51] [1954] AC 429. The Act was enacted to give effect to the recommendations of the Law Reform Committee, *Sixth Report (Court's Power to Sanction Variation of Trusts)* Cmnd 310 (1957).

introduction of the Variation of Trusts Act 1958, a revolutionary[52] enhancement of the court's jurisdiction to approve the variation of beneficial interests on behalf of those unable to give their consent.

24.20 The Act gives the court a broad discretionary jurisdiction to approve variations in respect of trusts of real and personal property whether created before or after the passing of the Act and whether arising under a will, a settlement, or other disposition but does not apply to property settled by Act of Parliament.[53] The jurisdiction is therefore very wide and applies even to trusts of which the proper law is not that of England and Wales.[54]

24.21 Section 1(1) of the Variation of Trusts Act 1958 provides as follows:

> Where property, whether real or personal, is held on trusts arising, whether before or after the passing of this Act, under any will, settlement or other disposition, the court may if it thinks fit by order approve on behalf of—
>
> (a) any person having, directly or indirectly, an interest, whether vested or contingent, under the trusts who by reason of infancy or other incapacity is incapable of assenting, or
>
> (b) any person (whether ascertained or not) who may become entitled, directly or indirectly, to an interest under the trusts as being at a future date or on the happening of a future event a person of any specified description or a member of any specified class of persons, so however that this paragraph shall not include any person who would be of that description, or a member of that class, as the case may be, if the said date had fallen or the said event had happened at the date of the application to the court, or
>
> (c) any person unborn, or
>
> (d) any person in respect of any discretionary interest of his under protective trusts where the interest of the principal beneficiary has not failed or determined,
>
> any arrangement (by whomsoever proposed, and whether or not there is any other person beneficially interested who is capable of assenting thereto) varying or revoking all or any of the trusts, or enlarging the powers of the trustees of managing or administering any of the property subject to the trusts:
> Provided that except by virtue of paragraph (d) of this subsection the court shall not approve an arrangement on behalf of any person unless the carrying out thereof would be for the benefit of that person.

---

[52] *Re Steed's Will Trusts, Sandford v Stevenson* [1960] 1 All ER 487, 493, *per* Lord Evershed MR. A striking example of the revolutionary nature of the jurisdiction is *Chapman v Chapman* itself: In *Re Chapman's Settlement Trusts (No 2)* [1959] 2 All ER 47n the arrangement which was not approved under the previous regime in *Chapman v Chapman* [1954] AC 429 was approved under the Act.

[53] Variation of Trusts Act 1958, s 1(6).

[54] *Re Ker's Settlement Trusts* [1963] Ch 533 (where the proper law was that of Northern Ireland); *Re Paget's Settlement, Baillie v De Brossard* [1965] 1 All ER 58 (where the proper law was that of New York); *Re Barton, Tod v Barton & Ors* [2002] WTLR 469.

F. The Variation of Trusts Act 1958

24.22 The section gives the court a discretionary[55] jurisdiction to approve arrangements on behalf of four classes of persons listed in paragraphs (a) to (d). Under the Variation of Trusts Act 1958 the court does not make a variation nor can it bind persons who are *sui juris* but unwilling to consent.[56] The court merely supplies the necessary consent on behalf of persons who cannot provide consent themselves. The 1958 Act has thus been viewed by the courts as a statutory extension of the consent principle embodied in the rule in *Saunders v Vautier*[57] discussed earlier in this chapter.[58] The principle recognizes the rights of beneficiaries, who are *sui juris* and together absolutely entitled to the trust property, to exercise their proprietary rights to overbear and defeat the intention of a testator or settlor to subject property to the continuing trusts, powers, and limitations of a will or trust instrument.

24.23 The nature of the court's jurisdiction has been explained by Lord Reid in the following way:[59]

> Under the Variation of Trusts Act the court does not itself amend or vary the trusts of the original settlement. The beneficiaries are not bound by variations because the court has made the variation. Each beneficiary is bound because he has consented to the variation. If he was not of full age when the arrangement was made he is bound because the court was authorised by the Act to approve of it on his behalf and did so by making an order. If he was of full age and did not in fact consent he is not affected by the order of the court and he is not bound. So the arrangement must be regarded as an arrangement made by the beneficiaries themselves. The court merely acted on behalf of or as representing those beneficiaries who were not in a position to give their own consent and approval.

24.24 In *Goulding v James*[60] Mummery LJ identified three propositions derived from three decisions of Megarry J.[61] First, what varies the trust is not the court, but the agreement or consensus of the beneficiaries. Secondly, there is no real difference in principle in the rearrangement of the trusts between the case where the court is exercising its jurisdiction on behalf of persons under the Variation of Trusts Act 1958 and the case where the resettlement is made by virtue of the doctrine in *Saunders v Vautier*[62] by all the adult beneficiaries joining together. Thirdly, the court is merely contributing on behalf of infants and unborn and unascertained persons the binding assents to the arrangement which they, unlike an adult beneficiary, cannot give.

---

[55] See the words 'if it thinks fit' in s 1(1). Since the jurisdiction is discretionary, reasons must be given in support of an application: *Re Oakes' Settlement Trusts* [1959] 2 All ER 58.
[56] *Knocker v Youle* [1986] 2 All ER 914; *Re Suffert's Settlement* [1960] 3 All ER 561.
[57] (1841) 4 Beav 115.   [58] See paras 24.03–24.04 above.
[59] *Re Holmden's Settlement Trusts, IRC v Holmden* [1968] 1 All ER 148, 151.
[60] [1997] 2 All ER 239.
[61] *Re Holt's Settlement* [1969] 1 Ch 100, 120C–D; *Re Ball's Settlement Trusts* [1968] 1 WLR 899, 905E; and *Spens v Inland Revenue Commissioners* [1970] 1 WLR 1173, 1184A–D.
[62] (1841) 4 Beav 115.

Benefit

24.25 Except in the case of a person falling within paragraph (1)(d)[63] the court cannot approve an arrangement on behalf of any person unless the carrying out of that arrangement would be for the benefit of that person[64] but the proviso does not *require* the court to approve a variation on the basis that there is benefit[65] for the power remains discretionary. In exercising its discretion, the function of the court is to protect those who cannot protect themselves.[66] Nonetheless, the benefit need not be certain so, when considering the question of benefit as regards, for example, unborn persons on whose behalf approval is sought, the court should be prepared to take the sort of risk that an adult would be prepared to take[67] or to 'take a broad view, but not a galloping, gambling view'.[68]

24.26 Benefit is not limited to financial benefit[69] but extends to moral or social benefit.[70] However, approval will not be given for an arrangement which deprives the persons on whose behalf approval is sought of an interest under the settlement without providing any compensation simply because doing so is for the general benefit of the family including those persons.[71]

24.27 The court is also concerned whether the arrangement as a whole, in all the circumstances, is such that it is proper to approve it. The court's concern involves, *inter alia*, a practical and businesslike consideration of the arrangement, including

---

[63] See below at paras 24.36–24.38. [64] Variation of Trusts Act 1958, s1(1) proviso.

[65] *Re Van Gruisen's Will Trusts, Bagger v Dean* [1964] 1 All ER 843.

[66] *Re Weston's Settlement Trusts* [1969] 1 Ch 223, 245B, Lord Denning MR. In that case it was the settlor himself who applied for the approval of an arrangement for the export of his trust to Jersey, where he had gone to live. But he was unable to persuade either Stamp J or the Court of Appeal to approve the arrangement. They held that it was not for the benefit of the specified class and refused to approve it.

[67] *Re Holt's Settlement, Wilson v Holt* [1968] 1 All ER 470 distinguishing *Re Cohen's Settlement Trusts, Eliot-Cohen v Cohen* [1965] 3 All ER 139. *Re Weston's Settlement Trusts* [1969] 1 Ch 223 ('There are many things in life worth more than money'). *Re Druce's Settlement Trusts, Pothecary v Druce* [1962] 1 All ER 563.

[68] *Re Robinson's Settlement Trusts, Heard v Heard* [1976] 3 All ER 61, 64f, *per* Templeman J. See also: *Re Brook's Settlement, Brook v Brook* [1968] 3 All ER 416 in which Stamp J refused to approve a variation.

[69] *Re C L* [1968] 1 All ER 1104 which concerned a patient under the jurisdiction of the Court of Protection. Cross J held that it was not always necessary for there to be some element of financial advantage to an adult patient when authorizing a gift.

[70] *Re Holt's Settlement, Wilson v Holt* [1968] 1 All ER 470, 479H, *per* Megarry J, following *Re Towler's Settlement Trusts* [1964] Ch 158.

[71] *Re Tinker's Settlement* [1960] 3 All ER 85 (distinguished in *Re C L* [1968] 1 All ER 1104) in which Russell J refused to approve an arrangement the intention of which was simply to rectify an error. The proposed arrangement was not for the benefit of unborn children whose interest were being cut down and that it was not beneficial to them as members of the family viewed as a whole that something which was reasonable and fair should be done. Similarly, in *Re Ball's Settlement Trusts, Ball v Ball* [1968] 2 All ER 438, Megarry J said that he could not see 'how it could be said that it is for the benefit of a person to destroy even the smallest hope of receiving a beneficial interest if nothing is put in its place'.

the total amounts of the advantages which the various parties obtain, and their bargaining strength.[72]

The jurisdiction has been exercised to postpone a right to capital and introduce **24.28** protective trusts in the meantime.[73] It has also been held beneficial to approve an arrangement which involved the deletion of the forfeiture provision which would take effect on a beneficiary practising Roman Catholicism.[74] Benefit can, and often does, comprise purely financial benefit in the form of tax advantages.[75]

The arrangement

It is the arrangement and not the order of the court which varies the trusts.[76] **24.29** Under the Variation of Trusts Act 1958 the court has jurisdiction to approve any arrangement varying or revoking all or any of the trusts, or enlarging the powers of the trustees of managing or administering any of the property subject to the trusts.[77] Arrangement is used here with a wide meaning. It is not limited to a contractual agreement but covers any proposal which any person may put forward for varying or revoking the trusts.[78]

While it has been said that the Act does not authorize the approval of an arrange- **24.30** ment which has the effect of creating a complete resettlement[79] 'varying' has been given such a wide meaning that a revocation coupled with a new declaration of trust will still be construed as a variation if the new trusts can be recognized as the former trusts[80] or if the substratum of the original trusts remains.[81] An arrangement may be proposed by any person, whether or not there is any other person beneficially interested who is capable of assenting to it. Some authority is to the effect that arrangements should be proposed by persons other than the trustees but the trustees may propose a variation if it is for the benefit of the persons

---

[72] *Re Van Gruisen's Will Trusts* [1964] 1 WLR 449, 449–450, *per* Ungoed-Thomas J.

[73] *Re Towler's Settlement Trusts* [1964] Ch 158.

[74] *Re Remnant* [1970] Ch 560. Pennycuick J approved the variation, because it was beneficial to all concerned although the testator's intention would be defeated.

[75] In *Re Weston's Settlement Trusts* [1969] 1 Ch 223 approval of the export of a settlement to Jersey for tax purposes was refused but the majority of decisions support the proposition. See: *Re Clitheroe's Settlement Trusts* [1959] 3 All ER 789; *Re Drewe's Settlement* [1966] 2 All ER 844; and *Re Sainsbury's Settlement* [1967] 1 All ER 878. The jurisdiction is available to approve variations exporting settlements to other jurisdictions.

[76] *Re Holt's Settlement, Wilson v Holt* [1968] 1 All ER 470.

[77] Many applications in the years following the commencement of the Variation of Trusts Act 1958 concerned enlarging the powers of the trustees of managing or administering the property subject to the trusts. Examples include *Re Thompson's Will Trusts (Practice Note)* [1960] 3 All ER 378; *Re Clarke's Will Trusts* [1961] 3 All ER 1133; and *Re Lister's Will Trusts* [1962] 3 All ER 737. Following the commencement of the Trustee Act 2000 few applications of this nature will be necessary.

[78] *Re Steed's Will Trusts, Sandford v Stevenson* [1960] 1 All ER 487, 492G, *per* Lord Evershed MR.

[79] *Re Towler's Settlement Trusts* [1964] Ch 158, 162, *per* Wilberforce J.

[80] *Re Holt's Settlement, Wilson v Holt* [1968] 1 All ER 470.

[81] *Re Ball's Settlement Trusts, Ball v Ball* [1968] 2 All ER 438.

on whose behalf approval is sought.[82] In some cases the settlor proposes the arrangement.[83]

Minors and other persons under an incapacity

24.31 Under paragraph 1(1)(a) the court may approve an arrangement on behalf of 'any person having, directly or indirectly, an interest, whether vested or contingent, under the trusts who by reason of infancy or other incapacity is incapable of assenting'.

24.32 The Act does not confer authority on the court to approve an arrangement on behalf of a person who is a patient within the meaning of the Part VII of the Mental Health Act 1983.[84] In such a case the Court of Protection or other authority having jurisdiction under Part VII should determine whether or not the arrangement is for the benefit of the patient and give consent on behalf of such a person.[85]

Persons with contingent interests

24.33 The Act also includes any person (whether ascertained or not) who may become entitled,[86] directly or indirectly, to an interest under the trusts as being at a future date or on the happening of a future event a person of any specified description or a member of any specified class of persons.[87] However, the Act does not include within this head persons or members of a class who would satisfy the contingency if the date had fallen or the event had happened on which the contingency depended at the date of the application to the court.[88]

Persons unborn

24.34 Under paragraph 1(1)(c) the court may approve an arrangement on behalf of 'any person unborn'. Often the interests of unborn persons and minors are provided for on an actuarial basis but, even if it is shown that actuarially the provisions for the infants and unborn persons are more beneficial for them under the arrangement than under the trusts to be varied, that is not conclusive. The court is not merely concerned with this actuarial calculation, even assuming that it satisfies the

---

[82] *Re Druce's Settlement Trusts, Pothecary v Druce* [1962] 1 All ER 563.
[83] *Re Weston's Settlement Trusts* [1969] 1 Ch 223; *Re Lloyd's Settlement, Lloyd v Leeper* [1967] 2 All ER 314.   [84] Variation of Trusts Act 1958, s 1(6).
[85] Variation of Trusts Act 1958, s 1(3). See, for example, *Re C L* [1968] 1 All ER 1104.
[86] This does not include persons with an actual but remote interest: *Knocker v Youle* [1986] 2 All ER 914.   [87] Variation of Trusts Act 1958, s 1(1)(b).
[88] *Re Suffert's Settlement, Suffert v Martyn-Linnington* [1961] Ch 1, [1960] 3 All ER 561; *Re Moncrieff's Settlement Trusts* [1962] 3 All ER 838n.

statutory requirement that the arrangement must be for the benefit of the infants and unborn persons.[89]

Not all proposed variations on behalf of minors and unborn persons need to come before the court. In *Re Pettifor's Will Trusts*[90] the court held that is was not necessary to seek its approval on behalf of the unborn children of a woman aged 78, describing the application as misconceived. A refusal at first instance to give approval has been overturned on appeal.[91] **24.35**

Variation of protective trusts

In the case of protective trusts, where the interest of the principal beneficiary has not failed or determined, the court may approve an order on behalf of any person[92] in respect of any discretionary interest under those trusts. For these purposes 'protective trusts' means the trusts specified in paragraphs (i) and (ii) of subsection (1) of section 33 of the Trustee Act 1925 or any like trusts, 'the principal beneficiary' has the same meaning as in Trustee Act 1925, section 33(1), and 'discretionary interest' means an interest arising under the trust specified in Trustee Act 1925, section 33(1)(ii), or any like trust.[93] The words 'any like trust' do not require identity but similarity. Similarity in form or detail or wording is not necessary: similarity in substance will suffice.[94] **24.36**

Examples of variations of protective trusts include the conversion of a protected life interest into an absolute life interest,[95] and the apportionment of capital between an applicant with a protected life interest and certain discretionary beneficiaries among whom the applicant had a power of appointment.[96] The court has refused to enlarge a protected interest into an absolute interest.[97] **24.37**

Where an application is made under the Variation of Trusts Act 1958 for the approval of a variation of protective trusts, the court may approve an order on behalf of any person in respect of any discretionary interest under those trusts although the arrangement is not for the benefit of that person.[98] However, because the power is discretionary, the court may insist that the arrangement **24.38**

---

[89] *Re Van Gruisen's Will Trusts* [1964] 1 WLR 449, 449–450, *per* Ungoed-Thomas J.
[90] *Re Pettifor's Will Trusts, Roberts v Roberts* [1966] Ch 257.
[91] *Goulding v James* [1997] 2 All ER 239.
[92] This includes unborn or unascertained persons: *Re Turner's Will Trusts, Bridgman v Turner* [1959] 2 All ER 689, [1960] Ch 122.
[93] Variation of Trusts Act 1958, s 1(2). For protective trusts and s 33 of the Trustee Act 1925, see paras 9.10–9.19 above.
[94] *Re Wallace's Settlements, Fane v Wallace, Chance v Wallace, Wallace v Beaumont* [1968] 2 All ER 209.
[95] *Re Burney's Settlement Trusts* [1961] 1 All ER 856; *Re Baker's Settlement Trusts* [1964] 1 All ER 482.
[96] *Re Robertson's Will Trusts* [1960] 3 All ER 146.
[97] *Re Steed's Will Trusts* [1960] 1 All ER 487.
[98] Variation of Trusts Act 1958, s 1(1) proviso.

should benefit members of the discretionary class (including unborn persons)[99] since approval is given at the discretion of the court.[100]

Procedure on an application under the Variation of Trusts Act 1958

24.39 Section 1 of the Variation of Trusts Act 1958 gives the High Court (and in some limited circumstances the county court) jurisdiction to entertain applications for the variation of existing trusts. The jurisdiction of the county court to hear applications for the variation of trusts pursuant to the 1958 Act is (as with the rest of its equity jurisdiction) limited to cases in which the value of the fund does not exceed £30,000.[101] The costs of bringing an application under the Variation of Trusts Act 1958 are generally of the same order as or exceed the limit of the county court jurisdiction so it is rarely commercially sensible to even contemplate applying in the county court. Applications in the High Court should be brought in the Chancery Division[102] and are ordinarily heard by a High Court Judge.[103] Exceptionally, an application to break protective trusts where the interest of the principal beneficiary has not failed or determined can be determined by a Master in the Chancery Division.[104]

Parties

24.40 There are no fixed rules as to who ought to be the claimant. Usually this is the person who is likely to derive a benefit from the variation but there is no reason why a person who is being deprived of an immediate interest cannot make the claim, particularly in the case of an application to break protective trusts which must necessarily involve the trustees acting on behalf of persons who are likely to be deprived of their 'interests' under the discretionary trusts arising on termination or forfeiture of the protected interest who cannot therefore make the application themselves.

24.41 All trustees must be parties[105] and, where the application is made by trustees, any who do not consent must be made defendants.[106] The claimant may make parties to the application any persons with an interest under the trust, who it is appropriate to make parties having regard to the nature of the order sought.[107] In practice, anybody whose interest under the trust is likely to be affected by the variation

[99] *Re Poole's Settlements' Trusts, Poole v Poole* [1959] 2 All ER 340.
[100] *Re Baker's Settlement, Benyon-Tinker v Baker (Practice Note)* [1964] 1 All ER 482; *Re: Burney's Settlement Trusts* [1961] 1 All ER 856.
[101] County Courts Act 1984, s 23(b)(iii).   [102] CPR, rr 64.1, 64.2(c).
[103] *Practice Direction—Allocation of Cases to Levels of Judiciary* 1999 PD 2B 5.1(c).
[104] ibid.
[105] Trustees should ordinarily act as watchdogs, only applying in clear cases of benefit: *Re Druce's Settlement Trusts, Pothecary v Druce* [1962] 1 All ER 563; *Re Wallace's Settlements, Fane v Wallace, Chance v Wallace, Wallace v Beaumont* [1968] 2 All ER 209.
[106] CPR, r 64.4(1)(a), (b).   [107] CPR, r 64.4(1)(c).

ought to be made a party. In addition to any persons who are necessary and proper defendants to the claim, the settlor and any other person who provided property for the purposes of the trusts to which the application relates must, if still alive and not the claimant, be made a party.[108] In addition, the court may order additional persons to be made parties to a claim.[109]

Mode of application

Application is by Part 8 Claim Form,[110] which should be supported by evidence in the form of a witness statement or affidavit setting out the reasons for the application.[111] The witness statement should exhibit the proposed arrangement. Witness statements must also be filed on behalf of the defendants to the application and, where appropriate, counsel's opinion should be exhibited. **24.42**

Counsel's opinion

In the case of an application brought pursuant to section 1(1)(a) to (c) of the Variation of Trusts Act 1958 it is necessary to show that the arrangement for which the court's approval is sought on behalf of any person falling within those sub-clauses is for the benefit of that person. In cases in which children or unborn beneficiaries will be affected by a proposed arrangement under the Variation of Trusts Act 1958, the evidence filed in support of the application must show that their litigation friends or the trustees support the arrangements as being in the interests of the children or unborn beneficiaries.[112] In addition, the evidence must also be accompanied by a written opinion to the effect that the proposed variation is for each of the affected parties' benefit by the advocate (usually chancery counsel) who will appear on the hearing of the application.[113] However, as the proviso to section 1 makes clear, it is not necessary to show that an arrangement which falls within paragraph (d) is for the benefit of any of the affected parties and it follows that in such a case it is not necessary to obtain counsel's opinion on their behalf.[114] A written opinion filed with the evidence must, if it is given on formal instructions, be accompanied by a copy of those instructions; or, otherwise state fully the basis on which it is given.[115] Only one opinion needs to be filed on behalf of all children or unborn beneficiaries whose interests are similar.[116] **24.43**

---

[108] CPR, r 64.4(2).   [109] Under CPR, r 19.2, CPR, r 64.4(2)(b).
[110] CPR, r 64.3.   [111] *Re Oakes' Settlement Trusts* [1952] 2 All ER 58.
[112] *Practice Direction—Estates, Trusts and Charities* PD 64 4.1(a).
[113] *Practice Direction—Estates, Trusts and Charities* PD 64 4.1(2).
[114] Chancery Division Practice Guide Chapter 26.32; *Practice Direction—Estates, Trusts and Charities* PD 64 4.3.   [115] *Practice Direction—Estates, Trusts and Charities* PD 64 4.2.
[116] *Practice Direction—Estates, Trusts and Charities* PD 64 4.4.

The hearing

24.44 Hearings of applications under the Variation of Trusts Act 1958 are, in the first instance, listed by the court as hearings in private.[117] The application may be listed for hearing in the General List without any direction by a Master on the lodgement of a certificate of readiness signed by advocates for all the parties stating that the evidence is complete and has been filed and that the application is ready for hearing, giving an estimated length of the hearing.[118] Bundles and skeleton arguments should be filed in the ordinary way although, where the matters to be drawn to the attention of the court are fully covered in the instructions and written opinion, it should not be necessary for a separate skeleton argument to be lodged, but the court needs to be informed that this is the case.[119]

Consequences of order

24.45 An order under the Variation of Trusts Act 1958 provides the necessary approval of an arrangement on behalf of those persons who cannot consent themselves but it is the arrangement made with the consent of all parties and not the order of the court which varies the trusts.[120] The variation has immediate effect but a memorandum of the order should be endorsed on the probate or settlement.[121]

G. Powers of Amendment: Purpose and Nature of a Power of Amendment[122]

24.46 In the absence of a power to amend, make alterations to, or modifications of, the terms and provisions of a trust cannot easily[123] be made in the future to take account of, and react to, changes in social or economic circumstances or in legislation. Both the beneficial and administrative terms and provisions of a trust are capable of being amended by the exercise of powers of various kinds, the most common being powers of appointment and powers of advancement.[124] However, it may not be desirable or possible to make an appointment of the kind required. In some instances,

---

[117] CPR, r 39.2(3)(c); *Practice Direction—Miscellaneous Provisions Relating to Hearings* PD 39 1.5(11). [118] Chancery Division Practice Guide Chapter 6.27.

[119] Chancery Division Practice Guide Chapter 26.26.

[120] *Re Holt's Settlement, Wilson v Holt* [1968] 1 All ER 470.

[121] *Re Rouse's Will Trusts* [1959] 2 All ER 47n, 51F, *per* Vaisey J.

[122] For a detailed discussion of powers of amendment, see GW Thomas, *Powers* (Sweet & Maxwell, 1998) ('*Thomas*') Ch 14.

[123] In the absence of a power of amendment, application must be made to the court, eg under the Variation of Trusts Act 1958 or s 57 of the Trustee Act 1925: see paras 24.16–24.45 above. See also s 69 of the Pensions Act 1995, conferring limited powers on the Occupational Pensions Regulatory Authority.

[124] *Re Rank's Settlement* [1979] 1 WLR 1242; *Bond v Pickford* [1983] STC 517, 522a–b.

for example, changes are required in the administrative powers of the trustees, without affecting existing beneficial interests (whether previously appointed or in default of appointment), but the scope of the available power of appointment may not permit this.[125] A power of appointment may be exercisable only with the consent of some person (for example the settlor himself), or only in accordance with some specified formality (for example by deed), or may only be exercisable at some future date (for instance when a named individual attains his majority).[126] In such instances, it would be considered too cumbersome and inflexible to require that all minor changes in administrative provisions should be fettered by such restrictions. Similarly, in the case of pension schemes (some of which can last indefinitely),[127] changes must frequently be made to the provisions of the trust deeds and rules in order to deal with new legislative requirements, changes in the circumstances of the employer, fluctuations in the size and composition of the classes of beneficiaries, and so forth. It is good practice, therefore, to include appropriate wide powers of amendment when drafting settlements and similar documents. On the other hand, if a power of amendment or modification is completely unrestricted, it may be that the trusts can be revoked entirely,[128] with unintended consequences, for example a pension scheme might fail to secure the approval of the Inland Revenue,[129] or a settlor may be subject to adverse tax consequences.[130]

A power to amend may expressly bear that description or it may take the form of a **24.47** power to add to, or to vary, modify, or alter the terms or provisions in question. Whatever its description, and whatever its scope, the exercise of any such power will cause some change to occur. In this sense, any power to amend resembles a power to appoint or a power to revoke. A power of appointment may be wide enough to permit an addition to, or a variation, modification, alteration, or amendment of administrative provisions, without there having to be an appointment of the trust fund itself or any dealing with the beneficial interests.[131] It may also be said that the exercise of a power of revocation clearly results in a variation or modification of (though not necessarily an addition to) the relevant trusts, powers, or provisions.[132] However, a revocation, whether partial or total, nullifies existing provisions, rather than modifies

---

[125] *Re Falconer's Trusts* [1908] 1 Ch 410.
[126] *Thomas*, paras 5-134 – 5-171; *Gas & Fuel Corporation of Victoria v Fitzmaurice* [1991] PLR 137.
[127] Pension Schemes Act 1993, s 163(1).
[128] *Matter of Woodward* (1954) 284 App Div 459, 132 NYS (2d) 266; *Lipic v Wheeler* (1951) 362 Mo 499, 242 SW (2d) 43; *Stahler v Sevinor* (1949) 324 Mass 18, 84 NE (2d) 447.
[129] Income and Corporation Taxes Act 1988, ss 590(6), 591B, 610, and 612; see also Pension Schemes Act 1993, ss 37 and 72.   [130] ICTA 1988, ss 672 and 675.
[131] *Re Rank's Settlement* [1979] 1 WLR 1242 (wide enough); *Re Falconer's Trusts* [1908] 1 Ch 410 (not wide enough).
[132] See, for example, *Long v Cleveland Trust Company* (1951) 59 Ohio Abs 324, 97 NE (2d) 107; *O'Hagan v Kracke* (1937) 165 Misc 4, 300 NY Supp 351, affirmed (1938) 253 App Div 632, 3 NYS (2d) 401.

them,[133] and, despite the possibility of overlap, powers of amendment usually perform a different function and merit separate treatment.

24.48   Moreover, in broad terms, those general principles which apply to powers of appointment and powers of revocation (such as the doctrine of fraud on a power, the rules against delegation, and so forth) also apply to powers of amendment (of whatever kind). Similarly, powers of amendment are subject to the rules relating to conflict of interests, so that such a power cannot be exercised (in the absence of a clear direction to the contrary) so as to confer an unauthorized benefit on the donee of the power, for example by amending the provisions of a settlement so as to introduce a power of charging for trustees, where none existed previously, or to create a new provision for payment of a pension scheme's assets to the employer.[134] These general principles are discussed in other chapters.[135]

H. Scope of Powers of Amendment

24.49   As with all other powers, the scope of a power of amendment will depend on its express terms, or on what may properly be implied. Thus, it seems clear that a simple power to add to the provisions of a settlement would not authorize any other kind of amendment, such as an exclusion or revocation, unless this would be a necessary consequence or implication of making the addition in question. Similarly, where an employer who sets up a pension scheme reserves a power to 'amend' it, this might be wide enough to authorize the employer to amend the beneficial interests themselves, but it is not necessarily so, for example if the amendment must be without prejudice to pension benefits secured by contributions already paid.[136] It is unusual, in fact, to find a power of amendment of any kind which is not subject to some limitation or restriction. For example, on the creation of a discretionary trust, a settlor may reserve to himself, or may confer on the trustees, a power to add new members to (or exclude existing members from) the class of discretionary objects, but it is invariably the case that such a power expressly prohibits the addition of the settlor or any spouse of his or hers.[137] A second example is the common

---

133   *National Newark & Essex Banking Co v Rosahl* (1925) 97 NJ Eq 74, 128 Atl 586.

134   *Burt v FMC Superannuation and Pension Scheme Trustees Ltd* [1995] OPLR 385; *Sulpetro Ltd v Sulpetro Ltd Retirement Plan Fund* (1990) 73 Alberta LR 44; *Re Pension Plan of Employees of Steams Catalytic Ltd* (Alberta Court of QB, 22 February 1990: noted in (1992) 44 British Pension Lawyers 23). Cf *Re Vauxhall Pension Fund* [1989] PLR 49.

135   See Chapters 11, 15, 18, and 19, and also paras 10.99–10.120 above.

136   *Re Alfred Herbert Ltd Pension and Life Assurance Scheme's Trusts* [1960] 1 WLR 271, esp 274; *UEB Industries Ltd v WS Brabant and Others* [1991] PLR 109 (NZ CA); *Lloyds Bank Pension Trust Corporation Ltd v Lloyds Bank plc* [1996] PLR 263. Cf *Ritchie v Blakeley* [1985] 1 NZLR 630.

137   Such a power may also be conferred on the trustees, subject to the same limitations, but it must then not be a power which the trustees are obliged to exercise: otherwise, the settlement may fail for uncertainty of objects: *Re Manisty's Settlement* [1974] Ch 17; *Re Hay's Settlement Trusts* [1982] 1 WLR 202.

practice of including in a settlement (of any kind) a power for the trustees to add to or vary only the administrative or managerial powers and provisions of the settlement. Clearly, such a power does not permit any interference with the beneficial interests in the trust fund.

In all cases, the scope of the relevant power is determined by the construction of **24.50** the words in which it is couched, in accordance with the surrounding context, and also of such extrinsic evidence (if any) as may be properly admissible. A power of amendment or variation in a trust instrument ought not to be construed in a narrow or unreal way.[138] It will have been created in order to provide flexibility, whether in relation to specific matters or more generally. Such a power ought, therefore, to be construed liberally so as to permit any amendment which is not prohibited by an express direction to the contrary or by some necessary implication, provided always that any such amendment does not derogate from the fundamental purposes for which the power was created. Thus, a power of amendment will undoubtedly be capable of making amendments which are essentially ancillary to, and for the better execution of, such fundamental purposes, for example so as to substitute an easier form of communication or service for the one originally stipulated, or so as to make other powers exercisable in writing rather than by deed, or, indeed, introduce other amendments which are not simply administrative or managerial in nature. It does not follow, of course, that the power of amendment itself can be amended in this way. Indeed, it is probably the case that there is an implied (albeit rebuttable) presumption, in the absence of an express direction to that effect, that a power of amendment (like any other kind of power) cannot be used to extend its own scope or amend its own terms. Moreover, a power of amendment is not likely to be held to extend to varying the trust in a way which would destroy its 'substratum'.[139] The underlying purpose for the furtherance of which the power was initially created or conferred will obviously be paramount.[140] However, this general principle may not always be a particularly helpful consideration where the evident purpose of the power is to ensure maximum flexibility.[141] In the case of most modern pension scheme trusts, for example, the courts are likely to interpret their provisions, including the scope of powers of amendment, so as to give reasonable and practical effect to the particular scheme, bearing in mind that it has to be operated against a constantly changing commercial background.[142]

---

[138] *Kearns v Hill* [1991] PLR 161 (Australia, CA).
[139] *Re Dyer* [1935] VLR 273; *Re Ball's Settlement Trusts* [1968] 1 WLR 899, 904; *Kearns v Hill* [1991] PLR 161.
[140] *Duke of Bedford v Marquess of Abercorn* (1836) 1 My & Cr 312.
[141] *Kearns v Hill, supra.*
[142] *Re Courage Group's Pension Schemes* [1987] 1 WLR 495, 505–506; *Mihlenstedt v Barclays Bank International Ltd* [1989] IRLR 522; *Mettoy Pension Trustees Ltd v Evans* [1990] 1 WLR 1587, 1610–1611; *Imperial Group Pension Trust Ltd v Imperial Tobacco Ltd* [1991] 1 WLR 589. See also

24.51 Where the power of amendment is subject to express restrictions, those restrictions must be complied with and cannot be amended, removed or annulled by means of an exercise of the power.[143] Similarly, the power may be subject to some implied restriction, such as the obligation of an employer, which is implied by both the contract of employment and the trust deed and rules of a pension scheme, to act in good faith and so as not seriously to damage the relationship of confidence between the employer and the employees and ex-employees.[144] It is also material, of course, whether the power of amendment is a fiduciary or a non-fiduciary power. A fiduciary power cannot be exercised by the fiduciary donee (whether he is a trustee or not) in favour of himself or itself,[145] whereas a non-fiduciary power may be so exercised.[146] Moreover, in the case of occupational pension schemes, different considerations may apply depending on whether the power of amendment is exercisable while the scheme is still in operation or following the winding up of the scheme. As Vinelott J observed in *British Coal Corporation v British Coal Staff Superannuation Scheme Trustees Ltd*:[147]

> ... the position is quite different when the question relates to the exercise of a power of amendment of a pension fund which has not been wound up. The employer, if he has a power of amendment, is entitled to exercise it in any way which will further the purposes of the pension scheme to ensure that the legitimate expectations of the members and pensioners is met without, so far as possible, imposing any undue burden on the employer or building up an unnecessary large surplus. The employer himself has an interest in maintaining a pension fund which is satisfactory to existing and attractive to future employees, and he has an interest in ensuring that it is effectively managed ... If the assets of the scheme are so large that all legitimate expectations of the members and pensioners can be met without continued contribution by him at the rate originally provided, he can by amendment reduce or suspend contributions for a period. What he cannot do is to set limits to the benefits provided for members or pensioners for a collateral purpose without regard to their legitimate expectations.

Cowan v Scargill [1985] Ch 270, 292; *Wilson v Law Debenture Trust Corpn plc* [1995] 2 All ER 337, 347; *Schmidt v Air Products of Canada Ltd* [1994] 2 SCR 611; *Bathgate v National Hockey League Pension Society* (1994) 16 OR (3d) 761, 766. Whether there is a useful analogy between a pension scheme and a members' club, as suggested by Millett J in *Re Courage, supra*, is doubtful: see *Thomas*, para 14-38.

[143] *British Coal Corporation v British Coal Staff Superannuation Scheme Trustees Ltd* [1994] OPLR 51 (power of amendment limited so as to prevent 'making any of the moneys of the scheme payable to any of the employers'). Cf *Aitken v Christy Hunt plc* [1991] PLR 1.

[144] *Imperial Group Pension Trust Ltd v Imperial Tobacco Ltd* [1991] 1 WLR 589. See further paras 11.92–11.103 above.

[145] *Mettoy Pension Trustees Ltd v Evans* [1990] 1 WLR 1587; *Icarus (Hertford) Ltd v Driscoll* [1990] PLR 1; *Re William Makin & Son Ltd* [1993] OPLR 171. See also *Thomas*, paras 6-63–6-59 and 11-45–11-52.

[146] *Imperial Group Pension Trust Ltd v Imperial Tobacco Ltd, supra*; *British Coal Corporation v British Coal Staff Superannuation Scheme Trustees Ltd, supra*.

[147] [1994] OPLR 51.

Entrenched restrictions

It is not always clear, however, whether a particular restriction or requirement **24.52**
imposed on the exercise (or even the scope) of a power of amendment is an
entrenched provision which cannot, therefore, be annulled, overridden, or ignored
in any circumstances, or whether it is one which will operate and bind only for as
long as it is allowed to remain in force. *Aitken v Christy Hunt plc*[148] is a good illustration of this difficulty. Here, company A acquired the business of company B,
and was substituted for company B for the purposes of its pension scheme. Three
years later, the business was closed down. At the date of the hearing, only two members of the scheme were employed by company A, although there were other members who were entitled either to pensions in payment or deferred pensions. The
scheme's assets substantially exceeded its liabilities. Company A then became a
wholly-owned subsidiary of company C, whose employees, together with those of
its subsidiaries, were covered by its group pension scheme. Company A proposed
to the trustees of the scheme that all the assets and liabilities of the scheme be transferred to company C's group scheme, equivalent pensions being given to members
of the scheme. The trustees wanted to use the entire fund for the benefit of scheme
members, and feared that a significant part of the surplus assets of the scheme
would be used for the benefit of members of company C's scheme, and hence indirectly of company C. The trustees therefore exercised a power of amendment and
amended the scheme's rules (a) so as to remove the requirement for company A's
consent to an augmentation of benefits, and (b) so as to prohibit the admission of
employees to membership after 1 August 1989. Company A challenged these
amendments. Ferris J held that both amendments were valid.

The effect of amendment (a) (which involved the deletion of the words 'subject to **24.53**
the consent of the company' in the relevant regulation) was that the power to augment pensions which had become payable would thenceforth be exercisable by the
trustees, with the advice of the scheme's actuary, but without the need to obtain the
consent of the company. The company argued that the requirement for consent was
entrenched; and that, if it were otherwise, trustees (who may have no connection
with the company) could unilaterally increase the burden so far as the company was
concerned: in effect, the trustees would have a blank cheque in favour of the fund.
At first sight, the provision requiring the company's consent to any amendment
would indeed appear to be entrenched and therefore not capable of being annulled
by the unilateral action of the trustees. Nevertheless, Ferris J concluded that, as a
matter of construction of the terms of the power, the trustees could amend the
scheme's regulations or rules so as to delete the requirement for consent. He pointed
out that, while the requirement remained in existence, it had force and substance:
any amendment of the regulations proposed by the trustees would have required

---

[148] [1991] PLR 1.

prior consultation with the company. Moreover, in deciding whether or not to delete the requirement, the trustees would have had to weigh up the risk that the company would retaliate by declining to pay further contributions (as it could do). However, this did not make the requirement for consent an irremovable entrenched provision. Nevertheless, the trustees did *not* have any power to amend the *trust deed* and could not, therefore, amend the power of amendment itself.

24.54   Even an express prohibition on the return of surplus funds to an employer on the termination of a pension scheme will not necessarily prevent an amendment of the scheme in order to enable a return of surplus prior to termination,[149] although in some cases it may do so.[150] It may depend, for example, on whether there is an intention to make an immediate payment to the employer,[151] or on whether the amendment is but a part of a larger transaction which benefits the scheme in other ways, such as the improvement of benefits for members and beneficiaries.[152] While the scheme is a continuing one, circumstances may change, and any number of considerations may arise, before any payment is made to the employer.[153] Even a power of amendment intended to provide maximum flexibility may have a different effect in different contexts.

24.55   On the other hand, an exercise of a power of amendment which has the effect of introducing restrictions on the power itself (as opposed to purporting to remove existing restrictions) seems more easily justified. In the absence of express directions to the contrary, and provided that it does not derogate from the fundamental purposes for which the power was created, the narrowing of the scope of the power of amendment as to the future ought to be a valid and effective exercise, akin to an execution of a wide overriding power of appointment which, *inter alia*, creates a narrower power of appointment, or transfers the subject matter of the original power to the trustees of a different settlement under which there is a similar, but narrower, power.

I. Retrospective Effect

24.56   It is generally considered that, in the absence of express provision to the contrary, a power of amendment cannot be exercised so as to have retrospective effect.

---

[149] *Hockin v Bank of British Columbia* (1990) 71 DLR (4th) 11; *Lock v Westpac Banking Corporation & Others* [1991] PLR 167; *Mettoy Pension Trustees Ltd v Evans* [1990] 1 WLR 1587. Cf *Wilson v Metro-Goldwyn Mayer* (1980) 18 NSWLR 730.

[150] *UEB Industries Ltd v WS Brabant and Others* [1991] PLR 109; *Sulpetro Ltd v Sulpetro Ltd Retirement Plan Fund* (1990) 73 Alberta LR 44.

[151] *Mettoy Pension Trustees Ltd v Evans* [1990] 1 WLR 1587.

[152] *Lock v Westpac Banking Corporation & Others, supra.* See also *BHLSPF Pty Ltd v Brashs Pty Ltd* (2001) 4 ITELR 696.

[153] See also the provisions of ss 37 and 76 of the Pensions Act 1995.

However, it is not obvious why this should be so, particularly if the power of amendment is found in the context of a pension scheme, where the need for retrospective amendments at some point during its existence can almost be presumed. In the context of registered friendly societies and building societies, for example, if the rules of such a society contain no power of amendment at all, neither prospective nor retrospective amendments would seem to be possible,[154] and the same result would probably apply in other contexts. Where a power of amendment exists, and where the members of such a society are bound by the 'rules for the time being', any amendment of the rules will bind the members as to the future, even to the extent of depriving them in some instances of vested interests and rights.[155]

Where the secondary contract (be it a mortgage, an insurance policy, or whatever) **24.57** is itself expressly made subject to the rules of the society for the time being, an amendment to those rules may also amend the provisions of that secondary contract.[156] Of course, in these cases, the relevant amendments have only prospective effect, and they do not provide support for the view that amendments may be made which have retrospective effect, although, in certain circumstances, a different view may be taken. As Wright J stated, in *R v Brabrook*:[157] 'It seems much too wide a proposition to say that he has power to refuse to sanction anything that is retrospective. Mere retrospectiveness is not necessarily wrong.'

A similar view was adopted more recently by the Supreme Court of Western Australia **24.58** in *Graham Australia Pty Ltd v Perpetual Trustees Ltd*.[158] Here, GA held units in a unit trust. The trust deed provided that unitholders could redeem units by requesting the manager to repurchase all or any units at a price calculated by reference to the value of a unit at a date at least seven days before the request was made (and not its current value). When the value of investments in the fund fell dramatically, GA asked the manager of the fund to repurchase its units. At a meeting of unitholders, a resolution was passed approving amendments to the trust deed so as to substitute 'current

---

[154] *Souter v Davies* (1895) Diprose and Gammon 69 (vested annuity of a member of a friendly society could not be taken away).

[155] *Smith v Galloway* [1898] 1 QB 71; *Strohmenger v Finsbury Permanent Investment Building Society* [1897] 2 Ch 467; *Pepe v City and Suburban Permanent Building Society* (1884) 9 App Cas 519; *Re Norwich and Norfolk Provident Permanent Benefit Building Society (Smith's Case)* (1875) 1 Ch D 481; *Rosenberg v Northumberland Building Society* (1889) 22 Ch D 373; *Page v Liverpool Victoria Society* (1927) 43 TLR 712; *Dixon v Thompson* and *Stooke v Mutual Provident Alliance* (both 1891) in Diprose and Gammon, 46 and 195 respectively; *Batten v City and Suburban Permanent Building Society* [1895] 2 Ch 441; *Davies v Second Chatham Permanent Benefit Building Society* (1889) 61 LT(NS) 680; *Sibun v Pearce* [1890] 44 Ch D 354; *Walker v General Mutual Building Society* (1887) 36 Ch D 777; *Sixth West Kent Mutual Building Society v Hills* [1899] 2 Ch 60.

[156] *Rosenberg v Northumberland Building Society* (1889) 22 Ch D 373. See also the cases listed in n 155 above.

[157] (1893) 69 LT 718, 719. See also *Hole v Garnsey* [1930] AC 472.

[158] [1992] PLR 193.

realisation value' as the measure for determining the price at which units had to be repurchased. A supplemental deed was executed to give effect to these amendments. The manager then made payments out of the fund on the amended basis. The court held that, as a matter of construction of the provisions of the trust deed, the requisite majority of unitholders had a power to amend the trust deed. This power extended to allowing amendments to be made so as to defeat vested or accrued rights of a unitholder (even where such person remained a unitholder only because of a breach of contract by the manager). The court noted that, as far as companies are concerned, the existing rights of shareholders could be altered, within the limits set by statute and the memorandum of association,[159] and so too in the case of building societies.[160] Moreover, none of the cases referred to said that retrospective amendments could not be made.[161] As Malcolm CJ indicated: 'What is within power and lawful is a matter of construction of the relevant instrument.'[162]

24.59 In certain restricted circumstances and for certain limited purposes, an occupational pension scheme may be amended, with retrospective effect, under the provisions of section 69 of the Pensions Act 1995. Where an order is made by the Occupational Pensions Regulatory Authority under section 69, authorizing the modification of an occupational pension scheme (other than a public service pension scheme), or actually modifying such a scheme, for the purposes specified in section 69(3), such an order may enable those exercising any power conferred by the order to exercise it retrospectively (whether or not the power could otherwise be so exercised) and, similarly, an order may modify a scheme retrospectively.[163] For these purposes, 'retrospectively' means with effect from a date before that on which the power is exercised or, as the case may be, the order is made.[164]

J. Duration of Powers of Amendment

24.60 Another common source of uncertainty and difficulty, in the context of pension schemes, is the question whether a power of amendment continues to be exercisable after the occurrence of a winding-up event. In *Re ABC Television Ltd, Pension Scheme*,[165] one of the regulations of the scheme (Rule 44(1)) provided: 'The

---

[159] *Alien v Gold Reefs of West Africa Ltd* [1900] 1 Ch 656, esp 673 (where it was said that the observations of Rigby LJ in *James v Buena Ventura Nitrate Grounds Syndicate* [1896] 1 Ch 456, 466, did not indicate that such alterations could not be retrospective); *Andrews v Gas Meter Co* [1897] 1 Ch 361; *British Equitable Assurance Co Ltd v Balfy* [1906] AC 35; *Peters'American Delicacy Co Ltd v Heath* (1939) 61 CLR 457; *Southern Foundries (1926) Ltd v Shirlaw* [1940] AC 710.
[160] The court referred to several of the cases listed in n 155 above, but not to *R v Brabrook, supra.*
[161] Not even *Dawkins v Antrobus* (1881) 17 Ch D 615 or *Hole v Garnsey* [1930] AC 472.
[162] [1992] PLR 193, 206.   [163] Section 71(1).   [164] Section 71(4).
[165] Decision of Foster J, 22 May 1973: not reported officially, but the judgment is printed in Inglis-Jones, *The Law of Occupational Pension Schemes*. See also *Buschau v Rogers Communications Inc* (2002) 5 ITELR 27 (BC).

Pension Scheme shall be wound up and the trusts of the Pension Scheme shall cease and determine and the Pension Fund shall be dissolved upon [*inter alia*] the employer ceasing to carry on business [which had happened].' Another provision of the scheme directed the trustee to apply any surplus funds 'in making such increases in such pensions as the Trustee may consider fair as between the respective Members for whom the same are to be provided . . .'. Foster J held, on the construction of other provisions, that the members who could benefit from an application of surplus funds were limited in number, with the result that such application did not exhaust that surplus. A further question therefore became relevant, namely whether the winding-up provisions could be altered by means of the power of amendment so as to include and make eligible for benefit those members who had been found to be excluded on the construction of the existing rules. Foster J held that the wording of Rule 44(1) was clear and that, once the scheme was wound up, all the previous trusts, powers, and provisions (including the power of amendment) came to an end.

Knox J came to a similar conclusion in *Re Dan Jones & Sons (Porth) Ltd Employees'* **24.61** *Pension Fund*:[166] he held that, once the relevant winding-up event had occurred and the trusts of the scheme determined, it ceased to be possible thereafter to operate machinery for varying those trusts.[167] In *Thrells Ltd v Lomas*,[168] the rules of the scheme provided that, if the employer were wound up, the scheme was also to be wound up, whereupon the trustee (which was also the employer) was directed to secure the benefits of pensioners and members of the scheme. Another rule provided that the employer 'may from time to time alter or modify all or any of the provisions of these Rules provided that no such alteration or modification shall be made which reduces the benefits of a member already accrued at the date of such alteration or modification'. Despite the fact that the terms of the power of alteration were open-ended (subject to the limitation which the power itself contained), Nicholls V-C held that the terms of the rule providing for the consequences of a winding up were inconsistent with the employer retaining any power thereafter to change the rules so far as those consequences were concerned.

There is no reason why a power of amendment (or any other power) should not **25.62** expressly be made exercisable after the winding up of a scheme has commenced (although it is surprising how rarely this is done in practice, particularly in view of the apparent reluctance of the courts to favour survivorship of such a power). Such a provision will almost certainly need to be carefully drafted and probably subjected to various limitations, such as a prohibition on any amendment which

---

[166] [1989] PLR 21.
[167] Whether it was necessary to reach a conclusion on this point seems doubtful, for the deed by which an amendment of the rules was purported to be made was clearly ineffective on other grounds.   [168] [1993] 2 All ER 546.

would adversely affect the accrued rights and interests of members of the scheme (and which might then be better described as a power of revocation), or which would increase the liabilities of contributors to the scheme (at least, without their respective consents). It may also be prudent to distinguish between trusts and powers, or between amendments which would have a dispositive effect (such as the alteration of benefits or the addition of new beneficiaries) and those which would be administrative and managerial only (thereby enabling the creation of powers which would assist in the process of winding up). In any event, in the absence of some clear, express provision in the scheme documentation, the question whether a particular power continues to be exercisable after a winding-up event has occurred may involve a difficult question of construction of all relevant provisions. It would appear (from the above-mentioned decisions) that it may then be difficult to establish that any such power has survived.

24.63 It is not unusual for a pension scheme to be 'closed', without being wound up. This may occur, for example, when an employer exercises a power to prohibit further new members from being admitted to the scheme. A 'closed' scheme cannot continue to operate if the powers conferred by the scheme cease to be exercisable after the date of closure. Investment of the scheme's funds, appointments of new trustees, and other essential administrative matters, must necessarily continue to be possible. There is no reason in principle why a power of amendment should not also continue to be exercisable, unless there is a clear indication to the contrary in a particular case. The closure of a scheme may also happen when a winding-up event has occurred if the trustees exercise a power (which is often conferred in such circumstances) to continue to operate the scheme as a closed scheme thereafter. In this instance, too, the continuing availability of most of the scheme's powers will probably be essential, and there is no obvious reason why a power of amendment should no longer be exercisable. In *Re Edward Jones Benevolent Fund*,[169] where a winding-up event had occurred and the trustees had elected to continue the scheme as a closed scheme, the judge held that a power of amendment continued to be exercisable.

> I can see no reason why the power to alter—limited, as it is, by certain safeguards—should cease to exist merely because the company has determined its contributions and the Trustees have decided, as they are entitled to do, to continue the Fund on a closed basis. The proviso to Rule 27 explains what is meant by continuing the Fund on a closed basis. It means that no further benefits will accrue after the date of the termination of contributions and that liability to provide benefits to pensioners and other former Members of the Fund existing at the date of termination is preserved in and retained by the Fund . . . the proviso has the effect of stopping the clock, but it does not have the effect of excluding powers to augment benefits, and there is no

---

[169] Decision of Chadwick QC, 8 March 1985: not reported officially, but the judgment is printed in Inglis-Jones, *supra*.

reason why it should have the effect of excluding powers of alteration. Indeed, as it appears to me, it is in just the circumstances that the Fund is being operated as a closed Fund that powers of augmentation and alteration are most likely to be required.

Whether a power (including a power of alteration) continues to be exercisable **24.64** after the closure of a scheme is, of course, a question of construction of the relevant provisions in each case. However, it would seem to be a safe presumption that, by continuing a scheme as a closed scheme, the powers of that scheme remain unaffected or, alternatively, if they cease to be exercisable on a winding-up event, they are revived on an election to have a continuing, closed scheme.

In any event, these are questions to which the process of construction may yield **24.65** different answers in each particular case. It ought to be a matter of elementary prudence, however, to ensure that powers of amendment are drafted sufficiently clearly to ensure that such questions of construction do not arise, even if, in many cases, the resolution of uncertainty may be possible by virtue of statutory provisions.

K. Statutory Provisions

There are various statutory provisions dealing with the amendment of trusts. In **24.66** particular, section 57 of the Trustee Act 1925, section 64 of the Settled Land Act 1925, and the Variation of Trusts Act 1958 are dealt with in Sections D to F of this chapter.

Part D

TRUSTS IMPLIED BY LAW

25

AN INTRODUCTION TO TRUSTS
IMPLIED BY LAW

A. An Overview of the Various Species of Trusts Implied by Law

The scope of trusts implied by law

This chapter is concerned to introduce this **Part D Trusts Implied by Law** with **25.01** an analysis of the nature of trusts implied by law. The three types of trusts implied by law with which we are concerned are resulting trusts, constructive trusts, and implied trusts.[1] The common thread which runs through these three forms of trust is that they arise by operation of law rather than by the deliberate act of a settlor in the manner of a declaration of an express trust, as considered in Part B. Thus far in this book we have focused on express trusts which have been consciously created by their settlors who have demonstrated sufficient certainty of

---

[1] This last category, as will be explored below, seems to be a label without content in English trusts law and many of the ideas which we will identify with it have already been subsumed by English cases under the heading 'express trusts', see para 25.41: see for example *Paul v Constance* [1977] 1 WLR 527.

intention to create such a trust.[2] By extension, the obligations of trustees in express trusts have been considered on the basis of either the express provisions in the trust instrument prepared by the settlor or on the basis of those default obligations which are imposed by the general law of trusts in the absence of such a trust instrument.[3] By contrast, trusts implied by law arise by operation of law: that is, through the ministry of the courts in recognizing the rights of the claimant as a beneficiary under a constructive, resulting, or implied trust, rather than as a result of some action taken by a settlor deliberately to constitute an express trust. Trusts implied by law are said to arise 'by operation of law' in that they will, generally, be imposed by the courts contrary to the wishes of the defendant. The obligations of trustees in relation to trusts implied by law are not hedged in by a trust instrument nor has the office of trustee been accepted voluntarily: rather, equity implies[4] the existence of a trust from the circumstances and thus imposes obligations of trusteeship on the defendant either to prevent him from benefiting from his unconscionable conduct[5] or in recognition of some pre-existing rights of the claimant beneficiary.[6] The claimant is protected by acquiring the rights of a beneficiary under a trust implied by law and the defendant is compelled to recognize the claimant's rights or to compensate the claimant by the same means.[7]

---

[2] See para 3.01; and the requirements of certainty of intention, of subject matter, and of the identity of the objects of the trust which stem from *Knight v Knight* (1840) 3 Beav 148; *Knight v Boughton* (1840) 11 Cl & F in 513.

[3] Principally by means of the Trustee Act 1925, on which see para 10.01, and the Trustee Act 2000, on which see paras 10.01 *et seq*.

[4] The question whether trusts implied by law are implied by the courts or are merely inferred from the circumstances is considered below at para 25.03.

[5] For example in relation to the acceptance of bribes (*Attorney-General for Hong Kong v Reid* [1994] 1 AC 324) or taking benefits from unlawful killing (*In the Estate of Crippen* [1911] P 108) or in any of the other forms of constructive trust which arise on this basis. Similarly, in relation to resulting trusts, the purchase price resulting trusts which seek to prevent the legal owner of property from denying the rights of other contributors to the purchase price (*Dyer v Dyer* (1788) 2 Cox Eq Cas 92; *Tinsley v Milligan* [1994] 1 AC 340).

[6] As considered below this is generally considered to be the means by which trusts implied by law come into existence. A good example being automatic resulting trusts (*Vandervell v IRC* [1967] 2 AC 291) which literally recognize the continuation of property rights in the hands of their last owner. Alternatively, common intention constructive trusts (*Lloyds Bank v Rosset* [1991] 1 AC 107) and constructive trusts imposed in support of contract (*Neville v Wilson* [1997] Ch 144) recognize that certain forms of agreement give a claimant a valid, consensually acquired right in property such that equity will deem ownership to have passed to the claimant. It is suggested that the rights in these contexts are being recognized by the courts in that they came into existence on the formation of the agreement and therefore were in existence before the constructive trust was imposed. As is considered below, however, there are forms of constructive trust which appear to grant entirely new rights, as opposed to recognizing existing rights, in the form of personal liabilities to account as a constructive trustee in the event of the knowing receipt of property in breach of trust (*Re Montagu* [1987] Ch 264) or dishonest assistance in a breach of trust (*Royal Brunei Airlines v Tan* [1995] 2 AC 378) or the acquisition of proprietary rights in bribes paid to a fiduciary by some third party (*Attorney-General for Hong Kong v Reid* [1994] 1 AC 324).

[7] Here the distinction between personal claims to equitable compensation and proprietary claims to identified property is evident, as considered below at para 25.10. The trust implied by law may be

In essence, then, when equity imposes trusts implied by law it is operating either in judgment on the unconscionability of the defendant's actions[8] or to further some principle of the law of property which requires the recognition of the property rights of the beneficiaries.[9] These various motivations for such trusts are considered in the following sections of this chapter.

This chapter will consider, in turn, resulting trusts, constructive trusts, implied trusts, and, by way of comparison, rights created by equitable estoppel.[10] The purpose of these discussions is to outline the manner in which each of these forms of trusts implied by law is structured and to suggest the principles on which each functions. The subsequent chapters in this Part D will then analyse those trusts in detail. The approach taken in this book is to identify those circumstances in which trusts have been implied by law in the decided cases, to classify them, and to consider the potential for development in those doctrines. This chapter aims to identify the three principal classes of trusts implied by law and their interaction with other equitable doctrines like estoppel and remedies for breach of trust. First, there is a recap of the conceptual underpinning of all trusts on the basis of conscience. **25.02**

Trusts implied by law function on various bases but always in recognition of the defendant's equitable duties of good conscience

That constructive trusts arise either to protect substantive rights or to provide a remedy

Trusts implied by law are the means by which equity achieves a variety of objectives intended principally to ensure that the defendant obeys the requirements of good conscience.[11] The central, conceptual complexity in trusts implied by law is knowing whether they simply give effect to pre-existing property rights, or whether they make awards either of rights in property or of equitable compensation to effect remedies in favour of any given claimant.[12] Trusts implied by law are avowedly concerned to give effect to substantive property rights by preventing the defendant from denying the rights of the claimant in equity, or from taking a benefit from property while knowingly acting contrary to the rights of another.[13] So, by way of example, purchase price resulting trusts give effect to the common **25.03**

---

a device to commence a tracing claim into a mixed fund in equity or a device to grant relief on third parties who have participated in a breach of trust. The distinctions here are considered below.

[8] Principally through the medium of the constructive trust and the purchase price resulting trust.

[9] This second category is particularly evident in relation to automatic resulting trusts: see para 26.20.

[10] The doctrine of proprietary estoppel (and the nascent category of equitable estoppel) is considered in Chapter 56.

[11] *Westdeutsche Landesbank v Islington* [1996] AC 669.

[12] See C Rotherham, *Proprietary Remedies in Context* (Oxford: Hart Publishing, 2002) ch 1.

[13] *Westdeutsche Landesbank v Islington* [1996] AC 669. See para 27.01.

intention[14] of the parties by requiring the legal owner of property to recognize the title of some other person who contributed to the purchase price of property;[15] common intention constructive trusts similarly give effect to arrangements or to conduct intended by the common intention of the parties to establish co-ownership of the home;[16] and constructive trusts which transfer the equitable interest in property which was to have been transferred under the terms of a contract are acting in support of the claimant's rights under the doctrine of specific performance.[17] All of these forms of trust implied by law are concerned to prevent the defendant from unconscionably denying the rights of the claimant while possibly taking a benefit himself. Other forms of trusts implied by law are concerned with ensuring the recognition of pre-existing property rights which have not been voluntarily given up—such as automatic resulting trusts in cases of some failure to dispose effectively of rights in property,[18] or specific restitution of property passed away by trustees in breach of trust,[19] or, by a more complex stream of logic, constructive trusts imposed in an equitable tracing claim[20] to vindicate the pre-existing rights of the claimant.[21] All of these forms of trusts implied by law are readily explicable as giving effect to substantive, pre-existing property rights and therefore as operating on an institutional basis.[22]

25.04   Nevertheless, there are also forms of trust implied by law which use the language of constructive trust merely as a formula with which to provide relief to the claimant without being concerned with the recognition of pre-existing rights.[23] The two principal examples of this phenomenon are the remedies for personal liability to account as a constructive trustee for receipt of property knowingly in

---

[14] *Westdeutsche Landesbank v Islington* [1996] AC 669.

[15] *Dyer v Dyer* (1788) 2 Cox Eq Cas 92; *Tinsley v Milligan* [1994] 1 AC 340. See para 26.72.

[16] *Pettitt v Pettitt* [1970] AC 777; *Gissing v Gissing* [1971] AC 886; *Lloyds Bank v Rosset* [1991] 1 AC 107. See para 56.01.

[17] Further to the notion that equity looks upon as done that which ought to have been done (*Walsh v Lonsdale* (1882) 21 Ch D 9, *Attorney-General for Hong Kong v Reid* [1994] 1 AC 324), a contract to transfer property from the defendant to the claimant grants the claimant a right of specific performance to require the transfer of that property (*Walsh v Lonsdale* (1882) 21 Ch D 9) and therefore the equitable title in that property is deemed to pass automatically on constructive trust at the time of the formation of the contract (*Neville v Wilson* [1997] Ch 144).

[18] *Vandervell v IRC* [1967] 2 AC 291; *Westdeutsche Landesbank v Islington* [1996] AC 669. See Chapter 56.

[19] *Target Holdings v Redferns* [1996] 1 AC 421. See para 32.01. See also the discussion of specific restitution in relation to following and common law tracing claims at para 32.11.

[20] *Westdeutsche Landesbank v Islington* [1996] AC 669.

[21] *Foskett v McKeown* [2001] 1 AC 102.

[22] That is, as considered in the various discussions below, a case can be made out to explain that these trusts arise on an institutional and not on a remedial basis: see para 25.12.

[23] Adopting the words of Ungoed Thomas J in *Selangor v Cradock (No 3)* [1968] 1 WLR 1555, 1579.

breach of trust[24] and for dishonestly assisting in a breach of trust,[25] which describe the defendant as being liable as though a constructive trustee of the trust property at issue. As Professor Hayton has described this concept, the defendant is treated as having constructive trusteeship imposed upon him.[26] In consequence, the constructive trustee becomes liable to account to the beneficiaries of the trust as though he had been formally constituted as a trustee of an express trust and thus liable under ordinary principles of breach of trust. Interposing a deemed trust[27] might therefore be considered to be a shorthand means of justifying the imposition of liability on the knowing recipient or dishonest assistant of trust property, particularly in circumstances in which the beneficiaries would otherwise be left with only an insufficient remedy personally against trustees without the means to pay under breach of trust principles[28] or against property which cannot be traced. Alternatively, this form of liability would be better described as a recognition that a defendant who has committed a wrong by participating in a breach of trust ought properly to be construed as owing the same duties to the beneficiaries as an express trustee and therefore as being properly described as being a constructive trustee.[29]

Similarly the constructive trust imposed in relation to the receipt of bribes is a **25.05** form of constructive trust which gives rise both to a proprietary constructive trust, which grants property rights to the claimant in property in which that claimant has never previously had rights, and also effectively to a remedy for the wrong committed by the defendant.[30] These alternative grounds of liability, stemming from a constructive trust, arise out of the decision of the Privy Council in *Attorney-General for Hong Kong v Reid*.[31] The constructive trust in this context is said to arise over a bribe received by a public official[32] or an employee or other fiduciary[33] immediately upon the receipt of that bribe because its recipient ought to have accounted to the beneficiary for that bribe and therefore, given that equity treats as done that which ought to have been done,[34] the equitable title in that

---

[24] *Re Montagu* [1987] Ch 264; *Polly Peck International v Nadir (No 2)* [1992] 4 All ER 769; *Polly Peck v Nadir* [1992] 4 All ER 769, [1993] BCLC 187.

[25] *Royal Brunei Airlines v Tan* [1995] 2 AC 378; *Twinsectra Ltd v Yardley* [2002] UKHL 12, [2002] 2 AC 164; *Dubai Aluminium v Salaam* [2002] 3 WLR 1913.

[26] A Underhill and DJ Hayton, *Law of Trusts and Trustees* (16th edn, Butterworths, 2002) ('*Underhill and Hayton*') 324.

[27] In the sense that the defendant is 'construed' to be a trustee and thus becomes a 'constructive' trustee. [28] See Chapter 32.

[29] One who is construed to be a trustee, otherwise than by his appointment in relation to an express trust, thus becomes a constructive trustee.

[30] *Attorney-General for Hong Kong v Reid* [1994] 1 AC 324. [31] [1994] 1 AC 324.

[32] *Reading v Attorney-General* [1951] 1 All ER 617; *Attorney-General for Hong Kong v Reid* [1994] 1 AC 324. Cf *Attorney-General v Blake* [2001] AC 268.

[33] cf *Boardman v Phipps* [1967] 2 AC 46. [34] cf *Walsh v Lonsdale* (1882) 21 Ch D 9.

bribe is deemed to pass automatically to the beneficiary on constructive trust, thus founding an equitable tracing claim into any property acquired with that bribe.[35] The beneficiary previously had no right in the property constituting the bribe and therefore the constructive trust arises in general terms to prevent the constructive trustee from taking an unconscionable benefit from the breach of his duty.[36] The alternative basis of liability in relation to that same wrong of taking the bribe arises from the same concept, it is said,[37] in the event that any property acquired with the bribe decreases in value: the constructive trustee is obliged to make good the decrease in the value of that property on a personal basis.[38]

The principle common to all of these forms of trust implied by law

25.06 The common thread which equity has weaved through all of these various heads of liability is that of acting *in personam* against the conscience of the defendant.[39] The term 'in personam' in this context does not relate solely to a personal claim for money but rather it reflects the core equitable principle that the courts of equity act against the individual defendant by measuring that person's conscience.[40] This centrality of the notion of conscience emerges from the speech of Lord Browne-Wilkinson in the House of Lords in *Westdeutsche Landesbank v Islington*,[41] as is considered below.[42] The use of conscience in this context is a slightly muddied combination of the recognition that the Lords Chancellor acted for centuries as the keeper of the monarch's conscience[43] when serving writs through the Chancery,[44] together with the jurisdiction embodied by the courts of equity within English jurisprudence which was concerned both to act on a moral

---

[35] *Attorney-General for Hong Kong v Reid* [1994] 1 AC 324.

[36] In the opinion of Lord Templeman there emerges a clear condemnation of the immorality of the receipt of bribes in public life which, it is suggested, founds this form of liability, on which see para 29.11.

[37] *Attorney-General for Hong Kong v Reid* [1994] 1 AC 324.

[38] *Attorney-General for Hong Kong v Reid* [1994] 1 AC 324, and see para 29.09.

[39] As Lord Ellesmere put it in the *Earl of Oxford's Case* (1615) Ch Cas 1, the role of the Courts of Chancery was 'to correct men's consciences for frauds, breaches of trust, wrongs and oppressions of what nature soever they be'. Furthermore, the role of equity was to correct any injustice which would result from the rigid application of the common law. As Lord Ellesmere put it, the second goal of the Court of Chancery was 'to soften and to mollify the extremity of the law'.

[40] *Ewing v Orr Ewing (No 1)* (1883) 9 App Cas 34, 40, *per* Lord Selborne.

[41] [1996] AC 669.

[42] See para 25.39.

[43] They also acted, of course, as keepers of the Great Seal of England.

[44] See, for example, GW Thomas, 'James I, equity and Lord Keeper John Williams' (1976) English Historical Rev 506; and AS Hudson, *Equity & Trusts* (3rd edn, Cavendish Publishing, 2003) ('*Hudson*') 6 *et seq*, 969 *et seq*, 977 *et seq*, and 991.

basis[45] and to mitigate the rigour of the common law.[46] The development of the trust itself was a means of recognizing that the common law owner of property owed a complex set of obligations to those who had rights in equity against that property, whether those rights were the rights of ownership associated with the rights of beneficiaries against a trust fund[47] or rights of another order associated with equitable leases,[48] equitable easements,[49] and so forth.

What remains significant is that the trust is concerned to impose obligations of good conscience on the defendant. Those obligations may arise in the form of the conscionability of recognizing that the claimant had pre-existing rights in property held on trust for him[50] or in requiring the claimant to obey the terms of a contract by virtue of which he was to have transferred identified property to the claimant[51] or in requiring him to hold on constructive trust property which he knew to have been transferred to him by mistake.[52] These examples, and the many others considered in this **Part D Trusts Implied by Law**, function on the basis of recognizing the pre-existing rights of another person in property and therefore the conscience with which equity is concerned is that form of conscience which prevents one person from interfering with property belonging to another.[53] **25.07**

The notion of conscience in the law of trusts

The idea of conscience in equity has a long and meandering history. As rendered by modern courts there is a particular resonance of a moral jurisdiction being exercised over the defendant to ensure that he has observed some objective notion of good conscience.[54] The historical roots of the idea of conscience are different from **25.08**

---

[45] The determination of some Lords Chancellor that their jurisdiction was a moral one emerges, for example, in the words of Lord Cowper LC in the following passage from *Dudley (Lord) v Dudley (Lady)* (1705) Prec Ch 241, 244: 'Now equity is no part of the law, but a moral virtue, which qualifies, moderates, and reforms the rigour, hardness, and edge of the law, and is an universal truth; it does also assist the law where it is defective and weak in the constitution (which is the life of the law) and defends the law from crafty evasions, delusions, and new subtleties, invested and contrived to evade and delude the common law, whereby such as have undoubted right are made remediless: and this is the office of equity, to support and protect the common law from shifts and crafty contrivances against the justice of the law. Equity therefore does not destroy the law, nor create it, but assist it.' Sentiments associated with the ethical philosophy of Aristotle (on which see *Hudson*, ch 1), even if Aristotle is not accepted as being in any sense the intellectual progenitor of the equitable jurisdiction in England and Wales. Although see *Jones v Maynard* [1951] Ch 572, 575, *per* Vaisey J, considering Plato's notion of equality. [46] ibid.

[47] *Saunders v Vautier* (1841) 4 Beav 241. [48] *Walsh v Lonsdale* (1882) 21 Ch D 9.

[49] *Ives (ER) Investment Ltd v High* [1967] 2 QB 379.

[50] See the obligations imposed on a trustee under an express trust as considered in Part C generally; *Westdeutsche Landesbank v Islington* [1996] AC 669. [51] *Neville v Wilson* [1997] Ch 144.

[52] *Westdeutsche Landesbank v Islington* [1996] AC 669.

[53] Ideas in their early conception in the English tradition identified with John Locke, *Second Treatise on Government*, 1690 (ed CB Macpherson, Indianapolis: Hackett, 1980) 18 and esp 22, para 35.

[54] On the feasibility of this notion see *Hudson* 977.

that, however. That the medieval Lords Chancellor were the keepers of the monarch's conscience recognized that those early Lords Chancellor were generally ecclesiastics and that the notion of conscience in that sense was a theological one. John Seldon's waspish remark that this power of the Lord Chancellor to act in good conscience suggested that what constituted good conscience would differ from Chancellor to Chancellor as would the length of any individual Chancellor's foot so that the latter would be an equally good measure as the former.[55] In this sense, the maxim that 'equality is equity' was significant. Whereas this doctrine has tended to be rendered in modern cases so as to order equal division of property between the parties to litigation,[56] its earlier roots were in the suggestion that equity should treat all those who came before it in equal fashion. To ensure that equity would treat all litigants equally it was necessary for a body of principles to be developed and to be binding in all subsequent cases, rather than allowing the Lords Chancellor and the courts of equity to dispose of any given case in any way which they saw fit.

25.09   Consequently, equity has tended to develop a series of core principles against which all cases will be judged[57] as opposed simply to deciding each individual case entirely in the abstract by reference to purely moral principles. Nevertheless, the narrow line between conscience as exercised through rules and conscience as a moral standard persists in the modern law of trusts nowhere more obviously than in relation to trusts implied by law where the courts are implementing a notion of good conscience when imposing trusteeship on defendants. That notion of good conscience is, however, imposed variously to prevent a defendant knowingly dealing unconscionably with property in the broadest terms,[58] or having acted dishonestly in assistance of a breach of trust,[59] or having wilfully and knowingly received property by way of a breach of trust,[60] or having acted otherwise than an honest person would have acted together with the knowledge that his actions would have been considered to be dishonest by other people,[61] or to prevent a trustee from taking any unauthorized benefit from his fiduciary office,[62] or to punish fiduciaries who take bribes in the discharge of their functions.[63] It is suggested, through this Part D, that these various notions of conscience are subtly and significantly different; but it is also suggested that the possibility which they offer to English law either to prevent the

---

[55]   *Table Talk of John Seldon* (F Pollock (ed) 1927) 43.

[56]   See, for example, *Midland Bank v Cooke* [1995] 4 All ER 562 and J McGhee, *Snell's Equity* (30th edn, Sweet & Maxwell, 2000) ('*Snell*') 36, citing, for example, *Petit v Smith* (1695) 1 P Wms 7, 9, *per* Lord Somers LC and *Re Bradberry* [1943] Ch 35, 40.

[57]   See, for example, *Snell* 27 and *Hudson* 18.

[58]   *Westdeutsche Landesbank Girozentrale v Islington LBC* [1996] AC 669, HL.

[59]   *Royal Brunei Airlines v Tan* [1995] 2 AC 378.   [60]   *Re Montagu* [1987] Ch 264.

[61]   *Twinsectra Ltd v Yardley* [2002] UKHL 12, [2002] 2 AC 164, [2002] 2 All ER 377, HL.

[62]   *Boardman v Phipps* [1967] 2 AC 46.

[63]   *Attorney-General for Hong Kong v Reid* [1994] 1 AC 324, [1993] 3 WLR 1143.

defendant from benefiting from unconscionable behaviour or to prevent the claimant from suffering uncompensated detriment as a result of such behaviour is an important part of ensuring ethical and moral behaviour on the part of litigants. In the loosest sense, equity is discharging the function which Aristotle perceived of supplementing the common law; equity is also maintaining a collection of equitable maxims by means of rules of precedent and procedure; and more generally equity is ensuring that English private law retains a moral base.

Rights *in rem* and rights *in personam*

There is a significant distinction between rights which arise 'in rem' and rights **25.10** which arise 'in personam'. Rights *in rem* are, literally, rights 'in a thing' or rights in an identified item of property. They will be referred to in this book as 'proprietary rights'. Such proprietary rights entitle the claimant to a right in property which will entitle the owner of those rights to hold them no matter what the value of the property in question. Thus some right of ownership of property which increases in value means that the owner's rights become more valuable, and rights in relation to property which decreases in value in turn become less valuable. In the event of an insolvency, the owner of proprietary rights is entitled to retain those rights regardless of the claims of other creditors in the insolvency.[64] Rights *in personam*, in contrast, do not create rights in property but rather create only rights owed personally between the parties, usually to pay amounts of money. Such rights will be referred to in this book as 'personal rights'. In the event that the defendant is not sufficiently in funds to satisfy a personal claim, the claimant will be in the position of an unsecured creditor without any rights in any identified property.[65]

It is important to distinguish between personal rights in the form of a remedy and **25.11** the general notion that equity acts *in personam*. The jurisdiction of equity is to ensure the good conscience of any given defendant. A court of equity will therefore, in effect, interrogate the behaviour of that defendant and consider whether or not it satisfies the requirements which equity would ordinarily make of such a person in such circumstances.[66] In that sense, equity is acting *in personam* in its concern always with the conscience of the individual as opposed to a rigorous and always inflexible obedience to a code of technical legal rules.[67] This is a different concept from the personal remedy.

---

[64] *Re Goldcorp Exchange Ltd* [1995] 1 AC 74.
[65] Assuming, that is, that the claimant has not previously acquired some secured right.
[66] See, for example, the complexities introduced both to the objective and subjective notions of 'dishonesty' relevant to claims for dishonest assistance in a breach of trust in *Twinsectra Ltd v Yardley* [2002] UKHL 12, [2002] 2 AC 164.   [67] See *Snell* 41; *Hudson* 16.

Institutional and remedial trusts

25.12 English trusts operate on an institutional basis and not on a remedial basis. That is the accepted position. An institutional trust is one which arises automatically when the defendant deals with property in the knowledge that his actions are unconscionable. The claimant's rights as a beneficiary under a constructive or other trust are imposed from that moment. They are not created from the date of a judgment at trial. Therefore, the court's role is to recognize the existence of this pre-existing right. By contrast an American remedial constructive trust arises at the date of the court's order at the end of a trial. That it is 'remedial' in nature means that its terms and its extent are at the discretion of the court. When a court imposes a remedial trust it is perfectly possibly creating new rights in property as a remedy, and not recognizing the pre-existence of that right in property.

25.13 That a trust is institutional is significant in the following contexts. First, a court has no discretion as to the form nor the terms of an institutional trust: rather, the court's role is limited to observing the existence of that trust. Secondly, that an institutional trust comes into effect at the time of the defendant's knowledge of his unconscionable act is significant because that right will be deemed to have come into existence automatically. Suppose A mistakenly paid money to B on 1 February and made B aware of the mistake on the 2 February. A constructive trust would obtain over that money[68] only at the time that B knew of the mistake and consequently had knowledge of some factor which would affect his conscience in relation to his dealings with that money. Then suppose that B went into bankruptcy on 3 February and that A's claim to establish a constructive trust over the money was decided by a court on 1 December. A remedial constructive trust would, seemingly, operate only prospectively from the date of judgment on 1 December to grant A some property right in the money held by B. An institutional constructive trust, by contrast, would operate retrospectively such that the court would recognize that A held an equitable interest under a constructive trust in the money as of 2 February such that A would have a secured right in B's bankruptcy in the form of his proprietary right in the money before 3 February. Consequently, the institutional trust device is limited in its avowed reluctance to create new property rights but it does offer a significant protection in the context of bankruptcy and similar events.

25.14 The term 'institutional' was imported into the English lexicon by Professor Maudsley[69] adopting the distinction suggested by Professor Pound in the American context between 'substantive'[70] and 'remedial' rights in property.[71] It reflects the

---

[68] Provided that it was held separately from all other money: *Westdeutsche Landesbank v Islington* [1996] AC 669; *Re Goldcorp Exchange Ltd* [1995] AC 74.

[69] RH Maudsley, 'Proprietary Remedies for the Recovery of Money' (1959) 75 LQR 234, 237.

[70] Where 'substantive' is the comparator to 'institutional'.

[71] R Pound, 'The Progress of Law' (1920) 33 Harv L Rev 420, 421.

stated determination of the English courts not to award proprietary rights *de novo* but rather to protect existing property rights by means of ordinary property law and where necessary by trusts implied by law. A clear statement of this English position was set out by Nourse LJ in *Re Polly Peck (in administration)(No 2)*:[72]

> You cannot grant a proprietary right to A who has not had it beforehand, without taking some proprietary right away from B. No English court has ever had the power to do that, except with the authority of Parliament.

In consequence the English courts are said to be recognizing pre-existing property rights when imposing trusts implied by law. The earlier discussion[73] at the beginning of this section relating to institutional and remedial trusts did show, however, that there are forms of trust implied by law which arise otherwise than in recognition of pre-existing rights. The doctrine of equitable tracing will permit pre-existing property rights to be followed into property for which they have been substituted. The example of equitable tracing could, however, be explained as vindicating the pre-existing rights of the claimant, albeit in property in which he had not previously had any rights. That form of constructive trust which applies in relation to a bribe, however, grants a right in property which the claimant had not previously owned. Consequently, we might question whether the imposition of trust in furtherance of equity's determination to ensure that a fiduciary acts in good conscience arises out of that pre-existing relationship.[74]

That trusts are said to arise on an institutional basis is considered in greater detail below in relation to constructive trusts.[75]

Fiduciary liability

The definition of a 'fiduciary relationship'

25.15 Those on whom the office of trustee is imposed by operation of law in any manner considered in this **Part D Trusts Implied by Law** occupy the status of fiduciaries. Consequently, it would be useful to spend some time considering what it means to describe a person as being a fiduciary. Professor Kennedy has described the term 'fiduciary' as being 'of ancient pedigree, and somewhat shrouded in mystery, it cannot be an overstatement that the fiduciary relationship is a legal concept of indistinct features and defining characteristics'.[76] So, we begin

---

[72] [1998] 3 All ER 812, 831.   [73] See para 25.12.

[74] See C Rotherham, *Proprietary Remedies in Context* (Hart, 2002) ch 1 generally, which argues that the courts do frequently create new property rights and that their coyness about seeming to do so expressly is misplaced. See also AS Hudson, 'The Unbearable Lightness of Property' in AS Hudson (ed), *New Perspectives on Property Law, Obligations and Restitution* (Cavendish, 2004) 1 and 23.

[75] See para 25.33.

[76] I Kennedy, 'The fiduciary relationship—doctors and patients' in *Wrongs and Remedies in the 21st Century* (Clarendon Press, 1996) 111.

by acknowledging that the term fiduciary is difficult to define despite being familiar to lawyers for some centuries. A little like an elephant, we think we would know one when we saw one but find it difficult to describe in the abstract. A dictionary definition of the word 'fiduciary', beyond a somewhat coy reference to it having a specifically legal sense, is 'relating to or based on a trust'. However, the etymology of the word 'fiduciary' is more enlightening: 'Late 16th century, via Latin *fiduciarius* "(holding) in a trust" from, ultimately, *fides* "trust".'[77] In this sense the word 'trust' has a link in the Latin with 'faith: *fide*' which is also the root of the English word 'confide', literally to have faith in someone or to have confidence in someone. There is therefore a clear connection between the ordinary use of the word 'fiduciary' with notions of 'faith', 'belief', 'confidence' and 'trust'.

25.16 In *Reading v R*[78] Asquith LJ proposed the following summary of those circumstances in which a fiduciary relationship can be said to exist:

> A consideration of the authorities suggests that for the present purpose a 'fiduciary relation' exists (a) whenever the plaintiff entrusts to the defendant property, including intangible property as, for instance, confidential information, and relies on the defendant to deal with such property for the benefit of the plaintiff or for purposes authorised by him, and not otherwise ... and (b) whenever the plaintiff entrusts to the defendant a job to be performed, for instance, the negotiation of a contract on his behalf or for his benefit, and relies on the defendant to procure for the plaintiff the best terms available ...

More simply yet Lord Browne-Wilkinson has described a fiduciary relationship as coming into existence by reference to the following principle: 'The paradigm of the circumstances in which equity will find a fiduciary relationship is where one party, A, has assumed to act in relation to the property or affairs of another, B.'[79]

25.17 The essence of the fiduciary relationship is often said to be one of loyalty and consequently one which precludes the fiduciary from advancing his personal interests at the expense of, or in conflict with, the interests of the object of his fiduciary obligations.[80] Those sentiments have been expressed by Millett LJ in the following terms:

> A fiduciary is someone who has undertaken to act for or on behalf of another in a particular matter in circumstances which give rise to a relationship of trust and confidence. The distinguishing obligation of a fiduciary is the obligation of loyalty. The principal is entitled to the single-minded loyalty of his fiduciary. The core liability has several facets. A fiduciary must act in good faith; he must not make a profit out of his trust; he must not place himself in a position where his duty and his interest may conflict; he may not act for his own benefit or the benefit of a third person

---

[77] *Encarta World Dictionary* (Bloomsbury, 1999).   [78] [1949] 2 KB 232, 236.
[79] *White v Jones* [1995] 2 AC 207, 271.
[80] On which see Chapter 29 on the imposition of constructive trusts in relation to the abuse of fiduciary office generally.

without the informed consent of his principal. This is not intended to be an exhaustive list, but it is sufficient to indicate the nature of fiduciary obligations. They are the defining characteristics of the fiduciary.[81]

What emerges further from this discussion is that the obligations of a fiduciary, while being subject to general rules, are nevertheless sensitive to context and capable of arising in entirely novel situations.[82] This notion is considered in the next section.

The nature of a fiduciary's obligations are sensitive to context

There are four established categories of fiduciary relationship: trustee and **25.18** beneficiary,[83] company directors in relation to the company,[84] partners *inter se* (within the terms of the 1890 Partnership Act),[85] and principal and agent.[86] Nevertheless, the range of potential fiduciary offices are infinite and may extend from an errand boy obliged to return change to the person who sent him on the errand, up to the situation in which one person reposes all of his most confidential and intimate affairs and property into the hands of another.[87] Examples of other situations in which fiduciary relationships have been found are as follows:[88] first, where a solicitor acts on behalf of his client[89] when advising that client as to the client's affairs within the scope of the solicitor's retainer;[90] secondly, in relation to

---

[81] *Bristol and West Building Society v Mothew* [1998] Ch 1, 18, *per* Millett LJ.

[82] *Collings v Lee* [2001] 2 All ER 332. See also *Sphere Drake Insurance Ltd v Euro International Underwriting Ltd* [2003] EWHC 1636.

[83] This category is generally simply assumed to be axiomatic of the fiduciary relationship, see *Ex parte Dale* (1879) 121 Ch D 772, 778, *per* Fry LJ; *Re Coomber* [1911] 1 Ch 723, 728 *per* Fletcher-Moulton LJ.

[84] *Selangor United Rubber Estates Ltd v Cradock (No 3)* [1968] 1 WLR 1555. Cf *Lindgren v L&P Estates Ltd* [1968] Ch 572 in relation to directors-elect.

[85] *Bentley v Craven* (1853) 18 Beav 75. See also *Holiday Inns Inc v Yorkstone Properties (Harlington)* (1974) 232 EG 951.

[86] *Lowther v Lowther* (1806) 13 Ves 95,103, *per* Lord Erskine; *Powell & Thomas v Evans Jones & Co* [1905] 1 KB 11. See also *Re Hallett's Estate* (1880) 13 Ch D 696 in relation to relationships of bailment.

[87] *Re Coomber* [1911] 1 Ch 723, 728, *per* Fletcher Moulton LJ. So, in *Hooper v Gorvin* [2001] WTLR 575, where a person undertook to act on behalf of himself and fellow leaseholders in negotiations as to their property, he was deemed to have accepted a fiduciary liability in relation to those negotiations even though he had not undertaken to act formally as the agent of the other parties.

[88] These examples have arisen primarily in England and Wales, whereas other jurisdictions have accepted that a doctor may owe fiduciary duties to his patient (*McInerney v MacDonald* (1992) 93 DLR (4th) 415) and that a parent who has abused his child is taken to have breached fiduciary duties to that child (*M(K) v M(H)* (1993) 96 DLR (4th) 449; *H v R* [1996] 1 NZLR 299).

[89] *Nocton v Lord Ashburton* [1914] AC 932; *McMaster v Byrne* [1952] 1 All ER 1363; *Brown v IRC* [1965] AC 244; *Boardman v Phipps* [1967] 2 AC 46; *Maguire v Makaronis* (1997) 144 ALR 729. By contrast, the Law Society owes no fiduciary duties to the solicitors whom it represents: *Swain v Law Society* [1983] 1 AC 598.

[90] *Bolkiah (Prince Jefri) v KPMG* [1999] 2 AC 222. This limitation has two senses, it is suggested. First, that the fiduciary obligations terminate when the retainer terminates: *Bolkiah v KPMG, op cit.* Secondly, that the solicitor is obliged to observe the obligations of a fiduciary in relation to the

senior employees holding sensitive positions with reference to their employers,[91] or where any employee exploits his office to generate a personal profit by way of a bribe;[92] thirdly, between the promoter of a company and the company itself;[93] and fourthly those who occupy public office whether or not as members of the secret service,[94] or as members of the armed forces using their rank to obtain passage for contraband through army roadblocks,[95] or an Attorney-General in particular when taking a bribe not to prosecute an alleged criminal.[96]

25.19 It will be observed, then, that whereas the four classic examples of fiduciary relationship will give rise to the duties considered in this Part D of this book, many of the other forms of fiduciary relationship which have been identified in the decided cases have arisen not simply because the fiduciary occupies such-and-such a position but rather have come to have the obligations of a fiduciary imposed upon them because they have acted inappropriately. In consequence, it might be thought that these fiduciary duties are latent in a wide number of relationships and are called actively to notice only when the officer acts unconscionably, such as the Attorney-General whose fiduciary duties were called to attention only when he took a bribe.[97] In that sense the equitable duties attendant on a fiduciary office are imposed to prevent the fiduciary from taking an unconscionable benefit from their office and so to hold them to act in good conscience.

25.20 From an understanding that the number of fiduciary offices is potentially infinite, and that the category of fiduciary relationships is therefore an elastic one, it should be recognized that the obligations befitting a fiduciary will differ from circumstance to circumstance. As Lord Browne-Wilkinson has held:

> ... the phrase 'fiduciary duties' is a dangerous one, giving rise to a mistaken assumption that all fiduciaries owe the same duties in all circumstances. That is not the case. Although so far as I am aware, every fiduciary is under a duty not to make a profit

---

client's legal affairs but not as to his choice of socks, where the latter falls outwith the scope of the duties forming a part of his retainer.

[91] *Canadian Aero-Services Ltd v O'Malley* (1973) 40 DLR (3d) 371, 381, *per* Laskin J; *Sybron Corporation v Rochem Ltd* [1984] Ch 112, 127, *per* Stephenson LJ; *Neary v Dean of Westminster* [1999] IRLR 288. However, this does not relate to ordinary employees and does not form a necessary part of the employment contract: *Nottingham University v Fishel* [2000] IRLR 471.
[92] *Attorney-General for Hong Kong v Reid* [1994] 1 AC 324.
[93] *Erlanger v New Sombrero Phosphate Company* (1878) 3 App Cas 1218. See AS Hudson, 'Capital Issues' in G Morse (ed) *Palmer's Company Law* (Sweet & Maxwell) para 5-113.
[94] A contentious category whereby it was accepted in *Attorney-General v Guardian Newspapers Ltd (No 2)* [1990] 1 AC 109 that such a person would be a fiduciary (in that case, when publishing his memoirs), but whereas in *Attorney-General v Blake* [1998] 1 All ER 833, CA, [2000] 4 All ER 385, HL it was considered that such a person would not always be fiduciary of necessity although his position may be akin to that of a fiduciary.
[95] *Reading v Attorney-General* [1951] 1 All ER 617.
[96] *Attorney-General for Hong Kong v Reid* [1994] 1 AC 324.
[97] *Attorney-General for Hong Kong v Reid* [1994] 1 AC 324. Indeed, in this example, the constructive trust took effect only from the moment at which the bribe was received.

from his position (unless such profit is authorised), the fiduciary duties owed, for example, by an express trustee are not the same as those owed by an agent.[98]

So it is with the precise obligations borne by a constructive trustee:[99] the precise obligations of the trustee will fall to be defined from context to context. The precise nature of the trusteeship borne in each context will emerge throughout the chapters of this **Part D Trusts Implied by Law.**

One important point to recognize is that the office of fiduciary can be imposed in addition to other legal obligations. So, for example, commercial partners have contractual obligations between them as set out in their partnership agreement. Similarly, agents stand in a contractual relationship to their principals. And yet both partners and agents bear fiduciary obligations above and beyond their contractual bonds. A professional trustee may only agree to act if sufficient limitations on her potential liability for breach of duty are included in a contract created between herself and the settlor.[100] In consequence, the professional trustee will be authorized to take a commission from the management of the fund and the trustee's general obligations to achieve the best possible return for the fund will be circumscribed by a contractual variation on the usual legend 'this investment may go down as well as up', to the effect that the trustees do not guarantee any particular rate of return.

25.21

In consequence, when considering the nature of fiduciary obligations it will frequently be necessary to examine the context to decide precisely what those fiduciary obligations mean in that particular situation. Such an atomization of fiduciary obligations into particular factual circumstances contributes to our difficulty in defining precisely what is meant by labelling someone as a fiduciary. We must return to the general ideas of good faith and loyalty outlined above for a more general understanding of what it means to be a fiduciary. A beneficiary is entitled (in the legal sense of having a 'right') to expect that the fiduciary will not permit that beneficiary to suffer loss. So, where does that insight take us? It means that the fiduciary responsibility is something greater than either contractual or tortious liability even though the content of the fiduciary liability may be limited by the fiduciary's express contractual refusal to adopt certain forms of liability. Otherwise, to be a fiduciary attracts liability for all loss suffered by the beneficiary and is not restricted simply to contractually anticipated forms of loss or even to the tests of causation and remoteness of damage under the duty of care in the tort of negligence. The following section examines the particular benefits which result from successfully identifying a defendant as owing fiduciary duties to a claimant.

---

[98] *Henderson v Merrett Syndicates* [1995] 2 AC 145, 206.

[99] Whether under a resulting trust or a constructive trust.

[100] For the court's willingness to accept the efficacy of such provisions, see *Armitage v Nurse* [1998] Ch 241.

Examples of the stringency and adaptability of fiduciary obligations imposed by means of trusts implied by law

25.22 The responsibilities of the fiduciary are based on a standard of utmost good faith in general terms. The older case law took the straightforward attitude that if there were any loss suffered by a beneficiary, then the fiduciary would be strictly liable for that loss.[101] This attitude has been promulgated by the decisions in *Regal v Gulliver*[102] (concerning directors of a company) and *Boardman v Phipps*[103] (concerning a solicitor advising trustees) which imposed strict liability for all unauthorized gains made by the fiduciaries deriving, however obliquely it would seem, from their fiduciary duty. The company directors in *Regal v Gulliver* were prevented from making a profit from a business opportunity which it was felt by the court ought to have been exploited on behalf of the company rather than on behalf of the directors personally. At one level this personal gain for the directors constituted a fraud on the shareholders who might otherwise have benefited in increased dividends from the investment in question. In *Boardman v Phipps* the obligations of fiduciary office were extended to a solicitor using his own money to exploit an opportunity which the trust could not have taken and which the solicitor for himself realized—the only nexus with the trust was the fact that he learned of the possibility while attending a meeting on behalf of his clients,[104] the trustees. Despite the indirect link between the solicitor's personal profits and the proprietary rights of the beneficiaries (who had all benefited directly from the solicitor's skills) the court held that the strict rule against fiduciaries profiting from their office should be upheld.

25.23 The requirement of good faith required by a court of equity is therefore a strict requirement. We should also consider the instructive example of *Attorney-General for Hong Kong v Reid*,[105] in which a public official was required to hold property on constructive trust for an unestablished category of beneficiaries in circumstances in which that property had never belonged to any person who could possibly have been considered to be a claimant. The money used to bribe the Attorney-General had only ever belonged to those whom the Attorney-General had refused to prosecute. In some general sense the bribes were held on trust for the people or the government of Hong Kong. The niceties of trusts—that is, the need for title in property and for identified beneficiaries—were overlooked in the court's enthusiasm to find a justification for taking the proceeds of the bribes from the defendant.

25.24 The case of *Attorney-General for Hong Kong v Reid*,[106] considered at length in Chapter 29 on constructive trusts, demonstrates two important facets of fiduciary

---

[101] *Keech v Sandford* (1726) Sel Cas Ch 61.   [102] [1967] 2 AC 134n.
[103] [1967] 2 AC 46.   [104] Together with the use of confidential information.
[105] [1994] 1 AC 324.
[106] *Attorney-General for Hong Kong v Reid* [1994] 1 AC 324; [1993] 3 WLR 1143.

responsibility. First, liability as a fiduciary can be imposed in entirely novel circumstances, there is no need to demonstrate a close analogy with any existing category of fiduciary relationship. In *Reid* there was no prior case law relating specifically to the position of an Attorney-General although there were cases relating to people in public office more generally defined (for example, the army sergeant in *Reading v Attorney-General*[107]). It would be disingenuous to suggest that *Reid* broke entirely new territory: rather it resolved the long-running skirmish in the academic journals in relation to the legal treatment of bribes.[108] Nevertheless, that a constructive trust was imposed was a novel departure for the law—albeit one well trailed in the scholarly literature. That constructive trust was founded on equity's determination that that which ought to have been done is looked upon as having been done: in other words, that the bribes once received ought to have been held on trust from the moment of their receipt. Secondly, the liability imposed on a trustee is not necessarily linked to any pre-existing relationship but may arise in relation to some subsequent act and relate only to that act. The liability imposed on the defendant in *Reid* was imposed not only in relation to property used in breach of the fiduciary duty but also in relation to an obligation to make good any loss on the investment of such property. The strict nature of fiduciary liability was observed once again. Beyond any precise contractual obligations owed by the Attorney-General to the government which employed him, there were the fiduciary obligations of a constructive trust in the receipt of the bribes alone—that action of receipt of a bribe generated fiduciary obligations (to hold the bribes on constructive trust) from that moment onwards.[109] *Boardman* was a slightly different situation because the solicitor was already in a fiduciary relationship to his client before making unauthorized profits; although it could be argued that the constructive trust was a new aspect to those fiduciary obligations once the unauthorized profits had been made.

The beneficiary acquires a range of equitable claims in relation to trusts implied **25.25** by law. The fiduciary will hold any property received in breach of some duty on trust for the beneficiary.[110] That also grants the beneficiary rights to any property acquired with that original property whether in the form of an income stream (such as dividends from shares) or in the form of substitute property (that is, a replacement capital asset). The beneficiary is also entitled to be compensated for any loss made by the fiduciary in dealing with property which was held on a constructive trust for the beneficiary as a result of some breach of duty.[111] The beneficiary can acquire compound interest on any judgment received against

---

[107] [1951] 1 All ER 617.
[108] eg RH Maudsley, 'Proprietary Remedies for the Recovery of Money' (1959) 75 LQR 234.
[109] cf *Attorney-General v Blake* [2000] 4 All ER 385.
[110] As considered above in relation to *Attorney-General for Hong Kong v Reid* [1994] 1 AC 324 and *Boardman v Phipps* [1967] 2 AC 46.   [111] *Boardman v Phipps* [1967] 2 AC 46.

e fiduciary for breach of duty.[112] Furthermore, the general result of finding that
: fiduciary is indeed a fiduciary is that everything is assumed against the
nuuciary. This is what *Boardman v Phipps* and *Regal v Gulliver* indicate: the
fiduciary will always be liable for any loss suffered by the beneficiary and also
responsible for generating the best possible return for that beneficiary.[113]

25.26 Consequently, fiduciary obligations can arise either in prescribed circumstances
or in novel situations, but those obligations can always be shaped and limited by
agreement between the parties. Fiduciary obligations in the form of trusts implied
by law can be imposed on defendants outside those well-established categories,
generally with a purpose typically limited to dealings with specific property. What
is important to note is that the fiduciary duty raises in the court a heightened
suspicion of anything which may conceivably benefit the fiduciary without
sufficient authorization under cover of an abstract standard of good faith and
loyalty.[114]

B. Resulting Trusts

The nature of resulting trusts

25.27 The resulting trust, as discussed in Chapter 26, is a limited doctrine which arises
in only two contexts.[115] The function of the first form of resulting trust is to
restore the equitable interest in property to its previous, beneficial owner where
some attempted disposition of those property rights has failed.[116] The purpose of
this category of resulting trust is to ensure that there is some recognized owner of
property such that it cannot exist in a vacuum without some person being responsible for it.[117] The second form of resulting trust arises in circumstances in which
two or more people have contributed to the purchase price of property with an
intention that each of those contributors should take some proprietary right in

---

[112] *Westdeutsche Landesbank v Islington* [1996] AC 669.
[113] See generally Chapter 32 on breach of trust.
[114] See, for example, *Keech v Sandford* (1726) Sel Cas Ch 61, *per* Lord King LC, in which the
court imposed a constructive trust on a trustee who renewed a lease in circumstances in which the
infant beneficiary for whom the lease had previously been held could not have done so, while
expressly providing that it was not necessary for the imposition of the trust that the trustee have
behaved wrongly but rather that it was the policy of the court to remove even the possibility that a
trustee might be able to benefit from his fiduciary office on an unauthorized basis: 'it is very proper
that rule should be strictly pursued'.
[115] *Westdeutsche Landesbank v Islington* [1996] AC 669.
[116] *Essery v Cowlard* (1884) 26 Ch D 191; *Vandervell v IRC* [1967] 2 AC 291.
[117] Thus ensuring that the property cannot simply be abandoned and thus have no owner: see
generally AH Hudson 'Abandonment', in Palmer and McKendrick (eds), *Interest in Goods* (LLP,
1993).

that property.[118] The purpose of this second category of resulting trust is to prevent any such contributor, or group of contributors, seeking unconscionably to deny the proprietary rights of any other contributor. This second form of resulting trust frequently operates in tandem with certain categories of presumption used by equity in situations in which the parties' intentions cannot be proved.[119] In both situations the resulting trust is imposed by operation of law over the property at issue.

There has been much judicial and academic comment on the true nature of the **25.28** resulting trust. On the basis of English authority it is possible to restrict the discussion of the resulting trust to those two categories outlined above, subject to one or two reservations considered below. The resulting trust could be considered to be an extension of express trust principles in the sense that the first form of resulting trust functions in response to the settlor's intentions (or lack of them) and that the second form of resulting trust functions so as to effect the common intention of all who contribute to the purchase price of property.[120] The doctrine of resulting trust is therefore a doctrine of limited application. The detail of the operation of both forms of resulting trust is considered in Chapter 26.

The traditional approach to the conceptual understanding of the resulting trust[121] **25.29** is that of Megarry J in *Re Vandervell (No 2)*[122] which established a broad division between automatic and presumed resulting trusts. This division remains viable, despite a minor doubt cast on the assumed breadth of the automatic resulting trust by Lord Browne-Wilkinson in *Westdeutsche Landesbank Girozentrale v Islington London Borough Council*.[123] The approach taken in this book, and broadly similar to that adopted by others,[124] is to divide between the two categories of resulting trust already identified because that accords with leading English authority and because it permits us to retain much of the traditional division made by Megarry J in *Re Vandervell (No 2)*. The utility of retaining the approach set out by Megarry J is that it has formed the basis of many of the decisions which fall to be considered in Chapter 26, as well as providing a fuller account of those forms of resulting trust identified by Lord Browne-Wilkinson than was set out in the leading case of

---

[118] *Westdeutsche Landesbank v Islington* [1996] AC 669.   [119] See para 26.79.

[120] *Westdeutsche Landesbank v Islington* [1996] AC 669. See below at para 26.72.

[121] *Underhill and Hayton* 329; *Hudson* 304. Broadly J Martin, *Hanbury and Martin's Modern Equity* (16th edn, Sweet & Maxwell, 2001) ('*Martin*') 237 is similar in its division between conveyance to trustees, no declaration of trust, voluntary conveyance and the presumptions, and purchase money resulting trusts.

[122] [1974] Ch 269.   [123] [1996] AC 669.

[124] Albeit that those others tend to divide the material among different chapters rather than contain it in one chapter: see, for example, J Mowbray et al, *Lewin on Trusts* (17th edn, Sweet & Maxwell 2000) ('*Lewin*'). There are similarities with P Pettit, *Equity and Trusts* (9th edn, Butterworths, 2001) ('*Pettit*').

Westdeutsche Landesbank Girozentrale v Islington London Borough Council[125] (hereafter '*Westdeutsche Landesbank v Islington*').

25.30 There is one other account of the resulting trust[126] which has suggested that the resulting trust is a means of achieving restitution of unjust enrichment. One form of this thesis divided the resulting trust between apparent gifts, trusts which fail, vitiated intention, and qualified intention.[127] This mooted restructuring of the resulting trust has been rejected by the House of Lords[128] and not adopted by any English court.

Persistent questions as to the nature of resulting trusts

25.31 One issue which continues to vex judges and academic commentators alike is the part that common intention plays in resulting trusts. By 'common intention' is meant the intention of all of the parties in the formation of the resulting trust: settlor, trustees, and beneficiaries. It is said, on occasion,[129] that a resulting trust comes into existence to give effect to the common intention of the parties, whether that is an automatic resulting trust or a presumed resulting trust. The answer to this question is simply put. Common intention plays no part in those resulting trusts which effect a restoration of the equitable interest to the settlor where the settlor has failed to exhaust the whole of the beneficial interest. The intention of the trustee is unimportant because the trustees are not capable, *qua* trustees, of declaring the terms of a trust;[130] and the beneficiaries are volunteers who have no power *qua* beneficiaries to declare the terms of the trust. Therefore, it is only the intention of the settlor which can be of any significance. Failure to exhaust the beneficial interest in the property gives rise automatically to the resulting trust.[131] In relation to purchase price resulting trusts, the *common* intention of the parties is of greater importance. Lord Browne-Wilkinson explained the foundations of the resulting trust in the following terms:

> Both types of resulting trust are traditionally regarded as examples of trusts giving effect to the common intention of the parties. A resulting trust is not imposed by law

---

[125] [1996] AC 669.

[126] See P Birks, 'Restitution and resulting trusts' in Goldstein (ed), *Equity: Contemporary Legal Developments* (Jerusalem, 1992) 335; R Chambers, *Resulting Trusts* (Clarendon Press, 1997). The restitutionary theory functioned, broadly, on the basis that the resulting trust should be remodelled so as to achieve restitution of unjust enrichment by ensuring that equitable title in property results back to its original owner on the happening of some unjust factor: See generally P Birks, *Introduction to the Law of Restitution* (Clarendon Press, 1992); R Chambers, *op cit*. It was an important part of this theory that the resulting trust comes into existence because the transferor did not intend the transferee to take the property beneficially: R Chambers, *op cit*. It is clear on the authorities that this approach is not English law (*Westdeutsche Landesbank v Islington* [1996] AC 669).

[127] R Chambers, *Resulting Trusts* (Clarendon Press, 1997).

[128] *Westdeutsche Landesbank v Islington* [1996] AC 669.

[129] *Westdeutsche Landesbank v Islington* [1996] AC 669.

[130] *Re Brook's ST* [1939] 1 Ch 993.   [131] *Vandervell v IRC* [1967] 2 AC 291.

against the intentions of the trustee (as is a constructive trust) but gives effect to his presumed intention.[132]

It is clear that not all resulting trusts are imposed by the courts to enforce the *common* intention of the parties.[133] For example, in *Vandervell v IRC*[134] Mr Vandervell directed that shares held on trust for himself as beneficiary should be transferred away from that trust for the benefit of the Royal College of Surgeons. As considered below,[135] the whole of the equitable interest in those shares was not disposed of because the trust retained an option to repurchase the shares and so was accepted by the House of Lords as having failed to declare a valid trust over that part of the equitable interest represented by the option. In that case there was only the intention of Mr Vandervell which was important in the imposition of the resulting trust. It is the title holder in property who decides how that property is to be treated—it cannot be the intention of a volunteer recipient which is important. In a case like *Westdeutsche Landesbank v Islington*, where there was a vitiated commercial contract, it might seem appropriate to talk of a common intention between both contracting parties—but that is not true of *all* cases.

The reference to 'common intention' in the creation of a resulting trust is a commonly used one.[136] Its meaning is that a resulting trust is a mixture of the intention of the settlor and the trustee's knowledge that the trustee is not intended to take the property beneficially. However, to read references to 'common intention' as requiring some quasi-contractual examination of the intentions of the various parties involved in the constitution, operation, and management of the trust is to misunderstand the function of the trust. Trusts arise, as Lord Browne-Wilkinson made clear in *Westdeutsche Landesbank v Islington*,[137] to control the conscience of the trustee. Therefore, the only common intention which is of importance is the recognition by the trustee that the settlor did not intend him to take any beneficial interest in the property *qua* trustee. The trustee is consequently obliged to hold the property on trust for some other person. Where no beneficiary has been vested with any equitable interest under express trust principles, the equitable interest must pass instead to the settlor on resulting trust. The 'common intention' here is the understanding between settlor and trustee that the trustee is not to have any beneficial interest in the trust property: it does not connote any more general reference to the parties' intentions as to the identity of the beneficiaries of the property. This idea is expressed as follows by Peter Gibson J in *Carreras Rothmans Ltd v Freeman Mathews Treasure Ltd*:[138]

25.32

> The principle in all these cases is that the equity fastens on the conscience of the person who receives from another property transferred for a specific purpose only and

---

[132] [1996] AC 669.   [133] Chambers, *op cit.*   [134] [1967] 2 AC 291.
[135] See para 25.32.
[136] See also *Carreras Rothmans Ltd v Freeman Mathews Treasure Ltd* [1985] Ch 207.
[137] [1996] AC 669.   [138] [1985] Ch 207, 217.

not, therefore, for the recipient's own purposes, so that such person will not be permitted to treat the property as his own or to use it for other than the stated purpose ... if the common intention is that property is transferred for a specific purpose and not so as to become the property of the transferee, the transferee cannot keep the property if for any reason that purpose cannot be fulfilled.

The intention of the trustee is meaningless in relation to the settlor's decision as to the terms of the trust and as to the identity of the beneficiaries under that trust. The only issue is the original title holder's intention as settlor concerning the ownership of the equitable interest. Where the settlor does not make his intention sufficiently clear or otherwise fails to exhaust the whole of the beneficial interest, then the problem as to the equitable ownership of the property left over is resolved by returning the title to the settlor on resulting trust.

C. Constructive Trusts

The classification and scope of constructive trusts

The core notion of the constructive trust

25.33   Constructive trusts arise by operation of law such that the defendant is construed to be liable as a trustee[139] in circumstances in which the defendant has knowledge of factors which affect his conscience and so justify the imposition of such liability.[140] The trustee will not be liable until he knows of the factor which is said to affect his conscience but, once he does know, he becomes constructive trustee of the property in question immediately, automatically, and will similarly be constructive trustee of any property which is substituted for that original property. Liability as a constructive trustee can be either proprietary or personal.[141]

25.34   Before essaying that programme of categorization, which the preceding paragraph requires, however, it is worth recalling the words of Edmund-Davies LJ in *Carl Zeiss Stiftung v Herbert Smith & Co* that

> English law provides no clear and all-embracing definition of a constructive trust. Its boundaries have been left perhaps deliberately vague so as not to restrict the court by technicalities in deciding what the justice of a particular case might demand.[142]

This statement indicates that the constructive trust is not a certain or rigid doctrine. Rather, its edges are blurred and the full scope of its core principles are

---

[139]   cf *Soar v Ashwell* [1893] 2 QB 390, 393, *per* Lord Esher MR.
[140]   *Westdeutsche Landesbank v Islington LBC* [1996] AC 669, *infra.*
[141]   See para 27.01.   [142]   [1969] 2 Ch 276, 300.

difficult to define. In *Paragon Finance plc v DB Thackerar & Co*[143] Millett LJ did attempt a general definition of the doctrine of constructive trust:

> A constructive trust arises by operation of law whenever the circumstances are such that it would be unconscionable for the owner of property (usually but not necessarily the legal estate) to assert his own beneficial interest in the property and deny the beneficial interest of another.[144]

Similarly in Irish law, Costello J has described the constructive trust as arising:

> ... when the circumstances render it inequitable for the legal owner of property to deny the title of another to it. It is a trust which comes into existence irrespective of the will of the parties and arises by operation of law. The principle is that where a person who holds property in circumstances which in equity and good conscience should be held or enjoyed by another he will be compelled to hold the property in trust for another.[145]

All constructive trusts arise by operation of law on the basis of the core principle that the defendant who has title to or possession of property will be construed to be a trustee of that property for another person where good conscience requires it.[146] That is, in circumstances in which the defendant has knowledge of some factor in relation to that property which the court considers should have affected his conscience, then he will be a constructive trustee of that property.[147] As a matter of vocabulary, that someone is *construed* to be a trustee means that that person is a constructive trustee. That core principle correlates with the core role of equity as a jurisdiction which acts *in personam* against the conscience of the individual defendant.[148] While that is the core principle on which constructive trusts will be described in this Part D of this book, there are a variety of subspecies of constructive trust considered in Chapters 27 through 30 in which that core principle is put to work in particular contexts.[149]

That the constructive trust is said to arise by operation of law means that it does **25.35** not arise in furtherance of the intentions of the parties in general or any settlor in particular.[150] However, there may be situations in which a constructive trust is imposed to ensure performance of a specifically enforceable contract[151] or otherwise to prevent a defendant from reneging unconscionably on some other form of voluntary agreement.[152] In such situations it might be said that the constructive

---

[143] [1999] 1 All ER 400.   [144] cf *Westdeutsche Landesbank v Islington LBC* [1996] AC 669.
[145] *HKN Invest OY v Incotrade PVT Ltd* [1993] 3 IR 152, 162, *per* Costello J. See also *Kelly v Cahill* [2001] IEHC 2, [2001] 2 ILRM 205.   [146] See para 27.01.
[147] The objective notion that the court is permitted to decide that the defendant's conscience ought to have been affected, rather than restricting itself to asking whether or not the defendant's conscience actually was affected, is considered in *Hudson* 977 and at para 30.35 of this book. It is suggested there that it is entirely in keeping with the nature of equity as a jurisdiction which seeks to inquire into the consciences of defendants that the courts should evaluate the conscionability of the defendant's actions on an objective rather than on a subjective basis.
[148] *Snell* 41.   [149] See para 27.03.
[150] *Westdeutsche Landesbank v Islington LBC* [1996] AC 669.
[151] *Chinn v Collins* [1981] AC 533; *Neville v Wilson* [1997] Ch 144.
[152] *Banner Homes Group plc v Luff Development Ltd* [2000] Ch 372; *Pallant v Morgan* [1953] Ch 43.

trust is being imposed in furtherance of some demonstrable agreement, arrangement, or understanding between the parties;[153] the more significant point is that the imposition of the constructive trust does not itself require the consent of all material parties.[154] Rather, the constructive trust, in general terms, is imposed as a response to some unconscionable act of the defendant related to property,[155] whether or not that property was formerly part of a trust fund if it accrued in conflict with some fiduciary office.[156] Therefore the discussion of constructive trusts in this book will consider both the manner in which constructive trusts arise further to a notion of responding to unconscionable actions in general terms[157] and the circumstances in which constructive trusts have been imposed by the case law by extrapolation from that central principle.

25.36 Proprietary constructive trusts arise such that the defendant is taken to hold identified property on trust, whether because the defendant occupied a fiduciary relationship in relation to the claimant[158] or because the defendant has acted knowingly contrary to conscience such that a constructive trust is imposed over property and against him for the first time.[159] It is suggested that proprietary constructive trusts imposed on persons who did not formerly occupy a fiduciary office operate by means of construing that person to have acted in a way in which the imposition of such a trust is appropriate and that the constructive trust itself operates so as to make that person liable to treat that constructive trust fund as though he had been appointed an express trustee of it.[160] As considered above, constructive trusts of either type are described as being 'institutional' and to arise by operation of law, which is to say that such constructive trusts are considered to take effect from the date of the activity which was contrary to conscience and not from the date of any court order.[161]

25.37 Personal liability to account to the claimant as a constructive trustee arises in two circumstances: first, where the defendant has received trust property into his possession or control knowing that he did so further to a breach of trust[162] or,

---

[153] eg *Lloyds Bank v Rosset* [1991] 1 AC 107; *Grant v Edwards* [1986] Ch 638; *Westdeutsche Landesbank v Islington LBC* [1996] AC 669.

[154] *Westdeutsche Landesbank v Islington LBC* [1996] AC 669; *Banner Homes Group plc v Luff Developments Ltd* [2000] Ch 372; *Lonrho plc v Fayed (No 2)* [1991] 4 All ER 961.

[155] *Westdeutsche Landesbank v Islington LBC* [1996] AC 669.

[156] *Boardman v Phipps* [1967] 2 AC 46; *Reading v Attorney-General* [1951] 1 All ER 617; *Attorney-General for Hong Kong v Reid* [1994] 1 AC 324;   [157] Set out at para 27.01.

[158] *Boardman v Phipps* [1967] 2 AC 46.

[159] *Westdeutsche Landesbank v Islington LBC* [1996] AC 669.

[160] As to the extent of a constructive trustee's fiduciary duties, see para 27.11 below.

[161] See para 27.05.

[162] *Twinsectra v Yardley* [2002] UKHL 12, HL, [2002] 2 All ER 377; *Bank of Credit and Commerce International v Akindele* [2001] Ch 437.

secondly, where the defendant has dishonestly assisted in a breach of trust perhaps without receiving any such property.[163] That such a person is described as being a constructive trustee is to say that that person is construed to be liable to account to the beneficiaries of a trust potentially for any loss suffered by that trust as a result of the breach of trust: the extent of the liability to make good the loss suffered by the trust is equivalent to the liability which would be faced by some person who was an express trustee of that trust.[164] Hence, the assertion that such a person is *construed* to be a trustee of that trust. In neither circumstance, however, is there any property which is held on trust by the defendant.[165] Rather this form of liability is purely a personal liability to account to the beneficiaries for their loss.[166]

The various species of constructive trust considered in this Part D

There are a great many examples of the constructive trust which are set out in the chapters to follow. This discussion categorizes the various forms of constructive trust and seeks to identify the themes that are common to the cases in each category. Those categories identify constructive trusts being imposed in the following circumstances. First, in response to unconscionable behaviour (as considered in Chapter 27) constructive trusts have been imposed in response to the following forms of behaviour: unlawful killing;[167] theft;[168] fraud, void, and voidable contracts;[169] undue influence and constructive fraud;[170] where statute has been used as an engine of fraud;[171] bribes;[172] unconscionable dealing with property;[173] in the enforcement of voluntary agreements.[174] Secondly, to enforce agreements whether in the form of binding contracts[175] (including specifically enforceable contracts, commercial joint ventures, agreements to stay out of the market, part performance of agreements, and a purchaser's undertakings) or other voluntarily assumed liability (in the form of common intention constructive trusts,[176] secret

25.38

---

[163] *Royal Brunei Airlines v Tan* [1995] 2 AC 378; *Twinsectra v Yardley* [1999] Lloyd's Rep Bank 438, CA.

[164] *Target Holdings v Redferns* [1996] 1 AC 421, [1995] 3 WLR 352, [1995] 3 All ER 785.

[165] *Twinsectra v Yardley* [2002] UKHL 12, HL, [2002] 2 All ER 377.

[166] This personal liability has led some to describe this remedy as being a wrong, akin to tort: P Birks, 'Receipt' in P Birks and A Pretto (eds), *Breach of Trust* (Hart, 2002) 213. That this form of liability is remedial rather than institutional might be true—depending on one's view of whether the liability for breach of trust arises institutionally or remedially. However, to equate that liability to wrongs such as tort is to overlook the fact that the remedy is based on the equitable remedy of account which does not correspond to common law notions of reasonableness and foreseeability.

[167] *In the Estate of Crippen* [1911] P 108.

[168] *Westdeutsche Landesbank v Islington* [1996] AC 669.　　　[169] See paras 27.24–27.26.

[170] See para 27.29.　　　[171] See para 27.34; *Rochefoucauld v Boustead* [1897] 1 Ch 196.

[172] *Attorney-General for Hong Kong v Reid* [1994] 1 AC 324.　　　[173] See para 27.45.

[174] See para 27.65.　　　[175] See para 28.02; *Neville v Wilson* [1997] Ch 144.

[176] *Lloyds Bank v Rosset* [1991] 1 AC 107.

trusts,[177] mutual wills,[178] or incompletely constituted transfers[179]) as considered in Chapter 28. Thirdly, in response to abuse of fiduciary position (as considered in Chapter 29) in circumstances such as the accrual to a person of unauthorized profits from a fiduciary office,[180] the acceptance of bribes,[181] or the permission of conflicts of interest.[182] Fourthly, where third parties are construed to be liable as though express trustees in relation to some breach of trust (as considered in Chapter 30) either on the basis of meddling with the trust to the extent that one is deemed to have become a trustee by virtue of one's own wrong (or, as a trustee de son tort),[183] personal liability to account as a constructive trustee for knowing receipt of property in breach of trust,[184] or personal liability to account as a constructive trustee for dishonest assistance in a breach of trust.[185]

The utility of the institutional constructive trust

25.39   Lord Browne-Wilkinson sets out the difference between institutional and remedial constructive trusts in *Westdeutsche Landesbank v Islington*. The purpose of that distinction was to explain the basis on which Goulding J ought to have decided the case of *Chase Manhattan v Israel-British Bank (London) Ltd*[186] in which a paying bank mistakenly made a payment twice to a recipient bank just before the recipient bank went into insolvency. The question at issue was whether or not the recipient bank could have been deemed to have become a constructive trustee of the second payment before going into insolvency, thus preserving the payer bank's proprietary rights in that money. Lord Browne-Wilkinson held in *Westdeutsche Landesbank v Islington* that:

> First, [the decision of Goulding J] is based on a concept of retaining an equitable property in money where, prior to the payment to the recipient bank, there was no existing equitable interest. Further I cannot understand how the recipient's 'conscience' can be affected at a time when he is not aware of any mistake. Finally, the judge found that the law of England and that of New York were in substance the same. I find this a surprising conclusion since the New York law of constructive trusts has for a long time been influenced by the concept of a *remedial* constructive trust,

---

[177] *Sellack v Harris* (1708) 2 Eq Ca Ab 46; *McCormick v Grogan* (1869) LR 4 HL 82; *Jones v Badley* (1868) 3 Ch App 362; *Blackwell v Blackwell* [1929] AC 318.
[178] *Dufour v Pereira* (1769) 1 Dick 419; *Stone v Hoskins* [1905] P 194; *Re Goodchild (deceased)* [1996] 1 WLR 694.   [179] See para 28.61.
[180] *Keech v Sandford* (1726) Sel Cas Ch 61; *Boardman v Phipps* [1967] 2 AC 46.
[181] *Attorney-General for Hong Kong v Reid* [1994] 1 AC 324. See para 29.07.
[182] See para 29.51.
[183] *Mara v Browne* [1896] 1 Ch 199, 209; *Carl Zeiss Stiftung v Herbert Smith (No 2)* [1969] 2 Ch 276, 289.
[184] *Barnes v Addy* (1874) 9 Ch App 244; *Blyth v Fladgate* [1891] 1 Ch 337; *Re Montagu* [1987] Ch 264.
[185] See para 30.01. *Barnes v Addy* (1874) 9 Ch App 244; *Royal Brunei Airlines v Tan* [1995] 2 AC 378; *Twinsectra Ltd v Yardley* [2002] UKHL 12, [2002] 2 AC 164.
[186] [1981] 1 Ch 105.

whereas hitherto English law has for the most part only recognised an institutional constructive trust. In the present context, that distinction is of fundamental importance. Under an institutional constructive trust, the trust arises by operation of law as from the date of the circumstances which give rise to it: the function of the court is merely to declare that such trust has arisen in the past. The consequences that flow from such trust having arisen (including the possibly unfair consequences to third parties who in the interim have received the trust property) are also determined by rules of law, not under a discretion. A remedial constructive trust, as I understand it, is different. It is a judicial remedy giving rise to an enforceable equitable obligation: the extent to which it operates retrospectively to the prejudice of third parties lies in the discretion of the court. Thus for the law of New York to hold that there is a remedial constructive trust where a payment has been made under a void contract gives rise to different consequences from holding that an institutional constructive trust arises in English law…[187]

In considering *Chase Manhattan*,[188] the problem which arose was the use of a seemingly remedial constructive trust with reference to a void contract. Lord Browne-Wilkinson held that English law will only impose an institutional constructive trust. The institutional constructive trust is defined as arising by operation of law without the scope for discretionary application on a case-by-case basis: **25.40**

> Under an institutional constructive trust, the trust arises by operation of law as from the date of the circumstances which give rise to it: the function of the court is merely to declare that such trust has arisen in the past. The consequences that flow from such trust having arisen … are also determined by rules of law, not under a discretion.

However, in delivering judgment in *Chase Manhattan v Israel-British Bank (London) Ltd*, Goulding J had sought to provide that there was no distinction between English and New York law, even though New York law would apply a remedial constructive trust as Lord Browne-Wilkinson explained in the following way:

> A remedial constructive trust, as I understand it, is different. It is a judicial remedy giving rise to an enforceable equitable obligation: the extent to which it operates retrospectively to the prejudice of third parties lies in the discretion of the court.

While the institutional constructive trust is found to be the English law approach, it is held possible for the remedial constructive trust to be introduced in future: 'Although the resulting trust is an unsuitable basis for developing proprietary restitutionary remedies, the remedial constructive trust, if introduced into English law, may provide a more satisfactory road forward.'[189]

---

[187] [1996] 2 All ER 961, 997.   [188] [1981] 1 Ch 105.
[189] cf P Birks, *Introduction to the Law of Restitution* (Clarendon Press, 1992).

D. Implied Trusts

25.41   There are situations in which trusts are imposed by operation of law which seek to give effect to the deliberate acts of the settlor in intending to achieve a result which he did not know or realize would be defined by equity as creating a trust. There are forms of trusts, dubbed 'implied trusts' for these purposes, in which the settlor will not have intended to create an express trust consciously. Instead, the courts recognize that the proper analysis of the settlor's actions was the establishment of a trust. One example of this type of trust arose in *Paul v Constance*[190] where Constance placed an amount of capital, in the form of a personal injury award, and joint bingo winnings won with his partner, Paul, into a bank account. While the bank account was held in Constance's sole name, the money in it was used jointly and Constance gave Paul to believe that the money was as much hers as his. Having found that the parties were unsophisticated and that they had no notion of the concept of trusts, Scarman LJ held that Constance's actions ought nevertheless to be interpreted as an intention to create an express trust. In cases such as *Paul v Constance*[191] the settlor was unaware that his actions would be so analysed, although the court was clear that his action should be taken to be an express trust, as opposed to a constructive trust. As a result, that category of trusts which fell between express trusts and constructive trusts appeared to disappear. That such a category exists is evident from s 53(2) of the Law of Property Act 1925 where there is a reference to 'implied, resulting and constructive trusts'. It is suggested that implied trusts ought to embrace this category of express trusts which are created unconsciously. The reason why such a category is required rests simply on the difficulty of knowing the obligations which are to be imposed in such situations in which the protagonists do not know that a trust of any sort has been created.

E. Proprietary Estoppel, Trusts Implied by Law in Relation to the Home, and Other Equitable Doctrines

The doctrine of proprietary estoppel

25.42   The doctrine of proprietary estoppel functions on the basis of some representation having been made in relation to property in reliance on which the claimant acts to her detriment.[192] The aim of the equity is to do the minimum necessary[193] in the light of the unconscionability of allowing the defendant to benefit or the

---

[190] [1977] 1 WLR 527.   [191] [1977] 1 WLR 527.

[192] *Re Basham* [1986] 1 WLR 1498.

[193] *Crabb v Arun DC* [1976] 1 Ch 179; *Pascoe v Turner* [1979] 1 WLR 431; *Bawden v Bawden* [1997] EWCA Civ 2664, *per* Robert Walker LJ.

claimant to suffer from the claimant's uncompensated detrimental reliance on the defendant's representation.[194] In consequence, if a representation has been made to some person in reliance on which she acts to her detriment, then the person who has suffered that detriment is entitled to a claim in proprietary estoppel for one of the range of rights considered in Chapter 56 and outlined in the discussion which follows.[195] This doctrine has supported the award of rights in property in situations as various as such rights not having been granted by will contrary to a representation which prompted the claimant to suffer some detriment[196] and the award of rights in property where the claimant had only a licence to occupy until it was coupled with his detrimental reliance on the defendant's representation.[197]

The doctrine of proprietary estoppel operates on a remedial basis[198] as is evidenced by the fact that the court may either make an award of some rights in property or alternatively merely an award of money sufficient to compensate the claimant for any detriment which she has suffered.[199] At their largest, when rights in property have been awarded on the basis of proprietary estoppel, they have amounted to the entire fee simple absolute in possession where that was deemed to be the minimum equity necessary to prevent the claimant from suffering detriment.[200] It is suggested, therefore, that even though the constructive trust appears to be a flexible doctrine, its avowedly institutional nature does not match the scope of remedy permitted by proprietary estoppel:[201] that is, in so far as those doctrines are currently constituted. What has become clear is that proprietary estoppel will give a claimant a substantive form of action with which to acquire rights in property which he had not had before and that it will not operate like promissory estoppel merely so as to defend that claimant from suffering detriment at the hands of the defendant.[202] **25.43**

What remains unclear is whether the aim of the equity is to give effect to the claimant's expectations—expectations which have been created by the defendant's representations—or to remedy the detriment suffered by the claimant. Suppose a claimant has acted on representations that he will receive a property worth £100,000 on the defendant's death and that the claimant incurs detriment **25.44**

---

[194] *Jennings v Rice* [2002] EWCA Civ 159.   [195] See para 56.91.
[196] *Re Basham* [1986] 1 WLR 1498.
[197] *Ramsden v Dyson* (1866) LR 1 HL 129, 170, *per* Lord Kingsdown; *Western Fish Products Ltd v Penrith DC* [1981] 2 All ER 204; *Brinnand v Ewens* [1987] 2 EGLR 67. However, see *Errington v Errington* [1952] 1 QB 290 as explained in *Ashburn Anstalt v Arnold* [1988] 2 WLR 706 as awarding rights in property further to a contractual licence on the basis of constructive trust.
[198] See para 56.87.   [199] *Baker v Baker* (1993) 25 HLR 408.
[200] *Pascoe v Turner* [1979] 2 All ER 945.
[201] As illustrated by *Sledmore v Dalby* (1996) 72 P & CR 196, *per* Roch J. See also *Campbell v Griffin* [2001] EWCA Civ 990, [2001] WTLR 981.
[202] See, for example, *Hearn v Younger* [2002] WTLR 1317 in particular, as well as the cases considered in this section in general whereby claimants establish rights in property which had not previously been vested with them.

to the value of £20,000 in reliance on that representation—perhaps in solving a boundary dispute relating to the property.[203] To give effect to the claimant's expectations would require a remedy to the value of £100,000, whether in cash or by means of an order for the transfer of the absolute title in that property. By contrast, an order intended only to compensate that claimant's detriment would be satisfied by an order for a payment of £20,000 by way of equitable compensation or a charge for that amount over the property. The purpose of the equity has been expressed as being a requirement 'to do justice'[204] or, more traditionally, to do the minimum equity necessary between the parties.

25.45   The evaluation of the minimum equity necessary in any given case would depend upon the circumstances. In the example just given, an elderly widow with no other means of protecting her rights in a property which had long been home and which she had been promised would be available for the rest of her life might lead the court to make an order for the transfer of the fee simple;[205] whereas a situation in which the claimant required money to help pay for an alternative home would be satisfied by an order for the payment of an amount of money equivalent to the cost of such a home;[206] or whereas a situation in which the claimant had always had an alternative home and his own income could be satisfied by an order for the payment of an amount of money equivalent to the detriment suffered. What is evident is that proprietary estoppel is not restricted to the purpose of most forms of the institutional constructive trust in giving effect to pre-existing property rights, but rather provides the claimant with new rights in property or to compensation in proportion to the equity required by the circumstances.[207] The source of these rights, then, is in the unconscionability of the defendant's actions and the concomitant need to do equity in response.

25.46   There is no single doctrine of estoppel and nor would it be possible simply to mould one from the raw material of the decided cases as they stand at present, despite some indications to the contrary by Lord Denning.[208] First, there is a distinction between those forms of estoppel recognized at common law and those recognized in equity; between proprietary estoppel which grants new rights in property,[209] promissory estoppel which functions merely as a shield,[210] and

---

[203]   As in *Re Basham* [1986] 1 WLR 1498.
[204]   *Jennings v Rice* [2002] EWCA Civ 159, para 36, *per* Aldous LJ.
[205]   *Pascoe v Turner* [1979] 2 All ER 945.   [206]   *Baker v Baker* (1993) 25 HLR 408.
[207]   See the discussion of those constructive trusts which provide for new rights in property at para 25.24.
[208]   *Amalgamated Investment & Property Co Ltd v Texas Commerce International Bank Ltd* [1982] QB 84. A view which also appealed to other judges: eg *Hiscox v Outhwaite (No 1)* [1992] 1 AC 562, 574, *per* Lord Donaldson; *John v George and Walton* (1996) 71 P & CR 375, 385, *per* Morritt LJ.
[209]   *Hearn v Younger* [2002] WTLR 1317.
[210]   See, for example, *Combe v Combe* [1951] 2 KB 215; *Brikom Investments Ltd v Carr* [1979] QB 467; *Hudson* 489.

estoppel by representation considered in this book to function as a defence to equitable tracing.[211] Secondly, there is no single explanation for the manner in which all estoppels operate given that estoppel is based on a range of bases varying from honesty[212] to common sense[213] to common fairness.[214] What emerges from this list is that common principles underpinning all estoppel can only be identified at the most rarefied levels—that of fairness, justice, and so forth.[215]

Nevertheless, a powerful argument has been put by Professor Cooke for the estab- **25.47**
lishment of a single doctrine of estoppel predicated on good conscience.[216] In general terms, Cooke considers the doctrine of estoppel to be a means of preventing a person from changing her mind in circumstances where it would be unconscionable so to do:[217] leaving us with a problem familiar to trusts lawyers of knowing what constitutes unconscionable behaviour in any particular context. The tension here between the historical truth that there are many forms of estoppel and the nagging sense nevertheless that they are all based on similar notions of conscionability is encapsulated in Lord Denning's apparent shift in emphasis when in 1980 he likened the many forms of this doctrine to 'a big house with many rooms' where 'each room is used differently from the others'[218] and then in 1981 when his lordship suggested that while 'the doctrine of estoppel ... has evolved during the last 150 years in a sequence of separate developments ... [a]ll these can now be seen to merge into one general principle shorn of limitations'.[219] It is this drift from separation between many technical forms of estoppel towards the recognition of a central operating principle which Cooke observes.

An early incarnation of the doctrine of proprietary estoppel was observable in the **25.48**
decision of the House of Lords in *Ramsden v Dyson*.[220] In the speech of Lord Cranworth the doctrine was stated as operating on the basis of some mistake being formulated in the claimant's mind by the defendant such that the claimant acts detrimentally in reliance on it.[221] Most of the modern cases are concerned with

---

[211] On this last category of estoppel see para 33.92.
[212] *Re Exchange Securities & Commodities Ltd* [1988] Ch 46, 54, *per* Harman J.
[213] *London Joint Stock Bank Ltd v Macmillan* [1918] AC 777, 818, *per* Lord Haldane.
[214] *Lyle-Meller v A Lewis & Co* [1956] 1 WLR 29, 44, *per* Morris LJ.
[215] The arguments for an all-embracing estoppel are based on such concepts: see eg the various dicta of Lord Denning in *Amalgamated Investment & Property Co Ltd (In Liquidation) v Texas Commerce International Bank Ltd* [1982] 1 QB 84; *Lyle-Meller v A Lewis & Co* [1956] 1 WLR 29; *Moorgate Mercantile Co Ltd v Twitchings* [1976] 1 QB 225.
[216] E Cooke, *The Modern Law of Estoppel* (Clarendon Press, 2000).
[217] eg *Amalgamated Investment and Property Co Ltd v Texas Commerce International Bank Ltd* [1982] 1 QB 84, 104, *per* Robert Goff J.
[218] *McIlkenny v Chief Constable of the West Midlands* [1980] 1 QB 283, 317.
[219] *Amalgamated Investment and Property Co Ltd v Texas Commerce International Bank Ltd* [1982] 1 QB 84, 122.   [220] (1866) LR 1 HL 129.
[221] ibid 140: '... if a stranger begins to build on my land supposing it to be his own, and I, perceiving his mistake, abstain from setting him right, and leave him to persevere in his error, a Court of equity will not allow me afterwards to assert my title to the land on which he had expended money

frustration of an expectation which the defendant permitted the claimant to form by means of either an express representation or some implied assurance that she would acquire rights in property.[222] The remedy is addressed to compensate the claimant for any detriment which was suffered in reliance on that representation or assurance. The source of this 'expectation approach' is typically identified with the speech of Lord Kingsdown in *Ramsden v Dyson*[223] where his lordship referred to a situation in which the claimant was:

> ... under an expectation, created or encouraged by [the defendant], that he shall have a certain interest ... upon the faith of such promise or expectation, with the knowledge of the landlord ... lays out money upon land, a Court of equity will compel the landlord to give effect to such promise or expectation.

Interestingly this early conception of the doctrine refers to a remedy aimed at giving 'effect to such promise' rather than at allowing the detriment suffered by the claimant to pass without compensation. This doctrine was restated significantly in *Taylors Fashions v Liverpool Victoria Trustees Co Ltd*[224] by Oliver J such that

> ... it would be unconscionable for a party to be permitted to deny that which, knowingly or unknowingly, he has allowed or encouraged another to assume to his detriment ...[225]

Oliver J preferred this focus on the detriment suffered by the claimant as opposed to some 'formula serving as a universal yardstick for every form of unconscionable behaviour'.[226] This approach has received general approbation[227] in preference to those few cases which have sought to apply the approach set out in *Wilmot v Barber* which expressed the doctrine of proprietary estoppel as being concerned exclusively with the defendant knowingly exploiting some mistaken apprehension of the claimant which caused that claimant detriment.[228] Thus the underpinning of the doctrine has been expressed by the Court of Appeal as being concerned to do the minimum equity necessary to respond to the defendant's unconscionability.[229]

25.49   It is suggested that there are broadly two forms of proprietary estoppel in its modern form, both of which operate on the basis of there having been some assurance

---

on the supposition that the land was his own'. See the extrapolation of this test in *Wilmot v Barber* (1880) 15 Ch D 96.

[222] For example, *Re Basham* [1986] 1 WLR 1498 considered below and *Sledmore v Dalby* (1996) 72 P & CR 196.   [223] (1866) LR 1 HL 129, 170.

[224] [1982] QB 133.   [225] ibid, 151.   [226] ibid.

[227] *Habib Bank Ltd v Habib Bank AG Zurich* [1981] 1 WLR 1265, CA; *Amalgamated Investment & Property Co Ltd v Texas Commerce International Bank* [1982] QB 84, CA; *Attorney-General of Hong Kong v Humphrey's Estate (Queen's Gardens) Ltd* [1987] 1 AC 114, PC; *Lim Teng Huan v Ang Swee Chuan* [1992] 1 WLR 113, PC; *Lloyds Bank v Carrick* [1996] 4 All ER 630, CA.

[228] *Coombes v Smith* [1986] 1 WLR 808; *Matharu v Matharu* (1994) 16 P & CR 93; also *Orgee v Orgee* (5 November 1997).   [229] *Jennings v Rice* [2002] EWCA Civ 159.

made to the claimant by the defendant on which the claimant relies to her detriment as considered above. The first form is an estoppel which operates in circumstances in which the representation made by the defendant was to the effect that the claimant would receive some rights in property, and in reliance on which the claimant suffered detriment. Clear examples of this form of estoppel have arisen. In *Re Basham*,[230] a testator gave his stepdaughter to believe that she would acquire title in a home and in reliance on which she acted to her detriment in a number of ways directed at the acquisition of those rights which she had been, effectively, promised. Similarly, in *Gillett v Holt*[231] an older man had made vague representations over a number of years to the effect that a younger man would eventually acquire all of the older man's land. While those representations were vague it was accepted that their accumulated effect over such a long period of time, coupled with the many acts of detriment incurred by the claimant in reliance on those representations, were sufficient to entitle the claimant to rights in that property under proprietary estoppel principles.

The second form of proprietary estoppel will subvert ostensibly mandatory rules of **25.50** law,[232] such as formal rules as to the means by which trusts may be created or rights in property transferred, in circumstances in which the claimant has acted to his detriment in reliance on representations made to him by the landowner to the effect that those property rights would be transferred to him. While this second form of estoppel may seem initially to be very similar to the first, it is suggested that it operates more broadly to exhume generally equitable doctrines such as the doctrine of part performance to give effect to the fundamental aim of the equitable jurisdiction to prevent one person taking an unconscionable benefit from the detriment suffered by another person. An example of this form of proprietary estoppel is provided by *Yaxley v Gotts*[233] in which a joint venture was formed for the acquisition of land. The joint venture did not comply with the requirement in section 2 of the Law of Property (Miscellaneous Provisions) Act 1989 that the terms of any purported contract for the transfer of any interest in land be in writing. The defendant therefore contended that the claimant could have acquired no right in contract to the land because there was no writing in accordance with the formal requirements of the statute. However, the court was prepared to uphold that between the parties there had been a representation that there would be a joint venture between the parties in reliance on which the claimant had acted to its detriment. It was held by the Court of Appeal that a constructive trust had

---

[230] [1986] 1 WLR 1498.   [231] [2001] Ch 210, [2000] 2 All ER 289.

[232] That is, civil law rules which preclude the validity of certain acts or which require a certain action in certain circumstances. Although those rights can be overreached: *Birmingham Midshires Mortgage Services Ltd v Sabherwal* (2000) 80 P & CR 256.

[233] [2000] 1 All ER 711; Smith, 'Oral contracts for the sale of land' (2000) 116 LQR 11; Tee, 'A merry-go-round for the millennium' (2000) CLJ 23.

arisen between the parties on the basis of their common intention—and that this constructive trust was indistinguishable in this form from a proprietary estoppel.[234]

Trusts implied by law in the home

Rights in the home distinct from other trusts implied by law

25.51   Trusts implied by law as they apply to the home have taken a form which is distinct from other forms of trusts implied by law. This area of the law receives its own lengthy consideration in Chapter 56 and, by extension, in Chapter 57. While built on concepts of resulting trust, constructive trust, and proprietary estoppel, the various means by which rights in the home are established have developed their own conceptual frameworks. If an express trust has been validly created in the conveyance or in some other form then that trust will be decisive of the parties' rights in the property.[235] The more complex questions arise in that great number of cases in which no such formal expression of the parties' rights in the home is created. This discussion refers, then, to situations in which there is no such declaration of trust.

25.52   In circumstances in which two or more people contribute to the purchase price of their home, provided that all of them intended that each contributor should take an interest in the property, the doctrine of purchase price resulting trusts will found an equitable interest for each contributor expressed as that proportion of the total cost of the home contributed by each person.[236] The legal owners of the home, recorded at the Land Registry as being the proprietors of that property in relation to registered land, will consequently hold the property on trust for all of the contributors to the purchase price who were intended to take some equitable interest in that property.

25.53   Alternatively, the House of Lords in the person of Lord Bridge in the case of *Lloyds Bank v Rosset*[237] has held, ostensibly eschewing the label 'resulting trust', that a common intention constructive trust can be founded in circumstances in which there has been some agreement, arrangement, or understanding between the parties as to their various rights in the home, or else that there has been conduct by the parties which justifies the recognition of such a right in circumstances in which the claimant has either contributed to the purchase price of the property or to any mortgage repayments.[238]

---

[234] [2000] 1 All ER 711, 721 *et seq, per* Robert Walker LJ.

[235] *Goodman v Gallant* [1986] FLR 106; *Re Gorman* [1990] 1 WLR 616; *Harwood v Harwood* [1991] 2 FLR 274.

[236] *Dyer v Dyer* (1788) 2 Cox Eq Cas 92; *Springette v Defoe* [1992] 2 FLR 388; *Tinsley v Milligan* [1994] 1 AC 340. Cf *Westdeutsche Landesbank v Islington LBC* [1996] AC 669.

[237] [1991] 1 AC 170   [238] *Ivin v Blake* [1995] 1 FLR 70.

This doctrine of common intention constructive trust constituted a narrowing of **25.54** earlier House of Lords decisions[239] and has not commanded respect in the lower courts.[240] Lord Bridge referred in his speech to 'constructive trust or proprietary estoppel' on five occasions. This raises an issue as to whether he intended to merge those two doctrines into one composite set of rules as to the acquisition of rights in the home. This could be said to be a constructive trust in that it creates rights for the claimant by operation of law. Alternatively, it could be said to arise by dint of proprietary estoppel because it creates rights to prevent the claimant suffering detriment.

In the Court of Appeal the doctrine of resulting trust has continued to be used.[241] **25.55** Flexibility has been added to the notion that a resulting trust crystallizes at the date of acquisition such that no alteration in those equitable interests is possible by means of accepting that constructive trust principles can justify the recalibration of a resulting trust.[242] In differently constituted Courts of Appeal,[243] however, the rigour of the decision in *Lloyds Bank v Rosset* has been impliedly rejected in favour of a survey of all of the circumstances of the case so as to take into account a much wider range of contributions to the life of the family than were permitted by that decision of the House of Lords.[244] These cases have proceeded on the basis that if it is too difficult to unravel the niceties of the proprietary rights of parties who have been in a long-term romantic relationship, particularly if it has spawned children and has seen the partners throw their lots in together, then the court may have recourse to the maxim that equality is equity and simply divide the property in half between the partners. Furthermore the doctrine of proprietary estoppel offers a very different, remedial approach to rights in property, as mentioned in the preceding section.

Resulting trust, constructive trust, or proprietary estoppel?

The hidden motive behind Lord Bridge's speech in *Lloyds Bank v Rosset* may have **25.56** been an elision of the categories of common intention constructive trust and proprietary estoppel, as mentioned above. The decision of Nourse LJ in *Stokes v Anderson*[245] makes the case for the contrary argument. His lordship, in following *Lloyds Bank v Rosset* and *Grant v Edwards*,[246] held that the 'court must supply the common intention by reference to that which all the material circumstances have shown to be fair'.[247] At that stage, his lordship did not see any reason for the elision

[239] *Pettitt v Pettitt* [1970] 1 AC 777; *Gissing v Gissing* [1971] 1 AC 886.
[240] As set out in para 56.01.   [241] *Springette v Defoe* [1992] 2 FLR 388, (1992) HLR 552.
[242] *Huntingford v Hobbs* [1993] 1 FLR 936.
[243] *Midland Bank v Cooke* [1995] 4 All ER 562. See also *Hammond v Mitchell* [1991] 1 WLR 1127.
[244] See also the decision of the Court of Appeal in *Burns v Burns* [1984] Ch 317 in relation to the narrow view of those factors which may be taken into account in relation to the establishment of a right in the home.   [245] [1991] 1 FLR 391.
[246] [1986] Ch 638.   [247] [1991] 1 FLR 391, 400.

of the common intention principles established originally in *Gissing v Gissing*[248] with the doctrine of proprietary estoppel. As considered above, the proprietary estoppel doctrine operates entirely at the discretion of the court and is prospective, whereas the constructive trust as an institutional trust operates retrospectively: with the result that any attempt to merge these concepts would have to address these differences.[249] Consequently, the doctrines appear to have significant differences between them. Nevertheless, in cases such as *Yaxley v Gotts*,[250] the narrow distinction between them has been commented on by the judiciary. In truth it would require only a slight recalibration of the foundations of one or other doctrine to subsume them, for example, under a general principle of unconscionability in the manner identified with constructive trusts in Chapter 27.[251]

Other equitable doctrines of significance

25.57 Whereas this Part D will focus on trusts implied by law, necessarily the concepts considered here are hemmed in by other equitable doctrines. In Chapter 33 the doctrine of equitable tracing considers the manner in which constructive trusts might be used to vindicate the property rights of beneficiaries whose trust property passes away from the trustees in breach of that trust, together with equitable liens, charges by way of subrogation, and other forms of equitable charge. Similarly, the doctrine of personal liability to account as constructive trustees for those who knowingly receive trust property in breach of trust or who dishonestly assist a breach of trust is bound up with that range of claims considered in Chapter 32 which relate to liability for breach of trust. The equitable doctrines of account and of equitable compensation also surround these claims. The doctrine of proprietary estoppel has been outlined in the preceding section. In Part J the alternative means of taking security in commercial transactions, such as floating charges, fixed charges, and *Quistclose* trusts are considered in detail alongside the ordinary principles of trusts implied by law. Consequently, the material considered in this Part D fits into larger conceptual categories, and particularly those issues considered in Parts H, I and J of this book.

---

[248] [1971] AC 886.
[249] Notwithstanding D Hayton, 'Equitable rights of cohabitees' [1990] Conv 370.
[250] [2000] 1 All ER 711.   [251] See para 27.01.

26

RESULTING TRUSTS

A. The Forms of Resulting Trust

The two categories of resulting trust

26.01 Resulting trusts arise in two different contexts. The first form of resulting trust restores the equitable interest in property to its previous, beneficial owner where some attempted disposition of that property has failed. The function of this type of resulting trust is either to restore the equitable title in property to its previous beneficial owner, or to recognize that such title remains with that person in equity. The second form of resulting trust arises in circumstances in which two or more people have contributed to the purchase price of property with an intention that each of those contributors should take some proprietary right in that property. The purpose of this category of resulting trust is to prevent any such contributor, or group of contributors, seeking unconscionably to deny the proprietary rights of any other contributor. This second form of resulting trust frequently operates in tandem with certain categories of presumption which are used by equity to resolve situations in which the parties' intentions cannot be proved conclusively. In both situations the resulting trust is imposed by operation of law over the property at issue. The two forms of resulting trust, and the various subcategories to which they give rise, are best understood as being conceptually distinct from one another, except to the extent that both respond to prevention of any unconscionable assertion of beneficial ownership by their trustees.

26.02 The manner in which the topic of resulting trusts ought to be divided is a matter of some debate. The traditional approach[1] is that of Megarry J in *Re Vandervell (No 2)*[2] which divides between automatic and presumed resulting trusts. This division remains viable, despite a minor doubt cast on the assumed breadth of the automatic resulting trust by Lord Browne-Wilkinson in the leading case of *Westdeutsche Landesbank Girozentrale v Islington London Borough Council* (hereafter '*Westdeutsche Landesbank v Islington*').[3] Other accounts[4] have advanced a (now-discredited[5]) account of the resulting trust as being a means of achieving restitution of unjust enrichment, perhaps to be divided between apparent gifts, trusts which fail, vitiated intention, and qualified intention.[6] The approach taken

---

[1] A Underhill and DJ Hayton, *Law of Trusts and Trustees* (16th edn, Butterworths, 2002) ('*Underhill and Hayton*') 329; AS Hudson, *Equity & Trusts* (3rd edn, Cavendish Publishing, 2003) ('*Hudson*') 304. Broadly J Martin, *Hanbury and Martin, Modern Equity* (16th edn, Sweet & Maxwell, 2001) ('*Martin*') 238 is similar in its division between conveyance to trustees, no declaration of trust, voluntary conveyance and the presumptions, and purchase money resulting trusts.

[2] [1974] Ch 269.

[3] [1996] AC 669. See also *Allen v Rea Brothers Trustees Ltd* (2002) 4 ITELR 627.

[4] P Birks, 'Restitution and resulting trusts' in Goldstein (ed), *Equity: Contemporary Legal Developments* (Jerusalem, 1992) 335.   [5] *Westdeutsche Landesbank v Islington* [1996] AC 669.

[6] R Chambers, *Resulting Trusts* (Clarendon Press, 1997). An approach which receives reserved support in *Carlton v Goodman* [2002] EWCA Civ 545.

in this book, and broadly similar to that adopted by others,[7] is to divide between the two categories of resulting trust already identified at the beginning of this chapter,[8] together with an analysis of matters such as presumptions relating to resulting trust and the interaction of illegality, mistake, and resulting trust.

Issues in the creation of resulting trusts

Limitations on the creation of resulting trusts

The resulting trust is a doctrine of limited application. Its scope is restricted to those two categories, outlined immediately above, concerning the acquisition of property and the prevention of any vacuum in the equitable ownership of property after a failed disposition of it. In relation to this latter form of resulting trust, it is tempting to suppose that it may be available in all situations in which there is a dispute as to the ownership of property. This approach could be identified, in a slightly different form, in the assertion that the doctrine of resulting trust be expanded greatly so as to effect restitution of property in any circumstance in which the defendant had gained some unjust enrichment at the expense of the claimant.[9] This suggested approach was rejected by the House of Lords in *Westdeutsche Landesbank v Islington*[10] in favour of recognizing the limited ambit of the resulting trust outlined above.   **26.03**

There are a number of questions as to the creation of resulting trusts which are logically anterior to a dissection of the categories of such trusts in the decided cases. The first question is as to the conceptual basis on which the resulting trust operates: specifically whether its function is to return property to the claimant, or whether it operates on the conscience of the trustee, or whether it vindicates the claimant's property rights. The second question concerns the time at which a resulting trust comes into existence. The third question concerns the nature of the obligations of the trustee under a resulting trust.   **26.04**

Whether resulting trust is predicated on a preceding transfer of property or on conscience

The traditional rationale for the resulting trust is that the equitable interest returns to the claimant only after it has been transferred away.[11] The term 'resulting' trust is taken from the Latin 'resalire' meaning 'to jump back'. Therefore, a resulting   **26.05**

---

[7] Albeit that those others tend to divide the material among different chapters rather than contain it in one chapter: J Mowbray et al, *Lewin on Trusts* (17th edn, Sweet & Maxwell, 2000) ('*Lewin*') generally. There are similarities with P Pettit, *Equity and Trusts* (9th edn, Butterworths, 2001) ('*Pettit*') 159.

[8] See para 26.01.

[9] P Birks, 'Restitution and resulting trusts' in Goldstein (ed), *Equity: Contemporary Legal Developments* (Jerusalem, 1992) 335.   [10] [1996] AC 669.

[11] *Re Vandervell's Trusts (No 2)* [1974] Ch 269.

trust sees rights in property jump back to the claimant who had previously transferred them away. However, it is not always clear on the decided cases that there
has indeed been any transfer away of property on this model; rather, it does appear
that in some cases the transfer had failed and therefore that there had been no
effective transfer of property away from the beneficiary under the resulting trust
in any event.

26.06 The most detailed judicial explanation of the operation of resulting trusts was
provided by Megarry J in *Re Vandervell (No 2)*.[12] The core of the resulting trust
was said to be that title in the property at issue must have been transferred away
from the claimant before the equitable interest could return to him on resulting
trust. In setting a series of numbered principles on which the resulting trust operates, his lordship began by holding that:

(1) If a transaction fails to make any effective disposition of any interest it does nothing. This is so at law and in equity, and has nothing to do with resulting trusts.[13]

Thus, if the settlor has failed to transfer away any interest in the property which
forms the trust fund, then the situation remains exactly the same: the purported
settlor remains absolute beneficial owner of all of the property sought to be settled
on trust. This notion is continued in the next paragraph of that judgment:

(2) Normally the mere existence of some unexpressed intention in the breast of the
owner of the property does nothing: there must at least be some expression of
that intention before it can effect any result. To yearn is not to transfer.[14]

Building on the requirement that there must have been some intention to transfer, it was required that there have been some transfer away of rights in property:

(3) Before any doctrine of resulting trust can come into play, there must at least be
some effective transaction which transfers or creates some interest in property.[15]

Therefore, for there to be any question of resulting trust (in the sense of *returning*
property rights to the settlor) it is necessary that those rights must have passed
away in the first place. The further principles of the law on resulting trusts are considered below. At this stage, however, there are questions as to whether or not a
transfer of property is always required and as to the time at which resulting trusts
come into existence.

26.07 In the case of *Westdeutsche Landesbank v Islington*,[16] however, an investment bank
transferred money to a local authority under a contract which was subsequently
declared to have been void *ab initio*. What was remarkable about that decision was
that the void contract was nevertheless held to have transferred good title in the

---

[12] [1974] Ch 269, 294; [1974] 1 All ER 47, 64.
[13] [1974] Ch 269, 294; [1974] 1 All ER 47, 64.
[14] [1974] Ch 269, 294; [1974] 1 All ER 47, 64.
[15] [1974] Ch 269, 294; [1974] 1 All ER 47, 64.   [16] [1996] AC 669.

money to the local authority. There was no resulting trust nor any constructive trust found in that case because the local authority neither knew of the void nature of the contract before the money had been dissipated, nor did the local authority have the money in its possession when the void nature of the contract was brought to light, in the wake of the decision of the House of Lords in *Hazell v Hammersmith & Fulham*.[17] Consequently, the resulting trust must now be understood as being organized around the impact on the conscience of the trustee and not simply on the validity of the transfer of property.

The question therefore arises whether or not a resulting trust can arise without some preceding transfer of property.

Whether resulting trusts require some preceding transfer of property

Whereas it was said by Megarry J in *Re Vandervell's Trusts (No 2)* that there must **26.08** have been some transfer of property before a resulting trust can be imposed, it is not clear that all forms of resulting trust do in fact *return* property rights to their previous owners: instead, there are situations in which it would appear on closer analysis that no rights ever leave the claimant and therefore that the resulting trust is, in truth, vindicating the continued presence of the property rights in the hands of the claimant. The answer to the question whether or not any property rights do in fact return to the claimant is an equivocal and contextual one which demonstrates that some resulting trusts do involve a return of property rights and that others do not. It is arguable that not all resulting trusts ought to be considered to be '*resulting* trusts' at all on that model because no title in fact leaves the settlor.

In this regard we might observe a distinction between automatic resulting trusts **26.09** and presumed resulting trusts. In relation to automatic resulting trusts there are cases in which the failure of the settlor's purported disposition of his property must suggest that no transfer of property was ever effected. So, in *Essery v Cowland*[18] property was to have been held on the terms of a marriage settlement but, because the marriage never took place, the marriage settlement was held to have failed. In consequence, equitable title in the property was found to have resulted back to the settlors. In that context there was never a trust and therefore it is not meaningful to say that title left the settlors only to be returned to them by means of resulting trust. An alternative analysis might be that the order of the court recognized that the settlors remained the equitable owners of the property on the basis that the marriage settlement was never properly constituted. Similarly, the decision of the House of Lords in *Vandervell v IRC*[19] concerned a purported transfer of a parcel of shares from a trust to the benefit of an educational institution. The transfer failed to account for an equitable interest in the form of

---

[17] [1992] 2 AC 1, [1991] 2 WLR 372, [1991] 1 All ER 545.   [18] (1884) 26 Ch D 191.
[19] *Vandervell v IRC* [1967] 2 AC 291, HL.

an option to repurchase those shares. Ownership of that option was not allocated and therefore it was held to return to the trust on resulting trust. This decision could be explained as recognizing that the equitable interest which was constituted by the option to repurchase the shares had never left the trust, as opposed to the more traditional explanation that title had somehow moved away from the original settlement only to be returned when it was realized that its ownership had not been explained with sufficient clarity.

26.10 The significance of a resulting trust analysis is not that it necessarily requires a transfer of property in all cases but rather that it operates so as to control the conscience of the common law owner of that property. Thus, if property were transferred away from its absolute owner without identifying its equitable owner, equity uses the resulting trust to oblige the person holding the legal title to recognize the continued rights of the previous, absolute owner of the property. This prevents this legal owner from asserting beneficial rights in the property. In situations in which the absolute owner had otherwise intended to make an outright transfer of property, rather than having intended to declare some form of trust, equity intervenes to impose a trust in order to prevent any unconscionable behaviour being committed by whoever has possession of that property. What equity is doing is justifying the imposition of fiduciary duties on the legal owner of property, whether or not that person had accepted the responsibilities of an express trustee, by supposing that the previous owner's rights in the property continue in existence so as to prevent unconscionable behaviour.

26.11 This explanation, predicated on the prevention of unconscionable activities, is the only means of explaining how presumed resulting trusts share any common heritage with the automatic resulting trusts considered hitherto. Presumed resulting trusts arise either to recognize that it would be unconscionable to deny the proprietary rights of someone who contributed to the purchase price of property on the common understanding that that person was to acquire some rights in that property, or in response to the presumptions which equity has developed in deciding contested disputes to property between spouses and between parents and their children. In the former category it is evidently a concern to prevent the unconscionable denial of another's property rights which motivates the courts to declare that the transfer of money or money's worth to acquire property generates an equitable interest under resulting trust in that property. In the latter form of presumed resulting trust the presumption operates in favour of deeming there to have been an intention to make a gift of property where the circumstances are otherwise unclear. This is an approach based on convenience and has more to do with English social history than the operation of equitable principle: as considered below.[20]

---

[20] See para 26.79.

In conclusion, there will be circumstances in which there has been some transfer **26.12** of property and circumstances in which there will not have been such a transfer of property: both leading potentially to the imposition of a resulting trust to resolve gaps in title and to prevent the common law owner of that property taking a beneficial right in it contrary to good conscience. Beyond that general observation, the resulting trust can only be rendered comprehensible by examining the various forms which they have taken in the decided cases. The further problem is in identifying the point in time at which such a trust comes into existence.

When a resulting trust comes into existence

The difficulty is knowing precisely when a resulting trust comes into existence. It **26.13** is important to know when a resulting trust comes into existence, for example, in insolvency proceedings to decide whether or not a creditor has a secured interest in property, or in relation to tax proceedings to identify whether or not the defendant had a proprietary right in the property at issue at the time when a liability to tax fell to be allocated. Ordinarily, it could be understood that a resulting trust is deemed to have come into effect immediately at the time when there is some unallocated portion of the beneficial interest in property. However, despite the initial attraction of the preceding analysis, it is not always immediately obvious when the resulting trust comes into existence.

It could be that the resulting trust comes into existence at one of two different **26.14** times. The first time a resulting trust might come into existence, for example in relation to an automatic resulting trust imposed because a declaration of trust has failed to exhaust all of the beneficial interest in the trust fund, could be said to be immediately on the declaration of trust which, subsequently, is recognized as having failed to exhaust the beneficial interest in the trust property. The difficulty with this analysis is that it is not always possible to know at the date of the declaration whether or not it would subsequently fail to exhaust the entire beneficial interest. For example, where a resulting trust is imposed on the basis that the completion of the purpose underpinning an express trust failed to use up all of the trust property, then it would not be possible to know that the imposition of the resulting trust was appropriate until the event which made it clear that that purpose had been achieved. Therefore, it could be argued that the resulting trust could only, logically, be said to have come into existence at that later date. What is clearly the case is that the resulting trust will only be capable of proof at the time when the trust purpose, to pursue the earlier example, has proved incapable of exhausting the entire beneficial interest. Consequently, the imposition of the resulting trust, even if it is deemed to have come into effect at the time the property was transferred away by the settlor, is being imposed retrospectively in response to the failure of the settlor's intentions.

26.15   Therefore, it is suggested that the time at which a resulting trust is imposed will be dependent on context. That resulting trusts operate by operation of law means that it would be possible for the courts to deem that the resulting trust ought to be recognized as having come into existence from the moment that the purported transfer of property was made. This would be to recognise that trusts are institutional devices in English law which come into existence retrospectively from the time when the trustee's conscience was affected and not prospectively from the date of any court order.[21] To do otherwise would be to render resulting trusts a remedial device.

The obligations of the trustee

26.16   There is no common usage of the term 'resulting trustee'.[22] Occasionally, the trustee is referred to as a 'constructive trustee':[23] but that is not to suggest that the resulting trust is a form of constructive trust; rather it is to recognize that the court is construing a person to be a trustee, as opposed to giving effect to some express trust obligation.

26.17   The automatic resulting trust is frequently a bare trust in which the legal owner of property is holding the unallocated portion of property effectively to the order of its previous, absolute owner by way of resulting trust. So, in the failed marriage settlement in *Essery v Cowlard*[24] the property was 'returned to its previous owners' by means of the trustees holding the property not on the terms of the ineffective settlement but rather as nominees prior to returning that property to its settlors. The obligations of the trustee in such a circumstance are therefore limited to obeying the orders of the beneficiary under the resulting trust and to taking reasonable care to ensure that the property at issue is not devalued, lost, or otherwise harmed by any act or omission of the trustee.

26.18   This second category of obligation is the crux of the matter. It is self-evident that the trustee must obey the orders of the beneficiaries in this context. What is more complex is knowing how extensive the trustee's obligations are in relation to the maintenance of the property. It is suggested that a resulting trust is primarily a nominee relationship whereby the trustee is obliged to return property to its previous owner. Therefore, there would be no necessary obligations to invest the trust fund nor to turn it to greater profit for the beneficiary. As such a resulting trust ought to last for only as long as it takes for the beneficiary to decide the manner in which he wishes to take receipt of that property. However, there are two potential, complicating factors. First, the trustee may have been acting in a professional context in which he already bore obligations under an express trust or some express investment contract to invest the property either for the beneficiary of the resulting

---

[21] *Westdeutsche Landesbank v Islington* [1996] AC 669.   [22] Chambers, *op cit*.
[23] *Lewin* 186.   [24] (1884) 26 Ch D 191.

trust or for the purported beneficiaries of the failed transfer. In that situation, a professional trustee bearing investment obligations under contract would still be responsible for the investment of the trust property. It is suggested that disputes in such a context are capable of resolution only by reference to the law of contract and any investment agreement between settlor and trustee. It is not the resulting trust which imposes such investment obligations. Secondly, the trustee may not wish to accept any obligations to maintain the property. It would seem unreasonable to impose greater obligations on the trustee to invest the property than were imposed on him under the original transfer arrangement. Nevertheless, it may be that it is not possible to return the property to the settlor's order immediately where the transfer of the property requires some formality to be completed before some administrative action which needs to be taken which would affect its value: for example, voting at an extraordinary general meeting in relation to a shareholding in a private company. In such a situation, the trustee may wish to relinquish any fiduciary office which he has not accepted in the manner in which a fiduciary obligation under an express trust might be accepted or repudiated. Such matters are little discussed in the decided cases. The principal focus of equity in these contexts is to prevent the trustee from taking an unconscionable benefit from his status as trustee and not, primarily, to impose complex obligations on such people. What emerges from this discussion is that the content of the trustee's obligations will depend on context but, in relation to a resulting trust, are likely to be limited to the obligations of a nominee in relation to a bare trust.

To whom the property results

Property results to the settlor of an *inter vivos* trust.[25] That is, the property results **26.19** to the person who provided the property which was settled on trust, and not to any other person who may have been identified in a trust instrument as being a settlor of that property without having in fact provided the property.[26] Where there are a number of settlors then the very property which they provided is returned to them if that property is separately identifiable,[27] or if the property is not separately identifiable then it is returned to them in proportion to their original contribution to the fund.[28] In relation to testamentary trusts which fail such that there is surplus property, the deceased person was treated before 1926 as having died intestate as to his personal property and such that his real property passed to his heir.[29] Property passed under testamentary trusts after 1926 are disposed of

---

[25] *Cogan v Stephens* (1835) LJ Ch 17; *Curteis v Wormald* (1878) 10 Ch D 172; *Re Vandervell's Trusts (No 2)* [1974] Ch 269.

[26] *Re Vandervell's Trusts (No 2)* [1974] Ch 269, 284, *per* Megarry J.

[27] *Re West Sussex Constabulary, etc, Fund* [1971] Ch 1, [1970] 1 All ER 544.

[28] *Re Trusts of the Abbott Fund* [1900] 2 Ch 326.

[29] *Ackroyd v Smithson* (1780) 1 Bro CC 503.

in accordance with the intestacy rules in favour of the statutory next of kin without any distinction being made between real and personal property.[30]

B. Resulting Trusts Where the Beneficial Interest Is Not Exhausted

Introduction

26.20   Resulting trusts arise automatically by operation of law in circumstances in which the beneficial interest in property settled on trust has not been exhausted. If property is transferred to some person who is not intended to take the beneficial interest, or part of the beneficial interest, in that property, it is important to know who is to take ownership of that unallocated beneficial interest. Where some part of the equitable interest in property is unallocated by the settlor after transferring property to the trustee, the equitable interest in that unallocated part automatically results back to the settlor. So, for example, if S purported to transfer the entirety of the equitable interest in land on which three houses were built to T to hold on trust, but where S failed to declare a trust over one of those houses, then the equitable interest in that one house would be held by T on resulting trust for S.[31] This is the simplest form of resulting trust. More examples of automatic resulting trusts are considered below.

Recognition of the title in property of its previous, beneficial owner

26.21   Resulting trusts which recognize the equitable title of the previous beneficial owner of property fall into many types, in the manner in which this chapter divides them.[32] In short, they arise whenever there is a 'gap', or vacuum, in the equitable title. That is, where the absolute owner of the property at issue purports to settle, transfer, or otherwise dispose of his rights in that property but fails to do so completely, leaving some portion of the equitable interest unallocated. This failure to deal with the entire equitable interest may be through a failure to make his intentions sufficiently clear, or a failure to constitute the trust properly, or through mistake, or because the trust's purpose is complete before all of the property has been

---

[30]   Administration of Estates Act 1925, ss 46–49, as amended.

[31]   See, for example, *Vandervell v IRC* [1967] 2 AC 291, HL, in which such a remaining, unallocated equitable interest was subjected to a resulting trust.

[32]   As considered below, the distinction is made here between resulting trusts which 'recognize the previous title of the claimant' and the more usual formulation that rights are 'restored to the claimant' on the basis that it is not always clear in relation to resulting trusts that any rights have necessarily left the claimant: rather, we might understand resulting trusts as being merely declarations that if the previous owner of the property is to be recognized as taking the equitable interest in the property on resulting trust, then maybe that is simply to vindicate the claimant's continued ownership of the property in equity throughout.

exhausted, or because it becomes impossible for the trust's purpose to be carried out. It is said, in effect, that equity causes the equitable title to pass on resulting trust to the previous owner of the property automatically on the failure of the disposition of the property.[33]

Thus, this form of resulting trust is activated by operation of law. That is, without **26.22** necessarily requiring the deliberate action of any of the parties to create such a trust: instead, equity infers the existence of a trust from the circumstances. As considered below, this resulting trust may also give effect to the common intention of the parties but it is not essential that the imposition of such a trust be in accordance with the intentions of all of the parties. Rather, the doctrine of resulting trust is concerned solely with the absence of any intention, expressed with sufficient certainty, on the part of the settlor to dispose of the whole of the equitable interest in the property at issue. In such circumstances, Megarry J understood this type of resulting trust to be an 'automatic resulting trust'[34] and as operating on the following principles:

> ... where the transfer to B is made on trusts which leave some or all of the beneficial interest undisposed of. Here B automatically holds on a resulting trust for A to the extent that the beneficial interest has not been carried to him or others. The resulting trust here does not depend on any intentions or presumptions but is the automatic consequence of A's failure to dispose of what is vested in him. Since *ex hypothesi* the transfer is on trust, the resulting trust does not establish the trust but merely carries back to A the beneficial interest that has not been disposed of. Such resulting trusts may be called 'automatic resulting trusts'.[35]

The automatic resulting trust operates on the basis of the equitable principle that equity abhors a vacuum. In practice this means that property rights must belong to some person because they cannot exist in a vacuum without an owner. Where there is no other equitable owner, those equitable rights are deemed to result automatically to the settlor: this appears sensible in principle given that the settlor was the last person to own those proprietary rights and is therefore the most logical person to be considered to be the owner of them after the failed transfer. In *Westdeutsche Landesbank v Islington*, Lord Browne-Wilkinson explained that this form of resulting trust arose:

> Where A transfers property to B *on express trusts*, but the trusts declared do not exhaust the whole beneficial interest.[36]

Therefore, as outlined above, where the settlor has purported to create an express trust but has failed to identify the person for whom that property is to be held,[37]

---

[33] *Vandervell v IRC* [1967] 2 AC 291.   [34] ibid.   [35] ibid.
[36] [1996] 2 All ER 961, 990–991; *Underhill and Hayton* 329 *et seq, White v Vandervell Trustees Ltd* [1974] Ch 269, 288 *et seq; Barclays Bank Ltd v Quistclose Investments Ltd* [1970] AC 567.
[37] *Vandervell v IRC* [1967] 2 AC 291.

and where the property is more than is required to 'exhaust the whole beneficial interest', then such a resulting trust arises. Lord Browne-Wilkinson's formulation is confined to the declaration of express trusts where there is some part of the equitable interest left unallocated. It is suggested that other of the categories of automatic resulting trust considered above, such as the impossibility of completing the trust's purpose, can also be understood to be a failure to exhaust the whole beneficial interest. In any event, the result is that the equitable interest in the property at issue results to its previous owner. This is said to prevent a vacuum in the ownership of the property because it ensures that there is no question left unanswered as to who is to exercise the rights and bear the obligations of the ownership of the property: the property is understood to be the property, in equity, of its previous beneficial owner. Thus, any gap in the ownership is filled.[38]

No declaration of trust, by mistake

26.23 The most straightforward form of resulting trust is that which arises when a settlor seeks to create a trust but does not declare the manner in which all of the property at issue is to be held on trust. If the settlor failed to declare any terms of the trust then there would not be any identifiable express trust binding over any property even if the legal title in that property had been transferred to trustees. Rather, the trust fund would be held on bare trust by the trustee but for no identified beneficiary nor on any identified terms. The doctrine of resulting trust would operate so as to recognize that the entire equitable interest resulted to the settlor. Alternatively, if it was only in relation to a portion of the trust fund that there was no declaration of the identity of the beneficiary over that property or no effective terms on which to form the basis of a trust, then the resulting trust will take effect over that unallocated portion of property alone.[39]

26.24 The clearest authority for this proposition is the decision of the House of Lords in *Vandervell v IRC*.[40] Mr Vandervell sought a tax efficient method of benefiting the Royal College of Surgeons (hereafter, the 'RCS') by means of a transfer of shares to the RCS such that the annual dividend on those shares would be paid to the RCS. Those shares were held on trust, *inter alia*, for Vandervell personally. Vandervell wanted to recover the shares after the dividend had been paid to the RCS. Therefore, Vandervell reserved an option for his trust to repurchase the shares from the RCS on payment of £5,000. The option was subsequently held to constitute a form of equitable interest in those shares. However, the owner of this equitable interest was not identified and thus leaving a vacuum in its ownership.

---

[38] This accords with the policy of English property law that, in general terms, property cannot be abandoned such that there is always some person who can bear the incidents of ownership and take the benefits of the rights of ownership of that property. See para 26.61.

[39] *Vandervell v IRC* [1966] Ch 261, [1967] 2 AC 291.

[40] [1966] Ch 261, [1967] 2 AC 291.

Consequently, it was held that the unallocated equitable interest personified by the option to repurchase the shares must be held on resulting trust for Vandervell's settlement.

In a subtly different context, a purported resettlement of a life interest under a set-   **26.25**
tlement which fails to identify the beneficiaries who receive the equitable interest in that property will cause the property at issue to pass back to the life tenant on resulting trust.[41] There are further contexts in which this same principle could arise. Where the equitable interest in property has not been disposed of properly, in accordance with the formalities for transfer appropriate to that form of property, that equitable interest will be held on resulting trust for the settlor. Therefore, it is assumed that a valid declaration of trust has been effected but that the formality necessary for the transfer of that equitable interest onto trust has not been effected. The principle is therefore akin to that in *Vandervell* considered above in that the settlor would be deemed to be the beneficiary under a resulting trust over that property. By way of example, suppose that S wished to transfer land onto trust and so transferred the legal title to T to hold on trust but that S did not comply with the requirements of section 53(1)(b) of the Law of Property Act 1925 that the declaration of trust be manifested and proved by some signed writing: in such a situation T would similarly hold the land on resulting trust for S. This issue is considered below in relation to 'failure of trust'.

Failure of trust

Where a trust fails for any reason, the equitable interests purportedly allocated by   **26.26**
the failed trust must pass to someone, on the basis that equity abhors a vacuum in the equitable ownership. A trust may fail because some condition precedent fails—for example, that the beneficiaries must marry, but they do not—or because some condition subsequent in the trusts fails—for example, that the beneficiaries must remain married, but they do not. In such situations where the trust fails, the equitable title in the trust fund passes automatically on resulting trust to the previous beneficial owner.[42] The trust may also fail for any of the reasons considered in Part B where there is uncertainty as to the identity of the beneficiaries,[43] or by reason of lapse,[44] or by reason of offending the rules against perpetuities and accumulations.[45] The court will effect the retransfer of the property to the settlor or to the settlor's estate by means of a resulting trust.[46]

---

[41] *Re Guinness's Settlement* [1966] 2 All ER 497; *Re Scott* [1975] 2 All ER 1033.

[42] *Vandervell v IRC, op cit; Chichester Diocesan Fund v Simpson* [1941] Ch 253; *Re Ames' Settlement* [1964] Ch 217.

[43] See para 4.01. *Morice v Bishop of Durham* (1804) 9 Ves 399, affirmed at (1805) 10 Ves 522; *Re Osmund* [1944] Ch 66, [1944] 1 All ER 12; *Re Pugh's Will Trusts* [1967] 3 All ER 337; *Re Atkinson's Will Trusts* [1978] 1 All ER 1275.   [44] *Ackroyd v Smithson* (1780) 1 Bro CC 503.

[45] *Tregonwell v Sydenham* (1815) 3 Dow 194; *Re Drummond's Settlement* [1986] 3 All ER 45; *Air Jamaica v Charlton* [1999] 1 WLR 1399.   [46] *Re Sayer* [1957] Ch 423, [1956] 3 All ER 600.

26.27   It was said in Chapter 5[47] that, once an express trust is created, that trust cannot be undone by the settlor.[48] However, there may be some trusts which only come into existence for a given reason: where that reason is not fulfilled it may be that the trust is deemed to have been ineffectively constituted. For example, in a situation in which a couple had intended to marry and to have certain property held on the terms of a marriage settlement, but where the marriage never took place in spite of the fact that the couple lived together and had children, it has been held that the marriage settlement must fail because there was no marriage which could call that settlement into being.[49] In consequence, the property purportedly held on the terms of the marriage settlement passed back to the couple on resulting trust.[50] In consequence it can be seen that where the trust fails for any reason the property intended to be held on trust will be held by the trustees on resulting trust instead. This principle can be distinguished from that in *Paul v Paul*,[51] where the two parties to a marriage settlement saw their marriage fail but were nevertheless prevented from unpacking the settlement and recovering the settled property *qua* settlors for fear of causing prejudice to the other beneficiaries, on the basis that the marriage took effect in *Paul v Paul* and therefore the trusts did not fail even though the marriage subsequently did; in the resulting trusts cases, the marriage failed to come into existence *ab initio* such that that condition precedent to the settlement was not fulfilled.[52]

26.28   This principle is illustrated in *Re Cochrane's Settlement Trusts*[53] in which a marriage settlement was created. Both of the parties to the marriage brought property to the marriage settlement. Under the terms of the marriage settlement, the income of the trust was to be paid to the wife provided that she continued to reside with her husband. In the event that either of them should die, the trust provided that the survivor acquired the entirety of the property in the fund beneficially. The wife left her husband who subsequently died. The issue therefore arose whether the wife would be entitled to succeed to the entirety of the trust fund, or whether her interest ceased once she left her husband. It was held that the wife received the equitable interest in the property which she had contributed to the marriage settlement on resulting trust but that the property which the husband had contributed to the

---

[47] See para 5.59.   [48] *Paul v Paul* (1882) 20 Ch D 742.
[49] *Essery v Cowlard* (1884) 26 Ch D 191.   [50] ibid.
[51] (1882) 20 Ch D 742.
[52] The other possible approach to this question, not taken in the decided cases, would have been to suggest that an implied condition subsequent (ie that the marriage continue in existence) was breached when the marriage did fail, such that a resulting trust could have been inferred. Such a condition subsequent is not inferred in the decided cases because there is no basis on which such an intention could be imputed to the parties, let alone was it included explicitly in the settlement, and it is not clear whether a marriage which lasted for a decent length of time could be said to have failed or succeeded if it either failed to produce children or if the parties eventually decided to separate.
[53] [1955] Ch 309.

marriage settlement passed to his estate on resulting trust after his death. The basis for this decision was the failure of the purpose of the marriage settlement (that is, that they should stay together) giving rise to a return of the property to the original settlors on resulting trust. Whereas in *Paul v Paul*[54] the court did not focus on the failure of the underlying purpose of the settlement, to provide for the progeny of the married couple, but rather focused on the rights of the various beneficiaries under the terms of the settlement, those cases in which a resulting trust has been found have been predicated on the failure of the settlement's underlying purpose and the concomitant need to restore the property to its previous, beneficial owners.

Similarly in *Re Ames' Settlement*[55] a marriage was declared null and void. The question arose as to the treatment of property held on a marriage settlement. The marriage settlement itself provided for beneficiaries to whom the property should pass on failure of the marriage and so forth. On the basis that the marriage was held to have been void *ab initio*—that is, treated as though it had never taken place— the marriage settlement was treated as having failed. On the basis that the marriage had never been valid it was held that the marriage settlement had similarly never been in existence and therefore that no term of the marriage settlement as to default beneficiaries could be effective. In consequence Vaisey J declared that the property held on the terms of that marriage settlement was held on resulting trust.   **26.29**

There are settlements which seem to be effectively constituted at the outset but for the settlor's failure to provide for the identity of the beneficiaries with sufficient certainty.[56] The result of such a failure to provide for the identity of the beneficiary is that the property to be settled on trust results to the settlor.[57] In circumstances in which a life interest failed to take effect, without there being a remainder interest capable of taking the place of the life interest, then the life interest passes on resulting trust to the settlor. This rule applies in relation to settlements which were effected by will and to settlements which were effected *inter vivos*.[58] Whereas the principle was developed originally in relation to real property,[59] it has expanded to cover personal property too.[60]   **26.30**

Another category of cases further illustrates this point. The traditional rule relating to gifts made to charity in circumstances in which that charitable purpose fails is that any property purportedly passed under such a failed gift is held on   **26.31**

---

[54] (1882) 20 Ch D 742.   [55] [1964] Ch 217.
[56] *Re Guinness's Settlement* [1966] 2 All ER 497; *Re Scott* [1975] 2 All ER 1033.
[57] *Vandervell v IRC* [1967] 2 AC 291; *Re Leek* [1967] Ch 1061, [1967] 2 All ER 1160.
[58] *Re Flower's Settlement Trusts* [1957] 1 All ER 462. Cf *Re Davies* [1957] 3 All ER 52; *Re Harker's Will Trusts* [1969] 3 All ER 1.
[59] *Re Scott* [1911] 2 Ch 374; including equitable interests in land: *Re Conyngham* [1921] 1 Ch 491. Cf *Re Hatfeild's Will Trusts* [1958] Ch 469, [1957] 2 All ER 261.
[60] *Re Hodge* [1943] Ch 469, [1943] 2 All ER 304.

resulting trust for the donor.[61] Where the gift itself is found to be worded so as not to disclose a charitable purpose (for example where it is expressed to be provided for a 'benevolent or charitable purpose' and therefore not for a purely charitable purpose) then that property is held on resulting trust for the donor.[62] In similar fashion if a gift is purportedly made to someone who is not able to receive that gift on grounds of their own incapacity to act, then that gift will be held on resulting trust for the donor because no completed gift will have been made.[63]

The rule in *Hancock v Watson*: failure of engrafted trust

26.32   A different approach obtains to property left by will in the form of an absolute gift but yet subject to testamentary trusts which fail. Suppose that a testator had left 'all my money to B absolutely but so that the bulk of the money shall be held on trust for X on reaching the age of majority'. In that situation, the testator has made an absolute gift of the money in favour of B but subject to a trust over a part of that money. On the terms of the trust in this example, the subject matter of the trust in favour of X is too uncertain and the trust will therefore be held to be void. It might have been expected that, on the failure of the trust, the entire gift ought to fail and that the property ought to be held on resulting trust as part of the testator's residuary estate. A different approach is taken, forming an exception to the operation of the resulting trust as considered thus far. The rule in *Hancock v Watson*[64] enforces the absolute gift and avoids the trust power which would otherwise have been held invalid on grounds of uncertainty of subject matter.[65] This result is achieved by finding that, in circumstances in which property has been left to a legatee as an absolute gift but subject to some trust which has failed, then the legatee takes the property absolutely. Therefore, this principle will preclude the imposition of a resulting trust in circumstances in which an absolute, testamentary gift is made to a person subject to a trust which fails. Rather, the absolute gift takes effect without the trust to the exclusion of any residuary beneficiary under resulting trust principles.

26.33   The principle was expressed by Lord Davey in *Hancock v Watson* in the following terms:

> ... it is settled law that if you find an absolute gift to a legatee in the first instance, and trusts are engrafted or imposed on that absolute interest which fail, either from lapse or invalidity or any other reason, then the absolute gift takes effect so far as the trusts have failed to the exclusion of the residuary legatee or next-of-kin as the case may be.[66]

---

[61] *Chichester Diocesan Fund v Simpson* [1944] AC 341.
[62] *Morice v Bishop of Durham* (1805) 10 Ves 522.
[63] *Simpson v Simpson* [1992] 1 FLR 601.   [64] [1902] AC 14.
[65] *Re Goldcorp* [1995] 1 AC 74.
[66] [1902] AC 14, 22. See also *Fyfe v Irwin* [1939] 2 All ER 271.

The rule may come into operation in a variety of circumstances in which trusts are held to be invalid. This rule also operates so as to circumvent the principle that the subject matter of a trust must be sufficiently certain before any trust can be imposed on it.[67]

The rule in *Hancock v Watson* is derived from the older cases of *Sprange v Barnard*[68]   **26.34**
and *Lassence v Tierney*.[69] In the case of *Sprange v Barnard*[70] a testatrix had left property to her husband 'for his sole use', subject only to a provision that 'all that is remaining in the stock, that he has not necessary use for, to be divided equally between' named beneficiaries. It was held the trust power over 'all that is remaining' was void for uncertainty because it could not have been known what was necessary for the husband's use. Therefore, the husband took the property absolutely beneficially. Similarly in *Palmer v Simmonds*[71] a testatrix had left money to her husband for 'his use and benefit' subject to a trust to take effect on the husband's death 'to leave the bulk of my residuary estate' to named relatives. This trust over 'the bulk' of the deceased wife's estate was held to be void for uncertainty of subject matter.[72] In consequence, the husband took his wife's estate absolutely beneficially free from the trust. In both cases the principle embodied subsequently in the rule in *Hancock v Watson* provided for the gift to continue in effect even though the trusts attached to them were held to have been void for uncertainty.

Peter Gibson J presented the following summary of the principles in this area in   **26.35**
Watson v Holland:[73]

(1) in each case the court must ascertain from the language of the instrument as a whole whether there has been an initial absolute beneficial gift onto which inconsistent trusts have been engrafted;
(2) if the instrument discloses no separate initial gift but merely a gift coupled with a series of limitations over so as to form one system of trusts, then the rule will not apply;
(3) in most of the cases where the rule has been held to apply, the engrafted inconsistent trusts have been separated from the absolute gift either by being placed in a separate clause or sentence or by being introduced by words implying a contrast, such as a proviso or words such as 'but so that'. But this is not an essential requirement, and in an appropriate context the engrafted trusts may be introduced by the word 'and' or the words 'and so that' . . .;
(4) references in parts of the instrument, other than the initial gift claimed to be absolute, to the share of the donee are usually treated as indicative that the share is owned by the donee . . .;
(5) if a donor, by the trusts which follow the initial gift, has sought to provide for every eventuality by creating what prima facie are exhaustive trusts, it is the more difficult to construe the initial gift as an absolute gift.[74]

---

[67] *Westdeutsche Landesbank v Islington* [1996] AC 669.
[68] (1789) 2 Bro CC 585.   [69] (1849) 1 Mac & G 551.   [70] (1789) 2 Bro CC 585.
[71] (1854) 2 Drew 221.   [72] See para 3.11.   [73] [1985] 1 All ER 290, 300.
[74] *Lassence v Tierney* (1849) 1 Mac & G 551; *Re Burton's Settlement Trusts* [1955] Ch 348.

This rule has been held to be equally applicable to *inter vivos* settlements[75] and to accrued shares.[76]

Approaches to the question of resulting trusts arising over surplus property on completion of the trust's purpose

26.36   When there is surplus property remaining after the purpose of the trust has been performed, the surplus property is returned to the settlor on resulting trust principles, unless there is some specific provision in the trust instrument, or, if there was no instrument, in the settlor's declaration of the trust and directions to the trustees, to suggest that any surplus should be held in some other manner.[77] Examples of this principle in operation in the decided cases are considered in the following sections of this chapter. At a simple level, this principle can be seen to be similar to the principle in the immediately preceding sections of this chapter in the sense that it is dealing with property which, although settled on trust initially, has been demonstrated by events not to have been settled in a way which has employed the entire fund: with the result that a portion of that fund is in a position similar to that if it had not been settled in the first place because there are no further trust provisions to dictate how it should be used henceforth.

26.37   The rule can be summarized in the following way. If a trust's objectives are performed but there is still money or other property remaining to be held on trust by the trustees, then that property is to be held on resulting trust for the people who subscribed it in the first place.[78] Suppose, for example, that S created a trust over a sum of money so that his elderly father B's fees for his nursing home care could be paid out of the trust. If the fees were paid in full by the time that B died but there was still money left over, there would be two theoretical possibilities: either the surplus money could pass into B's estate absolutely or that surplus money could be returned to S. The case law has taken the view that the surplus money should pass back to S on resulting trust. There are two alternative principles to consider. First, could B invoke the rule in *Saunders v Vautier*[79] as the absolutely entitled beneficiary so that the property became vested in him absolutely? In principle there is no reason why this rule should not operate unless S structured the trust so that B took no vested right in the trust property but was entitled only to the benefit of the nursing care and accommodation acquired with the trust money. Secondly, on a different point, the rules set out below in relation to unincorporated associations suggest that where money is given to such an association it will not pass back to the settlor on resulting trust.[80] Instead that

---

[75] *Doyle v Crean* [1905] 1 IR 352; *Re Burton's Settlement Trusts* [1955] Ch 348. Cf *Re Connell's Settlement* [1915] 1 Ch 867.

[76] *Re Litt's Will Trusts* [1946] Ch 154, [1946] 1 All ER 314.

[77] *Re Trusts of the Abbott Fund* [1900] Ch 326.   [78] ibid.   [79] (1841) 4 Beav 115.

[80] *Re Bucks Constabulary Benevolent Fund* [1978] 1 WLR 641, [1979] 1 All ER 623.

property will be distributed according to the terms of the contract between the members of that association, as considered below.[81] The manner in which this core principle has been applied in different contexts is considered in the following sections of this chapter.

Surplus property after performance of trust

As considered in the preceding paragraph, the following issue arises: what happens once the purpose of the trust has been performed and there is still property left over? Many of the cases in this area have already been considered in Chapter 6 above in relation to the distinction between purpose trusts and trusts for the benefit of people. Related issues arose, such as: should the property be distributed among potential human beneficiaries, or does it fall instead to be held for the donor of the property on resulting trust? The general rule is that such property will be held on resulting trust for the settlor,[82] unless the court can find an intention to benefit specific individuals instead.[83]   **26.38**

Thus in *Re Trusts of the Abbott Fund*[84] a trust fund was created in favour of two elderly   **26.39** ladies, and subscriptions were sought from the public. The aim underlying the trust was not fully performed before the two ladies died. It was held that the trust property remaining undistributed at the time of death should be held on resulting trust for the subscribers to the fund. A similar approach was taken in *Re Gillingham Bus Disaster Fund*[85] in considering a subscription fund for which money was raised from the public in the wake of a bus crash. The victims of the crash did not require all of the money raised. The issue arose as to the treatment of the surplus money raised from the public but not needed by the victims of the disaster. The court held that the surplus should be held on resulting trust for the subscribers.[86] Had the money been held on a charitable trust, then it could have been applied cy pres.[87]

Many of the deciding cases relate to the creation of settlements for the express pur-   **26.40** pose of meeting the settlor's debts with his creditors. Frequently, on the decided cases, those debts would have been met while still leaving surplus capital in the trust fund. The general rule in such cases is that the surplus funds are held on resulting trust for the settlor.[88] These forms of settlement often begin to function satisfactorily and only demonstrate a surplus over time. For example, where a tenant for life sought to release his interest under a settlement but failed to declare the terms on which his interest was to have been held, the purported resettlement of that life interest failed and the property at issue resulted back to the life tenant.[89] In circumstances in which a voluntary

---

[81] See para 26.42.   [82] *Re Trusts of the Abbott Fund* [1900] Ch 326.
[83] *Re Osoba* [1979] 2 All ER 393.   [84] [1900] Ch 326.   [85] [1958] Ch 300.
[86] *Re Hillier* [1954] 1 WLR 9; affirmed in part [1954] 1 WLR 700.
[87] See, for example, *Hudson* 824.
[88] *King v Denison* (1813) 1 Ves & B 260; *Watson v Hayes* (1839) 5 My & Cr 125.
[89] *Re Guinness's Settlement* [1966] 2 All ER 497; *Re Scott* [1975] 2 All ER 1033.

arrangement has been created for the benefit of creditors, then that arrangement will be binding as to the destination of any property held upon trust under the arrangement: there will be no resulting trust over such property.[90]

26.41   The only exceptions to this basic principle have involved situations in which the court could interpret the terms of the settlement so as to imply that the residue should be applied for another purpose,[91] or settlements in which the settlor's interest, or the possibility of any resulting trust passing property back to the settlor, have been expressly excluded by the settlement itself:[92] these examples are considered below.[93]

Surplus property upon dissolution of an unincorporated association

26.42   This area of the law has seen the emergence of a contractual approach to the allocation of rights in property on the dissolution of unincorporated associations. The context of the unincorporated association was considered in Chapter 6 in relation to purpose trusts. In that chapter an unincorporated association was defined as an association of people which does not itself have legal personality—thus raising problems as to the manner in which property subscribed to such an association is to be treated by the law. A particular problem arises on the dissolution of an unincorporated association as to the ownership of such property formerly held for the purposes of that association. There are two competing approaches: first, that the property should be held on resulting trust for the people who subscribed it or, secondly, that the contract executed between the members of the association ought to be decisive of the manner in which that property is then distributed.

26.43   The classical, equitable view is typified by the decision in *Re West Sussex, etc Fund Trusts*[94] which held that a resulting trust will be imposed in circumstances in which money has been raised from the public for the purposes of an unincorporated association but in which that association was wound up before all of the money was used, thus leaving a surplus. In that case it was held that, in relation to large donations attributable to identified individuals, such gifts should be held on trust for their donors. However, in relation to property in respect of which it would be difficult or impracticable to trace its donor, the classical view was that the property should pass *bona vacantia* to the Crown.[95] *Re West Sussex* must be considered to be of doubtful authority on these points in the light of the development of a more modern view, considered below.[96]

---

[90] *Shierson v Tomlinson* [2002] EWCA Civ 404, [2002] 3 All ER 474.
[91] *Re Akeroyd's Settlement* [1893] 3 Ch 363; *Re Cochrane* [1955] Ch 309, [1955] 1 All ER 222. See also *Re Cory* [1955] 2 All ER 630; *Re Follett* [1955] 2 All ER 22.
[92] *Croome v Croome* (1889) 61 LT 814; *Smith v Cooke* [1891] AC 297.
[93] See para 26.50.   [94] [1971] Ch 1.
[95] *Westdeutsche Landesbank v Islington* [1996] AC 669.
[96] *Re Bucks Constabulary Benevolent Fund* [1978] 1 WLR 641.

In relation to other contributions, such as payment for entertainments or partici-   **26.44**
pation in raffles, the approach taken by the court was that the contract between
the donor and the association for the provision of the entertainment disposed of
any right which the donor might claim to have had in the property: on the basis
that the subscribers had got what they paid for.[97] On older authority, in circumstances in which the donor could not be said to have retained any equitable interest on the basis that her intention had been to make an outright transfer of the
property, it has been held that any property left in the hands of a moribund association would not be held on resulting trust for that donor but rather would pass
bona vacantia to the Crown.[98] This approach was accepted as being conceivable
still in *Westdeutsche Landesbank v Islington*.[99] This notion of a donor ceasing to
have any title in property transferred finds its resolution in a more modern view.

The modern view, propounded by Walton J in *Re Bucks Constabulary Fund*,[100] is   **26.45**
that the dissolution of an unincorporated association and the distribution of property held for its purposes is a matter purely of contract. This approach is predicated
on an understanding of unincorporated associations as being based on a contract
between the association's members, possibly in the form of that association's constitution or club rules which detail such matters as the payment of subscriptions,
the various offices within the association, the members' various entitlements to use
the association's facilities, and the manner in which any surplus property is to be
deployed.[101] Therefore, it was held that it is the contract between the members
which should decide how the property is to be distributed without the need for the
intervention of any equitable doctrines (like resulting trust). Where there are
specific contractual provisions dealing with the distribution of the property, those
provisions would be decisive; whereas if there were no specific provisions, the
property should be divided among the members in equal shares.[102]

This alteration in approach indicates two things. First, it demonstrates the   **26.46**
important role played by contract in English law in allocating rights in property.
Secondly, it demonstrates that where a person intends to make a gift of property
to another person, that donor retains no further property in the gift because the
intention to make a gift itself terminates those property rights in the hands of the
donor if the gift is completely constituted.

Surplus property on winding up of a pension fund

Occupational pension fund trusts, considered in detail in Part H of this book, occa-   **26.47**
sionally generate surplus funds when the trust capital is invested over and above those

---

[97] ibid.   [98] *Cunnack v Edwards* [1896] 2 Ch 679; *Braithwaite v A-G* [1909] 1 Ch 510.
[99] [1996] AC 669.   [100] [1979] 1 All ER 623.
[101] *Conservative and Unionist Central Office v Burrell* [1982] 2 All ER 1.
[102] *Re Bucks Constabulary Fund* (1979), see also *Re GKN Sports Club* [1982] 1 WLR 774.

amounts needed to satisfy pensioners and the future needs of the fund, leading to disputes as to the ownership of that surplus.[103] The instrument and the rules creating the fund are incorporated by reference and their terms are also contained in part in employees' contracts of employment and form not only a trust instrument but also a contract between the employer, the employees who contribute to the fund, and the trustees of the fund. From this complex matrix of legal documentation it may be difficult to ascertain who owns the beneficial interest in the surplus funds, although a well-drafted set of scheme rules will make title in the surplus clear.[104]

26.48 In just such a dispute, in *Davis v Richards & Wallington Industries Ltd*[105] Scott J applied the contractual approach adopted in *Re Bucks Constabulary Fund*, which led to the finding that, where a pension trust deed provided that any surplus in the pension fund belonged to the employer, when the pension fund was wound up the surplus passed to the employer rather than being held on resulting trust for those people who had contributed funds to the pension trust. It was considered that to declare the employer to be the owner of the surplus would be to enforce the contractual intention bound up in the deed: another example of the primacy of contract law over property law in this context.[106]

26.49 However, Lord Millett was confronted with a trust instrument in *Air Jamaica v Charlton*[107] which provided that no moneys were to be returned to the company in any circumstances. That provision had been inserted for tax reasons to prevent the company being treated as beneficially entitled for tax purposes in any of the money held under the terms of the pension trust. The trust was subsequently held to have been void for offending the rule against perpetuity. In spite of the express term in the trust instrument, Lord Millett held that the surplus in the pension fund could be treated as belonging in equity to the company and the members of the pension fund scheme on resulting trust principles. Consequently, the funds remaining in the pension trust would not be treated as *bona vacantia* such that they would have passed to the government of Jamaica: the finding of a resulting trust instead provided that the company and the members of the scheme took title in them in accordance with the size of their contributions to the scheme.

Instances in which a resulting trust has not been found

Express exclusion of the settlor

26.50 The foregoing discussion of occupational pension funds has disclosed an ambivalent approach to situations in which the trust instrument expressly excluded the

---

[103] See AS Hudson, *The Law on Investment Entities* (London: Sweet & Maxwell, 2000) 153.
[104] cf *Air Jamaica v Charlton* [1999] 1 WLR 1399, considered below at para 26.49.
[105] [1990] 1 WLR 1511.
[106] See Part H of this book generally in relation to occupational pension funds.
[107] [1999] 1 WLR 1399.

possibility of the property passing back to the settlor. Such a provision will frequently be important to prevent the settlor being deemed to be the beneficial owner for tax purposes of property which he had intended to transfer away onto trust. On the older authorities, the principle was clearly established that an express intention to exclude the settlor from any future right in the trust property would prevent the operation of a resulting trust. So, in *Smith v Cooke*,[108] a trust deed provided expressly that none of the proceeds of sale of trust property were to be payable to the settlors, but rather the purpose of the trust was to settle property, to order the trustees to sell it, and to pay the sale proceeds to the settlors' creditors. In the event there was a surplus but the express prevention of any property passing back to the settlors was held to have precluded the operation of a resulting trust. It is suggested that the trust provision would need to be explicit for this analysis to operate. Indeed, if the trust instrument provided expressly who should take any surplus or gave some indication as to the manner in which such a surplus should be disposed of, then that would be a principled basis on which to avoid a resulting trust precisely because the trust would not be incomplete as to that portion of the fund.[109]

The decision in *Air Jamaica v Charlton*,[110] considered in paragraph 26.49, does **26.51** pose a problem in this context precisely because the Privy Council in that case was prepared to overlook just such an express provision on the basis that it was contained in the instrument for tax planning purposes, whereas the claim was one which arose from the inefficacy of the trust rather than as to the tax treatment of its income. In that case, however, the Privy Council did not support the notion that trust instruments should be interpreted in accordance with their tax treatment.[111]

Inference that some other person was intended to take beneficially

There is a miscellaneous collection of cases in which the courts have interpreted **26.52** the trust instrument or the settlor's intention to suggest that a particular person was intended to take the property purportedly settled on trust absolutely, rather than imposing a resulting trust over it. These seemingly exceptional cases arise in two contexts. The first arises in situations in which, even though the purpose for which the property in question was transferred to the donee failed subsequently, nevertheless it was found on the facts that the transferor intended to divest himself absolutely of any rights in the property. The best example of this approach was in *Westdeutsche Landesbank v Islington*[112] itself, the leading case which has given us the most recent authority on the nature of resulting trusts. In that case, a bank

---

[108] [1891] AC 297.
[109] See also *King v Denison* (1813) 1 Ves & B 260; *Wood v Cox* (1837) 2 My & Cr 684; *Croome v Croome* (1889) 61 LT 814; *Re West* [1900] 1 Ch 84. Cf *Re Foord* [1922] 2 Ch 519.
[110] [1999] 1 WLR 1399.
[111] ibid. Cf *Davis v Richard and Wallington Industries Ltd* [1990] 1 WLR 1511.
[112] [1996] AC 669.

transferred money to a local authority under a contractual arrangement which both parties considered to be one which the local authority could perform lawfully. It transpired that the arrangement was beyond the powers of the local authority and therefore void *ab initio*. The bank claimed, *inter alia*, that the failure of the contractual purpose ought to have entitled it to recover the property transferred to the local authority on the basis of restitution of unjust enrichment. A similar, and more traditionally equitable, claim might have been to argue that the purpose for which the property was transferred had failed and therefore that the bank ought to be recognized as the owner of the property in equity on resulting trusts principles. The House of Lords took the view, impliedly, that the bank had intended to transfer away absolute title in the money it had paid to the local authority and therefore that it could not claim to have retained any equitable interest in it. The limitation of the resulting trust to the two categories discussed at the beginning of this chapter[113] meant that there was no possibility of a resulting trust being found in that case. Thus an intention to transfer title to another person may negate the possibility of there being a resulting trust.

26.53   Otherwise, the second form of ostensible exception to the resulting trust principle is that in which the settlor had intended to grant a beneficial interest in the property to some other person, even if that intention was not made explicit. This category is difficult to conceptualize precisely because the settlors in the cases had not excluded their own rights under resulting trust nor had they provided for some person who would be entitled to any failed disposition of property. Rather, it seems that the courts have formed the impression in some cases that the most conscionable outcome was the finding of a beneficial interest in some person other than the settlor. For example, where a father left money on trust for the maintenance of his wife and the education of his daughters, it was found that the three women identified in the agreement took the property as joint tenants and that the trust fund did not pass back to the settlor on resulting trust when it failed.[114]

Where the recipient takes as a trustee and not as a beneficiary

26.54   A partial exception to the operation of resulting trusts arises in relation to purported transfers of property onto trust in circumstances in which the recipient is expressed on the face of the trust to take the property as a trustee. In *Re Rees's Will Trusts*[115] property was passed to the testator's 'trustees absolutely' with a proviso that they were to follow the instructions which he had given to them. It transpired that the settlor's instructions had been insufficient to exhaust the whole of the fund. Whereas it might have been expected that the surplus property would have

---

[113] See para 26.01.   [114] *Re Osoba* [1979] 2 All ER 393.
[115] [1950] Ch 204, [1949] 2 All ER 1003; *Re Pugh's Will Trusts* [1967] 3 All ER 337. Cf *Re Tyler's Fund Trusts* [1967] 3 All ER 389.

passed automatically on resulting trust back to the testator's estate, it was held instead that the testator would be treated as having died intestate in relation to the surplus property so that it passed to his statutory next of kin on intestacy principles. There are reported cases in which the testator has passed property by will to a fiancée ostensibly so that the fiancée should hold the property as trustee to discharge duties which the testator had communicated to her in advance.[116] In that circumstance, the court held that surplus property could be deemed to pass to the fiancée beneficially, rather than passing either on resulting trust or under the intestacy rules, on the basis that it could be assumed that the testator would have intended to provide for his fiancée. It is suggested that this latter approach bears the hallmarks of the presumption of advancement which would suggest a gift of property or of resulting trust, even of surplus property which was not disposed of under a trust. The courts may admit parol evidence of the settlor's intention to benefit the claimant by way of a gift, even if that person is named in the settlement as being a trustee, and so rebut the presumption of a resulting trust.[117]

Failed gifts made for a charitable purpose

Whereas a failed gift onto trust would ordinarily pass on resulting trust back to its **26.55** settlor, gifts on trust to a charity may occupy a different position. In circumstances in which there is a trust for charitable purposes, then the cy pres doctrine will cause the property to be applied to charitable purposes similar to that expressed in the original settlement rather than being passed on resulting trust back to the settlor.[118] It is not necessary for the trust to be interpreted as disclosing an intention to dispose of the property absolutely[119] but the disposition must disclose a general charitable intention to invoke the cy pres jurisdiction.[120] The reader is referred to the section dealing with the dissolution of unincorporated associations for a consideration of the manner in which various forms of property subscribed to such associations may be distributed when the association is wound up.[121]

Transfers intended as an outright gift

When the owner of property intends to transfer that property away absolutely, **26.56** then on leading authority there will not be a resulting trust over that property.[122] However, it is not always the case, simply because the owner of property wishes to divest himself of that property, that he will not be recognized as the equitable

---

[116] *Irvine v Sullivan* (1869) LR 8 Eq 673.

[117] See *Fowkes v Pascoe* (1875) 10 Ch App 343.

[118] *Re Wokingham's Fire Brigade Trusts* [1951] Ch 373, [1951] 1 All ER 454; *Re Ulverston and District New Hospital Building Trusts* [1956] Ch 622; *Re Cooper's Conveyance* [1956] 3 All ER 28.

[119] *Re Welsh Hospital (Netley) Fund* [1921] 1 Ch 655; *Re North Devon and West Somerset Relief Fund Trusts* [1953] 2 All ER 1032; *Re British School of Egyptian Archaeology* [1954] 1 All ER 887.

[120] *Re University of London Medical Sciences Institute Fund* [1909] 2 Ch 1.

[121] See para 26.42.

[122] *Westdeutsche Landesbank v Islington* [1996] AC 669.

owner of that property on resulting trust principles. So, in *Vandervell v IRC*[123] the beneficiary under a trust had given a direction to his trustees to transfer a parcel of shares out of the trust with the intention of divesting himself of his entire equitable interest in property: nevertheless the unallocated part of the equitable interest passed back to him on resulting trust. In *Westdeutsche Landesbank v Islington*[124] a bank intended to transfer absolute title in money to a local authority under an interest rate swap contract, the contract was subsequently held to have been void *ab initio*, but the absence of any knowledge of the unenforceability of the contract in the local authority precluded the imposition of any kind of trust, not least a resulting trust. The difference between these cases, it is suggested, revolves around the property being subject to a trust and also some part of the equitable interest in that trust being unallocated. The resulting trust therefore resolves the problem of there being a gap in the ownership of the property. The doctrine of resulting trust will not be used to recover property which was intended to be the subject of a gift or other outright transfer.

Transfers effected under contract law principles

26.57 As discussed in relation to the winding up of unincorporated associations,[125] there will not be a resulting trust in situations in which property was transferred in consideration for some contractual benefit[126] or for a purpose which is controlled by contractual stipulations.[127] As considered in the preceding paragraph, an intention to transfer property absolutely under a contract will negate the finding of a resulting trust.[128]

Gifts for moribund purposes: property passing *bona vacantia* to the Crown

26.58 Both Lord Browne-Wilkinson[129] and Megarry J[130] frame their explanation of the resulting trust as being based on a failure of an express trust to exhaust the whole of the beneficial interest in property. What these explanations do not cover, on a literal interpretation, are gifts or other outright transfers of property otherwise than on trust. The question therefore arises: should property purportedly transferred by means of an incomplete or an imperfect gift be treated as being held on resulting trust as though a failure to exhaust the whole of the beneficial interest under a trust?

26.59 There are two different analyses of what happens to property when it is the subject of a failed gift. If the transfer is ineffective, then there is simply no transfer of

---

[123] [1967] 2 AC 291.   [124] [1996] AC 669.   [125] See para 26.42.
[126] *Re Bucks Constabulary Benevolent Fund* [1978] 1 WLR 641, [1979] 1 All ER 623.
[127] *Re Bucks Constabulary Benevolent Fund* [1978] 1 WLR 641, [1979] 1 All ER 623; *Re GKN Sports Club* [1982] 1 WLR 774.
[128] *Westdeutsche Landesbank v Islington* [1996] AC 669.
[129] *Westdeutsche Landesbank v Islington* [1996] AC 669.
[130] *Re Vandervell's Trusts* [1974] Ch 269.

the property away from the purported donor. The more difficult application of this rule, however, is in circumstances in which the property has been transferred away for a period of time such that it cannot be transferred back to the donor. An example might be an outright transfer of property to an unincorporated association where that association ceases to be active and the purpose of the transfer becomes moribund. In such a situation the property will pass *bona vacantia* to the Crown.

The alternative analysis, evidently, would be that the remaining property not used **26.60** passes back on resulting trust to the donor. This resulting trust analysis fits with that set out by Megarry J in *Re Vandervell's Trusts (No 2)*.[131] However Lord Browne-Wilkinson took issue with Megarry J. Lord Browne-Wilkinson in his speech in *Westdeutsche Landesbank v Islington*[132] doubted that the division set out by Megarry J between automatic and presumed resulting trusts could be said to be correct in all circumstances:

> Megarry J in *Re Vandervell's Trusts (No 2)*[133] suggests that a resulting trust [imposed because it does not exhaust the entire beneficial interest] does not depend on intention but operates automatically. I am not convinced that this is right. If the settlor has expressly, or by necessary implication, abandoned any beneficial interest in the trust property, there is in my view no resulting trust: the undisposed-of equitable interest vests in the Crown as *bona vacantia*.[134]

Lord Browne-Wilkinson was therefore taking issue with the categorization of some transfers of property as constituting an automatic resulting trust. His lordship considered that where the settlor's intention had been to divest himself absolutely of his right, then there should not be a resulting trust in favour of the settlor.

There are two issues which arise here. The first is that English property law has **26.61** never expressly recognized that it is possible to 'abandon' rights in property.[135] English law has taken the view that one cannot dispose of property other than by transferring or terminating rights in it. What is not possible is simply to say that those rights of ownership which continue to exist simply belong to no one. Therefore, Lord Browne-Wilkinson is either altering the principle that it is impossible to abandon rights in property or is suggesting that where rights are purportedly disposed of it is incorrect to apply a resulting trust analysis to those rights. Secondly, it is not clear why those rights ought to revert to the Crown in preference to the original title holder (or her estate) recovering any title in property which was not adequately disposed of. The intervention of rights of the

---

[131] [1974] Ch 269.   [132] [1996] AC 669.   [133] [1974] Ch 269.
[134] See *Re West Sussex Constabulary's Widows, Children and Benevolent (1930) Fund Trusts* [1971] Ch 1.
[135] Except to the extent considered by AH Hudson, 'Abandonment' in N Palmer and E McKendrick (eds), *Interest in Goods* (LLP, 1993).

Crown here is a remedy of convenience or of merely historical interest rather than a logical outcome in property law terms in the modern era.

26.62 As considered above,[136] the Privy Council in *Air Jamaica v Charlton*[137] has interpreted a void pension fund trust as giving rise to a resulting trust in favour of the contributors to the fund and not as requiring that the property pass *bona vacantia*. It is suggested that the *bona vacantia* principle operates in truth as a vestige of feudal property law whereby any gap in the ownership of property which could not be resolved otherwise would be resolved by recognizing that the Crown held a default title in all property in the jurisdiction and therefore that if the property was not owned by any other person it would make most sense for it to revert directly to the Crown. This is not how modern social relations are understood. Particularly in a world of global markets in which property held on trust might not be susceptible to transfer to the British Crown and in which the ownership of private property has acquired a central place in our society, another rule would be preferable to the quaintness of the *bona vacantia* rule. The approach taken in *Air Jamaica v Charlton* had the merit of recognizing that private property ought properly to remain private and that the resulting trust is at its most useful when resolving gaps in the ownership of property by returning property to its last known owner.

Recovery of property by means of resulting trust on grounds of mistake

26.63 Where property is transferred by a person who is acting under the influence of a mistake, the transferor will wish to argue that that property should be held on trust by the transferee for the benefit of the transferor. In such a circumstance the transferor would seek to establish a resulting trust in her favour. Exactly this problem arose in *Westdeutsche Landesbank v Islington*.[138] A bank made an outright transfer of money to a local authority further to a contract which was subsequently found to have been void because it was beyond the local authority's powers. Both the bank and the local authority were operating under a mistake as to the validity of the contract. The bank sought to recover the payments made under the contract by arguing that the mistake ought to have founded a resulting trust because of the injustice of the local authority retaining the bank's money and consequently being liable to it only on the basis of a common law claim for money had and received, rather than liable to hold the property on resulting trust and so to account to it for compound interest (as opposed to simple interest). The House of Lords held, unanimously on this point, that the payment was not held on resulting trust for the bank because the bank had intended to make an outright transfer of the property to the local authority under the contract. More importantly, in relation to the law on resulting trusts, because the local authority did not realize the parties' mistake there was nothing to affect its conscience and therefore nothing which would cause a court

---

[136] See para 26.47.   [137] [1999] 1 WLR 1399.   [138] [1996] AC 669.

of equity to impose a trust on it. Furthermore, in that case, the money at issue had been dissipated and was therefore impossible to trace such that there was no property over which a trust could have been imposed in any event.

Therefore, mistake will give rise to a proprietary remedy in equity only in circum- **26.64** stances in which the defendant has knowledge of the factors which are said to affect his conscience and only if the property claimed is identifiable separately from all other property. The limitation on the categories of resulting trust set out by Lord Browne-Wilkinson (considered above[139]) meant that a resulting trust would not be an appropriate proprietary remedy even if the defendant had had sufficient knowledge of factors affecting his conscience. It is more likely that a constructive trust would be imposed in such a situation, provided that all of the foregoing pro-visos have been satisfied. At common law, the finding of a mistake will, as evidenced by the appeal in *Westdeutsche Landesbank v Islington*, found a claim for money had and received. This personal claim in restitution is considered in Chapter 55.[140]

There are instances in which property has been transferred by mistake and the **26.65** court has declared the recipient to be a trustee for the transferor.[141] Those cases, decided before the appeal in *Westdeutsche Landesbank v Islington*, have tended not to be explicit about the nature of the trust in this situation.[142] In many such cases it has been held that when the transferee has knowledge of the mistake, that transferee holds the property on constructive trust for the transferor rather than on resulting trust.[143] In two cases, the trust was expressly identified as a resulting trust.[144] As Millett J held in *El Ajou v Dollar Land Holdings*: 'having been induced to purchase shares by false and fraudulent misrepresentations, [the vic-tims of fraud] are entitled to . . . revest the equitable title to the purchase money in themselves . . . But . . . the trust which is operating in these cases is not some new model remedial constructive trust, but an old-fashioned institutional result-ing trust.'[145] It is suggested, however, that these dicta were delivered in the shadow of a belief that the principle of unjust enrichment[146] would found a

---

[139] See para 26.01. [140] See para 55.02.

[141] *Chase Manhattan Bank NA v Israel-British Bank (London) Ltd* [1981] Ch 105; *Leuty v Hillas* (1858) 2 De G & J 110; *Craddock Brothers v Hunt* [1923] 2 Ch 136, CA; *Blacklocks v JB Developments (Godalming) Ltd* [1982] Ch 183.

[142] On this see R Chambers, *op cit*, 23, where the argument is made that the trusts ought to be considered to have been resulting trusts because the equitable interest in property is being returned to its original equitable owner.

[143] *Westdeutsche Landesbank v Islington* [1996] AC 669 in considering *Chase Manhattan Bank NA v Israel-British Bank (London) Ltd* [1981] Ch 105.

[144] *El Ajou v Dollar Land Holdings* [1993] 3 All ER 717; *Clelland v Clelland* [1945] 3 DLR 664, BCCA.   [145] [1993] 3 All ER 717, 734.

[146] The position in English law relating to recovery on grounds of mistake at common law for money had and received has been greatly expanded by the decision of the House of Lords in *Kleinwort Benson v Lincoln CC* [1998] 4 All ER 513 which reversed the old rule that there could be no recovery on grounds of mistake of law. It is now clear that recovery can take place as a result of a mistake of law as well as a mistake of fact.

general form of resulting trust in such situations, a position subsequently rejected by the House of Lords.[147]

Resulting trusts under void contracts

26.66 The issues surrounding the imposition of proprietary rights in relation to void commercial contracts are considered in Chapter 55 in detail. The issues surrounding the imposition of resulting trusts are the same as those considered in the preceding paragraph relating to resulting trusts in circumstances in which property was transferred on the basis of a mistake. The decision in *Westdeutsche Landesbank v Islington*[148] limited the operation of the resulting trust to those two categories set out at the beginning of this chapter and therefore resulting trusts will not be imposed over property transferred under the terms of a contract which was subsequently declared to have been void *ab initio*.

C. *Quistclose* Trusts

26.67 The material covered in this section receives a more detailed treatment in Chapters 9 and 49.[149] The reader is referred to that discussion for a closer analysis of the practicalities of this doctrine within the context of contracts of loan and financial transactions. This section considers only the general principles on which *Quistclose* trusts operate akin to the resulting trust. While these trusts are commonly known as *Quistclose* trusts their source can be traced to the older principle established in *Hassall v Smither*[150] that equitable title vests in a lender where conditions are attached to the use of loan moneys by their borrower.[151]

26.68 A *Quistclose* trust[152] arises in a situation in which L lends money to B, a borrower, subject to a condition that B will use that money only for a specified purpose. In the event that the loan moneys are used for some other purpose in breach of that condition, equity deems a trust to have been created over the loan moneys in favour of L. L's rights under that trust will defeat the rights of any third person to whom B may have transferred those moneys in breach of that condition. This trust is considered in most of the cases as being a form of automatic resulting trust such that the equitable title in the loan moneys passes back automatically on resulting trust to L as soon as those moneys are misapplied.[153] As will emerge, the proper categorization of this form of trust is a matter for debate.

---

[147] *Westdeutsche Landesbank v Islington* [1996] AC 669.   [148] [1996] AC 669.

[149] See para 49.14.   [150] (1806) 12 Ves 119.

[151] See now also *Twinsectra Ltd v Yardley* [2002] UKHL 12, [2002] 2 AC 164, [2002] 2 All ER 377.

[152] *Barclay's Bank v Quistclose Investments Ltd* [1970] AC 567.

[153] *Twinsectra Ltd v Yardley* [1999] Lloyd's Rep Bank 438; *R v Common Professional Examination Board, ex p Mealing-McCleod* The Times, 2 May 2000.

In the case of *Barclays Bank v Quistclose*[154] itself a contract was formed by which Q   **26.69**
lent money to a company for the limited purpose of paying a dividend on its share
premium account. The borrower subsequently went into insolvency having misapplied the money in discharging its overdraft with the bank. The bank contended
that the money held in the share dividend account with it should be set off against
the company's overdraft with the bank in its general account on the basis that the
money belonged beneficially to the company. It was held that the loan money, held
separately in a share dividend bank account, should be treated as having been held
on resulting trust for the lender. The House of Lords held unanimously that the
money in the share dividend account was held on trust for the lender on the basis
that the specified purpose of the loan had not been performed.

Lord Wilberforce upheld the resulting trust in favour of the lender on the basis   **26.70**
that it was an implied term of the loan contract that the money be returned to the
lender in the event that it was not used for the purpose for which it was lent. Lord
Wilberforce found that there were two trusts: a primary trust (to use the money to
pay the dividend) and a secondary trust (to return the money to the lender if it was
not used to pay the dividend). As his lordship held:

> In the present case the intention to create a secondary trust for the benefit of the
> lender, to arise if the primary trust, to pay the dividend, could not be carried out, is
> clear and I can find no reason why the law should not give effect to it.

The principle has been alternatively stated in *Carreras Rothmans Ltd v Freeman
Mathews Treasure Ltd* to be that:[155]

> . . . equity fastens on the conscience of the person who receives from another prop-
> erty transferred for a specific purpose only and not therefore for the recipient's own
> purposes, so that such person will not be permitted to treat the property as his own
> or to use it for other than the stated purpose.

However, this statement could be taken to be authority for any number of understandings of the *Quistclose* arrangement. As considered in *Westdeutsche
Landesbank v Islington*,[156] to define the *Quistclose* trust as operating solely on the
conscience of the recipient of the money is merely to place the situation within the
general understanding of the trust as part of equity, rather than to allocate it to any
particular trust categorization.

In the House of Lords in *Twinsectra v Yardley*,[157] in his minority opinion,   **26.71**
Lord Millett considered the nature of the *Quistclose* trust as being akin to a retention of title clause. In Lord Millett's opinion the title in the loan moneys remains
in the lender throughout the transaction. As mentioned above, this would
depend, in fact, on the terms of the loan contract. Lord Millett's definition would

---

[154] *Barclays Bank v Quistclose Investments Ltd* [1970] AC 567.
[155] [1985] Ch 207, 222.   [156] [1996] AC 669.   [157] [2002] 2 All ER 377, 398.

not explain, for example, loan contracts which clearly identify a separate trust bank account in which the loan moneys are to be held such that the loan moneys are held on express trust, rather than being retained absolutely by the lender. What is difficult in Lord Millett's structure is how we conceptualize the permission which the borrower has to transfer title in the loan moneys for the contractually stipulated purpose. Perhaps the borrower is acting as the lender's agent or more satisfactorily is acting under a power to spend the money on the specified purpose. In this analysis the *Quistclose* trust is just another means by which commercial people retain title in property.[158]

D. Purchase Price Resulting Trusts

The nature of purchase price resulting trusts as presumed resulting trusts

26.72 The purchase price resulting trust has long been accepted as arising on the basis that if one contributed to the purchase price of property then it could be presumed that one intended to take some beneficial interest in the property.[159] This presumption could be rebutted if, for example, the contribution to the purchase price was made as part of a loan contract,[160] by way of gift, or in some other way which suggested that the contributor was not intended to acquire beneficial rights in the property. Purchase price resulting trusts arise so as to recognize that a person who has contributed to the purchase price of property (with an intention that he should acquire proprietary rights in that property) acquired an equitable interest in that property in proportion to the size of her contribution. That equitable interest is held on resulting trust for the contributor. Lord Browne-Wilkinson described this form of resulting trust in the following terms:

> ... where A makes a voluntary payment to B or pays (wholly or in part) for the purchase of property which is vested either in B alone or in the joint names of A and B, there is a presumption that A did not intend to make a gift to B: the money or property is held on trust for A (if he is the sole provider of the money) or in the case of a joint purchase by A and B in shares proportionate to their contributions. It is important to stress that this is only a *presumption*, which presumption is easily rebutted either by the counter-presumption of advancement or by direct evidence of A's intention to make an outright transfer.[161]

The resulting trust comes into existence in circumstances in which that person has provided part of the purchase price of property with an intention to take an

---

[158] [2002] 2 All ER 377, 398.

[159] This concept applies to personal property as well as to real property: *Rider v Kidder* (1805) 10 Ves Jr 360; *Shephard v Cartwright* [1955] AC 431; *Abrahams v Abrahams* [2000] WTLR 593.

[160] *Aveling v Knipe* (1815) 19 Ves 441; *Hussey v Palmer* [1972] 3 All ER 744, 749, *per* Cairns LJ. But see *Re Sharpe (a bankrupt)* [1980] 1 All ER 198; *Spence v Browne* [1988] Fam Law 291.

[161] *Underhill and Hayton* 329 *et seq*; *White v Vandervell Trustees Ltd* [1974] Ch 269, 288 *et seq*.

equitable interest in that property;[162] or where another person has acquired property for the claimant using money provided by the claimant.[163] If, however, one person were intended to be the sole occupant of the property and where that person pays for all of the mortgage repayments, the deposit, and the insurance premiums, then that person will be the sole owner of that property, and no other person will be entitled to any interest on resulting trust principles even if the mortgage were also taken out in that other person's name (given that that other person made no contribution to the mortgage repayments).[164] This first category affirms the long-standing principle in *Dyer v Dyer*[165] that, where a person contributes to the acquisition of property, that person receives a corresponding proportion of the total equitable interest in that property on resulting trust. This resulting trust is said to be a *presumed resulting trust* because it will not always be the case that the contributor is intended to acquire an equitable interest in the purchased property at all. In short, equity presumes that there is a resulting trust although that presumption can be rebutted if it can be proved that the contributor intended something other than the acquisition of property rights.

For example, if A Bank lends money by way of mortgage to B so that B can buy a **26.73** house, it will typically be the case that A Bank will have a loan contract with B entitling A Bank to a personal claim to repayment but not that A Bank would acquire any proprietary right in the house beyond the rights of a mortgagee. When there is an ordinary contract of loan the lender does not acquire a right in any property bought with that money; rather the lender is entitled to a chose in action entitling her to repayment of the loan in cash.[166] However, if A and B are husband and wife, and A contributes 50 per cent of the purchase price of the acquisition of the matrimonial home, it will be presumed by equity that A should acquire 50 per cent of the total equitable interest in that matrimonial home because a couple's intention is more likely to be that both acquire equitable title in the home.

There are other situations in which presumptions of advancement operate to **26.74** deem that rights in property have passed by way of gift between husband and wife, and between father and child.[167] A resulting trust will arise in favour of the donor

---

[162] *Dyer v Dyer* (1788) 2 Cox Eq Cas 92. This principle was expressed by Vinelott J in *Re Gorman* [1990] 2 FLR 284, 291: 'In circumstances of this kind, the court is concerned to ascertain, so far as is possible, from the evidence, what was the intention of the parties when the property was purchased, or what intention is to be imputed to them.' [163] ibid.
[164] *Carlton v Goodman* [2002] EWCA Civ 545: in that case, the parties' intentions on the acquisition of the property were unclear except to the extent that only one of the parties was ever intended to occupy the property. [165] (1788) 2 Cox Eq Cas 92.
[166] Thus a mortgagee or chargee over property has only a personal right to receive a sum of money and in default of payment a right to possession of that property: the mortgagee does not take an equitable interest in the property. [167] *Bennet v Bennet* (1879) 10 Ch D 474.

where that presumption of advancement can be rebutted on the facts.[168] As a final member of this category of resulting trusts, *Quistclose* trusts[169] arise where money has been lent to be used for a specified purpose so as to prevent that property being used for any other purpose. As was considered in the previous section, this form of trust has been identified judicially as being a form of resulting trust.[170] Lord Browne-Wilkinson did not make specific reference to these forms of trust in the passages quoted immediately above, however that is not to suggest that they have necessarily been removed from the canon of resulting trust: other cases,[171] including cases in which Lord Browne-Wilkinson has given speeches,[172] have suggested that the forms of presumed resulting trusts continue in existence.

Contribution to the purchase price of property founding a resulting trust

26.75 The clearest form of presumed resulting trust, accepted both by Lord Browne-Wilkinson in *Westdeutsche Landesbank v Islington*[173] and by Megarry J in *Vandervell (No 21)*,[174] is the situation in which a person contributes to the acquisition price of property and is therefore presumed to take a corresponding equitable interest in that property. The core principle in respect of purchase cases can be identified from the judgment of Eyre CB in *Dyer v Dyer*[175] where his lordship held that:

> The clear result of all the cases, without a single exception, is that the trust of a legal estate, whether freehold, copyhold or leasehold; whether taken in the names of the purchasers and others jointly, or in the names of other without that of the purchaser; whether in one name or several; whether jointly or successive—results to the man who advances the purchase money.

Where a contribution to the purchase price is intended to acquire some property right for the contributor then that contributor receives a correspondingly proportionate equitable interest in the property on resulting trust.[176] However, where the financial contribution is not directed at the acquisition of the property, that contribution will not ground an equitable interest under a resulting trust.[177]

---

[168] *Fowkes v Pascoe* (1875) LR 10 Ch App Cas 343.

[169] *Barclays Bank v Quistclose Investments Ltd* [1970] AC 567.

[170] Such a categorization is open to question, however, see para 49.14.

[171] *Tribe v Tribe* [1995] 4 All ER 236, [1995] 3 WLR 913.

[172] eg *Tinsley v Milligan* [1994] 1 AC 340.

[173] [1996] AC 669.

[174] [1974] Ch 269.

[175] (1788) 2 Cox Eq Cas 92.

[176] In the words of Dillon LJ: '... it has been consistently held that where the purchase money for property acquired by two or more persons in their joint names has been provided by those persons in unequal amounts, they will be beneficially entitled as between themselves in the proportions in which they provided the purchase money': *Walker v Hall* [1984] FLR 126, 133.

[177] *Winkworth v Edward Baron* [1987] 1 All ER 114, 118

It is a prerequisite that the claimant demonstrate that the contribution to the   **26.76**
purchase price is not made for any other purpose other than acquisition of a right
in the property. For example, where it could be demonstrated that the contributor intended only to make a loan to some other person for the purpose of buying
a house, then that would not acquire the lender any rights in the property.
Similarly an intention to make a gift of money to someone so that they could buy
a house would not grant the donor any right in the property. Thus, in *Sekhon v
Alissa*[178] a mother transferred title in a house into her daughter's name with the
intention of avoiding capital gains tax. It was held that she had no intention to
benefit her daughter; rather she had the intention of tax avoidance (or evasion on
those facts) which rebutted the presumption of intention to benefit the daughter.
Therefore, whereas the property had been transferred to the name of her daughter, a resulting trust over the property was necessarily said to arise in favour of the
mother on the basis of the true, demonstrable intentions of the parties.

Resulting trusts and common intention constructive trusts

In relation to real property constituting a home a number of specific rules have   **26.77**
been developed. Some of those adaptations for that context include an understanding of the nature of the contribution which will give rise to a resulting trust.
Therefore, contributions to the mortgage will suffice to create some equitable
interest for the contributor[179] in proportion to the size of the contribution relative
to the total value of the land,[180] whereas contributions only to domestic expenses
will not.[181] These particular principles are considered in Chapter 56. In that chapter it will emerge that the arithmetical certainties often associated with resulting
trusts will often be disturbed in line with some greater notion of justice.[182] It has
been suggested that the presumptions of advancement should not have any part
to play in decisions as to rights in the family home where other considerations
such as the rights of children come into play.[183]

The development of the common intention constructive trust in relation to the   **26.78**
family home has complicated the basis on which the resulting trust would ordinarily operate. Common intention constructive trusts are considered in detail in
Chapter 56.[184] That form of common intention constructive trust described by
Lord Bridge in the House of Lords in *Lloyds Bank v Rosset*[185] provided that a situation in which a person contributed to the purchase price of the home or paid

---

[178] [1989] 2 FLR 94.
[179] *Lloyds Bank v Rosset* [1991] 1 All ER 1111.
[180] *Springette v Dafoe* [1992] 2 FLR 388.
[181] *Burns v Burns* [1984] 1 All ER 244; *Nixon v Nixon* [1969] 1 WLR 1676.
[182] W Swadling, 'A hard look at *Hodgson v Marks*' in Birks and Rose (eds), *Resulting Trusts and Equitable Compensation* (Mansfield Press, 2000) 61.
[183] *Pettit v Pettit* [1970] AC 777; *Gissing v Gissing* [1971] AC 886; *Calverley v Green* (1984) 155 CLR 242.   [184] See para 56.24.   [185] [1991] 1 AC 117.

indirectly towards the purchase price by way of contributions to the repayments of a mortgage should be considered to be a form of constructive trust predicated on the common intention of the parties inferred from their conduct. This form of trust would ordinarily have been a resulting trust which would have crystallized the rights of the parties on the acquisition of the property on ordinary trusts law principles. However, the law in relation to the acquisition of property rights in the home has taken a different turn from the rest of the law of trusts, developing its own jargon. For example, some cases which have been decided expressly on the basis of resulting trusts principles have nevertheless found that the resulting trust formed by the parties on the acquisition of the property can be altered by interposing constructive trust principles of unconscionability in the event that the parties' subsequent behaviour required it.[186] Oddly, given the clarity of the principles considered thus far, the Court of Appeal in *Pratt v Medwin*[187] entertained the notion that the beneficial ownership of an insurance policy in common could be held on the basis of a common intention constructive trust—even though that doctrine has only previously been employed in relation to real property—rather than a resulting trust. That, it is suggested, is a novel step too far.

E. General Presumptions of Resulting Trust

Introduction

26.79 There are property law disputes in which it is impossible for the courts to know with any certainty which conclusion is correct. Aside from epistemological questions as to the possibility of ever knowing anything with complete certainty, the court is called upon to believe the evidence of one party or another, or, in the event that neither party's evidence is sufficiently compelling, the court will presume one interpretation of the facts to be the correct interpretation in line with one of the equitable presumptions developed in the case law. There are situations in which English law presumes that particular personal relationships give rise to outright gifts when property passes between people who are in such relationships, or alternatively that a resulting trust ought to be imposed. As Lord Upjohn held in *Vandervell v IRC*:[188]

> In reality the so-called presumption of a resulting trust is no more than a long-stop to provide an answer where the relevant facts and circumstances fail to reach a solution.

---

[186] See *Huntingford v Hobbs* [1993] 1 FLR 936, discussed at para 56.54.

[187] [2003] EWCA Civ 906—particularly in the judgment of Arden LJ at para 2; citing in this regard S Worthington, *Equity* (Clarendon Press, 2003) 239. A fuller argument proposing that the common intention constructive trust might be developed in *commercial* contexts to deal equitably with property dealt with as part of transactions comprising void or otherwise ineffective contracts was made by AS Hudson, *Swaps, Restitution and Trusts* (Sweet & Maxwell, 1999) 203.

[188] [1967] 2 AC 291, 313.

The situations in which such a presumption is important are those cases in which **26.80** neither party is able to prove to the courts' satisfaction what their true intentions were. Suppose two people S and T who are not related to one another. In a situation in which S hands his watch to T and passes legal title to T there are a number of possible explanations of the parties' intentions. It may be that S is making an outright gift of the watch to T. Alternatively, it may be that S has asked T to look after his watch while S goes swimming. Yet again, it may be that S has asked T to be trustee of the watch for S for life and then for his children after S's death. If the parties fall out and the matter comes to court, it will be very difficult for the judge to decide what S intended in respect of the watch: T may well insist that S made a gift of the watch whereas S may argue that T was only to have it for safekeeping. In such situations equity has developed presumptions as to what the parties intended. This means that, if neither party can prove conclusively what was intended, then the court will rely on its presumption to determine what it will deem to have been intended. In the hypothetical case just given of S and T, equity would presume that S did not intend to make a gift of the valuable watch to T because T is not a person for whom S would usually be expected by the equitable presumptions to provide, not being S's child nor spouse.[189] Therefore, T might hold that watch on resulting trust for S or as a bailee.

Suppose, alternatively, that S and T are husband and wife and therefore fall **26.81** within one of the categories covered by the presumptions.[190] Where S transfers property to T, the presumption is that S intended to make a gift of that property to T. This process of assuming an intention to make a gift when a husband passes property to his wife is known as 'the presumption of advancement'. The other relationship which gives rise to a presumption of advancement is the situation between father and child. However, if S and T were not married, and consequently did not fall within any of the categories of presumption, then where S transferred property to T without intending T to take that property beneficially (because there was no presumption of advancement) there would be a presumption that S's intention was to create a resulting trust over that property in favour of S on the basis that S would not be presumed to intend to make a gift of that property to T.

Presumed resulting trusts constitute a means by which equity will supplement **26.82** unclear factual circumstances by presuming that the equitable interest in property results back to its previous owner. This means that, in a case where the evidence adduced by the witnesses will not conclusively support one or other of the parties, the court will rely on one of its case law presumptions to imply an answer. The presumptions have been described by Nourse LJ as being best thought of as

---

[189] *Bennet v Bennet* (1879) 10 Ch D 474. See also *Winstanley v Winstanley* (1999) 2 ITLER 269 CA. [190] ibid.

'a judicial instrument of last resort comparable to the contra proferentem rule in the construction of deeds and contracts'.[191] Those presumptions operate in the following manner:

> (4) Where A effectually transfers to B (or creates in his favour) any interest in any property, whether legal or equitable, a resulting trust for A may arise in two distinct classes of case ... (a) The first class of case is where the transfer to B is not made on any trust. If, of course, it appears from the transfer that B is intended to hold on certain trusts, that will be decisive, and the case is not within this category; and similarly if it appears that B is intended to take beneficially. But in other cases there is a rebuttable presumption that B holds on a resulting trust for A. The question is not one of the automatic consequences of a dispositive failure by A, but one of presumption: the property has been carried to B, and from the absence of consideration and any presumption of advancement B is presumed not only to hold the entire interest on trust, but also to hold the beneficial interest for A absolutely. The presumption thus establishes both that B is to take on trust and also what that trust is. Such resulting trusts may be called 'presumed resulting trusts'.[192]

This first category of presumed resulting trust arises where no trust is created. Rather, there are a number of situations in which the common law raises a presumption that property passes between prescribed categories of individual. The example which arises most frequently is the situation in which property is transferred from father to child. The presumption which the law applies is that the father intends to make an outright gift of that property. This presumption can be displaced by evidence that that was not the father's intention. Where such rebuttal of the presumption takes place, the child holds the property on resulting trust for the father.

26.83 In more modern cases, even where a presumption of advancement exists, the courts are likely to accept evidence to disprove (or, rebut) any such intention to make an advancement of the property. The court would often prefer to find a conclusive answer on the facts and the evidence given by witnesses rather than simply have recourse to the presumption. In such a case where there is sufficient evidence, the presumption of a gift between S and T would be rebutted. In its place, a resulting trust comes into existence because T holds the legal title in the property after the transfer in circumstances in which T was never intended to take that property beneficially.

26.84 The importance of the resulting trust in this context is that, if the presumption does not operate to transfer property between the purported donor and donee, the principle of resulting trust provides that the equitable interest in the property be held on resulting trust for the donor. The cases which we will consider in the following sections therefore consider whether a presumption applies, or whether

---

[191] *McGrath v Wallis* [1995] 2 FLR 114, 121; *Ali v Khan* [2002] EWCA Civ 974.
[192] *Bennet v Bennet* (1879) 10 Ch D 474.

that presumption can be rebutted so that a resulting trust arises. In short, where S transfers legal title to T, S will want to rebut any presumption that a gift has been made and demonstrate that the property should be held on resulting trust for S.

Presumption of advancement—special relationships

This section considers some of the specific relationships which the case law considers give effect to deemed outright transfers of property in the absence of evidence to the contrary by way of presumption.

Father and child

Where a father transfers property to a child, it is presumed that the father intends **26.85** to make an outright gift of that property to that child.[193] In the absence of any cogent evidence to rebut this presumption of advancement no resulting trust will be imposed on the property in favour of the father.[194] The presumption is that a father would want to care for his child and therefore would make transfers of property to that child for the purposes of its maintenance. Under the ancient principle from the time of Coke that there were automatic obligations of maintenance on fathers in relation to their children, on husbands in relation to their wives, and on masters in relation to their servants, the relationship of mother and child does not give rise to a presumption of advancement because there was not thought to be any necessary implication that a mother is required to provide for the financial well-being of the child.[195] In Australia, the presumption has been held to apply equally to mothers as to fathers.[196] There is another presumption which arises where the donor stands *in loco patris* to the child (that is, as though the child's father).[197]

Husband and wife

Where a husband makes a transfer of property to his wife, the presumption is that **26.86** the husband intends to make an outright gift of such property.[198] In determining title to property, a transfer made on the breakdown of a relationship will frequently create the following type of conflict between the parties: one party will assert a resulting trust over the property whereas the other will wish to argue that the property was the subject of an outright gift. The husband will seek to argue that he intended the property to be held on resulting trust for him, whereas his

---

[193] *Bennet v Bennet* (1879) 10 ChD 474; *McGrath v Wallis* [1995] 2 FLR 114; *Ali v Khan* [2002] EWCA Civ 974.   [194] Rebuttal of the presumption is considered at para 26.96.

[195] ibid.

[196] *Brown v Brown* (1993) 31 NSWLR 582, 591. Cf *Gross v French* (1975) EG 39, CA.

[197] *Re Paradise Motor Company Ltd* [1968] 2 All ER 625.

[198] *Tinker v Tinker* [1970] P 136. This presumption does not apply in relation to transfers from wife to husband: *Abrahams v Abrahams* [2000] WTLR 593. Nor does it necessarily encompass those acting *in loco parentis*: *Tucker v Burrow* (1865) 2 Hem & M 515.

wife will argue that the presumption of advancement should apply to the effect that she take the property as a result of an outright gift. The husband's reasons for effecting a transfer not meant as a gift might be to avoid creditors (as discussed immediately below) or to avoid tax. Usually a combination of their conflicting evidence and the fact that few couples will have recorded in writing their true intentions will mean that the court will be hard-pressed on the facts to decide conclusively how the property should be treated. It should be noted that rules relating to divorced couples apply equally to couples who were previously engaged.[199]

26.87 Aside from the context of divorce, there is also the problem of insolvency. To avoid creditors on a bankruptcy being able to gain access to property, the person who fears bankruptcy will frequently transfer as much of his real and personal property as possible into the names of his spouse or children. The intention is to deceive the creditors into thinking that that property is owned absolutely by the spouse or child and not by the bankrupt personally. Aside from the insolvency legislation considered below, the issue will arise between the couple as to whether the property so transferred should be deemed subject to the presumption of outright gift or held under resulting trust for the transferor on the basis that his sole intention in effecting the transfer was to avoid his creditors.

26.88 The clearest modern application of the presumption of advancement between husband and wife is in the decision of the Court of Appeal in *Tinker v Tinker*.[200] Mr Tinker transferred land into the name of Mrs Tinker, avowedly to put the land out of the reach of the creditors of his garage business. Mr Tinker then sought to recover the property from his wife when their relationship broke down. Lord Denning held that Mr Tinker could not argue against his wife that the property was held on resulting trust for him, while also arguing against his creditors that the property was vested in his wife. Lord Denning found therefore that the presumption fell to be applied that the transfer was intended to effect an outright advancement in favour of his wife. It was clear on the evidence before the Court of Appeal that the wife was intended to acquire the beneficial interest under the transfer and that the husband sought to avoid the rights of his creditors as a priority. Similarly,[201] where a father sought to transfer property, comprising a nightclub and penthouse flat in Clapham, to his daughter on the basis that she would hold it on bare trust for him so that it would escape liability to inheritance tax, it was held that there would be no trust found in his favour. There were two principal reasons for this: first, that the stated intention that the daughter hold the property on bare trust would not have achieved his stated intention of avoiding inheritance tax such that his intentions were impossible to divine from the circumstances and, secondly, that his intention, to the extent that it could be understood, was solely to avoid his creditors.

---

[199] Law Reform (Miscellaneous Provisions) Act 1970, s 2(1).   [200] [1970] P 136.
[201] *Collier v Collier* [2002] EWCA Civ 1095.

Despite the application of the presumption as set out in *Tinker*, the modern view **26.89**
is to move away from its automatic application, particularly in respect of the
family home. In *Pettit v Pettit*[202] Lord Diplock held that:

> It would in my view be an abuse of the legal technique for ascertaining or imputing
> intention to apply to transactions between the post-war generation of married cou-
> ples 'presumptions' which are based upon inferences of fact which an earlier genera-
> tion of judges drew as the most likely intentions of that generation of spouses
> belonging to the propertied classes of a different social era.[203]

Similarly, in *Gissing v Gissing*[204] it was held that the principles determining equitable title to the family home as between the respective contributions of husband
and wife raised different concerns from the application of the age-old presumptions. The details of the rules concerning implied trusts in respect of the family
home are considered in Chapter 56. The foregoing principles were applied by
Goff J in *Re Densham*[205] where a husband was convicted of theft from his employers and made bankrupt. The issue arose as to whether or not his wife would
acquire an equitable interest in the property on the basis that their joint savings
had been put towards the purchase. His lordship held that the wife did acquire an
equitable interest in that property on resulting trust principles given that her
money had been applied in its purchase.

Voluntary gift

The first applicable category of presumption is where one party makes a gift voluntarily. That is, without any consideration having been provided by the donee.

Personal property

The law relating to the transfer of personalty from one person to another may raise **26.90**
the difficulties considered above where there is a dispute as to title in that property.
If there is no special relationship between the parties and no juristic cause for the
transfer, such as a contractual obligation to transfer the property, then there will
be a presumption of resulting trust which can in turn be rebutted.[206] Cotton LJ
put that proposition in the following form:[207]

> The rule is well settled that where there is a transfer by a person into his own name jointly
> with that of a person who is not his child, or his adopted child, then there is prima facie
> a resulting trust for the transferor. But that is a presumption capable of being rebutted
> by showing that at the time the transferor intended a benefit to the transferee, and in the
> present case there is ample evidence that at the time of the transfer, and for some time
> previously, the plaintiff intended to confer a benefit by this transfer on her late husband's
> godson.

---

[202] [1970] AC 777.   [203] ibid 824.   [204] [1971] AC 886.
[205] [1975] 3 All ER 726.
[206] *Wheeler v Smith* (1859) 1 Giff 300; *Fowkes v Pascoe* (1875) 10 Ch App 343.
[207] *Standing v Bowring* (1885) 31 Ch D 282.

The presumption in respect of personalty is that a voluntary transfer gives rise to a resulting trust. By way of example, the case of *Re Vinogradoff*[208] concerned a grandmother who was the absolute owner of a bond, in the form of a war loan, for £800 in her name. The grandmother transferred the bond into the joint names of herself and her granddaughter. Unfortunately she did not make plain her reasons for doing this. In consequence, it was unclear whether the grandmother continued to own the bond outright or whether she was now a joint tenant of it with her granddaughter. The grandmother continued to receive the dividends from the bond until her death. When the grandmother died the issue arose whether or not the bond formed part of the dead woman's estate or belonged to her granddaughter beneficially. Farwell J held that the property should be presumed to be held on resulting trust for the grandmother. His reasoning was that she did not fall within the usual category of the presumptions because she was not the child's father but rather only her grandmother. Furthermore, the fact that she continued to receive the dividends on her own without passing any of them to her granddaughter suggested that she had not intended to make a gift in her granddaughter's favour such that her granddaughter could claim the war loan absolutely on her grandmother's death.[209]

26.91 The intention to confer a benefit on another person may rebut this presumption of resulting trust. So in *Standing v Bowring*[210] it was held that a godmother's transfer of property into the name of herself and her godson would constitute an irrevocable transfer of that property on the basis that she had evidenced an intention to have that property pass to her godson on her death and also on the basis that she had been advised that the transfer would be irrevocable. Similarly, in *Fowkes v Pascoe*,[211] when a wealthy widow transferred two parcels of property into the names of herself and variously her close friend and her daughter-in-law's child, it was found that her intention must have been to effect gifts of that property.

26.92 The only means of reconciling these cases is on the basis that the facts in *Standing v Bowring* and *Fowkes v Pascoe* disclosed an intention to make a gift of the property whereas *Re Vinogradoff* was genuinely considered to fail to raise any clear

[208] [1935] WN 68.
[209] Aside from the tortured logic of these presumptions, there are a number of possible objections to this decision in principle. First, the granddaughter was a minor at the time of the purported transfer and therefore could not have acted as a trustee in any event because she was under age. Secondly, it is not clear how this resulting trust can be said to accord with the intention of the settlor. Her intention in transferring the war loan into their joint names was ostensibly to benefit her granddaughter in some form. A resulting trust does not achieve that objective because it returns all of the equitable interest to the grandmother. While the testamentary rules of the Wills Act had not been observed (thus preventing a testamentary gift), it is not clear why there could not have been an *inter vivos* gift of rights in the property either by means of the creation of a joint tenancy or a trust in favour of the grandmother and the granddaughter in remainder. [210] (1885) 31 Ch D 282.
[211] (1875) 10 Ch App 343.

conclusion on the facts with the result that the court was required to have recourse to the presumption of resulting trust. In *Westdeutsche Landesbank v Islington*[212] Lord Browne-Wilkinson explained *Re Vinogradoff*[213] and related cases as operating in circumstances where there was no intention to make an immediate gift. His lordship held that the conscience of the recipient is affected when she discovers the intention of the settlor not to create any personal benefit in the recipient's favour. The resulting trust is said to be imposed at the moment of the acquisition of this knowledge. As such, the resulting trust comes closer to the constructive trust set out by Lord Browne-Wilkinson in that same case.[214]

The recognition of resulting trusts in real property

The resulting use, and latterly resulting trust, was developed originally in relation **26.93** to real property as a presumption that certain devices to avoid married women's property legislation were intended to avoid the legislation and to retain equitable title in the transferor. In this context, prior to the enactment of section 60(3) of the Law of Property Act 1925, it had been necessary to specify a particular use governing the land in the conveyance. Where no such use was specified, the property was subject to a resulting trust in favour of the transferor. Section 60(3) provided that:

> In a voluntary conveyance a resulting trust for the grantor shall not be implied merely by reason that the property is not expressed to be conveyed for the use or benefit of the grantee.

As a result there is no automatic resulting trust on the ground that no use is specified. However, this does not prevent the possibility of a resulting trust being imposed, as was the case in *Hodgson v Marks*.[215] Rather it restricts the automatic imposition of such a resulting trust. Section 60 is not considered to raise a presumption of a resulting trust on the voluntary conveyance of land of necessity.[216]

In *Hodgson v Marks*[217] Mrs Hodgson was an elderly woman who had a lodger, **26.94** Evans, a man who turned out to be a rogue.[218] Evans put it about that Mrs Hodgson's nephew disapproved of Evans and that the nephew wanted to throw the lodger out. Nevertheless, Mrs Hodgson transferred her freehold interest in the house to Evans so that he would be protected from her nephew. The transfer was accompanied by an oral agreement that Mrs Hodgson would remain beneficial owner of the property, while Evans became the registered proprietor of the property.

---

[212] [1996] AC 669.   [213] [1935] WN 68.

[214] As Prof Martin points out, it is difficult to see how *Re Vinogradoff* supports this analysis given the infancy of the resulting trustee at all times during the case: *Martin* 246.   [215] [1971] Ch 892.

[216] *Lohia v Lohia* [2001] WTLR 101; *Ali v Khan* [2002] EWCA Civ 974.

[217] [1971] Ch 892.

[218] Readers may be reminded of the bounders played by the actor Terry-Thomas in films like *School for Scoundrels* in Ungoed-Thomas J's description of Evans as 'a very ingratiating person, tall, smart, pleasant, self-assured, 50 years of age, apparently dignified by greying hair and giving the impression . . . of a retired colonel'.

Without Mrs Hodgson's knowledge, Evans sold the freehold to Marks, a bona fide purchaser for value without notice of Mrs Hodgson's rights. The question was whether or not Mrs Hodgson was protected against the purchaser, Marks. The Court of Appeal held that Mrs Hodgson had an overriding interest under section 70(1)(g) of the Land Registration Act 1925. Further, Mrs Hodgson could not have claimed a declaration of an ordinary express trust under section 53(1)(b) of the Law of Property Act 1925 in the form of the oral agreement. However, the oral agreement did prove Mrs Hodgson's intention in respect of the equitable interest and therefore formed 'a resulting trust of the beneficial interest to the plaintiff, which would not, of course, be affected by section 53(1)'.[219]

26.95 The resulting trust recognized in *Hodgson v Marks* is a device which might in the future be recognized as that sort of constructive trust at large explained by Lord Browne-Wilkinson in *Westdeutsche Landesbank*,[220] if indeed it would be recognized at all. It is doubtful whether this case would now be followed, given that the imposition of a resulting as opposed to a constructive trust or some estoppel-based right would generally be more likely if a court was minded to protect Mrs Hodgson.[221] The basis of the decision was that Mrs Hodgson did not intend to transfer the whole of the equitable interest, which she had held beneficially, to Evans. Rather, she intended to reserve some of those rights to herself during her lifetime. Consequently, it was said that those rights ought to be restored to her by means of resulting trust when Evans breached their arrangement.[222]

Rebutting the presumption

26.96 Given the judicial reluctance to apply the ancient presumptions to cases involving family homes, this section considers the situations in which courts have found that the presumptions have been successfully rebutted.[223]

Generally

26.97 The application of the presumptions is clearly capable of outcomes which bear little or no relation to the intentions of the parties. Therefore, the courts have frequently sought to rebut the presumptions. In the old authority of *Finch v Finch*[224]

---

[219] ibid, [1971] 1 Ch 892, 933, *per* Russell LJ.   [220] [1996] AC 669.

[221] *Hodgson v Marks* [1971] Ch 892, *per* Russell LJ; Birks, 'Restitution and resulting trusts' in Goldstein (ed), *Equity: Contemporary Legal Developments* (Jesusalem, 1992) 335 and Chambers, *op cit*, 25.

[222] It has been suggested by Swadling, *op cit*, 61, that the decision in *Hodgson v Marks* ought to be understood as being predicated on the doctrine in *Rochefoucauld v Boustead* [1897] 1 Ch 196, considered in para 28.66. That thesis is predicated itself on an understanding of *Rochefoucauld v Boustead* as having been an express trust, rather than the more usual interpretation that it was a constructive trust or an application of the general equitable principle that statute cannot be used as an engine of fraud: see *Hudson* para 1.3.17 and also para 5.2.2.

[223] [1970] AC 777, 824, *per* Lord Diplock.   [224] (1808) 15 Ves Jr 43.

Lord Eldon suggested that the court should not accept a rebuttal of the presumption unless there was sufficient evidence to justify such rebuttal. The more modern approach indicated by cases like *McGrath v Wallis*[225] is to accept a rebuttal of the presumption of advancement in family cases on the basis of comparatively slight evidence—even in a situation where an unexecuted deed of trust was the only direct evidence indicating the fact that a father intended a division of the equitable interest rather than an outright transfer when conveying land into his son's name.[226]

26.98 The clearest general statement of principle surrounding rebuttals of the presumptions was made by James LJ in *Fowkes v Pascoe*[227] where his lordship held as follows:

> Where the Court of Chancery is asked, as an equitable assumption of presumption, to take away from a man that which by the common law of the land he is entitled to, he surely has a right to say: 'Listen to my story as to how I came to have it, and judge that story with reference to all the surrounding facts and circumstances'.[228]

In that case a woman had purchased shares in the names of herself and her grandson. There was no personal nexus which would have brought the woman and the grandson (even though he was her grandson) within the ambit of the usual presumption of advancement. Therefore, the usual presumption in such a case as this would have been that the property was held on resulting trust for the settlor. Nevertheless, the court illustrated English law's occasional willingness to infer such presumptions of advancement. On the facts the Court of Appeal was prepared to hold that the woman's intention must have been to make a gift to her grandson of half of the value of those shares. Therefore, the presumption of a resulting trust in favour of the woman was rebutted.

Bank accounts

26.99 Where property is paid into a bank account by a husband with the intention that that property shall be held on a joint tenancy basis by the husband and his wife, then the account is so held on joint tenancy and will pass absolutely to the survivor of the two.[229] Similarly, property acquired with funds taken from that joint bank account would belong to them both as joint tenants[230] unless it was expressly taken in the name of one or other of them.[231] In circumstances in which the parties' intention is that the money be their joint property and that anything acquired with that money is also their joint property then the principles of the concept of joint tenancy[232] mean that the acquired property is treated as

---

[225] [1995] 2 FLR 114.   [226] ibid.   [227] (1875) 10 Ch App Cas 343.   [228] ibid 349.
[229] *Marshall v Crutwell* (1875) LR 20 Eq 328; *Young v Sealey* [1949] Ch 278, [1949] 1 All ER 92; *Re Figgis* [1969] Ch 123, [1968] 1 All ER 999.
[230] *Jones v Maynard* [1951] Ch 572; *Rimmer v Rimmer* [1953], 1 QB 63, [1952] 2 All ER 863.
[231] *Re Bishop* [1965] Ch 450.
[232] See, for example, *Re Young* (1885) 28 Ch D 705; *Gage v King* [1961] 1 QB 188, [1960] 3 All ER 62.

theirs jointly and not held on resulting trust in proportion to their contributions to the account.[233] If the parties exhibit no such intention that the money held in the account is to be theirs jointly in this fashion, then the property may be treated as belonging to them either in proportion to their proven contributions to the fund or else attributed to one or other of them.[234] The difficulty arises in situations where either the intentions of the husband are not made clear or in situations in which the husband transfers the bank account into the joint names of himself and his wife but continues to use the account for his own personal use. In the latter circumstance it would appear that the presumption of advancement is to be rebutted.[235] These same factual issues would arise in relation to any purported joint tenancy over a bank account but the question of the presumption of advancement will only arise in relation to bank accounts held jointly between husband and wife or father and child.

26.100 It has been held possible for a husband to rebut the presumption of advancement to his wife in circumstances where he agreed merely to guarantee her bank account.[236] For the wife it would be contended that such a guarantee was to be interpreted as an advancement made by the husband for the wife's benefit. The husband would argue that this was merely a guarantee, that no money had actually been transferred until the wife's account fell into arrears, and that any money spent in that way was intended to be returned to the husband in any event. In a decided case the court accepted that the husband could recover the amount of the guarantee from his wife when it was called in because there had been no intention to make a gift of the sum to her.[237]

26.101 In circumstances in which bank accounts are opened in joint names with the intention that money is to be used jointly, or even jointly and severally, the owners of the account will be joint tenants. In *Re Figgis*[238] Megarry J was called upon to consider joint bank accounts which had been held for fifty years. The accounts in question comprised a current account and a deposit account. Megarry J held that a current account might be held in common for the sake of convenience so that bills and ordinary expenditure could be paid out of it. The deposit account was a different matter because money in that account would usually be held for a longer period of time and only used in capital amount for specific purposes. It would, however, be possible for either type of account to be deemed at a later stage to have become an advancement in favour of the wife if the circumstances of

---

[233] *Jones v Maynard* [1951] Ch 572, [1951] 1 All ER 802; *Rimmer v Rimmer* [1953] 1 QB 63, [1952] 2 All ER 863; *Re Bishop* [1965] Ch 450, [1965] 1 All ER 249.

[234] *Re Cohen* [1953] Ch 88, [1953] 1 All ER 378. Cf *Jones v Maynard* [1951] Ch 572, [1951] 1 All ER 802, *per* Vaisey J to the effect that, if investments were acquired with money from the account in the sole name of one party, then they would be considered to be the sole property of that person.

[235] *Young v Sealey* [1949] Ch 278.   [236] *Anson v Anson* [1953] 1 QB 636.   [237] ibid.

[238] [1969] Ch 123.

the case suggested that that was the better inference. Megarry J held, therefore, that the presumption of advancement should operate in the wife's favour even though the accounts had only been operated by the wife during the First World War and during her husband's final illness. A different result was reached in *Marshall v Crutwell*[239] where the account was opened merely for the sake of convenience and contained only money provided by the husband without there having been any further, material involvement by his wife.[240] Consequently, in this latter case the presumption of advancement was found to have no part to play. The position in relation to portfolio investment products may constitute a different context because, whereas a bank account is considered to retain its character as a chose in action albeit of a fluctuating value, a portfolio of investments will constitute a fluctuating body of property and not simply of fluctuating value, with the consequence that only an account standing for the holding of such investments could be the subject matter of a joint tenancy.[241]

Tax avoidance

The expression 'tax avoidance' connotes the lawful organization of a person's tax affairs so as to reduce his liability to tax. A common tax avoidance strategy is for a taxpayer to transfer property to a family member so as to reduce his own, personal liability to tax. Subsequently, the taxpayer may seek to have that property retransferred to him once the revenue authorities have been satisfied as to its provenance. The family member may refuse to retransfer the property thus requiring the taxpayer to come to court alleging that the property is held on resulting trust for the taxpayer. The problem raised in this regard is, in common with the discussion of *Tinker v Tinker*[242] above,[243] that the taxpayer will have told the Inland Revenue that he has no title in that property but will seek to convince the property law court that the property was nevertheless held on resulting trust for him, with the result that he is seeking to demonstrate two logically incompatible things. It is suggested that Lord Denning's approach in *Tinker v Tinker* is the only possible one: that is, to require the taxpayer either genuinely to give up any title to the property or to accept both equitable ownership of the property and therefore liability for any tax accruing from it. This approach is in accordance with the equitable principle that one cannot rely upon an illegal act, here rendering a false return to the Inland Revenue when one is the owner of property owing a liability in tax, when asserting an equitable claim to property.[244]

26.102

---

[239] (1875) LR 20 Eq 328. See also *Thompson v Thompson* (1970) 114 Sol Jo 455; *Hoddinott v Hoddinott* [1949] 2 KB 406; *Heseltine v Heseltine* [1971] 1 All ER 952.

[240] cf *Re Harrison* [1918] 2 Ch 59.   [241] *Aroso v Coutts & Co* [2001] WTLR 797.

[242] [1970] P 136, [1970] 1 All ER 540.   [243] See para 26.88.

[244] See, for example, the discussion of the principle deriving from *Gascoigne v Gascoigne* [1918] 1 KB 223 below at para 26.107.

26.103 However, there are cases in which the taxpayer has succeeded in putting property beyond the reach of the Inland Revenue initially while establishing an equitable right to property. So, in *Sekhon v Alissa*[245] a mother, who had transferred property into her daughter's name with the intention to evade or avoid liability to capital gains tax, sought to argue that the property should be held on resulting trust for her because she had no intention to benefit her daughter by the transfer. The mother, in the event, did not have to carry out any illegal action in evading liability to tax in respect of the transfer. Therefore, it was held that the mother was entitled to rely on her intention to rebut any argument that she intended to transfer the money outright to her daughter and thus demonstrate that the equitable interest in the house should remain with her on resulting trust. Similarly, in *Heseltine v Heseltine*[246] a wife successfully transferred property to her husband in a manner which avoided liability to estate duty but was taken by the court to have intended to commit no wrong and therefore to be entitled to enforce a resulting trust over that property against her husband. It remains unclear whether there is a presumption of gift in cases involving mother and daughter which mirrors the established rule in cases between father and child. It would appear that there remains a distinction in relation to the operation of the presumptions between transfers from fathers and those from mothers which is difficult to explain in the modern context.

26.104 In *Shephard v Cartwright*,[247] in circumstances in which a father divided shares in his successful companies between his three children, the issue arose as to whether those transfers of shares constituted advancements or whether the father was entitled to rely on his intention to divide them between his children so as to reduce the amount of tax payable on dividends declared over those shares. In that context Viscount Simonds held that the father could not pray in aid his subsequent treatment of the shares and the dividends, nor could he rely on the fact that the children signed documents at their father's instruction plainly without understanding what those documents meant. In consequence, the father's executors were required to hold the shares on trust for the children to give effect to the presumed advancement.

26.105 The decision in *Shephard* can be contrasted with that in *Warren v Gurney*[248] in which a father bought a house which was conveyed into his daughter Catherine's name prior to her marriage. The father retained the title deeds to the property (which title deeds Morton LJ accepted were 'the sinews of the land', thus adopting Coke's phrase) and this the court took to indicate that the father did not intend to part with all of the rights in the house in favour of Catherine. Rather, the father had written a document headed 'my wish' which purported to have the house divided equally between his three daughters. The court took the retention

---

[245] [1989] 2 FLR 94.   [246] [1971] 1 All ER 952.   [247] [1955] AC 431.
[248] [1944] 2 All ER 472.

of the title deeds and the document together to rebut any presumption of advancement in favour of Catherine. In consequence Catherine was deemed to hold the house on resulting trust for her father. The difference between these two cases is difficult to isolate in the abstract. Rather it is only on the facts of each individual set of facts that one can consider them and one must put oneself in the position of the judge deciding that particular case on the basis of the evidence presented to him.

The situation of tax avoidance should now be considered in the light of the doctrine in *Furniss v Dawson*,[249] whereby the court will ignore artificial steps which form part of a scheme designed solely to avoid tax. The courts' reluctance to support tax avoidance schemes is also evident from the decision in *Vandervell v IRC*.[250]   **26.106**

F. Illegality and Resulting Trust

Seeking to establish proprietary rights under resulting trust but not coming to equity with clean hands

The law of trusts is predicated on the notion of good conscience.[251] Consequently,   **26.107** there will be a problem in circumstances in which a person who has acted unconscionably, for example in committing an illegal act, wishes to have an equitable interest, such as a resulting trust, declared in his favour. In short the problem in this context is this: where a person seeks to rebut the presumption of advancement but is required to rely on some illegal or unlawful act to demonstrate the existence of that resulting trust, will that illegality preclude the operation of the equitable resulting trust? The illegality usually arises in situations in which the claimant was seeking to put property beyond the reach of his creditors, or to defraud some other person, by purporting to transfer that property to an associate and pretending as a result that he had no rights in that property. Once the illegal purpose has been carried out or once it becomes clear that he will not have to carry out his illegal purpose, the claimant will seek to recover title in the property. No resulting trust will arise over property in favour of a person who has committed an illegal act in relation to that property.[252] Suppose, for example, that a husband had transferred property to his wife with the intention of putting that property unlawfully beyond the reach of his creditors, could the husband claim that the presumption should be rebutted in favour of a resulting trust? It is a core principle of equity that one who comes to equity (for example, to prove a resulting trust) must come with

---

[249] [1984] AC 474.   [250] [1967] 2 AC 291.
[251] *Westdeutsche Landesbank v Islington* [1996] AC 669, see para 1.04.
[252] *Tinsley v Milligan* [1994] 1 AC 340; *Tribe v Tribe* [1995] 3 WLR 913. See also *Ali v Khan* [2002] EWCA Civ 974 and *Halley v Law Society* [2003] EWCA Civ 97, [2003] WTLR 845.

clean hands.[253] In consequence equity will not, in general terms, permit a resulting trust in circumstances in which the claimant was required to rely on an illegal act to prove the existence of that resulting trust. Therefore, the presumption of advancement would apply, or else the common law title would be decisive of the question.[254] Recent cases have seemed to dilute this principle, however, in situations in which the proprietary interest expressed in the form of the resulting trust can be established without relying on an illegal purpose,[255] or where an intended illegal purpose is inadvertently not carried out.[256]

Resulting trust allowed where illegality not required to demonstrate the proprietary interest

The principle that equity will not award a resulting trust to those who come to equity without clean hands

26.108 Equity will not intervene to find an equitable interest on resulting trust in favour of a person who had transferred property away in furtherance of an illegal purpose. This is an extension of the core equitable principle that 'he who comes to equity must come with clean hands'.[257] This principle is illustrated by the decision in *Gascoigne v Gascoigne*[258] where the court automatically effected the presumption of advancement in connection with the transfer of property by a husband to his wife with the intention of avoiding creditors. The claimant had leased land and built a house on it using his own money. The property was transferred into the name of his wife with the intention of eluding his creditors. This transfer raised the presumption of advancement which the claimant was required to rebut to demonstrate that his wife was intended to hold the property on resulting trust for the claimant. The only reference to actual fraud in the judgment of Lush J was that the plaintiff had refused to pay taxes in respect of the land on the basis that it belonged equitably and in law to his wife, the defendant. It was held, however, that the court would not allow a transferor to rely on an illegal or fraudulent purpose to rebut the presumption of advancement and establish an entitlement to the imposition of an equitable interest under a resulting trust. This approach was adopted as an instinctive response by the courts in these types of case to the effect that a person 'is not entitled to rely on his own fraud or illegality in order to assist a claim or rebut a presumption'.[259]

---

[253] *Jones v Lenthal* (1669) 1 Ch Cas 154; *Evroy v Nicholas* (1733) 2 Eq Ca Abr 488; *Coatsworth v Johnson* (1886) 54 LT 520; *Guinness v Saunders* [1990] 2 WLR 324; *Quadrant Visual Communications v Hutchison Telephone* [1993] BCLC 442.
[254] *Muckleston v Brown* (1801) 6 Ves 52.   [255] *Tinsley v Milligan* [1994] 1 AC 340.
[256] *Tribe v Tribe* [1995] 3 WLR 913.
[257] *Jones v Lenthal* (1669) 1 Ch Cas 154; *Evroy v Nicholas* (1733) 2 Eq Ca Abr 488; *Coatsworth v Johnson* (1886) 54 LT 520; *Guinness v Saunders* [1990] 2 WLR 324; *Quadrant Visual Communications v Hutchison Telephone* [1993] BCLC 442.   [258] [1918] 1 KB 223.
[259] *Tinsley v Milligan* [1994] 1 AC 340, [1993] 3 All ER 65, *per* Lord Jauncey. See also *Chettiar v Chettiar* [1962] AC 294, 302, [1962] 1 All ER 494, 498; *Tinker v Tinker* [1970] 2 WLR 136, 143, *per* Salmon LJ.

The long-established principles of equity in this context were subtly redrawn by **26.109**
the House of Lords in the case of *Tinsley v Milligan*.[260] The appeal concerned a
couple who had concocted a fraudulent scheme to ensure that one of them would
receive state benefits to which she would not otherwise have been entitled.
Milligan and Tinsley used the house as a lodging house which they ran as a joint
business venture. This business provided the bulk of both parties' income. The
property was registered in the sole name of Tinsley although both parties accepted
that the property was owned jointly in equity. The purpose for the registration in
Tinsley's sole name was to enable Milligan to claim state benefits with Tinsley's full
knowledge and assent. The relationship broke down and Tinsley moved out.
Tinsley claimed absolute title to the house. Milligan claimed that the house was
held on trust for the parties in equal shares. Tinsley argued that Milligan would be
required to rely on her illegal conduct to establish this claim and that equity
should not therefore operate to give Milligan the benefits of her wrongdoing. It
was held that Milligan was entitled to an equitable interest in the property on
resulting trust in proportion to her contribution to the purchase price.[261] In short
the rationale for this decision was that Milligan was able to prove that her interest
arose from the contribution to the purchase price (a lawful act) and not from the
fraud on the social security system (an unlawful act). That thinking requires some
closer examination.

In *Tinsley v Milligan* Lord Browne-Wilkinson held that the following were the **26.110**
core applicable principles:

(1) Property in chattels and land can pass under a contract which is illegal and therefore
would have been unenforceable as a contract.
(2) A plaintiff can at law enforce property rights so acquired provided that he does
not need to rely on the illegal contract for any purpose other than providing the
basis of his claim to a property right.
(3) It is irrelevant that the illegality of the underlying agreement was either pleaded
or emerged in evidence: if the plaintiff has acquired legal title under the illegal
contract that is enough.

His lordship considered the long-standing principle of Lord Eldon in *Muckleston
v Brown*[262] that, in cases where the plaintiff seeks to rely on illegality to establish a
trust, the proper response is to say 'let the estate lie, where it falls' with the owner
at common law rather than holding it on resulting trust. However, his lordship
found that the earlier cases also showed that the plaintiff ought to be entitled to
rely on a resulting trust where she did not have to rely on her illegality to prove
it.[263] Relying on principles of trusts of homes set out in *Gissing v Gissing*[264] and
Lloyds Bank v Rosset,[265] Milligan was able to argue that she had acquired an

---

[260] [1994] 1 AC 340.   [261] *Dyer v Dyer* (1788) 2 Cox Eq Cas 92.
[262] (1801) 6 Ves 52, 68–69.   [263] *Ali v Khan* [2002] EWCA Civ 974.
[264] [1971] AC 886.   [265] [1991] 1 AC 107; see para 56.24.

equitable interest in the property. The illegality was raised by Tinsley in seeking to rebut Milligan's claim. Milligan did not have to rely on her own illegality because she was entitled to an equitable share in the property in any event because she had contributed to the purchase price. The illegality was therefore not the *source* of her equitable rights: rather her contribution to the purchase price was the source of those rights.

26.111 Lord Browne-Wilkinson did describe the cases on trusts of homes as establishing the rule that the 'creation of such an equitable interest does not depend upon a contractual obligation but on a common intention acted upon by the parties to their detriment'. The form of trust which his lordship appears to have in mind is a common intention constructive trust [266] rather than a resulting trust as normally understood. It is submitted that the appropriate form of trust on the facts was a purchase price resulting trust arising from Milligan's contribution to the acquisition of the property. To return to the earlier discussion of the nature of resulting trusts, it does appear that his lordship is seeking to develop a resulting trust based on 'the common intention of the parties' rather than one which, *strictu sensu*, gives effect to the intention of the settlor alone. The whole drift of the law on resulting trust is therefore moving towards the establishment of remedial and discretionary principles rather than straightforward operation of legal principle.

The dissenting view: denying a resulting trust as part of a larger transaction involving an illegal purpose

26.112 The dissenting speech of Lord Goff in *Tinsley v Milligan* cited a number of authorities including *Tinker v Tinker*[267] and *Re Emery*[268] as establishing the proposition that equity will not assist someone who transfers property to another in furtherance of a fraudulent or illegal design to establish an interest in the property disposed of. This approach is founded primarily on the ancient equitable maxim that 'he who comes to equity must come with clean hands' and the fear that an extension of principle propounded by Lord Browne-Wilkinson would 'open the door to far more unmeritorious cases'. While there is a moral attraction to this approach, it does not deal with the fundamental property law issue 'who else can assert title to the property?'[269] Where the recipient has knowledge of the illegality bound up in the transfer, then there would appear to be no objection to removing any proprietary rights transferred. However, where there was no intention to transfer rights absolutely to the recipient, it would appear to cut to the heart of the nature of the resulting trust if the intentions of the settlor are not to be observed. Indeed the distinction between

---

[266] See para 56.24.　　[267] [1970] 2 WLR 331.　　[268] [1959] Ch 410.
[269] Furthermore, Tinsley would have acquired complete title in this property despite being a conspirator in Milligan's illegal actions thus making it equally undesirable that Milligan's rights be ignored.

Lords Goff and Browne-Wilkinson is that the former prefers a moral approach to the law whereas the latter prefers an approach based on an amoral intellectual rigour.

The question of intention and the failure of the illegal purpose

As a further dilution to the notion that one must come to equity with clean hands, **26.113** the courts have accepted that even where there was an intention to carry out an illegal act there might nevertheless be a resulting trust if the illegal purpose was not carried through. This principle does draw on older dicta of Lord Romilly MR : [270]

> Where the purpose for which the assignment was given is not carried into execution, and nothing is done under it, the mere intention to effect an illegal object when the assignment was executed does not deprive the assignor of his right to recover the property from the assignee who has given no consideration for it.

Remarkably, the failure to carry out the illegal purpose might have been inadvertent and not the result of a change of heart by the person who had intended to carry that purpose into effect. So, in *Tribe v Tribe* [271] T owned 459 out of a total of 500 shares in a family company. He was also the tenant of two leases used by the family company as licensees for the conduct of its business. The lessor served a notice of dilapidations on T which, it appeared at the time, would have required T to meet the cost of extensive works on the properties. T was advised that the costs of these works could lead him to lose the assets of the business and would cause him to go into bankruptcy. To avoid liability to his creditors, T purported to sell his shares in the family business to his son for £78,030. To put your assets beyond the reach of creditors in expectation of bankruptcy in this way was an illegal act. T transferred the shares to his son. In the event, no money was actually paid by the son in consideration for the transfer of the shares. Meanwhile, the lessor agreed to a surrender of the lease which meant that T was not required to sell any assets to repair the property or to satisfy his creditors. T then sought to recover his shares once he knew that his creditors would not need access to them but T's son refused to retransfer the shares to his father.

The issue arose whether the shares were held on resulting trust for T or whether **26.114** the presumption of advancement should lead the court to find that equitable ownership had been passed to T's son. T was therefore required to plead his own illegal act (that is, intentionally putting his assets beyond the reach of his creditors) to rebut the presumption of advancement. The Court of Appeal held that T was entitled to a resulting trust in his favour because his illegal purpose had not been carried into effect. The lessor had not required T to pay for refurbishment works which would have put T into insolvency and therefore T had not had any

---

[270] *Symes v Hughes* (1870) LR 9 Eq 475. Cf *Chettiar v Chettiar* [1962] AC 294, [1962] 1 All ER 494, PC. [271] [1995] 4 All ER 236; [1995] 3 WLR 913; [1995] 2 FLR 966.

creditors on insolvency to deceive. Therefore, despite T doing acts in the full expectation that they would turn out to be illegal acts, T was entitled to rebut the presumption of advancement to his son because he had not actually carried through his illegal purpose by staying solvent.

26.115   The current status of the law is set out in the judgment of Millett LJ in *Tribe v Tribe*:

(1) Title to property passes both at law and in equity even if the transfer is made for an illegal purpose. The fact that title has passed to the transferee does not preclude the transferor from bringing an action for restitution.

(2) The Transferor's action will fail if it would be illegal for him to retain any interest in the property.

(3) Subject to (2) the transferor can recover the property if he can do so without relying on the illegal purpose. This will normally be the case where the property was transferred without consideration in circumstances where the transferor can rely on an express declaration of trust or a resulting trust in his favour.

(4) It will almost invariably be so where the illegal purpose has not been carried out. It may be otherwise where the illegal purpose has been carried out and the transferee can rely on the transferor's conduct as inconsistent with his retention of a beneficial interest.

(5) The transferor can lead evidence of the illegal purpose whenever it is necessary for him to do so provided that he has withdrawn from the transaction before the illegal purpose has been wholly or partly carried in to effect. It will be necessary for him to do so (i) if he brings an action at law or (ii) if he brings proceedings in equity and needs to rebut the presumption of advancement.

(6) The only way in which a man can protect his property from his creditors is by divesting himself of all beneficial interest in it. Evidence that he transferred the property in order to protect it from his creditors, therefore, does nothing by itself to rebut the presumption of advancement; it reinforces it. To rebut the presumption it is necessary to show that he intended to retain a beneficial interest and conceal it from his creditors.

(7) The court should not conclude that this was his intention without compelling circumstantial evidence to this effect. The identity of the transferee and the circumstances in which the transfer was made would be highly relevant. It is unlikely that the court would reach such a conclusion where the transfer was made in the absence of an imminent and perceived threat from known creditors.

This new approach does not repudiate the equitable principle that 'he who comes to equity must come with clean hands', rather it looks to the factual question of whether or not an illegal purpose has actually been performed as opposed to examining simply the question as to what the claimant intended to do: it could be said that equity in this context now looks to the *actus reus* and not to the *mens rea*, to the question of what has actually been done and not to the question of what the claimant sought to do. If the illegal purpose were carried into effect, then there would not be a resulting trust.[272] Consequently, this statement of the law relating

---

[272]   *Collier v Collier* [2002] EWCA Civ 1095.

to resulting trusts and illegality still applies the principle in *Gascoigne v Gascoigne*[273] that a claimant cannot rely on an illegal act in seeking to establish a resulting trust. What is important to rebut the finding of a resulting trust is that there is a direct link between the interest sought under the resulting trust and the illegal act. What is plain is that the equitable principle here is being drawn very tightly. The ancient principle that 'he who comes to equity must come with clean hands' is being adapted by Lord Browne-Wilkinson's more focused approach in *Tinsley v Milligan* identifying the source of the interest under resulting trust and seeing if that flows directly from an illegal act. Lord Goff favoured a more broad-brush approach which required action in good faith throughout, in line with the classical understanding of the principles of equity.

Conveyances of property, illegality, and fraud

In *Tinsley v Milligan* Lord Jauncey held that:[274]   **26.116**

> ... it has, however, for some years been recognised that a completely executed trans-fer of property or of an interest in property made in pursuance of an unlawful agree-ment is valid and the court will assist the transferee in the protection of his interest provided that he does not require to found on the unlawful agreement.

A presumption of a resulting trust may be supported to rebut the defendant's con-tention that a transfer of property was not intended to be a gift even though that rebuttal was dependent upon an illegal purpose.[275] The general principle remains, however, that no title to property can be maintained if the person asserting that claim must rely on an illegality to make it out.[276]

From the discussion of *Tribe v Tribe*[277] in the previous section it is clear that an illegal   **26.117** design will not vitiate a transfer nor will it preclude the imposition of a resulting trust if the illegal purpose is not carried into effect.[278] This principle has been applied so as to permit a finding of a resulting trust thus returning property to their original own-ers in situations in which a man considered that he would forfeit property because he had mistakenly thought he would be guilty of bigamy,[279] and in which a man mis-takenly thought that he would be forced into bankruptcy by business debts. If the ille-gal purpose were effected, however, then there would not be a resulting trust.[280]

---

[273] [1918] 1 KB 223. See also *McEvoy v Belfast Banking Co Ltd* [1934] NI 67; *Re Emery's Investments' Trusts* [1959] Ch 410, [1959] 1 All ER 577.

[274] [1994] 1 AC 340, [1993] 3 All ER 65, citing in support: *Ayerst v Jenkins* (1873) LR 16 Eq 275. See also *Alexander v Rayson* [1936] 1 KB 169; *Bowmakers Ltd v Marnet Instruments Ltd* [1945] KB 65; *Sajan Singh v Sardara Ali* [1960] AC 167.

[275] *Silverwood v Silverwood* (1997) 74 P & CR 453.

[276] *Lowson v Coombes* [1999] Ch 373; [1999] Conv 242 (M Thompson); [1999] LMCLQ 465 (I Cotterill).   [277] [1995] 4 All ER 236; [1995] 3 WLR 913.

[278] *Symes v Hughes* (1870) LR 9 Eq 475.

[279] *Davies v Otty (No 2)* (1865) 35 Beav 208. Cf *Sekhon v Alissa* [1989] 2 FLR 94; *Rowan v Dann* (1991) 64 P & CR 202.   [280] *Collier v Collier* [2002] EWCA Civ 1095.

Where a settlement is created for an illegal consideration

26.118 No contract created to carry out an illegal purpose will be enforceable under the law of contract.[281] On the decided cases there were settlements, such as a marriage settlement, which were created in consideration for some illegal act. The best known of these cases was *Ayerst v Jenkins*[282] in which a widower wished to marry his deceased wife's sister. To encourage her into the marriage, it seemed, he made a settlement in the woman's favour. For the widower to have married his sister-in-law would have been illegal at the time, being an unlawful marriage. In consequence, the settlement was effected, it was alleged, for an unlawful consideration. It was held by the House of Lords that equity would not support an illegal purpose in the following terms:

> Relief is sought by the [widower's personal] representative, not merely of a particeps criminis, but of a voluntary and sole donor, on the naked ground of the illegality of his own intention and purpose. . . I know of no doctrine of public policy which requires, or authorises, a court of equity to give assistance to such a plaintiff under such circumstances. When the immediate or direct effect of an estoppel in equity against relief to a particular plaintiff might be to effectuate an unlawful object, or to defeat a legal prohibition, or to protect a fraud, such an estoppel may well be regarded as against public policy.[283]

The decision in *Tinsley v Milligan*, however, has opened the possibility that a contract or arrangement formed as part of a larger, illegal transaction might nevertheless attract equity's support provided that the property rights at issue were acquired lawfully. Similarly, if it can be demonstrated that the defendant sought to transfer the legal estate in land to enable the transferee to raise money on its security, then the equity of redemption in the property is held on a resulting trust for the transferor.[284]

Illegality under the Insolvency Act 1986 and resulting trust

26.119 One of the more common forms of illegality in this context is the avoidance of creditors when the transferor fears bankruptcy. Under section 423 of the Insolvency Act 1986, the court is empowered to reverse any action which puts assets beyond the reach of creditors with the intention of avoiding or weakening their claims. The section also covers sales at an undervalue in this context. The most important recent case in this context was that of *Midland Bank v Wyatt*,[285] in which Mr Wyatt had decided to set up a textile business which subsequently ran

---

[281] *Holman v Johnson* (1775) 1 Cowp 341, 343, *per* Lord Mansfield CJ; *Pearce v Brooks* (1866) LR 1 Exch 213, 217, *per* Pollock CB; *Alexander v Rayson* [1936] 1 KB 169, 182; *Bowmakers Ltd v Marnet Instruments Ltd* [1945] KB 65.

[282] (1873) LR 16 Eq 275. See also *Alexander v Rayson* [1936] 1 KB 169; *Bowmakers Ltd v Marnet Instruments Ltd* [1945] KB 65; *Sajan Singh v Sardara Ali* [1960] AC 167.

[283] (1873) LR 16 Eq 275, *per* Lord Selborne.

[284] *Haigh v Kaye* (1872) LR 7 Ch 473; *Re Duke of Marlborough* [1894] 2 Ch 133; *Ali v Khan* [2002] EWCA Civ 974.   [285] [1995] 1 FLR 697.

into financial problems, thus driving him to perform illegal acts to put his personal property beyond the reach of his creditors. The family home had been bought in 1981 and registered in the joint names of Mr Wyatt and his wife; the house was subject to a mortgage in favour of Midland Bank. From the outset, Mr Wyatt considered his textiles venture to be commercially risky and therefore created an express trust in 1987, on advice from his solicitor, under which his interest in the family home was held by him on trust for his wife and two daughters. Mr Wyatt was subsequently divorced from his wife in 1989. The business went into receivership in 1991. Mr Wyatt had used the house as security for a number of loans for his ailing business after 1987. All the lenders and creditors were unaware of the trust, thinking that the equitable interest was held by both Mr and Mrs Wyatt. Interestingly, Mrs Wyatt's solicitors were not made aware of the express trust when preparing the divorce arrangements. Midland Bank sought a charging order over the family home against Mr Wyatt's interest in the house. Mr Wyatt argued that the house was held on the terms of the express trust declared in 1987 and that the bank could not therefore realize its purported security. The bank contended that the trust was either void as a sham or voidable further to section 423 of the Insolvency Act 1986.

It was held that it was not necessary to establish a fraudulent motive to show that **26.120** there is a sham. Nor was it necessary to show that the declaration of trust should have no effect. It would be enough to set aside the purported express trust that, acting on mistaken advice, the transaction was not in substance what it appeared to be on its face. On the facts, it was clear that at the time of creating the trust Mr Wyatt had no intention of endowing his wife or the children with his interest in the house. This was demonstrated by the fact that Mr Wyatt continued to treat the house as being entirely his own and by the fact that his wife's solicitors were unaware of the purported express trust. Rather, the purpose of the transaction was to provide a safeguard against the commercial risk of the business. The transaction was therefore not what it purported to be. As such it must be held to have been a sham. Consequently, the express trust was held to have been void and unenforceable.

The transaction in *Midland Bank v Wyatt* was also capable of being rendered void **26.121** under section 423 of the 1986 Act because it sought to transfer the property gratuitously to Mrs Wyatt and the children with the purpose of avoiding creditors. The shortcoming with this second point is that there were no specific creditors which were to have been avoided. It is not evident how one could draw the line between a lawful arrangement of one's affairs and an unlawful avoidance of hitherto unknown, potential creditors. In applying the rule in *Re Butterworth*[286] it was held not necessary to show that the sole motive of the settlement was the avoidance of creditors. It was sufficient that such motive was one of a number of

---

[286] (1882) 19 Ch D 588.

identifiable motives. It would appear that all is to be presumed against the bankrupt and in favour of the creditors in an insolvency situation.

26.122   The decision in *Midland Bank v Wyatt*[287] confirmed the decision in *Re Butterworth*[288] that the creditors whom the defendant sought to avoid need not have been creditors at the time of the transaction which sought to put property beyond their reach: it is sufficient that they become creditors after the transfer or sale at an undervalue. In this case it was sufficient that the trust was purportedly created with the intention of avoiding any creditors, whether current or prospective creditors. There is no need that the transaction be dishonest; it is sufficient that there was intention to put assets out of the reach of creditors. In relation to a claim to establish a resulting trust, it is possible to set aside a transfer as a sham transfer and establish a resulting trust instead. From the point of view of a creditor in a bankruptcy, the creditor will be entitled to any property held in the bankrupt's estate. It is consequently in the creditor's best interests to demonstrate that the bankrupt has property held on resulting trust for him because a bankrupt is required to transfer to the creditors any property in which the bankrupt has beneficial title. Using section 423 of the Insolvency Act 1986 the court has the power to recognize that property may continue to be vested in the bankrupt's estate so that it can be realized in the administration of the bankruptcy in satisfaction of the creditor's rights. The means by which the property is recognized as remaining a part of the bankrupt's estate is the recognition of a resulting trust.

26.123   This case illustrates the difficult line between organizing your affairs legitimately so that the failure of a business does not mean losing your house and personal property, and creating unlawful arrangements to outwit your creditors once you have realized that your business is on the brink of insolvency. This case also indicates the ability of the court to look behind sham transactions where necessary in this context.

Attempts to avoid the rule against perpetuities and accumulations

26.124   No trust which seeks to avoid the rule against perpetuities or against remoteness of vesting will be lawful. So, for example, in circumstances in which a settlor purports to evade those rules by means of specifying an unlawful perpetuities period, it was held that the trust property would be held on resulting trust for the settlor's estate from the end of the lawful perpetuities period.[289] The underlying purpose of the imposition of a resulting trust in this regard is to prevent the circumvention of the law and thus to prevent the trustees from holding the trust property for the purposes originally identified by the settlor so as to breach the perpetuities rules.[290]

---

[287] [1995] 1 FLR 697; [1995] 3 FCR 11.   [288] (1882) 19 Ch D 588.
[289] *Re Travis* [1900] 2 Ch 541.
[290] *Carrick v Errington* (1726) 2 P Wms 361; *Tregonwell v Sydenham* (1815) 3 Dow 194; *Gibbs v Rumsey* (1813) 2 Ves & B 294.

27

CONSTRUCTIVE TRUSTS IN RESPONSE TO UNCONSCIONABLE BEHAVIOUR

A. The General Constructive Trust

Constructive trusts arising from knowledge of some factor affecting the defendant's conscience

27.01 A constructive trust is generally said to arise by operation of law.[1] By that is meant that a constructive trust arises automatically, retrospectively from the time of the circumstances which gave rise to it, and consequently without the discretion of the court; in a word, that it arises on an 'institutional'[2] or substantive[3] basis.[4] The constructive trusts which are considered in this chapter and in Chapters 28 through 30 arise on a variety of bases. The common principle running through all of these species of constructive trust is that the liability of any person to act as a constructive trustee is predicated on that person having knowledge of some factor which is deemed to affect their conscience sufficiently to justify the imposition of that office.[5]

27.02 Constructive trusts, it is suggested, can be observed as arising in any of the categories as set out below. However, it is also suggested that constructive trusts are not confined to those categories but rather can arise *sui generis* on the basis of a principle of general application, as set out by Lord Browne-Wilkinson in *Westdeutsche Landesbank v Islington*[6] on the basis that a proprietary constructive trust will be imposed on any person who knows that her actions in respect of specific property are unconscionable.[7] Such unconscionable behaviour is more difficult to define: examples are given in the discussion to follow. The property at issue may be property already held on trust, or may be property in relation to which the defendant already occupies a fiduciary position[8] or property in relation to which the defendant is deemed to come to occupy a fiduciary position,[9] or it may be property

---

[1] See, for example, J Mowbray et al, *Lewin on Trusts* (17th edn, Sweet & Maxwell, 2000) ('*Lewin*') 181; J Martin, *Hanbury and Martin's Modern Equity* (16th edn, Sweet & Maxwell, 2001) ('*Martin*') 297; A Oakley, *Parker and Mellows' The Modern Law of Trusts* (8th edn, Sweet & Maxwell, 2003) ('*Parker and Mellows*') 312. By contrast see A Underhill and DJ Hayton, *Law of Trusts and Trustees* (16th edn, Butterworths, 2002) ('*Underhill and Hayton*') 323, which identifies instead the various contexts in which constructive trusts arise, as opposed to commencing with the bald statement that constructive trusts arise by operation of law.
[2] RH Maudsley, ' Proprietary Remedies for the Recovery of Money' (1959) 75 LQR 234, 237.
[3] R Pound, 'The Progress of Law' (1920) 33 Harv L Rev 420, 421.
[4] RH Maudsley, 'Proprietary Remedies for the Recovery of Money' (1959) 75 LQR 234.
[5] *Westdeutsche Landesbank Girozentrale v Islington LBC* [1996] AC 669; *French v Mason* The Times, 13 November 1998; *Paragon Finance v DB Thackerar & Co* [1999] 1 All ER 400, 408, per Millett LJ. This general principle is identified as being the core of the constructive trust in AS Hudson, *Equity & Trusts* (3rd edn, Cavendish Publishing, 2003) ('*Hudson*') 347; P Pettit, *Equity and Trusts* (9th edn, Butterworths, 2001) ('*Pettit*') 135.   [6] [1996] AC 669.
[7] *Westdeutsche Landesbank Girozentrale v Islington LBC* [1996] AC 669.
[8] For example, *Boardman v Phipps* ([1967] 2 AC 46) where the defendant was held to have occupied a fiduciary relationship in relation to the trust fund before dealing with that property (including, possibly, confidential information said to form part of the trust's assets).
[9] For example, *Attorney-General for Hong Kong v Reid* ([1944] 1 AC 324, [1993] 3 WLR 1143) where the defendant was found to be constructive trustee of bribes received in the performance of

which has never been voluntarily transferred by its owner to its recipient.[10] It is important that the trustee has knowledge of the unconscionability of the treatment of that property. This issue is separate from the distinction between *in rem* and *in personam* rights. For the imposition of a proprietary constructive trust, the legal owner of property will be liable if she has knowledge of some factor which affects the conscionability of asserting beneficial title to that property.[11]

The observable species of constructive trust

Broadly speaking, constructive trusts arise in four contexts: in response to unconscionable behaviour in general terms, considered in this chapter;[12] to enforce agreements (whether in the form of legally enforceable contracts or non-contractual, voluntarily assumed liability), considered in Chapter 28;[13] in response to abuse of fiduciary position, considered in Chapter 29;[14] and where strangers to the trust are construed to be personally liable to account to the beneficiaries as though trustees under an express trust, considered in Chapter 30.[15] The discussions of these various categories of constructive trust have been broken into separate chapters for ease of reference in what would otherwise become a very long single chapter. That they have been separated in this way is not intended to dilute the central concept that constructive trusts arise on the basis of the intellectual kernel considered in this chapter of the defendant's knowledge of some factor which affects his conscience in relation to the treatment or use of property. **27.03**

The general potential application of the constructive trust

This section considers the manner in which constructive trusts may be said to come into existence in general terms and not necessarily only the limited categories considered in the remainder of this chapter. That is to say the constructive trust will arise in general terms to enforce the conscience of a defendant in relation to that defendant's treatment of either the claimant's property or the abuse of some fiduciary duty owed to the claimant.[16] Section 53(2) of the Law of Property Act 1925 provides that 'implied[17] resulting[18] or constructive trusts' do not require **27.04**

---

a public office: that public office was held to have been a fiduciary office, *infra*, and the property over which the constructive trust took effect was property which had never belonged previously to the objects of the fiduciary office nor to the fiduciary before its payment to him by way of a bribe.

[10] For example, in a case of theft where the thief is taken to be a constructive trustee of the stolen property: *Westdeutsche Landesbank v Islington* [1996] AC 669.

[11] *Westdeutsche Landesbank Girozentrale v Islington LBC* [1996] AC 669.

[12] See para 27.05. [13] See para 28.01. [14] See para 29.01. [15] See para 30.01.

[16] A policy evident in the line of cases from *Keech v Sandford* (1726) Sel Cas Ch 61 through *Boardman v Phipps* [1967] 2 AC 46, and in *Attorney-General for Hong Kong v Reid* [1994] 1 AC 324, [1993] 3 WLR 1143. [17] See para 25.41. [18] See Chapter 26 generally.

formalities in their creation. Rather the constructive trust is recognized as coming into existence by operation of law. It is therefore important to recognize the principles upon which such constructive trusts may come into existence in general terms.

Constructive trusts are based on the knowledge and the conscience of the trustee

27.05 The most detailed recent statement of the core principles in the area of trusts implied by law was made by Lord Browne-Wilkinson in *Westdeutsche Landesbank v Islington*[19] where his lordship went back to basics: identifying the root of any form of trust as being in policing the good conscience of the defendant. The first of his lordship's 'Relevant Principles of Trust Law' was identified as being that:

> (i) Equity operates on the conscience of the owner of the legal interest. In the case of a trust, the conscience of the legal owner requires him to carry out the purposes for which the property was vested in him (express or implied trust) or which the law imposes on him by reason of his unconscionable conduct (constructive trust).[20]

This notion of the conscience of the legal owner is said to underpin all trusts. It is suggested that it operates as the main underpinning principle in relation to all constructive trusts. A defendant is construed to be a trustee in relation to specified property in circumstances in which, as legal owner of that property, that person acts contrary to good conscience. This, it is suggested, is the core of the notion of the trust and is furthermore at the root of the equitable jurisdiction when it acts *in personam* against an individual defendant: not in the sense of imposing only personal rights and obligations but rather in the sense of concerning itself with the good conscience of that individual, in isolation from the common law or statute, and so justifying the imposition of proprietary obligations in the ways considered below. His lordship continued with his second principle of the law of trusts:

> (ii) Since the equitable jurisdiction to enforce trusts depends upon the conscience of the holder of the legal interest being affected, he cannot be a trustee of the property if and so long as he is ignorant of the facts alleged to affect his conscience, ie until he is aware that he is intended to hold the property for the benefit of others in the case of an express or implied trust, or, in the case of a constructive trust, of the factors which are alleged to affect his conscience.[21]

As a result of the requirement that the conscience of the holder of the legal interest is affected 'he cannot be a trustee of the property if and so long as he is ignorant of the facts alleged to affect his conscience'. Therefore, the defendant must have knowledge of the factors which are suggested to give rise to the constructive trust.[22]

---

[19] *Westdeutsche Landesbank Girozentrale v Islington LBC* [1994] 4 All ER 890, Hobhouse J, CA; and reversed on appeal [1996] AC 669, HL.   [20] [1996] AC 669, [1996] 2 All ER 961, 988.
[21] [1996] AC 669, [1996] 2 All ER 961, 988.   [22] [1996] 2 All ER 961, 988.

Lord Browne-Wilkinson has considered the difference between proprietary and personal claims in the following passage from his leading speech in *Westdeutsche Landesbank v Islington*, in which a bank was seeking (*inter alia*) to establish a constructive trust over money it had paid to a local authority (emphasis added):

> The bank contended that where, *under a pre-existing* trust, B is entitled to an equitable interest in trust property, if the trust property comes into the hands of a third party, X (not being a purchaser for value of the legal interest without notice), B is entitled to enforce his equitable interest against the property in the hands of X because X is a trustee for B. In my view the third party, X, is not necessarily a trustee for B: B's equitable right is enforceable against the property in just the same way as any other specifically enforceable equitable right can be enforced against a third party. Even if the third party, X, is not aware that what he has received is trust property B is entitled to assert his title in that property. If X has the necessary degree of knowledge, X may himself become a constructive trustee for B on the basis of knowing receipt. But unless he has the requisite knowledge he is not personally liable to account as trustee.[23] Therefore, innocent receipt of property by X subject to an existing equitable interest does not by itself make X a trustee despite the severance of the legal and equitable titles. *Underhill and Hayton, Law of Trusts and Trustees*,[24] whilst accepting that X is under no personal liability to account unless and until he becomes aware of B's rights, does describe X as being a constructive trustee. This may only be a question of semantics: on either footing, in the present case the local authority could not have become accountable for profits until it knew that the contract was void.

Thus, there will be no constructive trust without knowledge of the matters said to affect one's conscience.[25]

27.06 The example given by Lord Browne-Wilkinson in his leading speech in *Westdeutsche Landesbank v Islington*[26] was the factual matrix from the earlier case of *Chase Manhattan v Israel-British Bank*.[27] The decision of Goulding J in the *Chase Manhattan* case had long been a cause for controversy and had been taken variously as demonstrating a tentative exploration of the principle of unjust enrichment in this area of the law [28] and as a form of remedial constructive trust.[29] Lord Browne-Wilkinson instead took the opportunity to explain the general application of the constructive trust by explaining his preferred analysis of the factual matrix in *Chase Manhattan v Israel-British Bank*. In that case, Chase Manhattan made a payment perfectly properly to the Israel-British Bank. Mistakenly, however, that same payment was made a second time. Between the making of the first payment and Chase Manhattan's attempt to recover the second

---

[23] *In re Diplock; Diplock v Wintle* [1948] Ch 465, 478; *In re Montagu's Settlement Trusts* [1987] Ch 264.   [24] *Underhill and Hayton*, in the 15th edn, 369–370.

[25] See the discussion at para 33.67 in relation to the requirement of knowledge, however, in relation to constructive trusts imposed in response to equitable tracing claims.

[26] [1996] AC 669.   [27] [1980] 2 WLR 202.

[28] eg *Martin* in the 13th edn (1989), 628.

[29] eg *Westdeutsche Landesbank v Islington* [1996] AC 669. See also *Mountney v Treharne* [2002] EWCA Civ 1174.

payment, the Israel-British Bank went into insolvency. The question was whether the second payment was held on constructive trust for Chase Manhattan such that it could recover its money as a preferred creditor in the insolvency. Lord Browne-Wilkinson held that the proper analysis was to ask whether the Israel-British Bank had knowledge of the mistake at any time before its insolvency. If the Israel-British Bank knew of the mistake then that bank would become a constructive trustee of that payment from the moment of its knowledge: the rationale being that it would be contrary to conscience to seek to retain a payment which it knew had been paid to it under a mistake. In the event that the bank never knew of the mistake, then it would never be a constructive trustee of the second payment. Similarly, it could not be a constructive trustee of the second payment until such time as it had knowledge of the mistake.

27.07   That approach was applied in the House of Lords' decision in *Westdeutsche Landesbank v Islington LBC* itself. That case concerned payments made under an interest rate swap contract whereby the parties created a contract intended to last for ten years during which time the bank would pay a lump sum to the local authority at the outset and thereafter the parties would be required to account one to another for fixed and floating rates of interest on identified payment dates.[30] The purpose of the transaction therefore was to provide the local authority with off balance sheet loan capital outside the rate-capping legislation and to swap the floating rate interest cost the local authority bore on its onbalance sheet debt for a fixed rate.[31] Five years into the life of the transaction, the decision in the House of Lords in *Hazell v Hammersmith & Fulham LBC*[32] held that any interest rate swap contract entered into by a local authority was void *ab initio* on the ground that it was *ultra vires* the local authority. Before judgment had been handed down in that appeal, the local authority had already paid the moneys into its general bank accounts and dissipated them on its general, income expenses. Therefore, the bank was left with the problem of seeking to recover both the lump sum paid under the interest rate swap and the balance of payments of interest which it had made under that same transaction. This appeal raised fundamental questions of the relationship between equity and the common law.[33]

27.08   In relation to its argument based on constructive trust, the bank was seeking to establish that the local authority ought to be considered to be constructive trustee

---

[30] By virtue of 'payment netting' only the party owing a larger amount on that payment date would actually be called upon to transfer the amount of that surplus to its counterparty, thus achieving a set-off between their obligations.

[31] For a full analysis of financial derivatives transactions, such as interest rate swaps, see AS Hudson, *The Law on Financial Derivatives* (3rd edn, Sweet & Maxwell, 2002) ch 1.

[32] [1991] 1 AC 1.

[33] AS Hudson, *Swaps, Restitution and Trusts* (Sweet & Maxwell, 1999). See generally P Birks and F Rose (eds), *Lessons of the swaps litigation* (Mansfield Press, 2001).

of the money which it had received from the bank. Consequently, the bank sought to establish that it retained a proprietary right in that money not only entitling it to a beneficial right in it but also a right to receive compound interest on its judgment. However, Lord Browne-Wilkinson held that, at the time of entering into the transaction and at the time that the local authority had mixed the contract moneys with its general funds, both parties had believed that the interest rate swap transaction constituted a valid contract. Therefore, at no point before the moneys had been spent did the local authority know of any factor which ought to have affected its conscience in relation to that money. In consequence, the local authority was not a constructive trustee of that money at any time.[34]

The nature of the beneficiary's rights under a constructive trust

The beneficiary acquires proprietary rights in the property held on constructive trust—except in relation to cases where the defendant is made personally liable to account on grounds of knowing receipt or dishonest assistance.[35] In this respect the third fundamental principle identified by Lord Browne-Wilkinson in *Westdeutsche Landesbank v Islington* operated as follows: **27.09**

> (iii) In order to establish a trust there must be identifiable trust property. The only apparent exception to this rule is a constructive trust imposed on a person who dishonestly assists in a breach of trust who may come under fiduciary duties even if he does not receive identifiable trust property.[36]

The constructive trust comes into effect at the date knowledge of matters affecting the defendant's conscience is acquired and 'as from the date of its establishment the beneficiary has, in equity, a proprietary interest in the trust property'. It is trite law that the identity of the property to be held on an express trust must be certain or else the trust will be void.[37] There had been a question whether the property which is the subject of the constructive trust must be certain in the same way. Older authorities consider that the property must be certain under a constructive trust.[38] This view was upheld by Lord Browne-Wilkinson in *Westdeutsche Landesbank v Islington* although his lordship still accepted that there was one evident exception to this principle in relation to personal liability to account as a dishonest assistant.[39] Other authorities have suggested that a trust may be implied in any situation in which a person is required to hold property separate from all other property:[40] it is suggested that this latter proposition will be dependent upon the context.

---

[34] This conclusion had the effect that, in tandem with the court holding that no resulting trust arose, there was no possibility of any right of tracing into the local authority's funds nor of establishing a proprietary right to compound interest.   [35] See para 30.01.
[36] [1996] AC 669.   [37] *Re Goldcorp* [1994] 3 WLR 199.
[38] *Re Barney* [1892] 2 Ch 265, 273.   [39] [1996] AC 669.
[40] See, for example, the statement of Channell J in *Henry v Hammond* [1913] 2 KB 515, 521: 'It is clear that if the terms upon which the person receives the money are that he is bound to keep

27.10 His lordship's fourth fundamental principle sets out the manner in which the proprietary rights of the beneficiaries operate under a proprietary constructive trust:

> (iv) Once a trust is established, as from the date of its establishment the beneficiary has, in equity, a proprietary interest in the trust property, which proprietary interest will be enforceable in equity against any subsequent holder of the property (whether the original property or substituted property into which it can be traced) other than a purchaser for value of the legal interest without notice.

So the proprietary interest is 'enforceable in equity against any subsequent holder of the property' such that the beneficiary can trace those property rights through into 'the original property or substituted property into which it can be traced'. The only category of defendant who will not be liable in this way is equity's darling: or, the 'purchaser for value of the legal interest without notice'. The role of equity's darling is considered below.[41]

The extent of the trustee's obligations under a constructive trust

27.11 In general terms the office of trustee under a constructive trust is necessarily different from that under an express trust. The parties will not necessarily know with certainty whether or not a constructive trust exists until a court declares that such a trust does in fact exist.[42] That is to say, the very existence of a constructive trust will often be contested until the court makes an order declaring that it does exist. What is therefore at issue is the liability which ought to attach to the constructive trustee for the period between the time when the constructive trust actually came into existence and the time at which the court made the order confirming its existence.[43] We do know that in theory the office of trustee will arise as soon as the trustee has knowledge of some factor affecting his conscience because constructive trusts are institutional trusts.[44] What remains unclear is the extent to which a constructive trustee would be liable, for example, for a failure to make the best possible return on a trust investment and so forth, as would be

---

it separate, either in a bank or elsewhere, and to hand that money so kept as a separate fund to the person entitled to it, then he is a trustee of that money and must hand it over to the person who is the cestui que trust. If on the other hand he is not bound to keep the money separate, but is entitled to mix it with his own money and deal with it as he pleases, and when called upon to hand over an equivalent amount of money, then, in my opinion, he is not a trustee of the money, but merely a debtor.' However, the mere payment of money into a separate bank account without anything more will not necessarily constitute the owner of that account a trustee for any other person who may have a contractual interest in it: *DP Mann v Coutts & Co* [2003] EWHC 2138 (Comm). See also *King v Hutton* (1900) 83 LT 68 in relation to the receipt of moneys by an agent.

[41] See para 33.95.

[42] That is not to doubt that constructive trusts arise on an institutional basis (see para 25.12) but rather to suggest as a matter of practicality that many constructive trustees would not know they occupied such an office until they were informed of the fact.

[43] The precise nature of the trustee's obligations was considered in Chapter 10.

[44] *Westdeutsche Landesbank Girozentrale v Islington LBC* [1994] 4 All ER 890, Hobhouse J, CA; and reversed on appeal [1996] AC 669, HL.

required of a trustee under an express trust. As Millett J put the matter in *Lonrho v Fayed (No 2)*[45]

> ... it is a mistake to suppose that in every situation in which a constructive trust arises the legal owner is necessarily subject to all the fiduciary obligations and disabilities of an express trustee.

At one level this analysis could suggest that constructive trustees ought properly to bear no fiduciary obligations at all. Instead, their role might well be that of a bare trustee required only to hold the property to the beneficiary's order such that the property can be delivered up to the beneficiary. In consequence, there would be no other obligations as to maintenance, investment, or treatment of the property.

However, it is suggested that the obligations to be imposed on a constructive **27.12**
trustee will depend on the context of the case. Undoubtedly, they will extend to stewardship and maintenance of the property to the beneficiary's account but they will probably not extend so far as to impose positive obligations relating to the investment of the fund unless the constructive trustee already occupied some fiduciary position in relation to the beneficiary. For example, consider the trustee in *Keech v Sandford*[46] who was held to be a constructive trustee of a new lease acquired by way of a renewal of a former lease which he had held on the terms of an express trust previously for an infant beneficiary. In such a situation, the obligations of the trustee were clear under the terms of the express trust and the purpose of the constructive trust was to ensure that the infant beneficiary continued to receive the benefit of the lease which had previously been held on trust for him while also ensuring that there was no possibility of the trustee being able to take a personal benefit from the trust property. Therefore, the extent and the terms of the trustee's trusteeship were set out in the express trust and could therefore be reasonably read into the constructive trust where that constructive trust was intended to perpetuate the benefits accruing to the infant under the original express trust.

That analysis based on *Keech v Sandford* is a very different situation from suggest- **27.13**
ing that someone who had received an overpayment of change from a shop and who had been made aware of the mistake by store staff (so as to become a constructive trustee of that money) should be made liable as a trustee for a failure to generate the best available investment return from that overpayment of change while acting as constructive trustee of it before returning it to the shop. In the latter situation, no general obligation to make an investment of the money could reasonably be inferred from the circumstances. The more difficult question, it is suggested, arises in situations like that in *Chase Manhattan v Israel-British Bank*[47]

---

[45] [1992] 1 WLR 1; [1991] 4 All ER 961.   [46] (1726) Sel Cas Ch 61.
[47] [1981] 1 Ch 105, considered above at para 27.06.

in which a commercial bank received a mistaken payment and would have been held to have been constructive trustee of that mistaken payment from the moment that it had knowledge of said mistake. In the event that the property mistakenly received by the bank was separately identifiable property from the other property which it held in its accounts, would that bank as a commercial entity be expected to act in a professional manner in relation to the maintenance of that property; that is, to bear a higher standard of responsibility than the member of the public receiving an overpayment in a shop commensurate with its standing as a commercial bank experienced in handling moneys held on trust? Were it demonstrable that one bank acting as custodian of funds for a client or for someone as a commercial trustee would be expected to account for compound interest on such a deposit, that would give good ground to the payer who made a mistake to seek compound interest from the bank. The argument against such liability would be that it constituted a liability which the recipient bank would not have voluntarily assumed and by which it therefore ought not to be bound. Alternatively, the bank would be benefiting from retention of the moneys if they were being applied (as is the practice with commercial banks) to invest in money market deposits instead of being held statically in one particular place and not turned to account. Suppose further that the property were not an overpayment of cash but rather a holding of debt securities in relation to which a bank would ordinarily be expected to exercise the rights of the bondholder to receive a coupon and to enforce covenants contained in the bond contract. If the bank failed to enforce the rights of the bondholder as one might ordinarily expect of a custodian of such securities, ought that bank acting as constructive trustee of the property to be liable as though an express trustee over that property? It is suggested that, in that context, if the bank knew of the constructive trust (perhaps there had already been a court order against it to that effect) then its failure to maintain the property as a commercial custodian ought to attract the same liability as would be borne by an express trustee. Further, however, it is suggested that such a person with knowledge of a factor affecting its conscience in relation to such a holding of debt securities ought properly to be liable for the maintenance of those securities as though an express trustee or else the equitable doctrine of constructive trust is robbed of any tangible effect and the beneficiaries left to bear the risk of any impact on the value of that property, if the constructive trustee failed to maintain those securities.

27.14   It is suggested, therefore, that the better reading of Millett J's remarks in *Lonrho v Fayed (No 2)*[48] quoted earlier is that the extent of the constructive trustee's liability ought to be dependent on the context. A constructive trustee facing liability within the larger framework of an existing trust can readily have the obligations of one translated to the other, whereas a non-professional trustee acting as a mere

---

[48] [1992] 1 WLR 1; [1991] 4 All ER 961.

vessel holding property to the order of its rightful owner—as with the overpayment in the shop example—ought not to bear onerous obligations where no such office has been voluntarily accepted and where the imposition of such an office would be inappropriate. The more difficult intermediary case could, it is suggested, be resolved by recognition that the risk of damage or loss to property is more readily allocated to a person who has been subjected to constructive trusteeship because he has committed an unconscionable action (as with fraud or unlawful killing, considered below) or voluntarily agreed to the arrangement in some form (as with common intention constructive trusts, secret trusts, mutual wills, and so forth, considered below). That, it is suggested, would be the most suitable principle by reference to which the extent of such liability could be decided.

Profits from unlawful acts in general terms

A range of unconscionable actions, ranging from the illegal to the lawful-   **27.15**
but-unethical fall under the umbrella of acts performed otherwise than in good conscience which will ground a constructive trust. The remainder of this chapter, however, focuses on equity's treatment of rights in property which arise from unlawful acts—that is, acts which are contrary to the criminal law through to acts which are not lawful even if their commission does not lead to the imposition of a criminal penalty. In short, equity takes a particularly strict line in relation to property acquired as a result of unlawful activities. The approach of equity in this context could be said to be based on the proposition that 'no system of jurisprudence can with reason include among the rights which it enforces rights directly resulting to the person asserting them from the crime of that person':[49] or, in other words, a criminal will not be entitled to retain the fruits of his criminal activities. Since *Bridgman v Green*[50] it has been held that the profits of crime will be held on what is now known as a constructive trust. Two themes emerge. First, equity provides a response for the victim to that unlawful act both by means of proprietary constructive trust and also by means of additional personal liability to account in excess of the value of the property held on constructive trust. Secondly, this proprietary constructive trust will be ineffective against a bona fide purchaser for value of that property without knowledge of the unlawful act.[51]

B. Unlawful Killing

Profits from killing

It is a well-established principle of equity that any benefit taken from killing   **27.16**
another person will make the killer a constructive trustee of any property realized

---

[49] *Cleaver v Mutual Reserve Fund Life Association* [1892] 1 QB 147, 156.
[50] (1755) 24 Beav 382.   [51] *Westdeutsche Landesbank v Islington LBC* [1996] AC 669.

through that killing. This principle applies in general terms to all forms of killing which constitute a criminal offence.[52] In consequence a person guilty of murder will fall within the principle,[53] as will a person convicted of inciting others to murder her husband,[54] and (controversially because it does not require intention) death by reckless driving.[55] It has been held that the principle will not cover involuntary manslaughter where there was no intention to kill[56] or killing for which there is a defence such as insanity.[57] It is not necessarily a prerequisite of the application of this principle that there have been criminal proceedings to establish the guilt of the defendant provided that the criminal activity is proved at the civil proceedings to the criminal standard of proof.[58]

27.17　A murderer will not be entitled to take good title in property which is acquired solely by murdering its previous owner. Therefore, equity will intervene and find that the murderer holds any property so acquired as a constructive trustee for the victim's estate. In general terms a murderer, as with a thief considered below, will not acquire good title in property acquired by way of murder.[59]

Problems with constructive trusts in relation to unlawful killing

27.18　However, two problems emerge. First, what if the proceeds of crime are said to be passed to a third person? In the case of *In the Estate of Crippen*[60] Dr Crippen had murdered his wife. Crippen had intended to flee the country with his mistress but was, equally famously, captured on the boat while in flight by virtue of wireless telegraphy. The *Crippen* appeal itself considered the question whether or not property which would ordinarily have passed to Crippen as his wife's next of kin ought to pass to his mistress as Crippen's next of kin. It was held that, given the context of the murder, no rights would transfer to the mistress because Crippen was deemed to hold them on constructive trust for his wife's estate and therefore could not pass them to his mistress beneficially. Thus, the murderer becomes constructive trustee of all rights and interests in property which would have vested in him under the deceased's will[61] or even as next of kin in relation to a deceased who did not leave a will.[62] The criminal will not acquire rights under any life assurance policy which has been taken out over the life of the deceased.[63] Similarly, a murderer will not be entitled to take a beneficial interest under the widow's pension entitlements of his murdered wife.[64]

---

[52]　*Gray v Barr* [1971] 2 QB 554.　　[53]　*In the Estate of Crippen* [1911] P 108.
[54]　*Evans v Evans* [1989] 1 FLR 351.　　[55]　*R v Seymour (Edward)* [1983] AC 493.
[56]　*Re K (deceased)* [1986] Ch 180; *Re H (deceased)* [1990] 1 FLR 441.
[57]　*Re Holgate* (1971) unreported; Criminal Procedure (Insanity) Act 1964, s1.
[58]　*Re Sigsworth* [1935] 1 Ch 89.　　[59]　*Parker and Mellows* 356.　　[60]　[1911] P 108.
[61]　*Re Sigsworth* [1935] 1 Ch 89.　　[62]　*In the Estate of Crippen* [1911] P 108.
[63]　*Cleaver v Mutual Reserve Fund Life Association* [1892] 1 QB 147.
[64]　*R v Chief National Insurance Commissioner, ex p Connor* [1981] 1 QB 758.

Secondly, what of the murderer who would have received that property in any event **27.19** and only hastened its acquisition by killing its previous owner? In such circumstances the killer would not be acquiring property in which he would not otherwise have had any interest (as, for example, with the situation where a murderer steals property from the victim) but rather where the murderer would have acquired that interest in the fullness of time in any event. Suppose, for example, that a joint tenant would have been entitled to an absolute interest as a survivor on the death of the other joint tenant in any event but that he killed the victim so as to acquire that interest at an earlier date. It has been held that in such a situation the killer would acquire the entire legal interest on the survivorship principle but that the killer would hold the equitable interest on constructive trust for himself and for the representatives of the deceased as tenants in common.[65] It has been suggested obiter that, where a remainder beneficiary killed the life tenant, that remainder beneficiary should be prevented from taking the entire beneficial interest until a period suggested by actuarial estimate would have been the time when the life tenant would probably have died.[66] What emerges from *Crippen*[67] is that the murderer will be deprived of any such interest which the murderer would otherwise have been entitled to if, for example, the victim had coincidentally been killed accidentally on the day of the planned murder before the assassin had carried out her plan. Thus, the doctrine of constructive trust will intervene so as to prevent the killer from acquiring any rights in property to which the killer would otherwise have been entitled in any event at a later date.

One issue which should be borne in mind is that the courts do not have any prin- **27.20** cipled argument based on the recognition of pre-existing property rights to justify this principle of denying beneficial title in property to the defendant and instead diverting that beneficial title to some other person.[68] Rather, the courts are concerned with the punishment of the defendant. Exceptionally in the case of *Re K* (*deceased*)[69] a wife, who had been the victim of domestic violence, picked up a shotgun during an attack by her husband and that shotgun went off accidentally, killing her husband. Under the Forfeiture Act 1982 the court exercised its discretion to make an order not to oblige the wife to hold property received as a result of her husband's death on constructive trust. The underlying purpose of this principle which has been accepted in Commonwealth jurisdictions is that the criminal should simply not benefit from his wrong: so in Canada,[70] South Africa,[71] Australia,[72] and New Zealand.[73] The purpose of the constructive trust in these circumstances is to prevent a murderer from taking a benefit from that crime. This is, as said above, to do with retribution and not restitution.

---

[65] *Re K (deceased)* [1986] Fam 180.   [66] *Re Calloway* [1956] Ch 559.
[67] *In the Estate of Crippen* [1911] P 108.   [68] Youdan (1973) 89 LQR 235.
[69] [1986] Fam 180.   [70] *Schobelt v Barber* (1967) 59 DLR (2d) 519 (Ont).
[71] *Re Barrowcliff* [1927] SASR 147.   [72] *Rosmanis v Jurewitsch* (1970) 70 SR (NSW) 407.
[73] *Re Pechar* [1969] NZLR 574.

C. Theft and Dealings With Stolen Property

Property acquired by means of theft held on constructive trust

27.21   The further issue with reference to cases of theft is as follows: what are the obligations of a thief in relation to the original owner of the stolen property? A thief will hold the stolen property on constructive trust for the victim of that crime.[74] The basis of that constructive trust, drawing on *Attorney-General for Hong Kong v Reid*,[75] would appear to arise on the basis that the thief ought to return the property to its original owner;[76] in furtherance of the principle that equity looks upon as done that which ought to have been done, the thief is therefore deemed to have returned equitable title to the original owner of the property, thus generating a constructive trust over that property.[77] This grants a right to trace that property at common law and in equity.[78] That the thief holds the stolen property on constructive trust has been upheld, albeit obiter, in England[79] and also in Australia[80] and Canada.[81] In consequence the victim of the crime acquires an equitable interest which can be protected against the thief and is also able to establish a common law tracing claim to recover the stolen property,[82] or an equitable tracing claim in any substitute property,[83] as considered in Chapter 33.[84]

Purchase of stolen property by third party

27.22   The more difficult context arises when the stolen property has been transferred to a third party. If the property were passed to someone who had notice of the fact that it were stolen there would clearly be an offence of handling stolen goods[85] and the wrongful recipient of those goods must hold them on constructive trust

---

[74] *Westdeutsche Landesbank v Islington* [1996] AC 669.
[75] *Attorney-General v Reid* [1994] 1 AC 324; [1994] 1 All ER 1.
[76] *Parker v Taswell* (1858) 27 LJ Ch 812; *Walsh v Lonsdale* (1882) 21 Ch D 9.
[77] *Attorney-General v Reid* [1994] 1 AC 324; [1994] 1 All ER 1.
[78] *Banque Belge pour L'Etranger v Hambrouck* [1921] 1 KB 321; *Twinsectra Ltd v Yardley* [1999] Lloyd's Rep Bank 438, CA.
[79] *Lipkin Gorman v Karpnale* [1991] 2 AC 548, *per* Lord Templeman; *Westdeutsche Landesbank v Islington* [1996] AC 669, *per* Lord Browne-Wilkinson.
[80] *Black v S Freedman & Co* (1910) 12 CLR 105.
[81] *Lennox Industries (Canada) Ltd v The Queen* (1987) 34 DLR 297.
[82] *Jones (FC) & Sons v Jones* [1996] 3 WLR 703.
[83] *Bishopsgate v Homan* [1995] 1 WLR 31; *Ghana Commercial Bank v C* The Times, 3 March 1997.
[84] It might be thought that this constructive trust resembles a resulting trust but there is no suggestion that the victim of a theft could have voluntarily transferred any title to the thief: the trust must be one which is imposed by operation of law regardless of the wishes of the parties. Indeed it is suggested that the preferable explanation of the property law treatment of stolen property would be to find that the property rights in the stolen goods never leave the victim of crime because it is only the original owner of property who can transfer title in that property and clearly a victim of crime does not consent to the transfer of title to a thief. In this sense it is contended that the better approach in principle is for the court to make a declaration vindicating the property rights of the victim of the crime: cf *Foskett v McKeown* [2000] 3 All ER 97.   [85] Theft Act 1968, s 22.

for their original owner.[86] The complication arises when the thief then purports to sell that property to an innocent third party. There are two competing principles in play. First, the innocent purchaser would claim to be a bona fide purchaser for value of the property without notice of the victim's rights and therefore entitled to the protection of equity as being equity's darling. This approach was accepted by Lord Browne-Wilkinson in *Westdeutsche Landesbank Islington*.[87] It is a principle which operates to protect free markets in property by assuring the recipient of property that she can acquire good title in that property regardless of the root of title of that property: always provided that the purchaser does not have notice of the theft.[88] The alternative view would be that the thief never acquires title to the property and can therefore never transfer title to another person. That is, the commercial law *nemo dat* doctrine which suggests that one who does not have good title cannot give good title to anyone else.[89] In short, given that the victim of crime does not consent to the transfer of title to the thief, it would be said that no title can pass to the purchaser. That would be to reinforce the principle of caveat emptor (that is, 'let the buyer beware').

Profits from theft

Thus far, as has been explained, any property taken or received by means of theft **27.23** will be held on constructive trust for its original owner. A further issue arises: if the thief makes a profit, for example, from the sale of the goods or from some other commercial opportunity made available to him as a result of the theft, how are those profits to be treated? Further to the decision of the Privy Council in *Attorney-General for Hong Kong v Reid*,[90] by analogy with the position of the recipient of a bribe in that case, because the stolen property was to be held on constructive trust for its rightful owner equity will deem any property derived from that stolen property to be similarly held on constructive trust. Such derivations of property could take a number of forms. First, they might constitute the traceable proceeds of the stolen property which, further to the establishment of the constructive trust, would activate equitable tracing into such funds.[91] Secondly, those derivations might be in the form of income derived from the capital nature of the property, such as dividends on a shareholding. By extension of the rationale in *Reid*, such property will be deemed to belong to the equitable owner of the

---

[86] *Att-Gen for Hong Kong v Reid* [1994] 1 AC 324; [1994] 1 All ER 1, *infra*.

[87] [1996] AC 669.

[88] What is, perhaps, less clear is the interest which must be purchased to attract this defence. It is suggested that the underlying purpose of this doctrine is to ensure that the purchaser can acquire good title, provided he has acted in good faith, and so not be exposed to the risk of some third party asserting a prior title. Therefore, the title which the purchaser must have acquired, it is suggested, is whatever title was contracted for with the result that in equity there will not be any retransfer of the property. That may not apply to any failure to transfer legal title, for example taking possession of chattels.

[89] See para 27.53.   [90] [1994] 1 AC 324.   [91] See para 33.35; see also para 29.73.

capital property and therefore to be held on constructive trust. The better solution, it is suggested, would be to treat the original, stolen property as continuing to remain absolutely the property of its previous owner from whom it was stolen.[91A] The conceptual difficulty with finding that a constructive trust is imposed over the property is that the thief thus appears to have acquired good title at common law by dint of having stolen that property, albeit that the constructive trust is intended simply to impose obligations on the thief as to the maintenance and return of the stolen property and is therefore best thought of in any event as a mere conceit intended to achieve that goal.

D. Fraud

Acquisition of property by fraud

27.24 The principle that a statute or a rule of common law cannot be used as an engine of fraud is considered below. Similarly, where a criminal or a person not convicted of a criminal offence acquires interests in property by means of fraud, the fraudster will be required to hold the property so acquired at common law on constructive trust for the original owner of that property.[92] Also, where property is acquired by ordinary fraud, the fraudster will similarly not be entitled to take good title in that property,[93] except in relation to merely voidable contracts as considered below. That much is in line with the general principle set out above[94] whereby it would be unconscionable for the fraudster to retain property acquired by fraud[95] unless the victim acquiesced in the fraud.[96] So central is the equitable contempt for fraud that constructive trusts arise to prevent fraud in a number of contexts: secret trusts,[97] mutual wills,[98] to prevent abuse of statute,[99] and undue influence.[100]

27.25 Beyond saying that fraud is necessarily bound up with a number of the doctrines considered elsewhere in this chapter, it is worth considering what is meant more specifically by fraud. Fraudulent conduct in this context will include representing to the occupant of a cottage that she will be entitled to live in that cottage for the rest of her life and then seeking to evict her.[101] At the other end of the

---

[91A] See *Halley v Law Society* [2003] EWCA Civ 97, [2003] WTLR 845.

[92] *Rochefoucauld v Boustead* [1897] 1 Ch 196.   [93] ibid.

[94] See para 27.01; *Westdeutsche Landesbank v Islington* [1996] AC 669, *infra*.

[95] *Westdeutsche Landesbank v Islington* [1996] AC 669; *El Ajou v Dollar Land Holdings* [1993] 3 All ER 717; *Kuwait Oil Tanker Co SAK v Al Bader (No 3)* The Independent, 11 January 1999; *Lonrho v Al Fayed (No 2)* [1992] 1 WLR 1.   [96] *Lonrho v Fayed (No 2)* [1992] 1 WLR 1.

[97] *McCormick v Grogan* (1869) LR 4 HL 82; *Jones v Badley* (1868) 3 Ch App 362, 364, and *Blackwell v Blackwell* [1929] AC 318.   [98] *Dufour v Pereira* (1769) 1 Dick 419.

[99] *Rochefoucauld v Boustead* [1897] 1 Ch 196.

[100] *Barclay's Bank v O'Brien* [1994] 1 AC 180; *Royal Bank of Scotland v Etridge (No 2)* [2002] AC 773.

[101] *Bannister v Bannister* [1948] 2 All ER 133; *Neale v Willis* (1968) 110 SJ 521; *Binions v Evans* [1972] Ch 359.

spectrum there are forms of fraud which will constitute criminal offences such as obtaining pecuniary advantage by deception.[102] A defendant is not prevented from relying on his rights where, for example, the interest is not registered as required by some rule of formality[103] unless there is some unconscionability in that action.[104] Otherwise, property acquired by means of 'constructive fraud', such as duress or undue influence, will not vest in the person exerting that fraud in equity.[105] The remedy applied in cases of undue influence is that of setting aside the transaction, whereas transactions created by means of fraudulent misrepresentation are merely voidable.[106] Furthermore, a person seeking to rely on his own fraud or wrongdoing will not be able to rely on equitable remedies himself.[107] These various forms of fraudulent conduct are considered variously throughout this chapter.

Void and merely voidable contracts

It is not necessarily the case, however, that a contract procured by way of fraudu- **27.26**
lent misrepresentation will found a constructive trust over any property passed under that contract.[108] In *Lonrho v Al Fayed (No 2)*[109] Millett J held:

> A contract obtained by fraudulent misrepresentation is voidable, not void, even in equity. The representee may elect to avoid it, but until he does so, the representor is not a constructive trustee of the property transferred pursuant to the contract, and no fiduciary relationship exists between him and the representee. It may well be that if the representee elects to avoid the contract and set aside a transfer of property made pursuant to it, the beneficial interest in the property will be treated as having remained vested in him throughout, at least to the extent necessary to support any tracing claim.[110]

At first blush, this statement would appear to contradict the principle that a person who perpetrates a fraud will be required to hold any property acquired by virtue of that fraud on constructive trust for the representee. The distinction is made, however, between cases of theft and fraud where there has not been any consensual transfer, and cases where there is an underlying transaction which is voidable on grounds of misrepresentation.[111] The logic of this proposition is that such a voidable transaction might be affirmed by the representee and that it would

---

[102] Theft Act, s 16. See also the Proceeds of Crime Act 2002, creating a public body to seize the proceeds of crime and to administer them, as opposed to the property law question as to who has rightful title to such property under private law.
[103] *Midland Bank Trust Company v Green* [1981] AC 513.
[104] *Peffer v Rigg* [1977] 1 WLR 285.   [105] *Barclays Bank v O'Brien* [1993] 3 WLR 786.
[106] *Lonrho v Al Fayed (No 2)* [1992] 1 WLR 1; [1991] 4 All ER 961.
[107] *Guinness v Saunders* [1990] 2 WLR 324.
[108] *Daly v Sydney Stock Exchange Ltd* (1986) 160 CLR 371, 387.
[109] [1992] 1 WLR 1; [1991] 4 All ER 961.   [110] ibid 11; 971.
[111] *Bristol and West Building Society v Mothew* [1998] Ch 1, 23; *Twinsectra Ltd v Yardley* [1999] Lloyd's Rep Bank 438.

be contrary to principle if the equitable interest was held for the representee. The right to rescind the transaction is a mere equity and not an equitable interest.[112] However, it is suggested that this is no reason to absolve the representor of his fraud; instead, the constructive trust could be terminable at the instance of the representee in the same way that the transaction itself is capable of being affirmed.[113] This point is considered in greater detail in relation to 'Undue Influence and Constructive Fraud' immediately below.[114]

27.27 In general terms then, with the exception of fraudulent misrepresentation,[115] the commission of fraud in the round will constitute a form of unconscionable behaviour which will found a constructive trust. So in *Collings v Lee*[116] an estate agent purported to take a transfer of a house from the vendors in favour of a non-existent, arm's length purchaser but in fact procured a transfer of the land into a name which was an alias of his own. Subsequently, he refused to pay the purchase price to the vendors claiming not to be the transferee of the property. It was held that the estate agent was constructive trustee of the property in favour of the vendors so that the vendors retained an overriding interest in that property.[117] Whereas in *Lonhro v Fayed* the transferor had intended that the entire interest pass to the transferee in spite of the fraudulent misrepresentation, on these facts it was found that there had not been any such intention and furthermore the agent had breached his fiduciary duties to the parties.[118]

27.28 Similarly, in *JJ Harrison (Properties) Ltd v Harrison*[119] a director of a company procured the transfer of land owned by the company to himself personally. The transfer was made at an undervalue and therefore constituted a breach of the director's duties to the company. It was held that, whereas a director of a company is not ordinarily a trustee of the company's property (because the company is the absolute owner of its own property), in circumstances in which a director has unconscionably procured the transfer of the company's property to himself in breach of his fiduciary duties then that director will be a constructive trustee of that property in favour of the company.[120] These are instances of fraudulent conduct which have led to the imposition of a constructive trust.

---

[112] *Bristol and West Building Society v Mothew* [1998] Ch 1, 23; *Twinsectra Ltd v Yardley* [1999] Lloyd's Rep Bank 438.
[113] Such an argument was raised before the Court of Appeal in *Twinsectra Ltd v Yardley* [1999] Lloyd's Rep Bank 438 building on the general principle set out in *Westdeutsche Landesbank v Islington* [1996] AC 669 but rejected by the court, [1999] Lloyd's Rep Bank 438, 461, *per* Potter LJ.
[114] See para 27.29.   [115] Considered immediately below at para 27.29.
[116] (2001) 82 P & CR 27.
[117] Law of Property Act 1925, s 70(1)(g). See now Land Registration Act 2002.
[118] See also *Daly v Sydney Stock Exchange* (1986) 160 CLR 371, 389–390, *per* Brennan J; *Agip v Jackson* [1990] Ch 265, 290, *per* Millett J.   [119] [2002] 1 BCLC 162, [2001] WTLR 1327.
[120] Applying *Russell v Wakefield Waterworks Co* (1875) LR 20 Eq 474, 479, *per* Lord Jessel MR; *Belmont Finance Corporation v Williams Furniture Ltd and others (No 2)* [1980] 1 All ER 393, 405, *per* Buckley LJ.

E. Undue Influence and Constructive Fraud

Acquisition of property by undue influence or other constructive fraud

The doctrines of undue influence and of duress are themselves part of the more **27.29** general doctrine of constructive fraud.[121] The question is whether a person who acquires property by means of undue influence or other constructive fraud falls to be considered to be a constructive trustee of that property for the object of the fraud as beneficiary.[122] The issue relates specifically to the period of time after undue influence has given rise to a right to rescind the transaction. In short, where a transaction is procured by means of constructive fraud, that transaction will be set aside *in toto*,[123] except to the extent that the claimant has taken any benefit from the transaction.[124] The further question is as to title in any property acquired by virtue of the constructive fraud. On the authorities it is clear that undue influence will give rise to a mere equity which will bind anyone who takes a gratuitous transfer of the property at issue.[125] However, someone who purchases the property in good faith without notice of the rights of the beneficiary of the undue influence will not be bound by such a mere equity.[126] This approach is in parallel to the principle that '[a] contract obtained by fraudulent misrepresentation is voidable, not void, even in equity'.[127]

However, in relation to fraudulent misrepresentations, '[i] t may well be that if the **27.30** representee elects to avoid the contract and set aside a transfer of property made pursuant to it' the result will be that 'the beneficial interest in the property will be treated as having remained vested in him throughout, at least to the extent necessary to support any tracing claim'.[128] Therefore some equitable interest may accrue to the person subjugated to the undue influence. It is suggested that in accordance with the general principle set out in *Westdeutsche Landesbank v Islington*,[129] considered above,[130] it is unfortunate to require the wronged party to bear the risk of the person carrying on the undue influence selling or dealing with the property. It is suggested that the imposition of a constructive trust prevents the wrongdoer from dealing with the property and so failing to be accountable to the wronged party as though a trustee of that property. The imposition of a constructive trust would ensure that the wronged party is put in a position equivalent to that if the property were returned to it so as to put it in the position it would have been in but for the commission of the constructive fraud. The wrong in this

---

[121] J McGhee, *Snell's Equity* (30th edn, Sweet & Maxwell, 2000) ('*Snell*') 610.
[122] A Oakley, *Constructive Trusts* (3rd edn, Sweet & Maxwell, 1997) ('*Oakley*') 35 *et seq.*
[123] *TSB v Camfield* [1995] 1 WLR 430, [1995] 1 All ER 951.
[124] *Midland Bank v Greene* [1994] 2 FLR 827. [125] *Goddard v Carlisle* (1821) 9 Price 169.
[126] *Lancashire Loans v Black* [1934] 1 KB 380.
[127] *Lonrho v Al Fayed (No 2)* [1992] 1 WLR 1, 11; [1991] 4 All ER 961, 971.
[128] ibid 11; 971. [129] [1996] AC 669. [130] See para 27.01.

context is being committed in relation to property which, necessarily, has not been consensually transferred to the wrongdoer; as opposed to a contract set aside for undue influence where no property had been transferred and where no question of making restitution of the value of the property transferred arises (particularly if the property had a fluctuating value). It is suggested that this approach recognizing the non-consensual nature of the transaction by virtue of the commission of the undue influence is in line with the dicta of Lord Scott in *Royal Bank of Scotland v Etridge (No 2)*[131] relating to the basis of this doctrine in a failure to give free consent.

Frauds on a power do not give rise to a constructive trust

27.31　A fraud on a power arises in any situation in which the holder of a power seeks to make an excessive distribution from the fund over which that power is exercisable.[132] By 'excessive' in this context is meant any distribution which constitutes the exercise of a power in favour of a stranger to that power's objects or in some other way which is not consistent with the terms and scope of the power.[133] The name given to this doctrine is something of a misnomer given that the term fraud as used here does not 'carry the sense of deceit which the word "fraud" bears in other contexts'.[134] A fraud on a power does not give rise to a constructive trust.[135] Dishonesty is not a requirement of the doctrine's application.[136] That a fraud on a power could be committed without the need for knowing wrongdoing means, necessarily, that it does not generate a constructive trust automatically. A constructive trust will be applied only in circumstances in which some act is performed knowingly contrary to the conscience of the person performing it.[137] There will be cases in which there is both a fraud on a power and also some breach of fiduciary duty or an act committed knowingly contrary to conscience: in such circumstances a constructive trust would arise due to the equitable wrong committed and not simply by virtue of the fraud on the power.

Unconscionable bargains

27.32　In line with the discussions above of setting aside contracts procured by undue influence[138] and the mere voidability of contracts procured by fraudulent misrepresentation,[139] unconscionable bargains which were formerly covered by the Moneylenders Act and the ancient laws of usury are now the business of the

---

131　[2002] AC 773, [2001] 4 All ER 449.
132　*Aleyn v Belchier* (1758) 1 Eden 132; *Cloutte v Storey* [1911] 1 Ch 18; *Re Courage's Group's Pension Schemes* [1987] 1 WLR 495.
133　G W Thomas, *Powers* (Sweet & Maxwell, 1998) ('*Thomas*') 453.
134　*Re Dick* [1953] Ch 343, 360.　　135　*Thomas* 454.
136　*Kearns v Hill* [1991] PLR 161.
137　*Westdeutsche Landesbank v Islington* [1996] AC 669; para 27.01.　138　See para 27.29.
139　See para 27.26.

Unfair Contract Terms Act 1977 and the Consumer Credit Act 1974. Such transactions will not give rise automatically to constructive trusts for the reasons given in relation to contracts acquired by undue influence and fraudulent misrepresentation: that is, that those contracts are capable of being affirmed and therefore do not give rise automatically to rights under constructive trust.[140]

The lacuna in relation to merely voidable transactions

27.33 The policy grounds for the voidability of such transactions is that they have not been procured voluntarily by the contracting parties but rather only as a result of the unconscionable pressure placed on one of them. As such, it could be argued that such unconscionable transactions ought to impose a constructive trust on the other contracting party to prevent that person from disposing of any property procured through the transaction. That the prevailing authorities do not impose constructive trusts in such circumstances suggested two things. First, that the use of the term 'unconscionable' in these circumstances is intended to be different from the term 'conscience' used in relation to constructive trusts: the former seeming to indicate a vitiated consent on the part of the claimant and the latter some moral turpitude on the part of the defendant. In any event, the authorities contain no further discussion of the two concepts than that. Secondly, it suggests that common law damages and rescission are considered to be adequate remedies in the context. However, in the event that the party responsible for the unconscionable aspects of the transaction goes into insolvency or sells the property at an undervalue to a bona fide purchaser, the claimant will evidently not receive an adequate remedy for his loss when, evidently, he did not voluntarily assume the risk of such loss given the fact that his consent was necessarily vitiated by the undue influence, fraud, or other unconscionable feature of the transaction. Only the imposition of a constructive trust would provide a full remedy in such circumstances. And yet, presumably, any sale proceeds received from the sale of the property would, ordinarily, be required to be held on constructive trust for the claimant in the event that the transaction was avoided and the claimant sought restitution of his property.

F. Statute Used as an Engine of Fraud

27.34 It is a central principle of equity that statute cannot be used as an engine of fraud. Where a person seeks to rely on a literal application of a statutory or common law rule to take possession of property and where reliance on that rule is unconscionable in the context, such property will be held on constructive trust by that

---

[140] cf *Twinsectra Ltd v Yardley* [1999] Lloyd's Rep Bank 438.

person. Millett LJ in *Paragon Finance plc v Thakerar & Co*[141] has accepted that 'well-known examples' of constructive trusts which are 'coloured from the first by the trust and confidence by means of which he obtained it' include the doctrine that statute may not be used as an engine of fraud, as set out *inter alia* in *Rochefoucauld v Boustead*.[142] In the *Rochefoucauld* case itself the trustee had orally agreed to acquire property for the plaintiff and to hold that property on trust for the plaintiff, on the basis that the plaintiff would refund the purchase price to the trustee, but the trust was improperly recorded. The trustee subsequently went bankrupt and it was argued on behalf of his creditors that the absence of a formally valid trust over the land ought to have entitled the trustee to retain the land for himself. Nevertheless, it was held that for the trustee to have relied on the statutory formalities for the creation of a trust in this context would have been to perpetrate a fraud on the claimant for whose benefit that property had been acquired. Consequently a trust was recognized by the court in a form which is now recognized as being a constructive trust, given that no formally valid express trust was ever created.

27.35 The same principle was put into practice in *Lyus v Prowsa Developments*[143] where A sold land to B on the express understanding that B would hold the land on trust to give effect to a licence conferred by A on C. It was held, applying the principle against common law rights being used as an engine of fraud, that C acquired enforceable rights under trust against B to compel B to carry out the terms of that trust. In similar vein, it was held in *Bannister v Bannister*[144] that '[t]he fraud which brings the principle into play arises as soon as the absolute character of the conveyance is set up for the purpose of defeating the beneficial interest'. Consequently, the principle against permitting common law to be used as an engine of fraud is concerned to protect the person who is intended to receive the beneficial interest in that property as well as to regulate the conscience of the common law owner of property. The principle identified in this section is in line with one of the core principles of equity that equity will act *in personam* against a person who would otherwise be permitted to commit an unconscionable act by the strict application of common law rules, and furthermore it is in line with the principle set out by Lord Browne-Wilkinson in *Westdeutsche Landesbank*[145] that the essential nature of the trust is its regulation of the conscience of the common law owner of property.

27.36 While the *Rochefoucauld* doctrine operated in its original form on the basis of a general equitable principle that statute will not be used as an engine of fraud, Millett LJ in *Paragon Finance v DB Thackerar*[146] placed this principle four-square

---

[141] *Paragon Finance plc v Thakerar & Co* [1999] 1 All ER 400.   [142] [1897] 1 Ch 196.
[143] [1982] 1 WLR 1044.   [144] [1948] WN 261.   [145] [1996] AC 669.
[146] [1999] 1 All ER 400.

under the heading of constructive trust, an approach which is in line with cases like *Lyus v Prowsa*.[147] It is one of the core motivations of equity to balance out injustices in the literal application of common law and statutory rules. In such circumstances there is no finding of any intention to create an express trust over the property in question. Therefore, on the basis that a trust has been imposed by the courts to require the legal owner of that property to deal with it in a particular manner for the benefit of the beneficiary, the only viable explanation of the nature of that trust is that it forms a constructive trust in order to regulate the conscience of that common law owner which arises by operation of law.[148] Aspects of this doctrine are considered further in Chapter 28.[149]

G. Bribery

Profits from bribery held on constructive trust

The principle considered in this section is that any bribe (or other profit from an unlawful activity) will be held on constructive trust for the victim of that act. On the decided cases this principle has meant that a person acting in a fiduciary position who commits an unlawful act, such as receiving a bribe to breach his duty, will be required to hold any property received on constructive trust for the beneficiary of that fiduciary duty. A good illustration of this principle is found in *Reading v A-G*,[150] a case concerning a British army sergeant stationed in Cairo who received payments to ride in uniform in civilian lorries carrying contraband so that those lorries would not be stopped at army checkpoints. It was held by the Court of Appeal that the sergeant occupied a fiduciary position in relation to the Crown in respect of the misuse of his uniform and his position as a soldier in the British Army. Therefore, it was held that any money paid to him for riding in the lorry in breach of his fiduciary duty was held on constructive trust for the Crown. **27.37**

The fundamental conceptual problem with this principle is that profits made from, for example, bribes will not have been the property of the beneficiary before they were received by the fiduciary. Furthermore, the fiduciary duty recognized by the court in *Reading* and that recognized in *Attorney-General for Hong Kong v Reid*[151] (considered below and relating to an Attorney-General who took bribes not to prosecute certain criminals) are not classically understood categories of fiduciary duty.[152] Rather the duties of a fiduciary are imposed on the defendant to punish his unconscionable act in taking a bribe and not to vindicate some pre-existing property right. Consequently, it can be difficult to justify the **27.38**

---

[147] [1982] 1 WLR 1044.   [148] See *Oakley* 53 *et seq.*   [149] See para 28.66.
[150] [1951] 1 All ER 617.   [151] [1994] 1 AC 324.
[152] The categories of fiduciary are not closed: *Collings v Lee* [2001] 2 All ER 332.

reallocation of title in such bribes to the beneficiaries on constructive trust. What emerges here again is that the court is as concerned to punish the wrongdoer as to protect rights in property.[153] The court will require that the property be held on constructive trust on the basis that the fiduciary should be required to come to equity with clean hands. One who commits an unlawful act will be treated as having acted prima facie unconscionably.

Constructive trust where equity looks upon as done that which ought to have been done

27.39   Until 1994 it was an accepted but much contested facet of English law that a fiduciary who received bribes was liable only to a personal claim to render the cash equivalent of the bribe to the beneficiary of that power and not to account for any profits made on that bribe as a trustee. In the formerly leading case of *Lister v Stubbs*[154] the Court of Appeal held that to allow an order which entitled an employer to an equitable interest in property which an employee had acquired with bribes would be to confuse the plaintiff's entitlement to the cash amount of the bribes with ownership of the property acquired with them. The plaintiff had never had any proprietary right in the bribes and therefore could not claim title to the property acquired with the bribes. However, it was held that the plaintiff was entitled to require the defendant to account to the plaintiff for the value of the original bribe to prevent the fiduciary from making unauthorized profits from his office. The claim was found to be only a personal claim between debtor and creditor for a sum of money equal to the bribes.[155]

27.40   A different approach was taken by the Privy Council in *A-G Hong Kong v Reid*.[156] The former Attorney-General for Hong Kong had accepted bribes not to prosecute certain individuals accused of having committed crimes within his jurisdiction. The bribes which he had received had been profitably invested. The issue arose, similarly to *Lister v Stubbs*,[157] whether or not the property bought with the bribes and the increase in value of those investments should be held on constructive trust for the Attorney-General's employer, or whether the Attorney-General owed only an amount of cash equal to the bribes paid to him originally.

27.41   Lord Templeman, giving the leading opinion of the Privy Council, overruled *Lister v Stubbs* and took a very much stricter view of the law. He held that a proprietary constructive trust is imposed as soon as the bribe is received by the recipient of the bribe. This means that the employer is entitled to any profit generated by the cash bribe received from the moment of its receipt. Similarly, Lord Templeman held

---

[153] cf the discussion of theft above.   [154] (1890) 45 Ch D 1.

[155] See for example R Goff and G Jones, *The Law of Restitution* (6th edn, Sweet & Maxwell, 2002) ('*Goff & Jones*') 85.   [156] [1994] 1 AC 324; [1994] 1 All ER 1.

[157] (1890) 45 Ch D 1.

that the constructive trustee is liable to the beneficiary for any *decrease* in value in the investments acquired with the bribe as well as for any increase in value in such investments. Lord Templeman's policy motivation is clear: to punish the wrong-doer, particularly a wrongdoer in public office. He considered bribery to be an 'evil practice which threatens the foundations of any civilised society'.[158] As such, the imposition of a proprietary constructive trust was the only way in which the wrongdoer could be fully deprived of the value of his malfeasance. This, it is suggested, is less 'restitution' than 'retribution':[159] there is no proprietary right in the loss on the investments, rather there is a policy motivation both to disgorge the wrongdoer's profits and to impose punitive costs also. This is neither simply compensation nor restitution, then, but rather it is control of the defendant's conscience.

The manner in which Lord Templeman constructs his proprietary remedy **27.42** accords with the underlying theme of this book that equity acts *in personam* against the defendant, even when awarding a proprietary remedy.[160] Lord Templeman started from the premise that equity acts *in personam*. The defendant had acted unconscionably in accepting the bribe in breach of his fiduciary duty. In consequence of that breach of duty it was held that the bribe should have been deemed to pass to the beneficiary of the fiduciary power at the instant when it was received by the wrongdoer. Given that equity considers as done that which ought to have been done[161] it was held that the bribe should have been considered to have been the property of the beneficiary from the moment of its receipt. The means by which title passes to the beneficiary in equity in such circumstances is by means of a proprietary constructive trust. As such the bribe, any property acquired with the bribe, and any profit derived from such property fell to be considered as the property of the person wronged. In this circuitous way, Lord Templeman justified the imposition of a proprietary remedy in *Attorney-General for Hong Kong v Reid*[162] as opposed to the personal claim upheld in *Lister v Stubbs*.[163] This approach clearly accords with the speech of Lord Browne-Wilkinson in *Westdeutsche Landesbank*[164] that a trustee is a person required by good conscience to hold property on trust for another.

The nature of the trust

There is no requirement of any pre-existing proprietary right in the claimant for **27.43** the establishment of a constructive trust. Instead it is the fiduciary relationship of good faith which means that the defendant is deemed to hold any property

---

[158] [1994] 1 AC 324.   [159] P Jaffey, *The Nature and Scope of Restitution* (Hart, 2000).
[160] See para 1.39.
[161] *Parker v Taswell* (1858) 27 LJ Ch 812; *Walsh v Lonsdale* (1882) 21 Ch D 9.
[162] [1994] 1 AC 324; [1994] 1 All ER 1.   [163] (1890) 45 Ch D 1.   [164] [1996] AC 669.

received in breach of that duty as a constructive trustee. In *Reid* itself it is not difficult to see why on policy grounds the court would wish to impose a constructive trust so as to recover the proceeds of his unlawful act from the defendant although it is notable that the position of Attorney-General[165] and of an army sergeant[166] had not previously been held to fall within the established fiduciary relationships. In both of these contexts it is difficult to identify the beneficiaries of these trusts other than 'the State' or 'the Crown'.

27.44   A second very important issue arises from the judgment. Lord Templeman held that the defendant's liability does not stop with holding the bribe and any property bought with it on constructive trust, but also includes a liability to make good any diminution in the value of those investments from the constructive trustee's own pocket. By holding that the fiduciary is obliged not only to hold the bribes or any substitute property on constructive trust but also to account to the beneficiaries for any diminution in the value of those investments, the decision in *Attorney-General for Hong Kong v Reid*[167] reaches far beyond the simple rules of property law. The additional personal liability to account which is imposed on the malfeasant fiduciary places this particular claim in the category of a wrong for which the defendant is liable to account to the claimant akin to an action for breach of trust. As considered below,[168] trustees are liable not only to replace trust property when they commit a breach of trust but also to account personally to the beneficiaries for any further, outstanding loss.[169]

H. Unconscionable Dealings With Property

Constructive trust arising on interference with any right in property

27.45   In this section we consider a range of constructive trusts which are imposed in dealing with property: whether sales, joint ventures, theft, or agreements to stay out of the market. While this proposition might otherwise be considered to be merely a restatement of the general principle[170] on which constructive trusts arise, the particular focus of this section will be on circumstances in which there has been some contract to sell, joint venture to develop, or agreement to keep out of a market. In short, it will focus on breaches of otherwise consensual dealings with land, as opposed to the unlawful acts considered previously in this chapter. The source of the constructive trusts in this section comes from a judicial acceptance

---

[165] *Attorney-General v Reid* [1994] 1 AC 324; [1994] 1 All ER 1.
[166] *Reading v Attorney-General* [1951] 1 All ER 617.
[167] *Reading v Attorney-General* [1951] 1 All ER 617.   [168] See para 32.01.
[169] This final element of Lord Templeman's opinion suggests that the fiduciary is liable for an equitable remedy beyond the proprietary concept of the constructive trust considered above.
[170] See para 27.01.

that breach of such agreements constitutes unconscionable behaviour which will found a constructive trust over any property right which accrues to the person who breaks that agreement unconscionably.

Continuing from the general principle for constructive trusts identified above,[171] this group of constructive trusts is concerned with interference with pre-existing rights in property whether those rights are in the form of absolute title, legal title, or equitable title. In his leading speech in *Westdeutsche Landesbank v Islington*[172] Lord Browne-Wilkinson explained the potential ambit of this principle by reinterpreting the decision of Goulding J in *Chase Manhattan v Israel-British Bank*.[173] In *Chase Manhattan* the unconscionable act which led to the imposition of a constructive trust was the knowledge of the recipient of a payment that the payer had mistakenly made a payment twice and would therefore require repayment. Conscience here does not require that there has been some dishonesty or theft practised by the defendant, only that there be some treatment of property in which the claimant has rights which is considered to be wrong, unconscionable, or unethical in a broad sense.[174] **27.46**

As will emerge from the discussion to follow, constructive trusts can be said to arise in relation not only to people who held the legal title in property but also in situations in which the intermeddler had no prior interest in the property at all but nevertheless took the property into his possession in some way that would be considered unconscionable. An example of this latter operation of the constructive trust considered previously in this chapter[175] is the thief who takes the stolen property into his possession in circumstances in which, by definition, he acquires no right voluntarily from the victim of the crime but which will nevertheless be said to render him a constructive trustee of that property in favour of the victim of the crime;[176] or alternatively, where property comes into the defendant's possession in breach of a contract to use that property for another, specified purpose, as considered below.[177] The alchemy by which the wrongdoer could be said to acquire the legal title in the property could only be said to rest on some assumption that mere possession of such property would constitute transfer of a title at common law—that point is not considered in the authorities—but is more readily explicable as part of equity's jurisdiction to restrain unconscionable behaviour in general and to use constructive trusts in particular to restrain such behaviour in relation to identifiable property. **27.47**

Interaction between constructive trust of new property and existing express trust

By contrast with the foregoing, where an express trustee of property commits a breach of trust, for example by investing in unauthorized investments, such that **27.48**

---

[171] See para 27.01. [172] [1996] AC 669. [173] [1980] 2 WLR 202.
[174] See *Hudson*, Ch 37 generally. [175] See para 27.21.
[176] *Westdeutsche Landesbank v Islington* [1996] AC 669. [177] See para 26.67.

other property is brought within the trust fund, then that trust will continue to be an express trust over those unauthorized investments such that the trustee is obliged usually to replace those investments with authorized investments of the same value [178] unless the beneficiaries are able to elect to retain those unauthorized investments.[179] Alternatively, it could be argued that where those investments could not have formed part of the trust fund because they were not of a type which the trustees were authorized to hold, then it could only be a new, constructive trust which would be imposed over those investments to create rights over them in favour of the beneficiaries. So, for example, where a lease was held on trust for an infant but where that infant was not legally capable of taking a renewal of that lease, if the trustee purported to take out such a new lease in his own name then that new lease would be held on constructive trust by the trustee for the infant as beneficiary.[180] The trust would be a new, constructive trust as opposed to a continuation of the old express trust because the new lease constituted property different from the original lease. That is, the property is brought within the trust fund by operation of law rather than being contained within the terms of an express trust.

Constructive trusts in relation to land

27.49 Constructive trusts will arise in a number of contexts in relation to land. Those constructive trusts arise on different bases and therefore are considered separately in the next chapter: they are grouped together here for ease of reference. Constructive trusts may arise in relation to land in three principal ways. First, by means of a common intention constructive trust where the parties either form some agreement by means of express discussions or demonstrate a common intention by their conduct in contributing jointly to the purchase price or mortgage over a property.[181] This category is considered below at paragraph 28.23.

27.50 Secondly, by entering into a contract for the transfer of rights in land there is an automatic transfer of the equitable interest in that land as soon as there is a binding contract in effect.[182] That contract would have to be in writing in one document signed by the parties which contained all the terms of the contract.[183] However, proprietary estoppel will now offer a means of evading this statutory requirement for a written contract in circumstances in which the transferor made assurances to the transferee that the transferee would receive title in this land and where that transferee acted to her detriment in reliance on those assurances.[184] This category is considered below at paragraph 28.13.

---

[178] *Re Massingberd's Settlement* (1890) 63 LT 296.   [179] *Re Oatway* [1903] 2 Ch 356.
[180] *Keech v Sandford* (1726) Sel Cas Ch 61.   [181] *Lloyds Bank v Rosset* [1990] 1 All ER 1111.
[182] *Lysaght v Edwards* (1876) 2 Ch D 499.
[183] Law of Property (Miscellaneous) Provisions Act 1989, s 2.
[184] *Yaxley v Gotts* [2000] Ch 162; [1999] 3 WLR 1217.

Thirdly, where a party to a partnership created to exploit the development poten-   **27.51**
tial of land seeks exploit that land alone, then that person will hold that land or
any benefit derived from it on constructive trust for the other partners. Such a
constructive trust may arise even if no binding contract has been formed at the
time that the unilateral exploitation of the land took place.[185] So in *Banner Homes
Group plc v Luff Development Ltd*[186] it was held that the defendant could establish
a constructive trust even in the absence of a binding contract to the effect that the
claimant and defendant would exploit the land jointly if the defendant had
refrained from exploiting any personal interests in that land in reliance on the
negotiations being conducted between the claimant and defendant. The source of
the constructive trust was therefore the unconscionability of repudiating the other
party's reasonable expectations formed during the negotiations for the contract.

All of these categories of constructive trust over land suggest a similarity between   **27.52**
constructive trust and proprietary estoppel. In the first and third of these claims
(where estoppel can be defined as a claim) it is necessary that the claimant must
have suffered some detriment to found its claim.[187] The second arises on the basis
of the principle in *Walsh v Lonsdale*.[188]

Acquisition of title from one who does not have good title: *nemo dat quod non habet*

Commercial law gives greater prominence to the *nemo dat* principle than does   **27.53**
trusts law. Trusts law, as was discussed above,[189] deals with a case of theft (by way
of example) by declaring that the thief is to be construed to be a trustee of the
stolen property.[190] By contrast, suppose the thief sells the stolen goods to a third
party. Commercial law provides that, further to the *nemo dat* principle, because
the thief does not have good title in the stolen property he cannot transmit title to
the purchaser (subject to exceptions considered below[191]). Trusts law, however,
provides that the purchaser can resist the original owner's claim for delivery up of
his property from the constructive trustee on grounds of being equity's darling.[192]
What is problematic about the foregoing is not that equity chooses to take a strict
line with those who commit unlawful acts, but rather the way in which equity
chooses to treat such people who have come into possession of property from their
unlawful activities. That equity imposes a constructive trust in such circumstances means that the wrongdoer is accepted as having legal title in the property
such that he is capable of being a trustee of it, even if only a bare trustee.[193] This
means that common law is blind, apparently, to such wrongdoing and that it is

---

[185] *Pallant v Morgan* [1953] Ch 43.   [186] [2000] Ch 372, [2000] 2 WLR 772.
[187] *Grant v Edwards* [1986] Ch 638.   [188] (1882) 21 Ch D 9.   [189] See para 27.21.
[190] *Westdeutsche Landesbank v Islington* [1996] AC 669.   [191] See para 27.57.
[192] See, for example, *Westdeutsche Landesbank v Islington* [1996] AC 669.
[193] See para 27.11.

only equity which is capable of remedying it. Another approach would be to say that the wrongdoer acquires no title in the property at all.

27.54 There is consequently an oddity in calling a thief a constructive trustee and thereby assuming that the thief takes legal title in the stolen property necessary to establish him as a trustee of that property. Even if such a constructive trustee is only to operate as a bare trustee holding the property to the victim of crime's order, that is nevertheless to accept that some (albeit restricted) title vests in the thief. The alternative analysis would be to find that the thief took no title in the stolen property and therefore that the only order required was an order that the thief return the goods to the victim of the crime. It is suggested that such an approach would be in line with the commercial law principle that *nemo dat quod non habet*. Furthermore, it is difficult to justify in the abstract the operation of the defence of bona fide purchaser for value without notice of the victim of crime's rights. Where the thief purports to transfer title to the third party purchaser, if the *nemo dat* principle were employed, it would not be possible to justify the passing of any property rights to a third party purchaser of the stolen goods solely within the logic of property law. The logic of the bona fide purchaser defence is predicated entirely on a judicial determination to maintain free markets by reassuring any purchaser that a purchase in good faith will vest him with good title no matter what the history of the seller's acquisition of the goods in question.

27.55 The *nemo dat* principle provides, quite simply, that one cannot give what one does not have. Therefore, one who does not have good title cannot purport to transfer title to another person and furthermore that one cannot purport to transfer a greater title than the title which one has oneself. The root of the modern *nemo dat* principle is contained in the speech of Lord Cairns in *Cundy v Lindsay* in the following terms:

> If it turns out that the chattel has been found by the person who professed to sell it, the purchaser will not obtain a title good as against the real owner. If it turns out that the chattel has been stolen by the person who has professed to sell it, the purchaser will not obtain a title. If it turns out that the chattel has come into the hands of the person who professed to sell it, by a de facto [voidable] contract, that is to say, a contract which has purported to pass the property to him from the owner of the property, there the purchaser will obtain a good title.[194]

In that case a rogue impersonated a well-known firm to order a quantity of linen from Lindsay which was then sold on by that rogue to Cundy. Cundy acted in good faith. The question was whether or not the rogue could pass good title to Cundy. It was held that there was no meeting of minds sufficient to form a contract between Lindsay and the rogue because Lindsay thought it was dealing with a reputable firm well known to it rather than with the rogue. In consequence it was

---

[194] (1878) 3 App Cas 459.

held that the rogue did not acquire good title and could therefore not have passed title to Cundy.[195]

There is a clear conflict between the principle that a property owner should only **27.56** lose rights in property voluntarily and the judicial desire to enforce commercial bargains. As Lord Denning put the matter in a subsequent case:

> In the development of our law, two principles have striven for mastery. The first is for the protection of property: no one can give a better title than he himself possesses. The second is for the protection of commercial transactions: the person who takes in good faith and for value without notice should get a good title. The first principle has held sway for a long time, but it has been modified by the common law itself and by statute so as to meet the needs of our own times.[196]

It is suggested that this tension is replicated in the law relating to constructive trusts over property acquired further to criminal activity which is then sold on to a third party acting in good faith.

The *nemo dat* principle and sales through agents

As mentioned above one of the most common situations in which the *nemo dat* **27.57** rule is circumvented by the common law (as opposed to equity) is in relation to sales by agents. Suppose that the title holder does not sell property directly but rather uses an agent to contract a sale. Clearly, where the agent acts within the terms of her agency (that is, she acts with the permission of the principal) then that principal has consented to the sale and has no recourse to recover her property from its purchaser. The problem arises when the agent acts outwith the terms of the agency and where the purchaser is acting in good faith. There are broadly three contexts which are important in relation to agents.

First, the situation in which the agent acts under *apparent authority*. Where the **27.58** agent is acting beyond the terms of her authority but in a situation in which that agent appears to the third party purchaser to be acting lawfully, then that sale will be binding on the principal.[197] The question is in deciding what is meant by 'apparent authority'. It will be important to look at the context. In short, if the agent is acting as a professional 'mercantile agent' (as considered below) then the purchaser will usually receive good title. A mercantile agent would include a second hand car dealer selling the principal's car from her own car lot, but would not include the principal's next door neighbour asked to contract a sale of the same vehicle because the former would appear to the purchaser to be entitled to sell whereas there would be nothing to suggest that the latter was acting in the course

---

195 *Jerome v Bentley & Co* [1952] 2 All ER 114.
196 *Bishopsgate Motor Finance Corporation Ltd v Transport Brakes Ltd* [1949] 1 KB 322.
197 *Rainbow v Howkins* [1904] 2 KB 322.

of his ordinary business.[198] The question is whether the agent is acting in a professional capacity such that the purchaser could demonstrate that she relied on the agent's authority reasonably: in the absence of such good faith or if the circumstances clearly indicated that the agent did not have an absolute authority to sell, the purchaser would not acquire good title.[199] The purchaser would be required to demonstrate that she also acted in good faith in the context and therefore could not assert good title if inquiries would have revealed that the agent did not have the authority to sell the property.[200] The case law indicates that the onus is on the purchaser to ensure that the agent has sufficient authority to transfer title to the purchaser.[201]

27.59   Secondly, building on the case law considered above, under section 21(1) of the Sale of Goods Act 1979 '… where goods are sold by a person who is not their owner, and who does not sell them under the authority or with the consent of the owner, the buyer acquires no better title to the goods than the seller had …'. Therefore, a purchaser will not acquire good title if the agent did not have good title herself. The section does contain a caveat to this general principle in the following terms: '… unless the owner of the goods is by his conduct precluded from denying the seller's authority to sell'. In consequence, where the agent has ostensible authority to sell, the purchaser will take good title. The seller owes no duty to any potential purchaser to protect the purchaser.[202] In one case where a car was put in the possession of a shyster who fraudulently absconded with payment for that car, it was held that section 21(1) applied only to a sale and not to an agreement for which no payment had been made such that the purchaser did not acquire good title because no payment had been made to the owner for the car.[203] These cases emphasize context over everything else: that is, to decide whether the purchaser takes good title or not will depend on the context in which the sale was made.

27.60   Thirdly, and similarly, under section 2(1) of the Factors Act 1889 where a mercantile agent is appointed and effects a sale of property that sale will be effective against the owner of the property. The question is then what constitutes a mercantile agent. In section 1(1) of the 1889 Act it is defined to mean '… a mercantile agent having in the course of his business as such agent authority either to sell goods or to consign goods for the purpose of sale …'. It will include a situation in which a manufacturer of jewellery delivered thousands of pounds worth of jewellery to a person who ran a jewellery shop to sell those items of jewellery so that a purchaser would reasonably assume that the jeweller was acting properly in the

[198] *Turner v Sampson* (1911) 27 TLR 200.
[199] *Astley Industrial Trust Ltd v Miller* [1968] 2 All ER 36.
[200] *Pearson v Young* [1951] 1 KB 275.
[201] *Central Newbury Car Auctions Ltd v Unity Finance Ltd* [1957] 1 QB 371.
[202] *Moorgate Mercantile Co v Twitching* [1977] AC 890.
[203] *Shaw v Commissioner of Police of the Metropolis* [1987] 3 All ER 405.

course of his ordinary business.[204] However, where property is passed to someone who is a personal friend or adviser for them to sell, but where that person is not in the business of selling such property, that person will not be a mercantile agent. So, where jewellery was passed to a lawyer with instructions that it be sold on certain terms, that lawyer would not be a mercantile agent[205] whereas a person who owned shops selling artefacts who was entrusted with selling two tapestries held in the owner's house on certain terms would be a mercantile agent because the purchaser might reasonably suppose that seller to be the agent of the owner given that he had access to the owner's house and was in the business of selling such goods.[206]

Fourthly, a common law estoppel will arise further to the *nemo dat* principle where **27.61** the owner of property makes some representation to the claimant that the claimant would receive some rights in that property. This estoppel is said to be different from equitable estoppel and to be a form of 'common law estoppel'.[207] The estoppel is built on the proviso in section 21(1) of the Sale of Goods Act 1979 that no title passes to the claimant unless 'the owner of the goods is by his conduct precluded from denying the seller's authority to sell'. That expression 'precluded from denying' is taken to introduce the estoppel. The roots of this estoppel are found in the words of Ashurst J in *Lickbarrow v Mason* that 'wherever one of two innocent persons must suffer by the acts of a third, he who has enabled such third person to occasion the loss must sustain it'.[208] That principle has been taken in the case of *Commonwealth Trust v Akotey*[209] to enforce the rights of a third party when the title holder in property had not consented to its being sold. The court was concerned that the third party purchaser receive good title even though the intermediary which purported to sell it a consignment of cocoa had not received good title itself: the title holder contested the intermediary's rights to no avail because the court wanted to protect the innocent third party from disappointment. As a result of such aberrant extensions of the principle, cases such as *Farquharson Bros & Co v King & Co*[210] have doubted the apparent breadth of Ashurst J's statement in *Lickbarrow v Mason*. That leaves the estoppel in an ambiguous position both without a clear intellectual foundation and without a clear remedy attached to it.

Agents occupy a fiduciary relationship to their principals. Therefore, the remedies **27.62** available for abuse of fiduciary office ought to be available to the principal. Where the agent makes some unauthorized profit, that profit should be held on constructive trust for the principal from the moment that it is received.[211] Furthermore, if the agent makes any loss in his dealings with that unauthorized

---

[204] *Weiner v Harris* [1910] 1 KB 285.   [205] *Budberg v Jerwood* (1934) 51 TLR 99.
[206] *Lowther v Harris* [1927] 1 KB 393.
[207] *Eastern Distributors Ltd v Goldring* [1957] 2 QB 600.   [208] (1787) 2 TR 63.
[209] [1926] AC 72.   [210] [1902] AC 325.   [211] *Boardman v Phipps* [1967] 2 AC 46.

profit, then that loss should be made good to the principal by the agent personally.[212] Where no property remains in the hands of the agent but the agent had received the property, then the agent would be liable in knowing receipt for the entire loss suffered by the principal.[213] If the agent does not receive property then the agent would still be liable for breach of the agency agreement on general principles of breach of contract, or potentially for negligence in breach of its duty of care. It would be possible that even if it were only an employee or adviser to the agent, that the employee or adviser would be personally liable for dishonest assistance in a breach of duty even if the agent itself did not consciously breach its duty.[214]

Acquisition of property by fraud

Acquisition of property by means of merely voidable contracts

27.63 Common law fraud will not found a constructive trust because the plaintiff may choose to affirm any fraudulent transaction, even though the defendant's actions would be axiomatically unconscionable, as considered above in relation to fraudulent conduct in general. This same principle applies in relation to situations in which the defendant acquires property by fraud—as opposed to defrauding the plaintiff in general terms—and the plaintiff seeks to establish rights over that property. So, in *Re Ciro Citterio Menswear plc (in administration)*[215] two directors acquired land which was paid for as to about £250,000 with funds supplied by the company. This transfer of money was in breach of the rules in section 330 of the Companies Act 1985 governing loans to company directors. The company subsequently went into insolvent administration. It was held that a director would not automatically be constructive trustee of moneys loaned to her by the company in breach of the statutory code because such a loan could be made for proper purposes. The effect of the 1985 Act prohibiting such loans was merely to make them voidable and not void: therefore, the loan would not found a constructive trust automatically because the company may choose to affirm the loan subsequently.

Acquisition of property by means of void contracts

27.64 As considered above in relation to fraudulent conduct,[216] if the defendant's conduct was fraudulent at the time he acquired the property at issue—and therefore both unconscionable and knowingly so—and if the transaction comprising the fraud was void, then the defendant would be liable to be a constructive trustee of that property.[217] This principle is demonstrated, it is suggested, by *Westdeutsche*

---

[212] *Att-Gen for Hong Kong v Reid* [1994] 1 AC 324.
[213] *Twinsectra Ltd v Yardley* [1999] Lloyd's Rep Bank 438, CA.
[214] *Royal Brunei Airlines v Tan* [1995] 2 AC 378.   [215] [2002] 2 All ER 717.
[216] See para 27.24.   [217] *Westdeutsche Landesbank v Islington* [1996] AC 669.

Landesbank v Islington[218] a case in which a bank had advanced money to a local authority under the terms of an interest rate swap contract which was subsequently held to have been void *ab initio* because it was *ultra vires* the local authority. On the facts the local authority had disposed of the money advanced to it before either party to the transaction had known that their contract was void *ab initio*. It was held that there was no constructive trust on those facts for two reasons: first, because there was no traceable property over which a trust could be enforced and, secondly, because the defendant did not know that the property had been passed to it under a void transaction at any time before it disposed of that property. Two points are evident from this decision. First, as discussed at the outset of this chapter, no constructive trust will take effect unless the defendant has sufficient knowledge of the factors which are said to be unconscionable. Secondly, that a void transaction may pass good title in property—on these facts, the money paid by the bank and paid away by the local authority—and so preserve the defendant from being a constructive trustee because there is no money in his possession over which the trust could bite and from being liable to account as though a constructive trustee because he had insufficient knowledge of the factors which might otherwise have affected his conscience so as to make him liable in that fashion.[219]

I. Enforcement of Voluntary Agreements

The question of enforcement of voluntary agreements is considered in the **27.65** following chapter. Briefly put, English equity has long accepted that various forms of repudiation of either binding contracts or informal agreements, arrangements, or understandings will constitute unconscionable behaviour. However, unlike the foregoing forms of unconscionable behaviour considered in this section, constructive trusts raised to procure the enforcement of voluntary agreements, of either type, do not arise by operation of law contrary to the wishes of the parties. While it could logically be said that, by the time litigation has arisen, at least one party does not wish the constructive trust to be imposed nor the contract to be enforced, nevertheless the purpose of the constructive trust is to give effect to the parties' earlier, voluntary agreement and therefore the purpose underlying the constructive trust is different from the foregoing which has focused on questions of public policy, in truth, aimed at preventing the defendant from taking some benefit from his unconscionable action.

---

[218] [1996] AC 669.
[219] There may be other factors which would justify the imposition of a constructive trust, for example if the director was also committing criminal offences relating to insider dealing collateral to the loan contract, as in *Guinness plc v Saunders* [1990] 1 All ER 652.

28

CONSTRUCTIVE TRUSTS TO ENFORCE AGREEMENTS

A. Constructive Trusts Used to Supplement Agreements

This chapter focuses on a different sense in which constructive trusts are used **28.01** from those considered in the previous chapter. Where parties have entered either into a contract which is binding at common law or into one of another series of informal agreements considered in this chapter, equity will prevent the defendant from seeking unconscionably to renege on that agreement by means of the doctrine of specific performance or, in certain circumstances considered in this chapter, by means of a constructive trust. The mechanisms by which these constructive trusts are effected differ depending on whether the agreement is a legally binding contract or some more informal understanding between the parties. In the former, the existence of a contract binding at common law which entitles the contracting parties to specific performance activates the equitable principle that equity looks upon as done that which ought to have been done.[1] In consequence, equity will impose a constructive trust over any property which was required to have been transferred further to that agreement. In the latter circumstance, equity will intervene in limited circumstances to prevent a party to an informal agreement from reneging unconscionably on that agreement.[2] This principle, it is suggested, underpins the common intention constructive trust,[3] the secret trust,[4] the mutual will,[5] and situations in which an imperfect transfer will be deemed to have been perfected in equity where to do otherwise would be unconscionable.[6] The discussion to follow divides between these two circumstances.

A. CONTRACTS

B. Specifically Enforceable Contracts

Contracts for sale of property establishing constructive trusts in general terms

28.02   In circumstances in which a contract is created to effect the sale or other transfer of property, that contract will operate so as to transfer equitable title in that property from the original owner to the other contracting party.[7] The transfer of equitable title should be understood as taking effect by means of a constructive trust.[8]

---

[1] *Walsh v Lonsdale* (1882) 21 Ch D 9; *Attorney-General for Hong Kong v Reid* [1994] 1 AC 324, [1993] 3 WLR 1143.

[2] *Chinn v Collins* [1981] AC 533; *Neville v Wilson* [1997] Ch 144.

[3] *Gissing v Gissing* [1971] AC 886; *Cowcher v Cowcher* [1972] 1 All ER 948; *Grant v Edwards* [1986] Ch 638; *Lloyds Bank v Rosset* [1991] 1 AC 107, [1990] 1 All ER 1111, [1990] 2 WLR 867.

[4] *Blackwell v Blackwell* [1929] AC 318; *Ottaway v Norman* [1972] 2 WLR 50.

[5] *Dufour v Pereira* (1769) 1 Dick 419; *Re Dale* [1994] Ch 31; *Re Goodchild* [1997] 1 WLR 1216, [1997] 3 All ER 63.

[6] *Re Rose* [1952] Ch 499, [1952] 1 All ER 1217. See also *Pennington v Waine* [2002] EWCA Civ 227.

[7] *Lysaght v Edwards* (1876) 2 Ch D 499; *Oughtred v IRC* [1960] AC 206; *Neville v Wilson* [1997] Ch 144.

[8] *Chinn v Collins* [1981] AC 533; *Neville v Wilson* [1997] Ch 144. Historically this automatic transfer of title in equity might have been understood as operating on the more general, equitable principle that equity looks upon as done that which ought to have been done (*Walsh v Lonsdale* (1882) 21 Ch D 9) without requiring the mechanism of constructive trust. Alternatively, such a constructive trust may be understood as coming into effect, as considered in the main text above, in response to the operation of that same ancient equitable principle (*Attorney-General for Hong Kong v Reid* [1994] 1 AC 324).

The rationale behind the operation of this principle is as follows. Once the contract is formally created the contracting parties acquire rights of specific performance to force the other party to perform its part of the bargain. On the basis that each party has a right in equity to specific performance, and on the basis further that the contract is one to transfer title in property, it is said that the party so entitled acquires a right to the entire equitable interest in that property.[9] The automatic vesting of the equitable interest is said to arise due to the equitable principle that equity looks upon as done that which ought to have been done: therefore, equity considers that because the contract requires transfer of title then transfer of title must be deemed to have taken place automatically.[10]

Contract for the sale of land

Contracts for the sale of land have their own formalities which shape the doctrine that equitable title passes automatically on the creation of a contract accordingly. Further to section 2 of the Law of Property (Miscellaneous Provisions) Act 1989, any contract for the sale or transfer of an interest in land must be effected in writing in one document containing all of the terms of the contract and signed by all of the parties. Therefore, a formal requirement to the efficacy of this doctrine is the use of writing.[11] However, once that contract has been created, the equitable interest in the land is deemed to have transferred automatically to the purchaser of that interest.[12] It is suggested that the modern understanding of such an event would be that the vendor holds the property on constructive trust for the purchaser until completion of the sale or transfer.[13] **28.03**

The precise nature and scope of that constructive trust is worthy of closer examination. The constructive trust in these circumstances frequently grants more complex rights to the trustee than an ordinary bare trust although the rights of the beneficiary are typically limited to those of a beneficiary under a bare trust. In *Lloyds Bank v Carrick*[14] the defendant vendor contracted with his sister-in-law to sell a lease over a residential property to her. The transaction required the sister-in-law to sell her own home, to pay those sale proceeds to the defendant and then to **28.04**

---

[9] *Chinn v Collins* [1981] AC 533; *Neville v Wilson* [1997] Ch 144.

[10] *Walsh v Lonsdale* (1882) 21 Ch D 9.

[11] As becomes clear in the next section, that would have the effect of preventing the stamp duty avoidance techniques discussed there in relation to land transactions.

[12] *Lysaght v Edwards* (1876) 2 Ch D 499. No similar obligation is owed to a further, sub-purchaser: *Berkley v Earl Poulett* (1977) 242 EG 39. Although a sale to another person would require the vendor to hold the sale proceeds on trust for the initial purchaser under contract, *Lake v Bayliss* [1974] 1 WLR 1073; *Shaw v Foster* (1872) 5 HL 321.

[13] This operates in parallel, it is suggested, to the doctrine which provides that the vendor acts as trustee of the fee simple absolute in possession over land between the time of completion of sale and the re-registration of the proprietorship of that land in the name of the purchaser.

[14] [1996] 4 All ER 630.

move into property over which the defendant was lessee, at which time he would assign his interest in the lease to her. The defendant took out a charge with the claimant bank without informing his sister-in-law. The question turned on whether or not the sister-in-law had a right under a merely bare trust such that her right did not require registration and so could not be unenforceable against the bank for want of registration. It was held that the contract became specifically enforceable when the sister-in-law began to perform her obligations under the contract by entering into possession of the lease and paying the purchase price.[15] Consequently, it was held that the sister-in-law's interest arose by virtue of the specific enforceability of the contract and therefore was void as against the bank for want of registration.[16] Her right was the right of a person under a bare trust in relation to that interest in property for which she had contracted. This right would, however, grant a priority right in the vendor's insolvency.[17]

28.05 The fiduciary obligations of the vendor are limited. This constructive trust is limited to equity transferring the equitable title in the property which has been contracted to be sold and does impose no greater obligations on the trustee than that. Where the purchase price for the property remains unpaid it does not constitute the vendor a constructive trustee in general terms of, for example, all rents and other income received in relation to that property.[18] Furthermore, the vendor is entitled to protect his interests in the property prior to sale and therefore is not obliged to act only in the best interests of the purchaser, as would be the case with an ordinary trustee.[19] Indeed the vendor in such circumstances has been described as being a mere 'quasi-trustee' as a result, *inter alia*, of these limitations on his obligations.[20]

Contract for sale of personalty

28.06 The basis of the doctrine, that the equitable title in property passes on constructive trust when a contract is created for the transfer of that property, is that an automatic transfer of equitable title occurs where otherwise the former owner of that title would seek to renege on his obligations under that contract at common

---

[15] Significantly, however, this particular contract remained executory at the time that the charge was created in favour of the bank, [1996] 4 All ER 630, 637.

[16] ibid.

[17] *Freevale Ltd v Metrostore (Holdings) Ltd* [1984] 1 All ER 495; *Re Coregrange Ltd* [1984] BCLC 453; subject always to any statutory power to disclaim contracts *inter alia* as a fraud on the creditors of the insolvent person.

[18] *Rayner v Preston* (1881) 18 Ch D 1, 6, *per* Cotton LJ. The precise point in that case having been altered by Law of Property Act 1925, s 47. Also *J Sainsbury plc v O'Connor (Inspector of Taxes)* [1991] STC 318. Cf *Paine v Meller* (1801) 6 Ves Jr 349.

[19] *Shaw v Foster* (1872) LR 5 HL 321, 338, *per* Lord Cairns. See also *Royal Bristol and Permanent Building Society v Bomash* (1887) 35 Ch D 390.

[20] *Cumberland Consolidated Holdings Ltd v Ireland* [1946] KB 264, 269, *per* Lord Greene MR; *Berkley v Poulett* (1977) 242 EG 39.

law. In its earliest manifestations the equitable principle that equity looks upon as done that which ought to have been done[21] had the effect, for example, that once negotiations for a lease[22] had hardened into a contract that a formally valid lease should be granted, even though the parties had not yet executed a lease which would have been valid at common law, then there was held to be a lease in place by virtue of that agreement which took effect in equity.[23]

The notion of automatic transfer has been used particularly in tax planning to **28.07** effect automatic transfers of the equitable interest in property—and thereby the most valuable part of the absolute title in that property in the context of any liability to tax—without the need to effect transfer by means of any documentation or other act which might itself trigger liability to tax or stamp duty before the more valuable part of the title had been disposed of. This reversal of the core understanding of the *Walsh v Lonsdale*[24] principle into an offensive rather than a defensive mechanism has the weight of authority. Many of the decided cases relating to personalty consequently concern tax planning matters. Thus, in *Oughtred v IRC*[25] a mother and son wished to exchange title in valuable shareholdings so that the mother could consolidate a larger shareholding in one particular company. However, to have effected documentary transfers of the shares, necessary to transfer legal title, would have attracted liability to stamp duty. Therefore, the two created a contract between themselves to exchange shares. This structure has been held[26] to effect an automatic transfer of the equitable interest such that stamp duty levied on the document of transfer of the legal title is levied on a nil amount on the basis that all of the value in the shareholdings moves with the equitable interest.[27] Until the document transfers legal title to the intended recipient, the legal owner is constituted a constructive trustee of that property.[28] This principle has been upheld in subsequent cases.[29]

C. Partnerships and Commercial Joint Ventures

Where a partnership is formed to exploit a commercial opportunity, where one of **28.08** the partners seeks to exploit that venture unilaterally to the consequent disadvantage of the other partners, any benefit so obtained will be held on constructive

---

[21] *Parker v Taswell* (1858) 27 LJ Ch 812.
[22] At that time considered to be a chattel real and not real property.
[23] *Walsh v Lonsdale* (1882) 21 Ch D 9.   [24] (1882) 21 Ch D 9.   [25] [1960] AC 206.
[26] The leading speech of Lord Radcliffe in *Oughtred v IRC* [1960] AC 206 itself was somewhat elliptic on this point. His lordship's intention was to find the taxpayers liable to stamp duty under the then applicable stamp duty legislation at the least, although his lordship did appear to concede that the equitable interest in the shares did pass on the creation of the contract, even if that had no effect on the stamp duty position ultimately.
[27] See *Chinn v Collins* [1981] AC 533; *Neville v Wilson* [1997] Ch 144.
[28] *Chinn v Collins* [1981] AC 533; *Neville v Wilson* [1997] Ch 144.
[29] *Chinn v Collins* [1981] AC 533; *Neville v Wilson* [1997] Ch 144.

trust, as was considered in Chapter 27.[30] Either this constructive trust could be said to arise so as to prevent the unconscionable breach of a contract or, in this context, as an extension to the principle that a fiduciary (such as a partner) cannot retain unauthorized, 'secret' profits derived from that fiduciary office.[31] So, by entering into negotiations for a joint venture to exploit land and subsequently seeking to exploit that land alone when those negotiations had precluded the claimant from exploiting any interest in that land.[32]

28.09 In its earliest incarnation, this constructive trust was considered to be a device which operated on a general equitable basis. By way of illustration, in *Chattock v Muller*[33] two people were interested in bidding at auction to acquire a parcel of land adjoining the defendant's land. To avoid bidding against one another the parties came to a non-contractual agreement that only one of them should bid and that the property would subsequently be divided between them.[34] The defendant wrote to the plaintiff after this arrangement had been forged between them suggesting that he, the defendant, had had an offer from the auctioneer to buy the property. The plaintiff replied that he would not make an offer for the property himself as a result. In time the defendant acquired the property but decided to transfer it to his son as opposed to the plaintiff. It was held by Malins V-C that equity precluded the defendant from keeping the property for himself, even though he had not entered into a formal contract with the plaintiff, because his actions in the context of their arrangement had caused the plaintiff not to bid for the property on his own account on the basis that he would receive a part of it in any event. The defendant was considered to be acting, in this context, partly as the plaintiff's agent when bidding at the auction. Similarly, in *Pallant v Morgan*[35] the owners of adjoining land decided that they would bid at auction for woodland which abutted their land so that they could ensure its preservation. While the parties had not formed a binding contract as to the manner in which the property would be divided between them, it was agreed that the plaintiff's agent would refrain from bidding in relation to identified lots of the woodland and that identified lots, if acquired by the defendant, would be transferred subsequently to the plaintiff. The defendant acquired all of the relevant lots and then refused to transfer any part of them to the plaintiff. Harman J declared that there could not be any specific performance because there was no binding agreement capable of such enforcement but declared further that it would have been 'tantamount to sanctioning a fraud' on the defendant's part if the defendant were entitled to retain ownership of the identified lots. It was declared that the land was held by the

---

[30] See para 27.03.　　[31] *Boardman v Phipps* [1967] 2 AC 46.
[32] *Pallant v Morgan* [1953] Ch 43.　　[33] (1878) 8 Ch D 177.
[34] While there was no formal contract between the parties, there was a written memorandum which was sufficient to satisfy the court that there was no conflict with the Statute of Frauds 1677.
[35] [1953] Ch 43, [1952] 2 All ER 951.

defendant on trust for himself and the plaintiff jointly.[36] These cases appear to have been decided on a generally equitable basis rather than by specific reference to the doctrine of constructive trust.

Consequently, the basis of this doctrine was transformed from a general equity **28.10** into a trust which came into existence to prevent an unconscionable or quasi-fraudulent action on the part of the common law owner of the property. Its modern form, therefore, is as a constructive trust over that property.[37] So in *Banner Homes Group plc v Luff Development Ltd*[38] two commercial parties entered into what was described as a 'joint venture' to exploit the development prospects of land in Berkshire. It was held that no binding contract had been formed between the parties when the defendant sought to exploit the site alone without the involvement of the claimant. Extensive negotiations were conducted between the claimant and the defendant and their respective lawyers with reference to documentation to create a joint venture partnership or company. The defendant continued the negotiations while privately nursing reservations about going into business with the claimant. The defendant decided, however, that it should 'keep [the claimant] on board' unless or until a better prospect emerged. It was held that the defendant could establish a constructive trust even in the absence of a binding contract to the effect that the claimant and defendant would exploit the land jointly if the defendant had refrained from exploiting any personal interests in that land in reliance on the negotiations being conducted between the claimant and defendant.[39]

In relation to all of these categories of constructive trust over land there is a similarity between the constructive trust and proprietary estoppel. Indeed some cases **28.11** before *Banner Homes v Luff Development* had suggested that the equity in *Pallant v Morgan* bore great similarities to the doctrine of proprietary estoppel.[40]

---

[36] See also the dicta of Megarry J in relation to an application for interlocutory relief as part of the litigation in *Holiday Inns Inc v Broadhead* (unreported) quoted in *Banner Homes Group plc v Luff Development Ltd* [2000] 2 All ER 117, 131, to the effect that the equity in *Pallant v Morgan* substitutes an alternative form of remedy to specific performance where specific performance was itself not available.

[37] As explained in *Banner Homes Group plc v Luff Development Ltd* [2000] Ch 372, 137, per Chadwick LJ, in reliance on dicta in *Lonrho plc v Fayed (No 2)* [1991] 4 All ER 961, 969, per Millett J and *Paragon Finance plc v DB Thackerar & Co (a firm)* [1999] 1 All ER 400, 408, per Millett LJ as to the nature of the constructive trust. See also *London & Regional Investments Ltd v TBI Plc & Anor* [2002] EWCA Civ 355.

[38] [2000] Ch 372, [2000] 2 WLR 772, [2000] 2 All ER 117.

[39] It has been held, however, that this doctrine will not found a remedial constructive trust in support of a contract: *Thames Cruises Ltd v George Wheeler Launches Ltd* [2003] EWHC 3093.

[40] *Holiday Inns Inc v Broadhead* (1974) 232 EG 951, 1087, per Goff J; applying *Plimmer v Wellington Corporation* (1884) 9 App Cas 699; *Inwards v Baker* [1965] 2 QB 29, [1965] 1 All ER 446; *Ward v Kirkland* [1966] 1 All ER 609. See also Oliver J in *Time Products Ltd v Combined English Stores Group plc* (unreported) rehearsed in *Banner Homes Group plc v Luff Development Ltd* [2000] 2 All ER 117, 134.

The common feature in all of these claims (where estoppel can be defined as a claim) is that the claimant must have suffered some detriment to found its claim.[41] The claimant seeks to hold the defendant to a putative bargain which has not crystallized into a formal contract on the basis that sufficient representation has been made such that the claimant suffered detriment in reliance on those representations. In the course of commercial dealings prior to contract it may be a difficult matter to know in the abstract at what point the parties have progressed sufficiently far with their negotiations to know that they have made some actionable representation, because the representation in this context will manifest itself in such a weight of discussion, negotiation, and emergence of a common, commercial purpose between the parties,[42] such that the claimant can credibly suggest that he had become convinced that his actions in reliance on that commonality of purpose were reasonable and that the detriment which he suffered was deserving of compensation. In this sense it is important that in *Banner Homes v Luff Development* there had been long-standing negotiations between the parties and that the defendant was aware that the claimant was suffering detriment in the form of incurring expense in reliance on their emerging common purpose. A constructive trust analysis of this situation would suggest that it would be unconscionable for the defendant to renege on those arrangements,[43] whereas a proprietary estoppel analysis would seek to compensate the claimant for the detriment suffered in reliance on the representation.[44] The distinctions between these doctrines were considered in Chapter 25.[45]

D. Agreements to Stay Out of the Market

Constructive trusts to 'keep out of the market'

28.12   A constructive trust will be imposed in circumstances in which the claimant has refrained from exploiting some commercial opportunity[46] in reliance on some agreement or pre-contractual understanding reached with the defendant.[47] In general terms this is referred to as the claimant 'keeping out of the market'. The basis of the trust is that the claimant will have suffered detriment by failing to exploit a commercial opportunity. The conscience of the defendant is affected where the claimant's decision not to exploit that commercial opportunity is based on some understanding reached with the defendant or some assurance made by

---

[41] *Grant v Edwards* [1986] Ch 638.
[42] As in *Gillett v Holt* [2000] 2 All ER 289 where the 'representation' was formed over a number of years in the form of an understanding between the parties as opposed to a single statement.
[43] *Westdeutsche Landesbank v Islington* [1996] AC 669.
[44] *Lim v Ang* [1992] 1 WLR. 113.   [45] See para 25.42.
[46] In relation to specific property or, potentially it is suggested, otherwise.
[47] *Chattock v Muller* (1878) 8 Ch D 177; *Pallant v Morgan* [1952] 2 All ER 951.

the defendant that they would reach some other agreement: the defendant must then exploit that opportunity in some way in contravention of the parties' understanding. The trust bites on any property which the defendant realizes from exploiting the opportunity. This constructive trust will bind a purchaser of property who had previously procured the claimant's agreement not to bid for property at auction on the basis that the purchaser would sell part of that land to the claimant;[48] or bind a purchaser of land at auction who had previously agreed with the claimant not to bid against the claimant for part of that land at auction;[49] or would bind a defendant who acquired development land on its own account where it had reached an understanding with the claimant that that land would be exploited as a joint venture with the claimant.[50] This form of constructive trust is identified in the cases as arising on the basis of that form of constructive trust considered in the preceding section.[51]

E. Part Performance of Agreements

The old equitable doctrine of part performance was repealed by section 3 of the **28.13** Law of Property (Miscellaneous Provisions) Act 1989. It is suggested, however, that a constructive trust or proprietary estoppel arising to prevent the unconscionable repudiation of a contract which one of the parties relied upon when performing his obligations in part does found a right similar in form to that repealed doctrine. So, in recent cases the application of proprietary estoppel has been explained as arising by means of the imposition of a constructive trust on the property at issue.[52] It is not suggested here that the doctrine of proprietary estoppel necessarily equates exactly with that of constructive trust, although a number of judges[53] and commentators[54] have indicated that the two doctrines are susceptible to merger. What is suggested in this brief section is that a person who is estopped from denying another person rights in property to which he would have been otherwise entitled under contract is in a comparable position to one who may become a constructive trustee of that property for the claimant. That there has been judicial commentary suggesting an elision between these two doctrines only emphasizes that apparent similarity.[55]

---

[48] *Chattock v Miller* (1878) 8 Ch D 177. [49] *Pallant v Morgan* [1952] 2 All ER 951.
[50] *Banner Homes v Luff Developments* [2000] Ch 372; [2000] 2 WLR 772.
[51] See para 28.08. [52] *Yaxley v Gotts* [2000] 1 All ER 711.
[53] *Lloyds Bank v Rosset* [1991] AC 1.
[54] D Hayton, 'Constructive trusts: a bold approach' (1993) 99 LQR 485 contending for a remedial constructive trust. Cf E Cooke, *The Modern Law of Estoppel* (Clarendon Press, 1999) considered below, in which Prof Cooke contends that estoppel is based generally on the avoidance of unconscionability, which it is suggested is broadly in line with the constructive trust.
[55] For example see *Yaxley v Gotts* [2000] 1 All ER 711.

28.14 An example of this broader proprietary estoppel is provided by *Yaxley v Gotts* [56] in which a joint venture was formed for the acquisition of land. The joint venture did not comply with the requirement in section 2 of the Law of Property (Miscellaneous Provisions) Act 1989 that the terms of any purported contract for the transfer of any interest in land be in writing. The defendant therefore contended that the claimant could have acquired no right in contract to the land because there was no writing in accordance with the formal requirements of the statute. However, the court was prepared to uphold that between the parties there had been a representation that there would be a joint venture between the parties in reliance on which the claimant had acted to its detriment. It was held by the Court of Appeal that a constructive trust had arisen between the parties on the basis of their common intention—and that this constructive trust was indistinguishable in this form from a proprietary estoppel. [57]

28.15 The general issue arose as to whether or not the general public policy underpinning the statutory formalities ought to be rigidly adhered to so as to preclude the activation of any estoppel on the basis that it was a principle of fundamentally important social policy. [58] It was held that in deciding whether or not a parliamentary purpose was being frustrated, one should 'look at the circumstances in each case and decide in what way the equity can be satisfied'. [59] The court is able to apply the doctrine of proprietary estoppel where it was necessary to do the minimum equity necessary between the parties. [60] In effect this opens the way for the return of the part performance doctrine [61] in the guise of proprietary estoppel and constructive trust. While the doctrine of the creation of equitable mortgages by deposit of title deeds was deemed to have been removed by the 1989 Act [62] the equitable doctrine of proprietary estoppel remained intact [63] even where it would appear to offend the principle that an ineffective contract ought not to be effected by means of equitable doctrine. [64]

28.16 A constructive trust may arise in two ways in this context. First, suppose that a person has been promised a share in land together with third parties on the death

---

[56] [2000] 1 All ER 711; R Smith, 'Oral contracts for the sale of land' (2000) 116 LQR 11; Tee, 'A merry-go-round for the millennium' [2000] CLJ 23.

[57] [2001] 1 All ER 721 *et seq, per* Robert Walker LJ.

[58] *Kok Hoong v Leong Cheong Kweng Mines Ltd* [1964] AC 993; *Godden v Merthyr Tydfil Housing Association* [1997] NPC 1.

[59] *Plimmer v Mayor of Wellington* (1884) 9 App Cas 699, 714, *per* Sir Arthur Hobhouse.

[60] *Crabb v Arun DC* [1976] Ch 179, 198, *per* Scarman LJ. It is interesting to note that their lordships are prepared to find a means of eluding straightforwardly mandatory norms of statute to give effect to some higher purpose contained in the case law.

[61] Whereby any contract which had been partly performed would be perfected by equity.

[62] *United Bank of Kuwait plc v Sahib* [1997] Ch 107.

[63] *King v Jackson* [1998] 1 EGLR 30; and *McCausland v Duncan Lawrie Ltd* [1997] 1 WLR 38, *infra.*

[64] *Westdeutsche Landesbank v Islington LBC, Kleinwort Benson v Sandwell BC* [1994] 4 All ER 890.

of the absolute owner of that land. Further to authority, if the owner made a representation to the claimant that if he performed certain detrimental acts, then the claimant would be entitled to a claim against that property in the event that he performed those acts in reliance on that representation.[65] Prior to the resolution of the parties' claims to that land but once proprietary estoppel has been awarded preventing a winding up of the estate which overlooked the claimant's rights, the testator's personal representatives will be constructive trustees of that property for the claimant. Therefore, to prevent use of property in contravention of that estoppel, it is suggested that the legal owner of that property ought properly to be understood as being a constructive trustee until the court's remedy for the detrimental reliance on which the estoppel was based is effected. Secondly, it is also possible that a person who represents to another that that other will be vested with title in that property on the performance of certain detrimental acts, will be a constructive trustee of that property for that other person as soon as those acts are performed in reliance on the representation.[66] This second model of constructive trust differs from the first in that it is not merely a stopgap between the order of proprietary estoppel and the carrying out of the court-appointed remedy, but rather it is suggested that this would be creative of a substantive proprietary right.

The doctrine of part performance finds new expression in cases such as *Yaxley v* **28.17**
Gotts [67] where, in spite of the formal requirements for the creation of a contract for the sale of interests in land,[68] it was held that where one party had begun to perform its part of a bargain in reliance on its counterpart obeying the parties' agreement then that other party is estopped from repudiating the transaction. Whereas the Law of Property (Miscellaneous Provisions) Act 1989 was enacted *inter alia* to repeal section 40 of the Law of Property Act 1925 and the doctrine of part performance, the expanding doctrine of proprietary estoppel has reintroduced its effect by another means. In relation to constructive trusts, the party who is estopped from denying its representation is consequently a constructive trustee of any property interest which was to have been passed in connection with that representation on which detrimental reliance is placed.

F. Contractual Undertakings and Licences

Ordinary contractual provisions will not grant rights in property by operation of law

The operation of constructive trusts has been extended into regions relating **28.18**
to contractual provisions where subsequent authorities decided it ought not to

---

[65] *Re Basham* [1986] 1 WLR 1498; *Gillett v Holt* [2000] 2 All ER 289.
[66] *Yaxley v Gotts* [2000] 1 All ER 711.   [67] ibid.
[68] Law of Property (Miscellaneous Provisions) Act 1989, s 2.

have gone. Briefly put, a constructive trust will not arise, without more, where a contractual provision provides that the claimant is to be entitled to the use of property but without the creation of some substantive legal right in his favour.[69] The most significant example of this tendency to enlarge such contractual rights into proprietary rights arose in relation to contractual licences, as considered immediately below, in which such licences were held to have created such equitable proprietary rights capable of resisting any action brought by the licensor to evict the occupants.[70] In general terms, a constructive trust will only arise over property on the basis of agreements if that agreement is in the form of a contract for the sale of property,[71] or if it arises in relation to co-owned property by means of a common intention constructive trust,[72] or if one of the contracting parties would otherwise be able to use statute as an instrument of a fraud to defeat some other person's rights in property.[73] Otherwise a merely personal right will not be enlarged into a proprietary right over property simply by reason of the contract containing that personal right being broken. The one doctrine which offers protection is that of proprietary estoppel, considered immediately below in relation to contractual licences.[74]

Contractual licences

28.19 A slew of cases in the 1970s sought to enlarge the personal right granted by means of a contractual licence into a right in property. In particular the purpose behind this mooted doctrine was to enlarge the implied permission which spouses and children had to occupy their homes into a proprietary right to occupy the property.[75] However, it was subsequently held that there was no such general doctrine of contractual licences binding as property rights and that those authorities which had so held were explicable entirely on their own facts in terms of constructive trusts granting property rights.[76] Such a constructive trust arises only where it is satisfied that 'the conscience of the estate owner is affected'[77] but that a contract will not by itself be sufficient to achieve that.[78] Where the line rests between a constructive trust and mere contractual licence is difficult to establish in the abstract although it is clear that the general principle for the operation of constructive trusts[79] operates in this context in the sense that liability will arise in

---

[69] *Ashburn Anstalt v Arnold* [1989] Ch 1, [1988] 2 All ER 147.   [70] See para 28.20.

[71] *Neville v Wilson* [1997] Ch 144.

[72] *Lloyds Bank v Rosset* [1991] 1 AC 107, [1990] 1 All ER 1111, [1990] 2 WLR 867: see para 56.24.

[73] *Lyus v Prowsa Developments Ltd* [1982] 1 WLR 1044, [1982] 2 All ER 953: see para 27.34.

[74] See para 28.19.

[75] *Errington v Errington and Woods* [1952] 1 KB 290; *Binions v Evans* [1972] Ch 359; *DHN Food Distributors Ltd v Tower Hamlets Borough Council* [1976] 1 WLR 852; *Re Sharpe* [1980] 1 WLR 219.

[76] *Ashburn Anstalt v Arnold* [1989] Ch 1, 23, [1988] 2 All ER 147, 165, *per* Fox LJ.

[77] ibid.   [78] ibid.   [79] See para 27.01.

circumstances in which the conscience of the defendant is affected.[80] However, it will not be sufficient to establish behaviour contrary to conscience that some term of the contract was breached:[81] this is particularly so where damages would be an adequate remedy. To establish a right in property by means of a constructive trust, it would be necessary to demonstrate some detriment suffered by the claimant not remediable in contract by payment of common law damages—an approach which indicates that such a right is closer to proprietary estoppel[82] or to common intention constructive trusts.[83]

Estoppel licences

A contractual licence may be elevated effectively to the level of a property right **28.20** against the other contracting party where the claimant has relied on a representation by that other contracting party to his detriment in relation to that property. In such a situation, that contracting party would be estopped from reneging on the representation. So, for example, where a prospective tenant entered into a verbal agreement with a landlord in which the landlord assured that person that she would be granted an interest in the land in the future, with the result that she expended money in reliance on that assurance, that prospective tenant would acquire rights in the land under proprietary estoppel principles.[84] Any detriment suffered must have been in the expectation of receiving some right in the property of which the landlord was aware.[85] It is important that the landlord have acquiesced in the claimant's actions and not merely that the claimant have acted without the landlord's knowledge.[86] There is a drift in the cases which focuses on the unconscionable act of the defendant in more general terms concerning the promise of some interest in the property,[87] and even a principle of unjust enrichment.[88] More generally, it has been suggested that proprietary estoppel ought to arise more generally in cases of unconscionability.[89] In short, a licensee may acquire estoppel rights against property where a right holder in that property has made some assurance to that licensee that she would acquire some rights in the property whether by way of a lease or otherwise.

---

[80] *Ashburn Anstalt v Arnold* [1989] Ch 1, 23, [1988] 2 All ER 147, 165, *per* Fox LJ.
[81] ibid.   [82] *Gillett v Holt* [2000] 2 All ER 289.
[83] *Grant v Edwards* [1986] Ch 638; K Gray and S Gray, *Elements of Land Law* (Butterworths, 2000) 182.
[84] *Ramsden v Dyson* (1866) LR 1 HL 129, 170, *per* Lord Kingsdown.
[85] *Western Fish Products Ltd v Penrith DC* [1981] 2 All ER 204; *Brinnand v Ewens* [1987] 2 EGLR 67.
[86] *Jones v Stones* [1999] 1 WLR 1739.
[87] *Taylors Fashions Ltd v Liverpool Victoria Trustees Co Ltd* [1982] QB 133; *Elitestone Ltd v Morris* (1995) 73 P & CR 259; *Lloyds Bank v Carrick* [1996] 4 All ER 630.
[88] *Sledmore v Dalby* (1996) 72 P & CR 196, 208, *per* Hobhouse LJ.
[89] E Cooke, *The Modern Law of Estoppel* (Clarendon Press, 1999).

28.21   The remedy available to a claimant is effectively drawn on the same canvas as for proprietary estoppel.[90] This may lead to the acquisition of limited rights of secure occupation. Where a licensee had spent £700 on improvements to the bungalow in reliance on representations made to them that they would be able to remain in occupation, the court held that they could remain in secure occupation until their expenditure had been reimbursed[91] or generally 'for as long as they wish to occupy the property'.[92] Alternatively, the claimant may simply be entitled to an amount of money to compensate her for her detriment.[93] In exceptional cases a transfer of the entire fee simple has been ordered to protect the claimant from suffering detriment:[94] this may be because the contribution was so large that a transfer of the fee simple was the only suitable remedy[95] or because that would be the only means of securing the claimant's occupation in the light of a representation that she could occupy in perpetuity.[96] What is most significant is that the court will have complete freedom to frame its remedy once it has found that an estoppel is both available and appropriate.[97]

B. VOLUNTARILY ASSUMED LIABILITY

28.22   The categories of constructive trust assembled in this section are said to arise on the basis of voluntary assumption of liability where a person is deemed to be a constructive trustee because of some relationship or some course of dealing into which they entered voluntarily. The constructive trusts considered in this section arise not contrary to the intentions of the parties but rather in accordance with their common intention (whether expressed or implied) by operation of law. The common intention constructive trust properly so-called arises only in relation to trusts of homes by fastening on either an agreement of the parties or the conduct of the parties.[98] Equity recognizes that title passes automatically on the creation of the contract without the need for further formality, irrespective of the position at common law or under statute. It is suggested that a similar analysis applies to secret trusts[99] and mutual wills.[100]

---

[90] See para 25.42.
[91] *Dodsworth v Dodsworth* (1973) 228 EG 1115; *Burrows and Burrows v Sharpe* (1991) 23 HLR 82.   [92] *Inwards v Baker* [1965] 2 QB 29.
[93] *Baker v Baker* (1993) 25 HLR 408.
[94] *Pascoe v Turner* [1979] 1 WLR 431; *Voyce v Voyce* (1991) 62 P & CR 290.
[95] *Dillwyn v Llewelyn* (1862) 4 De GF & J 517.   [96] *Pascoe v Turner* [1979] 1 WLR 431.
[97] An approach approved as long ago as *Lord Cawdor v Lewis* (1835) 1 Y & C Ex 427, 433; *Plimmer v Wellington Corporation* (1884) 9 App Cas 699, 713.
[98] This form of trust is considered in great detail in Chapter 56 at para 56.24.
[99] See para 28.32.   [100] See para 28.55.

G. Common Intention Constructive Trusts

Common intention constructive trusts and the home

The question of the common intention constructive trust is considered in detail **28.23** in Chapter 56 in relation to trusts of the family home. The common intention constructive trust has been held to exist only in relation to the disputes over the family home.[101] The decision of the House of Lords in *Gissing v Gissing*[102] held that when deciding which members of a household should have which equitable interests in the home, the court should consider the common intention of the parties which may have been expressed outwith any formal conveyance of the property. This marked a profound change in the law relating to rights in the family home which had previously operated on the basis of the rules relating to presumptions of resulting trust and the unenforceability of agreements between husband and wife.[103]

The House of Lords' decision in *Lloyds Bank v Rosset*[104] provided a more rigid **28.24** statement of the nature of this common intention constructive trust. As a result of that decision it can be said that the common intention constructive trust arises in two situations. First, where a person contributes to the purchase price of the home, this might be expressed as a constructive trust based on the mutual conduct of the parties evidenced by their contribution to the purchase price or to the mortgage repayments in respect of the property (referred to here as a 'common intention constructive trust by mutual conduct').[105] Secondly, where there is no such contribution nor an express declaration of trust, the equitable interest in the home will be allocated according to the common intention of the parties by means of constructive trust (referred to here as a 'common intention constructive trust by agreement'),[106] based on an express agreement, arrangement, or understanding between the parties which need not constitute an express declaration of trust. The first form of constructive trust appears to be identical to that form of resulting trust accepted in *Dyer v Dyer*.[107] This doctrine, however, is somewhat problematic within the trusts law canon[108] mixing, as it does, the language of constructive

---

[101] However, see an argument for its broader utility in commercial situations in AS Hudson, 'Law of finance' in Birks (ed) *Lessons from the Swaps Cases* (Mansfield, 2000).

[102] [1971] AC 886.

[103] *National and Provincial Building Society v Ainsworth* [1965] AC 1175. Cf *Caunce v Caunce* [1969] 1 WLR 286.   [104] [1991] 1 AC 107.

[105] ibid.   [106] ibid.   [107] (1788) 2 Cox Eq Cas 92.

[108] Further, Lord Bridge clearly intends to compact constructive trust and proprietary estoppel together in this single doctrine: an approach which is criticized by AS Hudson, *Equity & Trusts* (3rd edn, Cavendish Publishing, 2003) ('*Hudson*') 437 *et seq* and outlined at para 56.26 below. The common intention constructive trust grants the successful claimant an equitable proprietary right in the home which will be calculated as a proportion of the total equity which corresponds to the claimant's financial contribution to the property: *Huntingford v Hobbs* [1993] 1 FLR 936.

trust with that of proprietary estoppel,[109] while also being reminiscent of the structure of the purchase price resulting trust.[110]

28.25 While the common intention constructive trust has been applied only in rela-tion to the home it might be argued that such a trust would apply similarly in relation to commercial contracts where the parties evince an intention as to the allocation of title in property.[111] In commercial contracts it is more likely, even if the contract is not formally valid, that the parties will have applied their minds more closely to issues of title in property than is commonly the case in family home situations. Commonwealth jurisdictions have turned against the common intention constructive trust in relation to the home precisely because it requires the court to try to find a common intention which has frequently never actually been formed explicitly by the parties.[112] The difficulty of finding such an intention in many cases has caused the English Court of Appeal to favour allocating equal shares in circumstances in which the home has been held by a family for a long period of time—particularly when the litigation is commenced by mortgagees seeking to enforce their security and dispossess the family.[113]

28.26 The manner in which common intention constructive trusts can be imposed will differ from context to context. The decision of Bagnall J in *Cowcher v Cowcher*[114] identified a difference between those cases in which the parties have established a 'money consensus' which is clear only as to how much money each would contribute to the purchase and those cases in which the parties have estab-lished an 'interest consensus' which is clear as to the size of the equitable interest each party is to receive regardless of their financial contribution. This distinction led Waite LJ to declare that he considered the variety of approaches on the authorities to be 'mystifying' in *Midland Bank v Cooke*.[115] What is clear[116] is that the equitable interest is not to be allocated simply by means of identifying what is 'reasonable, fair and just in all the circumstances',[117] thus distinguishing the common intention constructive trust from the new model constructive trust formerly advanced by Lord Denning.[118]

---

[109] See para 56.94.   [110] See para 56.39.
[111] AS Hudson, *Swaps, Restitution and Trusts* (Sweet & Maxwell, 1999) 203.
[112] See para 56.100.   [113] See *Midland Bank v Cooke* [1995] 4 All ER 562.
[114] [1972] 1 All ER 948, 951, 954–955.   [115] [1995] 4 All ER 562.
[116] Except, perhaps, for the decisions in *Hammond v Mitchell* [1991] 1 WLR 1127 and *Midland Bank v Cooke* [1995] 4 All ER 562 where the maxim 'equality is equity' was deployed liberally.
[117] [1972] 1 All ER 948, 954.
[118] *Hussey v Palmer* [1972] 1 WLR 1286; *Cooke v Head* [1972] 1 WLR 518; *Eves v Eves* [1975] 1 WLR 1338: imposed wherever 'justice and good conscience require'. *Hazell v Hazell* [1972] 1 WLR 301—look at all circumstances, including overall contribution to the family budget.

Common intention evidenced by agreement

The first limb of the test set out by Lord Bridge in *Lloyds Bank v Rosset*[119] provided   **28.27**
that there would be an agreement between the parties sufficient to constitute a
common intention on the following terms, in the words of Lord Bridge:

> The first and fundamental question which must always be resolved is whether, inde-
> pendently of any inference to be drawn from the conduct of the parties in the course
> of sharing the house as their home and managing their joint affairs, there has at any
> time prior to acquisition, or exceptionally at some later date, been any agreement,
> arrangement or understanding reached between them that the property is to be
> shared beneficially.[120]

This is the court's first inquiry.[121] The type of situation which is envisaged by
Lord Bridge is an occasion on which the couple sat down to discuss how the
rights in the property were to be divided between them. The issue remains as to
the nature of conversation or consensus which would be sufficient to constitute
such an 'agreement'. It is clear that it need not form a binding contract.[122] In the
words of Lord Bridge:

> The finding of an agreement or arrangement to share in this sense can only, I think,
> be based on evidence of express discussions between the partners, however imper-
> fectly remembered and however imprecise their terms.[123]

Two points are worthy of note. First, the discussions are expected to have been carried out in advance of the purchase. Subsequent discussions between the parties
are not important, or at least are of less importance. Secondly, the assumption is
that there are express discussions, rather than an emerging but unspoken intention between the parties. When there are fundamental changes in a personal relationship it is not always the case that the parties will have an express discussion as
to *rights in the property* which each is intended to receive. In circumstances in
which there has been no agreement between people to the effect that they would
own property in common, and in which no agreement could reasonably be
implied, there can be no constructive trust to that effect.[124]

Common intention evidenced by conduct

The second form of common intention constructive trust arises in the absence of   **28.28**
an express agreement or arrangement to share the beneficial ownership. Where
there is no such agreement the court will consider the conduct of the
parties: the form of conduct which is envisaged is contribution to the purchase

---

[119] [1991] 1 AC 107, [1990] 1 All ER 1111, [1990] 2 WLR 867.
[120] [1990] 1 All ER 1111, 1116.   [121] *Savill v Goodall* [1993] 1 FLR 755.
[122] See now in any event Law of Property (Miscellaneous Provisions) Act 1989, s 2.
[123] [1990] 1 All ER 1111, 1117.   [124] *Robinson v Reeve* [2002] EWHC 1179.

price of the property or to the repayment of the mortgage with which it was acquired:

> In sharp contrast with [the common intention constructive trust by agreement] is the very different one where there is no evidence to support a finding of an agreement or arrangement to share, however reasonable it might have been for the parties to reach such an arrangement if they had applied their minds to the question, and where the court must rely entirely on the conduct of the parties both as the basis from which to infer a common intention to share the property beneficially and as the conduct relied on to give rise to a constructive trust. In this situation direct contributions to the purchase price by the partner who is not the legal owner, whether initially or by payment of mortgage instalments, will readily justify the inference necessary to the creation of a constructive trust. But as I read the authorities it is at least extremely doubtful whether anything less will do.[125]

Thus the parties' conduct in respect of the property is capable of forming a common intention sufficient for the finding of a constructive trust. The type of conduct envisaged by Lord Bridge is, however, very limited. He has in mind 'direct contributions to the purchase price' only. Any other conduct which indicates a common intention to own the property jointly in some way, such as selecting the decorations together, or sending out invitations to the house-warming party in joint names, or contributing to the ordinary running expenses of a household will not be sufficient to evidence a common intention.

The requirement of detriment

28.29   It is a significant element of the common intention constructive trust that the claimant have suffered detriment before an equitable interest will be established.[126] This element suggests a similarity with proprietary estoppel which is predicated on many authorities on ensuring that no uncompensated detriment is suffered.[127] However, what precisely constitutes detriment is less clear. In *Grant v Edwards*[128] it was held that detriment will encompass any acts which are of purely personal disadvantage, such as leaving one emotional relationship to move in with the defendant and commence a relationship with that person. Browne-Wilkinson V-C suggested that there were three key principles in this regard: first, an understanding of the nature of the substantive right such that there must be a common intention that the claimant is to have a beneficial interest *and* that the claimant must have acted to her detriment; secondly, proof of the common intention, requiring direct evidence or inferred common intention; and, thirdly, the need for the quantification of the size of that right. The requirement for detriment in the context was mirrored in *Midland Bank v Dobson*[129] where it was held insufficient to create an equitable interest that there be simply a common intention unless

---

[125] [2002] EWHC 1179.   [126] *Cowcher v Cowcher* [1972] 1 All ER 948.
[127] *Lim v Ang* [1992] 1 WLR 113.   [128] [1986] Ch 638.   [129] [1986] 1 FLR 171.

there was also some detriment suffered by the claimant. However, in *Coombes v Smith*[130] it was held that the detriment must be directed at the acquisition of proprietary rights in the home and would not include merely personal disadvantage such as leaving one relationship for another.

On conveyance of property

A constructive trust will be imposed in the situation in which a contract has been 28.30
formed for the transfer of specified property. Once such a binding contract has been formed for the transfer of property it is said that equitable title in that property passes to the buyer automatically on the creation of the contract.[131] The contract effects a transfer of the equitable title automatically without the need for signed writing.[132] For this constructive trust to be effective it is necessary that the contract is capable of being specifically enforced, as considered above.[133] On the basis that equity would award specific performance, equity will recognize as done that which ought to have been done. Therefore, if the transfer ought to have been specifically enforced, equity will recognize the transferor as holding the property on constructive trust for the transferee until the transfer is actually enforced.[134] The constructive trust arises from this equitable principle on the basis that it would be unconscionable for one of the contracting parties to refute their specifically enforceable obligation to transfer title to the other party.[135] This rule applies to land in the same way that it applies to other items of property[136] provided that the contract is in writing containing all of the terms of the agreement in one document which must be signed by all the parties.[137] Furthermore, in the period of time between the formation of a contract for the sale of land and the registration of the buyer as proprietor on the land register, the former proprietor holds the interests which are the subject of the sale on constructive trust for the buyer until re-registration. Similarly, a contract to grant a lease creates leasehold rights which will be recognized by equity.[138]

H. Secret Trusts

A fuller, contextual discussion of the doctrine of secret trusts is contained in 28.31
Chapter 34 in relation to private client trusts. This section aims merely to set out the general principles on which secret trusts operate.

---

[130] [1986] 1 WLR 808.   [131] *Chinn v Collins* [1981] AC 533.
[132] See also *Neville v Wilson* [1997] Ch 144.   [133] See para 28.02.
[134] *Walsh v Lonsdale* (1882) 21 Ch D 9.   [135] *Neville v Wilson* [1997] Ch 144.
[136] *Lysaght v Edwards* (1876) 2 Ch D 499; *Rayner v Preston* (1881) 18 Ch D 1.
[137] Law of Property (Miscellaneous Provisions) Act 1989, s 2.
[138] *Parker v Taswell* (1858) 27 LJ Ch 812; *Walsh v Lonsdale* (1882) 21 Ch D 9.

The basis of the secret trust

28.32 Secret trusts arise in three sets of circumstances. First, where a testator enters into an arrangement with another person that that other person will receive a legacy in the testator's will but where that legacy is intended to be held on trust by the legatee for a third person as beneficiary, but also where that arrangement is neither contained in a contract nor an immediate, *inter vivos* express trust, and where that underlying purpose is not mentioned in the will (a fully secret trust). Secondly, where a testator enters into an identical arrangement to the first with a legatee, but the existence of the arrangement is disclosed in the will itself (a half-secret trust). Thirdly, where a person is encouraged not to make a will benefiting a third person in reliance on an arrangement made with the next of kin (entitled under the Intestacy Rules to take the dead person's estate that the next of kin would hold some portion of that estate on trust for the third person (a secret trust on intestacy). An intention to impose a merely moral obligation on a person will not amount to a secret trust.[139] The 'secret trust' is so named precisely because the circumstances which give rise to such arrangements have often tended to be secret because they were the part of some subterfuge aimed frequently at benefiting a mistress or illegitimate child without needing to disclose that beneficiary's existence to other family members on the face of the will. However, there is also a tendency for some testators to seek to retain some flexibility in their testamentary arrangements by using informal devices like the secret trust to enable them to alter the effect of their wills without needing to prepare a new will.

28.33 The secret trust is, controversially perhaps, included within this discussion of constructive trusts on the basis that secret trusts will be identified in the following discussion as responding most clearly to the core principle of constructive trusts identified above: that is, constructive trusts operate based on the trustee's knowledge of some factor which affects his conscience in relation to testamentary property. A fuller discussion of this categorization is set out below.[140] A secret trust is not an express trust because it does not respond to the formalities necessary for the creation of a will trust and therefore would be an unconstituted trust.[141] Such an express trust is not then formalized on death precisely because the trust remains outwith the formalities contained in the Wills Act. Nor is there an *inter vivos* express trust at the time the testator communicates its intention to the intended secret trustee because the testator does not intend the trust to be constituted before death and the testator is in any event able to dismantle the trust contrary to the ordinary rule in *Paul v Paul*[142] relating to express trusts. That this does not appear to observe the usual divisions drawn between fully secret and half-secret trusts, considered below,[143] reflects the contention below

---

[139] *Kasperbauer v Griffith* [2000] 1 WTLR 333.   [140] See para 28.49.
[141] See para 5.01.   [142] (1882) 20 Ch D 742.   [143] See para 28.37.

that in practice the difference between those two categories is frequently paper-thin: for example, in a case where there is some fleeting mention in the will of some expectation the testator has of one of the named legatees but which would not disclose the existence of the secret to anyone who did not previously know of it. In consequence, the argument made out below is that secret trusts conform most readily to the general pattern of the constructive trust.

The key feature of the secret trust is that it operates 'dehors the will' and in contravention of the provisions of the Wills Act 1837. Section 9 of the 1837 Act provides as follows: **28.34**

> No will shall be valid unless—
>
> (a) it is in writing and signed by the testator, or by some other person in his presence and by his direction; and
> (b) it appears that the testator intended by his signature to give effect to the will; and
> (c) the signature is made or acknowledged by the testator in the presence of two or more witnesses present at the same time; and
> (d) each witness either—
>
>   (i) attests and signs the will; or
>   (ii) acknowledges his signature, in the presence of the testator (but not necessarily in the presence of any other witness),
>
> but no form of attestation shall be necessary.

These provisions clearly set out the means by which a will is to be created if it is to be valid on death. Their purpose is to prevent frauds perpetrated by people who might otherwise claim that they were entitled to property held in the deceased's estate. As a result of the 1837 Act only those people who are identified in a properly executed will as having rights against the testator's property will be entitled to receive such property on the testator's death. In the event that no will is effected, or if the will is invalid, the intestacy rules will allocate title to the next of kin.[144]

Furthermore, if the testatrix wishes to alter the terms of her will, any alteration or any new will must conform to the provisions of the Act or else they will not be valid. Similarly, if the testator wishes to create some arrangement outside the precise terms of the will, that arrangement will be similarly invalid if it does not comply with the terms of the will.[145] Therefore, a secret trust (being an arrangement for the organization of title in property after the testator's death outside the terms of the will) will be strictly invalid under the terms of the Wills Act 1837. **28.35**

However, equity takes a different approach and holds that a properly created secret trust will be valid *in equity* if it is properly created. The requirements for the proper creation of a secret trust are considered below. The secret trust is a doctrine **28.36**

---

[144] Those rules being effected under the Administration of Estates Act 1925.
[145] *Re Edwards* [1948] Ch 440.

which seeks to provide justice in circumstances in which a literal application of the Wills Act would permit unconscionable behaviour on the part of the person intended to act as trustee of the secret trust.

Distinguishing between fully secret and half-secret trusts

28.37　The 'fully secret trust' is a trust which is not referred to at all in the terms of the will. In such a situation the testator will have communicated the terms of the arrangement to the intended secret trustee. The property intended to pass to the beneficiary of the arrangement will then be left to the secret trustee without any mention being made in the will as to the reason why the property is being left to the secret trustee. As will emerge from the discussion to follow it is often very difficult to prove the existence of a fully secret trust unless the testator had mentioned the detail of the arrangement to someone else. By contrast, the 'half-secret trust' is a trust the *existence* but *not the terms* of which is disclosed in the will. If all of the terms of the secret trust were disclosed in the will it would be a testamentary trust and not a secret trust at all. The manner in which the half-secret trust is disclosed in the terms of the will differs from case to case. Where the will makes reference to the testator's wishes having been set out in another document, such an explicit mention of another document may bring into play the probate doctrine of incorporation by reference which would require that that other document be construed as forming a part of the will.[146]

28.38　One further point should be noted on the distinction between a fully secret trust and a half-secret trust. Given that so much turns on the division made between the two, it is important to note that in many circumstances it will be difficult to know whether the trust is fully secret or half-secret. It would be possible for a will to be phrased so that the testator's cryptic reminder to the named legatee that he is to observe their agreement might be interpreted by the other legatees as the sentimental wanderings of a soul *in extremis*. For example, if the following provision appeared in the will—'I leave a sum of money to my closest friend, Bob, and hope that he will remember all that we discussed'—it could either be a reminder or else a last, fond farewell. When creating strict divisions between categories of secret trust this grey area between the two ostensibly clear categories should be borne in mind.

28.39　There is a third class of secret trust which arises when a dying person is encouraged not to make a will and thereby to leave property so that it passes on intestacy to a particular person whom the deceased believed would enforce a secret trust. If the next of kin had induced the dying person not to make a will in reliance on his

---

[146] *In the goods of Smart* [1902] P 238; *Re Jones* [1942] Ch 238; as interpreted by *Re Edwards WT* [1948] Ch 440.

promise to give effect to the dying person's wishes, then that next of kin would be required to hold the property received on trust for the intended beneficiaries.[147] This doctrine similarly prevents the recipient of property from perpetrating a fraud and consequently corresponds to the general species of constructive trust as considered above.[148]

The roots of the secret trust in the prevention of fraud

The original purpose of the doctrine of secret trusts in the early case law was to **28.40** prevent statute or common law being used as an instrument of fraud.[149] So, in *McCormick v Grogan*,[150] Lord Westbury set out the basis of the secret trust in the following terms:[151]

> . . . the court has, from a very early period, decided that even an Act of Parliament shall not be used as an instrument of fraud; and that equity will fasten on the individual who gets a title under that Act, and impose upon him a personal obligation, because he applies the Act as an instrument for accomplishing a fraud. In this way a court of equity has dealt with the Statute of Frauds, and in this manner, also, it deals with the Statute of Wills.

Thus, the legal owner of property may be made subject to a 'personal obligation' which requires that person to hold the specific property on trust for the person whom the testator had intended to receive equitable title in the property. Perhaps Lord Westbury's reference to a 'personal obligation' is better rendered as a 'fiduciary obligation arising from equity's jurisdiction to act *in personam* against the conscience of the trustee' to act as a trustee. Notably, the obligation is applied by operation of law to avoid fraud and so corresponds to those constructive trusts identified above as being intended for the prevention of fraud.[152]

One important facet of the early cases on secret trusts before *McCormick v* **28.41** *Grogan*[153] (in relation to fully secret trusts) and *Blackwell v Blackwell*[154] (in relation to half-secret trusts) was that it was necessary for the claimant to demonstrate that the secret trustee was perpetrating a fraud by suggesting that the legacy left to her on the terms of the will was intended in fact for the claimant beneficially. The difficulty with proving fraud was that the high standard of proof for fraud requires the claimant to prove almost beyond a reasonable doubt that the defendant was acting fraudulently, beyond the ordinary standard of proof in civil claims requiring proof only on the balance of probabilities.[155] With the advent of the more

---

[147] *Sellack v Harris* (1708) 2 Eq Ca Ab 46.   [148] See para 27.01.
[149] *McCormick v Grogan* (1869) LR 4 HL 82; *Jones v Badley* (1868) 3 Ch App 362, 364, and *Blackwell v Blackwell* [1929] AC 318.
[150] (1869) LR 4 HL 82.   [151] (1869) LR 4 HL 82, 97.   [152] See para 27.34.
[153] (1869) LR 4 HL 82.   [154] [1929] AC 318.
[155] *Peek v Gurney* (1873) LR 6; *Re Snowden* [1979] 2 WLR 654.

complex tests set out in *McCormick v Grogan*[156] and *Blackwell v Blackwell*[157] respectively, the need to prove actual fraud was removed.

Fully secret trusts

28.42   In the leading case of *Ottaway v Norman*,[158] Ottaway devised his bungalow, half his residuary estate, and a sum of money to Miss Hodges for her to use during her lifetime provided always that she was, in turn, to bequeath this property to the claimant after her death. She failed to do this in her will. Rather, she left the property by her own will to Mr and Mrs Norman. After Hodges's death the claimant brought an action against Hodges's executors claiming entitlement under secret trust principles to the property which had been left in Ottaway's will. Brightman J set out the elements necessary to prove the existence of a fully secret trust in the following terms:

> It will be convenient to call the person on whom such a trust is imposed the 'primary donee' and the beneficiary under that trust the 'secondary donee'. The essential elements which must be proved to exist are: (i) the intention of the testator to subject the primary donee to an obligation in favour of the secondary donee; (ii) communication of that intention to the primary donee; and (iii) the acceptance of that obligation by the primary donee either expressly or by acquiescence. It is immaterial whether these elements precede or succeed the will of the donor.[159]

As suggested in *Wallgrave v Tebbs*,[160] in circumstances in which the secret trustee-legatee 'expressly promises' or 'by silence implies' that he is accepting the obligation requested of him by the testator then he will be bound by that obligation.

28.43   It is therefore important that there be sufficient intention to create a secret trust such that the legatee under the will (or the next of kin on intestacy) will be trustee of that property for another.[161] However, if the deceased merely intended to impose a moral obligation on the legatee as to the use of property, that will not be sufficient to create a secret trust.[162] For example, where a testatrix left her estate to her elder brother with the words 'he shall know what to do', it was held by Megarry V-C that the deceased woman had only intended to impose a moral obligation on him which was insufficient to impose a positive trust obligation on her brother.[163] Similarly, where the testator left a letter which read, *inter alia*, 'I do not wish you to act strictly to the foregoing instructions, but leave it entirely to your own good judgment to do as you think I would if living, and as the parties are deserving', it was held that the legatee was absolved of any trusteeship.[164]

---

[156] (1869) LR 4 HL 82.   [157] [1929] AC 318.   [158] [1972] 2 WLR 50.
[159] [1972] 2 WLR 50.   [160] (1855) 25 LJ Ch 241.
[161] *Ottaway v Norman* [1972] 2 WLR 50, *per* Brightman J.
[162] *Re Snowden* [1979] 2 All ER 172.   [163] *Re Snowden* [1979] 2 All ER 172.
[164] *McCormick v Grogan* (1869) LR 4 HL 82.

Where the settlor intends to create a secret trust, it is important that this intention **28.44**
is communicated to the trustee and that the terms of the secret trust are similarly
communicated to the secret trustee. Without such communication of the trust to
the secret trustee, there can be no trust.[165] Communication and acceptance can be
effectuated at any time during the life of the testator. Under fully secret trusts there
need be communication only before death. However, more complex issues fall to
be considered. In the case of *Re Boyes*,[166] the testator informed the intended
trustee that he intended to leave property to him under a secret trust arrangement.
The testator also informed the trustee that the terms of the trust would be communicated to the trustee before the testator's death. In the event, the terms of the
trust were not communicated. After the testator's death, two unattested documents were found among the testator's effects which purported to direct the
trustee to hold the property on trust for the testator's mistress and child. Kay J held
that presentation of these two unattested documents was insufficient to constitute
communication of the terms of the trust to the trustee. It appears that communication of both the intention and of the terms requires that the trustee must be able
to know with sufficient certainty the terms of the trust before the death of the
testator, an approach which was approved in *Moss v Cooper*,[167] and also in *Re
Bateman WT*.[168]

The office of trustee under a fully secret trust can be accepted in one of two ways. **28.45**
In the words of Wood V-C in *Wallgrave v Tebbs*:[169]

> Where a person, knowing that a testator in making a disposition in his favour intends
> it to be applied for purposes other than his own benefit, either *expressly promises*, or
> *by silence implies*, that he will carry on the testator's intention into effect, and the
> property is left to him *upon the faith of that promise or understanding*, it is in effect a
> case of trust; and in such a case, the court will not allow the devisee to set up the
> [Wills Act] . . .

What is significant is whether or not the trustee's actions induced the testator to
pursue the secret trust arrangement. Importantly, the trustee is not required to
have expressly promised but rather it is enough that the trustee 'by silence implies'
that he will act as trustee.

In *Wallgrave v Tebbs*[170] itself a testator had left £12,000 'unto and to the use of **28.46**
Tebbs and Martin, their heirs and assigns, for ever, as joint tenants'. Oral and
written evidence was presented to the court which demonstrated both that the
testator had intended Tebbs and Martin to hold the property on secret trust and
that the purposes of that trust were in breach of the Statute of Mortmain. At no

---

[165] *Ottaway v Norman* [1972] 2 WLR 50.   [166] (1884) 26 Ch D 531.
[167] (1861) 1 J & H 352.
[168] [1970] 1 WLR 1463 which approved *Re Keen* [1937] Ch 236.
[169] (1855) 25 LJ Ch 241 (emphasis added).   [170] (1855) 25 LJ Ch 241.

time had the testator's true intentions been communicated to Tebbs or to Martin. In consequence, Tebbs and Martin sought an order from the court that they were entitled to take beneficial title in the property left to them by will. Wood V-C held that they could indeed take beneficial title and were not required to act as trustees because there had been 'no such promise or undertaking on the part of the devisees' which could have constituted acceptance of the office. Where the terms of the trust are not disclosed, it has been held that the trustee must hold on resulting trust for the testator to prevent his own unjust enrichment.[171]

Half-secret trusts

28.47 A half-secret trust is a trust under which the *existence* of the trust is disclosed in a document, such as a will, but the *terms* of the trust remain secret. In short, it is the situation in which the existence of the trust is disclosed by the will, or other instrument, but the terms are not. Lord Sumner set out the core principles in *Blackwell v Blackwell*[172] in the following terms:

> The necessary elements [to create a half-secret trust], on which the question turns, are intention, communication and acquiescence. The testator intends his absolute gift to be employed as he and not as the donee desires; he tells the proposed donee of this intention and, either by express promise or by the tacit promise, which is satisfied by acquiescence, the proposed donee encourages him to bequeath the money on the faith that his intentions will be carried out.

Furthermore, there is no need for the plaintiff to prove actual fraud on the part of the defendant (secret trustee).

28.48 Thus, communication must be before or at the time of the execution of the will.[173] Lord Sumner held in *Blackwell* that '[a] testator cannot reserve to himself a power of making future unwitnessed dispositions by merely naming a trustee and leaving the purposes of the trust to be supplied afterwards'.[174] The rationale for this rule is that the trustee must know of the terms of the trust and be able to disclaim the obligations of trusteeship. Similarly, the testator is not entitled to use the secret trust as a means of delaying the point in time at which he will finally decide the terms on which he wishes his estate to be left. Where communication occurs after the will, the trust will fail and the legatee will hold on resulting trust for the residuary estate.[175] Therefore, there is a distinction between half-secret trusts and fully secret trusts in that the settlor must communicate before the execution of the will in the former, but need not communicate the existence or terms of the trust until the time of death in the latter.[176]

---

[171] *Re Boyes* (1884) 26 Ch D 531.   [172] *Re Boyes* (1884) 26 Ch D 531.
[173] *Blackwell v Blackwell* [1929] AC 318.   [174] *Blackwell v Blackwell* [1929] AC 318, 339.
[175] *Re Keen* [1937] Ch 236, *Re Bateman's WT* [1970] 1 WLR 1463.
[176] *Re Spence* [1949] WN 237.

The secret trust as a constructive trust

There is a problem of categorizing the secret trust: whether the secret trust is con- **28.49**
sidered to be a constructive or an express trust may be important in relation to the
need for formalities. The traditional view is presented as the 'fraud theory' which
correlates with the equitable doctrine illustrated in *Rochefoucauld v Boustead*[177]
which precludes a person from relying on their common law rights to perpetrate
a fraud. It is that equitable doctrine which explains the underpinning of the secret
trust.[178] In *McCormick v Grogan*,[179] Lord Westbury set out the basis of the secret
trust as a means of preventing fraudulent reliance on common law or statutory
rights[180] so that, as a matter of historical fact, the doctrine was based on equity's
concern to prevent fraud. That the secret trust is based on fraud also imports the
higher standard of proof used in fraud cases than in ordinary civil cases.[181]

A more modern view of the nature of the secret trust is that the trust was created **28.50**
and declared *inter vivos* between the testator and the trustee, with the property
vesting upon the death of the testator. This approach justifies the classification of
the secret trust as a form of express trust. In short, it is argued that the testator
sought to declare a trust while alive but did not completely constitute that trust
until the point of death when the will transferred title in the trust fund to the
trustee. This approach would conflict with the rule in *Milroy v Lord*[182] that a
trust cannot be used to perfect a transfer which was intended to take effect by
other means. Furthermore, this approach is objectionable on the basis that it
requires the implication of an express trust which, by definition, was not
required to comply with the formalities for the creation of an express trust such
that no formally valid express trust was actually created. The secret trust arises
when there has been an intention to create a secret trust, communication of that
intention, and acceptance by the trustee of that office.

There is a third category of commentators[183] who take the view that the two **28.51**
types of secret trust ought to be considered as operating differently: the fully
secret trust as a constructive trust and the half-secret trust as an express trust.[184]
One further explanation of the operation of secret trusts would be, quite simply,
that they constitute an exception to the Wills Act which defies straightforward
definition. As Megarry V-C stated the matter in *re Snowden*:[185] 'the whole basis
of secret trusts ... is that they operate outside the will, changing nothing that is

---

[177] [1897] 1 Ch 196.   [178] *McCormick v Grogan* (1869) LR 4 HL 82.
[179] *McCormick v Grogan* (1869) LR 4 HL 82.
[180] *McCormick v Grogan* (1869) LR 4 HL 82, 97.   [181] *Re Snowden* [1979] 2 WLR 654.
[182] (1862) 4 De GF & J 264.
[183] A Oakley, *Constructive Trusts* (3rd edn, Sweet & Maxwell, 1997) ('*Oakley*') 243.
[184] J Martin, *Hanbury and Martin's Modern Equity* (16th edn, Sweet & Maxwell, 2001) ('*Martin*')
153.
[185] [1979] 2 All ER 172, 177.

written in it, and allowing it to operate according to its tenor, but then fastening a trust on to the property in the hands of the recipient'.

28.52　In truth, what is happening when courts impose secret trusts is that the court is imposing the office of trustee on the recipient of a gift on the basis that it would be unconscionable for that person to retain an absolute interest in the property. The primary motivating factor behind equity's response here is that the secret trustee is aware that she was not intended to take beneficial title in the property but rather to hold it on trust for another person. As considered above, there will be no finding of secret trust where the recipient had not had the testator's intention communicated to her and where that office had not been accepted.[186] Secret trusts will only be imposed on those who have knowledge of the unconscionability of retaining absolute title in the property.

28.53　Consequently, the imposition of a secret trust falls four-square within the test for a constructive trust as set out by Lord Browne-Wilkinson in *Westdeutsche Landesbank v Islington*:[187] that is, a constructive trust is imposed on a person who has knowledge of some factor affecting his conscience in relation to the use of property. Thus, the recipient of a testamentary gift who knows that he has acquiesced in an arrangement whereby the testator intended him only to take that property in a fiduciary capacity will be a constructive trustee of that property from the moment that legal title passes into his hands. In exactly that way, outwith the formalities for express trusts, equity imposes a constructive trust on anyone who accepts the office of secret trustee, whether that trust is disclosed in the will or not. As stated above, this is the only feature common both to fully secret and half-secret trusts. A secret trust therefore always conforms to a species of constructive trust which operates as an exception to the rules as to the creation of valid, express will trusts. That there is no need for any formality in the creation of constructive trusts is established by section 53(2) of the Law of Property Act 1925.

I.　Mutual Wills

28.54　A fuller, contextual discussion of the doctrine of mutual wills is contained in Chapter 34 in relation to private client trusts. This section aims to set out the general principles on which mutual wills operate.

Mutual wills as a means of avoiding fraud

28.55　As with secret trusts, equity is prepared to effect testamentary arrangements which do not comply *strictu sensu* with English probate law and section 9 of the Wills Act

---

[186]　*Wallgrave v Tebbs* (1855) 25 LJ Ch 241; *Blackwell v Blackwell* [1929] AC 318.
[187]　[1996] AC 669.

1837. The doctrine of mutual wills applies to wills created by two or more people in a particular form with the intention that the provisions of those wills shall be irrevocably binding. Ordinarily a will would be capable of amendment or repeal; mutual wills are subtly different because the parties intend that their wills be binding on them both and not capable of amendment. When the first of the parties to the mutual wills dies the arrangement becomes binding on any surviving parties. In the event that any survivor should have attempted to change his will or to break the mutual will arrangement, his personal representatives after his death would be required to hold his estate as constructive trustees subject to the terms of the mutual wills. Lord Camden expressed the doctrine in the following way in *Dufour v Pereira*:[188]

> ... he, that dies first, does by his death carry the agreement on his part into execution. If the other then refuses, he is guilty of a fraud, can never unbind himself, and becomes a trustee of course. For no man shall deceive another to his prejudice.

The essence of the doctrine is therefore the prevention of a fraud being committed by the survivor in failing to comply with the terms of the mutual will arrangement. For example, a husband and wife may agree that the survivor be obliged to leave all the matrimonial home to their only child absolutely. Thus, if the husband were to predecease his wife, and if his wife were to have a further child by a subsequent marriage and purport to leave the home after her death on trust for her two children in equal shares, then her personal representatives would be obliged to hold that property on constructive trust for the child of her first marriage.

It is frequently the case that mutual wills are effectuated with the intention that X **28.56** shall benefit Y and that Y shall benefit X no matter who dies first. In effect, they are 'mutual' in the sense that they are mutually beneficial and not simply mutually binding. However, in the wake of the decision in *Re Dale*[189] it was held that there was no requirement that each party to the arrangement take a personal benefit. Rather it is possible that there be benefits to third parties.

The question which arises is how this intention to create mutual wills would arise. **28.57** In *Re Hagger*,[190] a husband and wife made separate wills but both of those wills contained recitals that the parties had agreed to the disposal of their property in accordance with those wills and that they intended their wills to be irrevocable. It was held that this constituted sufficient intention to create mutual wills. That case should be juxtaposed with that of *Re Oldham*[191] in which a husband and wife created substantially similar wills with identical treatment of their property but those wills were not expressed as being irrevocable nor was their any evidence of such an intention and therefore it was held that there were not mutual wills.

---

[188] (1769) 1 Dick 419.   [189] [1994] Ch 31.   [190] [1930] 2 Ch 190.
[191] [1925] Ch 75.

The requirement of irrevocable intention

28.58 The most important aspects in establishing a mutual will arrangement are an intention expressed by the parties that their wills be irrevocable[192] and that the parties considered that their wills would be binding on one another after death.[193] This is so even if a literal reading of the terms of the wills indicates something other than a mutual will. There will be a mutual will arrangement where evidence from the couple's solicitor indicates that their true intention was to bind one another irrevocably.[194] In general terms the court is entitled to infer such an intention from the general circumstances of the case.[195]

28.59 The mutual wills do not become binding, as intimated above, until one of the parties dies because the arrangement can be broken up to that moment by all the parties in any event.[196] Where the parties terminate the agreement before the death of any of them, then all of the parties are relieved of their obligations under it.[197] Until the death of one of the parties the arrangement takes effect simply as a contract between the parties and has no effect in equity.[198] In the event that the first to die did not leave property as obliged to under the agreement, the survivor is entitled to damages for breach of contract from the deceased's estate.

The obligations of the survivor

28.60 The obligations of the survivor under the arrangement will clearly depend on the terms of the will and of the parties' intention under the mutual wills arrangement. It is generally assumed that the survivor (that is, not the first party to die) acquires the property as its absolute owner during her lifetime subject to a fiduciary duty to settle the property by will in accordance with the arrangement after her death.[199] In this respect the obligation of the survivor is a form of 'floating' trust,[200] or one that is 'in suspense':[201] that is, it will not become fully binding until death. The weakness in this arrangement is that it will not be binding on bona fide purchasers without notice of the mutual will arrangement.[202]

---

[192] *Re Green* (1951) Ch 158; *Re Cleaver* [1981] 1 WLR 939.
[193] *Re Goodchild (deceased)* [1996] 1 WLR 694.
[194] *Re Goodchild (deceased)* [1996] 1 WLR 694.
[195] *Dufour v Pereira* (1769) 1 Dick 419; *Stone v Hoskins* [1905] P 194.
[196] *Martin* 308.
[197] *Stone v Hoskins* [1905] P 194.
[198] *Robinson v Ommanney* (1883) 23 Ch D 285.
[199] *Birmingham v Renfrew* (1936) 57 CLR 666; *Re Cleaver* [1981] 1 WLR 939; *Goodchild v Goodchild* [1996] 1 WLR 694.
[200] DJ Hayton, 'Constructive trusts' (1985) Malaya L Rev 313.
[201] *Ottaway v Norman* [1972] Ch 698.
[202] *Pilcher v Rawlins* (1872) LR 7 Ch App 259.

J. Constructive Trusts Used to Perfect Imperfect Transfers

As was discussed in Chapter 5,[203] an imperfect gift will not be perfected simply by **28.61**
interpreting the donor to be a trustee of the property which was to have been the
subject matter of that gift,[204] nor will an incompletely constituted trust be rendered effective so as to aid a volunteer:[205] in neither case will equity perfect an
imperfect transfer of property. That much was made evident in the judgment of
Turner LJ in *Milroy v Lord*.[206] Turner LJ expressed this principle in terms that for
a settlement to be effective 'the settlor must have done everything which, according to the nature of the property comprised in the settlement, was necessary to be
done in order to transfer the property and render the settlement binding upon
him'.[207] The rigour of this principle that equity will not assist a volunteer by perfecting an imperfect gift appears to have been diluted by a statement of Lord
Browne-Wilkinson to the effect that 'although equity will not aid a volunteer, it
will not strive officiously to defeat a gift'.[208] In the case of *Re Rose*[209] the *Milroy v
Lord* principle was extended so that equity would deem title to have passed from
the donor to the donee, even if the gift had not been formally completed, provided
that the donor had done everything that was necessary for the donor to have done
to effect a transfer of the property. In *Re Rose* itself the donor had completed all of
the transfer documents relevant to transfer a parcel of shares such that the only
formality which remained to effect that transfer was a resolution of the company's
board of directors: that is, the donor had done everything which he had to do to
effect that transfer and it was only actions of other persons which remained outstanding. This principle has been accepted as forming part of English law[210] even
though it appeared to conflict with earlier English authority in the manner considered immediately below.[211]

The Privy Council has subsequently accepted that, when a man lying on his **28.62**
deathbed sought to declare a trust over his own property with himself as one of
nine trustees, a valid trust was created over that property even though the deceased
person had not transferred the legal title in the trust property to all nine trustees
as trustees.[212] There would have been no issue of formality had the deceased simply declared himself to be sole trustee of that property because transfer of title

---

[203] See para 5.01. [204] *Milroy v Lord* (1862) 4 De GF & J 264.
[205] *Re Brook's ST* [1939] 1 Ch 993. [206] (1862) 4 De GF & J 264.
[207] ibid.
[208] *T Choithram International SA v Pagarani* [2001] 2 All ER 492, 501; applied in *Pennington v
Waine* [2002] 4 All ER 215. [209] [1952] Ch 499.
[210] *Vandervell v IRC* [1967] 2 AC 291, HL; *Mascall v Mascall* (1984) 50 P & CR 119; *Brown &
Root Technology v Sun Alliance and London Assurance Co* [1996] Ch 51. See also *Corin v Patton*
(1990) 169 CLR 540. [211] *Richards v Delbridge* (1874) LR 18 Eq 11; *Re Fry* [1946] Ch 312.
[212] *T Choithram International SA v Pagarani* [2001] 1 WLR 1. See also M Halliwell [2003] The
Conveyancer 192.

would have been necessary to constitute the trust. Latterly the Court of Appeal has applied this principle so as to perfect a gift of shares in circumstances in which the donor had neither effected a declaration of trust over the shares nor done everything which was necessary for her to do to effect a transfer of the shares.[213] This decision extends the principle beyond its former boundaries where it could be demonstrated that the donor had indeed done everything necessary for her to have done to finalize the transfer. In that case Clarke LJ accepted that the principle operated in general terms and that the equity identified by the Court of Appeal in *Re Rose*[214] was capable of such general application. The principle to which the courts have had recourse in finding that the equitable interest has passed in such a situation is that a court of equity should not be officious in defeating a gift.[215]

28.63 It is suggested that this principle is in general terms best understood as a form of constructive trust in the modern context, as it has latterly been explained by the Court of Appeal,[216] even though the manner in which Lord Evershed MR explained it in *Re Rose*[217] was as an equitable acceptance of the unconscionability of the donor purporting to retain the shares and any dividends paid under them once he had completed and sent off the share transfer forms. Equity accepts that the equitable ownership of property passes to the anticipated donee of property when the intended donor has done everything which was necessary for him to do to effect such a transfer. Consequently, the legal title remains in the donor while the equitable title passes to the donee. This happens by operation of law and not by the will of the parties because the donor intended to make a gift or to declare an express trust, neither of which were completed. In consequence, it is suggested that a constructive trust arising by operation of law is the best explanation of this phenomenon.

28.64 In the case *Re Rose*[218] itself, however, the equity was explained as having arisen in a different fashion. In the case of *Re Rose*,[219] Mr Rose had intended to transfer one block of shares to his wife beneficially and another to his wife and another woman on trust for them both. He had completed the appropriate transfer forms. The only formality which remained to be performed was the acceptance by the company of the transfer of ownership: this was an action outwith Mr Rose's own control. It was held that Mr Rose had succeeded in transferring equitable title in the shares to his wife when he had completed all the formalities required of him. The classification of this trust is not straightforward. It cannot be deemed an express

---

[213] *Pennington v Waine* [2002] 1 WLR 2075.   [214] [1952] Ch 499.
[215] *T Choithram International SA v Pagarani* [2001] 1 WLR 1; *Pennington v Waine* [2002] 1 WLR 2075.
[216] *Pennington v Waine* [2002] 1 WLR 2075, 2088, *per* Arden LJ.
[217] [1952] Ch 499.   [218] [1952] Ch 499.   [219] [1952] Ch 499.

trust because there was no intention on the part of Mr Rose to create express trusts over all of the shares. Nor does the equitable interest result back to Mr Rose. Rather, it must be said that the equitable interest passes as a result of a constructive trust by operation of law.

Lord Evershed's judgment is couched in the language of gift and not trust: his **28.65** lordship refers throughout to 'donor', 'donee' and 'gift' rather than to 'trust' or 'trustee'. Therefore, it is not immediately apparent how this judgment is authority for a proposition based on the law of trust. A partial answer is offered by Lord Evershed's explanation as to how title passes to Mrs Rose from her husband when he argues that, after Mr Rose had purported to transfer title to his wife by doing everything necessary for him to do, it would have been inequitable for him to have reneged on that promise:

> ... if Mr Rose had received a dividend between [completion of the document and consent being granted by the board of directors] and Mrs Rose had claimed to have that dividend handed to her, what would Mr Rose's answer have been? It could no longer be that the purported gift was imperfect; it had been made perfect. I am not suggesting that the perfection was retroactive. But what else could he say? How could he... deny the proposition that he had... transferred the shares to his wife? ... therefore the transfer was valid and effectual in equity from March 30, 1943, and accordingly the shares were not assessable for estate duty.

Therefore, it was argued that Mr Rose would have been compelled to hand over the dividend if one had been received between the time when he had done everything necessary for him to do to transfer title and the date at which the company formally consented to the transfer of the shares. The reason why he is so compelled is not immediately obvious from these dicta. In the language of the twenty-first century we would explain it as being contrary to good conscience for Mr Rose to refuse to acknowledge that equitable title had passed and in consequence that a constructive trust had been created over the shareholding. However, on its face, the rationale is more obscure. Nevertheless, despite these conceptual difficulties, the *Re Rose* principle has been followed in numerous other cases.[220] As such it is suggested that this phenomenon is explicable only as a constructive trust. It has been accepted by some of the commentators that this form of trust constitutes a constructive trust primarily because it does not satisfy the formalities for the creation of an express trust because no title has been vested in a trustee.[221]

---

[220] *Vandervell v IRC* [1967] 2 AC 291, HL; *Mascall v Mascall* (1984) 50 P & CR 119; *Brown & Root Technology v Sun Alliance and London Assurance Co* [1996] Ch 51. See also *Corin v Patton* (1990) 169 CLR 540.

[221] Further, it is to be doubted whether this doctrine could be considered to be an express trust at all given that the transferor had no intention to create a trust: rather, he intended in *Re Rose* to make a gift of the property. As such the trust is being imposed against the intentions of the parties and therefore can only be described as taking effect by operation of law as a constructive trust.

K. A Survey of Constructive Trusts Used to Supplement Agreements

28.66   The most significant trend in the cases considered in this chapter has been the transformation of the various equities in cases such as that in *Walsh v Lonsdale*,[222] *Rochefoucauld v Boustead*,[223] *Re Rose*,[224] and *Chattock v Millar*,[225] which prevented the defendant from retaining property or denying the transfer of property to the claimant, into the modern constructive trust. Whereas those older equities appeared to arise on a general basis that there was something 'wrong' and therefore inequitable in the defendant's attempt to retain rights in property, the constructive trust is a comparatively predictable device which creates equitable proprietary rights in the form of a constructive trust for the claimant in circumstances in which the defendant has acted unconscionably.[226] So, the equitable principle that equity looks upon as done that which ought to have been done or the principle that equity must not be used as an engine of fraud, together with the more specific equities considered above, have coalesced in recent cases and in recent scholarship under the general banner 'constructive trust'. While the constructive trust is itself an ostensibly open-textured device, it is nevertheless developing as a means of understanding all of these formerly distinct doctrines by reference to one central concept of unconscionability, in the form of the institutional constructive trust.

28.67   In the examples considered in this chapter the manifestation of that unconscionability has been on the subversion of either a contract or a non-contractual promise by the defendant. Reneging on a contract or on certain types of promise are considered by equity to be unconscionable. In relation to commercial contracts, equity is supporting the law of contract by developing property law rules which transfer automatically sufficient title in an asset which is to be transferred under the terms of such a contract to the appropriate contracting party. Equity also creates a penumbra of moral principles which prevent participants in commercial and similar activity—such as those in *Rochefoucauld v Boustead* or *Lyus v Prowsa Developments*—from attempting to evade moral responsibilities which the court deems them to have assumed in relation to those with whom they have negotiated. So, in *Pallant v Morgan* the defendant is not permitted to renege on the impression which his negotiations have created in the mind of his counterparty, in *Re Rose* the deceased was prevented from reneging on his stated intention to transfer shares to his wife, and in *Walsh v Lonsdale* a pattern of negotiation is

---

[222] (1882) 21 Ch D 9.   [223] [1897] 1 Ch 196.   [224] [1952] Ch 499.
[225] (1878) 8 Ch D 177; referred to commonly in the cases before *Banner Homes Group v Luff Development* in [2000] Ch 372 as the 'equity in *Pallant v Morgan*' [1953] Ch 43.
[226] *Westdeutsche Landesbank v Islington* [1996] AC 669; *Paragon Finance plc v DB Thackerar & Co (a firm)* [1999] 1 All ER 400.

said to create enforceable proprietary rights even though the lease envisaged by both parties had not been formally created in law. Equity is generating a form of commercial morality in effect in these cases. It is an ancient form of equity which, in its modern conception, is concerned to act *in personam* against the defendant's conscience.[227] It is akin to proprietary estoppel in that it functions on the basis of the plaintiff acting in reliance on some promise or assurance made by the defendant. The distinction between the doctrines, however, is that proprietary estoppel is concerned to prevent the plaintiff suffering detriment [228] whereas the constructive trust is focused on the conscionability of the defendant's behaviour alone. The result is that proprietary estoppel is a remedial doctrine which fits its remedy to compensate the defendant's detriment, whereas the institutional constructive trust provides property rights for the plaintiff[229] or else entitles the plaintiff to receive an account from the defendant for breach of duty.[230]

---

[227] See *Attorney-General for Hong Kong v Reid* [1994] 1 AC 324.

[228] That seems to be the majority judicial opinion—see Lord Browne-Wilkinson in *Lim v Ang* [1992] 1 WLR 113—even if it is not the unanimous judicial view: see para 25.42.

[229] It remains a difficult question whether or not the courts are in truth creating novel property rights or merely vindicating pre-existing property rights: on which see C Rotherham, *Proprietary Remedies in Context* (Hart Publishing, 2002) Ch 1 generally.

[230] On which see para 32.01.

29

CONSTRUCTIVE TRUSTS IN RESPONSE TO ABUSE OF FIDUCIARY POSITION

A. The Principle that Constructive Trusts Arise in Response to Abuse of Fiduciary Position

The general principle that a constructive trust will be imposed in response to an abuse of a fiduciary office

29.01 A person who occupies a fiduciary office owes obligations of the utmost good faith and loyalty to the beneficiaries of that relationship.[1] In the event that such a fiduciary takes a benefit from that relationship which is not authorized by the instrument imposing that office on him, or where that benefit has not been authorized by the beneficiaries of the relationship, then he may open himself up both to personal liability for breach of trust,[2] as considered in Chapter 32, and also to a proprietary obligation to hold any benefit so obtained on constructive trust for the beneficiaries of the relationship.[3] This chapter is concerned with the latter head of liability. The defendant fiduciary will hold any unauthorized benefit or profit which he has received on constructive trust for the benefit of the beneficiary of his relationship from the moment of its receipt.[4] This liability to hold property on constructive trust is a proprietary liability such that, if the property received by way of the unauthorized profit is substituted by some other property, then the beneficiaries will be entitled to enforce their constructive trust over that substitute property[5] and similarly if the property received by way of unauthorized profit should increase in value or attract any income then, given that the right is a right in the property, that increase in value or income stream shall be similarly held on constructive trust by the fiduciary.[6]

29.02 As to the foundation of such a liability, simply put, a fiduciary must not permit his personal interests to interfere with his obligations to the beneficiaries. If he does allow such a conflict of interests then, it is suggested, the court will assume everything against him.[7] The foundation of the principle in this context can be found in the speech of Lord Cranworth LC in *Aberdeen Railway Co v Blaikie Bros*:[8]

> [I]t is a rule of universal application, that no one, having such [fiduciary] duties to discharge, shall be allowed to enter into engagements in which he has, or can have, a personal interest conflicting, or which possibly may conflict, with the interests of those whom he is bound to protect.

---

[1] *Re Coomber* [1911] 1 Ch 723; *Bristol and West Building Society v Mothew* [1998] Ch 1. See also the nature of a relationship of trust and confidence identified with such a relationship in *White v Jones* [1995] 2 AC 207.   [2] *Target Holdings v Redferns* [1996] 1 AC 421.
[3] *Regal v Gulliver* [1942] 1 All ER 378 *Boardman v Phipps* [1967] 2 AC 46; *Bristol and West Building Society v Mothew* [1998] Ch 1.
[4] *Attorney-General for Hong Kong v Reid* [1994] 1 AC 324.
[5] In relation to the tracing of the original proprietary rights into substitute property, see para 33.01 below.
[6] *Attorney-General for Hong Kong v Reid* [1994] 1 AC 324.   [7] See para 29.51.
[8] (1854) 2 Eq Rep 1281, 1 Macq 461, [1843–60] All ER Rep 249, HL. Approved in *Boardman v Phipps* [1967] 2 AC 46, 124, *per* Lord Upjohn.

Fiduciaries, in particular trustees, are thus held to a standard of the utmost good faith and loyalty such that the trustee need not be demonstrated to have acted dishonestly to be liable as a constructive trustee,[9] all that is required is that he acted outwith the terms of his fiduciary duties.[10] This discussion therefore relates to that in Chapter 10 as to the extent of the mandatory portion of a fiduciary's duties to beneficiaries. When a constructive trust comes into existence entirely by operation of law[11] there will generally be no opportunity for the defendant to have excluded his liability by agreement and therefore he will be reliant on demonstrating that his conflict of interest was authorized, in the manner considered below,[12] by the beneficiaries; whereas a constructive trust imposed on someone who is a trustee under an existing express trust, perhaps to prevent that trustee from taking personal profits from the trust fund, will be subject to any provision purporting to exclude his liability under the trust instrument.[13] These principles are considered in greater detail in the course of this chapter.

That the office must be a fiduciary office

A constructive trust will be imposed only if the office in question is a fiduciary office. The meaning of 'fiduciary' in this sense is considered in paragraph 29.05 below. In general terms, however, a constructive trust will not be imposed on this basis unless there is some fiduciary relationship between claimant and defendant.[14] It is the presence of the fiduciary duty which makes the defendant's generation of a personal profit subject to a constructive trust on account of the sensitivity of the relationship between the fiduciary and the beneficiary even though that was something which would have been perfectly conscionable, and consequently not actionable, in an ordinary person.   **29.03**

Furthermore, there is a requirement that there be identified property before a proprietary constructive trust of the sort considered in this chapter will be imposed. So, in *Re Goldcorp Exchange Ltd*[15] that a bullion exchange breached its contractual obligations to its customers in failing to set identified bullion aside to meet those customers' orders did not render it subject to a constructive trust because there was no identifiable property which could have constituted the subject matter of such a constructive trust. As Lord Mustill said:[16]   **29.04**

> No doubt the fact that one person is placed in a particular position vis-à-vis another through the medium of a contract does not necessarily mean that he does not also

---

[9] As has been evident ever since *Keech v Sandford* (1726) Sel Cas Ch 61.

[10] As, for example, in *Armitage v Nurse* [1998] Ch 241 where the terms of a trustee's appointment were limited by contract and so his liability did not include, in that case, liability for gross negligence under the terms of the trust instrument.   [11] See para 27.01.

[12] See para 29.60.   [13] *Armitage v Nurse* [1998] Ch 241.

[14] *Manchester Trust v Furness* [1895] 2 QB 539; *Re Wait* [1927] 1 Ch 606.

[15] [1995] 1 AC 74.   [16] [1995] 1 AC 74.

owe fiduciary duties to that other by virtue of being in that position. But the essence of a fiduciary relationship is that it creates obligations of a different character from those deriving from the contract itself.

In consequence, his lordship held that simply because there is some reliance between people which is typical of ordinary contracting parties there will not necessarily be obligations which are of that quality sufficient to create a fiduciary relationship between them. To imply fiduciary obligations too freely in commercial transactions, it is feared, would do violence to the certainty which the judiciary consider to be necessary in interpreting commercial contracts.[17]

The meaning of a 'fiduciary obligation' in this context

29.05   The meaning of the term 'fiduciary' was considered in detail in Chapter 25.[18] In that discussion it was suggested that while there are a range of recognized categories of fiduciary duty, nevertheless fiduciary duties are capable of being implied generally in situations other than those traditional categories. In this context, a fiduciary has been defined in the following terms:

> A fiduciary is someone who has undertaken to act for or on behalf of another in a particular matter in circumstances which give rise to a relationship of trust and confidence. The distinguishing obligation of a fiduciary is the obligation of loyalty. The principal is entitled to the single-minded loyalty of his fiduciary. The core liability has several facets. A fiduciary must act in good faith; he must not make a profit out of his trust; he must not place himself in a position where his duty and his interest may conflict; he may not act for his own benefit or the benefit of a third person without the informed consent of his principal. This is not intended to be an exhaustive list, but it is sufficient to indicate the nature of fiduciary obligations. They are the defining characteristics of the fiduciary.[19]

These dicta identify the core obligation of loyalty owed by the fiduciary to his beneficiary. Such obligations of loyalty include a standard of the utmost good faith such that the fiduciary is not permitted to advance his own, personal position when acting in his fiduciary capacity, whether in the form of making some personal profit or dealing on his own account with the object of his fiduciary office. Consequently, for the purposes of this chapter, that fiduciary will be prevented from making any profit from his office which is not authorized by the terms of that office or to which no informed consent has been given:[20] in the event that any such profit is made, the fiduciary will be deemed to hold that profit on constructive trust for the objects of his fiduciary obligations.[21]

---

[17] On which see *Manchester Trust v Furness* [1895] 2 QB 539, 545, *per* Lindley LJ; *Re Wait* [1927] 1 Ch 606, 634, *per* Atkin LJ.   [18] See para 25.15.

[19] *Bristol and West Building Society v Mothew* [1998] Ch 1, 18, *per* Millett LJ.

[20] As considered below at para 29.60.

[21] *Boardman v Phipps* [1967] 2 AC 46; *Attorney-General for Hong Kong v Reid* [1994] 1 AC 324; *Bristol and West Building Society v Mothew* [1998] Ch 1.

There are four established categories of fiduciary relationship: trustee and **29.06** beneficiary,[22] company directors in relation to the company,[23] partners *inter se* (within the terms of the 1890 Partnership Act),[24] and principal and agent.[25] Of significance in relation to the decided cases discussed in this chapter are other situations in which fiduciary relationships have been found, as follows. First, a solicitor will owe fiduciary duties to his client[26] when advising that client[27] or when attending a meeting on behalf of that client particularly when investing on the basis of confidential information acquired when on that client's business.[28] Secondly, senior employees, such as the board of directors, will owe fiduciary duties to their employers.[29] This obligation will not obtain as a necessary part of a contract of employment in relation to employees who do not hold important positions within the employer's organization.[30] However, any employee who exploits his office so as to receive a bribe will hold that bribe on constructive trust as a fiduciary.[31] Thirdly, those who hold a public office will generally be subject to fiduciary obligations, whether they are members of the secret service[32] or the armed forces,[33] or an Attorney-General when dealing with suspected criminals.[34] Other categories of fiduciary duty were considered in Chapter 25 and the reader is therefore referred back to that discussion.[35]

---

[22] This category is generally simply assumed to be axiomatic of the fiduciary relationship, see *Ex parte Dale* (1879) 121 Ch D 772, 778, *per* Fry LJ; *Re Coomber* [1911] 1 Ch 723, 728, *per* Fletcher-Moulton LJ.

[23] *Selangor United Rubber Estates Ltd v Cradock (No 3)* [1968] 1 WLR 1555. Cf *Lindgren v L&P Estates Ltd* [1968] Ch 572 in relation to directors-elect.

[24] *Bentley v Craven* (1853) 18 Beav 75. See also *Holiday Inns Inc v Yorkstone Properties (Harlington)* (1974) 232 EG 951.

[25] *Lowther v Lowther* (1806) 13 Ves 95, 103, *per* Lord Erskine; *Powell & Thomas v Evans Jones & Co* [1905] 1 KB 11. See also *Re Hallett's Estate* (1880) 13 Ch D 696 in relation to relationships of bailment; and *Re Stapylton Fletcher* [1994] 1 WLR 1181.

[26] *Bolkiah (Prince Jefri) v KPMG* [1999] 2 AC 222. This limitation has two senses, it is suggested. First, that the fiduciary obligations terminate when the retainer terminates: *Bolkiah v KPMG, op cit.* Secondly, that the solicitor is obliged to observe the obligations of a fiduciary in relation to the client's legal affairs but not as to his choice of socks, where the latter falls outwith the scope of the duties forming a part of his retainer.

[27] *Nocton v Lord Ashburton* [1914] AC 932; *McMaster v Byrne* [1952] 1 All ER 1363; *Brown v IRC* [1965] AC 244; *Boardman v Phipps* [1967] 2 AC 46; *Maguire v Makaronis* (1997) 144 ALR 729. By contrast, the Law Society owes no fiduciary duties to the solicitors whom it represents: *Swain v Law Society* [1983] 1 AC 598.   [28] *Boardman v Phipps* [1967] 2 AC 46.

[29] *Canadian Aero-Services Ltd v O'Malley* (1973) 40 DLR (3d) 371, 381, *per* Laskin J; *Sybron Corporation v Rochem Ltd* [1984] Ch 112, 127, *per* Stephenson LJ; *Neary v Dean of Westminster* [1999] IRLR 288. See also *Tesco Stores Ltd v Pook* [2003] EWHC 823.

[30] *Nottingham University v Fishel* [2000] IRLR 471.

[31] *Attorney-General for Hong Kong v Reid* [1994] 1 AC 324.

[32] A contentious category whereby it was accepted in *Attorney-General v Guardian Newspapers Ltd (No 2)* [1990] 1 AC 109 that such a person would be a fiduciary (in that case, when publishing his memoirs), but whereas in *Attorney-General v Blake* [1998] 1 All ER 833 CA, [2000] 4 All ER 385, HL it was considered that such a person would not always be fiduciary of necessity although his position may be akin to that of a fiduciary.   [33] *Reading v Attorney-General* [1951] 1 All ER 617.

[34] *Attorney-General for Hong Kong v Reid* [1994] 1 AC 324.   [35] See para 25.15.

B. Constructive Trusts Over Bribes Accepted by a Fiduciary

The general principle

29.07   In circumstances in which a bribe is received by an employee or by anyone acting in a fiduciary capacity then that bribe is deemed to be held on constructive trust from the moment of its receipt.[36] As considered above, the categories of fiduciary office are not closed;[37] rather, the courts will accept new categories of fiduciary beyond the familiar quartet of trustee, company director, partner, and agent.

The principle in relation to those occupying a public office

29.08   One example of a general category of situations in which a constructive trust will be imposed in relation to the receipt of bribes is the circumstance in which it is the holder of a public office who receives that bribe.[38] These cases are predicated primarily on the notion, set out below, that the holders of public office should not be permitted to benefit from the abuse of such an office and that they should be discouraged from so doing by having any profit they make held on constructive trust and also by bearing a further, personal duty to make good out of their own funds any diminution in the value of any investment made with that profit.[39] So, in *Reading v A-G*[40] a British army sergeant was held subject to this principle when he assisted smugglers to move through army checkpoints by using his army rank and uniform to obtain free passage for them.[41] The payments which he received from the smugglers were held on constructive trust. In consequence, any property acquired with those payments could also have been subjected to a constructive trust on tracing principles. The finding of a fiduciary relationship in that case was a useful mechanism by which the Court of Appeal could justify the State taking title in the payments received by the soldier.

29.09   In truth, it is suggested, the imposition of constructive trusts by virtue of a loose form of fiduciary duty over public officers is a part of public policy concerned to

---

[36] *Attorney-General for Hong Kong v Reid* [1994] 1 AC 324.

[37] *Collings v Lee* [2001] 2 All ER 332.

[38] Exceptionally in *The Estate of Dr Anandh v Barnet Primary Health Care Trust* [2004] EWCA Civ 5 the deceased had been an employee of the Health Care Trust and had taken property illegally from the Trust, *inter alia*, in breach of contract. It was held in that case that the court would not consider questions of constructive trust because the pleadings disclosed a sufficient basis for recovery on the basis of a claim for damages for breach of contract.

[39] *Attorney-General for Hong Kong v Reid* [1994] 1 AC 324.   [40] [1951] 1 All ER 617.

[41] See also *Attorney-General v Goddard* [1929] LJ (KB) 743 (in which a police officer had accepted bribes not to prosecute those living off the immoral earnings of prostitutes); *Brinks v Abu-Saleh (No 3)* [1996] CLC 133 (in which a security guard informed armed robbers about the movements of security vans); and *Jersey City v Hague* (1955) 155 At (2d) 8 (in which a town mayor had extorted a portion of the wages of those employed by the municipality). See also *Snepp v United States* 444 US 507 in which a secret service agent was required to account as a constructive trustee for bribes received in the discharge of his duties.

prevent corruption by such officials. So, in *Attorney-General for Hong Kong v Reid*[42] a public prosecutor took bribes not to prosecute certain criminals and, as discussed below, held the property bought with those bribes on constructive trust because the bribes were deemed to have been held on constructive trust from the moment of their receipt. As Lord Templeman has expressed this principle:[43]

> A bribe is a gift accepted by a fiduciary as an inducement to him to betray his trust. A secret benefit, which may or may not constitute a bribe, is a benefit which the fiduciary derives from trust property or obtains from knowledge which he acquires in the course of acting as fiduciary. A fiduciary is not always accountable for a secret benefit but he is undoubtedly accountable for a secret benefit which consists of a bribe. In addition a person who provides the bribe and the fiduciary who accepts the bribe may each be guilty of a criminal offence. In the present case the first respondent was clearly guilty of a criminal offence.

The fiduciary is thus liable to account to the beneficiaries for the receipt of the bribe. The moral underpinnings of the imposition of a constructive trust on such a bribe emerges from the following passage which continues on from the passage just quoted:

> Bribery is an evil practice which threatens the foundations of any civilised society. In particular bribery of policemen and prosecutors brings the administration of justice into disrepute. Where bribes are accepted by a trustee, servant, agent or other fiduciary, loss and damage are caused to the beneficiaries, master or principal whose interests have been betrayed. The amount of loss or damage resulting from the acceptance of a bribe may or may not be quantifiable. In the present case the amount of harm caused to the administration of justice in Hong Kong[44] by the first respondent in return for bribes cannot be quantified.

The basis on which the proprietary right comes into existence is then expressed in the following passage, which continues from that quoted immediately above: **29.10**

> When a bribe is offered and accepted in money or in kind, the money or property constituting the bribe belongs in law to the recipient. Money paid to the false fiduciary belongs to him. The legal estate in freehold property conveyed to the false fiduciary by way of bribe vests in him. Equity, however, which acts in personam, insists that it is unconscionable for a fiduciary to obtain and retain a benefit in breach of duty. The provider of a bribe cannot recover it because he committed a criminal offence when he paid the bribe. The false fiduciary who received the bribe in breach of duty must pay and account for the bribe to the person to whom that duty was owed. In the present case, as soon as the first respondent received a bribe in breach of the duties he owed to the Government of Hong Kong, he became a debtor in equity to the Crown for the amount of that bribe. So much is admitted. But, if the bribe consists of property which increases in value or if a cash bribe is invested advantageously, the false fiduciary will receive a benefit from his breach of duty unless he is

---

[42] [1994] 1 AC 324.   [43] [1994] 1 AC 324, 330–331, [1994] 1 All ER 1, 4–5.
[44] By virtue of the respondent having been Attorney-General in Hong Kong and having taken bribes from criminals not to prosecute them.

accountable not only for the original amount or value of the bribe but also for the increased value of the property representing the bribe. As soon as the bribe was received it should have been paid or transferred instanter to the person who suffered from the breach of duty. Equity considers as done that which ought to have been done. As soon as the bribe was received, whether in cash or in kind, the false fiduciary held the bribe on a constructive trust for the person injured …

When a bribe is accepted by a fiduciary in breach of his duty then he holds that bribe in trust for the person to whom the duty was owed. If the property representing the bribe decreases in value the fiduciary must pay the difference between that value and the initial amount of the bribe because he should not have accepted the bribe or incurred the risk of loss. If the property increases in value, the fiduciary is not entitled to any surplus in excess of the initial value of the bribe because he is not allowed by any means to make a profit out of a breach of duty.[45]

Thus the policy underpinning the earliest cases on constructive trusts on unauthorized profits taken by fiduciaries[46] is perpetuated here: a fiduciary, especially one holding a public office, must not be permitted to benefit from a breach of his office.

The principle in general terms

29.11   The cases considered in the preceding section concerned fiduciaries holding a public office and receiving a bribe to commit a breach of that office. However, any fiduciary bears a duty not to permit any conflict of interest, whether in terms of taking unauthorized profits from his office or taking bribes or otherwise acting contrary to the interests of the beneficiaries.

29.12   The constructive trust arises in the following manner. As a matter of public policy, bribes ought not to be paid or received by fiduciaries. Therefore, it is suggested that, if a fiduciary did accept a bribe, that bribe ought to be paid immediately to the beneficiary of the fiduciary office as a debt owed in equity to the beneficiary.[47] Equity looks upon as done that which ought to have been done[48] and therefore equity deems the bribe to have been passed to that beneficiary and thus rendering the fiduciary constructive trustee of the bribe.[49] The trust is a constructive trust because no express trust would ever have been declared over that property.[50] Where the bribe is invested the beneficiary retains equitable proprietary rights in any substitute property and any increase in value of that property.[51] In the event that the investment decreases in value, the fiduciary is personally liable to account

---

[45] [1994] 1 AC 324, 331–332, [1994] 1 All ER 1, 5.

[46] See *Keech v Sandford* (1726) Sel Cas Ch 61.

[47] *Attorney-General for Hong Kong v Reid* [1994] 1 AC 324.

[48] cf *Walsh v Lonsdale* (1882) 21 Ch D 9.

[49] *Attorney-General for Hong Kong v Reid* [1994] 1 AC 324. See also *Daraydon Holdings Ltd v Sollard International Ltd* [2004] EWHC 622.

[50] As in *Keech v Sandford* (1726) Sel Cas Ch 61.

[51] *Keech v Sandford* (1726) Sel Cas Ch 61.

to the beneficiary for that loss.[52] This approach correlates with the speech of Lord Browne-Wilkinson in *Westdeutsche Landesbank v Islington*[53] that a trustee is a person required by good conscience to hold property on trust for another.

The principle in this case has been accepted in other jurisdictions. So in **29.13** Singapore, the principle in *Lister v Stubbs*,[54] which had held that the recipient of a bribe was accountable for it only as though a debt at common law rather than under an equitable proprietary claim, was rejected even before the decision of the Privy Council in *Attorney-General for Hong Kong v Reid*. In *Sumitomo Bank v Thahir*[55] the general assistant to the president of the Indonesian state-owned enterprise Pertamina received bribes from two German contractors in relation to tenders for construction work in Java. Those bribes were paid into seventeen bank accounts which had been opened in Singapore specifically for the purpose of holding those bribes. After the general assistant's death, his widow claimed the moneys held in those accounts. However, the Singaporean court held that to find that the general assistant had owed merely a debt to Pertamina would be wrong in principle and that such 'undesirable and unjust consequences should not be imported and perpetuated' as part of the law of Singapore. Instead, the bribes were required to be held on a proprietary constructive trust for Pertamina and ultimately were ordered to be paid to Pertamina.

Before the Grand Court of the Cayman Islands in *Corporacion Nacional Del Cobre* **29.14** *De Chile v Interglobal Inc*[56] a Chilean, state-owned company which traded, *inter alia*, in metals futures sought to recover sums acquired by the head of its futures department through trading outwith the limits of his mandate to bind that company. By virtue of his contract of employment the manager was expressly forbidden from engaging in any conduct which would conflict with his employer's interests. Nevertheless, the manager had entered into a large number of futures transactions purportedly on behalf of his employer but which in fact resulted in all payments from those transactions being paid into bank accounts held jointly by the manager and his wife in the Cayman Islands. It emerged during the discovery process that these payments were in fact bribes intended to induce the manager to enter into futures contracts with those paying the bribes. The manager was convicted in Chile of criminal fraud and of presenting false documents in the course of those criminal proceedings. It was held that, further to the decision in *Attorney-General for Hong Kong v Reid*, the manager was acting as a fiduciary in relation to his employer and that any bribes received in the course of his fiduciary office were therefore to be treated as being held on constructive trust for that employer from the moment of their receipt. Ultimately, the Grand Court held that the contents

---

[52] *Keech v Sandford* (1726) Sel Cas Ch 61.   [53] [1996] AC 669.   [54] (1890) 45 Ch D 1.
[55] [1993] 1 SLR 735.   [56] (2003) 5 ITELR 744, [2002] CILR 298.

of the bank accounts, which were apparently accepted as having come entirely from these payments, were ordered to be paid to the plaintiff company.[57]

29.15   In general terms, it is suggested that any employee receiving a bribe would be rendered a fiduciary where that bribe was paid to encourage that person to abuse their office of employment, any powers that office carries (for example to order payment of money, or to order the release of property), or capabilities associated with it (for example access to information or physical access to premises). That a bribe is paid to such a person necessarily implies that that person is considered by the person making the bribe to occupy a situation which carries with it powers or capabilities to assist the person paying the bribe unconscionably. If the payer considered the payee to be someone who was worth bribing or inducing to act in a given fashion, then it is to be presumed that the payee occupied a fiduciary position so as to make that bribe worthwhile: that is, the defendant may be considered to be a fiduciary if his duties imbue him with a trust or confidence which he is able to turn to account in this manner. By way of illustration, in *Brinks v Abu-Saleh (No 3)*[58] a security guard received a bribe from armed robbers to disclose information as to the security arrangements in place in relation to the guarding of consignments of bullion at a warehouse near Heathrow Airport. In this context a security guard would not be sufficiently senior to constitute the operating mind and will of the company which employs him in relation to the transfer of the company's money between bank accounts but nevertheless his role as security guard would render him a fiduciary when he knowingly disclosed information to criminals who intended to steal from the company in return for cash. The security guard was indeed held to have been a fiduciary and would ordinarily have held any property received on constructive trust.[59]

29.16   The conceptually more difficult situation might arise in relation to a bribe which was paid not to take advantage of any of the recipient's powers or capabilities but rather to induce that person to remain silent, perhaps while a robbery was in progress. In this situation there is no active abuse of the employee's responsibilities but rather a passive omission to inform the employers of any matter which ought otherwise to be reported or to take some other action, such as calling the police. However, it is suggested that silence about matters such as the theft of the employer's property or about abuse of the employer's property ought ordinarily to constitute unconscionable behaviour and so fall within this principle such that any benefit taken by such a person is held on constructive trust from the moment of its receipt.

---

[57] See also *Cayman Islands New Bureau Ltd v Cohen* [1988–89] CILR 196.

[58] [1996] CLC 133.

[59] In that case, the claimant's purpose was not to impose a constructive trust on the security guard, rather the claim sought to demonstrate the existence of a fiduciary duty as part of more complex litigation.

The appropriate use and treatment of constructive trusts imposed over bribes

It is a notable feature of these cases that the finding of a proprietary constructive   **29.17**
trust is generally followed by an order that the subject matter of that trust be transferred absolutely to the beneficiary of that trust. This corresponds with the broadest common sense: in circumstances in which the entirety of a fund of money or
other property is found to be held on a bare constructive trust, that is in circumstances in which there are no other persons identified as being beneficiaries under
that same constructive trust in relation to that property, then the most appropriate resolution of the situation is to order an outright transfer of that property to
the person who has been identified in equity as being its rightful owner. Two problems arise, however: the first practical and the second conceptual.

That the subject matter of the constructive trust should be ordered to be trans-   **29.18**
ferred outright to the beneficiary would not be the case in circumstances in which
there was more than one equitable owner of that property. In the event that the
property at issue was money, then the only issue is the identification of the shares
in which each party to the litigation is entitled to take that property. If the property is not fungible in the same way as money, then the manner in which division
could be made is more complex. The reader is referred to Chapter 33 in relation
to tracing on the issue of the division of property in circumstances in which there
are competing claims to it. The conceptual problem relates to whether or not the
beneficiary could be said to have an automatic right to have the subject matter of
the trust fund delivered to him. As considered in Chapter 1, the principle in
Saunders v Vautier[60] may either suggest that all of the beneficiaries acting together
are entitled to call for delivery up of the trust fund, or else that they are entitled
only to give directions to the trustees to the extent permitted by the trust instrument. In relation to a constructive trust, there is no trust instrument to provide for
the detailed terms of that trust and in consequence the courts feel themselves at
liberty, often, to order delivery up of the absolute title in property even though the
constructive trust itself only operates to convey equitable title to the plaintiff.

C. Unauthorized Profits from Fiduciary Office

The rule against secret, or unauthorized, profits from a fiduciary office

A trustee or fiduciary will be a constructive trustee of any personal profits made   **29.19**
from that office, even where he has acted in good faith.[61] The rule is a strict rule

---

[60] (1841) 4 Beav 115.
[61] *William v Barton* [1927] 2 Ch 9 (where in good faith a trustee used a partnership of which he
was a member to value securities held by the trust and so earned himself a commission for which he
was required to account to the trust); *Regal v Gulliver* [1942] 1 All ER 378; *Boardman v Phipps*
[1967] 2 AC 46.

that no profit can be made by a trustee or fiduciary which is not authorized by the terms of the trust.[62] A fiduciary who profits from that office will be required to account for those profits.[63] There is no defence of good faith in favour of the trustee[64] although he may be able to rely either on his having received authorization to retain his personal profit or on the doctrine of equitable accounting effectively to reward him for any benefit which his efforts may have generated for the objects of his fiduciary duties,[65] as considered below.[66]

29.20   The rule that a fiduciary cannot take an unauthorized, personal benefit from the fiduciary office emerges from the old case of *Keech v Sandford*[67] in which the benefit of a lease with rights to receive profits from a market was settled on trust for an infant. The trustee sought to renew the lease on its expiry but his request was refused on the grounds that an infant could not be bound by such a lease. Therefore, the trustee sought to renew the lease in his own name with the intention that its benefit could then be passed on to the infant. As such the trustee was benefiting personally, although purporting to act in the interest of the beneficiary, by use of a right not available to the beneficiary nor to the trust. An application was made on behalf of the infant to the court for the benefit of the lease to be held on trust for him. The Lord Chancellor held that the lease must be held by the trustee for the infant. While there had been no allegation of fraud in that case the Lord Chancellor, Lord King, considered that the principle that a trustee must not take an unauthorized profit from a trust should be 'strictly pursued' because there were risks of fraud in allowing trustees to take, for example, the benefit of renewed leases which they had previously held on trust. As his lordship expressed the point:

> This may seem hard, that the trustee is the only person of all mankind who might not have the lease: but it is very proper that rule should be strictly pursued, and not in the least relaxed; for it is very obvious what would be the consequence of letting trustees have the lease, on refusal to renew to cestui que use. So decreed that the lease should be assigned to the infant, and that the trustee should be indemnified from any covenants comprised in the lease, and an account of the profits made since the renewal.[68]

This form of trust is said to be a constructive trust because the renewed lease is in fact a different lease from the old one and therefore a different piece of property

---

[62] *Boardman v Phipps* [1967] 2 AC 46; *Regal v Gulliver* [1942] 1 All ER 378.
[63] *Boardman v Phipps* [1967] 2 AC 46; *Regal v Gulliver* [1942] 1 All ER 378.
[64] *Keech v Sandford* (1726) Sel Cas Ch 61.
[65] *Boardman v Phipps* [1967] 2 AC 46; *Guinness v Saunders* [1990] 2 AC 663.
[66] See para 29.59.   [67] (1726) 2 Eq Cas Abr 741.
[68] (1726) 2 Eq Cas King 61. See also *Ex parte Grace* (1799) 1 Bos & P 376; *Rawe v Chichester* (1773) Amb 715. However, see *Re Biss* [1903] 2 Ch 40, in which case the Court of Appeal held that a widow, acting as administratrix of her deceased husband's estate, who sought an order regarding the renewal of a lease, which had been held previously by her husband, and now in favour of their son personally, was not entitled to have that lease held on constructive trust for the estate precisely because the son had not owed any fiduciary obligations towards his dead father nor to his estate.

from that originally held on trust: therefore the infant's trust would be acquiring rights in this particular lease for the first time. Given that the trust only referred to the original piece of property, a trust which attaches to a separate piece of property must be a constructive trust arising by operation of law and by order of the court, not strictly by the action of a settlor in creating a trust.

The central principle in this context remains the prevention of any fiduciary permitting a conflict between his personal and his fiduciary capacities.[69] Lord Upjohn made that point in the following fashion in the House of Lords in *Phipps v Boardman*:[70]

> Rules of equity have to be applied to such a great diversity of circumstances that they can be stated only in the most general terms and applied with particular attention to the exact circumstances of each case. The relevant rule for the decision of this case is the fundamental rule of equity that a person in a fiduciary capacity must not make a profit out of his trust, which is part of the wider rule that a trustee must not place himself in a position where his duty and his interest may conflict. I believe that the rule is best stated in *Bray v Ford* by Lord Herschell,[71] who plainly recognised its limitations:
>
>> 'It is an inflexible rule of the court of equity that a person in a fiduciary position, such as the plaintiff's, is not, unless otherwise expressly provided, entitled to make a profit; he is not allowed to put himself in a position where his interest and duty conflict. It does not appear to me that this rule is, as has been said, founded upon principles of morality. I regard it rather as based on the consideration that, human nature being what it is, there is danger, in such circumstances, of the person holding a fiduciary position being swayed by interest rather than by duty, and thus prejudicing those whom he was bound to protect. It has, therefore, been deemed expedient to lay down this positive rule. But I am satisfied that it might be departed from in many cases, without any breach of morality, without any wrong being inflicted, and without any consciousness of wrong-doing. Indeed, it is obvious that it might sometimes be to the advantage of the beneficiaries that their trustee should act for them professionally rather than a stranger, even though the trustee were paid for his services.'

That same point was expressed in the following manner by Lord Cranworth LC, in *Aberdeen Ry Co v Blaikie Brothers* where he said of fiduciaries that:[72]

> ... it is a rule of universal application that no one having such duties to discharge shall be allowed to enter into engagements in which he has or can have a personal interest conflicting or which possibly may conflict with the interests of those whom he is bound to protect.

It is evidently possible to avoid a constructive trust in these circumstances where the **29.21** individual renewing the lease can demonstrate that he does not occupy a fiduciary position in respect of that property. So in *Re Biss*[73] a son was entitled to take possession of a renewed lease where, acting in good faith, he had sought a renewal in

---

[69] As expressed most recently in *Bhullar v Bhullar* [2003] EWCA Civ 424, para 268, *per* Parker LJ.
[70] [1966] 3 All ER 721.   [71] [1895–99] All ER Rep 1011; [1896] AC 51.
[72] [1843–60] All ER Rep 249, 252.   [73] [1903] 2 Ch 40.

his own name of a lease which had formerly been held by his father's business after his father had died intestate. It was held that the son did not occupy a fiduciary position in respect of his father's business unlike the trustee in *Keech v Sandford*[74] who clearly occupied the fiduciary position of trustee in relation to the infant's settlement. Therefore, the son in *Re Biss*[75] would not be subject to a constructive trust over the renewed lease in his own name. While the decision in *Keech v Sandford* relates specifically to leases, its ratio has been broadened out into a more general principle that fiduciaries cannot profit personally from their office whatever the nature of the property at issue.

Constructive trust taking effect over any unauthorized profit

29.22 The continued rigour of this rule against fiduciaries taking unauthorized benefits from their offices is best illustrated by the decision of the House of Lords in the leading case of *Boardman v Phipps*.[76] The respondent, Boardman, was solicitor to the trustees of a trust: referred to here as 'the Phipps family trust'. As such he was not a trustee but he was held to be in a fiduciary capacity as adviser to the Phipps family trust. The trust fund included a minority shareholding in a private company. While making inquiries as to the performance of the company on behalf of the trust, Boardman and the one active trustee learned of the potential for profit in controlling the company through confidential information. Being a private company, Boardman would have been unable to find out this information or to acquire shares in the company without the initial introduction given to him as solicitor to the trustees of the Phipps family trust. Boardman and the trustees considered that the Phipps family trust would benefit if the trust controlled the company by acquiring a majority shareholding in it. The trust was not able to acquire these extra shares itself both because the trustees did not consider the trust was in sufficient funds for the purpose and because the trust would have required the leave of the court to make such an acquisition. Therefore, Boardman and one of the trustees, Fox, decided to acquire the shares personally. Boardman informed the active trustees that he intended to do this. However, it was held that Boardman had not provided them with enough information to be able to advance any defence that he had gained their consent to his plans. Together with the Phipps family trust's shareholding Boardman and the trustees were able, in effect, to take control of the company. With a great amount of work on Boardman's part the company generated a large profit for the trust, and for Boardman personally, as shareholders. The issue arose whether Boardman was entitled to keep the profit on his own shares or whether he was required to hold the profit on constructive trust for the beneficiaries of the trust.

---

[74] (1726) 2 Eq Cas Abr 741.   [75] [1903] 2 Ch 40.
[76] [1967] 2 AC 46. See also *Blair v Vallely* [2000] WTLR 615; *Ward v Brunt* [2000] WTLR 731.

It was held that Boardman was obliged to hold all of the property he acquired on **29.23** constructive trust for the Phipps family trust. It is difficult to identify one single ratio from the ruminations of the House of Lords but some principles are evident. It was accepted that Boardman occupied a fiduciary relationship although it is not entirely clear whether that was on the basis that he was a solicitor acting in his clients' affairs, or that he was a trustee de son tort[77] who had assumed the responsibilities of a trustee by virtue of taking charge of the powers of the trustees of the Phipps family trust, or simply that the powers which he was purporting to exercise were those of a trustee and therefore generative of fiduciary duties of necessity. That Boardman was a fiduciary was, however, accepted by the court. The House of Lords was operating on the basis of the principle in *Keech v Sandford* that no fiduciary should be permitted to take any unauthorized personal advantage, or secret profit, from his office. The House was moved also by the decision of the House of Lords in *Regal v Gulliver*,[78] considered below,[79] in which directors of a company who pursued on their personal accounts a business opportunity which had been available to the company of which they were the directors—even though the company might not have been in a position to take advantage of that opportunity at the time it arose—were held to be constructive trustees of the profits which their investment generated for the benefit of the company. Some of their lordships sought to justify the finding of a constructive trust not simply on the application of the principle in *Keech v Sandford*—although it is suggested that, on principle, that ought to have been sufficient—but rather on the basis that Boardman was using trust property to generate that profit for himself, where the trust property in question was held by some of their lordships to be the confidential information acquired at the shareholders' meeting of the target company which Boardman could not have acquired unless he had been representing the trust due to the restricted nature of shareholders' meetings in private companies. Had Boardman deliberately speculated with the trust's property and then purported to keep the profits for himself then he would have been subject to a constructive trust without any question.[80]

The appeal in *Boardman v Phipps* raises a number of questions as to the basis **29.24** of this form of constructive trust; the circumstances in which profits deriving from the exploitation of confidential information will give rise to such a constructive trust; the operation of this principle in relation to the exploitation of corporate opportunities by the officers of companies; the treatment of conflicts of interest between fiduciaries' personal capacity and their fiduciary capacity; and whether Boardman was entitled to argue that his profit had been authorized or that it

---

[77] See para 30.03.   [78] *Regal v Gulliver* [1942] 1 All ER 378, [1967] 2 AC 134n.
[79] See para 29.40.
[80] *Reid-Newfoundland Co v Anglo-American Telegraph Co* [1912] AC 555. Cf *Attorney-General v Blake* [1997] Ch 84.

ought to have entitled him to some form of compensation for his efforts (in effect, the range of defences open to someone in Boardman's position). Those issues are considered in turn in the sections to follow, beginning at paragraph 29.26.

The application of this principle to pension fund trusts

29.25   Occupational pension funds are considered in detail in Part H. Trustees of pension funds are also frequently beneficiaries under those trusts. Consequently, there is a theoretical conflict of interest between the trustee's position as both a fiduciary and a beneficiary under the trust when deciding how to exercise their powers under the trust instrument. In consequence recent cases have held that the rule in *Keech v Sandford* will not be employed with such rigour that the courts are not permitted to approve the actions of pension fund trustees acting in the bona fide exercise of their express powers under the trust instrument to grant benefits to beneficiaries under the trust, including themselves by implication.[81] It is suggested, however, that there is no meaningful limitation of the principle in *Keech v Sandford* if the trustees are activating their ordinary powers under the trust instrument or under statute for the benefit of the beneficiaries generally and in good faith because the trustees would be taking a benefit in such circumstances in their capacity as beneficiaries and not by means of any abuse of their fiduciary office.

D. Constructive Trusts and Confidential Information

Constructive trust over confidential information used by a fiduciary to earn an unauthorized profit

29.26   A majority of the House of Lords in *Boardman v Phipps*[82] held that Boardman should hold the profits on constructive trust for the beneficiaries of the existing trust. There is an issue as to the identity of the property which is to be held on trust. Mr Boardman had acquired his shares in a personal capacity: they had never belonged to the Phipps family trust. Some of their lordships indicated that they would have been prepared to find for Boardman if he could have demonstrated that he had made it clear to the trustees that he was acting on his own behalf, even though he had first acquired the confidential information as a fiduciary of the Phipps family trust. However, Lords Hodson and Guest held that the confidential information itself, obtained while on trust business, was to be considered the property of the Phipps family trust. Therefore, the profit which was generated for Boardman personally was derived from trust property (the confidential

---

[81] *Re Drexel Lambert Pension Plan* [1995] 1 WLR 32, 41, *per* Scott V-C; *Edge v Pensions Ombudsman* [1998] Ch 512, 539, *per* Scott V-C.   [82] [1967] 2 AC 46.

information) and therefore ought to have been considered to be the property belonging to the trust.[83]

29.27 It is peculiar that some of their lordships held that the trust was founded on this proprietary nexus between the information and the profit, rather than simply finding that the status of fiduciary required that the property be held on trust.[84] A more recent Australian decision has expressed the view that this rule is based on the fiduciary's obligation to permit no conflict between his personal benefit and his duties to others.[85]

The equitable obligation of confidence in intellectual property law

29.28 It is in intellectual property law that the greatest pressure has arisen for the recognition of confidential information in relation to a patented or other technical process or in relation to copyright.[86] The principal goal of litigation predicated on the protection of confidential information is to enjoin the recipient of that information from misusing or publishing it. However, it is suggested, given the belief of some of their lordships in *Boardman v Phipps* to this effect,[87] that the misuse of confidential information by a fiduciary might itself cause such a fiduciary to be constructive trustee of any profit realized by using that information for the benefit of the owner of the confidential information. Therefore, this section gives an overview of some of the instances in which the equitable obligation of confidence will arise.

29.29 Confidential information may include information which is subject to copyright so as to prevent any other person from profiting from or otherwise exploiting that copyright,[88] and similarly in relation to patented processes and also know-how.[89] Otherwise there is no conceptual restriction on the types of information which may fall within the category of 'confidential information', whether technical, industrial, commercial, or personal information: but it will not include 'trivial tittle-tattle'.[90] At its broadest, confidential information may include any information forming part of a personal relationship giving a ground for preventing its publication.[91] In general terms the communication of the information by one

---

[83] cf *Satnam Investments Ltd v Dunlop Heywood & Co Ltd* [1999] 3 All ER 652 where confidential information held by S was disclosed to third parties leading to the acquisition of a development site by those third parties, it was held that there was no constructive trust over the defendant because he was not in a fiduciary position in relation to S; applied *Brisby v Lomaxhall* (unreported, 2000).

[84] As in *Attorney-General for Hong Kong v Reid* [1994] 1 AC 324; [1994] 1 All ER 1 considered above.   [85] Deane J in *Chan v Zacharia* (1984) 154 CLR 178.

[86] *Douglas v Hello* [2001] EMLR 199, 251, *per* Keane LJ.   [87] See para 29.26.

[88] See, for example, *Prince Albert v Strange* (1849) 2 De G & Sm 652.

[89] See, for example, *Morison v Moat* (1851) 9 Hare 241; *Potters-Ballotini v Weston-Baker* [1977] RPC 202.   [90] *Coco v AN Clark (Engineers)* [1969] RPC 41, 48, *per* Megarry J.

[91] See *Barrymore v News Group Newspapers* [1997] FSR 600, 602 suggesting that such information may be confidential: cf *M & N Mackenzie v News Group Newspapers* (unreported, 18 January 1988).

person to another in a situation in which its recipient was aware that the information was being passed to him in confidence would raise the 'equitable obligation of confidence'.[92] In deciding whether or not the recipient ought to have understood that the information was being passed to him in confidence, the court will take into account standard practice in the industry or market in which that information was passed.[93] The test is whether or not a reasonable person would have considered that the information was being passed in confidence.[94] Therefore, an ordinary conversation during which confidential information was blurted out would not create any duty of confidence,[95] whereas the transfer of information expressly for a limited purpose would impose an obligation on its recipient to use that information only for that limited purpose,[96] and the transfer of information which was encrypted would not necessarily suggest to a reasonable person that simply because the information was encrypted meant that it was not to be disclosed to any other person.[97]

29.30 Obligations of confidence may be imposed on employees during their employment in relation to members of the security services when dealing with state secrets[98] or employees in the private sector dealing with industrial processes and secrets.[99] After employment, provisions in the contract of employment in reasonable restraint of trade will prevent use of confidential information.[100] It is not necessary that there have been some pre-existing relationship between the parties for the obligation of confidence to arise, rather it must have been obvious to a reasonable person who had acquired that information that it was of a type which ought to treated in confidence.[101]

---

[92] *Coco v AN Clark (Engineers)* [1969] RPC 41, 48, *per* Megarry J. See also *Seager v Copydex* [1967] 2 All ER 415.

[93] *Fraser v Thames TV* [1983] 2 All ER 101, 121; *De Maudsley v Palumbo* [1996] FSR 447, 457.

[94] *English & American v Herbert Smith* [1988] FSR 232; *Attorney-General v Guardian (No 2)* [1990] AC 109, 281, *per* Lord Goff.

[95] *Coco v AN Clark (Engineers)* [1969] RPC 41; *De Maudsley v Palumbo* [1996] FSR 447.

[96] *Carflow Products v Linwood Securities* [1996] FSR 424.

[97] *Mars v Teknowledge* [2000] FSR 138.   [98] *Attorney-General v Blake* [1998] 1 All ER 833.

[99] *Hivac v Park Royal Scientific Instruments* [1946] Ch 169.

[100] *Mitchel v Reynolds* (1711) 1 P Wms 181; *Mont v Mills* [1993] FSR 577. That is unless the information acquired is in the form of personal skills and attributes: *Herbert Morris v Saxelby* [1916] AC 688; *Attwood v Lamont* [1920] 3 KB 571. This doctrine may have been founded in *Dier's Case* (1414) 2 Hen V 5.

[101] *Attorney-General v Guardian (No 2)* [1990] AC 109; *Hellewell v Chief Constable of Derbyshire* [1995] 1 WLR 804. This may raise questions as to the manner in which the information was acquired (*Shelley Films v Rex Features* [1994] EMLR 134, in which a photographer who had taken photographs of actor Robert De Niro on the set of the film *Frankenstein*, without permission and having come uninvited onto the film set, was held to have known that the photographs and the information in them were acquired in breach of confidence; and the *Spycatcher* case [1995] 1 WLR 804, 807, *per* Lord Goff) and as to the intrinsic quality of the information itself (*Attorney-General v Guardian (No 2)* [1990] AC 109, 281, *per* Lord Goff).

Chinese walls: the preservation of confidential information by professional advisers

In certain circumstances a financial institution, or an accountancy firm, or a **29.31** solicitors' firm may be involved in complex transactions or litigation in which that organization is dealing with confidential information which cannot be allowed to pass from limited personnel to the rest of that organization's personnel, or else that some personnel from within that organization are involved in advising one party to a transaction while other personnel from within that same organization are advising different parties to that same transaction. The possibilities for conflicts of interest or for breaches of confidentiality are self-evident. Furthermore, professional advisers such as solicitors and accountants providing advice during litigation owe duties of confidentiality to their clients. In consequence, such organizations, provided that there is not thought to be any ethical objection to officers from the same organization dealing with both sides to the same transaction, will be obliged to ensure that their personnel and their resources and activities are segregated. These divisions are known as 'Chinese walls'.

Following on from the preceding discussions of the fair dealing and of the self- **29.32** dealing principle, a firm of professional advisers who fail to establish suitable Chinese walls will be potentially liable for breach of those principles and consequently to hold any benefit taken from those transactions on constructive trust for their clients.[102] There is also the potential for liability for fraud or negligence, where appropriate, and for any individual within the firm to be liable similarly for tort or for assistance in a breach of the firm's fiduciary duties.[103]

There is nothing new in the notion that a professional adviser like a solicitor will **29.33** be involved in advising numerous parties to the same transaction, as with solicitors who advise mortgagees, mortgagors, and those who cohabit with mortgagors about the effect of proposed mortgage contracts.[104] In a subtly different sense, however, the purpose of Chinese walls is to prevent various officers or departments within large organizations from breaching any duties of confidentiality or from breaching any duties of the utmost loyalty to all those people who are relying on those various parts of that organization. The way in which Chinese walls operate are by means of physical barriers within the workplace. Therefore, the personnel from one department might have their electronic 'swipe cards', which permit their holder to pass through security doors, reprogrammed so that they are denied access to parts of the workplace where sensitive material is kept. Similarly,

---

[102] See para 29.31. See also P Graham, 'The Statutory Regulation of Financial Services in the United Kingdom and the Development of Chinese Walls in Managing Conflicts of Interest' in E McKendrick (ed), *Commercial Aspects of Trusts and Fiduciary Obligations* (Oxford University Press, 1992) 43.   [103] See paras 30.16 and 30.64.
[104] *Halifax Mortgage Services Ltd v Stepsky* [1996] Ch 1, [1996] 2 All ER 277.

certain documents and meetings relating to matters concerning the confidential transaction will be restricted to geographical parts of the building. There will also be prohibitions on personnel from the various sectors discussing the transaction and from meeting at all in some circumstances.

29.34 The presence of these barriers impact on the question whether or not an organization can be deemed to have acted dishonestly or otherwise with knowledge which would give rise to a constructive trust[105] over any gain realized by that organization. Where a company, or limited liability partnership, is sued on this basis, the claimant will have to demonstrate that the company had knowledge of the factors which are alleged to affect its conscience. The presence of an effective Chinese wall will prevent the claimant from demonstrating that a combination of the knowledge of personnel from different departments segregated by that Chinese wall can be assumed such that the company can consequently be deemed to have the requisite knowledge in aggregate.[106] The complexities of demonstrating that a company has knowledge of some matter even where there are no Chinese walls are demonstrable in particular in relation to large companies.[107] Where, for example, a company owning a supermarket chain has many hundreds of branches employing many hundreds of middle managers, the company will not have the criminal liability or other knowledge attributed to the entire organization as a result of an individual middle manager having had such knowledge because such a middle manager could not be said to have constituted a controlling mind of the company.[108] Nevertheless, cases involving Chinese walls have tended to take the view that each employee is an agent of the organization and so their knowledge can be attributed to the organization: such that, the aggregate of the knowledge of two employees, which, if that knowledge had been held consciously in the mind of one person, would have amounted to knowledge of some dishonest or wrongful design, is deemed to attribute such aggregated knowledge to the organization.[109] This appears to be based on a judicial assumption, particularly in relation to solicitors' firms, that Chinese walls cannot be assumed to operate effectively at holding confidential information in a vacuum.[110]

29.35 To overcome the objection to an organization acting in this fashion and so raising an assumption that it would be acting in breach of its duties of confidentiality, the

---

[105] See para 30.64.

[106] *Galmerrow Securities Ltd v National Westminster Bank plc* [2002] WTLR 125.

[107] See, for example, *Lloyds Bank Ltd v Savory & Co* [1933] AC 201; *Harrods Ltd v Lemon* [1931] 2 KB 157; *El Ajou v Dollar Land Holdings plc* [1994] 2 All ER 685.

[108] See *Tesco Supermarkets Ltd v Nattrass* [1972] AC 153, [1971] 2 All ER 127 (liability for criminal offences in relation to trades description legislation); *Meridian Global v Securities Commission* [1995] 3 All ER 918; *Williams v Natural Life Health Foods Ltd* [1998] 2 All ER 577, [1998] 1 WLR 830 (liability in tort).   [109] *Harrods Ltd v Lemon* [1931] 1 KB 157.

[110] *National Mutual Holdings Pty Ltd v Sentry Corp* (1989) 87 ALR 539, 555, *per* Gummow J; *David Lee & Co (Lincoln) Ltd v Coward Chance and Others* [1990] 3 WLR 1278; *Re a firm of solicitors* [1992] 1 All ER 353.

organization in question needs to demonstrate that the arrangements which it puts in place to prevent information passing within the organization are sufficient for the purpose.[111] In general terms the courts will be unimpressed by temporary or ad hoc arrangements which are put in place to deal with one isolated transaction but rather would require a demonstration that the culture of an organization and the manner in which it was run and managed led to the establishment of suitable Chinese walls.[112]

E. Constructive Trusts in Relation to Abuse of Fiduciary Office in Commercial Situations

The judicial reluctance to imply fiduciary obligations in commercial contexts

Whereas the courts are astute in enforcing duties of utmost loyalty and good faith on those who occupy fiduciary offices, the judiciary has nevertheless expressed itself to be reluctant to imply such fiduciary obligations in commercial situations.[113] The policy underlying this attitude is concerned to preserve the certainty which is said to obtain in the interpretation of commercial contracts in the absence of any further obligations on the contracting parties imposed by operation of law or otherwise by courts of equity, particularly obligations as stringent as those imposed on fiduciaries.[114] As Sir Anthony Mason made this point when writing extrajudicially:[115] **29.36**

> ... there is strong resistance, especially in the United Kingdom, to the infiltration of equity into commercial transactions ... [arising] from apprehensions about the disruptive impact of equitable proprietary remedies, assisted by the doctrine of notice, on the certainty and security of commercial transactions.

Similar sentiments, bearing a suspicion of the imposition of flexible equitable doctrine, are evident from the following observation of Lord Browne-Wilkinson:

> ... wise judges have often warned against the wholesale importation into commercial law of equitable principles inconsistent with the certainty and speed which are essential requirements for the orderly conduct of business affairs.[116]

These principles are derived from older authorities such as *Barnes v Addy*[117] as well as being discernible in more modern ones such as *Scandinavian Trading* **29.37**

---

[111] *Bolkiah v KPMG* [1999] 2 AC 222.
[112] See, for example, *Re Firm of Solicitors* [2000] 1 Lloyds Rep 31; *Hazelwood International v Addleshaw Booth* [2000] Lloyd's Rep PN 298; *Laker Airways v FLS Aerospace Ltd* [2000] 1 WLR 113, *Koch Shipping Inc v Richard Butler* [2002] EWCA Civ 1280.
[113] *Kelly v Cooper* [1993] AC 205.
[114] *Manchester Trust v Furness* [1895] 2 QB 539, 545, *per* Lindley LJ; *Re Wait* [1927] 1 Ch 606, 634, *per* Atkin LJ.   [115] A Mason, 'Equity's role in the twentieth century' (1997/98) 8 KCLJ 1.
[116] [1996] AC 669.   [117] (1874) 9 Ch App 244.

Tanker Co AB v Flota Petrolera Ecuatoriana.[118] This issue of certainty is typically linked by the judiciary to a need to protect the integrity of commercial contracts and not to allow other considerations to intrude unless absolutely necessary. The problem is said to be the intervention of some legal principle outwith the expectation of the parties. As Robert Goff LJ has said:[119]

> It is of the utmost importance in commercial transactions that, if any particular event occurs which may affect the parties' respective rights under a commercial contract, they should know where they stand. The court should so far as possible desist from placing obstacles in the way of either party ascertaining his legal position, if necessary with the aid of advice from a qualified lawyer, because it may be commercially desirable for action to be taken without delay, action which may be irrecoverable and which may have far-reaching consequences. It is for this reason, of course, that the English courts have time and again asserted the need for certainty in commercial transactions—the simple reason that the parties to such transactions are entitled to know where they stand, and to act accordingly.

29.38   The essence of commercial certainty is therefore said to be the minimal use of discretionary remedies. Leggatt LJ was moved by similar concerns in *Scandinavian Trading v Flota Petrolera Ecuatoriana*:[120]

> ...tempting though it may be to follow the path which Lloyd J was inclined to follow in *the Afovos*,[121] we do not feel that it would be right to do so. The policy which favours certainty in commercial transactions is so antipathetic to the form of equitable intervention invoked by the charterers in the present case that we do not think it would be right to extend that jurisdiction to relieve time charterers from the consequences of withdrawal.

29.39   Alternatively, it might be argued that equity offers a particularly valuable means by which our social mores and culture can express affirmation or disapprobation for certain forms of commercial activity and that it will not always be possible simply to accept that whatever is provided for in a contract will always be considered by a court to be conscionable. The imposition of fiduciary obligations are an important means of ensuring that commercial certainty is protected by holding contracting parties to the standards of loyalty and good faith which are appropriate from context to context. Nevertheless, this see-sawing between enforcing minimum standards of good faith through fiduciary law and permitting commercial people to suffer all the consequences which may flow from the failings of their own, freely contracted transactions informs the law in this area. It is evidenced by the two contexts considered in following sections relating to the exploitation of a company's opportunities by its own directors and the realization of a profit by one partner at the expense of another.

---

[118] [1983] 2 WLR 248.
[119] *Scandinavian Trading v Flota Petrolera Ecuatoriana* [1983] 2 WLR 248, 257.
[120] [1983] 2 WLR 248, 258. See also the same judge in *Westdeutsche Landesbank v Islington* [1994] 4 All ER 890.   [121] [1980] 2 Lloyd's Rep 469.

The corporate opportunity doctrine

Many of the cases discussed thus far have related specifically to company law and **29.40** the exploitation of a company's business opportunities by its directors to the detriment both of the company, as the beneficiary of the directors' fiduciary duties, and of the shareholders who would otherwise have benefited from any profits realized by the directors. Therefore, it will be useful to identify some of the differences between company law and trusts law in this regard. The modern company grew out of the law of trusts and of partnership in the late nineteenth century.[122] The principle difference between the two institutions is that companies have distinct legal personality[123] whereas trusts do not.[124] Therefore, a company is absolute owner of its own property; the directors of the company take no title in the company's property and are therefore not trustees in that sense of the term.[125] Directors are nevertheless fiduciaries.[126] Directors owe their fiduciary duties to the company but do not owe fiduciary duties directly to the shareholders of the company in the same way that trustees owe duties to their beneficiaries. Significantly, whereas beneficiaries are the equitable owners of the property held on trust, shareholders are not recognized as having any equitable ownership of the company's property. Rather, any rights of ownership which the shareholders might have are restricted to ownership of their individual shares in the company and to any rights they may have to the company's property under the company's constitution if the company is wound up. Thus, a director will be obliged to hold any secret profits earned on his own account from his fiduciary duties on constructive trust for the company. The key principle in this context remains the policy against fiduciaries permitting any conflict between their personal and their fiduciary interests.[127] The pursuit of such an opportunity and the realization of any profits or the acquisition of any property from that opportunity will render the fiduciary a constructive trustee of such property. Whether or not the opportunity is one which the company would have exploited has been held not to be the central point: rather, the fiduciary's obligation has been found to be to communicate that information to the company in the first place.[128] Therefore, in circumstances in which a director is acting in a fiduciary capacity and encounters an opportunity

---

[122] On which see AS Hudson, *Equity v Trusts* (3rd edn, Cavendish Publishing, 2003) ('*Hudson*') para 25.1.   [123] *Saloman v A Saloman & Co Ltd* [1897] AC 22.

[124] *Smith v Anderson* (1880) 15 Ch D 247.

[125] Although the courts in company law cases do occasionally express the role of company directors as being akin to that of a trustee on occasion: eg *Re Lands Allotment Co* [1894] 1 Ch 616; *Re Duckwari plc* [1999] Ch 253, [1998] 2 BCLC 315.

[126] *Selangor United Rubber Estates Ltd v Cradock (No 3)* [1968] 1 WLR 1555.

[127] *Bhullar v Bhullar* [2003] EWCA Civ 424. See also *Dilmun v Sutton* [2004] EWHC 52 (Chancery) a case in which a managing director pursued a land development opportunity without disclosing it to the company.

[128] *Bhullar v Bhullar* [2003] EWCA Civ 424, para 41, *per* Parker LJ.

which could be exploited by the company, then that director is not entitled to pursue that opportunity on his own account. As is considered below,[129] there may be a defence for a fiduciary who obtains clear authorization to pursue that opportunity on his own account.[130]

29.41 This core principle has been expressed in the following manner in the decided cases. Delivering his speech in the House of Lords in *Regal Hastings v Gulliver*,[131] Lord Macmillan identified the central principle as being that directors are liable to account as constructive trustees for profits received in a personal capacity from their fiduciary office if:

> (i) what the directors did was so related to the affairs of the company that it can properly be said to have been done in the course of their management and in utilisation of their opportunities and special knowledge as directors and (ii) what they did resulted in profit for themselves.

In his decision in *Island Export v Umunna*,[132] Hutchison J held that:

> Descending from the generality, the fiduciary relationship goes at least this far: a director or a senior officer like [the defendants] is precluded from obtaining for himself, either secretly or without the approval of the company (which would have to be properly manifested on full disclosure of the facts), any property or business advantage either belonging to the company or for which it has been negotiating; and especially is this so when the director or officer is a participant in the negotiations on behalf of the company.

It has been accepted that this latter formulation of the fiduciary duty of a director is absolutely in accord with the line of authority exemplified by *Regal (Hastings) Ltd v Gulliver*.[133] In the Canadian case of *Canadian Aero Services v O'Malley*,[134] Laskin J identified the fundamental ethical principle at issue here:

> An examination of the case law in this Court and in the Courts of other like jurisdictions on the fiduciary duties of directors and senior officers shows the pervasiveness of a strict ethic in this area of the law. In my opinion, this ethic disqualifies a director or senior officer from usurping for himself or diverting to another person or company with whom or with which he is associated a maturing business opportunity which his company is actively pursuing; he is also precluded from so acting even after his resignation where the resignation may fairly be said to have been prompted or influenced by a wish to acquire for himself the opportunity sought by the company, or where it was his position with the company rather than a fresh initiative that led him to the opportunity which he later acquired.

29.42 The leading case in this context is that of *Regal v Gulliver*[135] in which the appellant company owned a cinema in Hastings and learned of the possibility of

---

[129] See para 29.60.
[130] *Queensland Mines v Hudson* (1977) 18 ALR 1. Cf *IDC v Cooley* [1972] 1 WLR 443.
[131] [1967] 2 AC 134n, 153.
[132] [1986] BCLC 460. On which see also *Canadian Aero Services v O'Malley* (1973) 40 DLR (3d) (Can SC) 371.   [133] *Bhullar v Bhullar* [2003] EWCA Civ 424.
[134] (1973) 40 DLR (3d) (Can SC) 371, 382.   [135] [1942] 1 All ER 378.

acquiring leases over two more and then selling their business in operating all three to third parties. Whereas the directors of the company had originally intended to create a subsidiary company to take out leases over the cinemas, it transpired that the lessor required either personal guarantees from the directors or that the company's paid up capital be increased. The directors decided that they would prefer to take the leases in their own names rather than give the guarantees in favour of the company and rather than raise the necessary capital for the company. The shares in the company were subsequently sold to the claimants and the company, under this new control, sought to recover the profits which the directors had earned personally from exploiting on their own accounts the opportunity which would otherwise have been exploited by the company. It was held by the House of Lords that the directors should account to the company for their profits. As Lord Russell held:

> ... the directors standing in a fiduciary relationship to Regal in regard to the exercise of their powers as directors, and having obtained these shares by reason and only by reason of the fact that they were directors of Regal and in the course of the execution of that office, are accountable for the profits which they have made out of them. The equitable rule laid down in *Keech v Sandford* and *Ex p James*[136] and similar authorities applies to them in full force.

Lord Russell held, further, that the directors could have protected themselves only if they had procured an antecedent or subsequent resolution of the shareholders in general meeting to approve the directors' actions: the directors were not, however, able to authorize themselves to exploit these leases on their own account. However, the general principle in company law is that the minority shareholders will not be entitled to disturb a resolution of the majority shareholders.[137] Such a resolution of the shareholders would only be effective if it was not procured by means of the control exercised over the company by the directors[138] or where the directors held the majority of shares in the company and were therefore deemed by the court to be seeking to make 'a present to themselves' by purporting to affirm the contract.[139]

Company law has, in consequence, developed a concept known as the 'corporate opportunity' doctrine whereby the directors will be liable to hold any profits on constructive trust for the company if those profits were made from an opportunity which the company could have exploited or which the company would have exploited but for the actions of the directors in diverting the opportunity for their   **29.43**

---

136 (1803) 8 Ves 337.
137 *Foss v Harbottle* (1843) 2 Hare 461; *Mozley v Alston* (1847) 1 Ph 790.
138 *Prudential Assurance Co Ltd v Newman Industries Ltd (No 2)* [1981] Ch 257, Vinelott J; reversed in part on the facts on appeal to the Court of Appeal at [1982] Ch 204 on the question, in that case, as to whether or not the litigation brought by the minority shareholders was something to which the company should be exposed when the shareholders were in any event entitled to affirm the transaction.   139 *Cook v Deeks* [1916] AC 554.

own, personal benefits.[140] Therefore, in *Queensland Mines v Hudson*, a company's managing director sought authorization to develop a business opportunity for his own benefit only once the board of directors had decided that it was not an opportunity which the company ought to have pursued. The rejection of the opportunity by the board of directors meant that Hudson was not appropriating a corporate opportunity for his own purposes but rather that the company had given up that opportunity through the board of directors. In *Regal v Gulliver*, even though there was a suggestion that the directors considered the company to be unable to procure the requisite finance to pursue the opportunity at issue in that case, the court nevertheless decided that the opportunity was one which the company would have wanted to pursue and therefore that it was a corporate opportunity.

29.44   More recent developments in company law have suggested that this corporate opportunity doctrine may have the effect that a director may be absolved from liability for secret profits if the company is not intending to pursue the opportunity.[141] So, in *Island Export Finance Ltd v Umanna*[142] the company had a contract with the government of Cameroon to supply the government with post boxes. Mr Umanna resigned from the company once the contract was completed, having worked on that contract and acquired a great deal of expertise in that particular activity. The company ceased pursuing this line of business and after his resignation Mr Umanna entered into a similar contract on his own behalf. The company sued him for the personal profits which he made for himself under this second contract. The court held that Mr Umanna's fiduciary obligations towards the company did not cease once he resigned from its employment. This makes sense: if it were not the case, then no fiduciary could ever be bound by their fiduciary office if they had the good sense to resign immediately before breaching their duties. However, in this instance the court found that the company had not been seeking to develop this sort of business opportunity at the time Mr Umanna had done so and therefore he had not interfered with a corporate opportunity.

29.45   So, what does this mean for the doctrine of constructive trust in relation to secret profits? Given that company law is based historically in trusts law, there is no surprise that the *Keech v Sandford*[143] doctrine has been extended to preclude company directors from making unauthorized profits from their fiduciary offices.

---

[140] See the discussion of opportunities which will be corporate and those which are personal in *Bhullar v Bhullar* [2003] EWCA Civ 424, a case in which a company director acquired real property adjacent to premises owned by the company purportedly for himself, although in the company's name. It was held that the possibility of acquiring such a property, akin to the many others which the business had acquired, so close to its existing premises was an opportunity of which the company should have been informed, that the defendant should be considered to have been acting in a fiduciary capacity throughout, and therefore that he should hold the property on constructive trust for the company and thus be obliged to transfer it to the company at his own cost.

[141] See generally J Lowry and R Edmonds, 'The Corporate Opportunity Doctrine' [1998] MLR 515.   [142] [1986] BCC 460.   [143] (1726) Sel Cas Ch 61.

One significant difference between company law and trusts law is that the trustees would, it appears, be required to seek authorization from the beneficiaries as equitable owners of the trust fund, whereas company shareholders do not have equivalent equitable title in the company's property and therefore the directors' duties are not owed to the shareholders in the same way that trustees owe their duties to beneficiaries.[144] Consequently, for company directors to seek authorization requires that to acquire authorization they approach either the board of directors—as the organ of management in the company—or the company's shareholders in general meeting. This bifurcation in control of the company is a feature of modern company law. The directors are taken to be the management of the company with control of its day-to-day affairs but the Companies Act 1985 reserves a variety of powers, including the power to remove individual directors from office,[145] for the exclusive competence of the company's shareholders in general meeting or extraordinary general meetings. Nevertheless, the stricter approach derived from *Keech v Sanford* considered above still appears to hold sway for the most part.[146] There will only be a defence to liability for constructive trust in exceptional cases where either the director has acquired authorization from the board of directors, without the board acting in bad faith in so doing,[147] or where the company is not pursuing the opportunity in question.

The approximation of investment trust structures to companies

The context of the trust may be very different from that of a company. The general principle is evident from cases like *Boardman v Phipps*[148] in which everything will be assumed against the trustee to ensure the protection of the beneficiaries. However, it remains to be seen whether or not in the future the courts may yet come to treat family trusts differently from commercial, investment trusts. The trust in *Boardman v Phipps* was a family trust in relation to which it might be inappropriate to think in terms of the trust having any 'corporate purpose' and making informed decisions as to which opportunities it would pursue and would not pursue. Nevertheless, the Phipps family trust was investing in private companies. Indeed in many such trusts the trustees are necessarily making decisions whether or not to invest in one opportunity or another on behalf of the beneficiaries. In relation to pension funds, the Pensions Act 1995 requires the trustees to draw up investment strategies and the Trustee Act 2000 requires ordinary trustees to have regard to 'standard investment criteria'[149] and to the diversification of investments.[150] In consequence, different types of trustees are already required by

29.46

---

[144] *Percival v Wright* [1902] 2 Ch 421. Cf. *Allen v Hyatt* (1914) 30 TLR 444, where the directors undertook exceptionally to act as the agents of the shareholders as well as in the capacity of directors of the company. [145] Companies Act 1985, s 303.
[146] *IDC v Cooley* [1972] 1 WLR 443, *Carlton v Halestrap* (1988) 4 BCC 538.
[147] As in *Regal v Gulliver* [1942] 1 All ER 378, [1967] 2 AC 134n. [148] [1967] 2 AC 46.
[149] Trustee Act 2000, s 4(1). [150] ibid, s 4(2).

statute to choose between opportunities which they wish to pursue and those which they do not. In relation to unit trust structures and similar structures which are created solely for speculation and investment of capital, the gap between trusts and companies carrying on trading activities is narrower than the gap between family trusts created simply to maintain assets like real property and trading companies. Therefore, one might be tempted to suggest that the advances in company law in relation to the *Keech v Sandford* principle could be adopted into trusts law in relation to commercial trusts structures, particularly given the suggestion that trusts law might yet come to differentiate between commercial trusts and traditional trusts.

29.47 At present it appears, however, that the *Boardman v Phipps* principle will continue to apply across the whole of trusts law. In consequence, it would appear that profits can only be authorized either in the terms of the trust itself or by the agreement of all of the beneficiaries. This position mirrors that for a trustee's liability for breach trust whereby the only defences available in the case law refer to the acquiescence of the beneficiaries in the trustee's actions.[151] To draw parallels between breach of trust and liability as a constructive trustee for secret profits also highlights the link between these two areas as species of equitable wrong:[152] that is, imposing liability on the defendant on account of the defendant's unconscionable action in breaching a trust or making unauthorized profits respectively.

The general principle in relation to partnerships and joint ventures

29.48 Partners who generate personal profits in breach of their partnership agreement will hold those profits on constructive trust for the benefit of the partnership (in the person of the various partners) and be liable to account to the other partners or to provide them with equitable compensation for any further loss suffered by the partners.[153] Therefore, in circumstances in which a partnership held land for their common benefit, if one partner sought to keep personal profits derived from that profit for himself then those profits would be held on constructive trust for the benefit of the partnership in proportion to the shares identified for those partners under their partnership agreement or, in the absence of such provision, in proportion to their capital contribution to the property.[154]

---

[151] *Lyall v Edwards* (1861) 6 H & N 337; *BCCI v Ali* [2000] 3 All ER 51.

[152] The expression 'equitable wrong' used, for example, by Lord Nicholls in discussing personal liability to account as a constructive trustee in *Dubai Aluminium v Salaam* [2003] 1 All ER 97, para 9.

[153] *Thompson's Trustee v Heaton* [1974] 1 WLR 605; *Popat v Shonchintra* [1995] 1 WLR 908, appealed at [1997] 1 WLR 1367; *Tang Man Sit v Capacious Investments* [1996] 1 AC 514.

[154] *Protheroe v Protheroe* [1968] 1 WLR 519; *Thompson's Trustee v Heaton* [1974] 1 WLR 605; *Popat v Shonchintra* [1997] 1 WLR 1367. Cf *Savage v Dunningham* [1974] Ch 181 where it was held that there would not be any constructive trust if there was no longer any fiduciary responsibility owed between the parties.

The same principle will apply in relation to joint ventures—a form of legal rela-   **29.49**
tionship recognized in other jurisdictions than England and Wales but which constitutes merely a form of contract, possibly a partnership, in England and
Wales—as in *Tang Man Sit v Capacious Investments*[155] in which one party to such
an agreement leased houses and kept the rents for himself whereas the joint venture agreement envisaged that the properties would have been sold to the claimant
with vacant possession. The defendant was deemed to have been in a fiduciary
relationship with the claimant. The claimant was held to be entitled to elect
between the various remedies open to him covering constructive trust, account,
and equitable compensation. The remedy of equitable compensation on these
facts enabled the claimant to recover the loss suffered as a result of the occupation
of the property.

Where a joint venture is formed on the understanding that property is to be used   **29.50**
for the purposes of the venturers jointly, but where one of the venturers decides
instead to exploit the opportunity on his own account, he will be required to hold
any benefit taken from that transaction on constructive trust for the other venturers in proportion to their understanding of their transaction.[156] This form of
liability is considered in Chapter 28.[157]

F. Conflicts of Interest

Profits derived from conflicts of interest giving rise to constructive trusts in general terms

The authorities are clear that if a trustee gains a profit from some conflict between   **29.51**
his personal and his fiduciary capacities, then he will hold any such profit on proprietary constructive trust for the beneficiaries of that relationship. Coupled with
the duty not to realize any unauthorized profit from that office is an obligation not
to permit any conflict between the individual's personal and fiduciary interests.[158]
These two duties are connected: earning a personal profit is, for a fiduciary, to permit a conflict between personal and fiduciary capacities.[159] Writing extrajudicially
Sir Peter Millett has summarized the obligation of the fiduciary to avoid conflicts
of interest of this nature in the following terms:

> [The fiduciary] must not place himself in a position where his interest may conflict
> with his duty. If he has done so, equity insists on treating him as having acted in
> accordance with his duty; he will not be allowed to say that he preferred his own

---

[155] [1996] 1 AC 514.
[156] *Pallant v Morgan* [1953] Ch 43; *Banner Homes Group plc v Luff Development Ltd* [2000] Ch 372.
[157] See para 28.08.   [158] *Bray v Ford* [1896] AC 44, 51, *per* Lord Herschell.
[159] *Swain v Law Society* [1982] 1 WLR 17, 29, *per* Stephenson LJ; *Chan v Zacharia* (1984) 53
ALR 417, 433, *per* Deane J.

interest to that of his principal. He must not obtain a profit for himself out of his fiduciary position. If he has done so, equity insists on treating him as having obtained it for his principal; he will not be allowed to say that he obtained it for himself. He must not accept a bribe. If he has done so, equity insists on treating it as a legitimate payment intended for the benefit of the principal; he will not be allowed to say that it was a bribe.[160]

Consequently the fiduciary is deemed to have acted in accordance with his duty in the sense that any profit which he has generated for himself will be treated as having been earned for the beneficiaries and so held on constructive trust for them.[161] As Lord Cohen held in *Boardman v Phipps*: 'an agent is, in my opinion, liable to account for profits which he makes out of the trust property if there is a possibility of conflict between his interest and his duty to his principal'. The nature of this constructive trust could therefore be characterized as being a proprietary institution or arise simply out of conflict of duty and act *in personam* in relation to that fiduciary's unconscionable conduct. Lord Upjohn dissented from this view on the basis that a solicitor ought to be able to act both on his own account and for his client provided that at no time does he allow a conflict of interest to develop between his duty to the client and his own desire for personal profit. As such, his lordship held, there ought to have been no objection to Boardman making some personal profit from these transactions.

The self-dealing principle

29.52   The foregoing section considered the obligations of fiduciaries when making unauthorized profits from their office in general terms. This section considers the obligations of fiduciaries when dealing with the beneficiaries of their power as a third party. For example, where a trustee seeks to buy property from the trust. In that instance the trustee would be acting on behalf of the trust as well as acting on her own behalf. Such a transaction bears the risk that the trustee will acquire the property from the trust at an advantageous price and thus exploit the beneficiaries. By the same token it might be that the price which the trustee obtains would have been the same price which the beneficiaries would have obtained on the open market. The self-dealing principle entitles the beneficiary to avoid any such transaction on the basis, set out in the *Keech v Sandford*[162] rule, that even the possibility of fraud or bad faith being exercised by the trustee is to be resisted:[163] this is referred to for present purposes as the principle in *Lacey*.[164]

---

[160] P Millett, 'Bribes, and secret commissions' [1993] RLR 7.
[161] Compare this notion with the 'honest trustee doctrine' applied in relation to equitable tracing claims in situations in which the trustee has mixed trust property with his own property such that the court will assume that any valuable property acquired from that mixed fund was intended to have been acquired for the beneficiaries rather than for the trustee: *Re Hallett's Estate* (1880) 13 Ch D 695. See para 33.39.
[162] (1726) 2 Eq Cas Abr 741.   [163] *Franks v Bollans* (1868) 3 Ch App 717.
[164] *Ex parte Lacey* (1802) 6 Ves 625.

Megarry V-C in *Tito v Waddell (No 2)*[165] enunciated the self-dealing principle in **29.53** the following terms: 'if a trustee purchases trust property from himself, any beneficiary may have the sale set aside *ex debito justitiae*, however fair the transaction'. The right of the beneficiary is therefore to set aside the transaction with the effect that the transaction is void.[166] There is no defence against the exercise of such a right that the transaction was entered into on a basis equivalent to that between parties acting at arm's length.[167] Even in situations in which the trustee bids at an open auction the sale may nevertheless be set aside on the basis that the trustee may have affected the behaviour of other bidders,[168] or in situations in which a trustee pays the full price for land identified by an independent valuer the sale may nevertheless be set aside.[169] The same principle applies to purchases by directors from their companies[170] although most articles of association in English companies expressly permit such transactions.[171] Where the beneficiary acquiesces in the transaction, then that beneficiary is precluded from seeking to have that transaction set aside.[172] A transaction which is nevertheless voidable on the basis of this principle may be affirmed by express provision in the trust instrument.[173]

By contrast, in *Holder v Holder*[174] it was doubted by Harman LJ, speaking obiter, **29.54** whether the court was bound to apply the principle in *Ex parte Lacey*[175] as a strict rule. In that case it was suggested that the mischief of the principle would not be affected where the trustee had ceased to act in effect as a trustee and therefore could not be deemed to be both the seller of the interest (on behalf of the trust) and also the buyer (on his own account). Courts in subsequent cases have not interpreted *Holder* as casting any doubt on the general applicability of the *Lacey* principle.[176]

The strict application of the *Lacey* principle was demonstrated in *Wright v* **29.55** *Morgan*[177] in which a will bequeathed rights in property to a person who was both legatee and one of two trustees of the will trusts. The will permitted sale of the property to that legatee of the property. The legatee sought to transfer the property to his co-trustee subject to an independent valuation of the open market price for the property. The issue arose whether this transfer to the co-trustee should be

---

[165] [1977] Ch 106. Cf *Prince Jefri Bolkiah v KPMG* [1999] 1 All ER 517—with reference to 'Chinese walls'. [166] *Franks v Bollans* (1868) 3 Ch App 717.

[167] *Wright v Morgan* [1926] AC 788; *Re Mulholland's Will Trusts* [1949] 1 All ER 460. See, however, *Re Postlethwaite* (1888) 37 WR 200, 60 LT 514 in which a sale by a trustee to a third party, in which it was suspected that the trustee intended to acquire the property from the third party in due course, was not avoided because there was no agreement between the trustee and the third party to effect such a further purchase. The beneficiaries would be able to object to such a subsequent purchase by the fiduciary: *Tennant v Trenchard* (1869) 4 Ch App 537.

[168] *Whelpdale v Cookson* (1747) 1 Ves Sen 9. [169] *Wright v Morgan* [1926] AC 788.

[170] *Aberdeen Railway Co v Blaikie Brothers* (1854) 1 Macq 461.

[171] See P Jaffey, *The Nature and Scope of Restitution* (Hart, 2000).

[172] *Holder v Holder* [1968] Ch 353.

[173] *Wright v Morgan* [1926] AC 788; *Sargeant v National Westminster Bank* (1990) P & CR 518.

[174] [1968] Ch 353. [175] (1802) 6 Ves 625.

[176] See, for example, *Re Thompson's Settlement* [1986] Ch 99. [177] [1926] AC 788.

set aside. It was held that the transaction was voidable even though there had been an independent valuation of the price.[178] The reasoning stated for applying the principle in spite of the independent valuation was that the trustees nevertheless could have delayed the sale and so applied a value which was no longer the open market value. Similarly, where fiduciaries acquired leases from a company and a partnership on their own account it was held that those transactions were voidable at the instance of the beneficiaries of the powers.[179]

29.56   In financial market practice it is common for fiduciaries to act as market makers whereby they sell to their customers securities and other financial instruments from their own personal holdings or in relation to transactions in which they stand to earn a profit. That the fiduciary is permitted to earn such profits within the terms of their office is set out expressly in a conduct of business agreement between the parties.[180] The more traditional legal treatment of situations in which fiduciaries make a profit from selling their own property (or securities owned by them at the time of their sale) considers such profits in the same light as any other unauthorized profit[181] and as liable to be set aside in the same manner[182] if the beneficiary elects so to do.[183]

29.57   The only advisable course of action for a trustee wishing to enter into a transaction tainted with self-dealing would be to acquire the leave of the court in advance of the transaction to acquire those interests.[184] The court will require the trustee to demonstrate that the transaction is in the interests of the beneficiaries and that the trustee will not take any unconscionable advantage from the transaction.[185] It might be thought that such an application has the effect merely of adopting the obiter remarks of Harman LJ in *Holder v Holder*[186] to the effect that the court could treat the *Lacey* principle as merely a rule of practice and accept as valid any transaction which was shown not to be to the unconscionable advantage of the trustee nor to the concomitant disadvantage of the beneficiaries. Unsurprisingly, however, the trustee will not be able to avoid the effect of this principle simply by selling to an associate or a connected company or similar person—although the authorities on this point relate primarily to sales to relatives,[187] the trustee's

---

[178] See also *Whelpdale v Cookson* (1747) 1 Ves Sen 9; *Sargeant v National Westminster Bank* (1990) 61 P & CR 518.   [179] *Re Thompson's Settlement* [1986] Ch 99.

[180] See Chapter 47 in relation to the FSA's Conduct of Business Regulations.

[181] *Bentley v Craven* (1853) 18 Beav 75; *Armstrong v Jackson* [1917] 2 KB 822; *Cook v Evatt (No 2)* [1992] 1 NZLR 676.   [182] *Gillett v Peppercone* (1840) 3 Beav 78.

[183] *Re Cape Breton Co* (1885) 29 Ch D 795; *Cavendish Bentinck v Fenn* (1887) 12 App Cas 652. Cf *Swindle v Harrison* [1997] 4 All ER 705.

[184] See *Holder v Holder* [1968] Ch 353, 371, *per* Cross J; *O'Sullivan v Management Agency and Music* [1985] QB 428, 466.

[185] *Campbell v Walker* (1800) 5 Ves 678; *Farmer v Dean* (1863) 32 Beav 327.

[186] [1968] Ch 353.

[187] *Coles v Trecothick* (1804) 9 Ves 234—which may be permitted where the transaction appears to be conducted as though at arm's length.

children,[188] and the trustee's spouse.[189] It is suggested that in any event such a transaction would be a sham transaction and therefore capable of being set aside in any event[190] or treated as an attempt to effect a fraud on the power.[191]

The fair-dealing principle

The fair-dealing principle validates acquisitions by trustees of the interests of their **29.58** beneficiaries and will be enforceable provided that the trustee does not acquire any advantage attributable to his fiduciary office.[192] This principle also applies to fiduciary relationships such as acquisitions by agents of the interests of their principals.[193] To demonstrate that the transaction was not procured as a result of any abuse of position the trustee will be required to demonstrate that no details were concealed, that the price obtained was fair, and that the beneficiary was not required to rely entirely on the trustee's advice.[194] The fair-dealing principle is necessarily less strict than the self-dealing principle because the trustee is able to seek justification of the former by demonstrating that the transaction was not procured in bad faith. It is an unconscious aspect of the principle nevertheless that the beneficiaries are required to authorize the transaction rather than permitting the trustee to act entirely alone: this accords with the principles on authorization considered below.[195] Where the beneficiary is an infant the trustee will not be able to demonstrate that the beneficiary made an informed decision.[196]

G. Defences and Vitiation of Absolute Liability to Hold Property on Constructive Trust

Defences to liability to hold property received in breach of fiduciary duty on constructive trust

There is one principal means of avoiding liability to hold a profit on constructive **29.59** trust on grounds of breach of one's fiduciary duty: that is, to demonstrate that the profit was authorized either by the terms of one's office or by the beneficiaries of one's duties. There is one principal means of minimizing the effects of the duty to hold property on constructive trust on those grounds: that is, to seek some equitable accounting to compensate one for the effort or expense expended by the fiduciary in generating that profit. Each is considered in turn in the paragraphs to follow.

---

[188] *Gregory v Gregory* (1821) Jac 631.
[189] *Ferraby v Hobson* (1847) 2 Ph 255; *Burrell v Burrell's Trustee* 1915 SC 333.
[190] *Street v Mountford* [1985] 2 WLR 877; *Midland Bank v Wyatt* [1995] 1 FLR 697.
[191] *Rochefoucauld v Boustead* [1897] 1 Ch 196.
[192] *Chalmer v Bradley* (1819) 1 J & W 51; *Tito v Waddell (No 2)* [1977] Ch 106.
[193] *Edwards v Meyrick* (1842) 2 Hare 60.   [194] *Coles v Bradley* (1804) 9 Ves 234.
[195] See para 29.60.   [196] *Sanderson v Walker* (1807) 13 Ves 601.

Authorization for fiduciary's profits

Establishing authorization

29.60 A fiduciary who would otherwise be made a constructive trustee of some profit made from his fiduciary office may be spared that equitable obligation if his profit had been authorized,[197] or possibly subsequently affirmed.[198] The issue arose in the case of *Boardman v Phipps*,[199] considered above,[200] as to the possibility of Mr Boardman being relieved of any liability to hold the profits he had made for himself on constructive trust for the beneficiaries of the Phipps family trust if he had made it known to the trustees and beneficiaries that he would be acquiring shares on his own behalf on the basis that the Phipps family trust could not and would not acquire those shares. In the Privy Council decision in *Queensland Mines v Hudson*[201] the defendant had been managing director of the plaintiff company and had therefore been in a fiduciary relationship to that company. The defendant had learned of some potentially profitable mining contracts. The company decided not to pursue these possibilities after having been made aware of all the relevant facts. The managing director resigned and pursued the business possibilities offered by the contracts on his own account. The company sought to recover the profits generated by the company from the director. The court held that the repudiation of the contracts by the company meant that the director was entitled to pursue them on his own account without a conflict with his fiduciary responsibility to the company. A disclosure to receive informed authorization must be full and frank and it must be made in advance of the pursuit of that opportunity.[202]

29.61 The mainstream English law has, however, remained rigidly on the course identified in *Keech v Sandford*.[203] In similar circumstances to *Queensland Mines v Hudson*, in *Industrial Development Consultants Ltd v Cooley*[204] a managing director was offered a contract by a third party. The offer was made expressly on the basis that the third party would deal only with the managing director but not with his employer company. Without disclosing this fact to the company, the managing director left his employment and entered into a contract with the third party within a week of his resignation. It was held that the managing director occupied a fiduciary position in relation to his employer company throughout. He was therefore required to disclose all information to the company and to account for the profits he made under the contract under constructive trusteeship. The issue in *Regal v Gulliver*[205] became whether or not the directors could be said to have given authority to themselves as private individuals to pursue a business opportunity in their own names. On the one hand, the directors were solely

---

[197] *Parker v McKenna* (1874) LR 10 Ch 96, *per* James LJ; *Queensland Mines v Hudson* (1977) 18 ALR1. [198] *Regal v Gulliver* [1942] 1 All ER 378, [1967] 2 AC 134n.
[199] [1967] 2 AC 46. [200] See para 29.19. [201] (1977) 18 ALR 1.
[202] *Dilmun v Sutton* [2004] EWHC 52 (Chancery), para 50, *per* Peter Smith J.
[203] (1726) Sel Cas Ch 61. [204] [1972] 2 All ER 162. [205] [1942] 1 All ER 378.

responsible for the management of the company and therefore it could have been said that they were perfectly competent to grant this authorization. However, the House of Lords was concerned, among other things, to prevent the management from perpetrating a fraud on the shareholders by diverting a business opportunity to themselves which ought properly to have been exploited on behalf of the company.

This rule is clearly set out in a number of contexts other than simply in relation to **29.62** trusts and trustees. In *Regal v Gulliver,*[206] which was approved by the House of Lords in *Boardman v Phipps*, it was held that directors of companies are fiduciaries and therefore similarly liable to account for profits made in the conduct of their duties. In *Regal v Gulliver*[207] four directors of the plaintiff company subscribed for shares in a subsidiary company which the board of directors had intended to be acquired by the plaintiff company itself. The directors had acquired the shares personally because the company was not able to afford them, even though it did have the legal capacity to have acquired them. It was held that the directors' profits on these shares were profits made from their offices as directors. Therefore, they were required to account for them to the company. The question which arises is, therefore, from whom can the fiduciaries acquire authorization for their actions?

From whom can authorization be obtained?

In seeking to advance an excuse that the profit had been authorized, the question **29.63** arises as to who it is that can grant such authorization. It will be necessary also that the fiduciary can demonstrate that he has made a full disclosure of the profit which he proposed to make. The question then arises as to whom the fiduciary owes this duty of disclosure so as to authorize the profits. There appear to be three possibilities. The duty of the solicitor to a trust could be said to be owed to the trustees, or simply to all of the beneficiaries, or to those beneficiaries affected by the profit making. In *Boardman v Phipps* there appeared to be an assumption on the part of the House of Lords that this obligation was owed by the fiduciary to the trustees and that it was the relationship primarily with the active trustee that was of most importance. In *Queensland Mines v Hudson* the assumption was that consent could be acquired from the other directors (although it was the case that the two majority shareholders were represented on that board in any event).

The strict application of *Regal v Gulliver* appears to suggest that fiduciaries cannot **29.64** simply rely on the permission of other fiduciaries. In consequence the duty of disclosure would be a duty to disclose to the shareholders of a company or to the beneficiaries of a trust respectively. This was the approach taken in the New Zealand decision in *Equiticorp Industries Group Ltd v The Crown*[208] which held that it was the shareholders of a company who were competent to authorize a

---

[206] [1942] 1 All ER 378.   [207] [1942] 1 All ER 378.   [208] [1998] 2 NZLR 485.

fiduciary making such profits on a personal basis. However, even where no authorization is given if the fiduciary takes their benefit in a different capacity (for example, as a beneficiary under a will) from that of their fiduciary duty then there will be no liability to account. So, where, for example, partner in a farming partnership was offered the chance in the capacity of a beneficiary under the reversioner's will to acquire the reversion over the agricultural tenancy held by the partnership, she was not liable to account because she was benefiting from her status as a beneficiary and not exploiting her fiduciary office.[209]

29.65 Any other point of view would open itself up to abuse. If the trustees had delegated their authority to a particular fiduciary there may be grounds for suggesting that the duty is owed primarily to those trustees. This situation might arise in circumstances in which a solicitor is appointed as in *Boardman v Phipps* or where a fund manager is appointed for the delegation of investment obligations. The risk with this approach is that fiduciaries may make decisions in their own interests and thus grant one another permission to act in certain circumstances, without necessarily concerning themselves with the interests of the beneficiaries. The primary relationship of the trust is that between trustee and beneficiary so that trustees must be considered to owe their duties primarily to the beneficiaries.[210] As such, any fiduciary role in respect of a trust ought to be centred on an obligation ultimately owed to the beneficiaries. Therefore, if duties ought properly to be owed to the beneficiaries, it should be the beneficiaries who authorize such activities which are beyond the powers granted to the trustees under the trust.

Authorization by trust instrument

29.66 The fiduciary is, in general terms, permitted to make any profit which is permitted by the instrument enshrining the terms of his trusteeship.[211] The trust instrument may authorize any action which is otherwise potentially voidable.[212]

Equitable accounting

29.67 In circumstances in which a fiduciary is considered to be entitled to some recompense for work done for the beneficiaries, in spite of being held liable as a constructive trustee for procuring unauthorized profits, it will be possible for the fiduciary to acquire some equitable accounting. This doctrine of account permits a court of equity in its discretion to adjust any amount owed by one party to another or provides, in relation to a proprietary constructive trust in favour of the beneficiaries, for those beneficiaries, to pay some amount to that fiduciary.

---

[209] *Ward v Bryant* [2000] WTLR 731; *Hancock Family Memorial Foundation Ltd v Porteous* [2000] 1 WTLR 1113 (Sup Ct (WA)).

[210] See generally Chapter 1 of this book. Also see D Hayton, 'The irreducible core content of trusteeship' in A Oakley (ed), *Trends in Contemporary Trust Law* (OUP, 1996) 47.

[211] *Armitage v Nurse* [1998] Ch 241; *Walker v Stones* [2001] QB 902.

[212] *Wright v Morgan* [1926] AC 788; *Sargeant v National Westminster Bank* (1990) 61 P & CR 518.

The House of Lords in *Boardman v Phipps*[213] was conscious of the hard work done by Boardman to generate a windfall profit for the beneficiaries. Therefore, the court ordered that there ought to be some equitable accounting by the trust in recognition of the work done by the fiduciary. It was held that Boardman was entitled to be compensated on a 'liberal scale' for the work and skill involved in acquiring the shares for the Phipps family trust and turning the private company into profit. The precise amount of that recognition was something left to be ascertained after the hearing of the appeal.

As a general, equitable doctrine, the availability of equitable accounting will be **29.68** dependent on the good conscience of the claimant. In *Guinness v Saunders*[214] a director of Guinness, Ernest Saunders, had made profits in connection with a takeover bid for the company in breach of his fiduciary duty. The company sought to recover the payments made to Saunders among other issues as to Saunders' criminal activities in relation to a takeover bid. The company sought to recover the profits made by Saunders from his fiduciary office on constructive trust principles. Saunders, however, sought to suggest that his work for the company over the period of his directorship had enriched the shareholders such that his liability as a constructive trustee in relation to unauthorized or unlawful profits ought to take into account the broader context of his work for the company. Therefore, Saunders claimed entitlement to a *quantum meruit* or entitlement to some equitable accounting in recognition of his services. As to the issue of liability as constructive trustee of the profits, it was held that the appropriate remedy was the imposition of a constructive trust over the wrongfully acquired profits made by Saunders from his fiduciary duty. As to the question of equitable accounting for the work done as a director, Lord Templeman was not prepared to allow Saunders to take any personal benefit from such wrongful acts. Indeed, this accords with the core equitable principle that a plaintiff must come to equity with clean hands. Therefore, it is clear that equitable accounting will only be made available for defendant fiduciaries like Boardman who have acted in reasonably good faith to generate profits for the beneficiaries.

H. The Nature of the Equitable Response to Abuse of a Fiduciary Office

There are ostensibly three forms of remedy disclosed by the doctrines considered **29.69** in this chapter.[215] The first is that the profit acquired in breach of fiduciary duty

---

[213] [1967] 2 AC 46.   [214] [1990] 2 AC 663.
[215] *Warman International v Dwyer* (1995) 128 ALR 201; *Kao Lee & Yip v Koo Hoi Yan* [2003] WTLR 200.

be held on constructive trust, whereas the second is that the constructive trustee must account to beneficiaries for the profit made, and the third is that the constructive trustee may be liable to pay equitable compensation to the claimant. In truth, it is suggested, the three go together such that the beneficiaries may elect which of the three is more convenient for them. In this sense the spectrum of available equitable responses to the abuse of a fiduciary's position is similar to that for express trustees who have breached their trust. An express trustee may be liable to effect specific restitution of that part of the trust fund which has been passed away in breach of trust,[216] whereas the constructive trust is different in that it grants the beneficiaries rights in property such that they are entitled to take possession of any increase in the value of the property, or any substitute for that property by means of equitable tracing, together with compound interest.[217] In relation to a breach of trust when it is impossible to recover the very property which had previously formed the trust fund, then the trustee's liability is to account to the beneficiaries for the cash value of that property. In relation to a constructive trust imposed on a fiduciary who has received a secret or unauthorized profit, in circumstances in which the profit is received in cash without attracting any further income or increase in value, then an account for those profits may be sufficient remedy. The third form of remedy in both contexts, as considered in detail in Chapter 32 in relation to breach of trust,[218] is equitable compensation for any loss suffered by the constructive beneficiaries so as to include, without being limited to, the value of the profit earned by the fiduciary.[219] Equitable compensation takes the form of a payment of money but includes an amount for any provable loss suffered by the constructive beneficiaries consequent on the breach of the fiduciary's office. The beneficiaries are able to elect between these various remedies.[220]

29.70 The proprietary constructive trust is generally the best remedy of the three in that it acquires for the beneficiary rights in property which may increase in value, it grants the beneficiaries rights to compound interest, and it would found an equitable tracing claim. These three effects are the incidents of the finding of a proprietary right. It should be borne in mind, in relation for example to the receipt of a bribe or the earning of a secret profit by the fiduciary, that the beneficiaries would have had no prior proprietary right in the property and therefore would not have had any equitable proprietary interest capable of founding an equitable tracing claim[221] or of founding a right to compound as opposed to simple interest.[222] It would only be if the property which would have been held on constructive trust

---

[216] See para 32.11.
[217] *Westdeutsche Landesbank v Islington LBC* [1996] AC 669.   [218] See para 32.18.
[219] As suggested by *Nocton v Lord Ashburton* [1914] AC 932.
[220] *Tang v Capacious Investments* [1996] 1 AC 514.
[221] *Re Diplock's Estate* [1948] Ch 465. See para 33.30 in relation to the operation of equitable tracing claims.   [222] *Westdeutsche Landesbank Girozentrale v Islington LBC* [1996] AC 669, HL.

had decreased in value that a proprietary constructive trust would be the lesser remedy: in such circumstances the claimant would prefer an account from the constructive trustee as to the amount of the profit or bribe.[223] Supposing, however, that a constructive trust were imposed, then if the fiduciary had used trust property to generate a profit, then that profit is said to derive from that property. As such the trust would be entitled to an equitable proprietary right against the fiduciary over the profit.[224] So, as considered above,[225] the Privy Council in *Attorney-General for Hong Kong v Reid*[226] held that where a bribe is received in the course of employment all profits connected to that property are held on proprietary constructive trust by the fiduciary for the employer.[227]

It is not clear precisely what the majority of their lordships considered the appropriate remedy to be in *Boardman v Phipps*.[228] Lord Cohen held that the fiduciary should be 'accountable to the respondent for his share of the net profits which they derived from the transaction': however, it is not clear whether that accounting is on a proprietary or a personal basis. The reference to 'net profits' presumably refers to profits made after deducting the expense of making them. However, Lords Hodson and Guest affirmatively held that the confidential information obtained by Boardman was the property of the Phipps family trust and, therefore, the profits generated by the fiduciary ought properly to be considered to have been in equity the property of the Phipps trust throughout. It is suggested that the account applicable in this instance was to be considered to be at the election of the beneficiaries, as suggested by *Tang Man Sit v Capacious Investments*[229] considered above.[230]   **29.71**

As outlined above, the alternative approaches to the imposition of a constructive trust would be simply to make good the amount lost to the trust in money terms by means of account[231] or alternatively by means of equitable compensation[232] similar to those recognized in relation to breach of trust in *Target Holdings v Redferns*.[233] These approaches do not amount to proprietary remedies being only   **29.72**

---

[223] See also the liability to account for any diminution in the value of the constructive trust fund: *Attorney-General for Hong Kong v Reid* [1994] 1 AC 324.

[224] Prof Burrows has argued that this doctrine ought to be considered to be restitutionary although this form of constructive trust is more usually expressed as being a proprietary trust arising on the basis of good conscience. Prof Burrows's viewpoint is based on the premise that the fiduciary is unjustly enriched by making an unauthorized profit. The potential weakness with considering this constructive trust as being restitutionary is that there is no restitution, in the sense of some restoration, of property to the beneficiaries because the beneficiaries would have had no pre-existing rights in the property aside from the chimerical confidential information. As set out by Lord Templeman in *Reid* the constructive trust arises on the basis of equitable principle and not unjust enrichment: A Burrows, *The Law of Restitution* (Butterworths, 1993) 85.   [225] See para 29.07.

[226] [1994] 1 AC 324; [1994] 1 All ER 1.

[227] *Holder v Holder* [1968] Ch 353; *O'Sullivan v Management Agency and Music* [1985] QB 428; *Swindle v Harrison* [1997] 4 All ER 705.   [228] [1967] 2 AC 46.

[229] [1996] 1 AC 514.   [230] See para 29.07.

[231] *Nocton v Lord Ashburton* [1914] AC 932.   [232] *Swindle v Harrison* [1997] 4 All ER 705.

[233] [1996] 1 AC 421, [1995] 3 WLR 352, [1995] 3 All ER 785.

amounts of money by way of personal remedy. In relation to the self-dealing and fair-dealing principles, the beneficiary has a broader range of potential remedies than in other circumstances because there is not only the possibility of constructive trust, account, or equitable compensation but also the choice between affirming and repudiating the transaction effected by the trustee.[234] The options for the beneficiaries are as before. If the value of the property passed under the transaction has fallen, then the beneficiaries would not wish to recover that property. If the property has passed into the hands of a third party then the beneficiaries must have recourse to tracing claims, as considered in the following section.

I. Constructive Trusts Applied in Equitable Tracing Claims

Constructive trust applied in equitable tracing claims

29.73   Constructive trusts are frequently applied in equitable claims over property which has been identified as constituting the traceable proceeds of property passed away by the trustees from a trust in breach of that trust. The doctrine of equitable tracing is discussed in Chapter 33 and the particular question of the nature of constructive trusts recognized as responses to equitable tracing claims are considered there.[235] The process of tracing permits a claimant who was the beneficiary under an equitable proprietary or fiduciary relationship, such as a trust, to trace property which was lost to his trust fund into mixtures of property and into substitutes for his original trust property. The tracing process identifies that property against which a claim is brought. Once that property has been identified the claimant can choose from among a range of potential remedies, including the imposition of a constructive trust over that property. The claimant would be entitled, as considered in detail in Chapter 33, to a charge or a lien over that property but, particularly in the event that the property was itself intrinsically valuable or income generating, the claimant may also seek to have a constructive trust imposed over the property in his favour.

Constructive trust further to an equitable tracing claim imposed against a fiduciary

29.74   If property is taken from the trust fund by someone who owes fiduciary duties to the beneficiaries, such as a trustee, then that person is required to:

> ...account to the person to whom the obligation is owed for any benefit or gain (1) which has been obtained or received in circumstances where a conflict or significant possibility of conflict existed between his fiduciary duty and his personal interest in the pursuit or possible receipt of such a benefit or gain or (2) which was obtained or received by use or by reason of his fiduciary position or of opportunity or knowledge

---

[234] See the discussion in Chapter 25.   [235] See para 33.67.

resulting from it. Any such benefit or gain is held by the fiduciary as constructive trustee.[236]

Therefore, any fiduciary who receives trust property personally without authorization under the trust instrument or from the beneficiaries (in the manner considered above[237]) will be required to make specific restitution of the very property which was taken from the trust fund, as considered in Chapter 32 in relation to liability for breach of trust,[238] or to account to the beneficiaries for any traceable proceeds from that original trust property, whether in the form of profits from that original property or any substitute for that original property.[239]

Constructive trust further to an equitable tracing claim against an innocent party

Subtly different considerations obtain if trust property is passed to a person who **29.75** is not a fiduciary. The beneficiaries will still have a right to trace their property in equity but if they wish to impose a constructive trust over any substitute property or other traceable proceeds of their original property they will be required to demonstrate both that the defendant has knowledge of their rights and that the defendant's conscience has been affected so as to bring the constructive trust into existence. So, in *Westdeutsche Landesbank v Islington*[240] a bank transferred money to a local authority under an interest rate swap agreement which was subsequently held to have been void *ab initio*. By that time all of the money paid to the local authority had been dissipated and therefore the bank sought to trace into the general funds of the local authority and to impose a constructive trust in some property so that it could found a proprietary claim sufficient to grant it a right to compound interest. The tracing claim failed on the basis that no traceable proceeds of the original money paid by the bank remained in the local authority's accounts. It was held, furthermore, that there could not be a constructive trust in favour of the bank because the bank had not known at any time before it transferred the money out of its accounts to meet its ordinary expenses that the contract had been void *ab initio*. All of the money had been spent before either party knew that the contract had been void *ab initio*. Consequently, the local authority had not had its conscience affected while in possession of the money or its traceable proceeds and therefore there had never been a constructive trust over it. Incidentally this meant that the bank could not claim compound interest. However, this requirement of unconscionability seems to contradict the ordinary principles of equitable tracing, as considered in paragraph 33.67.

---

[236] *Chan v Zachariah* (1984) 154 CLR 178, 198, *per* Deane J. Approved in *Don King Productions Inc v Warren* [2000] Ch 291, 341, *per* Morritt LJ. See also *Gencor ACP Ltd v Dalby* [2001] WTLR 825, [2000] 2 BCLC 734.
[237] See para 29.07.   [238] See para 32.11.   [239] See para 33.01.
[240] [1996] AC 669.

29.76 For present purposes, however, to establish a constructive trust as part of a tracing claim a claimant would have to prove both that the property constituted the traceable proceeds of its original property and also that the defendant's conscience was affected by knowledge of the fact that the money had been paid to it, in this instance, under a mistake. The doctrine of equitable tracing generally does not discriminate between those contexts in which there is a defendant who was innocent about the manner in which property came into his hands[241] and one who knew that the property had come into his hands, for example, in breach of trust or under a mistake.[242] Rather, one has a right to trace one's property rights to vindicate one's rights and not so as to punish some wrong committed by the defendant.[243] In the latter example, there would be no doubt that a constructive trust could be imposed because the defendant had knowledge of the factor which affected his conscience. In the former example the claimant would have a right to bring an equitable tracing claim but before being entitled to impose a constructive trust over the property the claimant would have to bring his equitable ownership of that property to the attention of the innocent defendant, who would not otherwise have known that the property had come into his hands by means of a mistake or breach of trust or otherwise and so not have acted with knowledge of any unconscionable act on his part sufficient to justify the imposition of a constructive trust. Rather, the constructive trust would only come into existence at the time at which the claimant informed the defendant for the first time that the property belonged in equity to the claimant. The time at which the trust came into existence would be significant in cases of insolvency and so forth.[244] At that point, the claimant would be well advised to seek a freezing injunction over the property to prevent the defendant from transferring it beyond the claimant's reach.[245]

Situations in which the constructive trust itself may found an equitable tracing claim

29.77 Returning to the facts of the *Chase Manhattan v Israel-British Bank*[246] case considered above[247] where a payer mistakenly makes a payment twice and where the recipient goes into insolvency before repaying that money,[248] by way of example, suppose that the money comprising the second payment is paid mistakenly into a general bank account and mixed there with other moneys; and suppose further that no withdrawals had been made from that account which reduced it below the value of the second payment.[249] At that juncture, to establish a claim to a part of the mixed

---

[241] See *Re Diplock's Estate* [1948] Ch 465; *Foskett v McKeown* [2001] 1 AC 102, [2000] 3 All ER 97. See para 33.30.

[242] See *Allen v Rea Brothers Trustees Ltd* (2002) 4 ITELR 627, considered at para 33.67.

[243] See *Foskett v McKeown* [2001] 1 AC 102, [2000] 3 All ER 97.   [244] See para 25.12.

[245] See para 31.21.   [246] [1981] 1 Ch 105.   [247] See para 27.06.   [248] See para 25.12.

[249] So evading the principle of loss of the right to trace in *Roscoe v Winder* [1915] 1 Ch 62; *Bishopsgate v Homan* [1995] 1 WLR 31.

fund equal to the mistaken payment, the claimant would be required to establish an equitable tracing claim. To do that would require a demonstration that the claimant had some pre-existing equitable interest in the property.[250] To establish such a pre-existing equitable interest the claimant could point to the unconscionability of the recipient retaining the money after it had been informed of the mistake and therefore establish that that money ought to be held on constructive trust for it. At that juncture the equitable jurisdiction is available to the claimant who is seeking to bring an equitable tracing claim. The resolution of the equitable tracing claim may not, however, result in a finding of constructive trust. As is considered elsewhere in this book in relation to equitable tracing,[251] the claimant may be held entitled to an equitable charge, lien, or constructive trust. The court's view may be that the mixed fund should be subjected to a charge equal to the overpayment in favour of the claimant and a charge in favour of any other claimant to the fund for the remainder or subject to a lien. Alternatively, the court could take the approach that all of the contributors to the fund ought to be entitled to a share of the total fund in proportion to the size of their contribution to that same fund, thus suggesting the imposition of a constructive trust recognizing those various proportions. In either case, the role of the constructive trust in this instance may simply be to found the equitable jurisdiction for the tracing claim prior, potentially, to some other equitable remedy being imposed in vindication of the claimant's property rights.

The property which is held on trust will simply be whatever property comprises **29.78** the fund at the time that the action is brought; moreover, the precise property to which the claimant will have entitlement will not be identifiable until the trustee takes steps to separate an amount of the requisite value from the bulk of the fund. Therefore, the focus of such constructive trusts, while nominally concerned with the protection of rights in property, is in fact concerned with the protection of rights of a given value which derived originally from rights in identifiable property. This is a frequently unspoken schism in the treatment of constructive trusts. Where the claimant seeks rights, for example, in an identified item of tangible property, then it is that asset which is held on trust unless the trust is imposed pursuant to a tracing claim over the sale proceeds of that asset. The second use of the trust to take title in the sale proceeds of the asset or in some other substitute property would have two important features. First, it would be concerned not with the preservation of the claimant's link with the particular item of property which was that asset but rather, secondly, it would be concerned with the preservation of an entitlement to wealth equal in value to the asset.[252] There is a tension between

---

[250] *Re Diplock's Estate* [1948] Ch 465; *Boscawen v Bajwa* [1996] 1 WLR 328; *Westdeutsche Landesbank v Islington* [1996] AC 669.　　　　　　　　　　　　　　　　　[251] See para 33.30.

[252] Allowing always for the question of establishing the value of property: whether its replacement cost, the loss of amenity to the claimant, its resale value, or some measurement of its sentimental value. In any event, those values may fluctuate over time, creating further problems as to

protecting rights in property and maintaining the value of the claimant's balance sheet. The rules in relation to proprietary rights differ from context to context between protecting rights to value in this way and protecting a clear link in ownership between the claimant and a particular piece of property. So, if shares were taken from a trust fund before being sold and their sale proceeds were used to acquire an oil painting, the doctrine of constructive trust may either operate so as to preserve the beneficiary's rights to those particular shares or else seek to preserve the beneficiary's balance sheet by establishing rights of equivalent value in the sale proceeds or in the oil painting.

29.79 Such a use of the constructive trust indicates two things. First, that the constructive trust is indeed a flexible device. Secondly, that the constructive trust can be used remedially in cases of tracing as one of a range of potential responses[253] designed, *inter alia*, to vindicate the rights of the claimant in assets of a given value.[254] A constructive trust exhibiting either of these tendencies is a creature of equity which reacts in accordance with the diktats of good conscience to prevent inappropriate behaviour by those identified as being constructive trustees and to protect the rights, particularly in relation to property, of those who become beneficiaries under such constructive trusts.

The subject matter of a constructive trust

29.80 There are issues as to the subject matter of the constructive trust in situations, for example, in which fungible property such as money has been paid between parties to a commercial transaction. Fungible property presents greater problems than non-fungible property and modern, electronic systems of payment complicate these issues further, with the result that it will not always be clear how a constructive trust could operate. Suppose the following example: a customer goes into a shop, purchases items advertised for sale at £9 with a £10 note and receives £11 in change because the till operator mistakenly thought that he had tendered a £20 note. If the customer had knowledge of the matter which affected his conscience—here, that the till operator had made a mistake and that he was consequently not entitled to all of the money which he had received—then the customer would hold the money to which he was not entitled on trust for the shop.[255] Where the customer has notes and coins in his hands it would be a comparatively simple matter to point out to him the mistake that had been made, thus bringing the matter into his field of knowledge, and to identify precisely the money which could be susceptible to the trust. It is clear that the customer is

---

whether to take the highest intermediate value, the value at which a sale could be demonstrated to have been possible, or simply the demonstrable loss to the claimant: *Target Holdings v Redferns* [1996] 1 AC 421.

[253] C Rotherham, *Proprietary Remedies in Context* (Hart, 2002) ch 1.
[254] G Virgo, *Principles of the Law of Restitution* (OUP, 1999).
[255] *Westdeutsche Landesbank v Islington* [1996] AC 669.

entitled to £1 out of the total of £11. As a matter of common sense there is little difficulty with separating the £1 coin from the £10 note in the customer's hand, if that was how the change was given to him. However, if the change had, for example, been tendered by way of a single £5 note and six £1 coins—perhaps because the till operator had thought she had no £10 notes left—then there would be a more difficult question as to the identity of the property to be held on trust. It would not be clear which of the six £1 coins would be held on trust for the customer and which for the shop: a problem of uncertainty of subject matter, as considered in Chapter 3. A common sense answer would be to suggest that the whole fund of £11 is to be held on constructive trust by the customer for the shop and for himself as beneficiaries in the ratio 10:1.[256] In either case, a level of common sense is needed to displace the complexities of certainty of subject matter.

A more complex situation is the following. Suppose that payment had been made **29.81** with a credit card and that the till operator had mistakenly charged the customer £10 too little by mistake when keying the total into the credit card payment mechanism. If the customer acted in full knowledge of the mistake, it could be argued that there would not be any money—that is identifiable property—to hold on trust because payment by credit card constitutes a transaction including the connected lender in the person of the credit card provider who undertakes to pay the vendor in accordance with its contracts both with the vendor and purchaser separately. At that level, the supermarket's claim would be a purely personal claim. However, the purchaser here has knowingly provided value of a lower amount than that agreed with the vendor and thus acquired goods or services in an amount greater than that to which he is prima facie entitled. Here a personal claim for restitution in the amount of the underpayment would be appropriate, or alternatively an action for specific performance (limited always by the notion that specific performance will not be available where common law damages would be sufficient remedy), or an action for damages for breach of contract.

What remains unclear is whether or not a constructive trust would be imposed **29.82** over any goods received as part of the transaction, in effect to secure the possibility of rescission of the transaction. In principle, such a constructive trust would lie on the basis that the purchaser had acquired goods without the fully informed consent of the vendor and contrary to good conscience. Again, the precise terms of that constructive trust would be that the property is held on trust for both parties in proportion to the size of the purchaser's payment and continuing underpayment, except in the event that the purchaser tenders the remaining portion of

---

[256] A different common sense answer would be to choose a £1 coin to leave with the customer and recover all of the other moneys on that basis that it cannot matter in this instance who takes which coins. However, it is cases such as insolvency where such problems become more acute where the creditor needs to be able to demonstrate precisely which coins are held on trust so that he is raised to the level of a secured creditor: *Re Goldcorp* [1995] AC 74.

the purchase price. What is more difficult is to assert any proprietary right through the credit card payment mechanism because there is no property consensually tendered which could be held on trust. One issue which arises here is whether such a use of a constructive trust would be, in truth, a remedial constructive trust or whether that structure could be said to constitute a recognition of a proprietary right which the vendor retained in the goods and so operate institutionally by operation of law, as considered above.[257]

---

[257] See para 25.12.

30

THE LIABILITY OF STRANGERS TO ACCOUNT AS CONSTRUCTIVE TRUSTEES

A. Intermeddlers as Constructive Trustees

Equity provides relief for beneficiaries who suffer loss as the result of the activities **30.01** of third parties who are not trustees (referred to here either as intermeddlers or as strangers to the trust) by imposing on such people a liability to account to the beneficiaries as though they were trustees of the trust. It is of course possible that a trust may suffer losses as a result of the actions of third parties which are due to the negligence of some person to whom the trustees have delegated their responsibilities, in which case the issues will relate to the tort of negligence or potentially the tort of deceit, or the issues may arise in the law of contract to the extent that some delegate of the trustees' powers has sought to limit his liability by means of contract.[1] Those common law claims are not, however, the focus of this chapter. Rather, the forms of liability considered in this chapter relate to losses resulting from a breach of trust, whether or not the trustees knowingly breached their duties,[2] and whether by reference to a loss of property to the trust fund or otherwise.[3]

30.02 In circumstances in which a person interferes with the management of the trust in such a way that that person assumes the responsibilities of a trustee in fact and so causes loss to the trust, then that person will face the liability of a trustee de son tort[4] as a constructive trustee.[5] The expression 'trustee de son tort'[6] means, literally, a trustee as a result of his own wrong. Such a person will be treated as a constructive trustee in the sense that he will be subject to a proprietary liability to hold any property acquired by his actions on trust for the beneficiaries and also subject to a personal liability to provide equitable compensation to the beneficiaries for any other loss, in the same manner as an express trustee.[7] In contrast to the trustee de son tort are the two categories of personal liability to account for knowing receipt of property in breach of trust or dishonest assistance in any breach of trust. Such people are treated as though they are de facto trustees so that they can be rendered liable to account to the beneficiaries as though they had been appointed trustees for any loss which their actions occasion to the trust. This pairing of equitable claims differs from the liability of trustees de son tort in two ways. First, the liability is simply a personal liability to account and does not include a proprietary liability to hold any specific property on trust. Secondly, the third parties (or, strangers) are not deemed to be trustees who have meddled with the trust's business: rather, they are strangers who have either received property with knowledge that that was done in breach of trust or have dishonestly assisted in a breach of trust without receiving any trust property.[8] In short, this is a form of equitable wrong which those strangers have committed, or to which they have been party. It is important to distinguish this form of liability from the proprietary forms of

---

[1] *Armitage v Nurse* [1998] Ch 241.   [2] *Royal Brunei Airlines v Tan* [1995] 2 AC 378.
[3] Where the claimants have no right to the trust—where, for example, they did not qualify under the terms of a pension fund trust scheme to the rights of pensioners—they will have no right to enforce liability against the defendant to account as though a constructive trustee and their claim will be struck out as disclosing no cause of action: *Hudson v HM Treasury* [2003] EWCA Civ 1612.
[4] *Selangor United Rubber Ltd v Cradock (No 3)* [1968] 1 WLR 1555.
[5] The latter expression is preferred by Lord Millett in *Dubai Aluminium v Salaam* [2002] 3 WLR 1913.
[6] The upshot, in Lord Millett's view, of 'substituting dog Latin for bastard French': *Dubai Aluminium v Salaam* [2002] 3 WLR 1913, 1946.
[7] *Mara v Browne* [1896] 1 Ch 199, 209; *Carl Zeiss Stiftung v Herbert Smith (No 2)* [1969] 2 Ch 276, 289.
[8] P Birks, 'Persistent problems in misdirected money' [1993] LMCLQ 218; S Gardner, 'Rethinking family property' (1996) 112 LQR 56.

constructive trust which have been considered hitherto in this chapter. Each of these claims is considered in turn in this chapter.

B. Trustees De Son Tort

The liability of trustees de son tort as constructive trustees

The doctrine is comparatively straightforward to state. Where a person who has **30.03** not been officially appointed as a trustee of an express trust interferes with or involves himself in the business of the trust so as to appear to be acting as a trustee, then that person shall be construed to be a trustee of that trust.[9] On the basis that trustees de son tort are not expressly declared by the settlor to be trustees but rather are deemed to be constructive trustees by operation of law, due to their meddling with trust affairs, they are therefore constructive trustees.[10] Smith LJ stated the nature of this form of constructive trust in the following way:[11]

> . . . if one, not being a trustee and not having authority from a trustee, takes upon himself to intermeddle with trust matters or to do acts characteristic of the office of trustee, he may therefore make himself what is called in law trustee of his own wrong—ie a trustee de son tort, or, as it is also termed, a constructive trustee.

Therefore, a trustee de son tort is a trustee who intermeddles with trust business. What does not emerge from this formulation set out by Smith LJ is the usual prerequisite that the trustee de son tort must have trust property in his possession or control before this form of constructive trust will obtain.[12] If the property were not vested in the defendant then the appropriate form of liability would be that of a dishonest assistant and not a constructive trustee bearing proprietary obligations.[13] A dishonest assistant, as considered below, is one who assists in a breach of trust in a manner in which an honest person would not have acted or reckless as to some risk being occasioned to the trust fund.[14] Whereas the liability for dishonest assistance is a personal liability to account for any loss suffered by the trust fund,[15] a trustee de son tort will be responsible for the maintenance of the trust property in his possession as well as personally liable for loss to the trust arising from a breach of trust.

So in *Blyth v Fladgate*,[16] Exchequer bills in bearer form had been held on trust by **30.04** a sole trustee. That trustee had deposited the bills in the name of a firm of

---

[9] When one is construed to be a trustee, one becomes a 'constructive trustee'.
[10] C Harpum, 'Accessory liability for procuring or assisting a breach of trust' (1995) 111 LQR 545.
[11] *Mara v Browne* [1896] 1 Ch 199, 209.   [12] *Re Barney* [1892] 2 Ch 265.
[13] *James v Williams* [2000] Ch 1, [1999] 3 All ER 309, *per* Aldous LJ: 'there are many cases where executors de son tort could not be constructive trustees. Each case will depend upon its own facts.'
[14] *Royal Brunei Airlines v Tan* [1995] 2 AC 378.   [15] *Barnes v Addy* (1874) 9 Ch App 244.
[16] [1891] 1 Ch 337.

solicitors: thus putting the bills under the control of the solicitors. The trustee died and, before substitute trustees had been appointed, the solicitors sold the bills and invested the proceeds in a mortgage. As matters turned out, the security provided by way of mortgage was insufficient to cover the loan and accordingly the trust suffered a loss. It was held that the firm of solicitors had become constructive trustees by dint of their having dealt with the trust property then within their control.[17] As such they were held liable to account to the beneficiaries for the loss occasioned to the trust. Similarly, in circumstances in which an estate manager continued to collect rents in respect of that land after the death of his principal, the landlord, without informing the tenants of their landlord's death, that manager was held to be a constructive trustee of those profits which had been held separately in an identified bank account.[18] The nature of the liability of a trustee de son tort as a constructive trustee was approved by the House of Lords in *Dubai Aluminium Company Ltd v Salaam*,[19] a case which is considered below.[20]

30.05 While the responsibilities of constructive trustees will not always equate to those of an express trustee, it has been held that because a trustee de son tort acts as though an express trustee then the trustee de son tort is to be treated as bearing all the obligations of an express trustee.[21]

C. The Nature of the Liability of Non-Trustees to Account in Relation to Breaches of Trust

The imposition of an equitable claim on one construed to be liable as a trustee

30.06 The status of the trustee and the fiduciary are easily comprehensible and have formed the subject matter of this book thus far. The rule that a fiduciary cannot profit from that office is well established in equity.[22] The further question is: in what circumstances will a person who is neither a trustee nor a beneficiary under a trust be held liable in respect of any breach of that trust? Such a person is referred to in the following sections as being a 'stranger'[23] to the trust, having no office connected to it nor any equitable interest in it. Equity has always sought to impose fiduciary duties on those who misuse trust property, whether such a person is holding an office under that trust or not. This imposition of liability has extended to the imposition of the duties of a trustee on people who meddle with the trust

---

[17] *Re Bell's Indenture* [1980] 1 WLR 1217.

[18] *Lyell v Kennedy* (1889) 14 App Cas 437; see also *English v Dedham Vale Properties* [1978] 1 WLR 93.   [19] [2002] 3 WLR 1913, [2003] 1 All ER 97.

[20] See para 30.38.   [21] *Soar v Ashwell* [1893] 2 QB 390.

[22] *Boardman v Phipps* [1967] 2 AC 46.

[23] That being the term used by Lord Selborne in the leading case of *Barnes v Addy* (1874) 9 Ch App 244, 251–252.

fund. One of the practical reasons for pursuing this remedy is that the intermeddler[24] is frequently an adviser or professional who is solvent and therefore capable of making good the money lost to the trust if the property itself is lost, thus making a tracing claim impossible, and if the properly appointed trustees have insufficient funds to meet the beneficiaries' loss in an action for breach of trust, or if the trustees are seeking an indemnity against such an action.

In short, the applicable principles can be stated in the following terms. First, a **30.07** person who is neither a trustee nor a beneficiary will be personally liable to account to the trust for any loss suffered in a situation in which she dishonestly assists in a breach of trust, without receiving any proprietary right in that trust property herself.[25] The test for 'dishonesty' in this context extends beyond straightforward deceit and fraud into reckless risk taking with trust property and other unconscionable behaviour demonstrating a 'lack of probity'.[26] Secondly, a person who is neither a trustee nor a beneficiary will be personally liable to account to the trust for any loss suffered in a situation in which she receives trust property with knowledge that the property has been passed to her in breach of trust.[27] 'Knowledge' in this context includes actual knowledge, wilfully closing one's eyes to the breach of trust, or failing to make the inquiries which a reasonable person would have made.[28] These outline principles are considered in greater detail in the remainder of this chapter.

The range of claims, including personal liability to account as a constructive trustee, which may arise after a breach of trust

The receipt claim and the assistance claim

There are two distinct categories of liability in this context: strangers who *receive* **30.08** trust property transferred in breach of trust ('knowing receipt'), and strangers who do *not receive* trust property but merely assist its transfer in breach of trust ('dishonest assistance').[29] The distinction between 'knowing receipt' and 'knowing assistance' was rendered by Lord Selborne LC in *Barnes v Addy*[30] as the difference between two things: first, the liability of a person as 'recipient' of trust property or its traceable proceeds, and secondly, the liability of a person as 'accessory' to a trustee's breach of trust. Evidently there is a narrow line between the categories of claim. The claims for 'knowing receipt' and 'dishonest assistance' are personal

---

[24] The term 'intermeddler' here is borrowed from Smith LJ's reference to those who intermeddle with the trust property: *Mara v Browne* [1896] 1 Ch 199, 209.

[25] *Royal Brunei Airlines v Tan* [1995] 2 AC 378.   [26] See para 30.23.

[27] *Re Montagu's Settlements* [1987] Ch 264.   [28] *Re Montagu's Settlements* [1987] Ch 264.

[29] It is suggested that there is no reason in principle why a person who has received trust property ought not to face liability also for dishonest assistance in a breach of trust, although the courts will prevent double recovery under both heads of claim in relation to the same facts.

[30] (1874) LR 9 Ch App 244, 251–252.

claims to account to the beneficiaries as though trustees for the beneficiaries' loss. However, it may be the case that the beneficiaries of the trust will also seek a proprietary claim as part of the broader range of their litigation in respect of the property lost to the trust, in tandem with personal claims against those strangers who were involved in transferring that property in breach of trust.

30.09 These claims for knowing receipt and dishonest assistance are therefore best understood as part of the web of claims which may be brought by beneficiaries in the event of a breach of trust. For example, suppose that T is the trustee of a valuable oil painting. If T were to transfer that oil painting away in breach of trust then T would be personally liable for breach of trust. As a trustee T would be liable to restore the painting to the trust, or to make restitution to the beneficiaries in the form of cash, or to provide equitable compensation to the beneficiaries.[31] The beneficiaries would be required to proceed against their trustee in the first place.[32]

If the oil painting were particularly valuable then it might be that T would not be able to compensate the beneficiaries if T did not have sufficient money. Therefore, the beneficiaries would need to identify someone else who would be able to make good their loss. Suppose then that A, an art dealer, had organized the means by which T had sold the oil painting. A would face liability for dishonest assistance in a breach of trust: that is, the liability of one who assisted the breach of trust.[33] As will emerge from the discussion below it will be necessary to demonstrate that A acted dishonestly when assisting the breach of trust.[34] The test of dishonesty which equity uses has extended beyond the natural, vernacular meaning of that term. The precise nature of A's liability would be to make good all of the loss suffered by the beneficiaries *as though A had been a trustee*.[35] This form of liability can be understood as being the imposition of the office of a constructive trustee on the defendant. That is, because of A's unconscionable act he is construed to be a trustee bearing the liability to make good any loss suffered by the beneficiaries which arises from a breach of trust. Significantly, A did not receive the painting: rather, his liability is based on his act of assistance rather than any contact with the property itself.

Further, suppose that B operates a warehouse and art gallery in which oil paintings can be stored and displayed for purchasers. If B received the painting and stored it prior to facilitating its sale on T's order, B would face liability for knowing receipt

---

[31] *Target Holdings v Redferns* [1996] 1 AC 421; [1995] 3 WLR 352; [1995] 3 All ER 785.

[32] ibid.

[33] *Royal Brunei Airlines v Tan* [1995] 2 AC 378; *Smith New Court v Scrimgeour Vickers* [1997] AC 254; *Corporacion Nacional Del Cobre De Chile v Sogemin Metals* [1997] 1 WLR 1396; *Fortex Group Ltd v MacIntosh* [1998] 3 NZLR 171; *Twinsectra Ltd v Yardley* [1999] Lloyd's Rep Bank 438; *Dubai Aluminium v Salaam* [1999] 1 Lloyd's Rep 415; *Wolfgang Herbert Heinl v Jyske Bank* [1999] Lloyd's Rep Bank 511; *Thomas v Pearce* [2000] FSR 718.

[34] ibid.   [35] ibid.

of property in breach of trust. That is, a potential liability based on the receipt of the painting. It would be necessary that two things took place: to borrow from criminal law, there would need to be an *actus reus* of *receipt* of the painting and a *mens rea* of *knowledge* that the painting had been received in breach of trust. The applicable principles surrounding each of these terms is considered below. The significant factor at this stage is that the liability which B faces is based on receipt of the property and not simply on assisting with the breach of trust.[36]

These claims would impose on A and B respectively personal liability to account to the beneficiaries for the value of the property passed out of the trust fund.[37] As considered above, it should not be forgotten that in many cases these claims will form part of a much larger web of actions commenced by beneficiaries. The beneficiaries may also pursue a range of proprietary claims simultaneously to recover the painting itself by way of tracing.[38] The first would be a proprietary tracing claim at common law to recover their painting itself.[39] If the painting had been sold to someone who would have a good defence to such a tracing claim, then they would seek an equitable proprietary tracing claim to assert title to the money received for the sale of the painting or any other property acquired as its traceable substitute.[40] Frequently, all of these claims will be pursued simultaneously by the beneficiaries. As such, the issue considered in this chapter might constitute only one of a number of claims brought in relation to any one set of facts.

A good illustration of such a web of claims is the case of *Lipkin Gorman v Karpnale*[41] in which a partner in a firm of solicitors frequently drew money from the firm's client account and used it in the defendant's casino. When the firm of solicitors discovered that their money had been taken by this partner they had to find a means of recovering it. The partner himself owed his fellow partners a liability as a fiduciary but was unable personally to make good the loss to the partnership. Therefore, the firm proceeded against the casino under a range of personal and proprietary claims. Among the personal claims brought by the solicitors' firm were actions against the casino under the tort of negligence, an action for money had and received at common law, an action for conversion of cheques, an action for conversion of a banker's draft, and an action for knowing receipt in respect of the money taken from their client account. Among the proprietary claims were actions for common law tracing into the casino's bank accounts and

30.10

---

[36] *Grupo Toras v Al-Sabah* (CA, 2 November 2000).

[37] What remains unclear is the extent to which the equitable remedy of account in these cases will permit the court to hold the defendant only liable to the extent that the defendant is genuinely culpable in the same way that, eg, a common law court would invoke principles of contributory negligence to reduce the defendant's liability.

[38] Considered in Chapter 33.　　[39] *Jones, FC (A Firm) v Jones* [1996] 3 WLR 703.

[40] *Re Diplock's Estate* [1948] Ch 465; *Westdeutsche Landesbank v Islington LBC* [1996] AC 669, HL.

[41] [1991] 3 WLR 10.

for equitable tracing similarly into their bank accounts. The firm also claimed against the bank which held the firm's client account claiming dishonest assistance, conversion of cheques, conversion of a banker's draft, and breach of contract.

In the House of Lords the matter was ultimately settled on the basis of unjust enrichment on the part of the casino with an account taken of the casino's change of position on receipt of the moneys—thus establishing the case as a landmark decision among restitution lawyers. The claimants were able to establish proprietary claims with reference to those moneys which the casino had held separately from other of their moneys so as to be identifiable, but were only able to proceed for the remaining moneys under personal claims to the extent that the casino could be demonstrated to have had sufficient knowledge of the source of the partner's moneys or to have been otherwise negligent. The complex web of claims was essential to the firm's claims.

30.11 Similarly, in *Agip (Africa) Ltd v Jackson*[42] the defendant accountants arranged that money would be taken from the plaintiffs by means of forged payment orders to a series of dummy companies. The intention had been to launder the money through these shell companies. The plaintiffs pursued a number of claims simultaneously both personally against the accountants themselves, against their firm, against the companies and banks which received the money, and also brought proprietary claims against any property which constituted or had been derived from the original moneys taken.[43]

The nature of the remedy of personal liability to account as a constructive trustee

30.12 As mentioned above, the form of relief awarded in this type of claim is the imposition of a personal liability to account on the stranger who is found to be liable as a constructive trustee. In *Selangor v Cradock (No 3)*[44] it was suggested by Ungoed-Thomas J that this form of action is

> ... nothing more than a formula for equitable relief. The court of equity says that the defendant shall be liable in equity, as though he were a trustee.

In short, this is not a trust as ordinarily understood in that there is no specific property which is held on trust. The cases on dishonest assistance have been excluded by Lord Browne-Wilkinson from many of the rules which concern express trusts. In *Westdeutsche Landesbank v Islington*,[45] Lord Browne-Wilkinson held that:

> In order to establish a trust there must be identifiable trust property. The only apparent exception to this rule is a constructive trust imposed on a person who dishonestly assists in a breach of trust who may come under fiduciary duties even if he does not receive identifiable trust property.

---

[42] *Agip v Jackson* [1990] Ch 265, 286, *per* Millett J; CA [1991] Ch 547.
[43] What is often referred to as the 'search for the solvent defendant'.
[44] [1968] 1 WLR 1555, 1579.   [45] [1996] AC 669.

It does appear that this form of equitable relief is as much in the form of a remedy as an institutional trust. That means dishonest assistance is as much a form of equitable wrong (organized solely around a standard of good conscience) as a trust (under which identified property is held on trust for beneficiaries).

The material considered in this section sits awkwardly within a discussion of constructive trust because it is, in truth, a species of liability for breach of trust which the courts persist in labelling as a 'constructive trust'.[46] The utility of this label, however, is that it explains the form of liability which is imposed on the defendant: that is, the same liability to account to the beneficiaries as would be faced by a properly appointed express trustee who was guilty of a breach of trust. Thus, the significance of the liability to account as a constructive trustee is that equity uses it to isolate those people who have either received property in the knowledge that there has been a breach of trust or who dishonestly have assisted in a breach of trust, such that it can impose that personal liability to make good the beneficiaries' losses on those strangers which would ordinarily attach only to someone officially appointed as a trustee of that trust.[47]

A question as to the extent of the remedy

There is one underlying problem with the remedy of personal liability to account in this context. The liability attaches to the defendant either for receipt or for assistance provided that the relevant '*mens rea*' of either knowledge or dishonesty has been satisfied, as considered below. The defendant is then liable for the whole of the loss suffered by the beneficiaries: the remedy appearing to be an all-or-nothing remedy. There is no common law defence available to the defendant in the manner of the defence of contributory negligence in the law of tort under which the defendant can admit liability but nevertheless demonstrate that the claimant's loss was not due entirely to the defendant's actions. The defendant to a claim for liability to account in equity has not yet been awarded such a defence, although equitable defences such as release may be available in the ways considered below. However, the point made here is that there is no obvious defence on the cases which responds to the level of fault which might be considered to attach to any given defendant. It would seem, in general terms, possible for a court of equity to exercise its discretion so as to measure the extent of the defendant's culpability for the loss suffered by the beneficiaries, rather than assuming simply that the entire loss suffered by the trust should be recoverable from the defendant once dishonesty or knowledge has been established.

Suppose, for example, that the defendant was chauffeur to a fiduciary who intended to defraud a trust over which he was trustee and then to disappear to

30.13

30.14

30.15

---

[46] L Smith, 'Constructive trusts and constructive trustees' [1999] CLJ 294.
[47] *Target Holdings v Redferns* [1996] 1 AC 421; [1995] 3 WLR 352; [1995] 3 All ER 785.

Brazil. Suppose further that the fiduciary told the chauffeur of his entire plan while being driven to the offices where he intended to break into a safe and steal the trust's valuable movable property. If the chauffeur was uneasy as to whether or not his boss was joking and agreed to carry his boss's bag of tools to the office door and then waited outside (so that he could not actually know whether or not his boss was taking anything) before carrying a heavy Gladstone bag loaded with the trust's property down to the car past security, then we would have to say that he assisted the breach of trust in the colloquial sense of the term 'assist'. We might also say that he was dishonest for not doing what an honest person would have done:[48] that is, perhaps, to have asked his boss outright whether he had stolen the trust's property or whether he had merely been joking. In such a situation, then, the chauffeur may possibly be held to have acted dishonestly on Lord Nicholls's formulation that one is dishonest if one fails to act as an honest person would have acted.[49] The issue would be whether or not he would be able to claim that he was only partly responsible for the loss suffered by the beneficiaries because, while perhaps not perfectly honest, he was not the person who stole the trust's property.

By contrast, if the chauffeur had been in the office when the safe was opened and had helped his boss to load the trust's chattels into a Gladstone bag before receiving a small diamond from the haul for his services, then he would appear to have been more dishonest than on the previous set of facts and perhaps to be deserving of a greater measure of liability as a result. Alternatively, if he had asked his boss outright whether or not he had been joking and was reassured by his boss that indeed he had only been joking, before carrying the suspiciously heavy bag to the boot of the car, then we might consider him to have been less dishonest but still not to have done all that an honest person might have done: perhaps to alert security or to ask more questions. And yet, if his boss absconded, the claim based on personal liability to account may impose liability on the chauffeur for the entirety of the loss if he is considered to have been dishonest, or alternatively the court may absolve him entirely of any liability.[50] That the courts have not hitherto made such distinctions suggests that the focus of this form of liability is on the compensation of the beneficiaries and not on the punishment of the dishonest assistant. It is suggested in such a situation that a court of equity ought to be able to measure the extent to which that chauffeur had indeed acted unconscionably and require him to account to the beneficiaries only to that extent.

---

[48] The test laid down by Lord Nicholls for 'dishonesty' in *Royal Brunei Airlines v Tan* [1995] 2 AC 378.

[49] *Royal Brunei Airlines v Tan* [1995] 2 AC 378.

[50] *Royal Brunei Airlines v Tan* [1995] 2 AC 378.

D. Dishonest Assistance

The foundations of personal liability to account as a constructive trustee for dishonest assistance in a breach of trust

The doctrine of dishonest assistance concerns the liability of strangers who assist **30.16** either in a breach of trust or in the transfer of property away from a trust otherwise than in accordance with the purposes of a trust. The distinction from knowing receipt is that there is no requirement for the imposition of liability that the stranger have had possession or control of the property at any time. As considered above, some commentators have doubted whether or not this form of liability should really be described as a 'constructive trust' because there is no property which can be held on trust nor the traceable proceeds of any trust property.[51] However, the courts have continued to use the terminology of constructive trust and to talk of the imposition of constructive trusteeship despite this conceptual problem.[52] It is suggested that the reason for the continued use of the language of constructive trust is that the person who dishonestly assists the commission of the breach of trust is *construed* to be a trustee and made personally liable for the loss suffered by the beneficiaries as though she were an express trustee.

The core principles informing this area are contained in the speech of Lord **30.17** Selborne LC in *Barnes v Addy* where his lordship held:[53]

> . . . strangers are not to be made constructive trustees merely because they act as the agents of trustees in transactions within their legal powers, transactions, perhaps, of which a Court of Equity may disapprove, unless those agents receive and become chargeable with some part of the trust property, or unless they assist with knowledge in a dishonest and fraudulent design on the part of the trustee.

The decision in *Barnes v Addy* is a useful foundation for the modern law in this area because it cites no earlier authority. In consequence it is possible to see very clearly the roots of this form of liability in Lord Selborne's short and clear judgment. There were earlier cases on which the House of Lords in *Barnes v Addy* could have chosen to rely or to build, but they did not:[54] these other cases are referred to below in contexts in which Lord Nicholls, principally, has made reference to them.[55]

---

[51] A Oakley, *Constructive Trusts* (3rd edn, Sweet & Maxwell, 1997) ('*Oakley*') 186 *et seq.*
[52] *Agip v Jackson* [1991] Ch 547; *Polly Peck International v Nadir (No 2)* [1992] 4 All ER 769; *Westdeutsche Landesbank v Islington* [1996] AC 669.
[53] (1874) 9 Ch App 244, 251–252.
[54] *Fyler v Fyler* (1841) 3 Beav 550, 49 ER 1031; *A-G v Leicester Corp* (1844) 7 Beav 176, 49 ER 1031; *Eaves v Hickman* (1861) 7 Beav 176.
[55] *Royal Brunei Airlines v Tan* [1995] AC 97, 102.

The rationale behind the imposition of liability for dishonest assistance

30.18   The core notion underpinning the imposition of liability for dishonest assistance is therefore knowledge of a 'dishonest and fraudulent design'. Earlier in that same speech, Lord Selborne referred to the liability of those who are not express trustees (that is, strangers to the trust) as being based on proof that

> . . . they are found either making themselves trustees *de son tort*, or actually participating in any fraudulent conduct of the trustee to the injury of the *cestui que trust*.[56]

Much has been made in the judgments in recent cases of Lord Selborne's suggestion that liability may be predicated on the defendant making himself in effect an express trustee de son tort by interfering with the running of the trust.[57] Similarly, much is made of the difference which is evident in cases such as *Mara v Browne*[58] between liability as a trustee de son tort and liability where there is property held under a constructive trust. Nevertheless, what is clear from those nineteenth-century judgments is the fact that all of the judges use the formula of constructive trust to impose liability *as though the defendant were an express trustee.* This may indeed be a 'formula for equitable relief'[59] but the reason why that equitable relief is provided at all is to support a principle that beneficiaries are entitled to expect that their trustees will be able to fulfil their fiduciary duties properly without interference from strangers:[60] this is so whether those strangers procure a breach of trust from gullible trustees, or whether they conspire with those trustees to commit a breach of trust, or whether they otherwise assist in the breach of the trustees' obligations. In consequence, the principles in this area have maintained that such wrongdoing strangers should bear the same liabilities as if they had themselves been trustees.

That there must have been a breach of trust

The need for a breach of trust to found liability

30.19   The imposition of liability is to compensate the beneficiaries for loss caused by some breach of trust, in the manner considered in Chapter 32.[61] If there were no requirement that there have been some breach of trust in which the stranger had participated then the stranger might be liable in circumstances in which perfectly reasonable investments or other actions by the trustees cause a reduction in the value in the trust fund—for example, where the stranger advises investment in

---

[56] [1995] AC 97, 251.

[57] *Dubai Aluminium Company v Salaam* [2002] 3 WLR 1913 [2003] 1 All ER 97, para 140 ff, *per* Lord Millett.

[58] [1896] 1 Ch 199.   [59] *Selangor v Cradock (No 3)* [1968] 1 WLR 1555, 1579.

[60] *Royal Brunei Airlines v Tan* [1995] 3 All ER 97, 103, *per* Lord Nicholls.

[61] By analogy *El Ajou v Dollar Land Holdings* [1994] 1 BCLC 464, 478, *per* Hoffmann J; *Brown v Bennett* [1998] EWCA Civ 1881.

shares which lose value only slightly in market conditions in which most shares have lost more value[62]—but without any liability to account having been found. Rather, the doctrine of dishonest assistance is a translation of the liability of trustees to account for a breach of trust to strangers who have assisted in such a breach of trust.

The source of the liability on the dishonest assistant is therefore that of a loss being **30.20** caused to the trust due to some action which was caused by the breach of another person; that is, in some breach of the duties of the express trustee. These breaches of trust fall into three kinds. First, a breach of the express trustee's obligations under the general law of trusts, as considered in Parts B and C of this book. Secondly, a breach of some specific duty within the terms of the express trustee's duties contained in the trust instrument about which the stranger could have been expected to have known. A good example of this second category of liability would be the theft of trust property by the trustee with the intention of permanently depriving the trust of it. In such a situation it would be clear that the stranger ought to understand that such an action would constitute a breach of the trustee's duties. Thirdly, the breach of some duty in the trust instrument of which the stranger was unaware. This is the most difficult of the forms of breach to justify in the abstract. An example of this type of liability would be an obligation on the trustee to hold given portions of the trust property separately from one another and to invest no more than a given proportion of the total fund in any given type of investment. In such a situation, it would be possible for a dishonest assistant in the form of an investment advisor to advise the investment of trust property in a given investment which was within the class of investments identified by the sett-lor but, to continue the example, in excess of the thresholds in the trust instru-ment for any particular type of investment. More particularly, as is considered below as to the mental element necessary to constitute dishonest assistance, the defendant would seek to demonstrate in such a circumstance that she was not act-ing dishonestly in relation to a breach of duty of which she was not and perhaps could not have been aware.

Consequently, the question arises as to what factor it is about which the stranger **30.21** must be dishonest: whether as to the knowledge specifically that there was a breach of trust, or as to the general probity of their actions without necessarily knowing that there was a breach of trust. In the abstract it could be said that the assistant ought to be liable for failing to act as an honest person would have acted, for example in accepting money in suspicious circumstances on behalf of an employer, without that person knowing the terms of the trustee's fiduciary duties.

---

[62] See para 32.07 in relation to the notion of the carping beneficiary who ought not to be able to claim a loss where otherwise there is none: *Target Holdings v Redferns* [1996] 1 AC 421. See also *Nestle v National Westminster Bank* [1993] 1 WLR 1260.

In such a situation the stranger's failure to question the source of the money could be said to be justification enough for the imposition of general liability to account to the beneficiaries. Alternatively, it could be argued that if the stranger did not know that the action in question constituted a breach of the trustee's detailed obligations in the trust instrument, then the stranger ought not to be held liable for any losses which are suffered ultimately by the beneficiaries. While the courts have not distinguished between these separate contexts it is suggested that the question would be addressed by Lord Nicholls's general approach to the definition of dishonesty, considered in the next section, when he considers dishonesty to be established by asking what an honest person would have done in the stranger's circumstances.[63] In taking that approach, one need not answer the question whether or not the stranger is required to know that the trustee's actions were a breach of the terms of the trust instrument or of the general principles of the law of trusts because one need only consider whether or not an honest person in the stranger's position should have realized that the actions in question constituted a breach of trust.

The trustee need not have been dishonest

30.22 The trustee need not have acted dishonestly for the stranger to be held liable for dishonest assistance. In Lord Selborne's original formulation of this liability it was necessary to prove that the stranger had assisted 'with knowledge in a dishonest and fraudulent design on the part of the trustee'.[64] That formulation suggested two things. First, that the breach of trust was the trustee's fraudulent design in which the stranger participated. Secondly, that it was the design which needed to be dishonest and that the stranger must have participated in it knowingly. Consequently, if the stranger could have demonstrated that the trustee had not acted dishonestly then, on a literal interpretation of this formulation, there could not have been a dishonest design on the part of the trustee and therefore no liability on the stranger. It is frequently the case that those who advise trustees are the professionals—whether stockbrokers, lawyers, accountants, and so forth—and that the trustees are not professionals. That trustees frequently delegate their responsibilities so that they are able to retain professional advisers in circumstances in which the trustee has no expertise, and that statute creates a framework within which this can take place, is a recognition of trustees' comparative innocence in many areas of trust management. If such an adviser were to concoct a scheme to defraud a trust then it would be a serious shortcoming in the law of trusts if it had no means of holding such a person liable to account as though they were a trustee simply because the trustee could not be fixed with any dishonesty.[65]

---

[63] See para 30.23.   [64] *Barnes v Addy* (1874) LR 9 Ch App 244.

[65] It is suggested that equity needed to develop its own form of liability given that the rights of the beneficiaries are recognized only in equity, that liability in contract can be excluded by

Consequently, Lord Nicholls made it plain that it is not necessary for the trustee to have been dishonest for the stranger to be liable for dishonest assistance.[66] The stranger's liability is entirely independent of the trustee's liability.

The nature of 'dishonesty' in dishonest assistance

A secondary form of liability

The liability is a secondary form of liability in that the dishonest assistant will be sued once the trustee's liability has been established or if the trustee cannot be held liable for breach of trust for some reason. The liability is secondary then to the primary liability of the trustee.[67] Moreover, the liability of the dishonest assistance is based on fault: that is, the defendant is held liable both for the act of assisting in the breach of trust and also for her fault in doing so dishonestly. Without having been dishonest, the defendant will not be liable for having assisted in a breach of trust.[68]

30.23

The leading case for the test of dishonest assistance is generally taken to be[69] the decision of the Privy Council in *Royal Brunei Airlines v Tan*.[70] In that case, the appellant airline contracted an agency agreement with a travel agency, BLT. Under that agreement BLT was to sell tickets for the appellant. BLT held money received for the sale of these tickets on express trust for the appellant in a current account. The current account was used to defray some of BLT's expenses, such as salaries, and to reduce its overdraft. BLT was required to account to the appellant for these moneys within thirty days. The respondent, Tan, was the managing director and principal shareholder of BLT. From time to time amounts were paid out of the current account into deposit accounts controlled by Tan. BLT held the proceeds of the sale of tickets as trustee for the appellant. In time, BLT went into insolvency. Therefore, the appellant sought to proceed against Tan for knowingly assisting[71] in a breach of trust. The issue between the parties was whether 'the breach of trust which is a prerequisite to accessory liability must itself be a dishonest and fraudulent breach of trust by the trustee'.

30.24

---

contractual provision, and that the measure of liability for breach of trust is not dependent on common law concepts of foreseeability and causation which might limit liability in negligence—as considered in Chapter 32 and made plain in *Target Holdings v Redferns* [1996] 1 AC 421.

[66] *Royal Brunei Airlines v Tan* [1995] 2 AC 378.   [67] On which, see para 32.01.
[68] *Carr v Bower Cotton* [2002] EWCA Civ 1788. See also *Goose v Wilson Sandford & Co* [1998] EWCA Civ 245 in which the claim of constructive trusteeship simply could not, in the court's opinion, be made out on the facts. Dishonesty must be pleaded and proved: *Wakelin v Read* [2000] EWCA Civ 82.
[69] See the general support for this decision by the various judicial committees of the House of Lords in *Twinsectra Ltd v Yardley* [2002] UKHL 12, [2002] 2 AC 164 and in *Dubai Aluminium v Salaam* [2002] 3 WLR 1913, as considered below.   [70] [1995] 2 AC 378.
[71] The liability was generally referred to before the decision in *Royal Brunei Airlines v Tan* as being 'knowing assistance'.

30.25   Lord Nicholls in *Royal Brunei Airlines v Tan* held that a breach of trust by a trustee need not have been a dishonest act *on the part of the trustee*. Rather, it is sufficient that some accessory acted dishonestly for that accessory to be fixed with liability for the breach. The test as set out by Lord Nicholls created a test of 'dishonesty'. The express trustee's state of mind is unimportant. The scenario is posited that the express trustee may be honest but the stranger who is made constructive trustee is dishonest. Where the third party is acting dishonestly, that third party will be liable to account. Mr Tan was held to have acted dishonestly in procuring the breach of trust on these facts.

30.26   The appropriateness of this objective test has been doubted in subsequent decisions.[72] This section will be structured in the following way: first, to analyse the objective test set out in *Royal Brunei Airlines v Tan* and then, secondly, to consider the subjectivity which has questionably been introduced to it by the subsequent decision of the House of Lords in *Twinsectra v Yardley*.[73]

The objective test for 'dishonesty'

30.27   In describing the nature of the test for dishonesty in this context Lord Nicholls in *Royal Brunei Airlines v Tan* held the following:

> . . . acting dishonestly, or with a lack of probity, which is synonymous, means simply not acting as an honest person would in the circumstance. This is an objective standard.[74]

So, the question which the objective form of this test requires the court to ask is not what the defendant thought personally but rather what an honest person would have done if they had been placed in the same circumstances. The court will therefore be holding the defendant up to an objective notion of what constitutes honest behaviour. The interesting notion raised by this passage is that dishonesty can be an *active* state of mind or alternatively a *passive* 'lack of probity'. It is suggested that while some level of *active deceit* is the vernacular, ordinary meaning of 'dishonesty',[75] nevertheless the term 'dishonesty' in this context was considered by the Privy Council to encompass *passive* dishonesty (such as failing to make inquiries, or to ensure that a proposed risk is not too great). This test framed by Lord Nicholls in *Royal Brunei Airlines v Tan* was therefore based on an objective understanding of 'dishonesty'; whereas the judgment of Scott LJ in *Polly Peck v Nadir (No 2)*[76] set out a subjective test of 'knowledge' in cases of knowing receipt which required the court to inquire whether or not the defendant ought to have been suspicious that the property which he had received had been passed to him in breach of trust. Thus the advance made in *Royal Brunei Airlines v Tan* was to

---

[72] In particular *Twinsectra Ltd v Yardley* [2002] UKHL 12, [2002] 2 AC 164.
[73] [2002] 2 AC 164.   [74] [1995] 2 AC 378, 386.   [75] *R v Ghosh* [1982] QB 1053.
[76] [1992] 4 All ER 769.

move away from a subjective notion of the defendant's knowledge of a breach of trust to an objective notion of whether or not an honest person would consider the defendant to have been dishonest.[77]

It had been found as a fact by the Brunei Court of Appeal that BLT, the travel **30.28** agency company run by Mr Tan, had not itself acted dishonestly. The Privy Council took this to mean that it was not established that Tan, as BLT's directing mind, had intended to defraud the airline. Rather, the money was held to be lost 'in the ordinary course of a poorly run business with heavy overhead expenses'. Evidently it requires a stylized notion of 'dishonesty' to accommodate a situation in which the defendant had not acted fraudulently. Lord Nicholls accepted that Tan 'hoped, maybe expected, to be able to pay the airline'[78] and therefore he was not suggesting that Tan had necessarily been acting fraudulently. Nevertheless, Tan was found liable for dishonest assistance in the undoubted breach of trust caused by the transfer of money out of the trust account where it was held for the airline. The test for dishonesty therefore bites in circumstances in which a business is run incompetently so that an honest person would not consider it to have been operated honestly. There is a narrow line between an innocently chaotic maintenance of a business's affairs and accounts, and the situation in which the reasonable person would suspect that those operating the business were not seeking assiduously enough to maintain a separation between various clients' funds and the funds of the business so that their good faith should be called into question. Nevertheless, both situations may lead to a finding of dishonesty on this objective test.

The basis of Lord Nicholls's decision on the facts was that **30.29**

> Mr Tan had no right to employ the money in the business at all. That was the breach of trust. The company's inability to pay the airline was the consequence of that breach of trust.[79]

So, in effect, Lord Nicholls found that Tan was acting dishonestly in that he was using money in a way that was not permitted by the contract entered into with the airline. However, there is no finding of fact by the Brunei Court of Appeal that Tan had used the money in a way that was per se 'fraudulent', although Tan did have actual knowledge of the breach.

Introducing a measure of subjectivity to the test of 'dishonesty'

Lord Nicholls was clear in *Royal Brunei Airlines v Tan* that he did not intend the **30.30** test of dishonesty to be subjective. That means, his lordship did not want the

---

[77] This objective approach found favour in *Woodland-Ferrari v UCL Group Retirement Benefits Scheme* [2002] 3 All ER 670, [2002] EWHC 1354 (Ch D), Ferris J.
[78] *Royal Brunei Airlines v Tan* [1995] 2 AC 378, 390.   [79] ibid 390.

question 'has this person acted dishonestly?' to be answered by reference to whether or not the defendant herself considered her actions to have been dishonest or whether or not she knew that other people would have considered them to have been dishonest. This view emerges from the following passage:[80]

> . . . subjective characteristics of dishonesty do not mean that individuals are free to set their own standards of honesty in particular circumstances. The standard of what constitutes honest conduct is not subjective. Honesty is not an optional scale, with higher or lower values according to the moral standards of each individual. If a person knowingly appropriates another's property, he will not escape a finding of dishonesty simply because he sees nothing wrong in such behaviour.[81]

This approach to the notion of dishonesty is very different from that in the criminal law whereby conviction for a crime of dishonesty will require that the defendant personally knew that her actions were dishonest.[82] In the context of the criminal law we might consider it unsurprising if the courts require that a person not be convicted of a crime without knowing that they had committed some act which they knew to involve a criminal *mens rea*. Nevertheless, the civil law in the form of the doctrine of dishonest assistance as conceived of by Lord Nicholls sought to judge the behaviour of the defendant by means of a purely objective standard.

30.31   Nevertheless, a combined subjective-objective approach to the meaning of dishonesty emerged in the subsequent decision of the House of Lords in *Twinsectra Ltd v Yardley*.[83] In that case Yardley sought to borrow money from Twinsectra to acquire property. It was a term of the loan agreement that the money was to be used solely for that purpose. It was a further part of the agreement that the money would be paid to Sims, a solicitor acting on behalf of Yardley, such that Sims would hold the loan money on trust with the power to spend it only for the acquisition of the property identified in the loan contract. The terms of the trust took the form of a solicitor's undertaking that the money would be used for the prescribed purpose, although Yardley was entitled to use the loan moneys as collateral for other transactions. However, Sims was replaced as Yardley's solicitor for the purposes of this transaction by another solicitor, Leach. Yardley assured Sims that the money could be passed to Leach on the basis that Leach would now act as solicitor under the agreement. The loan moneys were subsequently misapplied by Yardley and the loan was not repaid. Twinsectra brought proceedings, *inter alia*, against Leach contending that Leach had dishonestly assisted in a breach of Sims's

---

[80] ibid, [1995] 3 All ER 95, 106.

[81] This last sentence contains an unfortunate reference to 'appropriation' whereas it is not necessary for the operation of the assistance liability that the defendant receive the property into his possession: the term 'appropriation' here should be read as referring to participation in the act of appropriation of property from the trust fund without passing possession or control of it to the defendant.

[82] *R v Ghosh* [1982] QB 1053.   [83] [2002] 2 All ER 377.

trust obligations. Leach's defence was that he considered himself entitled to use the money for whatever purposes Yardley directed him to use it and in consequence that he did not consider that he had done anything dishonest.

The majority of the House of Lords (with Lord Millett dissenting) held that **30.32** liability for dishonest assistance required *both* that the actions would have been considered dishonest by honest and reasonable people and *also* that the defendant herself realized that the actions would have been considered dishonest by honest and reasonable people. After reviewing the authorities, Lord Hutton gave the following exposition of the appropriate test:[84]

> There is, in my opinion, a further consideration [beyond that of deciding whether the test is one of knowledge or dishonesty as set out by Lord Nicholls] which supports the view that for liability as an accessory to arise the defendant must himself appreciate that what he was doing was dishonest by the standards of honest and reasonable men. A finding by the judge that a defendant has been dishonest is a grave finding, and it is particularly grave against a professional man, such as a solicitor. Notwithstanding that the issue arises in equity law [*sic*] and not in a criminal context, I think that it would be less than just for the law to permit a finding that a defendant had been 'dishonest' in assisting in a breach of trust where he knew of the facts which created the trust and its breach but had not been aware that what he was doing would be regarded by honest men as being dishonest.

This test, therefore, clearly adds an important second, subjective element to the test of dishonesty. Significantly, though, the second limb of the test is whether or not the defendant realized that *other people* would have considered her actions to have been dishonest and not that *the defendant herself* thought that the action was dishonest. Therefore, the subjective element is a qualified form of subjectivity.

Nevertheless, whereas Lord Hutton's analysis of this matter, with which Lord **30.33** Steyn seemed to concur and with which Lord Slynn may have concurred, introduced a subjective element to the test of dishonesty, Lord Nicholls's original test in *Royal Brunei Airlines v Tan* is approved in general terms. This combination of the alteration of the detail of that *Royal Brunei Airlines v Tan* test and the approval of that same test is, it is suggested, generative of some conceptual awkwardness. Lord Hutton approached the matter in the following way:[85]

> It would be open to your Lordships to depart from the principle stated by Lord Nicholls [in *Royal Brunei Airlines v Tan*] that dishonesty is a necessary ingredient of accessory liability and to hold that knowledge is a sufficient ingredient. But the statement of that principle by Lord Nicholls has been widely regarded as clarifying this area of the law and, as he observed, the tide of authority in England has flowed strongly in favour of the test of dishonesty. Therefore, I consider that the courts should continue to apply that test and that your Lordships should state that dishonesty requires knowledge by the defendant that what he was doing would be regarded

---

[84] ibid 387.   [85] ibid 387.

as dishonest by honest people, although he should not escape a finding of dishonesty because he sets his own standards of honesty and does not regard as dishonest what he knows would offend the normally accepted standards of honest conduct.

Therefore, the utility of the dishonesty test and its growing popularity are cited as the reasons for its retention. It is perhaps unfortunate that the gloss which Lord Hutton puts on that test, by way of the subjective element considered above, is expressed as requiring 'knowledge' that what he was doing would be considered dishonest: this is unfortunate because the test of dishonesty was developed precisely to move away from tests of knowledge which were bound up in the doctrines of knowledge and of 'knowing assistance' applied before the decision in *Royal Brunei Airlines v Tan*.

30.34   The effect, it is suggested, is to leave the law in a confused state. Nor is it entirely clear with which parts of Lord Hutton's analysis the other members of the judicial committee of the House of Lords were agreeing. Lord Steyn concurred with both Lord Hutton and Lord Hoffmann. Lord Slynn concurred with Lord Hoffmann at the beginning of his short speech but then expressed concurrence also with Lord Hutton, although it is not entirely clear with which parts he proposed to concur. Lord Hoffmann disposed of the matter first by analysing the terms of the under-taking given by Sims. Lord Hoffmann then appeared to express agreement with Lord Hutton that 'a dishonest state of mind' is to be conceived of as 'conscious-ness that one is transgressing ordinary standards of honest behaviour', but then proceeded in the next paragraph to express agreement with Lord Nicholls, who was against any such subjectivity, and to express regret that the trial judge used subjective-sounding expressions like 'the defendant shut his eyes to the obvious' (considered below).[86] In Lord Hoffmann's opinion, the trial judge's finding that the solicitor had not been dishonest was viable on the basis that the trial judge had formed the view that the solicitor had taken a narrow understanding of his pro-fessional responsibilities and therefore that he had not subjectively understood his actions to have been dishonest.[87] Lord Millett dissented by focusing primarily on the nature of this arrangement as a *Quistclose* trust, and his analysis of the concept of dishonesty is predicated on a close analysis of Lord Nicholls's leading opinion in *Royal Brunei Airlines v Tan*. In Lord Millett's view, Leach knew all of the facts which caused his action to be considered wrongful and therefore could be consid-ered to have acted dishonestly.

Necessary limits on the application of subjectivity in the test of dishonesty

30.35   It was suggested in *Twinsectra v Yardley* that in deciding what constitutes an object-ive notion of dishonest conduct one must nevertheless consider whether or not the defendant herself knew that her conduct would be considered to be dishonest.

---

[86] [2002] 2 All ER, 383.   [87] ibid 383.

What none of the courts has accepted is a notion that defendants can rely on a defence that their own moral code did not consider their wrongdoing to have been dishonest. In considering what is frequently referred to as the 'Robin Hood defence', on the basis that the defendant might suggest that subjectively she considered robbing from the rich to be acceptable if it was done to give money to the poor, Sir Christopher Slade has held that:[88]

> A person may in some cases act dishonestly, according to the ordinary use of language, even though he genuinely believes that his action is morally justified. The penniless thief, for example, who picks the pocket of the multimillionaire is dishonest even though he genuinely considers the theft is morally justified as a fair redistribution of wealth and that he is not therefore being dishonest.

Lord Nicholls, delivering a speech in the subsequent decision of the House of Lords in *Dubai Aluminium Company Ltd v Salaam*,[89] defined the doctrine of dishonest assistance as being the 'equitable wrong of dishonest assistance in a breach of trust or fiduciary duty'.[90] Lord Nicholls described the stranger's liability as being that of a 'constructive trustee'[91] whose 'misconduct ... gives rise to a liability in equity to make good resulting loss'.[92] This analysis is predicated both on Lord Nicholls's own decision in *Royal Brunei Airlines v Tan*[93] and on the older authority of *Mara v Browne*:[94] the latter authority in relation to the liability of a partnership for the wrong committed by one of its partners as considered below.[95]

No mention was made in Lord Nicholls's judgment in *Dubai Aluminium v Salaam* **30.36** of the changes suggested in *Twinsectra v Yardley* which purported to introduce a subjective element to the objective notion of dishonesty in *Royal Brunei Airlines v Tan*. It is suggested that the changes suggested by Lord Hutton in *Twinsectra v Yardley* did not have the clear support of the majority of the House of Lords in that case and furthermore that they were not to be followed in the future. As considered above,[96] the approach suggested by the objective approach is to hold the stranger liable for any loss which results from circumstances in which an honest person would have acted differently, without that stranger needing to know that there has been any breach of trust committed. The policy behind this principle is to protect the beneficiary from any form of harm. This is a development from the formulation used by Lord Selborne in *Barnes v Addy* in which his lordship held that the liability was affixed to any person who had assisted 'with knowledge in a dishonest and fraudulent design on the part of the trustee': this is a formulation which suggests a knowing assistance such that the stranger realizes that he is assisting in a breach of trust, and not that he is doing something which he is taken to have believed to be wrong without having actual knowledge that there has been any breach of trust.

---

[88] *Walker v Stones* [2000] 4 All ER 412, 444, *per* Sir Christopher Slade.
[89] [2002] 3 WLR 1913, [2003] 1 All ER 97.   [90] ibid, para 9.   [91] ibid, para 40.
[92] ibid.   [93] [1995] 2 AC 378.   [94] [1896] 1 Ch 199, 208, *per* Lord Herschell.
[95] cf *In re Bell's Indenture* [1980] 1 WLR 1217, 1230, *per* Vinelott J.   [96] See para 30.23.

30.37 By contrast the formulation of liability in *Royal Brunei Airlines v Tan* is doing something very different and is using a stylized notion of dishonesty to affix liability to account on a person who has acted dishonestly regardless of the trustee's own state of mind, whereas Lord Selborne envisaged that it was the trustee who had concocted a dishonest and fraudulent design in which he had conspired with the stranger. Lord Nicholls accepted that the modern world of trusts practice leaves beneficiaries open to the dishonesty of investment advisers, professionals retained by the trustees, and other third parties, unless such people can be made severally liable for any loss to the trust from the liability of the trustees. It is common for the trustees to be non-professionals, and therefore innocent of any complex fraud on the trust, such that strangers may escape liability if Lord Selborne's formulation were applied so as to require that the trustees have been dishonest before the strangers could be liable to account. If the stranger is to be liable on his own terms, without needing to proving any *mala animus* in the trustee, then it cannot matter whether or not the trustee knew that there had been any breach of the trustee's own obligations: rather, they bear all the loss consequent on their failure to act as an honest person would have done in the circumstances.

The role of equity in this context is to identify fault on the part of the stranger by reference to their having acted dishonestly such that they are liable to account for all of the loss which flows from their dishonesty. It is suggested further than once a court of equity applying notions of good conscience takes it upon itself to judge the propriety of a person's mental state, then it is entitled to do so by reference to an objective conception of the behaviour which it would have required from such a person: that is, it is entitled to apply a conception of what an honest person would have done without needing to trouble itself as to the individual defendant's understanding of the probity of their own actions.[97] By permitting subjectivity into this test even a solicitor, as in *Twinsectra v Yardley*, can avoid liability for losses to a trust caused by his own lack of knowledge of the terms of the trust instrument; whereas the objective approach enables the court to judge the defendant's behaviour in the abstract. It is suggested that the objective test for dishonesty advanced by Lord Nicholls is to be preferred. Equity, acting as it always has done *in personam* against the defendant's conscience, nevertheless operates objectively by means of judging the defendant's behaviour against its own measure of good conscience and not by delving, as though some psychoanalyst, into the innermost recesses of the defendant's internal conscience. Ever since Lord Ellesmere's day in the *Earl of Oxford's Case*,[98] equity has existed 'to *correct* men's consciences'[99] and not simply to inquire into their contents. Equity's role here is as an objective arbiter and not as a subjectively-motivated psychologist concerned only to learn what is in a conscience rather than to judge its contents.

---

[97] See A S Hudson, *Equity & Trusts* (3rd edn, Cavendish Publishing, 2003) ('*Hudson*') 977, para 37.2, in which the notion of conscience in equity is considered in greater detail.

[98] (1615) 1 Ch Rep 1.   [99] ibid (emphasis added).

Dishonest assistance in the breach of a fiduciary duty owed between partners

As outlined above, the majority of the House of Lords in *Dubai Aluminium* **30.38**
Company Ltd v Salaam reverted to purely objective notions of dishonesty in relation to the liability of partners between themselves.[100] This case involved a
fraudulent scheme whereby Dubai Aluminium Co Ltd was induced to pay out
US$50 million under a sham consultancy agreement. One of the fraudsters,
Salaam, was a client of a firm of solicitors, Amhurst Brown.[101] It was claimed by
Dubai Aluminium that Mr Amhurst, a partner of the Amhurst Brown firm of
solicitors, had been a dishonest assistant in the fraud in that Mr Amhurst had
advised Salaam throughout his various activities. The House of Lords was able to
proceed on the basis that the Amhurst Brown partners were innocent of the fraud
and to recognize that no fraud had been proved against Mr Amhurst himself
because all of the parties had agreed to settle. The remaining question was as to
the liability of the Amhurst Brown partnership under the Civil Liability
(Contribution) Act 1978 and, consequently, whether Mr Amhurst's liability was
for the equitable wrong of dishonest assistance as opposed to a common law liability under tort, where equitable and common law liabilities received different
treatment under the 1978 Act. Lord Nicholls gave a leading speech in *Dubai
Aluminium Company Ltd v Salaam*[102] with which Lord Slynn concurred. Lord
Millett gave a speech in slightly different terms. Lord Hutton concurred with
both Lord Nicholls and with Lord Millett. Lord Hobhouse gave a speech, without concurring with any of the others, focusing on the role of the 1978 Act and,
inter alia, its use in providing 'restitutionary remedies for unjust enrichment at
the expense of another'.[103]

Lord Nicholls expressed liability for dishonest assistance as being the 'equitable **30.39**
wrong of dishonest assistance in a breach of trust or fiduciary duty'[104] such that
the stranger's liability rested on a 'wrongful act'. If a partnership were held liable
for fraudulent misrepresentation his lordship considered it 'remarkable' to suggest
that the partnership should not be vicariously liable for an individual partner's
'dishonest participation . . . in conduct directed at the misappropriation of another's
property'.[105] The stranger is liable as a 'constructive trustee'[106] in circumstances in
which his 'misconduct . . . gives rise to a liability in equity to make good resulting
loss'.[107] This analysis is predicated both on Lord Nicholls's own decision in
Royal Brunei Airlines v Tan,[108] and on the older authority of *Mara v Browne*[109]
whereby a partnership was held liable for a breach of fiduciary duty committed

---

[100] [2002] 3 WLR 1913, [2003] 1 All ER 97.
[101] In fact, Amhurst were two successive partnerships but they were treated by the House of
Lords as being one partnership.
[102] [2002] 3 WLR 1913, [2003] 1 All ER 97.   [103] ibid, para 76.   [104] ibid, para 9.
[105] ibid, para 11.   [106] ibid, para 40.   [107] ibid.   [108] [1995] 2 AC 378.
[109] [1896] 1 Ch 199, 208, *per* Lord Herschell.

by one of the partners.[110] No mention was made in his lordship's speech of the approach taken in *Twinsectra v Yardley* which purported to introduce a subjective element to the objective notion of dishonesty in *Royal Brunei Airlines v Tan*.

30.40 By contrast, in Lord Millett's speech the particular facts of this case were disposed of by reference to old principle imposing vicarious liability on a partnership for the equitable wrongdoing of any one partner[111] contrasted with vicarious liability in tort.[112] As to the roots of the dishonest assistance claim in cases such as *Mara v Browne*,[113] Lord Millett placed this claim in the context of trusteeship having become 'more professional. Clients no longer look to their trustees to be philosophers, guides and friends...', with the effect that we do not need to consider the usage of 'constructive trust' and 'constructive trustee' in *Mara v Browne* as denoting a trust of identifiable property[114] and that we should recognize that 'meanings have changed over time'. Lord Millett suggested that we should consider the form of constructive trusteeship in *Mara v Browne* as equivalent to liability as a trustee de son tort.[115] The impact of such a definition of the liability for dishonest assistance would be to predicate it solely on the fault of the defendant for intermeddling with the operation of the trust or rendering himself an 'actual trustee',[116] and not simply by means of assisting in a breach of that trust without seeking to take over its management. What Lord Millett seeks to make of this understanding on the facts before him is that no partnership can accept that any individual partner is entitled to breach his fiduciary duties to a client and therefore the partnership cannot be said to accept any liability for the actions of an individual partner who acts dishonestly. Therefore Amhurst Brown could not be liable as a trustee de son tort in relation to Mr Amhurst's actions because it had never accepted any liability for Mr Amhurst acting outside the scope of his fiduciary duties.

30.41 However, it is suggested that Lord Millett's approach overlooks the broader explanation of this liability in *Barnes v Addy*[117] given by Lord Selborne to the effect that the defendant would be liable not only for rendering herself a trustee de son tort but also by 'actually participating in the fraudulent conduct of the trustee to the injury of the *cestui que trust*'[118] in committing a breach of trust. Therefore, the history of this claim has been predicated on a form of constructive trusteeship which

---

110 cf *In re Bell's Indenture* [1980] 1 WLR 1217, 1230, *per* Vinelott J.
111 *Brydges v Branfill* (1842) 12 Sim 369.
112 *Credit Lyonnais Bank Nederland NV v Export Credits Guarantee Department* [2000] 1 AC 486.
113 [1896] 1 Ch 199.
114 *Paragon Finance plc v DB Thakerar & Co* [1999] 1 All ER 400, 408; *Coulthard v Disco Mix Club Ltd* [2000] 1 WLR 707, 731.
115 [2002] 3 WLR 1913, [2003] 1 All ER 97, paras 135 and 138. Cf *Taylor v Davies* [1920] AC 636; *Clarkson v Davies* [1923] AC 100, 110.
116 *Taylor v Davies* [1920] AC 636, 651, *per* Viscount Cave.
117 (1873–74) LR 9 Ch App 244.   118 ibid 251.

undoubtedly involves assistance in a breach of trust, or where the strangers 'assist with knowledge in a dishonest and fraudulent design on the part of the trustees',[119] and not control of the trust by the defendant. The whole purpose of the dishonest assistance claim is that it is imposed on the defendant due to his wrongdoing and not due to his acceptance of liability as such: in this regard, Lord Millett's comments must be taken to relate solely to the partnership aspects of the case before him. The correct approach to this remedy is that the wrongdoing dishonest assistant in made 'accountable in equity' for the loss which her dishonesty has caused to the beneficiaries.[120]

Dishonesty and negligence

Lord Nicholls recognized the thin line between dishonest assistance and negligence in *Royal Brunei Airlines v Tan*[121] particularly in contexts in which the trustees are professionals, tendering their services under contract. In such a situation it is possible that the same person might be liable for breach of contract, for breach of a duty of care (ie the tort of negligence), and for breach of trust in a situation in which there has been a breach of a trust. However, the liability in equity rests on the dishonesty of the assistant and it is not enough that they have been negligent or that they have breached a contract. Given what has been said thus far in this section, it is still somewhat surprising that in *Twinsectra Ltd v Yardley*[122] a solicitor is able to contend that he did not consider his actions to be dishonest even though those actions constituted a breach of trust and a breach of the original solicitor's undertaking. There is only a narrow line here between common law negligence and dishonesty sufficient to found liability for an equitable wrong. The solicitor would appear to have been negligent in considering that paying money to Yardley which was only to have been used for the purpose of acquiring good title in property was something which could have been done lawfully. Potentially, Leach's liability at common law might also have been a tortious procuring of a breach of Sims's undertaking to Twinsectra. The jump to liability for dishonest assistance is a significant one. One might have thought that the professional nature of a solicitor's role and the reliance placed by Twinsectra on the undertakings given to it by the solicitor Sims might have raised the presumption that an honest person would have expected a solicitor in Leach's position to consider properly the nature of his obligations both to his client, Yardley, and to the lender, Twinsectra, who had paid the loan moneys into trust subject to a solicitor's undertaking. The solicitor, Leach, is considered by the House of Lords to be entitled to restrict his liability to common law claims in tort on the basis that his own lack of

30.42

---

[119] ibid 252.

[120] *Selangor United Rubber Estates Ltd v Cradock (No 3)* [1968] 1 WLR 1555, 1582, *per* Ungoed-Thomas J.

[121] [1995] 3 All ER 95, 108.   [122] [2002] 2 All ER 377.

diligence as a solicitor failed to bring to his conscious mind the self-evident fact that if he paid the money to Yardley he would be breaching the fiduciary obligations originally owed by Sims to Twinsectra. This is particularly so given that those fiduciary obligations could be said to have been passed to him when he assumed Sims's role as Yardley's solicitor. The exculpation of liability on Leach, it is suggested, weakens markedly the nature of a solicitor's fiduciary duties and also returns us to that form of thinking so evident in cases like *Armitage v Nurse*[123] whereby trustees are ever more capable of reducing their liabilities as trustees by reference to contractual exemption clauses, or the terms of their retainers, or (it appears) their own ignorance of their responsibilities in professional transactions.

Risk as dishonesty

30.43 Lord Nicholls expanded his discussion of 'dishonesty' to consider the taking of risk. Risk is expressly encompassed within the new test. Lord Nicholls held:

> All investment involves risk. Imprudence is not dishonesty, although imprudence may be carried recklessly to lengths which call into question the honesty of the person making the decision. This is especially so if the transaction serves another purpose in which that person has an interest of his own.[124]

Therefore, an investment adviser who is employed by the trust could be liable for 'dishonesty' if she advises the trust to take a risk which is considered by the court to have been a reckless risk. The thinking is that, if X advises the trustees to take a risk which is objectively too great, then X could be considered to have been dishonest in giving that advice. The basis of liability is that a third party 'takes a risk that a clearly unauthorised transaction will not cause loss . . . If the risk materialises and causes loss, those who knowingly took the risk will be accountable accordingly.'[125] For these purposes it is said that 'fraud includes taking a risk to the prejudice of another's rights, which risk is known to be one which there is no right to take'.[126] Therefore, there is enormous potential liability in respect of advisers who advise trustees in any matter to do with the investment or other management of their property.

30.44 There is a difference in principle where there is doubt whether the risk is authorized or not. In situations where an investment adviser retained by the trustees is unsure whether or not an investment is encompassed by the investment powers of the trust, the issue arises whether or not the investment adviser is acting dishonestly. The question is then how to deal with matters of degree relating to the authority of trustees and third parties. In Lord Nicholls's opinion, it will be obvious in most cases whether or not a proposed transaction would offend the normal

---

[123] [1998] Ch 241; para 21.2.4.   [124] *Royal Brunei Airlines v Tan* [1995] 2 AC 378, 387.
[125] *Royal Brunei Airlines v Tan* [1995] 2 AC 378, 387.
[126] *Royal Brunei Airlines v Tan* [1995] 2 AC 378, 387.

standards of honest conduct. It is suggested that this does not help us towards an understanding of how far this new test for dishonesty extends. The discussion of the potential liability of professional advisers in relation to commercial transactions is considered in Chapter 49, where it is suggested that regulatory norms governing, for example, the responsibilities of providers of financial services could be interpolated into a consideration of the appropriate level of risk in any particular context.[127] Similarly, it does not help us to understand how a test for dishonesty is necessarily more certain than a test based on unconscionability, such as that suggested by Lord Browne-Wilkinson in *Westdeutsche Landesbank v Islington*.[128]

It is not a failure to ascertain whether or not the investment is in breach of trust **30.45** which is decisive of the matter, but rather whether or not the *level of risk* assumed is in breach of trust. His lordship tells us that '. . . honesty is an objective standard'. Therefore it is for the court to measure the level of risk and, consequently, to assess the honesty of the stranger. The outcome would seem to depend upon 'the circumstances known to the third party at the time', which necessarily imports a subjective element. However, recklessness as to the ability of the trust to invest must similarly be a factor to be taken into account in deciding on the honesty of the third party investment manager.

Lord Nicholls's position could be criticized on the basis that it does not accom- **30.46** modate the situation in which the investment decision being made is in itself risky. An investment decision taken to achieve the best return for the trust will necessarily involve a higher level of risk than an investment which restricts its exposure to a risk level and a rate of return which is below the market average. There is no obvious distinction in financial terms here between a risky investment which is authorized and an equally risky investment which is probably unauthorized, although the distinction in terms of the resulting breach of trust is self-evident. Reference in general terms, as considered in Chapter 47, could be had to the regulatory norms governing the suitability of any investment for any given class of client in deciding the appropriate level of risk to be taken.

The test for dishonesty thus expresses a level of risk which the court considers to **30.47** be too great. Therefore, an accessory may be liable where the risk taken was in furtherance of a contractual obligation to invest property and to manage its level of risk. The court might consider that risk to be too great, whereas the market might consider a particular investment to be standard practice and even advisable in many circumstances: nevertheless, a court may decide subsequently that the very fact that such an investment caused a large loss meant that the risk posed by that investment must have been too great even though it was standard market practice at the time it was made. Alternatively, by comparison with *Nestle v National*

---

[127] See para 49.03. [128] [1996] AC 669.

Westminster Bank plc,[129] the investment manager may be able to defend its actions on the basis that its actions were reasonable, as evidenced by their use as standard market practice. The better of these two approaches would depend upon the extent to which the market could be demonstrated to have adopted this investment strategy, the size of the market place which employed that tactic, and the reasonableness of that market practice in the context of the particular client. As considered in Chapter 47, the Financial Services Authority's Conduct of Business Regulations require that the investment be suitable for the client in question in the context.[130]

No general principle of unconscionability

30.48 It does appear that the range of matters brought within the ambit of dishonest assistance (including dishonesty, recklessness, inappropriate risk taking, and fraud) points towards the creation of a general test of unconscionability, despite Lord Nicholls's express assertion that this was not the case. The example of an investment adviser who is 'dishonest' on this technical meaning, while only actually being reckless as to the form of the investment, could be described as acting unconscionably, given the nature of his client. The test for 'dishonesty' that covers such a context, to use Lord Nicholls's own words, 'means something different' from the natural use of 'dishonesty'. A better approach, it is suggested, would be to admit that the test is really one of unconscionability and thus to bring the issue back within the more formal ambit of constructive trusts as defined by Lord Browne-Wilkinson in *Westdeutsche Landesbank v Islington.*[131]

The corporate context of dishonest assistance

30.49 The use of companies to organize business activity creates a distinction between, on the one hand, the individuals who are employed by companies and partnerships to give advice to clients such as trustees and, on the other hand, the company which employs them as a distinct person or the partners who employ them. So, if property is taken from the trust fund in breach of trust by virtue of being invested in financial instruments which are forbidden to the trustees and is paid to the company which employs the individual investment adviser who procured those investments for the trust, then the company may be liable under a tracing claim to recover the property used to acquire the investments or under a personal liability connected to the receipt of that property but the individual investment adviser will not be so liable because such a person would not receive that property personally. It is suggested that this form of liability will be imposed on any individual employee in relation to any fiduciary relationship in which he gives investment or other advice. Liability for dishonest assistance would make such an investment

---

[129] [1993] 1 WLR 1260.   [130] See para 47.03.   [131] [1996] AC 669.

adviser personally liable for his participation in the breach of trust without needing to have taken any direct benefit from the transaction. The individual investment adviser is then held liable to account to the beneficiaries for any loss suffered if he has been dishonest, in the manner considered above. That the individual adviser receives a commission or other profit from the transaction which comprised the breach of trust would increase the likelihood of his being proved to have acted dishonestly.[132] The company which employs the adviser would only be fixed with any knowledge or dishonesty of the adviser if the adviser were a controlling mind of the company.[133] This issue is considered further in Chapter 47.[134]

Liability of investment advisers

The development of the law on dishonest assistance has ramifications for invest- **30.50**
ment advisers. The separateness of the stranger's liability from that of the trustee means that the investment adviser can be personally liable to account to the beneficiaries for any assistance in a breach of trust. The extent of the adviser's liability is for all of the loss suffered without the need to recover or prove liability against the trustee beyond the breach of trust itself. The extension of the concept of dishonesty beyond active deceit into failing to act as an honest person would have acted, or advising that the trust take risks with investments which are subsequently defined as having been reckless, has the effect that the investment adviser may be liable for such loss for failing to act as other people would have expected them to act. The most straightforward expression of the behaviour which would be expected of an honest person giving investment advice, it is suggested, is found in the Financial Services Authority's rulebooks, as considered in Chapter 47.[135] These regulations express the manner in which an investment adviser is required to conduct investment business of various types with expert and inexpert clients. As such they give a clear indication of what level of behaviour would be expected of a reasonable banker, fund manager, or other investment adviser. These issues are considered further in Chapters 47 and 52.

The nature of the claimant's remedy

The defendant is liable to account for the entire loss suffered by the beneficiaries **30.51**
as though an express trustee. There remains the possibility of the court deciding that the defendant was only liable in part for the loss suffered by the beneficiaries and therefore that she would be liable only for the loss which could be said to have been caused by the defendant's act. It is suggested that an equitable remedy

---

[132] *Royal Brunei Airlines v Tan* [1995] 2 AC 378.
[133] *Tesco Supermarkets v Nattrass* [1972] AC 153.   [134] See para 47.09.
[135] See, for example, the use to which the Bank of England London Code was put by the High Court when deciding the level of probity required of bankers when dealing with inexpert clients in *Bankers Trust v Dharmala* [1996] CLC 518.

of liability to account should permit a flexible obligation on the part of the defendant to account for the extent to which the defendant is culpable for the loss. This would be broadly in line with the remedy for a person who was expressly appointed as a trustee for whom there is only liability where there is some causal connection between the breach of trust and the loss.[136]

Defences

Concurrence and acquiescence by the beneficiaries in the breach of trust

30.52   Once a beneficiary concurs in a breach of trust, or acquiesces in a breach of trust, that beneficiary is estopped from seeking to recover compensation for that breach of trust from any trustees to whom that concurrence was proffered.[137] That one or more of the beneficiaries instigates the breach of trust does not necessarily mean that any such beneficiary is obliged to indemnify the trustees who acted on those beneficiaries' instigation.[138] The principles have been explained in the following manner:[139]

> The . . . court has to consider all the circumstances in which the concurrence of the ces-tui qui trust was given with a view to seeing whether it is fair and equitable that, having given his concurrence, he should afterwards turn round and sue the trustees; . . . subject to this, it is not necessary that he should know that what he is concurring in is a breach of trust, provided that he fully understand what he is concurring in, and . . . it is not necessary that he should himself have directly benefited by the breach of trust.

Therefore, the most significant, underlying factor is the fairness and equity in the beneficiary bringing an action for compensation for breach of trust. In essence, one cannot have known of and agreed to something in relation to which one subsequently seeks to recover compensation.

Release

30.53   In circumstances in which the beneficiaries agree formally to release the stranger from any liability then the equitable doctrine of release will operate so as to protect that stranger from any liability arising from her involvement in the breach of trust.[140] Nevertheless the beneficiaries may seek equitable relief in respect of any

---

[136]   *Target Holdings v Redferns* [1996] 1 AC 421.

[137]   *White v White* (1798–1804) 5 Ves Jr 554; *Evans v Benyon* (1888) 37 Ch D 329; *Re Pauling's Settlement Trusts* [1964] Ch 303, 335, [1962] 1 WLR 86, 106. Cf *Chillingworth v Chambers* [1896] 1 Ch 685.

[138]   *Raby v Ridehalgh* (1855) 7 De GM & G 104; *Butler v Butler* (1877) 7 Ch D, affirming (1877) 5 Ch D 554; *Sawyer v Sawyer* (1883) 28 Ch D 595; *Bolton v Curre* [1895] 1 Ch 544; *Chillingworth v Chambers* [1896] 1 Ch 685; *Fletcher v Collis* [1905] 2 Ch 24.

[139]   *Re Pauling's Settlement Trusts* [1962] 1 WLR 86, 108, *per* Wilberforce J. See also *Re Garnett* (1885) 31 Ch D 1, a case dealing with release but adopted for this purpose; and *Holder v Holder* [1968] Ch 353, *Re Freeston's Charity* [1978] Ch 741, relating specifically to acquiescence. See further *Spellson v George* (1992) 26 NSWLR 666.

[140]   *Lyall v Edwards* (1861) 6 H & N 337, 158 ER 139; *Ecclesiastical Commissioners for England v North Eastern Rly Co* (1877) 4 Ch D 845; *Turner v Turner* (1880) 14 Ch D 829.

factor which was not made known to them at the time of granting the release or which arises outside the terms of that release.[141]

E. Knowing Receipt

The foundations of personal liability to account as a constructive trustee for knowing receipt of property in breach of trust

The category of personal liability to account on grounds of knowing receipt of trust **30.54** property concerns strangers who receive some trust property when that property has been transferred away in breach of trust. This doctrine has been described as a receipt-based claim analogous to equitable compensation.[142] Where a person receives trust property in the knowledge that that property has been passed in breach of trust or otherwise misapplied, then the recipient will be personally liable to account to the trust for the value of the property passed away. It is a defence to demonstrate that the receipt was authorized by the terms of the trust or that the recipient has lawfully changed his position in reliance on the receipt of the property. It is incumbent on the claimant to demonstrate that the defendant had the requisite knowledge.[143] Whether or not there has been a receipt of property will generally be decided in accordance with the rules for tracing claims, as considered below.[144]

That there must have been a breach of trust

There must have been a breach of trust before the stranger will bear liability for **30.55** knowing receipt of property passed out of the trust fund.[145] If the property had been passed from the trust to the stranger within the terms of the trust then no liability could lie. This issue was considered above in relation to dishonest assistance and it is suggested that the same considerations apply in this context.[146]

The defendant must have received trust property in breach of trust

The nature of 'receipt'

The first question is what actions will constitute 'receipt' in this context. In the **30.56** decision of Millett J in *Agip v Jackson*,[147] his lordship held that:

---

[141] *BCCI v Ali* [2000] 3 All ER 51.

[142] *El Ajou v Dollar Land Holdings* [1993] 3 All ER 717; appealed [1994] 2 All ER 685.

[143] *Polly Peck International v Nadir (No 2)* [1992] 4 All ER 769, 777, *per* Scott LJ.

[144] *El Ajou v Dollar Land Holdings* [1993] BCLC 735 and below in Chapter 33.

[145] *Eagle Trust plc v SBC Securities Ltd* [1992] 4 All ER 488; *El Ajou v Dollar Land Holdings* [1994] 1 BCLC 464, 478, *per* Hoffmann J; *Brown v Bennett* [1998] EWCA Civ 1881.

[146] See para 30.19.

[147] *Agip v Jackson* [1990] Ch 265, 286, *per* Millett J; CA [1991] Ch 547.

... there is receipt of trust property when a company's funds are misapplied by any person whose fiduciary position gave him control of them or enabled him to misapply them.

Therefore anyone who has control of trust property or who takes it into his possession such that it could be misapplied will have received that property. Nevertheless, the cases are not precise in defining the manner in which the property must be 'received'. Seemingly, it is enough that the property passes through the stranger's hands, even if the stranger never acquires the rights of an equitable or common law owner of that property. For example, a bank through which payments are made appears to be capable of being accountable for knowing receipt of money paid in breach of trust, even though it did not have any rights of ownership over that money.[148] Receipt therefore is a question of possession and of control, but not one of ownership. The key feature establishing liability will therefore be the receipt of that property with knowledge that there has been some breach of trust: that is, the fact of receipt is comparatively easy to demonstrate in theory, whereas the mental element of knowledge is the more contested notion.

Receipt of money by banks when paid into bank accounts

30.57 There is a question as to whether or not a bank receives money which is paid into a bank account operated by that bank. In circumstances in which X Bank allows a cheque drawn on a trust account in breach of that trust to be paid to a third party's account held by X Bank, the bank may be liable for dishonest assistance if it can be demonstrated that its officers failed to act as an honest banker would have acted in relation to those funds. The bank would not, however, have received those moneys because the money would still be credited to the account of one of its clients, that is another person from the bank itself. By contrast, if that third party's account was overdrawn, then the credit of the cheque would make the bank potentially liable for knowing receipt where the funds are used to reduce the overdraft because in the latter instance the bank itself receives the money in discharge of the overdraft loan. Similarly, where the bank charges any fees in connection with the transfer, it will receive those sums if they are paid out of the money which belonged formerly to the trust.[149] So, in *Polly Peck International v Nadir (No 2)*, Scott LJ held that a bank was liable only for dishonest assistance because it had acted only as banker and could not have been considered in that instance to have 'received' funds paid into a bank account operated by it.[150] The risk for the bank is that a remedy based on dishonest assistance will require the bank to pay over funds which it has never received in the manner considered earlier in this chapter.

---

[148] *Polly Peck International v Nadir (No 2)* [1992] 4 All ER 769.   [149] See *Oakley* 186 *et seq*.
[150] *Polly Peck International v Nadir (No 2)* [1992] 4 All ER 769.

Trust property

It is required that the property which is received is property which was held subject **30.58** to a trust. It is suggested, furthermore, that property held under some other fiduciary relationship, whereby the legal owner of that property owed fiduciary duties to other people in relation to the use of that property, may also found liability for knowing receipt.[151] Therefore, the transfer of partnership property, or of property held subject to an agency agreement, or of company property by a director of that company, could found liability for knowing receipt.

The defendant must have had knowledge of the breach of trust

The nature of 'knowledge' in this sense

The second fundamental question which arises in relation to claims for knowing **30.59** receipt is what constitutes 'knowledge' in this context. As Lord Browne-Wilkinson held in *Westdeutsche Landesbank v Islington*:

> If X has the necessary degree of knowledge, X may himself become a constructive trustee for B on the basis of knowing receipt.[152] But unless he has the requisite degree of knowledge he is not personally liable to account as trustee.[153] Therefore, innocent receipt of property by X subject to an existing equitable interest does not by itself make X a trustee despite the severance of the legal and equitable titles.[154]

The key to liability for knowing receipt is that the defendant has acted wrongfully by receiving property with the requisite knowledge as to the breach of trust which led to his possession of the property.[155]

The three categories of knowledge

It is important to note that the test in this context is one of 'knowledge' and not **30.60** 'notice'. Rather than depend on the imputed notice as used in conveyancing law or in relation to undue influence, the courts have focused instead on whether or not the defendant has knowledge of material factors. If the defendant is to be fixed with personal liability to account, then it is thought that the defendant must be demonstrated to *know* those factors which will attach liability to her. The further question, however, is what a person can be taken to 'know'. The most significant judicial exposition of the various categories of knowledge was set out by

---

[151] As was contended impliedly, for example, in *Agip v Jackson* [1990] Ch 265, 286, *per* Millett J, [1991] Ch 547, CA; and *El Ajou v Dollar Land Holdings* [1993] 3 All ER 717 in relation to property not held on trust but rather subject initially to other fiduciary obligations.

[152] [1996] AC 669.

[153] *Re Diplock* [1948] Ch 465 and *Re Montagu's Settlement Trusts* [1987] Ch 264.

[154] [1996] 2 All ER 961, 990.

[155] The act is said to be wrongful in this context because the receipt of the property must have been knowing—or, under cases considered below, unconscionable or dishonest—and therefore has bound up with it the wrongful retention of the property and/or failure to return or account for that property to the trust.

Peter Gibson J in *Baden v Société Generale*[156] as follows: first, actual knowledge; secondly, wilfully shutting one's eyes to the obvious; thirdly, wilfully and recklessly failing to make inquiries which an honest person would have made; fourthly, knowledge of circumstances which would indicate the facts to an honest and reasonable man; and fifthly, knowledge of circumstances which would put an honest and reasonable man on inquiry. The fourth and fifth categories are the most interesting given that they are potentially the broadest. The first three categories of knowledge are taken to indicate forms of actual knowledge and very similar knowledge of the circumstances.[157] The actual knowledge categories encompass situations in which the defendant knew the material facts, regardless of whether or not he tried to ignore them. The last two are indicators of constructive notice.[158]

30.61 The five categories of knowledge set out in *Baden v Société Generale* were whittled down to the first three for the purposes of liability for knowing receipt by Megarry J in *Re Montagu*.[159] Those three are therefore as follows: actual knowledge; wilfully shutting one's eyes to the obvious; and wilfully and recklessly failing to make inquiries which an honest person would have made. The reason for this restriction was that these three forms of knowledge necessarily included an element of wilful or deliberate behaviour on the part of the defendant who cannot be proved to have actually known of the facts which were alleged.[160] As Scott LJ held in *Polly Peck*, these categories are not to be taken as rigid rules and 'one category may merge imperceptibly into another'.[161] Professor Hayton has rendered these three categories of knowledge slightly more memorably as actual knowledge, 'Nelsonian knowledge',[162] and 'naughty knowledge' respectively.[163] As Lord Browne-Wilkinson held in *Westdeutsche Landesbank v Islington*:

---

[156] [1993] 1 WLR 509.

[157] cf *White v White* [2001] 3 WLR 1571—'knowledge' in relation to knowledge as to whether or not a vehicle was uninsured.

[158] *Agip v Jackson* [1989] 3 WLR 1367, 1389, *per* Millett J.   [159] [1987] Ch 264.

[160] See, for example, *Papamichael v National Westminster Bank plc* [2003] EWHC 164 (Comm) in which case the claimant had won a large amount of money on the Greek national lottery. The claimant's husband, however, transferred that money from the couple's joint bank account to a foreign exchange trading account which the husband had created with an officer of the defendant bank. It was found on the facts that the bank officer had constructive knowledge of the source of the money and of the claimant's lack of consent to its transfer to the trading account. It was found that the bank officer and the bank itself, more significantly for the purposes of satisfying the claim, had knowingly received that money in breach of the husband's duties to his wife under that joint bank account.

[161] *Polly Peck International v Nadir (No 2)* [1992] 4 All ER 769.

[162] Although see *Twinsectra Ltd v Yardley* [2002] 2 All ER 377, 383, *per* Lord Hoffmann, criticizing the image which this nomenclature summons up of Admiral Nelson at Copenhagen.

[163] A Underhill and DJ Hayton, *Law of Trusts and Trustees* (16th edn, Butterworths, 2002) ('*Underhill and Hayton*') 974.

If X has the necessary degree of knowledge, X may himself become a constructive trustee for B on the basis of knowing receipt. But unless he has the requisite degree of knowledge he is not personally liable to account as trustee: *Re Diplock*[164] and *Re Montagu's Settlement Trusts*.[165] Therefore, innocent receipt of property by X subject to an existing equitable interest does not by itself make X a trustee despite the severance of the legal and equitable titles.[166]

Therefore, the defendant will be liable only if he has the requisite degree of knowledge disclosing a level of wilfulness if there is no proof of actual knowledge. Innocent receipt of property will not attract any liability on the basis that such carelessness would not suggest that want of probity necessary for the imposition of liability for knowing receipt of property in breach of trust.[167]

On the cases decided before *Royal Brunei Airlines v Tan* in relation to dishonest **30.62** assistance,[168] the primary distinction between knowing receipt and dishonest assistance was that dishonest assistance required that there be some fraud in the misapplication of trust funds.[169] The primary difference between dishonest assistance and knowing receipt since *Royal Brunei Airlines v Tan* is the introduction of a radical distinction between a test for dishonesty and a test for knowledge respectively.

Identifying the inquiries which an honest or reasonable defendant should have made

The courts have not tended to apply the *Baden* categories of knowledge slavishly **30.63** as though they were a strict test. Much of the reason for that, it is suggested, lies in the nature of the litigation. It would be a rare event for the parties to go to court if there were evidence of actual knowledge, perhaps in the form of letters or memoranda of meetings in which the information was divulged expressly. In other circumstances, then, the court's principal task is to establish on the facts whether or not the defendant could be deemed to have had sufficient knowledge of material facts. For example, in relation to the third category of knowledge—that one should have wilfully and recklessly failed to make the inquiries which a reasonable person would have made—it may be a difficult matter to identify what further questions or investigations would have been appropriate. In the event that appropriate inquiries were not made, the defendant is likely to be fixed with knowledge, in effect, by default of action rather than by reference to having knowledge.

The establishment of this type of constructive knowledge is best explained by Scott LJ in *Polly Peck International v Nadir (No 2)*[170] when his lordship held that the acid test was whether or not the defendant 'ought to have been suspicious' that trust

---

[164] [1948] Ch 465. [165] [1987] Ch 264. [166] [1996] 2 All ER 961, 990.
[167] *Re Montagu's Settlement* [1987] Ch 264.
[168] *Royal Brunei Airlines v Tan* [1995] 2 AC 378.
[169] See Vinelott J in *Eagle Trust plc v SBC Securities Ltd* [1992] 4 All ER 488, 499; Scott LJ in *Polly Peck International v Nadir (No 2)* [1992] 4 All ER 769, 777. [170] ibid.

property was being misapplied.[171] As considered below,[172] that case concerned the potential liability of a central bank. The bank was not deemed to have had the appropriate knowledge because the payments which passed through its hands were nothing out of the ordinary for a central bank. That is, there was nothing which should have caused the officers of the bank to have made any inquiries. Similarly, in *Macmillan v Bishopsgate*,[173] in the wake of collapse of Robert Maxwell's companies, the question arose whether or not the officers of a bank through which a company's money was passed should have been taken to have had sufficient knowledge of the breaches of trust which had caused the moneys to come to the bank. In the court's view, account officers should not be required to be detectives, with the consequence that such account officers are not obliged to inquire into the detail of otherwise unremarkable transactions, and therefore those account officers were not to be fixed with knowledge which they could only possibly have had if they had carried out extensive investigations in a situation in which they had no reason to believe that there had been any impropriety. It was held instead that those account officers were 'entitled to believe that they were dealing with honest men' unless they had some suspicion raised in their minds to the contrary. In *El Ajou v Dollar Land Holdings*,[174] Millett J held that liability for knowing receipt would attach 'in a situation in which any honest and reasonable man would have made inquiry'. In short, the issue is whether or not the circumstances would necessitate a person to be suspicious, such that their conscience would encourage them to make inquiries.

Whether a complex corporate person should be taken to have knowledge of a customer's breach of trust

30.64 Demonstrating that an individual did or did not have knowledge is a matter which can be comfortably left to trial court on examination of the appropriate witnesses, once the question 'what is meant by knowledge?' has been resolved adequately. A more difficult problem arises, however, when the claimant wishes to recover his loss from a corporation by contending that the knowledge of some individual should be attributed to that company on the basis, most frequently, that that individual was an employee of the company in question. In general terms a company will be taken to have had knowledge of some factor if it was reasonable for it to be taken to have had that knowledge, for example on the basis that the transaction in which the knowledge was acquired was one in which the company would typically be expected to have acquired that knowledge.[175] Nevertheless, as considered in the next section,[176]

---

[171] *Eagle Trust v SBC (No 2)* [1996] 1 BCLC 121; *Hillsdown plc v Pensions Ombudsman* [1997] 1 All ER 862.

[172] In detail in the following paragraph.

[173] [1996] 1 WLR 387. See also *United Mizrahi Bank Ltd v Doherty* [1998] 1 WLR 435; *Bank of Scotland v A Ltd,* The Times, 6 February 2001.

[174] *El Ajou v Dollar Land Holdings* [1993] 3 All ER 717; appealed [1994] 2 All ER 685.

[175] *Cowan de Groot Properties Ltd v Eagle Trust* [1992] 4 All ER 700.   [176] Para 30.66.

the problem remains that ordinary company law attributes knowledge to a company only when some controlling mind of that company can be demonstrated to have had the appropriate level of knowledge. In relation to large companies with many employees conducting many different types of tasks it may be that a large amount of important knowledge and a large number of very significant transactions are conducted without, for example, the board of directors acquiring actual knowledge of any of the detail of those activities. It would be a reprehensible gap in the law, however, if companies could avoid liability for actions carried out by its officers simply because the detail of the circumstances of those actions could not be demonstrated to have come to the actual knowledge of the company's executive decision-making body. Consequently, a better approach is to consider the nature of the company involved, whether or not that type of company is subject to any formal regulation or other legal requirements as to the supervision of its staff and of their dealings with third parties, and whether or not the circumstances are such that the company ought to be fixed with the knowledge of any of its officers.

The case of *Polly Peck International v Nadir (No 2)*[177] is a useful illustration of this sort of problem. The facts related to the actions of Asil Nadir in respect of the insolvency of the Polly Peck group of companies. This particular litigation referred to a claim brought by the administrators of the plaintiff company against a bank controlled by Nadir, by the name of IBK, and the Central Bank of Northern Cyprus. It was alleged that Nadir had been responsible for the misapplication of substantial funds in sterling which were the assets of the plaintiff company. It was claimed that the Central Bank ought exchanged the sterling amounts for Turkish lire either with actual knowledge of fraud on the plaintiff company or in circumstances in which the Central Bank ought to have been put on inquiry as to the source of those funds. The plaintiff claimed against the Central Bank personal liability to account as a constructive trustee as a result of knowing receipt of the sterling amounts which had been exchanged for lire. The Central Bank contended that it had no such knowledge, actual or constructive, of the source of the funds. It was argued on behalf of the Central Bank that large amounts of money passed through its systems as would be expected in relation to a central bank on a regular basis and that as such it should not be on notice as to the source of even large amounts of money.

The Court of Appeal held that there was no requirement to prove a fraudulent misapplication of funds to found a claim on knowing receipt. It was enough to demonstrate that the recipient had the requisite knowledge both that the funds were trust funds and that they were being misapplied.[178] On the facts of this case

---

[177] [1992] 4 All ER 769.

[178] An approach which was also taken by Vinelott J in *Eagle Trust plc v SBC Securities Ltd* [1992] 4 All ER 488, applying dicta of Stirling J in *Re Blundell, Blundell v Blundell* [1889–90] All ER Rep 837, 842 and of Lord Herschell LC in *Thomson v Clydesdale Bank Ltd* [1893] AC 282, 287.

it was held that the simple fact that the plaintiff company was exchanging amounts of money between sterling and lire via IBK was not enough to have put it on suspicion that there had been a breach of trust. In deciding whether or not the Central Bank ought to have been suspicious, Scott LJ preferred to approach the matter from the point of view of the 'honest and reasonable banker'[179] although he did express some reservations that this was not necessarily the only test.[180] It does appear, however, that the reasonableness of the recipient's belief falls to be judged from the perspective of the recipient itself. On the facts, it was held that there was no reason for suspicion because large amounts of money passed through the Central Bank's accounts regularly and there was nothing at the time of this transaction to cause the bank to be suspicious of this particular transaction.[181]

30.65 The context will therefore be significant in deciding the inquiries which an honest or reasonable person would have made or whether or not the defendant has wilfully turned a blind eye to the circumstances. In relation to financial institutions, such as banks or other providers of financial services, it is suggested that regard should be had to the applicable financial regulation. With regard to the spectre of money laundering, for example, whether by terrorist organizations, drug dealers, or others, the appropriate regulations require financial institutions to conduct due diligence as to the identity of their clients and the source of payments into new accounts which is dubbed 'know your client' regulation.[182] The minimum requirements of these regulations should be taken to inform the minimum standards expected of a reasonable banker in situations such as that in *Polly Peck International v Nadir (No 2)* and *Macmillan v Bishopsgate*. In consequence, it is possible to identify with some certainty and justification the inquiries which an honest and reasonable banker should have taken into account, or the matters to which such a person could not have failed to have had regard. In situations in which a financial institution had no actual knowledge of any breach of duty and in which it would not have been expected by applicable regulatory principles to have such knowledge, there will be no liability as a constructive trustee.[183] In relation to other markets which do not have such regulations, it is a more complex matter to identify those principles with regard to which a reasonable participant in such a market ought to behave. In many such situations, as in the banking context,[184] these regulations conflict with ordinary duties of confidentiality owed to customers. These matters are considered in greater detail in Chapter 47.

---

[179] [1992] 3 All ER 769, 778–780; *Finers v Miro* [1991] 1 WLR 35.   [180] ibid 778.
[181] See also *Allen v Rea Brothers Trustees Ltd* (2002) 4 ITELR 627.
[182] See, for example, W Blair and others, *Banking and Financial Services Regulation* (3rd edn, Butterworths, 2002) 282.
[183] *Britannic Asset Management v Pensions Ombudsman* [2002] EWCA 441 (Admin).
[184] *Tournier v National Provincial and Union Bank of England* [1924] 1 KB 461, CA.

Attributing the knowledge of any individual employee or a linked company to a defendant company

When considering the liability of companies for knowing receipt of property in breach of trust, there is the self-evident problem of deciding whether or not the company could be said to have knowledge of the breach of trust which one of its employees has attributed to the company generally. The classic statement of the difficulty in fixing a company with the knowledge possessed by any of its officers was set out by Lord Reid in *Tesco Supermarkets Ltd v Nattrass*[185] in the following terms: **30.66**

> A living person has a mind which can have knowledge or intention or be negligent and he has hands to carry out his intentions. A corporation has none of these: it must act through living persons, though not always one or the same person. Then the person who acts is not speaking or acting for the company. He is acting as the company and his mind which directs his acts is the mind of the company.

The issue, therefore, is as to the seniority or influence of the person who has the requisite knowledge of the breach of trust so as to fix the company with that same knowledge and make it liable to account to the beneficiaries of that trust relationship. If the person with the knowledge is a junior employee acting outside the limits of his authority, then the company might not be fixed with his knowledge. This analysis is particularly likely if the company is a large, public company which employs a large number of people in the same position as the person with the knowledge of the breach of trust, such that it might be considered unreasonable for the company to be held responsible for the oversight of the actions of each individual. By contrast, if the company is a small company in which its managing director is also the majority shareholder and the person who conducts the majority of the company's business, then if that managing director has knowledge of something it is likely that his knowledge will be attributed to the company as a whole. So, in *Tesco v Nattrass* itself, an individual branch of a supermarket chain committed an offence under the trades description legislation but the fault involved was found to be the fault of the manager of that particular branch, who was a junior manager within the scope of that supermarket company with branches nationwide, and so not a fault which was attributable to the company. It is only if specific regulation imposes an obligation on a company to oversee the actions of even its junior employees that such a company could be held to have knowledge of those junior employees attributed to the company in general: in relation to financial regulation, see Chapter 47 generally. Similarly, further to the principle in *Prudential Assurance v Newman (No 2)*[186] that a minority shareholder may displace the rule in *Foss v Harbottle*[187] to the effect that a decision of the majority of shareholders may be set aside if it had been oppressive of the minority,

---

[185] [1972] AC 153, [1971] 2 All ER 127.   [186] [1982] Ch 204.   [187] (1843) 2 Hare 461.

if someone who procures the oppression of minority shareholders in a way which causes the directors to breach their fiduciary duties, then that procurer shall be liable for knowing receipt or dishonest assistance as appropriate.[188]

The discussion of *Polly Peck International plc v Nadir*[189] in the previous section suggested that a corporate entity will not be taken to have had knowledge of something if it can demonstrate that it had acted reasonably and if there was nothing about the circumstances which should have caused that corporation to have been suspicious. So, where the controlling mind of a group of companies knew that the hazelnuts received into its warehouses had been passed there in breach of trust then that knowledge would be attributed to all of those companies.[190] If, however, the circumstances had been different and, for example, it could have been demonstrated to the judge's satisfaction that a bank officer had known that the source of funds was a woman whose husband had taken that money out of a bank account held jointly with his wife and used the money to open a foreign exchange trading account with the defendant bank, then the dishonesty of the bank's officer will be attributed to the bank.[191] As is considered in the following paragraph, there is a difficulty here with attributing the knowledge of an individual, dishonest employee to the senior management of a complex organization like a commercial or investment bank such that it could be proved that the 'controlling mind' of the corporation shared that dishonesty. However, it would be a greater evil to suggest that a bank, for example, could escape liability for the acts of a dishonest employee so that the bank's clients bear the risk of an employee of the bank stealing their money without any recourse against the bank itself. Consequently, it is suggested, that the bank should be attributed with any knowledge or dishonesty that attaches to any employee who comes into contact with client money in the ordinary course of his duties or who could be expected to be able to come into contact with client money, unless the bank can demonstrate that the manner in which the money is appropriated from the client was not a result of any lapse in the bank in observing the regulatory and legal obligations of a bank in the maintenance of client money and also that the bank could not have been expected to prevent an appropriation of that type in any event.[192] In relation to corporations which are not regulated formally in the manner in which banks are regulated, then it is suggested that general notions of reasonable commercial behaviour should apply *mutatis mutandis* in place of norms of formal banking regulation.

---

[188] *Shaker v Al-Bedrawi* [2002] EWCA Civ 1452.   [189] [1992] 4 All ER 769.

[190] *Bank of Tokyo Mitsubishi Ltd v Baskan Gida* [2004] EWHC 945.

[191] *Papamichael v National Westminster Bank plc* [2003] EWHC 164 (Comm).

[192] For example, in the event that the employee used his knowledge of the lay-out of the bank's vaults to effect a forcible entry, rather than that he used his knowledge of the bank's security systems to effect an entry to those vaults undetected because the bank's security system was inadequate in some manner.

One further, related issue in relation to companies is that of the use of subsidiary companies to effect dishonest designs coupled with a claim that the knowledge of one company ought not to be attributed automatically to another company given that two companies are two separate persons in legal terms. Company law is generally prepared to lift the veil of incorporation when fraud is involved and in relation to tracing or constructive trust claims the courts have been prepared to lift the veil of incorporation when property has passed dishonestly between group companies or companies under common control.[193]

Whether knowledge can be forgotten

By contrast with the foregoing inference of knowledge from the circumstances, **30.67** the subjective nature of the test of knowledge is bound up with the possibility that one might have had actual knowledge of a circumstance at one time but have forgotten that same knowledge by the time of the receipt of property to which that circumstance relates. The case of *Polly Peck International v Nadir (No 2)* can be compared with the earlier decision of Megarry J in *Re Montagu*[194] in which the 10th Duke of Manchester was a beneficiary under a settlement created by the 9th Duke, subject to the trustees appointing chattels to other persons. In breach of trust, the 10th Duke and the trustees lapsed into the habit of treating all of the valuable chattels held on trust as belonging absolutely beneficially to the 10th Duke. The 10th Duke made a number of disposals of these valuable chattels during his lifetime. The issue arose whether or not the 10th Duke's estate should have been held liable for knowing receipt of these chattels in breach of trust. There was no doubt that the property had been received in breach of trust.

His lordship took the view that there had been 'an honest muddle' in this case. Further, although the 10th Duke had undoubtedly had actual knowledge of the terms of the trust at one stage, it was held that one does not have the requisite knowledge on which to base a claim for knowing receipt if the defendant has genuinely forgotten the relevant factors. Megarry J went further, in support of the idea that one should only be liable for knowing receipt if one has knowledge of the relevant factors, in finding that the knowledge of a trustee-solicitor or other agent should not be imputed to the defendant. That is, you do not 'know' something simply because your agent knows it.[195] Therefore, while the Duke had forgotten the terms of the trust, he was not to have his lawyers' knowledge, that for the Duke to treat the property as his own personal property would have been in breach of trust, imputed to him. Megarry J thus narrowed the scope of the knowledge test to acts which the defendant conducted wilfully or deliberately, or to facts of which he

---

[193] See, for example, *Agip (Africa) Ltd v Jackson* [1992] 4 All ER 385, 401, *per* Millett J.
[194] [1987] Ch 264.
[195] This is in contrast to the doctrine of notice, as considered above, in relation to which the knowledge of an agent may be imputed to the principal.

had actual knowledge. Consequently, no liability for knowing receipt attached to the 10th Duke or his estate.

30.68   The decision of Megarry J in *Re Montagu* suggests a true sense of subjectivity in the sense that one will only be liable for matters which one genuinely, subjectively knows. It is suggested that such an approach would be unlikely to be applied to those commercial situations, such as *Polly Peck International v Nadir (No 2)*, in which the defendant's knowledge of the appropriate factors may be inferred from the inquiries which he failed to make: that is, from knowledge which he deliberately sought to avoid. It is suggested that these commercial notions of knowledge are important to prevent commercial people from avoiding their obligations to have regard to their regulatory norms. Nevertheless, they do suggest an objective dimension to the test of knowledge by reference to which commercial people are required to act which is in contradistinction to the original notion expressed by Lord Selborne in *Barnes v Addy*[196] of one being liable in ordinary circumstances only when one had knowledge of the factors at issue. In common, however, with the roots of equity as a jurisdiction which inquires into the consciences of defendants,[197] it is evident that a commercial person who consciously fails to observe his regulatory or similar obligations may not in good conscience seek to refuse liability to account for any loss stemming from that action.

Developments in the treatment of knowing receipt

30.69   The law in this area has undergone some changes of detail: at the time of writing it is not immediately apparent which strain of authority will be favoured in the future. In short the fault line in the cases is now between the adoption of the test of dishonesty propounded by Lord Nicholls in *Royal Brunei Airlines v Tan*[198] in place of a test based on 'knowledge', and a general test of 'unconscionability' for the imposition of liability for knowing receipt. The other House of Lords cases considered in relation to dishonest assistance above did not make anything more than passing reference to the law on knowing receipt, although the Courts of Appeal in those same cases did make more explicit reference to that type of claim.

Knowledge by means of 'dishonesty'

30.70   The first line of authority advocating the displacement of the test of knowledge with a test of dishonesty is found in the decision of the Court of Appeal in *Twinsectra Ltd v Yardley*,[199] in which Potter LJ made it clear that in his opinion the

---

[196]   (1874) 9 Ch App 244, 251–252.

[197]   See, for example, the words of Lord Ellesmere in the foundational *Earl of Oxford's Case* (1615) 1 Ch Rep 1 to the effect that the jurisdiction of equity as effected through the person of the Lord Chancellor in the seventeenth century was 'to correct men's consciences for frauds, breach of trusts, wrongs and oppressions, of what nature soever they be . . .'.

[198]   [1995] 2 AC 378.   [199]   [1999] Lloyd's Rep Bank 438.

applicable test for *both* knowing receipt and dishonest assistance was that of 'dishonesty' as set out in *Royal Brunei Airlines v Tan*, as considered above.[200] This confirmation of the position of English law[201] indicates a movement away from knowledge as the basis for the receipt-based claim. It is clear that the same test was being used by Potter LJ both for dishonest assistance and knowing receipt (even though he acknowledged that one claim is receipt-based and the other not).

At no point in any of the judgments was there a discussion in the Court of Appeal **30.71** of 'knowledge' as applying to Leach and the solicitor here. The discussion proceeded on the basis of their 'honesty' and/or 'dishonesty' in relation both to receipt and assistance. It appears therefore that the test in *Royal Brunei v Tan* was imported into the area of knowing receipt. In his judgment in the Court of Appeal in *Twinsectra v Yardley*, Potter LJ made frequent references to the old knowledge-orientated ideas of the defendant 'shutting his eyes to the obvious'.[202] However, the Court of Appeal in *Twinsectra*, followed by the High Court in *Bank of America v Arnell*[203] and the Court of Appeal in *Heinl and Others v Jyske Bank*,[204] were using the established *Baden* categories of knowledge within which to analyse the mental state of the defendant (for example the wilful shutting of one's eyes to the obvious) but were concerned with whether or not that person was *honest* or dishonest, as opposed to whether or not that person had *knowledge* of some breach of trust. Therefore a number of Court of Appeal decisions have focused on asking whether or not the defendant has been dishonest when she received property in breach of trust; what is not clear is whether or not there is any impact rendered by the amendment to the test of dishonesty in the House of Lords in *Twinsectra v Yardley*[205] to involve a subjective element.

Whichever test is used, there remains the problem of witness credibility for the **30.72** judge. In that sense the question which the judge will continue to ask himself, regardless which test is used, is: 'do I believe that this witness did or did not act like an honest person?' Beyond that there will clearly be an important distinction at the edges between asking whether or not the defendant also realized that other people would have considered her actions to have been dishonest.

At first blush it might appear that there is only a marginal distinction between a **30.73** test of *knowledge* and test of *dishonesty*, but it is suggested that it could make a significant difference in marginal cases. Indeed, it is suggested that the distinction may yet be a significant one. A test based on knowledge is concerned with the state

---

[200] The question of knowing receipt was not raised before the House of Lords.
[201] *Royal Brunei Airlines v Tan* was a Privy Council decision.
[202] There is mention of '"not dishonest"..., he was referring to the state of conscience, as opposed to "Nelsonian" dishonesty...': ibid 462 col 2.
[203] [1999] Lloyd's Rep Bank 399.   [204] [1999] Lloyd's Rep Bank 511.
[205] [2002] 2 All ER 377, on which see para 30.37.

of mind of the defendant and is concerned to establish precisely what that particular defendant knew. In that sense, a test of knowledge is in line with the core equitable principle that the court is concerned with the state of mind of the defendant as part of an *in personam* action. A test based on dishonesty (in the definition given to that term by Lord Nicholls[206]) is a test concerned not with the particular mental state of the defendant but rather with what an honest person would have done in the defendant's place. That is, the court will attempt to establish what an objective, reasonable person would have done in those circumstances. There is therefore a partial shift here in the *Twinsectra v Yardley* decision in the Court of Appeal: the trigger for liability is 'what an objective, honest person would have done' rather than 'what the defendant knew'.[207]

Knowledge by means of 'unconscionability'

30.74 The second alternative approach to the test for knowing receipt, which is based on 'unconscionability', was set out in the more recent Court of Appeal decision in *Houghton v Fayers*[208] in which it was held that, for a defendant to be liable in knowing receipt, it is enough to establish that he knew or ought to have known of the breach of trust or fiduciary duty. The test is whether or not the defendant acted in good conscience. Such an approach would seem to place English law into the same position as Canadian law.[209] This test is very broadly based: what is not clear is what is meant by good and bad conscience in this context. Certainly, defrauding a client would be in bad conscience. What is not clear is whether or not it would be in bad conscience to advise the use of a strategy which an adviser knew contained an even risk of failure to success when another strategy carried a lower risk of failure, but where that apparently safer strategy would have raised only a fraction of the profit of the riskier strategy.[210] Is it reckless to favour profit over prudence in such circumstances?

30.75 In this regard, after the decision of the Court of Appeal in *Twinsectra v Yardley*, differently constituted Courts of Appeal have handed down two further judgments. The first was in the case of *Bank of Credit and Commerce International (Overseas) Ltd v Akindele*[211] in which Nourse LJ held explicitly that dishonesty is not an ingredient for a claim based on knowing receipt. Significantly, there is no reference made

---

[206] *Royal Brunei Airlines v Tan* [1995] 2 AC 378.
[207] *Twinsectra v Yardley* [1999] Lloyd's Rep Bank 438, 464 col 2, *per* Potter LJ, quoting Lord Nicholls in *Royal Brunei Airlines v Tan* [1995] 2 AC 378.　　　　[208] [2000] 1 BCLC 571.
[209] *Citadel General Assurance v Lloyds Bank Canada* [1997] 3 SCR 805, (1997) 152 DLR (4th) 411.
[210] A conundrum considered in relation to the obligations of trustees when investing trust property between generating the maximum possible return and ensuring a prudent management of the trust assets. At this juncture the financier is in well-understood territory of establishing a risk-return strategy; whereas the lawyer is in a grey area of identifying what would constitute suitable behaviour and potential reputation risk if litigation were started. See paras 52.85 and 54.11.
[211] [2000] 4 All ER 221.

by the Court of Appeal to the decision of Potter LJ in *Twinsectra*, considered above. Instead, it was held in *Bank of Credit and Commerce International (Overseas) Ltd v Akindele* that the court is required to look to see whether or not the defendant has acted 'unconscionably' in the receipt of the property.[212] What is unclear then is whether the defendant must be demonstrated both to have had knowledge of the breach of trust and also to have acted unconscionably.[213] This test necessarily begs the question as to what form of behaviour will constitute 'unconscionable' behaviour. We are told it is not behaviour tantamount to that which would have founded dishonesty in *Royal Brunei Airlines v Tan* but there is no clue in the judgment itself as to precisely what it does cover. Clearly, deliberate fraud will be caught: beyond that, all is speculation. Further to *Westdeutsche Landesbank v Islington*[214] there would be an unconscionable act if the defendant seeks to retain property paid to her by mistake, if she knows of the mistake.

The further recent decision is another decision of the Court of Appeal in *Walker v Stones*[215] concerning a trustee's wrongful acquiescence in a division of a shareholding. The Court of Appeal (in the leading judgment of Sir Christopher Slade) approved the test of dishonesty asserted by Lord Nicholls in *Tan* for the purposes of deciding whether or not the *trustee* had acted dishonestly. Nourse LJ agreed with the correctness of this approach—presumably it is only with reference to knowing receipt that Nourse LJ does not approve of the test of dishonesty.   **30.76**

The present state of the law on knowing receipt

The developments considered in the preceding section leave the law on knowing receipt in a state of some perturbation. What is clear is that the test based on that form of dishonesty described by Lord Nicholls in *Royal Brunei Airlines v Tan*[216] will expand the potential liability of bankers because those bankers are liable simply if they fail to act as an honest banker would have done. Whereas a test based on 'knowledge' would mean that the banker would only be liable if it could be proved that *that particular banker* had had sufficient knowledge that there had been a breach of trust. Significantly, that banker would not necessarily be liable for knowing receipt simply because objectively 'honest bankers' might have behaved differently. The development in *Royal Brunei Airlines v Tan* and in *Twinsectra v Yardley* would have the effect of extending the norms of proper behaviour set out in banking regulation into the case law dealing with personal   **30.77**

---

[212] This formulation was considered, in relation to a takeover agreement, in *Criterion Properties plc v Stratford UK Properties plc* [2002] EWHC 496 and [2002] EWCA Civ 1783. See also R Nolan, 'How knowing is knowing receipt?' [2000] CLJ 421.
[213] *Satnam Investments Ltd v Dunlop Hayward and Co Ltd* [1999] 3 All ER 652, CA and *Criterion Properties Ltd v Stratford UK Properties* [2003] 1 WLR 218, CA: a development which is decried by Peter Smith J in *Dilmun v Sutton* [2004] EWHC 52 (Chancery) para 23.
[214] [1996] AC 669.   [215] [2000] 4 All ER 412.   [216] See para 30.23.

liability to account: that is, the banker would be liable to account if he could not demonstrate that he had acted in accordance with the standards of integrity and honesty set out in banking regulation.

30.78 Clearly there has been a movement away from the old tests based on knowledge because Potter LJ did not explicitly use the old knowledge tests, even though he was considering knowing receipt as well as dishonest assistance. The only way of understanding the route through this thicket, it seems to me, is Scott LJ's comment in *Polly Peck International v Nadir (No 2)* that the judge needs to decide whether or not the defendant 'ought to have been suspicious'[217] in the light of what an honest person would have done. By that it is suggested that, regardless of the niceties of the tests, in the bulk of cases the court will be concerned to decide whether or not the individual defendant ought to have realized that property was being passed to her in breach of trust. The practical application of these tests will always be a combination of subjective and objective factors.

30.79 For bankers and their advisers (a constituency which has given rise to many of the cases considered above) the case law has taken another step towards strict liability for all advisers if client funds lose money. The adviser can expect these principles to develop in parallel to the statutory principles of good regulatory practice set out for the Financial Services Authority in the Financial Services and Markets Act 2000 advocating a sensitivity to risk and some consideration for the nature of that risk in the light of the expertise of the individual client.[218]

Defences

Release, knowledge, or good faith

30.80 In effect the defences to liability for knowing receipt relate to the defendant having had insufficient knowledge of the breach of trust, as considered above, or demonstrating that the circumstances surrounding the receipt of the trust property vindicate his state of mind on the basis, for example, that he paid in good faith for the property or that he was released from liability. Therefore, the only available defences against a claim for knowing receipt are, first, that the defendant was a bona fide purchaser for value without notice, in which the defendant can demonstrate that she purchased the property in good faith: which would in any event cancel out a claim for knowing receipt in that 'bona fides' would require an absence of knowledge or dishonesty.[219] Alternatively, as considered above,[220] there will be a defence if the defendant had been formally released from liability by the beneficiaries. As suggested, both of these defences would be unavailable

---

[217] *Polly Peck International v Nadir (No 2)* [1992] 4 All ER 769.
[218] Financial Services and Markets Act 2000, s 2; and in particular the protection of consumers, ibid, s 4 *et seq.*
[219] *Westdeutsche Landesbank v Islington LBC* [1996] AC 669.   [220] See paras 30.52, 30.58.

where the defendant is demonstrated to have had sufficient knowledge of the breach of trust or to have acted dishonestly.

The limits on the suitability of the change of position defence in this context

It has been argued that the defence of change of position[221] ought to be available in relation to claims for knowing receipt.[222] However, it is suggested that if one has acted knowingly in breach of trust then one ought not to be able to escape liability to account simply because one has changed one's position in reliance on receipt of property which, by definition,[223] one knew was being paid to one under breach of trust. Rather, the liability should be imposed in any circumstances in which knowledge and receipt can be proved: the state of mind is sufficient. Failing to act as an honest person would have done—either by refusing receipt of the property or returning it to its rightful owners—is itself sufficient to impose liability. Change of position can only be effected as a result of one's wrongful act. Lord Goff's description of the defence of change of position, considered in Chapter 33,[224] predicates that defence on the comparative justice of denying the beneficiaries the return of their property when measured against the justice of imposing liability on a person who has changed her position in reliance on the receipt of the property.[225] The only possibility for the application of this defence, it is suggested, would be in circumstances in which the defendant changed his position in reliance on the receipt of the property before acquiring the requisite knowledge to make him liable to account to the beneficiaries for knowing receipt of it. The defence of change of position is predicated on there being some action for restitution of unjust enrichment: however, it is suggested in the next section that liability for knowing receipt does not arise on the basis of restitution of unjust enrichment in any event and therefore that the change of position defence is inappropriate. **30.81**

The juristic nature of liability for knowing receipt

The difference between the two claims was stated in the following terms by the Court of Appeal in *Grupo Toras v Al-Sabah*:[226] **30.82**

> The basis of liability in a case of knowing receipt is quite different from that in a case of dishonest assistance. One is a receipt-based liability which may on examination prove to be either a vindication of persistent property rights or a personal restitutionary claim based on unjust enrichment by subtraction; the other is a fault-based liability as an accessory to a breach of fiduciary duty.

---

[221] *Lipkin Gorman v Karpnale* [1991] 3 WLR 10. [222] *Underhill and Hayton* 978.

[223] That is, if one did not have that knowledge, then one would not be liable for knowing receipt in any event. [224] See para 33.79.

[225] *Lipkin Gorman v Karpnale* [1991] 3 WLR 10: see para 33.79.

[226] *Grupo Toras v Al-Sabah* (CA, 2 November 2000).

The suggestion made here is that knowing receipt is a property law claim which seeks to vindicate the property rights of the claimant. The form of vindication is not a restoration of the original property to the claimant but rather a cash payment equivalent to the value of that lost property to the beneficiary. It is said that the claim is based on reversal of unjust enrichment:[227] this is simply not a tenable position. It is said that the unjust enrichment takes effect by way of subtraction of the enrichment: however, the measure of liability is the loss to the beneficiaries and not the level of the enrichment gained by the defendant. It may well be that the defendant received property worth £10,000 but was only enriched by £500 (for example, by way of a commission): in that circumstance the claimant would be entitled to only £500 by way of subtraction of the unjust enrichment. Whereas the remedy of knowing receipt entitles the beneficiaries to recover their entire loss, that is £10,000, from the defendant and not merely the extent of his enrichment. Similarly, the claim for dishonest assistance realizes a remedy equal to the loss suffered by the beneficiaries.

30.83 It has been suggested that the knowing receipt claim is restitutionary in many contexts.[228] Knowing receipt is predicated on the knowledge of the defendant that there has been some breach of trust. In consequence, knowing receipt is concerned to impose liability not to return property to the claimant—because that would constitute a tracing claim—but rather to compensate the beneficiaries for the loss which they suffered in part because of the defendant's receipt of property in breach of trust. That liability is faced not because the defendant retains some traceable proceeds of that trust property in her hands but rather because her knowledge of the breach of trust constituted that receipt a wrongful act. Where alternative tests of dishonesty or of unconscionability are imposed, rather than one of knowledge, that merely underlines the assertion that the claim is fault-based and is consequently not within the restitutionary canon. There may be circumstances in which the defendant looks to be effecting restitution where the loss is equal to the value of the property received but it is perfectly possible that the liability which the defendant bears as though a trustee is greater than the value of the property received in breach of trust.

---

[227] See also P Millett, 'Restitution and constructive trusts' (1998) 114 LQR, 399: arguing for replacing constructive trusteeship by restitution. Also Fox, 'Constructive notice and knowing receipt: an economic analysis' [1998] CLJ 391: considering what form of 'notice' is required in knowing receipt. L Smith, 'Constructive trusts and constructive trustees' [1999] CLJ 294.

[228] P Birks, 'Receipt' in P Birks and A Pretto (eds), *Breach of Trust* (Hart, 2002) 213.

BREACH OF TRUST

Part I

BREACH OF TRUST

31

AVOIDANCE OF BREACH OF TRUST

A. Prevention of Breach of Trust

The purpose of this chapter

The purpose of this chapter is to consider the powers recognized by the general law **31.01**
of trusts, whether vested in the beneficiaries or otherwise, to control the actions of
the trustees and to prevent breaches of trust. The trust has been described in this
book as being a combination of the property rights in the trust fund owed variously
by the trustees and the beneficiaries, and a bundle of obligations owed by the
trustees to the beneficiaries. Those obligations are expressed in the trust instrument
and are either supplemented or embodied, where there is no trust instrument, in
the fiduciary duties which the general law of trusts imposes on trustees. Those
fiduciary duties have been considered in detail in Part C in relation to express trusts
and in Part D in relation to trust duties implied by law. Chapter 32 considers the
liability of trustees for breach of trust in general terms, assuming that such a breach
of trust had taken place, whereas this chapter considers how the trustees' fiduciary
duties might be controlled by the beneficiaries to prevent any breach of trust.

A survey of this chapter

Once a breach of trust claim has reached the doors of the court it is sometimes too **31.02**
late to prevent the beneficiaries from suffering some level of loss in the value of

their trust fund and it is always too late to have saved the parties the stress involved with such litigation. Therefore, the most effective means of preventing the beneficiaries from suffering loss as result of a breach of trust is to structure the management of the trust so that meaningful breaches of trust are not possible. This chapter therefore divides, in effect, into two unequal halves. The first, smaller half considers the manner in which a trust might be structured to prevent a breach of trust by means of the selection of reliable trustees, the inclusion of powers enabling active control of the trustees by the beneficiaries, and so forth. The second, larger half considers formal legal means of preventing the trustees from carrying through a breach of trust by means of injunctions and stop notices, and also by means of court appointed and other functionaries who can displace the trustees, such as the judicial trustee, receivers, and the Public Trustee.

31.03　It is accepted that there is little that can be done in the event of fraud and theft perpetrated on the beneficiaries by the trustees but there are a number of devices which can be employed to minimize the risks of a breach of trust and to minimize the losses that might result. Throughout this chapter it will be evident that much will depend upon the nature of the trust involved. A large pension fund or commercial investment trust will be subject to formal, statutory regulation by a public official and therefore there is a context in which those trustees will be required to operate which provides much of the scrutiny and oversight which is recommended in this chapter. Such large trusts are also likely to be created as part of a fasciculus of contractual and trust terms, operating often in the shadow of a principal parliamentary statute, which define and limit the obligations of the professional trustees which such trusts usually have. Thus, unit trusts[1] and occupational pension trusts[2] are governed by mandatory statutory rules as to some of the forms of obligation which their trustees must bear but always subject, at the margins, to the limitation and moulding of those liabilities in the terms of the instruments which govern them. By contrast, smaller trusts created between family members in relation to a will or a trust of land will require the trust instrument to contain the entirety of the trustees' obligations and will require the settlor to consider carefully who is to act as trustee and how their liabilities will be managed potentially over many generations. In consequence the matters considered in this chapter will need to be adapted to any particular context.

Limits of the doctrine of breach of trust

31.04　The doctrine of breach of trust is considered in Chapter 32. One shortcoming in the approach to breach of trust typified by the leading case of *Target Holdings v Redferns*[3] is that the beneficiary is not able to bring an action against a trustee for breach of trust unless that beneficiary has suffered some financial loss directly as a

---

[1] See Chapter 51.　　[2] See Part H.　　[3] [1996] AC 421.

result of the breach of trust. Therefore, the remedies considered there are of use only once some loss has been occasioned, although the trustees will be required to bear the costs of any action brought prophylactically to prevent a breach of trust from taking place.[4] Whereas the doctrine of breach of trust focuses on the remedying of financial loss, there may be breaches of trust which generate no loss and therefore which preclude the beneficiaries from any substantive action. In those sorts of situation, however, the beneficiaries will still be entitled, for example, to require that the trustees replace unauthorized investments with authorized investments[5] and to reconstitute the trust as it would have been but for the breach of trust.[6] Nevertheless, the doctrine of breach of trust remains focused primarily on the recovery of loss or of property, whereas the material considered here is concerned with a broader context of the prevention of unconscionable action by the trustees before loss is caused.

Practical means of preventing a breach of trust

Retention of settlor as one of the trustees

The simplest means for the settlor to ensure that the trustees continue to act in the **31.05** manner anticipated by the settlor would be for the settlor to appoint himself as the sole trustee. In that way there would be no possibility of the trustee acting contrary to the wishes of the settlor. However, there may be practical and fiscal problems with the settlor retaining control over the trust in this fashion. The practical problems would relate to those situations in which there is more than one trustee and the impossibility of the settlor living for the entire perpetuity period of the trust: at some point it would be necessary for the mantle of trusteeship to be passed to someone other than the settlor. The fiscal problems ought not to arise provided that the settlor is suitably prevented from taking any benefit from the settled property.[7]

Appointment of reliable trustees

Alternatively, from the perspective of ensuring the proper performance of the **31.06** trust, any trustees selected other than the settlor must be sufficiently reliable. Professional trustees may be retained by the settlor, perhaps on the basis of contractual stipulation as to their powers. The settlor may then rely on a letter of wishes outwith the trust instrument which would provide guidelines in accordance with which the trustees could then be expected to exercise any powers or discretions. The settlor may consider the appointment of trustees who are not known to one another and therefore who are unlikely to act in league with one

---

[4] ibid.   [5] *Re Massingberd's Settlement* (1890) 63 LT 296.
[6] *Target Holdings v Redferns* [1996] AC 421.
[7] See, however, GW Thomas, *Taxation of Trusts* (Sweet & Maxwell, 1981) 192–194 discussing *Pearson v IRC* [1981] AC 753, [1980] 2 All ER 479.

another to defraud the beneficiaries. This is the theory behind the structure of the fiduciary duties in unit trusts[8] whereby one trustee acts as custodian of the trust property and the other makes the investment and management decisions as to the use of the trust property. In effect, the settlor is thrown back into the position of one who is required to 'trust' in the vernacular sense of that term:[9] that is, the settlor is required to depend upon the trustees once the ship is put to sea.[10]

Replacement of trustees

31.07 The trustees can be replaced in the manner discussed in Chapter 22.[11]

Protective provisions in the trust instrument

31.08 It is a straightforward business for the settlor to take some steps to prevent the trustees misbehaving with the trust property. As considered above, the settlor could make herself one of the trustees or the sole trustee. The settlor could thus, acting in a capacity as trustee, make herself a co-signatory to any transfer of trust property or payment out of the trust's bank accounts. Alternatively, if the settlor did not wish to act as a trustee, or if the trust was intended to be a testamentary trust, or if for some fiscal reason the settlor did not wish to appear to be a person retaining an interest in the trust, then the trust instrument should specify which trustees are empowered to deal with which trust property in which circumstances, or alternatively the trustees could be obliged to act jointly in relation to the management of the trust. In such circumstances, if the trustees had no particular connection one with another and no interests in common, then the settlor might feel more comfortable in relying on the honesty of each to keep control over the other.

31.09 The nature of the trust property will be important in relation to the number of trustees who may be required, for example, to ensure that the interests of any third person in relation to land are overreached. It may be that financial investments would be managed by professional trustees without requiring those trustees to seek the consent of non-professional members of a board of trustees to each individual transaction. The nature of the property would then govern the settlor's preparedness to have some or all of the trustees act unsupervised. As with the delegation of investment activity to professional investment managers,[12] the settlor would need to be confident that the specified investment manager would be reliable and that appropriate conduct of business agreements had been created between the parties. Similarly, if the trust's investment portfolio comprised a range of short-term investments then the board of trustees as a whole may need only to review the activities of the trustees managing the investments periodically; whereas if the

---

[8] See para 51.16.
[9] R Cotterrell, 'Trusting in law: legal and moral concepts of trust' (1993) 46(2) Current Legal Problems 75. [10] See *Paul v Paul* (1882) 20 Ch D 742.
[11] See para 22.01. [12] See para 52.04.

trust's investment portfolio consisted of one significant asset it may be preferable
for the board of trustees to vote on each significant action taken in respect of that
asset.

Beneficiaries' right to receive information from the trustees

Entitlement to receive accounts

An important part of the ability of the beneficiaries to control the trustees and to **31.10**
take action to prevent breaches of trust is the access to information as to the administration of the trust. Under the general law of trusts the beneficiaries will only have
limited rights to information, whether in the form of accounts or the reasons for the
making of management decisions and the exercise of the trustees' discretion.
Therefore, a trust instrument which obliged the trustees to make regular reports of
a specified kind to the beneficiaries, similar perhaps to the duties of company directors to have audited accounts prepared for the company and its shareholders, would
arm the beneficiaries with the necessary information to control the trustees
adequately and to forewarn the beneficiaries of any breaches of trust. The following
discussion, then, refers to the position under the general law in outline.[13]

The trustees' principal obligation is to provide accounts to the beneficiaries. **31.11**
Therefore, the trustees are required to show the trust accounts to beneficiaries on
demand.[14] A beneficiary can call for accounts whether or not his interest is in
possession[15] and whether the beneficiary is merely the object of a discretionary
trust.[16] The beneficiaries and objects of a power are entitled to know the nature
of their rights and the trustees are under a duty to inform them of that information:
the trustees must take reasonable steps to inform them of this information, rather
than waiting for the beneficiaries to approach them.[17] The objects of a power are
also entitled to be informed of the identity of the trustees who hold the power over
them.[18] The trustees, while obliged to provide accounts, are not required to give
reasons for the exercise of their discretion,[19] nor the details of the management of
any business operated by the trust,[20] nor to disclose any documentation setting

---

[13] See more generally para 32.01.
[14] *Armitage v Nurse* [1998] Ch 241, 261, *per* Millett LJ. See also *Wilson v Law Debenture Trust
Corporation* [1995] 2 All ER 337. [15] *Armitage v Nurse* [1998] Ch 241, 261.
[16] *Chaine Nickson v Bank of Ireland* [1976] IR 393; *Spellson v George* (1987) 11 NSWLR 300;
Re Murphy's Settlement [1998] 3 All ER 1. The objects of a power of appointment may be similarly
entitled if the settlor demonstrated an intention so to do: *Re Murphy's Settlement* [1998] 3 All ER 1;
although a settlor can exclude such a person from the right to receive accounts: see *Re Angora Trust*
[2001] WTLR 1081, Manx CA. Cf *Re Manisty's Settlement* [1974] Ch 17.
[17] *Stuart-Hutcheson v Spread Trustee Co Ltd* [2002] WTLR 1213.
[18] *Re Murphy's Settlement* [1998] 3 All ER 1.
[19] *Re Londonderry's Settlement* [1965] 2 WLR 229.
[20] *Re Rabbaiotti's Settlement* [2000] WTLR 953; *Rouse v 100F Australian Trustees Ltd* [2000]
WTLR 111.

out the settlor's instructions to the trustees where that would relate to the exercise of the trustees' discretion.[21] Consequently, in relation to discretionary trusts or powers of appointment, the beneficiaries can know whether or not they have rights under the trust but not the reason why.[22]

31.12 As mentioned above, trustees are required to give accounts and to provide details as to the decisions which have been made in accordance with the management of the trust.[23] The beneficiaries, or the class of objects of a power, are entitled to be informed of a decision, but are not entitled to be given the reasons as to why that decision was taken, as considered above. In similar vein, the beneficiaries are entitled to accounts which disclose the investment policy of the trust and to minutes of meetings not relating to confidential matters. As Lord Wrenbury held in *O'Rourke v Darbishire*:[24]

> A beneficiary has a right of access to the documents which he desires to inspect upon what has been called in the judgments in this case a proprietary right. The beneficiary is entitled to see all trust documents, because they are trust documents, and because he is a beneficiary. They are, in this sense, his own.

The question is then as to the nature of documents which can properly be described as 'trust documents'. The contents of that category have been found to be incapable of precise definition but do not include documents relating to the basis on which the trustees have made their decisions as to the use of their discretion.[25] This obligation to provide information (albeit of limited types) as to management accounts is an important part of the control of the conscience of the trustee by the court and by the beneficiaries. Without such information it would be impossible in many circumstances to commence litigation for breach of trust or to prevent a breach of trust in advance. What clearly limits the power of beneficiaries is the lack of any entitlement to see documentation as to the rationale underpinning trustees' decisions and the lack of a right (in the absence of any such provision in the trust instrument) to receive reasons for trustees' decisions.

Stop notices

31.13 Stop notices may be sought to prevent dealings with securities to acquire sufficient warning of intended dealings with securities held on trust.[26] The purpose of such a stop notice would be to overcome the fact that securities are held in the name of

---

[21] *Hartigan v Rydge* (1992) 29 NSWLR 405.

[22] *Klug v Klug* [1918] 2 Ch 67. In exceptional circumstances in which the trustees fail to explain the reasons for their decision to exercise their discretion in a particular way, the court may set aside that decision or require reasons to be given: *Re Beloved Wilkes Charity* (1851) 3 Mac & G 440. All this unless the contrary is contained in the trust instrument. The court will look at the adequacy of reasons where they are given. [23] *Re Londonderry* [1965] 2 WLR 229.

[24] [1920] AC 581. [25] *Re Londonderry* [1965] Ch 918, per Danckwerts LJ.

[26] CPR Pt 50, r 50.1.

the trustees and do not disclose the existence of a trust. The stop notice therefore gives the beneficiaries a right to information as to any dealing with the trust property to which they would not otherwise be entitled.[27]

B. The Nature of the Beneficiaries' Rights in the Trust Property

The beneficiaries have two forms of right against the trustees: first, proprietary **31.14** rights in the trust property recognized by equity and, secondly, rights against the trustees personally. The principle in *Saunders v Vautier*[28] suggests that all of the beneficiaries acting in concert are entitled to direct the trustees as to how the trustees should deal with the trust property. Further, the beneficiaries might also be entitled to call for delivery up of the trust property provided that the beneficiaries have suitably vested rights in the trust property.[29] Beneficiaries who are the objects of discretionary trusts could, on one analysis, be said to have no property right in the trust fund until property is appointed to them. However, it has been accepted that the objects of such a power are entitled to seek an interim injunction to prevent the trustees from committing a breach of trust,[30] whereas a person who is merely within a class of people subject to a power of appointment, such that no property might ever be advanced to that class of person will not be.[31] The cumulative effect of these rights in the beneficiaries has the effect of granting them sufficient *locus standi* to freeze trust property such that the trustees can be restrained from dissipating the fund contrary to their personal interests or in breach of trust.[32] The following section considers the manner in which the trustees can be restrained by means of injunction from committing a breach of trust prior to the hearing of the substantive merits of the various parties' powers and rights.

C. Restraining the Trustees

Interim injunctions

The general principles on which injunctions will be awarded to prevent a breach of trust

The most effective means of preventing a breach of trust is to enjoin the trustees **31.15** from carrying into effect any decision or strategy which would cause loss to

---

[27] See J Mowbray et al, *Lewin on Trusts* (17th edn, Sweet & Maxwell, 2000) ('*Lewin*') para 38-06.
[28] (1841) 4 Beav 115.   [29] See para 32.11.
[30] *Gartside v IRC* [1968] AC 553, 602, *per* Lord Reid; *Re Munro's Settlement Trusts* [1963] 1 WLR 145, 149.
[31] *Davis v Angel* (1862) 10 WR 772; *Molyneux v Fletcher* [1898] 1 QB 648, 655; *Re Brook's Settlement Trusts* [1939] 1 Ch 993.
[32] *Etty v Bridges* (1843) 2 Y & C Ch 486; *Hobbs v Wayet* (1887) 36 Ch D 256. See also *Wilkins v Sibley* (1863) 4 Giff 442.

the beneficiaries or which would be in breach of their powers.[33] Necessarily, this strategy requires that the beneficiaries have sufficient information to bring an application for an injunction before the trustees carry their decision into effect and then that an interim injunction is sought to prevent that action being carried out.[34] The entitlements of the beneficiaries to receive such information were considered above.[35] The beneficiaries' general purpose is to freeze the trust property before any breach of trust can take place:[36] the specific principles relating to freezing injunctions are considered below.[37] Any beneficiary is entitled to seek an injunction,[38] no matter how small that interest,[39] provided that the beneficiary does have an interest in property.[40] A person who has no proprietary right in the trust fund will generally not be entitled to seek such an injunction.[41] As considered above, it is a narrow line between having a right in property which gives the applicant sufficient *locus standi* to prevent the trustees' actions[42] and being someone with merely an expectation of some right in property.[43] The example of a person who is a remainder beneficiary is taken to be possessed of sufficient rights to prevent the trustees, for example, from disposing of the capital of the fund despite that interest not being in possession,[44] whereas a person who has a lively expectation of being the object of an advancement at some point in the future, but without any current proprietary right in the trust fund, will not have sufficient rights to seek such an injunction.[45] As considered above,[46] the line has been drawn on the authorities between someone who is the object of a discretionary trust and thus who has proprietary rights sufficient to justify the award of an injunction to prevent a breach of trust,[47] and someone who is merely the hopeful member of a class of people who fell within a power of appointment and so does not.[48]

---

[33] CPR Pt 25, r 25(1).

[34] *Etty v Bridges* (1843) 2 Y & C Ch 486; *Hobbs v Wayet* (1887) 36 Ch D 256. See also *Wilkins v Sibley* (1863) 4 Giff 442.   [35] See para 12.01.

[36] *Balls v Strutt* (1841) 1 Hare 146; *Noad v Buckhouse* (1843) 2 Y&C Ch 529; *Fletcher v Fletcher* (1844) 4 Hare 67; *Earl Talbot v Hope-Scott* (1858) 4 K&J 13; *Dickins v Harris* (1866) 14 LT 98; *Dance v Goldingham* (1873) 8 Ch App 902.   [37] See para 31.21.

[38] *Sandford v Jodrell* (1854) 2 Sm & G 176; *Dance v Goldingham* (1873) 8 Ch App 902.

[39] *Dance v Goldingham* (1873) 8 Ch App 902; *Bartlett v Bartlett* (1845) 4 Hare 631; *Governesses' Benevolent Institution v Rushbridger* (1854) 18 Beav 467; *Wheelwright v Walker (No 2)* (1883) 31 WR 912; *Re Parsons* (1890) 45 Ch D 51, 59.

[40] See, for example, *Re Ralli's Will Trusts* [1964] 2 WLR 144.

[41] *Clowes v Hilliard* (1876) 4 Ch D 413; *Re Parsons* (1890) 45 Ch D 51; *Re Brook's Settlement Trusts* [1939] 1 Ch 993.   [42] *Re Ralli's Will Trusts* [1964] 2 WLR 144.

[43] *Re Brook's Settlement Trusts* [1939] 1 Ch 993.   [44] *Re Ralli's Will Trusts* [1964] 2 WLR 144.

[45] *Davis v Angel* (1862) 10 WR 772; *Molyneux v Fletcher* [1898] 1 QB 648, 655; *Re Brook's Settlement Trusts* [1939] 1 Ch 993.   [46] See para 4.08.

[47] *Gartside v IRC* [1968] AC 553, 602, *per* Lord Reid; *Re Munro's Settlement Trusts* [1963] 1 WLR 145, 149.

[48] *Davis v Angel* (1862) 10 WR 772; *Molyneux v Fletcher* [1898] 1 QB 648, 655; *Re Brook's Settlement Trusts* [1939] 1 Ch 993.

The trustees are entitled to bring an action for an injunction when acting on behalf of the beneficiaries' interests.[49] An application for an injunction may be brought by some of the trustees against defaulting trustees, for example in circumstances in which new trustees or judicial trustees are seeking to establish a claim for breach of trust against the former trustees;[50] although it is not necessary that the applicant trustees have acted in good faith throughout[51] if they are seeking to recover property for the beneficiaries.[52] This situation may arise in circumstances in which the trust fund is large and where there are a number of trustees, possibly carrying out different duties or having had different responsibilities delegated to them. In general terms the beneficiaries do not need to be joined to any proceedings seeking an injunction unless the proceedings involve matters relating to which any of those beneficiaries may be required to give their consent.[53]

31.16

In general terms the award of an injunction will only be made if it can be demonstrated that common law damages would not be a sufficient remedy.[54] The general approach of the courts in relation to applications for interim injunctions to prevent a breach of trust is that the injunction should be awarded so that the trust fund is not dissipated before any substantive action can be heard to decide the proper treatment of that property.[55] In general terms, there are four requirements which must be satisfied before a court will award damages instead of an injunction in circumstances where an injunction might otherwise be awarded: first, that the harm suffered by the applicant must have been comparatively slight; secondly, that the harm suffered must be capable of being quantified in financial terms; thirdly, that the harm suffered must be such that it can be compensated adequately by payment of damages; and, fourthly, that it must have been oppressive to the respondent to have granted the injunction sought.[56] The potential loss of a part of the trust fund will typically constitute sufficient harm and will not be

31.17

---

[49] *Forest of Dean Coal Mining Co* (1878) 10 Ch D 450; *Re Cross* (1881) 20 Ch D 109; *Re Bennett* [1906] 1 Ch 216; *Space Investments Ltd v Canadian Imperial Bank of Commerce Trust Co. (Bahamas) Ltd* [1986] 1 WLR 1072, [1986] 3 All ER 75; *Young v Murphy* [1996] 1 VR 279. for example, where acting on behalf of a person *in vitro* or otherwise without competence to act: *Yunghanns v Candoora No 19 Pty Ltd* (2000) 2 ITELR 589. [50] *Hayim v Citibank NA* [1987] AC 730.
[51] *Franco v Franco* (1796) 3 Ves Jr 76; *May v Selby* (1842) 1 Y & C Ch 23; *Butler v Butler* (1877) 7 Ch D 116. [52] *Re Cross* (1881) 20 Ch D 109; *Williams v Barton* [1927] 2 Ch 9.
[53] See, for example, *Butler v Butler* (1877) 7 Ch D 116, 120, affirming (1877) 5 Ch D 554, *per* James LJ.
[54] *Jaggard v Sawyer* [1995] 1 WLR 269, [1995] 2 All ER 189. Section 37(1) of the Supreme Court Act 1981 provides that 'The High Court may by order (whether interlocutory or final) grant an injunction . . . in all cases in which it appears to the court to be just and convenient to do so.'
[55] *Foley v Burnell* (1783) 1 Bro CC 274; *Middleton v Dodswell* (1806) 13 Ves Jr 266; *Balls v Strutt* (1841) 1 Hare 146; *Fletcher v Fletcher* (1844) 4 Hare 67; *Earl Talbot v Hope-Scott* (1858) 4 K & J 139; *Re Blaksley's Trusts* (1883) 23 Ch D 549; *Waller v Waller* [1967] 1 WLR 451; *Bankers Trust Co v Shapira* [1980] 1 WLR 1274.
[56] *Shelfer v City of London Electric Lighting Co* [1895] 1 Ch 287; *Jaggard v Sawyer* [1995] 1 WLR 269, [1995] 2 All ER 189.

oppressive to the trustees who are obliged to recognize the rights of the beneficiaries in any event.[57]

31.18   The circumstances in which an injunction brought to prevent an alleged breach of trust might be refused might include the following sorts of factor. If the potential breach of trust involved the misuse of a comparatively small amount of money the beneficiary might be capable of being compensated by an order for compensation by way of money, particularly if the money has been applied for the benefit of another beneficiary who might be caused an inappropriate amount of harm if the money were recovered. If the breach concerned an alleged misuse of the trustees' powers under a discretionary trust, then the injunction might be refused if the applicant had a weak prima facie case to be entitled to an appointment of property. If the trust contained a power for the maintenance of the beneficiaries then one of the beneficiaries might require an advancement of money in an emergency, such that a delay in the trustees' use of a power which, ostensibly, they might use validly would cause hardship to that beneficiary.[58] These circumstances would need to be extreme, it is suggested, to justify the apparent presumption in the cases that the trust fund should be held intact until the court had the opportunity to consider the merits of the case and to hear all the appropriate witnesses at its leisure.[59]

The general equitable principles on which injunctions are awarded

31.19   There are a number of general equitable principles bound up with the award of an injunction. First, the applicant must come to equity with clean hands and so it is a key part of any equitable remedy that the applicant is not seeking that remedy to advance some inequitable purpose.[60] Secondly, the applicant must not delay in seeking the remedy. As Millett LJ put it in *Jaggard v Sawyer*: 'If the applicant delays proceedings until it is no longer possible for him to obtain an injunction, he destroys his own bargaining position and devalues his right.'[61] Delay will typically

---

[57] *Fletcher v Fletcher* (1844) 4 Hare 67; *Bankers Trust Co v Shapira* [1980] 1 WLR 124.

[58] In *Jaggard v Swayer* [1995] 1 WLR 269, [1995] 2 All ER 189 Millett LJ did acknowledge the utility of an award of damages to guard against potential future loss when his lordship held that a court 'can in my judgment properly award damages "once and for all" in respect of future wrongs because it awards them in substitution for an injunction and to compensate for those future wrongs which an injunction would have prevented'.

[59] There is also a further issue which arises from the decision of Millett LJ in *Jaggard v Sawyer* [1995] 1 WLR 269, [1995] 2 All ER 189 which relates to the nature of an injunction and damages as being either compensatory or restitutionary. If these remedies are to be compensatory, that would require measuring the loss suffered by the applicant and providing for a remedy which adequately compensates the applicant for her loss. Alternatively, a restitutionary remedy is concerned to take from the respondent the gain which the respondent has made by passing that gain to the applicant. Therefore, the restitutionary remedy would not necessarily require a calculation of the loss suffered by the applicant, but would instead be concerned to take from the respondent the gain made at the applicant's expense. This is unlike the remedy to account in relation to a breach of trust which is concerned to effect compensation.   [60] *Tinsley v Milligan* [1994] 1 AC 340, *per* Lord Goff.

[61] *Jaggard v Sawyer* [1995] 1 WLR 269, [1995] 2 All ER 189.

be taken as a sign of acquiescence in the actions of the defendant and thus disqualify the claimant from obtaining an injunction[62] and from damages in connection with any such injunction.[63] Thirdly, the trust fund must be capable of reconstitution or protection by means of the injunction at the time of the application on the basis that equity will not act in vain.[64] Fourthly, it is required by the general law that some right of the applicant must be affected: a matter which is self-evident in relation to applications by a beneficiary to prevent a breach of trust.[65]

The requirements for the award of interim injunctions

The classic test for the availability of an interim injunction was contained in **31.20** *American Cyanamid v Ethicon Ltd.*[66] In the words of Lord Diplock, 'The court must weigh one need against another and determine where "the balance of convenience" lies.' Therefore, in considering the mutual benefits and burdens that may result from the award of an injunction on an interlocutory basis, the court is required to consider, in all the circumstances, whether it would be more convenient on balance to award or deny the award of an interim injunction. There are four elements to the test: first, that the balance of convenience indicates the grant of an award; secondly, apparently, that the applicant can demonstrate a good prima facie case; thirdly, that there is a serious question to be resolved at trial; and, fourthly, that there is an undertaking for damages in the event that the applicant does not succeed at trial. Subsequent cases have cast doubt on the breadth of the applicability of the *American Cyanamid* principle.[67] Lord Diplock himself identified the importance of the applicant showing, not only a likelihood of suffering loss if the injunction is not granted, but also a likelihood that the applicant would succeed at full trial:[68]

> To justify the grant of such [an interim injunction] the applicant must satisfy the court first that there is a strong *prima facie* case that he will be entitled to a final order restraining the defendant from doing what he is threatening to do, and secondly that he will suffer irreparable injury which cannot be compensated by a subsequent award of damages in the action if the defendant is not prevented from doing it between the date of the application for the interim injunction and the date of the final order made on trial of the action.

The explanation proffered by Laddie J[69] of this requirement, and the tension between satisfying the court that one will win at trial while needing only to establish a prima facie case, was that Lord Diplock must have required the court to consider the comparative strengths of the parties' cases but without needing to resolve

---

62 *Jaggard v Sawyer* [1995] 1 WLR 269, [1995] 2 All ER 189.
63 *Jaggard v Sawyer* [1995] 1 WLR 269, [1995] 2 All ER 189.
64 See CPR Pt 25, r 25.1(1)(c)(i).
65 *Paton v British Pregnancy Advisory Service Trustees* [1979] QB 276.
66 [1975] AC 396, [1975] 1 All ER 504.   67 [1975] AC 396, [1975] 1 All ER 504.
68 [1975] AC 295, 360.   69 [1975] AC 295, 360.

any difficult issues of fact or law. Lord Diplock's conviction was that, in most cases, it will be apparent which party is more likely to win at trial.

Freezing injunctions to prevent breaches of trust

Freezing injunctions to prevent breaches of trust in general terms

31.21 Freezing injunctions are awarded to prevent the respondent from removing assets from the reach of the court before the completion of litigation to avoid settlement of a final judgment. Thus, a beneficiary could seek a freezing order against trustees of an express trust or against someone against whom a constructive trust is alleged, or against whom an equitable tracing claim is to be brought in relation to property passed away in breach of trust.[70] Therefore, in circumstances in which a director of a company sought to divert money from a company in breach of his fiduciary duties and to take that money out of the jurisdiction, the bank through which the payment was being made was prevented by means of a freezing order from dealing with moneys held in the applicable bank account.[71]

31.22 There are three types of injunction at issue here: first, injunctions to prevent assets from being put beyond the reach of the court in general terms,[72] secondly, injunctions to prevent assets being removed from the jurisdiction, and, thirdly, worldwide freezing injunctions taking effect over assets held outside the jurisdiction, perhaps ordering that assets be brought within the jurisdiction.[73]

Freezing injunctions to retain the trust fund intact

31.23 The freezing injunction usually requires that the applicant can demonstrate 'a good arguable case'[74] but that is not required in relation to a freezing order in relation to a trust in recognition of the relationship necessarily bound up with the existence of a trust: that is, the beneficiaries' proprietary rights in the trust fund and the trustees' fiduciary duties.[75] If the applicant is subsequently shown to have withheld important information from the court, the freezing injunction will generally be discharged;[76] whereas an injunction which subsequently appears to have been too stringent will be relaxed.[77] The applicant is also usually required to give

---

[70] *A v C* [1981] QB 956, 959; *Polly Peck International plc v Nadir (No 2)* [1992] 4 All ER 769, 784.
[71] *Polly Peck International plc v Nadir (No 2)* [1992] 4 All ER 769.
[72] This could involve, for example, disposing of assets such that there would be no effective tracing claim against them.   [73] *Derby & Co Ltd v Weldon (No 6)* [1990] 1 WLR 1139.
[74] *Third Chandris Shipping Corp v Unimarine SA* [1979] QB 645.
[75] *Derby & Co Ltd v Weldon* [1990] Ch 48, 57, *per* Parker LJ. The test differs from the standard test for interlocutory injunctions precisely because of the effect which a freezing injunction will have on the defendant in circumstances in which the defendant is typically not present in court at the original application. A 'good, arguable case' connotes a higher standard than merely a 'prima facie case'. This is a particularly important element of the application process given that the hearing is usually *ex parte*, and the court requires some evidence that the applicant is likely to succeed at trial.
[76] *Ali & Fahd v Moneim* [1989] 2 All ER 404; *Dubai Bank Ltd v Galadari* [1990] 1 Lloyd's Rep 120.
[77] *PCW (Underwriting Agencies) Ltd v Dixon* [1983] 2 Lloyd's Rep 197.

an undertaking in damages to the effect that, if the applicant is unsuccessful at trial, the applicant will be able to compensate the defendant adequately.[78] Furthermore, the court can grant an order requiring any person with knowledge of the location of trust assets which are held on trust or which constitute the traceable proceeds of the trust property passed away in breach of trust to divulge any information which they may have.[79]

The applicant is required to demonstrate three things, applying the general principles for such an order to the prevention of a breach of trust: something less than a good arguable case;[80] that there are assets within the jurisdiction; and, ordinarily, that there is a real risk of the dissipation of those assets which would otherwise make final judgment nugatory.[81] However, in relation to trusts this third requirement of the dissipation of assets does not require that the potential loss be irremediable before a beneficiary is entitled to a freezing order:[82] rather, the nature of a beneficiary's rights put such an applicant in a different category from the ordinary applicant. Therefore a beneficiary can act in order to prevent an abuse of the trust property by virtue of his rights in that property. Injunctions have been ordered to prevent the trustees from making an undesirable sale of trust property, such that the property would be put beyond the reach of the beneficiaries in an equitable tracing claim by transferring it to equity's darling by means of the sale.[83]

31.24

Freezing injunctions to keep assets within the jurisdiction

The ordinary focus of a freezing order relates to the preservation of assets within the jurisdiction to prevent the defendant from spiriting property beyond the reach of the court. The potentially very broad ambit of the freezing injunction has been limited by the courts. As Kerr LJ held in *Z Ltd v A-Z*:[84]

31.25

> *Mareva* [or, freezing] injunctions should be granted . . . when it appears to the court that there is a combination of two circumstances. First, when it appears likely that the applicant will recover judgment against the defendant for a certain or approximate sum. Secondly, when there are also reasons to believe that the defendant has assets within the jurisdiction to meet the judgment, in whole or in part, but may well

---

[78] *Third Chandris Shipping Corp v Unimarine SA* [1979] QB 645. This undertaking is an undertaking made to the court, rather than to the defendant (given the *ex parte* nature of the procedure): *Balkanbank v Taher* [1994] 4 All ER 239.

[79] CPR Pt 25, r 25.1(1)(g). See *Norwich Pharmacal Co v Customs and Excise Commissioners* [1974] AC 133; *Ashianti v Kashi* [1987] QB 888.   [80] *Derby & Co Ltd v Weldon* [1990] Ch 48.

[81] *Mareva Compania Naviera SA v International Bulk Carriers SA* [1975] 2 Lloyd's Rep 509; *Re BCCI SA (No 9)* [1994] 3 All ER 764; *Derby & Co v Weldon (Nos 3 and 4)* [1990] Ch 65. It is now referred to as an 'asset freezing order' in the reforms to the Rules of the Supreme Court.

[82] *Attorney-General v Foundling Hospital Governors* (1793) 2 Ves Jr 42; *Re Chertsey Market* (1818) 6 Price 261; *Reeve v Parkins* (1820) 2 Jac & W 390; *Corporation of Ludlow v Greenhouse* (1827) 1 Bli NS 17; *Marshall v Sladden* (1851) 4 De G & Sm 468.

[83] *Dance v Goldingham* (1873) 8 Ch App 902; *Hodges v Smith* [1950] WN 455.

[84] [1982] QB 558, 585.

take steps designed to ensure that these are no longer available or traceable when judgment is given against him.[85]

The award of an order to keep assets in the jurisdiction will then be made in accordance with those principles set out in the preceding paragraph. Therefore the applicant must prove a combination of a likelihood of success at trial,[86] tempered by the assumption that the rights of a beneficiary should be protected as considered above, and that the defendant has some assets within the jurisdiction of the court to meet that judgment. However, a freezing injunction will not be awarded where such an injunction would displace remedies which might be ordered at full trial of the issue.[87]

Freezing injunctions over assets outside the jurisdiction

31.26   By contrast with those freezing orders which try to keep assets within the jurisdiction, the English courts have recognized the jurisdiction to grant freezing injunctions over assets held outside England and Wales: the so-called worldwide freezing injunction. In *Derby v Weldon*[88] the Court of Appeal was of the view that the defendants were a corporation with sufficient know-how to put assets beyond the reach of the applicant even if the applicant was successful at trial. Therefore, the Court of Appeal held, exceptionally, that the freeze on the defendant's assets would be required to be global in scope for the applicant to be certain of receiving adequate compensation in the event of success at trial. In one of the cases arising out of the collapse of the Bank of Credit and Commerce International, Rattee J awarded a worldwide freezing injunction on the basis that, in the context of 'the complex international nature of the financial dealings' concerned in a case in which neither respondent was resident in England and Wales, it was necessary to make the injunction similarly international.[89] In a comparative relaxation of the principle, the Court of Appeal in *Credit Suisse Fides Trust v Cuoghi*[90] has held that the worldwide freezing injunction can be granted in circumstances in which 'it would be expedient', rather than being limited to a situation in which exceptional circumstances justify the order. However, it remains the case that the applicant is required to demonstrate a likelihood of assets being put beyond its reach in circumstances in which the respondent is both able and likely to act in that way. Many of the cases in which the injunction has been granted with worldwide effect have therefore involved financial institutions for which movements of assets around the world are, logistically, comparatively straightforward.[91]

---

[85] However, at general law, a freezing injunction will not be awarded where such an injunction would displace remedies which might be ordered at full trial of the issue: *Derby & Co v Weldon (Nos 3 and 4)* [1990] Ch 65, 76.   [86] Considered below at para 31.26.

[87] *Balkanbank v Taher* [1994] 4 All ER 239.

[88] *Derby & Co v Weldon (Nos 3 and 4)* [1990] Ch 65, 76.

[89] *Re Bank of Credit and Commerce International SA (No 9)* [1994] 3 All ER 764.

[90] [1997] 3 All ER 724.   [91] *Practice Direction* [1994] 4 All ER 52.

Freezing injunctions to bring assets within the jurisdiction

In relation specifically to trusts, the courts may make a freezing order in relation **31.27** to assets which are held in a jurisdiction which does not recognize the trust concept and which might not therefore enforce an order of an English court made on trusts principles.[92] The purpose of such an order would be to require that the assets be brought within the jurisdiction so that the order of the English court could be made subject to any subsequent order of the court.[93] The burden of proof in such circumstances is lower than that required for an ordinary freezing injunction.[94]

D. Payment into Court

On the ordering of an interim injunction, of the type considered in the foregoing **31.28** section, but before the making of an order for an account the trustees can be compelled to pay into court amounts of money or specified property which have been passed away under breach of trust.[95] The trustee[96] must be demonstrated to have those assets either in his possession[97] or under his control.[98] Before such an order for a payment into court has been made, there must be some admission by the trustee that a breach of trust has been committed.[99] Once the trustee has been found liable for a breach of trust and an order for an account has been made against him, then an order for payment into court will usually be made against the trustee without any other formality.[100] The amount to be paid into court, once the account has been ordered, will be decided in accordance with all the facts of the case particularly in the light of the nature of the account.[101]

E. Orders for Accounts

The liability of a defaulting trustee is to account to the beneficiaries. The princi- **31.29** ples on which such an order will be made are considered in Chapter 32.

---

[92] *Derby & Co Ltd v Weldon (No 6)* [1990] 1 WLR 1139. CPR Pt 25, r 25.1(1)(g).
[93] *Derby & Co Ltd v Weldon (No 6)* [1990] 1 WLR 1139. CPR Pt 25, r 25.1(1)(g).
[94] *Derby & Co Ltd v Weldon* [1990] Ch 48, 57, *per* Parker LJ.
[95] *Jervis v White* (1802) 6 Ves Jr 738; *Freeman v Cox* (1878) 8 Ch D 148; *Hampden v Wallis* (1884) 27 Ch D 251; *Porrett v White* (1885) 31 Ch D 51; *Re Benson* [1899] 1 Ch 39.
[96] An expression which appears to include constructive trustees, *Staniar v Evans* (1887) 34 Ch D 470, and also agents, *Dunne v English* (1874) LR 18 Eq 524.
[97] *Hollis v Burton* [1892] 3 Ch 226; *Nutter v Holland* [1894] 3 Ch 408; *Crompton and Evans Union Bank v Burton* [1895] 2 Ch 711.
[98] *Re Benson* [1899] 1 Ch 39.   [99] *Re Benson* [1899] 1 Ch 39.
[100] See *London Syndicate v Lord* (1878) 8 Ch D 84, 92, *per* Bagallay LJ; *Hampden v Wallis* (1884) 27 Ch D 251, 257; *Strafford v Sutcliffe* [1942] Ch 80.
[101] *Wanklyn v Wilson* (1887) 35 Ch D 180; *Green v Weatherill* [1929] 2 Ch 213.

F. Appointment of a Judicial Trustee

31.30   Judicial trustees are appointed by the court under the Judicial Trustees Act 1896. The 1896 Act gives the court the discretionary power to appoint a person to act as a judicial trustee on an application from, or on behalf of, the settlor, or one of the beneficiaries, or one of the trustees. The court is empowered to act on its own discretion in so doing. The role of the judicial trustee and the means of seeking the appointment of such a person were considered in Chapter 23.[102]

G. Appointment of a Receiver

31.31   In circumstances in which a trustee goes into insolvency the court will appoint a receiver to take charge of the trust property and an injunction will be awarded to prevent the dissipation of the trust fund.[103] Receivers have also been appointed in circumstances in which the trust's affairs were considered to be in disarray[104] or where it was alleged that the trustees were dissipating the trust property to their own benefit[105] or more generally where the trustees were behaving wrongly or fraudulently in misapplying the trust property.[106] A receiver may not be needed if the malfeasing trustee could be replaced leaving sufficient trustees still in office,[107] unless it is one of the co-trustees who applies for the appointment of a receiver.[108] It is more common to appoint a judicial trustee in modern contexts than to appoint a receiver.[109]

H. The Role of the Public Trustee

31.32   The Public Trustee may be able to assist the beneficiaries, as considered in Chapter 23.[110]

---

[102]   See para 23.01.
[103]   *Havers v Havers* (1740) Barn Ch 22; *Scott v Becher* (1816–17) 4 Price 346; *Mansfield v Shaw* (1818) 3 Madd 100; *Middleton v Dodswell* (1806) 13 Ves Jr 266.
[104]   *Attorney-General v Schonfield* [1980] 1 WLR 1182.
[105]   *Clarke v Heathfield* [1985] ICR 203.
[106]   *Richards v Perkins* (1838) 3 Y & C Ex 299; *Evans v Coventry* (1854) 5 De GM & G 911. See also *Derby & Co v Weldon (No 3)* [1990] Ch 65.   [107]   *Bowen v Philips* [1897] 1 Ch 174.
[108]   *Re Fowler* (1881) 16 Ch D 723.
[109]   The quaint nature of appointments of receivers in the past has focused on the personal foibles of trustees, such as drunkenness and bad character: *Everett v Prythergch* (1841) 12 Sim 363.
[110]   See para 23.01.

32

TRUSTEES' LIABILITY FOR
BREACH OF TRUST

A. Introduction

The extent of the trustees' liability for breach of trust

32.01 This chapter is concerned with the liability faced by trustees for breaches of trust. In the event of a breach of trust the trustees will face the primary liability either to restore trust property passed away in breach of trust, or to provide value equivalent to the value of any property passed away in breach of trust, or to pay equitable compensation to the trust to compensate the beneficiaries' loss.[1] It is not a prerequisite of liability that the trustee have taken any benefit from the breach of trust.[2] There is an important distinction to be made here between proprietary liability and personal liability. A trustee's liability is primarily a proprietary liability to effect specific restitution of any property, that is to recover the very property which was transferred out of the trust fund.[3] Trustees face a secondary liability, in the form of a personal liability, to reconstitute the cash value of the trust fund if the specific property or its traceable proceeds cannot be recovered.[4] The trustee also bears a liability to provide equitable compensation for any other loss consequent on the breach of trust.[5] These principles are considered in greater detail in the following sections of this chapter.

32.02 A trustee will be so liable in any situation in which the breach of trust has caused some loss to the trust.[6] There will be no liability in respect of a breach of trust where that breach resulted in no loss to the trust.[7] The measurement of compensation will

---

[1] *Nocton v Lord Ashburton* [1914] AC 932; *Target Holdings v Redferns* [1996] 1 AC 421, [1995] 3 WLR 352, [1995] 3 All ER 785; *Mahoney v Purnell* [1996] 3 All ER 61; *Bristol & West Building Society v Mothew* [1998] Ch 1; *Swindle v Harrison* [1997] 4 All ER 705; *Nationwide v Balmer Radmore* [1999] Lloyds Rep PN 241.

[2] *Dornford v Dornford* (1806) 12 Ves Jr 127, 129; *Adair v Shaw* (1803) Sch & Lef 243, 272; *Lord Montfort v Lord Cadogan* (1810) 17 Ves Jr 485, 489.

[3] *Nocton v Lord Ashburton* [1914] AC 932. See para 32.11.

[4] *Target Holdings v Redferns* [1996] 1 AC 421. See para 32.15.

[5] *Target Holdings v Redferns* [1996] 1 AC 421. See para 32.14.

[6] *Target Holdings v Redferns* [1996] 1 AC 421.

[7] *Target Holdings v Redferns* [1996] 1 AC 421.

be the actual, demonstrable loss to the trust, rather than some intermediate value of the property lost to the trust.[8] This liability stems from the beneficiaries' 'basic right ... to have the trust duly administered in accordance with the provisions of the trust instrument, if any, and the general law'.[9]

This chapter will focus on the liability of those who are identified as express **32.03** trustees and subsequently on those who have constructive trusteeship imposed on them despite not having been express trustees.[10] The reader is referred back to the general discussion of the duties of trustees in Part C above which constitute a necessary prologue in many cases to the question of whether or not those duties have been breached.

The many facets of litigation seeking to establish liability for breach of trust

The principal liability for any breach of trust will always lie with the trustees in **32.04** that the beneficiaries are required to proceed first against the trustee for breach of trust no matter who else may bear obligations to effect restitution to the trust[11] and even if the underlying cause of the loss to the trust is the dishonesty or failure of a third party.[12] There are a narrow class of defences which may exclude or reduce the liability of any individual trustee.[13] Nevertheless, despite the principal liability of the trustees, when a trust is breached there are a number of people who might potentially be made liable for that breach. From the perspective of the beneficiaries seeking to recover property passed away in breach of trust or to recover any loss suffered by the trust fund as a result of any breach of trust, the law is very protective of them and entitles them to proceed against the trustees in the first place so that it is for the trustees to proceed on their own account against any third party themselves to recover any further loss. The trustees' responsibility for so doing is only excluded by the defences considered below.[14]

Whereas the trustees personally will be liable for any breach of trust, the extent to **32.05** which the trustees will be able to meet the beneficiaries' claims will be restricted by three things: first, the availability of any defences to liability for breach of trust; secondly, whether or not they have the trust property over which specific restitution is sought in their possession; thirdly, the extent to which their own, personal means will enable them to meet those claims. Consequently, the beneficiaries may seek to impose liability on people other than the trustees, or the trustees may seek

---

[8] *Target Holdings v Redferns* [1996] 1 AC 421.
[9] *Target Holdings v Redferns* [1996] 1 AC 421, [1995] 3 All ER 785, 793.
[10] That is, by way of knowing receipt or dishonest assistance, as considered in Chapter 30.
[11] *Target Holdings v Redferns* [1996] 1 AC 421.
[12] *Target Holdings v Redferns* [1996] 1 AC 421, [1995] 3 All ER 785, 794, *per* Lord Browne-Wilkinson.
[13] See para 32.76.   [14] See para 32.79.

to have other people joined as third parties to any claim brought against them by the beneficiaries for breach of trust. In the event that the trust property has passed into the possession of some third party, a tracing claim will need to be brought at common law to recover that property provided that it has not been mixed with other property,[15] or else an equitable tracing claim will need to be brought to enforce a claim to a fund into which the trust property or its traceable proceeds have been mixed.[16] The manner in which a tracing claim is brought is considered in Chapter 33. Where the trust's traceable proceeds cannot be identified in the hands of any third person, or insufficient property remains in the hands of such a person so as to satisfy the beneficiaries' claims, then the beneficiaries will seek to proceed against any third person who either assisted dishonestly in the breach of trust[17] or who received property knowing of the breach of trust.[18] These liabilities will establish personal liability against such strangers to the trust and are discussed in detail in Chapter 30.

The liability of strangers to the trust in relation to a breach of trust

32.06 While the discussion of 'breach of trust' in most trusts law texts usually refers only to the liability of the trustees themselves for breach of trust, one could classify among the available claims arising in relation to a breach of trust issues such as tracing rights in trust property, knowing receipt of property in breach of trust, and dishonest assistance in a breach of trust. A person who is neither a trustee nor a beneficiary will be personally liable to account to the trust for any loss suffered in a situation in which she dishonestly assists in a breach of trust, without receiving any proprietary right in that trust property herself.[19] The test for 'dishonesty' in this context extends beyond straightforward deceit and fraud into reckless risk taking with trust property and other unconscionable behaviour demonstrating a 'lack of probity'.[20] A person who is neither a trustee nor a beneficiary will be personally liable to account to the trust for any loss suffered in a situation in which she receives trust property with knowledge that the property has been passed to her in breach of trust.[21] 'Knowledge' in this context includes actual knowledge, wilfully closing one's eyes to the breach of trust, or failing to make the inquiries which a reasonable person would have made.[22] In the contexts of knowing receipt

---

[15] See para 33.21.   [16] See para 33.30.
[17] *Royal Brunei Airlines v Tan* [1995] 2 AC 378.
[18] *Re Montagu* [1987] Ch 264; *Agip v Jackson* [1990] Ch 265, 286, *per* Millett J; CA [1991] Ch 547; *Lipkin Gorman v Karpnale* [1991] 2 AC 548; *El Ajou v Dollar Land Holdings* [1993] 3 All ER 717, appealed [1994] 2 All ER 685.   [19] *Royal Brunei Airlines v Tan* [1995] 2 AC 378.
[20] *Royal Brunei Airlines v Tan* [1995] 2 AC 378; *Twinsectra Ltd v Yardley* [1999] Lloyd's Rep Bank 438; *Bank of America v Kevin Peter Arnell* [1999] Lloyd's Rep Bank 399.
[21] *Re Montagu* [1987] Ch 264; *Agip v Jackson* [1990] Ch 265, 286, *per* Millett J; CA [1991] Ch 547; *Lipkin Gorman v Karpnale* [1991] 2 AC 548; *El Ajou v Dollar Land Holdings* [1993] 3 All ER 717, appealed [1994] 2 All ER 685.
[22] *Re Montagu* [1987] Ch 264.

and dishonest assistance, as they are discussed in this book, the personal liability to account as a constructive trustee provides the beneficiary with a remedy in money against that person equal to the loss to the trust if the defendant has either received the trust property in the knowledge of the breach of trust[23] or if she has assisted in that breach of trust. Indeed it was as a species of constructive trust that they have already been considered.[24] Where it is a particularly valuable or important item of property that is lost to the trust fund, the principles considered in Chapter 33 on tracing and proprietary claims will apply to require the trustee to deliver up that specific property if in her possession or under her control, or to enable the trust property to be identified and recovered (common law tracing),[25] or its traceable substitute to be acquired and added to the trust fund (equitable tracing).[26] Tracing will be explained in Chapter 33 as being the process by which a beneficiary who is affected by a misapplication of trust property is able to claim title either to their original property or a substitute for it[27] in the hands of another person. The nature of the precise claim and the nature of the appropriate remedy to the property is then a further question.[28] There are some logically anterior questions in the context of the liability of the trustees for breach of trust, however. Namely, in what circumstances will a breach arise and what forms of claim may flow from that?

B. Components of the Trustees' Liability for Breach of Trust

Loss as a foundation for the claim

The effect of the House of Lords decision in *Target Holdings v Redferns*[29] is that a   **32.07** trustee will be liable to account to the beneficiaries, in the manner considered in the two following paragraphs, for any breach of trust if the beneficiaries have suffered some loss and if that loss can be demonstrated to have some causal link with the trustees' breach of trust. This marked an important development in the law relating to breach of trust because it required the demonstration of a connected loss and not merely the demonstration that there had been a breach of trust. Whereas previously a trustee might have been liable for any loss which was suffered by the beneficiaries, the effect of *Target Holdings v Redferns* was to identify the central importance of the causal connection between the breach of trust and the loss. If there is no such causal connection between the breach of trust and the loss suffered by the beneficiaries, then the trustees bear no liability in this context.

---

[23] *Re Montagu* [1987] Ch 264.   [24] See Chapter 30.
[25] *FC Jones & Sons (A Firm) v Jones* [1996] 3 WLR 703.
[26] *Re Diplock's Estate* [1948] Ch 465; *Boscawen v Bajwa* [1996] 1 WLR 328.
[27] eg the sale proceeds of the original property taken in breach of trust.
[28] *Boscawen v Bajwa* [1996] 1 WLR 328.   [29] [1996] 1 AC 421.

32.08 By way of illustration, in the case of *Target Holdings v Redferns*[30] itself the claimant
sought to recoup a loss from its solicitors on the basis that the solicitors had committed a breach of trust when the solicitors took money held on trust for the
claimant in its client account and used that money to pay the solicitors' own
expenses. It was held, however, that the solicitors bore no liability to the claimant
because the claimant's loss had been caused by a fraudulent over-valuation of
property which it had taken as security for a loan made to third parties. The solicitors had restored sufficient funds to its client account to meet all of its obligations
to the claimant in good time. There was, consequently, no causal connection
between the loss which the claimant had suffered and the breach of trust which the
solicitors had committed, and therefore the claimant had no ground for recovery
against the solicitors in relation to the loss it had suffered by virtue of the fraudulent over-valuation of the land which had induced it to enter into the loan
contract. This case is considered in greater detail below.[31]

32.09 The particular concerns of the House of Lords in this sense were twofold. First,
the House of Lords was concerned that the trustees should only be liable for any
loss which their breach of trust has caused. It would not be sufficient to establish
liability in the trustees that the beneficiary had suffered some unconnected loss
which could not be demonstrated to have resulted from the trustees' breach of
their obligations. Secondly, by extension, if the beneficiary were able to recover a
loss from the trustees in any situation in which they committed a technical breach
of their trust obligations, then it would be possible that the trustees might be liable
to the beneficiaries while the transaction which the trustees might have contracted
on behalf of the trust might have generated a gain for the beneficiaries. Suppose,
by way of example, that the trust instrument restricted the trustees to making
investments in shares quoted on the FTSE-100 list maintained by the London
Stock Exchange but that the trustees invested in *x* shares which were listed instead
on the London Stock Exchange's Alternative Investment Market. To have invested
in the *x* shares clearly constituted a breach of the trustees' obligations, thus generating a potential liability for breach of trust if the trust suffered a loss. Suppose,
however, that the *x* shares rose in value such that the trust earned a profit from the
transaction. It was just such a situation which Lord Browne-Wilkinson considered in *Target Holdings v Redferns*[32] might lead to the beneficiaries achieving an
unjustified double benefit if they were both able to enforce an action for breach of
trust against the trustees and to retain the increase in the value of their trust fund
caused by the investment in *x* shares. Rather, Lord Browne-Wilkinson required
that an action for breach of trust be based on the compensation of any loss suffered
by the beneficiaries. This emerging principle ran contrary to the former approach
which did not permit a trustee to plead some intervening act which allegedly

[30] [1996] 1 AC 421.   [31] See para 32.70.   [32] [1996] 1 AC 421.

caused the loss.[33] The trustees would be required to dispose of the unauthorized investments in favour of authorized investments,[34] as considered below.[35]

The issue then arose as to the rights which must be affected to found a claim for **32.10** breach of trust. Lord Browne-Wilkinson considered the position which would arise in relation to a technical breach of trust by the trustee carried out with the consent of one beneficiary but not the other. His lordship considered the question whether there could be liability in such circumstances on a strict liability basis even though there had been in fact no loss suffered by the beneficiary who had not consented to the breach. His lordship held:[36]

> A carping beneficiary could insist that the unauthorised investment be sold and the proceeds invested in authorised investments: but the trustee would be under no liability to pay compensation either to the trust fund or to the beneficiary because the breach has caused no loss to the trust fund. Therefore, in each case the first question is to ask what are the rights of the beneficiary only if some relevant right has been infringed so as to give rise to a loss is it necessary to consider the extent of the trustee's liability to compensate for such loss.

Therefore, there must be a loss which flows directly from the breach of trust. It is not enough that there is some breach of trust if no loss is actually suffered as a result of it. Furthermore, in a trust in which different beneficiaries took different rights in different property under the trust, these dicta would suggest that only a beneficiary affected by the breach of trust could bring an action. For example, if land were held on trust such that it could be made available for the occupation of one class of beneficiaries only, in the event that the trustees breached their obligations to ensure that the property be available for the occupation of those beneficiaries, it would not be open to beneficiaries from another class to seek to enforce an action against the trustees because they would not have a 'relevant right' in that context to support such an action.

Liability to effect specific restitution of the trust property

The trustee faces a liability to effect specific restitution of any trust property which **32.11** is passed away in breach of trust.[37] This is an action *in personam* ordering the trustee to restore the trust fund: the reference to its being 'in personam' meaning that it is a claim brought against the trustee's conscience within the equitable jurisdiction.[38] This means that the trustee is obliged to recover the very property which had formed a part of the trust fund before the breach of trust from whomsoever has it in their possession. This principle operates most effectively in relation

---

[33] cf *Kellaway v Johnson* (1842) 5 Beav 319; *Magnus v Queensland National Bank* (1888) 37 Ch D 466; *Re Brogden* (1888) 38 Ch D 546.   [34] *Re Massingberd's Settlement* (1890) 63 LT 296.
[35] See para 32.12.   [36] [1995] 3 All ER 785, 793.
[37] *Nocton v Lord Ashburton* [1914] AC 932, 952, *per* Lord Haldane LC.
[38] *Target Holdings v Redferns* [1996] 1 AC 421. See para 32.27.

to tangible property such as chattels. The trustees would therefore be required to recover those chattels and restore them to the trust fund. The trustees are liable to bear the costs of recovering the property. In the event that the property is intangible, the process of recovering the very property which had previously comprised a part of the trust fund is then more complex if that property is mixed with other property. If the intangible property were held distinct from all other property then the process of reclaiming it would be comparatively straightforward.[39] If the property is mixed with other property in such a way that it was impossible to separate that property off from the remainder of the fund and thus to recover the same property as had been passed away, then the beneficiaries would be required to bring an equitable tracing claim to establish a claim by way of constructive trust, lien, or charge proportionate to the total value of the claim.[40] Regardless of the feasibilities of mounting a tracing claim in equity, however, if specific restitution of the original property were not possible, then the trustee would nevertheless be required to compensate the beneficiaries in the first place for the value of the property lost to the fund:[41] this aspect of the remedy is considered in the next paragraph. As considered above, it is likely that the trustees themselves would seek to bring a claim against whoever is in possession of the trust property to offset their own liability to the beneficiaries.

Replacing unauthorized investments with authorized investments

32.12 Whereas the discussion thus far has focused on the recovery of the very property taken from the trust fund, there are situations in which trust instruments specify with some precision the property in which the trustees can invest. In situations in which the trustees have invested in property not permitted by the trust instrument, their obligation will be to replace those unauthorized investments with authorized investments.[42] This is different from providing specific restitution because the trustees are not recovering property which has been passed away from the trust in breach of their duties but rather the trustees are acquiring the assets of a type which they ought to have acquired beforehand.[43] In circumstances in which the trustees have acquired unauthorized investments, the beneficiaries have a right to elect whether they wish to receive equitable compensation in cash from the trustees, or whether they wish to have the unauthorized investments replaced with authorized investments.[44] If the beneficiaries elect to replace unauthorized

---

[39] *FC Jones & Sons (A firm) v Jones* [1996] 3 WLR 703; see para 33.21.
[40] See para 33.30.
[41] *Caffrey v Darby* (1801) 6 Ves Jr 488; *Clough v Bond* (1838) 3 Myl & Cr 490; *Target Holdings v Redferns* [1996] AC 421.   [42] *Re Massingberd's Settlement* (1890) 63 LT 296.
[43] See para 32.11.
[44] See *Wright v Morgan* [1926] AC 788. See also *Docker v Soames* (1834) 2 My & K 655; *Watts v Girdlestone* (1843) 6 Beav 188; *Byreshall v Bradford* (1844) 6 Mass 235; *Shepherd v Mouls* (1845) 4 Hare 500; *Re Patten and Edmunton Union* (1883) 52 LJ Ch 787; *Re Jenkins and H E Randall's Contract* [1903] 2 Ch 362.

with authorized investments, then the trustees will be obliged to bear the cost of replacing those unauthorized with authorized investments personally.[45] Alternatively, if the beneficiaries elect to take compensation in cash, then the trustees will be able to retain those investments for themselves.[46]

This is distinct from the remedy considered in the next paragraph which relates to making good the loss to the trust in cash terms because it obliges the trustees to acquire property of a class identified in the trust instrument.[47] In circumstances in which the trustees failed to acquire a specific form of investment required to be acquired by them under the terms of the trust instrument, then the trustees are required to acquire assets of the kind which were supposed to have been acquired by the trustees.[48] The general obligations in relation to breaches of trust in relation to the acquisition of investments are considered below.[49] **32.13**

Personal liability to account for breach of trust and to effect equitable compensation

From Lord Browne-Wilkinson's account of the available actions in *Target Holdings v Redferns*,[50] beyond that for specific restitution of the trust property considered in paragraph 32.12, the following equitable remedy is available, as explained in the speech of Lord Browne-Wilkinson:[51] **32.14**

> If specific restitution of the trust property is not possible, then the liability of the trustee is to pay sufficient compensation to the trust estate to put it back to what it would have been had the breach not been committed.

This remedy should perhaps be considered to cover two slightly different grounds of claim: first, an action against the trustee to pay property of equivalent value to the trust fund; and, secondly, an action for equitable compensation also to recover other losses not represented narrowly by the replacement of the value of the property lost to the fund. The following two sections consider these subtly different remedies independently from one another, before a third section following considers the basis on which a valuation of the trustees' liability is conducted.

Restoration of the trust fund in cash terms

The first of these two strands in the further cause of action, as set out in the preceding paragraph, is then for restoration of an amount of money equal to the value **32.15**

---

[45] *Re Massingberd's Settlement* (1890) 63 LT 296.
[46] *Knott v Cottee* (1892) 16 Beav 77; *Head v Gould* [1898] 2 Ch 250.
[47] See para 32.14.
[48] *Shepherd v Mouls* (1845) 4 Hare 500, *per* Wigram V-C; *Robinson v Robinson* (1851) 1 De GM & G 247, 256. See also *Byrchall v Bradford* (1821) 6 Madd 13.   [49] See para 32.47.
[50] [1996] AC 421.
[51] *Caffrey v Darby* (1801) 6 Ves 488, [1775–1802] All ER Rep 507; *Clough v Bond* (1838) 3 My & Cr 490, (1838) 40 ER 1016.

of the property lost to the trust fund by the breach of trust.[52] As Lord Browne-Wilkinson described this liability in *Target Holdings v Redferns*: [53]

> The equitable rules of compensation for breach of trust have been largely developed in relation to such traditional trusts, where the only way in which all the beneficiaries rights can be protected is to restore to the trust fund what ought to be there. In such a case the basic rule is that a trustee in breach of trust must restore or pay to the trust estate either the assets which have been lost to the estate by reason of the breach or compensation for such loss. Courts of Equity did not award damages but, in acting in personam, ordered the defaulting trustee to restore the trust estate.[54]

The issue of valuation is considered below; however, valuation will be an amount to return the trust to the position it had occupied before the transaction which constituted the breach of trust. As Lord Browne-Wilkinson rendered the appropriate valuation: it is that required to 'put [the trust fund] back to what it would have been had the breach not been committed'.[55] In other words, the aim of this second remedy is to calculate the amount of money which is necessary to restore the value of the trust fund. It is important to note that there is a difference between personal compensation for loss suffered as a breach of trust, and compensation equivalent to the value of property lost to the trust.[56] This concept is rendered as restitution in *Swindle v Harrison*,[57] but this should not be confused with restitution of unjust enrichment but rather refers to an older, equitable sense of the term 'restitution' connected to the recovery of property held on trust.

32.16   It is possible that this could take a number of forms other than straightforwardly paying cash. For example, it might permit the acquisition of an annuity which would generate similar levels of income to any trust capital misapplied in breach of trust. The level of compensation, as a matter of evidence, must equate to the loss which the beneficiary can demonstrate was caused by the breach of trust such that the trust fund is placed back in the position it would have occupied but for the breach.[58] This might include any loss which the trust would have suffered subsequently as a result of the nature of the trust property—for example, accounting for a large fall in the value of such property subsequently.

32.17   However, what is important to note is that, while tracing revolves around the assertion of proprietary rights either in a specific item of property or in its substitute, Lord Browne-Wilkinson expressed the jurisdiction of equity in this context to be in the form of an action *in personam* against the trustee to recover the trust

---

[52] See para 32.14.   [53] [1996] 1 AC 421, [1995] 3 All ER 785, 793.

[54] See *Nocton v Lord Ashburton* [1914] AC 932, 952, 958, *per* Viscount Haldane LC.

[55] *Target Holdings v Redferns* [1996] 1 AC 421.

[56] *Swindle v Harrison* [1997] 4 All ER 705; *Bristol & West BS v Mothew* [1996] 4 All ER 698.

[57] [1997] 4 All ER 705. This usage is 'confusing' in that the trustee will not necessarily have been personally enriched as is ordinarily required for the establishment of liability for restitution for unjust enrichment.   [58] *Target Holdings v Redferns* [1996] 1 AC 421.

estate.[59] In accordance with the decision of Lord Nicholls in *Attorney-General for Hong Kong v Reid*,[60] the court is providing for an action *in personam* against a particular person who is identified as a trustee, seemingly, acting on the principle that 'equity looks upon as done that which ought to have been done' such that the trustee is required to continue to hold that item of specific property on trust for the beneficiaries (unless the property has passed out of the trustee's control or possession).[61] Where property has passed out of the trustee's control or possession, the action converts to an action in money to recover the equivalent cash value of the specific assets misapplied in breach of trust, as considered in the immediately following section. Therefore, it is suggested that the action is not strictly a personal action, but rather an action in relation to specific property which is brought against the trustee personally, subject to a personal action to account in money if the specific property cannot be recovered.

Restitution of the general losses to the trust fund by way of equitable compensation

The machinations of equitable compensation

Compensation is an equitable remedy which gives rise to a right which is purely personal in nature, giving no right to any specific property. In relation to breach of trust, by reference to which some loss has been caused to the trust, it is that loss which is made good by compensation. The court is therefore awarding a payment of money instead of some proprietary right which relies on the beneficiaries showing that a loss has resulted from the breach of trust. Rather than recognize some proprietary right in the beneficiary and impose a trust or charge to recognize the right as being proprietary, compensation requires only that the loss to the trust is calculated in cash terms and that that amount is accounted for by the trustee to the trust fund.   **32.18**

Whereas the operation of the equitable doctrine of compensation is avowedly not based on common law notions of foreseeability and remoteness of damage, there has nevertheless been a convergence of the principles on which those two distinct jurisdictions operate as a result of the decision in *Target Holdings v Redferns*,[62] in which case Lord Browne-Wilkinson held the following:[63]   **32.19**

---

[59] [1996] 1 AC 421 [1995] 3 All ER 785, 793.
[60] *Attorney-General for Hong Kong v Reid* [1994] 1 AC 324, [1993] 3 WLR 1143.
[61] The distinction between an *in personam* and an *in rem* action in this context is that an action *in personam* in equity binds only the particular defendant whereas an action *in rem* would bind any successors in title or assignees from the defendant (other than the bona fide purchaser for value).
[62] [1996] 1 AC 421.
[63] [1996] 1 AC 421 [1995] 3 All ER 785, 792.

At common law there are two principles fundamental to the award of damages. First, that the defendant's wrongful act must cause the damage complained of. Second, that the plaintiff is to be put 'in the same position as he would have been in if he had not sustained the wrong for which he is now getting his compensation or reparation'.[64] Although, as will appear, in many ways equity approaches liability for making good a breach of trust from a different starting point, in my judgment those two principles are applicable as much in equity as at common law. Under both systems liability is fault based: the defendant is only liable for the consequences of the legal wrong he has done to the plaintiff and to make good the damage caused by his wrong or to pay by way of compensation more than the loss suffered from such wrong.

32.20 Compensation for breach is therefore based on fault and loss, rather than on any strict liability of the trustee.[65] This is surprising given the drift in the law relating to knowing receipt and dishonest assistance towards an ever stricter liability for strangers to the trust who could not be expected to have such intimate knowledge of the terms of the trust as the trustee. The distinction between fault-based common law damages and fault-based equitable compensation is then a further issue. Lord Browne-Wilkinson put it in the following terms:[66]

> The detailed rules of equity as to causation and the quantification of the loss differ, at least ostensibly, from those applicable at common law. But the principles underlying both systems are the same. On the assumptions that had to be made in the present case until the factual issues are resolved (ie that the transaction would have gone through even if there had been no breach of trust), the result reached by the Court of Appeal does not accord with those principles. Redferns as trustees have been held liable to compensate Target for a loss caused otherwise than by the breach of trust.

Equitable compensation therefore arises on the basis of the trustee's equitable obligations to the beneficiaries. There is, however, an awkward distinction remaining between the need to demonstrate that there is some causal connection between the loss suffered by the beneficiaries and the breach of trust, and the determination that the means of establishing an entitlement to equitable compensation does not require the demonstration of sufficient proximity or common law causation between the loss and the breach of trust.

Distinguishing between 'restorative' and 'compensatory' remedies

32.21 There is a distinction made between compensation awarded for breach of the trustees' duty of skill and care,[67] and compensation awarded for breach of the general fiduciary duty borne by trustees not to permit conflict or not to deal with the trust property personally.[68] In relation to the former (breach of the duty of skill and care) the court will import analogous (if not identical) principles to those of

---

[64] See *Livingstone v Rawyards Coal Co* (1880) 5 App Cas 25, 39, *per* Lord Blackburn.
[65] Pawlowski, 'Equitable wrongs: common law damages or equitable compensation?' (2000) 6(9) T & T 20.   [66] *Target Holdings v Redferns* [1996] AC 421, [1995] 3 All ER 785, 792.
[67] See para 10.39.   [68] See para 10.99.

causation and remoteness of damage.[69] In this context, the award of equitable compensation is being made to compensate the beneficiaries for their losses in general terms and is not limited simply to the restoration of the trust fund. However, in relation to duties to avoid conflicts of interest and to refrain from self-dealing, equitable compensation is awarded in lieu of rescission of the contract which the trustee had entered into in breach of his fiduciary duty:[70] compensation in this instance will be calculated according to the value of the property lost to the trust, less the price paid to the trustee, plus interest.[71] Therefore, the purpose of equitable compensation in this context is to restore the value of the trust fund, rather than to compensate the beneficiaries for any other aspect of their loss in more general terms.

By way of illustration of this principle, in the case of *Swindle v Harrison*[72] a solicitor **32.22** named Mr Swindle failed to disclose all of the material facts in connection with a purchase of property to his client, Mrs Harrison, as he was required to do in furtherance of his fiduciary duties to her, with the result that she lost money in the transaction. Mrs Harrison sought compensation from the solicitors for her loss. The Court of Appeal held that Mrs Harrison was only entitled to restorative compensation, that is an amount of compensation to put the trust into the position which it had occupied before the transaction. The aim of this restorative remedy is to achieve rescission of the transaction. The Court of Appeal held that this restorative remedy is only available where the plaintiff has been induced into the contract by some fraud or unconscionable act on the part of the fiduciary. On the facts of *Swindle v Harrison*, Mrs Harrison wished to enter into the transaction of her own volition and therefore restorative remedies were not available.

It is suggested that, perhaps, this distinction between compensatory and restorative **32.23** compensation is somewhat artificial, although it is clearly established on the decided cases. To return to first principles, the basis of the trust is the operation of equity acting *in personam* on the conscience of the trustee as the legal owner of the property[73] and therefore it is suggested that good conscience requires the trustee not only to restore the value of the trust fund but also to account to the beneficiaries for any other benefit which would have accrued to them but for the trustees' breach of trust.[74] Consequently, it is suggested that it is in common with the principle in *Target Holdings v Redferns* and of the law of trusts in general that the trustee be liable to account to the trust for any loss of property or loss of opportunity which is caused by the trustee's breach of trust.

---

[69] *Bristol & West BS v Mothew* [1996] 4 All ER 698, *per* Millett LJ. That such common law principles are included by analogy is perhaps not surprising, given the similarities between negligence at common law and liability to equitable compensation of breach of the duty of skill and care.
[70] *Bristol & West BS v Mothew* [1996] 4 All ER 698.　　[71] *Holder v Holder* [1968] Ch 353.
[72] [1997] 4 All ER 705.
[73] *Westdeutsche Landesbank v Islington* [1996] AC 669; see para 27.01.
[74] cf *Attorney-General for Hong Kong v Reid* [1994] 1 AC 1.

Equitable compensation for an opportunity lost due to a breach of trust

32.24 The more difficult situation is that in which the beneficiaries seek to recover some lost opportunity caused by the breach of trust. While it is commonly said that the trustee will not be liable for such opportunity cost,[75] it might well be the case that the development of a causal link for the liability of trustees[76] will lead to liability for losses which are foreseeable as a result of the breach of trust. Nevertheless, the trustees will, on old authority, be liable for any omission to act such that property is not brought into the trust, provided that the trustees have acted with wilful default.[77] In consequence, it is suggested that trustees will be liable for failing to realize some opportunities in the form of property which the trustees ought to have gathered into the trust. An example of the easier case, it is suggested, would involve a situation in which the trustees failed to collect the rents from trust land leased out to third parties: in which case the trustees would have failed to realize an opportunity which ought to have accrued to the trust. A more difficult situation might be that in which a valuable oil painting held on trust was to have been sold to a dealer for £100,000 but the trustee sold it instead in breach of trust for only £75,000; it would be reasonable to suppose that the beneficiary ought to have some action against the trustee for the lost opportunity of the more valuable sale.[78]

32.25 The issue which remains is that compensation will not achieve restitution of specific property; only a payment of money equal to the loss. In *Target Holdings v Redferns* Lord Browne-Wilkinson held that:[79]

> If specific restitution of the trust property is not possible, then the liability of the trustee is to pay sufficient compensation to the trust estate to put it back to what it would have been had the breach not been committed.[80] Even if the immediate cause of the loss is the dishonesty or failure of a third party, the trustee is liable to make good that loss to the trust estate if, but for the breach, such loss would not have occurred.[81]

Therefore, provided that some causal connection between the breach of trust and the loss suffered by the beneficiaries can be demonstrated, compensation will be available to the beneficiary for all of the loss that is consequent on the breach of trust. It is suggested that there is nothing on the face of these dicta which ought to

---

[75] *Palmer v Jones* (1862) 1 Vern 144.

[76] *Target Holdings v Redferns* [1996] 1 AC 421, [1995] 3 WLR 352, [1995] 3 All ER 785.

[77] *Palmer v Jones* (1682) 1 Vern 144; *Harnard v Webster* (1725) Sel Ch Cas 53; *Pybus v Smith* (1790) 1 Ves Jr 189. See para 30.61.

[78] J Mowbray et al, *Lewin on Trusts* (17th edn, Sweet & Maxwell, 2000) ('*Lewin*') 1194; *Kingdon v Castleman* (1877) 46 LJ Ch 448; cf *Hobday v Peters (No 3)* (1860) 28 Beav 603.

[79] [1996] AC 421 [1995] 3 All ER 785, 792.

[80] *Caffrey v Darby* (1801) 6 Ves 488, [1775–1802] All ER Rep 507; *Clough v Bond* (1838) 3 My & Cr 490, (1838) 40 ER 1016.

[81] *Re Dawson, Union Fidelity Trustee Co Ltd (No 2)* [1980] 2 All ER 92 [1980] Ch 515.

exclude liability in relation to an opportunity which the trustees ought to have realized for the trust. The trustee is personally liable, even where the source of the misfeasance is with some third party.[82]

Equitable compensation in relation to exhausted trusts

Beneficiaries will be entitled to equitable compensation only if their interests are **32.26** in possession at the time or if they have some substantive right by reference to which they can establish that they have suffered loss. So, in circumstances in which the trust property has become vested absolutely in possession in some beneficiaries as a result of some exercise of the trustees' discretion, then the compensation attributable to those equitable interests is payable directly to those people who were absolutely entitled to the property at issue.[83] Similarly, if the trusts have terminated, for example if the trust property had been held by way of succession but has subsequently vested in possession, then the owner of that absolute interest will be entitled to receive compensation directly.[84] If the trust property has become vested absolutely in possession the beneficiary would not be entitled to have the trust property reconstituted but rather his remedy is limited to that of equitable compensation because the trust has become, in effect, wound up.[85]

That the action against the trustees is *in personam*

Courts of equity have never awarded damages but, in acting *in personam*, have ordered the defaulting trustee to restore the trust estate by way of compensation.[86] **32.27** The equitable rules of compensation for breach of trust have been largely developed in relation to traditional family settlements, such that the only way in which all the beneficiaries' rights can be protected is to restore to the trust fund property of a value equal to that which ought to have been there. In such a case the basic rule is that a trustee in breach of trust must restore or pay to the trust estate either the assets which have been lost to the estate by reason of the breach, or compensation in cash in an amount equal to that loss. As Lord Browne-Wilkinson explained this matter in *Target Holdings v Redferns*:[87]

> The equitable rules of compensation for breach of trust have been largely developed in relation to such traditional trusts, where the only way in which all the beneficiaries' rights can be protected is to restore to the trust fund what ought to be there. In such a case the basic rule is that a trustee in breach of trust must restore or

---

[82] *Target Holdings v Redferns* [1996] AC 421, [1995] 3 All ER 785, 794.
[83] *Bartlett v Barclays Bank Trust Co Ltd (No 2)* [1980] Ch 515, 543–544, [1980] 2 All ER 92, 95–96.
[84] *Bartlett v Barclays Bank Trust Co Ltd (No 2)* [1980] Ch 515, 543–544, [1980] 2 All ER 92, 95–96.
[85] *Target Holdings v Redferns* [1996] AC 421, [1995] 3 All ER 785, 795.
[86] *Nocton v Lord Ashburton* [1914] AC 932, 952, 958, *per* Viscount Haldane LC.
[87] [1996] 1 AC 421; [1995] 3 All ER 785, 793.

pay to the trust estate either the assets which have been lost to the estate by reason of the breach or compensation for such loss. Courts of Equity did not award damages but, in acting in personam, ordered the defaulting trustee to restore the trust estate.[88]

Therefore, the remedy of compensation is available on a personal basis from the trustee to achieve restitution of the loss suffered by the trust fund, as well as on a proprietary basis to achieve specific restitution of the trust property where that is possible. The significance of this principle having been developed in relation to family trusts is that the trustees in such cases were generally treated as though they occupied a position of special tenderness in relation to the beneficiaries.[89] Those principles apply even in cases such as *Target Holdings v Redferns* in which commercial questions are at issue. Lord Browne-Wilkinson expressed some reservations as to the suitability of some of those traditional principles in complex commercial cases.[90] Consequently, the trustees were to be held personally liable if any of the beneficiaries' personal fortunes were lost through the misfeasance of the trustees. It is perhaps questionable whether the same rule ought to apply to commercial situations, where perhaps a claim based on contract might be preferable.

Identifying the value to be compensated

Valuation of the loss to the trust

32.28 The appropriate valuation to be the subject of equitable compensation as a result of a breach of trust is that required to 'put [the trust fund] back to what it would have been had the breach not been committed';[91] that is, an amount such that the plaintiff is placed 'in the same position as he would have been in if he had not sustained the wrong for which he is now getting his compensation or reparation'.[92] The valuation is therefore that required to identify a level of compensation which is capable of restoring the value of the trust fund. The claimant beneficiary is therefore required to prove the level of compensation which equates to the loss caused to the trust by the breach of trust.[93]

32.29 This is a comparatively straightforward matter in relation to property which has a steady open market value or the value of which has remained constant between the time of the commission of the breach of trust and the date of trial. The more difficult question relates to compensation in respect of property which fluctuates in value between the date of the breach and the date of judgment. The beneficiary

---

[88] See *Nocton v Lord Ashburton* [1914] AC 932, 952, 958, *per* Viscount Haldane LC.
[89] [1996] 1 AC 421.   [90] ibid.
[91] *Target Holdings v Redferns* [1996] 1 AC 421, [1995] 3 All ER 785, 794; citing with approval *Caffrey v Darby* (1801) 6 Ves 488, [1775–1802] All ER Rep 507; *Clough v Bond* (1838) 3 My & Cr 490, 40 ER 1016.
[92] *Livingstone v Rawyards Coal Co* (1880) 5 App Cas 25, 39, *per* Lord Blackburn.
[93] The editors of *Lewin on Trusts* take the view that the value to be taken is the value of the property at trial: *op cit*, 1194. It is suggested, however, that the value is the loss to the beneficiaries at trial, an amount which may be greater than the value of the property which was taken from the trust fund.

would clearly prefer to claim the highest value for that property between the commission of the breach and the date of judgment. This approach, dubbed 'the highest intermediate balance' approach, was adopted in *Jaffray v Marshall*.[94] In that case it was taken that everything was to be presumed against the wrongdoing trustee. Therefore, if there had been an opportunity to realize the assets during a continuing breach of trust, this would lead to the quantum of the compensation payable by the trustee being an obligation to make good the lost opportunity at the highest point of its fluctuating market value. There was no distinction made in that case between shares and other types of property. The approach in *Jaffray v Marshall* was based on a strict liability on the part of the trustee for any breach of trust, holding the trustee accountable for the highest possible loss in the circumstances.

However, Lord Browne-Wilkinson in *Target Holdings v Redferns* overruled the **32.30** decision in *Jaffray v Marshall* as being wrong in principle. *Jaffray v Marshall*[95] was said to be wrongly decided in principle by Lord Browne-Wilkinson in *Target Holdings v Redferns* on the basis that its award of compensation was assessed on the basis of an assumption of an impossible sale (that is, a sale which might not have been possible to effect in practice, even if an open-market value could have been estimated for that time).

As considered above, in *Target Holdings v Redferns* it was decided that the **32.31** appropriate value was the loss to the beneficiaries by the date of trial. It has been held more generally by the courts that the measure of compensation for breach of trust would be 'fair compensation'. That is to say, the difference between proper performance of the trust obligations and what the trustee actually achieved, not the least that could have been achieved.[96] It has been held that the trustee will not be liable for speculative or unliquidated losses: the beneficiary must be able to demonstrate that amounts have been lost.[97] However, it is not clear how this will interact with the principles of equitable compensation and their potentially broader ambit.[98]

Liability for amounts which might otherwise have been lost in taxation

The trustees' liability for amounts lost to the trust by way of breach of trust will be **32.32** amounts which, if not so lost, would have been prima facie liable to taxation as part the trust's capital or income, as appropriate. No such exculpatory principle

---

[94] [1994] 1 All ER 143, [1993] 1 WLR 1285; see also *Nant-y-glo and Blaina Ironworks Co v Grave* (1878) 12 Ch D 738.   [95] [1994] 1 All ER 143, [1993] 1 WLR 1285.
[96] *Nestle v National Westminster Bank plc* [1994] 1 All ER 118; [1993] 1 WLR 1260, CA.
[97] *Palmer v Jones* (1862) 1 Vern 144.
[98] C Ricketts, 'Compensating for loss in equity' in Birks and Rose (eds), *Restitution and Equity*, vol 1 (Oxford: Mansfield, 2000) 172.

applies to liability for equitable compensation as for common law damages under the *Gourley*[99] principle.[100]

The exclusion of causation, foreseeability, and remoteness

The distinction between equitable compensation and common law damages

32.33 While there remains some distinction between the common law and equity in this context, Lord Browne-Wilkinson did not find it necessary to probe that difference on the facts of *Target Holdings v Redferns* on the basis that there was no proof that the loss to the trust was caused in any way by the breach of trust itself. As his lordship explained this matter:

> ... the common law rules of remoteness of damage and causation do not apply. However, there does have to be some causal connection between the breach of trust and the loss to the trust estate for which compensation is recoverable, viz the fact that the loss would not have occurred but for the breach.[101]

In line with the older authorities in this area, the distinction between the common law and equitable codes would be that the common law will impose liability to pay damages only where there is sufficient proximity and foreseeability, whereas equity will award compensation where the loss can be shown to have been derived from the breach of trust. The difference would therefore be that compensation may be awarded even where the loss was not strictly foreseeable, provided that it did result from the breach of trust.[102]

32.34 Suppose that the trustees invested in a company's shares contrary to their limited, express investment powers in the trust instrument but nevertheless on the basis that the trustees genuinely expected that their investment in those shares would generate a better return for the trust than the investments which they were authorized to make. If the company which was the subject of their investment fell unexpectedly into insolvency as a result of terrorist activity in their production plants, such that the trust's investment was rendered worthless, it is suggested that the trustees would be liable for the loss caused to the beneficiaries because it resulted from their breach of trust in investing in unauthorized investments. Under common law, it would be arguable that the terrorist activity was unforeseeable and that no liability should attach to the trustees as a result. The distinction between equity and common law is therefore evident.

---

[99] *British Transport Commission v Gourley* [1956] AC 185.

[100] *Re Bell's Indenture* [1980] 1 WLR 1217; *Bartlett v Barclay's Bank Trust Co Ltd* [1980] Ch 515; *John v James* [1986] STC 352, 361, *per* Nicholls LJ. Cf *O'Sullivan v Management Agency and Music Ltd* [1985] QB 428, which was decided *per incuriam Re Bell's Indenture* and *Bartlett v Barclay's Bank*.

[101] See also *Re Miller's Deed Trusts* (1978) 75 LS Gaz 454; *Nestle v National Westminster Bank plc* [1994] 1 All ER 118, [1993] 1 WLR 1260.

[102] *Clough v Bond* (1838) 3 My & C 490, (1838) 8 LJ Ch 51, (1838) 2 Jur 958; *Re Massingberd's Settlement* (1890) 63 LT 296.

The third limb of the available remedies for breach of trust set out in *Target*   **32.35**
Holdings v Redferns demonstrates an apparent overlap with common law damages
and the need for evidence of a link between loss and remedy.[103] The important
initial point is that the suit must be brought against the trustee in cases of breach
of trust, before the matter is pursued against others who may have orchestrated the
breach of trust in fact. As Lord Browne-Wilkinson continued:

> Even if the immediate cause of the loss is the dishonesty or failure of a third party, the
> trustee is liable to make good that loss to the trust estate if, but for the breach, such
> loss would not have occurred.[104]

One of the more complex issues to arise out of the *Target Holdings v Redferns*[105]   **32.36**
litigation was the distinction between equitable compensation and common law
damages. In short, Lord Browne-Wilkinson held that there is only a slight, if
significant, difference between the two doctrines. Both are dependent, first, on
the fault of the defendant and, secondly, on a nexus between the loss suffered by
the plaintiff and the defendant's wrongdoing. This point emerges from the speech
of Lord Browne-Wilkinson in *Target Holdings v Redferns*:[106]

> At common law there are two principles fundamental to the award of damages. First,
> that the defendant's wrongful act must cause the damage complained of. Second,
> that the plaintiff is to be put 'in the same position as he would have been in if he had
> not sustained the wrong for which he is now getting his compensation or reparation'
> ...Although, as will appear, in many ways equity approaches liability for making
> good a breach of trust from a different starting point, in my judgment those two
> principles are applicable as much in equity as at common law. Under both systems
> liability is fault based: the defendant is only liable for the consequences of the legal
> wrong he has done to the plaintiff and to make good the damage caused by his wrong
> or to pay by way of compensation more than the loss suffered from such wrong. The
> detailed rules of equity as to causation and the quantification of the loss differ, at least
> ostensibly, from those applicable at common law. But the principles underlying both
> systems are the same.

The subtle distinction between these two doctrines relates to the relative evidential   **32.37**
burdens in cases of equitable compensation in contradistinction to cases involving
common law damages. The common law rules of remoteness of damage and causation do not apply in relation to equitable compensation thus making it easier for
claimants to establish a right to equitable compensation provided that there is some
causal connection between the claim and the loss and provided that there is some
right suitable to call the equitable jurisdiction into play. That there does have to be
some causal connection between the breach of trust and the loss to the trust estate

---

[103] See also *Bristol & West v Mothew* [1996] 4 All ER 698.
[104] *Re Dawson, Union Fidelity Trustee Co Ltd (No 2)* [1980] 2 All ER 92, [1980] Ch 515.
[105] [1996] 1 AC 421.   [106] [1996] 1 AC 421, [1995] 3 All ER 785, 792.

for which compensation is recoverable requires simply some evidence of the fact that the loss would not have occurred but for the breach.[107]

Exceptions to the requirement for a causal connection: power of sale in relation to mortgages

32.38   There are contexts in which the obligations of a trustee may be equivocal. It may not be clear on what basis a trustee is required to act in a particular situation. For example, a person who is made a constructive trustee over property may not obviously know the detail of the duties bound up in her trusteeship. Suppose a person who exercises the statutory power of sale characteristic of a mortgagee and then that the trustee holds the sale proceeds partly on trust for herself and partly on trust for that other person as required by statute:[108] in what circumstances can there be said to have been a breach of trust committed if the precise terms of the trusteeship are not known?

32.39   The question of the precise fiduciary duties attaching to a statutory power of sale was considered in *Parker Tweedale v Dunbar*.[109] The issue arose in relation to the fiduciary duty that a mortgagee owes to the mortgagor in respect of sale proceeds received when the mortgagee had exercised its statutory power of sale under section 101 of the Law of Property Act 1925. The question arose as to the manner in which the trustee in such circumstances was required to deal with that property. The mortgagor claimed that the mortgagee had not ensured that the sale was conducted in the most beneficial manner in the interests of the mortgagor. The mortgagor contended that the mortgagee had committed a breach of its fiduciary duty to the mortgagor. It was held, however, that the mortgagee did not owe a duty to the beneficiary in respect to the conduct of the sale of the property (other than to avoid negligence). The duty was only in respect of the proceeds of the sale once the sale had been completed. That is, the mortgagee was a trustee of the sale proceeds only once the property had been sold but the mortgagee was not required to act as a trustee in the manner in which the property was sold.

32.40   The manner in which such powers of sale operate has been a cause of some difficulty in recent years. In one reported case it was suggested that in certain circumstances even mortgagees exercising their statutory power of sale were required to act as though fiduciaries. Thus the view of Nicholls V-C in *Palk v Mortgage Services Funding plc*[110] was that the mortgagee should be considered to occupy a position 'analogous to a fiduciary duty'. That is, a duty which is almost a fiduciary duty to consider the question whether or not a sale in the manner intended by the mortgagee would be oppressive to the mortgagor or not. The importance of the

---

[107]   *Re Miller's Deed Trusts* (1978) 75 LS Gaz 454; *Nestle v National Westminster Bank plc* [1994] 1 All ER 118, [1993] 1 WLR 1260.   [108]   Law of Property Act 1925, s 105.
[109]   *Parker Tweedale v Dunbar Bank plc* [1991] Ch 12.   [110]   [1993] 2 WLR 415.

decision in *Palk v Mortgage Services Funding plc* was that it enabled a mortgagor who had become trapped in a negative equity situation to procure an order for an immediate sale of the property, rather than be forced to wait for the mortgagee to decide that it should exercise its power of sale. Given that the mortgagor was being locked into an ever-increasing debt over the property, while the open market value continued to fall, it was held that it would be oppressive to force the mortgagor to continue to wait for an upturn in the housing market. As such the mortgagor was entitled to an order for sale over the property.[111]

However, this conflicted with the stricter approach taken in *Cuckmere Brick v* **32.41** *Mutual Finance Ltd*[112] and *China and South Sea Bank Ltd v Tan Soon Gin*[113] that there was no trust imposed over the manner in which the property was to be sold. Rather, the mortgagee is entitled to exercise its power of sale entirely in its own interests. Thus, the mortgagee was held to bear the obligations of a trustee only in relation to the manner in which the sale proceeds were applied in discharge of the mortgage, with the surplus being paid to the mortgagor as required by section 105 of the Law of Property Act 1925. In the subsequent decision in the Court of Appeal in *Cheltenham & Gloucester BS v Krausz*,[114] Millett LJ held that the approach taken in *Palk v Mortgage Services Funding plc* should be restricted to issues as to the terms on which a sale would be carried out and not as to the decision whether or not a sale should be conducted at all. Further, it was held that there would be no obligation to exercise the power of sale in any event in circumstances where sale at such a time would not discharge the mortgage debt.

Therefore, the courts are prepared to take a proactive attitude to the manner in **32.42** which property and rights in relation to property are used by those who are fiduciaries to some extent over that property. In relation to the law of mortgages, the decision in relation to *Cuckmere Brick v Mutual Finance Ltd*[115] is consistent with a general judicial policy of protecting the interests of mortgagees to preserve a fluid housing market.

Limitations inherent in the provision of equitable compensation

The true purpose of the provision of equitable compensation was said in *Target* **32.43** *Holdings v Redferns*[116] to be to make good the loss, even though the right of action based on breach of trust technically arose immediately. This is a possible weakness with the decision in *Target Holdings* in that there would have been a valid action against the trustee solicitors, who committed the breach of trust in misusing client money but had replaced those funds before they were required to use them for the purposes of their customer's loan contract, if such an action had been brought

111 See also *Wight v Olswang (No 2)* [2000] WTLR 783.   112 [1971] Ch 949.
113 [1990] 1 AC 536.   114 [1997] 1 All ER 21.   115 [1971] Ch 949.
116 [1996] AC 421.

before the solicitors had acquired the mortgage security for Target, but that action appeared to dissolve on the facts of that case precisely because the solicitors had remedied the breach before it came to light.[117] The more complex problem might arise in circumstances in which property with only sentimental value is disposed of. Perhaps the property is intrinsically valuable but in a way which the decision in *Target Holdings* does not consider because that decision assumes the only significant value to be an open market value. The requirement to demonstrate loss which can be quantifiable in terms of money compensation gives the beneficiary no effective remedy. This approach indicates that the right of the beneficiary is to be measured in amounts in terms of resale value and not in relation to the intrinsic value of taking a proprietary right over specific, identified trust property.

The availability of set-off in the event of breach of trust

32.44   The trustees may wish to set off a loss caused by one breach of trust against a gain which the trustees have procured for the benefit of the trust: self-evidently, if they were able to do so it would reduce their liability to the beneficiaries. The trustees will not be entitled to claim that any of the gains or successful investment which the trustees have transacted on behalf of the trust can be set off against the loss suffered by the beneficiaries as a result of the trustees' breach of trust.[118] The trustees will not be entitled to set off any loss suffered in one breach of trust against a gain made under an unconnected breach of trust.[119] Thus, each breach of trust will be treated distinctly one from another.[120] The trustees will be entitled, however, to set off any gain made from the breach of trust itself against any loss which resulted from that same breach of trust.[121] In essence, this principle could be said to be merely a part of the process of valuing the loss suffered by the trust.[122] Consequently, a profit resulting from the transaction which constituted the breach of trust cannot give the beneficiaries a right to compensation greater than the loss they have suffered due to the breach of trust:[123] setting off gain against loss is a necessary part of that process. The trustees will be liable to bear personally any

---

[117]   Maybe that case could be thought of in terms of the solicitors having breached their trust but then provided compensation—in the form of using other funds to acquire the security which their clients had instructed them to acquire—before their clients learned of the breach.

[118]   See *Wiles v Gresham* (1854) 2 Drew 258; *Re Deare* (1895) 11 TLR 183; *Dimes v Scott* (1824–28) 4 Russ 195. The principle would seem self-evident that the trustees cannot simply look back over the life of the trust's investment performance and claim to write off a present loss caused by breach of trust against previous gains established within the trustees' powers.

[119]   *Wiles v Gresham* (1854) 2 Drew 258, 271; *Re Deare* (1895) 11 TLR 183; *Dimes v Scott* (1824–28) 4 Russ 195.   [120]   This follows, it is suggested, from the cases cited above.

[121]   *Fletcher v Green* (1864) 33 Beav 426; *Vyse v Foster* (1872) 8 Ch App 309, affirmed at (1874) LR 7 HL 318; *Bartlett v Barclay's Bank Trust Co Ltd (No 2)* [1980] Ch 515.

[122]   See para 32.54.

[123]   See para 32.54: *Target Holdings v Redferns* [1996] AC 421, [1995] 3 All ER 785, 793, where Lord Browne-Wilkinson sought to exclude the possibility of the 'carping beneficiary' recovering compensation for a technical breach of trust if he had not suffered any loss.

costs involved in the replacement of unauthorized investments with authorized investments[124] or other costs connected with putting the breach of trust to rights.

The manner of the trustees' obligation to account to the beneficiaries

The beneficiaries are required to plead and to prove at trial any breach of trust **32.45** committed by the trustees. The beneficiaries are not permitted to use cross-examination and the remainder of the trial process as a means of embarking on a fishing expedition seeking evidence.[125] Rather, in circumstances in which the trustees have committed some act which has constituted the breach of trust, then the beneficiaries must plead both the identity of the property which has been received by the trustees and also the location of that property.[126] As part of the process of bringing a claim to court, however, the beneficiaries will be able to use the discovery and interrogatories process to flesh out the details of the breach of trust which they are seeking to establish. The limit of the beneficiaries' recovery by way of account from the trustees will typically be restricted to an amount of compensation equal to those items pleaded.[127]

A different approach obtains in circumstances in which the trustees' breach of **32.46** trust is caused by some omission, rather than any action. In such a situation the beneficiaries[128] must demonstrate that the trustees were guilty of some wilful default in their failure to act.[129] In this context, the term 'wilful default' connotes a wrongful omission, rather than a deliberate policy of not acting, such that an existing or imminent breach of trust can be proved at trial.[130] The court can make any of the orders considered in Chapter 31 relating to the avoidance of breaches of trust to prevent the trustees from continuing in their omission. The court can make an order in this regard at any stage during the litigation process.[131] The trustees' liability is for any loss actually suffered by the beneficiaries and also for any amount which the trustees ought to have gathered into the trust fund.[132]

---

[124] *Re Massingberd's Settlement* (1890) 63 LT 296.
[125] *Re Wrightson* [1908] 1 Ch 789; *Bartlett v Barclay's Bank Trust Co Ltd (No 2)* [1980] Ch 515. See also *Coope v Carter* (1852) 2 De GM & G 292; *Askew v Woodhead* (1873) 28 LT 465 preventing a claim in respect of omissions by way of wilful default in relation to matters which are only revealed during the trial process. Cf *Re Owens* (1882) 47 LT 61.   [126] *Re Stevens* [1898] 1 Ch 162.
[127] *Re Stevens* [1898] 1 Ch 162. Cf *Campbell v Gillespie* [1900] 1 Ch 255.
[128] Excluding any beneficiary such as a remainderman whose interest has not yet vested: *Whitney v Smith* (1869) Ch App 513.
[129] *Lord Kensington v Bouverie* (1855) 7 De GM & G 134, at 156; *Sleight v Lawson* (1857) 3 K&J 292; *Barber v Mackrell* (1879) 12 Ch D 534; *Smith v Armitage* (1883) 24 Ch D 727. Cf *Mayer v Murray* (1878) 8 Ch D 424. See now CPR [Civil Procedure Rules 1998] Pt 16, 11.2(7) Practice Direction.
[130] *Re Tebbs* [1976] 1 WLR 924; *Bartlett v Barclay's Bank Trust Co Ltd (No 2)* [1980] Ch 515.
[131] *Job v Job* (1877) 6 Ch D 562; *Mayer v Murray* (1878) 8 Ch D 424; and also *Re Symons* (1882) 21 Ch D 757; *Laming v Gee* (1878) 10 Ch D 715.
[132] *Palmer v Jones* (1682) 1 Vern 144; *Harnard v Webster* (1725) Sel Ch Cas 53; *Pybus v Smith* (1790) 1 Ves Jr 189; *Re Stevens* [1898] 1 Ch 162, at 172; *Bartlett v Barclay's Bank Trust Co Ltd (No 2)* [1980] Ch 515, 546.

C. Breach of Trust and Investment of the Trust Fund

The particular context of breach of trust and investment of the trust fund

32.47 Among the trustees most complex obligations are those in connection with the investment of the trust fund. The particular context of the investment of trusts is considered in Chapter 52.[133] Trustees, in ordinary circumstances, are required to balance the need to generate the best possible return on capital for the beneficiaries[134] with the need to choose investments prudently.[135] As will emerge from the following sections, the trustees' liability for breach of trust in relation to the investment of the trust fund will depend upon whether or not the trustees have acted in the manner in which other trustees in their circumstances would have done,[136] whether by demonstrating that the actions which the trustees have taken were in line with the actions taken by other trustees in similar circumstances[137] or that their omissions to act were in line with the omissions of trustees in similar circumstances.[138]

32.48 Failure to invest in the manner required by the trust instrument by reason of delay has led to trustees being held liable to account to the beneficiaries for interest[139] and costs[140] over the period of the delay. Contrariwise, failure to sell property in the manner and at the time required by the trust instrument will render the trustees liable to compensate the beneficiaries for the value which they would have received had they disposed of the property in the manner and at the time required by the trust instrument.[141] In many of the older cases, the trustee was held liable for failing to act as required by the trust instrument because he failed to accumulate the trust's income[142] or to deposit the trust's cash capital appropriately:[143] in consequence the award of interest was the appropriate measure of the beneficiaries' loss. The quantum of interest to be awarded in such circumstances

---

[133] See para 52. 01.   [134] *Cowan v Scargill* [1985] Ch 270.

[135] *Speight v Gaunt* (1883) 9 App Cas 1.

[136] *Nestle v National Westminster Bank plc* [1993] 1 WLR 1260; *Wight v Olswang (No 2)* [2000] WTLR 783, (2000) 2 ITELR 689.

[137] *Nestle v National Westminster Bank plc* [1993] 1 WLR 1260.

[138] *Wight v Olswang (No 2)* [2000] WTLR 783, (2000) 2 ITELR 689.

[139] *Attorney-General v Alford* (1855) 4 De GM & G 843, *Stafford v Fiddon* (1857) 23 Beav 386; *Chugg v Chugg* (1874) WN 185. On the court's willingness to make such an award at the end of the proceedings, whether or not it was pleaded, see *Turner v Turner* (1819) 1 J & W 39; *Hollingworth v Shakeshaft* (1851) 14 Beav 492.

[140] *Tickner v Smith* (1855) 3 Sm & G 42.   [141] *Fry v Fry* (1859) 27 Beav 144.

[142] *Raphael v Boehm* (1803–1805) 11 Ves Jr 92; *Dornford v Dornford* (1806) 12 Ves Jr 127; *Browne v Sansome* (1825) 1 McCle & Yo 427; *Knott v Cottee* (1852) 16 Beav 77; *Wilson v Peake* (1856) 3 Jur 155; *Re Emmett's Estate* (1881) 17 Ch D 142; *Re Barclay* [1899] 1 Ch 674.

[143] *Franklin v Frith* (1792) 3 Bro CC 433; *Treves v Townshend* (1784) 1 Bro CC 384; *Re Hilliard* (1790) 1 Ves Jr 89; *Rocke v Hart* (1805) 11 Ves Jr 58; *Ashburnham v Thompson* (1807) 13 Ves Jr 403.

is compound interest.[144] It is suggested that in circumstances in which the trust instrument specified with precision that a particular investment, other than cash held in bank accounts, was to be acquired, it is possible to hold the trustees liable for the return which the investment would have generated for the beneficiaries had the trustees not been dilatory in the performance of their duties, particularly during times when interest rates generate a much lower return than open market interest rates and where the market return on the investment specified in the trust instrument would equate more closely to the beneficiaries' true loss. In such situations the beneficiaries have a right to elect whether to receive compensation in cash[145] or to require delivery up of the assets which were supposed to have been acquired by the trustees.[146]

Compensation for loss caused by investment in breach of trust

In circumstances in which the trustees invest the trust property in investments which are beyond their express investment powers, the trustees will be liable both to compensate the beneficiaries for all of the loss consequent on that investment and also to bear the cost of replacing the unauthorized investments with authorized investments.[147] This form of liability will obtain particularly in circumstances in which there are express powers of investment and limits on those investment powers contained in a trust instrument; whereas, in situations in which there is no trust instrument, the powers of the trustees are expressed by the Trustee Act 2000 to be those of the absolute owner of the trust property. Where the trustees have the expansive powers given to them under the Trustee Act 2000, which are considered in Chapter 52,[148] the trustees cannot be held to be liable for breaching the letter of their duties because they have no express fetters on their powers, being deemed by the 2000 Act to be the absolute owners of that property. This statutory restriction on their liabilities will be effective only if the trustees observe the requirements contained in the 2000 Act that they take appropriate professional investment advice[149] and that they prepare appropriate investment criteria.[150] The liability of the trustees then will be based on their failure to act sufficiently prudently or to generate a suitable return on capital for the trust: these heads of liability are considered in the two following sections.

32.49

---

[144] *Raphael v Boehm* (1803–1805) 11 Ves Jr 92; *Dornford v Dornford* (1806) 12 Ves Jr 89; *Browne v Sansome* (1825) 1 McCle & Yo 427; *Knott v Cottee* (1852) 16 Beav 77; *Wilson v Peake* (1856) 3 Jur 155; *Re Emmett's Estate* (1881) 17 Ch D 142; *Re Barclay* [1899] 1 Ch 674; *Wallersteiner v Moir (No 2)* [1975] QB 373, 397, *per* Buckley LJ; *Belmont Finance Corporation v Williams Furniture Ltd (No 2)* [1980] 1 All ER 393.

[145] *Head v Gould* [1898] 2 Ch 250, *per* Kekewich J, where the unauthorized investments were then unobtainable.

[146] *Shepherd v Mouls* (1845) 4 Hare 500, *per* Wigram V-C; *Robinson v Robinson* (1851) 1 De GM & G 247, 256. See also *Byrchall v Bradford* (1821) 6 Madd 13.

[147] *Re Massingberd's Settlement* (1890) 63 LT 296.   [148] See para 52.01.

[149] See para 52.04.   [150] See para 52.47.

Breach of trust through failure to act with sufficient prudence

32.50   The trustees are obliged, when investing the trust fund, to act prudently, as though they were acting for someone for whom they felt morally bound to provide.[151] In circumstances in which the trustees cause a loss to the trust due to their imprudent investment decisions, the trustees will be liable to compensate the beneficiaries for the loss which they have caused to them. This general principle operates even if the trustees have exercised some discretion which is vested in them and selected investments which were strictly within their powers as trustees: the factor which generates liability in the trustees is their failure to act prudently in selecting investments. The trustees will generally be able to demonstrate that they acted with sufficient prudence if they can demonstrate that their investment strategy was deployed by all reasonable trustees in a similar context to their own[152] or if they can demonstrate that they diversified the trust's investments sufficiently to minimize the risk of loss.[153]

32.51   One difficulty in this context would arise in relation to the selection of the components of an investment portfolio. The ideology underlying portfolio investment is that acquiring a variety of investments will ensure that the trust is not exposed to a downturn in any one market: gains in one area are expected to outweigh the losses in another area. It is, nevertheless, possible to act imprudently in putting a portfolio together by virtue of including too large a concentration of investments which could be adversely affected by similar factors (such as movements in interest rates which affect equity markets, property markets, and so on, albeit in subtly different ways), or by including one particular investment which generates a loss entirely out of proportion to its cost when acquired for the fund (such as a house which develops unexpectedly serious faults requiring repair, or an oil futures contract which obliges the investor to pay an abnormally high price for oil due to the commencement of war in oil producing countries). Deciding whether or not any particular investment ought to have been included in a portfolio will be a difficult matter. There is a tendency to measure the rationality of acquiring a particular investment through the all-knowing spectacles of hindsight. A small holding of futures call contracts, which compel the buyer to acquire goods at the contractually stipulated price no matter what their market value, may have seemed to have been a sensible investment at the time they were acquired, even though the most pessimistic assessment of the risks which they bore may subsequently turn out to be the loss borne by the trust. Therefore, the decided cases have tended to focus on market expectation at the time when the investment strategies were formed.[154] The nature of portfolio investment and its interaction with the trustees' duties of investment are considered in detail in Chapter 52.[155]

---

[151] *Speight v Gaunt* (1883) 9 App Cas 1; *Learoyd v Whiteley* (1887) 12 App Cas 727.
[152] *Nestle v National Westminster Bank plc* [1993] 1 WLR 1260.
[153] *Bartlett v Barclays Bank Trust Co Ltd (No 2)* [1980] Ch 515.
[154] *Nestle v National Westminster Bank plc* [1993] 1 WLR 1260.   [155] See para 52. 38.

Breach of trust through failure to generate a sufficiently large return on capital

There is a long discussion in Chapter 52 as to the manner in which the obligations **32.52** of trustees should be measured.[156] Establishing a breach of trust founded on a failure to generate an adequate return on capital is a very different matter from showing that it was a trustee's breach of trust in selecting unauthorized investments which then generated a loss. If the trustees apply the trust property in unauthorized investments which then do generate a loss, it is a comparatively easy matter to hold those trustees liable to compensate the beneficiaries for that loss and to require them to replace the unauthorized investments with authorized investments.[157] It is a different question to contend that the trustees, while investing in authorized investments, simply failed to select investments which generated a sufficiently large profit. The liability which is to be imposed on the trustees in this situation is a liability due to their having failed to act adequately and not a question of their having failed to act properly. Consequently, where the trustees have demonstrated that other trustees managing the affairs of trusts of a similar kind have adopted similar investment strategies to their own and have achieved similar returns to their own, the courts have not felt able to find that those trustees have breached their obligations simply on the basis that the return generated was too small.[158]

In other jurisdictions there have been instances in which trustees have been held **32.53** liable for failing to generate a sufficiently large return on the basis that their performance compared to the market was inadequate.[159] The level of compensation payable by the trustees in such a situation has been discounted to the general performance of investors in that market to reflect the comparatively small size of the trust fund at issue. It is suggested in Chapter 52[160] that, while such mathematical comparisons with the performance of market indices are beguiling, they may tend to ignore the logically anterior question as to the investment strategy which a reasonable trustee in the circumstances of the defendant ought to have adopted. The first question is to decide which sorts of investment strategy would have been appropriate for the trustees of a trust fund of the size of that managed by the trustees, while taking into account other factors such as the level of risk acceptable to the beneficiaries, and also considering whether the trust is a commercial trust offering investment products to the public or a private trust seeking to maintain a family's wealth over the generations. Only once such factors have been established can it be appropriate to consider the performance of other market participants because that initial assessment informs the second question as to the nature of the other market participants with whom a mathematical comparison should be made.[161]

---

[156] See para 52. 15.   [157] *Re Massingberd's Settlement* (1890) 63 LT 296.
[158] *National Westminster Bank plc* [1993] 1 WLR 1260.
[159] *Re Mulligan* [1998] NZLR 481.   [160] See para 52. 85.
[161] See para 52. 85.

Establishing the value to be restored to the trust fund

32.54 The principal form of breach of trust connected to the investment of the trust fund relates to the acquisition of investments which are outwith those classes of investments which the trustees are permitted to make in their trust instrument. The trustees face two consequent forms of liability: first, to make good any loss which results to the trust from those unauthorized investments losing value and, secondly, to bear the cost of replacing those unauthorized investments with authorized investments.[162] The obligation to acquire property of the authorized type will include the cost of acquiring not only that property but also to make good to the trust any other income or rights which would have accrued to the trust had the trustees exercised their investment powers properly.[163]

32.55 So, for example, if the trust instrument limited the trustees' investment powers expressly to the acquisition of government bonds but the trustees nevertheless acquired mortgages over land in breach of their powers, then the trustees would be obliged to bear the cost of unwinding the mortgages and of acquiring the amount of government bonds which the trust would have acquired had the trustees invested as they were required to do.[164] That the trustees' liability is to acquire property to the value which the trust would have held had the trustees exercised their powers properly is straightforward in the example just given because the trustees could only invest in one form of security. The job of carrying out the task of reconstituting the trust fund in authorized investments is simple if the trustees are required simply to calculate the value of those government bonds at the time when the trustees ought to have acquired them, and then require the trustees to purchase the same number of those bonds at the date of the court judgment no matter what the market value or cost of acquiring them.

32.56 That the trustees are obliged to make good any income or other rights attaching to the property would mean that, in relation to securities such as the government bonds in the previous example or to shares, the trustees would be obliged to account to the trust for any payment of interest or dividend which accrued to those securities during the time when the trust ought to have owned them. So, if the property at issue was a parcel of shares which shares were the subject of a further rights issue after the time when the trustees ought to have acquired them under the terms of the trust instrument, then the trustees are obliged to acquire those further shares which had been granted to subscribers under the rights issue.[165]

---

[162] *Re Massingberd's Settlement* (1890) 63 LT 296.
[163] *Briggs v Massey* (1882) 50 LJ Ch 747, on appeal 51 LJ Ch 447.
[164] *Pride v Fooks* (1840) 2 Beav 430; *Re Barclay* [1899] 1 Ch 674. Cf *Byrchall v Byrchall* (1821) 6 Madd 235.
[165] *Briggs v Massey* (1882) 50 LJ Ch 747.

In a more modern context the question of replacing portfolio investments in this manner is a more complex proposition. If the trustees would have been entitled to acquire, for example, any share quoted on the London Stock Exchange then it would be impossible to know which share the trustees ought to have acquired given that they would have had a choice of many hundreds of shares, all quoted at different prices and all changing value in different fashions. In such a situation, the court could estimate the return which the trustees could have made for the trust by taking the amount of money which the trustees had available to them to invest and assuming a notional investment which would have generated the same return as an index of shares quoted on the London Stock Exchange like the FTSE-100. In the context of the Trustee Act 2000, which provides a long-stop set of investment powers if there is no express provision to the contrary in the trust instrument, the trustees are deemed to be the absolute owners of the trust property and therefore could, potentially, have invested in any investment: consequently, it would be very difficult indeed to second guess the investment which the trustees would have made if they had not made the investment which constituted a breach of trust of some sort. **32.57**

Breach of the obligation to maintain investments

The duties of trustees in relation to the investment of the fund are considered in detail in Chapter 52. This section considers a range of duties which arise from the general law of trusts as to the obligations of the trustees not simply to acquire investments but also, in given circumstances, to take action to maintain those investments. There are a number of examples of such failures to maintain investment property on the decided cases. A trustee who holds a covenant to call for the transfer, but who fails to exercise that covenant, will be liable for breach of trust for all losses which accrue to the trust as a result.[166] A trustee who permitted a residential home held under a trust for sale to deteriorate and who neglected to sell that property was similarly liable for breach of trust and for the restoration of the value of the property,[167] as would be a trustee who held shares on a trust for sale but who failed to sell those shares in good time.[168] A trustee who failed to maintain the premiums under an insurance policy so that the policy lapsed was liable for breach of trust,[169] as was a trustee who failed to give contractually required notices to the policy provider so as to maintain the policy.[170] A trustee has also been held liable for breach of trust for failing to maintain a life insurance policy up to the death of the insured with the result that the early surrender realized only £897 whereas the **32.58**

---

[166] *Fenwick v Greenwell* (1847) 10 Beav 412; *Cleary v Fitzgerald* (1881) 7 LR Ir 229.

[167] *Devaynes v Robinson* (1857) 24 Beav 86.

[168] *Sculthorpe v Tipper* (1871) LR 13 Eq 232.

[169] *Marriott v Kinnersley* (1830) Taml 470. Cf *Hobday v Peters (No 3)* (1860) 28 Beav 603.

[170] *Kingdon v Castleman* (1877) 46 LJ Ch 448.

proper maintenance of the policy would have realized about £5,000.[171] In circumstances in which trustees fail to notify the trustee in bankruptcy of the trust's interest in the bankrupt's estate, such that property is lost to the trust, then the trustee will similarly be liable for breach of trust.[172]

32.59 The application of these general principles to the situation in which trust property included a controlling interest in a company was considered in *Re Lucking's WT*[173] where it was held that the trustee should not simply consider the information he receives as shareholder, but should ensure that he is represented on the board. The extent of such representation will depend upon the circumstances: he may be required to act as managing director or he may only need to ensure that he has a nominee on the board who can report back. This principle was interpreted more liberally in *Bartlett v Barclay's Bank Trust Co Ltd*[174] in which it was held that the trustee need not always be represented on the board if the circumstances did not require this, provided that the trustee retained a sufficient flow of information from the company in accordance with the size of the shareholding. Other methods of control over the company's affairs may be sufficient depending on the context. The beneficiaries' source of recovery will be against the trustees and not against any directors of the company nor against the company itself.[175] Nevertheless, the trustees do bear an obligation to protect the beneficiaries' interests in so far as that is possible,[176] something which will frequently depend upon the size and nature of the company. In relation to a public limited company quoted on the London Stock Exchange it will be impossible to exercise control over the board of directors, even as a single institutional investor, given the number of shareholders and the expense of acquiring a sufficiently significant shareholding in such a company. By contrast, in relation to a small private company, it is more feasible for a trust to own a significant shareholding and so to exercise control over the company's decision-making processes.

D. Responsibility of the Trustees Between Themselves

Limitations on responsibility

32.60 In commercial contexts it is common for trustees either to require that the settlor set out the terms of their obligations in detail in the trust instrument or otherwise by means of a contract effected with the settlor. In this way the responsibility of

---

[171] *Re Deane* (1889) 42 Ch D 351.   [172] *Macnamara v Carey* (1867) 1 IR Eq 9.

[173] [1968] 1 WLR 866.   [174] [1980] Ch 515.

[175] *Prudential Assurance Co Ltd v Newman Industries Ltd* [1982] Ch 204.

[176] *Re Lucking's Will Trusts* [1968] 1 WLR 866. See also *Walker v Stones* [2000] WTLR 975, 1000, in which case the beneficiaries were able to proceed against defendants who had dishonestly assisted in the taking of the company's property.

any individual trustee may be limited in relation to any negligence or any breach of duty committed in the course of discharging his duties under the trust, excluding liability resulting from fraud or other dishonesty.[177] The defences available to trustees in general terms are considered in detail below.[178]

No trustee liable for the defaults of any other trustee

The core principle relating to the liability of trustees is that no individual trustee **32.61** is necessarily liable for the defaults of any other trustee,[179] unless that trustee knows of the breach of trust and conceals it,[180] or takes no steps to safeguard the position of the beneficiaries.[181] Section 30(1) of the Trustee Act 1925 previously provided the following in this regard, prior to its repeal by the Trustee Act 2000:

> A trustee shall be chargeable only for money and securities actually received by him notwithstanding his signing any receipt for the sake of conformity, and *shall be answerable and accountable only for his own acts, receipts, neglects, or defaults, and not for those of any other trustee*, nor for any banker, broker, or other person with whom any trust money or securities may be deposited, nor for any other loss, unless same happens through his own wilful default.[182]

The effect of the Trustee Act 2000 in this regard is considered in detail in Chapter 52.[183] Consequently, there is no current, statutory rehearsal of this principle.

Contribution between the trustees

Trustees may be liable to make contributions alongside the other trustees in situ- **32.62** ations in which they are liable for a breach of trust in common with those other trustees further to the Civil Liability (Contribution) Act 1978. The 1978 Act displaced the inherent power of the courts of equity to order a trustee to make such a contribution. The Act operates[184] so that any trustee who is made liable to compensate the beneficiaries for any breach of trust is entitled to recover a contribution towards his liability from the other trustees who are also liable for that same breach[185] and whose responsibility, impliedly, is not excluded by the trust instrument or by contract. The relevant liability in this sense is any liability for breach

---

[177] *Armitage v Nurse* [1998] Ch 241. See also the exclusion of a liability to contribute in relation to any prior agreement in Civil Liability (Contribution) Act 1978, s 2(3).

[178] See para 32. 76.

[179] *Townley v Sherborne* (1633) Bridg 35, 2 W & TLC (9th edn) 577; Trustee Act 1925, s 30(1).

[180] *Boardman v Mosman* (1799) 1 Bro CC 68.

[181] *Brice v Stokes* (1805) 11 Ves Jr 319; *Walker v Symonds* (1818) 3 Sw 1; *Oliver v Court* (1820) 8 Price 127; *Booth v Booth* (1838) 1 Beav 125; *Gough v Smith* [1872] WN 18.

[182] Emphasis added.   [183] See para 52. 04.

[184] The relevant acts must have occurred after 1978 for the Act to be effective.

[185] Civil Liability (Contribution) Act 1978, ss 1(1), 6(1). See *Friends Provident Life Office v Hillier Parker May & Rowden* [1997] QB 85. The trustee must have become a trustee after 1978: Civil Liability (Contribution) Act 1978, s 7(2); *Lampitt v Poole Borough Council* [1991] 2 QB 545.

of trust which could be established before a court in England and Wales.[186] The acceptance of liability for breach of trust by a trustee, accompanied by a payment into court or by way of a settlement in good faith with the beneficiaries, will be sufficient to establish a liability to make a contribution, provided that the liability accepted by the trustee seeking the contribution was itself good in law.[187]

32.63   The amount of the contribution to be made is such as the court considers to be just and equitable in the circumstances.[188] In assessing the extent of the justice and equity of any trustee making a contribution, the court will look to the fault which would attach to that trustee in regard to the breach of trust.[189] As a result it is open to the court to absolve the trustee from liability altogether or to require him to provide a complete indemnity to the other trustees or anything in between.[190]

32.64   In exercising their inherent jurisdiction in this context, the courts do not hold the trustees who were active in the commission of the breach of trust entirely at fault when the other trustees were also inactive in the exercise of their duties.[191] In this regard, the active trustee will be absolved from complete fault provided that he was acting in good faith and also if the inactive trustees were neglecting their duties rather than having matters concealed from them in bad faith by the active trustee. The policy behind this principle is that excusing the inactive trustees would be likely to act as an 'opiate on the consciences of the trustees' whereas it is in the interests of the beneficiaries to have all of the trustees taking an active part in the management of the trust so that they exercise control over one another.[192] The courts will generally apportion liability between the trustees[193] except in circumstances in which one trustee has acted fraudulently[194] or has demonstrated wilful default.[195] It may be that the first trustee acted deliberately to defraud the beneficiary whereas the other trustees would claim to be less culpable because they did not act deliberately, or because the first trustee's action was the primary factor in causing the loss, or on the basis of some similar explanation. In such a situation the court will typically require that the trustee who is most culpable will bear the

---

[186] Civil Liability (Contribution) Act 1978, s 6(1); *R A Lister Ltd v Thompson Shipping Ltd* [1987] 1 WLR 1614.   [187] Civil Liability (Contribution) Act 1978, s 1(4).

[188] Civil Liability (Contribution) Act 1978, s 2(1).

[189] Civil Liability (Contribution) Act 1978, s 2(1). Cf *Baker v Willoughby* [1970] AC 467; *Madden v Quirk* [1989] 1 WLR 702.

[190] Civil Liability (Contribution) Act 1978, s 2(2). See *Bacon v Camphausen* (1888) 58 LT 851; *Ramskill v Edwards* (1885) 31 Ch D 100.

[191] *Bahin v Hughes* (1886) 31 Ch D 390; *Robinson v Harkin* [1896] 2 Ch 415, 425.

[192] *Bahin v Hughes* (1886) 31 Ch D 390, 398, *per* Frey LJ.

[193] See *Bacon v Camphausen* (1888) 58 LT 851; *Ramskill v Edwards* (1885) 31 Ch D 100.

[194] *Charitable Corporation v Sutton* (1742) 2 Atk 400; *Lingard v Bromley* (1812) 1 V & B 114; *Tarleton v Hornby* (1833) 1 Y & C 333; *Attorney-General v Wilson* (1840) Cr & Ph 1.

[195] *Scotney v Lomer* (1886) 29 Ch D 535.

larger share of the loss.[196] Similarly, a trustee who takes some personal benefit from the breach of trust will generally be liable to bear a proportionately increased share of the liability,[197] although not necessarily the complete liability.[198] In the event that there has been no loss suffered but there are costs incurred in righting the breach of trust, then those costs can be recovered from the trustee against whom the action is to be taken.[199] It has been suggested that the courts will typically take into account the following factors: how large a role each trustee played in causing the loss, the level of moral blameworthiness attaching to each trustee, and the extent to which each trustee had taken some personal benefit from the breach of trust.[200] Although, it should not be forgotten that each trustee to a claim for breach of trust is potentially liable for the entire loss if, for example, the other trustees are bankrupt at the time of the trial.

The procedural rules relating to the joinder of parties to litigation relating to breach of trust are covered in Part 20 of the Civil Procedure Rules. There must be at least one trustee joined to the litigation to take receipt on behalf of the trust of any compensation which is ordered.[201]   **32.65**

Allocating claims between defendants for various aspects of breach of trust

There are two issues considered in short compass in this section. First, how does the claimant decide which of a potentially large number of claims to pursue? Secondly, how does the court decide how liability for loss suffered by the claimant is to be allocated between a large number of defendants? In general terms in relation to breach of trust there is a difficulty in deciding which of a number of defendants will be required to make good the claimant's loss. Suppose, for example, that a claimant can successfully demonstrate that she has valid claims in respect of a loss to her of x against her trustees, against a knowing recipient of property in breach of trust, and against a dishonest assistant to that breach of trust. The court will prevent the claimant from recovering more than x from all of those various defendants. If it were the case that there were only one defendant, then that defendant would be liable to make good the entire loss. In seeking to allocate contributions for the trustees' liability for a breach of trust, as considered in the preceding   **32.66**

---

[196] *Monetary Fund v Hashim* The Times, 11 October 1994; *Dairy Containers Ltd v NZI Bank Ltd* [1995] 2 NZLR 30; *Re Mulligan* [1998] 1 NZLR 481; *Dubai Aluminium Co Ltd v Salaam* [1999] 1 Lloyd's Rep 415.

[197] *Lockhart v Reilly* (1857) 25 LJ Ch 697; *Thompson v Finch* (1856) 8 De GM & G 560; *Blyth v Fladgate* [1891] 1 Ch 337; *Re Turner* [1897] 1 Ch 536.

[198] *Butler v Butler* (1877) 7 Ch D, affirming (1877) 5 Ch D 554.

[199] *Re Linsley* [1904] 2 Ch 785.

[200] C Mitchell, 'Apportioning liability for trust losses' in Birks and Rose (eds), *Restitution and Equity, Vol 1* (Oxford: Mansfield, 2000) 211.

[201] *Re Jordan* [1904] 1 Ch 260, although there is no obligation to join the personal representatives of any deceased person: *Re Harrison* [1891] 2 Ch 349.

section, a third party who colludes with the trustees and so gains a personal benefit from the breach of trust will be liable to make a contribution.[202]

Election between remedies

32.67   There is a need for the beneficiaries to decide, in many cases, whether to proceed in relation to a restitutionary proprietary claim for some property held in the trustee's hands, for a claim equal to the value of some specific property lost to the trust, or for a compensatory claim in relation to the breach of trust *simpliciter*.[203] These are substantively different remedies and the beneficiary will be required to elect between them to remove the possibility of multiple recovery in respect of the same loss.[204] It is important to note that there is a difference between personal compensation for loss suffered as a breach of trust, and compensation equivalent to the value of property lost to the trust,[205] as considered in the next section.

32.68   As considered above, there is a possibility of a number of remedies ranging from those associated with tracing claims, to those associated with restoration of the value of specific property, to those based on compensation.[206] There is then a question as to the remedy which the beneficiary is required to pursue in all the circumstances. The equitable doctrine of election arises in such situations to provide that it is open to the claimant to elect between alternative remedies.[207] In *Tang v Capacious Investments* the possibility of parallel remedies arose in relation to a breach of trust such that the plaintiff beneficiary was theoretically entitled to claim both an account of profits from the malfeasant trustee or to claim damages representing the lost profits to the trust. It was held that these two remedies existed in the alternative and therefore that the plaintiff could claim both, not being required to elect between them until judgment was awarded in its favour. Clearly, the court would not permit double recovery in respect of the same loss, thus requiring the beneficiary to elect between those remedies ultimately.

Limitation period

32.69   One point which has arisen recently is whether there is any limitation period on an action for account brought against a trustee. It has been held that the appropriate

---

[202]   See *Howe v Earl of Dartmouth* (1802) 7 Ves Jr 137. See also *Trafford v Boehm* (1746) 3 Atk 440; *Lord Montfort v Lord Cadogan* (1810) 17 Ves Jr 485; *Booth v Booth* (1838) 1 Beav 125; *Tickner v Old* (1874) LR 18 Eq 422. See also *Moxham v Grant* [1900] 1 QB 88.

[203]   *Target Holdings v Redferns* [1996] 1 AC 421; [1995] 3 WLR 352; [1995] 3 All ER 785.

[204]   *Tang v Capacious Investments* [1996] 1 AC 514.

[205]   *Swindle v Harrison* [1997] 4 All ER 705; *Bristol & West BS v Mothew* [1996] 4 All ER 698.

[206]   *Target Holdings v Redferns* [1996] 1 AC 421.

[207]   *Tang v Capacious Investments Ltd* [1996] 1 All ER 193. See Birks, 'Rights, Wrongs and remedies' (2002) OJLS1, 8.

period is that for common law fraud unless there has been a dishonest breach of fiduciary duty, in which case there is no period applicable.[208]

E. The Leading Case: *Target Holdings v Redferns*

The leading case on the principal liability for breach of trust: *Target Holdings v Redferns*

The purpose of this section is to analyse the factual matrix in the leading case of **32.70** *Target Holdings v Redferns* which has led to subtle but significant alterations in the test for establishing the liability of trustees for breach of trust. This modified test is significant because it appears to have limited slightly but significantly the potential liability of express trustees. As such it forms a useful bridge between the preceding discussion of the components of the trustees' liability for breach of trust and the remedies and defences available for breach of trust considered in the following sections.

The House of Lords has sought to apply the principles in the foregoing cases in a **32.71** slightly more applied manner, softening slightly the strict liability approach towards trustees' liability in relation to a breach of trust by introducing a requirement of causation and also by introducing a form of proprietary liability for the trustee in addition to the existing personal liabilities. The leading decision is that of the House of Lords in *Target Holdings v Redferns*[209] and it is from this case that the core test is drawn.

Target were seeking to enter into an investment with people who subsequently **32.72** turned out to be fraudsters. As part of the transaction, Target wanted a mortgage over a piece of land (referred to as 'the Property' from here onwards). To achieve this they required a valuation of the Property and the legal services of Redferns, a firm of solicitors, to ensure that they would acquire a valid legal charge over the Property. To facilitate this underlying purpose, the valuer provided a fraudulently high valuation of the Property's free market value. The aim of this fraudulently high valuation, concocted between a number of people who were not parties to the litigation, was to convince Target that their investment would be secured in a way that it was not so that Target would enter into other deals in reliance on the valuation of the security over the Property. When the investment subsequently failed and Target sought to take their security interest they found out for the first time that the Property did not have an open market value equivalent to that which they had been told. The fraudsters could not be found or were insolvent and therefore could not be sued for return

---

[208] *Coulthard v Disco Mix Club Ltd* [2000] 1 WLR 707; *Paragon Finance v DB Thackerar* [1999] 1 All ER 400; *Raja v Lloyds TSB Bank plc* The Times, 16 May 2000; *Cia de Seguros Imperio v Heath (REBX) Ltd* [2001] 1 WLR 112.   [209] [1996] 1 AC 421.

of the money obtained by their deception. When Target came, ultimately, to enforce their security, they were left with no obvious, available defendant.

Target had paid the loan moneys necessary to acquire the mortgage interest to Redferns, the solicitors. The agreement was that the solicitors were to hold the money as trustees on trust in their client account, to be paid out if the security was acquired or to be returned to Target if it was not. Redferns were not a party to the fraudulent valuation. In breach of that trust the solicitors paid the trust fund away to defray other personal expenses of their solicitors' firm, wholly unconnected to the fraudulent valuation of the Property. In time, however, the solicitors had enough money in their client account to pay for the acquisition of the mortgage security. This payment was made and Target therefore acquired the mortgage security which they had sought from the outset. However, it was when Target attempted to enforce their security later, when the underlying commercial transaction broke down, that Target realized that they had been given a fraudulently high valuation over the Property.

Consequently, Target began to search for someone they could sue to recover the loss they had made on the transaction. It is important to remember that the loss suffered by Target was the difference between the real value of the Property and the fraudulently high valuation of the Property which Target had been given when creating their mortgage security. Given that the parties to the transaction were not able to make good Target's loss, Target was forced to sue the first solvent person who came within their reach. Therefore, Target sought to sue Redferns, the solicitors, for breach of their trust obligations in respect of the money held in the client account.

32.73 Target's arguments fell into two parts: first that Target was entitled at the date of the trial to have the trust fund restored on a restitutionary basis; and secondly that immediately after the moneys had been paid away by Redferns on their own expenses, there had been an *immediate* loss to the trust fund which Redferns were required to make good. It is important to consider these arguments one at a time. Argument A obliged the trustee to restore the trust fund. The trust fund was made up of the money provided by Target to acquire the mortgage security. Target sought restitution of that fund from Redferns because it was Redferns who had paid away the property that had formerly been in the trust fund in breach of that express trust. This argument proceeded on the basis that there was a strict liability for a trustee to restore a trust fund *in any circumstances* in which there has been a misapplication of such property in breach of trust. This raises argument B under which Target maintained that there was a loss to the trust at the very moment Redferns made the payment of the money away in breach of trust.

Redferns counter-argued that, while there had been a breach of trust, the money was restored to the trust fund before Redferns were required to acquire the mortgage security. Target's argument on this form of strict liability was therefore being made irrespective of the fact that Redferns had made good the money taken from the client account before the date of acquisition. Target was in effect not asking for the restoration of the trust fund, but a payment equal to the loss suffered as a result of the Property not being worth the value represented by the fraudulent valuation.

Lord Browne-Wilkinson took the view that the loss suffered by Target had there- **32.74** fore been caused by the fraudulent valuation of the Property and not by Redferns' breach of trust. The breach of trust had been remedied by Redferns acquiring the mortgage security which Target had required from them. Redferns had provided the service which Target had required originally. The loss arose from different circumstances: to wit the fraud of other people. Therefore, Target would not be entitled to claim compensation for breach of trust against Redferns in respect of the loss caused by the insufficiency of the value of the mortgage security. Having cut the long story short, however, it is important to probe the more detailed elements of the decision, a process beginning immediately below.

Liability for breach of trust after termination of the trust

Where property is paid away in breach of trust, the question arises at what point **32.75** the trust terminates and furthermore as to the nature of the claim which can be brought when the trust property has been paid away. It may be said that a trust terminates when all of the trust property is consumed or transferred away.[210] It is not clear, however, in the wake of *Westdeutsche Landesbank v Islington*[211] how this position can be maintained on principle. It would appear that the trust, that is in the form of the equitable obligations borne by the trustees in relation to the trust property, does not come to an end when the property is transferred away. A trust should be thought of not simply as constituting title to property but as also including obligations of trusteeship to the beneficiaries which are imposed on the

---

[210] R Davern, 'The problem with bare trusts in contractual contexts' (1997/98) 8 KCLJ 86. Davern's point is that the trust in *Target Holdings v Redferns* terminated at the date of transfer and therefore there is no need to raise the argument that there be reconstitution of the trust fund, on the basis that there would be no fund to reconstitute in any event. The argument runs that, once the trust is dead, it cannot be brought back to life. The issue is then whether the trust had transformed into a chose in action against the trustee personally equal to the value of the trust fund. However, this would be to overlook the fact that equity will still give effect to many of those equitable obligations that made up the trust by means of equitable tracing claims, personal claims for dishonest assistance or knowing receipt, or subrogation claims. It must be the case that property acquired as a result of such a claim must be held on trust in the same manner that the property was held on trust before the unconscionable event which gave rise to the claim. Otherwise, when the fund property is got in, it would not be subject to the terms of that same express trust. It could not be established, on principle, that breach of trust would be remedied by an order to deal with property otherwise than in accordance with the trust that was originally breached. Further to *Target Holdings v Redferns* there is no liability to reconstitute the trust fund where the underlying commercial transaction has been performed. [211] [1996] AC 669.

trustee personally. Therefore, the trustees' obligations must necessarily continue while there is some order either for reconstitution of the fund or for the payment of compensation. The fact that such an order would be operative on the trustee must imply that obligations which arose by virtue of the trust continue to be operative too. The imposition of any equitable remedy on a trustee, whether personal or proprietary, suggests that such trusteeship must necessarily continue in existence.

Lord Browne-Wilkinson's discussion of the core content of trusteeship[212] in *Westdeutsche Landesbank v Islington*[213] has been described as resting on three separate platforms: first, that legal title in the trust property is held by the trustee; secondly, that the equitable interest is held by another person; and thirdly, that the trustee has incurred personal obligations with respect to that trust property. In Lord Browne-Wilkinson's opinion, it is not enough to constitute a trust that the legal title is held by one person and that there is some equitable title held by another person. Rather, it is said that there is also a need for obligations to have been imposed on the trustee in respect of that property sufficient to constitute him a trustee rather than being simply a party to a charge or some other equitable device. Consequently, it is suggested that a trust will continue while such obligations are in existence, even though its business may appear to have been completed. For example, even after a discretionary trust fund has been divided between some of the beneficiaries, it would be contrary to principle to suggest that a beneficiary who was properly entitled to some of that property should have no recourse against that trustee in breach of trust simply because all the fund has already been transferred away.

F. Trustees' Defences to Breach of Trust

There are, potentially, a large number of defences to an action for breach of trust: this section highlights the most significant of them.

Lack of a causal link between breach and loss

32.76   The claimant is required to prove a causal link between the loss suffered and the breach of trust.[214] For example, in *Nestle v National Westminster Bank plc (No 2)*[215] the bank had acted as trustee of a will trust for sixty years. The plaintiff contended that the bank had generated a rate of return on the trust property which was lower than comparable investment indices. The bank demonstrated that it had

---

212   P Birks, 'Trusts raised to avoid unjust enrichment' [1996] RLR 3.
213   [1996] AC 669.
214   *Nestle v National Westminster Bank plc (No 2)* [1993] 1 WLR 1260, [1994] 1 All ER 118.
215   [1993] 1 WLR 1260, [1994] 1 All ER 118.

acted prudently and in accordance with investment market practice throughout the period of its trusteeship. In consequence, it was not possible to demonstrate that the plaintiff had suffered any particular level of loss nor that the trustee had breached its fiduciary duties in general terms.

There is a defence for the trustee where the trustee can demonstrate that there was **32.77** a good reason for the sale or misapplication of the trust property.[216] Therefore, if a trustee were to breach the precise terms of a trust by investing in property out-with the investment powers contained in the trust deed, in circumstances in which the trustee would be able to demonstrate that the technical breach of trust protected the beneficiaries from losses which they would otherwise have suffered, it will be open to that trustee to maintain that the breach of trust is therefore not actionable. At one level it would be necessary for the beneficiary to demonstrate loss in any event. On the authority of *Nestle v National Westminster Bank plc*,[217] even if a small loss had been suffered it is open to a trustee to demonstrate that the investment strategy applied was adopted both for the long-term benefit of the beneficiaries and to guard against future risk to the fund. If proven, such an argument would constitute a good defence to an action for compensation for breach of trust arising out of such a loss.[218] The trustee would be establishing a defence that his actions were reasonable and therefore that he had committed no breach, rather than that the trust had suffered no loss. Evidently, the trustee would be required to prove that the adopted course of action was indeed well founded in accordance with market practice and further that any loss caused by his actions was a reasonable consequence of those actions necessary to achieve the trust's objectives.[219]

Breach committed by another trustee

An individual trustee may claim that a breach of trust was the sole responsibility **32.78** of another trustee or trustees. The general principle in this context is that one trustee is not held to be liable for the actions or omissions of any other trustee.[220] So, for example, a trustee will only be liable for custody of money where that trustee has given a receipt for that property and not otherwise.[221] A trustee will only be liable in this context for any wilful default[222] or for a failure to ensure, for example, that trust money has been properly invested.[223] Liability will not attach to a trustee who has attempted to ascertain that the other trustee has carried out

---

[216] [1993] 1 WLR 1260, [1994] 1 All ER 118.
[217] [1993] 1 WLR 1260, [1994] 1 All ER 118.
[218] [1993] 1 WLR 1260, [1994] 1 All ER 118.
[219] On these issues see, generally, Chapter 52 in relation to the investment of trust funds.
[220] *Townley v Sherborne* (1633) Bridg 35; (1633) W & TLC 577.
[221] Trustee Act 1925, s 30(1); *Re Fryer* (1857) 3 K & J 317; *Brice v Stokes* (1805) 11 Ves Jr 319.
[222] *Re Vickery* [1931] 1 Ch 572, 582.   [223] *Thompson v Finch* (1856) 22 Beav 316.

his obligations properly.[224] There is an obligation on a trustee to take action to protect the beneficiaries in the event that she learns of a breach of trust committed by another trustee,[225] for example by beginning an action for restoration of the trust fund.[226]

Contributory negligence

32.79   The trustee cannot claim as a defence that any one or more of the beneficiaries were contributorily negligent in relation to the breach of trust.[227] This principle may have been destabilized in one context as a result of the decision in *Target Holdings v Redferns* in that a trustee may now claim that his breach of duty did not cause the entirety of the loss suffered, whereas *Target Holdings* requires that there be some connection between breach and loss. It is unclear, however, the extent to which this aspect of the judgment in *Target Holdings* will be developed. Lord Browne-Wilkinson's intention was to require the demonstration of some causal link between breach and loss but, in eschewing the common law notions of foreseeability and causation, he did not adopt any notion of a sliding scale of responsibility due to any contributory negligence by any other person: the principal liability is still borne by the trustee. The trustee may be successful, however, in establishing that the beneficiaries permitted the situation to continue such that it was the beneficiaries' own fault which caused the loss or which caused some part of the loss such that there was no causal connection between the breach of trust and the loss.[228] This approach is similar to the defence of acquiescence considered below in that the beneficiaries would be taken to be somehow complicit in their own loss. In line with principle in such a situation, there will be no liability for breach of trust if a causal connection cannot be established between the trustees' breach of trust and the loss suffered by the beneficiaries. More generally, in common with the defence of acquiescence, if the beneficiaries actively consent to the action comprising the breach of trust, rather than inadvertently contributing to it, then the trustee would have a defence to an action for breach of trust.[229]

Failure by the beneficiary to alleviate loss

32.80   Failure by the beneficiary to minimize her own loss does not constitute a full defence to a claim for breach of trust but it may serve to reduce the trustee's

---

[224] *Thompson v Finch* (1856) 22 Beav 316; *Hanbury v Kirkland* (1829) 3 Sim 265. Cf *Re Munton* [1927] 1 Ch 262.

[225] *Brice v Stokes* (1805) 11 Ves Jr 319; *Oliver v Court* (1820) 8 Price 127, 166; *Booth v Booth* (1838) 1 Beav 125; *Gough v Smith* [1872] WN 18.

[226] *Earl Powlet v Herbert* (1791) 1 Ves Jr 297.   [227] (1888) 37 Ch D 466.

[228] *Corporacion Nacional Del Cobre de Chile v Sogemin Metals Ltd* [1997] 1 WLR 1396, 1403; *Canson Enterprises Ltd v Boughton & Co* (1991) 85 DLR (4th) 129, 161.

[229] *Re Pauling's Settlement Trusts* [1964] Ch 303.

liability. Where the beneficiary fails to take straightforward measures to protect herself against further loss, after due notice and opportunity to do so, then the trustee will not be liable for any further loss arising after the beneficiary could have taken action to protect herself.[230]

Concurrence and acquiescence by the beneficiaries in the breach of trust

Once a beneficiary concurs in a breach of trust, or acquiesces in a breach of trust, that beneficiary is estopped from seeking to recover compensation for that breach of trust from any trustees to whom that concurrence was proffered.[231] A minor cannot concur in such a breach of trust.[232] Matters are made more complex if the beneficiary who gives concurrence is also a trustee: in such a circumstance, the trustee-beneficiary could not seek compensation for the entirety of his loss from any other trustee.[233] However, there appears to be no obstacle to a contribution from that fellow trustee[234] other than, potentially, the general equitable principle that he who comes to equity comes with clean hands where the trustee-beneficiary has participated in the breach of trust.[235] **32.81**

Even if one or more of the beneficiaries instigates the breach of trust, that does not necessarily require that any such beneficiary is obliged to indemnify the trustees who acted at those beneficiaries' instigation.[236] However, there is a power for the court to impound the interest of any beneficiary who is at fault in some way for the breach of trust either to compensate the other beneficiaries or to indemnify the trustees who acted at his instigation.[237] **32.82**

For a beneficiary to be taken to have concurred or to have acquiesced in a breach of trust, it is necessary that the beneficiary has had sufficient knowledge of the breach of trust. Clearly, it would be impossible for a beneficiary to have concurred or acquiesced in some activity of which they knew nothing or the nature of which **32.83**

---

[230] *Corporacion Nacional Del Cobre de Chile v Sogemin Metals Ltd* [1997] 1 WLR 1396, 1403; *Canson Enterprises Ltd v Boughton & Co* (1991) 85 DLR (4th) 129, 161.

[231] *White v White* (1798–1804) 5 Ves Jr 554; *Evans v Benyon* (1888) 37 Ch D 329; *Re Pauling's Settlement Trusts* [1964] Ch 303, 335, [1962] 1 WLR 86, 106. Cf *Chillingworth v Chambers* [1896] 1 Ch 685. [232] *Buckeridge v Glasse* (1841) Cr & Ph 126; *Re Somerset* [1894] 1 Ch 231.

[233] *Butler v Carter* (1868) LR 5 Eq 276, 281.

[234] See para 10.98. See also *Lewin*, para 39-60.

[235] *Jones v Lenthal* (1669) 1 Ch Cas 154; *Guinness v Saunders* [1990] 2 WLR 324.

[236] *Raby v Ridehalgh* (1855) 7 De G & G 104; *Butler v Butler* (1877) 7 Ch D, affirming (1877) 5 Ch D 554; *Sawyer v Sawyer* (1883) 28 Ch D 595; *Bolton v Curre* [1895] 1 Ch 544; *Chillingworth v Chambers* [1896] 1 Ch 685; *Fletcher v Collis* [1905] 2 Ch 24.

[237] Trustee Act 1925, s 62. *Jacubs v Rylance* (1874) LR 17 Eq 341; *Doering v Doering* (1889) 42 Ch D 203; *Re Dacre* [1916] 1 Ch 344. See also *Lincoln v Wright* (1841) 4 Beav 427, 431, *per* Lord Langdale; *Fuller v Knight* (1843) 6 Beav 205.

they did not understand. The principles have been explained in the following manner:[238]

> The... court has to consider all the circumstances in which the concurrence of the cestui que trust was given with a view to seeing whether it is fair and equitable that, having given his concurrence, he should afterwards turn round and sue the trustees; ... subject to this, it is not necessary that he should know that what he is concurring in is a breach of trust, provided that he fully understand what he is concurring in, and ... it is not necessary that he should himself have directly benefited by the breach of trust.

Therefore, the most significant, underlying factor is the fairness and equity in the beneficiary bringing an action for compensation for breach of trust. In essence, one cannot have known of and agreed to something in relation to which one subsequently seeks to recover compensation.

Release

32.84 Where the beneficiaries agree formally to release the trustee from any liability then the equitable doctrine of release will operate so as to protect that trustee from any liability arising from her breach of trust.[239] However, that does not prevent the beneficiaries from seeking equitable relief in respect of any factor which was not made known to them at the time of granting the release or which arises outside the terms of that release.[240] Therefore, in a situation in which employees signed a release form in respect of any breach of duty by their employer, it was held that this would not prevent a claim for relief in relation to stigma caused to their careers when it subsequently emerged that their employer bank had been dealing dishonestly.[241]

Trustee exemption clause

32.85 In circumstances in which the trustee and the settler agree on a clause exempting the trustee from liability on the basis that the trustee's agreement to act as a trustee is dependent on such an exclusion of his liability, then that provision will generally be enforced.[242] This position was considered in Chapter 21 on the rights of trustees.[243] The question in recent cases has been as to the form of exemption

---

[238] *Re Pauling's Settlement Trusts* [1962] 1 WLR 86, 108, *per* Wilberforce J. See also *Re Garnett* (1885) 31 Ch D 1, a case dealing with release but adopted for this purpose; and *Holder v Holder* [1968] Ch 353, *Re Freeston's Charity* [1978] Ch 741, relating specifically to acquiescence. See further *Spellson v George* (1992) 26 NSWLR 666.

[239] *Lyall v Edwards* (1861) 6 H & N 337, 158 ER 139; *Ecclesiastical Commissioners for England v North Eastern Rly Co* (1877) 4 Ch D 845; *Turner v Turner* (1880) 14 Ch D 829.

[240] *BCCI v Ali* [2000] 3 All ER 51.

[241] *BCCI v Ali* [2000] 3 All ER 51. Cf *Malik v BCCI* [1997] 3 All ER 1.

[242] *Armitage v Nurse* [1998] Ch 241; *Bogg v Raper* The Times, 12 April 1998; *Wight v Olswang* [2000] WTLR 783; *Walker v Stones* [2001] QB 902.   [243] See para 21.10.

clause which will be enforced. A typical form of exemption clause is one which excludes the trustee's liability except in the event of the trustee's dishonesty. It was held in *Armitage v Nurse*[244] that such an exemption clause would be effective even to the exclusion of liability for the trustee's own negligence in the performance of her duties. Clearly, this approach greatly limits the extent of the trustee's liability if the trustee was sufficiently well advised to have insisted on such a contractual provision from the outset. Ordinarily, as considered above, the trustee would be liable for all loss resulting from her breach of trust without needing to identify fault or foreseeability: that a breach of trust had led to a loss in the beneficiaries was sufficient to impose liability.[245] A more restricted approach to this issue was taken in *Walker v Stones*[246] in which an exemption clause, which sought to exclude the trustee's liability for all actions except dishonesty, was held to be effective in general terms but not so as to exclude liability in circumstances in which the trustee could not reasonably have believed that her actions would be considered to be honest. Underlying these decisions is a fundamental difference of opinion as to the minimum content of trusteeship. In *Armitage v Nurse* the court took the view that exclusion clauses ought to be upheld because otherwise professional trustees would have refused to hold the office in question, whereas in *Walker v Stones* the court doubts the breadth of that proposition and prefers instead to look objectively at the probity of the trustee's actions.[247] Nevertheless, the principle is generally accepted that trustee exemption clauses will be effective to limit the trustee's liability; the only exception to that principle will be if the trustee has acted dishonestly. It does appear that liability for acting negligently can be excluded.[248]

Action not in connection with fiduciary duties or permitted by terms of trust

Most obviously the trustee will not be liable for breach of trust in circumstances **32.86** in which either the terms of the trust permit the action complained of[249] or if the action complained of is not connected to the trustee's fiduciary duties.[250] For example, in *Ward v Brunt*[251] a family farm business was left without anyone to run it after Norman Ward died. Norman had left the farm to be held equally for his grandchildren such that the farm business was to be run by them as partners. Susan, one of the beneficiaries under this arrangement, gave up her work as a teacher to take over the running of the farm because no one else was prepared to do so. Susan was thus a fiduciary in relation to the other partners. Norman's executors offered Susan an option to purchase the freehold over the farm, in accordance with the terms of Norman's will, which Susan subsequently agreed to exercise.

---

[244] [1998] Ch 241.   [245] *Target Holdings v Redferns* [1996] 1 AC 421.
[246] [2001] QB 902.   [247] See para 21.24.   [248] *Armitage v Nurse* [1998] Ch 241.
[249] *Galmerrow Securities Ltd v National Westminster Bank plc* [2002] WTLR 125.
[250] *Ward v Brunt* [2000] WTLR 731.   [251] *Ward v Brunt* [2000] WTLR 731.

Thus, Susan acquired the freehold over the land and Susan personally became land-lord to the business which she had agreed to run on behalf of the partnership. In time, Susan decided to serve a notice to quit on the farm business. The other beneficiaries contended that this service of the notice to quit was in breach of Susan's fiduciary duties as manager of the trust's business. It was held that Susan did not breach her fiduciary duties to the partnership in acquiring the freehold of the farm for herself and in consequence she was entitled to exercise all of the rights of a free-holder to serve a notice to quit on tenants of the property. Furthermore, Susan was not liable for the profits which she made from having a freehold with vacant posses-sion after the termination of the lease. Therefore, there is no liability for breach of trust, even if the fiduciary is acting contrary to the interests of the beneficiaries, pro-vided that the powers which the fiduciary is exercising accrue to her in a personal capacity or derive from her beneficial capacity. In this case Susan's powers accrue to her in a personal capacity and derive from her beneficial ownership of the freehold.

It is suggested that in circumstances such as this it would be necessary for the for-mer fiduciary to show that she did not acquire for herself the larger rights of, for example a freeholder, in a personal capacity either at an undervalue or in connec-tion with some transaction which contravened the prohibition on trustees self-dealing with trust property, or with the intention of defeating or devaluing the interests of the beneficiaries so that the fiduciary could generate some personal profit at the expense of those beneficiaries. In short, the fiduciary would need to demonstrate that the rights which she sought to exercise were not part of some long-term plan on her part to generate a personal profit due to some information or other factor under her control which was unconscionable and in contravention of her fiduciary obligations. In this sense the facts in *Ward v Brunt* are remarkable for disclosing no such design and for permitting the trustee to act in the manner that she did. The court was clearly able to distinguish between the things done at the time she was a fiduciary and things done once she had acquired the freehold from the trust business.

Excuses for breach of trust

32.87 There is a power for the court in section 61 of the Trustee Act 1925 to grant par-tial or total relief for breach of trust. That section provides that:

> If it appears to the court that a trustee . . . is or may be personally liable for any breach of trust . . . but has acted honestly and reasonably, and ought fairly to be excused for the breach of trust and for omitting to obtain the directions of the court in the mat-ter in which he committed such breach, then the court may relieve him either wholly or partly from personal liability for the same.

Therefore, the question is whether or not a trustee has acted honestly such that the court considers it appropriate to relieve her of her liability. This provision was directed primarily at the perceived harshness of the case law on breach of trust which tended to hold amateur trustees liable for the whole of any loss suffered by beneficiaries in circumstances in which there was no reason to suppose that those trustees had held themselves out as having any particular competence to manage the trust to any particular standard. So, in *Re Evans (dec'd)*[252] a daughter acted as administrator in her deceased father's estate, holding that estate on trust for herself and her brother beneficially as next of kin under the intestacy rules. When she came to distribute the estate she assumed her brother was dead because she had not heard from him for thirty years. The defendant bought an insurance policy to pay out half the value of the estate in the event that her brother reappeared. Her brother did reappear four years later and claimed that the defendant had breached the trust by taking all of the fund for herself beneficially and claimed further that the insurance policy would be insufficient to meet his total loss. The judge concluded that the defendant ought to be granted partial relief: her liability was limited to the amount which could be met from the sale of a house forming part of the estate. Otherwise, the approach of the courts has been to take a case-by-case approach to relief under this provision dependent usually on whether or not the trustee has acted reasonably[253] in the manner in which she might have handled her own property,[254] or whether the trustee acted unreasonably by leaving the trust property in the hands of a third party without good reason,[255] or on an erroneous understanding of the law.[256]

Limitation

There is no single, statutory limitation period for actions for breach of trust in the way that there are statutory limitation periods for common law actions. Under section 21 of the Limitation Act 1980 there is no limitation period in relation to an action by a beneficiary[257] against trustees in relation to fraud or a fraudulent breach of trust committed in whole by or with the connivance of a trustee.[258] In relation to an action by a beneficiary seeking to recover property by way of specific restitution from the trustee or which had been in the trustee's possession, that action will be statute-barred if it is brought after six years from the date on which the cause of action accrued.[259] Such a right of action in relation to a person with only a future interest in property will not be deemed to have accrued until that interest falls in,[260] and someone interested under a discretionary trust or under a power of appointment does not have such an interest until the trustees exercise their discretion or appoint property (as appropriate).[261]

32.88

---

[252] [1999] 2 All ER 777.   [253] *Chapman v Browne* [1902] 1 Ch 785.
[254] *Re Stuart* [1897] 2 Ch 583; *Re Barker* (1898) 77 LT 712.
[255] *Wynne v Tempest* (1897) 13 TLR 360; *Re Second East Dulwich etc Building Society* (1899) 68 LJ Ch 196.   [256] *Ward-Smith v Jebb* (1964) 108 Sol Jo 919.
[257] Such an action will not include an action in relation to a charitable trust: *A-G v Cooke* [1988] Ch 414.   [258] *Miller v Bain* [2002] BCLC 266.
[259] Limitation Act 1980, s 21(2).   [260] Limitation Act 1980, s 21(3).
[261] *Armitage v Nurse* [1998] Ch 241.

The starting assumption should be that a six year limitation period will apply—under one or other provision of the Act, applied directly or by analogy—unless it is specifically excluded by the Act or established case-law. Personal claims against fiduciaries will normally be subject to limits by analogy with claims in tort or contract.[262] By contrast, claims for breach of fiduciary duty, in the special sense explained in *Bristol and West Building Society v Mothew*,[263] will normally be covered by section 21. The six-year time-limit under section 21(3), will apply, directly or by analogy, unless excluded by subsection 21(1)(a) (fraud) or (b) (Class 1 trust).[264]

So where one manages property on behalf of another, one will be found to bear trustee-like obligations for the purposes of the 1980 Act.[265] In this context it has been held that a director of a company with trustee-like responsibilities personally over property which belongs in equity to the company may be treated as a constructive trustee within section 21 of the 1980 Act against whom claims are being made by a beneficiary, in the form of a company in this sense, for which he is then liable to account to the company, or alternatively by applying the same statutory limitation period which applies in relation to the recovery of property on grounds of breach of trust.[266]

32.89 In relation to resulting, constructive, and implied trustees, the Court of Appeal has suggested that there are two classes of constructive trustee for this purpose: those who hold property in their possession on constructive trust due to their own breach of trust and confidence, and secondly those who are merely personally liable to account as though a constructive trustee on grounds of dishonest assistance in a breach of trust.[267] It has been suggested that this second category of constructive trustee should be treated differently under section 21 of the 1980 Act from the former category such that the open-ended liability borne by trustees for breach of trust should attach only to the former category.[268] However, a different Court of Appeal did find that an executor de son tort had no defence in the form of a statute bar.[269]

32.90 This perpetual liability[270] is subject to the principle of laches whereby equity 'refuse its aid to stale demands'.[271] An exception to the general rule is the rule against conflicts of interest founded on the self-dealing and fair-dealing principles.[272]

---

[262] Limitation Act 1980 Act ss 2, 5; see *Cia De Seguros Imperio v Heath (REBX) Ltd* [2001] 1 WLR 112.   [263] [1998] Ch 1.

[264] *Gwembe Valley Development Co Ltd v Koshy* [2003] EWCA Civ 104, para 111. See also *DEG-Deutsche v Koshy* [2002] 1 BCLC 478, Rimer J.

[265] *Gwembe Valley Development Co Ltd v Koshy* [2003] EWCA Civ 104.   [266] ibid.

[267] *Paragon Finance plc v DB Thackerar & Co* [1999] 1 All ER 400, 408.

[268] See W Swadling, 'Limitation' in P Birks and A Pretto (eds), *Breach of Trust* (Hart, 2002) ch 11, and A Underhill and DJ Hayton, *Law of Trust and Trustees* (16th edn, Butterworths, 2002) ('*Underhill and Hayton*') 924.

[269] *James v Williams* [2000] Ch 1 CA: *per incuriam Paragon Finance v DB Thackerar & Co* [1999] 1 All ER 400.   [270] As it is referred to in *Underhill and Hayton* 923.

[271] *Smith v Clay* (1767) 3 Bro CC 639, 29 ER 743; *Nelson v Rye* [1996] 1 WLR 1378. See generally G Watt 'Laches, estoppel and election' in P Birks and A Pretto (eds), *Breach of Trust* (Hart, 2002) ch 12.   [272] *Tito v Waddell (No 2)* [1977] Ch 106.

33

TRACING AND PROPRIETARY CLAIMS

A. The Principles of Tracing

The process of identifying the subject matter of a tracing claim and the establishment of the appropriate remedy

33.01 This chapter is concerned with the recovery of property which has been transferred away from a trust in breach of that trust or, if that original property cannot be recovered in its original form,[1] with the establishment of some other proprietary right on behalf of the beneficiaries of that trust by means of tracing.[2] The process of tracing enables beneficiaries to track the movement of any property passed away in breach of trust, and either to obtain recovery of that specific property or to have the traceable proceeds of that property treated as though it had been previously a part of that trust fund. The term 'traceable proceeds' includes any mixture of property into which that original property was passed, or any property which was substituted for that original property, or any property which was acquired by turning the original property to account. The purpose of a claim based on tracing, then, is to provide the claimant with some right in property,[3] as opposed to merely a personal right against a trustee or some other person. Tracing is itself merely the process of identifying the property over which a proprietary claim can be brought. Once the property which is to be the subject matter of the claim has been identified by means of tracing, then a further question arises as to which form of remedy would be most appropriate[4] in recognition of the value lost to the trust, as considered below.[5]

33.02 Tracing can be effected at common law or in equity. Tracing at common law is limited to the recovery of property taken from the claimant or to a substitute for that property which has been kept separate from all other property. Consequently, in situations in which the claimant seeks to identify a specific item of property (or, its 'clean' substitute) in the hands of the defendant in which the claimant has retained proprietary rights, the claimant will bring a common law tracing claim to require the return of that specific item of property.[6] Common law tracing can operate in two senses, considered below in greater detail:[7] first, by means of a 'following claim'[8] which achieves specific restitution[9] of the property which has been passed away from the trust; or secondly, by means of the establishment of a claim against a fund of property which has not been mixed with any other property

---

[1] See para 33.15.   [2] See para 33.21 and 33.30.

[3] Including the right to compound interest which is dependent on the establishment of some proprietary right: *Westdeutsche Landesbank v Islington* [1996] AC 669.

[4] *Boscawen v Bajwa* [1996] 1 WLR 328.   [5] *Boscawen v Bajwa* [1996] 1 WLR 328.

[6] *FC Jones & Sons (A Firm) v Jones* [1996] 3 WLR 703—considered below at para 33.21.

[7] See para 33.06.   [8] See para 33.15.

[9] In the sense that that term is used in relation to recovery of the very property which has been passed away in breach of trust by a trustee: *Target Holdings v Redferns* [1996] 1 AC 421, [1995] 3 WLR 352, [1995] 3 All ER 785.

and which contains both the original trust property and any accretions, such as interest, which have been added to that property.[10] Common law tracing will not permit a claimant to trace after his property once it has become inextricably mixed with other property.

By contrast, tracing in equity permits the claimant to establish proprietary claims **33.03** over any substitute for the claimant's property even if it has been mixed with other property. The equitable jurisdiction will only be capable of being invoked, however, if the claimant occupied some position recognized by equity, such as being a beneficiary under an express or a constructive trust, which will invoke that equitable jurisdiction.[11] In the oldest sense of the division between common law and equity, this requirement was, in effect, a reason why a court of equity would agree that it had the jurisdiction to hear the case: that the claimant was, for example, a beneficiary under a trust would mean that that person was seeking to protect equitable rights which were the business of a court of equity. The range of remedies which are available to the claimant in equity are much broader than that available in the limited concept of tracing at common law, whether those equitable remedies are in the form of constructive trust, equitable charge, lien, subrogation, or some other.[12] The practical effect of describing tracing as being merely the process of identifying the subject matter of a further claim is to recognize that the remedy which will be imposed will be the remedy most appropriate in the circumstances. Typically, the choice of remedy will depend upon the manner in which the traced property is held, as considered below.[13] It is equitable tracing which will constitute the principal focus of this chapter both because it is the broader jurisdiction and because it will be available generally in relation to pre-existing trusts. There are a range of defences to tracing claims,[14] including change of position,[15] bona fide purchase of the property for value,[16] estoppel by representation,[17] and passing on.[18]

Common conceptual difficulties in establishing proprietary rights by means of tracing

There are two principal conceptual problems with establishing proprietary rights **33.04** by means of claims based on tracing. The first problem is that a tracing claim entitles the claimant to establish a right to property which has been substituted

---

[10] *FC Jones & sons (A Firm) v Jones* [1996] 3 WLR 703.

[11] *Boscawen v Bajwa* [1996] 1 WLR 328.

[12] See for example the claim in *Re Diplock's Estate* [1948] Ch 465.

[13] See para 33.58.   [14] See paras 33.78 *et seq.*

[15] *Lipkin Gorman v Karpnale* [1991] 2 AC 548; *Scottish Equitable v Derby* [2001] 3 All ER 818.

[16] *Westdeutsche Landesbank v Islington* [1996] AC 669.

[17] *National Westminster Bank plc v Somer International (UK) Ltd* [2001] Lloyds Rep Bank 263.

[18] *Kleinwort Benson v Birmingham City Council* [1996] 4 All ER 733, CA.

for the property which was originally taken from the trust: that is, the claimant is staking a claim to property in which he had no previous rights of ownership. Whereas civil law jurisdictions recognize only a dominium in the single owner of property which is subject to personal claims akin to debt in favour of claimants seeking redress if property is taken from them in breach of duty, common law jurisdictions recognize that ownership rights in property, once taken involuntarily from their owner, can be traced into other property for which those original rights have been substituted.

33.05 The second difficulty is that tracing claims are dependent upon the possibility of there being some property which can be identified as being the subject matter of a claim. Many of the decided cases have involved complex commercial transactions in which the property claimed was in the form of money held in electronic bank accounts[19] or other intangible assets which were the subject of money laundering schemes and passed from account to account and through a variety of shell companies[20] which were wound up once the assets had passed through them.[21] In these cases it is evident that the tracing rules which were created originally in relation to tangible, movable property, and which provided that the claimant would lose his right to trace if the property had ceased to exist,[22] are difficult to apply to situations in which other forms of property, principally intangible property, are at issue.

The three, distinct heads of claim

33.06 The subject matter of this chapter divides between three distinct heads of claim. All three are concerned to provide the claimant with some proprietary remedy once the claimant has identified the property which is the subject matter of his claim as being either his own property or its traceable substitute. The purpose of these claims differs, as considered in the discussion to follow, between the recognition of the claimant's continued ownership of property, his entitlement to any profit derived from that property, or an equitable entitlement to claim title to property which has been substituted for his original property, always provided that the defendant has no good defence to that claim.

33.07 The first category of claim is a claim to recover the original property which had been held on trust before being transferred away in breach of trust. This form of claim is referred to as a following claim[23] and effects specific restitution[24] of the original property.[25] At the first level it might be that all the owner is seeking

---

[19] *Westdeutsche Landesbank v Islington* [1996] AC 669.
[20] That is, companies which carried on no trade and which had no tangible assets, but which were, rather, devices used to hold and to conceal assets.
[21] *Agip (Africa) v Jackson* [1990] Ch 265, 286, *per* Millett J; CA [1991] Ch 547.
[22] *Roscoe v Winder* [1915] 1 Ch 62.   [23] See para 33.15.   [24] See para 33.20.
[25] See para 33.18.

to do is to recover property which he can prove to be his own property from the defendant.

The second is a claim to recover property for which his original property has been substituted or to claim property which has accrued to his original property. An example of the former context would be the situation in which the claimant's money is used to purchase securities such that the securities are a substitute for the claimant's money.[26] This claim is a claim to property which the claimant did not own but which is recognized at law or in equity as standing for the claimant's own property as a result of having replaced it. An example of the latter would a claimant's rights to trace his ownership of the original property not only into the substitute property but also into any profit realized by virtue of the ownership of that substitute property. For example, if the substitute property was a holding of bonds, then the owner of bonds would be entitled to receive periodical payments of coupon interest. Ownership of the substitute property will entitle the claimant to assert ownership to any profits which accrue to that property,[27] just as, to employ the familiar metaphor, the owner of a tree is taken to be the owner of the fruits of that tree. Ownership of the former generally implies ownership of the latter. The courts have tended not to consider the possibility of accounting to the defendant for the exercise of his skill in choosing a profitable substitute for the claimant's property.[28] **33.08**

The third category of claim is that in which the claimant can only trace his original property into a mixture of property. In such circumstances the owner may not be able to recover his original property because that property has been mixed with other property, or it cannot be found, or some other person has acquired good title to it by virtue, for example, of having purchased it in good faith.[29] In such a situation the owner may seek to establish property rights against some other property which the defendant has acquired by using the original property. Therefore, the claimant is seeking to assert title to substitute property, which might take the form of sale proceeds received on the sale of the original property, or of property acquired with those sale proceeds, or of some composite property in which the original property has been combined in some way. **33.09**

There is an important point of distinction to be made between seeking to establish title in the original item of property which was previously owned, and seeking to establish title to substitute property (or, traceable proceeds) which is not the exact property which was previously owned. Clearly, the former case requires the **33.10**

---

[26] *Jones (FC) & Sons v Jones* [1996] 3 WLR 703.
[27] *Jones (FC) & Sons v Jones* [1996] 3 WLR 703.
[28] See for example *Jones (FC) & Sons v Jones* [1996] 3 WLR 703 in which the defendant acquired no benefit in recognition of her successful investment strategy, as considered below.
[29] *Westdeutsche Landesbank v Islington* [1996] AC 669.

claimant to say 'That property is mine and I want it back.' In many cases this will be a case of fact and proof. Suppose my car is taken from me—a car which I will be able to identify by its registration plates and chassis number—I will wish to have that very car returned to me once I have proved that the car in the defendant's possession bears my number plates and chassis number and is therefore demonstrably my car. However, suppose that my car was taken from me and sold to someone who has moved such that I cannot now find my car. In that case I would be forced to bring an action against the person who took the car from me to recover the sale proceeds of the car from her: that is, money which had never previously belonged to me but which is clearly derived directly from the sale of my property. To establish such a claim would required me to *trace* my property rights from the car into the cash which the defendant has received. The former situation is clearly a process which recognizes my original ownership whereas the latter situation involves the proposition that it is somehow 'right' that the defendant give up the money which was received from the wrongful sale of my car. That process of following and tracing rights in property in these ways is our principal focus in this chapter.

Tracing within the general context of claims for breaches of trust

33.11   Tracing claims operate in tandem with other principles concerned to compensate the beneficiaries for any breach of trust, as considered elsewhere in this book. Any trustee will be liable under the principles considered in Chapter 32 to effect specific restitution of the trust property[30] or, if the trust property cannot be recovered, to restore the value of the fund personally in cash and to compensate the beneficiaries for any further loss by way of equitable compensation.[31] The former liability is an obligation to recover specific property whereas the latter is a personal liability to effect equitable compensation. As considered in Chapter 30, third parties who are not trustees (or, who are strangers to the trust) will be personally liable to account to the beneficiaries for any loss suffered by the trust if they have either received trust property knowing that the property had been passed to them in breach of trust or if they dishonestly assisted the breach of trust. These personal liabilities to account do not entitle the beneficiaries to any right in property and are dependent on the defendant being able to pay.

33.12   Tracing, by contrast, may be claimed against identified property which can in turn be subsumed within the trust fund, thus attracting to the fund any increase in its value or any income attributable to it, or subjected to a charge or lien to ensure the restoration of lost value to the trust fund. The flexibility inherent in this selection of remedies means that a loss merely of money can be remedied with the protection against the defendant's insolvency which is ensured by a proprietary remedy,

---

[30] See para 33.20.   [31] See para 32.18.

whereas a loss of another form of property with some inherent value can be recovered for the trust again without bearing the risk of the defendant's insolvency. Furthermore, in circumstances in which the property claimed[32] is particularly valuable, or likely to increase in value, the establishment of a proprietary claim will enable the claimant to claim entitlement to any profits derived from that property.[33] Such a proprietary claim will also entitle the claimant to recover compound interest (rather than merely simple interest) on the property recovered.[34]

The beneficiaries' principal source of action in relation to any breach of trust would be against the trustees in the first place, even if the trustees might claim that some third person induced their breach of trust,[35] as considered in Chapter 30.[36] Consequently, the trustees will bring a tracing claim to recover trust property themselves.[37] It is common for tracing claims, whether at common law or in equity, to be brought together with a claim for breach of trust against the trustees,[38] a claim for knowing receipt against any person who had the trust property under their control or in their possession,[39] and a claim for dishonest assistance against any person who participated in the breach of trust.[40] In this manner the beneficiaries increase their chances of effecting recovery against one or more of a variety of defendants. The beneficiaries then have a power to elect which of the available remedies they wish to enforce.[41] The tracing claim and any claim for specific restitution brought against the trustees[42] are the only remedies within this assortment which will recover property for the beneficiaries as opposed merely to cash compensation equal to their loss.[43] Therefore, a tracing claim will enable the beneficiaries both to re-establish the property held in their trust fund and consequently to re-establish the underlying purpose[44] for which the trust was established. **33.13**

That tracing is merely a process of identification

Tracing is a process. The process of tracing does not in itself provide a remedy.[45] It does nothing more than trace a right in the original item of property held on trust[46] into subsequent items of property or value which are the traceable **33.14**

---

[32] Whether the original trust property or its traceable substitute.
[33] *Attorney-General for Hong Kong v Reid* [1994] 1 AC 324.
[34] *Westdeutsche Landesbank v Islington* [1996] AC 669.
[35] *Target Holdings v Redferns* [1996] 1 AC 421.   [36] See para 30.01.
[37] See para 33.11.   [38] See para 32.01.   [39] See para 30.55.
[40] See para 30.16.   [41] *Tang v Capacious Investments* [1996] 1 AC 514.
[42] See para 33.15.   [43] *Target Holdings v Redferns* [1996] 1 AC 421.
[44] The term 'purpose' in this sense connoting the underlying motivation of the settlor to provide benefits for the beneficiaries, and not an abstract purpose which would render the trust void under the beneficiary principle: *Morice v Bishop of Durham* (1805) 10 Ves 522; *Leahy v Att-Gen for New South Wales* [1959] AC 457. See para 6.01.
[45] *Boscawen v Bajwa* [1996] 1 WLR 328. Also see L Smith, *The Law of Tracing* (Clarendon Press, 1997).
[46] Or subject to some other fiduciary relationship recognized by equity.

proceeds of that original property. Having conducted the tracing process, there is then the further issue as to the form of remedy which should be granted or the form of trust which arises. Therefore, the lawyer is required to do two things, one after the other: first trace into the appropriate property and secondly identify the best remedy to bring against that property. The remedy which the court will then impose is a separate issue. As outlined above, the court may make an order for compensation;[47] an order that the property be restored by direct transfer to the original owner;[48] or an order that the property be held, possibly, on resulting trust[49] or, more likely, on constructive trust,[50] or subject to a charge[51] or lien.[52] The nature of the remedy which is eventually granted is a separate issue from the issue whether or not the claimant can establish a tracing claim against identified property in the first place. The distinction is made plain in *Boscawen v Bajwa* in the judgment of Millett LJ when his lordship held that: [53]

> Tracing properly so-called, however, is neither a claim nor a remedy but a process... It is the process by which the plaintiff traces what has happened to his property, identifies the persons who have handled it or received it, and justifies his claim that the money which they handled or received (and if necessary which they still retain) can properly be regarded as representing his property. He needs to do this because his claim is based on the retention by him of a beneficial interest in the property which the defendant handled or received. Unless he can prove this, he cannot (in the traditional language of equity) raise an equity against the defendant or (in the modern language of restitution) show that the defendant's unjust enrichment was at his expense...

This is an important first point. Paragraph 33.58, and those following, consider the nature of the equitable remedies which may be available; whereas **Part D Trusts Implied by Law** has already considered in detail the nature of the constructive trusts which may be awarded, and whereas paragraph 33.62[54] considers more specifically the nature of the constructive trust which is usually imposed in relation to tracing claims. Common law remedies may be available in relation to common law tracing, encompassing remedies such as the simple common law restitution of property used by the Court of Appeal[55] and an action for money had and received.[56] The following discussion will consider simple following claims, tracing at common law, and then tracing into mixed funds in equity, before moving on to consider the manner in which the courts have used trusts and equitable remedies to address questions of tracing.

---

[47] *Target Holdings v Redferns* [1996] 1 AC 421, [1995] 3 WLR 352, [1995] 3 All ER 785.
[48] *Foskett v McKeown* [2000] 3 All ER 97.
[49] *El Ajou v Dollar Land Holdings* [1993] 3 All ER 717.
[50] *Westdeutsche Landesbank v Islington* [1996] AC 669.
[51] *Barlow Clowes International Ltd (In Liquidation) v Vaughan* [1992] 4 All ER 22.
[52] See *Foskett v McKeown* [2001] 1 AC 102, [2000] 3 All ER 97.   [53] [1995] 4 All ER 769.
[54] See also para 29.73.   [55] *FC Jones & sons (A Firm) v Jones* [1996] 3 WLR 703.
[56] cf *Westdeutsche Landesbank v Islington* [1996] AC 669.

B. Following and Effecting Specific Restitution

The nature of following claims

As considered above,[57] the owner of property may require an order simply that he **33.15** remains the owner of specific property which has been taken out of his possession without his consent or without any juristic reason or excuse.[58] Such orders have been described as being 'following claims'.[59] They are to be distinguished from tracing claims in which substitute property is claimed in place of the original property, as considered in the next paragraph, and are to be distinguished from claims in which the original property has accrued interest, profits, or similar property.[60] The subject matter of a following claim has been described as being similar to an order by the court, in effect, recognizing or vindicating the claimant's continued ownership of his property even though it has passed into the possession of another person.[61]

The clearest example of a following claim would relate to a chattel taken from the **33.16** claimant's possession. If the claimant were the absolute owner of, for example, a car which was taken from him by the defendant, then the claimant would be able to identify the car by its registration number, chassis number, and so forth. The court would then be called upon simply to recognize that the claimant remained the owner of that car. A following claim is a very limited device which would not function in a number of circumstances. Suppose, for example, that the defendant had purchased the car from some third person who had taken it from the claimant. In that situation, equity would protect a bona fide purchaser for value without notice of the claimant's rights to the car and preclude the owner from seeking recovery of his property. If the car had been stolen, equity would treat the holder of the car as being constructive trustee of it and consequently would invoke the equitable tracing jurisdiction.[62] In contrast, common law principles of commercial law would apply the principle that *nemo dat quod non habet* (that no one can give what he does not own) and therefore would order that no person can take the car from its owner and purport to transfer good title in it to the defendant if he did not have good title in the car himself.[63] Consequently, the following claim

---

[57] See para 33.11.
[58] Examples of a good juristic reason not operating on the basis of the consent of the owner of property would include the vesting of that person's estate in a trustee in bankruptcy or some statutory confiscation of property.
[59] *Foskett v McKeown* [2001] 1 AC 102.
[60] *FC Jones & sons (A Firm) v Jones* [1996] 3 WLR 703. See para 33.21.
[61] G Virgo, *Principles of the Law of Restitution* (Oxford University Press, 1999).
[62] *Westdeutsche Landesbank v Islington* [1996] AC 669.
[63] As Lord Cairns expressed this matter in *Cundy v Lindsay* (1878) 3 App Cas 459: 'If it turns out that the chattel has been found by the person who professed to sell it, the purchaser will not obtain a title good as against the real owner. If it turns out that the chattel has been stolen by the person who

will only function if there is no competing claim to ownership of the property in question. Akin to the Roman law concept of *vindicatio* it functions as a judicial recognition of some person's ownership of property but is not a means of resolving contested claims to the ownership of property.

33.17 It is not clear on which conceptual basis such following claims arise. At first blush, they are similar to common law tracing claims, considered below,[64] in which the common law will order the return of property to its rightful owner provided that it is identifiable as the claimant's original property and provided further that it has not been mixed with any other property.[65] It is suggested that such an order could be considered to be a common law equivalent to the equitable order of specific restitution made against a trustee who commits a breach of trust and is compelled to restore the very property which was taken from the trust fund to that trust.[66] If the following claim were considered to be an equitable device, it would only be available to those claimants who stood in some fiduciary nexus with the defendant, such as the relationship of trustee and beneficiary. The award of an order in a following claim is ostensibly intended to be a simple, a fortiori device in which the ownership of the absolute owner of property is recognized as continuing in existence unless there is some juristic reason to suppose that his ownership has terminated.

The distinction between following and tracing

33.18 The distinction between following and tracing has been expressed in the following manner by Lord Millett:[67]

> [Following and tracing] are both exercises in locating assets which are or may be taken to represent an asset belonging to the [claimants] and to which they assert ownership. The processes of following and tracing are, however distinct. Following is the process of following the same asset as it moves from hand to hand. Tracing is the process of identifying a new asset as the substitute for the old.

A following claim requires simply that a specific piece of property is followed and identified by its original absolute or common law owner, thus being returned to that original owner.[68] In short, following claims appear to have more in common with a principle of vindicating the rights of the original owner in the very property

---

has professed to sell it, the purchaser will not obtain a title. If it turns out that the chattel has come into the hands of the person who professed to sell it, by a de facto [voidable] contract, that is to say, a contract which has purported to pass the property to him from the owner of the property, there the purchaser will obtain a good title.' See generally AS Hudson, *Equity & Trusts* (3rd edn, Cavendish Publishing, 2003) *('Hudson')* 688, 753.

[64] See para 33.21.

[65] *Lipkin Gorman v Karpnale* [1991] 2 AC 548; *Agip v Jackson* [1990] Ch 265, 286, *per* Millett J; CA [1991] Ch 547; *FC Jones & sons (A Firm) v Jones* [1996] 3 WLR 703.

[66] See para 33.25.   [67] *Foskett v McKeown* [2001] 1 AC 102.

[68] See L Smith, *The Law of Tracing* (Clarendon Press, 1997) 1.14.

which was taken from him as opposed to the establishment of a derivative action[69] in other property which is said to represent the property taken. On the other hand, a tracing claim concerns the identification of some property against which the claimant may assert proprietary rights because the claimant's original property has been substituted by a wrongdoer by the property claimed.

There is also a distinction between common law tracing and equitable tracing, as **33.19** suggested above. This chapter will focus on equitable tracing for the most part, after first considering common law tracing. In short the common law will only allow tracing into the original property which was taken from its original owner. Latterly, this jurisdiction has been extended to include 'clean substitutions' where the original property is substituted by other property but where that substitute property is kept distinct from all other property.[70] It is suggested that claims involving clean substitutions differ from following claims because the claimant is seeking to do more than recover the very property which he previously owned because he is also claiming ownership of property which has accrued to his original property or been substituted for his original property in either case after it has left his possession. By way of further contrast, equitable tracing is a more extensive jurisdiction again because it entitles the claimant to rights not only in property substituted for the original property taken in breach of trust but also in mixtures into which such property is passed.[71]

The nature of specific restitution

As considered in relation to the liability of a trustee for breach of trust, the trustee **33.20** is liable to effect specific restitution of property which passes out of the trust fund into the possession of another person.[72] This does not relate to the restitution of unjust enrichment but rather to the recovery of property taken in breach of trust. The similarities between following claims and claims for specific restitution brought against trustees emphasize the role of tracing claims and following claims as part of the resolution of complex litigation arising from a breach of trust. The beneficiaries will bring a claim for specific restitution against the trustees if the trust property is capable of recovery and the trustees will bring a following claim against any person who has that trust property in his possession. Therefore, the following claim and the claim for specific restitution operate in tandem. In either

---

[69] In the sense, that is, of a right in one item of property leading to a right to claim ownership of property which has been substituted for that original property, such that the second claim is derived from the first.

[70] *FC Jones & sons (A Firm) v Jones* [1996] 3 WLR 703.

[71] It is a prerequisite of equitable tracing, on the current understanding of the authorities, that there have been some pre-existing equitable or fiduciary relationship to invoke the equitable jurisdiction.

[72] *Target Holdings v Redferns* [1996] 1 AC 421, [1995] 3 WLR 352, [1995] 3 All ER 785.

case, it is a prerequisite of the success of the claim that the trust property be capable of identification. In the event that the trust property cannot be identified separate from all other property and free from any other claims to ownership (as outlined in the previous paragraph), then the beneficiaries will be obliged to pursue a tracing claim at common law or in equity, and to bring a claim for equitable compensation against the trustees.[73]

C. Tracing at Common Law

The nature of common law tracing claims

33.21 The common law tracing process permits the claimant to identify a particular item of property which has passed into the possession of another person and to seek a remedy to recognize that that property is owned at common law by the claimant. What is required is that the claimant is able to demonstrate that the property claimed is the very property taken from the claimant,[74] or is a clean substitute for the original property taken from the claimant, or that the property claimed has not been mixed with any other property but rather has been held separately from all other property and only mixed with any profits which have accrued to that original property.[75] A clean substitution of property in this sense means that the original property taken from the claimant was replaced by other property without the substitute property which becomes the subject matter of the common law claim being mixed with any other property.

33.22 By way of example, if the original property was money which was taken from the claimant and then used to pay the entire purchase price for a parcel of securities, and those securities were then held separately from all other assets owned by the defendant, then those securities would be a clean substitute for the claimant's money.[76] In circumstances in which a partner in a solicitors' firm took money from client bank accounts held by the firm and used it opening a gambling account with a casino, it was held that solicitors' firm had a right to claim in common law tracing in respect of those moneys which where identifiable as having come from their client account by virtue of having been held separately in an account for the partner,[77] but money which had been mixed into the casino's general accounts could not be the subject of a common law tracing claim.[78] As considered

---

[73] Subject always to the prevention of double recovery by election between remedies: *Tang v Capacious Investments* [1996] 1 AC 514.

[74] See the discussion of following claims in the previous section.

[75] *FC Jones & sons (A Firm) v Jones* [1996] 3 WLR 703.

[76] *FC Jones & sons (A Firm) v Jones* [1996] 3 WLR 703.

[77] *Lipkin Gorman v Karpnale* [1991] 2 AC 548.

[78] *Banque Belge pour L'Étranger v Hambrouk* [1921] 1 KB 321.

below, only a tracing claim brought in equity could be imposed on moneys which had passed into a mixed account. Similarly it has been held that common law tracing cannot take effect between telegraphic transfers between electronic bank accounts where the moneys have been mixed because no property will be clearly identifiable.[79]

Similarly, in *Agip (Africa) Ltd v Jackson*[80] the defendant accountants arranged that money would be taken from the plaintiff by means of forged payment orders made out in favour of a series of shell companies.[81] The accountants' intention had been to launder the money through the shell companies by means of passing the money through a number of bank accounts in a number of different currencies belonging to a number of different companies such that those companies were wound up after the money had passed through their accounts.[82] The plaintiff pursued a number of claims simultaneously against the defendant. One of the claims was for money had and received at common law in relation to the money taken from them and another was for common law tracing against the bank accounts into which the moneys had passed. It was held that for common law tracing to be available it would be necessary for the plaintiff to demonstrate that the money claimed was the very money which had been wrongfully taken from the trust by the defendants' fraud, or its clean substitute, which had been held in either case separately from all other moneys. However, on the basis that money had been moved through numerous companies, currencies, and bank accounts, it was held that it was no longer possible for the original money to be identified and consequently that common law tracing would not be available to the plaintiff in relation to those sums.[83]   **33.23**

The limitations of common law tracing

As is obvious from the cases considered in the preceding section,[84] the common law tracing process is very brittle. If the property becomes unidentifiable or if it   **33.24**

---

[79] *El Ajou v Dollar Land Holdings* [1993] 3 All ER 717. This approach has been followed in *Nimmo v Westpac Banking Corporation* [1993] 3 NZLR 218; *Bank Tejarat v Hong Kong and Shanghai Banking Corporation (CI) Ltd* [1995] 1 Lloyd's Rep 239. Cf Birks (1995) 9 Trusts Law International 91. It has also been accepted that telegraphic transfer does not involve a transfer of property but rather simply an adjustment in the value of the choses in action constituted by the bank accounts: *R v Preddy* [1996] AC 815.

[80] [1991] Ch 547, 566, *per* Fox LJ, [1991] 3 WLR 116, [1992] 4 All ER 451.

[81] That is, companies created solely to carry out the defendants' fraudulent purpose by means of holding assets but which did not carry on a trade nor any other such activity.

[82] This is standard practice in money laundering. By transferring the money into different accounts, by combining it with other money and by changing it into different currencies, it becomes very difficult to prove where the original money went. The device of running the various companies insolvent means that the tracing process must be conducted through the complexities of such companies' windings up, which adds further complexity.

[83] *Agip v Jackson* is considered in greater detail below at para 33.32.

[84] *Lipkin Gorman v Karpnale* [1991] 2 AC 548; *Agip v Jackson* [1990] Ch 265, affirmed by the Court of Appeal [1991] Ch 547.

becomes mixed with any other property, then the common law tracing claim will fail.[85] A rogue seeking to avoid a common law tracing claim will therefore take money, for example, divide it up into randomly sized portions, pay it into bank accounts which already contain other money, convert that money into different currencies, and move it into yet other bank accounts perhaps in other jurisdictions. This type of subterfuge puts that property beyond the reach of common law tracing because the common law tracing process fails once the property claimed has been mixed with other property. The claimant is consequently required to rely on equitable tracing, as considered below.[86] It is these limitations which have led many leading academics and judges to recommend that the distinction between common law tracing and equitable tracing should be removed.[87] In *Agip (Africa) v Jackson* Millett J sought to preclude common law tracing from operation in circumstances where there had been anything other than clean, physical substitutions. Speaking extrajudicially he has said:[88]

> A unified and comprehensive restitutionary remedy should be developed based on equitable principles, and attempts to rationalise and develop the common law action for money had and received should be abandoned.

However, a more recent decision of the Court of Appeal has suggested that common law tracing may have a broader ambit than had previously been thought, as considered below.[89]

Asserting title to profits derived from property subject to specific restitution

33.25 In circumstances in which the claimant's property is taken from him and held separately from all other property so as to be the subject matter of a common law tracing claim or a following claim, that property may attract income by way of interest, dividend, or some similar accrual. The profits attracted by the original property will themselves be subject to a tracing claim at common law, provided that they have not been mixed with any property other than the original property.[90]

Asserting title to substitute property and to profits derived from substitute property

33.26 The leading case in relation to common law tracing, which suggested a much broader role for common law tracing than had seemed possible previously, is that of *FC Jones & Sons (A firm) v Jones*. The Court of Appeal's decision in *FC*

---

[85] *Lipkin Gorman v Karpnale* [1991] 2 AC 548; *Agip v Jackson* [1991] Ch 547.
[86] See para 33.30.
[87] For example P Birks, 'Tracing, claiming and defences' in *Laundering and Tracing* (Clarendon Press, 1995) 289; L Smith, *The Law of Tracing* (Clarendon Press, 1997).
[88] P Millett, 'Tracing the proceeds of fraud' (1991) 107 LQR 71, 85.
[89] *FC Jones & sons (A Firm) v Jones* [1996] 3 WLR 703.
[90] *FC Jones & sons (A Firm) v Jones* [1996] 3 WLR 703.

Jones & Sons (A firm) v Jones[91] concerned an amount of £11,700 which was paid from a partnership bank account to Mrs Jones, who was the wife of one of the partners. This advance was the subject matter of a loan lawfully made by the partnership to Mrs Jones. Mrs Jones invested the money in potato futures[92] and made a large profit. Ultimately she held a balance of £49,860 constituting both her capital stake in her futures investments and the profits which she accrued from those investments. All of the money was held separately from her other property in a single bank account. Subsequently, it transpired that the partnership had committed an act of bankruptcy under the Bankruptcy Act 1914, such that it was deemed to have been technically bankrupt before it had made the payment to Mrs Jones. Consequently, all of the partnership's property was deemed to have passed retrospectively to the Official Receiver. This meant that the Official Receiver was the rightful owner of the £11,700 before it had been paid to Mrs Jones. Therefore, it was claimed that Mrs Jones had had no title to the original £11,700 and that the Official Receiver should be entitled to trace into Mrs Jones's bank account to recover the money from her.

33.27 An ordinary understanding of common law tracing might have suggested that the Official Receiver could have recovered the £11,700, being the original property, but that it could not recover any further amounts unless it could demonstrate equitable title in the property (under equitable tracing principles). On these facts there could be no equitable tracing because the partnership had retained no equitable interest in the money lent to Mrs Jones.[93] There was no doubt that the Official Receiver was entitled to the £11,700 before the date of its transfer to Mrs Jones, and that the sum of £11,700 ought to have been recoverable by the Official Receiver. The more difficult problem was to decide whether or not the Official Receiver ought to be entitled to the entire £49,860 which Mrs Jones had generated from that initial £11,700 in her investments in potato futures. Furthermore, the combination of the conversion of the original £11,700 into futures contracts and then its mixture with profits made on those investments would ordinarily have meant that common law tracing would have offered no redress for the Official Receiver winding up the partnership's assets because the original property had been substituted for other property which had in turn been mixed into a general fund (on these facts the mixture of the futures contracts and the profits derived from those investments).

33.28 Nevertheless, the Court of Appeal held that all of the £49,860 was to be paid to the Official Receiver as part of a common law tracing claim. The rationales behind

---

[91] [1996] 3 WLR 703, [1996] 4 All ER 721.

[92] ie, a form of derivatives contract traded on the commodities markets which speculates on the value of potatoes in the future.

[93] *Re Diplock's Estate* [1948] Ch 465.

that decision suggest a significant development in the scope of common law tracing. Millett LJ was prepared to allow a proprietary, common law claim on the basis that the money at issue in this case was perfectly identifiable in a single bank account. Here the £11,700 originally held and the £49,860 in profits generated ultimately had been held in a single bank account and not mixed with any other moneys. On the facts, there could not have been a claim in equity against Mrs Jones because she had never been in any fiduciary relationship with the Official Receiver (a necessary prerequisite of an equitable tracing claim).[94] The nature of the common law tracing right was explained by Millett LJ as being a proprietary right to claim whatever was held in the bank account, whether the amount at the time of the claim was more or less than the original amount deposited. Furthermore, it was held that it was immaterial whether or not those amounts constituted profits on the original money, or simply the original money, or a combination of the two. Nourse LJ reached the same conclusion, albeit by a different route. His lordship expressed himself to be willing to grant the personal claim for money had and received, but on these facts that was explained as being a right entitling the Official Receiver to a right in property representing the original property (which may therefore have been more than the original money taken from the partnership's assets) and not merely the original property. Furthermore, his lordship held that the action for money had and received was based on conscience, making it seem more like an equitable claim than a common law claim.[95]

33.29 The decision of the Court of Appeal in *FC Jones & Sons (A Firm) v Jones* seemed to confirm the existence of a proprietary remedy at common law in relation to a common law tracing claim. The common law generally recognizes two personal remedies:[96] common law damages[97] and money had and received.[98] The common law does have property law concepts, of which the most obvious example considered in this book has been the legal title held by the trustee of a trust fund. The remedy

---

[94] As considered below at para 33.35.

[95] Following *Taylor v Plumer* (1815) 3 M & S 562, on which see L Smith, *The Law of Tracing* (Clarendon Press, 1997) 162 *et seq*, in which case the Court of Appeal accepted the founding case on common law tracing had in fact used equitable tracing rules. Smith has taken this to be justification for the amalgamation of common law tracing with equitable tracing in the future (considered at the end of this chapter). However, the Court of Appeal held that the principle of common law tracing remained valid nonetheless. See, however, P Millett, 'Tracing the proceeds of fraud' (1991) 107 LQR 71, 85 in which Millett surprisingly argued for the elimination of common law tracing shortly before extending its ambit greatly in *FC Jones & sons (A Firm) v Jones* [1996] 3 WLR 703.

[96] There are other common law principles to do with identification of assets under which mixtures of tangible property will be divided on the basis of the old Roman rules of *commixio* and *confusio* (*Indian Oil Corp Ltd v Greenstone Shipping SA* [1987] 3 All ER 893) provided that they have not become capable of separation, in which case the claimants would become tenants in common of the combined mass (*Buckley v Gross* (1863) 3 B & S 566). See also *Greenwood v Bennett* [1973] QB 195.

[97] As provided in relation to breach of contract and to compensate tortious loss.

[98] Or 'a personal claim in restitution', *per* Lord Goff in *Westdeutsche Landesbank v Islington* [1996] AC 669.

awarded in *FC Jones & Sons (A firm) v Jones* appears both to mirror that form of vindication which has already been identified with following claims[99] and specific restitution for breach of trust,[100] and also to entitle the claimant to the fruits of the property which he claims as well as to the property itself in the form of profits or other accruals. Nevertheless, it appears that common law tracing will not permit a claim to pass through interbank clearing systems because the original property in such situations is not capable of being identified sufficiently clearly.[101]

D. The Foundations of Tracing in Equity

The nature of tracing in equity

Equitable tracing is the only means by which a claimant can trace into mixtures of property, in circumstances in which a part of that mixture represents or comprises money in which the claimant previously held some equitable proprietary right. Particular difficulties have arisen in recent cases in relation to money passed through electronically-held bank accounts: the challenge posed by those cases to the general principles considered in this section are considered towards the end of this chapter.[102]   **33.30**

It is important to understand the elements necessary to found an equitable tracing claim. The first requirement is that the claimant has some pre-existing equitable interest in the property before the claim can commence.[103] This requirement, considered in detail below, is a prerequisite of calling the equitable jurisdiction into play. The second requirement is that it be possible to identify the traceable proceeds of the claimant's property, or property in which he had some equitable interest, in the pool of property against which the tracing claim is brought. This requirement has two effects. If the claimant cannot demonstrate that his property ever formed a part of the mixture against which the tracing claim is brought, then he cannot claim against it simply because he can demonstrate that the owner of that mixture of property received the traceable proceeds of his property and holds it in some unidentified place: the claimant must be able to prove that the property claimed contains property which had its source in the claimant's hands. Furthermore, the claimant will lose his right to trace against that mixture if it can be proved that his property was taken from the mixture, for example by virtue   **33.31**

---

[99] See para 33.15.   [100] See para 32.11.

[101] *FC Jones & sons (A Firm) v Jones* [1997] Ch 159, 168.

[102] See para 33.97. English law treats each payment of money as being distinct tangible property such that, when a bank account containing such money is run overdrawn, that property is said to disappear. Consequently, there can be no tracing claim in respect of property which has ceased to exist.

[103] *Re Diplock's Estate* [1948] Ch 465.

of the contents or value of the pooled property having fallen to zero between the time when the claimant's property entered the pool and the time at which the tracing claim was brought. In explaining the ability to trace into a mixed fund, Millett LJ held that[104]

> ... equity's power to charge a mixed fund with the repayment of trust moneys enables the claimant to follow the money, not because it is his, but because it is derived from a fund which is treated as if it were subject to a charge in his favour.

It is unclear whether or not a further requirement is that the recipient's conscience is affected in respect of that proprietary right such that a constructive trust or some other equitable remedy can be imposed.[105] It has been held by the House of Lords that a constructive trust will only be imposed in circumstances in which the defendant's conscience has been affected,[106] whereas older authorities have permitted tracing in equity against innocent volunteers[107] on the principle, it is suggested, that equity will not assist a volunteer.[108] The older rule is more closely in line with the principle that equitable tracing operates in recognition of the beneficiaries' rights in property and not on the basis that the defendant, who may have been innocent of the breach of trust, has acted unconscionably. More generally, the courts of equity have demonstrated themselves to be assiduous in their protection of beneficiaries under fiduciary relationships (whether in the form of trusts, companies, partnerships, agency relationships, or otherwise), a tendency which is in keeping with equity's role as the supervisor of the defendant's conscience.[109] Furthermore, the continued division between common law and equitable tracing permits the use of those sorts of discretionary remedy which are based on the conscience of the defendant and which are not predicated on the logical recognition of property rights exemplified by common law tracing claims[110] and following claims,[111] considered above.

The benefits of equitable tracing

33.32 The benefits of equitable tracing over common law tracing appear in money laundering cases like *Agip (Africa) v Jackson*[112] which demonstrated that a claimant

---

[104] *Foskett v McKeown* [2001] 1 AC 102.

[105] *Foskett v McKeown* [2001] 1 AC 102, [2000] 3 All ER 97.

[106] *Westdeutsche Landesbank v Islington* [1996] AC 669. See para 29.73, in relation to the nature of the constructive trust imposed in satisfaction of tracing claims.

[107] *Re Diplock's Estate* [1948] Ch 465; *Foskett v McKeown* [2000] 3 All ER 97. See para 33.36 in relation to the older authorities on innocent volunteers having no protection against equitable tracing claims, despite there being no impact on their conscience to justify the imposition of a constructive trust or other equitable remedy.

[108] See for example *Milroy v Lord* (1862) 4 De GF & J 264.

[109] See para 1.04, and also para 33.39 where it is argued that a trustee mixing property with his own property is treated differently from combinations of the property of innocent volunteers.

[110] See para 33.21.   [111] See para 33.15.

[112] [1991] Ch 547, 566, *per* Fox LJ, [1991] 3 WLR 116, [1992] 4 All ER 451.

may be able to trace through mixtures of property as well as through the orchestrated bankruptcies of front companies designed to obscure the movement of those funds stolen from the claimant. In that case, on instructions from the plaintiff oil exploration company, the Banque du Sud in Tunis transmitted a payment to Lloyds Bank in London, to be passed on to a specified person. The plaintiff's chief accountant fraudulently altered the payment instruction so that the money was in fact passed on to a company called Baker Oil Ltd. Before the fraud was uncovered, Lloyds Bank had paid out under the chief accountant's instruction to Baker Oil before receiving payment from Banque du Sud via the New York payment system. The account was then closed and the money was transferred via the Isle of Man to a number of recipients controlled by the fraudsters. The defendants were independent accountants who ran a number of shell companies[113] through which the moneys were paid: their intention being to pass the moneys through those companies so that the funds would become, in effect, untraceable in practice with the ultimate intention that the defendants would keep those moneys. The issue arose whether or not the value received by Baker Oil constituted the traceable proceeds of the property transferred from Tunis.

It was held that either a principal or an agent can sue on the equitable tracing **33.33** claim, the role of plaintiff was not restricted to the Banque du Sud. The bank had not paid Baker Oil with 'its own money' but rather on instruction from the plaintiff (albeit that they were fraudulent instructions). Further, it was impossible to trace the money at common law where the value had been transferred by 'telegraphic transfer' thus making it impossible to identify the specific money which had been misapplied. Therefore, it was important for the plaintiff to demonstrate that it could trace in equity. On these facts, because it was the plaintiff's fiduciary who had acted fraudulently, it was held that the plaintiff had a right to trace the money in equity stemming from that fiduciary relationship. There was also personal liability to account imposed on those persons who had knowingly received misapplied funds or who had dishonestly assisted in the misapplication of the funds.

This case demonstrates the ability of equity to trace into complex mixtures of **33.34** property outwith the jurisdiction of the common law. It is also possible for equity to make a variety of awards of trusts and other remedies, as considered below.[114] Futher, it is also possible for the equitable jurisdiction to make awards for discovery of documents during litigation to assist in the tracing process and also for injunctions which will prevent a defendant from dissipating property after the date of the injunction.[115]

---

[113] That is, companies created solely to carry out the defendants' fraudulent purpose by means of holding assets but which did not carry on a trade nor any other such activity.
[114] See para 33.58.
[115] *Bankers Trust Co v Shapiro* [1980] 1 WLR 1274; *In Re DPR Futures Ltd* [1989] 1 WLR 778.

The need for a prior equitable interest in the property claimed before the equitable jurisdiction can be invoked

33.35   As considered in outline above, it is a prerequisite for an equitable tracing claim that the claimant had some equitable interest in the original property, or that the person who transferred that property away had some fiduciary relationship to the claimant (such as being a trustee).[116] Therefore, before starting an equitable tracing claim, one must always ensure that there is a pre-existing equitable interest.[117] An example of the application of this principle was the decision of the Court of Appeal in *Boscawen v Bajwa*.[118] In that case a building society advanced money under a putative mortgage contract to the vendor's solicitors such that the vendor's solicitors were to hold that money on trust pending completion of the sale. The sale was never completed but the solicitors paid the money to the vendor believing that it had been. Those moneys were immediately applied to discharge the vendor's mortgage with another building society. To effect a remedy in favour of the first building society, that building society needed to trace its money in equity into the second building society's discharged mortgage so that it could receive the equitable remedy of subrogation and so compel the vendor to owe the same obligations to it as he had owed to the second building society under the discharged mortgage. The presence of the trust obligations owed by the solicitors to the building society entitled the building society to claim in equity and so to receive an order for its subrogation to the rights of the second building society.

That equitable tracing will be available against an innocent volunteer

33.36   The case which is commonly taken to be authority for the proposition that equitable tracing will only be available to a claimant who can demonstrate an equitable relationship with the property rights which are to be traced, is the Court of Appeal's decision in *Re Diplock*.[119] It is also authority for the important proposition that, just as equity will not assist a volunteer, it is no defence to an equitable tracing claim that the defendant was an innocent volunteer.[120] In *Re Diplock* itself the defendants had been the recipients of grants made to them by the personal representatives of a deceased testator in accordance with the terms of a residuary

---

[116]   *Re Diplock's Estate* [1948] Ch 465.

[117]   Prof Smith has argued that the precise decision of the Court of Appeal in *Re Diplock* did not establish a rule that there must be a pre-existing proprietary base for an equitable tracing claim: L Smith, *The Law of Tracing* (Clarendon Press, 1997) 126 *et seq*. It is argued that it is in subsequent cases that *Diplock* has been taken to establish that point. What is clear is that English law does currently require a pre-existing equitable proprietary base, although the provenance and desirability of that rule must be called into question: *Westdeutsche Landesbank v Islington* [1996] AC 669. Despite these academic arguments, the modern understanding is that the equitable jurisdiction will only be invoked if the claimant can demonstrate some pre-existing equitable interest to justify its invocation.

[118]   [1995] 4 All ER 769.   [119]   [1948] Ch 465.

[120]   That is, equity will not assist a volunteer by holding that their being a volunteer will in itself be a defence to an equitable tracing claim.

bequest in that will. The gift was afterwards held by the House of Lords to have been void on the basis that its charitable purpose failed. The residue was therefore to have passed under the intestacy rules rather than to the defendants under the terms of the will. The next of kin, entitled on intestacy, brought an action to recover the money which had been paid away by the personal representatives. It was found that the recipients of the money had acted in good faith and had every reason to think that it was their property. They were held nevertheless to be subject to the rights of the residuary beneficiaries to trace after the money in equity even though they had not themselves acted unconscionably. However, property rights were held to bind even 'volunteers provided that as a result of what has gone before some equitable proprietary interest has been created and attaches to the property in the hands of the volunteer'.[121] Therefore, it would not matter that the ultimate recipients were innocent of any breach of trust provided that there had been some preceding breach of an equitable duty by someone else. In effect this approach distinguishes between the source of the property rights in the hands of persons under a fiduciary duty and the further question of the remedy which might then be sought against the volunteers who then held the property. As the matter was put in *Re Diplock*:

> ... once the proprietary interest has been created by equity as a result of the wrongful or unauthorised dealing by the original recipient of the money, that interest will persist and operate against an innocent third party who is a volunteer, provided only that the means of identification or disentanglement remain. For such purpose it cannot make any difference whether the mixing was done by the original recipient [that is, the fiduciary] or by the innocent third party.[122]

What emerges from these dicta is that the court will seek to protect the beneficiary under the original fiduciary duty rather than allow the subsequent innocent volunteer to retain any rights in the windfall which he has received.

This approach was applied by the House of Lords in *Foskett v McKeown*[123] in circumstances in which a trustee took money from a trust and used it to pay the premiums on an existing insurance policy which the trustee had previously taken out in his personal capacity in favour of his children. It was held that the beneficiaries under the trust were entitled to trace in equity into the proceeds of the insurance policy after the trustee's death: thus illustrating that the limitation on the children's rights in the lump sum paid on the maturity of the insurance policy was subject to the beneficiaries' right to trace even though the children had played no part in the breach of trust. Therefore, the innocent volunteer is prima facie liable in a tracing claim, with the precise remedy to be decided, as considered below.[124]

33.37

---

[121] *Re Diplock* [1948] Ch 465, 530. [122] ibid 536. [123] [2000] 3 All ER 97.
[124] See para 33.58.

33.38 The order made in *Re Diplock* was that the innocent volunteers and the beneficiary claimants should take a pro rata share under an equitable charge in the property held in that commingled fund. This principle was encapsulated in the following terms:

> Where an innocent volunteer (as distinct from a purchaser for value without notice) mixes 'money' of his own with 'money' which in equity belongs to another person, or is found in possession of such a mixture, although that other person cannot claim a charge on the mass superior to the claim of the volunteer, he is entitled, nevertheless, to a charge ranking *pari passu* with the claim of the volunteer... Such a person is not in conscience bound to give precedence to the equitable owner of the other of the two funds.[125]

Therefore, it is not simply a question of an equitable notion of conscience which gives rise to this claim and the remedy recognizes the continued rights of the innocent volunteer in that part of the fund not derived from the trust. The claim arises to vindicate the property rights of the beneficiaries of the original trust which were mistakenly paid away. In that sense, the equitable tracing claim is predicated on the existence of the original equitable relationship, consequently recognizing the original duties of good conscience owed to the claimant-beneficiary, and is merely enforcing that person's property rights by means of equitable tracing. This has been expressed by some commentators as being the situation in which the claimants achieve restitution of that property by means of having the equitable interest in that property passed back to them to be held on the terms of the original trust;[126] however, there is now clear authority that tracing does not arise on the basis of restitution of unjust enrichment.[127]

E. Equitable Tracing into Mixed Funds

Tracing into mixtures of property in equity

33.39 As considered in the previous section, the principal benefit of tracing in equity is that the claimant is able to trace into mixtures of property in a manner which is not permitted at common law.[128] The process of tracing, and identifying property over which a remedy is sought, is a separate activity from the issue of imposing a remedy or trust over that property. In relation to mixtures of trust and other money held in bank accounts, a variety of approaches have been taken in the courts from the application of the old first-in, first-out principle, to the establishment of proportionate shares in any substitute property. One of the more problematic issues

---

[125] [1948] Ch 465, 524.
[126] L Smith, *The Law of Tracing* (Clarendon Press, 1997) generally.
[127] *Boscawen v Bajwa* [1995] 4 All ER 769, 776.
[128] As considered above in the discussion of common law tracing.

in equitable tracing claims is that of identifying title in property in funds which are made up both of trust property and other property. Where it is impossible to separate one item of property from another, it will be impossible to effect a common law tracing or a following claim.[129] However, where the property is fungible, such as money in a bank account, such segregation cannot be easily performed. These are considered in detail in the section to follow.

Mixture of trust money with trustee's own money

The court's determination to prioritize the position of the beneficiary

It is suggested that, when the courts are dealing with situations involving the mis-   **33.40** use of the trust property by the trustee or in which the trustee has permitted the trust property to be mixed with his own property, then the courts will interpret the facts of the case in whichever manner will generate the best available result for the beneficiaries. This is the most cogent explanation for the broad range of different approaches which the courts have adopted when dealing with trustees who have allowed trust property to be mixed with their own property, as opposed to the property of some innocent, third person.[130] It is suggested that this approach is in keeping with the trustee's fiduciary obligations of loyalty towards the beneficiaries, to deal with the trust fund in accordance with the terms of his trusteeship, and to exercise that level of skill and care commensurate with his office.[131]

The assumption that the trustee has dealt properly with the trust property

In circumstances in which the trustee has mixed trust property with his own   **33.41** money in breach of trust, he will be liable to effect specific restitution of the trust property or to pay equitable compensation to the beneficiaries, as considered in Chapter 32. If the trustee makes investments out of a mixture of property, or uses that property in different ways, the problem is in deciding whether any given application of property taken from that mixture constituted property belonging to the trust or property belonging to the trustee in his personal capacity. The approach taken by the courts in general terms is to assume the best interpretation of the facts from the perspective of the beneficiaries such that it will be deemed that trust property was used for any purpose which generated a profit or no loss, rather than any purpose which demonstrated a loss.[132] In that sense the court assumes that the trustee has acted honestly and so sought to do the best for the trust, thus relegating his own needs to those of the beneficiaries. An illustration of

---

[129] *FC Jones & sons (A Firm) v Jones* [1996] 3 WLR 703, [1997] Ch 159.

[130] On which see para 33.45.

[131] The fiduciary obligations of trustees in general terms were considered in Parts C and D of this book.

[132] *Re Hallett's Estate* (1880) 13 Ch D 696.

this principle would be in relation to investment of property, given that the trustee is required to invest trust property to achieve the best possible return for the trust.[133] By suggesting that the trustee is required to behave honestly in respect of the trust property, the court may choose to assume, in relation to a range of investments made out of a fund containing trust property and the trustee's own property, that the trustee intended to use trust property to make successful investments and his own money for any inferior investments.

This approach is most clearly exhibited in *Re Hallett's Estate*.[134] Hallett was a solicitor who was a bailee of Russian bonds for one of his clients, Cotterill. Hallett also held securities of that type on express trust for his own marriage settlement (so that he was among the beneficiaries of that marriage settlement). Hallett sold the bonds and paid all the proceeds of sale into his own bank account. Hallett died subsequently. Therefore, it was left to the trustees of the marriage settlement and Cotterill to claim proprietary rights over the remaining contents of Hallett's bank account. It was held that it could be assumed that, where a trustee has money in a personal bank account to which trust money is added, the trustee is acting honestly when paying money out of that bank account. Therefore, it is assumed that the trustee is paying out his own money on investments which lose money and not the trust money. It was held that:

> . . . where a man does an act which may be rightfully performed . . . he is not allowed to say against the person entitled to the property or the right that he has done it wrongfully.

Therefore, it is said that the trustee has rightfully dissipated his own moneys such that the trust money remains intact. The beneficiaries were entitled to claim either equitable title in the assets acquired by the trustee or a lien over that asset.[135] In the more modern language of the law of trusts we might argue that this approach recognizes that the basis of the trust is the conscience of the trustee[136] and that the trustee owes fiduciary duties of the utmost loyalty to the beneficiaries.[137] Therefore, not only is the court assuming that the trustee was acting honestly but it was also applying the tenets of equity so as to require him to act honestly: that is, by holding that any benefit to derive from the property held would be passed to the beneficiaries. By the same token, it might be said that an investment in successful investments would be deemed to be an investment made out of the trust property.[138] Similarly, if a director of a company diverted property from that company to contribute to his own pension fund, then those moneys would be subject

---

[133] *Cowan v Scargill* [1985] Ch 270.   [134] (1880) 13 Ch D 695.

[135] It is clear though that the beneficiary will not now be confined to claiming a lien: *Re Tilley's Will Trusts, Burgin v Croad* [1967] 2 All ER 303, 308, [1967] Ch 1179, 1186; *Scott v Scott* (1963) 109 CLR 649; *Foskett v McKeown* [2000] 3 All ER 97, 123, *per* Lord Millett.

[136] cf *Westdeutsche Landesbank v Islington LBC* [1996] AC 669.   [137] See para 25.15.

[138] See *Re Oatway* [1903] 2 Ch 356 below.

to an equitable tracing claim and the pension fund held subject to a charge in favour of the company.[139]

The power of the beneficiaries to elect which property held by the trustee should be subsumed within the trust fund

By contradistinction to the approach suggested by *Re Hallett's Estate* in the pre- **33.42** ceding paragraph, there is an alternative approach based on the beneficiaries' right to elect which property they wish to have subsumed within the trust fund as a result of any equitable tracing claim. This principle appears most clearly in the case of *Re Oatway*.[140] In that case, the trustee held £4,077 in his personal bank account. The trustee then added £3,000 of trust money to this account. Out of the £7,077 held in the account, £2,137 was spent on purchasing shares. The remainder of the money in the bank account was then dissipated. The beneficiaries sought to trace from the £3,000 taken out of the bank account into the shares acquired with that money. The beneficiaries then sought to impose a charge over those shares. The shares themselves had risen in value to £2,474. The beneficiaries also sought a further accounting in cash to make up the balance of the £3,000 taken from the trust fund.

It was held that where a trustee has wrongfully mixed his own money and trust money, then the trustee is not entitled to say that the investment was made with his own money and that the trust money has been dissipated. Importantly, though, the beneficiaries are entitled to elect either that the property be subject to a charge as security for amounts owed to them by the trustee, or that the unauthorized investment be adopted as part of the trust fund. It is therefore clear that the courts are prepared to protect the beneficiaries at all costs from the misfeasance of the trustee—re-emphasizing the strictness of the trustee's obligations to the beneficiaries.[141]

This approach was doubted in *Foskett v McKeown*[142] by the House of Lords on the **33.43** basis, in effect, of fault by Lord Millett.[143] His lordship held that:

> The primary rule in regard to a mixed fund, therefore, is that gains and losses are borne by the contributors rateably.[144] The beneficiary's right to elect instead to enforce a lien to obtain repayment is an exception to the primary rule, exercisable where the fund is deficient and the claim is made against the wrongdoer and those claiming through him.

Lord Millett relied on similar principles which apply in relation to physical mixtures where it is said that if the mixture is the fault of the defendant then it is open

---

[139] *Clark v Cutland* [2003] EWCA Civ 810.   [140] [1903] 2 Ch 356.
[141] See now *Foskett v McKeown* [2000] 3 All ER 97, 123, *per* Lord Millett.
[142] [2000] 3 All ER 97.   [143] ibid 124.   [144] That is, in proportionate shares.

to the claimant to 'claim the goods'.[145] Importantly, even where the defendant is not at fault in the commingling of property, such an innocent volunteer is not entitled to occupy a better position than the person who was responsible simply by reason of her innocence.[146] This situation of innocent volunteers is considered immediately below.

33.44   There is one anomalous case, given the general trend in the cases to assume everything against the trustee who acts wrongfully. In *Re Tilley's Will Trusts*[147] a trustee took money which she held on trust and paid it into her own personal bank account. The trustee made investments on her own behalf from that bank account. The moneys she took from the trust settled her overdraft on that account in part so that she was able to continue her investment activities. The court held that the beneficiaries had no rights to trace into the investments which the trustee had made with the money taken from that account but rather the court was convinced on the facts that the trust money had simply served to reduce her overdraft but not to pay for her investments. An alternative and, it is suggested, preferable analysis, more in keeping with the decision of the House of Lords in *Foskett v McKeown*, would have been to find that, if the trust money made the investment possible, then the trust should be taken to have contributed traceable funds to the acquisition of those investments.

Mixture of two trust funds or mixture with innocent volunteer's money

The general principle

33.45   This section considers the situation in which trust property is misapplied such that the trust property is mixed with property belonging to an innocent third party. Therefore, rather than consider the issues which arose in the previous section concerning the obligations of the wrongdoing trustee, it is now necessary to decide how property belonging to innocent parties should be allocated between them. It was held in *Re Diplock*[148] that the entitlement of the beneficiary to the mixed fund should rank *pari passu* (or equally) with the rights of the innocent volunteer:

> Where an innocent volunteer (as distinct from a purchaser for value without notice) mixes 'money' of his own with 'money' which in equity belongs to another person, or is found in possession of such a mixture, although that other person cannot claim a charge on the mass superior to the claim of the volunteer, he is entitled, nevertheless, to a charge ranking *pari passu* with the claim of the volunteer... Such a person is not

---

[145] *Lupton v White, White v Lupton* (1808) 15 Ves 432, [1803–13] All ER Rep 336; *Sandeman & Sons v Tyzack and Branfoot Steamship Co Ltd* [1913] AC 680, 695, [1911–13] All ER Rep 1013, 1020, *per* Lord Molton.
[146] *Jones v De Marchant* (1916) 28 DLR 561; *Foskett v McKeown* [2000] 3 All ER 97.
[147] *Re Tilley's Will Trusts, Burgin v Croad* [1967] Ch 1179.   [148] [1948] Ch 465, 524.

in conscience bound to give precedence to the equitable owner of the other of the two funds.

In *Re Diplock,* charities had been the innocent recipients of property which had been paid to them under a term in a trust document which required that property be applied for charitable or benevolent purposes. After the advancement had been made it was held that this term of the trust was ineffective to create a charitable purpose trust because its purpose was not exclusively charitable. In consequence the moneys which had been advanced to the charities had been advanced technically in breach of trust. Therefore, the claimants seeking to establish their beneficial interest under the trust sought to recover those moneys which would be held on trust for themselves in remainder. It was no objection to the claim for recovery of the money by means of tracing that the recipients of the money had been entirely innocent: in that sense tracing operates to vindicate the claimants' property rights and not to punish them for any intentionally wrongful act. Nevertheless, even in that case there was a breach of trust which would render it unconscionable for the defendants to have asserted a right to retain those moneys, particularly in circumstances in which they had been paid to them mistakenly and in which they had not changed their position in reliance on those funds.

Therefore, none of the innocent contributors to the fund is considered as taking **33.46** any greater right than any other contributor to the fund. Rather, each person has an equal charge over that property. This principle was adopted in *Foskett v McKeown*[149] by the House of Lords,[150] a case in which Lord Millett held that:

> The primary rule in regard to a mixed fund, therefore, is that gains and losses are borne by the contributors rateably.[151] The beneficiary's right to elect instead to enforce a lien to obtain repayment is an exception to the primary rule, exercisable where the fund is deficient and the claim is made against the wrongdoer and those claiming through him.

As considered above,[152] when considering rights to payments made under an insurance policy to which a trust had unwittingly contributed premium payments, Lord Millett applied principles more usually applied to physical mixtures of chattels which suggest that if the creation of a mixture of property is the fault of the defendant then it is open to the claimant to 'claim the goods'.[153] This idea suggests, further, that equitable tracing operates on the basis of fault, or possibly of conscience more generally. Perhaps it should be understood as separating out those cases in which fault can be identified from those cases in which neither party

---

[149] [2000] 3 All ER 97.

[150] ibid 124. Applied in *Bracken Pastries Ltd v Gutteridge* [2003] EWHC 1064, [2003] 2 BCLC 84.

[151] That is, in proportionate shares.   [152] See para 33.45.

[153] *Lupton v White, White v Lupton* (1808) 15 Ves 432, [1803–13] All ER Rep 336; *Sandeman & Sons v Tyzack and Branfoot Steamship Co Ltd* [1913] AC 680, 695, [1911–13] All ER Rep 1013, 1020, *per* Lord Molton.

can be considered to be at fault. It was held, in common with the decision in *Re Diplock*,[154] that even where the defendant was not at fault in the commingling of property, he would nevertheless not be entitled to occupy a better position than the person who was responsible for that commingling simply by reason of his innocence.[155] This suggests that, in general terms, the doctrine of equitable tracing is not concerned with the conscience of the defendant. The general principle could be expressed to be that where property subject to one express trust is transferred improperly and without valuable consideration to the trustees of another trust, that property or its traceable proceeds still belongs in equity to the first trust and its trustees have a proprietary claim to recover that property.[156]

33.47 In the case of *Foskett v McKeown* itself, a trustee had been misusing the trust's funds to pay part of the premiums on a life assurance policy, of about £20,000, which he had taken out in favour of his wife and children. When the trustee died and the breach of trust was discovered, it was held that the beneficiaries of the trust were entitled to trace into the moneys paid out under the life assurance policy on the basis that their money had been mixed with the trustee's own money to pay for the life assurance policy premiums, which were to pay a lump sum to the trustee's children on the trustee's death. Whereas the Court of Appeal had held that the beneficiaries were entitled only to an amount of money equal to the two premiums, an amount of about £20,000, the House of Lords held that they were entitled to a two-fifths share of the lump sum payable on the maturity of the policy, worth about £400,000. Consequently, the beneficiaries were entitled to the proceeds of the insurance policy in proportion to the size of the contribution made by the trust fund to the total amount of the insurance policy premiums.

33.48 If trust property were used to contribute x to an investment fund, it would ordinarily be assumed that the trust would be entitled to recoup the proportionate profits, y, which the investment fund made from the participation of the trust fund's x, as well as its being entitled to recoup the amount of x. If the trust's contribution of x was considered by other innocent volunteers to be buying those volunteers a pension or a lump sum on which their maintenance would be based, with a value of z, then those volunteers would be disappointed to receive only z less y taken by the trust in recognition of its anticipated share of the profits. However, the trust would be similarly disadvantaged if it received only a return of x contributed by it at the outset when it would have expected that its trustee would have invested x to generate a profit, and thus income, for the trust. That was essentially the issue in *Foskett v McKeown*. In such situations one or other of the innocent

---

[154] [1948] Ch 465.

[155] *Jones v De Marchant* (1916) 28 DLR 561; *Foskett v McKeown* [2001] 1 AC 102, [2000] 3 All ER 97.

[156] *Foskett v McKeown* [2001] 1 AC 102; *Allen v Rea Brothers Trustees Ltd* (2002) 4 ITELR 627; *Clark v Cutland* [2003] EWCA Civ 810.

parties is bound to receive less than they would have wished. The approach taken by the courts is that the trustee owes fiduciary duties to the beneficiaries and that the beneficiaries are therefore entitled to that proportion of the profit attributable to the contribution of x. Thus the beneficiaries receive y from the investment fund and an amount of x, whereas the innocent volunteers are entitled only to the surplus which z offers them less y to which the beneficiaries are entitled.

The decision in *Foskett v McKeown* was possible because the property at issue was **33.49** capable of easy division. A more difficult situation might be that in which the property cannot be divided between the parties rateably because, for example, it is a tangible chattel like an oil painting, which cannot reasonably be cut into pieces and divided, or a large item of industrial machinery. Page Wood V-C has held quite simply that 'if a man mixes trust funds with his own, the whole will be treated as the trust property, except so far as he may be able to distinguish what is his own'.[157] Therefore, if it were a valuable oil painting which the trust had lost to the innocent volunteers, the beneficiaries might have been entitled to recover the entire property as opposed to only having a right to a pro rata share or a lien to make good their loss. If the painting had belonged entirely to the trust fund, this would be simply a following claim to recover the painting. If the painting had been bought with money taken from the trust fund and money taken from the innocent volunteers, then it would appear more equitable to order a sale of the painting and a rateable division of the sale proceeds between the beneficiaries and the innocent volunteers in proportion to their contributions to the purchase price of the painting.

Furthermore, it does not matter what the market value of the assets contributed **33.50** to the fund were at the time of their contribution: what matters is the value which they constitute as a proportion of the total fund at the time of making the claim. Suppose, for example, that a trustee took 1,000 shares from a trust at a time when those shares were worth 100p and later that a third party's money was used to acquire a further 1,000 shares of the same type which were worth only 90p at the time when they were acquired. Suppose further that at the time of making the claim those shares had risen in value to 150p. The courts would not take the third party's contribution to have been £900 (the value of her shares at the time of their contribution) and the trust's shares £1,000. Rather, each is taken to have contributed one-half of all of the property in the mixed fund of 2,000 shares.[158] The purpose of a tracing claim is to recognize the claimant's property rights and it is then for other doctrines such as breach of trust to look to the compensation of any of the parties for any loss which remains outstanding.[158A]

---

[157] *Frith v Cartland* (1865) 2 Hem & M 417, 420, (1865) 71 ER 525, 526; *Foskett v McKeown* [2000] 3 All ER 97, 125.

[158] *Foskett v McKeown* [2000] 3 All ER 97, *per* Lord Millett.

[158A] In relation to equitable compensation see para 32.14.

33.51 The question then is as to the range of other remedies which the courts may choose to offer. On the cases relating to money in bank accounts much has turned on whether or not the claimants can establish rights either to money subsisting in bank accounts or in relation to moneys used to buy assets of substantial value. Typically in the cases involving money in bank accounts some money has simply been dissipated whereas other money has acquired profitable investments. It is to this type of issue which we now turn.

Payments made in and out of the fund

33.52 The rule in *Re Diplock* which was considered above[159] applies satisfactorily to funds the property in which does not change its character. Suppose that the property making up the fund constitutes two cars of equal value contributed one each by the two innocent parties. In that circumstance it is easy to divide the fund between two claimants so that they receive one car each. If the fund were a house which was bought with the aggregate proceeds of the property belonging to the two innocent parties, *Re Diplock* would require that each person take an equal charge over that house. The more difficult situation, however, is that in which the fund containing the mixed property is used in separate parcels to acquire different items of property. The most common example on the decided cases is that of a current bank account from which payments are made to acquire different items of property. The problem will lie in deciding which of the innocent contributors to the fund ought to take which right in which piece of property. There are two competing approaches to deal with situations of this sort: the first-in, first-out approach and the proportionate share approach.

The first-in, first-out approach to current bank accounts

33.53 The long-standing rule relating to title in property paid out of current bank accounts is that in *Clayton's Case*.[160] In relation to current bank accounts, the decision in *Clayton's Case* held that the appropriate principle is 'first in, first out' such that in deciding which property has been used to acquire which items of property it is deemed that money first deposited is used first. The reason for this rule is a rigid application of accounting principles. Suppose an empty bank account to which one person unwittingly contributes £1,000 and another person £2,000; further suppose that, after both amounts have been paid into that account,[161] £1,000 is used from that account to acquire shares which treble in value and £2,000 the following day to acquire shares which become worthless. The first-in, first-out principle provides that the first money paid into the account is deemed

---

[159] See para 33.45.   [160] (1816) 1 Mer 572.

[161] If the shares were bought with money from that account after only the £1,000 had been paid in and before the £2,000 was paid in, then there would be no problem with suggesting that the profitable shares in the above example were acquired only with that initial £1,000.

to acquire the first parcel of shares, and so the contributor of the £1,000 is therefore taken to own shares worth £3,000; whereas the contributor of £2,000 is deemed to have acquired the next parcel of property and so to be the owner of the worthless shares.[162]

The result of this approach, evidently, is that the property which each contributor acquires may be entirely arbitrary. The only way of understanding this rule is to recall that it derives from a case decided early in the nineteenth century when there was comparatively little litigation concerning intangible property. The metaphor which this principle conjures up is that of a wholesaler of soft fruit. If we ran a business as wholesalers of soft fruit—oranges, pears, and so forth—we would have a large warehouse in which the fruit was stored. When an order came in for a consignment of oranges, we would be foolish to ship out the fruit which had arrived in our warehouse most recently because that would leave older fruit at the rear of the warehouse at greater risk of rotting. Instead, the first fruit to have arrived in our warehouse would be the first fruit which we would ship out: first in, first out. This way of thinking carried on into elementary bookkeeping in which the assumption was that the first money to be paid into a bank account would similarly be the first money to be paid out. In a world of intangible property it is an approach which appears anachronistic. A different approach is suggested in the next section. **33.54**

Proportionate share

The alternative approach would be to decide that each contributor should take proportionate shares in all of the property acquired with the proceeds of the fund. This is the approach taken in most Commonwealth jurisdictions.[163] On the facts above, each party contributed to the bank account in the ratio 1:2 (in that one person provided £1,000 and the other provided £2,000). Therefore, the two parcels of shares would be deemed to be held one-third for the first party and two-thirds for the other party. The result is the elimination of any differential movements in value across this property in circumstances in which it is pure chance which beneficiaries would take rights in which property. **33.55**

A slightly different twist on this approach was adopted in *Barlow Clowes International v Vaughan*.[164] In that case investors in the collapsed Barlow Clowes **33.56**

---

[162] An analogy might be drawn with a warehouse full of soft fruit. Clearly the longer the fruit remains in the warehouse the more it will rot. Therefore, the older fruit will be moved out of the warehouse before the newer fruit. *Clayton's Case* adopts a similar approach to money. The money which has sat in the account longest is taken to have moved out of the account first and the newer money is not moved out of the account until all the old money has gone.

[163] *Re Ontario Securities Commission* (1985) 30 DLR (4th) 30; *Re Registered Securities* [1991] 1 NZLR 545.

[164] [1992] 4 All ER 22, [1992] BCLC 910; noted in Birks [1993] LMCLQ 218.

organization had their losses met in part by the Department of Trade and Industry. The Secretary of State for Trade and Industry then sought to recover, in effect, the amounts which had been paid away to those former investors by tracing the compensation paid to the investors into the assets of Barlow Clowes. At first instance, Peter Gibson J found that the rule in *Clayton's Case*[165] should be applied. *Clayton's Case* asserts the rule (as considered immediately above) that tracing claims into mixed funds in current bank accounts are to be treated as the money first paid into the bank account to be first paid out of the account. The majority of the Court of Appeal favoured a distribution between the rights of the various investors on a *pari passu* basis, considering *Clayton's Case* too formalistic and arbitrary. Leggatt and Woolf LJJ approved an approach culled from the Canadian cases[166] which recognizes that if a contribution is made to a fund for a long period of time, it makes a greater contribution to the value of the fund than an investment of the same amount which formed part of the fund for a shorter period of time. Consequently, in considering the value of the contributors to an investment fund, it is appropriate to weight the proportion which each contributors is deemed to have contributed to the fund by recognition of the time value of that contribution. It is suggested that this approach is the more sensible approximation to the contribution which each good faith investor has made to the total fund. On the facts of *Barlow Clowes v Vaughan* the process of calculating these separate entitlements to take into account the time value of each contribution was taken to have been too complicated given the large number of investors and the huge range of investments made by the funds at issue, and therefore it was not applied in that case.[167]

Which approach is to be preferred?

33.57 The rolling charge approach recognized by the Canadian cases was approved by the English Court of Appeal but not applied by it in *Barlow Clowes*; and the rule in *Clayton's Case* was criticized by Leggatt LJ in *Barlow Clowes* as having 'nothing to do' with tracing property rights through into property but it has not yet been overruled. Indeed, it does appear to effect somewhat arbitrary results in many circumstances, as considered above. The rule in *Clayton's Case* derives from a time when money was considered to be a tangible item of property like cattle, land, and so forth. As mentioned above, the first-in, first-out rule mimics the way in which goods in a warehouse would be accounted for. In *Clayton's Case* money is being

---

[165] (1816) 1 Mer 572.

[166] *Re Ontario Securities Commission* (1985) 30 DLR (4th) 30. Considered also in *Russell-Cooke Trust Co v Prentis* [2002] EWHC 2227.

[167] Rather than look to which investors contributed their money first and which last on the *Clayton's Case* principle, a more equitable approach would resort to the resulting trust principle that each should take according to the proportionate size of their contributions. See para 33.59.

treated in the same fashion—thus denying that it is in fact intangible and the application of that rule generates arbitrary results in many circumstances.

F. Equity's Responses to Tracing Claims: Trusts and Other Equitable Remedies

The available equitable responses to tracing claims

Having considered the nature of the tracing process, it is important to consider **33.58** the types of claim and the forms of remedy which might be imposed as a result of it. The principal remedies are the equitable charge,[168] the constructive trust,[169] the lien,[170] and a charge by way of subrogation;[171] although resulting trust,[172] equitable compensation,[173] and even a charge over the swollen assets of the defendant have been, somewhat heretically, considered to be possible on the basis of recent cases.[174] The structure is simple: first, the tracing process is carried out in accordance with the principles considered thus far in this chapter; secondly, having identified the property which is to be the subject matter of the claim, the plaintiff then seeks to impose a trust or some equitable remedy over that property. The various possibilities are considered in this section.

Selecting the most appropriate remedy

Equitable tracing potentially gives rise to a range of equitable remedies and trusts. **33.59** The principal issue is whether the most appropriate remedy is to award the claimant a charge over the traced property, or a possessory lien over that property, or to award proprietary rights over that property in the form of a trust. The decision as to which remedy will be the most appropriate will depend on the circumstances: one remedy will appear more appropriate in some circumstances than in others. If property can be identified as belonging entirely in equity to the claimant, then a constructive trust would appear to be an appropriate remedy. If the property identified at the end of the tracing process belongs to more than one person in equity, and if all of the potential claimants want to share in the property itself rather than simply in a proportion of its value in cash, then a charge in favour

---

[168] *Re Tilley's Will Trusts* [1967] Ch 1178.
[169] *Westdeutsche Landesbank v Islington LBC* [1996] AC 669, *infra*.
[170] *Foskett v McKeown* [2001] 1 AC 102.   [171] *Boscawen v Bajwa* [1996] 1 WLR 328.
[172] *El Ajou v Dollar Land Holdings* [1993] 3 All ER 717.
[173] *Target Holdings v Redferns* [1996] 1 AC 421, [1995] 3 WLR 352, [1995] 3 All ER 785.
[174] Contrary to Prof Birks's argument that it is not appropriate to talk of 'rights' and 'remedies' but rather only of 'rights' which necessarily imply their remedies (P Birks, 'Rights, wrongs and remedies' (2000) OJLS 1), this is one context in which the rights of the claimant may lead to the realization of any one of a number of remedies dependent on the context, one of which (equitable compensation) necessarily involves some judicial discretion; see generally K Barker, 'Rescuing remedialism in unjust enrichment law: why remedies are right' [1998] CLJ 301, 319.

of each equitable owner equivalent to their proportionate title in the property would also appear to be appropriate.[175] If the property is incapable of division, then it would only be possible to satisfy the claimants' various interests if the property were sold and the sale proceeds divided between the claimants in recognition of their rights under a charge. By contrast, if the property were capable of division between the parties and also intrinsically valuable, then the property could be held on constructive trust for all of the claimants as beneficiaries such that each would be entitled to demand delivery of their share from the constructive trustee.[176] For a constructive trust to be imposed in favour of each claimant individually then the property would need to be segregated into individual lots; if the property were not so segregated, then it would not be possible to impose a trust over that property.[177] If the equitable owners are concerned only to recover the cash value of their share in the property, or if the value of the fund will not satisfy the tracing claim, then a lien would be a sufficient remedy to secure the defendant's obligation to satisfy the tracing claim in cash. The lien will therefore not be appropriate in all circumstances; the claimant's right to elect to enforce a lien, rather than to obtain title in identified property, is an exception to the primary rule that the claimant will take title in property and is exercisable where the fund is deficient to satisfy the claimant's rights.[178] Each of these claims is considered below.

33.60 Therefore, if the traceable proceeds of the claimant's original property were mixed with property belonging to other innocent parties, then the more appropriate approach would be to award a charge to each party in proportion to their contribution to the total fund. Alternatively, the claimant might be awarded a lien in circumstances in which compensation in money would be appropriate but so that the claimant would have the protection of a lien in the event that payment were not made.

33.61 The advantage of the constructive trust is that the claimant acquires equitable title in specific property. However, a fixed charge does grant property rights which will be enforceable in the event of an insolvency by means of granting the claimant a right to be paid an amount of money but, if the debtor defaults, giving the claimant a right to seize the specified property to realize its claim.[179] The shortcoming of a charge is that, once the repossessed property is sold, the claimant is only entitled to recover the amount of the debt and is not entitled to take absolute title in the property: having to account to the debtor instead for any surplus. Were

---

[175] See *Re Hallett's Estate* (1880) 13 Ch D 696, 709, *per* Lord Jessel MR, in which there was a suggestion that, in the event that there was a mixed fund of property, then only a charge would be an appropriate remedy.

[176] Further to the principle in *Saunders v Vautier* (1841) 4 Beav 115.

[177] *MacJordan Construction Ltd v Brookmount Erostin Ltd* [1992] BCLC 350.

[178] *Foskett v McKeown* [2001] 1 AC 102, [2000] 3 All ER 97.

[179] *Re Tilley* [1967] Ch 1178; *Paul Davies Pty Ltd v Davies* (1983) 1 NSWLR 440.

the claimant to establish a right under a trust, as considered below, then the claimant would be entitled to take title in the property and thus take title in any increase in value in that property.

Constructive trusts recognized in response to equitable tracing claims

Constructive trusts, tracing, and unconscionable behaviour

A constructive trust is imposed in circumstances in which the defendant deals knowingly and unconscionably with property.[180] Thus, the House of Lords held (unanimously on this point) in *Westdeutsche Landesbank v Islington LBC*[181] that there will not be an equitable proprietary right in the form of a trust without there being knowledge of some factor which affects the conscience of the legal owner of property. For the imposition of a constructive trust as a result of an equitable tracing claim it is therefore required that there be a pre-existing equitable interest sufficient to ground the equitable tracing claim, that there be identifiable property which can be the subject matter of the trust, and that the defendant have acted unconscionably with knowledge that his actions were unconscionable.[182]   **33.62**

The leading case on the nature of constructive trusts in equitable tracing claims is *Westdeutsche Landesbank v Islington*.[183] In that case a bank paid money to a local authority under an interest rate swap contract which was subsequently found to have been void *ab initio*. The principal question was whether or not the bank could demonstrate that the local authority should be required, by virtue of their common mistake as to the validity of the contract or the failure of consideration when the contract was avoided, to be treated as a constructive trustee of the moneys paid to it such that the bank would be able to trace its money into the local authority's general funds. It was held that the local authority would not be treated as having been a constructive trustee of the moneys paid to it by the bank because, from the time it received the money until the time at which it dissipated those moneys, it had no knowledge that the contract was void *ab initio* and therefore could not have dealt unconscionably with the money.[184] There was no constructive trust, nor any trust of any other kind,[185] and therefore no equitable interest sufficient to found an equitable tracing claim. Furthermore, there could not have been a constructive trust because there was no property over which such a trust could have been imposed, or in relation to which an equitable tracing claim could have been commenced, once the local authority had spent the money paid to it by the bank.[186]   **33.63**

---

[180] See para 27.01.   [181] [1996] AC 669, [1996] 2 All ER 961.

[182] *Westdeutsche Landesbank v Islington* [1996] AC 669.   [183] [1996] AC 669.

[184] See generally the discussion of this principle at para 27.05.

[185] Particularly no resulting trust, as considered at para 26.03.

[186] The moneys had been paid into the local authority's general bank accounts and those accounts had subsequently gone overdrawn, this terminating any possible right of tracing, as considered below at para 33.73.

33.64 There is a difficulty with describing a constructive trust as being a 'remedy' in relation to an equitable tracing claim because constructive trusts arise by operation of law on an institutional basis: that is, constructive trusts arise automatically and retrospectively, they do not arise at the discretion of the court only prospectively from the date of the court judgment, and so are not 'remedies'. A constructive trust may itself found an equitable tracing claim. If a person is found to be a constructive trustee over property, then the beneficiary under that trust has a sufficient equitable interest to found a tracing claim.[187]

33.65 In this sense it is important to recognize that constructive trusts may arise either in recognition of a pre-existing proprietary right or to impose an equitable obligation over a defendant in relation to property which the claimant had not previously owned. The recognition of pre-existing property rights is evident from the decision in *Westdeutsche Landesbank v Islington*.[188] By contrast, that constructive trusts may arise in satisfaction of a form of general, equitable obligation is demonstrated by Lord Templeman in *Attorney-General for Hong Kong v Reid*[189] where his lordship held that a person who receives a bribe in breach of some office holds that bribe on constructive trust from the moment he receives it, with the result that any property which is acquired with that property or any profit derived from that property is similarly held on constructive trust. The first constructive trust over the bribe itself arises as a result of equity acting *in personam* against the defendant such that his unconscionable receipt of that property causes him to be deemed to be a constructive trustee of that property for those beneficiaries to whom fiduciary duties were owed. On the basis, then, that equity looks upon as done that which ought to have been done, the property held on trust is to be treated as having been the property of the claimant from the moment when the conscience of the defendant was affected by knowledge that his act was unconscionable, thus giving rise to a proprietary right in equity. This constructive trust arises over property in which the beneficiaries previously had no proprietary rights but founds equitable proprietary rights by operation of law and consequently a right to commence an equitable tracing claim if the constructive trustee passes that property away or deals with it in some way.

---

[187] Another, esoteric interpretation of the operation of an avowedly constructive trust in relation to a tracing claim arose in relation to counsel's submission that there could be no equitable tracing claim because there was only ever an outright transfer of the property and so that the facts were incapable of creating a trust. It was held that '[i]t is beyond argument that the equitable proprietary interest in the money was at all times vested in NLM. It never passed to Eye Group, or to the intermediary or to Mrs Smalley. All that did pass was the legal title to be held at each stage on trust for NLM': *Smalley v Bracken Partners* [2003] EWCA Civ 1875, para 30, *per* Mantell LJ. How the legal title alone can be held on trust is not entirely clear. In the decision of Mummery LJ, the trust was founded on the fact that the legal title was in one place and the beneficial interest in another.
[188] [1996] AC 669.   [189] [1994] 1 AC 324, [1993] 3 WLR 1143.

Constructive trusts, tracing, and theft

One particular context in which tracing becomes important, other than the **33.66** straightforward breaches of fiduciary duty considered above, is when property is stolen. No system of law will permit a thief to obtain or retain any proprietary rights in the proceeds of the crime. A thief is construed as holding the stolen property on constructive trust for the victim of the crime (that is, the rightful owner of the stolen property) from the moment that he takes it into his possession.[190] When property was stolen from a pension fund, the thief holds the stolen property on constructive trust for the victims of the theft;[191] when accountants stole money from a client and passed that money into shell companies, the accountants would be treated as constructive trustees of those moneys;[192] similarly, it was held in *Westdeutsche Landesbank v Islington* that, if a bag of coins was stolen, the thief would be treated as holding that stolen property on constructive trust for the victim of the crime.[193] The principal benefit to the victim of crime which stems from the imposition of the office of constructive trustee on the thief is that, if the thief sells or otherwise transfers the property away, the victim of crime is able to found an equitable tracing claim in order to establish title in the traceable proceeds of the stolen property in the thief's hands. If the stolen property were still held separately in the thief's hands then a following claim would be sufficient to recover it. This potential to bring a tracing claim is significant if the thief were to mix the stolen property with other property or if the thief were to pass the stolen property to someone who has a good defence to a following claim.[194] For example, if a thief steals my property and sells it to a bona fide purchaser, this sale to a bona fide

---

[190] *Westdeutsche Landesbank v Islington* [1996] AC 669.

[191] *Bishopsgate v Maxwell* [1993] Ch 1, 70.

[192] *Agip (Africa) Ltd v Jackson* [1990] Ch 265; affirmed by the Court of Appeal [1991] Ch 547.

[193] *Westdeutsche Landesbank v Islington* [1996] AC 669.

[194] The other means of conceiving of the law in this area is that the victim of the crime is the only person who could release her rights in the property which was stolen. Therefore, those rights must be considered to have continued in existence, despite the theft. Consequently, the courts should not be concerned to grant new property rights to the claimant under constructive trust, but rather should simply be recognizing that those rights have always continued in existence such that the claimant ought to be entitled to a declaration that those rights have continued to exist. The conceptual problem with the imposition of a constructive trust on the thief is the apparent recognition that the thief acquired legal title in the stolen property. Indeed, the further problem with *Attorney-General for Hong Kong v Reid* is that the employer had no pre-existing rights in either the stolen property or its proceeds, and therefore ought only to receive a right *in personam* against the defendant in the manner in which Lord Templeman explained it. In both of these situations, equity appears to be acting in a way which punishes the criminal, in effect, and which grants the victim of crime a right to trace her stolen property in equity by granting her an equitable interest in the property by means of the constructive trusts device. Without the grant of a constructive trust, the victim would be considered to have had held only an absolute title in the property such that there was no distinct equitable interest capable of founding equitable tracing: *Westdeutsche Landesbank v Islington* [1996] AC 669.

purchaser would have the result that the bona fide purchaser[195] would take good title in equity to the property.[196] The victim of crime will then wish to establish title in the proceeds which the thief has realized from the sale of the stolen goods.

Tensions between the general doctrine of constructive trust and the imposition of constructive trusts in response to equitable tracing claims

33.67 There is a tension in the nature of constructive trusts between those constructive trusts imposed on a person who deals with property knowing that his actions are unconscionable, and those constructive trusts which are imposed in relation to equitable tracing claims.[197] It has been suggested that, in the light of the speech of Lord Browne-Wilkinson in *Westdeutsche Landesbank v Islington*,[198] there is no requirement to demonstrate a prior equitable interest in the property on the basis that his lordship only requires that a defendant have knowledge of a factor which affects her conscience for there to be a proprietary remedy imposed.[199] Equitable tracing claims entitle the claimant to a remedy even if the defendant is an innocent volunteer.[200] It may be that the defendant has acted unconscionably in coming into possession of the property but that is not a prerequisite of the claim. It could be contended that the constructive trust is imposed on the basis of good conscience once the defendant becomes aware that the property which he holds has been taken in breach of trust and therefore that it does comply with the requirement that the defendant have acted unconscionably in the knowledge that his actions were unconscionable.

This point might become clearer with an illustration, taken by extrapolation from one decided case, *Allan v Rea Brothers Trustees Ltd*.[201] Suppose that property was transferred to one pension trust fund, A, from another pension trust fund, B. It was found that the money had been received by the trustees of the A trust in breach of the terms of the B trust, but the consciences of the trustees of A were not affected for so long as they did not know that the transfer to them had been conducted in breach of the terms of the B trust because the terms of the trust in that case were not known to the parties at the time of the transaction. Consequently, it was suggested that there would not be any trust over the transferred moneys in favour of the B trust because the trustees of A had not had knowledge at the

---

[195] ie, a bona fide purchaser for value without notice of the victim's rights in the property; or 'equity's darling'.

[196] *Pilcher v Rawlins* (1872) LR 7 Ch App 259; *Westdeutsche Landesbank v Islington* [1996] AC 669.

[197] See specifically the discussion of the nature of constructive trusts in equitable tracing claims at paras 29.73 *et seq*.

[198] [1996] 2 WLR 802, 838–839 in relation to a part of the speech headed 'The stolen bag of coins'.

[199] P Birks, 'Trusts raised to avoid unjust enrichment: the *Westdeutsche* case' [1996] RLR 3,10.

[200] *Re Diplock's Estate* [1948] Ch 465; *Foskett v McKeown* [2001] 1 AC 102, [2000] 3 All ER 97.

[201] *Allen v Rea Brothers Trustees Ltd* (2002) 4 ITELR 627, where this issue emerges at para 46.

material time of any factor which ought to have affected their consciences. However, in that case it was acknowledged,[202] nevertheless, that the property remained in equity the property of the B trust, further to the decision in *Foskett v McKeown*, regardless of the knowledge of the trustees of the A trust. Clearly, there is a tension here between the question whether or not a person can be held liable to hold property on constructive trust further to an equitable tracing claim so as to vindicate the claimant's property rights in the trust property, or whether such a constructive trust can only come into existence if the defendant's conscience is affected. It is suggested that the courts have taken the approach that a constructive trust will be imposed further to an equitable tracing claim so as to vindicate the claimant's property rights.[203] In practice, it is suggested that, for an equitable tracing claim to be successful, it would be necessary in any event for the defendant to have under his control or in his possession the traceable proceeds of some property belonging in equity to the claimant; therefore the commencement of proceedings to assert title to that property and any communications prior to the service of proceedings will have furnished the defendant with sufficient knowledge to be obliged to hold that property on constructive trust for the claimant; and that the defendant would be required to make out a defence of change of position, of having purchased that property in good faith, or of estoppel by representation to resist the tracing claim. In this way, it is suggested, the conceptual problem as to whether or not the mooted imposition of a constructive trust in a claim for equitable tracing would be trumped by a lack of sufficient knowledge disappears in practice.

Equitable charges and charges by way of subrogation

Charges imposed in equitable tracing claims

An equitable charge will give the claimant a proportionate right in a fund of   **33.68**
property equal to a given value but without the need for the claimant to segregate property within that fund as would be required for the creation of a trust.[204] Charges can be fixed over specific property or they can float over a pool of property such that the legal owner of that fund can continue to deal with it. The means of identifying the difference between a fixed and a floating charge is the following one:

> A [fixed, or] specific charge... is one that without more fastens on ascertained and definite property or property capable of being ascertained and defined; a floating charge, on the other hand, is ambulatory and shifting in its nature, hovering over and so to speak floating with the property which it is intended to affect until some event

---

[202] *Allan v Rea Brothers Trustees Ltd* [2002] EWCA Civ 85, para 52, *per* Robert Walker LJ.
[203] *Re Diplock; Diplock v Wintle* [1948] Ch 465; *Foskett v McKeown* [2001] AC 102.
[204] *Re Goldcorp* [1995] 1 AC 74.

occurs or some act is done which causes it to settle and fasten on the subject of the charge within its reach and grasp.[205]

It is more likely that a court would order a fixed charge so as to freeze the fund held by the defendant with each claimant to a beneficial share of that fund entitled to a specified proportion of it. A charge, then, offers a means of granting property rights to the claimant without the need for the formalities necessary for a trust.[206]

Charge by way of subrogation

33.69 The equitable remedy of subrogation[207] permits a claimant to trace his property rights in circumstances in which his property has been used to discharge the defendant's obligations to a third person.[208] Whereas the ordinary rules of tracing would consider the claimant to have lost his right to trace once the property has been dissipated, as with the discharge of a debt, the remedy of subrogation permits the claimant to a charge such that the obligations discharged with the claimant's money are owed instead to the claimant.

33.70 The leading case in this context is *Boscawen v Bajwa*,[209] in which the Abbey National Building Society paid mortgage moneys to Bajwa expecting that they would be secured over the land which Bajwa was selling. Bajwa's solicitors were acting as trustee of the mortgage moneys with a power to apply those moneys only on completion of the sale. Those solicitors mistakenly believed that the sale had been completed and so paid the mortgage moneys to discharge Bajwa's existing mortgage with the Halifax Building Society. The sale was never completed. Therefore, the Abbey National did not acquire the mortgage security it was expecting. The Abbey National was able to trace its money in equity because that money was held on trust by the solicitors. The money could be identified as having discharged Bajwa's mortgage and therefore the court awarded subrogation with the effect that the mortgage moneys which Bajwa had previously owed to the Halifax were owed instead to Abbey National on the same terms: consequently, Abbey National was subrogated to the rights of Halifax. In relation to tracing generally, the remedy of subrogation allows the claimant to trace her property into the defendant's possession and then, even if that property has been used to pay off a debt and ostensibly has therefore disappeared, the claimant can become the

---

[205] *Illingworth v Houldsworth* [1904] AC 355, 358, *per* Lord Macnaghten.
[206] *Clough Mill v Martin* [1984] 3 All ER 982.
[207] See *Crantrave Ltd v Lloyds Bank plc* [2000] 4 All ER 473.
[208] See *Re Byfield* [1982] 1 Ch 267, 272, *per* Goulding J. See also *McCullough v Marsden* (1919) 45 DLR 645, where beneficiaries were subrogated to the rights of a mortgagee where a trustee misappropriated trust property to pay off a mortgage.
[209] [1996] 1 WLR 328. See now also *Liberty Mutual Insurance Company (UK) Ltd v HSBC Bank plc* [2002] EWCA Civ 691.

defendant's creditor for the debt which was discharged.[210] Millett LJ described the remedy of subrogation in the following terms:

> Subrogation . . . is a remedy, not a cause of action . . . Once the equity is established the court satisfies it by declaring that the property in question is subject to a charge by way of subrogation in the one case or a constructive trust in the other.[211]

Therefore subrogation is available where appropriate, or alternatively a constructive trust, to supply the claimant's proprietary remedy.[212] Subrogation, in effect, secures a payment of money to the claimant, as opposed to establishing title in identified property in the way that a constructive trust does.[213]

Whether a charge must be imposed on specific property or can be imposed over the defendant's entire estate

Exceptionally there has been a suggestion in obiter dicta in the Privy Council to the effect that a charge might be available over all of the defendant's assets. The charge would be of a value sufficient to secure the plaintiff's claim but, instead of taking effect over specific property, it would be a charge which took effect over the entirety of the defendant's estate. This form of charge is a common feature of tracing remedies in the USA but has not been applied in England and Wales on the basis, it is suggested, that it contravenes the central requirement of property law that there be some identified property which forms the subject matter of that claim.[214] Lord Templeman held in *Space Investments Ltd v CIBC Trust Co (Bahamas) Ltd*:[215] **33.71**

> In these circumstances [where money has passed in breach of fiduciary duty into the assets of the defendant, such that the specific money cannot be traced] it is impossible for the beneficiaries interested in trust money misappropriated from their trust to trace their money to any particular asset belonging to the trustee bank. But equity allows the beneficiaries, or a new trustee appointed in place of an insolvent bank

---

[210] *Gertsch v Aspasia* (2000) 2 ITELR 342.   [211] [1995] 4 All ER 769, 776–777.

[212] *Banque Financiere de la Cité v Parc (Battersea) Ltd* [1999] AC 221 establishes subrogation as being predicated on the restitution of unjust enrichment.

[213] '[Subrogation] is available in a wide variety of different factual situations in which it is required to reverse the defendant's unjust enrichment. Equity lawyers speak of a right of subrogation, or of an equity of subrogation, but this merely reflects the fact that it is not a remedy which the court has a general discretion to impose whenever it thinks it just to do so. The equity arises from the conduct of the parties on well settled principles and in defined circumstances which make it unconscionable for the defendant to deny the proprietary interest claimed by the plaintiff. A constructive trust arises in the same way. Once the equity is established the court satisfies it by declaring that the property in question is subject to a charge by way of subrogation in the one case or a constructive trust in the other': *Boscawen v Bajwa* [1996] 1 WLR 328, 335, *per* Millett LJ ; approved by Lord Hoffmann in *Banque Financiere de la Cité v Parc (Battersea) Ltd* [1999] AC 221, 233.

[214] See for example *Illingworth v Houldsworth* [1904] AC 355 and *Re Goldcorp Exchange Ltd* [1995] 1 AC 74 and the discussion at para 3.01.

[215] [1986] 3 All ER 75, 76–77, [1986] 1 WLR 1072, 1074.

trustee . . . to trace the trust money to all the assets of the bank and to recover the trust money by the exercise of an equitable charge over all the assets of the bank . . . that equitable charge secures for the beneficiaries and the trust priority over the claims of customers . . . and . . . all other unsecured creditors.

The importance of this 'swollen assets' approach is that it is not necessary to identify specific property over which the tracing claim is to be exercised. On the facts of the *Space Investments* case itself, money was paid by one bank to another as a result of an unjust factor, which would have entitled the payer to recover that property in ordinary circumstances. However, the money passed into the general accounts of the payee, so that it could not be separated from the general assets of the payee. The traditional approach of English equity would be to say: 'if the payment cannot be identified separately from other property then there is no right to trace into that property'. By contrast, Lord Templeman's approach suggests that it is possible to say: 'my money can be demonstrated to have passed into that person's estate and therefore I should be entitled to a charge over the whole of that person's estate.' The difficulty with this approach is that it is not clear which assets would be subject to the charge and, in the event of an insolvency, this would contravene the *pari passu* principle to the effect that no single creditor is entitled to take any preferential right to property unless they had some pre-existing right in specified property.[216] Thus, it was held in *Bishopsgate v Homan*[217] by Dillon LJ that the swollen assets approach should not be interpreted in any event to give rights in an overdrawn account by asserting rights over all the assets of the bank. This approach perhaps recognizes more accurately the true nature of the sets of property rights represented by electronic bank accounts, as considered above.

Liens

33.72 A lien is a right only to detain property and not a right to sell it.[218] If the claimant wishes to sell the property to recover amounts owed to it by the defendant, then she must apply to the court for such permission.[219] Liens can arise both at common law or in equity. Common law liens are frequently annexed to a contractual right in some way. By contrast general, equitable liens can be imposed by the courts otherwise than by means of an express contractual provision.[220] Rather, an equitable lien is a right accepted by equity to detain property which then gives rise to an equitable charge,[221] such an equitable charge in turn granting its holder a proprietary right in the manner considered above.[222]

---

[216] *Re Goldcorp Exchange Ltd* [1995] 1 AC 74.   [217] [1995] 1 WLR 31.
[218] *Hammonds v Barclay* (1802) 2 East 227.   [219] *Larner v Fawcett* [1950] 2 All ER 727.
[220] *In re Welsh Irish Ferries Ltd* [1986] Ch 471.
[221] ibid; *In re Kent & Sussex Sawmills Ltd* [1947] Ch 177.   [222] See para 33.68.

G. Loss of the Right to Trace

The general rule

A tracing claim is necessarily a proprietary claim by which the claimant seeks to establish a right to property in the form of a constructive trust or a payment of compensation for the loss of property secured by means of a charge or lien, as considered above.[223] The claimant in a tracing claim will lose the right to trace if there is no property against which that claim can be brought. A following claim will fail once the original property belonging to the claimant cannot be located or is subject to some ownership rights in some other person. A common law tracing claim will fail once the original property or any clean substitute for the property being traced is mixed with other property.[224] An equitable tracing claim will fail if the original property or any of its traceable proceeds ceases to exist or is dissipated.[225] In relation to bank accounts, if money is paid out of a bank account then it can be traced into the next bank account in which it comes to rest.[226] However, once a bank account goes overdrawn then there is no possibility of tracing into that bank account because there is no vestige of the money being traced left in the account.[227] Similarly, the claimant cannot bring a claim against any bank account greater than the lowest balance held in the account after the traced moneys were paid into it.[228]

33.73

This last principle is demonstrated most clearly in *Bishopsgate Investment Management v Homan.*[229] Here, in the aftermath of newspaper mogul Robert Maxwell's death, it transpired that amounts belonging to pension trust funds under his control had been misapplied. The amounts had been paid into accounts held by MCC (a company controlled by Maxwell) and other companies. Those accounts had gone overdrawn since the initial deposit of the money. The pension fund trustees sought an order granting them an equitable charge over all the accounts held by MCC, in line with dicta of Lord Templeman in *Space Investments v CIBC Trust Co (Bahamas) Ltd.*[230] It was held that it is impossible to trace money into an overdrawn account on the basis that the property from which the traceable substitute derives is said to have disappeared. Further, on the facts of that case it was also held that there could be no equitable remedy enforced against an asset which was

33.74

---

[223] See para 33.58.   [224] *Lipkin Gorman v Karpnale* [1991] 2 AC 548.
[225] *Roscoe v Winder* [1915] 1 Ch 62; *Bishopsgate v Homan* [1995] 1 WLR 31; *Westdeutsche Landesbank v Islington* [1996] AC 669.
[226] *Agip (Africa) Ltd v Jackson* [1990] Ch 265, HC, on appeal [1991] Ch 547 CA; *El Ajou v Dollar Land Holdings* [1993] 3 All ER 717, HC, on appeal [1994] 2 All ER 685, CA.
[227] *Bishopsgate v Homan* [1995] 1 WLR 31; *Westdeutsche Landesbank v Islington* [1996] AC 669.
[228] *Westdeutsche Landesbank v Islington* [1996] AC 669. See para 33.74.
[229] [1995] Ch 211, [1995] 1 All ER 347, [1994] 3 WLR 1270.
[230] *Space Investments Ltd v Canadian Imperial Bank of Commerce Trust Co (Bahamas) Ltd* [1986] 1 WLR 1072; [1986] 3 All ER 75.

acquired before the misappropriation of the money took place. This is because it is not possible to trace into property which had been acquired without the aid of the misapplied property: that is, if a person bought a car on 1 January, and then subsequently misappropriated cash from a trust fund on 1 February, it could not be said that that trust property made it possible to acquire the car.

Lowest intermediate balance

33.75　The principle set out above does not account for the circumstance which is more generally the case when property is taken away from a fund, such as a bank account, and new property added to that fund. The question arises whether the claimant ought to be able to trace into any property held in a fund to which her own property has been added, or whether the claimant should be restricted to tracing only into property which can be demonstrated to have derived from the original misappropriated property. The rule is that the claimant has only a right to claim the lowest intermediate balance of that property.[231] The reference to lowest intermediate balance means that the claimant will be entitled to trace into only the lowest value of the property held between the date of its misapplication and the date of the claim being brought. By way of example, the case of *Roscoe v Winder*[232] concerned money being taken from a trust, paid into a bank account, and mixed with other money such that sums were paid into and out of that account on numerous occasions, causing fluctuating balances in that account over time. The main issue is then to ascertain which level in the bank account should be considered to be the one against which the claimant could claim. The court held that, assuming the trust money was the last to be paid out of the account, the claimant could only assert a claim against the lowest level in that account because (by definition) any money paid into the account after that lowest level had been reached could not be said to have been derived from the trust.

33.76　Suppose the following: £100 is taken from a trust fund and added to a bank account already containing £50 on 1 January. Then suppose that £130 is taken out of the account on 1 February, before £200 is paid into the account on 1 March. If a claim were brought on 1 April, the beneficiary would be entitled to trace into only the £20 which was left in the account on 1 February on the basis that that is the only money which could possibly be said to have derived from the original £100. That £20 is the lowest intermediate balance of the fund. The £200 paid in subsequently had not come from the trust by definition and therefore there could be no claim against it. The £20 is the lowest intermediate balance against which a claim based on tracing can be established.

231　*Roscoe v Winder* [1915] 1 Ch 62.　　232　ibid.

Tracing into property which has been dissipated

When property has been dissipated, such that there is no property left against **33.77** which a tracing claim can be brought, then the tracing claim will fail.[233] However, the remedy of subrogation, considered above,[234] may enable a claimant to assert a proprietary claim in relation to property which has been used to discharge a debt.[235] So, in a case in which solicitors misapplied money which they held on trust so as to discharge a third person's mortgage, in the mistaken belief that they were acquiring a mortgage security for the beneficiary, the beneficiary was entitled to be subrogated to the rights of the third person's mortgagee.

H. Defences to Tracing Claims

The range of defences to tracing claims

While the preceding discussion has considered the contexts in which a claimant **33.78** will be able to mount a tracing claim, there will be situations in which the recipient of the traceable proceeds of the claimant's property will be able to resist the claim. There are a number of defences apparently available: change of position,[236] passing on,[237] estoppel by representation,[238] and bona fide purchaser for value without notice.[239]

Change of position

The basis of the defence of change of position

The defence of change of position will be available to a defendant who has received **33.79** property and, on the faith of the receipt of that property, suffered some change in their personal circumstances.[240] The clearest judicial statement of the manner in which the defence of change of position might operate can be extracted from the (partially dissenting) speech of Lord Goff in *Westdeutsche Landesbank v Islington*:[241]

> Where an innocent defendant's position is so changed that he will suffer an injustice
> if called upon to repay or to repay in full, the injustice of requiring him so to repay
> outweighs the injustice of denying the plaintiff restitution.

Thus the court is required to consider whether it would be more inequitable to permit the defendant to retain the property or whether it would be more inequitable to require the defendant to return the property to the claimant on the

---

[233] *Westdeutsche Landesbank v Islington* [1996] AC 669.   [234] See para 33.69.
[235] *Boscawen v Bajwa* [1996] 1 WLR 328.   [236] See para 33.79.
[237] See para 33.90.   [238] See para 33.92.   [239] See para 33.95.
[240] *Lipkin Gorman v Karpnale* [1991] 2 AC 548.   [241] [1996] AC 669.

basis that the defendant had acted in reliance on having acquired rights in that property.[242]

33.80 The foundations of the defence were set out in the following terms by Lord Goff in his speech in the House of Lords in *Lipkin Gorman v Karpnale*:[243]

> I am most anxious that, in recognising this defence to actions of restitution, nothing should be said at this stage to inhibit the development of the defence on a case by case basis, in the usual way. It is, of course, plain that the defence is not open to one who has changed his position in bad faith, as where the defendant has paid away the money with knowledge of the facts entitling the plaintiff to restitution; and it is commonly accepted that the defence should not be open to a wrongdoer. These are matters which can, in due course, be considered in depth in cases where they arise for consideration. They do not arise in the present case. Here there is no doubt that the respondents have acted in good faith throughout, and the action is not founded upon any wrongdoing of the respondents. It is not however appropriate in the present case to attempt to identify all those actions in restitution to which change of position may be a defence. A prominent example will, no doubt, be found in those cases where the plaintiff is seeking repayment of money paid under a mistake of fact but I can see no reason why the defence should not also be available in principle in a case such as the present, where the plaintiff's money has been paid by a thief to an innocent donee, and the plaintiff then seeks repayment from the donee in an action for money had and received. At present I do not wish to state the principle any less broadly than this: that the defence is available to a person whose position has so changed that it would be inequitable in all the circumstances to require him to make restitution, or alternatively to make restitution in full. I wish to stress however that the mere fact that the defendant has spent the money, in whole or in part, does not of itself render it inequitable that he should be called upon to repay, because the expenditure might in any event have been incurred by him in the ordinary course of things. I fear that the mistaken assumption that mere expenditure of money may be regarded as amounting to a change of position for present purposes has led in the past to opposition by some to recognition of a defence which in fact is likely to be available only on comparatively rare occasions. In this connection I have particularly in mind the speech of Lord Simonds in *Ministry of Health v Simpson*.[244]

The key themes to emerge from this passage of Lord Goff's speech are as follows. There are no boundaries placed on the future development of the defence although it is not anticipated that it will develop into a defence of very general application. For example, simply that the defendant has spent money will not in and of itself demonstrate a change of position. At the very least the expenditure of money would need to be balanced, as with any other detrimental act, against the injustice of permitting the claimant to trace their property rights into the property in the defendant's hands. Bad faith will obviate reliance on the defence, which is in line with the defence in general terms being concerned with balancing the

---

[242] *Scottish Equitable v Derby* [2000] 3 All ER 793, HC, [2001] 3 All ER 818, CA.
[243] [1991] 2 AC 548, 580.   [244] [1951] AC 251, 276.

inequity of requiring the defendant to make restitution against the inequity of denying the vindication of the claimant's proprietary rights.

What constitutes bad faith in such circumstances remains a difficult question. If a **33.81** commercial person receives money which was paid by mistake, without making any inquiries of the payer, and then uses that money in a way which would otherwise constitute a change of position, it would be doubtful that such a person will be found to have acted in good faith.[245] Equally if the recipient has said or done something which has encouraged the payer to make that payment, whether innocently or deliberately, then the recipient will be unlikely to make out the defence of change of position successfully.[246] Change of position will be available to the extent that a defendant made payments unknowingly to the fictitious subsidiary company of a third party, as part of a scheme to defraud the defendant and the claimant, but a defendant will not be able to rely on that defence in relation to commissions received as part of the process of making those same payments.[247] That the defence of change of position is predicated on the balance of justice between the parties, rather than on proving the fault or deliberate action of either party,[248] suggests that even innocent actions of this sort may cause the defence of change of position to be unavailable. It has been held by Sedley LJ in *Niru Battery Manufacturing Company v Milestone Trading Ltd*[249] that the defence of change of position is not dependent upon the demonstration of an absence of bad faith in equal and opposite manner to the obligation to prove dishonesty in a claim for dishonest assistance.[250] Bad faith in this context is therefore not to be taken to be equivalent to dishonesty.[251]

By way of illustration of this principle suppose the following facts: a publisher has **33.82** received a valuable piece of desktop computer equipment which was transferred to him in breach of trust. The publisher is unaware of the breach of trust and therefore invests a large amount of money on a lease for suitable premises and on promotional work in reliance on his ownership of the desktop publishing equipment which will enable him to reduce the costs of hiring typesetters. Subsequently, the beneficiaries under the trust bring a claim to follow their trust property. Lord Goff's explanation of the defence of change of position would make this circumstance a difficult one. The issue would be whether or not the publisher's expenditure on setting up his business and his reliance on the costs savings secured by his ownership of the equipment could be said to outweigh the

---

[245] *Niru Battery Mfg Co v Milestone Trading Ltd* [2002] EWHC 1425 (Comm), para 135, *per* Moore-Bick J.

[246] See *Larner v London County Council* [1949] 2 KB 683, 688, *per* Lord Denning.

[247] *Maersk Air Ltd v Expeditors International (UK) Ltd* [2003] 1 Lloyds Rep 491.

[248] See *Dextra Bank and Trust Company Ltd v Bank of Jamaica* [2002] 1 All ER (Comm) 193, para 142.

[249] [2003] EWCA Civ 1446.   [250] ibid, para 179.   [251] ibid, para 182.

value of the equipment to the trust. Clearly, expenditure of a few thousand pounds would not justify the publisher retaining equipment worth several millions. The publisher would then be required to seek a remedy from the person who transferred the property to her initially. However, if the equipment was only worth an amount equivalent to the publisher's expenditure on it, then it might be unjust to deny the publisher his continued possession of the equipment given his change of position (spending those sums) in reliance on his receipt of the equipment.[252]

33.83 The defence of change of position would appear to include, however, all sums expended by the defendant in reliance on any representation or payment made by the claimant, including the cost of financing a proposed transaction between the parties.[253] Furthermore, where the defendant forgoes an opportunity to take a benefit from another source in reliance on the payment received from the claimant, then the defendant is entitled to include such a reliance within her defence of change of position.[254] It has been suggested that even receipt of a payment of money in reliance on an agreement not to contest a divorce petition might constitute a change of position.[255] What the defendant cannot do is seek to rely on the benefit of a contract which turned out to have been void[256] nor to have acted in good faith reliance on a payment in circumstances in which she has acquiesced in the action which rendered such payment void.[257] In any event, the defendant is required to have acted in good faith in seeking to assert a defence of change of position.[258] However, if the defendant has had the benefit of money paid to her, for example in that she has earned interest on that money or has saved herself banking charges by not going overdrawn to the extent of that payment, then the defendant will be required to account for any such benefit in reducing the worth to her of the change of position defence.[259] Where for example the defendant

---

[252] It has been suggested by R Goff and G Jones, *The Law of Restitution* (6th edn, Sweet & Maxwell, 2002)('*Goff and Jones*') 829, that estoppel is a comparatively 'clumsy, indeed inappropriate' defence when compared to the symmetrical balancing act which Lord Goff's conception of the defence of change of position permits. It is suggested that the defence of estoppel in these circumstances ought to permit the court to identify an appropriate defence which takes into account the defendant's reliance on the receipt of the property in good faith; however, this description of the current state of the defences is well made.

[253] *Sanwa Australia Finance Ltd v Finchill Pty Ltd* [2001] NSWCA 466.

[254] *Palmer v Blue Circle Southern Cement Ltd* [2001] RLR 137.

[255] *X v X (Y and Z intervening)* [2002] 1 FLR 508, as considered in *Commerzbank v Price* [2003] EWCA Civ 1633, para 68, *per* Munby J.

[256] *South Tyneside Metropolitan Borough Council v Svenska International plc* [1995] 1 All ER 545.

[257] *Standard Bank London Ltd v The Bank of Tokyo Ltd* [1995] 2 Lloyd's Rep 169, *infra*.

[258] *Lipkin Gorman v Karpnale* [1991] 2 AC 548; *South Tyneside Metropolitan Borough Council v Svenska International plc* [1995] 1 All ER 545; *Euroactividade AG v Moeller* (unreported, 1 February 2001). See also *Lloyds Bank v Independent Insurance* [1999] 2 WLR 986; *Friend's Provident v Hillier Parker* [1995] 4 All ER 260.

[259] *Pearce v Lloyds Bank plc* (unreported, 23 November 2001).

received £10,000 from the claimant and thus earned interest on that £10,000, the claimant will be entitled to reduce the amount which the defendant claims is represented by her change of position to account for that interest earned.

Change of position in relation to mistaken and to windfall payments

In recent years there have been a slew of cases on change of position. So, in *Scottish* **33.84** *Equitable v Derby*,[260] where a pensioner received a payment of about £172,400 from a pension fund of which he was a member by mistake, the issue arose whether the pension fund could recover the money. The pensioner had not taken any steps nor refrained from any action on receipt of the windfall from the pension fund, except for an expenditure of about £9,600 on his family's home. The pensioner contended, however, that to repay the money to the pension fund at a time when he was separating from his wife would cause him great financial hardship. In effect he was arguing that it would have been unfair for him to have repaid the money because he had come to consider that money as being 'his' since his receipt of it. The change of position which he hastily alleged was the disappointment this would cause him and his wife who were dividing their property on divorce on the basis that he owned this large windfall. However, it was held in the High Court that because his hardship was not causally linked to the mistaken payment to him (the hardship having resulted from his separation whereas the payment was caused by an unrelated administrative error), the pensioner was not entitled to rely on the defence of change of position, except in relation to the £9,600 which he had spent in reliance on his receipt of the money.[261] The Court of Appeal held that the sums claimed by the claimant were so large that they bore no relation to the detriment which the defendant pensioner was claiming he had suffered by way of a change of position.[262] Therefore, the pensioner was not entitled to retain the full £172,400 but he could retain the £9,600 which he had spent in good faith. The Court of Appeal also considered the question of estoppel by representation, which is discussed below.

Similar issues arose in *Philip Collins Ltd v Davis*[263] where overpayments were **33.85** made to one of Phil Collins's backing singers by mistake. The singer sought to retain that money simply on the basis that she thought she was due it, even though her contract provided expressly to the contrary. The employer proposed to recover the money by withholding it from future royalties which would otherwise have been paid to the singer. The singer contended that she had changed her day-to-day lifestyle in reliance on the receipt of the money. It was held that the singer bore the burden of proving that the defence applied to her. On these facts she was entitled to resist recovery of half of the overpayments in that she had changed her lifestyle

---

[260] [2000] 3 All ER 793.   [261] [2000] 3 All ER 793.   [262] [2001] 3 All ER 818.
[263] [2000] 3 All ER 808.

in reliance on having received them. It might be suggested that this is a thin premise on which to deny the claimant recovery of money which had been paid mistakenly, to which the defendant had no entitlement, and to which one might have expected the defendant to realize she had no entitlement.[264]

33.86 It is not sufficient for the defendant to argue that his expectations in receiving the windfall would be disappointed by return of the money to the payer (in that he would have less money than he had otherwise thought): rather there must be some change in position (by the taking of steps which would not otherwise have been taken, or refraining from some action which would otherwise have been taken) linked to the receipt of that money in circumstances in which it could not be alleged by the defendant that she had any good reason to assume that the money was rightfully hers.[265] Therefore, where a payment is made mistakenly without any representation that the defendant was entitled to that money to which she would not otherwise be entitled, and where the sum of money was so large that the defendant ought reasonably to have realized that there had been a mistake, then there should be no defence of change of position.[266] What is required is that the transfer of the property which is being traced should be referable in some way to the change of position.[267]

Change of position as an equitable defence concerned to effect justice

33.87 The general principle on which the courts are currently recognizing the operation of the defence of change of position has been variously expressed that 'the essential question is whether on the facts of a particular case it would in all the circumstances be inequitable or unconscionable, and thus unjust, to allow the recipient of money paid under a mistake of fact to deny restitution to the payer'[268] and in terms that '... courts ... are not tied to a single rigid standard in deciding whether

---

[264] Indeed this final element—as to the conscionability or reasonableness (where those two terms are taken to be broadly similar in this sense) of the defendant failing to notice that she has received an overpayment—might be considered an important element of this defence in the future. Such an approach would recognize the importance of proof of a link between the conscionability of the change of position, or the hardship that the claimant would suffer, and the receipt of the money. See, for example, *Lloyds Bank v Independent Insurance* [1999] 2 WLR 986; *Home Office v Ayres* [1992] ICR 175.

[265] What is not addressed, ibid, is what would have happened if the pensioner had separated from his wife *because* he had received this money and could therefore support himself with the money received.

[266] *State Bank of New South Wales v Swiss Bank Corporation* (1995) 39 NSWLR 350: a case in which a bank received a very large electronic payment transfer from another bank without any clear instruction as to which account or customer that amount was to have been credited—it was held that, while not dishonest, the recipient bank could not credibly claim that it was entitled to rely on the receipt of so large an amount without any identified payee, so as to have changed its position. See also *Philip Collins Ltd v Davis* [2000] 3 All ER 808.

[267] *Philip Collins Ltd v Davis* [2000] 3 All ER 808, 827f, *per* Jonathan Parker J.

[268] *Niru Battery Manufacturing Co and anor v Milestone Trading Ltd and ors* [2003] EWCA Civ 1446, para 162, *per* Clarke LJ.

a defence of change of position succeeds. They are to decide whether it is equitable to uphold the defence. Since the doctrine of restitution is centrally concerned with the distribution of loss among parties whose rights are not met by some stronger doctrine of law, one is by definition looking for the least unjust solution to a residual problem.'[269] The keynote of the defence of change of position has become its transformation into a general, equitable form of defence which is 'founded on a principle of justice designed to protect the defendant from a claim to restitution in respect of a benefit received by him in circumstances in which it would be inequitable to pursue that claim, or to pursue it in full'.[270]

Whether future liabilities will amount to a change of position

Thus far our focus has been on a defendant who has changed his position after **33.88** receipt of the traced property but before the action comes to court. What has not been considered thus far in this discussion is the position in relation to a defendant who has generated liabilities which will change his position only in the future. The authorities are in conflict. In *Lipkin Gorman v Karpnale*[271] it was accepted without much discussion that such future liabilities would found the defence of change of position, although in *South Tyneside Metropolitan BC v Svenska International plc*[272] it was held by Clarke J that the change of position must have taken place after receipt of the property. In this latter case the bank had entered into hedging transactions in anticipation of amounts which it would receive from the local authority under an interest rate swap contract which was subsequently held to have been void *ab initio*. It was held that the bank could not claim that its hedging policy—involving the creation of financial instruments with third parties the effect of which was expected to cancel out the effect of any loss suffered under the swap contract with the local authority—could found a defence of change of position because those hedging contracts were created before its obligation to effect restitution of payments arose. This decision was considered to have been reached on 'exceptional' circumstances by the Privy Council in *Dextra Bank and Trust Co v Bank of Jamaica*.[273]

In *Dextra Bank and Trust Co v Bank of Jamaica*[274] the Privy Council was prepared to hold that incurring a future liability would constitute a change of position. Dextra had been approached by W who induced it to lend US$ 3 million to the Bank of Jamaica secured by a note issued by the Bank of Jamaica, although W had no authority to execute this transaction. W in turn convinced the Bank of Jamaica

---

[269] *Niru Battery Manufacturing Co and anor v Milestone Trading Ltd and ors* [2003] EWCA Civ 1446, para 192, *per* Sedley LJ.
[270] *Dextra Bank and Trust Co v Bank of Jamaica* [2002] 1 All ER (Comm) 193, para 38, *per* Lord Bingham and Lord Goff giving the advice of the Privy Council.
[271] [1991] 2 AC 548.   [272] [1995] 1 All ER 545.
[273] [2002] 1 All ER (Comm) 193.   [274] [2002] 1 All ER (Comm) 193.

that the money was to be used in a foreign exchange transaction to acquire its equivalent in Jamaican dollars. This was a fraudulent conspiracy. The Bank of Jamaica paid out the equivalent of US$ 3 million in Jamaican dollars to the conspirators, all the while believing that it was making payment to Dextra. The argument was raised, *inter alia*, that the Bank of Jamaica could have relied on the defence of change of position to Dextra's action in restitution. During the transaction, the Bank of Jamaica had paid Jamaican dollars before Dextra's cheque had cleared into the Bank of Jamaica's accounts and therefore the change of position was in relation to a future payment at that stage. The Privy Council was of the opinion that there was no objection to such a claim. Their lordships preferred to permit the defence to be broadly understood, on the following terms:[275]

> It is surely no abuse of language to say, in the second case as in the first, that the defendant has incurred expenditure in reliance on the plaintiff's payment or, as it is sometimes said, on the faith of the payment. It is true that, in the second case, the defendant relied on the payment being made to him in the future (as well as relying on such payment, when made, being a valid payment); but, provided that his change of position was in good faith, it should provide, pro tanto at least, a good defence because it would be inequitable to require the defendant to make restitution, or to make restitution in full. In particular it does not, in their Lordships' opinion, assist to rationalise the defence of change of position as concerned to protect the security of receipt and then to derive from that rationalisation a limitation on the defence. The defence should be regarded as founded on a principle of justice designed to protect the defendant from a claim to restitution in respect of a benefit received by him in circumstances in which it would be inequitable to pursue that claim, or to pursue it in full.

33.89　That a change of position can take place before the property is received has been accepted in *Commerzbank AG v Price*[276] in which case a merchant banker took the decision not to seek alternative employment on the basis that he would receive a severance payment from the bank which employed him at the time: it was no objection to his reliance on the defence of change of position that his alleged change of position took place before his receipt of the property. A future liability has been held not to amount to a factor sufficient to found the defence of change of position in *Pearce v Lloyds Bank*.[277] In that case the defendant's bank had set off amounts in the defendant's bank account against forged payment instructions which it had received from third parties out of that same account. The defendant contended that the bank ought not to have been entitled to set off those amounts because the defendant would have been liable to pay value added tax on the payments which had passed in and out of that account. At the time, however, these future liabilities to value added tax had not been discharged. It was held that such future liabilities could not found a defence of change of position.

---

[275] [2002] 1 All ER (Comm) 193, para 38, *per* Lord Bingham and Lord Goff.
[276] [2003] EWCA Civ 1633.　　[277] [2001] EWCA Civ 1097.

It is suggested that the approach taken in *Dextra Bank and Trust Company v Bank of Jamaica* is to be preferred. Once a liability becomes legally enforceable, whether or not it has been discharged, then the defendant can be considered to have changed his position in the sense that his balance sheet will show that he owes a liability and not that the assets necessary to discharge that liability constitute free funds.

Passing on

The defence of passing on bears some similarity to the defence of change of position. Passing on requires that the defendant has passed the property on or that some expense has been incurred such that the value of the property has effectively been passed on to some third person. The defendant will therefore claim that she does not have possession of the property, nor of its traceable proceeds because that property has been transferred to another person without receipt of any traceable proceeds. Given that tracing is a proprietary claim, it is necessary for there to be some traceable proceeds in the hands of the defendant. Otherwise to impose a liability on the defendant to account to the claimant with some property which was not the traceable proceeds of the claimant's original property would be to impose a personal claim on the defendant rather than a proprietary claim. **33.90**

The defence of passing on was raised before the Court of Appeal in *Kleinwort Benson v Birmingham CC*.[278] That case concerned an interest rate swap in which the bank claimed that the defence of passing on should have been available to it on the basis that the contract with the local authority (which was subsequently held to have been void *ab initio*) had caused the bank to incur extra expense to manage the risk of the transaction. The Court of Appeal held, however, that there was no necessary link between the contract with the local authority and the bank's decision to incur that expense by means of a hedging strategy over which the local authority had no control. Therefore, the passing on defence is available, where the property has been passed on, but not where there is no link between the expenditure and the liability incurred. **33.91**

Estoppel by representation

Estoppel by representation is a defence which is similar, at least at first blush, to that of change of position. The significant difference between the two defences is that the estoppel is predicated on some representation being made by the claimant, as opposed to a balancing of the competing equities of the case as suggested by the defence of change of position.[279] Where the defendant to a tracing **33.92**

---

[278] [1996] 4 All ER 733; AS Hudson, 'Proprietary rights in financial transactions' (1997) *Amicus Curiae*, 2 November, 27.
[279] *Goff and Jones* 829.

action can demonstrate that some representation has been made to her, that that representation was deliberately or accidentally false, and that the claimant knew the representation would be acted upon, then the estoppel defence will be available if the defendant then acts to her detriment in reliance upon the representation. There is no defence to the estoppel. This estoppel has been recognized both at common law and in equity.[280]

33.93   A good example of this defence in action arose in *National Westminster Bank plc v Somer International*.[281] Somer held a US dollar account with the bank into which it paid moneys received from foreign clients. Somer was expecting to receive a sum of between US$70,000 and US$78,000 from one of its clients and informed the bank of this. Subsequently the bank received a payment of US$76,708 which was intended for another of its account holders but which it mistakenly credited to Somer's US dollar account. The bank informed Somer that the money had been paid into its dollar account and Somer assumed that it was the payment which it was expecting to receive from its own client. In reliance on the receipt of the money, Somer shipped £13,180 worth of goods to the client from which it was expecting the payment. Subsequently, the bank sought to recover the mistaken payment. Somer argued that it was entitled to an estoppel by representation because the bank had represented to it that the money belonged to Somer, that Somer had acted to its detriment in reliance on that representation, and that it was therefore entitled to retain the whole of the moneys paid to it by the bank.

33.94   Previously, the doctrine of estoppel by representation had operated as a rule of evidence to the effect that a defendant would have been entitled to retain the whole of a mistaken payment.[282] The Court of Appeal held that the doctrine of estoppel by representation operated on equitable principles such that it was possible to operate outwith any strict rule requiring that the defendant be entitled to retain the whole of the payment. Rather, where the court considered the retention of the whole of the payment to be unconscionable, it would be possible to limit the defendant's entitlement to rely on the estoppel only to the extent that it had suffered detriment. Therefore, on these facts, Somer could retain only an amount equal to the value of the goods which it had shipped in reliance on the representation.[283] This mooted development is, however, at odds with earlier authority and the flexibility of the older, purely evidential form of the estoppel by representation and consequently this development awaits confirmation by a higher court.[284]

---

[280] *Jordan v Money* (1854) V HLC 185, 10 ER 868.   [281] [2002] QB 1286, CA.

[282] *Avon County Council v Howlett* [1983] 1 WLR 605.

[283] *Scottish Equitable v Derby* [2001] 3 All ER 818 applied.

[284] See *Avon County Council v Howlett* [1983] 1 WLR 605, 622, *per* Slade LJ.

Bona fide purchaser for value without notice of the claimant's rights

The availability of the defence of equity's darling involves the perennial problem **33.95**
of deciding between the person who has lost their property to a wrongdoing
fiduciary, and the person who buys that property in all innocence. Suppose the
example of the painting held on trust for beneficiaries which is transferred away in
breach of trust by T. Suppose then that the painting is purchased by E in good
faith for its full market price. E will necessarily take the view that she has paid an
open market price for property in circumstances in which she could not have
known that the property ought properly to have been held on trust. By the same
token, the beneficiaries would argue that it is they who ought to be entitled to
recover their property from E. From a strict, analytical viewpoint, the property
lawyer ought to find for the beneficiaries. At no time do the beneficiaries relinquish their property rights in the painting before E purchases it. Therefore, those
rights ought to be considered as subsisting. E cannot acquire good title on the
basis that the beneficial title still properly remains in the beneficiaries. The
approach of equity, though, is to protect free markets by ensuring that the bona
fide purchaser for value without notice of the rights of a beneficial owner is entitled to assert good title in property in such situations. Such a person is rightly
referred to as 'equity's darling'. Consequently, a good defence to a tracing claim
would appear to be an assertion that you are a purchaser acting in good faith
without notice of the rights of the beneficiary.[285]

Consensual transfer

The matter is usually little discussed in relation to defences to a tracing claim but **33.96**
if the original owner of the property had either made a perfect gift of the property
to the defendant or had entered into a contract to transfer the property to the
defendant, then the defendant ought to be recognized as having a complete
defence to any tracing claim. The second proposition is clearly an extension of the
bona fide purchaser principle, potentially, into cases in which the contract transferring the property might not constitute a contract of sale. The former proposition seems to be common sense. In the event that there has been a transfer of
absolute title from the claimant to the defendant without any duress or undue
influence, then the common law would recognize the defendant's ownership of
that property. It would only be cases of vitiated consent, such as undue influence,
which would prevent a claim being founded on tracing. Thus it is possible to sever
a claimant's ties with her original property or its traceable proceeds where she can
be taken to have agreed to transfer title in it. The only complication here is
where there was an intention to transfer that property away which the claimant

---

[285] *Westdeutsche Landesbank v Islington LBC* [1996] AC 669, *per* Lord Browne-Wilkinson.

subsequently sought to disavow, as in *National Westminster Bank v Somer*[286] in which the claimant appears to have an intention to transfer property at the outset but subsequently realized a mistake and so sought to reverse that transfer. This issue has been considered in the preceding section.

I. Tracing Money Held in Bank Accounts

Particular problems connected with tracing through electronic bank accounts

33.97 One of the most vexed problems in tracing claims is that of establishing proprietary rights in amounts of money which are held in electronic bank accounts. Electronic bank accounts are choses in action between the depositor and the bank. The bank owes, by way of debt, the amount of money in the account to the depositor (provided that the account is in credit) under the terms of their contract. Therefore, these accounts are not tangible property. Rather, they are debts with value attached to them (that value being the amount of the deposit plus interest). Nevertheless the manner in which property law considers money in bank accounts is as though it were tangible property. For example, the analysis of the tracing of electronic payments in *Westdeutsche Landesbank v Islington*[287] was conducted on the basis that this electronic money was nevertheless tangible property akin to a bag of coins where the coins themselves were intrinsically valuable and not simply representations of value. When considering the way in which tracing applies to money held in bank accounts, conceiving of that money as being tangible rather than being simply an amount of value, creates problems particularly in relation to the loss of the right to trace.[288] When money is paid out of a bank account and into another account, there is no ability to trace that amount into the first bank account even if there is further money paid into it subsequently.[289] In *Westdeutsche Landesbank v Islington LBC*[290] the specific property provided by the payer was not capable of identification, given that it had been paid into bank accounts which had subsequently been run into overdraft on a number of occasions.[291]

Tracing money at common law

33.98 Money can be traced at common law provided that it is not mixed with other money. Therefore, in *FC Jones & Sons (A firm) v Jones*[292] the claimant was able to

---

[286] [2002] QB 1286, CA.   [287] [1996] AC 669.
[288] See now *Lloyds Bank plc v Independent Insurance Co Ltd* [1999] 2 WLR 986, CA.
[289] *Roscoe v Winder* [1915] 1 Ch 62; *Westdeutsche Landesbank v Islington* [1996] AC 669.
[290] [1996] AC 669, [1996] 2 All ER 961.
[291] In general *Hudson* 921; AS Hudson, 'Money as property in financial transactions' (1999) vol 14:06 Journal of International Banking Law 170.   [292] [1996] 3 WLR 703.

trace money into a bank account in which it was combined only with profits derived from that money. The scope of the tracing claim in that case entitled the claimant not only to the original money paid into the account but also through the futures contracts which were acquired with that money and into the money replaced in the account when the futures contracts were sold. The key element was that the money was not mixed with other money at any stage and therefore the money ultimately claimed could be demonstrated to have derived entirely from the original money.

Tracing money in equity

Tracing into current accounts

In relation to current accounts the long-standing principle set out in *Clayton's* **33.99** *Case*[293] is that tracing can proceed in equity into a mixture but that property acquired with money from that current account is deemed to be paid out sequentially so that the first money paid into the account is deemed to have been applied first when purchasing property with the money held in the account. As considered above,[294] the preferred approach is one which treats contributions to the bank account as entitling the various contributors to a rolling charge such that each takes a proportionate right in any property acquired with the money held in the account. This principle is akin to a purchase price resulting trust.[295] On principle it would seem correct that interest earned on an interest-bearing account should be considered to be the fruits of any contributor to that account rateably.[296]

Property rights in money

The difficulty caused by these various analyses of money, as Millett J held in *Agip* **33.100** *(Africa) Ltd v Jackson,*[297] is that it is impossible to maintain an action for tracing at common law where money was moved between accounts by means of 'telegraphic transfer' (that is, electronically without the transfer of notes or coins) and mixed with other money. His lordship held that the property which was being dealt with in *Agip (Africa) Ltd v Jackson* was really a transmission of electrons between computers which evidenced debts of money in the form of bank accounts. Similarly, the issues before the House of Lords in *Westdeutsche Landesbank v Islington*[298] were concerned with the payment, and sought-after repayment, of amounts of money represented by electronic bank accounts and telegraphic transfers. Indeed Lord Goff makes the following point early in his judgment:

> . . . the basic question is whether the law can restore the parties to the position they were in before they entered into the transaction. I feel bound to say that, in the

---

[293] (1816) 1 Mer 572.   [294] See paras 33.45 *et seq.*
[295] See para 26.72; *Dyer v Dyer* (1788) 2 Cox Eq Cas 92.
[296] *Banton v CIBC Trust Corporation* (1999) 182 DLR (4th) 486.
[297] [1990] Ch 265, 286, *per* Millett J; CA [1991] Ch 547.   [298] [1996] AC 669.

present case, *there ought to be no difficulty about that at all. This is because the case is concerned solely with money. All that has to be done is to order that each party should pay back the money that it has received*—or more sensibly strike a balance, and order that the party who has received most should repay the balance; and then to make an appropriate order for interest in respect of that balance. It should be as simple as that. And yet we find ourselves faced with a mass of difficult problems, and struggling to reconcile a number of difficult cases.[299]

The practical problem appears to be straightforward ('pay back the money') and yet a number of complex issues of legal analysis arise concerning the proprietary and personal nature of the remedies, and the applicable codes of rules under which they should be awarded. Nothing but a stream of electrons passes between the banks' computers as a result of telegraphic transfers. The very nature of interbank clearing systems creates problems of identifying property.[300] The broader issues of property law involved in money laundering and tracing property in money are generated by the very intangibility of the property involved.[301]

Claims to compound interest predicated on proprietary rights in electronic money

33.101   The general issue arises: what constitutes a proprietary claim with respect to electronic bank accounts? Having the use of the property would connote an ability to earn compound interest on it.[302] It is submitted that to arrive at any other measure of the proprietary rights attached to money would be too speculative because it is impossible to know how the money would have been invested if it had not been applied to the transaction between the bank and the local authority. In the context of financial contracts, compound interest is the appropriate measure of proprietary title. Therefore, there are difficulties with the approaches of Lord Goff and Lord Woolf to the question whether or not the House of Lords in *Westdeutsche Landesbank v Islington*[303] should award compound interest on the basis that their lordships' approach expressly disavowed the need to find pre-existing proprietary rights. This approach appears, in the light of traditional property law, to be counter-intuitive because the award of compound interest would have been tantamount to a proprietary remedy, being (as it was) a recognition that compound interest was the return which the bank would have received on the money transferred to the local authority *if the bank had retained ownership of it*. The award of compound interest would therefore have been a measurement of the return generated by continued ownership.

---

[299] Emphasis added.
[300] A Oakley *Constructive Trusts* (3rd edn, Sweet & Maxwell, 1997) ('*Oakley*') 377.
[301] P Birks, *Introduction to the Law of Restitution* (Clarendon Press, 1989) 258; P Millett, 'Tracing the proceeds of fraud' (1991) 107 LQR 71; C Harpum (1991) 50 CLJ 409; Goulding [1992] Conv 367; W Swadling [1994] All ER Rev 259.
[302] *Westdeutsche Landesbank v Islington* [1996] AC 669.   [303] [1996] AC 669.

In the House of Lords in *Westdeutsche Landesbank v Islington* Lord Browne-Wilkinson was not able to begin his analysis at the place where Millett J in *Agip* placed the modern performance of financial contracts by electronic transfer. Rather, there was a perceived need to retreat into the history of money as a chattel—where the intrinsic worth of coins were equal to their face value. This required Lord Browne-Wilkinson to begin his disavowal of the possibility of equitable tracing in that case with an analysis of rights in the money paid to the local authority as being equivalent to title in a stolen bag of coins, such that the claimant to those coins would be seeking to identify the very coins which had been stolen from her and not any other coins of equivalent value, before progressing to consider the applicability of equitable tracing rules to the interest rate swap payments made in that case.

33.102

Tracing payments made by mistake

A common situation in relation to electronic payments is that in which a payment is made mistakenly. At common law, the payer would be entitled to recover the payment on the basis of money had and received.[304] However, a common law remedy would only be useful if the defendant were able to pay it. In the event that the defendant were insolvent or if the claimant wished to recover compound interest on the amount owed to him, then the claimant would need to demonstrate that he had a proprietary right in the mistaken payment to take a secured interest in the insolvency or to recover compound interest.[305]

33.103

In *Chase Manhattan Bank NA v Israel-British Bank (London) Ltd*[306] a payment between banks was made twice by mistake. The recipient bank went into insolvency before repaying the second, mistaken payment. The issue arose whether the payer had a proprietary right in the payment so that it could be traced by the payer and deemed to be held on trust for it. It was held by Goulding J that the property should be held on trust for the payer and that the payer could therefore trace into the assets of the recipient bank as a result of the equitable interest founded under the trust. The precise basis for the extended fiduciary duty imposed by Goulding J is difficult to identify being an uncomfortable combination of restitution of unjust enrichment and constructive trust.[307] The rationale of that judgment was overruled and explained in different terms by Lord Browne-Wilkinson in *Westdeutsche Landesbank v Islington*[308] where his lordship declared that he was

33.104

---

[304] *Westdeutsche Landesbank v Islington* [1996] AC 669.

[305] That is, suppose the absence of a contract or any other juristic reason entitling the defendant to retain that money.

[306] [1981] Ch 105, [1980] 2 WLR 202, [1979] 3 All ER 1025.

[307] Old editions of Prof Martin's *Modern Equity* have suggested that Goulding J stopped short of adopting the principle of unjust enrichment as the basis for this trust: *Modern Equity* (13th edn, 1989) 628.   [308] [1996] AC 669.

prepared to accept that this decision was correct on the basis that a constructive trust arose at the time when the property had been received *and* the recipient knew of the mistake. It was held that the combination of knowledge of the mistake and the effect on the recipient's conscience would be sufficient to justify the creation of a constructive trust. By the same token, ignorance of the mistake would not have given rise to an equitable proprietary right.

33.105   In *Lloyds Bank plc v Independent Insurance Co Ltd*[309] a bank made a mistake in relation to a payment into an account held by one of its clients. However, the bank's mistake was not as to a countermand but rather as to how much money was paid through its customer's account. It was held, applying the decision in *Barclays Bank v Simms*,[310] that the bank could not recover against the payee because the payment discharged a debt owed by the bank's customer to the payee.

Tracing into property passed under a void contract

33.106   The decision in *Westdeutsche Landesbank v Islington* both avoided the interest rate swap contract purportedly entered into between the parties while at the same time implicitly accepting that the transfer of property under that void contract is nevertheless valid. So it is that the bank is deemed to have transferred title in the money paid to the local authority even though the contract which purported to transfer that title was itself held to have been void *ab initio*. The alternative view of this situation might be that a mistake as to the validity of the contract[311] (or other vitiating factor[312]) would lead to the contract being rescinded at the claimant's election and thus giving rise to a right to trace after that money.[313] The House of Lords in *Westdeutsche Landesbank v Islington* held that there is no such right to trace where the intention of the parties was to transfer outright the title in the property[314] and where the money or its traceable proceeds had been dissipated.[315]

Commercial attitudes to tracing property

33.107   The law of tracing has developed in recent years in accordance with commercial understandings of 'conscience' rather than straightforwardly in line with the

---

[309] [1999] 2 WLR 986, CA.   [310] [1980] QB 677.

[311] Now a valid ground for avoidance of a contract: *Kleinwort Benson v Lincoln City Council* [1998] 4 All ER 513.

[312] Such as misrepresentation or undue influence: J Martin, *Hanbury and Martin's Modern Equity* (16th edn, Sweet & Maxwell, 2001) ('*Martin*') 666.

[313] *Daly v Sydney Stock Exchange* (1986) 160 CLR 371; *Lonrho plc v Fayed (No 2)* [1992] 1 WLR 1; *El Ajou v Dollar Land Holdings* [1993] 3 All ER 717; *Halifax Building Society v Thomas* [1996] Ch 217.

[314] Although, necessarily, that intention would not have been present but for the mistake which the parties had made as to the validity of the contract.

[315] See also *Re Goldcorp Exchange Ltd* [1995] 1 AC 74.

nineteenth-century cases. An example of this phenomenon is the decision in *Re Ontario Securities*[316] and that in *Barlow Clowes v Vaughan*[317] in which the courts considered the possibility of using actuarial calculations in establishing a rolling charge over a complex investment fund as opposed to the more straightforwardly equitable approaches adopted in *Re Hallett's Estate*[318] and *Re Oatway*.[319] Much of the reason for change in the law of tracing has been occasioned in these recent cases by the fact that the property involved money held in electronic bank accounts as opposed to tangible property.

Professor Goode has described money as fungible in that any unit of account is capable of being exchanged for any other unit of account.[320] Such a conception means that resolving personal claims for money are merely a matter of calculating damage, whereas the justification for proprietary claims like tracing—and the possibilities for acquiring the status of secured creditor in an insolvency or of acquiring rights to compound interest on one's judgment—are more complex. The focus of a property law claim is on the identification of property in which the claimant has (or may claim to have) some property right; whereas a claim for damages is concerned to compensate the claimant for some loss which she has suffered. A claim to ownership is a claim to have a pre-existing right of ownership recognized by the court as part of a broader social recognition that private property rights are to be protected by the law: this is not necessarily predicated on the defendant's fault but rather it is predicated on the claimant's pre-existing right to property. Rights to compensation flow from a different form of injustice based on the defendant bearing some responsibility to compensate the claimant where the defendant was at fault for the harm suffered by the claimant. **33.108**

Professor Goode's understanding of money as being fungible is really built on a commercial lawyer's understanding of tracing as being simply one of many ways in which a commercial actor might try to recover money from a counterparty to a contract or from some other person who has caused the claimant loss. The issue which arises in relation to commercial tracing more than any other is the possibility of establishing proprietary rights in relation to money held in electronic bank accounts. So, in relation to this electronic money the issue remains whether or not it must be segregated from other property before any proprietary claim in tracing can be established.[321] This has caused complications with deciding whether or not the original property or its traceable proceeds continue to exist if the money is passed through enough companies and bank accounts, as in *El Ajou v Dollar Land Holdings*[322] or *Agip (Africa) Ltd v Jackson*.[323] Thus, where a bank account goes **33.109**

---

[316] (1985) 30 DLR (4th) 30.   [317] [1992] 4 All ER 22.   [318] (1880) 13 Ch D 695.
[319] [1903] 2 Ch 356.   [320] R Goode, *Commercial Law* (2nd edn, Penguin, 1997) 491.
[321] *Re Goldcorp* [1995] 1 AC 74; *Boscawen v Bajwa* [1996] 1 WLR 328.
[322] [1994] 2 All ER 685.   [323] [1991] Ch 547.

overdrawn, the money that was held in that bank account is said to disappear from that particular bank account at the moment that the account goes into over-draft.[324] This demonstrates that property law has overlooked Goode's assertion that the nature of money is such that it ought not to matter which part of the fund is allocated subject to the proprietary base required to found an equitable tracing claim. Rather property law continues to cling to the notion that all property is capable of being identified separately from all other property even if it is intangible in form.[325]

33.110   This issue of the severability of intangible property repays a little attention. The Court of Appeal has accepted that where a fund of identical units is impressed with a trust equal to 5 per cent of their total value, there is no requirement to seg-regate out a fund equal to that 5 per cent.[326] This decision, is however, in opposi-tion to the speech of Lord Browne-Wilkinson in *Westdeutsche Landesbank v Islington*[327] and the speech of Lord Mustill in *Re Goldcorp*.[328] As such there is a fundamental difficulty with deciding whether or not money is a form of property which, at English law, is required to be segregated in order for there to be a bind-ing trust over it. Without the possibility of a binding trust, the efficacy of standard market means of taking security is negated.

---

[324] *Boscawen v Bajwa* [1996] 1 WLR 328; *Roscoe v Winder* [1915] 1 Ch 62.
[325] AS Hudson, 'The Unbearable Lightness of Property' in AS Hudson (ed), *New Perspectives on Property Law, Obligations and Restitution* (Cavendish, 2004) 11.
[326] *Hunter v Moss* [1994] 1 WLR 452.   [327] [1996] AC 669.   [328] [1995] AC 74.

SECTION TWO

SPECIFIC TRUSTS

PRIVATE CLIENT TRUSTS

34

PRIVATE CLIENT TRUSTS: INHERITANCE TAX AND INTEREST IN POSSESSION TRUSTS

A. Introduction

Among the principal motives for making a settlement are the protection of the beneficiaries and the preservation of the settled property through the generations. This was particularly true of the now obsolescent strict settlement[1] which was formerly the principal device for preserving family estates for future generations. Since the advent of estate duty, however, tax considerations have increasingly come to influence the form of settlements. The rise and development of the discretionary settlement since World War II owed much to the fact that, unlike the life interest settlement, it enabled property to be transmitted from generation to generation effectively without charge to the very high rates of duty then prevailing. The introduction of capital transfer tax (now inheritance tax) has likewise had a profound effect on the form of settlements currently in use; indeed one form of settlement, the so-called accumulation and maintenance settlement,[2] is very much a creature of the legislation. An account is given below and in the following three chapters of the four types of private trust which are now most often encountered, being the interest in possession trust, the discretionary trust, the accumulation and

34.01

---

[1] ie a settlement created under the Settled Land Act 1925 and earlier legislation. Strict settlements cannot in general be created after 1 January 1997: Trusts of Land and Appointment of Trustees Act 1996, s 2.　　[2] See Chapter 35 below.

maintenance trust, and the disabled trust.[3] Thus there follows a résumé of certain inheritance tax factors as they affect testamentary trusts and rearrangements of the dispositions of the estates of deceased persons. Since inheritance tax is such an important underlying influence, a brief account of its principal features is given first.

B. Inheritance Tax

34.02   Capital transfer tax, from which inheritance tax derives and with which it has many features in common, was introduced by the Finance Act 1975. The tax was in principle charged on all transfers of property, whether *inter vivos* or on death, though with exemptions, for example for gifts to spouses and to charity, and reliefs, for example for transfers of business or agricultural property. The legislation was consolidated in the Capital Transfer Tax Act 1984. The Finance Act 1986 introduced major reforms, changed the name of the tax to inheritance tax, and also gave the 1984 Act the alternative title of the Inheritance Tax Act 1984 ('IHTA 1984') by which it is now invariably known. Inheritance tax, as its name implies, is primarily a tax on property passing on death, though, like estate duty, it is also charged on gifts of property within seven years of the donor's death. In certain events, however, lifetime gifts continue to attract an immediate charge to tax, though at a lower rate.

34.03   The rules for charging inheritance tax on settled property are set out in Part III of the IHTA 1984. This Part provides two quite different methods of charging tax according to whether there is an interest in possession in the settled property or not. If there is an interest in possession (as is usually the case with a life interest settlement), the person entitled to that interest is treated for most inheritance tax purposes as if he were the owner of the settled property (or that part of it) in which the interest subsists.[4] In such a case the settled property (or part) forms part of the life tenant's estate for inheritance tax purposes.[5] Settled property in which there is no interest in possession (as is the case with the conventional form of discretionary settlement) is defined as 'relevant property' by the Act.[6] Relevant property is subject to a periodic charge to inheritance tax during the subsistence of the discretionary trust;[7] there is also an 'exit' charge whenever property ceases to be relevant property.[8] The creation of a settlement will normally give rise to a transfer of value on the part of the settlor, ie a disposition as a result of which the value of his estate

---

[3]   Other trusts for which express provision is made, ie trusts of property held on temporary charitable trusts, newspaper trusts, employee trusts, charitable trusts, and trusts of maintenance funds for historic buildings, are outside the scope of this work.   [4]   IHTA 1984, s 49(1).
[5]   IHTA 1984, ss 5(1) and 49(1).   [6]   IHTA 1984, s 58(1).
[7]   IHTA 1984, ss 64, 66, and 67.   [8]   IHTA 1984, ss 65, 68, and 69.

immediately after the disposition is less than it would have been but for the disposition.[9] However, whereas the settlement of property on discretionary trusts will give rise to a chargeable transfer, the settlement of property on interest in possession trusts for the benefit of persons other than the settlor or his or her spouse or on accumulation and maintenance trusts (or other forms of favoured non-interest in possession trusts such as disabled trusts[10]) will give rise to a potentially exempt transfer which will become a chargeable transfer only if the settlor dies within seven years.[11]

Interest in possession

It will be apparent from the foregoing account that the term 'interest in possession in settled property' is of critical importance in determining how settled property is taxed. An interest in possession is clearly to be distinguished from a reversionary interest. But in its application to interests which are not reversionary the term has no settled and invariable legal meaning. It is perhaps surprising therefore that it is nowhere defined in the legislation.[12] The Inland Revenue expressed its view at an early stage. In a Press Release dated 12 February 1976 the Revenue stated its opinion that **34.04**

> . . . an interest in possession in settled property exists where the person having the interest has the immediate entitlement (subject to any prior claim by the trustees for expenses or other outgoings properly payable out of income) to any income produced by that property as the income arises; but that a discretion or power, in whatever form, which can be exercised after income arises so as to withhold it from that person negatives the existence of an interest in possession. For this purpose a power to accumulate income is regarded as a power to withhold it, unless any accumulations must be held solely for the person having the interest or his personal representatives.
> On the other hand the existence of a mere power of revocation or appointment, the exercise of which would determine the interest wholly or in part (but which, so long as it remains unexercised, does not affect the beneficiary's immediate entitlement to income) does not in the Board's view prevent the interest from being an interest in possession.

The rival contention was that a trust (as distinct from a power) to pay the income of settled property to a beneficiary conferred an interest in possession on that beneficiary even if his interest was defeasible by the exercise of a power which was exercisable over income already accrued, for example a power of accumulation. Such a trust conferred an interest, albeit a defeasible interest, and since such interest was

---

[9] IHTA 1984, s 3(1). A self-settlement under which the settlor takes an immediate interest in possession will not give rise to a transfer of value as the value of his 'estate' will not be diminished.
[10] See paras 36.05 *et seq* below.   [11] IHTA 1984, s 3A.
[12] A 'qualifying interest in possession' is defined by IHTA 1984, s 59(1) for the purposes of the code for the taxation of discretionary trusts as 'an interest in possession to which an individual . . . is beneficially entitled', but this is a circular definition which is of no assistance.

not a reversionary interest, it followed, according to this argument, that it was an interest in possession. The analogy was drawn with the settled land legislation which provides that a person entitled to an interest in settled land for life is to be treated as the owner of the settled land having the powers of a tenant for life even though his interest is subject to a power of accumulation.[13]

34.05   The matter was finally resolved by litigation. In *Pearson v IRC* the facts were that a trust fund was settled on a beneficiary for life subject to an overriding power of appointment among a discretionary class and subject also to a power to accumulate income for 21 years. Both Fox J and the Court of Appeal favoured the rival contention mentioned above and held that the life tenant's interest was an interest in possession.[14] But on further appeal the House of Lords, reversing the courts below by a bare majority, upheld the Revenue view.[15] It was held that the true test was whether the interest in question conferred a 'present right to present enjoyment', in other words an indefeasible right to the trust income which was not dependent on the trustees' decision whether or not to exercise a power, for example a power to accumulate it.[16] According to this test a beneficiary has an interest in possession only if he is entitled to call for the trust income as it arises. Income which can be distributed to others or accumulated does not satisfy this test. On the other hand, the mere existence of an overriding power of appointment which is exercisable prospectively only and cannot therefore affect the destination of income which has already accrued is not inconsistent with the existence of an interest in possession.[17]

Dispositive and administrative powers

34.06   The decision of the House of Lords in *Pearson v IRC* is also important in establishing the significance of the distinction between 'dispositive' and 'administrative' powers. It is only powers of the former kind, such as powers to accumulate income or to distribute income among a class of beneficiaries, that are capable of negativing interests in possession. Administrative powers, such as powers to pay trust expenses out of income, are not. Indeed in *Pearson v IRC* it was held that an express power for the trustees to pay out of income liabilities which would otherwise have been chargeable to capital was administrative rather than dispositive and that the existence of such a power was not inconsistent with the existence of an interest in possession even though the exercise of the power would trench on income for the benefit of capital.[18] In *Miller v IRC*[19] the Court of Session, applying this reasoning, held that powers for the trustees of a life interest trust to appropriate revenue for

---

[13]   SLA 1925, s 20(1)(viii).   [14]   [1980] Ch 1.   [15]   [1981] AC 753.
[16]   ibid 772H–773C, 780G, 781G–782A, and 787B–C.
[17]   ibid 774C–D, 780E–F, and 787C–D.
[18]   ibid 774G–775B, 775F, 784H–785C, and 787B–C.   [19]   [1987] STC 108.

the purpose of making good any depreciation in the capital value of the trust assets and for any other purpose they might deem advisable or necessary were powers directed to the preservation of the trust estate; they were accordingly held to be administrative rather than dispositive in nature and to be consistent with the existence of an interest in possession in the settled property which was accordingly taxable on the life tenant's death.

Where trustees are under a duty to pay or apply the trust income to or for the **34.07** benefit of the life tenant without any power to accumulate it, the beneficiary is regarded as having an interest in possession even though the trustees can in the exercise of their powers apply the income for the benefit of the beneficiary in, for example, the payment of his debts or other outgoings. Although such powers are in a sense exercisable so as to divert income away from the beneficiary, they are to be regarded as ancillary to or in aid of the beneficial interest of the beneficiary and as being therefore consistent with the existence of an interest in possession.[20]

Minors

Where property is settled on a minor beneficiary, then, subject to any prior inter- **34.08** est or charge, section 31 of the Trustee Act 1925 ('TA 1925'), unless modified or excluded,[21] will apply to the trust income. The section will apply whether the minor's interest is vested or contingent,[22] though in the latter case only if the interest carries the intermediate income of the settled property.[23] Where the section applies, the trustees have power during the beneficiary's minority to pay to the minor's parent or guardian or otherwise apply for or towards the minor's maintenance, education, or benefit the whole or such part (if any) of the trust income as may in all the circumstances be reasonable whether or not there is any other fund applicable to that purpose or any person bound by law to provide for his maintenance or education.[24] In exercising this power, however, the trustees are directed to have regard to the minor's age and requirements and generally to the circumstances of the case and, so far as practicable, to ensure that where other funds are available for maintenance purposes a proportionate part only of each fund is paid or applied for the purpose.[25] On attaining majority the beneficiary, even if he does not have a vested interest in trust income,[26] will become entitled to call for the income[27] and will thenceforth be entitled to an interest in possession in the settled property.

---

[20] cf *Lord Inglewood v IRC* [1983] STC 133, 139e–f, *per* Fox LJ, CA.
[21] TA 1925, s 69(2); see *Re Turner's Will Trusts* [1937] Ch 15, CA.
[22] TA 1925, s 31(1).   [23] TA 1925, s 31(3).   [24] TA 1925, s 31(1)(i).
[25] TA 1925, s 31(1), proviso.
[26] eg where the property and its income is settled on the beneficiary contingently on attaining the age of 25.   [27] TA 1925, s 31(1)(ii).

34.09 Income which is not applied during the beneficiary's minority is accumulated, with power for the trustees during the beneficiary's minority to resort to the accumulations and apply them as income of the current year.[28] The destination of any accumulations so made varies according to the nature of the minor's interest. This part of the section has two limbs. The first limb provides that where the minor attains the age of 18 or marries under that age and has a vested interest in the trust income during his minority or until his marriage,[29] or where on attaining 18 or marrying under that age the minor becomes entitled to the settled property in fee simple, absolute or determinable, or absolutely,[30] or for an entailed interest,[31] the accumulations are to be held on trust for the beneficiary absolutely.[32] Where the minor has an absolute interest, he will be entitled to the income (including accumulated income) in any event, but in all other cases the minor will have an interest in any accumulated income contingently on attaining his majority or marrying under that age,[33] but will not have an interest in possession in the meantime. On attaining his majority the minor will become entitled to call for the income[34] and will accordingly become entitled to an interest in possession. If the minor marries before attaining his majority, then although the trustees will continue to have power to apply the income for his benefit during his minority,[35] he will be entitled to the income which has already been accumulated[36] and he will likewise be entitled to all future income which is not applied for his benefit. As a married minor he will be entitled to give a good receipt for such income and for any accumulated income.[37] A minor having a vested interest in the trust income who marries before attaining his majority will thus become entitled to an interest in possession.[38]

34.10 In all other cases, for example where a beneficiary has an interest in capital contingently on attaining 18 or 25 which carries the intermediate income, statutory accumulations of income are held as an accretion to the capital from which they arose.[39] In the case of property held on trust for a class of beneficiaries in undivided shares the accumulated income of a particular beneficiary's share will be held as an accretion to that beneficiary's share rather than to corpus generally.[40] In these cases accumulated income will be added to capital even though the beneficiary had a vested interest in such income. If therefore a minor having

---

[28] TA 1925, s 31(2).   [29] TA 1925, s 31(2)(i)(a).

[30] A defeasibly vested interest in personalty as distinct from realty does not fall within this limb of s 31(2): *Re Sharp's Settlement Trusts* [1973] Ch 331.

[31] It has not been possible to create entailed interests after 1996: Trusts of Land and Appointment of Trustees Act 1996, s 2(6), Sch 1, para 5. Entailed interests created before 1997, however, continue to be valid.   [32] TA 1925, s 31(2)(i).

[33] TA 1925, s 31(2)(i)(a).   [34] ibid, s 31(1)(ii).   [35] ibid, s 31(1)(i).

[36] ibid, s 31(2)(i)(a).   [37] LPA 1925, s 21.

[38] cf *Stanley v IRC* [1944] KB 255, 259–260, CA.   [39] TA 1925, s 31(2)(ii).

[40] *Re Joel's Will Trusts* [1967] Ch 14. See para 35.21 below as to the potential significance of this factor in the context of flexible accumulation and maintenance trusts.

a vested interest in settled property dies under 18 and unmarried (and therefore without attaining a vested interest in accumulated income under the first limb), such accumulations will be held as an accretion to capital and not as part of his estate.

Non-income producing assets and enjoyment of assets in specie

The discussion thus far assumes that the assets comprised in the settled fund actu- **34.11** ally produce income. But what if an asset is non-income producing, for instance a life insurance policy or a capital growth bond which pays no dividend or an interest-free loan which has been made out of the trust assets in favour of the income beneficiary? The answer is that the 'present right to present enjoyment', which is the defining characteristic of an interest in possession, includes the right to call for the income, if any, of the settled property and that a beneficiary who would be entitled to call for the income of the settled property if it produced any is entitled to an interest in possession in such property.[41] The same is true of assets which are enjoyed in specie such as chattels. A more common example is a dwelling house occupied by a beneficiary; if in such case the trusts are so framed as to confer a right of occupation on the beneficiary, he will be treated as having an interest in possession in the dwelling house[42] or that part of it which he in fact occupies.[43]

Where land, whether or not being or including a dwelling house, is comprised in **34.12** a settlement, the matter is complicated by statute. Section 12(1) of the Trusts of Land and Appointment of Trustees Act 1996 ('TLATA 1996') provides that a beneficiary who is entitled to an interest in possession in land subject to a trust of land[44] is entitled by virtue of his interest to occupy that land if either (a) the purposes of the trust include making the land available for his occupation (or for the occupation of beneficiaries of a class of which he is a member or of beneficiaries in general) or (b) the land is held by the trustees so as to be so available. The beneficiary does not, however, have a right to occupy land which is unavailable or unsuitable for occupation by him.[45] Section 12 is subject to section 13. This section applies where two or more beneficiaries have the right to occupy land and confers on the trustees power to restrict or exclude the entitlement of any one or

---

[41] cf IHTA 1984, s 50(1) in which the words 'the income (if any)' contemplate that a person may have an interest in possession in assets not yielding income. Cf also *Re Kilpatrick's Policies* [1966] Ch 730, [1966] 2 All ER 149, CA (in which a settlor who settled a number of single premium insurance policies on his life on trust for himself for life was held to have an interest in possession in such policies for estate duty purposes).
[42] *IRC v Lloyds Private Banking Ltd* [1998] STC 559 and cf IHTA 1984, ss 46 and 50(5). See also para 36.02 below.
[43] *Cook v IRC* [2002] STC (SCD) 318 (widower given a right of residence in a house which was divided into two flats, one of which was let, held to have an interest in possession in the flat which he actually occupied). [44] As defined by TLATA 1996, s 1.
[45] TLATA 1996, s 12(2).

more (but not all) of them to occupy it. Trustees may impose reasonable conditions on any beneficiary in occupation and may also make provision for compensating payments to any beneficiary whose occupation has been excluded or restricted. The exercise of this power may affect the extent of the beneficiaries' respective interests in possession in the land and possibly also in the other assets comprised in the settlement.

Sole object of discretionary trust

34.13 Discretionary income trusts of which there is only one living object raise peculiar problems. It might be thought that a beneficiary in this position would have an interest in possession. But this is by no means always the case. The capital transfer tax implications of such a situation were considered in *Re Trafford's Settlement, Moore v IRC*[46] in which property was settled on discretionary trusts for the benefit of the settlor and any wife and issue of his. The settlor never married and never had children. The Revenue claimed tax on his death on the footing that he had an interest in possession in the settled property.[47] It was accepted that a sole object of a discretionary class which was *closed* would have an interest in possession.[48] But it was held[49] that where income accruing to the trustees of a discretionary trust was distributable in favour of a class which was not closed, the sole member of that class for the time being could not claim an immediate entitlement to the income so long as there existed a possibility that another member of the class could come into existence within a reasonable time. It was accordingly held that the settlor in that case had no interest in possession at his death.[50] As it happens, the settlor was known to have had no intention of marrying and the decision may, as the judge recognized, seem contrary to common sense.[51] On the other hand the judge was influenced by the 'remarkable and unsatisfactory' results which would flow from acceptance of the Crown's argument.[52] The decision is, moreover, consistent with the principle that while the court may in the exercise of its administrative jurisdiction authorize the distribution of trust assets if satisfied on the evidence that a given individual is incapable of having children, unless and until such jurisdiction is exercised beneficial entitlements will be ascertained on the footing that every individual is capable of having children until the end of his or her life, however unrealistic that prospect may be.[53]

---

[46] [1985] Ch 32, [1984] 1 All ER 1108.
[47] The settlement was created in 1951 long before the introduction of the gift with reservation provisions by FA 1986.
[48] [1985] Ch 32, [1984]1 All ER 1108, at 38E–39E, 1113e–1114c.
[49] ibid at 40E–41A, 1115a–d, following *Re Weir's Settlement, MacPherson v IRC* [1971] Ch 145, [1970] 1 All ER 297, CA.
[50] Given the circumstances of the case the term of 'a reasonable time' was generously construed.
[51] ibid 40E–F, 1115a.   [52] ibid 41B–F, 1115d–h.   [53] See *Figg v Clarke* [1997] STC 247.

C. Interest in Possession Trusts

A simple example of an interest in possession settlement is a settlement under 34.14 which property is settled on a beneficiary for life with remainder to his children. The range of interest in possession settlements is, however, a wide one and settlements within this category are capable of being very elaborate. Despite the adoption by the House of Lords in *Pearson v IRC* of a narrow interpretation of the term 'interest in possession', it is possible to retain a great degree of flexibility in a settlement conferring a life interest which qualifies as an interest in possession by incorporating wide overriding powers of appointment or application under which capital may be distributed to, or appointed or resettled on trusts for the benefit of, the life tenant or other persons. Provided that such powers are exercisable prospectively only, their existence will not prejudice the existence of an interest in possession.[54] If the exercise of such powers terminates the interest in possession, this may give rise to a chargeable transfer or potentially exempt transfer for inheritance tax purposes, but if the power is exercised in such manner that the life tenant becomes entitled to, or to another interest in possession in, the settled property, there will be no charge to inheritance tax.[55] The same result will follow if the settlor's spouse becomes so entitled.[56]

The interest in possession trust is most commonly used as a means of providing 34.15 for an adult beneficiary without giving him complete dominion over the property. A self-settlement on interest in possession trusts is also commonly used as a means of protecting property from inheritance tax by settlors who are resident but not domiciled in the United Kingdom.[57] Provided that the settled property is situated outside the jurisdiction it will rank as excluded property for inheritance tax purposes and will accordingly be exempt from tax.[58] Other fiscal advantages of such a settlement are that income tax and capital gains tax will be chargeable only if the income or amounts representing gains are remitted to the United Kingdom.[59]

Reverter to settlor

Although settled property will ordinarily be chargeable to inheritance tax on the 34.16 death of the life tenant,[60] the charge is excluded if the property then reverts to the settlor or his spouse or, if the settlor has died not more than two years earlier, to his widow (or widower).[61] This exception enables an employer to make provision for a retired employee, for example by settling a dwelling house on the employee for

---

[54] See para 34.05.   [55] IHTA 1984, s 53(2).   [56] IHTA 1984, s 18(1).
[57] ie domiciled at common law or in the extended statutory sense: IHTA 1984, ss 48(3) and 267(1).   [58] IHTA 1984, ss 3(2), 48(3).
[59] ICTA 1988, s 65(4), (5); TCGA 1992, s 12.   [60] IHTA 1984, ss 5(1) and 49(1).
[61] IHTA 1984, s 54. The charge is also excluded on the termination of the life tenant's interest during his life: s 53(3), (4).

life. A reverter to settlor settlement is also frequently employed where a person settles a life policy on discretionary trusts for the benefit of his spouse and children. If on his death the proceeds of the policy are distributed to the children, they can make provision for the surviving spouse by settling the proceeds on the spouse for life with remainder to themselves. If on the death of the spouse the settled property reverts to them,[62] it will not be taxable as part of the spouse's estate.[63] When the interest in possession terminates on the life tenant's death and on the same occasion the settlor becomes absolutely entitled to the trust assets, there is no capital gains tax-free revaluation of the trust assest;[64] no chargeable gain accrues on such occasion and the settlor is deemed to reacquire the trust assets on a no gain no loss basis.[65]

Protective trusts

34.17 Protective trusts require particular mention in the context of interest in possession settlements. The term 'protective trusts' is a shorthand reference to trusts in the terms set out in section 33 of the Trustee Act 1925. Where property is settled on protective trusts it is held on trust for the 'principal beneficiary' for life or any less period (the 'trust period') until he does or attempts to do or suffers any act or thing, or until any event happens, other than an advance under any statutory[66] or express power, whereby if the income were payable during the trust period to the principal beneficiary absolutely, he would be deprived of the right to receive it.[67] If that event occurs, a discretionary trust of the income during the residue of the trust period arises in favour of a class consisting of the principal beneficiary, his or her spouse and remoter issue, or, if there is no spouse or issue in existence, the person or persons who would be entitled to the settled property if the principal beneficiary were dead.[68]

34.18 Where settled property is held on protective trusts, the principal beneficiary is entitled to an interest in the income terminable on forfeiture which will constitute an interest in possession provided that the other requirements for an interest in possession are satisfied. On the subsequent forfeiture of the interest, the discretionary income trusts will come into effect and the interest in possession will terminate.[69] One accidental by-product of these provisions is that under the law formerly in force it was not possible to settle property on protective trusts for the

---

[62] Or to their spouses or, if they have died not more than two years earlier, to their widows or widowers.
[63] This consequence also follows where the life interest is surrendered or otherwise terminated before his death: IHTA 1984, s 53(3), (4).   [64] Under TCGA 1992, s 71.
[65] TCGA 1992, s 73(1).   [66] TA 1925, s 32.   [67] TA 1925, s 33(1)(i).
[68] TA 1925, s 33(i)(ii).
[69] Exceptionally the discretionary trusts will take effect from the outset, eg where the beneficiary is already bankrupt: *Trappes v Meredith* (1871) 7 Ch App 248; *Re Evans* [1920] 2 Ch 304. CA; *Re Walker* [1939] Ch 974.

benefit of minors and at the same time comply with the requirements for accumulation and maintenance settlements in that it could not be said with certainty that the minor beneficiary would necessarily become entitled to an interest in possession on or before attaining 18 or other specified age.[70] One further feature of the protected life interest under the former code is that the spouse exemption was not capable of applying on the death of a protected life tenant whose interest had been forfeited.

Under the capital transfer tax legislation as originally introduced in 1975, special **34.19** provision was made for property held on protective trusts or on 'trusts to the like effect'.[71] This provided that there was to be no charge to tax on the forfeiture of a protected life interest[72] and, further, that a distribution of capital to the principal beneficiary should also not give rise to a charge.[73] After a forfeiture the settled property became subject to the capital transfer tax code for discretionary trusts which, as mentioned above,[74] subjected the settled property to periodic and exit charges. In relation to existing settlements,[75] however, generous transitional reliefs were available in respect of distributions made before 1 April 1980.[76] A popular device for minimizing the tax charge on the transmission of property from one generation to the next[77] involved making use of the provisions relating to protective trusts in conjunction with the provisions giving transitional relief. Under a scheme of this kind the beneficiary entitled to the income of settled property absolutely would resettle his interest on protective trusts for his own benefit and then deliberately commit a forfeiture of his interest thereby bringing discretionary income trusts into effect. The settled property would then be distributed to the remainder beneficiaries at relatively much lower rates of tax.[78]

The Inland Revenue made an early attempt to restrict the use of this device by **34.20** expressing the view[79] that the expression 'trusts . . . to the like effect' in the capital transfer tax legislation was a reference to trusts which were 'not materially different' from those specified in section 33. Minor variations or the addition of administrative powers would not be regarded as material. But the extension of the list of potential beneficiaries under the discretionary income trust to, for example, mothers and sisters would not be regarded as a minor variation. The Revenue view was clearly at odds not only with common sense but also with judicial authority. In *Re Wallace's Settlements*[80] Megarry J considered the meaning of the words 'like trusts' in the context of the Variation of Trusts Act 1958 and held that the word

---

[70] See para 35.03 below.   [71] FA 1975, Sch 5, para 18(1).
[72] FA 1975, Sch 5, para 18(2)(a).   [73] FA 1975, Sch 5, para 18(2)(b).
[74] See para 34.03 above.   [75] ie settlements made before 27 March 1974.
[76] FA 1975, Sch 5, para 14.
[77] Under capital transfer tax, lifetime transfers were ordinarily chargeable to tax, though at lower rates than transfers on or within 3 years of the transferor's death: FA 1975, s 37.
[78] The tax efficacy of this type of scheme was established in *Thomas v IRC* [1981] STC 382.
[79] Statement of Practice E7 (3 March 1976).   [80] [1968] 1 WLR 711.

'like' required 'not identity but similarity' and went on to say '"similarity" in substance suffices without the need for similarity in form or detail or wording'.[81]

34.21 The provisions relating to the inheritance tax treatment of protective trusts were radically reformed in 1978.[82] Under the amended provisions which continue in force[83] the forfeiture of a protected life interest occurring after 11 April 1978 is disregarded and the principal beneficiary is treated as continuing to be entitled to an interest in possession for the remainder of the trust period. This reform elimin-ates the protective trust trap already referred to[84] and also means that the spouse exemption[85] is capable of applying on the termination of a forfeited life interest. Distributions of settled property subject to a protected life interest which was for-feited prior to 12 April 1978 continued to attract tax under the discretionary code.[86] Under the current provisions[87] tax is charged at a rate which increases to a maximum of 30 per cent with the length of time since the date of the forfeiture.[88]

Power to augment income

34.22 The existence or exercise of a power to resort to capital in order to augment out of capital the income of a beneficiary entitled to an interest in possession in the settled property is neutral for inheritance tax purposes. Since the beneficiary is already treated as entitled to the settled property,[89] the exercise of the power so as to give him an absolute interest in capital will not affect the value of his 'estate'[90] for inheritance tax purposes.[91] If there is a direction to trustees to resort to capital so far as necessary to maintain his income at a particular level, the capital so paid is liable to be treated as income in the beneficiary's hands for income tax pur-poses.[92] It is preferable in such cases to confer an unrestricted power on the trustees to pay capital to the beneficiary. Capital distributed to an income beneficiary under such a power will not ordinarily be treated as income in his hands even if the power is exercised on a recurrent basis.[93]

---

[81] [1968] 1 WLR 716D–F.   [82] FA 1978, s 71.   [83] IHTA 1978, s 88.
[84] See para 34.18 above.   [85] IHTA, s 18.   [86] FA 1982, s 118.
[87] IHTA 1984, s 73.   [88] IHTA 1984, s 73(3) applying s 70(3)–(10).
[89] IHTA 1984, s 49(1).   [90] As defined by IHTA 1984, ss 5(1) and 49(1).
[91] See Revenue Statement of Practice E6.
[92] *Brodie's Trustees v IRC* (1933) 17 TC 432; *Cunard's Trustees v IRC* (1946) 27 TC 122, CA.
[93] *Stevenson v Wishart* [1987] 1 WLR 1204, CA.

35

ACCUMULATION AND MAINTENANCE TRUSTS

A. Introduction

Of the various classes of non-interest in possession trust which enjoy favoured **35.01** treatment for inheritance tax purposes the most commonly encountered is the so-called accumulation and maintenance trust. As already mentioned, this type of trust is very much the creation of the capital transfer tax/inheritance tax legislation.[1] The accumulation and maintenance settlement is technically the most interesting of the forms of settlement considered in Part F. It also gives rise to the greatest number of problems. There is anecdotal evidence that of the settlements claiming to be accumulation and maintenance settlements which are considered by the Revenue about half are thought to be defective.

B. Conditions

An accumulation and maintenance trust must satisfy the following conditions:[2] **35.02**

(a) one or more persons (referred to as 'beneficiaries') will, on or before attaining a specified age not exceeding 25, become entitled to, or to an interest in possession in, the settled property or part of it;[3]

---

[1] FA 1975 Sch 5, para 15. This was replaced by FA 1982, s 114 which has now been re-enacted as IHTA 1984, s 71.
[2] IHTA 1984, s 71(1), (2).   [3] ibid, s 71(1)(a).

(b) no interest in possession subsists in the settled property or part and the income from it is to be accumulated so far as not applied for the maintenance, education, or benefit of a beneficiary;[4] and

(c) either :

    (i) not more than 25 years have elapsed since the day on which the settlement was made, or if it was later, since the time (or latest time) when the first two conditions above were satisfied with respect to the property or part,[5] or

    (ii) all the persons who are or have been beneficiaries are or were either grandchildren of a common grandparent or children, widows, or widowers of such grandchildren who were themselves beneficiaries but died before the time when, had they survived, they would have become entitled as mentioned above.[6]

These conditions call for a number of comments.

Condition (a)

35.03   The word 'will' requires that the beneficiaries are *bound* under the trusts of the settlement to become entitled to or to an interest in possession in the settled property on attaining a specified age not exceeding 25 if they so long live; the existence of an overriding power of appointment exercisable in favour of persons who are not 'beneficiaries' is thus inconsistent with the existence of accumulation and maintenance trusts.[7] On the other hand the incorporation of the statutory power of advancement, which can in theory be exercised so as to divert capital away from a beneficiary,[8] is compatible with this requirement as such a power is regarded as ancillary to or in aid of the beneficial interest of the beneficiary and as therefore being consistent with the existence of accumulation and maintenance trusts.[9]

35.04   The Revenue originally argued[10] that the reference to a 'specified age not exceeding 25' required that the age had to be specified and that it was not sufficient if the trust specified a date, for example the end of an accumulation period, at which the beneficiary was to become entitled to or to an interest in possession in the settled property even if that date was bound to occur before the beneficiary's twenty-fifth birthday. However, the Revenue subsequently accepted that the condition is satisfied even if no age is specified provided that it is clear that a beneficiary will in fact become entitled by 25.[11]

---

[4] IHTA 1984, s 71(1)(b).   [5] ibid, s 71(2)(a).   [6] ibid, s 71(2)(b).
[7] *Lord Inglewood v IRC* [1983] STC 133, CA.
[8] See *Re Clore's Settlement Trust* [1966] 1 WLR 955 and *Re Hampden Settlement Trusts* [1977] TR 177.   [9] *Lord Inglewood v IRC* [1983] STC 133, 139e–f, per Fox LJ, CA.
[10] In reliance on *White v Whitcher* [1928] 1 KB 453, a decision on the similar wording of Income Tax Act 1918, s 25.
[11] Revenue Concession F8 (2 September 1977).

The term 'beneficiaries' is not defined as persons who are for the time being under **35.05** 25 but is restricted to persons who have not attained the age at which they become entitled to or to an interest in possession in the property. A person who attains the specified age ceases to be a 'beneficiary' for the purposes of the section. This may be the age of 25 but this is not necessarily so. This is a potentially significant factor in the context of 'flexible' accumulation and maintenance settlements.[12]

The class of 'beneficiaries' for the purposes of the section may include unborn per- **35.06** sons but the conditions will not be satisfied unless during the subsistence of the trust there is or has been a living beneficiary.[13] This means that the provisions of section 71 will not apply unless there is a living beneficiary or until a beneficiary is born, but that so long as there has been a living beneficiary, the fact that there ceases to be any member of the class will not necessarily mean that the trusts will cease to qualify as accumulation and maintenance trusts pending the birth of future members of the class. It is essential that there should be no interest in possession in the meantime. A trust to distribute the income to persons other than beneficiaries would infringe condition (b); in practice therefore a trust to accumulate the income is the only form of intermediate trust which will continue to satisfy section 71. Where a settlor wishes to settle property on accumulation and maintenance trusts for the benefit of a class of beneficiaries, for instance grandchildren, none of whom are as yet in existence, it may be possible to do so by creating a so-called 'peg-life trust' for a composite class including as a beneficiary a living child who is not a member of the primary class and giving that child a small fraction of the fund in the event that members of the primary class subsequently come into existence.

Condition (b)

This condition requires that no interest in possession in the settled property **35.07** should subsist and the income from it should be accumulated so far as not applied for the maintenance, education, or benefit of a beneficiary. The wording of the latter part of this condition closely resembles and is clearly framed by reference to section 31 of the Trustee Act 1925 which gives power to trustees to apply income for the benefit of a minor beneficiary and directs that any income not so applied is to be accumulated. An initial question was whether a *power* to accumulate income coupled with a *trust* to apply unaccumulated income for maintenance purposes satisfied the requirements of condition (b). The Revenue, it seems, takes the view that the latter arrangement of powers and trusts satisfies the condition.[14] The cautious draftsman may nevertheless employ the former alternative.

---

[12] See para 35.18 below.   [13] IHTA 1984, s 71(7).
[14] Consistently with the observation made by Lord Wilberforce in *McPhail v Doulton* [1971] AC 424, 448H, HL that a logician would find it difficult to understand the difference between the two. Cf *IRC v Berrill* [1981] STC 784, 793.

35.08 The foregoing problem will not arise if, as is usually the case, section 31 is incorporated. However, the accumulation trust in the section normally operates only until the income beneficiary attains his majority.[15] Where a permissible accumulation period is available,[16] it will be possible to extend the operation of section 31 and defer the vesting of interests in possession. In practice the only available period will be the period of 21 years in gross from the date of the disposition.[17] Where in the case of a settlement the class is closed at the date of its creation and all the members have then already attained 4, the operation of the section can be expressly extended to age 25 in all cases. Where, however, the class is not closed, this simple solution will not be available; it will, however, be possible to defer the vesting of interests in possession for the maximum period consistent with the accumulation rules by defining a 'specified age' at which interests in possession vest which will be 25 in the case of any beneficiary who is 4 or more at the date of the settlement and in the case of any beneficiary who is either less than 4 at that date or is born within 3 years of the execution of the settlement the age which such beneficiary will attain on the twenty-first anniversary of the settlement. In relation to subsequently born beneficiaries the 'specified age' will remain 18.

Condition (c)

35.09 The advantages which are enjoyed by maintenance and accumulation settlements were intended to benefit relatively short-term trusts in favour of children. However, the exemption as originally enacted was subsequently thought to be expressed too widely and what were in substance relatively long-term discretionary trusts were capable of being framed so as to fall within the qualifying definition. Accordingly, condition (c) above was added[18] with the consequence that the relief is limited to a 25-year period or to settlements in favour of one generation, in the latter case with the addition of certain substituted beneficiaries.

35.10 Framing trusts falling within condition (c)(ii) above,[19] and so outside the 25-year restriction, is not always an easy task. For example, if a settlor wishes to benefit the children of two different families without the requisite common ancestry, it may be preferable to create two distinct funds, one for each set of children, instead of a single one for all of them. If the primary class of beneficiaries is confined to grandchildren of a common grandparent, care must be taken to ensure that any substitutional proviso applying to the share of a beneficiary who fails to attain an

---

[15] Or, where the income interest is vested, until he marries, if earlier: TA 1925, s 31(2)(i)(a).

[16] The Law Commission has proposed the abolition of the rules against excessive accumulation, but these proposals require primary legislation and have yet to be implemented.

[17] LPA 1925, s 163(1)(b) in the case of a will; Perpetuity and Accumulations Act 1964, s 13(1)(a) in the case of a settlement.   [18] By Finance Act 1976, s 106(1).

[19] IHTA 1984, s 71(2)(b).

interest in possession is not too widely drawn, in particular that it is confined to his children and does not extend to his issue generally; for otherwise it will be subject to the 25-year rule.

For the purposes of the common grandparent rule the expression 'children' includes a person's illegitimate and adopted children and his stepchildren.[20] A person can become another person's stepchild at any age. If therefore the class of beneficiaries under a settlement intended to be an accumulation and maintenance settlement includes future stepchildren, it is essential to impose a limit on the age up to which a stepchild can become eligible so as to ensure compliance with condition (a). Although under English law only minors may be adopted,[21] adoptions under foreign systems of law may permit the adoption of adults. Statute already makes provision for the recognition of 'overseas adoptions',[22] but these are confined to cases where a minor is adopted.[23] The existing provisions are, however, to be replaced by provisions which contemplate the recognition of an overseas adoption where the 'child' is a minor when the application to adopt is made though not necessarily when the adoption order itself is made.[24] In any event foreign adoptions may be recognized in appropriate circumstances at common law.[25] The cautious view is that one should impose an age limit where future adopted children are included in the class of beneficiaries. The same considerations apply in relation to legitimated children, at any rate where illegitimate children are excluded from the class. **35.11**

The 25-year restriction will not apply if the beneficiaries are a closed class of living persons. But if the accumulation and maintenance trusts are for an open class of beneficiaries not having a common grandparent and are therefore capable of enduring beyond the 25-year limit, it will be necessary to incorporate a power for the trustees to accelerate the vesting of interests in possession in the beneficiaries or those of them who have not already attained such an interest by the relevant time or to include a provision producing the same effect automatically on the twenty-fifth anniversary of the settlement or the time when the accumulation trusts first came into effect. **35.12**

In relation to accumulation and maintenance settlements created before 15 April 1976 in respect of which conditions (a) and (b) were satisfied on that date the common grandparent rule is treated as satisfied if it was satisfied on that date or if **35.13**

---

[20] IHTA 1984, s 71(8).
[21] Adoption Act 1976, ss 12 and 72(1) (definition of 'child'). These provisions will be replaced by the Adoption and Children Act 2002, ss 46 and 144(1), when brought into force.
[22] Adoption Act 1976, ss 38(1)(d) and 72(2).
[23] ibid, s 72(1) (definition of 'child') and (2).
[24] Adoption and Children Act 2002, ss 66(1)(d) and 87(1), (6) (definition of 'child').
[25] *Re Valentine's Settlement* [1965] Ch 226, CA.

it was satisfied in respect of the period beginning with 1 April 1977 and either (a) there was no living beneficiary on 15 April 1976 or (b) the beneficiaries on 1 April 1977 included a living beneficiary or (c) there was no power under the settlement whereby it could have been satisfied in respect of the period beginning with 1 April 1977 and the trusts of the settlement could not have been varied at any time after 15 April 1976.[26] It should be noted that if an accumulation and maintenance settlement falling within case (c) above is varied, the transitional application of the common grandparent rule automatically ceases. It is therefore essential to ensure that immediate absolute interests or interests in possession are conferred to avoid a heavy inheritance tax charge.

C. Engrafted Trusts

35.14 As has already been noted, the provisions of section 71 of the IHTA 1984 are closely modelled on those of section 31 of the Trustee Act 1925. A simple trust of capital and income for a minor contingently on attaining 18 or 25 will qualify as an accumulation and maintenance trust.[27] But it is not necessary for the minor to become absolutely entitled. He can also consistently with the requirements for an accumulation and maintenance settlement become entitled to an interest in possession. This can be achieved simply by settling property on the minor for life. If section 31 applies, the vesting of an interest in possession will automatically be deferred until age 18. The age at which the vesting of an interest in possession occurs can be further deferred in the case of a living beneficiary or a beneficiary born within three years of the settlement by modifying the operation of the section in reliance on the statutory 21-year accumulation period in gross. It should be noted, however, that since a minor with a vested interest in income becomes entitled to the income on marrying, it will be necessary in such a case to exclude the reference to marriage in the relevant provisions[28] if it is intended to defer the age of vesting to the maximum age consistent with the rules against excessive accumulation.

35.15 Where property is settled on long-term trusts for the benefit of a class of minor and unborn beneficiaries it is the usual practice not to settle the property on immediate life interest trusts but instead to incorporate an initial trust for the members of the primary class contingently upon attaining 18 or 25 or, where the vesting of interests in possession is deferred for as long as possible consistently with the rules against excessive accumulation, a 'specified age' at which the particular beneficiary

---

[26] IHTA 1984, s 71(6).
[27] There may be advantages if the accumulation and maintenance trusts determine on the same occasion as the minor becomes absolutely entitled, as holdover relief for capital gains tax will be available under TCGA 1992, s 260.   [28] In TA 1925, s 31(2)(i)(a); see para 34.09 above.

attains an interest in possession. The share of a beneficiary who attains a vested interest under the initial trust will be settled on continuing trusts for his benefit, for example on trust for life with remainders over for the benefit of his spouse and issue. Such trusts may attract the rule in *Lassence v Tierney*[29] under which the interest to which the beneficiary becomes entitled on attaining 18 or 25 or the intermediate age specified in the trust instrument will take effect absolutely if the engrafted trusts fail. The application of the doctrine depends upon there being an initial unqualified gift; if there is any contrary indication, for example words such as 'subject to the direction for the retention and settlement of the beneficiary's share hereinafter contained', the doctrine will be excluded.[30]

Where a settlor creates a peg-life trust[31] for the benefit of a class which is not **35.16** confined to the grandchildren of a common grandparent, two points should be borne in mind. First, if no member of the intended class came into existence, the peg-life will become entitled to the entire fund. Secondly, if the income of the fund is substantial, trust income which is accumulated before the arrival of a member of the intended class will under section 31 be held on trust for the peg-life absolutely on attaining his majority.[32] It is therefore desirable to modify section 31 so as to ensure that accumulations of income are held as an accretion to corpus generally rather than as an accretion to the particular beneficiary's share.

D. Flexible Trusts

Despite the technical requirements which have to be satisfied an accumulation **35.17** and maintenance trust is capable of being a very flexible instrument. Flexibility can be achieved essentially in two ways, first by incorporating powers of appointment or application over capital and secondly by conferring a power to vary the shares of the beneficial class. Powers to appoint or apply capital are capable of coexisting with accumulation and maintenance trusts provided that they can only be exercised after the vesting of an interest in possession in the share over which the power is being exercised. Such powers may be exercisable in favour of a class which includes but is not confined to members of the primary class.[33]

Powers of variation give rise to greater theoretical difficulty. It has always been **35.18** accepted that the shares of a class of beneficiaries do not have to be equal, but under the law as originally enacted[34] it was unclear whether it was possible consistently with these provisions to vary beneficial shares. The Revenue expressed the view at

---

[29] (1849) 1 Mac & G 551. [30] *Re Cohen's Will Trusts* [1936] 1 All ER 103.
[31] See para 35.06 above. [32] *Re Joel's Will Trusts* [1967] Ch 14; and see para 34.10 above.
[33] See Revenue Statement of Practice E1, §2. [34] FA 1975, Sch 5, para 15.

an early stage that it was.[35] The currently expressed view of the Revenue is in substantially the same terms:

> . . . a trust which otherwise satisfies the requirements of s 71(1)(a) would not be disqualified by the existence of a power to vary or determine the respective share of members of the class (even to the extent of excluding some members altogether) provided the power is exercisable only in favour of a person under 25 who is a member of the class.[36]

The Revenue view is not easy to reconcile with the terms of the legislation in two respects. First, as has already been seen,[37] the term 'beneficiaries' as defined in section 71(1)(a) is restricted to persons who have not reached the age at which they become entitled to interests in possession. This may be 25, but this is by no means necessarily the case. It follows from the Revenue view that a power to vary shares could be exercised adversely to the interests of a beneficiary who has not attained an interest in possession and in favour of one who already has. This does not appear to be consistent with the section. Though in practice it is safe to rely on the Revenue view, the cautious draftsman may nevertheless wish to confine a power to vary shares to the shares of beneficiaries who have not attained the 'specified age' at which interests in possession vest.

35.19   The Revenue view that it is possible to exclude a beneficiary altogether is also difficult to square with the legislation. Section 71(1)(a) requires that 'one or more persons' 'will' (ie are bound to[38]) become entitled to or to an interest in possession in the settled property on or before attaining a specified age not exceeding 25. It is not easy to see why, if a single beneficiary must necessarily attain an interest in the property on or before attaining 25 if he so long lives, two or more beneficiaries should not likewise all be required to satisfy the same condition. The Revenue view is convenient and may in practice be relied on. But once again the cautious draftsman may prefer not to exclude any beneficiary altogether and to provide that all primary beneficiaries are to take a share of a minimum percentage or value. Since powers of appointment are now presumed to be exclusive,[39] it is necessary to make express provision. A power of variation which is qualified in this way provides a rare instance of a non-exclusive power in a modern trust instrument.

35.20   Powers of variations which are exclusive give rise to another interesting conundrum. Suppose that property is settled on such one or more of three minor beneficiaries, A, B, and C, as attain 18 as the trustees may appoint and that the settlement includes a direction for the retention and settlement of the share of any beneficiary who attains 18. Suppose that the trustees exercise the power of variation so as wholly to exclude

---

[35]   Revenue Press Release dated 19 January 1976.
[36]   Revenue Statement of Practice E1, §4.   [37]   See para 35.05 above.
[38]   See para 35.03 above.   [39]   LPA 1925, s 158.

B and C and that A attains 18 but that the trusts engrafted on his share fail. Do B and C take any interest under the initial trusts in default? In principle the answer is that they do not, more particularly if the scheme of trusts attracts the rule in *Lassence v Tierney*.[40] There is no reported case on the point though there is one unreported decision.[41] It follows that, unless the engrafted trusts incorporate an overriding power under which they may benefit, beneficiaries who are excluded in circumstances similar to those outlined above will altogether cease to be eligible to benefit under the settlement.

Powers of variation raise a further point. As already noticed, income accumulated **35.21** under section 31 of the Trustee Act 1925 during a beneficiary's minority in cases where (as will usually be the case) the beneficiary does not have a vested interest in the income[42] will form an accretion to the beneficiary's share rather than an accretion to corpus generally.[43] If the power of variation is non-exclusive and the beneficiary in question retains a share, however small, then the accumulations will continue to form part of that share. And even if the beneficiary's share is altogether extinguished, it would seem that any accumulations of the income of the extinguished share, unless also diverted to the other beneficiaries under the power of variation, will continue to be held on contingent trusts for the beneficiary. In such a case it is wise to ensure that the power of variation is not merely exercisable over the original capital of the trust fund but also extends to accumulations of income.

---

[40] See para 35.15 above.

[41] *Re Fortescue's Will Trusts* (Ch D, 19 November 1998) in which Jacob J, without giving judgment, made a declaration consistent with the argument set out in the text.

[42] Or other qualifying interest: see para 34.09 above.

[43] See para 34.10 above.

36

DISCRETIONARY TRUSTS AND DISABLED TRUSTS

A. Discretionary Trusts

The antithesis of the interest in possession trust in the context of inheritance tax **36.01** is the conventional discretionary trust. Formerly very popular on account of its inherent estate duty advantages, the discretionary trust lost most of its former appeal with the introduction of capital transfer tax and with it a system of charging discretionary trusts to tax which was widely considered to be very unfavourable. The law has since been modified, and as currently in force[1] has caused discretionary trusts to regain some of their former popularity. Where a charge to inheritance tax will arise on the death of a person in any event, for example because no spouse exemption will be available, a discretionary trust of residue can be included without additional charge to tax. The availability of generous reliefs is another consideration. Discretionary trusts may, for example, be used without tax penalty where the property settled qualifies for 100 per cent business property relief, for instance unquoted shares in a trading company,[2] or 100 per cent agricultural property relief, for example agricultural property carrying the right to vacant possession or the right to obtain it within twelve months.[3] They may also be used without tax penalty where the value of the property settled does not exceed the settlor's nil-rate band.[4] The main non-fiscal reasons for employing discretionary trusts are to protect beneficiaries from their own improvidence or to

---

[1] IHTA 1984, Part III, Ch III.   [2] ibid, ss 104(1)(a) and 105(1)(bb) and (3).
[3] ibid, s 116(2)(a).   [4] Currently (ie in relation to transfers on or after 6 April 2004) £263,000.

provide for a disabled beneficiary in a way which does not prejudice his entitlement to social security benefits. The inheritance tax advantages of short-term
discretionary trusts created by will are discussed elsewhere.[5]

Occupation of dwelling house

36.02   A matter which formerly gave rise to some difficulty was whether an interest in
possession is created if trustees allow a discretionary beneficiary to have the free
use of a house or chattels or to borrow trust moneys interest free. The Inland
Revenue originally indicated in 1975 that trustees allowing a beneficiary the free
use of a house in normal circumstances would not be regarded as creating an interest in possession.[6] Subsequently, however, *Sansom v Peay*[7] was decided. In that
case beneficiaries were permitted by the trustees of a discretionary settlement to
occupy a house under a power contained in the settlement. It was held that such
beneficiaries were 'entitled to occupy it under the terms of the settlement' within
the relevant capital gains tax legislation[8] with the consequence that the house was
exempt from capital gains tax on its disposal by the trustees. The wording of the
legislation is not identical with any provision in the inheritance tax legislation but
the similarities are striking.[9] The Inland Revenue therefore announced that it
would in future normally regard someone having the use of a house held on trust
by permission of the trustees as having an interest in possession, particularly
where the power is exercised to provide a permanent home for a beneficiary.[10]
Therefore, this type of power should normally only be exercised after careful consideration of the potential inheritance tax consequences.

Chattels and loans

36.03   The beneficial enjoyment of chattels by a beneficiary may also confer an interest
in possession on that beneficiary.[11] The making of interest-free loans to a
beneficiary is more problematical. There is clearly an argument in favour of the
view that an interest in possession is thereby created. But the better view is that the
debt created by the loan is a distinct asset from the moneys loaned which, unlike
a dwelling house which a beneficiary is permitted to occupy or a chattel which he
is permitted to enjoy, become his property. This view has not been challenged by
the Revenue and is impliedly accepted in relation to the debt and charge schemes
referred to elsewhere.[12]

---

[5] See paras 37.30 *et seq* below.
[6] See Revenue letter in the Law Society's Gazette, 6 August 1975.
[7] [1976] 1 WLR 1073.   [8] FA 1965, s 29(9), since re-enacted as TCGA 1992, s 225.
[9] See especially IHTA 1984, s 50(5).   [10] Revenue Statement of Practice SP 10/79.
[11] See para 34.11 above.   [12] See para 37.08 *et seq* below.

Letter of wishes

In the case of any settlement which confers wide discretions, but particularly so in **36.04** the case of a fully discretionary settlement, it is desirable to invite the settlor to set out in a letter of wishes how he contemplates that the trust will be administered and the property distributed over the longer term. Such a letter has no binding force but enables the settlor to exert some influence, albeit of an indirect, non-binding kind, over the future of the trust and provides trustees with guidance as to how they are expected to exercise their discretions. This may be of considerable assistance to them in deciding between the competing claims of beneficiaries at a later date.

B. Disabled Trusts

Disabled trusts, like accumulation and maintenance trusts, owe their existence to **36.05** fiscal legislation, principally inheritance tax.

Inheritance tax

Section 89 of the IHTA 1984 provides that for the purposes of inheritance tax a **36.06** disabled trust must satisfy the following conditions:[13]

(a) during the life of the disabled person no interest in the settled property subsists; and

(b) the trusts must secure that not less half of the settled property which is applied during his life is applied for his benefit.

Where these conditions are satisfied the disabled person is treated as having an interest in possession in the settled property.[14] A disabled person settling property on disabled trusts for his own benefit will thus make no transfer of value of that property[15] and a person settling property on disabled trusts for the benefit of another (not being his spouse) makes a potentially exempt transfer of the property.[16]

Condition (a)

Condition (a), the income condition, simply requires that during the disabled **36.07** person's life there should be no interest in possession. This can be achieved by imposing a trust or power to accumulate income during any available accumulation period[17] or a discretionary income trust. It is a curious feature of this condition that

---

[13] IHTA 1984, s 89(1).
[14] IHTA 1984, s 89(2). The section applies only to settlements created after 9 March 1981.
[15] See para 34.03 above.   [16] IHTA 1984, s 3A(1)(c).
[17] See para 36.12 and n 30 below.

it does not in terms require that income or any specified proportion of it should be applied for the disabled person's benefit nor even that he should be a member of the discretionary income class.

Condition (b)

36.08 Condition (b), the capital condition, which requires that not less than half the settled property which is applied during the disabled person's life is applied for his benefit, would in strictness require the exclusion of the statutory power of advancement if, as is usually the case, the capital trusts taking effect on the disabled person's death are for the benefit of other persons. However, it is expressly provided[18] that trusts which otherwise qualify as disabled trusts are not to be treated as disqualified by reason only that the statutory power of advancement[19] applies. If the inclusion of the statutory power is permissible consistently with the existence of disabled trusts, it is arguable that the exercise of such power must likewise be permissible even if such exercise infringes condition (b). It is wise, however, to ensure conformity with the condition by not modifying or extending the statutory power and by making express provision excluding the exercise of the power during the disabled person's life.

Disabled person

36.09 A disabled person for the purposes of section 89 is a person who is either

(a) incapable by reason of mental disorder[20] of administering his property or managing his affairs; or

(b) in receipt of an attendance allowance;[21] or

(c) in receipt of a disability living allowance[22] by virtue of entitlement to the care component at the highest or middle rate.

It is essential that the disabled person suffers from mental disorder or is in actual receipt of either of the benefits mentioned above at the time property is transferred into settlement. If thereafter property is added to the settlement, it is necessary that he should satisfy one of the conditions at that time. But it is immaterial that the disabled person ceases to satisfy one of these conditions after the commencement of the settlement or the addition of further property.[23]

---

[18] IHTA 1984, s 89(3).

[19] Under TA 1925, s 32 or Trustee Act (Northern Ireland) 1958, s 33.

[20] Within the meaning of the Mental Health Act 1983.

[21] Under the Social Security Contributions and Benefits Act 1992, s 64 or the Social Security Contributions and Benefits (Northern Ireland) Act 1992, s 64.

[22] Under the Social Security Contributions and Benefits Act 1992, s 71 or the Social Security Contributions and Benefits (Northern Ireland) Act 1992, s 71.   [23] IHTA 1984, s 89(4).

C. Capital Gains Tax

The capital gains tax legislation[24] provides that the trustees of trusts for the benefit **36.10** of mentally disabled persons created on or after 10 March 1981 qualify for the full exemption for annual gains[25] instead of being entitled, along with trustees of other trusts, to one half.[26]

D. Mentally Disabled Person

For these purposes a mentally disabled person must satisfy the following **36.11** conditions:[27]

(a) that during the life of a mentally disabled person not less than half the settled property which is applied is applied for his benefit; and
(b) that the mentally disabled person is entitled to not less than half the income arising from the settled property or that no such income may be applied for the benefit of any other person.

The term 'mentally disabled person' as defined in the legislation[28] is not wholly appropriate as it is identical with the inheritance tax definition of 'disabled person'[29] and therefore includes persons who are in receipt of attendance allowance or disability living allowance and who may well not be mentally disabled.

Conditions (a) and (b)

Of the two conditions which must be satisfied, condition (a), the capital condi- **36.12** tion, is identical with the corresponding inheritance tax condition. But the terms of condition (b), the income condition, are usually impossible to reconcile with the terms of the corresponding inheritance tax condition. To comply with the capital gains tax condition the trust must confer an interest in possession in at least half the fund after the initial 21-year accumulation period has expired.[30] Such a requirement is inconsistent with the inheritance tax requirement that the trust must secure that there is no interest in possession in the settled property throughout the disabled person's life. Since inheritance tax factors are likely to be more significant, trusts complying with the inheritance tax conditions are likely to be preferred.

---

[24] TCGA 1992, s 3, Sch 1, para 1.
[25] £8,200 for the year 2004 – 2005 subject to being increased in subsequent years by reference to the RPI: TCGA 1992, s 3(2), (3).   [26] TCGA 1992, s 3, Sch 1, para 2.
[27] TCGA 1992, Sch 1, para 1(1).   [28] In Sch 1, para 1(6).   [29] See para 36.09 above.
[30] Unless the disabled person is the settlor in which event the life of the settlor under LPA 1925, s 164(1)(a) may be adopted.

E. Disabled Trust or Discretionary Trust?

36.13 Despite the inheritance tax advantages of a disabled trust, there may be counter-vailing advantages in providing for a disabled person by way of a discretionary trust. One particular factor is the availability of state or local authority benefits. Such benefits are complex and are frequently modified or amended by statutory instrument. A detailed consideration of them is beyond the scope of this work, but the essential point is that, if the disabled person is in receipt of means-tested state benefits or is in the care of a local authority, there is a greater risk of the capital and income under a trust which is tailor-made for his benefit being taken into account for the purpose of assessing his liability to contribute than under a fully discretionary trust which is not overtly tailor-made for him. Where large funds are involved, there may be an inheritance tax penalty in creating a discretionary trust, but not if the value of the fund does not exceed the nil-rate band or if the trust is a testamentary trust of the estate of a surviving parent of the disabled person on which inheritance tax will be payable in any event.

37

TESTAMENTARY TRUSTS

A. Introduction

By and large the form of testamentary trusts is governed by similar considerations **37.01**
to those governing *inter vivos* trusts. Certain differences have already been noted,
in particular the fact that although the creation of a lifetime discretionary trust
constitutes a chargeable transfer which may give rise to an immediate charge to
inheritance tax, there is no disincentive to the creation of a discretionary trust by
will if inheritance tax is to be paid on the testator's death in any event.[1] There are,
however, factors which are peculiar to will trusts.

B. Estates in Administration

In strict point of law the estate of a deceased person devolving on his personal rep- **37.02**
resentative 'comes to him in full ownership, without distinction between legal and
equitable interests' with the consequence that trusts do not attach to the assets
comprised in an estate until the administration is complete and residue is ascertained.[2] Until that time a beneficiary has no right to any particular asset comprised

---

[1] See further para 37.30 *et seq* below as to the inheritance tax treatment of testamentary discretionary trusts which are brought to an end within two years of the death.

[2] *Commr of Stamp Duties (Queensland) v Livingston* [1965] AC 694, 707–708 PC; see also *Re
Hayes' Will Trusts* [1971] 1 WLR 358, 764–765. This principle does not apply in relation to property which is specifically given: *IRC v Hawley* [1928] 1 KB 578, 583; see also *Re Neeld decd* [1962]

in the unadministered estate, but only a chose in action, being the right to due administration.[3] For inheritance tax purposes, however, a person will be treated as entitled to an interest in possession in residue if he would be so entitled if residue had been ascertained immediately after the deceased person's death.[4]

Commorientes

37.03 It is common to insert in a will a provision making the gifts taken under it conditional on surviving the testator by a specified period. Section 92 of the IHTA 1984 provides that where the period so specified does not exceed six months, then the disposition taking effect at the end of the period or, if the beneficiary dies within that period, the disposition taking effect on his death is treated for inheritance tax purposes as having taken effect on the testator's death. It appears not to matter whether or not the interest carries the intermediate income or that it is an income interest only.

37.04 Section 92 applies to property devolving under a will 'or otherwise' and accordingly applies where a provision of the sort described above is included in a settlement, for example a provision making a gift in remainder subject to surviving the life tenant by a specified period not exceeding six months. The intestacy rules now incorporate a 28-day survival period where an intestate's husband or wife takes an interest in the intestate's estate.[5] If the husband or wife dies within that period, section 92 will apply and the trusts in default will be treated as having taken effect on the intestate's death.

37.05 Although the inclusion of a survival period in a will is a popular device, there is one circumstance, happily a rare one, in which its use can be prejudicial, namely where spouses die in circumstances where it cannot be known which of them survived the other, for instance where both spouses perish in a road accident or an air crash. The younger of the spouses is deemed to have survived the older for succession purposes generally,[6] though not in the case of intestate succession.[7] For inheritance tax purposes, however, the spouses are treated as having died at the same instant[8] with the consequence that the estate of the older spouse will not be aggregated with that of the younger spouse for the purpose of determining the rate

---

Ch 643, 687–688, CA. A specific donee is thus entitled to an equitable interest in property specifically given to him subject to the personal representative's right to resort to it for administration purposes.

[3] The rights of a beneficiary solely entitled to residue may, however, enable him to direct how the assets comprised in residue are dealt with: *Re Leigh's Will Trusts* [1970] Ch 277.

[4] IHTA 1984, s 91.

[5] AEA 1925, s 47(2A) (introduced as respects the death of a person intestate on or after 1 January 1996 by the Law Reform (Succession) Act 1995).

[6] LPA 1925, s 185. See *Hickman v Peacey* [1945] AC 304, HL as to the effect of this provision.

[7] AEA 1925, s 46(3); and see now s 46(2A) referred to above.   [8] IHTA 1984, s 4(2).

of tax on the latter's death. However, to the extent that the estate of the older spouse becomes comprised in the estate of the younger spouse, the spouse exemption[9] will still apply. Where spouses leave their estates to each other and survivorship provisions are included, the will of the older spouse should therefore exclude the operation of the clause if they should die in circumstances rendering uncertain which of them survived the other.

Chattels

A specific gift of personal chattels by will often confers a discretion on an individual or the executors as to the manner in which such chattels are to be distributed with a request that the individual or the executors give effect to any memorandum of wishes which the testator may leave with his papers. When the discretion is conferred on an individual and there is a default trust in his favour, there is no difficulty as the power of distribution is tantamount to a general power of appointment. Where the discretion is conferred on executors and the class of potential recipients is defined, no problem arises either. But it is now a common practice to confer on the executors what is tantamount to a general power of appointment with a default gift over on the trusts of residue. Although what is tantamount to a general power which is vested in executors or trustees does not on the face of it satisfy the requirement of certainty of objects, such powers are in the light of the authorities[10] valid, but it is thought that a *trust* to distribute which is not confined to an ascertainable class would not be. The inheritance tax provisions relating to the distribution of chattels and other personal property in accordance with the testator's wishes are considered elsewhere.[11]

37.06

Nil-rate band legacies

If a testator leaves his entire estate to his spouse and the spouse survives him, the estate will be wholly exempt from inheritance tax,[12] but the entire joint estate will be taxable on the survivor's death so far as not expended or distributed in the meantime. If the couple have children, the testator is able without incurring a charge to tax to leave them a legacy equal to the nil-rate band prevailing at his death or so much of it as has not been exhausted by chargeable lifetime gifts made by him within seven years of his death or by gifts with reservation which are treated as part of his taxable estate on his death. This solution will not only avoid a charge to inheritance tax on the testator's death but will enable the surviving

37.07

[9] Under IHTA 1984, s 18(1).
[10] *Re Manisty's Settlement* [1974] Ch 17; *Re Hay's Settlement Trusts* [1982] 1 WLR 202; *Re Beatty decd* [1990] 1 WLR 1503. [11] See para 37.29 below.
[12] In the unusual, though possible, situation that the testator dies domiciled in the United Kingdom (or treated as so domiciled for inheritance tax purposes: IHTA 1984, s 267) and his spouse is domiciled outside the jurisdiction, the exemption is limited to £55,000: IHTA 1984, s 18(2).

spouse to make potentially exempt transfers in favour of the children with a view to reducing the value of the remainder of the joint estate on the survivor's death. Where, however, the testator's estate is relatively modest in value, it may not be desirable to deprive the surviving spouse of access to the income and capital of the nil-rate band legacy. In such circumstances a device which is frequently resorted to is to settle the nil-rate band legacy on discretionary trusts for the benefit of a class of whom the surviving spouse is a member. Such a scheme enables the survivor to enjoy part or even the whole of the income of the discretionary fund without the fund forming part of his or her estate on death for inheritance tax purposes save to the extent that capital has been advanced to him or her in the meantime. A nil-rate band discretionary legacy is administratively inconvenient but is unlikely to attract any or any significant periodic or exit charges.[13] However, the creation of an investment fund in satisfaction of the nil-rate band discretionary legacy will not be possible if there are insufficient liquid assets in the estate to fund the legacy.

Debt and charge schemes

37.08 Where there are insufficient liquid assets and effectively the only available asset to incorporate in the nil-rate band legacy is the matrimonial home or a share of it, the difficulty which will arise is that the surviving spouse's continued beneficial occupation of the home will ordinarily give him or her an interest in possession in it[14] thus nullifying the inheritance tax advantages of the scheme. Possible solutions in such situations which have been developed in recent years involve the constitution of a nil-rate band discretionary fund by a debt or charge. These schemes presuppose that the testator's will leaves a nil-rate band discretionary legacy of which the surviving spouse is an object and leaves residue to the surviving spouse. The essential feature of such schemes is that the discretionary fund is constituted by the surviving spouse entering into a personal obligation to pay the amount of the nil-rate band to the trustees of the will in consideration of their distributing the estate to him or by the trustees taking a charge over the house to secure the relevant sum and distributing the estate to the surviving spouse subject to the charge. If the fund is constituted by the personal obligation of the surviving spouse, the debt is interest free and payable on demand and, if by way of charge, the charge is interest free and enforceable on demand. The surviving spouse in effect has the benefit of the income of the notional fund, but he also owns the entire house or share of it and will be entitled to claim the principal private residence relief for capital gains tax purposes[15] in the event of its sale during his lifetime.

---

[13] If the will creates other trusts, these will normally be taken into account in computing the rate of tax: IHTA 1984, ss 64, 65(3), 66(4)(c), 68(5)(b), and 69(1). Where, however, property is settled on trusts under which the surviving spouse takes an immediate interest in possession, this consequence does not follow: ibid, s 80. [14] See para 36.02 above.

[15] TCGA 1992, s 225.

The thinking behind the debt and charge schemes is that the debt or charge which **37.09** forms the discretionary fund is a legitimate deduction in valuing the estate of the surviving spouse for inheritance tax purposes on his death. In the case of a debt scheme the debt has been incurred by the surviving spouse for full value, ie in exchange for having the estate distributed to him. In the case of a charge scheme the estate, including the house, is distributed to him subject to the charge and his estate will be correspondingly reduced in value on his death when the charge is redeemed. An important assumption underlying both schemes is that the benefit of the debt or the benefit of the charge is an asset of the discretionary fund in which the surviving spouse has no interest in possession[16] and which does not therefore form part of his taxable estate.

The debt and charge schemes are both artificial in that they involve the creation of **37.10** a notional discretionary fund of which the surviving spouse effectively has the full use. But they have not as yet been challenged by the Revenue and appear to be accepted in the context of testamentary trusts. This is impliedly confirmed by the fact that the legislative reforms recently introduced by the Revenue[17] imposing an income tax charge on the free use of property are intended only to apply to an asset formerly owned by the user and are therefore effectively confined to *inter vivos* schemes.

C. Alteration of Dispositions Taking Effect on Death

The statutory jurisdiction to vary trusts generally is considered elsewhere in this **37.11** work.[18] But there are important provisions authorizing the alteration of the dispositions of a deceased person's estate taking effect on his death without adverse tax consequences.

Variations and disclaimers

Section 142(1) of the IHTA 1984 provides as follows: **37.12**

  (1) Where within the period of two years after a person's death—
       (*a*) any of the dispositions (whether effected by will, under the law relating to intestacy or otherwise[19]) of the property comprised in his estate immediately before his death are varied, or
       (*b*) the benefit conferred by any of those dispositions is disclaimed,

---

[16] See para 37.07 above.   [17] FA 2004, s 184 and Sch 15.
[18] See paras 24.19 *et seq* above.   [19] See further para 37.20 below.

by an instrument in writing made by the persons or any of the persons who benefit or would benefit under the dispositions, this Act shall apply as if the variation had been effected by the deceased or, as the case may be, the disclaimed benefit had never been conferred.

37.13 There are distinctions between these two methods of varying testamentary trusts.

Variations

37.14 Variations must (a) be effected by an instrument in writing,[20] (b) be made within two years of the death, (c) be made by the person or persons who benefit or would benefit under the relevant disposition, and (d) contain a statement by such person or persons and, if the variation results in additional tax being payable, by the deceased's personal representatives that section 142(1) is intended to apply.[21] Where the persons benefiting under the disposition are under age or unborn, it will be possible to effect a variation within the section only by promoting a variation under the Variation of Trusts Act 1958[22] or, where some issue concerning the estate or its devolution has arisen, by way of a compromise of that issue approved by the court.

37.15 Variations operate as assignments and there is no restriction on the class of persons or purposes who or which may benefit under them.[23] Variations can and frequently do create elaborate systems of trusts which are read back to the death for inheritance tax purposes. It is no objection that the beneficiary has already received a benefit prior to the variation. It is not possible, however, to vary a disposition which has already been varied.[24]

Disclaimers

37.16 The law of disclaimer is relatively obscure and its effects are frequently not fully understood. The basic principle is summarized in the colourful dictum that 'a Man cannot have an Estate put into him in Spight of his Teeth'.[25] The corollary of this principle is that a person who has accepted property or an interest in it cannot thereafter disclaim it.[26] It also follows that since a disclaimer operates not by way of conveyance or assignment but by way of avoidance, it may be effected

---

[20] In practice variations are usually effected by deed.
[21] IHTA 1984, s 142(1), (2), (2A). The latter requirement, introduced by FA 2000 in relation to instruments made after 31 July 2000, replaces the requirement that notice in writing should be given to the Revenue within six months.   [22] As to which see paras 24.19 *et seq* above.
[23] Under FA 1975, s 47(1) (repealed by FA 1980, s 80, Sch 13, Pt V as regards variations made on or after 11 April 1978) variations had to be effected by 'deed of family arrangement or similar instrument' which implied some restriction of uncertain scope on the identity of the persons eligible to benefit under the variation.   [24] *Russell v IRC* [1981] 1 WLR 834.
[25] *Thomson v Leach* (1690) 2 Vent 198, 206, *per* Ventris J, cited with approval by Abbott CJ in *Townson v Tickell* (1819) 3 B & Ald 31, 37 and applied in *Re Stratton's Disclaimer* [1958] Ch 42, 50–51, CA and *Re Gulbenkian's Settlement (No 2)* [1970] Ch 408, 418.
[26] *Re Wimperis* [1913] 1 Ch 502.

informally, even by word of mouth.[27] To be effective for inheritance tax purposes, however, a disclaimer must be made in writing[28] and, since an informal disclaimer can be retracted if no one has altered his position on the faith of it,[29] disclaimers are almost invariably effected by deed, a deed being irrevocable unless a power of revocation is expressly incorporated.[30]

As with variations, disclaimers must be made within two years of the death and must be made by the person disclaiming the benefit and, if the disclaimer results in additional inheritance tax being payable, by the personal representatives as well.[31] There is, however, no requirement that a disclaimer must contain a statement that section 142(1) is intended to apply. If therefore a benefit from the estate is disclaimed within two years of the death, the provisions of section 142 will apply automatically. Since, unlike variations, disclaimers operate by way of avoidance, they cannot control the subsequent devolution of the interest which has been renounced. This can lead to unexpected results.[32] If, for example, a testator leaves his estate to his wife with a gift over to his children in the event of her predeceasing him and his wife survives him, a disclaimer by her of her absolute interest will not operate to accelerate the interest of the children and the estate will be undisposed of.[33] Deeds of variation are therefore normally to be preferred. **37.17**

Consideration

Section 142(1) of the IHTA 1984 does not apply to a variation or disclaimer made for any consideration in money or money's worth other than consideration consisting of the making in relation to another of the dispositions a variation or disclaimer to which the subsection applies.[34] If therefore the donee under a variation agrees to pay the costs of the variation out of his own rather than estate moneys to which he is entitled, such payment may take the transaction outside the scope of the section. **37.18**

Interests in possession

It is provided by section 142(4) of the IHTA 1984 that where a variation to which the section applies results in property being held in trust for a person for a period which ends not more than two years after the death, the Act is to apply as if the disposition taking effect at the end of such period had had effect from the beginning of the period.[35] It will be recalled that for inheritance tax purposes a beneficiary on **37.19**

---

[27] *Townson v Tickell* (1819) 3 B & Ald 31, 38.   [28] IHTA 1984, s 142(1).
[29] *Re Young* [1913] 1 Ch 272; *Re Cranstoun* [1949] Ch 523. It is otherwise with gifts *inter vivos*: *Re Paradise Motor Co Ltd* [1968] 1 WLR 1125, 1143E, CA.
[30] *Re Beesty's Will Trusts* [1966] Ch 223, 232–233.   [31] IHTA 1984, s 142(1).
[32] cf *Re Scott decd* [1975] 1 WLR 1260 and see the Law Commission's Consultation Paper No 172 *The Forfeiture Rule and the Law of Succession*, Pt III.
[33] cf *Re Sinclair decd* [1985] Ch 446, CA.   [34] IHTA 1984, s 142(3).
[35] IHTA 1984, s 142(4).

whom a life interest is conferred in property comprised in the estate of a deceased person which would otherwise qualify as an interest in possession will be treated as having such an interest notwithstanding that the administration is not complete.[36] This provision means that if a variation effected within two years results in the termination of an interest in possession for the future only without disturbing the beneficiary's entitlement to income which has already accrued in the meantime, the disposition taking effect on the making of the variation will be treated as having taken effect on the death. The provision also means that where a short-term interest in possession is conferred by the variation, for example a short-term interest in favour of a surviving spouse to secure the application of the spouse exemption, such interest must endure for more than two years.[37] It is also provided by section 142(4) that the subsection is not to affect the application of the Act in relation to any distribution or application of property occurring before the termination of the short-term interest in possession. This rather obscure provision appears to mean that any distribution or application of capital already made by trustees under powers conferred by the will or the general law before the termination of the short-term interest in possession cannot be retrospectively varied for the purposes of section 142(1). If, however, the variation does not create a short-term interest in possession, intermediate distributions of capital can be varied.

Meaning of 'estate'

37.20 For the purposes of section 142 of the IHTA 1984 'estate' does not have its usual inheritance meaning but is modified[38] so as to include excluded property and to exclude settled property in which the deceased had an interest in possession[39] or property subject to reservation in which he was treated as having an interest in possession[40] immediately before his death. The section can apply to property, other than settled property, which does not pass under a deceased person's will or on his intestacy, for example joint property. It will also include property (not being settled property) over which the deceased has a general power of disposition,[41] for instance property passing under a nomination, but not settled property in which the deceased had an interest in possession and a general power of appointment by will. The exclusion of settled property means that the only relevant relieving provision in relation to settled property is the right of a beneficiary to disclaim an interest in it.[42] It is to be noted that if the settled property has vested

---

[36] IHTA 1984, s 91: see para 37.02 above.

[37] The Revenue view is that the use of the word 'results' in the subsection requires that the interest must be expressly limited to a fixed period not exceeding two years and that the subsection does not apply if the interest, though capable of enduring for longer, in fact ends within that period. If therefore in order to utilize the spouse exemption a variation confers on a surviving spouse an interest in possession in part of the testator's estate for a period in excess of two years, that interest will not be disregarded merely because the period is terminable or that it actually determines on her death within the two-year period.

[38] IHTA 1984, s 142(5).   [39] IHTA 1984, s 49(1).   [40] FA 1986, s 102.

[41] IHTA 1984, s 5(2).   [42] IHTA 1984, s 93.

absolutely, for example on the death of a life tenant, the absolutely entitled beneficiary will not be able to invoke this provision as the property will no longer be settled.

Variations before grant of probate or completion of administration

There is no requirement that probate of a will should have been obtained before a **37.21** variation is made; indeed it is often convenient for a variation to precede the grant of probate if it results in a reduction in the amount of inheritance tax payable on the death. Initially the Revenue did not accept that a variation could be made before the completion of the administration on the grounds that no beneficiary has an interest in unadministered estate.[43] However, a beneficiary possesses a chose in action, namely the right to have the estate duly administered, a right which is transmissible,[44] and the Revenue appears to have abandoned its initial opposition.

Double death variations

Where a beneficiary of the estate of a deceased person dies within two years it may **37.22** be desirable for his personal representatives and the beneficiaries of his estate to vary the dispositions of the deceased's estate. Where the deceased and the surviving beneficiary are husband and wife, such a variation may well be desirable to take advantage of the nil-rate band exemption on the death of the first to die and thereby avoid an unnecessarily large charge to tax on the joint estate on the death of the survivor. As has already been noted,[45] where spouses die in circumstances rendering it uncertain which of them survived the other, a significant inheritance tax saving will be made if the estate of the older spouse devolves on the younger. If the older spouse leaves no will or if his will does not already provide for this to happen, it may be possible to effect a variation producing this result.[46]

While double death variations are accepted as effective for inheritance tax pur- **37.23** poses, certain limitations should be noted. If, for example, the surviving beneficiary's interest is terminable on his death, for example if he is given a right to occupy a dwelling house belonging to the deceased and he dies before the variation is made, it will not be possible to extinguish his terminable interest by variation after his death and invoke section 142. This is because there is nothing left to give up or vary.[47]

---

[43] See para 37.02 above.   [44] *Re Leigh's Will Trusts* [1970] Ch 277.
[45] See para 37.05 above.
[46] It is essential that the estate is either given or treated by the variation as having been given *by will* for the scheme to be effective: see para 37.05 above.
[47] *Soutter's Executry v IRC* [2002] STC (SCD) 385 in which the executors, having fallen into 'the *Frankland* trap' (see para 37.34 below), unsuccessfully attempted to retrieve the situation in reliance on IHTA 1984, s 143.

37.24   It may possibly be otherwise if the interest is a life interest in a fund of investments and the variation operates as an assignment of the income accruing during the beneficiary's life since the deceased's death. Provided that the trust assets have produced some income, it cannot be said that the variation has no operative effect at all. But the moral is that where the surviving beneficiary has a limited interest which he wishes to extinguish, effect should be given to that wish as expeditiously as possible.

37.25   There is a further limitation. Section 142(1) requires the variation to be made by the persons who 'benefit'. The Revenue takes the view that this means the persons who are beneficiaries of the surviving beneficiary's estate. In other words it will not be sufficient if the personal representatives of the surviving beneficiary make the variation alone, even in cases where the administration of the surviving beneficiary's estate is incomplete and the legal and equitable interest in the surviving beneficiary's property is therefore vested in them.[48]

Fiscal consequences of variations and disclaimers

37.26   A variation or disclaimer falling within section 142 of the IHTA 1984 does not constitute a transfer of value on the part of the beneficiary making the variation or disclaiming the benefit[49] and also has the effect that for inheritance tax purposes the varied disposition is treated as effected by the deceased or the disclaimed benefit as never having been conferred. This means that if a beneficiary on whom the estate of a deceased devolves resettles it on discretionary trusts for the benefit of a class of which he is a member by way of a variation to which section 142 applies, the gift with reservation provisions[50] will not apply. It also means that if the deceased was not domiciled in the United Kingdom at the time of death but the beneficiary making the variation was, the property settled by the variation, so long as not situate in the United Kingdom, will be excluded property for inheritance tax purposes.[51]

37.27   There is no income tax provision corresponding with section 142. Accordingly a beneficiary who resettles property by way of a variation to which the section applies will be the settlor of the property so resettled for income tax purposes. It seems that the Revenue view is that income to which an unmarried minor child of the settlor is absolutely entitled is not paid to or applied for his benefit[52] and that under the earlier legislation it was therefore not taxable as the settlor's income. The consequence was that until recently the disclaimer of an interest in the estate of a deceased person by a beneficiary in favour of his minor children would result in the income of the property being treated as his children's for income tax purposes.[53]

---

[48] See para 37.02 above.   [49] IHTA 1984, s 17(a).   [50] FA 1986, s 102.
[51] IHTA 1984, s 48(3).   [52] Within what is now ICTA 1988, s 660B(1)(a).
[53] The hiatus has now been filled by statute: see ICTA 1988, s 660B(1)(b) (inserted by FA 1999, s 64(1), (5)).

By contrast there is a capital gains tax provision in terms similar to those of section **37.28** 142, namely section 62(6) of the Taxation of Chargeable Gains Act 1992.[54] This provision is, however, more limited in its effect. Whereas the effect of a variation under section 142 is that the varied disposition is treated for all the purposes of inheritance tax as made by the deceased, the varied disposition is treated for capital gains tax purposes as if effected by the deceased only for the purposes of section 62. This means that a donee who has assets transferred to him under the variation will be treated as receiving them 'as legatee' under section 62(4).[55] But for all other capital gains tax purposes, and in particular for the purpose of identifying the settlor of the property settled by the variation, the deeming provision does not apply and the beneficiary making the variation will be treated as settlor.[56]

Compliance with testator's request

Section 143 of the IHTA 1984 provides as follows: **37.29**

> Where a testator expresses a wish that property bequeathed by his will should be transferred by the legatee to other persons, and the legatee transfers the property in accordance with that wish within two years of the death of the testator, this Act shall have effect as if the property transferred had been bequeathed by the will to the transferee.

This section was probably designed to give inheritance tax relief in cases where the donee of personal chattels is given a discretion to dispose of them in accordance with the deceased's known wishes. Curiously, the section is not confined to personal chattels but extends to 'property bequeathed', an imprecise phrase which suggests, however, that personal property of any kind is included.[57] The section does not prescribe the manner in which the testator should communicate his wishes and wishes expressed orally appear to suffice. As the references to 'testator' and 'will' indicate, its operation is confined to gifts by will. It has been held that 'legatee' does not include a trustee and that the section does not overlap with section 144[58] and is confined to cases in which the property is given to a donee personally and not in a fiduciary capacity.[59] Distributions of property made within two years automatically attract the operation of the section. Such distributions are not transfers of value for inheritance tax purposes.[60]

---

[54] See also TCGA 1992, s 62(10).
[55] And will thus be deemed to acquire them at their value on death.
[56] *Marshall v Kerr* [1995] 1 AC 148, HL.
[57] Cf *Re Beatty decd* [1990] 1 WLR 1503 in which the exercise of a power conferred on trustees to distribute personal chattels and a legacy of £1.5m in accordance with the wishes of the testatrix 'of which they shall be aware' was upheld.   [58] See para 37.30 *et seq* below.
[59] *Harding v IRC* [1997] STC (SCD) 321.   [60] IHTA 1984, s 17(b).

Distribution etc from property settled by will

37.30   Section 144 of the IHTA 1984 provides as follows:

(1) This section applies where property comprised in a person's estate immediately before his death is settled by his will and, within the period of two years after his death and before any interest in possession has subsisted in the property, there occurs—

  (a) an event on which tax would (apart from this section) be chargeable under any provision, other than section 64 or 79, of Chapter III of Part III of this Act, or

  (b) an event on which tax would be so chargeable but for section 75 or 76 above or paragraph 16(1) of Schedule 4 to this Act.

(2) Where this section applies by virtue of an event within paragraph *(a)* of subsection (1) above, tax shall not be charged under the provision in question on that event; and in every case in which this section applies in relation to an event, this Act shall have effect as if the will had provided that on the testator's death the property should be held as it is held after the event.

37.31   The section in effect provides that where property is settled by will on discretionary trusts, during the two-year period following the testator's death no charge to inheritance tax will arise, other than a charge under section 64 (under which a periodic charge may arise where the interest settled was subject to discretionary trusts prior to the death) or section 79 (which imposes a charge where exemption from the periodic charge has been obtained in relation to works of art comprised in a settlement and a chargeable event occurs). The events mentioned in section 144(1)(b)[61] are events on which property ceases to be relevant property but without an exit charge arising.

37.32   Section 144 applies where 'property comprised in a person's estate immediately before his death is settled by his will'. These words restrict the scope of the section to property which the testator has power to dispose of by will. The word 'estate' is not otherwise modified by the section which, unlike section 142, therefore extends to settled property in which the testator had an interest in possession and over which he has a general testamentary power of appointment which he exercises by his will so as to make the settled property part of his estate.

37.33   It was originally the Revenue view that where a deceased person's estate was settled by will on discretionary trusts his trustees could not exercise their power of appointment until probate had been granted, the administration was complete,

---

[61]   ie a distribution to an employee trust (s 75), to a charitable trust (s 76), or to a maintenance fund (Sch 4, § 16(1)).

and the trusts constituted. This view has been relaxed[62] and the Revenue appear to accept the validity of an appointment or distribution where the will expressly authorizes the executors to exercise their power before the grant of probate and before the administration is complete.

Where section 144 applies, it operates for inheritance tax purposes both to relieve the appointed or applied property from any exit charge and also to treat the trusts then taking effect as having taken effect on the testator's death. The exit charge would probably not be very large and on the whole the latter consequence is more significant as it enables the testator's trustees to appoint trusts in favour of a surviving spouse or charity which will operate so as to exempt the property so appointed from inheritance tax on the testator's death. One particular hazard of section 144 ('the *Frankland* trap') is that it only applies if the occasion on which the property ceases to be relevant property would (but for the section) have resulted in a charge to inheritance tax. No exit charge arises on a distribution occurring during the first quarter following the commencement of the settlement.[63] If therefore the testator's residuary estate is held on discretionary trusts and the trustees exercise their power of appointment in favour of the testator's spouse within three months of his death, the section will not apply and the spouse exemption will not apply.[64] To guard against the risk of a premature exercise the will should expressly provide that no powers of appointment or application are capable of being exercised before the expiration of three months following the death. **37.34**

Redemption of surviving spouse's life interest

Under section 47A of the Administration of Estates Act 1925[65] the surviving spouse of a person dying intestate has the right to elect to have his or her life interest in the intestate's residuary estate capitalized. This election is to be made within twelve months of the grant of probate but the court has power to extend time.[66] The rules for calculating the capital sum are contained in tables scheduled to the Intestate Succession (Interest and Capitalisation) Order 1977.[67] **37.35**

Section 145 of the IHTA 1984 provides that where an election is made under section 47A of the 1925 Act, the IHTA 1984 is to apply as if the surviving spouse, instead of being entitled to the life interest, had been entitled to a sum equal to the capital value mentioned in section 47A. This provision applies automatically if an election is made and does not impose a time limit within which the election must be made. Its effect is that the surviving spouse is treated as not having made **37.36**

---

[62] See para 37.21 above.   [63] IHTA 1984, s 65(4).
[64] *Frankland v IRC* [1997] STC 1450, CA.
[65] As amended by the AJA 1977, s 32, Sch 5, Pt VI.   [66] AEA 1925, s 47A(5).
[67] SI 1977/491 made under powers conferred by AEA 1925, s 47A(2), (3).

a transfer of value[68] and that there is no charge to inheritance tax on the termination of the life interest. A consequence is that the spouse exemption on the intestate's death will no longer extend to the entirety of the fund in which the life interest subsisted but will be limited to the value of the capital sum.

Family provision

37.37   The Inheritance (Provision for Family and Dependants) Act 1975 confers a wide jurisdiction on the court to make orders in favour of a deceased person's dependants that reasonable financial provision be made out of his estate. A detailed consideration of this Act is outside the scope of this work but certain tax considerations should be noted. First, section 19(1) provides that where an order under the Act is made, then for all purposes, 'including the purposes of capital transfer tax' the will or the rules of intestate succession as they apply to the estate are to have effect subject to the order. In effect therefore the terms of an order will be read back to the death for the purposes of all forms of tax, a consequence which is replicated for the purposes of inheritance tax by section 146(1) of the IHTA 1984. If therefore a surviving spouse makes a successful application for provision, the order may result in a reduction in the amount of inheritance tax payable on the deceased's death.

37.38   Many claims for provision are settled. The 1975 Act does not in terms cater for consent orders. By contrast section 146(8) of the IHTA 1984 expressly provides that where an order is made staying or dismissing proceedings under the 1975 Act on terms set out in or scheduled to the order, section 146 is to have effect as if the consent order were an order under the 1975 Act. This provision gives considerable scope for the settlement of claims by surviving spouses on terms which take advantage of the spouse exemption. Claims by spouses are frequently compromised on terms which take advantage of the exemption despite the judicial observation that where the effect of the order is to confer a substantial advantage on the parties at the expense of the Revenue the court should be satisfied that the order is not only within its jurisdiction but that it is also one which may properly be made.[69]

37.39   There is no provision in the income tax and capital gains tax legislation which corresponds with section 146(8). However, the same result can be achieved, at any rate in cases where minor or unborn beneficiaries are involved and the court's

---

[68] IHTA 1984, s 17(c).
[69] *Re Goodchild decd* [1997] 1 WLR 1216, 1231, *per* Morritt LJ, CA.

approval to the compromise is required, by inviting the court to exercise its jurisdiction and make an order in the manner proposed rather than simply staying the
proceedings on agreed terms in a Tomlin order.[70] Such an order is thought to be
an 'order' for the purposes of section 19(1) of the 1975 Act and therefore to have
effect for all tax purposes.

---

[70] ie a form of consent order reciting the agreement of the parties to settle proceedings on terms
set out in a schedule and staying the proceedings save for the purpose of enforcing the agreed terms
for which purposes the parties are given liberty to apply. This form of order is named after Tomlin J
who settled it in its current form: *Practice Direction* [1927] WN 290.

Part G

INTERNATIONAL TRUSTS

38

OFFSHORE ASSET PROTECTION TRUSTS

A. Offshore Trusts[1]

'Offshore trusts' (sometimes misleadingly called 'international trusts') are the increasingly novel creations produced in various 'offshore' financial centres, of which there are said to be around 45 at present. 'Offshore' is not a technical term. Although many offshore centres are located in the Caribbean, they are found all over the world—in the Isle of Man, the Channel Islands, various Pacific Islands, and also in several 'onshore' locations, such as Alaska and Delaware, Nevada and Rhode Island, and various Latin American countries such as Venezuela and Panama. In broad terms, they are all simply jurisdictions which have deliberately set out to create and develop a financial services industry catering for, and specializing in, the financial, business, and investment needs of individual and corporate clients domiciled and resident in other jurisdictions. Specific, tailor-made offshore trusts legislation has been enacted, whose overall aim and purpose is to enable owners of property to do things in the relevant offshore jurisdiction that they could not accomplish at home.

38.01

Offshore trusts are created for a wide range of purposes, of which the most common include the avoidance of taxation in the domestic forum (although this has become

38.02

---

[1] See, generally, J Glasson, *The International Trust* (Jordans, 2002) and esp the overview by D Waters in Ch 14: J Glasson (ed), *International Trust Laws* (Jordans, loose-leaf). See also [1996] Private Client Business 226 (Part I) and 302 (Part II) (P Willoughby).

increasingly difficult, especially for US citizens); the avoidance of forced heirship laws—something which has traditionally been catered for by the classic English trust;[2] or as a substitute for prenuptial contracts and to minimize the impact of the 'community of property' regimes of certain states (like California). The two most popular purposes—and certainly the ones that have had the greatest impact on the law of trusts—are asset protection and the creation of non-charitable purpose trusts as commercial vehicles.

38.03   This chapter will focus on asset protection trusts and the following chapter will deal with non-charitable purpose trusts. In each case, there is an introduction to the particular topic, followed by a brief overview of the ways in which offshore legislation has attempted to deal with specific problems, and then by a more detailed examination of the specific provisions adopted by some of the main offshore jurisdictions. There is then a third chapter dealing specifically with the unique STAR trust of the Cayman Islands: this is dealt with separately because it is a peculiar form of trust, intended to be of general utility and not limited to any specific purpose, whether it be asset protection or for non-charitable purposes.

B. Offshore Asset Protection Trusts[3]

38.04   The preservation of wealth and providing protection against creditors have long been among the primary uses of trusts. Many of these concerns could be met by means of tried and tested methods within the client's home jurisdiction, for example, by incorporation, transfers of assets to a spouse (which is itself a risky strategy in view of prevailing divorce rates), or even by means of discretionary trust. However, in many jurisdictions—England and Wales and the USA among them[4]—there are specific provisions which are designed to prevent a person from transferring or disposing of assets in order to defeat or defraud the claims of creditors or, where any such disposition has been made, to enable a creditor to have it set aside. The scope of such provisions, the readiness with which the courts have

---

[2] Even in England, where freedom of testation is a basic norm, the Inheritance (Provision for Family and Dependants) Act 1975 enables specified categories of claimants to apply to the court for reasonable financial provision from the estate of a deceased person—and the Act contains special provisions to prevent avoidance.

[3] This section is based on GW Thomas, 'Asset Protection Trusts' (being Chapter 7 (337–478) of J Glasson (ed), *The International Trust* (Jordans, 2002)).

[4] In England, the Insolvency Act 1986. In the USA, the 'fraudulent conveyance' law of some States is derived from the Statute of Eliz I (1572), whereas other States have adopted a version of the Uniform Fraudulent Conveyance Act and the Uniform Fraudulent Transfers Act 1984. In addition, at a federal level, there are additional provisions, including the Bankruptcy Code 1976, the Money Laundering Control Act 1986, the Internal Revenue Code 1986, the Financial Institutions Reform, Recovery and Enforcement Act 1989, and the Crime Control Act 1990.

interpreted and applied them in favour of creditors, and the fact that many of them apply irrespective of the transferor's bankruptcy, pose serious obstacles to anyone who wishes to safeguard assets against potential creditors. As we have seen,[5] in England, the Insolvency Act 1986 now governs 'transactions at an undervalue', but English law has been 'pro-creditor', as opposed to 'pro-debtor', for centuries. Although the relevant bankruptcy provisions can be traced back to the mid-nineteenth century, the more far-reaching, and even draconian, provisions that applied independently of bankruptcy can be traced back to a statute of Elizabeth I in 1571 (13 Eliz I, c 5), and beyond.

The two most significant English statutory provisions prior to the Insolvency Act **38.05** 1986 were section 172 of the Law of Property Act 1925 (based largely on the 1571 Statute) and section 42 of the Bankruptcy Act 1914.[6] Establishing an 'intent to defraud' was central to both the 1571 Statute and section 172(1) of the 1925 Act and a large body of case law developed around the meaning and extent of this requirement, how it was to be established, and upon whom the burden of proof lay.[7] In particular, these statutes were construed widely so as to protect future or subsequent, unascertained creditors and it was not necessary that a settlor should actually be indebted at the time he created a settlement.[8] Section 172 was not subject to any time limit and applied irrespective of bankruptcy. Section 42(1) of the Bankruptcy Act 1914, on the other hand, provided for the setting aside of settlements created by someone who was subsequently declared bankrupt. It imposed fixed time limits: a settlement was automatically void as against a trustee in bankruptcy if the settlor became bankrupt within two years of the creation; after two years and within ten years of that date, it was void only if the beneficiaries failed to establish one of the exceptions specified in the section; and, after the expiry of the ten-year period, section 42 ceased to apply to the settlement. Unlike section 172, section 42 did not require an intent to defraud to be established. These provisions severely restricted the scope for disposing of property so as to avoid the claims of creditors. As we have seen, the Insolvency Act 1986 (which has replaced these earlier provisions) has maintained this policy and, if anything, has made asset protection even more difficult to attain.

These older English statutes also form the basis of almost identical legislation **38.06** in several overseas jurisdictions. For example, in the context of bankruptcy,

---

[5] See paras 9.21–9.53 above.
[6] For a detailed description and discussion of the relevant pre-1925 (English) law, being the provisions of the 1571 Statute (13 Eliz I, c 5), s 42 of the Bankruptcy Act 1914 and s 172 of the Law of Property Act 1925. See GW Thomas, *op cit,* 338–370.
[7] See, for example, *Lloyds Bank Ltd v Marcan* [1973] 1 WLR 339. Various 'badges of fraud' were laid down, originally in *Twyne's Case* (1602) 3 Co Rep 80b.
[8] See, for example, *Stileman v Ashdown* (1742) 2 Atk 477; *Holmes v Penney* (1856) 3 K & J 90; *Crossley v Elworthy* (1871) LR 12 Eq 158; *Freeman v Pope* (1870) 5 Ch App 538; *Mackay v Douglas* (1872) LR 14 Eq 106; *Re Butterworth* (1882) 19 Ch D 588; *Re Wise* (1886) 17 QBD 290.

section 71 of the Bahamian Bankruptcy Act 1870 is similar to section 91 of the English Bankruptcy Act 1869 (and applies, as did the 1869 Act, only to 'traders'); section 45(1) of the Bermudian Bankruptcy Act 1989 and section 107 of the Cayman Islands' Bankruptcy Law (Revised) are similar to section 42 of the English Bankruptcy Act 1914 (save that, in Bermuda, there is a more lenient time limit of five rather than ten years). In relation to the setting aside of transactions intended to defraud creditors (irrespective of bankruptcy), each of the Australian states has legislation based on the 1571 Statute of Elizabeth I (where an 'intent to defraud' is central) and English case law on the 1571 Statute and section 172 of the English Law of Property Act 1925 has been followed; section 149 of the Belize Law of Property Act and section 81 of the British Virgin Islands' Conveyancing and Law of Property Act are also similar to section 172. Similar provisions are also in force in Gibraltar, Guernsey, Hong Kong, and New Zealand.

38.07 Several offshore centres have introduced legislation to counteract the restrictions imposed by English and US law and which is deliberately designed to be 'pro-debtor', by encouraging and making specific provision for the creation of asset protection trusts. The precise terms of such legislation varies from jurisdiction to jurisdiction, but, in broad terms, the intention is to provide a settlor with a high degree of protection from or against claims by future unidentified creditors. In many jurisdictions, such protection is afforded only to 'foreign' settlors or debtors, and, for their own domestic purposes, many have retained their original, English-based restrictive legislation. In any event, the purpose, as well as the typical form and scope, of this new legislation tends to be explicable only by reference to the old, English-based statutes which it seeks to counter and to the problems to which the 'old' law gave rise.

38.08 In its simplest form, an asset protection trust consists of little more than a bank account held by trustees in a jurisdiction which does not recognize or assist in enforcing the judgments of the debtor's domestic forum, thereby forcing the creditor to bring his claim, *de novo*, in the more hostile offshore location. More complex strategies include dividing the relevant assets between underlying companies (and, in the USA, family limited partnerships) and transferring them out of the domestic jurisdiction. The basic aim is not necessarily to ensure that assets remain completely invulnerable to attack from creditors, but to discourage and hinder claims made by creditors, and thereby encourage early settlement on terms favourable to the debtor. The choice of offshore jurisdiction for a particular transaction is, therefore, crucial. It must obviously have favourable (and preferably sophisticated) asset protection legislation, which must include appropriate rules about recognition and enforcement of foreign judgments, as well as a sympathetic judiciary. It must have political stability, sophisticated and reliable local financial and legal services, international banking services, favourable tax laws, modern telecommunications facilities, and probably physical accessibility and no language barriers. Needless to say, specialist legal and financial advice from those with expertise in, and familiarity with, the offshore world in general, and asset protection in particular, are clearly essential. Otherwise, the entire transaction may unravel and fail, sometimes many years after it was entered into.[9]

General survey of asset protection provisions[10]

The general approach is not to prohibit creditors from trying to set aside disposi-   **38.09**
tions into a trust: rather, it is a matter of making life very much more difficult for them. In the Bahamas, for example, the burden of proving an intent to defraud lies on the creditor seeking to set aside the disposition, which means that he has to prove that the transferor 'wilfully' intended to defeat an obligation owed to the creditor. There is also a two-year time limit: the creditor must commence proceedings within two years of the date of the relevant disposition. Even if he were to succeed, the disposition would be set aside only to the extent necessary to satisfy the obligation owed to that creditor: the entire disposition will not necessarily be set aside and the success of one creditor will not enure for the benefit of another. There are also other provisions to safeguard any distributions made from the trust to a beneficiary.

Similarly, in the Cook Islands, a creditor can have a disposition to an 'international   **38.10**
trust' set aside only if he can prove (and the burden is on the creditor) beyond reasonable doubt (so it is a high standard) that the settlor intended to defraud him (and not some other creditor), and, indeed, that this was also the settlor's 'principal intent'. Again, there is a two-year time limit for bringing proceedings.

Other jurisdictions have adopted a similar anti-creditor approach, thereby   **38.11**
effectively reversing the position in England. In addition, if an effective creditor-proof trust is to be created, confidentiality becomes a crucial factor. If the creditor is denied access to information about the trust—who created it, who put money into it, what and where its assets are, who controls them, and what has happened

---

[9] For a useful survey of the difficulties that may arise (particularly from an ill-considered use of offshore legislation) see [1996] Private Client Business 226 and 302 (P Willoughby). See also *Re Stephen Jay Lawrence* (2002) 5 ITELR 1 for a salutary lesson in the consequences of a settlor retaining too much control over his trust.
[10] In recent years, 'offshore' jurisdictions have been subjected to a series of investigations and criticism: see, in particular, the Financial Stability Forum's *Report of the Working Group on Offshore Centres* (available at www.fsforum.org.uk); the Financial Action Task Force's *Review to Identify Non-Cooperative Countries or Territories* (available at www.oecd.org/fatf); the OECD's Reports entitled *Harmful Tax Competition* (1998) and *Towards Global Tax Cooperation* (2000) (both available at www.oecd.org); Andrew Edwards, *Review of Financial Regulation in the Crown Dependencies* (Cmnd 4109); (1999) 3 Jersey LR 22 (Powell); [1999] Private Client Business 345 (Hay). Although these investigations focus, as their titles suggest, on financial stability and tax issues, their effect has been to make several offshore jurisdictions somewhat nervous about their activities and products; and this may well introduce a note of caution into their application of their legislation dealing with asset protection trusts.

to them—then life becomes very difficult indeed for him, if not impossible. Several of the offshore statutes therefore have enacted stringent provisions to ensure and protect the confidentiality of matters relating to the trust.

C. Asset Protection Legislation of Specific Jurisdictions

The Bahamas

38.12 Section 71 of the Bahamian Bankruptcy Act is identical to section 42 of the English Bankruptcy Act 1914 (including the same two-year and ten-year time limits, and subject to the same exceptions) but, unlike section 42, section 71 expressly applies only to 'traders' (as did section 91 of the English Bankruptcy Act 1869). However, the Fraudulent Dispositions Act 1991 ('FDA' 1991) came into effect on 5 April 1991 ('the appointed date')[11] and replaced 'the law in effect prior to the appointed date'.[12] The previous law was the same as English law—ie any disposition made with intent to defraud creditors was void—and English case law was followed. The FDA 1991, however, seeks to strike a fairer balance between the protection of assets and the protection of creditors. Its main purpose is to avoid the situation where a person's assets are held subject to possible claims by creditors who are entirely unknown to him and whose identity cannot seriously be within his contemplation.[13]

38.13 The FDA 1991 applies, with effect from the appointed date, to every disposition of property made after the appointed date by any person, and whether or not the property which is the subject matter of the disposition is situate in The Bahamas or elsewhere.[14] Subject to the provisions of the FDA 1991, every disposition of property made 'with an intent to defraud and at an undervalue shall be voidable at the instance of a creditor thereby prejudiced'.[15] A 'disposition', for these purposes, means 'any disposition or series thereof, however effected, and (without prejudice to the generality thereof) includes any transaction, gift, grant or transfer of property of any nature whatsoever'.[16] The word 'property' is not defined anywhere (not even by reference to another statute);[17] but it seems safe to assume that it encompasses every kind of property, including cash. An 'intent to defraud' means 'an intention of a transferor *wilfully* to defeat an obligation owed to a creditor'.[18] An 'obligation' is defined as 'an obligation or liability (which shall include a contingent liability) which existed on or prior to the date of a relevant disposition

---

[11] The Fraudulent Dispositions Act 1991 ('FDA'), ss 1(2), 2.   [12] ibid, s 3(1).
[13] In fact, neither the 1571 Act nor the LPA 1925, s 172, was ever wide enough to assist a subsequent creditor who could not be seriously within the debtor's contemplation.
[14] FDA 1991, s 3(1).   [15] ibid, s 4(1).   [16] ibid, s 2.
[17] Such as, eg, the Trusts (Choice of Governing Law) Act 1989, s 2.
[18] FDA 1991, s 2 (emphasis added).

and of which the transferor had *actual* notice'.[19] The disposition must also be made at an 'undervalue', which means that either no consideration was provided for it or the value of such consideration as was provided for the disposition was 'significantly less' than the value of the property which was the subject matter of the disposition.[20] A 'creditor' means, quite simply, 'a person to whom an obligation is owed'.[21]

The burden of establishing an intent to defraud for the purposes of the FDA 1991 **38.14** lies on the creditor seeking to set aside the disposition.[22] In any event, no action or proceedings can be commenced under the Act unless commenced within two years of the date of the relevant disposition.[23]

Thus, the FDA 1991 departs materially from (pre- and post-1986) English law in **38.15** some crucial aspects. It is true that the obligation owed to the creditor may not only be an accrued liability (such as a debt the date for payment of which has already passed, or a final award of damages which has already been made but not yet satisfied) but it may also be a contingent liability—and, thus far, this accords with the pre-1986 and existing English law. However, the relevant liability (contingent or otherwise) must be one which already exists on or prior to the date of the relevant disposition. In this respect, the FDA 1991 clearly restricts the range of creditors who may seek to set aside that disposition. Moreover, the additional requirement that the transferor must also have had actual notice of the relevant obligation or liability makes the creditor's task even harder.

Precisely what constitutes a 'contingent' liability is not made clear in the Act. **38.16** However, it seems clear that it includes, for example, a debt (or liability) which has actually been incurred—and is known by the transferor to have been incurred— but which is not repayable (or to be discharged otherwise) until some future date. On the other hand, a transferor who makes a disposition of property immediately before entering upon a trading venture or other hazardous activity would seem not to be caught by the Act: although it may still be accurate to categorize his liabilities to his future creditors (say, suppliers of goods and services) as 'contingent' liabilities (as in *Re Butterworth*[24] and associated cases), such liabilities will not exist on or prior to the date of the disposition and, therefore, the transferor will not have actual knowledge of them unless and until they are actually incurred.

Similarly, if any obligations are owed at the date of the disposition, but they are all **38.17** subsequently discharged, it is impossible for anyone who became a creditor thereafter to seek to have the disposition set aside under the FDA 1991. Indeed, it would also seem that, where a transferor may have committed a tort (say, some act

---

[19] ibid, (emphasis added).   [20] ibid.   [21] ibid.   [22] ibid, s 4(2).
[23] ibid, s 4(3). A 'relevant disposition' means a disposition to which s 4(1) applies.
[24] (1882) 19 Ch D 588.

of medical negligence) prior to the date of the relevant disposition, but in respect of which no writ had been issued and no notice of any impending claim had been given before that date, the victim who subsequently obtains judgment would encounter great difficulty in his attempt to have the disposition set aside: either the transferor was not under any liability—actual or contingent—to anyone at the relevant time or, alternatively, he did not have actual notice of any such liability.[25] Whether the same would be true of a transferor who had already been notified of an impending claim (although no proceedings had yet been commenced)—or even one who made the relevant disposition in circumstances in which it was obvious to him that he had committed a tort or other actionable wrong and was clearly at risk of being sued—is less clear, but prudence would suggest that any disposition made in such circumstances should be assumed to be vulnerable under the terms of the Act.

38.18 There is no intent to defraud, for the purposes of the FDA 1991, unless the transferor 'wilfully' intended to defeat an obligation owed to a creditor. In other words, it appears that, even if a creditor can establish the existence of an obligation within the compass of the statute, this alone will not be sufficient: he must also establish that the transferor wilfully made the disposition which he seeks to set aside in order to defeat that obligation. In broad terms, the word 'wilfully' implies that a person 'knows what he is doing, and intends to do what he is doing, and is a free agent',[26] although, of course, the precise meaning can vary according to the particular context. In the context of the FDA 1991, it seems clear that the word implies that the transferor must *deliberately* and *knowingly*[27] intend to defeat an obligation to his creditor, and it would not be sufficient, for example, if he acted under an honest mistake, by accident, or inadvertently.[28] Therefore, the word seems to connote dishonesty.[29] Mere indebtedness at the time of the disposition would not, by itself, be sufficient grounds on which it could be impeached. Nor could an intent to defraud be imputed or inferred on the basis that the transferor must be presumed to have intended the natural consequences of his own acts.[30] Such factors—presumably along with the traditional 'badges of fraud'[31]—may

---

[25] cf the English cases of *Barling v Bishopp* (1860) 29 Beav 417; *Crossley v Elworthy* (1871) LR 12 Eq 158; and *Re Wise* (1886) 17 QBD 290.

[26] cf *Re Young and Harston's Contract* (1885) 31 Ch D 168, 175, *per* Bowen LJ. See also *Lomas v Peck* [1947] 2 All ER 574, 575, *per* Lord Goddard CJ: 'If a man permits a thing to be done, it means that he gives permission for it to be done, and if a man gives permission for a thing to be done, he knows what is to be done or is being done, and, if he knows that, it follows that it is wilful.'

[27] cf *Re Senior* [1899] 1 QB 283, esp 290–291; *Hall v Jordan* [1947] 1 All ER 826; *Re Piche* (1967) 10 Cr LQ 107.

[28] cf *Smith v Barnham* (1876) 1 Ex D 419; *Graham v Belfast & Northern Counties Railway* [1901] 2 Ir R 19.

[29] cf *Lloyds Bank Ltd v Marcan* [1973] 1 WLR 339, 1392, *per* Cairns LJ.

[30] See GW Thomas, *op cit*, 353–355.

[31] ibid 345–347; and *Twyne's Case* (1602) 3 Co Rep 80b.

well still be relevant as items of evidence adduced in support of an allegation of wilful conduct on the part of the transferor, but they are clearly not sufficient or conclusive in themselves.

Thus, by way of summary, in order to set aside a disposition under the FDA 1991, **38.19** a creditor must prove that:

(a) the transferor owed him an obligation (ie that he is a creditor);
(b) not only did the obligation or liability exist on or before the date of the disposition but also the transferor then[32] had actual knowledge of it;
(c) the disposition was made at an undervalue; and
(d) the transferor made the disposition wilfully in order to defeat his obligations to the creditor.

The creditor must also bring proceedings within two years of the date of the disposition.

It will probably be very difficult for any creditor to satisfy all these requirements.[33] **38.20** If he does succeed in doing so, the disposition shall be set aside under the FDA 1991, but only to the extent necessary to satisfy the obligation owed to that creditor (ie 'the creditor at whose instance the disposition had been set aside') together with such costs as the court may allow.[34] In other words, the entire disposition will not necessarily be set aside; and the success of one creditor will not enure for the benefit of another.

Moreover, even in the event that a disposition is set aside, there is a measure of pro- **38.21** tection for the transferee (ie 'the person to whom a relevant disposition is made' and any successor in title).[35] Section 5(1) of the Act provides that, in that event, unless the court is satisfied that the transferee 'has acted in bad faith', the transferee shall have a first and paramount charge over the property which is the subject matter of the disposition, of an amount equal to the entire costs properly incurred by the transferee in the defence of the action or proceedings to set aside (and not merely such costs as might otherwise be allowed by the court); and the relevant disposition shall be set aside subject to the proper fees, costs, pre-existing rights, claims, and interests of the transferee (and of any predecessor transferee which has not acted in bad faith).

Moreover, unless the court is satisfied that a beneficiary of a trust has acted in bad **38.22** faith, the disposition shall only be set aside subject to the right of such a

---

[32] The word 'then' does not appear in the definition of 'obligation', but it seems clear that this is intended to be the time at which the transferor 'had' actual notice.
[33] See, however, *The Private Trust Corporation v Grupo Torras SA* (1997/98) 1 OFLR 443 (Court of Appeal of The Bahamas).
[34] FDA 1991, s 6.   [35] ibid, s 2.

beneficiary to retain any distribution made consequent upon the prior exercise of a trust, power, or discretion vested in the trustee of such trust or any other person, and otherwise properly exercised. Thus, it appears that a distribution to a beneficiary by trustees who are themselves acting in bad faith could not be set aside or prejudiced, provided the beneficiary himself is not also acting in bad faith.

38.23   However, the trust, power, or discretion must also be 'otherwise properly exercised'. Thus, a fraudulent exercise of a power by trustees (in the sense of a 'fraud on a power'), for example an appointment to a beneficiary on condition that he transfers the appointed property to a non-object, would not be validated under section 5(1)(b); and the property thus fraudulently appointed could be set aside by the court. The burden of proving that a transferee or beneficiary has acted in bad faith again lies on the person making the allegation.[36]

38.24   Precisely what constitutes 'bad faith' for these purposes is unclear. In some contexts, the words 'in good faith' have been construed to mean 'not only the absence of notice, but genuine and honest absence of notice'.[37] In other contexts, they have been construed as meaning 'honestly and with no ulterior motive'.[38] In either case, there seems to be a requirement of honesty; and it might therefore be argued that, in section 5 of the FDA 1991, the expression 'bad faith' requires the claiming creditor to prove that the transferee or beneficiary had acted 'dishonestly' and was not simply an 'honestly blundering and careless' individual. However, this does not necessarily require proof of actual conscious and deliberate dishonesty. As Lord Blackburn stated in *Jones v Gordon*:[39]

> if the facts and circumstances are such that the jury, or whoever has to try the question, came to the conclusion that he was not honestly blundering and careless, but that he must have had a suspicion that there was something wrong, and that he refrained from asking questions, not because he was an honest blunderer or a stupid man, but because he thought in his own secret mind—I suspect there is something wrong, and if I ask questions and make farther enquiries, it will no longer be my suspecting it, but my knowing it, and then I shall not be able to recover—I think that is dishonesty.

Thus, actual knowledge on the part of a transferee or beneficiary (as opposed to a transferor) may not be required; and wilfully closing one's eyes to the obvious, or even refraining from pursuing one's suspicions, may be sufficient to constitute 'bad faith'.

38.25   It seems clear from the definition of 'transferee', which includes not only the person to whom a relevant disposition is made but also any successor in title,[40] that

---

[36] FDA 1991, s 5(2).

[37] See, eg, *Midland Bank Trust Co v Green* [1981] AC 513, 528, *per* Lord Wilberforce.

[38] See, eg, *Smith v Morrison* [1974] 1 WLR 659; *Central Estates (Belgravia) Ltd v Woolgar* [1972] 1 QB 48.

[39] (1877) 2 App Cas 616, 629. See also *Tatam v Haslar* (1889) 23 QBD 345; and also GW Thomas, *op cit*, 402–408.

[40] FDA 1991, s 2.

any 'bad faith' on the part of a transferee need not be shown to relate to, or exist at the date of, the relevant disposition itself, but that it may be present at any subsequent time. Thus, for example, the transferee could lose the limited protection accorded by section 5(1)(a) not only in a case where, with full knowledge of the transferor's circumstances and obligations, he colluded with the transferor in making the relevant disposition which gave effect to the latter's intent to defraud creditors,[41] but also in the case where the transferee subsequently committed some act—such as the exercise of a power or discretion whereby property which was the subject matter of the disposition was distributed to a beneficiary—with a deliberate intent to defeat (or perhaps even unduly delay) a creditor seeking to have the disposition set aside.

However, it is not clear whether the court must be satisfied that the transferee or **38.26** beneficiary has acted in 'bad faith' (whichever way it is construed, and irrespective of the time at which he may have so acted) in relation to the particular creditor who succeeded in having the disposition set aside or whether it is sufficient that he has done so in relation to some other creditor (or anyone else). Suppose, for example, that a transferee-trustee knowingly and deliberately colluded with the transferor in defrauding Creditor A, but the disposition was subsequently set aside at the instance of Creditor B. Is the transferee deprived of the protection accorded by section 5 on the basis that he acted in bad faith towards Creditor A, or must the court be satisfied that he acted in bad faith towards Creditor B? The provisions of section 6 (which would limit the avoidance of the disposition only to the extent necessary to satisfy the obligation owed to Creditor B) might suggest that bad faith in relation to Creditor B must be established. On the other hand, sections 5 and 6 are clearly aimed at different ends. Section 6 simply ensures that the benefit of setting aside the relevant disposition accrues only to Creditor B, but section 5 could affect the amount which Creditor B might be able to recover; and, in such circumstances, it might be said to be unreasonable that the transferee-trustee is protected by his bad faith towards Creditor A.

Section 7(a) of the FDA 1991 declares that nothing in the Act shall validate any **38.27** disposition of property which is neither owned by the transferor nor the subject of a power in that behalf vested in the transferor. This is self-evident and merely declaratory. Reliance on the FDA 1991 is clearly not required in order to impeach a purported disposition of property which does not belong to the transferor, or over which he has no lawful power of disposition. An 'intent to defraud' is defined by reference to the intent of a 'transferor'; and a 'transferor' is defined in terms of ownership of (or holding of a power over) property.[42] In *The Private Trust*

---

[41] It must be remembered that the provisions of s 5 come into operation only when a disposition has been set aside, ie after the requisite intent to defraud has been established.

[42] FDA 1991, s 2.

Corporation v Grupo Torras SA,[43] the appellant (PTC) was the trustee of a Bahamian trust of which Sheikh Fahad Al Sabah was the 'primary beneficiary'. The respondents were alleging, in proceedings in England, that the Sheikh had defrauded them of approximately US$450 million while he was employed in their London office. The English court had granted a worldwide injunction against the Sheikh. In the course of the English proceedings, a connection was discovered between the Sheikh and the Bahamian trust. The respondents sought, and were granted, a *Mareva* injunction against the appellants in The Bahamas and an order for discovery. The Bahamian Court of Appeal, dismissing the appellant's appeal, held that the terms of the trust and the circumstances justified an assumption that the Sheikh had substantial and effective control over the trust funds. A *Mareva* injunction and an order for discovery were calculated to discover and immobilize the trust assets and would therefore be upheld.

38.28   It is not at all clear why the court came to this conclusion. It may have been because, on the evidence, there was a strong prima facie case that the Sheikh had purported to create a trust with someone else's money which he had acquired through fraud, ie he fell squarely within section 7(a) of the FDA 1991 (which was not in fact referred to). Consequently, the alleged trust would be void and the trustee, having notice of the alleged fraud, would hold the trust assets on constructive trusts for the true owner. If this were the case, however, the provisions of the trust (including the flee clause) would have had no effect, and would not have required the detailed consideration which the court gave them. Much the greater part of the judgment is devoted to an examination of the specific terms of the trust, for example the fact that the trustee's discretion to invest was subject to the prior consent of the settlor; that the trustee had power to add to the class of beneficiaries, subject to the prior consent of the protector; and that the power to appoint the original protector (but not successors) was vested in the Sheikh. In the circumstances, these were held to justify an assumption that the Sheikh 'had substantial and effective control over the trust funds'. However, the relevant provisions were not in any way unusual for a discretionary trust under which the settlor is himself an object.[44] Moreover, the crucial dispositive discretions were vested in the trustee, which clearly owed fiduciary obligations (to the Sheikh and to other beneficiaries) and which the court accepted had not been a party to the Sheikh's fraud. Consequently, it is difficult to see how the so-called 'trust fund' could be said to be property which effectively belonged to the Sheikh (or over which he had effective control). It would have made much more sense to say that the property had never belonged to the Sheikh in the first place.

---

[43] (1997/98) 1 OFLR 443. See also *Meespierson (Bahamas) Ltd v Grupo Torras SA*, Civil appeal No 41 of 1998 (Bahamian CA, 16 April 1999): Bahamian courts have no jurisdiction to grant a free-standing *Mareva* injunction where there is no substantive claim against the defendants in the jurisdiction.
[44] cf the Cook Islands' International Trusts Act 1984, ss 13A and 13C.

In any event, the court did not refer to or discuss any provision of the 1991 Act **38.29** and for present purposes, therefore, it has limited significance. Nevertheless, the readiness with which the court seems to have reached its conclusion, as well as the lack of clarity and conviction in the reasoning underlying the judgment, might well be seen as seriously undermining the claims of The Bahamas to be an effective and reliable jurisdiction in which to base any asset protection strategy.[45]

Finally, section 8 of the FDA 1991 declares that nothing in the Act creates or **38.30** enables any right, claim, or interest on behalf of a creditor or person, which right, claim, or interest would be avoided or defeated by the Trusts (Choice of Governing Law) Act 1989. This Act provides *inter alia* that, in the creation of a trust, a settlor, whether or not he is resident in The Bahamas, may expressly declare in the trust instrument that the laws of The Bahamas shall be the governing law of the trust, and such an express declaration is valid, effective, and conclusive regardless of any other circumstances.[46] Subject to certain exceptions, all questions arising in regard to a trust which is for the time being governed by the laws of The Bahamas, or in regard to any disposition of property upon the trusts thereof, will be determined in accordance with the laws of The Bahamas, without reference to the laws of any other jurisdiction with which the trust or disposition may be connected.[47] Section 7(2) then declares that this general rule shall not validate *inter alia* any trust or disposition of immovable property situate in a jurisdiction other than The Bahamas in which such trust or disposition is invalid according to the laws of such jurisdiction.[48] In particular, section 8 of the TGLA 1989 declares that no trust governed by the laws of The Bahamas, and no disposition of property to be held on a trust that is valid under the laws of The Bahamas, is void, voidable, liable to be set aside, or defective in any manner by reference to a foreign law.

There is no Bahamian statute similar to the English Recognition of Trusts Act **38.31** 1987 and The Bahamas have not adopted the Hague Convention on the Law Applicable to Trusts and their Recognition 1985.

Belize

The legal system of Belize (formerly British Honduras) is based on that of England, **38.32** together with local legislation. Prior to 1992, the principal trust legislation was the Trusts Act 1923, which was repealed by the Trusts Act 1992 ('TA 1992'). The

---

[45] On the other hand, see *Meespierson (Bahamas) Ltd v Gruppo Torras SA*, Civil Appeal No 41 of 1998 (Bahamian CA, 16 April 1999) and *B v T* (1999) 4 ITELR 523.

[46] TGLA 1989, s 4(1),(2).   [47] ibid, s 7(1).

[48] Section 7(2)(b) provides that s 7 shall take effect subject to any express term of a trust or disposition to the contrary. However, it is difficult to see how such an express term could override the provisions of s 7(2)(a).

TA 1992, which came into force on 18 May 1992,[49] provides a code dealing with the definition of a trust, the validity of trusts, the proper law of trusts, the creation and maximum duration of a trust, and so forth.

38.33   Under section 57 of the TA 1992, the court[50] has jurisdiction in respect of any matters where:

(a) the proper law of trust is the law of Belize;

(b) a trustee of the trust is resident in Belize (and, presumably, only one of several trustees need be so resident);

(c) any property of the trust is situated in Belize; and

(d) any part of the administration of the trust is carried on in Belize.

On the application of a trustee, beneficiary, a settlor or his personal representatives, a protector,[51] or, with the leave of the court, any other person, the court may *inter alia* make a declaration as to the validity or enforceability of a trust.[52] A trustee (but apparently not anyone else) may apply to the court for directions as to how he should or might act in any of the affairs of the trust and the court may make such order as it thinks fit.[53]

38.34   The TA 1992 also provides for the optional registration of trusts.[54] The settlor or trustee of a trust may, but (subject to the terms of the trust) shall not be obliged to, apply for registration of the trust on a register maintained by the Registrar of the court, upon payment of the specified registration fee and conforming with the procedures laid down. The register is not open for inspection except that the trustees of a trust (which, presumably, means all the trustees where there are several)[55] may in writing authorize a person to inspect the entry of that trust on the register.[56] This facility for secrecy is apparently available to all trusts, irrespective of whether the proper law is the law of Belize.[57] In addition, if the trust is an 'exempt trust', it will not be subject to taxation in Belize[58] and will be regarded as not resident in Belize for the purposes of exchange control regulations.[59]

38.35   A trust is an 'exempt trust' in any year if:

(a) the settlor is not resident in Belize during that year;

(b) none of the beneficiaries is resident in Belize during that year; and

(c) the trust property does not include any land situated in Belize.[60]

---

[49] The day appointed by Order of the Attorney-General of Belize published in the *Belize Government Gazette*: see TA 1992, s 70.

[50] ie the Supreme Court of a Judge thereof: see ibid, s 68(1).

[51] Section 16 deals with the appointment and powers of a protector and provides that, in the exercise of his office, he owes a fiduciary duty to the beneficiaries, but he is not to be accounted or regarded as a trustee.

[52] TA 1992, s 58(1)(b).   [53] ibid, s 59.   [54] ibid, s 63.   [55] ibid, s 29.

[56] ibid, s 63(7).   [57] ibid, s 66(3).   [58] ibid, s 64.   [59] ibid, s 65.

[60] ibid, s 64(1).

For present purposes, the main provision of relevance is section 7 of the TA 1992. Section 7(2) provides that a trust will be 'invalid and unenforceable' *inter alia* to the extent that:

(a) it purports to do anything contrary to the law of Belize; or
(b) it purports to confer any right or power or impose any obligation the exercise of which or the carrying out of which is contrary to the law of Belize.

It will also be 'invalid and unenforceable' to the extent that:

(a) the court declares that the trust was established by duress, fraud, mistake, undue influence, or misrepresentation; or
(b) the trust is immoral or contrary to public policy.

38.36 Where a trust is created for two or more purposes of which some are 'lawful' and others are not, or where some of the terms of the trust are 'invalid' and others are not, the consequences differ according to whether or not those purposes or terms can be separated. If they cannot be separated, the trust is invalid. If they can be separated, the court may declare that the trust is valid as to the terms which are valid and the purposes which are lawful. Where a trust is partially invalid, the court may declare what property is to be held subject to the trust. Property provided by a settlor and as to which a trust is invalid shall be held by the trustee on trust for the settlor absolutely, or, if he is dead, as if it had formed part of his estate at his death.[61]

38.37 Section 149 of the (Belize) Law of Property Act 1925[62] is identical to section 172 of the English Law of Property Act 1925. Consequently, a transfer of property made with intent to defraud creditors is voidable in Belize, as it was in England, at the instance of any person thereby prejudiced. Moreover, a trust created with such an intent could be said to fall within the first two limbs of section 7(1)(a) of the TA 1992 (being contrary to the law of Belize or conferring a right or power or imposing an obligation the exercise or carrying out of which is contrary to the law of Belize); and it may even fall within section 7(1)(b)(i) (being established by fraud). If so, such a trust would apparently be 'invalid and unenforceable', but it is not clear whether this means that it is void or simply voidable (as under section 149 of the Belize Law of Property Act and section 172 of the English Act). Nor is it clear how the 'purposes' of such a trust could be separated under subsections (3)–(5).

38.38 Section 7(6) of the TA 1992 provides that where a trust is 'created' under the law of Belize, the court shall not vary it or set it aside or recognize the validity of any

---

[61] ibid, s 7(3)–(5) inclusive.   [62] Chapter 154 of the Revised Laws of Belize.

claim against the trust property pursuant to the law of another jurisdiction or the order of a court of another jurisdiction in respect of *inter alia* the claims of creditors in an insolvency. Thus, subsection (6) seems to apply only to a trust actually created under the law of Belize, and not to a trust the proper law of which was originally the law of a jurisdiction other than Belize but which has been changed to that of Belize.[63] Section 7(7) then declares that subsection (6) has effect notwithstanding the provisions of section 149 of the Law of Property Act, section 42 of the Bankruptcy Act, and the provisions of the Reciprocal Enforcement of Judgments Act.

38.39 Section 3(1) of the latter Act[64] provides that, where a judgment[65] has been obtained in the High Court in England, the judgment creditor may apply to the Supreme Court in Belize at any time within twelve months after the date of judgment or such longer period as may be allowed to register the judgment; and it will be registered accordingly 'if in all the circumstances of the case [the Supreme Court] thinks it is just and convenient that the judgment should be enforced' in Belize. Section 3(2)(f) declares expressly, however, that no judgment shall be ordered to be registered if it was in respect of a cause of action which, for reasons of public policy or for some other similar reason, could not have been entertained by the registering court. Part II of the Act deals with reciprocal enforcement of judgments in relation to other foreign countries and a 'judgment' in this context is defined so as to include compensation or damages to an injured party as well as a payment of a sum of money.[66]

38.40 A judgment creditor within Part II may apply for registration of the judgment (within six years of the date of judgment) 'subject to proof of . . . the other provisions' of the Act. Whether this latter requirement includes section 3(2)(f) is unclear. The implication (especially in section 9(2)) is that the judgment must have been capable of being given originally in Belize. Thus, the precise manner in which the Reciprocal Enforcement of Judgments Act is intended to interact with the TA 1992 is not entirely free from doubt.

38.41 However, the effect of the provisions of the TA 1992 seems to be that section 7(6) clearly does not prevent a Belize court from varying or setting aside a Belize trust, or recognizing a claim against property held in a Belize trust,[67] at the instance of a

---

[63] But see TA 1992, s 66(3). Section 4 of the Act deals with the proper law of a trust and clearly recognizes that the proper law may be changed to or from the law of Belize.

[64] Chapter 133.

[65] A 'judgment' refers to any judgment or order 'whereby any sum of money is made payable': Reciprocal Enforcement of Judgments Act, s 2.

[66] ibid, s 7.

[67] If the proper law of a trust is changed from the law of Belize to the law of another jurisdiction, no provision of the law of Belize (which must include s 149) shall operate so as to render the trust void, invalid, or unlawful or to render void, invalid, or unlawful any functions conferred on the trustee under the new law: TA 1992, s 4(6). Cf the jurisdiction conferred on the court by s 57 of the Act.

creditor pursuant to section 149 of the Law of Property Act 1925, provided that the creditor is not relying on the law of another jurisdiction or the order of a court in another jurisdiction. On the other hand, the enforcement of a law of a foreign jurisdiction or an order of a foreign court purporting to set aside a Belize trust in favour of creditors is not likely to be furthered or assisted in Belize if and in so far as it is contrary to Belize public policy or tends to undermine the provisions of the TA 1992.

Section 7(6)(c) refers only to the claims of creditors 'in an insolvency'. Section **38.42** 68(1) of the Act provides that, unless the context otherwise requires, the word 'insolvency' includes the making of an administration order, the appointment of a receiver, and the bankruptcy of any person. However, sections 423–425 of the English Insolvency Act 1986, under which an English court may set aside a transaction at an undervalue (for example a Belize trust created by a settlor domiciled in England), or make such order as it thinks fit to protect the victims of such a transaction, can operate entirely independently of insolvency. In such circumstances, it is not clear that section 7(6) of the TA 1992 would apply so as to prevent a Belize court from recognizing the validity of the order of the English court setting aside the trust.

Section 12(4) of the TA 1992 declares that any rule of law or public policy which **38.43** prevents a settlor from establishing a protective or spendthrift trust[68] of which he is a beneficiary is abolished. Thus, the so-called rule in *Re Burroughs Fowler*[69] no longer has any effect in Belize.

The Cayman Islands

On bankruptcy

Section 107 of the Bankruptcy Law (Revised) contains provisions which are iden- **38.44** tical to those in section 42 of the English Bankruptcy Act 1914 (with the same two-year and ten-year time limits, and subject to the same exceptions).[70] Only 'debtors' may be declared bankrupt under the Law. 'Debtors' are defined so as to include any person, whether a British subject or not, who at the time when any act of bankruptcy was done or suffered by him:

(a) was personally present in the Islands; or
(b) ordinarily resided or had a place of residence in the Islands; or
(c) was carrying on business in the Islands, personally or by means of an agent or manager; or
(d) was a member of a firm or partnership which carried on business in the Islands.[71]

---

[68] Section 12 deals generally with protective and spendthrift trusts.   [69] [1916] 2 Ch 251.
[70] See GW Thomas, *op cit*, 363–370.   [71] Bankruptcy Law (Revised), s 2.

38.45 A settlor with no relevant Cayman Islands connection at the date of the settlement may become subject to the Bankruptcy Law if he acquires a relevant connection at any time up until the tenth anniversary of the settlement. If property is added to an existing settlement, the 10-year period runs from the date of the addition and not the date of the original settlement.[72]

Irrespective of bankruptcy

38.46 Prior to the Fraudulent Dispositions Law 1989 ('the 1989 Law'), the position in the Cayman Islands was governed by provisions of the English Statute of Elizabeth I (1571).[73] However, section 3 of the 1989 Law provides that, with effect from 'the appointed date' (being 1 May 1990)[74] the 1989 Law shall apply in place of the law in effect prior to the appointed date to every disposition of property made before or after the appointed date by any person, and whether or not the property, the subject of the disposition, is situate in the Islands or elsewhere.

38.47 The provisions of the 1989 Law are virtually identical with those of the Bahamian Fraudulent Dispositions Act 1991 (which seem to have been modelled on the 1989 Law and which have already been described above). Thus, section 4(1) of the 1989 Law declares that, subject to the provisions of the Law, every disposition of property 'made with an intent to defraud and at an undervalue' shall be voidable at the instance of a creditor thereby prejudiced. The definitions of the key terms in section 2 are almost identical to the definitions of the same terms in the Bahamian legislation.[75] However, there are three differences, at least two of which (and probably all three) seem to render the Cayman Islands legislation more advantageous to a creditor than the Bahamian legislation which followed it.

38.48 First, although the definition of 'obligation' in the 1989 Law refers to an obligation or liability (including a contingent liability) which existed on or prior to the date of the relevant disposition, it must nonetheless be an obligation of which the transferor 'had notice'. This is virtually identical with the definition in the Bahamian Act, save that the latter expressly refers to such an obligation or liability

---

[72] ibid, s 14.

[73] The settlers who settled the Cayman Islands (between 1658 and 1734) were deemed to have brought with them English law in effect at the date of settlement. See now Interpretation Act 1963, s 40. The Cayman Islands' Special Trust (Alternative Regime) Law 1997, coupled with the Perpetuities (Amendment) Law 1997, provides the most sophisticated and flexible vehicle of all the offshore jurisdictions. These so-called STAR trusts may be used *inter alia* for the purpose of asset protection. However, STAR trusts are subject to the same rules and provisions as to 'fraudulent dispositions' as ordinary trusts and therefore do not require special treatment here. STAR trusts are dealt with in Chapter 40 below.

[74] Fraudulent Dispositions (Commencement) Law, s 2.

[75] The word 'disposition' is defined by reference to the Trusts (Foreign Element) Law 1987, s 2(1), where the word is given the same meaning as in the Bahamian legislation.

of which the transferor 'had actual notice'. This suggests that, for the purposes of the 1989 Law, constructive (and even imputed) notice may be sufficient.

Secondly, section 4(3) of the 1989 Law declares that no action or proceeding shall be commenced pursuant to the 1989 Law unless commenced within six years of the date of the relevant disposition. The relevant period under section 4(3) of the Bahamian Fraudulent Dispositions Act 1991 is two years. (Thus, the Cayman Islands legislation is more favourable to a creditor than that in The Bahamas.) **38.49**

Thirdly, section 5 of the 1989 Law (which accords a degree of protection to a transferee and a beneficiary of a trust to whom a distribution has been made) applies 'if the Court is satisfied that the transferee [or beneficiary] has not acted in bad faith', whereas its counterpart, in section 5 of the Bahamian Act, applies, 'unless the court is satisfied that the transferee [or beneficiary] has acted in bad faith'. In addition, whereas the Bahamian legislation includes an additional provision (in section 5(2)) to the effect that the burden of proving that the transferee (or beneficiary) has acted in bad faith shall lie upon the person making the allegation, there is no such provision in the 1989 Law. This subtle difference therefore has the effect that, under the 1989 Law, the burden of proof on the question of protection for a transferee (or beneficiary) is effectively reversed: it is for the transferee (or beneficiary) to establish that he has not acted in bad faith, and not for the creditor to prove that the transferee (or beneficiary) has done so. **38.50**

As a further point, section 6 of the Trusts (Foreign Element) Law 1987 provides for the exclusion of foreign law in respect of a trust governed by the law of the Cayman Islands, or a disposition of property to be held upon the trusts thereof.[76] However, it is difficult to see how this provision is relevant to the question of 'asset protection'. Section 6 declares that a Cayman Islands trust will not be void, voidable, liable to be set aside, or defective in any fashion, by reason that the trust or disposition avoids or defeats rights, claims, or interests conferred by foreign law, but this provision seems to be confined to such rights, claims, or interests as are conferred by reason of personal relationship with the settlor, or by way of heirship rights. The rights and interests of creditors in an insolvency, for example, are not referred to and cannot, it seems, be included by implication. **38.51**

Similarly, the alternative head under which a trust shall not be void, voidable, or liable to be set aside, namely that it contravenes any rule of foreign law or foreign judicial or administrative order or action, seems to be confined to such rules, orders, or actions as are intended to recognize, protect, enforce, or give effect to 'any such rights, claims or interests'. (In contrast, section 8 of the Bahamian Trusts (Choice of Governing Law) Act 1989, provides generally that a Bahamian trust **38.52**

---

[76] See *Re the Lemos Trust Settlement* (1992–93) CILR 26 and *Lemos v Coutts & Co (Cayman) Ltd* (1992–93) CILR 5.

shall not be void, voidable, or set aside 'by reference to a foreign law'.) Thus, there seems to be no obvious reason why an order of a foreign court (such as an order made by an English court under section 423 of the Insolvency Act 1986) should not be enforced in the Cayman Islands, even if it relates to the setting aside of a disposition to a Cayman Islands trust.

The Cook Islands

38.53   The Cook Islands have a separate legislative regime for offshore entities.[77] The governing legislation for international trusts, which has been emulated in other jurisdictions, is the International Trusts Act 1984 ('ITA 1984') (as amended by a series of Amending Acts).[78]

38.54   An international trust is a trust which is registered under the ITA 1984 and in respect of which:

(a) at least one of the trustees, including a custodian trustee, or in the case of a disposition granting powers of appointment, maintenance or advancement, at least one of the donors or holders of the power of appointment or power of maintenance or power of advancement is either:

    (i) a registered foreign company; or
    (ii) an international company; or
    (iii) a trustee company;

    and shall include, where the context so permits, a trust which is established or settled under the laws of another jurisdiction but which, subject to paras (a) and (b) of this definition, is subsequently registered as an international trust under the ITA 1984; and

(b) the beneficiaries are at all times non-resident.[79]

---

[77]   Provided the requirements of the ITA 1984 are complied with (eg those relating to registration), an international trust enjoys many advantages, such as, eg, freedom from the rules against perpetuities, remoteness of vesting, and excessive accumulations: see ss 6 and 9 of the ITA 1984. The 1984 Act does not apply to a beneficiary who is domiciled or ordinarily resident in the Cook Islands: see s 22(1).

[78]   The International Trusts Amendment Act 1985, the International Trusts Amendment Act 1989, the International Trusts Amendment (No 2) Act 1989, the International Trusts Amendment Act 1991, the International Trusts Amendment Act 1995–96, the International Trusts Amendment (No 2) Act 1995–96, and the International Trusts Amendment Act 1999. References in this section are to the 1984 Act as amended.

[79]   ITA 1984, s 2. A 'non-resident' is defined (also in s 2) as: (a) an individual not domiciled in the Cook Islands; (b) an individual not ordinarily resident in the Cook Islands; (c) an international company; (d) a foreign company; (e) a trustee company; (f) a subsidiary of a trustee company being either an international company or a foreign company.

A trust registered under the ITA 1984 is a valid trust notwithstanding that it may be invalid according to the law of the settlor's[80] domicile or residence or place of current incorporation.[81] **38.55**

Section 13A deals specifically with bankruptcy and allied matters. It provides that, notwithstanding any provision of the law of the settlor's domicile or place of ordinary residence or the settlor's current place of incorporation, and notwithstanding further that an international trust is voluntary and without valuable consideration being given for the same, or is made on or for the benefit of the settlor, settlor's spouse, or children of the settlor, or any of them, an international trust and a disposition to an international trust shall not be void or voidable in the event of the settlor's bankruptcy, insolvency, or liquidation (other than in the case of an international company registered pursuant to the International Companies Act 1981–82 that is in liquidation) or in any action or proceedings at the suit of creditors of the settlor, but shall remain valid and subsisting and take effect according to its tenor, subject to the provisions of section 13B. **38.56**

Section 13B then deals with international trusts, and dispositions to international trusts, made or alleged to have been made with the intention of defrauding creditors. The provisions of section 13B[82] are declared to apply to all actions and proceedings brought in the High Court of the Cook Islands in which fraud, deceit, unconscionable conduct, or any other inequitable conduct (however described) or any species of unjust enrichment is alleged, against any party (whether a party to the proceedings or not), with regard to the settlement or establishment of an international trust or the disposition of property to such a trust, or receipt of property by or for such a trust (or subsequent disposition of property from such a trust with the intention of prejudicing creditors of the settlor of such property or such trust); and the remedy conferred by section 13B(1) (see below) shall be the sole remedy available in such an action or proceedings, to the exclusion of any other relief or remedy against any party to the relevant action or proceeding.[83] It is also expressly provided that the provisions of section 13B operate to the exclusion of **38.57**

---

[80] A 'settlor' is defined in s 2 and in relation to an international trust means and includes an assignor of property to an international trust and each and every person who, directly or indirectly, on behalf of himself or any other(s), as owner, or as the holder of a power in that behalf, disposes of property to be held in such trust or declares or otherwise creates such trust. This definition, coupled with the definition of 'disposition', has the effect that the donee of a power of appointment could be a settlor for the purposes of the ITA 1984.

[81] ibid, s 5(2).

[82] Amendments to section 13B were prompted, at least in part, by the recent interlocutory decision of the Cook Islands Court of Appeal in *South Orange Grove Owners Association v Orange Grove Partners* (1995) No 208/94 (as to which see below). The amended s 13B(8), in particular, seems to apply only to every international trust settled or established on or after 8 September 1989, and to every disposition of property to such trust made on or after that date: see the International Trusts Amendment Act 1995–96, s 27(2). See also *A v B* (2002) 4 ITELR 877.

[83] ITA 1984, s 13B(9).

any other remedy, principle, or rule of law, whether provided for by statute or founded in equity or in common law, including (for the avoidance of doubt) the imposition of a constructive trust upon any interested party or the recognition and enforcement of any constructive trust imposed or recognized by the laws of any other jurisdiction.[84] Indeed, the provisions of section 13B apply not only to every international trust but also to every trust which, having been registered as an international trust, is no longer so registered (and in respect to all dispositions to such a trust).[85] Thus, the ITA 1984 provides a fairly comprehensive code for international trusts which may be—and is clearly intended to be—of considerable assistance to those who seek to avoid or defeat their creditors.[86]

38.58   Section 13B(1) provides that, where it is proven 'beyond reasonable doubt' by a creditor that an international trust settled or established, or property disposed to an international trust:

(a) was so settled, established, or disposed by or on behalf of the settlor 'with principal intent' to defraud 'that creditor' of the settlor; and

(b) did at the time such settlement, establishment, or disposition took place render the settlor insolvent or without property by which that creditor's claim (if successful) could have been satisfied,

then such settlement, establishment, or disposition shall not be void or voidable, but the international trust shall be liable to satisfy the creditor's claim out of the property which, but for the settlement, establishment, or disposition, would have been available to satisfy the creditor's claim; and such liability shall only be to the extent of the interest that the settlor had in the property prior to the settlement, establishment, or disposition and any accumulation to the property (if any) subsequent thereto.

38.59   Thus, it is clear that a creditor who invokes the provisions of section 13B must establish that the settlor intended to defraud him, and not some other creditor. It

---

[84] ITA 1984, s 13B(10).

[85] ibid, s 13B(11). This is subject to s 16(6), dealing with deregistration and the consequences thereof.

[86] The recent amendments to the 1984 Act have clearly strengthened the usefulness of the Cook Islands legislation for this purpose. However, any such legislation is seriously at risk unless it is interpreted and applied by a sympathetic judiciary, and the attitude of the Cook Islands judiciary to the legislation, as manifested in the *Orange Grove* case, seems to be anything but sympathetic. Although the Court of Appeal cannot be criticized for indicating that Cook Islands legislation was not intended to assist fraudsters, it does nonetheless appear to have favoured the interests of creditors rather than those of the settlors. On the other hand, on 11 August 1999, the High Court rejected an application by the US Federal Trade Commission (following the decision in *Federal Trade Commission (FTC) v Affordable Media LLC and Anderson* 179F 2d 1228 (9 Cir, 1999) (the *Anderson* case)) to have a Cook Islands trustee removed and its own appointee appointed as a new trustee and protector of a Cook Islands trust.

is not clear, however, whether this burden can be discharged by showing that the settlor intended to defraud a class or category of creditors of which that particular creditor was a member, although it may be inferred from other parts of section 13B (for example, subsections (1)(b) and (2)) that a creditor who invokes section 13B must have been a creditor at the date of the settlement or disposition. A 'creditor' is not defined but is stated to include 'any person who alleges a cause of action'.[87] This must be read in the context of the other (somewhat convoluted) provisions of section 13B (which are dealt with below).

It is clear, however, that an intent to defraud a creditor must have been the settlor's **38.60** 'principal intent'. Although it is not entirely beyond debate, this seems to require that such an intent must be the chief or paramount intention, and to indicate that it is not sufficient that it was an important consideration or motivation on the settlor's part, if it was not indeed his primary intent. It also appears that the creditor must establish both limbs of subsection (1) (which are joined by the word 'and'). In other words, proving a clear intent to defraud would not seem to suffice in itself if the settlor was not rendered insolvent or unable to satisfy the creditor's claim.[88] Similarly, proving that, as a direct result of the settlement or disposition, the settlor was rendered insolvent or unable to satisfy the creditor's claim would seem not to suffice if a principal intent to defraud could not be established.

In determining whether the creation of an international trust, or a disposition to **38.61** an international trust, has rendered the settlor insolvent or without property by which a creditor's claim (if successful) may be satisfied, regard shall be had to the fair market value of the settlor's property (not being property of or relating to the trust) at the time immediately after the creation of the settlement or the disposition. In the event that the fair market value of such property exceeded the value of the creditor's claim at that time, then the trust or disposition shall, for all purposes (and not just for the purposes of the ITA 1984), be deemed not to have been created or made with intent to defraud the creditor.[89]

The ITA 1984 also imposes certain time limits. The creation of, and a disposition **38.62** to, an international trust shall for all purposes be deemed not to have been made with intent to defraud a creditor of a settlor:

(a) if it occurred *after* the expiration of two years from the date on which the creditor's cause of action accrued; or
(b) where it occurred before the expiration of two years from the date on which the creditor's cause of action accrued, if that creditor fails to commence, in a court of competent jurisdiction, proceedings in respect of that creditor's

---

[87] ITA 1984, s 13B(12).
[88] See also the concluding words of s 13B(2) (although it is not clear that they add anything).
[89] ITA 1984, s 13B(2).

cause of action before the expiration of one year from the date on which the international trust was created or the relevant disposition made.[90]

38.63 In addition, the creation of, or a disposition to, an international trust shall not be fraudulent as against a creditor of a settlor if it occurred before that creditor's cause of action against the settlor accrued.[91] For these purposes (and also for the purposes of section 13K, dealing with the commencement of proceedings) the date on which the cause of action accrued shall be determined in accordance with the recently amended provisions of section 13B(8). This provides, first, that it shall be the date of that act or omission which is relied upon to establish (wholly or partly) the cause of action. If there is more than one act, or the omission is a continuing one, then the date of the first act, or the date that the omission first occurred, as the case may be, shall be the date on which the cause of action accrued.

38.64 It is then provided further that the term 'cause of action' means the earlier cause of action capable of assertion by a creditor against the settlor of an international trust, by which that creditor has established (or may establish) an enforceable claim against that settlor.[92] Where a creditor has or asserts (or could have asserted) multiple or successive causes of action against a settlor (whether by virtue of the nature of the relevant circumstances of the case, or by reason of having attained the status of a judgment creditor in respect of one or more of such causes of action, or by reason of asserting or being able to assert an allegedly fraudulent settlement of or disposition to an international trust, or otherwise) the entitlement of such a creditor to relief under section 13B shall be determined, and the periods referred to in section 13B shall be calculated, by reference to one only of

---

[90] ITA 1984, s 13B(3). It is provided further that these latter provisions shall not have effect if (and subject also to subsection (5)) at the time of the creation of the international trust or of the relevant disposition, proceedings in respect of that creditor's cause of action against that settlor have already been commenced in a court of competent jurisdiction. It is difficult to see how this proviso fits in with subsection (3)(b). It also seems that the creditor has one year from the date of the relevant disposition to commence proceedings *in the Cook Islands*, and it is *not* the case that, provided he commences domestic proceedings within one year, he will have a further two years in which to commence proceedings in the Cook Islands: the second *Orange Grove* case (1996) 1 OFLR 3, CA.

[91] ibid, s 13B(4).

[92] ITA 1984, s 13B(8)(b). Prior to the International Trusts Amendment Act 1995–96, s 13B(8)(b) of the 1984 Act declared that, in the case of an action upon a judgment, the date of the cause of action accruing should be the date of that act or omission (or, where there was more than one act or the omission was a continuing one, the date of the first act or the date that the omission first occurred, as the case may be) which gave rise to the judgment itself. In *515 South Orange Grove Association v Orange Grove Partners* (1995) No 208/94, where the issue was whether proceedings for a *Mareva* injunction taken in the Cook Islands to enforce a Californian judgment had been commenced in time, the Cook Islands Court of Appeal held that the effect of this provision, coupled with s 13B(3), was that the relevant time limit before which a creditor had to bring proceedings under s 13B was the expiration of two years from the date of the finding of the Californian jury and not from the date when the original cause of action accrued. There were two *Orange Grove* cases, in fact (dealing with two identical trusts). It is believed that both cases were settled.

that creditor's causes of action, being that cause of action which accrued first in time in accordance with subsection (8)(b).[93] However, nothing in subsection (8)(b) or (c) shall apply so as to affect the rights (or requirement) of a creditor to commence separate proceedings under section 13B in relation to a cause of action where the court is satisfied (having regard to subsection (8)(c)) that both the circumstances out of which the cause of action arose and the subject matter of that cause of action are wholly unrelated to those of the other cause of action.[94]

A creditor seeking to enforce a claim under section 13B in reliance on a foreign judg- **38.65** ment may not enforce such a claim until such time as it (*sic*) can demonstrate to the reasonable satisfaction of the court that (a) it has exhausted all remedies available to it against the settlor's remaining property and (b) all rights of appeal against that foreign judgment have been exhausted.[95] For the purposes of assessing the liability of an international trust to a creditor under section 13B, where the amount of that creditor's claim against the settlor is wholly or partly in any way related to or evidenced by a foreign judgment, the court in making any award in favour of that creditor shall disregard and exclude any amount awarded in that foreign judgment to that creditor which comprises any form of exemplary, vindictive, retributory, or punitive damages (by whatever name) or is an amount of damages arrived at by doubling, trebling, or otherwise multiplying a sum assessed as compensation for the loss or damage (which types of damage are together called 'punitive damages').[96] The burden of proving that an amount awarded in a foreign judgment does not wholly or partly comprise punitive damages rests on the creditor.[97] However, the above-mentioned provisions of subsection (14) shall not apply if, at the time of the settlement, establishment, or disposition (as the case may be), an award of punitive damages has already been made in a foreign judgment against the settlor.[98]

The burden of proving an intent to defraud on the part of the settlor lies on the **38.66** creditor.[99] This burden is a heavy one, for the opening words of section 13B(1) make it clear that it must be proved 'beyond reasonable doubt' (and not just on a balance of probabilities) that an international trust was created, or a disposition to an international trust was made, not only with the principal intent to defraud but also that it resulted in the insolvency of the settlor or rendered him unable to satisfy the creditor's claim. In addition, a settlor shall not have imputed to him an intent to defraud a creditor, solely by reason that the settlor:

(a) has settled or established a trust or has disposed of property to such trust within two years from the date of that creditor's cause of action accruing;

---

[93] ITA 1984, s 13B(8)(c). [94] ibid, s 13B(8)(d). [95] ibid, s 13B(13).
[96] ibid, s 13B(14), inserted by the International Trusts Amendment Act 1999.
[97] ibid, s 13B(15), inserted by the International Trusts Amendment Act 1999.
[98] ibid, s 13B(16), inserted by the International Trusts Amendment Act 1999.
[99] ibid, s 13B(7).

(b) has retained, possesses, or acquires any of the powers or benefits referred to in section 13C(a)–(f);

(c) is a beneficiary, trustee, or protector;

(d) has settled or established a trust, or has disposed of property to such trust, at a time when proceedings in respect of that creditor's cause of action against the settlor have already been commenced in a court of competent jurisdiction.[100]

38.67 In any event that an international trust is liable to satisfy a creditor's claim in the manner provided for in section 13B(1), that creditor's rights to recovery shall be limited to that property referred to in subsection (1), or to the proceeds of that property, to the exclusion of any rights against the trustees of the international trust or any of them, against any other property of the international trust, or any of them; and, where the international trust is unable to satisfy the creditor's claim by reason of the fact that the property referred to in subsection (1) has been disposed of, other than to a bona fide purchaser for value, then any such disposition shall be void.[101] There are no special provisions in the ITA 1984 (unlike the legislation in force in The Bahamas and Bermuda, for example) giving protection (in respect of the costs of defending an action brought by a creditor or any other costs) to a transferee who has not given value but has acted in good faith (or not acted in bad faith) or to a beneficiary who has (in good faith or otherwise) received a distribution from an international trust.

38.68 Section 13C deals with the retention of control and benefit by a settlor. It provides that an international trust shall not be declared invalid, nor a disposition declared void or be affected in any way by reason of the fact that the settlor, and if more than one, any of them, retains, possesses, or acquires:

(a) a power to revoke the trust;

(b) a power of disposition over property of the trust;

(c) a power to amend the trust;

(d) any benefit, interest, or property from the trust;

(e) the power to remove or appoint a trustee or protector;

(f) the power to direct a trustee or protector on any matter;

or is a beneficiary of the trust, either solely or together with others.[102]

---

[100] ITA 1984, s 13B(5).   [101] ibid, s 13B(6).

[102] ibid, s 13C(a)–(g). If the settlor retains such control, he is clearly at considerable risk of being compelled by the courts of his domestic jurisdiction to exercise his powers to repatriate the trust assets and of being penalized for contempt if he fails to do so: see, eg, *Ex parte Coffelt* 389 SW 2d 234 (7 Cir, 1989); and especially *Federal Trade Commission (FTC) v Affordable Media LLC and Anderson* 179 F 3d 1228 (9 Cir, 1999) (the *Andersen* case), where the settlors were protectors, co-trustees, and beneficiaries of a Cook Islands trust. Following the decision in the latter case, the FTC brought

Furthermore, section 13D deals specifically with the non-enforcement of foreign **38.69** judgments. It is provided that, notwithstanding the provisions of any treaty or statute, or any rule of law or equity, to the contrary, no proceedings for or in relation to the enforcement or recognition of a judgment obtained in a jurisdiction other than the Cook Islands against any interested party shall be in any way entertained, recognized, or enforced by any court in the Cook Islands to the extent that the judgment:

(a) is based upon the application of any law inconsistent with the provisions of the ITA 1984 (or of the Trustee Companies Act 1981–82); or
(b) relates to a matter or particular aspect that is governed by the law of the Cook Islands.

In determining the governing law of an international trust, regard shall first be had **38.70** to the terms of that trust and to any evidence therein as to the intention of the parties. The other circumstances of an international trust may be taken into account only if the terms of the trust fail to provide such evidence.[103] A term of an international trust expressly selecting the laws of the Cook Islands to govern the trust is valid, effective, and conclusive regardless of any other circumstances.[104] Similarly, where a trust instrument[105] so provides, or where, in accordance with the powers contained in a trust instrument, the law of the Cook Islands is chosen to govern a particular aspect of an international trust, and law other than that of the Cook Islands is chosen to govern other aspects of that trust, then the choice of Cook Islands law and the choice of that other law as to their respective aspects shall be valid, effective, and conclusive regardless of any other circumstances.[106]

Where a trust instrument contains a power to change the governing law of **38.71** that trust, the law may be changed to or from the law of the Cook Islands in accordance with that power, and that change shall be valid, effective, and conclusive according to the terms of such power; and such a change in governing law shall not affect the legality or validity of, or render any person liable for, any thing done before the change.[107] A change in the governing law of a trust shall not of itself interrupt the continuity of the relationships whether in equity or law established by the trust and, without limitation, will not constitute a resettlement of the trust.[108]

---

proceedings in the Cook Islands to have the Cook Islands trustee removed, its own appointee appointed as trustee and protector, and the trust assets repatriated. The High Court of the Islands found in favour of the existing trustee and rejected the application (decision of 11 August 1999). See also *Re W Family Trust* (18 July 1999) HC of CI.

[103] ITA 1984, s 13G(1).   [104] ibid, s 13G(2).

[105] A 'trust instrument', 'instrument', or 'registered instrument' means the deed, trust agreement, will, codicil, settlement, or instrument establishing or creating a trust and includes any variation or amendment to such deed, trust agreement, will, codicil, settlement, or instrument: see ibid, s 2.

[106] ibid, s 13G(3).   [107] ibid, s 13G(4), (5).   [108] ibid, s 13G(6).

The disposition of any property to or from a trust in accordance with the governing law of that trust at the time of the disposition shall not be affected or invalidated by a subsequent change from that governing law to some other law.[109] Where the donee of a power to change the governing law of a trust exercises that power in accordance with the terms of that power, then such exercise shall be deemed to have been proper.[110] The location of the interested parties, selection or imposition of jurisdiction, place of administration, or the situation of the property of the trust, will not affect the validity or effect of a choice of the governing law of a trust made in accordance with the trust instrument.[111]

38.72 Finally, where the governing law of a trust is changed to or from the law of the Cook Islands, the trustees are empowered to make all such consequential alterations or additions to the trust instrument as they consider necessary or desirable to ensure that the provisions, rights, liabilities, powers, and obligations of and under the trust instrument shall be as valid and effective under the new governing law as they were under the previous governing law.[112]

38.73 All questions arising in regard to an international trust which is for the time being governed by the laws of the Cook Islands, or in regard to any disposition of property upon the trusts thereof—including *inter alia* any aspect of the validity of the trust or disposition or the interpretation or effect thereof and the existence and extent of powers conferred or retained—are to be determined (subject to certain specified exceptions) according to the laws of the Cook Islands, without reference to the laws of any other jurisdictions with which an international trust or disposition may be connected.[113] In addition, it is expressly declared that no international trust governed by the laws of the Cook Islands, and no disposition of property to be held upon the trusts thereof, is void, voidable, liable to be set aside, or defective in any fashion, nor may relief be had under section 13B of the ITA 1984, nor is the capacity of any settlor to be questioned, by reason *inter alia* that:

(a) the international trust or disposition avoids or defeats rights, claims, or interests conferred by the law of a foreign jurisdiction upon any person or contravenes any rules of foreign law or any foreign judicial or administrative order or action intended to recognize, protect, enforce, or give effect to any such rights, claims, or interests; or

(b) the laws of the Cook Islands or the provisions of the ITA 1984 are inconsistent with any foreign law.[114]

No action or proceedings, 'whether pursuant to this Act or at common law or in equity', to set aside the settlement of an international trust or to set aside any

---

[109] ITA 1984, s 13G(8). [110] ibid, s 13G(9). [111] ibid, s 13G(10).
[112] ibid, s 13G(11).
[113] ibid, s 13H(1). The specified exceptions are set out in subsection (2). [114] ibid, s 13I.

disposition to any international trust, or to seek relief or remedy under section 13B, shall be commenced, unless such action or proceedings is or are commenced (a) in the High Court of the Cook Islands and (b) before the expiration of two years from the date of the settlement of the international trust or the disposition to the international trust, as the case may be.[115] No action or proceedings, whether pursuant to the ITA 1984 or at common law or in equity, shall be commenced by any person:

(a) claiming to have had an interest in property before that property was settled upon or disposed to an international trust; and[116]
(b) seeking to derive a legal or equitable interest in property, unless such action or proceedings is or are commenced:
   (i) in the High Court of the Cook Islands; and
   (ii) before the expiration of two years from the date that such property was thus settled or disposed of.[117]

No action or proceeding (whether substantive or interlocutory in nature) to **38.74** which either section 13K or section 13B applies shall be commenced, and no order shall be made or granted by the court in respect of or relating to such action or proceeding (including any injunction or order that would have the effect of preventing the exercise of, or the granting or restoring of any right, duty, obligation, or power, or of preserving, granting custody of, detaining, or inspecting any property, including for the avoidance of doubt any *Anton Piller* or any *Mareva* injunction) unless the court, having regard to the affidavit filed pursuant to subsection (4), shall first be satisfied, beyond reasonable doubt, that:

(a) commencement of the action or proceedings is not precluded by the provisions of subsections (1) and (2); and
(b) the remedy or relief sought is not precluded by the provisions of subsection (6);

and in any action or proceedings to which section 13B applies, that:

(c) the remedy or relief sought is not precluded by the provisions of section 13B; and
(d) the evidence as disclosed by the affidavit demonstrates the ability of the plaintiff to prove those matters necessary to establish a right to relief under section 13B(1).[118]

---

[115] ibid, s 13K(1).   [116] The 'and' actually seems to indicate 'or'.
[117] ITA 1984, s 13K(2).   [118] ibid, s 13K(3).

In every action or proceeding to which section 13K or section 13B applies, the plaintiff must, upon commencement of such proceedings, file an affidavit deposing as to the matters specified in subsection (4). These include:

(a) the facts and circumstances giving rise to the action or proceedings;

(b) whether an action or proceedings have been commenced in any other jurisdiction between any of the parties to the action or proceedings, or by any party against the settlor of any relevant trust or of property upon any relevant trust;

(c) such of the circumstances of the plaintiff as are or may be relevant to determine the quantum of security to be paid by the plaintiff;

(d) the date upon which the international trust or property, in respect of which the action or proceedings are brought, was settled or disposed of;

and, in any case to which section 13B applies:

(e) the facts and circumstances of the creditor's cause of action (and, in the case of multiple or successive causes of action, those of the first in time to accrue);

(f) the date on which that creditor's cause of action accrued; and

(g) whether an action or proceedings have been commenced in any jurisdiction in respect of that creditor's cause of action and the date of commencement of such action or proceedings.[119]

38.75 Notwithstanding any other provision of the ITA 1984, the provisions of sections 13A–13K inclusive shall apply to every international trust governed, or expressed to be wholly or partly governed, by the law of the Cook Islands. This includes a trust that formerly was not wholly or partly governed by the law of the Cook Islands, but in respect of which the governing law of the trust has been changed (whether before or after registration) so that the trust, or any aspect of it, is governed or expressed to be governed by the law of the Cook Islands; and, without limiting the generality of the foregoing and notwithstanding any other law to the contrary, after the date of registration:

(a) the settlement or establishment of such trust;

(b) every disposition to such trust, including any disposition occurring before the date of registration or change of law; and

(c) every proceeding commenced after the date of registration concerning such settlement, establishment, or disposition,

shall be subject to the provisions of sections 13A–13K inclusive as if, upon the date that such settlement, establishment, or disposition occurred, the trust was an international trust governed wholly and exclusively by the law of the Cook Islands.[120]

---

[119] ITA 1984, s 13K(4).   [120] ibid, s 13K(5).

It is also provided that, in any action or proceedings (whether commenced **38.76** pursuant to the ITA 1984 or at common law or in equity) wherein the usual or appropriate remedy (whether sought or not) would be either:

(a) the setting aside of the settlement of, or disposition to, an international trust; or

(b) the award of a legal or equitable interest in property settled upon or disposed of to an international trust,

but the grant of such a remedy is or would be precluded by section 13B or section 13K(1) or (2), then neither damages nor any other relief or remedy which is effectively an alternative to or consequential upon a precluded remedy shall be awarded.[121]

It is an offence for a person to divulge or communicate to any other person infor- **38.77** mation relating to the establishment, constitution, business undertakings, or affairs of an international trust. In addition, all judicial proceedings, other than criminal proceedings, relating to international trusts, must, unless ordered otherwise, be heard in camera and no details of the proceedings shall be published by any person without leave of the court or person presiding.[122] These provisions are subject to those of section 23(3) which provides that every decision of the court in respect of any proceedings concerning the application or interpretation of the ITA 1984 must be published or reported for the purposes of affording a record of those proceedings, provided that in every case:

(a) the written decision of the court shall be edited to such extent as shall be necessary to preserve secrecy in respect of the identity of the trust, of every interested party, and of the subject matter of the proceedings; and

(b) no such report shall be reported or published unless or until a judge of the court shall have ascertained the views of the parties to the proceedings as to the adequacy of any editing undertaken, and certified in writing to the Registrar of the Court that the decision as edited may be released for publication or reporting.[123]

Unless excluded by the terms of a trust instrument, a trustee or an officer or **38.78** employee of a trustee company may divulge or make available information

---

[121] ibid, s 13K(6).   [122] ibid, s 23(1),(2).
[123] ibid, s 23(3). This seems to be a response to the approach adopted by the Court of Appeal in *515 South Orange Grove Association v Orange Grove Partners* (1995) No 208/94, where an attempt to prevent the publication of the judgment (under s 23(2)) was rejected and publication authorized both within and outside the Cook Islands.

relating to the establishment, constitution, business undertakings, or affairs of an international trust:

(a) to any person or class of persons as that trustee, officer, or employee considers necessary from time to time, in its complete discretion, for carrying out the management and administration of the trust assets in the ordinary course of business; or

(b) to a legal practitioner:

(i) for the purpose of obtaining legal advice relating to the establishment, constitution, business undertakings, or affairs of an international trust; or

(ii) for the purpose of prosecuting or defending any litigation relating to the establishment, constitution, business undertakings, or affairs of an international trust.

38.79 Although there is no legislation (other than those provisions in the ITA 1984 itself) providing specifically for the enforcement of a foreign judgment (other than New Zealand judgments) in the Cook Islands, there is a possibility that a foreign judgment which is registered in New Zealand will be moved to the High Court of the Cook Islands. Under the common law of the Cook Islands, a foreign judgment may be enforced in accordance with general principles of the conflict of laws—subject, of course, to the express provisions of the ITA 1984. However, in view of the express provisions of the ITA 1984 (and especially those in sections 13D and 13I), it seems most unlikely that a court in the Cook Islands would assist in the enforcement of a foreign court order which set aside, or purported to set aside, an international trust on the grounds that it defrauded creditors (unless, of course, the creditor could equally well have made out his case before a court in the Cook Islands).

38.80 There is no bankruptcy statute in the Cook Islands to govern individual bankruptcies.

Cyprus

38.81 Cyprus has also enacted legislation dealing specifically with 'international trusts'. The key provisions are to be found in the International Trusts Law 1992 ('the 1992 Law') which applies to all 'international trusts' created after 24 July 1992 (when the 1992 Law came into force).[124]

38.82 An 'international trust', for the purposes of the 1992 Law, is defined as a trust in respect of which:

(a) the settlor is not a permanent resident in the Republic of Cyprus ('the Republic');

---

[124] Date of publication in the *Official Gazette*. See also s 13.

(b) at least one of the trustees for the time is, during the whole duration of the trust, a permanent resident in the Republic;

(c) no beneficiary (other than a charitable institution) is a permanent resident of the Republic;

(d) the trust property does not include any immovable property situated in the Republic.[125]

The expressions 'immovable property' and 'trust' have the meanings ascribed thereto in section 3 of the Trustee Law 1955.[126]

38.83 Section 3(2) of the 1992 Law provides that an international trust shall not be void or voidable in the event of the settlor's bankruptcy or liquidation of his property or in any action or proceedings against the settlor at the suit of his creditors, notwithstanding any provision of the law of the Republic or of the law of any other country and notwithstanding further that the trust is voluntary and without consideration having been given for the same, or is made for the benefit of the settlor, the spouse or children of the settlor or any of them, unless and to the extent that it is proven to the satisfaction of the court[127] that the international trust was made 'with the intent to defraud the creditors of the settlor at the time of the transfer of his assets to the trust'. The burden of establishing such an intent on the part of the settlor lies on such creditors.[128] Moreover, an action against a trustee of the international trust pursuant to the provisions of section 3(2) must be brought within two years from the date when the transfer or disposal of assets was made to the trust.[129]

38.84 The provisions of the 1992 Law are not as detailed as those in the Cook Islands legislation (or those of most other offshore jurisdictions, in fact) and may well be less advantageous to a debtor (an expression which is not defined). As we have seen,[130] in the Cook Islands' International Trusts Act 1984, the creditor must be able to establish the grounds of his claim 'beyond reasonable doubt'. In contrast, no standard of proof is mentioned in the 1992 Law and it may therefore reasonably be assumed that the ordinary civil standard (on a balance of probabilities) applies. In Cyprus, the 1992 Law refers simply to an 'intent to defraud' (as did section 172 of the English Law of Property Act 1925), whereas the comparable Cook Islands legislation refers to 'the principal intent to defraud'. It may therefore not be necessary for the creditor to establish that the settlor had no other intention or purpose, provided that an intent to defraud was one of his intentions. Section 13B(1)(b) of the Cook Islands' ITA 1984 requires proof that the settlement or disposition rendered

---

[125] International Trusts Law 1992, s 2.   [126] ibid.
[127] Meaning the President of the District Court or the Senior Judge of the district where the trustees of the international trust (or any one of them who resides in the Republic) have their residence: ibid, s 2.
[128] ibid, s 3(2).   [129] ibid, s 3(3).   [130] See paras 38.58–38.60 above.

the settlor insolvent or without property by which the creditor's claim could have been satisfied. In Cyprus, such a result would probably be highly material in determining whether the settlor had the requisite intent to defraud, but it does not seem to be necessary to establish that the transfer of assets itself rendered him insolvent.

38.85 Indeed, in broad terms, the Cyprus legislation is very similar to section 172 of the English Law of Property Act 1925, save that there is an express time limit (of two years) for bringing any claim to set aside the transfer of assets (whereas section 172 was subject to no time limit at all). In the absence of a definition of a 'creditor' and also of some indication of the nature or extent of the obligations in respect of which a transferor might find himself liable to a creditor, it is difficult to see how far the 1992 Law will differ, in its effects, from either section 172 or the Cook Islands legislation. It is clear that, for the purposes of the 1992 Law, a creditor must have been a creditor of the settlor at the date of the transfer of assets. Thus, a transferor who settles his property on the eve of embarking on a trade or other hazardous venture would not be at risk from a person who became a creditor after that date—in other words, the settlement under challenge in *Re Butterworth*[131] would not have been set aside under the 1992 Law. Beyond this, however, many of the difficult questions which arose in relation to section 172 might still be pertinent in relation to the 1992 Law.

38.86 For example, in the English cases it was not entirely clear whether the 1571 Act or section 172 (as the case may be) could be of assistance to a person who had a cause of action against the transferor at the date of the relevant transfer of assets but who had not as yet obtained judgment. Was it sufficient that a cause of action had accrued by then? Did the cause of action have to have reasonable or realistic prospects of success? Would a person who had a cause of action against the settlor, but who was unknown to the settlor (for example because no claim had as yet been raised or made) be a creditor for these purposes?[132] The Cook Islands legislation makes express provision for such cases and clearly intends to include, within the class of potential claimants, those who had an accrued cause of action against the settlor (subject to the limitations specified). It is not clear, however, whether the 1992 Law has a similar intent or what its effect might actually be.

Gibraltar

38.87 In broad terms, the laws of Gibraltar are similar to, and indeed are derived from, those of England and Wales. Thus Gibraltar trust law is based almost entirely on English trust law. The same is also broadly true in matters of insolvency. Section 42 of the Bankruptcy Ordinance contains provisions similar to those of the

---

[131] (1882) 19 Ch D 588.
[132] See GW Thomas, *op cit*, 356–360.

English Bankruptcy Act 1914. A bankruptcy petition may not be presented in Gibraltar unless the debtor is domiciled in Gibraltar, or within a year before the presentation of the petition was ordinarily resident or had a dwelling house or place of business in Gibraltar, or carried on a business in Gibraltar, either personally or by means of an agent or manager.[133] Moreover, the (English) 1571 Act still applies in Gibraltar.[134]

However, the provisions of both the Bankruptcy Ordinance and the 1571 Act **38.88** are subject to important amendments, introduced in 1990, which are intended to provide a greater degree of protection for settled property against the claims of creditors. Section 42A(1) of the Bankruptcy Ordinance provides that, if:

(a) under or by virtue of any disposition made in respect of property the same becomes settled property; and
(b) the settlor is an individual; and
(c) the settlor is not insolvent at the date of the disposition;
(d) the settlor does not become insolvent in consequence thereof; and
(e) the disposition is registered in accordance with the requirements of any regulations,

such disposition shall not be voidable at the instance of or upon application by any creditor of the settlor.

A 'disposition' is defined in conventional terms as any disposition or series thereof, **38.89** howsoever effected, and (without prejudice to the generality thereof) includes any transaction, gift, grant, or transfer of property of any nature whatsoever.[135] 'Settled property' means any property held in or upon trust, other than any property held by any person as nominee for another person, or as trustee for any other person who is absolutely entitled to the beneficial interest in such property. 'The settlor', in relation to any settled property, includes the maker of any disposition of property which in consequence thereof becomes settled property. A 'creditor' is not defined, but the word 'insolvent' means, in respect of a settlor, any settlor whose liabilities, both actual and contingent or prospective, exceed the value of his assets. It is further provided that no claim by creditors shall be deemed to be a

---

[133] In other words, this is similar to the English Bankruptcy Act 1914, s 4(d) (as applied to Gibraltar) and not entirely dissimilar from the English Insolvency Act 1986, s 265(1).

[134] Incorporated into Gibraltar law by the English Law (Application) Ordinance. See *Hess v Line Trust Corporation Ltd* (1998/99) 1 ITELR 249 (Gibraltar Court of Appeal): claim under the 1571 Act struck out on the grounds that the settled property (shares in a Swiss company) was not amenable to execution by the Gibraltar court, and the claimant did not have an existing and quantifiable claim as creditor against the alleged fraudulent person.

[135] In order to be effective, the particular disposition must, of course, comply with the rules of law applicable to dispositions of that kind: *Pehrsson's Trustee in Bankruptcy v Von Greyerz* (1999) 2 ITELR 230, PC.

contingent or prospective liability of a settlor who, at the time of making the disposition, does not have actual notice of such claim or of the facts or circumstances which may render him liable to such claim.[136]

38.90 In order that section 42A shall apply to a disposition, it must be registered in accordance with the requirements of the relevant regulations. Section 42A(4) empowers the Financial and Development Secretary to make regulations for the establishment of a register of dispositions and for all matters incidental to the maintenance of such register.[137] These regulations—the Bankruptcy (Register of Dispositions) Regulations 1990[138]—came into effect on 1 December 1990. The regulations established a register, set out what must be entered thereon, laid down registration requirements, stipulated the conditions that have to be met by trustees, and so forth.

38.91 The regulations also make provisions for the secrecy of registered dispositions. Every person having an official duty in the administration of the regulations must regard and deal with all documents, information, and declarations relating to dispositions which have been registered, or in respect of which application for registration has been made, as secret and confidential. Any communication of, or attempt to communicate, such information or anything contained in such document or declaration is an offence in respect of which the guilty party is liable on summary conviction to a fine of £1,000. It is also provided that no person employed in carrying out the provisions of the regulations shall be required to produce in any court or before any authority or person for any purpose whatsoever any document or declaration in his possession in pursuance of the regulations, or to divulge or communicate to any court any matter or thing coming to his notice in the performance of his duties under the regulations, except as may be necessary for the purpose of carrying into effect the provisions of the regulations or for the purposes of any criminal or civil proceedings in which such document, declaration, matter, or thing is material.[139]

38.92 If section 42A applies to a disposition or settlement, then neither the (English) 1571 Act nor section 42 of the Bankruptcy Ordinance may do so.

38.93 The interpretation of section 42A is not free from difficulty. Although it is clear that a relevant liability need not be an actual or accrued liability, it is not entirely

---

[136] All these terms are defined in the Bankruptcy Ordinance, s 42A(3).

[137] Section 42A(4) provides further that, without prejudice to the foregoing, such regulations may include the matters specified in paras (a)–(g).

[138] Legal Notice No 158 of 1990. See also the Registered Trust Ordinance 1999.

[139] See Bankruptcy (Register of Dispositions) Regulations 1990, reg 9. The concluding words of reg 9(3) are very wide in their ambit and seem to contradict the restrictions laid down in the earlier parts of reg 9.

clear whether a 'contingent' liability differs from a 'prospective' one.[140] The location of the words 'both', 'and', and 'or' in the phrase 'both actual and contingent or prospective' suggests that they are not intended to indicate different concepts. On the other hand, it seems likely that what is contemplated is a differentiation of actual, probable, and possible liabilities. Suppose, for example, that, prior to the date of the disposition, the settlor has guaranteed another's liability. If performance of the guarantee has already been demanded, but not satisfied, the settlor is under an actual or accrued liability. If the question of performance has not yet arisen (or performance has not yet been demanded), the settlor is presumably under a contingent liability (ie his liability may become an actual liability if, but only if, the guaranteed person fails to meet his original liability). In addition, there may also be a liability which will probably (say, at a certain time in the future) become an actual liability.

The requirement that the settlor must have had actual knowledge at the time of making the disposition seems straightforward at first sight, but it, too, may be problematic. It does not apply, for example, to an actual or accrued liability. Consequently, it may be sufficient for a creditor to establish that a settlor had constructive (or even imputed) notice of such liability at the relevant time or, indeed, that no notice at all is required, ie the mere existence of the liability suffices. In addition, the requirement is not tied specifically to the contingent or prospective liability itself, but only to 'such claim' or to the facts or circumstances which 'may' render the settlor liable to 'such a claim'. **38.94**

The word 'claim' is not defined, and it is not clear whether (and, if so, how) a 'liability' differs from, or is identical with, a 'claim' in this context, although it would seem that the intention is that a 'claim' indicates a state of affairs (of which the settlor had actual notice) which will or might lead to an actual liability. In other words, 'claim' seems to indicate both a cause of action and a claim that has actually been made (the writ having been served). Thus, a settlor who, at the date of the disposition, has actual notice of a claim against him (say, for some negligent act or omission, or for breach of some contract)—whether the writ has been issued or simply notice given that proceedings are about to be commenced—can reasonably be said to be under a contingent or prospective liability. **38.95**

However, actual knowledge of 'facts or circumstances which may render him liable to such a claim' seems to be a very wide concept, and seems to suggest that the settlor need not necessarily have actual knowledge that a claim will (or even **38.96**

---

[140] It is also not obvious why the expression 'shall be deemed to be' has been used: the intention, it seems, is to ensure that a contingent or prospective liability of which the settlor does not have actual notice shall not actually be a contingent or prospective liability for these purposes (and not to identify and exclude a state of affairs which, by some deeming process, might otherwise be regarded as such a liability).

may) be made on the basis of such known facts and circumstances. For instance, a settlor may create a settlement when he is about to embark on a trade or other hazardous venture—as in *Re Butterworth*.[141] He may subsequently become insolvent, leaving many of his suppliers unpaid. At the date of the disposition, he may not have had an intention of defrauding such creditors (as would have been required under section 172 of the English Law of Property Act 1925). Nevertheless, it still seems to be arguable that he then had actual knowledge of facts and circumstances which may render him liable to claims from such creditors. If this is correct, then there must be many cases in which section 42A of the Bankruptcy Ordinance will provide a settlor with no greater protection than did section 172 in England.

38.97   Such uncertainties would also seem to affect the question of the insolvency of the settlor. It is clear that the settlor must not be insolvent at the date of the disposition. However, it must also be the case that he has not become insolvent in consequence thereof. There is no time limit during which such 'consequential' insolvency must be shown to have arisen. Indeed, in the case of a contingent or prospective liability, the question of 'consequential' insolvency must be determined *ex post facto* and may even be open-ended (subject to any limitation period applicable to the specific cause of action). If the settlor was under an actual liability at the time of the disposition, it should not be difficult to conclude whether or not, by and in consequence of that disposition, he was rendered incapable of discharging that liability, ie whether it rendered him insolvent or not. However, if, at the date of the disposition, the settlor simply had actual knowledge of facts or circumstances which may render him liable to a claim by a creditor, it is difficult to see how that liability can be quantified, in order to determine the effect of the disposition on his solvency, until the creditor has obtained final judgment. Thus, the absence of a time limit for bringing an application to set aside a particular disposition could add to the uncertainty surrounding the insolvency of the settlor and the avoidability of the settlement.

38.98   In this sense, at least, the complete abandonment of any requirement of an intent to defraud (which, of course, never applied in bankruptcy cases, but which was—and presumably still is—central in relation to the 1571 Act), and its replacement by an almost mathematical requirement of insolvency, can be said to be detrimental, rather than helpful, to the debtor. For example, it would be quite possible, in appropriate circumstances, to find that a settlor or transferor did not have an intention to defraud his creditors, despite the fact that his disposition rendered him insolvent (especially in relation to future creditors) and, in consequence, for that disposition not to be set aside. However, where the criterion is the insolvency of the settlor or transferor (whether caused by or as a result of that disposition), all

---

[141]   (1882) 19 Ch D 588.

that is required is factual proof of such insolvency, and it becomes irrelevant whether or not he intended to defraud his creditors.

The Isle of Man

In broad terms, the law of the Isle of Man in relation to settlements by individuals **38.99** who are adjudicated bankrupt is similar to that in section 42 of the English Bankruptcy Act 1914 (with the same two-year and ten-year limits). There are also similar preconditions (concerning domicile, residence, and place of business) for the presentation of a bankruptcy petition in the Isle of Man; and it may be impossible to bankrupt in the Isle of Man a non-Manx settlor of a Manx trust.

A disposition to a Manx trust may be capable of being set aside (irrespective of **38.100** bankruptcy) under the Statute of Fraudulent Assignments 1736, which provides that:

> . . . all fraudulent assignments or transfers of the debtor's goods and effects shall be void and of no effect against his just creditors, any custom or practice to the contrary notwithstanding.

Until recently, the scope of this provision was uncertain. Does it require some **38.101** form of dishonesty on the part of the transferor of property, and does it apply to future debts as well as existing ones? It seems to have been assumed generally that its effect in Manx law was substantially the same as that of the 1571 Act on English law. Indeed, a statement to this effect seems to have been made by Kneen CR in *Re Corrin's Bankruptcy*,[142] but there is no report or transcript of the judgment in this case. In *Corlett v Radcliffe*,[143] the Judicial Committee of the Privy Council, on appeal from the Court of Chancery of the Isle of Man, considered the relationship between the (English) 1571 Act and the (Isle of Man) 1736 Statute, but in a somewhat inconclusive manner. Lord Chelmsford stated:[144]

> Each case must depend upon its own circumstances, and in all the question is one of fact, whether the transaction was *bona fide*, or was a contrivance to defraud creditors. It may, however, be stated generally that a deed is void against creditors when the debtor is in a state of insolvency, or when the effect of the deed is to leave the debtor without the means of paying his present debts. If this is the condition of the debtor, or the consequence of his act, it is not sufficient to render a deed valid that it should be made upon good consideration: for as is said in *Twyne's Case*,[145] 'a good consideration does not suffice if it be not also *bona fide*'.

Although the words 'whether the transaction was *bona fide*, or was a contrivance to defraud creditors' suggest that dishonesty was required if a transaction was to be caught by the 1736 Statute, this was by no means clear. Such a requirement would have distinguished Manx law from English law; and, indeed, the (Manx)

---

[142] (1912) unreported: it is referred to 'with caution' in *Re Heginbotham's Petition* (1999) 2 ITELR 95.
[143] (1859) 14 Moo PCC 121.   [144] ibid, 135.   [145] (1602) 3 Co Rep 80b.

1736 Statute and the (English) 1571 Act are in very different terms. However, it is the 1571 Act that refers to an 'intent' to 'delay, hinder or defraud creditors', whereas the 1736 Statute makes no reference to any such 'intent'.

38.102   Some of these questions were resolved recently by the High Court of the Isle of Man (Common Law Division) in *Re Heginbotham's Petition*.[146] The petitioner had been awarded damages in default of defence to his counterclaim against a company; and his petition alleged that the company had transferred its assets (a property management portfolio, which generated a monthly income of £200, and a trading name)[147] to other companies, with 'no reasonable commercial ground or purpose', but solely to avoid the consequences of the litigation and of any judgment entered against it, and had therefore made a fraudulent transfer within the meaning of the 1736 Statute.

38.103   Deemster Cain held that, despite the absence of any reference to an 'intent' to defraud in the 1736 Statute, the expression 'fraudulent assignments or transfers' must impute an intent by the debtor to assign or transfer his goods or effects fraudulently, ie in the context of the relationship of debtor and creditor. This did not necessarily involve actual deceit, but there had to be dishonesty.[148] The next question was whether the intent to defraud applied only to existing creditors of the debtor at the date of the assignment or transfer or also to future creditors. In *Corlett v Radcliffe*, Lord Chelmsford referred to a debtor 'in a state of insolvency' and to the case 'when the effect of the deed is to leave the debtor without the means of paying his present debts'.[149] On this basis, Deemster Cain concluded:[150]

> A state of insolvency implies an inability to pay existing, or present, debts. A person is not in a 'state of insolvency' merely because he may not be able to pay contingent or future debts, which may never materialise . . . The expression 'present debts' must have been a reference to the debts of the debtor at the date of the deed or other transaction. It cannot have been a reference to debts which that person might possibly incur at some future date. I would construe that term 'present debts', however, to include known and ascertained debts which are to fall due on a date in the future. A transaction or contrivance designed to deprive known and ascertained future

---

[146]   (1999) 2 ITELR 95. See also P Dougherty, 'Asset Protection Trusts in the Isle of Man' (1999) 7 Journal of International Trust and Corporate Planning 177.

[147]   The 1736 Statute refers to the debtor's 'goods and effects'. It was conceded in *Corlett v Radcliffe* (1859) 14 Moo PCC 121 that lands liable to be taken for sale in execution for debt were considered by law to be goods, chattels, or effects. In *Heginbotham* the property was intangible (business rights and goodwill) but there is no discussion in the case whether this constituted 'goods and effects' for the purposes of the Statute.

[148]   Adopting the observations of Cairns LJ in *Lloyds Bank Ltd v Marcan* [1973] 1 WLR 339, 1392.

[149]   See (1859) 14 Moo PCC 121, 135.

[150]   (1999) 2 ITELR 95, 112. It is doubtful, in fact, whether Lord Chelmsford's observations were intended to have such wide application. *Corlett* decided that Manx and English law were the same only on the point that a deed is void against creditors when the debtor is in a state of insolvency or when the effect of the deed is to leave the debtor without the means of paying his present debts. It does not actually purport to decide anything on wider questions, such as similarities (if any) in the law relating to future creditors.

creditors of 'timely recourse to property which would otherwise be applicable for their benefit'[151] would not be honest in the context of the relationship of debtor and creditor and would not therefore be bona fide.

Thus, the (Manx) 1736 Statute has clearly not been construed as broadly as the (English) 1571 Act. The former does not assist future, unknown, or unascertained creditors. Indeed, *Re Heginbotham* seems to suggest that only known or ascertained existing creditors are protected.

On the facts of *Re Heginbotham's Petition* itself, it was held that the transfer of **38.104** assets to other companies was a bona fide transaction and was not a contrivance to defraud the then present creditors or known and ascertained future creditors. At the time when the assets were transferred, the petitioner had served neither a defence in the action against him nor his counterclaim. Even if the existence of the counterclaim had been known, this would not have created a 'present' debt nor a 'known and ascertained future debt'. The petitioner was therefore not a creditor for the purposes of the 1736 Statute and the transactions were not void.

Jersey

Bankruptcy ('desastre') in Jersey is governed by the Bankruptcy (Desastre) (Jersey) **38.105** Law 1990, the provisions of which are broadly similar to those of the English Insolvency Act 1986 as far as transactions at an undervalue are concerned. In Jersey, however, the definition of 'undervalue' depends largely on whether there has been a lack or insufficiency of 'cause' (which is broadly similar to, but not identical with, 'consideration' in English law).[152]

Until recently, Jersey law in relation to the setting aside of a disposition to defraud **38.106** creditors was in a state of uncertainty, there being very little by way of authority on the matter. A Jersey court had held that a gratuitous transfer of assets by a person to a third party in order to defeat the claims of his creditors may be set aside,[153] and there seems to be no reason, in principle, why the same should not apply to a transfer of assets to trustees. Moreover, a disposition which defrauds creditors may be set aside in Jersey on the grounds that it is contrary to public policy,[154] although this will probably not be allowed where the action is essentially one to enforce the revenue laws of a foreign country.[155]

---

[151] As Pennycuick V-C said in *Lloyds Bank Ltd v Marcan* [1973] 1 WLR 1387.
[152] See Bankruptcy (Desastre) (Jersey) Law 1990, Art 17.
[153] See, eg, *Golder v Societe des Magasins Concorde Ltd* [1967] JJ 721. The disposition must not, of course, be a complete sham: *Rahman v Chase Bank (CI) Trust Company Ltd* [1991] JLR 103.
[154] Trusts (Jersey) Law 1989, Art 10(2)(b)(ii).
[155] *In the Matter of Tucker* [1987–88] JLR 473 (an application by an English trustee in bankruptcy for an order from the Royal Court to act in aid of and be an auxiliary to the English High Court (pursuant to the Bankruptcy Act 1914, s 122) was rejected on the grounds that the sole creditor was the UK Inland Revenue and the application was an indirect attempt to enforce a foreign revenue law). Cf, however, *Le Marquand and Backhurst v Chiltmead Ltd* [1987–88] JLR 86. See also *Re Roy Clifford Tucker* (Guernsey CA, 27 September 1988).

38.107 In addition, a Jersey court had shown itself willing to comply with a request from a foreign court (Florida) to direct trustees to exercise their discretion in a particular manner.[156] On this basis, it might have seemed somewhat imprudent to rely on the laws of Jersey for asset protection purposes. Recently, however, the Jersey courts have had to deal with complex litigation involving a series of claims made by a company, Grupo Torras SA, in an attempt to recover substantial sums of money lost as a result of the fraudulent activities of its chairman, one Sheikh Fahad. Two major judgments delivered recently in the course of this litigation have addressed and clarified many issues relevant to asset protection trusts and the way in which they may be dealt with under Jersey law. They merit close attention.

38.108 The background to this litigation may be summarized as follows.[157] Grupo Torras SA ('GT') was a company owned by the Kuwait Investment Office. At all material times, Sheikh Fahad was its chairman. Between May 1988 and October 1990, the Sheikh conspired with others to defraud GT of some US$430 million, of which his personal share was $120 million. GT obtained judgment against the Sheikh in respect of the fraud in the English High Court for a total, with accrued interest, of some $800 million.[158] This judgment was registered in Jersey under the Judgments (Reciprocal Enforcement) (Jersey) Law 1960 and was therefore enforceable within the jurisdiction of the Jersey courts. Sheikh Fahad was hopelessly insolvent. He had been declared bankrupt in The Bahamas, where he now resided. GT was unable to recover its judgment debt from Sheikh Fahad's personal assets.

38.109 Between 1981 and 1994, the Sheikh set up a number of trusts in different jurisdictions. GT now sought to recover its judgment debt from those trusts. Two of them were situated in Jersey, in that the trustee was resident in the island and the trusts were governed by Jersey law. The first was the Esteem Settlement, established in 1981. At about the same time, Sheikh Fahad also acquired ownership of a Liechtenstein Anstalt called Ceyla ('Ceyla'). In August 1992, Sheikh Fahad also established the Number 52 Trust. Prior to the commencement of the fraud, Sheikh Fahad contributed assets to the Esteem Settlement and to Ceyla from time to time. These transfers were not subject to attack. Between 1988 and 1992, after he had begun to defraud GT, he contributed more of his own funds to the Esteem Settlement and to Ceyla. In April 1992, he contributed £4.4 million of monies which he had stolen from GT. In August 1992, he contributed £4 million of his own funds to the Number 52 Trust. In 1999, the Royal Court gave directions on

---

[156] *Cadwell v Cadwell* (unreported) 8 August 1989. See also the Judgment (Reciprocal Enforcement) (Jersey) Law 1960; *Le Marquand and Backhurst v Chiltmead Ltd* [1987–88] JLR 86; and *Compass Trustees Ltd v McBarnett* (2002) 5 ITELR 44.

[157] For a more detailed account of the litigation and discussion of the various judgments, see GW Thomas, *op cit*, 457–474. See also the recent decision in *Abacus (CI) Ltd and Grupo Torras SA v Sheikh Fahad Mohammad al Sabah* (2004) ITELR 368; [2003] JRC 092.

[158] *Grupo Torras SA v Sheikh Fahad Mohammed Al Sabah* [1999] CLC 1469. For other proceedings in England arising from the 'Grupo Torras litigation', see (2001) Lloyd's Rep Bank 36; [2001]

the procedure to be followed in order to resolve any questions as to the validity of the two trusts or of transfers of assets to those trusts in the light of the judgment of the English High Court. These proceedings were known as 'the 1999 Action'. In the 1999 Action, GT claimed all the assets in the two trusts on a number of grounds.

(1) It alleged that the general circumstances surrounding the use of the trusts by Sheikh Fahad enabled the trusts to be set aside in law on three grounds: namely, that they were contrary to public policy; that the 'veil' of the trusts should be lifted; or that a remedial constructive trust in favour of GT should be imposed on the assets of the trusts.
(2) It alleged that all transfers of assets to the trusts at any time after the fraud began in 1988 were made with the intention of defrauding creditors; such transfers were therefore liable to be set aside.
(3) It alleged a proprietary claim over certain of the trust assets in respect of £1,267,686.

In April 2000, before any of the above claims had been tried, the trustee of the trusts sought directions of the court ('the 2000 Proceedings') as to whether the assets of the two trusts should, pursuant to the discretionary powers conferred on the trustee by the trust deeds, be distributed wholly or partly to Sheikh Fahad, such distribution to be effected by way of payment to GT as his judgment creditor. (In so applying, the trustee surrendered its discretion to the court.) The Esteem Settlement was a discretionary trust for the benefit of the settlor (Sheikh Fahad), his children and remoter issue and those who married them. The Sheikh himself specifically objected to this course of action. The Jersey Court of Appeal ordered that the 2000 Proceedings should be heard before the 1999 Action.

The Royal Court held that: (i) the trustee, and therefore the court,[159] could make **38.110** a distribution for the benefit of a beneficiary against the objections of that beneficiary; (ii) on the facts of the case, a distribution by way of payment to Grupo Torras in reduction of the Sheikh's debt would not have been a payment for the benefit of the Sheikh; (iii) on the assumption (contrary to the court's conclusion) that such a payment would be for the benefit of the Sheikh, any benefit to him would in reality be minimal[160] and it would be a wholly wrong exercise of discretion to pay out all or most of the trust fund so as to confer a very intangible benefit on him

CLC 221; [1999] CLC 885; [1997] 3 WLR 1143; The Times, 13 October 1997; The Times, 17 April 1997; [1995] CLC 1025; Lawtel Doc No C0100019 (11 October 2000); Lawtel Doc No C0006852 (13 May 1998).

[159] It is not suggested, of course, that the court could exercise such a discretion or power where it had not been surrendered by the trustee to the court.

[160] Even if all the funds in all the relevant settlements (of which the Esteem Settlement was but one) were distributed in payment of the Sheikh's debts, he would still have owed US$583 million.

and cause a material disadvantage to the other beneficiaries. Grupo Torras, who had been joined as a party to the application, appealed.

38.111 The Court of Appeal upheld the decision.[161] It was held that where an inferior court had exercised a discretion on behalf of a trustee, an appeal court should not interfere with it and substitute its own discretion unless: (i) it could be shown that the inferior court had erred in law in relation to an issue that affected the exercise of its discretion or (put another way) had misdirected itself with regard to the principles in accordance with which its discretion had been exercised; or (ii) the court below had taken into account matters which it ought not to have taken into account or had failed to take into account matters which it ought to have done; or (iii) the decision of the inferior court was plainly wrong or (put another way) it appeared on other grounds that injustice would result from the manner in which the discretion had been exercised. The Court of Appeal concluded that the court below had been entitled to come to the conclusion that the payment of a small proportion of the beneficiary's indebtedness was of no material benefit. The fact that his debt arose out of fraud could not characterize a reduction in the debt as a benefit in circumstances where it would not be of benefit for a non-fraudulent beneficiary. Although there was no rigid rule that in no case would the reduction of a beneficiary's debts be of benefit to him, in the circumstances of this case the court had been justified in concluding that there was no sufficient benefit to justify the proposed distribution and that the interests of other beneficiaries would be prejudiced thereby.

38.112 Consequently, although the decision certainly does not preclude a creditor from applying to a Jersey court for an order that trust funds be distributed to him in payment of a beneficiary's debts—especially where a tangible and material 'benefit' to that beneficiary can be shown—the fact remains that it has severely restricted the chances of success of any such application. If the trustee, in the proper exercise of his discretion, decides not to make such a distribution, there is nothing that the creditor can do to challenge and overturn that decision. In these circumstances, the creditor would probably be better advised to seek the setting aside of the settlement.

38.113 In any event, following the failure of Grupo Torras in the 2000 Proceedings, the Royal Court ordered (on 12 February 2001) that the claims referred to in paragraphs (2) and (3) above be tried as separate issues prior to the trial of the remaining issues in the 1999 Action. By the time of the hearing, following further amendment to its pleadings, GT's claims fell under three headings:

(i) a proprietary tracing claim in respect of £1.276 million (being the balance of the £ 4.4 million referred to above) and the tracing of this sum into the assets of the Esteem Settlement;

---

[161] *Abacus (CI) Ltd v Al Sabah* (2000) 4 ITELR 555, Gloster JA, Sumption and Rokison JJA.

(ii) alternatively, a claim in restitution for the sum of £1.276 million against the Esteem Settlement;

(iii) a claim to set aside all transfers made into the Esteem Settlement, the Number 52 Trust and Ceyla at any time after the fraud began in May 1988, on the basis that these transfers were made in fraud of GT as a creditor of Sheikh Fahad. (This part of the claim is referred to as the 'Pauline action'.)

These claims raised a number of complex and novel issues of Jersey law, which the Royal Court identified as follows:

(I) Does Jersey law recognize the ability to trace assets and, if so, in what circumstances?

(II) Does Jersey law recognize a claim in restitution even where there is no fault on the part of an innocent recipient?

(III) Although the case of *Golder v Société des Magasins Concorde Limited*[162] establishes that Jersey law recognizes a right of action to set aside gifts made in fraud of creditors, what are the limits of and principles underlying such an action?

(IV) What limitation period is applicable to the Pauline action?[163]

Each of these claims was then considered. A brief summary of the Royal Court's findings follows.

(I) Does Jersey law recognize the ability to trace assets and, if so, in what circumstances?

The answer to this first question depended on the answers to a series of other, subsidiary questions. The first of these was: does the victim of fraud have an equitable proprietary interest in the proceeds of the fraud? It was acknowledged that, under English law and many other common law jurisdictions, the position was clear:[164] a person in the position of Sheikh Fahad, who, as a director, defrauds the company of which he is a director, holds the proceeds on constructive trust for the company which has an equitable proprietary interest in the property in question. It was argued, however, that there was no justification for importing this concept into Jersey law. The Jersey law of property was very different and was essentially based on the civil law, which does not recognize differences between legal and equitable ownership. Even in the case of express trusts, the Trusts (Jersey) Law 1984 ('the 1984 Law') does not state clearly that beneficiaries have an equitable proprietary interest in the trust assets rather than a personal right against the trustee. Even if

38.114

---

[162] [1973] JJ 721.

[163] Claim (iii) was referred to as 'the Pauline action', the title apparently being derived from the action of the same name in Roman law. The Royal Court was anxious, however, to point out that it was not considering the exact nature of the action in Roman law and how that would have applied to this particular case, but endeavouring to establish the parameters and principle of Jersey law.

[164] The court referred to *Westdeutsche Landesbank Girozentrale v Islington London Borough Council* [1996] AC 669, 716; *Black v S Freedman & Co* (1910) 12 CLR 105, 110; *Lipkin Gorman v Karpnale Limited* [1991] 2 AC 548, 565.

beneficiaries under an express trust do have such a proprietary interest, the same is not necessarily true in respect of a constructive trust. In the court's view, a beneficiary under an express Jersey trust has an equitable proprietary interest in the trust property. It was true that nowhere does the 1984 Law state specifically that a beneficiary under an express trust has an equitable proprietary interest in the trust fund. However, the 1984 Law is not a codification. Trusts were recognized and enforced by the Jersey courts well before the passing of the 1984 Law and, in doing so, they looked to English law for guidance on trust matters and, by and large, adopted English principles, save where it was appropriate to differ. A Jersey trust is essentially the same animal as is found in English law subject to certain local modifications.[165]

38.115 It was then argued, relying in particular on Articles 29 and 50 of the 1984 Law, that, even if a beneficiary under an express trust has a proprietary interest, there was no reason to follow English law in holding that the position was the same outside the context of an express trust. If the notion of equitable property interests were current in Jersey, it was difficult to see why express provision had to be made for a constructive trust in the limited and simple case of a profit made by a trustee on trust property. Similarly, it would not have been necessary to have included Articles 50(3) in a jurisdiction which already recognized the notion of an equitable proprietary interest arising in the event of an alienation or conversion of trust property. Thus there was no counterpart in the English Trustee Act 1925, no doubt because it was basic jurisprudence that trust beneficiaries can assert proprietary interests in the traceable proceeds of an unauthorized disposition. However, the court pointed out that the flaw in this argument was that the 1984 Law was not a codification, nor was it enacted in a vacuum. There was already a customary law of trusts in existence. Many of the provisions of the 1984 Law were simply reflections of the pre-existing law or of English principles. There was no implication that, because a provision was included in the 1984 Law, it was something which did not exist beforehand. The court was, therefore, in no doubt that it was already the law of Jersey that the making of a profit from a breach of trust gave rise to a constructive trust, but it was clearly reasonable and sensible to reflect that principle in the statute. A beneficiary under a constructive trust did have an equitable proprietary interest in the assets which are the subject of that trust.

38.116 The question then arose as to whether Jersey law should follow English law in holding that a constructive trust exists in circumstances such as the present. The constructive trust had been used by the courts of England and other jurisdictions as a mechanism to assist in fashioning appropriate remedies to deal with problems of commercial fraud. It accorded with the interests of justice. If the fraudster did

---

[165] The court approved of the summary of the position expressed in Matthews and Sowden, *Jersey Law of Trusts* (3rd edn) para 1.20.

not hold the property on constructive trust, the victim had to prove his claim alongside ordinary creditors of the fraudster, because the assets belonged to the fraudster and would be available for such creditors. The Royal Court had no doubt that Jersey law should draw on the experience of English law and other jurisdictions to impose a constructive trust in a case such as the present. Therefore, in Jersey too, when property is obtained by fraud, equity imposes a constructive trust on the fraudulent recipient so that the victim has a proprietary interest in such property.[166]

Does Jersey law permit tracing?[167] It was argued that Jersey law should be slow to adopt English rules in relation to tracing. It was clear[168] that, under English law, tracing was part of the law of property, not part of the law of unjust enrichment. However, the Jersey law of property had wholly different origins from that of England. It did not appear that countries based on the civil law had adopted the concept of tracing. However, both of the two previous Jersey cases dealing with the issue of tracing, namely *Re the Viscount; In the matter of PKT Consultants (Jersey) Limited*[169] and *Royal Bank of Scotland Limited v Khan*,[170] strongly supported the view that tracing did form a part of Jersey law. In the court's judgment, tracing offered an effective method of vindicating and safeguarding proprietary rights, particularly in cases of fraud. **38.117**

Although the rules of tracing that should be applied ought, as a starting point, to be the English rules, the court emphasized that it was not bound by them and, indeed, ought to depart from them if convinced that there was a better alternative. The court adverted to the debate in England as to whether the time has come for the common law tracing rules to be subsumed into the more flexible rules of equitable tracing. In particular, this would allow tracing through a mixed fund. Although it had not heard argument on this point, it expressed the preliminary view that the differences between the two systems of tracing in England had a historical origin which had no application in Jersey. On the face of it, there seemed to be little reason to incorporate such technical distinctions into Jersey law and some advantage in applying the more flexible rules of equitable tracing (as constituting the Jersey rules of tracing) to all tracing actions. In particular, in the case of a current account where trust monies had been mixed with monies belonging to an innocent third party, English law applied the 'first in, first out' (FIFO) basis (or the rule in *Clayton's Case*[171]). However, this rule worked in a haphazard manner and **38.118**

---

[166] The court recognized that this conclusion raised questions concerning Art 10(2)(a)(iii) of the 1984 Law, but these were not sufficient to negate the conclusion.

[167] The court adopted the meaning of 'tracing' (as opposed to 'following') now current in England and referred to L Smith, *The Law of Tracing* (OUP, 1997) 6; *Foskett v McKeown* [2000] 2 WLR 1299, 1304.

[168] From *Foskett v McKeown* [2000] 2 WLR 1299, 1322.

[169] Unreported, 1 August 1991.   [170] 1999/183: unreported, 19 October 1999.

[171] (1816) 1 Mer 572. See paras 33.45–33.57 above.

had been much criticized.[172] Consequently, the Royal Court concluded that it saw no advantage in adopting into Jersey law a rule which had been much criticized and which could clearly produce capricious and arbitrary results. The 'Apportionment Method' (as suggested in *Barlow Clowes*[173]) was more likely to produce a fair result and there was no reason not to adopt it. As a general rule, therefore, monies to be traced through a mixed bank account (whether current or deposit) should be dealt with under Jersey law by application of the Apportionment Method.

38.119 Could tracing extend to improvements in pre-existing property? On the assumption that English law—and specifically *Re Diplock*[174]—prohibited tracing money into improvements in land already owned by a third party (and the Royal Court was not convinced that English law went this far), there was no reason why this principle should be applied in Jersey. If the English court held that, where funds being traced are mixed with an innocent recipient's funds and used to purchase real property, the funds can be traced into that property; but that where the funds being traced are used to improve an asset already owned, they cannot be traced, then it was hard to see the logic of this distinction. If the funds being traced had added value, why should the innocent volunteer benefit from that increase in value to which he had contributed nothing, but the beneficiaries whose funds have been used to add value not be entitled to anything? Fairness surely dictated that they should be able to recover that increased value. This would leave the innocent volunteer in no worse position than he was previously in the sense that he would be left with the value of the unimproved property. Consequently, the position in Jersey was held to be that, where funds being traced had been spent on improvements to property already owned by an innocent volunteer, the claimant could trace into the increased value of the property which was attributable to those funds. Clearly if, as envisaged in *Diplock*, there had been no increase in value attributable to the funds, there could be no tracing as the funds would have been lost.

38.120 Finally, in relation to the tracing claim, the Royal Court held that:

(a) under Jersey law (as under English law) a plaintiff's equitable title is defeated and the right to trace is lost, either in whole or in part, in circumstances where it would be inequitable to allow the plaintiff to trace; and

(b) although the concept of the equitable charge (being the appropriate remedy for enforcing a tracing exercise through a mixed fund) was not known to Jersey law, the court did not foresee any insurmountable difficulty in the way of fashioning remedies which ensure that effect can be given to a tracing decision and was prepared to do so in an appropriate case. Indeed, it saw no reason why the court should not have such a power.

---

[172] *Barlow Clowes International Limited (in liquidation) v Vaughan* [1992] BCLC 910; *Re Walter J Schmidt & Co, ex parte Feuerbach* (1923) 298 F 314, 316.
[173] [1992] BCLC 910.   [174] [1948] 2 All ER 318, esp 360.

(II) Does Jersey law recognize a claim in restitution even where there is no fault on the part of an innocent recipient?[175]

As an alternative to its proprietary tracing claim, GT brought a claim in restitu-   **38.121**
tion based upon unjust enrichment. It accepted that the claim arose only if it did
not succeed in its tracing claim. In the light of the court's conclusions on the tracing claim, it did not strictly need to consider the restitutionary claim.
Nevertheless, the court thought it right to express its conclusions.

All parties agreed that, were this case being heard in England, a claim in restitu-   **38.122**
tion could not succeed. Under English law, where the property in question or its
identified proceeds were still in the hands of the innocent recipient (applying the
relevant tracing rules), the plaintiff was entitled to recover the property or those
proceeds as a proprietary claim. But if the recipient did not still have the property
or its identifiable proceeds, then no claim lay against the recipient unless he had
been at fault in some way. If he was guilty of fault, equity treated him as a constructive trustee. The nature and degree of fault had been the subject of conflicting
decisions in England,[176] but these did not bind the Royal Court and it declined to
follow them. It held that, under the law of Jersey, where property in respect of
which a person (a beneficiary) has an equitable proprietary interest (because the
property has been taken from the beneficiary by a person who is in a fiduciary
position towards that beneficiary) is received by an innocent volunteer, the
beneficiary has a personal claim in restitution against the recipient even where the
recipient has not been guilty of any 'fault' in receiving the property. In other
words, the state of mind required for a 'knowing receipt' claim under English law
is not required in Jersey. It is a strict restitutionary liability. However, the claim is
based upon unjust enrichment and, accordingly, the beneficiary can only succeed
to the extent that the recipient remains unjustly enriched. A defence of change of
position is therefore available. The court also emphasized that the liability is a
personal one; the recipient is not a constructive trustee for the beneficiary.

(III) Although the Jersey law recognizes a right of action to set aside gifts made in fraud of creditors, what are the limits of and principles underlying such an action?[177]

The third claim (referred to in the 1999 Action as 'the Pauline action') differed from   **38.123**
the proprietary tracing claim and the claim in restitution, in that it was based on an
acceptance by GT that Sheikh Fahad had transferred his own assets to the relevant

---

[175] The court heard further argument on the question of change of position and delivered its conclusions on 11 March 2002.

[176] Referring to *Re Montague's Settlement Trust* [1987] Ch 264 and *Belmont Finance Corporation v Williams Furniture Limited (No2)* [1980] 2 All ER 393. For the current state of English law, see paras 30.55–30.88 above.

[177] The court heard further argument on the question of entitlement to profits earned on an asset alienated in fraud of creditors, but subsequently recovered in a Pauline action, and delivered its conclusions on 12 March 2002.

settlements but it was alleged, instead, that he had done so in order to defraud GT as his creditor and that, in the circumstances, the transfers could be set aside.

38.124   It was clear that Jersey law recognized an ability, in certain circumstances, to set aside a transfer undertaken in fraud of creditors. There was judicial authority to this effect, namely *Golder v Société des Magasins Concorde Limited*.[178] The issue before the court in the 1999 Action was essentially whether Jersey law allowed recovery in circumstances that went beyond those which existed in *Golder*.

38.125   The first question that needed to be addressed was: who is a creditor? The defendants contended that only a person who is a creditor at the time of the transaction under attack could bring a Pauline action and that a person did not become a creditor until he has a certain claim. GT's claim did not arise out of contract, but out of tort. GT did not have a certain claim until the English court delivered judgment in its favour (June 1999). Any disposal made by Sheikh Fahad before that time could not be attacked by GT because GT was not then a creditor. This contention thus gave rise to two subsidiary questions:

38.126   (a) **Does the claim of a creditor have to pre-date the transaction under attack?** In dealing with this issue in the present case, the court considered a number of treatises by a variety of jurists—not only writers on Jersey law (such as Poingdestre and Le Geyt) but also French jurists (such as Pothier, Domat, Dalloz, Planiol, and Ripert) writing both before and after the introduction of the Code Civil.[179] It was also referred to a number of cases decided under the English 1571 Act—decisions which the court did not find helpful. Having surveyed such authorities, the court concluded that the law of Jersey was as stated by Poingdestre, and, implicitly, by the Royal Court in Golder, namely that only a creditor whose debt preceded the transaction in question could bring a Pauline action. Just as it was right that creditors should be protected from fraudulent debtors, so was it important that security of receipt and an assumption of validity of transactions be considered. To set aside transactions at the instance of a person whose claim did not exist at the time of the transaction was a major interference with the freedom for a person to deal with his assets freely and for persons who transact with him to be able to rely on what has been done.

38.127   (b) **When can the debt of a creditor be said to arise, particularly in cases of tort?** The defendants argued that a person claiming in tort did not rely upon the debtor's creditworthiness and the implied undertaking that his patrimony was available to support his obligations. The Pauline action was therefore not available to a person claiming in tort until he becomes a judgment creditor (as in Golder). Moreover,

---

[178] [1973] JJ 721.

[179] In the absence of judicial authority, considerable weight is attached to writers on the law of Jersey (in the present case, Poingdestre and Le Geyt), on the law of Normandy, and also on French law.

they relied on the fact that, in the Bankruptcy (Desastre) (Jersey) Law 1990, Article 29 was drawn more narrowly than the equivalent provision in the Insolvency Act 1986 of the United Kingdom and only allowed proof in a desastre of:

> . . . certain debts and liabilities, present or future, certain or contingent, to which the debtor is subject at the time of the declaration, or to which he becomes subject before payment of the final dividend by reason of any obligation incurred before the time of the declaration . . .

Thus a claim for liability in tort, particularly where the proceedings had not yet been brought, was not provable in a bankruptcy. The claimant could not, therefore, be classified as a creditor. It would be wholly illogical, said the defendants, for a person who could not claim in a bankruptcy to be treated as a creditor for setting aside a transaction in a Pauline action. In addition, the defendants relied upon the fact that the Pauline action originally envisaged a claim based in contract.

In the event, however, the court was clearly struck by the fact that the consequences of holding that a claimant had not become a creditor until the date of judgment in his favour were unreasonable and unacceptable. On this issue, therefore, it opted to have regard to modern French writers (Dalloz in particular) and held that, for the purposes of a Pauline action under Jersey law, a person was deemed to become a creditor when the facts giving rise to his cause of action occur, even if the validity of the cause of action was not established until later. All the facts necessary to give rise to the cause of action must have occurred before a person can be deemed to be a creditor. He cannot, in the court's judgment, be considered a creditor when only some of the facts which support his cause of action have occurred. However, once liability to the creditor is established, it relates back to the date of the facts which give rise to that liability. **38.128**

Is insolvency on the part of a debtor required? If so, at what stage? It was clear **38.129** that a Pauline action arises as a result of a disposal by the debtor to the prejudice of his creditors. All the texts agreed that it was necessary to show actual prejudice to the creditor. It was accepted by all parties that there must be insolvency at the date of the action; otherwise there were sufficient assets to meet the claim and therefore no prejudice. However, the court also concluded that the weight of relevant authority was overwhelmingly in favour of the view that a creditor must also show that the debtor was insolvent at the time of the disposition or became insolvent as a result of it. The English cases, which turned on the terms of an English statute which had no application in Jersey, were not of assistance.

However, the court also added that it believed that the principles set out in Dalloz **38.130** and approved in *Golder* had to be applied with common sense having regard to the modern world. Nowadays, insolvency, particularly when the action was being heard many years after the disposition in question, cannot be measured with precision. Assets were more fluid. Furthermore, it was extremely unlikely that the creditor bringing the action would have access to all the information concerning the financial affairs of the debtor so many years ago. In addition, as the present case showed, the debtor's assets may be spread throughout the world and may be held through the medium of companies. Accordingly, the court held that, once the plaintiff had established insolvency on the part of the debtor at the time of the action, the burden then shifted to those seeking to uphold the disposition to prove that he was not also insolvent at the time of or as a result of the disposition. Furthermore, a broad common-sense approach had to be taken to the question of insolvency resulting from the disposition. It was not a question of carrying out a meticulous balance-sheet exercise the instant following the disposition. In most cases this was simply not practical and was an unfair and unrealistic burden on the creditor. It was more a question of seeing whether, within a reasonably short period following the disposition, the debtor became insolvent so that it could be said that the disposition contributed to or exacerbated the insolvency. The court must simply be satisfied that there was a close connection in time and effect between the disposition and the subsequent insolvency.

38.131 **How was insolvency to be measured?** A claim which was contingent, but was later found to be due, should be brought into account when calculating insolvency at the time of the disposition. Once the liability is established by law, it relates back to the facts which give rise to the liability. Accordingly, the liability is to be taken into account from that time for the purpose of calculating solvency. Balance-sheet solvency should be calculated as it always is, namely by calculating the value of all the debtor's assets and deducting his liabilities. There should not be excluded from the debtor's assets those items which are inalienable, difficult to distrain upon, or concealed.

38.132 On the other hand, if the court had been required to decide the issue, it would have held that assets in a revocable trust are not to be counted as assets of the debtor for these purposes: unless and until revoked, the assets are held by the trustees upon the trusts set out in the trust deed; and the trustees owe fiduciary duties to the beneficiaries, and the assets cannot properly be considered to be those of the debtor merely because he has a power of revocation.

38.133 **The difference between transactions 'lucrative' and 'onereuse'.** In *Golder*, the Royal Court approved the statement of Poingdestre that there were two types of alienation to be considered in a Pauline action. The first was an alienation to a *volunteer* which Poingdestre called '*alienations faites pour cause lucrative*'. The second was an alienation made *for value* which he calls '*alienations faites pour cause onereuse*'. In the first case, the alienation was voidable when the alienor alone was guilty of an intention to defeat his creditor but, for the alienation to be voidable in the second case, both the alienor and the alienee must be privy to the real nature of the transaction. An alienation did not become '*onereuse*' simply because there was some 'cause' given. A transaction only becomes '*onereuse*' if the 'cause' given by the recipient was commensurate and proportionate to the value of the thing alienated; if the price is not commensurate or proportionate in this way, it was a transaction '*lucrative*'.

What is the required state of mind on the part of the debtor? In *Golder*, the court had approved the following statement from Dalloz: **38.134**

> ... the creditor in order to succeed had to prove the intention to defeat creditors and their actual defeat by showing that their debtor is insolvent and that his insolvency was due to the act which is challenged.

The court in the present proceedings concluded that *Golder* correctly stated the law of Jersey on this point. It was clear that, at all times until well after the introduction of the Code Civil in France, the Pauline action required the two elements of *prejudice* to creditors and an *intention* on the part of the debtor to cause that prejudice. Dishonesty was required. It was accepted that, during the latter part of the nineteenth century and the twentieth century, French law had changed, and it was now enough that the debtor foresaw that prejudice would or might result from the transaction. This was very far removed from any normal meaning of 'intention'. On the contrary, a requirement merely to be aware that a particular result might follow was really a requirement of recklessness rather than intention. A debtor may indeed wish not to prejudice his creditors but may be prepared for other reasons (for example tax advantages) to go ahead and take the risk of its transpiring that they are in fact prejudiced. **38.135**

The court concluded that it was not open to it to substitute a test of recklessness for a test of intention. Recklessness had never been sufficient until recent developments in French law. All the sources which carried weight in Jersey required intention. Accordingly, the court held that, in order to succeed in a Pauline action in Jersey, it must be shown that the transaction in question was undertaken by the debtor with the intention (object) of defeating his creditors. Of course, in order to ascertain the state of a person's mind the court had to consider all the evidence and draw inferences. The fact that the defeat of creditors was the natural result of a transaction was undoubtedly a material factor in assessing whether the necessary state of mind on the part of the debtor was established. The weight to be given to this factor will vary according to the circumstances, not least by reference to the degree of certainty that prejudice to the creditors will result from the transaction.

In the event that the debtor had more than one purpose in relation to the transaction, there was no reason to require that an intention to defraud creditors was his dominant purpose. In reality, when there was more than one purpose, it would often be a very artificial exercise to try and establish which purpose was dominant. The requirements of a Pauline action were satisfied under Jersey law if, where there was more than one purpose, a *substantial* purpose of the transaction was to defeat creditors. **38.136**

38.137 The nature of the claim—possible defences. According to the Royal Court, the Pauline action has always been a revocatory action. The creditor is not entitled to compensation from an innocent volunteer: he is entitled to reclaim the property. Where the original property is no longer in the hands of the recipient, it is clear that, in the case of innocent receipt, there is no liability beyond the enrichment (if any) which the recipient still enjoys. If, and to the extent that, the recipient no longer retains any benefit, then no recovery is permitted from him. Accordingly, it was held that, once a creditor has established that all the other conditions of a Pauline action are satisfied, the court must consider whether, in reliance upon the receipt, an innocent recipient has so changed his position that it would be inequitable to require him to make restitution or to make restitution in full. The underlying principle is that an order for restitution should not result in an innocent recipient being worse off as a result of the transactions in question than he would have been if those transactions had not occurred. The burden of showing that it would be inequitable to order restitution lies upon the recipient.

(IV) What is the limitation period?

38.138 There was no judicial authority on the prescriptive period for a Pauline action. After considering a number of analogous authorities and relevant writers, the Royal Court concluded that a creditor has no title in the thing alienated. Indeed, he is not asserting any claim on his part to the thing itself. The creditor sues the defendant either to return the thing itself to the debtor's patrimony, if he still has it, or to return such value originating from the thing as may remain in the recipient's hands. In those circumstances, it is a claim for money. It went on to hold that a 10-year period (referred to by Le Geyt) should be a general period which should be taken to apply to all personal actions and all actions concerning movables save to the extent that they had already been held to be subject to a different period (for instance tort, actions concerning estates, etc) or that some other period was, by analogy, clearly more applicable. The court also expressed the view (although the point did not have to be decided) that one prescriptive period should cover Pauline actions against innocent and fraudulent recipients (and that period in each case should be ten years).

Judgment

38.139 The court found that 'a substantial purpose' of Sheikh Fahad in making several of the transfers to the No 52 Trust, Ceyla, and the Esteem Settlement was to defeat GT's claim against him. He therefore had the necessary intent to defraud. Indeed, the court added that, had it been necessary to do so, it would also have found this to have been his dominant purpose, with his tax planning purpose being of lower significance.

Subsequent proceedings

38.140 Although the Royal Court held that Sheikh Fahad's transfers into trust after 1990 were made with an intent to defraud creditors, the trustees and beneficiaries could rely on a defence of change of position. In the circumstances, the effect was that there were no remaining assets in the No 52 Trust but substantial assets remained in the Esteem Settlement. Sheikh Fahad's trustee in bankruptcy was joined as a plaintiff in the 1999 Action and, in the final chapter in the Grupo Torras litigation in Jersey, claimed the remaining assets in the Esteem Settlement on the grounds that it was a sham,[180] that it infringed the maxim *donner et retenir ne vaut*,[181] that it infringed public policy,[182] that the veil of the trust should be pierced so that its assets became available to the settlor's creditors, and that the court should declare that the trustee held the trust assets on a remedial constructive trust for the creditors. The Royal Court dismissed all these additional claims.[183]

The Esteem Settlement as a sham.   The court held that, in order to be a sham,   **38.141**
both the trustee and settlor must intend that the true arrangement is otherwise than it is made to appear.[184] A 'unilateral' sham intention on the part of the settlor alone was not sufficient. In fact, in this particular case, there was no evidence of a sham intention on the part of either.[185]

Donner et retenir ne vaut.   This claim was based on the allegation that Sheikh   **38.142**
Fahad exercised control and dominion over the trust assets. However, the maxim could apply only if he was capable of freely disposing of the assets at all times. The Royal Court held that he had not reserved any powers in the trust deed to enable him to exercise such control; and the trustee had been appointed as a genuine trustee and not simply as the settlor's nominee.

Piercing the veil.   There was no authority to support this allegation and the   **38.143**
court held that there is no such cause of action. A trust is fundamentally different from a company: it has no separate legal personality and is essentially a description of the obligations owed by a trustee to beneficiaries, and the concept of a 'veil' could not be applied to such a relationship.[186]

Public policy.   A trust can, of course, be declared void because it is against public   **38.144**
policy. However, it was conceded here that the Esteem Settlement was initially valid and the claim alleged only that it subsequently became invalid. The court expressed the view that a particular action or decision by a trustee might be against public policy, but, in such an event, it would normally be the action or decision that would be struck down and not the trust itself, although it also conceded that, in exceptional circumstances, the trust itself might also be declared invalid. In this particular case, however, there was no basis for such a conclusion.[187]

---

[180] *Abacus (CI) Ltd and Grupo Torras SA v al Sabah* (2004) ITELR 368, paras 41–54; [2003] JRC 092.   [181] ibid, paras 61–73.
[182] ibid, paras 74–124.   [183] ibid.
[184] Having referred, with approval, to *Snook v West London Riding Investments Ltd* [1967] 2 QB 786; *Hitch v Stone* [2001] STC 214.
[185] *Abacus (CI) Ltd and Grupo Torras SA v al Sabah* (2004) ITELR 368, paras 41–60.
[186] ibid, paras 74–124.   [187] ibid, paras 125–135.

38.145 **Remedial constructive trust.** The trustee in bankruptcy's claim was based on the fact that a remedial constructive trust had been imposed in Australia (on the ground of unconscionability),[188] Canada (on the ground of unjust enrichment),[189] and New Zealand (on both grounds).[190] However, the Royal Court noted the fact that, in England, the remedial constructive trust had been rejected[191] and inclined to the view that it was also not a remedy available in Jersey:[192] in any event, if it were available in Jersey, one would not be imposed on the facts of this case.[193]

38.146 Ultimately, the position which the Royal Court sought to adopt was one in which a balance was struck between the settlor's right to dispose of property and certainty and security of receipt for the recipent-trustee, on the one hand, and the rights of creditors on the other. This balance is difficult to strike at the best of times, but the task would not be made easier by creating novel causes of action, and in this instance the court declined to do so.

---

[188] *Muschinski v Dodds* (1985) 160 CLR 583.

[189] *Pettkus v Becker* (1980) 117 DLR (3d) 257; *LAC Minerals Ltd v International Corona Resources Ltd* (1989) 61 DLR (4th) 14.

[190] *Commonwealth Reserves v Chodar* (2001) 3 ITELR 549.

[191] *Re Polly Peck International plc (No 2)* [1998] 3 All ER 812.

[192] The court also expressed the view that, if the remedial constructive trust were part of Jersey law, it would be preferable if it were based on unjust enrichment.

[193] *Abacus (CI) Ltd and Grupo Torras SA v al Sabah* (2004) ITELR 368, paras 136–151.

39

OFFSHORE PURPOSE TRUSTS[1]

A. Introduction

Another prominent use for offshore trusts is the creation of non-charitable pur- **39.01**
pose trusts. As we have seen,[2] the creation of non-charitable purpose trusts is not
possible under English trusts law: at least, there is sufficient doubt and uncertainty
on the point to make it a very risky enterprise. Offshore trusts legislation, however, has now introduced provisions which enable such trusts to be created and
provide them with substantial protection. Clearly, there is no great demand for
offshore trusts for a specific pet, or even for the promotion of fox-hunting—and,
even if there were, they would be small trusts indeed. Offshore legislation is motivated by the fact that non-charitable purpose trusts play an important role in various
commercial transactions, for instance as a means of effecting off-balance-sheet
transactions, or financing complex and large-scale commercial transactions.[3] The
overall aim and purpose of offshore trusts legislation, then, is to enable owners of
property to do things in the relevant offshore jurisdiction that they could not
accomplish at home—which essentially means filling the gaps and curing the
defects that have proved problematic in relation to the traditional English trust.

In broad terms, all this has been accomplished in a variety of different ways. For **39.02**
example, some offshore centres have extended the definition of what constitutes

---

[1] This section is based on GW Thomas, 'Purpose Trusts' (being Chapter 6 (237–336) of
J Glasson (ed), *The International Trust* (Jordans, 2002)). [2] See Chapter 6 above.
[3] See, for example, P Matthews, 'The New Trust: Obligations without Rights?' in AJ Oakley
(ed), *Trends in Contemporary Trust Law* (Oxford, 1996) 1, 18–22.

a 'charitable purpose' in a way that is intended to resolve some of the problems encountered in the English law of charities. Belize and Labuan, for instance, have adopted the *Pemsel*[4] classification of charities, but Belize has added to it the protection of the environment and the advancement of human rights and fundamental freedoms as acceptable charitable purposes, while Labuan has added the promotion of art, science, and religion. (Neither, however, mentions sport and recreation.) The Cook Islands and Cyprus—both of which have introduced an 'international trust'—also adopt the *Pemsel* classification of charities but have relaxed it to the extent that a trust need only be 'substantially' for one of those purposes (ie there is no need for a purpose to be exclusively charitable).

39.03   Some jurisdictions also provide extended perpetuity and accumulation periods. Trusts need not be subject to a perpetuity period at all in the Cook Islands and Cyprus. Elsewhere, there are still perpetuity periods—120 years in Belize, 100 years in Bermuda and Labuan, and just 80 years in the Isle of Man. Given that a perpetuity period of at least 80 years is possible in England—and probably well over 100 years if a 'royal lives' clause is used—this may not be a great advantage. There is an advantage, however, as far as accumulation of income is concerned: there is no accumulation period at all in the Cook Islands and Cyprus; and elsewhere (as in Belize) it can match the duration of the trust itself. The availability of an extended accumulation period is likely to be one of the major attractions of these offshore jurisdictions.

39.04   Most offshore jurisdictions have clearly taken note of the fact that, in the reported English decisions, the reason why non-charitable purpose trusts may have been held void could have been something other than the application of the beneficiary principle—such as uncertainty or lack of specificity in the description of the purpose, the fact that the particular purpose was contrary to public policy or immoral, and so on.[5] Consequently, virtually all the offshore statutes provide, in essentially similar terms, that non-charitable purpose trusts are valid, provided the purpose is specific, reasonable, and capable of fulfilment; that it is not immoral, unlawful, or contrary to public policy; and that its terms are sufficiently certain. This is the case, for example, in Belize, Bermuda, British Virgin Islands, and the Isle of Man. This is not true of all the offshore jurisdictions, however. The Cook Islands, Cyprus, Jersey, and Labuan all recognize the validity of non-charitable purpose trusts but do not impose the same, or indeed any, such restrictions. Equally important, of course, is the fact that, in several jurisdictions, non-charitable purpose trusts can last in perpetuity.

39.05   Hand in hand with the recognition of non-charitable purpose trusts must go the question of enforcement. A purpose cannot enforce a trust. Offshore legislation

---

[4] *Commissioners for Special Purposes of Income Tax v Pemsel* [1891] AC 531.
[5] See para 6.25 above.

therefore had to, and does, provide an enforcement mechanism for non-charitable purpose trusts. The precise method varies slightly from place to place; and one can see potential problems with most of the mechanisms used. In Bermuda, for example, the original non-charitable purpose trusts legislation made provision for the appointment of a protector. Under the revised legislation (the Trusts (Special Provisions) Amendment Act 1998, section 12B)[6] there is no longer a need to appoint a protector: now the Supreme Court can make an order on the application of 'any person interested' under the trust, the settlor, a trustee, or any other person considered to have sufficient interest in enforcement; and, failing any such person, on the application of the Attorney-General. Despite its somewhat convoluted nature, this seems a feeble mechanism: the trust instrument may not have appointed anyone; the settlor may be dead (or even ruled out by the trust instrument); the trustees may have adopted an erroneous view of their duties or just be unwilling to act (especially if the underlying problem is that they are in breach of trust); and there may be no other person with a sufficient interest and willing to act. So how will the Attorney-General find out about any breach?

Similar problems arise in the British Virgin Islands, where the mechanism is slightly different. Here, at least one trustee must be a 'designated person' (who must be a barrister, solicitor, or accountant-auditor practising in the British Virgin Islands).[7] Also, the trust instrument must appoint a protector (with a mechanism for appointing his successor) as enforcer. In the British Virgin Islands, the Attorney-General has no standing to enforce a trust which is not exclusively charitable. Again, what happens if the enforcer is dead, unwilling, incapable, or refusing to act? There is no provision in the legislation outlining the duties of the enforcer nor imposing any sanction on him for not acting. The trustee who is also the 'designated person' must inform the Attorney-General of the fact (and will be liable to a fine if he fails to do so); and only then can the Attorney-General act, by applying to court for the appointment of a new enforcer. If it is a 'mixed' trust (ie one with human beneficiaries and non-charitable purposes), do the human beneficiaries have any standing at all to enforce the trust or have their rights been displaced by the Act's provisions for an enforcer? What if the trustees (especially a sole trustee who is also the designated person) and the enforcer decide not to support the 'purpose' but to preserve capital and accumulate income for the human remainderman? Is this a breach of trust for which they may be liable, for example is there any duty to maintain an even hand? Must they invest in the normal way? More important still, who is going to complain? **39.06**

Other offshore jurisdictions have similar enforcement mechanisms—using one or more of the combination of an enforcer, a protector, a designated person (who may or may not be a trustee), and with or without the involvement of the **39.07**

---

[6] See paras 39.27–39.32 below.   [7] See para 39.66 below.

Attorney-General of the particular jurisdiction. However, all of them seem to raise the same kinds of questions as the legislation of Bermuda and the British Virgin Islands as to the duties and liabilities of both enforcers and trustees. Above all, ultimately, they all lead back to the core problem of all non-charitable purpose trusts: what happens when the specified enforcement mechanism (however complicated it may be) breaks down?

B. Non-Charitable Purpose Trusts Legislation of Specific Jurisdictions

Belize

39.08 The law of non-charitable purpose trusts in Belize is governed largely by sections 14 to 16 of the Belize Trusts Act 1992 ('TA 1992') which came into force on 18 May 1992.[8]

Charitable purposes

39.09 Under section 14 of TA 1992, the following purposes shall be regarded as charitable:

(a) the relief of poverty;
(b) the advancement of education;
(c) the advancement of religion;
(d) the protection of the environment;
(e) the advancement of human rights and fundamental freedoms;
(f) any other purposes which are beneficial to the community.

39.10 Categories (a), (b), (c), and (f) correspond with Lord Macnaghten's classification of charitable purposes in *Commissioners for Special Purposes of Income Tax v Pemsel*.[9] In England, categories (d) and (e) may be charitable, although particular cases within category (e) (and possibly category (d) as well) may fall foul of the prohibition on political purposes qualifying as charitable. Even in Belize, the scope of category (e) is not defined: it is not clear how 'human rights' or 'fundamental freedoms' will be construed (the two terms being intended, presumably, to convey different meanings) nor whether a trust intended to advance these objectives by changing the law of Belize or of another country would be regarded as charitable.[10] Somewhat surprisingly, the TA 1992 does not deal expressly with recreational charities, which in England have caused some difficulty.

---

[8] See para 38.32 above.   [9] [1891] AC 531, 583.
[10] cf *National Anti-Vivisection Society v IRC* [1948] AC 31; *McGovern v A-G* [1982] Ch 321. See also ss 14(3) and 15(1)(b) of TA 1992; paras 39.12–39.17 below.

Section 14(2) provides that a purpose shall not be regarded as charitable unless the **39.11**
fulfilment of that purpose is for the benefit of the community or a substantial
section of the community, having regard to the type and nature of the purpose.
This reproduces the requirement of public benefit which applies to all charitable
trusts in England other than trusts for the relief of poverty. It may be that trusts for
poor relations (which are, anomalously, valid charitable trusts in England) are not
valid in Belize, although they may be covered by the final words of section 14(2)
('having regard to the type and nature of the purpose'); or, alternatively, they may
be valid private trusts either as being trusts for the benefit of individuals or as being
non-charitable purpose trusts.

Section 14(3) provides that a purpose may be regarded as charitable whether it is to **39.12**
be carried out in Belize or elsewhere and whether it is beneficial to the community
in Belize or elsewhere.

Non-charitable purposes

The combined effect of section 15(1) and section 7(2) is that trusts for non- **39.13**
charitable purposes are valid in Belize, provided that:

(a) the purpose is specific, reasonable, and capable of fulfilment;[11]
(b) the purpose is not immoral, unlawful, or contrary to public policy;[12]
(c) the terms of the trust are not so uncertain that its performance is rendered
      impossible;[13]
(d) the terms of the trust provide for the appointment of a protector who is
      capable of enforcing the trust and for the appointment of a successor to any
      protector.[14]

Section 7(3) makes provision for trusts which are created for two or more pur- **39.14**
poses, of which some are lawful and others are not, or where some of the terms of
the trust are invalid and others are not. If the trust purposes or terms can be 'separated', the court may declare that the trust is valid as to the terms which are valid
and the purposes which are lawful,[15] the invalid terms or the unlawful purposes
being, in effect, struck out of the trust instrument. If no such separation is possible, the trust is invalid.[16]

---

[11] TA 1992, s 15(1)(a).   [12] ibid, s 15(1)(b).
[13] ibid, s 7(2)(b)(iii). To the extent that the court declares that the terms of the trust are so uncertain that its performance is rendered impossible, the trust is invalid and unenforceable. A charitable
trust, on the other hand, is deemed always to be capable of performance (ibid), with the result that
questions of initial impossibility and general charitable intention appear to play no part in the law
of charity of Belize.   [14] ibid, s 15(1)(c).
[15] ibid, s 7(3)(b). Where a trust is partially invalid the court may declare what property is to be
held subject to the trust (s 7(4)), ie subject to so much of the trust as the court declares to be valid.
Property as to which a trust is invalid is, subject to any order of the court, to be held on a resulting
trust for the settlor or his estate (s 7(5)).   [16] ibid, s 7(3)(a).

39.15   The enforcement of non-charitable purpose trusts in Belize is dealt with by sections 16(2) and 15(1)(c) and (2). Section 16(2) provides that a protector of a trust shall have the following powers:

(a) (unless the terms of the trust otherwise provide) power to remove a trustee and to appoint a new or additional trustee;

(b) such further powers as are conferred on the protector by the terms of the trust or the TA 1992.

Section 15(1)(c) requires a trust for non-charitable purposes to appoint a protector and to confer on him power to enforce the trust. Section 15(2) empowers the Attorney-General to appoint a protector, where he has reason to believe that there is no protector of a trust for non-charitable purposes or the protector is unwilling or incapable of acting. A protector appointed by the Attorney-General is empowered from the date of his appointment to exercise the functions of protector of the trust.

39.16   The protector may be the settlor or a trustee.[17] Where there is more than one protector then, subject to the terms of the trust, any functions conferred on the protectors may be exercised if more than one-half of the protectors for the time being agree on their exercise.[18]

39.17   In the exercise of his office, a protector is not to be accounted or regarded as a trustee[19] but, subject to the terms of the trust, 'shall owe a fiduciary duty... to the purpose for which the trust is created'.[20] Given that a purpose cannot sue for breach of duty and, indeed, that no duty can sensibly be said to be owed to any 'purpose', and given that the role of the Attorney-General is apparently confined to the appointment of a protector where none is acting or the protector is unwilling or incapable, the effect of the imposition of this fiduciary duty is unclear.

Duration of trusts and the rule against perpetuities

39.18   Section 6 of the TA 1992 confines the duration of all trusts (other than trusts established exclusively for a charitable purpose or purposes) to a period of 120 years from the date of their creation and provides that a trust shall terminate on the 120th anniversary of its creation unless terminated sooner. Trusts for non-charitable purposes are accordingly subject to a maximum duration of 120 years. The TA 1992 provides that, subject to the terms of the trust and to any order of the court, undistributed income or capital at the compulsory termination of the trust (not being a trust established for a charitable purpose) is to be held on a resulting trust for the settlor or his estate.[21] If the terms of the trust provide (as

---

[17] TA 1992, s 16(3).   [18] ibid, s 16(6).   [19] ibid, s 16(4).   [20] ibid, s 16(5).

[21] ibid, s 44(1). The words 'subject to any order of the court' in s 44(1) (which are also found in s 7(5)) suggest that a resulting trust is not an automatic or necessary consequence of the termination (or invalidity) of a trust, though the scope of the court's power is unclear.

they may) for the trust property to vest in a particular person or persons, then it must be distributed to him or them within a reasonable time[22] subject to any retention by the trustee of sufficient assets to meet existing, future, contingent, or other liabilities.[23]

Section 6(3) provides that 'the rule of law known as the rule against perpetuities **39.19** shall not apply to any trust to which this section applies'. The effect of this provision, taken together with section 66(3), seems to be that the rule against perpetuities should not apply to any trust the proper law of which is the law of Belize. Section 6(1) provides for a maximum duration of 120 years; section 6(2) then removes that restriction from charitable trusts; and section 6(3) is intended to abolish the rule with respect to all trusts governed by the law of Belize. All this is expressed in such a way that section 6 seems to have the odd result that the rule against perpetuities continues to apply in the case of exclusively charitable trusts with regard to the vesting of interests (as under English law), but does not apply to any other trusts, whether as regards the vesting of interests or the duration of the trust, subject only to the statutory maximum duration of 120 years.

Accumulation

The terms of a non-charitable purpose trust may direct or authorize the **39.20** accumulation of all or part of the income of the trust for a period not exceeding the maximum duration of the trust,[24] ie for a period which may endure for 120 years.

Variation of trusts

Although the TA 1992 contains provisions for the variation of trusts,[25] they do **39.21** not authorize the court to approve a variation in respect of a trust for non-charitable purposes. A settlor who wishes to create a Belize trust for one or more non-charitable purposes, with or without an ultimate trust for ascertainable human beneficiaries, should consider the desirability of conferring on the trustees or protector an express power of variation.

Bermuda

The general non-statutory law of Bermuda follows English law. Until the **39.22** enactment of the Trusts (Special Provisions) Act 1989 ('TSPA 1989')[26] a trust for a purpose could exist only if its purposes were exclusively charitable within one of the four recognized heads of charity (the relief of poverty, the advancement of

---

[22] ibid, s 46(1).   [23] ibid, s 46(2).   [24] ibid, s 6(4).
[25] ibid, s 45(2) (charitable trusts) and s 48 (non-charitable trusts).
[26] The Trusts (Special Provisions) Act 1989 came into force on 31 January 1990, the day appointed by the Premier of Bermuda pursuant to s 1.

education, the advancement of religion, or other purposes beneficial to the community)[27] and it was for public benefit. As in England, a charitable trust established under the law of Bermuda may exist in perpetuity.

39.23 Part II of the TSPA 1989 contained special provisions governing the creation, validity, administration, and enforcement of purpose trusts, provisions which were subsequently adopted, in substantially the same form, by other jurisdictions. However, the original Part II of the TSPA 1989 has now been replaced in its entirety by a new Part II substituted by the Trusts (Special Provisions) Amendment Act 1998 ('TSPAA 1998'), which came into force on 1 September 1998.

Meaning of a 'purpose trust'

39.24 In the original legislation,[28] a 'trust for a purpose or purposes' was defined as any trust other than a trust for the benefit of particular persons (whether or not immediately ascertainable), or of some aggregate of persons ascertained by reference to some personal relationship. This rather odd definition raised numerous points of construction and sometimes proved difficult to satisfy. However, the TSPAA 1998 has now substituted a new section 12A, which provides that a trust may be created for a non-charitable purpose or purposes, provided that the conditions set out in section 12A(2) are satisfied. Such a trust is now referred to as a 'purpose trust' and the conditions laid down are that the purpose or purposes are:

(a) sufficiently certain to allow the trust to be carried out;

(b) lawful; and

(c) not contrary to public policy.

39.25 Under the original legislation (section 13(l)(a) and (b)), the purpose or purposes had to be 'specific, reasonable and possible' and not be 'immoral, contrary to public policy or unlawful'. Whether there is any change of substance here is doubtful: a trust which is 'sufficiently certain' for the purposes of limb (a) of the new definition is likely to be one which would also have been 'specific, reasonable and possible', and an 'immoral' purpose would seem to be against public policy in any event. Consequently, trusts for 'philanthropic purposes', for 'the promotion of democratic values', and the like are likely to be insufficiently certain to be valid. Similarly, trusts 'for artistic purposes'[29] or 'to present artistic dramatic works'[30] or 'for good works'[31] might be considered too vague, and a trust to block up a house for a lengthy period

---

[27] A purpose which falls within the first three categories is charitable regardless of the place where the purpose is pursued or effected. A purpose may be charitable within the fourth category only if it is of benefit to the community of Bermuda.

[28] TSPA 1989, s 12(1).   [29] *Re Ogden* (1909) 25 TLR 382.

[30] *Associated Artists Ltd v IRC* [1956] 2 All ER 583.   [31] *Re How* [1930] 1 Ch 66.

might be considered unreasonable.[32] And schools for prostitutes or pickpockets would presumably be against public policy and be void.[33] The applicable test of 'certainty of objects' of a purpose trust—and particularly a discretionary purpose trust—is not laid down in the TSPAA 1998, but, presumably, the principles established in English law in relation to trusts for beneficiaries will apply, ie the 'complete list' test in the case of a purpose trust where there is no discretion as to the application of income or capital[34] and the 'any given postulant test' in the case of a discretionary trust for purposes.[35] It is also likely that a discretionary trust for purposes will fail for 'administrative unworkability'[36] in Bermuda, as in England.

39.26 A purpose trust may only be created in writing.[37] A purpose trust which does not comply with section 12A is invalid.[38]

Enforcement

39.27 The absence of any beneficiary who can claim a beneficial interest—at least, so as to enforce the primary trusts, as opposed to preventing misapplication—clearly presents a fundamental problem of enforcement for any purpose trust, whether or not it is created by statute. (The TSPAA 1998 says nothing about the location of the beneficial interest under a purpose trust.) Whereas the TSPA 1989 declared that the instrument creating a trust for purposes had to appoint a person to enforce the trust, and also had to make provision for the appointment of his successor,[39] the new legislation imposes no such requirement. Instead, section 12B(1) of the TSPAA 1998 simply provides that the Supreme Court may make such order as it considers expedient for the enforcement of a purpose trust on the application of any of the following persons:

(a) any person appointed by or under the trust for the purposes of the subsection;
(b) the settlor, unless the trust instrument provides otherwise;
(c) a trustee of the trust;
(d) any other person whom the court considers has sufficient interest in the enforcement of the trust.

In addition, where the Attorney-General satisfies the court that there is no such person who is able and willing to make an application under section 12B(1), the Attorney-General himself may make an application for enforcement of the trust (which he could not do under the TSPA 1989).

39.28 As an enforcement mechanism, this provision seems rather feeble—it is certainly weaker than that provided in the TSPA 1989. The court cannot act unless, and

---

[32] *Brown v Burdett* (1882) 21 Ch D 667.   [33] *Re Pinion* [1965] Ch 85, 105.
[34] *IRC v Broadway Cottages Trust* [1955] Ch 20.   [35] *McPhail v Doulton* [1971] AC 424.
[36] *R v District Auditor, ex parte West Yorkshire Metropolitan County Council* (1986) 26 RVR 202.
[37] TSPAA 1998, s 12A(3).   [38] ibid, s 12C.   [39] TSPA 1989, s 13(1)(e).

until, some authorized person makes an application to it. However, there may not be any such person. For example, the trust instrument may not have appointed anyone; the settlor may be dead, or ruled out by the trust instrument (for example for tax reasons); the trustees may have taken an erroneous view of their duties or wilfully be refusing to act; and there may not be any person who has a sufficient interest to complain (especially where the purpose trust is perpetual). It is not at all clear how, in such a case, the Attorney-General (any more than the court) will have notice of any breach of trust or of the need to make an application to the court in respect of any matter connected with the enforcement of the trust. The TSPA 1989 contained detailed provisions requiring one of the trustees to be a 'designated person', whose duties, the performance of which was backed by criminal sanctions, included the supervision of the (compulsorily appointed) enforcer and the reporting to the Attorney-General of any refusal or failure to act on the part of the enforcer. Perhaps none of these provisions would have prevented a trustee and enforcer from committing a breach of trust if they were intent on doing so. Nevertheless, the TSPAA 1998 has removed one layer of protection entirely while weakening another. It is also rather bizarre to find a trustee of a purpose trust listed as one of the persons who may apply to the court for enforcement of the trust: if he is a sole trustee, he is hardly likely to bring proceedings against himself; and if he is one of several trustees complaining against his co-trustees, he would presumably have a right to bring proceedings in any event.

39.29　It remains to be seen who will be regarded as having a 'sufficient interest' for the purposes of section 12B(1)(d). It seems clear that any such person need not have a proprietary 'interest' under the trust, although he may perhaps do so (say, as an ultimate remainderman), but exactly what kind of 'interest' it must be, and when it will be regarded as 'sufficient', are matters which remain ambiguous (probably deliberately so). It seems likely that such a person must be someone who, either expressly or by necessary implication, derives, or may derive, some benefit or advantage, whether directly or indirectly, from the purposes of the trust. Thus, employees of a company such as that under scrutiny in *Re Denley*,[40] and members of an unincorporated association such as that involved in *Re Lipinski*,[41] would probably qualify as persons with a 'sufficient interest'. However, the court will clearly have to look at the specific purposes of each trust and the particular circumstances of each case.

39.30　The new provisions do not make clear whether an enforcer owes any positive obligations at all, and, if so, what they might be. If a trust instrument appoints an enforcer, presumably it may expressly impose a duty on him to ensure that the purpose trust is executed properly, but there is no indication that it must do so: it may simply confer authority on the enforcer to apply to the court in the event that

---

[40] [1969] 1 Ch 373.　　[41] [1976] Ch 235.

he becomes aware of a breach of trust, without requiring him to do so. Certainly, it is very unlikely that anyone within section 12B(l)(b) (ie a settlor) or (d) (ie a person with a sufficient interest) is intended, without more, to be under a duty to supervise the carrying out of the purpose trust, or to make application to the court. It is not even clear whether the Attorney-General, once apprised of the absence of any other qualifying complainant, is under such a duty. Nor is there any indication that the enforcer (whoever he might be) has a right to compel the trustees to disclose information concerning the trust, without which he might well find it impossible to determine whether or not the purpose trust is in need of being enforced.

These uncertainties are compounded by the absence of any guidance as to the **39.31** duties of the trustees themselves. Are they subject to the same laws governing the investment of trust funds that apply to trustees of private trusts? If, for example, the purpose of the trust is to retain shares in a private family company, could the appointed person apply to the court for an order that such shares be sold or otherwise dealt with in cases of emergency (say, when the value of the shares is in danger of falling drastically)? Suppose, for example, that the purpose is to provide and maintain a sports ground for employees of a particular company. The value of the land increases greatly (as a result of development potential) or some dramatic change occurs to the company (because its workforce is reduced considerably, or it is relocated to another part of the country). Are the trustees failing to carry out their trust if they refuse to sell the land and acquire a new sports ground elsewhere? Is the appointed person under a duty to apply to the court in such circumstances? Are the trustees obliged to maintain an even balance between the non-charitable purposes and the ultimate human remaindermen (if any)? In short, there may be considerable ambiguity as to what the duties of the trustees ought to be in relation to the carrying out of the purpose trust and a corresponding uncertainty as to the need for enforcement or the existence of any ground upon which a complaint to the court could be founded.

It has already been indicated that the TSPAA 1998, unlike its predecessor, no **39.32** longer requires the appointment of a 'designated person'. One of the trustees of a trust for purposes formerly had to be such a person (who had to be a Bermudan lawyer, chartered accountant, trust corporation, or person designated by the Minister of Finance). The 'designated person' was required, *inter alia*, to keep at his office a copy of the trust instrument, a register of certain details appertaining to the trust, and such documents as were sufficient to show the true financial position of each trust in each financial year. A number of criminal sanctions applied in the event that such duties were not performed. All such requirements have now been swept away. There is no longer any requirement to appoint a 'designated person' (or a similar officer) and all such duties and sanctions have therefore ceased to be relevant.

Perpetuity

39.33 Whereas under the original legislation[42] a trust for purposes could not be created for a term exceeding 100 years, and the trust instrument had to specify the event upon the happening of which the trust terminated, section 12A(4) and (5) of the TSPAA 1998 now provides that the rule of law (known as the rule against excessive duration or the rule against perpetual trusts), which limits the time during which the capital of the trust may remain unexpendable to the perpetuity period under the rule against perpetuities, shall not apply to a purpose trust; but the rule against perpetuities (also known as the rule against remoteness of vesting), as modified by the Perpetuities and Accumulations Act 1989,[43] shall apply to a purpose trust. Thus, a purpose trust of indefinite duration can now be created in Bermuda: it will continue until all its capital has been distributed or expended. However, if the purpose trust is not of indefinite duration, the date of its termination and the vesting of interests at that time must all occur within a perpetuity period not exceeding 100 years (as under the TSPA 1989).[44]

Variation of a purpose trust

39.34 There was no provision in the TSPA 1989 for the variation of a trust for purposes. Section 12B(2) of the TSPAA 1998 now provides that the court may, upon the application of certain persons and if it thinks fit, approve a scheme to vary any of the purposes of the trust, or to enlarge or otherwise vary any of the powers of the trustees of the trust.[45] The persons who may make such an application are:

(a) any person appointed by or under the trust for these purposes;
(b) the settlor, unless the trust instrument provides otherwise;
(c) a trustee of the trust.

This is yet another provision in the TSPAA 1998 which has yielded simplicity at the expense of certainty and clarity. It may be reasonable to seek the enlargement or variation of the powers of trustees, but it is not at all clear how the purposes of a non-charitable purpose trust can or ought to be varied. Whereas, in the case of a trust for beneficiaries, the court would be expected to protect the interests of those beneficiaries, on behalf of whom it approves a scheme varying the trusts, by

---

[42] TSPA 1989, s 13(1).

[43] The Bermuda Act is in identical terms to the English Perpetuities and Accumulations Act 1964.

[44] The doubt whether s 1(1) of the English Perpetuities and Accumulations Act 1964 applies to purpose trusts did not, however, arise, for the 100-year trust period in the case of purpose trusts in Bermuda was authorized by TSPA 1989, s 13(1). Section 13(1) has now been repealed by the TSPAA 1998. However, TSPAA 1998, s 12A(5) seems to have the same effect.

[45] TSPAA 1998, s 12B(3) provides that, where any costs are incurred in connection with any application under s 12B (ie both applications for enforcement and applications for variation), the court may make such order as it considers just as to payment of those costs (including payment out of the trust property).

ensuring that the scheme is for their benefit,[46] there is no such requirement in section 12B(2) of the TSPAA 1998. Indeed, there is no guidance at all as to the manner in which the court is expected to exercise its jurisdiction. The intention may be to confer authority on the court to make a kind of cy pres scheme in respect of a purpose trust, in the same way that such a scheme can be made in relation to a charitable trust. However, whereas, in the latter case, the charitable purpose in question must have become impossible or impracticable (assuming Bermudan law is the same in this respect as English law), no such precondition is laid down in the TSPAA 1998 for a (non-charitable) purpose trust. There is not even a requirement that the court must have regard to the intentions of the settlor or to the spirit of the gift. Suppose, for example, that the purpose of the trust is to retain shares in a private family company, but the value of those shares is suddenly in danger of falling drastically. Could the court vary the purpose in such a case? If so, by reference to what criteria would it be able to do so?

Land

No interest in land in Bermuda shall be held, directly or indirectly, in a purpose trust.[47] The word 'indirectly' raises a doubt as to whether ownership by the trustees of shares in a company possessing land in Bermuda would amount to a breach of this prohibition (a doubt also raised under the TSPA 1989). There is no sanction for a breach of the prohibition: it does not appear to affect the validity of the trust (unlike a failure to comply with section 12A). **39.35**

Purpose trusts pre-September 1998

The substitution by the TSPAA 1998 of a new Part II for the TSPA 1989 applies in relation to: **39.36**

(a) trusts created after the coming into force of the TSPAA 1998 (on 1 September 1998); and

(b) trusts for non-charitable purposes validly subsisting immediately before that date.[48]

Special provision is made in order to bring existing purpose trusts within the new regime. Existing purpose trusts are *deemed* to satisfy the conditions set out in section 12A(2) of the TSPAA 1998 (ie the conditions which a purpose trust must satisfy in order to be valid). There does not seem to be a material difference between these new conditions and the requirement in the TSPA 1989 that purposes had to be 'specific, reasonable and possible', so this provision probably serves only to remove any lingering doubt as to validity. The person appointed (and required

---

[46] See, eg, the English Variation of Trusts Act 1958, s 1: see paras 24.19–24.25 above.
[47] TSPAA 1998, s 12D.   [48] ibid, s 4(1)(a) and (b).

to be appointed under section 13(1) and (2) of the TSPA 1989) as an enforcer by the trust instrument of a pre-September 1998 trust for purposes is deemed to have been appointed as a person who, for the purposes of section 12B(1) of the TSPAA 1998, may apply to the court for the enforcement of a purpose trust.[49] Moreover, a pre-September 1998 trust instrument is *deemed* to have provided that the settlor shall not make an application to the court for either the enforcement or the variation of a purpose trust.[50]

39.37 Other than the above-mentioned provisions, the TSPAA 1998 is silent about several aspects of pre-September 1998 trusts for purposes. Nothing is said about the role or status of any 'designated person' appointed by the trust instrument of an existing purpose trust. It seems clear that the statutory duties imposed on a 'designated person' by the TSPA 1989 no longer apply, but it is not clear whether any such duties expressly imposed by the trust instrument itself remain in force or have also been annulled, by implication, by the TSPAA 1998. Indeed, does any such creature as a 'designated person' continue in existence, or has the TSPAA 1998 provided, again by implication, for enforced retirement or removal?

The British Virgin Islands

39.38 The general trusts law of the British Virgin Islands is largely derived from English law, but supplemented by statute.[51] The main governing statute is the Trustee Ordinance (c 303). This has been amended by the Trustee (Amendment) Act 1993 (1993/7) ('TAA 1993'), most of which came into force on 1 November 1993, and recently by the Trustee (Amendment) Act 2003 ('TAA 2003'), which at the date of writing has not yet been brought into force.[52] Sections 84 and 84A of the TAA 1993 contain special provisions governing the creation, validity, and enforcement of purpose trusts. Section 84, which has itself been amended by the TAA 2003,[53] applies only to purpose trusts created before the coming into force of the new section 84A (which is inserted by section 12 of the TAA 2003).[54] In broad terms, the new section 84A introduces a new and simplified definition of a purpose trust; and both the amendments to section 84 and section 84A introduce new provisions in relation to the enforcement of purpose trusts, as well as other minor amendments. Because these two sets of provisions will eventually coexist, they are distinguished below (where necessary) as 'section 84 purpose trusts' and 'section 84A purpose trusts'.

---

[49] TSPAA 1998, s 4(2)(b).   [50] ibid, s 4(2)(c).
[51] The Common Law (Declaration of Application) Act 1705 (c 13); the West Indies Act 1967; the West Indies Associated States Supreme Court Order 1967, SI 1967/223, as amended by the Anguilla, Montserrat and Virgin Islands (Supreme Court) Order 1983, SI 1983/1108.
[52] The TAA 2003 will come into force on such date or dates as the Governor may, by proclamation published in the *Gazette*, appoint: TAA 2003, s 1(2).   [53] TAA 2003, s 11.
[54] TAA 1993, s 84(22). Section 84A (inserted into TAA 1993 by TAA 2003, s 12) applies only to trusts created on or after the date on which the section comes into force: s 84A(29).

Meaning of a section 84 purpose trust

One of the key features of the new section 84A is the introduction of a simplified   **39.39**
concept of 'purpose trust'. The central concept in section 84 of the TAA 1993 (the
existing provision) is a 'trust for any purpose'. This is defined in a somewhat
convoluted manner, as follows:[55]

> Trust for any purpose means a trust other than a trust—
>
> (i) that is for the benefit of particular persons whether or not immediately ascertainable; or
> (ii) that is for the benefit of some aggregate of persons ascertained by reference to some personal relationship.

The effect of the definition is that every trust which is not for the benefit of
particular persons whether or not immediately ascertainable or for the benefit of
some aggregate of persons ascertained by reference to some personal relationship
is a trust for a purpose or purposes, the validity of which (unless charitable)
depends entirely[56] on the conditions for validity laid down in section 84 of the
TAA 1993.

The definition raises several questions of construction. The phrase 'particular   **39.40**
persons' clearly is not confined to *named* persons, for it includes those who may
not be immediately ascertainable. It is less clear, however, whether the word
'particular' is intended only to signify a particular individual differentiated from all
other persons, such as the settlor's eldest son, or whether the expression 'particular
persons' also includes the members of a class of individuals, such as the settlor's
children or grandchildren.

It is yet more difficult to see what is meant by 'some aggregate of persons ascer-   **39.41**
tained by reference to some personal relationship'. It may be that a class of persons
related by blood to a common *propositus*—for example the settlor's issue—falls
within these words, although the word 'aggregate' seems inappropriate to describe
a class of persons. Indeed, an 'aggregate of persons' suggests a quasi-corporate
body, not composed of individuals. But limb (b) of the definition cannot refer to
members of an unincorporated association, for their relationship *inter se* is contractual, and not personal.

The definition clearly seems to result in a trust for the maintenance or education   **39.42**
or advancement of a class of related persons (for example the *Re Compton*[57] type
of case of a trust for the education of descendants of a common ancestor) not
being a 'trust for a purpose or purposes': the descendants of a common ancestor
are either 'particular persons' within limb (a) of the definition or 'an aggregate of

---

[55] TAA 1993, s 84(1)(b).
[56] This is subject to the possibility that some non-charitable purpose trusts may be valid under
the general law.   [57] [1945] Ch 123.

persons ascertained by reference to some personal relationship' within limb (b); and a trust for maintenance or education is presumably a trust for the benefit of the persons who are to be maintained or educated and therefore not a trust for a purpose or purposes. All such trusts fall outside the definition of a 'trust for a purpose or purposes' and their validity (or invalidity) is unaffected by the requirements of the TAA 1993.

39.43 But the definition leaves a case such as *Oppenheim*[58] (a perpetual trust for the education of children of employees of a particular company) uncertain: limb (b) seems to be inapplicable, for although the beneficiaries are in part ascertained by reference to their personal relationship to their parents, they can only be ascertained in the first place by ascertaining the relationship between their parents and the company employing them, and it seems at least doubtful whether such a relationship is a 'personal relationship' within the meaning of the definition; on the other hand, if a class comprising the children of present and future employees of a particular employer is a class of 'particular persons' within limb (a), it is difficult to conceive of a case to which limb (b) was intended to apply.

39.44 The word 'benefit' in the definition clearly leaves open the question whether the benefit which takes the trust outside the scope of section 84 must be a direct and tangible benefit (in the sense of conferring some legal or equitable interest on some person) or whether such benefit may be indirect (which might then mean that the *Re Denley*[59] type of trust would not be a 'trust for a purpose or purposes').

39.45 In any event, the definition clearly includes trusts for specific animals, tombs, and monuments. The purposes of unincorporated associations may also be included, in so far as the trust is construed as one for purposes and not one for the members.

39.46 Examples of other non-charitable purposes which would qualify would seem to include: (a) furthering a particular profession, industry, trade union, trade association, or other group where the primary objective is the promotion of its/their purposes and not to make a gift to the members;[60] (b) maintaining a particular building; (c) purposes which are not exclusively charitable; (d) holding shares in a family trading or investment company where the primary intention is to retain the shares and not necessarily to benefit any individuals; (e) providing fringe benefits (for example education) for the employees, or children of employees, of a particular company or for any other group which does not constitute a section of the public (and which does not fall within paragraphs (a) or (b) in the definition of 'trust for a purpose or purposes' in section 84(1)); (f) supporting yacht racing[61] or any

---

[58] *Oppenheim v Tobacco Securities Trust Co Ltd* [1951] AC 297.   [59] [1969] 1 Ch 373.
[60] *Re Mead* [1961] 1 WLR 1244; *General Medical Council v IRC* (1928) 97 LJKB 578; *Geologists' Association v IRC* (1928) 14 TC 271; *R v IRS, ex parte Headmasters' Conference* (1925) 41 TLR 651; *Re Barnett* (1908) 24 TLR 788.   [61] *Re Nottage* [1895] 2 Ch 649.

other sport or recreation; (g) promoting political propaganda (whether masquerading as education or not).[62] Indeed, subject to the requirement of certainty, gifts to promote any non-charitable purpose, such as anti-vivisection,[63] or the promotion of political parties, political dogma, changes in the law of a country[64] (presumably other than the British Virgin Islands), the promotion of temperance by political means,[65] the improvement of international relations,[66] or a trust to provide pensions for and donations to present and past employees and the education and benefit of their dependants[67] would seem to qualify under the TAA 1993.

Section 84(2) of the TAA 1993 then authorizes the creation of a 'trust for any purpose', whether charitable or not, provided the purpose is 'specific, reasonable and possible' and is not immoral, contrary to public policy, or unlawful.[68] Thus, a trust for 'philanthropic purposes', for 'the promotion of democratic values', and the like might be insufficiently certain to be valid. Similarly, trusts for 'artistic purposes'[69] or 'to present artistic dramatic works'[70] or 'for good works'[71] might be considered too vague, and a trust to block up a house for a lengthy period might be considered unreasonable.[72] And schools for prostitutes or pickpockets would be void on grounds of immorality or public policy.[73] **39.47**

Meaning of a section 84A purpose trust

The new section 84A (which is not yet in force and will apply only to trusts created after it comes into force) simplifies matters greatly. A 'purpose trust' is defined simply as a trust for a purpose or purposes, not being a trust for exclusively charitable purposes, which satisfies the conditions in section 84A(3).[74] The conditions referred to are that the purpose or purposes are specific, reasonable, and possible, and the purpose or purposes are not immoral, contrary to public policy, or unlawful.[75] There is no longer any requirement equivalent to section 84(1)(b) of the TAA 1993. **39.48**

Enforcement

In broad terms, the scheme of enforcement of a British Virgin Islands purpose trust is as follows. A purpose trust must have (a) an enforcer (who may not be a trustee) and (b) a trustee who is also a designated person. The role of the enforcer, **39.49**

---

[62] *Bonar Law Memorial Trust v IRC* (1933) 17 TC 508; *Re Hopkinson* [1949] 1 All ER 346; *Re Bushnell* [1975] 1 All ER 721.

[63] *National Anti-Vivisection Society v IRC* [1948] AC 31.

[64] *McGovern v A-G* [1982] Ch 321.

[65] *IRC v Temperance Council of Christian Churches of England and Wales* (1926) 136 LT 27.

[66] *Re Strakosch* [1949] Ch 529; *Buxton v Public Trustee* (1962) 41 TC 235.

[67] *Re Saxone Shoe Co Ltd's Trust Deed* [1962] 1 WLR 943. [68] TAA 1993, s 84(2)(a), (b).

[69] *Re Ogden* (1909) 25 TLR 382. [70] *Associated Artists Ltd v IRC* [1956] 2 All ER 583.

[71] *Re How* [1930] 1 Ch 66. [72] *Brown v Burdett* (1882) 21 Ch D 667.

[73] *Re Pinion* [1965] Ch 85, 105.

[74] TAA 1993, s 84A(1), (2), (4) (TAA 2003, s 12). Thus, a trust with 'mixed' purposes, charitable and non-charitable, is a 'purpose trust' within section 84A.

[75] TAA 1993, s 84A(3)(a), (b).

as the title implies, is to act as a 'watchdog' of the trustees: he is the person who is ultimately responsible for enforcing the purpose trust. The designated person-trustee is responsible for ensuring that there is always an enforcer in place. The circle is then completed by ensuring that the enforcer and the trustee(s) must (and other specified persons may) in turn ensure that there is always a designated person in place. It is a simple and practical mechanism, based on mutual reinforcement. The details of the scheme are as follows.

Enforcement of a section 84 purpose trust

39.50 Section 84(2)(d) of the TAA 1993 declared that the trust instrument of a section 84 purpose trust must appoint a person, who may be a protector, to enforce the trust and must provide for the appointment of his successor. It is not clear whether this refers simply to the immediate successor of the original enforcer, or requires some mechanism that can ensure that an enforcer is appointable, whenever required, throughout the duration of the trust, or something in between.[76] The person so appointed must be a party to the trust instrument or give his consent in writing, addressed to the trustee who is a 'designated person', to act as enforcer of the trust.[77]

39.51 Although the TAA 1993 does not say so in terms, it seems likely from the scheme of section 84(2) that the enforcer of a section 84 purpose trust cannot also be a trustee who is a designated person, and may not be able to be a trustee at all.[78] There would seem to be no reason why the settlor should not reserve power to enforce the trust to himself as the named enforcer and/or power to appoint a successor/enforcer.

39.52 Of course, circumstances may arise in which an enforcer, just like a trustee, may be unwilling or unable to act. The solution to this problem, in relation to a section 84 purpose trust, is provided by section 84(5) of the TAA 1993 (which is modelled on the statutory power to appoint new trustees in section 36(1) of the Trustee Ordinance[79]). It provides that, where he has reason to believe that a person appointed to enforce the trust is dead, is unwilling, refuses, or is unfit to act, or is incapable of acting, a trustee who is a designated person must as soon as practicable inform the Attorney-General in writing of the fact and send him a copy of the instrument creating the trust.[80]

---

[76] Would it suffice, for example, if a power to appoint an enforcer was reserved by the settlor himself or conferred on some other person (not in his capacity as an office holder) who may, and probably will, die before the termination of the trust?   [77] TAA 1993, s 84(2)(e).

[78] This point is dealt with expressly in relation to a section 84A purpose trust: see s 84A(18) and paras 39.58–39.70 below. The amendments to s 84 (inserted by TAA 2003, s 11) do not address this issue in relation to a s 84 purpose trust, presumably on the basis that it is better to let sleeping dogs lie.

[79] Which is similar to s 36(1) of the English Trustee Act 1925: see paras 22.42–22.54 above.

[80] Oddly, what is missing here is any requirement that the designated person should also be satisfied that the existing enforcer will not be removed, and/or another enforcer appointed, pursuant to some provision in the trust instrument. Common sense would suggest that involving the Attorney-General should be the designated person's last resort.

Where a designated person fails to carry out this duty, he commits an offence and **39.53** is liable on summary conviction to a fine not exceeding $5,000,[81] although it is a defence to a charge of committing such an offence to prove that the designated person took all reasonable steps and exercised all due diligence to avoid committing the offence.[82] This particular duty is not imposed on any other trustee.

On being informed by a designated person of the matters specified above, the Attorney-General must (in the case of a section 84 purpose trust) within 90 days, **39.54** apply to the court for the appointment of a person to enforce the trust.[83] The Attorney-General has no standing to enforce a purpose trust (other than a charitable trust) directly. Common sense would suggest, however, that, in the first instance, the Attorney-General (and why not the designated person?) should satisfy himself that the existing enforcer will not be removed, and/or another enforcer appointed, pursuant to some provision in the trust instrument: surely, an application to the court should be his last resort?

Section 84(6) seems to require the Attorney-General to nominate or recom- **39.55** mend a person, or perhaps a choice of persons, to the court, whose power then seems to be limited to the approval or non-approval of that choice. In order to be a valid purpose trust at all, the trust instrument must make provision for the appointment of a successor to the appointed enforcer.[84] If the problem is that the named appointor is simply refusing or unwilling to act, it must also be implied, presumably, that the court has power to remove the refusing or unwilling appointor. The court does not have power, apparently, to make provision for the appointment of a successor to its appointed enforcer. In any event, an order of the court declaring a person to be the person to enforce the trust is conclusive evidence of the appointment and the appointment takes effect from the date of the order.[85]

The TAA 1993 makes no provision as to the qualifications of the person so **39.56** appointed or as to the manner in which he is to enforce the trust, nor does it impose any sanction on him in the event that he fails to enforce it. The circumstances in which the enforcer should intervene to enforce the trust are not made clear. Although this may be said to ensure maximum flexibility, it also tends to underline one of the fundamental weaknesses of the purpose trust: what is it that an enforcer is supposed to be enforcing?[86]

Costs incurred by the Attorney-General in applying to the court for the appoint- **39.57** ment of an enforcer may be ordered to be paid out of the assets of the trust.[87] Where any costs are incurred by the person who has been appointed to enforce the trust in connection with enforcement, the court may make such order as it

---

[81] TAA 1993, s 84(9).   [82] ibid, s 84(10).   [83] ibid, s 84(6).
[84] ibid, s 84(2)(d).   [85] ibid, s 84(7).   [86] See further paras 39.58 *et seq* below.
[87] ibid, s 84(8).

considers just as to payment of those costs, including payment out of the property of the trust.[88]

Enforcement of section 84A purpose trust

39.58 An attempt has been made to address some of these uncertainties in the case of the new section 84A purpose trust.

39.59 Section 84A(3)(d) provides, in similar but not identical terms, that the trust instrument of a section 84A purpose trust must appoint a person as enforcer of the trust and must also provide for the appointment of another enforcer on any occasion on which there is no enforcer, or no enforcer able and willing to act. The reference to 'any occasion' suggests that appropriate provision must be made in the trust instrument for ensuring that an enforcer is appointable, whenever required, throughout the duration of the trust. The person so appointed must be a party to the trust instrument or give his consent in writing, addressed to the trustee who is a 'designated person', to act as enforcer of the trust.[89]

39.60 Section 84A(18) provides expressly that a person may not be or become a trustee of a section 84A purpose trust while he is the enforcer of that trust.[90] There would seem to be no reason, however, why the settlor should not reserve power to enforce the trust to himself as the named enforcer and/or power to appoint a successor/enforcer, provided that additional provision is also made to cover the eventuality that the settlor will die (or become incapable) before the termination of the trust.

39.61 Clearly, in the first instance, it would be expected that, as the need arises, a new enforcer would be appointed pursuant to the provisions of the trust instrument.[91] However, the possibility of some failure in the basic enforcement mechanism is dealt with by section 84A(10), which provides:

> Where a trustee of a purpose trust who is a designated person has reason to believe that there is no enforcer of the trust, or no enforcer able and willing to act, and that no enforcer is likely in the immediate future to be appointed, that trustee shall as soon as practicable inform the Attorney-General in writing of the fact and send him a copy of the instrument creating the trust.

This is broadly in line with section 84(5).[92] There now seems to be a requirement that, before he invoke the assistance of the Attorney-General, the designated person should first be satisfied that the existing enforcer will not be removed and/or another enforcer appointed pursuant to some provision in the trust instrument.

---

[88] TAA 1993, s 84(19). There is no specific provision for payment of the costs of a designated person.
[89] TAA 1993, s 84A(3)(e).
[90] The amendments to s 84 (inserted by TAA 2003, s 11) do not address this issue in relation to a s 84 purpose trust, presumably on the basis that it is better to let sleeping dogs lie.
[91] TAA 1993, s 84(3)(d).   [92] See para 39.52 above.

It remains the case that, where a designated person fails to carry out this duty, he **39.62** commits an offence and is liable on summary conviction to a fine not exceeding $5,000;[93] and the same defence is available to him.[94] This particular duty is still not imposed on any other trustee.

On being informed by a designated person of the matters specified above, **39.63** the Attorney-General must, 'with all reasonable speed but in any event within ninety days', apply to the court for the appointment of an enforcer under section 84A(9).[95] Common sense suggests that the Attorney-General would first need to satisfy himself that the matter cannot be resolved by means of the appropriate provisions in the trust instrument, without legal proceedings, but this is not made explicit anywhere.[96] Presumably, in appropriate circumstances, the Attorney-General may make an application to the court of his own motion, without prior notification by a trustee, for instance where the enforcer and all the trustees are dead. Moreover, the strong implication of the detailed statutory enforcement code is that no one else other than the Attorney-General (not even a human beneficiary of, or a 'person interested' in, the trust) is able to make an application for the removal or replacement of a 'failing' enforcer. Presumably, this is deliberate, so as to prevent a multiplicity of applications, some of which may even be frivolous.

The court's power is no longer restricted (if it ever was) to the approval or non- **39.64** approval of the person(s) nominated by the Attorney-General: indeed, the Attorney-General is no longer required to nominate any person (merely to apply for the appointment of 'an enforcer'). Section 84A(9) now confers a wider power on the court (the model for which is section 42(1) of the Trustee Ordinance[97]):

> The Court may, whenever it is expedient to appoint an enforcer of a purpose trust and it is found inexpedient so to do without the assistance of the Court, make an order appointing an enforcer either to fill a vacancy or in substitution for the existing enforcer.

Thus, not only is expediency the governing criterion but also the court explicitly has power to substitute one enforcer for another.

The Attorney-General still has no standing to enforce a purpose trust (other than **39.65** a charitable trust) directly. Costs incurred by the Attorney-General in applying to the court may be ordered to be paid out of the assets of the trust.[98] Where any costs

---

[93] TAA 1993, s 84A(13).   [94] ibid, s 84(10); s 84A(14).
[95] ibid, s 84A(11). There is a subtle difference in wording here in comparison with s 84(6), but probably no difference in substance.
[96] Indeed, a much simpler solution, not requiring the inconvenience and costs of an application to court, would have been to provide that the Attorney-General himself could exercise the relevant powers in the trust instrument and remove and/or appoint an enforcer.
[97] Which is similar to s 41(1) of the English Trustee Act 1925: see paras 22.58–22.68 above.
[98] ibid, s 84A(12).

are incurred by the person who has been appointed to enforce the trust in connection with enforcement, the court may make such order as it considers just as to payment of those costs, including payment out of the property of the trust.[99]

Designated person

39.66   At least one of the trustees of both a section 84 purpose trust and a section 84A purpose trust must be a 'designated person'.[100] It is the trustee who is a designated person who is subjected to a specific duty to ensure that the trust has an enforcer. For both trusts a 'designated person' is defined in identical terms, ie as a barrister or solicitor practising in the Territory of the British Virgin Islands, an accountant practising in the Territory who qualifies as an auditor for the purposes of the Banks and Trust Companies Act 1990, a licensee under the Banks and Trust Companies Act 1990, or such other person as may be designated by order of the Minister of Finance.[101]

39.67   In addition to his duties in relation to an enforcer, the trustee of a purpose trust (of a section 84 purpose trust or a section 84A purpose trust) who is also a designated person shall keep in the British Virgin Islands Territory a documentary record of

(a) the terms of the trust;

(b) the identity of any other trustees and the enforcer of the trust;

(c) all settlements of the property upon the trust and the identity of settlors;

(d) the accounts of the trust; and

(e) all distributions or applications of the trust property.[102]

There was originally no specific provision for ensuring that there was at all times a trustee who was a designated person, which was a strange omission given that it is the designated person who acts as the 'watchdog' of the enforcer.

39.68   However, this omission is now remedied in relation to both a section 84 purpose trust and a section 84A purpose trust. Section 84(12) and (13) provides:

> (12) Where any of the persons specified in subsection (13) has reason to believe that no trustee of a trust to which subsection (2) applies is a designated person or that no designated person is likely in the immediate future to be appointed as a trustee pursuant to the terms of the trust instrument, that person shall use all reasonable endeavours to secure the appointment of a designated person as a trustee of the trust and if such endeavours fail to result in such an appointment he shall make an application to the Court for the appointment of a designated person pursuant to the provisions of subsection (14).

---

[99] TAA 1993, s 84A(26). There is still no specific provision for payment of the costs of a designated person.
[100] ibid, s 84(2)(c); s 84A(3)(c). It seems somewhat odd that the legislation does not require a purpose trust to have at least two trustees—which would make its enforcement mechanism work more easily. As things stand, there can be a sole trustee, as long as he is also a designated person.
[101] TAA 1993, s 84(1)(a); s 84A(1).   [102] ibid, s 84(21); s 84A(28).

(13) The persons referred to in subsection (12) are

(a) any trustee of the trust who is not a designated person;[103]
(b) any person who has been appointed to enforce the trust.

Section 84A(19) and (20) are in essentially identical terms in relation to **39.69** section 84A purpose trusts. Whether there are any sanctions that may be brought to bear on a trustee or enforcer who fails to carry out this duty is unclear: there does not seem to be any criminal penalty equivalent to that imposed on a designated person who fails in his duty in relation to an enforcer;[104] and the provisions of section 84(20) and section 84A(27) (which do apply to a trustee and an enforcer) apply only where there is 'an intention . . . to defeat the trust' (and which therefore do not seem relevant to this issue).

In any event, a trustee or enforcer of a purpose trust who 'has reason to believe' **39.70** that no trustee is a designated person, or that no such person is likely to be appointed as a trustee under the trust instrument in the immediate future, is under a duty, in the first instance, to 'use all reasonable endeavours' to secure the appointment of such person as trustee; and then, if such endeavours fail, the trustee or enforcer is under a duty to apply to the court for the appointment of such person as trustee. One simple solution would be for the trust instrument to confer a power to appoint a designated person on one of the trustees, thereby enabling him to act and fill the vacancy without legal proceedings.

In relation to a section 84 purpose trust, section 84(14) provides: **39.71**

(14) If, at any time following its creation, a trust to which subsection (2) applies does not have at least one trustee who is a designated person, on the application in relation to the trust by

(a) any existing trustee of the trust,
(b) a person who has been appointed to enforce the trust, or
(c) the Attorney-General,

the Court shall make an order appointing a designated person as a trustee of the trust.

Thus, the Attorney-General may, but (unlike the enforcer and trustee) need not, apply for the appointment of a designated person. In relation to a section 84A purpose trust, section 84A(21) makes similar, but not quite identical, provision, in that an application may also be made by the settlor, unless the trust instrument provides otherwise, and not just by the three parties specified in paragraphs (a), (b),

---

[103] It is not clear what the words 'who is not a designated person' add to 'any trustee'. A purpose trust need have only one trustee-designated person. If there is such a trustee, then there is no cause for concern and subsection (12) does not apply. If there is no such trustee, then, by definition, 'any trustee' of the trust will not be a 'designated person' in any event.
[104] See TAA 1993, s 84(9); s 84A(13).

and (c) above. Thus, a reasonably simple method is provided for ensuring that, at all times, a purpose trust has a trustee who is a designated person. It remains possible in theory (though unlikely in practice) that a sole trustee–designated person and the enforcer are both dead, in which case the statutory mechanism may break down. Matters would have been simpler if the legislation had required a purpose trust to have at least two trustees at all times, but it does not do so.

Duties of the enforcer

39.72 The duties of an enforcer (whether of a section 84 purpose trust or a section 84A purpose trust) are not spelled out anywhere in the TAA 1993. Section 84(2)(d) merely states that an enforcer's role is 'to enforce the trust'. Section 84A(3)(d) merely refers to an 'enforcer', although section 84A(17) then declares: 'An enforcer of a trust appointed in accordance with the provisions of this section shall have both the power and the duty of enforcing it.'[105] The enforcement of a trust implies the protection of the trust assets and taking steps to ensure that the trustees (existing or substituted) carry out the duties imposed on them, and not taking over and actually implementing those duties in place of the trustees. However, this is not made clear in the legislation. Moreover, even after making due allowance for the fact that different kinds of trust involve different kinds of duties (for example depending on whether or not they involve the exercise of dispositive discretions), there is a fundamental problem here. It is not at all clear what duties are owed by the trustees of a purpose trust themselves; and it is, therefore, difficult to establish when the trust needs to be enforced and when an enforcer is supposed to intervene.

39.73 Enforcers clearly need proper information in order to fulfil their role. Section 84(11) provides that an enforcer of a section 84 purpose trust

> ... shall be entitled, in addition to any documents, information or other rights specifically provided for in the trust instrument, to
>
> (a) annual accounts of the trust;
> (b) copies of the trust instrument and deeds and other written instruments executed pursuant to the trust instrument; and
> (c) counsel's opinions and legal advice received by the trustees.

Section 84A(15) now provides that, in relation to a section 84A purpose trust, a trustee of such trust 'shall provide' the enforcer of the trust with the same things as are mentioned in paragraphs (a), (b), and (c) above and also (d) such, if any,

---

[105] This is a somewhat curious provision. First, a 'duty' to enforce necessarily implies a 'power' to do so. Secondly, it is confined to an enforcer appointed 'in accordance with the provisions' of s 84A. Enforcers will initially (and mostly) be appointed in, or pursuant to the provisions of, the trust instrument and not in accordance with s 84A, in which cases it is unclear whether the enforcers are still required to be under a duty to enforce or whether it will be sufficient to empower them to do so.

other documents and information as the trust instrument requires to be provided. Thus, what was originally an entitlement on the part of the enforcer (if he requested it) has now become a positive duty for the trustee.

The prevention of the misapplication of funds by the trustees, and the recovery of **39.74** misapplied funds, are presumably among the enforcer's tasks (although this role could already be undertaken by the ultimate remaindermen). Compelling the trustees to apply or distribute income or capital, or to consider the exercise of their dispositive powers and discretions, must be other functions. Beyond this, however, matters become rather uncertain, because it is unclear what the duties of the trustees themselves are supposed to be in relation to a purpose trust. Thus, in relation to a section 84 purpose trust, are the trustees obliged to maintain an even balance between the non-charitable purpose and the ultimate human remaindermen? Are they subject to the same laws governing the investment of trust funds that apply to trustees of private trusts? If, for example, the purpose of the trust is to retain shares in a private family company, could the enforcer ask for those shares to be sold or otherwise dealt with in cases of emergency (ie when the value of the shares is in danger of falling drastically)? If the purpose is to provide and maintain a sports ground for employees of a particular company, could the enforcer ask for the sale of the land if its value increases greatly (as a result of development) or if some dramatic change happens to the company (ie because its workforce is reduced considerably, or it is relocated to another part of the country)?

Similar questions may arise in relation to a section 84A purpose trust, although **39.75** section 84A(16)(c) now provides that the trust instrument *may* (but still need not)

> . . . provide that, for so long as the trust is a purpose trust, the trustees owe no duty
>
> (i) to any persons entitled to such assets when the trust ceases to be a purpose trust; or
> (ii) in relation to any purposes for which such assets are then to be applied.

However, this leaves open questions such as whether the ultimate (human) remaindermen themselves have any standing at all, or whether the 'policing' role of the enforcer is entirely exclusive. It also does not address the fundamental issue of the content of the duties (if any) owed by a trustee or enforcer towards the trust's purposes (or, if this is a meaningless concept, the duties owed during such time as the trust is a purpose trust). For example, what is the sanction or liability if the trustees and the enforcer acquiesce in the retention of trust assets, or the accumulation of trust income, for the benefit of the human remaindermen ultimately entitled to the trust assets, thereby wholly or partially defeating the intentions of the settlor in relation to the trust's purposes? In particular, the TAA 1993 understandably imposes no obligation on a trustee who is a designated person (and who may be the sole trustee) to report breaches of trust to the Attorney-General, but neither is he under any obligation to report any failure to enforce the trust by a fit and capable enforcer who cannot be described as refusing to act.

39.76 This seems to be the weakness of the British Virgin Islands purpose trust (like all other purpose trusts). The enforcement mechanism is effective in the sense that it ought to ensure that there are always both an enforcer and a trustee who is a designated person in place and that these two persons remain separate. However, even this mechanism cannot ultimately guarantee that the trustees will actually carry out their trusts in favour of non-charitable purposes. If the enforcer and the designated person ignore the purpose trusts and favour human beneficiaries (remaindermen or not) exclusively, there is still no one to complain of a breach of trust.

Termination and disposal of surplus assets

39.77 Under section 84 of the TAA 1993, it is also a requirement for a valid purpose trust that the trust instrument specifies the event upon the happening of which the trust terminates and also provides for the disposition of surplus assets of the trust upon its termination.[106] This requirement seems confined, however, to cases where the trust is terminable. The TAA 1993 makes no express provision for the disposal of the trust property in the event that a perpetual non-charitable purpose trust fails by reason of a failure of objects or purposes. There is nothing corresponding to the cy pres jurisdiction applicable to charitable trusts.

39.78 This is no longer a *requirement* in relation to purpose trusts which will be subject to the TAA 2003, section 84A. Instead, section 84A(16) provides that the instrument declaring or evidencing a purpose trust *may*, but *need not*, specify an event or date upon the happening or occurrence of which the trust ceases to be a purpose trust and provide for the disposition of assets of the trust when the trust ceases to be a purpose trust. In the case of a terminable purpose trust, it will obviously be prudent to make such provision, although it will not be a relevant consideration in the case of a perpetual purpose trust.

Power to vary purposes of the trust

39.79 The court now has powers to vary a purpose trust. In relation to a section 84A purpose trust, section 84A(22) provides that, on an application in relation to a purpose trust by

(a) any person appointed by the instrument declaring or evidencing the trust for the purposes of this subsection,

(b) the settlor, unless the trust instrument provides otherwise,

(c) a trustee of the trust, or

(d) the enforcer of the trust,

the court may in such manner as it thinks fit vary any of the purposes of the trust, or enlarge or otherwise vary any of the powers of the trustees or other provisions

---

[106] TAA 1993, s 84(2)(f).

of the trust. In relation to a section 84 purpose trust, section 84(15) makes similar provision, save that only a trustee of the trust and its enforcer may apply to the court.

In exercising the powers conferred upon it by section 84A(22) or section 84(15), **39.80** the court shall have regard to such factors as the court thinks material, which may include

(a) such changes in circumstances since the trust was created as are in the opinion of the court relevant; and

(b) such factors and proposals as are set out in the application.[107]

The 'changes in circumstances' referred to in paragraph (a) above may include the fact that the execution of the trust in accordance with its terms has become in whole or in part

(a) impossible or impracticable;

(b) unlawful or contrary to public policy; or

(c) obsolete in that, by reason of changed circumstances, it fails to achieve the intention of the settlor and the spirit of the gift.[108]

It seems clear that this statutory power is exercisable only after the creation of a valid purpose trust and not so as to render the purpose trust valid in the first place.

Where any costs are incurred in connection with an application for variation of **39.81** the purpose trust, the court may make such order as it considers just as to payment of those costs, including payment out of the property of the trust.[109]

Effect of satisfying the statutory conditions

A 'trust for any purpose' to which section 84 of the TAA 1993 applies is not **39.82** subject to the rule against perpetuities and remoteness of vesting.[110] It is further provided that,

> for the avoidance of doubt, the rule against perpetuities and remoteness of vesting includes the rule against inalienability, the rule against perpetual trusts, any rule prohibiting a trust under which trust property would, apart from that rule, be inalienable beyond a permissible period, and any rule prohibiting a trust or power under which trust property would, apart from that rule, be capable of application for a purpose beyond a permissible period.[111]

The effect is to authorize perpetual non-charitable purpose trusts.

---

[107] ibid, s 84(16); s 84A(23). [108] ibid, s 84(17); s 84A(24).
[109] ibid, s 84(18); s 84A(25). [110] ibid, s 84(3).
[111] Words added to s 84(3) by TAA 2003, s 11(a).

39.83 The exemption of a 'trust for any purpose' from the rule against remoteness of vesting is puzzling. It appears to enable such a trust to take effect at a remote future time, for example after a prior trust creating a series of life interests in favour of specified persons born during a 100-year trust period.[112] In English law, even charitable trusts are subject to the rule against remoteness of vesting, save as regards a passing from one charitable trust to another.[113] It is arguable that the point does not in fact arise, for the TAA 1993 seems to proceed on the basis that the trust will take effect at the moment of its creation: see, for example, section 84(2)(e), requiring the enforcer to be a party to the trust instrument or to consent in writing to act as the enforcer. However, the more obvious meaning of these provisions is that a 'trust for any purpose' may include both existing non-charitable purposes and those which may come into being at any time thereafter.

39.84 Similarly, section 84A(5) of the TAA 2003 provides that no rule against trusts or powers of excessive duration shall apply to a purpose trust. The expression 'rule against trusts or powers of excessive duration' is defined in the same terms as the amendment to section 84(5).[114] Thus, the focus here is, as it should be, on inalienability and perpetual duration and not on remoteness of vesting. The odd feature of section 84 would therefore seem to have been avoided and, presumably, purpose trusts to which section 84A apply are subject to the rule against remoteness of vesting.[115]

Relationship with charitable trusts

39.85 Nothing in the TAA 1993 affects the existing law with respect to trusts established for charitable purposes.[116] It follows that a trust for charitable purposes is valid in the British Virgin Islands notwithstanding that (a) its purposes are not specific, (b) its trustees do not include a 'designated person', and (c) it makes no provision for the appointment of a person to enforce the trust. Apart from section 84, charitable trusts in the British Virgin Islands are enforceable by the Attorney-General.

39.86 The definition of a section 84 purpose trust seems wide enough to include charitable purpose trusts and, therefore, to enable a trust for purposes which are exclusively charitable to comply with the statutory requirements for the creation of a 'trust for any purpose', including the appointment of a person to enforce the trust. It is unclear what powers of enforcement the enforcer of such a trust would have, and

---

[112] The maximum perpetuity period under the Trustee Ordinance is 100 years: TAA 1993, s 68(1). It seems a strange policy (which is not confined to the British Virgin Islands) to insist upon a limited perpetuity period for trusts for humans but to have none at all for trusts for non-charitable purposes.

[113] See Picarda, *The Law and Practice Relating to Charities* (2nd edn Butterworths, 1995), 265–274. [114] Section 84A(1).

[115] This is on the assumption that the words 'includes, but without limitation' in the definition of 'rule against trusts or powers of excessive duration' are not intended to signify that the rule against remoteness of vesting might also be in contemplation. This seems unlikely, however.

[116] TAA 1993, s 84(4); s 84A(6).

whether they would affect the powers of enforcement normally vested in the Attorney-General. However, this is not the case with a section 84A purpose trust. Section 84A(7) reaffirms this by declaring that nothing in section 84A shall affect the ability of the Attorney-General to enforce a charitable trust; and section 84A(8) provides that any purported appointment of an enforcer of a charitable trust shall be of no effect.

In order for a trust to be a valid charitable trust in the British Virgin Islands, apart **39.87** from section 84 of the TAA 1993, its purposes must be exclusively charitable. A trust for purposes which include both charitable and non-charitable purposes can be valid under section 84 or section 84A. It is, therefore, possible in the British Virgin Islands to create a perpetual trust, for example, for philanthropic purposes but which, by reason of the inclusion of one or more non-charitable purposes, would be void under English law.

The Cook Islands

The Cook Islands have a separate legislative regime for offshore entities. The gov- **39.88** erning legislation for international trusts is the International Trusts Act 1984 ('ITA 1984').[117] A trust registered under the ITA 1984 is a valid trust notwithstanding that it may be invalid according to the law of the settlor's domicile or residence or place of current incorporation.[118] The definition of an 'international trust' is set out in an earlier chapter.[119]

Perpetuity period and duration of an international trust

Under section 6(1), both the rule against perpetuities or remoteness of vesting and **39.89** the rule against perpetual trusts or against inalienability have no application to an 'international trust'.[120] However, notwithstanding this general disapplication, a trust instrument may make provision for vesting of all or any part of the property of the trust upon such terms as are prescribed by the trust instrument, including, but not limited to, provision for:

(a) a period within which the property of a trust shall vest in any beneficiary of the trust; or

(b) the happening of an event upon which the property of the trust shall vest in any beneficiary of the trust; or

(c) the property of the trust not to vest in any beneficiary of the trust or the trust not to terminate.[121]

---

[117] As amended by the International Trusts Amendment Acts 1985, 1989, 1991, and 1995–96, the International Trusts Amendment (No 2) Acts 1989 and 1995–96, and the International Trusts Amendment Act 1999. References in this section to the ITA 1984 are to the ITA 1984 as amended.
[118] ITA 1984, s 5(2).   [119] See para 38.54 above.
[120] The rule against excessive accumulations also does not apply. Income of settled property may or shall be validly accumulated if the disposition of the accumulated income is itself valid: ITA 1984, s 9(1).   [121] ibid, s 6(2).

39.90 Section 6(3) provides that, where a trust would otherwise be held by the court to be void for uncertainty, because of its terms relating to termination of the trust or vesting of the property of the trust, and such uncertainty would be removed by imposing a date for termination of that trust, then the trust shall terminate on the date 100 years from the date of creation of the trust; and the property of the trust shall vest in the beneficiaries on that date, unless termination or vesting occurs earlier in accordance with the trust instrument.[122] Just what this ambiguous provision is aimed at is not at all clear. It seems to be intended to deal with some form of uncertainty, which can be cured by the imposition of a date for the termination of the trust and not with any form of uncertainty (such as uncertainty of objects) which might be fatal to the trust, but which cannot be cured simply by the adoption of a termination date. Since a trust may be perpetual, there is actually no need to stipulate any termination date (or vesting date) in the trust instrument, so, presumably, what is intended to be covered is the case where an attempt has been made to specify a termination date (or vesting date), but it is one which is too uncertain to be workable—which may be due, for example, to the conceptual uncertainty of the words used or to difficulty in determining whether some specified precondition or triggering event has actually occurred. If the trust instrument provides that the trust shall be perpetual unless, say, the trustees decide to terminate it at some point in the exercise of a power or discretion conferred on them, but the terms in which their power or discretion are couched are uncertain, will it be the case that the trust remains a perpetual trust, but with no effective power to terminate, or will it be converted into a 100-year trust by section 6(3)?[123] It is also not clear whether the words 'would . . . be held by the court' actually require an application to, and a determination by, the court or whether, in a plain case or where the powers of 'variation' conferred by section 6(5) might be available (see below), it is sufficient to treat the trust as a 100-year trust without any such formal determination.

39.91 Where a period or an event is specified within, or at the end of, or upon which the property of a trust shall vest in a beneficiary (or where section 6(3) applies), the property of the trust then remaining shall vest in the beneficiary in accordance with the provision which specifies that period or event (or in accordance with section 6(3)) and such vesting shall apply in relation to all property then remaining of that trust and every general or special power of appointment under that trust shall be exercised in a manner consistent therewith.[124]

39.92 Without limiting any other rights conferred on trustees to vary a trust instrument, the trustees of an international trust may, with the prior consent of 'the

---

[122] ITA 1984, s 6(3).   [123] The provisions of s 6(4) do not seem to be relevant to this question.
[124] ibid, s 6(4).

interested parties', or if permitted by the trust instrument, vary the terms of the trust instrument to make provision:

(a) for a period being not less than the existing period provided for in the trust instrument within which the property of the trust shall vest in any beneficiary of the trust; or

(b) for the happening of an event being an event that will occur beyond the period within which the property of the trust would otherwise vest in the beneficiaries and upon the happening of which the property of the trust shall vest in any beneficiary of the trust; or

(c) to remove the period within which the property of the trust shall vest in any beneficiary.[125]

An 'interested party' means, in relation to any trust, any settlor, donor, trustee, protector, beneficiary and any person claiming through any one of such persons.[126] It is not specified whether 'the interested parties' whose consent is required means *all* such interested parties or a majority or just some of them (for example only those who may be directly affected by any proposed change), nor indeed whether they must all be adult and *sui juris*. The interrelationship of section 6(3) and (5) is not at all clear. If the termination date (or vesting date) of the trust is 'uncertain' (in the sense contemplated by section 6(3), whatever that might be), will this preclude the trustees (even with the consent of all 'interested parties') from exercising the powers conferred on them under section 6(5) to remove or extend such period? Presumably, this will be the case: otherwise section 6(3) would seem to be otiose. Even so, if a 100-year time limit is imposed under section 6(3), will such limit then be extendable or removable by the trustees in accordance with section 6(5)?[127]

Finally, it is provided[128] that, except where there is express provision to the contrary contained in the trust instrument, where the proper law of an international trust is to be changed from that of the Cook Islands to that of another jurisdiction, the trustees may with the consent of the interested parties, or if permitted by the trust instrument, vary the terms of the trust instrument to provide for a lesser period in which the then remaining property of the trust shall vest in any beneficiary so as not to infringe the law of that other jurisdiction. **39.93**

International charitable trusts

Section 12(1) provides that, notwithstanding any rule of law to the contrary, an international trust shall be deemed to be charitable or for charitable **39.94**

---

[125] ibid, s 6(5).   [126] ibid, s 2(1).
[127] ibid: s 6(4) is of no assistance, it seems, for (as we have seen) it provides only that 'every general or special power of appointment under the trust' shall be exercised in a manner consistent with the original or imposed termination date.   [128] ibid, s 6(6).

purposes where it is a trust *substantially* for one or more of the following objects or purposes:

(a) the relief of poverty;
(b) the advancement of education;
(c) the advancement of religion;
(d) other purposes beneficial to the community,

notwithstanding that the object or purpose may not be of a public nature or for the benefit of the public, but may be for the benefit of a section of the public or members of the public, or that it may also benefit privately one or more persons or objects or persons within a class of persons or is liable to be defeated whether by the exercise of a power of appointment or disposition or that the trustee has the power to defer the enjoyment of any charity or other beneficiary of the trust for any period not exceeding the term of the trust, and notwithstanding further that the trust may be discretionary or contingent upon the happening of any event.

39.95 In relation to 'international trusts', section 12(1) radically alters the law relating to the validity of charitable trusts. First, and most obviously, it dispenses with the requirement that a trust, in order to be a valid charitable trust, must have exclusively charitable objects or purposes: it is enough that the trust is 'substantially' for one or more of the objects comprised in the traditional four heads of charity. The meaning of the word 'substantially', which has been judicially described as being chameleon-like,[129] is capable of giving rise to difficult questions of fact and degree. Secondly, it may be that section 12(1) was intended to dilute or remove the requirement in English law that a trust to be charitable must be for the benefit of the public or of a sufficient section thereof. However, the language of section 12(1) arguably does not remove altogether the need for some public benefit: the phrase 'notwithstanding that the object or purpose may not be of a public nature or for the benefit of the public, but, may be for the benefit of a section of the public or members of the public', suggests that, while an international trust may remain charitable notwithstanding that its object or purpose is not of a public nature or for the benefit of the public, it must nevertheless be for the benefit of 'a section of the public or members of the public'.

39.96 The extent of the dilution of the English requirement of public benefit is left unclear: in England a trust may be charitable if it is for the benefit of a sufficient section of the public; and it is unclear:

(a) whether the expression 'a section of the public or members of the public' can mean anything different from a sufficient section of the public;

---

[129] See *R v Monopolies and Mergers Commission, ex parte South Yorkshire Transport Ltd* [1992] 1 WLR 291, 299, 302; *Re Baden's Deed Trusts (No 2)* [1973] Ch 9, 24.

(b) how 'members of the public' differ from 'a section of the public', and
(c) how an object or purpose can at the same time be for the benefit of a section
of the public or members of the public while not being of a public nature.

The uncertainty whether there is any continuing requirement for any public benefit
makes it difficult to say whether trusts which failed in England for want of a public
benefit, such as *Williams' Trustees v IRC*,[130] *IRC v Baddeley*,[131] *Re Compton*,[132] and
Oppenheim v Tobacco Securities Trust Co Ltd[133] would be charitable under the laws
of the Cook Islands if created as international trusts.

Purpose trusts

Section 12(2) provides that, notwithstanding any rule of law or equity to the con- **39.97**
trary, a trust settled or established by a non-resident of the Cook Islands shall not
be void or voidable by virtue of the fact that the trust fund shall be held for a purpose or purposes, whether charitable or not. And any trust so created shall be
enforceable on the terms set out in the trust instrument or by the person or persons named in the instrument establishing the trust as the person or persons
appointed to enforce the trust and the trust shall be enforceable at the instance of
the person or persons so named notwithstanding that such person or persons are
not beneficiaries under the trust.[134]

There is no requirement, however, that an enforcer be appointed by the trust **39.98**
instrument; and there is no stipulation (as in certain other jurisdictions, such as
the British Virgin Islands) that one of the trustees must be a 'designated person' for
enforcement purposes. However, recent amendments to the legislation now make
provision for replacement of enforcers. Section 12(3) provides that a person
appointed to enforce the trust may resign or be removed or replaced in accordance
with the trust instrument. Section 12(4) then provides further that, if the person
appointed to enforce the trust resigns, or is removed, or is unwilling, refusing,
unfit, or unable to act, and if no successor can be appointed in accordance with the
trust instrument, the trustees shall forthwith apply to the court for directions or
for another person or persons to be appointed by the court to enforce the trust.
The court shall be empowered to make an order appointing a person or persons to
enforce the trust on such terms it sees fit, and pending appointment by the court

---

[130] [1947] AC 447. [131] [1955] AC 572. [132] [1945] Ch 123.
[133] [1951] AC 297.
[134] The word 'trust' is defined in ITA 1984, s 2(1). Section 12 is not expressly confined to an
international trust. However, apart from the title of the Act, s 5(1) declares that the Act applies,
unless the context otherwise requires and subject to s 15, to (a) international trusts, (b) all registered
instruments (whether they take effect on, before, or after the commencement of the Act), (c) any disposition to or by an international trust, and (d) all questions and matters relating to or concerning
an international trust.

the Attorney-General shall be entitled, on such terms as he may require, to enforce the trust with the same rights and powers as the person appointed under the trust instrument to enforce the trust.[135]

Cyprus

39.99 Cyprus has enacted legislation similar to, but not identical with, that of the Cook Islands, providing for 'international trusts' and authorizing the creation of certain non-charitable purpose trusts. The provisions are to be found in the International Trusts Law 1992 ('ITL 1992') which came into force on 24 July 1992.[136] The principal differences from the law of the Cook Islands are (a) that the ITL 1992 only validates purpose trusts (as defined) which are also international trusts, and (b) that they are not required to be registered.[137]

39.100 The definition of an 'international trust' is set out in an earlier chapter.[138]

International charitable trusts

39.101 Section 7(1) provides that, subject to the Constitution of the Republic of Cyprus and notwithstanding the existence of any contrary legal provision of the law of Cyprus or any other law, an international trust shall be deemed to be charitable where the trust has as its 'main purpose' the achievement of one or more of the following:

(a) the relief of poverty;
(b) the advancement of education;
(c) the advancement of religion;
(d) other purposes beneficial to the community.

The 'main purpose' requirement corresponds to the requirement under the law of the Cook Islands that the trust be 'substantially' for one or more of the stipulated objects or purposes. It is not clear that the difference in language has avoided (indeed, it may have increased) the difficulties in identifying those multi-purpose trusts which qualify as charitable trusts and those which do not.

39.102 By section 7(2) an international trust established for one or more of the above-mentioned objects or purposes is deemed to be charitable notwithstanding that the object or purpose may not be of a public nature or for the benefit of the public,

---

[135] For a discussion of some problems concerning enforcement generally, see the sections dealing with Bermuda, the British Virgin Islands, and the chapter on the Cayman Islands' STAR trust.

[136] Date of publication in the *Official Gazette*.

[137] ITL 1992, s 15.

[138] See para 38.82 above. A trust still qualifies as an international trust notwithstanding that the settlor or the trustee or a beneficiary is a partnership or company qualifying under s 8Y and s 28A of the Cyprus Income Tax Laws: ibid, s 2.

but may benefit a section of the public, or that it may benefit particularly one or more persons or objects or persons within a class of persons or is liable to be modified or terminated whether by the exercise of a power of appointment or the disposition of assets, or that the trustee has the power to defer the distribution of benefits to any charity of the trust for a period not exceeding the period of the trust, and notwithstanding that the trust 'is or is considered to be in the category of discretionary trusts'. This provision is in very similar, though not identical, terms to the corresponding provision of the law of the Cook Islands.[139]

International purpose trusts

Section 7(3) of the Act provides that, notwithstanding the existence of any contrary **39.103** legal provision of the law of Cyprus or of any other country, an international trust shall not be void or voidable by reason only that it is a 'purpose trust' provided that, where it is a non-perpetual or terminable trust, the instrument creating the trust specifies the event or events upon the happening of which the trust terminates, and provides for the disposition of its net assets upon its termination.[140] The expression 'purpose trust' is defined to mean a trust other than 'a trust with beneficiaries being particular natural or legal persons whether or not immediately ascertainable' and other than 'a trust with beneficiaries being an aggregate of particular natural or legal persons ascertainable by reference to some personal attribute or relationship'.[141]

This definition closely follows the definition of the expression 'trust for any **39.104** purpose' in the original section 84 of the British Virgin Islands' legislation of 1993;[142] and it raises the same difficult questions of construction.[143]

An international trust which is a purpose trust is enforceable by the settlor or his **39.105** personal representatives or by the person or persons named in the instrument establishing the trust as the person or persons appointed to enforce the trust and the trust is enforceable at the instance of the person or persons so named notwithstanding that such person or persons are not beneficiaries under the trust.[144]

---

[139] See paras 38.54, 39.88, 39.94–39.96
[140] The Act seems to make no provision for the disposal of the trust property in the event that a perpetual non-charitable international purpose trust fails by reason of a failure of objects or purposes. There is nothing corresponding to the cy pres jurisdiction applicable to charitable trusts; and the requirement in s 7(3) that the trust instrument must provide for the disposition of its net assets upon its termination seems to be confined to cases where the trust is terminable.
[141] ITL 1992, s 2.
[142] Section 84 of TAA 1993 has been amended, and a new s 84A introduced, by ss 11 and 12 of TAA 2003.
[143] See paras 39.40–39.44 above. It is also similar to the definition of 'a trust for a purpose or purposes' in the original Bermuda legislation (TSPA 1989, s 12(1)) which was replaced by a simpler definition in s 12A of the TSPAA 1998.
[144] The word 'trust' is defined in the ITA 1992, s 2, by reference to the Cyprus Trustee Law and includes trusts created by will.

39.106   As with the legislation of the Cook Islands there is no requirement that one of the
trustees be a 'designated person'. Although there may be a nominated enforcer, there
is no requirement to this effect; there is no involvement by the Attorney-General in
ensuring that there is someone who is able and willing to act as the enforcer; there is
no provision for a substitute enforcer; and there are no criminal sanctions.[145]

Perpetuity and accumulation periods

39.107   The duration of an international trust which is a purpose trust is not subject to
any perpetuity period.[146] Additionally, section 6 of the Act provides that, in an
instrument creating an international trust, a 'direction' for the accumulation of
income is valid 'for any period within the period of the duration of the trust'. The
expression 'direction' connotes a trust to accumulate as opposed to a mere power
to do so.[147]

39.108   Section 6 would appear to authorize a perpetual trust to accumulate income in a
perpetual international non-charitable purpose trust, but not a similar power to
accumulate. It may, however, be doubtful whether a perpetual trust for non-
charitable purposes, with a trust to accumulate the income in perpetuity, could
indeed qualify as a purpose trust at all. On the other hand, an international trust
for non-charitable purposes to terminate at the end of a period of, for example,
250 years, with a trust in remainder for the issue of the settlor living at the end of
the trust period and containing a trust to accumulate the income for 50 years
would apparently be a valid trust in Cyprus;[148] and if that is so, it is difficult to see
on what basis a similar trust with a direction to accumulate the income for, say,
200 years would not be likewise a valid trust. The possibility of the creation of
such trusts principally for the benefit of human ultimate beneficiaries might be of
considerable interest to a modern-day Thellusson.[149]

Confidentiality

39.109   The Act contains provisions for confidentiality in relation to international trusts,
including purpose trusts.[150]

---

[145] For a discussion of some problems concerning enforcement generally, see the sections dealing with Bermuda, the British Virgin Islands, and the chapter on the Cayman Islands' STAR trust.
[146] ITL 1992, s 5(2).
[147] The decision in the English case of *Re Robb* [1953] Ch 459 that the prohibition on excessive
accumulation contained in the Law of Property Act 1925, s 164 (which refers to a 'direction' to accumulate) applies to powers as well as trusts does not appear to be inconsistent with the view expressed
in the text.
[148] However long the trust period, the trust in remainder for issue would not, it seems, be void
for perpetuity, given the opening words of ITL 1992, s 7(3): 'Notwithstanding the existence of any
contrary legal provision of the law of the Republic or of any other country ...', coupled with the
requirement that the trust instrument provide for the disposition of the net assets of the trust on its
termination.
[149] cf *Thellusson v Woodford* (1799) 4 Ves 227; (1805) 11 Ves 112.   [150] See ITL 1992, s 11.

Isle of Man

Requirements of a 'purpose trust'

The Purpose Trusts Act 1996 ('PTA 1996') provides that a person may create a **39.110** valid purpose trust, for a period not exceeding 80 years, provided the conditions laid down in the Act are complied with.[151] A 'purpose trust' is defined[152] as:

> a trust for a purpose or purposes other than a trust:
>
> (a) that is for the benefit of particular persons whether or not immediately ascertainable; or
> (b) that is for the benefit of some aggregate of persons ascertained by reference to some personal relationship; or
> (c) that is for charitable purposes.

A trust shall not be treated as being for charitable purposes by reason only of the fact that the instrument creating the trust contains a gift or bequest of any part of the trust assets to a charity.

The conditions with which the purposes must comply are as follows. They must be **39.111** 'certain, reasonable and possible'; and they must not be 'unlawful, contrary to public policy or immoral'.[153] The trust must be created: (a) by deed; or (b) by a will which is capable of being and is admitted to probate in the Isle of Man, or in respect of which letters of administration in the Island are capable of being and are granted.[154] There must be two or more trustees, at least one of whom is a 'designated person'.[155] The instrument creating the trust must appoint a person who is independent of the trustees to enforce the trust (referred to in the Act as 'the enforcer'); and it must also provide for the appointment, as soon as is practicable, of such a person as enforcer in the event of a vacancy in the office of enforcer or in the event of an enforcer ceasing to be independent of the trustees, or if for any reason the enforcer is incapable, unable or unwilling to act as enforcer.[156] The instrument creating the trust must provide for the enforcer to have an absolute right of access to any information or document relating to the trust, the assets of the trust, or to the administration of the trust.[157] Finally, the instrument creating the trust must specify the event upon the happening of which the trust terminates and provide for the disposition of surplus assets of the trust upon its termination.[158] Trusts for a non-charitable purpose or purposes which do not comply with these conditions are invalid.[159] No land or any interest in land in the Isle of Man shall be held, directly or indirectly, in a purpose trust.[160]

---

[151] Purpose Trusts Act 1996, s 1(1). The provisions of the Act are similar to, and evidently modelled on, those in Part II of the Bermudan Trusts (Special Provisions) Act 1989, which has now been repealed, and also those of s 84 of the British Virgin Islands' Trustee Ordinance. See paras 39.39–39.47 above.   [152] PTA 1996, s 9.
[153] ibid, s 1(1)(a).   [154] ibid, s 1(1)(b).   [155] ibid, s 1(1)(c).   [156] ibid, s 1(1)(d).
[157] ibid, s 1(1)(e).   [158] ibid, s 1(1)(f).
[159] ibid, s 1(3). Section 4 of the Act provides that neither the creation, variation, termination or validity of any trust created under or in accordance with any statutory provision or any other law nor any trust for charitable purposes or the law relating to such trusts is affected.   [160] ibid, s 5.

Designated person

39.112   A 'designated person' is defined as a person in the Isle of Man who is:

(a)   an advocate;

(b)   a legal practitioner registered under the Legal Practitioners Registration Act 1986;

(c)   a person qualified under section 14(1)(a) of the Companies Act 1982 for appointment as auditor of a public company;

(d)   a member of the Chartered Institute of Management Accountants;

(e)   a member of the Institute of Chartered Secretaries and Administrators;

(f)   a fellow or associate member of the Institute of Bankers; or

(g)   a trust corporation (as defined in section 65A of the Trustee Act 1961).[161]

39.113   Section 2(1) of the Act provides that every designated person shall keep in the Island:

(a)   a copy of the instrument which created or evidenced each purpose trust of which he is a trustee and also copies of amending and supplemental instruments;

(b)   a register of each such trust specifying in respect of each such trust the name of the person who created the trust, a summary of the purpose or purposes of the trust, and the name and address of the enforcer of the trust; and

(c)   such documents as are sufficient to show the true financial position of each such trust at the end of the trust's last financial year together with details of all applications of principal and income during the financial year.

A designated person shall permit the Attorney-General or a person authorized by him to inspect the instruments, registers, and documents referred to above.[162] However, these provisions do not create an obligation to make such instruments, registers, and documents available for public inspection.[163]

39.114   Under section 6 of the Act, a designated person is guilty of an offence and is liable on summary conviction to a fine not exceeding £5,000 where he:

(a)   fails to comply with the above obligations;[164]

(b)   makes, or authorizes the making of, an untrue statement in an instrument, register, or document referred to in section 2(1) of the Act;[165]

(c)   refuses to permit the Attorney-General or a person authorized by him to inspect such an instrument, register, or document (in which case he is also liable to a further fine of £500 for every day on which his refusal continues);[166] and

(d)   fails to comply with the provisions of section 3(1) relating to the appointment of a replacement enforcer.[167]

---

[161] PTA 1996, s 9.   [162] ibid, s 2(2).   [163] ibid, s 2(3).   [164] ibid, s 6(1).
[165] ibid, s 6(2).   [166] ibid, s 6(3).   [167] ibid, s 6(4).

In proceedings against a designated person for an offence under section 6(1), **39.115**
(2), or (4),[168] it shall be a defence for him to satisfy the court that he took all
reasonable steps and exercised all due diligence to avoid committing the
offence.[169] However, he is not entitled to rely on such a defence if he relied on
information given by another, unless he shows that it is reasonable in all
the circumstances for him to have relied on the information, having regard, in
particular, to:

(a) the steps which he took, and those which might reasonably have been taken,
for the purpose of verifying the information; and
(b) whether he had any reason to disbelieve the information.[170]

Where an offence under the Act is committed by a body corporate and is proved **39.116**
to have been committed with the consent or connivance of, or to be attributable
to neglect on the part of, a director, manager, secretary, or other similar officer of
the body corporate or a person who was purporting to act in such capacity, he, as
well as the body corporate, is guilty of the offence and liable to be proceeded
against and punished accordingly.[171] Where the affairs of a body corporate are
managed by its members, the last-mentioned provision applies in relation to the
acts and defaults of a member in connection with his functions of management as
if he were a director of the body corporate.[172]

Enforcer

The High Court may on the application of the enforcer of a trust make such **39.117**
orders as it considers necessary or expedient to enable or assist an enforcer:

(a) to enforce a trust; or
(b) to gain access to any information or document which relates to a trust, the
assets of a trust, or the administration of a trust.[173]

As discussed previously, the trust instrument itself ought to make provision for the **39.118**
appointment of an enforcer in the event of a vacancy or in the event of the enforcer
ceasing to be independent of the trustees or for any reason being incapable,
unable, or unwilling to act.[174] Subject to such express provisions, section 3(1) of
the Act provides that, where a trustee who is a designated person has reason to
believe that:

(a) there is a vacancy in the office of enforcer; or
(b) the enforcer has ceased to be independent of the trustees; or

---

[168] ie, a refusal to permit inspection of an instrument, register, or document (see s 6(3)) is
excluded from the scope of the defences referred to in s 7.   [169] ibid, s 7(1).
[170] ibid, s 7(2).   [171] ibid, s 8(1).   [172] ibid, s 8(2).   [173] ibid, s 1(2).
[174] ibid, s 1(1)(d)(ii).

(c) the enforcer is for any reason incapable, unable or unwilling to act as enforcer,

then that trustee 'shall' (ie it is a duty) as soon as practicable:

> (i) give written notice of, and the grounds for, his belief to the Attorney-General, and
>
> (ii) provide the Attorney-General with a copy of the instrument by which the trust was created.

On receipt of such a notice, the Attorney-General 'may' apply to the High Court for the appointment of a person as the enforcer of the trust and the High Court may by order declare that person to be the enforcer.[175] Such an order of the High Court is conclusive evidence of the appointment of an enforcer of a trust.[176] The High Court may also order that the costs and expenses of the Attorney-General shall be paid out of the assets of the trust.[177]

Jersey

Trusts and purpose trusts

39.119 Jersey trusts are governed by the Trusts (Jersey) Law 1984 ('TJL 1984') which came into force on 23 March 1984, and by three subsequent amending statutes.[178] Article 2 of the TJL 1984 declares that a trust exists where a person (known as a trustee) holds or has vested in him or is deemed to hold or have vested in him property (of which he is not the owner in his own right):

(a) for the benefit of any person (known as a beneficiary) whether or not yet ascertained or in existence; or

(b) for any purpose which is not for the benefit only of the trustee; or

(c) for a combination of (a) and (b) above.

The proper law of a trust shall be the law of the jurisdiction expressed by the terms of the trust as the proper law, or, failing that, be implied from the terms of the trust, and, failing either of these, the law with which the trust at the time it was created had the closest connection.[179] The court[180] has jurisdiction where the trust is a Jersey trust (meaning a trust whose proper law is the law of Jersey),[181] or where a trustee of a foreign trust (meaning a trust whose proper law is the law

---

[175] PTA 1996, s 3(2). Presumably, this is in place of (and not in addition to) any previous enforcer who was/is not independent of the trustees.　　　　　　　　　　　　　　[176] ibid, s 3(3).

[177] ibid, s 3(4).

[178] The Trusts (Amendment) (Jersey) Law 1989, which came into force on 21 July 1989; the Trusts (Amendment No 2) (Jersey) Law 1991, which came into force on 9 October 1991; and the Trusts (Amendment) (Jersey) Law 1996, which came into force on 24 May 1996.

[179] TJL 1984, Art 4. See also Trusts (Amendment No 2) (Jersey) Law 1991, Art 1.

[180] Defined in ibid, Art 1(1) as the Inferior Number of the Royal Court.

[181] A Jersey trust, which is not a trust for charitable purposes, may continue until the 100th anniversary of the date on which it came into existence, and if not sooner terminated shall then terminate: ibid, Art 11.

of some jurisdiction other than Jersey) is resident in Jersey, or where any trust property of a foreign trust is situated in Jersey, or the administration of any trust property of a foreign trust is carried out in Jersey.[182]

Article 9(1) of the TJL 1984 (which applies only to a Jersey trust) declares that a **39.120** beneficiary shall be:

(a) identifiable by name; or
(b) ascertainable by reference to:

    (i) a class, or
    (ii) a relationship to some person, whether or not living at the time of the creation of the trust or at the time which under the terms of the trust is the time by reference to which members of a class are to be determined.[183]

Article 10(2)(a)(iv) declares that a Jersey trust shall be invalid if it is created for a purpose in relation to which there is no beneficiary, not being a charitable purpose. Thus, non-charitable purpose trusts per se are not valid in Jersey. Moreover, those few anomalous non-charitable purpose trusts recognized in English law would also not be valid in Jersey.

However, the Trusts (Amendment No 3) (Jersey) Law 1996 ('the 1996 Law'), **39.121** which came into force on 24 May 1996, has modified the position by inserting in the TJL 1984 a new Article 10A which provides that non-charitable purpose trusts may now be created in Jersey, provided they satisfy the relevant statutory provisions. Article 10A declares that a trust shall not be invalid to any extent by reason of Article 10(2)(a)(iv) (see preceding paragraph) if the terms of the trust provide for the appointment of an enforcer in relation to its non-charitable purposes, and for the appointment of a new enforcer at any time when there is none. Article 10B(1) then declares that it shall be the duty of an 'enforcer' to enforce the trust in relation to its non-charitable purposes; but a trustee of that trust cannot be appointed as an enforcer of it.[184] Article 17(4) of the TJL 1984 applies to an enforcer as it applies to a trustee, ie except with the approval of the court or as permitted by the TJL 1984 or expressly provided by the terms of the trust, he shall not directly or indirectly profit from his appointment or cause or permit any other person to profit directly or indirectly from such appointment or on his own account enter into any transaction with the trustees or relating to the trust property which may result in such profit.[185] Beyond this, there is very little indication

---

[182] ibid, Art 5.

[183] Beneficiaries may be added or excluded (Art 9(2)); obligations may be imposed as a condition of benefit (Art 9(3)); a beneficiary may irrevocably disclaim his whole interest (or, subject to the terms of the trust, part thereof) in writing (Art 9(4) – (9)).

[184] TJL 1984, Art 10B(1) and (2) (inserted by the 1996 Law, Art 3). An action by the enforcer alleging breach of trust must be brought within three years of delivery of final accounts or first having knowledge of the breach: ibid, Art 53(2) (as amended by the 1996 Law, Art 9).

[185] TJL 1984, Art 10B(3).

as to the duties of an enforcer. Although he may not be a trustee, it seems clear that the intention is that he should occupy a fiduciary position and must act in good faith (although it is unclear as to whom he owes such duties).

39.122   Where there is more than one purpose, or at least one beneficiary and one purpose, then, subject to the terms of the trust, a trustee shall be impartial and shall not execute the trust for the advantage of one at the expense of another. The meaning of this vaguely worded provision is unclear. It is consistent with the view that the trustees must ensure equal distribution among the purposes and beneficiaries (an unequal distribution inevitably being an advantage to one at the expense of another), but it seems unlikely that this was intended. Does it mean that the trustees may not make illusory or exclusive appointments (both of which have been permitted in England since the early nineteenth century and now by section 158 of the Law of Property Act 1925)? Does it mean that the trustees must maintain an 'even hand' as between objects and beneficiaries?

39.123   A trustee of a trust for non-charitable purposes shall, at any time when there is no enforcer in relation to them, take such steps as may be necessary to secure the appointment of a new enforcer.[186] Where the trustee of a trust for non-charitable purposes has reason to believe that the enforcer in relation to them is unwilling or refuses to act, or is unfit to act or incapable of acting, he shall apply to the court for the removal of the enforcer and the appointment of a replacement.[187]

39.124   In order to assist an enforcer in fulfilling his duty to enforce the non-charitable purposes of a trust, he is given the same rights as a beneficiary to compel a trustee to disclose any document which 'relates to or forms part of the accounts of the trust'.[188] This provision, expressed in narrow terms, has been construed widely by the Jersey court and it has been held[189] to include all documents and correspondence relating to the administration of the trust property or to the execution of the trust (as in *Re Londonderry's Settlement*).[190] However, an enforcer, like a beneficiary, has no right (subject to an order of the court) to compel a trustee to disclose any document which discloses the trustee's deliberations as to the manner in which he has exercised a power or discretion or performed a duty conferred or imposed upon him; or discloses the reason for any particular exercise of such power or discretion or performance of duty or the material upon which such reason shall or might have been based; or relates to the exercise or proposed exercise of such power or discretion or the performance or proposed performance of such duty.[191]

---

[186]   TJL 1984, Art 17(7) (inserted by the 1996 Law, Art 4).
[187]   ibid, Art 17(8) (inserted by the 1996 Law, Art 4).
[188]   ibid, Art 25 (inserted by the 1996 Law, Art 6).
[189]   *West v Lazard Brothers & Company (Jersey) Ltd* [1987–88] JLR 414.
[190]   [1965] Ch 918. Cf *Schmidt v Rosewood Trust Ltd* [2003] 2 WLR 1442 (PC, on appeal from Isle of Man).   [191]   TJL 1984, Art 25(a) – (c).

Failure or termination of trusts

Where property is held by trustees for a purpose (which may be a charitable or **39.125** non-charitable purpose) which has ceased to exist or is no longer applicable, that property shall be held for such other purpose (charitable or non-charitable) as the court may declare to be consistent with the original intention of the settlor (meaning the person who provided that property).[192]

Resignation and removal of enforcer

An enforcer may resign his office by notice in writing delivered to the trustee; and **39.126** his resignation takes effect on the delivery of such notice.[193] An enforcer shall cease to be the enforcer of the trust in relation to its non-charitable purposes immediately upon:

(a) his removal from office by the court;
(b) his resignation becoming effective;
(c) the coming into effect of a provision in the terms of a trust under which he is removed from office or otherwise ceases to hold office; or
(d) his appointment as a trustee of the trust.[194]

Validity of purpose trusts

The 1996 Law provides no assistance on the question of what kind of non- **39.127** charitable purpose is valid and acceptable in Jersey, the implication being that there are very few restrictions at all. Article 10(2) of the TJL 1984 declares that a trust shall be invalid if it purports to do anything, the doing of which is contrary to the law of Jersey; or it purports to confer any right or power or impose any obligation the exercise or carrying out of which is contrary to the law of Jersey; or it purports to apply directly to immovable property situated in Jersey; or it is created for a purpose in relation to which there is no beneficiary, not being a charitable purpose and not being a trust which satisfies the requirements of the 1996 Law. In addition, a trust shall be invalid to the extent that the court declares that it is immoral or contrary to public policy or the terms of the trust are so uncertain that its performance is rendered impossible.[195] Thus, trusts for conceptually uncertain objects, such as 'objects of benevolence and liberality',[196] or 'some useful memorial',[197] or 'the maintenance of good understanding between nations',[198] may be declared invalid in Jersey, as they have been in England, but this is not entirely clear. Similarly, Jersey public policy, like that of England and Scotland, is

---

[192] ibid, Art 38(2) (as amended by the 1996 Law, Art 7). An application to the court *may* (but apparently need not) be made by the Attorney-General.
[193] TJL 1984, Art 10C(1), (2).   [194] ibid, Art 10C(4).
[195] ibid, Art 10(2)(b)(ii) and (iii).   [196] *Morice v Bishop of Durham* (1804) 9 Ves 399.
[197] *Re Endacott* [1960] Ch 232.   [198] *Re Astor's Settlement Trusts* [1952] Ch 534.

likely to prohibit trusts which are capricious, useless, wasteful, or harmful.[199] However, this remains to be seen. Beyond these general restrictions, which are applicable to all Jersey trusts, there is no indication of any limit on the nature of the non-charitable purposes that may be created.

39.127A Where a Jersey trust is created for two or more purposes, of which some are lawful and others are unlawful, then, if those purposes cannot be separated, the trust shall be invalid.[200] However, where those purposes can be separated, the court may declare that the trust is valid as to the purposes which are lawful; and, in the case of such partial validity, the court may also declare what property is trust property and what property is not trust property.[201] Property as to which a trust is wholly or partially invalid shall, subject to any order of the court, be held by the trustees in trust for the settlor absolutely (the settlor being the person who provided that property) or, if he is dead, for his personal representative.[202]

Registration and filing

39.128 Jersey has no requirements for the registration or filing of trust instruments.

Labuan

39.129 Labuan is a capital territory of Malaysia. Malaysian trust law is based on English law, but, in its application to Labuan, it has been modified extensively by statute. The main statute is the Labuan Offshore Trusts Act 1996 ('LOTA 1996') which deals with the creation, recognition, and administration of Labuan 'offshore trusts'. The Trustee Act 1949 and the Trustee (Incorporation) Act 1952, which are the main statutes governing Malaysian domestic trusts, do not apply.

39.130 In many respects, the provisions of the LOTA 1996 are similar to, if not identical with, those enacted for similar purposes in other jurisdictions, for example Belize and Bermuda. Following a lengthy series of elaborate and often convoluted definitions (section 2), the LOTA 1996 deals with the existence of a trust (section 3), charitable and purpose trusts (section 4), spendthrift or protective trusts (section 5), and then the proper law of a trust (section 6). Part II (sections 7 to 21) of the LOTA 1996 deals with the creation and recognition of offshore trusts; Part III (sections 22 to 25) with the beneficiaries of offshore trusts; Part IV (sections 26 to 46) with the trustees of offshore trusts; and Part V (sections 47 to 62) with miscellaneous matters, such as the variation of trusts, the general powers of the courts, limitation of actions, and so forth.

---

[199] See *Brown v Burdett* (1882) 21 Ch D 667; *M'Caig v University of Glasgow* 1907 SC 231; *M'Caig's Trustees v Kirk Session of United Free Church of Lismore* 1915 SC 426; *Aitken's Trustee v Aitken* 1927 SC 374.
[200] TJL 1984, Art 10(3)(a).   [201] ibid, Art 10(3)(b), (4).
[202] ibid, Art 10(6), (7). See also Art 10(5).

Existence of a 'trust' and an 'offshore trust'

Section 3 of the LOTA 1996[203] (which is virtually identical with section 2 of the **39.131**
Belize Trusts Act 1992) declares that a trust exists where a person holds or has
vested in him[204] property of which he is not the owner in his own right and is
under an obligation as a trustee to deal with that property:

(a) for the benefit of any beneficiary, whether or not ascertained or in existence;

(b) for any purpose which is not for the benefit of the trustee;[205] or

(c) for both such benefit and purpose mentioned in paragraphs (a) and (b).

Section 7(1) then provides that a trust is an 'offshore trust' where:

(a) the settlor is a qualified person at the time the trust is created;[206]

(b) the trust property[207] does not include any immovable property[208] situated in
Malaysia, unless otherwise allowed by the relevant authorities[209] and laws for
the time being in force;

(c) subject to section 7(2) and (3), all the beneficiaries[210] under the trust are
qualified persons at the time the trust is created or at the time any one or more
of them otherwise become entitled to be beneficiaries under the trust; and

(d) at least one of the trustees is a trust company.[211]

The key concept in this definition is 'a qualified person' (a requirement which
applies to both the settlor and the beneficiaries of an offshore trust). This means
'a person who is not a resident of Malaysia'. A 'resident' is someone:

(a) who is a citizen or permanent resident of Malaysia; or

---

[203] LOTA 1996, s 2(1) provides, in addition, that 'trust' includes 'the trust property and the rights, powers, duties, interests, relationships and other obligations under a trust'.

[204] Belize Trusts Act 1992, s 2 also extends to the case where a trustee 'is deemed' to hold property or have it vested in him.

[205] Belize Trusts Act 1992, s 2(b) refers to a purpose which is 'not for the benefit only' of the trustee. Thus, where a trustee is one of several persons who benefit from a purpose trust of the kind at issue in *Re Denley* [1969] 1 Ch 373 (sports ground for employees of a company), such a trust would fall within this provision, but not, it seems, within LOTA 1996, s 3(b).

[206] Where the trust is created by will, this is the time at which the will takes effect: LOTA 1996, s 7(4), ie on death.

[207] The expression 'trust property' is defined (somewhat unnecessarily) as 'the property for the time being held on trust': ibid, s 2(1).

[208] 'Immovable property situated in Malaysia' includes shares, stocks, or debentures in or of a company whose assets include immovable property situated in Malaysia, other than a public company quoted on the official list of a stock exchange of any country or jurisdiction therein: ibid.

[209] Which are not defined, which presumably include, but are not synonymous with, 'the Authority' and the 'Minister', both of which terms are defined in LOTA 1996, s 2(1).

[210] A 'beneficiary' means 'a person entitled to benefit under a trust or in whose favour a discretion to distribute property held in trust may be exercised': ibid.

[211] A 'trust company' means 'a company registered under s 4 of the Labuan Trust Companies Act 1990 to carry on business as a trust company': ibid.

(b) who has established a place of business and is operating in Malaysia (other than an offshore company or a foreign offshore company incorporated or registered under the Offshore Companies Act 1953).

There is even an extended definition of 'Malaysia'.[212]

39.132 A trust shall remain as an offshore trust notwithstanding that one or more of the beneficiaries who are qualified persons at the time the trust is created subsequently become resident in Malaysia at the time they otherwise become entitled to be beneficiaries.[213] Moreover, a trust shall be an offshore trust notwithstanding that a person who is not a qualified person benefits together with any other persons as members of a class of persons who are beneficiaries under a trust for a charitable purpose.[214]

39.133 Subject to section 4(3) (see below), a beneficiary must be:

(a) identifiable by name; or
(b) ascertainable by reference to a class or to a relationship to some persons, whether or not living at the time, which under the terms of the offshore trust is the time by reference to which members of a class are to be determined.[215]

Where there are no beneficiaries thus identifiable or ascertainable, the trust is not valid unless the purpose is a charitable purpose.[216] A settlor or trustee of an offshore trust may also be a beneficiary of the trust but, if he is the sole trustee, he shall not also be a beneficiary thereunder.[217]

Creation of an offshore trust

39.134 An offshore trust must be created by will or other instrument in writing, including a unilateral declaration of trust.[218] For this purpose, a unilateral declaration of trust is a declaration in writing by a trust company stating:

(a) that it is the trustee of an offshore trust;
(b) the name of the trust;
(c) the terms of the trust; and
(d) the names, or information enabling the identification, of all the beneficiaries.[219]

---

[212] It means the territories of the Federation of Malaysia, the territorial waters of Malaysia, and the seabed and subsoil of the territorial waters, and includes any area extending beyond the limits of the territorial waters of Malaysia, and the seabed and subsoil of any such area, which has been or may hereafter be designated under the laws of Malaysia and in accordance with international law as an area over which Malaysia has sovereign rights for the purposes of exploring and exploiting the natural resources, whether living or non-living. In the context of LOTA, this is surely overkill.

[213] LOTA 1996, s 7(3).   [214] ibid, s 7(2).   [215] Labuan Trust Companies Act 1990, s 22(1).
[216] ibid, s 22(2).   [217] ibid, s 22(3).   [218] LOTA 1996, s 8(1).
[219] ibid, s 8(2). The rather odd requirement that the unilateral declaration of trust be made by a trust company, and not the settlor himself, seems merely to provide for evidence of the trusts.

Given the definition of 'beneficiary' in section 2(1), the identification of any purpose, whether charitable or non-charitable, would not seem to be necessary (unless this is regarded as being required by 'the terms of the trust'). A unilateral declaration of trust need not contain the name of the settlor, but in such a case the declaration shall contain a statement by the trust company that the settlor is 'a qualified person' on the date of the making of the declaration.[220]

Charitable and non-charitable purpose trusts

A trust is regarded as a trust for charitable purposes under the LOTA 1996 where: **39.135**

(a)   the trust is made for any one or more of the purposes specified in section 4(1); and

(b)   the fulfilment of such purpose or purposes is for the benefit of the community or a substantial section of the community, having regard to the type and nature of the purpose or purposes.

The specified charitable purposes are:

(a)   the relief or eradication of poverty;
(b)   the advancement of education;
(c)   the promotion of art, science, and religion;
(d)   the protection of the environment;
(e)   the advancement of human rights and fundamental freedoms; and
(f)   any other purposes which are beneficial to the community.

This list is based firmly on the fourfold classification of charities found in English law,[221] under which five of the six listed categories are clearly charitable. Whether a particular purpose is 'beneficial to the community', and therefore falls within category (f), will probably give rise to the same uncertainties and difficulties as are encountered in English law in relation to the fourth category of the *Pemsel* classification. As in the case of the Belize Trusts Act 1992, section 14 of the LOTA 1996 surprisingly does not deal expressly with recreational charities, which have caused some difficulty in England and which, presumably, remain non-charitable in Labuan. Category (e) would be regarded as a political purpose and not charitable under English law[222] and therefore represents a new departure. A purpose may be regarded as charitable whether it is to be carried out in Malaysia or elsewhere and whether it is beneficial to the community in Malaysia or elsewhere.[223] As in the case of Belize, regard must be given to the type and nature of the purpose, so that, for example, trusts for the relief of poor relations

---

[220]   ibid, s 8(3).
[221]   *Commissioners for Special Purposes of Income Tax v Pemsel* [1891] AC 531, 583; *Scottish Burial Reform and Cremation Society Ltd v Glasgow Corporation* [1968] AC 138.
[222]   *McGovern v Attorney-General* [1982] Ch 321.   [223]   LOTA 1996, s 4(2).

(which are valid charitable trusts in England, although anomalous) are presumably also charitable in Labuan.

39.136   Notwithstanding any law to the contrary (and section 22(1) in particular), a trust (which apparently need not be an offshore trust) may be created or established for a particular purpose or purposes, *whether charitable or not.* There is no express restriction on the kind of non-charitable purpose which is permissible: unlike other jurisdictions (for instance Belize, Bermuda, and the British Virgin Islands), the LOTA 1996 does not specify that such purposes must be specific, reasonable, or capable of fulfilment, or even not be against public policy. Section 9(2)(d) provides that an offshore trust shall be invalid and unenforceable where the court declares that the object for which it was created has failed or that the terms of the trust are such that its performance is not possible, but there is little guidance (beyond that which is an actual offence) as to the kind of purpose or object that might cause such failure or impossibility.

39.137   There is a requirement that the trust property must vest in natural persons within the perpetuity period applying or expressed to apply to the trust.[224] Section 16 of the LOTA 1996 provides that an offshore trust shall, unless otherwise stated in and subject to the terms of the trust, continue to exist for a period not exceeding 100 years (but it may be terminated at any time in accordance with the provisions of the LOTA 1996). (The wording suggests that a period in excess of 100 years could be created expressly. However, this is clearly not what is intended.)

39.138   The settlor of a trust may give to the trustee a letter of his wishes (or the trustee may prepare a memorandum of the wishes of the settlor) with regard to the exercise of any functions conferred on the trustee by the terms of the trust.[225] The trustee may then have regard to such letter (or memorandum) in exercising any such functions, but shall not be accountable for his failure or refusal to do so. No fiduciary duty or obligation shall be imposed on the trustee merely by the giving to him of a letter of wishes (or preparation of a memorandum).[226]

Enforcement

39.139   In so far as enforcement of a trust created or established for a purpose is concerned, section 4(3) provides that it shall be enforceable by the settlor or his personal representatives, or by the person or persons named in the instrument creating or establishing the trust as the person or persons appointed to enforce the trust; and the trust shall be enforceable at the instance of the person or persons so named, notwithstanding that such person or persons are not beneficiaries under the trust. The role of enforcer in relation to a purpose trust would seem to require some form of supervision or monitoring of the trustees' activities, but this is not

---

[224] LOTA 1996, s 4(3).   [225] ibid, s 34(1).   [226] ibid, s 34(4), (5).

made clear. Indeed, the LOTA 1996 is silent on a number of matters. Are the enforcer's duties fiduciary in nature (akin to those of a protector)? Must he be entirely independent of, and have no connection with, the purposes of the trust? What are his duties and powers in the event that he concludes that the trustees are failing to carry out their trusts? Can he remove the trustees or must he apply to the court for directions and assistance?

An offshore trust, validly created in accordance with or as provided by the LOTA 1996, shall be recognized and be enforceable in accordance with its terms by the courts in Malaysia situated at Labuan, or at such other place as may be designated by the Chief Justice of the Federal Court notwithstanding the provisions of any other law.[227] An offshore trust is not valid and is unenforceable in Labuan where: **39.140**

(a) it requires, purports, or encourages the doing of any act, which is an offence under the laws of Malaysia or which, if carried out in Malaysia, would be such an offence (provided that such act is also punishable as a criminal offence in the other country or jurisdiction where the act takes place);

(b) it has income accruing or derived or originating from an operation, transaction, or other activity which is or would be an offence of the kind referred to in (a) above;

(c) it comprises property the receipt, ownership, or control of which is or would be such an offence; or

(d) the court declares that the object for which it was created has failed or that the terms of the trust are such that its performance is not possible.[228]

There is no indication that the failure of the trust's object or the impossibility of performance must be established *ab initio,* so that the question of invalidity or unenforceability may arise (probably unexpectedly) during the lifetime of the trust.

Where an offshore trust is created for two or more purposes, of which some are lawful and others are unlawful, then the whole trust is invalid if the unlawful purposes cannot be properly separated. However, where the unlawful purposes can be properly separated, the court may make a finding that the trust is valid with respect to the lawful purpose or purposes which do not affect the validity of the trust to the extent and under the conditions as may be determined by it.[229] Where the trustee of an offshore trust is of the opinion that the trust is or may be, in whole or in part, invalid, he shall [*sic*] seek directives from the court as to the validity of the trust and as to any matter concerning the trust property and his obligations in **39.141**

---

[227] ibid, s 9(1).
[228] ibid, s 9(2). It is difficult to see what paras (b) and (c) add to the widely worded para (a).
[229] ibid, s 9(3).

relation to the trust.[230] A settlor or beneficiary of an offshore trust may also request such directives as to such matters.[231]

Registration

39.142   The provisions of the LOTA 1996 dealing with registration are optional and not compulsory. Section 12(1) merely provides that every offshore trust validly created in accordance with or as provided by the Act, whether in Labuan or abroad, 'may be registered' with the Labuan Offshore Financial Services Authority. If the offshore trust is registered, responsibility for its registration and any subsequent changes in connection therewith rests with the trustee of the trust.[232] Registration is effected by filing with the Authority:

(a)   a statement containing the name of the offshore trust, the date of its creation, the name and address of the trust company acting as trustee, the address of the registered office of the offshore trust, and the proper law of the offshore trust; and

(b)   a declaration by the trust company acting as trustee of the offshore trust that the trust satisfies the conditions of the LOTA 1996 in order that it be an offshore trust.[233]

39.143   On being satisfied that all the requirements of the LOTA 1996 for the existence of an offshore trust have been complied with and upon payment of the prescribed fee, the Authority may register the trust and issue a certificate of registration accordingly.[234] Any subsequent change in the particulars of a registered offshore trust must be notified to, and registered with, the Authority in the prescribed form (within one month of the change) and shall not have effect until it is so registered.[235] The trustee of such a trust must also notify the Authority of the termination of the trust in the prescribed form within one month of the termination.[236] Moreover, the trustee of the registered offshore trust must notify the Authority in the prescribed form as to whether the trust is still in existence, and whether he is still the trustee thereof, not later than one month after every anniversary of the registration of the trust in Labuan.[237] Any trustee who fails to comply with these requirements shall be guilty of an offence and be liable to a fine of 10,000 ringgit.[238] In view of the fact registration is not compulsory, it is difficult to see why trustees would voluntarily subject themselves to such controls and potential penalties, unless public disclosure is specifically required.

39.144   The trustee of a registered offshore trust 'may furnish' the Authority with a copy of the trust instrument or any amendment thereto, which has been certified by the

---

[230] LOTA 1996, s 9(4).   [231] ibid, s 9(5).
[232] ibid, s 12(2).   [233] ibid, s 12(3).   [234] ibid, s 12(4).   [235] ibid, s 12(5).
[236] ibid, s 12(6).   [237] ibid, s 12(7).   [238] ibid, s 12(8).

trustee, and the Authority shall register and file that copy as a true copy.[239] Every trust instrument must include the name by which the offshore trust is to be known and registered and such name shall remain unchanged until the termination of the trust, unless the Authority, having regard to the circumstances of the case, thinks it fit to authorize a change in the name.[240]

---

[239] ibid, s 13.   [240] ibid, s 14(1).

40

THE CAYMAN ISLANDS' STAR TRUST;
THE BRITISH VIRGIN ISLANDS
SPECIAL TRUSTS ACT 2003

A. The Cayman Islands' STAR Trust[1]

Introduction

The most ambitious and sophisticated offshore legislation is currently to be found **40.01** in the form of the Cayman Islands' Special Trusts (Alternative Regime) Law 1997, now substantially incorporated into Part VIII of the Trusts Law (2001 Revision).

---

[1] A Duckworth, *STAR Trusts: the Special Trusts (Alternative Regime) Law 1997* (Gostick Hall Pubs, 1997); P Matthews, 'Shooting STAR: The New Special Trusts Regime from the Cayman Islands' (1998) 11 Trust Law Int 67; A Duckworth, 'STAR WARS: The Colony Strikes Back' (1998) 12 Trust Law Int 16; P Matthews, 'STAR: Big Bang or Red Dwarf' (1999) 13 Trust Law Int 98; A Duckworth, 'STAR WARS: Smiting the Bull' (1999) 13 Trust Law Int 158. See also (1998) 8 Offshore Taxation Review 43 (DJ Hayton); Huxley, 'Rhodes, Arakan, Grand Cayman: Three Versions of Offshore' in Edge (ed), *Comparative Law in Global Perspective* (Transnational Pubs Inc, 2001).

Although the STAR legislation is clearly intended to make it easier to create both non-charitable purpose trusts and asset protection trusts, it is certainly not confined to these purposes. Trusts of all kinds may be established under STAR, ie trusts for people as well as trusts for charitable and non-charitable purposes, or, indeed, all or any combination of these. These all-embracing qualities, as well as the original and unique features, of STAR trusts make it more convenient, if not necessary, to give them separate consideration.

Trusts subject To STAR

40.02 STAR applies only to a 'special trust'. A 'trust' is said to include 'a trust of a power, as well as a trust of property' (and 'trustee' has a correspondingly extended meaning);[2] and 'a power is said to be held in trust if granted or reserved subject to any duty, expressed or implied, qualified or unqualified, to exercise the power or to consider its exercise'.[3] In addition, a 'power' includes an administrative power as well as a dispositive power. Consequently, for the purposes of STAR, the expression 'trust' is intended to include not just 'fixed' and discretionary trusts (which trustees are obliged to carry into effect),[4] but also all powers (whether dispositive or administrative) conferred on trustees *qua* trustees (the exercise of which such trustees are under a duty to consider from time to time, although not obliged actually to exercise them).[5] Thus, on this wide definition, any power conferred on any fiduciary (such as a protector or a management committee, and not just on a trustee) would be included. However, only 'special', as opposed to 'ordinary', trusts and powers are covered: the word 'special', in reference to a trust or a power, signifies that it is a trust or power which is subject to STAR.[6] Nothing in STAR affects an 'ordinary' power, directly or by inference.[7] Indeed, even 'special' trusts and powers are subject to the same general law in every respect as 'ordinary' trusts and powers, save as provided in STAR itself.[8]

40.03 In order to be subject to STAR (and therefore regarded as 'special'):

(a) a trust or power must be created by or on the terms of a written instrument (testamentary or *inter vivos*); and

(b) the instrument must contain a declaration to the effect that STAR is to apply.[9]

Where a trust or power is created by written instrument in exercise of a special power (within the meaning of STAR, and therefore not necessarily a 'special' power in the 'ordinary' sense) and the instrument contains no declaration as to the

---

[2] Trusts Law (2001) Revision, s 95(1).　　[3] ibid, s 95(2).
[4] *IRC v Broadway Cottages Trust* [1955] Ch 20; *McPhail v Doulton* [1971] AC 424.
[5] *Re Gestetner Settlement* [1953] Ch 672; *Re Gulbenkian's Settlements* [1970] AC 508. See also paras 11.03–11.29 above.　　[6] Trusts Law (2001) Revision, s 95(1).
[7] ibid, s 97.　　[8] ibid, s 98.　　[9] ibid, s 96(1).

application of STAR, then, subject to evidence of a contrary intention, STAR shall be *deemed* to be intended to apply (and the instrument shall be deemed to contain a declaration to that effect).[10] What this seems to mean is that, where a particular power is subject to STAR, then any trust or other power which is created by its exercise will itself be subject to STAR, unless the contrary is expressed. A trust or power created by the exercise of an 'ordinary' power may also be subject to STAR, but this clearly requires an express declaration within section 96(1)(b). Any trust or power which does not meet the requirements of section 96(1), or is not deemed to do so under section 96(2), is an 'ordinary' trust or power and is not subject to STAR.[11]

Objects of special trusts

STAR provides that the objects of a special trust or power may be persons or purposes or both[12] (as was always the case for ordinary powers). The persons may be of any number[13] (and presumably may be corporations as well as human beings); and the purposes may be of any number or kind, charitable or non-charitable, provided they are 'lawful and not contrary to public policy'.[14] In broad terms, this expression is likely to be interpreted in the same way as under English law. In addition, it is expressly provided that no land nor any interest in land in the Cayman Islands shall be subject, directly or indirectly, to a special trust; but a special trust may hold an interest in a company, partnership, or other entity which holds such land, or an interest in such land, for the purposes of its business.[15]   **40.04**

A special trust is not rendered void by uncertainty as to its objects or mode of execution.[16] The terms of a special trust may give the trustee or any other person power to resolve an uncertainty as to its objects or mode of execution.[17] It is not clear whether 'uncertainty' refers only to evidential uncertainty, in which case the trustee or other person can merely determine whether or not any given object falls within the description of the clearly defined class of objects as a whole, or also extends to include conceptual uncertainty as well, so that the trustee or other person can determine the meaning of the words used by the settlor to describe or define the class of objects itself. If a special trust has multiple objects and there is no allocation of the trust property between them, the trustee, subject to evidence of contrary intention, has discretion to allocate the trust property.[18] It is not made clear, however, whether, in any such case, a trust for several objects which is not a fixed trust will effectively become a discretionary trust, ie one where the trustee must exercise his discretion, or whether the statute simply confers on the trustee a power to select which he is not obliged to exercise. It is also difficult to see how, in   **40.05**

---

[10] ibid, s 96(2).   [11] ibid, s 96(3).   [12] ibid, s 99(1).   [13] ibid, s 99(2).
[14] ibid, s 99(3).   [15] ibid, s 16.   [16] ibid, s 103(1), which is subject to s 103(4).
[17] ibid, s 103(2).   [18] ibid, s 103(3).

the absence of reasonably specific criteria, the trustees would be expected to exercise their discretion.

40.06 If an uncertainty as to the objects or mode of execution of a special trust cannot be resolved, or has not been resolved pursuant to the terms of the trust, the court:

(a) may resolve the uncertainty:
   (i) by reforming the trust,
   (ii) by settling a plan for its administration, or
   (iii) in any other way which the court deems appropriate; or
(b) in so far as the objects of the trust are uncertain and the general intent of the trust cannot be found from the admissible evidence as a matter of probability, may declare the trust void.[19]

Cy pres application

40.07 A STAR trust may be a perpetual trust. STAR also clearly contemplates that a trust may be reformed in accordance with the express terms of the trust itself. In addition, it creates a mechanism for the court to reform the trust cy pres, if the execution of a special trust in accordance with its terms becomes in whole or in part impossible or impracticable, unlawful or contrary to public policy, or obsolete (because of changed circumstances) in that it fails to achieve the general intent of the special trust. In any such case, the trustees shall [*sic*], unless the trust is reformed pursuant to its own terms, apply to the court to reform the trust cy pres or, if or in so far as the court is of the opinion that it cannot be reformed consistently with the general intent of the trust, the trustees shall dispose of the trust property as though the trust or the relevant part of it has failed.[20]

Enforcement

40.08 It might have been thought that, where a STAR trust has a person as a beneficiary, it would be enforceable by that beneficiary, and only in the case of a STAR trust partly or exclusively in favour of a purpose would it be necessary to provide some specific mechanism for enforcement. However, this is not the approach adopted by STAR. The *only* persons who have standing to enforce a STAR trust are such persons, whether or not beneficiaries, as are appointed to be enforcers:

(a) by or pursuant to the terms of the trust; or
(b) by order of the court.[21]

---

[19] Trusts Law (2001) Revision, s 103(4).
[20] ibid, s 104(1). Section 72 (jurisdiction of the court to vary trusts) does not apply to special trusts (s 104(2)).   [21] ibid. s 100(2).

In other words, a beneficiary of a STAR trust does not have any right, simply by virtue of his status as a beneficiary, to enforce that trust, although such a right may be conferred upon him expressly by the trust instrument or by the court (in which case, of course, he will then have that right in an entirely different capacity). Nor does he have an enforceable right, as beneficiary, against a trustee or against an enforcer, or an enforceable right to the trust property.[22] A 'beneficiary' means 'a person who will or may derive a benefit or advantage, directly or indirectly, from the execution of a special trust'.[23] An 'enforcer' is 'a person who has standing to enforce a special trust'; and 'standing to enforce' means 'the right or duty to bring an action for the enforcement of a special trust'.[24] The expression 'right or duty' in this context seems to be intended to distinguish between an enforcer who is under a duty to enforce, and an enforcer who has authority or power to do so, but is under no such duty.[25] A right or duty to enforce a trust is presumed, subject to evidence of a contrary intention, to extend to every trust which is created by, or on the terms of, the same instrument, or pursuant to a power so created.[26]

If an enforcer with a duty to enforce is unable, unwilling, or unfit to do so, the court may, on the application of a trustee (or another enforcer), appoint an enforcer (or another enforcer).[27] In such a case, the enforcer himself may be guilty of, and liable for, a breach of duty, but it is not clear whether a trustee is obliged to make an application to the court in such circumstances and would be liable for breach of duty if he failed to do so.[28] The court may also intervene, on the application of a trustee (or enforcer), if the terms of the trust require the appointment of an enforcer but: **40.09**

(a) it is impossible to make the appointment without the court's assistance or
(b) it is difficult or inexpedient to make the appointment without the court's assistance.[29]

The trust instrument may impose an obligation to appoint an enforcer on a trustee and, in circumstances where the court's assistance is required, the trustee would presumably be under a duty to seek such assistance. However, if the trustee is not under a duty to appoint an enforcer, is he nonetheless under an implied duty to make an application to the court in these circumstances? Common sense would **40.10**

---

[22] ibid, s 100(1).
[23] ibid, s 95(1). STAR distinguishes (rightly) between an 'object' and a 'beneficiary' of a trust. An 'object' which is a purpose could not enforce a trust, in any event, so the provisions of s 100 could (and are expressed to) apply only to 'beneficiaries'.   [24] ibid, s 95(1).
[25] ibid, s 101(1), which declares that standing to enforce a special trust may be granted or reserved as a right or as a duty.   [26] ibid, s 100(3).   [27] ibid, s 100(4)(b).
[28] A duty to do what was required in order to enforce and implement the trust would, of course, be inherent in the office of trustee in relation to any 'ordinary' trust; but the allocation of duties under a 'special' STAR trust is not always clear.   [29] ibid, s 104(4)(a).

suggest that the provisions of section 100(4)(a) and (b) could be given compre-hensive (as opposed to partial) effect only by construing them as imposing, by implication, a duty on a trustee to make the requisite application to the court. However, the provisions of section 100(5) (which are expressed to apply only to the circumstances described in section 100(4)(c) seem to suggest otherwise. Limb (i) of section 100(4)(c) and section 100(5), taken together, have the effect that, in the event that there is no enforcer who is of full capacity and who is also a beneficiary, the trustee *shall* within thirty days apply to the court for the appoint-ment of an enforcer, or for the administration of the special trust under the direc-tion of the court, or for such other order as the court shall think fit. If the trustee knowingly fails to do so, he shall be guilty of an offence and shall be liable on sum-mary conviction to a fine not exceeding $10,000. The same applies to limb (ii) of section 100(4)(c), which applies to the case where there is no enforcer 'of full capacity' who 'has a duty to enforce and is fit and willing to do so'. Although this provision, too, is not clearly expressed, the intention, it seems, is to ensure that a trustee must apply to the court if there is no effective enforcer; and there will be an effective enforcer only where there is either:

(a)   a person who benefits under the terms of the trust and who is of full age and sound mind; or

(b)   a person who has undertaken a duty to enforce the trust who is also of full age and sound mind.

40.11   Subject to evidence of a contrary intention, an enforcer is deemed to have a fiduciary duty to act responsibly with a view to the proper execution of the trust.[30] To whom this fiduciary duty is owed is unclear. In the case of a pure purpose trust, it cannot sensibly be said to be owed to the trust's purposes; nor does it make sense to say that an enforcer owes such a duty to himself; and there is no indication that the duty is owed to the settlor. Presumably what is meant is that an enforcer is sub-ject to a statutory duty to act and to conduct himself with the same degree of responsibility *as if* he had been appointed an enforcer of a trust for persons.[31] A trustee (or another enforcer), or any person expressly authorized by the terms of the special trust, has standing to bring an action for the enforcement of the duty (if any) of an enforcer.[32] Thus, an enforcer who fails to carry out his duty (if any) to enforce the trust can be brought to book by the appropriate authorized person and, in determining whether the enforcer should be held liable, as well as the extent of his liability, he will be judged as one deemed to owe fiduciary duties (for example to address his mind from time to time to the question of proper enforce-ment of the trust) and not as an ordinary individual owing no fiduciary obliga-tions at all (which would enable him to ignore the trust and its enforcement

---

[30]   Trusts Law (2001) Revision, s 101(2).   [31]   See also s 102, referred to below.   [32]   ibid, s 101(3).

entirely). Whether this enforcement mechanism will work or not remains to be seen: it certainly appears to be capable of operating in a circular (and possibly self-defeating) manner, in that the enforcer is supposed to ensure that the trustee carries out the trust, while it may be the trustee who has the task of ensuring that the enforcer fulfils his obligation to enforce.

Section 102 of the Trusts Law (2001 Revision) provides that, subject to the terms of his appointment, an enforcer has the same rights as a beneficiary of an ordinary trust: **40.12**

(a) to bring administrative and other actions, and make applications to the court, concerning the trust; and

(b) to be informed of the terms of the trust, to receive information concerning the trust and its administration from the trustee, and to inspect and take copies of trust documents.

It also provides that, in the performance of his duties (if any), an enforcer has the rights of a trustee of an ordinary trust to protection and indemnity and to make applications to the court for an opinion, advice, or direction or for relief from personal liability. And also, in the event of a breach of trust, an enforcer has, on behalf of the trust, the same personal and proprietary remedies against the trustee and against third parties as a beneficiary of an ordinary trust. The enforcer clearly does not have a proprietary interest under the trust: he is simply given statutory remedies which are equivalent to the remedies that would be available to a beneficiary who had such an interest. In the exercise of any and all of these functions, an enforcer is deemed to have a fiduciary duty to act responsibly (subject to evidence of a contrary intention).[33]

Section 100 does not affect:

(a) the enforcement by a trustee, enforcer, or any other person involved in the administration of a trust of a right to remuneration or indemnity; or

(b) the enforcement of a trustee's duties by a co-trustee or a successor trustee.[34]

Nature of a STAR trust

The unusual, indeed unique, form and structure of a STAR trust raises interesting and difficult questions as to the nature of a trust—indeed, whether a STAR trust is a trust at all—and also as to ownership of the beneficial interest in the trust property. As Millett LJ said in *Armitage v Nurse*,[35] in English law, there must exist **40.13**

---

[33] ibid, s 101(2).   [34] ibid, s 100(6). Section 83 does not apply to special trusts: s 100(7).
[35] [1997] 2 All ER 705, 713.

'an irreducible core of obligations owed by the trustees to the beneficiaries and enforceable by them which is fundamental to the concept of a trust. If the beneficiaries have no rights enforceable against the trustees there are no trusts.' (There may be some debate as to what that core of obligations may amount to or needs to be, but it is plain that, whatever the answer to that question may be, the core of obligations is regarded as owed to and enforceable by beneficiaries.) In the case of a STAR trust, however, the fundamental defining features or characteristics of a trust (as traditionally understood in England) are expressly excluded. For example, a 'beneficiary' is simply someone who will or may derive a benefit or advantage, directly or indirectly, from the execution of a special trust. Such a 'beneficiary' may well have a full proprietary interest in the trust fund, but he may equally be no more than an object of a mere power (and therefore not a beneficiary in the English trust law sense at all). Moreover, a beneficiary of a STAR trust has no right to enforce the trust, has no enforceable right against a trustee or an enforcer, and has no enforceable right to the trust property itself[36] (which effectively excludes the rule in *Saunders v Vautier*).[37] Consequently, it is arguable that, in English law, the trustee of a STAR trust, under which no person is both a beneficiary and an enforcer, would hold the legal title on resulting trust for the settlor, but with a power to benefit 'beneficiaries' who are, in reality, no more than the objects of that power. The settlor's beneficial interest under such a resulting trust would form part of his estate (for the purposes of taxation, succession, insolvency, and so forth).[38] The settlor, as resulting beneficiary, would have rights of enforcement, to information, to an account, and so on—and the statutory provisions excluding all these rights would have no effect. This would indeed be a trust, but certainly not the kind of trust that the settlor intended.

40.14 Alternatively, it is arguable that the trustee of such a STAR trust has vested in him both the legal *and* beneficial ownership of the trust property, to the exclusion of both the 'beneficiaries' and the settlor, but to be subject, like the executor of an unadministered estate, to fiduciary obligations (but towards whom is not entirely clear). This might derive some support from *Carreras Rothmans Ltd v Freeman Matthews Treasure Ltd*,[39] but this is weak support for such a far-reaching analysis. In the case of a STAR trust, this 'suspended' beneficial ownership could and probably would last indefinitely and not just for a short period while some precondition was being met (for example the estate being administered). In any event, neither analysis solves the problem presented by the exclusion of the normal and essential rights of beneficiaries. In each case, if a valid trust were to be acknowledged at all, it would have to be on the basis that the key elements of a STAR trust

---

36 Trusts Law (2001 Revision), s 100(1). Cf *Lawrence v Berbrier* (2002) 5 ITELR 9 (Ontario).
37 (1841) 4 Beav 115.
38 (1998) 8 Offshore Taxation Review 43, 45 (DJ Hayton). Cf (2000) 117 LQR 96 (DJ Hayton).
39 [1985] Ch 207. See also paras 9.74–9.85 above.

had no effect. It is therefore just as possible that a STAR trust would not be recognized as a trust at all—it would then be some form of contractual relationship, perhaps some form of agency, between settlor and trustees.

As far as the Cayman Islands themselves are concerned, a STAR trust and its peculiar characteristics are laid down by statute. Therefore, it is difficult to see how the question of initial validity could arise. Specific features of the STAR legislation will no doubt lead, on occasion, to problems of construction and interpretation and so on—but it is unlikely that the fundamental question of validity that would concern an English trusts lawyer would need to be raised and addressed at all within the Cayman Islands themselves. The duties, powers, rights, and remedies imposed or conferred on various parties are statutory in origin and nature and, as such, they are enforceable in the domestic forum without any need to fit them into a traditional analysis. Section 90 of the Trusts Law (2001 Revision) provides that all questions arising in regard to a trust which is for the time being governed by the laws of the Islands, including questions as to any aspect of the validity of the trust, or the interpretation or effect thereof, are to be determined by the laws of the Islands.

40.15

Conflict of laws

It may be a different matter, of course, when the same questions are raised in another jurisdiction, ie when they have to be addressed in the context of a conflict of laws. Article 2 of the Hague Convention on Trusts refers to trusts 'for the benefit of a beneficiary or for a specified purpose', which might suggest that signatories to the Convention will recognize non-charitable purpose trusts as well as charitable ones, provided they are created in accordance with the law specified in Chapter II of the Convention.[40] It is possible that the Convention's drafting committee intended to include not just charities but also Scots public purposes and anomalous English non-charitable purpose trusts as well. However, this must be doubtful. In 1982–1983, when the Convention was being negotiated, only Liechtenstein and Nauru, both of which have specially introduced trusts legislation and, in any event, neither of which was represented at the negotiations, recognized non-charitable purpose trusts; and the reference in the Convention to 'a specified purpose' may have been intended to include only charitable and public purpose trusts.[41]

40.16

---

[40] See J Glasson (ed), *International Trust Laws* (Jordans, loose-leaf) Section C, Appendix 51. Many 'trust-law jurisdictions' have *not* ratified the Convention (eg the USA, Ontario, New Zealand, South Africa) and very few 'non-trust jurisdictions' have done so (eg Italy, The Netherlands).

[41] Von Overbeck, *Explanatory Report on the Convention*, para 39. See also (1987) 36 ICLQ 260 (DJ Hayton); (1987) 35 Am Jo Comp Law 307 (Gaillard and Troutmann); (1999) 32 Vanderbilt Jo Transnat Law 999 (Dyer); *Fothergill v Monarch Airlines Ltd* [1981] AC 251, 278, 283, 294–295.

40.17 In any event, Article 18 declares that the provisions of the Convention may be disregarded when their application would be manifestly incompatible with public policy. An English court might hold that the beneficiary principle is a rule of public policy (to prevent property becoming economically ownerless) and (under Article 18) hold that a STAR trust was 'manifestly incompatible with public policy', so that, at best, there can be no more than a resulting trust for the settlor (although charities must then be acknowledged to be an exception, also justified by public policy). Thus, it may well be the case that a perpetual STAR trust of English land would not be recognized by an English court (even if a similar effect could be engineered by conveying such land into the ownership of a holding company, the shares in which are owned by a STAR trust). It is noteworthy that the STAR legislation itself—just like that of other offshore jurisdictions—prohibits ownership by a STAR trust of land in the Cayman Islands, although it can own shares in a company which owns such land. Similarly, it is conceivable that the arrangement created by a particular STAR trust would be regarded as no more than a contractual relationship or as a resulting trust for the settlor, or even, in certain circumstances, as just a sham not involving any effective disposition of property at all.

40.18 It is suggested that any such response is unlikely—or, at least, that it would be one of last resort—especially given that the trustees (and indeed the enforcer) of a STAR trust are liable, under the domestic forum, to stringent statutory duties (some of which carry criminal penalties) in relation to the property subject to the trust. It is not obvious why an English court would refuse to recognize and assist in the enforcement of trust-like obligations, which are valid and effective in another jurisdiction, unless there are compelling English public policy reasons for not doing so. After all, what is regarded as a contract in civil law countries differs appreciably from an English contract, and yet no one would suggest that these differences on their own would justify an English court in refusing to recognize and assist in the enforcement of a civil law contract. How an English court actually will respond when faced with a STAR trust remains to be seen, however. This uncertainty, added to the fact that STAR trusts are unique to the Cayman Islands and not duplicated or mirrored in any other jurisdiction, may prove to be one practical restriction too many for settlors and their advisers and discourage the creation of STAR trusts in the first place.

Unlawful acceptance

40.19 Section 107 of the Trusts Law (2001 Revision) provides that a person who, as trustee, accepts a settlement of property upon a special trust, without taking steps to ensure that the settlor, or the person making the settlement on his behalf, understands who will have standing to enforce the trust, is guilty of an offence and liable on summary conviction to a fine not exceeding $10,000, or to imprisonment for a period not exceeding one year, or to both, or on conviction on indictment to a fine not exceeding $100,000, or to imprisonment for a period not exceeding five years, or both.

Trusteeship

Section 105(1) declares that, except as authorized by an order of the court or per- **40.20** mitted by or pursuant to section 105:

(a) the trustee of a special trust shall be or include a trust corporation; and
(b) the trustee shall keep in the Islands at the office of the trust corporation a documentary record of:
   (i) the terms of the special trust,
   (ii) the identity of the trustee and the enforcers,
   (iii) all settlements of the property upon the special trust and the identity of the settlors,
   (iv) the property subject to the special trust at the end of each of its accounting years, and
   (v) all distributions or applications of the trust property.[42]

A 'trust corporation' for these purposes means a body corporate licensed to conduct trust business, with or without restriction, under the Banks and Trust Companies Law (2000 Second Revision).[43] Section 105(3) provides that the court may authorize non-compliance with section 105(1) on such terms as it thinks fit if it is satisfied that the execution of the trust will not be prejudiced.

Land

No land nor any interest in land in the Islands shall be subject, directly or indi- **40.21** rectly, to a special trust, but a special trust may hold an interest in a company, partnership, or other entity which holds land in the Islands, or an interest in such land for the purposes of its business.

B. VISTA Trusts

Trusts of shares in corporate businesses—the current problem

It has become increasingly evident in recent years that the familiar rule which **40.22** requires a trustee to act prudently in relation to trust investments[44] is impeding

---

[42] Trusts Law (2001) Revision, s 105(1). Section 105(4)–(8) contains criminal sanctions for breaches of s 105(1).   [43] ibid, s 105(2).
[44] In some jurisdictions this may be the so-called prudent man of business rule as stated by Lindley J in *Re Whiteley* (1886) 33 Ch D 347, 355. In others it may have a statutory basis.

the use of trusts as vehicles for holding controlling interests in companies. The problem is particularly acute when trusts are needed to provide for succession to incorporated family businesses.[45]

40.23   The problem arises from the specific obligations that the duty of prudence places on trustees when the trust fund consists of a controlling shareholding in a company. The obligations are, briefly, as follows:

A.   To monitor the conduct of the directors of the company and to intervene where necessary in the company's business (for example to prevent the company from entering into an unduly speculative venture).[46]

B.   To exploit the shareholding to maximum financial advantage—which may require the trustees to accept a financially attractive takeover bid for the company, or to seek out and take opportunities for spreading the trust's financial risk by selling the company or its underlying assets and reinvesting in a diversified portfolio.

40.24   Experience has shown that these obligations fail to meet the requirements of the typical settlor of family company shares, and pose significant difficulties for trustees. The reasons, in summary, are these.

1.   The prudence required of trustees when monitoring a company's affairs is incompatible with the entrepreneurial flare and quick decision taking required to run a successful business.

2.   Trustees rarely have, or can be expected to have, the skills appropriate for assessing business decisions made by directors. If the trustees delegate the assessment task to, or act on advice from, a person with suitable skills[47] that person may be doing no more than second-guessing the directors.

3.   The cost of trust administration is increased substantially, and often disproportionately, by the monitoring procedures necessary to ensure that trustees are acting prudently.

4.   Case law on the duty of prudence has not yet answered crucial questions on the precise responsibilities of a trustee controlling an entrepreneurial business (which by its nature carries a significantly higher level of risk than that carried by a balanced investment portfolio).[48]

---

[45]   In international situations, trusts, as a general rule, are preferred to wills as succession vehicles because they are likely to be less susceptible to the delays and uncertainties arising from conflict of laws rules.

[46]   *Bartlett v Barclays Bank Trust Co Ltd* [1980] Ch 515. See also *Re Lucking's Will Trusts* [1967] 3 All ER 726, [1968] 1 WLR 866.

[47]   And such a person may in practice be difficult to find.

[48]   The leading case on the duty of monitoring, *Bartlett v Barclays Bank Trust Co Ltd* [1980] Ch 515, arose out of the failure of a hazardous development project. But where is the dividing line between hazardous speculation and reasonable commercial judgement? Does it vary according to

5. Indemnity insurance for trustees with controlling shareholdings may be prohibitively expensive, if not unobtainable.

6. A settlor with an established corporate business may not view the business merely in investment terms[49] and hence may not wish the company or its assets to be sold for the sake of short-term gain or diversification.

7. In so far as the business is seen by the settlor as an investment he or she may wish to take a longer view in terms of profit generation than a prudent trustee would be prepared to allow. He may also prefer to leave to the directors, rather than to the trustees/shareholders, the question of whether the company expands, contracts, or even goes out of business.

8. The trustees' obligation to intervene extends, when appropriate, to the appointment and dismissal of directors—a potential source of conflict if the settlor wishes, reasonably enough,[50] to remain at the helm and to nominate successors.

The Virgin Islands Special Trusts Act 2003—overview

A number of possible non-legislative solutions to these difficulties, such as the **40.25** 'non intervention' clause in trust instruments, requirements for consent, and complex structuring (for example involving voting and non-voting shares), have been put forward, but all of these suffer from significant drawbacks. The Virgin Islands Special Trusts Act 2003[51] ('VISTA'), which came into force on 1 March 2004, enables special new British Virgin Islands trusts (known as 'VISTA trusts') to be created which circumvent the difficulties.

The aim of VISTA is to enable a shareholder to establish a trust of his company **40.26** that disengages the trustee from management responsibility and permits the company and its business to be retained as long as the directors think fit. This is achieved in general terms by: first, authorizing the entire removal of the trustee's monitoring and intervention obligations (except to the extent that the settlor otherwise requires); secondly, by permitting the settlor to confer on the trustee a role more suited to a trustee's abilities, namely a duty to intervene to resolve specific problems (for example a deadlocked board); thirdly, by allowing trust instruments to lay down rules for the appointment and removal of directors (so reducing the

---

the nature of the business (some businesses being inherently more risky than others)? If a trustee, on a safety first principle, adopts a too cautious approach may he incur liability for losses which follow from his not being prepared to adopt the level of risk customary for the business in question?

[49] Other factors in his mind may include, for example, family tradition, social concerns for employees or the environment, and career opportunities for descendants.

[50] Because (a) the settlor is settling his or her own assets and should be free to decide the terms on which he or she does so, and (b) as economic commentators have pointed out, some of the most successful companies are those whose owners have remained at the helm.   [51] No 10 of 2003.

trustee's ability to intervene in management by appointing directors of its own choice); fourthly, by giving both beneficiaries and directors the right to apply to the court if trustees fail to comply with the requirements for non-intervention or the requirements for director appointment and removal; and, lastly, by prohibiting the sale of shares without directors' approval.

Primary purpose of the Act

40.27 The primary purpose of the Act is stated in section 3 as being 'to enable a trust of company shares to be established under which

(a) the shares may be retained indefinitely; and

(b) the management of the company may be carried out by its directors without any power of intervention being exercised by the trustee'.

Section 3 provides a positive statement of the intention behind the Act and should be seen as a background to, and an aid to interpretation of, its subsequent provisions.

When the Act will apply

40.28 The provisions of VISTA will *only* apply to a trust if (a) there is a direction in the trust instrument to the effect that its provisions apply to all (or to specified) shares in British Virgin Islands companies which are comprised in the trust fund *and* (b) the conditions listed in section 4(4) of the Act are satisfied. In the absence of such a direction, or if those conditions are not satisfied, VISTA will not apply to a British Virgin Islands trust.

40.29 The conditions listed in section 4(4) of VISTA are as follows:

(a) the trust must be created by or on the terms of a written testamentary or *inter vivos* instrument;

(b) a 'designated trustee' (ie a holder of a trust licence under the British Virgin Islands Banks and Trust Companies Act, 1990[52]) must be the sole trustee of the trust;

(c) the terms of the trust must require that any successor trustee[53] is a designated trustee (as defined in paragraph (b) above) acting as sole trustee; and

(d) the trust must not be created in the exercise of a power conferred by another trust.[54]

---

[52] No 9 of 1990.
[53] This condition is not expressed in such a way that it only applies *for so long as* the trust is subject to VISTA.   [54] Even, it would appear, another VISTA trust.

Who may be the trustee of and what property may be made subject to a VISTA trust

As indicated in Section 4 (4) of VISTA above, a 'designated trustee' must be the **40.30** sole trustee of a VISTA trust. This will (*inter alia*) ensure that VISTA trusts are always subject to British Virgin Islands regulatory control. In order to prevent a conflict of interest, section 13 of the Act prohibits a trustee from being a director of a company in which shares subject to a VISTA trust are held.

In general[55] VISTA will only apply (directly)[56] to shares in British Virgin Islands **40.31** companies (not being companies which hold licences pursuant to, or which are otherwise regulated by, specified British Virgin Islands regulatory statutes); such shares are defined by the Act[57] as 'Virgin Islands shares'. It cannot therefore apply (directly) to shares in foreign companies or to other property.[58] Shares which are held on a VISTA trust are defined[59] by the Act as 'designated shares'.

Whether VISTA applies to all Virgin Islands shares which are held on trust or only **40.32** to specified Virgin Islands shares will depend on the wording of the direction which is contained in the trust instrument,[60] and section 4(2) of VISTA effectively enables VISTA to apply to Virgin Islands shares which are added to the trust fund (whether by way of additional settlement of by way of reinvestment) after the trust's original creation. However, as a result of section 4(3) of VISTA, the Act cannot apply to shares which are added to the trust fund by a trustee of another trust in the exercise of a power in that other trust.[61]

Differences between VISTA trusts and other British Virgin Islands trusts

The main differences between VISTA trusts and other British Virgin Islands **40.33** trusts which are not subject to VISTA[62] are as follows:

(a) Trust to retain

Section 5 of VISTA gives effect to one of the main purposes of the Act by provid- **40.34** ing that designated shares will (subject to section 9)[63] be held on 'trust to retain' and that the trustee's statutory duty to retain the shares has precedence over any duty to preserve or enhance the value of the trust fund. This means that trustees will not be able to dispose of the shares in exercising their administrative powers

---

[55] In view of the definition of 'connected companies' which is effectively included in s 2(2), certain provisions of the Act may also affect trustees' powers and duties in relation to underlying companies.
[56] The Act might, however, have an effect on the underlying assets of the trust, given the trustees' diluted powers and responsibilities as shareholders of the companies which hold such assets. See paras 40.41–40.55 below. [57] VISTA, s 2(1). [58] See n 56 above.
[59] In s 2(1). [60] See VISTA, s 4(1). [61] Even, *semble*, another VISTA trust.
[62] See Christopher J McKenzie's chapter on British Virgin Islands trusts in Glasson (ed), *International Trust Laws* (Jordans, loose-leaf). [63] See paras 40.35–40.38 below.

unless section 9[64] of the Act applies to the trust, or unless ordered or authorized to do so by the court pursuant to section 11.[65]

(b) Power of disposal

40.35 Although the objective of the Act is that shares in a VISTA trust should be capable of being held indefinitely, it would be unduly restrictive to impose a total ban on sale, for example if there is a significant change in circumstances after the trust is originally created. A limited power of sale is therefore contained in section 9.

40.36 Section 9(2) of VISTA confers on trustees the power (in the management or administration of the trust fund) to sell or otherwise dispose[66] of designated shares in such manner and upon such terms and conditions as they (acting in their fiduciary capacity) think fit. However subsection (2) of that section also makes it clear (consistently with the spirit of the Act) that the existence of this power will not carry an implied duty to exercise it for the purpose of preserving or enhancing the value of the assets of the trust (or to consider its exercise for that purpose) and will not make the trustee liable (in consequence of not exercising the power) for losses of the kind referred to in paragraph 40.40 below.

40.37 Moreover the power which is conferred on trustees of VISTA trusts by section 9(2) is both capable of exclusion by the trust instrument and subject to the provisions of subsection (3) of that section which specifies that (unless the trust instrument provides to the contrary) the trustee of a VISTA trust cannot exercise the statutory power of sale or disposal[67] in the management or administration of the trust fund without the consent of the sole director or a majority of the directors of the company (the shares of which are held on a VISTA trust) and without such other consents, if any, as are required by the trust instrument. The requirement for directors' consent is consistent with the overall policy of ensuring that the company is managed by directors chosen in accordance with the rules laid down by the settlor, since once the trust has been created the trustee will in general have no power other than to enforce those rules.

40.38 An application to confer a power of sale or disposal on the trustee cannot be made to the court pursuant to section 59 of the Trustee Act[68] (which is the British Virgin Islands equivalent to section 57 of the English Trustee Act 1925).[69]

(c) Residuary power of the court to order the sale or disposal of designated shares

40.39 Section 11 of VISTA contains a provision which enables 'interested persons' (as defined in paragraph 40.51 below) to apply to the court to order or authorize the

---

[64] ibid.   [65] See para 40.39 below.
[66] This term is defined very widely by VISTA, s 2(3) to include certain other transactions which affect the shares, namely liquidation of the company, cancellation of the shares or of any rights attached to them, and the creation of any interest in the shares.   [67] See n 66 above.
[68] Cap 303.   [69] VISTA, s 9(5).

sale or disposal[70] (on such terms as it thinks fit) of designated shares (without the consent of those referred to in section 9(3)[71] of the Act) on showing that the retention of the shares is no longer compatible with the wishes of the settlor.[72] The provisions of this section are equivalent to the court's inherent salvage jurisdiction to authorize trustees to carry out transactions not expressly authorized by the settlement in circumstances which could not reasonably have been predicted by the settlor, and the court's power will generally be a power of last resort.

(d) Statutory protection from liability for losses resulting from retaining shares

Section 5(3) of VISTA reinforces one of the main objectives of the Act by making it clear that a trustee of a VISTA trust will not be liable for losses arising directly or indirectly from holding, rather than disposing of, designated shares. In particular such a trustee will not be liable for losses arising from the absence or inadequacy of financial return from any designated shares, a decrease in value of any designated shares, speculative or imprudent activities of the company (or any underlying company) or depletion of such a company's assets by disposition, any act or omission of the directors of such a company (regardless of whether it is made or carried out in good faith), liquidation or receivership of such a company, share market fluctuation, the loss of opportunity to make gains from reinvestment of the proceeds of designated shares, and the liabilities and expenses of such a company (including directors' remuneration and expenses). 40.40

(e) Restrictions on the exercise of trustees' voting[73] and other powers

Section 6 of VISTA gives effect to the other main objective of the Act, ie the intention that, as a general rule, the management of the company should be in the hands of the directors without intervention by the trustee. The section provides that voting or other powers in respect of designated shares cannot be exercised by the trustee of a VISTA trust so as to interfere with the management or conduct of any business of the company, and, in particular, that the trustee is required to leave the conduct of every such business, and all decisions as to the payment or non-payment of dividends to the company's directors, and cannot require the declaration or payment of any dividend by the company or exercise any power which it may have of compelling any such declaration or payment. In addition section 6(3) provides that such a trustee shall take no steps to instigate or support any action by the company against any of its directors for breach of duty to the company, to procure the appointment or removal of directors, or (subject to the other 40.41

---

[70] See n 66 above.   [71] See para 40.37 above.   [72] See para 40.59 below.
[73] References in VISTA to voting powers in respect of shares include references to powers to direct the voting of shares held by a nominee. See VISTA, s 2(2)(a). The relevant definition takes account of the fact that the shares in a trust will often in practice be held by a nominee rather than the trustee itself.

provisions of the Act) to apply to the court for any form of remedy or relief in relation to the company;[74] the subsection also limits the trustee's powers to take steps to wind up the company.

40.42 Importantly section 6 of VISTA is, however, subject to any provisions to the contrary in the trust instrument (so that the settlor can, in an individual case, give the trustee greater responsibility)[75] and to the relevant provisions of sections 7 and 8 of the Act (which relate, *inter alia*, to voting powers in relation to directors and provide for intervention in prescribed circumstances).[76]

(f) Removal of trustees' duties

40.43 Section 15 of VISTA makes it clear, furthermore, that a trustee of a VISTA trust has no 'fiduciary responsibility or duty of care in respect of the assets of, or the conduct of the affairs of, the company'[77] in which designated shares are held, except when acting on an 'intervention call'[78] (pursuant to section 8). In particular such a trustee is not required to make any enquiry as to whether any facts exist which would, or may, whether with or without any other information, form the basis of an intervention call; nor is it obliged to inform any interested person[79] of any fact of which it becomes aware, or which it suspects, concerning the assets of such a company or the conduct of its affairs; and it is also exonerated from liability as an accessory to a director's breach of duty by reason of any omission on its part to take action where it is aware, or suspects, that there will be such a breach (or by reason of any act or omission in compliance with the provisions of section 7 of the Act, which essentially deal with trustees' obligations in relation to the appointment, removal, and remuneration of directors).[80] The provisions of section 15 will apply to a trust in all cases in which a VISTA trust is created and cannot be overridden by a trust instrument.

(g) Voting[81] powers relating to directors

40.44 Section 7 of VISTA contains provisions relating to the exercise by trustees of VISTA trusts of any powers which they may have as shareholders of companies in which designated shares are held to appoint, remove, and determine the remuneration of directors. Subsection (1) provides that the trust instrument may

---

[74] This being the case VISTA will in general only be appropriate where the entire shareholding in a company is held on the trusts of a VISTA trust: partial shareholding should be held by British Virgin Islands companies *all* of the shares of which are held by the trustees of a VISTA trust.

[75] There is, however, a question mark over what, if any, liability that greater responsibility carries in view of the provisions of s 15 (discussed at para 40.43 below).

[76] See paras 40.44–40.49 and 40.50–40.55 below.

[77] It may well be, however, that trustees will have a duty if they do act rather than decline to do so.

[78] See paras 40.50–40.55 below.

[79] See the definition which is referred to in para 40.51 below.

[80] See paras 40.44–40.49 below.

[81] See n 73 above.

contain rules (which are defined in the Act as the 'office of director rules') for determining the manner in which such powers should be exercised and that it may make provision for the office of director rules to be amended. Those rules will not, however, override the provisions in the company's memorandum and articles of association relating to the appointment and removal of directors; it will therefore be essential for draftsmen to ensure that the office of director rules are compatible with the relevant provisions in the company's articles.

In particular the office of director rules may require the trustee to ensure that a   **40.45**
particular person[82] holds (or retains) office as a director, require any person to be appointed to the office of director at some future date (or upon some future event), require the removal of a director in specified circumstances, prescribe the minimum and maximum number of directors to hold office[83] at any time or times, and require the trustee (in relation to the appointment and removal of directors) to act generally (or in any specified circumstances) on the decision of a third person or a committee.

If office of director rules are contained in a trust instrument, a trustee is (*inter alia*)   **40.46**
obliged by section 7(3) of VISTA to exercise any voting powers which it has to ensure (in so far as its voting powers are sufficient to enable this to be achieved) that the identity of the directors of a company in which designated shares are held conforms with such rules. However, there are three qualifications to this statutory obligation. First, consistently with the general policy of the Act of obviating the need for trustees to enquire into the company's affairs, the trustee has no duty either to act pursuant to subsection (3) unless it receives actual notice that circumstances requiring such action have arisen or to enquire as to whether such circumstances exist. Secondly, the provisions of subsection (3) are subject to those of section 8 of the Act (which may in certain circumstances require trustees to intervene if complaints are made). Thirdly, the trustee is not obliged to follow the office of director rules in (what is defined[84] in the Act as) an 'exempted case'. An exempted case is one for which the office of director rules make no provision or in which the trustee concludes in good faith that it would be impossible, unlawful, or plainly inconsistent with the wishes of the settlor to ensure compliance with the rules.

Subsection (4) of section 7 of the Act makes it clear that directors owe no fiduciary   **40.47**
or other obligations under the trust (or, for that matter, to the trustee), but that the provisions of that subsection do not affect any duty which a director owes (*qua* director) to the company.

---

[82] Persons for whose appointment the office of director rules may provide include both ascertained and unascertained persons and any settlor or protector of the trust. See para 40.51 and n 91 below for meaning of 'protector'.
[83] Subject to the requirements of the company's memorandum and articles of association.
[84] In s 7(8).

40.48 Subsection (6) makes it clear that the trustee shall incur no liability for securing, sanctioning, or not opposing the appointment of a director where that appointment is in conformity with the office of director rules and further exoneration provisions are included in subsection (7) which deals with certain appointments (contrary to the rules or in exempted cases) which are consistent with the wishes of the settlor.[85]

40.49 Although the inclusion of office of director rules in trust instruments is optional under VISTA, it will invariably be essential to include them, since such rules, if carefully drafted, will help ensure that the company, at any given time, has a functioning board of directors (or sole director when required) and that the persons appointed as directors meet the criteria laid by the settlor. How elaborate the rules should be will naturally depend on the circumstances.

(h) Intervention in the management of the company in prescribed circumstances

40.50 It will be apparent that prohibiting the trustee from interfering in the conduct of the business of a company may not be appropriate in all cases. For example, if, after the death of the settlor, his two children are appointed sole directors, in accordance with the office of director rules, and if some years later they are deadlocked, it would be reasonable for the trustee to intervene to resolve the situation. VISTA therefore enables them to intervene in prescribed circumstances.

40.51 Thus, although section 6(2)[86] of VISTA will in general prevent trustees of VISTA trusts from exercising their voting and other powers to interfere in the management or conduct of the affairs of a company, the provisions of that subsection are (*inter alia*) subject to the provisions of section 8 of the Act which effectively enable a trustee to intervene if an 'interested person' requests it to do so. However such a request (which is defined[87] in the Act as an 'intervention call') must be made in writing, the trustees may only intervene 'to deal with the complaint', and the complaint must be one concerning the conduct of the company's affairs on a ground for complaint which is 'permitted'. A ground for complaint is permitted if it is expressed as such in the trust instrument;[88] the trust instrument may specify one or more such grounds for complaint, but need not specify any (so that, in the latter case, section 8 of the Act would be inapplicable to the trust). An 'interested person' is defined[89] as a beneficiary, an object of a discretionary power, a parent or legal guardian[90] of either, (in the case of a charitable trust) the Attorney-General,

---

[85] See para 40.59 below. Subsection (10) further provides that where, on any question concerning the appointment of a director, a trustee makes an application to the court for directions, the court shall not seek to reduce 'business risk', except to the extent, if at all, that the court concludes that a reduction would be consistent with the wishes of the settlor. (See the definition of 'business risk' which is referred to in paras 40.50–40.55 below and para 40.59 below in relation to the settlor's wishes.)

[86] See paras 40.41–40.42 above.   [87] In s 2(1).   [88] Section 2(2)(f).

[89] In s 2(1).

[90] ie a person legally recognized as a minor's guardian in any jurisdiction with which the minor has a substantial connection (VISTA, s 2(1)). (This definition should reduce the difficulty, in international situations, in determining who qualifies as a legal guardian.)

(in the case of a non-charitable purpose trust) the enforcer, a protector (which is defined[91] as any person or committee whose consent is requisite to the exercise of any power), or an 'appointed enquirer' (as defined below).

Upon receiving an intervention call, a trustee is required (but only if it is satisfied that the complaint is substantiated) to take such action as it considers appropriate to deal with it in the interests of the trust, and after taking this action the trustee's obligation to intervene will be at an end (that is, unless and until there is another intervention call). This action may include changing the directors of the company (disregarding the office of director rules[92] if, in the trustee's opinion, it is expedient to do so for the purposes of dealing with the complaint), procuring action by the company to recover any losses caused by the conduct giving rise to the complaint, and taking legal and other advice. When considering taking the action in question, the trustee is, however, required to have regard to the settlor's wishes and to the efficient functioning of the company, but must disregard 'business risk' except to the extent that the ground for complaint consists of or arises from any disagreement among the directors as to business risk, or unless any wishes of the settlor require business risk to be considered. 'Business risk' is in effect defined[93] in the Act as any risk attached to any business of the company, or an underlying company, when conducted in the manner in which it has in fact been conducted or any risk which can be expected to be attached to any projected business of the company, and for these purposes 'business' is defined[94] to include the holding of shares or other assets and non-commercial activities. **40.52**

Where one or more permitted grounds for complaint are specified in a trust instrument, there are further provisions in section 8 of VISTA which enable interested persons (as defined above) to require trustees to provide them with (and which facilitate trustees in obtaining) certain information in relation to the affairs of companies (and underlying companies) so that they can judge whether intervention calls are necessary. Furthermore the Act contains provisions[95] which effectively enable trust instruments to appoint 'appointed enquirers'[96] to make intervention calls, and imposing certain duties on such appointed enquirers, but these provisions are not mandatory. Where no such appointed enquirer is appointed, the trustee is (but only in circumstances in which the trust instrument specifies one or more permitted grounds for complaint) required[97] to use all reasonable endeavours to ensure that at least one interested person (as defined above) of full capacity who (in the reasonable opinion of the trustee) has acquired or is likely to acquire a substantial equitable interest in the designated shares (or his or **40.53**

---

[91] In s 2(2)(b).   [92] See paras 40.44–40.49 above.   [93] In s 2(1).   [94] ibid.
[95] Section 2(2)(c) and s 8(8).
[96] This term is defined in s 2(2)(c) as any person who by, or under any power conferred by, the terms of a trust is appointed to make intervention calls.   [97] By subsection (8)(c).

her parent or 'legal guardian')[98] is provided with certain documents and information in relation to the trust (and in relation to any company in which designated shares are held).

40.54   There are also provisions in section 8 which deal with expenses which are incurred in relation to intervention calls[99] and provisions which are designed to prevent repeated 'nuisance' intervention calls from being effective.[100]

40.55   Although the inclusion in the trust instrument of permitted grounds for complaint is optional under VISTA, it is difficult to conceive of a situation in which it would not be appropriate, indeed vital, for such grounds to be specified to cater for circumstances which the settlor might not have foreseen. It would, however, be essential to ensure that these and any other permitted grounds for complaint should be defined with certainty in the trust instrument in order both to ensure that the legal validity of the provisions is upheld and to enable the trustee to know when it is able to intervene.

Enforcement

40.56   Section 10 of VISTA contains enforcement provisions which are tailored to the particular characteristics of a VISTA trust. The section enables applications to the court to be made for relief[101] where there is a breach of any duty imposed by the Act on a trustee. Such applications may be made by 'interested persons' (as defined above),[102] directors of companies in which designated shares are held, and persons who would be their directors had the trustee complied with section 7[103] of the Act (for example by following the office of director rules).

40.57   Subsection (4) further provides that where there is a breach of duty or obligation imposed by the Act on the trustee of a trust, the breach shall be, and be actionable in civil proceedings as, a breach of trust.

Validity of provisions in trust instruments excluding beneficiaries' powers of direction and variation by the court

40.58   Section 12 of VISTA enables a VISTA trust instrument to prevent beneficiaries from thwarting the intentions of the settlor and the purposes of the Act (ie that the directors should continue to run the company) by including provisions excluding the rights of a beneficiary who is solely interested in designated shares (and those

---

[98] See n 90 above.   [99] In subsection (9).   [100] In subsection (7).

[101] By (a) making such order as it considers appropriate to attain, as nearly as may be, the outcome that the court considers would have been, or would most likely have been, attained in respect of the trust, the company, its directors, and generally if the breach had not occurred, and (b) by making supplementary or incidental orders, but there is a proviso to the statutory provision which will have the effect of protecting certain acquired property rights.

[102] See para 40.51 above.   [103] See paras 40.44–40.49 above.

of *sui juris* beneficiaries who are collectively entitled to such shares)[104] to require the trustees to transfer the shares to them or to terminate or modify the trust. However, such exclusion of entitlement (during which section 58 of the Trustee Act[105] will not apply to the trust) is limited in duration to a maximum of twenty years after the trust's creation.

Identifying the settlor for the purposes of the Act and ascertaining the settlor's wishes

As will be clear from the above commentary, there are a number of provisions in the Act which expressly refer to the wishes of the settlor. First, there are those in section 7(7) which exonerate the trustee against liability for securing, sanctioning, or not opposing the appointment of a director of the trustee's own selection in certain circumstances where there are no office of director rules and in an 'exempted case'.[106] Secondly, there is the definition of an exempted case in section 7(8).[107] Thirdly, there are the factors which are set out in section 8(5) to which the trustee should have regard after an intervention call has been made.[108] Fourthly, there are the circumstances in which the court may order or authorize a disposal of designated shares in section 11.[109]   **40.59**

Section 4(6) and (7) of VISTA specifies who should be regarded as the 'settlor' for the purposes of the Act. As a result of subsection (6), in order to ensure that in most cases the trustee will not need to consider the wishes of more than one settlor, any references in the Act to the 'settlor' will be regarded solely as references to the trust's original settlor, even if other persons subsequently add property to the trust fund, unless the trust instrument includes a provision to the effect that subsection (6) shall not apply to the trust, in which case each person who has settled property on trust will be regarded as the settlor in relation to the property which he or she has provided[110] (ie as would be the case in relation to non-VISTA trusts). Obviously anyone who adds property to a VISTA trust which has been created by someone else will need to be advised of the position unless subsection (6) has been excluded, in which case the trustee would need to ensure that property settled by different persons is carefully segregated in case it becomes necessary at any stage to ascertain the wishes of at least one of the settlors.   **40.60**

Section 14 of VISTA specifies how the settlor's wishes should be ascertained where this is necessary for the purposes of the Act. Subsection (2) provides that, where   **40.61**

---

[104] Under what is often described as the rule in '*Saunders v Vautier*'.

[105] This is the British Virgin Islands equivalent to the English Variation of Trusts Act 1958 which effectively allows the court to participate in a *Saunders v Vautier* exercise on behalf of certain categories of persons, eg minors, and such participation would, therefore, be inconsistent with the exclusion of the rule.   [106] See para 40.46 above.

[107] ibid.   [108] See para 40.52 above.   [109] See para 40.39 above.
[110] VISTA, s 4(7).

the settlor is alive, he or she shall, where possible and practicable, be consulted as to his wishes. Where the settlor is dead, or where consultation is impossible or impracticable, subsection (3) provides that the settlor's wishes shall be taken to be such wishes as he or she has most recently communicated to the trustee or (failing that) those that the court (or the trustee in good faith) believes (from the evidence available) most likely to have been the settlor's wishes. Given the provisions of section 14, a carefully crafted letter of wishes covering all relevant matters (updated where necessary) will almost always be a crucial requirement when setting up a VISTA trust.

When a VISTA trust should be set up

40.62   VISTA provides opportunities for many individuals who would otherwise wish to set up trusts to hold shares in their companies but who previously felt disinclined to do so as a result of the existing prudent trustee rules.

40.63   Examples of more sophisticated applications of the Act include blind trusts for politicians, trusts dealing with matrimonial settlements, and trusts for commercial purposes (such as charitable and non-charitable purpose trusts for securitizations and other off-balance-sheet transactions).

40.64   While, as indicated in paragraph 40.30 above, the Act can only apply to designated shares (ie shares in British Virgin Islands companies), there is obviously no reason why other property such as shares in foreign companies and other assets which the settlor intends trustees to retain (and to have restricted duties in connection with) should not be held through a British Virgin Islands company the shares of which are held on a VISTA trust.

40.65   Essentially the Act sets up a special trust system which is ideally suited to the ownership of shares in private companies, just as the English Settled Land Act 1925[111] and the English Trusts of Land and Appointment of Trustees Act 1996 set up special trust systems the provisions of which were specifically crafted to deal with the unique features of particular types of assets.[112]

---

[111] There are analogies between VISTA and the English Settled Land Act 1925, eg in that the duties of trustees of Settled Land Act settlements were in practice fairly thin and in that that Act was designed to permit the beneficiaries in possession (rather than the trustees) to manage the property.

[112] In those cases land.

41

INTERNATIONAL TRUSTS:
CHOICE OF LAW

A. Introduction to Chapters 41 and 42

International trust issues

41.01 When a trust has links with two or more countries issues may arise as to:

(1) the choice of law (or laws) to govern the validity, interpretation, administration, and effect of the trust;[1]

(2) which courts can exercise jurisdiction over the trust, and what remedies are available in those courts;

(3) whether judgments or orders relating to the trust obtained in one country will be recognized or enforced in another.

Scope of Chapters 41 and 42

41.02 The present chapter considers choice of law issues.[2] Jurisdiction, remedies, enforcement, and recognition are dealt with in Chapter 42.

A section on forced heirship is included at the end of this chapter; and a section on payment by trustees of foreign taxes is included at the end of Chapter 42.

Except where otherwise stated, the law under discussion is the law of England and Wales.

Conflict of laws

41.03 The legal rules discussed in this and the following chapter fall within the branch of English law known as the conflict of laws, also called private international law. This is an area of law notorious for its uncertainties and competing theories. In the case

---

[1] Including issues relating to the validity of dispositions into the trust.
[2] Including the corollary provisions on 'recognition' of trusts in Article 11 of the Hague Trusts Convention.

of trusts, the Hague Trusts Convention has brought welcome clarification to certain issues, but on others the rules remain debatable (especially, as will be seen, in relation to the capacity of a settlor to create a trust and in relation to the assignment to trustees of intangible property).

It should of course be kept in mind that conflict of laws rules in England may differ from those applicable in other jurisdictions.[3]

Specialist works

References in this chapter to specialist works should be taken to be references to, in particular, J Harris, *The Hague Trusts Convention—Scope , Application, and Preliminary Issues* (Hart, 2002) ('Harris *Hague Trusts Convention*'), L Collins (ed), *Dicey and Morris, The Conflict of Laws* (13th edn, Sweet & Maxwell, 2000) ('*Dicey and Morris*'), and North and Fawcett, *Cheshire and North's Private International Law* (13th edn, Butterworths, 1999) ('*Cheshire and North*'). **41.04**

Glossary of conflict of laws terms

Some common technical conflict of laws terms are explained below. They are used without further definition in this chapter, and in Chapter 42. Other terms (for example capacity,[4] renvoi,[5] and characterization,[6] are explained in the text). **41.05**

Applicable law	See 'proper law'.
Choice of law rules	Rules for determining which country's law is to be applied to an issue before the court, for example an issue of validity of a trust, disposition, or contract. In a case before an English court, the court applies its own law to determine the relevant choice of law rule.
Country	In the conflict of laws, the term 'country' normally refers to a territorial unit that has its own system of law. Thus England and Wales comprise one country, and Scotland another. Each state of the USA and of Australia, and each province of Canada is a country.
Domestic (or internal) law	The term refers to the law of a country not including its conflict of laws rules.
Domicile	The term generally refers to domicile under English common law rules as amended by statute.[7] However, in relation to jurisdiction the term domicile has a narrower legislative definition.[8]
Essential (or material) validity	The validity of a transaction ignoring formal requirements and assuming capacity. For example, a disposition in a will made by a person of full capacity and which is formally valid under the Wills Act 1963 may fail to meet the requirements for essential validity because the disposition is one not permitted under the law of the testator's domicile.

---

[3] For details of conflicts rules for trusts in a range of other jurisdictions, see Glasson (ed), *International Trust Laws* (Jordans, loose-leaf).   [4] See para 41.12 below.
[5] See para 41.32 below.   [6] See para 41.17 below.
[7] Set out, for example, in *Dicey and Morris*, Ch 6.   [8] See Chapter 42 of this book.

Formal validity	Validity in terms of formal requirements, for example a requirement for writing, or notarial attestation.
Governing law	See 'proper law'.
Immovable property	Essentially the term refers to land and buildings, but certain property involving or related to land or buildings may be included. In case of doubt it appears settled that the law of the place in which the property is situated determines whether it should be classified as movable or immovable.[9] A particular jurisdiction may classify certain items connected with land as immovable (for example title deeds) or may classify certain temporary buildings as movable. Under English law the term includes rent charges and, almost certainly,[10] a mortgagee's interest in land in England including the mortgagee's right to repayment of the debt. The English court will apply its own rules in deciding where property is situated.[11]
	The distinction between immovable and movable property is not the same as that between realty and personalty, so that, for example, leasehold land is immovable under English law.[12]
Internal law	See 'domestic law'.
Lex fori	The law of the forum, ie the court seised of the matter. The lex fori governs, *inter alia*, matters of procedure.
Lex loci actus, as regards any legal act	The law of the country in which the act is concluded.
Lex situs, as regards any property	The law of the country in which the property is situated.
Movable property	Any property which is not immovable as defined above. The expression covers both *tangible* property (ie physical objects) and *intangible* property (ie choses in action such as shares, debts, insurance policies, and intellectual property).
	There are situs rules for determining the location of intangible property[13] (sometimes open to the charge of artificiality).
Personal law	The law with which an individual is regarded as connected for conflict of laws purposes and which may determine certain matters related to that individual, for instance his capacity to make a will of movable property. Under English law an individual's personal law is the law of his domicile (ascertained under common law rules as amended by statute). Under other systems of law, an individual's personal law might be, typically, the law of his nationality, his habitual residence, or his religion.

---

[9] *Re Hoyles* [1911] 1 Ch 179, 185; *Re Berchtold* [1923] 1 Ch 192, 199; *Macdonald v Macdonald* 1932 SC (HL) 79, 84; *Re Cutcliffe* [1940] Ch 565, 571.

[10] See cases cited and discussion in *Dicey and Morris*, 22-012, n 21.

[11] The English *situs* rules, which are not discussed in this chapter, can be found in the specialist works.   [12] See further *Dicey and Morris*, 22-007.

[13] See *Dicey and Morris*, 22-025 – 22-051.

Proper law, as regards a contract, disposition, or trust	The law governing the contract, disposition, or trust or some aspect of it. The terms 'proper law', 'governing law', and 'applicable law' tend to be used interchangeably.

CHOICE OF LAW

B. Choice of Law: Introduction

This section is concerned with choice of law rules for trust issues when more than one country's law has some claim in the matter, for example because the trust property is in one country and the trustees are in another, or because one country's law has been chosen by the settlor as the law to govern the trust and the trust's connections are otherwise with another country. **41.06**

With certain exceptions, choice of law questions relating to trusts are nowadays governed by rules contained in the 1985 Hague Convention on the Law Applicable to Trusts and their Recognition ('the Hague Trusts Convention'). The exceptions are these. First, Article 4 of the Convention excludes from the Convention 'preliminary issues relating to the validity of wills or of other acts by virtue of which assets are transferred to the trustee'.[14] Secondly, certain trusts fall outside the scope of the Convention.[15] Thirdly, there are situations in which, under the Convention, non-Convention rules can or must be applied.[16] **41.07**

The preliminary issues falling under the first exception (Article 4) include, in particular:[17] **41.08**

(1) the capacity of the settlor[18] to create the trust;
(2) the essential and formal validity of the disposition to the trustee of the intended trust property;
(3) issues arising from any requirement for perfection of the trustee's title, for example by registration;
(4) issues relating to the settlor's title to the intended trust property; and
(5) issues as to priority between a disposition to the trustee and another disposition.

---

[14] Often called 'rocket launching' issues, ie issues that must be satisfactorily dealt with before the trust 'rocket' gets off the ground.

[15] See paras 41.75–41.80 below.

[16] See paras 41.69–41.72 below.

[17] There is no exhaustive list of preliminary issues. The list in this paragraph includes those that most commonly arise on the creation of a trust.

[18] Capacity to act as trustee (which is now a Hague Trusts Convention issue) and capacity to act as beneficiary are considered at para 41.55 below.

Items (1) to (4) are discussed in the next part of this section (paragraphs 41.11 to 41.37). Item (5), which will only occasionally arise in a trust context, is not discussed in the present work.[19]

41.09 The rules laid down by the Hague Trusts Convention are discussed in the third part of this section (paragraphs 41.38 to 41.85).

41.10 The law to be applied to trusts which fall outside the scope of the Convention is considered in the fourth part of this section (paragraph 41.86).

C. Preliminary Issues Excluded from the Hague Trusts Convention

(1) Choice of Law Rules for Settlor's Capacity to Create a Trust and for Validity of Settlor's Disposal to Trustee

(1) The choice of law process

41.11 To arrive at the law which must ultimately be applied to an issue, the basic process is this:

1. Identify the category of issue, ie is it one of capacity,[20] formal validity, or essential validity.
2. Determine, in accordance with the *lex situs*,[21] whether the property to which the issue relates is movable or immovable. If the former decide whether it is tangible or intangible.
3. Determine under the choice of law rules set out below which country's law should be applied to the issue.
4. Determine whether, under the doctrine of renvoi,[22] that country's law should be displaced by the law of another country.

This process does, however, need to be used with caution. The conflict of laws is an underdeveloped area of law where authority is often scarce or contradictory, where theories abound,[23] where many of the older decisions on conflict of laws are 'faulty and dangerous guides',[24] and where courts may be tempted to look for

---

[19] There is considerable uncertainty in this area of law. See, eg, J Collier, *Conflict of Laws* (3rd edn, Cambridge University Press, 2001) ('*Collier*') 257–259.

[20] On the meaning of which, see para 41.12.   [21] See glossary in para 41.05 above.

[22] See para 41.32 below.

[23] Chapter 1 of *Cheshire and North* includes a helpful general discussion of current theories.

[24] *Cheshire and North* 19.

ways of departing from so-called 'rules' in order to do justice, as they see it, in a particular case.[25]

(2) Settlor's capacity

(a) Definition and background matters

The meaning of capacity.   Capacity concerns the legal competence or qualification **41.12** of a person to enter into a transaction. Under every system of law a person may be expected to lack capacity if he is a minor, or he is mentally incompetent. Since this form of incapacity can, as a general rule, be readily detected, it rarely causes problems for trust practitioners.

More difficult is incapacity imposed by the law of a particular country on a specific category of adult individuals[26] regardless of their mental competence. Incapacity of this type is not apparent without knowledge of the law of the country in question.

'Personal' and 'proprietary' incapacity.   The different types of incapacity **41.13** described under the previous heading can be referred to, respectively, as 'personal' and 'proprietary'. However, this terminology is liable to be confusing, partly because there appears to be no legal distinction in English law between the two types[27] and partly because the term 'proprietary capacity' is also sometimes used[28] when speaking of a general restriction on disposal (for instance one designed to preserve the rights of spouse or children) to which the rules on essential validity, rather than capacity, may be best applied.[29]

Capacity to dispose and capacity to declare a trust.   With most trusts[30] it is **41.14** necessary to consider as distinct issues (a) the capacity of the settlor to transfer the

---

[25] 'There is no sacred principle that pervades all decisions ... Private international law is no more an exact science than is any other part of the law of England; it is not scientifically founded on the reasoning of jurists, but is beaten out on the anvil of experience', *Cheshire and North* 32.

[26] eg by reference to marital status, insolvency, criminal conviction, or religion. Some forms of exchange control legislation may, or may arguably, create incapacities. A corporation's capacity may be limited by its constitution (but see further para 41.25).

[27] Harris, for example, writes 'An alleged restriction on distribution of property imposed upon a particular person of full age and sound mind of which he is the sole owner is no less a question of capacity than an alleged restriction imposed on minors and should be governed by the same law.' (Harris, *Hague Trusts Convention* 10). See also Clarkson and Hill, *Jaffey on the Conflict of Laws* I (2nd edn, Butterworths, 2002) ('*Jaffey*') 243: 'Rules relating to capacity define classes of person who lack power which people in general have to make or be bound by a contract ... The commonest kind of incapacity to contract is that of a minor. Others who may lack capacity under a particular legal system are married women, corporations, and mentally disordered people.'

[28] As by *Dicey and Morris*, 27-023.   [29] See para 41.16 below.

[30] For the less usual case of a settlor declaring a trust of his own property, see discussion at para 41.24.

intended trust property to the trustee and (b) the capacity of the settlor to declare a trust of that property.[31] Both these aspects of capacity are discussed below.

41.15 **Contractual capacity.** Some discussion of the law relating to contractual capacity is necessary in the present context because contract law may be influential[32] when a court is considering those aspects of trust capacity on which the law remains unclear.[33]

It has been submitted[34] that capacity to enter into a contract is not a distinct issue but merely a facet of essential validity. The difficulty with this view is that, in general, the law governing the essential validity of a contract can be selected by the parties to the contract. If, therefore, capacity were merely a facet of essential validity this would permit a contracting party to choose a law that gives him capacity in preference to a law that does not. Both *Dicey and Morris*[35] and *Cheshire and North*[36] resist the idea that capacity to enter into a contract can be so easily acquired. They cite *Cooper v Cooper*,[37] a case involving a contract to enter into a marriage settlement, where it was stated:[38]

> It is difficult to suppose that [a minor] could confer capacity on herself by contemplating a different country as the place where the contract was to be fulfilled.

In a previous era a likely approach would have been to apply the law of domicile to the issue of contractual capacity on the basis of the maxim *mobilia sequuntur personam* (meaning that movables, wherever situated, follow the law of the owner's domicile). But the maxim has to a large degree fallen out of favour, except in relation to succession to movables.[39]

---

[31] This may sometimes be referred to as capacity to create the trust structure or capacity to impose equitable obligations on the trustee.

[32] The English cases relating to capacity to make a marriage settlement *contract* (see n 39 below) are usually cited by commentators in any discussion of trust capacity; and in a leading Australian case, *Augustus v Permanent Trustee Co (Canberra) Ltd* (1971) 124 CLR 245, it was held that the proper law of a trust was to be determined by the same considerations as for a contract.

[33] As will be seen there is a particular lack of clarity in relation to *inter vivos* trusts of movable property.

[34] Sykes and Pryles, *Australian Private International Law* (3rd edn, The Law Book Co, 1991) ('*Sykes and Pryles*') 614, 694, and 715.

[35] See *Dicey and Morris*, Rule 179, discussed at para 32R-213 *et seq*.   [36] 592–594.

[37] (1888) 13 App Cas 88.   [38] *Per* Lord Macnaghten at 108.

[39] Although *Re Cooke's Trusts* (1887) 56 LT 737, *Cooper v Cooper* (1888) 13 App Cas 88, and *Viditz v O'Hagan* [1900] 2 Ch 87 (CA) appear to support the proposition that the capacity of a party to a marriage settlement contract is governed by the law of his or her domicile, the judgments have been widely criticized; and *Dicey and Morris* consider it arguable that, properly considered, they are authority for the view that capacity is governed by the proper law of the contract (para 28-037), although this, on their view would be the proper law objectively ascertained (para 28-040). Per contra J Mowbray et al, *Lewin on Trusts* (17th edn, Sweet & Maxwell, 2000) ('*Lewin*'), suggest (at para 11-61) that *Viditz v O'Hagan* relates to incapacity as determined by the law of domicile. Matthews says: 'Although the position for commercial contracts may be distinguished, under English law capacity to make a *contract to create a trust* is, as a matter of authority, still governed by

Thus *Dicey and Morris*[40] say 'all modern writers and most modern judges have discarded the test of domicile, and it has been said that all that the maxim *mobilia sequuntur personam* means today is that succession to movables is governed by the personal law of the deceased'. *Cheshire and North*[41] point out that the domicile test is capable of leading to situations which are commercially impracticable, and contrary to both natural justice and the normal expectations of the parties. *Sykes and Pryles*[42] describe the concept that domicile should determine contractual capacity as an outrage to all policy considerations. 'It would amount to allowing the itinerant domiciliary to carry around the disabling incapacity in his baggage and use it to escape liability for it in all jurisdictions, even those which do not recognise the status at all.'

Further, the notorious imprecision[43] of the concept of domicile under English law means that the application of the law of domicile to contractual capacity fails the test suggested in recent years in the Court of Appeal,[44] namely that 'if at all possible the rules of conflict should be simple and easy to apply'.

In *Male v Roberts* (1800) 3 Esp 173 it was held that the *lex loci actus* governed contractual capacity, although, as pointed out in *Jaffey*[45] this was at a time when it was generally assumed that contracts were governed by the law of the country where they were made. Today it would be hard to find any support for the *lex loci actus*.

The approach to the problem of contractual capacity proposed by *Dicey and Morris* is to confer capacity on a person entering into a contract if he has capacity either under the law of his domicile and residence *or* under the governing law of the contract objectively ascertained, by which *Dicey and Morris* mean the law with which the contract is most closely connected not necessarily that chosen by the parties. *Cheshire and North*[46] also advance arguments in favour of the application of the objectively ascertained governing law.[47] However, there is little authority to support this objective test[48] and, as Harris points out,[49] this approach lacks

---

the law of the contracting person's domicile at that time … but this must be admitted to be a conservative approach' (P Matthews, 'Capacity to create a trust: the onshore problem, and the offshore solutions' (2002) 6(2) Edinburgh Law Review 176–198, ('Matthews *Capacity*') 179, emphasis in original). See also n 77 below on Professor Matthews' argument that *Viditz v O'Hagan* is authority on dispositions as well as contracts.

[40] At para 24-002. [41] 939. [42] 344.
[43] Cheerfully exploited by tax planners.
[44] *Macmillan Inc v Bishopsgate Trust (No 3)* [1996] 1 WLR 387, 392, *per* Staughton LJ.
[45] 243. [46] 592–594.
[47] Referring to domicile, rather than domicile and residence.
[48] The Canadian appeal case *Charron v Montreal Trusts Co* (1958) DLR (2d) supports the objective approach, but is not regarded as strong authority as the primary issue was one of essential validity. See commentary in *Jaffey* 534. In *Bodley Head Ltd v Flegon*, Brightman J supported the idea of the proper law of the contract as governing capacity; *Cheshire and North* suggest (593) that, although the point was not discussed in the judgment, this must be regarded as a reference to the law with which the contract is most substantially connected. [49] Harris, *Hague Trusts Convention* 14.

commercial convenience, since to identify the law of closest connection is an uncertain process, and makes the proffering of advice 'immensely difficult and fraught with danger'.[50]

Harris, however, does agree with *Dicey and Morris*, and with *Cheshire and North* that English law probably does not permit unfettered freedom in relation to the choice of law to govern capacity to contract and, that being so, it cannot be expected that freedom of choice should be allowed to govern all issues relating to the capacity of a settlor to dispose of property on trust.[51]

41.16 **The interface between capacity and essential validity.**   Essential validity is concerned with the question of whether a transaction can be entered into at all. Capacity, on the other hand, is concerned with restrictions which prohibit a particular class of persons from entering into a transaction. The two concepts may, however, become difficult to disentangle in the case of a provision of the following type: *that no person domiciled in country X may enter into a given transaction.* Put this way it appears to be a question of capacity, ie affecting a class of persons, namely those domiciled in X. The better approach,[52] however, may be to regard many rules of this type as rules of essential validity on the basis that under the *domestic* law of country X they apply generally, but would not be applied by the courts of country X to transnational issues where under the *conflict of laws* rules of country X a foreign law would be applicable.[53]

41.17 **The problem of characterization.**   A further difficulty with capacity is that what English law regards as capacity may not be so regarded in other countries (which may, for example, adopt a narrower view of its meaning—perhaps one that equates more closely to capacity of the first type referred to in paragraph 41.13 above).

Deciding how to categorize the issue in these circumstances involves the process of characterization. Characterization is a difficult doctrine, beyond the scope of this work to discuss in detail,[54] but the general point may be made that the approach most favoured in English law is to characterize issues by reference to English categories, albeit that this may result in a foreign law being applied in circumstances where the foreign court would not apply that law (because it would categorize the issue differently).

---

[50] Harris, *Hague Trusts Convention* 15.   [51] ibid 15.

[52] See *Bodley Head Ltd v Flegon* [1972] 1 WLR 680, and discussion of this decision in Harris, *Hague Trusts Convention* 8. See also *Dicey and Morris*, para 27-023 in relation to 'proprietary capacity', and para 41.13 above.

[53] As Harris points out the distinction is often acutely difficult to make (Harris, *Hague Trusts Convention* 8).

[54] See the standard conflicts works and, in a trust context, Harris, *Hague Trusts Convention* 8–9.

(b) Capacity to dispose of property to a trustee—choice of law rules for particular transactions

41.18 Note. The rules on all preliminary issues discussed in this chapter are stated initially without regard to the possible effect of the doctrine of renvoi. At the end of each rule, there is an indication of whether renvoi applies or may apply. For discussion of renvoi, see paragraph 41.32.

Inter vivos transactions

Capacity to transfer immovable property. It appears to be universally accepted **41.19** (although not without some criticism[55]) that all aspects of the *inter vivos* transfer of immovables, including capacity, are governed by the law of the *situs*.

In *Nelson v Bridport*[56] Lord Langdale MR said,[57] in relation to a purported devise by Lord Nelson of his estate in Sicily contrary to the law of Sicily, 'The incidents to real estate, the right of alienating or limiting it, and the course of succession to it, depend entirely on the law of the country where the estate is situated.'

In *Bank of Africa Ltd v Cohen*[58] the court held that rules of South African law, designed to protect married women, deprived a woman domiciled in England of capacity to enter into an agreement to mortgage her land in South Africa. The case has been criticized, partly on the grounds that the South African rule was not necessarily intended to protect non-South African domiciliaries.[59]

There is no English authority on transfers of English land by a foreign domiciliary, but application of the law of the *situs* is supported by the Canadian decision *Landry v Lachapelle*.[60]

The doctrine of renvoi in principle applies—see paragraph 41.32.

Capacity to transfer tangible movable property. Of the possible candidates for **41.20** applicable law on capacity to transfer tangible movable property, the law of the *situs* is firmly favoured by *Dicey and Morris*[61] and by Harris,[62] and, arguably, there is some authority to back it.[63] The views of Matthews, who supports a domicile

---

[55] For discussion, see *Cheshire and North* 929–930.   [56] (1846) 8 Beav 547.
[57] ibid 570.   [58] [1909] 2 Ch 129.
[59] For discussion, and other grounds for criticism, see *Dicey and Morris* 960, and *Cheshire and North* 932.   [60] (1937) 2 DLR 504.
[61] 24-005. 'If the *lex situs* says that no title passes to the transferee because the parties lack capacity to transfer or because of some defect of form or essential validity in the transfer, then other jurisdictions should, it is submitted, accept the fact that no title has passed, no matter what the applicable law of the transfer may say.'
[62] Harris, *Hague Trusts Convention* 16. 'Given the "mandatory" characteristics of capacity rules, one might expect that the *lex situs* has an even stronger claim [than in relation to essential validity] in relation to capacity to transfer tangible movables.'
[63] See *Re Korvine's Trusts* [1921] 1 Ch 343, *MacMillan Inc v Bishopsgate Investment Trust plc (No 3)* [1996] 1 WLR 387, and *Glencore International AG v Metro Trading International Inc* discussed at para 41.21 below.

related test for movables generally, are discussed under the next heading.

The doctrine of renvoi may apply—see paragraph 41.32.

41.21   *Capacity to transfer intangible movable property.*   The Rome Convention on the Law applicable to Contractual Obligations, 1980, in force in England by virtue of the Contracts (Applicable Law) Act 1990, has some relevance to assignments of intangibles.[64] But it can be largely disregarded for present purposes. This is partly because the Convention has only a limited application to questions of capacity [65] and partly because a disposition to a trust appears to be expressly excluded by Article 1(2)(g).[66] In the absence of any applicable Rome Convention rules, the common law rules, which have been described as a 'highly unsatisfactory and retrograde jurisprudence',[67] need to be examined.

The only cases in which the issue of capacity to transfer intangibles appears to have been considered are *Lee v Abdy*[68] and *Republica de Guatemala v Nunez*.[69] They both support the application of the law of the place of execution. In the second of these cases the law of the transferor's domicile was suggested as an alternative possibility.[70] Both decisions are criticized by *Cheshire and North*,[71] and their value as authority today must be doubtful.

There is no consensus among English commentators as to the law that should in principle govern capacity to transfer intangible movables. *Dicey and Morris*[72] suggest that questions of validity of an assignment of a right, against persons other

---

[64] See Art 12. The scope of Art 12 is debatable—see Mark Moshinsky, 'The Assignment of Debt in Conflict of Laws' (1992) 109 LQR 591, 614–616.

[65] The Convention (Art 11) merely provides some measure of protection for persons dealing unknowingly with an incapacitated person.

[66] Article 1(2)(g) provides that the rules of the convention shall not apply to 'the constitution of trusts and the relationship between settlors, trustees, and beneficiaries'. There is perhaps room for argument about whether the reference in Article 1(2)(g) to 'constitution' is a reference to the terms of the trust rather than to the act of constituting the trust. The official report on the Convention, which the English court is entitled to consider in ascertaining the meaning or effect of any provision of the Convention, states that Art 1(2)(g) 'concerns "trusts" in the sense in which they are understood in common law countries' and that 'the English word "trust" is properly used to define the scope of the exclusion'. This strongly suggests that 'constitution' is intended to have the same meaning as it has to a lawyer in a common law jurisdiction and therefore that a disposition to the trustees, when it forms part of the process of constitution in this sense, is outside the scope of the convention. Even if it could be successfully argued that trusts are not outside the Convention, it would in most cases be impossible to apply it. This is because the law to be applied is that which 'applies to the contract between the assignor and assignee' and it would be unusual for a transfer to a trust to be preceded by a contract.   [67] Fletcher, *Conflict of Laws and European Community Law* (1982), 176.

[68] (1886) 17 QBD 309.   [69] [1927] 1 KB 669, 689.   [70] *Per* Scrutton LJ, 689.

[71] 959–960. 'It is a little surprising to meet the suggestion that the capacity of a person to enter into a commercial contract is determined by the law of his domicil; little less surprising is the suggestion that the determining law is the law of the place of acting, if that expression is to be taken literally.' *Cheshire and North* go on to raise the possibility that the judges, when referring to the law of the place of acting, might in the context of the time have really only been indicating the law governing the assignment. See also Harris, *Hague Trusts Convention* 16.   [72] At para 24-061.

than the parties, are to be governed by the law under which the right is created or otherwise arises, but do not specify whether this includes questions of capacity. *Cheshire and North*,[73] suggest that capacity to enter into a *contractual* assignment of a debt should be subject to the law of the country with which the assignment itself is more closely connected. However, if that were the rule, and if it were extended to non-contractual assignments, it would lead to considerable uncertainty—see discussion in paragraph 41.15 above in relation to the objective test for contractual capacity.

Harris[74] submits that the *lex situs* is to be preferred. He writes: 'Given that the *situs* of an intangible is actually likely to be more enduring than that of a tangible movable, and that the *lex situs* can sensibly be applied to capacity to transfer the latter, it is difficult to see in principle why the *lex situs* ought not also to be applied to the transfer of intangibles.'

Matthews,[75] on the other hand, argues for domicile either as the sole test or as the test with some modification—without suggesting any distinction in this connection between tangible and intangible movables. Professor Matthews's argument rests on the propositions (a) that the domicile test is supported by two English decisions reported in 1900, and by a Scottish case reported in 1950,[76] (b) that it is established in civil law countries that an individual's personal law governs questions of capacity, and (c) that there is no authority to support the *lex situs*. It is suggested, with respect, that there are difficulties with each proposition. As to (a), the two English decisions seem at best inconclusive authority,[77] and might in any

---

[73] 959. [74] Harris, *Hague Trusts Convention* 16. [75] 176 *et seq.*

[76] *Pouey v Hordern* [1900] 1 Ch 492, better reported at 16 TLR 191; *Viditz v O'Hagan* [1900] 2 Ch 87; and *Black v Black's Trustees* 1950 SLT (Notes) 32. See next footnote for discussion.

[77] In the *Pouey* case Farwell J considered the validity of a power of appointment under a settlement made by a settlor whose domiciliary law was French. An earlier challenge in the same proceedings to the validity of the settlement had not succeeded because, as appears from the report at 16 TLR 191, 192, the challenging party was barred for reasons of judgment estoppel. Professor Matthews comments that 'the report is unclear, but it appears that, without those reasons, the challenge would have succeeded'. But one could argue that Farwell J is, on this issue, either neutral, or tending towards the *lex situs*. In his judgment on the validity of the power of appointment issue he refers to 'any' disability a person may have under his or her domiciliary law; and, in his judgment dealing with the challenge to the validity of the settlement the judge makes the point that the trust money was located in England, suggesting that the *lex situs* was a factor in arriving at his decision on that issue.

The second case cited by Professor Matthews, *Viditz v O'Hagan*, is often described as 'difficult'. In terms of its judgments this is a case merely on domicile as a test for contractual capacity, and as indicated above (n 39) much criticized on that score. Professor Matthews makes the fair point that the decision resulted in a trust of existing property being set aside, consistently with the test for that being the law of domicile. However, this seems to have resulted more from the fact that the settlor was held to have power to revoke. One commentator writes 'it may be suggested that what was in issue was capacity to revoke, governed by Austrian law... In that case, the decision is not very relevant' (*Collier*, 280).

event be regarded as 'faulty and dangerous guides'[78] since the issues were not fully ventilated; the Scottish case, which has civil law connotations, must be of doubtful value in determining the law in England. As to (b), in civil law countries the personal law is generally the law of nationality or habitual residence, thus avoiding the uncertainty of the domicile concept. As to (c), there is arguably some authority on the issue. In *Re Korvine's Trusts*[79] a *donatio mortis causa* of tangible movables made by a Russian domiciliary was held valid because the items were situated in England and the *lex situs* applied. Although capacity was not mentioned it seems implicit in the decision that any lack of capacity under the law of his domicile was irrelevant to the consideration. In *MacMillan Inc v Bishopsgate Investment Trust plc (No 3)*,[80] Auld LJ said, without making any exception for capacity, 'In general, disputes about the ownership of land *and of tangible and intangible movables*, including negotiable instruments, are governed by the lex situs' (emphasis added).[81] In *Glencore International AG v Metro Trading International Inc*[82] Moore-Bick J said (in relation to tangible movables): '[The *lex situs* rule] reflects the natural expectation that a transaction which is effective to transfer title to goods by the law of the country in which they are situated will vest a good title in the transferee which will be recognised generally. Any other rule would require extensive and probably fruitless enquiries into the provenance of the goods and expose the transferee to great uncertainty.' While capacity was not in question in the *Glencore* case, the rationale of Moore-Bick J's statement applies as much to capacity as it does to other validity issues.[83]

For the rules on determining the *situs* of intangible movables, see the specialist works.

The doctrine of renvoi may apply—see paragraph 41.32.

Testamentary dispositions

41.22 *Capacity to make a testamentary disposition of immovable property.* There appears to be no English authority on what law determines capacity to make a will of immovables. *Dicey and Morris* suggest it would be the *lex situs* citing *Bank of Africa v Cohen* (discussed at paragraph 41.19 above).

The doctrine of renvoi almost certainly applies—see paragraph 41.32.

41.23 *Capacity to make a testamentary disposition of movable property (tangible and intangible).* It appears settled that testamentary capacity in relation to movables

---

[78] A description which *Cheshire and North* would apply to many of the older conflicts decisions. *Cheshire and North* 19.   [79] [1921] 1 Ch 343.
[80] [1996] 1 WLR 387.   [81] ibid 410.   [82] [2001] Lloyds Rep 284, 294.
[83] The rationale, it is submitted, is applicable as much to voluntary transfers of movables as to commercial transfers. If this were not the case the need to make 'extensive and probably fruitless enquiries' would simply pass to the person seeking to obtain title from the volunteer.

is governed by the law of the testator's domicile.[84] There is, however, a continuing debate over whether this is the domicile at the time of the will or the domicile at death. Both *Dicey and Morris*,[85] and *Cheshire and North*[86] argue in favour of taking the domicile at the time of the will.

The doctrine of renvoi may apply—see paragraph 41.32.

(c) Choice of law rule on capacity to declare a trust (alternatively expressed as capacity to create the trust structure or capacity to impose equitable obligations on the trustee)

There is little authority on this aspect of capacity.[87] It is in fact only in relatively **41.24** recent writings[88] that the significance of the distinction between (on the one hand) capacity to transfer property to a trustee and (on the other hand) capacity to declare a trust of that property has come to be appreciated.

The text of the Hague Trusts Convention is unsatisfactory on the issue. Article 4, as we have seen, states that the Convention does not apply to 'preliminary issues relating to . . . acts by virtue of which assets are transferred to the trustee', which, exclusion, on the face of it, does not extend to the declaration of trust. However, the Explanatory Report on the Convention[89] indicates that the intention of Article 4 was to include the situation in which an owner declared a trust of his own property and, that being so (although the matter is not expressly addressed) it can hardly have been intended that declarations of trust where there *was* a transfer to a trustee were not to be covered by Article 4. Moreover, although the text of the Convention makes no express mention of capacity (except in relation to trustees), the Explanatory Report states that 'a consensus emerged that this was not to be governed by the Convention'. Since the Explanatory Report is a recognized aid to construction,[90] it seems likely, although not beyond argument,[91] that the Convention has no application to the issue of capacity to declare a trust.

As already discussed, a settlor probably does not have unfettered freedom of choice as to the law to govern his capacity to transfer property to trustees. But, as Harris has pointed out, this restriction on choice does not need to extend to the

---

[84] *In bonis Maraver* (1828) 1 Hagg Ecc 498; *In bonis Gutteriez* (1869) 38 LJP & M 48; *In the Estate of Fuld (No 3)* [1968] P 675,696; *Re Lewal's Settlement* [1918] 2 Ch 391.

[85] At para 27-022.   [86] 986–987.

[87] *Pouey v Hordern* [1900] 1 Ch 492 sometimes cited in this context is not very helpful because the validity of the settlement in question was grounded on judgment estoppel. See discussion in n 77 above.

[88] See, for example, Harris *Hague Trusts Convention* 17–19, and Matthews, *Capacity* 187–189.

[89] Alfred E Von Overbeck, *Explanatory Report on the Hague Trusts Convention*, English Translation by the Permanent Bureau, Hague Conference on Private International Law ('*Overbeck*'), para 57.   [90] See para 41.40 below.

[91] See PE Nygh, *Conflicts of Law in Australia* (6th edn, 1995) ('*Nygh*') 518, and Matthews, *Capacity* 189.

creation of the trust structure, because the law applicable to the issue of capacity to dispose[92] can:

> sensibly be confined to the question of whether the settlor can dispose of his property *at all.* Once he is able to do so, it should not be that law's concern whether he makes an outright transfer of the property or transfers on trust.[93]

Objections to freedom of choice having been removed, Harris suggests that the proper law of the trust (a law which is capable of being chosen by the settlor)[94] is the law most suited to govern capacity to create the trust structure, whether the creation is *inter vivos* or testamentary.[95]

Professor Harris's suggestion offers practicality and certainty, in contrast to the other main contenders, namely the proper law objectively ascertained and the law of the domicile of the settlor. [96] Supporters of the proper law, apart from Harris, include the Australian conflicts writers, Sykes and Pryles[97] and Nygh.[98]

Professor Matthews, however, suggests that the test should be the same as for contracts to create a trust which, on a conservative view of the law relating to contractual capacity,[99] brings domicile back into play. He counters the criticism mentioned above[100] that this would allow 'an itinerant domiciliary to carry around the disabling incapacity in his baggage and use it to escape liability for it in other jurisdictions...' by saying[101] that 'whatever force this argument may have in the context of *commercial contracts*, where the contracting parties commonly undertake substantial liabilities, it has none in the context of trusts, where the settlor in creating the trust undertakes no (or no significant) liability at all'. Although the point on liabilities is a fair one, the domicile test, when applied to a trust, is unsatisfactory for different reasons. Given that a trust may last for 100 years or more it would, it is submitted, be an oppressive rule under which the acts of the trustees and the entitlements of the beneficiaries can be called into question long after the trust's creation on the grounds of an alleged incapacity under the law of the settlor's domicile—a domicile which will often be uncertain or disputed or in a country which has no law of trusts and no established conflicts rule by reference to which capacity to enter into a foreign trust can readily be ascertained. Domicile

---

[92] On Harris's view the *lex situs.*   [93] Harris, *Hague Trusts Convention* 18.

[94] Hague Trusts Convention, Art 6.

[95] Harris, *Hague Trusts Convention* 20 (as to *inter vivos* trusts), 52 (as to testamentary trusts).

[96] These laws are discussed in relation to contractual capacity at para 41.15 above.

[97] 715, but on the basis of their view referred to above (para 41.15) that capacity is a facet of essential validity.

[98] *Nygh* 518, although, having concluded that in relation to wills capacity is excluded from the Convention by Art 4, Professor Nygh proposes the proper law to govern capacity only in relation to *inter vivos* settlements.   [99] See n 39 above.

[100] At para 41.15 above.   [101] Matthews, *Capacity* 188, emphasis in original.

signally fails the test that 'if at all possible the rules of conflict should be simple and easy to apply'.[102]

Renvoi should not apply if, as suggested, capacity to declare the trust is governed by the proper law. If the proper law is the law identified as the applicable law under the Hague Trusts Convention's rules, then Article 17 excludes renvoi. If, exceptionally, the proper law is identified under common law rules, that law implicitly excludes renvoi.[103] If the proper law test does not apply, there may be scope for debate over the application of renvoi. For discussion of renvoi, see paragraph 41.32 below.

(d) Special cases

Corporate capacity.   In the case of a corporate settlor, the corporation needs of course to be able to enter into the relevant transaction under the rules of its constitution. However, it is probable[104] that this is insufficient, and that capacity under the law applied according to the relevant choice of law rule (see discussion above) is additionally required.   **41.25**

Penal rules and public policy.   A foreign rule on capacity will not be enforced in an English court where it is penal[105] or infringes public policy.[106]   **41.26**

(3) Essential and formal validity of the transfer to the trustees[107]

(a) Preliminary points

(i) The rules below are discussed on the assumption that the settlor has good title to the intended trust property. The title question is considered at paragraph 41.37 below.   **41.27**

(ii) Professor Harris[108] has pointed out that one could argue that, technically, two questions arise as to the passing of property on the creation of a trust: (a) the transfer of the legal title to the trustee, and (b) the transfer of equitable title to the beneficiary. However, Harris rejects this argument. It might preclude, for example, a trust of property situated in a country not recognizing equitable ownership, and so run counter to the philosophy of the Hague Trusts Convention.[109] The particular interest of the beneficiary, suggests Harris, might be considered as an

---

[102]   *Macmillan Inc v Bishopsgate Trust (No 3)* [1996] 1 WLR 387, 392, *per* Staughton LJ.

[103]   Because domestic law rules are the ones needed to determine a trust's validity, and govern its administration etc.

[104]   For discussion, see Harris, *Hague Trusts Convention* 19–20.

[105]   *Regazzoni v K C Sethia (1944) Ltd* [1956] 2 QB 490; *Re Herbert Wagg & Co Ltd* [1956] Ch 323; *Oppenheimer v Catermole* [1976] AC 249. See also cases discussed in *Cheshire and North* 128–132.   [106]   See further para 41.72 below.

[107]   See also heading 'Perfection of title', para 41.36 below.

[108]   Harris, *Hague Trusts Convention* 24–25. See also *Sykes and Pryles* 712.

[109]   Which, as will be seen, contemplates the location of property in non-trust states.

aspect of the relationship between trustee and beneficiary, which Article 8(g) of the Convention states to be within the Convention's scope.[110] The following discussion proceeds on the basis that Harris is correct and that only the passing of the legal title[111] needs to be considered.

(b) Choice of law rules for validity of inter vivos transactions

41.28 **Transfer of immovable property.**   There is no doubt that the law of the *situs* applies to both the formal and the essential validity of a transfer of immovables.[112] The reason is that ultimately only that law can control the means of transfer.

Renvoi almost certainly applies—see paragraph 41.32

41.29 **Transfer of tangible movable property.**[113]   In general the law of the *situs* at the time of transfer can be expected to apply to issues of both formal and essential validity. See *Cammell v Sewell*[114] and *Winkworth v Christie*[115] as to commercial transfers—there is little in the way of authority on gifts and transfers to trustees but on principle, it is suggested, they should be treated similarly.[116]

Exceptions to the general rule include goods in transit, goods with a casual or unknown presence, situations where the law of the *situs* is contrary to public policy or where the general rule is overridden by a mandatory English provision, and general assignments under insolvency law.

The application of renvoi is an open question—see paragraph 41.32 below.

41.30 **Transfer of intangible movables.**   As *Dicey and Morris* point out, intangible movables cover a 'very wide spectrum of property and rights' and the rules 'are not easy to state with certainty'.[117] A full discussion cannot be attempted here, but a few general points are worth making.

1. While the Rome Convention has some application to assignment of intangibles,[118] it seems to be wholly excluded in the case of a transfer to a trustee as part of the constitution of a trust.[119]
2. In the case of a trust the assignment to the trustee will usually be non-contractual, so that rules for contractual assignments[120] will not necessarily apply.

---

[110] See para 41.60
[111] Which for the purposes of this discussion may be taken to include title to an equitable interest which is being transferred into trust.   [112] *Nelson v Bridport* (1846) 8 Beav 547.
[113] For fuller discussion see the relevant sections of *Dicey and Morris*, and *Cheshire and North*. See also Harris, *Hague Trusts Convention* 28–30.   [114] (1858) H & N 616.
[115] [1980] Ch 496.   [116] This accords with the view of *Cheshire and North* 952–953.
[117] *Dicey and Morris* 24-047.   [118] See para 41.21 above.
[119] ibid and n 66 above.
[120] On which see *Raiffeisen Zentralbank Osterrieich Ag v Five Star General Trading* [2001] QB 85, and discussion of that case in *Jaffey* 492, and Harris, *Hague Trusts Convention* 32 .

3. There is a case for applying the *lex situs* to some at least of the issues concerning the validity of a transfer of intangibles. Notwithstanding the artificiality of some *situs* rules, they provide 'a ready way to locate intangible property and hence provide a straightforward choice of law rule'.[121] However, support for the *lex situs* is not universal.[122]

4. The practical advice in case of doubt must be for the settlor to ensure that his transfer to the trustee conforms with the requirements of every law that may have some claim in the matter.

5. Questions relating to the *assignability* of an intangible are generally governed by the law under which the intangible is constituted.[123]

As in the case of tangibles, the application of renvoi is debatable—see paragraph 41.32.

(c) Choice of law rules for testamentary dispositions

The testamentary disposition of property to a trustee requires a valid will or other **41.31** testamentary instrument and a vesting, after the testator's death, of the intended trust property in the trustee. These matters are governed by laws on succession and estate administration—large topics beyond the scope of this work. The comments below are for general guidance on the position under English law. They assume that the settlor has the requisite testamentary capacity, and capacity to declare the trust.[124]

1. A will disposing of property to a trustee must be formally valid, and the disposition to the trustee must, it is considered,[125] be essentially valid.

---

[121] Harris, *Hague Trusts Convention* 31. See also Collier, 256–257 and *Macmillan Inc v Bishopsgate Investment Trust plc* (No 3) [1996] 1 WLR 387 CA. For the rules on determining the *situs* of intangible movables, see specialist works.

[122] See in relation to debts *Jaffey* n 495. See also *Dicey and Morris*, para 24-050 and *Cheshire and North* 963.

[123] See *Trendtex v Credit Suisse* [1982] AC 679, and *Dicey and Morris*, para 24-061.

[124] On both of which see earlier discussion of capacity.

[125] The authors of *Lewin* consider at 11.08 the common situation where executors and trustees are the same people. They refer to Art 4 of the Hague Trusts Convention which excludes from the Convention a will or act 'by virtue of which assets are transferred to the trustee'. They go on to say (emphasis added) 'if the will makes the executors as such into trustees, it is not thought there is any transfer or act by which the assets are transferred to them other than the will itself, *whose validity is conclusively established by the probate*, even though the executors hold the assets (after they have cleared the estate and assented to the gift) in the capacity of trustees rather than executors. The Convention again specifies the law to govern the validity, construction and effect of the trusts declared, and there is nothing more for it to do.' The difficulty with this approach seems to be that, since probate of a will is no guarantee that the dispositions under it are essentially valid, it could lead to valid trusts of essentially invalid testamentary dispositions—not a result likely to have been intended by Art 4. The better view, it is suggested, is that even if the executors and trustees are the same people, there remains a requirement for essential validity of the testamentary disposition under the relevant succession law.

2. Essential validity rules will govern such matters as forced heirship and perpetuity, to the extent that these fall outside the Hague Trusts Convention.[126]

3. The essential validity of a will of immovable property is governed by the *lex situs.*[127]

4. The essential validity of a will of movable property is governed by the law of the testator's domicile at his death.[128]

5. A will is formally valid if it complies with one of the laws specified in section 1 of the Wills Act 1963. In the case of immovable property compliance with the requirements of the internal law of the *situs* is also sufficient—see section 2(1)(b).

As regards essential validity, renvoi applies, almost certainly, in relation to immovables and, debatably, in relation to movables—see paragraph 41.32. In the case of formal validity, the laws specified in the Wills Act 1963 are domestic laws,[129] thus excluding renvoi for both movables and immovables.

(2) Further Matters

(1) Renvoi

41.32 The doctrine of renvoi requires that when a particular country's law is applied to a given issue (for example of capacity or essential validity) the law so applied is not merely that country's domestic law, but includes that country's conflict of law rules. Thus, if the court of country A decides that an issue is to be governed by the law of country B, the court will not necessarily apply the domestic law of country B, because the courts of country B might, under country B's conflict of law rules, have referred the matter back to the law of country A or to a third country.

The doctrine takes two forms: (1) single (or partial) renvoi, and (2) total renvoi (sometimes referred to as double renvoi or the foreign court theory).

Where single renvoi is adopted, if country A refers the matter to the law of country B, which refers it back to the law of country A, then the matter will be determined by the law of country A.

In the case of total renvoi, country A does whatever the court in country B would do. Thus, if A refers to B, and B refers to A, the law of A might refer it back again to B. If B would accept this reference back and determine the matter according to

---

[126] See paras 41.87 and 41.59 below.

[127] See *Dicey and Morris*, Rule 138, and cases cited in support.

[128] See *Dicey and Morris*, Rule 137, and cases cited in support.

[129] Sections 1 and 2(1)(b) of the Act refer to 'internal' laws. Section 6 defines 'internal law' in relation to any territory or state as the law which would apply in a case where no question of the law in force in any other territory or state arose.

its own domestic law, then it is B's domestic law that will be applied in country A. If on the first reference from A, B would refer to the domestic law of country C, then that law will be applied in A.

The doctrine is much debated,[130] and the extent of its application in English law remains to be determined. A few general points can be made.

1. In England renvoi has sometimes, but not always, been applied to the testamentary succession to movables.[131] In that context, total renvoi appears to be favoured.[132] It remains open to the Court of Appeal to reject this approach or indeed renvoi altogether.[133]

2. Total renvoi will almost certainly be applied in England to most[134] issues relating to *inter vivos* and testamentary dispositions of foreign immovable property, on the basis that it is futile for an English court to make an order which would have no chance of being recognized or enforced in the country in which the property is situated.[135] (Note also the European rule, discussed in the next chapter,[136] on exclusive jurisdiction over immovable property.)

3. As recently confirmed in *Glencore International AG v Metro Trading International Inc*[137] the application of the doctrine of renvoi in relation to *inter vivos* transactions in movables remains an open question. Although its application can give rise to difficulties,[138] a substantial case can be made[139] for renvoi where the issue is one to be determined by the *lex situs*—because, as with immovables, it is the *situs* which has practical control over the asset. The case is perhaps stronger for tangible than for intangible movables, where the *situs* rules can be artificial.

(2) Settlors declaring trusts of their own property

The focus of the previous discussion has been on the most common method of **41.33** constituting a trust, namely a transfer of property by the settlor to the trustee coupled with a declaration by the settlor as to the trusts on which the property is to be held. The analysis of the situation in which a settlor constitutes a trust merely by declaring himself a trustee of certain property is more difficult.

---

[130] See, for example, *Dicey and Morris*, Ch 4.   [131] ibid.   [132] ibid.
[133] A course favoured by *Lewin*, 11-10.
[134] Note that, in relation to the formal validity of wills, the exclusion of renvoi under the Wills Act 1963 extends to immovables.   [135] *Dicey and Morris,* para 4-022.
[136] At para 42.20.
[137] [2001] 1 Lloyds Rep 384, 397. See also *Winkworth v Christie, Manson & Woods* [1980] Ch 496, 514.
[138] For example the potential for a never-ending passing back and forth between countries A and B if they both adopt double renvoi. On this and other difficulties, see *Dicey and Morris* 4-027–4-031.
[139] See *Dicey and Morris* 24-007, and Harris, *Hague Trusts Convention* 29–30.

As we have seen,[140] a declaration of trust certainly raises the issue of whether there is capacity to declare it. There is no distinction here between a declaration coupled with a transfer, and a declaration on its own. The same choice of law rule should apply, which on the view preferred by the present author would be the proper law of the trust.[141]

Not so obvious is whether a declaration of trust involves a transfer of property issue. At first glance, it does not because there is no transfer from settlor to trustee. However, Harris points out that there is a proprietary alienation involved. This gives the *situs* a legitimate interest, especially if the beneficiaries could call for the legal title under the *Saunders v Vautier*[142] principle.

While this topic cannot be said to be free from doubt the Harris solution would be to allocate to the *lex situs* the question of whether *any* property right has passed, but to allocate to the proper law of the trust the question of whether the title the would-be beneficiary has received is equitable.[143]

(3) Perpetuities and accumulations

41.34   There are arguments as to the extent to which, if at all, the law on perpetuities and accumulations is a matter for consideration when determining the validity of a transfer to the trustee, as distinct from being a trust matter governed by the proper law in accordance with the Hague Trusts Convention. The issue is discussed in the Hague Convention section of this chapter.[144]

(4) Community of property regimes

41.35   Many countries provide for community of property between spouses. The law on the topic is extensive and, of course, varies from country to country. For present purposes, practitioners need to be aware of the potential effect of a matrimonial property regime on a settlor's ability to settle property. For example, is the consent of the spouse required before property is settled? Local advice should be obtained where necessary.

(5) Perfection of title

41.36   Where any law applicable to the validity of a disposition to a trustee requires some further step to be taken (for example entry on a share register or registration at a Land Registry) before title is effectively transferred that step should of course be

---

[140] At para 41.24 above.   [141] See discussion in para 41.24 above.
[142] (1841) Cr & Ph 240; 19 LJ Ch 354; 4 Beav 115.
[143] Harris, *Hague Trusts Convention* 25. 'Otherwise', as Harris says (ibid),' no valid trust could be made whenever assets were situated in a country in which the concept of equitable ownership was unknown'.   [144] See para 41.59.

taken as part of the process for constituting the trust (albeit that in some cases the failure to take such step may not be fatal).[145]

(6) Settlor's title

The foregoing rules on capacity and validity will of course also be relevant in **41.37** establishing the settlor's title to the intended trust property (ie in determining the effect of any transfer to the settlor or to any prior owner), but other factors may also need to be considered, for example the effect of a community of property regime,[146] the possibility that the settlor may have lost title through government expropriation or in some other way,[147] and the possibility that the title has become encumbered. In view of the countless number of matters that can affect title, one can only recommend that, in circumstances where verification of title appears necessary or advisable, every issue relating to title should be checked under every law which conceivably has some claim to determine the matter.

D. The Hague Trusts Convention

(1) Preliminary

So far as English law is concerned, the importance of the Hague Trusts Convention **41.38** lies in its introduction of new, and on the whole clearer, choice of law rules for trust issues.[148] Paragraphs 41.41 to 41.82 discuss the nature, con-sequences, and limitations of these rules when applied in England. Paragraphs 41.83 to 41.85 consider the implications of the Convention for an English trust abroad.

(2) The Convention in English Law

The Hague Trusts Convention was concluded on 1 July 1985. Its provisions, **41.39** with some exclusions,[149] were incorporated into the law of the United Kingdom by section 1(1) of the Recognition of Trusts Act 1987, which came into force on 1 August 1987.[150]

The Convention itself applies only to trusts[151] created voluntarily and evidenced in writing.[152] However, under the 1987 Act the provisions of the Convention adopted by the UK are extended so as to have effect, so far as practicable, 'in

---

[145] See paras 5.39–5.44 above.   [146] See para 41.35 above.
[147] eg insolvency, adverse possession, or undisclosed disposition.
[148] Other than the preliminary issues discussed in paras 41.11–41.37.
[149] Which, where significant, are referred to in the discussion below.
[150] SI 1987/1177. Whether, and if so to what extent, the Act has retrospective effect is considered at para 41.81 below.
[151] As to the meaning of which under the Convention, see Art 2 and para 41.74 below.
[152] Article 3.

relation to any other trusts of property arising under the law of any part of the United Kingdom or by virtue of a judicial decision whether in the United Kingdom or elsewhere'.[153]

(3) Interpretation of the Convention—the Overbeck Report

41.40　The Explanatory Report on the Convention written by Professor Alfred E von Overbeck,[154] is likely to be referred to by the court on matters of interpretation.[155] Thus in *Re Barton, Tod v Barton*,[156] Lawrence Collins J said:

> If there were any ambiguity in the convention I have no doubt that resort could be had to the [Overbeck] report . . . either as an essential part of the travaux preparatoires[157] or because of Professor von Overbeck's standing in the field of private international law.

(4) Choice of Law Rules Under the Convention

(1) Preliminary

41.41　The rules discussed below apply under English law to trusts which fall within the scope of the Convention as extended by the Recognition of Trusts Act 1987. In practice this will be the vast majority of expressly created trusts. Issues relating to whether a trust is, or is not, within the extended scope of the Convention are left for later discussion.[158]

So far as England is concerned,[159] there is no requirement for reciprocity in the application of the Convention rules. Thus, it makes no difference whether or not the law ascertained under the Convention is that of a state which has ratified the Convention.

England has not adopted Article 25, which gives priority to other international agreements.[160]

(2) Ascertaining a trust's governing law under the Convention—overview

41.42　Under the Convention rules, determining the governing law of a trust will in many cases be a more straightforward process then in the past. However, the gain

---

[153] Section 1(2). Article 20 allows states to declare that the provisions of the Convention will be extended to trusts declared by judicial decisions. The UK has made this declaration.

[154] An English translation of the report is reproduced in Glasson (ed), *International Trust Laws* (Jordans, loose-leaf), and in Harris, *Hague Trusts Convention*. It can also be downloaded from http://www.hcch.net/e/conventions/expl30e.html.

[155] Although, in contrast to the Expert Reports on the Brussels and Lugano Conventions (referred to at para 42.15 below), it has no statutory status.

[156] [2002] EWHC 264 (Ch); [2002] WTLR 469; (2002) 4 ITELR 715. See also *Charalambous v Charalambous* [2004] EWCA (Civ) 1030, 30 July 2004.

[157] On the standing of which see *Dicey and Morris* 1-024 et seq.

[158] Paragraphs 41.75 – 41.80 below.

[159] The UK having not made the reservation provided for in Art 21. For text of this Article, see para 41.85 below.　　　　[160] The text of Art 25 is reproduced at para 41.85 below.

in clarity is offset to some degree[161] by provisions in the Convention which allow the governing law, in certain circumstances, to be overridden.[162]

Articles 6 and 7 of the Convention are the principal articles concerned with ascertaining the law to govern a trust. They are supplemented by Articles 9 (dépeçage),[163] 17 (exclusion of renvoi), 10 (change of law), and 5 (ineffectual choice of law). The scope of the applicable law, once ascertained, is dealt with in Article 8.[164] Article 23 of the Convention, which is concerned with multi-legal system states, does not apply under English law, although the effect of this exclusion may not be significant.[165]

Reduced to essentials, Articles 6 and 7 say this:

- A settlor may choose the governing law for his trust (Article 6).
- He may do this by express or implied choice (Article 6).
- If the settlor fails to make a choice, or if the law chosen does not provide for trusts or the category of trust involved, the trust is governed by the law with which the trust is most closely connected (Article 7).

(3) Express choice of law—Article 6[166]

Article 6 allows complete freedom of choice of governing law.[167] This is striking **41.43** for two reasons.

First, there is no requirement that there be any connection between the trust and the chosen governing law. Thus under English law a British national who is domiciled and resident in England may, when creating a trust of shares in a company registered in England and Wales with English resident beneficiaries and with English resident trustees, choose the law of, say, Bermuda to govern the trust. That will be a perfectly valid choice of law under English law so far as Article 6 is concerned.

---

[161] Some would argue to such a degree as to wipe out the advantages of the Convention, but it remains to be seen how these provisions will be applied in practice. See further para 41.85 below.

[162] See discussion below of Chapter IV of the Convention—paras 41.69–41.72.

[163] The term 'dépeçage' (or 'dismemberment') refers, in this context, to the splitting of a trust into separate aspects governed by separate laws.

[164] Considered at paras 41.51–41.63 below. See also Art 11 on 'recognition' considered at paras 41.64–41.68.   [165] See para 41.49 below.

[166] In most cases trust practitioners will be concerned with an express choice of law under Art 6: since the inclusion of a choice of law clause in a professionally drawn trust instrument is nowadays commonplace where there is, or is likely to be, an overseas connection.

[167] Described in conflict of laws language as 'party autonomy', and comparable with the freedom of parties to a contract to choose the law to apply to their relationship. See discussion in Harris, *Hague Trusts Convention* 167–168.

Secondly, the *lex situs* is given no part to play under Article 6, albeit that the country in which property is situated is normally regarded as having a legitimate interest in the creation of rights in that property,[168] especially if it is immovable.[169] (In the illustration in the previous paragraph, it would make no difference to the validity of the settlor's choice if the trust property consisted of English land.)

The freedom offered by Article 6 is not, however, one that can or should be exercised without restraint because (i) there are circumstances in which a chosen law can be overridden under Chapter IV of the Convention,[170] (ii) the choice of an unconnected foreign law will not necessarily be recognized in a country which has not adopted the Convention rules,[171] and (iii) in certain circumstances Article 13[172] of the Convention allows even a country bound by the Convention[173] to refuse recognition of the trust.

Article 6 fell for consideration recently in *Re Barton, Tod v Barton*,[174] where Lawrence Collins J held, as a matter of construction, that a choice of law expressed to apply to a will extended to a trust arising under that will.

(4) Implied choice of law—Article 6

41.44   Article 6 requires the law chosen by the settlor to 'be express *or be implied in the terms of the instrument creating or the writing evidencing the trust, interpreted, if necessary, in the light of the circumstances of the case*' (emphasis added).

Comments on implied choice

- Factors relevant to an implied choice under Article 6 are those which indicate an intention on the part of the settlor—not necessarily those which, under Article 7, show an objective connection with a particular law.
- The requirement under Article 6 is to look *first* at the trust instrument. If, and only if, this does not show a clear intention one looks at the circumstances of the case.
- The circumstances of the case are relevant only to the extent that they assist in interpreting the trust instrument.
- Provisions in a trust instrument which are likely to indicate the settlor's intention include a choice of court clause for resolution of disputes, references to

---

[168] See discussion in Harris, *Hague Trusts Convention* 169–178.
[169] cf *Re Piercy* [1895] 1 Ch 192.
[170] See paras 41.69–41.72 below.
[171] Thus in the USA it has been known for choices of foreign law to be disregarded. See decisions discussed in (1999) 7 Journal of International Trust and Corporate Planning 3.
[172] See further on Art 13, para 41.85 below.
[173] But not England and Wales, Scotland, or Northern Ireland, since the UK has not adopted Art 13.
[174] [2002] EWHC 264 (Ch); [2002] WTLR 469; (2002) 4 ITELR 715.

charitable trusts under a particular law,[175] and references to statutory provisions of a particular law.[176]

- The wording of Article 6 does not cover an implied choice in an oral trust that is not evidenced in writing (even though such a trust, by virtue of section 1(2) of the Recognition of Trusts Act 1987, may be subject to the provisions of the Convention as adopted by the UK).

(5) Choice of law: objective test—Article 7

Article 7 provides as follows: **41.45**

Where no applicable law has been chosen, a trust shall be governed by the law with which it is most closely connected.
In ascertaining the law with which a trust is most closely connected reference shall be made in particular to—
(a) the place of administration of the trust designated by the settlor;
(b) the situs of the assets of the trust;
(c) the place of residence or business of the trustee;
(d) the objects of the trust and the places where they are to be fulfilled.

As regards the factors listed at (a) to (d) above, the Explanatory Report on the Convention[177] says:

These criteria are all in principle on the same footing; however, the conference has given them their places by order of importance so that it might be said that there is among them a certain implicit hierarchy.

This seems, as Harris[178] comments, a case of: 'all factors being equal, but some being more equal than others'.

However, it seems likely that in many cases the specified factors will be of little assistance and that the court will be compelled to look further afield for guidance. This was illustrated recently in *Chellaram v Chellaram (No 2)*,[179] where Lawrence Collins J said:[180]

In ascertaining [the law of closest connection under Article 7] reference is to be made 'in particular' to (a) the place of administration designated by the settler—no such place was designated; (b) the situs of the assets of the trust—this was Bermuda if account only is taken of the shares . . . which were settled, but many other countries (especially in Asia and Africa) if the underlying assets are taken into account; (c) the place of residence or business of the trustees—Mr Rupchand and Mr Bharwani were

[175] See *Re Barton, Tod v Barton* [2002] WTLR 469, [36]; (2002) 4 ITELR 715, [36].
[176] Note, however, that references to statutory provisions on trust administration may indicate that the law in question is intended to apply to administration, but not *automatically* to other aspects of the trust. See para 41.46 below.   [177] *Overbeck*, para 72.
[178] Harris, *Hague Trusts Convention* 217.
[179] [2002] EWHC 632; [2002] 3 All ER 17; and (2002) 4 ITELR 729.   [180] ibid [166].

resident in London at the date of the settlements, and the evidence of Ram's evidence was inconclusive, although he then had substantial London connections; (d) the objects of the trust and the places where they were to be fulfilled—there was no one place to which these factors could point.

In the end the judge indicated a preference for Indian law as the governing law on the basis of factors *none of which* were listed in Article 7, namely the fact that the settlements were drafted by Indian lawyers for a family of Indian origin with strong Indian ties.[181]

In *Chellaram (No 2)* Lawrence Collins J[182] doubted if there was any significant difference between Article 7 and the likely approach at common law.[183] A similar view was taken in *Re Carapiet's Trusts*.[184] In this case the question arose of whether or not Article 7 should be applied because the trust in question pre-dated the coming into force of the Recognition of Trusts Act 1987. Jacob J[185] found it unnecessary to decide this question,[186] counsel having all agreed that 'whether the Act applied or the previous common law applied, the position was the same'.

(6) Dépeçage—Article 9

41.46   Article 9 reads:

> In applying this Chapter[187] a severable aspect of a trust, particularly matters of administration, may be governed by a different law.

The idea of different laws applying to different aspects of a trust is not new. At one time, for example, *Dicey and Morris* advocated that questions of trust administration be governed by the law of the place of administration.[188] However, in *Chellaram v Chellaram*[189] this approach was criticized by Scott J:[190]

> I find myself unable to accept the distinction drawn . . . in Dicey and Morris between 'validity, interpretation and effect' on the one hand and 'administration' on the other hand. The rights and duties of trustees, for example, may be regarded as matters of administration but they also concern the effect of the settlement. The rights of the trustees are enjoyed as against the beneficiaries; the duties of the trustees are owed to the beneficiaries. If the rights of the beneficiaries are to be ascertained by applying the proper law of the settlement, I do not understand how the duties of the trustees can be ascertained by applying a different law, and vice-versa. In my judgment, a conclusion that the law of the place of administration of a settlement governs such matters as the rights and duties of the trustees, can only be right if that law is the proper law governing the settlement.

---

181   ibid, [167].   182   ibid, [166].   183   See para 41.86 below.
184   [2002] EWHC 1304 (Ch); [2002] WTLR 989.   185   ibid, [3].
186   Which is considered at para 41.81 below.
187   Chapter IV, which comprises Arts 6–10.   188   *Dicey and Morris* 29-012.
189   [1985] Ch 409.
190   ibid 432. On the difficulties of distinguishing administration from other aspects of a trust, see also P Matthews, *Trusts: Migration and Change of Proper Law* (Key Haven, 1997) ('Matthews *Migration*') Section 15 and Harris, *Hague Trusts Convention* 283–289.

If, notwithstanding Scott J's comments, administration *can* be viewed as a sufficiently distinct aspect of a trust[191] to be capable of being governed by a different law (something which, in any event, Article 9 now arguably requires), difficulties relating to the actual application of a different law need to be considered. The first is that the borderline of the term 'administration' is far from clear leaving open to debate whether certain provisions (for instance, the power of maintenance) are administrative or not. Of course one might try to define in the trust instrument what is, and what is not, to be regarded as administration, but this would be an unusual and probably thankless task.

Secondly there is the question (in the absence of definition) of which law is to be applied to determine what administration means. Probably, as argued by Harris,[192] this is the law governing construction,[193] but the issue is not beyond debate.[194]

Thirdly, even in the case of powers which are clearly intended to be administrative, there is scope for argument over whether fiduciary duties associated with the exercise of those powers (the trustees' duties of loyalty) are themselves administrative.[195]

Against this background, and bearing in mind that in modern trust practice it does not usually cause severe problems for the administration of a trust in country A to be governed by the law of country B,[196] it is suggested that to apply a separate law to administration is rarely a 'game worth the candle'.

It is of course possible under Article 9 to choose a separate law to govern an aspect of a trust other than administration—possibly, it may be suggested, matters of construction or validity. However, it is again difficult to see the overall benefits of so doing.[197]

---

[191] A Underhill and DJ Hayton, *Law of Trusts and Trustees* (16th edn, Butterworths, 2002) ('*Underhill and Hayton*') submit (at 1038) that certain provisions of a trust are administrative on any view. These include powers of investment, right to remuneration, the acquisition and disposal of assets, and, more questionably perhaps, the appointment and removal of trustees. But note that the view has also been advanced that *everything* after the initial setting up of the trust is properly termed administrative.   [192] Harris, *Hague Trusts Convention* 289.

[193] The identification of which may itself be a matter for argument. Where the settlor does not specify a law to govern construction and only subjects the administration of the trust to a separate law, Harris's view is that it may be assumed that construction is to be subjected to the same law as that which governs validity (Harris, *Hague Trusts Convention* 289). Another way of looking at it may be that any law specified under Arts 6 or 7 (apart from a law expressly limited to administration) will generally extend to construction by virtue of the first paragraph of Art 8.

[194] Harris, *Hague Trusts Convention* 288.

[195] See L Barnard, [1992] CLJ 474, 483–484, considered in Harris *Hague Trusts Convention* 252–253.

[196] Laws on trust administration in different jurisdictions usually have a lot in common. Where advice on local law is needed it is readily obtainable and routinely sought.

[197] It needs to be kept in mind, as pointed out by *Underhill and Hayton*, that 'validity often hinges on a matter of construction'—*Underhill and Hayton* 1040.

(7) Change of law—Article 10[198]

41.47   Article 10 provides:

> The law applicable to the validity of the trust shall determine whether that law or the law governing a severable aspect of the trust may be replaced by another law.

Comments on Article 10

1. Article 10 recognizes the possibility that the law applicable to a trust, or to a severable aspect of it, may be changed, while referring the question of whether it can, in fact, be changed to the law applicable to the validity of the trust (ie the law arrived at under Article 6 or 7).

2. The question of whether, and if so in what manner and with what consequences, English law permits the law of a trust to be changed has given rise to considerable discussion.[199]

Some commentators,[200] have expressed the view that a change of proper law can be effected by the exercise of an express power for that purpose given in the trust instrument. However, there is no substantial authority in English law to support this view,[201] and it raises difficult questions.

A power to change proper law is a special power which, as such, derives its lifeblood from the law governing the trust—that is to say, the initial governing law. Accordingly mandatory provisions of that law (for instance in relation to perpetuity, accumulations, the exercise of powers, the effect of bankruptcy[202]) cannot be avoided by changing to a law under which they do not apply or are less onerous.

At the most, it is thought, such a power (if valid at all[203]) permits—and should be restricted to—change to a law which does not involve infringement of mandatory provisions of the initial governing law (or, for that matter, infringement of

---

[198]   The author is extremely grateful to Edward Nugee QC for his guidance on this topic, which included drawing the author's attention to, and explaining the implications of, the decision of Plowman J in *Re Levick*.

[199]   Matthews, *Migration* 67 *et seq*; Harris, *Hague Trusts Convention* 297–310; *Underhill and Hayton* 1040; E Campbell, *Changing the terms of Trusts* (Butterworths, 2002) ('*Campbell*') 8.5 *et seq*.

[200]   *Lewin* 11-42; *Underhill and Hayton* 1039; *Dicey and Morris* 29-020; Harris, *Hague Trusts Convention* 297.

[201]   Although Lawrence Collins J said recently in *Chellaram v Chellaram (No 2)* (referring to *Lewin* and to *Dicey and Morris*) that governing law could probably be changed by the exercise of a power reserved in the trust instrument, the point does not appear to have been fully argued. *Chellaram v Chellaram (No 2)* [2002] EWHC 632 [146] [160]; [2002] 3 All ER 17 [146] [160]; (2002) 4 ITELR 729 [146] [160].

[202]   Matthews gives the example of a life interest determinable on bankruptcy which is valid under law A but not under law B. Matthews, *Migration* 68.

[203]   And there seems no reason in principle why it should not be.

provisions contained in the trust instrument which do not allow of variation). Even then the old law will not have been eradicated, since the new law will operate under its umbrella.

The umbrella concept is illustrated by *Re Levick's Will Trusts*.[204] The case involved a will by a South African domiciliary which created a trust governed by the law of England. The testator died in 1937. The testator's son, who had a life interest in part of the trust fund, died in 1961. The question was whether certain American assets passing on the life tenant's death were subject to UK estate duty. This turned on whether the law regulating the disposition under which the assets passed was English law. Plowman J held that the law regulating the disposition was in fact the law of the domicile, South Africa, since it was that law on which the validity of the will and the dispositions under it depended. As regards the application of English law to the trust, the judge said this (emphasis added):[205]

> . . . in my opinion, as a matter of construction, the testator did intend to set up an English trust in the sense that he intended his will to operate according to English law *so far as the law of South Africa allowed that to happen*. But . . . it is, in my judgment, the very fact that one has to refer to the law of South Africa for this purpose, which makes the law of that country the proper law regulating the disposition.

Also to be considered is the question[206] of whether the effect of a change in the law is to replace the original trust with a new one (with potentially adverse tax consequences). The argument in favour of a new trust is essentially that the legal framework under which the trust exists has been replaced. As against this a number of arguments can be deployed. The first is that the new law, as discussed above, applies under the umbrella of the old.[207] Secondly, it is arguable that the very existence of Article 10 indicates that the Convention sees the trust after the change of law as being the same one as before.[208] Thirdly, on the basis of current authority[209] one might expect an English court to apply a 'common-sense' rather than a legalistic

---

[204] [1963] 1 WLR 311.   [205] ibid 319.

[206] See Matthews, *Migration* 75–77, *Underhill and Hayton* 1040, Harris, *Hague Trusts Convention* 304–306.

[207] It is true that this has not prevented the courts from taking the view that a settlement created by the exercise of a special power does, in the *right circumstances*, replace the original settlement. See discussion in the tax cases *Hart v Briscoe* [1979] Ch 1, *Roome v Edwards* [1982] AC 279, *Bond v Pickford* [1983] STC 517, *Swires v Renton* [1991] STC 490. However, the circumstances in question are very different from those now under consideration. (Even when the right circumstances do exist, the link between the old and new settlements is not entirely broken because the validity and effect of the new settlement cannot be determined without looking at the old—see *Pilkington v IRC* [1964] AC 612, 642, HL).

[208] See Harris, *Hague Trusts Convention* 305. 'It may be said to be implicit in Article 10 that the "one trust" approach is adopted for Convention purposes . . .'.

[209] See particularly *Roome v Edwards* [1982] AC 279, 292–293. In considering the question of whether, following the exercise of a power, a separate settlement had been created, Lord Wilberforce said: 'Since "settlement" and "trust" are legal terms, which are also used by businessmen or laymen in a business or practical sense, I think that the question of whether a particular set of facts amounts

approach to the question of whether or not a new trust has come into existence, in which case if the trust is essentially the same in terms of its property and the relationship between trustees and beneficiaries the court might feel no pressing reason to conclude that the trust after the change of law is 'new'.

3. Another possible way, it is sometimes said, of changing the law is by collective decision of the beneficiaries. However, this is an application of the rule in *Saunders v Vautier*,[210] under which the old settlement is brought to an end and a new one created.[211] It is the same principle at work when a change of law is effected under the Variation of Trusts Act 1958.[212]

4. Whether, under English law, the governing law can be changed[213] by exercise of an implied power is an open question, but it seems on the whole unlikely. *Underhill and Hayton*[214] say 'An example of where such implication might be drawn is where the trust instrument authorises the trustees to retire in favour of foreign trustees in another trust State and to transfer the assets to those new trustees: can one not necessarily infer that at least the law governing administration was then intended by the settlor to change to the law of the new State of administration?' However, such an inference would, it is suggested, not be legitimate if the court accepted the views expressed earlier[215] on the problems attached to separating administration from other aspects of a trust.[216]

(8) Exclusion of renvoi—Article 17

41.48 Article 17 reads:

> In the Convention the word 'law' means the rules of law in force in a State other than its rules of conflict of laws.

The effect of this provision is to exclude the doctrine of 'renvoi'[217] when applying the rules discussed above in Articles 6, 7, and 9.[218]

---

to the settlement should be approached by asking what a person with knowledge of the legal context of the word under established doctrine and applying this knowledge in a practical and common-sense manner to the facts under examination, would conclude.'

[210] (1841) Cr & Ph 240. See paras 7.05–7.07 above.
[211] See *Duke of Marlborough v A-G* (No 1) [1845] Ch 78, 84.
[212] *Re Holt's Settlement* [1969] 1 Ch 100, 120.
[213] Albeit under the umbrella of the original law as suggested above.   [214] 1039.
[215] Paragraph 41.46 above.
[216] See also *Re Hewett's Settlement* [1915] 1 Ch 228, 233–234, from which it appears that a change in residence of trustees does not itself alter the governing law.
[217] Discussed at para 41.32 above.
[218] For arguments for and against this approach, see Harris, *Hague Trusts Convention* 387–389. Note also that the exclusion of renvoi can lead to the law of country A governing a trust, when country A would not itself apply that law, eg because country A's law is expressly chosen pursuant to Article 6, but country A would determine governing law solely on the basis of closest connection (*Underhill and Hayton* 1037).

On the face of it Article 17 applies also to references to 'law' in Articles other than those concerned with choice of law rules for trusts. Whether it should be so construed is open to debate, because it could lead to outcomes arguably not intended by the drafters.[219]

Section 1(4) of the Recognition of Trusts Act 1987 provides that 'in Article 17 the reference to a State includes a reference to a country or territory (whether or not a party to the Convention and whether or not forming part of the United Kingdom) which has its own system of law'.[220]

(9) Multi-legal system states

Article 23 of the Convention seeks to make provision for states that comprise several territorial units, each with its own rules of law in respect of trusts.[221] States of this kind include the United Kingdom itself (which has separate trust laws for England and Wales, Scotland, and Northern Ireland), the USA, Canada, and Australia.

41.49

However, Article 23 is not among the provisions adopted by the Recognition of Trusts Act 1987. Accordingly English law will need to address, without the aid of the Convention, the question of whether a territorial unit within a state can itself be a state within the meaning of the Convention. There is a difficulty here in that the word 'state',[222] may be used[223] to signify 'the whole of a territory subject to one sovereign power',[224] thus excluding geographical areas forming part of that territory, for example Scotland, or states of the USA, or provinces of Canada.

If, in applying the Convention rules, one were to construe 'state' in the manner just mentioned this would of course fail to cater for a choice under Article 6 of, say, British Columbian law. However, Harris[225] submits that 'it is almost certain that the English court will regard each territorial unit as a "state" for Convention purposes in any event, since it can only sensibly apply the Convention by identifying the law of a place having one system of law, such as British Columbia'.

If the law expressed to be chosen under Article 6 is the law of a state separated into different territorial units (for instance the law of 'Canada' or of the 'USA'), then the choice is meaningless and the governing law will require to be determined under Article 7.[226]

---

[219] For example, excluding *renvoi* in relation to questions of title to immovable property under the designated law referred to in Art 15. See Harris, *Hague Trusts Convention* 389, who submits that Art 17 should be construed as referring only to the choice of law rules for trusts.

[220] On this provision see also the next heading.

[221] Although the language used could be improved upon.

[222] As distinct from the word 'country'. [223] As in *Dicey and Morris*. See 1-064.

[224] ibid. [225] 409. [226] *Overbeck*, para 176.

There is also the question of whether the Convention applies to intra-UK conflicts. Although it is a pity that the position on this is not clearly stated, the provisions mentioned below suggest that the Convention will so apply.[227]

- The UK has not adopted Article 24 which states that the Convention does *not* necessarily apply to conflicts solely between territorial units within a state.
- Section 1(2) of the Recognition of Trusts Act 1987 extends the adopted provisions of the Convention to trusts arising 'under *any part* of the United Kingdom'(emphasis added);
- Section 1(4) extends the meaning of state in Article 17 (the Article excluding renvoi) to territories having their own system of law.

(10) Ineffectual choice of law—Articles 5 and 6

41.50 Article 5 reads:

> The Convention does not apply to the extent that the law specified by Chapter II [ie Articles 6–10] does not provide for trusts or the category of trusts involved.

This provision needs to be read in conjunction with the second paragraph of Article 6 which reads:

> Where the law chosen under the previous paragraph [settlor's express or implied choice] does not provide for trusts or the category of trusts involved, the choice shall not be effective and the law specified in Article 7 shall apply.

The overall position, therefore, is that if the settlor chooses the law of a non-trust state or one that does not have the particular category of trust, one looks to Article 7. If the law arrived at under Article 7 is again of such a state the Convention does not apply. As the Explanatory Report on the Convention points out, this is likely to be a rare occurrence.[228]

(5) Scope of the Governing Law—Article 8

(1) Preliminary

41.51 Article 8 of the Convention provides for the law specified by Article 6 or 7 to govern the validity of the trust, its construction, its effects, and the administration of the trust. Article 8 then lists certain matters that, in particular, the law is to govern.

---

[227] Harris comments 'Indeed, any other solution, which required application of the common law to intra-United Kingdom trusts conflicts, would create a schism in the private international law of trusts in England for no obvious reason or benefit.' Harris, *Hague Trusts Convention* 411.

[228] *Overbeck*, para 61.

(2) Validity

In relation to validity, the reference to the law specified by Article 6 or 7 is strictly **41.52** a reference to the *putative* governing law, since there can only be a governing law when validity has been established.[229] It should be remembered of course that Article 8 does not extend to questions of validity arising from preliminary issues excluded by Article 4.[230]

It seems that Article 8 may not be intended to cover formal, as distinct from essential, validity,[231] since the view was taken during the drafting that matters of form relate to preliminary issues (excluded by Article 4) and not to the trust itself.[232] This reasoning is difficult to follow. In English law, for example, the formal requirement concerning an *inter vivos* trust of land in section 53(1)(b) of the Law of Property Act 1925 clearly relates to the trust itself.[233]

Assuming Article 8 does not cover formal validity then one needs to look outside the Convention to establish which law governs the matter. The best candidate seems to be the law that applies to essential validity, ie the same law as is applicable under Article 8.[234]

(3) Construction and administration

These are matters which could, by virtue of Article 9, be governed by a different **41.53** law than that which governs validity.[235]

(4) Effects

This has been described as a 'rather vague' term.[236] It is probably concerned **41.54** primarily with the sort of matters listed in paragraphs (a) to (j) of Article 8 and those referred to in Article 11.[237] It may include, or include in part, the capacity of beneficiaries (discussed in the next paragraph).

---

[229] See further discussion of this issue in Harris, *Hague Trusts Convention* 276.
[230] As to which, see paras 41.11 *et seq* above and para 41.82 below.
[231] *Overbeck* para 82.   [232] ibid, para 83.
[233] Section 53(1)(b) reads: 'A declaration of trust respecting any land or any interest therein must be manifested and proved by some writing signed by some person who is able to declare such trust or by his will.'
[234] Since, as demonstrated by Harris, other candidates for law to govern formal validity have significant drawbacks. See Harris, *Hague Trusts Convention* 274–276.
[235] Although the present author is no enthusiast for this idea. See para 41.46 above.
[236] Harris, *Hague Trusts Convention* 234.   [237] Discussed at paras 41.64–41.68 below.

(5) Particular matters listed in Article 8 which the law specified by Article 6 or 7 is to govern[238]

(a) The appointment, resignation, and removal of trustees, the capacity to act as trustee, and the devolution of the office of trustee

41.55 The inclusion in paragraph (a) of 'appointment, resignation, and removal of trustees' seems to have changed the law. The matter is discussed in the next chapter at para 42.42.

The reference to capacity in Article 8 is exceptional, since issues of capacity are, as a general rule, not determined by international conventions.[239] The Article is thought to refer only to issues of capacity related to the office of trustee, not to capacity to receive a transfer of the trust property.[240]

Capacity of beneficiaries is not referred to, and the conflicts rules in this area are unclear. While it has been said that 'beneficiaries do not always need to have capacity',[241] Harris[242] takes the view that rules are required on the issue and has suggested how they might be formulated.[243]

The subject of distributions by trustees of trust property where the person entitled is mentally disordered or a minor is considered below.[244]

(b) The rights and duties of trustees among themselves

41.56 Despite this provision, it appears that the provisions of the Civil Liability (Contribution) Act 1978 continue to apply to a claim by one trustee sued for breach of trust for a contribution from the others.[245]

---

[238] The list is not intended to be exhaustive—*Overbeck*, para 81.

[239] Not least because of the difficulties of arriving at a consensus on this difficult area of law (discussed in para 41.12 *et seq* above).

[240] An issue which Harris suggests tends to point to the *lex situs* in the case of *inter vivos* transfers. In the case of testamentary transfers of movables it points to the law of the testator's last domicile. See Harris, *Hague Trusts Convention* 238–239.

[241] See *Overbeck*, para 59, second para. The statement quoted perhaps stems from the fact that when speaking of beneficiary incapacity we are usually thinking of mental disorder or minority: these, however, relate to the question of capacity to give a good receipt for trust property not to the ability to be a beneficiary at all.   [242] Harris, *Hague Trusts Convention* 21–23.

[243] The Harris suggested rules are: (a) The capacity of a beneficiary at all to receive a benefit *inter vivos* is determined by the *lex situs* at the time of the purported transfer of property to the trustee. (b) The capacity of a person who may, according to rule (a), obtain a benefit, to assert a beneficial interest under a trust, including the question of whether he is presently entitled to that benefit, is governed by the proper law of the trust. In the case of a testamentary disposition of movables, the law of the deceased's last domicile would be applicable under (a). Ibid 23.

[244] Paragraph 41.62 below.

[245] *Arab Monetary Fund v Hashim (No 9)* The Times, 11 October 1994. See also discussion in Harris, *Hague Trusts Convention* 239.

(c) The right of trustees to delegate in whole or in part the discharge of their duties or the exercise of their powers

Although not stated here the law governing the trust should also apply to the question of whether trustees are liable to beneficiaries for acts of a delegate.[246] **41.57**

(d) The powers of trustees to administer or to dispose of trust assets, to create security interests in the trust assets, or to acquire new assets

Cases decided pre-Convention[247] held that, where there was an English grant of administration relating to a foreign domiciliary's estate, English statutory powers to postpone sale of assets and of maintenance and advancement were applicable. *Dicey and Morris*[248] suggests that these decisions are unaffected by the Convention. This view is challenged by Harris in the light of the wording of Article 8(d).[249] Resolution of the question seems to turn on (a) whether these cases are essentially matters of estate administration rather than trust law and (b) whether an English court would, in any event, invoke Article 16 (mandatory provisions of the forum) to override Article 8(d).[250] **41.58**

(e) The powers of investment of trustees

(f) Restrictions upon the duration of the trust, and upon the power to accumulate the income of the trust

The question arises of whether restrictions of this kind relate to issues which are excluded from the Convention by Article 4. As Harris[251] says 'A trust which fails to comply with the law of perpetuities is arguably never launched in the first place'. **41.59**

An argument in favour of perpetuities being an Article 4 issue is that the *lex situs* of a country imposes such restrictions to prevent property within its boundaries from being tied up indefinitely and that this is a matter of *property* law.[252] Against this both perpetuity and accumulation rules are in practice 'predominantly trust focussed'[253] and accordingly, it might be said, matters for the trust's governing law.[254]

---

[246] This follows, it is considered, from the general opening wording of Art 8. See also discussion in Harris, *Hague Trusts Convention* 240.   [247] *Re Wilks* [1935] Ch 635; *Re Kehr* [1952] Ch 26.
[248] 29-021.   [249] Harris *Hague Trusts Convention* 241–242.
[250] A course to which strong objections can be advanced. See Harris, *Hague Trusts Convention* 242.
[251] Harris, *Hague Trusts Convention* 244.
[252] Although, as Harris points out, it is a question of construction of the law in question to determine its nature. Harris, *Hague Trusts Convention* 154.
[253] Harris, *Hague Trusts Convention* 155.
[254] For further discussion, see D Hayton (1987) 36 ICLQ 260; Matthews, *Migration*; Harris, *Hague Trusts Convention* 154–155.

A further question is whether an English court would allow circumvention of English rules on perpetuities or accumulations[255] by the simple means of choosing a foreign law to govern a trust of property situated in England. There is scope under Chapter IV of the Convention for an English court to override the foreign law in this situation. See discussion later in this chapter.[256]

(g) The relationships between the trustees and the beneficiaries including the personal liability of the trustees to the beneficiary

41.60 The main question that arises on Article 8(g) is whether the liability referred to extends to fiduciary liabilities of trustees which are not trust specific, for instance duties which could equally apply as between agent and principal such as the duty to account for profits. An Australian case,[257] *Paramasivam v Flynn*, points to the *lex fori* to determine such issues, but the decision has been termed 'rather anachronistic'.[258] There are a variety of arguments that can be brought to bear on the matter.[259] The present writer's view is that, since the trustees and beneficiaries may regard the difference between a fiduciary duty which is trust specific and one which is not as a technicality, the court will lean heavily towards applying the governing law to both categories of duty.[260]

Article 8(g) is not intended to cover the liability of trustees to third parties.[261]

(h) The variation or termination of the trust

41.61 See the next chapter[262] for discussion of the difficulties to which this provision gives rise in relation to the Variation of Trusts Act 1958 and the Matrimonial Causes Act 1973.

In *Re Barton, Tod v Barton*[263] Lawrence Collins J held that there was no doubt that the question of whether a settlement could be terminated under the rule in *Saunders v Vautier*[264] was to be referred to the governing law.

(i) Distribution of the trust assets

41.62 This includes the question of how to deal with assets when a person absolutely entitled is not of sound mind or is a minor. If in such a case the beneficiary is resident or domiciled abroad it may be necessary, notwithstanding that English law

---

[255] Assuming of course that they are treated as matters subject to the governing law of the trust rather than excluded (Article 4) issues.   [256] Paras 41.69–41.72 below.
[257] (1998–1999) 160 ALR 203.   [258] Harris, *Hague Trusts Convention* 247.
[259] See discussion in Harris, *Hague Trusts Convention* 246–253.
[260] cf Privy Council's refusal in *Schmidt v Rosewood Trust Ltd* [2003] WTLR 565 to differentiate between objects of discretionary trusts and objects of discretionary powers in the context of a trustee's duty of disclosure.   [261] See *Overbeck*, para 87.
[262] Paras 42.43 and 42.44.
[263] [2002] EWHC 264 (Ch), [38]; [2002] WTLR 469, [38]; (2002) 4 ITELR 715, [38].
[264] (1841) 4 Beav 115.

governs the trust, to refer to a foreign law in order to determine whether, and if so how, distributions can be made.

Pre-Convention English case law[265] shows that where a foreign person suffering from mental incapacity is entitled to property situated in England (whether or not trust property), the court is prepared to sanction the transfer of the property to a person (for example a curator) who under the domiciliary law of the mentally disordered person has authority to receive and give a good discharge for the property. The court will of course wish to be satisfied on issues of entitlement and authority.[266]

A question for a trustee is whether to seek approval of the court before transferring property to a curator etc. Although it is said[267] that the court 'has a discretion as to directing the property to be handed over to the curator or other authorised person' that probably applies only where a question of entitlement or authority does arise.[268] Thus, in the leading case, *Didisheim v London and Westminster Bank*[269] the Court of Appeal said (emphasis added):

> If the title of the lunatic is clear, and the authority to act for him is equally clear, we fail to see what discretion the Court has in the matter. *The trustees may properly say that they cannot safely act without the sanction of the Court, but we fail to see what other discretion there is.* Where the lunacy jurisdiction is being exercised, as it was in *In re Stark* ((1874) 2 Mac & G 174, 42 ER 67), other considerations at once arise. If, as in *In re Garnier* ((1872) LR 13 Eq 532), the lunatic were an Englishman temporarily abroad, and confined as a lunatic abroad, we should feel considerable difficulty in holding that the Courts of this country were bound to recognise the title of a foreign curator to sue in this country. But here we are dealing with an alien domiciled abroad, and over whom the Courts of this country have no jurisdiction except such as is conferred by the fact that she has property here.

In one case[270] the applicant for permission to transfer was compelled to bear its own costs in the action on grounds that, having regard to the Court of Appeal's decision in *Didisheim*, it was showing undue and unreasonable excess of caution in involving the court.

However, precisely on what basis the authority of a foreign curator etc is to be determined is unclear[271] and will in some cases justify an application to the court.

---

[265] eg *Didisheim v London and Westminster Bank* [1900] 2 Ch 15; *Thiery v Chalmers, Guthrie & Co* [1900] 1 Ch 80; *Re de Linden* [1897] 1 Ch 453; *Pelegrin v Coutts & Co* [1915] 1 Ch 696.

[266] *Re Barlow's Will* (1887) 36 Ch D 287 as explained in *Didisheim v London and Westminster Bank* [1900] 2 Ch 15, 49.

[267] *Halsbury's Laws of England,* 'Mental Health,' para 1426.

[268] This statement appears to accord with the view taken by Hale J in *Re S (hospital patient: foreign curator)* [1995] 4 All ER 30, 34.

[269] [1900] 2 Ch 15.

[270] *Pelegrin v Coutts & Co* [1915] 1 Ch 696.

[271] See Hale J in *Re S (hospital patient: foreign curator)* [1995] 4 All ER 30, 35. The judge goes on to say 'It may be that, because of our own expansive jurisdiction, we will accept that others may for

Where the Court of Protection in England is involved in a beneficiary's affairs,[272] then naturally trustees should look to that court for directions. Note also the court's power, under section 100 of the Mental Health Act 1983, to make directions in relation to transfers to a foreign curator etc of shares and the right to dividends.

As to beneficiaries who are foreign minors, in some cases a parent or guardian may have authority under the law of the minor's domicile to deal with, and give a good receipt for, the minor's property. Authority is slight on the question of whether a trustee of a trust governed by English law may transfer funds to the parent or guardian in such a case and get a good receipt.

In *Re Chatard's Settlement*[273] a fund to which French minors had become entitled was paid into court by the trustee. Kekewich J held that the court was not bound to pay out the fund to the father (and guardian) of the minors as of right, but that evidence ought to be provided showing that the fund would be applied for the benefit of the children. However, he also commented (emphasis added): 'if the fund had not been paid into court *the trustee would have had a legal discharge if he had paid the money of the infants to their guardian*'.[274]

Nowadays a trustee should also consider section 1(1) of the Children Act 1989, which provides:

> When a court determines any question with respect to . . . the administration of a child's property or the application of any income arising from it, the child's welfare shall be the court's paramount consideration.

In relation to both mental capacity and minority, mention should be made of Article 15 of the Convention (discussed later in this chapter).[275] Article 15 arguably makes it mandatory for an English court to apply a foreign law relating to the protection of minors or incapable parties if that is the law designated by English conflicts rules.[276] However, the argument can only succeed in English proceedings if this is what the court would regard itself as bound to do anyway (ie regardless of Article 15). In a case in which the court considers it retains discretion to refuse to sanction a transfer of funds, Article 15 would not apply (because the

---

similar reasons adopt the same approach. But we will reserve the right to invoke our own jurisdiction if called upon to do so in an appropriate case.'

[272] Or an application to the court has been or is proposed to be made.

[273] [1899] 1 Ch 612. See also cases referred to in the report. The authors of *Lewin* are of the view that 'the authority of the parent or guardian of a foreign domiciled minor to give a good receipt for trust income or capital payable to a minor is governed by the law of the domicile'.

[274] The judge for this purpose assumes the truth of the still-to-be proved statement in the Petition as to the entitlement and right of the guardian under French law to receive and give a discharge for the money.   [275] See para 41.70 below.

[276] See para (4) of Art 15. The issue for determination, it is suggested, is one of entitlement to property rather than of trust administration. It can, and does, arise in other than trust contexts.

law conferring the discretion, not the foreign law, would be designated under English conflicts rules). In summary it is not thought likely that Article 15 will have any significant impact on the outcome of any given case.

English law does not recognize a foreign disability where it regards it as penal—see paragraph 41.26 above.

(j) The duty of trustees to account for their administration

This will cover duties to provide information to beneficiaries and duties to keep accounting records.   **41.63**

(6) 'Recognition' of Trusts— Chapter III (Articles 11–14)

(1) Preliminary

Strictly it makes little sense to speak of recognition in this context since recognition is no more than a self-evident consequence of a trust's validity. However, it was considered desirable to set out the typical effects of a trust for the benefit of countries not familiar with the concept.[277] This is done in Article 11. Article 12 provides for registration by a trustee of trust assets in his capacity as trustee. Article 13 (not adopted in England) contains a provision for refusal of recognition in stated circumstances.[278] Article 14 permits the application of rules of law more favourable to recognition.[279]   **41.64**

(2) Consequences of 'recognition'—Article 11

Article 11 reads: **41.65**

> A trust created in accordance with the law specified in the preceding Chapter [Articles 6–10] shall be recognised as a trust.
> Such recognition shall imply, as a minimum, that the trust property constitutes a separate fund, that the trustee may sue and be sued in his capacity as trustee, and that he may appear or act in this capacity before a notary or any person acting in an official capacity.
> In so far as the law applicable to a trust requires or provides, such recognition shall imply in particular—
> (a) that personal creditors of the trustee shall have no recourse against the trust assets;
> (b) that the trust assets shall not form part of the trustee's estate upon his insolvency or bankruptcy;
> (c) that the trust assets shall not form part of the matrimonial property of the trustee or his spouse nor part of the trustee's estate upon his death;
> (d) that the trust assets may be recovered when the trustee, in breach of trust, has mingled trust assets with his own property or has alienated trust assets. However,

---

[277] *Overbeck*, para 31.   [278] See para 41.85 below.   [279] See para 41.68 below.

the rights and obligations of any third party holder of the assets shall remain
subject to the law determined by the choice of law rules of the forum.

Comments on Article 11

(i)   Article 11 does not affect the rules concerning recognition of foreign judg-
      ments (discussed in the next chapter).

(ii) The third paragraph of Article 11 applies (as one would expect) 'in so far
      as the law applicable to the trust requires or provides'. The fact that these or
      similar words do not appear in the second paragraph indicates that under the
      Convention a trust has the consequences referred to in this paragraph even
      if contrary to the trust's governing law.[280]

(iii) All the provisions of Article 11 are subject to the Articles in Chapter IV con-
      cerning mandatory provisions,[281] overriding rules,[282] and public policy.[283]

(iv) Where trust assets are being followed or traced, the potentially limiting
      effect of the final words of Article 11(d) should be kept in mind (especially
      where the assets are situated in a country which is unfamiliar with principles
      of following or tracing).[284]

(3) Registration—Article 12

41.66 Article 12 provides as follows:

> Where the trustee desires to register assets, movable or immovable, or documents of
> title to them, he shall be entitled, in so far as this is not prohibited by or inconsistent
> with the law of the State where registration is sought, to do so in his capacity as
> trustee or in such other way that existence of the trust is disclosed.

The words 'in so far as this is not prohibited by or inconsistent with the law of the
State where registration is sought' should be sufficient to justify refusing to enter,
for example, reference to a trust on a register of English company shares.[285]

(4) Denial of recognition—Article 13

41.67 This Article has not been adopted by the UK. It is considered under the heading
'The English Trust Abroad'.[286]

---

[280] See discussion in M Lupoi, *Trusts—a Comparative Study* (Cambridge University Press, 2000)
('*Lupoi*') 354, and Harris, *Hague Trusts Convention* 313.   [281] See para 41.70 below.
[282] See para 41.71 below.   [283] See para 41.72 below.
[284] For a detailed consideration of tracing in an international setting, which includes consideration of the position under the Hague Trusts Convention, see Harris, 'Tracing and the Conflict of
Laws' [2002] British Yearbook of International Law 65.
[285] See Companies Act 1985, s 360.   [286] Paras 41.83–41.85 below.

(5) Adoption of rules more favourable to recognition—Article 14

The Article reads:

41.68

> The Convention shall not prevent the application of rules of law more favourable to the recognition of trusts.

Thus in the case of England the application of common law conflict rules to trusts outside the scope of the Convention[287] is not adversely affected by the Convention.[288]

(7) Limitations on Governing Law (and on Article 11)—Chapter IV
(Articles 15, 16, and 18)

(1) Overview

Articles 15 and 16[289] make provision for a court[290] to apply to a trust issue, instead of the governing law ascertained under Article 6 or 7, either a mandatory law designated by the forum's own conflicts rules (Article 15), or its own overriding rules (Article 16).

41.69

Article 18[291] makes provision for the Convention to be disregarded where its application would be manifestly incompatible with public policy.

(2) Preservation of mandatory rules—Article 15

Article 15 reads:

41.70

> The Convention does not prevent the application of provisions of the law designated by the conflicts rules of the forum, in so far as those provisions cannot be derogated from by voluntary act, relating in particular to the following matters—
>
> (a) the protection of minors and incapable parties;
> (b) the personal and proprietary effects of marriage;
> (c) succession rights, testate and intestate, especially the indefeasible shares of spouses and relatives;
> (d) the transfer of title to property and security interests in property;
> (e) the protection of creditors in matters of insolvency.

Comments on Article 15

(i) Article 15[292] 'preserves the mandatory[293] rules of the law designated by the conflicts rules of the forum for matters other than trusts'.

---

[287] As extended by s 1(2) of the Recognition of Trusts Act 1987.
[288] See para 41.86 below.   [289] Discussed more fully at paras 41.70 and 41.71 below.
[290] That is, the court of a country which has adopted the provisions of the Convention.
[291] Discussed at para 41.72 below.   [292] See *Overbeck*, 136.
[293] Article 15 itself does not use the term 'mandatory', but refers to provisions that 'cannot be derogated from by voluntary act'. The term 'voluntary act' is probably used in the sense of prior agreement.

(ii) [Note. Shortly before publication, and too late for detailed consideration, the Court of Appeal allowed the application of Article 15 in circumstances under consideration below. See *Charalambous v Charalambous* [2004] EWCA (Civ) 1030, 30 July 2004.] By way of example, in England it has been suggested that Article 15 might be invoked when a court is asked to vary a foreign trust by way of ancillary relief in divorce proceedings.[294] The thinking is as follows.[295]

The English court has power to vary trusts under section 24 of the Matrimonial Causes Act 1973—a provision of English law which, under Article 8(h), should not be applied to a trust governed by a foreign law. However, Article 15 enables a court to override Article 8(h) (and to apply section 24) if it is established that:

(a) section 24 is a provision which 'cannot be derogated from by voluntary act';[296]

(b) section 24 is a provision of 'the law designated by the conflicts rules of the forum' (that is to say, English conflicts rules).

As to (a) there can be no doubt that English law is such a provision. As to (b) it appears that normally the law designated by the English conflicts rules *is* in fact English law.[297]

Although ancillary relief on divorce is not one of the matters specifically listed in Article 15[298] this is no bar to the application of the Article.[299]

(iii) The question arises of whether an English court is bound to invoke Article 15 or has a discretion not to do so.

The inclusion in Article 15 of the words 'does not prevent'[300] helps support an argument for discretion while section 1(3) of the Recognition of Trusts

---

[294] See also paras 42.43 – 42.44 below.

[295] See also Harris, *Hague Trusts Convention* 264–267, where the application of Art 15 in relation to trust variation is more fully considered.   [296] See n 293 above.

[297] *Dicey and Morris*, rule 86(7). At 18-194 *Dicey and Morris* say: 'It has never been doubted that the court, when making an order for financial provision under the Matrimonial Causes Act 1973 and the Magistrates Court Act 1978 or their predecessors, always applies its own law, irrespective of the domicile of the parties.' For legislative exceptions, see ibid, 18-195.

[298] Unless it could be successfully argued that it falls within (b) 'the personal and proprietary effects of marriage'. [This argument did in fact succeed in the *Charalambous* case referred to in the note at the beginning of the current discussion.]

[299] 'It should be emphasised that the enumeration of the first paragraph of Article 15 is by way of example. Mandatory rules in matters which are not listed may therefore also override the trust's rules.' *Overbeck*, para 139. The Report adds (emphasis added): '*Not without reason, it was said that a hostile judge might always find in article 15 a means of frustrating the trust.*'

[300] *Underhill and Hayton* point out (1046) that Art 15 is 'based on a French text then translated into English'. In the French text the words are 'la Convention ne fait pas obstacle à'. Compare Art 16, where the opening words in English are similar to those of Art 15, but the French is 'La Convention ne porte pas atteinte'.

Act points the other way. Section 1(3) reads (emphasis added):

In accordance with Article 15 and 16 such provisions of the law as are there mentioned *shall*, to the extent there specified, apply to the exclusion of the other provisions of the Convention.

Professor Hayton[301] is of the clear view that Article 15 is mandatory,[302] but arguments to the contrary have also been advanced.[303]

(iv) Other areas where Article 15 may call for consideration include:

    a. *English land legislation.* An English court would possibly regard certain provisions of the Trusts of Land and Appointment of Trustees Act 1996[304] as mandatory.

    b. *Perpetuities and accumulations.*[305] Would an English court invoke Article 15 so as to require the application of English perpetuity and accumulation rules to trusts governed by a foreign law of property, especially land, situated in England? In so far as perpetuities and accumulations are preliminary issues the question is not governed by the Convention at all.[306] If they are trust matters, then Article 15 will be inapplicable, it is suggested, because Article 15 is concerned, according to the Explanatory Report,[307] with mandatory rules for 'matters other than trusts'.[308] See, however, (vi) below.

(v) In the courts of foreign Convention countries the reference in Article 15(c) to 'the indefeasible shares of spouses and relatives' may be of crucial significance in forced heirship cases. (Forced heirship is discussed later in this chapter.)[309]

(vi) Article 15 should be considered in conjunction with Articles 16 and 18. One or both of these Articles may apply even if Article 15 does not.

(vii) In some cases the matters listed in Article 15 will be Article 4 issues and thus outside its scope. So for example the reference in paragraph (d) to transfer of title to property will not include the transfer of title to the trustee to constitute the trust.

---

[301] Professor Hayton headed the UK delegation to the Fifteenth Session of the Hague Conference which settled the terms of the draft Convention.

[302] See D Hayton, 'The International Recognition of Trusts' in Glasson (ed), *The International Trust* (Jordans, 2002) ('*Hayton in Glasson*') 133.

[303] See Harris, *Hague Trusts Convention* 362.   [304] eg s 12 conferring rights of occupation.

[305] Any consideration of these issues should also take account of the Law Commission's recommendations to modify the existing perpetuity rules and to abolish the rules against excessive accumulations except in relation to charities. See Law Commission, *The Rules against Perpetuities and Excessive Accumulations* (Law Com No 251, 1998).

[306] See discussion at para 41.59 above.   [307] *Overbeck* 136.

[308] See also Lawrence Collins J in *Re Barton, Tod v Barton* [2002] WTLR 469, [42]; (2002) 4 ITELR 715, [42].   [309] Paragraph 41.87 below.

(3) Overriding rules of the forum—Article 16

41.71   Article 16 reads (so far as adopted in England)[310] as follows:

> The Convention does not prevent the application of those provisions of the law of the forum which must be applied even to international situations, irrespective of rules of conflict of laws.

Comments on Article 16

(a) The Explanatory Report[311] states that Article 16 is concerned with 'provisions known among legal authors under the name of "laws of immediate application" and designated in the Rome Convention as "mandatory rules" '. It goes on to say that they are 'in fact special mandatory rules and this idea is expressed in article 16 as follows: "provisions ... which must [312] be applied even in international situations, irrespective of rules of conflict of laws" '.

(b) It is difficult to assess the potential scope of Article 16. Much will depend on the view individual jurisdictions take of it and there is, as yet, no English case law. As has been pointed out,[313] 'an obstreperous attitude, which holds that any number of provisions of the law of property, insolvency, family law and succession are of international application, may dilute the Convention to the point of ineffectiveness'.

(c) Examples given in the Explanatory Report[314] of laws within Article 16 are 'laws ... intended to protect the cultural heritage of a country, public health, certain vital economic interests, the protection of employees or the weaker party to another contract'. Also mentioned, at the specific request of the French delegation, are currency exchange regulations.

(d) One cannot rule out the possibility of argument in an English court that Article 16 should be invoked in the type of case considered in the discussion of Article 15 (variation of a foreign trust on divorce,[315] application of legislative

---

[310] The remainder of Article 16 reads:

If another State has a sufficiently close connection with a case, then, in exceptional circumstances, effect may also be given to rules of that State which have the same character as mentioned in the preceding paragraph.

Any Contracting State may, by way of reservation, declare that it will not apply the second paragraph of this article.

The reservation referred to above was made by the UK. See Full Status Report on Convention at http://www.hcch.net/e/status/stat30e.html.   [311] *Overbeck*, para 149.

[312] The word 'must,' coupled with the different opening phrase in the French version from that discussed in relation to Art 15 (see n 299 above), indicates that Art 16 is mandatory.

[313] In Harris, *Hague Trusts Convention* 381.   [314] *Overbeck*, para 149.

[315] *Underhill and Hayton* (1049) suggest the possibility of Art 16 applying here. However, Harris, *Hague Trusts Convention* (268) submits that Art 16 does not apply to variation.

provisions relating to land, application[316] of perpetuity and accumulation rules[317]).

(e) An important difference between Article 15 and Article 16 is that the latter is not restricted to matters other than trusts.[318] Thus if the law on perpetuity were held by an English court to be a provision of the kind referred to in Article 16 it would be no answer to say that the provision relates to a trust matter.

(4) Public policy—Article 18

Article 18 reads: **41.72**

> The provisions of the Convention may be disregarded when their application would be manifestly incompatible with public policy (ordre public). [Note. The words 'ordre public', while appearing in the English translation of the Convention, do not appear in Article 18 as scheduled to the Recognition of Trusts Act 1987.]

The inclusion of an article on public policy is standard practice in international conventions on conflicts issues. The word 'manifestly' indicates an intention that the provision should not be invoked lightly. There are, as yet, no guidelines on how an English court would apply this provision. As in relation to Article 16, one cannot rule out argument that Article 18 should be invoked in matters of the kind discussed in relation to Article 15 (variation of a foreign trust on divorce,[319] application[320] of perpetuity and accumulation rules[321]).

(8) What Trusts Are Subject to the Convention

(1) Preliminary

As previously mentioned, the Convention itself applies only to trusts[322] created **41.73**
voluntarily and evidenced in writing,[323] but under the Recognition of Trusts Act 1987 the provisions of the Convention adopted in the UK are extended so as to

---

[316] Where a Convention issue—see para 41.59 above.

[317] The authors of *Lewin* (11.34) submit 'Article 16 is not in point because . . . it preserves only provisions "which must be applied even to international situations, irrespective of the rules of conflict of laws", which section 164 and the English rule against perpetuities are not.'

[318] This assumes the position on Art 15 to be as stated in *Overbeck*, para 136.

[319] A possibility suggested by *Cheshire and North* 1043, n 14. See, however, Harris, *Hague Trusts Convention* 268–269.   [320] Where a Convention issue—see para 41.59 above.

[321] *Underhill and Hayton* suggest that while English public policy might be infringed if a foreign trust prevents alienation for a period exceeding that permitted under the Perpetuities and Accumulations Act 1964, the fact that, in the case of freely alienable trust property, the interests of the beneficiaries in the changing investments representing the trust fund from time to time may arise outside the perpetuity period laid down in that Act should not be grounds for invoking Art 18. *Underhill and Hayton* 1051 (and n 3).

[322] As to the meaning of which under the Convention, see Art 2 and para 41.74 below.

[323] Article 3.

have effect, so far as practicable, 'in relation to any other trusts of property arising under the law of any part of the United Kingdom or by virtue of a judicial decision whether in the United Kingdom or elsewhere'.[324]

(2) What is a trust for the purpose of the Convention?

41.74 The Convention does not aim for a precise definition of the term 'trust'. Rather it sets out, in Article 2, a general description; it follows this with a list of a trust's characteristics; and it concludes with provisions to take account of the fact that a settlor may retain rights or powers or be a beneficiary.

Article 2 reads:

> For the purposes of this Convention, the term 'trust' refers to the legal relationship created—*inter vivos* or on death—by a person, the settlor, when assets have been placed under the control of a trustee for the benefit of a beneficiary or for a specified purpose.[325]

> A trust has the following characteristics—

> (a) the assets constitute a separate fund and are not a part of the trustee's own estate;
> (b) title to the trust assets stands in the name of the trustee or in the name of another person on behalf of the trustee;
> (c) the trustee has the power and the duty, in respect of which he is accountable, to manage, employ or dispose of the assets in accordance with the terms of the trust and the special duties imposed upon him by law.

> The reservation by the settlor of certain rights and powers, and the fact that the trustee may himself have rights as a beneficiary, are not necessarily inconsistent with the existence of a trust.

Article 2 is framed in broad terms so as to embrace analogous institutions in non-common law countries.[326] There is a danger that this goes too far: for example, the question is debated of whether Article 2 includes some forms of agency.[327]

Professor Lupoi has written in relation to Article 2:[328]

> Before the Hague Convention you would know a trust when you met one. That is no longer so…The shapeless trust has come into this world.

---

[324] Section 1(2).   [325] On which see para 40.16 above.

[326] See *Overbeck*, para 36. However, some institutions comparable to trusts will not qualify. Thus, Hayton writes (*Hayton in Glasson* 125): 'It is clear that if there is an Anstalt, Stiftung or Foundation that has legal personality and has legal beneficial ownership of assets, then in the absence of a separate fund of such assets separate from its own assets, there can be no trust within Art 2.'

[327] See *Hayton in Glasson* 124, Harris, *Hague Trusts Convention* 106.

[328] Lupoi, 'The Shapeless Trust' in *Trusts and Trustees* vol 1, 15. See also *Lupoi* 339.

Notwithstanding the difficulties with Article 2 (and subject to what is said in the next paragraph) it seems clear that it covers the trust concept as it is known in English law.[329]

The fact that Article 2 refers to assets placed under the control of the trustee raises the question of whether a trust declared by a settlor of his own property is within the Convention. The general view appears to be that the Convention does, or at least should, apply to trusts of this kind.[330] However, the point remains an open one. It appears[331] that attempts at the drafting stage to include wording to deal with the issue were unsuccessful. On the other hand, the commentary in the Explanatory Report[332] on Article 4 refers to the exclusion under that Article of acts by which a trust is declared by a settlor of his own property which would hardly have been necessary if such trusts were not intended to be within the Convention in the first place.

(3) What trusts are not within the Convention?

(a) Trusts outside the Convention categories (as extended)

A trust is outside the Convention (as extended) if it does not fall within any of the **41.75** categories specified in (i) to (iii) below.

(i) Trusts created voluntarily and evidenced in writing;[333]
(ii) Trusts of property arising under the law of some part of the United Kingdom;[334]
(iii) Trusts of property arising by virtue of a judicial decision whether in the United Kingdom or elsewhere.

Thus excluded trusts include voluntary trusts created orally and not evidenced in writing when the governing law[335] is that of a country outside the UK (for example an oral express trust governed by the law of the Republic of Ireland).

The position in respect of trusts arising by operation of law (constructive and resulting) is more complicated. First, as is plain, categories (ii) and (iii) above will

---

[329] Harris says: 'Clearly, the paradigm English express trust falls within Article 2 and is the prime concern of the Convention, as the Preamble indicates'(Harris, *Hague Trusts Convention* 104). As to constructive and resulting trusts, see discussion below.
[330] See *Lewin*, 11-32, *Underhill and Hayton* 1015, *Lupoi* 335 ('on balance'), Harris, *Hague Trusts Convention* 106.   [331] *Lupoi* 335
[332] *Overbeck* para 57.   [333] Article 3.
[334] Recognition of Trusts Act 1897, s 1(2). In applying this provision it must be assumed, as can hardly be otherwise, that the reference in s 1(2) to 'the law of some part of the United Kingdom' is a reference to the law which would be applicable *if* the Convention's choice of law rules applied.
[335] This would have to be the governing law determined by applying common law conflicts rules, and presupposes that the Convention rules do not lead to a law of a part of the United Kingdom being applied.

cover many constructive and resulting trusts. Note, however, that while (iii) covers remedial constructive trusts (not currently imposed under English law) it does not extend to constructive trusts confirmed by a court but arising from pre-existing circumstances (the 'institutional' constructive trust).[336] In cases outside (ii) and (iii) the position is as follows.

41.76 Constructive trusts (except as above). Constructive trusts, when not created by judicial decision, will often fall outside the Convention because they are not created voluntarily. Sometimes, however, the voluntary element will be, or arguably be, present, for instance in the case of constructive trusts arising from mutual wills.

41.77 Resulting trusts (except as above). A resulting trust is thought to fall within the Convention if it arises from an express trust which does so.[337]

A resulting trust of the kind sometimes presumed by circumstances (for example where property which A has paid for is vested in A and B) will normally fall outside the Convention for lack of evidence in writing (irrespective of whether a court would regard such a trust as created 'voluntarily').[338]

(b) Exclusion by Article 5

41.78 A trust may fall outside the scope of the Convention by virtue of Article 5,[339] but will not then be a valid trust in English eyes unless, conceivably,[340] it is saved under common law conflict rules.

(c) Trusts declared by settlor of own property

41.79 See above[341] as to the possibility of a trust declared by a settlor of his own property being outside the Convention.

(d) Old trusts

41.80 See discussion under the next heading.

(9) The Time Factor—To What Extent Does the Convention Apply to Old Trusts?

41.81 Article 22 of the Convention reads:

The Convention applies to trusts regardless of the date on which they were created.

---

[336] *Underhill and Hayton* argue (1022) that this anomaly might be removed by a purposive construction of s 1(2). [337] See *Overbeck*, para 51.

[338] Although *Underhill and Hayton* (1018) mention the possibility that 'evidenced in writing' imposes a requirement only of *sufficiency* of evidence.

[339] Discussed at para 41.50 above.

[340] One would need to try to argue that under common law conflict rules, discussed below, the court should apply the law of the *trust* state of closest connection. [341] Paragraph 41.74.

However, a Contracting State may reserve the right not to apply the Convention to trusts created before the date on which, in relation to that State, the Convention enters into force.

To this English law has added:

Article 22 shall not be construed as affecting the law to be applied in relation to anything done or omitted before the coming into force of this Act.

The meaning of this provision, contained in section 1(5) of the Recognition of Trusts Act 1987, is a matter for debate. It seems clear that breaches of trust committed before 1 August 1987 (when the Act came into force) are outside the scope of the Convention.[342] But does the Convention have any application in respect of a pre-Act trust?

Underhill and Hayton[343] submit that it does, arguing that section 1(5) was enacted:

... out of an abundance of caution in case (which [the UK] did not believe) the Convention rules differed from the common law rules on which there is a paucity of authority ... so that breaches of trust committed before such date (*but not after*) are to be judged according to the common law rules applicable before that date [emphasis added].

However, it can also be contended, as in *Lewin*,[344] that the wording of section 1(5) puts the Convention

... out of view when choosing the law to govern the validity of trusts declared before the Act, leaving the pre-Act common law rules to govern the choice of law to test the validity of pre-Act declarations of trust.

Section 1(5) has been referred to in two recent decisions. In the first, *Chellaram v Chellaram (No 2)*,[345] the judge, Lawrence Collins J, *did* regard provisions of the Convention as applicable to a pre-Act trust.[346]

In the second, *Re Carapiet's Trusts*,[347] the judge, Jacob J, commented[348] that 'the Act is obscure in its retrospective effect' (but was able to decide the case without addressing the issue).[349]

---

[342] The view taken by Lawrence Collins J in *Chellaram v Chellaram (No 2)* [2002] EWHC 632 [164]; [2002] 3 All ER 17 [164]; and (2002) 4 ITELR 729 [164].   [343] 1013.

[344] 11-28.

[345] *Chellaram v Chellaram (No 2)* [2002] EWHC 632; [2002] 3 All ER 17; and (2002) 4 ITELR 729.

[346] See particularly at para [160], considering Arts 6 and 10. At para [166] the judge considers Art 7 but also comments that he doubts whether there is any significant difference between Art 7 and the likely approach at common law.

[347] [2002] EWHC 1304 (Ch) [3]; [2002] WTLR 989 [3].   [348] ibid.   [349] ibid.

On balance the present writer thinks that section 1(5) would have been differently worded had a total exclusion of pre-Act trusts been intended.

(10) Article 4—Revisited

41.82   Article 4 has been referred to at various places in this chapter. Under this heading the main points are gathered together.

Article 4 reads:

> The Convention does not apply to preliminary issues relating to the validity of wills or of other acts by virtue of which assets are transferred to the trustee.

The following comments on Article 4 are of relevance:

(a) Some matters on Article 4 are quite clear. In particular, Article 4 applies to (and so excludes from the Convention):

  (i) The capacity to transfer property *inter vivos* to a trustee;[350]
  (ii) The essential and formal validity of a transfer *inter vivos* to a trustee;[351]
  (iii) The capacity to make a will or other testamentary disposition under which a trust is created;[352]
  (iv) The formal validity of such a will;[353]
  (v) Issues concerning the title of the settlor to the intended trust property;[354]
  (vi) Issues concerning priority as between *inter vivos* transfers to a trustee.[355]

(b) There is scope for debate over whether Article 4 covers capacity of a settlor to subject property to a trust,[356] whether the property is transferred to a trustee or the settlor declares a trust of his own property.[357]

(c) Issues relating to perpetuities and accumulations could arguably fall either inside or outside Article 4, or partly one and partly the other.[358]

(d) Whether an issue relating to a forced heirship claim falls within Article 4 will depend on the particular circumstances, but often crucial elements in such a claim will fall within the Article.[359]

(e) There is a question of the significance of Article 4 in relation to the essential validity of certain testamentary dispositions.[360]

---

[350] See paras 41.19–41.21 above.   [351] See paras 41.28–41.30 above.
[352] See paras 41.22–41.23 above.   [353] See para 41.31 above.
[354] See para 41.37 above.   [355] See para 41.08 above.
[356] Or, in other terms, to declare the trust or create the trust structure.
[357] See para 41.24 above.   [358] See para 41.59 above.
[359] See para 41.87 below.
[360] See para 41.31 above, esp n 125.

(11) The English Trust Abroad

(1) Non-Convention countries[361]

The numerous non-Convention territories which have the trust concept (includ- **41.83**
ing, for example, the USA, India, and South Africa) are likely[362] to give effect to a
trust governed by English law subject to any local overriding rules. Beware, however, of the possibility that local choice of law rules will lead to the application of
a law other than English.[363]

In non-Convention countries which do not have the trust (for example most of
the civil law countries of continental Europe) the outcome for a trust is often
unpredictable. A typical civil law approach is to decide the matter by reference to
some local analogue of the trust or of the category of trust in question, for instance
mandate or contract. (In Switzerland statutory provisions relating to companies
may apply.)[364]

(2) Convention countries

For the English trust abroad the value of the Convention is likely to be most **41.84**
evident in those Convention countries which do not have the trust as part of
their domestic law because (as mentioned above) that country's attitude to
trusts might otherwise have been unpredictable.

The states which have ratified the Convention[365] are: Australia, Canada (as to
certain territories),[366] Hong Kong, Italy, Luxembourg,[367] Malta, The Netherlands
(as to the Kingdom in Europe), and the United Kingdom (as to certain territories).[368]

---

[361] See on this topic generally, *Hayton in Glasson* 136 *et seq*. In relation to Switzerland, a county
with considerable exposure to trusts which has not yet adopted the Convention, see Alfred E
Overbeck, 'Digest for Switzerland' in Glasson (ed), *International Trust Laws* (Jordans, loose-leaf)
Section A, Chap 52.

[362] Although it is dangerous to generalize and advice on a particular country's attitude should
always be taken.

[363] Thus in the USA it has been known for choices of foreign law to be disregarded. See decisions
discussed in (1999) 7 Journal of International Trust and Corporate Planning, 3. For US position
generally see W Fratcher, *Scott on Trusts* (4th edn, Little, Brown, 1987) ('*Scott*'), vol VA, Chap 14.
See also the US Uniform Trust Code (especially ss 107 and 403) enacted at the time of writing in
four states. For text, commentary, and current status, see http://www.nccusl.org/nccusl/
DesktopDefault.aspx.

[364] 'It is generally agreed that Articles 150–155 [of the Swiss Statute on Private International Law]
dealing with companies applies to most trusts . . .'.: Alfred E Overbeck, 'Digest for Switzerland' in
Glasson (ed), *International Trust Laws* (Jordans, loose-leaf) Section A, Chap 52, para A52.7.

[365] Written on 15 January 2004.

[366] The initial ratification covered Alberta, British Columbia, New Brunswick, Newfoundland,
and Prince Edward Island. It has since been extended to Manitoba and Saskatchewan.

[367] The most recent ratification. The Convention came into force in relation to Luxembourg on
1 January 2004.

[368] The initial ratification covered the United Kingdom of Great Britain and Northern Ireland,
the Isle of Man, Bermuda, British Antarctic Territory, British Virgin Islands, Falkland Islands,

Switzerland is giving ratification serious consideration. The USA has signed, but not yet ratified, the Convention.

A full status report on the Convention regularly updated is to be found at http://www.hcch.net/e/status/stat30e.html.

41.85 In considering how the Convention might be applied to an English trust in a Convention country, matters to be kept in mind include, in particular, the following.

a. The Convention is open to a range of interpretations. The manner in which its text was hammered out by lawyers from both trust and non-trust cultures, and against time constraints, often led, in the words of Professor Hayton[369] (who headed the UK delegation) 'to curiously expressed English provisions and to matters being "fudged" by the use of "grey" open-textured language capable of being interpreted narrowly or broadly, while some dangerous areas ... were skirted round, leaving it open for countries to develop these areas as they thought fit as they became more accustomed to . . . trusts'.[370]

b. None of the provisions of the Convention introduce the trust concept into the domestic law of the countries which ratify it. Rather (as we have seen in the discussion of the Convention, as it applies in England) the Convention provides those countries with conflict of laws rules which they can apply when asked to give effect to a foreign trust.

c. Articles 15 and 16 have the potential to undermine the Convention, especially in non-trust countries. Thus the Explanatory Report[371] says:

> Not without reason, it was said that a hostile judge might always find in Article 15 a means of frustrating the trust.

> As regards Article 16, note its potentially broader effect in those countries which have adopted its second paragraph.[372]

Gibraltar, Saint Helena, Saint Helena Dependencies, South Georgia and the South Sandwich Islands, United Kingdom Sovereign Base Areas of Akrotiri and Dhekelia in the Island of Cyprus. The Convention has since been extended to Hong Kong (now China, Hong Kong Special Administrative Region), Montserrat, Jersey, Guernsey (but not the Islands of Alderney and Sark), and the Turks and Caicos. See Glasson (ed), *International Trust Laws* (Jordans, loose-leaf) for details of the Convention's implementation in a number of these jurisdictions.

[369] *Hayton in Glasson* 123.

[370] For criticism of the Convention see, eg, J Schoenblum, 'The Hague Convention on Trusts: Much Ado about Very Little'(1994) 3 Journal of International Trust and Corporate Planning 5; and *Lupoi*, Ch 6. For other sides of the argument, see, eg, D Hayton, 'The Hague Convention on Trusts: a Little is Better than nothing but why so Little?' (1994) 3 Journal of International Trust and Corporate Planning 23; Harris, *Hague Trusts Convention* 421–427.

[371] *Overbeck* 139.   [372] Reproduced at para 41.71 above, n 310.

It should be said that the fears over these Articles have not, so far, materialized, and indeed Italy (an early ratifier of the Convention) is becoming increasingly comfortable with the notion of foreign trusts.[373]

d. The Convention contains various provisions which the UK has not adopted but other states may have done. Details of the most important of these (apart from the second paragraph of Article 16 mentioned above) are given below.

i. Article 13:

No State shall be bound to recognise a trust the significant elements of which, except for the choice of applicable law, the place of administration and the habitual residence of the trustee, are more closely connected with States which do not have the institution of the trust or the category of trust involved.

See comments below.

ii. Article 19:

Nothing in the Convention shall prejudice the powers of the States in fiscal matters.

iii. Article 21

Any Contracting State may reserve the right to apply the provisions of Chapter III [comprising Articles 11 to 14] only to trusts the validity of which is governed by the law of a Contracting State.

This introduces a requirement for reciprocity which the United Kingdom has rejected.

iv. Article 23:

For the purpose of identifying the law applicable under the Convention, where a State comprises several territorial units each of which has its own rules of law in respect of trusts, any reference to the law of that State is to be construed as referring to the law in force in the territorial unit in question.

v. Article 24:

A State within which different territorial units have their own rules of law in respect of trusts is not bound to apply the Convention to conflicts solely between the laws of such units.[374]

---

[373] 'In Italy, 10 years after the approval of the law of ratification of [the Hague Trusts Convention] the attitude among practitioners and academics has completely changed: the word "trust" is no longer absent from the Italian legal vocabulary, and the use of a trust is becoming one of a number of possible structures for holding property by private individuals or economic entrepreneurs, primarily in the areas of estate planning and closely held family businesses . . . Limited in number, but significant in their implications, judicial decisions and the practice of some public offices are confirming the legitimate use of trusts in Italy': F Albisinni and R Gambino, 'Digest for Italy' in Glasson (ed), *International Trust Laws* (Jordans, loose-leaf) Section A, Chap 51.

[374] See also para 41.49 above.

vi Article 25:

> The Convention shall not affect any other international instrument containing pro-
> visions on matters governed by this Convention to which a contracting state is, or
> becomes, a Party.

e. Article 13 has the capability of being a particular barrier to the recognition of
English law trusts.

Thus if a resident and national of non-trust country A creates a trust and
chooses English law to govern it, then notwithstanding that the trustees are
resident in England, and the trust is administered in England, and notwithstanding that the choice of English law conforms with Article 6, the trust may
be denied recognition by a court of *Convention* country B if the court takes
the view that the residence and nationality of the settlor in country A makes
country A the place of closest connection (for this purpose *disregarding* as
connecting factors the chosen law, the residence of the trustees, and the place
of administration).

E. Trusts Falling Outside the Convention[375]

41.86 Outside the Convention the governing law of a trust needs to be ascertained
under common law conflicts rules. These rules are famously unclear, although, in
the light of case law in the second half of the twentieth century,[376] they almost certainly closely resemble the rules of the Convention. Thus, it is apparent that the
settlor can choose (expressly or by implication[377]) the law to govern a trust[378]
(including a testamentary trust),[379] although possibly not a law with which there
is no connection.[380] In the absence of choice the law of closest connection governs
the trust: and this appears to be essentially the same rule as applies under Article 7.[381]

In respect of immovable property, the rules of the *lex situs* need to be considered
because, as Hayton[382] says, 'the court of the *situs* will apply its local law and is

---

[375] See paras 41.75 – 41.80 above as to reasons for them so doing.
[376] The authority of older cases may be doubtful. Hayton: 'Old cases emphasise distinctions that
are increasingly being seen to be obsolete, the distinction between movables and immovables, and
between marriage settlements and other settlements …' — *Hayton in Glasson* 143.
[377] See *Re Iveagh* [1954] Ch 364, 376.
[378] See *Augustus v Permanent Trustee Co* (1971) 124 CLR 245; *Re Lord Cable* [1977] 1 WLR 7.
[379] See *Re Lord Cable* [1977] 1 WLR 7, 20, although this may be under the umbrella of the law
applicable to the will's essential validity (see *Re Levick's Will Trusts* [1963] 1 WLR 311 discussed at
para 41.47 above).
[380] This appears to be a general view rather than anything based on authority. What is the consequence of attempting to choose an unconnected law is undecided.
[381] See *Re Carapiet's Trusts* [2002] EWHC 1304 (Ch) [3], [2002] WTLR 989 [3]; *Chellaram v
Chellaram (No 2)* [2002] EWHC 632 [166]; [2002] 3 All ER 17 [166]; and (2002) 4 ITELR 729
[166].   [382] *Hayton in Gasson* 147.

the controlling main jurisdiction'.[383] However, within those constraints the English courts have shown a willingness to apply English law to trusts of foreign immovables.[384]

There can be no expectation that an English court will, under non-Convention rules, allow the choice of a foreign law (even when there is a significant connection) to avoid rules of English law that in the particular circumstances the court regards as overriding (for instance rules relating to creditor protection). However, in relation to the English rules on perpetuities it is thought likely that an English court would raise no objection to their avoidance in the case of a trust administered in, and governed by the law of, a foreign country whose perpetuity provisions are different and with which country there is a significant connection, for example trustees and trust property in that country.[385]

FORCED HEIRSHIP CLAIMS UNDER ENGLISH LAW—A NOTE[386]

Forced heirship refers to the rights of children and other relatives to an indefeasible share in a deceased person's estate. Such rights are likely to exist in particular in civil law and Moslem countries.   **41.87**

In recent years an increasing number of *inter vivos*[387] trusts of movable property have been entered into by settlors from forced heirship regimes. This has raised the question of whether those trusts can survive challenge if their terms are incompatible with the forced heirship rules applicable in the settlor's home country.

By way of illustration:

In 1988[388] Etienne creates a trust of £500k[389] expressed to be governed by the law of England.
Etienne is at all relevant times domiciled and permanently resident in, and a citizen of, France.

---

[383] For the approach to immovables in the USA, see *Scott*, vol VA, paras 651–652.

[384] See Case C–294/2 *Webb v Webb* [1994] ECR 1–1717, [1994] QB 696. See also *Re Piercy* [1895] 1 Ch 83 where a half-way house solution was adopted: the *lex situs* applying while the foreign land was unsold but the trusts of the English will applying to the proceeds of sale.

[385] This accords with the view of *Lewin,* para 11-55.

[386] See also discussion in A Duckworth, 'Forced Heirship and the Trust' in Glasson (ed), *The International Trust* (Jordans, 2002) ('*Duckworth in Glasson*'); *Lewin,* paras 11-59 to 11-61; *Underhill and Hayton* 1047–1048, Harris, *Hague Trusts Convention* 54–56.

[387] Testamentary trusts of movables are of course an entirely different proposition because of the application of the law of last domicile.

[388] ie after the coming into force of the Recognition of Trusts Act 1987.

[389] For the purpose of illustration, the fund is assumed to remain constant in value, and exchange control issues are disregarded.

The principal beneficiary of the trust is Mary, a person for whom Etienne feels morally obliged to provide.

At all relevant times, Mary and the trustees are resident in England, the trust property is situated in England, and the trust administration is conducted in England.

Etienne dies, a widower,[390] in 2003 (15 years after the creation of the trust).

Etienne's estate (disregarding the trust) consists of money in a French bank account to the value (in sterling) of £700k.

Etienne has had three children all of whom survive him.

Under French law,[391] Etiennes's children are entitled to a minimum share of three-quarters of his estate, *to include* for this purpose the money transferred to his English trust. The process of adding back funds in this way to the estate is generally referred to as 'clawback'.

Thus, on the figures, Etienne's children's claim is for £900k [75 per cent of (700+500)].

Since this leaves a shortfall in the French estate of £200k, Etienne's children look to the English trust to make this good.

The question considered below is whether in English law a claim against the trust by Etienne's children for £200k (or claims of a similar nature from other jurisdictions) might succeed.

(1) It should be said at once that the children's claim raises complex issues. This, and the uncertainty as to how those issues will be resolved, have led most offshore regimes to pass legislation designed to protect trusts against forced heirship attack.[392] In England, however, there is no legislation of this nature. The following summarizes the current position in English law (as it appears to the author).

(2) The first task is to examine the nature of the particular forced heirship rules. They vary considerably from country to country. Not all confer a right of clawback. When they do they may or may not have a time limit for exercise of the right.[393]

(3) The next step is to consider whether the transfer of movable property into trust was effective, ie whether it was essentially and formally valid and whether the settlor had capacity to make it and had good title. These of course are preliminary issues within Article 4 to which the rules discussed in paragraphs 41.11 *et seq* above will apply. In the majority of cases, it is considered, the application of these rules will lead to the conclusion that the transfer into trust of the assets (especially if situate in the UK at the time) was fully effective.[394]

---

[390] For simplicity, to avoid the need to consider the spouse's position.

[391] As understood by the writer.

[392] See *Duckworth in Glasson* for commentary on some of these laws (as of 1993). For the text of legislation in a range of offshore jurisdictions see Glasson (ed), *International Trust Laws* (Jordans, loose-leaf).   [393] France, it is understood, confers a right of clawback without time limit.

[394] See also discussion in *Lewin*, 11-59 to 11-61.

(4) Assuming the transfer into trust to be effective the question is then whether the rules of the Hague Trusts Convention could assist Etienne's children in their claim. The rules to be considered are those in Articles 15, 16, and 18.

(5) Article 15, as we have seen, authorizes a country to apply 'provisions of law designated by the conflicts rules of the forum, in so far as those provisions cannot be derogated from by voluntary act, relating in particular to . . . (c) succession rights, testate and intestate, especially the indefeasible shares of spouses and relatives'. The questions are,[395] therefore,

(i) whether French law on succession and indefeasible shares (which cannot be derogated from by voluntary act), is, in proceedings before an English court, the law designated by English law in relation to the children's claim, and, if so,

(ii) whether the effect of application of French law will be to give effect to that claim.

The answer to question (i) is arguably 'yes'.[396] But the answer to question (ii) is considered to be 'no',[397] because an English court will only apply a foreign succession law to assets in the deceased's estate, and those assets do not include property in a trust created during the deceased's lifetime.[398]

Of course if, as may be argued, the issue is not one of succession, then Article 15(c) does not come into play at all.

(6) Article 16, as already discussed, concerns overriding rules of the forum. Foreign laws on indefeasible shares do not fall into this category under English law.

(7) Article 18 can be invoked where the application of the provisions of the Convention would be manifestly incompatible with public policy. Maintaining the inviolability of foreign indefeasible shares is not thought to be part of English public policy.

(8) At this point in the discussion, the conclusion is that an English *inter vivos* trust of movable property is likely, in many (probably most) cases, to survive challenge by foreign heirs. But in view of the boundless ingenuity of lawyers, one needs to consider whether there might be other lines of attack. Duckworth[399] looks at the possibility of claims by heirs under a number of

---

[395] Paragraph (d) of Art 15 relating to 'transfer of title to property' needs also to be considered. Presumably this provision does not affect the transfer to the trustee since that is excluded under Art 4.

[396] *Duckworth in Glasson* 182; Harris, *Hague Trusts Convention* 55.

[397] A conclusion which appears to have general support. See *Lewin*, 11-59 to 11-61; *Underhill and Hayton* 1047–1048, Harris, *Hague Trusts Convention* 54-56.

[398] Two cases (albeit a century old and so not necessarily reliable on conflicts matters) lend support to this view. They are *Pouey v Hordern* [1900] 1 Ch 492, better reported at 16 TLR 191, and *Re Mégret* [1901] 1 Ch 547.   [399] *Duckworth in Glasson* 173 *et seq.*

heads: assertion of a proprietary interest of some kind, tort, restitution, direct enforcement of the heir's rights. While none seem promising from an heir's standpoint, it has to be acknowledged that this is legal territory which, in a forced heirship context, is almost wholly unexplored.

(9) Another possibility to be considered is that, in our example, Etienne's children obtain a judgment in France (or another country) against the trust which they seek to enforce in England. The obtaining of a foreign judgment enforceable in England would, it is thought, face considerable, if not insuperable, difficulties. The rules on jurisdiction and enforcement are discussed in the next chapter. In the present context, the main points to keep in mind are these:

(a) Enforcement in England is under either the European rules or the traditional rules.[400]

(b) The European rules do not apply to matters of succession. As mentioned above, forced heirship rules are arguably to be classified as relating to succession. If, however, the European rules did apply there would remain difficulties arising from the jurisdictional requirement that proceedings should take place in the country of domicile of the defendant or of the trust (in our example likely to be England[401] in each case).

(c) The traditional rules require, *inter alia,* the defendant to be resident, possibly merely present,[402] in the jurisdiction in which proceedings are taken (unless the defendant submits to jurisdiction). A further matter to be noted is the requirement that the judgment must be for a fixed sum of money. As discussed later[403] it is thought that this contemplates actions for fixed sums which are actions in debt. A judgment requiring payment out of a trust fund appears not to fall into this category.[404] If the foreign court gave a judgment in debt against the trustee (ie under which he was personally liable) enforcement might, arguably, be resisted on public policy grounds.

(10) There is a further Convention relevant in this area—the Hague Succession Convention[405] concluded in 1989. It has not been ratified by the United Kingdom, and indeed has not entered into force. If the provisions of this

---

[400] The traditional rules include the common law rules and the statutory rules derived from them.
[401] England, specifically, rather than the UK because of the application of the Civil Jurisdiction and Judgments Act 1982, s 10 and the Civil Jurisdiction and Judgments Order 2001, SI 2001/3929, Sch 1 para 7(2). [402] See para 42.49 below. [403] ibid.
[404] ibid. A judgment obtained against a beneficiary might of course be a different matter.
[405] More fully: The Convention on the Law Applicable to Succession to the Estates of Deceased Persons. See http://www.hcch.net/e/conventions/menu32e.html.

Convention were to become part of English law they debatably[406] would allow clawback in English law. As far as the author is aware, there is no immediate sign of this happening.

(11) Needless to say a forced heirship claim is likely to be successful if made against trust assets[407] situated in the country whose law is the deceased's personal law (France in our case) and very possibly in any country which adopts forced heirship as part of its law and is for that reason sympathetic to the claim. Trustees may increase their exposure to a potential claim if they are resident in or travel to any such country.

---

[406] See *Duckworth in Glasson* (1993) 213–216; Harris, *Hague Trusts Convention* 56–59; D Hayton, 'Trusts and Forced Heirship Problems' (1993) 3 Journal of International Trust and Corporate Planning 8.

[407] And very probably against assets held by trustees through underlying companies. See *Caron v Odell* (1986) 75 Rev ce de dr int priv 66, and discussion of this case in *Hayton in Glasson* 142.

42

JURISDICTION, REMEDIES, AND THE RECOGNITION AND ENFORCEMENT OF FOREIGN JUDGMENTS

A. Jurisdiction and Remedies

Scope of section A

This section discusses first the jurisdiction of the English courts over trusts with an overseas connection, and secondly[1] the remedies available when this jurisdiction is exercised.

42.01

Jurisdiction—preliminary points

Jurisdictional Rules

Nowadays trust jurisdictional issues between England and countries outside the United Kingdom[2] are governed for the most part either by harmonized European rules that have been introduced into English law at various times since 1987 or by traditional rules of *in personam* jurisdiction arising under the common law. Both

42.02

---

[1] From para 42.41 below.
[2] For jurisdiction as between different parts of the UK, see para 42.14 below.

sets of rules are considered below. The European rules should be regarded as the first point of reference. The common law rules, while still of considerable importance, are best seen as residual.[3]

Certain jurisdiction areas have their own rules. These include matrimonial proceedings, insolvency, and areas covered by international Convention. Although the rules in these areas are not generally relevant in a trust context, there are exceptions (for example, when it is proposed to vary a trust in matrimonial proceedings—see para 42.44 below). The rules in question are too extensive and varied to cover here. Readers should check the position when required in specialist works. (Note that the expression 'European rules' in this chapter does not extend to Brussels Regulations relating to these excluded areas.)

Limits of discussion

42.03 This section is not an exhaustive survey of the European and common law rules (which are extensive and notoriously complex[4]). The aim is to give broad guidance on the trust jurisdictional issues that are most likely to come up in practice, and to provide a basis for more detailed research.

Conflict of laws meanings

42.04 The subject matter of this chapter, like that of the previous chapter, falls within the branch of English law known as the conflict of laws. In a conflict of laws context, terms may not be given the same meaning as they are given under English domestic law. For example, because certain obligations that in England are regarded as equitable are largely unknown in continental Europe they may, especially in the interpretation of the European rules, need to be equated with some other concept. Thus it is possible that the liability of a fiduciary to account for profits will be classified as contractual, or that liability arising from knowing receipt of trust property or assistance in breach of trust will be regarded as tortious.[5]

Service of process—Civil Procedure Rules

42.05 Whether the legal basis of the English court's jurisdiction is the European regime or the common law, there is a requirement for service of process on the defendant.[6] The rules relating to service will generally be found in Part 6 of the Civil Procedure Rules.

---

[3] Briggs and Rees, *Civil Jurisdiction and Judgments* (3rd edn, LLP, 2002) ('*Briggs and Rees*') paras 1.02–1.03. J Harris, 'Transnational Trusts Litigation—Jurisdiction and Enforcement of Foreign Judgments' in J Glasson (ed), *The International Trust* (Jordan, 2002) ('Harris, *Transnational Trusts Litigation*') 10.

[4] A 'minefield and a public disgrace', *Briggs and Rees*, para 2.01, in relation to the current set of European rules.

[5] Harris, *Transnational Trusts Litigation* 11; also at 26–29 (European rules), and at 46–48 (common law). *Casio Computer Co Ltd v Sayo* [2001] EWCA Civ 661, [2001] IL Pr 43; *Dexter v Harley* The Times, 2 April 2001.   [6] *Briggs and Rees*, para 5.01.

Under common law, service has an additional significance in that jurisdiction is dependent on it.[7] See further paragraphs 42.30 to 42.35 below.

Arbitration

The topic of arbitration is not considered in this chapter.   **42.06**

The Hague Conference draft convention

A worldwide convention on jurisdiction and enforcement of judgments has recently   **42.07**
been under discussion at the Hague Conference on Private International Law.
However, it now seems likely that any convention will be limited to jurisdiction
agreements[8]—possibly with little if any relevance to trusts.[9]

The Hague Trusts Convention

Despite an argument to the contrary, the better view seems to be that the Hague   **42.08**
Trusts Convention[10] has no application to the subject matter of this chapter.

The contrary argument arises from the fact that in the United Kingdom section
1(2) of the Recognition of Trusts Act 1987 extends the operation of the
Convention[11] to 'trusts of property arising...by virtue of a judicial decision
whether in the United Kingdom or elsewhere'. This, it might be suggested,
involves recognition of a judgment of a foreign court creating a trust even if, under
normal rules, the judgment would not qualify for recognition, for example on
grounds of jurisdictional incompetency under common law rules. But that would
be a surprising result.[12] The alternative view is that 'the Convention is about
choice of law rules and the impact of trusts conforming to those rules: it is *not* about
the *jurisdiction* of any courts to rule on trusts matters ... Section 1(2) ... extends
the application of the Convention, but it does not otherwise alter the position'.[13]

Chapter III of the Convention contains provisions relating to the recognition of
trusts but is considered irrelevant to recognition of foreign trust judgments.[14]

---

[7] See *Briggs and Rees*, para 4.02.
[8] At least in the first instance. See Preliminary Document 22, *Report on the Work of the Informal Working Group on the Judgments Project* http://www.hcch.net/e/workprog/jdgm.html. See also L Collins (ed), *Dicey and Morris, The Conflict of Laws* (13th edn, Sweet & Maxwell, 2000) ('*Dicey and Morris*'), Third Supp 11-006–11-007.
[9] Preliminary Document 22, ibid: 'The [working] group felt that the question whether trusts should be excluded from the scope of the Convention required further consultation. It was pointed out, however, that the limitation of the Convention to choice of court clauses, and thereby to litigation between the contracting parties, would in all likelihood already limit the possible application of the Convention to litigation concerning trusts, even if they were not as such excluded from scope.'
[10] Discussed in Chapter 41.
[11] So far as its provisions are adopted in the UK—see para 41.39.
[12] Notwithstanding the fact that the extension is said to have been motivated by the desire to meet the UK's obligations under the Brussels Convention, Art 5(6)—see *Dicey and Morris*, 29-004.
[13] J Harris, *The Hague Trusts Convention—Scope, Application, and Preliminary Issues* (Hart, 2002) ('Harris, *Hague Trusts Convention*') 149, emphasis in original.
[14] See discussion in Harris, *Hague Trusts Convention*, 312.

Specialist works

42.09 References in this chapter to specialist works are references to, in particular, *Briggs and Rees, Dicey and Morris,* North and Fawcett, *Cheshire and North; Private International Law* (13th edn, Butterworth, 1999) ('*Cheshire and North*'), and Harris *Transnational Trusts Litigation.*

The European rules

Overview

42.10 Until recently the European rules on jurisdiction applicable in England to 'civil and commercial matters' (an expression which includes trusts)[15] were the two sets of near-identical rules laid down by the Brussels Convention[16] and by the Lugano Convention. The former applied as between European Union member states, and the latter as between those states and members of the European Free Trade Area.

Since 1 March 2002 the Brussels Convention rules have been largely displaced by rules contained in a Regulation of the European Union ('the Brussels Regulation').[17] The rules in the Brussels Regulation are similar in many respects to the Convention rules—differences are noted in this chapter where relevant to the discussion.

The broad position today[18] for proceedings instituted on or after 1 March 2002[19] is as follows:

(a) The new Brussels Regulation applies as between member states of the European Union except Denmark (which opted out of it).

(b) The Brussels Convention applies as between Denmark and the other member states of the European Union.

(c) The Lugano Convention applies as between member states of the European Union and Switzerland, Poland,[20] Norway, and Iceland.

The rules under the Brussels and Lugano Conventions are introduced into English law by the Civil Jurisdiction and Judgments Act 1982 (as amended).

The Brussels Regulation applies directly in the United Kingdom without the need for implementing legislation.[21] However, certain matters left by the

---

[15] See further para 42.19 below. Note also discussion in para 42.19 of possible exclusion from the European rules of testamentary trusts.

[16] A term used here to designate the 1968 Brussels Convention as amended over the years by four Accession Conventions. For more detail, see eg *Briggs and Rees*, Ch 1.

[17] Council Regulation (EC) 44/2001 on Jurisdiction and the Recognition and Enforcement of Judgments in Civil and Commercial Matters.

[18] January 2004.

[19] For position in relation to earlier proceedings, reference should be made to *Briggs and Rees* or other specialist works.

[20] But note Poland's accession to the European Unions on 1 May 2004. See EU Treaty of Accession 2003, http://www.europa.eu.int/enlargement/negotiations/treaty-of-accession-2003/index.htm.

[21] European Communities Act 1972, s 2(1).

Regulation to national law are dealt with in the Civil Jurisdiction and Judgments Order 2001.[22]

'Member state' and 'contracting state'

In the following provisions of this chapter the expression 'member state' refers, as in the Brussels Regulation,[23] to a member state of the European Union *other* than Denmark. The expression 'contracting state' refers, according to context, to a state which is a contracting party to the Brussels and/or Lugano Conventions. **42.11**

Where to find the European rules

The Brussels Regulation can be downloaded in PDF format from the Eur-Lex website, http://europa.eu.int/eur-lex/en/. The Convention texts can be found in the appendices to the Civil Jurisdiction and Judgments Act 1982 (as amended). **42.12**

Briggs and Rees reproduce the full text of the Brussels Regulation, the latest text of the Brussels Convention, and those parts of the Lugano Convention that differ from the Brussels Convention.

The loose-leaf work J Glasson (ed), *International Trust Laws* (Jordans) reproduces the Brussels Regulation, Brussels Convention, and related UK legislation.

The text of the Brussels Regulation also appears as an appendix to the Third (2003) Supplement to *Dicey and Morris*.

The modern role of the common law jurisdictional rules

Common law rules apply to civil and commercial matters only where the relevant European rules have no application or those rules require application of the common law. In the latter case, as will be seen,[24] the European rules retain a significant role. **42.13**

Jurisdiction within the UK

The allocation between different parts of the UK (England and Wales, Scotland, and Northern Ireland) of jurisdiction on those matters which, as between the UK and a member state of the EU, would fall within the Brussels Regulation is governed by rules laid down by the Civil Jurisdiction and Judgments Act 1982 (as amended).[25] These rules are a modified version of those contained in the Regulation. **42.14**

Interpretation of the European rules

Interpretation of the rules of the Brussels Regulation and Brussels Convention is ultimately a matter for the European Court of Justice, which aims for a European **42.15**

---

[22] SI 2001/3929.   [23] Article 1(3).   [24] Paragraph 42.29 below.
[25] See Sch 4 of the Civil Jurisdiction and Judgments Act 1982 as substituted by the Civil Jurisdiction and Judgments Order 2001, SI 2001/3929. In relation to trusts, see also s 10(2) of the 1982 Act, the Civil Jurisdiction and Judgments Order 2001, SI 2001/3929, sch 1, para 7(2), and para 42.22 below.

autonomous meaning for basic definitional terms.[26] The powers of the European court do not extend to the interpretation of the Lugano Convention. In relation to application of the Brussels Regulation in the United Kingdom, only the House of Lords will be able to make a reference to the European Court.[27]

The text of the Regulation and Conventions is written in various official languages. Each text is equally authentic.

Since the Brussels Regulation is new, existing case law on interpretation relates solely to the Conventions. It can be expected, however, that decisions on the Conventions will carry equal weight in the interpretation of terms used in the Regulation.

The Conventions are supplemented by the Expert Reports listed below, which are used as an aid to interpretation.[28] There is no equivalent Report for the Brussels Regulation—however, it is likely that courts will continue to have recourse to the Expert Reports on the Conventions.[29]

- The Brussels Convention: Jenard [1979] OJ C59/1.
- Accession of UK: Schlosser [1979] OJ C59/71.
- Accession of Greece: Evrigenis and Kerameus [1986] OJ C298/1.
- Accession of Portugal and Spain: report of Almeida Cruz, Desantes Real, and Jenard [1990] OJ C189/35.
- The Lugano Convention: Jenard and Moller [1990] OJ C189/57.

Process for determining jurisdiction under the European rules

42.16 At the heart of the Brussels Regulation and of the Brussels and Lugano Conventions is the concept that, with certain exceptions, a defendant is entitled to be sued only in the state in which he is domiciled.[30] The exceptions either confer exclusive jurisdiction on one state (as in the case of a dispute relating to legal title to land) or confer jurisdiction on more than one state (as in the case of certain trusts). However, these essentially simple ideas can give rise to much complication in their application.

Briggs and Rees have shown that in applying the rules the safest practice is to ask a series of questions in a prescribed order.[31] Discussion here is limited to those questions which have, or are likely in certain situations to have, trust significance. To simplify matters further, the discussion proceeds on certain assumptions—listed in paragraph 42.17.

---

[26] For examples, see *Briggs and Rees*, para 2.04.
[27] For reasons given in *Dicey and Morris*, Third Supp 11-043–11-054.
[28] Civil Jurisdiction and Judgments Act, ss 3(3) and 3B(2).
[29] An approach 'justifiable in practice if not in law', *Briggs and Rees*, para 1.13.
[30] As to definition of domicile for this purpose, see para 42.21 below.
[31] *Briggs and Rees*, para 2.08.

Readers asking the selected questions in the order in which they appear in paragraphs 42.19 to 42.23, and taking account of the supplementary commentary in paragraphs 42.24 to 42.27, can expect to arrive at the answer to most trust jurisdictional questions arising from the Regulation or Conventions. However, before reaching a final conclusion readers must be advised, given the complexity of the topic, to consider the full set of questions set out in *Briggs and Rees*,[32] the complete text of the European rules, and all other relevant legal sources including case law, the Civil Jurisdiction and Judgments Act 1982 (as amended), the Civil Jurisdiction and Judgments Order 2001,[33] the Civil Procedure Rules, the Expert Reports[34] (especially Schlosser and Jenard), and specialist commentaries.[35]

In general, the remainder of this section refers only to the Brussels Regulation. This is done for ease of reading. It may be assumed, except where otherwise indicated, that the position is similar under the Conventions (although Article numbers may differ).

Assumptions for discussion of jurisdictional questions under European rules

The discussion in paragraphs 42.19 to 42.23 proceeds on the assumptions listed below.   **42.17**

(a) There is no valid choice of court clause (as to which see paragraph 42.24).
(b) There has been no voluntary submission to jurisdiction (as to which see paragraph 42.25).
(c) The doctrine *forum non conveniens* does not fall to be considered (as to which see paragraph 42.26).
(d) The proceedings under consideration are instituted on or after 1 March 2002.[36]

Questions to assist in determining jurisdiction under the European rules

Notes   **42.18**

1. For the basis on which the questions below are selected, the assumptions made, and a cautionary note, see paragraphs 42.16 and 42.17.
2. The questions should be asked in the order in which they appear.

(A) Does the subject matter of the claim fall within the scope of the Brussels   **42.19**
Regulation? Article 1 of the Brussels Regulation provides for the Regulation to apply in civil and commercial matters whatever the nature of the tribunal. The

---

[32] ibid.   [33] SI 2001/3929.   [34] See para 42.15 above.
[35] Especially, *Briggs and Rees, Dicey and Morris, Cheshire and North*, and, specifically on trusts, Harris *Transnational Trusts Litigation*.
[36] See *Briggs and Rees* or other specialist works for the rules applicable to earlier proceedings.

expression 'civil and commercial matters' is not defined but the fact that there are references to trusts elsewhere in the Regulation makes it clear that trusts are intended to fall within the term.[37]

Article 1 is stated not to extend to 'revenue,[38] customs or administrative matters'.

In addition certain matters are excluded from the scope of the Regulation, including:

(a) the status or legal capacity[39] of legal persons;
(b) rights in property arising out of a matrimonial relationship, wills, and succession;
(c) bankruptcy.[40]

The exclusion relating to matrimonial matters does not extend to maintenance.[41] This may be of significance where the court wishes to make an order against trustees in exercise of powers under matrimonial legislation.[42] To bring the case within the ambit of the Regulation would seem to require the court to be satisfied that the order was made for the purpose of maintenance, as distinct from being a decision on property rights. Although it is argued in Rayden and Jackson[43] that all financial orders made under the 1973 Act are technically maintenance, this argument seems difficult to sustain in the light of the European case law[44] and the fact that the expression 'maintenance' for the purpose of the Conventions will be given a European autonomous meaning, rather than whatever meaning it may have under English law.

The question arises of whether the exclusion of 'wills and succession' extends to trusts arising under wills. *Dicey and Morris* say that it does,[45] and the Schlosser Report[46] seems to support this view stating:

> The expression 'wills and succession' covers all claims to testate or intestate succession to an estate. It includes disputes as to the validity or interpretation of the terms of a will setting up a trust, even where the trust takes effect on a date subsequent to the death of the testator... The [Brussels] Convention does not, therefore, apply to

---

[37] But note possible inclusion of testamentary trusts within the 'wills and succession' exclusion—see later in this paragraph.

[38] For discussion of a trustee's position when faced with a foreign revenue claim, see paras 42.51 *et seq*.

[39] Important in the context of the discussion on capacity in Chapter 41.

[40] For a limit on this exclusion in the eyes of an English court, see *Re Hayward (decd)* [1997] Ch 45.

[41] See Brussels Regulation, Art 5(2). See *Dicey and Morris*, 18-190, for a discussion of the uncertainties to which this gives rise, and of the English jurisdictional rules.

[42] See para 42.44 below.

[43] Rayden and Jackson, *Divorce and Family Matters* (17th edn) 34.82, n 2.

[44] *Van de Boogaard v Laumen* (case C–220/295) [1997] All ER (EC) 517, ECJ.

[45] Third Supplement (2003) S11-277 (in the context of a discussion of Art 5(6)).

[46] An authorized aid to interpretation of the Brussels Convention and a likely aid to interpretation of the Brussels Regulation—see para 42.15 above.

any disputes concerning the creation, interpretation and administration of trusts arising under the law of succession including wills.[47]

However, arguably the conclusion reached in the third sentence in this passage does not follow from the earlier part of the passage. There does not seem to be any rational basis for treating a will trust differently from an *inter vivos* trust once the former has become fully established and can be said to have an existence independent of its creating document.[48]

If the answer to question (A) is 'no', the Regulation has no application. If 'yes', then question (B) should be considered.

(B) Does the Regulation provide for a particular state to have exclusive jurisdiction?   By way of exception to the normal rule that jurisdiction is based on the defendant's domicile,[49] Article 22 of the Regulation contains provisions which confer exclusive jurisdiction on the courts of a particular member state. The exclusive jurisdiction provisions most likely to be of relevance in a trust context are those contained in Article 22(1) and (3).   **42.20**

Article 22(1) provides that, in the case of proceedings 'which have as their objects rights *in rem* in immovable property or tenancies of immovable property' the court of the member state in which the property is situated shall have exclusive jurisdiction.

The scope of a similarly worded exclusive jurisdiction provision under the Brussels Convention[50] was considered by the European Court of Justice in *Webb v Webb*.[51] The facts were that a father, who had bought a flat in France in the name of his son, was seeking a declaration in the English court that the son held the flat in trust for his father together with an order for the son to execute documents to vest the legal title in the father. The son claimed that as the father was seeking to exercise a right *in rem*, the case should be heard in France. The European Court

---

[47] Schlosser Report [1979] OJ C59/71, para 52. At para 112, Schlosser states even more unequivocally that 'if a trust has been established by a will, disputes arising from the internal relationships are outside the scope of the [Brussels] Convention'. However, this statement refers back to, and probably stands or falls by, para 52.

[48] Or, as A Underhill and DJ Hayton, *Law of Trusts and Trustees* (16th edn, Butterworths, 2002) ('*Underhill and Hayton*') say (1057) 'once the law concerning wills and succession has been fully applied (so becoming *functus officio*)'. Cf *Re Barton, Tod v Barton* [2002] WTLR 469, (2002) 4 ITELR 715 where the law of the testator's domicile applicable to the validity of a will was treated as *functus officio* when considering the validity of a variation by the beneficiaries of a trust arising under the will. In the Hague Trusts Convention the distinction between a will and trusts arising under it is given express recognition by Art 4—see para 41.82 above.

[49] See para 42.08.   [50] Article 16 (1) of the Brussels Convention.

[51] (C–294/2) [1994] ECR 1–1717. Applied in *Ashurst v Pollard* [2001] 2 WLR 722.

held, in a much criticized judgment,[52] that the father's action did not constitute an action *in rem* within the meaning of the Convention since the father was exercising rights against the son alone.

Webb was distinguished by Rattee J in *Re Hayward (Decd).*[53] Here the claim of a trustee in bankruptcy claiming an interest in property in Minorca was held to fall within the exclusive jurisdiction provision since the trustee was asserting a right to legal ownership.

As Harris points out[54] the two cases do not sit comfortably together. It seems that it may be open to a claimant to evade the operation of the exclusive jurisdiction provision by asserting an equitable rather than legal right, and subsequently invoking the right to terminate the trust under the *Saunders v Vautier*[55] principle.

Article 22(3) provides that in proceedings which have as their object the validity of entries in public registers, the courts of the member state in which the register is kept should have exclusive jurisdiction.[56]

If the answer to question (B) is yes, the state on which jurisdiction is conferred will have jurisdiction even if none of the parties to the proceedings is domiciled in a member state. If the answer is 'no', question(C) should be considered.

42.21 **(C) Is the defendant domiciled in a member state?** Domicile is the cornerstone of the European jurisdictional rules. Subject to specific exceptions (for example as in paragraph 42.20) domicile in a particular state gives jurisdiction to the courts of that state on matters within the Regulation.[57]

However, 'domicile' for the purposes of the Regulation does not refer to the concept of domicile as it is understood in English common law. As regards individuals, each member state applies its own law in deciding whether the individual is domiciled in that state; and United Kingdom law[58] provides that an individual is domiciled for the purpose of the Regulation in the United Kingdom if he resides there and the nature and circumstances of his residence indicate that he has a substantial connection with the United Kingdom (a substantial connection being presumed after three months unless the contrary is proved).

---

[52] See, for example, Harris, *Transnational Trusts Litigation* 18–19, and J Harris, 'Ordering the Sale of Land Situated Overseas' [2001] LMCLQ 205.

[53] [1997] Ch 45, cf *Ashurst v Pollard* [2001] 2 WLR 722.

[54] Harris, *Transnational Trusts Litigation* 19.   [55] (1841) 4 Beav 115.

[56] In *Re Hayward (decd)* [1997] Ch 45, discussed above in the context of Art 22(1), the proceedings were held also to fall within the Brussels Convention equivalent of Art 22(3).

[57] Article 2.

[58] See Civil Jurisdiction and Judgments Order 2001, SI 2001/3929, Sch 1, para 9.

In relation to companies or other legal persons or associations of natural or legal persons, there is a European autonomous definition of domicile.[59] This provides that a company is domiciled at the place where it has its: (a) statutory seat;[60] or (b) central administration; or (c) principal place of business.

If the answer to question (C) is 'no', then, by virtue of Article 4, the common law rules may apply to jurisdiction.[61] If 'yes', then question (D) should be considered.

(D) Does a member state other than the state of the defendant's domicile have   **42.22** **jurisdiction?** Article 5 of the Regulation provides that in certain situations a person domiciled in one member state may be sued in another member state. In particular, so far as trusts are concerned, Article 5(6) provides that a settlor, trustee, or beneficiary of a trust created by the operation of a statute, or by written instrument, or created orally and evidenced in writing, may, if domiciled in any member state, be sued in the member state in which the trust is 'domiciled'.[62]

The Regulation also provides that in order to determine 'whether a trust is domiciled in the member state whose courts are seised of the matter, the court shall apply its rules of private international law'.[63] In the case of the UK it is provided[64] that a trust is domiciled in a part of the United Kingdom if and only if the system of law of that part is the system of law with which the trust has the closest and most real connection. This objective test suggests that the court should consider matters such as place of administration, *situs* of trust assets, residence of the trustees, as well as governing law.[65] However, in *Chellaram v Chellaram (No 2)*[66] Lawrence Collins J thought that Article 5(6) 'was probably limited to claims in relation to trusts governed by English law'.

---

[59] Article 60. This is one of the departures from the rules under the Conventions, where corporate domicile is left to national laws.
[60] For the purposes of the UK and Ireland, the statutory seat means 'the registered office or, where there is no such office anywhere, the place of incorporation, or where there is no such place anywhere, the place under the law of which the formation took place'. See Brussels Regulation, Art 60(2).
[61] See para 42.28 below.
[62] Where any proceedings are brought in the United Kingdom under this provision they shall be brought in the courts of the part of the United Kingdom in which the trust is domiciled—Civil Jurisdiction and Judgments Order 2001, SI 2001/3929, Sch 1, para 7(2), re-enacting, for the purposes of the Regulation, the Civil Jurisdiction and Judgments Act 1982, s 10(2) (which applies for the purposes of the Conventions).
[63] Article 60(3).
[64] Civil Jurisdiction and Judgments Order 2001, SI 2001/3929, Sch 1, para 12(3), re-enacting, for the purposes of the Regulation, the Civil Jurisdiction and Judgments Act 1982, s 45(3) (which applies for the purposes of the Conventions).
[65] cf Hague Trusts Convention, Art 7.
[66] [2002] EWHC 632, [141]; [2002] 3 All ER 17 [141]; (2002) 4 ITELR 729 [141].

Article 5(6) probably applies only to matters arising from the internal relationship of the trust (for example disputes between the trustees or between the trustees and the beneficiaries).[67]

Of the remaining provisions of Article 5 the one most likely to be relevant in a trust context is Article 5(2), which allows proceedings for maintenance to be instituted in the place where the maintenance creditor is domiciled or habitually resident.

If the answer to question (D) is 'yes', then consider question (E).

42.23 **(E)   If the courts of more than one member state have jurisdiction, which state may exercise it in practice?**   In a trust context this situation might arise, for example, where the defendant is a trustee domiciled in the United Kingdom[68] of a trust domiciled in the Republic of Ireland.[69] By virtue of Article 5, both states have jurisdiction. (Note also Article 6—allowing composite actions.)

The Regulation seeks to solve this problem by providing that only the first court seized of a case may hear it.[70] There are also provisions for proceedings to be stayed or jurisdiction declined where related actions are pending in different courts.[71] There are areas of complication and uncertainty in the application of these provisions, discussed in the specialist works.

Further matters for consideration under the European rules

42.24 **Choice of court clause.**   Article 23(4) of the Brussels Regulation provides as follows:

> The court or courts of a Member State on which a trust instrument has conferred jurisdiction shall have exclusive jurisdiction in any proceedings brought against a settlor, trustee or beneficiary if relations between those persons or their rights or obligations under the trust are involved.

Article 23(4) takes effect subject to other provisions in the Conventions for exclusive jurisdiction (for example in relation to actions *in rem* and the validity of entries in public registers—discussed above).[72]

It will be noted that Article 23(4) confers *exclusive* jurisdiction. Although non-exclusive jurisdiction clauses are expressly contemplated in Article 23 in relation to agreements,[73] the status of such a clause under Article 23(4) is unclear.[74]

---

[67] The corresponding provision of the Brussels Convention was inserted specifically to make better provision for internal disputes—see Schlosser Report [1979] OJ C59/71, paras 109–120. Cf Art 23(4).

[68] Under the Civil Jurisdiction and Judgments Order 2001, SI 2001/3929, Sch 1, para 9.

[69] ibid, para 12.   [70] Article 27.   [71] Article 28.   [72] See para 42.20 above.

[73] See Art 23(1). This is a change, no such provision being included in Art 17 of the Conventions, the Article which corresponds to Art 23 of the Regulation. See *Kurz v Stella Musical GmbH* [1992] Ch 196 and discussion in *Dicey and Morris*, para 12.07, and *Cheshire and North*, 239–240, in relation to the effect of non-exclusive jurisdiction clauses under the Convention wording.

[74] See the discussion referred to in the previous footnote, and query whether anything now turns on the fact that the opportunity was not taken to include in Art 23(4) wording corresponding to that included in Art 23(1).

The question has been raised as to whether Article 23(4) binds beneficiaries and successor trustees who have not executed the trust instrument. It seems likely that it does, since it is one of the terms on the basis of which a beneficiary takes his interest, and a trustee accepts appointment. Moreover, Schlosser[75] shows that the fact that a trust 'need not be established by contract' and could be a 'unilateral legal instrument' was the particular reason for introducing this provision into the European rules. This question is discussed further in relation to the common law rules.[76]

Submission to jurisdiction.   Article 24 of the Brussels Regulation makes provision for the court of a member state to have jurisdiction if the defendant has entered into an appearance before that court. This rule does not apply where appearance was entered to contest the jurisdiction, or where another court has exclusive jurisdiction under Article 22.[77] It is not clear whether under this Article the defendant must be domiciled in a member state, but it may make little practical difference in England.[78]   **42.25**

Doctrine of *forum non conveniens*.   At common law, the doctrine *forum non conveniens* may cause an English court to stay proceedings if another court is a more appropriate venue for the litigation—see paragraph 42.30. The question is whether there is any room for the application of the doctrine under the European rules. Although there are English decisions supporting the view that the doctrine can in certain circumstances be applied,[79] the question is controversial and remains to be finally determined by the European Court.[80]   **42.26**

Foreign immovable property.   While, as we have seen,[81] the European rules give exclusive jurisdiction in proceedings which have as their object rights *in rem* in immovable property to the member state or contracting state in which the property is situated, there is no express mention in the European rules of immovable property situated in other states. On the face of it, if jurisdiction in a dispute concerning legal title to land in, say, New York is allocated to the United Kingdom under the Brussels Regulation (for instance because the defendant is domiciled in the United Kingdom) the United Kingdom court[82] is bound by the Regulation   **42.27**

---

[75] Schlosser Report [1979] OJ C59/71, para 178.   [76] Paragraph 42.38 below.
[77] See para 42.20 above .
[78] See discussion in Clarkson and Hill, *Jaffey on the Conflict of Laws* (2nd edn, Butterworths, 2002) ('*Jaffey*') 79 and *Cheshire and North* 246. Cf *Briggs and Rees*, para 2.64.
[79] *Re Harrods (Buenos Aires) Ltd* [1992] Ch 72; *Ace Insurance SA-NV v Zurich Insurance Co* [2001] Lloyds Rep 618. And see comments of Lawrence Collins J in *Chellaram v Chellaram (No 2)* [2002] EWHC 632, [132]; [2002] 3 All ER 17 [132]; and (2002) 4 ITELR 729 [132].
[80] See discussion in, for example, Harris, *Transnational Trusts Litigation* 42.
[81] Paragraph 42.20 above.
[82] Of that part of the United Kingdom to which jurisdiction is allocated under the Civil Jurisdiction and Judgments Act 1982 (as amended).

to accept jurisdiction. However, this would be contrary to 'a rule of the conflict of laws of great antiquity and widespread application'.[83] It has been suggested that a so-called 'reflexive' interpretation of Article 22 might prevent jurisdiction being taken under the Regulation in such circumstances.[84]

Jurisdiction at common law

Application

42.28 The traditional common law rules on *in personam* jurisdiction apply in the following situations:[85]

(1) where the subject matter of the proceedings is outside the scope—as stated in Article 1[86]—of the Regulation or the Conventions; and

(2) where (a) the defendant is not domiciled in a member state (or contracting state in the case of the Conventions),[87] and (b) jurisdiction is not allocated under Articles 22[88] or 23 of the Regulation (or Convention equivalents).[89]

In case (1) above, the common law rules apply simply because neither the Regulation nor the Conventions have any application. However, in case (2) they apply because of the requirement in Article 4 of the Regulation (and the Conventions equivalent) that in such a case jurisdiction of a member or contracting state should be determined by the law of that state. This difference is significant as explained in the following paragraph.

Relationship of common law rules with the Regulation and Conventions

42.29 In case (2) in the preceding paragraph, although common law rules apply they do so only by virtue of the Regulation/Conventions. As *Briggs and Rees*[90] say, the Regulation and Conventions 'borrow and incorporate the rules for the taking of jurisdiction from the rules of national law'. In consequence the Regulation still has application in relation to (a) recognition and enforcement,[91] (b) interim relief, (c) the rules on multiple and related proceedings,[92] and arguably, suggest *Briggs and Rees*,[93] (d) the court's discretion to decline to hear a case of which it is seized on *forum non conveniens* grounds.

---

[83] *Briggs and Rees*, para 2.60.   [84] ibid.
[85] This statement disregards special areas of jurisdiction (see para 42.02 above) including jurisdiction arising from international conventions apart from Brussels and Lugano. For details of these conventions, see *Dicey and Morris*, Ch 15. As to intra–UK jurisdiction see para 42.14 above.
[86] Discussed at para 42.19.
[87] Except possibly where he has submitted under Art 24—see para 42.25.
[88] See para 42.20 above.   [89] Subject to a possible query arising from the fact that the Convention equivalent of Art 23 is not referred to in Art 24 of the Convention. See *Cheshire and North*, 198. For discussion of Art 23, see para 42.24 above.   [90] At para 4.01.
[91] See Section B of this chapter.   [92] See para 42.23 above.
[93] *Briggs and Rees*, para 4.01. This is a difficult area on which views differ. Reference should be made to specialist works.

Nature of the common law rules

Whereas the European rules are generally mandatory, at common law the English court has a large measure of discretion on jurisdictional issues. The position, put shortly, is as follows: **42.30**

(1) With certain exceptions,[94] the court has jurisdiction if process has been properly served on the defendant or he has submitted[95] to the jurisdiction.
(2) Service is of right if the defendant is present in the jurisdiction.
(3) Service requires the permission of the court if the defendant is out of the jurisdiction.
(4) In case (2) the court may[96] stay proceedings on *forum non conveniens* grounds (ie that the English court is not the appropriate forum) or, probably,[97] when, in trust proceedings, there is a clause in the trust instrument conferring jurisdiction on the courts of another country.
(5) In case (3) the application for permission is governed by the Civil Procedure Rules (see paragraphs 42.33 to 42.34 below).

The criteria currently applied by the court when considering a *forum non conveniens* issue are largely based on principles established in *Spilliada Maritime Corp v Cansulex Ltd*[98] Readers are referred to the specialist works for further details of this topic.[99]

Service of process

The rules on service, including method of service, are generally to be found in Part 6 of the Civil Procedure Rules. Selected aspects of the rules are considered below. **42.31**

Service in the jurisdiction. Broadly service can be made on any individual present in the jurisdiction.[100] Special rules apply for companies.[101] **42.32**

Service out of the jurisdiction. As mentioned earlier, service out of the jurisdiction generally requires permission of the court. Among the requirements are that the claimant must show that his application falls within one of the heads specified in Rule 6.20. Some of these heads are discussed below, selected on the basis of relevance, or likely potential relevance, to proceedings relating to trusts. **42.33**

It is for the applicant to satisfy the court that he has a good arguable case *on the facts* that his case falls within one or more of these heads.[102] Relevant issues of law,

---

[94] See para 42.35 below.   [95] For law on submission, see specialist conflicts works.
[96] Subject to the *Briggs and Rees* argument mentioned in para 42.29 above.
[97] See paras 42.36–42.39 below.   [98] [1987] AC 460.
[99] For examples of recent decisions on *forum non conveniens* relevant to the subject matter of this chapter, see *Chellaram v Chellaram (No 2)* [2002] EWHC 632; [2002] 3 All ER 17; (2002) 4 ITELR 729, and *Hindocha (Widow of Gheewala) v Juthabhai & ors,* [2003] UKPC 77.
[100] *Maharanee of Baroda v Wildenstein* [1972] 2 QB 283.
[101] Civil Procedure Rules 6.2(2).
[102] See *Seaconsar Far East Ltd v Bank Markazi Iran* [1994] 1 AC 438, a case on the Rules of the Supreme Court Order 11 which the Civil Procedure Rules have replaced.

for instance as to the proper law of the trust, must be decided at this stage by the court.[103] The application must include in its support written evidence that the claimant believes that his claim has a reasonable prospect of success.[104]

The claim having been brought successfully within one of the heads, the court still has a discretion to refuse permission to serve out. At this stage the court will need to be satisfied that, among other things, England is the proper place to bring the claim[105] (considering the same factors as those which it would consider in deciding whether to grant a stay on *forum non conveniens* grounds in favour of a defendant who has been served within the jurisdiction)[106] and that there is a serious issue to decide.[107]

42.34 **Selected heads[108] under Rule 6.20 (claimant applying for permission to serve out of the jurisdiction).**

(1) Rule 6.20(1). *The claim is 'made for a remedy against a person domiciled[109] within the jurisdiction'.*

Note domicile in the jurisdiction will often cause the Brussels Regulation or one of the Conventions to apply—a possible exception is where the trust is testamentary.[110]

(2) Rule 6.20(2). *The claim is 'made for an injunction ordering the defendant to do or refrain from doing an act within the jurisdiction'.*

The injunction must be a genuine part of the substantive relief sought and not claimed merely to bring the case within the rule. There must also be a reasonable prospect of an injunction being granted.[111]

(3) Rule 6.20(3). *The claim is 'made against someone on whom the claim form has been or will be served and—*

   (a) *there is between the claimant and that person a real issue which it is reasonable for the court to try; and*
   (b) *the claimant wishes to serve the claim form on another person who is a necessary or proper party to that claim'.*

(4) Rule 6.20(10). *The 'whole subject matter of a claim relates to property located within the jurisdiction'.*

---

[103] See *Dicey and Morris* Supp 11-127, and *Chellaram v Chellaram (No 2)* [2002] EWHC 632 [136]; [2002] 3 All ER 17 [136]; (2002) 4 ITELR 729 [136]. Cf *Maubeni Hong Kong and South China Ltd v Mongolian Government* [2002] All ER (Comm) 873.
[104] Civil Procedure Rules 6.21(1)(b).   [105] Civil Procedure Rules 6.21(2A).
[106] See para 42.30 above.   [107] See further Harris, *Transnational Trusts Litigation* 49.
[108] See para 42.32 above.
[109] For this purpose the definition of domicile is similar to that used under the European rules. See CPR r 6.18(g).   [110] See para 42.19 above.
[111] White Book on Civil Procedure 2002, 6.21.26.

(5) Rule 6.20(11). *The claim is 'made for any remedy which might be obtained in proceedings to execute the trusts of a written instrument where—*

    (a) *the trusts ought to be executed according to English law; and*

    (b) *the person on whom the claim form is to be served is a trustee of the trusts'.*

The Hague Trusts Convention[112] will generally determine whether English law governs the trusts. On the basis of *Chellaram v Chellaram (No 2)*[113] it appears that the time for ascertaining proper law is the time at which the claimant applies for permission to serve out, and that if different laws govern validity and administration it is enough for one of these to be English law.

(6) Rule 6.20(14). *The claim is 'made against the defendant as constructive trustee where the defendant's alleged liability arises out of acts committed within the jurisdiction'.*

There is some debate as to whether this covers a person becoming constructive trustee by reason of knowing receipt if the receipt itself is outside the jurisdiction.[114]

(7) Rule 6.20(15). *The claim is 'made for restitution where the defendant's alleged liability arises out of acts committed within the jurisdiction'.*

Claims not justiciable in England

There are certain limits on the common law jurisdiction of the English courts. **42.35** The most important of these in the present context is the general exclusionary rule relating to foreign immovables.[115] This bars the court from adjudicating on property rights in foreign immovables, regardless of the residence or domicile of the parties. However, there are limits on this exclusion. Under the *Penn v Baltimore*[116] principle personal obligations relating to foreign immovable property, including those arising under trusts, will in certain circumstances be enforced in an English court.[117] In addition, the court has in the past adjudicated on a question of title to foreign immovable property if the question arises in relation to the administration of an estate or trust which includes English property,[118] although the basis for jurisdiction in these circumstances is

---

[112] Considered in Chapter 41.

[113] [2002] EWHC 632, paras 151, 141; corresponding paras in [2002] 3 All ER 17; and (2002) 4 ITELR 141.

[114] See *ISC Technologies Ltd v Radcliffe*, 7 December 1990, *ISC Technologies v Guerin* [1992] 2 Lloyds Rep 430, *Polly Peck International plc v Nadir* The Times, 17 March 1993, and discussion in *Briggs and Rees*, para 4,47; also Harris, *Transnational Trusts Litigation* 45–46.

[115] *British South Africa Co v Companhia de Moçambique.*[1893] AC 602, HL.

[116] (1750) 1 Ves Sen 444.

[117] For more detailed discussion of this point and the topic of non-justiciability generally see *Cheshire and North*, Ch 14.

[118] As in *Re Duke of Wellington* [1948] Ch 118, and *Nelson v Bridport* (1846) 8 Beav 547.

unclear.[119] Formerly the general exclusionary rule extended to actions in trespass to foreign land even if no question of title was involved; however, section 30(1) of the Civil Jurisdiction and Judgments Act 1982 now provides[120] as follows:

> The jurisdiction of any court in England and Wales or Northern Ireland to entertain proceedings for trespass to, or any other tort affecting, immovable property shall extend to cases in which the property in question is situated outside that part of the United Kingdom unless the proceedings are principally concerned with a question of title to, or the right to possession of, that property.

Supplementary matters

Jurisdiction clauses in trust instruments

42.36 **Preliminary.** The ability to select a court under the European rules has already been discussed.[121] At common law, the effect of a jurisdiction clause in a trust instrument would fall for consideration when the court is being asked either to order proceedings to be stayed or for permission to serve process out of the jurisdiction.

There appears to be no reported English decision to indicate the court's likely attitude to a jurisdiction clause in a trust instrument where the European rules are inapplicable. In principle the clause should carry significant weight, as it does in the case of a jurisdiction clause in a contract.

Recent overseas cases offer some guidance. They are considered below under the headings: (1) What constitutes a jurisdiction clause? (2) On whom is a jurisdiction clause binding? (3) What is the effect of a jurisdiction clause?

So far as English law is concerned there is a possible procedural hurdle where England is the chosen court under a jurisdiction clause and where it is necessary to make application to serve process out of the jurisdiction.[122] Although a clause in a *contract* selecting the English court is specified in the Civil Procedure Rules as a ground on which application to serve out of the jurisdiction may be made,[123] no corresponding ground is specified in relation to trusts. Of course, this will not be a problem if one of the other grounds specified in Rule 6.20 of the Civil Procedure Rules is available,[124] but that will not always be the case.[125]

---

[119] *Cheshire and North* 383–384.

[120] This provision takes effect subject to the European rules and to the provisions in the 1982 Act concerning intra-UK jurisdiction—see 1982 Act, s 30(2) as amended.

[121] Paragraph 42.24.

[122] For requirements for service out of the jurisdiction, see paras 42.33–42.34 above.

[123] Rule 6.20(5)(d).

[124] Often this will be Rule 6.20(11): '. . . the claim is being made for any remedy which might be obtained in proceedings to execute the trusts of a written instrument where—(a) the trusts ought to be executed according to English law; and (b) the person on whom the claim form is to be served is a trustee of the trusts'. It would be unusual for a jurisdiction clause in favour of the English court to appear in a trust that was *not* to be executed according to English law.

[125] For example, the rule mentioned in the previous footnote will not be available if the claim is against a protector of the trust.

What constitutes a jurisdiction clause? In *Koonmen v Bender,*[126] the Jersey **42.37**
Court of Appeal considered a trust instrument which defined the 'proper law' as
the law to the 'exclusive jurisdiction' of which the rights of all parties and the construction and effect of the relevant provisions shall from time to time be subject
'and by which such rights, construction and effect shall be construed and regulated'. The court interpreted this as an exclusive jurisdiction clause on the basis
that if 'exclusive jurisdiction' did not refer to 'the jurisdiction of the relevant forum
or court, it would be redundant'.

Professor Matthews[127] has questioned the correctness of this interpretation.
He submits that:

> the 'jurisdiction' referred to is not (as a litigation or arbitration lawyer might think)
> the jurisdiction or competence of the forum, but instead (as a non-contentious trusts
> draftsman would have considered) the jurisdiction, meaning 'scope' or 'province of
> application,' *of the law itself.* It answers the question, *Which* law governs *what* aspects
> of the trust? And the answer given here is, *all* aspects of this trust, including the rights
> of the parties, are subject to the law identified as the proper law [original italics].[128]

In the *Koonmen* case the Court of Appeal felt that it was supported in its interpretation of the 'exclusive jurisdiction' provision by a subsequent clause which, after
declaring the proper law to be the law of Anguilla, stated that Anguilla should be
the 'forum for the administration' of the settlement.[129] On this Professor
Matthews[130] makes the important point that the expression 'forum for administration' refers merely to the court which is to deal with those aspects of trust
administration and construction that require the assistance of the court (for
example questions arising on the scope of an investment power or on distribution
of trust assets where there are contingent claims)—the sort of question which

---

[126] (2004) 6 ITELR 568; (2004) 18 Trust Law International 44.

[127] P Matthews, 'What is a Jurisdiction Clause?' (2003) Jersey Law Review 232 ('Matthews,
Jurisdiction Clauses') 241.

[128] Accepting the force of this argument in the context of the clause under consideration in
Koonmen it will only be available, it is thought, in a limited number of cases. A slight change in wording can put the matter beyond doubt. Thus in the *EMM Capricorn* case discussed below the relevant
clause reads (emphasis added):

> This Declaration has been made by the Original Trustee in the Island of Guernsey and the trusts hereby
> created are established under the law of the Island of Guernsey and *the rights of all parties* and the con-
> struction and effect of each and every provision hereof *shall be subject to the exclusive jurisdiction of the
> Royal Courts of the Island of Guernsey* and construed and regulated only according to the law of the Island
> of Guernsey notwithstanding that one or more of the Trustees may be or become from time to time
> resident or domiciled elsewhere than in the Island of Guernsey.

[129] A further factor in the case was that expert evidence had been obtained from Anguilla to the
effect that the clauses in the trust instrument made Anguilla the 'forum of choice'. The court's conclusion that there was no meaningful distinction between 'forum of choice' and 'exclusive jurisdiction' is also criticized by Professor Matthews. See Matthews, *Jurisdiction Clauses* 244.

[130] Matthews, *Jurisdiction Clauses* 242.

falls, in England, under Part 64 of the Civil Procedure Rules. 'There could not be any suggestion', he says,[131] 'that this "forum for administration" was *automatically* intended also to be the exclusive jurisdiction for the resolution of *contentious disputes involving beneficiaries*' (emphasis added).

The term 'forum for administration' crops up again in a recent British Columbian case, *Green v Jernigan*,[132] involving a trust governed by the law of the Island of Nevis. Here the original trust deed had been amended in what the court termed a 'curious manner' in that 'rather than rescinding and replacing clauses, the trustee and the settlor agreed to add articles to the trust deed'. To some extent, the added articles appeared to contradict the original articles of the trust deed, although they did not explicitly purport to replace them. Having decided that, despite these problems, the courts of the Island of Nevis were intended to have jurisdiction in respect of trust disputes, the judge, Groberman J, said:

> The only matter that is not entirely without question is whether the deed reflects an intention to make Nevis the *exclusive* venue for dealing with the interpretation of, and disputes arising under, the deed. I am convinced that it does, and that the reference [in both the original trust deed and one of the added provisions] to Nevis being the 'forum for administration' of the trust was intended to make the courts the exclusive venue for legal disputes under the deed [original italics].[133]

The Matthews argument, referred to above, as to the restricted meaning of 'forum for administration' does not appear to have been deployed in *Green v Jernigan*.

The difficulties thrown up by these cases can of course be avoided by suitable drafting.

42.38   On whom is a jurisdiction clause binding?   On one view jurisdiction clauses are essentially contractual.[134] In a trust context this raises the question of how they can be binding on non-parties to the trust deed, especially beneficiaries and successor trustees. Various suggestions have been made as to the basis on which a non-party might be regarded as contractually bound, but none are without difficulty.[135]

The solution, it is suggested, is that in a trust context a jurisdiction clause is binding by virtue of trust, rather than contract, law. A beneficiary takes his interest subject to the terms of the trust including any jurisdiction clause. A successor trustee accepts appointment on the basis of the terms of the trust including any such clause.

This view is supported by the treatment of jurisdiction clauses in the European Rules. The need for a specific rule on trusts arose precisely *because* trusts could be non-contractual.[136]

---

131 Matthews, *Jurisdiction Clauses* 243.   132 [2003] BCSC 1097; (2003) 6 ITELR 330.
133 [2003] BCSC 1097 [41]; (2003) 6 ITELR 330 [41].
134 Matthews, *Jurisdiction Clauses* 235.
135 See discussion in Matthews, *Jurisdiction Clauses* 246–248.
136 Schlosser Report [1979] OJ C59/71, para 178.

It also draws support from two Jersey decisions. In the first, *EMM Capricorn Trustees Ltd v Compass Trustees Ltd*,[137] it was said: 'The fact is the beneficiaries and the trustee assume their rights and obligations under the terms of the trust deed. One cannot simply ignore an important provision of the trust deed, namely an exclusive jurisdiction clause.' In the second, *Koonmen v Bender*,[138] the Jersey Court of Appeal said 'that, as an important element in the structure of the trust in respect of which any would be beneficiary claims any interest, it should prima facie be binding on such beneficiary'.[139]

What is the effect of a jurisdiction clause?   In *Green v Jernigan*[140] the judge in   **42.39** British Columbia, Groberman J, having decided that there was an exclusive jurisdiction clause in favour of the Island of Nevis,[141] held that he should give effect to such a clause, and should stay proceedings in British Columbia, unless there was a strong cause to depart from it. The judge also decided that there was no such strong cause despite the concern of the plaintiffs[142] that Nevis was a small jurisdiction, with a small Bar, and with close connections between corporate entities such as the main defendants and the Island's political authorities; and despite the further concern about restrictions in Nevis on discovery arising from tight secrecy provisions under its Exempt Trust Ordinance. Groberman J:

> The parties to the trust have clearly and consciously chosen to govern their affairs according to the laws of Nevis, and particularly under the secretive provisions of the Exempt Trust Ordinance. I do not, of course, know why the plaintiffs have chosen to do so, but it would be surprising if they did not have cogent reasons for wishing to place their significant assets in a secretive offshore trust. I have no hesitation in finding that having expressly chosen such a vehicle for their investments, the plaintiffs are stuck with dealing with those investments under the laws of Nevis and in its courts, even though they may now see those laws as disadvantageous or distasteful.

It appears that the principal parties in the *Jernigan* case were also parties to the original trust deed and its amending deeds, so that there was no need to consider whether, if this had not been the case, the same weight would have been given to the jurisdiction provisions. However, this question did fall for consideration in the Jersey case, *EMM Capricorn Trustees Ltd v Compass Trustees Ltd*.[143] Here, the court was considering the principles on which it should consider an application for staying proceedings where a trust contained a clause conferring exclusive jurisdiction on a foreign court. The court took the view that the general approach

---

[137] [2001] JLR 205; (2001) 4 ITELR 42. However, see para 42.39 on the court's view as to the weight to be given to a non-contractual jurisdiction clause.

[138] (2004) 6 ITELR 568 [49]; (2004) 18 Trust Law International 44 [49].

[139] Note, however, criticism of this statement in its particular context in Matthews, *Jurisdiction Clauses* 246.

[140] [2003] BCSC 1097; (2003) 6 ITELR 330.   [141] See para 42.37 above.

[142] On which admissible evidence was minimal.

[143] (2001) 4 ITELR 42. The Jersey court's jurisdiction in this case was statutory.

should be the same as for a jurisdiction clause in a contract, but giving the jurisdiction clause less weight because it was non-contractual.[144] Whether this is the right approach (bearing in mind, as the court acknowledged, that 'the beneficiaries and the trustee assume their rights and obligations under the terms of the trust deed')[145] seems questionable.[146]

It is not thought that the point referred to at (d) in paragraph 42.29 above would prevent an English court from staying proceedings to give effect to a jurisdiction clause in favour of a non-member and non-contracting state.

Anti-suit injunctions and interim relief

42.40 The English court will, in some circumstances, grant at common law an order preventing a person from pursuing proceedings in another country, or will grant injunctive or other interim relief in England to a claimant in foreign proceedings. Specialist publications should be consulted on these topics.

Remedies available when an English court takes jurisdiction

42.41 We assume here that a trust related action is before an English court in circumstances where the court is bound to exercise jurisdiction or is entitled and willing to do so.

In proceedings against a trustee equity acts *in personam*. Accordingly it 'acts upon the person whom it finds within its jurisdiction and compels him to perform the duty which he owes to the [claimant]'.[147]

While generally the remedies available in the case of a trust with foreign connections are the same as for a domestic trust, there are some practical and legal constraints. Enforcement of an English court's order may be difficult or impossible if the trustee and the trust property are abroad. As already noted there are limits on the court's powers over foreign immovables.[148] In addition, as illustrated below, the Hague Trusts Convention may sometimes affect, or arguably affect, what the court can do.

Impact of Hague Trusts Convention on remedies

42.42 **Removal of trustees.** Before the coming into force of the Hague Trusts Convention, there was authority for the view that an English court would, if thought appropriate for the good administration of a trust, order the removal of a trustee, regardless of whether the governing law of the trust was English.[149] Now, however,

---

[144] On the facts, it declined to grant a stay.   [145] (2001) 4 ITELR 34, [18].

[146] See Harris, *Transnational Trusts Litigation* 85.

[147] Lord Blackburn in *Ewing v Orr Ewing* (1883) 9 App Cas 34, 45–46. See also *Chellaram v Chellaram* [1985] Ch 409.

[148] For the possibility of the court acting *in personam* against a trustee in respect of foreign immovable property, see paragraphs 42.20 and 42.35 above. See also paragraph 42.35 above as to court's limited jurisdiction to adjudicate on title to foreign land.

[149] *Chellaram v Chellaram* [1985] Ch 409.

Article 8 of the Convention provides for the law applicable to the trust to govern, *inter alia*, the appointment, resignation, and removal of trustees.[150] The apparent outcome is that, while the English court retains its power to order the removal of trustees of a trust governed by a foreign law, it should apply the foreign law when deciding whether to do so. The consequences in practice seem difficult to predict.

Applications under the Variation of Trust Act 1958.   Before the coming into   **42.43**
force of the Recognition of Trusts Act 1987, case law[151] had established that the English court had power under the Variation of Trusts Act 1958 to approve a variation of a trust with foreign connections, including one governed by a foreign law, but with a discretion for the power not to be exercised.[152]

One effect of the Recognition of Trusts Act 1987 has been to incorporate into English law Article 8 of the Hague Trusts Convention which provides that the law applicable to a trust (as determined under Articles 6 and 7) should govern, among other things, 'the variation and termination of the trust'.[153] The effect of this provision in relation to applications under the 1958 Act is currently the subject of debate.

Harris[154] argues that the 1958 Act is not jurisdictional in nature (as suggested by *Cheshire and North*[155]) but is concerned with the substantive question of whether the court may alter the rights of parties. Such a question 'ought to be : (i) considered even in respect of trusts unconnected with England, and (ii) determined exclusively by the applicable law of the trust, in accordance with the Hague Trusts Convention requirements'. He acknowledges the difficulty, pointed out by J Mowbray et al in *Lewin on Trusts* (17th edn, Sweet & Maxwell, 2000) ('*Lewin*'),[156] that could arise if the power under the foreign applicable law is exercisable only by the courts of the foreign state, but says[157] 'arguably, [the English court] should not be deterred from varying such a settlement, provided that the substantive conditions of the applicable law for varying the trust are met'.

Lewin also raises the question of whether the Convention provision is intended to apply to variations by the court, as distinct from variations under a power in the trust instrument. The authors regard the position as generally obscure. 'The only conclusion that can be safely reached is that an application to a court to vary trusts should preferably be made in the jurisdiction of their governing law.'[158] This conclusion is supported by E Campbell in *Changing the Terms of Trusts* (Butterworths,

---

[150] Article 8(a).
[151] *Re Ker's Settlement Trusts* [1963] Ch 553; *Re Paget's Settlement* [1965] 1 WLR 1046.
[152] 'Obviously...where there are substantial foreign elements in a case, the court must consider carefully whether it is proper for it to exercise the jurisdiction'—Cross J in *Re Paget's Settlement* [1965] 1 WLR 1046, 1050.
[153] Article 8(h).   [154] Harris, *The Hague Trusts Convention* 263–264.
[155] 1042–1043.   [156] At para 11-40.
[157] Harris, *Hague Trusts Convention* 264, n 845.   [158] *Lewin* at para 11-40.

2002) (*'Campbell'*),[159] who also poses the question[160] 'how could the English court assume the discretionary jurisdiction of a foreign court?'

Underhill and Hayton[161] submit that the test that an English court should apply is to 'ask whether (assuming that it has *in personam* jurisdiction over the defendant) it is a natural forum in which to grant the particular variation order sought'. In deciding this it should give weight to the governing law and objective connection with England but, as against this, should consider, *inter alia*, the philosophy of paragraph (h) of Article 8 that the 'mere fact that a foreign law governs the trust is nothing like a conclusive reason for the forum not to exercise the jurisdiction to vary in accordance with such law'.

While the law remains to be clarified, it would be strange if the effect of the Hague Trusts Convention were to make it less, rather than more, likely that the English court would act in a foreign element case.

42.44 **Applications for variation under the Matrimonial Causes Act 1973.** Section 24 of the Matrimonial Causes Act 1973[162] gives the English court power in the context of divorce or other matrimonial proceedings to make an order varying for the benefit of the parties to the marriage and of the children of the family or either or any of them any antenuptial or post-nuptial settlement (including one made by will) made on the parties to the marriage. The court may also make an order extinguishing or reducing the interest of either of the parties to the marriage under any such settlement.

It is well established that (leaving aside the Hague Trusts Convention discussed in the next paragraph) the English court will, under this provision, vary a settlement which comprises property situated abroad and is governed by foreign law and the trustees of which reside abroad.[163] Moreover, the English court may seek to join foreign trustees as parties (on the basis that this will facilitate enforcement of any variation order it might make[164]) and, if appropriate, to change trustees or protector.[165]

As we have seen,[166] Article 8 of the Convention provides for the applicable law of a trust to govern 'the variation or termination of the trust'. Accordingly if the Convention stopped at Article 8 the English court would, on the face of it,[167] be

---

[159] 8.24.   [160] 8.23.   [161] 1044–1045.

[162] See also the powers contained in s 17 of the Matrimonial and Family Proceedings Act 1984 applicable in relation to foreign decrees.

[163] *Dicey and Morris*, para 18.159, and see cases on earlier statutory provisions cited in n 67 ibid.

[164] See *T v T* [1996] 2 FLR 357. The impact of the Hague Trusts Convention does not appear to have been considered in this case.

[165] See *E v E* [1990] 2 FLR 233. Again, the impact of the Hague Trusts Convention does not appear to have been considered.

[166] At paras 41.61 and 42.43 above.

[167] Subject to the question raised in paragraph 42.43 above as to whether Article 8(h) is intended to apply to variations made by a court.

precluded from applying section 24 to a settlement governed by an overseas law. However it is highly likely that an English matrimonial court would find an escape route either by invoking Article 15 (which allows the court to apply its own mandatory provisions)[168] or (but less attractively) by invoking Article 18 (the standard public policy provision)[169] or Article 16 (overriding rules of the forum).[170]

[Note. Shortly before publication, and too late for detailed consideration, the Court of Appeal confirmed that Article 15 could be invoked in these circumstances. See *Charalambous v Charalambous* [2004] EWCA (Civ) 1030, 30 July 2004.]

B. Recognition and Enforcement of Judgments

Preliminary

This section considers the circumstances in which a judgment or order obtained abroad in relation to a trust will be recognized or enforced in England. As in the previous section, this is not a detailed survey but an attempt to highlight points which are likely to be of relevance in a trust context.   **42.45**

The particular question of enforcement of foreign tax judgments is considered separately.[171]

The general position

There are four principal sets of rules[172] under which a foreign[173] *in personam*   **42.46** judgment or order might achieve recognition or be enforced in England:

(1) The European Rules discussed in Section A of this chapter (the Brussels Regulation and the Brussels and Lugano Conventions);
(2) The common law rules on recognition and enforcement;
(3) The Administration of Justice Act 1920; and
(4) The Foreign Judgments (Reciprocal Enforcement) Act 1933.

The European Rules are considered briefly at paragraph 42.48, the common law rules at paragraph 42.49, and the statutory provisions at paragraph 42.50.

---

[168] See further discussion at para 41.70 above.
[169] See further discussion at para 41.72 above.
[170] See further discussion at para 41.71 above.   [171] At paras 42.52 *et seq.*
[172] This chapter does not consider enforcement in areas of jurisdiction not discussed in section A—see para 42.02 above.
[173] In relation to recognition and enforcement in an English court of judgments obtained in another part of the UK, see Civil Jurisdiction and Judgments Act 1982 (as amended).

'Recognition' and 'enforcement'

42.47 Enforcement requires the court to acknowledge the obligation imposed by the foreign judgment on the defendant and to take positive steps to give effect to the remedy granted by the foreign court. Thus enforcement requires recognition, but recognition does not necessarily lead to enforceability. Ordinarily recognition by itself is a negative process, whereby the defendant may be able to plead the existence of the foreign judgment as a defence to the plaintiff seeking to bring the same cause of action against him.[174]

The European rules

42.48 The complexity of the European rules on jurisdiction discussed in Section A of this chapter gives way to a relatively simple regime for enforcement and recognition of judgments. Only a few points will be made, leaving the detail for more specialist works:

(1) The application and scope of the European rules for this purpose is the same as for jurisdiction.[175] (For ease of reading, the following paragraphs will refer solely to the rules under the Brussels Regulation).

(2) Article 33(1) of the Brussels Regulation provides that 'a judgment given in a Member State shall be recognised in the other Member States without any special procedure being required'.

(3) 'Judgment' is widely defined in Article 32 to include decree, order, etc.[176]

(4) There are limited circumstances in which recognition can be resisted.[177]

(5) Section 2 of Chapter III of the Regulation sets out a procedure under which a judgment given in a member state and enforceable in that state can be enforced in another member state. In England registration is required.

(6) If a judgment given in a member state falls within the scope—as defined in Article 1—of the Regulation, it generally[178] makes no difference for enforcement purposes that, by virtue of Article 4, jurisdiction was taken by that state under its traditional (non-Convention) rules. The result could be, for example, that the judgment of a French court which has taken jurisdiction in proceedings against a habitual resident of New York on grounds of the defendant's French citizenship is enforceable in England, regardless of the fact that in English proceedings citizenship is not a basis for jurisdiction.

---

[174] See *Briggs and Rees*, paras 7.57 *et seq.*   [175] See Section A of this Chapter.

[176] But believed not to include a purely procedural ruling. See Schlosser Report [1979] OJ C59/71, para 187.

[177] See Brussels Regulation, Arts 34, 35, and 72, and *Briggs and Rees*, paras 7.11–7.17.

[178] This is subject to certain treaties entered into pursuant to Art 59 of the Brussels Convention exempting certain persons from the Convention regime when jurisdiction is taken under Art 4 on grounds specified in Art 3. These remain effective under the Regulation—see Art 72. The UK has entered into such treaties with Canada and Australia. See further *Briggs and Rees*, para 7.11.

The common law rules

The common law rules on recognition and enforcement are a great deal **42.49** more restrictive than those under the European rules. The requirements are, in summary, that:

For recognition

(1) The foreign judgment is an *in personam* judgment given by a competent court, applying English criteria to determine competency.
(2) The judgment is final and conclusive upon the merits of the claim.

For enforcement, in addition to the above

(3) The judgment is for a fixed sum of money.
(4) Enforcement will not involve enforcement of foreign penal or revenue or other public law, or a judgment for multiple damages.

As regards requirement (1) the English criteria for competency applied in this context are that the foreign court was one in whose jurisdiction the defendant was present (or possibly resident)[179] when proceedings were instituted, or to whose jurisdiction the defendant submitted.[180]

Requirement (3) may be of some practical significance in a trust context. Assume, say, an order by a foreign court purporting to vary a trust by requiring the trustee to pay a fixed sum of money to X.[181] Is this a judgment for a fixed sum of money within (3) above? It is thought not, because it seems that the action for a fixed sum contemplated by the common law rules is an action in debt.[182] A requirement for a trustee to make a payment from a trust fund is not an action in debt because it involves no personal liability on the part of the trustee.

Recognition and enforcement of the foreign judgment may be resisted on certain specified grounds, for example the judgment was procured by fraud.

The rules under the 1920 and 1933 statutes

The Administration of Justice Act 1920 and the Foreign Judgments (Reciprocal **42.50** Enforcement) Act 1933 each provide for a reciprocal recognition and enforcement

---

[179] This is a matter for debate following the decision in *Adams v Cape Industries plc* [1990] Ch 433. See *Briggs and Rees*, para 7.42.
[180] See Civil Jurisdiction and Judgments Act 1982, s 33 as to circumstances in which an appearance in proceedings does not amount to submission.
[181] By way of example, see *E v E* [1990] 2 FLR 233.   [182] See *Briggs and Rees*, para 7.53.

regime as between the UK and certain other countries. The criteria for enforcement follow, for the most part, the common law. Readers are referred to the specialist works for details of the current application of these statutes, the extent to which they depart from common law rules, and their relationship with those rules.

It is believed that the point made at 42.49 concerning requirement (3) is equally applicable to the enforcement of judgments under the statutes.

C. Payment by Trustees of Foreign Taxes[183]

Introduction

42.51 The well-known rule that one country will not enforce the revenue laws of another ('the non-enforceability rule') frequently poses difficulties for trustees. In some instances the use of trust funds to discharge an unenforceable tax liability gives rise to a breach of trust.[184] In other instances a foreign tax claim can legitimately be paid out of trust moneys.

This chapter considers:

- the general application of the non-enforceability rule;
- limitations on the scope of the rule;
- circumstances in which trustees might be permitted or required to provide funds to discharge a non-enforceable foreign tax;
- express powers to pay foreign taxes.

The non-enforceability rule—general application[185]

42.52 The non-enforceability rule, as expressed by *Dicey and Morris*,[186] is that:

> English courts have no jurisdiction to entertain an action ... for the enforcement, either directly or indirectly, of a ... revenue ... law of a foreign State ...

The rule is recognized in many parts of the world.[187] In England it can be traced back to before 1775[188] although it was not until 1955 that the rule became finally established.[189] In 1999 the Court of Appeal confirmed that the rule retains its vigour.[190]

---

[183] Section C was co-written by Christopher Sly and John Glasson. It is based on a longer piece by the same authors, 'Payments by Trustees of Foreign Taxes' in J Glasson (ed), *The International Trust* (Jordans, 2002) ('*Sly and Glasson in Glasson*'), in which fuller discussion of some of the cases can be found.

[184] Possibly even where non-payment would leave the trustees personally liable for the tax in another jurisdiction. See *Stringham v Dubois* [1993] 3 WWR 273, discussed at para 42.61 below.

[185] See also *Dicey and Morris*, 5-018R *et seq*; *Cheshire and North* 107 *et seq*; P Baker, 'Transnational Enforcement of Tax Liability' in *Tolleys International Tax Planning* (4th edn, Butterworths, 1999) ('*Baker*') 34-1; and Lawrence, *International Estate Planning*, 765 *et seq*.

[186] *Dicey and Morris*, 5-018R (Rule 3).

[187] For information on individual jurisdictions, see *Baker*, Appendix.

[188] *Holman v Johnson* (1775) 1 Cowp 341, 343.

[189] *Government of India, Ministry of Finance (Revenue Division) v Taylor and Another* [1955] AC 491.

[190] *QRS 1 Aps and Others v Frandsen* [1999] STC 616.

The question of whether a particular imposition falls within the expression 'revenue law' is decided by the courts of the jurisdiction in which enforcement is sought. In England and Wales the expression includes laws imposing income taxes, capital gains taxes, inheritance or succession taxes, and customs duties.[191]

Despite the non-enforceability rule, the English courts will *recognize* foreign revenue laws and, as will be seen below,[192] recognition may be enough to allow a tax claim to be satisfied out of trust funds.

The non-enforceability rule is reflected in the European rules[193] on jurisdiction and enforcement of foreign judgments,which do not apply to revenue matters. However, this is counterbalanced to a large extent by the fact that the European Union has now adopted machinery for member states to assist one another in tax recovery.[194]

The Foreign Judgments (Reciprocal Enforcement) Act 1933 does not extend to judgments for any sum payable in respect of taxes or other charges of a like nature.[195]

The provisions for reciprocal enforcement contained in the Administration of Justice Act 1920 do not expressly exclude judgments in respect of tax claims. However, *Dicey and Morris*[196] comment that 'it seems safe to conclude that [such a judgment] would not be enforced under the 1920 Act, either because it would be contrary to public policy or because the court would exercise its discretion not to register the judgment'.[197]

An application for a grant of probate or letters of administration may fail if it is made for the purpose of remitting funds to pay foreign tax.[198]

The position as stated in the previous paragraphs represents the law before the introduction of legislation on money laundering and proceeds of crime. (See discussion below.) The application of this legislation to overseas tax evasion (combined with other initiatives, for example by the OECD) reflects a sea change in attitudes. It remains to be seen whether, in the new climate, English courts will be more responsive to the idea of modifying the effect of the traditional rule—in particular, by authorizing or even ordering the payment of a foreign tax in cases where trustees have incurred legal responsibility for the payment in the foreign state.

---

[191] See further *Dicey and Morris*, 5-028.

[192] See paras 42.61–42.62 below, discussing *Re Lord Cable, Decd; Garratt and Others v Walters and Others* [1977] 1 WLR 7, and para 42.61 below, discussing *Re Reid* (1970) 17 DLR (3d) 199.

[193] See Sections A and B of this chapter.   [194] See para 42.56 below.

[195] Section 1 (2).   [196] At 14. 164.

[197] But query whether this conclusion needs to be reviewed in the light of the Proceeds of Crime Act 2002 discussed at para 42.54 below.

[198] This is on the basis of two overseas authorities, *Bath v British and Malaysian Trustees Ltd and the Trustees Executors and Agency Company Ltd* (1969) 90 WN 9 NSW 44; *Clapham v Le Mesurier* [1991] JLR 5.

Limitations on the scope of the non-enforceability rule

Judicial limitations

42.53 Although the non-enforceability rule extends to indirect enforcement, the expression 'indirect' has been held[199] not to extend to the oral examination of witnesses in England under the Evidence (Proceedings in Other Jurisdictions) Act 1975 for the purpose of obtaining information relevant to the assessment of tax in Norway.

Courts have sometimes, but not always, declined to apply the rule in an insolvency context where the liquidator or trustee in bankruptcy is seeking recovery for the benefit of a foreign revenue authority.[200]

Limitations under domestic and international legislation

42.54 (a) **Legislation relating to criminal proceedings and money laundering.** Inroads into the non-enforceability principle have been made, for example, in legislation relating to mutual assistance in criminal matters. Thus, in *R v Chief Metropolitan Stipendiary Magistrate, ex parte Secretary of State for the Home Department*[201] the court held that the doctrine did not prevent the extradition of a person for an offence arising from tax evasion, if the offence was an extradition crime under the Extradition Act 1870.

More recently Part 5 of the Proceeds of Crime Act 2002 (in force since 30 December 2002) introduced provisions for (*inter alia*) recovery in civil proceedings of the proceeds of crime which are not limited to acts in the UK. A recovery order may be obtained against trustees in respect of property which they have 'obtained through unlawful conduct'. Unlawful conduct is defined to include conduct which:

(a) occurs in a country outside the UK and is unlawful under the criminal law of that country, and
(b) if it occurred in a part of theUK, would be unlawful under the criminal law of that part.

The precise operation of Part 5 in a trust context remains to be determined. Plainly recovery action could well prove successful where the placing of property

---

[199] *Re State of Norway's Application; Re State of Norway's Application (No 2)* [1990] 1 AC 723. See also, in the Isle of Man, *Re the Attorney-General of the Isle of Man* (1997/1998) 1 OFLR 419.

[200] See *Buchanan v McVey* [1954] IR 89, [1955] AC 516n; *Ayres v Evans* (1981) 39 ALR 129; *Priestly v Clegg* (1985) (3) SA 950; *Le Marquand and Backhurst v Chilmead Ltd (in Liquidation)* [1987–88] JLR 86, Butterworths Offshore Cases vol 1, 507; *QRS 1 Aps and Others v Frandsen* [1999] STC 616. For discussion of these cases see *Baker*, 34-4–34-8, and *Sly and Glasson in Glasson*, B2.11*et seq*. Insolvency cases may also turn on the interpretation of statutory provisions—see para 42.55 below. [201] [1989] 1 All ER 151.

in a trust was, or was associated with, overseas criminal tax evasion. If the placing of assets into trust was not *ipso facto* unlawful within the definition, then the application of Part 5 in respect of undischarged overseas tax liabilities imposed on trustees *after* the creation of the trust may be less clear. Relevant to this issue is the meaning which the courts decide to give to section 242(1) which provides that '[a] person obtains property through unlawful conduct (whether his own conduct or another's) if he obtains property by or *in return* for the conduct' (emphasis added).

By way of more general observation, the widespread promulgation of anti-money laundering legislation, full treatment of which is beyond the scope of this chapter, should be carefully considered by trustees in a tax liability context.

In the UK the Criminal Justice Act 1993 introduced to the UK 'all crimes' money laundering legislation for the first time, thus making it an offence to assist in the retention or disposal of the proceeds of criminal conduct. Initially, there was debate over the extent to which these provisions extended to the proceeds of foreign tax crime. Nowadays, however, it is generally accepted that foreign tax evasion is covered. The 1993 Act must now be read in conjunction with the Proceeds of Crime Act 2002 (discussed above in relation to Part 5).

All crimes money laundering legislation has also now been introduced in a large number of overseas jurisdictions, including many offshore financial centres. In most of these jurisdictions, the legislation extends to foreign fiscal crime.

In consequence of these developments trustees everywhere now need to take adequate precautions to protect themselves from criminal liability in all relevant jurisdictions including liability arising from tax offences.

(b) Insolvency legislation. Insolvency legislation (although normally outside of the scope of this chapter) may sometimes have an impact or alleged impact on the operation of the non-enforceability principle in situations where recovery is being sought for the benefit of a foreign revenue authority.[202] **42.55**

(c) European Directives on Assistance and Recovery. The Mutual Assistance Directive[203] lays down specific rules for collaboration between member states with regard to exchange of information and other assistance in relation to taxation matters.[204] **42.56**

---

[202] See (a) cases on the now repealed s 122 of the Bankruptcy Act 1914, (b) the Insolvency Act 1986, s 426, and (c) the Regulation on Insolvency Proceedings (EC) 1346/2000, [2000] OJ L160/1. For further information and discussion, see *Baker*, and *Sly and Glasson in Glasson*.

[203] Directive (EEC) 77/799, [1977] OJ L336/15.

[204] For an example of this Directive's application, see Case C–20/98 *WN v Staatssecretaris van Financien* [2000] ECR I–2847.

The Mutual Assistance and Recovery Directive[205] makes a major inroad into the non-enforceability principle by providing (in relation to certain taxes) that, where recovery of a debt by a taxation authority in one member state is unsuccessful, that authority can request another member state to attempt recovery if the debtor resides or has assets there.

42.57   **(d) OECD/EC Multilateral Convention on Mutual Assistance (1988).**   The OECD/Council of Europe Multilateral Convention on Mutual Administrative Assistance in Tax Matters extends the powers of co-operation between those countries that ratify it. It has so far not been ratified by the UK.

42.58   **(e) Double tax conventions.**   Double tax conventions between individual countries usually include provision for mutual assistance in relation to tax claims including, in some cases, tax recovery.[206]

When trustees can, or should, provide funds to discharge a non-enforceable foreign tax

42.59   This section considers situations in which trustees may be authorized or obliged to discharge a foreign tax in the absence of any express power so to do in the trust instrument. (Note, however, that if the trust instrument does contain a power to discharge foreign taxes, this section does not automatically cease to be relevant— see paragraph 42.66 below.)

Payment required to achieve a fair and proper administration

42.60   If executors or trustees in jurisdiction A fail to pay tax due in jurisdiction B, the revenue authorities in jurisdiction B may have power to enforce payment of the whole amount due against beneficiaries or assets in jurisdiction B, possibly leaving the beneficiaries resident in jurisdiction B bearing an unfair proportion of the tax. Judicial decisions in Scotland and New York[207] suggest that the courts recognize as a general principle that executors (and by analogy trustees) have a duty to pay foreign taxes if unfairness of this kind would otherwise result and if payment would be consistent with the intention or presumed intention of the testator (or settlor).[208]

---

[205] Directive (EEC) 76/308, [1976] OJ L73/18 as substantially extended by Directive (EC) 2001/44, [2001] OJ L175/17. In relation to the application of the Directive in the UK see also Finance Act 2002, s 134 and sch 39. Inheritance tax is, it is thought, outside the scope of the Directive as presently worded.

[206] See further *Baker*, 34-66–34-68.

[207] *Scottish National Orchestra Society Ltd v Thomson's Executor* 1969 SLT 325; *In Re Hollins* 139 NYS 713 (Surr Ct NY Co 1913). See also the Jersey decision *Re Marc Bolan Charitable Trust* [1981] JJ 117 where payment of UK taxes was authorized by the court on grounds that it benefited the UK resident beneficiaries of the trust.

[208] Compare the South African decision, *Jones v Borland* 1969 (4) SA 29, where on the facts an intention for the tax to be paid was not presumed. See also the Jersey case *Re Sidney Walmesley (decd)* [1983] JJ 35 where, on the facts, the court refused to authorize payment.

However, it may be unwise for trustees to make payment without the sanction of the court. In a decision in 1984[209] a Canadian court refused to allow payment of UK inheritance tax despite the fact that enforcement by the Capital Taxes Office against UK assets would have wiped out the entitlement of the UK resident charitable beneficiary.[210]

Payment where liability can be enforced in a foreign jurisdiction

A well-established principle of trust law[211] is that a trustee is entitled to be indemnified from the trust fund for liabilities which he has properly incurred in the administration of the trust. This raises the question of whether, and if so in what circumstances, trustees can rely on this principle in order to pay from the trust fund a foreign tax which is unenforceable against them in their home jurisdiction, but which they nonetheless find themselves obliged to pay. There are no clearly established guidelines[212] and in most cases the trustee will be best advised to seek the directions of the court. The court might be expected to look sympathetically at a trustee's plight if there is no fault on his part. However, this sympathy might be lost if enforcement has been triggered by the trustee's own conduct, for instance if he has invested in property in the foreign jurisdiction against which enforcement action can be taken or if he allows himself to be served with proceedings by visiting the jurisdiction. **42.61**

A situation in which an executor or trustee might reasonably expect a sympathetic hearing is where he is charged with the administration of an estate or trust fund which is located partly in one jurisdiction and partly in another. Whether this expectation is justified is uncertain. Canadian cases point in opposite directions.

In *Re Reid*[213] the British Columbia Court of Appeal permitted a UK executor company, which had been compelled to pay UK estate duty to a value greater than that of the UK assets, to reimburse itself out of Canadian assets. But in *Stringham v Dubois*[214] the Alberta Court of Appeal declined to follow *Re Reid*, and refused to allow a US executor to sell Canadian property in order to pay US estate taxes due in respect of the estate of a US domiciliary, even though the US executor could apparently be liable for the estate tax in any event.

The English case, *Re Lord Cable*,[215] which concerned, in part, remission of funds from England to meet Indian tax liabilities, is consistent with *Re Reid*, although in

---

[209] *Re Fudger* (1984) 18 ETR 12 (Ontario Supreme Court).

[210] *Re Fudger* is arguably distinguishable on its facts from the Scottish and New York authorities. See discussion in *Sly and Glasson in Glasson*.

[211] Currently given statutory force by the Trustee Act 2000, s 31.

[212] Although trustee exposure to liability is usually regarded by the courts as an important factor. See *Re Lord Cable* [1977] 1 WLR 7; *Re Marc Bolan Charitable Trust* [1981] JJ 117; *Re Sidney Walmesley (decd)* [1983] JJ 35; *Balkin v Peck* [1998] NSW SC 337; cf *Stringham v Dubois* [1993] 3 WWR 273; *Air India v Caribjet* [2002] 2 All ER (Cm) 76.   [213] (1970) 17 DLR (3d) 199.

[214] [1993] 3 WWR 273.   [215] [1977] 1 WLR 7. See also *Balkin v Peck* [1998] NSW SC 337.

Cable an additional consideration was that the trust in question was governed by Indian law.

All the foregoing should now be read in the context of the comment made earlier that, in the light of current attitudes to money laundering and OECD (and similar) initiatives, English courts will possibly be more willing to consider authorizing or ordering the payment by trustees of a non-enforceable foreign tax.

Tax paid under legislation forming part of the proper law of the trust

42.62   *Re Lord Cable,*[216] supports the proposition that a trustee is entitled to pay a particular state's taxes if the law of that state is also the law governing the trust (although, as mentioned in the previous paragraph, this was not the sole consideration).

Tax paid under a dispositive power to benefit a beneficiary

42.63   There are occasions when it would be appropriate to use a dispositive power either to pay a foreign tax or to enable a beneficiary so to do. Take, for example, a discretionary trust which is administered in the Isle of Man, but which has UK resident beneficiaries and a UK domiciled settlor. Distributions out of the trust are potentially subject to UK inheritance tax. If the trustees wish to make a distribution to a UK beneficiary of a sum net of tax, they can achieve this by fixing the distribution at such an amount as will leave the beneficiary with that sum after the tax has been paid (whether payment is made by the trustees or by the beneficiary). There can hardly be doubt, in the authors' view, that this is a proper exercise of a dispositive power in favour of that beneficiary notwithstanding that the UK Inland Revenue also benefits.

Payment by trustees to indemnify settlor

42.64   Under UK tax legislation a settlor of a non-resident trust may be personally liable to tax in respect of the income and gains of the trust. The relevant taxing legislation does, however, give the settlor a statutory right of reimbursement by the foreign trustees.[217] Although the settlor may be able to obtain judgment in the UK in respect of the indemnity,[218] enforceability against overseas trustees is uncertain. This may turn on the proper law of the settlement. If the proper law is English, the overseas court may accept the argument that the right of indemnity, being granted by an English statute, is enforceable notwithstanding that this might otherwise appear to be the indirect enforcement of a foreign revenue claim.[219] It might also

---

[216] [1977] 1 WLR 7.

[217] See, for example, Income and Corporation Taxes Act 1988, s 660D and Taxation of Chargeable Gains Act 1992, sch 5, para 6.

[218] See *Prestwich v Royal Bank of Canada Trust Company (Jersey) Limited* (1998/99) 1 ITLR 565 (also noted at (1998) 1 ITELR 671) where the court accepted jurisdiction in respect of a claim for indemnity by a UK settlor against a Jersey trustee.

[219] cf *Re Lord Cable* [1977] 1 WLR 7.

be possible to argue (irrespective of the governing law) that the settlor's reimbursement claim concerns not the direct or indirect enforcement of tax, but merely the incidence of tax already paid.[220] These arguments were accepted in a Guernsey case, *Kleinwort Benson (Guernsey) Trustees Ltd v Wilson.*[221]

The question of enforceability of the statutory right of reimbursement against Jersey trustees was expressly left open by the Jersey Royal Court in *Re Colin Douglas 1990 Settlement.*[222]

Tax paid for the benefit or protection of trust property

If trustees properly acquire property in a particular jurisdiction by way of investment, or for use or occupation by a beneficiary, there is unlikely, in the authors' view, to be an objection to the payment of taxes and other fiscal liabilities relating to the property if payment is necessary to prevent enforcement action against the property.   **42.65**

Express powers to pay foreign taxes

In light of the problems that can arise for trustees faced with a foreign tax claim, it is not unusual to see in a trust instrument an express power to pay foreign taxes. Such a power may be fiduciary, in the sense that it must be exercised solely for the benefit of some or all of the beneficiaries, or it may be intended for the protection of the trustees from personal liability for fiscal claims (or partly one and partly the other).   **42.66**

The nature and scope of the power in any particular case is of course a matter for construction of the trust instrument.[223] In practice it is rare to see the question of the power's fiduciary status expressly addressed in the power itself. One is therefore left to make inferences from the wording of the clause and the context in which it appears. Typically, the power is contained among the administrative powers of the trust instrument. But this may not be a conclusive indication of fiduciary intent because the 'administrative' schedule to a trust instrument often extends to trustee protection provisions.

Interpreting the scope of the power is further complicated if, as is usual, the power includes a provision permitting trustees to pay a foreign tax irrespective of whether payment will be to the disadvantage of any of the beneficiaries. At first

---

[220] See discussion of this argument in *Lewin*, 21-12A.
[221] (2003) 17 Trust Law International, 198. The case concerned two English law settlements. *Air India v Caribjet* [2002] 2 All ER (Comm) 76 provides further support for the 'incidence' argument.
[222] (2000) 2 ITELR 682. In *Re T's Settlement* (2002) 41 ITELR 820 the Jersey court expressed some doubt as to whether it could give effect to the statutory right of reimbursement.
[223] Also to be considered, if the power is intended to be exercisable for the protection of the trustees, is whether a power of this nature is permissible under the governing law of the trust, and whether any necessary requirements of that law (eg as to obtaining the settlor's informed consent) have been complied with.

glance this seems wide enough to entitle the trustees to use the power for their own protection. However, as it seems to the authors, such a provision is consistent with the purpose being merely to permit trustees to deal with the kind of situation arising in the Scottish and New York decisions[224] discussed above.[225] That is to say, the power is to be exercised solely to ensure a fair and proper administration as between the beneficiaries, even though one or more beneficiaries might be disadvantaged. In both the Scottish and New York cases the executors were discharging a fiduciary responsibility rather than acting in their own interests.[226]

To the extent that, on a proper construction, the power is fiduciary then paragraphs 42.59 to 42.65 above remain relevant.

---

[224] *Scottish National Orchestra Society Ltd v Thomson's Executor* 1969 SLT 325; *In Re Hollins* 139 NYS 713 (Surr Ct NY Co 1913).

[225] At para 42.60 above.

[226] Observations by the Barbados Court of Appeal in *Bank of Nova Scotia v Tremblay* (1998/99) 1 ITELR 673, 690–692 lend support to the view expressed in this paragraph.

Part H

OCCUPATIONAL PENSION SCHEME TRUSTS

43

NATURE AND STRUCTURE OF OCCUPATIONAL PENSION SCHEME TRUSTS

A. Introduction

Occupational pension schemes represent an important economic and social force **43.01** in the UK. In 1998, the Government estimated the financial assets in occupational pension schemes to be worth £640 billion.[1] This makes occupational pension scheme trustees one of the largest institutional investors in the UK. In addition, the financial importance of occupational pension schemes is matched by their social importance as they represent one of the largest assets many people own.

The importance of occupational pension schemes has resulted in increasing **43.02** attention being paid to them by successive governments and a growing volume of legislation, largely designed to protect the interests of scheme beneficiaries.

---

[1] *New Contract for Welfare Partnerships in Pensions,* DSS Green Paper (1998), Chapter 2, para 21 (Cm 4179).

This means that although they are based on the classic trust model discussed elsewhere in this book, it is no longer possible to analyse the rights and duties of the parties to an occupational pension scheme solely in terms of trust law, as in many areas legislation has made the trust provisions largely redundant.

43.03 The increase in statutory obligations for both employer and trustees needs to be viewed in the context of occupational pension provision being a voluntary benefit provided by employers. The compliance issues created by the large volume of pensions legislation give rise to cost issues and, as a result, an increasing number of occupational pension schemes are being closed to new members or wound up.

43.04 This chapter looks at the key legislative provisions which govern occupational pension schemes as at 1 December 2003 and how they interact with trust law. However, at the date of writing, the law is undergoing substantial review, partly with the aim of simplifying the existing legislative regime and partly to increase the security of scheme beneficiaries. A new Pensions Act is expected as a result. In addition, the tax framework for occupational pension schemes is also under review. Therefore, within the next few years, it is likely that the law discussed below will have undergone significant change and, to reflect this, the key proposals are also discussed.

B. Structure of UK Pension Provision

43.05 Before considering the legal regime for occupational pension schemes in detail, it is useful to understand the general pensions framework in the UK. There are three tiers of pension provision:

(a) Basic state pension, which with effect from 6 October 2003 has been supplemented by a two tier pension credit. The basic or old-age pension is a flat-rate pension payable at state pension age, (currently 65 for a man and 60 for a woman but to be equalized at age 65 over a ten-year period starting on 6 April 2010). The full basic state pension is payable to those who have a full record of National Insurance contributions and, for those who do not, it is reduced pro rata.[2] The Pension Credit has two basic components: (i) the guarantee credit which provides a guaranteed income level for those aged 60 or over; and (ii) the savings credit which gives pensioners over age 65 around sixty pence for every pound of income they have from pensions and other savings above a threshold level (up to prescribed limits).[3]

---

[2] Social Security Benefits and Contributions Act 1992 and for the 2003/4 rates see the Social Security Benefits Up-rating Order 2003, SI 2003/526.

[3] State Pension Credit Act 2002 and State Pension Credit Regulations 2002, SI 2002/1792.

(b) On top of the basic pension, there is a supplementary state pension which is linked to an individual's earnings. Up until 6 April 2002 this was the State Earnings Related Pension Scheme, or SERPS. The way SERPS is calculated is extremely complex, but in simplified terms it is based on an individual's career average earnings between two points: a lower earnings limit and an upper earnings limit[4] (band earnings). The annual SERPS benefit is a fraction of revalued band earnings, the fraction varying depending on the individual's age and National Insurance contributions record.

From 6 April 2002, SERPS was replaced with the state second pension. The basic aim of the state second pension is to ensure that limited state resources are spent on those who need them most rather than providing better benefits for higher earners. The calculation of state second pension is even more complex than SERPS with three different rates of accrual, lower earners benefiting from higher rates of accrual.[5] The lowest state second pension accrual rate is the same as the SERPS accrual rate.

(c) Private pension schemes including personal and occupational pension schemes. If private pension arrangements comply with certain requirements, notably limits on benefits and contributions, they can apply to the Inland Revenue for exempt approval (see below), which if granted means that both contributions and investments can benefit from valuable tax concessions.

Many occupational pension schemes have benefit designs which take the two tiers **43.06** of state pension benefits into account and aim to provide members with an overall benefits package, for example it is not unusual for occupational pension schemes to contain an earnings offset to reflect the element of income perceived to be pensioned through basic state pension. In addition, membership of the state second pension arrangement is optional; it is possible to 'contract-out' of this tier of state benefits provided that specified alternative pension arrangements are made through either a personal or occupational scheme (see below).

C. Types of Occupational Pension Scheme

There are two main types of occupational pension scheme and the legislative pro- **43.07** visions applicable differ depending on which type of scheme is being considered. This section considers those two main types; however, there are others and, in the future, these other types may become more common.

---

[4] The 2003/4 levels of the lower and upper earnings limits are set out in the Social Security (Contributions) (Amendment) Order 2003, SI 2003/193 and the weekly rates are £77 and £595 respectively.

[5] Sections 33–35 of the Child Support, Pensions and Social Security Act 2000 which amend the Social Security Contributions and Benefits Act 1992. In the medium term, it is proposed to replace the current arrangement with a flat rate benefit.

Final salary/defined benefit schemes

43.08   Final salary or defined benefit schemes provide benefits on retirement based on the member's salary at or near retirement and the number of years he has worked. A typical formula for calculation of pension might be: *1/60th x final pensionable salary x number of years' pensionable service*. There is a considerable amount of flexibility as to what constitutes pensionable salary. For example, it might include bonuses or be restricted to basic salary. It could be salary in the year immediately prior to retirement or salary averaged over a three-year period or the best three-year period ending in the last ten.[6] Trustees need to be aware of the benefits which their scheme provides as they are responsible for ensuring they are paid out in a correct manner.

43.09   The major advantage of a final salary scheme to a beneficiary is the relative certainty of the level of benefits he will receive depending on pensionable salary at retirement and the number of years' pensionable service (assuming the continued solvency of the employer). For an employee who moves jobs frequently, a final salary scheme may not be so advantageous as if he leaves before completing two years' service he will only be entitled to a return of his own contributions. If he leaves after two years, he has the option to transfer his accrued benefits to another scheme, but the transfer value may not represent a good return on his investment, or he can leave his benefits in his former employer's scheme as deferred benefits to be taken at retirement but there is a chance that their value may not have kept pace with inflation.

43.10   For the employer, the difficulty with final salary schemes is their unpredictability. Costs will vary depending upon a number of fluctuating elements such as the investment return on the scheme's assets and increases in the pay of the scheme members. The employees' contributions are fixed so it is the employer who meets the balance of such costs. The employer will also usually meet the costs of running the scheme. In addition, as will be seen, the legislative regime applicable to final salary schemes is considerably more complex than that for money purchase schemes.

Money purchase/defined contribution schemes

43.11   In a money purchase or defined contribution scheme the fixed element is not the emerging benefit but rather the level of contributions payable by employer and employee. A money purchase scheme is therefore more closely equivalent to a conventional savings plan (albeit with generous tax reliefs) and to a personal pension plan.

43.12   The member's pension is dependent upon the level of contributions paid into the scheme, the return achieved on those contributions when invested, and whatever

---

6   Practice Notes on the Approval of Occupational Pension Schemes, IR 12 (2001), definition of 'Remuneration'.

the aggregate amount will secure by way of pension at the time the member retires. This last element will depend upon the annuity rates in force at the relevant time as the member's money purchase account must be used to purchase an annuity.[7]

For the employee, there is no certainty of benefit and they bear the investment risk, so, if the value of investments falls, the fund available to purchase an annuity will shrink. However, such a scheme is conceptually simpler than a final salary scheme and it can therefore be perceived as being more attractive. Many schemes also offer investment options to the scheme members so they can have a degree of control over their benefits. Finally, money purchase benefits are often said to be more advantageous for mobile employees as early leavers can simply transfer their accumulated fund to a new scheme rather than be dependent on the level of a transfer payment determined by the trustees.   **43.13**

For the employer, the major advantage of this type of scheme is financial certainty, contributions are fixed and there is no issue of having to fund a particular level of benefits. In addition, the legislative regime is simpler. Such a scheme is easier to explain to the workforce and the running costs are lower than those of a final salary scheme. However, in the longer term, particularly for a more stable and mature workforce, a money purchase scheme rarely provides as good a benefit as that provided by a final salary scheme.   **43.14**

Contracted-out schemes

Both final salary and money purchase occupational schemes may be contracted-out of SERPS and the state second pension arrangements.   **43.15**

At retirement, an employee will normally receive both the basic old age pension and a SERPS/state second pension together with a supplementary pension from any occupational or personal pension scheme of which he is a member. However, if an individual is in a contracted-out occupational pension scheme, his SERPS/state second pension entitlement will be reduced. For service up to April 2002, an individual will only receive the basic state old-age pension for periods of contracted-out service. The occupational pension scheme replaces SERPS/state second pension and the scheme receives a rebate of employee and employer National Insurance contributions. However from April 2002, employees contracted-out of the state second pension via an occupational pension scheme will receive a state second pension top-up if they earn less than a specified amount.[8] This is because   **43.16**

---

[7] Purchase of an annuity can be deferred up to age 75 and the member can, with the consent of the trustees, elect to receive a pension in the form of income drawdown. If a decision is made to use this flexibility it is the trustees' responsibility to ensure that any necessary rule amendments are made and issue relevant announcements to the scheme members. IR 12 (2001) (n 6 above), Appendix XII.

[8] Child Support, Pensions and Social Security Act 2000, Sch 4 and is £25,600 at the date of writing.

the National Insurance rebates paid in respect of contracted-out employees continue to reflect the rate that benefits would have accrued under SERPS and therefore, without a top-up, lower earning employees benefiting from the enhanced state second pension accrual rates would be worse off in a contracted-out scheme.

43.17 Contracting-out is extremely complex and is chief among the Government's current targets for simplification.[9] In general terms, if a contracted-out occupational pension scheme is a final salary scheme, for the period up to 6 April 1997 it has to guarantee that the scheme will be able to provide a pension (loosely) equivalent to an employee's foregone SERPS entitlement. This element of pension is called the Guaranteed Minimum Pension ('GMP'). Because GMPs are based on SERPS, they are calculated by reference to the different state retirement ages for men and women. It has therefore been claimed that they are discriminatory on grounds of sex. The Pensions Ombudsman has supported this view[10] and required a scheme to equalize GMPs (although he failed to give any direction as to how this might be achieved). His determination was overturned on appeal but, unfortunately, the decision was based on the Ombudsman's lack of jurisdiction rather than the substantive issue.[11] The issue may therefore be raised again and, in the meantime, trustees whose schemes have GMPs need to be aware of the potential sex discrimination issues. The Government is aware of this issue but, in the passage of the Pensions Act 1995 through Parliament, it was decided that, although there 'can be no doubt that equality must be provided in the overall rate of pensions accrued since 1990...we have concluded that contracted-out salary-related schemes should have the freedom and flexibility to make their own arrangements as to how that should be achieved, rather than having arrangements imposed on them by government'.[12] Unfortunately there is no clearly correct way of achieving this so the Government's stance leaves trustees exposed whatever they resolve to do.

43.18 Fortunately, this problem does not arise in respect of service after 6 April 1997 when the test for contracted-out salary related schemes was changed (partly to resolve this issue going forward). Now the benefits provided in such schemes must be at least broadly equivalent to a package of benefits laid down in legislation. This is known as the reference scheme test, because the scheme actuary has to certify that pensions provided by the scheme are at least broadly equivalent to the pensions provided under a hypothetical reference scheme. A scheme will fail the test if the pensions of more than 10 per cent of its employees or their spouses are not broadly equivalent to the reference scheme benefits. In broad terms, the 'reference

---

[9] *Simplicity, Security and Choice: Working and Saving For Retirement–Action on Occupational Pensions* (Cm 5835), Ch 3 paras 23–26   [10] Determination H00177.
[11] *Marsh & McLennan Companies UK Ltd v Pensions Ombudsman* [2001] OPLR 221.
[12] *Per* Lord Mackay of Ardbrecknish, *Hansard*, HL (series 55) vol 562, col 703 (13 March 1995).

scheme' provides a pension of one-eightieth of 90 per cent of the member's average earnings between the upper and lower earnings limits for each year of service, with a spouse's pension of half that amount.[13]

Occupational pension schemes can also be contracted-out on a money purchase **43.19** basis. The National Insurance rebate in respect of those employees in contracted-out money purchase schemes is age related. This is partly because the Government did not want individuals who contracted-out of SERPS/state second pension when they were younger to contract-in again when they were older because the SERPS/state second pension benefit had become more valuable than the rebate. If the contracted-out benefits are in money purchase form, the scheme does not guarantee any particular level of benefits, instead it must guarantee that a basic minimum level of contributions will be paid to the trustees of the scheme. The minimum contribution is equal to the amount the employee and employer save in National Insurance contributions by being contracted-out of SERPS/state second pension. These contributions, once invested in the private scheme, provide 'protected rights' for the member.

Where a scheme is contracted-out, the trustees must comply with a variety of **43.20** additional requirements to ensure the scheme can remain contracted-out, in particular there are detailed requirements to supply information to the Inland Revenue and to ensure that the scheme provides the benefits which contracting-out requires.[14] Both the trustees and the employer must sign the election to contract-out, so the trustees must be satisfied the scheme meets the requirements for contracting-out.[15]

D. Taxation

Legislative framework

If an occupational pension scheme is to enjoy the favourable tax treatment avail- **43.21** able it must obtain exempt approval from the Inland Revenue.

Exempt approval can be either automatic or discretionary. If a scheme complies **43.22** with the stringent requirements in the Income and Corporation Taxes Act 1988 ('ICTA'), section 590, it qualifies for automatic tax approval by the Inland Revenue. However, in practice, the requirements of section 590 are so prescriptive

---

[13] Pension Schemes Act 1993, s 12A as amended by Pensions Act 1995, s 136.

[14] Pension Schemes Act 1993, Pt III and the Occupational Pension Schemes (Contracting-out) Regulations 1997, SI 1996/1172.

[15] Contracted-out Guidance for Salary Related Pension Schemes and Salary Related Overseas Schemes CA14C and Contracted-out Guidance for Money Purchase Pension Schemes and Money Purchase Overseas Schemes CA14D.

it is never used and schemes instead rely on the Inland Revenue's discretionary ability to give tax approval contained in section 591. Detailed guidance on the manner in which the Inland Revenue will exercise this discretion and the things it will expect from a scheme are contained in guidance notes issued by the Inland Revenue.[16]

43.23 An application for tax approval must be made by the scheme trustees.[17] Once approval has been granted, the scheme administrator for tax purposes (which is almost always the scheme trustees[18]) is under a variety of obligations in relation to the scheme if approval is to be maintained. Chief among these obligations is a requirement to disclose various events to the Inland Revenue so they can monitor continued compliance with Revenue requirements. The trustees used to have to enter into an undertaking with the Revenue that they would comply with these requirements, but now the requirements have for the most part been included in regulations[19] and trustees are liable to fines if they fail to comply.

Tax relief

43.24 The advantages of tax approval are such that almost all schemes are set up with a view to obtaining it and consequently to satisfying Inland Revenue requirements (the exception is those schemes which are set up to provide higher paid employees with benefits above the limits permitted by the Inland Revenue).

43.25 If an occupational pension scheme obtains tax approval, the employer's contributions to it are tax deductible. In addition, there is no benefit in kind tax charge on the employee in respect of the employer's contributions and the employee's own contributions are deducted from his gross income and so also enjoy tax relief.[20]

43.26 Once money is in the scheme, investment returns are fully tax free (provided that the scheme is not doing anything that the Revenue interprets as trading as the proceeds of trading activities would be taxable).[21]

Tax treatment of benefits

43.27 Generally speaking, because tax relief is given on the money paid into an occupational pension scheme, money coming out is subject to tax. Pension is treated as

---

[16] Practice Notes on the Approval of Occupational Pension Schemes, IR12 (2001).

[17] ICTA 1988, s 604 (as amended by Finance Act 1998, Sch 15, para 3) and IR12 (2001), PN 16.3.

[18] ICTA 1988, s 611AA (as amended by Finance Act 1994, s 103(1)) provides the definition of administrator.

[19] The Retirement Benefit Schemes (Information Powers) Regulations 1995, SI 1995/3103 as amended by The Retirement Benefits Schemes (Information Powers) (Amendment) Regulations 2002, SI 2002/3006. [20] ICTA 1988, s 593.

[21] The exemption is provided under ICTA 1988, s 592. For an example of what can constitute 'trade' see *Clark v British Telecom Pension Scheme Trustees* [2000] OPLR 53.

the income of the recipient and is taxable at the marginal rates applicable to the individual. A member who leaves scheme membership with less than two years' pensionable service, and who is therefore entitled to a refund of his own contributions to the scheme rather than a pension, is liable to a 20 per cent tax charge[22] on the refund.

There are, however, payments from an occupational pension scheme which are not **43.28** generally subject to tax. A lump sum of up to four times the member's remuneration at the date of his death may be payable on death in service. Scheme documentation is always drafted to ensure that trustees have a discretion as to the recipient of this benefit, and this discretionary element means that the benefit does not form part of the deceased member's estate, and is not therefore subject to Inheritance Tax. It is tax-free in the hands of the recipient.[23] In addition, on retirement a scheme member may 'commute' part of his pension. This means that he will receive a lump sum in exchange for taking a smaller pension. The lump sum is calculated on the basis of an Inland Revenue formula (the maximum being two and a quarter multiplied by the initial annual rate of pension), and is tax-free.[24]

Inland Revenue limits

The very generous tax regime means that the Revenue places strict limits on the **43.29** benefits that may be taken from and the contributions which can be paid to an exempt approved scheme. The form of these limits dictates the form of benefits provided by occupational pension schemes. Failure to comply with these limits can result in withdrawal of Revenue approval, and accordingly the scheme trustees need to ensure that benefits and contributions are within these limits.

Limits on contributions

It is a condition of approval that the employer must contribute to the scheme, but **43.30** there are generally no upper limits on the contributions an employer may pay into the scheme for the benefit of his employees.

A member's contributions to an occupational pension scheme are generally **43.31** restricted to a maximum of 15 per cent of annual remuneration (see below for limits on remuneration). That maximum relates to aggregate contributions to all schemes of which an individual may be a member. However, members who earn below a certain threshold[25] may also (subject to certain conditions) be able to join personal pension schemes (including stakeholder schemes) and contribute up to £3,600 a year, regardless of how much they are paying into their occupational pension scheme.[26]

---

[22] ICTA 1988, s 598.   [23] IR12 (2001) PN 11.2.   [24] ibid, PN 8.7.
[25] ibid, s 632B(4) (as amended by Finance Act 2000, Sch 13, Pt I, para 8), currently £30,000.
[26] ibid and The Personal Pension Schemes (Concurrent Membership) Order 2000, SI 2000/2318.

43.32   An occupational money purchase scheme can make a one-off election for the personal pension tax regime to apply to it.[27] Maximum contributions to a personal pension plan (including stakeholder schemes) are determined on a sliding scale depending on the member's age. The scale starts at 17.5 per cent of remuneration and rises to a maximum of 40 per cent for the age band 61–74[28] (these limits apply to aggregate contributions from employers and employees). In addition, from 6 April 2001 a member has been able to contribute up to £3,600 a year to a personal pension plan regardless of earnings.

Limits on benefits

43.33   Broadly speaking, the maximum pension a member may take on retirement is two-thirds of his final remuneration (see below for limits on remuneration) and there are limits on how fast this pension can be earned. The maximum pension a member's spouse or dependant may receive after the member's death is two-thirds of the member's pension. The maximum lump sum that may be payable on a member's death in service is four times his total remuneration at the date of death.[29]

43.34   The earliest a member can take his benefits unless he is retiring on grounds of ill health is age 50 (although this will of course depend on what the scheme rules provide) and the latest (irrespective of whether the member remains in employment) is age 75.[30]

Limits on remuneration

43.35   The most significant limit on remuneration for pension purposes is the earnings cap which was introduced in the Finance Act 1989. This limits the amount of salary that can be treated as pensionable when calculating maximum benefits and employee contributions. For 2003/04 the earnings cap is set at £99,000,[31] and (usually) increases each year in line with the increase in the retail prices index.

43.36   The cap is a particular problem for high earners when moving jobs, especially if they have been in their existing job since before 1989 as in such cases the cap will not previously have applied to them. High earners in a strong bargaining position will negotiate top-up benefits in the form of unapproved arrangements to cushion them from some or all of the effect of the cap. As a result the cap has been criticized for contributing to senior executives being disinterested in occupational pension provision.

---

[27] ICTA 1988, s 631A (inserted by Finance Act 2000, Sch 13, Pt I, para 7).
[28] Inland Revenue Guidance Notes IR76 (2000) Personal Pension Schemes Guidance Notes (Including Stakeholder Pension Schemes), PN 4.4.
[29] IR12 (2001) PN 11.2.   [30] IR12 (2001), PN 6.1.
[31] The Retirement Benefit Schemes (Indexation of Earnings Cap) Order 2003, SI 2003/843.

The future of Inland Revenue limits

The requirements for discretionary approval are lengthy and complex and have **43.37** for many years dictated the form of the benefits provided by occupational pension schemes. So extensive are these provisions that the Pensions Law Review Committee observed that:

> because of the vacuum in the general law relating to pension schemes, tax legislation and Inland Revenue discretionary powers have been used to bring in matters of pension policy and not merely of fiscal policy. Thus the conditions of approval of schemes for the purpose of tax relief are made the vehicle for rules about funding and the segregation of assets, and restrictions on alienation of pensions, which should form part of the general law. In short, the tax tail wags the pensions dog . . . [32]

At the date of writing, an extensive review of the tax regime is being undertaken. **43.38** A consultation paper was published in December 2002 which advocated a radical simplification of the existing tax regime.[33] The key proposal was to replace the majority of the existing Inland Revenue limits with a single lifetime limit on the value of pension benefits which can be accrued of £1.4 million together with an annual limit on increases in value in a member's accrued pension benefits of £200,000.

E. Nature of the Pension Trust

This section looks at the structure of occupational pension schemes and the rela- **43.39** tionship of the parties to the pensions trust.

Trusts as a vehicle for occupational pension schemes

Occupational pension schemes are generally established under trust. There are **43.40** three reasons typically given for doing so:

(a) There has been a requirement since the Finance Act 1921 that, in order for a pension scheme to benefit from various tax reliefs associated with exempt approval, the assets of the scheme must be held separately from those of the sponsoring employer. This requirement is currently to be found in ICTA, section 592(1) which requires a scheme to be established under irrevocable trust in order for it to be exempt approved for tax purposes.[34]

---

[32] *Pension Law Reform: Pension Law Review Committee Report 1993* (Cm 2342), Volume 1, para 4.1.6.

[33] HM Treasury/Inland Revenue Consultation Document December 2002, Simplifying the Taxation of Pensions: Increasing Choice and Flexibility for All.

[34] For further guidance on what is required for exempt approval for occupational pension schemes see IR12(2001), PN 2.3–2.5.

(b) To protect the employees' accrued pension benefits from the sponsoring employer's creditors in the event of the employer's insolvency.

(c) Prior to the Contracts (Rights of Third Parties) Act 1999, to ensure that contingent beneficiaries such as spouses and children would be able to enforce any entitlement they have to benefits under the pension scheme in the event of the member's death.

43.41 Over the years there have been numerous criticisms of the suitability of trusts as a vehicle for occupational pension schemes. In 1992 the Field Report said:

> ... there is still too much flexibility within the [pensions] legal framework which could result in loss of benefits whether by innocent errors or by design. And yet for the majority of the population the 'ownership' of an occupational pension is second only in value to the ownership of their home ... While it is understandable that the growth in occupational pension schemes should have been piecemeal it is less understandable why the political parties have allowed a system of pension provision to arise for which the legal basis is medieval trust law. With the knowledge of hindsight, we believe that this has proved to be an error of major importance ... We believe that pension funds should be governed by laws analogous to those governing companies.[35]

43.42 This recommendation was not acted upon and the issue was considered again in 1993. On this occasion, the Pensions Law Review Committee observed that:

> ... trust law in itself is broadly satisfactory and should continue to provide the foundation for interests, rights and duties arising in relation to pension schemes. But some of the principles of trust law require modification in their application to pensions. In particular, some curbs need to be placed on the permissible content of scheme rules, especially in relation to certain of the powers that can be reserved to the employer and the trustees and the scope of exemptions given to trustees from liability for breach of duty. Trust law also requires statutory reinforcement in other ways. This is reflected in the growing volume of legislation enacted in recent times to strengthen the rights of scheme members and the duties of employers, trustees, auditors and actuaries.[36]

43.43 The effect of recommendations such as these is that there has been an ever increasing volume of pensions legislation aimed at regulating the rights and duties of the parties to the pensions trust and codifying some of the applicable trust law principles.

Relationship of parties

43.44 Lord Walker has observed that a family trust can be envisaged as a linear process where the settlor's bounty proceeds through the trustees to the beneficiaries.

---

[35] *Social Security Committee Second Report—The Operation of Pension Funds*, 4 March 1992, paras 7 and 8.
[36] *Pension Law Reform: Pension Law Review Committee Report 1993* (Cm 2342), vol 1, para 4.1.14.

A pensions trust is more aptly envisaged as a triangle with trustees at the apex and the employer and members at the bottom corners, linked to the trustees by fiduciary and contractual obligations. The relationship between employer and employee is based on the contract of employment and the mutual duties and responsibilities that are typically implied into that contract.[37] It has also been suggested that, at the heart of the classic trust model, there is a separation of the roles of trustee, settlor, and beneficiary, whereas in a pensions trust there is a blurring of these roles in so far as there is no strict segregation of the interests or even of the identities of each of the parties.[38]

Beneficiaries are not volunteers

It is often argued that principles of law derived from the context of private family **43.45** trusts should not apply to pension scheme beneficiaries because they are not 'volunteers'. This idea has been examined a number of times in pensions cases. In *Kerr v British Leyland (Staff) Trustees Ltd,*[39] involving an assertion that a claim for incapacity benefit had been wrongly rejected by the scheme trustees, Fox L J said that:

> The beneficiaries here are not volunteers. Their rights derive from contractual and commercial origins. They have purchased their rights as part of their employment. Consistently with that, the power of the trustee to decline acceptance of the claim cannot be simply an uncontrolled discretion. It seems to me that the duty of this trustee was to give properly informed consideration to the application.
>
> If the discretion were in a will or in a private settlement in favour of beneficiaries who were volunteers, the conclusion that the person on whom it was conferred owed no duty to the objects of it would not be startling. However, in deciding between a construction of the deed of 1983 [that is the relevant pension scheme] which would lead to a like conclusion and a construction of it leading to the conclusion that the employer did owe a duty to the objects of the discretion, one must in my view have regard to the fact that the beneficiaries under a pension scheme are not volunteers. As I pointed out earlier, their rights are derived from the contracts of employment of the members as well as from the trust instrument. Those rights have been earned by the service of the members under those contracts as well as by their contributions. I do not mean by that that, on some default by the trustees, a member would have an alternative right of action against the employer in contract for payment of the benefits due to him under the scheme. I mean only that, in construing the trust instrument, one must bear in mind as an important part of the background, the origin of the beneficiaries' rights under it.

The point was considered again in *Imperial Group Pension Trust Ltd v Imperial* **43.46** *Tobacco Ltd,*[40] which concerned the exercise of a power to increase benefits.

---

[37] R Walker, 'Some trust principles in the pensions context' [1996] PLR 107.

[38] M Milner, 'Pension Trusts: a new trust form?' (1997) 61 Conv 89.

[39] High Court, 26 March 1986 and cited with approval on this point in *Stannard v Fisons Pension Trust Ltd* [1991] PLR 225.   [40] [1991] 1 WLR 589.

In determining that an employer's power to withhold consent to benefit increases must be exercised in good faith, it was held that:

> Pension scheme trusts are of quite a different nature to traditional trusts. The traditional trust is one under which the settlor, by way of bounty, transfers property to trustees to be administered for the beneficiaries as objects of his bounty. Normally, there is no legal relationship between the parties apart from the trust. The beneficiaries have given no consideration for what they receive. The settlor, as donor, can impose such limits on his bounty as he chooses, including imposing a requirement that the consent of himself or some other person shall be required to the exercise of the powers.
> ...Pension benefits are part of the consideration which an employee receives in return for the rendering of his services. In many cases, including the present, membership of the pension scheme is a requirement of employment. In contributory schemes, such as this, the employee is himself bound to pay for his or her contributions. Beneficiaries of the scheme, the members, far from being volunteers have given valuable consideration. The company employer is not conferring a bounty. In my judgment, the scheme is established against the background of such employment and falls to be interpreted against that background.[41]

43.47 The conclusion to be drawn from these cases is that an occupational pension scheme member has a right to the benefits provided under the scheme; he has provided consideration for them in the form of his services to the employer. The practical result of this is that the exercise of any discretionary powers in occupational pension schemes by either employers or trustees must take into account the nature of the pensions trust and have due regard for the fact that the members have purchased their rights under it.

Relationship between beneficiaries and trustees

43.48 The relationship between pension scheme trustees and scheme beneficiaries can be more complex than the relationship between other forms of trustee and beneficiary as a result of duties imposed on trustees by the legislative requirements aimed at protecting members' benefits. These requirements are considered in the following chapters.

43.49 In addition, the relationship between pension scheme trustees and beneficiaries has on occasion been found to have a basis in contract as well as trust law. An illustration of this can be found in *Nicol and Andrew v Brinkley*.[42] This concerned an overgenerous statement of the pensionable service which would be provided on a transfer into a scheme. In upholding a determination of the Pensions Ombudsman,[43] the court held that:

> The transferring members were members of the new scheme [and] already entitled to benefits in respect of service after 1 September, 1987, when the letters inviting

---

[41] [1991] 1 WLR 597.   [42] [1996] OPLR 361.   [43] Determination B10084.

them to agree a transfer payment from the SUITS scheme in respect of service while members of that scheme were sent out. However, to the extent to which they were invited to agree a transfer from the SUITS scheme, they were in no different position to that of a stranger to the new scheme invited to join on specified terms as to the benefits that would be provided in exchange for a payment into the scheme. The offer and acceptance of the offer, in my judgment, clearly gave rise to a contract. It is absurd to suppose that the terms of that contract can now be altered.

The Pensions Ombudsman has found contracts to exist between trustees and beneficiaries on a number of other occasions. Finding a contractual relationship is usually to the advantage of the complainant member because the scheme (or the employer, depending on the facts) will be bound to provide benefits based on the incorrect information rather than simply being liable for loss flowing from the misquotation.[44]   **43.50**

The employer

The majority of employers retain a significant role under their pension scheme   **43.51**
trust documentation. Typical examples of the powers which employers retain in the trust deed (either individually or jointly with the trustees) include: augmenting benefits, granting the right to take an early retirement pension, determining the level of increase to pensions in payment (in excess of statutory requirements), admitting employees to the scheme who do not conform to membership requirements, appointment and removal of trustees, and amending the scheme.

Prior to the Pensions Act 1995, the balance of power in the scheme was largely deter-   **43.52**
mined by the employer and its advisers when the scheme was initially established as they were responsible for drafting the scheme's initial documentation. This meant that, in many schemes, the balance was very heavily skewed in favour of the employer. However, the Pensions Act 1995 has changed the position and reserves a significant number of powers to the trustees in whole or in part, irrespective of what the scheme trust deed provides. These powers include amending the scheme, determining contribution rates (up to certain levels), appointing trustees, and distributing surplus.

Relationship between employer and trustees

Because of the employer's continued involvement in the scheme, the trustees and   **43.53**
the employer have an ongoing relationship. The employer is not only the settlor of the scheme, but is also generally a residuary beneficiary in the event that the scheme winds up with surplus assets.

This means that when the trustees are making decisions in relation to the scheme,   **43.54**
they need to take the employer's interests into account as well as those of other

---

[44] Examples of determinations where the Pensions Ombudsman has found contracts to exist can be found in Determinations K00117, K00377, K00541.

beneficiaries. The issue of the extent to which the trustees can take into account the interests of the employer when exercising their powers was considered in *Edge v Pensions Ombudsman*,[45] which concerned a distribution of surplus by the trustees in an ongoing scheme. It was held in *Edge* that:

> First, the proposition that the trustees were not entitled, when deciding how to reduce the £29.9m surplus, to take any account of the position of the employers is one with which I emphatically disagree. The employers play a critical part in this pension scheme. They have to pay contributions sufficient to keep the scheme solvent. They have to employ employees who are willing to join the scheme and pay contributions. The £29.9m was an actuarially calculated figure based on future projections and estimates of the sums that would be coming into the open fund from employers' contributions and from members contributions. It seems to me obvious that the continued viability of the respective employers was something that, in the interests of the pension scheme and its members as a whole, the trustees were entitled to want to promote. Otherwise, if one or more of the employers went into decline or collapsed, the financial projections, on the basis of which the actuarial calculations had been made, would become invalidated.[46]

Therefore, trustees should consider the position of the employer when exercising their powers and the effect their decisions will have on it, although clearly they need to balance this consideration with the interests of the scheme members.

Relationship between employer and beneficiaries

43.55 Clearly there is a contractual relationship between the employer and the employees who are active members of its pension scheme. Consideration of this relationship is outside the scope of this chapter. However, the contractual relationship does have consequences for the pension scheme; in particular, when agreeing to scheme amendments, the employer needs to bear in mind what contractual entitlements the members have. Even though an amendment may be permitted under the scheme rules, it may be in breach of contract and render the employer liable to claims and damages as a result (this is examined further in the last chapter in this Part).

43.56 In addition to the express contractual terms, the employment relationship is subject to an implied duty of mutual trust and confidence which translates loosely as a duty to act in good faith and not to damage the employment relationship.[47] This duty has been held to apply to the exercise of an employer's powers under an occupational pension scheme as much as to any other element of the employment relationship. In *Imperial Group Pension Trust Ltd v Imperial Tobacco Ltd*[48] it was held:

> In every contract of employment there is an implied term 'that the employers will not, without reasonable and proper cause, conduct themselves in a manner

---

[45] *Edge v Pensions Ombudsman* [1998] 2 Ch 512.   [46] ibid 537.
[47] See paras 11.92–11.103 above.   [48] [1991] 1 WLR 589.

calculated or likely to destroy or seriously damage the relationship of confidence and trust between employer and employee'. . . I will call this implied term 'the implied obligation of good faith'. In my judgment, that obligation of an employer applies as much to the exercise of his rights and powers under a pension scheme as they do to the other rights and powers of an employer. Say, in purported exercise of its right to give or withhold consent, the company were to say, capriciously, that it would consent to an increase in the pension benefits of members of union A but not of the members of union B. In my judgment, the members of union B would have a good claim in contract for breach of the implied obligation of good faith . . . Construed against the background of the contract of employment, in my judgment the pension trust deed and rules themselves are to be taken as being impliedly subject to the limitation that the rights and powers of the company can only be exercised in accordance with the implied obligation of good faith.

44

TRUSTEESHIP AND DUTIES OF TRUSTEES OF OCCUPATIONAL PENSION SCHEME TRUSTS

A. Appointment and Removal of Trustees[1]

One of the key elements in the successful operation of a pension scheme is the identity of the trustees.   **44.01**

Provisions of the trust deed

In all well-drafted schemes, the trust deed and rules will contain provisions relat-   **44.02** ing to the appointment and removal of trustees and, typically, the power will be the employer's.

---

[1] For the appointment, removal, and retirement of trustees generally, see Chapter 22 above.

44.03   Questions have arisen about the extent to which the employer's power of appointment and removal is a fiduciary power which must therefore be exercised in the
best interests of the pension scheme beneficiaries. This is important as in the event
that a dispute arises between the trustees and employer about the way in which the
scheme is run, the employer may be tempted to resolve the problem by removing
the current trustees and replacing them with some more favourably inclined
towards the employer's proposals.

44.04   The nature of the employer's power has been considered on a number of occasions,[2] in particular in *Simpson Curtis Pension Trustees Ltd v Readson Ltd.*[3] In this
case, administrative receivers had been appointed to the sponsoring employer and
the receivers purported to exercise the employer's power under the pension
scheme to appoint and remove trustees. The court held that the power of appointment of new trustees was not in the true sense an asset of the employer company
and accepted the argument that the power was fiduciary to the extent that it had
to be exercised bona fide for the benefit of the scheme beneficiaries and should not
be used by an employer for his own gain or benefit. The court went on to consider
the power of removal and suggested that it might be different from the power of
appointment. However, the issue was not considered in any detail as all of the
directors of the original trustee company had resigned and it was no longer
capable of acting.

Requirements for member nominated trustees and directors

44.05   The provisions in the trust deed on the appointment and removal of trustees must
now be read in connection with the requirements of sections 16–21 of the
Pensions Act 1995 and The Occupational Pension Schemes (Member-nominated
Trustees and Directors) Regulations[4] ('the MNT Regulations').

44.06   These provisions were introduced in 1997 following a recommendation by
the Pensions Law Review Committee which said that it was not appropriate for
the employer to have the sole power of appointment as 'however scrupulous the
employer may be, there is no substitute for the discipline of another voice in the
decision-making process, who can ensure that the employer-appointed trustees
do not allow themselves, consciously or unconsciously, to be unduly influenced
by the wishes and concerns of the employer'.[5] Having member trustees would, in
the view of the Committee 'impose the discipline of another view, bringing to the

---

[2] A review of the authorities in the context of pension schemes by David Pollard can be found
at (1991) 37 British Pension Lawyer 1. See also GW Thomas, *Powers* (Sweet & Maxwell, 1998)
('*Thomas*') 194–211, where the issue is treated as one of capacity.   [3] [1994] OPLR 231.
[4] SI 1996/1216 as amended by the Occupational Pension Schemes (Member-nominated
Trustees and Directors) Amendment Regulations 2002, SI 2002/2327.
[5] *Pension Law Reform: Pension Law Review Committee Report 1993* (Cm 2342), vol 1, para 4.5.19.

trustee board a different experience and perspective, and [help] to ensure that the interests and views of scheme members as potential beneficiaries are constantly kept in mind' and encourage confidence in the way schemes were being run in the post-Maxwell era.

At first glance the idea appears fairly straightforward. However, the notion that member nominated trustees ('MNTs') would be able to represent the interests of scheme members on the trustee board is a dramatic departure from the traditional trust law concept that trustees are impartial and should be acting in the best interests of the scheme membership as a whole. It seems to be an acknowledgement of the idea that employer appointed trustees, at least in part, represent the interests of the employer and MNTs represent the interests of the members. **44.07**

It is the trustees' responsibility for ensuring compliance with the MNT requirements. Basically, they must ensure that at least one-third of their number are nominated by the members (with a minimum of two where the scheme has 100 or more members, and a minimum of one if less). There are certain exemptions to this requirement, in particular unapproved schemes, single member schemes, schemes which provide death benefits only, and small self-administered schemes.[6] **44.08**

Trustees have some flexibility in the way in which they implement the MNT requirements. In particular, they can put forward their own mechanism for the selection and appointment of MNTs (referred to in the legislation as 'appropriate rules') which must be approved by the members under a statutory consultation procedure.[7] Alternatively they can implement a set of prescribed statutory rules which set out a mechanism for the appointment and removal of MNTs. In either case, there are certain basic features which the arrangements implemented must contain; in particular, the MNTs must hold office for between three and six years, may only be removed by all of the other trustees, and they must have the same functions as other trustees (although this latter is not true in the case of member nominated directors). **44.09**

It is possible for the employer to 'opt out' of the MNT requirements by proposing its own alternative arrangements for the appointment of trustees. To go down this route, the employer's proposals must also be approved by the scheme members in a statutory consultation procedure.[8] The employer has almost unlimited flexibility in the form its opt-out takes; in particular there is no requirement for it to secure that one-third of the trustees (or indeed any) are nominated by the members, although clearly the proposals should be designed with a view to getting them through the statutory consultation procedure. **44.10**

---

[6] The Occupational Pension Schemes (Member-nominated Trustees and Directors) Regulations 1996, SI 1996/1216, regs 4 and 6.
[7] ibid, Sch 1.   [8] Pensions Act 1995, ss 17 and 19.

44.11 The statutory consultation procedure is not a particularly difficult hurdle for employers and trustees to surmount. It focuses on a certain level of members objecting to the proposals rather than a certain number giving them positive approval. Generally speaking at least 10 per cent of eligible members (or if less, 10,000 eligible members) must object to the proposed rules or arrangements.[9] Eligible members for this purpose are defined in section 21(8) of the Pensions Act 1995 as including active (ie employed) and pensioner members and may include deferred members (ie those members who have left employment but are not yet in receipt of pension) at the discretion of the trustees.

44.12 Once in place, MNT arrangements were originally intended to last for six years but this has now been extended to ten years while new legislation is being considered.[10] However, the scheme trustees must monitor the composition of the scheme to ensure that the MNT arrangements remain appropriate. Regulation 20 of the MNT regulations provides that, if either the accrued rights of a group of members have been or are to be transferred to or from the scheme without consent or there is a change in the identity or ownership of the participating employers to the scheme, the trustees must consider if the MNT arrangements in place remain appropriate. If the trustees consider they are not appropriate, they must give notice to the employer and then new arrangements must be put in place.

44.13 When the Government started a review of pensions legislation in December 1998, they said that the MNT arrangements had 'had time to bed down and the feedback we have received is that the requirements are too inflexible and complex, difficult and costly to implement. And many schemes still do not have trustees who have been nominated and selected by scheme members.'[11] As a result, legislation is now in place in the Child Support, Pensions and Social Security Act 2000 which will remove the ability of employers to opt out of the MNT requirements.[12] However, at the date of writing the legislation has not been brought into force as it has been delayed pending a general review of pensions legislation with a view to simplification.

Conflicts of interest[13]

44.14 As the trustees are typically appointed or nominated by either the employer or members or their representatives, the issue of conflicts of interest is an important

---

[9] See The Occupational Pension Schemes (Member-nominated Trustees and Directors) Regulations 1996, SI 1996/1216, Sch 1, para 8.
[10] The Occupational Pension Schemes (Member-nominated Trustees and Directors) Amendment Regulations 2002, SI 2002/2327.
[11] *A New Contract for Welfare Partnerships in Pensions 1998* (Cm 4179), Ch 8, para 28.
[12] Child Support, Pensions and Social Security Act 2000, ss 43–46.
[13] For trustees' duty not to place themselves in a position where their duty and self-interest conflict, see paras 10.99–10.116 above.

one in pension schemes. Clearly, member trustees will often have a personal interest in the decisions being taken by the trustees in relation to benefits and employer trustees will have an interest in the costs of such decisions.

There has been some case law discussion about the extent to which member **44.15** trustees can participate in such decisions. In *British Coal Corporation v British Coal Staff Superannuation Scheme Trustees Ltd*, Vinelott J said;

> I find the idea that a person who has a power to distribute a fund amongst a class which includes himself should be able to apply the fund or any part of it for his own benefit equally outrageous. This does not rest on any technical rule of trust law. Common sense dictates that no man should be asked to exercise a discretion as to the application of a fund amongst a class of which he is a member. He cannot be expected fairly to weigh his own merits against the merits of others.[14]

This general rule of avoiding conflict was considered again in a pensions context in *Manning v Drexel Burnham Lambert*,[15] where it was held that this general rule did not apply in such a way as to deny the court the jurisdiction to give directions sought in relation to a scheme of distribution proposed by trustees where some of the trustees would benefit in their capacity as members. The court did not rule on the question, which remains unanswered, whether an express provision in the trust deed could circumvent this general rule.

If this position had been maintained, it would have made a nonsense of the stated **44.16** aims of the MNT regime. Therefore, section 39 of the Pensions Act 1995 provides that 'No rule of law that a trustee may not exercise the powers vested in him so as to give rise to a conflict between his personal interest and his duties to the beneficiaries shall apply to a trustee of a trust scheme, who is also a member of the scheme, exercising the powers vested in him in any manner, merely because their exercise in that manner benefits, or may benefit, him as a member of the scheme.' In addition, the Pensions Act made changes to employment legislation to protect employees from suffering any detriment as a result of their activities as a pension scheme trustee[16] and employers are now required to give employees any necessary time off during working hours to perform their duties as a trustee.[17]

The position is more complex in relation to employer appointed trustees as there **44.17** are no statutory provisions allowing them to take part in decisions which might affect the employer (for example setting the employer contribution rate). On the face of it, any director who is also a trustee of the company's scheme automatically faces a potential conflict of interest. However, this conflict could be resolved by arguing that, in appointing an individual as a trustee, the employer impliedly waives some of the duties that would normally be owed to it by that individual.

---

[14] [1995] 1 All ER 912.   [15] [1995] 1 WLR 32.
[16] Employment Rights Act 1996, ss 46–49.   [17] ibid, ss 58–60.

This might include a waiver of the duty to provide the employer with all the information received by the individual in his role as trustee. In other words responsibilities to the trust are effectively given precedence over those to the employer. However, the individual will still need to avoid taking part in decisions directly relating to the employer.

Independent trustees

44.18   Many larger pension schemes appoint professional independent trustees to take over some of the day-to-day tasks that it is not possible for lay trustees to do effectively, or to provide an experienced and informed view at trustees' meetings.

44.19   In addition, there are circumstances where the appointment of an independent trustee will be required. Sections 22–26C of the Pensions Act 1995[18] set out these circumstances. Section 23 provides that where the employer in relation to the scheme has become insolvent, the insolvency practitioner must satisfy himself that at all times at least one of the trustees of the scheme is an independent person, and, if at any time he is not so satisfied, he must appoint or secure the appointment of an independent person as a trustee of the scheme. If the insolvency practitioner fails in this duty then the members can apply to court for the appointment of an independent trustee. These requirements are examined in further detail in the winding-up section below.

Occupational Pensions Regulatory Authority

44.20   In certain circumstances the Occupational Pensions Regulatory Authority ('Opra') has the power to appoint and remove trustees. The power of appointment is in section 7 of the Pensions Act 1995 and it gives Opra the power to appoint trustees where necessary '(a) to secure that the trustees as a whole have, or exercise, the necessary knowledge and skill for the proper administration of the scheme, (b) to secure that the number of trustees is sufficient for the proper administration of the scheme, or (c) to secure the proper use or application of the assets of the scheme'.

44.21   In addition, Opra can appoint a trustee to replace someone who is disqualified from being a trustee (see below) or who has been removed by Opra. Opra will also consider exercising its powers where an insolvency practitioner has failed in its duty to appoint an independent trustee on an employer's insolvency.

44.22   The powers of any trustees appointed by Opra may be narrower than those of other scheme trustees or they may be able to exercise some powers to the exclusion of the other trustees.[19] Opra may appoint a professional trustee or an individual

---

[18]   As amended by the Child Support, Pensions and Social Security Act 2000, s 47.
[19]   Pensions Act 1995, s 8(4) as amended by the Welfare Reform and Pensions Act 1999, s 18.

who already has a connection with the scheme[20] and Opra may order that the trustee be paid fees and expenses out of the scheme's resources. In addition, Opra may also specify the number of trustees needed to administer the scheme properly.

Sections 4–6 of the Pensions Act 1995 give Opra powers to suspend and remove **44.23** individuals from acting as pension scheme trustees or to prohibit them from becoming a trustee of a particular scheme where they have breached a specific obligation or have been in serious or persistent breach of any of the statutory requirements enforced by Opra. If a person continues to act as a trustee when they have been suspended or prohibited from doing so by Opra, they can be liable to a fine or imprisonment.[21] However, section 7 of the Pensions Act 1995 provides that things 'done by a person purporting to act as trustee of a trust scheme while prohibited from being a trustee of the scheme under section 3 or suspended in relation to the scheme under section 4 are not invalid merely because of that prohibition or suspension'.

Disqualification

Section 29 of the Pensions Act 1995 provides for people to be disqualified from **44.24** being an occupational pension scheme trustee. The circumstances where someone will be disqualified as a trustee include where they have been convicted of any offence involving dishonesty or deception, are an undischarged bankrupt, or subject to a disqualification order under the Company Directors Disqualification Act 1996. A company will be disqualified from being a director if any of its directors fall into any of these categories.

The consequences of disqualification are set out in section 30 of the Pensions Act **44.25** 1995. A person acting as a pension scheme trustee while disqualified is guilty of a criminal offence. However, disqualification does not affect the validity of actions done while a trustee.

Opra maintains a register of disqualified trustees which is publicly available for **44.26** inspection and should be checked before any new trustee is appointed.

B. Duties of Trustees of Occupational Pension Schemes

Occupational pension scheme trustees are of course subject to the general trust **44.27** law duties discussed elsewhere in this book.[22] However, the statutory regime applicable to pension schemes means that these duties are subject to considerable

---

[20] Guidance on the type of trustees that Opra will appoint in particular cases can be found in Opra Note 5: Appointment of Trustees by Opra.   [21] Pensions Act 1995, s 7(1).
[22] See Chapters 10 and 11 above.

modification. This section looks at how statute has modified the duties applicable to occupational pension scheme trustees.

Duty to carry out the terms of the trust[23]

44.28 Pension scheme trust deeds are typically complex documents containing detailed provisions in relation to the amount and circumstances in which benefits are payable and the balance of power between trustees and employers. All trustees must know what the terms of the trust are. However, in the case of pension scheme trustees, failure to do so not only amounts to breach of trust; the Pensions Ombudsman has said that it is the first duty of a trustee to familiarize himself with the trust documentation[24] and that failure to do so also amounts to maladministration (see section on regulators below).

44.29 Trustees must be aware of what powers they have been given under the scheme as they have a duty to consider the exercise of their powers in relevant situations. Again failure to do so amounts to both breach of trust and maladministration. The Pensions Ombudsman has said (in a case dealing with the exercise of an amendment power) 'the power of amendment is an important tool to ensure that a pension scheme fulfils its purpose over long periods of time. It is not given to trustees as a personal power, to be exercised in accordance with the interests of each individual trustee or the party which appointed him. It is a fiduciary power. A fiduciary power carries duties. In particular, a duty to consider whether that power should be exercised.'[25]

Duty to act in the best interests of the beneficiaries[26]

44.30 The requirement to act in the best interests of scheme beneficiaries forms an important part of the trustees' duties in any trust. The interests which trustees should take into account are strictly those as scheme beneficiaries and not any wider social or personal considerations. This was clearly illustrated in *Cowan v Scargill* where it was held that:

> The starting point is the duty of trustees to exercise their powers in the best interests of the present and future beneficiaries of the trust, holding the scales impartially between different classes of beneficiaries. This duty of the trustees towards their beneficiaries is paramount. They must, of course, obey the law; but subject to that, they must put the interests of their beneficiaries first. When the purpose of the trust is to provide financial benefits for the beneficiaries, as is usually the case, the best interests of the beneficiaries are normally their best financial interests.[27]

---

[23] See also paras 10.07–10.08 above.
[24] See for example determinations G00472 and G00030.
[25] *Packwood v British Airways Pension Scheme* [1995] OPLR 369.
[26] See also paras 10.13–10.31 above.
[27] *Cowan v Scargill* [1985] Ch 270.

Trustees must take into account what is in the best interests of the beneficiaries of **44.31**
the scheme as a whole. They are not generally representatives of a specific interest
group. This may seem somewhat peculiar given the nature of trustee appointments and the Pensions Act requirements in relation to MNTs (although, as discussed above, the Government does seem to envisage that trustees will be partisan
to a degree). A common temptation for employers and employer nominated
trustees is to consider the interests of the active members ahead of those of other
members. Not unreasonably, for commercial reasons, it is active members, ie
employees, whose interests the company will normally seek to promote ahead of
former employees. An employer may consider deferred members to be no longer
of any interest. The trustees cannot.

However, there is no requirement for trustees to treat all members equally.[28] This **44.32**
was emphasized in *Edge v Pensions Ombudsman*.[29] The results of an actuarial valuation showed a surplus which the trustees could not use without the employers'
consent. However, unusually, the employers could not reduce their contributions
below the level of member contributions, so the employers could not get full
advantage of the surplus without the trustees' agreement either. In the end,
one-third of the surplus was used as a reserve, one-third to improve the benefits of
members in service (including reducing their contributions), and the other third
on reducing the employers' contributions. A pensioner complained to the
Pensions Ombudsman who found that the trustees had breached their duty of
impartiality by agreeing to benefit improvements which only advantaged the
active members and not the pensioners. He thought the trustees had acted with
'undue partiality' towards the active members.[30] On appeal, the court disagreed.
Trustees are entitled to choose and prefer some beneficiaries over others and it was
not for the Ombudsman to decide that their partiality was 'undue'. Trustees have
to consider all beneficiaries fairly, but do not need to treat them equally.
The Court of Appeal supported these views.

Duty to act with reasonable care

The statutory duty of care set out in section 1 of the Trustee Act 2000[31] is of **44.33**
limited application to occupational pension scheme trustees. Section 36 of the
Trustee Act 2000 provides that the section 1 duty does not apply to occupational
pension schemes in relation to investment powers or delegating such investment
powers.

                                                                              44.34

The reason for the exclusion of occupational pension investment powers from
section 1 of the Trustee Act 2000 is that legislation was already in place in relation
to investment duties in the Pensions Act. Although the Pensions Act 1995 does

---

[28] See also paras 10.13–10.31 above.   [29] [1998] Ch 512 and [2000] Ch 602.
[30] Determination C11545.   [31] See also paras 10.32–10.34 above.

not provide a statutory threshold of care, section 33 provides that liability for breach of an obligation under any rule of law to take care or exercise skill in the performance of any investment functions cannot be excluded or restricted by any instrument or agreement. However, if the trustees delegate their investment powers in certain ways (see below), they will not be liable for the acts of their delegates.

44.35 The relatively low threshold of the duty of care has been criticized in a pensions context where the trustees are dealing with large amounts of members' money. Therefore, there are proposals that the duty of care applicable to pension scheme trustees should be codified and strengthened. At the date of writing the proposals aim to ensure that '. . .legislation will. . .provide that trustees be required to be familiar with the issues or have relevant knowledge across the full range of their responsibilities. The Codes of Practice. . .will provide guidance on how this legal requirement could be satisfied. These may cover relevant training, qualifications and experience, as well as relevant governance issues, which might include record keeping and skills audits.'[32] The codes of practice referred to will be issued by the pensions regulator and would not represent the law, but the regulator's view of it. It is intended that they 'should have evidential value in proceedings where it will be determined whether a breach of the legislative provision had occurred, including decisions by the Pensions Ombudsman'. It has been argued that raising the standard of the duty of care could be problematic for member trustees who would usually have no knowledge of the requirements of running an occupational pension scheme and, as a result, would need to be trained how to be a trustee.

Duty to act jointly[33]

44.36 To avoid the necessity of trustee decisions being made unanimously by often large trustee bodies and the potential problem that this could result in crucial decisions not being taken at all, section 32 of the Pensions Act 1995 provides that decisions may be taken by agreement of the majority unless the trust deed and rules say otherwise.

Duty to see that sums owed are paid

44.37 Scheme rules may provide for both employee and employer contributions and trustees have a duty to gather such contributions in.

44.38 Employee contributions will be deducted from pay by the employer. The only authority that the employer has for deducting contributions from pay is for onward transmission to the scheme and employers must therefore pay the money to the trustees. Using that money, as some employers have done in times of financial distress, for the general purposes of the business is tantamount to theft.

---

[32] *Simplicity, Security and Choice: Working and Saving For Retirement—Action on Occupational Pensions 3* (Cm 5835, 2003), Ch 2, paras 26 and 27.   [33] See para 10.98 above.

While in such circumstances this money would always have been treated as a debt owed to the scheme, trustees found it difficult in practice to take steps to recover it; in addition, there was no real mechanism to enforce prompt payment of member contributions to the scheme. This issue was addressed in the Pensions Act 1995 which requires employers to pass over member contributions to the scheme within nineteen days of the end of the month in which they were deducted. Failure to comply with this requirement can result in fines, or criminal sanctions if anyone is 'knowingly concerned in the fraudulent evasion' of the requirement[34] and, in addition, reports must be made to Opra and the scheme members unless payment is made within a further ten days and the default is only the first or second default by that employer in the last twelve months.

Failure by the employer to pay over contributions due from it amounts to statutory debt owed to the scheme which the trustees can enforce.[35]   **44.39**

However, ensuring compliance with the statutory requirements and time periods   **44.40**
in relation to payment of contributions to the scheme, does not appear sufficient to discharge the trustees' duties. In one determination,[36] the Pensions Ombudsman decided that a systematic delay of at least ten days between additional voluntary contributions being deducted from a member's salary and being paid over to the insurance company was 'an unnecessary and unreasonable delay which constituted maladministration causing injustice'. When it was pointed out that the payment period was actually shorter than the Pensions Act 1995 time limits relating to contributions deducted from salary, the Pensions Ombudsman said that 'the existence of such long-stop sanctions does not absolve trustees or managers of their responsibility to ensure that good practices are established for all areas of pension scheme administration'.

Duty of disclosure[37]

Trustees have always had a duty to permit any beneficiary to inspect the scheme's   **44.41**
trust deed and rules, the scheme accounts, and documents relating to the scheme's investments. Beneficiaries are even entitled to minutes of trustees' administrative decisions, and legal advice relating to them. In addition, in occupational pension schemes, trustees must comply with a variety of statutory disclosure obligations, the majority of which are set out in the Disclosure Regulations.[38] These Regulations set out in detail a large amount of information to be provided to members either automatically or on request and within specified time frames.

---

[34] Pensions Act 1995, s 49 (as amended by the Welfare Reform Act 1999) and The Occupational Pension Schemes (Scheme Administration) Regulations 1996, SI 1996/1715, reg 16.
[35] Pensions Act 1995, s 59(2) (final salary schemes) and s 88(2) (money purchase schemes).
[36] Determination G00543.   [37] See also Chapter 12 above.
[38] The Occupational Pension Schemes (Disclosure of Information) Regulations 1996, SI 1996/1655.

44.42 Trustees of schemes which provide money purchase benefits have additional obligations under the Disclosure Regulations. With effect from 6 April 2003, members entitled to (but not yet receiving) money purchase benefits (including members of final salary schemes, where for example there are money purchase additional voluntary contributions) will need to be given a statutory money purchase illustration as part of their annual benefit statement. There are some exceptions to this requirement, in particular where:

(a) the member is within 2 years of retirement;

(b) the value of the member's money purchase benefits under the scheme were less than £5,000 on the first illustration date falling after 5 April 2003, and no contributions have been made after 5 April 2003, or, in the opinion of the trustees, are likely to be made; or

(c) there is a money purchase underpin which, in the opinion of the trustees, is unlikely to apply.

44.43 The statutory money purchase illustration is an illustration of the amount of pension likely to have accrued to the member at retirement in respect of money purchase benefits under the scheme. It must be calculated according to requirements in the Disclosure Regulations[39] and actuarial guidance.[40] Less helpfully for members, the Disclosure Regulations also require a statutory money purchase illustration to contain various caveats to the effect that the illustration is based on assumptions and is not therefore guaranteed. The intention behind these requirements is to ensure that members of money purchase schemes have a realistic expectation of the level of benefits their money purchase accounts are likely to provide them at retirement.

44.44 Trustees do not have to disclose the reasons for the exercise of their discretions. This was settled in relation to private trusts in *Re Londonderry's Will Trusts*.[41] However, it was then re-examined and applied in the context of a pension scheme in *Wilson v The Law Debenture Trust Corporation plc*,[42] although the position may have been affected by the decision of the Privy Council in *Schmidt v Rosewood Trust Ltd*.[43] Moreover, the issue has also been considered by the Pensions Ombudsman in a few cases and he has said:

> It is not good trust administration for trustees to seek to make themselves unaccountable to their beneficiaries, myself or the courts by omitting to keep proper records of their decisions. It opens the way to conflict of interest, hidden negligence,

---

[39] SI 1996/1655, reg 5 (as amended by The Occupational and Personal Pension Schemes (Disclosure of Information) Amendment Regulations 2002, SI 2002/1383).

[40] Actuarial Guidance Note GN34, Illustration of Defined Contribution Pension Scheme Benefits and Technical Memorandum TM1, Statutory Money Purchase Illustrations.

[41] [1965] Ch 918.   [42] [1995] 2 All ER 337. See para 12.10 above.

[43] [2003] 2 WLR 1442. See the discussion in paras 12.14–12.19 above.

and even corruption, although there is no suggestion of this on the part of the Trustee here. Trustees should keep proper records of their decisions (and the Pensions Act 1995 has now introduced such a requirement). Whilst there are circumstances, as set out in *Re Londonderry's Settlement* and *Wilson v The Law Debenture Trust Corporation plc* why such records need not always be revealed to a beneficiary, this does not justify trustees in deliberately omitting to keep any record of their deliberations.[44]

Duty not to delegate[45]

The general rule that trustees cannot delegate their powers unless the terms of the trust specifically allow them to do so applies to occupational pension scheme trustees except in the case of investment powers.   **44.45**

In relation to investment, Section 34(2) of the Pensions Act 1995 provides that any 'discretion of the trustees of a trust scheme to make any decision about investments . . . may be delegated by or on behalf of the trustees to a fund manager to whom subsection (3) applies . . .'. The effect of this provision is that the delegation must be to someone who is authorized to carry out regulated investment activities under the Financial Services and Markets Act 2000.[46] No other delegation of investment powers is permitted except under the provisions of section 25 of the Trustee Act 1925 (delegation of trusts for period not exceeding twelve months) or section 34(5) of the Pensions Act 1995. Section 34(5) permits (where the trust documentation allows) delegation of investment powers to two or more of the trustees or to an unauthorized fund manager (provided the investment is not one regulated by the Financial Services and Markets Act 2000).   **44.46**

The Pensions Act 1995 encourages the delegation of investment powers; section 34(4) provides trustees with a statutory exoneration from liability for the acts of properly appointed, authorized investment managers providing the trustees have taken all such steps as are reasonable to satisfy themselves that the fund manager has the appropriate knowledge and experience for managing the investments of the scheme and that he is carrying out his work competently and complying with the requirements in section 36 on choosing investments (discussed in the investment section below). If a delegation is made to an unauthorized fund manager, there is no statutory exoneration, but the trustees may relay on an exoneration provision in the scheme rules providing they satisfy themselves of the same things.   **44.47**

---

[44] Determinations F00898, F00899, F00900 and G00221.

[45] See generally Chapter 15 above.

[46] These requirements tie in with the Financial Services and Markets Act 2000 (Carrying on Regulated Activities by way of Business) Order 2001, SI 2001/1177, art 4, which states anyone who carries out day-to-day investment activities for an occupational pension scheme is generally to be regarded as undertaking a business activity and therefore requires authorization under the Financial Services and Markets Act 2000.

44.48 These restrictions on the ability of trustees to delegate their investment powers potentially cause problems in money purchase schemes where there are investment options and trustees leave the decision of which of several investment options a member's fund will be invested in to individual members. Clearly, the vast majority of members do not fall within the meaning of the term 'fund manager' in section 34. As such, delegation to them of decisions regarding investment is not permitted. This problem can be dealt with by drafting scheme documentation to ensure that there is no delegation of trustees' investment powers. This can be achieved by providing that the member can indicate an investment preference which the trustees are not obliged to follow. This means that the investment power remains the trustees', although the trustees would in each case have to consider whether it was appropriate to follow the member's direction. Alternatively, the investment provisions in the trust may give the trustees power to select the investment vehicles, but leave the decision as to how an individual's money purchase account should be invested to the member. This means that there is no delegation of the investment power as the power to choose between the various investments is always and only the member's.

Duty to hold meetings and keep records

44.49 The Pensions Act 1995 requires the trustees to keep proper records of all their meetings including the date, time, and venue, the names of the trustees invited and those who attended, the decisions made, and, if a decision has been taken by the trustees since the last meeting, a record of that decision too.[47]

44.50 There is no minimum number of trustees that need to be present to make a trustee meeting valid. However, if decisions are to be taken by majority, then unless all the trustees otherwise agree, a meeting requires at least ten business days' notice, unless it is necessary as a matter of urgency to make a decision.[48]

Duty to appoint professional advisers

44.51 Section 47 of the Pensions Act 1995 requires that, with some minor exceptions, trustees must appoint a scheme auditor, a scheme actuary, and a fund manager. Money purchase schemes do not have to appoint an actuary. The appointment must be in writing and state the date the appointment is due to take effect, to whom the professional adviser is to report, and from whom they are to take instructions. The adviser must acknowledge his appointment within one month and confirm that he will notify the trustees of any conflict of interest to which he is subject in relation to the scheme immediately he becomes aware of its existence. An adviser may resign at any time by giving written notice to the trustees and the

---

[47] Pensions Act 1995, s 49 and The Occupational Pension Schemes (Scheme Administration) Regulations 1996, SI 1996/1715, Pt III.   [48] ibid, s 32 and regs 9–10.

trustees are able to remove professional advisers. In the case of an auditor or actuary, they must provide the trustees with a statement specifying any circumstances connected with their removal which, in their opinion, significantly affect the interests of the members, prospective members, or beneficiaries under the scheme.[49]

There is no requirement to appoint a legal adviser to the scheme. However, **44.52** section 47(3) of the Pensions Act 1995 provides that, if 'in exercising any of his functions [a trustee] places reliance on the skill or judgement' of a legal adviser, auditor, actuary, or fund manager who has not been appointed by or on behalf of them, the trustee can be liable to fines or be prohibited from being a trustee. Accordingly, trustees cannot rely upon the advice of the employer's solicitors or auditors, unless they formally appoint them as their own advisers as well.

Duty to have dispute resolution procedure

Trustees are required to have their own internal dispute resolution procedure **44.53** under section 50 of the Pensions Act 1995. This gives members the ability to require decisions affecting them to be reviewed by the trustees without the need to lodge a claim with the Pensions Ombudsman or start court proceedings.

Duty to invest[50]

As pension schemes are primarily financial trusts, investment of the trust assets is **44.54** one of the most important powers which pension scheme trustees have; and it is in this area, perhaps more than any other, where the legal position relating to occupational pension schemes is different from that applicable to other trusts.

Permitted range of investments

Prior to the Pensions Act 1995, the investments which trustees were allowed to **44.55** purchase were determined by provisions in the trust deed and the Trustee Investment Act 1961. The provisions in the Trustee Investment Act 1961 were generally felt to be too narrow and restrictive for occupational pension schemes where the nature of the long-term liabilities meant that large-scale equity investment outside the scope of the investments permitted by the Act was often felt to be appropriate. Therefore, the majority of schemes did not rely on the statutory provisions, but had trust deeds containing wide investment powers, often permitting almost any type of investment at all.

---

[49] ibid, reg 5 as amended by The Occupational Pension Schemes (Reference Scheme and Miscellaneous Amendments) Regulations 1997, SI 1997/819, The Personal and Occupational Pension Schemes (Miscellaneous Amendments) (No 2) Regulations 1997, SI 1997/3038, and The Personal and Occupational Pension Schemes (Miscellaneous Amendments) Regulations 1999, SI 1999/3198.

[50] On trustees' duties in relation to investment, see generally paras 10.58–10.84 above.

44.56 To reflect the realities of pension scheme investment, section 34(1) of the Pensions Act 1995 provides that the 'trustees of a trust scheme have, subject to any restriction imposed by the scheme, the same power to make an investment of any kind as if they were absolutely entitled to the assets of the scheme'. The Pensions Act 1995 does not define what is meant by investment so pension scheme trustees must give some thought as to whether a particular disposition of scheme assets can truly be seen as an 'investment'. There has been some judicial consideration of the meaning of 'investment'. It has been said that in a trust context an investment needs to produce income;[51] however, it is hard to imagine a court taking a view that an asset purchased with the intention of generating money from capital appreciation would not constitute an investment.

44.57 The wide statutory investment power may be restricted by provisions in the trust deed. Common restrictions include an absolute prohibition on investing in the shares of the sponsoring employer or types of investment which are usually associated with a high degree of risk. The one form of prohibition which it is not possible to have in the trust deed is one which permits particular types of investment, only with the consent of the employer; section 35(4) provides that the scheme may not 'impose restrictions (however expressed) on any power to make investments by reference to the consent of the employer'.

44.58 Further limits on the wide statutory investment powers can be found in section 40 of the Pensions Act 1995 and The Occupational Pension Schemes (Investment) Regulations 1996.[52] These provisions impose restrictions on the amount of scheme assets which can be invested in employer related investments. Employer related investments include shares or other securities issued by the employer, land which is occupied, used by, or subject to a lease in favour of the employer, property which is used for the purposes of any business carried on by the employer, and loans to the employer.[53] No more than 5 per cent of the market value of the scheme assets can be invested in employer related investments and none of them can be invested in employer related loans. Failure to comply with these requirements renders the trustees liable to both civil and criminal sanctions, irrespective of whether the investment was permitted under the trust deed. The reason for this prohibition reflects the need to keep the scheme assets separate from those of the employer to protect them from the employer's creditors in the event of the employer's insolvency.

Considerations when selecting investments

44.59 Section 36 of the Pensions Act 1995 provides 'The trustees or fund manager must have regard: (a) to the need for diversification of investments, in so far as appropriate

---

[51] See for example *Re Wragg* [1919] 2 Ch 58.   [52] SI 1996/3127.

[53] Details of what constitutes an employer related investment can be found in The Occupational Pension Schemes (Investment) Regulations 1996, SI 1996/3127, reg 4.

to the circumstances of the scheme, and (b) to the suitability to the scheme of investments of the description of investment proposed and of the investment proposed as an investment of that description'. This provision is not very different from the statutory provisions in relation to other types of trust which can be found in section 4(3) of the Trustee Act 2000 (which does not apply to occupational pension schemes by virtue of section 36(3) of the Trustee Act 2000).

In addition, section 35 of the Pensions Act 1995 provides that trustees must have a statement of investment principles. This statement must set out their policy in relation to a range of issues including the kinds of investments to be held, the balance between different kinds of investments, risk, the expected return, and the realization of investments. This should not be an unduly onerous requirement for trustees as these considerations really only represent what a prudent trustee should be taking into account when investing fund assets in any event and are designed to ensure that even where trustees have delegated day-to-day investment decisions, they still focus on investments at a strategic level.   **44.60**

With effect from 3 July 2000, the statement of investment principles must also specify the extent (if at all) to which social, environmental, or ethical considerations are taken into account in the selection, retention, and realization of investments and the trustees' policy (if any) in relation to the exercise of the rights (including voting rights) attaching to investments.[54] This requirement has caused concern as there is a question mark over the validity of ethical investment in a pensions context. In *Cowan v Scargill*, the court held that the duty to act in the best interests of the scheme beneficiaries normally means 'their best financial interests' and an investment power 'must be exercised so as to yield the best return for the beneficiaries, judged in relation to the risks of the investments in question; and the prospects of the yield of income and capital appreciation both have to be considered in judging the return from the investment'.[55] This has been interpreted as preventing any kind of ethical investment of pension fund assets as the trustees' primary concern clearly needed to be financial rather than ethical. However, to stick to this strict interpretation of the case would render the requirement to state ethical policy in the statement of investment principles a nonsense. The practical view is therefore that expressed by the Pension Law Review Committee, that trustees: **44.61**

> ... are perfectly entitled to have a policy on ethical investment and to pursue that policy, so long as they treat the interests of the beneficiaries as paramount and the investment policy is consistent with the standards of care and prudence required by law. This means that trustees are free to avoid certain kinds of prudent investment which they consider the scheme members would regard as objectionable, so long as they

---

[54] The Occupational Pension Schemes (Investment, and Assignment, Forfeiture, Bankruptcy etc) Amendment Regulations 1999, SI 1999/1849, reg 2(4).   [55] [1985] Ch 270, 286–287.

make equally advantageous investments elsewhere, and that they are entitled to put funds into investments which they believe the members would regard as desirable, so long as these are proper investments on other grounds. What trustees are not entitled to do is to subordinate the interests of the beneficiaries to ethical or social demands and thereby deprive the beneficiaries of investment income or opportunities they would otherwise have enjoyed.[56]

44.62 When drafting their statement of investment principles, trustees are required to obtain and consider the written advice of a person who is reasonably believed by them to be qualified by his ability in and practical experience of financial matters and to have the 'appropriate knowledge and experience' of the management of the investments of pension schemes. They must also consult the employer, which is the logical result of the employer (in a final salary scheme) bearing the investment risk. However, the obligation is only consultation and ultimately the trustees are free to ignore the employer's wishes. To ensure that investment decisions are actually made with regard to the statement of investment principles, section 36 requires the trustees, or the fund manager to whom any investment powers have been delegated, to exercise such powers with a view to giving effect to the principles contained in the statement in so far as reasonably practicable.

44.63 As well as obtaining advice when drafting the statement of investment principles, section 36 provides that, before investing in any manner (other than in a manner mentioned in Part I, Schedule 1 of the Trustee Investment Act 1961), the trustees must obtain and consider 'proper advice' from a suitably qualified person on the question of whether the investment is satisfactory having regard to the principles of diversification and suitability and the provisions of the statement of investment principles. Proper advice means, in the case of an investment regulated by the Financial Services and Markets Act 2000, from a person authorized under that Act and, in any other case, 'the advice of a person who is reasonably believed by the trustees to be qualified by his ability in and practical experience of financial matters and to have the appropriate knowledge and experience of the management of the investments of trust schemes' and the advice must be confirmed in writing. Finally, section 36 also provides that trustees retaining any investment must determine at what intervals the circumstances, in particular the nature of the investment, make it desirable to obtain proper advice and to obtain and consider such advice accordingly. Failure to obtain such advice renders the trustees liable to a fine or to being prohibited from being trustees.

Code of practice

44.64 In addition to the legislative requirements on investment, in March 2001 the Government published a set of principles which in their view represent investment best practice and which trustees should have regard to when making investment

---

[56] *Pension Law Reform: Pension Law Review Committee Report 1993* (Cm 2342), vol 1, para 4.9.18.

decisions.[57] The Government has also said that it 'expects that pension funds will publicly disclose their compliance with these [principles] on a voluntary basis'.

These investment principles, referred to as the 'Myners' principles' include the following: **44.65**

(a) Decisions should be taken only by persons or organizations with the skills, information, and resources necessary to take them effectively. Where trustees elect to take investment decisions, they must have sufficient expertise and appropriate training to be able to evaluate critically any advice they take.

(b) Trustees should assess whether they have the right set of skills, both individually and collectively, and the right structures and processes to carry out their role effectively. They should draw up a forward-looking business plan.

(c) Trustees should set out an overall investment objective for the fund that represents their best judgement of what is necessary to meet the fund's liabilities given their understanding of the contributions likely to be received from employer(s) and employees.

(d) The mandate given by the trustees to their fund managers and the scheme trust deed should incorporate the principle of the US Department of Labor Interpretative Bulletin on activism (that is exercising the votes attaching to shares held by the trust). Trustees should also ensure that managers have an explicit strategy, elucidating the circumstances in which they will intervene in a company; the approach they will use in doing so; and how they measure the effectiveness of this strategy.

(e) Trustees should arrange for measurement of the performance of the fund and make formal assessment of their own procedures and decisions as trustees. They should also arrange for a formal assessment of performance and decision making delegated to advisers and managers.

Compliance with these principles is currently voluntary, but the Government is undertaking a review to see whether they have been effective in changing investment practice and, depending on the outcome, has indicated that legislation may follow. **44.66**

C. Funding

Prior to the Pensions Act 1995 there were no legal requirements for pension schemes to have a minimum funding level. This meant that, in the case of final salary schemes, employers could make a promise to their employees that they **44.67**

---

[57] Myners Review: Institutional Investment in the UK, The Government's Response, October 2001.

would receive a certain benefit on retirement, but were not obliged to ensure that there were sufficient assets in the pension scheme to meet the promise. This problem was brought into particularly stark relief by the so-called Maxwell affair where hundreds of millions of pounds were withdrawn from Maxwell Group pension schemes over a period of time to keep various companies afloat, leaving insufficient assets in the schemes to pay benefits as they fell due.

44.68 Funding is not an issue for money purchase schemes where the benefits the member receives are dependent on the amount of money in the fund, rather than at a promised level.

The Minimum Funding Requirement

44.69 The Pensions Law Review Committee said 'that the purpose of a funded pension scheme is that, no matter what happens to the sponsoring employer, the scheme members' accrued rights will be inviolate. We have therefore concluded that the introduction of a statutory minimum solvency requirement is necessary to provide security for the accrued pension rights of scheme members.'[58] This resulted in the Pensions Act provisions in relation to the Minimum Funding Requirement, and the imposition of a number of statutory duties in relation to scheme funding.

44.70 The key provisions in relation to the Minimum Funding Requirement ('MFR') can be found in sections 56–61 of the Pensions Act 1995 and The Occupational Pension Schemes (Minimum Funding Requirement) Regulations ('the MFR Regulations').[59] The effect of the MFR and associated requirements has been to dramatically shift the balance of power in final salary schemes in favour of trustees.

44.71 The concept behind the MFR is straightforward. At its most basic it requires the assets of a final salary scheme to be sufficient to meet the liabilities and the trustees are required to ensure that contributions are paid at a level capable of securing this. However, in practice, the MFR has proved to be of labyrinthine complexity and has failed to be flexible enough to meet the needs of individual schemes.

MFR valuations

44.72 The scheme assets and liabilities must be valued by the scheme actuary in the manner required by the MFR Regulations and Actuarial Guidance Note GN27, Retirement Benefit Schemes, Minimum Funding Requirement. The value of the liabilities is then set off against the value of the assets to determine the scheme's funding level.

---

[58] *Pension Law Reform: Pension Law Review Committee Report 1993* (Cm 2342), vol 1, para 4.4.16.
[59] The Occupational Pension Schemes (Minimum Funding Requirement) Regulations 1996, SI 1996/1536.

The value of the assets is determined in accordance with the MFR Regulations, **44.73** regulation 4. In general terms, it is the figure shown in the scheme's audited accounts. However, if the scheme actuary has any reason to believe that this figure does not reflect the market value of the assets, he can make such adjustments as he considers necessary.

To value the liabilities, the scheme actuary assumes that all the active members of **44.74** the scheme leave service and become entitled to deferred pensions based on their service up to the valuation date and their current pensionable pay. The value of the scheme's liabilities is then calculated on the assumption that it is 'equal to the amount required to be invested in investments of an appropriate description in order to meet those liabilities, and that calculation shall be made by reference to the yield on such investments (as indicated in such indices are specified in the guidance given in [actuarial guidance note] GN27)'.[60] Investments of the 'appropriate description' are, in the case of pensioner liabilities, gilt-edged securities[61] and, in the case of non-pensioner members, equities and in the ten years prior to retirement it is assumed that liabilities are met from a mixture of equities and gilts. It is also possible for the trustees to adopt a gilts-matching policy for liabilities in respect of pensioner members, pension credit members (that is those members who acquire benefits under the scheme as a result of a divorce order made against a scheme member), or deferred members by stating in their statement of investment principles that their policy is to meet all liabilities in respect of such members from investments in gilt-edged securities; this has the effect of potentially increasing the value of the scheme's liabilities. Trustees must consider whether to structure the scheme's investments to match the MFR assumptions (which may have an adverse effect on the investment returns they would otherwise have earned).

MFR valuations are generally carried out at three-year intervals. However, if it **44.75** appears to the trustees (having consulted the scheme actuary) that there has been an event in the interim which could have had a significant effect on the value of the scheme's assets or liabilities such that the scheme could fail to meet the MFR, then a valuation is required within six months. This means that the trustees must ensure that they are aware of events which could affect the scheme's funding position.

Each MFR valuation must contain a statement from the scheme actuary setting **44.76** out the funding level of the scheme and the percentage of liabilities which could be satisfied if the scheme was wound up.

Contributions

As part of the MFR process, the trustees must prepare and revise from time to time **44.77** a schedule of contributions showing the contributions required to ensure the

---

[60] ibid, reg 7(2)
[61] Unless pensioner liabilities exceed £100 million, in which case an easement is given, ibid, reg 7(4).

scheme remains fully funded on the MFR basis or, if the last MFR valuation showed the scheme was underfunded, to bring the scheme up to 100 per cent funded. Section 58 of the Pensions Act 1995 provides that the schedule must show the rates of contributions payable to the scheme by or on behalf of the employer and the active members of the scheme, and the dates on or before which such contributions should be paid.

44.78 The schedule of contributions should be prepared within twelve weeks from the signing of each MFR valuation. The trustees have eight weeks to agree it with the employer; if they are unable to reach agreement within that period, then the trustees must themselves determine the rates of contributions necessary, in their opinion, to ensure the scheme meets the MFR. This means that, even where the scheme documentation provides that employer contributions are determined by the employer, the power is effectively the trustees' at least up to the level necessary to meet the MFR.

44.79 The schedule must show the contributions due over a five-year period. However, where the valuation showed that the MFR was not met, this is extended to ten years and must show the contributions necessary to bring the scheme up to the MFR level. In certain circumstances, an application may be made to Opra to extend the period of the schedule of contributions, including where as a result of 'exceptional general economic or financial circumstances there has been . . . a substantial decrease in the value of the scheme assets'.[62]

44.80 The schedule will need to be certified by the scheme actuary who must state whether in his opinion the level of contributions shown is sufficient to ensure the scheme remains fully funded on the MFR basis or will be fully funded at the end of the schedule period. If the actuary does not believe the contribution level will enable the MFR to be met, he must say so. Annual re-certification will be required from the actuary unless the scheme was fully funded at the last actuarial valuation.

44.81 If the employer fails to pay the contributions due under the schedule of contributions, the amount is treated as a debt owed to the scheme.[63] If contributions are not paid over by the due date, reports must be given by the trustees to Opra and the members within prescribed time limits (30 days to get the report to Opra and 90 days to members).[64] In addition, trustees who fail to comply with the requirements are subject to fines under the Pensions Act 1995. Trustees therefore need to ensure that they monitor the collection of contributions.

---

[62] ibid, reg 25.   [63] Pensions Act 1995, s 59.
[64] The Occupational Pension Schemes (Minimum Funding Requirement) Regulations 1996, SI 1996/1536, reg 23. Reports do not need to be made if payment is made within 10 days of the due date and the default is only the first or second in the last 12 months.

Shortfalls

Where the MFR valuation shows that a scheme is between 90 and 100 per cent **44.82** funded on the MFR basis, it now has ten years to reach 100 per cent funded. Where there is a serious under-provision and the scheme was under 90 per cent funded on the MFR basis, the scheme must reach the 90 per cent level within three years and 100 per cent within ten years.

A serious funding under-provision can be dealt with through contributions or **44.83** the employer can pay a lump sum into the scheme. Alternatively, the employer may enter into other arrangements with the trustees within twelve weeks of the MFR valuation, which will guarantee to bring the scheme's assets up to at least 90 per cent of the liabilities if the employer becomes insolvent or the scheme starts to wind up within ten years. These arrangements include arranging a letter of credit in favour of the trustees, lodging the appropriate amount in a deposit account with the trustees, or giving the trustees a charge over an asset of the employer, providing the asset is not subject to any other charge. These alternatives are intended to avoid the strict requirement to eliminate the serious shortfall within three years.

If it appears to the trustees that the MFR is not met on two successive valuations, **44.84** they have three months to prepare a report explaining why the MFR was not met at the second valuation. The report must be made available to members, prospective members, and their spouses, and recognized trade unions within one month. In the case of failure to address a serious under-provision, section 60(4) requires the trustee to notify both Opra and the scheme membership.

The future of the MFR

The MFR has been subject to criticism almost since its introduction in April **44.85** 1997. One of the key problems arose following the abolition of the Advance Corporation Tax Credit given to exempt approved schemes from July 1997.[65] The effect of this was to make the MFR assumptions in relation to investment values inaccurate. Another problem is that even if trustees match the MFR liability profile it is not guaranteed that they will be 100 per cent funded on the MFR basis as actuarial guidance Note GN27 contains assumptions about the rate of return on equities, gilts; and dividend growth; clearly if experience does not reflect the assumptions the MFR position will deteriorate as time passes.

---

[65] Finance (No 2) Act 1997, s 19. This tax credit meant that pension schemes received a tax credit to reflect corporation tax already paid on dividends by the declaring company, but as exempt approved schemes do not have to pay tax on dividend income there was no tax liability to set the tax credit against and instead it represented extra income for schemes.

44.86   In addition, from the members' perspective, the protection provided by the MFR can be illusory as, if the scheme is wound up, even if it is 100 per cent funded on the MFR basis, there may well be insufficient funds to purchase annuities to secure members' benefits as buyout costs can exceed the MFR value of the scheme's liabilities.

44.87   Because of the problems with the MFR, the Government has proposed that it should be replaced with a scheme specific funding requirement which will allow schemes greater flexibility to match their investment strategy to the profile of their members.[66] The trustees will be required to draw up a statement of funding principles with the scheme actuary setting out the funding strategy for the scheme. As now, trustees will be required to obtain a full actuarial valuation at least every three years and, following the valuation, they must put a schedule of contributions in place, setting out how much the employer and employees will pay into the scheme.

Other methods of valuing scheme assets

44.88   As well as valuing the assets on the MFR basis, the Inland Revenue requires that the assets of the scheme should be valued on a statutory basis to ensure that the scheme does not have an excessive surplus. Schedule 22 of ICTA provides that, if a scheme is more that 105 per cent funded on a prescribed basis,[67] either tax is payable on the excess funding or the trustees must submit proposals to the Inland Revenue to reduce the funding to an acceptable level within five years. It is very rare for a scheme to be in statutory surplus as the valuation requirements are so conservative. However, if such a surplus does arise, the options for reducing it to an acceptable rate are an augmentation of benefits, an employer and/or employee contribution holiday, or a refund of surplus to the employer. Failure to reduce a statutory surplus within required time limits can result in withdrawal of Revenue approval.

44.89   In practice, refunds of surplus to an employer in an ongoing scheme are rare as section 37 of the Pensions Act 1995 has imposed stringent conditions on doing so. Section 37 provides that, where there is a surplus for the purposes of Schedule 22, the power to refund surplus can only be exercised by the trustees (irrespective of what the scheme rules provide) and the following conditions must also be met:

(a)   The trustees must be satisfied that 'it is in the interests of the members that the power be exercised in the manner so proposed'. This may be difficult for

---

[66]   DWP/Treasury Consultation Document, *The Minimum Funding Requirement—The Next Stage of Reform*, September 2001.
[67]   Set out in The Pension Schemes Surpluses (Valuation) Regulations 1986, SI 1986/412.

the trustees and is almost certainly not something they should agree to without negotiating with the employer about the possibility of some of the surplus being used for benefit improvements or a member contribution holiday (as these issues will probably require employer consent).

(b) Where the power is conferred by the trust deed on the employer, the employer must have asked for or consented to it being exercised.

(c) Limited price indexation increases (inflation up to 5 per cent) must be applied to all pensions payable under the scheme (rather than just post-April 1997 benefits as would otherwise be required).

(d) Notice must be given to the members of the scheme of the proposal to exercise the power and members have a right to make representations to the trustees which they must then consider (although they do not need to act on them).[68]

(e) Section 601 of ICTA requires the trustees to deduct tax at 35 per cent from any payment of surplus to employer.

As well as complying with these statutory requirements, there is extensive case law on the considerations which trustees should take into account when exercising a power to allocate surplus in an ongoing scheme.[69] A helpful summary of the position was given by Chadwick LJ in *Edge v Pensions Ombudsman*; he said that trustees must: **44.90**

> ... act in a way which appears to them fair and equitable in all the circumstances; and so leads to a reasonable expectation amongst beneficiaries that is what will be done ... The obligation to consider, properly, the question whether to increase benefits (and, if so, which benefits) will usually require the trustees to consider (amongst other matters) the circumstances in which the surplus has arisen. In deciding what is fair and equitable in all the circumstances, the trustees may be expected to give weight to the claims of those whose contributions are, or will be, the effective source of the surplus ... The need to consider the circumstances in which the surplus has arisen does not lead to the conclusion that the trustees are bound to take any particular course as a result of that consideration. They are not constrained by any rule of law either to increase benefits or to reduce contributions or to adopt any particular combination of those options. Nor does the need to consider the circumstances in which the surplus has arisen lead to the conclusion that the trustees are not required to take—or are prohibited from taking—any other matters into account in deciding what course to adopt. They must, for example, always have in mind the main purpose of the scheme—to provide retirement and other benefits for employees of the participating employers. They must consider the effect that any course which they are minded to take will have on the financial ability of the employers to make the contributions which that course will entail. They must be careful not to impose burdens which imperil the continuity and proper development of the employers' business or the employment of the members who work in that business. The main purpose of the

---

[68] For detailed requirements see The Occupational Pension Schemes (Payments to Employers) Regulations 1996, SI 1996/2156.

[69] On trustees' duties in relation to the exercise of their powers, see Chapter 11 above.

scheme is not served by putting an employer out of business. They must also consider the level of benefits under their scheme relative to the benefits under comparable schemes; or in the pensions market generally. They should ask themselves whether the scheme is attractive to the members whose willingness to continue paying contributions is essential to its future funding. Are the benefits seen by the members to be good value in relation to the contributions; would the members find it more attractive to pay higher contributions for higher benefits; or to pay lower contributions and accept lower benefits? The main purpose of the scheme is not served by setting contributions and benefits at levels which deter employees from joining; or which causes resentment. And they must ask themselves whether the benefits enjoyed by members in pension have kept up with increases in the cost of living; so that the expectations of those members during their service—that they were making adequate provision for their retirement through contributions to an occupational pensions scheme—are not defeated by inflation.[70]

44.91 The other basis on which final salary schemes are valued is on a discontinuation basis.[71] The triennial actuarial valuation must include a 'discontinuance statement' which gives an indication of the solvency position of a scheme if it were to be discontinued at the valuation date and, in particular, if there were no further contributions due from the employer(s). The actuary should state whether or not, in his opinion, the assets would have been sufficient at the valuation date to cover liabilities arising (including any dependants' contingent benefits) in respect of pensions in payment, preserved benefits for members whose pensionable service has ceased, and accrued benefits for members in pensionable service.

Money purchase schemes

44.92 The MFR does not apply to money purchase schemes as there are no promised benefits and therefore no minimum funding level necessary to secure them. However, section 87 of the Pensions Act 1995 provides that the trustees must ensure that there is prepared, maintained, and from time to time revised a payment schedule showing the rates of contributions payable to the scheme by or on behalf of the employer and the active members of the scheme. It must also state the due dates agreed for such contributions. It works in a very similar way to a final salary scheme schedule of contributions with the same results if the contributions are not paid across in accordance with the payment schedule.[72] In addition, employers who fail to pay contributions by the due date are also subject to fines.[73]

---

[70] [2000] Ch 602, 626.

[71] Details of the discontinuance basis are set out in Actuarial Guidance Note GN9, Retirement Benefit Schemes—Actuarial Reports.

[72] The Occupational Pensions Schemes (Administration) Regulations 1996, SI 1996/1715, regs 17–21.   [73] Section 88(3) of the Pensions Act 1995.

45

LEGISLATION AFFECTING BENEFITS

A. Introduction

In addition to general trust law requirements, employees and trustees need to be concerned with various legislative provisions aimed at the protection of scheme members and their dependants and ensuring that benefits under occupational pension schemes are treated in a manner consistent with other employment benefits.

45.01

The responsibility for ensuring compliance with these requirements varies as in some cases they are imposed on the scheme trustees and in other cases they relate to the employment relationship between the employees and the scheme members. This chapter examines the impact of the ever-increasing volume of 'protective' legislation and looks at what should be done to ensure compliance with it.

45.02

B. Sex Discrimination

Article 141 of the EC Treaty (Article 119 of the Treaty of Rome, as amended) establishes the principle that men and women should receive equal pay for work of equal value. The meaning of pay has been interpreted fairly widely. In *Barber v*

45.03

Guardian Royal Exchange Assurance Group,[1] the European Court of Justice ('ECJ') held that the concept of pay, within the meaning of Article 141, included any kind of consideration, whether in cash or in kind, whether immediate or future, provided that the worker receives it, albeit indirectly, in respect of his employment from his employer and the equal pay principle must be applied to each element of the remuneration package. In consequence, the ECJ held that rights under a contracted-out occupational pension scheme constituted consideration paid by the employer to the worker in respect of his employment and therefore fell within the scope of Article 141.

45.04 In *Barber*, the common practice of having different retirement ages for men and women was found to be contrary to Article 141. However, to avoid an undue financial burden being imposed on the pensions industry, a temporal limitation was imposed on the impact of the *Barber* judgement and the requirement to equalize retirement ages for men and women only applies to service after the 17 May 1990.[2]

45.05 *Barber* left several issues unresolved, some of which were considered in *Coloroll*.[3] It was held in *Coloroll* that the duty to ensure that pension schemes treated men and women equally for the purposes of Article 141 was not just the employer's but also the trustees'. However, the court acknowledged that trustees were also bound by the terms of their trust documentation and there could well be a conflict between a duty to secure equal treatment and the express terms of the trust deed. It was not clear whether or not the effect of this judgment was to ensure that Article 141 overrides the terms of the trust deed. However, happily for pension scheme trustees, many of the difficulties which this conflict could have created have been resolved by the Pensions Act 1995. Section 62 provides that an occupational pension scheme which does not include an equal treatment rule shall be treated as including one. An equal treatment rule provides that a woman employed in like or equivalent work to a man shall not be treated less favourably than that man in relation to the terms on which she can become a member of the scheme or the way she is treated under it. In addition, in the event that the employer or anyone else will not give any consents necessary to amend the scheme to remove any inequalities, section 65 gives the trustees a unilateral power of amendment to enable them to ensure that the scheme complies with the equal treatment rule.

45.06 One of the difficulties for trustees is that sex discrimination does not have to be direct (that is a provision which expressly differentiates between people on

---

[1] [1991] 1 QB 344; Case C–262/88 *Barber v Guardian Royal Exchange Assurance Group* [1990] ECR I–1889.

[2] To avoid any potential for doubt this date was confirmed at the request of the Dutch government in the Maastricht Protocol (amending the Treaty of Rome).

[3] [1994] OPLR 179; Case C–200/91 *Coloroll Pension Trustees Ltd' v Russell* [1994] ECR I–4389.

grounds of sex). It can be indirect (a sex neutral condition, the consequences of which adversely affect proportionately more members of one sex than another) and therefore difficult to recognize. In broad terms, the test of whether indirect discrimination has taken place looks at whether a requirement or condition which is applied equally to men and women (a) has a disparate effect on the sexes; (b) is such that the proportion of one sex who can comply with it is considerably smaller than the proportion of the other sex who can comply with it; and (c) cannot be objectively justified on grounds other than sex.[4]

One indirect discrimination issue which has caused pension schemes a consider- **45.07**
able amount of difficulty is the rights of part-time employees. The question was first considered by the ECJ in 1986 in *Bilka Kaufhaus*.[5] The ECJ held that not admitting part-time employees to occupational pension schemes could amount to indirect sex discrimination (as the majority of part-time employees tend to be women) unless such exclusion could be objectively justified. The issue was considered again in 1994 in the cases of *Vroege* and *Fisscher*,[6] where the ECJ ruled that part-time employees could bring indirect discrimination claims for exclusion from their employers' occupational pension schemes in respect of employment periods dating back to April 1976.[7] The court also held that time limits under national law could be applied to such claims provided that they did not render virtually impossible or excessively difficult the exercise of community law rights (the 'effectiveness principle') and were no less favourable than those for similar actions of a domestic nature (the 'equivalence principle'). As a result, the Government enacted regulations with effect from 31 May 1995 which provided that part-timer claims must be made within six months after leaving service and backdated membership could be awarded for a maximum period of two years immediately preceding the date of the claim. The validity of these time limits was considered in *Preston*[8] and the ECJ held that the two-year time limit was contrary to the effectiveness principle but the six-month time limit was not. The matter was then remitted back to the House of Lords and, in February 2001, they decided that part-timers could be allowed to claim backdated service for periods as far back as April 1976[9] but claims still have to be made within six months of leaving service.

---

[4] For an example of how to determine whether there has been indirect sex discrimination see *R v Secretary of State, ex parte Seymour-Smith and Perez* [1999] 2AC 554.
[5] Case 170/84 *Bilka-Kaufhaus v Weber von Hartz* [1986] ECR 1607.
[6] Case C–57/93 *Vroege v NCIV Instituut voor Volkshuisvesting BV* [1994] ECR I–4541 and Case C–128/93 *Fisscher v Voorhuis Hengelo VB* [1994] ECR I–4583.
[7] The date of the ECJ's decision in Case 43/75 *Defrenne v Belgium* [1976] ECR 455, where it ruled that Art 141 (then Art 119) could be relied on by an individual to bring a claim irrespective of whether it had been enacted in the relevant domestic jurisdiction.
[8] Case C–78/98 *Preston v Wolverhampton Healthcare NHS Trust* [2000] ECR I–3201.
[9] *Preston v Wolverhampton NHS Healthcare Trust* [2001] 2 AC 455. It needs to be borne in mind that claims to the Pensions Ombudsman have different time limits to those settled on by the House of Lords, which was only considering claims to employment tribunals. The Ombudsman has not

45.08 However, even if indirect sex discrimination can be demonstrated it is still possible that employers may claim that the treatment was 'objectively justified' and no action is therefore required. Objective justification has not really been tested in a pensions context, but it seems unlikely that cost savings would suffice.

C. Part-Time Workers

45.09 The position of part-time employees going forward is different: they no longer have to prove indirect sex discrimination in relation to their treatment in respect of service after July 2000.

45.10 The Part-Time Workers (Prevention of Less Favourable Treatment) Regulations 2000[10] were introduced with effect from 1 July 2000 and, in general terms, prohibit employers from treating part-time workers differently from full-time workers simply because they work part-time. The Regulations provide that a part-time worker has the right not to be treated less favourably by his employer than a full-time worker who works under the same type of contract and who is engaged in the same or broadly similar work, unless the discrimination can be objectively justified. The Regulations do not impose obligations directly on the pension scheme trustees.

45.11 The effect of the Regulations for pension schemes is that employers must not discriminate between full-time and part-time workers over access to their schemes unless different treatment is justified on objective grounds.

D. Fixed-Term Employees

45.12 Legislation was put in place to protect fixed-term workers from 1 October 2002.[11] The Fixed-term Employees Regulations introduced similar requirements for fixed-term employees as those applicable to part-time workers discussed above. Under the Regulations, fixed-term employees have the right not to be treated less favourably by their employer than comparable permanent employees. The terms of the Regulations are wide enough to cover rights under occupational pension schemes. There is again an 'objective justification' defence and the Regulations

---

previously considered himself bound by the *Preston* case or the related regulations and has instead applied his normal three-year statutory time limit to both eligibility to bring a claim and the period in respect of which he directs compensation.

[10] Part-time Workers (Prevention of Less Favourable Treatment) Regulations 2000, SI 2000/1551 implementing Council Directive (EC) 97/81 concerning the framework agreement on part-time work concluded by UNICE, CEEP and the ETUC [1998] OJ L131.

[11] The Fixed-term Employees (Prevention of Less Favourable Treatment) Regulations 2002, SI 2002/2034 implementing Council Directive (EC) 99/70 concerning the framework agreement on fixed-term work concluded by ETUC, UNICE and CEEP [1999] OJ L175.

provide that treatment can be taken to be justified on objective grounds where the terms of the fixed term employee's contract of employment, taken as a whole, are at least as favourable as the comparable permanent employee.

Again, this is an obligation on the employer rather than the trustees. The type of **45.13** situation it is likely to apply to in occupational pension schemes is where the scheme is only open to permanent staff. The objective justification may well be that the contract was less than two years and the fixed-term workers would not therefore become entitled to any vested benefits under the scheme (see below on rights of early leavers).

E. Age Discrimination

In 2000, a European Equal Treatment Directive[12] was issued, establishing a **45.14** general framework for combating discrimination on various grounds including age. When the Directive is implemented into UK law it will have the effect of outlawing age discrimination.

Article 6 of the Directive permits member states to allow differences in treatment **45.15** on grounds of age if 'they are objectively and reasonably justified by a legitimate aim, including legitimate employment policy...and if the means of achieving that aim are appropriate and necessary'. Article 6 also specifically allows member states to permit occupational pension schemes to fix 'ages for admission or entitlement to retirement or invalidity benefits...and the use...of age criteria in actuarial calculations' providing that there is no sex discrimination.

There is as yet no UK legislation on age discrimination, but when the age provi- **45.16** sions of the Directive are implemented in the UK (which they must be by 2 December 2006) it could affect matters such as the requirement to use money purchase funds to purchase annuities at age 75, age related employer contributions, and winding-up priorities (which favour pensioners over the generally younger deferred members). It will certainly prevent the employer from specifying fixed retirement ages.

F. Sexual Orientation

The Equal Treatment Directive also contains provisions in relation to discri- **45.17** mination on grounds of sexual orientation. Regulations[13] came into force on

---

[12] Council Directive (EC) 2000/78 establishing a general framework for equal treatment in employment and occupation [2000] OJ L303.
[13] The Employment Equality (Sexual Orientation) Regulations 2003, SI 2003/1661.

1 December 2003, which provide that it is unlawful to discriminate on grounds of sexual orientation in relation to terms of employment offered, which includes pension provision. However, there is a provision in Regulation 25 allowing discrimination where access to benefits is dependent on marital status. This means that the Regulations will not prevent occupational pension schemes providing death benefits for legal spouses only.

45.18 Additional Regulations[14] make it unlawful for trustees or managers of occupational pension schemes to discriminate against members or prospective members on grounds of sexual orientation. Regulation 3(3) includes an equal treatment rule in all occupational pension schemes and gives trustees 'power to alter the scheme so as to secure conformity with the non-discrimination rule'.

G. Disability

45.19 Disability discrimination is prevented by the Disability Discrimination Act 1995. However, the Act will be amended to reflect the Equal Treatment Directive with effect from 1 October 2004. An employer, or the trustees of an occupational pension scheme, discriminate against a disabled person if, for a reason relating to the disabled person's disability, they treat that person less favourably than they would treat someone who did not have a disability and they cannot show that the treatment in question is justified. Treatment can only be justified if the reason for it is material to the circumstances of a particular case and is essential. Section 17 of the Act inserts into every occupational pension scheme a provision 'requiring the trustees or managers of the scheme to refrain from any act or omission which, if done in relation to a person by an employer, would amount to unlawful discrimination'. This is not quite the same as the equal treatment rule in the Pensions Act for sex discrimination which inserts an equality provision in the scheme rules, this simply prevents the trustees from acting in a discriminatory way. Section 17(2) provides that the non-discrimination provision is overriding.

45.20 It is currently possible for less favourable treatment towards a disabled person to be justified in a pensions context if the reason for it is 'material' and 'substantial'.[15] This means that where a disabled person's health could lead to a substantial increase in the cost of providing benefits under the pension scheme because, for example, they suffer from a degenerative disease and are likely to retire early on health grounds, it may be justifiable to treat them less favourably by applying different eligibility conditions. Before restricting the benefit, however, trustees

---

[14] The Employment Equality (Sexual Orientation) (Amendment) Regulations 2003, SI 2003/2827.
[15] The Disability Discrimination (Employment) Regulations 1996, SI 1996/1456, reg 4.

should consider obtaining actuarial and possibly medical advice on whether there is a substantial increase in cost.

The position will be different from 1 October 2004. Regulations were issued in 2003 **45.21** which are due to come into force on 1 October 2004 and will amend the Disability Discrimination Act 1995 in relation to trustees' duties under occupational pension schemes.[16] They will give trustees the power to make unilateral amendments to the scheme to ensure compliance with the non-discrimination rule and impose a duty on trustees to make reasonable adjustments where 'a provision, criterion or practice (including a scheme rule) applied by or on behalf of the trustees or managers of an occupational pension scheme, or . . . any physical feature of premises occupied by the trustees or managers . . . places a relevant disabled person at a substantial disadvantage in comparison with persons who are not disabled' (a suggested example of the impact of this is that a booklet would have to be in a form accessible to a blind member if that member would otherwise be at a substantial disadvantage to other members).

H. Maternity and Family Leave

The position for occupational pension schemes in relation to maternity is **45.22** complex. The requirements derive in part from the Social Security Act 1989, Schedule 5 and in part from the Employment Rights Act 1996 (as amended by the Employment Relations Act 1999).

Schedule 5 to the Social Security Act 1989 provides that every 'employment- **45.23** related benefit scheme shall comply with the principle of equal treatment' and the 'principle of equal treatment is that persons of the one sex shall not, on the basis of sex, be treated less favourably than persons of the other sex in any respect relating to an employment-related benefit scheme';[17] and 'where the scheme includes any unfair maternity provisions, it shall to that extent be regarded as according less favourable treatment to women on the basis of sex'. Unfair maternity provisions are defined as being provisions which relate to the accrual of benefits or continuing membership of the scheme during a period of paid maternity absence (whether statutory or contractual). This means that while a woman is receiving any pay at all she must continue to accrue benefits as normal under the scheme and the accrual must be based on the salary she would have been earning if she were not on maternity leave; however, she is only obliged to pay contributions based on the salary she actually receives.

---

[16] The Disability Discrimination Act 1995 (Pensions) Regulations 2003, SI 2003/2770. Note, that provisions amending the Disability Discrimination Act in relation to employers' obligations are set out in The Disability Discrimination Act 1995 (Amendment) Regulations 2003, SI 2003/1673.

[17] This provision was brought into force on 23 June 1994 for the purposes only of the unfair maternity and family leave provisions in Sch 5, paras 5 and 6.

45.24   In addition, section 71 of the Employment Rights Act 1996 provides that a member on ordinary maternity leave (generally 26 weeks) is entitled to the benefit of the terms and conditions of employment which would have applied if she had not been absent (except in so far as they relate to remuneration, but this is very narrowly construed as wages or salary).[18] Section 75A of the Employment Rights Act 1996 makes similar provisions in relation to ordinary adoption leave.

45.25   There are some questions about the correct way to treat a member of a money purchase scheme who is on paid maternity leave. Clearly the employer must maintain its own contributions at the pre-maternity leave level. However, the employee's contributions will be based only on the pay she is actually receiving which, without any additional employer contributions, would result in her resulting benefits being lower. The question is therefore whether the employer is under a duty to make up the employee's contributions. The Schedule 5 equal treatment requirements only apply to 'employment related benefit schemes' which means a scheme which provides service related benefits. It is questionable how this applies to money purchase schemes. However, the Pregnant Workers Directive,[19] which Schedule 5 implements, makes no distinction between final salary and money purchase schemes and the safest interpretation would therefore seem to be to apply Schedule 5 to both and say that the employer should make up any shortfall in the employee's own contributions during periods of paid maternity absence. The position is even less clear in relation to additional voluntary contributions and is something that individual employers will need to take a view on.

45.26   The position is different if the member is on unpaid 'additional maternity leave' (generally a further 26 weeks); there are no requirements for this period to be counted as pensionable. Continuity of qualifying service is, however, maintained for the purpose of determining whether the member is entitled to a vested benefit under the scheme. Similar provisions apply in relation to parental leave, unpaid adoption leave, and paternity leave.[20]

I. Pensions Increases

45.27   Sections 51–55 of the Pensions Act 1995 contain requirements in relation to increases to pensions in payment. These requirements apply to both money

---

[18] The Maternity and Parental Leave etc Regulations 1999, SI 1999/3312, reg 9(3).

[19] Council Directive (EEC) 92/85 on the introduction of measures to encourage improvements in the safety and health at work of pregnant workers and workers who have recently given birth or are breastfeeding [1992] OJ L348.

[20] See the Maternity Regulations and The Paternity and Adoption Leave Regulations 2002, SI 2002/2788.

purchase and final salary schemes and provide for 'limited price indexation' ('LPI') on pensions in payment. LPI requires pensions to be increased by the lesser of 5 per cent or the percentage annual increase in the retail prices index. The requirement only applies to, in the case of final salary schemes, pension benefits accrued on or after 6 April 1997 and, in the case of money purchase schemes, payments made in respect of employment after 6 April 1997. The statutory requirement only applies where the annual rate of the pension would not otherwise be increased each year by at least the LPI amount.

Section 51(2) of the Child Support, Pensions and Social Security Act 2000 **45.28** introduced an exception to this basic requirement for pensions under money purchase schemes which are used to purchase investment linked annuities. The idea being that this would allow for greater flexibility in relation to the annuity product which had to be purchased.

There are different increase requirements in relation to Guaranteed Minimum **45.29** Pensions ('GMPs'). Section 109 of the Pension Schemes Act 1993 provides that GMPs should be increased each year they are in payment by the lesser of 3 per cent or the percentage annual increase in the retail prices index. Any increases to GMPs above this level can be offset against the LPI requirements.

The LPI requirements have been criticized on the basis that they provide an **45.30** unnecessary level of prescription on the form that a voluntary benefit provided by the employer must take and represent a disproportionate level of costs. When the Government consulted on the possibility of abolishing the LPI requirements the response it received from the pensions industry was along the lines that the 'continued existence [of LPI] is a major factor prompting the closure of defined benefit schemes . . . schemes should no longer be required to provide guaranteed increases for future service'. However, consumer organizations and trade unions 'stressed that it was important that the purchasing power of pensions was broadly maintained'. The Government has said that the 5 per cent cap is excessive in the current climate as LPI was only intended to provide partial inflation proofing but, because inflation is currently well below 5 per cent, it has ended up providing full cover. Therefore, the proposal is that the 5 per cent cap should be reduced to 2.5 per cent.

J. Early Leavers

Another area where scheme design is affected by legislation aimed at protecting **45.31** members' benefits is in relation to the benefits payable to or in respect of those individuals who leave service before normal retirement date. It was once commonplace to provide such former employees with no pension benefits. However, as employees have earned their pension benefits and they amount to deferred pay, this was clearly not acceptable. Therefore, legislation was introduced to protect the rights of such individuals. The key provisions are currently in Part IV of the Pensions Act 1993 and The Occupational Pension Schemes (Preservation of Benefit) Regulations.[21]

45.32 These requirements do not override contrary provisions in the scheme documentation. Section 132 of the Pension Schemes Act 1993 provides that it is the 'responsibility of the trustees and managers of the scheme to take such steps as are open to them for bringing the rules of the scheme into conformity with [these] requirements'.

Short-Service Benefit

45.33 The basic requirement to protect the benefits of early leavers is that if such a member has a least two years' qualifying service he is entitled to receive his benefits under the scheme in one of a number of ways. Qualifying service is defined in section 71 of the Pension Schemes Act 1993 as meaning '2 years (whether a single period of that duration or two or more periods, continuous or discontinuous, totalling 2 years) in which the member was at all times employed either: (a) in pensionable service under the scheme; or (b) in service in employment which was contracted-out by reference to the scheme; or (c) in linked qualifying service under another scheme'.

45.34 The benefit that an early leaver is entitled to is his 'short service benefit' and it must be calculated in the same way as his benefits would have been calculated if he had remained in service until retirement (his 'long service benefit'). A scheme must not contain any rule which results, or can result, in a member being treated less favourably for any purpose relating to short service benefit than he is, or is entitled to be, treated for the corresponding purpose relating to long service benefit.[22] Careful thought therefore needs to be given to the benefit structure in schemes to ensure that there is no such discrimination.

45.35 A short service benefit may be provided in a number of ways including a pension from the scheme (including an early retirement pension) or a transfer to another pension arrangement or be bought out with an insurance policy.

Revaluation

45.36 For so long as the benefit is retained in the scheme, it must be revalued each year to ensure that when it comes into payment it has retained a degree of meaningful value. The revaluation requirements are currently contained in Part IV, Chapter II

---

[21] SI 1991/167.   [22] Pension Schemes Act 1993, s 72.

of the Pension Scheme Act 1993.[23] The short service benefit (in excess of any GMP entitlement) must be revalued each year from the date of leaving until retirement by the lesser of 5 per cent a year compound or the percentage annual increase in the retail prices index.

Individual Transfer Payments

Members have a statutory entitlement to take their benefits from their former **45.37** employer's scheme and transfer them to another approved pension arrangement. The basic right is set out in section 94 of the Pension Schemes Act 1993 and varies slightly dependent on whether an individual is a member of a final salary or money purchase scheme. Section 94 provides that a money purchase scheme member 'acquires a right, when his pensionable service terminates . . . to the cash equivalent at the relevant date of any benefits which have accrued to or in respect of him under the applicable rules'. The position is slightly more complex in the case of a final salary scheme member. A final salary member has the right to require a guaranteed statement of what their cash equivalent is worth. The trustees must supply a transfer value quotation on request and the transfer value must normally be calculated within three months of the date of the request and the amount must be guaranteed for a further three months. The transfer value quotation must be issued within ten working days of the date at which it has been calculated. The normal time limit for calculating the transfer value may be extended to six months if the trustees decide that, for reasons beyond their control, they are unable to obtain the information required to calculate the transfer value within three months. A member who has received a quotation and wishes to transfer his benefits must submit a written application within the three-month guarantee period. The normal time limit for paying a guaranteed transfer value is six months from the guarantee date.

The provisions in relation to the calculation of cash equivalents are set out in **45.38** section 97 of the Pension Schemes Act 1993, The Occupational Pension Schemes (Transfer Values) Regulations 1996[24] and Actuarial Guidance Note GN11 Retirement Benefit Schemes—Transfer Values. The position is fairly straightforward in a money purchase scheme as it is easy to attach a value to a member's money purchase account. It is much more difficult to put a value on a member's accrued rights in a final salary scheme as what is being valued is a right to the

---

[23] These requirements only relate to those who leave service after 1 January 1991. For those who left service before this date, the revaluation requirements only apply to post 31 December 1984 service (although many schemes disregard this distinction).

[24] SI 1996/1847 as amended by The Occupational Pension Schemes (Transfer Values and Miscellaneous Amendment) Regulations 2003, SI 2003/1727.

payment of an annual pension in the future. As a result the rules for calculating the cash equivalent transfer value in a final salary scheme are complex.

45.39   The calculation of a final salary scheme transfer value must be carried out by the scheme actuary, be consistent with the principles set out in Actuarial Guidance Note GN11,[25] and generally provide, as a minimum, an amount consistent with the methods and assumptions adopted in calculating the Minimum Finding Requirement ('MFR'). GN11 requires that a cash equivalent should represent the expected cost of providing the member's accrued benefits in the scheme and should be assessed having regard to market rates of return on equities, gilts, or other assets as appropriate. This is referred to as the 'fair value' test. Under GN11, if the immediate payment of a full cash equivalent transfer value would reduce the security of other members' benefits, the actuary should advise the trustees as to any reduced cash equivalent transfer value which would be appropriate having regard to the provisions of the relevant provisions of the Transfer Regulations.

45.40   Unfortunately, it became very difficult for actuaries to certify that the MFR basis for calculating transfer values satisfied the fair value test and, as a result, the Transfer Regulations were amended.[26] Under the revised Transfer Regulations, trustees are able to reduce transfer values by the level of underfunding shown on the actuary's GN11 basis as well as where the last actuarial valuation showed an MFR deficit or where the scheme is winding up with an MFR deficit. The difficulty for the trustees is how to balance the interests of departing members with those who are remaining behind to ensure that the departing member is not better or worse off than the remaining members. For example, if a transfer value is reduced to reflect a shortfall on the GN11 basis, what weight should the trustees give the fact that members will generally receive their benefits in full unless a winding up is triggered and then, if the employer is solvent, it will have to make up any shortfall (as discussed below)?

45.41   The payment of transfer payments over and above the statutory entitlements will usually be a discretion of the trustees, as will a decision whether or not to accept a transfer payment into the scheme. Both will require balancing the interests of the transferring members against those of the other scheme members.

Bulk Transfers

45.42   Bulk transfers usually occur where part of the employer's business is being sold or the employer is reorganizing its pension arrangements and a number of

---

[25] GN11 is given statutory force by The Occupational Pension Scheme (Transfer Values) Regulations 1996, SI 1996/1847, reg 8(4).
[26] The Occupational Pensions Schemes (Transfer Values and Miscellaneous Amendments) Regulations 2003, SI 2003/1727.

schemes are being merged. Additional considerations apply in the case of bulk transfers.

In the case of bulk transfers, trustees will need to consider whether member **45.43** consent needs to be obtained to the transfer. Consent will usually be required unless the requirements in The Occupational Pension Schemes (Preservation of Benefits) Regulations[27] are satisfied. These broadly require the trustees to obtain a certificate from the scheme actuary confirming the transfer credits to be acquired for each member under the receiving scheme are broadly no less favourable than the rights to be transferred and, where it is the established custom for discretionary benefits to be awarded under the transferring scheme, there is good cause to believe that the award of discretionary benefits under the receiving scheme will (making allowance for any amount by which transfer credits under the receiving scheme are more favourable than the rights to be transferred) be broadly no less favourable.[28] The actuary is not, however, required to certify whether the transfer payment is reasonable in all the circumstances. This is an issue for the scheme trustees.

When determining the amount of any bulk transfer payment, there is a duty to **45.44** balance the interests of the transferring members and the remaining ones. Where the power is given to the trustees and the transfer arises on the sale of part of the employer's business, the employer may have already agreed a transfer payment with the purchaser. However, such an agreement does not bind the trustees and they must determine what they think an appropriate transfer value is and they must ensure that they take into account all the considerations which are relevant at the time of the transfer. The considerations to be made by trustees when determining bulk transfers were considered in the *Fisons* case.[29] A substantial part of the Fisons business was sold and, at the time of the sale, the pension scheme was in deficit. However, by the time a bulk transfer came to be made the scheme was in surplus. A member complained when the trustees transferred a sum calculated on the basis agreed at the time of the sale. The case came to court and the trustees were required to reconsider their transfer arrangements as, by the time of the transfer, there had been a change in circumstances. The court emphasized the importance of trustees taking into account the position of the transferring members. In particular, where a scheme is in surplus, they should consider the chance of the transferring members enjoying the benefit of that surplus.

Where the issue of a transfer has arisen as a result of a proposed scheme merger, **45.45** both receiving and transferring trustees need to think very carefully as to whether

---

[27] SI 1991/167, reg 12.
[28] Details of what the actuary will take into account when giving his certificate are to be found in Actuarial Guidance Note GN16, Retirement Benefit Schemes–Bulk Transfers for the requirements in relation to such certificates.   [29] *Stannard v Fisons Pension Trust Limited,* [1991] PLR 225.

the merger is in the interests of their members. The best achievable in any situation will depend upon the respective bargaining powers of the trustees and the employer. So, for example, if on winding up the trustees have unilateral power to use surplus to improve benefits, they will have a much stronger bargaining position than if this is subject to employer consent. The other major factor is the financial state of the two schemes. The trustees of a scheme in surplus should be very wary about receiving monies and liabilities from, or transferring them to, a scheme with a deficit. Any such transfer could affect the security of members' benefits.

K. Divorce

45.46   Trustees have a duty to implement the provisions in relation to the treatment of pension benefits on a member's divorce. They can be faced with two different types of court order: an earmarking order which provides that part of the member's pension and/or a part of a lump sum benefit may be paid to the member's former spouse or a pension sharing order which splits the member's benefits between him and his former spouse, giving her a pension in her own right.

45.47   In relation to earmarking, the court can order that part of a member's pension or part of any lump sum payable to or in respect of the member should be paid to the member's former spouse. This includes any lump sum death benefit payable in respect of the member and an order allocating part of the lump sum death benefit to the former spouse overrides any discretion which the trustees have in the scheme documentation to allocate the death benefit.[30] The problem with earmarking is that the former spouse must wait until the member receives his benefits before anything is payable to her and she will not be entitled to a dependant's pension on the member's death.

45.48   Pension sharing gives rise to more complex issues from the trustees' perspective. A pension sharing order will result in a percentage of the member's cash equivalent being shared with the former spouse. The cash equivalent will be calculated as if an active member had left service the day before the effective date of the pension sharing order. The member's pension rights are then debited by the specified percentage and the former spouse acquires a corresponding pension 'credit'.[31]

45.49   Trustees must allow the former spouse to transfer the pension credit to a suitable pension arrangement of her choice. In the absence of a choice being made by the former spouse, the trustees may either retain the pension credit within the scheme or transfer it to a 'qualifying arrangement' (which can include another occupational scheme, a personal pension plan, an insurance contract, and a stakeholder

---

[30] Pensions Act 1995, ss 166–167 amending the Matrimonial Causes Act 1973.
[31] For details on the calculation of the pension credit and debit see The Pension Sharing (Valuation) Regulations 2000, SI 2000/1052.

arrangement).[32] If the credit is retained in the scheme there is considerable flexibility as to exactly what benefits will be provided, but in general terms the former spouse will be treated in much the same way as an early leaver.

When the trustees are making a decision what to do with pension credit benefits, **45.50** there are some difficult considerations for them. If one views the matter solely considering the interests of the former spouse, there may be good reasons for offering an internal transfer, at least as an option. But if the former spouse is retained in the scheme, must the trustees offer her the best available benefit—for example, could final salary scheme trustees consider offering a money purchase benefit? Trustees will also need to consider the interests of other beneficiaries; if there is additional expense in retaining pension credit benefits in the scheme, then this may affect the security of other members' benefits. Trustees may be initially tempted to decide to have nothing to do with the former spouse's benefits and, as scheme rules must be amended to accommodate pension sharing, introduce a rule allowing only for pension credit benefits to be transferred out rather than retained in the scheme. However, they must not fetter the discretions which legislation has given them and so, while they can form a policy to transfer pension credits out, they must keep it under review and not take any irreversible step to prevent internal transfers.

Underfunded schemes have a different problem. A reduced pension credit transfer **45.51** can be offered if the scheme is underfunded on the MFR basis, but the former spouse cannot be compelled to accept it. If she does not, either a full transfer value must be used to secure the credit, or she must be given benefits within the scheme (with the same priority on wind up as the member's benefits would have).

Dealing with pension sharing orders will undoubtedly add to the administration **45.52** costs of the scheme. In recognition of this, the legislation allows trustees to impose charges on the divorcing parties, although they need not do so. If charges are imposed, they will fall on the member unless the trustees are informed otherwise. Charges can be recovered directly from the parties, or by deducting them from the former spouse's pension credit or the member's benefits. The trustees will have the right to delay the implementation of a pension sharing order if charges have been invoiced but remain unpaid. Charges are limited to the costs incurred in implementing the order and further charges can be made if the former spouse's benefits are retained in the scheme rather than transferred out.[33]

A detailed consideration of the requirements of implementing a pension sharing **45.53** or earmarking order is outside the scope of this chapter. However, there are

---

[32] Welfare Reform and Pensions Act 1999, Sch 5 and reg 7 of The Pension Sharing (Implementation and Discharge of Liability) Regulations 2000, SI 2000/1053.
[33] The Pensions on Divorce etc (Charging) Regulations 2000, SI 2000/1049.

detailed requirements in relation to the information that the scheme trustees are obliged to provide to the parties and time limits for implementing the orders.[34]

L. Inalienability of Pension Rights

45.54 Section 91(1) of the Pensions Act 1995 provides that as a general rule any entitlement to pension under an occupational pension scheme cannot be assigned, commuted, surrendered, or charged and no lien or set-off can be exercised in respect of it. Any agreement attempting to effect any of these things is unenforceable.

45.55 However, this general prohibition does not prevent a charge or lien on, or set-off against a person's benefits to allow the employer to obtain the discharge of a monetary obligation due to it or to discharge a monetary obligation due from the person to the scheme. In either case the obligations must arise out of a criminal, negligent, or fraudulent act or omission by the person or, if the person is a trustee of an occupational pension scheme and the obligation is due to the scheme, arising out of a breach of trust by him.

45.56 Section 92 of the Pensions Act 1995 contains a general prohibition on forfeiture of rights under an occupational pension scheme. There used to be an exception for bankruptcy, and scheme rules typically provided that, in the event of an attempted assignment of benefits on a member's bankruptcy, the trustees could forfeit a member's benefits to ensure that they were not paid to the member's trustee in bankruptcy.[35] Typically, in these cases, the trustees would also have a discretion to pay the forfeited benefits to one of the member's dependants. However, where the petition for bankruptcy was made after 29 May 2000, the position has changed. Legislation now provides that the vast majority of pension rights do not form part of the member's estate and therefore they will not vest in the member's trustee in bankruptcy.[36] Perversely, a member may actually be worse off under this new regime. Because the member remains entitled to receive the benefits (rather than the scheme trustees exercising a power to pay the benefits to the member's dependants) a trustee in bankruptcy may be entitled to obtain an income payments order to the effect that the bankrupt must pay to the trustee in bankruptcy an agreed amount which is deemed to be above the income which the bankrupt requires by way of subsistence allowance. Once their pension comes into payment, an income

---

[34] See in particular The Pension Sharing (Implementation and Discharge of Liability) Regulations 2000, SI 2000/1053 and The Pensions on Divorce etc (Provision of Information) Regulations 2000, SI 2000/1048.

[35] The principle that a provision in a trust instrument purporting to forfeit an absolute interest is void as contrary to the nature of such an interest was dealt with by drafting the scheme rules to ensure that the members did not have an absolute interest in their benefits under the scheme but a conditional interest which continued only so long as they did not become bankrupt. This approach was approved in *Re Scientific Investment Plan* [1998] OPLR 41.

[36] Welfare Reform and Pensions Act 1999, s 11, amending s 91 of the Pensions Act 1995.

payments order can apply to a bankrupt's pension benefits and may bind scheme trustees. This could apply even if the income payments order pre-dates the bankrupt's retirement or if the bankrupt retires after his bankruptcy is discharged.

Section 15 of the Welfare Reform and Pensions Act 1999 also makes provision for **45.57** dealing with excessive contributions. A trustee in bankruptcy may apply to the court for an order that contributions made to a pension scheme prior to bankruptcy were excessive and designed to put assets out of reach of creditors. When considering such an order, the trustee in bankruptcy can request the trustees of a pension scheme to provide any information which he reasonably requires. The pension scheme has nine weeks from receipt of the request to provide the information. The court may also require an affidavit from the pension scheme with details of the bankrupt's dealings with the scheme. Where there have been excessive contributions, the court may order the pension scheme to pay the excessive element of the contributions to the trustee in bankruptcy and reduce the bankrupt's pension rights accordingly.[37]

M. European Law

As well as a myriad of UK legislative provisions, European law has also had a **45.58** significant impact on occupational pension schemes. Until recently, it was primarily European law on employment that was relevant; however, recently, Europe has passed specific legislation in relation to occupational pension schemes.

In June 2003, the first European Pensions Directive was published.[38] The **45.59** Directive provides a framework for the operation and supervision of occupational pension schemes. It also allows schemes established in one EU member state to be sponsored by employers in other member states.

Member states must implement the Directive by September 2005. By and large it **45.60** should not have a great deal of impact on the current legislative regime in the UK as most of its provisions are already largely reflected in UK law. At the date of writing, the Department of Work and Pensions has published a consultation paper focusing on the key areas in which the Directive will impact on UK law.[39] The areas it focuses on are discussed below.

The Directive establishes the prudent man approach in relation to investment **45.61** powers in line with the approach already adopted in the UK. It also provides for

---

[37] The Occupational and Personal Pension Schemes (Bankruptcy) (No 2) Regulations 2002, SI 2002/836.

[38] Council Directive (EC) 2003/41 on the activities and supervision of institutions for occupational retirement provision.

[39] *Implementing the European Directive on the Activities and Supervision of Institutions for Occupational Retirement Provision: a Consultation Paper,* 28 October 2003.

some liberalization of the quantitative investment restrictions currently applied in some countries (there are no such restrictive requirements in the UK).

45.62 Schemes will be supervised and regulated by national regulators (such as the Occupational Pensions Regulatory Authority ('Opra'). They will need to be registered (as they must already be in the UK) and must fulfil a number of minimum conditions, such as being run by people of good repute and having properly constituted scheme rules. The regulators will be able to carry out inspections and intervene to help protect members' rights (this may be slightly more proactive than the role currently carried out by Opra).

45.63 There are significant disclosure requirements (which are broadly in line with those already in UK legislation, in particular in the Disclosure Regulations). There are also disclosure requirements in relation to the regulator, who will also have powers to require schemes to provide certain information.

45.64 Certain schemes (such as final salary schemes) will have to value their accrued liabilities annually. A triennial valuation is permitted if the scheme provides members and/or the competent authorities with a report setting out the adjusted development of the scheme's liabilities and changes in risks covered. The Directive lays down a framework for how this calculation is to be done. Schemes must hold 'sufficient and appropriate assets' to cover accrued liabilities. If a scheme is underfunded, it must adopt a recovery plan and there are rules about how the recovery plan must be drawn up.

45.65 There are a number of optional elements in the Directive which member states can choose whether to adopt. In particular, the extent to which the Directive should apply to pension schemes with fewer than 100 members.

45.66 The provisions likely to have the most impact in the UK are those which relate to funding. A concern has been voiced that the provisions in the Directive relating to ensuring that there are sufficient assets to cover liabilities could replicate many of the problems currently being experienced with the MFR and might cause difficulties in relation to the proposals to replace the MFR with a scheme specific solvency standard.

N. Transfer of Undertakings

45.67 Another element of European law which is likely to have an impact on pension schemes in the future is the Acquired Rights Directive.[40] Member states are required under the Directive to adopt the measures necessary to ensure that

---

[40] Council Directive (EEC) 77/187 as amended by Council Directive (EC) 98/50.

employment rights are protected on the transfer of an undertaking. However, the Directive also provides that employees' rights to old age, invalidity, or survivors' benefits under supplementary company or inter-company pension schemes outside the statutory social security schemes in member states are exempt from this general requirement.

The provisions of the Acquired Rights Directive are implemented in UK law in **45.68** the Transfer of Undertakings (Protection of Employment) Regulations 1981[41] ('TUPE') and the exemption for old age benefits is contained in Regulation 7. Regulation 7 provides that terms in a contract of employment which relate to occupational pension schemes will not transfer to the new owner of the business. However, this exemption does not apply to terms of the pension scheme which do not relate to 'benefits for old age, invalidity or survivors'.

The meaning of benefits relating to old age and the scope of the pensions exemp- **45.69** tion have been considered on several occasions by the ECJ who have interpreted this more narrowly than UK schemes might have hoped. The ECJ has held that:

> Given the general objective of safeguarding the rights of employees in the event of transfers of undertakings pursued by the Directive . . . the exception . . . must be interpreted strictly. That exception can therefore apply only to the benefits listed exhaustively in that provision and they must be construed in a narrow sense. In that connection, it is only benefits paid from the time when an employee reaches the end of his normal working life as laid down by the general structure of the pension scheme in question, and not benefits paid in circumstances such as those in point in the main proceedings (dismissal for redundancy) that can be classified as old-age benefits, even if they are calculated by reference to the rules for calculating normal pension benefits.[42]

This means that employees who are members of pension schemes which provide benefits on redundancy or restructuring and who transfer to new employers may retain the right to some of their specific pre-transfer pension benefits. This would mean that the new employer would need to replicate these benefits. It is, however, worth noting that TUPE operates to preserve rights under the contract of employment between employer and employee and is not therefore an issue which scheme trustees need to be directly concerned with.

The interpretation of the pensions exemption may cease to be of so much **45.70** relevance in the future as changes to TUPE are currently under review. As pension benefits are regarded as pay, it seems anomalous that they should be excluded from the general transfer of employment rights. The Government feels the current provisions leave 'many employees vulnerable to having detrimental changes made to their future pension entitlement' and have put forward proposals to deal with this

---

[41] SI 1981/1794.
[42] Case C–164/00 *Beckmann v Dynamco Whicheloe Macfarlane*, 4 June 2002, paras 29–31.

issue.[43] Their current proposals aim 'to ensure that workers who already enjoy pensions contributions will not have them withdrawn by reason of a transfer, or because a company is taken over. In achieving this we want to make sure that we do not place an excessive burden on the new employer...The Government proposes a flexible and worthwhile provision for a contribution to a stakeholder pension. We envisage that this will consist of an obligation to match employee contributions up to a level of 6 per cent. Moving forward with TUPE in this way will bolster confidence in pensions.'[44]

45.71 These proposals are not consistent with the treatment of other employment rights under TUPE and indeed there is a possibility that an employee could be better off after the transfer, if for example he had previously been a member of a scheme where employers provided matching contributions up to a lower percentage. However, it does attempt to address concerns about business becoming over-regulated and avoids the usual problems which have been put forward with incorporating pensions into TUPE, for example whether the obligation to provide pension benefits would be subject to the powers of amendment and winding up in the transferring scheme and, if so, whether there would be any time following the transfer during which these powers could not be exercised.

---

[43] *A new contract for welfare: partnership in pensions*, chapter 8, paras 63 and 64.
[44] Cm 5835, June 2003, *Simplicity, Security and Choice: Working and Saving For Retirement—Action on Occupational Pensions*, Chapter 2, paras 30–31.

46

AMENDMENT, TERMINATION, AND REGULATION OF OCCUPATIONAL PENSION SCHEMES

A. Amendment of Pension Scheme Trusts: Introduction

Pensions and trust legislation does not confer a general statutory power on **46.01** trustees to amend their scheme trust deed and rules (although there is a limited statutory power discussed below). Therefore they are largely dependent on what their trust documentation provides.[1]

B. Express Power of Amendment

All well-drafted pension trust deeds include an amendment power. A typical **46.02** pension scheme amendment provision will be a joint power to be exercised

---

[1] For powers of amendment of trusts generally, see Chapter 24, paras 24.46 *et seq* above.

by the trustees and principal employer, although on occasion the documentation may provide that the employer may exercise the power alone. Trustees should always ensure that any amendment power in the scheme actually permits the proposed change as many powers have express limitations. Some amendment powers prohibit adverse amendments to accrued rights. Furthermore, particularly in older scheme rules it is not unusual to find amendment powers which prohibit changes which would result in payments to the employer, except on winding up.

46.03 Unfortunately, it may not always be straightforward to determine what a restriction on an amendment power actually means. In *Lloyds Bank Pension Trust Corporation Limited v Lloyds Bank plc*,[2] an amendment power prevented amendments which would decrease the pecuniary benefits secured to or in respect of any member. It was proposed to use the amendment power to reduce future accrual rates in the scheme, but the court held that 'the natural interpretation of "the pecuniary benefits secured . . ." was that it referred to benefits accrued to date by past service and to all future benefits promised under the Scheme', so the proposed amendment was not permitted. However, the court is generally reluctant to imply restrictions over and above those expressed in the scheme documentation unless it is obvious that such restrictions should be implied.[3] In addition to express limitations on amendment powers, they must only be exercised for the purposes for which they were granted.[4]

46.04 It is also generally accepted that schemes' amendment powers cannot themselves be amended. As a result, problems can sometimes occur where trustees have merely signed at the bottom of a standard updating trust deed which contains the drafter's pro forma amendment power. Future amendments made on the basis of the new amendment power could be invalid.

C. Statutory Provisions on Amendment

46.05 Pensions legislation requires trustees to do a number of things which may conflict with their scheme documentation (for example the implementation of the member nominated trustee requirements). Therefore, even though trustees have a statutory power to do such things, for the sake of clarity, some may wish to bring their scheme documentation in line with statutory requirements.

---

² [1996] OPLR 181.
³ *Capital Cranfield Trust Corporation v Sagar*, High Court Chancery Division, 19 February 2001.
⁴ See *Re Courage Group's Pension Schemes* [1987] 1 All ER 528; and see generally Chapters 11 and 19 (esp para 19.28) above.

Section 68 of the Pensions Act 1995

To enable this to be achieved section 68 of the Pensions Act 1995 provides that the **46.06**
trustees can amend the scheme by resolution in a limited number of circumstances. These circumstances are:

(a) to extend the class of persons who may receive benefits under the scheme in
respect of the death of a member;

(b) to enable the scheme to conform with the member nominated trustee
requirements (including amendments to provisions relating to the number or
category of trustees or provision for the transfer or vesting of property);

(c) to enable the scheme to comply with such terms and conditions as may be
imposed by the Compensation Board in relation to any payment made by
them;

(d) to enable the scheme to conform with the requirement in section 37(2)
(trustees to exercise powers to distribute surplus in ongoing scheme), section
76(2) (assets in a final salary scheme on a wind up to be distributed in accordance with a statutory priority order), and sections 91 or 92 of the Pensions
Act 1995 (inalienability of pension rights);

(e) to enable the scheme to accommodate persons with pension credits or pension credit rights in relation to divorcing members; and

(f) to enable the total amount of a debt due to the scheme from the employers
under section 75 of the Pensions Act 1995 (see winding up below) to be
apportioned among the employers in different proportions than the amount
of the scheme's liabilities attributable to employment with that employer
bears to the total amount of the scheme's liabilities attributable to employment with any of the employers.

The amendment referred to in paragraph (a) above requires the consent of the **46.07**
employer as it does not reflect a statutory requirement, its purpose being seemingly to allow amendments to be made which could otherwise be challenged by
contingent beneficiaries under section 67 of the Pensions Act 1995 (see below).
However, the amendments in paragraphs (b) to (f) can be made unilaterally by
the trustees.

Section 69 of the Pensions Act 1995

In addition, the trustees or employer can apply to the Occupational Pensions **46.08**
Regulatory Authority ('Opra') for a modification order under section 69 of
the Pensions Act 1995. Such an order will only be granted where its purpose
is to:

(a) reduce an excessive statutory surplus as required by Schedule 22 of ICTA
(reduction of pension fund surpluses in certain exempt approved schemes);

(b) enable excess assets in a scheme which is being wound up to be distributed to the employer, after all liabilities have been discharged; or

(c) enable the scheme to satisfy the contracting-out requirements.

46.09 A modification order may only be made if it is not otherwise possible to achieve the desired aim, or if, without the modification order, the procedure to achieve such aim would be unduly complex or protracted, or involve the obtaining of consents which cannot be obtained, or can only be obtained with undue delay or difficulty.

Section 67 of the Pensions Act 1995

46.10 Regardless of what the scheme documentation provides, regard must be had to the requirements of section 67 of the Pensions Act 1995. This section provides that an amendment power cannot be exercised 'on any occasion in a manner which would or might affect any entitlement, accrued right or pension credit right of any member of the scheme acquired before the power is exercised' unless specified requirements are satisfied. Accrued rights are defined in section 124 of the Pensions Act 1995 as being 'the rights which have accrued to or in respect of [the member] at that time to future benefits under the scheme, and . . . at any time when the pensionable service of a member of an occupational pension scheme is continuing, his accrued rights are to be determined as if he had opted, immediately before that time, to terminate that service'. Member is also defined in section 124 and includes active, pensioner, deferred and pension credit members and the Modification Regulations extend this definition to include widows and widowers.[5]

46.11 The specified requirements referred to in section 67 are that:

(a) the trustees have satisfied themselves that: (i) the certification requirements, or (ii) the requirements for consent . . . are met in respect of that member, and (b) where the power is exercised by a person other than the trustees, the trustees have approved the exercise of the power in that manner on that occasion.

The effect of this is that trustees must be involved in all decisions in relation to amendments affecting accrued rights. In the absence of member consent, they must also obtain a certificate from the scheme actuary which confirms that the amendment power is not exercised 'in any manner which, in [his] opinion . . . would adversely affect any member of the scheme (without his consent) in respect of his entitlement, accrued rights or pension credit rights . . . acquired before the power is exercised'.[6] These certificates can be difficult to obtain and should be in place before an amendment is made.

46.12 While this seems straightforward, determining the actual amendments to which section 67 applies has proved problematic as it can be difficult to determine what

---

[5] The Occupational Pension Schemes (Modification of Schemes) Regulations 1996, SI 1996/2517, reg 2.   [6] Ibid, reg 3.

'accrued rights' actually are and also whether a proposed amendment might have an adverse effect on them.[7] For example, if the intention is to abandon fixed increases to pensions in payment and move to full limited price indexation increases (ie inflation up to 5 per cent), this change may or may not adversely affect accrued rights depending on the level of inflation. This would seem to require certification under section 67 as the section looks at amendments which 'would or might' affect a member's entitlement or accrued rights. Another difficult amendment would, for example, be where a spouse's pension was amended to be a spouse's or children's pension determined at the discretion of the trustees. This could actually result in a reduction in the benefit payable on the member's death as children's pensions can only be payable for a limited time,[8] whereas the spouse's pension would usually be for life; in addition it potentially takes away the pension the spouse would have been entitled to. There is no easy answer to this question and it serves to illustrate the difficulties in determining the scope of section 67.

The section 67 test is not an aggregate one, it is generally interpreted as applying **46.13** individually to each member and each benefit. This means an improvement for one group of members cannot be offset against a reduction in the value of accrued rights for another.

There has been some judicial attention given to the effect which section 67 has on **46.14** the ability to correct mistakes in trust deeds. Where the mistake has purported to give excessive benefits, the actuary may be unable to provide the requisite certificate to allow the scheme to be amended to correct the position. This issue was considered in *South West Trains v Wightman*[9] where changes to remuneration packages that included a change to the pension scheme had been agreed through a binding collective bargaining arrangement. These were communicated to the workforce and came into effect. Unfortunately, the pension changes were not made until after section 67 came into force. One of the trustees refused to sign the deed introducing the change on the basis that, in doing so, he would be reducing the accrued rights and entitlements that had built up between the change of the remuneration package and the proposed execution of the deed of amendment. The court held that the binding contractual obligations of the individual members would prevent them from claiming the pension on the unchanged basis and the result of this for the documentation of the scheme was that:

> SWT [South West Trains] can (in law), would (out of self interest), and probably should (out of duty to its other employees), injunct any driver seeking the payment of a pension on a more generous basis than that agreed with SWT, and given, indeed,

[7] For a detailed consideration of these questions see the Joint Opinion of Nicholas Warren QC and Paul Newman on section 67, prepared for the Institute and Faculty of Actuaries.
[8] See the definition of 'Dependent' in IR12 (2001) for limits on children's pensions.
[9] [1998] PLR 113, para 20.

1483

that it is well arguable that the Trustee could refuse to pay a pension on such a basis in any event, it appears to me that it is obviously sensible to permit, indeed to support, the execution of the Deed in order to regularise the position. The Deed's execution will, in truth, be no more than an administrative, or tidying up, act, which makes the position clear for the future.

Because the 'tidying up' deed was simply reflecting the legal position rather than modifying it, section 67 did not prevent its execution. It should, however, be noted that the change that the court decided had in effect altered the pension arrangements took place before 6 April 1997. It is not therefore certain whether such reasoning could apply to a similar set of facts taking place today.

46.15   Section 67 has been criticized as being overly complex and the Government has put forward proposals for amending it. Under the Government's proposals, schemes will be able to make a rule change which affects accrued rights if:

(a) there is a power in the scheme rules to make the change;

(b) the change does not involve converting defined benefit rights into defined contribution rights;

(c) the trustees approve the change;

(d) the total actuarial value of members' accrued rights at the point of any change is maintained;

(e) pensions already in payment are not reduced; and

(f) members are consulted before a change is made.[10]

It is not wholly clear that this will simplify the current position and it could legitimately be asked what purpose section 67 or any amended provision serves at all as even without the requirements of section 67 trustees would be likely to have difficulties claiming an amendment which adversely affected accrued rights was in the best interest of the scheme beneficiaries.

46.16   Finally, it is worth briefly mentioning amendments to future service benefits which are outside the scope of section 67. A simple improvement to active members' future service benefits is unlikely to cause any difficulty for scheme trustees. However, a reduction in the rate of future service accrual can be more problematic for example, can it ever be said to be in the best interests of the members to reduce benefits and therefore could the trustees ever agree to such an amendment (if the scheme documentation required them to do so)? It is arguable that a reduction in future service benefits is permissible because such benefits are really part of the employment package and therefore are a matter for negotiation between employees and the employer. Moreover, the employer will usually have the right to wind

---

[10] *Simplicity, Security and Choice: Working and Saving For Retirement—Action on Occupational Pensions* (Cm 5835, 2003), Ch 3, para 17.

up the scheme and therefore could terminate it if necessary and start up a new scheme.

D. Termination of a Pension Scheme

Pension scheme trusts are set up with a view to lasting many years; indeed, so long is their life expected to be that they are exempt from the perpetuities rule[11] (although this exemption does not override any perpetuity periods which have been included in the scheme's trust deed). However, it is no longer safe for employees to assume that their company pension arrangement is guaranteed to exist on their retirement. The long-term existence of an occupational pension scheme depends upon the continued solvency and support of the principal employer. Figures published by Opra indicate that, between 1 April 2002 and 31 March 2003, 1,575 schemes were in wind up and 4,192 schemes notified them during the period that a wind up had been completed.

46.17

Because there is no requirement for employers to enter into an open-ended commitment to continue to contribute to or operate an occupational pension scheme, Inland Revenue guidance provides that it is necessary for discretionary tax approval that the rules of the scheme 'specify what is to happen if the employer's contributions cease.[12]

46.18

This section looks at the winding up of the whole scheme. However, many schemes provide that, in the event a participating employer leaves the scheme, there will be a 'partial winding up' of the scheme in respect of the assets and liabilities of the scheme relating to that employer. Partial wind ups are becoming increasingly uncommon and are not dealt with in this section but the majority of the provisions relating to a full wind up are the same as for a partial wind up.

46.19

Commencing a wind up

For reasons discussed below, it is important to determine exactly when the winding up of a scheme commenced. The scheme's trust deed will typically provide that a winding up is triggered when the principal employer gives the trustees notice that it wishes to terminate the scheme, on an insolvency practitioner being appointed in respect of the principal employer, or on a cessation of contributions by the employers. More unusually, some schemes permit trustees to trigger a winding up.

46.20

Once there has been an event triggering a winding up, there may be provisions in the trust deed which allow the trustees to defer the winding up and run the scheme as a

46.21

---

[11] Section 163 of the Pensions Act 1993.   [12] IR12 (2001), PN 14.2.

closed scheme. Even if there is no such power in the scheme documentation, section 38 of the Pensions Act 1995 provides that, in the case of a final salary scheme:

(1)… the trustees may determine (a) that the scheme is not for the time being to be wound up but that no new members are to be admitted to it, or (b) that the scheme is not for the time being to be wound up but that no new members, except pension credit members, are to be admitted to it.

(2) Where the trustees make a determination under subsection (1), they may also determine (a) that no further contributions are to be paid towards the scheme, or (b) that no new benefits are to accrue to, or in respect of, members of the scheme.

When deciding whether to exercise such a power the trustees will need to consider whether it is in the interests of the scheme members to continue the scheme and what will happen to the funding position and the security of members' benefits if they operate the scheme as a closed scheme.

Exercise of powers during wind up

46.22   There has been much debate about the extent to which the powers of both trustees and employers remain intact once a scheme starts winding up. If an independent trustee has been appointed following the employer's insolvency under section 23 of the Pensions Act 1995, section 25(2) of the Pensions Act 1995 gives them the sole power to exercise any discretionary power vested in the trustees and any discretionary power conferred on the employer (otherwise than as trustee of the scheme) but only as trustee of the power. It is not completely clear what powers an employer holds as 'trustee of the power' as this is not a categorization generally used in pension scheme documentation.[13]

46.23   It is particularly important to determine where the employer's powers end up in winding up as, if the employer has become insolvent, the functions of the directors will have vested in an insolvency practitioner who owes a duty to the employer's creditors to realize as much money as possible and any pension scheme surplus will look very appetizing to them indeed. In addition, if the employer goes into liquidation and ceases to exist, a question arises as to who can exercise any of the employer's residual powers; this is particularly important where the scheme documentation will not allow the winding up to be completed without the involvement of the employer. This issue was considered in the *Capital Cranfield* case,[14] where the employer had been dissolved and any distribution of surplus on completion of the wind up required its approval. It was held that:

Given that the principal employer is dissolved and, therefore, as a matter of law, does not exist, two alternatives are possible. The first is that the power . . . is not exercisable.

---

[13]   See the fourfold categorization of powers in *Mettoy Pension Trust Limited v Evans* [1990] 1 WLR 1587: see para 17.14 above. H Arthur, *Pensions and Trusteeship* (1st edn, 1998) 328–329, considers that powers in categories 2 and 4 will pass to the independent trustee. See also GW Thomas, *Powers* (Sweet & Maxwell, 1998) '*Thomas*', 5-34 – 5-98, 6-99 – 6-100, 14-17 – 14-41, 15-14 – 15-20.

[14]   *Capital Cranfield Trust Corporation v Sagar*, High Court Chancery Division, 19 February 2001.

The second is that it can be exercised without the need for consent. It seems to me that those two alternatives only have to be put forward for one to see which of the two is correct, namely the latter. This view receives support from an observation of Scott J in *Davis v Richard & Wallington Ltd* [1990] WLR 1511, where a pensions trust deed required, in effect, a varying deed to be signed by a number of different companies and one of those companies was no longer in the employers' group. Mr Justice Scott said at p1532C: 'It is a matter of common sense that execution of the deed would not be required of companies that had lost their legal existence'.[15]

In addition, irrespective of whom particular powers rest with, there is a question as to whether particular powers can be exercised at all. In particular, in *Re ABC Television Pension Scheme*,[16] it was held that, once a scheme has started to wind up, the terms of the trust cannot be amended (unless there is a specific power in the trust deed to do so).

Distributing the assets

Distributing the assets in a money purchase scheme which is winding up is fairly straightforward. Each member is entitled to the benefits which can be secured with the accrued value of their money purchase accounts. The value in these accounts may be reduced if money is needed to meet the expenses of winding up and in some cases there may even be surplus assets in the scheme, where for example members have left before completing two years' qualifying service and the employer's contributions in respect of them are retained in the scheme. **46.24**

Unsurprisingly the position in final salary schemes is much more complex as there is unlikely to be exactly the right amount of assets to secure the accrued liabilities and meet the scheme expenses without any surplus or deficit. Prior to the Pensions Act 1995, the method of valuing liabilities on a winding up and the treatment of any surplus or deficit was dealt with by provisions in the scheme rules; however, since April 1997, such provisions are overridden by legislation. **46.25**

Section 73 of the Pensions Act 1995 provides a statutory priority order for securing liabilities. Unfortunately it does not just provide one set of priorities; the priority order differs depending on when the winding up commences. For schemes where winding up commenced prior to April 2007, the order is basically: scheme expenses; additional voluntary contributions; pensions in payment; contracted-out benefits and refunds of contributions for members with less than two years' service; increases on pensions in payment; increases in respect of contracted-out benefits; other benefits; and, lastly, increases on such benefits. The priority order is simplified for wind ups which begin after 5 April 2007: scheme expenses; additional **46.26**

---

[15] ibid, para 62.   [16] High Court, 22 May 1973.

voluntary contributions; pensions in payment; other benefits; and, lastly, increases on all benefits.[17]

46.27 Benefits which fall into the statutory priority order must be valued on the same basis that they would be valued in a Minimum Funding Requirement ('MFR') valuation, details of which are set out in the Deficiency Regulations[18] which in turn refer to the MFR Regulations[19] and Actuarial Guidance Notes GN27 and GN19. In particular, paragraphs 3.3 and 3.4 of GN27 provide that: 'The value of the liabilities must not be limited to the value of the assets, even where the scheme rules may so provide. In particular, in the valuation of the liabilities in hybrid schemes which give a money purchase benefit subject to a defined benefit promise, the value of the defined benefit promise must not be limited to the value of the assets of the scheme, even if the rules of the scheme restrict the benefit promise where there are not sufficient assets in the scheme.'

46.28 The MFR value does not necessarily represent the true cost of the benefits and, therefore, members' benefits may not be fully secured after the statutory priority order has been exhausted. If this is the case, and there are still assets in the scheme, the trustees will need to resort to the provisions of the scheme to determine the way in which the excess assets should be distributed. Usually this will mean going through any pre-Pensions Act 1995 priorities set out in the trust deed and then distributing the balance in accordance with the provisions in the winding-up rule on distribution of surplus.

46.29 The position is slightly different if the scheme is winding up with a solvent employer. From March 2002, the value of liabilities in respect of pensions in payment will be calculated on the basis of the cost of purchasing annuities to secure them and taking into account the expenses incurred in securing them.[20] In addition, the Government has said that a solvent employer who chooses to wind up a scheme should 'ensure that there are sufficient funds in the scheme to meet the full costs of the rights accrued by scheme members unless doing so would put the company itself at risk, in which case the trustees, exercising their fiduciary duties, can agree a lower amount'. They are therefore proposing to require all liabilities to be valued at full buyout cost in the same way that pensioner liabilities are currently

---

[17] The draft Occupational Pensions Schemes (Winding Up) (Amendment) Regulations 2004 will, if brought into force, amend this position. The 2007 priorities will be brought into force and an additional category will be introduced to attempt to make the distribution of assets fairer for members with long service. Deferred benefits will be split into two categories, the first category will be the member's accrued rights reduced by 2.5% for each year of service less than 40. The reduction is referred to as the postponed proportion and will be paid out in a new lower category.

[18] The Occupational Pension Schemes (Deficiency on Winding Up etc) Regulations 1996, SI 1996/3128.   [19] SI 1996/1536.

[20] See The Occupational Pension Schemes (Minimum Funding Requirement and Miscellaneous Amendments) Regulations 2002.

valued.[21] The effect of this proposal could make the debt on the employer (discussed below) so large that it may make it impossible for solvent employers ever to terminate final salary schemes (which is presumably the Government's intention).

Debt on the employer

Section 75 of the Pensions Act 1995 provides that if, 'in the case of an occupa- **46.30**
tional pension scheme which is not a money purchase scheme, the value at the applicable time of the assets of the scheme is less than the amount at that time of the liabilities of the scheme, an amount equal to the difference shall be treated as a debt due from the employer to the trustees or managers of the scheme'.

The 'applicable time' for determining the value of the debt due from the employer **46.31**
under section 75 is dependent of a number of things. If an employer goes into liquidation, the debt crystallizes immediately before the resolution or court order commencing the liquidation is made.[22] If an employer is not going into liquidation, the trustees can determine when the applicable time is.[23] It is clearly therefore of great importance for the trustees to ensure that they crystallize the debt due from the employer at the right time and the longer they wait the greater the risk that there will be unanticipated changes in the value of the scheme assets or the solvency of the employer.

There is additional scope for the trustees to capitalize on the debt due from the **46.32**
employer. As discussed above, the assets and liabilities of the scheme are valued in accordance with the MFR Regulations and if the trustees have included a gilts matching policy in their statement of investment principles (as permitted under the MFR Regulations—see above) it can increase the value of the liabilities and hence the debt due from the employers.

Where there is a multi-employer scheme, the debt will be shared among the **46.33**
employers either in accordance with the scheme rules, or, if they are silent, on a basis determined by the scheme actuary, after consultation with the trustees, as representing the proportion that the scheme's liabilities attributable to employment with each employer bears to the total amount of the scheme's liabilities.

The amount of the section 75 debt can be quite significant and payment could **46.34**
threaten the solvency of the employer. Although it is not possible for trustees to

---

[21] Cm 5835, June 2003, *Simplicity, Security and Choice: Working and Saving For Retirement—Action on Occupational Pensions*, Ch 2, para 13.

[22] This means that the provision applies equally to an insolvent company forced into liquidation and a solvent company going into voluntary liquidation, hence the reference in s 75(2) to a 'relevant insolvency event' is somewhat misleading.

[23] There has been some discussion as to whether it is possible for trustees to determine the amount of the debt under s 75 on several occasions. Obiter comments by Charles Aldous QC in *Bradstock Group Pension Scheme Trustees Limited v Bradstock Group plc and Others* [2002] PLR 327 suggest that this is not possible.

contract out of section 75, *Bradstock*[24] makes it clear that the trustees can compromise a section 75 debt. In *Bradstock*, it was held that compromising the debt:

> . . . is not a case of contracting out of the provision but rather of enforcing it by means which the trustees honestly and reasonably believe secures the largest amount towards the shortfall. In other words it is giving effect to the legislation in the best practical way, consistent with the exercise of the trustees' general powers. This is the very opposite of contracting out. Here the Trustee has agreed to the compromise in the knowledge of the funding deficit and the Employers' financial position, seeking to obtain payment of as much of the shortfall as it believes it can reasonably recover. Trustees can compromise a claim under Section 75 just as they could decide not to enforce it if in doing so they would incur costs which were disproportionate to any reasonably expected recovery. There is no overriding statutory purpose or public interest to require trustees to enforce the claim to a Section 75 debt to the point of forcing the employer into liquidation, regardless of the recovery. Indeed it would be contrary to the purpose of the MFR legislation if trustees were to be prevented from compromising the debt and forced to take steps which would produce less for the Scheme when this would be a conflict with their ordinary duties as trustees towards their members.

Surplus assets

46.35   It is increasingly rare for there to be any surplus assets on a wind up as the reasons for winding up a final salary scheme are usually connected with the employer finding it too expensive to continue to contribute to the scheme or being in financial difficulties. If the scheme does have a surplus, the starting place for determining how it should be allocated will be the provisions of the trust deed. The power to distribute surplus can be drafted to be either the employer's or the trustees' and can require member benefits to be augmented or the full amount to be refunded to the employers.

46.36   Whatever the scheme documentation provides, regard needs to be had to sections 76–77 of the Pensions Act 1995. Section 76 provides that, where the power to distribute surplus is given to either the employer or the trustees, it cannot be exercised unless:

(a)   the liabilities of the scheme have been fully discharged,

(b)   where there is any power under the scheme to distribute surplus assets to anyone other than the employer, the power has been exercised or a decision has been made not to exercise it,

(c)   the annual rates of all pensions under the scheme are increased by limited price indexation (as opposed to just post-April 1997 benefits which would otherwise be the case), and

---

[24] [2002] PLR 327, Obiter at para 15. See also *Owens Corning Fibreglass (UK) Ltd* [2002] PLR 323.

(d) notice has been given to the members of the scheme of the proposal to exercise the power.[25]

Failure to comply with these requirements renders the trustees liable to fines. If **46.37** the scheme rules prohibit payments of surplus to the employer, section 77 allows such a payment to be made if members' benefits have been augmented to the maximum levels permitted by the Inland Revenue and full limited price indexation increases have been granted on such benefits. In the event that all else fails, 'any surplus is held on resulting trust for those who provided it'.[26]

Where the trustees are considering how to distribute any surplus, what they do will **46.38** depend very much upon what the scheme documentation provides. However, where the trustees have a discretion how to distribute surplus (subject to the Pensions Act requirements already discussed), they should not start from the proposition that either employers or members are entitled to it. Warner J said in *Mettoy Pension Trustees v Evans*:

> In my opinion it is not correct to say that the rights of the beneficiaries under the scheme are satisfied when they have received their mandatory benefits and that anything more lies in the bounty of the employer. I think the beneficiaries have a right to be considered for discretionary benefits . . . One cannot in my opinion, in construing a provision in the rules of a 'balance of cost' pension scheme relating to surplus, start from an assumption that any surplus belongs morally to the employer.[27]

Information requirements

Anyone who has the power under the scheme to wind up the scheme or defer a **46.39** wind up must keep records of any determination or decision they make (although Opra have said that they would in any event expect that trustees or managers would maintain their own record of the decision as a matter of good practice).[28] A record must also be made specifying the date the first steps to wind up the scheme will be taken as well as the date on which that decision was taken.

While a winding up is ongoing, the trustees must make periodic reports to Opra. **46.40** The first report must be made when the scheme has been winding up for three years. Reports about the progress of the winding up must then be made at least annually until the winding up is complete. Transitional reporting provisions apply for

---

[25] Details of notification requirements are set out in The Occupational Pension Schemes (Payments to Employers) Regulations 1996, SI 1996/2156.

[26] *Per* Millett LJ in *Air Jamaica v Charlton* [1999] OPLR 11. In that case, as both employer and employees had made contributions, it was held that 'the surplus must be treated as provided as to one half by the Company and as to one half by the Members'. This Privy Council decision casts doubt on the earlier decision of *Davis v Richards & Wallington* [1990] 1 WLR 1511 which held, where the members had got their promised benefits, any resulting trust was solely for the employer.

[27] [1990] 1 WLR 1587. See also para 17.14 above.

[28] Section 49A of the Pensions Act 1995 as amended by s 49(3) of the Child Support, Pensions and Social Security Act 2000; Winding Up Regulations, reg 11.

schemes that started to wind up before 1 April 2002.[29] The contents of the report must include details in relation to whether an independent trustee has been appointed, the date when it is estimated that the winding up will be complete, the progress being made in winding the scheme up including the steps completed and those still to be taken with an estimate from the person making the report as to when each of these remaining steps will be completed, and a statement as to whether any particular issues are hindering the winding up or delaying its completion.[30]

46.41   In addition, under the Disclosure Regulations, when the trustees have started to wind up a scheme, they must inform the members within one month of doing so and explain why. While the winding up is ongoing, they must also tell the members once a year what action is being taken to establish the scheme's liabilities and to recover any assets, when it is anticipated final details will be known, and (where the trustees have sufficient information) an indication of the extent to which, if at all, the actuarial value of accrued rights or benefits to which such person is entitled is likely to be reduced.[31]

Completing a wind up

46.42   The winding up of a pension scheme is completed when all of the assets have been disposed of and all of the liabilities secured.

46.43   The trustees will be discharged from liability under the scheme either in accordance with the terms of the trust or, in the case of final salary scheme trustees, a statutory discharge is available under section 74 of the Pensions Act 1995. The discharge can be obtained if the trustees secure the liabilities in respect of the scheme beneficiaries in one of a number of prescribed ways, including making a transfer to an occupational or personal pension scheme and purchasing buyout policies.[32] Where benefits are being transferred, trustees will need to obtain members' consent, or, if this is not practical and the transfer is to another occupational pension scheme, they can obtain a certificate from the scheme actuary confirming that the benefits to be acquired for each member under the receiving scheme are, broadly, no less favourable than the rights to be transferred.[33]

The Pensions Compensation Board

46.44   If a scheme has insufficient assets to secure all of its liabilities, there is a possibility that a payment could be obtained from the Pensions Compensation Board.[34]

---

[29]   Section 72A of the Pensions Act 1995 as amended by s 49(1) Child Support, Pensions and Social Security Act 2000.

[30]   The Occupational Pension Scheme (Winding up Notices and Reports) Regulations 2002, SI 2002/459, reg 10.   [31]   SI 1996/1655, reg 5(10).

[32]   For requirements see s 74 of the Pensions Act 1995 and Winding Up Regulations, reg 6.

[33]   Winding Up Regulations, reg 6 and The Occupational Pension Schemes (Preservation of Benefits) Regulations 1991, SI 1991/167, reg 12.

[34]   Established in accordance with s 78 of the Pensions Act 1995.

Under section 81 of the Pensions Act 1995 (as amended by section 17 of the   **46.45**
Welfare Reform and Pensions Act 1999), applications can be made to the
Compensation Board for payments to be made where:

(a) the employer is insolvent (the definition of which covers the appointment of
    any insolvency practitioner);
(b) the value of the assets has been reduced and it is reasonably believed that this
    is due to an offence involving dishonesty; and
(c) if the scheme is salary related, the funding level is not sufficient to provide full
    benefits for pensioners and those within ten years of retirement, 90 per cent
    of benefits for other members, and the full amount of other liabilities (such as
    expenses).[35]

There is no obligation on the Board to make any award but it will do if it believes   **46.46**
that it is reasonable to do so. It is unlikely, therefore, that an award will be made if
those suffering are the employees who are implicated in the dishonesty that has
caused the original loss. Applications to the Board should be made within one year
of the insolvency event or such later time as the reduction in value became or
should have become apparent, although the Board may extend this period. The
amount of the payment is discretionary but it cannot exceed the extent of the
shortfall at the date of the application (plus interest).

The protection provided by the Compensation Board has proved to be limited in   **46.47**
practice because of the requirement for an offence involving dishonesty. It is therefore proposed that a new Pensions Protection Fund ('PPF') be introduced. The
aim of the PPF would be to ensure that final salary scheme members are guaranteed to receive a certain amount of their benefits.

It is intended that the PPF will pay a maximum of 100 per cent of pensions in pay-   **46.48**
ment, and 90 per cent of the benefits of those still working. There will be a cap on
the maximum amount guaranteed by the PPF. The PPF will be funded by a levy
on occupational pension schemes and, where the funding level of a scheme being
wound up is such that a claim on the PPF needs to be made, it seems that all of the
scheme assets will be transferred to the PPF and the PPF will complete the distribution of the assets. PPF benefits will form an additional element of the section
73 priority order discussed above.

To minimize the risk that the employer could choose to fund to a low level, or the   **46.49**
trustees hold a higher risk portfolio than appropriate because of the existence of

---

[35] The Occupational Pension Schemes (Pensions Compensation Provisions) Regulations 1997, SI
1997/665, as amended by The Occupational Pension Schemes (Pension Compensation Provisions)
Amendment Regulations 2001, SI 2001/1218.

the compensation scheme, the Government proposes that pension schemes which are underfunded will pay a higher premium to the compensation fund compared with well-funded schemes. This risk-based premium will be on top of a flat-rate levy payable by all employers with defined benefit schemes (other than those public service schemes where benefits are guaranteed by government).

46.50   The Government has also indicated that it will introduce various 'moral hazard' provisions to ensure that solvent employers or solvent parent companies of insolvent subsidiaries cannot walk away from pension liabilities. By contrast, it is also possible that some support may also be given to pensioners who have historically lost out because of insolvent employers with underfunded pension schemes.

E. Regulation

46.51   This section looks at the various bodies that regulate occupational pension schemes and the impact which they have on the way in which schemes are operated.

Pensions Ombudsman

46.52   Traditionally the Pensions Ombudsman's jurisdiction covers two types of grievance: disputes of fact or law and maladministration. Section 146(1)(a) of the Pension Schemes Act 1993 provides that the Ombudsman may investigate a complaint made 'by or on behalf of an actual or potential beneficiary of an occupational or personal pension scheme who alleges that he has sustained injustice in consequence of maladministration in connection with any act or omission of a person responsible for the management of the scheme'; regulations extend this to acts or omissions of administrators (that is anyone concerned with the administration of the scheme).[36] The Pensions Ombudsman can also investigate complaints of maladministration brought by trustees and managers against employers and vice versa or by the trustees or managers of one scheme against the trustees or managers of another.

46.53   Maladministration has no statutory meaning but has been the subject of judicial interpretation. In *Legal and General Assurance Society v Pensions Ombudsman*,[37] it was held that 'the concept of "maladministration" is broad and includes bias, inattention, delay, incompetence, ineptitude, perversity, turpitude and arbitrariness . . . It is concerned with the decision-making process rather than the merits of a decision.'

---

[36] The Personal and Occupational Pension Schemes (Pensions Ombudsman) Regulations 1996, SI 1996/2475, reg 2. For an analysis of the meaning of 'administrator' see *Britannic Asset Management v Pensions Ombudsman*, Court of Appeal, 14 October 2002 and *Ewing v Arthur Cox*, Court of Appeal, 4 February 2000.   [37] [2000] 2 All ER 577.

In addition to making determinations in relation to disputes of fact or law and 46.54
maladministration, the Ombudsman habitually makes awards for distress and
inconvenience and this practice has been approved by the courts,[38] although, in
City and County of Swansea v Johnson,[39] the court held that 'in the absence of very
exceptional circumstances (not proved here) an award in excess of £1000 ought
not to be considered as appropriate by way of damages for distress'.

Provisions in section 53 of the Child Support, Pensions and Social Security Act 46.55
2000 were introduced (with effect from 1 December 2000) to extend the
Ombudsman's jurisdiction by allowing him to:

(a) investigate complaints made by a statutory independent trustee (ie appointed
    on the sponsoring employer's insolvency) alleging maladministration by the
    other trustees, or former trustees;
(b) consider disputes between trustees of the same scheme brought by at least half
    of the trustees;
(c) consider a question from a sole trustee about the carrying out of his functions; and
(d) investigate a complaint where the subject matter has previously gone before
    an employment tribunal or a court, and the case has been discontinued (this
    will not apply to any cases referred to the Ombudsman before these provi-
    sions come into force).

The current position is that the Ombudsman cannot accept a case if the investi- 46.56
gation of it would impact upon the interests, particularly the financial interests, of
those not directly involved in the case.[40] This is because, particularly where large
classes of individuals are concerned, it is impractical for them all to be consulted
in the investigation. Accordingly they cannot be bound by his determinations. To
overcome this, section 54 of the Child Support, Pensions and Social Security Act
2000 provides that the Ombudsman will be able to:

(a) link to a case those whose interests may be affected by the complaint or dis-
    pute or its outcome;
(b) give actual or potential beneficiaries the opportunity to make representations;
(c) appoint a person to represent a group of those who have the same interest in
    a complaint, for instance, all the pensioner members, and it will then be this
    appointed person who will make representations on behalf of that group and
    the group will be bound by the determination.

Unfortunately it now appears that the provisions in section 54 will not be brought 46.57
into force as a result of the Government's attempts to simplify pensions

---

[38] See, for example, Walker J in *Westminster City Council v Haywood* [1996] 3 WLR 583.
[39] [1999] 1 All ER 863.   [40] *Edge v Pensions Ombudsman* [1999] 4 All ER 546.

legislation. However, it seems that the Government does still endorse the principles behind section 54 and may well bring similar legislation into force.

Occupational Pensions Regulatory Authority

46.58 Opra was set up in April 1997, under section 1 of the Pensions Act 1995. It was set up as a result of a recommendation by the Pensions Law Review Committee which had observed that a 'major weakness of the present law governing occupational pension schemes is that there is no statutory authority with overall responsibility for their supervision and for enforcement of the legal responsibilities of those who administer them. The new legal framework we have recommended depends for its effectiveness on proper supervisory and enforcement machinery. We therefore recommend that the Pensions Regulator should have wide-ranging functions and powers.'[41]

46.59 Opra's primary role is to ensure that schemes are operated in compliance with the requirements of the Pensions Act 1995 and other pensions legislation. However, it has had mixed success. It relies on trustees and their professional advisers reporting breaches of the legislative requirements to them. This means that there are a large number of reports in relation to relatively minor breaches of fairly well run schemes. However, particularly badly run schemes are the ones most likely not to make reports to Opra or to have the advisers in place to do so. As a result, proposals are currently in place to replace Opra with a more proactive regulator, able to target areas where there is particular risk to scheme members.[42]

46.60 There are a variety of legislative breaches which Opra can pursue criminal sanctions for.[43] They include the following:

   (a) acting as an actuary or an auditor of the scheme while a trustee of a scheme or connected or in association with a trustee—section 28 of the Pensions Act 1995;

   (b) purporting to be a trustee while suspended, prohibited, or disqualified—sections 6 and 30 of the Pensions Act 1995;

   (c) trustees knowingly receiving a reimbursement from scheme assets for any fine imposed as a result of criminal proceedings or an Opra penalty—section 31 of the Pensions Act 1995;

   (d) making an investment in breach of the restrictions on employer related investments—section 40 of the Pensions Act 1995; and

   (e) being knowingly concerned in the fraudulent evasion of the requirement to pay employees' contributions within prescribed time limits—section 49 of the Pensions Act 1995.

---

[41] Paragraph 4.19.22

[42] Cm 5835, June 2003, *Simplicity, Security and Choice: Working and Saving For Retirement—Action on Occupational Pensions*, Chapter 2, paras 19–23.

[43] Opra Note 1, Section 48(1)—Reporting to Opra (revised October 2003), Appendix 3.

Opra seems to have found these criminal sanctions of limited use in practice and few criminal prosecutions have ever been brought under these provisions.

Many of the statutory requirements for trustees attract fines for non-compliance. **46.61** Under section 10 of the Pensions Act 1995, the maximum fine per offence that can be imposed is £5,000 in the case of an individual trustee and £50,000 in any other case. Legislation may specify a lower penalty for particular breaches. In addition, section 31 of the Pensions Act 1995 provides that trustees cannot recover fines from the scheme's assets or insure themselves against them out of scheme monies. However, there appears to be no reason why the employer cannot insure them directly out of company assets.

There are a variety of other sanctions and steps available to Opra which are set out **46.62** in sections 1–15 and sections 98–109 of the Pensions Act 1995, as well as the provisions already discussed; these most notably include orders to wind up a scheme where it is deemed necessary to protect the interests of scheme members as a whole.

Opra may also make directions in relation to occupational pension schemes. This **46.63** power enables them to require trustees to circulate a statement produced by Opra to scheme members or to include such a statement in the scheme's annual report. In addition, Opra may direct trustees to take specific action to pay benefits where an employer, as paying agent, fails to maintain a separate bank account.

Opra is not for the most part a proactive regulator. As mentioned, it relies on **46.64** reports from people connected with schemes to ensure that they comply with the relevant legislative requirements. Section 48(1) of the Pensions Act 1995 provides that:

> If the auditor or actuary of any occupational pension scheme has reasonable cause to believe that: (a) any duty relevant to the administration of the scheme imposed by any enactment or rule of law on the trustees or managers, the employer, any professional adviser or any prescribed person acting in connection with the scheme has not been or is not being complied with, and (b) the failure to comply is likely to be of material significance in the exercise by the Authority of any of their functions, he must immediately give a written report of the matter to the Authority.

Opra has given guidance as to when it expects reports to be made to it and what **46.65** amounts to 'material significance'.[44] It categorizes breaches as follows:

(a) Opra will always expect to receive a report in what they classify as 'red' scenarios, which involve breaches which Opra will always regard as materially significant because of the significant risk they constitute to members' interests. The areas that are of particular concern are ensuring that 'trustees have

---

[44] Opra Note 1, Section 48(1)—Reporting to Opra (revised October 2003), Appendix 4.

properly considered their investment policy and the assets are invested appropriately; payments out of the scheme are legitimate and timely; and members receive good quality information, which is neither materially misleading nor coercive, without delay'.

(b) Opra does not expect to receive reports in what they classify as 'green' scenarios, which involve breaches which it does not regard as materially significant because their experience has shown that such breaches do not constitute any significant risk to members' interests. However, trustees remain under a duty to put matters right and to comply in the future.

(c) Finally, there are scenarios which involve breaches where the risk to members' interests is less clear. Opra classifies these as 'amber' breaches and says that 'only by taking into account the context of the breach in relation to the scheme can the scheme auditor or scheme actuary decide whether the breach constitutes a significant immediate or potential risk to members' interests, and is therefore likely to be of material significance to Opra and should be reported'.

Inland Revenue

46.66 The Inland Revenue has two functions in relation to pension schemes. The Inland Revenue Savings, Pensions, Share Schemes section ('IR SPSS') ensures that tax approved schemes satisfy all of the requirements in relation to continuing tax approval. To this end IR SPSS requires certain information to be submitted to it. The most draconian sanction available for failure to comply with Inland Revenue requirements is a withdrawal of tax approval which can happen for serious breaches such as payment of excessive benefits or a persistent failure to furnish information.[45] This would result in back tax becoming due from the trustees, company and/or the members and is unusual. Under the Taxes Management Act 1970, IR SPSS can fine trustees for failing to comply with its information providing requirements. Section 98 of the Taxes Management Act 1970 provides for an initial penalty of up to £3,000 and a daily penalty of up to £60 for as long as the failure continues.

46.67 The other function which the Inland Revenue has is overseeing contracting-out through the National Insurance Contributions Office. For failure to comply with the various contracting-out requirements, a scheme's contracting-out certificate can be cancelled.

F. Shift from Final Salary to Money Purchase Schemes

46.68 As a final issue, it is worth considering briefly how some of the issues discussed in the preceding pages impact on the shift currently being seen away from final salary provision towards money purchase schemes.

---

[45] See IR 12 2001, Part 19

Reasons

There are a number of reasons for this trend, including: **46.69**

(a) The growing complexity of pensions legislation and the amount of regulation that schemes have to comply with. As the majority of regulations apply equally to final salary and money purchase schemes (other than things such as the MFR), complexity may be more of a factor in making employers consider whether occupational pension schemes in general are something that they want to provide.

(b) The performance of equity markets in recent years has made final salary provision an increasingly expensive option for employers as they have to meet the balance of the cost of benefits.

(c) The accounting standard FRS 17 which sets out the way employer companies must account for pension costs in their annual accounts appears to have had an astonishing impact on employers. Compliance with FRS 17 changes the way that pension funds are dealt with in employing company accounts, in particular it requires assets to be valued at their market value and the immediate recognition of the full value of pension scheme surpluses and deficits on the employer's balance sheet. (The former accounting standard SSAP 24 allowed for long-term smoothed actuarial values to be used.)

The common theme underlying all of these various factors is cost. Employers, **46.70** under no obligation to provide occupational pension provision at all, understandably do not want to provide the most costly of the pensions alternatives.

Options

If an employer wishes to move from final salary to money purchase pension pro- **46.71** vision, there are a number of ways it can do this. It is important to establish which method is being used and what is happening both to the existing final salary arrangement and to any new money purchase arrangement.

The basic options in relation to the final salary arrangement are to close it to new **46.72** members but allow continued accrual for existing members, close it to all future accrual, or wind it up and buy out or transfer members' benefits (the requirements for which have been considered elsewhere).

The options in relation to the new money purchase arrangement include setting **46.73** up a money purchase section under the trusts of the existing final salary scheme which has advantages in terms of regulatory compliance. In addition, if the final salary scheme was in surplus, there is a possibility that, if the scheme documentation permits, the final salary surplus may be used to fund contributions to the money purchase section. Alternatively, a new money purchase scheme can be set up which has the advantage that it will not inherit any problems that there may have been with the existing final salary scheme documentation.

46.74   If the members of the final salary scheme are to be offered membership of the money purchase scheme, they can be offered the chance to transfer their accrued final salary rights into the money purchase arrangement. However, in the absence of members agreeing to this, it is unlikely that a transfer could be made without consent as an actuarial certificate would be required to the effect that the transfer credits the members would acquire would be broadly no less favourable than the rights being transferred.[46] The problem with this is illustrated by Actuarial Guidance Note GN16 which provides that 'A transfer from a defined benefit scheme to a defined contribution scheme, or vice versa, would represent a major change in the nature of the rights of members. A certificate is therefore unlikely to be given, other than in exceptional circumstances, for transfers where one of the schemes is a defined contribution scheme.'[47] In addition, it is quite difficult to see how such a transfer could be in the best interests of scheme members and therefore how the trustees could exercise any transfer power they had.

46.75   If the decision is made to close the final salary scheme to new members, the employer and the trustees will need to make sure that there is power to do so. Consideration will also need to be given to how to deal with the position of any employees who have not yet joined the scheme but who were in the process of satisfying waiting periods and whose contracts of employment provide that they can join a final salary scheme.

46.76   If all future accrual is to cease under the scheme, the trust deed needs to be carefully checked as some schemes provide that once the employer ceases to contribute, the winding-up provisions will be triggered. The trustees may have power under the scheme rules to delay such a winding up and to continue to run the scheme as a closed scheme, but to exercise this power they must presumably believe that there is some advantage to the members in doing so. Trustees would need to ensure that they had taken appropriate advice (legal, investment, and actuarial) and that they reviewed the situation from time to time. Consideration must also be given to what happens to final salary benefits accrued up to the date of closure. In particular, the power of amendment in the scheme rules may not allow the final salary link to be removed from accrued service, so benefits at retirement will have to be determined by reference to salary at retirement.[48]

46.77   If it is decided to amend the final salary scheme to include a money purchase section, there are two key issues which need to be considered: whether the amendment can or should be made (which will require consideration of the provisions in the scheme documentation, the trustees' duties, and section 67 of the Pensions

---

[46] The Occupational Pension Schemes (Preservation of Benefit) Regulations 1991, SI 1991/167, reg 12.

[47] Actuarial Guidance Note GN16, Retirement Benefits Schemes, Bulk Transfers, para 2.9.

[48] *Lloyds Bank Pension Trust Corporation Limited v Lloyds Bank Plc* [1996] OPLR 181.

Act 1995) and what the amendment may allow the trustees to do. Consideration of the express provisions in the scheme's amendment power is the starting point. Any procedures or formal requirements set out in the scheme rules should be complied with. The amendment power may also contain provisions which restrict or prohibit certain amendments and the exact meaning of such provisions needs to be considered with great care. In addition, when exercising any power under the scheme, trustees need to have regard to their general trust law duties, including a duty to act in the best interests of the beneficiaries. It could be argued that amending the scheme to prevent future final salary accrual is clearly not in the members' interests. However, the trustees are entitled to have regard to additional factors such as the continuing financial viability of the employer.

Cross subsidies

One of the key benefits of setting up a money purchase section in an existing final salary scheme is the possibility that an existing final salary surplus may be used to fund contributions to the money purchase section. Whether or not this is possible has been considered by the courts on several occasions. In *Barclays Bank plc v Barclays Pension Funds Trustees Limited*,[49] the bank decided that it would provide benefits for future recruits on a money purchase basis and established a money purchase section in the existing final salary scheme. The scheme had a very large surplus which was used in part to reduce and then suspend the bank's contributions. Money purchase members were, however, credited with employer contributions at the full rate by using the surplus. A member of the final salary section complained to the Pensions Ombudsman that the bank's use of surplus constituted maladministration. Relying on the earlier case of *Kemble v Hicks*,[50] the Ombudsman upheld the complaint on the basis that the money purchase section formed a separate trust to the pre-existing final salary trust and there could be no legal basis for the payment of the bank's contributions due to one trust out of the surplus of another.[51] The bank appealed. On appeal, it was held that, as a matter of law, an employer or any other person could set up a pension scheme which had a money purchase section and a final salary section. On the facts, the bank had said in the original deed of amendment that it wished 'to alter and amend the provisions of the trust deed' and to 'introduce a new benefit structure'. Such terminology, while not being conclusive, was consistent with the notion that there continued to be a single trust fund rather than the creation of an entirely new and separate fund. **46.78**

The court went on to consider the question of whether the bank had power to use surplus to credit the money purchase members' accounts. The decision in *Kemble v Hicks* was distinguished on the facts. In *Kemble* an announcement which was incorporated into the scheme rules said that 'the Company will *pay* contributions **46.79**

---

[49] [2001] OPLR 37.   [50] [1999] OPLR 1.   [51] Determination H00530.

into the new money purchase plan'. This wording was said in *Barclays* to impose 'an unequivocal obligation on the employer to actually pay into the fund, at least in relation to contributions relating to members of the money purchase scheme'. By contrast the rules in the Barclays scheme provided that the bank would 'pay such contributions to the Fund as the Bank after consulting the Trustees and the Actuary decides are necessary to pay the benefits under the Fund' and in the case of the money purchase members, the bank's contributions would be 'credited to… [the] Member's Account'. The court therefore decided the bank was not obliged under the terms of the scheme to pay contributions in respect of the money purchase section members if they could be funded out of surplus.

PART I

TRUSTS IN FINANCIAL TRANSACTIONS

47

TRUSTEES IN THE LAW OF FINANCE

A. The Role of Trustees in Relation to Investment Entities

The contexts in which trusts interact with financial transactions

There are three contexts in which trusts interact with financial transactions. First, **47.01** where a trust is used to provide security for financial activities. Secondly, where a trust is taken over a financial transaction as a trust fund. Thirdly, where trusts law is used to provide a remedy for breach of a financial transaction. Similarly, there are three contexts in which the law of trusts interacts with investment contracts: the unit trust, the issue of eurobonds, and the issue of debenture stock. Beyond those, the law of trusts has been important in the genesis of many modern financial techniques ranging from the early forms of the modern company through to taking security in financial transactions. The importance of the trust has been wedded to the significance of Anglo-American jurisdictions in creating the norms which have attended these markets. As a result, the development of the unit trust, for example, in England and Wales was predicated on the common use of the trust structure. More generally, however, the trust has been important in developing investment structures simply as a means of allowing an investment manager or promoter to hold assets on behalf of a range of investors.

The following sections of this chapter introduce the material to appear in subsequent chapters.

B. The Financial Services and Markets Act 2000

The scope of the Financial Services and Markets Act 2000

47.02   The significance of the Financial Services and Markets Act 2000 ('FSMA 2000") for present purposes is that it is the principal legislation concerning the regulation of financial activity in the United Kingdom. In consequence, for the context of trusts law, it provides both for the substantive principles underpinning institutions such as the unit trust and other collective investment schemes, and it also provides for the foundational principles on which financial regulation of such institutions is to be carried on. At the same time as the FSMA 2000 was introduced, the enactment of the Trustee Act 2000 provided the basis for the investment principles underpinning ordinary trusts. The consequence has been a radical overhaul of the principles on which ordinary trusts and regulated trusts, such as unit trusts, are regulated. This section aims to highlight some of the principal points of significance for trustees from that legislation.

47.03   FSMA 2000 came into full force and effect as from 1 December 2001, after the passage of that Act on 14 June 2000.[1] By that Act, the Financial Services Authority ('FSA') was created as the single principal regulator for financial activity in the United Kingdom, absorbing within it the functions of a range of the previous self-regulatory organizations and regulatory bodies considered below.[2]

47.04   In relation to the detail of financial regulatory principles, FSMA 2000 is primarily enabling legislation in that it transfers the power to make regulations covering a range of issues previously covered by primary legislation either to the Treasury or to the FSA. Given the enabling nature of much of the legislation it will therefore always be important to look to the regulatory rulebooks published by the FSA when considering the detail of financial regulation from time to time.

47.05   The question as to the circumstances in which trustees will be regulated by FSMA 2000 are considered in the following three sections. The remainder of this chapter then considers the general scheme for financial regulation introduced by the Act relating to the scope of the FSA's powers, the penalties for market abuse, and so forth.

The requirement for authorization

47.06   Any person who carries on a regulated activity in the United Kingdom is required to obtain authorization to do so from the FSA.[3] Therefore, one is not entitled to carry on investment activity as a business without authorization,[4] nor is one entitled to advertise the sale of any investment without FSA authorization,[5] nor is one

---

[1] Financial Services and Markets Act 2000, s 1(1).   [2] Para 47.05.
[3] Financial Services and Markets Act 2000, s 19.   [4] ibid.
[5] Financial Services and Markets Act 2000, s 21.

entitled (in effect) to do any preparatory or inchoate act connected with engaging in investment activity.[6] The penalties for acting without authorization vary from the unenforceability of any agreements formed by an unauthorized person[7] to criminal penalties for the breach of the code prohibiting financial promotion and advertisement.[8] Authorization then carries with it subjection to the FSA's general rules as to the conduct of investment activity, considered in outline below.

The circumstances in which trustees will be regulated under FSMA 2000

Trustees will be regulated under FSMA 2000 by the FSA in circumstances in which they are conducting 'regulated activities'[9] of a specified kind[10] and always providing that they do so 'by way of business'.[11] The next section considers those investment activities which constitute 'regulated activities', whereas this section considers what is meant by carrying on investment 'by way of business'. **47.07**

The meaning of 'activities carried on by way of business' is defined by Treasury regulation, further to section 419 of FSMA 2000. However, the appropriate regulation is very vague about the content of 'business' for these purposes,[12] providing only that it applies to those dealing in investments either as principal or as agent, or safeguarding or administering investments, or advising on investments within the context of the Regulated Activities Order. The FSA rulebooks are similarly non-committal as to the meaning of the term 'business'.[13] The possible meanings of those otherwise undefined terms are ventilated in the next section. The definition of the term 'business' is therefore left to common law definition. This section will therefore consider the definitions found in financial services law and other legal fields before considering how they might apply to trustees. **47.08**

The only case in which the meaning of 'business' was considered within the financial services context was (in relation to section 63 of the old Financial Services Act 1986) in the case of *Morgan Grenfell & Co v Welwyn Hatfield DC*.[14] In that case, Hobhouse J suggested that there was no reason to impose a narrow meaning on that term for these purposes and that 'it should not be given a technical construction but rather one which conformed to what in ordinary parlance would be described as a business transaction as opposed to something personal or casual'.[15] **47.09**

---

[6] Financial Services and Markets Act 2000, s 26.
[7] Financial Services and Markets Act 2000, s 26.
[8] Financial Services and Markets Act 2000, ss 21, 23.
[9] Financial Services and Markets Act 2000, s 22(2), giving effect to s 22(1) by way of Sch 2.
[10] That is, those listed in Financial Services and Markets Act 2000, Sch 2, as considered below.
[11] Financial Services and Markets Act 2000, s 22(1).
[12] The Financial Services and Markets Act 2000 (Carrying on Regulated Activities by Way of Business) Order 2001, para 3.
[13] FSA, *AUTH Module*, Block 3, Chapter 2 (Regulatory Processes). [14] [1995] 1 All ER 1.
[15] ibid.

47.10   This has been the tenor of most of the case law considering the meaning of the term 'business' in other contexts.[16] The frequency of the investment activity might be a guide, but not conclusive of the question whether or not a business of investment is being carried on.[17] While many of the decided cases on the meaning of the term 'business' have emphasized the frequency with which the activity must be carried on to constitute a business, there are three other factors which must be of importance: whether or not the trustee takes a personal benefit beyond any fee ordinarily accruing to him under the terms of the trust, the amount of money involved in the trust fund, and the quantity and sophistication of the investment choices made.[18] Therefore, it is suggested that there are four general badges of business in this context: time, volume, profit, and quality.[19]

Time

47.11   Time in this sense refers to the frequency with which the trustee enters into investment transactions. In the course of a business it would be expected that there would be many more transactions entered into than in the course of investment carried on otherwise than as a business activity. Therefore, where speculative investment activity is carried on both frequently and over a long period of time, then that would indicate that a business is being carried on.[20] In many of the early cases on whether or not associations were carrying on unlawful investment activity as companies, one of the decisive factors was the repetition of investment activity indicating a pattern of business.[21] There will be business activities, possibly including investment, which occur only occasionally but which, for example, involve dealings with capital assets and therefore would still indicate a business is being carried on albeit that the nature of the property being invested militates against a high volume of transactions being conducted in a short space of time.[22]

Volume

47.12   The term 'volume' in this context refers both to the quantity of investment transactions entered into by a trustee and also the size of those transactions. Where, for

---

[16]   *American Leaf Blending Co Sdn Bhd v Director General of Inland Revenue* [1979] AC 676.
[17]   *Morgan Grenfell & Co v Welwyn Hatfield DC* [1995] 1 All ER 1.
[18]   *Re Brauch* [1978] 1 Ch 316, in which case it was accepted that for a business to be being conducted the defendant would need to be acting on behalf of other people. Cf *R v Wilson* [1997] 1 All ER 119, in which to be carrying on an insurance business one had to be acting for one's own benefit and not for the benefit of others.
[19]   eg *Calkin v IRC* [1984] 1 NZLR 1: in which the New Zealand Court of Appeal considered that the term 'business' concerned 'the nature of the activities carried on including the period over which they are engaged in, the scale of operation and the volume of transactions, the commitment of time, money and effort, the pattern of activity and the financial results'.
[20]   *Re Debtor, ex p Debtor (No 490 pf 1935)* [1936] Ch 237.
[21]   *Smith v Anderson* [1880] 15 Ch D 247.
[22]   *American Leaf Blending Co Sdn Bhd v Director General of Inland Revenue* [1979] AC 676; *Morgan Grenfell & Co v Welwyn Hatfield DC* [1995] 1 All ER 1.

example, a financial institution conducted many hundreds of investment transactions in a single day, there would be no doubt that the volume of trades constituted a business even if they were for comparatively small amounts. Indeed, where there is an intention to carry on a large number of transactions in the future, then the fact that a person has only conducted a few transactions would not prevent that activity from being considered to be a business.[23] Therefore, the number and size of transactions which a trustee intended to conduct would be important in deciding whether or not that person was carrying on a business activity.

Profit

It is an axiomatic part of a business purpose that it is conducted with a view to profit. What is more complex is knowing whether or not the generation of profit in itself necessarily indicates a business.[24] However, where the activity is undertaken purely for pleasure or for one's own, personal benefit, then it is less likely that there is a business in operation. In the sense of personal benefit meaning that one is benefiting in one's personal capacity rather than the benefit of a business. So the management of a covenant taking effect over leasehold land would not necessarily connote a business activity unless it constitutes a duty or an occupation of that land, as opposed to pleasure.[25]

47.13

Quality

In spite of the formulaic principles considered in this discussion, it is suggested that it is the question of the quality of the trustee's investment activities which will be decisive of whether or not he is acting in the course of a business.[26] As such, 'business' would generally connote 'the fundamental notion of the exercise of an activity in an organised and coherent way and one which is directed to an end result'.[27] Consequently, whereas a trustee may appear to enter into a large number of transactions in a given period on behalf of the trust, whereas a trustee may enter into such transactions involving the entirety of the trust fund, and whereas these transactions may be conducted solely with a view to profit, nevertheless they may not constitute a business if the transactions were of a quality that did not correlate with those of a market professional. Thus, a small family trust might change through a range of investments during a bull or a bear market in which there is a large amount of press publicity but nevertheless not convert those who are investing their little all into business people who require formal regulation. As Hobhouse J has held in the context of financial services legislation: '[the term "business"] should not be given

47.14

---

[23] *Re Griffin, ex p Board of Trade* (1890) 60 LJ QB 235; *CIR v Marine Steam Turbine Co Ltd* [1920] 1 KB 193. [24] *R v Crayden* [1978] 1 WLR 604.
[25] *Rolls v Miller* (1884) 27 Ch D 71, 88, *per* Lindley LJ.
[26] *Morgan Grenfell & Co v Welwyn Hatfield DC* [1995] 1 All ER 1.
[27] *Calkin v IRC* [1984] 1 NZLR 1.

a technical construction but rather one which conformed to what in ordinary parlance would be described as a business transaction as opposed to something personal or casual'.[28] At the simplest level, then, the opening of a bank account and the deposit of the trust moneys therein could not, in itself, be considered to constitute a business activity, even though it falls literally within the statute's list of investment activities, because it is not of the quality necessary to constitute a business.

47.15 It is suggested that any trustee who is already regulated by the FSA and who is offering his services professionally to the service of the beneficiaries of a trust falls to be regulated by the FSA in his capacity as a trustee in any event. The more difficult question is the potential liability of a person, at the other end of the scale, who is not a professional and who agrees to act as a trustee as some personal favour to the settlor or to the beneficiaries but with no understanding of what that role entails. Within Schedule 2 of the Act, it is a regulated activity even to make a deposit with a bank if that is so done in the course of a business. A single bank deposit will not constitute a business.[29] What is more difficult is to know at what point a decision by that trustee to keep changing the bank with which that deposit is made in search of the best available rate of interest will constitute a business. Where a trustee does not have a professional qualification nor any employment in any capacity which would ordinarily involve conducting business in investment, it must be unlikely at the very least that such a person would be considered to be carrying on such a business if he occasionally organized bank deposits and perhaps invested the trust fund in publicly quoted shares or in a general investment fund operated by a high street financial institution.

47.16 The reason why trustees may wish to avoid regulation by the FSA are twofold. First, regulation does subject the trustee to official oversight by the FSA and to compliance with regulatory standards outwith the scope of the terms of the trust. Whereas the trust deed itself may contain provisions excluding the trustee's liability for a variety of losses which might be suffered by the beneficiaries, the financial regulatory code may not permit such excuses particularly if they relate to the trustees' integrity. Secondly, the financial regulatory code contains a range of positive obligations, including duties to consider the conduct of business with the beneficiaries when considering the investment of trust property in, for example, high-risk investments whereas the beneficiaries may be inexpert and thus prefer a low-risk investment portfolio. In this sense it will be tempting for a trustee to rely on the provisions of the trust deed and on the broad powers permitted to trustees under the Trustee Act 2000 to deal with property as though its absolute owner, albeit subject to a duty of care.

47.17 The trustee may seek to argue that his relationship with the beneficiary is not one of investment manager and client but rather one in which the beneficial owner of

---

[28] *Morgan Grenfell & Co v Welwyn Hatfield DC* [1995] 1 All ER 1.   [29] See ibid.

property has assigned legal title in that property to the trustee and effectively abandoned responsibility for the fate of the trust fund to the trustee, subject always to the terms of the trust. The presence of the terms of the trust might, in itself, encourage a trustee to suggest that a particular bargain had been struck with the beneficial owner of that property subject only to the law of trusts and deliberately cocooned from any broader norms of financial services law. Given the apparent lassitude of trusts law in allowing trustees to limit their liability even for gross negligence, a trustee would evidently prefer this form of liability. Nevertheless, it is suggested, the purpose of the financial services regulation introduced by the Financial Services Act 1986 and extended by FSMA 2000 is the protection of investors from behaviour which offends the mandatory norms of financial regulation. It has yet to happen that the courts have examined the general norms of financial services law when considering the investment obligations of trustees. It is suggested that the law of trusts ought to incorporate those norms as set out in the FSA rulebooks, established under the auspices of FSMA 2000, in cases dealing with professional trustees acting in the course of their businesses. In particular, norms as to the suitability of the investments acquired for the beneficiaries and as to the suitability of the manner in which the trustees conduct their management of the trust's affairs are ripe for importation.[30] There are cases in which regulatory norms have been imported by the commercial courts in developing the common law liability of financial institutions to their clients in negligence and fraud.[31]

Those forms of investment activity regulated under FSMA 2000

In relation to trustees, regulation by the FSA under FSMA 2000 will have effect if **47.18** those trustees are carrying on any of the activities identified in Schedule 2 to the Act.[32] There is no single provision which deals with trustees. There are a number of provisions which, even on a narrow interpretation of the legislation, would appear to cover the situation in which the trustee is acting as a manager of investments in relation to a trust fund. The further question will be whether or not a trustee who is not acting in a professional capacity will be similarly liable to regulation under the Act.

Those acting as an agent on behalf of another, as well as those acting as principal, **47.19** in 'buying, selling, subscribing for or underwriting investments or offering or agreeing to do so',[33] are conducting a 'regulated activity'. Consequently, trustees

---

[30] AS Hudson, *The Law on Financial Derivatives* (3rd edn, Sweet & Maxwell, 2002) 271–316, esp 314.

[31] eg *Bankers Trust v Dharmala* [1996] CLC 518 in which Mance J looked to the Bank of England London Code to decide on the appropriate standard of conduct for a bank when selling complex derivatives products to a comparatively inexpert financial institution from Indonesia; *Morgan Stanley v Puglisi* [1998] CLC 481.

[32] Financial Services and Markets Act 2000, s 22(2).

[33] Financial Services and Markets Act 2000, Sch 2, para 2(1).

acting in this way may find themselves liable in general terms in relation to dealings in securities. A narrow interpretation of that provision would suggest that an 'agent' relates to those whose obligations are governed solely by contract and does not cover those who are acting as express trustees, subject for example to a trust deed. The limitation of this provision would mean that the liability of trustees would be covered by narrower, subsequent provisions.

47.20 More closely analogous to the role of trustee is that category of regulated activity considered in paragraph 5 which relates to 'safeguarding and administering assets belonging to another which consist of or include investments or offering or agreeing to do so'.[34] Once more, there is no clear use of the term 'trustee' here but the 'safeguarding of assets'[35] is the manner in which the Act defines the obligations of the trustee of a unit trust[36] and therefore could apply equally to a trustee. However, the form of trustee implied by the term 'safekeeping' would, as with the trustee of a unit trust, suggest a person who acts as custodian of the trust property and not someone who also has active investment powers to buy, sell, and otherwise deal with the trust property. The term 'administering' might connote this broader sense of an active trusteeship as opposed to the narrower role of a custodian fiduciary responsible merely for the 'safekeeping' but not the investment of trust property.[36A]

47.21 For the purposes of paragraph 5, the trust property must include, but need not comprise in its entirety, 'investments'. The term 'investments' is defined in Part II of Schedule 2 of the Act as including securities in the form of shares or debt securities in companies, government and public securities, warrants and other instruments entitling their holder to subscribe for investments, certificates representing securities, units in collective investment schemes, options to buy or to sell property, futures contracts, contracts for differences, contracts of insurance or participation in Lloyd's syndicates, deposits in relation to which any sum of money is paid on terms that money shall be repaid, loans secured on land, or any right in an investment. These provisions are drawn deliberately broadly, it is suggested, with the aim of encapsulating any form of investment conducted, *inter alia*, by trustees from ordinary bank deposits to complex financial derivatives. It should be remembered, as considered above, that such activities must nevertheless be conducted 'by way of business'.[37]

47.22 The third available heading under which the business of trusteeship might fall is paragraph 6 of Schedule 2 relating to the management of investments. Where a

---

[34] Financial Services and Markets Act 2000, Sch 2, para 5(1).
[35] Or, arranging for the safeguarding or administering of assets: Financial Services and Markets Act 2000, Sch 2, para 5(2). [36] Financial Services and Markets Act 2000, s 237(2).
[36A] The term 'safekeeping' is used in the body of the Act and in the title to the Financial Services and Markets Act 2000, Sch 2, para 5(1), and yet the term 'safeguarding' appears in the body of ibid para 5(1) as though to emphasize a non-technical usage.
[37] Financial Services and Markets Act 2000, s 22(1).

person conducts a business of 'managing, or offering or agreeing to manage, assets belonging to another person', then that constitutes a regulated activity.[38] As part of this head of regulated activity, it may be the case that the person involved retains some discretion as to the arrangements for the investment of the assets. Thus, trustees of discretionary trusts or trustees with powers to select the investment property, or trustees with the general investment powers of the absolute owner of property would all fall within this head of liability.

The Financial Services Authority's general duties

The FSMA 2000 provides for overtly political and macroeconomic objectives **47.23** relating to the manner in which the FSA exercises its regulatory powers. In short, the new regulatory body is charged with the preservation of the integrity of financial markets in the UK, the education of investors, and the place of the UK within the global economy, as well as the oversight of the operations of market participants which characterized the previous legislative code. The FSA not only centralizes the power of a number of previously distinct regulatory bodies but it also grants that body a quasi-judicial function in relation to market abuse[39] and overtly macroeconomic objectives in the way in which those powers are exercised.[40]

The FSA's general duties are the promulgation of 'market confidence, public **47.24** awareness, the protection of consumers, and the reduction of financial crime'.[41] More accurately, there is no governing verb in relation to that list of objectives as an aid to interpretation as to whether the FSA is required merely to advocate, more significantly to advance, or most strenuously to require that those objectives are put to work in the financial markets. These core regulatory objectives place emphasis on the risks associated with financial activity and need for the FSA to appreciate the role which risk plays in the provision of financial services and the concomitant risk that is assumed by citizens using such services. So it is that the principle dealing with 'public awareness' requires that the FSA promote public understanding of the financial system.[42] That purpose of generating awareness is said to include 'promoting awareness of the benefits and risks associated with different kinds of investment or other financial dealing'.[43]

The second principle relates to the 'protection of consumers'.[44] The definition **47.25** given that objective is the provision of 'the appropriate degree of protection for

---

[38] Financial Services and Markets Act 2000, Sch 2, para 6(1).   [39] See para 47.32.
[40] The FSA is itself a body corporate governed by its chair and governing body, capable of being removed by the Treasury, Financial Services and Markets Act 2000, Sch 1, para 2.
[41] Financial Services and Markets Act 2000, s 2(2).
[42] Financial Services and Markets Act 2000, s 4(1).
[43] Financial Services and Markets Act 2000, s 4(2).
[44] Financial Services and Markets Act 2000, s 5(1).

consumers'. This standard of appropriateness includes consideration of:

(a) . . . the different degrees of *risk* involved in different kinds of investment or other transaction;
(b) the differing degrees of *experience and expertise* that different consumers may have in relation to different kinds of regulated activity;
(c) the needs that consumers may have for advice and accurate information; and
(d) the general principle that consumers should *take responsibility* for their decisions.[45]

In carrying out its duties the FSA is required to comply with a range of statutory principles of behaviour.[46] In contradistinction to the potentially far-reaching ramifications of creating a single financial regulator for all markets, there is a sense in the legislation that the regulator will be required to act in a manner which is sensitive to the needs of market participants. So, the FSA is not permitted to restrain activity simply because it deems that activity to be undesirable but rather the regulator's ability to act is restricted by a requirement that its action be in proportion to the general benefits to the markets of its action, in the following terms: 'a burden or restriction which is imposed on a person, or on the carrying on of an activity, should be *proportionate* to the benefits, considered in general terms, which are expected to result from the imposition of that burden or restriction . . .'.[47]

Conduct of Business Rules

FSA regulation of the manner in which investment business is conducted by professional investment advisers

47.26 The FSA's conduct of business rules prioritize the need for the sellers of financial products—that is, those who are authorized under the Act to do so—to categorize their customers according to the level of their expertise.[48] Consequently, the manner in which business is done and the type of business which can be done with inexpert customers differs from that with more expert customers. In effect, the seller of financial products is required to maintain the suitability of both the means by which the product is sold and the nature of the product itself. The rules themselves are contained in the FSA's *Conduct of Business Sourcebook*.[49] There is a different code for business done with inexpert customers and business done with market professionals; the latter is contained in the Inter-Professionals Conduct code which is supplemental to the main code on conduct of business. The principles contained in the code generally refer to conduct of business by authorized persons in regulated activities, in relation to non-regulated activity, in relation to client money accounts, and in relation to financial promotion.

---

[45] Financial Services and Markets Act 2000, s 5(2).
[46] Financial Services and Markets Act 2000, s 2(3).
[47] Financial Services and Markets Act 2000, s 2(3)(c).
[48] FSA Rulebook, *Conduct of Business Sourcebook* ('COB'), generally.
[49] Published in February 2000 as FSA *Consultation Paper 45*.

The approach of financial services regulation in the UK is to focus on regulating **47.27** those who are participating in the market, rather than regulating the conduct of the market itself. That is, the regulations identify categories of market participant and set out specific prerequisites to transaction, documentation, and procedures in relation to each. The markets do not create codes of conduct to be applied generically across the whole of a particular market place. As considered above, different forms of trustee will receive different treatment under these provisions as will different forms of beneficiary with different risk appetite.

The general requirement which underpins the Conduct of Business code is that, **47.28** when the seller communicates information to a customer, it must do so in a way which is 'clear, fair and not misleading'.[50] The regulations provide that the seller must have regard to the level of knowledge which the buyer has of the transaction at issue when making written or oral communications.[51] Further, the seller must ensure that its officers do not take any inducements or 'soft commissions' in effecting transactions.[52]

The classification of customers

Customers are divided between three categories: market counterparties, intermedi- **47.29** ate customers, and private customers. The categories are set out in chapter 4 of the FSA Conduct of Business rules. The purpose of the provisions, as outlined above, is to ensure that 'clients are appropriately recognised so that the regulatory protections are focused on those clients who need them most'[53] with the result that there can be a regulatory 'light-touch' in relation to dealings between market professionals. Therefore, the client must be categorized before any transactions are conducted.[54]

At the outset, the seller must provide a private customer with its terms of business before any designated business is conducted,[55] whereas intermediate customers must only be so informed within a reasonable period of the beginning of desig- nated business being conducted.[56] Those terms of business should include men- tion of the commencement of the terms of business, the applicable regulator, the investment objectives, any restrictions on the relevant designated business, which services will be provided, how payment for services will be effected, disclosure of any polarization, whether the seller is to act as investment manager, any conflicts of interest, and whether or not the client has a right to withdraw.[57]

Suitability

The philosophy underpinning the FSA's Conduct of Business Regulations is that **47.30** the treatment of the client, the investments and financial products which are sold

---

[50] COB, 2.1.3. [51] COB, 2.1.4. [52] COB, 2.2.3. [53] COB, 4.1.3.
[54] COB, 4.1.4. [55] Except where the client is habitually resident outside the UK.
[56] COB, 4.2.5. [57] COB, 4.2.15.

to that client, and the manner in which business is conducted with that client must all be suitable for that context. Therefore, the trustee's allocation of the client to a particular category of expertise operates both to set the level at which the service provider will pitch his treatment of the client and also to ensure that the service provider has considered the nature of those services which will be provided, as considered below. In the pre-2000 Securities and Investment Board's 'Conduct of Investment Business Rules',[58] which preceded the FSA's code, there was specific mention of the concept of suitability.[59]

47.31 It is important, then, not only that the product is suitable for its purpose, but also that the product is appropriate for the particular client and also that the advice to buy a particular product is given in a suitable way.[60] In relation to private customers, the seller is required to keep its treatment of such customers under regular review.[61] The polarization rules require that the seller be giving independent advice wherever possible and that in circumstances in which it is acting otherwise than entirely in the clients interests—for example, if it is a market maker or acting as a discretionary fiduciary of some sort—then that status must be communicated adequately to the client in the context of the buyer's level of expertise.[62] The test adopted throughout chapter 5 of COB is that the seller must have taken 'reasonable steps'—the expression adopted by the case law for example in relation to the enforcement of domestic mortgages against co-habitees of the mortgagor[63]—in relation to its treatment of that client. An example would be the manner in which its officers induce clients to enter into particular transactions.[64] The type of reasonable steps which will be suitable are not susceptible of general definition but rather:

> will vary greatly, depending on the needs and priorities of the private customer, the type of investment or service being offered, and the nature of the relationship between the firm and the private customer and, in particular, whether the firm is giving a personal recommendation or acting as a discretionary investment manager.[65]

In so doing the firm is required to ensure that the product is the most suitable of that type of product for the purpose,[66] although another product would not be more suitable simply because it would be available at a lower price.[67]

C. Market Abuse

The market abuse code

47.32 The code on 'market abuse' expands the powers of the Financial Services Authority to prosecute those market participants—whether authorized or unauthorized

---

[58] SIB Rules, Ch III, Pt 2.
[59] AS Hudson, *Swaps, Restitution and Trusts* (Sweet & Maxwell, 1999) 200.   [60] COB, 5.2.4.
[61] COB, 5.2.6.   [62] COB, chapter 5.   [63] *Barclays Bank v O'Brien* [1994] AC 180.
[64] COB, 5.1.11, 5.1.13.   [65] COB, 5.3.4.   [66] COB, 5.3.6(1).   [67] COB, 5.3.7.

under the legislation—outside the ambit of the ordinary criminal law for misfeasance in financial dealings. The importance of this regime is that it carries punitive penalties but that it does not replicate all of the protections and rights which are characteristic of the criminal law. Its legislative purpose was to make successful prosecutions for market abuse easier to obtain than had been the case under the pre-existing criminal law.

The market abuse regime relates to 'qualifying investments' traded on LIFFE, the London Stock Exchange, and other markets[68] where the behaviour in question would be regarded by 'a regular user of that market' as a failure 'to observe the standard of behaviour reasonably expected of a person in . . . their position in relation to the market'.[69] A 'regular user' is someone who is a 'reasonable person who regularly deals on that market in investments of the kind in question'; the term 'regular user' appears frequently in this code.[70] More specifically, the behaviour in question must exhibit three further features. First, it must be based on information which is 'not generally available to those using the market' but which would be considered by a 'regular user' of the market to be 'relevant' to entering into transactions on that market.[71] Secondly, it must be 'likely to give a regular user of the market a false or misleading impression' as to the supply of, demand for, and value of the investments in question.[72] Thirdly, the behaviour must be of a kind that would be 'likely. . . to distort the market' in question.[73]   **47.33**

To supplement this statutory code then there is a code of conduct which is required   **47.34**
to be created by the FSA under the auspices of FSMA 2000.[74] This code ('MAR 1')[75] requires that the instrument in question be one which is traded on an existing market and in which there is a continuing market. It is important to recognize that the types of behaviour which the FSA intends to encompass within this regime relate not only to dealing directly in shares and other instruments but also to any behaviour which affects their value more generally.[76] Further, that behaviour may take place in another jurisdiction but nevertheless have an impact on instruments traded in the United Kingdom and so fall within the market abuse code.[77]

The standard used by the legislation of a hypothetical 'reasonable user' of the market is intended to replicate the 'reasonable man' test used frequently by the

---

[68] Financial Services and Markets Act 2000, s 118(1).
[69] Financial Services and Markets Act 2000, s 118(3).
[70] Financial Services and Markets Act 2000, s 118(10).
[71] Financial Services and Markets Act 2000, s 118(2)(a).
[72] Financial Services and Markets Act 2000, s 118(2)(b).
[73] Financial Services and Markets Act 2000, s 118(2)(c).
[74] Financial Services and Markets Act 2000, s 119.
[75] Published under the Financial Services Authority, Market Conduct Sourcebook Instrument 2001 ('MAR 1').   [76] MAR 1, 1.11.8E.
[77] MAR 1, 1.2.9G.

common law to establish a level of objectivity but while also retaining some recognition of the particular context within which that defendant is operating; thus creating a test more akin to the 'average trader on the Stock Exchange' than 'the man on the Clapham omnibus'.[78]

Offences relating to market abuse

47.35 The offence of making misleading statements is contained in section 397 of FSMA 2000.[79] That offence is committed in one of three circumstances. First, where a person makes a statement, promise, or forecast which 'he knows to be misleading, false or deceptive in a material particular'.[80] What is not made clear in this context is what will constitute knowledge; that is, whether one can be taken to 'know' a statement is misleading only if you have actual knowledge, or whether it would be sufficient to have constructive notice of its misleading nature, or whether it would be sufficient that one has wilfully and recklessly failed to make the inquiries which an honest and reasonable person would have made in that context.[81] Secondly, where such a person 'dishonestly conceals any material facts' in relation to a statement, promise, or forecast.[82] Again, it is unclear whether dishonesty in this context would require actual fraud or whether it could be established in circumstances in which the defendant fails to act as an honest person would have acted in the circumstances.[83] It is suggested that the latter would accord most closely with the 'reasonable user' test within the market abuse code more generally. Thirdly, where such a person 'recklessly makes (dishonestly or otherwise) a statement, promise or forecast which is misleading, false or deceptive in a material particular'.[84]

Insider dealing

47.36 The legislative code on insider dealing was established under Part V of the Criminal Justice Act 1993. Further to the enactment of FSMA 2000, the FSA has the power to prosecute any allegations of insider dealing.[85]

Financial promotion

47.37 The financial promotion code provides that no person shall 'in the course of business, communicate an invitation or inducement to engage in investment

---

[78] cf *Polly Peck v Nadir* [1992] 4 All ER 769 where an objective test of reasonableness is used in relation to a claim for knowing receipt but where that objectivity is tempered by making reference to a 'reasonable banker' in relation to financial transactions and not simply to an average person who may or may not have any banking knowledge.   [79] cf *R v De Berenger* (1814) 3 M & S 66.

[80] Financial Services and Markets Act 2000, s 397(1)(a).   [81] eg *Re Montagu* [1987] Ch 264.

[82] Financial Services and Markets Act 2000, s 397(1)(b).

[83] eg *Royal Brunei Airlines v Tan* [1995] 2 AC 378.

[84] Financial Services and Markets Act 2000, s 397(1)(c).

[85] Financial Services and Markets Act 2000, s 402.

activity'.[86] This general prohibition is then hedged in with exceptions where the communication is made by an authorized person or is an authorized communication. Further exceptions are provided for by Treasury regulation. Breach of this central prohibition on financial promotion constitutes an offence;[87] although it is a defence to that offence for the accused to show that he took 'all reasonable precautions and exercised all due diligence to avoid committing the offence'.[88]

Any agreement entered into by an authorized person in contravention of the general prohibition on inviting or inducing another person to engage in investment activity under section 21(1) of FSMA 2000 will be 'unenforceable against the other party'.[89] That agreement must have been made after the Act came into force. The counterparty is entitled to recover any money or other property transferred under the agreement and also compensation for any loss sustained in connection with having 'parted with it'.[90] An unenforceable agreement resulting from an unlawful communication under section 21 of FSMA 2000 may, however, be enforced by a court or a court may order that money or property transferred under the agreement is to be retained[91] provided that the court is satisfied that it would be 'just and equitable' to do so.[92]

---

[86] Financial Services and Markets Act 2000, s 21(1).
[87] Financial Services and Markets Act 2000, s 23(1).
[88] Financial Services and Markets Act 2000, s 23(3).
[89] Financial Services and Markets Act 2000, s 26(1); except in relation to the acceptance of deposits, s 26(4).   [90] Financial Services and Markets Act 2000, s 26(2).
[91] cf *Westdeutsche Landesbank v Islington LBC* [1996] AC 669, where a transfer of property under a contract void *ab initio* was nevertheless held to have been a good transfer of title in spite of the void nature of that contract, thus requiring the claimant to seek restitution at common law or in equity.
[92] Financial Services and Markets Act 2000, s 30(4).

48

TRUSTS OF FINANCIAL
INSTRUMENTS AND OF MONEY

A. Financial Instruments as the Subject Matter of a Trust

A financial transaction is itself an item of property if by 'financial transaction' is meant an obligation created between two parties requiring the payment of money or the transfer of other assets, whether or not calculated by reference to some extraneous market rate and whether or not requiring reciprocal payments to be made between those parties. Financial transactions of this type fall into two distinct categories: those instruments which are freely transferable in the financial market place generally and those non-transferable transactions which are negotiated privately between two (or more) contracting parties.[1] All financial transactions, of whatever sort, are bundles of personal rights and duties which, as choses in action, acquire the status of intangible property. **48.01**

What is more complex is identifying precisely the manner in which they constitute property. For example, a bond which entitles the bondholder to receive a payment of interest annually at a fixed rate over a period of ten years might be said to **48.02**

---

[1] Commonly referred to as 'over-the-counter' transactions, indicating that they are transacted off-exchange. Cf AS Hudson, *The Law on Financial Derivatives* (3rd edn, Sweet & Maxwell, 2002) 1.

constitute a single executory right to receive ten payments of interest or rather as a series of rights each to receive a single amount of interest payable by instalments. Furthermore, the bond is itself a transferable security which can be sold for a capital amount. The right to receive interest goes with the ownership of the bond: this would suggest that the rights to interest are several and therefore that the bond can be transferred, for example five years into its life, and carry with it entitlement only to those remaining five interest payments. By contrast, an ordinary share carries with it no entitlement to receive any cash flow unless and until a dividend is declared, or unless a winding up has been ordered and the shareholder has a right to participate in that winding up. The principal value in a share in a publicly limited company, other than the dividend, is in its resale value (something which might not apply in relation to shares in private companies which are not transferable).

48.03 In relation to securities, then, the property in question is both the transferable capital value of the security and the future income stream (contingent or otherwise) which flows from it. In relation to ordinary lending transactions or privately-contracted financial derivatives, however, there is no such security issued. Therefore, the property in question would be the benefit flowing from that contract. In this instance, the commercial value of the contract would be the present market value of the future cash flow, both income and capital, payable by the borrower over the remaining life of the loan.[2] The legal property deriving from the contracts is conceptualized in general terms as being a chose in action whereas a more accurate conceptualization might be to recognize the cash flow deriving from the contract as being the property at issue.[3] This latter approach, conceiving of the cash flow as being at the heart of the relationship, accords most closely with commercial practice.

B. Certainty of Subject Matter in Trusts of Financial Instruments

The principle of certainty of subject matter

48.04 It is an essential prerequisite of a validly constituted express trust that the subject matter of that trust be certain.[4] This principle was considered in Chapter 3 on certainty of subject matter.[5] In seeking to apply the rule as to certainty of subject matter to the constitution of trusts of financial transactions one encounters the

---

[2] The market value of such a loan would vary depending on the level of security provided for that loan.

[3] *Don King Productions Inc v Warren* [1998] 2 All ER 608, Lightman J; affirmed [2000] Ch 291, CA; *Re Celtic Extraction Ltd (in liq), Re Bluestone Chemicals Ltd (in liq)* [1999] 4 All ER 684; *Swift v Dairywise Farms* [2000] 1 All ER 320.

[4] *Re London Wine Co (Shippers) Ltd* [1986] PCC 121; *Re Goldcorp* [1995] 1 AC 74; *Westdeutsche Landesbank Girozentrale v Islington LBC* [1996] AC 669, HL.   [5] See para 3.01.

problem discussed at paragraph 48.15 of seeking to apply that principle to intangible property. The discussion in the previous section identified financial transactions as being items of intangible property made up of bundles of contractual obligations. Many of the cases concerning the requirement of certainty of subject matter concerned the difficulty in establishing trusts of such contractual obligations so as, in many of the cases, to take secured rights in the event of another person's insolvency. The problem is a familiar one then to the law of trusts.

To establish a trust over tangible property, that property must be separately **48.05** identifiable from all other property. In relation to land, that is a question of identifying with sufficiently clarity which land is at issue. In relation to chattels, that is similarly a question of identifying which chattels are intended to be held on trust. The question in the example of chattels is more likely to be complicated by mixtures of chattels, in which the property to be held on trust may be commingled with property not to be held on trust, or by the settlor failing to segregate those chattels which are to be held on trust from the chattels which are not. So, in *Re London Wine Co (Shippers) Ltd*[6] a trust was purportedly created over bottles of wine held in a cellar. In the event, when the wine shippers who held possession of the wine bottles went into liquidation, those bottles which were to have been held on trust had not been segregated from those bottles not to have been held on trust, nor had the bottles to be held on trust been labelled or identified as such. In consequence the trust failed for want of certainty as to the subject matter of the trust.

In *Re Goldcorp Exchange Ltd*[7] a bullion exchange went into liquidation and its customers sought to take possession of the bullion which they had ordered and left on deposit with the exchange. Their claims centred on the contention that their contracts with the exchange gave rise to trusts which rendered them secured creditors in the exchange's insolvency. It was held that the only customers who could establish a trust over any property held by the exchange would be those customers who could demonstrate that there was bullion held to their account separately from the exchange's general stock of bullion. By contrast, those customers who were left bringing a claim *ex bulk* against the bullion held by the exchange did not have such proprietary rights because they could not ascertain which bullion would form the subject matter of their trust distinct from the other bullion held by the exchange. From the perspective of establishing trusts over financial instruments, this case is instructive. The unsuccessful claimants claimed that the terms of their contracts gave rise to trusts because they required the exchange to hold bullion of equivalent value and quality to their order for them. This claim confused, in the manner of the great philosophers, 'is' with 'ought'. The claimants argued that because the contract provided that the exchange 'ought' to have held bullion separately to

---

[6] [1986] PCC 121.   [7] [1995] 1 AC 74.

their account, then the court should deem that that 'is' what happened. Instead, the court held that unless there had in fact been segregation of the property to make sufficiently certain which property constituted the trust fund, there could be no such fund. The claimants even sought to rely on the doctrine in *Walsh v Lonsdale*[8] whereby a person who is subject to a specifically enforceable contractual obligation to transfer property to another is deemed to have transferred equitable title in that property automatically.[9] Again, this line of argument failed because the claimants could still not demonstrate which property was to be held on trust.

48.06 Three issues follow on from this analysis. First, to what extent is this principle different in relation to intangible property, such as financial instruments? Secondly, to what extent do the terms of a financial instrument influence the possibility of imposition of trust over that property? Thirdly, how can non-transferable, over-the-counter financial instruments be subject to a trust? These issues are considered in turn in the following sections.

Establishing trusts over intangible property

48.07 To establish an express trust or a constructive trust over intangible property, that property should be segregated from all other property. Segregation in this sense requires that the property which is to be the subject matter of the trust be separately identifiable from all other property. In situations in which the property at issue is money contained in a bank account, for example, that money should be placed in a bank account before the declaration of the trust and not mixed with any other moneys. In consequence it would be possible to say with sufficient certainty that the money held in that bank account was segregated. If that money were in a bank account together with other money—in practice, if the amount of money held in that bank account is greater than the amount which was to have been held on trust—then there could not be a valid trust because the property to be held on trust would be uncertain.[10]

In *Hunter v Moss*[11] the Court of Appeal held that it was not necessary to segregate the property comprising the trust fund if the property was intangible property, like ordinary shares, with each unit being indistinguishable from another unit. While Dillon LJ, in giving the leading judgment, did not express the matter quite so baldly, he did suggest that there were instances in which trusts would be imposed even though the trustee did not know which property would be subject to the trust—the example given was of an executor who does not know at the time

---

[8] *Walsh v Lonsdale* (1882) 21 Ch D 9.
[9] This is, in effect, a precursor of the modern constructive trust: *Chinn v Collins* [1981] AC 533; *Neville v Wilson* [1997] Ch 144.
[10] *MacJordan Construction Ltd v Brookmount Erostin Ltd* [1992] BCLC 350.
[11] [1994] 1 WLR 452.

of the creation of a will trust which property will constitute the trust fund[12]—and that the situation in front of him was distinguishable from the *Re London Wine Co* decision (considered immediately above) on the basis that *Re London Wine* considered the declaration of a trust over chattels whereas his case did not.

It is from this latter reasoning that one subsequent case has extrapolated the suggestion that intangible property falls to be treated differently from tangible property.[13] So, the decision of Neuberger J in *Re Harvard Securities (Holland v Newbury)*[14] concerned a dealer in financial securities who held securities as nominee for his clients. While the terms of the contracts entered into with his clients suggested that the dealer held the securities on bare trust for each of his clients, the securities were not numbered and were not segregated. In consequence, none of the clients was able to identify which securities were held on bare trust for which client. Neuberger J distinguished *Re Wait*,[15] *Re London Wine*,[16] and *Re Goldcorp*[17] on the basis that those cases concerned chattels; and decided to apply *Hunter v Moss*[18] because that case similarly concerned intangible securities. It was therefore held that the trusts were not invalid for uncertainty of subject matter because the securities were intangible property and therefore did not require segregation.

This second strand of authority, to the effect that intangible property such as **48.08** financial instruments should be treated differently from tangible property, contains a number of problems. First, these authorities reverse the ordinary requirement of English property law that there be specific and identifiable property which is the subject of the property right.[19] Thus, when considering rights in an asset like a share which is held on a register, the property right involved is not the share (because that is a piece of property which is not distinguishable from other shares) but rather is the chose in action represented by the entry on the register (because that is a transferable right between the shareholder, the registry, and the company).[20] Furthermore, in cases involving insolvency, this second approach would breach the *pari passu* principle in insolvency law[21] by permitting an otherwise unsecured creditor to enlarge a contractual right into a proprietary right, without more. Thirdly, it is not immediately obvious why intangible property

---

[12] However, it is suggested that this analogy is a false one because, first, the trust is not properly constituted until the testator's death and, secondly, at the time of the testator's death his executor will know that the testator's entire estate falls under the terms of the will: consequently, the executor does know with sufficient certainty which property falls under the will trust because it constitutes any property to which the testator is entitled.

[13] *Re Harvard Securities Ltd; Holland v Newbury* [1997] 2 BCLC 369.

[14] [1997] 2 BCLC 369.   [15] [1927] 1 Ch 606.   [16] [1986] PCC 121.

[17] [1995] AC 74.   [18] [1994] 1 WLR 452.

[19] *Westdeutsche Landesbank v Islington LBC* [1996] AC 669, *per* Lord Browne-Wilkinson, expressly approving *Re Goldcorp*.

[20] AS Hudson, *The Law on Investment Entities* (Sweet & Maxwell, 2000).

[21] *Stein v Blake* [1996] 1 AC 243, HL; *Re BCCI (No 8)* [1995] Ch 46.

8

requires a different principle simply because its units may be identical: there are many forms of mass-manufactured chattel, for example, which are of the same value, exhibit the same properties, and are (to all intents and purposes) identical.

Establishing trusts over mixed funds

48.09   If the settlor intended to create a trust over part of the money held in an account or over some only of the securities comprising part of a holding, then the settlor would need to settle the whole of that fund on trust and to give the trustees discretion as to the manner in which the contents of the trust fund would be distributed between the various beneficiaries who would require recourse to those securities. It is a peculiar feature of this area of law, perhaps, that the principle of certainty of subject matter refers only to property which comprises the total trust fund but does not extend any further so as to require certainty at the time at which the trust is created as to which property the trustees will advance to which beneficiary. Rather, it is sufficient that the trustees have sufficiently clear discretion as to how they will exercise their powers of advancement or maintenance of the trust fund and that the identity of the beneficiaries be sufficiently certain.[22]

Subtly different issues arose in two cases. In *Re Golay Morris v Bridgewater and Others*[23] it was held that a provision that a 'reasonable income' be provided out of a fund could be held to be valid if one could make an objective measurement of what would constitute a reasonable income in any particular case. A contrary approach was demonstrated in *Re Kolb's Will Trusts*,[24] in which the testator had directed trustees in his will to invest in 'blue chip' stocks, when Cross J held that insufficient power had been given to the trustees to decide what was meant by 'blue chip'. A possible distinction between *Golay* and *Kolb* might be to examine whether or not on the facts of any particular case the trustees have sufficient power to enable them to decide which property is intended to fall within the trust fund and which property should not.

Establishing trusts where the subject matter of the trust is not certain

48.10   There are two conflicting lines of authority as to the treatment of intangible property. In relation to money held in electronic bank accounts, there is authority to the effect that any purported trust over money held in a bank account which is mixed with other money will not be valid.[25] Where a subcontractor in a large building development was contractually entitled to a stage payment, the payer had gone into liquidation. The subcontractor claimed that it could identify the bank account in which the sum to be paid to it was then held, claimed that the amount was then due, and consequently claimed that a trust should be imposed

---

[22] See para 4.01.   [23] [1965] 1 WLR 969.   [24] [1962] Ch 531.
[25] *MacJordan Construction Ltd v Brookmount Erostin Ltd* [1992] BCLC 350.

over the bank account in which those moneys were held such that the claimant would be a secured creditor in the insolvency proceedings. The moneys were, however, mixed with other money and therefore the Court of Appeal held that they were not capable of forming the subject matter of a trust.[26] This contrasts with the authority of *Hunter v Moss* considered in paragraph 48.07 which suggested that a trust could be imposed are intangible property without the need for the segregation of that property.

Title in sale of goods contracts

Where the trust fails for uncertainty of subject matter, no trust will have been properly created because there was no fund of property ever impressed with a trust.[27] This latter proposition derives from the necessity that there be property over which the trust takes effect—where there is no such property, there can never be said to have been a trust at all. Whereas, where it is the identity of the beneficiaries which is uncertain, the trust fund may well be impressed with a trust and the trustee subject to fiduciary obligations but the settlor will receive the equitable interest in such property on resulting trust.[28] **48.11**

In general terms the approach of the case law to questions of the creation of trusts in commercial situations is the same as that for ordinary property situations. So, for example, in *Re Wait*[29] it was held that, when the claimant had rights to 500 tons of wheat out of a total shipment of 1,000 tons carried from Oregon, that claimant had no proprietary rights to any 500 tons out of the total 1,000 tons held by the shipper at the time of his bankruptcy because no such 500 tons had been segregated and held to the claimant's order. In short, the claimant had only a contractual right at common law to be delivered 500 tons of wheat but no equitable proprietary right in any identified 500 tons. **48.12**

However, in cases like *Re Staplyton*[30] there are clear distinctions drawn between rules of commercial law and norms of ordinary property law in relation to a store of wines kept in warehouses by a vintner for its customers but where those bottles of wine were not marked as being held for any particular customer. Following the decision in *Re London Wine* there could have been no question that any customer took rights in any particular bottles of wine—rather, all customers should have had only the rights of unsecured creditors against the entire stock of wine. In that case, Judge Baker QC applied dicta of the courts in *Re Wait* and in *Liggett v Kensington*[31] to the effect that contracts to carry or store goods for another do not necessarily create equitable interests in such goods. But, the judge applied section **48.13**

---

[26] This authority is perhaps obiter on this point given that there were also unresolved issues as to the claimant's contractual rights.   [27] *Westdeutsche Landesbank v Islington* [1996] AC 669.
[28] *Vandervell v IRC* [1967] 2 AC 291, HL.   [29] [1927] 1 Ch 606.
[30] [1994] 1 WLR 1181.   [31] [1993] 1 NZLR 257.

16 of the Sale of Goods Act 1979 to find that the wine claimed by the plaintiff was sufficiently 'ascertainable' for the purposes of commercial law.

48.14 Therefore, the approach taken by the application of commercial law statute is different from the position under ordinary principles of the law of trusts. Under the Sale of Goods (Amendment) Act 1995, the effect of *Re Goldcorp*[32] would be nullified. The 1995 Act provides that in relation to sales of goods (as with the contracts at the heart of the *Goldcorp* litigation) all of the purchasers would be deemed tenants in common in accordance with the proportionate size of their contractual entitlements.

C. Trusts of Non-Transferable Financial Instruments

Trusts over non-transferable property

48.15 There is authority for the proposition that a trust may take effect over a contract such as a financial instrument, even if that contract is not transferable, as one would ordinarily expect property to be, if there is some stream of income or future benefit over which the trust may take effect. In *Don King Productions Inc v Warren*[33] a partnership was formed between two boxing promoters and the various companies which were under their control to the effect that the benefit of any applicable promotion contract which any of the partners should enter into was to have been held on trust for the benefit of the partnership. One of the promoters entered into such a promotion contract but sought to retain the benefit of that contract for himself, and not to transfer its benefit to the partnership, on the basis, *inter alia*, that the contract was itself expressed to be not transferable. However, it was held, that contractual provision notwithstanding, that the contract would give rise to future benefits in the form of a cash flow. Therefore, it was held that the entitlement to receive this cash flow in itself constituted a valuable right which its owner could have contracted to transfer to other persons and therefore the right to the cash flow constituted a property right capable of forming the subject matter of a trust and of being subject to the partnership agreement.

The same point has been reached with other forms of intangible right. So, in *Swift v Dairywise Farms*[34] a milk quota licence was purportedly made the subject matter of a property right in spite of the fact that the licence was granted by a public body and expressed to be incapable of being transferred to any other person. Again, it was held that the valuable cash flow and other rights which flowed from the ownership of this licence were themselves capable of being transferred to

---

[32] [1995] AC 74.   [33] [1998] 2 All ER 608, Lightman J; affirmed [2000] Ch 291, CA.
[34] [2000] 1 All ER 320.

another person. Similarly, in the liquidation of a company which held waste management licences in relation to the extraction of minerals, it was held that the benefits which flowed from that licence were capable of being transferred and so of forming the subject matter of a trust even though the licence was itself expressed to be incapable of transfer.[35]

The subject matter of such a trust

It is important to identify the property at issue here. It is not the licence nor the promotions contract (in relation to the foregoing cases): rather, the property is the benefit which can be taken from that licence or contract. Where one stands to receive a benefit, it is possible to contract to transfer that benefit to another person or to use that anticipated benefit to found security for a loan. That these benefits are capable of being transferred or turned to account, even if the source of those benefits is not itself so transferred nor turned to account, then that is enough to constitute a distinct right from its source. The point is a familiar one to economists. The well-understood metaphor that is usually employed to explain the distinction between capital and income is that of the tree: it is said that the tree is the capital asset and that the fruit of the tree is income. Here, the promotions contract in *Don King* is the tree and the cash flow expected to be derived from it in the future is the fruit of that tree.

48.16

The difficulty with the analogy, however, is that the benefits which are purportedly being settled on trust or treated as property are items of future property. That is, they are not benefits in the hands of the settlor at the time of purporting to create the trust. This returns us to the discussion in paragraph 5.30 where the problem of 'after-acquired' property was considered. In that discussion it was said that a mere expectation that some money will be received will not in itself constitute a trust which will bite over that property if it is subsequently received.[36] Where the settlor has some right in the after-acquired property at the time of purporting to create the trust, then the trust will be valid.[37] In relation to financial instruments the question is one of the construction of the instrument. In the case of an instrument which entitles the settlor to receive a liquidated or an identifiable sum of money or item of property, then that contractual right itself can constitute the subject matter of a trust.[38] However, if the contractual right may not give rise to a right to any money because, perhaps, it is subject to a condition precedent such as the movement of market rates to a given level, then that instrument may not be capable of forming the subject matter of a trust because it may be interpreted to constitute merely an expectation and not a right to any property.

48.17

---

[35] *Re Celtic Extraction Ltd (in liq), Re Bluestone Chemicals Ltd (in liq)* [1999] 4 All ER 684.
[36] *Re Brook's Settlement Trusts* [1939] 1 Ch 993.   [37] *Re Ralli's WT* [1964] 2 WLR 144.
[38] *Fletcher v Fletcher* (1844) 4 Hare 67.

48.18 The case of *Re Ralli's Will Trusts*[39] is instructive in this regard. In that case it was held that the right of a beneficiary in remainder (that is, someone entitled to the vested beneficial interest in property only after the death of the life tenant) was a right capable of forming the subject matter of a trust in itself even though the remainder beneficiary could not have known which property would pass to her under the trust. The remainder beneficiary could know only that whatever property remained vested in the trust could pass to her but she could not have known in advance of the death of the life tenant either the precise identity of the property which would pass to her nor its value: such things could only have been known at the later date when her full rights in the beneficial interest vested in her. Nevertheless, it was held that those few rights which she held at the earlier date as remainder beneficiary were sufficient to found the trust obligation on her such that when she did receive the entire beneficial interest later, then that property passed into the trust which she had created some time earlier.

48.19 Therefore, in relation to financial instruments, the coupon to which a bondholder is entitled is property to which he has a current contractual right now even though he is only entitled to receive payment in the future on the payment date. Therefore, he is able to settle his right to receive coupon on trust, or to transfer it, for the benefit of another person immediately even though the property itself will only accrue subsequently. This is the logical conclusion from *Don King v Warren* considered above. The settlor need not have title in the property which is to constitute the total value of the fund in the future, provided that he has some valid right to that property now. It is that right which establishes the trust and it is the equitable obligations which that trust imposes on the settlor which compels him to transfer onto trust the full value which is received subsequently. In this way an uneasy accommodation is reached with the rule requiring certainty of subject matter, considered above.

48.20 In relation to financial transactions in which the counterparty has no right to receive any payment, then the contractual right may not itself be sufficient to found a trust before that property is vested in that counterparty. A transaction which provides that the counterparty is entitled to receive the difference between rates of interest, if rate x is greater than rate y, will only entitle that counterparty to any payment if x does indeed exceed y. In that instance it might be said that the counterparty has no right to any payment at all because all is contingent on x exceeding y, whereas it might be said in the alternative that the contract itself constitutes a chose in action which can be settled on trust and supplemented by any payment received if x does turn out to be greater than y. Whereas a trust which purported to transfer the benefit of a contract which had not yet been created

---

[39] [1964] 2 WLR 144.

would not similarly be capable of constituting the subject matter of a trust at that moment in time because there was no chose in action, even, which was capable of constituting the trust fund, let alone any benefit to be drawn from it in the future. This element of time is missing from the analysis in the *Don King v Warren* case, although that is explained by the extreme vagueness with which the agreements in those cases were effected, leaving Lightman J to draw inferences where the parties themselves had contracted only for confusion.

D. Trusts of Money

Issues concerning trusts of money

This sub-heading suggests a vast discussion to follow: however, its focus is only on **48.21** the problems surrounding the execution of trusts over money held in electronic bank accounts—a subject which was considered in detail in Chapter 33 and which is therefore considered only briefly here to underline the similarities in financial transactions between effecting trusts of financial instruments and securities and trusts over funds of electronically held money. The principal issue revolving around trusts of money is that of identifying the subject matter of the trust distinct from all other funds of money. A trust declared over a ten pound note clutched in the settlor's hand and the serial number of which is recorded would clearly be a trust which took effect over that note. The further point which the law of property accepts is that if a new bank account were declared over that 'ten pounds'—which in effect means a bank account over that amount of ten pounds—then the trust shifts from the ten pound note whose serial number had been recorded onto the chose in action constituted by the bank account held by the recipient bank. Thus a personal claim by the depositor against the bank with a value of ten pounds sterling is said, somewhat uncomfortably, to afford the beneficiary of the trust an equitable interest in that bank account or, even worse, 'in that ten pounds'. The fragility of this beneficial interest is indicated by the following proposition: if a further ten pounds were paid into that account which was not intended to form a part of the trust fund, then the beneficiary would have only an equitable tracing claim against the mixed fund contained in, or expressed by, the bank account to a maximum value of ten pounds, which claim might result in a constructive trust or a charge. If money moves out of this bank account, then the beneficiary is required to trace his equitable interest into successive items of property representing the original proprietary right 'in ten pounds'. That equity permits such claims to be carried on through successive items of property is testament to its flexibility and to its commercial appeal; that matters become so complex is testament to the complex nature of 'money' in any transaction involving bank accounts.

Quistclose **trusts**

48.22   The *Quistclose* trust is considered in detail in Chapter 49. In relation to trusts over money, the *Quistclose* trust is a particularly significant doctrine. If money is loaned on terms that the borrower is permitted only to use the property for identified purposes, then the lender is said to acquire an equitable interest in the loaned moneys[40] or alternatively to have a secondary trust which comes into existence once the moneys are misused.[41] In such circumstances, a claimant will only seek to pray the *Quistclose* trust in aid if the loan moneys have already been paid away. Therefore, there will not be any money in the borrower's hands representing the original loan moneys—unless the lender is acting in an exceptional case so as to acquire an injunction to prevent the moneys from being misused. In the former case, however, the *Quistclose* trust will be a means of identifying an equitable proprietary interest in the lender's hands so that the lender will be able to begin an equitable tracing claim against whatever fund has absorbed the loan moneys.

Tracing electronically held money

48.23   As considered immediately above, trusts will be implied by law over money as well as being expressly declared by a settlor. It has become increasingly common in a world of money held in electronic bank accounts for money to be transferred quickly and easily between bank accounts whether those accounts are held in the same jurisdiction or in different jurisdictions. The upshot of this technical feasibility of transferring money easily is that mistakes or fraud can spirit funds out of one account, through a series of other accounts and companies before the rightful owners of that property are aware of it.[42] The claimant will lose a right to trace money into any given account if that particular account has gone overdrawn since the money was paid into it—on the basis that no money which constituted a part of the original fund—could be said to be left in that account.[43] Consequently, it is suggested that trusts over money are in practice easy to lose and difficult to recover. The reader is referred to Chapter 33 for a consideration of tracing into electronically held bank accounts.

The ubiquity and obscurity of money

The value of property described in terms of money

48.24   Many of the trusts considered in this book concern either trusts of money or trusts containing property which has a value, that value being generally rendered in terms of an equivalent sum of money referred to as its 'market value'. The focus of

---

[40]   *Twinsectra Ltd v Yardley* [2002] UKHL 12, [2002] 2 AC 164.
[41]   *Barclay's Bank v Quistclose Investments Ltd* [1970] AC 567.
[42]   See, for example, *Agip v Jackson* [1990] Ch 265.
[43]   *Roscoe v Winder* [1915] 1 Ch 62; *Bishopsgate v Homan* [1995] 1 WLR 31.

property lawyers on the value of property is a one-dimensional concern with the amount of money which would be required to buy that property on the open market: it makes no reference to the exchange value nor to the sentimental value nor to the labour value of that property. Nor does such reference to the value of property take into consideration the fact that a measurement of the value of property in pounds sterling is in itself a variable value given that the value of sterling changes on foreign exchange markets. Therefore, the intrinsic value ascribed to property is in itself variable in a sense beyond that in which the value which an item will fetch on the open market is variable.

The nature of money

There is insufficient space in this book to consider the nature of money in very **48.25** great detail. Very often, however, the courts have tended to consider money as though it were a tangible item of property which once spent is said to disappear and so be incapable of being traced.[44] In truth, the 'money' which is at issue in financial transactions is in the form of lines of credit made available by banks to their clients. This money does not exist in any tangible form: its status as property is dependent upon its status as a form of chose in action. It has been recognized that in criminal law the appropriation of money from a bank account was not theft in that the chose in action constituted by the bank account remained in the hands of its owner but that it was only the value of that chose in action which had diminished.[45] Thus, property lawyers continue to talk of 'money' in a loose fashion which means, very often, an amount of value transferred from one bank account to another bank account such that the value of the former account diminishes and the latter increases by the same amount. The establishment of trusts over such items of property is necessarily a vexed business which depends, in effect, on the notional segregation of money into a distinct fund which an accountant could identify as having been derived from a single source in which the beneficiary of that trust had an equitable interest.

---

[44] *Westdeutsche Landesbank v Islington* [1996] AC 669.
[45] *R v Preddy* [1996] AC 815.

49

TRUSTS USED TO TAKE SECURITY IN COMMERCIAL TRANSACTIONS

A. Allocating Title in Property Subject to a Transaction

49.01 This chapter is concerned with the use of trusts to take security in commercial and financial transactions. In general terms, the trust permits one person to be the legal owner of property and another person to be the equitable owner of property: that much is trite law. In commercial terms such a structure means that two contracting parties can provide for the manner in which the title to property which is being used for the purposes of their transaction, or the title to any property which will be generated by that transaction, is to be allocated between them.

49.02 Broadly speaking there are three ways in which title in property might be held. First, the property might be dealt with as being the property absolutely of one transacting party or the other. This would not require the imposition of a trust: rather, at common law the identified person would be the absolute owner of all rights in that property subject only to a contractual obligation to use that property in a given way for the purposes of the contract.

Secondly, the parties might decide that one party is to be the legal owner of the property such that he is empowered to use that property as though its absolute owner throughout the life of the transaction but subject always to some right in the other contracting party in the property at the end of the transaction. In this context the common law owner of the property might be considered to be a trustee of that property for his counterparty, or else there might be some form of fixed or floating charge over that property, or the common law owner might be subject merely to a contractual obligation to assign absolute title in that property at the end of the transaction. The counterparty would prefer to have beneficial rights in the property throughout the transaction in the event of the common law owner's bankruptcy during the life of the transaction or the transfer of the property to some third person, such as a bona fide purchaser for value of the property, which might put the property beyond the counterparty's reach. Alternatively, the contract might specify the purposes for which the common law owner of the property is entitled to use that property such that his counterparty has an equitable interest in that property which will bite on any property used for any other purpose.[1]

Thirdly, the parties might lodge their property with either one of them or with some third party custodian such that the custodian would hold the property on trust for both parties so that the parties would have rights in the property contingent on their performance of that contract. For example, X might be absolutely entitled to an amount of money held on trust equal in value to an identified quantity of sugar of an identified quality delivered to Tilbury docks, whereas Y would be entitled to absolute title in any money held on trust in relation to which X fails to satisfy that condition precedent. In this way a trust would enable all of the contracting parties to have rights in property in different fashions at the same time.

49.03 This chapter considers these various structures and the manner in which the trust and other doctrines such as the floating charge, retention of title clauses, and the pledge shade into one another. It is suggested that there is a spectrum of techniques for taking security which moves from the outright retention or transfer of title in property, through the allocation of some right by way of charge over a floating or a fixed pool of property which is exercisable only on the happening of some event, through to contingent rights to take a beneficial interest in property under trust, to finally an identified equitable interest in identified property held on trust by some other person. Where on this spectrum any individual, contracting party finds itself will be a matter for negotiation between the parties and for the proper interpretation of the terms of any contract effected between them.

---

[1] *Barclay's Bank v Quistclose Investments Ltd* [1970] AC 567; *Twinsectra Ltd v Yardley* [2002] UKHL 12, [2002] 2 AC 164.

B. Techniques of Taking Security

Retention of outright title

The clearest means of taking security over property which is to be used in a **49.04**
commercial transaction is to retain absolute title in that property. In relation to a
machine being used as part of the manufacturing process it would be a comparatively easy matter to provide that the machine in question is not to be connected
to any other machine so that it is incapable of easy separation at the end of the
transaction. In such a situation, it would be a straightforward matter for the owner
of that machine to provide that the machine should not be considered at any time
to have passed to any other person. However, in a financial transaction in which X
is required to transfer possession of a fund of securities to Y such that Y can invest
those securities and then re-transfer securities of a like kind to X (the basic structure involved in repo and stock lending transactions in financial markets) it would
be impossible for X to retain title in those securities because the purpose of the
transaction is that Y be able to sell them or otherwise use them as though their
absolute owner. Therefore, there will be commercial contexts in which it is not
practicable to suggest that the owner of property retain title in that property: in
many such situations, commercial people will use 'collateralization' structures, by
way of trust or pledge, as considered below.[2]

Floating charges

The most important form of charge, for present purposes, is the floating charge. **49.05**
That is, a form of charge which has an identified value and which takes effect over
a fluctuating pool of property only crystallizing at a point in time identified in the
agreement which gives rise to it. Whereas a fixed charge requires that the property
at issue be held immobile for the purposes of establishing a property right in the
chargee, subject to the chargor's performance of the relevant payment obligations,

---

[2] Collateralization refers to a transaction in which the party seeking security from its counterparty requires that that counterparty lodge some assets of a specified type (referred to here as the 'collateral') with a third party, or hold those assets in a distinct fund, or transfer those assets to the
secured party for the life of the transaction. Suppose a situation in which the secured party takes
delivery of assets itself from the counterparty. In a retention of title structure, the assets would be lent
only by the party posting collateral such that that party posting collateral would not surrender title
in those assets to the secured party. Rather the secured party would acquire possession of those assets
with only a lien over them. That means that the assured party has possession of the assets but no
rights of ownership empowering him either to sell that property, to mortgage it, or to deal with it, in
any other way. A lien may crystallize into a proprietary right if the contract between the parties containing the lien entitles the secured party to convert those assets once the counterparty has failed to
perform the relevant obligations under the main agreement or where it has committed some event
of default under the main agreement. However, in the absence of any breach of the agreement or in
the absence of the commission of any event of default, the party posting collateral retains ownership
rights in the property.

the floating charge permits the chargor to continue to use the property for the purposes of the chargor's business without tying that property down. The contractual difficulty is in establishing that the floating charge crystallize at a time slightly before the chargor defaults on its contractual obligations or before the chargor is able to put the charged property beyond the reach of the chargee. The process of crystallization, then, refers to the chargee's rights being converted from a putative right in unidentified property up to a given value into a right over identified property—that is, all of the property in the pool at the moment of crystallization—to the extent necessary to meet the charged value.

49.06 A floating charge has a defined value which takes effect over a range of property but not over any specific property until the point in time at which it crystallizes,[3] by contrast with a fixed charge, in which the rights attach to identified property.[4] A floating charge will usually be identified by reference to the following factors:

> (1) If it is a charge on a class of assets of a company present and future; (2) if that class is one which, in the ordinary course of business of the company, would be changing from time to time; and (3) if you find that by the charge it is contemplated that, until some future step is taken by or on behalf of those interested in the charge, the company may carry on its business in the ordinary way so far as concerns the particular class of assets I am dealing with.[5]

An alternative expression of that same distinction is the following one:

> A [fixed, or] specific charge . . . is one that without more fastens on ascertained and definite property or property capable of being ascertained and defined; a floating charge, on the other hand, is ambulatory and shifting in its nature, hovering over and so to speak floating with the property which it is intended to effect until some event occurs or some act is done which causes it to settle and fasten on the subject of the charge within its reach and grasp.[6]

49.07 A floating charge comes into existence by virtue of some contractual provision which grants the chargee rights of a given value over a fund of property which is greater in size than that right or which contains property the identity of which may change from time to time.[7] So, in *Clough Mill v Martin*[8] a supplier of yarn had entered into a contract with a clothes manufacturer under which the supplier was granted proprietary rights in any unused yarn and, significantly, in any clothes made with that yarn until it received payment from the clothes manufacturer. It was held by the Court of Appeal that there was insufficient intention to create a

---

[3] *Re Yorkshire Woolcombers Association* [1903] 2 Ch 284; *Illingworth v Houldsworth* [1904] AC 355; *Evans v British Granite Quarries Ltd* [1910] 2 KB 979; *Re Bond Worth* [1980] 1 Ch 228.
[4] *Royal Trust Bank v National Westminster Bank plc* [1996] BCC 316.
[5] *Re Yorkshire Woolcombers Association Ltd* [1903] 2 Ch 284, 295, *per* Romer LJ.
[6] *Illingworth v Houldsworth* [1904] AC 355, 358, *per* Lord Macnaghten.
[7] Such as a stock of goods held in a warehouse by a manufacturer where some of those goods will be shipped out and other goods added to the fund from time to time.
[8] [1984] 3 All ER 982.

trust of any particular stock of clothing. In part, the court considered the fact that the identity of the property over which the supplier's proprietary rights were to have taken effect changed from time to time and that those proprietary rights took effect over a stock of property larger than the value of the rights which the supplier was to have received. It need not matter that the charge is expressed by contract to be a fixed charge if in fact the court considers that it can only be a floating charge due to the changeability of the fund of property held.[9] That the rights of the chargee do not bite until the charge itself has crystallized creates a complex form of right.[10] The right is necessarily contingent on the chargor committing some default under the terms of the contract giving rise to the charge. The chargor is able to dispose of the property held on trust and to deal with it in the ordinary course of events.[11]

A floating charge enables the owner of that property to continue to use it as **49.08** though unencumbered by any other rights. That is, to act as though he is the absolute owner of the pool of property subjected to the floating charge. The first distinction between trusts and floating charges is evident when the chargee seeks to enforce its rights. Where the contract provided that the secured party was en-titled to seize and to take possession of all of the chattels remaining in a warehouse on the crystallization of the applicable contractual provision, then the following problem arises. If the governing contractual provision purported to create a trust over 'the remaining part of what is left' among those chattels in that warehouse such that the secured party could take property up to a given value from that pool of property, there may be a problem as to whether or not there was sufficient cer-tainty as to the intention to create a trust and as to the subject matter of the trust, given that the identity of the precise property at issue could not be known.[12] Alternatively, if the analysis were taken that this governing provision constituted a mere floating charge then there would be no such problem of the validity of the arrangement because the secured party would only acquire a right of a given value over that general pool of property without having any proprietary right attaching to any particular part of it. Such a structure would be weaker than a proprietary trust right in the event of an insolvency because the right holder could not iden-tify any particular property to which the right attached.[13]

One particular, recurring problem with taking charges is that of taking charges **49.09** over book debts. A book debt is a form of intangible property which can take many forms: in essence, it is a record of an obligation owed by one person to another person kept on the creditor's books as an asset and on the debtor's book as

---

[9] *Re Armagh Shoes Ltd* [1984] BCLC 405; *Re Brightlife Ltd* [1987] Ch 200.
[10] *Re Woodroffes (Musical Instruments) Ltd* [1986] Ch 366.
[11] *Wallace v Evershed* [1899] 1 Ch 891.   [12] *Sprange v Bernard* (1789) 2 Bro CC 585.
[13] *Re Goldcorp* [1995] 1 AC 74.

a liability. The issue is this: if, for example, a bank holds an account for its customer, can it take a charge over that account even though the account is in itself a debt which it owes to its customer?[14] The importance of identifying an agreement as being or not being a book debt is that a book debt will require registration under section 396 of the Companies Act 1985.[15] Failure to register such a charge renders that charge unenforceable[16] and in consequence the charge holder loses its priority in relation to an insolvency.[17] Furthermore, every officer of the company in default is liable to a fine.[18] In circumstances where at the date of the creation of an agreement there is a charge over property, then that charge is registrable;[19] whereas if no charge is created at the time of the creation of the agreement then there will not be a book debt requiring registration as a charge, even if such a charge might be created subsequently.[20] Lord Millett in *Agnew v IRC ('The Brumark')*[21] advocated a two-step process whereby the court, first, should consider the rights and obligations which the parties granted each other under their agreement and then, secondly, should seek to categorize the charge only after such an identification of the true intentions of the parties.[22] The appropriate test was said to be, on the construction of the agreement, whether the assets were under the free use of the chargor such that they could be subtracted from the security offered to the chargee, or whether they were under the restrictive control of the chargee so that they could not be subtracted from the chargee's security.[23]

The distinction between charges and trusts

49.10 Charges and trusts are very different precisely because it is an essential part of a charge that those rights represented by the charge must cease to exist when the debt has been discharged.[24] That distinction has been expressed in the following terms:

> ... any contract which, by way of security for the payment of a debt, confers an interest in property defeasible or destructible upon payment of such debt, or appropriates such property for the discharge of the debt, must necessarily be regarded as creating a mortgage or charge, as the case may be. The existence of the equity of redemption is quite inconsistent with the existence of a bare trustee-beneficiary relationship.[25]

---

[14] *Shipley v Marshall* (1863) 14 CBNS 566; *Independent Automatic Sales Ltd v Knowles and Foster* [1962] 1 WLR 974. Cf G McCormack [1989] LMCLQ 198; G McCormack, *Reservation of Title* (2nd edn, Sweet & Maxwell, 1995) 105 *et seq*.   [15] Companies Act 1985, s 396(1)(e).
[16] *Re Bond Worth* [1980] Ch 228.   [17] ibid.   [18] Companies Act 1985, s 399(3).
[19] *Independent Automatic Sales Ltd v Knowles and Foster* [1962] 1 WLR 974.
[20] *Paul and Frank Ltd v Discount Bank (Overseas) Ltd* [1967] Ch 348.
[21] [2001] 2 BCLC 188, 199, *per* Lord Millett.
[22] ibid 201; where his lordship drew a parallel with the case of *Street v Mountford* [1985] AC 809 in which the courts look for the true intentions of the parties in the analysis of leases and licences before allocating any particular agreement to either category.   [23] ibid 200.
[24] See eg *Reeve v Lisle* [1902] AC 461; *Samuel v Jarrah Timber Corporation* [1904] AC 323.
[25] *Re Bond Worth* [1980] 1 Ch 228, 248, *per* Slade J. See also *Re George Inglefield Ltd* [1933] Ch 1.

The rights of a beneficiary under a trust are not capable of being terminated, in the ordinary course of events, simply by discharge of a debt. Rather, the rights of the beneficiary would continue in existence regardless of the discharge of a debt. However, it would be possible to structure a trust in commercial contracts such that the rights of the beneficiary do come to an end once the contractual purpose has been performed. In consequence, this form of trust may appear to be closer in form to the charge. It might be that the trust is structured as though a discretionary trust such that the trustee can determine the interests of the secured party once the transaction has terminated such that the entire equitable interest is vested in the counterparty who provided the security. The constant in the trust structure is the trusteeship borne by the legal owner of the property. That person owes the duties of a trustee to all of the beneficiaries throughout the life of the transaction not to dispose of the trust property without accounting to the beneficiaries, not to favour one beneficiary over another beneficiary except to the extent permitted in the terms of the trust, and so forth.[26] In relation to a floating charge, however, the chargor is entitled to turn the charged property to his own account and to deal with it as though its absolute owner throughout the life of the transaction: a trustee may not act in such a way, unless expressly permitted to do so by the terms of his trusteeship.

Pledge

Pledge transactions involve the pledgor transferring possession of assets to the secured party, or to some third party as bailee. In the ordinary sense of pledge, as used for example in pawnbroking transactions, those assets are generally required to be retained by the pawnbroker and not disposed of except in a manner provided for in the terms of the broking contract. So, disposal may only be permitted after the effluxion of a given period of time or on the pledgor's failure to make payment to recover those assets within a specified time. In that form of pledge structure typically used in financial contracts, the party providing the security transfers title in the assets to be pledged outright to the secured party. The assured party, on receiving those assets, is entitled to treat that property entirely as its own and therefore to sell it, mortgage it, or deal with it in any way that an absolute owner would be entitled to behave with it. The only obligation which the assured party bears is to return property of a like kind if its obligation to its counterparty under the transaction falls due. That obligation to return property of a like kind means that the original property posted as collateral does not have to be returned; rather, it is only similar property or its equivalent value in cash which is to be returned (as specified in the contract itself). The key to these various forms of pledging activity is in the detail of the contract governing the structure. In particular, it is significant to

49.11

---

[26] See generally Chapter 11.

know whether the secured party is obliged the return the very property transferred to him, in which case his obligation resembles a trust or bailment, or if the secured party is obliged to return only property of a like kind or value, in which case his obligations are merely personal and so offer a lesser form of protection to the pledgor.

The particular features of the trust

49.12　The most remarkable feature about a trust is that it enables more than one person to have rights in the same property simultaneously. As opposed to models used in civilian jurisdictions in which anyone claiming rights related to property can only establish personal claims against the absolute owner of that property, the trust recognizes that the trustee takes only legal title whereas he is obliged to hold the beneficial title in that property on trust for the beneficiaries of the arrangement. As a result the trustee is able to exercise all of the common law rights of transferring, mortgaging, and dealing with the property. The rights of the beneficiary are nevertheless rights in the trust property itself[27] although they do also express a range of rights which the beneficiary has against the trustee to ensure that the trustee observes his beneficial interest, that he acts fairly between the beneficiaries, and that he commits no breach of trust nor obtains any unauthorized profit without accounting to the beneficiaries.

49.13　Rights under a charge, as considered above, are necessarily terminated once the underlying performance obligation has been discharged, whereas the rights of a beneficiary do not necessarily terminate in that fashion. Similarly, a pledge arrangement will cease to be effective once the performance obligation has been discharged or, in the case of a pledge, the property has been redeemed. Outright transfers of property or retention of title in property similarly deal in absolutes: there is absolute ownership of property vested either in one person or in another, but there is no division of ownership in the manner permitted by a trust either between beneficiaries or between beneficiary and trustee.

C.　Taking Security in Ordinary Lending: *Quistclose* Trusts

The purpose of *Quistclose* trusts

49.14　The spectrum of legal techniques which might be used to take security in commercial transactions established at the beginning of this chapter indicated that the best form of security which a secured party could take would be absolute title in some property of equal worth to the obligations owed to it by its counterparty.

---

[27] *Saunders v Vautier* (1841) 4 Beav 115.

Similarly, retention of title structures indicate that a contracting party does not wish to part with title in property which might be used as part of the performance of a contract. A modified form of that type of protection is the *Quistclose* trust which seeks, in the broadest terms, to enable a person lending money to require that the loan moneys are used only for specified purposes and that, if they are not so used, that equitable title in those moneys shall be considered to crystallize in the hands of the lender: it is a moot point, considered below, whether the lender has such an equitable interest throughout the life of the transaction[28] or whether he acquires his rights under some secondary trust only on the happening of some condition precedent.[29] As with all of the structures considered thus far in this chapter, the devil is in the detail. As will emerge, that form of *Quistclose* trust considered in the decided cases is not the only form which could be devised by an appropriately drafted loan contract. In consequence, the rights which the lender of moneys may retain in those loan moneys will depend very much on the manner in which the loan contract, its covenants, and other provisions are constituted in the contract between lender and borrower.

The development of *Quistclose* trusts

The principle in underpinning the *Quistclose* trust derives from the decision in *Hassall v Smither*.[30] In short, where a transferor transfers property subject to a contractual provision that the transferee is entitled only to use that property for limited purposes, the transferee will hold the property on trust for the transferor in the event that the property is used for some purpose other than that set out in the contract. Significantly, in the event that the transferee purports to transfer rights to some third party in breach of that contractual provision then the transferor is deemed to have retained its rights under a trust which will preclude the transferee from acquiring rights in that property. At present the *Quistclose* arrangement has been applied only to loan moneys but there is no reason in principle why it should apply only to money and not to other forms of property.[31] **49.15**

In *Barclays Bank v Quistclose*[32] itself, a loan contract was formed by which Quistclose lent money to Rolls Razor Ltd solely for the payment of dividends to its shareholders. That money was held in a share dividend bank account separate from all other moneys. Quistclose was in financial difficulties at the time. After negotiation between Rolls Razor and the lender, the purpose of the loan was specified to be the payment of a dividend to Rolls Razor's shareholders and was to be used for no other purpose. In the event Rolls Razor went into insolvency before **49.16**

---

[28] *Twinsectra Ltd v Yardley* [2002] UKHL 12, [2002] 2 AC 164.
[29] *Barclay's Bank v Quistclose Investments Ltd* [1970] AC 567.
[30] (1806) 12 Ves 119; *Toovey v Milne* (1819) 2 B & Ald 683, 106 ER 514.
[31] S Worthington, *Proprietary Rights in Commercial Transactions* (Clarendon Press, 1996) 63.
[32] *Barclay's Bank v Quistclose Investments Ltd* [1970] AC 567.

the dividend was paid. Barclays Bank argued that it should be entitled to set off the money held in the share dividend account against the overdraft which Rolls Razor had taken out with the bank. Quistclose contended that the money in the share dividend account was held on trust for Quistclose and therefore that the bank was not entitled to set that money off against the outstanding overdraft on Rolls Razor's other account.

The House of Lords held that the loan money held separately in a share dividend bank account should be treated as having been held on trust for the lender. The House of Lords held unanimously that the money in the share dividend account was held on resulting trust for Quistclose on the basis that the specified purpose of the loan had not been performed. Lord Wilberforce upheld the resulting trust in favour of Quistclose on the basis that it was an implied term of the loan contract that the money be returned to the lender in the event that it was not used for the purpose for which it was lent. Lord Wilberforce found that there were two trusts: a primary trust (which empowered Rolls Razor to use the money to pay the dividend) and a secondary trust (which required Rolls Razor to return the money to the lender if it was not used to pay the dividend). As his lordship held:

> In the present case the intention to create a secondary trust for the benefit of the lender, to arise if the primary trust, to pay the dividend, could not be carried out, is clear and I can find no reason why the law should not give effect to it.

This bicameral trust structure is unique to the case law in this area—although it would be possible to create a complex express trust which mimicked it. What is significant is that the *Quistclose* trust will be imposed in circumstances in which the parties to a loan contract have been silent as to the precise construction which is to a be placed on their contract.

49.17 The House of Lords used the expression 'resulting trust' to describe this arrangement.[33] However, that same principle has been alternatively stated in *Carreras Rothmans Ltd v Freeman Mathews Treasure Ltd*[34] to be that:

> . . . equity fastens on the conscience on the person who receives from another property transferred for a specific purpose only and not therefore for the recipient's own purposes, so that such person will not be permitted to treat the property as his own or to use it for other than the stated purpose.

This statement could be taken to be authority for one of three competing understandings of the *Quistclose* arrangement. At first blush, the reference to the 'conscience' of the recipient equates most obviously to a constructive trust, although those dicta are capable of multiple analyses. Those possibilities are considered next.

---

[33] ibid, and *Westdeutsche Landesbank v Islington* [1996] AC 669, *per* Lord Browne-Wilkinson.
[34] [1985] Ch 207, 222.

Varying analyses of *Quistclose*-type structures in loan contracts

As has been considered above, the analysis of *Quistclose* trusts set out by Lord **49.18**
Wilberforce in *Barclays Bank v Quistclose* was that the failure to use the loan
moneys for the contractually stipulated purpose gave rise to a resulting trust. This
analysis was advanced through the 'primary trust'/'secondary trust' structure considered above. The principal reason for viewing this form of trust as being a resulting trust in favour of the lender appears to be that, if the court held otherwise, it
would permit the borrower to affirm the transaction in part (by taking the loan
moneys and passing that money to creditors on insolvency) but to refuse to be
bound by the condition that the property could only be used for a specified purpose.[35] In that sense it appears that title in the loan money passes away from the
lender to the borrower, only to result (or, return) back to the lender at the moment
when it is misapplied by the borrower. However, that analysis does not correspond
neatly with the notion that there exists a primary trust, governing the borrower's
initial use of the money, and shadowed by a secondary trust. Rather than the property *resulting* back to the lender, it might be said that the lender's rights were latent
in the property already and were activated by the borrower's wrongful act. In consequence, the *Quistclose* trust might not cause property to return to the lender but
rather would appear to vindicate the lender's ongoing title.[36]

Thus it could be said that the lender retains an equitable interest in the loan **49.19**
moneys throughout the life of the loan transaction, such that the borrower may
use the loan moneys for the contractually specified purpose.[37] Presumably on the
performance of that purpose the lender's equitable interest in the money must be
discharged. Whereas, if the borrower misuses the money then the lender's
equitable interest would empower him either to seek an injunction to prevent the
misuse of the loan moneys or else to launch an equitable tracing claim to recover
that money or to launch a claim for breach of trust against the borrower.

This latter analysis of the *Quistclose* trust is to be found in Lord Millett's minority **49.20**
speech in the House of Lords in *Twinsectra Ltd v Yardley*.[38] In that case Leach, himself a solicitor, had assumed the responsibilities of another solicitor to a man called
Yardley. Yardley's previous solicitor, Sims, had offered a solicitor's undertaking to
Twinsectra that, if Twinsectra agreed to lend money to Yardley for the purpose of

---

[35] *Re Rogers* (1891) 8 Morrell 243, 248 *per* Lindley LJ.
[36] See, for example, the explanation given by Lord Millett in *Twinsectra Ltd v Yardley* [2002]
UKHL 12, [2002] 2 AC 164, [2002] 2 All ER 377, HL.
[37] P Millett, 'The *Quistclose* trust: who can enforce it?' (1985) 101 LQR 269; J Priestly, 'The
Romalpa Clause and the *Quistclose* trust' in Finn (ed), *Equity and Commercial Transactions* (1987)
217, 237; M Bridge, 'The *Quistclose* trust in a world of secured transactions' (1992) 12 OJLS 333,
352. See also *General Communications Ltd v Development Finance Corp of New Zealand Ltd* [1990]
3 NZLR 406; *Re Australian Elizabethan Theatre Trust* (1991) 102 ALR 681.
[38] [2002] 2 All ER 377.

acquiring property, then Sims would hold that money in an account so that it would be applied solely for that purpose. The majority of the House of Lords focused on Leach's liability as a dishonest assistant to Sims's breach of trust when Leach paid the money to Yardley personally rather than using it for the purpose of acquiring that property. However, Lord Millett took the view Sims's undertaking gave rise to a *Quistclose* trust over the money such that it was to be used solely for the identified purpose. His lordship explained his view that a *Quistclose* trust operated in the following manner:

> On this analysis, the *Quistclose* trust is a simple, commercial arrangement akin ... to a retention of title clause (though with a different object) which enables the borrower to have recourse to the lender's money for a particular purpose without entrenching on the lender's property rights more than necessary to enable the purpose to be achieved. The money remains the property of the lender unless and until it is applied in accordance with his directions, and in so far as it is not so applied it must be returned to him. I am disposed, perhaps predisposed, to think that this is the only analysis which is consistent both with orthodox trust law and with commercial reality.[39]

The lender could therefore be taken to retain the equitable interest in loan moneys throughout the life of the contract.[40] However, a closer reading of Lord Millett's words, in particular the expression 'the money remains the property of the lender', requires that the property remains absolutely the property of the lender: that is, the entire title, both legal and equitable, would remain with the lender. It is suggested, however, that this latter analysis would mean that there was no trust because no title would have passed to the borrower sufficient to constitute a trust of any sort. Rather, the lender would remain the owner of all of the property rights in the borrowed money and the borrower would be merely the bailee of the borrowed money until such time as it was applied for the contractually specified purpose.[41] It is suggested that Lord Millett's expression 'the money remains the property of the lender' should be interpreted to mean that all of the equitable interest in the money remains vested in the lender, except that the borrower has a right to be vested automatically with the absolute interest in that money so as to be entitled to use it for the purpose identified in the loan contract. Consequently, the lender's equitable interest must be defeasible by the borrower's proper use of the money, with the result either that the borrower has the power as trustee of the money to defeat the lender's rights in that money or alternatively that the borrower itself has an equitable interest in the money which is contingent on the borrower's proper use of the loan moneys. This last analysis would suggest

---

[39] [2002] 2 All 377, 398–399.   [40] ibid, 398, para 80.

[41] As Lord Browne-Wilkinson reminded us in *Westdeutsche Landesbank v Islington* [1996] AC 669: if there is no separation of the equitable title from the legal title such that a trustee or trustees hold the equitable title for identified beneficiaries, then there is no trust: rather, absolute title remains with the outright 'owner' of the property—the person who civilian lawyers would consider to have dominium in the property.

that the lender does not hold all of the equitable interest, but rather all of the equitable interest except for that part represented by the borrower's contingent rights.

It is suggested, then, that the least satisfactory analysis of a *Quistclose* trust would be that the lender retains absolute title in the money because that would deny the existence of a trust. It would be the case that the lender retained absolute title in the loan moneys if the loan contract provided that the borrower had merely a facility with the lender such that the borrower could instruct the lender to make payment of the loan moneys to a third party identified in the loan agreement (in a manner similar, perhaps, to a letter of credit facility). In such a situation, however, there would be no trust but rather a contractual right to instruct the lender to transfer the money at the borrower's instruction in the manner provided for in the loan agreement. In accordance with commercial reality, this mimics a retention of title clause with title in the money only passing once the money is used for its specified purpose. Similarly, the borrower does not acquire full title in the property because that would defeat the purpose of the arrangement if the borrower were found to have entirely free use of the money.[42] However, for there to be a trust at all there must be a declaration of a trust such that there is a division between the ownership of the legal and the equitable titles in the loan moneys between two or more people. As considered earlier in this chapter, the commercial purpose of a *Quistclose* trust—that the borrower be prevented from using borrowed moneys for some purpose other than that agreed between borrower and lender—can be achieved by a number of devices by which the lender retains some proprietary rights in the loan moneys and thus makes those moneys available to the borrower but without vesting absolute title in the loan moneys in the borrower.

The nature of the *Quistclose* trust is dependent on the terms of the loan contract

While the preceding analysis of the *Twinsectra* model[43] of the *Quistclose* device might appear to present a step towards a settled understanding of the *Quistclose* trust, it is suggested nevertheless that the precise nature of any given *Quistclose* arrangement will depend upon the structure of the loan agreement which the parties have effected. It might of course be that the loan moneys are not to be advanced to the borrower until the contractually specified object has been performed or under terms whereby the bank insists on a payment facility which can only be used for the completion of that specified purpose, such as by way of a banker's draft in favour of the third party who will perform that purpose together with the borrower. The use of the loan moneys might be made available to the borrower subject to a trust arrangement made express in the loan contract that the funds were to be held by some custodian subject only to a power to use them for the contractually

49.21

---

[42] [2002] 2 All ER 377, 399, para 81.   [43] [2002] 2 All ER 377, 398–399.

specified purpose. In consequence, the commercial objective of a *Quistclose* trust would be achieved without the use of either a traditional *Quistclose* model (with its primary and secondary trust) or the *Twinsectra* model (with the retention of rights in the property by the lender).

49.22　Alternatively, then, a *Quistclose* trust could be conceived of on the basis that the loan moneys are subject to an express trust under which the borrower acts as trustee with a power to use the trust property for the purpose specified in the contract, but for no other. The benefit of such a structure would be that the borrower, as trustee, would bear personal liability for the breach of any trust as well as an obligation to reconstitute the trust fund in the event that the moneys were transferred away for some purpose other than that specified in the contract. For such an express trust analysis to be viable in any given circumstance, it would be necessary for there to be sufficient intention on the part of the contracting parties for the borrower to hold the loan moneys on trust from the outset of the transaction and not simply that the trust is enforced by the court subsequently to prevent the borrower unconscionably from seeking to apply those moneys otherwise than for the contractually agreed purpose. This analysis of a loan contract does not conform to the ordinary presumption of a loan contract that the lender intends to transfer outright all of the interest in the loan moneys but rather contains an express contractual provision which precludes the borrower from using the money for any purpose other than that provided for in the contract. A well-drafted contract may well provide that the borrower shall hold the loan moneys on trust for the lender until such time as the contractually stipulated purpose is performed. At that time the borrower would be obliged to transfer the money outright. Such a contract would clearly contain an express trust.

49.23　More frequently the decided cases have turned on contracts in which it is not clear what the parties intended. Such contracts may nevertheless disclose an express trust (such intention being capable of imputation by the court in an unconscious express trust or even an implied trust).[44] The lender does not part with equitable title in a *Quistclose* situation: rather, the lender retains equitable title in the loan moneys. That retention of title in which the borrower acquires legal title (and thus the ability to pay the loan moneys into its own bank account) coupled with the retention of the equitable title by the lender and the contractual limitation on the use of the property constitutes a *Quistclose* trust as a form of express trust.

The *Quistclose* trust as an equitable device enabling tracing where the loan moneys have been put beyond reach

49.24　Much of the debate surrounding *Quistclose* trusts proceeds on the basis of an abstract intellectual analysis of the structure itself. Primarily, the question has

---

[44] *Paul v Constance* [1977] 1 WLR 527.

been put as to whether a *Quistclose* trust is truly a resulting trust, or an express trust, or simply a different form of trust altogether.[45] For the purposes of this section, however, the more important question is as to the manner in which a contractual provision sets out to achieve the general aim of a *Quistclose* trust: that is, to provide security for the lender in relation to loan moneys which were to have been used only for a specified purpose. The assumption made by many of the judges when dealing with *Quistclose* trusts is that the borrower is obliged to keep the money separate from all other moneys, so as to use that money for the contractually specified purpose, and that consequently there will be some identifiable fund over which the *Quistclose* trust can take effect in a way that will avoid it being declared to be invalid under the principle that there be sufficient certainty of subject matter.[46] The principal difficulty, it is suggested, with the operation of *Quistclose* trusts is that the borrower who breaches the stipulation in the loan contract that the loan moneys be used only for a specified purpose will necessarily have paid those moneys away such that there may not be a fund over which such a trust can take effect. That problem is considered in this section.

It is suggested that the central issue in the design of a *Quistclose* structure is that it ought properly to be ineffective in the event that the loan moneys or their traceable equivalent are not identifiable in the hands of the borrower. Suppose, for example, that a loan is made to a borrower subject to an express contractual provision that the loan moneys are to be used solely to discharge sums owed to identified trade creditors. If those loan moneys were in fact dissipated by the borrower on general expenses otherwise than for those identified trade creditors, such that the moneys had passed into a general current account which had subsequently gone overdrawn, then it would be impossible to identify property which could be the subject matter of a trust in that general current account. In theory, the *Quistclose* trust would obtain because of its inclusion in the loan contract. However, where there is no identifiable subject matter of a trust, that trust will fail.[47] What the *Quistclose* trust analysis would provide is an equitable interest on

49.25

---

[45] Yet another explanation would be that the *Quistclose* trust is properly to be considered as a constructive trust on the basis that it would be unconscionable for the lender to assert title to that money if it was not used for the purpose for which it was lent, on which see the dicta from *Carreras Rothmans Ltd v Freeman Mathews Treasure Ltd* [1985] 1 Ch 207 reproduced above. The principal shortcoming with the analysis of this form of trust as a kind of constructive trust is that the equitable interest of the lender appears to exist *before* the borrower seeks to perform any unconscionable act in relation to the property. In the context of a *Quistclose* arrangement the rights of the lender arise under the contract and therefore pre-date the transfer of the loan moneys. A constructive trust would seem to require that the borrower misapply the loan moneys before her conscience could be affected so as to create a constructive trust: *Westdeutsche Landesbank v Islington LBC* [1996] AC 669. It is not the court imposing a constructive trust to grant rights, or restore pre-existing rights, to the lender. Rather, the lender would ordinarily appear to have retained its proprietary rights throughout the transaction.   [46] See para 3.01.

[47] See paras 3.01 *et seq.*

the basis of which the lender could seek to trace those funds in equity through other bank accounts.[48] Therefore, the *Quistclose* provision would, in practice, require more careful consideration than simply to provide that the loan moneys are only to be used for an identified purpose.

49.26 The lender would prefer to ensure that the borrower was not able in fact (whether or not able in law) to dissipate the loan moneys other than for the contractually prescribed purpose. Therefore, the most secure form of *Quistclose* trust would be one in which the loan moneys were held in a separate account operated by the lender from which payment could only be made on application to the lender for telegraphic transfer to the contractually identified recipient. Coupled with a *Quistclose* provision this structure would achieve three things. First, the lender would retain those equitable rights characteristic of the *Quistclose* trust as described by Lord Wilberforce himself. Secondly, the lender itself would be able to vet the purposes for which the moneys are intended to be used rather than rely on the good faith of the borrower under an ordinary outright transfer of loan moneys. Thirdly, the moneys retained in the account would constitute an identifiable fund which could be subjected to a trust without confusion as to its identity.

49.27 This structure is similar to a retention of title in the manner of the familiar *Romalpa* clause. In the event that the borrower is in a commercial position whereby a lender would wish to control the purposes for which the loan moneys were used, it is suggested that a provision in the form outlined above ought to be capable of negotiation. Alternatively, the *Romalpa* structure gives an example of the possibility of retaining absolute title in the loan moneys even after the loan contract has been formed. By using an express trust structure, it would be possible to transfer an equitable interest in the loan moneys to the borrower, with the lender retaining legal title as trustee and also a residuary equitable interest in the event that the borrower sought to breach the terms of the loan contract. Neither of these two possibilities seems to offer any particular advantage over the other— both offer the lender control over the loan moneys up to the point at which they are to be transferred from the borrower for an approved purpose.

D. Collateralization and Property-Based Security in Complex Financial Transactions

The context of complex financial transactions

49.28 The principal complexity which the global marketplaces in financial instruments have occasioned for the law of trusts (and for other areas of private law) is that of

---

[48] See para 33.97 above.

developing sophisticated choses in action which demand to be analysed as distinct items of property even though they are, in essence, typically only obligations to pay or receive cash flows packaged in the form of a single obligation. The very existence of money held in electronic bank accounts causes problems for trusts law: a clear example being the difficulty of tracing after moneys which exist only in virtual form and which are moved by means of telegraphic transfer.[49] The difficulty of subjecting such instruments to trusts was considered in Chapter 48.

The focus of this discussion is on the ways in which such financial instruments are themselves secured by means of trusts, pledge, and other, hybrid structures. There are two, principal forms of activity at issue here: collateralization (which is very similar to margin arrangements in clearing house trading exchanges) and stock lending. Both structures are used in subtly different ways in different financial markets and fall either side of that divide which is so familiar to lawyers between taking proprietary rights and taking merely personal rights over property. First, it would be useful to explain collateralization and stock lending.

Collateralization structures[50]

The development of collateralization techniques

The earliest collateralization structures offered participants in financial markets a **49.29** means of acquiring security against their counterparties' failure to pay under complex financial transactions. Principally in the financial derivatives markets, transactions could continue in existence for ten years or more and the counterparty's solvency over that period might be at issue. Therefore, the counterparty would be asked to provide assets—usually in the form of government bonds or commercial bonds—which would be held on trust by a third party custodian for the benefit of the other party ('the secured party') to the transaction. In the event that the counterparty failed to pay as required under the main agreement, the secured party would become absolutely entitled to the assets held on trust by the custodian. Over time, the custodian's role was assumed by the secured party itself: thus constituting the secured party trustee over the collateral assets, as well as being a contingent beneficiary in the fund containing those assets. As these structures became more sophisticated, the trustee would also be required to value the parties' outstanding obligations one to another under their main transaction and to return amounts of collateral assets held on trust which were surplus to the amounts still outstanding between the parties.

---

[49] *El Ajou v Dollar Land Holdings* [1993] 3 All ER 717; appealed [1994] 2 All ER 685.
[50] AS Hudson, *The Law on Financial Derivatives* (3rd edn, London: Sweet & Maxwell, 2002) 443 *et seq.*

49.30   This rudimentary collateral structure assumed, as was the case at the time, that a financial institution with a good credit rating was transacting with another entity of a lesser credit worth: it would have been rare for large financial institutions to have demanded collateral one from another. However, after the Russian banking moratorium and the instability in Pacific Rim economies in the 1990s, it became more common for all parties to complex financial transactions such as derivatives to demand collateral from each other in all transactions. Therefore, rather than the counterparty alone providing collateral assets to be held on trust, it became customary for both parties to transfer assets to the custodian equal to their exposure to the other party under the main transaction. In effect, both parties were prepaying their obligations under the main transaction. This was, clearly, an illiquid practice and therefore the parties would set off amounts owed under one transaction against amounts owed between them under other, similar transactions so that only one of the parties would be required to tender a smaller, net amount of collateral. EC Directives, recognizing the desirability of collateral in reducing the amount of risk exposure between financial institutions in volatile financial markets, allowed financial institutions to use the amount of collateral posted in their favour to reduce the amount of regulatory capital which they would be required to post with their regulator under the capital adequacy regulations. Consequently, collateral structures became a means of reducing bankers' costs in posting regulatory capital, which the financial institution would need to fund from its own resources, and thus an effective means of enhancing its liquidity.

49.31   Consequently, financial markets have begun to move away from the trust structure used for collateral arrangements and towards a form of 'pledge' of assets whereby the parties transfer outright the amount of collateral required from them by their collateral agreement, equal to the net exposure owed to their counterparty, subject only to an obligation on that counterparty to return assets of a like kind and of the same value in the event that all obligations under the main agreement were performed. This structure is more akin to stock lending[51] in which

---

[51] Alternative structures used in these markets revolve around stock lending and margin credit. It is suggested that while each has a different label from 'collateralization', nevertheless they raise the same legal issues as have been considered thus far. Margin credit is the system by which participants in an exchange or clearing house structure are required to post assets or money equal to a proportion of their exposure on that exchange. At the end of the trading day, the clearing house calculates its ordinary members' and its clearing members' obligations during that day's trading and requires them to settle all outstanding amounts through the clearing house or exchange. In this way, all members receive their profits from the clearing house, thus ensuring they are not exposed directly to the credit worth of their counterparties, and all members pay their losses to the clearing house. In the event that a member cannot meet its losses, then the clearing house has recourse to the margin which it has already posted. The terms on which margin is held reflect exactly the considerations above as the obligations of the custodian as a trustee and either its proprietary obligations to return the very property held on trust or its personal obligations to return assets of a like kind. Stock lending, conducted typically as part of the 'repo' markets, involves the 'loan' of securities at a given price for a given period of time to a counterparty such that the counterparty is obliged either to return the very

assets are described as being 'lent' between the parties, whereas in truth they are transferred outright by one person to another so that the recipient is able to invest those assets subject only to a personal obligation to transfer back assets of a like kind and of a like value at a specified time in the future.

Collateralization under a bare trust

The simplest form of collateralization structure was for a third party to be con- **49.32** tracted to act as custodian in the transaction. The custodian would be a nominee under a bare trust entitled to the receipt of a fee for its services. In such a situation the party who sought security (the secured party) would require the other party (the counterparty) to deliver assets (referred to as 'the collateral') to the custodian. The assets themselves could be any form of cash (in whichever currency) or securities (whether bonds or shares) as agreed between the parties. There is a tendency in financial markets not to use liquid currency in a structure as illiquid as a bare trust because it ties money up when that same money could otherwise be turned to account through investment. Therefore, it is usually bonds which are used in collateral structures as a matter of market practice. The value of the collateral required to be posted would be either assets of a value equal to the whole of the secured party's exposure to the counterparty or such proportion of that entire exposure as would satisfy the secured party's credit risk concerns as to the counterparty's performance of the contract. The parties' exposure one to another would vary over time depending not only on the terms of their contract but also on the profitability of their payment obligations when measured against movements in financial markets from time to time; such that, for example, an obligation to pay interest rate x on a borrowing of money which was unattractive at the time the contract was created might appear to be profitable to the counterparty if it is now able to lend out that same money at the higher market interest rate of y. Similarly, the value of the collateral posted between the parties will itself be of a variable value from time to time.

The consequence of the foregoing is that in these bare trust collateral structures, a **49.33** third party custodian would hold a fund of assets on trusts which were subject to two, alternative conditions precedent: if the counterparty failed to perform its contractual obligations then the property was held on trust for the secured party in an amount sufficient to meet the counterparty's default, or alternatively the assets were held on trust for the counterparty to the extent that the counterparty

---

securities that were lent to it, thus constituting it a trustee of those assets, or to return only securities of a like kind, thus imbuing it with only personal obligations to make payment of a given value. Identical legal issues therefore arise in all of these market sectors as to the manner in which property is passed between market counterparties and whether it is held on trust or merely subject to personal obligations to make repayment in kind. The discussion of collateral in this chapter will therefore stand for all such property-based obligations.

did perform its obligations under the contract. As the parties' exposures one to another altered over time with the movement in the amounts required to be paid by them under the financial instrument, the custodian would call for further collateral to be posted with it by the counterparty and it would return collateral to the counterparty as its exposure to the secured party fell with the completion of its contractual obligations. Therefore, the value of the collateral held in the trust fund would be required to alter in accordance with variations in the value of the parties' exposure one to another and also in accordance with variations in the market value of the collateral itself.

49.34 Typically, the fund would not have been a fixed fund. That is, the fund is usually established to operate in parallel to a large number of transactions between the two parties whereby transactions will be created and transactions will terminate during the continuing life of the collateral fund. The amount of collateral which either party is required to deposit in the fund is, usually, an amount equal to its outstanding obligations to its counterparty at any identified payment date. The value of such outstanding obligations includes not only amounts which stand to be paid at that valuation date but also any amounts owed in the future. The value used to establish the amount of collateral to be posted is then the mark to market value of all such obligations at the valuation date. The process of marking-to-market is the market's means of establishing a present value for replacing transactions which will mature only in the future.

The problem of certainty of subject matter

49.35 The principal difficulty in relation to the creation of valid collateral structures by means of trusts arises in relation to the principle of certainty of subject matter. It is common market practice for the collateral assets in question to be either government or corporate bonds, or other commercial paper. Such bonds once existed in bearer form but latterly such bonds are issued only under a global note which is held by a custodian such that the investors in a bond acquire only an entry on a register to prove their entitlement to the bonds held by the custodian. The de-materialization of such financial obligations, as this process of moving towards global bonds has been called, has had the effect that a purported trust will fail for uncertainty of subject matter on the basis that it will not be possible to know which bond from the stock held by the custodian is owned by the investor and therefore which bond is to be the subject matter of the trust.[52] Therefore, where a beneficiary attempts to assert rights under the law of trusts over a trust fund comprising a portion of a total holding of intangible securities, that trust will not be

---

[52] *Re Goldcorp* [1995] 1 AC 74; *Re London Wine (Shippers) Ltd* [1986] PCC 121; cf Goode 'Ownership and Obligation in Commercial Transactions' (1987) 103 LQR 433; Ryan, 'Taking Security Over Investment Portfolios held in Global Custody' [1990] 10 JIBL 404.

found valid unless the specific securities at issue are identified.[53] There is authority, however, that, with reference to a trust declared over a portion of a total holding of ordinary shares, there is no need to segregate those shares which are to be held on that trust.[54] It is suggested that this latter approach will only be effective where there is, for example, no issue of insolvency and a number of creditors seeking to claim rights in the shares which is greater than the number of shares available to be distributed among them.[55] In relation specifically to money, which might be thought to be the most obvious example of property which is interchangeable, there is a requirement that the fund be segregated within a bank account before any trust can be imposed equal to a liquidated sum held with other moneys in a bank account.[56] There is one final issue as to the role of the custodian of the global note as a trustee in itself. A trustee may or may not be appointed in respect of the global note. Further, the custodian may not be expressed to be a trustee and yet appear to have the trappings of a trustee in a jurisdiction where the trust concept is not recognized. The issue as to the enforceability of trustee obligations is therefore a vexed one. This issue arises generally with reference to bond issues and in particular in respect of depositary receipts.[57]

It is suggested that there are two potential means of avoiding this problem of certainty of subject matter. The first is to avoid the use of a trust and to use a pledge structure instead, in the form advanced by the appropriate standard market documentation.[58] This pledge structure, it is suggested, nevertheless serves only to reduce one's exposure to the risk of the other party's failure to pay to the amount of one's outstanding exposure to that person under the collateral structure having set-off all outstanding transactions and reduced them to one net figure: the pledge structure imposes only a personal obligation to repay collateral. If a trust structure is preferred, then the second means of avoiding the problem of certainty of subject matter is to have the trust take effect over the chose in action between the investor and the registrar maintaining the register of bondholders. Whereas such a chose in action is an abstract form of intangible property its identity is nevertheless certain and therefore easier to make the subject matter of a trust, perversely, than the bond **49.36**

---

[53] [1995] 1 AC 74.

[54] *Hunter v Moss* [1994] 1 WLR 452, [1994] 3 All ER 215; see also (1994) 110 LQR 335. Also possibly *Re Stapylton Fletcher Ltd* [1944] 1 WLR 1181 would be of some support as to the lack of need for segregation, although the case relates only to legal interests in the chattels at issue.

[55] See *Westdeutsche Landesbank v Islington LBC* [1996] AC 669, [1996] 2 All ER 961 *per* Lord Browne-Wilkinson approving the decision in *Re Goldcorp*, (n 52 above).

[56] *Mac-Jordan Construction Ltd v Brookmount Erostin Ltd* [1992] BCLC 350; *Re Jartray Development Ltd* (1982) 22 BLR 134; *Rayack Construction v Lampeter Meat Constructions Co Ltd* (1979) 12 BLR 30; *Nestle Oy v Lloyds Bank plc* [1983] 2 Lloyds Rep 658; *Concorde Constructions Co Ltd v Colgan Ltd* (1984) 29 BLR 120. cf *Swiss Bank v Lloyds Bank* [1979] 2 All ER 853, affirmed [1981] 2 All ER 449, whereby a claim to an unsegregated fund might nevertheless give rise to a charge.   [57] See J Benjamin, *The Law on Global Custody* (Butterworths, 1996) 41 *et seq.*

[58] See AS Hudson, *The Law of Financial Derivatives* (3rd edn, Sweet & Maxwell, 2002) 443 *et seq.*

itself. Otherwise, the claimant would be required to contend that the bond, even if held under a global note in a jurisdiction which does not recognize the trust, ought to be considered to be equally identifiable as a share held under a share register in the UK.

Breaches of collateral arrangements

49.37 In circumstances in which a trustee fails to maintain the property constituting the collateral separately from other assets, and thus breaches the terms of his fiduciary obligation,[59] issues will arise as to title in substitute assets or the traceable proceeds of the assets which were supposed to have been maintained as collateral. For example, where the custodian breaches an obligation to maintain the collateral assets separate from all other property, a mixture of assets would lead to issues of equitable tracing as to which assets were to be considered to be the property of the collateral provider.[60] Similarly, where the collateral is misapplied, the issue would arise as to whether or not the collateral provider could enforce a claim based on equitable tracing over property acquired by the trustee in consideration for the disposal of the collateral assets.[61] Where the trustee is liable for breach of trust, its obligation will be to restore the trust property, or its equivalent in money, and to provide compensation for any loss that results directly from the breach.[62]

49.38 Alternatively, a number of alternative claims suggest themselves in response to an attempt to demonstrate title in collateral assets. A claim for subrogation would entitle the collateral provider to be subrogated to the position of another person whose debt with the trustee was discharged by the use of the collateral assets.[63] It has been argued that it ought, in such circumstances, to be possible to trace backwards into the debt discharged[64] or to be subrogated to the rights of the party whose rights have been discharged. It is also possible that equitable set-off could

---

[59] The assumption made is that the collateral agreement will impose the office of trustee, or at least fiduciary obligations, on the custodian. However, it is to be remembered that the collateral arrangement used will need to be analysed to ensure that it does create a binding trust arrangement.

[60] Subject always to the defence of change position—*Lipkin Gorman v Karpnale* [1991] 3 WLR 10, [1992] 4 All ER 512, [1991] 2 AC 548; in circumstances where a fiduciary relationship existed before the misapplication of the property—*Boscawen v Bajwa* [1995] 4 All ER 769; or by means of the rejuvenated use of common law tracing to identify a clean substitution of and accretion to the misapplied property—*FC Jones & Sons (A Firm) v Jones* [1996] 3 WLR 703, [1996] 4 All ER 721.

[61] *Re Diplock* [1948] Ch 465; *Chase Manhattan Bank NA v Israel-British Bank (London) Ltd* [1981] Ch 105; [1980] 2 WLR 202; [1979] 3 All ER 1025 as explained in *Westdeutsche Landesbank v Islington LBC* [1996] AC 669, [1996] 2 All ER 961 *per* Lord Browne-Wilkinson. Where the collateral fund is subsumed into other funds, there is slight authority for the proposition that the collateral provider would be entitled to a charge over the entirety of the trustee's assets equal to the size of the loss, an approach favoured in many US jurisdictions: *Space Investments Ltd v Canadian Bank* [1986] 3 All ER 75, 76–77; [1986] 1 WLR 1072, 1074, *per* Lord Templeman.

[62] *Target Holdings v Redferns* [1996] 1 AC 421, [1995] 3 All ER 785 HL. See also *Bristol & West Building Society v Mothew* [1996] 4 All ER 698; *Swindle v Harrison* [1997] 4 All ER 705, CA.

[63] *Boscawen v Bajwa* [1995] 4 All ER 769.

[64] See L Smith, *The Law of Tracing* (Oxford, 1997) generally.

be used in circumstances in which the collateral agreement obligations can be set off against amounts owed under the transactions which were to be secured by the collateral agreement.[65] Such alternative claims would be important in circumstances where the right to trace into the collateral assets or into their substitute is lost due to destruction or disappearance of the assets.[66]

---

[65] See AS Hudson, *The Law of Financial Derivatives* (3rd edn, Sweet & Maxwell, 2002) ch 13.

[66] *Roscoe v Winder* [1915] 1 Ch 62; *Bishopsgate Investment Management v Homan* [1995] Ch 211, [1995] 1 All ER 347, [1994] 3 WLR 1270.

50

TRUSTS IN RELATION TO DEBT SECURITIES

A. Issues of Bonds and Eurobonds Requiring a Trustee

The use of a trustee in eurobond issues

The general practice in relation to the issue of debt securities is that a trustee has **50.01** tended to be used in the manner outlined below. Many debt securities issued by large companies which are to be offered for sale to the public in the United Kingdom are required to be entered onto the official list of the London Stock Exchange. The regulations governing the admission of securities to the official list are complex. The Financial Services Authority, acting as the UK Listing Authority ('UKLA')[1] for the purposes of the applicable EC directives,[2] created the latest version of the listing rules (at the time of writing) in a modified edition published in August 2002. These listing rules flesh out the general provisions contained in Part VI 'The Listing Rules' of the Financial Services and Markets Act 2000 ('FSMA 2000').

---

[1] Financial Services and Markets Act 2000, s 72(1); Official Listing of Securities (Change of Competent Authority) Regulations 2000, SI 2000/968, reg 3.

[2] The Admissions Directive (Directive (EEC) 79/279, [1979] OJ L66/21); The Listing Particulars Directive (Directive (EEC) 80/390, [1980] OJ L100/1), now consolidated into Directive (EC) 2001/34; The Interim Reports Directive (Directive (EEC) 82/121, [1982] OJ L48/26); The Prospectus (Public Offers) Directive (Directive 89/298, [1989] OJ L124/8).

50.02 The UKLA's listing rules stop short of providing an unequivocal requirement that each debt security be accompanied by a trust deed creating a trustee empowered to protect the interests of investors (in the manner considered below). In the listing rules there is a requirement that among the 'additional documents' which the UKLA may require to be lodged with it together with any application to the UKLA for the listing of any securities is: 'in the case of debt securities, a copy of the executed trust deed'.[3] Further, the listing rules contain a continuing obligation that, if there is no other obligation for the issuer to publish annual accounts, the trust deed contain a requirement that the trustee be informed annually as to whether or not there has been any event of default under the terms of the issue.[4] These provisions suggest that a trust structure is expected by the listing rules.

50.03 However, it is clear that the trust structure is not always obligatory. In the chapter of the listing rules which deals specifically with 'specialist securities (including eurobonds)', it is provided that 'where there is no trust deed the issuer must retain a copy of the fiscal agency agreement or equivalent document' as required in the rule quoted in the previous sentence.[5] Therefore, while the rules could be clearer on this point, it is clear that a trust deed is not always required, even if it is expected that in general terms there will be one. The reference to 'fiscal agency' is a reference to the practice in syndicated lending—a form of lending usually involving a syndicate of banks rather than smaller investors, which is considered below[6]—of using an agency contract structure rather than a trust to protect the interests of the investors. It is important, nevertheless, whichever structure is used, that the UKLA has the power to analyse the terms of the fiduciary's obligations (whether that fiduciary is a trustee or an agent). In relation to more complex asset-backed securities issues (that is, debt securities backed by equity securities) there is a requirement that there be a trustee 'or other appropriate independent party' in either case whose role is that of 'representing the interests of the holders of the asset-backed securities and with the right of access to appropriate information relating to the assets'.[7]

Consequently, a large number of bond issues are conducted in the market place without using the trust structure, many of which may not seek official listing if, for example, they are not to be offered for sale to the public. However, this chapter will consider those issues which do seek entry onto the official list and which use the trust structure. The rights acquired by the investor in the bonds are held on trust by the trustee in the manner considered in the following discussion. It is the nature of this particular form of trustee which forms the focus of this first section and the composition of the necessarily complex form of trust. A comparison

---

[3] *Listing Rules*, Chapter 7, para 7.9(f).   [4] *Listing Rules*, Chapter 23, para 23.32.
[5] *Listing Rules*, Chapter 23, para 23.14(i).   [6] At para 50.18.
[7] *Listing Rules*, Chapter 23, para 23.28(d). See *Law Debenture Trust Corporation plc v Ancona* [2004] EWHC 270 (Ch).

will be drawn with issues of bonds other than eurobonds prepared for listing on the London Stock Exchange and with the structure of syndicated lending.

The commercial basis of bond issues

As outlined at the beginning of this chapter, bond issues are a form of borrowing in relation to which the lender receives a security which is itself transferable. The company which is seeking to borrow money (the issuer) does so by issuing securities to lenders (or, investors) in the form of bonds. Historically, the bonds would take the form of bearer bonds which were physical pieces of paper the possession of which identified the holder as the owner of the bond and consequently the person entitled to receive the payments of interest and the repayment of the capital purchase price of the bond at the end of the transaction. In consequence, investors are frequently referred to as 'bondholders' in recognition of the tangible nature of the security. The way in which the investor would have received his periodic payments of interest would be by presentation of one of the coupons attached to the bearer bond, the redemption of which entitled the bearer to his payment of interest which was payable on identified dates throughout the life of the issue. The nomenclature 'coupon' to describe these payments of interest, again, reflects the tangible nature of the bearer bond. Akin to bank notes, possession of the physical bond carried the presumption that the bearer was its absolute owner. **50.04**

A significant change in the business of bond issues occurred in the late twentieth century after a spate of thefts of bearer bonds. Rather than print and distribute individual bonds to investors, ownership of the bonds was instead evidenced by means of a register of bondholders rather than by possession of a bearer bond. A 'global note' is now issued which stands for all of the individual bearer bonds which would otherwise have been issued. In a nod to the ancient practice of printing and distributing bearer bonds, such paper securities are still printed but held in a vault by a custodian institution rather than being distributed to investors. This process of removing the tangible bonds from circulation is commonly dubbed 'dematerialization'. The proprietary right of the investor is therefore in the chose in action against the registrar and not in any individual bond. **50.05**

The convoluted structure of ownership, therefore, is that the investor is notionally the owner of an individual bond but does not take that bond into his possession. Rather, the registrar recognizes that the bondholder is entitled to a given number of bonds (according to the size of his investment) and the title is represented by that entry on the register. The role of the trustee, however, obfuscates a simple suggestion that the investor's rights are expressed simply through the process of registration, as with a share. The trustee acquires rights to intercede if there is any irregularity with the payment of coupon to the investor and so the bond issue is declared to be held on express trust by the trustee, in the manner considered below. **50.06**

50.07 The trustee is not acting as an investment manager, however. The bond issue is managed either by a single lead manager or a group of managers depending on the size and complexity of the issue. It will be the responsibility of the lead manager to prepare a prospectus for the issue, to fix the issue price of the bonds, and to organize their placement in the market.[8] The bond issue will be extensively documented and will contain a series of provisions entitling the investors to terminate the issue early and recover their capital sums and other amounts in lieu of periodical interest.[9] The bond itself constitutes a personal claim exercisable by the investor against the issuer. The claim is both for the stream of interest payments to be made on the identified payment dates and for the repayment of the capital amount at the end of the issue. The bond is itself an item of property and is therefore transferable and capable of being used as security for lending in itself.

The two possible trusts

50.08 There are two trusts which could possibly be said to arise in bond issues. The more important, for present purposes, is the express trust which is declared in writing as part of the bond documentation process. A trustee is appointed to oversee the conduct of payments of coupon under the bond. As is considered in the next section of this chapter, there are difficult questions as to the nature of the property which is held on trust. In effect, the dematerialization of the bond discussed above means that there is a problem with identifying the form of property which is to be held on trust, given that the investor is not the owner of any separately identifiable bond. In any event, the commercial purpose of the express trust is not to interpose the legal title of a trustee over the bonds between the issuer and the investor. Rather, the trustee needs only some minor form of title to grant that trustee sufficient *locus standi* to intervene and compel payment by the issuer of any amount owed to the investors. The precise form of this proprietary interest is considered below.

50.09 The alternative form of trust is the nominee trust under which the custodian of the bearer bonds holds that property subject to the terms of the global note for the benefit ultimately of the investors. Commercially, the investors have little interest in ever taking possession of the bearer securities in any event. The purpose of this arrangement is to prevent theft of bearer bonds in the future. In the event that there were some difficulty with the issuer paying coupon or redeeming the bonds, it is unlikely that the bearer bond would have any market value in any event beyond the contractual rights which the investors have to receive periodical payments of

---

[8] *Listing Rules*, Chapter 23.
[9] P Wood, *Law and Practice of International Finance* (Clark Boardman, 1981); R Tennekoon, *The Law and Regulation of International Finance* (Butterworths, 1991); Brealey and Myers, *Principles of Corporate Finance* (5th edn, McGraw Hill, 1995).

coupon and the redemption value of each bond. Furthermore, as considered below, the custodian is typically organized under a system of law, resident in a jurisdiction, and operating under a contractual agreement in relation to which trusts law will not operate.

The following discussion will focus on the express appointment of the trustee, rather than the role of the custodian.

The structure of the trust in a eurobond issue

The question

The principal issue concerning the imposition of the trust over a eurobond issue   **50.10**
is the identity of the trust property. As considered in Chapter 3, for there to be a valid trust there must be identifiable property which is held on trust.[10] If there were no identifiable property over which the trust would take effect then the trust would be invalidly constituted and the trustee would have no *locus standi* to act in relation to the bond issue. This is so particularly given that the trust structure used in such instances replaces any explicit contractual mechanism which would give the trustee such standing and the trust also displaces the problem of identifying the lack of consideration extended by the trustee in obtaining its fiduciary rights and obligations.

The trust property could, in theory, be the bonds themselves. However, were that   **50.11**
the structure then the investor would only receive an equitable interest in the bond held on trust for it by the trustee.[11] Instead the parties' intention is that the investor takes absolute title in the bond so that the open market in bonds can operate without complications of assigning equitable interests on their disposition.[12] Therefore, typically the bonds are not the intended trust fund.[13] Standard bond documentation provides that when a bond is sold in the open market both title to the bond and to the coupon stream passes on sale. If the bond were held on trust, then only an equitable interest would be disposed of on sale of the bond.[14] This issue is considered in the following paragraph.

The subject matter of the trust

Following on from the preceding discussion, the subject matter of the trust must   **50.12**
be some property other than the bond itself. Or rather, the trust fund is something other than the bundle of rights to receive coupon and repayment of principal which are embodied by the bond. Nevertheless, to satisfy the requirement of

---

[10] *Re Goldcorp* [1995] 1 AC 74; *Westdeutsche Landesbank Girozentrale v Islington LBC* [1994] 4 All ER 890, Hobhouse J, CA; and reversed on appeal [1996] AC 669, HL.

[11] R Tennekoon, *The Law and Regulation of International Finance* (Butterworths, 1991) 226 *et seq.*

[12] Law of Property Act 1925, s 53(1)(c).

[13] R Tennekoon, *The Law and Regulation of International Finance* (Butterworths, 1991) 226.

[14] Requiring signed writing to effect the transfer: Law of Property Act 1925, s 53(1)(c).

trusts law that there be some identifiable trust fund before that trust can be valid, and to satisfy the commercial requirement that the investors transfer absolute title in the bonds, the trust fund must take effect over one of the many rights bundled up in the bond. The structure used is to hold the chose in action constituted by the issuer's obligation to pay coupon to the investors on trust.[15] The issuer gives an undertaking to pay coupon in the bond documentation both to the investors and to the trustee. That is the essential part of the structure: the trustee is able to hold that obligation to make payment on trust. Within the terms of that documentation, payment to the investor discharges any obligation to make payment to the trustee. This slight proprietary right is, being a chose in action, sufficient to constitute the subject matter of a trust.[16]

50.13 While that structure appears complex its effect is the creation of an obligation to make payment to the trustee. That is so even if that obligation is not expected to be honoured in practice. That obligation is itself a chose in action which is capable of constituting a trust fund. Under English law there is no objection to constituting a trust fund with such an obligation.[17] There is long-standing authority that covenants in a trust deed can themselves constitute a trust fund.[18] So, in *Fletcher v Fletcher*[19] a father entered into a covenant with a trustee to settle property not yet in his possession on trust for his children. The settlor thereby demonstrated an intention to transfer property by will to a trustee. Significantly, because he had no title in that property at the time of purporting to declare that trust, there was no valid trust. In consequence, the trustee sought to take a beneficial interest in the property passed to him by will which had come into the testator's ownership subsequent to the declaration of trust. The court held that the testator had demonstrated a sufficient intention that the benefit of the covenant entered into with the trustee—rather than the property subsequently acquired—was to have been held on trust by the trustee and that the property subsequently acquired passed onto the trust automatically. In a more modern example,[20] two boxing promoters and a variety of companies under their respective control entered into partnership agreements whereby, the court decided, they agreed to hold the benefit of any boxing promotion contract entered into with any boxer relating to fights in Europe on trust for the benefit of the partners. It was contended by one of the partners that the trust was not valid on the basis that the contract at issue

[15] R Tennekoon, *The Law and Regulation of International Finance* (Butterworths, 1991) 227.
[16] *Don King Productions Inc v Warren* [1998] 2 All ER 608, Lightman J; affirmed [2000] Ch 291, CA.
[17] *Fletcher v Fletcher* (1844) 4 Hare 67; *Don King Productions Inc v Warren* [1998] 2 All ER 608, Lightman J; affirmed [2000] Ch 291, CA; *Swift v Dairywise Farms* [2000] 1 All ER 320.
[18] *Tomlinson v Gill* (1756) Amb 330; *Fletcher v Fletcher* (1844) 4 Hare 67; *Lloyd's v Harper* (1880) 16 Ch D 290; *Les Affreteurs Reunis SA v Leopold Walford (London) Ltd* [1919] AC 801.
[19] (1844) 4 Hare 67.
[20] *Don King Productions Inc v Warren* [1998] 2 All ER 608, Lightman J; affirmed [2000] Ch 291, CA.

contained provisions on its own terms to the effect that it was not capable of transfer. In consequence it was argued that this non-transferable contract was not capable of forming the subject matter of a trust. It was held, however, that it was no objection to the efficacy of the trust that the property was not transferable because the benefit which was to flow from that contract in the future was capable of constituting the subject matter of the trust. In line with commercial practice in the financial markets, therefore, future cash flows become property in themselves where they constitute the benefit stemming from a contract.

By analogy, the chose in action constituted by the obligation to make payment under the bond documentation to the investors can itself constitute a cash flow which is capable of being the subject matter of a trust as is the chose in action that the issuer make payments of coupon interest to the investors. The obligation to make payment only constitutes an asset capable of becoming a trust fund in the hands of the trustee (as payee, rather than as a fiduciary) and in the hands of the investors.[21] Therefore, the trust is capable of being declared only by the trustee or by the investors. The more advisable course of action is for the trustee by way of contract to recognize itself as express trustee of the debt owed to it thus binding itself with an obligation to ensure the proper treatment of the investors. The reason why it is less complicated for the trustee to declare that trust is considered in the following section.   **50.14**

The impact of the development of global bonds

The foregoing structure has worked on the assumption that the beneficiaries under the transaction will remain easily identifiable. It has assumed that the investors will be those people to whom the bonds are issued from the outset. However, once the bonds have been issued they are capable of being traded in the open aftermarket. Therefore, the class of beneficiaries would need to be expressed to be the bondholders from time to time, as opposed to the initial subscribers for the bond.   **50.15**

As considered at the beginning of this chapter, the practice of the bond market, at the time of writing, is to issue bonds not in their bearer form (as has always formerly been bond market practice[22]) but rather in the form of entries in a register acknowledging that the beneficiary has a right to one bond out of the total issue of bonds.[23] A so-called 'global note' is issued to stand for the entirety of the bonds issued. The bonds are still expressed in the documentation as being bearer bonds, even though the

---

[21] *Vanderpitte v Preferred Accident Insurance Corpn of New York* [1933] AC 70.

[22] It was market practice until a spate of muggings of couriers taking bearer bonds between investment houses created the impetus to make the bonds invulnerable to theft in the street by developing dematerialized securities.

[23] For an excellent survey of this area see J Benjamin, *The Law of Global Custody* (Butterworths, 1994).

individual bonds are no longer issued and delivered to the bondholder personally. Instead those individual bonds in the European markets are lodged with one of two commercial custodians as considered above. Therefore, under the terms of the bond documentation, it could be said to be these custodians who are the beneficial owners of the bonds because they are in possession of the bonds in their bearer form. English law would have no difficulty in holding that these custodians necessarily hold any rights which they acquire in those bonds on trust for the investors who are recognized on the register of bondholders as having rights in the bonds.

The bonds are not identifiable as belonging to any individual investor because all of the bonds are held together and no certificate number is issued to any investor. Rather the investor simply has a chose in action against the registrar and the custodian to recognize a claim with a value equal to the number of bonds registered to the investor. In consequence, it is difficult to identify any individual investor as having any equitable interest in the bonds in any event. The investor receives a proportionate right in the entire fund (or, issue of bonds) and not any equitable interest in any separately identifiable bond. The neater structure for the purposes of English law would therefore be to identify the custodian as beneficiary under the trust of the claim vested in the eurobond trustee. That complete equitable interest is in turn held on trust by the custodian for the investors as a homogeneous beneficial class.[24] Consequently, another chose in action which could constitute the subject matter of a trust is the obligation borne by the custodian of the global note and the person maintaining the register of bondholders to recognize the title of the investor.

The nature of the trustee's obligations

50.16 The structure of the trust as set out above is clearly considerably more complex than is usual in the vanilla forms of trust[25] considered in Part B of this book. Indeed, it is questionable whether the trustee in these eurobond transactions is anything more than the holder of a fiduciary power. It is true that the trustee does hold some property on trust, in the form of one of the choses in action considered in the foregoing paragraphs. In relation to bonds it is clear that the personal claim evidenced by the bond is only a claim to a payment of a stream of interest and of principal. The 'property' is only the synthetic obligation to pay interest to the trustee: even though no party to the bond transaction expects that any payment will ever be made to the trustee beneficially.[26] The real value in the bond transaction is constituted by the

---

[24] This is subject to the point made in relation to collateralization below that Clearswift and Euroclear are resident in jurisdictions which do not recognize the legal efficacy of the trust. Therefore, there is the possibility that the bonds are resident in a jurisdiction in which the fiduciary obligations on the custodian are not enforceable. In consequence it appears that the trust will only be enforceable in England and Wales—this requiring a concomitant provision in the bond documentation.   [25] By 'vanilla' is meant ordinary trusts without any special features.

[26] The existence of the trustee is merely a device to protect the investors: using 'trust' as a complex euphemism for 'reliability' and 'solidity'.

bonds themselves and the anticipated stream of payments to be made by the issuer to each investor. Therefore, the trustee does not have legal title in the asset which contains the true value in the transaction.

It is this thinking which reduces the role of the trustee to that of a financial agent charged with the duty of supervising the issuer.[27] The presence of the trustee is not essential to the enforcement of the obligation incumbent on the issuer to make payment when due under the bond transaction. The interpolation of the trustee is an artificial device. The trustee exists not to take title in any property which is held for the benefit of the investor, nor to effect investment of that property in the usual way. Rather, the trustee is a fiduciary responsible for the proper performance of the bond transaction. The more significant role of the eurobond trustee is in relation to the exclusive powers conferred on the eurobond trustee by the documentation to the exclusion of the investors.

50.17

Comparison with syndicated lending

There is a similarity between the issue of bonds and ordinary syndicated lending. Syndicated lending involves ordinary bank lending but by a group of banks as opposed to one single lender. The principal distinction between syndicated lending and bond issues is that in a bond issue a security is issued to the investor by the issuer. The covenants contained in the legal documentation of these methods will be broadly similar (in that they will allow for early termination in certain circumstances, and so forth) but will contain significant differences (in that one method involves the issue of a security and that the other does not).

50.18

The role of the trustee in a eurobond issue bears comparison with the agents in syndicated loan transactions. So it is that Wood contrasts the role of eurobond trustee with that of the 'fiscal agent' in syndicated lending.[28] In syndicated lending the fiscal agent is a functionary who carries out the instructions of the borrower, arranging the availability of the credit and the making of payment. To continue with this analysis, the fiscal agent represents the issuer and not the investor; whereas the trustee exists to represent the interests of the investors.[29] Further the fiscal agent is responsible for making payment and for carrying out administrative obligations to do with the conversion of the global bond and so forth. The trustee, however, will bear all the usual fiduciary duties relating to the

50.19

---

[27] A long-held view: P Wood, *Law and Practice of International Finance* (Clark Boardman, 1981) para 9.12(3)(b). See now P Wood, *Law and Practice of International Finance* (London: Sweet & Maxwell, 1995) 168 *et seq*. See also R Tennekoon (n 15 above) 227.

[28] P Wood, *Law and Practice of International Finance* (Sweet & Maxwell, 1995) 168 *et seq*.

[29] It is my opinion that the trustee does not represent the investors straightforwardly. There are a number of events of default in which the trustee is required to judge whether or not there has been breach: the trustee is required to act impartially in these circumstances and therefore could not be said to be partial on behalf of the investors in all circumstances.

avoidance of conflicts of interest, due diligence, and so forth[30] as well as taking title in the issuer's obligation to pay.

Powers attaching to the trustee in eurobond documentation

Legal powers of the trustee

50.20 Thus far the trustee has been painted as something of a cypher. The eurobond trustee is in truth little more than an agent whose obligations are governed by the contract between the issuer and the investors.[31] There is, though, an express trust created over the obligation owed by the issuer to the trustee. That obligation is identical to the obligation owed to the investors although it is not expected that the trustee will ever be paid beneficially in the same way that the investors are expected by all the contracting parties to be paid.[32] The following sections consider four groups of powers which are conferred solely on the eurobond trustee by the bond documentation. Clearly these powers enhance the supervisory role of the eurobond trustee. However, it is suggested that this does not require that the eurobond trustee is necessarily a trustee rather than being merely an agent with supervisory powers. Consequently, it is only the use of trust structures as envisaged by the listing rules which raises that presumption.

Acceleration of obligations

50.21 Breach of payment and other covenants under the terms of the bond transaction lead to the issuer being required to make payment earlier than would otherwise have been required by the terms of the parties' agreement: a so-called 'acceleration of obligations' provision. The bond documentation, observing the supervisory role of the trustee, gives the eurobond trustee exclusive competence to call for acceleration of the bond obligations in the event of breach of a relevant condition of the agreement. The bond documentation will also provide for a range of obligations in relation to which the eurobond trustee has the discretion to judge whether or not the issuer is in breach of its contractual duties. The trustee's role as arbiter between the issuer, the investment banks leading the issue, and the investors will be significant in the event of a default under the terms of the bond contract. For example, once accelerated payments are recovered from the issuer, those payments are

---

[30] *Keech v Sandford* (1726) Sel Cas Ch 61; *Aberdeen Railway v Blaikie Bros* (1854) 1 Macq 461, HL; *Bray v Ford* [1896] AC 44; *Parker v McKenna* (1874) 10 Ch App 96; *Boardman v Phipps* [1967] 2 AC 46; and in relation to liability for breach of trust *Target Holdings v Redferns* [1996] 1 AC 421.
[31] Therefore, this is at first blush an instance of contract giving rise to rights in property.
[32] The rights of the trustee outside this express declaration of trust over the trustee's chose in action do nothing more than establish the eurobond trustee as being a de facto agent and the entire structure in truth one to do with contract and not property. It is a question of form and substance: like the unit trust, the contractual and regulatory context requires a trust structure despite the investors' principal concern being in the return provided for in the basic investment contract.

necessarily held on trust by the eurobond trustee for the investors in accordance with their proportionate equitable interests.

Enforcement proceedings brought by the trustee

The power to bring enforcement proceedings under the terms of the bond docu- **50.22**
mentation is vested in the trustee.[33] The restriction of these rights to the exclusive competence of the trustee is akin to an express contractual agreement to resolve disputes by arbitration. It would appear right in principle that the trustee would hold this power to bring enforcement proceedings on trust for the investors in the sense that the trustee only has the capacity to exercise this power acting as a fiduciary in the interests of the investors. In consequence it would seem to be in accordance with the principle that the investors could force the trustee to bring enforcement proceedings.

Notification of events of default

The trustee acts as an impartial arbiter in many circumstances. This constitutes an **50.23**
important distinction from the role of a trustee in ordinary circumstances where the trustee has an obligation to achieve the best possible return for the beneficiary.[34] For the trustee to be obliged to act impartially between the beneficiary and third parties who are strangers to the trust constitutes a difference from that position. In terms of the information which the trustee is required to give to the beneficiaries, there is no obligation on the trustees to notify the investors of any breach of trust (typically) until the eurobond trustee has actual knowledge of that breach. There is no obligation to seek out information on behalf of the trustees—which is a distinction from the ordinary law of trusts.[35]

Covenants between eurobond trustee and issuer

It is usual for covenants contained in the trust deed to be entered into between the **50.24**
trustee and the issuer. Surprisingly, this means that those covenants are not directly owed, in the documentation, by the issuer to the investors, thus reinforcing the role of the trustee in ensuring the performance of the issuer's contractual obligations. There is an obligation on the part of the issuer to make payment to the investors. Therefore, it would seem reasonable that any conditions included in the trust deed are understood by the investors to be implied into the obligation of the issuer to make payment. In that regard the ungainly legal structure does achieve the regulatory policy behind the provisions of the UKLA listing rules.

---

[33] It is significant that the documentation will vest this competence in the trustee whereas an alternative analysis of the structure (in the absence of the usual specific documentary provision to the contrary) would be that the investor has a straightforward right in contract and in specific performance to enforce the issuer's payment obligations.
[34] *Cowan v Scargill* [1985] Ch 270.   [35] cf *Learoyd v Whiteley* (1887) 12 App Cas 727.

B. The Debenture Trustee

The nature of a debenture

50.25   The true nature of a debenture is rather quixotic. As Chitty J held:[36]

> I cannot find any precise definition of the term [debenture], it is not either in law or commerce a strictly technical term, or what is called a term of art.

The general definition which has emerged from cases has been described as 'a document which either creates a debt or acknowledges it'.[37] As for the creation of a distinct legal category of 'debenture' within company law there is Part V, Chapter VIII of the Companies Act 1985 which is titled 'Debentures' but which contains no definition of that term. That Act does have an elliptical definition in section 744 in the following terms:

> 'debenture'... includes debenture stock, bonds and other securities of a company, whether constituting a charge on the assets of the company or not.

The Financial Services and Markets Act 2000 contains a reference to 'debentures, including debenture stock, loan stock, bonds, certificates of deposit and other instruments creating or acknowledging indebtedness...'[38] but no express definition. None of these provisions gets to the heart of the matter. Simply put, for present purposes, a debenture is a loan coupled with the issue of a transferable security evidencing that loan. The intention behind both the legislation and the little case law in this area is to keep that definition as broad as possible for the purposes of the Companies Acts. Debentures are a part of a company's debt and not a company's equity capital: the investor acquires no rights against the company's property other than those of a creditor and acquires rights to a payment of interest and not any participation in the profits of the company by way of a right to dividend.[39]

50.26   The principal difference between those debentures issued in the 1860s and unsecured bond issues at that time was that debentures were generally secured by means of a charge over some assets of the company.[40] The debenture therefore comprised three components: first, the company's obligation to repay; secondly, some security in favour of the debenture holder usually in the form of a fixed or floating charge; and, thirdly, the detailed covenants attached to the loan. This process was simplified by the turn of the twentieth century by means of the issue of a security to the investor and the interposition of a trustee between the company and the debenture holders so that the trustee could enforce the rights of the

---

[36]   *Levy v Abercorris Slate and Slab Company* (1883) 37 Ch D 260; 57 LJ Ch 202.
[37]   E Lomnicka and J Powell, *Encyclopedia of Financial Services Law* (Sweet & Maxwell, 1987–2003), para 2-779.   [38]   Financial Services and Markets Act 2000, Sch 2, para 12.
[39]   With the exception of convertible securities which are debt instruments capable of being converted into equity at the option of the right holder.
[40]   R Pennington, *Company law* (8th edn, Butterworths, 2001) 529.

debenture holders and to limit the company's negotiations for any alterations to the debenture agreement to garnering the consent of the trustee rather than that of each debenture holder individually.

The nature of the trustee in a debenture issue

On the issue of debenture stock, the practice is to do so by means of a deed **50.27** appointing trustees to hold that stock. The trust is structured as follows. The trustees take legal title in the debenture stock and so hold the benefit of the debenture, and the benefit of any charge effected as part of the debenture arrangement, on trust for the investors. Whether or not there would be any charge in the modern context would be a question for those managing the issue of the debenture stock in deciding both what level of interest would be required to attract investors and whether or not security would be similarly required to attract investors. Therefore, issues by companies of good credit worth will not require security; whereas issues by companies of lesser credit worth may.

By effecting the issue by way of trust, there is no need to register the common law **50.28** title of any debenture holder directly: rather, the trustee holds the legal title and the debenture holders are recognized as taking equitable title under this trust. It is common that part of the security for such debentures will be shares in subsidiary entities and so forth: it is therefore possible for the trustee to exercise all of the voting and other rights connected to such security on behalf of all of the debenture holders. The difficulty with such a structure is evidently twofold: first, it complicates the means by which the debenture holders will evidence their title and, secondly, it reduces the means by which the rights of the debenture holders are protected to the preparedness of the trustees to act assiduously.

51

UNIT TRUSTS

A. The Nature of a Unit Trust as a Collective Investment Scheme

Collective investment schemes

51.01 The unit trust is a form of collective investment scheme organized under the Undertaking for Collective Investment in Transferable Securities ('UCITS') Directive[1] which came into effect in 1985.[2] The purpose of the UCITS Directive was to 'co-ordinate' the various legal codes and legal models which existed in member states dealing with investment in common 'with a view to approximating the conditions of competition between those undertakings at Community level, while at the same time ensuring more effective and more uniform protection for unit holders', to make it easier for schemes to operate in different member states

---

[1] [1985] OJ L375/3.

[2] As amended, *inter alia*, by Directive (EC) 2001/108, [2002] OJ L041.

within the EU, and thus to facilitate the creation of a 'European capital market'.[3] The focus of the Directive is on open-ended investment vehicles which raise capital by promoting themselves to the public in the EU.[4] No collective investment scheme may carry on this form of activity unless it is authorized by the competent authorities designated for that purpose[5] in the member state in which it is situated.[6] Section 235 of the Financial Services and Markets Act 2000 ('FSMA 2000') provides that this form of activity comprises:

> ...any arrangements with respect to property of any description, including money, the purpose or effect of which is to enable persons taking part in the arrangements (whether by becoming owners of the property or any part of it or otherwise) to participate in or receive profits or income arising from the acquisition, holding, management or disposal of the property or sums paid out of such profits or income.

The focus of this definition is the right of any person who is a party to 'an arrangement', to participate in the profits received from the holding and management of property. At that level the definition could encompass a shareholding in an ordinary company or being a partner in an undertaking in common with a view to profit[7] or being a beneficiary in an ordinary trading trust.[8] In relation to the definition of the term 'arrangement' in its predecessor provision,[9] Laddie J has held that even actions preparatory to the establishment of a collective investment scheme, such as placing the investors' capital into a separate bank account, would constitute 'arrangements' for this purpose.[10] More generally those arrangements must have a certain purpose or effect, they must be effected so that the participants can take part in those arrangements, the arrangements must be managed by some other people,[11] the capital must be pooled or managed as a whole, and the arrangements must enable the participants to participate in the profits or income derived from their common capital in some way.[12] Open-ended investment companies and unit trusts are the two forms of collective investment scheme recognized in English law: this chapter will focus on authorized unit trusts.

51.02   Collective investment schemes, as their name suggests, effect investment of pooled money, or other property, contributed by a range of participants with a view to sharing out any profits rateably among those participants and returning

---

[3] As expressed in the preamble to the UCITS Directive.   [4] UCITS Directive, art 2(1).
[5] UCITS Directive, art 1A(8).   [6] UCITS Directive, art 4(1).
[7] Partnership Act 1890, s 1.
[8] That is some trust which carries on business activities: see Chapter 53.
[9] Financial Services Act 1986, s 75, since repealed.
[10] *The Russell-Cooke Trust Company v Prentis* [2002] EWHC 2227.
[11] Otherwise, if the participants all participated fully in the management of the scheme then they would simply appear to be in partnership or to have formed an unincorporated association or trading trust, rather than a collective investment scheme: see AS Hudson, *Palmer's Company Law* (ed, G Morse) para 5A-106.
[12] *The Russell-Cooke Trust Company v Elliott* [2002] EWHC 2227.

their original investment stake. As distinct from the non-regulated trusts used for investment purposes considered in Chapter 52, and the general law of trusts relating to the investment obligations of trustees in such contexts, collective investment schemes are regulated by the Financial Services Authority ('FSA') and the obligations of their fiduciary officers are defined by Part XVII of FSMA 2000. Unit trusts have, nevertheless, been in existence for some considerable time. In the wake of the South Sea Bubble in 1720,[13] which led to companies being declared to be unlawful, unit trusts surged in popularity as a means of sharing capital for investment purposes. Their structure borrowed from the model developed in the USA in the nineteenth century of having two fiduciary officers in place so that each could watch the other and so, it was hoped, prevent the possibility of corruption on the part of trustees or directors. This chapter focuses, however, on that form of unit trust shaped by the provisions of FSMA 2000.

The unit trust scheme is a trust under which the investment property is held on **51.03** trust for its participants.[14] By contrast, the open-ended investment company was introduced to English law in 1997 to offer a corporate equivalent to the unit trust and so permit British investment managers to mimic the corporate structure used elsewhere in Europe.[15] Prior to the enactment of specific legislation introducing the open-ended investment company, it had been a principle of company law that (with only very limited exceptions) a company could not purchase its own shares. As considered below, for an open-ended investment company to operate, it would be necessary for the company to be able to repurchase its own shares from participants in the collective investment scheme so that those participants would be able to redeem their investment.

---

[13] That is, the name usually given to the catastrophic collapse of the South Sea Company in that year which had offered to exchange its own shares for bills belonging to those who held government debt: it thus bought the preponderance of the national debt and a great deal else besides before the fraudulent company went bankrupt and brought down with it the government and the financial fortunes of many among the English royalty and aristocracy.

[14] Financial Services and Markets Act 2000, s 237(1).

[15] This new form of entity was created by the Open-Ended Investment Companies (Investment Companies with Variable Capital) Regulations 1996 ('Open-Ended Investment Companies Regulations 1996'). The Open-Ended Investment Companies Regulations 1996 were made on 11 November 1996 and came into force on 6 January 1997. The scope of the regulations is that they have effect with reference to any investment company with variable capital which has its head office in Great Britain. Further to the Open-Ended Investment Companies Regulations 1996, the SIB created The Financial Services (Open-Ended Investment Companies) Regulations 1997 ('the SIB Regulations 1997') to govern the administration and marketing of open-ended investment companies in the UK and across the EU. The SIB Regulations came into force on 16 January 1997. Those regulations have since been superseded by regulations passed further to the Financial Services and Markets Act 2000, s 236 contained in the FSA's *CIS Sourcebook*, being Block 5 to the FSA Rulebook. See AS Hudson, 'Open-ended investment companies', in G Morse (ed), *Palmer's Company Law* (Sweet & Maxwell) Part 5A.

The structure of a unit trust

The fundamentals of a unit trust

51.04 A unit trust is, at root, a network of investment contracts between investors, a scheme manager, and a trustee. The scheme manager will be a financial institution whose employees, in practice, will have conceived of, marketed, and managed the particular unit trust for which investment is sought from the public. The trustee acts simply as a custodian of the scheme property. The scheme manager will therefore have to be a person authorized by the FSA to conduct investment business. As is considered below, unit trusts are created to invest in different market sectors and marketed with an expectation of generating different returns on the investors' capital. The investors are typically members of the public who have no necessary connection with each other and who will, as considered below, not necessarily have any formal, legal connection one with another. The investors (or, 'participants') acquire units in the unit trust.[16] That is, a contribution of *x* will acquire a participant one unit and therefore the participant will contribute multiples of *x* and acquire a corresponding number of units. All of the moneys raised from participants will then be pooled and the scheme manager will make investments with it. The investments made will be those detailed in the contract executed between the scheme manager and each participant separately. Importantly, the participants are able to redeem their units on demand and to receive back their investment stake, subject to the terms of the deed governing the unit trust scheme.

51.05 The contract between the parties is the most significant legal relationship for the achievement of the parties' commercial purpose because it is that contract which expresses the rights and obligations of the scheme manager and also the rights of the participants. The parties' fundamental purpose is the accumulation of profit and this purpose is expressed in the provisions governing the scheme manager's investor powers, the participants' pro rata share of any profits that are made, and the right of the participants to redeem their units. In recognition of this profit motive, collective investment schemes are expressed in section 235(1) of FSMA 2000 to comprise: 'any arrangements with respect to property of any description …the purpose or effect of which is…to participate in or receive profits or income…'. Nevertheless, the legal structure extends beyond that of a mere contract. Open-ended investment companies take effect as companies and their participants take rights as shareholders under the applicable regulations, as well as their contractual rights. By contrast, in relation to a unit trust scheme, 'the property is held on trust for the participants'. Therefore, the trust structure constitutes an essential part of a unit trust.

---

[16] Technically, the participants acquire 'sub-units' within the entire 'unit trust'. However, for the purposes of this chapter, the more familiar term 'units' will be used to connote the participants' individual parcels of investment.

Whereas the precise nature of the rights of the participants as beneficiaries and of **51.06** the scheme manager as a form of trustee were considered to have been at issue by some commentators before the enactment of FSMA 2000,[17] the legislation makes the trust relationship explicit.[18] The precise constitution of the trust exhibits features peculiar to the unit trust, however. The role of trustee is discharged by the 'trustee', as person distinct from the scheme manager,[19] whereas the scheme manager takes no legal title in the scheme property and instead makes only the investment decisions.[20] The trustee bears no investment manager powers or duties. Rather the trustee is responsible merely for the safekeeping of the property, as considered below, and for delivering property to the scheme manager's order in accordance with the terms of the scheme rules governing the unit trust. The role of the trustee is to ensure that the scheme manager does not use the trust fund for any purpose outwith the terms of its investment powers as contained in the unit trust's scheme rules. The scheme manager and the trustee must be independent of each other and both must be bodies corporate incorporated in the United Kingdom, or another EC member state, and carry on business there.[21] That the proposed manager and trustee of the scheme are required to be different persons[22] embodies the nineteenth century, regulatory objective that each of the unit trust's officers can observe one another.

The trust structure

The unit trust is created under a deed of trust. The appointed managers of the **51.07** trust (that is, the 'scheme manager' referred to above) will usually be in the form of a management company. Those managers will be empowered by the trust deed to acquire securities or investments of a type specified in the trust deed. This power will be subject to a general duty to maintain a portfolio of investments to spread the risk of the total investment capital of the fund. Those securities are then transferred to the trustees appointed in the trust deed. The trustees will usually be a company which is, nevertheless, required to be distinct from the management company which acts as scheme manager. The fiduciary function is therefore divided between the investment management responsibilities of the managers and the custodian responsibilities of the trustees. The profits of the pooled capital

---

[17] K Fan Sin, *The Legal Nature of the Unit Trust* (Clarendon Press, 1997) 64; Vaughan, *The Regulation of Unit Trusts* (Oxford University Press, 1990).

[18] AS Hudson, *The Law on Investment Entities* (Sweet & Maxwell, 2000) 199.

[19] That the scheme manager and the trustee are distinct legal persons is a requirement of the legislation: Financial Services and Markets Act 2000, s 242(2).

[20] It is this particular feature of the structure which has caused some commentators to consider that the unit trust is to be analysed as a contract: K Fan Sin, *The Legal Nature of the Unit Trust* (Clarendon Press, 1997) 64. That approach is insupportable, however: AS Hudson, *The Law on Investment Entities* (Sweet & Maxwell, 2000) 199 *et seq.*

[21] Financial Services and Markets Act 2000, s 242(2).

[22] Financial Services and Markets Act 2000, s 242(2).

are then allocated equally between the units held. The investor-beneficiary (or, participant) will be entitled to a pro rata cash return for each unit held.

The nature of the participant's rights

51.08   The participant's principal right is his contractual entitlement to a share of the profits of the scheme in any period of account, which is quantifiable in terms of an investment return calculated directly by reference to the value of the underlying investments in which the scheme acquires interests. The participant has two forms of right. The first form of right is a contractual right against the scheme manager to receive a pro rata share of the total profits of the fund and to have his investment redeemed on demand. The participant also has the rights of a beneficiary under a trust in the scheme property. The presence of the trust ensures that the trustee and the scheme manager owe fiduciary obligations to the beneficiaries. The individual participant also has an equitable proprietary interest in the scheme property which offers the participant further security against any malfeasance by either the trustee or the scheme manager.

51.09   The anticipated return for the participant is to be provided by way of cash. Therefore, while the discussion below of the legal nature of the rights of the participants will follow the familiar path of rights under a trust, the intention of the parties is far more mercenary than the niceties of the law of trusts would otherwise suggest. The participant's intention is not to be a 'participant', or member, in the company law sense of that term (as borrowed from the early corporate investment models of the pre-runners to the joint stock company), but rather to be a cash 'investor' receiving a cash return. The old-fashioned 'participant' was indeed participating in a corporate or entrepreneurial activity: literally participating in the activities of the corporate entity. A participant in a unit trust, by contrast, is a passive investor who is interested only in a cash return on his investment.

B. The Unit Trust as a Species of Trust

51.10   The unit trust is a trust.[23] However, the most important element of this trust relationship from a commercial standpoint is the 'unit' in which the participant acquires rights. The approach of the case law has been to identify the rights of the participant in those units: that is a form of chose in action against the manager and the trustee of the unit trust. Unlike beneficiaries under an ordinary trust, therefore, the common understanding of the rights of the participant was that they were not rights attaching to the scheme property. Now section 237(1) of FSMA 2000 makes the legal nature of the unit trust quite clear when it provides that the term

---

[23]   Financial Services and Markets Act 2000, s 237.

... 'unit trust scheme' means a collective investment scheme under which the property is held on trust for the participants.

The question which remains outstanding is what was meant by the term 'property' under the 2000 Act in forming the trust fund.[24] It is not clear whether this refers to the scheme's investment property or simply to the chose in action created between the participant and the scheme manager by their initial contract of investment. The scheme manager acquires securities to be held on the terms of the unit trust. The manager is required to ensure that a broad portfolio of investments is maintained in the scheme. Rather than allow the investments acquired to be limited to a small range of securities, there is an obligation on the managers to acquire a range of investments which spreads the risk of the scheme. The securities acquired then form a single unit.[25] The units offered may be admitted to listing on the Stock Exchange.[26] The investors are expressed to be the beneficiaries under the trust deed. However, their rights are strictly to a pro rata share of the dividends, interest, or other income generated by the portfolio of securities which make up the unit.

The settlor in unit trust schemes

The Australian case law has provided that the scheme manager is a settlor of the unit trust.[27] In New Zealand there is authority for the proposition that when the manager brings the unit trust into existence that is an act which is sufficient to qualify the manager as a settlor.[28] The New Zealand authorities accept that there is a trust but that the value contributed to the unit trust results from the subscriptions of the participants and not from the original action of the manager in creating the trust. However, that is no different, it is suggested, to the creation of a pension fund trust.[29] There is English law authority for the proposition that the participant is not settling property when subscribing for units within section 164(1) of the Law of Property Act 1925.[30] Rather that contribution is in consideration for the receipt of contractual rights derived from the investment of the unit trust.

51.11

---

[24] Similarly, the expression the 'property in question' under the Financial Services Act 1986, now repealed.

[25] The managers then seek investors (or, participants)—those investors acquire, technically, rights in sub-units which are derived from that main unit. While they are in fact sub-units, the rights acquired by the participants are, however, generally referred to as 'units': Financial Services and Markets Act 2000, s 237(2); formerly Financial Services Act 1986, s 75(8).

[26] See generally AS Hudson, 'Offers of securities', in G Morse (ed), *Palmer's Company Law* (Sweet & Maxwell) Part 5, para 5.200 *et seq*.

[27] *Truesdale v FCT* (1969) 120 CLR 353, a case involving the tax effects of settlement; *Famel Pty Ltd v Burswood Management Ltd* (1989) 15 ACLR 572, *per* French J.

[28] *Baldwin v CIR* [1965] NZLR 1; *Tucker v CIR* [1965] NZLR 1027: both cases concerning the question of creating a trust in the context of taxation.   [29] Considered in Part H.

[30] *Re AEG Unit Trust (Managers) Ltd's Deed* [1957] 1 Ch 415, 420, *per* Wynn-Parry J.

The division of the fiduciary obligations in a unit trust

51.12 Unit trusts have two forms of officer: the scheme manager and the trustee. The trustee acts as a trustee and holds the trust property on trust for the participants.[31] There is a conceptual problem in the division of the functions normally associated with an ordinary trustee between the scheme manager and the trustee. Nevertheless, in an ordinary trust it would not be exceptional to provide that different trustees are to have subtly different responsibilities one from another. So, one trustee might be responsible for investment management, another trustee for custody of the trust fund, and yet another for the collection of income. In the context of a unit trust the division is simply made between the investment management function carried on by the manager and the custodian function carried on by the unit trustee. That does not prevent the unit trust from being described as a trust—rather, the unit trust perhaps looks more like a complex commercial trust than a simple institutional trust. Both scheme manager and trustee are to be considered to be fiduciaries.

51.13 The scheme manager falls to be considered to be a fiduciary because his investment obligations are owed entirely for the benefit of beneficiaries, to whom the scheme also owes direct contractual obligations. Powers of investment in relation to private express trusts have been held to be fiduciary powers in general.[32] Such a combination of obligations renders the scheme manager a fiduciary in relation to the participants in the unit trust scheme. The majority of commentators on unit trusts and a number of cases[33] have accepted that the rule in *Saunders v Vautier*[34] applies to unit trusts in the same way as it applies to ordinary trusts.[35] Only one commentator has expressed any concern at the extent of this proposition.[36] If it is true to say that the rule in *Saunders v Vautier* does apply to unit trusts then it is clear that the most important element of a trust, the vesting of absolute equitable title and ultimate control in the participants as beneficiaries, is present.

---

[31] Financial Services and Markets Act 2000, s 237(1).

[32] *Lord Vestey's Executors v IRC* [1949] 1 All ER 1108, 1115, *per* Lord Simonds.

[33] See, for example, *Re AEG Unit Trust (Managers) Ltd's Deed* [1957] Ch 415.

[34] (1841) 4 Beav 115.

[35] Walsh, 'Unit Trusts' in Grbich, Munn and Reicher (eds), *Modern Trusts and Taxation* (Butterworths Australia, 1978) 36, 71; Ford, 'Public Unit Trusts' in Austin and Vann (eds), *The Law of Public Company Finance* (Law Book Co, 1986) 400 *et seq*; Ford and Lee, *Principles of the Law of Trusts* (2nd edn, Law Book Co, 1990) 2304.5.

[36] Sin, *op cit*, 114 *et seq*. The basis for his concern is to rehearse his core thesis that the unit trust ought not to be considered to be a trust properly so-called because it lacks a settlor with a single donative intention—something which Sin asserts is at the heart of the rule in *Saunders v Vautier*. It is this writer's opinion that the cases on the *Saunders v Vautier* principle intend the rule to extend further than simply to effect the intentions of a settlor given that the rule plainly permits the beneficiary to ignore the settlor's express trust terms.

The scheme manager does assume the position of a person bearing all the hall-marks of a trustee by directing the 'trustee'[37] how to deal with the property. The trustee is then required to obey those directions.[38] The acid test would therefore appear to be: what would happen if there were a breach of the investment obligations of the unit trust? Given that the unit trustee is required to obey, the manager must be intermeddling in the affairs of the unit trust either as an express trustee entitled to direct the investment of the trust fund, or as a delegate of the person who is the trustee,[39] or as a trustee de son tort, or as a dishonest assistant in the treatment of the trust property. It would be contrary to principle to consider that someone who was delegated, or appointed in the trust document, to have the specific task of making investment decisions would not be the person who would be subject to the general trusts law obligations of investment. If there was a breach of the investment powers set out in the trust document, it would be remarkable if the person who was responsible for carrying out investment could argue that, while he has breached the investment obligations binding on the trustees, he was somehow responsible for those investment activities solely on the basis of contract. If this were the case, then the scheme manager would not be responsible under the law of trusts for breach of trust to reconstitute the trust fund or pay equitable compensation to the participants as an ordinary trustee would be required to do.[40] It would seem more sensible to suggest that the scheme manager bears the investment obligations of a trustee and therefore should be liable as a trustee for any breach of those obligations.

51.14

The last of the list of potential liabilities (the knowing or dishonest assistant[41]) creates only a personal liability to account as a stranger to the trust and therefore could arise without the manager being recognized as a trustee. The trustee de son tort would arise as a constructive trust where the manager interfered with the trust so as to be considered properly to be a constructive trustee. However, it would seem strange to deem the manager a trustee de son tort in a context in which the manager was acting in the way that the manager was expected to act under the express terms of the trust deed. It is suggested that it would be more consistent with principle to treat the manager as an express trustee in carrying out the obligations of a co-trustee.[42]

51.15

---

[37] That is, the person named as 'trustee' in unit trust jargon.
[38] See Sin, *op cit*; Maurice, 'The office of custodian trustee' (1960) 24 Conv 196; Stephenson, 'Co-trustees or several trustees?' (1942) 16 Temple ULQ 249, 250.
[39] Whoever that would be, because it appears that it is not the unit trustee.
[40] *Target Holdings v Redferns* [1996] 1 AC 421, [1995] 3 WLR 352, [1995] 3 All ER 785.
[41] Rendered now as 'dishonest assistant' by the Privy Council in *Royal Brunei Airlines v Tan* [1995] 2 AC 378.
[42] These forms of liability are considered generally in Chapter 11.

C. The Powers and Obligations of the Scheme Manager

Powers and obligations of the scheme manager

Permitted activities of managers

51.16   The activities in which a fund manager is allowed to engage are restricted by statute. The manager seeks subscriptions for the unit trust. This is a peculiar position for a trustee when compared to the simple institutional trust model of trusts because there is necessarily a conflict between the commercial need for the manager to attract investors and its obligation to invest for the benefit of the participants. The existence of a potential for conflict does not mean that the manager is not to be considered to be a trustee; rather, it increases the importance of considering him to be a trustee. A provision in the trust deed of a unit trust that any balance of the net income which is not used for distribution to the unit holders shall be added to the capital, and shall thereupon cease to be available for distribution, does not infringe section 164 of the Law of Property Act 1925, which re-enacts the restrictions formerly contained in the Thellusson Act.[43]

Restrictions on exclusion clauses

51.17   The scheme manager will wish to limit the extent to which it can be liable for any loss suffered by the participants or the trustee and,[44] significantly, to explain the risks which the participants are taking and the losses for which the manager would not be contractually liable.[45] This is the case with trustees in ordinary, private trusts. Nevertheless, there is a statutory restriction placed on the ability of the manager of a unit trust to seek to restrict its own liability in the following terms:

> Any provision of the trust deed of an authorised unit trust scheme is void in so far as it would have the effect of exempting the manager or trustee from liability for any failure to exercise due care and diligence in the discharge of his functions in respect of the scheme.[46]

So, any provision of the trust deed of an authorized unit trust scheme will be void if it has the effect of exempting the manager or trustee from liability for any failure in due care and diligence.

51.18   There is in consequence a question as to those obligations which the scheme manager is required to perform. As the settlor of the unit trust, it is open to the manager to define and limit those events for which it will be liable to perform in the detail of the contract, provided always that by so doing it does not create any exclusion

---

[43] *Re AEG Unit Trust (Managers) Ltd's Deed* [1957] Ch 415.
[44] Generally see P Matthews, 'The Efficacy of Trustee Exemption Clauses in English Law' [1989] Conv 42.   [45] See *Hayim v Citibank* [1987] AC 730.
[46] Financial Services and Markets Act 2000, s 253.

clauses which purport to exclude liability for any lapse in due care or diligence on the scheme manager's part.[47]

The more general question is then one of ordinary contract law as to whether or not the exclusion clause seeks to exclude liability in relation to something which constitutes a breach of a fundamental term of the contract.[48] It is only in the Australian cases that many of these issues have been considered. In relation to unit trusts, construction will be presumed against the manager because it is the manager who is responsible for the provisions of the terms of the unit trust deed.[49] Where the exemption clause is ambiguous, construction will similarly also be effected against the manager.[50]   **51.19**

One further issue is the extent of the liability which equity will impose on the trustee by virtue of the holding of that fiduciary office. In the absence of any case law on the topic it is unclear in the English law of trusts the extent to which exclusion clauses would be valid. On principle it is suggested that a trustee ought not to be able to limit its own liability for fraud[51] or negligence,[52] bad faith,[53] or for failures of performance in situations in which trustees 'from motives however laudable in themselves act in plain violation of the duty which they owe to the individuals beneficially interested in the funds which they administer'.[54] This is further to the general duties of trustees in managing the investments of a trust.[55]   **51.20**

Powers of control over managers and trustees

In any case in which the FSA has power to give a direction to the manager[56] in relation to an authorized unit trust scheme, the FSA is empowered to apply to the court for an order that the manager and the trustee wind up the scheme or the   **51.21**

---

[47] See also the Unfair Contract Terms Act 1977, s 1(2). In any event, exclusion of such liability would require explicit provision in the Australian context: *Commissioner for Railways (NSW) v Quinn* (1946) 72 CLR 345; *Davis v Pearce Parking Station Pty Ltd* (1954) 91 CLR 642; *Wilson v Darling Island Stevedoring & Lighterage Co Ltd* (1956) 95 CLR 43; *Port Jackson Stevedoring Pty Ltd v Salmond & Spraggon (Aust) Pty Ltd* (1978) 139 CLR 231.

[48] *Suisse Atlantique Societe d'Armement Maritime v NV Rotterdamsche Kolen Centrale* [1967] 1 AC 361; *Photo Production Ltd v Securicor Transport Ltd* [1980] AC 487, [1980] 1 All ER 556.

[49] *Davis v Pearce Parking Station Pty Ltd* (1954) 91 CLR 642.

[50] *Van der Sterren v Cibernetics (Holdings) Pty Ltd* [1970] ALR 751; *Darlington Futures v Delco Australia Ltd* (1986) 161 CLR 500; *Nissho Iwai Australia Ltd v Malaysian International Shipping Corporation* (1989) 167 CLR 219.

[51] To which the Court of Appeal in Jersey has restricted this principle: *Midland Bank Trustee (Jersey) Ltd v Federated Pension Services Ltd* [1996] Pen LR 179.

[52] This is the approach of the Scottish cases, being appeals to the House of Lords: *Knox v Mackinnon* (1888) 13 App Cas 753; *Rae v Meek* (1889) 14 App Cas 558; *Clarke v Clarke's Trustee* 1925 SC 693.

[53] This was the approach taken in their 15th edition by D Hayton in *Underhill and Hayton* 902.

[54] *Knox v Mackinnon* (1888) 13 App Cas 753, 765, *per* Lord Watson.

[55] *Speight v Gaunt* (1883) 9 App Cas 1; *Re Vickery* [1931] 1 Ch 572.

[56] Financial Services and Markets Act 2000, s 257(1).

fiduciaries cease all issues or redemptions under the scheme.[57] The only alternative means of controlling the manager and trustee is by means of exercise of the beneficiary powers of participants as beneficiaries in equity.[58] This is an issue which has been considered above.[59] This ability of the absolutely entitled beneficiaries to exert control over the trustee is an important part of the philosophy of the law of trusts in regulating the behaviour of the trustees in their management of the trust fund.[60] The beneficiary principle, so-called, gives any person with an equitable interest in the trust the power to call the trustees to account[61] and to hold the trustees to their duty to act evenly between the various classes of beneficiaries.[62]

The rights of the manager

51.22   The scheme manager seeks subscribers to the unit trust. Units which are unallocated will remain vested in the scheme manager until they are allocated. Similarly, when units are redeemed, the choses in action constituting the unsubscribed units will vest in the scheme manager. Therefore, the scheme manager has a beneficial interest in those unallocated units and therefore constitutes not only a trustee[63] but also a form of beneficiary.[64] It is also said that a right to remuneration from the trust entitles a trustee to be considered to have some beneficial interest against the property of that fund.[65] It is suggested, however, that these constitute mere personal, contractual rights against the totality of the trust fund to be remunerated and not proprietary rights in the manner of a beneficiary with a vested equitable interest.[66]

The obligations of the trustee

51.23   The unit trustee is properly considered to be a custodian or a bare trustee. Strictly it is the unit trustee who makes the investments on behalf of the unit trust under

---

[57] Financial Services and Markets Act 2000, s 257(2).

[58] *Saunders v Vautier* (1841) 4 Beav 115; *Gosling v Gosling* (1859) John 265; *Harbin v Masterman* [1894] 2 Ch 184, *per* Lindley LJ, approved by House of Lords in *Wharton v Masterman* [1895] AC 186; *Re Bowes* [1896] 1 Ch 507; *Re Brockbank* [1948] Ch 206; *Re AEG Unit Trust (Managers) Ltd's Deed* [1957] Ch 415; *Stephenson v Barclays Bank* [1975] 1 All ER 625, 637, *per* Walton J.

[59] See para 46.24.

[60] See in particular the discussion of *Re Denley* [1969] 1 Ch 373, *per* Goff J, expressing the requirement that the beneficiary principle is satisfied provided that there is some person in whose benefit the court can order performance.

[61] *Morice v Bishop of Durham* (1805) 10 Ves 522; *Re Denley* [1969] 1 Ch 373.

[62] *Re Barton's Trust* (1868) LR 5 Eq 238; *Re Bouch* (1885) 29 ChD 635; *Hill v Permanent Trustee Co of New South Wales* [1930] AC 720; *Re Doughty* [1947] 1 Ch 263; *Re Kleinwort's Settlements* [1951] 2 TLR 91; *Nestle v National Westminster Bank* [1994] 1 All ER 118.

[63] As argued above at para 46.23.

[64] *Parkes Management Ltd v Perpetual Trustee Co Ltd* [1977] CLC 29, NSW.

[65] *Re Pooley* (1888) 40 Ch D 1; *Re Thorley* [1891] 2 Ch 613; *Re Duke of Norfolk's Trusts* [1982] 1 Ch 61.

[66] *Application of Trust Company of Australia re Barclays Commercial Property Trust*, noted by Sin, *op cit*, 101.

the direction of the manager. It is on that basis that it is said that the unit trustee acts as a mere bare trustee having little role to play other than maintenance and stewardship of the property. The active management of the unit trust is carried on by the scheme manager.

D. The Nature of the Participants' Rights

The nature of the participants' rights in a collective investment scheme in general terms

The participants in a collective investment scheme are merely passive investors **51.24** and not managers of the scheme's activities. Section 235(2) of FSMA 2000 provides that:

> The arrangements [comprising the collective investment scheme] must be such that the persons who are to participate ('participants') do not have day-to-day control over the management of the property, whether or not they have the right to be consulted or to give directions.[67]

The marketing of such schemes to the public is conducted by expert fund managers for whom unit trusts are investment products made available to the inexpert, retail investor base. Such participants in a unit trust will not expect to have rights of direction or consultation in respect of the scheme's activities. A greater sense of this control of a collective investment scheme by expert managers on behalf of inexpert or passive investors emerges from the following provision:

> The arrangements must also have either or both of the following characteristics—
> (a) the contributions of the participants and the profits or income out of which payments are to be made to them are to be pooled;[68]
> (b) the property is managed as a whole by or on behalf of the operator of the scheme.[69]

This final part of section 235(3) of the Financial Services and Markets Act 2000 is considerably narrower in scope than is section 253(1) and presents two key features of the collective investment scheme: first, that it is concerned with the investment of pooled funds derived from the participants and, secondly, that the scheme manager carries on the management of the scheme on their behalf. The effect of this section 235 as a whole is therefore a form of telescoping down from the breadth of the opening definition to the two defining characteristics of the collective investment scheme.

---

[67] Financial Services and Markets Act 2000, s 235(2).
[68] References to pooling, however, do not constitute those separate pools as a single collective investment scheme unless their participants are entitled to exchange rights in one pool for rights in another: Financial Services and Markets Act 2000, s 235(4).
[69] Financial Services and Markets Act 2000, s 235(3).

The nature of the participants' rights in a unit trust in general terms

51.25 The definition of 'a unit trust scheme' given in FSMA 2000 is 'a collective investment scheme under which the property in question is held on trust for the participants'.[70] The nature of the obligations owed between the fiduciaries and the participants, between the participants themselves, and the rights of the participants in the scheme property are all the subject matter of the following discussion. The FSMA 2000 provides that:

> The participants must be entitled to have their units redeemed in accordance with the scheme at a price related to the net value of the property to which the units relate and determined in accordance with the scheme.[71]

Further:

> But a scheme shall be treated as complying with this subsection if it requires the manager to ensure that a participant is able to sell his units on an investment exchange at a price not significantly different from that mentioned in this subsection.[72]

Therefore, the central right of the participant is that of redemption of her units and the payment to her of their cash value. Without redemption of the unit, and payment out of the value of the unit, the unit trust would be commercially useless. The commercial purpose of the unit trust is the ability of the participant to redeem her units by ensuring that she is entitled to sell them for their market value at any given time.

51.26 The Australian courts have accepted that there is an analogy to be made between the allotment of shares in an ordinary company and an allotment of units in a unit trust.[73] Similarly, on a transfer of a unit, the transferor participant is entitled to have the transferee accepted as being a good transfer of the rights attaching to the unit to the transferee.[74] Under statute, good title attaches to the holder of the unit from the moment that person is entered on the register as owner of the unit.[75] The rights of the participants against the unit trustee are similarly a mixture of elements based on the law of contract, based on the issuance of the units in parallel to an issue of shares in company law,[76] and based on the law of trust given the custodianship duties of the unit trustee.[77]

---

[70] Financial Services and Markets Act 2000, s 237(1); formerly Financial Services Act 1986, s 75(8).

[71] Financial Services and Markets Act 2000, s 243(10).

[72] Financial Services and Markets Act 2000, s 243(11).

[73] *Graham Australia Pty Ltd v Corporate West Management Pty Ltd* (1990) 1 ACSR 682, 687.

[74] *Elkington v Moore Business Systems Australia Ltd* (1994) 15 ACSR 292, 296.

[75] Financial Services (Regulated Schemes) Regulations 1991, reg 6.03.

[76] *Elkington v Moore Business Systems Australia Ltd* (1994) 15 ACSR 292.

[77] *West Merchant Bank Ltd v Rural Agricultural Management Ltd*, noted in Sin, *op cit*, 82. See also K Fan Sin, 'Enforcing the Unit Trust Deed among Unitholders' (1997) 15 ACSR 292.

Rights of the participants against the scheme property

The manager and the trustee stand in the relationship of a trust against the participants. What is less clear is the nature of the property that is held on trust for those participants. Whereas section 237(1) of FSMA 2000 provides that the 'property' is held on trust for the participants, the answer is probably that it is the units, constituting choses in action between the manager and the unit trustee on the one hand and the participants on the other, which are the trust property but that they are capable of attaching to whatever property constitutes the trust's investments from time to time.[78]   **51.27**

The rights of the participants attach to the capital of the unit trust, any income stream owed to the manager and trustee, any income guarantees by way of options or otherwise, the obligations of the manager to the participants, the obligations of the unit trustee to the participants, and also to any voting and similar rights (if such are reserved to the participants in the scheme rules). Therefore, the precise rights of the participants arise from these various sources. It is not enough to say that the rights of the participants attach to the property in which the manager instructs the unit trustee to invest from time to time. In consequence, the rights of the participants are *primarily* contractual rights against the manager and the unit trustee to be paid a return calculated in accordance with the contractual formulae. However, the participants do have some proprietary right against the scheme property by virtue both of section 237 of FSMA 2000 and of the rule in *Saunders v Vautier*[79] permitting the beneficiaries (provided that they are *sui juris* and absolutely entitled) to terminate the trust. Hence the qualification that their rights are primarily, but not exclusively, contractual. Rather, the participant has[80] ultimately that kind of proprietary right,[81] when exercised in common with all the other participants, which is usually said to attach to a beneficiary under a trust.[82]   **51.28**

---

[78] The participants do not have rights in the underlying investments held by the trustee on behalf of the scheme. Rather the participants have only contractual rights against the manager and unit trustee *as to their cash flow entitlement* from the unit trust. There are, however, also rights in equity against the manager and unit trustee in relation to their management of the scheme property. In relation to an umbrella trust, the participant has rights in a trust which itself has interests in other trusts. An umbrella trust is a unit trust which carries investments in a range of different categories of unit trust. It is suggested that the form of equitable interest in such a trust will be different from an interest in a more straightforward securities trust. Added to that are the myriad complications of the specific contractual provisions of any unit trust which in themselves might alter the nature of the precise equitable interest under the unit trust.

[79] (1841) 4 Beav 115.

[80] Subject to any specific contractual, structural provision to the contrary.

[81] *Baker v Archer-Shee* [1927] AC 844

[82] *Costa and Duppe Properties Pty Ltd v Duppe* [1986] VR 90; *Softcorp Holdings Pty Ltd v Commissioner of Stamps* (1987) 18 ATR 813. These cases do turn on the construction of their various trust deeds but it is suggested that they also constitute the general rule in the absence of a specific provision to the contrary.

Rights against the scheme manager

51.29 The role of the manager is pivotal to the unit trust.[83] The manager therefore bears personal obligations in relation to investment which obligations are owed to the participants.[84] Those obligations are merely personal because the manager has no title in any of the trust property. However, the manager does have control over the trust property and therefore it is suggested that the manager ought to owe the proprietary obligations of a trustee to the participants in the event of breach of trust[85] or receipt of a bribe, as considered above.[86]

Rights between participants *inter se*

The question of the existence of a contract

51.30 Older authorities suggest that there was no contractual nexus between the participants to a unit trust; while modern Australian authorities suggest that there ought to be in certain circumstances, while relying on well-established contractual rules. It was said by James LJ in *Smith v Anderson*[87] that there are no rights or obligations owed between the participants in a unit trust.[88] This has been upheld in Australia even in circumstances in which the participants were given power to contest other people being accepted as participants—the court held that this did not constitute the creation of mutual contractual rights, merely a power to raise an objection.[89] In Australia the law generally does not accept contractual obligations being owed between members of an association simply by virtue of membership of that association without more.[90]

51.31 The general English law on unincorporated associations does accept that there are contractual obligations between members to an association.[91] That principle need not necessarily extend, however, to a supposition that participants in a unit trust necessarily have contractual obligations owed one to another. The participant forms a contractual nexus with the manager and with the unit trustee but not with the other participants—each investor contributes money in expectation of a return from the manager but in ignorance of the identity, size of investment, and

---

[83] *Parkes Management Ltd v Perpetual Trustee Co Ltd* [1977] CLC 29, NSW.

[84] Unlike in relation to a company where the rights are owed to the company.

[85] *Target Holdings v Redferns* [1996] 1 AC 421, [1995] 3 WLR 352, [1995] 3 All ER 785.

[86] *Att-Gen Hong Kong v Reid* [1994] 1 AC 324—indeed this form of constructive trust is instructive because in that case the defendant had not been trustee of any property for the claimants and yet he was held to be subject to a proprietary constructive trust over property (a bribe) which had never been the property of the claimants.   [87] (1880) 15 Ch D 247, 274.

[88] See also *AF & ME Pty Ltd v Aveling* (1994) 14 ACSR 499, *per* Heerey J.

[89] *AF & ME Pty Ltd v Aveling* (1994) 14 ACSR 499, *per* Heerey J.

[90] *Cameron v Hogan* (1934) 51 CLR 358, 370. However, Sin expresses reluctance to accept this principle, see Sin, (1997) *op cit* 85; and also *Woodford v Smith* [1970] 1 WLR 806; and *Grogan v MacKinnon* (1973) 2 NSWLR 290.

[91] See *Re Bucks Constabulary Widows and Orphans Friendly Society (No 2)* [1979] 1 WLR 937; *Universe Tankships Inc of Monrovia v International Transport Workers Federation* [1983] 1 AC 366.

nature of the other participants, let alone in expectation of the extension of any contractual obligation from them.[92] The only nexus with the other participants is in equity under the rule in *Saunders v Vautier*[93] under which the participants *qua* beneficiaries absolutely entitled to the trust fund are entitled to control the manager and unit trustee.

No partnership between participants

On the authorities there is no partnership between the participants to a unit trust on the basis that they are not carrying on a business with a view to profit within the terms of the Partnership Act 1890.[94] It was said in *Smith v Anderson* that the participants are making an investment and not carrying on the business of investment. Rather, that business activity is being carried on by the manager and the unit trustee on behalf of the participants. In consequence they are not involved in a business.[95]   **51.32**

E. The Regulation of Unit Trusts

The regulation of unit trusts

The regulation of unit trusts is provided for by statute and by FSA regulation. It is   **51.33** suggested that unit trusts, in consequence, are treated differently from ordinary trusts. The legislative policy underlines the assumption that there is something so significant about the activities of unit trusts that the ordinary law of trusts—particularly in the form of the duties imposed on trustees in the ordinary circumstances—is insufficient to preserve the rights of beneficiaries and to enforce the obligations of trustees. Unit trust schemes are regulated by the FSA under the FSMA 2000.[96] There is, however, a considerable body of secondary legislation that is important in practice.[97] Part XVII of the FSMA 2000 sets out the new regime for the recognition of overseas schemes. Unit trusts are regulated by the FSA under the terms of the CIS Sourcebook contained in the FSA Rulebook.

---

[92] An approach which found favour with James LJ in *Smith v Anderson* (1880) 15 Ch D 247. However, English law does permit contractual obligations to arise in situations in which those parties are in ignorance of one another, as in *Clarke v Dunraven* [1897] AC 59; *Borland Trustee v Steel Brothers & Co Ltd* [1901] 1 Ch 279. It is suggested that those cases concerned situations in which the parties could be reasonably said to have anticipated that the actions of each would affect the other and therefore that obligations ought to be owed. In relation to a unit trust, the actions of one participant do not affect the rights of any other—for example, each participant is entitled to redeem their units in the ordinary course of events and thus affect the total value of the scheme property without suffering any liability to any other participant. The company law case of *Rayfield v Hands* [1960] Ch 1, in which contractual rights were enforced between shareholders, is admittedly more difficult to square with this argument.   [93] (1841) 4 Beav 115.

[94] *Smith v Anderson* (1880) 15 Ch D 247; *Crowther v Thorley* (1884) 50 LT 43; *R v Siddall* (1885) 29 Ch D 1; but cf *Re Thomas* (1884) 14 QBD 379.   [95] ibid.

[96] Council Dir 85/611, noted by Frank Wooldridge in [1987] JBL 329–333; Financial Services and Markets Act 2000, s 1.   [97] Contained primarily in the *CIS Sourcebook*.

51.34 For a scheme manager to be permitted to promote a unit trust investment scheme to the public, that unit trust scheme must have been authorized by the FSA.[98] The scheme manager and the trustee are required to be different persons for this purpose.[99] The manner in which authorizations are to be made is set out by the FSA rulebook governing Collective Investment Schemes.[100] An application for authorization must include a copy of the scheme rules and a declaration signed by a solicitor to the effect that those scheme rules comply with the statutory requirements.[101] The detail of the authorization procedure is considered in the next section. The FSA makes its decision on all applications within six months of them being made.[102] When an application for authorization is refused, the applicant receives a decision notice detailing any reasons for the refusal and then has a right to petition the Tribunal created by the FSMA 2000.[103]

Authorization of unit trust schemes

51.35 Before unit trusts may be marketed to the public, they must receive authorization from the FSA. In the terms employed by the FSMA 2000, an authorized person—that is, a fund manager or other financial institution authorized to market investments to the public—may not communicate an invitation or inducement to participate in a unit trust[104] unless the scheme is an authorized unit trust scheme or is an authorized open-ended investment company.[105] Applications for authorization must be made by the scheme manager and the trustee to the Authority.[106] The Authority must then be satisfied that the proposed unit trust scheme complies with the criteria set out in section 243 of the FSMA 2000. Those criteria are as follows. First, the scheme manager and the trustee must be different people.[107] Secondly, both the manager and the trustee must be a body corporate incorporated either in the United Kingdom or in another EEA State.[108] Thirdly, both the manager and the trustee must have a place of business in the United Kingdom.[109] Fourthly, the affairs of the manager and of the trustee must be administered in the

---

[98] Financial Services and Markets Act 2000, s 242(1).
[99] Financial Services and Markets Act 2000, s 242(2).
[100] Financial Services and Markets Act 2000, s 242(3). Referred to here, and in those regulations, as 'CIS'. [101] Financial Services and Markets Act 2000, s 243(1).
[102] Financial Services and Markets Act 2000, s 244(1).
[103] Financial Services and Markets Act 2000, s 245(1).
[104] Financial Services and Markets Act 2000, s 238(1).
[105] Financial Services and Markets Act 2000, s 238(2).
[106] Financial Services and Markets Act 2000, s 242(1).
[107] Financial Services and Markets Act 2000, s 243(4). See also Financial Services and Markets Act 2000, s 242(2).
[108] Financial Services and Markets Act 2000, s 243(5)(a). Where the manager or trustee is incorporated in another EEA State, then that scheme must not be one which is not a 'recognised scheme' within Financial Services and Markets Act 2000, s 264(2) on the grounds that the scheme's operator or the authorities which will regulate the scheme in that state would not comply with 'the law in force in the United Kingdom'. [109] Financial Services and Markets Act 2000, s 243(5)(b).

country in which each is incorporated.[110] Fifthly, both manager and trustee must be authorized persons under the terms of the FSMA 2000 generally, and both must be authorized to act as manager and trustee of a unit trust respectively.[111] Sixthly, the name given to the scheme must not be undesirable nor misleading.[112] Seventhly, the scheme's purposes must be 'reasonably capable of being successfully carried into effect'.[113] Finally, the participants must be entitled to have their units redeemed under the scheme rules at a price which is related to the net value of scheme property and as calculated in accordance with the scheme's rules.[114]

Restrictions on promotion

An authorized person cannot promote a collective investment scheme in general terms.[115] Promotion in this sense connotes any situation in which such an authorized person seeks to 'communicate an invitation or inducement to participate' in such a scheme.[116] The terms 'communicate', 'invitation' and 'inducement' are not defined, it is suggested, so as to permit the broadest possible interpretation of those terms. This general prohibition does not apply to authorized unit trusts or to authorized open-ended investment companies or other recognized schemes.[117] If an unauthorized person sought to make such promotions then that person would be committing offences under the unlawful communications provisions of the FSMA 2000.[118] In general terms, within the 'financial promotion code' created by section 21 of the FSMA 2000, financial promotion may be permitted in specified circumstances by authorized persons and only if the content of the communication has been authorized.[119]   **51.36**

Promotion may not be made in general terms from outside the United Kingdom to the public in and having an effect in the United Kingdom.[120] An 'effect' will be communicated in this sense even if the communication is made available on a web-site which can be accessed from within the United Kingdom: it need not be intentionally delivered into the United Kingdom.

---

[110] Financial Services and Markets Act 2000, s 243(5).
[111] Financial Services and Markets Act 2000, s 243(7).
[112] Financial Services and Markets Act 2000, s 243(8).
[113] Financial Services and Markets Act 2000, s 243(9).
[114] Financial Services and Markets Act 2000, s 243(10) and (11).
[115] Financial Services and Markets Act 2000, s 238(1).
[116] Financial Services and Markets Act 2000, s 238(1).
[117] Financial Services and Markets Act 2000, s 238(4).
[118] Financial Services and Markets Act 2000, s 21.
[119] Financial Services and Markets Act 2000, s 21(2).
[120] Financial Services and Markets Act 2000, s 238(3).

The contents of scheme rules and of the prospectus

51.37 The unit trust scheme must have scheme rules which comply with section 247 of FSMA 2000. Those requirements include the following material. First, the scheme rules must contain the constitution of the scheme: dealing particularly with the management and the operation of the scheme's activities. The scheme must make plain the powers, duties, rights, and liabilities of the scheme manager and of the trustee.[121] The participants in the scheme must have their rights and duties made plain also.[122] The scheme rules are required to explain the manner in which the redemption of the participants' units can be carried out—this is clearly central to the participants' commercial purpose when investing in a unit trust.[123] Bound up with that is the requirement that the scheme rules explain how the expenses of the scheme will be calculated and the manner in which they will be met.[124]

51.38 When a unit trust scheme is offered to the public, the manager will be required to publish a prospectus which gives prospective investors all of the information which would reasonably be required by any reasonable person dealing reasonably frequently in the appropriate market place to make an informed decision as to whether or not to invest in the scheme. The prospectus must be drawn up by an authorized fund manager[125] and lodged both with the FSA and the trustee.[126] The *CIS Sourcebook* makes clear the material which must be included in the prospectus and any scheme particulars. Significantly the prospectus is not permitted to contain any material not required by the rules: a method of ensuring that investors are not blinded by too much information but rather that they have just enough material on which to make informed decisions without being confused.[127] In the event that there is any 'materially significant change in matters stated in' the prospectus, whether contained in the annual review or not, then the prospectus must be altered to take account of that matter.[128] However, before such a change can be made, the approval of the unitholders must be acquired.[129] Aside from any liability at common law or in equity, the scheme manager will be liable to pay compensation to any participant in the scheme in relation to any false or misleading statement in or omission from the prospectus.[130]

51.39 The material considered in this section is reproduced in the table in para 3.5.2 of the *CIS Sourcebook*. The specific matters referred to in paragraph 3.5 relating to open-ended investment companies, in outline, are as follows. A prominent statement that

---

[121] Financial Services and Markets Act 2000, s 247(1)(b).
[122] Financial Services and Markets Act 2000, s 247(1)(c).
[123] Financial Services and Markets Act 2000, s 247(2)(a).
[124] Financial Services and Markets Act 2000, s 247(2)(b).
[125] *CIS Sourcebook*, para 3.2.1(1).   [126] ibid, para 3.2.2.
[127] ibid, para 3.2.1(2).   [128] ibid, para 3.4.1.
[129] ibid, para 3.4.2.   [130] ibid, para 3.3.1.

the prospectus is a prospectus for the purposes of the *CIS Sourcebook*. The prospectus must also include basic information as to the name of the authorized fund, that the fund is an open-ended investment company, to which category the open-ended investment company belongs, the effective date of the FSA's authorization order at which time the open-ended investment company can commence business, the base currency for the fund, and any limitation on the duration of the open-ended investment company. Significantly, the prospectus must contain a statement that the shareholders of the open-ended investment company are not liable for the open-ended investment company's debts. The further category of information relates to the open-ended investment company's investment objectives and policy, including a list of eligible securities for the fund, a statement as to whether or not the fund will invest in land or in other funds, any sovereign securities in which the open-ended investment company may invest, and the open-ended investment company's policy in relation to its borrowing powers. The prospectus is required to give 'sufficient information' in relation to the investment objectives and policy of the company 'to enable a shareholder to ascertain' the investment objectives of the company, the company's investment policy in relation to those objectives, and 'the extent to which that policy does not envisage remaining fully invested at all times'.[131] In relation to distributions, the prospectus must provide information as to the open-ended investment company's annual and interim accounting periods, how distributable income is to be determined and paid, and the open-ended investment company's policy on income equalization.

51.40 With respect to the characteristics of units in the scheme the following information must be provided: the various classes of unit, the rights held by unitholders, and the manner in which those rights may be executed. Information must be provided as to the identity and structure of the scheme manager, as to its directors, and in relation to any sums payable to the trustee and other payments from the scheme property. The information required in respect of the scheme manager relates to its name, date, and place of incorporation, place of business and registered office, whether or not it is a subsidiary, the duration of its corporate status, the amount of its share capital which is fully paid up, whether it is authorized by the FSA to carry on investment business in the UK, and whether it holds any office in relation to other collective investment schemes.

51.41 The prospectus is also required to give particulars by means of a 'summary of the material provisions' of the contract between the participants and the scheme manager, particularly in relation to termination, compensation on termination, and indemnity. Where there is a capital charge in favour of the scheme manager's remuneration, the scheme's attitude to the priority of capital over income (or vice versa) must be identified. Where there are any restrictions on investment in transferable securities, the restriction must be identified.

---

[131] ibid, para 3.5.2(3.1).

51.42 The prospectus must provide information in relation to directors of the scheme manager and also of payments or remuneration made to them. The same information relating to identification must be made in relation to the trustee as for the scheme manager (in all material respects) together with a 'description of its principal business activity' and a summary of 'the material provisions of the contract between the company and the depositary which may be relevant to shareholders'. Where an investment adviser is retained in relation to the company, the same information is required in relation to it, including a 'description of its principal business activity' and a summary of 'the material provisions of the contract between the company and the depositary which may be relevant to shareholders'.

51.43 Payments made to the scheme manager out of scheme property must also be set out—whether such payments are in the capacity of scheme manager or otherwise and whether by way of remuneration for services or otherwise. The information is required to include the method for calculating the scheme manager's remuneration, when it will be paid, whether or not unitholders are notified of each such payment, and whether or not unitholders are notified of any change in the calculation of such payment. Other payments from the scheme property relating to the company's liability to reimburse any director other than the scheme manager, the trustee, or any third party, or to remunerate any third party, or payment of charges and expenses generally, must be set out in the prospectus. Such information as to other payments must also cover payments in respect of movable and immovable property, whether the company intends to have any interest in any immovable property occupied by it (or tangible, movable property used by it), and the amount of any costs to be amortized.

51.44 Similarly, information must be provided in relation to the trustee, in relation to the investment adviser retained in connection with the business of the open-ended investment company, and in relation to the auditor. In relation to the accounting and valuation policies of the fund, the prospectus must give the potential investors, and current investors, information as to amortization, as to the sale and redemption of shares, as to the valuation of scheme property, as to the dilution levy, and as to any charges in relation to the fund. In respect of the sale and redemption of shares, information must be given as to the times at which and procedure by which sale and redemption may take place, and as to restrictions on the issue and redemption of shares by the scheme manager. Further the prospectus must specify the dates and methods for the calculation of distributable income. Information must also be provided in relation to preliminary charges, and redemption charges. Information must be provided as to the arrangements for marketing in another member state where such sale and marketing is to take place.

52

INVESTMENT OF PRIVATE
EXPRESS TRUSTS

A. The Use of Trusts as Investment Vehicles

The scope of this chapter

52.01 This chapter considers trusts structures which are used as investment vehicles but which do not fall into any of those categories of trust which have their own regulatory codes like unit trusts,[1] trustees in debt securities transactions,[2] charitable purpose trusts, and occupational pension fund trusts.[3] The discussion of the investment of private trusts in this chapter is divided into three main parts: the provisions of the Trustee Act 2000, the role of express investment powers in trust deeds, and the impact of decided cases on the nature of those investment obligations. This discussion amplifies that set out in Chapter 10[4] which considered those principles only in outline terms within the context of the trustees' general duties and obligations. The purpose of this analysis, then, is to consider the context of investment powers and obligations in relation to express, private trusts in greater detail.

The utility of private trusts for investment purposes

52.02 The principal attraction of a trust for investment purposes has always been the possibility of pooling investment capital from a number of different sources, this was particularly so in that period of time between the outlawing of companies in the wake of the South Sea Bubble in 1720 and the passage of the Limited Liability Act in 1844. The trust, then, offered the most convenient means of collecting investment capital together and gave rise to the joint stock company: itself a combination of trusts law principles and principles of partnership law.[5] In other, non-commercial contexts, the trust offered the possibility for a single settlor to provide for the maintenance of a range of potential beneficiaries within his household or his extended family. In either case, the trust allowed the settlor or the investors to appoint professionals or trusted persons to act on their behalf in the investment and the stewardship of their property. The possibility both of the responsibilities borne by the trustees and the countervailing beneficial rights of the beneficiaries, where those beneficiaries might also have subtly different rights one from another,

---

[1] See the discussion in Chapter 51.   [2] See the discussion in Chapter 50.
[3] See the discussion in Part H of this book as to the obligations of trustees of occupational pension funds.
[4] See the discussion at para 10.58.
[5] See the context of the litigation in *Smith v Anderson* (1880) Ch D 247, considered by AS Hudson, *The Law on Investment Entities* (Sweet & Maxwell, 2000) 108. The property attributed to a joint stock company—itself originally a company of persons who contributed stock to a venture seeking to trade that stock overseas—was held on trust by the managers of the company for the members of the company; in turn those members were partners in the business of the company. It was only latterly that companies acquired their own legal personality: *Saloman v A Saloman & Co Ltd* [1897] AC 22.

offered settlors enormous freedom to shape their investment activities and their ulterior purposes.

B. Trustees as Authorized Persons Under FSMA 2000

The treatment of the trustee as a person requiring authorization under the **52.03**
Financial Services and Markets Act 2000 has already been considered in detail.[6]
The reader is referred to the discussion of this issue in Chapter 47.

C. Introduction to the Principles of the Trustee Act 2000

An introduction to trustees' investment obligations in the wake of the Trustee Act 2000

The underlying aim of the Trustee Act 2000 was to provide trustees with the same **52.04**
powers to invest property held on trust as the absolute owner of that property
would have had. Whereas the previous statutory regime dealing with the investment of trust funds, in the shape of the Trustee Investment Act 1961, had required
a risk averse treatment of the trust fund which greatly limited the ability of trustees
to manage the fund in the best financial interests of the beneficiaries, the Trustee
Act 2000 took a more modern approach to investment management. This modern approach recognized that trustees would be required to take risk in making
investment on behalf of the beneficiaries. What was considered important was
that the trustees both take appropriate professional advice and also that they frame
investment criteria in advance of making any investments: these principles are
considered below. In consequence, the Trustee Act 2000 enables trustees to make
a broader range of investment than had been permitted before but it also requires
trustees to have considered their investment choices carefully in advance. In the
event that the trustees' investment decisions should cause the beneficiaries loss,
the statute provides that trustees owe a duty of care in relation to any exercise of a
power of investment which has not been excluded by the trust instrument. The
effect of this duty of care is that the trustee owes a tortious duty to the beneficiaries
in the event of any investment decision made by the trustee causing loss to the
beneficiaries. Therefore, the permissiveness of the power to make investments is
counterbalanced by the creation of a duty of care over trustees.

The Trustee Act 2000 creates a statutory code for the investment powers and **52.05**
obligations of trustees which may nevertheless be excluded by express provision in
the trust instrument.[7] This is also true of the Trustee Act 1925 which makes more

---

[6] See the discussion at para 47.02.
[7] See para 47.02 in relation to the Financial Services and Markets Act 2000, Sch 1, para 7 and
other provisions referred to in the text to follow.

general provision with regard to the powers and duties of trustees. In consequence, the legislation is merely a means of supplementing the provisions of trust instruments but does not establish mandatory rules which all trustees will be required to observe in all situations. The decided cases on the obligations of trustees when investing trust property have also developed the manner in which the trustees' standards and duties of care are to be understood.

The meaning of 'trustee' in this context

52.06   The Trustee Act 2000 contains no definition of the term 'trustee'. Consequently, it is not clear whether or not it is to apply only to properly appointed trustees of express trusts or whether it refers also to constructive trustees, trustees of resulting trusts, or trustees of implied trusts like that in *Paul v Constance*.[8] The common feature between all those latter forms of trust being that the trustees would not know of their trusteeship until the court order which confirms it. Therefore, it is possible that there are trustees who do not know of their obligations and who are in breach of the positive obligations in the Trustee Act 2000 which apply in the absence of any clause in the trust instrument excluding the operation of that Act—such as to produce a policy statement for the investment of trust funds and so forth.[9] The structure of the Trustee Act 2000, and its references to exclusion of liability in the trust instrument, indicate that the legislative draftsperson was focused on express trusts formed by way of an instrument.[10] Paragraph 7 of Schedule 2 to the 2000 Act provides that the general duty of care owed by trustees when making investments on behalf of the trust, as considered below,[11] does not apply if it appears from the trust instrument that that duty of care is not meant to apply. While that provision is of significance in relation to express trusts, it gives little assistance in relation to constructive or implied trusts.

52.07   The difficulty with imposing the duties required by the Trustee Act 2000 on constructive trustees[12] is that such trustees might not know until the court order confirming their holding of such an office that they are indeed constructive trustees. Consequently, it is unlikely that such a person would have either prepared the required strategy for the investment of the trust property or even have done anything more with the trust fund than hold it intact as though for

---

[8] [1977] 1 WLR 527; that is, a trust which the court accepts as being an express trust even though neither the settlor, trustee, nor beneficiaries realized that a trust had been unconsciously created.

[9] Trustee Act 2000, s 4.

[10] eg ibid, ss 9, 22; Sch 1, para 7: all of which make reference to existing trust instruments or provisions.

[11] See the discussion at para 52.15.

[12] For this purpose, the term constructive trustee refers to trustees of constructive, resulting, or implied trusts: in any event, any person who is construed or implied to be a trustee, rather than one who has been properly appointed trustee of an express trust.

safekeeping. It could be said that constructive trustees' obligations as a constructive trustee arise as a result of their renewal of pre-existing duties as a trustee over property: an example of such a person would be the trustee in *Keech v Sandford*[13] who had been a trustee of a lease but who was found to be a constructive trustee of a replacement lease which was acquired when the original lease expired. In such a situation there would appear to be little prejudice in requiring the trustee to observe the fiduciary obligations which had been incumbent upon him in his previous role as express trustee. However, in other contexts it would seem that in relation to a person who cannot know until the court order declares him to be a constructive trustee that the imposition of positive duties of trusteeship would cause him prejudice. For example, a person who is taken to have acted unconscionably in relation to property might not be expected to comply with the duty to review the investments which the trust holds under the Trustee Act 2000, even though passive duties not to dispose of the property or turn it to his personal account could be enforced without prejudice to him (given the finding of unconscionable acquisition of the property at the outset). Nevertheless, there are circumstances in which trustees de son tort, as constructive trustees, are deemed to be subject to the duties of express trusts as a result of their activities intermeddling with the management of an express trust.[14] The imposition of the obligations under the Trustee Act 2000 would seem to stem from the fact that the trustee de son tort has effectively assumed the role of an express trustee and therefore might reasonably be obliged to comply with the duties of someone who was in fact an express trustee.

Repeal of the Trustee Investment Act 1961

In creating a general power of investment, the Trustee Act 2000 also provides that that power is both in addition to anything set out in the trust instrument but also capable of being excluded by any such trust instrument.[15] Therefore, the settlor could preclude the trustees from making particular forms of investment. In contradistinction to the 1961 code, this means that the trustee is presumed to be free to make any suitable investments in the absence of any express provision to the contrary, whereas the trustee was previously presumed to be capable only of making a limited range of investments in the absence of any provision to the contrary. The code created by the 1961 Act is now replaced by the Trustee Act 2000 in this regard.[16]

52.08

---

[13] (1726) Sel Cas Ch 61.
[14] *Taylor v Davies* [1920] AC 636; *Selangor United Rubber Estates Ltd v Cradock (No 3)* [1968] 1 WLR 1555; *Citadel General Assurance Co v Lloyds Bank Canada* (1997) 152 DLR (4th) 411; *Paragon Finance plc v DB Thackerar & Co* [1999] 1 All ER 4000.
[15] Trustee Act 2000, s 6(1).   [16] ibid, s 7(3).

D. The General Power of Investment

The scope of the general power of investment

52.09   The general power of investment[17] provides:[18]

> Subject to the provisions of this Part, a trustee may make any kind of investment that he could make if he were absolutely entitled to the assets of the trust.

Therefore, in relation to trusts to which this provision applies, the trustee is not constrained as to the investments which are made by reason only of his trustee-ship.[19] Rather, the trustee is treated as though the absolute owner of the property and consequently as someone able to make investments on that basis. As is considered below,[20] this provision will not apply to trusts which exclude its operation either expressly or by implication. Nor will this provision apply to occupational pension fund trusts nor to unit trusts. Furthermore, the trustee is not permitted to invest in land,[21] except in the ways identified explicitly in the Act[22] or in loans secured on land.[23] The particular context of investment in land is considered later in this chapter.[24]

52.10   The application of the whole Act, and with it the general investment power, has limited application. In effect, the operation of the Act is subject to any express provisions of any trust instrument, including provisions excluding the operation of the Act. Section 6(1) of the Trustee Act 2000 provides that the general investment power is:

(a) in addition to powers conferred on trustees otherwise than by [the Act], but

(b) subject to any restriction or exclusion imposed by the trust instrument or by any enactment or any provision of subordinate legislation.[25]

Thus the Act supplements trusts which have no express trust investment powers. This may be so whether the terms of the trust in question have no investment powers at all or whether the terms of the trust contain investment powers which are limited. In circumstances in which the trust instrument contains trust investment powers which conflict in some way with the terms of section 6(1), then the

---

[17] The name given to it by Trustee Act 2000, s 3(2).   [18] Trustee Act 2000, s 3(1).

[19] This is in contrast to older authorities which interpreted general powers of investment restrictively, often limited to powers to acquire securities open to trustees with special powers: *Cock v Goodfellow* (1722) 10 Mod 489; *Bethell v Abraham* (1873) LR 17 Eq 24; *Re Braithwaite* (1882) 21 Ch D 121. However, later authorities did occasionally take more permissive approaches: *Re Smith* [1896] 1 Ch 71; *Re McEachern's Settlement Trusts* [1939] Ch 858; *Re Harari's Settlement Trusts* [1949] WN 79.

[20] See the discussion at para 52.91.   [21] Trustee Act 2000, s 3(3).

[22] Trustee Act 2000, s 8.

[23] Trustee Act 2000, s 3(4), by which is meant any rights under contract which provides a person with credit and whereby the borrower's obligation is secured on the land.

[24] See para 52.66.   [25] Trustee Act 2000, s 6(1).

terms of the trust instrument take priority.[26] Significantly, this would permit the express terms of a trust to exclude the general power of investment and the standard investment criteria provisions. The term 'trust instrument' is not defined in the Act. It would naturally cover any deed of trust or document giving effect to the trust. What would be more difficult would be an orally declared trust in which the settlor's expression of the trust suggested an exclusion of the terms of the trust. Whereas such a conflict would not fall within the literal terms of section 6(1), the underlying principle of that provision would suggest that the settlor's intentions are to be effected and that the Act is to be considered to supply investment terms where otherwise there are none. A decisive factor might be whether or not there was any evidential doubt as to the settlor's intentions: the requirement for an instrument in section 6(1) has the advantage of operating only in circumstances in which the settlor's intention will be evident from the terms of the trust instrument. The trust instrument may impose restrictions on the trustees' powers to make investments and, beyond that, financial regulation may in effect preclude certain types of investment by persons who are considered to be insufficiently expert to make them.[27] There remain restrictions on the power of trustees to make investments in land unless by way of loans secured on land (such as mortgages).[28]

The meaning of 'investment'

The term 'investment' is not defined for the purposes of section 3 of the Trustee Act 2000. Its meaning in the general law of trusts has transformed from simply a consideration of income yield,[29] into a broader notion of the enhancement of capital value in parallel with income increase,[30] and also into the desirability of the diversity of investment risk by means of portfolio investment strategies.[31] The combination of income and capital gain requires that trustees seek the highest available return whether that is in the form of capital or income growth. During a steeply rising housing market and a weak share market, a focus on the capital growth in real property investments has been accepted as being a reasonable investment strategy for trustees.[32] The growing acceptance of portfolio investment strategies is considered below:[33] briefly put, in common with the combined strategy of seeking the highest available return in the form of capital and income

52.11

---

[26] No trust power created before 3 August 1961 is capable of restricting or excluding the general power of investment: Trustee Act 2000, s 7(2).

[27] Financial Services and Markets Act 2000.

[28] Trustee Act 2000, s 3(3).

[29] *Re Somerset* [1894] 1 Ch 231, 247; *Re Wragg* [1919] 2 Ch 58, 65.

[30] *Cowan v Scargill* [1985] Ch 270, 287; *Harries v Church Commissioners* [1992] 1 WLR 1241, 1246.

[31] See discussion below at para 52.38.

[32] *Harries v Church Commissioners* [1992] 1 WLR 1241, 1246; Lord Nicholls (1995) 14 Trusts Law Int 75, 83.

[33] See discussion at para 52.38.

growth,[34] portfolio investment strategies require that the trustees spread the trust's investments across a range of markets and differing investments so that the risk of a loss in any individual market will be absorbed by the investments in other markets.

52.12 The Financial Services and Markets Act 2000 ('FSMA 2000') defines 'investment' in more categorical terms. The meaning which that statute gives to that term is by means of a list of broadly defined market activities set out in Schedule 2 to that Act.[35] That list includes: securities in the form of shares or debt securities in companies, government, and public securities, warrants and other instruments entitling their holder to subscribe for investments, certificates representing securities, units in collective investment schemes, options to buy or to sell property, futures contracts, contracts for differences, contracts of insurance or participation in Lloyd's syndicates, deposits in relation to which any sum of money is paid on terms that money shall be repaid, loans secured on land, or any right in an investment.[36] The expansion of trustees' investment powers signalled by the Trustee Act 2000 makes no explicit reference to the enactment of FSMA 2000 even though that latter statute has effected wide-ranging change in the substantive law and regulation of financial services in the UK.[37] Nevertheless, that both of those statutes were enacted in the same year by the same administration and, given that trustees will be regulated by the Financial Services Authority ('FSA') under FSMA 2000, it is reasonable to suggest that those categories of investment falling within FSMA 2000 should inform the range of investments in which trustees are now permitted to invest with their enhanced capabilities.

52.13 Whereas the existing case law on trust investment has indicated that the courts are not eager to support trust investment while increasing the ratio of debt to other investments incurred by the trustees to facilitate increased investment,[38] it is suggested that where the trustees are regulated by the FSA on the basis that they are providing investment services to the trust[39] then it should be accepted that trustees will consider participation in the complete range of investment activities which are ordinarily envisaged by market professionals. This would include complex investments such as contracts for differences (such as financial derivatives) and potentially highly geared transactions, provided always that they are acquired in accordance with the conduct of business regulations produced by the FSA. The development by the courts of the legal principles relating to investment by

---

[34] *Cook v Medway Housing Society* [1997] STC 90, 98, *per* Lightman J.
[35] Financial Services and Markets Act 2000, s 22.
[36] Financial Services and Markets Act 2000, Sch 2, Pt II.
[37] See the discussion in Chapter 47.
[38] *Re Svenson-Taylor's Settlement* [1974] 1 WLR 1280, [1974] 3 All ER 397.
[39] Or, that non-professional trustees are taking advice from such FSA regulated persons as required by the Trustee Act 2000, s 5.

trustees, a term which appears to have been left deliberately at large in the drafting of the legislation, will require the courts to take a stance on the question whether they should continue the avowedly conservative approach of the old case law or whether they should dilute their policy of protecting beneficiaries in accepting that once the risk appetite of a trust has been suitably categorized by any FSA regulated service provider acting as trustee then the trust falls to be considered in exactly the same manner as any other investment transaction under FSMA 2000.

As considered in Chapter 47, an investment in securities necessarily combines the capital acquisition cost of the investment as well as an expectation that that security will generate an income stream (for example, the coupon payment on bonds or the dividend paid on shares). Investment should be taken to include capital and income components. This is true of investment in real property even if that property is intended to be leased so as to generate a rental income stream, the acquisition of valuable works of art, and so on. In each of these contexts there is a combination of capital outlay, expectation of income generation, and a hope of an increase in capital value. In consequence, the rigid distinction between income and capital which was a feature of the nineteenth-century cases on trust investment[40] does not mirror investment practice in a range of assets typically acquired by trustees in the modern market place. **52.14**

E. The Trustee's Standard of Care When Making Investments

The statutory duty of care

The duty to provide reasonable skill and care relative to context

The Trustee Act 2000 provides for a statutory duty of care which imposes a duty of 'such skill and care as is reasonable in the circumstances'.[41] The wording of that obligation is sensitive to context and provides for a level of subjectivity in framing its precise nature, by reference to the circumstances of the trust, of the trustee, and of the investment power at issue. Section 1 of the Act provides: **52.15**

(1) Whenever the duty under this subsection applies to a trustee, he must exercise such care and skill as is reasonable in the circumstances, having regard in particular—

   (a) to any special knowledge or experience that he has or holds himself out as having, and

   (b) if he acts as trustee in the course of a business or profession, to any special knowledge or experience that it is reasonable to expect of a person acting in the course of that kind of business or profession.

(2) In this Act the duty under subsection (1) is called 'the duty of care'.

---

[40] See, for example, *Re Somerset* [1894] 1 Ch 231, 247.   [41] Trustee Act 2000, s 1(1).

The governing adjective which qualifies the care which must be exercised by the trustee is 'reasonable'. The inclusion of this adjective ensures a great potential scope for the development of the duties of trustees; whereas the word 'prudent' used in the case law since the nineteenth century[42] suggested that caution was at a premium compared to other concerns. The underlying purpose of the Trustee Act 2000 is to liberate trustees from the overriding objective to be prudent in their investment activities above all else. Trustees may be expected to seek to generate greater profit for the trust now that they are imbued with a general investment power[43] and now that trustees providing investment advice as part of a business are regulated by the FSA.[44] With the increased participation of many ordinary citizens in financial market activity directly through share acquisitions in public limited companies, or indirectly through participation in unit trusts or occupational pension funds, it may be thought that the culture in which trustees are investing would also require a transformation in the standard expected of trustees when exercising their investment powers from caution to an assumption of investment risk commensurate with the nature of the trust which they are administering. It is to that end that the narrow formalism of the Trustee Investment Act 1961 was replaced by the trustees' general investment power under the Trustee Act 2000 together with its attendant safeguards in the form of the standard investment criteria and the duty to take advice, considered in the previous section of this chapter.

52.16 In the new regime it is of central significance that the nature of the duty of care[45] is relative to the context in which the trustee is acting. Financial services regulation, as considered above, concerns itself with the context of any investment relationship by requiring the service provider (for present purposes that is the trustee) to evaluate and to categorize the level of expertise of the client, and then to deal in a suitable manner with that client, selling him only financial instruments which are suitable for his purposes. The other sense in which the context is important, however, is in relation to the trustee's own level of experience. There is a significant distinction between a trustee who is an investment professional retained by the settlor precisely because of his expertise and who is subject to a formal conduct of business agreement, and a trustee who agrees to act as a trustee perhaps as a personal favour to the settlor without professing to have or indeed actually having any expertise in investment business whatsoever. The Trustee Act 2000 provides that where the trustee has, or holds himself out as having, any particular 'special knowledge or experience' then the standard of care expected of that trustee will be higher in the

---

42 *Learoyd v Whiteley* (1887) 12 App Cas 727.
43 Unless that power has been expressly excluded by the trust instrument: Trustee Act 2000, s 6.
44 See the discussion at para 52.03 above and at para 47.02 *et seq* more generally.
45 Trustee Act 2000, s 1(2).

light of those factors.[46] Furthermore, if the duties of trustee are performed 'in the course of a business or profession' then the standard of care expected from him will similarly be higher than would otherwise have been the case.[47]

The possible meanings of 'reasonable' care

The sense of the term 'reasonable' therefore becomes very significant. Whereas we can recognize the distinction between a professional and a non-professional trustee, that tells us nothing about the categories in between those two poles of being either an expert or an innocent, nor does it tell us how the obligations borne by those two extreme examples of trustees are to be framed. **52.17**

The most significant form of trustee in relation to investment powers will be the professional trustee who is retained to act as trustee precisely because he is a professional. It is precisely such trustees, ironically, who will not be covered by the Trustee Act 2000 because they will generally agree to act as trustees only if the trust instrument specifies their powers, their obligations, and the precise manner in which their fees will be calculated. Such trustees will also tend to act as market makers when selling securities to the trust—by which is meant that those trustees will insist on being able to sell investments which they already own to the trust without facing liability for making secret profits or for permitting a conflict of interest[48]—and therefore they will wish to exclude the operation of the general law of trusts in that sense. Nevertheless, suppose that such a trustee fell within the provisions of the Trustee Act 2000. It would be appropriate to ascertain the standard of his obligations by reference to standard market practice and by reference to standard market regulation. Thus, in cases such as *Bankers Trust v Dharmala*,[49] when searching for the appropriate measurement of the obligations of an expert financial services provider selling complex interest rate swaps to a comparatively inexpert counterparty for the purposes of undue influence, negligent misrepresentation, and fraud, the High Court has looked to the relevant regulatory rulebook for an expression of the principles by which the behaviour of such a service provider ought to be judged.[50] It is suggested therefore that an appropriate, objective measurement of the obligations of such professional trustees would be the provisions of the FSA's rulebook on conduct of business.[51] That rulebook expresses the manner in which such organizations and their employees are expected to behave, on penalty of sanction by the FSA, and therefore the appropriate rulebook constitutes a code of principles by which both professional trustee and beneficiary can expect the trustee reasonably to be judged. **52.18**

---

[46] ibid, s 1(1)(a).   [47] ibid, s 1(1)(b).   [48] *Boardman v Phipps* [1967] 2 AC 46.
[49] *Bankers Trust v Dharmala* [1996] CLC 518.
[50] For a discussion of this particular case and for this issue more generally, see AS Hudson, *The Law on Financial Derivatives* (3rd edn, Sweet & Maxwell, 2002) 276.
[51] See the discussion of this rulebook at para 47.26.

52.19 A difficult intermediary category of trustee would be an individual who is a professional investment manager but who agrees to act as a trustee in a personal capacity. In such a situation it could be argued that the individual is not acting in the course of a business and accordingly might not fall to be regulated by the FSA in that capacity. Nevertheless, in such a situation it would appear that the settlor would be relying on that person's expertise of investment management and that the trustee himself ought to be aware both of the settlor's reliance on his professionalism and of the risks associated with the assumption of such a role without professional indemnity insurance, a conduct of business agreement limiting his liability, and so forth. Therefore, it would seem reasonable to measure that individual by reference to the requirements of the FSA rulebooks and standard, financial market practice.

52.20 It is by reference to non-professional trustees that the most difficult problems arise. Two conflicting points of principle collide at this juncture. The first concerns the level of expectation expressed by the settlor and by the beneficiaries, and the reasonableness of their reliance on the particular trustee; the second is the protection of the trustee in relation to liabilities which he may not have understood he was assuming or which he may not have considered himself sufficiently skilled to assume. Suppose the trustee is selected by the settlor because he is both a relative or family friend and also because he is respected for his business acumen and success. In that situation, the trustee may well appreciate the reliance which is being placed on him and so be said to assume a comparatively high standard of care to match that expectation. Whereas there might not be such an expectation nor any such reliance in relation to a trustee who is invited to act, for example, as trustee of a will trust solely because he is a relative, because he is considered to be honest, and because there are few other family members of sufficient maturity to take on the role. Where this latter trustee was known to the family to have had no experience of investments at all, not even any on his own account, then it would not be reasonable to suppose that they expected any particularly high standard of care from him, nor that he undertook any such duty of care.

52.21 The difficult question for the courts will be whether they choose to measure reasonableness by reference to the need to compensate the beneficiary for any loss occasioned by the trustee's action or omission, or whether the courts choose to measure reasonableness by reference to the justice of holding the individual trustee only to obligations which he assumed voluntarily and in full cognizance of their ramifications. Orientating the notion of reasonableness around the beneficiaries' need for protection would mean that trustees could be found liable in circumstances in which they failed to take proper cognizance of any professional advice or where their ignorance of the Trustee Act 2000 itself caused them to make unfortunate decisions on their own initiative. The non-professional trustee is more likely to be held liable in the operation of such a principle which aims to compensate the beneficiary. If the operating principle were, instead, the level of the trustee's voluntary assumption of liability, then that might accord more closely with the central principle of trusts law that the trust operates on the conscience of the trustee: thus, where a trustee has not assumed an obligation voluntarily and in full cognizance of its meaning, then it would not be out of bad conscience that that trustee had exercised his investment powers improperly. Therefore, the likelihood of the trustee being found liable would clearly be reduced and the principle of good conscience would be maintained.

The next section considers the case law decided before the Trustee Act 2000 on the trustee's standard of care when exercising investment powers and considers its interaction with the statutory code.

The requirement that trustees effect investment as though a 'reasonable man of business'

Before the introduction of the statutory duty of care by the Trustee Act 2000, **52.22** trustees were required to exercise their investment powers as though investing as a prudent person of business investing on behalf of someone for whom they felt morally bound to provide. The statutory duty of care under the Trustee Act 2000 suggests that that obligation ought now to be considered to be an obligation to act as a reasonable person would act in the context. The effect of the Trustee Act on the standard of care owed by trustees in exercising investment powers may be significant as a result. In this section we shall consider the obligation to act prudently under the case law and then contrast that with the statutory duty of care.

The trustee's duty to act prudently and safely under the case law

In contrast to the statutory duty to act with reasonable care in the subjective **52.23** context of one's special knowledge and experience, the case law advanced a more objective standard orientated around the need to take caution, to protect the trust fund, and (latterly) to act in accordance with market practice. That obligation was more evidently in common with the more general duties of trusteeship incumbent on a trustee. The trustee's general duties of investment under the case law can be summarized in the following three core principles: the duty to act prudently and safely;[52] the duty to act fairly between beneficiaries;[53] and the duty to do the best for the beneficiaries financially.[54] The first of these three relates specifically to the decision as to investment whereas the other two are concerned more generally with the trustee's fiduciary duty to avoid conflict by acting loyally in the interests of all of the beneficiaries.

---

[52] *Learoyd v Whiteley* (1887) 12 App Cas 727.   [53] *Bartlett v Barclays Bank* [1980] Ch 515.
[54] *Cowan v Scargill* [1984] 3 WLR 501.

52.24 In the decided cases there was always a latent conflict between these principles. The principal assumption was that acting prudently in the selection of investments required a cautious approach preferred by nineteenth-century courts whereas the beneficiaries' own, more mercenary concerns might have been to realize as high a level of income return as possible. So, in *Learoyd v Whiteley*[55] it was held that the trustee must both act as a businessman of ordinary prudence while also avoiding all hazardous investments. Necessarily this would lead to a cautious investment policy whereby the trustee would eschew profitable investments if they presented a substantive amount of risk. It is a truism of modern financial theory that all investment necessarily involves some level of risk.[56] The business of investment management is therefore to measure the level of return achieved against the client's risk appetite and also against the return that that level of risk generates. It is usually expected that the greater the risk that is taken, the higher the return will be. In consequence, it is impossible for the trustees to make financial market investments which are completely risk-free: only investments which have a greater or lesser risk profile. A trustee who was concerned to act with the utmost prudence would be required to invest in leasing real property or in bank account deposits to minimize the level of risk: and even those forms of investment can never be entirely without risk.

52.25 In consequence, the old case law approach established in *Learoyd v Whiteley*[57] was modified in *Bartlett v Barclays Bank*,[58] in which a distinction was drawn between a prudent degree of risk and something which amounted to 'hazard'. The former, prudently taken risk, would be acceptable, whereas to put the trust fund in hazard would be unacceptable. The irony behind this search for the perfect conceptualization of the trustee's investment obligations is that it will only be possible to know whether or not an investment is a good one when it has expired: until then, all is speculation. Furthermore, the trustees were required to take advice where necessary. As this concept was put by Megarry V-C, the trustees are required to:

> take such care as an ordinary prudent man would take if he were minded to make an investment for the benefit of other people for whom he feels morally bound to provide. This duty includes the duty to seek advice on matters which the trustee does not understand, such as the making of investments, and, on receiving that advice, to act with the same degree of prudence. Although a trustee who takes advice on investments is not bound to accept and act on that advice, he is not entitled to reject it merely because he sincerely disagrees with it, unless in addition he is acting as an ordinary prudent man would act.[59]

The approach taken here is that the trustees are to focus primarily on the protection and maintenance of the trust fund, while also allowing it to grow steadily. The

---

[55] (1887) 12 App Cas 727.   [56] Lord Nicholls (1995) 9 Trusts Law Int 71.
[57] (1887) 12 App Cas 727.   [58] [1980] Ch 515.   [59] [1985] Ch 270, 289.

modern expectation of perpetual growth in investments, which has shored up the market in personal pensions and the UK housing market, suggests a contrary expectation: one that is considered in the following section.

The availability of equitable compensation for the trustees' failure to match a market return on the investment of the trust fund

Thus far we have supposed that the beneficiaries are seeking to recover some loss **52.26** occasioned by the trustees' breach of trust or their negligence. However, it may be that the beneficiaries are not complaining that they have suffered a loss. Rather, they may be complaining that, while the trustees may have generated a profit, the profit is nevertheless too small. This particular line of attack was taken in *Nestle v National Westminster Bank*[60] in which the beneficiaries argued not that the trustees had lost them money, but rather that the trustees' surfeit of caution had caused a much reduced return on their capital than average market investment would have realized. The beneficiaries adduced evidence that the average return in the financial markets was much greater over the period for which the trustees had been acting for the trust than the trustees had realized for the beneficiaries. The argument raised by the trustees was that they were acting not as ordinary investment managers but rather as trustees for a long-standing family trust who had conducted the trust's affairs in the manner in which all the professional trustees of similar funds had conducted the affairs of those trusts: that is to say, they had invested cautiously and for the long term, and not for potentially hazardous, short-term gain. Hoffmann J held that the trustees were entitled to have their actions measured in accordance with current portfolio theory: the theory that their investment risk be spread broadly. Furthermore, they were entitled to have their actions compared with other market professionals. On the basis that the trustees had spread the investments and invested in the same manner as other market professionals, they were held not to have breached their duties. In this manner the objectivity of the case law is fixed by reference to the activities or opinions not of any one trustee but rather by reference to the practice of the market.

It has been suggested that a failure to diversify a holding of government bonds into **52.27** shares would itself be a breach of trust which would open the trustees up to liability to pay equitable compensation to the beneficiaries.[61] Identifying the level of compensation payable would be a difficult matter.[62] It has been suggested that one might look to the average return which would have been obtained by a reasonable investment professional over the same period of time.[63] In relation to *Nestle v*

---

[60] [2000] WTLR 795.
[61] *Guerin v The Queen* [1984] 2 SCR 335, (1984) 13 DLR (4th) 321; cited with approval in *Nestle v National Westminster Bank plc* [1993] 1 WLR 1260, 1268, *per* Dillon LJ.
[62] See para 32.18.
[63] *Nestle v National Westminster Bank plc* [1993] 1 WLR 1260, 1268, *per* Dillon LJ and 1280, *per* Staughton LJ.

National Westminster Bank plc itself, the evidence suggested that this process of measuring the trustees against the average market performance would not, however, be an entirely objective matter: rather, the court would look to other trustees investing on behalf of a similar type of risk averse, family trust rather than taking as a comparator the entire equities market. It is suggested that such a process then becomes entirely circular. In deciding the question 'what sort of investment professionals should be taken as a comparator for the trustees in this instance?' the court will necessarily be asking the same general question 'is the investment performance of these trustees to be measured against the market generally or against a risk averse, specialist investment community which would have performed as weakly as this particular trust?' It is the general question which needs to be addressed first because the more specific question is dependent upon it.[64]

52.28   It has been held[65] that in relation to a particular trust a market professional ought to have diversified 40 per cent of the trust fund into the equities market and therefore that the trustees' failure to do so would make them liable to compensate the beneficiaries in an amount equal to the difference between 40 per cent of the fund's actual profits and the equities market return on 40 per cent of the value of the fund over the same time period. To meet the suggestion that the trust in that instance was too small, the court took the view that the average market return should be discounted by 25 per cent on the basis that such a small fund, even if invested in equities, could not have generated the average market return.[66] It is suggested, however, that over-reliance on straightforward, mathematical approaches would not deal adequately with the question as to the appropriate comparator for any given set of trustees bearing particular investment obligations with reference to a particular trust fund.

52.29   A more appropriate approach would be to break the test down into two questions. The first question is to consider what form of investment strategy the trustees should have adopted when compared to funds of a similar size and nature. The second further question then requires a mathematical measurement of the return which would have been generated by a reasonable fund of the type identified in

---

[64] The further point mentioned in *Nestle v National Westminster Bank plc* is that if the trustees choose investments which lose money from a selection of investment possibilities of which other possibilities would have made gains, the trustees will not be liable for a breach of trust provided that their investment decisions were reasonable in the context. The alternative view was advanced in *Robinson v Robinson* (1851) 1 De GM & G 247 to the effect that trustees could be liable for breach of trust if they selected the wrong investments. It is suggested that this goes too far and means that trustees could, in effect, become liable for breach of trust in any circumstance in which their investment choices lead to a loss without the trustees having acted negligently or inappropriately. It would replace a fault-based liability with a nearly strict liability.

[65] *Re Mulligan* [1998] NZLR 481.

[66] There are funds available in the market place now which mimic the return which would be earned on a given market index regardless of the size of the investment.

answer to the first question. The first question ensures that the trustees' investment decisions are being evaluated according to the nature of their trust before any finding of a breach of duty is made against them.

However, if the first question were taken to be whether or not the trustees measured up to an average return on investment, then it can be supposed that something approaching half of the participants[67] in the market place will necessarily appear to have failed to generate an average market return (that is because an average will generally be greater than half the sample and less than the other half of the sample) and so be potentially liable to their customers for breach of some duty of competence. A test which prioritizes mathematical matters over matters of strategy and context, as in this first question, will necessarily increase the incidence of liability for trustees and so encourage those trustees always to invest more adventurously so as to generate a return on capital which will place them in the top half of the market place's league table. This, it is suggested, would be contrary to the prudence which is typically expected from trustees, in balance with any duty to achieve a good return. In the first part, the question of size indicates the number of investments which could be compiled into a portfolio and also how diverse those investments could be, given that a large fund permits more investments to be acquired than a small fund; and the nature of the investment strategy covers matters such as the level of risk inherent in the investments, whether the investors wish to invest for long- or short-term return, and how risk averse are the investors. The second part, informed by the first, gives a better approximation, it is suggested, of the mean return of participants in the circumstances of the trustees at issue.

As a matter of general observation, trustees will not tend to be held liable for **52.30** failure to exercise their investment powers properly if they can demonstrate that they acted in accordance with market practice or as other market professionals would have done in their situation.[68] Trustees will be held liable for causing loss by contravening an express trust provision limiting their investment powers if that investment causes a loss to the beneficiaries,[69] or if they can be shown to have been negligent, dishonest, or fraudulent in their exercise of their investment powers.[70]

The duty to act fairly between beneficiaries

The trustee bears a range of fiduciary obligations of loyalty to all of the **52.31** beneficiaries.[71] Unlike unit trusts or occupational pension fund trusts in which

---

[67] That is, broadly, excluding the possibility of any particularly large successes or failures disturbing the statistical likelihood that the average performance will be equivalent to the performance of those actors in the middle of the sample's league table.

[68] *Nestle v National Westminster Bank plc* [2000] WTLR 795.

[69] *Target Holdings v Redferns* [1996] 1 AC 421, [1995] 3 WLR 352, [1995] 3 All ER 785.

[70] See the discussion of *Walker v Stones* [2001] QB 902, [2000] 4 All ER 412 in para 21.24.

[71] See the discussion at para 21.15.

the beneficiaries have broadly similar interests in the generation of steady income over a long period of time, in other forms of trust there are likely to be different classes of beneficiaries with interests which are at odds one with another. So, as Megarry V-C held:

> It is the duty of trustees to exercise their powers in the best interest of the present and future beneficiaries of the trust, holding the scales impartially between the different classes of beneficiaries.[72]

By way of illustration, in *Nestle v National Westminster Bank*[73] the court held that the trustees were entitled to invest cautiously in a way which would not simply generate high levels of income but which would also maintain the fund's capital. This distinction between the life tenant and the remainderman is the classic example of the different objectives of beneficiaries with different interest. Given the competing interests of different classes of beneficiaries, in *Nestle v National Westminster Bank* Hoffmann J held that:

> A trustee must act fairly in making investment decisions which may have different consequences for differing classes of beneficiaries ... The trustees have a wide discretion. They are, for example, entitled to take into account the income needs of the tenant for life or the fact that the tenant for life was a person known to the settlor and a primary object of the trust whereas the remainderman is a remoter relative or stranger. Of course, these cannot be allowed to become the overriding considerations but the concept of fairness between classes of beneficiaries does not require them to be excluded. It would be an inhuman rule which required trustees to adhere to some mechanical rule for preserving the real value of capital when the tenant for life was the testator's widow who had fallen upon hard times and the remainderman was young and well-off.[74]

In consequence, the rule permitted some reference to the precise issues which faced the trustee in the context of his own trust obligations and did not simply require that the trustees live up to an objective standard of proper performance. Ordinarily, then, the trustees and the life tenants are responsible to prevent the trust fund from falling into disrepair with the aim that the value of the trust fund be maintained for remainder beneficiaries. There are circumstances in which the preservation of the capital value of the asset may not depend upon the life tenant and the trustee maintaining that property if, for example in the case of real property, the real value of the capital asset is bound up in the development potential of the land and not in the state of repair of a house on that land occupied by the life tenant.[75]

---

[72] *Cowan v Scargill* [1985] Ch 270, 286.   [73] [1994] 1 All ER 118.
[74] *Nestle v National Westminster Bank plc* [2000] WTLR 795, 802.
[75] On the facts of an Australian case it was held that, where the life tenant had allowed a house on a large piece of land to fall into disrepair, there was no need to consider whether or not the life tenant was obliged to maintain the property so as to preserve its value for the capital beneficiaries, on the basis that the property's value rested on the development potential of the land rather than on the condition of the house on that land. Therefore, on these facts the life tenant's failure to maintain

*Aspects of the trustee's obligation to do the best for the beneficiaries financially,
or else to keep pace with the market*

As considered above,[76] there has been a movement in the law of trusts, perhaps, **52.32**
from a requirement of caution on the part of trustees when exercising their investment powers to a requirement that they act reasonably. There is a stream of
authority in the cases which suggests that the trustees' duty towards the
beneficiaries is a duty to act in the beneficiaries' best financial interests. There are
three different senses in which this duty could be said to operate. The first, simply
put, would be to require the trustees to seek the highest possible market return on
the trust's capital. It is suggested that such an approach would require the trustees
to seek the most risky available investments so as to acquire as high a return as possible. The second approach, subtly different from the first, would be to require the
trustees, when choosing between a range of available investments, to select that
investment which offered the highest available yield made possible by the investment criteria which the trustees have created for the trust. In this situation the
trustees would not be seeking investments which promised a high return at a
potentially unacceptable level of risk but rather, once a field of suitable investments had been identified, the trustees would be required to choose the most
remunerative of those suitable investments. The third approach would be to recognize that non-financial considerations ought not to be taken into account. This
third approach would therefore suggest that trustees ought not to allow ethical or
other considerations to sway their financial decisions.

Megarry V-C held that the trustees' obligations fell to be understood in the **52.33**
following way:

> When the purpose of the trust is to provide financial benefits for the beneficiaries, as
> is usually the case, the best interests of the beneficiaries are normally their best
> financial interests. The power must be exercised so as to yield the best return for the
> beneficiaries, judged in relation to the risks of the investments in question; and the
> prospects for the yield of income and capital appreciation both have to be considered
> in judging the return from the investment.[77]

These dicta suggest that the trustees should be guided by a combination of the
second and third approaches outlined above: that is, the trustees should seek the
most remunerative of the investments which are identified as being suitable for
the trust, while putting non-financial considerations from their minds.

A difficult question arises as to the meaning of the term 'non-financial' **52.34**
considerations. An example will make the point. If the trust is required by the
terms of the trust instrument to provide accommodation for beneficiaries while

---

the property had caused no loss to the remainder beneficiaries: *Perpetual Trustees WA Ltd v Darvell*
[2002] WTLR 1349.

[76] See para 52.09.   [77] *Cowan v Scargill* [1985] Ch 270, 286–287.

also investing in real property, then the trustees bear obligations to attend to financial considerations (the duty to invest in real property) and also to non-financial considerations (the duty to provide accommodation to beneficiaries). The issue then arises: in what circumstances can a trustee excuse herself from making the maximum reasonable return, for example through preferring collateral purposes such as non-financial, ethical, or moral considerations instead of the desire for financial profit? This issue arose in the case of *Cowan v Scargill*[78] in which the defendant was one of the trustees of the miners' pension fund and also President of the National Union of Mineworkers. The board of trustees was divided between executives of the trade union and executives from the Coal Board. The most profitable investment opportunities which were considered to be available to the trustees were in companies working in the oil industry and also in South Africa. The defendant, and the other trade union members of the board of trustees, refused to agree to the trust making such investments on the grounds that it was ethically wrong for the fund to invest in apartheid South Africa and also contrary to the interests of the beneficiaries, who were either working or retired coal mine workers, to invest in an industry which competed with the coal industry, in which all the beneficiaries worked or had worked previously. Megarry V-C held, in the passage quoted above, that it was the principal duty of the trustees to act in the best financial interests of the beneficiaries regardless of other considerations. As quoted above, the scope of the duty of investment was summarized by his lordship as the need to bear in mind both the prospects for the yield of income and also the potential for capital appreciation.

52.35 Specifically as to the question of non-financial considerations, Megarry V-C focused on the objections which the defendant trustee had raised in respect of the particular form of investment which had been suggested. In short those objections were that apartheid South Africa would have been an immoral investment and that investment in the oil industry would be contrary to the economic interests of the pensioners' communities. Megarry V-C held that 'the trustees must put on one side their own personal interests and views . . .', and later that '. . . if investments of this type would be more beneficial to the beneficiaries than other investments, the trustees must not refrain from making the investments by reasons of the views that they hold'.[79] As the matter was put further: 'trustees may even have to act dishonourably (though not illegally) if the interests of their beneficiaries require it'. Nevertheless, Megarry V-C was prepared to accept that a *sui juris* set of beneficiaries with strict views on moral matters, such as a condemnation of alcohol, would be entitled to prevent the trustees from investing in companies

---

[78] [1984] 3 WLR 501.

[79] Given that the trust is an institution based on conscience, there is perhaps an irony in that the trustee is not permitted to bring decisions of an ethical nature to bear on the scope of his investment powers.

involved in the production of alcohol. The moral relativism in this approach is perhaps difficult to distil into principle: apparently, one can take into account the beneficiaries' moral objections to alcohol but not their preference for one form of economic activity over another.

If the trust were expressed in terms that the trustees were precluded from investing **52.36** in certain types of industry, such as alcohol or the arms trade, then the trustees would be acting in breach of trust if they did otherwise. Alternatively, Megarry V-C suggests that the beneficiaries could express a common objection to a particular form of activity: this approach recognizes that the trust property is the property of the beneficiaries and consequently that the beneficiaries therefore have a good claim to restricting the trustees from using the property for purposes which they consider to be unethical or immoral.[80]

A different aspect of the trustees obligations to generate the best return for the **52.37** beneficiaries, as outlined above, is the level of risk which the trustees ought to take in seeking to generate a good investment return. It is suggested that the FSA *Conduct of Business Regulations*[81] do give a framework within which professional trustees can justify the decisions which they have made in correlating the expertise and risk appetite of their clients with the investments which were selected. The activities of a professional trustee in *Nestle v National Westminster Bank*,[82] as is considered in paragraph 52.39 are particularly instructive in this regard. In that case the trustees appeared not to have reviewed the investments acquired for the family trust fund in that case for a period of about 60 years with the result that the return which was obtained on the trust's capital was much less than had been obtained by other investments in financial markets over the same period of time. The trustees were able to demonstrate, however, that their investment decisions were in common with market practice for a trust fund of that kind being spread across a portfolio of low risk investments. There is now a statutory obligation under section 5 of the Trustee Act 2000 to review the trust's investment portfolio (considered above), which should remove the failure complained of in this case, unless the operation of that provision were excluded by the trust instrument.

Investment in accordance with portfolio investment theory

The standard of the duty—'current portfolio theory'

The courts have begun to accept the need to adapt to the manner in which **52.38** financial markets and finance professionals operate in the modern context; that is, that such professionals will typically only agree to act as trustees for a fee, in accordance with existing regulation of financial services, and on the terms of conduct of

---

[80] *Saunders v Vautier* (1841) 4 Beav 115. [81] See the discussion in Chapter 47.
[82] [1994] 1 All ER 118.

business letters entered into between the adviser and the lay client.[83] The Trustee Act 2000 requires that the trustees look to the diversification of the trust's assets.[84] In this way, principles of equity relating to the investment powers and obligations of trustees have altered.

52.39 So, in *Nestle v National Westminster Bank plc*[85] trustees had managed the investment of a family trust between 1922 and 1986. It was alleged by the beneficiaries that, while the trust amounted to £269,203 in 1986, if properly invested over that same period it should have amounted to over £1 million or even if it had risen only in line with the cost of living then it would have amounted to £400,000. The trustee bank defended its management of the trust on the basis that it had generated a broadly similar return on capital for its clients as other banks investing large family trusts had generated for theirs. On these facts the judge at first instance had found that the bank had done nothing less than what would have been expected of a trustee in managing such a fund. However, it was also found that the trustee would have been able to generate a much healthier return if it had realized that the fund would not have been subject to estate duty (such that the capital did not need to be maintained in the manner it was) and if it had realized that it should have switched a number of the investments into gilts (government index-linked securities). Importantly, the Court of Appeal held that there was no default committed by the trustee; rather, the plaintiff was contending that there had been a failure to do better, which is not the same thing. If the plaintiff could have demonstrated some misfeasance in the management of the trust, then liability would have been easier to demonstrate. However, the trustee could not be shown to have acted wrongly in a manner which caused loss: only to have acted less profitably, which did not cause loss so much as it failed to generate a larger return.

52.40 In effect, the trustee bank was able to demonstrate that its management of the trust was broadly in line with the management policies of other trustees of private, family trusts (in which the risk appetite is usually small) and therefore that it had acted perfectly properly. Hoffmann J in delivering judgment at first instance in *Nestle v National Westminster Bank plc* held that:

> Modern trustees acting within their investment powers are entitled to be judged by the standards of current portfolio theory, which emphasises the risk level of the entire portfolio rather than the risk attaching to each investment taken in isolation.[86]

In pursuing this point, his lordship found that a trustee is required to act fairly between all the beneficiaries of the trust fund which he was empowered to invest. However, the reference back to the behaviour of trustees acting in the context of

---

[83] FSA, *Conduct of Business Rules*.   [84] Trustee Act 2000, s 4(3).
[85] [1993] 1 WLR 1260, [1994] 1 All ER 118.
[86] *Nestle v National Westminster Bank plc* [2000] WTLR 795, 802.

the modern financial markets indicates the appropriateness of trustees balancing their investments between different types of product to manage the level of risk, as well as taking into account the necessary risk required to make the maximum return for the trust.

The position which the trustee is placed in by equity—that is, to achieve the highest return possible at the lowest reasonable level of risk—appears to be a deeply invidious one, unless some reference is made to common market practice. That is, unless the trustee is able to rely on the fact that comparable investors had adopted similar investment strategies. Otherwise, on every downturn in any given financial market all trustees would be prima facie liable for failing to generate a high investment return.[87] The duty to act evenly between different categories of beneficiaries requires a difficult balancing act between generating short-term return and protecting the integrity of the long-term fund.[88] High-risk short-term investments are necessary to satisfy the requirements of the rule to make the maximum possible return for the trust.[89] However, within that doctrine of maximum gain there is a requirement to act as a prudent person of business would act specifically with reference to someone for whom the trustee felt morally bound to provide.[90] The types of transaction available for the trustee's investment without stricture are similarly limited by statute[91] and by common law (aside from the requirement of prudence, there are prohibitions on lending on personal security).[92]   **52.41**

The trustee is similarly required to supervise professionals to whom delegation of the investment function is made, as considered below.[93] The principle in *Learoyd v Whiteley*[94] indicates that the trustee when investing trust property must not only act as a business person of ordinary prudence, but must also avoid all investments of a hazardous nature. Whereas in *Bartlett v Barclays Bank*,[95] a distinction was drawn between a prudent degree of risk and unacceptable hazard: the former would be acceptable whereas the latter would not. In consequence, it is difficult to establish liability for a trustee who fails to generate a large return on the trust's capital. It is only in circumstances in which the trustee can be shown to have made some mistake or to have acted wrongly that there will be any liability.   **52.42**

This reflection of current portfolio theory in the Trustee Act 2000 underlines the need for the trustee to walk a narrow line between modern market practice and long-established equitable obligations. In this field, perhaps as in no other, the   **52.43**

---

[87] See above the discussion of *Nestle v National Westminster Bank* (29 June 1988) [1993] 1 WLR 1260 in relation to 'current portfolio theory'.

[88] Lord Nicholls (1995) 9 Trusts Law Int 71.   [89] *Cowan v Scargill* [1985] Ch 270.

[90] *Speight v Gaunt* (1883) 22 Ch D 727.

[91] *Bartlett v Barclays Bank Trust Co Ltd* [1980] Ch 515.

[92] *Holmes v Dring* (1788) 2 Cox Eq Cas 1; *Khoo Tek Keong v Ch'ng Joo Tuan Neoh* [1934] AC 529.

[93] See para 52.62.   [94] (1887) 12 App Cas 727.   [95] [1980] Ch 515.

particular nature of the trust is significant. The trust occupies a place somewhere between rules of property and rules of personal obligation. Whereas equity operates on the property that is held as the trust fund by means of proprietary principles, there are also a raft of personal claims against the trustee in connection with the manner in which the function of minding the trust fund is carried out.[96] There are obligations for making too little profit, making profits for himself which were not open to the trust,[97] and taking risks to make greater profit which then caused loss to the trust.[98]

The significance of the shift to reasonableness in the statutory duty of care

52.44 The duty of care may not effect widespread change on the judicial understanding of the obligations of trustees when exercising their investment powers if the notion of 'reasonableness' in section 1 of the Trustee Act 2000 is taken to admit a very wide understanding of those obligations. What the language of 'duty of care' would suggest is a shift into tortious liability and away from fiduciary liability. However, as is clear from *Target Holdings v Redferns*[99] in relation to a trustee's liability for breach of trust, common law notions of causation, foreseeability, and contributory liability do not form part of liability for breach of trust. Therefore, the duty of care should not be developed too closely to common law notions of tortious or contractual liability.

52.45 What the duty of care does suggest is, as considered above, that the trustee must act reasonably in the context of his own trusteeship. That is, by reference to his own level of expertise and the nature of the trust. In contrast to the older principle in *Learoyd v Whiteley*, which suggested an objectivity in the prudence required of trustees, the duty of care as conceived of within the Trustee Act 2000 is comparatively subjective. This reflects the development of the liability for dishonesty of non-trustees assisting in a breach of trust[100] in which the House of Lords has suggested that the notion of dishonesty should both require that the defendant's conduct have been considered dishonest by reasonable people and also that the defendant himself have realized that his conduct would have been considered to have been dishonest by such people.[101]

52.46 The Trustee Act 2000 more generally was enacted in the context of the trustees' investment obligations being set out in contracts between the settlor and the trustees to the exclusion of the general law of trusts. In consequence, the obligations of

---

[96] As to the nature of trusteeship in this context see D Hayton, 'The irreducible core content of trusteeship', in A Oakley (ed), *Trends in Contemporary Trust Law* (Oxford University Press, 1996) 47, emphasizing the core of the nature of the trust being the ability of the beneficiary to enforce the trust by personal obligations enforceable against the trustee.

[97] *Cowan v Scargill* [1985] Ch 270.   [98] *Bartlett v Barclays Bank* [1980] Ch 515.

[99] [1996] 1 AC 421.

[100] *Twinsectra Ltd v Yardley* [2002] 2 WLR 802, [2002] 2 All ER 377.

[101] See the discussion at para 30.23.

trustees are conceived of less in terms of duties of active management of the trust's assets and ever more in terms of defence against liability for negligence.

F. The Process of Making Investment Decisions

The statutory duty of care in the process of making investment decisions

The Trustee Act 2000 creates a statutory duty of care to which trustees are subject when making investment decisions. The detail of the duty of care is considered below.[102] This section of this chapter is concerned with the statutory principles governing the mechanism by which trustees make investment decisions. The duties which those trustees bear in the investment-making process is subject always to the statutory duty of care,[103] whether in relation to the general power of investment or their obligations to review the fund's investments, as considered immediately below. Therefore, the trustees' liability for any malfeasance or loss occasioned through their investment decisions will fall to be assessed in accordance with the duty of care and with the principles of breach of trust under the general law of trust. The following paragraphs will consider the investment decision process before turning to the detail of the statutory duty of care.

52.47

Standard investment criteria under statute

The general power of investment provides that trustees are to be treated as though they were the absolute owners of the trust property, except in circumstances in which the trust instrument precludes such a power.[104] Beyond this general power of investment there is a fasciculus of provisions in the Trustee Act 2000 dealing with the standard of care required of the trustees by statute. The general duty of care created by the statute is considered below.[105] In this section we consider the level of care which is to be expected from the trustees and in the next section we consider the trustees' obligations to take advice as part of their duty of care when making investment decisions.

52.48

The Trustee Act 2000 requires that the trustees have regard to something described in the statute as the 'standard investment criteria'[106] when exercising their investment powers. Further, the trustees are required to review the trust's investments 'from time-to-time' and consider whether or not those investments should be varied in the light of the standard investment criteria.[107] Consideration of these standard investment criteria apply whether the trustees are making new investments or considering their existing investments.[108] The two 'standard

52.49

---

[102] See the discussion at para 52.48.   [103] Trustee Act 2000, Sch 1, para 1(b).
[104] Trustee Act 2000, s 6(1).   [105] See para 52.49.   [106] Trustee Act 2000, s 4(1).
[107] Trustee Act 2000, s 4(2).   [108] Trustee Act 2000, s 4(2).

investment criteria' encompass both the need to make 'suitable' investments and the need to maintain a diverse portfolio of investments to spread the fund's investment risk. Section 4(3) of the Trustee Act 2000 provides that the standard investment criteria are:

(a) the suitability to the trust of investments of the same kind as any particular investment proposed to be made or retained and of that particular investment as an investment of that kind, and

(b) the need for diversification of investments of the trust, in so far as is appropriate to the circumstances of the trust.[109]

The expression 'suitability'[110] is one familiar to investment regulation specialists[111] which requires that, in general terms, investment managers are required to consider whether or not the risk associated with a given investment is appropriate for the client proposing to make that investment. In line with the FSA Conduct of Business Regulations,[112] a regulated service provider is required to allocate each client to a regulatory category in accordance with their knowledge of financial investments. The Conduct of Business Regulations do not set out a specific definition of what will or will not be suitable in any particular context but rather provide that the steps which are required of any service provider:

> will vary greatly, depending on the needs and priorities of the private customer, the type of investment or service being offered, and the nature of the relationship between the firm and the private customer and, in particular, whether the firm is giving a personal recommendation or acting as a discretionary investment manager.[113]

Having categorized each client in this manner, the service provider is then required to treat them in a manner which is suitable to their expertise and also to ensure that the investments sold to them are suitable for their purposes. Therefore, the requirement under section 4(3)(a) of the Trustee Act 2000 that the trustee is required to consider whether the trust fund for which he is making an investment would be dealing in a suitable manner in making the proposed investment will differ depending on the nature of the trust. Where the trust is a small family trust with a comparatively weak risk appetite, then the investments to be made should be safe; whereas investments made on behalf of a trust fund created by two corporations who are expert in financial services (a not uncommon structure for highly leveraged hedge funds) could be considerably more adventurous, taking greater risks. It is presumed that the trustee would be liable for breach of trust in

---

[109] Trustee Act 2000, s 4(3).   [110] This term is considered in detail at para 54.03.
[111] See the discussion of suitability in AS Hudson, *Swaps, Restitution and Trusts* (Sweet & Maxwell, 1999) 192; AS Hudson, *The Law on Financial Derivatives* (3rd edn, Sweet & Maxwell, 2002) 275, 527. See also, for example, the old Securities and Investment Board Rulebook, Ch III, Part 2; Securities and Futures Authority Rulebook, as supplemented from time to time, Rule 5.31; New York Stock Exchange 'Know Your Customer Rule', CCH NYSE Guide, s 2152 (Art III, s 2).
[112] See the discussion at para 47.26.   [113] FSA, *Conduct of Business Rules*, para 5.3.4.

the event that an unsuitable investment were made which caused loss to the trust, assuming further that the trust instrument was silent as to the rectitude of the trustees investing in a particular type of instrument. However, even if the instrument in question was of a type which may have been within the trustees' express powers, it is suggested that to invest in a form of that investment which regulatory principles would have considered unsuitable for that type of client would mean that the manner in which the trustees exercised their power might be considered to have been a breach of trust.[114]

Secondly, the trustees must pay heed to 'the need for diversification of investments **52.50** of the trust, in so far as is appropriate to the circumstances of the trust'.[115] Two points arise from this provision. First, the question as to the amount of diversification necessary is dependent on the nature of the trust. A trust which requires the trustees to hold a single house on trust for the occupation of a named beneficiary does not require that the trustees make a range of investments: rather, the trustees are impliedly precluded from making a range of investments. Similarly, a trust with only a small amount of capital could not afford to buy a large number of investments. Secondly, the need for diversification is itself bound up with the need to dilute the risk of investing in only a small number of investments. This is frequently referred to as 'portfolio theory'[116] and is predicated on the notion that if an investor invests in a number of investments in different markets the impact of any individual market or investment suffering from a fall in value is balanced out by the investments made in other markets which will not have suffered from that particular fall in value. This process has already been considered in detail in this chapter in paragraph 52.38.

The obligation to take professional advice

Trustees are under a positive obligation to take professional advice on the **52.51** investments which they propose to make on behalf of the trust.[117] This advice must be taken before the exercise of any investment power.[118] Once the advice has been obtained, the trustees are required to consider it and its bearing on the manner in which their investment power should be exercised.[119] There is no statutory obligation on the trustees to follow the advice which they receive and so it is open to them to follow whichever path they consider appropriate. Megarry V-C held the following in relation to the trustees' obligations in relation to the advice they receive:

> Although a trustee who takes advice on investments is not bound to accept and act on that advice, he is not entitled to reject it merely because he sincerely disagrees with it, unless in addition he is acting as an ordinary prudent man would act.[120]

---

[114] *Target Holdings v Redferns* [1996] 1 AC 421; [1995] 3 WLR 352; [1995] 3 All ER 785.
[115] Trustee Act 2000, s 4(2)(b).   [116] Considered at para 52.38.
[117] Trustee Act 2000, s 5(1).   [118] ibid.   [119] ibid.   [120] [1985] Ch 270, 289.

Alternatively, there is nothing in the statute to preclude trustees from taking advice from a number of sources, or to take advice from one source as to a range of different investment decisions which could be taken, before then selecting the strategy which most appeals to them in the context of their fiduciary responsibilities.

52.52 The standard investment criteria considered above requires the trustees to review their investments from time to time and decide whether or not to vary those investments.[121] The trustees are also required to take qualified investment advice when carrying on this periodical process of review.[122]

52.53 These obligations to take advice will not apply only if it appears reasonable to the trustee in the circumstances to dispense with such advice[123] or if the terms of the trust dispense with the need for such advice (perhaps in circumstances in which the trustees themselves are adequately qualified to make those decisions without further advice). The type of advice which the trustee must acquire is 'proper advice'. The term 'proper advice' is defined as being advice from someone whom the trustee reasonably believes to be qualified to give such advice by virtue of his 'practical experience of financial and other matters' and by reference to his 'ability'.[124] The requirement of practical experience is a fairly comprehensible one. However, the requirement that a person's 'ability' makes them fit for the task is less clear. By 'ability' could be meant their personal characteristics, such as level-headedness or prudence, as well as their professional qualifications or work experience. If that were so, the trustees would seem to have a great deal of personal discretion, for example as to their views of an adviser's personal characteristics, as opposed to discretion which is required to be measured by reference to objective factors, such as a person's professional qualifications.

52.54 The Act requires that advice be taken and considered. The wording of the provisions in Part II of the Act are deliberately broad, in the ways considered above. Therefore, while there are a number of interesting questions of theory in the abstract raised by these provisions, the more immediate problem facing trustees will be the manner in which they demonstrate that they have complied with their statutory duties in the event of a complaint by beneficiaries either that the trust has suffered a loss or that the trust has failed to generate as great an income as it ought to have done.[125] The concept of loss in this regard is considered below in greater detail.[126] To this end, trustees would be well-advised to record their decisions and the reasons for their decisions in writing, drawing in detail on written advice provided to them by the advisers on whose advice they relied. Those advisers should be required by the trustees, as well as by any regulation

---

[121] Trustee Act 2000, s 4(2).   [122] ibid, s 5(2).   [123] ibid, s 5(3).
[124] ibid, s 5(4).   [125] *Nestle v National Westminster Bank plc* [2000] WTLR 795.
[126] See the discussion at para 52.81.

which covers them, to give full information as to the risks associated with any particular investment strategy, details of their professional qualifications to make such advice, and such other information as the trustees would require to complete a written record of their decision-making procedure. Evidently, a trust instrument which contained a procedure for the manner in which the trustees were required to go about making their investment decisions would make matters much easier than the Trustee Act 2000 which, necessarily, is broadly drafted so as to encompass all forms of trustees' decisions. Alternatively, a settlor's letter of wishes giving instructions of this sort would be of assistance to trustees.[127]

The interaction of the Trustee Act 2000 with trusts effected before 1961

52.55 The provisions of Part II of the Trustee Act 2000, relating to the general power of investment, the standard investment criteria, and the obligation to consult advisers, apply to trusts created either before or after the commencement of the Act.[128] No trust power created before 3 August 1961 is capable of restricting or excluding the general power of investment.[129] Furthermore, an investment power under section 3(2) of the Trustee Investment Act 1961 contained in a trust instrument effected after 3 August 1961 is to be treated as conferring a general power of investment on its trustees.[130] Otherwise, the trust instrument is able to exclude or restrict the operation of the general power of investment in the manner considered above.[131]

G. The Selection and Management of Particular Investments

The scope of this section

52.56 The discussion in this chapter hitherto has concerned itself with the identification of the trustee's powers of investment and of his duties in the exercise of those powers. What has not been considered yet is the case law which has governed the more precise obligations of trustees historically in relation to particular forms of investment. Thus far we have considered the general power of investment and the process by which investments should be chosen and the process by which the selection of those investments should be reviewed occasionally. The questions considered here relate to the manner in which trustees are required to oversee and manage those investments once they have been acquired. For example, once the trustees have decided to acquire a particular security or to acquire a valuable chattel there are then questions as to the maintenance of that asset, the need to insure it,

---

[127] *Public Trustee v Cooper* [2001] WTLR 901.   [128] Trustee Act 2000, s 7(1).
[129] Trustee Act 2000, s 7(2).   [130] Trustee Act 2000, s 7(3).
[131] See the discussion in para 52.09.

the manner in which the trustees should exercise any powers which are incidental to its ownership, and so forth.

The trustee's duty to manage investments, in general terms

52.57 Frequently the trustees will wish to appoint professionals to act on their behalf. The trustees will seek to delegate to such professionals their management responsibilities. The question will then arise as to any liability for breach of trust, or failure to achieve the best possible results for the trust, when the trustees' powers were being carried out by delegates: whether they are agents, custodians, or nominees. The trustees can only appoint agents, nominees or custodians in one of the following circumstances:[132] if those appointees carry on business in that capacity, or if the appointee is a body corporate (such as an ordinary company) controlled by the trustees themselves,[133] or the delegates are a body corporate recognized under Section 9 of the Administration of Justice Act 1985.[134] Charitable trustees are required to seek the guidance of the Charity Commissioners in this context.[135] It is open to the trustees to decide on the remuneration of such delegates.[136]

Agents and principals

52.58 The Trustee Act 2000 provides that the trustees are permitted to 'authorise any person to exercise any or all of their delegable functions as their agent'.[137] The trustees are entitled to delegate any of their fiduciary obligations to an agent except for those expressly ring-fenced by statute. The effect of these provisions is to establish a core of fiduciary obligations which are reserved only to the trustee. Those functions include: a decision as to the distribution of trust assets; the power to decide whether fees should be payable out of income or capital; any power to appoint some person to be a trustee; or any power to delegate trustee responsibilities.[138]

52.59 The trustees can appoint one of the trustees to act on their behalf.[139] The trustees are not entitled to authorize a beneficiary to act as their agent.[140] This latter provision is clearly in accordance with principle where there is more than one beneficiary because if one beneficiary could act as the trustee's agent then it would be possible for that beneficiary to advantage himself at the expense of the other

---

[132] Trustee Act 2000, s 19(1).

[133] As defined by analogy with Income and Corporation Taxes Act 1988, s 840: Trustee Act 2000, s 19(3).

[134] Trustee Act 2000, s 19(2).   [135] ibid, s 19(4).   [136] ibid, s 20.

[137] ibid, s 11(1).

[138] ibid, s 11(2). In relation to charitable trusts, the trustees are entitled to appoint agents in relation to raising funds (which does not include the conduct of a trade which forms the primary purpose of the trust), any function which involves a decision which the trustees have taken, or any function involving the investment of the trust's funds: Trustee Act 2000, s 11(3).

[139] Trustee Act 2000, s 12(1).   [140] ibid, s 12(3).

beneficiaries. However, there is no general rule of trusts law to preclude a trustee from being a beneficiary. Similarly, under the rule in *Saunders v Vautier*[141] an absolutely entitled beneficiary would be able to direct the trustees how to act with the property. The agent must nevertheless be subject to the same duties as the trustees when the agent is exercising those powers.[142] However, these powers can be excluded by the terms of the trust instrument, as considered above. Further, the trustees are empowered to decide on the level of the agent's remuneration.[143]

In relation to 'asset management functions' the trustees are only entitled to **52.60** appoint agents if the terms of the agency are 'evidenced in writing'.[144] The 'asset management functions' of the trustees relate to the investment of assets under the trust, the acquisition of property to be held on trust, and the management of interests in property held on trust.[145] Further to the obligation to detail the agency in writing, the trustees are required to prepare a written[146] 'policy statement' which guides the agent as to how to exercise the powers which are delegated to them.[147] The agent must then be obliged under the terms of the agency to act in accordance with the terms of the policy statement. The difficulty with this provision is that the trustees themselves are not required to have a policy statement for their own cognizance and therefore the trustees would be required to develop their own such policy statement from scratch, requiring the agent to act in 'the best interests of the trust'.[148]

Nominees and custodians

The trustees are empowered to appoint a nominee, or bare trustee, to act in **52.61** relation to any of the assets of the trust as they determine.[149] Similarly the trustees have a power to appoint a custodian to take custody of any trust assets which they may consider appropriate for such treatment.[150] If the trust acquires bearer securities[151] then it is mandatory that those securities be deposited with a custodian.[152] What is not immediately apparent is the difference between a nominee and a custodian within the terms of the Trustee Act 2000. Neither term is expressly defined. A 'nominee' could refer to a person who assumes all of the rights of the trustee. Alternatively, a nominee could be a person who holds title in the trust property on behalf of the trustees: in which case it would be difficult to distinguish them from a custodian. A 'custodian' could be a form of trustee required to hold, and possibly to maintain, the trust assets in the exercise of some trust discretion as to the manner in which those assets are maintained. In this sense a

---

[141] (1841) 4 Beav 115.   [142] Trustee Act 2000, s 13.   [143] ibid, s 14(1).
[144] ibid, s 15(1).   [145] ibid, s 15(5).   [146] ibid, s 15(4).   [147] ibid, s 15(2).
[148] ibid, s 15(3).   [149] ibid, s 16(1).   [150] ibid, s 17(1).
[151] ie, securities for which the holder of the security document is entitled to receive payment and which are, consequently, always vulnerable to theft and conversion into cash by the thief without much difficulty (a little like a banknote).
[152] Trustee Act 2000, s 18(1).

custodian is someone who is responsible for protecting the trust property from theft, fraudulent conversion, or other harm: as with bearer securities considered immediately above.[153] Alternatively a custodian may be simply a bailee of the trust property with no fiduciary powers over that property other than holding the property for safekeeping.[154]

The trustee's duty in relation to delegates

The delegation of trustee's capacities by power of attorney

52.62 Trustees are empowered to delegate their powers by means of a power of attorney.[155] The donor of the power (for example, the trustee transferring the power) is liable for acts of the donee (that is, the attorney acting on behalf of the trustee) as though they were his own acts.[156]

Liability for the acts of delegates

52.63 The Trustee Act 2000 provides for a code to decide the allocation of liability in circumstances in which agents, nominees, or custodians have been appointed validly under the terms of the Act. The trustees are required to 'keep under review' the arrangements under which the delegate acts and to consider any 'power of intervention' which they may have.[157] Such a power of intervention includes a power to revoke the delegate's authorization or a power to give directions to the delegate.[158] If the trustees decide that there is a need to intervene, then they are required to intervene.[159]

52.64 A trustee will not be liable for 'any act or default of the agent, nominee, or custodian unless he has failed to comply with the duty of care applicable to him.[160] Therefore, the trustee is in general terms not liable for any breach of duty carried on by the delegate unless the trustee failed to comply with his duty of care in relation to the appointment of suitable agents.[161] Under section 30 of the Trustee Act 1925, since repealed, it was provided that:

> A trustee shall be chargeable only for money and securities actually received by him notwithstanding his signing any receipt for the sake of conformity, and shall be answerable and accountable only for his own acts, receipts, neglects, or defaults, and not for those of any other trustee, nor for any banker, broker, or other person with whom any trust money or securities may be deposited, nor for any other loss, unless same happens through his own wilful default.

---

153 Perhaps in the sense of a 'custodian trustee' within the Public Trustee Act 1906.
154 An expression used in relation to unit trusts and open-ended investment companies.
155 Trustee Delegation Act 1999, s 5; by amendment to Trustee Act 1925, s 25.
156 Trustee Delegation Act 1999, s 5(7).   157 Trustee Act 2000, s 22(1).
158 ibid, s 22(4). Interestingly, the 2000 Act does not require that such powers be expressly included in the documentation required for any effective delegation.
159 ibid, s 22(1).   160 That is, the duty of care under Trustee Act 2000, Sch 1, para 3.
161 ibid, s 23(1).

The extent of this indemnity was clearly very broad, and much more so than the liability set out above. This provision was, however, repealed by the Trustee Act 2000 and no replacement provision included in that Act, although such a provision may be included in trust instruments. Liability is confined to personal receipts of the trustee. The classic statement of the trustee's obligation regarding the delegation of authority to invest is set out in *Speight v Gaunt*[162] in the decision of Lord Jessel MR:

> It seems to me that on general trust principles a trustee ought to conduct the business of the trust in the same manner that an ordinary prudent man of business would conduct his own, and that beyond that there is no liability or obligation on the trustee.

Exceptionally in *Re Vickery*,[163] where a trustee had given money to a solicitor who absconded with it, Maugham J considered the central issue to be whether or not the trustee was negligent in employing the solicitor or permitting money to remain in his hands. It was held that there was no liability on the trustee unless there had been some 'wilful default' by him, being something more than a mere lack of care. This test has come in for much academic criticism,[164] being based on *Re City Equitable Fire Insurance*[165] which was a company law case looking at the obligations of fiduciaries in the context of specific articles of association.

52.65

Investments in land

The acquisition of land

The power to invest in land is excluded from the general power of investment under the 2000 Act except in relation to loans secured on land.[166] Rather section 8 of the 2000 Act includes a specific power to acquire legal estates in land—that is, freehold or leasehold land—in the United Kingdom either as an investment, for occupation by a beneficiary, or for any other reason.[167] Thus, trustees are empowered to acquire freehold and leasehold land for any purpose.[168] The trustee has the powers of 'the absolute owner in relation to the land'.[169] This presumably means that the trustee is free to deal with the land on behalf of the trust in terms of conveying it, securing it, and so forth. It also supposes, for example, that even if property is acquired for the occupation of a beneficiary then the trustees have power to impose conditions as to the manner in which that property is occupied. It not clear whether or not the Act requires that the beneficiaries in question have an interest in possession and indeed if the trustees have the power to impose

52.66

---

[162] (1883) 9 App Cas 1.   [163] [1931] 1 Ch 572.
[164] G Jones (1968) 84 LQR 474; D Hayton, 'Investment management problems' (1990) 106 LQR 89.
[165] [1925] Ch 407.   [166] Trustee Act 2000, s 3(3).   [167] ibid, s 8(1).
[168] These particular powers do not apply to land that was settled land before 1996: Trustee Act 2000, s 10.
[169] Trustee Act 2000, s 8(3).

conditions—such as the defeasibility of the beneficiaries' rights of occupation—then the beneficiary need not have an interest in possession in that property but rather an interest only in the property as an investment asset within the context of his interests in the larger fund. However, it is not supposed that this could be taken to mean that the trustee is entitled to ignore the equitable interests of any beneficiaries who do have an interest in possession in that land when held on trust, just as an absolute owner of land unencumbered by any other rights need have no concern for any other person. The rights of the beneficiary would depend upon the structure of the trust: a trust which invests in a large number of buildings may make one of the properties available for the occupation of one beneficiary out of a large class, and thus deny that beneficiary any rights greater than a licence to occupy it, whereas a trust holding only one property on trust for one, absolutely-entitled beneficiary would suggest that the beneficiary would have an interest in possession in that property unless the context clearly required that the property was intended to be held solely as a short-term capital investment.

52.67 In line with the general scheme of the Trustee Act 2000, the legislation provides for additions to any terms of any trust instrument so that there are default provisions if a trust should lack them.[170] However, it is open to the settlor to exclude the operation of the statute in any particular circumstances: reinforcing yet again that the Act does not impose mandatory rules as to the behaviour of trustees.

When the trust property includes a mortgage

52.68 There has been much discussion as to whether power to invest in mortgages allows investment in equitable and second mortgages. In view of the objections to the latter put forward in *Chapman v Browne*[171] it seems unlikely that the latter, at least, are permissible notwithstanding the removal of the objection concerning protection by the Land Charges Act 1972.

52.69 Section 8 of the Trustee Act 1925 provides guidelines for a trustee investing in a mortgage to follow. If he does so, he will not subsequently be liable if the security later proves to be insufficient, always provided that: the trustee must invest on the basis of a report prepared by an able and independent surveyor or valuer as to the value of property;[172] the amount of the loan must not exceed two-thirds of the value as stated in the report;[173] and the report expressly advises the loan, in which case the trustee is entitled to presume that this advice is correct.[174] If the only aspect of non-compliance with section 8 is the amount loaned, section 9 of the Trustee Act 1925 offers some minimization of the trustee's liabilities in that the trustee will only be liable for the difference between the amount in fact lent and

---

[170] Trustee Act 2000, s 9. [171] (1801) 6 Ves 404. [172] Trustee Act 1925, s 8(1)(a).
[173] ibid, s 8(1)(b). [174] ibid, s 8(1)(c); *Shaw v Cates* [1909] 1 Ch 389.

the amount which should have been lent. In addition to following the general principles, a trustee must limit the investments to those authorized either by the trust instrument or by statute.

In relation to express powers to invest in land, for a power to be greater than that contained in the Trustee Act 2000,[175] that power would have to be explicit on the terms of the trust instrument.[176] A mere power, for example, to invest in ground-rents will not be deemed to be a power to acquire freehold or leasehold properties.[177] **52.70**

Investments in shares

General principles relating to shares and securities

When the trust is subscribing for shares[178] on their issue it is usual for those shares to be paid up soon afterwards.[179] The trustees are entitled to subscribe for partly paid up shares within a general power to invest in shares and to pay any remaining instalments on the shares out of the trust fund.[180] **52.71**

The general term 'securities' has been taken in trusts law to refer to any investment which was secured on property or, in relation to companies, on the companies' property or stock.[181] That term in modern market parlance refers more generally to any investment in which the evidence of the investment is capable of being transferred independently of the underlying rights, such as a share or a bond. The sense of the security connoting some generally transferable asset was accepted by some trusts law authorities in the early twentieth century.[182] **52.72**

It is a feature of trusts created in relation to securities that they are frequently expressed in vague terms. Valid trust investment powers include references to securities of a public company,[183] 'any railway or public company',[184] and **52.73**

---

[175] Trustee Act 2000, s 8(3).

[176] *Re Suenson-Taylor's Settlement Trusts* [1974] 1 WLR 1280.

[177] *Re Mordan* [1905] 1 Ch 515.

[178] The 'stocks' are generally taken to be synonymous with 'shares' in this context: *Morrice v Aylmer* (1874) 10 Ch App 148; *Re McEacharn's Settlement Trusts* [1939] Ch 858; *Re Boys* [1950] WN 134. Cf. *Re Willis* [1911] 2 Ch 563, where a reference to 'preference stock' was held not to import a right to acquire preference shares. A reference to 'ordinary preferred stock' may, nevertheless, connote a subclass of ordinary shares which carried a preferential right: *Re Powell-Cotton's Resettlement* [1957] Ch 159.

[179] AS Hudson, 'Capital Issues' in Morse (ed), *Palmer's Company Law* (London: Sweet & Maxwell) Part 5.

[180] *Re Johnson* [1886] WN 72.

[181] *Harris v Harris (No 1)* (1861) 29 Beav 107; *Murphy v Doyle* (1892) 29 LR Ir 333.

[182] *Re Rayner* [1904] 1 Ch 176; *Re Gent and Eason's Contract* [1905] 1 Ch 386; *Re Tapp and London Dock Co's Contract* (1905) 92 LT 829. This sense is then evident in later cases such as *Re Douglas's Will Trusts* [1959] 1 WLR 744; *Cordell v Moore* [1998] NIJB 207.

[183] *Re Lysaght* [1898] 1 Ch 115. Since Companies Act 1985, s 1, this term has had a statutory definition.

[184] *Re Sharp* (1890) 45 Ch D 286.

'public stocks of the Bank of England'.[185] Reference to companies trading overseas have been restricted to companies which are nevertheless incorporated in England and Wales.[186] Investment powers which have been held to be invalid include references in trust instruments to 'blue chip' stocks,[187] and references to 'any company incorporated by Act of Parliament' when the trust was intended to invest in a company incorporated under the Companies Act 1985.[188]

When the trust property includes a controlling interest in a company

52.74   The application of these general principles to the situation in which trust property includes a controlling interest in a company was considered in *Re Lucking's Will Trusts*.[189] It was said that the trustee should not simply consider the information she receives as shareholder, but should, in some way, ensure that she is represented on the board of directors of that company. The extent of such representation will depend upon the circumstances: she may be required to act as managing director if the trust owns a controlling interest in the company or she may only need to ensure that she has a nominee on the board who can report back to her if the context otherwise dictates. This principle was interpreted more liberally in *Bartlett v Barclays Bank*[190] in which it was said that the trustee need not always be represented on the board if the circumstances did not require this, provided that the trustee retained a sufficient flow of information from the company in accordance with the size of the shareholding, as is considered in the next paragraph. Other methods of control over the company's affairs may be sufficient depending on the context. The shortcomings in this assumption that the trustees can acquire such control or such an adequate flow of information are considered in the next section.

The duty to intervene in the affairs of the company

52.75   The extent of the trustee's obligation to intervene in the investments held by the trust is illustrated by *Bartlett v Barclays Bank*[191] in which, despite a near total shareholding, the trustees failed to be forewarned about a disastrous property speculation made by the company in which the trustee, a bank, had invested. The questions arose as to the scope of the duty of the trustee bank; the extent to which the trustee bank had been in breach of that duty; whether any such breach of duty had caused the loss suffered by the fund; and the extent to which the trustee bank was liable to make good that loss. It was held that the standard of observation and

---

[185]   *Re Hill* [1914] WN 132.
[186]   *Re Castlehow* [1903] 1 Ch 352; *Re Hilton* [1909] 2 Ch 548.
[187]   *Re Kolb's Will Trusts* [1962] Ch 531.
[188]   That is, the company was required to be a company created by its own Act of Parliament: *Re Smith* [1896] 2 Ch 590.   [189]   [1968] 1 WLR 866.   [190]   [1980] Ch 515.
[191]   *Bartlett v Barclays Bank* [1980] Ch 515.

control in relation to the investments was the 'same care as an ordinary prudent man of business would extend towards his own affairs'. Given that the trustees in that case had been investing in a private company, the trustees' obligation was to 'ensure an adequate flow of information in time to make use of their controlling interest'. In other words, it was recognized that in some situations the trustee will be required to intervene and ensure that she is able to amass sufficient information to manage the investment. Therefore, the principles will depend on context: where the trustee has access to some control of a company then the trustee would be expected to procure some control in return for that significant investment, whereas a trustee holding only a small investment in a large public company would not have such control (unless a trustee of a particularly large pension fund, for example) and therefore would not be expected to exert such control.

This quaint attitude to trustees taking control of companies could only apply to   **52.76**
limited categories of private companies where it would be possible to acquire such a controlling shareholding. Other issues arise, however, if trustees are to exercise such powers of control over companies in which they invest. In relation to private companies it would be important to acquire significant voting power and not simply to acquire shares which carry dividend rights with only limited voting powers. In relation to public limited companies it would generally be impossible to acquire such control on behalf of ordinary private trusts. The structure of the shareholding of such public companies is such that about 80 per cent of companies quoted on the FTSE-100 are owned by investment trusts, pension funds, and other institutional funds.[192] Even such institutional investors, who might themselves be acting as trustees, will only hold a small minority shareholding in any given company and therefore will only be able to exercise any control over the company's management by acting informally in concert with other institutional investors. Recent reports on corporate governance in public limited companies in the United Kingdom have emphasized the significance of the relationship between institutional shareholders and boards of directors in controlling the principal, structural decisions affecting companies.[193] However, even if the trustees of such an institutional investment fund sought to exercise influence with other, similar investors over the board of directors, those trustees would have no legal right to oblige either the other institutional investors nor, in the ordinary course of events, the company's management to act in any particular manner which would be of benefit to the trust. The rule in *Foss v Harbottle*[194] prevents minority shareholders from even commencing litigation to force a company to adopt any given course of action if the majority of the company's shareholders would simply

---

[192] J Parkinson, *Corporate Power and Responsibility* (Clarendon Press, 1993) 166.
[193] See, for example, Higgs, *Report on Corporate Governance*, 2003.
[194] (1843) 2 Hare 461.

vote to ratify the directors' actions, unless there is some evident oppression of minority shareholders.[195]

Investment by means of loan

52.77 Trustees may make loans. They may not lend, however, on a purely personal security,[196] unless specifically empowered by the terms of their trusteeship so to do.[197]

The power to vary investments

52.78 Section 57 of the Trustee Act 1925 gives the court power to vary the powers of investment under a trust. That section provides that:

> Where in the administration of any property vested in trustees [any investment] is in the opinion of the court expedient, but the same cannot be afforded by reason of the absence of any power for that purpose vested in the trustees by the trust instrument, if any, or by law, the court may by order confer upon the trustees, either generally or in any particular instance, the necessary power for the purpose . . .

Therefore, the court is entitled to permit investments of a broad range, from mortgages and loans through to purchase or sales of assets generally, where the court considers it to be expedient. That power can be exercisable on a one-off basis or can be effected by way of a variation of the terms of the trust. Such transactions must be for the benefit of all of the beneficiaries and not for any particular beneficiary.[198] In cases involving large funds, the court may permit a large expansion of the trust investment powers to enable the retention of a professional fund investment manager. Thus, in *Anker-Peterson v Anker-Peterson*,[199] a fund containing £4 million was expanded in this way such that the investment manager would be able to invest the fund in a commercially reasonable manner. Each case is treated on its own merits, and recourse to litigation may be necessary even after the Trustee Act 2000 if the trust instrument had some express restriction on investment.[200]

H. Express Powers of Investment

Priority of express powers of investment over statutory principles

52.79 An express power granted to a trustee to make an investment may be general, giving the trustees power to invest in whatever they wish, or alternatively it may be limited to specified types of investment. The trustee will nevertheless be subject to

---

[195] See, for example *Prudential Assurance v Newman* [1982] 1 All ER 354.
[196] *Holmes v Dring* (1788) 2 Cox 1.
[197] *Forbes v Ross* (1788) 2 Bro CC 430; *Paddon v Richardson* (1855) 7 De GM & G 563.
[198] *Re Craven's Estate* [1937] Ch 431.　　[199] (1991) LS Gaz 32.
[200] *Trustees of the British Museum v Attorney-General* [1984] 1 WLR 418.

certain limitations. Although in *Re Harari's Settlement Trusts*[201] it was held that such a power would not be interpreted restrictively, the case of *Re Power's Will Trusts*[202] established that the word 'invest' implied a yield of income and, thus, non-income producing property would not be permissible as an investment. Therefore, while there is a permissive approach to interpreting investment clauses, it is important that it is 'investment' which is taking place. In *Re Power* the trustee was relying on the investment provision to justify the acquisition of a house for the beneficiaries to live in. It was held that this acquisition did not include the necessary element of income generation for the trust. Thus in *Re Wragg*[203] the trustee was permitted to acquire real property on behalf of the trust on the basis that that property was expected to generate income for the trust. It should be remembered that the trustee will have powers of investment both under any express power and under the Trustee Act 2000, as considered above.[204]

Strict construction of powers of investment

The authorities are inconclusive on the manner in which powers of investment are to be construed. In general terms, provisions which have sought to enlarge the trustees' powers of investment have tended to be construed strictly.[205] Whereas, other forms of trust power have not always been construed restrictively.[206]   **52.80**

I. Breach of Investment Powers

The concept of 'loss' and breach of trust

The ingredients of liability for failure to comply with investment obligations

Having considered the scope of the trustees' obligations to invest the trust fund, issues relating to trustees' liability for a breach of their investment obligations arise. There are a number of possible heads of liability. The first relates to the trustees' obligations in circumstances in which the trustees simply invest in unauthorized investments, without the trust suffering loss. The second relates to the situation in which the trust suffers a loss as a result of the trustees' breach of their investment powers and obligations. The general law on breach of trust was considered in detail in Chapter 32.   **52.81**

In the absence of express terms in the trust instrument to the contrary, then a failure to comply with the terms of the Trustee Act 2000 would be sufficient to found a claim for breach of a trustee's obligations. Breach of trust in this context   **52.82**

---

[201] [1949] 1 All ER 430.   [202] [1951] Ch 1074; distinguishing *Re Wragg* [1919] 2 Ch 58.
[203] [1919] 2 Ch 58.   [204] See para 52.09.
[205] *Re Maryon-Wilson's Estate* [1912] 1 Ch 55; *Re Harari's Settlement Trusts* [1949] WN 79.
[206] *Re Peczenik's Settlement Trusts* [1964] 1 WLR 720.

would invoke the ordinary principles of breach of trust, given that the Trustee Act 2000 is merely supplying powers where otherwise there are none, thus invoking the ordinary principles of breach of trust.

52.83   The contractual context of the trustees' investment powers was made apparent in *Galmerrow Securities Ltd v National Westminster Bank*,[207] a case in which the fiduciaries in a unit trust, here the National Westminster bank, had expressly excluded their liability for the exercise of their investment obligations except in cases of negligence or fraud. The beneficiaries contended that the scheme managers had been negligent in their investment of the bulk of the fund in the real property market. The scheme managers contended that it would have been impossible to have amended their investment powers so as to have avoided the investment objectives of the unit trust and to have extracted the fund's investments from the real property market before it collapsed in 1974. The court held that:

> The venture was a speculation and like all speculations carried with it the risk of failure. It would not be right to visit the consequences of that misjudgment of the market upon NatWest which is not shown to have had any power open to it which would remedy or mitigate the consequence . . . it is not negligent to fail to act where no alternative course of conduct to the continuance of the present arrangement is proved to have been available to the person who has a power to act.

Therefore, the circumstances precluded the trustees from suffering liability because there was no other course of action open to them. The trust's objective of speculating on the property market was, quite simply, a speculation which failed. It was, perhaps, a result of the intractability of the terms of the trust and of the requirement that those terms be sufficiently rigid to attract the approval of the fund's regulators that this speculation could not be undone.

Breach of trustees' investment powers

52.84   The beneficiaries would therefore be required to demonstrate that there had been a breach of trust which generated loss. If the allegation is that the trustees were permitted only to invest in *x*, but that they actually invested in *y* and so caused a loss to the trust fund, then the trustees' liability for that loss would be easily demonstrated. The most significant means of holding trustees liable for any loss caused by a failure to comply with their investment powers in a trust instrument is by means of a claim for breach of trust. The general liability for breach of trust was considered in Chapter 32. In that regard, the leading case of *Target Holdings v Redferns*[208] identified three categories of liability for a trustee causing loss to the trust fund as a result of his breach of trust: first, a liability to replace the very

---

[207]   [2002] WTLR 125, 155.
[208]   [1996] 1 AC 421; [1995] 3 WLR 352; [1995] 3 All ER 785.

property that was taken from the trust fund; secondly, a personal liability to reconstitute the loss to the trust fund in cash; and, thirdly, a liability to pay equitable compensation to the beneficiaries.[209]

In most situations, however, professional trustees would be able to demonstrate that they had obeyed the terms of their investment powers in the trust instrument. In consequence, the beneficiaries' claim would be based on the trustees' failure to invest sufficiently well, rather than simply to invest in the correct forms of asset. This latter form of claim is more difficult to establish because it requires the beneficiaries to show that the trustees generated an unsatisfactory return on the trust's investment, rather than that they acted straightforwardly in breach of the terms of their duty. The courts general support for the exclusion of the trustees' liability for negligence was considered in Chapter 32.[210] The beneficiaries would therefore be required to show that no reasonable trustee acting with the minimum, reasonable level of care and skill would have generated such a poor return on the trust's capital.[211] In measuring the trustees' competence in this sense, it would be necessary to have regard to market conditions and to the element of speculative good or bad fortune which may attend any investment strategy.[212] However, it is suggested that it would be a matter which would relate to a professional trustee's competence, principally as to whether or not he had managed to assemble a portfolio of investments which insulated the trust against large losses. In that sense, the importance of a portfolio strategy is that the trust may make only a small profit or a small loss as a result of the failure of one component of the trust's investment portfolio, but if the trust suffered a large loss because a single form or category of investment constituted a large proportion of the total trust fund then the trustee ought to be recognized as bearing some liability for failing to calibrate the contents of the portfolio appropriately. Further to the obligations in the Trustee Act 2000 for non-professional trustees to take professional advice, such non-professional trustees ought to be found liable to a similar extent if they failed to follow the advice which they were given so as to ensure that the trust's portfolio was insulated against loss.

52.85

Where unauthorized investments acquired but no loss suffered

As considered above, matters are comparatively simple in circumstances in which the loss was caused by a clear infraction of the trustees' duties as set out in the trust

52.86

---

[209] ibid.

[210] *Armitage v Nurse* [1998] Ch 241, suggesting that a contractual exclusion of liability clause will excuse liability for negligence; *Walker v Stones* [2001] QB 902, [2000] 4 All ER 412, suggesting that such an exclusion of liability clause ought not to excuse liability for dishonesty.

[211] *Bristol & West Building Society v Mothew* [1998] Ch 1; *Wight v Olswang (No 2)* [2000] WTLR 783, approved at [2001] WTLR 291. See also *Re Mulligan* [1998] 1 NZLR 481.

[212] *Nestle v National Westminster Bank* [1994] 1 All ER 118, 133, *per* Staughton LJ.

instrument. However, where the trustees have made investments of the wrong type matters might be more complex. If the investments were of the wrong type and caused a loss to the trust, then the trustees' would be straightforwardly liable for the loss in the manner set out in *Target Holdings v Redferns*.[213] Alternatively, if the investments did not cause a loss but rather merely held their value or generated a profit which was less than might have been obtained if the trustees had acquired authorized investments, then the analysis might be different. In the context of investments in financial securities, the issue is whether the trustees are required to replace the stock which they have sold in breach of trust, or simply repay the cash equivalent of the sale. The answer suggested by the case of *Re Massingberd*[214] is that the trustees should replace the stock that is sold and not simply provide a mere cash equivalent equal to any notional loss to the fund. If the unauthorized investments have not made a loss, then it might simply be a question of obliging the trustees to acquire investments of an authorized kind by disposing of the unauthorized investments and to bear any incidental costs of so doing.[215]

Where unauthorized investment makes less profit than authorized investment

52.87   The issue nevertheless remains as to the value of unauthorized investments which must be replaced by authorized investments, particularly in circumstances in which the unauthorized investments generated a profit but arguably a lesser profit than authorized investments would have done. Usually, the trustee's duty is to restore the trust to the value before the breach of trust,[216] in which case the acquisition of an unauthorized investment which made a smaller profit than might have been made by an authorized investment would not disclose any loss. That is the first possible analysis. However, there is another possible analysis. The trustee might be held liable to account to the trust for the difference between the profit which was actually made from the unauthorized investments and the profit which would have been made by authorized investments on the basis that the trust lost the opportunity to make the larger profit. It has long been held that trustees can set off gains made, even through breaches of trust, against losses made through the same breach of trust, and therefore it is only for the difference in amounts of profit for which the trustee could be liable.[217]

52.88   It has been suggested in Australia that it would be open to the beneficiaries to surcharge the trustees' accounts for the failure to acquire the return on appropriate investments.[218] The requirement on the trustees is that the trust fund be

---

[213] [1996] 1 AC 421.   [214] (1890) 63 LT 296.   [215] ibid.
[216] *Nocton v Lord Ashburton* [1914] AC 932, 952, *per* Lord Haldane LC.
[217] *Wiles v Gresham* (1854) 2 Drew 258, 271; *Fletcher v Green* (1864) 33 Beav 426; *Vyse v Foster* (1872) 8 Ch App 309, affirmed at (1874) LR 7 HL 318; *Re Deare* (1895) 11 TLR 183.
[218] *Glazier v Australian Men's Health (No 2)* [2001] NSWC 6.

placed in the position it would have been in but for the trustees' breach of trust.[219] In that sense, the trust would have been in possession of a greater profit but for the trustees' breach of trust and therefore that the trustees be required to fund the difference between those two amounts.

The practical difficulty would be in demonstrating as a matter of fact that the **52.89** trustees would have been compelled to acquire a particular set of investments, which would have realized the profit contended for, from among the range of possible investments which would otherwise have been possible.[220] Suppose that within the class of authorized investments, investment *x* would have generated a larger profit than the unauthorized investments actually acquired, but that investment *y* from the class of authorized investments would have made a lower profit. How can the beneficiaries demonstrate that they have suffered an opportunity loss? After all, it is unlikely that *all* of the possible investments from the class of authorized investments would have generated the same level of profit and therefore the opportunity loss to the fund would be equally difficult to prove. Where some authorized investments would have generated a profit and others a loss, it is suggested that it would be impossible to prove as a matter of fact that the trust did in fact suffer a loss through the unauthorized investments.

In *Nestle v National Westminster Bank* the claimant beneficiary failed to demonstrate **52.90** that, even though the trustees had failed to conduct any significant review of the trust's investment portfolio in about sixty years, there had been any loss to the fund. Rather, the fund had increased in value but only by an amount which appeared to be much less than open market investments ought to have gained. The significant difference between that case and the present question is that it was not self-evident that the trustees had committed a breach of their duties of investment. The beneficiary's claim foundered when the trustees were able to demonstrate that they had acted in line with other trustees' investment policies in similar circumstances. What this demonstrates, perhaps, is that it is not enough for the beneficiaries to show that they have failed to realize as large a profit as they might have been entitled to, but rather that they must also prove that the trustees were at fault in exercising their investment powers otherwise than as required by the terms of their trusteeship.

---

[219] *Re Dawson* (1966) 2 NSWLR 211.

[220] If the unauthorized investments were in bonds, whereas the class of authorized investments was limited exclusively to share markets, it would be difficult to prove that the trustees would have acquired shares which made a profit as opposed to shares which made a loss. Furthermore, it would be impossible to know precisely which shares would have been acquired and, because different shares would make different levels of profit, it would be impossible to demonstrate with exactitude the extent of the trust's loss. Alternatively a broad-brush approach would be to use an index of bonds against an index of equities to estimate the loss.

J. Exclusion of the Trustee's Liability

Exclusion of liability under statute

52.91 It should be remembered that the provisions of the 2000 Act can be expressly or implied displaced by the trust instrument.[221] In consequence this duty of care may be limited by the express provisions of the trust, or even by a construction of those provisions which suggests that the settlor's intention was to exclude such a liability.[222]

52.92 The duty of care is not expressed by the 2000 Act to be a general duty in the form of an all-encompassing statutory tort. Rather, the Act provides that the duty will apply in certain limited circumstances.[223] The principal instance in which the statutory duty of care applies[224] is in relation to a trustee exercising a 'general power of investment'[225] under the Act or any other power of investment 'however conferred'.[226] Alternatively the duty of care applies when trustees are carrying out obligations under the Act in relation to exercising or reviewing powers of investment.[227] The duty of care also applies in relation to the acquisition of land,[228] which would logically appear to cover the use of appropriate advice and appropriate levels of care in selecting the land, contracting for its purchase, and insuring it.[229] It applies in general terms in relation to the appointment of agents, custodians, and nominees:[230] which would include the selection of reasonable agents with appropriate qualifications for the task for which they were engaged.

The validity of exclusion clauses under case law

52.93 A provision in a trust instrument, or a contractual provision entered into between a trustee and some person employed to act on behalf of the trust, which restricts the liability of either the trustee or that other person will be valid unless it purports to limit that person's core fiduciary liability. Professional trustees will not agree to act unless their obligations are limited by contract. Paradoxically this has the result that in the former situation the trustee is punished for a lack of expertise if the trust does not generate a reasonable return, whereas in the latter the professional trustee is absolved from any failure to generate a profit precisely by virtue of her

---

[221] Trustee Act 2000, Sch 1, para 7.   [222] cf para 52.93.   [223] Trustee Act 2000, s 2.
[224] ibid, Sch 1, para 1.   [225] As defined by ibid, s 3(2) and considered below.
[226] With the effect that this provision may be the only mandatory provision in the legislation because it appears to apply to powers of investment in general and not simply to that set out in Trustee Act 2000, s 3(2). However, the Act does permit an express exclusion in the trust to obviate the operation of any of the provisions in the Act and therefore it would appear possible to circumscribe the operation of this provision: Trustee Act 2000, Sch 1, para 7.
[227] Trustee Act 2000, ss 4, 5.   [228] ibid, Sch 1, para 2.
[229] ibid, Sch 1, para 5; Trustee Act 1925, s 19.   [230] ibid, Sch 1, para 3.

expertise in drafting her exclusion clauses appropriately.[231] The case of *Armitage v Nurse*[232] (decided before the enactment of the Trustee Act 2000 discussed above) held that a clause excluding a trustee's personal liability would be valid even where it purported to limit that trustee's liability for gross negligence. In explaining the limit of the trustee's obligations, Millett LJ had the following to say:

> [T]here is an irreducible core of obligations owed by the trustees to the beneficiaries and enforceable by them which is fundamental to the concept of a trust. If the beneficiaries have no rights enforceable against the trustees there are no trusts. But I do not accept the further submission that their core obligations include the duties of skill and care, prudence and diligence. The duty of trustees to perform the trusts honestly and in good faith for the benefit of the beneficiaries is the minimum necessary to give substance to the trusts, but in my opinion it is sufficient . . . a trustee who relied on the presence of a trustee exemption clause to justify what he proposed to do would thereby lose its protection: he would be acting recklessly in the proper sense of the term.

The approach of the court would have been different if the trustees had acted dishonestly or fraudulently: in such a situation the exclusion clause would have been of no effect.[233] To demonstrate that there has been fraud would be difficult to prove in a situation in which the trustee did not take any direct, personal benefit. The more likely ground for any claim brought by the beneficiaries would be that the trustee had breached a duty to act fairly between the beneficiaries or to do the best possible for the beneficiaries within the limits of current portfolio theory: all of which issues were considered immediately above.[234]

K. Professional Trustees' Duties When Conducting Investment Business

Limitation of liability

The principles relating to the trustees' ability to exclude or limit their liability by contract were considered in Chapter 21.[235] In relation to trustees who are regulated by the FSA there are regulations as to the conduct of investment business which prevent the regulated (or, authorized) person from relying on contractual provisions which are inappropriate for that type of customer, as described under the Conduct of Business Regulations. **52.94**

Such contractual exclusion clauses are also subject to the Unfair Contract Terms Act regime. One issue to arise under the Unfair Contract Terms Act 1977 ('UCTA') is that of trustees in the business of selling their services as investment **52.95**

---

[231] *Armitage v Nurse* [1998] Ch 241.   [232] [1998] Ch 241.
[233] *Walker v Stones* [2001] QB 902, [2000] 4 All ER 412.   [234] See para 52.38.
[235] See para 21.24.

managers seeking to rely on their standard documentation, particularly when dealing with inexpert customers. Under section 2(2) of UCTA, a trustee will not be able to restrict its liability for negligence unreasonably in its written agreement. The form of negligence which the Act seeks to cover is negligent breach of any obligation to exercise reasonable skill and care. Furthermore, section 13 of UCTA extends the application of section 2 to any circumstance in which the seller seeks to restrict its duties under the contract in respect of its tortious and non-tortious obligations. It has been held that this might extend as far as provisions which seek to exclude rights to set-off.[236] A further question might then relate to the use of the standard form contracts by trustees to limit their liabilities. The principal issue would be whether or not this could be said to constitute a standard form contract of the particular entity in question which would entitle the buyer to refute any provision in that contract which 'claimed to be entitled ... to render a contractual performance substantially different from that which was reasonably expected'.[237] Further to the Unfair Terms in Consumer Contract Regulations 1999, enacting the appropriate EC Council Directive,[238] 'unfair' terms are not binding on the consumer. Those regulations apply where there have been individually negotiated terms between one party acting in furtherance of its business as a seller or supplier and another party acting as a consumer. These regulations apply, however, only to natural persons and not to corporations,[239] unlike the 1977 Act.[240] No reference to this legislation has been made in those cases considering general attempts by trustees to limit their liabilities, as discussed in Chapter 32.[241]

Money laundering

52.96 The regulation of banks with a view to combating money laundering has long been a feature of international financial regulation but has been given new impetus by concerns about international terrorism. In England and Wales, the Proceeds of Crime Act 2002 seeks to make provision for the treatment of the proceeds of criminal activity and the Terrorism Act 2000 makes provision for the treatment of funds which it is suspected will be applied for the purposes of terrorism. There are also the Money Laundering Regulations 1993 at the European Union level. The regulations require that authorized persons, including regulated trustees, conduct due diligence as to their clients' identity and the source of their funds. Bound up with this is the need to report suspicious transactions, to train staff appropriately, and to

---

[236] *Stewart Gill Ltd v Horatio Myer & Co Ltd* [1992] QB 600.
[237] UCTA 1977, s 3(1).   [238] Council Directive (EEC) 93/13, [1993] OJ L95/29.
[239] Unfair Terms in Consumer Contract Regulations 1999, reg 3.
[240] *R & B Customs Brokers Ltd v United Dominions Trust Ltd* [1988] 1 WLR 321.
[241] See para 32.85.

keep records appropriately.[242] The details of these criminal statutes and of the appropriate financial regulation are beyond the scope of this work.[243]

Market abuse

The market abuse code was introduced by FSMA 2000 in order to expand the powers of the FSA to prosecute any market participants for any misfeasance in financial dealings. The importance of this regime is that it carries punitive penalties but that it does not replicate all of the protections and rights which are characteristic of the criminal law.[244] The market abuse regime relates to 'qualifying investments' traded on LIFFE, the London Stock Exchange, and other markets[245] where the behaviour in question would be regarded by 'a regular user of that market' as a failure 'to observe the standard of behaviour reasonably expected of a person in ... their position in relation to the market'.[246] A 'regular user' is someone who is a 'reasonable person who regularly deals on that market in investments of the kind in question'; the term 'regular user' appears frequently in this code.[247] More specifically, the behaviour in question must exhibit three further features. First, it must be based on information which is 'not generally available to those using the market' but which would be considered by a 'regular user' of the market to be 'relevant' to entering into transactions on that market.[248] Secondly, it must be 'likely to give a regular user of the market a false or misleading impression' as to the supply of, demand for, and value of the investments in question.[249] Thirdly, the behaviour must be of a kind that would be 'likely ... to distort the market' in question.[250]

52.97

To supplement this statutory code, then, there is a code of conduct which is required to be created by the FSA under the auspices of the FSMA 2000.[251] This code (referred to as 'MAR 1' in the FSA Rulebook)[252] requires that the instrument in question be one which is traded on an existing market and in which there is a continuing market. It is important to recognize that the types of behaviour which

52.98

---

[242] See W Blair, A Allison, G Morton, P Richards-Carpenter, G Walker, N Walmsley, *Banking and Financial Services Regulation* (3rd edn, Butterworths, 2003) 282.

[243] The reader is referred to the work cited in the previous footnote.

[244] This in itself may cause difficulties in relation to art 6 of the European Convention of Human Rights and its guarantees of a right to a fair trial. Its legislative purpose was therefore to make successful prosecutions for market abuse easier to obtain than had been the case under the pre-existing criminal law.

[245] Financial Services and Markets Act 2000, s 118(1).

[246] Financial Services and Markets Act 2000, s 118(3).

[247] Financial Services and Markets Act 2000, s 118(10).

[248] Financial Services and Markets Act 2000, s 118(2)(a).

[249] Financial Services and Markets Act 2000, s 118(2)(b).

[250] Financial Services and Markets Act 2000, s 118(2)(c).

[251] Financial Services and Markets Act 2000, s 119.

[252] Published under the Financial Services Authority, Market Conduct Sourcebook Instrument 2001 (MAR 1).

the FSA intends to encompass within this regime relate not only to dealing directly in shares and other instruments but also to any behaviour which affects their value more generally.[253] Further, that behaviour may take place in another jurisdiction but nevertheless have an impact on instruments traded in the United Kingdom and so fall within the market abuse code.[254]

52.99 The offence of making misleading statements is contained in section 397 of FSMA 2000.[255] That offence is committed in one of three circumstances. First, where a person makes a statement, promise, or forecast which 'he knows to be misleading, false or deceptive in a material particular'.[256] What is not made clear in this context is what will constitute knowledge; that is, whether one can be taken to 'know' a statement is misleading only if you have actual knowledge, or whether it would be sufficient to have constructive notice of its misleading nature, or whether it would be sufficient that one has wilfully and recklessly failed to make the inquiries which an honest and reasonable person would have made in that context.[257] Secondly, where such a person 'dishonestly conceals any material facts' in relation to a statement, promise, or forecast.[258] Again, it is unclear whether dishonesty in this context would require actual fraud or whether it could be established in circumstances in which the defendant fails to act as an honest person would have acted in the circumstances.[259] It is suggested that the latter would accord most closely with the 'reasonable user' test within the market abuse code more generally. Thirdly, where such a person 'recklessly makes (dishonestly or otherwise) a statement, promise or forecast which is misleading, false or deceptive in a material particular'.[260]

Insider dealing

52.100 The legislative code on insider dealing was established under Part V of the Criminal Justice Act 1993 and is intended to deal with any situation in which a market participant abuses price sensitive information which he acquires when acting as an insider when dealing in price-affected securities.[261] Further to the enactment of the FSMA 2000, the FSA has the power to prosecute any allegations of insider dealing.[262]

Chinese walls

52.101 The liability of firms of professional advisers in relation to the maintenance of Chinese walls both in relation to their potential liability for breach of the

---

[253] MAR 1, 1.11.8E.   [254] MAR 1, 1.2.9G.
[255] cf *R v De Berenger* (1814) 3 M & S 66.
[256] Financial Services and Markets Act 2000, s 397(1)(a).
[257] eg *Re Montagu's Settlement* [1987] Ch 264.
[258] Financial Services and Markets Act 2000, s 397(1)(b).
[259] eg *Royal Brunei Airlines v Tan* [1995] 2 AC 378.
[260] Financial Services and Markets Act 2000, s 397(1)(c).
[261] Criminal Justice Act 1993, s 52.   [262] Financial Services and Markets Act 2000, s 402.

prohibitions on fair dealing and on self-dealing were considered in Chapter 29.[263] There is also a consideration of the potential liabilities for sellers of financial services in Chapter 54 in relation to the provision of professional advice during commercial transactions.[264]

L. Distinction Between Capital and Income

Examples of the distinction between capital and income

There are many situations in which trustees will be called upon to distinguish **52.102** between capital and income in the management of the trust fund. The principal context is that in which there are different beneficiaries entitled either to the capital of the trust fund or to the income. The other significant context is that in which trust expenses are required to be attributed between capital and income beneficiaries.

The usual metaphor for the distinction between capital and income is the **52.103** distinction between ownership of a tree and ownership of the fruit borne by that tree. Ownership of the tree itself connotes ownership of capital: that is, the source from which income is derived. By contrast ownership of the fruit of the tree is a right to a stream of assets which flow from the capital source. It is then a distinction between source and product. Thus, quite literally, in relation to a trust of land, the sale of timber cut to improve the growth of other trees constituted capital: quite literally, the tree may be a capital asset.[265] The increase in regularity of a stream of assets will suggest that it is more likely to be income; the greater the size or value of the assets the more likely it is to be capital. Thus, ownership of freehold rights in land which is leased so as to generate a rental income will mean that the capital asset is the land itself whereas the rental payments constitute income[266] as would payments of interest on a mortgage even if payable as a lump sum.[267]

Similarly, ownership of shares will constitute ownership of capital whereas rights **52.104** to the dividend stream derived from those shares will constitute a right to income.[268] Where such income assets are securitized, or capitalized, and issued in a block then they are frequently taken to constitute capital on account of their size

---

[263] See para 29.51. [264] See para 54.05.
[265] *Earl of Cowley v Wellesley* (1866) 3 Beav 635. However, a different analysis would be possible in relation to ownership of land whereby regularly felled timber could be deemed to be the fruit which came from ownership of the land in which the trees grew.
[266] *Brigstocke v Brigstocke* (1878) 8 Ch D 363; *Sinclair v Lee* [1993] Ch 496, 506. This includes increases in rent or back payments: *Re Westminster* [1921] 1 Ch 585.
[267] *Re Lewis* [1907] 2 Ch 296; see also *Caulfield v Maguire* (1842) 2 Jo & La T 141 in relation to payment of interest by lump sun instalment.
[268] *De Gendre v Kent* (1867) LR 4 Eq 283.

and the one-off nature of their provision:[269] an alternative analysis would be that securitized assets are representations of income payments and therefore ought properly to be considered to be income assets still in spite of their large form.

52.105   There are contexts, nevertheless, in which a trust may buy and sell land on a regular basis and in such volume that there may be a suggestion that the parcels of land in which the trust deals are income assets: however, it is unlikely that assets involving such a large financial outlay either to buy or to sell would be considered to be anything other than capital assets because the cost of such assets is likely to constitute a large amount of money even in the context of a large trust fund. That there are a series of assets held by a trust does not in itself preclude an analysis of them as being capital assets: even though, in relation to a trading trust, they may be considered to be ordinary trading assets.

52.106   When the trust requires that capital expenses are to be met from the capital portion of the trust fund and the income expenses to be met from the income of that fund, then the trustees are required to make the appropriate apportionment.[270] In situations in which it is not clear whether the expenses accrue to the capital or to the income portion of the fund, then more difficult issues may arise. Section 31(1) of the Trustee Act 2000 suggests that the trustees are entitled to apportion those expenses between the various portions of the fund as they see fit. The position before the enactment of that provision would have been that the trustees were required to distinguish clearly between the two portions of the fund. All recurrent expenses of the trust, such as rates, taxes, interest on charges and other incumbrances, are to be applied to the income portion of the fund; whereas all costs, charges and expenses incurred for the benefit of the whole estate are borne by the capital portion of the fund.[271] What this does not take into account, perhaps, is the fact that there is some loss to the income beneficiaries too every time there is a reduction in the capital of the fund. Equally, if the income beneficiaries meet the interest payable on a capital liability, such as a mortgage, then income will similarly be meeting a capital liability: ordinarily, income beneficiaries will be required to meet such expenditure in any event, even if they are required to reimburse the capital beneficiaries subsequently in circumstances in which those capital beneficiaries met that expense initially due to a lack of income at the time.[272] Contrariwise, the capital beneficiaries will be charged with any expense met by the income beneficiaries due to a shortfall in the capital at the time.[273]

The rule in *Howe v Lord Dartmouth*

52.107   There is an implied duty to convert any residuary property, except real property and specific bequests, in circumstances in which that property is a wasting asset

---

[269] *Bouch v Sproule* (1887) 12 AC 385.   [270] *Carver v Duncan* [1985] AC 1082.
[271] *Carver v Duncan* [1985] AC 1082, 1120, *per* Lord Templeman.
[272] *Honywood v Honywood* [1902] 1 Ch 347.   [273] *Stott v Milne* (1885) 25 Ch D 710.

which will decrease in value. This is the first part of the rule in *Howe v Lord Dartmouth*[274] which provides that:

> If a testator gives his residuary personal estate in trust for, or directly to, persons in succession without imposing a trust for sale and it comprises wasting assets or unauthorised investments, then unless the tenant for life can show that the testator meant him to enjoy the income of those assets or investments in specie, they must be sold and the proceeds invested in authorised securities.

This duty is an implied duty and therefore may be disapplied. Within the trustees' ordinary discretion to effect investment, except in relation to provisions in a trust instrument expressly to the contrary, those trustees will be required to consider the nature of the property held on trust and to consider its replacement, that is its conversion into other assets from time to time so as to the preserve the profitability of the trust. Thus, the trustees may decide to retain authorized investments even if they may be considered to be wasting assets in the best interests of the trust. However, in relation to unauthorized investments, those assets must be converted into authorized investments.[275]

The second branch of the rule in *Howe v Lord Dartmouth*[276] requires that, once **52.108** unauthorized investments have been sold, those proceeds must be converted into authorized investments. In an action for a breach of trust in a failure to give effect to the first limb of this rule, the income beneficiary is entitled to recover from the trustees an amount of compensation equal to the return which the trust would have earned had the trustees acted properly under this principle. This rule will not apply if there is a clear, contrary intention in the trust instrument: for example, if a trustee had a power to postpone sale.[277]

---

[274] (1802) 7 Ves Jr 137. [275] *Re Gough* [1957] Ch 323.
[276] (1802) 7 Ves Jr 137. [277] See, for example, *Re Inman* [1915] 1 Ch 187.

TRUSTS USED IN COMMERCIAL CONTEXTS

PART I

TRUSTS USED IN COMMERCIAL
CONTEXTS

53

TRUSTS WHICH CONDUCT A BUSINESS

A. The Manner in Which a Trust Conducts a Business

Introduction

This chapter considers private trusts which conduct a business.[1] That is, trusts **53.01**
which carry on a trade. Whereas private trusts are required to be carried on for the
benefit of persons and not to conduct abstract purposes,[2] trusts conducting a
business must be organized so that their beneficiaries take the equitable interest in
the trust assets and so that their trustees take the legal title in those assets, also that
they conduct the business of the trust, and that they owe fiduciary obligations to
the beneficiaries. In consequence, trusts conducting a business must not be organized to achieve abstract purposes on pain of being found to be in breach of the
beneficiary principle and so to be invalid.[3] In situations in which business trusts
do satisfy the beneficiary principle, there are complex interactions between the
trustees and between the trustees and the beneficiaries, in that the trustees will
both owe the ordinary duties of trusteeship to the beneficiaries and also have a

---

[1] Focusing on private trusts means that it will not consider charitable trusts.
[2] *Re Denley* [1969] 1 Ch 373; *Re Lipinski's Will Trusts* [1976] Ch 235.
[3] *Leahy v Attorney-General for New South Wales* [1959] AC 457.

collateral purpose of managing the trust's business activities. The trustees may wish to invest for the benefit of the business whereas the beneficiaries may prefer to preserve their capital or to take an income benefit from the trust. The equilibrium that must be achieved between these contrasting obligations is considered below, together with the structural questions which surround business trusts.

Business trusts for 'trade', not 'investment'

53.02 The trusts considered in this chapter conduct trades but are not involved in investment. Trusts which are involved in investment were considered in detail in Chapter 52 and the interaction between the law of investment finance and the law of trusts was considered in Chapter 47, together with financial regulation under the Financial Services and Markets Act 2000. In the wake of the 'South Sea Bubble' crisis of 1720, in which the South Sea Company had collapsed spectacularly losing investment capital of much of English society broadly equal in amount to the national debt, investment companies were made unlawful.[4] In consequence, to avoid the illegality of company structures, trusts and partnerships were used to allow people to interact for trading or for investment purposes. It was unlawful for groups of people to come together to raise investment capital but not to trade.[5] The authorities began to distinguish between trading and investment activities in consequence.[6]

53.03 The definition of the term 'investment' was considered in Chapter 47.[7] In circumstances in which trustees are conducting investment business on behalf of beneficiaries, those trustees will be subject to regulation by the Financial Services Authority. Investment in this sense includes those forms of speculative activity set out in Schedule 1 of the Financial Services and Markets Act 2000, including, by way of example, the acquisition of shares to earn dividend income or to sell those shares at a profit. Where a group of individuals come together with a view to benefiting from investments made from their pooled funds that does not suggest that they are conducting a trade together.[8] Rather, trade would suppose a frequency of transacting and a quality of transacting to constitute their activities as a trade. This is necessarily a matter of degree and of an analysis of the circumstances of any particular case. This chapter is concerned with trading activities unconnected with the acquisition of investments.

---

[4] See AS Hudson, *The Law on Investment Entities* (London: Sweet & Maxwell, 2000) 103, 107; or for a stimulating, historical account of the crisis itself see M Balen, *A Very English Deceit* London: Fourth Estate, 2002).

[5] *Smith v Anderson* (1880) 15 Ch D 247.   [6] *Smith v Anderson* (1880) 15 Ch D 247.

[7] See paras 47.07 (the definition of investment business within Financial Services and Markets Act 2000) and 52.11 (the meaning of 'investment' within Trustee Act 2000).

[8] *Smith v Anderson* (1880) 15 Ch D 247.

Trusts structures used for trade

Transactions conducted through the trustee

A trust has no legal personality. It does not own property, nor does it contract with **53.04** third parties, nor does it sue in its own name. A trust does not conduct a trade in isolation from its human actors in the way that a company does. Therefore, the trust is required to trade through its trustee. This means that all business carried on in the name of the trust is in fact contracted for by the trustees personally in their capacity as trustees. Given that a trust is not an entity with separate legal personality, and that its transactions must be conducted through its trustee, this may give the impression to any third party dealing with the trust that all transactions are conducted with the trustees personally. The trustees are, of course, only transacting *qua* trustees and therefore are only permitted to transact within the terms of their authority. Therefore, creditors are in the position of a person who contracts with the trustees acting on behalf of other people, the beneficiaries, with whom that creditor cannot contract but in a way that the creditor will only be able to proceed against the trustees personally in the event that the trustees have acted outwith their authority. It is important for creditors both to satisfy themselves as to the extent of the trustees' authority and also to consider ways of securing their rights under their transactions.

The authority of the trustees to bind the trust

The question of the trustees' authority is significant. In the event that the trustees **53.05** enter into a contract which is outside the authority given to them by the terms of their trusteeship then that contract would, at first blush, be a contract which imposes obligations on the trustees personally in relation to the other party to that contract but which denies the trustees any right to recover any costs arising from that contract from the trust itself.[9] It has been suggested by Lord Millett in *Dubai Aluminium v Salaam*[10] that an agent who enters into a contract on behalf of another person outwith the terms of his authority will not bind his principal precisely because he was acting outwith the authority to act which that principal had given him. The doctrine of ostensible authority in contract law nevertheless appears to grant a third party a right to proceed against a principal in the event that that third party had contracted with an agent who appeared to have ostensible authority to act, even though the precise terms of the agent's authority did not grant him that right. The doctrine of ostensible authority provides that a third party contracting with an agent acting on behalf of a principal would be able to enforce any contract entered into with the agent in circumstances in which the principal in some way represented to the counterparty that the agent had authority to act in the way that it did.[11] This

---

[9] See para 21.24.   [10] *Dubai Aluminium v Salaam* [2002] 3 WLR 1913.
[11] *Freeman & Lockyer v Buckhurst Park Properties (Mangal) Ltd* [1964] 2 QB 480.

doctrine has been explained as being a subset of estoppel: effectively estopping the principal from reneging on an agreement entered into by its agent in circumstances in which the counterparty was reasonably entitled to rely on the agent's ostensible authority.[12]

In relation to trusts it is suggested that the beneficiaries may be able to insulate themselves from any breach by the trustees of their duties to the beneficiaries as encapsulated by the terms of their trusteeship. The central issue will be whether or not the circumstances suggest that the trustee can be considered to have been acting in a manner equivalent to a commercial agent conducting a business for his principal or, rather, whether the contracting party is a trustee who owes duties of maintenance and care on behalf of beneficiaries in which the settlor could not have intended that the trustees accept any liability which could be transmitted to the integrity of the beneficiaries' trust fund outwith the terms of the trustees' powers. In either event, the risk is born by the third party as to the internal relationship between the trustees and the beneficiaries as conceptualized in the terms of the trustees' authority. If the trustees could be made personally liable by means of the doctrine of breach of trust or personally liable in damages in contract to the third party, then no real issue would arise. It is only if the trustees are unable to defray the third party's claim that a real issue arises. The question of contracts created for the benefit of a third person were considered in Chapter 5;[13] and the question of the trustee's right to an indemnity is considered below.[14]

The authorities at common law as to the ostensible authority of agents are not in obvious accord. In one decided case, an employee of a bank has been held to have had his actual authority enlarged when a customer reasonably believed that that person had the authority to enter into contracts technically outwith his actual authority. The bank's officer had authorized loans to the customer when writing letters to that customer suggesting that he had such authority although that was unsubstantiated by any other officer of the bank.[15] Contrariwise, the Court of Appeal has held that in general terms an officer of a bank cannot act outwith his authority nor make representations outwith that authority.[16] In that case, however, it was held that a counterparty may rely on that officer's signature on the basis that the officer in question had suggested that he did have the authority to enter into that contract when in fact he did not. On those facts, the Court of Appeal was both mindful of the general principle that one should not go outside one's authority and yet aware of the fact that if someone has actual authority to enter into contracts of one kind it may not be obvious to third parties that that officer's authority

---

[12] *Rama Corporation Ltd v Proved Tin and General Investments Ltd* [1952] 2 QB 147.
[13] See para 5.62.   [14] See paras 21.10 and 53.24.
[15] *First Energy (UK) Ltd v Hungarian International Bank Ltd* [1993] 2 Lloyd's Rep 194.
[16] *Egyptian International Foreign Trade Co v Soplex Wholesale Supplies Ltd (The Raffaella)* [1985] 2 Lloyd's Rep 36.

precludes him from entering into other types of contract when the officer himself suggests that he can do so.

The trustees precluded from making unauthorized profits

That the trustees contract *qua* trustees means that they become personally liable **53.06** for any losses but are not entitled to take any unauthorized benefit from any business transactions.[17] The beneficiaries' role is entirely passive: that is, they are owed duties by the trustees and they are entitled in equity both to the trust property and consequently to any assets which flow from that property.

The capital and income structure of the trust

The trust might be organized for the maintenance of capital or for the generation **53.07** of income. In such a situation there may different classes of beneficiaries entitled either to capital or to income, whether as remainder beneficiaries and life tenants or otherwise. Alternatively, the trust might be organized as a discretionary trust such that the trustees are entitled to decide whether the trust's assets are used for the expansion of the business or to be distributed among the class of beneficiaries. In such a situation the trustees must balance their obligations to the beneficiaries with the needs of the business enterprise. These concerns mirror the management of ordinary companies in which shareholders have rights to dividends only when the directors decide that the money can be spared from the company's main business activities, in which company law is required to choose between the ownership rights of shareholders and the management duties of the directors, and in which different categories of shareholder may have different voting and dividend rights. As considered below,[18] the drafting of the trust instrument will be of singular importance in establishing the respective rights of different categories of beneficiary and the duties of the directors.

As a further dimension, the conduct of the business may require the addition of capital to the trust from time to time. This may necessitate providing for the manner in which new capital is to be settled on trust and the rights which such contributors will receive as beneficiaries as a result. In company structures there may be issues of shares or bonds, or ordinary borrowing. Contributions of capital which acquire the rights of a beneficiary would be similar to issues of shares in an ordinary company in that the investor acquires a right against the assets of the business enterprise. This would equate, as considered below,[19] to taking effective security against the assets of the trust by dint of having some equitable interest in them. By contrast, the trust may be empowered to borrow money in a manner which is similar to an issue of bonds (without the creation of transferable securities) or to ordinary lending.

---

[17] See the discussion at para 53.21 below.　　[18] See para 53.15.　　[19] See para 53.27.

The role of employees and business managers

53.08 Unit trusts, considered in Chapter 51 have two forms of trustee: the scheme manager and the trustee. In relation to a trading trust it may be that the trust chooses to adopt a similar structure such that the 'trustee' is a custodian for the trust's assets without any powers of management over the business activities conducted with the trust's assets. The custodian's responsibilities would mimic the role of the depositary in open-ended investment companies whose principal responsibility is that of the 'safekeeping' of the company's assets, subject to the directions of the company's management but always for the benefit of shareholders.[20] This is particularly so given that the trustee of a trading trust will frequently be a corporate entity in itself such that the company holds the trust property and the company's employees act as the managers of the trust's business. A custodian, then, holds the trust's assets subject to the directions of the manager. The manager may be expressed in the trust instrument of a trading trust also to be a trustee, albeit with different responsibilities from the custodian, or as another officer of the trust. It is suggested that a manager will always be acting in a fiduciary capacity in relation to the trust unless his powers to apply the business's assets are circumscribed by empowering the custodian to ignore or to affirm that manager's recommendations as to the deployment of the business's capital assets.

53.09 A trading trust which retains employees, for example, would need to distinguish between the capital assets which are to be preserved or applied only in the expectation of a long-term return for the beneficiaries and those items of circulating capital and income which are used to discharge the day-to-day expenses of the business, to maintain plant and machinery, or to pay staff's wages and other costs. In such a situation it may be possible for managers to act in a capacity which is junior to the control of the board of trustees and which does not require the authority of the board of trustees for expenditure of identified amounts for identified purposes, in all cases without rendering that manager a fiduciary in relation to the beneficiaries. Rather, the manager in this context would have a contractual nexus with the trustees and in relation to the trust's assets but not necessarily any fiduciary responsibility. Akin to a large company, there may be a tier of middle management who exercise only limited levels of management control but who do not constitute a fiduciary officer of the company.[21] Whereas, the manager may be held to owe fiduciary duties to the trust in the event that he sought to make an unauthorized, personal profit from his position or that he sought to disadvantage

---

[20] Financial Services and Markets Act 2000, s 237(2)(b).
[21] *Tesco Supermarkets Ltd v Nattrass* [1972] AC 153, [1971] 2 All ER 127, in which a failure by a branch manager to comply with the terms of the Trade Descriptions Act 1968 was not held to have been a default by a controlling mind of the company such that his default could have been attributed to the company as a whole. The comparatively junior status of this middle manager meant that, despite the control granted to him over activities in his branch of the Tesco supermarket chain, his omission did not impose a liability on the company.

the beneficiaries in some other way, that, it is suggested, would require the imposition of fiduciary liability as a response to such a specific breach of good conscience and not subject the manager to a more general fiduciary responsibility for all of the acts which he performs on behalf of the trust's business affairs.

So, in the context of modern companies, employees are generally not considered to be fiduciaries when carrying out their ordinary duties; rather, it is in relation to a limited category of misfeasance that relates to diverting corporate opportunities for private gain[22] or sharing confidential information with a competitor[23] that employees will face liability as constructive trustees. In company law terms this could be understood as being part of a general duty of fidelity which employees are said in some cases to owe to their employers.[24] More generally, it is suggested, that these forms of liability can be understood as being part of the general equitable principle that one should not act unconscionably in relation to another's property on pain of being held to be a constructive trustee of any profit made from that action[25] or personally liable to account for any breach of trust.[26] **53.10**

The commercial purpose of business trusts

Business enterprises are generally organized as a company, as a partnership, or by means of an entrepreneur acting as a sole trader. It is comparatively rare for such enterprises to be undertaken through a trust structure unless done as part of a family trust arrangement dealing with a family business, or to avoid regulation of some kind. The regulation most commonly at issue in relation to trusts is that of taxation. This book does not purport to encompass the detailed principles of the taxation of trusts. The secret to the use of trusts as a means of avoiding or minimizing the liability to tax is simply the sleight of hand achieved by means of property belonging to a settlor becoming at common law the property of the trustee, subject only to whatever qualified, discretionary, or contingent rights the settlor may choose to grant to the beneficiaries in equity. For tax purposes, a trust is a means of making it seem either that one person's property belongs to another or that the same item of property is owned by more than one person simultaneously. The legislation, case law, and literature on this topic is vast.[27] Contained within those legal principles, it should never be forgotten, are many elephant traps in the form of anti-avoidance principles and many cases dealing with sham trusts created **53.11**

---

[22] *Regal v Gulliver* [1942] 1 All ER 378, [1967] 2 AC 134n.
[23] *Hivac Ltd v Park Royal Scientific Investments Ltd* [1946] Ch 169.
[24] *Hivac Ltd v Park Royal Scientific Investments Ltd* [1946] Ch 169.
[25] *Regal v Gulliver* [1942] 1 All ER 378, [1967] 2 AC 134n; *Boardman v Phipps* [1967] 2 AC 46; *Attorney-General for Hong Kong v Reid* [1994] 1 AC 324, [1993] 3 WLR 1143; *Westdeutsche Landesbank Girozentrale v Islington LBC* [1996] AC 669, HL.
[26] See the discussion in Chapter 30.
[27] See GW Thomas, *Taxation and Trusts* (Sweet & Maxwell, 1981) generally.

solely for the purpose of avoiding liability to tax which have no underlying commercial purpose.[28]

53.12 The other principal motivation for the use of a trust to conduct a business is to generate income for beneficiaries otherwise than by means of those sorts of investment considered in Part I of this book. Thus a family business, for example, can be held on trust for the benefit of identified members of the family as beneficiaries and operated so as to generate income for them by their trustees. Whereas a trust structure does not lend itself easily to the constitution of complex business ventures in the manner that a company can, trusts do have the advantage of lacking many forms of public regulation, accounting rules, and so forth to which companies are prey. The advantage of a company is that it constitutes a nexus of contracts whereby creditors, employees, and so forth are able to transact simply with the company in full knowledge of its publicly available accounts and constitutive documents, whereas trusts are required to effect multi-layered contracts between the trustees and each individual creditor or employee always in the shadow of the limitations placed on the rights of each by the trust instrument. A declaration of an ordinary trust of chattels, however, can be created orally and so with the minimum of formality;[29] unlike a company organized under English law which requires an array of properly structured constitutional documentation to satisfy public officials at Companies House,[30] and a minimum number of directors,[31] company secretaries,[32] published and audited accounts,[33] and regular meetings organized and conducted according to statute and the company's own constitution.

53.13 There are, therefore, commercial uses for trusts beyond the avoidance of tax and the generation of income for beneficiaries in a quasi-familial context. One example is that of the hedge fund, a form of financial actor which is occasionally structured as a trust and which trades in speculation on a range of financial instruments. Hedge funds are usually joint ventures between banks or other financial institutions which are frequently created in jurisdictions in which the resultant entity will not be subjected to financial regulation with the express purpose of making high-risk, high-return investments in a way which the financial institutions would not wish or would not be able to do on their own balance sheets. The financial institutions contribute a given amount of investment capital and appoint, usually, traders from other institutions to act as their agents with clear guidelines as to their investment strategies. Hedge funds benefit from structures either as partnerships, as joint ventures (in jurisdictions which recognize that notion as a specific form of legal entity), or as trusts. These structures have the advantage of not being

---

[28] *Fitzwilliam v IRC* [1990] STC 65; *Hitch v Stone* [2001] STC 214. More generally see the 'artificial steps' doctrine in *Ramsay v IRC* [1982] AC 300; *Furniss v Dawson* [1984] AC 474.
[29] *M'Fadden v Jenkyns* (1842) 1 Ph 153.   [30] Companies Act 1985, s 2.
[31] Companies Act 1985, s 282.   [32] Companies Act 1985, ss 283, 286.
[33] Companies Act 1985, ss 235–237, where appropriate.

required to publish accounts or their constitutional documents. As a result, counterparties dealing with hedge funds usually have little publicly available information as to the hedge funds' credit worth, the authority of its traders, or the capacity of the fund itself. These issues require contractual agreement as to the disclosure of financial and legal information in practice.

The trust, therefore, offers confidentiality and the possibility of a high speculative **53.14**
return not permitted by ordinary financial regulation. The financial institutions who fund these hedge funds act as settlors and also hold equitable title in the assets and the profits of the fund. The traders they retain may either be employed by means of a contract with some specially created subsidiary of the settlors or are appointed to be trustees of the fund itself. It is also possible, through the trust mechanism, to decide the precise terms on which the settlors have title reserved to them as beneficiaries for tax purposes. The detail of the taxation of trusts will differ from jurisdiction to jurisdiction and from context to context.

B. The Role of the Trustee

Title in trading assets

The trust trades through its trustees, as considered above.[34] The legal title in the **53.15**
trust property is held by the trustees also. The trustees are empowered to deal with the trust property in whichever way the trust instrument provides: generally in the furtherance of the trust's business purpose and to advance the fruits of that enterprise to the beneficiaries as provided for by the trust.

The trust property in this context will be more difficult to establish than in ordinary **53.16**
situations and the equitable interests of the beneficiaries will be similarly opaque. Whereas, in ordinary trusts structures, the beneficiaries would be entitled to exercise their collective powers under the rule in *Saunders v Vautier*[35] to call for the trust property, in relation to trading trusts the purpose of the trust will require that the trust property is applied to the furtherance of the business. Therefore, the trust instrument will typically limit the beneficiaries' interests by permitting them only to receive income or only to wind up the trust's business activities in certain, limited circumstances. To prevent the beneficiaries at any time from claiming to constitute the entirety of the equitable interest in the fund and to be entitled to call for delivery up or the sale of the trust's assets, the settlor will generally ensure either that there is some parcel of the equitable interest which is held by some person who is directed not to agree to such a winding up (and so to prevent any other beneficiaries from constituting the entire equitable interest), or else make their equitable interests contingent on some event, including the continued operation of the business.

---

[34] See para 53.04.   [35] (1841) 4 Beav 115.

The management role of the trustees

53.17 The trustees bear a difficult, dual role which the trust instrument would be required to make plain. On the one hand, the trustees are required by the general law of trusts to avoid conflicts of interest,[36] to act faithfully in the interests of the beneficiaries,[37] and to act fairly between the beneficiaries.[38] On the other hand, however, the trustees will bear contractual duties to the creditors of the business, to whom they may owe personal liabilities (as considered in the next paragraph), and also duties to any employees of the business. Where the trustee is a corporate trustee, its officers will be required to balance their obligations to the company for which they work with their obligations to the trust which they serve. As such the trust instrument, as considered below,[39] will generally contain a range of exclusions from liability for those trustees so as to explain how they are expected to manage their duties to the company which employs them and the trust which retains that company as its trustee. There remains, however, the overriding problem of balancing the needs of the business, with its call on capital investment and the other assets of the trust, with the needs of the beneficiaries perhaps to advancements out of the trust's capital and to its income stream. The trustees will need to correlate the beneficiaries' desire for a stream of income with a manager's natural desire both to expand his business through investment and to use the business's assets to pay incentives to employees, to maintain the physical working environment, and to comply with the business's general legal and social obligations as an employer. All of these various claims on the business's assets and on the trustees' attention are considered in the following paragraphs.

The personal liability of trustees

53.18 In line with the ordinary law of trusts, subject to what is said in paragraphs 53.21–53.23 concerning the limitation and exclusion of liability, the trustees will be personally liable for any breach of trust or for any loss suffered by the trust[40] and also for any obligation owed to any third party by means of a contract entered into by the trustees on behalf of the trust.[41] That is so even if the trustee retires from his trusteeship,[42] unless the creditor has agreed to the replacement of one trustee with another. It is for this reason that settlors of trading trusts will tend to use companies as trustees so that the trustee has a limited liability due to its corporate status.

53.19 The difficulty with losses suffered by a trading trust, even in the absence of exclusion of liability provisions in the trust instrument, is that a trade is likely to suffer

---

[36] See para 10.99.   [37] See para 10.07.   [38] See para 10.13.
[39] See the discussion at para 53.24.   [40] *Target Holdings v Redferns* [1996] 1 AC 421.
[41] *Wightman v Townroe* (1813) 1 M & S 412.
[42] *Wightman v Townroe* (1813) 1 M & S 412; *Muir v City of Glasgow Bank* (1879) 4 App Cas 337.

loss not simply because of the culpable failures of its management but also because technological change, social change, or economic circumstances may cause general loss in the market in which that business operates. A typewriter repair business might become obsolete as the small businesses which once it served acquire computers with warranties that provided on-site repair from the manufacturer. A business selling luxury goods is likely to suffer a downturn during a general economic recession in which people are less inclined to buy its products. Whereas there are many things which a trustee or business manager can do to minimize the effect of these changes or even to reposition the business to take advantage of them, trading trusts are likely to suffer loss (or fail to generate profit growth) for reasons which are not the fault of the trustees. The trust instrument must identify how such changes in the business's fortunes are to be treated and at what point, if any, the trustees may become liable for any loss suffered by the trust as a result of a downturn in the profits earned by that trust's business. Otherwise, it may become a difficult matter for the law of trusts to decide what level of business competence is required of a trustee in such circumstances and whether or not a plea that mitigating factors in the market place caused the trust's loss ought to succeed.

By analogy from the general law on trust investment, trustees are required to act **53.20** as though prudent business persons acting in the interests of those for whom they feel morally bound to provide.[43] The Trustee Act 2000 does not appear to apply in this context but rather only to investment activity, as considered in Chapter 52[44] However, prudence does not answer this particular question. A requirement of prudence does not oblige trustees to be dynamic business managers. Rather, it suggests that they should avoid risk wherever possible. That is not how a business would meet changes in its market or challenges from outside. To meet such challenges the trustees would be required to apply the trust's assets to change the trust's business or to adapt it in some way. That requires the opposite of prudence: it requires active management of the business and the taking of appropriate levels of risk. The requirement of prudence in this sense might become closer to the requirement in the Trustee Act 2000 that the trustees understand that their duty of care to the beneficiaries requires that they act reasonably and that they take appropriate professional advice.[45]

The limitation and exclusion of the trustee's liability

The trustee may seek to limit his liability in two ways. The first form of limitation **53.21** of liability might be with regard to the beneficiaries so that the beneficiaries are not entitled to recover any loss suffered by the trust from the trustees personally.[46]

---

[43] *Learoyd v Whiteley* (1887) 12 App Cas 727.
[44] See DJ Hayton, 'Trading Trusts', in J Glasson (ed), *The International Trust* (London: Jordan Publishing, 2002) 479.
[45] See the discussion at para 52.15. [46] *Armitage v Nurse* [1998] Ch 241.

The other form of limitation, however, relates to liabilities owed by the trustee to creditors. In this section, it is this latter form of limitation of liability which is discussed.

53.22 The trustee will be personally liable to third party creditors for all obligations contracted for on behalf of the trust by any of the trustees,[47] unless the trustee has expressly limited his personal liability in any contract entered into with those creditors.[48] To exclude or limit his liability, the trustee would require an explicit term of the contract with that creditor to justify a departure from the ordinary principles of the law of trust.[49] It would be a requirement that the trustee be permitted by the trust instrument to limit his liability in this way by means of contract.[50]

53.23 Alternatively, the trustee would require that there be an express provision in such a contract to the effect that the trustee was acting only in his capacity as a trustee and not so as to give the creditors any access to his personal property or estate in the event that there be any breach of contract or other obligation owed to that creditor.[51] It is a matter for the construction of such contracts as to their efficacy. The trustee is most likely to structure the contract to the effect that the creditors would be able to proceed only against the assets of the trust in satisfaction of their obligations. If the trust is subject to a number of similar claims, there may not be sufficient property in the trust to satisfy those claims. If the contracts provide no guarantee that the trust will be able to meet their claims out of its assets, but rather restrict those creditors' rights to proceed against the trust fund to the extent that there are assets available to meet their claims, then the creditors' claims would be so limited, if unsecured.[52]

The trustee's right to indemnity

53.24 The preceding paragraphs considered the manner in which the trustee might exclude or limit his liability either to the beneficiaries or to third party creditors; this section considers the manner in which the trustees might secure an indemnity from the beneficiaries for either form of liability. Trustees are permitted to recover their expenses by the general law of trusts.[53] However, the question of an indemnity against liability occupies a different, exceptional context from the recovery of ordinary expenses.

---

[47] *Muir v City of Glasgow Bank* (1879) 4 App Cas 337.
[48] *Re Robinson's Settlement* [1912] 1 Ch 717; *Helvetica Insurance Co v Knight* [1982] 7 ACLR 225.
[49] *Muir v City of Glasgow Bank* (1879) 4 App Cas 337.
[50] *Octavo Investments Property Ltd v Knight* (1979) 144 CLR 360.
[51] *Re Robinson's Settlement* [1912] 1 Ch 717.
[52] *Swiss Bank Corporation v Lloyds Bank Ltd* [1980] 3 WLR 457.
[53] Trustee Act 1925, s 30(2).

If the trust instrument provides for an exclusion or an indemnity of liability, then the **53.25** trustees are entitled to rely on that provision;[54] contrariwise, the trustees will have no such right if the trust instrument expressly excludes it.[55] In general terms, where there is no such express trust provision, the trustee has a right to be indemnified by the trust fund.[56] This right also permits the trustee to retain the trust assets until the indemnity is met either by way of a lien[57] or alternatively as a form of 'preferred beneficiary'.[58] The right to an indemnity is effective provided that the trustee has not been guilty of a breach of trust in relation to those matters which cause him to seek the indemnity,[59] or if the expenses have otherwise been improperly incurred.[60] Provisions in the trust instrument seeking to exclude the right of indemnity might not be enforceable if it appears that the purpose of that provision was to exclude creditors' rights[61] for the benefit of the beneficiaries or of the settlor. The nature of the trustees' indemnity was considered in detail in Chapter 21.

Bankruptcy

In the event that it is not possible to meet the creditors' claims out of the assets of **53.26** the trust then, subject to what has been said above about the limitation of liability, it is possible for any individual acting as trustee to be made bankrupt or for any company acting as trustee to be placed in liquidation. The bankruptcy of an individual trustee may give grounds for that trustee to be removed from his office.[62]

C. The Rights of Beneficiaries

Title in the trust property

The meaning of 'property' in this sense

The property which comprises the trust fund will extend beyond a fund of money **53.27** expressed by the trust's capital account and its profits, and beyond any premises or plant, into the goodwill of the business and future cash flow.[63] The trust instrument will be required to identify how title in each of these assets is to be understood and how the trustees are entitled to deal with and account for each. If goodwill is

---

[54] *Trustee Act* 1925, s 15.
[55] *Trustee Act* 1925, s 69(2); *Re German Mining Co* (1854) 4 De GM & G 19.
[56] *Chief Commissioner of Stamp Duties v Buckle* (1998) 72 ALJR 243.
[57] *Jennings v Mather* [1902] 1 KB 1.
[58] *Chief Commissioner of Stamp Duties v Buckle* (1998) 72 ALJR 243.
[59] *Target Holdings v Redferns* [1996] 1 AC 421. Cf *Re Evans* (1887) Ch D 597; *Re British Power Traction and Lighting Co Ltd* [1910] 1 Ch 470.
[60] *Fraser v Murdoch* (1881) 6 App Cas 855; *Strickland v Simmons* (1884) 26 Ch D 245.
[61] *Re Johnson* (1880) 15 Ch D 548.   [62] *Trustee Act* 1925, s 36.
[63] *Don King Productions Inc v Warren* [1998] 2 All ER 608, Lightman J; affirmed [2000] Ch 291, CA.

accepted as being a part of the business's assets, then any action of the trustees which damaged that goodwill could be said to be a form of loss wrought on the trust by the trustees, even if there is no other, more tangible loss to the trust's assets.

The comparison with shareholders in a company or members of a co-operative

53.28 Shareholders in an ordinary company acquire rights to be consulted in company meetings and minority shareholders acquire rights not to be oppressed by majority control.[64] More generally, the shareholders acquire a right to a dividend if a dividend is declared and to participate in the assets of the business on a winding up. Similarly members in an industrial and provident society acquire statutory rights under the Industrial and Provident Societies Act 1965 to control the society's officers.[65] These societies are required to be organized for the benefit of the community on a co-operative basis. Significantly, the members of the society acquire no proprietary rights in the assets of the society but rather have democratic rights of control over the use of its assets. Beneficiaries have proprietary rights in the assets of the fund, unlike the members of companies or industrial and provident societies, but they do not ordinarily have rights *qua* beneficiaries to vote in the activities of the trust in formal meetings.

Trust, not partnership

53.29 The structure of the beneficiaries' rights must be careful to avoid the creation of a partnership. Whether or not a partnership has been created would be interpreted in the circumstances by the courts by reference to section 1 of the Partnership Act 1890 which provides that a 'partnership' is 'the relation which subsists between persons carrying on a business in common with a view of profit'. An important feature of a partnership is that the partners share the profits from their business enterprise by virtue of a contract between them. In many cases it is the liability in common to share in the losses of an enterprise which can be the clearest indication that there is a partnership in existence.[66] In consequence, the beneficiaries will not be partners simply by reason of the fact that they receive profits from a business but they might be construed to be partners if a contract between the beneficiaries and the trustees grants the beneficiaries powers over the activities of the trustees which suggest that they are equal participants in the conduct of the business *qua* beneficiaries. If the beneficiaries' powers are restricted to the receipt of the equitable interest in profits

---

[64] *Prudential Assurance Co Ltd v Newman Industries Ltd (No 2)* [1981] Ch 257, [1980] 2 All ER 841. See also the derivative action under Companies Act 1985, s 459.

[65] As amended in part by the Industrial and Provident Societies Act 2002.

[66] *Wise v Perpetual Trustee Co* [1903] AC 139, 149, whereby unincorporated associations are distinguished from partnerships on the basis that the subscribers to an association are not required to contribute any amounts to the association's losses beyond their original subscription to join the association.

and to the ordinary right to receive information from the trustees, then they would not be partners in common with the trustees.

Beneficiaries' control of the trustees

The beneficiaries' principal control over the trustees can be exercised through the rule in *Saunders v Vautier*[67] if they act together, provided that they are *sui juris* and that they constitute the whole of the equitable interest. Otherwise, the beneficiaries' only effective powers relate to the trustees' obligations to provide information to the beneficiaries and to carry out their duties properly. If the beneficiaries are given powers which are too extensive, then, as considered in the previous paragraph, this may render them partners with the trustees rather than simply beneficiaries. **53.30**

D. The Rights of Creditors

Activities beyond the powers of the trustees, or outwith the scope of the trust

When dealing with a trust which conducts a business, it is important for the creditor to know the details of the trustees' powers under the trust instrument to ensure that the trustees have the authority to bind the trust's assets by a contract with the creditors. If a trustee purports to act outwith the scope of his powers, then he does not have the capacity to bind the trust assets to that transaction.[68] This analysis applies whether the trustee has simply acted beyond the scope of either his own powers or the capacity of the trust,[69] or that he has acted in breach of trust.[70] By contrast, company law has excluded the operation of the *ultra vires* principle by statute[71] in relation to the activities of companies by providing that nothing in the memorandum of association or in the articles of association will cause any transaction purportedly entered into on behalf of the company to be avoided, unless the third party seeking to rely on the contract has acted in bad faith. **53.31**

Creditors' action against the trustee personally

The rights of the creditors against the trustees personally were considered above.[72] The basis of that claim will be the contractual nexus between the creditors and the trustees, and any tortious liability which may have been occasioned during any transaction. Consequently, the extent of the claim would be governed by the terms of that contract or by the law of tort. The creditors, however, are entitled to **53.32**

---

[67] (1841) 4 Beav 115.   [68] *Re Johnson* (1880) 15 Ch D 548, 552.
[69] *Re Johnson* (1880) 15 Ch D 548, 552.   [70] *Re Evans* (1887) 34 Ch D 597.
[71] Companies Act 1985, ss 35, 35A, and 35B.   [72] See para 53.01.

be subrogated to any right which the trustees have to be indemnified from the trust's assets[73] if any personal claim against the trustee will fail.[74]

Taking security in the trust assets

53.33   The means by which security is taken using trust structures was considered in Chapter 48.[75] The simplest means of so doing would be for a third party creditor to be admitted to the class of beneficiaries, with the value of his rights limited to the extent of his contractual claim, by means of the variation of the terms of the trust. While this is legally the clearest mechanism for securing the rights of the creditor, it may pose commercial and practical problems. Alternatively, the trustees could be required to hold assets on trust for the creditor outwith the terms of the business trust or subject to a charge. In general terms, the courts will not be astute to infer an intention to create a secured right, such as a charge, over a trust.[76] In consequence such a right would need to be created explicitly and plainly. Otherwise, the means by which the creditors' rights will be protected will be limited to contractual provisions: a solution which provides no security in the event that the trust has insufficient assets to meet any individual creditor's claims.

---

[73] *Re Oxley* [1914] 1 Ch 604.
[74] *Owen v Delamere* (1872) LR 15 Eq 134; *Fairland v Percy* [1875] LR 3 P & D 217.
[75] See the discussion at para 48.01.
[76] *Re State Fire Insurance Co* (1863) 1 De GJ & SM 634.

54

FIDUCIARY LIABILITY IN THE CREATION OF FINANCIAL AND COMMERCIAL TRANSACTIONS

A. The Scope of Fiduciary Liability in Commercial Transactions

Introduction

The purpose of this chapter is to consider the manner in which the law of trusts **54.01** conceives of the fiduciary liability of trustees and others when creating commercial, and particularly financial, contracts. Of particular significance here is the liability of those who act as advisers—whether as investment advisers or otherwise—to trustees or to others who owe fiduciary duties to third parties. Their liabilities are principally those of constructive trustees to the extent that they are involved in any breach of their clients' fiduciary duties or are possibly the obligations of fiduciaries in their own right depending upon the nature of their relationship with their clients. In modern financial markets and in other areas of commercial activity, it is increasingly common for the providers of services to occupy roles in relation to their clients which lead to them being categorized as fiduciaries, in the manner considered in Chapter 25, or which require those advisers to transact with people who themselves owe fiduciary duties to third parties. So, for example, in financial markets we have witnessed increasing volumes of investment in private pension funds and collective investment schemes as more ordinary members of the public, who would not previously have held any financial investments, have been forced to provide for their own pensions and other means of support outside the welfare state. Consequently, there is ever more financial services activity involving professional advisers whose clients are inexpert, retail customers in relation to whom the professional adviser is required by the financial regulation considered in this chapter to exercise a greater level of care than other categories of client when selling and dealing with financial services. This may render the adviser himself a fiduciary, as considered later in the chapter. Alternatively, the adviser may be dealing with the trustee of a fund who is in a fiduciary relationship to third parties such that the adviser may, even if not a fiduciary himself, face equitable obligations to compensate those third parties in the event that his advice generates a loss for them. While much of the discussion in this chapter focuses on financial services and on financial services regulation, it is suggested that the discussion relates more generally to other commercial activity albeit with the important caveat that other commercial markets may not be governed by the sort of formal regulation which informs the manner in which financial services providers treat their customers. Therefore, this chapter will consider the liabilities of investment advisers as fiduciaries, the duties owed by such advisers under Financial Services Authority regulation, and the liabilities which such persons may face in relation to the commission of equitable wrongs. The general principles relating to fiduciary liability imposed by the law of trusts which arise in this chapter have been considered variously in Section One of this book: this chapter, therefore, seeks to draw together some of those concepts relevant to this context and, in so doing, to extract some of the key themes which have informed the growing litigation in this area. The first section considers the classification of the various claims at issue in relation to commercial contracts and then the remainder of the chapter teases out those claims which relate to the law of trusts.

54.02   Under the general law, the full range of legal and equitable claims covering the breach of fiduciary liabilities in commercial transactions fall into three categories: first, claims for common law damages or for rescission arising from some failure of the contract to express the parties' free intentions (vitiated consent); secondly, claims for compensation for loss arising from torts, constructive trusteeship attracted by some involvement in a breach of trust, and other forms of misfeasance (wrongs and other misfeasance); and, thirdly, claims to rights in property or for loss arising on the basis of some unconscionable act by one or other of the parties (equitable recovery of property or profits, or restitution of unjust enrichment).[1] The focus of this chapter will be, as is considered in paragraph 54.05, on those claims which arise in equity in relation to the law of trusts. A more extended discussion of actions brought in relation to unconscionable behaviour and restitution is set out in Chapter 55, a discussion which deals with the recovery of property from transactions which are terminated involuntarily. This chapter will concentrate instead on claims arising directly from selling products or from unconscionable activity in the creation of contracts, and not on the termination of contracts which are considered in the next chapter.

Identifying the suitability of a commercial transaction in equity using regulatory rules

The financial services markets operate in the United Kingdom under the scrutiny **54.03** of the Financial Services Authority which creates regulatory rules under the auspices of the Financial Services and Markets Act 2000, as considered in Chapter 47. Those regulatory rules establish a quasi-legal context[2] in which the activities of persons authorized under the 2000 Act to sell financial services operate. Taken together, then, it is clear that the regulation of financial markets functions so as to inform the manner in which the substantive law treats financial market activity: although financial regulation operates in a manner which generates results akin to law but nevertheless outwith the substantive law.[3] For present purposes, it is sufficient to note that regulation can inform the manner in which common law courts and courts of equity will consider what is reasonable and what is conscionable in a commercial context, as well as what is formally lawful.[4]

---

[1] The tripartite division between consent, wrongs, and unjust enrichment is a modish one, commanding the particular support of restitution lawyers. It is not the aim of this book to argue one viewpoint rather than another: the author seeks to describe and anticipate events rather than state partisan intellectual opinions. See perhaps P Birks, 'Trusts Raised to Reverse Unjust Enrichment: The *Westdeutsche* Case' [1996] RLR 3, 26. Although this writer has doubted many of the claims made for restitution of unjust enrichment generally (see AS Hudson, *Equity & Trusts* (3rd edn, Cavendish Publishing, 2003) ('*Hudson*'), ch 34) it is a useful catch-all expression in relation to commercial contracts.

[2] The context is 'quasi-legal' in the sense that they do not create legal concepts akin to the contract or the trust but nevertheless in the sense that they do create norms with which market participants must comply if they are to be considered to be acting as a reasonable or a conscionable market participant would; they are also 'quasi-legal' in the sense that, while the regulations do not in themselves create offences which are overseen by the criminal law, nevertheless they do grant powers to the Financial Services Authority to punish entities which they regulate for infractions of the regulations.

[3] *Bankers Trust v Dharmala* [1996] CLC 518.

[4] *Dunford & Elliot Ltd v Johnson & Firth Brown Ltd* [1977] 1 Lloyd's Rep 505; *Re St Piran* [1981] 1 WLR 1300; *Re a Company* [1987] BCLC 382, 387; *Stafford v Conti* [1981] 1 All ER 691; *Crabtree v Hinchcliffe* [1972] AC 707, 730. On the interaction between financial regulation and the common law, see AS Hudson, 'The regulatory aspect of English law in derivatives markets' in AS Hudson (ed), *Modern Financial Techniques, Derivatives and Law* (London: Kluwer International, 1999) 69.

54.04 A useful idea in this context is that of 'suitability': that is, suitability as to the manner in which a product or a strategy is sold to a counterparty, and also suitability as to the intrinsic appropriateness of that transaction for the particular customer for whom it is provided or to whom it is sold.[5] The notion of suitability, then, obliges the seller of a financial instrument to act in a manner which is commercially suitable for the context: failure so to do will constitute a breach of those regulations.[6] The Financial Services Authority's Conduct of Business Regulations provide the following in relation to the manner in which financial instruments or investments are sold to ordinary private customers:[7]

> (1) A firm must take reasonable steps to ensure that it does not in the course of designated investment business—
>
>> (a) make any personal recommendation to a private customer to buy or sell a designated investment; or
>>
>> (b) effect a discretionary transaction for a private customer…
>
> unless the recommendation or transaction is suitable for the private customer having regard to the facts disclosed by him and other relevant facts about the private customer of which the firm is, or reasonably should be aware.

Therefore, authorized persons dealing in financial services in the UK are required to consider the suitability of the purpose of an investment for the particular investor. The firm is required to take reasonable steps to ensure that they act suitably and that the investment is suitable for the customer's general investment portfolio in circumstances in which the firm is acting as 'investment manager' for such a customer.[8] The proximity between the status of investment manager and that of trustee or agent, and thus fiduciary, is considered in greater detail below.[9] In either circumstance, the principles of fiduciary duty considered in this chapter are significant in relation to the sellers of financial services where the fiduciary is required to avoid conflicts of interest and to act in the best interests of the beneficiary, just as the seller of financial services is obliged in general terms to ensure that it provides only suitable investments for its customers. It is suggested that these concepts of fiduciary obligation and of suitability may bear features in common, in the manner considered in this chapter.

Within the context of suitability is the implicit obligation to avoid conflicts of interest.[10] The enforcement of a notion of suitability, as considered in the context of this section, is in the form of the collective term for a group of common law,

---

[5] FSA, *Conduct of Business Regulations*, reg 5.3.5.

[6] See W Blair et al, *Banking and Financial Services Regulation* (3rd edn London: Butterworths, 2002) 317; R Cranston, *Principles of Banking Law* (2nd edn, Oxford University Press, 2000) 212. Also see J Beatson 'Financial services and fiduciary duties' in E McKendrick (ed), *Commercial Aspects of Trusts and Fiduciary Obligations* (Clarendon Press, 1992) 55, 64.

[7] FSA, *Conduct of Business Regulations*, reg 5.3.5.

[8] ibid, reg 5.3.5(2).   [9] See para 54.05.

[10] See W Blair, *Financial Services: The New Core Rules* (Blackstone, 1991) 94.

statutory, and equitable claims to do with the liability of a seller of financial services, whether a bank or some other financial institution. Significantly, it is also the product of a creeping convergence of case law norms with regulatory norms in cases concerning the sale of financial instruments to purchasers who claimed that they had not understood the scope of their potential liabilities in relation to these products.[11] The combination of the particular regulations involved, as to the manner in which business is to be conducted with customers,[12] and the development of the case law requires the seller of a financial product both to ensure that the means by which a product is sold and the substance of the product itself are suitable for that particular customer.[13]

B. The Categories of Fiduciary Duty Arising in Commercial Contracts

The liability of commercial parties as fiduciaries

The general scope of fiduciary liability was considered in Chapter 25.[14] It is sug- **54.05** gested that, while the following discussion focuses primarily on the liabilities of financial institutions, its principles may nevertheless be applicable to commercial parties in general terms. The core of fiduciary liability in this context is easier to define by reference to what it is not. A person is not a fiduciary simply by virtue of giving advice to another person. A person is not a fiduciary simply by virtue of having greater bargaining strength when creating a transaction. Rather, fiduciary duties will only be imposed on a commercial person in circumstances in which there is a relationship of sufficient dependence by one party on the other, which that other party accepts, such that a relationship of trust and confidence is created.

The essence of the fiduciary relationship is often said to be one of loyalty and consequently one which precludes the fiduciary from advancing his personal interests

---

[11] *Bankers Trust v Dharmala* [1996] CLC 518; *Morgan Stanley v Puglisi* [1998] CLC 481.
[12] Financial Services Authority, *Conduct of Business Rules.*
[13] There has been some debate as to the need for a concept of suitability within the English common law to protect unsophisticated users of financial derivatives from the dangers inherent in the products and also to protect them from the attentions of experienced sellers: see, for example, S Greene, 'Suitability and the Emperor's new clothes' (1996) 3 EFSL 53; and Little, 'Suitability the Courts and the Code' (1996) 3 EFSL 119. Much of the argument circulates around the issues which typically arise in the debate as to the need to regulate financial derivatives because they are considered necessarily to be generative of risk and not of any evident benefit. The principal argument for the development of a distinct category of liability on grounds of suitability is that derivatives constitute a new risk which is deserving of a specific, tailor-made remedy. The counter-argument is that there is a sufficiency of common law and equity able to deal with these claims. This argument is capable, at its edges, of running into the anti-regulation argument that existing regulatory safeguards ought to be sufficient to protect the unwise or unwary when creating financial instruments. See AS Hudson, *Swaps, Restitution and Trusts* (Sweet & Maxwell, 1999) 196 *et seq.*   [14] See para 25.15.

at the expense of, or in conflict with, the interests of the object of his fiduciary obligations.[15] This creates difficulties in relation to financial advisers who are acting as market makers in the securities which they sell to their customers or who stand to earn a commission or other profit from some other financial instrument created for an individual customer.[16] The imposition of fiduciary liability nevertheless arises in contexts in which there is some duty of loyalty imposed on the defendant, as expressed by Millett LJ in the following terms:

> A fiduciary is someone who has undertaken to act for or on behalf of another in a particular matter in circumstances which give rise to a relationship of trust and confidence. The distinguishing obligation of a fiduciary is the obligation of loyalty. The principal is entitled to the single-minded loyalty of his fiduciary. The core liability has several facets. A fiduciary must act in good faith; he must not make a profit out of his trust; he must not place himself in a position where his duty and his interest may conflict; he may not act for his own benefit or the benefit of a third person without the informed consent of his principal. This is not intended to be an exhaustive list, but it is sufficient to indicate the nature of fiduciary obligations. They are the defining characteristics of the fiduciary.[17]

What emerges further from this discussion is that the obligations of a fiduciary, while being subject to general rules, are nevertheless sensitive to context and capable of arising in entirely novel situations.[18] As Lord Browne-Wilkinson has held:

> . . . the phrase 'fiduciary duties' is a dangerous one, giving rise to a mistaken assumption that all fiduciaries owe the same duties in all circumstances. That is not the case. Although so far as I am aware, every fiduciary is under a duty not to make a profit from his position (unless such profit is authorized), the fiduciary duties owed, for example, by an express trustee are not the same as those owed by an agent.[19]

Reliance in these situations is best considered by analogy with the relationships of trustee and beneficiary, where one person takes custody or some power over the property of another, or of agent and principal, where one person agrees to act on behalf of another, or where the parties become business partners. If one party were providing professional advice in the course of his business to that other person as his client, then a situation akin to the solicitor-client relationship may be created such that the adviser may be deemed to owe duties of loyalty and confidentiality to the client. In any event, the nature and the terms of the fiduciary responsibilities which are imposed in any of these situations will depend very much on the circumstances, on the relative expertise of the parties, the length of any relationship between the parties, and the parties' common understanding of the nature of their commercial interaction. It would not be supposed that one who sells goods to

---

[15] On which see Chapter 29 on the imposition of constructive trusts in relation to the abuse of fiduciary office generally.   [16] Such as an over-the-counter derivative.

[17] *Bristol and West Building Society v Mothew* [1998] Ch 1, 18, *per* Millett LJ.

[18] *Collings v Lee* [2001] 2 All ER 332.

[19] *Henderson v Merrett Syndicates* [1995] 2 AC 145, 206.

another acts in a fiduciary capacity unless the seller has been understood by both parties to have been the buyer's agent, perhaps acting in similar transactions over some period of time. In relation to the financial institutions, these difficulties are considered in greater detail.[20] The contexts in which fiduciary liability may and may not come into existence are considered in the following sections.

Where the client is dependent upon the financial adviser or bank such that a fiduciary duty may come into existence

Where a financial institution is acting as a trustee for a client, or as an agent of that client, or as a partner of that client, or as a director of a company for that client, then it will be in an express fiduciary relationship in connection with that client. That much is trite law. In consequence the trustee will be liable to account to the client for any loss which is connected to any breach of trust which the trustee commits.[21] By contrast, the relationship of banker and client in itself will not necessarily import a fiduciary relationship, although there are a number of situations in which a fiduciary relationship will arise, such as the situation in which: the bank induces business by agreeing to become financial adviser,[22] the bank advises a customer to enter into a transaction,[23] the bank has discretionary control of a customer's assets (but only to the extent of that discretionary control),[24] and the bank advises a person to enter into a transaction which is to their financial disadvantage without ensuring that they have taken independent advice.[25]

54.06

That banks occupy a fiduciary position in relation to their customers only in limited circumstances

In general terms, banks will not owe fiduciary duties to their customers but rather merely contractual obligations.[26] This is in spite of the bargaining power which banks might ordinarily be considered to have over their customers. As considered in the previous paragraph it will only be in circumstances in which banks act as advisers to their customers, such that the relationship becomes something other than an ordinary banker-customer relationship, that there will be any fiduciary

54.07

---

[20] See P Finn, 'Fiduciary Law and the Modern Commercial World', in E McKendrick (ed), *Commercial Aspects of Trusts and Fiduciary Obligations* (Oxford: Clarendon Press, 1992) 7.
[21] *Target Holdings v Redferns* [1996] 1 AC 421, [1995] 3 WLR 352, [1995] 3 All ER 785.
[22] *Woods v Martins Bank Ltd* [1959] 1 QB 55; *Standard Investments Ltd v Canadian Imperial Bank of Commerce* (1985) 22 DLR (4th) 410.
[23] *Lloyds Bank v Bundy* [1975] QB 326; *Royal Bank of Canada v Hinds* (1978) 88 DLR (3rd) 428.
[24] *Ata v American Express Bank*, unreported, 7 October 1996 (Rix J), 17 June 1998 (Court of Appeal).
[25] *National Westminster Bank plc v Morgan* [1985] AC 686; *Barclay's Bank v O'Brien* [1993] 3 WLR 786; *CIBC v Pitt* [1993] 3 WLR 786. Cf *Royal Bank of Scotland v Etridge (No 2)* [2002] AC 773 in relation to domestic mortgages.
[26] *National Westminster Bank plc v Morgan* [1983] 3 All ER 85. See the more detailed discussions in other jurisdictions in *Stewart v Phoenix National Bank* (1937) 64 P 2d 101; *Haywood v Bank of Nova Scotia* (1984) 45 OR (2d) 542; *Smith v Commonwealth Bank of Australia* (1991) 102 ALR 453.

duties imposed on the bank. One example of the imposition of just such a fiduciary relationship would be the context in which banks advise a customer who is vulnerable, as with the elderly customer in *Lloyds Bank v Bundy*,[27] to acquire a financial product (such as an endowment mortgage or a high interest overdraft) from the bank which causes the customer loss while making a gain for the bank. The general context in which a bank will have its contracts set aside and potentially be considered to be acting in a fiduciary capacity, in the words of Lord Denning, will be in the following context, where there is:[28]

> . . . inequality of bargaining power. By virtue of it, the English law gives relief to one who, without independent advice, enters into a contract upon terms which are very unfair or transfers property for a consideration which is grossly inadequate, when his bargaining power is grievously impaired by reason of his own needs or desires, or by his own ignorance or infirmity, coupled with undue influences or pressures brought to bear on him by or for the benefit of the other.

Therefore, whereas mere inequality of bargaining power will not in itself impose a fiduciary relationship on a bank, if it is coupled with an unfair exercise of such power in a manner which is oppressive of the customer, then the bank may be deemed to be a fiduciary. Considered more closely, this formulation suggested that the imposition of fiduciary liability is dependent on the bank acting unfairly and therefore as being a formula for providing relief rather than an office which the bank could be considered to have held throughout the parties' interaction. A little like the defendant who owes damages under the tort of negligence only once he has breached some duty of care, the bank in these circumstances would only appear to become a fiduciary once its actions have become oppressive of its client. The term 'oppressive' here is used because it is reminiscent of Lord Ellesmere's formulation of those factors which would cause equity to act in general terms[29] and also because Lord Nicholls uses it in *Palk v Mortgage Services Funding plc*[30] to denote the point at which a mortgagee's exercise of its right of sale over mortgaged property put it in a position analogous to that of a fiduciary.

There are a number of contexts in which a bank will owe implied duties of care to its customers, dependent generally upon the contracts created between them.[31]

---

[27] [1975] QB 326.

[28] *Lloyds Bank v Bundy* [1975] QB 326, 339, [1974] 3 All ER 757 765. See, however, *National Westminster Bank v Morgan* [1985] AC 686, 708, [1985] 1 All ER 821, 830 which sought to call the breadth of this principle into question, suggesting that each case must be considered on its own facts and in its own circumstances.

[29] As Lord Ellesmere put it in the *Earl of Oxford's Case* (1615) 1 Ch Rep 1, the purpose of the office of Lord Chancellor (always assuming that office still exists once this book is published) acting through the Courts of Chancery was 'to correct men's consciences for frauds, breaches of trust, wrongs and oppressions of what nature soever they be, and to soften and to mollify the extremity of the law, which is called summum jus'.   [30] [1993] 2 WLR 415.

[31] M Hapgood, *Paget's Law of Banking* (12th edn, Butterworths, 2003) 119. See in particular the sentiments expressed by Lord Scarman in *Cotton Mill Ltd v Liu Chong Hing Bank Ltd* [1986] AC 80,

These general duties often relate to technical matters as to the bank's implied duty to protect its customers from fraud relating to cheques and statutory obligations relating to negligence in clearing cheques. However, there are also obligations relating to the obligations to exercise due care and skill when advising customers as to investment choices.

Significant examples of general fiduciary duties incumbent on banks are the bank's general, contractual duty of confidentiality in respect of its customer's dealings[32] and also the recently developing law in relation to undue influence over loans secured by way of mortgage.[33] The bank's duty of confidentiality is expressed in the case law as being an implied contractual obligation, as opposed to a general fiduciary duty, which can be breached[34] when it is required by law, or in the discharge of a duty to the public, or where disclosure has been authorized, or in the bank's own interest.[35] It is suggested that this last ground for ignoring the duty would itself call into question its fiduciary character, although the point has not been considered expressly in decided cases. Breach of these duties is generally considered to be a matter giving rise to liability in contract[36] although it is suggested that in ordinary circumstances one would expect that a duty of confidentiality would constitute a fiduciary duty when combined with a relationship of some sensitivity in which the person owing the duty is acting as the agent of the other and has control of the other's financial affairs subject to contract. The particular context of undue influence, however, as it has developed in equity and, consequently, in banking law prevents the bank from exercising its contractual rights under the mortgage contract and has led some commentators to treat the bank in such situations as being a constructive trustee for the victim of the undue influence of any benefit arising to it from the transaction:[37] a matter considered in Chapter 27.[38]

54.08

105, [1985] 2 All ER 947, 956, to the effect that if banks wish to limit their liabilities it is for them to do so by changing the terms of their terms of business by contract (to the extent permitted now by FSA regulation, as considered above, para 47.01 *et seq*) and not to rely on the law to rein in their liabilities by a contraction in the law of negligence and also, it is suggested, of fiduciary duties.

[32] *Tournier v National Provincial and Union Bank of England* [1924] 1 KB 461.
[33] *Royal Bank of Scotland v Etridge (No 2)* [2001] UKHL 44, [2001] 3 WLR 1021, [2001] 4 All ER 449. [34] *Tournier v National Provincial and Union Bank of England* [1924] 1 KB 461.
[35] *Sutherland v Barclays Bank Ltd* (1938) 5 LDAB 163.
[36] See for example M Hapgood, *Paget's Law of Banking* (12th edn, London: Butterworths, 2003) 135, para 8.16.
[37] A Oakley, *Constructive Trusts* (3rd ed, Sweet & Maxwell, 1997) ('*Oakley*') 35. See also *Morris v Burroughs* (1737) 1 Atk 398. [38] See para 27.29. See also *Hudson* 665.

C. Advisers and Others Interfering With a Fiduciary Relationship

The liability of financial advisers acting as fiduciaries

54.09 This section considers the problem of advisers who themselves might not occupy fiduciary positions but who might be advising trustees or other people occupying fiduciary positions. The range of fiduciary relationships in the modern commercial world, ranging from pensions funds to unit trusts to commercial agents and company directors, makes the liability of such advisers as constructive trustees particularly important. The potential liability either for assistance in a breach of a fiduciary duty or for receipt of property transferred in breach of such a duty arises where the adviser had sufficient knowledge of the breach of duty.

Participation in a breach of a fiduciary duty

54.10 Dishonest assistance in some breach of a fiduciary duty will found a personal liability in the defendant to account to the claimant for the full extent of its loss as a constructive trustee.[39] Where a person dishonestly assists another in a breach of a fiduciary duty, then that dishonest assistant will be personally liable to account to the beneficiary of that duty for the value lost to the trust or other fiduciary relationship. The dishonest assistant itself will not need to be a fiduciary; simply that it assist in some breach of some other person's fiduciary duty. 'Dishonesty' in this context is a broad concept requiring that there be some element of fraud, lack of probity, or even reckless risk taking. It is not necessary that any fiduciary is itself dishonest; simply that the dishonest assistant is dishonest. The distinction from liability for 'knowing receipt', considered below, is that there is no requirement for the imposition of liability that the stranger have had possession or control of the property at any time.[40]

54.11 In describing the nature of the test for liability for dishonest assistance in *Royal Brunei Airlines v Tan*,[41] Lord Nicholls held that ' . . . acting dishonestly, or with a lack of probity, which is synonymous, means simply not acting as an honest person would in the circumstance. This is an objective standard.'[42] What is clear is that this test of 'dishonesty' does not require that there is any active *lying*.[43] Rather, it is sufficient that the assistant fails to live up to an objective standard of probity.[44]

---

[39] *Royal Brunei Airlines v Tan* [1995] 2 AC 378.

[40] *Agip (Africa) Ltd v Jackson* [1991] Ch 547; *Polly Peck International plc v Nadir (No 2)* [1992] 4 All ER 769; *Westdeutsche Landesbank v Islington* [1996] AC 669.

[41] [1995] 2 AC 378; *Twinsectra v Yardley* [2002] UKHL 12.   [42] [1995] 2 AC 378, 386.

[43] cf *Eagle Trust plc v SBC Securities Ltd* [1992] 4 All ER 488, 499, *per* Vinelott J; *Polly Peck International plc v Nadir (No 2)* [1992] 4 All ER 769, 777, *per* Scott LJ.

[44] This is to be contrasted with the action for knowing receipt which, in the judgment of Scott LJ in *Polly Peck International plc v Nadir (No 2)* [1992] 4 All ER 769, sets out a form of subjective test of whether or not the recipient 'ought to have been suspicious' and thereby have constructive notice of the breach of trust in those particular circumstances.

Indeed, with particular relevance to the context of investment advisers, Lord Nicholls expanded his discussion of 'dishonesty' to consider the taking of risk by that assistant, for example, when giving investment advice to a customer and failing to deal appropriately with the level of risk appropriate to that customer. Lord Nicholls held that:

> All investment involves risk. Imprudence is not dishonesty, although imprudence may be carried recklessly to lengths which call into question the honesty of the person making the decision. This is especially so if the transaction serves another purpose in which that person has an interest of his own.[45]

It may be that an investment adviser will be liable to account to the beneficiaries of his trustee customer for any loss caused by an investment strategy which is both a breach of trust and one which is considered to have been recklessly imprudent in that context. Furthermore, if the adviser stands to profit from the transaction by way of commission or by way of having acted as a market maker (that is, selling securities to the customer which the investment adviser owned himself at the time of the sale), then that will increase the likelihood that that investment adviser will be held to have been 'dishonest' in this stylized sense. The basis of this form of liability is that the investment adviser

> ... takes a risk that a clearly unauthorized transaction will not cause loss ... If the risk materialises and causes loss, those who knowingly took the risk will be accountable accordingly.[46]

An investment adviser may therefore be liable where the risk taken, for example in respect of an interest rate swap, is in furtherance of a contractual obligation to invest property and manage its level of risk. The court might consider that risk to be too great, even though the market might consider a plain interest rate swap to be standard practice and even advisable in many circumstances. If the FSA's Conduct of Business rulebook required a particular level of treatment for a particular type of client and the investment adviser failed to observe those obligations, then the likelihood that the adviser will be held to be have acted 'dishonestly' in this sense is all the greater.

The liability for the seller is that of making good the whole of the claimant's loss **54.12** where its property invested under some fiduciary relationship was found to have been invested imprudently or recklessly.[47] Therefore, the role of a commercial adviser is problematic. In terms of transactions such as that in *Bankers Trust v Dharmala*,[48] where the losses generated are very large in cash terms, it will appear *ex post facto* that the risk taken would have been unacceptable. This is particularly so where the transaction at issue is being used as part of a portfolio investment strategy but then generates a loss which is large in terms of the total size of the

---

[45] [1995] 2 AC 378, 387.   [46] [1995] 2 AC 378, 387.   [47] ibid.
[48] [1996] CLC 518.

portfolio, or which is disproportionate to the losses generated by the other assets making up the portfolio. On the basis that it is the court's decision on the level of risk that counts, it is therefore difficult to counsel an adviser as to the approach to be taken to the investment of trust property. It is not a failure to ascertain whether or not the investment is in breach of trust which is decisive of the matter, but rather whether or not the *level of risk* assumed is in breach of duty. Recklessness as to the ability of the trust to invest must similarly be a factor to be taken into account in deciding on the honesty of the third party investment manager. Similarly, where the bank charges any fees in connection with the transfer, it may be liable for knowing receipt of a part of that money.[49]

Receipt of property transferred in breach of a fiduciary duty

54.13 Knowing receipt of property passed away in breach of trust carries with it the same liability as that for dishonest assistance in the breach of trust to account to the beneficiaries for any loss suffered as a result of that breach of trust.[50] In contradistinction to dishonest assistance, knowing receipt requires that there have been some receipt of property of whatever form which has been transferred from the trust in breach of fiduciary duty. Where a person receives trust property in the knowledge that that property has been passed in breach of fiduciary duty, the recipient will be personally liable to account to the trust for the value of the property passed away.[51]

54.14 In relation to investment advice, trust property must therefore be demonstrated to have been received by that adviser for him to be liable for knowing receipt. Commonly the individual adviser will not receive trust property. If the adviser simply gives the client trustees advice as to which investments they ought to acquire, then no property will pass through the adviser's possession and therefore there will not be any liability for knowing receipt. More commonly, the adviser will act as an intermediary and so maintain accounts for its customers so that the adviser will organize that the money which it holds to its customer's account is invested in the requisite investments and that those investments may in turn be held by the adviser: in such a situation, the adviser will receive the trust property and so be liable for knowing receipt.

54.15 The more complex questions arise as follows. First, who was it who received the trust property? Typically, the individual who provides investment advice will be

---

[49] The liability in respect of deposit-taking banks can be difficult to conceptualize. For example, where X Bank allows a cheque drawn on A's account to be paid to a third party's account, the bank may be liable for dishonest assistance. Where the third party's account was overdrawn, the credit of the cheque will make the bank potentially liable for knowing receipt where the funds are used to reduce the overdraft because in the latter instance the bank receives the money in discharge of the overdraft loan. See *Oakley* 186 *et seq.*   [50] *Re Montagu* [1987] Ch, 264.
[51] *Per* Scott LJ in *Polly Peck International plc v Nadir (No 2)* [1992] 4 All ER 769.

employed by a financial institution and it will be that institution which holds the client's account and which will receive the trust property. Consequently, in relation to the second question, it will be necessary to show that the financial institution which receives the trust property had the requisite knowledge to justify the imposition of liability to account as a constructive trustee. The categories of knowledge applicable in this context are actual knowledge of the breach of trust; wilfully shutting one's eyes to the obvious fact that the property was paid away in breach of trust; and wilfully and recklessly failing to make inquiries which an honest person would have made so as to discover that the property was passed away in breach of trust.[52] As Scott LJ held in *Re Polly Peck plc v Nadir (No 2)*,[53] these categories are not to be taken as rigid rules and 'one category may merge imperceptibly into another'.[54] In that case, it was held that there was no requirement to prove a fraudulent misapplication of funds to found a claim on knowing receipt; rather, it was enough to demonstrate that the recipient had had the requisite knowledge both that the funds were trust funds and that they were being misapplied. Scott LJ approached the liability of commercial people from the perspective, in a case involving the liability of a bank, of an 'honest and reasonable banker'.[55] In that sense, it is important to look to regulatory norms to consider how a commercial person in the circumstances of the defendant might have been expected to act in any particular market.[56] These issues were considered in Chapter 47.[57]

Where the adviser intermeddles with the trust relationship

There may be other situations in which a financial institution may intermeddle **54.16** with a pre-existing fiduciary relationship to such an extent that it would be deemed to be a fiduciary itself. The likelihood of such a finding is increased where the adviser is making all of the investment decisions for that trust. However, it has been held that a trustee, and therefore by extension it is suggested a constructive trustee, may limit its liabilities for negligent dealings with the trust fund by means of contract in the form of a conduct of business letter.[58] In circumstances in which a solicitor interfered with the running of a trust to the extent where he was making its investment decisions, that solicitor has been held to be a constructive trustee in relation to that trust.[59] Where a person who has not been officially appointed as a trustee of an express trust interferes with or involves himself in the business of the trust so as to appear to be acting as a trustee, that person shall be

---

[52] The original five categories are restricted to three by *Re Montagu*, [1987] Ch 264.
[53] *Per* Scott LJ in *Polly Peck International plc v Nadir (No 2)* [1992] 4 All ER 769.
[54] *Per* Millett J in *Agip (Africa) Ltd v Jackson* [1989] 3 WLR 1367, 1389.
[55] *Op cit* 778–780.
[56] It does appear, however, that the reasonableness of the recipient's belief falls to be judged from the perspective of the recipient itself. [57] See para 52.18.
[58] *Armitage v Nurse* [1998] Ch 241. [59] *Boardman v Phipps* [1967] 2 AC 46.

deemed to be a trustee.[60] The trustee de son tort must have trust property in his possession or control before this form of constructive trust will obtain.[61] As such, a fiduciary will be liable to account to the beneficiaries as though a trustee for the loss occasioned to the trust.

The liability of a fiduciary for unauthorized profits

54.17   This section will consider that part of the law of trusts which will impose financial or fiduciary responsibility on the defendant in respect of some loss suffered as a result of some commercial transaction and which will require the fiduciary to account for some unauthorized profits made in respect of the transaction. There are two contexts in which this form of liability might be important. The first is where a seller is advising a customer as to its commercial strategy in circumstances where it occupies either an express or a constructive fiduciary relationship in respect of its client. As with the facts of the leading cases, often the use of information acquired from the fiduciary relationship to make profit is itself grounds for liability. The second situation is where, for example a market-making stockbroker, sells a product to its client in relation to which it makes a profit for itself. There is straightforwardly a conflict between the fiduciary obligations of protecting the beneficiary and the need to make profit.

54.18   A fiduciary will be constructive trustee of any unauthorized profits made from that office, even if the fiduciary has acted in good faith.[62] The rule is a strict rule that no profit can be made by a trustee or fiduciary which is not authorized by the terms of the office. A fiduciary who profits from that office will be required to account for those profits. The rule emerges from *Keech v Sandford*[63] in which it was held that a trustee who renewed a lease personally to protect the interest of an infant beneficiary was required to hold his interest under that lease on trust for the child. While there had been no allegation of fraud in that case, the Lord Chancellor considered that the rule should be 'strictly pursued' because there were risks of fraud in allowing trustees to take the benefit of renewed leases which they had previously held on trust.[64] The continued rigour of this rule is best illustrated by the decision of the House of Lords in *Boardman v Phipps*[65] in which a solicitor to a trust generated personal profits from the takeover of a private company, having learned of the opportunity while on trust business, and was required to hold those profits on constructive trust for the beneficiaries of that trust.[66] As Lord Cohen held in *Boardman v Phipps*: 'an agent is, in my opinion, liable to account for profits

---

[60] *Mara v Browne* [1896] 1 Ch 199, 209.   [61] *Re Barney* [1892] 2 Ch 265.
[62] *Boardman v Phipps* [1967] 2 AC 67.   [63] (1726) 2 Eq Cas Abr 741.
[64] See also *Re Biss* [1903] 2 Ch 40   [65] [1967] 2 AC 46.
[66] It is worth nothing that the trust was not out-of-pocket as a result of the transaction although the trust would clearly have generated more profit if the shares had been bought for the trust; that is, the trust was affected by an opportunity lost rather than a direct, out-of-pocket loss.

which he makes out of the trust property if there is a possibility of conflict between his interest and his duty to his principal'.[67] The nature of this constructive trust may therefore be a proprietary institution or arise simply out of conflict of duty. The issue for the adviser is the possible liability for profits made out of a transaction in respect of which that adviser was meant to act in fiduciary relation to the buyer. Two points arise from this decision. The first is the rigour with which the rule is applied to circumstances in which the solicitor did not take an opportunity which the trust was already enforcing for its own purposes for his own profit and for which he used his own money rather than any trust property.[68] The second is the manner in which the solicitor was deemed to be a fiduciary in relation to the trust.

To resist this claim the trustee must either have the profits authorized or, in recent company law cases, have demonstrated that the opportunity in question was not one which the company intended to pursue for itself. So, in *Queensland Mines v Hudson*[69] a managing director who pursued a business opportunity which the company did not want to pursue was absolved of liability as a constructive trustee because he had received authorization from the company's board of directors. The strictness of the rule from *Keech v Sandford* was illustrated in the very similar case of *Industrial Development Consultants Ltd v Cooley*[70] where a managing director acting similarly was held liable to hold the profits he made from exploiting such a spurned business opportunity as constructive trustee, in spite of purportedly receiving the authorization of the board of directors. As considered in Chapter 21,[71] it is a feature of commercial trusts arrangements that fiduciaries have their liabilities excluded by express contractual provision with the settlor.[72] **54.19**

Liability in respect of bribes or other unlawful profits

When a person commits an unlawful act or receives a bribe, that person is deemed to occupy a fiduciary position during the commission of such an act; for example, when acting as an employee in relation to her employer or as a trustee in relation to a client, the fiduciary is required to hold the traceable proceeds of **54.20**

---

[67] Some of their lordships held that the trust was founded on this proprietary nexus between the information and the profit, rather than simply finding that the status of fiduciary required property to be held on trust. Perhaps this indicates the role of the law on constructive trusts as being a part of property law rather than a law of personal obligations.

[68] Aside, that is, from the question as to whether or not the solicitor was using confidential information belonging to the trust. [69] (1977) 18 ALR 1.

[70] [1972] 2 All ER 162. [71] See para 21.24.

[72] *Armitage v Nurse* [1998] Ch 241.

the bribe on proprietary constructive trust for the beneficiaries of the fiduciary duty.[73] That proprietary constructive trust requires that any profits made are similarly to be held on constructive trust. Similarly, any losses made as a result of investing the bribe will be required to be made good by the constructive trustee.[74]

[73] *Attorney-General for Hong Kong v Reid* [1994] 1 AC 324.
[74] See also *Reading v A-G* [1951] AC 507.

55

TRUSTS AND THE TERMINATION OF CONTRACTS

A. Introduction

This chapter considers the effect of the involuntary termination of transactions by   **55.01**
virtue of some mistake between the parties, failure of consideration, supervening
illegality of the transaction, or some similar event. When a transaction terminates
involuntarily in such a fashion there will be questions as to the manner in which
any outstanding performance obligations under the contract will fall to be carried
out, questions as to restitution of any amounts of money paid under the transaction, and questions as to the recovery of any other property transferred under the
transaction. The issue of the performance of any outstanding obligations will be
resolved by contract law and the doctrine of specific performance; however, the
issues as to the recovery of money or other property transferred under the transaction will fall to be resolved by the law of trusts and the common law on money
had and received, and therefore form the focus of this chapter.

B. Effecting Recovery of Payments at Common Law

Before considering the role of the law of trusts in the establishment of proprietary   **55.02**
claims on the termination of a commercial contract, it is important to consider
the counterpart to such claims in the form of personal claims to recover money
owed to the claimant at common law. This section, therefore, considers briefly the
nature and the limits of such common law claims in an attempt to identify both
the advantages and the requirements for the maintenance of proprietary claims in
equity.

55.03 The leading case in this context is the decision of the House of Lords in *Westdeutsche Landesbank v Islington*.[1] In that case, a bank had made payments, comprising payments of a capital sum and of interest, to a local authority under a ten-year interest rate swap before the parties learned that the contract had been void *ab initio*. The bank sought an equitable proprietary claim against the amounts which had been paid to the local authority, a claim which will be considered below in greater detail, and also a claim at common law for money had and received. The House of Lords held unanimously that the bank was entitled to recover an amount equal to that which it had transferred to the local authority together with simple interest. In Lord Goff's opinion, the basis for that claim was based on the speech of Lord Mansfield in *Moses v Macferlan*,[2] where his lordship had held that the 'gist of the action for money had and received'[3] is that 'the defendant, upon the circumstances of the case, is obliged by the ties of natural justice and equity to refund the money'.[4]

55.04 The basis on which the claim for money had and received (or, the personal claim for restitution) was made in *Westdeutsche Landesbank v Islington* was unclear. There were a number of candidates for the role. One category of claim which gives rise to a personal claim for restitution is that of failure of consideration. A claim based on failure of consideration will be available where a contract is found to be unenforceable, regardless of whether there has been some purported partial performance of that contract or not. The failure of consideration in that case could be said to have arisen on the basis that the contract was *ultra vires* the local authority. To that effect, Morritt LJ held that:[5]

(1) A contract which is ultra vires one of the parties to it is and always has been devoid of any legal contractual effect.
(2) Payments made in purported performance thereof are necessarily made for a consideration which has totally failed and are therefore recoverable as money had and received.[6]

Alternatively, a common mistake as to the efficacy of the contract could have founded that claim. A mistake made by both parties in entering into a transaction will enable that contract to be rescinded.[7] However, where only one party to a

---

[1] [1996] AC 669.   [2] (1760) 2 Burr 1005, 1012.
[3] [1996] 2 All ER 961, 980. *South Tyneside MBC v Svenska International plc* [1995] 1 All ER 545.
[4] *Westdeutsche Landesbank v Islington* [1996] AC 669, [1996] 2 All ER 961, 980; *Guinness Mahon & Co Ltd v Kensington & Chelsea RLBC*, The Times, 2 March 1998, CA, *South Tyneside MBC v Svenska International plc* [1995] 1 All ER 545.   [5] [1998] 2 All ER 272, 284.
[6] These dicta appear in the wake of the decision of Lush J in *Brougham v Dwyer* which held that, in relation to the failure of the Birkbeck Building Society: '... the defendant had received moneys belonging to the building society under a transaction which had no validity of any sort ... The case appears to me to be on all fours with one in which money has been advanced on something which was thought to be a contract, but as to which it turns out there had been a total failure of consideration ...': (1913) 108 LT 504, 505. See also *Re Coltman* (1881) 19 Ch D 64, CA.
[7] *Cundy v Lindsay* (1878) 3 App Cas 459.

contract is acting under a mistake, the contract, typically, will not be rescinded[8] unless the party who was not operating under a mistake was aware that the other party was so operating.[9] Furthermore, it does appear that the mistake must have been operative on the minds of the contracting parties and must have induced them to enter into the contract.[10]

The long-standing principle that restitution could not be sought on the basis of a **55.05** mistake of law was overruled by a decision of the House of Lords in relation to interest rate swaps in *Kleinwort Benson v Lincoln City Council*.[11] The more difficult question was in deciding what sorts of circumstances would constitute a mistake of law. The question was put to the House of Lords whether a settled understanding of the law in a market place would suffice and further whether honest receipt of money by a person acting on such a settled understanding of the law ought to constitute a defence to an action for restitution of amounts paid to it. Lord Goff held for the majority it is not a part of English law that payments made under a settled understanding of the law among market participants is irrecoverable when that settled understanding of the law is subsequently held to have been incorrect. By analogy with the mistake of fact cases the possibilities seemed to include liability mistakes, causative mistakes, and fundamental mistakes. In *Nurdin and Peacock plc v D B Ramsden and Co Ltd*[12] Neuberger J held that Robert Goff J's causative test in *Barclays Bank v Simms*[13] should apply equally to a case where the money was paid under a mistake of law by deciding that issue on the basis of whether or not that mistake was operative on the actions of the parties.[14]

C. Proprietary Claims on Termination of a Commercial Contract

When proprietary claims will be available

The principal form of proprietary claim in relation to unenforceable contracts will **55.06** be a claim seeking to establish a constructive or resulting trust, by means of equitable tracing. The clearest judicial statement of the nature of the trust was that of Lord Browne-Wilkinson in *Westdeutsche Landesbank v Islington*.[15] That case concerned an interest rate swap in which moneys were transferred outright by a bank to a local authority as payments under that swap before the parties learned that the swap contract was outwith the capacity of the local authority and was therefore

---

[8] *Riverlate Properties Ltd v Paul* [1975] Ch 133.
[9] *Webster v Cecil* (1861) 30 Beav 62; *Cooper v Phibbs* (1867) LR 2 HL 149; *Hartog v Colin & Shields* [1939] 2 All ER 566.
[10] *Bell v Lever Bros* [1932] AC 161; *Oscar Chess v Williams* [1957] 1 WLR 370.
[11] [1998] 4 All ER 513.   [12] The Times, 18 February 1999.   [13] [1980] QB 677.
[14] Neuberger J added that '[i]t might also be that the payer had to go further and establish, for instance, that the mistake was directly connected to the overpayment and/or was connected to the payer/payee relationship.'   [15] [1996] AC 669.

void *ab initio*. The bank argued that the local authority should be deemed to hold those moneys on trust for it as a result of the injustice of allowing the local authority to retain the money on the basis either of the parties' mutual mistake or the failure of their contract. They sought to argue such a trust so that they could receive compound interest on their money rather than merely simple interest. Their argument failed in front of the House of Lords. In the leading speech of Lord Browne-Wilkinson in *Westdeutsche Landesbank v Islington*[16] the kernel of the trust concept was identified as being equity operating on the conscience of the person who is the owner of the legal title in property. By extension of that principle, it was held that a person 'cannot be a trustee of the property if and so long as he is ignorant of the facts alleged to affect his conscience'.[17] In consequence, it was held that no constructive trust had come into existence because the local authority did not know it lacked the legal capacity to enter into the interest rate swap contract at the time when that contract was purportedly created: the parties did not know that the swaps contract had been void *ab initio* until the House of Lords handed down its decision in *Hazell v Hammersmith & Fulham*[18] declaring the authority's incapacity to create such a contract some years after it had received and spent the money paid to it by the bank. To succeed in a claim that there be a constructive trust imposed, the bank would have had to show that the defendant had some knowledge of 'the factors which [were] alleged to affect his conscience' at the time he received the money or at some time before he disposed of it.[19]

55.07   The further problem which arose in *Westdeutsche Landesbank v Islington* related to equitable tracing. In the *Westdeutsche* case itself, the property, which the bank had transferred to the local authority before the void nature of the contract was known, had ceased to be identifiable when it was transferred into a bank account which subsequently went overdrawn. This was said to offend against the principle that there must be identifiable trust property before there can be a valid trust or an equitable tracing claim into that bank account: the overdraft on the account proved that the property which had been in that account had ceased to be there and that money was, as a matter of fact, impossible to trace after it had left that account.[20] As Lord Browne-Wilkinson held, in reliance on *Re Goldcorp Exchange Ltd (in receivership)*,[21] '[o]nce there ceased to be an identifiable trust fund, the local authority could not become a trustee' of the money it had received from the bank.

On the facts before him, Lord Browne-Wilkinson held that there was never a coming together of all of the factors necessary to found a trust or a tracing claim

---

[16] [1996] AC 669.   [17] ibid.   [18] [1991] 1 AC 1.
[19] [1996] AC 669, [1996] 2 All ER 961, 988.
[20] ibid. There is an exception to this principle in the case of personal liability imposed under constructive trust on a person who dishonestly assisted in a breach of trust.
[21] [1995] 1 AC 74.

in equity before the judgment in *Hazell v Hammersmith & Fulham LBC* was handed down. As his lordship held:

> There was therefore never a time at which both (a) there was defined trust property and (b) the conscience of the local authority in relation to such defined trust property was affected. The basic requirements of a trust were never satisfied.[22]

As such, equity will not grant any proprietary remedy to the payer under a void contract unless there had been either some effective, express retention of proprietary rights or some unconscionable act on the part of the recipient which would create a constructive trust while the defendant held the traceable proceeds of the original property in his possession.

Constructive trusts

The creation of proprietary rights under constructive trust

Where no express trust or other proprietary right has been created,[23] then the claimant will be required to demonstrate that the defendant holds the property sought on constructive trust for him. The need to demonstrate a proprietary right arises in three kinds of situation: the first is where the contract has sought to retain rights in particular property; the second is where the parties are attempting to establish rights in specific property after an event of default or the insolvency of their counterparty; the third is where the plaintiff is claiming compound interest. **55.08**

As considered in detail in Chapter 27, the clearest example of a constructive trust coming into existence was Lord Browne-Wilkinson's own reinterpretation of the facts of the decision in *Chase Manhattan v Israel-British Bank*.[24] In that case one bank had mistakenly made a payment to another bank twice: the first payment was properly owed but the second payment was made because of a clerical error. The recipient bank went into insolvency before the mistaken, second payment was returned to the payer bank. Lord Browne-Wilkinson explained that there could only be a trust of the second payment both if the recipient knew that the payment had been made to it under a mistake and also if it would have been unconscionable for the recipient to have retained the money. That the payment was made under a mistake meant that it would have been unconscionable for the recipient to have retained that payment: however, a trust would only come into existence at the time when the recipient realized that the payment had been made mistakenly or that the mistake was brought to its attention. Consequently, if the customer had not known before the time of its bankruptcy that the second payment had been made under a mistake, then the customer would not be taken **55.09**

---

[22] [1996] AC 669, [1996] 2 All ER 961, 988–989.
[23] Whether by retention of title or creation of a fixed charge or otherwise: para 11.03.
[24] [1981] 1 Ch 105—delivered by Lord Browne-Wilkinson in *Westdeutsche Landesbank Girozentrale v Islington LBC* [1996] AC 669, HL.

to hold that second payment on a constructive trust for the bank because its conscience would not have been affected at the material time.[25] If the constructive trust came into existence before the bankruptcy, then the constructive trust would establish the bank as a secured creditor in the bankruptcy, but not otherwise.[26] On this basis, on the facts of *Westdeutsche Landesbank v Islington* itself, the local authority was not taken to have been a constructive trustee of the money it received from the bank because it had not known that the contract under which those payments were made was void.

The role of constructive trust in commercial cases

55.10 In commercial situations, for example that in *Westdeutsche Landesbank v Islington*,[27] it is important for the parties to know who has which rights in property dealt with as part of a contract. A proprietary constructive trust will give a right *in rem* to the beneficiary. That is, a right in the property itself which is enforceable against any other person. The *in rem* right comes into operation from the moment that the proprietary right is validly created, under an express trust[28] or other security structure, or at the moment when the defendant has knowledge of the factor which fixes it with the obligation of acting as a trustee under a constructive trust.[29] The alternative is a mere *in personam* right entitling the successful plaintiff to a claim in money only and not to any specific property, which would arise in relation to constructive trusteeship on the basis of dishonest assistance in a breach of trust or on the basis of knowing receipt of property in breach of trust—both of which claims were considered in Chapter 30. In cases of insolvency this relegation of the claimant's rights to a merely personal claim would mean that the claimant would have no secured rights but only a debt claim *pari passu* with other unsecured creditors. The further shortcoming of the personal claim is that it grants only an entitlement to simple interest on the money claim and not compound interest.[30] The law relating to compound interest and the nature of the constructive trust is now the subject of a more concrete test than had been the case hitherto.[31]

Tracing

55.11 As considered in Chapter 33, tracing is the process by which a claimant seeks to establish title in some property in which he either had title previously or which has been acquired or constituted in some way with his original property. The former claim, establishing title in property owned previously by the claimant, is a

---

[25] ibid.   [26] *Re Goldcorp* [1995] 1 AC 74.   [27] [1996] AC 669.
[28] An express trust is validly created either on a valid declaration of trust by the settlor (*Richards v Delbridge* (1874) LR 18 Eq 11) or at the time when legal title in the trust property is transferred to the trustee (*Milroy v Lord* (1862) 4 De GF & J 264).
[29] *Westdeutsche Landesbank v Islington* [1996] AC 669, [1996] 2 All ER 961, 988.
[30] *Westdeutsche Landesbank v Islington* [1996] AC 669.
[31] *Westdeutsche Landesbank v Islington* [1996] AC 669.

straightforward process of common law tracing using a process which vindicates the claimant's rights in the property at issue.[32] The more complex claim is the latter in which the claimant seeks to establish equitable rights in property in which he has never previously held title or in which the claimant seeks to establish proprietary rights over a mixture of property. Tracing claims are of great importance on the termination of commercial contracts because it is through tracing that commercial parties will seek to recover property or money which was transferred during the course of the contract but which is unobtainable under contract law or which will establish a different quality of claim by virtue of establishing a proprietary right. It is frequently the case that the detective work of following the passage of amounts of money through electronic bank accounts leads to accounts in which money from a variety of sources has been mixed and deployed to acquire yet other property, title in which then falls to be allocated between those various sources for the money. The claimant therefore seeks to establish some rights over the money held in that account.[33] The advantage of such a proprietary claim, as opposed to a personal claim for money had and received considered above,[34] will be that it will grant the claimant a priority in an insolvency or that it will establish title in assets which themselves increase in value.

Common law tracing

In *Lipkin Gorman v Karpnale*[35] a firm of solicitors sought to trace after money taken from its accounts and its client accounts which one of its partners had stolen and gambled at a casino. The casino held an account for the partner and had also mixed much of the money which the partner had gambled in its own, general bank accounts. It was held that the plaintiff could trace at common law only after those moneys held in accounts only for the partner and not into the casino's general bank accounts because the very money which had been misappropriated was unidentifiable from other money held in those accounts. Similarly, in *Agip (Africa) Ltd v Jackson*[36] it was held that common law tracing was only possible after clean, physical substitutions of property.[37] Therefore, where money was passed through a series of bank accounts held by a series of companies and mixed with other moneys as these transactions were carried out, it was found to be impossible to support a tracing claim at common law.

55.12

---

[32] cf *FC Jones & Sons (A Firm) v Jones* [1996] 3 WLR 703.
[33] *Agip v Jackson* [1990] Ch 265, 286, *per* Millett J; CA [1991] Ch 547; *El Ajou v Dollar Land Holdings* [1993] 3 All ER 717; appealed [1994] 2 All ER 685; *Lipkin Gorman v Karpnale* [1991] 2 AC 548.   [34] See para 9.09.
[35] [1991] 3 WLR 10, [1992] 4 All ER 512, [1991] 2 AC 548.
[36] [1991] Ch 547, [1991] 3 WLR 116, [1992] 4 All ER 451.
[37] This approach was supported by Sir Peter Millett writing extrajudicially—Millett, 'Tracing the Proceeds of Fraud' (1991) 107 LQR 71—where his lordship argued that the proper approach for English law would be to do away with common law tracing completely on the basis that it is of restricted potential use, and of no use where property is mixed or no longer separately identifiable.

1687

55.13 An extension of this doctrine was signalled by the decision of the Court of Appeal in *FC Jones & Sons (A Firm) v Jones*,[38] a case which has suggested a broader role for common law tracing by holding that it does operate to provide rights not only to identifiable property but also to profits made from such property.[39] In that case money was borrowed from a partnership by the wife of one of the partners, but at a time when the partnership was technically bankrupt. The wife had invested the money successfully and so, when the Official Receiver sought to realize the partnership's assets, the Official Receiver sought to trace at common law into the profits which the wife had made on investing the loan moneys. The loan moneys had been kept in a bank account which was distinct from all other moneys and the profits had been mixed in this account too. It was held that all of the money held in that account was to be paid to the Official Receiver on the basis of a common law tracing claim. This decision expanded the scope of common law tracing from merely following the loan moneys into an establishment of title in the profits which were derived from the investment of the original money. The Court of Appeal held, variously, that the money at issue was perfectly identifiable, that it would be unconscionable to deny the Official Receiver's claim on behalf of the partnership's estate, and that there was no reason why the wife ought not to pay the profits to the Official Receiver on the basis that they were the fruits of the original loan moneys.

Equitable tracing

55.14 Equitable tracing operates, in contradistinction to common law tracing, by permitting the claimant to trace into mixed property which is alleged to be comprised in part by property in which the claimant has an equitable interest (or the traceable substitute of such property). It is a prerequisite for an equitable tracing claim that the plaintiff had some equitable interest in the original property, or that the person who transferred that property away had some fiduciary relationship with the plaintiff, such as being a trustee.[40] This section considers the manner in which equitable tracing claims are established in commercial situations, the defences which are available, and other situations in which the right to trace might be lost on the termination of commercial contracts.

55.15 Tracing, as considered in Chapter 33,[41] is the process of identifying the property against which a claim may be brought;[42] tracing is not in itself a remedy: rather it is the means by which the property against which a remedy may be asserted is identified. In equitable tracing, the stem from which the claim flowers is the property which was held on trust or subject to some other fiduciary relationship for the

---

[38] [1996] 3 WLR 703, [1996] 4 All ER 721.
[39] Ironically, Millett LJ gave the leading judgment in that Court of Appeal.
[40] *Re Diplock's Estate* [1948] Ch 465; *Boscawen v Bajwa* [1996] 1 WLR 328.
[41] See para 33.01. [42] *Boscawen v Bajwa* [1996] 1 WLR 328.

claimant.[43] As considered in Chapter 33, there are distinctions drawn between situations in which a fiduciary has mixed trust property with his own property, or whether the fiduciary mixed the property of innocent volunteers with each other: in the former context equity has tended to pursue its policy of holding trustees liable for all of the loss suffered by the beneficiaries[44] whereas the latter context requires the courts to arbitrate between the morally equivalent claims of innocent people whose property has been commingled without their consent.[45]

The remedies available in equitable tracing

55.16 The principal remedies available in the event of commercial tracing claims are a charge,[46] a lien,[47] or a constructive trust[48] over the pool of property over which the claim is brought. On the decided cases awards have been given of other remedies in the form of a resulting trust,[49] equitable compensation,[50] and subrogation.[51] The principal issue is therefore whether the appropriate remedy is to award a charge over the property or to award direct proprietary rights in property to the plaintiff in the form of a constructive trust. The advantage of the direct proprietary right is that the plaintiff acquires equitable title in specific property; although a charge does grant property rights which will be enforceable in the event of an insolvency.[52] These issues are considered in detail in Chapter 33.

The interaction of conscience-based trusts with commercial practice

55.17 Therefore, the tracing process itself has been predicated in many of the decided cases on morally comfortable choices, between the wrongdoer and the innocent, which are not available in commercial situations in which the protagonists are commercial parties who have contracted at arm's length. In consequence, the law is required to vindicate title in morally equivalent cases or to turn to regulatory norms which would support the notion that one party had acted unconscionably. An example of such regulatory norms would be the regulations generated by the Financial Services Authority in relation to financial services providers whose interactions with their customers were conducted in a manner which contravened the standards required of a regulated service provider. A useful example of this dilemma was the case of *Bankers Trust v Dharmala*[53] in which Bankers Trust sold two complex interest rate swap structures to Dharmala. Bankers Trust was an

---

[43] *Re Diplock's Estate* [1948] Ch 465; *Boscawen v Bajwa* [1996] 1 WLR 328.
[44] *Re Hallett's Estate* (1880) 13 Ch D 695.
[45] For example see the discussions of cases as disparate as *Re Diplock's Estate* [1948] Ch 465 and *Foskett v McKeown* [2000] 3 All ER 97.   [46] *Re Tilley's WT* [1967] Ch 1178.
[47] *Re Diplock's Estate* [1948] Ch 465.
[48] *Westdeutsche Landesbank Girozentrale v Islington LBC* [1996] AC 669, HL.
[49] *El Ajou v Dollar Land Holdings* [1993] 3 All ER 717; appealed [1994] 2 All ER 685.
[50] *Target Holdings v Redferns* [1996] 1 AC 421, [1995] 3 WLR 352, [1995] 3 All ER 785.
[51] *Boscawen v Bajwa* [1996] 1 WLR 328.   [52] *Re Tilley's WT* [1967] Ch 1178.
[53] [1996] CLC 518.

expert in such structures whereas Dharmala was a financial institution without expertise in the area of financial derivatives. Dharmala claimed that it had not understood that movements in US interest rates would affect the amounts which it owed under these interest rate swaps; it further alleged that it had been the victim of common law fraud and equitable, constructive fraud exerted over it by Bankers Trust. The resolution effected by Mance J to the identification of the standard of care owed generally by Bankers Trust to Dharmala was to examine the financial regulatory code with which Bankers Trust was required to comply when dealing with its customers. Akin to the Financial Services Authority *Conduct of Business Regulations*, the then Bank of England's *London Code* required Bankers Trust to evaluate the expertise of its customer and to deal with that customer suitably, so that inexperienced customers were not sold complex financial products without having had all the necessary risks explained to them. The resolution of this particular case was in the recognition that Dharmala was a financial institution, albeit an inexpert one in the markets at issue, and therefore that Dharmala could have been expected to have informed itself about the relevant risks in this context. In this sort of context, the notion of lapses of good conscience is clearly identifiable in relation to actual fraud, duress, and undue influence, but it is more difficult to establish in other contexts simply in which one party to a contract relies on its knowledge of the markets, or its conviction that the market would move so as to generate profits at the expense of its counterparty.

Part K

TRUSTS OF LAND AND OF THE HOME

56

TRUSTS OF THE FAMILY HOME

A. Introduction

The scope of this chapter

56.01   The purpose of this chapter is to consider the principles relating to the acquisition of rights in the home in equity by means of the trust and of proprietary estoppel. The detailed rules governing the operation of trusts of land, particularly in relation to the Trusts of Land and Appointment of Trustees Act 1996 and the Settled Land Act 1925, are considered in the next chapter. That discussion relates to trusts of land once they are in existence, whereas this chapter is concerned with the means by which such trusts come into existence. The law of trusts is the means by which disputes as to ownership of the home are decided by the law of property. The focus of this chapter is on the manner in which rights are acquired by means of express trusts and trusts implied by law both over the home and, tangentially, also in any personal property owned by members of a household.[1]

56.02   There are two categories of dispute which give rise to claims for rights in trust over the home. The first form of dispute which gives rise to the issues considered in this chapter is that of conflict between owners of property. Such disputes may arise on family breakdown (whether through divorce or the termination of non-marital relationships), or in circumstances in which other co-owners of property are in conflict over their various rights in that property: property law will decide those claims in circumstances in which the family courts do not have jurisdiction, as considered below.[2] The second form of dispute is generated by some third person outside the family nexus, typically a mortgagee or other creditor, seeking to enforce a proprietary right against one or other of the beneficial owners of the home such that the other beneficial owners will seek to assert their own interests so as to prevent that third party from taking possession of the home. The protagonists involved in claims in this area may be members of the same family, whether married or unmarried, or people sharing property without being involved in any form of familial or romantic relationship. The neutral expression 'cohabitee' will be used to refer to all protagonists in such disputes.

A summary of the law on trusts of homes

This section sets out a summary of the various doctrines in English law as to the allocation and acquisition of rights in the home.

Formally valid express trusts of land

56.03   In circumstances in which there has been an express trust declared over land, the terms of that trust will be decisive of the parties' equitable interests in land,[3] in the

---

[1] The principles governing the establishment of trusts over personal property and over real property were considered in Chapter 5.   [2] See para 56.09.
[3] *Goodman v Gallant* [1986] FLR 106; *Re Gorman* [1990] 1 WLR 616; *Harwood v Harwood* [1991] 2 FLR 274.

absence of any fraud, undue influence, or duress. Such a declaration of trust must satisfy the formal requirements in section 53(1)(b) of the Law of Property Act 1925.[4]

Purchase price resulting trusts, crystallizing on acquisition of the property

Where a person contributes to the purchase price of the home an amount of the **56.04** total equitable interest proportionate to the size of the contribution will be held on resulting trust for that person.[5] A resulting trust will crystallize at the time of the acquisition of the property, thus setting the parties' respective proprietary rights in a way which will not account for subsequent alterations in the parties' domestic arrangements, their understandings of their mutual ownership of the home, nor any financial contributions to the alteration or improvement of the property itself. The rigour of the purchase price resulting trust doctrine has been diluted in recent cases to account for indirect contributions to the purchase price.[6]

Constructive trust in recognition of the common intention of the parties

The doctrine of constructive trust offers an alternative means of thinking about **56.05** the ownership of rights in the home, which may permit a resulting trust to be re-calibrated to account for subsequent dealings with the property.[7] Constructive trusts in this context operate on the basis of the common intention of the parties and are dubbed 'common intention constructive trusts'.[8] Such a constructive trust may operate on the basis of the mutual conduct of the parties as evidenced by their contribution to the purchase price or the mortgage repayments.[9] The contributions which will found an equitable interest in property will be in the form of direct applications of money to the improvement of the property[10] which are not too small to be of relevance,[11] and contributions to the mortgage repayments.[12] Alternatively, where there is no such contribution nor an express declaration of trust, the equitable interest in the home may be allocated according to the common intention of the parties by means of a constructive trust which is based on an express agreement between the parties which need not constitute an express declaration of trust.[13] In either case the claimant must have suffered some detriment.[14]

---

[4] See para 56.12.
[5] *Dyer v Dyer* (1788) 2 Cox Eq Cas 92; *Springette v Defoe* [1992] 2 FLR 388; *Tinsley v Milligan* [1994] 1 AC 340. Cf *Westdeutsche Landesbank v Islington LBC* [1996] AC 669.
[6] *Springette v Defoe* [1992] 2 FLR 388; *Huntingford v Hobbs* [1993] 1 FLR 936; *McHardy v Warren* [1994] 2 FLR 338. See also *Bernard v Josephs* [1982] Ch 391.
[7] *Huntingford v Hobbs* [1993] 1 FLR 936.
[8] *Gissing v Gissing* [1971] AC 886; *Lloyds Bank v Rosset* [1990] 1 AC 107.
[9] *Lloyds Bank v Rosset* [1990] 1 AC 107.
[10] Matrimonial Property and Proceedings Act 1973, s 37.
[11] *Burns v Burns* [1984] Ch 317; *Lloyds Bank v Rosset* [1991] 1 AC 107, [1990] 1 All ER 1111, [1990] 2 WLR 867.   [12] *Lloyds Bank v Rosset* [1991] 1 AC 107.
[13] *Lloyds Bank v Rosset* [1991] 1 AC 107; *Ivin v Blake* [1995] 1 FLR 70.
[14] *Grant v Edwards* [1986] Ch 638; *Lloyds Bank v Rosset* [1991] 1 AC 107.

56.06 That form of common intention constructive trust established by the House of Lords in *Lloyds Bank v Rosset*[15] has not commanded the respect of the junior courts, in that conduct outwith the requirements outlined in that case have nevertheless founded rights in the home.[16] The constructive trust concept in this context was limited by *Lloyds Bank v Rosset* after having been described in *Cowcher v Cowcher*[17] as supporting rights created on the basis of common intention as to the money to be contributed to the acquisition of the property and also as to the interest which each party was to take in the property regardless of their financial contribution. Latterly, it has been suggested that when the circumstances of the case do not lead to any obvious conclusion then the principle that equality is equity should be applied so as to divide the property equally between parties to long-standing familial relationships.[18] The Australian cases, by way of contrast, have taken the view that the constructive trust should be concerned to avoid unconscionability.[19]

Proprietary estoppel: detrimental reliance on assurances as to rights in property

56.07 The doctrine of proprietary estoppel will grant an equitable interest to a person who has been induced to suffer detriment in reliance on a representation that he would acquire some rights in the property as a result of his detrimental reliance.[20] Whereas rights based on constructive trust and resulting trust are institutional trusts taking retrospective effect by operation of law, as opposed to remedial trusts seeking to compensate the claimant at the discretion of the court,[21] proprietary estoppel in contrast may give rise to a purely personal right[22] or, in seeking to secure the minimum equity necessary in the context,[23] may lead the court to award the claimant the fee simple absolute in possession.[24]

Conflicting authorities

56.08 In what follows it would be foolhardy to suggest that the way through the many authorities is clear, and misleading to suggest that any individual view of the law is without qualification. At present, English law appears to be peopled with a variety of approaches to the means by which people acquire proprietary rights in

---

[15] [1991] 1 AC 107. See para 56.24.
[16] See paras 56.47 *et seq*; especially *Hammond v Mitchell* [1991] 1 WLR 1127; *Springette v Defoe* [1992] 2 FLR 388; *Huntingford v Hobbs* [1993] 1 FLR 936; *Midland Bank v Cooke* [1995] 4 All ER 562. [17] [1972] 1 WLR 425.
[18] See in particular *Midland Bank v Cooke* [1995] 4 All ER 562. This approach was expressly disavowed in *Pettitt v Pettitt* [1970] AC 777. See para 56.80.
[19] *Baumgartner v Baumgartner* (1987) 164 CLR 137; *Bryson v Bryant* (1992) 29 NSWLR 188.
[20] *Taylors Fashions Ltd v Liverpool Victoria Trustees Co Ltd* [1982] 1 QB 133; *Re Basham (Deceased)* [1986] 1 WLR 1498; *Wayling v Jones* (1993) 69 P&CR 170; *Gillett v Holt* [2000] 2 All ER 289. [21] *Westdeutsche Landesbank v Islington LBC* [1996] AC 669.
[22] *Baker v Baker* (1993) 25 HLR 408. [23] *Crabb v Arun DC* [1976] Ch 179.
[24] *Pascoe v Turner* [1979] 2 All ER 945.

their homes. Consequently the discussion in this chapter picks the clearest path through the thicket of frequently conflicting decisions. It is possible, however, to identify clear rules in relation to express trusts over the home and to identify the key issues relating to the manner in which trusts implied by law, whether constructive, resulting, or implied, will allocate similar rights. The analysis set out in this chapter suggests that there are a number of judicial approaches to the acquisition of rights in the home which cannot be reconciled one with another. Approaches taken in other Commonwealth countries are, in this area, greatly different from the most recent English authorities. Therefore, much of the discussion to follow will focus on particular issues which have been resolved in individual cases and not simply on the general shape of the law.

B. The Distinction Between Family Law and Property Law Proceedings

The respective jurisdictions of family law and trusts law courts

56.09 By way of introduction it is useful to identify the narrow line between family law proceedings relating to rights in the home and property law proceedings. The jurisdiction of the family courts relates to matrimonial property disputes.[25] Family proceedings, however, do not include disputes arising over property on the death[26] or bankruptcy[27] of an owner of that property, or in relation to actions brought by creditors, such as mortgagees, seeking to take possession of their security.[28] Consequently, those matters which are excluded from family proceedings will generally fall within the jurisdiction of the Chancery courts as property law disputes which are generally decided on the basis of principles of trusts law and of estoppel as opposed to divorce law or child law concepts. Of course there will also be disputes as to the home which involve neither divorce law nor child law concepts and which would therefore not fall within the scope of family proceedings in any event.

56.10 The development of the family law jurisdiction has seen a development of the principles of the law of trusts specifically in relation to matrimonial disputes to achieve the best result for all members of the family without being limited to the recognition of the parties' pre-existing property rights in the manner that the law

[25] Matrimonial Causes Act 1973, ss 24, 25, 25A. See *Wachtel v Wachtel* [1973] Fam 72, 91, *per* Lord Denning.
[26] See Matrimonial Causes Act 1973, s 28(3); *D'Este v D'Este* [1973] Fam 55, in relation to marriage adjustment orders after the death of one of the parties to a marriage.
[27] See *Pettitt v Pettitt* [1970] AC 777, 803, *per* Lord Morris, 817, *per* Lord Upjohn; *Re Densham* [1975] 1 WLR 1519.
[28] See *Lloyds Bank v Rosset* [1991] 1 AC 107; *Midland Bank v Cooke* [1995] 4 All ER 562.

of trusts would be.[29] What is evident is that family law proceedings take an approach which is far more closely linked to responding to the circumstances and the needs of the family members whose situation has prompted the litigation than do property law proceedings which are more closely linked to the recognition of pre-existing property rights. This distinction can be observed at even the most superficial level between two House of Lords' cases. The former, in which the judicial committee was appraised of family law issues under section 25 of the Matrimonial and Family Proceedings Act 1984, was that in *White v White*.[30] Section 25 empowers the court to consider 'all the circumstances' when deciding the appropriate maintenance to be made for members of the family after divorce. In consequence the court took into account the needs of all family members and did not restrict itself to the recognition of pre-existing property rights. By contrast the House of Lords in *Lloyds Bank v Rosset*[31] limited the scope of equity's ability to order the recognition of proprietary rights to situations in which the claimant has either contributed to the purchase price or the mortgage over the property at issue or to situations in which the parties have reached an express agreement as to the respective interests in the property. Property law, therefore, does not consider as broad a range of circumstances in allocating rights in the home as family law. It does not, for example, consider the welfare of children who have not contributed to the purchase price of the home.[32]

The treatment of unmarried cohabitees and of married couples

56.11   The law of trusts is blind as to whether the protagonists who claim rights are married or unmarried,[33] of different sexes or the same sex.[34] The law of trusts does focus primarily on the financial contributions made by the parties[35] over and above other measurements of their common intentions.[36] In relation to family proceedings, family law has prioritized the needs of all members of the family, the welfare of any children,[37] and the most appropriate means of using family property as its guiding principles. Family law and child law do apply exclusively to married couples in many contexts: a trend which is evident in the case law.[38] In general terms the courts have not been willing to extend matrimonial rights to

---

[29] *Kowalczuk v Kowalczuk* [1973] 1 WLR 930, 934, *per* Lord Denning; *Richards v Dove* [1974] 1 All ER 888; *Bernard v Josephs* [1982] Ch 391; *Gordon v Douce* [1983] 1 WLR 563. On the applicable principles of family statute see Matrimonial Causes Act 1973, ss 24, 25, 25A.

[30] [2001] 1 AC 596, [2000] 3 WLR 1571, [2001] 1 All ER 1.

[31] [1991] 1 AC 107, [1990] 1 All ER 1111.

[32] The fundamental principle of child law contained in the Children Act 1989, s 1.

[33] *Hammond v Mitchell* [1991] 1 WLR 1127.

[34] *Wayling v Jones* (1995) 69 P & CR 170; *Tinsley v Milligan* [1993] 3 All ER 65.

[35] *Lloyds Bank v Rosset* [1990] 1 All ER 1111.

[36] Except in the family assets cases like *Midland Bank v Cooke* [1995] 4 All ER 562.

[37] Children Act 1989, s 1.   [38] *Windeler v Whitehall* [1990] FLR 505, Millett J.

non-married couples.[39] This includes claims brought by mistresses of married people[40] or the business partners of married people.[41] The approach of the courts in relation to cohabitants has been to consider their various claims for rights in property to be a matter for contract[42] or agreement[43] between them. This is to be contrasted with the situation in which the rights of children or the rights of children to occupy property are involved. In relation to married couples the courts used to be reluctant to enforce contracts between the parties on the basis that marriage constituted the couple as one person in law.[44] Early suggestions of an alteration to this traditional understanding were set forth in landmark decisions such as *National Provincial Bank v Ainsworth*[45] and *Pettitt v Pettitt*[46] where it was suggested that spouses could create legally enforceable rights between themselves; as well as *Williams & Glyn's Bank v Boland*[47] in which a wife acquired a novel right of actual occupation distinct from her marriage to her husband.[48]

C. Express Trusts of Homes

When attempting to decide which of a number of co-owners is to acquire equitable rights in the home, the most straightforward factual situation is that where there has been an express declaration of trust dealing with the whole of the equitable interest in the land. Such a trust may arise under the terms of the conveyance of the property to the co-owners,[49] or as a result of an express declaration of trust between the parties,[50] or in a situation in which the property is provided for the co-owners under a pre-existing settlement.[51] Where there has been an express trust declared over land, the terms of that trust will be decisive of the division of the equitable interest in land. Such a declaration of trust must satisfy the formal requirements of section 53(1)(b) of the Law of Property Act 1925.

56.12

---

[39] *Mossop v Mossop* [1989] Fam 77; *Windeler v Whitehall* [1990] FLR 505.

[40] *Dennis v MacDonald* [1981] 1 WLR 810, 814, Purchas J.

[41] *Harwood v Harwood* [1991] 2 FLR 274, husband's business partner claims rights in the matrimonial home.

[42] For rights to be created under contract the statutory requirements of Law of Property (Miscellaneous Provisions) Act 1989, s 2(1) would have to be satisfied. A formally ineffective contract would have no effect: *Hemmens v Wilson Browne* [1994] 2 FLR 101; *United Bank of Kuwait plc v Sahib* [1995] 2 All ER 973, Chadwick J; *Pitt v PHH Asset Management Ltd* [1993] 4 All ER 961, CA. Although see now *Yaxley v Gotts* [2000] 1 All ER 711 in which proprietary estoppel was used to avoid the provisions of the 1989 Act. See also *Jennings v Rice* [2002] EWCA Civ 159, [2003] 1 FCR 501; *Ottey v Grundy* [2003] EWCA Civ 1176.

[43] See para 56.24 as to common intention and so forth.

[44] *Hyman v Hyman* [1929] AC 601; *Sutton v Sutton* [1984] 184.   [45] [1965] AC 1175.

[46] [1970] AC 777.   [47] [1981] AC 487.

[48] See also *Tanner v Tanner* [1975] 1 WLR 1346; *Layton v Martin* [1986] 2 FLR 227.

[49] *Goodman v Gallant* [1986] FLR 106.   [50] *Lloyds Bank v Rosset* [1990] 1 AC 107.

[51] *Pettitt v Pettitt* [1970] AC 777.

56.13 The most straightforward authority in this context is the case of *Goodman v Gallant*[52] where the conveyance of property included the express trust which allocated the entire equitable interest between the parties. The trust provided that the property was to be held on trust for the parties as joint tenants. The issue arose as to what interest each party had on the break-up of the relationship given their differing financial contributions towards the property up to that time. It was held by the Court of Appeal that the express trust in the deed of conveyance was decisive of all of the interests of all parties to land, and therefore that the wife took a half of the interest in the property as the deed provided.[53] It was held by Slade LJ in *Goodman v Gallant* that:

> If, however, the relevant conveyance contains an express declaration of trust which comprehensively declares the beneficial interests in the property or its proceeds of sale, there is no room for the application of the doctrines of resulting implied or constructive trusts unless and until the conveyance is set aside or rectified; until that event *the declaration contained in the document speaks for itself.*[54]

The declaration of an express trust in a conveyance or other instrument relating to the transfer of rights in land[55] is thus conclusive of the matter and there is consequently no need to consider any surrounding circumstances in the context in which the equitable interest in the property has been allocated between the parties on express trust. This principle will apply even in circumstances in which the parties to a deed of conveyance had neither read nor necessarily understood it, provided that the declaration was formally valid.[56] The only exception to this rule would be in a situation in which, under the principle in *Saunders v Vautier*,[57] the absolutely entitled beneficiaries under such a trust had directed that the equitable interest be dealt with by the trustees in some other way. Commonwealth attitudes to this principle are less fixated on the necessary decisiveness of the deed of conveyance.[58]

---

[52] [1986] FLR 106; *Re Gorman* [1990] 1 WLR 616; *Harwood v Harwood* [1991] 2 FLR 274. A solicitor may even be negligent where she does not ensure that she has properly recorded the parties' intentions as to the beneficial interest in property: *Walker v Hall* [1984] FLR 126, 129, *per* Dillon LJ.

[53] A deed will bind all parties to that deed: *City of London Building Society v Flegg* [1988] AC 54. It is suggested that the binding nature of the declaration by way of deed is based on the doctrine of estoppel by deed: J Mee, *The Property Rights of Cohabitees* (Hart, 1999) 32.

[54] Emphasis added.

[55] For example, one sufficient to constitute a declaration of trust over land in the form of the manifestation or proof of such a declaration in signed writing (Law of Property Act 1925, s 53(1)(b)) or the disposition of an equitable interest in land being signed writing (Law of Property Act 1925, s 53(1)(c)).

[56] *Pink v Lawrence* (1978) 36 P & CR 98; although there is authority to suggest that there is an exception to this principle where cogent evidence could be advanced to demonstrate that the parties' intentions were other than that contained in the deed: *Huntingford v Hobbs* [1993] 1 FLR 936.

[57] (1841) 4 Beav 115.

[58] D Hayton, 'Remedial constructive trusts of homes; an overseas view' [1988] Conv 259.

It should be remembered that in order for there to be a valid declaration of trust   **56.14**
over land, the declaration must comply with section 53(1)(b) of the Law of
Property Act 1925:

> ... a declaration of trust respecting any land or any interest therein must be mani-
> fested and proved by some writing signed by some person who is able to declare such
> trust or by his will.

Failure to comply with that formal requirement will lead to a failure to create a
valid express trust over land. It should also be remembered that under section
53(2) of the same Act there is no requirement of formality in relation to constructive, resulting, or implied trusts. The following sections will consider the creation
of constructive and resulting trusts.

D. Common Intention as the Foundation for Beneficial Ownership of the Home

The emergence of the common intention constructive trust

The development of the notion of common intention

Two leading decisions in the 1970s provided that, in the absence of a declaration   **56.15**
of an express trust and even in cases involving disputes between married couples,
it would be the common intention of the parties which would found the parties'
rights in their home by means of resulting or constructive trust.[59] Consequently,
the specific context of the acquisition of rights in the home functioned on a
different basis from other forms of trusts implied by law. As considered below,[60]
the meaning of common intention in this context gave rise to a range of
conflicting forms of constructive trust and therefore led to a further attempt by
the House of Lords to rigidify the concept.[61] Despite the clarity of that judgment,
it did not provide the flexibility which the lower courts have subsequently
attracted to themselves. To achieve this, those lower courts have returned to the
earlier House of Lords' decisions. To understand the development of the common
intention constructive trust it is therefore necessary to begin with the 1970s cases.

The decision of the House of Lords in *Pettitt v Pettitt*[62] was the first to move away   **56.16**
from older notions of the nature of marriage and the Married Women's Property
Act 1882, replacing them instead with the allocation of equitable interests in the
family home under resulting trust principles. In that case Mrs Pettitt had been
bequeathed the entire beneficial interest in a cottage. Her husband performed
renovation works on that cottage which cost him £730 and which were agreed to

---

[59] *Pettitt v Pettitt* [1970] AC 777; *Gissing v Gissing* [1971] AC 886.   [60] See para 56.24.
[61] *Lloyds Bank v Rosset* [1991] 1 AC 107.   [62] [1970] AC 777.

have increased the value of the property by about £1,000. Mr Pettitt argued that he had acquired some equitable interest in the cottage by virtue of those works and sought an order under section 17 of the Married Women's Property Act 1882 to reflect those contentions. It was contended by Mr Pettitt that the presumption of advancement would require that the wife be deemed to have intended that some equitable interest pass to the husband in return for the work undertaken in the property.[63] It was held that Mr Pettitt had not performed sufficiently important works to be entitled to an equitable interest in the property: a stream of thought which persists to this day[64] and which denies equitable interests to those who perform only minor works of repair or alteration but who have not contributed directly to the purchase price of the property.

56.17 The second case was that of *Gissing v Gissing*.[65] This case continues to found notions of common intention around the Commonwealth.[66] In that case, Mrs Gissing had worked as a secretary and married in 1935. Her husband could not find work after the 1939–1945 war but she procured him a position with the firm where she worked herself. Her husband did well and prospered in his new position. The couple bought a house in 1951 which was registered in the husband's sole name. The purchase price was provided predominantly by way of a mortgage in the husband's name together with a loan from the couple's employers. Mrs Gissing spent £220 on laying a lawn at the house and on furnishings for the house. Her husband left her in 1961 to live with another woman. The wife sought a declaration that she had some equitable interest in the property. It was held, unanimously, that Mrs Gissing acquired no beneficial interest in the property on the grounds that she had made no contribution to the purchase price of the property. It was considered that spending money on ephemeral items such as soft furnishings was not a contribution of the same order as contributing to the purchase price and therefore would be insufficient to found any equitable interest in the home.

56.18 The development which was made in *Gissing v Gissing* was that the law of trusts would not look solely to any pre-existing or formally granted rights in property but rather that the law of trusts will consider the common intention of the parties as founding equitable proprietary rights in the home. The roots of the common intention concept were expressed in the following terms:

> I take it to be clear that if the court is satisfied that it was the common intention of both spouses that the contributing wife should have a share in the beneficial interest and that her contributions were made upon this understanding, the court in the

---

[63] While criticized in *Pettitt v Pettitt* [1970] 1 AC 777, 793, *per* Lord Reid the presumption is defended by Lord Upjohn, and considered by Deane J to be too well entrenched to be completely ignored: *Calverley v Green* (1984) 155 CLR 242, 266.
[64] *Lloyds Bank v Rosset* [1991] 1 AC 107.   [65] [1971] AC 886, [1970] 3 WLR 255.
[66] Cases as different as *Lloyds Bank v Rosset* [1991] 1 AC 107 and *Midland Bank v Cooke* [1995] 4 All ER 562 have all prayed *Gissing* in aid.

exercise of its equitable jurisdiction would not permit the husband in whom the legal estate was vested and who had accepted the benefit of the contributions to take the whole beneficial interest merely because at the time the wife made contributions there had been no express agreement as to how her share in it was to be quantified. In such a case the court must first do its best to discover from the conduct of the spouses whether any inference can reasonably be drawn as to the probable common understanding about the amount of the share of the contributing spouse upon which each must have acted in doing what each did, even though that understanding was never expressly stated by one spouse to the other or even consciously formulated in words by either of them independently.[67]

The focus of common intention in this conception is on preventing the defendant from taking the benefit of the claimant's contributions without granting her a right in property. In Australia this same general notion has given rise to the notion that it would be unconscionable for the defendant to deny the claimant such a right; and in Canada to the notion that the defendant would be unjustly enriched in denying the claimant such rights and that the law will effect restitution of that enrichment by recognizing her rights in the home. In English law the court will infer a common intention from the facts of the case even if no such intention has been manifested expressly.

The House of Lords in *Gissing v Gissing* accepted that the common intention of **56.19** the parties played an important part in the foundation of equitable rights in the home but a subsequent decision of the House of Lords betrayed a concern lest such common intentions be too loosely defined or too easily established. Thus the subsequent decision of the House of Lords in *Lloyds Bank v Rosset*[68] limited the bases on which 'constructive trusts and proprietary estoppel' would give rise to a right in the home. This case is considered in detail below[69] in relation to narrowing of the concept of the common intention constructive trust, although a brief account of the rationale adopted in that decision is given here. The first form of common intention constructive trust on the *Lloyds Bank v Rosset* model arises in circumstances in which a person contributes to the purchase price of the home: this trust is generally founded on the common intentions of the parties as to their rights in the home expressed by their respective contributions to the purchase price or the mortgage repayments ('common intention constructive trust by mutual conduct'). The second form of common intention constructive trust arises where there is no such contribution nor an express declaration of trust; rather, the equitable interest in the home will be allocated according to the common intention of the parties by means of constructive trust ('common intention constructive trust by agreement') based on an express agreement between the parties which need not constitute an express declaration of trust. The nature of each form of common intention constructive trust is considered in detail below.[70]

---

[67] *Gissing v Gissing* [1971] AC 886, 908, [1970] 2 All ER 780, 792, *per* Lord Diplock.
[68] [1991] 1 AC 107, [1990] 1 All ER 1111.   [69] See para 56.24.   [70] See para 56.24.

Common intention inferred from the circumstances

56.20 The acts which will give rise to the inference of a common intention will include contributions not only directly to the purchase price of the property but also to the repayment of the mortgage. Whereas the purchase price resulting trust model which had been used previously[71] generally required that the financial contributions which the parties made would be paid at the time of the acquisition of the property, the common intention constructive trust recognized that the majority of homes were acquired in whole or in part with a loan by way of mortgage in relation to which the parties' contributions would be paid over the life of the mortgage and not at the date of acquisition. Consequently, the common intention principle in *Gissing v Gissing* functioned by recognizing that

> [t]here is nothing inherently improbable in their acting on the understanding that the wife should be entitled to a share which was not to be quantified immediately upon the acquisition of the home but should be left to be determined when the mortgage was repaid or the property disposed of, on the basis of what would be fair having regard to the total contributions, direct or indirect, which each spouse had made by that date. Where this was the most likely inference from their conduct it would be for the court to give effect to that common intention of the parties by determining what in all the circumstances was a fair share.[72]

Whereas the decision in *Gissing v Gissing* did effect a broadening in the law, nevertheless it restricts its ambit to situations in which there has been some financial contribution to the acquisition of the property. Furthermore, Lord Diplock held that *Pettitt v Pettitt* was not correct to the extent that his lordship found it impossible to impute a common intention to a couple in circumstances where there was no direct evidence of any express agreement between the parties.[73] Those sentiments were expressed in the following terms:

> ... in the absence of agreement, and there being no question of any estoppel, one spouse who does work or expends money upon the property of the other has no claim whatever upon the property of the other.[74]

Therefore, the simple incurring of detriment would count for nothing unless there were some agreement between the parties which could found an equitable right for the contributor. Nevertheless it was not necessary that there be any formality in the agreement reached between the parties, rather the most general forms of agreement would be acceptable as founding such a common intention, as indicated when Lord Diplock acknowledged that:

> [the parties'] common intention is more likely to have been concerned with the economic realities of the transaction than with the unfamiliar technicalities of the English law of legal and equitable interests in land.[75]

---

[71] As considered in detail in Chapter 26.

[72] *Gissing v Gissing* [1971] AC 886, 909, [1970] 2 All ER 780, 793, *per* Lord Diplock; applied in *Midland Bank v Cooke* [1995] 4 All ER 562; *Drake v Whipp* [1996] 2 FCR 296.

[73] [1971] AC 886, 904.

[74] *Pettitt v Pettitt* [1970] AC 777, 818, [1969] 2 All ER 385, 410, *per* Lord Upjohn.

[75] ibid 906.

These dicta indicate that the court is to look to the circumstances as the parties saw them and not to restrict the parties to any particular legal formula.[76] The parties must, however, have reached some form of agreement for the equitable interest to arise on this model. It is suggested that subsequent decisions of the Court of Appeal have been prepared to infer agreements from the most slender materials when there was no evidence of any express agreement but rather a suggestion that the parties ought to be considered to have formed some unspoken understanding, for example, during the course of a long marriage.[77]

The various forms of constructive trust based on common intention

The immediate legacy of the decisions in *Gissing v Gissing* and in *Pettitt v Pettitt* was an uncertainty as to the ambit of this notion of common intention. Subsequent decisions in the lower courts, prior to the decision of the House of Lords in *Lloyds Bank v Rosset*, offered a variety of readings of the common intention idea. The decisions in cases such as *Cowcher v Cowcher*,[78] *Grant v Edwards*,[79] and *Coombes v Smith*[80] offered a variety of readings of the concept of 'common intention' which ranged from divisions between the forms of consensus, the need for common intention to be coupled with detriment, and proprietary estoppel respectively. **56.21**

The diversity evident in those cases was summarized in the decision of Bagnall J in *Cowcher v Cowcher*[81] which began by explaining that proprietary rights are not to be determined simply on the basis of what is considered to be 'reasonable, fair and just in all the circumstances', thus underlining the courts' determination to avoid the development of a remedial constructive trust approach in relation to family homes. That a decision appeared to be 'unfair' was considered not to make it 'unjust'. Consequently, the courts ought not to be concerned to do fairness between the parties, but rather to uncover their real intentions and reflect them through the constructive trust. The heart of the analysis is then that the cases resolve into the two basic categories considered above: 'interest consensus' and 'money consensus'. To take each concept one at a time. The *interest consensus* constituted an expression of the common intention of the parties as to the extent of one another's interest in the property regardless of their financial contributions. The interest consensus would therefore be an agreement as to the equitable interest which each party is to receive which would be derived from the conduct of the parties if no express agreement could be proved. Such conduct need not be evidenced solely at the date of acquisition but could also develop subsequently.[82] **56.22**

---

[76] cf *Lloyds Bank v Rosset* [1991] 1 AC 107. See para 56.24.
[77] See the discussion of *Midland Bank v Cooke* [1995] 4 All ER 562 below.
[78] [1972] 1 All ER 948.   [79] [1986] Ch 638.   [80] [1986] 1 WLR 808.
[81] [1972] 1 All ER 948, 948–951, 954–955.
[82] Although this is not permitted in *Lloyds Bank v Rosset* [1991] 1 AC 107, it is accepted in cases like *McHardy v Warren* [1994] 2 FLR 338.

The *money consensus* would derive from the parties agreeing how much money each would contribute to the purchase price of the property. The money consensus is not derived from conduct but rather is based on an express agreement as to the amount of money provided by each party for the purchase of the property.[83] It was held, furthermore, that the concepts of resulting and constructive trust could be taken to be synonymous although the category of constructive trust ought more usually to be reserved for situations in which a fiduciary had sought to benefit from his office.

56.23 This form of common intention constructive trust appears to be a mixture of a resulting trust (which measures the parties' contributions to the purchase price of the property) and a constructive trust properly so-called (which would evaluate the conscionability of allowing one party to take an unfair benefit from some understanding reached between the parties as to ownership of the property). The common intention constructive trust is different from the model of constructive trust considered in Chapter 27 in that the leading authority on the operation of the common intention constructive trust, *Lloyds Bank v Rosset*[84] considered immediately below, restricts its operation to a particular form of conduct to do with contribution to the purchase price and does not allow it to operate on the basis of a general test of good conscience (as do the courts in Australia).[85]

The narrow concept of the common intention constructive trust: *Lloyds Bank v Rosset*

56.24 The decision in the House of Lords in *Lloyds Bank v Rosset*[86] both ordered and obfuscated this area of law. In the light of the welter of contradictory and difficult authority, there was some momentum for rationalization of the law. Just such a rationalization was set out in what is now the leading authority on the operation of the constructive trust in this area in the speech of Lord Bridge in *Lloyds Bank v Rosset*.[87] Lord Bridge appointed himself the task of setting out the terms on which a claimant may acquire an equitable interest in the home on grounds of 'constructive trust or proprietary estoppel'.

56.25 The facts of *Lloyds Bank v Rosset* itself were as follows. A semi-derelict farmhouse was put in Mr Rosset's name. The house was to be the family home and renovated as a joint venture. His wife oversaw all of the building work. Mrs Rosset had been led to believe that the property was to be acquired without a mortgage. However Mr Rosset did acquire the property with a mortgage registered in his sole name. Mr Rosset fell into arrears on the mortgage and the mortgagee bank sought

---

83 *Springette v Defoe* (1992) HLR 552, [1992] 2 FLR 388.   84 [1991] 1 AC 107.
85 See *Baumgartner v Baumgartner* (1988) 62 AJLR 29. See para 56.36.
86 [1991] 1 AC 107. As applied in *Ip Man Shan Henry v Ching Hing Construction Co Ltd (No 2)* [2003] 1 HKC 256, 5 ITELR 771.   87 [1991] 1 AC 107.

repossession in lieu of money owed by Mr Rosset under the mortgage. Mrs Rosset sought to resist an order for sale in favour of the mortgagee, *inter alia*, because of her equitable interest in the property which she claimed granted her an overriding interest on grounds of actual occupation.[88] It was held that Mrs Rosset had acquired no equitable interest in the property. Lord Bridge delivered the only speech in the House of Lords in which he sought to redraw the basis on which a common intention constructive trust would be formed. The test fell into two halves and therefore created two distinct forms of common intention constructive trust: common intention based on conduct and common intention based on agreement.

The narrow formulation of the common intention constructive trust set out by **56.26** Lord Bridge in *Lloyds Bank v Rosset* is analysed in detail in the following sections of this chapter. There are two forms. The common intention constructive trust by agreement comes into existence in any situation in which there has been some express agreement, arrangement, or understanding between the parties in advance of the acquisition of the property. By contrast, the common intention constructive trust by conduct arises in circumstances in which the claimant has contributed to the purchase price of the property or to the mortgage repayments, but his lordship considered that it is at least extremely doubtful whether anything less than that would found an equitable interest in the property. The claimant is furthermore required to have suffered some detriment to justify the award of a right in property. Those rights come into existence on the basis of constructive trust or proprietary estoppel, a conceptualization which seems to suggest that constructive trusts and proprietary estoppel are to be taken to be equivalents and which appears to overlook the existence of the resulting trust. This bicameral test has been applied in few cases in England and Wales and has seen the rest of the Commonwealth develop their own, very different understandings of the manner in which claimants acquire rights in the home.[89] The detail of the *Rosset* principles are considered in the following sections.

E. Express Agreements as to Beneficial Ownership of the Home

Common intention constructive trusts evidenced by agreement

The form of agreement, arrangement, or understanding necessary to found common intention

Building on the advances made in *Gissing v Gissing*[90] it was accepted that common **56.27** intention could arise from some agreement between the parties. The issue is therefore

---

[88] Land Registration Act 1925, s 70(1)(g).
[89] See AS Hudson, *Equity & Trusts* (3rd edn, Cavendish Publishing, 2003) ('*Hudson*') 458.
[90] [1971] AC 886.

as to the form of agreement which the parties must reach to constitute a constructive trust. If that intention needed to be in writing then it might constitute evidence of an express declaration of trust. However, it is only in exceptional cases that the parties will have gone to such pains to make their intentions so clear. In most of the cases there will only be evidence as to conversations between the parties which may or may not have been explicit about their intentions as to rights in the property, some of which may have been conducted in anger or which are remembered differently by those who participated in them. On the basis that such an agreement would not be sufficient to constitute an express trust as it would not satisfy section 53(1)(b) of the Law of Property Act 1925, it would have to be enforced by some form of trust implied by law.[91] Lord Bridge suggested that the parties might conceivably discuss a variety of matters which might be thought to lead them to a variety of conclusions,

> [b]ut each of these conclusions would have to be the result of some agreement. Sometimes an agreement, though not put into express words, would be clearly implied from what the parties did. But there must be evidence which establishes an agreement before it can be held that one spouse has acquired a beneficial interest in property which previously belonged to the other ...[92]

Thus the first limb of the test in *Lloyds Bank v Rosset* provided that there must be some agreement between the parties sufficient to constitute a common intention on the following terms, even if that had to be inferred from the circumstances. Again, in the words of Lord Bridge:[93]

> The first and fundamental question which must always be resolved is whether, independently of any inference to be drawn from the conduct of the parties in the course of sharing the house as their home and managing their joint affairs, there has at any time prior to acquisition, or exceptionally at some later date, been any agreement, arrangement or understanding reached between them that the property is to be shared beneficially.

This is the court's first line of inquiry.[94] The type of situation which is envisaged by Lord Bridge is an occasion on which the couple sat down with the intention of discussing how the rights in the property would be divided between them. The issue remains as to the nature of the conversation or consensus which would be sufficient to constitute such an 'agreement'. It is clear that it need not form a binding contract.[95] There are other considerations, as set out in the following sections, relating to the time and the circumstances in which such agreements might be forged.

---

[91] Law of Property Act 1925, s 53(2), *infra*.
[92] *Pettitt v Pettitt* [1970] AC 777, 804, [1969] 2 All ER 385, 398, *per* Lord Morris. This was a view with which Lord Hodson agreed at 810, 403. However, Lord Reid and Lord Diplock did not consider that this was a valid distinction at 795, 390 and 822, 413 respectively. Cf *Jansen v Jansen* [1965] P 478, [1965] 3 All ER 363.   [93] [1991] 1 AC 117, [1990] 1 All ER 1111, 1116.
[94] *Savill v Goodall* [1993] 1 FLR 755.
[95] See now in any event Law of Property (Miscellaneous Provisions) Act 1989, s 2.

The time at which the agreement must be formulated

As to the time at which the agreement must be formulated, the discussions are **56.28**
expected to have been carried out in advance of the purchase. In the words of Lord
Bridge:[96]

> The finding of an agreement or arrangement to share in this sense can only, I think,
> be based on evidence of express discussions between the partners, however imper-
> fectly remembered and however imprecise their terms.

By inference, subsequent discussions between the parties are considered to be
unimportant, or are at least of less importance. It is suggested that this approach
does not seem to recognize the reality of relationships in which intentions alter over
the years with the birth of children, the death of family members, unemployment,
and so forth. Similarly, the agreement is related to each property individually (subject to what is said below about deposits and the use of sale proceeds of previous
properties).[97] Suppose a couple buy a house, then sell it and move to a second
house: it is not clear to what extent conversations about the second house can override agreements formulated as to title in the first house, although it is clear that the
courts will impute intentions relevant to the first house to subsequent purchases.[98]
Generally financial contributions to the first house are deemed to be transferred
pro tanto to the subsequent acquisition of a new home,[99] but it need not necessarily be the case that the parties' intentions must transfer in the same format because
to do so would restrict the ability of cohabitees to adapt to the changing circumstances of their lives and the thousand natural shocks to which flesh is heir.

Whether the agreement must be express or can be unspoken

The assumption is that there are express discussions, rather than an emerging but **56.29**
unspoken intention between the parties. For example, where one party ceases to
work to bring up children, thus interrupting the ability to earn money to be applied
to the mortgage instalments, the intention of the parties will have been impliedly
re-calibrated while the other partner assumes the burden of paying off the mortgage. It is unlikely that there will be an express discussion as to *rights in the property*
which each is intended to receive, although it is likely that the parties will adjust
their lifestyle to accommodate the need to meet their household expenses and so
forth. The second limb of the test is the only one which permits for this type of
flexibility, and it is that subject which is considered immediately below.

Illustrations of inferred agreements

An example of an agreement between parties would be the situation in which a **56.30**
husband and wife prepare a transfer form such that the entire interest in the

---

[96] [1991] 1 AC 117, [1990] 1 All ER 1111, 1116.   [97] See para 56.56.
[98] *McHardy v Warren* [1994] 2 FLR 338.
[99] *McHardy v Warren* [1994] 2 FLR 338; *Midland Bank v Cooke* [1995] 4 All ER 562.

property should be transferred to the wife. In the event the form is not presented to the Land Registry, there would be no transfer of title at common law. However, in just such a case, a court was prepared to find that this was evidence of the parties' intentions to transfer title to the wife which would consequently take effect in equity.[100] It is presumed that the result would have been different if the failure to present the form was a result of the parties having changed their minds: nevertheless it would still have constituted evidence that *at one time* their intention was to transfer rights to the wife. It would usually be the case that the intentions of the parties are more difficult to isolate. So when a woman left Poland, thus 'burning her boats' as the matter was described, to come and live in England with the defendant, it was held that she had understood that she would have a home for life even though there was no demonstrable intention that all of the rights in the property at issue would be transferred to her. The woman was held to be entitled to have the property held on trust for her occupation during her lifetime.[101] In general terms the courts will be reluctant to draw inferences of such agreements if they are not evident on the facts of the case.[102]

Agreements between spouses

56.31 Before the decision of the House of Lords in *Pettitt v Pettitt*[103] it had been a vexed question whether or not spouses could form enforceable contracts between themselves, such contracts having been considered immoral and contrary to the notion that husbands and wives formed one legal unit which could not have rights against one another. However, as Lord Reid held, just because an agreement may not be enforceable in itself, that does not mean that the performance of an act undertaken in reliance on such an agreement does not have legal consequences.[104] So, for example, even if husbands and wives could not form contracts between themselves as to the use of their home, their common intentions as to the use of that home embodied in the unenforceable contract may nevertheless raise rights in equity. The further issue in the *Pettitt* appeal was the extent to which the parties can reach some agreement as to the allocation of the total equitable interest in the property, without forming a binding contract or a formally valid express trust, and make that agreement both binding between themselves and binding on third parties. As we will see below in relation to the case of *Gissing v Gissing*,[105] the House of Lords came to accept that such an agreement would be enforceable in

---

[100] *Barclays Bank v Khaira* [1993] 1 FLR 343.
[101] *Ungarian v Lesnoff* [1990] Ch 206—under the Settled Land Act 1925. Also *Costello v Costello* [1996] 1 FLR 805. Cf *Dent v Dent* [1996] 1 All ER 659.
[102] '. . .our trust law does not allow property rights to be affected by telepathy', *Springette v Defoe* [1992] 2 FLR 388, 392, *per* Steyn LJ; *Evans v Hayward* [1995] 2 FLR 511. Although the family assets approach *is* prepared to permit such unspoken intentions to be enforced, as considered below.
[103] [1970] AC 777.   [104] [1970] AC 777.   [105] [1971] AC 886.

equity where it constituted a 'common intention' formed between the parties. These various forms of common intention are considered in more detail below.

F. Contributions to the Purchase Price of the Home

The various conceptual approaches to contributions to the purchase price

In circumstances in which a person contributes to the purchase price of the home **56.32** it is a long-standing principle of the law of trust that an amount of the total equitable interest in the home proportionate to the size of the contribution will be held on resulting trust for that person.[106] Lord Bridge's speech in *Lloyds Bank v Rosset*[107] described contributions to the purchase price as giving rise to a common intention constructive trust or to proprietary estoppel, but there was no reference to resulting trust.[108] Subsequent Court of Appeal decisions have described contributions to the purchase price as giving rise to rights under resulting trust[109] but subject to re-calibration on constructive trusts principles in the event that circumstances caused the parties to alter their common intention.[110] This section begins with a consideration of classical resulting trust principles before proceeding to consider common intention constructive trusts.

Purchase price resulting trusts

Acquisition of rights on resulting trust by contribution to the purchase price

The most straightforward rule in situations where there is no express trust over land **56.33** is that any person who contributes to the acquisition price of property will acquire an equitable interest in that property. That interest will be expressed as a percentage of the total equitable interest in the property, in proportion to the cost of acquiring the total interest in the property. The only exceptions to such a finding would occur in situations in which the contribution to the purchase price was made by way of a gift of money to the purchasers, or by way of a loan to the purchasers, either of which intentions would negate any presumption that the donor was intended to take an equitable interest in the property.[111] Otherwise banks lending money under mortgage agreements would acquire equitable interests in property beyond their statutory right to repossession.[112] Similarly, a gift of money involves an outright transfer

---

[106] *Dyer v Dyer* (1788) 2 Cox Eq Cas 92.   [107] [1991] 1 AC 107.
[108] *Lloyds Bank v Rosset* [1991] 1 AC 107, [1990] 1 All ER 1111; *Drake v Whipp* [1996] 2 FCR 296; *Yaxley v Gotts* [2000] Ch 162, [2000] 1 All ER 711; *Jennings v Rice* [2002] EWCA Civ 159, [2003] 1 FCR 501; *Hyett v Stanley* [2003] EWCA Civ 942; *Ottey v Grundy* [2003] EWCA Civ 1176.
[109] *Springette v Defoe* [1992] 2 FLR 388; *Huntingford v Hobbs* [1993] 1 FLR 936.
[110] *Huntingford v Hobbs* [1993] 1 FLR 936.
[111] *Grant v Edwards* [1986] Ch 638; *Hyett v Stanley* [2003] EWCA Civ 942.
[112] This would interfere with the equity of redemption necessary in the law of mortgages. For the mortgagee to acquire an equitable interest would mean that the mortgagor would not be able to recover unencumbered possession of his rights: *Samuel v Jarrah Timber Corp* [1904] AC 323.

to the donee but does not entitle the donor to any rights in property acquired with the money.[113] The core principle in this area was set out in *Dyer v Dyer*[114] where Eyre CB held that that there is a resulting trust in favour of a person who contributes to the purchase price of property in the following terms:

> The clear result of all the cases, without a single exception, is that the trust of a legal estate . . . results to the man who advances the purchase money.[115]

That principle received support in the speech of Lord Browne-Wilkinson in *Westdeutsche Landesbank v Islington LBC* when his lordship recognized the purchase price resulting trust as being one of only two forms of resulting trust in existence.[116] As Lord Browne-Wilkinson held in *Tinsley v Milligan*:

> Although for historical reasons legal estates and equitable estates have differing incidents, the person owning either type of estate has a right in property, a right *in rem* and not merely a right *in personam*.[117]

So, a gift of money to a couple on their wedding day to enable them to buy a house would not grant the donor any interest in the house which the couple subsequently bought with that money in circumstances in which the donor had intended to make an outright transfer of that money.[118] Consequently, it is always important to ascertain the purpose underlying the advancement of money to acquire the property.

The role of the presumption of advancement

56.34 The presumption of advancement[119] applies in relation to these resulting trusts, in theory at least, in the same way as it applies to all resulting trusts.[120] Where a husband transfers property to his wife it is presumed in the absence of cogent evidence to the contrary that his intention was to make a gift of that property to her.[121] The principle of advancement no longer applies to a married couple once separated or divorced,[122] or where some other intention underpinning the advancement (such as the acquisition of a mortgage loan) can be demonstrated.[123] That same presumption will not apply in relation to a transfer from wife to husband.[124]

---

[113] *Westdeutsche Landesbank v Islington LBC* [1996] AC 669.
[114] (1788) 2 Cox Eq Cas 92. See also *Dewar v Dewar* [1975] 1 WLR 1532, 1537; *Tinsley v Milligan* [1994] 1 AC 340, 371, contributing money to the purchase price raises a presumption that you are to acquire an equitable interest in that property. [115] ibid 93.
[116] [1996] AC 669.   [117] [1994] 1 AC 340.
[118] *McHardy v Warren* [1994] 2 FLR 338.   [119] See para 26.85.
[120] *Mercier v Mercier* [1903] 2 Ch 98; *Re Emery's Investment Trust* [1959] Ch 410. Cf *Silver v Silver* [1958] 1 WLR 259.
[121] *In Re Eykyn's Trusts* (1877) 6 Ch D 115; *Moate v Moate* [1948] 2 All ER 486 (transfers between fiancés); *Wirth v Wirth* (1956) 98 CLR 228; *Jenkins v Wynen* (1992) 1 Qd R 40. Cf *Eeles v Wilkins* unreported, 3 February 1988.
[122] *Wilson v Wilson* [1963] 1 WLR 601; *Cossey v Bach* [1992] NZLR 612.
[123] *Loades-Carter v Loades-Carter* (1966) 110 SJ 51—house conveyed to wife solely to obtain a mortgage, such that the presumption of advancement was rebutted.
[124] *Mercier v Mercier* [1903] 2 Ch 98.

By contrast to the presumption of advancement, the presumption of resulting trust on contribution to the purchase price of property functions in the following manner: **56.35**

> … the presumption [of resulting trust] operates by reference to the presumed intention of the party whose contribution exceeds his or her proportionate share; it cannot prevail over the actual intention of that party as established by the overall evidence, including the evidence of the parties' respective contributions.[125]

The presumptions in this context would ordinarily have been used in circumstances in which the intentions of the parties could not be satisfactorily divined from the evidence. However, it was held in the same case that:

> [w]e are concerned to discover the actual intention which the appellant had when the land was put in the names of the parties as tenants in common, and not to impute to her an intention which she did not possess …[126]

There is an increasing chorus of disapproval for the continued application of the **56.36** presumptions in trusts of homes cases,[127] with the result that the courts will be prepared to find that the presumptions have been rebutted on the balance of probabilities[128] even where the claimant had intended to commit an illegal act which did not come to fruition.[129] The presumption of advancement has been described as a judicial instrument of last resort:[130]

> …the presumption of advancement is not an immutable rule to be applied blindly where there is no direct evidence as to the common intention of the spouses. It is rather a guideline to be followed by the court in an appropriate case when it searches for the intention which ought, in the absence of evidence, to be imputed to the parties. It is proper for the trial judge to review the background of the case and to decide in appropriate circumstances that the guideline is not one which can sensibly be followed in the case before him.[131]

In *Pettitt v Pettitt* Lord Reid held that the presumptions should be taken to belong **56.37** to a different era and should not have any place in deciding modern cases concerning the family home.[132]

---

[125] *Muschinski v Dodds* (1985) 160 CLR 583, 612, *per* Deane J.
[126] *Muschinski v Dodds* (1985) 160 CLR 583, 593, *per* Gibbs CJ.
[127] *Silver v Silver* [1958] 1 WLR 259, 261; *Pettitt v Pettitt* [1970] 1 AC 777, 793, *per* Lord Reid; *Falconer v Falconer* [1970] 1 WLR 1333, 1335; *Harwood v Harwood* [1991] 2 FLR 274, 294; *McGrath v Wallis* [1995] 2 FLR 114, 115. Similarly in Canada: *Rathwell v Rathwell* [1978] 2 SCR 436, 452; *Mehta v Mehta* [1993] 6 WWR 457 (Man CA). Although it is considered too well established in the case law to be completely ignored by Deane J in *Calverley v Green* (1984) 155 CLR 242, 266.
[128] See eg *Barry v Barry* [1992] 2 FLR 233, 241, *per* Waite J, refusing to accept that the husband had 'scuttled his own hopes of ever establishing an interest in the matrimonial home' by arguing that the property had been transferred into his wife's name 'through family prudence'—further, *Tinker v Tinker* [1970] 2 WLR 331 showed a 'heffalump trap' from which many unwitting husbands have emerged with nothing intact but their honour. [129] *Tribe v Tribe* [1995] 4 All ER 236.
[130] *McGrath v Wallis* [1995] 3 FCR 661, 662, [1995] 2 FLR 114, 115, *per* Nourse LJ.
[131] *Neo Tai Kim v Foo Stie Wah* [1985] 1 MLJ 397, 399, *per* Lord Brightman. See also *Overseas Trust Bank Ltd v Lee See Ching John* [1999] 3 HKC 197, 201, *per* Godfrey JA.
[132] *Pettitt v Pettitt* [1970] 1 AC 777, 793.

56.38 However, vestiges of the old outlook continued. It was held by Lord Upjohn that:

> Nor can the meaning of the [Married Women's Property Act 1882] have changed merely by reason of a change in social outlook since the date of its enactment; it must continue to bear the meaning which upon its true construction in the light of the relevant surrounding circumstances it bore at that time.[133]

In Lord Upjohn's opinion the statute of 1882 was to be interpreted in accordance with the presumption and the social mores of the time in which it was enacted.[134] For Lord Upjohn it was not enough to argue that the world had changed between 1882 and 1970, and that the courts should treat rights in the home differently as a result.[135]

Common intention constructive trust in relation to contribution to the purchase price

Limitations on the use of resulting trusts

56.39 The importance of the development of the notion of common intention in *Gissing v Gissing* is that it breaks out of the mould which restricts the parties only to the acquisition of rights under resulting trusts. Instead of restricting the parties only to rights which flowed directly from a contribution to the purchase price, the focus on the broader common intention of the parties meant that there could be some other factor which would permit the founding of some equitable interest. Significantly, Lord Diplock's dicta restricted the possible forms of such common intention. To permit rights to be formed on the basis of common intention, even if only a narrow range of intentions can be included,[136] does mean that the parties are not limited only to rights founded on the *Dyer v Dyer*[137] principle.[138] This notion has been expressed in the following terms:

> However [the principle of resulting trust] could not apply if (1) there was a common intention to share the property beneficially found to exist on the application of the guidance given by Lord Bridge [in *Lloyds Bank v Rosset*[139]], whether by dint of a finding of an agreement, arrangement or understanding on evidence of express discussions between the partners or by ready inference from direct contributions to the purchase price by the partner who is not the legal owner, and (2) that partner has acted to his or her detriment in reliance on the common intention.[140]

The adoption of the language of 'common intention' by Lord Diplock opened the way for the use of the constructive trust for the granting of rights in land, rather

---

[133] *Pettitt v Pettitt* [1970] 1 AC 777, 813.   [134] cf *Caunce v Caunce* [1969] 1 WLR 286.
[135] This despite Larkin's lament that the 1960s in particular constituted such a sea change in our social life: 'Sexual intercourse began / In nineteen sixty-three / (Which was rather late for me) / Between the end of the Chatterley ban / And the Beatles' first LP.' Larkin, *Annus Mirabilis* (1974).
[136] As considered in para 56.24 above.   [137] (1788) 2 Cox Eq Cas 92.
[138] See para 56.33.   [139] [1991] 1 AC 107, [1990] 1 All ER 1111.
[140] *Drake v Whipp* [1996] 2 FCR 296, 299, *per* Peter Gibson LJ.

than the more mathematical precision of the purchase price resulting trust which would grant only an equitable interest in proportion to the plaintiff's contribution to the purchase price. This use of the constructive trust has been adopted by the courts in preference to the resulting trust—perhaps, in part, because of the comparatively large discretion which is given to the court.

Common intention constructive trust by conduct

Lord Bridge expressed a contribution to the purchase price of property or to the repayment of the mortgage as giving rise to a constructive trust or proprietary estoppel right.[141] This form of constructive trust is considered in the next section. **56.40**

G. Common Intention Evidenced by Other Conduct

Common intention constructive trust evidenced by conduct

A common intention constructive trust will arise by reference to the conduct of the parties, in the absence of an express agreement or arrangement to share the beneficial ownership. Where there is no such agreement the court will consider the conduct of the parties. In this situation it is payments towards the initial purchase price of the property or towards mortgage instalments 'which justify the inference necessary for the creation of a constructive trust'. As Lord Bridge set out the requirements for this form of constructive trust in *Lloyds Bank v Rosset*:[142] **56.41**

> In sharp contrast with [the common intention constructive trust by agreement] is the very different one where there is no evidence to support a finding of an agreement or arrangement to share, however reasonable it might have been for the parties to reach such an arrangement if they had applied their minds to the question, and where the court must rely entirely on the conduct of the parties both as the basis from which to infer a common intention to share the property beneficially and as the conduct relied on to give rise to a constructive trust. In this situation direct contributions to the purchase price by the partner who is not the legal owner, whether initially or by payment of mortgage instalments, will readily justify the inference necessary to the creation of a constructive trust. But as I read the authorities it is at least extremely doubtful whether anything less will do.

Thus the parties' conduct in respect of the property is capable of forming a common intention sufficient for the finding of a constructive trust. The type of conduct envisaged by Lord Bridge is, however, very limited. He has in mind 'direct contributions to the purchase price' only. Any other conduct which indicates a common intention to own the property jointly in some way, such as selecting the decorations together or sending out invitations to the house-warming party in

---

[141] *Lloyds Bank v Rosset* [1991] 1 AC 107.
[142] [1991] 1 AC 107, [1990] 1 All ER 1111, 1117.

joint names, will not be sufficient to evidence a common intention. Less flippantly, perhaps, it would also exclude from consideration a wife who took occasional part-time work to subsidize the payment of household bills while her husband was out of work and thus only able to meet the mortgage repayments.[143] A payment towards the purchase price of property which was intended only to be a loan would not acquire the payer any equitable interest in the property.[144]

56.42   One further problem arises: most people are not able to afford to buy their homes for cash and are therefore required to take out mortgages which are paid back over periods of (usually) 25 years. In recognition of the reality of those families who finance the purchase of the property by mortgage, rather than by cash purchase, Lord Bridge tells us that it is sufficient for the contributions to be made either 'initially [that is, by cash purchase or cash deposit] or by payment of mortgage instalments'.[145] The limitation of these means of contribution is underlined when Lord Bridge explicitly holds that 'it is at least extremely doubtful whether anything less will do'. It is suggested below that this last sentence is of pivotal importance because its literal interpretation suggests that non-financial contributions to the household or financial contributions directed otherwise than at the purchase price or the mortgage repayments will not acquire an interest in property.[146]

56.43   The decision of the Court of Appeal in *Ivin v Blake*[147] applied the approach of the House of Lords in *Lloyds Bank v Rosset*. B had run a pub from the time of her husband's death, in 1953, which became profitable enough for her to buy a house. She could not acquire a mortgage in her own name and therefore the mortgage was taken out in the name of her son, T. B's daughter, D, had given up her job to work in the pub full-time to help her mother, also in 1953. D's agreement to come and work in the pub, thus saving B from having to hire more staff, enabled B to cobble together enough money to buy the property and to generate sufficient income to meet the mortgage repayments. The issue arose whether or not T was required to hold the pub on constructive trust (in part) for D on the basis that D's contribution to the pub business had facilitated the acquisition of the house and also the making of mortgage payments over the house. The court held that there had been no intention at the time of the acquisition of the house that D would acquire any interest in the house and therefore there could be no constructive trust. Furthermore there had been no direct contribution by D to the purchase price of the house. Consequently, D had satisfied neither limb of the test set out in *Lloyds Bank v Rosset* and therefore it was held that D acquired no equitable interest in the property. On the basis that B had met all of the cash expenses of the

---

[143] Just such a set of circumstances, nevertheless, did found an equitable right in the home in *Midland Bank v Cooke* [1995] 4 All ER 562, as considered below.
[144] *Nel v Kean* [2003] WTLR 501.   [145] [1991] 1 AC 107, [1990] 1 All ER 1111, 1117.
[146] See para 56.32.   [147] [1995] 1 FLR 70.

purchase of the house which had not been provided by means of the mortgage, her equitable interest was said to have survived her death and that it fell to be apportioned according to her will with the rest of her estate.[148]

The need for detriment in the common intention constructive trust

It is held in *Lloyds Bank v Rosset* that it is necessary for the claimant to demonstrate **56.44** that he has suffered detriment before being able to demonstrate any right under a common intention constructive trust. The core principles of the common intention constructive trust were described in *Grant v Edwards*[149] by Browne-Wilkinson V-C in an attempt to develop the core principles previously set out by Lord Diplock in *Gissing v Gissing*. In his lordship's opinion there were three important factors to be established in each case. First, the nature of the substantive right which required that there must be a common intention that the claimant was to have a beneficial interest *and* that the claimant had acted to his detriment in acquiring such a right. Secondly, proof of the common intention, requiring direct evidence or inferred common intention. Thirdly, the quantification of the size of that right. The requirement for detriment in the context was mirrored in *Midland Bank v Dobson*[150] where it was held insufficient to create an equitable interest that there be simply a common intention unless there was also some detriment suffered by the claimant.

The significance of the requirement of detriment has been stressed in subsequent cases. For example, the Court of Appeal in *Chan Pui Chun v Leung Kam Ho*[151] considered a defendant who had promised that he would leave his wife and live with the claimant. To this end, he bought a house in Surrey for himself and his lover, the claimant, to occupy. While the facts were difficult to establish, it seemed that the defendant had offered the claimant shares in both the house and in his business. The court was of the opinion that the defendant had lied on a number of occasions. The claimant had agreed to work for the defendant's business and subsequently acquired a general power of attorney over the defendant's affairs while the defendant served a prison sentence. The mortgage on the Surrey home had been placed in the name of a company which the defendant controlled and the mortgage had been discharged using money from the defendant's business through various companies under his control. In time the claimant obtained a court order excluding the defendant from the Surrey home on grounds of his violence towards her and the issue arose whether or not she had acquired any equitable interest in the Surrey home. It was held that she had acquired such rights, in the form of an equal share in both the Surrey home and the businesses, on the basis

---

[148] Further, only occasional contributions to expenses do not acquire rights: *Kowalczuk v Kowalczuk* [1973] 1 WLR 930, 935, *per* Buckley LJ.   [149] [1986] Ch 638.
[150] [1986] 1 FLR 171.   [151] [2003] 1 FLR 23.

that she had suffered detriment in working for, and from time to time running, the defendant's businesses, and that she had acted always in reliance on his promise that he would marry her. Her right in the Surrey home stemmed, it was found, from her work for the businesses which had in turn defrayed the mortgage over the Surrey home.

56.45   In *Grant v Edwards*[152] it was held that there must be an agreement or conduct by the person who did not own the legal title in the property which could only be explained as being directed at acquiring rights in property. While the claimant in that case had not made a financial contribution directly towards the purchase of the property, the defendant had made excuses to her for not putting her on the legal title which was held to indicate an intention that she would otherwise have acquired rights in the property but for the defendant's subterfuge. In short, he had sought to keep her off the title through deceit, indicating that otherwise she would probably have had formal rights.[153] Further, it was found that her contributions to family expenses were more than would otherwise have been expected in the circumstances and thereby enabled the defendant to make the mortgage payments. It was held that this behaviour could not have been expected unless the claimant had understood that she would acquire an interest in the property. Consequently she acquired an equitable interest by dint of facilitating payment for the house and in accordance with, effectively, an imputed common intention. The roots of the modern approach are discernible in this double-barrelled focus on both any agreement made between the parties and also on an analysis of the parties' conduct in respect of the purchase of the property and on its mortgage repayments.

56.46   The conclusion reached in that case was that it is possible for purely personal acts to be evidence of an intention that a proprietary interest be acquired by the claimant. However, the court in *Coombes v Smith*[154] took the view that for the claimant to leave her partner to have children with the defendant would not lead to the acquisition of a right in property because that was purely personal detriment, not the sort necessary to acquire rights in property. As considered below, it is generally the case that detriment which is suffered merely as a part of a claimant's personal life (for example, where that person leaves her current partner on the promise that the defendant will give her a right in property) will not be sufficient to found a right in property. What is important to note is that detriment is an important part of demonstrating rights under a common intention constructive trust—a feature which makes it appear similar to proprietary estoppel.[155]

---

[152] [1986] Ch 638. See also *Driver v Yorke* (2003–04) 6 ITELR 80.
[153] See also *Eves v Eves* [1975] 1 WLR 1338.   [154] [1986] 1 WLR 808.
[155] As considered below at para 56.87.

H. Alteration of the Common Intention After Acquisition of the Property

The more difficult question is then as to those forms of agreement or activity **56.47** which will alter any common intention which the parties are deemed to have formed before the acquisition of the property. The ordinary vicissitudes of life mean that the settled understandings which Lord Bridge envisaged that people would form in relation to the ownership of their homes may well be unsettled by subsequent events, whether in the form of relationship breakdown, unemployment, death, or childbirth. Either one takes the common intention formed at the date of acquisition of the property as determinative of the parties' interests or else one permits other factors to alter the scope, value, and quality of those interests. Lord Diplock anticipated this problem in *Gissing v Gissing* and suggested the possibility that a 'fresh agreement' between the parties may intrude on their original common intention:

> ... in the branch of English law relating to constructive, implied or resulting trusts effect is given to the inferences as to the intentions of parties to a transaction which a reasonable man would draw from their words or conduct and not to any subjective intention or absence of intention which was not made manifest at the time of the transaction itself. It is for the court to determine what those inferences are. In drawing such an inference, what spouses said and did which led up to the acquisition of a matrimonial home and what they said and did while the acquisition was being carried through is on a different footing from what they said and did after the acquisition was completed. Unless it is alleged that there was some subsequent fresh agreement, acted on by the parties, to vary the original beneficial interests created when the matrimonial home was acquired, what they said and did after the acquisition was completed is relevant if it is explicable only upon the basis of their having manifested to one another at the time of the acquisition some particular common intention as to how the beneficial interests should be held. But it would in my view be unreasonably legalistic to treat the relevant transaction involved in the acquisition of a matrimonial home as restricted to the actual conveyance of the fee simple into the name of one or other spouse. Their common intention is more likely to have been concerned with the economic realities of the transaction than with the unfamiliar technicalities of the English law of legal and equitable interests in land.[156]

This passage therefore expresses a preference that the nature of the parties' equitable interests will generally be crystallized at the date of acquisition but that they are susceptible of alteration if there has been some further agreement between the parties on which all those parties act with the intention of altering the agreement, arrangement, or understanding formulated at the time of the acquisition. It was suggested by Viscount Simonds in an earlier decision of the House of Lords that the more traditional approach required that evidence as to subsequent statements

---

[156] *Gissing v Gissing* [1971] AC 886, 906, [1970] 2 All ER 780, 790, *per* Lord Diplock.

between the parties might only be adduced in evidence against the person who made them, as expressed in the following passage:

> It must then be asked by what evidence can the presumption be rebutted, and it would, I think, be very unfortunate if any doubt were cast…upon the well-settled law on this subject. It is, I think, correctly stated in substantially the same terms in every textbook that I have consulted and supported by authority extending over a long period of time. I will take, as an example, a passage from Snell's *Equity*, 24th edn, p 153, which is as follows: 'The acts and declarations of the parties before or at the time of the purchase, or so immediately after it as to constitute a part of the transaction, are admissible in evidence either for or against the party who did the act or made the declaration … But subsequent declarations are admissible as evidence only against the party who made them, and not in his favour.' I do not think it necessary to review the numerous cases of high authority upon which this statement is founded. It is possible to find in some earlier judgments reference to 'subsequent' event without the qualification contained in the textbook statement: it may even be possible to wonder in some cases how in the narration of facts certain events were admitted to consideration. But the burden of authority in favour of the broad proposition as stated in the passage I have cited is overwhelming and should not be disturbed.[157]

56.48 An alternative approach was taken by the Court of Appeal in *Midland Bank v Cooke* to the effect that the court ought not to restrict itself to any formulaic approach to the acquisition of proprietary rights but rather ought to be able to consider all of the surrounding circumstances of the case and to reach its decision on the basis of general equitable principles if the circumstances of the case do not indicate any particular rights.[158] Therefore, Waite LJ held as follows:

> When the court is proceeding, in cases like the present where the partner without legal title has successfully asserted an equitable interest through direct contribution, to determine (in the absence of express evidence of intention) what proportions the parties must be assumed to have intended for their beneficial ownership, the duty of the judge is to undertake a survey of the whole course of dealing between the parties relevant to their ownership and occupation of the property and their sharing of its burdens and advantages. That scrutiny will not confine itself to the limited range of acts of direct contribution of the sort that are needed to found a beneficial interest in the first place. It will take into consideration all conduct which throws light on the question what shares were intended. Only if that search proves inconclusive does the court fall back on the maxim that 'equality is equity'.[159]

This approach suggests that the court will not be restricted to those forms of conduct or to those agreements between the cohabitees to which the speech of Lord Bridge in *Lloyds Bank v Rosset*[160] would have required it to be. This deviation from

---

[157] *Shephard v Cartwright* [1955] AC 431, 445, [1954] 3 All ER 649, 652, *per* Viscount Simonds. Although it has been held in Australia that this formulation is not exhaustive of all the matters which might be considered: *Damberg v Damberg* [2001] NSWCA 87, (2001) 4 ITELR 65.
[158] [1995] 4 All ER 562.   [159] *Midland Bank v Cooke* [1995] 4 All ER 562, 574, *per* Waite LJ.
[160] [1991] 1 AC 107.

the literal application of the dicta in *Lloyds Bank v Rosset* by the lower courts is considered in the following sections.

I. Calculating the Size of a Beneficial Interest in the Home

Introduction

Variously constituted Courts of Appeal have taken into account many forms of contribution to the acquisition of the property—including the procuring of discounts on the purchase price[161]—and also contributions to the property subsequent to the date of acquisition—including the construction of conservatories,[162] participation in the family business,[163] and contribution to the running expenses of the household.[164] In effect the courts have created a balance sheet of these various items for each party[165] such that each contribution is aggregated and that the parties receive a proportionate share in the total equity in the property.[166] As considered above, there is some confusion as to whether or not that common intention constructive trust doctrine ought to be read as subsuming the doctrines of proprietary estoppel and resulting trust. However, that the Court of Appeal has concerned itself with calculation of the value of the cohabitees' various contributions to the property means that the various doctrinal questions considered above have not interfered with the courts' determination to reach what they considered to be the right conclusion on the facts in front of them.

56.49

Calculating the size of the equitable interest

The Court of Appeal in *Bernard v Josephs*[167] considered itself entitled to consider the mathematical equity contributed by each party across the range of transactions contributing to the acquisition of a home. Dealing simply with the issue of contributions made to the purchase price at the date of acquisition it is clear that a contribution can be made in a number of different ways. The following are some of the more common forms of contribution. First, by cash payment. Secondly, by agreeing to pay all or part of the interest payments on the mortgage throughout the life of the mortgage. Thirdly, to pay the whole or part of the capital cost of the mortgage throughout the life of the mortgage. Fourthly, agreeing to be liable to the lender for the mortgage debt in the event that the mortgagor goes into arrears, without actually making any payments. Fifthly, acting as guarantor or surety for the mortgage. Sixthly, obtaining a reduction or discount in the acquisition price

56.50

---

[161] *Springette v Defoe* [1992] 2 FLR 388.   [162] *Huntingford v Hobbs* [1993] 1 FLR 936.
[163] *Hammond v Mitchell* [1991] 1 WLR 1127.
[164] *Midland Bank v Cooke* [1995] 4 All ER 562.
[165] A concept developed in *Hudson* 439.   [166] *Bernard v Josephs* [1982] Ch 391.
[167] [1982] Ch 391; *Passee v Passee* [1988] 1 FLR 263.

by exercise of a pre-existing right in the property. Notably, the fourth and fifth items do not require that any payment be made at the time of acquisition. Indeed, the second and third options only require that periodic payments are made after the date of acquisition. There are then a number of alternative possible means by which contributions could be made after the date of acquisition. These are yet further possibilities. Seventhly, by undertaking to make only some of the mortgage repayments on an ad hoc basis—for example where a wife undertakes to pay the mortgage for a period of a couple of months while her husband finds work. Eighthly, by repaying some of the capital cost of the mortgage without acquiring a legal obligation to do so.

56.51 All eight of these possibilities (clearly there could be others) assume some level of agreement between the cohabitees: that is, some explicit or implicit understanding that both of them are contributing to the acquisition of the property at the outset or subsequently. Two further issues then arise. First, the situation where there is no express agreement but the parties fall into a pattern of shared expenditure which is dictated by, for example, whether or not they are in employment at any particular time during their joint occupation of the family home. A situation which may not constitute 'conduct' within the meaning ascribed to that term in *Lloyds Bank v Rosset*. Secondly, the situation where there is a casual agreement that one party will meet expenses related to the mortgage while the other meets 'domestic' expenditure such as utility bills, food shopping, and so forth. In this situation it may be that the mortgagor could not make those mortgage repayments unless the other party met the ordinary domestic expenditure: it should be remembered that under a literal application of the test in *Lloyds Bank v Rosset*[168] those payments for ordinary expenses would not acquire any interest in the property even though they were necessary to enable the mortgagor to make his mortgage payments.

56.52 As considered above, direct contribution to the purchase price will give rise to a resulting trust,[169] or a common intention constructive trust by conduct.[170] The second possibility will give rise to an equitable interest in the cohabitee's favour on resulting or constructive trust, where it can be proved that the cohabitee contributed to the price of the property after the acquisition. The size of the interest in such circumstances will be proportionate to the contribution to the total purchase price.[171] The Court of Appeal in *Huntingford v Hobbs* was prepared to look behind the documentation signed by the parties which suggested that they held the equitable interest in the property in equal shares. However, it was held that to look behind such documents there must be 'cogent evidence' that any documentation signed by the parties was not intended to constitute the final statement as

---

[168] See para 56.24.   [169] *Dyer v Dyer* (1788) 2 Cox Eq Cas 92.
[170] *Lloyds Bank v Rosset* [1990] 1 AC 107.   [171] *Huntingford v Hobbs* [1993] 1 FLR 936.

to their beneficial interests. Therefore, where a house cost £100,000 and X provides £40,000, where Y procures a mortgage for £60,000, Y is taken to have contributed 60 per cent of the purchase price.[172]

There is also the possibility of equitable accounting to take into account periods **56.53** of rent-free occupation and so forth by one or other of the parties.[173] So where, for example, one spouse quits the property until the litigation as to the equitable interest is resolved it will be possible for such a spouse to recover money from the spouse who remains in residence to defray part of the costs of his own rental obligations. It is possible for litigation to take a number of years to resolve during which time one spouse would have full use of the property while the other party would be required to find the financial wherewithal to live elsewhere. What is clear from this doctrine of equitable accounting is that equity will provide for items to be added to this 'balance sheet' which are outside the strict test in *Lloyds Bank v Rosset*. It is clear that Lord Bridge's leading speech in *Lloyds Bank v Rosset* does not account for the full picture. The question of what other sorts of contribution might be taken into account is considered in further detail below.

In *Suttill v Graham*,[174] a case considering section 17 of the Married Women's Property Act 1882, a husband remained in the home after the divorce and paid all mortgage instalments. It was held as a consequence that a person 'entitled to an equal share in equity of property of which he is a trustee, and which he himself occupies, is to be charged with at least an occupation rent so that if as here he seeks to charge his co-beneficiary trustee with half the outgoings he should be charged with half the occupation rent . . . it must be wrong that he should seek to charge the wife with half the mortgage interest which he has paid while living in the property rent free and resisting a sale of the property':[175] an approach which was expected to produce a fair result and to save costs in the majority of cases. By contrast in *Re Gorman*[176] the wife had remained in the property with the children after her divorce from her husband. Contrary to an agreement between the parties that the husband would pay off the considerable arrears on the mortgage, the wife in fact made a number of payments under the mortgage. Subsequently the husband was adjudicated bankrupt, and his trustee in bankruptcy applied to the court for an order for sale. It was held that the wife's payment of her former husband's share of the mortgage instalments could not entitle her to a greater than half share in the property, but she was entitled to bring such payments into the

---

[172] ibid; *Cowcher v Cowcher* [1972] 1 WLR 425.
[173] *Bernard v Josephs* [1982] Ch 391; *Huntingford v Hobbs* [1993] 1 FLR 936.
[174] [1977] 1 WLR 819.
[175] [1977] 1 WLR 819, 821–822, *per* Stamp LJ. Cf *M'Mahon v Burchell* in which it was said that: 'Where there was neither contract nor exclusion, nor anything received, occupation by one tenant in common created no liability for rent to the other tenants in common': (1846) 1 Coop t Cott 457, 475, 47 ER 951.   [176] [1990] 1 WLR 616.

equitable accounting which would take place after sale to determine the respective shares, and accordingly there would be an order for sale and for equitable accounts. Vinelott J held that the practice in *Suttill v Graham* was not a rule of law to be applied in all circumstances but rather that it was a rule of convenience and more readily applies between husband and wife, or cohabitees, than between a spouse and the trustee in bankruptcy of the other co-owner. His lordship continued that:[177]

> Moreover, although the practice as recorded in *Suttill v Graham* is to set the interest element in mortgage instalments against a notional occupation rent, leaving the party paying the mortgage instalments free to charge a due proportion of any capital repayments against the share of the other, I can see no reason why, if an account is taken, the party paying the instalments should not be entitled to set a due proportion of the whole of the instalments paid against the share of the other party. The mortgagee will normally have a charge on the property for principal and interest and a right to possession and sale to enforce his charge. The payment of instalments due under the mortgage operates to relieve the property from the charge and gives rise to an equitable right of contribution in the co-owner who has not paid his due proportion of the instalments.

In *Re Pavlou*,[178] Millett J set out the principles in the following manner:

> First, a court of equity will order an inquiry and payment of occupation rent, not only in the case where the co-owner in occupation has ousted the other, but in any other case in which it is necessary in order to do equity between the parties that an occupation rent should be paid. The fact that there has not been an ouster or forceful exclusion therefore is far from conclusive. Secondly, where it is a matrimonial home and the marriage has broken down, the party who leaves the property will, in most cases, be regarded as excluded from the family home, so that an occupation rent should be paid by the co-owner who remains. But that is not a rule of law; that is merely a statement of the prima facie conclusions to be drawn from the facts. The true position is that if a tenant in common leaves the property voluntarily, but would be welcome back and would be in a position to enjoy his or her right to occupy, it would normally not be fair or equitable to the remaining tenant in common to charge him or her with an occupation rent which he or she never expected to pay.[179]

Millett J approved the proposition set out by Vinelott J in *Re Gorman* that an occupation rent would not be charged of necessity, and it was not a rule of law but rather a rule of convenience which 'more readily applies between husband and wife or co-habitees than between a spouse and a trustee in bankruptcy of the other co-owner'.[180] So, in *Dennis v McDonald*[181] a wife had been forced to leave the matrimonial home by her husband's violence. In the light of the wife's effectively involuntary quitting of the home it was held that 'the basic principle that a tenant in common is not liable to pay an occupation rent by virtue merely of his being in sole occupation of the property does not apply in the case where an association

---

[177] [1990] 1 WLR 616, 627. [178] [1993] 1 WLR 1046. [179] ibid at 1050.
[180] ibid at 1051. See especially now *Byford v Butler* [2003] EWHC 1267 *per* Lawrence Collins J.
[181] [1982] Fam 63 (Purchas J and CA).

similar to a matrimonial association has broken down and one party is, for practical purposes, excluded from the family home'.[182] The Court of Appeal took the situation on these facts to be, in effect, an ouster of one tenant in common by the other.[183]

Purchase price resulting trust altered by subsequent agreement of the parties

The courts have not slavishly followed the very clear test set out in *Lloyds Bank v Rosset*. The decisions in subsequent cases have tended to favour an approach based on calculation of the proportionate interests acquired by the parties from the cash amounts which they have contributed to the purchase of the property. For example, the decision of the Court of Appeal in *Huntingford v Hobbs*,[184] particularly in the judgment of Sir Christopher Slade, demonstrated an attitude based not on 'an abstract notion of justice' but on a rough approximation to what each party had contributed with adjustments for outstanding obligations.   **56.54**

In *Huntingford v Hobbs*[185] itself there were two contributors to the purchase price of the property: one party had contributed cash whereas the other had undertaken to pay off the mortgage on the property. In part the Court of Appeal, without express reference to the doctrinal issues considered above, was relying on resulting trust principles to grant interests equivalent to the cash contributions made. However, the court did not restrict itself to resulting trust principles. Rather, it also inferred a common intention from the conduct of the parties that the plaintiff would be responsible for the mortgage and therefore that it would accord him with an interest in proportion to the size of that undertaking. This was despite the fact that both parties were legally responsible for the mortgage—that is, while only the person who makes the repayments is awarded the proprietary rights, both are potentially, legally liable under the terms of the mortgage contract. The court preferred to concentrate on the parties' agreement as to who should pay off the mortgage, rather than on their respective legal obligations which could have made them liable to the mortgagee to make repayments. It is clear that the court will not consider itself bound simply by the cash contributions made by the parties but rather will also consider any other understanding reached between them as to the equitable interests which they intended each to receive.[186]   **56.55**

Deposits and sale proceeds from previous properties

One of the common shortcomings of English property law is that the rules focus on specific items of property rather than taking into account the range of dealings   **56.56**

---

[182] ibid 71.   [183] ibid 80.   [184] [1993] 1 FCR 45.   [185] [1993] 1 FCR 45.
[186] *Drake v Whipp* [1996] 1 FLR 826—where a contribution of one-fifth of the purchase price (on a net basis) was enlarged to one-third of the entire equitable interest because the court inferred that to be the parties' underlying intention on the evidence despite the size of their direct proportions to the purchase price; *Killey v Clough* [1996] NPC 38.

between individuals which might impact on the property but which were perhaps not directly related to it. In this way, sales of properties generate capital to acquire further properties, typically after discharge of the mortgage. It is important therefore that focus on the particular land in issue does not ignore interests held previously in other properties. So if A and B acquired 55 Mercer Road with equal cash contributions on the basis of a tenancy in common, that 50:50 division in the equitable interest ought to be carried forward when 55 Mercer Road is sold and the proceeds used to buy 1 Acacia Avenue: that is, so that those parties then have a 50:50 share of the equitable interest in 1 Acacia Avenue.

56.57 Similarly, it will typically be the case that individuals buying a home will generate most of the capital to acquire the property by means of mortgage. Those individuals may be required to pay a deposit from their own funds by the mortgagee in order to take out that mortgage, or they may choose to do so thus reducing the size of their mortgage debt. Where these deposits are the only cash contributions made by the parties (otherwise than by way of mortgage), their proportionate size may be decisive of the parties' respective equitable interests, or may contribute to their part of the balance sheet. By way of illustration, if A and B each contribute £5,000 separately by way of mortgage deposit and borrow £90,000 by way of mortgage (making a total acquisition price of £100,000), then A and B would acquire half each of the equitable interest in the property—the mortgagee would not acquire any equitable interest in the property because the parties' common intention would have been that the mortgagee acquire only the rights of a secured lender and not those of a beneficiary under a resulting trust. As a consequence, the mortgage deposit will be a significant part of the allocation of the equitable interest in many such cases. Each party would be deemed to have an equitable interest in the property worth £50,000 (being half of the house worth £100,000) even though they had only paid £5,000 in cash. The right acquired, then, is a right to a proportion of the total value of the property and not a right to be compensated for the amount of cash actually paid.

56.58 So, in *Midland Bank v Cooke*[187] it was held that a common intention constructive trust can arise where cohabitees equally provide a deposit on a house purchased in the name of one or both of them.[188] In that case W had contributed nothing to the purchase price but was deemed to have contributed the deposit for the purchase of the property equally with H which had been given to them by way of wedding gift. The question arose whether or not W had any beneficial interest in the property in any event. Waite LJ held that the judge must survey the whole course of dealing between the parties. Further it was held that the court was not

---

[187] [1995] 4 All ER 562.
[188] The facts of this case are considered in greater detail below, at para 56.79 in relation to the family assets doctrine.

required to confine its survey to the limited range of acts of direct contribution of the sort that are needed to found a beneficial interest in the first place. If that survey is inconclusive, the court should fall back on the maxim 'equality is equity'. Part of the judgment of Waite LJ was that equal contribution to the original deposit was an indication that the parties intended to split the equitable interest in their home equally between them. However, as considered above, it is difficult to reconcile this focus on equality between the parties with the other cases in this area asserting a strict approach based on direct contributions to the purchase price (for example *Lloyds Bank v Rosset*) or the balance sheet cases (for example *Huntingford v Hobbs*[189]) which would consider such an equal division to be inequitable.

56.59 On the issue of deposits and subsequently purchased homes, in *McHardy v Warren*[190] H's parents had paid the whole of the deposit on the matrimonial home acquired by H and his wife, W. The legal title in the property was registered in H's sole name. The remainder of the purchase price of the property was provided entirely by means of a mortgage. The mortgage was taken out in H's name only. That house was sold and then two subsequent homes were bought (one after the other) out of the sale proceeds of the first home. The mortgagee sought to recover their security by seeking an order for the sale of the house. W sought to resist their claim on the basis that she had an equitable interest in the property too, grounded on the argument that the deposit provided by her father-in-law constituted a wedding gift to them both and therefore that she had acquired an equitable interest at that stage derived from her share of the wedding present. Consequently, she claimed that she had 50 per cent of the equitable interest in the original property, which translated into 50 per cent of all subsequent acquisitions.

56.60 It was contended on behalf of the mortgagee that W had only a right equal to the cash value of W's half of the deposit in proportion to the total purchase price of the house. That is, a right to half of the original £650 deposit out of the total value of the property. The central principle was held to be that the parties must have intended that there be equal title in the property to sustain W's argument. On the facts, the court felt that the only plausible conclusion to be drawn was that the intention of the father in putting up the deposit was to benefit H and W equally and that their intention must be that the property be held equally in equity. Therefore, the court held that W was entitled to an equal share of the house with H because W put up the deposit equally with H. That is, H and W held the entire equity in the property in equal shares: that is, half each on these facts. In consequence the building society could not claim that W was entitled merely to £325 (being half of the original deposit in cash terms) and were bound by her half share in the equitable interest in the property.

---

[189] [1993] 1 FCR 45.   [190] [1994] 2 FLR 338.

Non-cash contributions to the purchase price

56.61 Either on resulting trust principles or further to *Lloyds Bank v Rosset*, direct cash contributions to the purchase price, or to the mortgage repayments, will be taken into account in calculating an equitable interest.[191] The question arose in *Springette v Defoe*[192] whether or not a person who procures a discount on the purchase price of property is entitled to bring that discount on the price of the property into the calculation of his equitable interest in the property. The argument runs that getting a discount on the property constitutes an indirect contribution to the purchase price, being reliant on the use of some other right that person has.[193]

56.62 On the facts of *Springette v Defoe*, Miss Springette had been a tenant of the London Borough of Ealing for more than eleven years. She began to cohabit with Mr Defoe and they decided to purchase a house in 1982. Neither party was able to raise the necessary mortgage because their incomes, whether taken jointly or severally, were not large enough. However, Miss Springette was entitled to a discount of 41 per cent under the applicable right-to-buy legislation on the purchase price of her home from the council because she had been an Ealing council tenant for more than eleven years. The purchase price was therefore £14,445 with the discount. The parties took out a mortgage for £12,000. There was an agreement between the parties that they would meet the mortgage repayments half each. Mr Defoe provided £180 in cash. Miss Springette provided the balance of £2,526 in cash. Their relationship broke down in 1985. The issue arose as to the proportionate equitable interest which each should have in the house.

56.63 The Court of Appeal held that there should be a resulting trust imposed unless there was found to be sufficient specific evidence of a common intention to found a constructive trust. Such a common intention must be communicated between the parties and made manifest between them at the time of the transaction. On the facts of *Springette v Defoe* there was no evidence to support the contention that the parties had had any sort of discussion as to their respective interests (within Lord Bridge's test in *Lloyds Bank v Rosset*) nor that they had reached any such agreement.[194] Therefore, the presumption of resulting trust could not be displaced. The court performed a calculation exercise in the following terms, calculating the amount of value which each party had contributed to the purchase price. Miss Springette was taken to have contributed the aggregate of £10,045 by way of a discount on the property price, £6,000 being half of the mortgage payments, and £2,526 in cash: a total of £18,571; whereas Mr Defoe contributed £6,000 being half of the mortgage payments and £180 in cash: a total of £6,180.

---

[191] *Lloyds Bank v Rosset* [1990] 1 AC 107. [192] (1992) HLR 552, [1992] 2 FLR 388.
[193] cf *Evans v Hayward* [1995] 2 FLR 511, *per* Staughton LJ; *Ashe v Mumford* The Times, 15 November 2000. [194] cf J Mee, *The Property Rights of Cohabitees* (Hart, 1999).

Therefore, Springette was taken, after rounding, to have contributed 75 per cent of the equity and Defoe 25 per cent.

The effect of merely contributing 'value', not cash

Importantly, the court looked at the *value* contributed and not at the *amount of cash paid* in *Springette v Defoe*. It is interesting to see how this compares to Lord Bridge's insistence in *Lloyds Bank v Rosset* that it is 'at least extremely doubtful whether anything less' than a direct contribution to the mortgage or to the purchase price will do. If it is accepted that procuring a reduction in the purchase price is a sufficient contribution, why should it be impossible to argue that if A pays for the household costs, the car, and the children's clothes, thus enabling B to defray the mortgage, that A is making it possible for B to pay off the mortgage and thus making a financial contribution to the purchase? After all, once you accept that the contribution need not be made in cash but merely by some other form of 'value', at what point is the line to be drawn under the range of non-cash contributions which are possible? For example, could someone with a natural flair for negotiating discounts claim a share in the property simply by virtue of convincing the vendor that he should sell the property for less than would otherwise have been accepted?[195] **56.64**

It is suggested that what is significant about *Springette v Defoe* is that the contribution which is made by way of the discount on the sale price arose directly from a statutory entitlement: that is, Miss Springette had a right of a given value under statute which was deducted from the acquisition of the property and which made the purchase possible. Where, for example, a discount on the sale price is negotiated, that is not a contribution of some valuable right of the claimant but rather it would be an alteration in the contractual sale price without the transfer of any valuable rights on his part. It is suggested that the foundation of an equitable interest in the home requires a contribution of a valuable right, such as the right which Miss Springette owned, as opposed to the performance of some task of negligible value which did not constitute the transfer of a valuable right. **56.65**

The nature of the contribution acceptable is complicated even on the facts of *Lloyds Bank v Rosset*. It is accepted that the courts should allow the parties to include contingent or future liabilities, such as the mortgage obligations, as part of the calculation of their respective contributions. Rather than a straightforward application of the principle in *Dyer v Dyer*[196] that such a contribution denotes an interest under resulting trust, the parties are being permitted to include in the calculations amounts which they will have to pay in the future but which they have not paid yet under the mortgage contract. This issue is considered further below. **56.66**

---

[195] See *Evans v Hayward* [1995] 2 FLR 511, *per* Staughton LJ.   [196] (1788) 2 Cox Eq Cas 92.

Accounting for contributions and payments made after acquisition

Bringing deferred mortgage repayments into account immediately; and enabling the parties to reallocate responsibility for the mortgage

56.67   A mortgage constitutes a loan of money which contributes to the purchase price of property but which the mortgagor only pays for over the life of the mortgage by way of interest and capital repayments. Nevertheless, the courts have taken the approach that the amount contributed by way of mortgage is to be taken to constitute an immediate contribution to the purchase price of the property at the date of its acquisition. Typically, when matters come to court a part of the mortgage has been paid off but a large amount remains undischarged. The question of how to account for the fact that the mortgage remains undischarged was addressed in part in *Huntingford v Hobbs*.[197] The issue is the need to account for the amount of the mortgage which had been paid off by the time of the court hearing, and to discount that part of the mortgage which remained to be paid off in the future.

56.68   In *Huntingford v Hobbs*, the plaintiff and the defendant lived together but did not marry. The plaintiff was living on social security benefits; the defendant had been recently divorced and was living in her own former matrimonial home. The plaintiff moved in with the defendant but was uncomfortable living in his partner's matrimonial home and therefore they decided to sell up. The plaintiff wanted to move to Woking where he felt he had a better chance to make money as a music teacher. The parties also wanted to be able to provide a home for the defendant's 21-year-old daughter. The plaintiff and the defendant bought a property in which they lived for £63,250 in 1986. The defendant sold her previous property and put £38,860 towards the purchase of the new property. The remaining £25,000 was provided by way of endowment mortgage. The mortgage liability was undertaken in the names of both plaintiff and defendant. It was agreed between the plaintiff and the defendant that the plaintiff would make the mortgage repayments. In 1988 the plaintiff left the defendant. The plaintiff had paid £5,316.30 in mortgage interest and £1,480.25 in premium payments. After the purchase of the property, the plaintiff spent £2,000 on the construction of a conservatory but this did not increase the value of the property although it was found on the facts that it did make it easier to sell. The defendant did not have any real income. The plaintiff paid for most income expenses and household bills. The property was valued at £95,000 at the time of the hearing and there remained £25,000 in capital outstanding on the mortgage.

56.69   The plaintiff contended that the property was to be held in equity under a joint tenancy on the basis of the terms of the conveyance into the names of both plaintiff and defendant. Therefore, the plaintiff sought an order that the property should be sold and the sale proceeds divided in equal shares between the parties.

---

[197]   [1993] 1 FLR 936.

The Court of Appeal held that the property should be sold but that the sale should be postponed to give the defendant a chance to buy out the plaintiff. Further, it was found that the plaintiff must have been intended to have some equitable interest in the property. In terms of establishing the parties' respective balance sheets, the court decided as follows. The defendant should be deemed to have contributed the cash proceeds of sale of her previous home; whereas the plaintiff should be deemed to have contributed the whole amount of the mortgage (because he was to have made the mortgage repayments) and that the plaintiff should receive some credit for the cost of the conservatory. The issue then arose as to the remaining, unpaid capital left on the mortgage. The Court of Appeal held that the plaintiff should have deducted from his equitable interest an amount in recognition of the fact that he had not yet paid off the capital of the mortgage and that it was the defendant who would have to meet that cost.

56.70 Therefore, the Court of Appeal calculated that: the plaintiff should receive £2,000 in relation to the expenditure on the conservatory after acquisition and 39% being the portion contributed by the mortgage, whereas the defendant should receive £25,000 by way of contribution to the capital of the mortgage and 61% being a cash contribution to the purchase price of the property. Again, the court's approach was to look straightforwardly at the amounts of money contributed by the parties towards the property without taking a literal approach to whether such expenditure took place at the time of acquisition (for example, the money spent on the conservatory was applied after purchase) and whether such expenditure was directed at the purchase price and not merely at more ephemeral matters of building work on the property (for example, the money expended on the conservatory again).

Additions and alterations to the property made after acquisition; together with alterations to the parties' common intention

56.71 The Court of Appeal in *Huntingford v Hobbs* was prepared to accept that, while the parties' equitable interests calculated on resulting trust principles crystallized at the time of the acquisition of the property, it would be possible for the parties to advance cogent evidence of subsequent changes of intention which would take effect over that resulting trust by means of constructive trust principles. On the facts of *Huntingford v Hobbs* the defendant's contribution to the property by way of paying for the construction of the conservatory was made after the date of the acquisition of the property. Nevertheless, this contribution was taken into account in deciding the defendant's rights in the property. It should also be remembered that this contribution was taken into account even though it did not increase the value of the property but rather made it merely more saleable. Similarly, it was held that it would be possible to overturn even documentary evidence of the parties' intentions with cogent evidence of other intentions. A hybrid form of resulting and constructive trust is therefore formed—one which enables changes in the relationship between the parties to be accounted for in the equitable interests which the court will recognize as existing between the parties.

Recognition of the parties' underlying intentions

56.72 The courts have demonstrated themselves prepared to consider cogent evidence of the parties true intentions rather than to consider themselves bound by, for example, contributions made directly to the purchase price at the outset, whether under resulting trust principles or not. Therefore, where a wife had made a contribution of one-fifth of the purchase price of property (on a net basis), the court enlarged her share to one-third of the entire equitable interest because the court was prepared to find that that had been the parties' underlying intention on the evidence in place of the size of their direct proportions to the purchase price.[198]

Time of the creation of the interest

56.73 What emerges from the foregoing discussion is that the contribution does not need to be made before the purchase of the property. Rather, the various forms of contribution accepted in the foregoing cases demonstrate that the manner in which the court will draw up the parties' balance sheet will be by reference to a broad range of contributions and entitlements created at different times after acquisition. The Court of Appeal in *Huntingford v Hobbs*[199] upheld the principle that one can use cogent evidence to demonstrate that documentation identifying the rights of the parties was not intended to constitute the full extent of the parties' interests. Furthermore, it was held that, even though the resulting trust in that case crystallized on the date of the acquisition of the property, it was nevertheless possible to restructure those equitable interests on constructive trust principles. There was also the possibility of equitable accounting to take into account periods of rent-free occupation by one or other of the parties.[200] In contradistinction to the assertion made in *Lloyds Bank v Rosset* that the contribution to the purchase price, or the agreement giving rise to a common intention constructive trust, must occur at the date of the purchase, it has been held that a constructive trust arises from the date of the acts complained of.[201]

J. Contributions to the Running of the Home

Domestic chores and domestic expenses will not found property rights

56.74 In line with the House of Lords' decision in *Gissing v Gissing*, the Court of Appeal in *Burns v Burns*[202] held that a mere contribution to household expenses would

---

198 *Drake v Whipp* [1996] 1 FLR 826.   199 [1993] 1 FLR 936.
200 *Bernard v Josephs* [1982] Ch 391; *Huntingford v Hobbs* [1993] 1 FLR 936.
201 *Re Sharpe* [1980] 1 WLR 219.   202 [1984] Ch 317.

not be sufficient to acquire an interest in property. Rather, the claimant would have to demonstrate that her contributions were made to the purchase price of the property with a view to acquiring an interest in that property. A wife who had run the home, cared for the children, and paid some household bills (including utility bills and shopping bills) would not acquire rights in the property. This is contrary to the approach in *Midland Bank v Cooke*[203] and contrary to the more progressive approach taken in Canada.[204] The *Burns v Burns* approach has been applied in a number of cases, including *Lloyds Bank v Rosset* (where mere supervision of building work was not sufficient to found a right in the property) and *Nixon v Nixon*[205] (where contribution to household expenses was again considered inadequate to found a right in property). Therefore, to found a right in property there is a need for some substantive (typically financial) contribution to the property beyond mere work within the normal context of the family, such as housework.

Improvements to the property

Contributions to the maintenance of the property insufficient to found an equitable interest in property

The first issue before the House of Lords in *Pettitt v Pettitt*[206] was the question **56.75** whether or not a spouse could acquire rights in property by doing acts or defraying expenditure which enabled the other spouse to maintain the home. The simple answer was that only expenditure directed at the acquisition of rights in the property at the time of purchase could generate any such equitable interest.[207] Simply paying for repair or maintenance work to the premises would not constitute expenditure directed solely at the acquisition of rights in the property. Nor is it necessarily the case that carrying out improvements to a property will acquire an equitable interest in that property without more.[208] The focus of this thinking was therefore clearly on the direct acquisition of property rights and not on any more general question of justice between cohabitees. A part of the parties' common intention may be agreements as to the maintenance of the property:

> Effect must be given to the intention of the parties that they would use their respective funds over the period necessary to purchase the land, build the house and then improve and furnish it. The extent of their respective interests must therefore be determined as at the conclusion of these activities, even though the trust was created on the date of the first expenditure, or on the date on which agreement was reached as to the way in which the funds would be used.[209]

Nevertheless, contributions solely to the maintenance of the property will not be sufficient in themselves to found an equitable interest. So, in *Pettitt v Pettitt*,

---

[203] [1995] 4 All ER 562, considered below at para 56.80.
[204] Considered below at para 56.100.   [205] [1969] 1 WLR 1676.   [206] [1970] AC 777.
[207] [1970] AC 777, 794, *per* Lord Reid.   [208] *Woodman v Tracy* [2002] EWCA Civ 880.
[209] *Tracy v Bifield* (1998) 23 Fam LR 260, *per* Templeman J. See also *Latimer v Latimer* (1970) 114 Sol Jo 973; *Re Superyield Holdings Ltd* [2000] 2 HKC 90, 170.

Mr Pettitt's claim failed because the improvements were of a purely ephemeral nature[210] and because 'do-it-yourself' jobs in themselves would not ground rights in property.[211] Therefore, as considered above in relation to *Lloyds Bank v Rosset*, it is only contributions to the purchase price of the property, or substantial financial contributions to the property itself, which will grant rights under resulting trust to the contributor. The limitation on the forms of contribution formed part of the judicial concern that insubstantial contributions should not be accepted as creating rights in property. Adopting the words of Coke, Lord Hodson suggested that total judicial discretion in this area would not be appropriate because:

> ... this would be to substitute the uncertain and crooked cord of discretion for the golden and straight metwand of the law.[212]

In other words, the law should always strive for certainty and principle as opposed to permitting judges to do as they thought fit in any case. These words may appear ironic given the complexities which were to follow, as considered in the foregoing section in relation to the restructuring of common intention agreements and as discussed further below.

Contributions by spouses to the improvement of the matrimonial home

56.76 Statute gives us an example of detriment which is sufficient to acquire an equitable interest. Section 37 of the Matrimonial Proceedings and Property Act 1970 provides that:

> ... where a husband or a wife contributes in money or in money's worth to the improvement of real or personal property in which ... either or both of them has or have a beneficial interest, the husband or wife so contributing shall ... be treated as ... having then acquired by virtue of his or her contribution a share ... in that beneficial interest ... as may in all the circumstances seem just to any court ...

Therefore, under section 37 of the Matrimonial Proceedings and Property Act 1970, where a husband or wife contributes to the improvement of property that contributor will be awarded such equitable interest as appears to the court to be just. It is important to note that this statute is restricted to cases involving spouses, as opposed to other forms of cohabiting relationship.

56.77 Under section 23 of the Matrimonial Causes Act 1973, the court is entitled (as part of its powers in relation to financial settlement on divorce) to adjust the beneficial interests of the parties to the former marriage. As part of its powers, the court is required to bear in mind the welfare of any children of the relationship[213] and also the parties' respective financial contributions to the welfare and upbringing

---

[210] [1970] AC 777, 796, *per* Lord Reid.
[211] A view expressed in various cases like *Nixon v Nixon* [1969] 1 WLR 1676; *Burns v Burns* [1984] Ch 317. [212] [1970] AC 808. [213] Matrimonial Causes Act 1973, s 25(1).

of such children.[214] In effect, then there is a very broad discretion on the court to take into account a wide range of issues which properly form the subject matter of a family law text.

Participation in long-term relationships

Exceptionally, for a property law court, the Court of Appeal in *Midland Bank v Cooke*[215] upheld an equitable interest in Mrs Cooke who had made no direct contribution to the purchase price of the property and only occasional contributions to the repayment of the mortgage. Her contributions were found to be, in effect, her integral contribution to the family over a number of years as wife and mother to the couple's children and in finding work on those occasions when Mr Cooke was out of work. More akin, perhaps, to a decision in family proceedings, even though the matter was in relation to mortgage possession proceedings, Mrs Cooke was found to have become entitled to equitable rights in the home based on these informal contributions to the family which were sufficient to resist a mortgagee's claim for possession and sale.[216]   **56.78**

K. Situations in Which Equality is Equity

An approach based on the allocation of family assets

As considered at various points in the foregoing discussion, the decisions of Waite   **56.79**
LJ have propounded a form of family assets doctrine which is avowedly grounded in *Gissing v Gissing*[217] but which has eschewed the complexity of much of the other case law in favour of dividing property equally between couples who are terminating a long-term relationship.[218] The expression 'family assets' doctrine was originally used by Lord Denning in relation to the division of property on a divorce.[219] The phrase was considered to be a convenient short way of expressing an important concept. It referred to those things which were acquired by one or other or both of the parties, with the intention that there should be continuing provision for them and their children during their joint lives, and that the home be used for the benefit of the family as a whole.[220] While this attempt to introduce a new model constructive trust to give effect to family assets was championed by Lord Denning,[221] it did not find universal favour in the law of property and was

---

[214] ibid s 25(2).   [215] [1995] 4 All ER 562.
[216] *Hammond v Mitchell* [1991] 1 WLR 1127.   [217] [1971] AC 886.
[218] It has not been necessary in these cases that the couple have been married: see for example *Hammond v Mitchell* [1991] 1 WLR 1127.   [219] *Wachtel v Wachtel* [1973] Fam 72, 90.
[220] ibid.
[221] *Hussey v Palmer* [1972] 1 WLR 1286; *Cooke v Head* [1972] 1 WLR 518; *Eves v Eves* [1975] 1 WLR 1338: imposed wherever 'justice and good conscience require'. *Hazell v Hazell* [1972] 1 WLR 301—look at all circumstances, including overall contribution to the family budget.

discarded.[222] It is not suggested here that that thinking has been given effect to by the courts in retrospect. Rather, it is suggested here that there are similarities in a strain of decisions delivered by family courts in relation to rights in property which have echoes of Lord Denning's original approach.[223] The family assets approach advanced by Lord Denning has been rejected in a number of English decisions. It was been held in a range of cases[224] that English law on the home contains no such concept as the 'family assets' doctrine as a result of the decisions of the House of Lords in *Gissing* and *Pettitt*. What is meant by a family assets doctrine in *those cases* was that it was not possible to say that where a purchase was made out of the general assets of a family the equitable interest in the property so acquired should have been divided equally among those family members. However, the law of trusts of homes permits a number of seemingly irreconcilable doctrines, as will emerge from the following discussion. The family assets approach considered here is something quite different.

Long-term relationships in which equality is equity

56.80   The confusion which remains at the doctrinal level in the cases on trusts of homes is well illustrated by the decision of the Court of Appeal in *Midland Bank v Cooke*.[225] In 1971 a husband and wife purchased a house for £8,500. The house was registered in the husband's sole name. The purchase was funded as follows: the bulk of the purchase price, an amount of £6,450, was provided by means of mortgage taken out in the husband's name although Mrs Cooke was a signatory to a second mortgage subsequently taken out over the property. Mr Cooke made a cash contribution of £950 with the balance being provided by means of a wedding present made to the couple of £1,100. In 1978 the mortgage was replaced by a more general mortgage in favour of H which secured the repayment of his company's business overdraft. In 1979 W signed a consent form to subordinate any interest she may have to the bank's mortgage. Subsequently the bank sought forfeiture of the mortgage and possession of the house in default of payment. W claimed undue influence and an equitable interest in the house to override the bank's claim.

56.81   The Court of Appeal reverted to *Gissing v Gissing* without considering the detail of *Lloyds Bank v Rosset* (although accepting in passing that the test in *Lloyds Bank v Rosset* was ordinarily the test to be applied). Waite LJ had trouble with the different

---

[222]   *Ivin v Blake* [1995] 1 FLR 70; *MacFarlane v MacFarlane* [1972] NILR 59, 66; and *McHardy v Warren* [1994] 2 FLR 338.

[223]   *Hammond v Mitchell* [1991] 1 WLR 1127; *Midland Bank v Cooke* [1995] 4 All ER 562; *Drake v Whipp* [1996] 1 FLR 826; *Rowe v Prance* [1999] 2 FLR 787. Cf *Re B (Child: Property Transfer)* [1999] 2 FLR 418.

[224]   *Ivin v Blake* [1995] 1 FLR 70; *MacFarlane v MacFarlane* [1972] NILR 59, 66; and *McHardy v Warren* [1994] 2 FLR 338.   [225]   [1995] 4 All ER 562.

approaches adopted in *Springette v Defoe*[226] and *McHardy v Warren*.[227] The former calculated the interests of the parties on a strictly mathematical, resulting trust basis; whereas the latter looked to the intentions of all the parties as to whether or not the deposit should be considered as a proportionate part of the total purchase price or as establishing a half share of the equity in the property. His lordship claimed to find the difference between these two approaches 'mystifying'.[228]

The question then arose as to how the court should address this problem. Waite **56.82** LJ returned to the speech of Lord Diplock in *Gissing* and to the decision of Browne-Wilkinson V-C in *Grant v Edwards*, before holding the following:

> [T]he duty of the judge is to undertake a survey of the whole course of dealing between the parties relevant to their ownership and occupation of the property and their sharing of its burdens and advantages. That scrutiny will not confine itself to the limited range of acts of direct contribution of the sort that are needed to found a beneficial interest in the first place. It will take into consideration all conduct which throws light on the question what shares were intended. Only if that search proves inconclusive does the court fall back on the maxim that 'equality is equity'.

These dicta are particularly significant because they implicitly reject the formalism of Lord Bridge's approach in *Lloyds Bank v Rosset* ('that scrutiny will not confine itself to the limited range of acts of direct contribution of the sort that are needed to found a beneficial interest in the first place') and instead require the court to consider the whole course of dealing between the parties ('will take into consideration all conduct which throws light on the question what shares were intended'). It should be recalled that Mrs Cooke had contributed only those sorts of assistance (bar a handful of contributions to the mortgage which would have been dismissed as being *de minimis* in themselves) which would not have founded a right in property on a strict application of the principle in *Lloyds Bank v Rosset*. On these facts, the court considered that the matter could not be decided simply by reference to the cash contributions of the parties. Rather, the court accepted that the parties' situation constituted a clear example of a situation in which a couple 'had agreed to share everything equally': but again, in the form of a situation which would not have disclosed an agreement of the sort required by *Lloyds Bank v Rosset* to found an equitable interest in the home. It was the parties' instinctive sharing of the ups and downs of their married life which convinced the court that equal ownership of their home was equity's proper analysis of their situation. Facts indicating this shared attitude to all aspects of their relationship included evidence of the fact that Mrs Cooke had brought up the children, worked part-time and full-time to pay household bills, and had become a co-signatory to the second mortgage.

---

[226] [1992] 2 FLR 388.   [227] [1994] 2 FLR 338.
[228] The distinction is that identified by Bagnall J in *Cowcher v Cowcher* [1972] 1 WLR 425, 430 and considered at the beginning of this chapter.

56.83 What is not clear is how this decision is to be reconciled with the findings in *Burns v Burns*[229] and *Nixon v Nixon*[230] that activities revolving only around domestic chores could not constitute the acquisition of rights in property. Further, it is not obvious how the decision can be reconciled with the dicta of Lord Bridge in *Lloyds Bank v Rosset* that a common intention formed on the basis of conduct must be directed at the mortgage payments and that it 'is at least extremely doubtful that anything less will do'. Returning to *Gissing v Gissing*, as Lord Pearson held: 'I think that the decision of cases of this kind have been made more difficult by excessive application of the maxim "equality is equity".'[231] Therefore, Waite LJ's approaches in *Midland Bank v Cooke* above and also in *Hammond v Mitchell*[232] are fundamentally different from those earlier principles. Furthermore, the family assets approach is in line with the possibility of providing for equitable accounting so that the court can take account of expenditure made on property even if the claimant is not awarded the proprietary interest sought.[233] It is suggested that it marks a significant incursion of the principles and the intellectual approach of family law into this area of property law.[234]

Communal undertakings and common participation in a family business

56.84 In most cases involving long-term relationships and children there will be a complicated list of items of property and communal undertakings. Picking between real and personal property, and including matters like the value of voluntary work by one spouse in the other spouse's business, will all confuse the issue whether or not cohabitees have acquired any rights in property. There are also further issues as to title in the personal property which a couple will amass during the course of their relationship. The case of *Hammond v Mitchell* explores precisely this point. *Hammond v Mitchell*[235] was a decision of Waite J (as he then was) in which the question arose as to rights in real property, business ventures, and chattels. A couple who did not marry had a tempestuous relationship. It was said by Waite J that '[t]hey both shared a zest for the good life'[236] and that '[t]hey were too much in love at this time either to count the pennies or pay attention to who was providing them'.[237] The judgment details their romantic (in a very

[229] [1984] Ch 317.   [230] [1969] 1 WLR 1676.   [231] [1971] AC 886, 903.
[232] [1991] 1 WLR 1127.
[233] For a discussion of the operation of such equitable accounting in English law see E Cooke, *The Modern Law of Estoppel* (Oxford: Clarendon Press, 2000) 391; also *Re Pavlou* [1993] 2 FLR 751, Millett J; *Leake v Bruzzi* [1974] 1 WLR 1528, CA; not following *Cracknell v Cracknell* [1971] P 356; *Suttill v Graham* [1977] 1 WLR 819, CA; *Re Gorman* [1990] 2 FLR 284, Vinelott J.
[234] See the approaches taken in cases such as *Bedson v Bedson* [1965] 2 QB 666; *Re John's Assignment Trusts* [1970] 1 WLR 955; *Bernard v Josephs* [1982] Ch 391, 411; *Chhokar v Chhokar* [1984] FLR 313.   [235] [1991] 1 WLR 1127.   [236] [1991] 1 WLR 1127, 1129.
[237] ibid, 1130.

kitchen sink drama kind of a way) meeting as he, a second hand car dealer from Essex, gave a lift to her, a much younger hostess at the Playboy nightclub, in Epping Forest. These details informed his lordship's impression of the circumstances that it was perfectly reasonable for this couple not to allocate rights in any of the property which they subsequently acquired in any formal way. Consequently, there was no clear common intention formed between the parties although there was some evidence that Mr Hammond had promised Miss Mitchell that everything would be half hers. Ultimately their relationship lasted eleven years and spawned two children. Their property comprised a house, a large amount of movable property, and Hammond's participation in a restaurant venture in Spain. The couple both participated in a range of trading ventures working hand to mouth.

When the unmarried couple finally separated, the court was asked to decide the **56.85** parties' respective rights in the real and the personal property. Waite J was clear that he considered the question of finding a common intention 'detailed, time-consuming and laborious'.[238] He acknowledged that the first question for the court to address was whether or not there had been any agreement between the parties. Here there had been discussions as to the house. Echoing Lord Pearson in *Pettitt v Pettitt,* Waite J held that '[t]his is not an area where the maxim "equality is equity" falls to be applied unthinkingly'.[239] However, in the light of all the facts, it was found that Mitchell's share of the house should be one-half of the total interest, on the basis that it appeared that the couple had intended to muck in together and thereby share everything equally. The further question was whether or not there was any imputed intention which should be applied to the parties. It was found that, while she contributed personally to the business which he had set up in Valencia, this did not justify any reallocation of any proprietary rights in that venture to her without more. Her cash investment had not, it was found, been made with an intention to acquire any further property rights in that Spanish property but rather was intended simply to realize a cash return. With reference to the household chattels it was held that 'the parties must expect the courts to adopt a robust allegiance to the maxim "equality is equity"'.[240] Therefore, everything was divided equally.

The extraordinary facet of these decisions is that they eschew all of the carefully **56.86** prescribed rules in *Lloyds Bank v Rosset.* There is one further doctrine which offers even more scope to the judiciary to indulge their desire for the discretion to allocate proprietary rights between parties: that is the doctrine of proprietary estoppel which is considered next.

---

[238] ibid, 1130.   [239] ibid, 1137.   [240] ibid, 1138.

L. Interests in the Home Under Proprietary Estoppel

The doctrine of proprietary estoppel

The three requirements of proprietary estoppel

56.87   The doctrine of proprietary estoppel will grant an equitable interest to a person who has been induced to suffer detriment in reliance on a representation (or some assurance) that they would acquire some rights in the property as a result.[241] Whereas, rights based on constructive trust and resulting trust are 'institutional' trusts taking retrospective effect, proprietary estoppel may give a different kind of right. The clearest conception of the doctrine of proprietary estoppel in modern cases was set out by Edward Nugee QC in *Re Basham*.[242] That case supported the three stage requirement of representation, reliance, and detriment in the following terms:

> . . . where one person, A, has acted to his detriment on the birth of a belief, which was known to and encouraged by another person, B, then B cannot insist on his strict legal rights if to do so would be inconsistent with A's belief . . . where the belief is that A is going to be given a right in the future, it is properly to be regarded as giving rise to a species of constructive trust, which is the concept employed by a court of equity to prevent a person from relying on his legal rights where it would be unconscionable for him to do so. The rights to which proprietary estoppel gives rise, and the machinery by which effect is given to them, are similar in many respects to those involved in cases of secret trusts, mutual wills, and other comparable cases in which property is vested in B on the faith of an understanding that it will be dealt with in a particular manner . . . In cases of proprietary estoppel the factor which gives rise to the equitable obligation is A's alteration of his position on the faith of a similar understanding.

In short, proprietary estoppel will arise where the claimant has performed some act (arguably, which must be done in relation to the property) to her detriment in reliance upon a representation made to her by the cohabitee from whom the claimant would thereby seek to acquire an equitable interest in the property.[243]

The nature of the representation required to found the estoppel

56.88   It is clear from the cases that the representation made by the defendant need only amount to an assurance and it can be implied, rather than needing to be made expressly.[244] Therefore, it is sufficient that the defendant allowed the claimant to believe that her actions would acquire her property rights; it is not necessary that there be any express, single promise. The reliance is generally assumed (on an

---

[241]   *Re Basham* [1986] 1 WLR 1498; *Lissimore v Downing* [2003] 2 FLR 308.
[242]   [1986] 1 WLR 1498.
[243]   *Re Basham* [1986] 1 WLR 1498; *In Re Sharpe (A Bankrupt)* [1980] 1 WLR 219.
[244]   *Crabb v Arun DC* [1976] Ch 179.

evidential basis) where a representation has been made.[245] The question of what will constitute 'detriment' is considered below.

The flexible nature of the representation under the doctrine of proprietary estoppel is illustrated by the decision of the Court of Appeal in *Gillett v Holt*.[246] That case concerned a friendship between a farmer, Mr Holt, and a young boy of 12, Gillett, which lasted for 40 years during which time the boy worked for the farmer. Gillett left his real parents and moved in with Holt when aged 15: there was even a suggestion that the farmer would adopt the boy at one stage. On numerous occasions the claimant, Gillett, was assured by Holt that he would inherit the farm. The claimant's wife and family were described as being a form of surrogate family for the farmer. In time a third person, Wood, turned Holt against Gillett which led to Gillett being removed from Holt's will. Robert Walker LJ held that there was sufficient detriment by Gillett in the course of their relationship over 40 years evidenced by the following factors: working for Holt and not accepting other job offers, performing actions beyond what would ordinarily have been expected of an employee, taking no substantial steps to secure for his future by means of pension or otherwise, and spending money on a farmhouse (which he expected to inherit) which had been almost uninhabitable at the outset. The combination of these factors over such a long period of time were considered by the Court of Appeal to constitute ample evidence of detriment sufficient to found a proprietary estoppel. The court upheld the threefold test for proprietary estoppel which has become familiar in the cases: that there be a representation (or assurance), reliance, and detriment.[247] Each of those elements is considered in outline terms in the sections which follow.

It is important that the assurances of the representor have been intended by their maker to lead the claimant to believe that he would acquire rights in property. So, for example, it would not be sufficient that the representor was merely toying with the claimant without either of them forming a belief that the claimant would in fact acquire any rights in property. For, as Robert Walker LJ put it, 'it is notorious that some elderly persons of means derive enjoyment from the possession of testamentary power, and from dropping hints as to their intentions, without any question of any estoppel arising'.[248] On the facts of *Gillett v Holt*[249] it was clear that the assurances had been repeated frequently and were sincerely meant when made. It is clear that in general terms it will be sufficient if the defendant makes an express representation to the claimant[250] but it would also be sufficient to establish

---

[245] *Lim v Ang* [1992] 1 WLR 113; *Grant v Edwards* [1986] Ch 638.
[246] [2000] 2 All ER 289.
[247] *Taylors Fashions Ltd v Liverpool Victoria Trustees Co Ltd* [1982] 1 QB 133; *Re Basham (Deceased)* [1986] 1 WLR 1498; *Wayling v Jones* (1993) 69 P & CR 170; *Gillett v Holt* [2000] 2 All ER 289.　　　　　　　　　　　　[248] [2000] 2 All ER 289, 304.　　　[249] ibid.
[250] *Taylors Fashions Ltd v Liverpool Victoria Trustees Co Ltd* [1982] 1 QB 133; *Re Basham (Deceased)* [1986] 1 WLR 1498; *Wayling v Jones* (1993) 69 P & CR 170; *Gillett v Holt* [2000] 2 All ER 289.

an estoppel if some implied assurance were made in circumstances in which the defendant knew that the claimant was relying on the impression she had formed.[251]

The fulfilment of expectations

56.89 A typical situation in which proprietary estoppel claims arise is where promises are made by the absolute owner of land to another person that that other person will acquire an interest in the land if they perform acts which would otherwise be detrimental to them.[252] Typically, then, the person making the promise dies or deals with the property in some other fashion without transferring any right in the property to that other person. By way of example, in *Re Basham*[253] the claimant was 15 years old when her mother married the deceased. She worked unpaid in the deceased's business, cared for the deceased through his illness, sorted out a boundary dispute for the deceased, and refrained from moving away when her husband was offered employment with tied accommodation elsewhere. All of these acts were performed on the understanding that she would acquire an interest in property on the deceased's death. The deceased died intestate. It was held that the claimant had acquired an equitable interest on proprietary estoppel principles. It was found that proprietary estoppel arises where:

> A has acted to detriment on the faith of a belief which was known to and encouraged by B, that he either has or will receive a right over B's property, B cannot insist on strict legal rights so as to conflict with A's belief.

This case can be contrasted with *Layton v Martin*[254] in which a man had promised to provide for his mistress in his will. He died without leaving any of the promised bequests in his will and therefore the mistress sued his estate claiming rights on constructive trust. Her claim was rejected on the basis that she had not contributed in any way to the maintenance of his assets.[255] At one level it is a decision based on the absence of detriment. This can be compared with the decision in *Re Basham* in which the claimant was found to have made sufficient contributions to the defendant's assets.[256] Similarly, where a wife contributes to her husband's business activities generally it may be found that she has suffered detriment which will ground a right in property,[257] particularly if this evidences a common intention at some level which may be undocumented.[258] Other relatives will be entitled to rely on their contributions to the acquisition or maintenance of property where there

---

[251] *Crabb v Arun DC* [1976] Ch 179. [252] *Gillett v Holt* [2000] 2 All ER 289.
[253] [1986] 1 WLR 1498. [254] [1986] 1 FLR 171.
[255] See also *Midland Bank v Dobson* [1986] 1 FLR 171—wife's claim failed because there was no evidence that she had suffered any detriment.
[256] As noted by J Martin (1987) Conv 211; D Hayton (1986) C LJ 394, M Davey (1988) 8 Legal Studies 92, 101. [257] *Heseltine v Heseltine* [1971] 1 WLR 342.
[258] *Re Densham* [1975] 1 WLR 1519.

have been assurances made to them that they would be able to occupy that property as their home.[259] In such situations it is essential that the expenditure is made in reliance on a representation that it will accrue the contributor some right in the property.[260]

The avoidance of detriment

Another example of proprietary estoppel arose in the decision of Lord Denning in **56.90** *Greasley v Cooke*.[261] There a woman, Doris Cooke, had been led to believe that she could occupy property for the rest of her life. She had been the family's maid but then had formed an emotional relationship with one of the family and become his partner. In reliance on this understanding she looked after the Greasley family, acting as a housekeeper, instead of getting herself a job and providing for her own future. The issue arose whether or not she had acquired any equitable interest in the property. It was held by Lord Denning that she had suffered detriment in looking after the family and not getting a job in reliance on the representation made to her. Therefore, it was held that she had acquired a beneficial interest in the property under proprietary estoppel principles because she had acted to her detriment in continuing to work for the Greasleys in reliance on their assurance to her that she would acquire some proprietary rights as a result. The form of right which Lord Denning granted was an irrevocable licence to occupy the property for the rest of her life.[262] That such a particular remedy was awarded brings us to the more general question: what form of remedy can be awarded under proprietary estoppel principles?

The remedial nature of the interest awarded under proprietary estoppel

Proprietary estoppel is very different, in a number of ways, from the institutional **56.91** resulting and constructive trusts considered above. By one account, the aim of proprietary estoppel is to avoid detriment rather than to enforce the promise; by another, its purpose is to reinforce the expectation of the party who acted to her reliance on the representation.[263] A survey of the various possibilities was conducted by Robert Walker LJ in *Jennings v Rice*.[264] Whereas the common intention constructive trust appears to be quasi-contractual (in that it enforces an express or

---

[259] *Re Sharpe* [1980] 1 WLR 219—aunt acquires 'constructive trust' right on the basis of contributions to the acquisition of the property based on a promise that she could live there.
[260] *Thomas v Fuller-Brown* [1988] 1 FLR 237, *per* Slade LJ, spending money does not, by itself, acquire you rights in property.   [261] [1980] 1 WLR 1306.
[262] What is particularly satisfying about this case is that, had Charles Dickens sought to incorporate these events into a novel like *Nicholas Nickleby*, he could have found no better name for the Squeers-like family than 'the Greasleys'.
[263] E Cooke, 'Estoppel and the Protection of Expectations' [1997] 17 Legal Studies 258; S Gardner, 'The Remedial Discretion in Proprietary Estoppel' (1999) 115 LQR 438.
[264] [2002] EWCA Civ 159, [2003] 1 FCR 501.

implied agreement), estoppel is directed at preventing detriment being caused by a broken promise. In *Walton Stores v Maher*[265] Brennan J held that:

> The object of the equity is not to compel the party bound to fulfil the assumption or expectation: it is to avoid the detriment which, if the assumption or expectation goes unfulfilled, will be suffered by the party who has been induced to act or to abstain from acting thereon.[266]

In a similar vein, Lord Browne-Wilkinson has held in *Lim v Ang*[267] that the purpose of proprietary estoppel is to provide a response where 'it is unconscionable for the representor to go back on the assumption that he permitted the representee to make'. That is, to avoid the detriment caused by reneging on that representation. This approach is important because the court's intention is not merely to recognize that an institutional constructive trust exists between the parties, but rather to provide a remedy which prevents the claimant from suffering detriment.[268] The narrow line between proprietary estoppel and the (at the time of writing, heretical) remedial constructive trust is considered at the end of this chapter.

56.92   The determination of the courts to prevent detriment therefore requires the court both to identify the nature of the property rights which were the subject of the representation and to mould a remedy to prevent detriment resulting from the breach of promise. Typically, this requires the demonstration of a link between the detriment and a understanding that property rights were to have been acquired. Thus in *Wayling v Jones*[269] two gay men, A and B, lived together as a couple. A owned a hotel in which B worked for lower wages than he would otherwise have received in an arm's length arrangement. A promised to leave the hotel to B in his will. The hotel was sold and another acquired without any change in A's will having been made to reflect that assurance. B sought an interest in the proceeds of sale of the hotel. The issue turned on B's evidence as to whether or not he would have continued to work for low wages had A not made the representation as to the interest in the hotel. Initially, B's evidence suggested that it was as a result of his affection for A that B had accepted low wages. Before the Court of Appeal, B's evidence suggested that he accepted low wages from A in reliance on the assurance that B would acquire property rights in the hotel. Consequently, the Court of Appeal held that B was entitled to acquire proprietary rights under proprietary estoppel because his detrimental acts were directed at the acquisition of rights in property and were not merely the sentimental ephemera of their relationship.

56.93   Professor Hayton has expressed the view[270] that the court is not here giving effect to pre-existing rights but rather is fitting a remedy to a particular wrong.

[265] (1988) 62 AJLR 110.   [266] ibid 125.   [267] [1992] 1 WLR 113, 117.
[268] *Westdeutsche Landesbank v Islington LBC* [1996] AC 669.   [269] (1995) 69 P & CR 170.
[270] D Hayton, 'Equitable rights of cohabitees' [1990] Conv 370; D Hayton, 'Constructive trusts: a bold approach' (1993) 109 LQR 485.

This remedy may be in the form of a prospective, remedial constructive trust. Indeed, it was held in *Re Sharpe*[271] that proprietary estoppel right exists only from the date of the court order. The award appears to be remedial in its effect—providing a remedy for the detriment suffered.[272] However, it is worthy of note that, in a number of cases, the court appears to be awarding expectation loss (that is, giving to the claimant rights which the claimant had expected to receive), rather than simply avoiding detriment.[273]

The extent and nature of the interest awarded under proprietary estoppel

The nature of the remedy is at the discretion of the court. The decision of the Court of Appeal in *Pascoe v Turner*[274] is illustrative of the breadth of the remedy potentially available under a proprietary estoppel claim. The plaintiff and the defendant cohabited in a property which was registered in the name of the plaintiff alone. The plaintiff often told the defendant that the property and its contents were hers—however, the property was never conveyed to her. In reliance on these representations, the defendant spent money on redecoration and repairs to the property. While the amounts were not large, they constituted a large proportion of the defendant's savings. The defendant sought to assert rights under proprietary estoppel when the plaintiff sought an order to remove the defendant from the property. **56.94**

The decision of the Court of Appeal in *Pascoe v Turner* was that the size of the appropriate interest would be that required to do the 'minimum equity necessary' between the parties.[275] Therefore, it was decided to award the transfer of the freehold to the defendant, to fulfil the promise that a home would be available to her for the rest of her life, rather than (so it appears) merely to avoid the detriment which had actually been suffered in reliance on the representation. It is impossible to grant a larger interest in land than an outright assignment of the freehold. Therefore, the court apparently has within its power the ability to award any remedy which will prevent the detriment which would otherwise be suffered by the claimant. **56.95**

---

[271] *Re Sharpe (A Bankrupt)* [1980] 1 WLR 219.

[272] See also M Pawlowski, *The Doctrine of Proprietary Estoppel* (Sweet & Maxwell, 1996) generally.

[273] *Pascoe v Turner* [1979] 1 WLR 431; *Greasley v Cooke* [1980] 1 WLR 1306; and *Re Basham* [1986] 1 WLR 1498.

[274] [1979] 2 All ER 945, [1979] 1 WLR 431.

[275] Drawing on the dicta of Scarman LJ to that effect in *Crab v Arun DC* [1976] Ch 179, 198, drawing on older authorities such as *Duke of Beaufort v Patrick* (1853) 17 Beav 60 and *Plimmer v Wellington Corporation* (1884) 9 App Cas 699, 713, *per* Sir Arthur Hobhouse ('In fact the court must look at the circumstances in each case to decide in what way the equity can be satisfied'). See also, similar in tone, *Maddison v Alderson* (1883) 8 App Cas 467, 475, *per* Lord Selborne LC; and *Dillwyn v Llewelyn* (1862) 4 De GF & J 517, 522, *per* Lord Westbury ('The equity of the donee and the estate to be claimed by virtue of it depend on the transaction ...').

56.96 However, it is not the case that proprietary estoppel will always lead to an award of property rights.[276] For example, in *Baker v Baker*[277] the plaintiff was deemed entitled only to compensation in respect of the cost of giving up secure accommodation. The plaintiff was a 75-year-old man with a secure tenancy over a house in Finchley. The defendants were his son and daughter who rented accommodation in Bath. It was agreed that the plaintiff should vacate his flat and that the parties should buy a house together in Torquay. The plaintiff contributed £33,950 in return for which he was entitled to occupy the property rent-free. The defendants acquired the remainder of the purchase price by way of mortgage. The parties decided to terminate the relationship and the plaintiff was rehoused as a secure tenant with housing benefit.

56.97 It was held that there was no resulting trust in favour of the plaintiff (a matter accepted by the court, and presumably the parties, although the reason is not clear from the judgment). Therefore, he sought to establish rights on the basis of proprietary estoppel. It was held that the appropriate equitable response was to provide him with equitable compensation rather than with a proprietary interest in the Torquay house. The amount of compensation was valued in accordance with the annual value of the accommodation he enjoyed, capitalized for the remainder of his life. The amount of the award would then be discounted as an award of a capital sum. Some account was also taken of the costs of moving and so forth. The application of equitable compensation, while a matter of some complexity,[278] does not convey proprietary rights in the land at issue but only a right to receive equity's equivalent to common law damages to remedy the detriment suffered as a result of the failure of the representation. What is remarkable about this decision is that the court was concerned to consider the claimant's needs (here, for sheltered accommodation for the remainder of his life) and not simply to consider whether or not he had acquired rights in property. The strength of proprietary estoppel is that it enables the courts to achieve the most just result between the parties in novel situations.[279]

56.98 In conclusion it is clear that proprietary estoppel will provide an entitlement to a broad range of remedies the application of which are at the discretion of the court. The court's discretion will be exercised so as to prevent the detriment potentially suffered by the claimant. What is more difficult to isolate is the extent to which this remedial jurisdiction equates to restitution of unjust enrichment. The issue is therefore whether proprietary estoppel could be said to be about the reversal of unjust enrichment. The difficulty with any such analysis is that there is no necessary

---

[276] *Matharu v Matharu* [1994] 2 FLR 597, criticized by Battersby, (1995) CFLQ 59.
[277] (1993) 25 HLR 408.   [278] Considered above in Chapter 32.
[279] On the ability of proprietary estoppel to adapt to novel situations and to meet changing social mores see *Matharu v Matharu* (1994) 68 P & CR 93; *Sledmore v Dalby* (1996) 72 P & CR 196; Cooke and Hayton, 'Land law and trusts' in Hayton (ed), *Law's Futures* (Oxford: Hart, 2000) 433.

pre-existing proprietary base in the property at issue. Rather, it is sufficient that there is some representation made in relation to that property. Consequently, it is unclear how proprietary estoppel could be said to operate so as to *restore* property rights to their original owner where there was previously no such right.[280]

What is less clear, then, is the basis on which proprietary estoppel does arise. The **56.99** role of estoppel is to prevent a legal owner from relying on common law rights where that would be detrimental to another. Alternatively, proprietary estoppel might be bundled up with the constructive trust notion of preventing uncon-scionable conduct more broadly, in particular if the decision of the House of Lords in *Lloyds Bank v Rosset* is taken to have elided the concepts, an elision which was countenanced in *Yaxley v Gotts*.[281] Some authorities would describe propri-etary estoppel as raising a 'mere equity' which is binding only between the parties until the judgment is performed. More difficult explanations are that it provides a cause of action, thus infringing the notion that estoppel can only be a shield and not a sword, or that it operates to perfect imperfect gifts.[282] Both of these readings have some validity on the cases considered. Evidently, in many situations, propri-etary estoppel is the only means by which a claimant can sue *and* be awarded rights in land. For example, the award made in *Pascoe v Turner* which operates in the face of *Lloyds Bank v Rosset* which would not have awarded any proprietary rights to the claimant for mere decorative work on the building. Consequently, the doc-trine has the hallmarks of a de facto claim made to preclude unconscionability rather than to deal with the claimant's pre-existing property rights. As to the rule that equity will not perfect an imperfect gift, in any case where there is a represen-tation to transfer rights in property, and where that promise is not carried out, proprietary estoppel is perfecting that imperfect gift on proof of some detriment suffered by the claimant—that is the distinction between the successful claimant and the mere volunteer.

M. Restitution of Unjust Enrichment

The English law on allocation of rights in the home is not predicated on the **56.100** notion of restitution of unjust enrichment.[283] It was contended in *Pettitt v Pettitt* that the claimant should have been entitled to restitution for money expended on the home. It was held that a claim for restitution of unjust enrichment would result only in a 'money claim' in any event as opposed to a 'beneficial interest in

---

[280] Nor is proprietary estoppel restitutionary in the sense of reversing unjust enrichment because there is no requirement that the defendant have been enriched—simply that the claimant has suffered detriment which was directed at the acquisition of rights in the property.

[281] [2000] 1 All ER 711.

[282] As considered in Chapter 25; *Hearn v Younger* [2002] WTLR 1317.

[283] *Pettitt v Pettitt* [1970] AC 777, 795, *per* Lord Reid.

the property which has been improved'.[284] In Canada, by contrast, a far more expansive notion of the law of unjust enrichment than is usually employed in English law[285] has been developed.

56.101   The basis of this Canadian principle is found in *Pettkus v Becker*[286] in the leading judgment of Dickson J. The parties in that case were an unmarried couple who had lived together for nineteen years. The property at issue was the farm in which they had both lived and a bee-keeping business which had been established through their joint efforts. The woman claimed an entitlement to half of the business and to the land. The court was unanimous in holding that she should be entitled to a constructive trust to prevent any unjust enrichment on the part of her former partner. Dickson J set out the general underpinnings of the Canadian approach:

> . . . where one person in a relationship tantamount to spousal prejudices herself in the reasonable expectation of receiving an interest in property and the other person in the relationship freely accepts benefits conferred by the first person in circumstances where he knows or ought to have known of that reasonable expectation, it would be unjust to allow the recipient of the benefit to retain it.[287]

In the later case of *Peter v Beblow*[288] the test is more clearly stated. For there to be an unjust enrichment in the Canadian law relating to equitable rights in the home it was held that three conditions must be satisfied:

> (1) there has been an enrichment; (2) a corresponding deprivation has been suffered by the person who supplied the enrichment; and (3) there is an absence of any juristic reason for the enrichment itself.[289]

The effect of this test is said to be the creation of a presumption that the 'performance of domestic services will give rise to a claim for unjust enrichment'.[290] The principal driver away from the English common intention constructive trust was that, in the words of Dickson J, the courts were involved in the 'meaningless ritual' of searching for a 'fugitive common intention'.[291] On the facts of *Pettkus* there had been no common intention formed but the court wished to provide the claimant with a remedy. It was considered that a judgment in money by way of equitable compensation would have been inappropriate to prevent that unjust enrichment and the court therefore made an order for a constructive trust over the property at issue.

---

[284] [1970] AC 777, 795, *per* Lord Reid.   [285] *Lipkin Gorman v Karpnale* [1991] 2 AC 548.
[286] (1980) 117 DLR (3d) 257.   [287] (1980) 117 DLR (3d) 257, 274.
[288] *Peter v Beblow* (1993) 101 DLR (4th) 621.
[289] (1993) 101 DLR (4th) 621, 630, *per* Cory J.
[290] J Mee, *The Proprietary Rights of Cohabitees* (Hart, 1999) 192.
[291] (1980) 117 DLR (3d) 257, 269.

57

TRUSTS OF LAND

A. The Scope of This Chapter

This Part K of the book **Trusts of Land and of the Home** was concerned, in the **57.01**
preceding Chapter 56, with the manner in which beneficial rights of ownership are
acquired in relation to the home and this chapter is concerned with the manner in
which trusts operate over land once they have come into existence. In consequence, this chapter is concerned principally with the functioning of trusts of land
under the Trusts of Land and Appointment of Trustees Act 1996, with the law on

concurrent interests in and co-ownership of land, and also with the operation of settlements created under the Settled Land Act 1925 before 1997.

B. Concurrent Interests in Land

The different legal codes dealing with concurrent interests in land

57.02 This book does not consider the whole of English land law; however, some introduction is necessary to locate within the broader context of land law the analyses of trusts for sale, trusts of land, and Settled Land Act settlements in this chapter. Consequently, what follows in this section is an abbreviated account of the law relating to co-ownership (or, concurrent ownership of rights) in relation to land. English law maintains a multi-titular approach to ownership of property: that is, English law accepts that more than one person can have ownership rights in property at any one time, unlike a unititular system in which only one person has dominium over land. Whereas the effect of the Land Registration Act 2002 has been to effect a shift in this multi-titularity towards a system of land ownership which is closer to a unititular system,[1] it nevertheless remains a significant part of English land law that there can be more than one person with proprietary rights in relation to property. This chapter is concerned, necessarily, with contexts in which there is more than one person with rights in property: that is, situations in which there is co-ownership, rendered most specifically in the form of trusts of land where those whose names appear on the legal title of land hold that land for the benefit of others who have equitable interests in that property. The Trusts of Land and Appointment of Trustees Act 1996 has effected significant changes in the administration of the trusts which are the mechanisms by which the rights of the competing claims of the co-owners of land, that is those with concurrent interests in land, operate.

The structure of the law on co-ownership and the trust of land

57.03 An important part of the structure of the law on co-ownership of land is the relationship between the concepts of joint tenancy and tenancy in common. The ownership of rights in land reflects the division between the rights of those recorded on the legal title to land and the rights of those persons who either take other interests recognized at common law or who take interests recognized in equity. In relation to trusts of land, those recorded on the legal title (whether in registered or unregistered land) are the trustees of that land for the benefit of those with the equitable rights of co-owners of the property. Co-owners of the property, for present purposes, are those who are recognized as having beneficial rights in the property created in one of the ways considered in Chapter 56, by virtue of

---

[1] See E Cooke, 'The Land Registration Act 2002 and the nature of ownership' in AS Hudson (ed), *New Perspectives on Property Law, Obligations and Restitution* (London: Cavendish Publishing, 2003) 117.

having contributed to its purchase price with an intention of becoming an owner of the property, or in some other way which would found an equitable right of ownership.[2] By contrast, equity recognizes a range of other rights, such as equitable easements, rights under negative covenants, and equitable leases, which do not purport to grant their holder beneficial ownership of the home or of the land, but rather merely some right established by equity *in personam* against the legal owner of that property or limited categories of his heirs and assigns. This latter category of equitable right in the land is not the sort of right considered in this chapter because such rights are not concerned with rights in the ownership of the fee simple in land nor with rights under a trust of land.

The law on co-ownership in outline

A joint tenancy is a form of community of property whereby all of the joint tenants together own the entire interest in property in undivided shares but individually own nothing. On the death of one of the joint tenants, the doctrine of survivorship provides that the deceased person's rights do not pass into his estate but rather remain subsumed in those rights which continue to be held by the surviving joint tenants. The joint tenancy continues, then, notionally until there is only one surviving joint tenant who then becomes the absolute owner of the rights held under the joint tenancy.   **57.04**

If the co-owners are not joint tenants then they are tenants in common who hold their own, several shares in the property distinct one from another. Co-owners can become tenants in common by virtue either of the fact that they did not from the outset satisfy the requirements for the creation of a joint tenancy or because a pre-existing joint tenancy was severed. The effect of a person being a tenant in common is that that person is able to pass his share in property on death as part of his estate or to deal with his several share independently, to the extent that the law allows, of the rights of the other tenants in common. These principles are considered in greater detail below.   **57.05**

There is an important distinction between the joint tenancy at law and the joint tenancy in equity: a division which informs the structure of the following paragraphs. The owners of the legal title can only be joint tenants and that joint tenancy has been rendered by statute to be incapable of severance. Since 1925 severance can only operate in relation to an equitable joint tenancy.[3] By contrast, in equity the co-owners may be either joint tenants or tenants in common in accordance with the principles considered below.   **57.06**

---

[2] Notably, the trust for sale as provided for under the Law of Property Act 1925 did not account for the creation of a tenancy in common by virtue, for example, of a purchase price resulting trust in circumstances in which the parties had made unequal contributions of money towards that purchase price: see *Re Buchanan-Wollaston's Conveyance* [1939] Ch 217, affirmed at [1939] Ch 738; *Bull v Bull* [1955] 1 QB 234, [1955] 1 All ER 253; *Cook v Cook* [1962] P 181, [1962] 2 All ER 262, affirmed at [1962] P 235, [1962] 2 All ER 811; *William & Glyn's Bank v Boland* [1979] Ch 312, [1979] 2 All ER 697.   [3] Law of Property Act 1925, s 1(6).

Joint tenancy at law

57.07 The legal title in land can be held only on the basis of a joint tenancy when a conveyance of the property is made to co-owners:[4]

> ... where land is expressed to be conveyed to any persons in undivided shares and those persons are of full age, the conveyance shall operate ... as if the land had been expressed to be conveyed to the grantees, or, if there are more than four grantees, then to the first four named in the conveyance, as joint tenants in trust for the persons interested in the land.

Once those persons take as joint tenants it is then not possible to sever that joint tenancy:[5]

> ...no severance of a joint tenancy of a legal estate, so as to create a tenancy in common in land, shall be permissible.

The reason why the owners of the legal title were only permitted to be joint tenants in the Law of Property Act 1925 was to make the conveyancing process easier by ensuring that no single legal owner of property held different rights from any other. This has important ramifications not only for the transfer of property but also for the overreaching process, considered below.

Joint tenancy in equity

57.08 Where the parties have acquired their equitable interests in the property with unity of time, title, interest, and possession they will be taken to be joint tenants of that property, provided that they had sufficient intention to do so.[6] The result of the creation of a joint tenancy is that none of the parties takes any individual interest in the property: rather they all acquire the whole of the interest in the property.[7] The surviving joint tenants acquire the rights attributable to the deceased joint tenant: those rights do not pass into the estate of the deceased joint tenant unless that joint tenant had severed the joint tenancy before his death.[8] The process of severance is considered in the next paragraph. In the event that there is no joint tenancy created in equity, the equitable co-owners of the property are necessarily tenants in common with several shares.

Severance of a joint tenancy in equity

57.09 Severance of a joint tenancy is possible only in relation to an equitable joint tenancy and not a joint tenancy of the legal title.[9] The process of severance has been explained as occurring in the following way:[10]

---

[4] Law of Property Act 1925, s 34(2).   [5] Law of Property Act 1925, s 36(2).
[6] *Burgess v Rawnsley* [1975] Ch 429.
[7] *Hammersmith & Fulham LBC v Monk* [1992] 1 AC 478, [1992] 1 All ER 1.
[8] *Re Drapers Conveyance* [1969] 1 Ch 486; *Harris v Goddard* [1983] 1 WLR 1203.
[9] Law of Property Act 1925, s 36(2).
[10] *Harris v Goddard* [1983] 1 WLR 1203, 1210, *per* Dillon LJ.

> Severance . . . is the process of separating off the share of a joint tenant, so that the
> concurrent ownership will continue but the right of survivorship will no longer
> apply. [After severance has taken place] the parties will hold separate shares as tenants
> in common.

Severance then produces the following result:

> On severance the beneficial joint tenancy becomes a beneficial tenancy in common in
> undivided shares and right by survivorship no longer obtains. If there be two joint ten-
> ants, severance produces a beneficial tenancy in common in two equal shares. If there
> be three beneficial joint tenants and one only severs, he is entitled to a one-third undi-
> vided share and there is no longer survivorship between him and the other two, though
> the other two may remain inter se beneficial joint tenants of the other two-thirds.[11]

Severance will not, in itself, result in the joint tenants becoming entitled (as tenants in common) in unequal shares—not even where they contributed unequally
to the original purchase price;[12] although unequal shares may be produced by an
express agreement between them[13] or by means of an assignment or a declaration
of trust,[14] or by a court order under matrimonial legislation.[15]

Severance occurs in a number of ways in which the parties evidence sufficient   **57.10**
intention to deal with their own share[16] either by way of statutory notice[17] or by
way of the methods suggested by Page-Wood V-C in the following terms:[18]

> A joint tenancy may be severed in three ways: in the first place, an act of any one of
> the persons interested operating upon his own share may create a severance as to that
> share . . . Secondly, a joint tenancy may be severed by mutual agreement. And, in the
> third place, there may be a severance by any course of dealing sufficient to intimate
> that the interests of all were mutually treated as constituting a tenancy in common.

These means of severing a joint tenancy have been expanded upon by subsequent
cases and fall, it is suggested, into the following six categories.

First, severance will occur on the alienation by a joint tenant of his rights in the   **57.11**
property. Alienation can take place if that joint tenant effects a sale or mortgage of
his undivided share of the property[19] or where he purports to do so over the whole
of the property.[20] Alienation can also take place on the bankruptcy of one joint

---

[11] *Bedson v Bedson* [1965] 2 QB 666, 689, *per* Russell LJ. See also *Nielson-Jones v Fedden* [1975]
Ch 222, 228, *per* Walton J.   [12] *Goodman v Gallant* [1986] FLR 106, 118–119, *per* Slade LJ.
[13] *Barton v Morris* [1985] 1 WLR 1257, 1262, *per* Walton J.
[14] *Goodman v Gallant* [1986] FLR 106, 119.   [15] Matrimonial Causes Act 1983, ss 24, 24A.
[16] *Williams v Hensman* (1861) 1 J & H 546, 70 ER 862. For example, by dealing fraudulently
with the property: *Ahmed v Kendrick* (1988) 56 P & CR 120; except where that would permit the
fraudster to benefit from that fraud—*Penn v Bristol & West Building Society* [1995] 2 FLR 938.
[17] Law of Property Act 1925, s 36(2).   [18] *Williams v Hensman* (1861) 1 J & H 546, 557.
[19] *Cedar Holdings v Green* [1981] Ch 129, [1979] 3 All ER 117; *First National Securities Ltd v
Hegerty* [1985] QB 850, [1984] 3 All ER 641; *Ahmed v Kendrick* (1987) P & CR 120; *Monarch
Aluminium v Rickman* [1989] CLY 1526.
[20] *First National Securities Ltd v Hegerty* [1985] QB 850, [1984] 3 All ER 641; *Ahmed v Kendrick*
(1987) P & CR 120.

tenant when that joint tenant's interest in the land vests automatically in his trustee in bankruptcy.[21] Severance will not occur where one joint tenant creates a will which purports to transfer his share in the property severally as a part of his estate.[22]

57.12 Secondly, severance occurs when one joint tenant serves a notice of severance on the other joint tenants.[23] Under statute where a joint tenant '... shall give to the other joint tenants a notice in writing of such desire' to sever the joint tenancy, then that is sufficient to constitute a severance of that joint tenancy.[24] A notice in writing addressed to the other joint tenant, and delivered to her address by registered post or recorded delivery complies with the requirements as to giving notice in section 196(4) of the Law of Property Act 1925, and is therefore effective to sever the joint tenancy, even though the notice is not actually received by the addressee.[25]

57.13 Thirdly, the unilateral act of one joint tenant can effect severance in circumstances in which one joint tenant acquires some greater interest in the property than the other joint tenants. This alteration in that joint tenant's interest would operate to destroy the unity of interest between the joint tenants. So, if the joint tenant were to acquire an interest in reversion over the property, then that joint tenant would have a greater interest than the other joint tenants and thus sever the joint tenancy.[26] The same analysis would apply if that joint tenant received a release of another joint tenant's interest.[27] Clearly, this latter example intrudes more closely on the category of mutual conduct considered below.

57.14 Fourthly, severance will be effected if one joint tenant commits the homicide of another. So in *Re K*,[28] where one joint tenant killed the other joint tenant unlawfully, the joint tenancy was deemed to have been automatically severed such that the killer and the deceased became tenants in common and the deceased's portion of the property passed with her estate. As has been considered already in relation to constructive trusts in Chapter 27, the alternative analysis of this situation is that the killer would hold the property on constructive trust so that he would be unable to benefit from his unconscionable act.[29]

57.15 Fifthly, severance can take place by the mutual conduct of the parties,[30] or by their mutual agreement,[31] or by a suitable course of dealing.[32] Mutual conduct of the

---

[21] *Re Gorman* [1990] 2 FLR 284; *Re Pavlou* [1993] 2 FLR 751; *Re Dennis* [1993] Ch 72. Cf *Re Palmer* [1994] Ch 316. See also *Byford v Butler* [2003] EWHC 1267 (Chancery). [22] ibid.
[23] *Re 88 Berkeley Road* [1971] Ch 648. [24] Law of Property Act 1925, s 36(2).
[25] *Re 88 Berkeley Road* [1971] Ch 648. See also *Kinch v Bullard* [1999] 1 WLR. 42.
[26] *Wiscot's Case* (1599) 2 Co Rep 60. [27] *Re Schar* [1951] Ch 280, [1950] 2 All ER 1069.
[28] [1985] Ch 85, [1985] 1 All ER 403; affirmed at [1986] Ch 180, [1985] 2 All ER 833.
[29] See para 27.16. See also *Scholbelt v Barber* (1966) 60 DLR (2d) 519; *Re Pechar* [1969] NZLR 574.
[30] *McDowell v Hirschfield Lipson & Rumney and Smith* [1992] 2 FLR 126; *Gore and Snell v Carpenter* (1990) 60 P & CR 456, 462.
[31] *Nielson-Jones v Fedden* [1975] Ch 222; *Greenfield v Greenfield* (1979) 33 P & CR 570; *Hunter v Babbage* [1994] 2 FLR 806. Cf *Edwards v Hastings* [1996] NPC 87.
[32] *Burgess v Rawnsley* [1975] Ch 429, [1975] 3 All ER 142.

sort required to effect severance may include partition of a part of the property or sale of a part of the property. In relation to mutual agreement it is necessary that the joint tenants demonstrate sufficient intention to sever the joint tenancy. It is not a necessary requirement that there be a binding contract between the parties provided that their intention to sever the joint tenancy is evident. So, in *Burgess v Rawnsley*[33] the question at issue was not whether or not the parties had entered into some binding arrangement for the transfer of their interests *inter se*, but rather whether or not it had been made sufficiently clear between them that they intended their joint tenancy to be terminated. Lord Denning expressed the matter in that case as whether or not there was a course of dealing which would be suitable to sever the joint tenancy in the following terms:[34]

> It is sufficient if there is a course of dealing in which one party makes clear to the other that he desires that their shares should no longer be held jointly but be held in common. I emphasise that it must be clear to the other party.

It is then a matter for the party alleging severance of the joint tenancy to prove that there has been suitable mutual conduct, mutual agreement, or course of dealing.[35]

57.16 Finally, severance can be effected on divorce in limited circumstances. If death occurs before service of the final order then severance will not take place and the doctrine of survivorship will pass the deceased's undivided share to their spouse,[36] although there are authorities which have held that service of final divorce proceedings will constitute an act of severance[37] whereas merely seeking the advice of the court as to one's rights as a preparatory step to divorce proceedings will not.[38]

The relationship between joint tenancy in equity and trust of land

57.17 As considered in the following section of this chapter, the trust of land (that is, the doctrine introduced by the Trusts of Land and Appointment of Trustees Act 1996) arises in any situation in which there is a trust which consists of or includes land.[39] For there to be a trust of land, there must be a distinction between the legal owners and the equitable owners of that land: if there is no division in ownership then there is no trust at all, merely absolute ownership of property.[40] Therefore, for there to be a trust of land there must be two or more joint tenants of the legal title in property holding that property for the benefit of another person or persons as beneficiary either as joint tenants or tenants in common, as they are required to

---

[33] [1975] Ch 429.   [34] *Burgess v Rawnsley* [1975] Ch 429, 439, [1975] 3 All ER 142, 147.
[35] *McDowell v Hirschfield Lipson & Rumney and Smith* [1992] 2 FLR 126.
[36] *Re Palmer (decd)* [1994] 2 FLR 609.
[37] *Re Drapers Conveyance* [1969] 1 Ch 486. Criticized in *Nielson-Jones v Fedden* [1975] Ch 222, 237, *per* Walton J, but subsequently endorsed in *Burgess v Rawnsley* [1975] Ch 429, 439–440 and *Harris v Goddard* [1983] 1 WLR 1203, 1209–1210.   [38] *Harris v Goddard* [1983] 1 WLR 1203.
[39] Trusts of Land and Appointment of Trustees Act 1996, s 1(1)(a).
[40] *Westdeutsche Landesbank v Islington* [1996] AC 669.

do by statute.[41] In the event that there are two or more beneficiaries and those beneficiaries are joint tenants, then the doctrine of survivorship will govern the manner in which their property rights are passed on death, unless there is a severance of that joint tenancy. If there are two or more beneficiaries and those beneficiaries are tenants in common, then their rights are several and therefore they are at liberty to deal with the rights as they see fit within the law of trusts. If there is only one beneficiary (such that there will be no joint tenancy nor any tenancy in common[42]) then there will be a bare trust which in turn constitutes a trust of land.[43] Significantly, whether the beneficiaries are joint tenants or tenants in common, or whether there is a bare trust, the provisions of the Trusts of Land and Appointment of Trustees Act 1996 provide for rights of occupation of the trust property and for rights to be consulted by the trustees in favour of beneficiaries which were not a feature of the Law of Property Act 1925. The enhancement of the quality of the rights of beneficiaries under the 1996 Act reflects the distinction between the trust of land created under that Act and the pre-existing doctrine of trusts for sale, as considered in the next section.

C. The Trust of Land

The purpose of the Trusts of Land and Appointment of Trustees Act 1996

57.18   The introduction of the Trusts of Land and Appointment of Trustees Act 1996 ('TLATA 1996') was enacted further to the Law Commission Paper, *Transfer of Land: Trusts of Land*.[44] The fundamental technical aim of TLATA 1996 was to achieve the conversion of all settlements under the Settled Land Act 1925, all bare trusts, and all trusts for sale under the Law of Property Act 1925 into a composite form of trust defined to be the 'trust of land'. Within that re-composition of the property law understanding of rights in the home were some larger objectives concerned with the rights of beneficiaries under trusts of land to occupy the home and an extension of the categories of person whose rights should be taken into account when reaching decisions on applications for the sale of the home.

57.19   As part of this technical aim to reform the manner in which land was treated by the 1925 legislation, section 3 of TLATA 1996 set out the abolition of the doctrine of conversion. Significantly, this change altered the automatic assumption that the rights of any beneficiary under the old trust for sale were vested not in the property itself but rather in the proceeds of sale. This notion of conversion of

---

[41] Law of Property Act 1925, s 34(2).
[42] With the exceptional complications of there being simply one surviving joint tenant after a joint tenancy.   [43] Trusts of Land and Appointment of Trustees Act 1996, s 1.
[44] Law Com No 181.

rights flowed from the understanding of trusts for sale as being trusts whose purpose was the sale of the trust fund and its conversion into cash. Clearly, this ran contrary to the intention of most people acquiring land for their own occupation in which it was not supposed for a moment that their sole intention was to dispose of the property as though a mere investment (but rather their true intention must be to live in the property). Therefore, the common law developed the notion of a 'collateral purpose' under which the court would resist the obligation to sell the property in place of an implied ulterior objective for families (for example) to retain the property as their home.[45]

The meaning of 'trust of land'

The term 'trust of land' means 'any trust of property which consists of or includes land'.[46] Therefore, any trust which includes within a more general portfolio of property a parcel of land will become a trust of land, even if the remainder of the trust property is comprised of chattels and intangible property, or alternatively if the trust fund includes money which is intended to be applied for the acquisition of land, in the manner considered below. Trusts of land include not only express trusts but also constructive trusts, resulting trusts, 'implied trusts', bare trusts, and trusts for sale: indeed 'any description of trust'.[47] The reference to 'trusts for sale' is to trusts falling under the Law of Property Act 1925, a code repealed by the 1996 Act, and considered in the next paragraph. Trusts are caught within the scope of trusts of land whether they were created before or after the 1996 Act came into force.[48] In terms of trusts implied by law, the statute covers any trusts 'arising' before or after the coming into force of the Act, as well as any express trust consciously 'created' before or after the Act.[49] There are two forms of land which fall outwith the Act: land which was settled land under the Settled Land Act 1925 (before TLATA 1996 came into force) or land to which the Universities and Colleges Estates Act 1925[50] applies.[51] Settled land is considered below. The bulk of this chapter is concerned with the functions of trustees, the rights of beneficiaries, and the protection of purchasers under trusts of land, prior to a consideration of the strict settlement regime as amended by the 1996 Act.

57.20

---

[45] *Jones v Challenger* [1961] 1 QB 176. Cf *Re Citro* [1991] Ch 142.

[46] Trusts of Land and Appointment of Trustees Act 1996, s 1(1)(a).

[47] Trusts of Land and Appointment of Trustees Act 1996, s 1(2)(a).

[48] Trusts of Land and Appointment of Trustees Act 1996, s 1(2)(b).

[49] Trusts of Land and Appointment of Trustees Act 1996, s 1(2)(b).

[50] Where universities, generally bodies corporate, have land held on trust then this provision is of significance to them. Excluded from the scope of universities and colleges under the 1925 Act are those institutions of further education effected under the Education Reform Act 1988 as higher education or further education corporations.

[51] Trusts of Land and Appointment of Trustees Act 1996, s 1(3).

Trust for sale

Trusts for sale before 1997

57.21 The trust for sale was a feature of the Law of Property Act 1925 which provided that property held under 'an immediate binding trust for sale'[52] was to be deemed to be held for the purpose of effecting its sale. This obligation to effect sale was subject to a power in the trustees to delay such a sale. Subsequently, the courts provided that sale could be postponed indefinitely if some collateral purpose to that of effecting a sale could be established.[53] The most significant field in which trusts for sale operated on the decided cases was in relation to trusts of family homes. In such situations the 1925 Act created the presumption that the purpose of the domestic arrangement in the event of a dispute was that those who held the legal title in the home were obliged to sell it; consequently, the courts created the countervailing notion of a secondary or collateral purpose that the property was to have been used as a home and not simply as an asset to be sold which could in appropriate circumstances lead to an order under section 30 of the Law of Property Act 1925 that the home would not be sold.[54]

57.22 The most significant aspect of the trust for sale regime before 1997 was that the rights of the beneficiaries were deemed to have been converted from rights in the land into rights in the sale proceeds of that land on sale. Thus, the rights of the beneficiaries were effectively merely rights in personalty. The principle underlying this regime was explained by Cross LJ in the following terms:[55]

> The whole purpose of the trust for sale is to make sure, by shifting the equitable interest away from the land and into the proceeds of sale, that a purchaser of the land takes free from the equitable interests. To hold these to be equitable interests in the land itself would be to frustrate this purpose. Even to hold that they have equitable interests in the land for a limited period, namely, until the land is sold, would, we think, be inconsistent with the trust for sale being an 'immediate' trust for sale working an immediate conversion, which is what the Law of Property Act 1925 envisages.[56]

The doctrine of conversion has been abolished in part, as considered in the following paragraph. The manner in which TLATA 1996 seeks to provide for protection of purchasers, in the manner envisaged by Cross LJ, is considered below.

The doctrine of conversion

57.23 Before 1996, the equitable interest of a beneficiary under a trust for sale was deemed to have been converted into an equitable interest in the proceeds of the

---

[52] Law of Property Act 1925, s 205(1), in its unamended state before the enactment of the Trusts of Land and Appointment of Trustees Act 1996, s 25(2) and Sch 4.
[53] See, for example, *Jones v Challenger* [1961] 1 QB 176.
[54] *Jones v Challenger* [1961] 1 QB 176.
[55] *Irani Finance Ltd v Singh* [1971] Ch 59, 80, [1970] 3 All ER 199, 203.
[56] Law of Property Act 1925, s 205(1)(xxix).

sale of that property even before the power of sale had been executed by the trustees. Therefore, the rights of the beneficiaries under a trust for sale were effectively rights only in personalty rather than rights in the trust property. There was no statutory right to object to the sale: rather it was the case law, in the manner considered above, which supplied the only means of restraining the trustees' use of the power of sale under the trust for sale.

Similarly, rights under a trust in which the trustees were required to invest in land were themselves considered by the Law of Property Act 1925 to operate so that the land acquired by the trustees was held subject to a trust for sale.[57] More significantly, the doctrine of conversion required that the personalty with which the land would be acquired by the trustees was itself to be considered to be an interest in land.[58] This form of the doctrine of conversion was abolished by the 1996 Act.[59] **57.24**

The doctrine of conversion was abolished in part by TLATA 1996. Specifically, two aspects of the doctrine of conversion were abolished.[60] First, to the extent that a beneficial interest in land held on a trust for sale had previously been considered automatically to have been converted into a right only in personalty and, secondly, to the extent that a beneficial interest in personalty which was held under a trust for sale with a power to acquire land had itself previously been considered to have been converted into an interest in land.[61] The characteristics of the trust of land, considered below, mean that the doctrine of conversion could be of little application because the beneficiaries are 'beneficially entitled to an interest in possession in land subject to the trust'[62] and have rights of occupation as expressed by statute[63] which are not limited to rights to the proceeds of sale. The principal distinction between the pre-1996 trust for sale and the trust of land, then, is that any beneficiary under a trust of land has the rights set out in TLATA 1996 which are not limited by the doctrine of conversion. **57.25**

---

[57] Law of Property Act 1925, s 32.

[58] This facet of the doctrine was important in succession law in which realty would pass to the heir at law and personalty to the next of kin. This legal fiction, that the personalty with which the land was to be acquired was itself regarded as being an interest in land, meant that the personalty passed to the heir at law as though land. See *Lechmere v Earl of Carlisle* 3 P Wms 211 where Lord Lechmere had settled £30,000 to be spent on land and which, having been unspent but deemed to be land by the doctrine of conversion, passed to his heir at law. See also *Re Kempthorne* [1930] 1 Ch 268 for the often peculiar ramifications of this doctrine.

[59] Trusts of Land and Appointment of Trustees Act 1996, s 5(1); Sch 2, para 2.

[60] Leading to an academic dispute as to whether or not the marginal note in the legislation, dubbed the 'abolition of the doctrine of conversion', was incorrect. See P Pettit (1997) 113 LQR 207, 209, asserting that the marginal note was incorrect on the basis that certain facets of the doctrine of conversion continued in effect, for example in relation to specifically enforceable contracts for the sale of land. Alternatively, see C Harpum, 'The Law Commission and the Reform of Land Law' in S Bright and J Dewar (eds), *Land Law: Themes and Perspectives* (Oxford University Press, 1998) 151, 173.   [61] Trusts of Land and Appointment of Trustees Act 1996, s 3.

[62] Trusts of Land and Appointment of Trustees Act 1996, s 9.

[63] Trusts of Land and Appointment of Trustees Act 1996, s 12.

57.26   The doctrine of conversion continues in existence in at least three significant contexts. First, in relation to a trust created by will before 1997.[64] Secondly, in relation to administration of a dead person's estate by his personal representatives.[65] Thirdly, in relation to specifically enforceable contracts for the sale of land.[66]

Trusts for sale created after 1996

57.27   Trusts for sale may yet be created in the sense that a trust which provides expressly that the trustee is obliged to sell the trust property will be a trust for sale. Such a trust obliging the trustee to carry out a sale will still take effect as a trust of land subject to the provisions of TLATA 1996. The definition of a trust for sale after 1997 is in the following terms:

> 'Trust for sale', in relation to land, means an immediate trust for sale, whether or not exercisable at the request or with the consent of any person: 'trustees for sale' mean the persons (including a personal representative) holding land on trust for sale.[67]

The definition of trust for sale under the Law of Property Act 1925, as considered above, required that the trust be for an 'immediate binding trust for sale': that the trust for sale be 'binding' is no longer a part of that definition. Nevertheless, the trust for sale remains an immediate trust for sale rather than containing a provision equivalent to a mere power to effect a sale at some point in the future. Under the old form of trust for sale there was a power to postpone sale implied in statute[68] and enlarged upon by the case law, as discussed above. The Trusts of Land and Appointment of Trustees Act 1996 provides for a power to postpone sale to be read into any trust instrument whether or not the trust instrument itself seeks to exclude it.[69] Whereas the *ancien régime* included such a power which could have been excluded by the terms of the trust, the new regime maintains the power of postponement but makes its inclusion mandatory whether the trust was created before or after the Act came into effect.[70] The circumstances in which trusts for sale will be implied are governed by Schedule 2 to the 1996 Act interposing amendments to the Law of Property Act 1925 relating to mortgaged property held by trustees after redemption has been barred, in relation to land purchased by trustees of personal property, in relation to dispositions to tenants in common, and on intestacy.[71]

---

[64]   Trusts of Land and Appointment of Trustees Act 1996, s 3(2).
[65]   Trusts of Land and Appointment of Trustees Act 1996, s 18(3).
[66]   *Lysaght v Edwards* (1876) 2 Ch D 499, 506; *Lake v Bayliss* [1974] 1 WLR 1073, [1974] 2 All ER 1114.
[67]   Law of Property Act 1925, s 205(1), as amended by Trusts of Land and Appointment of Trustees Act 1996, s 25(2) and Sch 4.   [68]   Law of Property Act 1925, s 25(1).
[69]   Trusts of Land and Appointment of Trustees Act 1996, s 4(1).
[70]   Trusts of Land and Appointment of Trustees Act 1996, s 4(2).
[71]   Trusts of Land and Appointment of Trustees Act 1996, s 5(1). Section 1 of the Settled Land Act 1925 is disapplied in this context: Trusts of Land and Appointment of Trustees Act 1996, s 5(2).

Settlements under the Settled Land Act 1925

Land which was settled land under the Settled Land Act 1925 by virtue of a settlement effected before the 1996 Act came into force is not captured by the provisions of the 1996 Act.[72] Nevertheless, the 1996 Act prevents the creation of any new Settled Land Act settlements from 1 January 1997 onwards.[73] The exclusion of new Settled Land Act settlements does not mean that any variation of such a settlement, any alteration of any interest in such a settlement, or any person becoming entitled under such a settlement, converts that settlement into a trust of land, provided that the original settlement was in existence before 1 January 1997 and that the alteration in question was provided for in the instrument giving effect to that original settlement.[74] The definition of 'settled land' is imported[75] from section 205(1)(xxvi) of the Law of Property Act 1925 and section 2 of the Settled Land Act 1925 in the following terms: 'Land which is or is deemed to be the subject of a settlement is, for the purposes of this Act, settled land.' The scheme created by the Settled Land Act 1925 is considered below.[76]

57.28

Bare trust

The statutory systems of trusts of land before 1997 diverged between strict settlements and trusts for sale. Neither code, however, made any provision for bare trusts. As was considered earlier[77] a beneficiary under a bare trust is able to give directions to a nominee over a bare trust as to the treatment of the trust property.[78] By omitting bare trusts from both of the two statutory schemes, it was unclear whether or not the doctrine of overreaching could apply to them.[79] Transfer of the property to a purchaser could be guaranteed to take effect only with the agreement of the beneficiary[80] because the trustee had no statutory power of sale[81] and would be personally liable for breach of trust if a sale was effected without the concurrence of the beneficiary.[82] However, under TLATA 1996, any bare trust already in

57.29

---

[72] Trusts of Land and Appointment of Trustees Act 1996, s 1(3).
[73] Trusts of Land and Appointment of Trustees Act 1996, s 2(1).
[74] Trusts of Land and Appointment of Trustees Act 1996, s 2(2).
[75] Trusts of Land and Appointment of Trustees Act 1996, s 23(2).
[76] See para 57.75.   [77] See para 57.02.
[78] *Saunders v Vautier* (1841) 4 Beav 115; Cr & Ph 240. The question remains whether or not the beneficiary is able to command the trustee to terminate the trust and to deliver absolute title in the trust property to the beneficiary. It was suggested above at para 57.22 that this would depend upon the precise terms of the trust and principally whether or not the trust instrument precluded the beneficiary from having any such capability vested in him.
[79] In the negative, E Burn, *Cheshire and Burn's The Modern Law of Real Property* (16th edn, Butterworths, 2000) ('*Cheshire and Burn*') 231; uncertain but not necessarily negative C Harpum, *Megarry and Wade's The Law of Real property* (6th edn, Sweet & Maxwell, 2000)('*Megarry and Wade*') 441.   [80] *Lee v Soames* (1888) 34 WR 884.
[81] Unlike that conferred on trustees of land by Trusts of Land and Appointment of Trustees Act 1996, s 6(1), considered below.   [82] See *Hodgson v Marks* [1971] Ch 892.

existence or any bare trust created after the passage of the 1996 Act will fall under the definition of a 'trust of land'[83] and will consequently be capable of being over-reached.[84]

D. Trustees of Land

Functions of the trustees of land

General powers as though the absolute owner of the trust property

57.30   The trustees under a trust of land have the following extensive capabilities:[85]

> For the purposes of exercising their functions as trustees, the trustees of land have in relation to the land subject to the trust all the powers of an absolute owner.

Therefore, akin to the powers of trustees under the Trustee Act 2000, the trustees are entitled to deal with the property held under the trust as though its absolute owner.[86] The Law Commission sought to make the powers of the trustees of land as 'broadly based and as flexible as possible'.[87] The reference to 'functions' in section 6(1) is a reference to the powers and the obligations of the trustees considered in Part C **The Duties and Powers of Trustees** of this book and the terms of the trust instrument. There are, necessarily, restrictions on the scope of the trustees' powers such as the reference to the trustees being entitled to act as though the 'absolute owner' of the trust property. The trustees are required to act in the best interests of the beneficiaries and to avoid any conflict of interest between their personal and their fiduciary capacities. Within TLATA 1996, there is also an express restriction to the effect that:[88]

> The powers conferred by [section 6] shall not be exercised in contravention of, or of any order[89] made in pursuance of, any other enactment or any rule of law or equity.

Within the reference to the 'rule of ... equity' can be supposed to be a reference to the principles limiting the powers of trustees, as considered above in Part C of this

---

[83]   Trusts of Land and Appointment of Trustees Act 1996, s 1(2)(a).

[84]   Furthermore, the Trustee Act 2000 gives the trustees the power to act as though the absolute owner of the trust property: Trustee Act 2000, s 3(1); except to the extent that trustees are not permitted to invest in land under the 2000 Act otherwise than by way of loans secured on land: Trustee Act 2000, s 3(3). Cf *Re Pratt's WT* [1943] Ch 326 in relation to the now repealed Trustee Investments Act 1961.

[85]   Trusts of Land and Appointment of Trustees Act 1996, s 6(1). See also Trustee Act 2000, s 8(3) which grants trustees the power to acquire land for the occupation of beneficiaries or as an investment without the need for the existence of a trust of land.

[86]   The Law of Property Act 1925, s 28 by contrast provided that the trustees had 'all the powers of a tenant for life and the trustees of a settlement under the Settled Land Act 1925'.

[87]   Law Commission Report No 181, para 10.4.105.

[88]   Trusts of Land and Appointment of Trustees Act 1996, s 6(6).

[89]   Whether that be an order of the court or of the Charity Commissioners: Trusts of Land and Appointment of Trustees Act 1996, s 6(7).

book generally. In any event, the trustees are expressly required by statute to 'have regard to the rights of the beneficiaries'.[90] Furthermore, TLATA 1996 provides that the generality of the power does not operate so as to override any restriction, limitation, or condition placed on the trustees by any other 'enactment'.[91] It is suggested that these provisions add nothing which the general law of trusts would not have added in any event. It could not be supposed that trustees would be permitted, simply by virtue of section 6(1) of TLATA 1996, to circumvent their ordinary fiduciary obligations or any mandatory rules of statute applicable to them. The drafts person of the Trustee Act 2000, which has a similarly broad power of investment for trustees, did not consider it necessary to qualify that power in this manner.

The Trusts of Land and Appointment of Trustees Act 1996 contains two further, **57.31** express powers for trustees. First, provided that all of the beneficiaries under the trust of land are of full age and full capacity, the general powers of the trustees include a power 'to convey the land to the beneficiaries even though they have not required the trustees to do so'.[92] The beneficiaries are then required to do 'whatever is necessary' to ensure that it vests in them subject to the possibility that a court may order them so to do.[93] This is, in effect, the inverse of the rule in *Saunders v Vautier*[94] in that the trustee is able to compel a conveyance of full title in the property to the beneficiaries, as opposed to the beneficiaries calling for a conveyance of that title.

Secondly, the trustees have 'power to purchase a legal estate in any land in England **57.32** or Wales'.[95] The statute is clear to express the breadth of this principle. This power can be exercised by way of investment,[96] to provide that land for the occupation of any of the beneficiaries,[97] or for any other reason.[98]

The power to partition the land

The trustees have a power to partition all or any part of the land held under a trust **57.33** of land[99] by conveying that land under severalty[100] and to provide for the payment of any equality money whether by way of mortgage or otherwise.[101] The limitation on the utility of this provision rests in the requirement that the

---

[90] Trusts of Land and Appointment of Trustees Act 1996, s 6(5).
[91] Trusts of Land and Appointment of Trustees Act 1996, s 6(8).
[92] Trusts of Land and Appointment of Trustees Act 1996, s 6(2).
[93] Trusts of Land and Appointment of Trustees Act 1996, s 6(2)(a) and (b).
[94] (1841) 4 Beav 115.   [95] Trusts of Land and Appointment of Trustees Act 1996, s 6(3).
[96] Trusts of Land and Appointment of Trustees Act 1996, s 6(3)(a).
[97] Trusts of Land and Appointment of Trustees Act 1996, s 6(3)(b).
[98] Trusts of Land and Appointment of Trustees Act 1996, s 6(3)(c).
[99] Trusts of Land and Appointment of Trustees Act 1996, s 7(1).
[100] Trusts of Land and Appointment of Trustees Act 1996, s 7(2).
[101] Trusts of Land and Appointment of Trustees Act 1996, s 7(1).

beneficiaries be of full age and absolutely entitled in undivided shares to the land before the trustees are entitled to use this power. As considered among the general principles of trusts law earlier in this book,[102] the rule in *Saunders v Vautier*[103] would permit the beneficiaries to direct the trustees to partition the land in any event if they wished to do so. This is particularly so given that the statute requires that the trustees seek the consent of all of the beneficiaries before effecting such a partition,[104] except to the extent that the trustees may act on behalf of a beneficiary who is a minor in a manner not permitted by the rule in *Saunders v Vautier*.

The trustees' duty of care

57.34   The Trustee Act 2000, as considered in detail in Chapter 52,[105] imposes a duty of care on trustees in the following terms:[106]

> Whenever the duty under this subsection applies to a trustee, he must exercise such care and skill as is reasonable in the circumstances, having regard in particular—
>
> > (a) to any special knowledge or experience that he has or holds himself out as having, and
> >
> > (d) if he acts as trustee in the course of a business or profession, to any special knowledge or experience that it is reasonable to expect of a person acting in the course of that kind of business or profession.

The effect of this provision is to enlarge the potential liabilities of trustees of land, particularly those acting in furtherance of a business or profession, by imposing an implied duty to exercise reasonable skill and care in the discharge of their fiduciary obligations. The duty of care under the 2000 Act is imposed on trustees of land by means of an amendment to section 6 of the 1996 Act.[107]

Exclusion and restriction of the powers of trustees of land

57.35   Whereas the powers of trustees under the TLATA 1996 are extensive, the powers considered in the preceding paragraphs, as provided by section 8 of that Act,

> ... do not apply in the case of a trust of land created by a disposition in so far as provision to the effect that they do not apply is made by the disposition.[108]

The ostensible meaning of this provision is that the powers of the trustees to deal with the land as absolute owner or to partition the land can be excluded by the trust instrument itself. This is the approach taken both in the Trustee Act 1925 and in the Trustee Act 2000: that is, the powers of trustees contained in the

---

[102] See para 7.05.   [103] (1841) Cr & Ph 240, (1841) 4 Beav 115.
[104] Trusts of Land and Appointment of Trustees Act 1996, s 7(3).   [105] See para 52.15.
[106] Trustee Act 2000, s 1(1).
[107] By means of inserting a provision to that effect in the Trusts of Land and Appointment of Trustees Act 1996, s 6(9).   [108] Trusts of Land and Appointment of Trustees Act 1996, s 8(1).

legislation operate as a default setting but not as mandatory rules which would preclude the settlor from providing for something different in the terms of the trust itself. However, the terms of section 8(1) would appear to have the effect of enabling the settlor to postpone the trustees' right of sale of the property, for example, indefinitely.[109]

Another peculiar feature of section 8 is the requirement that the trust of land have **57.36** been created by a 'disposition'. At the simplest level, the vernacular sense of the word 'disposition' would suggest that a trust of land could be created, for the purposes of this provision, by any transfer of property onto trust whether by way of an express declaration of trust, by way of the implication of a trust by operation of law, or otherwise. However, the term 'disposition' has been the subject of detailed litigation in the sense that it is used in section 53(1)(c) of the Law of Property Act 1925. In that context the term is used ostensibly so as to provide for any transfer of an existing equitable interest to be effective only if evidenced and proved by some signed writing. From the leading cases of *Grey v IRC*[110] and *Vandervell v IRC*,[111] taken together with section 53(1)(b) of the 1925 Act, the impression emerges that a 'disposition' of an equitable interest does not include a declaration of trust. If the same analysis were applied in relation to section 8 of the 1996 Act then the powers of trustees under the 1996 Act would not apply, remarkably, if the trust of land at issue had been created by an express declaration of trust. It is suggested that the term 'disposition' in this context should therefore be given its broad, natural meaning so as to include trusts of land created by means of a declaration of trust.

Furthermore, in general terms the trustees are prevented from exercising either of **57.37** these powers without the consent of the beneficiaries if the consent of the beneficiaries is required.[112]

Delegation of the powers of trustees of land

The TLATA 1996 has given trustees of land much wider powers to delegate their **57.38** responsibilities than was possible under the 1925 Act. Section 9 provides that:[113]

> The trustees of land may, by power of attorney, delegate to any beneficiary or beneficiaries of full age and beneficially entitled to an interest in possession in land subject to the trust any of their functions as trustees which relate to the land.

The trustees are entitled to delegate their functions in relation to the land only when acting collectively; any trustee wishing to delegate his functions individually to some other person must comply with the procedure for so doing in the

---

[109] Provided always that such a provision conformed with the rule against perpetuities.
[110] [1960] AC 1.   [111] [1967] 2 AC 291.
[112] Trusts of Land and Appointment of Trustees Act 1996, s 8(2).
[113] Trusts of Land and Appointment of Trustees Act 1996, s 9(1).

Trustee Act or the Enduring Powers of Attorney Act 1985.[114] The delegation under section 9 of the 1996 Act, requiring the trustees to act as a body and not individually, must be agreed unanimously.[115] The delegation must be effected in the form of a deed[116] but it may be for a definite or an indefinite period of time.[117] Delegation of the trustees' powers to a beneficiary renders that beneficiary a trustee for those purposes under statute:[118] something which could have been deduced from the general law of trusts and the obligation on anyone acting in the capacity of a trustee to avoid conflicts of interest[119] subject to a potential liability for breach of trust on ordinary trusts law principles.[120] The trustees, nevertheless, become jointly and severally liable for the actions of such a beneficiary to whom the trustees' powers have been delegated[121] only to the extent that they have acted without reasonable care in their choice of delegate.[122]

57.39 Purchasers of the land dealing with a delegate exercising the powers of the trustees are given protection by section 9. It is assumed that the delegate was someone to whom the functions of the trustees could have been properly delegated provided that a purchaser, or indeed any third party dealing with the delegate, was acting in good faith.[123] This protection is then extended to cover those who acquire trust property in good faith from someone who dealt with the delegate.[124]

E. Beneficiaries Under a Trust of Land

The meaning of 'beneficiary'

57.40 The term 'beneficiary' for the purposes of the 1996 Act means

> ... a person who under the trust has an interest in property subject to the trust (including a person who has such an interest as a trustee or a personal representative).[125]

In consequence, the definition of 'beneficiary' is very wide-ranging. Falling within this definition are beneficiaries under express trusts, constructive trusts, or resulting trusts over the land. That the definition includes any person with a proprietary interest in the land has the effect that mortgagees and trustees in bankruptcy constitute beneficiaries under the terms of the Act. Similarly, trustees and personal representatives, who would ordinarily have no equitable proprietary interest in the trust property but rather only legal title in that property, are expressly defined

---

[114] See para 15.01.   [115] Trusts of Land and Appointment of Trustees Act 1996, s 9(3).
[116] Trusts of Land and Appointment of Trustees Act 1996, s 9(1).
[117] Trusts of Land and Appointment of Trustees Act 1996, s 9(5).
[118] Trusts of Land and Appointment of Trustees Act 1996, s 9(7).   [119] See para 29.51.
[120] See para 32.01.   [121] Trusts of Land and Appointment of Trustees Act 1996, s 9(8).
[122] Trusts of Land and Appointment of Trustees Act 1996, s 9(8).
[123] Trusts of Land and Appointment of Trustees Act 1996, s 9(2).
[124] Trusts of Land and Appointment of Trustees Act 1996, s 9(2).
[125] Trusts of Land and Appointment of Trustees Act 1996, s 22(1).

as falling within the definition of 'beneficiary'. The purpose behind this extensive definition is to grant *locus standi* to this broad range of people with interests in the property to commence proceedings under section 14 of the Act to seek an order for the sale of that property or some other order from the court, as considered below.[126] Excluded from the definition of 'beneficiary who is beneficially entitled' are those who acquire rights under the trust by virtue of being trustees or personal representatives,[127] and similarly excluded is a person who is a beneficiary who is considered to be 'beneficially entitled' solely by virtue of being an annuitant.[128]

Consents

It is frequently the case that trust instruments seek to protect the beneficiary from having the trust property sold away from underneath him by preventing any individual trustee from selling identified categories of trust assets without the consent of some other person. To that effect, section 10 of the 1996 Act provides as follows: **57.41**

> If a disposition creating a trust of land requires the consent of more than two persons to the exercise by the trustees of any function relating to the land, the consent of any two of them to the exercise of the function is sufficient in favour of a purchaser.[129]

In relation to minors whose consent is required by the trust instrument, the trustees are required to obtain the consent of 'a parent who has parental responsibility for him (within the meaning of the Children Act 1989)' or of a guardian.[130] Section 14(2) of TLATA 1996 permits the trustees to acquire an order from the court to relieve them of the requirement to obtain the consent of any person connected with the operation of the trustees' functions. This provision is considered below.[131]

Rights to consultation

The Trusts of Land and Appointment of Trustees Act 1996 provides for beneficiaries   **57.42**
to be consulted by the trustees in a manner which was only available under section 26(3) of the Law of Property Act 1925 in relation to trusts for sale implied by law. The new provision extends to all trusts of land. The new provisions apply to all trusts of land created after 1996 but only apply to trusts created before 1997 if there is a provision contained in a deed requiring such consultation.[132] Section 11 of TLATA 1996 provides:[133]

> The trustees of land shall in the exercise of any function relating to land subject to the trust—
>
> (a) so far as practicable, consult the beneficiaries of full age and beneficially entitled to an interest in possession in the land, and

---

[126] See para 57.58.   [127] Trusts of Land and Appointment of Trustees Act 1996, s 22(2).
[128] Trusts of Land and Appointment of Trustees Act 1996, s 22(3).
[129] Trusts of Land and Appointment of Trustees Act 1996, s 10(1).
[130] Trusts of Land and Appointment of Trustees Act 1996, s 10(3).   [131] See para 57.44.
[132] Trusts of Land and Appointment of Trustees Act 1996, s 11(3).
[133] Trusts of Land and Appointment of Trustees Act 1996, s 11(1).

(b) so far as consistent with the general interest of the trust, give effect to the
wishes of those beneficiaries, or (in case of dispute) of the majority (according
to the value of their combined interests).

Two issues arise from this provision. The expansive wording of this provision, particularly the terms 'so far as practicable' and 'so far as consistent', is not qualified
in the statute, nor has the wording received close analysis in decided cases. As to
the questions of practicality, it is not clear what types of trust business might
be considered too minor to require consultation with the beneficiaries nor how
far the practicalities of the situation (such as the detrimental effect of delay,
difficulties with obtaining responses from individual beneficiaries, and so on)
could be taken to absolve the trustees from any claim that they had failed to carry
on an effective consultation in deciding to desist from contacting the
beneficiaries. Clearly, the size of the trust, the extent of its property holdings, and
the number of beneficiaries who might need to be consulted will affect both the
possibility of the trustees being able to contact those beneficiaries and the range of
business activities (both large and small) which the trustees may have to manage:
some of which may be thought suitably significant to require consultation and
others not. For example, a decision as to the number of paper clips needed to conduct the trust's business would not be significant enough to require consultation,
whereas deciding whether or not to sell the only land held on trust would be
sufficiently significant. As to the questions of consistency with the general interest of the trust, the principal question will be that of identifying what the general
interests of the trust are: the more complex the trust, the more difficult the task of
establishing those interests; the greater the number of beneficiaries, the more
difficult the task of picking a path between their conflicting interests. It is suggested that in practice this statutory provision, while containing an obligation on
the trustees to seek consultation with the beneficiaries, nevertheless requires the
trustees simply to observe the general duty under trusts law to permit no conflict
of interest, to act fairly between the trustees, and to refrain from committing any
breaches of trust.[134] The effect of this provision is that, in conducting the proper
management of a trust of land, and, in relation to issues of appropriate
significance to the trust, the trustees must first consult with the beneficiaries and
then act in accordance with the ordinary principles of the law of trusts and the
terms of the trust instrument.

57.43 Failure to consult the beneficiaries when required to do so will itself constitute a
breach of trust.[135] What is more difficult to know is what happens if the trustees
decide to act in a way which is contrary to the majority opinion of the beneficiaries as
established by the process of consultation. Weighing the results of that consultation

---

[134] See, for example, *Rodway v Landy* [2001] Ch 703.
[135] *Re Jones* [1931] 1 Ch 375; *Crawley Borough Council v Ure* [1996] QB 13, [1996] 1 All ER 724.

and then refusing to act in accordance with the majority view will not necessarily constitute a breach of trust. Under general trusts law, the trustees are required to act in the interests of all of the beneficiaries and not to favour any particular group of beneficiaries.[136] Therefore, if the trustees can demonstrate that their decision was reasonable in all the circumstances, even though it did not give effect to the wishes of a simple majority of the beneficiaries, then they would not be liable for any breach of trust to any beneficiaries who formed a part of that majority: always provided that they had conducted the consultation in the first place.

Section 14(2) of TLATA 1996 permits the trustees to acquire an order from the court to relieve them of the requirement either to consult any person or to obtain the consent of any person connected with the operation of the trustees' functions. The trustees would therefore be well advised in practice to seek the permission of the court before dispensing with the requirement to consult with the beneficiaries. **57.44**

Rights of occupation

The beneficiaries' limited rights of occupation

One of the underlying aims of the changes introduced by TLATA 1996 was to grant beneficiaries under trusts of land a qualified right to occupy land held on trust for them. The contexts in which this right of occupation was permitted will, in some circumstances, limit the rights of some beneficiaries to occupy the land at the expense of others. The obligations of trusteeship under TLATA 1996 include duties to consult with the beneficiaries before taking any action under the statute.[137] Section 12 provides that: **57.45**

> A beneficiary who is beneficially entitled to an interest in possession in land subject to a trust of land is entitled by reason of his interest to occupy the land at any time if at that time—
>
> (a) the purposes of the trust include making the land available for his occupation (or for the occupation of beneficiaries of a class of which he is a member or of beneficiaries in general), or
> (b) the land is held by the trustees so as to be so available.

Therefore, the 1996 Act provides for a right of occupation to any beneficiary whose interest is in possession at the material time. What is clear is that no beneficiary has a right to occupy the land simply by virtue of being a beneficiary under a trust of land.[138] It is necessary that the interest must entitle the beneficiary to occupation. That is, within the purposes of the trust there must not be a provision which limits the beneficiary's rights to receipt of income only or which restricts those who can occupy the land to a restricted class of persons. The right

---

[136] See para 10.13.   [137] Trusts of Land and Appointment of Trustees Act 1996, s 11.
[138] *IRC v Eversden* [2002] STC 1109, para 25.

of occupation can be exercised at any time and therefore need not be permanent nor continuous.

57.46 The further caveats are then in the alternative. The first is that the purposes of the trust include making the land available for a beneficiary such as the applicant. Again, this serves merely to reinforce the purposes of the trust of land: excluding from occupation those beneficiaries who were never intended to occupy and permitting occupation by those beneficiaries who were intended to be entitled to occupy the property. The trustees are nevertheless required to act fairly and evenly between all of the potential occupants.[139] The second means of enforcing a right to occupy is that the trustees 'hold' the land to make it available for the beneficiary's occupation. The problem is what is meant by the term 'hold' in these circumstances. There are two possibilities: either the trustees must have made a formal decision that the property is to be held in a particular manner, or more generally that it must be merely practicable that the land is made available for the beneficiary's occupation given the nature and condition of the land. The case law has defined the notion of availability for occupation to be dependent on whether or not the trust instrument provides that the beneficiaries are entitled to occupy that land or that it would be a proper exercise of the trustees' powers as expressed in that trust instrument to make it available for the occupation of the beneficiaries.[140] Clearly, this second possibility is broader than the first: in effect, the land is available for occupation if there is nothing in the trust instrument to prevent the trustees from allowing beneficiaries to occupy it and if occupation is physically possible in the sense of the property being habitable and vacant. Nevertheless, it has also been held that just because the trustees have a power, as opposed to an obligation, to make the property available for the beneficiaries' occupation, that does not entitle the beneficiaries to go into occupation unless the trustees decide to exercise their power such that any of the beneficiaries are permitted to occupy it.[141] Depending on the terms of the trust instrument, which may contain a provision which explicitly prevents such a course of action, it would be possible for the trustees to sell the trust property and use the sale proceeds to acquire another property which could be made available for the beneficiaries' occupation further to the power contained in section 8(1)(c) of the Trustee Act 2000.[142]

The exclusion of beneficiaries from occupation of the property

57.47 The more contentious part of the legislation is that in section 13(1) of TLATA 1996 whereby the trustees have the right to exclude beneficiaries:

> Where two or more beneficiaries are entitled under s 12 to occupy land, the trustees of land may exclude or restrict the entitlement of any one or more (but not all) of them.

---

[139] *Rodway v Landy* [2001] Ch 703.   [140] *IRC v Eversden* [2002] STC 1109.
[141] *IRC v Eversden* [2002] STC 1109, affirmed at [2003] EWCA Civ 668.
[142] See para 57.45.

The limits placed on this power by the legislation are set out in section 13(2) in the following terms:

> Trustees may not under subsection (1)—
> (a) unreasonably exclude any beneficiary's entitlement to occupy land, or
> (b) restrict any such entitlement to an unreasonable extent.

The trustees therefore have a right to exclude beneficiaries where they see fit, in effect, provided that they are able to justify the reasonableness of their actions after the event. Any decision to exclude any of the beneficiaries from occupying the property must therefore be capable of being justified on the basis that it is not unreasonable. For beneficiaries seeking to overturn a decision of the trustees to exclude them from occupation of the property, perhaps to the benefit of other beneficiaries, it is not possible to ask the court to direct the trustees to make a decision which permits them to occupy the property but rather the Act permits the courts to evaluate whether or not the trustees have acted unreasonably. In common with the principles of judicial review, the court would not then replace the trustees' decision with their own decision but rather would require the trustees to make their decision again but in a manner which is not unreasonable: the court will not act in the place of the trustee and will not make the decision itself.

57.48 The trustees are expressly required, beyond the requirements to act reasonably, to take into account 'the intentions of the person or persons . . . who created the trust'[143] and 'the purposes for which the land is held . . .'[144] and 'the circumstances and wishes of each of the beneficiaries . . .'.[145] Therefore, at one level, it might be said that the section 13 power to exclude the beneficiaries merely achieves the application of the purposes of the trust.[146] It is possible for the trustees to effect a partition of the property, to require that the beneficiaries occupy different portions from one another, and to require further that the beneficiaries do not intrude on one another's portions.[147]

The effect of these provisions on the unity of possession

57.49 The argument has been made that the 1996 Act does violence to the concept of unity of possession, reawakening the spectre of *Bull v Bull*,[148] whereby a trustee who is also a beneficiary under a trust of land could abuse her powers as trustee to exclude other persons who were also beneficiaries but not trustees under the trust of land.[149] As to the merits of that argument, it seems that section 12 operates only where it is

---

[143] Trusts of Land and Appointment of Trustees Act 1996, s 13(4)(a).
[144] Trusts of Land and Appointment of Trustees Act 1996, s 13(4)(b).
[145] Trusts of Land and Appointment of Trustees Act 1996, s 13(4)(c).
[146] It is suggested that these intentions could be expressed in a document creating the trust or be divined in the same manner as a common intention is located in a constructive trust over a home: see para 56.39.   [147] *Rodway v Landy* [2001] EWCA Civ 471, [2001] Ch 703.
[148] [1955] 1 QB 234.
[149] Barnsley, 'Co-owners' Rights to Occupy Trust Land' (1998) 57 CLJ 123.

the underlying purpose of the trust that the claimant-beneficiary be entitled to occupy that property[150] or that the property is otherwise held so as to make that possible, in which case the trustees would be required to observe the terms of the trust in making any such decision.[151] Consequently, the exclusion of beneficiaries under section 13 will only apply where it is in accordance with the purpose of the trust.

57.50 Furthermore, an unconscionable breach of the trustees' duty to act fairly as between beneficiaries would lead to the court ordering a conscionable exercise of the power. In any event there is a power to make an order in relation to the trustees' functions under section 14 to preclude the trustee from acting in flagrant breach of trust or in a manner which was abusive of her fiduciary powers in permitting a personal interest and fiduciary power to come into conflict.[152]

57.51 Of course, the other way in which TLATA 1996 could be analysed would be as a statute containing a permissive provision in the form of section 12 which grants a qualified right of occupation, in relation to which it is necessary to protect the trustees from an action for breach of the duty of fairness by means of section 13 if some beneficiaries are granted a right of occupation rather than the others. That means, the trustee would be deemed to have a power to permit some person to occupy the land under section 12 while at the same time protecting the trustee from any action based on breach of trust under section 13 in permitting that occupation.

57.52 None of this would be of importance in relation to 'de facto unions' (that is, marriages and relationships of similar permanence)[153] because the purpose of the trust would clearly be to allow all parties to occupy the land as their home. Therefore, it is only in relation to atypical cases where land is acquired with a purpose that only some of the beneficiaries might occupy the property that the *Bull v Bull*[154] problem is of any great concern. It seems that the legislative purpose behind the TLATA 1996 in this context was to displace the concept of interests in possession as the decisive factor in the treatment of the home in favour of considering the advantages of permitting some persons to continue to occupy the home even if that led to the exclusion of some other beneficiaries.

Rights of occupation in the event of a beneficiary's bankruptcy

57.53 The rights of the parties to occupy the trust property are altered in the event that a beneficiary goes into bankruptcy such that his creditors will seek to take possession of his rights under the trust.[155] At first blush, any spouse of that bankrupt

---

[150] Trusts of Land and Appointment of Trustees Act 1996, s 12(1)(a).
[151] Trusts of Land and Appointment of Trustees Act 1996, s 12(1)(b).   [152] See para 10.99.
[153] See this expression deployed in *Gillies v Keogh* [1989] 2 NZLR 327.
[154] [1955] 1 QB 234.
[155] The right of a beneficiary to a share of a life interest which is defeasible by a power of the trustees will not, however, constitute a basis for possession or sale for a mortgagee: *Skyparks Group plc v Marks* [2001] WTLR 607.

person might seek to assert rights of occupation of that property. However, section 336 of the Insolvency Act 1986 provides that:

(1) Nothing occurring in the initial period of the bankruptcy (that is to say, the period beginning with the day of the presentation of the petition for the bankruptcy order and ending with the vesting of the bankrupt's estate in a trustee) is to be taken as having given rise to any [matrimonial home rights under Part IV of the Family Law Act 1996] in relation to a dwelling house comprised in the bankrupt's estate.

Thus, any rights which might otherwise arise under the Family Law Act 1996 are restricted. Similarly,

(2) Where a spouse's [matrimonial home rights under the Act of 1996] are a charge on the estate or interest of the other spouse, or of trustees for the other spouse, and the other spouse is adjudged bankrupt—

    (a) the charge continues to subsist notwithstanding the bankruptcy and, subject to the provisions of that Act, binds the trustee of the bankrupt's estate and persons deriving title under that trustee, and

    (b) any application for an order under [section 33 of that Act] shall be made to the court having jurisdiction in relation to the bankruptcy.

57.54 The powers of the court to make an order are then expressed in the following form:

(4) On such an application as is mentioned in subsection (2) . . . the court shall make such order under [section 33 of the Act of 1996] . . . as it thinks just and reasonable having regard to—

    (a) the interests of the bankrupt's creditors,

    (b) the conduct of the spouse or former spouse, so far as contributing to the bankruptcy,

    (c) the needs and financial resources of the spouse or former spouse,

    (d) the needs of any children, and

    (e) all the circumstances of the case other than the needs of the bankrupt.

Whereas the scope of those rights might seem expansive, and to be similar in form to those in section 15 (as considered below), they are limited by the following significant proviso which requires the court to give priority to the interests of the bankrupt's creditors:

(5) Where such an application is made after the end of the period of one year beginning with the first vesting under Chapter IV of this Part of the bankrupt's estate in a trustee, the court shall assume, unless the circumstances of the case are exceptional, that the interests of the bankrupt's creditors outweigh all other considerations.

57.55 Where a beneficiary is entitled to occupy trust property as his residence, there may be claims as to the bankrupt's right to remain in that property. Section 337(2) of the Insolvency Act 1986 provides a right for the bankrupt not to be evicted or, if not already in occupation, to go into occupation, in the following terms:[156]

---

[156] By virtue of s 337(1), this principle 'applies where—(a) a person who is entitled to occupy a dwelling house by virtue of a beneficial estate or interest is adjudged bankrupt, and (b) any persons

(2) Whether or not the bankrupt's spouse (if any) has rights of occupation under [matrimonial home rights under Part IV of the Family Law Act 1996]—

    (a) the bankrupt has the following rights as against the trustee of his estate—

        (i) if in occupation, a right not to be evicted or excluded from the dwelling house or any part of it, except with the leave of the court,

        (ii) if not in occupation, a right with the leave of the court to enter into and occupy the dwelling house, and

    (b) the bankrupt's rights are a charge, having the like priority as an equitable interest created immediately before the commencement of the bankruptcy, on so much of his estate or interest in the dwelling house as vests in the trustee.

57.56 Taking into account the foregoing rights of the bankrupt person to make an application to the court, the court in turn is empowered on such an application to 'make such order under [section 33 of the Act of 1996] as it thinks just and reasonable having regard to the interests of the creditors, to the bankrupt's financial resources, to the needs of the children and to all the circumstances of the case other than the needs of the bankrupt'.[157] Tellingly, the court's approach to the making of any order is made subject to following proviso:[158]

> (6) Where such an application is made after the end of the period of one year beginning with the first vesting . . . of the bankrupt's estate in a trustee, the court shall assume, unless the circumstances of the case are exceptional, that the interests of the bankrupt's creditors outweigh all other considerations.

Consequently, the core principle of insolvency law that, all else being equal, the rights of creditors are to be considered to be paramount is maintained.

57.57 A final provision, section 338 of the Insolvency Act 1986, deals in the following terms with the possibility that the bankrupt might argue that payments towards the discharge of the mortgage would vest the bankrupt with property rights:

> Where any premises comprised in a bankrupt's estate are occupied by him . . . on condition that he makes payments towards satisfying any liability arising under a mortgage of the premises or otherwise towards the outgoings of the premises, the bankrupt does not, by virtue of those payments, acquire any interest in the premises.

Therefore, the impact of insolvency law on the ownership of property is prevented from raising any presumption that a bankrupt person owns property simply because he defrays some part of the mortgage over that property: rather, that matter is left to the law of property as considered in Chapter 56.

---

under the age of 18 with whom that person had at some time occupied that dwelling house had their home with that person at the time when the bankruptcy petition was presented and at the commencement of the bankruptcy'.

[157] Insolvency Act 1986, s 335A(5).   [158] Insolvency Act 1986, s 335A(6).

The powers of the court to make orders for sale of the land

The powers of the court

A court which is seized of an application under section 14 of TLATA 1996 is free to **57.58** make any order which it sees fit, except in relation to the appointment or removal of trustees.[159] Section 14(1) provides that:

> Any person who is a trustee of land or has an interest in property subject to a trust of land may make an application to the court for an order under this section.[160]

Consequently, occupants of property cannot apply unless they can demonstrate that they have an 'interest in property' relating to the land in question. This would include mortgagees and other secured creditors but not children of a relationship solely on the basis of their occupation of the property. Subject to what is said in relation to section 15 below, children are entitled to have their interests taken into account but not to apply to the court in relation to the trustees' treatment of the land.[161] This provision replaces section 30 of the Law of Property Act 1925 which provided that the court was entitled to make any order it saw fit in response to an application. There was an extensive case law on the effect of section 30, particularly in relation to disputes between family members at a time of family breakdown or situations involving a mortgagee seeking repossession or sale of the home further to a mortgage loan contract. The more difficult area in the cases has been the question of whether or not to order a sale of land where the beneficiaries cannot come to a unanimous decision as to whether or not a sale should go ahead.

An application under section 14 can be brought by three categories of person. **57.59** First, the trustees may make an application. The trustees may seek to rely on this provision in circumstances in which they are unable to reach a unanimous decision between themselves, or alternatively in a situation in which the trustees were required to consult with the beneficiaries and that consultation did not generate a unanimous view. Secondly, by the beneficiaries (as the archetypal person with 'an interest in property'[162]) seeking an order to direct that the trustees deal with the property in a given way. The most common form of application in the decided cases relates to beneficiaries seeking a sale of the property, for example in the event of a relationship breakdown, and thus seeking an order that the trustees effect such a sale. The respondent to such an application will typically seek either to resist the application in its entirety or to agree to such an order only on terms, for example, as to his right or the right of any children of the relationship to continue in

---

[159] Trusts of Land and Appointment of Trustees Act 1996, s 14(3).

[160] Applications under this section may be made either before or after the commencement of this Act: Trusts of Land and Appointment of Trustees Act 1996, s 14(4).

[161] See for example Children Act 1989, s1 which establishes that the welfare of the child is paramount, as considered below.

[162] Trusts of Land and Appointment of Trustees Act 1996, s 14(1).

occupation of the home. Third, by any other person who has 'an interest in property'[163] such as a mortgagee with a right secured over the home.

57.60 The scope of any order which the court is entitled to make is set out in section 14(2) of TLATA 1996[164] in the following terms:

> ... the court may make any such order—
>
> (a) relating to the exercise by the trustees of their functions (including an order relieving them of any obligation to obtain the consent of, or to consult, any person in connection with the exercise of any of their functions), or
> (b) declaring the nature or extent of a person's interest in property subject to the trust, as the court thinks fit.[165]

The two provisions, section 30 of the 1925 Act and section 14 of the 1996 Act which replaced it, therefore operate in parallel to the extent that the court is empowered to make any such order as the court 'thinks fit' in relation to the trustees' functions. The 1996 version necessarily makes express reference to the court making orders as to the trustees' obligations to consult the beneficiaries and to obtain consent in circumstances where such consents are necessary: the obligations to obtain consent and to consult, respectively, were considered earlier.

Matters which the court is required to take into account when considering an application

57.61 Section 15 sets out those matters which are to be taken into account by the court in making an order in relation to section 14. There was no comparable provision in the 1925 Act to section 15, although three of the matters which are identified in section 15 were features of the case law on section 30. The one notable addition is a reference to the rights of any children. There are four categories of matter to be considered in relation to an exercise of a power under section 14:[166]

> (a) the intentions of the persons or persons (if any) who created the trust,
> (b) the purposes for which the property subject to the trust is held,
> (c) the welfare of any minor who occupies or might reasonably be expected to occupy any land subject to the trust as his home, and
> (d) the interests of any secured creditor or any beneficiary.

There is a balancing act to be conducted by the court between these four, potentially contradictory considerations. It does not appear that there is any significance in the ranking of these matters which the courts are required to take into account.[167] Each heading is considered in turn in the paragraphs to follow.

---

[163] Trusts of Land and Appointment of Trustees Act 1996, s 14(1).
[164] Formerly personified in s 30 of the Law of Property Act 1925.
[165] Trusts of Land and Appointment of Trustees Act 1996, s 14(2).
[166] Trusts of Land and Appointment of Trustees Act 1996, s 15(1).
[167] *A v B* (Family Division, 23 May 1997) *per* Cazalet J.

The purpose of the trust and the settlor's intention

Paragraph (a) of section 15 provides that the underlying purpose of the trust as **57.62** expressed by its settlor is to be applied by the court in reaching any decision. Nevertheless, the settlor's intentions may not be instructive as to any particular issue as to the purposes for which the property is being held under the trust. For example, a settlor's original intention that the property be leased so as to generate an income stream for the beneficiaries, subject to a power to use the property for the beneficiaries' occupation, might conflict with a decision taken by the trustees to permit one of the beneficiaries to occupy the property. Consequently, the terms of the trust instrument and the use to which those powers are being put by the trustees might not be capable of easy reconciliation. In such a situation, the attitude of English trusts law to the effect that all of the beneficiaries acting in concert are able to direct the trustees how to deal with the property may trump the settlor's original intentions.[168] An example would be the decision in *Re Bowes*[169] in which the settlor's original intention, to provide for the maintenance of large gardens on settled land, was overridden by the unanimous direction of the beneficiaries to the effect that the trust property should be applied for their personal benefit as opposed to its use solely for the abstract purpose of the maintenance of parkland. Thus, the trust's purposes may be different to the underlying purposes set out in paragraph (a). Those 'purposes' may vary from context to context.[170]

The rights of children in occupation of the property

The third paragraph of section 15 imports to trusts law a need to consider that **57.63** the rights of children in relation to their homes are to be taken into account. Under ordinary principles of trusts law, particularly those considered in Chapter 56, children do not have rights in the home under property law principles on the basis that they are unlikely to have made a financial contribution to the acquisition of the property.[171] Consequently, ordinary trusts law would not consider the rights of children in deciding the allocation of rights in the home. The inclusion of paragraph (c), therefore, requires that the position of the children be considered. The case law on section 30 of the 1925 Act did take into account the place of the children in making an order. For example, in *Re Holliday*[172] the needs of the children to finish their schooling were taken into account such that the order for sale of the property was made conditional on the children of the relationship reaching school-leaving age. This provision may also lead to the importation of elements of child law and of the case law under the Children Act 1989 to this area, under which the welfare of the

---

[168] *Saunders v Vautier* (1841) 4 Beav 115.   [169] [1896] 1 Ch 507.
[170] *Bankers Trust Co v Namdar* [1997] EGCS 20; *Barclays Bank v Hendricks* [1996] 1 FLR 258; *Mortgage Corporation v Shaire* [2000] 1 FLR 973; *Grindal v Hooper* The Times, 8 February 2000.
[171] As required, for example, by *Lloyds Bank v Rosset* [1991] 1 AC 1.
[172] [1981] 2 WLR 996.

child is made paramount.[173] The principles of child law have arisen since the principal cases on section 30 and therefore it is difficult to know how property law courts will deal with concepts developed originally by family courts in disposing of applications seeking the use of the family courts' broad, statutory discretion. Under sections 14 and 15 it would be possible for the court to import child law concepts given the express power for the court to make such order as it sees fit.[174]

The rights of any secured creditor of the beneficiaries

57.64 The fourth paragraph (d) of section 15 of the 1996 Act requires the court to consider the rights of any creditor of any beneficiary, not requiring that the beneficiary be bankrupt at the time. Therefore, mortgagees will be entitled to have their interests taken expressly into account. The courts have indicated that mortgagees ought to be protected with the same enthusiasm as bankruptcy creditors in these contexts.[175] The situation in relation to creditors in the event of bankruptcy is considered in the following paragraph. The courts have been concerned to protect the interests of mortgagees and other secured creditors otherwise than in a bankruptcy with the same diligence as they have protected creditors in a bankruptcy. In consequence, the courts have tended to order a sale of the land to meet the debts owed to those creditors.[176] The few situations in which a sale has been denied in relation to bankruptcy are considered in the following paragraph.

The situation in which one of the beneficiaries is bankrupt

57.65 The circumstances in which one of the beneficiaries is bankrupt are different from other circumstances. If one of the trustees of land is bankrupt, the trust property will not form a part of his estate simply because he is a trustee: it is only if the trustee also has some beneficial interest in the trust property that the trust property will be brought into account in the bankruptcy proceedings. If it is a beneficiary who is bankrupt, then the trustee in bankruptcy will be entitled to bring an application under section 14 as a person with an interest in the land by dint of the bankruptcy proceedings.

57.66 Section 335A of the Insolvency Act 1986 overrides any situation in which the 1986 Act is applicable, in place of the provisions of the 1996 Act.[177] Section 335A(1) provides that:

> Any application by a trustee of a bankrupt's estate under section 14 . . . for an order under that section for the sale of land shall be made to the court having jurisdiction in relation to the bankruptcy.

---

[173] *Bankers Trust Co v Namdar* [1997] EGCS 20; *Barclays Bank v Hendricks* [1996] 1 FLR 258; *Mortgage Corporation v Shaire* [2000] 1 FLR 973; *Grindal v Hooper* The Times, 8 February 2000.
[174] Trusts of Land and Appointment of Trustees Act 1996, s 14(2).
[175] *Lloyds Bank v Byrne* (1991) 23 HLR 472, [1993] 1 FLR 369.
[176] *Lloyds Bank v Byrne* (1991) 23 HLR 472, [1993] 1 FLR 369.
[177] Further to Trusts of Land and Appointment of Trustees Act 1996, s 15(4).

The application under section 14 is therefore subjugated to the hearing of the bankruptcy petition. That court's powers operate as follows:[178]

> ... the court shall make such order as it thinks just and reasonable having regard to—
>
> (a) the interests of the bankrupt's creditors;
> (b) where the application is made in respect of land which includes a dwelling house which is or has been the home of the bankrupt or the bankrupt's spouse or former spouse—
>
>> (i) the conduct of the spouse or former spouse, so far as contributing to the bankruptcy,
>> (ii) the needs and financial resources of the spouse or former spouse, and
>> (iii) the needs of any children; and
>
> (c) all the circumstances of the case other than the needs of the bankrupt.

57.67 The court is therefore empowered to make any order which it considers just and reasonable and, thereafter, appears to be subject to broadly similar considerations to those under section 15 of the 1996 Act. It is section 335A(3) of the 1986 Act which contains the sting in the tail:

> Where such an application [under section 14 of the 1996 Act] is made after the end of the period of one year beginning with the first vesting ... of the bankrupt's estate in a trustee, the court shall assume, unless the circumstances of the case are exceptional, that the interests of the bankrupt's creditors outweigh all other considerations.

The court is consequently obliged to assume that the interests of the creditors in the bankruptcy are to be given priority over all other considerations. Therefore, it is assumed that the property should be sold and the relevant proportion of the proceeds transferred to the trustee in bankruptcy to discharge the creditors' debts.

57.68 In the case of *Harrington v Bennett*[179] it was held that the requirements of section 335A of the Insolvency Act 1986 were fivefold. First, where the application is made more than one year after the vesting of the bankrupt's property in the trustee, the interests of creditors are paramount. Secondly, the court can only ignore the creditors' interests in exceptional circumstances, which circumstances will typically relate to the personal circumstances of the joint owners. Thirdly, the categories of exceptional circumstances are not closed, with the effect that it is open to the judge to decide what may constitute exceptional circumstances in future cases. Fourthly, the term 'exceptional' connotes circumstances 'outside the usual melancholy consequences of debt or improvidence'. Fifthly, that the sale proceeds may be used entirely to discharge the expenses of the trustee in bankruptcy is not an exceptional circumstance which may affect the interests of the creditors.

57.69 In the case of an application made by a trustee in bankruptcy under section 14, different criteria have been applied on the cases under section 30 from those

---

[178] Insolvency Act 1986, s 335A(2).   [179] [2000] BPIR 630.

considered in relation to the other paragraphs of section 15 which do not relate to bankruptcy. The court will generally order a sale of the property automatically in a situation in which one of the beneficiaries has fallen into bankruptcy. So, in the case of *Re Citro*[180] it was no answer to an application for sale on behalf of the bankrupt's creditors that the loss of the home which was the subject of the trust would require the family to leave the area in which they lived and to uproot their children from their schooling. It was held that a sale of the property would not be refused unless the circumstances were exceptional and that this form of hardship was, in the maudlin and yet lyrical view of the court, merely one of the melancholy features of life.

57.70 There have been a limited category of situations in which the courts have been prepared to forbear from ordering a sale of the property in the event of bankruptcy on the basis that the circumstances were exceptional. The first situation was that in *Re Holliday*,[181] a case in which the bankrupt had gone into bankruptcy on his own petition to rid himself of his creditors and one in which the debt was so small in comparison to the sale value of the house that there was thought to be no hardship to the creditors in waiting for the bankrupt's three children to reach school-leaving age before ordering a sale. However, that hardship will be caused to the children or to the family in general as a result of a sale in favour of a trustee in bankruptcy is considered, as mentioned in the preceding paragraphs, to be merely one of the melancholy vicissitudes of life.[182] A second situation in which a sale in favour of the creditors has been denied was that in which the bankrupt's spouse has been terminally ill.[183]

The interpretative role of the case law decided before 1997

57.71 The impact of the 1996 Act on this area of law is difficult to assess given the paucity of decided cases in this area since its enactment. The introduction of the statutory categories of matter to be taken into account by the courts in section 15 do not appear to have introduced any extraordinarily new concepts to these cases, with the exception of the explicit introduction of a requirement that the courts consider the rights of any minors. Therefore, it seems probable that the courts will continue to consider the case law decided under section 30 of the 1925 Act. The recent case of *Mortgage Corporation v Shaire*[184] has recognized, however, that the enactment of the 1996 Act could be read as intending to alter the manner in which such cases are considered by the courts. That intention might be to create equality between the rights of secured creditors such as mortgagees and the rights of occupants of the

---

[180] [1991] Ch 142.   [181] [1981] 2 WLR 996.   [182] *Re Citro* [1991] Ch 142, *supra*.
[183] *Claughton v Charalambous* [1999] 1 FLR 740; *Re Bremner* [1999] 1 FLR 912. Further *Re Raval* [1998] 2 FLR 718, in which a one-year suspension of the sale was granted due to a diagnosis of paranoid schizophrenia. See also *Skyparks Group plc v Marks* [2001] WTLR 607, in which a mortgagee was denied an order for possession and sale of mortgaged property against a contingent right of a beneficiary under a trust for sale.
[184] [2001] Ch 743, [2001] 4 All ER 364. See also *Bank of Ireland Home Mortgages Ltd v Bell* [2001] 2 All ER (Comm) 920; *First National Bank plc v Achampong*, 1 April 2003, unreported at para 61.

property and their families (including children), rather than simply assuming that the rights of creditors should still be treated as being paramount. In the case of *Mortgage Corporation v Shaire* itself only interlocutory questions were considered without any final decision on the merits being reached. Therefore the High Court did not reach any conclusions as to the proper interpretation of the new legislation. Other, as yet unreported,[185] cases have suggested, however, that the pre-1997 case law will continue to be of significance in interpreting the broadly similar matters to be taken into account under the 1996 Act.[186] It is suggested that the position in relation to bankruptcy will remain as it was before 1997 by virtue of section 335A of the Insolvency Act 1986 and that the remaining case law on section 30 of the 1925 Act will continue to be influential given that the provisions of section 30 and section 14 of the 1996 Act are so similar.

F. The Protection of Purchasers

When the purchase is contracted with a delegate of the trustees' powers

When a purchase is contracted with someone to whom the trustees have delegated their powers this raises the possibility that the sale may subsequently be repudiated by the trustees or the beneficiaries. In circumstances in which the purchaser has acted in good faith, the purchase is presumed to be valid.[187] These provisions were considered above.[188] **57.72**

When a consent is required prior to sale

The protection of purchasers against any provision of the trust instrument preventing the trustees from selling the trust property without the consent of the beneficiaries has already been considered.[189] Section 10 of the 1996 Act provides that, where two or more people are to give their consent in advance of a valid sale, consent being given by any two of them is sufficient to transfer good title to the purchaser.[190] **57.73**

Overreaching

The doctrine of overreaching provides that if the purchase price for property is paid to two trustees or a trust corporation, then the rights of the purchaser overreach the interests of the beneficiaries under that trust of land.[191] Overreaching will not operate in situations in which there is only one trustee of the trust of **57.74**

---

[185] In the materials available to me at the time of writing.
[186] *Wright v Johnson* (Court of Appeal, 2 November 1999) *per* Robert Walker LJ.
[187] Trusts of Land and Appointment of Trustees Act 1996, s 9(1).   [188] See para 15.35.
[189] See para 57.72.   [190] Trusts of Land and Appointment of Trustees Act 1996, s 10(1).
[191] Law of Property Act 1925, s 27.

land.[192] The particular problem which has arisen in land law is whether an over-riding interest[193] in relation to a person in actual occupation of land[194] would trump a purchaser who has paid purchase moneys over that land to two trustees so as to claim a right to overreach the rights of those beneficiaries. The House of Lords had held that an equitable interest acquired by a wife against her husband under an implied trust for sale coupled with actual occupation of that land constituted an overriding interest:[195] however, the doctrine of overreaching was not at issue in that case.[196] A subsequent decision of the House of Lords held that the proper management of the conveyancing system required that the doctrine of overreaching should take priority over an equitable interest coupled with actual occupation of the property.[197] The effect of this latter decision was to enhance the protection available to purchasers who pay the purchase moneys for land to two or more trustees, or to a trust corporation, by ensuring that their interests over-reach those of any beneficiary in actual occupation of the property under a trust for sale or, latterly, by extension under a trust of land.

G. Settled Land Act Settlements

The impact of the Trusts of Land and Appointment of Trustees Act 1996 on settled land

57.75 The TLATA 1996 does not effect changes on settlements created under the Settled Land Act 1925 before 1 January 1997.[198] The definition of 'settled land' for the purposes of TLATA 1996 is that contained in section 2 of the Settled Land Act 1925, as considered above.[199] As has been considered, the 1996 Act does prevent the creation of any new Settled Land Act settlements after 1 January, 1997.[200] However, there is no alteration on the proper functioning of existing Settled Land Act settlements. Alterations of interests in such settlements and the process by which people may become entitled for the first time under such settlements take effect as before, provided that such changes were provided for in the instrument giving effect to that original settlement.[201] People may become entitled under such settlements for the first time by means of the succession of a new

---

[192] *Williams & Glyn's Bank Ltd v Boland* [1981] AC 487.

[193] After the enactment of the Land Registration Act 2002, Sch 3, now rendered as 'interests which override'. [194] Law of Property Act 1925, s 70(1)(g).

[195] That was, under s 70(1)(g) of the 1925 Act.

[196] *Williams & Glyn's Bank Ltd v Boland* [1981] AC 487.

[197] *City of London Building Society v Flegg* [1988] AC 54.

[198] Trusts of Land and Appointment of Trustees Act 1996, s 1(3).

[199] Trusts of Land and Appointment of Trustees Act 1996, s 23(2). Necessarily, then, the original settlement must have been in existence before 1 January 1997 or else it would have taken effect as a trust of land. [200] Trusts of Land and Appointment of Trustees Act 1996, s 2(1).

[201] Trusts of Land and Appointment of Trustees Act 1996, s 2(2).

tenant for life on the termination of an interest in possession, by means of the exercise of a power of appointment under an existing settlement, or by means of a variation or derivation of an existing settlement. Any settlement of property which, by its own instrument, declares it not to be a Settled Land Act settlement will not take effect as such a settlement even if it could otherwise have taken effect under a Settled Land Act settlement.[202] There is, therefore, a means by which trustees of Settled Land Act settlements may convert appointments under such settlements to trusts of land.[203] However, the statute does not grant an explicit power to trustees to effect this conversion and therefore the trustees can only make such a change if the instrument establishing the settlement provides them with a power so to do.

There are two contexts in which settlements are taken out of the Settled Land Act **57.76** scheme. First, settlements which have 'no relevant property' subject to the settlement cease permanently to be Settled Land Act settlements and become trusts of land instead.[204] The term 'relevant property' in this sense refers to land and personal chattels, being 'heirlooms', falling within section 67 of the Settled Land Act 1925.[205] Secondly, land which is held on charitable, ecclesiastical, or public trusts is no longer to be considered to be held under the terms of the Settled Land Act, even if it had been previously.[206]

The structure of Settled Land Act settlements

The scope of Settled Land Act settlements

The purpose of Settled Land Act settlements (hereafter, 'SLA settlements') was to **57.77** enable the owners of large estates to structure the way in which their estates would pass to successive generations after their own demises. The means by which that was done was to identify an 'estate owner' in whom the legal estate would be vested. The dead hand of the testator, in consequence, rested on their land and hovered over the fate of future generations. This structure, of course, generated much of the background to some of the finest English novels, in particular Charles Dickens's *Bleak House*, and Jane Austen's *Sense and Sensibility* and *Pride and Prejudice*.

What is presented here is a truncated account on the law relating to SLA settlements. **57.78** That SLA settlements are limited now to those in effect before 1 January 1997 has the effect that this area of law will necessarily dwindle in importance. Much of the 1925 Act contained provisions concerned with the underlying legislative

---

[202] Trusts of Land and Appointment of Trustees Act 1996, s 2(3).
[203] Trusts of Land and Appointment of Trustees Act 1996, s 2(3).
[204] Trusts of Land and Appointment of Trustees Act 1996, s 2(4).
[205] Trusts of Land and Appointment of Trustees Act 1996, s 2(4).
[206] Trusts of Land and Appointment of Trustees Act 1996, s 2(5).

purpose of simplifying the conveyance of settled land and therefore the reader is referred to *Megarry & Wade's The Law of Real Property*[207] or *Emmett on Title*.

57.79 An important part of the dwindling importance of SLA settlements, aside from their relegation by statute to purely historical usage in the treatment of land by settlors, has been their aggressive treatment for tax purposes under the inheritance tax regime. Inheritance tax falls on the full value of the estate on the death of each life tenant, with the result that SLA settlements now appear to be a disadvantageous means of transferring property through the generations.[208]

The composition of SLA settlements

57.80 The tenant for life under an SLA settlement took on the role both of a beneficiary entitled to the use of property during his life and also that of legal owner of the property, creating self-evident possibilities for conflict between the tenant for life and the trustees of the settlement. The life tenant, as owner of the legal estate either in the form of the fee simple or of a term of years, constituted the 'estate owner' and was, in fulfilment of the legislative purpose behind the 1925 Act, able to transfer good title in the settlement land more easily than could have been achieved previously by virtue of the doctrine of overreaching. The doctrine of overreaching ensured that the rights of any other beneficiaries taking after the life tenant would be superseded by any such transfer. The presence of, and the rights of, any such people would be kept from the purchaser by dint of the 'curtain principle': with the purchaser left free to transact with the trustees of the settlement, confident that his purchase would overreach any beneficiaries interested under that settlement provided that the sale was conducted in accordance with statute. There would also be beneficiaries in remainder whose interests would only vest in them on the death of the life tenant or as otherwise provided for in the terms of the settlement. The rights and obligations of each member of this dramatis personae are considered in the sections to follow.

The definition of 'settlement' in this context

57.81 The definition of the term 'settlement' in this context covers not only trusts which were consciously intended by their settlors to fall within the Settled Land Act scheme but also those settlements which fell within the statutory definition by accident.[209] The definition of a 'settlement' contained in section 1 of the 1925 Act is as follows:

> (1) Any deed, will, agreement for a settlement or other agreement, Act of Parliament, or other instrument, or any number of instruments, whether made or passed before

---

[207] Sixth edition by C Harpum (Sweet & Maxwell, 2000).
[208] See *Ingram v IRC* [2000] 1 AC 293, 300, *per* Lord Hoffmann.
[209] *Bannister v Bannister* [1948] 2 All ER 133; *Ungurian v Lesnoff* [1990] Ch 206; *Costello v Costello* (1994) 70 P & CR 297.

or after, or partly before and partly after, the commencement of this Act, under or by virtue of which instrument or instruments any land, after the commencement of this Act, stands for the time being—

(i) limited in trust for any persons by way of succession; or

(ii) limited in trust for any person in possession—

   (a) for an entailed interest whether or not capable of being barred or defeated;

   (b) for an estate in fee simple or for a term of years absolute...;

   (c) for a base or determinable fee other than a fee which is made absolute by section 7 of the Law of Property Act 1925 or any corresponding interest in leasehold land;

   (d) being an infant, for an estate in fee simple or for a term of years absolute; or

(iii) limited in trust for any person for an estate in fee simple or for a term of years absolute contingently on the happening of any event; or

(iv) ...

(v) charged, whether voluntarily or in consideration of a marriage or by way of family arrangement, and whether immediately or after an interval, with the payment of any rentcharge for the life of any person or any less period, or of any capital, annual or periodical sums for the portions, advancement, maintenance or otherwise for the benefit of any persons with or without any term of years for securing or raising the same.

Excluded from this definition are trusts for sale[210] and bare trusts,[211] as was considered at the beginning of this chapter.

The tenant for life

The conveyancing process

The Settled Land Act 1925 identifies an 'estate owner'[212] who was generally the **57.82** tenant for life being 'the person of full age who is for the time being beneficially entitled under a settlement to possession of the settled land'.[213] There may have been situations in which there was more than one person entitled, in which case those people will take as joint tenants and constitute the tenant for life together, being entitled to operate the powers and to be subject to the obligations attendant on that status.[214] Alternatively, there may not have been a tenant for life entitled to take as a *sui juris* beneficiary on the grounds of being either a minor or of lacking sufficient mental competence or otherwise.[215] In such a situation, a 'statutory owner' would take the place of the tenant for life.[216]

---

[210] Settled Land Act 1925, s 1(7), as inserted by the Law of Property (Amendment) Act 1926. See para 57.21. [211] See para 57.29. [212] Settled Land Act 1925, s 117(1)(xi).

[213] Settled Land Act 1925, s 19(1). See Settled Land Act 1925, s 117(1)(xix) on the definition of 'possession', including not only physical possession but also entitlement to receive rents and profits.

[214] Settled Land Act 1925, s 19(2).

[215] See, for example, *Re Frewen* [1926] Ch 580; *Re Bird* [1927] 1 Ch 210; *Re Norton* [1929] 1 Ch 84.

[216] Settled Land Act 1925, ss 23, 26, 117(1)(xxvi).

57.83   There were two documents required for the tenant to acquire his interests in land. The first was a vesting deed which conveyed the settled land to the tenant for life or to the statutory owner. The second document was the trust instrument which declared the detailed terms of the trust, including the beneficial interest of the various vested and contingent beneficiaries.[217] Testamentary dispositions of property onto SLA settlements by means of will would constitute the will as the trust instrument.[218] The estate owner, in the form of the tenant for life or other statutory owner, took the legal title in the settled land: whereas the equitable interests in the settled property were allocated by the trust instrument.

The requirement of an instrument granting rights to the tenant for life

57.84   Significantly, section 1 of the Settled Land Act requires that the tenant for life take his interest under an instrument.[219] Consequently a person who acquires his rights by virtue of a licence or proprietary estoppel will not acquire the rights of a tenant for life under an SLA settlement if there is no instrument confirming the creation of those rights.[220] Assuming the presence of an adequate instrument, then a claimant will be entitled to enjoy the rights of a tenant for life under a licence to occupy property[221] (provided that that licence purports to grant an equitable proprietary right and not merely a purely personal right against the licensor), under proprietary estoppel,[222] or under an option to occupy land (once that option has been exercised).[223] A person with rights of occupation under a trust for sale will not, however, become a tenant for life because that would exclude the Law of Property Act 1925[224] and cross that divide which provides that trusts for sale do not fall within the scope of SLA settlements.[225] In the wake of the decision in *Yaxley v Gotts*[226] the question remains to be answered whether or not proprietary estoppel could be understood to operate so as to circumvent formal statutory requirements in circumstances in which someone who had relied to his detriment on an assurance made to him by the owner of property with the result that an interest which the claimant had been led to believe would have been

---

[217]   Settled Land Act 1925, ss 4, 117(1)(xxxi).   [218]   Settled Land Act 1925, s 6(a).

[219]   Settled Land Act 1925, s 1(1).

[220]   *Ivory v Palmer* [1975] ICR 340. Cf *Ungarian v Lesnoff* [1990] Ch 206 where such a right was held to have been created in the absence of an instrument, although this decision is considered to have been wrong by J Mowbray et al, the editors of *Lewin on Trusts* (17th edn, Sweet & Maxwell, 2000) ('*Lewin*') 1070.

[221]   *Bannister v Bannister* [1948] 2 All ER 133 as applied by *Binions v Evans* [1972] Ch 359; *Ivory v Palmer* [1975] ICR 340; *Chandler v Kerley* [1978] 1 WLR 693; *Dent v Dent* [1996] 1 WLR 683. The claimant will become tenant for life only on exercising his right of occupation: *Re Anderson* [1920] 1 Ch 175.   [222]   By analogy from *Binions v Evans* [1972] Ch 359.

[223]   *Re Gibbons* [1920] 1 Ch 372.

[224]   *Re Herklot's WT* [1964] 1 WLR 583; *Ayer v Benton* [1967] EGD 700; *Dodsworth v Dodsworth* [1973] EGD 233, 238.

[225]   Settled Land Act 1925, s 1(7), as inserted by the Law of Property (Amendment) Act 1926.

[226]   [2000] 1 All ER 711.

settled on trust for him would be so settled in spite of the formal requirement for the presence of an instrument so to do.

The powers of the tenant for life

The conflict between beneficial and fiduciary capacities of the tenant for life

The tenant for life is both a trustee and a beneficiary of the settled land. Whereas **57.85** the life tenant is able to enjoy his equitable interest in the land during his lifetime, self-evidently his possession of the legal title in that land cannot permit him to act entirely in the furtherance of his own interests in opposition to the interests of others who are or who may become beneficially entitled to the settled property in remainder or otherwise.

Section 16(1) of the 1925 Act provides that: **57.86**

> All equitable interests and powers in or over settled land (whether created before or after the date of any vesting instrument affecting the legal estate) shall be enforceable against the estate owner in whom the settled land is vested (but in the case of personal representatives without prejudice to their rights and powers for purposes of administration) in manner following (that is to say):—

> (i) The estate owner shall stand possessed of the settled land and the income thereof upon such trusts and subject to such powers and provisions as may be requisite for giving effect to the equitable interests and powers affecting the settled land or the income thereof of which he has notice according to their respective priorities . . .

On the positive side, then, the tenant for life is possessed of the powers of a trustee **57.87** under the settlement. However, he is also obliged in the exercise of those powers to have regard to the interests of other people with beneficial rights under the settlement and so bears fiduciary obligations in the use of his powers and responsibilities in relation to the settlement. To this effect, section 107(1) of the 1925 Act provides that:

> A tenant for life or statutory owner shall, in exercising any power under this Act, have regard to the interests of all parties entitled under the settlement, and shall, in relation to the exercise thereof by him, be deemed to be in the position and to have the duties and liabilities of a trustee for those parties.

Consequently, the tenant for life will be liable for his treatment of the settled prop- **57.88** erty as though an express trustee and liable to have his actions supervised by the courts.[227] It is this power in the court to supervise the actions and decisions of the tenant for life when acting in this fiduciary role which functions so as to restrain any decision by the tenant for life to sell the settled land.[228] Evidently, this is a

---

[227] *Re Duke of Marlborough's Settlement* (1886) 32 Ch D 1.
[228] *Wheelwright v Walker* (1883) 23 Ch D 752, 762, *per* Pearson J; *Thomas v Williams* (1883) 24 Ch D 558; *Re Chaytor's Settled Estate Act* (1884) 25 Ch D 651; *Hatton v Russell* (1888) 36 Ch D 334; *Mogridge v Clapp* [1892] 3 Ch 382; *Chandler v Bradley* [1897] 1 Ch 315.

significant issue in relation to the operation of SLA settlements where the settled land is the centrepiece of the trust and intended to sustain future generations of a family. Sale of a part of the trust fund might constitute a reasonable investment strategy if, for example, the fund contained a number of parcels of land. However, if the trust fund contained only one house, with the settlor having had the intention that that very house be maintained for the benefit of successive generations, then different considerations would apply. In such a situation, it is likely that the trust instrument will have been structured so as to hinder any individual from seeking a sale of the property. It could be expected that the sale would be opposed unless the sale were being effected so as to acquire a more desirable property to be held for future generations in the same manner: for example, if the original house was found to lie on a flood plain or to be liable to subsidence, then a change of property may be in the long-term interests of beneficiaries in remainder.

Furthermore, the tenant for life is entitled to lease the settled property provided that any lease is transacted in good faith.[229] Examples of acting in bad faith have included situations in which the tenant for life has taken a bribe from the prospective lessee.[230] Alternatively, if the tenant for life were to lease the property to his wife on advantageous terms that would render the lease determinable but that does not preclude the tenant for life leasing the property to members of his immediate family in good faith.[231] The guiding principle was expressed by Jenkins LJ in the following terms:

> It is no doubt true that a tenant for life is a trustee of his statutory powers. But he is also a beneficiary under the settlement, entitled to the whole of the income of the trust property, whether in the form of land or of capital money. A direction by him by which he gains some benefit involves no breach of trust, provided that the benefit which he gets does not go beyond what he is entitled to in right of his beneficial interest.[232]

These dicta illustrate the delicate path to be trodden by one who is both beneficiary and fiduciary required to bear in mind not only his own short-term interests but also the interests of others in the dim and distant future.

Restrictions on the powers of the tenant for life

57.89 The powers of the tenant for life as trustee may be defined either by the trust instrument or by statute. Section 108(1) of the 1925 Act provides that 'nothing in this Act shall take away, abridge, or prejudicially affect any power … exercisable by the tenant for life'. Where there is a conflict in relation to the powers of the tenant for life relating to the exercise of any power contained in the Act between the terms of a settlement and of the 1925 Act, then the provisions of the Act

---

[229] *Sutherland v Sutherland* [1893] 3 Ch 169; *Chandler v Bradley* [1897] 1 Ch 315; *Re Cornwallis* (1919) 88 LJ KB 1237.   [230] *Chandler v Bradley* [1897] 1 Ch 315.
[231] *Sutherland v Sutherland* [1893] 3 Ch 169; *Gilbey v Rush* [1906] 1 Ch 11.
[232] *Re Pelly's Will Trusts* [1957] Ch 1, 18.

prevail:[233] the terms of the trust instrument are able to grant greater powers to the tenant for life than are contained in the Act.[234] In the event of any uncertainty as to the effect of a power, the court is empowered to resolve that doubt.[235] Whereas these powers cannot be fettered,[236] they are also incapable of release or assignment[237] but not delegation.[238]

The role of trustees under SLA settlements

Prior to the enactment of the Trustee Act 2000, the role of the trustees has been limited in SLA settlements. The tenant for life has held the bulk of the fiduciary powers and responsibilities with the trustees being employed primarily with the performance of acts required by the tenant for life. The trustees' role, as a body, was as much that of an observer of the smooth transfer of the settlement property across the generations as anything else, whereas the tenant for life carried out those tasks which would have ordinarily accrued to the trustees of an express trust. For example, classically, whereas the trustees were required to take possession of all capital moneys[239] and to have them invested in their names,[240] they were nevertheless obliged to invest those moneys in accordance with the directions given to them by the tenant for life. This provision has since been amended by the Trustee Act 2000 to the effect that the trustees shall now exercise their own discretion in relation to the investment of capital funds in SLA settlements.[241] Otherwise the powers of the trustees are to act as statutory owners on behalf of a tenant for life during his minority[242] or to consent to certain transactions under the 1925 Act.[243] **57.90**

SLA settlements and the condition of the law of trusts

The passage of the law on SLA settlements into antiquity is perhaps illustrative of much in the law of trusts. Old models die as new ones are born. This ancient mechanism for the holding of land so that it could pass down the generations, always under the immortal eye of a board of disinterested trustees made up of a succession of different people but acting always as though one body in accordance with conscience and always without any conflict of interest, has succeeded in time to the creation of, what is hoped to be, a more streamlined form of trust of land. Whereas generations of Chancery lawyers will have come to understand the peculiarities of SLA settlements, just as they have come to understand so much of the **57.91**

---

[233] Settled Land Act 1925, s 108(2).   [234] Settled Land Act 1925, s 109(1).
[235] Settled Land Act 1925, s 108(3).   [236] Settled Land Act 1925, s 106.
[237] Settled Land Act 1925, s 104.   [238] Trustee Act 1925, s 25.
[239] Settled Land Act 1925, ss 94 and 95.   [240] Settled Land Act 1925, s 75.
[241] Trustee Act 2000, s 40 and Sch 2, Pt II.
[242] Settled Land Act 1925, s 26. See also Law of Property Act 1925, s 1(6).
[243] Among these forms of transactions are: sale of the main house (s 65), cutting and selling timber (s 66), compromising claims (s 58), and selling settled chattels (s 67).

equitable doctrine of trust, the legislative imperative was nevertheless to create a property management vehicle which could be more comprehensible to non-specialists even though, ironically, it is unlikely that many people other than the Chancery specialists would ever care to know anything at all about it before it was too late. The trust in general terms has evolved from being a means of administering the land owned by those who spent little time in England in the thirteenth century into a mechanism capable by turns of taking security over property in commercial transactions, of ensuring conscionable behaviour over property in general terms, of heeding the wishes of the dead long after they are gone, and of dealing with ownership of the home. The elegance of the central principle—that a person may be obliged by courts of equity to act in good conscience when dealing with property in which others have an interest—has proved itself to be resilient precisely because it is so simple at root and yet sufficiently subtle to adapt to change.

This book has considered the many shades of meaning and interpretation possible in the matrix of property rights, fiduciary obligations, and equitable claims which the trust encompasses: always shifting and adapting to each context. The trust may well be, as Maitland thought, English law's greatest contribution to jurisprudence.[244] Its seeming power rests perhaps in the fact that it is not an innate nor an a priori legal principle in the manner of punishment for wrongs, the enforcement of contractual bargains, or the protection of rights in property which occur in most human societies in one form or another. Rather, it is a singular concept which has been fashioned carefully over many centuries. It is a man-made, rather than a found object in that sense, and one which continues to be one of the most remarkable intellectual techniques for analysing our treatment of property and of one another. Whether Maitland was right or not, the trust has undoubtedly become one of the core concepts of English and Welsh law and one which promises to remain as such.

---

[244] Maitland, *Essays on Equity* (2nd edn, Cambridge University Press, 1936) 1.

INDEX

Index

Index

1865